Reference

AN

Almanack

For the Year of Our Lord

2018

ESTABLISHED 1868

BY

JOSEPH WHITAKER, FSA

CONTAINING AN ACCOUNT OF THE

ASTRONOMICAL AND OTHER PHENOMENA

AND

A vast Amount of INFORMATION respecting the
GOVERNMENT, FINANCES, POPULATION,
COMMERCE, and GENERAL STATISTICS of
the various Nations of the WORLD
with an INDEX containing
nearly 7,500
References

LONDON

OFFICE: 50 BEDFORD SQUARE
LONDON WC1B 3DP

The traditional design of the title page for Whitaker's Almanack which has appeared in each edition since 1868

BLOOMSBURY

LON • DELHI • SYDNEY

D030B296

Bloomsbury Publishing
An imprint of Bloomsbury Publishing Plc

50 Bedford Square	1385 Broadway
London	New York
WC1B 3DP	NY 10018
UK	USA

www.bloomsbury.com

WHITAKER'S, the W Trident logo and the Diana logo are trademarks
of Bloomsbury Publishing Plc

British Library Cataloguing-in-Publication Data
A catalogue record for this book is available from the British Library.

ISBN: PB: 978-1-4729-4803-8

www.whitakersalmanack.com

2 4 6 8 10 9 7 5 3 1

Typeset by QPM from David Lewis XML Associates Ltd
Printed and bound by CPI Group (UK) Ltd, Croydon, CR0 4YY

To find out more ab... ... will find extracts,
author interview... ...ur newsletters.

CONTENTS

4

TIME AND SPACE

Key events of 2017 started with Donald Trump being sworn in as the 45th President of the United States of America on 20 January, quickly followed by the announcement of a surprise snap General Election for the UK on 8 June which returned Theresa May as prime minister, but not with the majority she had hoped for. Negotiations between the Conservative Party and the Northern Ireland Democratic Unionist Party led to an agreement in which the ten DUP MPs agreed to back Theresa May's minority government in key Commons votes.

In Northern Ireland, the assembly collapsed on 9 January 2017 when the late Martin McGuinness resigned as Deputy First Minister. Under the joint protocols governing the NI power-sharing agreement, if either the first minister or the deputy resigns and a replacement is not nominated by the relevant party within seven days, then a snap election must be called. The assembly was formally dissolved at midnight on 25 January 2017 and elections were held on 2 March 2017 to elect the now 90 members of the legislative assembly. Following that election, negotiations to form an executive missed both the normal three-week deadline and an extended deadline of 29 June 2017 set by the Secretary of State for Northern Ireland. As both deadlines have passed the Northern Ireland secretary has a duty to set a date for a new election, but at the time of writing this duty is under review and the assembly remains suspended until an executive is formed.

On 29 March Theresa May announced that the UK had officially triggered Article 50 of the treaty on European union: 'in accordance with the wishes of the British people, the United Kingdom is leaving the European Union. This is an historic moment from which there can be no turning back.' Official negotiations between the EU and the UK to decide the terms of the UK's withdrawal from the EU began on 19 June 2017 and are set to be finalised by December 2017.

As always, a complete constituency-by-constituency list of the results from the 2017 General Election is included alongside a full list of MPs. The results of the NI Assembly election on 2 March can also be found in our chapter on Devolved Government.

All of this and much, much more about the UK can be found in this concise edition of *Whitaker's,* and regular updates to all the information will be available to our website subscribers throughout the year. Go to www.whitakersalmanack.com to subscribe to the whole site using discount code **WhitA2018Print**, or alternatively access individual sections of content for as little as £1 as and when required.

We hope you enjoy this edition; please do not hesitate to get in touch with us at: whitakersalmanackteam@bloomsbury.com with any comments or feedback, or stay up-to-date with all things Whitaker's by visiting our website and subscribing to our newsletter.

Ruth Northey
Executive Editor
www.whitakersalmanack.com

6

COVER PHOTOGRAPHS

Main image: Michel Barnier, chief negotiator for the European Union, meets Secretary of State for Exiting the European Union David Davis, ahead of the start of Brexit negotiations in Brussels, Belguim © Getty Images

Top, from left to right:
1. Lake District National Park became a UNESCO World Heritage site in 2017 © Getty Images
2. Newly elected 45th US President Donald Trump © Getty Images
3. Newly elected French President Emmanuel Macron © Getty Images
4. IPC World Para Athletics Championships 2017 London – Men's 400m T43 Final (left to right: Nick Rogers (USA), Hunter Woodhall (USA) and Johannes Floors (Germany) © Getty Images

SOURCES

Whitaker's was compiled with the assistance of the Press Association and the UK Hydrographic Office. Crown copyright material is reproduced with the permission of the Controller of Her Majesty's Stationery Office.

EDITORIAL STAFF

Executive Editor: Ruth Northey
Project Editor: James Robinson
Editorial Assistants: Millie Lean; George Salter
Head of Yearbooks: Katy McAdam

Thanks to Omer Ali, Lucy Beevor, John Bromham, Rob Hardy, Stephen Kershaw, Elizabeth Kingston, Hilary Marsden

CONTRIBUTORS (where not listed)
Sheridan Williams, Graham Relf (Astronomy); Anthea Lipsett, Caroline Macready (Education); Clive Longhurst (Insurance); Richard McMeeken, Chris Priestley (Legal Notes); Hilary Marsden (Taxation)

Terrestrial Magnetism data supplied by Dr Susan Macmillan of the British Geological Survey

Night Sky data supplied by John Flannery of the Irish Astronomical Society

THE YEAR 2018

THE YEAR 2018

CHRONOLOGICAL CYCLES AND ERAS

Dominical Letter	G
Epact	13
Golden Number (Lunar Cycle)	V
Julian Period	6731
Roman Indiction	11
Solar Cycle	11

	Beginning
*Muslim year AH 1439	22 Sep 2017
Japanese year Heisei 30	1 Jan
Roman year 2771 AUC	14Jan
Chinese year of the Dog	16 Feb
Regnal year 67	6 Feb
Sikh new year	14 Mar
Indian (Saka) year 1940	22 Mar
Hindu new year (Chaitra)	18 Mar
*Jewish year AM 5779	10 Sep

* Year begins at sunset on the previous day

RELIGIOUS CALENDARS

CHRISTIAN

Epiphany	6 Jan
Presentation of Christ in the Temple	2 Feb
Ash Wednesday	14 Feb
The Annunciation	25 Mar
Palm Sunday	25 Mar
Maundy Thursday	29 Mar
Good Friday	30 Mar
Easter Day (western churches)	1 Apr
Easter Day (Eastern Orthodox)	8 Apr
Rogation Sunday	6 May
Ascension Day	10 May
Pentecost (Whit Sunday)	20 May
Trinity Sunday	27 May
Corpus Christi	31 May
All Saints' Day	1 Nov
Advent Sunday	2 Dec
Christmas Day	25 Dec

HINDU

Makar Sankranti	14 Jan
Vasant Panchami (Sarasvati Puja)	22 Jan
Shivaratri	14 Feb
Holi	2 Mar
Chaitra (Spring new year)	18 Mar
Ram Navami	26 Mar
Raksha-bandhan	26 Aug
Krishna Janmashtami	3 Sep
Ganesh Chaturthi, first day	13 Sep
Navaratri festival (Durga Puja), first day	9 Oct
Dussehra	19 Oct
Diwali (New Year festival of lights), first day	7 Nov

JEWISH

Purim	1 Mar
Pesach (Passover), first day	31 Mar
Shavuot (Feast of Weeks), first day	20 May
Rosh Hashanah (Jewish new year)	10 Sep
Yom Kippur (Day of Atonement)	19 Sep
Succot (Feast of Tabernacles), first day	24 Sep
Hanukkah, first day	3 Dec

MUSLIM†

Al-Hijra (Muslim new year)	21 Sep 2017
Ashura	30 Sep 2017
Ramadan, first day	16 May
Eid-ul-Fitr	14 Jun
Hajj, first day	19 Aug
Eid-ul-Adha	21 Aug

† The Islamic calendar is lunar so religious dates may vary by one or two days locally and according to when the new Moon is first seen

SIKH

Birthday of Guru Gobind Singh Ji	5 Jan
‡Hola Mohalla	2 Mar
1 Chet (Sikh new year)	14 Mar
Baisakhi	14 Apr
Martyrdom of Guru Arjan Dev Ji	16 Jun
‡Birthday of Guru Nanak Dev Ji	23 Nov
Martyrdom of Guru Tegh Bahadur Ji	24 Nov

‡ Currently celebrated according to the lunar, rather than Nanakshahi, calendar, so the date varies annually

CIVIL CALENDAR

Duchess of Cambridge's birthday	9 Jan
Countess of Wessex's birthday	20 Jan
Accession of the Queen	6 Feb
Duke of York's birthday	19 Feb
St David's Day	1 Mar
Earl of Wessex's birthday	10 Mar
Commonwealth Day	12 Mar
St Patrick's Day	17 Mar
Birthday of the Queen	21 Apr
St George's Day	23 Apr
Europe Day	9 May
Coronation Day	2 Jun
The Queen's Official birthday	9 Jun
Duke of Edinburgh's birthday	10 Jun
Duke of Cambridge's birthday	21 Jun
Duchess of Cornwall's birthday	17 Jul
Princess Royal's birthday	15 Aug
Lord Mayor's Day	10 Nov
Remembrance Sunday	11 Nov
Prince of Wales' birthday	14 Nov
Wedding Day of the Queen	20 Nov
St Andrew's Day	30 Nov

LEGAL CALENDAR

LAW TERMS

Hilary Term	11 Jan to 28 Mar
Easter Term	10 Apr to 25 May
Trinity Term	5 Jun to 31 Jul
Michaelmas Term	1 Oct to 21 Dec

QUARTER DAYS	TERM DAYS
England, Wales and Northern Ireland	Scotland
Lady – 25 Mar	Candlemas – 28 Feb
Midsummer – 24 Jun	Whitsunday – 28 May
Michaelmas – 29 Sep	Lammas – 28 Aug
Christmas – 25 Dec	Martinmas – 28 Nov

2018

JANUARY
Sunday		7	14	21	28
Monday	1	8	15	22	29
Tuesday	2	9	16	23	30
Wednesday	3	10	17	24	31
Thursday	4	11	18	25	
Friday	5	12	19	26	
Saturday	6	13	20	27	

FEBRUARY
Sunday		4	11	18	25
Monday		5	12	19	26
Tuesday		6	13	20	27
Wednesday		7	14	21	28
Thursday	1	8	15	22	
Friday	2	9	16	23	
Saturday	3	10	17	24	

MARCH
Sunday		4	11	18	25
Monday		5	12	19	26
Tuesday		6	13	20	27
Wednesday		7	14	21	28
Thursday	1	8	15	22	29
Friday	2	9	16	23	30
Saturday	3	10	17	24	31

APRIL
Sunday	1	8	15	22	29
Monday	2	9	16	23	30
Tuesday	3	10	17	24	
Wednesday	4	11	18	25	
Thursday	5	12	19	26	
Friday	6	13	20	27	
Saturday	7	14	21	28	

MAY
Sunday		6	13	20	27
Monday		7	14	21	28
Tuesday	1	8	15	22	29
Wednesday	2	9	16	23	30
Thursday	3	10	17	24	31
Friday	4	11	18	25	
Saturday	5	12	19	26	

JUNE
Sunday		3	10	17	24
Monday		4	11	18	25
Tuesday		5	12	19	26
Wednesday		6	13	20	27
Thursday		7	14	21	28
Friday	1	8	15	22	29
Saturday	2	9	16	23	30

JULY
Sunday	1	8	15	22	29
Monday	2	9	16	23	30
Tuesday	3	10	17	24	31
Wednesday	4	11	18	25	
Thursday	5	12	19	26	
Friday	6	13	20	27	
Saturday	7	14	21	28	

AUGUST
Sunday		5	12	19	26
Monday		6	13	20	27
Tuesday		7	14	21	28
Wednesday	1	8	15	22	29
Thursday	2	9	16	23	30
Friday	3	10	17	24	31
Saturday	4	11	18	25	

SEPTEMBER
Sunday		2	9	16	23	30
Monday		3	10	17	24	
Tuesday		4	11	18	25	
Wednesday		5	12	19	26	
Thursday		6	13	20	27	
Friday		7	14	21	28	
Saturday	1	8	15	22	29	

OCTOBER
Sunday		7	14	21	28
Monday	1	8	15	22	29
Tuesday	2	9	16	23	30
Wednesday	3	10	17	24	31
Thursday	4	11	18	25	
Friday	5	12	19	26	
Saturday	6	13	20	27	

NOVEMBER
Sunday		4	11	18	25
Monday		5	12	19	26
Tuesday		6	13	20	27
Wednesday		7	14	21	28
Thursday	1	8	15	22	29
Friday	2	9	16	23	30
Saturday	3	10	17	24	

DECEMBER
Sunday		2	9	16	23	30
Monday		3	10	17	24	31
Tuesday		4	11	18	25	
Wednesday		5	12	19	26	
Thursday		6	13	20	27	
Friday		7	14	21	28	
Saturday	1	8	15	22	29	

PUBLIC HOLIDAYS	England and Wales	Scotland	Northern Ireland
New Year	1 January†	1, 2† January	1 January†
St Patrick's Day	—	—	19 March
*Good Friday	30 March	30 March	30 March
Easter Monday	2 April	—	2 April
Early May	7 May†	7 May	7 May†
Spring	28 May	28 May†	28 May
Battle of the Boyne	—	—	12 July‡
Summer	27 August	6 August	27 August
St Andrew's Day	—	30 November§	—
*Christmas	25, 26 December	25†, 26 December	25, 26 December

* In England, Wales and Northern Ireland, Christmas Day and Good Friday are common law holidays

† Subject to royal proclamation

‡ Subject to proclamation by the Secretary of State for Northern Ireland

§ The St Andrew's Day Holiday (Scotland) Bill was approved by parliament on 29 November 2006; it does not oblige employers to change their existing pattern of holidays but provides the legal framework in which the St Andrew's Day bank holiday could be substituted for an existing local holiday from another date in the year

Note: In the Channel Islands, Liberation Day is a bank and public holiday

2019

JANUARY
Sunday		6	13	20	27
Monday		7	14	21	28
Tuesday	1	8	15	22	29
Wednesday	2	9	16	23	30
Thursday	3	10	17	24	31
Friday	4	11	18	25	
Saturday	5	12	19	26	

FEBRUARY
Sunday		3	10	17	24
Monday		4	11	18	25
Tuesday		5	12	19	26
Wednesday		6	13	20	27
Thursday		7	14	21	28
Friday	1	8	15	22	
Saturday	2	9	16	23	

MARCH
Sunday		3	10	17	24	31
Monday		4	11	18	25
Tuesday		5	12	19	26
Wednesday		6	13	20	27
Thursday		7	14	21	28
Friday	1	8	15	22	29
Saturday	2	9	16	23	30

APRIL
Sunday		7	14	21	28
Monday	1	8	15	22	29
Tuesday	2	9	16	23	30
Wednesday	3	10	17	24	
Thursday	4	11	18	25	
Friday	5	12	19	26	
Saturday	6	13	20	27	

MAY
Sunday		5	12	19	26
Monday		6	13	20	27
Tuesday		7	14	21	28
Wednesday	1	8	15	22	29
Thursday	2	9	16	23	30
Friday	3	10	17	24	31
Saturday	4	11	18	25	

JUNE
Sunday		2	9	16	23	30
Monday		3	10	17	24
Tuesday		4	11	18	25
Wednesday		5	12	19	26
Thursday		6	13	20	27
Friday		7	14	21	28
Saturday	1	8	15	22	29

JULY
Sunday		7	14	21	28
Monday	1	8	15	22	29
Tuesday	2	9	16	23	30
Wednesday	3	10	17	24	31
Thursday	4	11	18	25	
Friday	5	12	19	26	
Saturday	6	13	20	27	

AUGUST
Sunday		4	11	18	25
Monday		5	12	19	26
Tuesday		6	13	20	27
Wednesday		7	14	21	28
Thursday	1	8	15	22	29
Friday	2	9	16	23	30
Saturday	3	10	17	24	31

SEPTEMBER
Sunday	1	8	15	22	29
Monday	2	9	16	23	30
Tuesday	3	10	17	24	
Wednesday	4	11	18	25	
Thursday	5	12	19	26	
Friday	6	13	20	27	
Saturday	7	14	21	28	

OCTOBER
Sunday		6	13	20	27
Monday		7	14	21	28
Tuesday	1	8	15	22	29
Wednesday	2	9	16	23	30
Thursday	3	10	17	24	31
Friday	4	11	18	25	
Saturday	5	12	19	26	

NOVEMBER
Sunday		3	10	17	24
Monday		4	11	18	25
Tuesday		5	12	19	26
Wednesday		6	13	20	27
Thursday		7	14	21	28
Friday	1	8	15	22	29
Saturday	2	9	16	23	30

DECEMBER
Sunday	1	8	15	22	29
Monday	2	9	16	23	30
Tuesday	3	10	17	24	31
Wednesday	4	11	18	25	
Thursday	5	12	19	26	
Friday	6	13	20	27	
Saturday	7	14	21	28	

PUBLIC HOLIDAYS	England and Wales	Scotland	Northern Ireland
New Year	1 January†	1, 2† January	1 January†
St Patrick's Day	—	—	18 March
*Good Friday	19 April	19 April	19 April
Easter Monday	22 April	—	22 April
Early May	6 May†	6 May	6 May†
Spring	27 May	27 May†	27 May
Battle of the Boyne	—	—	12 July‡
Summer	26 August	5 August	26 August
St Andrew's Day	—	2 December§	—
*Christmas	25, 26 December	25†, 26 December	25, 26 December

* In England, Wales and Northern Ireland, Christmas Day and Good Friday are common law holidays

† Subject to royal proclamation

‡ Subject to proclamation by the Secretary of State for Northern Ireland

§ The St Andrew's Day Holiday (Scotland) Bill was approved by parliament on 29 November 2006; it does not oblige employers to change their existing pattern of holidays but provides the legal framework in which the St Andrew's Day bank holiday could be substituted for an existing local holiday from another date in the year

Note: In the Channel Islands, Liberation Day is a bank and public holiday

FORTHCOMING EVENTS

* Provisional dates

JANUARY 2018

10–14	London Boat Show, Excel, London Docklands
12–21	London Short Film Festival
16–18	UK Open Dance Championships, Bournemouth
17–21	London Art Fair, Business Design Centre
18–4 Feb	Celtic Connections Music Festival, Glasgow

FEBRUARY

2	World Wetlands Day
7–25	Leicester Comedy Festival
18	British Academy Film Awards, Royal Opera House, London

MARCH

1	World Book Day
3	World Wildlife Day
8	International Women's Day
8–11	Crufts Dog Show, NEC, Birmingham
9–14	Belfast Children's Festival
14–20	BADA Antiques and Fine Art Fair, Duke of York Square, London
17–2 Apr	Ideal Home Show, Olympia, London
18	St Patrick's Day Parade, Piccadilly, London
21	World Poetry Day

APRIL

10–12	London Book Fair, Olympia, London
22	Earth Day
Late Apr	Stratford-upon-Avon Literary Festival

MAY

16–19	Museums at Night, London
19 May–26 Aug	Glyndebourne Festival
Mid May	Bath Festival
22–26	RHS Chelsea Flower Show, Royal Hospital, London
24–3 Jun	Hay Festival of Literature and the Arts, Hay-on-Wye

JUNE

Early-Jun	Strawberry Fair, Cambridge
6–10	RHS Chatsworth Flower Show, Derbyshire
9	Trooping the Colour, Horse Guards Parade, London
21–24	50th Isle of Wight Festival
21–24	Royal Highland Show, Edinburgh

JULY

3–8	RHS Hampton Court Palace Flower Show, Surrey
4–15	Cheltenham Music Festival
13–8 Sep	BBC Promenade Concerts, Royal Albert Hall, London
18–22	RHS Flower Show, Tatton Park, Cheshire
Mid-Jul	The Welsh Proms, St David's Hall, Cardiff
26–29	WOMAD Festival, Charlton Park, Wiltshire
28–4 Aug	Three Choirs Festival, Hereford

AUGUST

2–5	Cambridge Folk Festival
3–5	Brighton Pride, Brighton and Hove
3–11	National Eisteddfod of Wales, Anglesey
3–25	Edinburgh Military Tattoo, Edinburgh Castle
3–27	Edinburgh International Festival
Mid Aug	Brecon Jazz Festival
*25–26	Notting Hill Carnival, London

SEPTEMBER

1	Braemar Royal Highland Gathering, Aberdeenshire
*1–5 Nov	Blackpool Illuminations, Blackpool Promenade
8	International Literacy Day
*9–12	150th TUC Annual Congress
Mid Sept	Liberal Democrat Party Conference
Late Sept	Labour Party Conference

OCTOBER

Early Oct	Conservative Party Conference, Manchester
Early Oct	Frieze Art Fair, Regent's Park, London
Mid-Oct	Booker Prize Awards
Mid-Oct	BFI London Film Festival
25–27	Museums at Night, London

NOVEMBER

10 Nov	Lord Mayor's Procession and Show, City of London
Mid-Nov	CBI Annual Conference

SPORTS EVENTS

JANUARY 2018

6–14	Darts: BDO World Darts Championship, Lakeside
12–28	Bowls: World Indoor Bowls Championships, Great Yarmouth
14–21	Snooker: Masters, Alexandra Palace, London
15–28	Tennis: Australian Open, Melbourne, Australia

FEBRUARY

3–17 Mar	Rugby Union: Six Nations Championship, Europe
4	American Football: Super Bowl 52, Minneapolis, Minnesota, USA
9–25	XXIII Winter Olympic Games, Pyeongchang, South Korea
Mid Feb	Squash: British National Championships, Manchester
25	Football: EFL Cup Final, Wembley Stadium, London
28–4 Mar	Cycling: UCI Track Cycling World Championships, Appledorn, The Netherlands

MARCH

1–4	Athletics: European Indoor Championships, Birmingham
19–25 Apr	Figure Skating: World Championships, Milan, Italy
24	Rowing: The Boat Race, Putney to Mortlake, London
29–30 Sept	Baseball: Major League Baseball Season

APRIL

4–15	XXI Commonwealth Games, Gold Coast, Australia
5–8	Golf: Masters, Augusta, Georgia, USA
12–14	Horse Racing: Grand National, Aintree, Liverpool
21–7 May	Snooker: World Championship, Crucible Theatre, Sheffield
22	Athletics: London Marathon
26–6 May	Table Tennis: World Championships, Halmstad, Sweden

MAY

2–6	Equestrian: Badminton Horse Trials, Badminton
4–5	Horse Racing: Kentucky Derby, Louisville, Kentucky, USA
*5–6	Horse Racing: Guineas Festival, Newmarket
9–13	Equestrian: Royal Windsor Horse Show, Home Park, Windsor
11	Rugby Union: EuropeanChallenge Cup Final, Bilbao, Spain
12	Rugby Union: European Rugby Champions Cup Final, Bilbao, Spain
16	Football: UEFA Europa League Final, Leon, France
19	Football: FA Cup Final, Wembley Stadium, London
19	Football: Scottish Cup Final, Hampden Park, Glasgow
26	Football: UEFA Champions League Final, Olympic Stadium, Kiev, Ukraine

27	Motor Racing: Indianapolis 500, Indiana, USA
27–10 Jun	Tennis: French Open, Paris, France

JUNE

1	Horse Racing: The Derby, Epsom Downs
11–17	Golf: US Open, Southampton, New York, USA
14–15 July	Football: FIFA World Cup, Russia
19–23	Horse Racing: Royal Ascot

JULY

2–15	Tennis: Wimbledon Championships, All England Lawn Tennis Club, London
4–8	Rowing: Henley Royal Regatta, Henley-on-Thames
7–29	Cycling: Tour de France
15–22	Golf: Open Championship, Carnoustie
15–15 Aug	Fencing: World Championships, Wuxi, China
21–5 Aug	Hockey: Women's World Cup, London
29–4 Aug	Squash: World Masters Championships, Charlottesville, Virginia, USA
Late Jul	Horse Racing: King George VI and Queen Elizabeth Diamond Stakes, Ascot

AUGUST

3–12	Aquatics: European Championships, Glasgow
6–12	Golf: PGA Championship, Bellerive Country Club, Missouri, USA
15	Football: UEFA Super Cup final, Tallinn, Estonia
20–26	Athletics: European ParaAthletics Championships, Berlin, Germany
27–10 Sep	Tennis: US Open, New York
30–2 Sep	Equestrian: Burghley Horse Trials, Stamford, Lincolnshire

SEPTEMBER

Early Sep	Horse Racing: St Leger, Doncaster
Early Sep–Late Dec	American Football: NFL Season
9	Athletics: Great North Run, Newcastle
9–16	Rowing: World Championships, Plovdiv, Bulgaria
25–30	Golf: Ryder Cup, Paris, France

OCTOBER

Late Oct–Early Nov	Baseball: World Series

NOVEMBER

*4	Athletics: New York City Marathon, New York, USA
12–18	Tennis: ATP World Tour Finals, O2 Arena, London
24–3 Dec	Weightlifting: IWF World Championships, Lima, Peru
28–16 Dec	Hockey: Men's World Cup, Bhubaneswar, India

DECEMBER

7–11	Swimming: FINA World Swimming Championships (25m), Hangzhou, China

CENTENARIES

2017

1517

17 Jan — Henry Grey, 1st Duke of Suffolk and father of Lady Jane Grey, born

31 Oct — Martin Luther posted his Ninety-Five Theses on a church door in Wittenberg

21 Nov — Sikandar Lodi, Sultan of Delhi, died

1617

21 Mar — Pocahontas, Native American noblewoman, died

4 Apr — John Napier, mathematician who discovered logarithms, died

1717

19 Feb — David Garrick, actor and manager of the Drury Lane Theatre, born

13 May — Maria Theresa, Austrian Holy Roman Empress, born

24 Jun — The first Masonic Grand Lodge was founded in St. Paul's Churchyard

5 Sep — King George I issued the Act of Grace, pardoning all pirates

24 Sep — Horace Walpole, gothic novelist and son of Robert Walpole, born

1817

19 Jan — Argentine general José de San Martín led an army across the Andes into Chile

25 Jan — The Scotsman was published for the first time in Edinburgh

8 Mar — The New York Stock Exchange was founded

12 Jul — Henry David Thoreau, American author and naturalist, born

17 Jul — Premier of Handel's Water Music in London

18 Jul — Jane Austen, novelist, died

5 Nov — The British East India Company defeated the Maratha Empire at the battle of Khadki

22 Nov — The Roman emerald mines at Sikait, Egypt were discovered

7 Dec — William Bligh, captain of the HMS Bounty, died

1917

10 Jan — William Frederick Cody, American frontiersman known as Buffalo Bill, died

12 Jan — Maharishi Mahesh Yogi, guru and spiritual leader, born

2 Feb — Bread rationing was introduced in the UK

8 Mar — Ferdinand von Zeppelin, German airship inventor, died

20 Mar — Vera Lynn, actor and singer, born

9 Apr — The First World War Battle of Vimy Ridge began in France

25 Apr — Ella Fitzgerald, American jazz singer, born

29 May — John F. Kennedy, 35th president of the USA, born

7 Jun — Dean Martin, American singer and member of the 'Rat Pack', born

10 Jun — Eric Hobsbawm, historian, born

17 Jul — The British Royal Family adopted the surname Windsor

31 Jul — Battle of Passchendaele (Third Battle of Ypres) began in Flanders, Belgium

28 Aug — Jack Kirby, American comic book artist, born

8 Nov — Colin Blythe, cricketer, died

16 Dec — Arthur C. Clarke, science fiction author, born

2018

1518

29 Sep — Tintoretto, Italian painter, born

3 Oct — Cardinal Wolsey's Treaty of London temporarily assured peace in Europe

1618

20 Feb — Philip William, Prince of Orange, died

23 May — The Thirty Years War began, initiated by the Second Defenestration of Prague

29 Oct — Sir Walter Raleigh, English explorer, writer and courtier, executed on charges of treason

1718

7 May — The city of New Orleans was founded by Jean-Baptiste Le Moyne de Bienville

5 Jun — Thomas Chippendale, English furniture maker, born

18 Nov — Voltaire's first play, Oedipe, premiered in Paris

22 Nov — Edward Teach, English pirate known as 'Blackbeard', died

17 Dec — France, Britain, the Dutch Republic and the Holy Roman Empire declared war on Spain (War of the Quadruple Alliance 1718–20)

1818

11 Jan — Percy Bysshe Shelley's poem 'Ozymandias' was published under a pseudonym in The Examiner

12 Feb — Chile proclaimed independence from the Spanish Empire

14 Feb — Adopted birthday of Frederick Douglass, African American abolitionist author and statesman

11 Mar — Mary Shelley's novel Frankenstein was published anonymously

8 Apr — King Christian IX of Denmark, born

5 May — Karl Marx, German political philosopher, born

30 Jul — Emily Brontë, English novelist and author of Wuthering Heights, born

24 Dec — The Christmas Carol 'Silent Night' ('Stille Nacht') was performed for the first time in Austria

1918

25 Jan — The Ukranian People's Republic declared independence from Russia

1 Feb — Muriel Spark, Scottish author, born

6 Feb — The Representation of the People Act gave most UK women the vote

6 Feb — Gustav Klimt, Austrian painter, died

3 Mar — The Treaty of Brest-Litovsk was signed, ending Russian involvement in the First World War

25 Mar — Claude Debussy, French composer, died

1 Apr — The Royal Air Force was formed

8 Apr — Betty Ford, US First Lady, born

16 Apr — Spike Milligan, comedian, writer and actor, born

21 Apr — Manfred von Richthofen, German fighter pilot known as 'the Red Baron', died in combat

18 Jul — Tsar Nicholas II and his family were executed at Yekaterinburg, ending the Romanov dynasty

18 Jul — Nelson Mandela, South African president, born

29 Sep — Allied forces breached the German Hindenburg Line

17 Oct — Rita Hayworth, American actor, born

3 Nov — Poland declared independence from Russia

11 Nov — An armistice between the Allies and Germany was signed at Compiègne, France, ending the First World War

13 Nov	Allied occupation of Constantinople began
11 Dec	Aleksandr Solzhenitsyn, Russian writer, born
28 Dec	David Lloyd George's coalition government won the UK general election, while Sinn Fein claimed a landslide victory in Ireland

2019

1519

13 Mar	Conquistador Hernán Cortés landed in Mexico
28 Jun	Charles V became Holy Roman Emperor

1619

7 Jan	Nicholas Hilliard, painter, died
18 May	Hugo de Groot was given life imprisonment
10 Nov	Rene Descartes had dreams that inspired *Meditations on First Philosophy*

1719

23 Jan	The principality of Liechtenstein was established
25 Apr	Daniel Defoe published *Robinson Crusoe*
20 Aug	Christian Mayer, astronomer, born
11 Dec	A sighting of aurora borealis was recorded for the first time

1819

2 Mar	USA passed its first federal legislation on immigration
11 Mar	Sir Henry Tate, founder of the Tate Gallery, born
22 May	SS Savannah departed on the first steam propelled journey across the atlantic ocean
24 May	Queen Victoria, born
19 Aug	James Watt, developer of the steam engine, died

1919

1 Jan	Jerome Salinger, novelist, born
6 Jan	Theodore Roosevelt, 26th US President, died
21 Jan	Sinn Féin created its own parliament
25 Jan	The League of Nations was established
23 Mar	Benito Mussolini formed Fasci Italiani di Combattimento
13 Apr	The Amritsar massacre took place
29 May	Arthur Eddington validated Albert Einstein's theory of general relativity
20 Jul	Edmund Hillary, explorer and mountaineer, born
11 Aug	Germany established parliamentary democracy
19 Aug	Adolf Hitler joined the German Workers' Party
12 Sep	Afganistan became independent
22 Oct	Doris Lessing, Nobel Prize winning author, born
3 Dec	Pierre-Auguste Renoir, painter, died

THE UNITED KINGDOM

THE UK IN FIGURES

The United Kingdom comprises Great Britain (England, Wales and Scotland) and Northern Ireland. The Isle of Man and the Channel Islands are Crown dependencies with their own legislative systems and are not part of the UK.

ABBREVIATIONS
ONS   Office for National Statistics
NISRA   Northern Ireland Statistics and Research Agency

All data is for the UK unless otherwise stated.

AREA OF THE UNITED KINGDOM

	Sq. km	Sq. miles
United Kingdom	243,122	93,870
England	130,280	50,301
Wales	20,733	8,005
Scotland	77,958	30,100
Northern Ireland	14,150	5,463

Source: ONS (Crown copyright)

POPULATION

The first official census of population in England, Wales and Scotland was taken in 1801 and a census has been taken every ten years since, except in 1941 when there was no census because of the Second World War. The last official census in the UK was taken on 27 March 2011.

The first official census of population in Ireland was taken in 1841. However, all figures given below refer only to the area which is now Northern Ireland. Figures for Northern Ireland in 1921 and 1931 are estimates based on the censuses taken in 1926 and 1937 respectively.

Estimates of the population of England before 1801, calculated from the number of baptisms, burials and marriages, are:

1570	4,160,221	1670	5,773,646
1600	4,811,718	1700	6,045,008
1630	5,600,517	1750	6,517,035

Further details are available on the ONS website (W www.ons.gov.uk).

CENSUS RESULTS (THOUSANDS)

	United Kingdom			England and Wales			Scotland			Northern Ireland		
	Total	Male	Female	Total	Male	Female	Total	Male	Female	Total	Male	Female
1801	–	–	–	8,893	4,255	4,638	1,608	739	869	–	–	–
1811	13,368	6,368	7,000	10,165	4,874	5,291	1,806	826	980	–	–	–
1821	15,472	7,498	7,974	12,000	5,850	6,150	2,092	983	1,109	–	–	–
1831	17,835	8,647	9,188	13,897	6,771	7,126	2,364	1,114	1,250	–	–	–
1841	20,183	9,819	10,364	15,914	7,778	8,137	2,620	1,242	1,378	1,649	800	849
1851	22,259	10,855	11,404	17,928	8,781	9,146	2,889	1,376	1,513	1,443	698	745
1861	24,525	11,894	12,631	20,066	9,776	10,290	3,062	1,450	1,612	1,396	668	728
1871	27,431	13,309	14,122	22,712	11,059	11,653	3,360	1,603	1,757	1,359	647	712
1881	31,015	15,060	15,955	25,974	12,640	13,335	3,736	1,799	1,936	1,305	621	684
1891	34,264	16,593	17,671	29,003	14,060	14,942	4,026	1,943	2,083	1,236	590	646
1901	38,237	18,492	19,745	32,528	15,729	16,799	4,472	2,174	2,298	1,237	590	647
1911	42,082	20,357	21,725	36,070	17,446	18,625	4,761	2,309	2,452	1,251	603	648
1921	44,027	21,033	22,994	37,887	18,075	19,811	4,882	2,348	2,535	1,258	610	648
1931	46,038	22,060	23,978	39,952	19,133	20,819	4,843	2,326	2,517	1,243	601	642
1951	50,225	24,118	26,107	43,758	21,016	22,742	5,096	2,434	2,662	1,371	668	703
1961	52,709	25,481	27,228	46,105	22,304	23,801	5,179	2,483	2,697	1,425	694	731
1971	55,515	26,952	28,562	48,750	23,683	25,067	5,229	2,515	2,714	1,536	755	781
1981	55,848	27,104	28,742	49,155	23,873	25,281	5,131	2,466	2,664	1,533*	750	783
1991	56,467	27,344	29,123	49,890	24,182	25,707	4,999	2,392	2,607	1,578	769	809
2001	58,789	28,581	30,208	52,042	25,327	26,715	5,062	2,432	2,630	1,685	821	864
2011	63,182	31,028	32,153	56,076	27,574	28,502	5,295	2,567	2,728	1,810	887	923

* Figure includes 44,500 non-enumerated persons

ISLANDS

	Isle of Man			Jersey			Guernsey		
	Total	Male	Female	Total	Male	Female	Total	Male	Female
1901	54,752	25,496	29,256	52,576	23,940	28,636	40,446	19,652	20,794
1921	60,284	27,329	32,955	49,701	22,438	27,263	38,315	18,246	20,069
1951	55,123	25,749	29,464	57,296	27,282	30,014	43,652	21,221	22,431
1971	56,289	26,461	29,828	72,532	35,423	37,109	51,458	24,792	26,666
1991	69,788	33,693	36,095	84,082	40,862	43,220	58,867	28,297	30,570
2001	76,315	37,372	38,943	87,186	42,485	44,701	59,807	29,138	30,669
2006	80,058	39,523	40,535	–	–	–	–	–	–
2011	84,497	41,971	42,526	97,857	48,296	49,561	62,915	31,025	31,890

Source: Guernsey Annual Publication Bulletin, Isle of Man Government, States of Jersey Statistics Unit

RESIDENT POPULATION

ACTUAL AND PROJECTED BY COUNTRY
people, thousands

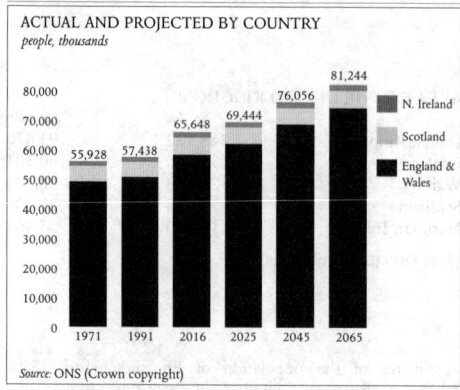

Source: ONS (Crown copyright)

PROJECTED AGE DISTRIBUTION, 2016 AND 2065
percentage

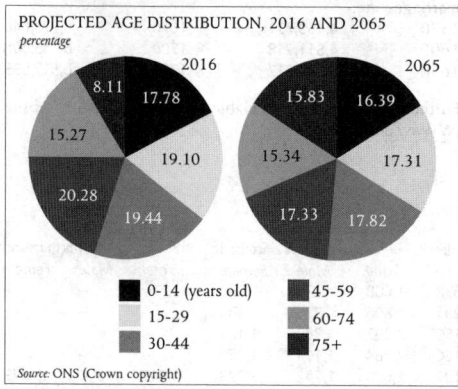

Source: ONS (Crown copyright)

NON-UK BORN RESIDENTS BY COUNTRY OF BIRTH
thousands

	2004	2016
Poland	94	911
India	505	833
Pakistan	285	534
Republic of Ireland	453	389
Romania	–	310
Germany	276	292
Bangladesh	228	227
China	152	211
South Africa	181	210
Italy	–	196

Source: ONS (Crown Copyright)

BY AGE AND SEX (UK), 2016
people, thousands

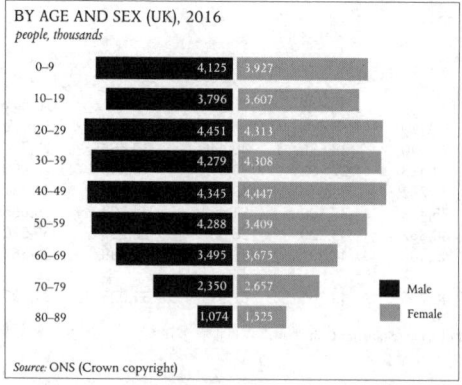

Source: ONS (Crown copyright)

ASYLUM

NATIONALITIES APPLYING FOR UK ASYLUM
year ending in March

Top 5 Nationalities	2015	2016
1) Iran	3,242	4,192
2) Pakistan	2,470	2,857
3) Iraq	2,216	2,666
4) Afghanistan	2,261	2,341
5) Bangladesh	1,110	1,939

Source: Home Office, National Statistics: Asylum

BIRTHS

	Live births 2016	Birth rate* 2016
United Kingdom	774,849	11.8
England and Wales	696,271	12.1
Scotland	54,488	10.2
Northern Ireland	24,090	13.0

* Live births per 1,000 population
Source: General Register Office for Scotland, NISRA, ONS (Crown copyright)

FERTILITY RATES
Total fertility rate is the average number of children which would be born to a woman if she experienced the age-specific fertility rates of the period in question throughout her child-bearing life span. The figures for the years 1960–2 are estimates.

	1960–2	2000	2016
United Kingdom	3.07	1.62	1.76
England and Wales	2.77	1.65	1.80
Scotland	2.98	1.48	1.52
Northern Ireland	3.47	1.75	1.95

Source: General Register Office for Scotland, NISRA, ONS (Crown copyright)

MATERNITY RATES FOR ENGLAND AND WALES 2015

	All maternities*	Singleton	All multiple†	Twins	Triplets
All ages	689,751	678,678	11,073	10,901	169
	23,925	23,780	145	142	2
20–24	107,603	106,590	1,013	1,006	7
25–29	196,363	193,758	2,605	2,571	33
30–34	214,870	211,163	3,707	3,644	62
35–39	118,524	115,863	2,661	2,619	41
40–44	26,474	25,736	738	722	16
45+	1,992	1,788	204	196	8

* Includes stillbirths
† Total includes rates for twins, triplets, quads and above
Source: ONS (Crown copyright)

TOP TEN BABY NAMES (ENGLAND AND WALES)

	1914		2016	
	Girls	Boys	Girls	Boys
1	Mary	John	Olivia	Oliver
2	Margaret	William	Amelia	Harry
3	Doris	George	Emily	George
4	Dorothy	Thomas	Isla	Jack
5	Kathleen	James	Ava	Jacob
6	Florence	Arthur	Isabella	Noah
7	Elsie	Frederick	Lily	Charlie
8	Edith	Albert	Jessica	Muhammad
9	Elizabeth	Charles	Ella	Thomas
10	Winifred	Robert	Mia	Oscar

Source: ONS (Crown copyright)

LIVE BIRTHS (ENGLAND AND WALES)
by age of mother and registration type

Outside marriage/civil partnership

Year	under 20	20–29	30–39	40+	All ages
1944	7,257	33,107	13,202	1,607	55,173
1964	17,372	32,633	11,589	1,746	63,340
1984	33,135	61,714	14,685	931	110,465
2004	41,031	141,232	80,385	6,352	269,724
2014	24,812	186,918	107,243	7,076	330,235

Within marriage/civil partnership

Year	under 20	20–29	30–39	40+	All ages
1944	17,468	362,252	284,314	32,271	696,305
1964	59,362	514,170	217,295	21,805	812,632
1984	21,373	347,772	151,010	6,198	526,353
2004	4,063	139,824	212,393	13,717	269,997
2014	1,165	122,515	223,570	17,748	364,998

Source: ONS (Crown copyright)

MARRIAGE AND DIVORCE

	Marriages 2015	Divorces 2015
United Kingdom	285,139	116,307
England and Wales	*247,372	*101,055
Scotland	†29,412	12,892
Northern Ireland	8,355	2,360

* Figures for England and Wales are for 2014
† Figures for Scotland are for 2016
Source: NISRA, ONS (Crown copyright), Scottish Government

LEGAL ABORTIONS

	2005	2016
England and Wales	186,416	185,596
Scotland	12,665	12,063

Source: Department of Health, NHS Scotland

DEATHS

INFANT MORTALITY RATE 2015*

United Kingdom	4.0
England and Wales	3.7
Scotland	3.2
Northern Ireland	5.1

* Deaths of infants under one year of age per 1,000 live births
Source: NISRA, ONS (Crown copyright), Scottish Government

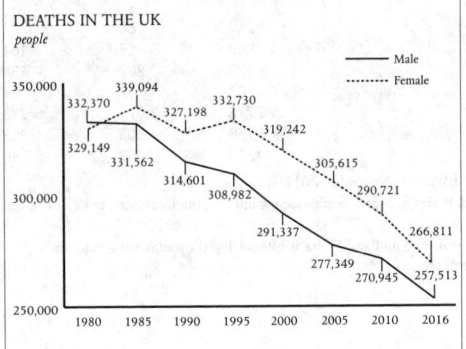

DEATHS IN THE UK
people

Source: ONS (Crown copyright)

EMPLOYMENT

MEDIAN FULL-TIME GROSS ANNUAL EARNINGS BY REGION (£)

Region	2005	2015
UK	22,888	27,645
England	23,280	27,872
North East	20,263	25,346
North West	21,777	25,681
Yorkshire and the Humber	21,506	25,180
East Midlands	21,494	25,003
West Midlands	21,447	25,779
East	22,883	27,299
London	29,882	35,333
South East	24,229	29,036
South West	21,279	25,982
Wales	20,634	24,733
Scotland	21,312	27,710
Northern Ireland	20,060	25,847

Source: ONS (Crown Copyright)

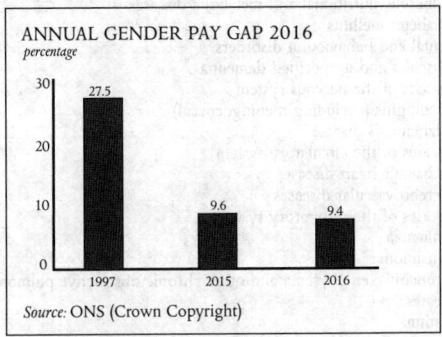

ANNUAL GENDER PAY GAP 2016
percentage

Source: ONS (Crown Copyright)

OVERSEAS VISITS TO THE UK

Year	Visits (thousands)	Spending (£m)
1980	12,419	2,961
1985	14,450	5,442
1990	18,017	7,748
1995	23,538	11,762
2000	25,207	12,806
2005	29,970	14,247
2010	29,804	16,714
2011	30,798	17,998
2012	31,085	18,640
2013	32,689	21,259
2014	34,380	21,851
2015	36,115	22,072
2016	37,610	22,544

DEATHS BY CAUSE, 2016

	England and Wales*	Scotland	N. Ireland
Total deaths	529,655	56,728	15,433
Deaths from natural causes	508,879	53,657	14,764
Certain infectious and parasitic diseases	5,783	753	175
Intestinal infectious diseases	1,363	144	53
Respiratory and other tuberculosis	281	17	6
Meningococcal infection	65	4	1
Viral hepatitis	282	26	2
Human immunodeficiency virus (HIV)	171	24	1
Neoplasms	147,757	16,245	4,666
Malignant neoplasms	144,330	15,901	4,539
Malignant neoplasm of trachea, bronchus and lung	30,520	4,068	990
Malignant melanoma of skin	2,210	162	63
Malignant neoplasm of breast	10,266	1,029	293
Malignant neoplasm of cervix uteri	720	106	19
Malignant neoplasm of prostate	10,579	894	262
Leukaemia	4,142	395	139
Diseases of the blood and blood-forming organs and certain disorders involving the immune mechanism	1,130	114	39
Endocrine, nutritional and metabolic diseases	7,669	1,149	294
Diabetes mellitus	5,582	879	160
Mental and behavioural disorders	48,317	4,427	1,392
Vascular and unspecified dementia	47,363	3,608	1,267
Diseases of the nervous system	28,373	3,418	925
Meningitis (excluding meningococcal)	155	4	2
Alzheimer's disease	14,323	1,963	493
Diseases of the circulatory system	138,614	15,132	3,630
Ischaemic heart diseases	60,818	6,697	1,825
Cerebrovascular diseases	34,883	4,142	988
Diseases of the respiratory system	75,534	7,296	1,973
Influenza	274	115	10
Pneumonia	29,601	1,800	794
Bronchitis, emphysema and other chronic obstructive pulmonary diseases	29,066	3,146	819
Asthma	1,302	121	44
Diseases of the digestive system	25,101	3,041	776
Gastric and duodenal ulcer	1,924	107	28
Diseases of the liver	7,974	1,088	304
Diseases of the skin and subcutaneous tissue	1,901	171	24
Diseases of the musculo-skeletal system and connective tissue	4,063	405	120
Osteoporosis	954	66	13
Diseases of the genitourinary system	9,359	1,091	251
Complications of pregnancy, childbirth and the puerperium	29	5	2
Certain conditions originating in the perinatal period*	190	97	66
Congenital malformations, deformations and chromosomal abnormalities†	1,257	180	72
Symptoms, signs and abnormal findings not classified elsewhere	11,849	485	161
Senility	8,179	207	136
Sudden infant death syndrome	101	18	4
Deaths from external causes	20,776	3,071	773
Suicide and intentional self-harm	4,150	603	305
Assault	‡299	53	30

* 2015 data; the provisional release date 2016 data concerning England and Wales is November 2017

† Excludes neonatal deaths (those at age under 28 days): for England and Wales neonatal deaths are included in the total number of deaths but excluded from the cause figures

‡ This will not be a true figure as registration of homicide and assault deaths in England and Wales is often delayed by adjourned inquests

Source: General Register Office for Scotland, NISRA, ONS (Crown copyright)

THE NATIONAL FLAG

The national flag of the United Kingdom is the Union Flag, generally known as the Union Jack.

The Union Flag is a combination of the cross of St George, patron saint of England, the cross of St Andrew, patron saint of Scotland and the cross of St Patrick, patron saint of Ireland.

Cross of St George: cross Gules in a field Argent (red cross on a white ground)

Cross of St Andrew: saltire Argent in a field Azure (white diagonal cross on a blue ground)

Cross of St Patrick: saltire Gules in a field Argent (red diagonal cross on a white ground)

A flag combining the cross of St George and the cross of St Andrew was first introduced by royal decree in 1606 following the conjoining of the English and Scottish crowns in 1603. In 1707 this flag became the flag of Great Britain after the parliaments of the two kingdoms were united. The cross of St Patrick was added in 1801 after the union of Great Britain and Ireland.

FLYING THE UNION FLAG

The correct orientation of the Union Flag when flying is with the broader diagonal band of white uppermost in the hoist (ie near the pole) and the narrower diagonal band of white uppermost in the fly (ie furthest from the pole).

The flying of the Union Flag on government buildings is decided by the Department for Culture, Media and Sport (DCMS) at the Queen's command. There is no formal definition of a government building but it is generally accepted to mean a building owned or used by the Crown and/or predominantly occupied or used by civil servants or the Armed Forces.

The Scottish or Welsh governments are responsible for drawing up their own flag-flying guidance for their buildings. In Northern Ireland, the flying of flags is constrained by The Flags Regulations (Northern Ireland) 2000 and the Police Emblems and Flag Regulations (Northern Ireland) 2002. Individuals, local authorities and other organisations may fly the Union Flag whenever they wish, subject to compliance with any local planning requirement.

FLAGS AT HALF-MAST

Flags are flown at half-mast (ie two-thirds up between the top and bottom of the flagstaff) on the following occasions:
- from the announcement of the death of the sovereign until the funeral
- the death or funeral of a member of the royal family*
- the funerals of foreign rulers*
- the funerals of prime ministers and ex-prime ministers of the UK*
- the funerals of first ministers and ex-first ministers of Scotland, Wales and Northern Ireland (unless otherwise commanded by the sovereign, this only applies to flags in their respective countries)*
- other occasions by special command from the Queen

* By special command from the Queen in each case

DAYS FOR FLYING FLAGS

On 25 March 2008 the DCMS announced that UK government departments in England, Scotland and Wales may fly the Union Flag on their buildings whenever they choose and not just on the designated days listed below. In addition, on the patron saints' days of Scotland and Wales, the appropriate national flag may be flown alongside the Union Flag on UK government buildings in the wider Whitehall area. When flying on designated days flags are hoisted from 8am to sunset.

Duchess of Cambridge's birthday	9 Jan
Countess of Wessex's birthday	20 Jan
Accession of the Queen	6 Feb
Duke of York's birthday	19 Feb
St David's Day (in Wales only)*	1 Mar
Earl of Wessex's birthday	10 Mar
Commonwealth Day (2018)	12 Mar
St Patrick's Day (in Northern Ireland only)†	17 Mar
The Queen's birthday	21 Apr
St George's Day (in England only)*	23 Apr
Europe Day†	9 May
Coronation Day	2 Jun
The Queen's official birthday (2018)	9 Jun
Duke of Edinburgh's birthday	10 Jun
Duke of Cambridge's birthday	21 June
Duchess of Cornwall's birthday	17 Jul
Princess Royal's birthday	15 Aug
Remembrance Day (2018)	11 Nov
Prince of Wales' birthday	14 Nov
Wedding Day of the Queen	20 Nov
St Andrew's Day (in Scotland only)*	30 Nov

Opening of parliament by the Queen‡
Prorogation of parliament by the Queen‡

* The appropriate national flag, or the European flag, may be flown in addition to the Union Flag (where there are two or more flagpoles), but not in a superior position
† Only the Union Flag should be flown
‡ Only in the Greater London area, whether or not the Queen performs the ceremony in person

THE ROYAL STANDARD

The Royal Standard comprises four quarterings – two for England (three lions passant), one for Scotland* (a lion rampant) and one for Ireland (a harp).

The Royal Standard is flown when the Queen is in residence at a royal palace, on transport being used by the Queen for official journeys and from Victoria Tower when the Queen attends parliament. It may also be flown on any building (excluding ecclesiastical buildings) during a visit by the Queen. If the Queen is to be present in a building, advice on flag flying can be obtained from the DCMS.

The Royal Standard is never flown at half-mast, even after the death of the sovereign, as the new monarch immediately succeeds to the throne.

* In Scotland a version with two Scottish quarterings is used

THE ROYAL FAMILY

THE SOVEREIGN

ELIZABETH II, by the Grace of God, of the United Kingdom of Great Britain and Northern Ireland and of her other Realms and Territories Queen, Head of the Commonwealth, Defender of the Faith
Her Majesty Elizabeth Alexandra Mary of Windsor, elder daughter of King George VI and of HM Queen Elizabeth the Queen Mother
Born 21 April 1926, at 17 Bruton Street, London W1
Ascended the throne 6 February 1952
Crowned 2 June 1953, at Westminster Abbey
Married 20 November 1947, in Westminster Abbey, HRH the Prince Philip, Duke of Edinburgh
Official residences Buckingham Palace, London SW1A 1AA; Windsor Castle, Berks; Palace of Holyroodhouse, Edinburgh
Private residences Sandringham, Norfolk; Balmoral Castle, Aberdeenshire

HUSBAND OF THE QUEEN

HRH THE PRINCE PHILIP, DUKE OF EDINBURGH, KG, KT, OM, GBE, Royal Victorian Chain, AK, QSO, PC, Ranger of Windsor Park
Born 10 June 1921, son of Prince and Princess Andrew of Greece and Denmark, naturalised a British subject 1947, created Duke of Edinburgh, Earl of Merioneth and Baron Greenwich 1947

CHILDREN OF THE QUEEN

HRH THE PRINCE OF WALES (Prince Charles Philip Arthur George), KG, KT, GCB, OM and Great Master of the Order of the Bath, AK, QSO, PC, ADC(P)
Born 14 November 1948, created Prince of Wales and Earl of Chester 1958, succeeded as Duke of Cornwall, Duke of Rothesay, Earl of Carrick and Baron Renfrew, Lord of the Isles and Great Steward of Scotland 1952
Married (1) 29 July 1981 Lady Diana Frances Spencer (Diana, Princess of Wales (1961–97), youngest daughter of the 8th Earl Spencer and the Hon. Mrs Shand Kydd), marriage dissolved 1996; (2) 9 April 2005 Mrs Camilla Rosemary Parker Bowles, now HRH the Duchess of Cornwall, GCVO, PC (*born* 17 July 1947, daughter of Major Bruce Shand and the Hon. Mrs Rosalind Shand)
Residences Clarence House, London SW1A 1BA; Highgrove, Doughton, Tetbury, Glos GL8 8TN; Birkhall, Ballater, Aberdeenshire
Issue
1. HRH Duke of Cambridge (Prince William Arthur Philip Louis), KG, KT, PC *born* 21 June 1982, *created* Duke of Cambridge, Earl of Strathearn and Baron Carrickfergus 2011 *married* 29 April 2011 Catherine Elizabeth Middleton, now HRH the Duchess of Cambridge (*born* 9 January 1982, elder daughter of Michael and Carole Middleton), and has issue, HRH Prince George of Cambridge (Prince George Alexander Louis), *born* 22 July 2013; HRH Princess Charlotte of Cambridge (Princess Charlotte Elizabeth Diana), *born* 2 May 2015 *Residence* Kensington Palace, London W8 4PU; Anmer Hall, Norfolk PE31 6RW
2. HRH Prince Henry of Wales (Prince Henry Charles Albert David), KCVO *born* 15 September 1984 *Residence* Nottingham Cottage, Kensington Palace, London W8 4PU

HRH THE PRINCESS ROYAL (Princess Anne Elizabeth Alice Louise), KG, KT, GCVO
Born 15 August 1950, declared the Princess Royal 1987
Married (1) 14 November 1973 Captain Mark Anthony Peter Phillips, CVO (*born* 22 September 1948); marriage dissolved 1992; (2) 12 December 1992 Vice-Adm. Sir Timothy James Hamilton Laurence, KCVO, CB, ADC (P) (*born* 1 March 1955)
Residence Gatcombe Park, Minchinhampton, Glos GL6 9AT
Issue
1. Peter Mark Andrew Phillips, *born* 15 November 1977, *married* 17 May 2008 Autumn Patricia Kelly, and has issue, Savannah Phillips, *born* 29 December 2010; Isla Elizabeth Phillips, *born* 29 March 2012
2. Zara Anne Elizabeth Tindall, MBE, *born* 15 May 1981, *married* 30 July 2011 Michael James Tindall, MBE, and has issue, Mia Grace Tindall, *born* 17 January 2014

HRH THE DUKE OF YORK (Prince Andrew Albert Christian Edward), KG, GCVO, ADC(P)
Born 19 February 1960, created Duke of York, Earl of Inverness and Baron Killyleagh 1986
Married 23 July 1986 Sarah Margaret Ferguson, now Sarah, Duchess of York (*born* 15 October 1959, younger daughter of Major Ronald Ferguson and Mrs Hector Barrantes), marriage dissolved 1996
Residence Royal Lodge, Windsor Great Park, Berks
Issue
1. HRH Princess Beatrice of York (Princess Beatrice Elizabeth Mary), *born* 8 August 1988
2. HRH Princess Eugenie of York (Princess Eugenie Victoria Helena), *born* 23 March 1990

HRH THE EARL OF WESSEX (Prince Edward Antony Richard Louis), KG, GCVO, ADC(P)
Born 10 March 1964, created Earl of Wessex, Viscount Severn 1999
Married 19 June 1999 Sophie Helen Rhys-Jones, now HRH the Countess of Wessex, GCVO (*born* 20 January 1965, daughter of Mr and Mrs Christopher Rhys-Jones)
Residence Bagshot Park, Bagshot, Surrey GU19 5HS
Issue
1. Lady Louise Mountbatten-Windsor (Louise Alice Elizabeth Mary Mountbatten-Windsor), *born* 8 November 2003
2. Viscount Severn (James Alexander Philip Theo Mountbatten-Windsor), *born* 17 December 2007

NEPHEW AND NIECE OF THE QUEEN

Children of HRH the Princess Margaret, Countess of Snowdon and the Earl of Snowdon (*see* House of Windsor):
EARL OF SNOWDON (DAVID ALBERT CHARLES ARMSTRONG-JONES), *born* 3 November 1961, *married* 8 October 1993 Hon. Serena Alleyne Stanhope, and has issue, Viscount Linley (Charles Patrick Inigo Armstrong-Jones), *born* 1 July 1999; Lady Margarita Armstrong-Jones (Margarita Elizabeth Alleyne Armstrong-Jones), *born* 14 May 2002
LADY SARAH CHATTO (Sarah Frances Elizabeth), *born* 1 May 1964, *married* 14 July 1994 Daniel Chatto, and has issue, Samuel David Benedict Chatto, *born* 28 July 1996; Arthur Robert Nathaniel Chatto, *born* 5 February 1999

COUSINS OF THE QUEEN

Child of HRH the Duke of Gloucester and HRH Princess Alice, Duchess of Gloucester (*see* House of Windsor):
HRH THE DUKE OF GLOUCESTER (Prince Richard Alexander Walter George), KG, GCVO, Grand Prior of the Order of St John of Jerusalem
Born 26 August 1944
Married 8 July 1972 Birgitte Eva van Deurs, now HRH the Duchess of Gloucester, GCVO (*born* 20 June 1946, daughter of Asger Henriksen and Vivian van Deurs)

Residence Kensington Palace, London W8 4PU

Issue

1. Earl of Ulster (Alexander Patrick Gregers Richard), *born* 24 October 1974 *married* 22 June 2002 Dr Claire Alexandra Booth, and has issue, Lord Culloden (Xan Richard Anders), *born* 12 March 2007; Lady Cosima Windsor (Cosima Rose Alexandra), *born* 20 May 2010
2. Lady Davina Lewis (Davina Elizabeth Alice Benedikte), *born* 19 November 1977 *married* 31 July 2004 Gary Christie Lewis, and has issue, Senna Kowhai Lewis, *born* 22 June 2010; Tane Mahuta Lewis, *born* 25 May 2012
3. Lady Rose Gilman (Rose Victoria Birgitte Louise), *born* 1 March 1980 *married* 19 July 2008 George Edward Gilman, and has issue, Lyla Beatrix Christabel Gilman, *born* 30 May 2010; Rufus Gilman, *born* 2 November 2012

Children of HRH the Duke of Kent and Princess Marina, Duchess of Kent (*see* House of Windsor):

HRH THE DUKE OF KENT (Prince Edward George Nicholas Paul Patrick), KG, GCMG, GCVO, ADC(P)

Born 9 October 1935

Married 8 June 1961 Katharine Lucy Mary Worsley, now HRH the Duchess of Kent, GCVO (*born* 22 February 1933, daughter of Sir William Worsley, Bt.)

Residence Wren House, Palace Green, London W8 4PY

Issue

1. Earl of St Andrews (George Philip Nicholas), *born* 26 June 1962, *married* 9 January 1988 Sylvana Tomaselli, and has issue, Lord Downpatrick (Edward Edmund Maximilian George), *born* 2 December 1988; Lady Marina-Charlotte Windsor (Marina-Charlotte Alexandra Katharine Helen), *born* 30 September 1992; Lady Amelia Windsor (Amelia Sophia Theodora Mary Margaret), *born* 24 August 1995
2. Lady Helen Taylor (Helen Marina Lucy), *born* 28 April 1964, *married* 18 July 1992 Timothy Verner Taylor, and has issue, Columbus George Donald Taylor, *born* 6 August 1994; Cassius Edward Taylor, *born* 26 December 1996; Eloise Olivia Katharine Taylor, *born* 3 March 2003; Estella Olga Elizabeth Taylor, *born* 21 December 2004
3. Lord Nicholas Windsor (Nicholas Charles Edward Jonathan), *born* 25 July 1970, *married* 4 November 2006

Princess Paola Doimi de Lupis Frankopan Subic Zrinski, and has issue, Albert Louis Philip Edward Windsor, *born* 22 September 2007; Leopold Ernest Augustus Guelph Windsor, *born* 8 September 2009; Louis Arthur Nicholas Felix Windsor, *born* 27 May 2014

HRH PRINCESS ALEXANDRA, THE HON. LADY OGILVY (Princess Alexandra Helen Elizabeth Olga Christabel), KG, GCVO

Born 25 December 1936

Married 24 April 1963 the Rt. Hon. Sir Angus Ogilvy, KCVO (1928–2004), second son of 12th Earl of Airlie

Residence Thatched House Lodge, Richmond Park, Surrey TW10 5HP

Issue

1. James Robert Bruce Ogilvy, *born* 29 February 1964, *married* 30 July 1988 Julia Rawlinson, and has issue, Flora Alexandra Ogilvy, *born* 15 December 1994; Alexander Charles Ogilvy, *born* 12 November 1996
2. Marina Victoria Alexandra Ogilvy, *born* 31 July 1966, *married* 2 February 1990 Paul Julian Mowatt (marriage dissolved 1997), and has issue, Zenouska May Mowatt, *born* 26 May 1990; Christian Alexander Mowatt, *born* 4 June 1993

HRH PRINCE MICHAEL OF KENT (Prince Michael George Charles Franklin), GCVO

Born 4 July 1942

Married 30 June 1978 Baroness Marie-Christine Agnes Hedwig Ida von Reibnitz, now HRH Princess Michael of Kent (*born* 15 January 1945, daughter of Baron Gunther von Reibnitz)

Residence Kensington Palace, London W8 4PU

Issue

1. Lord Frederick Windsor (Frederick Michael George David Louis), *born* 6 April 1979, *married* 12 September 2009 Sophie Winkleman, and has issue, Maud Elizabeth Daphne Marina Windsor, *born* 15 August 2013; Isabella Alexandra May Windsor *born* 16 January 2016
2. Lady Gabriella Windsor (Gabriella Marina Alexandra Ophelia), *born* 23 April 1981

ORDER OF SUCCESSION

The Succession to the Crown Act 2013 received royal assent on 25 April 2013 and makes provision for the order of succession to the Crown not to be dependent on gender and for those members of the royal family married to a Roman Catholic to retain the right of succession to the throne. The provisions of the Act came into force on 26 March 2015, following its ratification by all 15 Realms of the Commonwealth.

On the Act's commencement HRH Prince Michael of Kent and the Earl of St Andrews were restored to the succession. In addition, all male members of the royal family born after 28 October 2011 no longer precede any elder female siblings; and their place in the order of succession changed accordingly.

The following list includes all living descendants of the sons of King George V eligible to succeed to the Crown under the current legislation. Lord Nicholas Windsor, Lord Downpatrick and Lady Marina-Charlotte Windsor renounced their rights to the throne on converting to Roman Catholicism in 2001, 2003 and 2008 respectively. Their children remain in succession provided that they are in communion with the Church of England.

1	HRH the Prince of Wales
2	HRH the Duke of Cambridge
3	HRH Prince George of Cambridge
4	HRH Princess Charlotte of Cambridge
5	HRH Prince Henry of Wales
6	HRH the Duke of York
7	HRH Princess Beatrice of York
8	HRH Princess Eugenie of York
9	HRH the Earl of Wessex
10	Viscount Severn
11	Lady Louise Mountbatten-Windsor
12	HRH the Princess Royal
13	Peter Phillips
14	Savannah Phillips
15	Isla Phillips
16	Zara Tindall
17	Mia Tindall
18	Earl of Snowdon
19	Viscount Linley
20	Lady Margarita Armstrong-Jones
21	Lady Sarah Chatto
22	Samuel Chatto
23	Arthur Chatto
24	HRH the Duke of Gloucester
25	Earl of Ulster
26	Lord Culloden
27	Lady Cosima Windsor
28	Lady Davina Lewis
29	Senna Lewis
30	Tane Lewis
31	Lady Rose Gilman
32	Lyla Gilman
33	Rufus Gilman
34	HRH the Duke of Kent
35	Earl of St Andrews
36	Lady Amelia Windsor
37	Albert Windsor
38	Leopold Windsor
39	Louis Windsor
40	Lady Helen Taylor
41	Columbus Taylor
42	Cassius Taylor
43	Eloise Taylor
44	Estella Taylor
45	HRH Prince Michael of Kent
46	Lord Frederick Windsor
47	Maud Windsor
48	Isabella Windsor
49	Lady Gabriella Windsor
50	HRH Princess Alexandra, the Hon. Lady Ogilvy
51	James Ogilvy
52	Alexander Ogilvy
53	Flora Ogilvy
54	Marina Ogilvy
55	Christian Mowatt
56	Zenouska Mowatt

THE ROYAL HOUSEHOLD

The PRIVATE SECRETARY is responsible for:
- informing and advising the Queen on constitutional, governmental and political matters in the UK, her other Realms and the wider Commonwealth, including communications with the prime minister and government departments
- organising the Queen's domestic and overseas official programme
- the Queen's speeches, messages, patronage, photographs, portraits and official presents
- communications in connection with the role of the royal family
- dealing with correspondence to the Queen from members of the public
- royal travel policy
- coordinating and initiating research to support engagements by members of the royal family

The DIRECTOR OF ROYAL COMMUNICATIONS is in charge of Buckingham Palace's communications office and reports to the Private Secretary. The director is responsible for:
- developing communications strategies to enhance the public understanding of the role of the monarchy
- briefing the British and international media on the role and duties of the Queen and issues relating to the royal family
- responding to media enquiries
- arranging media facilities in the UK and overseas to support royal functions and engagements
- the management of the royal website

The Private Secretary is keeper of the royal archives and is responsible for the care of the records of the sovereign and the royal household from previous reigns, preserved in the royal archives at Windsor. As keeper, it is the Private Secretary's responsibility to ensure the proper management of the records of the present reign with a view to their transfer to the archives as and when appropriate. The Private Secretary is an *ex officio* trustee of the Royal Collection Trust.

The KEEPER OF THE PRIVY PURSE AND TREASURER TO THE QUEEN is responsible for:
- the Sovereign Grant, which is the money paid from the government's Consolidated Fund to meet official expenditure relating to the Queen's duties as Head of State and Head of the Commonwealth and is provided by the government in return for the net surplus from the Crown Estate and other hereditary revenues (*see also* Royal Finances)
- through the Director of Human Resources, the planning and management of personnel policy across the royal household, the allocation of employee and pensioner housing and the administration of all its pension schemes and private estates employees
- information systems and telecommunications
- property services at occupied royal palaces in England, comprising Buckingham Palace, St James's Palace, Clarence House, Marlborough House Mews, the residential and office areas of Kensington Palace, Windsor Castle and buildings in the Home and Great Parks of Windsor and Hampton Court Mews and Paddocks
- audit services
- health and safety; insurance matters
- the Privy Purse, which is mainly financed by the net income of the Duchy of Lancaster, and meets both official and private expenditure incurred by the Queen
- liaison with other members of the royal family and their households on financial matters
- the Queen's private estates at Sandringham and Balmoral, the Queen's Racing Establishment and the Royal Studs and liaison with the Ascot Authority

- the Home Park at Windsor and liaison with the Crown Estate Commissioners concerning the Home Park and the Great Park at Windsor
- the Royal Philatelic Collection
- administrative aspects of the Military Knights of Windsor
- administration of the Royal Victorian Order, of which the Keeper of the Privy Purse is secretary, Long and Faithful Service Medals, and the Queen's cups, medals and prizes, and policy on commemorative medals

The Keeper of the Privy Purse is one of three royal trustees (in respect of his responsibilities for the Sovereign Grant) and is Receiver-General of the Duchy of Lancaster and a member of the Duchy's Council.

The Keeper of the Privy Purse is an *ex officio* trustee of the Royal Collection Trust.

The DIRECTOR OF THE PROPERTY SECTION has day-to-day responsibility for the royal household's property section:
- fire and health and safety
- repairs and refurbishment of buildings and new building work
- utilities and telecommunications
- putting up stages, tents and other work in connection with ceremonial occasions, garden parties and other official functions

The property section is also responsible, on a sub-contract basis from the DCMS, for the maintenance of Marlborough House (which is occupied by the Commonwealth Secretariat).

The MASTER OF THE HOUSEHOLD is responsible for:
- delivering the majority of the official and private entertaining in the Queen's annual programme across all the occupied palaces and residences in the UK when required
- periodic support for entertaining by all other members of the royal family
- furnishings and internal decorative refurbishment of all the occupied palaces in the UK in conjunction with the Director, Royal Collection Trust
- all operational, domestic and kitchen staff in the royal household

The COMPTROLLER, LORD CHAMBERLAIN'S OFFICE is responsible for:
- the organisation of all ceremonial engagements, including state visits to the Queen in the UK, royal weddings and funerals, the state opening of parliament, Guards of Honour at Buckingham Palace, investitures, and the Garter and Thistle ceremonies
- garden parties at Buckingham Palace and the Palace of Holyroodhouse
- the Crown Jewels, which are part of the Royal Collection, when they are in use on state occasions
- coordination of the arrangements for the Queen to be represented at funerals and memorial services and at the arrival and departure of visiting heads of state
- delivery of all official and approved travel operations
- advising on matters of precedence, style and titles, dress, flying of flags, gun salutes, mourning and other ceremonial issues
- supervising the applications for Royal Warrants of Appointment
- advising on the commercial use of royal emblems and contemporary royal photographs
- the ecclesiastical household, the medical household, the bodyguards and certain ceremonial appointments such as Gentlemen Ushers and Pages of Honour
- the Lords in Waiting, who represent the Queen on various occasions and escort visiting heads of state during incoming state visits

- the Queen's bargemaster and watermen and the Queen's swans
- the Royal Almonry and Royal Maundy Service

The Comptroller is also responsible for the Royal Mews, assisted by the CROWN EQUERRY, who has day-to-day responsibility for:

- the provision of carriage processions for the state opening of parliament, state visits, Trooping of the Colour, Royal Ascot, the Garter Ceremony, the Thistle Service, the presentation of credentials to the Queen by incoming foreign ambassadors and high commissioners, and other state and ceremonial occasions
- the provision of chauffeur-driven cars
- coordinating travel arrangements by road in respect of the royal household
- supervision and administration of the Royal Mews at Buckingham Palace, Windsor Castle, Hampton Court and the Palace of Holyroodhouse

The Comptroller also has overall responsibility for the MARSHAL OF THE DIPLOMATIC CORPS, who is responsible for the relationship between the royal household and the Diplomatic Heads of Mission in London; and the SECRETARY OF THE CENTRAL CHANCERY OF THE ORDERS OF KNIGHTHOOD, who administers the Orders of Chivalry, makes arrangements for investitures and the distribution of insignia, and ensures the proper public notification of awards through *The London Gazette;* and the DIRECTOR OF OPERATIONS, ROYAL TRAVEL, who is responsible for the provision of travel arrangements by air and rail.

The DIRECTOR, ROYAL COLLECTION TRUST is responsible for:

- the administration and custodial control of the Royal Collection in all royal residences
- the care, display, conservation and restoration of items in the collection
- initiating and assisting research into the collection and publishing catalogues and books on the collection
- making the collection accessible to the public and educating and informing the public about the collection

The Royal Collection, which contains a large number of works of art, is held by the Queen as sovereign in trust for her successors and the nation and is not owned by her as an individual. The administration, conservation and presentation of the Royal Collection are funded by the Royal Collection Trust solely from income from visitors to Windsor Castle, Buckingham Palace and the Palace of Holyroodhouse. The Royal Collection Trust is chaired by the Prince of Wales. The Lord Chamberlain, the Private Secretary and the Keeper of the Privy Purse are *ex officio* trustees and there are three external trustees appointed by the Queen.

The Director, Royal Collection Trust is also at present the SURVEYOR OF THE QUEEN'S WORKS OF ART, responsible for paintings, miniatures and works of art on paper, including the watercolours, prints and drawings in the Print Room at Windsor Castle, and for the books, manuscripts, coins, medals and insignia in the Royal Library.

Royal Collection Enterprises Limited is the trading subsidiary of the Royal Collection Trust. The company, whose chair is the Keeper of the Privy Purse, is responsible for:

- managing access by the public to Windsor Castle (including Frogmore House), Buckingham Palace (including the Royal Mews and the Queen's Gallery) and the Palace of Holyroodhouse (including the Queen's Gallery)

- running shops at each location
- managing the images and intellectual property rights of the Royal Collection

The Director, Royal Collection Trust is also an *ex officio* trustee of Historic Royal Palaces.

PRIVATE SECRETARIES

THE QUEEN
Office: Buckingham Palace, London SW1A 1AA **T** 020-7930 4832
Private Secretary to the Queen, Edward Young, CVO

PRINCE PHILIP, THE DUKE OF EDINBURGH
Office: Buckingham Palace, London SW1A 1AA **T** 020-7930 4832
Private Secretary, Brig. Archie Miller-Bakewell

THE PRINCE OF WALES AND THE DUCHESS OF CORNWALL
Office: Clarence House, London SW1A 1BA **T** 020-7930 4832
Principal Private Secretary, Clive Alderton, LVO

THE DUKE AND DUCHESS OF CAMBRIDGE
Office: Kensington Palace, Palace Green, London W8 4PU **T** 020-7930 4832
Private Secretary to the Duke of Cambridge, Miguel Head, LVO
Private Secretary to the Duchess of Cambridge, Catherine Quinn

PRINCE HENRY OF WALES
Office, Kensington Palace, Palace Green, London W8 4PU **T** 020-7930 4832
Private Secretary, Ed Lane Fox

THE DUKE OF YORK
Office: Buckingham Palace, London SW1A 1AA **T** 020-7024 4227
Private Secretary, Amanda Thirsk, LVO

THE EARL AND COUNTESS OF WESSEX
Office: Bagshot Park, Surrey GU19 5PL **T** 01276-707040
Private Secretary, Tim Roberts

THE PRINCESS ROYAL
Office: Buckingham Palace, London SW1A 1AA **T** 020-7024 4199
Private Secretary, Capt. N. P. Wright, CVO, RN

THE DUKE AND DUCHESS OF GLOUCESTER
Office: Kensington Palace, London W8 4PU **T** 020-7368 1000
Private Secretary, Lt.-Col. Alastair Todd

THE DUKE OF KENT
Office: York House, St James's Palace, London SW1A 1BQ **T** 020-7930 4872
Private Secretary, Nicholas Marden

PRINCE AND PRINCESS MICHAEL OF KENT
Office: Kensington Palace, London W8 4PU
W www.princemichael.org.uk
Private Secretary, Camilla Rogers

PRINCESS ALEXANDRA, THE HON. LADY OGILVY
Office: Buckingham Palace, London SW1A 1AA **T** 020-7024 4270
Private Secretary, Diane Duke, LVO

SENIOR MANAGEMENT OF THE ROYAL HOUSEHOLD

Lord Chamberlain, Earl Peel, GCVO, PC

HEADS OF DEPARTMENT
Private Secretary to The Queen, Edward Young, CVO
Keeper of the Privy Purse, Sir Alan Reid, GCVO
Master of the Household, Vice-Adm. Tony Johnstone-Burt, CB, OBE
Comptroller, Lord Chamberlain's Office, Lt.-Col. Sir Andrew Ford, KCVO
Director of the Royal Collection, Jonathan Marsden, CVO

NON-EXECUTIVE MEMBERS
Private Secretary to the Duke of Edinburgh, Brig. Archie Miller-Bakewell
Principal Private Secretary to the Prince of Wales and the Duchess of Cornwall, Clive Alderton, LVO

ASTRONOMER ROYAL

The post of Astronomer Royal dates back to 1675, when astronomy had many practical applications in navigation. Today the post is largely honorary, although the Astronomer Royal is expected to be available for consultation on scientific matters for as long as the holder remains a professional astronomer. The Astronomer Royal receives a stipend of £100 a year and is a member of the royal household.

Astronomer Royal, Lord Rees of Ludlow, OM, *apptd* 1995

MASTER OF THE QUEEN'S MUSIC

The office of Master of the Queen's Music is an honour conferred on a musician of great distinction. The office was first created in 1626, when the master was responsible for the court musicians. Since the reign of King George V, the position has had no fixed duties, although the Master may choose to produce compositions to mark royal or state occasions. The Master of the Queen's Music is paid an annual stipend of £15,000. In 2004 the length of appointment was changed from life tenure to a ten-year term.

Master of the Queen's Music, Judith Weir, CBE, *apptd* 2014

POET LAUREATE

The post of Poet Laureate was officially established when John Dryden was appointed by royal warrant as Poet Laureate and Historiographer Royal in 1668. The post is attached to the royal household and was originally conferred on the holder for life; in 1999 the length of appointment was changed to a ten-year term. It is customary for the Poet Laureate to write verse to mark events of national importance. The postholder currently receives an honorarium of £5,750 a year.

The Poet Laureate, Dame Carol Ann Duffy, DBE, *apptd* 2009

ROYAL FINANCES

Dating back to the late 17th century the Civil List was originally used by the sovereign to supplement hereditary revenues for paying the salaries of judges, ambassadors and other government officers as well as the expenses of the royal household. In 1760, on the accession of George III, it was decided that the Civil List would be provided by parliament to cover all relevant expenditure in return for the king surrendering the hereditary revenues of the Crown. At that time parliament undertook to pay the salaries of judges, ambassadors etc. In 1831 parliament agreed also to meet the costs of the royal palaces in return for a reduction in the Civil List.

Until 1 April 2012 the Civil List met the central staff costs and running expenses of the Queen's official household. Annual grants-in-aid provided for the maintenance of the occupied royal palaces (see Royal Household for a list of occupied palaces) and royal travel.

THE SOVEREIGN GRANT

Under the Sovereign Grant Act 2011, which came into force on 1 April 2012, the funding previously provided by the Civil List and the grants-in-aid was consolidated in the Sovereign Grant, which was set at £42.8m for 2016–17. It is provided by HM Treasury from public funds in exchange for the surrender by the Queen of the revenue of the Crown Estate.

Official expenditure met by the Sovereign Grant in 2016–17 amounted to £41.9m. Royal travel accounted for £4.5m of the expenditure and property maintenance for £17.8m. The excess of Sovereign Grant over expenditure of £0.9m was transferred to the Sovereign Grant reserve. For 2016–17 the Sovereign Grant was calculated based on 15 per cent of the income account net surplus of the Crown Estate for the financial year two years previous. The Royal Trustees have agreed that from 2017–18, the Sovereign Grant will be calculated based on 25 per cent of the income account net surplus of the Crown Estate for the financial year two years previous. This provides for a Sovereign Grant of £76.1m for 2017–18. The additional grant will be used to fund the refurbishment of Buckingham Palace over a period of ten years.

The legislative requirement is for Sovereign Grant accounts to be audited by the Comptroller and Auditor-General, scrutinised by the National Audit Office, and submitted to parliament annually. They are then subjected to the same audit scrutiny as for any other government department. The annual report for the year to 31 March 2017, was published in June 2017.

	2015–16	2016–17
Sovereign Grant	£40,100,000	£42,800,000
Draw-down from/(transfer to) the reserve	(£300,000)	(£900,000)
Net Funding Receipts	£39,800,000	£41,900,000
Net Expenditure	(£39,800,000)	(£41,900,000)

PARLIAMENTARY ANNUITIES

The Civil List acts provided for other members of the royal family to receive parliamentary annuities from government funds to meet the expenses of carrying out their official duties. Since 1993 these annuities have been a statutory anomaly as the Queen reimbursed HM Treasury for all of them except those paid to the late Queen Elizabeth the Queen Mother and the Duke of Edinburgh. The Sovereign Grant Act 2011 repealed all the parliamentary annuities paid to the royal family, with the exception of the Duke of Edinburgh. The Duke of Edinburgh's annuity (£359,000) is now paid directly from the Consolidated Fund.

THE PRIVY PURSE

The funds received by the Privy Purse pay for official expenses incurred by the Queen as head of state and for some of the Queen's private expenditure. The revenues of the Duchy of Lancaster are the principal source of income for the privy purse. The revenues of the Duchy were retained by George III in 1760 when the hereditary revenues were surrendered. The Duchy Council reports to the Chancellor of the Duchy of Lancaster, who is accountable directly to the sovereign rather than to parliament. However the chancellor does answer parliamentary questions on matters relating to the Duchy's responsibilities.

THE DUCHY OF LANCASTER, 1 Lancaster Place, London WC2E 7ED
Chancellor of the Duchy of Lancaster, Rt. Hon. Sir Patrick McLoughlin, MP, *apptd* 2016
Chair of the Council, Sir Mark Hudson, KCVO
Chief Executive and Clerk, Nathan Thompson
Receiver-General, Sir Alan Reid, GCVO
Attorney-General, Robert Miles, QC

PERSONAL INCOME

The Queen's personal income derives mostly from investments, and is used to meet private expenditure.

PRINCE OF WALES' FUNDING

The Duchy Estate was created in 1337 by Edward III for his son and heir Prince Edward (the Black Prince) who became the Duke of Cornwall. The Duchy's primary function is to provide an income from its assets for the Prince of Wales. Under a 1337 charter, confirmed by subsequent legislation, the Prince of Wales is not entitled to the proceeds or profit on the sale of Duchy assets but only to the annual income which is generated. The Duchy is responsible for the sustainable and commercial management of its properties, investment portfolio and 53,266 hectares of land, based mostly in the south-west of England. The Prince of Wales has chosen to use a proportion of his income to meet the cost of his public and charitable work. The Duchy also funds the public, charitable and private activities of the Duchess of Cornwall, the Duke and Duchess of Cambridge and Prince Henry of Wales.

THE DUCHY OF CORNWALL, 10 Buckingham Gate, London SW1E 6LA T 020-7834 7346 W www.duchyofcornwall.org
Lord Warden of the Stannaries, Sir Nicholas Bacon, Bt., OBE
Receiver-General, Hon. James Leigh-Pemberton, CVO
Attorney-General, Jonathan Crow, QC
Secretary and Keeper of the Records, Alastair Martin

TAXATION

The sovereign is not legally liable to pay income tax or capital gains tax. In 1992 the Queen offered to pay income and capital gains tax on a voluntary basis from 6 April 1993, and the Prince of Wales offered to pay tax on a voluntary basis on his income from the Duchy of Cornwall (he was already taxed in all other respects).

The main provisions for the Queen and the Prince of Wales to pay tax, set out in a Memorandum of Understanding on Royal Taxation presented to parliament on 11 February 1993, are that the Queen will pay income tax and capital gains tax in respect of her private income and assets, and on the proportion of the income and capital gains of the Privy Purse used for private purposes. Inheritance tax will be paid on the Queen's assets, except for those which pass to the next sovereign, whether automatically or by gift or bequest. The Prince of Wales will pay income tax on income from the Duchy of Cornwall used for private purposes.

ROYAL SALUTES

ENGLAND

The basic royal salute is 21 rounds with an extra 20 rounds fired at Hyde Park because it is a royal park. At the Tower of London 62 rounds are fired on royal anniversaries (21 plus a further 20 because the Tower is a royal palace and a further 21 'for the City of London') and 41 on other occasions. When the Queen's official birthday coincides with the Duke of Edinburgh's birthday, 124 rounds are fired from the Tower (62 rounds for each birthday). Gun salutes occur on the following royal anniversaries:

- Accession Day
- The Queen's birthday
- Coronation Day
- Duke of Edinburgh's birthday
- The Queen's Official Birthday
- The Prince of Wales' birthday
- State opening of parliament

Gun salutes also occur when parliament is prorogued by the sovereign, on royal births and when a visiting head of state meets the sovereign in London, Windsor or Edinburgh.

In London, salutes are fired at Hyde Park and the Tower of London although on some occasions (state visits, state opening of parliament and the Queen's birthday parade) Green Park is used instead of Hyde Park. Other military saluting stations in England are at Colchester, Dover, Plymouth, Woolwich and York.

Constable of the Royal Palace and Fortress of London, Gen. Sir Nicholas Houghton, GCB, CBE, ADC

Lieutenant of the Tower of London, Lt.-Gen. Sir Simon Mayall, KBE, CB

Master Gunner of St James's Park, Lt.-Gen. Sir Andrew Gregory, KBE, CB

Resident Governor and Keeper of the Jewel House, Col. Richard Harrold, OBE

Master Gunner within the Tower, HRH Prince Michael of Kent, GCVO

SCOTLAND

Royal salutes are authorised at Edinburgh Castle and Stirling Castle. A salute of 21 guns is fired on the following occasions:

- the anniversaries of the birth, accession and coronation of the sovereign
- the anniversary of the birth of the Duke of Edinburgh

A salute of 21 guns is fired in Edinburgh on the occasion of the opening of the general assembly of the Church of Scotland. A salute of 21 guns may also be fired in Edinburgh on the arrival of HM The Queen or a member of the royal family who is a Royal Highness on an official visit.

Military saluting stations are also situated at Cardiff Castle in Wales, Hillsborough Castle in Northern Ireland and in Gibraltar.

MILITARY RANKS AND TITLES

THE QUEEN

ARMY
Colonel-in-Chief
The Life Guards; The Blues and Royals (Royal Horse Guards and 1st Dragoons); The Royal Scots Dragoon Guards (Carabiniers and Greys); The Royal Lancers; The Royal Tank Regiment; Corps of Royal Engineers; Grenadier Guards; Coldstream Guards; Scots Guards; Irish Guards; Welsh Guards; The Royal Regiment of Scotland; The Duke of Lancaster's Regiment (King's, Lancashire and Border); The Royal Welsh; Adjutant General's Corps; The Governor General's Horse Guards (of Canada); The King's Own Calgary Regiment (Royal Canadian Armoured Corps); Canadian Forces Military Engineering Branch; Le Royal 22e Regiment (of Canada); The Governor General's Foot Guards (of Canada); The Canadian Grenadier Guards; The Stormont, Dundas and Glengarry Highlanders; Le Régiment de la Chaudière (of Canada); The Royal New Brunswick Regiment; The North Shore (New Brunswick) Regiment; 48th Highlanders of Canada; The Argyll and Sutherland Highlanders of Canada (Princess Louise's); The Calgary Highlanders; Royal Australian Engineers; Royal Australian Infantry Corps; Royal Australian Army Ordnance Corps; Royal Australian Army Nursing Corps; The Corps of Royal New Zealand Engineers; Royal New Zealand Infantry Regiment; Malawi Rifles
Affiliated Colonel-in-Chief
The Queen's Gurkha Engineers
Captain-General
Royal Regiment of Artillery; The Honourable Artillery Company; Combined Cadet Force; Royal Regiment of Canadian Artillery; Royal Regiment of Australian Artillery; Royal Regiment of New Zealand Artillery; Royal New Zealand Armoured Corps
Royal Colonel
Balaklava Company, 5th Battalion The Royal Regiment of Scotland
Patron
Royal Army Chaplains' Department

ROYAL AIR FORCE
Air Commodore-in-Chief
Royal Auxiliary Air Force; Royal Air Force Regiment; Air Reserve (of Canada); Royal Australian Air Force Reserve; Territorial Air Force (of New Zealand)
Commandant-in-Chief
RAF College, Cranwell
Royal Honorary Air Commodore
RAF Marham; 603 (City of Edinburgh) Squadron Royal Auxiliary Air Force

TRI-SERVICE
Colonel-in-Chief
The Canadian Armed Forces Legal Branch

PRINCE PHILIP, DUKE OF EDINBURGH

ROYAL NAVY
Lord High Admiral of the United Kingdom
Admiral of the Fleet
Admiral of the Fleet, Royal Australian Navy
Admiral of the Fleet, Royal New Zealand Navy
Admiral, Royal Canadian Navy
Admiral, Royal Canadian Sea Cadets

ROYAL MARINES
Captain-General

ARMY
Field Marshal
Field Marshal, Australian Military Forces
Field Marshal, New Zealand Army
General, Royal Canadian Army
Colonel-in-Chief
The Queen's Royal Hussars (Queen's Own and Royal Irish); The Rifles; Corps of Royal Electrical and Mechanical Engineers; Intelligence Corps; Army Cadet Force Association; The Royal Canadian Regiment; The Royal Hamilton Light Infantry (Wentworth Regiment of Canada); The Cameron Highlanders of Ottawa; The Queen's Own Cameron Highlanders of Canada; The Seaforth Highlanders of Canada; The Royal Canadian Army Cadets; The Royal Australian Corps of Electrical and Mechanical Engineers; The Australian Army Cadet Corps
Colonel
Grenadier Guards
Royal Colonel
The Highlanders, 4th Battalion The Royal Regiment of Scotland
Honorary Colonel
The Trinidad and Tobago Regiment
Member
Honourable Artillery Company

ROYAL AIR FORCE
Marshal of the Royal Air Force
Marshal of the Royal Australian Air Force
Marshal of the Royal New Zealand Air Force
General, Royal Canadian Air Force
Air Commodore-in-Chief
Royal Canadian Air Cadets
Honorary Air Commodore
RAF Northolt

THE PRINCE OF WALES

ROYAL NAVY
Admiral of the Fleet
Admiral of the Fleet, Royal New Zealand Navy
Vice-Admiral
Royal Canadian Navy
Commodore-in-Chief
Royal Naval Command Plymouth; Fleet Atlantic, Royal Canadian Navy

ARMY
Field Marshal
Lieutenant-General
Canadian Army
Colonel-in-Chief
The Royal Dragoon Guards; The Parachute Regiment; The Royal Gurkha Rifles; Army Air Corps; The Royal Canadian Dragoons; Lord Strathcona's Horse (Royal Canadians); The Royal Regiment of Canada; Royal Winnipeg Rifles; Royal Australian Armoured Corps; The Royal Pacific Islands Regiment; 1st The Queen's Dragoon Guards; The Black Watch (Royal Highland Regiment) of Canada; The Toronto Scottish Regiment (Queen Elizabeth The Queen Mother's Own); The Mercian Regiment; 2nd Battalion The Irish Regiment of Canada
Royal Colonel
The Black Watch, 3rd Battalion The Royal Regiment of Scotland; 51st Highland, 7th Battalion The Royal Regiment of Scotland
Colonel
The Welsh Guards
Royal Honorary Colonel
The Queen's Own Yeomanry

ROYAL AIR FORCE
Marshal of the RAF
Lieutenant-General
   Royal Canadian Air Force
Honorary Air Commodore
   RAF Valley
Air Commodore-in-Chief
   Royal New Zealand Air Force
Colonel-in-Chief
   Air Reserve Canada

THE DUCHESS OF CORNWALL

ROYAL NAVY
Commodore-in-Chief
   Royal Naval Medical Services; Naval Chaplaincy Services

ARMY
Colonel-in-Chief
   Queen's Own Rifles of Canada; Royal Australian Corps of
   Military Police
Royal Colonel
   4th Battalion The Rifles

ROYAL AIR FORCE
Honorary Air Commodore
   RAF Halton; RAF Leeming

THE DUKE OF CAMBRIDGE

ROYAL NAVY
Lieutenant Commander
Commodore-in-Chief
   Scotland Command; Submarines Command

ARMY
Colonel
   Irish Guards
Major
   The Blues and Royals (Royal Horse Guards and 1st
   Dragoons)

ROYAL AIR FORCE
Squadron Leader
Honorary Air Commandant
   RAF Coningsby

THE DUCHESS OF CAMBRIDGE

ROYAL AIR FORCE
Honorary Air Commandant
   Air Cadets

PRINCE HENRY OF WALES

ROYAL NAVY
Commodore-in-Chief
   Small Ships and Diving Command

ARMY
Captain
   The Blues and Royals (Royal Horse Guards and 1st
   Dragoons)

ROYAL AIR FORCE
Honorary Air Commandant
   RAF Honington

THE DUKE OF YORK

ROYAL NAVY
Vice-Admiral
Commodore-in-Chief
   Fleet Air Arm
Admiral of the Marine Society and Sea Cadets

ARMY
Colonel-in-Chief
   The Royal Irish Regiment (27th (Inniskilling), 83rd, 87th
   and The Ulster Defence Regiment); The Yorkshire
   Regiment (14th/15th, 19th and 33rd/76th Foot); Small
   Arms School Corps; The Queen's York Rangers (First
   Americans); Royal New Zealand Army Logistics Regiment;
   The Royal Highland Fusiliers of Canada; The Princess
   Louise Fusiliers (Canada)
Deputy Colonel-in-Chief
   The Royal Lancers
Royal Colonel
   The Royal Highland Fusiliers, 2nd Battalion The Royal
   Regiment of Scotland

ROYAL AIR FORCE
Honorary Air Commodore
   RAF Lossiemouth

THE EARL OF WESSEX

ROYAL NAVY
Commodore-in-Chief
   Royal Fleet Auxiliary
Patron
   Royal Fleet Auxiliary Association

ARMY
Colonel-in-Chief
   Hastings and Prince Edward Regiment; Saskatchewan
   Dragoons; Prince Edward Island Regiment
Royal Colonel
   2nd Battalion, The Rifles
Royal Honorary Colonel
   Royal Wessex Yeomanry; The London Regiment

ROYAL AIR FORCE
Honorary Air Commodore
   RAF Waddington

THE COUNTESS OF WESSEX

ARMY
Colonel-in-Chief
   Corps of Army Music; Queen Alexandra's Royal Army
   Nursing Corps; The Lincoln and Welland Regiment; South
   Alberta Light Horse Regiment
Royal Colonel
   5th Battalion, The Rifles
Patron
   Queen Alexandra's Royal Army Nursing Corps Association

ROYAL AIR FORCE
Honorary Air Commodore
   RAF Wittering

ROYAL NAVY
Sponsor
   HMS *Daring*

THE PRINCESS ROYAL

ROYAL NAVY
Admiral (Chief Commandant for Women in the Royal Navy)
Commodore-in-Chief
   HM Naval Base Portsmouth; Fleet Pacific, Royal Canadian
   Navy

ARMY
Colonel-in-Chief
   The King's Royal Hussars; Royal Corps of Signals; Royal
   Logistic Corps; The Royal Army Veterinary Corps; 8th
   Canadian Hussars (Princess Louise's); Royal Newfoundland
   Regiment; Canadian Forces Communications and
   Electronics Branch; The Grey and Simcoe Foresters; The
   Royal Regina Rifles; Canadian Forces Medical Branch;

Royal Canadian Hussars; Royal Australian Corps of Signals; Royal Australian Corps of Transport; Royal New Zealand Corps of Signals; Royal New Zealand Nursing Corps

Affiliated Colonel-in-Chief
The Queen's Gurkha Signals; The Queen's Own Gurkha Transport Regiment

Royal Colonel
The Royal Scots Borderers, 1st Battalion The Royal Regiment of Scotland; 52nd Lowland, 6th Battalion The Royal Regiment of Scotland

Colonel
The Blues and Royals (Royal Horse Guards and 1st Dragoons)

Honorary Colonel
University of London Officers' Training Corps

Commandant-in-Chief
First Aid Nursing Yeomanry (Princess Royal's Volunteer Corps)

ROYAL AIR FORCE
Honorary Air Commodore
RAF Brize Norton; University of London Air Squadron

THE DUKE OF GLOUCESTER

ARMY
Colonel-in-Chief
The Royal Anglian Regiment; Royal Army Medical Corps; Royal New Zealand Army Medical Corps

Deputy Colonel-in-Chief
The Royal Logistic Corps

Royal Colonel
6th Battalion, The Rifles

Royal Honorary Colonel
Royal Monmouthshire Royal Engineers (Militia)

ROYAL AIR FORCE
Honorary Air Marshal
Honorary Air Commodore
RAF Odiham; No. 501 (County of Gloucester) Logistic Support Squadron

THE DUCHESS OF GLOUCESTER

ARMY
Colonel-in-Chief
Royal Army Dental Corps; Royal Australian Army Educational Corps; Royal New Zealand Army Educational Corps; Royal Canadian Dental Corps; The Bermuda Regiment

Deputy Colonel-in-Chief
Adjutant General's Corps

Royal Colonel
7th Battalion, The Rifles

Vice-Patron
Adjutant General's Corps Regimental Association

Patron
Royal Army Educational Corps Association; Army Families Federation

THE DUKE OF KENT

ARMY
Field Marshal
Colonel-in-Chief
The Royal Regiment of Fusiliers; Lorne Scots (Peel, Dufferin and Hamilton Regiment)

Deputy Colonel-in-Chief
The Royal Scots Dragoon Guards (Carabiniers and Greys)

Royal Colonel
1st Battalion The Rifles

Colonel
Scots Guards

ROYAL AIR FORCE
Honorary Air Chief Marshal

THE DUCHESS OF KENT

ARMY
Honorary Major-General
Deputy Colonel-in-Chief
The Royal Dragoon Guards; Adjutant General's Corps; The Royal Logistic Corps

PRINCE MICHAEL OF KENT

ROYAL NAVY
Honorary Vice-Admiral of the Royal Naval Reserves
Commodore-in-Chief of the Maritime Reserves

ARMY
Colonel-in-Chief
Essex and Kent Scottish Regiment (Ontario)

Royal Honorary Colonel
Honourable Artillery Company

Senior Colonel
King's Royal Hussars

ROYAL AIR FORCE
Honorary Air Marshal
RAF Benson

PRINCESS ALEXANDRA, THE HON. LADY OGILVY

ROYAL NAVY
Patron
Queen Alexandra's Royal Naval Nursing Service

ARMY
Colonel-in-Chief
The Canadian Scottish Regiment (Princess Mary's)

Deputy Colonel-in-Chief
The Royal Lancers

Royal Colonel
3rd Battalion The Rifles

Royal Honorary Colonel
The Royal Yeomanry

ROYAL AIR FORCE
Patron and Air Chief Commandant
Princess Mary's RAF Nursing Service

KINGS AND QUEENS

ENGLISH KINGS AND QUEENS 927 TO 1603

HOUSES OF CERDIC AND DENMARK

Reign

927–939   **ÆTHELSTAN**
Son of Edward the Elder, by Ecgwynn, and grandson of Alfred *acceded* to Wessex and Mercia *c.*924, established direct rule over Northumbria 927, effectively creating the Kingdom of England *reigned* 15 years

939–946   **EDMUND I**
born 921, son of Edward the Elder, by Eadgifu *married* (1) Ælfgifu (2) Æthelflæd *killed* aged 25 *reigned* 6 years

946–955   **EADRED**
Son of Edward the Elder, by Eadgifu *reigned* 9 years

955–959   **EADWIG**
born before 943, son of Edmund and Ælfgifu *married* Ælfgifu *reigned* 3 years

959–975   **EDGAR I**
born 943, son of Edmund and Ælfgifu *married* (1) Æthelflæd (2) Wulfthryth (3) Ælfthryth *died* aged 32 *reigned* 15 years

975–978   **EDWARD I (the Martyr)**
*born c.*962, son of Edgar and Æthelflæd *assassinated* aged *c.*16 *reigned* 2 years

978–1016   **ÆTHELRED (the Unready)**
born 968/969, son of Edgar and Ælfthryth *married* (1) Ælfgifu (2) Emma, daughter of Richard I, Count of Normandy, 1013–14 dispossessed of kingdom by Swegn Forkbeard (King of Denmark 987–1014) *died* aged *c.*47, *reigned* 38 years

1016   **EDMUND II (Ironside)**
(Apr–Nov)   *born* before 993, son of Æthelred and Ælfgifu *married* Ealdgyth *died* aged over 23 *reigned* 7 months

1016–1035   **CNUT (Canute)**
*born c.*995, son of Swegn Forkbeard, King of Denmark, and Gunhild *married* (1) Ælfgifu (2) Emma, widow of Æthelred the Unready. Gained submission of West Saxons 1015, Northumbrians 1016, Mercia 1016, King of all England after Edmund's death, King of Denmark 1019–35, King of Norway 1028–35 *died* aged *c.*40 *reigned* 19 years

1035–1040   **HAROLD I (Harefoot)**
born 1016/17, son of Cnut and Ælfgifu *married* Ælfgifu 1035 recognised as regent for himself and his brother Harthacnut; 1037 recognised as king *died* aged *c.*23 *reigned* 4 years

1040–1042   **HARTHACNUT (Harthacanute)**
*born c.*1018, son of Cnut and Emma. Titular king of Denmark from 1028, acknowledged King of England 1035–7 with Harold I as regent; effective king after Harold's death *died* aged *c.*24 *reigned* 2 years

1042–1066   **EDWARD II (the Confessor)**
born between 1002 and 1005, son of Æthelred the Unready and Emma *married* Eadgyth, daughter of Godwine, Earl of Wessex *died* aged over 60 *reigned* 23 years

1066   **HAROLD II (Godwinesson)**
(Jan–Oct)   *born c.*1020, son of Godwine, Earl of Wessex, and Gytha *married* (1) Eadgyth (2) Ealdgyth *killed* in battle aged *c.*46 *reigned* 10 months

THE HOUSE OF NORMANDY

1066–1087   **WILLIAM I (the Conqueror)**
born 1027/8, son of Robert I, Duke of Normandy; obtained the Crown by conquest *married* Matilda, daughter of Baldwin, Count of Flanders *died* aged *c.*60, *reigned* 20 years

1087–1100   **WILLIAM II (Rufus)**
born between 1056 and 1060, third son of William I; succeeded his father in England only *killed* aged *c.*40 *reigned* 12 years

1100–1135   **HENRY I (Beauclerk)**
born 1068, fourth son of William I *married* (1) Edith or Matilda, daughter of Malcolm III of Scotland (2) Adela, daughter of Godfrey, Count of Louvain *died* aged 67 *reigned* 35 years

1135–1154   **STEPHEN**
born not later than 1100, third son of Adela, daughter of William I, and Stephen, Count of Blois *married* Matilda, daughter of Eustace, Count of Boulogne. Feb–Nov 1141 held captive by adherents of Matilda, daughter of Henry I, who contested the Crown until 1153 *died* aged over 53 *reigned* 18 years

THE HOUSE OF ANJOU (PLANTAGENETS)

1154–1189   **HENRY II (Curtmantle)**
born 1133, son of Matilda, daughter of Henry I, and Geoffrey, Count of Anjou *married* Eleanor, daughter of William, Duke of Aquitaine, and divorced queen of Louis VII of France *died* aged 56 *reigned* 34 years

1189–1199   **RICHARD I (Coeur de Lion)**
born 1157, third son of Henry II *married* Berengaria, daughter of Sancho VI, King of Navarre *died* aged 42 *reigned* 9 years

1199–1216   **JOHN (Lackland)**
born 1167, fifth son of Henry II *married* (1) Isabella or Avisa, daughter of William, Earl of Gloucester (divorced) (2) Isabella, daughter of Aymer, Count of Angoulême *died* aged 48 *reigned* 17 years

1216–1272   **HENRY III**
born 1207, son of John and Isabella of Angoulême *married* Eleanor, daughter of Raymond, Count of Provence *died* aged 65 *reigned* 56 years

1272–1307   **EDWARD I (Longshanks)**
born 1239, eldest son of Henry III *married* (1) Eleanor, daughter of Ferdinand III, King of Castile (2) Margaret, daughter of Philip III of France *died* aged 68 *reigned* 34 years

1307–1327   **EDWARD II**
born 1284, eldest surviving son of Edward I and Eleanor *married* Isabella, daughter of Philip IV of France *deposed* Jan 1327 *killed* Sep 1327 aged 43 *reigned* 19 years

1327–1377   **EDWARD III**
born 1312, eldest son of Edward II *married* Philippa, daughter of William, Count of Hainault *died* aged 64 *reigned* 50 years

1377–1399   **RICHARD II**
born 1367, son of Edward (the Black Prince), eldest son of Edward III *married* (1) Anne, daughter of Emperor Charles IV (2) Isabelle, daughter of Charles VI of France *deposed* Sep 1399 *killed* Feb 1400 aged 33 *reigned* 22 years

THE HOUSE OF LANCASTER

1399–1413   HENRY IV
born 1366, son of John of Gaunt, fourth son of Edward III, and Blanche, daughter of Henry, Duke of Lancaster married (1) Mary, daughter of Humphrey, Earl of Hereford (2) Joan, daughter of Charles, King of Navarre, and widow of John, Duke of Brittany died aged c.47 reigned 13 years

1413–1422   HENRY V
born 1387, eldest surviving son of Henry IV and Mary married Catherine, daughter of Charles VI of France died aged 34 reigned 9 years

1422–1471   HENRY VI
born 1421, son of Henry V married Margaret, daughter of René, Duke of Anjou and Count of Provence deposed Mar 1461 restored Oct 1470 deposed Apr 1471 killed May 1471 aged 49 reigned 39 years

THE HOUSE OF YORK

1461–1483   EDWARD IV
born 1442, eldest son of Richard of York (grandson of Edmund, fifth son of Edward III; and son of Anne, great-granddaughter of Lionel, third son of Edward III) married Elizabeth Woodville, daughter of Richard, Lord Rivers, and widow of Sir John Grey acceded Mar 1461 deposed Oct 1470 restored Apr 1471 died aged 40 reigned 21 years

1483   EDWARD V
(Apr–Jun)
born 1470, eldest son of Edward IV deposed Jun 1483, died probably Jul–Sep 1483, aged 12 reigned 2 months

1483–1485   RICHARD III
born 1452, fourth son of Richard of York married Anne Neville, daughter of Richard, Earl of Warwick, and widow of Edward, Prince of Wales, son of Henry VI killed in battle aged 32 reigned 2 years

THE HOUSE OF TUDOR

1485–1509   HENRY VII
born 1457, son of Margaret Beaufort (great-granddaughter of John of Gaunt, fourth son of Edward III) and Edmund Tudor, Earl of Richmond married Elizabeth, daughter of Edward IV died aged 52 reigned 23 years

1509–1547   HENRY VIII
born 1491, second son of Henry VII married (1) Catherine, daughter of Ferdinand II, King of Aragon, and widow of his elder brother Arthur (divorced) (2) Anne, daughter of Sir Thomas Boleyn (executed) (3) Jane, daughter of Sir John Seymour (died in childbirth) (4) Anne, daughter of John, Duke of Cleves (divorced) (5) Catherine Howard, niece of the Duke of Norfolk (executed) (6) Catherine, daughter of Sir Thomas Parr and widow of Lord Latimer died aged 55 reigned 37 years

1547–1553   EDWARD VI
born 1537, son of Henry VIII and Jane Seymour died aged 15 reigned 6 years

1553   JANE
*(6/10–
19 Jul)
born 1537, daughter of Frances (daughter of Mary Tudor, the younger daughter of Henry VII) and Henry Grey, Duke of Suffolk married Lord Guildford Dudley, son of the Duke of Northumberland deposed Jul 1553 executed Feb 1554 aged 16 reigned 13/9 days

* Depending on whether the date of her predecessor's death (6 July) or that of her official proclamation as Queen (10 July) is taken as the beginning of her reign

1553–1558   MARY I
born 1516, daughter of Henry VIII and Catherine of Aragon married Philip II of Spain died aged 42 reigned 5 years

1558–1603   ELIZABETH I
born 1533, daughter of Henry VIII and Anne Boleyn died aged 69 reigned 44 years

BRITISH KINGS AND QUEENS SINCE 1603

THE HOUSE OF STUART

Reign

1603–1625   JAMES I (VI OF SCOTLAND)
born 1566, son of Mary, Queen of Scots (granddaughter of Margaret Tudor, elder daughter of Henry VII), and Henry Stewart, Lord Darnley married Anne, daughter of Frederick II of Denmark died aged 58 reigned 22 years

1625–1649   CHARLES I
born 1600, second son of James I married Henrietta Maria, daughter of Henry IV of France executed 1649 aged 48 reigned 23 years

INTERREGNUM 1649–1660

1649–1653   Government by a council of state
1653–1658   Oliver Cromwell, Lord Protector
1658–1659   Richard Cromwell, Lord Protector

Reign

1660–1685   CHARLES II
born 1630, eldest son of Charles I married Catherine, daughter of John of Portugal died aged 54 reigned 24 years

1685–1688   JAMES II (VII OF SCOTLAND)
born 1633, second son of Charles I married (1) Lady Anne Hyde, daughter of Edward, Earl of Clarendon (2) Mary, daughter of Alphonso, Duke of Modena. Reign ended with flight from kingdom Dec 1688 died 1701 aged 67 reigned 3 years

INTERREGNUM 11 Dec 1688 to 12 Feb 1689

Reign

1689–1702   WILLIAM III
born 1650, son of William II, Prince of Orange, and Mary Stuart, daughter of Charles I married Mary, elder daughter of James II died aged 51 reigned 13 years

and

1689–1694   MARY II
born 1662, elder daughter of James II and Anne died aged 32 reigned 5 years

1702–1714   ANNE
born 1665, younger daughter of James II and Anne married Prince George of Denmark, son of Frederick III of Denmark died aged 49 reigned 12 years

THE HOUSE OF HANOVER

1714–1727   GEORGE I (Elector of Hanover)
born 1660, son of Sophia (daughter of Frederick, Elector Palatine, and Elizabeth Stuart, daughter of James I) and Ernest Augustus, Elector of Hanover married Sophia Dorothea, daughter of George William, Duke of Lüneburg-Celle died aged 67 reigned 12 years

1727–1760   GEORGE II
born 1683, son of George I married Caroline, daughter of John Frederick, Margrave of Brandenburg-Anspach died aged 76 reigned 33 years

1760–1820 GEORGE III
born 1738, son of Frederick, eldest son of George II *married* Charlotte, daughter of Charles Louis, Duke of Mecklenburg-Strelitz *died* aged 81 *reigned* 59 years

REGENCY 1811–1820
Prince of Wales regent owing to the insanity of George III

Reign
1820–1830 GEORGE IV
born 1762, eldest son of George III *married* Caroline, daughter of Charles, Duke of Brunswick-Wolfenbüttel *died* aged 67 *reigned* 10 years

1830–1837 WILLIAM IV
born 1765, third son of George III *married* Adelaide, daughter of George, Duke of Saxe-Meiningen *died* aged 71 *reigned* 7 years

1837–1901 VICTORIA
born 1819, daughter of Edward, fourth son of George III *married* Prince Albert of Saxe-Coburg and Gotha *died* aged 81 *reigned* 63 years

THE HOUSE OF SAXE-COBURG AND GOTHA
1901–1910 EDWARD VII
born 1841, eldest son of Victoria and Albert *married* Alexandra, daughter of Christian IX of Denmark *died* aged 68 *reigned* 9 years

THE HOUSE OF WINDSOR
1910–1936 GEORGE V
born 1865, second son of Edward VII *married* Victoria Mary, daughter of Francis, Duke of Teck *died* aged 70 *reigned* 25 years

1936 EDWARD VIII
(20 Jan–11 Dec) born 1894, eldest son of George V *married* (1937) Mrs Wallis Simpson *abdicated* 1936 *died* 1972 aged 77 *reigned* 10 months

1936–1952 GEORGE VI
born 1895, second son of George V *married* Lady Elizabeth Bowes-Lyon, daughter of 14th Earl of Strathmore and Kinghorne *died* aged 56 *reigned* 15 years

1952– ELIZABETH II
born 1926, elder daughter of George VI *married* Philip, son of Prince Andrew of Greece

KINGS AND QUEENS OF SCOTS 1016 TO 1603

Reign
1016–1034 MALCOLM II
born c.954, son of Kenneth II *acceded* to Alba 1005, secured Lothian c.1016, obtained Strathclyde for his grandson Duncan c.1016, thus reigning over an area approximately the same as that governed by later rulers of Scotland *died* aged c.80 *reigned* 18 years

THE HOUSE OF ATHOLL
1034–1040 DUNCAN I
son of Bethoc, daughter of Malcolm II, and Crinan, Mormaer of Atholl *married* a cousin of Siward, Earl of Northumbria *reigned* 5 years

1040–1057 MACBETH
born c.1005, son of a daughter of Malcolm II and Finlaec, Mormaer of Moray *married* Gruoch, granddaughter of Kenneth III *killed* aged c.52 *reigned* 17 years

1057–1058 LULACH
(Aug–Mar) born c.1032, son of Gillacomgan, Mormaer of Moray, and Gruoch (and stepson of Macbeth) *died* aged c.26 *reigned* 7 months

1058–1093 MALCOLM III (Canmore)
born c.1031, elder son of Duncan I *married* (1) Ingiborg (2) Margaret (St Margaret), granddaughter of Edmund II of England *killed* in battle aged c.62 *reigned* 35 years

1093–1097 DONALD III BÁN
born c.1033, second son of Duncan I *deposed* May 1094 *restored* Nov 1094 *deposed* Oct 1097 *reigned* 3 years

1094 DUNCAN II
(May–Nov) born c.1060, elder son of Malcolm III and Ingiborg *married* Octreda of Dunbar *killed* aged c.34 *reigned* 6 months

1097–1107 EDGAR
born c.1074, second son of Malcolm III and Margaret *died* aged c.32 *reigned* 9 years

1107–1124 ALEXANDER I (the Fierce)
born c.1077, fifth son of Malcolm III and Margaret *married* Sybilla, illegitimate daughter of Henry I of England *died* aged c.47 *reigned* 17 years

1124–1153 DAVID I (the Saint)
born c.1085, sixth son of Malcolm III and Margaret *married* Matilda, daughter of Waltheof, Earl of Huntingdon *died* aged c.68 *reigned* 29 years

1153–1165 MALCOLM IV (the Maiden)
born c.1141, son of Henry, Earl of Huntingdon, second son of David I *died* aged c.24 *reigned* 12 years

1165–1214 WILLIAM I (the Lion)
born c.1142, brother of Malcolm IV *married* Ermengarde, daughter of Richard, Viscount of Beaumont *died* aged c.72 *reigned* 49 years

1214–1249 ALEXANDER II
born 1198, son of William I *married* (1) Joan, daughter of John, King of England (2) Marie, daughter of Ingelram de Coucy *died* aged 50 *reigned* 34 years

1249–1286 ALEXANDER III
born 1241, son of Alexander II and Marie *married* (1) Margaret, daughter of Henry III of England (2) Yolande, daughter of the Count of Dreux *killed* accidentally aged 44 *reigned* 36 years

1286–1290 MARGARET (the Maid of Norway)
born 1283, daughter of Margaret (daughter of Alexander III) and Eric II of Norway *died* aged 7 *reigned* 4 years

FIRST INTERREGNUM 1290–1292
Throne disputed by 13 competitors. Crown awarded to John Balliol by adjudication of Edward I of England

THE HOUSE OF BALLIOL
Reign
1292–1296 JOHN (Balliol)
born c.1250, son of Dervorguilla, great-great-granddaughter of David I, and John de Balliol *married* Isabella, daughter of John, Earl of Surrey *abdicated* 1296 *died* 1313 aged c.63 *reigned* 3 years

SECOND INTERREGNUM 1296–1306
Edward I of England declared John Balliol to have forfeited the throne for contumacy in 1296 and took the government of Scotland into his own hands

THE HOUSE OF BRUCE

Reign

1306–1329   ROBERT I (Bruce)
born 1274, son of Robert Bruce and Marjorie, Countess of Carrick, and great-grandson of the second daughter of David, Earl of Huntingdon, brother of William I *married* (1) Isabella, daughter of Donald, Earl of Mar (2) Elizabeth, daughter of Richard, Earl of Ulster *died* aged 54 *reigned* 23 years

1329–1371   DAVID II
born 1324, son of Robert I and Elizabeth *married* (1) Joanna, daughter of Edward II of England (2) Margaret Drummond, widow of Sir John Logie (divorced) *died* aged 46 *reigned* 41 years

1332 (Sep–Dec) Edward Balliol, son of John Balliol
1333–1336 Edward Balliol

THE HOUSE OF STEWART

1371–1390   ROBERT II (Stewart)
born 1316, son of Marjorie (daughter of Robert I) and Walter, High Steward of Scotland *married* (1) Elizabeth, daughter of Sir Robert Mure of Rowallan (2) Euphemia, daughter of Hugh, Earl of Ross *died* aged 74 *reigned* 19 years

1390–1406   ROBERT III
born c.1337, son of Robert II and Elizabeth *married* Annabella, daughter of Sir John Drummond of Stobhall *died* aged c.69 *reigned* 16 years

1406–1437   JAMES I
born 1394, son of Robert III *married* Joan Beaufort, daughter of John, Earl of Somerset *assassinated* aged 42 *reigned* 30 years

1437–1460   JAMES II
born 1430, son of James I *married* Mary, daughter of Arnold, Duke of Gueldres *killed* accidentally aged 29 *reigned* 23 years

1460–1488   JAMES III
born 1452, son of James II *married* Margaret, daughter of Christian I of Denmark *assassinated* aged 36 *reigned* 27 years

1488–1513   JAMES IV
born 1473, son of James III *married* Margaret Tudor, daughter of Henry VII of England *killed* in battle aged 40 *reigned* 25 years

1513–1542   JAMES V
born 1512, son of James IV *married* (1) Madeleine, daughter of Francis I of France (2) Mary of Lorraine, daughter of the Duc de Guise *died* aged 30 *reigned* 29 years

1542–1567   MARY
born 1542, daughter of James V and Mary *married* (1) the Dauphin, afterwards Francis II of France (2) Henry Stewart, Lord Darnley (3) James Hepburn, Earl of Bothwell *abdicated* 1567, prisoner in England from 1568, *executed* 1587 *reigned* 24 years

1567–1625   JAMES VI (and I of England)
born 1566, son of Mary, Queen of Scots, and Henry, Lord Darnley *acceded* 1567 to the Scottish throne *reigned* 58 years *succeeded* 1603 to the English throne, so joining the English and Scottish crowns in one person. The two kingdoms remained distinct until 1707 when the parliaments of the kingdoms became conjoined

WELSH SOVEREIGNS AND PRINCES

Wales was ruled by sovereign princes from the earliest times until the death of Llywelyn in 1282. The first English Prince of Wales was the son of Edward I, who was born in Caernarvon town on 25 April 1284. According to a discredited legend, he was presented to the Welsh chieftains as their prince, in fulfilment of a promise that they should have a prince who 'could not speak a word of English' and should be native born. This son, who afterwards became Edward II, was created 'Prince of Wales and Earl of Chester' at the Lincoln Parliament on 7 February 1301.

The title Prince of Wales is borne after individual conferment and is not inherited at birth, though some Princes have been declared and styled Prince of Wales but never formally so created (s.). The title was conferred on Prince Charles by the Queen on 26 July 1958. He was invested at Caernarvon on 1 July 1969.

INDEPENDENT PRINCES AD 844 TO 1282

844–878	Rhodri the Great
878–916	Anarawd, son of Rhodri
916–950	Hywel Dda, the Good
950–979	Iago ab Idwal (or Ieuaf)
979–985	Hywel ab Ieuaf, the Bad
985–986	Cadwallon, his brother
986–999	Maredudd ab Owain ap Hywel Dda
999–1005	Cynan ap Hywel ab Ieuaf
1005–1018	Aeddan ap Blegywyrd
1018–1023	Llywelyn ap Seisyll
1023–1039	Iago ab Idwal ap Meurig
1039–1063	Gruffydd ap Llywelyn ap Seisyll
1063–1075	Bleddyn ap Cynfyn
1075–1081	Trahaern ap Caradog
1081–1137	Gruffydd ap Cynan ab Iago
1137–1170	Owain Gwynedd
1170–1194	Dafydd ab Owain Gwynedd
1194–1240	Llywelyn Fawr, the Great
1240–1246	Dafydd ap Llywelyn
1246–1282	Llywelyn ap Gruffydd ap Llywelyn

ENGLISH PRINCES SINCE 1301

1301	Edward (Edward II)
1343	Edward the Black Prince, son of Edward III
1376	Richard (Richard II), son of the Black Prince
1399	Henry of Monmouth (Henry V)
1454	Edward of Westminster, son of Henry VI
1471	Edward of Westminster (Edward V)
1483	Edward, son of Richard III (d. 1484)
1489	Arthur Tudor, son of Henry VII
1504	Henry Tudor (Henry VIII)
1610	Henry Stuart, son of James I (d. 1612)
1616	Charles Stuart (Charles I)
c.1638 (s.)	Charles Stuart (Charles II)
1688 (s.)	James Francis Edward Stuart (The Old Pretender), son of James II (d. 1766)
1714	George Augustus (George II)
1729	Frederick Lewis, son of George II (d. 1751)
1751	George William Frederick (George III)
1762	George Augustus Frederick (George IV)
1841	Albert Edward (Edward VII)
1901	George (George V)
1910	Edward (Edward VIII)
1958	Charles, son of Elizabeth II

PRINCESSES ROYAL

The style Princess Royal is conferred at the sovereign's discretion on his or her eldest daughter. It is an honorary title, held for life, and cannot be inherited or passed on. It was first conferred on Princess Mary, daughter of Charles I, in approximately 1642.

c.1642	Princess Mary (1631–60), daughter of Charles I
1727	Princess Anne (1709–59), daughter of George II
1766	Princess Charlotte (1766–1828), daughter of George III
1840	Princess Victoria (1840–1901), daughter of Victoria
1905	Princess Louise (1867–1931), daughter of Edward VII
1932	Princess Mary (1897–1965), daughter of George V
1987	Princess Anne (b. 1950), daughter of Elizabeth II

DESCENDANTS OF QUEEN VICTORIA

I. HRH Princess Victoria Adelaide Mary Louisa, Princess Royal (1840–1901), *m* Friedrich III (1831–88), later German Emperor	II. HRH Prince Albert Edward (HM KING EDWARD VII) (1841–1910) *succeeded* 22 Jan 1901 *m* HRH Princess Alexandra of Denmark (1844–1925)	III. HRH Princess Alice Maud Mary (1843–78) *m* Prince Ludwig (1837–92), later Grand Duke of Hesse	IV. HRH Prince Alfred Ernest Albert, Duke of Edinburgh (1844–1900) *succeeded* as Duke of Saxe-Coburg and Gotha 1893 *m* Grand Duchess Marie Alexandrovna of Russia (1853–1920)

1. HIM Wilhelm II (1859–1941), later German Emperor *m* (1) Princess Augusta Victoria of Schleswig-Holstein-Sonderburg-Augustenburg (1858–1921) (2) Princess Hermine of Reuss (1887–1947). *Issue* Wilhelm (1882–1951); Eitel-Friedrich (1883–1942); Adalbert (1884–1948); August Wilhelm (1887–1949); Oskar (1888–1958); Joachim (1890–1920); Viktoria Luise (1892–1980)

2. Charlotte (1860–1919) *m* Bernhard, Duke of Saxe-Meiningen (1851–1928). *Issue* Feodora (1879–1945)

3. Heinrich (1862–1929) *m* Princess Irene of Hesse (*see* III.3). *Issue* Waldemar (1889–1945); Sigismund (1896–1978); Heinrich (1900–4)

4. Sigismund (1864–6)

5. Victoria (1866–1929) *m* (1) Prince Adolf of Schaumburg-Lippe (1859–1916) (2) Alexander Zubkov (1900–36)

6. Waldemar (1868–79)

7. Sophie (1870–1932) *m* Constantine I (1868–1923), later King of the Hellenes. *Issue* George II (1890–1947); Alexander I (1893–1920); Helena (1896–1982); Paul I (1901–64); Irene (1904–74); Katherine (1913–2007)

8. Margarethe (1872–1954) *m* Prince Friedrich Karl of Hesse (1868–1940). *Issue* Friedrich Wilhelm (1893–1916); Maximilian (1894–1914); Philipp (1896–1980); Wolfgang (1896–1989); Richard (1901–69); Christoph (1901–43)

1. Albert Victor, Duke of Clarence and Avondale (1864–92)

2. George (HM KING GEORGE V) (1865–1936) (*see* House of Windsor)

3. Louise (1867–1931), later Princess Royal *m* 1st Duke of Fife (1849–1912). *Issue* Alexandra (1891–1959); Maud (1893–1945)

4. Victoria (1868–1935)

5. Maud (1869–1938) *m* Prince Carl of Denmark (1872–1957), later King Haakon VII of Norway. *Issue* Olav V (1903–91)

6. Alexander (6–7 Apr 1871)

1. Victoria (1863–1950) *m* Prince Louis of Battenberg (1854–1921), later 1st Marquess of Milford Haven. *Issue* Alice (1885–1969); Louise (1889–1965); George (1892–1938); Louis (1900–79)

2. Elizabeth (1864–1918) *m* Grand Duke Sergius of Russia (1857–1905)

3. Irene (1866–1953) *m* Prince Heinrich of Prussia (*see* I.3)

4. Ernst Ludwig (1868–1937), Grand Duke of Hesse, *m* (1) Princess Victoria Melita of Saxe-Coburg (see IV.3) (2) Princess Eleonore of Solms-Hohensolms-Lich (1871–1937). *Issue* Elizabeth (1895–1903); George (1906–37); Ludwig (1908–68)

5. Frederick William (1870–3)

6. Alix (Tsaritsa of Russia) (1872–1918) *m* Nicholas II, Tsar of All the Russias (1868–1918). *Issue* Olga (1895–1918); Tatiana (1897–1918); Marie (1899–1918); Anastasia (1901–18); Alexis (1904–18)

7. Marie (1874–8)

QUEEN VICTORIA (Alexandrina Victoria) (1819–1901) *succeeded* 20 Jun 1837 *m* (Francis) Albert Augustus Charles Emmanuel, Duke of Saxony, Prince of Saxe-Coburg and Gotha (HRH Albert, Prince Consort) (1819–61)

VI. HRH Princess Louise Caroline Alberta (1848–1939) *m* Marquess of Lorne (1845–1914), later 9th Duke of Argyll

VII. HRH Prince Arthur William Patrick Albert, Duke of Connaught (1850–1942) *m* Princess Louisa of Prussia (1860–1917)

VIII. HRH Prince Leopold George Duncan Albert, Duke of Albany (1853–84) *m* Princess Helena of Waldeck (1861–1922)

IX. HRH Princess Beatrice Mary Victoria Feodore (1857–1944) *m* Prince Henry of Battenberg (1858–96)

1. Alfred, Prince of Saxe-Coburg (1874–99)

2. Marie (1875–1938) *m* Ferdinand (1865–1927), later King of Roumania. *Issue* Carol II (1893–1953); Elisabeth (1894–1956); Marie (1900–61); Nicolas (1903–78); Ileana (1909–91); Mircea (1913–16)

3. Victoria Melita (1876–1936) *m* (1) Grand Duke Ernst Ludwig of Hesse (*see* III.4) (2) Grand Duke Kirill of Russia (1876–1938). *Issue* Marie (1907–51); Kira (1909–67); Vladimir (1917–92)

4. Alexandra (1878–1942) *m* Ernst, Prince of Hohenlohe Langenburg (1863–1950). *Issue* Gottfried (1897–1960); Maria (1899–1967); Alexandra (1901–63); Irma (1902–86)

5. Beatrice (1884–1966) *m* Alfonso of Orleans, Infante of Spain (1886–1975). *Issue* Alvaro (1910–97); Alonso (1912–36); Ataulfo (1913–74)

1. Margaret (1882–1920) *m* Crown Prince Gustaf Adolf (1882–1973), later King of Sweden. *Issue* Gustaf Adolf (1906–47); Sigvard (1907–2002); Ingrid (1910–2000); Bertil (1912–97); Count Carl Bernadotte (1916–2012)

2. Arthur (1883–1938) *m* HH Duchess of Fife (1891–1959). *Issue* Alastair Arthur (1914–43)

3. (Victoria) Patricia (1886–1974) *m* Adm. Hon. Sir Alexander Ramsay (1881–1972). *Issue* Alexander (1919–2000)

1. Alice (1883–1981) *m* Prince Alexander of Teck (1874–1957), later 1st Earl of Athlone. *Issue* May (1906–94); Rupert (1907–28); Maurice (Mar–Sep 1910)

2. Charles Edward (1884–1954), Duke of Albany until title suspended 1917, Duke of Saxe-Coburg-Gotha *m* Princess Victoria Adelheid of Schleswig-Holstein-Sonderburg-Glücksburg (1885–1970). *Issue* Johann Leopold (1906–72); Sibylla (1908–72); Dietmar Hubertus (1909–43); Caroline (1912–83); Friedrich Josias (1918–98)

1. Alexander, 1st Marquess of Carisbrooke (1886–1960) *m* Lady Irene Denison (1890–1956). *Issue* Iris (1920–82)

2. Victoria Eugénie (1887–1969) *m* Alfonso XIII, King of Spain (1886–1941). *Issue* Alfonso (1907–38); Jaime (1908–75); Beatriz (1909–2002); Maria (1911–96); Juan (1913–93); Gonzalo (1914–34)

3. Maj. Lord Leopold Mountbatten (1889–1922)

4. Maurice (1891–1914)

V. HRH Princess Helena Augusta Victoria (1846–1923) *m* Prince Christian of Schleswig-Holstein-Sonderburg-Augustenburg (1831–1917)

1. Christian Victor (1867–1900)

2. Albert (1869–1931), later Duke of Schleswig-Holstein

3. Helena (1870–1948)

4. Marie Louise (1872–1956), *m* Prince Aribert of Anhalt (1864–1933)

5. Harold (12–20 May 1876)

THE HOUSE OF WINDSOR

King George V assumed by royal proclamation (17 July 1917) for his House and family, as well as for all descendants in the male line of Queen Victoria who are subjects of these realms, the name of Windsor.

KING GEORGE V

(George Frederick Ernest Albert), second son of King Edward VII *born* 3 June 1865 *married* 6 July 1893 HSH Princess Victoria Mary Augusta Louise Olga Pauline Claudine Agnes of Teck (Queen Mary *born* 26 May 1867 *died* 24 March 1953) *succeeded* to the throne 6 May 1910 *died* 20 January 1936. *Issue*
1. HRH PRINCE EDWARD Albert Christian George Andrew Patrick David *born* 23 June 1894 *succeeded* to the throne as King Edward VIII, 20 January 1936 *abdicated* 11 December 1936 *created* Duke of Windsor 1937 *married* 3 June 1937 Mrs Wallis Simpson (Her Grace The Duchess of Windsor *born* 19 June 1896 *died* 24 April 1986) *died* 28 May 1972
2. HRH PRINCE ALBERT Frederick Arthur George *born* 14 December 1895 *created* Duke of York 1920 *married* 26 April 1923 Lady Elizabeth Bowes-Lyon, youngest daughter of the 14th Earl of Strathmore and Kinghorne (HM Queen Elizabeth the Queen Mother *born* 4 August 1900 *died* 30 March 2002) *succeeded* to the throne as King George VI, 11 December 1936 *died* 6 February 1952. *Issue*
> (1) HRH Princess Elizabeth Alexandra Mary *succeeded* to the throne as Queen Elizabeth II, 6 February 1952 (*see* Royal Family)
> (2) HRH Princess Margaret Rose (later HRH The Princess Margaret, Countess of Snowdon) *born* 21 August 1930 *married* 6 May 1960 Anthony Charles Robert Armstrong-Jones, GCVO *created* Earl of Snowdon 1961 (1930–2017), *marriage dissolved* 1978, *died* 9 February 2002, having had issue (*see* Royal Family)
3. HRH PRINCESS (Victoria Alexandra Alice) MARY *born* 25 April 1897 *created* Princess Royal 1932 *married* 28 February 1922 Viscount Lascelles, later the 6th Earl of Harewood (1882–1947) *died* 28 March 1965. *Issue:*

(1) George Henry Hubert Lascelles, 7th Earl of Harewood, KBE *born* 7 February 1923 *died* 11 July 2011 *married* (1) 1949 Maria (Marion) Stein (marriage dissolved 1967) *issue (a)* David Henry George, 8th Earl of Harewood *born* 1950 *(b)* James Edward *born* 1953 *(c)* (Robert) Jeremy Hugh *born* 1955 (2) 1967 Patricia Tuckwell *issue (d)* Mark Hubert *born* 1964
(2) Gerald David Lascelles *born* 21 August 1924 *died* 27 February 1998 *married* (1) 1952 Angela Dowding (marriage dissolved 1978) *issue (a)* Henry Ulick *born* 1953 (2) 1978 Elizabeth Collingwood (Elizabeth Colvin) *issue (b)* Martin David *born* 1962
4. HRH PRINCE HENRY William Frederick Albert *born* 31 March 1900 *created* Duke of Gloucester, Earl of Ulster and Baron Culloden 1928 *married* 6 November 1935 Lady Alice Christabel Montagu-Douglas-Scott, daughter of the 7th Duke of Buccleuch and Queensberry (HRH Princess Alice, Duchess of Gloucester *born* 25 December 1901 *died* 29 October 2004) *died* 10 June 1974. *Issue*
> (1) HRH Prince William Henry Andrew Frederick *born* 18 December 1941 accidentally *killed* 28 August 1972
> (2) HRH Prince Richard Alexander Walter George (HRH The Duke of Gloucester, *see* Royal Family)
5. HRH PRINCE GEORGE Edward Alexander Edmund *born* 20 December 1902 *created* Duke of Kent, Earl of St Andrews and Baron Downpatrick 1934 *married* 29 November 1934 HRH Princess Marina of Greece and Denmark (*born* 30 November 1906 *died* 27 August 1968) *killed* on active service 25 August 1942. *Issue*
> (1) HRH Prince Edward George Nicholas Paul Patrick (HRH The Duke of Kent, *see* Royal Family)
> (2) HRH Princess Alexandra Helen Elizabeth Olga Christabel (HRH Princess Alexandra, the Hon. Lady Ogilvy, *see* Royal Family)
> (3) HRH Prince Michael George Charles Franklin (HRH Prince Michael of Kent, *see* Royal Family)
6. HRH PRINCE JOHN Charles Francis *born* 12 July 1905 *died* 18 January 1919

PRECEDENCE

ENGLAND AND WALES

The Sovereign
The Prince Philip, Duke of Edinburgh
The Prince of Wales
The Sovereign's younger sons
The Sovereign's grandsons
The Sovereign's cousins
Archbishop of Canterbury
Lord High Chancellor
Archbishop of York
The Prime Minister
Lord President of the Council
Speaker of the House of Commons
Speaker of the House of Lords
President of the Supreme Court
Lord Chief Justice of England and
    Wales
Lord Privy Seal
Ambassadors and High Commissioners
Lord Great Chamberlain
Earl Marshal
Lord Steward of the Household
Lord Chamberlain of the Household
Master of the Horse
Dukes, according to their patent of
    creation:
    1. of England
    2. of Scotland
    3. of Great Britain
    4. of Ireland
    5. those created since the Union
Eldest sons of Dukes of the Blood
    Royal
Ministers, Envoys, and other important
    overseas visitors
Marquesses, according to their patent
    of creation:
    1. of England
    2. of Scotland
    3. of Great Britain
    4. of Ireland
    5. those created since the Union
Dukes' eldest sons
Earls, according to their patent of
    creation:
    1. of England
    2. of Scotland
    3. of Great Britain
    4. of Ireland
    5. those created since the Union
Younger sons of Dukes of Blood
    Royal

Marquesses' eldest sons
Dukes' younger sons
Viscounts, according to their patent of
    creation:
    1. of England
    2. of Scotland
    3. of Great Britain
    4. of Ireland
    5. those created since the Union
Earls' eldest sons
Marquesses' younger sons
Bishop of London
Bishop of Durham
Bishop of Winchester
Other English Diocesan Bishops,
    according to seniority of
    consecration
Retired Church of England Diocesan
    Bishops, according to seniority of
    consecration
Suffragan Bishops, according to
    seniority of consecration
Secretaries of State, if of the degree of
    a Baron
Barons, according to their patent of
    creation:
    1. of England
    2. of Scotland (Lords of Parliament)
    3. of Great Britain
    4. of Ireland
    5. those created since the Union,
        including Life Barons
Master of the Rolls
Deputy President of the Supreme
    Court
Justices of the Supreme Court,
    according to seniority of
    appointment
Treasurer of the Household
Comptroller of the Household
Vice-Chamberlain of the Household
Secretaries of State under the degree of
    Baron
Viscounts' eldest sons
Earls' younger sons
Barons' eldest sons
Knights of the Garter
Privy Counsellors
Chancellor of the Order of the Garter
Chancellor of the Exchequer
Chancellor of the Duchy of Lancaster
President of the Queen's Bench
    Division
President of the Family Division

Chancellor of the High Court
Lord Justices of Appeal, according to
    seniority of appointment
Judges of the High Court, according to
    seniority of appointment
Viscounts' younger sons
Barons' younger sons
Sons of Life Peers
Baronets, according to date of patent
Knights of the Thistle
Knights Grand Cross of the Bath
Knights Grand Cross of St Michael
    and St George
Knights Grand Cross of the Royal
    Victorian Order
Knights Grand Cross of the British
    Empire
Knights Commanders of the Bath
Knights Commanders of St Michael
    and St George
Knights Commanders of the Royal
    Victorian Order
Knights Commanders of the British
    Empire
Knights Bachelor
Circuit Judges, according to priority
    and order of their respective
    appointments
Master of the Court of Protection
Companions of the Bath
Companions of St Michael and St
    George
Commanders of the Royal Victorian
    Order
Commanders of the British Empire
Companions of the Distinguished
    Service Order
Lieutenants of the Royal Victorian
    Order
Officers of the British Empire
Companions of the Imperial Service
    Order
Eldest sons of younger sons of peers
Baronets' eldest sons
Eldest sons of knights, in the same
    order as their fathers
Members of the Royal Victorian Order
Members of the British Empire
Baronets' younger sons
Knights' younger sons, in the same
    order as their fathers
Esquires
Gentlemen

WOMEN

Women take the same rank as their husbands or as their brothers; but the daughter of a peer marrying a commoner retains her title as Lady or Honourable. Daughters of peers rank next immediately after the wives of their elder brothers, and before their younger brothers' wives. Daughters of peers marrying peers of a lower degree take the same order of precedence as that of their husbands; thus the daughter of a

Duke marrying a Baron becomes of the rank of Baroness only, while her sisters married to commoners retain their rank and take precedence over the Baroness. Merely official rank on the husband's part does not give any similar precedence to the wife.
    Peeresses in their own right take the same precedence as peers of the same rank, ie from their date of creation.

SCOTLAND

The Sovereign
The Prince Philip, Duke of Edinburgh
The Lord High Commissioner to the
General Assembly of the Church of
Scotland (while that assembly is
sitting)
The Duke of Rothesay (eldest son of
the Sovereign)
The Sovereign's younger sons
The Sovereign's grandsons
The Sovereign's nephews
Lord-Lieutenants
Lord Provosts, during their term of
office*
Sheriffs Principal, during their term of
office and within the bounds of
their respective sheriffdoms
Lord Chancellor of Great Britain
Moderator of the General Assembly of
the Church of Scotland
Keeper of the Great Seal of Scotland
(the First Minister)
Presiding Officer
The Secretary of State for Scotland
Hereditary High Constable of Scotland
Hereditary Master of the Household in
Scotland
Dukes, as in England

Eldest sons of Dukes of the Blood
Royal
Marquesses, as in England
Dukes' eldest sons
Earls, as in England
Younger sons of Dukes of Blood
Royal
Marquesses' eldest sons
Dukes' younger sons
Lord Justice General
Lord Clerk Register
Lord Advocate
The Advocate General
Lord Justice Clerk
Viscounts, as in England
Earls' eldest sons
Marquesses' younger sons
Lords of Parliament or Barons, as in
England
Eldest sons of Viscounts
Earls' younger sons
Eldest sons of Lords of Parliament or
Barons
Knights and Ladies of the Garter
Knights and Ladies of the Thistle
Privy Counsellors
Senators of the College of Justice
(Lords of Session)
Viscounts' younger sons
Younger sons of Lords of Parliament
or Barons
Baronets

Knights and Dames Grand Cross of
orders, as in England
Knights and Dames Commanders of
orders, as in England
Solicitor-General for Scotland
Lord Lyon King of Arms
Sheriffs Principal, when not within
own county
Knights Bachelor
Sheriffs
Companions of Orders, as in England
Commanders of the Royal Victorian
Order
Commanders of the British Empire
Lieutenants of the Royal Victorian
Order
Companions of the Distinguished
Service Order
Officers of the British Empire
Companions of the Imperial Service
Order
Eldest sons of younger sons of peers
Eldest sons of baronets
Eldest sons of knights, as in England
Members of the Royal Victorian Order
Members of the British Empire
Baronets' younger sons
Knights' younger sons
Queen's Counsel
Esquires
Gentlemen

* The Lord Provosts of Aberdeen, Dundee, Edinburgh and Glasgow are Lord-Lieutenants for these cities *ex officio* and take precedence as such

THE PEERAGE

ABBREVIATIONS AND SYMBOLS

S.	Scottish title
I.	Irish title
**	hereditary peer remaining in the House of Lords
°	there is no 'of' in the title
b.	born
s.	succeeded
§	life peer disqualified from sitting in the House of Lords as a member of the judiciary
ℂ	life peer who has resigned permanently from the House of Lords

m.	married
c.p.	civil partnership
w.	widower or widow
M.	minor
†	heir not ascertained at time of going to press
‡	title not ascertained at time of going to press
F_	represents forename
S_	represents surname
cr.	created
E.	life peer expelled for absenteeism under section 2 of the House of Lords Reform Act 2014 (*see* below)

The rules which govern the creation and succession of peerages are extremely complicated. There are, technically, five separate peerages, the Peerage of England, of Scotland, of Ireland, of Great Britain, and of the United Kingdom. The Peerage of Great Britain dates from 1707 when an Act of Union combined the two kingdoms of England and Scotland and separate peerages were discontinued. The Peerage of the United Kingdom dates from 1801 when Great Britain and Ireland were combined under an Act of Union. Some Scottish peers have received additional peerages of Great Britain or of the UK since 1707, and some Irish peers additional peerages of the UK since 1801.

The Peerage of Ireland was not entirely discontinued from 1801 but holders of Irish peerages, whether pre-dating or created subsequent to the Union of 1801, were not entitled to sit in the House of Lords if they had no additional English, Scottish, Great Britain or UK peerage. However, they were eligible for election to the House of Commons and to vote in parliamentary elections. An Irish peer holding a peerage of a lower grade which enabled him to sit in the House of Lords was introduced there by the title which enabled him to sit, though for all other purposes he was known by his higher title.

In the Peerage of Scotland there is no rank of Baron; the equivalent rank is Lord of Parliament, abbreviated to 'Lord' (the female equivalent is 'Lady').

All peers of England, Scotland, Great Britain or the UK who were 21 years or over, and of British, Irish or Commonwealth nationality were entitled to sit in the House of Lords until the House of Lords Act 1999, when hereditary peers lost the right to sit. However, section two of the act provided an exception for 90 hereditary peers plus the holders of the office of Earl Marshal and Lord Great Chamberlain to remain as members of the House of Lords for their lifetime or pending further reform. Of the 90 hereditary peers, 75 were elected by the hereditary peers in their political party, or Crossbench grouping, and the remaining 15 by the whole house. Until 7 November 2002 any vacancy arising due to the death of one of the 90 excepted hereditary peers was filled by the runner-up to the original election. From 7 November 2002 any vacancy due to a death – or, from 2014, a permanent retirement – has been filled by holding a by-election. By-elections are conducted in accordance with arrangements made by the Clerk of the Parliaments and have to take place within three months of a vacancy occurring. If the vacancy is among the 75, only the excepted hereditary peers in the relevant party or Crossbench grouping are entitled to vote. If the vacancy is among the other 15, the whole house is entitled to vote.

In the list below, peers currently holding one of the 92 hereditary places in the House of Lords are indicated by **.

HEREDITARY WOMEN PEERS

Most hereditary peerages pass on death to the nearest male heir, but there are exceptions, and several are held by women. A woman peer in her own right retains her title after marriage, and if her husband's rank is the superior she is designated by the two titles jointly, the inferior one second. Her hereditary claim still holds good in spite of any marriage whether higher or lower. No rank held by a woman can confer any title or even precedence upon her husband but the rank of a hereditary woman peer in her own right is inherited by her eldest son (or in some cases daughter).

After the Peerage Act 1963, hereditary women peers in their own right were entitled to sit in the House of Lords, subject to the same qualifications as men, until the House of Lords Act 1999.

LIFE PEERS

From 1876 to 2009 non-hereditary or life peerages were conferred on certain eminent judges to enable the judicial functions of the House of Lords to be carried out. These lords were known as Lords of Appeal in Ordinary or law lords. The judicial role of the House of Lords as the highest appeal court in the UK ended on 30 July 2009 and since 1 October 2009, under the Constitutional Reform Act 2005, any peer who holds a senior judicial office is disqualified from sitting in the House of Lords until they retire from that office. In the list of life peerages which follows, members of the judiciary who are currently disqualified from sitting and voting in the House of Lords until retirement, are marked by a '§'.

Under the Constitutional Reform and Governance Act 2010, five peers permanently resigned from the House of Lords.

Since 1958 life peerages have been conferred upon distinguished men and women from all walks of life, giving them seats in the House of Lords in the degree of Baron or Baroness. They are addressed in the same way as hereditary lords and barons, and their children have similar courtesy titles.

HOUSE OF LORDS REFORM ACT 2014

The House of Lords Reform Act 2014 makes provision for a member of the House of Lords who is a peer to retire or resign by giving notice in writing to the Clerk of Parliaments. Resignations may not be rescinded. A number of life peers and elected hereditary peers have already retired permanently under this provision. The Act also makes provision for the expulsion of peers who do not attend the House of Lords for an entire parliamentary session which is longer than six months (indicated by an 'E.' in the following list). Peers on leave of absence or subject to a suspension or disqualification which results in absenteeism for an entire session will not be expelled. The House can also resolve that a peer should not be expelled by reason of special circumstances.

All life peers who have resigned permanently from the House of Lords are indicated by a 'ℂ' in the following list.

PEERAGES EXTINCT 21 SEPTEMBER 2016 TO 31 AUGUST 2017
BARONY: Gladwyn (cr.1960); Lyell (cr. 1914)
LIFE PEERAGES: Armstrong-Jones (cr. 1999); Bagri (cr. 1997); Borrie (cr. 1996); Dixon (cr. 1997); Goodhart (cr. 1997); Hart of Chilton (cr. 2004); Heyhoe Flint (cr. 2011); Jenkin of Roding (cr. 1987); Joffe (cr. 2000); McCluskey (cr. 1976); Prior (cr. 1987); Prys-Davies (cr. 1982); Sandberg (cr. 1997); Soulsby of Swaffham Prior (cr. 1990); Taylor of Blackburn (cr. 1978); Thomas of Swynnerton (cr. 1981); Waddington (cr. 1990); Wall of New Barnet (cr. 2004); Williams of Baglan (cr. 2010)

DISCLAIMER OF PEERAGES
The Peerage Act 1963 enables peers to disclaim their peerages for life. Peers alive in 1963 could disclaim within twelve months after the passing of the act (31 July 1963); a person subsequently succeeding to a peerage may disclaim within 12 months (one month if an MP) after the date of succession, or of reaching 21, if later. The disclaimer is irrevocable but does not affect the descent of the peerage after the disclaimant's death, and children of a disclaimed peer may, if they wish, retain their precedence and any courtesy titles and styles borne as children of a peer. The disclaimer permitted the disclaimant to sit in the House of Commons if elected as an MP. As the House of Lords Act 1999 removed the automatic right of hereditary peers to sit in the House of Lords, they are now entitled to sit in the House of Commons without having to disclaim their titles.
The following peerages are currently disclaimed:
EARLDOM: Selkirk (1994)
BARONIES: Sanderson of Ayot (1971); Silkin (2002)
PEERS WHO ARE MINORS (ie under 21 years of age)
EARLDOM: St Germans (b. 2004)
BARONY: Rodney (b. 1999)

FORMS OF ADDRESS
Forms of address are given under the style for each individual rank of the peerage. Both formal and social forms of address are given where usage differs; nowadays, the social form is generally preferred to the formal, which increasingly is used only for official documents and on very formal occasions.

ROLL OF THE PEERAGE

Crown Office, House of Lords, London SW1A 0PW
T 020-7219 4687 E hereditary.claims@justice.gsi.gov.uk

The Roll of the Peerage is kept at the Crown Office and maintained by the Registrar and Assistant Registrar of the Peerage in accordance with the terms of a 2004 royal warrant. The roll records the names of all living life peers and hereditary peers who have proved their succession to the satisfaction of the Lord Chancellor. The Roll of the Peerage is maintained in addition to the Clerk of the Parliaments' register of hereditary peers eligible to stand for election in House of Lords' by-elections.
  A person whose name is not entered on the Roll of the Peerage can not be addressed or mentioned by the title of a peer in any official document.
  Registrar, Mrs Ceri King

HEREDITARY PEERS

PEERS OF THE BLOOD ROYAL

Style, His Royal Highness the Duke of _/His Royal Highness the Earl of_/His Royal Highness the Lord_
Style of address (formal) May it please your Royal Highness; *(informal)* Sir

Created	Title, order of succession, name, etc	Heir
	Dukes	
1947	Edinburgh (1st), HRH the Prince Philip, Duke of Edinburgh	The Prince of Wales *
1337	Cornwall, HRH the Prince of Wales, s. 1952	‡
1398 S.	Rothesay, HRH the Prince of Wales, s. 1952	‡
2011	Cambridge (1st), HRH Prince William of Wales	HRH Prince George of Cambridge
1986	York (1st), Prince Andrew, HRH the Duke of York	None
1928	Gloucester (2nd), Prince Richard, HRH the Duke of Gloucester, s. 1974	Earl of Ulster
1934	Kent (2nd), Prince Edward, HRH the Duke of Kent, s. 1942	Earl of St Andrews
	Earl	
1999	Wessex (1st), Prince Edward, HRH the Earl of Wessex	Viscount Severn

* In June 1999 Buckingham Palace announced that the current Earl of Wessex will be granted the Dukedom of Edinburgh when the title reverts to the Crown. The title will only revert to the Crown on both the death of the current Duke of Edinburgh and the Prince of Wales' succession as king
‡ The title is held by the sovereign's eldest son from the moment of his birth or the sovereign's accession

DUKES

Coronet, Eight strawberry leaves

Style, His Grace the Duke of _
Envelope (formal), His Grace the Duke of _; *(social),* The Duke of _. *Letter (formal),* My Lord Duke; *(social),* Dear Duke. *Spoken (formal),* Your Grace; *(social),* Duke
Wife's style, Her Grace the Duchess of _
Envelope (formal), Her Grace the Duchess of _; *(social),* The Duchess of _. *Letter (formal),* Dear Madam; *(social),* Dear Duchess. *Spoken,* Duchess
Eldest son's style, Takes his father's second title as a courtesy title (*see* Courtesy Titles)
Younger sons' style, 'Lord' before forename (F_) and surname (S_)
Envelope, Lord F_ S_. *Letter (formal),* My Lord; *(social),* Dear Lord F_. *Spoken (formal),* My Lord; *(social),* Lord F_
Daughters' style, 'Lady' before forename (F_) and surname (S_)
Envelope, Lady F_ S_. *Letter (formal),* Dear Madam; *(social),* Dear Lady F_. *Spoken,* Lady F_

Created	Title, order of succession, name, etc	Heir
1868 I.	*Abercorn (5th),* James Hamilton, KG, *b.* 1934, *s.* 1979, *m.*	Marquess of Hamilton, *b.* 1969
1701 S.	*Argyll (13th),* Torquhil Ian Campbell, *b.* 1968, *s.* 2001 *m.*	Marquess of Lorne, *b.* 2004
1703 S.	*Atholl (12th),* Bruce George Ronald Murray, *b.* 1960, *s.* 2012, *m.*	Marquis of Tullibardine, *b.* 1985
1682	*Beaufort (12th),* Henry John Fitzroy Somerset, *b.* 1952, *s.* 2017, *m.*	Marquess of Worcester, *b.* 1989
1694	*Bedford (15th),* Andrew Ian Henry Russell, *b.* 1962, *s.* 2003, *m.*	Marquess of Tavistock, *b.* 2005
1663 S.	*Buccleuch (10th) and Queensberry (12th) (S. 1684),* Richard Walter John Montagu Douglas Scott, KBE, *b.* 1954, *s.* 2007, *m.*	Earl of Dalkeith, *b.* 1984
1694	*Devonshire (12th),* Peregrine Andrew Morny Cavendish, KCVO, CBE, *b.* 1944, *s.* 2004, *m.*	Earl of Burlington, *b.* 1969
1900	*Fife (4th),* David Charles Carnegie, *b.* 1961, *s.* 2015, *m.*	Earl of Southesk, *b.* 1989
1675	*Grafton (12th),* Henry Oliver Charles FitzRoy, *b.* 1978, *s.* 2011, *m.*	Earl of Euston, *b.* 2012
1643 S.	*Hamilton (16th) and Brandon (13th) (1711),* Alexander Douglas Douglas-Hamilton, *b.* 1978, *s.* 2010, *m. Premier Peer of Scotland*	Marquess of Douglas and Clydesdale, *b.* 2012
1766 I.	*Leinster (9th),* Maurice FitzGerald, *b.* 1948, *s.* 2004, *m. Premier Duke, Marquess and Earl of Ireland*	Edward F., *b.* 1988
1719	*Manchester (13th),* Alexander Charles David Drogo Montagu, *b.* 1962, *s.* 2002, *m.*	Lord Kimble W. D. M., *b.* 1964
1702	*Marlborough (12th),* Charles James Spencer-Churchill, *b.* 1955, *s.* 2014, *m.*	Marquess of Blandford, *b.* 1992
1707 S. **	*Montrose (8th),* James Graham, *b.* 1935, *s.* 1992, *w.*	Marquis of Graham, *b.* 1973
1483 **	*Norfolk (18th),* Edward William Fitzalan-Howard, *b.* 1956, *s.* 2002, *m. Premier Duke and Earl Marshal*	Earl of Arundel and Surrey, *b.* 1987
1766	*Northumberland (12th),* Ralph George Algernon Percy, *b.* 1956, *s.* 1995, *m.*	Earl Percy, *b.* 1984
1675	*Richmond (11th), Gordon (6th) (1876) and Lennox (11th) (S. 1675),* Charles Henry Gordon Lennox, *b.* 1955, *s.* 2017, *m.*	Earl of March and Kinrara, *b.* 1994
1707 S.	*Roxburghe (10th),* Guy David Innes-Ker, *b.* 1954, *s.* 1974, *m. Premier Baronet of Scotland*	Marquis of Bowmont and Cessford, *b.* 1981
1703	*Rutland (11th),* David Charles Robert Manners, *b.* 1959, *s.* 1999, *m.*	Marquess of Granby, *b.* 1999
1684	*St Albans (14th),* Murray de Vere Beauclerk, *b.* 1939, *s.* 1988, *m.*	Earl of Burford, *b.* 1965
1547 **	*Somerset (19th),* John Michael Edward Seymour, *b.* 1952, *s.* 1984, *m.*	Lord Seymour, *b.* 1982
1833	*Sutherland (7th),* Francis Ronald Egerton, *b.* 1940, *s.* 2000, *m.*	Marquess of Stafford, *b.* 1975
1814 **	*Wellington (9th),* Arthur Charles Valerian Wellesley, OBE, *b.* 1945, *s.* 2014, *m.*	Marquess of Douro, *b.* 1978
1874	*Westminster (7th) and 9th Marquess of Westminster (1831),* Hugh Richard Louis Grosvenor, *b.* 1991, *s.* 2016	To Marquessate only, Earl of Wilton (*see* that title)

MARQUESSES

Coronet, Four strawberry leaves alternating with four silver balls

Style, The Most Hon. the Marquess (of) _ . In Scotland the spelling 'Marquis' is preferred for pre-Union creations
Envelope (formal), The Most Hon. the Marquess of _; (social), The Marquess of _. Letter (formal), My Lord; (social), Dear Lord _.
Spoken (formal), My Lord; (social), Lord _
Wife's style, The Most Hon. the Marchioness (of) _
Envelope (formal), The Most Hon. the Marchioness of _; (social), The Marchioness of _. Letter (formal), Madam; (social), Dear
Lady _. Spoken, Lady _
Eldest son's style, Takes his father's second title as a courtesy title (see Courtesy Titles)
Younger sons' style, 'Lord' before forename and surname, as for Duke's younger sons
Daughters' style, 'Lady' before forename and surname, as for Duke's daughter

Created	Title, order of succession, name, etc	Heir
1915	Aberdeen and Temair (7th), Alexander George Gordon, b. 1955, s. 2002, m.	Earl of Haddo, b. 1983
1876	Abergavenny (6th) and 10th Earl of Abergavenny (1784), Christopher George Charles Nevill, b. 1955, s. 2000, m.	To Earldom only, David M. R. N., b. 1941
1821	Ailesbury (8th), Michael Sidney Cedric Brudenell-Bruce, b. 1926, s. 1974	Earl of Cardigan, b. 1952
1831	Ailsa (9th), David Thomas Kennedy, b. 1958, s. 2015, m.	Earl of Cassilis, b. 1995
1815	Anglesey (8th), Charles Alexander Vaughan Paget, b. 1950, s. 2013, m.	Earl of Uxbridge, b. 1986
1789	Bath (7th), Alexander George Thynn, b. 1932, s. 1992, m.	Viscount Weymouth, b. 1974
1826	Bristol (8th), Frederick William Augustus Hervey, b. 1979, s. 1999	Timothy H. H., b. 1960
1796	Bute (7th), John Colum Crichton-Stuart, b. 1958, s. 1993, m.	Earl of Dumfries, b. 1989
1812 °	Camden (6th), David George Edward Henry Pratt, b. 1930, s. 1983	Earl of Brecknock, b. 1965
1815 **	Cholmondeley (7th), David George Philip Cholmondeley, KCVO, b. 1960, s. 1990, m. Lord Great Chamberlain	Earl of Rocksavage, b. 2010
1816 I. °	Conyngham (8th), Henry Vivian Pierpoint Conyngham, b. 1951, s. 2009, m.	Earl of Mount Charles, b. 1975
1791 I.	Donegall (8th), Arthur Patrick Chichester, b. 1952, s. 2007, m.	Earl of Belfast, b. 1990
1789 I.	Downshire (9th), (Arthur Francis) Nicholas Wills Hill, b. 1959, s. 2003, m.	Earl of Hillsborough, b. 1996
1801 I.	Ely (9th), Charles John Tottenham, b. 1943, s. 2006, m.	Lord Timothy C. T., b. 1948
1801	Exeter (8th), (William) Michael Anthony Cecil, b. 1935, s. 1988, m.	Lord Burghley, b. 1970
1800 I.	Headfort (7th), Thomas Michael Ronald Christopher Taylour, b. 1959, s. 2005, w.	Earl of Bective, b. 1989
1793	Hertford (9th), Henry Jocelyn Seymour, b. 1958, s. 1997, m.	Earl of Yarmouth, b. 1993
1599 S.	Huntly (13th), Granville Charles Gomer Gordon, b. 1944, s. 1987, m. Premier Marquess of Scotland	Earl of Aboyne, b. 1973
1784	Lansdowne (9th), Charles Maurice Mercer Nairne Petty-Fitzmaurice, LVO, b. 1941, s. 1999, m.	Earl of Kerry, b. 1970
1902	Linlithgow (4th), Adrian John Charles Hope, b. 1946, s. 1987, m.	Earl of Hopetoun, b. 1969
1816 I.	Londonderry (10th), Frederick Aubrey Vane-Tempest-Stewart, b. 1972, s. 2012	Lord Reginald A. V.-T.-S., b. 1977
1701 S.	Lothian (13th) and Baron Kerr of Monteviot (life peerage, 2010), Michael Andrew Foster Jude Kerr (Michael Ancram), PC, QC, b. 1945, s. 2004, m.	Lord Ralph W. F. J. K., b. 1957
1917	Milford Haven (4th), George Ivar Louis Mountbatten, b. 1961, s. 1970, m.	Earl of Medina, b. 1991
1838	Normanby (5th), Constantine Edmund Walter Phipps, b. 1954, s. 1994, m.	Earl of Mulgrave, b. 1994
1812	Northampton (7th), Spencer Douglas David Compton, b. 1946, s. 1978, m.	Earl Compton, b. 1973
1682 S.	Queensberry (12th), David Harrington Angus Douglas, b. 1929, s. 1954, m.	Viscount Drumlanrig, b. 1967
1926	Reading (4th), Simon Charles Henry Rufus Isaacs, b. 1942, s. 1980, m.	Viscount Erleigh, b. 1986
1789	Salisbury (7th) and Baron Gascoyne-Cecil (life peerage, 1999), Robert Michael James Gascoyne-Cecil, KCVO, PC, b. 1946, s. 2003, m.	Viscount Cranborne, b. 1970
1800 I.	Sligo (12th), Sebastian Ulick Browne, b. 1964, s. 2014, m.	Earl of Altamont, b. 1988
1787 °	Townshend (8th), Charles George Townshend, b. 1945, s. 2010, m.	Viscount Raynham, b. 1977
1694 S.	Tweeddale (14th), Charles David Montagu Hay, b. 1947, s. 2005	(Lord) Alistair J. M. H., b. 1955
1789 I.	Waterford (9th), Henry Nicholas de la Poer Beresford, b. 1958, s. 2015, m.	Earl of Tyrone, b. 1987
1551	Winchester (18th), Nigel George Paulet, b. 1941, s. 1968, m. Premier Marquess of England	Earl of Wiltshire, b. 1969
1892	Zetland (4th), Lawrence Mark Dundas, b. 1937, s. 1989, m.	Earl of Ronaldshay, b. 1965

EARLS

Coronet, Eight silver balls on stalks alternating with eight gold strawberry leaves

Style, The Rt. Hon. the Earl (of) _
Envelope (formal), The Rt. Hon. the Earl (of) _; *(social)*, The Earl (of) _. *Letter (formal)*, My Lord; *(social)*, Dear Lord _. *Spoken (formal)*, My Lord; *(social)*, Lord _.
Wife's style, The Rt. Hon. the Countess (of) _
Envelope (formal), The Rt. Hon. the Countess (of) _; *(social)*, The Countess (of) _. *Letter (formal)*, Madam; *(social)*, Lady _. *Spoken (formal)*, Madam; *(social)*, Lady _.
Eldest son's style, Takes his father's second title as a courtesy title (*see* Courtesy Titles)
Younger sons' style, 'The Hon.' before forename and surname, as for Baron's children
Daughters' style, 'Lady' before forename and surname, as for Duke's daughter

Created	Title, order of succession, name, etc	Heir
1639 S.	*Airlie (13th)*, David George Coke Patrick Ogilvy, KT, GCVO, PC, Royal Victorian Chain, b. 1926, s. 1968, m.	Lord Ogilvy, b. 1958
1696	*Albemarle (10th)*, Rufus Arnold Alexis Keppel, b. 1965, s. 1979	Viscount Bury, b. 2003
1952 °	*Alexander of Tunis (2nd)*, Shane William Desmond Alexander, b. 1935, s. 1969, m.	Hon. Brian J. A., CMG, b. 1939
1662 S.	*Annandale and Hartfell (11th)*, Patrick Andrew Wentworth Hope Johnstone, b. 1941, s. 1983, m. claim established 1985	Lord Johnstone, b. 1971
1789 I. °	*Annesley (12th)*, Michael Robert Annesley, b. 1933, s. 2011, m.	Viscount Glerawly, b. 1957
1785 I.	*Antrim (9th)*, Alexander Randal Mark McDonnell, b. 1935, s. 1977, m.	Viscount Dunluce, b. 1967
1762 I. **	*Arran (9th) and 5th UK Baron Sudley (1884)*, Arthur Desmond Colquhoun Gore, b. 1938, s. 1983, m.	To Earldom only, William H. G., b. 1950
1955 ° **	*Attlee (3rd)*, John Richard Attlee, b. 1956, s. 1991, m.	None
1714	*Aylesford (12th)*, Charles Heneage Finch-Knightley, b. 1947, s. 2008, m.	Lord Guernsey, b. 1985
1937 ° **	*Baldwin of Bewdley (4th)*, Edward Alfred Alexander Baldwin, b. 1938, s. 1976, w.	Viscount Corvedale, b. 1973
1922	*Balfour (5th)*, Roderick Francis Arthur Balfour, b. 1948, s. 2003, m.	Charles G. Y. B., b. 1951
1772 °	*Bathurst (9th)*, Allen Christopher Bertram Bathurst, b. 1961, s. 2011, m.	Lord Apsley, b. 1990
1919 °	*Beatty (3rd)*, David Beatty, b. 1946, s. 1972, m.	Viscount Borodale, b. 1973
1797 I.	*Belmore (8th)*, John Armar Lowry-Corry, b. 1951, s. 1960, m.	Viscount Corry, b. 1985
1739 I.	*Bessborough (12th)*, Myles Fitzhugh Longfield Ponsonby, b. 1941, s. 2002, m.	Viscount Duncannon, b. 1974
1815	*Bradford (7th)*, Richard Thomas Orlando Bridgeman, b. 1947, s. 1981, m.	Viscount Newport, b. 1980
1469 S.	*Buchan (17th)*, Malcolm Harry Erskine, b. 1930, s. 1984, m.	Lord Cardross, b. 1960
1746	*Buckinghamshire (10th)*, (George) Miles Hobart-Hampden, b. 1944, s. 1983, m.	Sir John V. Hobart, Bt., b. 1945
1800 °	*Cadogan (8th)*, Charles Gerald John Cadogan, KBE, b. 1937, s. 1997, m.	Viscount Chelsea, b. 1966
1878 °	*Cairns (6th)*, Simon Dallas Cairns, CVO, CBE, b. 1939, s. 1989, m.	Viscount Garmoyle, b. 1965
1455 S. **	*Caithness (20th)*, Malcolm Ian Sinclair, PC, b. 1948, s. 1965, w.	Lord Berriedale, b. 1981
1800 I.	*Caledon (7th)*, Nicholas James Alexander, KCVO, b. 1955, s. 1980, m.	Viscount Alexander, b. 1990
1661	*Carlisle (13th)*, George William Beaumont Howard, b. 1949, s. 1994	Hon. Philip C. W. H., b. 1963
1793	*Carnarvon (8th)*, George Reginald Oliver Molyneux Herbert, b. 1956, s. 2001, m.	Lord Porchester, b. 1992
1748 I.	*Carrick (11th)*, Arion Thomas Piers Hamilton Butler, b. 1975, s. 2008, m.	Hon. Piers E. T. L. B., b. 1979
1800 I.°	*Castle Stewart (8th)*, Arthur Patrick Avondale Stuart, b. 1928, s. 1961, m.	Viscount Stuart, b. 1953
1814 ° **	*Cathcart (7th)*, Charles Alan Andrew Cathcart, b. 1952, s. 1999, m.	Lord Greenock, b. 1986
1647 I.	*Cavan (13th)*, Roger Cavan Lambart, b. 1944, s. 1988 (claim to the peerage not yet established)	Cavan C. E. L., b. 1957
1827 °	*Cawdor (7th)*, Colin Robert Vaughan Campbell, b. 1962, s. 1993, m.	Viscount Emlyn, b. 1998
1801	*Chichester (9th)*, John Nicholas Pelham, b. 1944, s. 1944, m.	Richard A. H. P., b. 1952
1803 I. **	*Clancarty (9th)*, Nicholas Power Richard Le Poer Trench, b. 1952, s. 1995, m.	None
1776 I.	*Clanwilliam (8th)*, Patrick James Meade, b. 1960, s. 2009, m.	Lord Gillford, b. 1998
1776	*Clarendon (8th)*, George Edward Laurence Villiers, b. 1976, s. 2009, m.	Lord Hyde, b. 2008
1620 I. **	*Cork and Orrery (15th)*, John Richard Boyle, b. 1945, s. 2003, m.	Viscount Dungarvan, b. 1978
1850	*Cottenham (9th)*, Mark John Henry Pepys, b. 1983, s. 2000, m.	Hon. Sam R. P., b. 1986
1762 I. **	*Courtown (9th)*, James Patrick Montagu Burgoyne Winthrop Stopford, b. 1954, s. 1975, m.	Viscount Stopford, b. 1988
1697	*Coventry (13th)*, George William Coventry, b. 1939, s. 2004, m.	David D. S. C., b. 1973
1857 °	*Cowley (8th)*, Garret Graham Wellesley, b. 1965, s. 2016, m.	Viscount Dangan, b. 1991
1892	*Cranbrook (5th)*, Gathorne Gathorne-Hardy, b. 1933, s. 1978, m.	Lord Medway, b. 1968

1801	*Craven (9th),* Benjamin Robert Joseph Craven, *b.* 1989, *s.* 1990	Rupert J. E. C., *b.* 1926
1398 S.	*Crawford (29th) and Balcarres (12th) (S. 1651) and Baron Balniel (life peerage, 1974),* Robert Alexander Lindsay, KT, GCVO, PC, *b.* 1927, *s.* 1975, *m.* Premier Earl on Union Roll	Lord Balniel, *b.* 1958
1861	*Cromartie (5th),* John Ruaridh Blunt Grant Mackenzie, *b.* 1948, *s.* 1989, *m.*	Viscount Tarbat, *b.* 1987
1901	*Cromer (4th),* Evelyn Rowland Esmond Baring, *b.* 1946, *s.* 1991, *m.*	Viscount Errington, *b.* 1994
1633 S.	*Dalhousie (17th),* James Hubert Ramsay, *b.* 1948, *s.* 1999, *m. Lord Steward*	Lord Ramsay, *b.* 1981
1725 I.	*Darnley (12th),* Ivo Donald Stuart Bligh, *b.* 1968, *s.* 2017, *m.*	Lord Clifton, *b.* 1999
1711	*Dartmouth (10th),* William Legge, MEP, *b.* 1949, *s.* 1997, *m.*	Hon. Rupert L., *b.* 1951
1761 °	*De La Warr (11th),* William Herbrand Sackville, *b.* 1948, *s.* 1988, *m.*	Lord Buckhurst, *b.* 1979
1622	*Denbigh (12th) and Desmond (11th) (I. 1622),* Alexander Stephen Rudolph Feilding, *b.* 1970, *s.* 1995, *m.*	Viscount Feilding, *b.* 2005
1485	*Derby (19th),* Edward Richard William Stanley, *b.* 1962, *s.* 1994, *m.*	Lord Stanley, *b.* 1998
1553	*Devon (19th),* Charles Peregrine Courtenay, *b.* 1975, *s.* 2015, *m.*	Lord Courtenay, *b.* 2009
1800 I.	*Donoughmore (8th),* Richard Michael John Hely-Hutchinson, *b.* 1927, *s.* 1981, *w.*	Viscount Suirdale, *b.* 1952
1661 I.	*Drogheda (12th),* Henry Dermot Ponsonby Moore, *b.* 1937, *s.* 1989, *m.*	Viscount Moore, *b.* 1983
1837	*Ducie (7th),* David Leslie Moreton, *b.* 1951, *s.* 1991, *m.*	Lord Moreton, *b.* 1981
1860	*Dudley (5th),* William Humble David Jeremy Ward, *b.* 1947, *s.* 2013	Hon. Leander G. D. W., *b.* 1971
1660 S. **	*Dundee (12th),* Alexander Henry Scrymgeour, *b.* 1949, *s.* 1983, *m.*	Lord Scrymgeour, *b.* 1982
1669 S.	*Dundonald (15th),* Iain Alexander Douglas Blair Cochrane, *b.* 1961, *s.* 1986, *m.*	Lord Cochrane, *b.* 1991
1686 S.	*Dunmore (12th),* Malcolm Kenneth Murray, *b.* 1946, *s.* 1995, *m.*	Hon. Geoffrey C. M., *b.* 1949
1833	*Durham (7th),* Edward Richard Lambton, *b.* 1961, *s.* 2006, *m.*	Viscount Lambton, *b.* 1985
1643 S.	*Dysart (13th),* John Peter Grant of Rothiemurchus, *b.* 1946, *s.* 2011, *m.*	Lord Huntingtower, *b.* 1977
1837	*Effingham (7th),* David Mowbray Algernon Howard, *b.* 1939, *s.* 1996, *m.*	Lord Howard of Effingham, *b.* 1971
1507 S.	*Eglinton (18th) and Winton (9th) (S. 1600),* Archibald George Montgomerie, *b.* 1939, *s.* 1966, *m.*	Lord Montgomerie, *b.* 1966
1821	*Eldon (6th),* John Francis Thomas Marie Joseph Columba Fidelis Scott, *b.* 1962, *s.* 2017, *m.*	Viscount Encombe, *b.* 1996
1633 S.	*Elgin (11th) and Kincardine (15th) (S. 1647),* Andrew Douglas Alexander Thomas Bruce, KT, *b.* 1924, *s.* 1968, *m.*	Lord Bruce, *b.* 1961
1789 I.	*Enniskillen (7th),* Andrew John Galbraith Cole, *b.* 1942, *s.* 1989, *m.*	Berkeley A. C., *b.* 1949
1789 I.	*Erne (7th),* John Henry Michael Ninian Crichton, *b.* 1971, *s.* 2016	Charles D. B. C., *b.* 1953
1452 S. **	*Erroll (24th),* Merlin Sereld Victor Gilbert Hay, *b.* 1948, *s.* 1978, *m.* Hereditary Lord High Constable and Knight Marischal of Scotland	Lord Hay, *b.* 1984
1661	*Essex (11th),* Frederick Paul de Vere Capell, *b.* 1944, *s.* 2005	William J. C., *b.* 1952
1711 °	*Ferrers (14th),* Robert William Saswalo Shirley, *b.* 1952, *s.* 2012, *m.*	Viscount Tamworth, *b.* 1984
1789 °	*Fortescue (8th),* Charles Hugh Richard Fortescue, *b.* 1951, *s.* 1993, *m.*	John A. F. F., *b.* 1955
1841	*Gainsborough (6th),* Anthony Baptist Noel, *b.* 1950, *s.* 2009, *m.*	Viscount Campden, *b.* 1977
1623 S.	*Galloway (13th),* Randolph Keith Reginald Stewart, *b.* 1928, *s.* 1978, *w.*	Andrew C. S., *b.* 1949
1703 S.**	*Glasgow (10th),* Patrick Robin Archibald Boyle, *b.* 1939, *s.* 1984, *m.*	Viscount of Kelburn, *b.* 1978
1806 I.	*Gosford (7th),* Charles David Nicholas Alexander John Sparrow Acheson, *b.* 1942, *s.* 1966, *m.*	Nicholas H. C. A., *b.* 1947
1945	*Gowrie (2nd),* Alexander Patrick Greysteil Hore Ruthven, PC, *b.* 1939, *s.* 1955, *m.*	Viscount Ruthven of Canberra, *b.* 1964
1684 I.	*Granard (10th),* Peter Arthur Edward Hastings Forbes, *b.* 1957, *s.* 1992, *m.*	Viscount Forbes, *b.* 1981
1833 °	*Granville (6th),* Granville George Fergus Leveson-Gower, *b.* 1959, *s.* 1996, *m.*	Lord Leveson, *b.* 1999
1806 °	*Grey (7th),* Philip Kent Grey, *b.* 1940, *s.* 2013, *m.*	Viscount Howick, *b.* 1968
1752	*Guilford (10th),* Piers Edward Brownlow North, *b.* 1971, *s.* 1999, *m.*	Lord North, *b.* 2002
1619 S.	*Haddington (14th),* George Edmund Baldred Baillie-Hamilton, *b.* 1985, *s.* 2016	Thomas R. Hamilton-Baillie, *b.* 1948
1919 °	*Haig (3rd),* Alexander Douglas Derrick Haig, *b.* 1961, *s.* 2009, *m.*	None
1944	*Halifax (3rd),* Charles Edward Peter Neil Wood, *b.* 1944, *s.* 1980, *m.*	Lord Irwin, *b.* 1977
1754	*Hardwicke (10th),* Joseph Philip Sebastian Yorke, *b.* 1971, *s.* 1974, *m.*	Viscount Royston, *b.* 2009
1812	*Harewood (8th),* David Henry George Lascelles, *b.* 1950, *s.* 2011, *m.*	Viscount Lascelles, *b.* 1978
1742	*Harrington (12th),* Charles Henry Leicester Stanhope, *b.* 1945, *s.* 2009, *m.*	Viscount Petersham, *b.* 1967
1809	*Harrowby (8th),* Dudley Adrian Conroy Ryder, *b.* 1951, *s.* 2007, *m.*	Viscount Sandon, *b.* 1981
1605 S. **	*Home (15th),* David Alexander Cospatrick Douglas-Home, KT, CVO, CBE, *b.* 1943, *s.* 1995, *m.*	Lord Dunglass, *b.* 1987
1821 ° **	*Howe (7th),* Frederick Richard Penn Curzon, PC, *b.* 1951, *s.* 1984, *m.*	Viscount Curzon, *b.* 1994
1529	*Huntingdon (16th),* William Edward Robin Hood Hastings Bass, LVO, *b.* 1948, *s.* 1990, *m.*	Hon. Simon A. R. H. H. B., *b.* 1950
1885	*Iddesleigh (5th),* John Stafford Northcote, *b.* 1957, *s.* 2004, *m.*	Viscount St Cyres, *b.* 1985
1756	*Ilchester (10th),* Robin Maurice Fox-Strangways, *b.* 1942, *s.* 2006, *m.*	Lord Stavordale, *b.* 1972
1929	*Inchcape (4th),* (Kenneth) Peter (Lyle) Mackay, *b.* 1943, *s.* 1994, *m.*	Viscount Glenapp, *b.* 1979
1919	*Iveagh (4th),* Arthur Edward Rory Guinness, *b.* 1969, *s.* 1992, *m.*	Viscount Elveden, *b.* 2003
1925 °	*Jellicoe (3rd),* Patrick John Bernard Jellicoe, *b.* 1950, *s.* 2007	Hon. Nicholas C. J., *b.* 1953
1697	*Jersey (10th),* George Francis William Child Villiers, *b.* 1976, *s.* 1998, *m.*	Viscount Villiers, *b.* 2015
1822 I.	*Kilmorey (6th),* Sir Richard Francis Needham, PC, *b.* 1942, *s.* 1977, *m.* (Does not use title)	Viscount Newry and Mourne, *b.* 1966

1866	*Kimberley (5th),* John Armine Wodehouse, *b.* 1951, *s.* 2002, *m.*	Lord Wodehouse, *b.* 1978
1768 I.	*Kingston (12th),* Robert Charles Henry King-Tenison, *b.* 1969, *s.* 2002, *m.*	Viscount Kingsborough, *b.* 2000
1633 S. **	*Kinnoull (16th),* Charles William Harley Hay, *b.* 1962, *s.* 2013, *m.*	Viscount Dupplin, *b.* 2011
1677 S.	*Kintore (14th),* James William Falconer Keith, *b.* 1976, *s.* 2004, *m.*	Lord Inverurie, *b.* 2010
1624 S.	*Lauderdale (18th),* Ian Maitland, *b.* 1937, *s.* 2008, *m.*	Viscount Maitland, *b.* 1965
1837	*Leicester (8th),* Thomas Edward Coke, *b.* 1965, *s.* 2015, *m.*	Viscount Coke, *b.* 2003
1641 S.	*Leven (15th) and Melville (14th) (S. 1690),* Alexander Ian Leslie Melville, *b.* 1984, *s.* 2012	Hon. Archibald R. L. M., *b.* 1957
1831	*Lichfield (6th),* Thomas William Robert Hugh Anson, *b.* 1978, *s.* 2005, *m.*	Viscount Anson, *b.* 2011
1803 I.	*Limerick (7th),* Edmund Christopher Pery, *b.* 1963, *s.* 2003, *m.*	Viscount Glentworth, *b.* 1991
1572	*Lincoln (19th),* Robert Edward Fiennes-Clinton, *b.* 1972, *s.* 2001	Hon. William J. Howson, *b.* 1980
1633 S. **	*Lindsay (16th),* James Randolph Lindesay-Bethune, *b.* 1955, *s.* 1989, *m.*	Viscount Garnock, *b.* 1990
1626	*Lindsey (14th) and Abingdon (9th) (1682),* Richard Henry Rupert Bertie, *b.* 1931, *s.* 1963, *m.*	Lord Norreys, *b.* 1958
1776 I.	*Lisburne (9th),* David John Francis Malet Vaughan, *b.* 1945, *s.* 2014, *m.*	Hon. Michael J. W. M. V., *b.* 1948
1822 I.**	*Listowel (6th),* Francis Michael Hare, *b.* 1964, *s.* 1997, *m.*	Hon. Timothy P. H., *b.* 1966
1905 **	*Liverpool (5th),* Edward Peter Bertram Savile Foljambe, *b.* 1944, *s.* 1969, *m.*	Viscount Hawkesbury, *b.* 1972
1945 °	*Lloyd George of Dwyfor (4th),* David Richard Owen Lloyd George, *b.* 1951, *s.* 2010, *m.*	Viscount Gwynedd, *b.* 1986
1785 I.	*Longford (8th),* Thomas Frank Dermot Pakenham, *b.* 1933, *s.* 2001, *m.* (Does not use title)	Edward M. P., *b.* 1970
1807	*Lonsdale (8th),* Hugh Clayton Lowther, *b.* 1949, *s.* 2006, *m.*	Hon. William J. L., *b.* 1957
1633 S.	*Loudoun (15th),* Simon Michael Abney-Hastings, *b.* 1974, *s.* 2012, *m.*	Hon. Marcus W. A.-H., *b.* 1981
1838	*Lovelace (5th),* Peter Axel William Locke King, *b.* 1951, *s.* 1964, *m.*	None
1795 I.	*Lucan (8th),* George Charles Bingham, *b.* 1967, *s.* 2016, *m.*	Hon. Hugh B., *b.* 1939
1880 **	*Lytton (5th),* John Peter Michael Scawen Lytton, *b.* 1950, *s.* 1985, *m.*	Viscount Knebworth, *b.* 1989
1721	*Macclesfield (9th),* Richard Timothy George Mansfield Parker, *b.* 1943, *s.* 1992, *m.*	Hon. J. David G. P., *b.* 1945
1800	*Malmesbury (7th),* James Carleton Harris, *b.* 1946, *s.* 2000, *m.*	Viscount FitzHarris, *b.* 1970
1776	*Mansfield (8th) and Mansfield (9th) (1792),* Alexander David Mungo Murray, *b.* 1956, *s.* 2015, *m.*	Viscount Stormont, *b.* 1988
1565 S.	*Mar (14th) and Kellie (16th) (S. 1616) and Baron Erskine of Alloa Tower (life peerage, 2000),* James Thorne Erskine, *b.* 1949, *s.* 1994, *m.*	Hon. Alexander D. E., *b.* 1952
1785 I.	*Mayo (11th),* Charles Diarmuidh John Bourke, *b.* 1953, *s.* 2006, *m.*	Lord Naas, *b.* 1985
1627 I.	*Meath (15th),* John Anthony Brabazon, *b.* 1941, *s.* 1998, *m.*	Lord Ardee, *b.* 1977
1766 I.	*Mexborough (8th),* John Christopher George Savile, *b.* 1931, *s.* 1980, *m.*	Viscount Pollington, *b.* 1959
1813	*Minto (7th),* Gilbert Timothy George Lariston Elliot-Murray-Kynynmound, *b.* 1953, *s.* 2005, *m.*	Viscount Melgund, *b.* 1984
1562 S.	*Moray (21st),* John Douglas Stuart, *b.* 1966, *s.* 2011, *m.*	Lord Doune, *b.* 2002
1815	*Morley (7th),* Mark Lionel Parker, *b.* 1956, *s.* 2015, *m.*	Hon. Nigel G. P., *b.* 1931
1458 S.	*Morton (22nd),* John Stewart Sholto Douglas, *b.* 1952, *s.* 2016, *m.*	Lord Aberdour, *b.* 1986
1789	*Mount Edgcumbe (8th),* Robert Charles Edgcumbe, *b.* 1939, *s.* 1982	Piers V. E., *b.* 1946
1947 °	*Mountbatten of Burma (3rd),* Norton Louis Philip Knatchbull, *b.* 1947, *s.* 2017, *m.*	Lord Romsey, *b.* 1981
1805 °	*Nelson (10th),* Simon John Horatio Nelson, *b.* 1971, *s.* 2009, *m.*	Viscount Merton, *b.* 2010
1660 S.	*Newburgh (12th),* Don Filippo Giambattista Camillo Francesco Aldo Maria Rospigliosi, *b.* 1942, *s.* 1986, *m.*	Princess Donna Benedetta F. M. R., *b.* 1974
1827 I.	*Norbury (7th),* Richard James Graham-Toler, *b.* 1967, *s.* 2000	None
1806 I.	*Normanton (6th),* Shaun James Christian Welbore Ellis Agar, *b.* 1945, *s.* 1967, *m.*	Viscount Somerton, *b.* 1982
1647 S.	*Northesk (15th),* Patrick Charles Carnegy, *b.* 1940, *s.* 2010, *m.*	Hon. Colin D. C., *b.* 1942
1801	*Onslow (8th),* Rupert Charles William Bullard Onslow, *b.* 1967, *s.* 2011, *m.*	Anthony E. E. O., *b.* 1955
1696 S.	*Orkney (9th),* (Oliver) Peter St John, *b.* 1938, *s.* 1998, *m.*	Viscount Kirkwall, *b.* 1969
1328 I.	*Ormonde and Ossory (I. 1527),* The 25th/18th Earl (7th Marquess) died in 1988	†Viscount Mountgarret *b.* 1961 (*see* that title)
1925 **	*Oxford and Asquith (3rd),* Raymond Benedict Bartholomew Michael Asquith, OBE, *b.* 1952, *s.* 2011, *m.*	Viscount Asquith, *b.* 1979
1929 ° **	*Peel (3rd),* William James Robert Peel, GCVO, PC, *b.* 1947, *s.* 1969, *m.* Lord Chamberlain	Viscount Clanfield, *b.* 1976
1551	*Pembroke (18th) and Montgomery (15th) (1605),* William Alexander Sidney Herbert, *b.* 1978, *s.* 2003, *m.*	Lord Herbert, *b.* 2012
1605 S.	*Perth (18th),* John Eric Drummond, *b.* 1935, *s.* 2002, *m.*	Viscount Strathallan, *b.* 1965
1905	*Plymouth (3rd),* Other Robert Ivor Windsor-Clive, *b.* 1923, *s.* 1943, *w.*	Viscount Windsor, *b.* 1951
1785 I.	*Portarlington (7th),* George Lionel Yuill Seymour Dawson-Damer, *b.* 1938, *s.* 1959, *m.*	Viscount Carlow, *b.* 1965
1689	*Portland (12th),* Count Timothy Charles Robert Noel Bentinck, *b.* 1953, *s.* 1997, *m.*	Viscount Woodstock, *b.* 1984
1743	*Portsmouth (10th),* Quentin Gerard Carew Wallop, *b.* 1954, *s.* 1984, *m.*	Viscount Lymington, *b.* 1981
1804	*Powis (8th),* John George Herbert, *b.* 1952, *s.* 1993, *m.*	Viscount Clive, *b.* 1979
1765	*Radnor (9th),* William Pleydell-Bouverie, *b.* 1955, *s.* 2008, *m.*	Viscount Folkestone, *b.* 1999
1831 I.	*Ranfurly (7th),* Gerald Françoys Needham Knox, *b.* 1929, *s.* 1988, *m.*	Viscount Northland, *b.* 1957
1771 I.	*Roden (10th),* Robert John Jocelyn, *b.* 1938, *s.* 1993, *m.*	Viscount Jocelyn, *b.* 1989
1801	*Romney (8th),* Julian Charles Marsham, *b.* 1948, *s.* 2004, *m.*	Viscount Marsham, *b.* 1977

1703 S.	*Rosebery (7th)*, Neil Archibald Primrose, *b.* 1929, *s.* 1974, *m.*	Lord Dalmeny, *b.* 1967
1806 I.	*Rosse (7th)*, William Brendan Parsons, *b.* 1936, *s.* 1979, *m.*	Lord Oxmantown, *b.* 1969
1801 **	*Rosslyn (7th)*, Peter St Clair-Erskine, CVO, QPM, *b.* 1958, *s.* 1977, *m.*	Lord Loughborough, *b.* 1986
1457 S.	*Rothes (22nd)*, James Malcolm David Leslie, *b.* 1958, *s.* 2005, *m.*	Hon. Alexander J. L., *b.* 1962
1861 °	*Russell (7th)*, John Francis Russell, *b.* 1971, *s.* 2014, *m.*	None
1915 °	*St Aldwyn (3rd)*, Michael Henry Hicks Beach, *b.* 1950, *s.* 1992, *m.*	Hon. David S. H. B., *b.* 1955
1815 M.	*St Germans (11th)*, Albert Charger Eliot, *b.* 2004, *s.* 2016	Hon. Louis R. E., *b.* 1968
1660 **	*Sandwich (11th)*, John Edward Hollister Montagu, *b.* 1943, *s.* 1995, *m.*	Viscount Hinchingbrooke, *b.* 1969
1690	*Scarbrough (13th)*, Richard Osbert Lumley, *b.* 1973, *s.* 2004, *m.*	Hon. Thomas H. L., *b.* 1980
1701 S.	*Seafield (13th)*, Ian Derek Francis Ogilvie-Grant, *b.* 1939, *s.* 1969, *m.*	Viscount Reidhaven, *b.* 1963
1882 **	*Selborne (4th)*, John Roundell Palmer, GBE, *b.* 1940, *s.* 1971, *m.*	Viscount Wolmer, *b.* 1971
1646 S.	*Selkirk (11th)*, Disclaimed for life 1994 (*see* Lord Selkirk of Douglas, Life Peers)	Master of Selkirk, *b.* 1978
1672	*Shaftesbury (12th)*, Nicholas Edmund Anthony Ashley-Cooper, *b.* 1979, *s.* 2005, *m.*	Lord Ashley, *b.* 2011
1756 I.	*Shannon (10th)*, Richard Henry John Boyle, *b.* 1960, *s.* 2013	Robert F. B., *b.* 1930
1442 **	*Shrewsbury and Waterford (22nd) (I. 1446)*, Charles Henry John Benedict Crofton Chetwynd Chetwynd-Talbot, *b.* 1952, *s.* 1980, *m. Premier Earl of England and Ireland*	Viscount Ingestre, *b.* 1978
1961	*Snowdon (2nd)*, David Albert Charles Armstrong-Jones, *b.* 1961, *s.* 2017, *m.*	Viscount Linley, *b.* 1999
1765 °	*Spencer (9th)*, Charles Edward Maurice Spencer, *b.* 1964, *s.* 1992, *m.*	Viscount Althorp, *b.* 1994
1703 S.**	*Stair (14th)*, John David James Dalrymple, *b.* 1961, *s.* 1996, *m.*	Viscount Dalrymple, *b.* 2008
1984	*Stockton (2nd)*, Alexander Daniel Alan Macmillan, *b.* 1943, *s.* 1986, *m.*	Viscount Macmillan of Ovenden, *b.* 1974
1821	*Stradbroke (6th)*, Robert Keith Rous, *b.* 1937, *s.* 1983, *m.*	Viscount Dunwich, *b.* 1961
1847	*Strafford (9th)*, William Robert Byng, *b.* 1964, *s.* 2016, *m.*	Viscount Enfield, *b.* 1998
1606 S.	*Strathmore and Kinghorne (19th) (S. 1677)*, Simon Patrick Bowes Lyon, *b.* 1986, *s.* 2016	Hon. John F. B. L., *b.* 1988
1603	*Suffolk (21st) and Berkshire (14th) (1626)*, Michael John James George Robert Howard, *b.* 1935, *s.* 1941, *m.*	Viscount Andover, *b.* 1974
1955	*Swinton (3rd)*, Nicholas John Cunliffe-Lister, *b.* 1939, *s.* 2006, *m.*	Lord Masham, *b.* 1970
1714	*Tankerville (10th)*, Peter Grey Bennet, *b.* 1956, *s.* 1980	Adrian G. B., *b.* 1958
1822 °	*Temple of Stowe (9th)*, James Grenville Temple-Gore-Langton, *b.* 1955, *s.* 2013, *m.*	Hon. Robert C. T.-G.-L., *b.* 1957
1815	*Verulam (7th)*, John Duncan Grimston, *b.* 1951, *s.* 1973, *m.*	Viscount Grimston, *b.* 1978
1729 °	*Waldegrave (13th)*, James Sherbrooke Waldegrave, *b.* 1940, *s.* 1995, *m.*	Viscount Chewton, *b.* 1986
1759	*Warwick (9th) and Brooke (9th) (1746)*, Guy David Greville, *b.* 1957, *s.* 1996, *m.*	Lord Brooke, *b.* 1982
1633 S.	*Wemyss (13th) and March (9th) (S. 1697)*, James Donald Charteris, *b.* 1948, *s.* 2008, *m.*	Lord Elcho, *b.* 1984
1621 I.	*Westmeath (13th)*, William Anthony Nugent, *b.* 1928, *s.* 1971, *m.*	Sean C. W. N., *b.* 1965
1624	*Westmorland (16th)*, Anthony David Francis Henry Fane, *b.* 1951, *s.* 1993, *m.*	Hon. Harry St C. F., *b.* 1953
1876	*Wharncliffe (5th)*, Richard Alan Montagu Stuart Wortley, *b.* 1953, *s.* 1987, *m.*	Viscount Carlton, *b.* 1980
1801	*Wilton (8th)*, Francis Egerton Grosvenor, *b.* 1934, *s.* 1999, *m.*	Viscount Grey de Wilton, *b.* 1959
1628	*Winchilsea (17th) and Nottingham (12th) (1681)*, Daniel James Hatfield Finch Hatton, *b.* 1967, *s.* 1999, *m.*	Viscount Maidstone, *b.* 1998
1766 I. °	*Winterton (8th)*, (Donald) David Turnour, *b.* 1943, *s.* 1991, *m.*	Robert C. T., *b.* 1950
1956	*Woolton (3rd)*, Simon Frederick Marquis, *b.* 1958, *s.* 1969, *m.*	None
1837	*Yarborough (8th)*, Charles John Pelham, *b.* 1963, *s.* 1991, *m.*	Lord Worsley, *b.* 1990

COUNTESSES IN THEIR OWN RIGHT

Style, The Rt. Hon. the Countess (of) _
Envelope (formal), The Rt. Hon. the Countess (of) _; (social), The Countess (of) _. Letter (formal), Madam; (social), Lady _. Spoken (formal), Madam; (social), Lady _.
Husband, Untitled
Children's style, As for children of an Earl
In Scotland, the heir to a Countess may be styled 'The Master/Mistress of _ (title of peer)'

Created	Title, order of succession, name, etc	Heir
c.1115 S. **	Mar (31st), Margaret of Mar, b. 1940, s. 1975, m. Premier Earldom of Scotland	Mistress of Mar, b. 1963
c.1235 S.	Sutherland (24th), Elizabeth Millicent Sutherland, b. 1921, s. 1963, w.	Lord Strathnaver, b. 1947

VISCOUNTS

Coronet, Sixteen silver balls

Style, The Rt. Hon. the Viscount _
Envelope (formal), The Rt. Hon. the Viscount _; (social), The Viscount _. Letter (formal), My Lord; (social), Dear Lord _. Spoken, Lord _.
Wife's style, The Rt. Hon. the Viscountess _
Envelope (formal), The Rt. Hon. the Viscountess _; (social), The Viscountess _. Letter (formal), Madam; (social), Dear Lady _. Spoken, Lady _.
Children's style, 'The Hon.' before forename and surname, as for Baron's children
In Scotland, the heir to a Viscount may be styled 'The Master/Mistress of _ (title of peer)'

Created	Title, order of succession, name, etc	Heir
1945	Addison (4th), William Matthew Wand Addison, b. 1945, s. 1992, m.	Hon. Paul W. A., b. 1973
1946	Alanbrooke (3rd), Alan Victor Harold Brooke, b. 1932, s. 1972	None
1919	Allenby (4th), Henry Jaffray Hynman Allenby, b. 1968, s. 2014, m.	Hon. Harry M. E. A., b. 2000
1911	Allendale (4th), Wentworth Peter Ismay Beaumont, b. 1948, s. 2002, m.	Hon. Wentworth A. I. B., b. 1979
1642 S.	of Arbuthnott (17th), John Keith Oxley Arbuthnott, b. 1950, s. 2012, m.	Master of Arbuthnott, b. 1977
1751 I.	Ashbrook (11th), Michael Llowarch Warburton Flower, b. 1935, s. 1995, m.	Hon. Rowland F. W. F., b. 1975
1917 **	Astor (4th), William Waldorf Astor, b. 1951, s. 1966, m.	Hon. William W. A., b. 1979
1781 I.	Bangor (8th), William Maxwell David Ward, b. 1948, s. 1993, m.	Hon. E. Nicholas W., b. 1953
1925	Bearsted (5th), Nicholas Alan Samuel, b. 1950, s. 1996, m.	Hon. Harry R. S., b. 1988
1963	Blakenham (2nd), Michael John Hare, b. 1938, s. 1982, m.	Hon. Caspar J. H., b. 1972
1935	Bledisloe (4th), Rupert Edward Ludlow Bathurst, b. 1964, s. 2009, m.	Hon. Benjamin B., b. 2004
1712	Bolingbroke (9th) and St John (10th) (1716), Nicholas Alexander Mowbray St John, b. 1974, s. 2011, m.	German A. St J., b. 1980
1960	Boyd of Merton (2nd), Simon Donald Rupert Neville Lennox-Boyd, b. 1939, s. 1983, m.	Hon. Benjamin A. L.-B., b. 1964
1717 I.	Boyne (11th), Gustavus Michael Stucley Hamilton-Russell, b. 1965, s. 1995, m.	Hon. Gustavus A. E. H.-R., b. 1999
1929	Brentford (4th), Crispin William Joynson-Hicks, b. 1933, s. 1983, m.	Hon. Paul W. J.-H., MBE, b. 1971
1929 **	Bridgeman (3rd), Robin John Orlando Bridgeman, b. 1930, s. 1982, m.	Hon. Luke R. O. B., b. 1971
1868	Bridport (4th) and 7th Duke, Bronte in Sicily, 1799, Alexander Nelson Hood, b. 1948, s. 1969, m.	Hon. Peregrine A. N. H., b. 1974
1952 **	Brookeborough (3rd), Alan Henry Brooke, b. 1952, s. 1987, m.	Hon. Christopher A. B., b. 1954
1933	Buckmaster (4th), Adrian Charles Buckmaster, b. 1949, s. 2007, m.	Hon. Andrew N. B., b. 1980
1939	Caldecote (3rd), Piers James Hampden Inskip, b. 1947, s. 1999, m.	Hon. Thomas J. H. I., b. 1985
1941	Camrose (5th), Jonathan William Berry, b. 1970, s. 2016, m.	Hon. Hugo W. B., b. 2000
1954	Chandos (3rd) and Baron Lyttelton of Aldershot (life peerage, 2000), Thomas Orlando Lyttelton, b. 1953, s. 1980, m.	Hon. Oliver A. L., b. 1986
1665 I.	Charlemont (15th), John Dodd Caulfeild, b. 1966, s. 2001, m.	Hon. Shane A. C., b. 1996

1921	*Chelmsford (4th)*, Frederic Corin Piers Thesiger, *b.* 1962, *s.* 1999, *m.*	Hon. Frederic T., *b.* 2006
1717 I.	*Chetwynd (11th)*, Adam Douglas Chetwynd, *b.* 1969, *s.* 2015, *m.*	Hon. Connor A. C., *b.* 2001
1911	*Chilston (4th)*, Alastair George Akers-Douglas, *b.* 1946, *s.* 1982, *m.*	Hon. Oliver I. A.-D., *b.* 1973
1902	*Churchill (3rd) and 5th UK Baron Churchill (1815)*, Victor George Spencer, OBE, *b.* 1934, *s.* 1973	To Barony only, Richard H. R. S., *b.* 1926
1718	*Cobham (12th)*, Christopher Charles Lyttelton, *b.* 1947, *s.* 2006, *m.*	Hon. Oliver C. L., *b.* 1976
1902 **	*Colville of Culross (5th)*, Charles Mark Townshend Colville, *b.* 1959, *s.* 2010	Master of Colville, *b.* 1961
1826	*Combermere (6th)*, Thomas Robert Wellington Stapleton-Cotton, *b.* 1969, *s.* 2000, *m.*	Hon. Laszlo M. W. S.-C., *b.* 2010
1917	*Cowdray (4th)*, Michael Orlando Weetman Pearson, *b.* 1944, *s.* 1995, *m.*	Hon. Peregrine J. D. P., *b.* 1994
1927 **	*Craigavon (3rd)*, Janric Fraser Craig, *b.* 1944, *s.* 1974	None
1943	*Daventry (4th)*, James Edward FitzRoy Newdegate, *b.* 1960, *s.* 2000, *m.*	Hon. Humphrey J. F. N., *b.* 1995
1937	*Davidson (3rd)*, Malcolm William Mackenzie Davidson, *b.* 1934, *s.* 2012, *m.*	Hon. John N. A. D., *b.* 1971
1956	*De L'Isle (2nd)*, Philip John Algernon Sidney, MBE, *b.* 1945, *s.* 1991, *m.*	Hon. Philip W. E. S., *b.* 1985
1776 I.	*de Vesci (7th)*, Thomas Eustace Vesey, *b.* 1955, *s.* 1983, *m.*	Hon. Oliver I. V., *b.* 1991
1917	*Devonport (3rd)*, Terence Kearley, *b.* 1944, *s.* 1973, *m.*	Chester D. H. K., *b.* 1932
1964	*Dilhorne (2nd)*, John Mervyn Manningham-Buller, *b.* 1932, *s.* 1980, *m.*	Hon. James E. M.-B., *b.* 1956
1622 I.	*Dillon (22nd)*, Henry Benedict Charles Dillon, *b.* 1973, *s.* 1982	Thomas A. L. D., *b.* 1983
1785 I.	*Doneraile (10th)*, Richard Allen St Leger, *b.* 1946, *s.* 1983, *m.*	Hon. Nathaniel W. R. St J. St L., *b.* 1971
1680 I.	*Downe (12th)*, Richard Henry Dawnay, *b.* 1967, *s.* 2002	Thomas P. D., *b.* 1978
1959	*Dunrossil (3rd)*, Andrew William Reginald Morrison, *b.* 1953, *s.* 2000, *m.*	Hon. Callum A. B. M., *b.* 1994
1964 **	*Eccles (2nd)*, John Dawson Eccles, CBE, *b.* 1931, *s.* 1999, *m.*	Hon. William D. E., *b.* 1960
1897	*Esher (5th)*, Christopher Lionel Baliol Brett, *b.* 1936, *s.* 2004, *m.*	Hon. Matthew C. A. B., *b.* 1963
1816	*Exmouth (10th)*, Paul Edward Pellew, *b.* 1940, *s.* 1970, *m.*	Hon. Edward F. P., *b.* 1978
1620 S.**	*of Falkland (15th)*, Lucius Edward William Plantagenet Cary, *b.* 1935, *s.* 1984, *m. Premier Scottish Viscount on the Roll*	Master of Falkland, *b.* 1963
1720	*Falmouth (9th)*, George Hugh Boscawen, *b.* 1919, *s.* 1962, *w.*	Hon. Evelyn A. H. B., *b.* 1955
1720 I.	*Gage (8th)*, (Henry) Nicolas Gage, *b.* 1934, *s.* 1993, *m.*	Hon. Henry W. G., *b.* 1975
1727 I.	*Galway (12th)*, George Rupert Monckton-Arundell, CD, *b.* 1922, *s.* 1980, *m.*	Hon. J. Philip M.-A., *b.* 1952
1478 I.	*Gormanston (17th)*, Jenico Nicholas Dudley Preston, *b.* 1939, *s.* 1940, *m. Premier Viscount of Ireland*	Hon. Jenico F. T. P., *b.* 1974
1816 I.	*Gort (9th)*, Foley Robert Standish Prendergast Vereker, *b.* 1951, *s.* 1995, *m.*	Hon. Robert F. P. V., *b.* 1993
1900 **	*Goschen (4th)*, Giles John Harry Goschen, *b.* 1965, *s.* 1977, *m.*	Hon. Alexander J. E. G., *b.* 2001
1849	*Gough (5th)*, Shane Hugh Maryon Gough, *b.* 1941, *s.* 1951	None
1929	*Hailsham (3rd) and Baron Hailsham of Kettlethorpe (life peerage, 2015)*, Douglas Martin Hogg, PC, QC, *b.* 1945, *s.* 2001, *m.*	Hon. Quintin J. N. M. H., *b.* 1973
1891	*Hambleden (5th)*, William Henry Bernard Smith, *b.* 1955, *s.* 2012, *m.*	Hon. Bernardo J. S., *b.* 1957
1884	*Hampden (7th)*, Francis Anthony Brand, *b.* 1970, *s.* 2008, *m.*	Hon. Lucian A. B., *b.* 2005
1936 **	*Hanworth (3rd)*, David Stephen Geoffrey Pollock, *b.* 1946, *s.* 1996, *m.*	Harold W. C. P., *b.* 1988
1791 I.	*Harberton (11th)*, Henry Robert Pomeroy, *b.* 1958, *s.* 2004, *m.*	Hon. Patrick C. P., *b.* 1995
1846	*Hardinge (8th)*, Thomas Henry de Montarville Hardinge, *b.* 1993, *s.* 2014	Hon. Jamie A. D. H., *b.* 1996
1791 I.	*Hawarden (9th)*, (Robert) Connan Wyndham Leslie Maude, *b.* 1961, *s.* 1991, *m.*	Hon. Varian J. C. E. M., *b.* 1997
1960	*Head (2nd)*, Richard Antony Head, *b.* 1937, *s.* 1983, *m.*	Hon. Henry J. H., *b.* 1980
1550	*Hereford (19th)*, Charles Robin de Bohun Devereux, *b.* 1975, *s.* 2004, *m. Premier Viscount of England*	Hon. Henry W. de B. D., *b.* 2015
1842	*Hill (19th)*, Peter David Raymond Charles Clegg-Hill, *b.* 1945, *s.* 2003, *m.*	Hon. Michael C. D. C.-H., *b.* 1988
1796	*Hood (8th)*, Henry Lyttelton Alexander Hood, *b.* 1958, *s.* 1999, *m.*	Hon. Archibald L. S. H., *b.* 1993
1945	*Kemsley (3rd)*, Richard Gomer Berry, *b.* 1951, *s.* 1999, *m.*	Hon. Luke G. B., *b.* 1998
1911	*Knollys (3rd)*, David Francis Dudley Knollys, *b.* 1931, *s.* 1966, *m.*	Hon. Patrick N. M. K., *b.* 1962
1895	*Knutsford (6th)*, Michael Holland-Hibbert, *b.* 1926, *s.* 1986, *m.*	Hon. Henry T. H.-H., *b.* 1959
1954	*Leathers (3rd)*, Christopher Graeme Leathers, *b.* 1941, *s.* 1996, *m.*	Hon. James F. L., *b.* 1969
1781 I.	*Lifford (9th)*, (Edward) James Wingfield Hewitt, *b.* 1949, *s.* 1987, *m.*	Hon. James T. W. H., *b.* 1979
1921	*Long (5th)*, James Richard Long, *b.* 1960, *s.* 2017	None
1957	*Mackintosh of Halifax (3rd)*, (John) Clive Mackintosh, *b.* 1958, *s.* 1980, *m.*	Hon. Thomas H. G. M., *b.* 1985
1955	*Malvern (3rd)*, Ashley Kevin Godfrey Huggins, *b.* 1949, *s.* 1978	Hon. M. James H., *b.* 1928
1945	*Marchwood (3rd)*, David George Staveley Penny, *b.* 1936, *s.* 1979, *w.*	Hon. Peter G. W. P., *b.* 1965
1942	*Margesson (3rd)*, Richard Francis David Margesson, *b.* 1960, *s.* 2014, *m.*	None
1660 I.	*Massereene (14th) and Ferrard (7th) (I. 1797)*, John David Clotworthy Whyte-Melville Foster Skeffington, *b.* 1940, *s.* 1992, *m.*	Hon. Charles J. C. W.-M. F. S., *b.* 1973
1802	*Melville (10th)*, Robert Henry Kirkpatrick Dundas, *b.* 1984, *s.* 2011	Hon. James D. B. D., *b.* 1986
1916	*Mersey (5th) and 14th Lord Nairne (S. 1681)*, Edward John Hallam Bigham, *b.* 1966, *s.* 2006, *m.*	Hon. David E. H. B., *b.* 1938 (to Viscountcy); Mistress of Nairne, *b.* 2003 (to Lordship of Nairne)
1717 I.	*Midleton (12th)*, Alan Henry Brodrick, *b.* 1949, *s.* 1988, *m.*	Hon. Ashley R. B., *b.* 1980
1962	*Mills (3rd)*, Christopher Philip Roger Mills, *b.* 1956, *s.* 1988, *m.*	None
1716 I.	*Molesworth (12th)*, Robert Bysse Kelham Molesworth, *b.* 1959, *s.* 1997	Hon. William J. C. M., *b.* 1960
1801 I.	*Monck (7th)*, Charles Stanley Monck, *b.* 1953, *s.* 1982 (Does not use title)	Hon. George S. M., *b.* 1957

1957	*Monckton of Brenchley (3rd)*, Christopher Walter Monckton, *b.* 1952, *s.* 2006, *m.*	Hon. Timothy D. R. M., *b.* 1955
1946	*Montgomery of Alamein (2nd)*, David Bernard Montgomery, CMG, CBE, *b.* 1928, *s.* 1976, *m.*	Hon. Henry D. M., *b.* 1954
1550 I.	*Mountgarret (18th)*, Piers James Richard Butler, *b.* 1961, *s.* 2004, *m.*	Hon. Theo O. S. B., *b.* 2015
1952	*Norwich (2nd)*, John Julius Cooper, CVO, *b.* 1929, *s.* 1954, *m.*	Hon. Jason C. D. B. C., *b.* 1959
1651 S.	*of Oxfuird (14th)*, Ian Arthur Alexander Makgill, *b.* 1969, *s.* 2003, *m.*	Master of Oxfuird, *b.* 2012
1873	*Portman (10th)*, Christopher Edward Berkeley Portman, *b.* 1958, *s.* 1999, *m.*	Hon. Luke O. B. P., *b.* 1984
1743 I.	*Powerscourt (11th)*, Mervyn Anthony Wingfield, *b.* 1963, *s.* 2015, *m.*	Hon. Guy C. P. W., *b.* 1940
1900 **	*Ridley (5th)*, Matthew White Ridley, *b.* 1958, *s.* 2012, *m.*	Hon. Matthew W. R., *b.* 1993
1960	*Rochdale (3rd)*, Jonathan Hugo Durival Kemp, *b.* 1961, *s.* 2015, *m.*	George T. K., *b.* 2001
1919	*Rothermere (4th)*, (Harold) Jonathan Esmond Vere Harmsworth, *b.* 1967, *s.* 1998, *m.*	Hon. Vere R. J. H. H., *b.* 1994
1937	*Runciman of Doxford (3rd)*, Walter Garrison (Garry) Runciman, CBE, *b.* 1934, *s.* 1989, *m.*	Hon. David W. R., *b.* 1967
1918	*St Davids (4th)*, Rhodri Colwyn Philipps, *b.* 1966, *s.* 2009, *m.*	Hon. Roland A. J. E. P., *b.* 1970
1801	*St Vincent (8th)*, Edward Robert James Jervis, *b.* 1951, *s.* 2006, *m.*	Hon. James R. A. J., *b.* 1982
1937	*Samuel (5th)*, Jonathan Herbert Samuel, *b.* 1965, *s.* 2014, *m.*	Hon. Benjamin A. S., *b.* 1983
1911	*Scarsdale (4th)*, Peter Ghislain Nathaniel Curzon, *b.* 1949, *s.* 2000, *m.*	Hon. David J. N. C., *b.* 1958
1905	*Selby (6th)*, Christopher Rolf Thomas Gully, *b.* 1993, *s.* 2001	Hon. (James) Edward H. G. G., *b.* 1945
1805	*Sidmouth (8th)*, Jeremy Francis Addington, *b.* 1947, *s.* 2005, *w.*	Hon. John A., *b.* 1990
1940 **	*Simon (3rd)*, Jan David Simon, *b.* 1940, *s.* 1993, *m.*	None
1960 **	*Slim (2nd)*, John Douglas Slim, OBE, *b.* 1927, *s.* 1970, *m.*	Hon. Mark W. R. S., *b.* 1960
1954	*Soulbury (4th)*, Oliver Peter Ramsbotham, *b.* 1943, *s.* 2010, *m.*	Hon. Edward H. R., *b.* 1966
1776 I.	*Southwell (7th)*, Pyers Anthony Joseph Southwell, *b.* 1930, *s.* 1960, *m.*	Hon. Richard A. P. S., *b.* 1956
1942	*Stansgate (3rd)*, Stephen Michael Wedgwood Benn, *b.* 1951, *s.* 2014, *m.*	Hon. Daniel J. W. B., *b.* 1991
1959	*Stuart of Findhorn (3rd)*, Dominic Stuart, *b.* 1948, *s.* 1999, *m.*	Hon. Andrew M. S., *b.* 1957
1957	*Tenby (3rd)*, William Lloyd George, *b.* 1927, *s.* 1983, *m.*	Hon. Timothy H. G. L. G., *b.* 1962
1952 **	*Thurso (3rd)*, John Archibald Sinclair, PC, *b.* 1953, *s.* 1995, *m.*	Hon. James A. R. S., *b.* 1984
1721	*Torrington (11th)*, Timothy Howard St George Byng, *b.* 1943, *s.* 1961, *m.*	Colin H. Cranmer-Byng, *b.* 1960
1936 **	*Trenchard (3rd)*, Hugh Trenchard, *b.* 1951, *s.* 1987, *m.*	Hon. Alexander T. T., *b.* 1978
1921 **	*Ullswater (2nd)*, Nicholas James Christopher Lowther, LVO, PC, *b.* 1942, *s.* 1949, *m.*	Hon. Benjamin J. L., *b.* 1975
1642 I.	*Valentia (16th)*, Frances William Dighton Annesley, *b.* 1959, *s.* 2005, *m.*	Hon. Peter J. A., *b.* 1967
1952 **	*Waverley (3rd)*, John Desmond Forbes Anderson, *b.* 1949, *s.* 1990, *m.*	Hon. Forbes A. R. A., *b.* 1996
1938	*Weir (3rd)*, William Kenneth James Weir, *b.* 1933, *s.* 1975, *m.*	Hon. James W. H. W., *b.* 1965
1918	*Wimborne (4th)*, Ivor Mervyn Vigors Guest, *b.* 1968, *s.* 1993, *m.*	Hon. Julian J. G., *b.* 1945
1923 **	*Younger of Leckie (5th)*, James Edward George Younger, *b.* 1955, *s.* 2003, *m.*	Hon. Alexander W. G. Y., *b.* 1993

BARONS/LORDS

Coronet, Six silver balls

Style, The Rt. Hon. the Lord _
   Envelope (formal), The Rt. Hon. Lord _; *(social)*, The Lord _. *Letter (formal)*, My Lord; *(social)*, Dear Lord _. *Spoken*, Lord _.
In the Peerage of Scotland there is no rank of Baron; the equivalent rank is Lord of Parliament and Scottish peers should always be styled 'Lord', never 'Baron'.

Wife's style, The Rt. Hon. the Lady _
   Envelope (formal), The Rt. Hon. Lady _; *(social)*, The Lady _. *Letter (formal)*, My Lady; *(social)*, Dear Lady _. *Spoken*, Lady _
Children's style, 'The Hon.' before forename (F_) and surname (S_)
Envelope, The Hon. F_ S_. *Letter*, Dear Mr/Miss/Mrs S_. *Spoken*, Mr/Miss/Mrs S_
In Scotland, the heir to a Lord may be styled 'The Master/Mistress of _ (title of peer)'

Created	*Title, order of succession, name, etc*	*Heir*
1911	*Aberconway (4th)*, (Henry) Charles McLaren, *b.* 1948, *s.* 2003, *m.*	Hon. Charles S. M., *b.* 1984
1873 **	*Aberdare (5th)*, Alastair John Lyndhurst Bruce, *b.* 1947, *s.* 2005, *m.*	Hon. Hector M. N. B., *b.* 1974
1835	*Abinger (9th)*, James Harry Scarlett, *b.* 1959, *s.* 2002, *m.*	Hon. Peter R. S., *b.* 1961
1869	*Acton (5th)*, John Charles Ferdinand Harold Lyon-Dalberg-Acton, *b.* 1966, *s.* 2010, *m.*	Hon. Robert P. L.-D.-A., *b.* 1946
1887 **	*Addington (6th)*, Dominic Bryce Hubbard, *b.* 1963, *s.* 1982, *m.*	Hon. Michael W. L. H., *b.* 1965

1896	Aldenham (6th) and Hunsdon of Hunsdon (4th) (1923), Vicary Tyser Gibbs, b. 1948, s. 1986, m.	Hon. Humphrey W. F. G., b. 1989
1962	Aldington (2nd), Charles Harold Stuart Low, b. 1948, s. 2000, m.	Hon. Philip T. A. L., b. 1990
1945	Altrincham (3rd), Anthony Ulick David Dundas Grigg, b. 1934, s. 2001, m.	Hon. (Edward) Sebastian G., b. 1965
1929	Alvingham (2nd), Maj.-Gen. Robert Guy Eardley Yerburgh, CBE, b. 1926, s. 1955, m.	Capt. Hon. Robert R. G. Y., b. 1956
1892	Amherst of Hackney (5th), Hugh William Amherst Cecil, b. 1968, s. 2009, m.	Hon. Jack W. A. C., b. 2001
1881	Ampthill (5th), David Whitney Erskine Russell, b. 1947, s. 2011, m.	Hon. Anthony J. M. R., b. 1952
1947	Amwell (3rd), Keith Norman Montague, b. 1943, s. 1990, m.	Hon. Ian K. M., b. 1973
1863	Annaly (6th), Luke Richard White, b. 1954, s. 1990, m.	Hon. Luke H. W., b. 1990
1885	Ashbourne (4th), Edward Barry Greynville Gibson, b. 1933, s. 1983, m.	Hon. Edward C. d'O. G., b. 1967
1835	Ashburton (7th), John Francis Harcourt Baring, KG, KCVO, b. 1928, s. 1991, m.	Hon. Mark F. R. B., b. 1958
1892	Ashcombe (5th), Mark Edward Cubitt, b. 1964, s. 2013, m.	Hon. Richard R. A. C., b. 1995
1911 **	Ashton of Hyde (4th), Thomas Henry Ashton, b. 1958, s. 2008, m.	Hon. John E. A., b. 1966
1800 I.	Ashtown (8th), Roderick Nigel Godolphin Trench, b. 1944, s. 2010, m.	Hon. Timothy R. H. T., b. 1968
1956 **	Astor of Hever (3rd), John Jacob Astor, PC, b. 1946, s. 1984, m.	Hon. Charles G. J. A., b. 1990
1789 I.	Auckland (10th) and Auckland (10th) (1793), Robert Ian Burnard Eden, b. 1962, s. 1997, m.	Henry V. E., b. 1958
1313	Audley, Barony in abeyance between three co-heiresses since 1997	
1900	Avebury (5th), Lyulph Ambrose Lubbock, b. 1954, s. 2016, m.	Hon. Alexander L. R. L., b. 1985
1718 I.	Aylmer (14th), (Anthony) Julian Aylmer, b. 1951, s. 2006, m.	Hon. Michael H. A., b. 1991
1929	Baden-Powell (3rd), Robert Crause Baden-Powell, b. 1936, s. 1962, w.	Hon. David M. B.-P., b. 1940
1780	Bagot (10th), (Charles Hugh) Shaun Bagot, b. 1944, s. 2001, m.	Richard C. V. B., b. 1941
1953	Baillieu (3rd), James William Latham Baillieu, b. 1950, s. 1973, m.	Hon. Robert L. B., b. 1979
1607 S.	Balfour of Burleigh (8th), Robert Bruce, b. 1927, s. 1967, m.	Hon. Victoria B., b. 1973
1924	Banbury of Southam (3rd), Charles William Banbury, b. 1953, s. 1981, m.	None
1698	Barnard (12th), Henry Francis Cecil Vane, b. 1959, s. 2016, m.	Hon. William H. C. V., b. 2005
1887	Basing (6th), Stuart Anthony Whitfield Sclater-Booth, b. 1969, s. 2007, m.	Hon. Luke W. S.-B., b. 2000
1917	Beaverbrook (3rd), Maxwell William Humphrey Aitken, b. 1951, s. 1985, m.	Hon. Maxwell F. A., b. 1977
1647 S.	Belhaven and Stenton (13th), Robert Anthony Carmichael Hamilton, b. 1927, s. 1961, m.	Master of Belhaven, b. 1953
1848 I.	Bellew (8th), Bryan Edward Bellew, b. 1943, s. 2010, m.	Hon. Anthony R. B. B., b. 1972
1856	Belper (5th), Richard Henry Strutt, b. 1941, s. 1999, m.	Hon. Michael H. S., b. 1969
1421	Berkeley (18th) and Gueterbock (life peerage, 2000), Anthony Fitzhardinge Gueterbock, OBE, b. 1939, s. 1992, m.	Hon. Thomas F. G., b. 1969
1922	Bethell (5th), James Nicholas Bethell, b. 1967, s. 2007, m.	Hon. Jacob N. D. B., b. 2006
1938	Bicester (4th), Hugh Charles Vivian Smith, b. 1934, s. 2014	Charles J. V. S., b. 1963
1903	Biddulph (5th), (Anthony) Nicholas Colin Maitland Biddulph, b. 1959, s. 1988, m.	Hon. Robert J. M. B., b. 1994
1958	Birkett (3rd), Thomas Birkett, b. 1982, s. 2015	None
1907	Blyth (5th), James Audley Ian Blyth, b. 1970, s. 2009, m.	Hon. Hugo A. J. B., b. 2006
1797	Bolton (8th), Harry Algar Nigel Orde-Powlett, b. 1954, s. 2001, w.	Hon. Thomas O.-P., MC, b. 1979
1452 S.	Borthwick (24th), John Hugh Borthwick, b. 1940, s. 1996, m.	Hon. James H. A. B. of Glengelt, b. 1940
1922 **	Borwick (5th), (Geoffrey Robert) James Borwick, b. 1955, s. 2007, m.	Hon. Edwin D. W. B., b. 1984
1761	Boston (11th), George William Eustace Boteler Irby, b. 1971, s. 2007, m.	Hon. Thomas W. G. B. I., b. 1999
1942 **	Brabazon of Tara (3rd), Ivon Anthony Moore-Brabazon, PC, b. 1946, s. 1974, m.	Hon. Benjamin R. M.-B., b. 1983
1925	Bradbury (3rd), John Bradbury, b. 1940, s. 1994, m.	Hon. John B., b. 1973
1962	Brain (3rd), Michael Cottrell Brain, b. 1928, s. 2014, m.	Hon. Thomas R. B., b. 1965
1938	Brassey of Apethorpe (4th), Edward Brassey, b. 1964, s. 2015, m.	Hon. Christian B., b. 2003
1788	Braybrooke (11th), Richard Ralph Neville, b. 1977, s. 2017	John N., b. 1944
1957	Bridges (3rd), Mark Thomas Bridges, CVO, b. 1954, s. 2017, m.	Hon. Miles E. F. B., b. 1992
1945	Broadbridge (4th), Martin Hugh Broadbridge, b. 1929, s. 2000, w.	Air Vice-Marshal Hon. Richard J. M. B., b. 1959
1933	Brocket (3rd), Charles Ronald George Nall-Cain, b. 1952, s. 1967, m.	Hon. Alexander C. C. N.-C., b. 1984
1860 **	Brougham and Vaux (5th), Michael John Brougham, CBE, b. 1938, s. 1967	Hon. Charles W. B., b. 1971
1776	Brownlow (7th), Edward John Peregrine Cust, b. 1936, s. 1978, m.	Hon. Peregrine E. Q. C., b. 1974
1942	Bruntisfield (3rd), Michael John Victor Warrender, b. 1949, s. 2007, m.	Hon. John M. P. C. W., b. 1996
1950	Burden (4th), Fraser William Elsworth Burden, b. 1964, s. 2000, m.	Hon. Ian S. B., b. 1967
1529	Burgh (8th), (Alexander) Gregory Disney Leith, b. 1958, s. 2001, m.	Hon. Alexander J. S. L., b. 1986
1903	Burnham (7th), Harry Frederick Alan Lawson, b. 1968, s. 2005	None
1897	Burton (4th), Evan Michael Ronald Baillie, b. 1949, s. 2013, m.	Hon. James E. B., b. 1975
1643	Byron (13th), Robert James Byron, b. 1950, s. 1989, m.	Hon. Charles R. G. B., b. 1990
1937	Cadman (3rd), John Anthony Cadman, b. 1938, s. 1966, m.	Hon. Nicholas A. J. C., b. 1977
1945	Calverley (3rd), Charles Rodney Muff, b. 1946, s. 1971, m.	Hon. Jonathan E. Brown, b. 1975
1383	Camoys (7th), (Ralph) Thomas Campion George Sherman Stonor, GCVO, PC, b. 1940, s. 1976, m.	Hon. R. William R. T. S., b. 1974
1715 I.	Carbery (12th), Michael Peter Evans-Freke, b. 1942, s. 2012, m.	Hon. Dominic R. C. E.-F., b. 1969
1834 I.	Carew (7th) and Carew (7th) (1838), Patrick Thomas Conolly-Carew, b. 1938, s. 1994, m.	Hon. William P. C.-C., b. 1973

Date	Peer	Heir
1916	Carnock (5th), Adam Nicolson, b. 1957, s. 2008, m.	Hon. Thomas N., b. 1984
1796 I.	Carrington (6th) and Carrington (6th) (1797) and Carington of Upton (life peerage, 1999), Peter Alexander Rupert Carington, KG, GCMG, CH, MC, PC, b. 1919, s. 1938, w.	Hon. Rupert F. J. C., b. 1948
1812 I.	Castlemaine (8th), Roland Thomas John Handcock, MBE, b. 1943, s. 1973, m.	Hon. Ronan M. E. H., b. 1989
1936	Catto (3rd), Innes Gordon Catto, b. 1950, s. 2001, m.	Hon. Alexander G. C., b. 1952
1918	Cawley (4th), John Francis Cawley, b. 1946, s. 2001, m.	Hon. William R. H. C., b. 1981
1858	Chesham (7th), Charles Gray Compton Cavendish, b. 1974, s. 2009, m.	Hon. Oliver N. B. C., b. 2007
1945	Chetwode (2nd), Philip Chetwode, b. 1937, s. 1950, m.	Hon. Roger C., b. 1968
1945	Chorley (3rd), Nicholas Rupert Debenham Chorley, b. 1966, s. 2016, m.	Hon. Patrick A. C. C., b. 2000
1858	Churston (5th), John Francis Yarde-Buller, b. 1934, s. 1991, m.	Hon. Benjamin F. A. Y.-B., b. 1974
1800 I.	Clanmorris (8th), Simon John Ward Bingham, b. 1937, s. 1988, m.	Robert D. de B. B., b. 1942
1672	Clifford of Chudleigh (14th), Thomas Hugh Clifford, b. 1948, s. 1988, m.	Hon. Alexander T. H. C., b. 1985
1299	Clinton (22nd), Gerard Nevile Mark Fane Trefusis, b. 1934, s. 1965, m.	Hon. Charles P. R. F. T., b. 1962
1955	Clitheroe (2nd), Ralph John Assheton, b. 1929, s. 1984, m.	Hon. Ralph C. A., b. 1962
1919	Clwyd (4th), (John) Murray Roberts, b. 1971, s. 2006, m.	Hon. John D. R., b. 2006
1948	Clydesmuir (3rd), David Ronald Colville, b. 1949, s. 1996, m.	Hon. Richard C., b. 1980
1960	Cobbold (2nd), David Antony Fromanteel Lytton Cobbold, b. 1937, s. 1987, m.	Hon. Henry F. L. C., b. 1962
1919	Cochrane of Cults (4th), (Ralph Henry) Vere Cochrane, b. 1926, s. 1990, m.	Hon. Thomas H. V. C., b. 1957
1954	Coleraine (2nd), (James) Martin (Bonar) Law, b. 1931, s. 1980, m.	Hon. James P. B. L., b. 1975
1873	Coleridge (5th), William Duke Coleridge, b. 1937, s. 1984, m.	Hon. James D. C., b. 1967
1946 **	Colgrain (4th), Alastair Colin Leckie Campbell, b. 1951, s. 2008, m.	Hon. Thomas C. D. C., b. 1984
1917 **	Colwyn (3rd), (Ian) Anthony Hamilton-Smith, CBE, b. 1942, s. 1966, m.	Hon. Craig P. H.-S., b. 1968
1956	Colyton (2nd), Alisdair John Munro Hopkinson, b. 1958, s. 1996, m.	Hon. James P. M. H., b. 1983
1841	Congleton (9th), John Patrick Christian Parnell, b. 1959, s. 2015, m.	Hon. Christopher J. E. P., b. 1987
1927	Cornwallis (4th), Fiennes Wykeham Jeremy Cornwallis, b. 1946, s. 2010, m.	Hon. Fiennes A. W. M. C., b. 1987
1874	Cottesloe (5th), John Tapling Fremantle, b. 1927, s. 1994, w.	Hon. Thomas F. H. F., b. 1966
1929 **	Craigmyle (4th), Thomas Columba Shaw, b. 1960, s. 1998, m.	Hon. Alexander F. S., b. 1988
1899	Cranworth (3rd), Philip Bertram Gurdon, b. 1940, s. 1964, m.	Hon. Sacha W. R. G., b. 1970
1959 **	Crathorne (2nd), Charles James Dugdale, KCVO, b. 1939, s. 1977, w.	Hon. Thomas A. J. D., b. 1977
1892	Crawshaw (5th), David Gerald Brooks, b. 1934, s. 1997, m.	Hon. John P. B., b. 1938
1940	Croft (3rd), Bernard William Henry Page Croft, b. 1949, s. 1997, m.	None
1797 I.	Crofton (8th), Edward Harry Piers Crofton, b. 1988, s. 2007	Hon. Charles M. G. C., b. 1988
1375 **	Cromwell (7th), Godfrey John Bewicke-Copley, b. 1960, s. 1982, m.	Hon. David G. B.-C., b. 1997
1947	Crook (3rd), Robert Douglas Edwin Crook, b. 1955, s. 2001, m.	Hon. Matthew R. C., b. 1990
1920	Cullen of Ashbourne (4th), Michael John Cokayne, b. 1950, s. 2016, m.	None
1914	Cunliffe (3rd), Roger Cunliffe, b. 1932, s. 1963, m.	Hon. Henry C., b. 1962
1332	Darcy de Knayth (19th), Caspar David Ingrams, b. 1962, s. 2008, m.	Hon. Thomas R. I., b. 1999
1927	Daresbury (4th), Peter Gilbert Greenall, b. 1953, s. 1996, m.	Hon. Thomas E. G., b. 1984
1924	Darling (3rd), (Robert) Julian Henry Darling, b. 1944, s. 2003, m.	Hon. Robert J. C. D., b. 1972
1946	Darwen (4th), Paul Davies, b. 1962, s. 2011, m.	Hon. Oscar K. D., b. 1996
1932	Davies (3rd), David Davies, b. 1940, s. 1944, m.	Hon. David D. D., b. 1975
1812 I.	Decies (7th), Marcus Hugh Tristram de la Poer Beresford, b. 1948, s. 1992, m.	Hon. Robert M. D. de la P. B., b. 1988
1299	de Clifford (27th), John Edward Southwell Russell, b. 1928, s. 1982, m.	Miles E. S. R., b. 1966
1851	De Freyne (8th), Fulke Charles Arthur John French, b. 1957, s. 2009, m.	Hon. Alexander J. C. F., b. 1988
1821	Delamere (5th), Hugh George Cholmondeley, b. 1934, s. 1979, m.	Hugh C., b. 1998
1838 **	de Mauley (7th), Rupert Charles Ponsonby, b. 1957, s. 2002, m.	Ashley G. P., b. 1959
1937 **	Denham (2nd), Bertram Stanley Mitford Bowyer, KBE, PC, b. 1927, s. 1948, m.	Hon. Richard G. G. B., b. 1959
1834	Denman (6th), Richard Thomas Stewart Denman, b. 1946, s. 2012, m.	Hon. Robert D., b. 1995
1887	De Ramsey (4th), John Ailwyn Fellowes, b. 1942, s. 1993, m.	Hon. Freddie J. F., b. 1978
1264	de Ros (28th), Peter Trevor Maxwell, b. 1958, s. 1983, m. Premier Baron of England	Hon. Finbar J. M., b. 1988
1881	Derwent (5th), Robin Evelyn Leo Vanden-Bempde-Johnstone, LVO, b. 1930, s. 1986, m.	Hon. Francis P. H. V.-B.-J., b. 1965
1831	de Saumarez (7th), Eric Douglas Saumarez, b. 1956, s. 1991, m.	Hon. Victor T. S., b. 1956
1910	de Villiers (4th), Alexander Charles de Villiers, b. 1940, s. 2001, m.	None
1930	Dickinson (2nd), Richard Clavering Hyett Dickinson, b. 1926, s. 1943, m.	Hon. Martin H. D., b. 1961
1620 I.	Digby (12th) and Digby (5th) (1765), Edward Henry Kenelm Digby, KCVO, b. 1924, s. 1964, m.	Hon. Henry N. K. D., b. 1954
1615	Dormer (18th), William Robert Dormer, b. 1960, s. 2016, m.	Hon. Hugo E. G. D., b. 1995
1943	Dowding (3rd), Piers Hugh Tremenheere Dowding, b. 1948, s. 1992, m.	Hon. Mark D. J. D., b. 1949
1439	Dudley (15th), Jim Anthony Hill Wallace, b. 1930, s. 2002, m.	Hon. Jeremy W. G. W., b. 1964
1800 I.	Dufferin and Clandeboye (11th), John Francis Blackwood, b. 1944, s. 1991, m. (claim to the peerage not yet established)	Hon. Francis S. B., b. 1979
1929	Dulverton (3rd), (Gilbert) Michael Hamilton Wills, b. 1944, s. 1992, m.	Hon. Robert A. H. W., b. 1983
1800 I.	Dunalley (7th), Henry Francis Cornelius Prittie, b. 1948, s. 1992, m.	Hon. Joel H. P., b. 1981
1324 I.	Dunboyne (30th), Richard Pierce Theobald Butler, b. 1983, s. 2013, m.	Michael J. B., b. 1944
1892	Dunleath (6th), Brian Henry Mulholland, b. 1950, s. 1997, m.	Hon. Andrew H. M., b. 1981

1439 I.	*Dunsany (21st)*, Randal Plunkett, *b.* 1983, *s.* 2011	Hon. Oliver P., *b.* 1985
1780	*Dynevor (10th)*, Hugo Griffith Uryan Rhys, *b.* 1966, *s.* 2008	Robert D. A. R., *b.* 1963
1963	*Egremont (2nd) and Leconfield (7th) (1859)*, John Max Henry Scawen Wyndham, *b.* 1948, *s.* 1972, *m.*	Hon. George R. V. W., *b.* 1983
1643 S.	*Elibank (14th)*, Alan D'Ardis Erskine-Murray, *b.* 1923, *s.* 1973, *w.*	Master of Elibank, *b.* 1964
1802	*Ellenborough (9th)*, Rupert Edward Henry Law, *b.* 1955, *s.* 2013, *m.*	Hon. James R. T. L., *b.* 1983
1509 S.	*Elphinstone (19th) and Elphinstone (5th) (1885)*, Alexander Mountstuart Elphinstone, *b.* 1980, *s.* 1994, *m.*	Master of Elphinstone, *b.* 2011
1934 **	*Elton (2nd)*, Rodney Elton, TD, *b.* 1930, *s.* 1973, *m.*	Hon. Edward P. E., *b.* 1966
1627 S. **	*Fairfax of Cameron (14th)*, Nicholas John Albert Fairfax, *b.* 1956, *s.* 1964, *m.*	Hon. Edward N. T. F., *b.* 1984
1961	*Fairhaven (3rd)*, Ailwyn Henry George Broughton, *b.* 1936, *s.* 1973, *m.*	Maj. Hon. James H. A. B., *b.* 1963
1916	*Faringdon (3rd)*, Charles Michael Henderson, KCVO, *b.* 1937, *s.* 1977, *m.*	Hon. James H. H., *b.* 1961
1756 I.	*Farnham (13th)*, Simon Kenlis Maxwell, *b.* 1933, *s.* 2001, *w.*	Hon. Robin S. M., *b.* 1965
1856 I.	*Fermoy (6th)*, Maurice Burke Roche, *b.* 1967, *s.* 1984, *m.*	Hon. E. Hugh B. R., *b.* 1972
1826	*Feversham (7th)*, Jasper Orlando Slingsby Duncombe, *b.* 1968, *s.* 2009, *m.*	Hon. Orlando B. D., *b.* 2009
1798 I.	*ffrench (8th)*, Robuck John Peter Charles Mario ffrench, *b.* 1956, *s.* 1986, *m.*	None
1909	*Fisher (4th)*, Patrick Vavasseur Fisher, *b.* 1953, *s.* 2012, *m.*	Hon. Benjamin C. V. F., *b.* 1986
1295	*Fitzwalter (22nd)*, Julian Brook Plumptre, *b.* 1952, *s.* 2004, *m.*	Hon. Edward B. P., *b.* 1989
1776	*Foley (9th)*, Thomas Henry Foley, *b.* 1961, *s.* 2012	Rupert T. F., *b.* 1970
1445 S.	*Forbes (23rd)*, Malcolm Nigel Forbes, *b.* 1946, *s.* 2013, *m. Premier Lord of Scotland*	Master of Forbes, *b.* 1970
1821	*Forester (9th)*, Charles Richard George Weld-Forester, *b.* 1975, *s.* 2004, *m.*	Hon. Brook G. P. W.-F., *b.* 2014
1922	*Forres (4th)*, Alastair Stephen Grant Williamson, *b.* 1946, *s.* 1978, *m.*	Hon. George A. M. W., *b.* 1972
1917	*Forteviot (4th)*, John James Evelyn Dewar, *b.* 1938, *s.* 1993, *w.*	Hon. Alexander J. E. D., *b.* 1971
1951 **	*Freyberg (3rd)*, Valerian Bernard Freyberg, *b.* 1970, *s.* 1993, *m.*	Hon. Joseph J. F., *b.* 2007
1917	*Gainford (4th)*, George Pease, *b.* 1926, *s.* 2013, *m.*	Hon. Adrian C. P., *b.* 1960
1818 I.	*Garvagh (6th)*, Spencer George Stratford de Redcliffe Canning, *b.* 1953, *s.* 2013, *m.*	Hon. Stratford G. E. de R. C., *b.* 1990
1942 **	*Geddes (3rd)*, Euan Michael Ross Geddes, *b.* 1937, *s.* 1975, *m.*	Hon. James G. N. G., *b.* 1969
1876	*Gerard (5th)*, Anthony Robert Hugo Gerard, *b.* 1949, *s.* 1992, *m.*	Hon. Rupert B. C. G., *b.* 1981
1824	*Gifford (6th)*, Anthony Maurice Gifford, QC, *b.* 1940, *s.* 1961, *m.*	Hon. Thomas A. G., *b.* 1967
1917	*Gisborough (3rd)*, Thomas Richard John Long Chaloner, *b.* 1927, *s.* 1951, *m.*	Hon. T. Peregrine L. C., *b.* 1961
1899	*Glanusk (5th)*, Christopher Russell Bailey, *b.* 1942, *s.* 1997, *m.*	Hon. Charles H. B., *b.* 1976
1918 **	*Glenarthur (4th)*, Simon Mark Arthur, *b.* 1944, *s.* 1976, *m.*	Hon. Edward A. A., *b.* 1973
1911	*Glenconner (4th)*, Cody Charles Edward Tennant, *b.* 1994, *s.* 2010	Euan L. T., *b.* 1983
1964	*Glendevon (3rd)*, Jonathan Charles Hope, *b.* 1952, *s.* 2009	None
1922	*Glendyne (4th)*, John Nivison, *b.* 1960, *s.* 2008	None
1939 **	*Glentoran (3rd)*, (Thomas) Robin (Valerian) Dixon, CBE, *b.* 1935, *s.* 1995, *m.*	Hon. Daniel G. D., *b.* 1959
1909	*Gorell (5th)*, John Picton Gorell Barnes, *b.* 1959, *s.* 2007, *m.*	Hon. Oliver G. B., *b.* 1993
1953 **	*Grantchester (3rd)*, Christopher John Suenson-Taylor, *b.* 1951, *s.* 1995, *m.*	Hon. Jesse D. S.-T., *b.* 1977
1782	*Grantley (8th)*, Richard William Brinsley Norton, *b.* 1956, *s.* 1995	Hon. Francis J. H. N., *b.* 1960
1794 I.	*Graves (10th)*, Timothy Evelyn Graves, *b.* 1960, *s.* 2002, *m.*	None
1445 S.	*Gray (23rd)*, Andrew Godfrey Diarmid Stuart Campbell-Gray, *b.* 1964, *s.* 2003, *m.*	Master of Gray, *b.* 1996
1950	*Greenhill (3rd)*, Malcolm Greenhill, *b.* 1924, *s.* 1989	None
1927 **	*Greenway (4th)*, Ambrose Charles Drexel Greenway, *b.* 1941, *s.* 1975, *m.*	Nicholas W. P. G., *b.* 1988
1902	*Grenfell (3rd) and Grenfell of Kilvey (life peerage, 2000)*, Julian Pascoe Francis St Leger Grenfell, *b.* 1935, *s.* 1976, *m.*	Richard A. St L. G., *b.* 1966
1944	*Gretton (4th)*, John Lysander Gretton, *b.* 1975, *s.* 1989, *m.*	Hon. John F. B. G., *b.* 2008
1397	*Grey of Codnor (6th)*, Richard Henry Cornwall-Legh, *b.* 1936, *s.* 1996, *m.*	Hon. Richard S. C. C.-L., *b.* 1976
1955	*Gridley (3rd)*, Richard David Arnold Gridley, *b.* 1956, *s.* 1996, *m.*	Peter A. C. G., *b.* 1940
1964	*Grimston of Westbury (3rd)*, Robert John Sylvester Grimston, *b.* 1951, *s.* 2003, *m.*	Hon. Gerald C. W. G., *b.* 1953
1886	*Grimthorpe (5th)*, Edward John Beckett, *b.* 1954, *s.* 2003, *m.*	Hon. Harry M. B., *b.* 1993
1945	*Hacking (3rd)*, Douglas David Hacking, *b.* 1938, *s.* 1971, *m.*	Hon. Douglas F. H., *b.* 1968
1950	*Haden-Guest (5th)*, Christopher Haden-Guest, *b.* 1948, *s.* 1996, *m.*	Hon. Nicholas H.-G., *b.* 1951
1886	*Hamilton of Dalzell (5th)*, Gavin Goulburn Hamilton, *b.* 1968, *s.* 2006, *m.*	Hon. Francis A. J. G. H., *b.* 2009
1874	*Hampton (7th)*, John Humphrey Arnott Pakington, *b.* 1964, *s.* 2003, *m.*	Hon. Charles R. C. P., *b.* 2005
1939	*Hankey (3rd)*, Donald Robin Alers Hankey, *b.* 1938, *s.* 1996, *m.*	Hon. Alexander M. A. H., *b.* 1947
1958	*Harding of Petherton (3rd)*, William Allan John Harding, *b.* 1969, *s.* 2016, *m.*	Hon. Angus J. E. H., *b.* 2001
1910	*Hardinge of Penshurst (4th)*, Julian Alexander Hardinge, *b.* 1945, *s.* 1997, *m.*	Hon. Hugh F. H., *b.* 1948
1876	*Harlech (7th)*, Jasset David Cody Ormsby-Gore, *b.* 1986, *s.* 2016	None
1939	*Harmsworth (3rd)*, Thomas Harold Raymond Harmsworth, *b.* 1939, *s.* 1990, *m.*	Hon. Dominic M. E. H., *b.* 1973
1815	*Harris (8th)*, Anthony Harris, *b.* 1942, *s.* 1996, *m.*	Rear-Adm. Michael G. T. H., *b.* 1941
1954	*Harvey of Tasburgh (3rd)*, Charles John Giuseppe Harvey, *b.* 1951, *s.* 2010, *m.*	Hon. John H., *b.* 1993

1295	*Hastings (23rd)*, Delaval Thomas Harold Astley, *b.* 1960, *s.* 2007, *m.*	Hon. Jacob A. A., *b.* 1991
1835	*Hatherton (8th)*, Edward Charles Littleton, *b.* 1950, *s.* 1985, *m.*	Hon. Thomas E. L., *b.* 1977
1776	*Hawke (12th)*, William Martin Theodore Hawke, *b.* 1995, *s.* 2009	None
1927	*Hayter (4th)*, George William Michael Chubb, *b.* 1943, *s.* 2003, *m.*	Hon. Thomas F. F. C., *b.* 1986
1945	*Hazlerigg (3rd)*, Arthur Grey Hazlerigg, *b.* 1951, *s.* 2002, *m.*	Hon. Arthur W. G. H., *b.* 1987
1943	*Hemingford (3rd)*, (Dennis) Nicholas Herbert, *b.* 1934, *s.* 1982, *m.*	Hon. Christopher D. C. H., *b.* 1973
1906	*Hemphill (6th)*, Charles Andrew Martyn Martyn-Hemphill, *b.* 1954, *s.* 2012, *m.*	Hon. Richard P. L. M.-H., *b.* 1990
1799 I. **	*Henley (8th) and Northington (6th) (1885)*, Oliver Michael Robert Eden, PC, *b.* 1953, *s.* 1977, *m.*	Hon. John W. O. E., *b.* 1988
1800 I.	*Henniker (9th) and Hartismere (6th) (1866)*, Mark Ian Philip Chandos Henniker-Major, *b.* 1947, *s.* 2004, *m.*	Hon. Edward G. M. H.-M., *b.* 1985
1461	*Herbert (19th)*, David John Seyfried Herbert, *b.* 1952, *s.* 2002, *m.* Title called out of abeyance 2002	Hon. Oliver R. S. H., *b.* 1976
1935	*Hesketh (3rd)*, Thomas Alexander Fermor-Hesketh, KBE, PC, *b.* 1950, *s.* 1955, *m.*	Hon. Frederick H. F.-H., *b.* 1988
1828	*Heytesbury (7th)*, James William Holmes à Court, *b.* 1967, *s.* 2004, *m.*	Peter M. H. H. à. C., *b.* 1968
1886	*Hindlip (6th)*, Charles Henry Allsopp, *b.* 1940, *s.* 1993, *w.*	Hon. Henry W. A., *b.* 1973
1950	*Hives (3rd)*, Matthew Peter Hives, *b.* 1971, *s.* 1997	Hon. Michael B. H., *b.* 1926
1912	*Hollenden (4th)*, Ian Hampden Hope-Morley, *b.* 1946, *s.* 1999, *m.*	Hon. Edward H.-M., *b.* 1981
1897	*Holm Patrick (4th)*, Hans James David Hamilton, *b.* 1955, *s.* 1991, *m.*	Hon. Ion H. J. H., *b.* 1956
1797 I.	*Hotham (8th)*, Henry Durand Hotham, *b.* 1940, *s.* 1967, *m.*	Hon. William B. H., *b.* 1972
1881	*Hothfield (6th)*, Anthony Charles Sackville Tufton, *b.* 1939, *s.* 1991, *m.*	Hon. William S. T., *b.* 1977
1930	*Howard of Penrith (3rd)*, Philip Esme Howard, *b.* 1945, *s.* 1999, *m.*	Hon. Thomas P. H., *b.* 1974
1960	*Howick of Glendale (2nd)*, Charles Evelyn Baring, *b.* 1937, *s.* 1973, *m.*	Hon. David E. C. B., *b.* 1975
1796 I.	*Huntingfield (7th)*, Joshua Charles Vanneck, *b.* 1954, *s.* 1994, *w.*	Hon. Gerard C. A. V., *b.* 1985
1866 **	*Hylton (5th)*, Raymond Hervey Jolliffe, *b.* 1932, *s.* 1967, *m.*	Hon. William H. M. J., *b.* 1967
1933	*Iliffe (3rd)*, Robert Peter Richard Iliffe, *b.* 1944, *s.* 1996, *m.*	Hon. Edward R. I., *b.* 1968
1543 I.	*Inchiquin (18th)*, Conor Myles John O'Brien, *b.* 1943, *s.* 1982, *m.*	Conor J. A. O'B., *b.* 1952
1962	*Inchyra (3rd)*, Christian James Charles Hoyer Millar, *b.* 1962, *s.* 2011, *m.*	Hon. Jake C. R. M., *b.* 1996
1964 **	*Inglewood (2nd)*, (William) Richard Fletcher-Vane, *b.* 1951, *s.* 1989, *m.*	Hon. Henry W. F. F.-V., *b.* 1990
1919	*Inverforth (4th)*, Andrew Peter Weir, *b.* 1966, *s.* 1982, *m.*	Hon. Benjamin A. W., *b.* 1997
1941	*Ironside (2nd)*, Edmund Oslac Ironside, *b.* 1924, *s.* 1959, *w.*	Hon. Charles E. G. I., *b.* 1956
1952	*Jeffreys (3rd)*, Christopher Henry Mark Jeffreys, *b.* 1957, *s.* 1986, *m.*	Hon. Arthur M. H. J., *b.* 1989
1906	*Joicey (5th)*, James Michael Joicey, *b.* 1953, *s.* 1993, *m.*	Hon. William J. J., *b.* 1990
1937	*Kenilworth (4th)*, (John) Randle Siddeley, *b.* 1954, *s.* 1981, *m.*	Hon. William R. J. S., *b.* 1992
1935	*Kennet (3rd)*, William Aldus Thoby Young, *b.* 1957, *s.* 2009, *m.*	Hon. Archibald W. K. Y., *b.* 1992
1776 I.	*Kensington (8th) and Kensington (5th) (1886)*, Hugh Ivor Edwardes, *b.* 1933, *s.* 1981, *m.*	Hon. W. Owen A. E., *b.* 1964
1951	*Kenswood (2nd)*, John Michael Howard Whitfield, *b.* 1930, *s.* 1963, *m.*	Hon. Michael C. W., *b.* 1955
1788	*Kenyon (6th)*, Lloyd Tyrell-Kenyon, *b.* 1947, *s.* 1993, *m.*	Hon. Lloyd N. T.-K., *b.* 1972
1947	*Kershaw (4th)*, Edward John Kershaw, *b.* 1936, *s.* 1962, *m.*	Hon. John C. E. K., *b.* 1971
1943	*Keyes (3rd)*, Charles William Packe Keyes, *b.* 1951, *s.* 2005, *m.*	Hon. (Leopold R.) J. K., *b.* 1956
1909	*Kilbracken (4th)*, Christopher John Godley, *b.* 1945, *s.* 2006, *m.*	Hon. James J. G., *b.* 1972
1900	*Killanin (4th)*, (George) Redmond Fitzpatrick Morris, *b.* 1947, *s.* 1999, *m.*	Hon. Luke M. G. M., *b.* 1975
1943	*Killearn (3rd)*, Victor Miles George Aldous Lampson, *b.* 1941, *s.* 1996, *m.*	Hon. Miles H. M. L., *b.* 1977
1789 I.	*Kilmaine (8th)*, John Francis Sandford Browne, *b.* 1983, *s.* 2013	Revd Aubrey R. C. B., *b.* 1931
1831	*Kilmarnock (8th)*, Dr Robin Jordan Boyd, *b.* 1941, *s.* 2009, *m.*	Hon. Simon J. B., *b.* 1978
1941	*Kindersley (4th)*, Rupert John Molesworth Kindersley, *b.* 1955, *s.* 2013, *m.*	Hon. Frederick H. M. K., *b.* 1987
1223 I.	*Kingsale (36th)*, Nevinson Mark de Courcy, *b.* 1958, *s.* 2005, *m. Premier Baron of Ireland*	Joseph K. C. de C., *b.* 1955
1902	*Kinross (5th)*, Christopher Patrick Balfour, *b.* 1949, *s.* 1985, *m.*	Hon. Alan I. B., *b.* 1978
1951	*Kirkwood (3rd)*, David Harvie Kirkwood, PHD, *b.* 1931, *s.* 1970, *m.*	Hon. James S. K., *b.* 1937
1800 I.	*Langford (9th)*, Col. Geoffrey Alexander Rowley-Conwy, OBE, *b.* 1912, *s.* 1953, *m.*	Hon. Owain G. R.-C., *b.* 1958
1942	*Latham (2nd)*, Dominic Charles Latham, *b.* 1954, *s.* 1970	Anthony M. L., *b.* 1954
1431	*Latymer (9th)*, Crispin James Alan Nevill Money-Coutts, *b.* 1955, *s.* 2003, *m.*	Hon. Drummond W. T. M.-C., *b.* 1986
1869	*Lawrence (5th)*, David John Downer Lawrence, *b.* 1937, *s.* 1968	None
1947	*Layton (3rd)*, Geoffrey Michael Layton, *b.* 1947, *s.* 1989, *m.*	Jonathan F. L., *b.* 1942
1839	*Leigh (6th)*, Christopher Dudley Piers Leigh, *b.* 1960, *s.* 2003, *m.*	Hon. Rupert D. L., *b.* 1994
1962	*Leighton of St Mellons (3rd)*, Robert William Henry Leighton Seager, *b.* 1955, *s.* 1998, *m.*	Hon. Simon J. L. S., *b.* 1957
1797	*Lilford (8th)*, Mark Vernon Powys, *b.* 1975, *s.* 2005, *m.*	Robert C. L. P., *b.* 1930
1945	*Lindsay of Birker (3rd)*, James Francis Lindsay, *b.* 1945, *s.* 1994, *m.*	Alexander S. L., *b.* 1940
1758 I.	*Lisle (9th)*, (John) Nicholas Geoffrey Lysaght, *b.* 1960, *s.* 2003	Hon. David J. L., *b.* 1963
1850	*Londesborough (9th)*, Richard John Denison, *b.* 1959, *s.* 1968, *m.*	Hon. James F. D., *b.* 1990
1541 I.	*Louth (17th)*, Jonathan Oliver Plunkett, *b.* 1952, *s.* 2013, *m.*	Hon. Matthew O. P., *b.* 1982
1458 S.	*Lovat (16th) and Lovat (5th) (1837)*, Simon Fraser, *b.* 1977, *s.* 1995, *m.*	Hon. Jack F., *b.* 1984
1946	*Lucas of Chilworth (3rd)*, Simon William Lucas, *b.* 1957, *s.* 2001, *m.*	Hon. John R. M. L., *b.* 1995
1663 **	*Lucas (11th) and Dingwall (14th) (S. 1609)*, Ralph Matthew Palmer, *b.* 1951, *s.* 1991, *m.*	Hon. Lewis E. P., *b.* 1987

1929	*Luke (4th)*, Ian James St John Lawson Johnston, *b.* 1963, *s.* 2016, *m.*	Hon. Samuel A. J. St J. L. J., *b.* 2000
1859	*Lyveden (7th)*, Jack Leslie Vernon, *b.* 1938, *s.* 1999, *m.*	Hon. Colin R. V., *b.* 1967
1959	*MacAndrew (3rd)*, Christopher Anthony Colin MacAndrew, *b.* 1945, *s.* 1989, *m.*	Hon. Oliver C. J. M., *b.* 1983
1776 I.	*Macdonald (8th)*, Godfrey James Macdonald of Macdonald, *b.* 1947, *s.* 1970, *m.*	Hon. Godfrey E. H. T. M., *b.* 1982
1937	*McGowan (4th)*, Harry John Charles McGowan, *b.* 1971, *s.* 2003, *m.*	Hon. Dominic J. W. M., *b.* 1951
1922	*Maclay (3rd)*, Joseph Paton Maclay, *b.* 1942, *s.* 1969, *m.*	Hon. Joseph P. M., *b.* 1977
1955	*McNair (3rd)*, Duncan James McNair, *b.* 1947, *s.* 1989, *m.*	Hon. William S. A. M., *b.* 1958
1951	*Macpherson of Drumochter (3rd)*, James Anthony Macpherson, *b.* 1979, *s.* 2008, *m.*	Hon. Daniel T. M., *b.* 2013
1937 **	*Mancroft (3rd)*, Benjamin Lloyd Stormont Mancroft, *b.* 1957, *s.* 1987, *m.*	Hon. Arthur L. S. M., *b.* 1995
1807	*Manners (6th)*, John Hugh Robert Manners, *b.* 1956, *s.* 2008, *m.*	Hon. John A. D. M., *b.* 2011
1922	*Manton (4th)*, Miles Ronald Marcus Watson, *b.* 1958, *s.* 2003, *m.*	Hon. Thomas N. C. D. W., *b.* 1985
1908	*Marchamley (4th)*, William Francis Whiteley, *b.* 1968, *s.* 1994, *m.*	Hon. Leon W., *b.* 2004
1965	*Margadale (3rd)*, Alastair John Morrison, *b.* 1958, *s.* 2003, *m.*	Hon. Declan J. M., *b.* 1993
1961	*Marks of Broughton (3rd)*, Simon Richard Marks, *b.* 1950, *s.* 1998, *m.*	Hon. Michael M., *b.* 1989
1964	*Martonmere (2nd)*, John Stephen Robinson, *b.* 1963, *s.* 1989, *m.*	Hon. James I. R., *b.* 2003
1776 I.	*Massy (10th)*, David Hamon Somerset Massy, *b.* 1947, *s.* 1995	Hon. John H. S. M., *b.* 1950
1935	*May (4th)*, Jasper Bertram St John May, *b.* 1965, *s.* 2006	None
1928	*Melchett (4th)*, Peter Robert Henry Mond, *b.* 1948, *s.* 1973	None
1925	*Merrivale (4th)*, Derek John Philip Duke, *b.* 1948, *s.* 2007, *m.*	Hon. Thomas D., *b.* 1980
1911	*Merthyr (5th)*, David Trevor Lewis, *b.* 1977, *s.* 2015, *m.*	Hon. Peter H. L., *b.* 1937
1919	*Meston (3rd)*, James Meston, QC, *b.* 1950, *s.* 1984, *m.*	Hon. Thomas J. D. M., *b.* 1977
1838	*Methuen (8th)*, James Paul Archibald Methuen-Campbell, *b.* 1952, *s.* 2014	Thomas R. M. M.-C., *b.* 1977
1711	*Middleton (13th)*, Michael Charles James Willoughby, *b.* 1948, *s.* 2011, *m.*	Hon. James W. M. W., *b.* 1976
1939	*Milford (4th)*, Guy Wogan Philipps, QC, *b.* 1961, *s.* 1999, *m.*	Hon. Archie S. P., *b.* 1997
1933	*Milne (3rd)*, George Alexander Milne, *b.* 1941, *s.* 2005	Hon. Iain C. L. M., *b.* 1949
1951	*Milner of Leeds (3rd)*, Richard James Milner, *b.* 1959, *s.* 2003, *m.*	None
1947	*Milverton (2nd)*, Revd Fraser Arthur Richard Richards, *b.* 1930, *s.* 1978, *m.*	Hon. Michael H. R., *b.* 1936
1873	*Moncreiff (6th)*, Rhoderick Harry Wellwood Moncreiff, *b.* 1954, *s.* 2002, *m.*	Hon. Harry J. W. M., *b.* 1986
1884	*Monk Bretton (3rd)*, John Charles Dodson, *b.* 1924, *s.* 1933, *m.*	Hon. Christopher M. D., *b.* 1958
1885	*Monkswell (5th)*, Gerard Collier, *b.* 1947, *s.* 1984, *m.*	Hon. James A. C., *b.* 1977
1728	*Monson (12th)*, Nicholas John Monson, *b.* 1955, *s.* 2011, *m.*	Hon. Andrew A. J. M., *b.* 1959
1885	*Montagu of Beaulieu (4th)*, Ralph Douglas-Scott-Montagu, *b.* 1961, *s.* 2015, *m.*	Hon. Jonathan D. D.-S.-M., *b.* 1975
1839	*Monteagle of Brandon (7th)*, Charles James Spring Rice, *b.* 1953, *s.* 2013, *m.*	Hon. Michael S. R., *b.* 1935
1943	*Moran (3rd)*, James McMoran Wilson, *b.* 1952, *s.* 2014, *m.*	Hon. David A. M. W., *b.* 1990
1918	*Morris (4th)*, Thomas Anthony Salmon Morris, *b.* 1982, *s.* 2011	Hon. John M. M., *b.* 1983
1950	*Morris of Kenwood (3rd)*, Jonathan David Morris, *b.* 1968, *s.* 2004, *m.*	Hon. Benjamin J. M., *b.* 1998
1831	*Mostyn (7th)*, Gregory Philip Roger Lloyd-Mostyn, *b.* 1984, *s.* 2011	Roger H. L.-M., *b.* 1941
1933	*Mottistone (6th)*, Christopher David Peter Seely, *b.* 1974, *s.* 2013	Hon. Richard W. A. S., *b.* 1988
1945 **	*Mountevans (4th)*, Jeffrey Richard de Corban Evans, *b.* 1948, *s.* 2014, *m.*	Hon. Alexander R. A. E., *b.* 1975
1283	*Mowbray (27th)*, Segrave (28th) (1295) and Stourton (24th) (1448), Edward William Stephen Stourton, *b.* 1953, *s.* 2006, *m.*	Hon. James C. P. S., *b.* 1991
1932	*Moyne (3rd)*, Jonathan Bryan Guinness, *b.* 1930, *s.* 1992, *m.*	Hon. Valentine G. B. G., *b.* 1959
1929 **	*Moynihan (4th)*, Colin Berkeley Moynihan, *b.* 1955, *s.* 1997, *m.*	Hon. Nicholas E. B. M., *b.* 1994
1781 I.	*Muskerry (9th)*, Robert Fitzmaurice Deane, *b.* 1948, *s.* 1988, *m.*	Hon. Jonathan F. D., *b.* 1986
1627 S.	*Napier (15th) and Ettrick (6th) (1872)*, Francis David Charles Napier, *b.* 1962, *s.* 2012, *m.*	Master of Napier, *b.* 1996
1868	*Napier of Magdala (6th)*, Robert Alan Napier, *b.* 1940, *s.* 1987, *m.*	Hon. James R. N., *b.* 1966
1940	*Nathan (3rd)*, Rupert Harry Bernard Nathan, *b.* 1957, *s.* 2007, *m.*	Hon. Alasdair H. St J. N., *b.* 1999
1960	*Nelson of Stafford (4th)*, Alistair William Henry Nelson, *b.* 1973, *s.* 2006, *m.*	Hon. James J. N., *b.* 1947
1959	*Netherthorpe (3rd)*, James Frederick Turner, *b.* 1964, *s.* 1982, *m.*	Hon. Andrew J. E. T., *b.* 1993
1946	*Newall (2nd)*, Francis Storer Eaton Newall, *b.* 1930, *s.* 1963, *m.*	Hon. Richard H. E. N., *b.* 1961
1776 I.	*Newborough (8th)*, Robert Vaughan Wynn, *b.* 1949, *s.* 1998, *m.*	Antony C. V. W., *b.* 1949
1892	*Newton (5th)*, Richard Thomas Legh, *b.* 1950, *s.* 1992, *m.*	Hon. Piers R. L., *b.* 1979
1930	*Noel-Buxton (4th)*, Charles Connal Noel-Buxton, *b.* 1975, *s.* 2013, *m.*	Hon. Simon C. N.-B., *b.* 1943
1957	*Norrie (2nd)*, (George) Willoughby Moke Norrie, *b.* 1936, *s.* 1977, *m.*	Hon. Mark W. J. N., *b.* 1972
1884 **	*Northbourne (5th)*, Christopher George Walter James, *b.* 1926, *s.* 1982, *m.*	Hon. Charles W. H. J., *b.* 1960
1866 **	*Northbrook (6th)*, Francis Thomas Baring, *b.* 1954, *s.* 1990, *m.*	To the Baronetcy, Peter B., *b.* 1939
1878	*Norton (8th)*, James Nigel Arden Adderley, *b.* 1947, *s.* 1993, *m.*	Hon. Edward J. A. A., *b.* 1982
1906	*Nunburnholme (6th)*, Stephen Charles Yanath Wilson, *b.* 1973, *s.* 2000, *m.*	Hon. Charles T. C. W., *b.* 2002
1950	*Ogmore (3rd)*, Morgan Rees-Williams, *b.* 1937, *s.* 2004, *m.*	Hon. Tudor D. R.-W., *b.* 1991
1870	*O'Hagan (4th)*, Charles Towneley Strachey, *b.* 1945, *s.* 1961, *m.*	Hon. Richard T. S., *b.* 1950
1868	*O'Neill (4th)*, Raymond Arthur Clanaboy O'Neill, KCVO, TD, *b.* 1933, *s.* 1944, *w.*	Hon. Shane S. C. O'N., *b.* 1965
1836 I.	*Oranmore and Browne (5th) and Mereworth (3rd) (1926)*, Dominick Geoffrey Thomas Browne, *b.* 1929, *s.* 2002	Shaun D. B., *b.* 1964

1933 **	*Palmer (4th)*, Adrian Bailie Nottage Palmer, *b.* 1951, *s.* 1990, *m.*	Hon. Hugo B. R. P., *b.* 1980
1914	*Parmoor (5th)*, Michael Leonard Seddon Cripps, *b.* 1942, *s.* 2008, *m.*	Hon. Henry W. A. C., *b.* 1976
1937	*Pender (4th)*, Henry John Richard Denison-Pender, *b.* 1968, *s.* 2016, *m.*	Hon. Miles J. C. D.-P., *b.* 2000
1866	*Penrhyn (7th)*, Simon Douglas-Pennant, *b.* 1938, *s.* 2003, *m.*	Hon. Edward S. D.-P., *b.* 1966
1603	*Petre (18th)*, John Patrick Lionel Petre, KCVO, *b.* 1942, *s.* 1989, *m.*	Hon. Dominic W. P., *b.* 1966
1918	*Phillimore (5th)*, Francis Stephen Phillimore, *b.* 1944, *s.* 1994, *m.*	Hon. Tristan A. S. P., *b.* 1977
1945	*Piercy (3rd)*, James William Piercy, *b.* 1946, *s.* 1981	Hon. Mark E. P. P., *b.* 1953
1827	*Plunket (9th)*, Tyrone Shaun Terence Plunket, *b.* 1966, *s.* 2013, *m.*	Hon. Rory P. R. P., *b.* 2001
1831	*Poltimore (7th)*, Mark Coplestone Bampfylde, *b.* 1957, *s.* 1978, *m.*	Hon. Henry A. W. B., *b.* 1985
1690 S.	*Polwarth (11th)*, Andrew Walter Hepburne-Scott, *b.* 1947, *s.* 2005, *m.*	Master of Polwarth, *b.* 1973
1930	*Ponsonby of Shulbrede (4th) and Ponsonby of Roehampton (life peerage, 2000)*, Frederick Matthew Thomas Ponsonby, *b.* 1958, *s.* 1990, *m.*	Hon. Cameron J. J. P., *b.* 1995
1958	*Poole (2nd)*, David Charles Poole, *b.* 1945, *s.* 1993, *m.*	Hon. Oliver J. P., *b.* 1972
1852	*Raglan (6th)*, Geoffrey Somerset, *b.* 1932, *s.* 2010, *m.*	Inigo A. F. S., *b.* 2004
1932	*Rankeillour (5th)*, Michael Richard Hope, *b.* 1940, *s.* 2005, *m.*	Hon. James F. H., *b.* 1968
1953	*Rathcavan (3rd)*, Hugh Detmar Torrens O'Neill, *b.* 1939, *s.* 1994, *m.*	Hon. François H. N. O'N., *b.* 1984
1916	*Rathcreedan (3rd)*, Christopher John Norton, *b.* 1949, *s.* 1990, *m.*	Hon. Adam G. N., *b.* 1952
1868 I.	*Rathdonnell (5th)*, Thomas Benjamin McClintock-Bunbury, *b.* 1938, *s.* 1959, *m.*	Hon. William L. M.-B., *b.* 1966
1911	*Ravensdale (4th)*, Daniel Nicholas Mosley, *b.* 1982, *s.* 2017, *m.*	Hon. Ivo A. R. M., *b.* 1951
1821	*Ravensworth (9th)*, Thomas Arthur Hamish Liddell, *b.* 1954, *s.* 2004, *m.*	Hon. Henry A. T. L., *b.* 1987
1821	*Rayleigh (6th)*, John Gerald Strutt, *b.* 1960, *s.* 1988, *m.*	Hon. John F. S., *b.* 1993
1937 **	*Rea (3rd)*, John Nicolas Rea, MD, *b.* 1928, *s.* 1981, *m.*	Hon. Matthew J. R., *b.* 1956
1628 S.	*Reay (15th)*, Aeneas Simon Mackay, *b.* 1965, *s.* 2013, *m.*	Master of Reay, *b.* 2010
1902	*Redesdale (6th) and Mitford (life peerage, 2000)*, Rupert Bertram Mitford, *b.* 1967, *s.* 1991, *m.*	Hon. Bertram D. M., *b.* 2000
1940	*Reith (3rd)*, James Harry John Reith, *b.* 1971, *s.* 2016, *m.*	Hon. Harry J. J. R., *b.* 2006
1928	*Remnant (3rd)*, James Wogan Remnant, CVO, *b.* 1930, *s.* 1967, *m.*	Hon. Philip J. R., CBE, *b.* 1954
1806 I.	*Rendlesham (9th)*, Charles William Brooke Thellusson, *b.* 1954, *s.* 1999, *m.*	Hon. Peter R. T., *b.* 1920
1933	*Rennell (4th)*, James Roderick David Tremayne Rodd, *b.* 1978, *s.* 2006	None
1964	*Renwick (2nd)*, Harry Andrew Renwick, *b.* 1935, *s.* 1973, *m.*	Hon. Robert J. R., *b.* 1966
1885	*Revelstoke (7th)*, Alexander Rupert Baring, *b.* 1970, *s.* 2012	Hon. Thomas J. B., *b.* 1971
1905	*Ritchie of Dundee (6th)*, Charles Rupert Rendall Ritchie, *b.* 1958, *s.* 2008, *m.*	Hon. Sebastian R., *b.* 2004
1935	*Riverdale (3rd)*, Anthony Robert Balfour, *b.* 1960, *s.* 1998	Arthur M. B., *b.* 1938
1961	*Robertson of Oakridge (3rd)*, William Brian Elworthy Robertson, *b.* 1975, *s.* 2009, *m.*	None
1938	*Roborough (4th)*, Massey John Henry Lopes, *b.* 1969, *s.* 2015, *m.*	Hon. Henry M. P. L., *b.* 1997
1931	*Rochester (3rd)*, David Charles Lamb, *b.* 1944, *s.* 2017, *m.*	Hon. Daniel L., *b.* 1971
1934	*Rockley (4th)*, Anthony Robert Cecil, *b.* 1961, *s.* 2011, *m.*	Hon. William E. C., *b.* 1996
1782 M.	*Rodney (11th)*, John George Brydges Rodney, *b.* 1999, *s.* 2011	Nicholas S. H. R., *b.* 1947
1651 S.	*Rollo (14th) and Dunning (5th) (1869)*, David Eric Howard Rollo, *b.* 1943, *s.* 1997, *m.*	Master of Rollo, *b.* 1972
1959	*Rootes (3rd)*, Nicholas Geoffrey Rootes, *b.* 1951, *s.* 1992, *m.*	William B. R., *b.* 1944
1796 I.	*Rossmore (7th) and Rossmore (6th) (1838)*, William Warner Westenra, *b.* 1931, *s.* 1958, *m.*	Hon. Benedict W. W., *b.* 1983
1939 **	*Rotherwick (3rd)*, (Herbert) Robin Cayzer, *b.* 1954, *s.* 1996, *m.*	Hon. H. Robin C., *b.* 1989
1885	*Rothschild (4th)*, (Nathaniel Charles) Jacob Rothschild, OM, GBE, *b.* 1936, *s.* 1990, *m.*	Hon. Nathaniel P. V. J. R., *b.* 1971
1911	*Rowallan (4th)*, John Polson Cameron Corbett, *b.* 1947, *s.* 1993, *m.*	Hon. Jason W. P. C. C., *b.* 1972
1947	*Rugby (4th)*, Robert Charles Maffey, *b.* 1951, *s.* 1990, *m.*	Hon. Timothy J. H. M., *b.* 1975
1919 **	*Russell of Liverpool (3rd)*, Simon Gordon Jared Russell, *b.* 1952, *s.* 1981, *m.*	Hon. Edward C. S. R., *b.* 1985
1876	*Sackville (7th)*, Robert Bertrand Sackville-West, *b.* 1958, *s.* 2004, *m.*	Hon. Arthur S.-W., *b.* 2000
1964	*St Helens (2nd)*, Richard Francis Hughes-Young, *b.* 1945, *s.* 1980, *m.*	Hon. Henry T. H.-Y., *b.* 1986
1559 **	*St John of Bletso (21st)*, Anthony Tudor St John, *b.* 1957, *s.* 1978, *m.*	Hon. Oliver B. St J., *b.* 1995
1887	*St Levan (5th)*, James Piers Southwell St Aubyn, *b.* 1950, *s.* 2013, *m.*	Hon. Hugh J. St A., *b.* 1983
1885	*St Oswald (6th)*, Charles Rowland Andrew Winn, *b.* 1959, *s.* 1999, *m.*	Hon. Rowland C. S. H. W., *b.* 1986
1960	*Sanderson of Ayot (2nd)*, Alan Lindsay Sanderson, *b.* 1931, *s.* 1971, *m.* Disclaimed for life 1971.	Hon. Michael S., *b.* 1959
1945	*Sandford (3rd)*, James John Mowbray Edmondson, *b.* 1949, *s.* 2009, *m.*	Hon. Devon J. E., *b.* 1986
1871	*Sandhurst (6th)*, Guy Rees John Mansfield, QC, *b.* 1949, *s.* 2002, *m.*	Hon. Edward J. M., *b.* 1982
1888	*Savile (4th)*, John Anthony Thornhill Lumley-Savile, *b.* 1947, *s.* 2008, *m.*	Hon. James G. A. L.-S., *b.* 1975
1447	*Saye and Sele (21st)*, Nathaniel Thomas Allen Fiennes, *b.* 1920, *s.* 1968, *m.*	Hon. Martin G. F., *b.* 1961
1826	*Seaford (6th)*, Colin Humphrey Felton Ellis, *b.* 1946, *s.* 1999, *m.*	Hon. Benjamin F. T. E., *b.* 1976
1932 **	*Selsdon (3rd)*, Malcolm McEacharn Mitchell-Thomson, *b.* 1937, *s.* 1963, *m.*	Hon. Callum M. M. M.-T., *b.* 1969
1489 S.	*Sempill (21st)*, James William Stuart Whitemore Sempill, *b.* 1949, *s.* 1995, *m.*	Master of Sempill, *b.* 1979
1916	*Shaughnessy (5th)*, Charles George Patrick Shaughnessy, *b.* 1955, *s.* 2007, *m.*	David J. S., *b.* 1957
1946	*Shepherd (3rd)*, Graham George Shepherd, *b.* 1949, *s.* 2001, *m.*	Hon. Patrick M. S., *b.* 1980
1964	*Sherfield (3rd)*, Dwight William Makins, *b.* 1951, *s.* 2006, *m.*	None
1902	*Shuttleworth (5th)*, Charles Geoffrey Nicholas Kay-Shuttleworth, KG, KCVO, *b.* 1948, *s.* 1975, *m.*	Hon. Thomas E. K.-S., *b.* 1976
1950	*Silkin (3rd)*, Christopher Lewis Silkin, *b.* 1947, *s.* 2001. Disclaimed for life 2002.	Rory L. S., *b.* 1954

1963	*Silsoe (3rd)*, Simon Rupert Trustram Eve, *b.* 1966, *s.* 2005	Hon. Peter N. T. E., OBE, *b.* 1930
1947	*Simon of Wythenshawe (3rd)*, Matthew Simon, *b.* 1955, *s.* 2002, *w.* In dormancy since 2016 when the 3rd baron officially reassigned his gender.	Michael B. S., *b.* 1970
1449 S.	*Sinclair (18th)*, Matthew Murray Kennedy St Clair, *b.* 1968, *s.* 2004, *m.*	Master of Sinclair, *b.* 2007
1957	*Sinclair of Cleeve (3rd)*, John Lawrence Robert Sinclair, *b.* 1953, *s.* 1985, *m.*	None
1919	*Sinha (6th)*, Arup Kumar Sinha, *b.* 1966, *s.* 1999, *m.*	Hon. Dilip K. S., *b.* 1967
1828 **	*Skelmersdale (7th)*, Roger Bootle-Wilbraham, *b.* 1945, *s.* 1973, *m.*	Hon. Andrew B.-W., *b.* 1977
1916	*Somerleyton (4th)*, Hugh Francis Saville Crossley, *b.* 1971, *s.* 2012, *m.*	Hon. John de B. T. S. C., *b.* 2010
1784	*Somers (9th)*, Philip Sebastian Somers Cocks, *b.* 1948, *s.* 1995	Jonathan B. C., *b.* 1985
1780	*Southampton (7th)*, Edward Charles FitzRoy, *b.* 1955, *s.* 2015, *m.*	Hon. Charles E. M. F., *b.* 1983
1959	*Spens (4th)*, Patrick Nathaniel George Spens, *b.* 1968, *s.* 2001, *m.*	Hon. Peter L. S., *b.* 2000
1640	*Stafford (15th)*, Francis Melfort William Fitzherbert, *b.* 1954, *s.* 1986, *m.*	Hon. Benjamin J. B. F., *b.* 1983
1938	*Stamp (4th)*, Trevor Charles Bosworth Stamp, MD, *b.* 1935, *s.* 1987, *m.*	Hon. Nicholas C. T. S., *b.* 1978
1839	*Stanley of Alderley (9th), Sheffield (9th) (I. 1738) and Eddisbury (8th) (1848)*, Richard Oliver Stanley, *b.* 1956, *s.* 2013, *m.*	Hon. Charles E. S., *b.* 1960
1318	*Strabolgi (12th)*, Andrew David Whitley Kenworthy, *b.* 1967, *s.* 2010, *m.*	Hon. Joel B. K., *b.* 2004
1628	*Strange (17th)*, Adam Humphrey Drummond of Megginch, *b.* 1953, *s.* 2005, *m.*	Hon. John A. H. D. of M., *b.* 1992
1955	*Strathalmond (3rd)*, William Roberton Fraser, *b.* 1947, *s.* 1976, *m.*	Hon. William G. F., *b.* 1976
1936	*Strathcarron (3rd)*, Ian David Patrick Macpherson, *b.* 1949, *s.* 2006, *m.*	Hon. Rory D. A. M., *b.* 1982
1955 **	*Strathclyde (2nd)*, Thomas Galloway Dunlop du Roy de Blicquy Galbraith, CH, PC, *b.* 1960, *s.* 1985, *m.*	Hon. Charles W. du R. de B. G., *b.* 1962
1900	*Strathcona and Mount Royal (4th)*, Donald Euan Palmer Howard, *b.* 1923, *s.* 1959, *m.*	Hon. D. Alexander S. H., *b.* 1961
1836	*Stratheden (7th) and Campbell (7th) (1841)*, David Anthony Campbell, *b.* 1963, *s.* 2011, *m.*	None
1884	*Strathspey (6th)*, James Patrick Trevor Grant of Grant, *b.* 1943, *s.* 1992	Hon. Michael P. F. G., *b.* 1953
1838	*Sudeley (7th)*, Merlin Charles Sainthill Hanbury-Tracy, *b.* 1939, *s.* 1941, *m.*	Nicholas E. J. H.-T., *b.* 1959
1786	*Suffield (13th)*, John Edward Richard Harbord-Hamond, *b.* 1956, *s.* 2016, *m.*	Hon. Sam C. A. H.-H., *b.* 1989
1893	*Swansea (5th)*, Richard Anthony Hussey Vivian, *b.* 1957, *s.* 2005, *m.*	Hon. James H. H. V., *b.* 1999
1907	*Swaythling (5th)*, Charles Edgar Samuel Montagu, *b.* 1954, *s.* 1998, *m.*	Rupert A. S. M., *b.* 1965
1919 **	*Swinfen (3rd)*, Roger Mynors Swinfen Eady, MBE, *b.* 1938, *s.* 1977, *m.*	Hon. Charles R. P. S. E., *b.* 1971
1831 I.	*Talbot of Malahide (11th)*, Richard John Tennant Arundell, *b.* 1957, *s.* 2016, *m.*	Hon. John R. A., *b.* 1998
1946	*Tedder (3rd)*, Robin John Tedder, *b.* 1955, *s.* 1994, *m.*	Hon. Benjamin J. T., *b.* 1985
1884	*Tennyson (6th)*, David Harold Alexander Tennyson, *b.* 1960, *s.* 2006	Alan J. D. T., *b.* 1965
1918	*Terrington (6th)*, Christopher Richard James Woodhouse, MB, *b.* 1946, *s.* 2001, *m.*	Hon. Jack H. L. W., *b.* 1978
1940	*Teviot (2nd)*, Charles John Kerr, *b.* 1934, *s.* 1968, *m.*	Hon. Charles R. K., *b.* 1971
1616	*Teynham (20th)*, John Christopher Ingham Roper-Curzon, *b.* 1928, *s.* 1972, *m.*	Hon. David J. H. I. R.-C., *b.* 1965
1964	*Thomson of Fleet (3rd)*, David Kenneth Roy Thomson, *b.* 1957, *s.* 2006, *m.*	Hon. Benjamin T., *b.* 2006
1792 **	*Thurlow (9th)*, Roualeyn Robert Hovell-Thurlow-Cumming-Bruce, *b.* 1952, *s.* 2013, *m.*	Hon. Nicholas E. H.-T.-C.-B., *b.* 1986
1876	*Tollemache (5th)*, Timothy John Edward Tollemache, KCVO, *b.* 1939, *s.* 1975, *m.*	Hon. Edward J. H. T., *b.* 1976
1564 S.	*Torphichen (15th)*, James Andrew Douglas Sandilands, *b.* 1946, *s.* 1975, *m.*	Robert P. S., *b.* 1950
1947 **	*Trefgarne (2nd)*, David Garro Trefgarne, PC, *b.* 1941, *s.* 1960, *m.*	Hon. George G. T., *b.* 1970
1921 **	*Trevethin (5th) and Oaksey (3rd) (1947)*, Patrick John Tristram Lawrence, QC, *b.* 1960, *s.* 2012, *m.*	Hon. Oliver J. T. L., *b.* 1990
1880	*Trevor (5th)*, Marke Charles Hill-Trevor, *b.* 1970, *s.* 1997, *m.*	Hon. Iain R. H.-T., *b.* 1971
1461 I.	*Trimlestown (21st)*, Raymond Charles Barnewall, *b.* 1930, *s.* 1997	None
1940	*Tryon (3rd)*, Anthony George Merrik Tryon, OBE, *b.* 1940, *s.* 1976, *w.*	Hon. Charles G. B. T., *b.* 1976
1935	*Tweedsmuir (4th)*, John William de l'Aigle (Toby) Buchan, *b.* 1950, *s.* 2008, *m.*	Hon. John A. G. B., *b.* 1986
1523 **	*Vaux of Harrowden (12th)*, Richard Hubert Gordon Gilbey, *b.* 1965, *s.* 2014, *m.*	Hon. Alexander J. C. G., *b.* 2000
1800 I.	*Ventry (8th)*, Andrew Wesley Daubeny de Moleyns, *b.* 1943, *s.* 1987, *m.*	Hon. Francis W. D. de M., *b.* 1965
1762	*Vernon (11th)*, Anthony William Vernon-Harcourt, *b.* 1939, *s.* 2000, *m.*	Hon. Simon A. V.-H., *b.* 1969
1922	*Vestey (3rd)*, Samuel George Armstrong Vestey, KCVO, *b.* 1941, *s.* 1954, *m.*	Hon. William G. V., *b.* 1983
1841	*Vivian (7th)*, Charles Crespigny Hussey Vivian, *b.* 1966, *s.* 2004, *m.*	Thomas C. B. V., *b.* 1971
1934	*Wakehurst (3rd)*, (John) Christopher Loder, *b.* 1925, *s.* 1970, *m.*	Hon. Timothy W. L., *b.* 1958
1723	*Walpole (10th) and Walpole of Wolterton (8th) (1756)*, Robert Horatio Walpole, *b.* 1938, *s.* 1989, *m.*	Hon. Jonathan R. H. W., *b.* 1967
1780	*Walsingham (9th)*, John de Grey, MC, *b.* 1925, *s.* 1965, *m.*	Hon. Robert de G., *b.* 1969
1936	*Wardington (3rd)*, William Simon Pease, *b.* 1925, *s.* 2005, *m.*	None
1792 I.	*Waterpark (8th)*, Roderick Alexander Cavendish, *b.* 1959, *s.* 2013, *m.*	Hon. Luke F. C., *b.* 1990
1942	*Wedgwood (5th)*, Antony John Wedgwood, *b.* 1944, *s.* 2014, *m.*	Hon. Josiah T. A. W., *b.* 1978
1861	*Westbury (6th)*, Richard Nicholas Bethell, MBE, *b.* 1950, *s.* 2001, *m.*	Hon. Alexander B., *b.* 1986
1944	*Westwood (3rd)*, (William) Gavin Westwood, *b.* 1944, *s.* 1991, *m.*	Hon. W. Fergus W., *b.* 1972
1544/5	*Wharton (12th)*, Myles Christopher David Robertson, *b.* 1964, *s.* 2000, *m.*	Hon. Meghan Z. M. R., *b.* 2006

1935	*Wigram (3rd)*, Andrew Francis Clive Wigram, MVO, *b.* 1949, *s.* 2017, *m.*	Hon. Harry R. C. W., *b.* 1977
1491 **	*Willoughby de Broke (21st)*, Leopold David Verney, *b.* 1938, *s.* 1986, *m.*	Hon. Rupert G. V., *b.* 1966
1937	*Windlesham (4th)*, James Rupert Hennessy, *b.* 1968, *s.* 2010, *m.*	Hon. George R. J. H., *b.* 2006
1951	*Wise (3rd)*, Christopher John Clayton Wise, *b.* 1949, *s.* 2012, *m.*	Hon. Thomas C. C. W., *b.* 1989
1869	*Wolverton (8th)*, Miles John Glyn, *b.* 1966, *s.* 2011	Jonathan C. G., *b.* 1990
1928	*Wraxall (4th)*, Antony Hubert Gibbs, *b.* 1958, *s.* 2017, *m.*	Hon. Orlando H. G., *b.* 1995
1915	*Wrenbury (4th)*, William Edward Buckley, *b.* 1966, *s.* 2014, *m.*	Hon. Jamie P. B., *b.* 2001
1838	*Wrottesley (6th)*, Clifton Hugh Lancelot de Verdon Wrottesley, *b.* 1968, *s.* 1977, *m.*	Hon. Victor E. F. de V. W., *b.* 2004
1829	*Wynford (9th)*, John Philip Robert Best, *b.* 1950, *s.* 2002, *m.*	Hon. Harry R. F. B., *b.* 1987
1308	*Zouche (18th)*, James Assheton Frankland, *b.* 1943, *s.* 1965, *m.*	Hon. William T. A. F., *b.* 1984

BARONESSES/LADIES IN THEIR OWN RIGHT

Style, The Rt. Hon. the Lady _ , *or* The Rt. Hon. the Baroness _ , according to her preference. Either style may be used, except in the case of Scottish titles (indicated by S.), which are not baronies and whose holders are always addressed as Lady.
Envelope, may be addressed in same way as a Baron's wife or, if she prefers *(formal),* The Rt. Hon. the Baroness _; *(social),* The Baroness _. Otherwise as for a Baron's wife
Husband, Untitled
Children's style, As for children of a Baron
In Scotland, the heir to a Lady may be styled 'The Master/Mistress of _ (title of peer)'

Created	Title, order of succession, name, etc	Heir
1664	*Arlington (11th)*, Jennifer Jane Forwood, *b.* 1939, *s.* 1999, *w.* Title called out of abeyance 1999	Hon. Patrick J. D. F., *b.* 1967
1455	*Berners (16th)*, Pamela Vivien Kirkham, *b.* 1929, *s.* 1995, *m.* Title called out of abeyance 1995	Hon. Rupert W. T. K., *b.* 1953
1529	*Braye (8th)*, Mary Penelope Aubrey-Fletcher, *b.* 1941, *s.* 1985, *m.*	Linda K. C. Fothergill, *b.* 1930
1321	*Dacre (29th)*, Emily Beamish, *b.* 1983, *s.* 2014, *m.*	Three co-heiresses
1283	*Fauconberg (10th) and Conyers (16th) (1509)*, Baronies in abeyance between two co-heiresses since 2013	
1490 S.	*Herries of Terregles (16th)*, (Theresa) Jane Kerr, Marchioness of Lothian, *b.* 1945, *s.* 2017, *m.*	Lady Clare T. Hurd, *b.* 1979
1597	*Howard de Walden (10th)*, Mary Hazel Caridwen Czernin, *b.* 1935, *s.* 2004, *m.* Title called out of abeyance 2004	Hon. Peter J. J. C., *b.* 1966
1602 S.	*Kinloss (13th)*, Teresa Mary Nugent Freeman-Grenville, *b.* 1957, *s.* 2012	Mistress of Kinloss, *b.* 1960
1445 S.	*Saltoun (20th)*, Flora Marjory Fraser, *b.* 1930, *s.* 1979, *w.*	Hon. Katharine I. M. I. F., *b.* 1957
1313	*Willoughby de Eresby (27th)*, (Nancy) Jane Marie Heathcote-Drummond-Willoughby, *b.* 1934, *s.* 1983	Two co-heirs

LIFE PEERS

Style, The Rt. Hon. the Lord _ /The Rt. Hon. the Lady _ , *or* The Rt. Hon. the Baroness _ , according to her preference
Envelope (formal), The Rt. Hon. Lord _/Lady_/Baroness_; *(social),* The Lord _/Lady_/Baroness_ *Letter (formal),* My Lord/Lady; *(social),* Dear Lord/Lady _. *Spoken,* Lord/Lady _
Wife's style, The Rt. Hon. the Lady _
Husband, Untitled
Children's style, 'The Hon.' before forename (F_) and surname (S_)
   Envelope, The Hon. F_ S_. *Letter,* Dear Mr/Miss/Mrs S_. *Spoken,* Mr/Miss/Mrs S_

NEW LIFE PEERAGES
31 October 2016 to 31 August 2017:

Ian James Duncan; Laura Lee Wyld

SYMBOLS
* Hereditary peer who has been granted a life peerage. For further details, please refer to the Hereditary Peers section. For example, life peer *Balniel* can be found under his hereditary title *Earl of Crawford and Balcarres*
§ Members of the Judiciary currently disqualified from sitting or voting in the House of Lords until they retire from that office. For further information *see* Law Courts and Offices
‡ Title not confirmed at time of going to press
℄ Peer who has permanently resigned from the House of Lords
E. Peer who has been expelled for absenteeism, under section 2 of the House of Lords Reform Act 2014, for failing to attend a sitting of the House during a session lasting six months or longer *see* page 45

CREATED UNDER THE APPELLATE JURISDICTION ACT 1876 (AS AMENDED)

BARONS
Created

2004   *Brown of Eaton-under-Heywood,* Simon Denis Brown, PC, *b.* 1937, *m.*
1991   ℄*Browne-Wilkinson,* Nicolas Christopher Henry Browne-Wilkinson, PC, *b.* 1930, *m.*
2004   *Carswell,* Robert Douglas Carswell, PC, *b.* 1934, *m.*
2009   *Collins of Mapesbury,* Lawrence Antony Collins, PC, *b.* 1941
1995   *Hoffmann,* Leonard Hubert Hoffmann, PC, *b.* 1934, *m.*
1997   *Hutton,* (James) Brian (Edward) Hutton, PC, *b.* 1931, *m.*
2009   §*Kerr of Tonaghmore,* Brian Francis Kerr, PC, *b.* 1948, *m.*
1993   ℄*Lloyd of Berwick,* Anthony John Leslie Lloyd, PC, *b.* 1929, *m.*
2005   §*Mance,* Jonathan Hugh Mance, PC, *b.* 1943, *m.*
1998   ℄*Millett,* Peter Julian Millett, PC, *b.* 1932, *m.*
2007   *Neuberger of Abbotsbury,* David Edmond Neuberger, PC, *b.* 1948, *m.*
1994   ℄*Nicholls of Birkenhead,* Donald James Nicholls, PC, *b.* 1933, *m.*
1999   *Phillips of Worth Matravers,* Nicholas Addison Phillips, KG, PC, *b.* 1938, *m.*
1997   *Saville of Newdigate,* Mark Oliver Saville, PC, *b.* 1936, *m.*
2000   ℄*Scott of Foscote,* Richard Rashleigh Folliott Scott, PC, *b.* 1934, *m.*
1995   *Steyn,* Johan van Zyl Steyn, PC, *b.* 1932, *m.*
2003   *Walker of Gestingthorpe,* Robert Walker, PC, *b.* 1938, *m.*

1992   *Woolf,* Harry Kenneth Woolf, CH, PC, *b.* 1933, *m.*

BARONESSES
2004   §*Hale of Richmond,* Brenda Marjorie Hale, DBE, PC, *b.* 1945, *m.* President of the Supreme Court

CREATED UNDER THE LIFE PEERAGES ACT 1958

BARONS
Created

2001   *Adebowale,* Victor Olufemi Adebowale, CBE, *b.* 1962
2005   *Adonis,* Andrew Adonis, PC, *b.* 1963, *m.*
2011   *Ahmad of Wimbledon,* Tariq Mahmood Ahmad, *b.* 1968, *m.*
1998   *Ahmed,* Nazir Ahmed, *b.* 1957, *m.*
1996   *Alderdice,* John Thomas Alderdice, *b.* 1955, *m.*
2010   *Allan of Hallam,* Richard Beecroft Allan, *b.* 1966
2013   *Allen of Kensington,* Charles Lamb Allen, CBE, *b.* 1957
1998   *Alli,* Waheed Alli, *b.* 1964
2004   *Alliance,* David Alliance, CBE, *b.* 1932
1997   *Alton of Liverpool,* David Patrick Paul Alton, *b.* 1951, *m.*
2005   *Anderson of Swansea,* Donald Anderson, PC, *b.* 1939, *m.*
2015   *Arbuthnot of Edrom,* James Norwich Arbuthnot, PC, *b.* 1952, *m.*
1992   *Archer of Weston-super-Mare,* Jeffrey Howard Archer, *b.* 1940, *m.*
1988   *Armstrong of Ilminster,* Robert Temple Armstrong, GCB, CVO, *b.* 1927, *m.*
2000   ℄*Ashcroft,* Michael Anthony Ashcroft, KCMG, PC, *b.* 1946, *m.*
2001   *Ashdown of Norton-sub-Hamdon,* Jeremy John Durham (Paddy) Ashdown, GCMG, CH, KBE, PC, *b.* 1941, *m.*
1998   *Bach,* William Stephen Goulden Bach, *b.* 1946, *m.*
1997   *Baker of Dorking,* Kenneth Wilfred Baker, CH, PC, *b.* 1934, *m.*
2013   *Balfe,* Richard Andrew Balfe, *b.* 1944, *m.*
1974   **Balniel,* The Earl of Crawford and Balcarres, KT, GCVO, PC, *b.* 1927, *m.* *(see* Hereditary Peers)
2013   *Bamford,* Anthony Paul Bamford, *b.* 1945, *m.*
1992   ℄*Barber of Tewkesbury,* Derek Coates Barber, *b.* 1918, *m.*
2015   *Barker of Battle,* Gregory Leonard George Barker, PC, *b.* 1966, *m.*
1997   *Bassam of Brighton,* (John) Steven Bassam, PC, *b.* 1953
2008   *Bates,* Michael Walton Bates, PC, *b.* 1961
2010   *Beecham,* Jeremy Hugh Beecham, *b.* 1944, *m.*
2015   *Beith,* Alan James Beith, PC, *b.* 1943, *m.*
1998   *Bell,* Timothy John Leigh Bell, *b.* 1941, *m.*
2013   *Berkeley of Knighton,* Michael Fitzhardinge Berkeley, CBE, *b.* 1948, *m.*
2001   *Best,* Richard Stuart Best, OBE, *b.* 1945, *m.*
2007   *Bew,* Prof. Paul Anthony Elliott Bew, *b.* 1950, *m.*
2001   *Bhatia,* Amirali Alibhai Bhatia, OBE, *b.* 1932, *m.*
2004   *Bhattacharyya,* Prof. (Sushantha) Kumar Bhattacharyya, CBE, *b.* 1932, *m.*
2010   *Bichard,* Michael George Bichard, KCB, *b.* 1947
2006   *Bilimoria,* Karan Faridoon Bilimoria, CBE, *b.* 1961, *m.*
2015   *Bird,* John Anthony Bird, MBE, *b.* 1946, *m.*
2000   *Birt,* John Francis Hodgess Birt, *b.* 1944, *m.*
2010   *Black of Brentwood,* Guy Vaughan Black, *b.* 1964, *m.*
2001   *Black of Crossharbour,* Conrad Moffat Black, *b.* 1944, *m.*
1997   *Blackwell,* Norman Roy Blackwell, *b.* 1952, *m.*
2010   *Blair of Boughton,* Ian Warwick Blair, QPM, *b.* 1953, *m.*

2011   *Blencathra,* David John Maclean, PC, *b.* 1953
2015   *Blunkett,* David Blunkett, PC, *b.* 1947, *m.*
1995   *Blyth of Rowington,* James Blyth, *b.* 1940, *m.*
2010   *Boateng,* Paul Yaw Boateng, PC, *b.* 1951, *m.*
2010   *Boswell of Aynho,* Timothy Eric Boswell, *b.* 1942, *m.*
2013   *Bourne of Aberystwyth,* Nicholas Henry Bourne, *b.* 1952
1996   *Bowness,* Peter Spencer Bowness, CBE, *b.* 1943, *m.*
2003   *Boyce,* Michael Boyce, KG, GCB, OBE, *b.* 1943, *m.*
2006   §*Boyd of Duncansby,* Colin David Boyd, PC, *b.* 1953, *m.*
2006   *Bradley,* Keith John Charles Bradley, PC, *b.* 1950, *m.*
1999   *Bradshaw,* William Peter Bradshaw, *b.* 1936, *m.*
1998   *Bragg,* Melvyn Bragg, *b.* 1939, *m.*
1987   *Bramall,* Edwin Noel Westby Bramall, KG, GCB, OBE, MC, *b.* 1923, *w.*
2000   *Brennan,* Daniel Joseph Brennan, QC, *b.* 1942, *m.*
2015   *Bridges of Headley,* James George Robert Bridges, MBE, *b.* 1970, *m.*
2004   *Broers,* Prof. Alec (Nigel) Broers, *b.* 1938, *m.*
1997   *Brooke of Alverthorpe,* Clive Brooke, *b.* 1942, *m.*
2001   ℂ*Brooke of Sutton Mandeville,* Peter Leonard Brooke, CH, PC, *b.* 1934, *m.*
1998   *Brookman,* David Keith Brookman, *b.* 1937, *m.*
2006   *Browne of Belmont,* Wallace Hamilton Browne, *b.* 1947
2010   *Browne of Ladyton,* Desmond Henry Browne, PC, *b.* 1952
2001   *Browne of Madingley,* Edmund John Phillip Browne, *b.* 1948
2015   *Bruce of Bennachie,* Malcolm Gray Bruce, PC, *b.* 1944, *m.*
2006   *Burnett,* John Patrick Aubone Burnett, *b.* 1945, *m.*
1998   *Burns,* Terence Burns, GCB, *b.* 1944, *m.*
1998   *Butler of Brockwell,* (Frederick Edward) Robin Butler, KG, GCB, CVO, PC, *b.* 1938, *m.*
2016   *Caine,* Jonathan Michael Caine, *b.* 1966
2014   *Callanan,* Martin John Callanan, *b.* 1961, *m.*
2004   *Cameron of Dillington,* Ewen (James Hanning) Cameron, *b.* 1949, *m.*
1984   ℂ*Cameron of Lochbroom,* Kenneth John Cameron, PC, *b.* 1931, *m.*
2015   *Campbell of Pittenweem,* (Walter) Menzies Campbell, CH, CBE, PC, QC, *b.* 1941, *m.*
2001   *Campbell-Savours,* Dale Norman Campbell-Savours, *b.* 1943, *m.*
2002   *Carey of Clifton,* Rt. Revd George Leonard Carey, PC, Royal Victorian Chain, *b.* 1935, *m.*
1999   **Carington of Upton,* Lord Carrington, KG, GCMG, CH, MC, PC, *b.* 1919, *w.* *(see* Hereditary Peers)
1999   *Carlile of Berriew,* Alexander Charles Carlile, CBE, QC, *b.* 1948, *m.*
2013   *Carrington of Fulham,* Matthew Hadrian Marshall Carrington, *b.* 1947, *m.*
2008   *Carter of Barnes,* Stephen Andrew Carter, CBE, *b.* 1964, *m.*
2004   *Carter of Coles,* Patrick Robert Carter, *b.* 1946, *m.*
2014   *Cashman,* Michael Maurice Cashman, CBE, *b.* 1950
1990   *Cavendish of Furness,* (Richard) Hugh Cavendish, *b.* 1941, *m.*
1996   *Chadlington,* Peter Selwyn Gummer, *b.* 1942, *m.*
1964   ℂ*Chalfont,* (Alun) Arthur Gwynne Jones, OBE, MC, PC, *b.* 1919, *w.*
2005   *Chidgey,* David William George Chidgey, *b.* 1942, *m.*
1998   *Christopher,* Anthony Martin Grosvenor Christopher, CBE, *b.* 1925, *m.*
2001   *Clark of Windermere,* David George Clark, PC, PHD, *b.* 1939, *m.*
1998   *Clarke of Hampstead,* Anthony James Clarke, CBE, *b.* 1932, *m.*
2009   *Clarke of Stone-Cum-Ebony,* Anthony Peter Clarke, PC, *b.* 1943, *m.*
1998   *Clement-Jones,* Timothy Francis Clement-Jones, CBE, *b.* 1949, *m.*

1990   *Clinton-Davis,* Stanley Clinton Clinton-Davis, PC, *b.* 1928, *m.*
2000   *Coe,* Sebastian Newbold Coe, CH, KBE, *b.* 1956, *m.*
2011   *Collins of Highbury,* Raymond Edward Harry Collins, *b.* 1954
2001   *Condon,* Paul Leslie Condon, QPM, *b.* 1947, *m.*
2014   *Cooper of Windrush,* Andrew Timothy Cooper, *b.* 1963, *m.*
1997   *Cope of Berkeley,* John Ambrose Cope, PC, *b.* 1937, *m.*
2010   *Cormack,* Patrick Thomas Cormack, *b.* 1939, *m.*
2006   *Cotter,* Brian Joseph Michael Cotter, *b.* 1938, *m.*
1991   *Craig of Radley,* David Brownrigg Craig, GCB, OBE, *b.* 1929, *m.*
1987   *Crickhowell,* (Roger) Nicholas Edwards, PC, *b.* 1934, *m.*
2006   *Crisp,* (Edmund) Nigel (Ramsay) Crisp, KCB, *b.* 1952, *m.*
2003   *Cullen of Whitekirk,* William Douglas Cullen, KT, PC, *b.* 1935, *m.*
2005   *Cunningham of Felling,* John Anderson Cunningham, PC, *b.* 1939, *m.*
1996   *Currie of Marylebone,* David Anthony Currie, *b.* 1946, *m.*
2011   *Curry of Kirkharle,* Donald Thomas Younger Curry, CBE, *b.* 1944, *m.*
2011   *Dannatt,* (Francis) Richard Dannatt, GCB, CBE, MC, *b.* 1950, *m.*
2015   *Darling of Roulanish,* Alistair Maclean Darling, PC, *b.* 1953, *m.*
2007   *Darzi of Denham,* Ara Warkes Darzi, OM, KBE, PC, *b.* 1960, *m.*
2006   *Davidson of Glen Clova,* Neil Forbes Davidson, QC, *b.* 1950, *m.*
2009   *Davies of Abersoch,* Evan Mervyn Davies, CBE, *b.* 1952, *m.*
1997   *Davies of Coity,* (David) Garfield Davies, CBE, *b.* 1935, *m.*
1997   *Davies of Oldham,* Bryan Davies, PC, *b.* 1939, *m.*
2010   *Davies of Stamford,* John Quentin Davies, *b.* 1944, *m.*
2006   *Dear,* Geoffrey (James) Dear, QPM, *b.* 1937, *m.*
2010   *Deben,* John Selwyn Gummer, PC, *b.* 1939, *m.*
2012   *Deighton,* Paul Clive Deighton, KBE, *b.* 1956, *m.*
1991   *Desai,* Prof. Meghnad Jagdishchandra Desai, PHD, *b.* 1940, *m.*
1997   *Dholakia,* Navnit Dholakia, OBE, PC, *b.* 1937, *m.*
1993   *Dixon-Smith,* Robert William Dixon-Smith, *b.* 1834, *m.*
2010   *Dobbs,* Michael John Dobbs, *b.* 1948, *m.*
1985   *Donoughue,* Bernard Donoughue, DPHIL, *b.* 1934
2004   *Drayson,* Paul Rudd Drayson, PC, *b.* 1960, *m.*
1994   *Dubs,* Alfred Dubs, *b.* 1932, *m.*
2017   *Duncan of Springbank,* Ian James Duncan, *b.* 1973
2015   *Dunlop,* Andrew James Dunlop, *b.* 1959, *m.*
2004   *Dykes,* Hugh John Maxwell Dykes, *b.* 1939, *m.*
1995   *Eames,* Rt. Revd Robert Henry Alexander Eames, OM, PHD, *b.* 1937, *m.*
1992   *Eatwell,* John Leonard Eatwell, PHD, *b.* 1945
1983   ℂ*Eden of Winton,* John Benedict Eden, PC, *b.* 1925, *m.*
2011   ℂ*Edmiston,* Robert Norman Edmiston, *b.* 1946, *m.*
1999   *Elder,* Thomas Murray Elder, *b.* 1950
1992   *Elis-Thomas,* Dafydd Elis Elis-Thomas, PC, *b.* 1946, *m.*
1981   *Elystan-Morgan,* Dafydd Elystan Elystan-Morgan, *b.* 1932, *w.*
2011   *Empey,* Reginald Norman Morgan Empey, OBE, *b.* 1947, *m.*
2000   ℂ**Erskine of Alloa Tower,* Earl of Mar and Kellie, *b.* 1949, *m. (see* Hereditary Peers)
1998   *Evans of Watford,* David Charles Evans, *b.* 1942, *m.*
2014   *Evans of Weardale,* Jonathan Douglas Evans, KCB, *b.* 1958

1997   *Falconer of Thoroton,* Charles Leslie Falconer, PC, QC, *b.* 1951, *m.*
2014   *Farmer,* Michael Stahel Farmer, *b.* 1944, *m.*
1999   *Faulkner of Worcester,* Richard Oliver Faulkner, *b.* 1946, *m.*
2010   *Faulks,* Edward Peter Lawless Faulks, QC, *b.* 1950, *m.*
2001   *Fearn,* Ronald Cyril Fearn, OBE, *b.* 1931, *m.*
1996   ℂ*Feldman,* Basil Feldman, *b.* 1926, *m.*
2010   *Feldman of Elstree,* Andrew Simon Feldman, PC, *b.* 1966, *m.*
1999   *Fellowes,* Robert Fellowes, GCB, GCVO, PC, *b.* 1941, *m.*
2011   *Fellowes of West Stafford,* Julian Alexander Fellowes, *b.* 1949, *m.*
1999   *Filkin,* David Geoffrey Nigel Filkin, CBE, *b.* 1944
2011   *Fink,* Stanley Fink, *b.* 1957, *m.*
2013   *Finkelstein,* Daniel William Finkelstein, OBE, *b.* 1962, *m.*
2011   *Flight,* Howard Emerson Flight, *b.* 1948, *m.*
1999   *Forsyth of Drumlean,* Michael Bruce Forsyth, PC, *b.* 1954, *m.*
2015   *Foster of Bath,* Donald Michael Ellison Foster, PC, *b.* 1947, *m.*
2005   *Foster of Bishop Auckland,* Derek Foster, PC, *b.* 1937, *m.*
1999   ℂ*Foster of Thames Bank,* Norman Robert Foster, OM, *b.* 1935, *m.*
2005   *Foulkes of Cumnock,* George Foulkes, PC, *b.* 1942, *m.*
2001   *Fowler,* (Peter) Norman Fowler, PC, *b.* 1938, *m. Lord Speaker*
2014   *Fox,* Christopher Francis Fox, *b.* 1957, *m.*
2011   *Framlingham,* Michael Nicholson Lord, *b.* 1938, *m.*
2016   *Fraser of Corriegarth,* (Alexander) Andrew (Macdonell) Fraser, *b.* 1946, *m.*
1997   *Freeman,* Roger Norman Freeman, PC, *b.* 1942, *m.*
2009   *Freud,* David Anthony Freud, PC, *b.* 1950, *m.*
2016   *Gadhia,* Jitesh Kishorekumar Gadhia, *b.* 1970, *m.*
2010   *Gardiner of Kimble,* John Gardiner, *b.* 1956, *m.*
1997   *Garel-Jones,* (William Armand Thomas) Tristan Garel-Jones, PC, *b.* 1941, *m.*
1999   ℂ*Gascoyne-Cecil,* The Marquess of Salisbury, KCVO, PC, *b.* 1946, *m.* (*see* Hereditary Peers)
2010   *German,* Michael James German, OBE, *b.* 1945, *m.*
2004   *Giddens,* Prof. Anthony Giddens, *b.* 1938, *m.*
2015   *Gilbert of Panteg,* Stephen Gilbert, *b.* 1963
2011   *Glasman,* Maurice Mark Glasman, *b.* 1961, *m.*
2011   *Glendonbrook,* Michael David Bishop, CBE, *b.* 1942
2014   *Goddard of Stockport,* David Goddard, *b.* 1952
2011   *Gold,* David Laurence Gold, *b.* 1951, *m.*
1999   *Goldsmith,* Peter Henry Goldsmith, PC, QC, *b.* 1950, *m.*
2005   *Goodlad,* Alastair Robertson Goodlad, KCMG, PC, *b.* 1943, *m.*
1997   *Gordon of Strathblane,* James Stuart Gordon, CBE, *b.* 1936, *m.*
1999   *Grabiner,* Anthony Stephen Grabiner, QC, *b.* 1945, *m.*
2011   *Grade of Yarmouth,* Michael Ian Grade, CBE, *b.* 1943, *m.*
1983   *Graham of Edmonton,* (Thomas) Edward Graham, PC, *b.* 1925, *m.*
2000   *Greaves,* Anthony Robert Greaves, *b.* 1942, *m.*
2014   *Green of Deddington,* Andrew Fleming Green, KCMG, *b.* 1941, *m.*
2010   *Green of Hurstpierpoint,* Stephen Keith Green, *b.* 1948, *m.*
2000   ℂ*Grenfell of Kilvey,* Lord Grenfell, *b.* 1935, *m.* (*see* Hereditary Peers)
2004   *Griffiths of Burry Port,* Revd Dr Leslie John Griffiths, *b.* 1942, *m.*
1991   *Griffiths of Fforestfach,* Brian Griffiths, *b.* 1941, *m.*
2001   *Grocott,* Bruce Joseph Grocott, PC, *b.* 1940, *m.*

2000   *Gueterbock,* Lord Berkeley, OBE, *b.* 1939, *m.* (*see* Hereditary Peers)
2000   *Guthrie of Craigiebank,* Charles Ronald Llewelyn Guthrie, GCB, LVO, OBE, *b.* 1938, *m.*
1995   *Habgood,* Rt. Revd John Stapylton Habgood, PC, PHD, *b.* 1927, *w.*
2015   *Hague of Richmond,* William Jefferson Hague, PC, *b.* 1961, *m.*
2015   *Hailsham of Kettlethorpe,* Viscount Hailsham, PC, QC, *b.* 1945, *m.* (*see* Hereditary Peers)
2015   *Hain,* Peter Gerald Hain, PC, *b.* 1950, *m.*
2010   *Hall of Birkenhead,* Anthony William Hall, CBE, *b.* 1951, *m.*
2007   *Hameed,* Dr Khalid Hameed, CBE, *b.* 1941, *m.*
2005   *Hamilton of Epsom,* Archibald Gavin Hamilton, PC, *b.* 1941, *m.*
2001   *Hannay of Chiswick,* David Hugh Alexander Hannay, GCMG, CH, *b.* 1935, *w.*
1998   *Hanningfield,* Paul Edward Winston White, *b.* 1940
1997   ℂ*Hardie,* Andrew Rutherford Hardie, PC, QC, *b.* 1946, *m.*
2006   *Harries of Pentregarth,* Rt. Revd Richard Douglas Harries, *b.* 1936, *m.*
1998   *Harris of Haringey,* (Jonathan) Toby Harris, *b.* 1953, *m.*
1996   *Harris of Peckham,* Philip Charles Harris, *b.* 1942, *m.*
1999   *Harrison,* Lyndon Henry Arthur Harrison, *b.* 1947, *m.*
1993   *Haskel,* Simon Haskel, *b.* 1934, *m.*
1998   *Haskins,* Christopher Robin Haskins, *b.* 1937, *m.*
2005   *Hastings of Scarisbrick,* Michael John Hastings, CBE, *b.* 1958, *m.*
1997   ℂ*Hattersley,* Roy Sidney George Hattersley, PC, *b.* 1932
2013   *Haughey,* William Haughey, OBE, *b.* 1956, *m.*
2004   *Haworth,* Alan Robert Haworth, *b.* 1948, *m.*
2014   *Hay of Ballyore,* William Alexander Hay, *b.* 1950, *m.*
2015   *Hayward,* Robert Antony Hayward, OBE, *b.* 1949
2010   *Hennessy of Nympsfield,* Prof. Peter John Hennessy, *b.* 1947, *m.*
2001   *Heseltine,* Michael Ray Dibdin Heseltine, CH, PC, *b.* 1933, *m.*
1997   *Higgins,* Terence Langley Higgins, KBE, PC, *b.* 1928, *m.*
2010   *Hill of Oareford,* Jonathan Hopkin Hill, CBE, PC, *b.* 1960, *m.*
2000   *Hodgson of Astley Abbotts,* Robin Granville Hodgson, CBE, *b.* 1942, *m.*
1991   *Hollick,* Clive Richard Hollick, *b.* 1945, *m.*
2013   *Holmes of Richmond,* Christopher Holmes, MBE, *b.* 1971
1995   *Hope of Craighead,* (James Arthur) David Hope, KT, PC, *b.* 1938, *m.*
2005   ℂ*Hope of Thornes,* Rt. Revd David Michael Hope, KCVO, PC, *b.* 1940
2013   *Horam,* John Rhodes Horam, *b.* 1939, *m.*
2010   *Howard of Lympne,* Michael Howard, CH, PC, QC, *b.* 1941, *m.*
2004   *Howard of Rising,* Greville Patrick Charles Howard, *b.* 1941, *m.*
2005   *Howarth of Newport,* Alan Thomas Howarth, CBE, PC, *b.* 1944
1997   *Howell of Guildford,* David Arthur Russell Howell, PC, *b.* 1936, *m.*
1978   *Howie of Troon,* William Howie, *b.* 1924, *w.*
1997   *Hoyle,* (Eric) Douglas Harvey Hoyle, *b.* 1930, *w.*
1997   *Hughes of Woodside,* Robert Hughes, *b.* 1932, *m.*
2000   *Hunt of Chesterton,* Julian Charles Roland Hunt, CB, *b.* 1941, *m.*
1997   *Hunt of Kings Heath,* Philip Alexander Hunt, OBE, PC, *b.* 1949, *m.*
1997   *Hunt of Wirral,* David James Fletcher Hunt, MBE, PC, *b.* 1942, *m.*

1997 ¢Hurd of Westwell, Douglas Richard Hurd, CH, CBE, PC, b. 1930, w.

2011 Hussain, Qurban Hussain, b. 1956, m.

1978 Hutchinson of Lullington, Jeremy Nicolas Hutchinson, QC, b. 1915, w.

2010 Hutton of Furness, John Matthew Patrick Hutton, PC, b. 1955, m.

1999 Imbert, Peter Michael Imbert, CVO, QPM, b. 1933, m.

1997 ¢Inge, Peter Anthony Inge, KG, GCB, PC, b. 1935, m.

1987 Irvine of Lairg, Alexander Andrew Mackay Irvine, PC, QC, b. 1940, m.

2006 James of Blackheath, David Noel James, CBE, b. 1937, m.

2007 Janvrin, Robin Berry Janvrin, GCB, GCVO, PC, b. 1946, m.

2006 Jay of Ewelme, Michael (Hastings) Jay, GCMG, b. 1946, m.

2001 Jones, (Stephen) Barry Jones, PC, b. 1937, m.

2007 Jones of Birmingham, Digby Marritt Jones, b. 1955, m.

2005 Jones of Cheltenham, Nigel David Jones, b. 1948, m.

1997 Jopling, (Thomas) Michael Jopling, PC, b. 1930, m.

2000 Jordan, William Brian Jordan, CBE, b. 1936, m.

1991 Judd, Frank Ashcroft Judd, b. 1935, m.

2008 Judge, Igor Judge, PC, b. 1941, m.

2010 Kakkar, Prof. Ajay Kumar Kakkar, PC, b. 1964

2004 Kalms, Harold Stanley Kalms, b. 1931, m.

2015 Keen of Elie, Richard Sanderson Keen, QC, b. 1954, m.

2010 Kennedy of Southwark, Roy Francis Kennedy, b. 1962, m.

2004 Kerr of Kinlochard, John (Olav) Kerr, GCMG, b. 1942, m.

2010 *Kerr of Monteviot, Marquess of Lothian (Michael Ancram), PC, QC, b. 1945, m. (see Hereditary Peers)

2015 Kerslake, Robert Walter Kerslake, b. 1955, m.

2011 Kestenbaum, Jonathan Andrew Kestenbaum, b. 1959, m.

2001 Kilclooney, John David Taylor, PC (NI), b. 1937, m.

2001 King of Bridgwater, Thomas Jeremy King, CH, PC, b. 1933, m.

2013 King of Lothbury, Mervyn Allister King, KG, GBE, b. 1948

2005 Kinnock, Neil Gordon Kinnock, PC, b. 1942, m.

1999 Kirkham, Graham Kirkham, b. 1944, m.

1975 Kirkhill, John Farquharson Smith, b. 1930, m.

2016 Kirkhope of Harrogate, Timothy John Robert Kirkhope, b. 1945, m.

2005 Kirkwood of Kirkhope, Archibald Johnstone Kirkwood, b. 1946, m.

2010 Knight of Weymouth, James Philip Knight, PC, b. 1965, m.

2007 Krebs, Prof. John (Richard) Krebs, FRS, b. 1945, m.

2004 ¢Laidlaw, Irvine Alan Stewart Laidlaw, b. 1942, m.

1999 Laird, John Dunn Laird, b. 1944, m.

1998 Laming, (William) Herbert Laming, CBE, PC, b. 1936, w.

1998 Lamont of Lerwick, Norman Stewart Hughson Lamont, PC, b. 1942, m.

1997 Lang of Monkton, Ian Bruce Lang, PC, b. 1940, m.

2015 Lansley, Andrew David Lansley, CBE, PC, b. 1956, m.

1992 Lawson of Blaby, Nigel Lawson, PC, b. 1932, m.

2000 Layard, Peter Richard Grenville Layard, b. 1934, m.

1999 Lea of Crondall, David Edward Lea, OBE, b. 1937

2006 Lee of Trafford, John Robert Louis Lee, b. 1942, m.

2013 Leigh of Hurley, Howard Darryl Leigh, b. 1959, m.

2004 Leitch, Alexander Park Leitch, b. 1947, m.

2014 Lennie, Christopher John Lennie, b. 1953, m.

1993 Lester of Herne Hill, Anthony Paul Lester, QC, b. 1936, m.

1997 Levene of Portsoken, Peter Keith Levene, KBE, b. 1941, m.

1997 Levy, Michael Abraham Levy, b. 1944, m.

2010 Lexden, Alistair Basil Cooke, OBE, b. 1945

2010 Liddle, Roger John Liddle, b. 1947, m.

2010 Lingfield, Robert George Alexander Balchin, b. 1942, m.

1999 Lipsey, David Lawrence Lipsey, b. 1948, m.

2014 Lisvane, Robert James Rogers, KCB, b. 1950, m.

2015 Livermore, Spencer Elliot Livermore, b. 1975

2013 Livingston of Parkhead, Ian Paul Livingston, b. 1964, m.

2016 Llewellyn of Steep, Edward David Gerard Llewellyn, OBE, PC, b. 1965, m.

1997 Lloyd-Webber, Andrew Lloyd Webber, b. 1948, m.

2011 Loomba, Rajinder Paul Loomba, CBE, b. 1943, m.

2006 Low of Dalston, Prof. Colin MacKenzie Low, CBE, b. 1942, m.

2000 Luce, Richard Napier Luce, KG, GCVO, PC, b. 1936, m.

2015 Lupton, James Roger Crompton Lupton, CBE, b. 1955, m.

2000 *Lyttelton of Aldershot, The Viscount Chandos, b. 1953, m. (see Hereditary Peers)

2010 McAvoy, Thomas McLaughlin McAvoy, PC, b. 1943, m.

1989 McColl of Dulwich, Ian McColl, CBE, FRCS, FRCSE, b. 1933, m.

2010 McConnell of Glenscorrodale, Dr Jack Wilson McConnell, PC, b. 1960, m.

2010 Macdonald of River Glaven, Kenneth Donald John Macdonald, QC, b. 1953, m.

1998 ¢Macdonald of Tradeston, Angus John Macdonald, CBE, PC, b. 1940, m.

2010 McFall of Alcluith, John Francis McFall, PC, b. 1944, m.

1991 ¢Macfarlane of Bearsden, Norman Somerville Macfarlane, KT, FRSE, b. 1926, m.

2001 MacGregor of Pulham Market, John Roddick Russell MacGregor, CBE, PC, b. 1937, m.

2016 McInnes of Kilwinning, Mark McInnes, CBE, b. 1976

1979 Mackay of Clashfern, James Peter Hymers Mackay, KT, PC, FRSE, b. 1927, m.

1995 ¢Mackay of Drumadoon, Donald Sage Mackay, PC, b. 1946, m.

1999 MacKenzie of Culkein, Hector Uisdean MacKenzie, b. 1940

1998 Mackenzie of Framwellgate, Brian Mackenzie, OBE, b. 1943, m.

2004 McKenzie of Luton, William David McKenzie, b. 1946, m.

1996 MacLaurin of Knebworth, Ian Charter MacLaurin, b. 1937, m.

2001 Maclennan of Rogart, Robert Adam Ross Maclennan, PC, b. 1936, m.

1995 McNally, Tom McNally, PC, b. 1943, m.

2016 Macpherson of Earl's Court, Nicholas Ian Macpherson, GCB, b. 1959, m.

2011 Magan of Castletown, George Morgan Magan, b. 1945, m.

2001 Maginnis of Drumglass, Kenneth Wiggins Maginnis, b. 1938, m.

2015 Mair, Prof. Robert James Mair, CBE, PHD, FRS, b. 1950, m.

2007 Malloch-Brown, George Mark Malloch Brown, KCMG, PC, b. 1953, m.

2008 Mandelson, Peter Benjamin Mandelson, PC, b. 1953

2011 Marks of Henley-on-Thames, Jonathan Clive Marks, QC, b. 1952, m.

2006 Marland, Jonathan Peter Marland, b. 1956, m.

1991 Marlesford, Mark Shuldham Schreiber, b. 1931, m.

2009 Martin of Springburn, Michael Martin, PC, b. 1945, m.

2015 Maude of Horsham, Francis Anthony Aylmer Maude, TD, PC, b. 1953, m.

2005   *Mawhinney,* Brian Stanley Mawhinney, PC, *b.* 1940, *m.*

2007   *Mawson,* Revd Andrew Mawson, OBE, *b.* 1954, *m.*

2004   *Maxton,* John Alston Maxton, *b.* 1936, *m.*

2001   ⟨*May of Oxford,* Robert McCredie May, OM, *b.* 1936, *m.*

2013   *Mendelsohn,* Jonathan Neil Mendelsohn, *b.* 1966, *m.*

2000   *Mitchell,* Parry Andrew Mitchell, *b.* 1943, *m.*

2000   **Mitford,* Lord Redesdale, *b.* 1967, *m.* (*see* Hereditary Peers)

2008   *Mogg,* John (Frederick) Mogg, KCMG, *b.* 1943, *m.*

2010   *Monks,* John Stephen Monks, *b.* 1945, *m.*

2005   *Moonie,* Dr Lewis George Moonie, *b.* 1947, *m.*

1992   *Moore of Lower Marsh,* John Edward Michael Moore, PC, *b.* 1937, *w.*

2000   *Morgan,* Kenneth Owen Morgan, *b.* 1934, *m.*

2001   *Morris of Aberavon,* John Morris, KG, PC, QC, *b.* 1931, *m.*

2006   *Morris of Handsworth,* William Manuel Morris, *b.* 1938, *m.*

2006   *Morrow,* Maurice George Morrow, *b.* 1948, *m.*

2015   *Murphy of Torfaen,* Paul Peter Murphy, PC, *b.* 1948

2008   *Myners,* Paul Myners, CBE, *b.* 1948, *m.*

1997   *Naseby,* Michael Wolfgang Laurence Morris, PC, *b.* 1936, *m.*

2013   *Nash,* John Alfred Stoddard Nash, *b.* 1949

1997   *Newby,* Richard Mark Newby, OBE, PC, *b.* 1953, *m.*

1994   ⟨*Nickson,* David Wigley Nickson, KBE, FRSE, *b.* 1929, *m.*

1998   *Norton of Louth,* Philip Norton, *b.* 1951

2000   *Oakeshott of Seagrove Bay,* Matthew Alan Oakeshott, *b.* 1947, *m.*

2015   *Oates,* Jonathan Oates, *b.* 1969, *c.p.*

2012   *O'Donnell,* Augustine Thomas (Gus) O'Donnell, GCB, *b.* 1952, *m.*

2005   *O'Neill of Clackmannan,* Martin John O'Neill, *b.* 1945, *m.*

2015   *O'Neill of Gatley,* Terence James O'Neill, *b.* 1957, *m.*

2015   *O'Shaughnessy,* James Richard O'Shaughnessy, *b.* 1976, *m.*

2001   *Ouseley,* Herman George Ouseley, *b.* 1945, *m.*

1992   *Owen,* David Anthony Llewellyn Owen, CH, PC, *b.* 1938, *m.*

1999   *Oxburgh,* Ernest Ronald Oxburgh, KBE, FRS, PHD, *b.* 1934, *m.*

2013   *Paddick,* Brian Leonard Paddick, *b.* 1958, *m.*

2011   *Palmer of Childs Hill,* Monroe Edward Palmer, OBE, *b.* 1938, *m.*

1991   *Palumbo,* Peter Garth Palumbo, *b.* 1935, *m.*

2013   *Palumbo of Southwark,* James Rudolph Palumbo, *b.* 1963

2008   *Pannick,* David Philip Pannick, QC, *b.* 1956, *m.*

2000   *Parekh,* Bhikhu Chhotalal Parekh, *b.* 1935, *m.*

1999   *Patel,* Narendra Babubhai Patel, KT, *b.* 1938

2000   *Patel of Blackburn,* Adam Hafejee Patel, *b.* 1940

2006   *Patel of Bradford,* Prof. Kamlesh Kumar Patel, OBE, *b.* 1960, *m.*

1997   *Patten,* John Haggitt Charles Patten, PC, *b.* 1945, *m.*

2005   *Patten of Barnes,* Christopher Francis Patten, CH, PC, *b.* 1944, *m.*

1996   *Paul,* Swraj Paul, PC, *b.* 1931, *m.*

1990   *Pearson of Rannoch,* Malcolm Everard MacLaren Pearson, *b.* 1942, *m.*

2001   *Pendry,* Thomas Pendry, PC, *b.* 1934, *m.*

1998   ⟨*Phillips of Sudbury,* Andrew Wyndham Phillips, OBE, *b.* 1939, *m.*

1992   *Plant of Highfield,* Prof. Raymond Plant, PHD, *b.* 1945, *m.*

1987   *Plumb,* (Charles) Henry Plumb, *b.* 1925, *m.*

2015   *Polak,* Stuart Polak, CBE, *b.* 1961

2000   **Ponsonby of Roehampton,* Lord Ponsonby of Shulbrede, *b.* 1958, *m.* (*see* Hereditary Peers)

2010   *Popat,* Dolar Amarshi Popat, *b.* 1953, *m.*

2015   *Porter of Spalding,* Gary Andrew Porter, CBE, *b.* 1960, *m.*

2000   *Powell of Bayswater,* Charles David Powell, KCMG, *b.* 1941, *m.*

2010   *Prescott,* John Leslie Prescott, *b.* 1938, *m.*

2016   *Price,* Mark Ian Price, CVO, *b.* 1961, *m.*

2015   *Prior of Brampton,* David Gifford Leathes Prior, *b.* 1954, *m.*

2013   *Purvis of Tweed,* Jeremy Purvis, *b.* 1974

1997   *Puttnam,* David Terence Puttnam, CBE, *b.* 1941, *m.*

1994   *Quirk,* Prof. (Charles) Randolph Quirk, CBE, FBA, *b.* 1920, *m.*

2001   *Radice,* Giles Heneage Radice, PC, *b.* 1936, *m.*

2005   *Ramsbotham,* David John Ramsbotham, GCB, CBE, *b.* 1934, *m.*

2004   *Rana,* Dr Diljit Singh Rana, MBE, *b.* 1938, *m.*

1997   *Razzall,* (Edward) Timothy Razzall, CBE, *b.* 1943, *m.*

2005   *Rees of Ludlow,* Prof. Martin John Rees, OM, *b.* 1942, *m.*

2010   *Reid of Cardowan,* Dr John Reid, PC, *b.* 1947, *m.*

1991   *Renfrew of Kaimsthorn,* (Andrew) Colin Renfrew, FBA, *b.* 1937, *m.*

1999   *Rennard,* Christopher John Rennard, MBE, *b.* 1960

1997   ⟨*Renton of Mount Harry,* (Ronald) Timothy Renton, PC, *b.* 1932, *m.*

1997   *Renwick of Clifton,* Robin William Renwick, KCMG, *b.* 1937, *m.*

2010   *Ribeiro,* Bernard Francisco Ribeiro, CBE, *b.* 1944, *m.*

1990   *Richard,* Ivor Seward Richard, PC, QC, *b.* 1932, *m.*

2014   *Richards of Herstmonceux,* David Julian Richards, GCB, CBE, DSO, *b.* 1952, *m.*

2016   *Ricketts,* Peter (Forbes) Ricketts, GCMG, GCVO, *b.* 1952, *m.*

2010   *Risby,* Richard John Grenville Spring, *b.* 1946, *m.*

2015   *Robathan,* Andrew Robathan, PC, *b.* 1951, *m.*

2004   *Roberts of Llandudno,* Revd John Roger Roberts, *b.* 1935, *m.*

1999   *Robertson of Port Ellen,* George Islay MacNeill Robertson, KT, GCMG, PC, *b.* 1946, *m.*

1992   *Rodgers of Quarry Bank,* William Thomas Rodgers, PC, *b.* 1928, *w.*

1999   *Rogan,* Dennis Robert David Rogan, *b.* 1942, *m.*

1996   *Rogers of Riverside,* Richard George Rogers, CH, RA, RIBA, *b.* 1933, *m.*

2001   *Rooker,* Jeffrey William Rooker, PC, *b.* 1941, *m.*

2014   *Rose of Monewden,* Stuart Alan Ransom Rose, *b.* 1949

2004   *Rosser,* Richard Andrew Rosser, *b.* 1944, *m.*

2006   *Rowe-Beddoe,* David (Sydney) Rowe-Beddoe, *b.* 1937, *m.*

2004   *Rowlands,* Edward Rowlands, CBE, *b.* 1940, *m.*

1997   *Ryder of Wensum,* Richard Andrew Ryder, OBE, PC, *b.* 1949, *m.*

1996   *Saatchi,* Maurice Saatchi, *b.* 1946, *w.*

2009   *Sacks,* Chief Rabbi Dr Jonathan Henry Sacks, *b.* 1948, *m.*

1989   *Sainsbury of Preston Candover,* John Davan Sainsbury, KG, *b.* 1927, *m.*

1997   *Sainsbury of Turville,* David John Sainsbury, *b.* 1940, *m.*

1985   *Sanderson of Bowden,* Charles Russell Sanderson, *b.* 1933, *m.*

2010   *Sassoon,* James Meyer Sassoon, *b.* 1955, *m.*

1998   *Sawyer,* Lawrence (Tom) Sawyer, *b.* 1943

2014   *Scriven,* Paul James Scriven, *b.* 1966

1997   *Selkirk of Douglas,* James Alexander Douglas-Hamilton, PC, QC, *b.* 1942, *m.*

1996   ⟨*Sewel,* John Buttifant Sewel, CBE, *b.* 1946

2010   *Sharkey,* John Kevin Sharkey, *b.* 1947, *m.*

1999   ⟨*Sharman,* Colin Morven Sharman, OBE, *b.* 1943, *m.*

1994   ⟨*Shaw of Northstead,* Michael Norman Shaw, *b.* 1920, *m.*

2011   *Wood of Anfield,* Stewart Martin Wood, *b.* 1968, *m.*

1999   *Woolmer of Leeds,* Kenneth John Woolmer, *b.* 1940, *m.*

2013   *Wrigglesworth,* Ian William Wrigglesworth, *b.* 1939, *m.*

1994   *Wright of Richmond,* Patrick Richard Henry Wright, GCMG, *b.* 1931, *m.*

2015   *Young of Cookham,* George Samuel Knatchbull Young, CH, PC, *b.* 1941, *m.*

1984   *Young of Graffham,* David Ivor Young, CH, PC, *b.* 1932, *m.*

2004   *Young of Norwood Green,* Anthony (Ian) Young, *b.* 1942, *m.*

BARONESSES

Created

2005   *Adams of Craigielea,* Katherine Patricia Irene Adams, *b.* 1947, *w.*

2007   *Afshar,* Prof. Haleh Afshar, OBE, *b.* 1944, *m.*

2015   *Altmann,* Dr Rosalind Miriam Altmann, CBE, *b.* 1956, *m.*

1997   *Amos,* Valerie Ann Amos, CH, PC, *b.* 1954

2000   *Andrews,* Elizabeth Kay Andrews, OBE, *b.* 1943, *m.*

1996   *Anelay of St Johns,* Joyce Anne Anelay, DBE, PC, *b.* 1947, *m.*

2010   *Armstrong of Hill Top,* Hilary Jane Armstrong, PC, *b.* 1945, *m.*

1999   *Ashton of Upholland,* Catherine Margaret Ashton, GCMG, PC, *b.* 1956, *m.*

2011   *Bakewell,* Joan Dawson Bakewell, DBE, *b.* 1933, *w.*

2013   *Bakewell of Hardington Mandeville,* Catherine Mary Bakewell, MBE, *b.* 1949

1999   *Barker,* Elizabeth Jean Barker, *b.* 1961

2010   *Benjamin,* Floella Karen Yunies Benjamin, OBE, *b.* 1949, *m.*

2011   *Berridge,* Elizabeth Rose Berridge, *b.* 1972

2016   *Bertin,* Gabrielle Louise Bertin, *b.* 1978, *m.*

2000   *Billingham,* Angela Theodora Billingham, DPHIL, *b.* 1939, *w.*

1987   *Blackstone,* Tessa Ann Vosper Blackstone, PC, PHD, *b.* 1942

1999   *Blood,* May Blood, MBE, *b.* 1938

2016   *Bloomfield of Hinton Waldrist,* Olivia Caroline Bloomfield, *b.* 1960, *m.*

2004   *Bonham-Carter of Yarnbury,* Jane Bonham Carter, *b.* 1957, *w.*

2000   *Boothroyd,* Betty Boothroyd, OM, PC, *b.* 1929

2005   *Bottomley of Nettlestone,* Virginia Hilda Brunette Maxwell Bottomley, PC, *b.* 1948, *m.*

2015   *Bowles of Berkhamsted,* Sharon Margaret Bowles, *b.* 1953, *m.*

2014   *Brady,* Karren Rita Brady, CBE, *b.* 1969, *m.*

2011   *Brinton,* Sarah Virginia Brinton, *b.* 1955, *m.*

2015   *Brown of Cambridge,* Prof. Julia Elizabeth King, DBE, PHD, FRENG, *b.* 1954, *m.*

2010   *Browning,* Angela Frances Browning, *b.* 1946, *m.*

2015   *Burt of Solihull,* Lorely Jane Burt, *b.* 1954, *m.*

1998   *Buscombe,* Peta Jane Buscombe, *b.* 1954, *m.*

2006   *Butler-Sloss,* (Ann) Elizabeth (Oldfield) Butler-Sloss, GBE, PC, *b.* 1933, *m.*

1996   *Byford,* Hazel Byford, DBE, *b.* 1941, *w.*

2008   *Campbell of Loughborough,* Susan Catherine Campbell, CBE, *b.* 1948

2007   *Campbell of Surbiton,* Jane Susan Campbell, DBE, *b.* 1959, *m.*

2016   *Cavendish of Little Venice,* Hilary Camilla Cavendish, *b.* 1968, *m.*

2016   *Chakrabarti,* Sharmishta Chakrabarti, CBE, *b.* 1969

1992   *Chalker of Wallasey,* Lynda Chalker, PC, *b.* 1942

2014   *Chisholm of Owlpen,* Caroline Elizabeth (Carlyn) Chisholm, *b.* 1951, *m.*

2005   §*Clark of Calton,* Dr Lynda Margaret Clark, PC, *b.* 1949

2000   *Cohen of Pimlico,* Janet Cohen, *b.* 1940, *m.*

2005   *Corston,* Jean Ann Corston, PC, *b.* 1942, *w.*

2007   *Coussins,* Jean Coussins, *b.* 1950

2016   *Couttie,* Philippa Marion Roe, *b.* 1962, *m.*

1982   *Cox,* Caroline Anne Cox, *b.* 1937, *m.*

1998   *Crawley,* Christine Mary Crawley, *b.* 1950, *m.*

1990   *Cumberlege,* Julia Frances Cumberlege, CBE, *b.* 1943, *m.*

1993   *Dean of Thornton-le-Fylde,* Brenda Dean, PC, *b.* 1943, *m.*

2005   *Deech,* Ruth Lynn Deech, DBE, *b.* 1943, *m.*

2010   *Donaghy,* Rita Margaret Donaghy, CBE, *b.* 1944, *m.*

2010   *Doocey,* Elizabeth Deirdre Doocey, OBE, *b.* 1948, *m.*

2010   *Drake,* Jean Lesley Patricia Drake, CBE, *b.* 1948

2004   *D'Souza,* Dr Frances Gertrude Claire D'Souza, CMG, PC, *b.* 1944, *m.*

1990   ℂ*Dunn,* Lydia Selina Dunn, DBE, *b.* 1940, *m.*

2010   *Eaton,* Ellen Margaret Eaton, DBE, *b.* 1942, *m.*

1990   *Eccles of Moulton,* Diana Catherine Eccles, *b.* 1933, *m.*

1997   *Emerton,* Audrey Caroline Emerton, DBE, *b.* 1935

2014   *Evans of Bowes Park,* Natalie Jessica Evans, PC, *b.* 1975, *m.*

1974   *Falkender,* Marcia Matilda Falkender, CBE, *b.* 1932

2004   *Falkner of Margravine,* Kishwer Falkner, *b.* 1955, *m.*

2015   *Fall,* Catherine Susan Fall, *b.* 1967

1994   *Farrington of Ribbleton,* Josephine Farrington, *b.* 1940, *m.*

2015   *Featherstone,* Lynne Choona Featherstone, PC, *b.* 1951

2001   *Finlay of Llandaff,* Ilora Gillian Finlay, *b.* 1949, *m.*

2015   *Finn,* Simone Jari Finn, *b.* 1968

1990   *Flather,* Shreela Flather, *b.* 1934, *m.*

1997   *Fookes,* Janet Evelyn Fookes, DBE, *b.* 1936

2006   *Ford,* Margaret Anne Ford, *b.* 1957, *m.*

2005   *Fritchie,* Irene Tordoff Fritchie, DBE, *b.* 1942, *m.*

1999   *Gale,* Anita Gale, *b.* 1940

2007   *Garden of Frognal,* Susan Elizabeth Garden, PC, *b.* 1944, *w.*

1981   *Gardner of Parkes,* (Rachel) Trixie (Anne) Gardner, *b.* 1927, *w.*

2000   *Gibson of Market Rasen,* Anne Gibson, OBE, *b.* 1940, *m.*

2013   *Goldie,* Annabel MacNicholl Goldie, *b.* 1950

2001   *Golding,* Llinos Golding, *b.* 1933, *w.*

1998   *Goudie,* Mary Teresa Goudie, *b.* 1946, *m.*

1993   *Gould of Potternewton,* Joyce Brenda Gould, *b.* 1932, *m.*

2001   *Greenfield,* Susan Adele Greenfield, CBE, *b.* 1950, *m.*

2000   *Greengross,* Sally Ralea Greengross, OBE, *b.* 1935, *m.*

2013   *Grender,* Rosalind Mary Grender, MBE, *b.* 1962

2010   *Grey-Thompson,* Tanni Carys Davina Grey-Thompson, DBE, *b.* 1969, *m.*

1991   *Hamwee,* Sally Rachel Hamwee, *b.* 1947

1999   *Hanham,* Joan Brownlow Hanham, CBE, *b.* 1939, *m.*

2014   *Harding of Winscombe,* Diana Mary (Dido) Harding, *b.* 1967, *m.*

1999   *Harris of Richmond,* Angela Felicity Harris, *b.* 1944

1996   *Hayman,* Helene Valerie Hayman, GBE, PC, *b.* 1949, *m.*

2010   *Hayter of Kentish Town,* Dr Dianne Hayter, *b.* 1949, *m.*

2010   *Healy of Primrose Hill,* Anna Healy, *b.* 1955, *m.*

2014   *Helic,* Arminka Helic, *b.* 1968

2004   *Henig,* Ruth Beatrice Henig, CBE, *b.* 1943, *m.*

1991   *Hilton of Eggardon,* Jennifer Hilton, QPM, *b.* 1936

2013   *Hodgson of Abinger,* Fiona Ferelith Hodgson, CBE, *b.* 1954, *m.*

1995   *Hogg,* Sarah Elizabeth Mary Hogg, *b.* 1946, *m.*

2010   *Hollins,* Prof. Sheila Clare Hollins, *b.* 1946, *m.*

1990   *Hollis of Heigham,* Patricia Lesley Hollis, PC, DPHIL, *b.* 1941, *m.*

1985	*Hooper,* Gloria Dorothy Hooper, CMG, *b.* 1939
2001	*Howarth of Breckland,* Valerie Georgina Howarth, OBE, *b.* 1940
2001	*Howe of Idlicote,* Elspeth Rosamond Morton Howe, CBE, *b.* 1932, *w.*
1999	*Howells of St Davids,* Rosalind Patricia-Anne Howells, OBE, *b.* 1931, *m.*
2010	*Hughes of Stretford,* Beverley Hughes, PC, *b.* 1950, *m.*
2013	*Humphreys,* Christine Mary Humphreys, *b.* 1947
2010	*Hussein-Ece,* Meral Hussein Ece, OBE, *b.* 1953
2014	*Janke,* Barbara Lilian Janke, *b.* 1947, *m.*
1992	*Jay of Paddington,* Margaret Ann Jay, PC, *b.* 1939, *m.*
2011	*Jenkin of Kennington,* Anne Caroline Jenkin, *b.* 1955, *m.*
2010	*Jolly,* Judith Anne Jolly, *b.* 1951, *m.*
2013	*Jones of Moulsecoomb,* Jennifer Helen Jones, *b.* 1949
2006	*Jones of Whitchurch,* Margaret Beryl Jones, *b.* 1955
2015	*Jowell,* Tessa Jane Helen Douglas Jowell, DBE, PC, *b.* 1947, *m.*
2013	*Kennedy of Cradley,* Alicia Pamela Kennedy, *b.* 1969, *m.*
1997	*Kennedy of the Shaws,* Helena Ann Kennedy, QC, *b.* 1950, *m.*
2012	*Kidron,* Beeban Tania Kidron, OBE, *b.* 1961, *m.*
2011	*King of Bow,* Oona Tamsyn King, *b.* 1967, *m.*
2006	*Kingsmill,* Denise Patricia Byrne Kingsmill, CBE, *b.* 1947, *m.*
2009	*Kinnock of Holyhead,* Glenys Elizabeth Kinnock, *b.* 1944, *m.*
1997	☾*Knight of Collingtree,* (Joan Christabel) Jill Knight, DBE, *b.* 1927, *w.*
2010	*Kramer,* Susan Veronica Kramer, PC, *b.* 1950, *w.*
2013	*Lane-Fox of Soho,* Martha Lane Fox, CBE, *b.* 1973
2013	*Lawrence of Clarendon,* Doreen Delceita Lawrence, OBE, *b.* 1952
2010	*Liddell of Coatdyke,* Helen Lawrie Liddell, PC, *b.* 1950, *m.*
1997	☾*Linklater of Butterstone,* Veronica Linklater, *b.* 1943, *m.*
2011	*Lister of Burtersett,* Margot Ruth Aline Lister, CBE, *b.* 1949, *m.*
1978	☾*Lockwood,* Betty Lockwood, *b.* 1924, *w.*
1997	*Ludford,* Sarah Ann Ludford, *b.* 1951
2004	*McDonagh,* Margaret Josephine McDonagh, *b.* 1961
2015	*McGregor-Smith,* Ruby McGregor-Smith, CBE, *b.* 1963
1999	*McIntosh of Hudnall,* Genista Mary McIntosh, *b.* 1946
2015	*McIntosh of Pickering,* Anne Caroline Ballingall McIntosh, *b.* 1954, *m.*
1997	*Maddock,* Diana Margaret Maddock, *b.* 1945, *m.*
1991	*Mallalieu,* Ann Mallalieu, QC, *b.* 1945
2008	*Manningham-Buller,* Elizabeth (Lydia) Manningham-Buller, LG, DCB, *b.* 1948, *m.*
2013	*Manzoor,* Zahida Parveen Manzoor, CBE, *b.* 1958, *m.*
1970	*Masham of Ilton,* Susan Lilian Primrose Cunliffe-Lister, *b.* 1935, *w.*
1999	*Massey of Darwen,* Doreen Elizabeth Massey, *b.* 1938, *m.*
2006	*Meacher,* Molly Christine Meacher, *b.* 1940, *m.*
1998	*Miller of Chilthorne Domer,* Susan Elizabeth Miller, *b.* 1954
2014	*Mobarik,* Nosheena Shaheen Mobarik, CBE, *b.* 1957, *m.*
2015	*Mone,* Michelle Georgina Mone, OBE, *b.* 1971
2004	*Morgan of Drefelin,* Delyth Jane Morgan, *b.* 1961, *m.*
2011	*Morgan of Ely,* Mair Eluned Morgan, *b.* 1967, *m.*
2001	*Morgan of Huyton,* Sally Morgan, *b.* 1959, *m.*
2004	*Morris of Bolton,* Patricia Morris, OBE, *b.* 1953
2005	*Morris of Yardley,* Estelle Morris, PC, *b.* 1952
2004	*Murphy,* Elaine Murphy, *b.* 1947, *m.*
2004	*Neuberger,* Rabbi Julia (Babette Sarah) Neuberger, DBE, *b.* 1950, *m.*
2007	*Neville-Jones,* (Lilian) Pauline Neville-Jones, DCMG, PC, *b.* 1939
2013	*Neville-Rolfe,* Lucy Jeanne Neville-Rolfe, DBE, CMG, *b.* 1953, *m.*
2010	*Newlove,* Helen Margaret Newlove, *b.* 1961, *w.*
1997	*Nicholson of Winterbourne,* Emma Harriet Nicholson, *b.* 1941, *m.*
1982	*Nicol,* Olive Mary Wendy Nicol, *b.* 1923, *m.*
2000	*Noakes,* Sheila Valerie Masters, DBE, *b.* 1949, *m.*
2000	*Northover,* Lindsay Patricia Granshaw, PC, *b.* 1954
2010	*Nye,* Susan Nye, *b.* 1955, *m.*
1991	*O'Cathain,* Detta O'Cathain, OBE, *b.* 1938, *w.*
2009	*O'Loan,* Nuala Patricia O'Loan, DBE, *b.* 1951, *m.*
1999	*O'Neill of Bengarve,* Onora Sylvia O'Neill, CH, CBE, FRS, FBA, *b.* 1941
1989	*Oppenheim-Barnes,* Sally Oppenheim-Barnes, PC, *b.* 1930, *m.*
2006	*Paisley of St George's,* Eileen Emily Paisley, *b.* 1931, *w.*
2010	*Parminter,* Kathryn Jane Parminter, *b.* 1964, *m.*
1991	☾*Perry of Southwark,* Pauline Perry, *b.* 1931, *m.*
2015	*Pidding,* Emma Samantha Pidding, CBE, *b.* 1966
2014	*Pinnock,* Kathryn Mary Pinnock, *b.* 1946, *m.*
1997	*Pitkeathley,* Jill Elizabeth Pitkeathley, OBE, *b.* 1940
1999	*Prashar,* Usha Kumari Prashar, CBE, PC, *b.* 1948, *m.*
2015	*Primarolo,* Dawn Primarolo, DBE, PC, *b.* 1954, *m.*
2004	*Prosser,* Margaret Theresa Prosser, OBE, *b.* 1937
2006	*Quin,* Joyce Gwendoline Quin, PC, *b.* 1944
1996	*Ramsay of Cartvale,* Margaret Mildred (Meta) Ramsay, *b.* 1936
2011	*Randerson,* Jennifer Elizabeth Randerson, *b.* 1948, *m.*
1994	*Rawlings,* Patricia Elizabeth Rawlings, *b.* 1939
2014	*Rebuck,* Gail Ruth Rebuck, DBE, *b.* 1952, *w.*
2015	*Redfern,* Elizabeth Marie Redfern, *b.* 1947
1998	*Richardson of Calow,* Kathleen Margaret Richardson, OBE, *b.* 1938, *m.*
2015	*Rock,* Kate Harriet Alexandra Rock, *b.* 1968, *m.*
2004	*Royall of Blaisdon,* Janet Anne Royall, PC, *b.* 1955, *m.*
1997	*Scotland of Asthal,* Patricia Janet Scotland, PC, QC, *b.* 1955, *m.*
2015	*Scott of Bybrook,* Jane Antoinette Scott, OBE, *b.* 1947, *m.*
2000	*Scott of Needham Market,* Rosalind Carol Scott, *b.* 1957
1991	*Seccombe,* Joan Anna Dalziel Seccombe, DBE, *b.* 1930, *w.*
2010	*Shackleton of Belgravia,* Fiona Sara Shackleton, LVO, *b.* 1956, *m.*
1998	☾*Sharp of Guildford,* Margaret Lucy Sharp, *b.* 1938, *m.*
1973	*Sharples,* Pamela Sharples, *b.* 1923, *w.*
2015	*Sheehan,* Shaista Ahmad Sheehan, *b.* 1959, *m.*
2005	*Shephard of Northwold,* Gillian Patricia Shephard, PC, *b.* 1940, *m.*
2010	*Sherlock,* Maeve Christina Mary Sherlock, OBE, *b.* 1960
2014	*Shields,* Joanna Shields, OBE, *b.* 1962, *m.*
2010	*Smith of Basildon,* Angela Evans Smith, PC, *b.* 1959, *m.*
1995	*Smith of Gilmorehill,* Elizabeth Margaret Smith, *b.* 1940, *w.*
2014	*Smith of Newnham,* Dr Julie Elizabeth Smith, *b.* 1969
2010	*Stedman-Scott,* Deborah Stedman-Scott, OBE, *b.* 1955
1999	*Stern,* Vivien Helen Stern, CBE, *b.* 1941
2011	*Stowell of Beeston,* Tina Wendy Stowell, MBE, PC, *b.* 1967
2015	*Stroud,* Philippa Claire Stroud, *b.* 1965, *m.*
2016	*Sugg,* Elizabeth Grace Sugg, CBE, *b.* 1977
2013	*Suttie,* Alison Mary Suttie, *b.* 1968
1996	*Symons of Vernham Dean,* Elizabeth Conway Symons, PC, *b.* 1951, *m.*

2005   *Taylor of Bolton*, Winifred Ann Taylor, PC, *b.* 1947, *m.*

1994   **E.***Thomas of Walliswood*, Susan Petronella Thomas, OBE, *b.* 1935, *m.*

2006   *Thomas of Winchester*, Celia Marjorie Thomas, MBE, *b.* 1945

2015   *Thornhill*, Dorothy Thornhill, MBE, *b.* 1955, *m.*

1998   *Thornton*, (Dorothea) Glenys Thornton, *b.* 1952, *m.*

2005   *Tonge*, Dr Jennifer Louise Tonge, *b.* 1941, *m.*

1980   *Trumpington*, Jean Alys Barker, DCVO, PC, *b.* 1922, *w.*

1985   **E.***Turner of Camden*, Muriel Winifred Turner, *b.* 1927, *m.*

2011   *Tyler of Enfield*, Claire Tyler, *b.* 1957

1998   *Uddin*, Manzila Pola Uddin, *b.* 1959, *m.*

2007   *Vadera*, Shriti Vadera, PC, *b.* 1962

2005   *Valentine*, Josephine Clare Valentine, *b.* 1958, *m.*

2016   *Vere of Norbiton*, Charlotte Sarah Emily Vere, *b.* 1969

2006   *Verma*, Sandip Verma, *b.* 1959, *m.*

2000   *Walmsley*, Joan Margaret Walmsley, *b.* 1943

1985   ❮*Warnock*, Helen Mary Warnock, DBE, CH, *b.* 1924, *w.*

2007   *Warsi*, Sayeeda Hussain Warsi, PC, *b.* 1971

1999   *Warwick of Undercliffe*, Diana Mary Warwick, *b.* 1945, *m.*

2015   *Watkins of Tavistock*, Mary Jane Watkins, PHD, *b.* 1955

2010   *Wheatcroft*, Patience Jane Wheatcroft, *b.* 1951, *m.*

2010   *Wheeler*, Margaret Eileen Joyce Wheeler, MBE, *b.* 1949

1999   *Whitaker*, Janet Alison Whitaker, *b.* 1936

1996   *Wilcox*, Judith Ann Wilcox, *b.* 1940, *w.*

1999   ❮*Wilkins*, Rosalie Catherine Wilkins, *b.* 1946

1993   ❮*Williams of Crosby*, Shirley Vivien Teresa Brittain Williams, CH, PC, *b.* 1930, *w.*

2013   *Williams of Trafford*, Susan Frances Maria Williams, *b.* 1967, *m.*

2014   *Wolf of Dulwich*, Alison Margaret Wolf, CBE, *b.* 1949, *m.*

2011   *Worthington*, Bryony Katherine Worthington, *b.* 1971, *m.*

2017   *Wyld*, Laura Lee Wyld, *b.* 1978

2004   *Young of Hornsey*, Prof. Margaret Omolola Young, OBE, *b.* 1951, *m.*

1997   *Young of Old Scone*, Barbara Scott Young, *b.* 1948

COURTESY TITLES

The heir apparent to a Duke, Marquess or Earl uses the highest of his father's other titles as a courtesy title. For example, the Marquess of Blandford is heir to the Dukedom of Marlborough, and Viscount Amberley to the Earldom of Russell. Titles of second heirs (when in use) are also given, and the courtesy title of the father of a second heir is indicated by * eg Earl of Mornington, eldest son of *Marquess of Douro.

The holder of a courtesy title is not styled 'the Most Hon.' or 'the Rt. Hon.', and in correspondence 'the' is omitted before the title. The heir apparent to a Scottish title may use the title 'Master'.

MARQUESSES

Blandford – *Marlborough, D.*
Bowmont and Cessford – *Roxburghe, D.*
Douglas and Clydesdale – *Hamilton and Brandon, D.*
*Douro – *Wellington, D.*
Graham – *Montrose, D.*
Granby – *Rutland, D.*
*Hamilton – *Abercorn, D.*
Lorne – *Argyll, D.*
Stafford – *Sutherland, D.*
Tavistock – *Bedford, D.*
Tullibardine – *Atholl, D.*
Worcester – *Beaufort, D.*

EARLS

*Aboyne – *Huntly, M.*
Altamont – *Sligo, M.*
Arundel and Surrey – *Norfolk, D.*
Bective – *Headfort, M.*
Belfast – *Donegall, M.*
Brecknock – *Camden, M.*
*Burford – *St Albans, D.*
*Burlington – *Devonshire, D.*
*Cardigan – *Ailesbury, M.*
Cassilis – *Ailsa, M.*
Compton – *Northampton, M.*
Dalkeith – *Buccleuch and Queensberry, D.*
Dumfries – *Bute, M.*
Euston – *Grafton, D.*
*Haddo – *Aberdeen and Temair, M.*
Hillsborough – *Downshire, M.*
*Hopetoun – *Linlithgow, M.*

Kerry – *Lansdowne, M.*
March and Kinrara – *Richmond, Gordon and Lennox, D.*
Medina – *Milford Haven, M.*
Mornington – *Douro, M.*
Mount Charles – *Conyngham, M.*
Mulgrave – *Normanby, M.*
Percy – *Northumberland, D.*
Rocksavage – *Cholmondeley, M.*
Ronaldshay – *Zetland, M.*
*St Andrews – *Kent, D.*
Southesk – *Fife, D.*
*Tyrone – *Waterford, M.*
*Ulster – *Gloucester, D.*
Uxbridge – *Anglesey, M.*
*Wiltshire – *Winchester, M.*
Yarmouth – *Hertford, M.*

VISCOUNTS

Aithrie – *Hopetoun, E.*
Alexander – *Caledon, E.*
Althorp – *Spencer, E.*
Andover – *Suffolk and Berkshire, E.*
Anson – *Lichfield, E.*
Asquith – *Oxford and Asquith, E.*
Borodale – *Beatty, E.*
Bury – *Albemarle, E.*
Campden – *Gainsborough, E.*
Carlow – *Portarlington, E.*
Carlton – *Wharncliffe, E.*
Chelsea – *Cadogan, E.*
Chewton – *Waldegrave, E.*
Clanfield – *Peel, E.*

Clive – *Powis, E.*
Coke – *Leicester, E.*
Corry – *Belmore, E.*
Corvedale – *Baldwin of Bewdley, E.*
Cranborne – *Salisbury, M.*
Curzon – *Howe, E.*
Dalrymple – *Stair, E.*
Dangan – *Cowley, E.*
Drumlanrig – *Queensberry, M.*
Duncannon – *Bessborough, E.*
Dungarvan – *Cork and Orrery, E.*
Dunluce – *Antrim, E.*
Dunwich – *Stradbroke, E.*
Dupplin – *Kinnoull, E.*
Elveden – *Iveagh, E.*
Emlyn – *Cawdor, E.*
Encombe – *Eldon, E.*
Enfield – *Strafford, E.*
Erleigh – *Reading, M.*
Errington – *Cromer, E.*
Feilding – *Denbigh and Desmond, E.*
FitzHarris – *Malmesbury, E.*
Folkestone – *Radnor, E.*
Forbes – *Granard, E.*
Garmoyle – *Cairns, E.*
Garnock – *Lindsay, E.*
Glenapp – *Inchcape, E.*
Glentworth – *Limerick, E.*
Glerawly – *Annesley, E.*
Grey de Wilton – *Wilton, E.*
Grimston – *Verulam, E.*
Gwynedd – *Lloyd George of Dwyfor, E.*
Hawkesbury – *Liverpool, E.*

Hinchingbrooke – *Sandwich, E.*
Howick – *Grey, E.*
Ikerrin – *Carrick, E.*
Ingestre – *Shrewsbury and Waterford, E.*
Jocelyn – *Roden, E.*
Kelburn – *Glasgow, E.*
Kingsborough – *Kingston, E.*
Kirkwall – *Orkney, E.*
Knebworth – *Lytton, E.*
Lambton – *Durham, E.*
Lascelles – *Harewood, E.*
Linley – *Snowdon, E.*
Lymington – *Portsmouth, E.*
Macmillan of Ovenden – *Stockton, E.*
Maidstone – *Winchilsea and Nottingham, E.*
Maitland – *Lauderdale, E.*
Marsham – *Romney, E.*
Melgund – *Minto, E.*
Merton – *Nelson, E.*
Moore – *Drogheda, E.*
Newport – *Bradford, E.*
Newry and Mourne – *Kilmorey, E.*
Northland – *Ranfurly, E.*
Petersham – *Harrington, E.*
Pollington – *Mexborough, E.*
Raynham – *Townshend, M.*
Reidhaven – *Seafield, E.*
Royston – *Hardwicke, E.*
Ruthven of Canberra – *Gowrie, E.*
St Cyres – *Iddesleigh, E.*
Sandon – *Harrowby, E.*
Savernake – *Cardigan, E.*

Severn – *Wessex*, E.
Slane – *Mount Charles*, E.
Somerton – *Normanton*, E.
Stopford – *Courtown*, E.
Stormont – *Mansfield and Mansfield*, E.
Strabane – *Hamilton*, M.
Strathallan – *Perth*, E.
Stuart – *Castle Stewart*, E.
Suirdale – *Donoughmore*, E.
Tamworth – *Ferrers*, E.
Tarbat – *Cromartie*, E.
Villiers – *Jersey*, E.
Weymouth – *Bath*, M.
Windsor – *Plymouth*, E.
Wolmer – *Selborne*, E.
Woodstock – *Portland*, E.

BARONS (LORDS)
Aberdour – *Morton*, E.
Apsley – *Bathurst*, E.
Ardee – *Meath*, E.

Ashley – *Shaftesbury*, E.
Balniel – *Crawford and Balcarres*, E.
Berriedale – *Caithness*, E.
Brooke – *Warwick and Brooke*, E.
Bruce – *Elgin and Kincardine*, E.
Buckhurst – *De La Warr*, E.
Burghley – *Exeter*, M.
Cardross – *Buchan*, E.
Cavendish – *Burlington*, E.
Clifton – *Darnley*, E.
Cochrane – *Dundonald*, E.
Courtenay – *Devon*, E.
Culloden – * *Ulster*, E.
Dalmeny – *Rosebery*, E.
Doune – *Moray*, E.
Downpatrick – *St Andrews*, E.
Dunglass – *Home*, E.
Elcho – *Wemyss and March*, E.
Gillford – *Clanwilliam*, E.

Greenock – *Cathcart*, E.
Guernsey – *Aylesford*, E.
Hay – *Erroll*, E.
Herbert – *Pembroke and Montgomery*, E.
Howard of Effingham – *Effingham*, E.
Huntingtower – *Dysart*, E.
Hyde – *Clarendon*, E.
Inverurie – *Kintore*, E.
Irwin – *Halifax*, E.
Johnstone – *Annandale and Hartfell*, E.
Leveson – *Granville*, E.
Loughborough – *Rosslyn*, E.
Masham – *Swinton*, E.
Medway – *Cranbrook*, E.
Montgomerie – *Eglinton and Winton*, E.
Moreton – *Ducie*, E.
Naas – *Mayo*, E.

Norreys – *Lindsey and Abingdon*, E.
North – *Guilford*, E.
Ogilvy – *Airlie*, E.
Oxmantown – *Rosse*, E.
Porchester – *Carnarvon*, E.
Ramsay – *Dalhousie*, E.
Romsey – *Mountbatten of Burma*, E.
St John – *Wiltshire*, E.
Scrymgeour – *Dundee*, E.
Seymour – *Somerset*, D.
Stanley – *Derby*, E.
Stavordale – *Ilchester*, E.
Strathavon – *Aboyne*, E.
Strathnaver – *Sutherland*, C.
Vere of Hanworth – *Burford*, E.
Wodehouse – *Kimberley*, E.
Worsley – *Yarborough*, E.

PEERS' SURNAMES

The following symbols indicate the rank of the peer holding each title:

C. Countess
D. Duke
E. Earl
M. Marquess
V. Viscount
* Life Peer

Where no designation is given, the title is that of a hereditary Baron or Baroness.
Abney-Hastings – *Loudoun*, E.
Acheson – *Gosford*, E.
Adams – *A. of Craigielea*
Adderley – *Norton*
Addington – *Sidmouth*, V.
Agar – *Normanton*, E.
Ahmad – *A. of Wimbledon*
Aitken – *Beaverbrook*
Akers-Douglas – *Chilston*, V.
Alexander – *A. of Tunis*, E.
Alexander – *Caledon*, E.
Allan – *A. of Hallam*
Allen – *A. of Kensington*
Allsopp – *Hindlip*
Alton – *A. of Liverpool*
Anderson – *A. of Swansea*
Anderson – *Waverley*, V.
Anelay – *A. of St Johns*
Annesley – *Valentia*, V.
Anson – *Lichfield*, E.
Arbuthnot – *A. of Edrom*
Archer – *A. of Weston-super-Mare*
Armstrong – *A. of Hill Top*
Armstrong – *A. of Ilminster*
Armstrong-Jones – *Snowdon*, E.
Arthur – *Glenarthur*
Arundell – *Talbot of Malahide*
Ashdown – *A. of Norton-sub-Hamdon*
Ashley-Cooper – *Shaftesbury*, E.

Ashton – *A. of Hyde*
Ashton – *A. of Upholland*
Asquith – *Oxford and Asquith*, E.
Assheton – *Clitheroe*
Astley – *Hastings*
Astor – *A. of Hever*
Aubrey-Fletcher – *Braye*
Bailey – *Glanusk*
Baillie – *Burton*
Baillie Hamilton – *Haddington*, E.
Baker – *B. of Dorking*
Bakewell – *B. of Hardington Mandeville*
Balchin – *Lingfield*
Baldwin – *B. of Bewdley*, E.
Balfour – *Kinross*
Balfour – *Riverdale*
Bampfylde – *Poltimore*
Banbury – *B. of Southam*
Barber – *B. of Tewkesbury*
Baring – *Ashburton*
Baring – *Cromer*, E.
Baring – *Howick of Glendale*
Baring – *Northbrook*
Baring – *Revelstoke*
Barker – *B. of Battle*
Barker – *Trumpington*
Barnes – *Gorell*
Barnewall – *Trimlestown*
Bassam – *B. of Brighton*
Bathurst – *Bledisloe*, V.
Beamish – *Dacre*
Beauclerk – *St Albans*, D.
Beaumont – *Allendale*, V.
Beckett – *Grimthorpe*
Benn – *Stansgate*, V.
Bennet – *Tankerville*, E.
Bentinck – *Portland*, E.
Beresford – *Decies*
Beresford – *Waterford*, M.
Berkeley – *B. of Knighton*
Berry – *Camrose*, V.
Berry – *Kemsley*, V.

Bertie – *Lindsey and Abingdon*, E.
Best – *Wynford*
Bethell – *Westbury*
Bewicke-Copley – *Cromwell*
Bigham – *Mersey*, V.
Bingham – *Clanmorris*
Bingham – *Lucan*, E.
Bishop – *Glendonbrook*
Black – *B. of Brentwood*
Black – *B. of Crossharbour*
Blackwood – *Dufferin and Clandeboye*
Blair – *B. of Boughton*
Bligh – *Darnley*, E.
Bloomfield – *B. of Hinton Waldrist*
Blyth – *B. of Rowington*
Bonham Carter – *B.-C. of Yarnbury*
Bootle-Wilbraham – *Skelmersdale*
Boscawen – *Falmouth*, V.
Boswell – *B. of Aynho*
Bottomley – *B. of Nettlestone*
Bourke – *Mayo*, E.
Bourne – *B. of Aberystwyth*
Bowes Lyon – *Strathmore and Kinghorne*, E.
Bowles – *B. of Berkhamsted*
Bowyer – *Denham*
Boyd – *B. of Duncansby*
Boyd – *Kilmarnock*
Boyle – *Cork and Orrery*, E.
Boyle – *Glasgow*, E.
Boyle – *Shannon*, E.
Brabazon – *Meath*, E.
Brand – *Hampden*, V.
Brassey – *B. of Apethorpe*
Brett – *Esher*, V.
Bridgeman – *Bradford*, E.
Brodrick – *Midleton*, V.
Brooke – *Alanbrooke*, V.
Brooke – *B. of Alverthorpe*
Brooke – *B. of Sutton Mandeville*

Brooke – *Brookeborough*, V.
Brooks – *Crawshaw*
Brougham – *Brougham and Vaux*
Broughton – *Fairhaven*
Brown – *B. of Eaton-under-Heywood*
Browne – *B. of Belmont*
Browne – *B. of Ladyton*
Browne – *B. of Madingley*
Browne – *Kilmaine*
Browne – *Oranmore and Browne*
Browne – *Sligo*, M.
Bruce – *Aberdare*
Bruce – *Balfour of Burleigh*
Bruce – *B. of Bennachie*
Bruce – *Elgin and Kincardine*, E.
Brudenell-Bruce – *Ailesbury*, M.
Buchan – *Tweedsmuir*
Buckley – *Wrenbury*
Burt – *B. of Solihull*
Butler – *B. of Brockwell*
Butler – *Carrick*, E.
Butler – *Dunboyne*
Butler – *Mountgarret*, V.
Byng – *Strafford*, E.
Byng – *Torrington*, V.
Cameron – *C. of Dillington*
Cameron – *C. of Lochbroom*
Campbell – *Argyll*, D.
Campbell – *C. of Loughborough*
Campbell – *C. of Pittenweem*
Campbell – *C. of Surbiton*
Campbell – *Cawdor*, E.
Campbell – *Colgrain*
Campbell – *Stratheden and Campbell*
Campbell-Gray – *Gray*
Canning – *Garvagh*
Capell – *Essex*, E.
Carey – *C. of Clifton*
Carington – *Carrington*

Herbert – *Pembroke and Montgomery, E.*
Herbert – *Powis, E.*
Hervey – *Bristol, M.*
Hewitt – *Lifford, V.*
Hicks Beach – *St Aldwyn, E.*
Hill – *Downshire, M.*
Hill – *H. of Oareford*
Hill-Trevor – *Trevor*
Hilton – *H. of Eggardon*
Hobart-Hampden – *Buckinghamshire, E.*
Hodgson – *H. of Abinger*
Hodgson – *H. of Astley Abbotts*
Hogg – *Hailsham, V.*
Holland-Hibbert – *Knutsford, V.*
Hollis – *H. of Heigham*
Holmes – *H. of Richmond*
Holmes à Court – *Heytesbury*
Hood – *Bridport, V.*
Hope – *Glendevon*
Hope – *H. of Craighead*
Hope – *H. of Thornes*
Hope – *Linlithgow, M.*
Hope – *Rankeillour*
Hope Johnstone – *Annandale and Hartfell, E.*
Hope-Morley – *Hollenden*
Hopkinson – *Colyton*
Hore Ruthven – *Gowrie, E.*
Hovell-Thurlow-Cumming-Bruce – *Thurlow*
Howard – *Carlisle, E.*
Howard – *Effingham, E.*
Howard – *H. of Lympne*
Howard – *H. of Penrith*
Howard – *H. of Rising*
Howard – *Strathcona and Mount Royal*
Howard – *Suffolk and Berkshire, E.*
Howarth – *H. of Breckland*
Howarth – *H. of Newport*
Howe – *H. of Idlicote*
Howell – *H. of Guildford*
Howells – *H. of St. Davids*
Howie – *H. of Troon*
Hubbard – *Addington*
Huggins – *Malvern, V.*
Hughes – *H. of Stretford*
Hughes – *H. of Woodside*
Hughes-Young – *St Helens*
Hunt – *H. of Chesterton*
Hunt – *H. of Kings Heath*
Hunt – *H. of Wirral*
Hurd – *H. of Westwell*
Hutchinson – *H. of Lullington*
Hutton – *H. of Furness*
Ingrams – *Darcy de Knayth*
Innes-Ker – *Roxburghe, D.*
Inskip – *Caldecote, V.*
Irby – *Boston*
Irvine – *I. of Lairg*
Isaacs – *Reading, M.*
James – *J. of Blackheath*
James – *Northbourne*
Jay – *J. of Ewelme*
Jay – *J. of Paddington*
Jenkin – *J. of Kennington*
Jervis – *St Vincent, V.*
Jocelyn – *Roden, E.*

Jolliffe – *Hylton*
Jones – *J. of Birmingham*
Jones – *J. of Cheltenham*
Jones – *J. of Moulsecoomb*
Jones – *J. of Whitchurch*
Joynson-Hicks – *Brentford, V.*
Kay-Shuttleworth – *Shuttleworth*
Kearley – *Devonport, V.*
Keith – *Kintore, E.*
Kemp – *Rochdale, V.*
Kennedy – *Ailsa, M.*
Kennedy – *K. of Cradley*
Kennedy – *K. of Southwark*
Kennedy – *K. of the Shaws*
Kenworthy – *Strabolgi*
Keppel – *Albemarle, E.*
Kerr – *Herries of Terregles*
Kerr – *K. of Kinlochard*
Kerr – *K. of Tonaghmore*
Kerr – *Lothian, M. / K. of Monteviot*
Kerr – *Teviot*
King – *Brown of Cambridge*
King – *K. of Bow*
King – *K. of Lothbury*
King – *Lovelace, E.*
King-Tenison – *Kingston, E.*
Kinnock – *K. of Holyhead*
Kirkham – *Berners*
Kirkhope – *K. of Harrogate*
Kirkwood – *K. of Kirkhope*
Knatchbull – *Brabourne*
Knatchbull – *Mountbatten of Burma, C.*
Knight – *K. of Collingtree*
Knight – *K. of Weymouth*
Knox – *Ranfurly, E.*
Lamb – *Rochester*
Lambart – *Cavan, E.*
Lambton – *Durham, E.*
Lamont – *L. of Lerwick*
Lampson – *Killearn*
Lane Fox – *L.-F. of Soho*
Lang – *L. of Monkton*
Lascelles – *Harewood, E.*
Law – *Coleraine*
Law – *Ellenborough*
Lawrence – *L. of Clarendon*
Lawrence – *Trevethin and Oaksey*
Lawson – *Burnham*
Lawson – *L. of Blaby*
Lawson Johnston – *Luke*
Lea – *L. of Crondall*
Lee – *L. of Trafford*
Legge – *Dartmouth, E.*
Legh – *Newton*
Leigh – *L. of Hurley*
Leith – *Burgh*
Lennox-Boyd – *Boyd of Merton, V.*
Le Poer Trench – *Clancarty, E.*
Leslie – *Rothes, E.*
Leslie Melville – *Leven and Melville, E.*
Lester – *L. of Herne Hill*
Levene – *L. of Portsoken*
Leveson-Gower – *Granville, E.*
Lewis – *Merthyr*
Liddell – *L. of Coatdyke*
Liddell – *Ravensworth*
Lindesay-Bethune – *Lindsay, E.*

Lindsay – *Crawford and Balcarres, E.*
Lindsay – *L. of Birker*
Linklater – *L. of Butterstone*
Lister – *L. of Burtersett*
Littleton – *Hatherton*
Livingston – *L. of Parkhead*
Llewellyn – *L. of Steep*
Lloyd – *L. of Berwick*
Lloyd George – *Lloyd George of Dwyfor, E.*
Lloyd George – *Tenby, V.*
Lloyd-Mostyn – *Mostyn*
Loder – *Wakehurst*
Lopes – *Roborough*
Lord – *Framlingham*
Low – *Aldington*
Low – *L. of Dalston*
Lowry-Corry – *Belmore, E.*
Lowther – *Lonsdale, E.*
Lowther – *Ullswater, V.*
Lubbock – *Avebury*
Lucas – *L. of Chilworth*
Lumley – *Scarbrough, E.*
Lumley-Savile – *Savile*
Lyon-Dalberg-Acton – *Acton*
Lysaght – *Lisle*
Lyttelton – *Chandos, V.*
Lyttelton – *Cobham, V.*
Lytton Cobbold – *Cobbold*
McClintock-Bunbury – *Rathdonnell*
McColl – *M. of Dulwich*
McConnell – *M. of Glenscorrodale*
Macdonald – *M. of River Glaven*
Macdonald – *M. of Tradeston*
McDonnell – *Antrim, E.*
McFall – *M. of Alcluith*
Macfarlane – *M. of Bearsden*
MacGregor – *M. of Pulham Market*
McInnes – *M. of Kilwinning*
McIntosh – *M. of Hudnall*
McIntosh – *M. of Pickering*
Mackay – *Inchcape, E.*
Mackay – *M. of Clashfern*
Mackay – *M. of Drumadoon*
Mackay – *Reay*
Mackay – *Tanlaw*
Mackenzie – *Cromartie, E.*
MacKenzie – *M. of Culkein*
Mackenzie – *M. of Framwellgate*
McKenzie – *M. of Luton*
Mackintosh – *M. of Halifax, V.*
McLaren – *Aberconway*
MacLaurin – *M. of Knebworth*
Maclean – *Blencathra*
Maclennan – *M. of Rogart*
Macmillan – *Stockton, E.*
Macpherson – *M. of Drumochter*
Macpherson – *M. of Earl's Court*
Macpherson – *Strathcarron*
Maffey – *Rugby*
Magan – *M. of Castletown*
Maginnis – *M. of Drumglass*
Maitland – *Lauderdale, E.*
Makgill – *Oxfuird, V.*

Makins – *Sherfield*
Manners – *Rutland, D.*
Manningham-Buller – *Dilhorne, V.*
Mansfield – *Sandhurst*
Marks – *M. of Broughton*
Marks – *M. of Henley-on-Thames*
Marquis – *Woolton, E.*
Marsham – *Romney, E.*
Martin – *M. of Springburn*
Martyn-Hemphill – *Hemphill*
Massey – *M. of Darwen*
Masters – *Noakes*
Maude – *Hawarden, V.*
Maude – *M. of Horsham*
Maxwell – *de Ros*
Maxwell – *Farnham*
May – *M. of Oxford*
Meade – *Clanwilliam, E.*
Mercer Nairne Petty-Fitzmaurice – *Lansdowne, M.*
Methuen-Campbell – *Methuen*
Millar – *Inchyra*
Miller – *M. of Chilthorne Domer*
Milner – *M. of Leeds*
Mitchell-Thomson – *Selsdon*
Mitford – *Redesdale*
Monckton – *M. of Brenchley, V.*
Monckton-Arundell – *Galway, V.*
Mond – *Melchett*
Money-Coutts – *Latymer*
Montagu – *Manchester, D.*
Montagu – *Sandwich, E.*
Montagu – *Swaythling*
Montagu Douglas Scott – *Buccleuch and Queensberry, D.*
Montagu Stuart Wortley – *Wharncliffe, E.*
Montague – *Amwell*
Montgomerie – *Eglinton and Winton, E.*
Montgomery – *M. of Alamein, V.*
Moore – *Drogheda, E.*
Moore – *M. of Lower Marsh*
Moore-Brabazon – *Brabazon of Tara*
Moreton – *Ducie, E.*
Morgan – *M. of Drefelin*
Morgan – *M. of Ely*
Morgan – *M. of Huyton*
Morris – *Killanin*
Morris – *M. of Aberavon*
Morris – *M. of Bolton*
Morris – *M. of Handsworth*
Morris – *M. of Kenwood*
Morris – *M. of Yardley*
Morris – *Naseby*
Morrison – *Dunrossil, V.*
Morrison – *Margadale*
Mosley – *Ravensdale*
Mountbatten – *Milford Haven, M.*
Muff – *Calverley*
Mulholland – *Dunleath*
Murphy – *M. of Torfaen*
Murray – *Atholl, D.*

Murray – *Dunmore, E.*
Murray – *Mansfield and Mansfield, E.*
Nall-Cain – *Brocket*
Napier – *Napier and Ettrick*
Napier – *N. of Magdala*
Needham – *Kilmorey, E.*
Nelson – *N. of Stafford*
Neuberger – *N. of Abbotsbury*★
Nevill – *Abergavenny, M.*
Neville – *Braybrooke*
Nicholls – *N. of Birkenhead*★
Nicolson – *Carnock*
Nicolson – *N. of Winterbourne*★
Nivison – *Glendyne*
Noel – *Gainsborough, E.*
North – *Guilford, E.*
Northcote – *Iddesleigh, E.*
Norton – *Grantley*
Norton – *N. of Louth*★
Norton – *Rathcreedan*
Nugent – *Westmeath, E.*
Oakeshott – *O. of Seagrove Bay*★
O'Brien – *Inchiquin*
Ogilvie-Grant – *Seafield, E.*
Ogilvy – *Airlie, E.*
O'Neill – *O'N. of Bengarve*★
O'Neill – *O'N. of Clackmannan*★
O'Neill – *O'N. of Gatley*★
O'Neill – *Rathcavan*
Orde-Powlett – *Bolton*
Ormsby-Gore – *Harlech*
Paget – *Anglesey, M.*
Paisley – *P. of St George's*★
Pakenham – *Longford, E.*
Pakington – *Hampton*
Palmer – *Lucas and Dingwall*
Palmer – *P. of Childs Hill*★
Palmer – *Selborne, E.*
Palumbo – *P. of Southwark*★
Parker – *Macclesfield, E.*
Parker – *Morley, E.*
Parnell – *Congleton*
Parsons – *Rosse, E.*
Patel – *P. of Blackburn*★
Patel – *P. of Bradford*★
Patten – *P. of Barnes*★
Paulet – *Winchester, M.*
Pearson – *Cowdray, V.*
Pearson – *P. of Rannoch*★
Pease – *Gainford*
Pease – *Wardington*
Pelham – *Chichester, E.*
Pelham – *Yarborough, E.*
Pellew – *Exmouth, V.*
Penny – *Marchwood, V.*
Pepys – *Cottenham, E.*
Percy – *Northumberland, D.*
Perry – *P. of Southwark*★
Pery – *Limerick, E.*
Philipps – *Milford*
Philipps – *St Davids, V.*
Phillips – *P. of Sudbury*★
Phillips – *P. of Worth Matravers*★
Phipps – *Normanby, M.*
Plant – *P. of Highfield*★
Pleydell-Bouverie – *Radnor, E.*
Plumptre – *Fitzwalter*
Plunkett – *Dunsany*

Plunkett – *Louth*
Pollock – *Hanworth, V.*
Pomeroy – *Harberton, V.*
Ponsonby – *Bessborough, E.*
Ponsonby – *de Mauley*
Ponsonby – *P. of Shulbrede*
Porter – *P. of Spalding*★
Powell – *P. of Bayswater*★
Powys – *Lilford*
Pratt – *Camden, M.*
Preston – *Gormanston, V.*
Primrose – *Rosebery, E.*
Prittie – *Dunalley*
Purvis – *P. of Tweed*★
Ramsay – *Dalhousie, E.*
Ramsay – *R. of Cartvale*★
Ramsbotham – *Soulbury, V.*
Rees – *R. of Ludlow*★
Rees-Williams – *Ogmore*
Reid – *R. of Cardowan*★
Renfrew – *R. of Kaimsthorn*★
Renton – *R. of Mount Harry*★
Renwick – *R. of Clifton*★
Rhys – *Dynevor*
Richards – *Milverton*
Richards – *R. of Herstmonceux*★
Richardson – *R. of Calow*★
Ritchie – *R. of Dundee*
Roberts – *Chwyd*
Roberts – *R. of Llandudno*★
Robertson – *R. of Oakridge*
Robertson – *R. of Port Ellen*★
Robertson – *Wharton*
Robinson – *Martonmere*
Roche – *Fermoy*
Rodd – *Rennell*
Rodgers – *R. of Quarry Bank*★
Roe – *Couttie*★
Rogers – *Lisvane*★
Rogers – *R. of Riverside*★
Roper-Curzon – *Teynham*
Rose – *R. of Monewden*★
Rospigliosi – *Newburgh, E.*
Rous – *Stradbroke, E.*
Rowley-Conwy – *Langford*
Royall – *R. of Blaisdon*★
Runciman – *R. of Doxford, V.*
Russell – *Ampthill*
Russell – *Bedford, D.*
Russell – *de Clifford*
Russell – *R. of Liverpool*
Ryder – *Harrowby, E.*
Ryder – *R. of Wensum*★
Sackville – *De La Warr, E.*
Sackville-West – *Sackville*
Sainsbury – *S. of Preston Candover*★
Sainsbury – *S. of Turville*★
St Aubyn – *St Levan*
St Clair – *Sinclair*
St Clair-Erskine – *Rosslyn, E.*
St John – *Bolingbroke and St John, V.*
St John – *St John of Bletso*
St Leger – *Doneraile, V.*
Samuel – *Bearsted, V.*
Sanderson – *S. of Ayot*
Sanderson – *S. of Bowden*★
Sandilands – *Torphichen*
Saumarez – *de Saumarez*
Savile – *Mexborough, E.*
Saville – *S. of Newdigate*★
Scarlett – *Abinger*

Schreiber – *Marlesford*★
Sclater-Booth – *Basing*
Scotland – *S. of Asthal*★
Scott – *Eldon, E.*
Scott – *S. of Bybrook*★
Scott – *S. of Foscote*★
Scott – *S. of Needham Market*★
Scrymgeour – *Dundee, E.*
Seager – *Leighton of St Mellons*
Seely – *Mottistone*
Seymour – *Hertford, M.*
Seymour – *Somerset, D.*
Shackleton – *S. of Belgravia*★
Sharp – *S. of Guildford*★
Shaw – *Craigmyle*
Shaw – *S. of Northstead*★
Shephard – *S. of Northwold*★
Sherbourne – *S. of Didsbury*★
Shirley – *Ferrers, E.*
Shutt – *S. of Greetland*★
Siddeley – *Kenilworth*
Sidney – *De L'Isle, V.*
Simon – *S. of Highbury*★
Simon – *S. of Wythenshawe*
Simpson – *S. of Dunkeld*★
Sinclair – *Caithness, E.*
Sinclair – *S. of Cleeve*
Sinclair – *Thurso, V.*
Singh – *S. of Wimbledon*★
Skeffington – *Massereene and Ferrard, V.*
Smith – *Bicester*
Smith – *Hambleden, V.*
Smith – *Kirkhill*
Smith – *S. of Basildon*★
Smith – *S. of Clifton*★
Smith – *S. of Finsbury*★
Smith – *S. of Gilmorehill*★
Smith – *S. of Hindhead*★
Smith – *S. of Kelvin*★
Smith – *S. of Leigh*★
Smith – *S. of Newnham*★
Somerset – *Beaufort, D.*
Somerset – *Raglan*
Spencer – *Churchill, V.*
Spencer-Churchill – *Marlborough, D.*
Spring – *Risby*★
Spring Rice – *Monteagle of Brandon*
Stanhope – *Harrington, E.*
Stanley – *Derby, E.*
Stanley – *S. of Alderley and Sheffield*
Stapleton-Cotton – *Combermere, V.*
Steel – *S. of Aikwood*★
Sterling – *S. of Plaistow*★
Stern – *S. of Brentford*★
Stevens – *S. of Kirkwhelpington*★
Stevens – *S. of Ludgate*★
Stevenson – *S. of Balmacara*★
Stevenson – *S. of Coddenham*★
Stewart – *Galloway, E.*
Stewart – *Stewartby*★
Stoddart – *S. of Swindon*★
Stone – *S. of Blackheath*★
Stoneham – *S. of Droxford*★
Stonor – *Camoys*
Stopford – *Courtown, E.*
Stourton – *Mowbray, Segrave and S.*

Stowell – *S. of Beeston*★
Strachey – *O'Hagan*
Strutt – *Belper*
Strutt – *Rayleigh*
Stuart – *Castle Stewart, E.*
Stuart – *Moray, E.*
Stuart – *S. of Findhorn, V.*
Suenson-Taylor – *Grantchester*
Sutherland – *S. of Houndwood*★
Symons – *S. of Vernham Dean*★
Taylor – *Kilclooney*★
Taylor – *T. of Bolton*★
Taylor – *T. of Goss Moor*★
Taylor – *T. of Holbeach*★
Taylor – *T. of Warwick*★
Taylour – *Headfort, M.*
Temple-Gore-Langton – *Temple of Stowe, E.*
Tennant – *Glenconner*
Thellusson – *Rendlesham*
Thesiger – *Chelmsford, V.*
Thomas – *T. of Cwmgiedd*★
Thomas – *T. of Gresford*★
Thomas – *T. of Macclesfield*★
Thomas – *T. of Walliswood*★
Thomas – *T. of Winchester*★
Thomson – *T. of Fleet*
Thynn – *Bath, M.*
Tottenham – *Ely, M.*
Trefusis – *Clinton*
Trench – *Ashtown*
Tufton – *Hothfield*
Turner – *Netherthorpe*
Turner – *T. of Camden*★
Turner – *T. of Ecchinswell*★
Turnour – *Winterton, E.*
Tyler – *T. of Enfield*★
Tyrell-Kenyon – *Kenyon*
Vallance – *V. of Tummel*★
Vanden-Bempde-Johnstone – *Derwent*
Vane – *Barnard*
Vane-Tempest-Stewart – *Londonderry, M.*
Vanneck – *Huntingfield*
Vaughan – *Lisburne, E.*
Vere – *V. of Norbiton*★
Vereker – *Gort, V.*
Verney – *Willoughby de Broke*
Vernon – *Lyveden*
Vesey – *de Vesci, V.*
Villiers – *Clarendon, E.*
Vincent – *V. of Coleshill*★
Vivian – *Swansea*
Wade – *W. of Chorlton*★
Waldegrave – *W. of North Hill*★
Walker – *W. of Aldringham*★
Walker – *W. of Gestingthorpe*★
Wallace – *Dudley*
Wallace – *W. of Saltaire*★
Wallace – *W. of Tankerness*★
Wallop – *Portsmouth, E.*
Ward – *Bangor, V.*
Ward – *Dudley, E.*
Warrender – *Bruntisfield*
Warwick – *W. of Undercliffe*★
Watkins – *W. of Tavistock*★
Watson – *Manton*
Watson – *W. of Invergowrie*★
Watson – *W. of Richmond*★
Webber – *Lloyd-Webber*★
Weir – *Inverforth*

Weld-Forester – *Forester*
Wellesley – *Cowley, E.*
Wellesley – *Wellington, D.*
West – *W. of Spithead★*
Westenra – *Rossmore*
White – *Annaly*
White – *Hanningfield★*
Whiteley – *Marchamley*
Whitfield – *Kenswood*
Williams – *W. of Crosby★*
Williams – *W. of Elvel★*
Williams – *W. of Oystermouth★*
Williams – *W. of Trafford★*

Williamson – *Forres*
Willis – *W. of Knaresborough★*
Willoughby – *Middleton*
Wills – *Dulverton*
Wilson – *Moran*
Wilson – *Nunburnholme*
Wilson – *W. of Dinton★*
Wilson – *W. of Tillyorn★*
Windsor – *Gloucester, D.*
Windsor – *Kent, D.*
Windsor-Clive – *Plymouth, E.*
Wingfield – *Powerscourt, V.*
Winn – *St Oswald*

Wodehouse – *Kimberley, E.*
Wolf – *W. of Dulwich★*
Wolfson – *W. of Aspley Guise★*
Wolfson – *W. of Sunningdale★*
Wood – *Halifax, E.*
Wood – *W. of Anfield★*
Woodhouse – *Terrington*
Woolmer – *W. of Leeds★*
Wright – *W. of Richmond★*
Wyndham – *Egremont and Leconfield*
Wynn – *Newborough*
Yarde-Buller – *Churston*

Yerburgh – *Alvingham*
Yorke – *Hardwicke, E.*
Young – *Kennet*
Young – *Y. of Cookham★*
Young – *Y. of Graffham★*
Young – *Y. of Hornsey★*
Young – *Y. of Norwood Green★*
Young – *Y. of Old Scone★*
Younger – *Y. of Leckie, V.*

LORDS SPIRITUAL

The Lords Spiritual are the Archbishops of Canterbury and York and 24 other diocesan bishops of the Church of England. The Bishops of London, Durham and Winchester always have seats in the House of Lords; the other 21 seats were previously filled by the remaining diocesan bishops in order of seniority. However, the Lords Spiritual (Women) Act 2015 provides for vacancies among the remaining 21 places to be filled by any female diocesan bishop in office at the time and, only if there is no female diocesan bishop without a seat, by the longest serving male diocesan bishop. The provision will remain in place for ten years from 2015, equivalent to two fixed-term parliaments. At the end of this period, the provision under the Act will end and the previous arrangements under which vacancies are filled according to length of service as a diocesan bishop will be restored.

The Bishop of Sodor and Man and the Bishop of Gibraltar in Europe are not eligible to sit in the House of Lords.

ARCHBISHOPS

Style, The Most Revd and Rt. Hon. the Lord Archbishop of_
Addressed as Archbishop *or* Your Grace

INTRODUCED TO HOUSE OF LORDS
2012   *Canterbury* (105th), Justin Portal Welby, PC, *b.* 1956, *m., cons.* 2011, *elected* 2011, *trans.* 2013
2006   *York* (97th), John Mugabi Tucker Sentamu, PC, PHD, *b.* 1949, *m., cons.* 1996, *elected* 2002, *trans.* 2005

BISHOPS

Style, The Rt. Revd the Lord Bishop of _
Addressed as Bishop *or* My Lord
elected date of confirmation as diocesan bishop

INTRODUCED TO HOUSE OF LORDS
as at November 2017
2014   *Durham* (74th), Paul Roger Butler, *b.* 1955, *m., cons.* 2004, *elected* 2009, *trans.* 2014
2012   *Winchester* (97th), Timothy John Dakin, *b.* 1958, *m., cons.* 2012, *elected* 2012
2001   *Chester* (40th), Peter Robert Forster, PHD, *b.* 1950, *m., cons.* 1996, *elected* 1996
2004   *Norwich* (71st), Graham Richard James, *b.* 1951, *m., cons.* 1993, *elected* 1999
2010   *Derby* (7th), Alastair Llewellyn John Redfern, PHD, *b.* 1948, *m., cons.* 1997, *elected* 2005
2010   *Birmingham* (9th), David Andrew Urquhart, *b.* 1952, *cons.* 2000, *elected* 2006
2012   *Worcester* (113th), John Geoffrey Inge, PHD, *b.* 1955, *m., cons.* 2003, *elected* 2007
2013   *Coventry* (9th), Christopher John Cocksworth, PHD, *b.* 1959, *m., cons.* 2008, *elected* 2008
2013   *Oxford* (44th), Stephen John Lindsey Croft, PHD, *b.* 1957, *m., cons.* 2009, *elected* 2009, *trans.* 2016

2013   *Carlisle* (66th), James William Scobie Newcome, *b.* 1953, *m., cons.* 2002, *elected* 2009
2013   *St Albans* (10th), Alan Gregory Clayton Smith, PHD, *b.* 1957, *cons.* 2001, *elected* 2009
2014   *Peterborough* (38th), Donald Spargo Allister, *b.* 1952, *m., cons.* 2010, *elected* 2010
2014   *Portsmouth* (9th), Christopher Richard James Foster, *b.* 1953, *m., cons.* 2001, *elected* 2010
2014   *Chelmsford* (10th), Stephen Geoffrey Cottrell, *b.* 1958, *m., cons.* 2004, *elected* 2010
2014   *Rochester* (107th), James Henry Langstaff, *b.* 1956, *m., cons.* 2004, *elected* 2010
2014   *Ely* (69th), Stephen David Conway, *b.* 1957, *cons.* 2006, *elected* 2010
2014   *Southwark* (10th), Christopher Thomas James Chessun, *b.* 1956, *cons.* 2005, *elected* 2011
2015   *Leeds* (1st), Nicholas Baines, *b.* 1957, *m., cons.* 2003, *elected* 2011, *trans.* 2014
2015   *Salisbury* (78th), Nicholas Roderick Holtam, *b.* 1954, *m., cons.* 2011, *elected* 2011
2015   *Gloucester* (41st), Rachel Treweek, *b.* 1963, *m., cons.* 2015, *elected* 2015
2016   *Newcastle* (12th), Christine Elizabeth Hardman, *b.* 1951, *m., cons.* 2015, *elected* 2015
2017   *Lincoln* (72nd), Christopher Lowson, *b.* 1953, *m., cons.* 2011, *elected* 2011
2017   *Chichester* (103rd), Martin Clive Warner, PHD, *b.* 1958, *cons.* 2010, *elected* 2012

BISHOPS AWAITING SEATS, in order of seniority
as at November 2017
Blackburn (9th), Julian Tudor Henderson, *b.* 1954, *m., cons.* 2013, *elected* 2013
Manchester (12th), David Stuart Walker, *b.* 1957, *m., cons.* 2000, *elected* 2013
Bath and Wells (79th), Peter Hancock, *b.* 1955, *m., cons.* 2010, *elected* 2014
Exeter (71st), Robert Ronald Atwell, *b.* 1954, *cons.* 2008, *elected* 2014
Liverpool (8th), Paul Bayes, *b.* 1953, *m., cons.* 2010, *elected* 2014
Hereford (105th), Richard Michael Cokayne Frith, *b.* 1949, *m., cons.* 1998, *elected* 2014
Guildford (10th), Andrew John Watson *b.* 1961, *m., cons.* 2008, *elected* 2014
St Edmundsbury and Ipswich (11th), Martin Alan Seeley *b.* 1954, *m., cons.* 2015, *elected* 2015
Southwell and Nottingham (12th), Paul Gavin Williams, *b.* 1968, *m., cons.* 2009, *elected* 2015
Leicester (7th), Martyn James Snow, *b.* 1968, *m., cons.* 2013, *elected* 2016
Lichfield (99th), Michael Geoffrey Ipgrave, OBE, PHD, *b.* 1958, *m., cons.* 2012, *elected* 2016
Sheffield (8th), Peter Wilcox, DPHIL, *b.* 1961, *m., cons.* 2017, *elected* 2017
London (133rd), vacant
Bristol (56th), vacant
Truro (16th), vacant

ORDERS OF CHIVALRY

THE MOST NOBLE ORDER OF THE GARTER (1348)

KG
Ribbon, Blue
Motto, Honi soit qui mal y pense (*Shame on him who thinks evil of it*)

The number of Knights and Ladies Companion is limited to 24

SOVEREIGN OF THE ORDER
The Queen

LADIES OF THE ORDER
HRH The Princess Royal, 1994
HRH Princess Alexandra, The Hon. Lady Ogilvy, 2003

ROYAL KNIGHTS
HRH The Prince Philip, Duke of Edinburgh, 1947
HRH The Prince of Wales, 1958
HRH The Duke of Kent, 1985
HRH The Duke of Gloucester, 1997
HRH The Duke of York, 2006
HRH The Earl of Wessex, 2006
HRH The Duke of Cambridge, 2008

EXTRA KNIGHTS COMPANION AND LADIES
Grand Duke Jean of Luxembourg, 1972
HM The Queen of Denmark, 1979
HM The King of Sweden, 1983
HM King Juan Carlos, 1988
HRH Princess Beatrix of the Netherlands, 1989
HIM The Emperor of Japan, 1998
HM The King of Norway, 2001
HM The King of Spain, 2017

KNIGHTS AND LADIES COMPANION
Lord Carrington, 1985
Lord Bramall, 1990
Lord Sainsbury of Preston Candover, 1992
Lord Ashburton, 1994
Sir Ninian Stephen, 1994
Sir Timothy Colman, 1996
Duke of Abercorn, 1999
Sir William Gladstone, 1999
Lord Inge, 2001
Sir Anthony Acland, 2001
Lord Butler of Brockwell, 2003
Lord Morris of Aberavon, 2003

Sir John Major, 2005
Lord Luce, 2008
Sir Thomas Dunne, 2008
Lord Phillips of Worth Matravers, 2011
Lord Boyce, 2011
Lord Stirrup, 2013
Baroness Manningham-Buller, 2014
Lord King of Lothbury, 2014
Lord Shuttleworth, 2016
Sir David Brewer, 2016

Prelate, Bishop of Winchester
Chancellor, Duke of Abercorn, KG
Register, Dean of Windsor
Garter King of Arms, Thomas Woodcock, CVO
Gentleman Usher of the Black Rod, Lt.-Gen. David Leakey, CMG, CBE
Secretary, Patric Dickinson, LVO

THE MOST ANCIENT AND MOST NOBLE ORDER OF THE THISTLE (REVIVED 1687)

KT
Ribbon, Green
Motto, Nemo me impune lacessit (*No one provokes me with impunity*)

The number of Knights and Ladies of the Thistle is limited to 16

SOVEREIGN OF THE ORDER
The Queen

ROYAL KNIGHTS
HRH The Prince Philip, Duke of Edinburgh, 1952
HRH The Prince of Wales, Duke of Rothesay, 1977
HRH The Duke of Cambridge, Earl of Strathearn, 2012

ROYAL LADY OF THE ORDER
HRH The Princess Royal, 2000

KNIGHTS AND LADIES
Earl of Elgin and Kincardine, 1981
Earl of Airlie, 1985
Earl of Crawford and Balcarres, 1996
Lord Macfarlane of Bearsden, 1996
Lord Mackay of Clashfern, 1997
Lord Wilson of Tillyorn, 2000
Lord Sutherland of Houndwood, 2002
Sir Eric Anderson, 2002
Lord Steel of Aikwood, 2004
Lord Robertson of Port Ellen, 2004

Lord Cullen of Whitekirk, 2007
Lord Hope of Craighead, 2009
Lord Patel, 2009
Earl of Home, 2013
Lord Smith of Kelvin, 2013

Chancellor, Earl of Airlie, KT, GCVO, PC
Dean, Very Revd Prof. Iain Torrance, TD
Secretary, Mrs C. Roads, LVO
Lord Lyon King of Arms, Dr Joseph Morrow, QC
Gentleman Usher of the Green Rod, Rear-Adm. Christopher Layman, CB, DSO, LVO

THE MOST HONOURABLE ORDER OF THE BATH (1725)

GCB   GCB *Civil*
Military

GCB Knight (or Dame) Grand Cross
KCB Knight Commander
DCB Dame Commander
CB   Companion

Ribbon, Crimson
Motto, Tria juncta in uno (*Three joined in one*)

Remodelled 1815, and enlarged many times since. The order is divided into civil and military divisions. Women became eligible for the order from 1 January 1971.

THE SOVEREIGN

GREAT MASTER AND FIRST OR PRINCIPAL KNIGHT GRAND CROSS
HRH The Prince of Wales, KG, KT, GCB, OM

Dean of the Order, Dean of Westminster
Bath King of Arms, Admiral of the Fleet, the Lord Boyce, KG, GCB, OBE
Registrar and Secretary, Rear-Adm. Iain Henderson, CB, CBE
Genealogist, Thomas Woodcock, CVO
Gentleman Usher of the Scarlet Rod, Maj.-Gen. Charles Vyvyan, CB, CBE
Deputy Secretary, Secretary of the Central Chancery of the Orders of Knighthood

Chancery, Central Chancery of the Orders of Knighthood, St James's Palace, London SW1A 1BH

THE ORDER OF MERIT (1902)

OM *Military*   OM *Civil*

OM
Ribbon, Blue and crimson

This order is designed as a special distinction for eminent men and women without conferring a knighthood upon them. The order is limited in numbers to 24, with the addition of foreign honorary members.

THE SOVEREIGN
HRH The Prince Philip, Duke of
  Edinburgh, 1968
Sir Michael Atiyah, 1992
Sir Aaron Klug, 1995
Lord Foster of Thames Bank, 1997
Prof. Sir Roger Penrose, 2000
Sir Tom Stoppard, 2000
HRH The Prince of Wales, 2002
Lord May of Oxford, 2002
Lord Rothschild, 2002
Sir David Attenborough, 2005
Baroness Boothroyd, 2005
Sir Michael Howard, 2005
Sir Timothy Berners-Lee 2007
Lord Eames, 2007
Lord Rees of Ludlow, 2007
Rt. Hon. Jean Chrétien, QC, 2009
Robert Neil MacGregor, 2010
Hon. John Howard, 2012
David Hockney, 2012
Sir Simon Rattle, 2013
Prof. Sir Magdi Yacoub, 2013
Lord Darzi of Denham, 2016
Prof. Dame Ann Dowling, 2016
Sir James Dyson, 2016

Secretary and Registrar, Lord Fellowes,
  GCB, GCVO, PC, QSO

Chancery, Central Chancery of the Orders
  of Knighthood, St James's Palace,
  London SW1A 1BH

THE MOST DISTINGUISHED ORDER OF ST MICHAEL AND ST GEORGE (1818)

GCMG   KCMG

GCMG   Knight (or Dame) Grand
       Cross
KCMG   Knight Commander
DCMG   Dame Commander
CMG   Companion

Ribbon, Saxon blue, with scarlet centre
Motto, Auspicium melioris aevi (*Token of
a better age*)

THE SOVEREIGN

GRAND MASTER
HRH The Duke of Kent, KG, GCMG,
  GCVO, ADC

Prelate, Rt. Revd David Urquhart
Chancellor, Lord Robertson of Port
  Ellen, KT, GCMG, PC
Secretary, Permanent Under-Secretary
  of State at the Foreign and
  Commonwealth Office and Head of
  the Diplomatic Service
Registrar, Sir David Manning, GCMG,
  KCVO
King of Arms, Sir Jeremy Greenstock,
  GCMG
Usher of the Blue Rod, Dame DeAnne
  Julius, DCMG, CBE
Dean, Dean of St Paul's
Deputy Secretary, Secretary of the
  Central Chancery of the Orders of
  Knighthood
Hon. Genealogist, Timothy Duke

Chancery, Central Chancery of the Orders
  of Knighthood, St James's Palace,
  London SW1A 1BH

THE IMPERIAL ORDER OF THE CROWN OF INDIA (1877) FOR LADIES

CI

Badge, the royal cipher of Queen Victoria in jewels within an oval, surmounted by an heraldic crown and attached to a bow of light blue watered ribbon, edged white

The honour does not confer any rank or title upon the recipient

No conferments have been made since 1947

HM The Queen, 1947

THE ROYAL VICTORIAN ORDER (1896)

GCVO   KCVO

GCVO   Knight or Dame Grand
       Cross
KCVO   Knight Commander
DCVO   Dame Commander
CVO   Commander
LVO   Lieutenant
MVO   Member

Ribbon, Blue, with red and white edges

Motto, Victoria

THE SOVEREIGN

GRAND MASTER
HRH The Princess Royal, KG, KT,
  GCVO

Chancellor, Lord Chamberlain
Secretary, Keeper of the Privy Purse
Registrar, Secretary of the Central
  Chancery of the Orders of
  Knighthood
Chaplain, Chaplain of the Queen's
  Chapel of the Savoy
Hon. Genealogist, David White

THE MOST EXCELLENT ORDER OF THE BRITISH EMPIRE (1917)

GBE   KBE

The order was divided into military and civil divisions in December 1918

GBE   Knight or Dame Grand Cross
KBE   Knight Commander
DBE   Dame Commander
CBE   Commander
OBE   Officer
MBE   Member

Ribbon, Rose pink edged with pearl grey with vertical pearl stripe in centre (military division); without vertical pearl stripe (civil division)
Motto, For God and the Empire

THE SOVEREIGN

GRAND MASTER
HRH The Prince Philip, Duke of Edinburgh, KG, KT, OM, GBE, PC

Prelate, Bishop of London
King of Arms, Lt.-Gen. Sir Robert Fulton, KBE
Registrar, Secretary of the Central Chancery of the Orders of Knighthood
Secretary, Secretary of the Cabinet and Head of the Home Civil Service
Dean, Dean of St Paul's
Lady Usher of the Purple Rod, Dame Amelia Chilcott Fawcett, DBE
Chancery, Central Chancery of the Orders of Knighthood, St James's Palace, London SW1A 1BH

ORDER OF THE COMPANIONS OF HONOUR (1917)

CH

Ribbon, Carmine, with gold edges

This order consists of one class only and carries with it no title. The number of awards is limited to 65 (excluding honorary members).

Amos, Baroness, 2016
Anthony, John, 1981

Ashdown of Norton-sub-Hamdon, Lord, 2015
Attenborough, Sir David, 1995
Baker, Dame Janet, 1993
Baker of Dorking, Lord, 1992
Bannister, Sir Roger, 2016
Birtwistle, Sir Harrison, 2000
Brenner, Sydney, 1986
Brook, Peter, 1998
Brooke of Sutton Mandeville, Lord, 1992
Campbell of Pittenweem, Lord, 2013
Carrington, Lord, 1983
Clarke, Kenneth, 2014
Coe, Lord, 2012
Conran, Sir Terence, 2017
De Chastelain, Gen. John, 1999
Dench, Dame Judi, 2005
Elder, Sir Mark, 2017
Eyre, Sir Richard, 2016
Glennie, Dame Evelyn, 2016
Grey, Dame Beryl, 2017
Hannay of Chiswick, Lord, 2003
Hawking, Prof. Stephen, 1989
Heseltine, Lord, 1997
Higgs, Prof. Peter, 2012
Hockney, David, 1997
Howard, Sir Michael, 2002
Howard of Lympne, Lord, 2011
Hurd of Westwell, Lord, 1995
Jeffreys, Sir Alec, 2016
King of Bridgwater, Lord, 1992
Lovelock, Prof. James, 2002
Lynn, Dame Vera, 2016
McCartney, Sir Paul, 2017
McKellen, Sir Ian Murray, 2008
McKenzie, Prof. Dan Peter, 2003
Major, Sir John, 1998
O'Neill of Bengarve, Baroness, 2013
Osborne, George, 2016
Owen, Lord, 1994
Patten of Barnes, Lord, 1997
Peters, Dame Mary, 2015
Riley, Bridget, 1998
Rogers of Riverside, Lord, 2008
Rowling, Joanne, 2017
Serota, Sir Nicholas, 2013
Shirley, Dame Stephanie, 2017
Smith, Delia, 2017
Smith, Dame Margaret (Maggie), 2014
Smith of Kelvin, Lord, 2016
Somare, Sir Michael, 1978
Stern of Brentford, Lord, 2017
Strathclyde, Lord, 2013
Strong, Sir Roy, 2016
Sulston, Sir John, 2017
Tebbit, Lord, 1987
Warnock, Baroness, 2016
Williams of Crosby, Baroness, 2016
Woolf, Lord, 2015
Young of Cookham, Lord, 2012
Young of Graffham, Lord, 2015

Honorary Members, Bernard Haitink, 2002; Prof. Amartya Sen, 2000; Most Revd Desmond Tutu, 2015
Secretary and Registrar, Secretary of the Central Chancery of the Orders of Knighthood

THE DISTINGUISHED SERVICE ORDER (1886)

DSO

Ribbon, Red, with blue edges

Bestowed in recognition of especial services in action of commissioned officers in the Navy, Army and Royal Air Force and (since 1942) Mercantile Marine. The members are Companions only. A bar may be awarded for any additional act of service.

THE IMPERIAL SERVICE ORDER (1902)

ISO

Ribbon, Crimson, with blue centre

Appointment as companion of this order is open to members of the civil services whose eligibility is determined by the grade they hold. The order consists of the sovereign and companions to a number not exceeding 1,900, of whom 1,300 may belong to the home civil services and 600 to overseas civil services. The then prime minister announced in March 1993 that he would make no further recommendations for appointments to the order.

Secretary, Head of the Home Civil Service
Registrar, Secretary of the Central Chancery of the Orders of Knighthood

THE ROYAL VICTORIAN CHAIN (1902)

It confers no precedence on its holders

HM The Queen

HM The Queen of Denmark, 1974
HM The King of Sweden, 1975
HRH Princess Beatrix of the Netherlands, 1982
Gen. Antonio Eanes, 1985
HM King Juan Carlos, 1986
HM The King of Norway, 1994
Earl of Airlie, 1997
Rt. Revd and Rt. Hon. Lord Carey of Clifton, 2002
HRH Prince Philip, Duke of Edinburgh, 2007
HM The Sultan of Oman, 2010
Rt. Revd and Rt. Hon. Lord Williams of Oystermouth, 2012

BARONETAGE AND KNIGHTAGE

BARONETS

Style, 'Sir' before forename and surname, followed by 'Bt.'
  Envelope, Sir F_ S_, Bt. *Letter (formal),* Dear Sir; *(social),* Dear Sir F_. *Spoken,* Sir F_
Wife's style, 'Lady' followed by surname
  Envelope, Lady S_. *Letter (formal),* Dear Madam; *(social),* Dear Lady S_. *Spoken,* Lady S_
Style of Baronetess, 'Dame' before forename and surname, followed by 'Btss.' (*see also* Dames)

There are five different creations of baronetcies: Baronets of England (creations dating from 1611); Baronets of Ireland (creations dating from 1619); Baronets of Scotland or Nova Scotia (creations dating from 1625); Baronets of Great Britain (creations after the Act of Union 1707 which combined the kingdoms of England and Scotland); and Baronets of the United Kingdom (creations after the union of Great Britain and Ireland in 1801).

Badge of Baronets of the UK

Badge of Baronets of Nova Scotia

Badge of Ulster

The patent of creation limits the destination of a baronetcy, usually to male descendants of the first baronet. In some cases, however, special remainders have allowed baronetcies to pass, in the absence of sons, to another relative. In the case of baronetcies of Scotland or Nova Scotia, a special remainder of 'heirs male and of tailzie' allows the baronetcy to descend to heirs general, including women. There are four existing Scottish baronetcies with such a remainder.

The Official Roll of the Baronetage is kept at the Crown Office and maintained by the Registrar and Assistant Registrar of the Baronetage. Anyone who considers that he or she is entitled to be entered on the roll may apply through the Crown Office to prove their succession. Every person succeeding to a baronetcy must exhibit proofs of succession to the Lord Chancellor. A person whose name is not entered on the official roll will not be addressed or mentioned by the title of baronet or baronetess in any official document, nor will he or she be accorded precedence as a baronet or baronetess.

The Standing Council of the Baronetage, established in 1898 as the Honourable Society of the Baronetage, is responsible for maintaining the interests of the Baronetage and for publishing the Official Roll of the Baronetage as established by royal warrant in 1910 (W www.baronetage.org/official-roll-of-the-baronets).

OFFICIAL ROLL OF THE BARONETAGE, Crown Office, House of Lords, London SW1A 0PW **T** 020-7219 4687
  E hereditary.claims@justice.gsi.gov.uk
  Registrar, Mrs Ceri King

STANDING COUNCIL OF THE BARONETAGE, Forestside, Martin's Corner, Waterlooville, Hampshire PO7 4RA
  E secretary@baronetage.org **W** www.baronetage.org
Chair, Sir Nicholas Thompson, Bt.
  Secretary, Cdr Perry Abbott, OBE, RN

BARONETCIES IDENTIFIED AS EXTINCT SINCE SEPTEMBER 2016
Campbell (cr. 1808); De la Bère (cr. 1953); Evans (cr. 1920); Fayrer (cr. 1896); White (cr. 1937)

KNIGHTS

Style, 'Sir' before forename and surname, followed by appropriate post-nominal initials if a Knight Grand Cross or Knight Commander
  Envelope, Sir F_ S_. *Letter (formal),* Dear Sir; *(social),* Dear Sir F_. *Spoken,* Sir F_
Wife's style, 'Lady' followed by surname
  Envelope, Lady S_. *Letter (formal),* Dear Madam; *(social),* Dear Lady S_. *Spoken,* Lady S_

The prefix 'Sir' is not used by knights who are clerics of the Church of England, who do not receive the accolade. Their wives are entitled to precedence as the wife of a knight but not to the style of 'Lady'.

ORDERS OF KNIGHTHOOD
Knight Grand Cross and Knight Commander are the higher classes of the Orders of Chivalry (*see* Orders of Chivalry). Honorary knighthoods of these orders may be conferred on men who are citizens of countries of which the Queen is not head of state. As a rule, the prefix 'Sir' is not used by honorary knights.

KNIGHTS BACHELOR

The Knights Bachelor do not constitute a royal order, but comprise the surviving representation of the ancient state orders of knighthood. The Register of Knights Bachelor, instituted by James I in the 17th century, lapsed, and in 1908 a voluntary association under the title of the Society of Knights (now the Imperial Society of Knights Bachelor) was formed with the primary objectives of continuing the various registers dating from 1257 and obtaining the uniform registration of every created Knight Bachelor. In 1926 a design for a badge to be worn by Knights Bachelor was approved and adopted; in 1974 a neck badge and miniature were added.

THE IMPERIAL SOCIETY OF KNIGHTS BACHELOR, Magnesia House, 6 Playhouse Yard, London EC4V 5EX
  Knight Principal, Sir Colin Berry
  Prelate, vacant
  Registrar, Sir Michael Hirst
  Hon. Treasurer, Sir Clive Thompson
  Clerk to the Council, Col. Simon Doughty

LIST OF BARONETS AND KNIGHTS *as at 31 August 2017*

†   Not registered on the Official Roll of the Baronetage
( )   The date of creation of the baronetcy is given in parentheses
I   Baronet of Ireland
NS   Baronet of Nova Scotia
S   Baronet of Scotland

A full entry in italic type indicates that the recipient of a knighthood died during the year in which the honour was conferred. The name is included for purposes of record. Peers are not included in this list.

Aaronson, Sir Michael John, Kt., CBE
†Abdy, Sir Robert Etienne Eric, Bt. (1850)
Abed, *Dr* Sir Fazle Hasan, KCMG
Acher, Sir Gerald, Kt., CBE, LVO
Ackroyd, Sir Timothy Robert Whyte, Bt. (1956)
Acland, Sir Antony Arthur, KG, GCMG, GCVO
Acland, *Lt.-Col.* Sir (Christopher) Guy (Dyke), Bt. (1890), LVO
†Acland, Sir Dominic Dyke, Bt. (1678)
Adams, Sir Geoffrey Doyne, KCMG
Adams, Sir William James, KCMG
Adjaye, Sir David Frank, Kt., OBE
Adsetts, Sir William Norman, Kt., OBE
Adye, Sir John Anthony, KCMG
Aga Khan IV, HH Prince Karim, KBE
Agnew, Sir Crispin Hamlyn, Bt. (S. 1629)
Agnew, Sir George Anthony, Bt. (1895)
Agnew, Sir Rudolph Ion Joseph, Kt.
Agnew, Sir Theodore, Kt.
Agnew-Somerville, Sir James Lockett Charles, Bt. (1957)
Ah Koy, Sir James Michael, KBE
Aikens, *Rt. Hon.* Sir Richard John Pearson, Kt.
Ainslie, Sir Charles Benedict, Kt., CBE
†Ainsworth, Sir Anthony Thomas Hugh, Bt. (1917)
Aird, Sir (George) John, Bt. (1901)
Airy, *Maj.-Gen.* Sir Christopher John, KCVO, CBE
Aitchison, Sir Charles Walter de Lancey, Bt. (1938)
Ajegbo, Sir Keith Onyema, Kt., OBE
Akenhead, *Hon.* Sir Robert, Kt.
Akers-Jones, Sir David, KBE, CMG
Alberti, *Prof.* Sir Kurt George Matthew Mayer, Kt.
Albu, Sir George, Bt. (1912)
Alcock, *Air Chief Marshal* Sir (Robert James) Michael, GCB, KBE
Aldous, *Rt. Hon.* Sir William, Kt.
Aldridge, Sir Rodney Malcolm, Kt., OBE
Alexander, *Rt. Hon.* Sir Daniel (Grian), Kt.
Alexander, Sir Douglas, Bt. (1921)
Alexander, Sir Richard, Bt. (1945)
Alghanim, Sir Kutayba Yusuf, KCMG
Allan, *Hon.* Sir Alexander Claud Stuart, KCB
Allen, Sir Errol Newton Fitzrose, KCMG
Allen, *Prof.* Sir Geoffrey, Kt., PHD, FRS

Allen, Sir Mark John Spurgeon, Kt., CMG
Allen, *Hon.* Sir Peter Austin Philip Jermyn, Kt.
Allen, Sir Thomas Boaz, Kt., CBE
Allen, *Hon.* Sir William Clifford, KCMG
Allen, Sir William Guilford, Kt.
Alleyne, Sir George Allanmoore Ogarren, Kt.
Alleyne, *Revd* John Olpherts Campbell, Bt. (1769)
Allinson, Sir (Walter) Leonard, KCVO, CMG
Allison, *Air Chief Marshal* Sir John Shakespeare, KCB, CBE
Altman, Sir Paul Bernard, Kt.
Amess, Sir David Anthony Andrew, Kt.
Amet, *Hon.* Sir Arnold Karibone, Kt.
Amory, Sir Ian Heathcoat, Bt. (1874)
Anderson, *Dr* Sir James Iain Walker, Kt., CBE
Anderson, Sir John Anthony, KBE
Anderson, Sir Leith Reinsford Steven, Kt., CBE
Anderson, *Prof.* Sir Roy Malcolm, Kt.
Anderson, *Air Marshal* Sir Timothy Michael, KCB, DSO
Anderson, Sir (William) Eric Kinloch, KT
Anderton, Sir (Cyril) James, Kt., CBE, QPM
Andrew, Sir Robert John, KCB
Andrew, Sir Warwick, Kt.
Andrews, Sir Ian Charles Franklin, Kt., CBE, TD
Angest, Sir Henry, Kt.
Annesley, Sir Hugh Norman, Kt., QPM
Anson, Sir John, KCB
Anson, *Rear-Adm.* Sir Peter, Bt. (1831), CB
Anstruther, Sir Sebastian Paten Campbell, Bt. (S. 1694 and S. 1700)
Anstruther-Gough-Calthorpe, Sir Euan Hamilton, Bt. (1929)
Antrobus, Sir Edward Philip, Bt. (1815)
Appleyard, Sir Leonard Vincent, KCMG
Arbib, Sir Martyn, Kt.
Arbuthnot, Sir Keith Robert Charles, Bt. (1823)
Arbuthnot, Sir William Reierson, Bt. (1964)
Arbuthnott, *Prof.* Sir John Peebles, Kt., PHD, FRSE

†Archdale, Sir Nicholas Edward, Bt. (1928)
Arculus, Sir Thomas David Guy, Kt.
Armitage, *Air Chief Marshal* Sir Michael John, KCB, CBE
Armitt, Sir John Alexander, Kt., CBE
Armour, *Prof.* Sir James, Kt., CBE
Armstrong, Sir Christopher John Edmund Stuart, Bt. (1841), MBE
Armstrong, Sir Richard, Kt., CBE
Armytage, Sir John Martin, Bt. (1738)
Arnold, *Hon.* Sir Richard David, Kt.
Arnold, Sir Thomas Richard, Kt.
Arnott, Sir Alexander John Maxwell, Bt. (1896)
Arthur, *Lt.-Gen.* Sir (John) Norman Stewart, KCB, CVO
Arthur, Sir Michael Anthony, KCMG
†Arthur, Sir Benjamin Nathan, Bt. (1841)
Arulkumaran, *Prof.* Sir Sabaratnam, Kt.
Asbridge, Sir Jonathan Elliott, Kt.
Ash, *Prof.* Sir Eric Albert, Kt., CBE, FRS, FRENG
Ashburnham, Sir James Fleetwood, Bt. (1661)
Ashworth, *Dr* Sir John Michael, Kt.
Aske, Sir Robert John Bingham, Bt. (1922)
Askew, Sir Bryan, Kt.
Asquith, *Hon.* Sir Dominic Anthony Gerard, KCMG
Astill, *Hon.* Sir Michael John, Kt.
Astley-Cooper, Sir Alexander Paston, Bt. (1821)
Astwood, *Hon.* Sir James Rufus, KBE
Atiyah, Sir Michael Francis, Kt., OM, PHD, FRS
Atkins, *Rt. Hon.* Sir Robert James, Kt.
Atkinson, Sir Frederick John, KCB
Atkinson, Sir William Samuel, Kt.
Atopare, Sir Sailas, GCMG
Attenborough, Sir David Frederick, Kt., OM, CH, CVO, CBE, FRS
Aubrey-Fletcher, Sir Henry Egerton, Bt. (1782)
Audland, Sir Christopher John, KCMG
Augier, *Prof.* Sir Fitzroy Richard, Kt.
Auld, *Rt. Hon.* Sir Robin Ernest, Kt.
Austin, Sir Peter John, Bt. (1894)
Austin, *Air Marshal* Sir Roger Mark, KCB, AFC
Austen-Smith, *Air Marshal* Sir Roy David, KBE, CB, CVO, DFC
Avei, Sir Moi, KBE
Ayaz, *Dr* Sir Iftikhar Ahmad, KBE
Ayckbourn, Sir Alan, Kt., CBE
Aykroyd, Sir Henry Robert George, Bt. (1920)

Aykroyd, Sir James Alexander
Frederic, Bt. (1929)
Aylmer, Sir Richard John, Bt. (I. 1622)
Aylward, *Prof.* Sir Mansel, Kt., CB
Aynsley-Green, *Prof.* Sir Albert, Kt.

Bacha, Sir Bhinod, Kt., CMG
Backhouse, Sir Alfred James Stott, Bt.
(1901)
Bacon, Sir Nicholas Hickman
Ponsonby, Bt., OBE (1611 and
1627), *Premier Baronet of England*
Baddeley, Sir John Wolsey Beresford,
Bt. (1922)
Badge, Sir Peter Gilmour Noto, Kt.
Bagge, Sir (John) Jeremy Picton, Bt.
(1867)
Baggott, Sir Matthew David, Kt., CBE,
QPM
Bagnall, *Air Chief Marshal* Sir Anthony,
GBE, KCB
Bai, Sir Brown, KBE
Bailey, Sir Alan Marshall, KCB
Bailey, Sir Brian Harry, Kt., OBE
Bailey, Sir John Bilsland, KCB
Bailey, Sir John Richard, Bt. (1919)
Bailhache, Sir Philip Martin, Kt.
Bailhache, Sir William, Kt.
Baillie, Sir Adrian Louis, Bt. (1823)
Bain, *Prof.* Sir George Sayers, Kt.
Baird, Sir Charles William Stuart, Bt.
(1809)
†Baird, Sir James Andrew Gardiner,
Bt. (S. 1695)
Baird, *Air Marshal* Sir John Alexander,
KBE
Baird, *Vice-Adm.* Sir Thomas Henry
Eustace, KCB
Bairsto, *Air Marshal* Sir Peter Edward,
KBE, CB
Baker, *Hon.* Sir Andrew William, Kt.
Baker, Sir Bryan William, Kt.
Baker, *Hon.* Sir Jeremy Russell, Kt.
Baker, *Prof.* Sir John Hamilton, Kt.,
QC
Baker, Sir John William, Kt., CBE
Baker, *Hon.* Sir Jonathan Leslie, Kt.
Baker, *Rt. Hon.* Sir (Thomas) Scott
(Gillespie), Kt.
Balasubramanian, *Prof.* Sir Shankar, Kt.
Baldry, Sir Antony Brian, Kt.
Baldwin, *Prof.* Sir Jack Edward, Kt.,
FRS
Ball, Sir Christopher John Elinger, Kt.
Ball, *Prof.* Sir John Macleod, Kt.
Ball, Sir Richard Bentley, Bt. (1911)
Ball, *Prof.* Sir Robert James, Kt., PHD
Ballantyne, *Dr* Sir Frederick Nathaniel,
GCMG
Band, *Adm.* Sir Jonathon, GCB
Banham, Sir John Michael Middlecott,
Kt.
Bannerman, Sir David Gordon, Bt. (S.
1682), OBE
Bannister, Sir Roger Gilbert, Kt., CH,
CBE, DM, FRCP
Barber, Sir Brendan, Kt.
Barber, Sir Michael Bayldon, Kt.
Barber, Sir (Thomas) David, Bt. (1960)
Barclay, Sir Robert Colraine, Bt. (S.
1668)
Barclay, Sir David Rowat, Kt.
Barclay, Sir Frederick Hugh, Kt.

Barder, Sir Brian Leon, KCMG
Baring, Sir John Francis, Bt. (1911)
Barker, *Hon.* Sir (Richard) Ian, Kt.
Barling, *Hon.* Sir Gerald Edward, Kt.
Barlow, Sir Christopher Hilaro, Bt.
(1803)
Barlow, Sir Frank, Kt., CBE
Barlow, Sir James Alan, Bt. (1902)
Barlow, Sir John Kemp, Bt. (1907)
Barnes, *The Most Revd* Brian James,
KBE
Barnes, Sir (James) David (Francis), Kt.,
CBE
Barnett, *Hon.* Sir Michael Lancelot
Patrick, Kt.
Barnett, *Prof.* Sir Richard Robert, Kt.
Barnewall, Sir Reginald Robert, Bt. (I.
1623)
†Barran, Sir John Ruthven, Bt. (1895)
Barrett, Sir Stephen Jeremy, KCMG
Barrett-Lennard, Sir Peter John, Bt.
(1801)
†Barrington, Sir Benjamin, Bt. (1831)
Barrington, Sir Nicholas John, KCMG,
CVO
Barrington-Ward, *Rt. Revd* Simon,
KCMG
Barron, Rt. Hon. Sir Kevin, Kt.
Barrons, *Gen.* Sir Richard, KCB, CBE,
ADC
Barrow, Sir Anthony John Grenfell, Bt.
(1835)
Barrow, Sir Timothy Earle, KCMG,
LVO, MBE
Barry, Sir (Lawrence) Edward
(Anthony Tress), Bt. (1899)
Barter, Sir Peter Leslie Charles, Kt.,
OBE
Bartlett, Sir Andrew Alan, Bt. (1913)
Barttelot, *Col.* Sir Brian Walter de
Stopham, Bt. (1875), OBE
Bate, *Prof.* Sir Andrew Jonathan, Kt.,
CBE
Bates, Sir James Geoffrey, Bt. (1880)
Bates, Sir Richard Dawson Hoult, Bt.
(1937)
Batho, Sir Peter Ghislain, Bt. (1928)
Bathurst, *Admiral of the Fleet* Sir (David)
Benjamin, GCB
Battersby, *Prof.* Sir Alan Rushton, Kt.,
FRS
Battishill, Sir Anthony Michael
William, GCB
Baulcombe, *Prof.* Sir David Charles,
Kt., FRS
Baxendell, Sir Peter Brian, Kt., CBE,
FRENG
Bayley, Sir Hugh Nigel Edward, Kt.
Bayne, Sir Nicholas Peter, KCMG
Baynes, Sir Christopher Rory, Bt.
(1801)
Bazalgette, Sir Peter Lytton, Kt.
Bazley, Sir Thomas John Sebastian, Bt.
(1869)
Beach, *Gen.* Sir (William Gerald)
Hugh, GBE, KCB, MC
Beache, *Hon.* Sir Vincent Ian, KCMG
Beale, *Lt.-Gen.* Sir Peter John, KBE,
FRCP
Beamish, Sir Adrian John, KCMG
Beamish, Sir David Richard, KCB
Bean, *Dr* Sir Charles Richard, Kt.
Bean, *Rt. Hon.* Sir David Michael, Kt.

Bear, Sir Michael David, Kt.
Beatson, *Rt. Hon.* Sir Jack, Kt.
Beavis, *Air Chief Marshal* Sir Michael
Gordon, KCB, CBE, AFC
Beck, Sir Edgar Philip, Kt.
Beckett, Sir Richard Gervase, Bt.
(1921), QC
Beckwith, Sir John Lionel, Kt., CBE
Beddington, *Prof.* Sir John Rex, Kt.,
CMG
Beecham, Sir Robert Adrian, Bt.
(1914)
Beevor, Sir Antony James, Kt.
Beevor, Sir Thomas Hugh Cunliffe, Bt.
(1784)
Behan, Sir David, Kt., CBE
Beldam, *Rt. Hon.* Sir (Alexander) Roy
(Asplan), Kt.
Belgrave, *HE* Sir Elliott Fitzroy,
GCMG
Bell, Sir David Charles Maurice, Kt.
Bell, Sir David Robert, KCB
Bell, *Prof.* Sir John Irving, GBE
Bell, Sir John Lowthian, Bt. (1885)
Bell, *Prof.* Sir Peter Robert Frank, Kt.
Bell, *Hon.* Sir Rodger, Kt.
Bellamy, *Hon.* Sir Christopher William,
Kt.
Bellingham, Sir Anthony Edward
Norman, Bt. (1796)
Bellingham, Sir Henry Campbell, Kt.
Bender, Sir Brian Geoffrey, KCB
Benjamin, Sir George William John,
Kt., CBE
Benn, Sir (James) Jonathan, Bt. (1914)
Bennett, *Air Vice-Marshal* Sir Erik
Peter, KBE, CB
Bennett, *Hon.* Sir Hugh Peter Derwyn,
Kt.
Bennett, *Gen.* Sir Phillip Harvey, KBE,
DSO
Bennett, Sir Ronald Wilfrid Murdoch,
Bt. (1929)
Benson, Sir Christopher John, Kt.
Beresford, Sir (Alexander) Paul, Kt.
Beresford-Peirse, Sir Henry Njers de la
Poer, Bt. (1814)
Berghuser, *Hon.* Sir Eric, Kt., MBE
Beringer, Sir John Evelyn, Kt.,
CBE
Berman, Sir Franklin Delow, KCMG
Berners-Lee, Sir Timothy John, OM,
KBE, FRS
Bernard, Sir Dallas Edmund, Bt.
(1954)
Berney, Sir Julian Reedham Stuart, Bt.
(1620)
Bernstein, Sir Howard, Kt.
Berragan, *Lt.-Gen.* Sir Gerald William,
KBE, CB
Berridge, *Prof.* Sir Michael John, Kt.,
FRS
Berriman, Sir David, Kt.
Berry, *Prof.* Sir Colin Leonard, Kt.,
FRCPATH
Berry, *Prof.* Sir Michael Victor, Kt.,
FRS
Berthoud, Sir Martin Seymour, KCVO,
CMG
Berwick, *Prof.* Sir George Thomas, Kt.,
CBE
Best-Shaw, Sir Thomas Joshua, Bt.
(1665)

Bethel, Sir Baltron Benjamin, KCMG
Bethlehem, Sir Daniel, KCMG
Bett, Sir Michael, Kt., CBE
Bettison, Sir Norman George, Kt.,
QPM
Bevan, Sir James David, KCMG
Bevan, Sir Martyn Evan Evans, Bt.
(1958)
Bevan, Sir Nicolas, Kt., CB
Beverley, Lt.-Gen. Sir Henry York La
Roche, KCB, OBE, RM
Bhadeshia, Prof. Sir Harshad Kumar
Dharamshi, Kt., FRS
Bibby, Sir Michael James, Bt. (1959)
Bickersteth, Rt. Revd John Monier,
KCVO
Biddulph, Sir Ian D'Olier, Bt. (1664)
Biggam, Sir Robin Adair, Kt.
Bilas, Sir Angmai Simon, Kt., OBE
Bill, Lt.-Gen. Sir David Robert, KCB
Billière, Gen. Sir Peter Edgar de la
Cour de la, KCB, KBE, DSO, MC
Bindman, Sir Geoffrey Lionel, Kt.
Bingham, Hon. Sir Eardley Max, Kt.
Birch, Sir John Allan, KCVO, CMG
Birch, Sir Roger, Kt., CBE, QPM
Bird, Prof. Sir Adrian Peter, Kt., CBE,
FRS, FRSE
Bird, Sir Richard Geoffrey Chapman,
Bt. (1922)
Birkett, Sir Peter, Kt.
Birkin, Sir John Christian William, Bt.
(1905)
Birkin, Sir (John) Derek, Kt., TD
Birkmyre, Sir James, Bt. (1921)
Birrell, Sir James Drake, Kt.
Birss, Hon. Sir Colin Ian, Kt.
Birt, Sir Michael, Kt.
Birtwistle, Sir Harrison, Kt., CH
Bischoff, Sir Winfried Franz Wilhelm,
Kt.
Black, Prof. Sir Nicholas Andrew, Kt.
Black, Sir Robert David, Bt. (1922)
Blackburn, Vice-Adm. Sir David
Anthony James, KCVO, CB
Blackburne, Hon. Sir William Anthony,
Kt.
Blackett, Sir Hugh Francis, Bt. (1673)
Blackham, Vice-Adm. Sir Jeremy Joe,
KCB
Blackman, Sir Frank Milton, KCVO,
OBE
†Blair, Sir Patrick David Hunter, Bt.
(1786)
Blair, Hon. Sir William James Lynton,
Kt.
†Blake, Sir Charles Valentine Bruce,
Bt. (I. 1622)
Blake, Sir Francis Michael, Bt. (1907)
Blake, Hon. Sir Nicholas John Gorrod,
Kt.
Blake, Sir Peter Thomas, Kt., CBE
Blake, Sir Quentin Saxby, Kt., CBE
Blakemore, Prof. Sir Colin Brian, Kt.,
FRS
Blaker, Sir John, Bt. (1919)
Blakiston, Sir Ferguson Arthur James,
Bt. (1763)
Blanch, Sir Malcolm, KCVO
Bland, Lt.-Col. Sir Simon Claud
Michael, KCVO
Blank, Sir Maurice Victor, Kt.
Blatherwick, Sir David Elliott Spiby,
KCMG, OBE

Blavatnik, Sir Leonard, Kt.
Blennerhassett, Sir (Marmaduke)
Adrian Francis William, Bt. (1809)
Blewitt, Maj. Sir Shane Gabriel Basil,
GCVO
Blofeld, Hon. Sir John Christopher
Calthorpe, Kt.
Blois, Sir Charles Nicholas Gervase,
Bt. (1686)
Blom-Cooper, Sir Louis Jacques, Kt.,
QC
Blomefield, Sir Thomas Charles
Peregrine, Bt. (1807)
Bloom, Prof. Sir Stephen Robert, Kt.
Bloomfield, Sir Kenneth Percy, KCB
Bundell, Prof. Sir Richard William, Kt.,
CBE, FBA
Blundell, Sir Thomas Leon, Kt., FRS
†Blunden, Sir Hubert Chisholm, Bt. (I.
1766)
Blunt, Sir David Richard Reginald
Harvey, Bt. (1720)
Blyth, Sir Charles (Chay), Kt., CBE,
BEM
Boardman, Prof. Sir John, Kt., FSA,
FBA
Bodey, Hon. Sir David Roderick
Lessiter, Kt.
Bodmer, Sir Walter Fred, Kt., PHD,
FRS
Body, Sir Richard Bernard Frank
Stewart, Kt.
Bogle, Sir Nigel, Kt.
Bogan, Sir Nagora, KBE
Boileau, Sir Nicolas Edmond George,
Bt. (1838)
Boleat, Sir Mark John, Kt.
Boles, Sir Richard Fortescue, Bt.
(1922)
Bollom, Air Marshal Sir Simon John,
KBE, CB
Bona, Sir Kina, KBE
Bonallack, Sir Michael Francis, Kt.,
OBE
Bond, Sir John Reginald Hartnell, Kt.
Bond, Prof. Sir Michael Richard, Kt.,
FRCPSYCH, FRCPGLAS, FRCSE
Bone, Prof. Sir (James) Drummond, Kt.,
FRSE
Bone, Sir Roger Bridgland, KCMG
Bonfield, Sir Peter Leahy, Kt., CBE,
FRENG
Bonham, Sir George Martin Antony,
Bt. (1852)
Bonington, Sir Christian John Storey,
Kt., CVO, CBE
Bonsor, Sir Nicholas Cosmo, Bt.
(1925)
Boord, Sir Nicolas John Charles, Bt.
(1896)
Boorman, Lt.-Gen. Sir Derek, KCB
Booth, Sir Clive, Kt.
Booth, Sir Douglas Allen, Bt. (1916)
Boothby, Sir Brooke Charles, Bt.
(1660)
Bore, Sir Albert, Kt.
Boreel, Sir Stephan Gerard, Bt. (1645)
Borthwick, Sir Antony Thomas, Bt.
(1908)
Borysiewicz, Prof. Sir Leszek
Krzysztof, Kt.
Bosher, Sir Robin, Kt.
Bossom, Sir Bruce Charles, Bt. (1953)

Bostock, Sir David John, KCMG
Boswell, Lt.-Gen. Sir Alexander
Crawford Simpson, KCB, CBE
Botham, Sir Ian Terence, Kt., OBE
Bottomley, Sir Peter James, Kt.
Bottoms, Prof. Sir Anthony Edward,
Kt.
Boughey, Sir John George Fletcher, Bt.
(1798)
†Boulton, Sir John Gibson, Bt. (1944)
Bouraga, Sir Phillip, KBE
Bourn, Sir John Bryant, KCB
Bourne, Sir Matthew Christopher, Kt.,
OBE
Bowater, Sir Euan David Vansittart, Bt.
(1939)
†Bowater, Sir Michael Patrick, Bt.
(1914)
Bowden, Sir Andrew, Kt., MBE
Bowden, Sir Nicholas Richard, Bt.
(1915)
Bowen, Sir Barry Manfield, KCMG
Bowen, Sir Geoffrey Fraser, Kt.
Bowen, Sir George Edward Michael,
Bt. (1921)
Bowes Lyon, Sir Simon Alexander,
KCVO
Bowlby, Sir Richard Peregrine
Longstaff, Bt. (1923)
Bowman, Sir Edwin Geoffrey, KCB
Bowman, Sir Jeffery Haverstock, Kt.
Bowness, Sir Alan, Kt., CBE
Bowyer-Smyth, Sir Thomas Weyland,
Bt. (1661)
Boyce, Sir Graham Hugh, KCMG
Boyce, Sir Robert Charles Leslie, Bt.
(1952)
Boyd, Sir Alexander Walter, Bt. (1916)
Boyd, Sir John Dixon Ikle, KCMG
Boyd, Sir Michael, Kt.
Boyd, Prof. Sir Robert David Hugh,
Kt.
Boyd-Carpenter, Sir (Marsom) Henry,
KCVO
Boyd-Carpenter, Lt.-Gen. Hon. Sir
Thomas Patrick John, KBE
Boyle, Prof. Sir Roger Michael, Kt.,
CBE
Boyle, Sir Simon Hugh Patrick, KCVO
Boyle, Sir Stephen Gurney, Bt. (1904)
Bracewell-Smith, Sir Charles, Bt.
(1947)
Bradford, Sir Edward Alexander Slade,
Bt. (1902)
Bradshaw, Lt.-Gen. Sir Adrian, KCB,
OBE
Brady, Prof. Sir John Michael, Kt., FRS
Brailsford, Sir David John, Kt., CBE
Braithwaite, Sir Rodric Quentin,
GCMG
Bramley, Prof. Sir Paul Anthony, Kt.
Branagh, Sir Kenneth Charles, Kt.
Branson, Sir Richard Charles Nicholas,
Kt.
Bratza, Hon. Sir Nicolas Dušan, Kt.
Brazier, Sir Julian William Hendy, Kt.,
TD
Breckenridge, Prof. Sir Alasdair Muir,
Kt., CBE
Brennan, Hon. Sir (Francis) Gerard,
KBE
Brenton, Sir Anthony Russell, KCMG
Brewer, Sir David William, KG, CMG,
CVO

Brierley, Sir Ronald Alfred, Kt.

Briggs, *Rt. Hon.* Sir Michael Townley Featherstone, Kt.

Brighouse, *Prof.* Sir Timothy Robert Peter, Kt.

Bright, Sir Graham Frank James, Kt.

Bright, Sir Keith, Kt.

Brigstocke, *Adm.* Sir John Richard, KCB

Brinckman, Sir Theodore George Roderick, Bt. (1831)

†Brisco, Sir Campbell Howard, Bt. (1782)

Briscoe, Sir Brian Anthony, Kt.

Briscoe, Sir John Geoffrey James, Bt. (1910)

Brittan, Sir Samuel, Kt.

Britton, Sir Paul John James, Kt., CB

†Broadbent, Sir Andrew George, Bt. (1893)

Broadbent, Sir Richard John, KCB

Brocklebank, Sir Aubrey Thomas, Bt. (1885)

Brodie, Sir Benjamin David Ross, Bt. (1834)

Bromhead, Sir John Desmond Gonville, Bt. (1806)

Bromley, Sir Michael Roger, KBE

Bromley, Sir Rupert Charles, Bt. (1757)

Bromley-Davenport, Sir William Arthur, KCVO

Brook, *Prof.* Sir Richard John, Kt., OBE

Brooke, Sir Alistair Weston, Bt. (1919)

Brooke, Sir Francis George Windham, Bt. (1903)

Brooke, *Rt. Hon.* Sir Henry, Kt.

Brooke, Sir Richard Christopher, Bt. (1662)

Brooke, Sir Rodney George, Kt., CBE

Brooking, Sir Trevor David, Kt., CBE

Brooksbank, Sir (Edward) Nicholas, Bt. (1919)

Broomfield, Sir Nigel Hugh Robert Allen, KCMG

†Broughton, Sir David Delves, Bt. (1661)

Broughton, Sir Martin Faulkner, Kt.

Broun, Sir Wayne Hercules, Bt. (S. 1686)

Brown, Sir (Austen) Patrick, KCB

Brown, *Adm.* Sir Brian Thomas, KCB, CBE

Brown, Sir David, Kt.

Brown, Sir Ewan, Kt., CBE

Brown, Sir George Francis Richmond, Bt. (1863)

Brown, Sir Mervyn, KCMG, OBE

Brown, Sir Peter Randolph, Kt.

Brown, *Rt. Hon.* Sir Stephen, GBE

Brown, Sir Stephen David Reid, KCVO

Brownrigg, Sir Nicholas (Gawen), Bt. (1816)

Browse, *Prof.* Sir Norman Leslie, Kt., MD, FRCS

Bruce, Sir (Francis) Michael Ian, Bt. (s. 1628)

Bruce-Clifton, Sir Hervey Hamish Peter, Bt. (1804)

Bruce-Gardner, Sir Robert Henry, Bt. (1945)

Brunner, Sir Hugo Laurence Joseph, KCVO

†Brunner, Sir Nicholas Felix Minturn, Bt. (1895)

†Brunton, Sir James Lauder, Bt. (1908)

Bryant, *Air Chief Marshal* Sir Simon, KCB, CBE, ADC

Bubb, Sir Stephen John Limrick, Kt.

Buchan-Hepburn, Sir John Alastair Trant Kidd, Bt. (1815)

Buchanan, Sir Andrew George, Bt. (1878), KCVO

Buchanan-Jardine, Sir John Christopher Rupert, Bt. (1885)

Buckland, Sir Ross, Kt.

Buckley, *Dr* Sir George William, Kt.

Buckley, Sir Michael Sidney, Kt.

Buckley, *Lt.-Cdr.* Sir (Peter) Richard, KCVO

Buckley, *Hon.* Sir Roger John, Kt.

Bucknall, *Lt.-Gen.* Sir James Jeffrey Corfield, KCB, CBE

†Buckworth-Herne-Soame, Sir Richard John, Bt. (1697)

Budd, Sir Alan Peter, GBE

Budd, Sir Colin Richard, KCMG

Buffini, Sir Damon Marcus, Kt.

Bull, Sir George Jeffrey, Kt.

Bull, Sir Simeon George, Bt. (1922)

Bullock, Sir Stephen Michael, Kt.

Bultin, Sir Bato, Kt., MBE

Bunbury, Sir Michael William, Bt. (1681), KCVO

Bunyard, Sir Robert Sidney, Kt., CBE, QPM

Burbidge, Sir Peter Dudley, Bt. (1916)

Burden, Sir Anthony Thomas, Kt., QPM

†Burdett, Sir Crispin Peter, Bt. (1665)

Burgen, Sir Arnold Stanley Vincent, Kt., FRS

Burgess, Sir (Joseph) Stuart, Kt., CBE, PHD, FRSC

Burgess, *Prof.* Sir Robert George, Kt.

Burke, Sir James Stanley Gilbert, Bt. (I. 1797)

Burke, Sir (Thomas) Kerry, Kt.

Burn, *Prof.* Sir John, Kt.

Burnell-Nugent, *Vice-Adm.* Sir James Michael, KCB, CBE, ADC

Burnett, Sir Charles David, Bt. (1913)

Burnett, *Rt. Hon.* Sir Ian Duncan, Kt.

Burnett, Sir Walter John, Kt.

Burney, Sir Nigel Dennistoun, Bt. (1921)

Burns, *Dr* Sir Henry, Kt.

Burns, Sir (Robert) Andrew, KCMG

Burns, *Rt. Hon.* Sir Simon Hugh McGuigan, Kt.

Burnton, *Rt. Hon.* Sir Stanley Jeffrey, Kt.

Burrell, Sir Charles Raymond, Bt. (1774)

Burridge, *Air Chief Marshal* Sir Brian Kevin, KCB, CBE, ADC

Burt, Sir Peter Alexander, Kt.

Burton, *Lt.-Gen.* Sir Edmund Fortescue Gerard, KBE

Burton, Sir Graham Stuart, KCMG

Burton, *Hon.* Sir Michael John, Kt.

Burton, Sir Michael St Edmund, KCVO, CMG

Butler, *Hon.* Sir Arlington Griffith, KCMG

Butler, *Dr* Sir David Edgeworth, Kt., CBE

Butler, Sir Percy James, Kt., CBE

Butler, Sir Reginald Richard Michael, Bt. (1922)

Butler, Sir Richard Pierce, Bt. (I. 1628)

Butterfield, *Hon.* Sir Alexander Neil Logie, Kt.

Butterfill, Sir John Valentine, Kt.

Buxton, Sir Crispin Charles Gerard, Bt. (1840)

Buxton, *Rt. Hon.* Sir Richard Joseph, Kt.

Buzzard, Sir Anthony Farquhar, Bt. (1929)

Byatt, Sir Ian Charles Rayner, Kt.

Byford, Sir Lawrence, Kt., CBE, QPM

Byron, *Rt. Hon.* Sir Charles Michael Dennis, Kt.

Cable, *Rt. Hon.* Sir (John) Vincent, Kt., PHD

†Cable-Alexander, Sir Patrick Desmond William, Bt. (1809)

Cadbury, Sir (Nicholas) Dominic, Kt.

Cadogan, *Prof.* Sir John Ivan George, Kt., CBE, FRS, FRSE

Cahn, Sir Albert Jonas, Bt. (1934)

Cahn, Sir Andrew Thomas, KCMG

Caine, Sir Michael (Maurice Micklewhite), Kt., CBE

Caines, Sir John, KCB

Cairns, *Very Revd* John Ballantyne, KCVO

Caldwell, Sir Edward George, KCB

Callaghan, Sir William Henry, Kt.

Callan, Sir Ivan Roy, KCVO, CMG

Callender, Sir Colin Nigel, Kt., CBE

Callman, *His Hon.* Sir Clive Vernon, Kt.

Calman, *Prof.* Sir Kenneth Charles, KCB, MD, FRCP, FRCS, FRSE

Calne, *Prof.* Sir Roy Yorke, Kt., FRS

Calvert-Smith, Sir David, Kt., QC

Cameron, Sir Hugh Roy Graham, Kt., QPM

Campbell, *Prof.* Sir Colin Murray, Kt.

Campbell, Sir Ian Tofts, Kt., CBE, VRD

Campbell, Sir James Alexander Moffat Bain, Bt. (S. 1668)

Campbell, Sir John Park, Kt., OBE

Campbell, Sir Lachlan Philip Kemeys, Bt. (1815)

Campbell, *Dr* Sir Philip Henry Montgomery, Kt.

Campbell, Sir Roderick Duncan Hamilton, Bt. (1831)

Campbell, Sir Louis Auchinbreck, Bt. (S. 1628)

Campbell, *Dr* Sir Simon Fraser, Kt., CBE

Campbell, *Rt. Hon.* Sir William Anthony, Kt.

†Campbell-Orde, Sir John Simon Arthur, Bt. (1790)

Cannadine, *Prof.* Sir David Nicholas, Kt.

Capewell, *Lt.-Gen.* Sir David Andrew, KCB, OBE, RM

†Carden, Sir Christopher Robert, Bt. (1887)

†Carden, Sir John Craven, Bt. (I. 1787)

Carew, Sir Rivers Verain, Bt. (1661)

Carey, Sir de Vic Graham, Kt.

Carleton-Smith, *Maj.-Gen.* Sir Michael Edward, Kt., CBE

Carlisle, Sir James Beethoven, GCMG

Carlisle, Sir John Michael, Kt.

Carlisle, Sir Kenneth Melville, Kt.

Carnegie, Sir Roderick Howard, Kt.

Carnwath, *Rt. Hon.* Sir Robert John Anderson, Kt., CVO (Lord Carnwath of Notting Hill)

Carr, *Hon.* Sir Henry James, Kt.

Carr, Sir Peter Derek, Kt., CBE

Carr, Sir Roger Martyn, Kt.

Carrick, *Hon.* Sir John Leslie, KCMG

Carrick, Sir Roger John, KCMG, LVO

Carruthers, Sir Ian James, Kt., OBE

Carsberg, *Prof.* Sir Bryan Victor, Kt.

Carter, Sir Andrew Nicholas, Kt., OBE

Carter, Sir David Anthony, Kt.

Carter, *Prof.* Sir David Craig, Kt., FRCSE, FRCSGLAS, FRCPE

Carter, Sir Edward Charles, KCMG

Carter, Sir John Gordon Thomas, Kt.

Carter, *Lt.-Gen.* Sir Nicholas Patrick, KCB, CBE, DSO

Cartledge, Sir Bryan George, KCMG

Caruna, *Hon.* Sir Peter Richard, KCMG, QC

†Cary, Sir Nicholas Robert Hugh, Bt. (1955)

Cash, Sir Andrew John, Kt., OBE

Cash, Sir William Nigel Paul, Kt.

Cass, Sir Geoffrey Arthur, Kt.

Cassel, Sir Timothy Felix Harold, Bt. (1920)

Cassels, *Adm.* Sir Simon Alastair

Cassillis, KCB, CBE

Cassidi, *Adm.* Sir (Arthur) Desmond, GCB

Castell, Sir William Martin, Kt.

Catto, *Prof.* Sir Graeme Robertson Dawson, Kt.

Cave, Sir John Charles, Bt. (1896)

Cave-Browne-Cave, Sir John Robert Charles, Bt. (1641)

Cayley, Sir Digby William David, Bt. (1661)

Cazalet, *Hon.* Sir Edward Stephen, Kt.

Cazalet, Sir Peter Grenville, Kt.

Chadwick, *Rt. Hon.* Sir John Murray, Kt.

Chadwick, Sir Joshua Kenneth Burton, Bt. (1935)

Chadwyck-Healey, Sir Charles Edward, Bt. (1919)

Chakrabarti, Sir Sumantra, KCB

Chalmers, Sir Iain Geoffrey, Kt.

Chalmers, Sir Neil Robert, Kt.

Chalstrey, Sir (Leonard) John, Kt., MD, FRCS

Chan, *Rt. Hon.* Sir Julius, GCMG, KBE

Chan, Sir Thomas Kok, Kt., OBE

Chance, Sir (George) Jeremy ffolliott, Bt. (1900)

Chandler, Sir Colin Michael, Kt.

Chantler, *Prof.* Sir Cyril, GBE, MD, FRCP

Chaplin, Sir Malcolm Hilbery, Kt., CBE

Chapman, Sir David Robert Macgowan, Bt. (1958)

Chapman, Sir Frank, Kt.

Chapman, Sir George Alan, Kt.

Chapple, *Field Marshal* Sir John Lyon, GCB, CBE

Charles, *Hon.* Sir Arthur William Hessin, Kt.

Charlton, Sir Robert (Bobby), Kt., CBE

Charnley, Sir (William) John, Kt., CB, FRENG

Chartres, *Rt. Revd and Rt. Hon.* Richard John Carew, KCVO

†Chaytor, Sir Bruce Gordon, Bt. (1831)

Checketts, *Sqn. Ldr.* Sir David John, KCVO

Checkland, Sir Michael, Kt.

Cheshire, Sir Ian Michael, Kt.

Cheshire, *Air Chief Marshal* Sir John Anthony, KBE, CB

Chessells, Sir Arthur David (Tim), Kt.

†Chetwynd, Sir Peter James Talbot, Bt. (1795)

Cheyne, Sir Patrick John Lister, Bt. (1908)

Chichester, Sir James Henry Edward, Bt. (1641)

Chilcot, *Rt. Hon.* Sir John Anthony, GCB

Child, Sir (Coles John) Jeremy, Bt. (1919)

Chinn, Sir Trevor Edwin, Kt., CVO

†Chinubhai, Sir Prashant, Bt. (1913)

Chipperfield, *Prof.* Sir David Alan, Kt., CBE

Chipperfield, Sir Geoffrey Howes, KCB

Chisholm, Sir John Alexander Raymond, Kt., FRENG

†Chitty, Sir Andrew Edward Willes, Bt. (1924)

Cholmeley, Sir Hugh John Frederick Sebastian, Bt. (1806)

Chow, Sir Chung Kong, Kt.

Chow, Sir Henry Francis, Kt., OBE

Christopher, Sir Duncan Robin Carmichael, KBE, CMG

Chung, Sir Sze-yuen, GBE, GCMG, FRENG

Clark, *Prof.* Sir Christopher Munro, Kt.

Clark, Sir Francis Drake, Bt. (1886)

Clark, Sir Jonathan George, Bt. (1917)

Clark, Sir Terence Joseph, KBE, CMG, CVO

Clark, Sir Timothy Charles, KBE

Clarke, Sir (Charles Mansfield) Tobias, Bt. (1831)

Clarke, *Rt. Hon.* Sir Christopher Simon Courtenay Stephenson, Kt.

Clarke, *Hon.* Sir David Clive, Kt.

Clarke, Sir Jonathan Dennis, Kt.

Clarke, Sir Paul Robert Virgo, KCVO

Clarke, Sir Rupert Grant Alexander, Bt. (1882)

Clary, *Prof.* Sir David Charles, Kt.

Clay, Sir Edward, KCMG

Clay, Sir Richard Henry, Bt. (1841)

Clayton, Sir David Robert, Bt. (1732)

Cleaver, Sir Anthony Brian, Kt.

Clementi, Sir David Cecil, Kt.

Clerk, Sir Robert Maxwell, Bt. (S. 1679), OBE

Clerke, Sir Francis Ludlow Longueville, Bt. (1660)

Clifford, Sir Roger Joseph, Bt. (1887)

Clifford, Sir Timothy Peter Plint, Kt.

Coates, Sir Anthony Robert Milnes, Bt. (1911)

Coates, Sir David Frederick Charlton, Bt. (1921)

†Coats, Sir Alexander James Stuart, Bt. (1905)

Cobb, *Hon.* Sir Stephen William Scott, Kt.

Cochrane, Sir (Henry) Marc (Sursock), Bt. (1903)

†Cockburn, Sir Charles Christopher, Bt. (S. 1671)

Cockburn-Campbell, Sir Alexander Thomas, Bt. (1821)

Cockell, Sir Merrick, Kt.

Cockshaw, Sir Alan, Kt., FRENG.

Codrington, Sir Christopher George Wayne, Bt. (1876)

Codrington, Sir Giles Peter, Bt. (1721)

Codron, Sir Michael Victor, Kt., CBE

Coghill, Sir Patrick Kendal Farley, Bt. (1778)

Coghlin, *Rt. Hon.* Sir Patrick, Kt.

Cohen, Sir Ivor Harold, Kt., CBE, TD

Cohen, *Prof.* Sir Philip, Kt., PHD, FRS

Cohen, Sir Ronald, Kt.

Cole, Sir (Robert) William, Kt.

Coleman, Sir Robert John, KCMG

Coleridge, *Hon.* Sir Paul James Duke, Kt.

Coles, Sir (Arthur) John, GCMG

Colfox, Sir Philip John, Bt. (1939)

Collas, Sir Richard John, Kt.

Collett, Sir Ian Seymour, Bt. (1934)

Collier, Sir Paul, Kt., CBE

Collins, Sir Alan Stanley, KCVO, CMG

Collins, *Hon.* Sir Andrew David, Kt.

Collins, Sir Bryan Thomas Alfred, Kt., OBE, QFSM

Collins, *Dr* Sir David John, Kt., CBE

Collins, Sir John Alexander, Kt

Collins, Sir Kenneth Darlingston, Kt.

Collins, *Dr* Sir Kevan Arthur, Kt.

Collins, *Prof.* Sir Rory Edwards, Kt.

Collyear, Sir John Gowen, Kt.

Colman, Sir Michael Jeremiah, Bt. (1907)

Colman, Sir Timothy, KG

Colquhoun of Luss, Sir Malcolm Rory, Bt. (1786)

Colt, Sir Edward William Dutton, Bt. (1694)

Colthurst, Sir Charles St John, Bt. (I. 1744)

Colton, *Hon.* Sir Adrian George Patrick, Kt.

Conant, Sir John Ernest Michael, Bt. (1954)

Conner, *Rt Revd* David John, KCVO

Connery, Sir Sean, Kt.

Connolly, William (Billy), Kt., CBE

Connor, Sir William Joseph, Kt.

Conran, Sir Terence Orby, Kt., CH

Cons, *Hon.* Sir Derek, Kt.

Constantinou, Sir Kosta George, Kt., OBE

Constantinou, Sir Theophilus George, Kt., CBE

Conway, *Prof.* Sir Gordon Richard, KCMG, FRS

Cook, Sir Andrew, Kt., CBE

Cook, Sir Christopher Wymondham Rayner Herbert, Bt. (1886)

Cook, *Prof.* Sir Peter Frederic Chester, Kt.

Cooke, *Hon.* Sir Jeremy Lionel, Kt.

Cooke, *Prof.* Sir Ronald Urwick, Kt.

†Cooke-Yarborough, Sir Anthony Edmund, Bt. (1661)

Cooksey, Sir David James Scott, GBE

Cooper, *Prof.* Sir Cary Lynn, Kt., CBE

Cooper, *Gen.* Sir George Leslie Conroy, GCB, MC

Cooper, Sir Richard Adrian, Bt. (1905)

Cooper, Sir Robert Francis, KCMG, MVO

Cooper, *Maj.-Gen.* Sir Simon Christie, GCVO

Cooper, Sir William Daniel Charles, Bt. (1863)

Coote, Sir Nicholas Patrick, Bt. (I. 1621), *Premier Baronet of Ireland*

Corbett, *Maj.-Gen.* Sir Robert John Swan, KCVO, CB

Corder, Vice-Adm. Sir Ian Fergus, KBE, CB

Cordy-Simpson, *Lt.-Gen.* Sir Roderick Alexander, KBE, CB

Corness, Sir Colin Ross, Kt.

Corry, Sir James Michael, Bt. (1885)

Cortazzi, Sir (Henry Arthur) Hugh, GCMG

Cory, Sir (Clinton Charles) Donald, Bt. (1919)

Cory-Wright, Sir Richard Michael, Bt. (1903)

Cossons, Sir Neil, Kt., OBE

Cotter, Sir Patrick Laurence Delaval, Bt. (I. 1763)

Cotterell, Sir John Henry Geers, Bt. (1805)

†Cotts, Sir Richard Crichton Mitchell, Bt. (1921)

Coulson, *Hon.* Sir Peter David William, Kt.

Couper, Sir James George, Bt. (1841)

Courtenay, Sir Thomas Daniel, Kt.

Cousins, *Air Chief Marshal* Sir David, KCB, AFC

Coville, *Air Marshal* Sir Christopher Charles Cotton, KCB

Cowan, *Gen.* Sir Samuel, KCB, CBE

Coward, *Lt.-Gen.* Sir Gary Robert, KBE, CB, OBE

Coward, *Vice-Adm.* Sir John Francis, KCB, DSO

Cowdery, Sir Clive, Kt.

Cowper-Coles, Sir Sherard Louis, KCMG, LVO

Cox, Sir Alan George, Kt., CBE

Cox, *Prof.* Sir David Roxbee, Kt.

Cox, Sir George Edwin, Kt.

Craft, *Prof.* Sir Alan William, Kt.

Cragg, *Prof.* Sir Anthony Douglas, Kt., CBE

Cragnolini, Sir Luciano, Kt.

Craig, Sir (Albert) James (Macqueen), GCMG

Craig-Cooper, Sir (Frederick Howard) Michael, Kt., CBE, TD

Craig-Martin, Sir Michael, Kt., CBE

Crane, *Prof.* Sir Peter Robert, Kt.

Cranston, *Hon.* Sir Ross Frederick, Kt.

Craufurd, Sir Robert James, Bt. (1781)

Crausby, Sir David Anthony, Kt.

Craven, Sir John Anthony, Kt.

Craven, Sir Philip Lee, Kt., MBE

Crawford, *Prof.* Sir Frederick William, Kt., FRENG

Crawford, Sir Robert William Kenneth, Kt., CBE

Crawley-Boevey, Sir Thomas Michael Blake, Bt. (1784)

Cresswell, *Hon.* Sir Peter John, Kt.

Crew, Sir (Michael) Edward, Kt., QPM

Crewe, *Prof.* Sir Ivor Martin, Kt.

Crisp, Sir John Charles, Bt. (1913)

Critchett, Sir Charles George Montague, Bt. (1908)

Crittin, *Hon.* Sir John Luke, KBE

Croft, Sir Owen Glendower, Bt. (1671)

Croft, Sir Thomas Stephen Hutton, Bt. (1818)

Crofton, Sir Edward Morgan, Bt. (1801)

Crofton, Sir Julian Malby, Bt. (1838)

Crombie, Sir Alexander, Kt.

Crompton, Sir Dan, Kt., CBE, QPM

Cropper, Sir James Anthony, KCVO

Crosby, Sir Lynton Keith, Kt.

Crossley, Sir Sloan Nicholas, Bt. (1909)

Crowe, Sir Brian Lee, KCMG

Cruickshank, Sir Donald Gordon, Kt.

Cubie, *Dr* Sir Andrew, Kt., CBE

Cubitt, Sir Hugh Guy, Kt., CBE

Cubitt, *Maj.-Gen.* Sir William George, KCVO, CBE

Cullen, Sir (Edward) John, Kt., FRENG

Culme-Seymour, Sir Michael Patrick, Bt. (1809)

Culpin, Sir Robert Paul, Kt.

Cummins, Sir Michael John Austin, Kt.

Cunliffe, *Prof.* Sir Barrington, Kt., CBE

Cunliffe, Sir David Ellis, Bt. (1759)

Cunliffe, Sir Jonathan Stephen, Kt., CB

Cunliffe-Owen, Sir Hugo Dudley, Bt. (1920)

Cunningham, *Lt.-Gen.* Sir Hugh Patrick, KBE

Cunningham, *Prof.* Sir John, KCVO

Cunningham, Sir Roger Keith, Kt., CBE

Cunningham, Sir Thomas Anthony, Kt.

Cunynghame, Sir Andrew David Francis, Bt. (S. 1702)

Curran, *Prof.* Sir Paul James, Kt.

†Currie, Sir Bradley Mark Higgins, Bt. (1847)

Curtain, Sir Michael, KBE

Curtis, Sir Barry John, Kt.

Curtis, *Hon.* Sir Richard Herbert, Kt.

Curtis, Sir Edward Philip, Bt. (1802)

Cuschieri, *Prof.* Sir Alfred, Kt.

Dain, Sir David John Michael, KCVO

Dales, Sir Richard Nigel, KCVO

Dalrymple-Hay, Sir Malcolm John Robert, Bt. (1798)

†Dalrymple-White, Sir Jan Hew, Bt. (1926)

Dalton, Sir David Nigel, Kt.

Dalton, *Vice-Adm.* Sir Geoffrey Thomas James Oliver, GCB

Dalton, Sir Richard John, KCMG

Dalton, *Air Chief Marshal* Sir Stephen Gary George, GCB

†Dalyell, Sir Gordon Wheatley, Bt. (NS 1685)

Dancer, Sir Eric, KCVO, CBE

Daniel, Sir John Sagar, Kt., DSC

Darell, Sir Guy Jeffrey Adair, Bt. (1795)

Darrington, Sir Michael John, Kt.

Darroch, Sir Nigel Kim, KCMG

Dasgupta, *Prof.* Sir Partha Sarathi, Kt.

Dashwood, *Prof.* Sir (Arthur) Alan, KCMG, CBE, QC

Dashwood, Sir Edward John Francis, Bt. (1707), *Premier Baronet of Great Britain*

Dashwood, Sir Frederick George Mahon, Bt. (1684)

Daunt, Sir Timothy Lewis Achilles, KCMG

Davey, *Rt. Hon.* Sir Edward Jonathan, Kt.

David, *His Hon.* Sir Robin (Robert) Daniel George, Kt.

Davidson, Sir Martin Stuart, KCMG

Davies, *Prof.* Sir David Evan Naughton, Kt., CBE, FRS, FRENG

Davies, Sir David John, Kt.

Davies, Sir Frank John, Kt., CBE

Davies, *Prof.* Sir Graeme John, Kt., FRENG

Davies, Sir John Howard, Kt.

Davies, Sir John Michael, KCB

Davies, Sir Raymond Douglas, Kt.

Davies, Sir Rhys Everson, Kt., QC

Davis, Sir Andrew Frank, Kt., CBE

Davis, Sir Crispin Henry Lamert, Kt.

Davis, Sir John Gilbert, Bt. (1946)

Davis, Sir Michael Lawrence, Kt.

Davis, *Rt. Hon.* Sir Nigel Anthony Lamert, Kt.

Davis, Sir Peter John, Kt.

Davis, *Hon.* Sir William Easthope, Kt.

Davis-Goff, Sir Robert (William), Bt. (1905)

Davson, Sir George Trenchard Simon, Bt. (1927)

Dawanincura, Sir John Norbert, Kt., OBE

Dawbarn, Sir Simon Yelverton, KCVO, CMG

Dawson, *Hon.* Sir Daryl Michael, KBE, CB

Dawson, Sir Nicholas Anthony Trevor, Bt. (1920)

Dawtry, Sir Alan (Graham), Kt., CBE, TD

Day, Sir Barry Stuart, Kt., OBE

Day, *Air Chief Marshal* Sir John Romney, KCB, OBE, ADC

Day, Sir Jonathan Stephen, Kt., CBE

Day, Sir (Judson) Graham, Kt.

Day, Sir Michael John, Kt., OBE

Day, Sir Simon James, Kt.

Day-Lewis, Sir Daniel Michael Blake, Kt.

Deane, *Hon.* Sir William Patrick, KBE

Dearlove, Sir Richard Billing, KCMG, OBE

Deaton, *Prof.* Sir Angus Stewart, Kt.

†Debenham, Sir Thomas Adam, Bt. (1931)

Deegan, Sir Michael, Kt., CBE
Deeny, *Hon.* Sir Donnell Justin Patrick, Kt.
De Haan, Sir Roger Michael, Kt., CBE
De Halpert, *Rear-Adm.* Sir Jeremy Michael, KCVO, CB
de Hoghton, Sir (Richard) Bernard (Cuthbert), Bt. (1611)
de la Rue, Sir Andrew George Ilay, Bt. (1898)
Dellow, Sir John Albert, Kt., CBE
Delves, *Lt.-Gen.* Sir Cedric Norman George, KBE
Denholm, Sir John Ferguson (Ian), Kt., CBE
Denison-Smith, *Lt.-Gen.* Sir Anthony Arthur, KBE
Denny, Sir Charles Alistair Maurice, Bt. (1913)
†Denny, Sir Piers Anthony de Waltham, Bt. (I. 1782)
De Silva, *Rt. Hon.* Sir (George) Desmond Lorenz, Kt., QC
de Trafford, Sir John Humphrey, Bt. (1841)
Devane, Sir Ciaran Gearoid, Kt.
Deverell, *Lt.-Gen.* Sir Christopher Michael, KCB, MBE
Deverell, *Gen.* Sir John Freegard, KCB, OBE
Devereux, Sir Robert, KCB
De Ville, Sir Harold Godfrey Oscar, Kt., CBE
Devine, *Prof.* Sir Thomas Martin, Kt., OBE, FRSE
Devitt, Sir James Hugh Thomas, Bt. (1916)
Dewey, Sir Rupert Grahame, Bt. (1917)
De Witt, Sir Ronald Wayne, Kt.
Diamond, *Prof.* Sir Ian David, Kt., FRSE
Dick-Lauder, Sir Piers Robert, Bt. (S. 1690)
Dilke, Revd Charles John Wentworth, Bt. (1862)
Dilnot, Sir Andrew William, Kt., CBE
Dillon, Sir Andrew Patrick, Kt., CBE
Dilley, Sir Philip Graham, Kt.
Dillwyn-Venables-Llewelyn, Sir John Michael, Bt. (1890)
Dingemans, *Hon.* Sir James Michael, Kt.
Dion, Sir Leo, KBE
Dixon, Sir Jeremy, Kt.
Dixon, Sir Jonathan Mark, Bt. (1919)
Dixon, *Dr* Sir Michael, Kt.
Dixon, Sir Peter John Bellett, Kt.
Djanogly, Sir Harry Ari Simon, Kt., CBE
Dobson, *Vice-Adm.* Sir David Stuart, KBE
Dodd, Sir Kenneth Arthur, Kt., OBE
Dollery, Sir Colin Terence, Kt.
Don-Wauchope, Sir Roger (Hamilton), Bt. (S. 1667)
Donald, Sir Alan Ewen, KCMG
Donaldson, *Prof.* Sir Liam Joseph, Kt.
Donaldson, *Rt. Hon.* Sir Jeffrey Mark, Kt.
Donaldson, *Prof.* Sir Simon Kirwan, Kt.
Donnelly, Sir Joseph Brian, KBE, CMG

Donnelly, Sir Martin Eugene, KCB, CMG
Dorman, Sir Philip Henry Keppel, Bt. (1923)
Douglas, *Prof.* Sir Neil James, Kt.
Douglas, *Hon.* Sir Roger Owen, Kt.
Dove, *Hon.* Sir Ian William, Kt.
Dowell, Sir Anthony James, Kt., CBE
Dowling, Sir Robert, Kt.
Downes, *Prof.* Sir Charles Peter, Kt., OBE, FRSE
Downey, Sir Gordon Stanley, KCB
Doyle, Sir Reginald Derek Henry, Kt., CBE
D'Oyly, Sir Hadley Gregory, Bt. (1663)
Drewry, *Lt.-Gen.* Sir Christopher Francis, KCB, CBE
Drinkwater, Sir John Muir, Kt., QC
Dryden, Sir John Stephen Gyles, Bt. (1733 and 1795)
Duberly, Sir Archibald Hugh, KCVO, CBE
Duckworth, Sir James Edward Dyce, Bt. (1909)
du Cros, Sir Julian Claude Arthur Mallet, Bt. (1916)
Dudley-Williams, Sir Alastair Edgcumbe James, Bt. (1964)
Duff, *Prof.* Sir Gordon William, Kt.
Duff-Gordon, Sir Andrew Cosmo Lewis, Bt. (1813)
Duffell, *Lt.-Gen.* Sir Peter Royson, KCB, CBE, MC
Duffy, Sir (Albert) (Edward) Patrick, Kt., PHD
†Dugdale, Sir (William) Matthew Stratford, Bt. (1936)
Duggin, Sir Thomas Joseph, Kt.
Dunbar, Sir Edward Horace, Bt. (S. 1700)
Dunbar, Sir James Michael, Bt. (S. 1694)
Dunbar, Sir Robert Drummond Cospatrick, Bt. (S. 1698)
Dunbar of Hempriggs, Sir Richard Francis, Bt. (S. 1706)
Dunbar-Nasmith, *Prof.* Sir James Duncan, Kt., CBE
Duncan, *Rt. Hon.* Sir Alan James Carter, KCMG
Duncan, Sir James Blair, Kt.
Dunford, *Dr* Sir John Ernest, Kt., OBE
Dunlop, Sir Thomas, Bt. (1916)
Dunne, Sir Martin, KCVO
Dunne, Sir Thomas Raymond, KG, KCVO
Dunning, Sir Simon William Patrick, Bt. (1930)
Dunnington-Jefferson, Sir John Alexander, Bt. (1958)
Dunstone, Sir Charles William, Kt., CVO
Dunt, *Vice-Adm.* Sir John Hugh, KCB
Duntze, Sir Daniel Evans, Bt. (1774)
Dupre, Sir Tumun, Kt., MBE
Durand, Sir Edward Alan Christopher David Percy, Bt. (1892)
Durie, Sir David Robert Campbell, KCMG
Durrant, Sir William Alexander Estridge, Bt. (1784)
Duthie, Sir Robert Grieve (Robin), Kt., CBE

Dutton, *Lt.-Gen.* Sir James Benjamin, KCB, CBE
Dwyer, Sir Joseph Anthony, Kt.
Dyke, Sir David William Hart, Bt. (1677)
Dymock, *Vice-Adm.* Sir Anthony Knox, KBE, CB
Dyson, Sir James, Kt., OM, CBE
Dyson, *Rt. Hon.* Sir John Anthony, Kt. (Lord Dyson)

Eady, *Hon.* Sir David, Kt.
†Eardley-Wilmot, Sir Benjamin John Assheton, Bt. (1821)
Earle, Sir (Hardman) George (Algernon), Bt. (1869)
Eastwood, *Prof.* Sir David Stephen, Kt.
Eaton, *Adm.* Sir Kenneth John, GBE, KCB
Eberle, *Adm.* Sir James Henry Fuller, GCB
Ebrahim, Sir (Mahomed) Currimbhoy, Bt. (1910)
Eddington, Sir Roderick Ian, Kt.
Eder, *Hon.* Sir Henry Bernard, Kt.
Edis, *Hon.* Sir Andrew Jeremy Coulter, Kt.
Edge, *Capt.* Sir (Philip) Malcolm, KCVO
†Edge, Sir William, Bt. (1937)
Edmonstone, Sir Archibald Bruce Charles, Bt. (1774)
Edward, *Rt. Hon.* Sir David Alexander Ogilvy, KCMG
Edwardes, Sir Michael Owen, Kt.
Edwards, Sir Christopher John Churchill, Bt. (1866)
Edwards, *Prof.* Sir Christopher Richard Watkin, Kt.
Edwards, Sir Gareth Owen, Kt., CBE
Edwards, Sir Llewellyn Roy, Kt.
Edwards, *Prof.* Sir Michael, OBE
Edwards, Sir Robert Paul, Kt.
†Edwards-Moss, Sir David John, Bt. (1868)
Edwards-Stuart, *Hon.* Sir Antony James Cobham, Kt.
Egan, Sir John Leopold, Kt.
Egerton, Sir William de Malpas, Bt. (1617)
Ehrman, Sir William Geoffrey, KCMG
Eichelbaum, *Rt. Hon.* Sir Thomas, GBE
Elder, Sir Mark Philip, Kt., CH, CBE
Eldon, Sir Stewart Graham, KCMG, OBE
Elias, *Rt. Hon.* Sir Patrick, Kt.
Eliott of Stobs, Sir Rodney Gilbert Charles, Bt. (S. 1666)
Elliot, Sir Gerald Henry, Kt.
Elliott, Sir Clive Christopher Hugh, Bt. (1917)
Elliott, Sir David Murray, KCMG, CB
Elliott, *Prof.* Sir John Huxtable, Kt., FBA
Elliott, *Prof.* Sir Roger James, Kt., FRS
Ellis, Sir Herbert Douglas, Kt., OBE
Ellis, Sir Vernon James, Kt.
Ellwood, Sir Peter Brian, Kt., CBE
†Elphinston, Sir Alexander, Bt. (S. 1701)
Elphinstone, Sir John Howard Main, Bt. (1816)
Elton, Sir Arnold, Kt., CBE

Elton, Sir Charles Abraham Grierson, Bt. (1717)
Elvidge, Sir John, KCB
Elwes, Dr Sir Henry William, KCVO
Elwes, Sir Jeremy Vernon, Kt., CBE
Elwood, Sir Brian George Conway, Kt., CBE
Elworthy, Air Cdre. Hon. Sir Timothy Charles, KCVO, CBE
Enderby, Prof. Sir John Edwin, Kt. CBE, FRS
English, Sir Terence Alexander Hawthorne, KBE, FRCS
Ennals, Sir Paul Martin, Kt., CBE
Epstein, Prof. Sir (Michael) Anthony, Kt., CBE, FRS
Errington, Sir Robin Davenport, Bt. (1963)
Erskine, Sir (Thomas) Peter Neil, Bt. (1821)
Erskine-Hill, Sir Alexander Roger, Bt. (1945)
Esmonde, Sir Thomas Francis Grattan, Bt. (I. 1629)
†Esplen, Sir William John Harry, Bt. (1921)
Esquivel, Rt. Hon. Sir Manuel, KCMG
Essenhigh, Adm. Sir Nigel Richard, GCB
Etherington, Sir Stuart James, Kt.
Etherton, Rt. Hon. Sir Terence Michael Elkan Barnet, Kt.
Evans, Rt. Hon. Sir Anthony Howell Meurig, Kt., RD
Evans, Prof. Sir Christopher Thomas, Kt., OBE
Evans, Air Chief Marshal Sir David George, GCB, CBE
Evans, Hon. Sir David Roderick, Kt.
Evans, Sir Harold Matthew, Kt.
Evans, Prof. Sir John Grimley, Kt., FRCP
Evans, Sir John Stanley, Kt., QPM
Evans, Sir Malcolm David, KCMG, OBE
Evans, Prof. Sir Martin John, Kt., FRS
Evans, Sir Richard Harry, Kt., CBE
Evans, Prof. Sir Richard John, Kt.
Evans, Sir Robert, Kt., CBE, FRENG
Evans-Lombe, Hon. Sir Edward Christopher, Kt.
†Evans-Tipping, Sir David Gwynne, Bt. (1913)
Everard, Sir Henry Peter Charles, Bt. (1911)
Everard, Lt.-Gen. Sir James Rupert, KCB, CBE
Everington, Dr Sir Anthony Herbert, Kt., OBE
Every, Sir Henry John Michael, Bt. (1641)
Ewart, Sir William Michael, Bt. (1887)
Eyre, Sir Reginald Edwin, Kt.
Eyre, Sir Richard Charles Hastings, Kt., CH, CBE

Fagge, Sir John Christopher Frederick, Bt. (1660)
Fahy, Sir Peter, Kt., QPM
†Fairbairn, Sir Robert William, Bt. (1869)
Fairlie-Cuninghame, Sir Robert Henry, Bt. (S. 1630)

Fairweather, Sir Patrick Stanislaus, KCMG
Faldo, Sir Nicholas Alexander, Kt., MBE
†Falkiner, Sir Benjamin Simon Patrick, Bt. (I. 1778)
Fall, Sir Brian James Proetel, GCVO, KCMG
Fallon, Rt. Hon. Sir Michael Cathel, KCB
Fang, Prof. Sir Harry, Kt., CBE
Farah, Sir Mohamed (Mo) Muktar Jama, Kt., CBE
Fareed, Sir Djamil Sheik, Kt.
Farmer, Sir Thomas, Kt., CVO, CBE
Farquhar, Sir Michael Fitzroy Henry, Bt. (1796)
Farquharson, Sir Angus Durie Miller, KCVO, OBE
Farrell, Sir Terence, Kt., CBE
Farrer, Sir (Charles) Matthew, GCVO
Farrington, Sir Henry William, Bt. (1818)
Faull, Sir Jonathan Michael Howard, KCMG
Fay, Sir (Humphrey) Michael Gerard, Kt.
Feachem, Prof. Sir Richard George Andrew, KBE
Fean, Sir Thomas Vincent, KCVO
Feilden, Sir Henry Rudyard, Bt. (1846)
Feldmann, Prof. Sir Marc, Kt.
Fell, Sir David, KCB
Fender, Sir Brian Edward Frederick, Kt., CMG, PHD
Fenwick, Sir Leonard Raymond, Kt., CBE
Fergus, Sir Howard Archibald, KBE
Ferguson, Sir Alexander Chapman, Kt., CBE
Ferguson-Davie, Sir Michael, Bt. (1847)
Fergusson, Rt. Hon. Sir Alexander Charles Onslow, Kt.
Fergusson of Kilkerran, Sir Charles, Bt. (S. 1703)
Ferris, Hon. Sir Francis Mursell, Kt., TD
Fersht, Prof. Sir Alan Roy, Kt., FRS
ffolkes, Sir Robert Francis Alexander, Bt. (1774), OBE
Field, Sir Malcolm David, Kt.
Field, Hon. Sir Richard Alan, Kt.
Fielding, Sir Leslie, KCMG
Fields, Sir Allan Clifford, KCMG
Fiennes, Sir Ranulph Twisleton-Wykeham, Bt. (1916), OBE
Figgis, Sir Anthony St John Howard, KCVO, CMG
Finlay, Sir David Ronald James Bell, Bt. (1964)
Finlayson, Sir Garet Orlando, KCMG, OBE
Fish, Prof. Sir David Royden, Kt.
†Fison, Sir Charles William, Bt. (1905)
Fittall, Sir William Robert, Kt.
FitzGerald, Sir Adrian James Andrew Denis, Bt. (1880)
†Fitzgerald, Sir Andrew Peter, Bt. (1903)
FitzHerbert, Sir Richard Ranulph, Bt. (1784)

Fitzpatrick, Air Marshal Sir John Bernard, KBE, CB
Flanagan, Sir Ronald, GBE, QPM
Flaux, Rt. Hon. Sir Julian Martin, Kt.
Floud, Prof. Sir Roderick Castle, Kt.
Floyd, Rt. Hon. Sir Christopher David, Kt.
Floyd, Sir Giles Henry Charles, Bt. (1816)
Foley, Lt.-Gen. Sir John Paul, KCB, OBE, MC
Follett, Prof. Sir Brian Keith, Kt., FRS
Forbes of Craigievar, Sir Andrew Iain Ochoncar, Bt. (S. 1630)
Forbes, Adm. Sir Ian Andrew, KCB, CBE
Forbes, Sir James Thomas Stewart, Bt. (1823)
Forbes, Vice-Adm. Sir John Morrison, KCB
Forbes, Hon. Sir Thayne John, Kt.
†Forbes Adam, Revd Stephen Timothy Beilby, Bt. (1917)
Forbes-Leith, Sir George Ian David, Bt. (1923)
Ford, Lt.-Col. Sir Andrew Charles, KCVO
Ford, Sir Andrew Russell, Bt. (1929)
Ford, Sir John Archibald, KCMG, MC
Forestier-Walker, Sir Michael Leolin, Bt. (1835)
Forrest, Prof. Sir (Andrew) Patrick (McEwen), Kt.
Forte, Hon. Sir Rocco John Vincent, Kt.
Forwood, Hon. Sir Nicholas James, Kt., QC
Forwood, Sir Peter Noel, Bt. (1895)
Foskett, Hon. Sir David Robert, Kt.
Foster, Sir Andrew William, Kt.
Foster, Prof. Sir Christopher David, Kt.
Foster, Sir Saxby Gregory, Bt. (1930)
Foulkes, Sir Arthur Alexander, GCMG
Fountain, Hon. Sir Cyril Stanley Smith, Kt.
Fowke, Sir David Frederick Gustavus, Bt. (1814)
Fowler, Sir (Edward) Michael Coulson, Kt.
Fox, Sir Christopher, Kt., QPM
Fox, Sir Paul Leonard, Kt., CBE
Francis, Sir Horace William Alexander, Kt., CBE, FRENG
Francis, Hon. Sir Peter Nicholas, Kt.
Francis, Sir Robert Anthony, Kt., QC
Frank, Sir Robert Andrew, Bt. (1920)
Franklin, Sir Michael David Milroy, KCB, CMG
Fraser, Sir Charles Annand, KCVO
Fraser, Sir Iain Michael Duncan, Bt. (1943)
Fraser, Sir James Murdo, KBE
Fraser, Hon. Sir Peter Donald, Kt.
Fraser, Sir Simon James, GCMG
Fraser, Sir William Kerr, GCB
Frayling, Prof. Sir Christopher John, Kt.
Frederick, Sir Christopher St John, Bt. (1723)
Freedman, Rt. Hon. Prof. Sir Lawrence David, KCMG, CBE
Freeman, Sir James Robin, Bt. (1945)
French, Air Marshal Sir Joseph Charles, KCB, CBE

Frere, *Vice-Adm.* Sir Richard Tobias, KCB

Friend, *Prof.* Sir Richard Henry, Kt.

Froggatt, Sir Peter, Kt.

Fry, Sir Graham Holbrook, KCMG

Fry, *Lt.-Gen.* Sir Robert Allan, KCB, CBE

Fry, *Dr* Sir Roger Gordon, Kt., CBE

Fulford, *Rt. Hon.* Sir Adrian Bruce, Kt.

Fuller, Sir James Henry Fleetwood, Bt. (1910)

Fulton, *Lt.-Gen.* Sir Robert Henry Gervase, KBE

Furness, Sir Stephen Roberts, Bt. (1913)

Gage, *Rt. Hon.* Sir William Marcus, Kt, QC

Gains, Sir John Christopher, Kt.

Gainsford, Sir Ian Derek, Kt.

Gale, Sir Roger James, Kt.

Galsworthy, Sir Anthony Charles, KCMG

Galway, Sir James, Kt., OBE

Gamble, Sir David Hugh Norman, Bt. (1897)

Gambon, Sir Michael John, Kt., CBE

Gammell, Sir William Benjamin Bowring, Kt.

Gardiner, Sir John Eliot, Kt., CBE

Gardner, *Prof.* Sir Richard Lavenham, Kt.

Gardner, Sir Roy Alan, Kt.

Garland, *Hon.* Sir Patrick Neville, Kt.

Garland, *Hon.* Sir Ransley Victor, KBE

Garland, *Dr* Sir Trevor, KBE

Garnett, *Adm.* Sir Ian David Graham, KCB

Garnham, *Hon.* Sir Neil Stephen, Kt.

Garnier, Sir Edward Henry, Kt., QC

Garnier, *Rear-Adm.* Sir John, KCVO, CBE

Garrard, Sir David Eardley, Kt.

Garrett, Sir Anthony Peter, Kt., CBE

Garrick, Sir Ronald, Kt., CBE, FRENG

Garthwaite, Sir (William) Mark (Charles), Bt. (1919)

Garwood, *Air Marshal* Sir Richard Frank, KBE, CB, DFC

Gass, Sir Simon Lawrance, KCMG, CVO

Geidt, *Rt. Hon.* Sir Christopher, KCB, KCVO, OBE

Geim, *Prof.* Sir Andre Konstantin, Kt.

Geno, Sir Makena Viora, KBE

Gent, Sir Christopher Charles, Kt.

George, *Prof.* Sir Charles Frederick, Kt., MD, FRCP

Gerken, *Vice-Adm.* Sir Robert William Frank, KCB, CBE

Gershon, Sir Peter Oliver, Kt., CBE

Gethin, Sir Richard Joseph St Lawrence, Bt. (I. 1665)

Gibbings, Sir Peter Walter, Kt.

Gibbons, Sir William Edward Doran, Bt. (1752)

Gibbs, *Hon.* Sir Richard John Hedley, Kt.

Gibbs, Sir Roger Geoffrey, Kt.

†Gibson, *Revd* Christopher Herbert, Bt. (1931)

Gibson, Sir Ian, Kt., CBE

Gibson, Sir Kenneth Archibald, Kt.

Gibson, *Rt. Hon.* Sir Peter Leslie, Kt.

Gibson-Craig-Carmichael, Sir David Peter William, Bt. (S. 1702 and 1831)

Gieve, Sir Edward John Watson, KCB

Giffard, Sir (Charles) Sydney (Rycroft), KCMG

Gifford, Sir Michael Roger, Kt.

Gilbart, *Hon.* Sir Andrew James, Kt.

Gilbart-Denham, *Lt.-Col.* Sir Seymour Vivian, KCVO

Gilbert, *Air Chief Marshal* Sir Joseph Alfred, KCB, CBE

†Gilbey, Sir Walter Gavin, Bt. (1893)

Gill, Sir Anthony Keith, Kt.

Gill, Sir Robin Denys, KCVO

Gillam, Sir Patrick John, Kt.

Gillen, *Hon.* Sir John de Winter, Kt.

Gillett, Sir Nicholas Danvers Penrose, Bt. (1959)

Gillinson, Sir Clive Daniel, Kt., CBE

Gilmore, *Prof.* Sir Ian Thomas, Kt.

Gilmour, *Hon.* Sir David Robert, Bt. (1926)

Gilmour, Sir John Nicholas, Bt. (1897)

Gina, Sir Lloyd Maepeza, KBE

Giordano, Sir Richard Vincent, KBE

Girolami, Sir Paul, Kt.

Girvan, *Rt. Hon.* Sir (Frederick) Paul, Kt.

Gladstone, Sir (Erskine) William, Bt. (1846), KG

Glean, Sir Carlyle Arnold, GCMG

Globe, *Hon.* Sir Henry Brian, Kt.

Glover, Sir Victor Joseph Patrick, Kt.

Glyn, Sir Richard Lindsay, Bt. (1759 and 1800)

Gobbo, Sir James Augustine, Kt., AC

Godfray, *Prof.* Sir Hugh Charles Jonathan, Kt., CBE

Goldberg, *Prof.* Sir David Paul Brandes, Kt.

Goldring, *Rt. Hon.* Sir John Bernard, Kt.

Gomersall, Sir Stephen John, KCMG

Gonsalves-Sabola, *Hon.* Sir Joaquim Claudino, Kt

Gooch, Sir Arthur Brian Sherlock Heywood, Bt. (1746)

Gooch, Sir Miles Peter, Bt. (1866)

Good, Sir John James Griffen, Kt., CBE

Goodall, *Air Marshal* Sir Roderick Harvey, KBE, CB, AFC

Goode, *Prof.* Sir Royston Miles, Kt., CBE, QC

Goodenough, Sir Anthony Michael, KCMG

Goodenough, Sir William McLernon, Bt. (1943)

Goodhart, Sir Robert Anthony Gordon, Bt. (1911)

Goodison, Sir Nicholas Proctor, Kt.

Goodson, Sir Alan Reginald, Bt. (1922)

Goodwin, Sir Frederick, KBE

Goold, Sir George William, Bt. (1801)

Gordon, Sir Donald, Kt.

Gordon, Sir Gerald Henry, Kt., CBE, QC

Gordon, Sir Robert James, Bt. (S. 1706)

Gordon-Cumming, Sir Alexander Alastair Penrose, Bt. (1804)

Gore, Sir Hugh Frederick Corbet, Bt. (I. 1622)

Gore-Booth, Sir Josslyn Henry Robert, Bt. (I. 1760)

Goring, Sir William Burton Nigel, Bt. (1678)

Gormley, Sir Antony Mark David, Kt., OBE

Gormley, Sir Paul Brendan, KCMG, MBE

Goschen, Sir (Edward) Alexander, Bt. (1916)

Gosling, Sir (Frederick) Donald, KCVO

Goss, *Hon.* Sir James Richard William, Kt.

Goulden, Sir (Peter) John, GCMG

Goulding, Sir (William) Lingard Walter, Bt. (1904)

Gourlay, Sir Simon Alexander, Kt.

Gowans, Sir James Learmonth, Kt., CBE, FRCP, FRS

Gowers, *Prof.* Sir William Timothy, Kt.

Gozney, Sir Richard Hugh Turton, KCMG

Graaff, Sir De Villiers, Bt. (1911)

Graham, Sir Alexander Michael, GBE

Graham, Sir James Bellingham, Bt. (1662)

Graham, Sir James Fergus Surtees, Bt. (1783)

Graham, Sir James Thompson, Kt., CMG

Graham, Sir John Alexander Noble, Bt. (1906), GCMG

Graham, Sir John Alistair, Kt.

Graham, Sir John Moodie, Bt. (1964)

Graham, Sir Peter, KCB, QC

Graham, *Lt.-Gen.* Sir Peter Walter, KCB, CBE

†Graham, Sir Ralph Stuart, Bt. (1629)

Graham-Moon, Sir Peter Wilfred Giles, Bt. (1855)

Graham-Smith, *Prof.* Sir Francis, Kt.

Grainge, Sir Lucian Charles, Kt., CBE

Grange, Sir Kenneth Henry, Kt., CBE

Grant, Sir Archibald, Bt. (S. 1705)

Grant, *Dr* Sir David, Kt., CBE

Grant, Sir Ian David, Kt., CBE

Grant, Sir John Douglas Kelso, KCMG

Grant, *Prof.* Sir Malcolm John, Kt., CBE

Grant, Sir Patrick Alexander Benedict, Bt. (S. 1688)

Grant, Sir Paul Joseph Patrick, Kt.

Grant, *Lt.-Gen.* Sir Scott Carnegie, KCB

Grant-Suttie, Sir James Edward, Bt. (S. 1702)

Granville-Chapman, *Gen.* Sir Timothy John, GBE, KCB, ADC

Grattan-Bellew, Sir Henry Charles, Bt. (1838)

Gray, Sir Bernard Peter, Kt.

Gray, *Hon.* Sir Charles Anthony St John, Kt.

Gray, Sir Charles Ireland, Kt., CBE

Gray, *Prof.* Sir Denis John Pereira, Kt., OBE, FRCGP

Gray, *Dr* Sir John Armstrong Muir, Kt., CBE

Gray, Sir Robert McDowall (Robin), Kt.

Gray, Sir William Hume, Bt. (1917)

Graydon, *Air Chief Marshal* Sir Michael James, GCB, CBE

Grayson, Sir Jeremy Brian Vincent Harrington, Bt. (1922)

Green, Sir Allan David, KCB, QC

Green, Sir Edward Patrick Lycett, Bt. (1886)

Green, Sir Gregory David, KCMG

Green, *Hon.* Sir Guy Stephen Montague, KBE

Green, *Prof.* Sir Malcolm, Kt.

Green, *Hon.* Sir Nicholas Nigel, Kt.

Green, Sir Philip Green, Kt.

Green-Price, Sir Robert John, Bt. (1874)

Greenaway, *Prof.* Sir David, Kt.

Greenaway, Sir Thomas Edward Burdick, Bt. (1933)

Greenbury, Sir Richard, Kt.

Greener, Sir Anthony Armitage, Kt.

Greengross, Sir Alan David, Kt.

Greenstock, Sir Jeremy Quentin, GCMG

Greenwell, Sir Edward Bernard, Bt. (1906)

Greenwood, *Prof.* Sir Brian Mellor, Kt., CBE

Greenwood, *Prof.* Sir Christopher John, Kt., CMG

Gregory, *Lt.-Gen.* Sir Andrew Richard, KBE, CB

Gregory, *Prof.* Sir Michael John, Kt., CBE

Gregson, Sir Peter Lewis, GCB

Grey, Sir Anthony Dysart, Bt. (1814)

Grice, Sir Paul Edward, Kt.

Griffiths, Sir Michael, Kt.

Grigson, *Hon.* Sir Geoffrey Douglas, Kt.

Grimshaw, Sir Nicholas Thomas, Kt., CBE

Grimstone, Sir Gerald Edgar, Kt.

Grimwade, Sir Andrew Sheppard, Kt., CBE

Grose, *Vice-Adm.* Sir Alan, KBE

Gross, *Rt. Hon.* Sir Peter Henry, Kt.

Grossart, Sir Angus McFarlane McLeod, Kt., CBE

Grotrian, Sir Philip Christian Brent, Bt. (1934)

Grove, Sir Charles Gerald, Bt. (1874)

Grundy, Sir Mark, Kt.

Guinness, Sir Howard Christian Sheldon, Kt., VRD

Guinness, Sir John Ralph Sidney, Kt., CB

Guinness, Sir Kenelm Edward Lee, Bt. (1867)

Guise, Sir Christopher James, Bt. (1783)

Gull, Sir Rupert William Cameron, Bt. (1872)

Gumbs, Sir Emile Rudolph, Kt.

Gunning, Sir Charles Theodore, Bt. (1778)

Gunston, Sir John Wellesley, Bt. (1938)

Gurdon, *Prof.* Sir John Bertrand, Kt., DPHIL, FRS

Guthrie, Sir Malcolm Connop, Bt. (1936)

Haddacks, *Vice-Adm.* Sir Paul Kenneth, KCB

Haddon-Cave, *Hon.* Sir Charles Anthony, Kt.

Hadlee, Sir Richard John, Kt., MBE

Hagart-Alexander, Sir Claud, Bt. (1886)

Haines, *Prof.* Sir Andrew Paul, Kt.

Haji-Ioannou, Sir Stelios, Kt.

Halberg, Sir Murray Gordon, Kt., MBE

Hall, *Dr* Sir Andrew James, Kt.

Hall, Sir David Christopher, Bt. (1923)

Hall, *Prof.* Sir David Michael Baldock, Kt.

Hall, Sir Ernest, Kt., OBE

Hall, Sir Geoffrey, Kt.

Hall, Sir Graham Joseph, Kt.

Hall, Sir Iain Robert, Kt.

Hall, Sir John, Kt.

Hall, Sir John Bernard, Bt. (1919)

Hall, Sir John Douglas Hoste, Bt. (S. 1687)

Hall, HE *Prof.* Sir Kenneth Octavius, GCMG

Hall, Sir Peter Edward, KBE, CMG

Hall, *Revd* Wesley Winfield, Kt.

Hall, Sir William Joseph, KCVO

Halpern, Sir Ralph Mark, Kt.

Halsey, *Revd* John Walter Brooke, Bt. (1920)

Halstead, Sir Ronald, Kt., CBE

Hamblen, *Rt. Hon.* Sir Nicholas Archibald, Kt.

Hambling, Sir Herbert Peter Hugh, Bt. (1924)

Hamilton, Sir Andrew Caradoc, Bt. (S. 1646)

Hamilton, Sir David, Kt.

Hamilton, Sir Nigel, KCB

Hamilton-Dalrymple, *Maj.* Sir Hew Fleetwood, Bt. (S. 1698), GCVO

Hamilton-Spencer-Smith, Sir John, Bt. (1804)

Hammick, Sir Jeremy Charles, Bt. (1834)

Hammond, Sir Anthony Hilgrove, KCB, QC

Hampel, Sir Ronald Claus, Kt.

Hampson, Sir Stuart, Kt., CVO

Hampton, Sir (Leslie) Geoffrey, Kt.

Hampton, Sir Philip Roy, Kt.

Hanham, Sir William John Edward, Bt. (1667)

Hankes-Drielsma, Sir Claude Dunbar, KCVO

Hanley, *Rt. Hon.* Sir Jeremy James, KCMG

Hanmer, Sir Wyndham Richard Guy, Bt. (1774)

Hannam, Sir John Gordon, Kt.

Hanson, Sir (Charles) Rupert (Patrick), Bt. (1918)

Harcourt-Smith, *Air Chief Marshal* Sir David, GBE, KCB, DFC

Hardie Boys, *Rt. Hon.* Sir Michael, GCMG

Harding, *Marshal of the Royal Air Force* Sir Peter Robin, GCB

Hardy, Sir David William, Kt.

Hardy, Sir James Gilbert, Kt., OBE

Hardy, Sir Richard Charles Chandos, Bt. (1876)

Hare, Sir David, Kt., FRSL

Hare, Sir Nicholas Patrick, Bt. (1818)

Haren, *Dr* Sir Patrick Hugh, Kt.

Harford, Sir Mark John, Bt. (1934)

Harington, Sir David Richard, Bt. (1611)

Harkness, *Very Revd* James, KCVO, CB, OBE

Harley, *Gen.* Sir Alexander George Hamilton, KBE, CB

Harman, *Hon.* Sir Jeremiah LeRoy, Kt.

Harman, Sir John Andrew, Kt.

Harmsworth, Sir Hildebrand Harold, Bt. (1922)

Harper, *Air Marshal* Sir Christopher Nigel, KBE

Harper, Sir Ewan William, Kt., CBE

Harper, *Prof.* Sir Peter Stanley, Kt., CBE

Harris, Sir Christopher John Ashford, Bt. (1932)

Harris, *Air Marshal* Sir John Hulme, KCB, CBE

Harris, *Prof.* Sir Martin Best, Kt., CBE

Harris, Sir Michael Frank, Kt.

Harris, Sir (Theodore) Wilson, Kt.

Harris, Sir Thomas George, KBE, CMG

Harrison, *Prof.* Sir Brian Howard, Kt.

Harrison, Sir David, Kt., CBE, FRENG

Harrison, *Hon.* Sir Michael Guy Vicat, Kt.

Harrison, Sir Michael James Harwood, Bt. (1961)

Harrison, Sir (Robert) Colin, Bt. (1922)

Harrison, Sir Terence, Kt., FRENG

Harrop, Sir Peter John, KCB

Hart, *Hon.* Sir Anthony Ronald, Kt.

Hart, Sir Graham Allan, KCB

Hartwell, Sir (Francis) Anthony Charles Peter, Bt. (1805)

Harvey, Sir Charles Richard Musgrave, Bt. (1933)

Harvey, Sir Nicholas Barton, Kt.

Harvie, Sir John Smith, Kt., CBE

Harvie-Watt, Sir James, Bt. (1945)

Harwood, Sir Ronald, Kt., CBE

Haselhurst, *Rt. Hon.* Sir Alan Gordon Barraclough, Kt.

Hastie, *Cdre* Sir Robert Cameron, KCVO, CBE, RD

Hastings, Sir Max Macdonald, Kt.

Hastings, *Dr* Sir William George, Kt., CBE

Hatter, Sir Maurice, Kt.

Havelock-Allan, Sir (Anthony) Mark David, Bt. (1858), QC

Hawkes, Sir John Garry, Kt., CBE

Hawkhead, Sir Anthony Gerard, Kt., CBE

Hawkins, Sir Richard Caesar, Bt. (1778)

Hawley, Sir James Appleton, KCVO, TD

Haworth, Sir Philip, Bt. (1911)

Hay, Sir John Erroll Audley, Bt. (S. 1663)

†Hay, Sir Ronald Frederick Hamilton, Bt. (S. 1703)

Hayden, *Hon.* Sir Anthony Paul, Kt.

Hayes, Sir Brian, Kt., CBE, QPM

Hayes, Sir Brian David, GCB

Hayman-Joyce, *Lt.-Gen.* Sir Robert John, KCB, CBE

Hayter, Sir Paul David Grenville, KCB, LVO

Head, Sir Patrick, Kt.

Head, Sir Richard Douglas Somerville, Bt. (1838)

Heald, *Rt. Hon.* Sir Oliver, Kt.

Heap, Sir Peter William, KCMG

Heap, *Prof.* Sir Robert Brian, Kt., CBE, FRS

Hearne, Sir Graham James, Kt., CBE

Heathcote, Sir Simon Robert Mark, Bt. (1733), OBE

†Heathcote, Sir Timothy Gilbert, Bt. (1733)

Heber-Percy, Sir Algernon Eustace Hugh, KCVO

Hedley, *Hon.* Sir Mark, Kt.

Hegarty, Sir John Kevin, Kt.

Heiser, Sir Terence Michael, GCB

Heller, Sir Michael Aron, Kt.

Hempleman-Adams, *Dr* Sir David Kim, KCVO, OBE

Henderson, *Rt Hon.* Sir Launcelot Dinadin James, Kt.

Henderson, *Maj.* Sir Richard Yates, KCVO

Hendry, *Prof.* Sir David Forbes, Kt.

Hendy, Sir Peter Gerard, Kt., CBE

Hennessy, Sir James Patrick Ivan, KBE, CMG

†Henniker, Sir Adrian Chandos, Bt. (1813)

Henniker-Heaton, Sir Yvo Robert, Bt. (1912)

Henriques, *Hon.* Sir Richard Henry Quixano, Kt.

Henry, Sir Lenworth George, Kt., CBE

†Henry, Sir Patrick Denis, Bt. (1923)

Henshaw, Sir David George, Kt.

Herbecq, Sir John Edward, KCB

Herbert, *Adm.* Sir Peter Geoffrey Marshall, KCB, OBE

Heron, Sir Conrad Frederick, KCB, OBE

†Heron-Maxwell, Sir Nigel Mellor, Bt. (S. 1683)

Hervey, Sir Roger Blaise Ramsay, KCVO, CMG

Hervey-Bathurst, Sir Frederick William John, Bt. (1818)

Heseltine, *Rt. Hon.* Sir William Frederick Payne, GCB, GCVO

Hewetson, Sir Christopher Raynor, Kt., TD

Hewett, Sir Richard Mark John, Bt. (1813)

Hewitt, Sir (Cyrus) Lenox (Simson), Kt., OBE

Hewitt, Sir Nicholas Charles Joseph, Bt. (1921)

Heygate, Sir Richard John Gage, Bt. (1831)

Heywood, Sir Jeremy John, KCB, CVO

Heywood, Sir Peter, Bt. (1838)

Hickey, Sir John Tongri, Kt., CBE

Hickinbottom, *Rt. Hon.* Sir Gary Robert, Kt.

Hickman, Sir (Richard) Glenn, Bt. (1903)

Hicks, Sir Robert, Kt.

Hielscher, Sir Leo Arthur, Kt.

Higgins, Sir David Hartmann, Kt.

Higgins, *Rt. Hon.* Sir Malachy Joseph, Kt.

Hildyard, *Hon.* Sir Robert Henry Thoroton, Kt.

Hill, Sir Brian John, Kt.

Hill, *Rt. Revd Dr* Christopher John, KCVO

Hill, Sir James Frederick, Bt. (1917), OBE

Hill, Sir John Alfred Rowley, Bt. (I. 1779)

Hill, *Vice-Adm.* Sir Robert Charles Finch, KBE, FRENG

Hill-Norton, *Vice-Adm. Hon.* Sir Nicholas John, KCB

Hill-Wood, Sir Samuel Thomas, Bt. (1921)

Hillhouse, Sir (Robert) Russell, KCB

Hillier, *Air Marshal* Sir Stephen John, KCB, CBE, DFC

Hills, Sir John Robert, Kt., CBE

Hilly, Sir Francis Billy, KCMG

Hine, *Air Chief Marshal* Sir Patrick Bardon, GCB, GBE

Hintze, Sir Michael, Kt.

Hirsch, *Prof.* Sir Peter Bernhard, Kt., PHD, FRS

Hirst, Sir Michael William, Kt.

Hoare, *Prof.* Sir Charles Anthony Richard, Kt., FRS

Hoare, Sir Charles James, Bt. (I. 1784)

Hoare, Sir David John, Bt. (1786)

Hobart, Sir John Vere, Bt. (1914)

Hobbs, *Maj.-Gen.* Sir Michael Frederick, KCVO, CBE

Hobhouse, Sir Charles John Spinney, Bt. (1812)

†Hodge, Sir Andrew Rowland, Bt. (1921)

Hodge, Sir James William, KCVO, CMG

Hodgkinson, Sir Michael Stewart, Kt.

Hodson, Sir Michael Robin Adderley, Bt. (I. 1789)

Hogan-Howe, Sir Bernard, Kt., QPM

Hogg, Sir Christopher Anthony, Kt.

Hogg, Sir Piers Michael James, Bt. (1846)

Hohn, Sir Christopher, KCMG

Holcroft, Sir Charles Anthony Culcheth, Bt. (1921)

Holden, Sir John David, Bt. (1919)

Holden, Sir Paul, Bt. (1893)

Holden-Brown, Sir Derrick, Kt.

Holder, Sir John Henry, Bt. (1898)

Holderness, Sir Martin William, Bt. (1920)

Holdgate, Sir Martin Wyatt, Kt., CB, PHD

Holgate, *Hon.* Sir David John, Kt.

Holland, *Hon.* Sir Christopher John, Kt.

Holland, Sir John Anthony, Kt.

Holm, Sir Ian (Holm Cuthbert), Kt.,CBE

Holman, *Hon.* Sir Edward James, Kt.

Holman, *Prof.* Sir John Stranger, Kt.

Holmes, Sir John Eaton, GCVO, KBE, CMG

Holroyd, Sir Michael De Courcy Fraser, Kt., CBE

Holroyde, *Hon.* Sir Timothy Victor, Kt.

Home, Sir William Dundas, Bt. (S. 1671)

Honywood, Sir Filmer Courtenay William, Bt. (1660)

†Hood, Sir John Joseph Harold, Bt. (1922)

Hooper, *Rt. Hon.* Sir Anthony, Kt.

Hope, Sir Alexander Archibald Douglas, Bt. (S. 1628), OBE

Hope-Dunbar, Sir David, Bt. (S. 1664)

Hopkin, *Prof.* Sir Deian Rhys, Kt.

Hopkin, Sir Royston Oliver, KCMG

Hopkins, Sir Anthony Philip, Kt., CBE

Hopkins, Sir Michael John, Kt., CBE, RA, RIBA

Hopwood, *Prof.* Sir David Alan, Kt., FRS

Hordern, *Rt. Hon.* Sir Peter Maudslay, Kt.

Horlick, *Vice-Adm.* Sir Edwin John, KBE, FRENG

Horlick, Sir James Cunliffe William, Bt. (1914)

Horn-Smith, Sir Julian Michael, Kt.

Horne, Sir Alan Gray Antony, Bt. (1929)

Horner, *Hon.* Sir Thomas Mark, Kt.

Horsbrugh-Porter, Sir Andrew Alexander Marshall, Bt. (1902)

Horsfall, Sir Edward John Wright, Bt. (1909)

Hort, Sir Andrew Edwin Fenton, Bt. (1767)

Hosker, Sir Gerald Albery, KCB, QC

Hoskins, *Prof.* Sir Brian John, Kt., CBE, FRS

Hoskyns, Sir Robin Chevallier, Bt. (1676)

Hotung, Sir Joseph Edward, Kt.

Houghton, *Gen.* Sir John Nicholas Reynolds, GCB, CBE

Houghton, Sir John Theodore, Kt., CBE, FRS

Houghton, Sir Stephen Geoffrey, Kt., CBE

Houldsworth, Sir Richard Thomas Reginald, Bt. (1887)

Hourston, Sir Gordon Minto, Kt.

Housden, Sir Peter James, KCB

House, Sir Stephen, Kt., QPM

Houssemayne du Boulay, Sir Roger William, KCVO, CMG

Houstoun-Boswall, Sir (Thomas) Alford, Bt. (1836)

Howard, Sir David Howarth Seymour, Bt. (1955)

Howard, *Dr* Sir Laurence, KCVO, OBE

Howard, *Prof.* Sir Michael Eliot, Kt., OM, CH, CBE, MC

Howard-Lawson, Sir John Philip, Bt. (1841)

Howarth, Sir (James) Gerald Douglas, Kt.

Howells, Sir Eric Waldo Benjamin, Kt., CBE

Howes, Sir Christopher Kingston, KCVO, CB

Howlett, *Gen.* Sir Geoffrey Hugh Whitby, KBE, MC

Hoy, Sir Christopher Andrew, Kt., MBE

Hudson, Sir Mark, KCVO

Hugh-Jones, Sir Wynn Normington, Kt., LVO

Hughes, *Rt. Hon.* Sir Anthony Philip Gilson, Kt. (Lord Hughes of Ombersley)

Hughes, *Rt. Hon.* Sir Simon Henry Ward, Kt.

Hughes, Sir Thomas Collingwood, Bt. (1773)

Hughes, Sir Trevor Poulton, KCB

Hughes-Hallett, Sir Thomas Michael Sydney, Kt.

Hughes-Morgan, Sir (Ian) Parry David, Bt. (1925)

Hull, *Prof.* Sir David, Kt.

Hulme, Sir Philip William, Kt.

Hulse, Sir Edward Jeremy Westrow, Bt. (1739)

Hum, Sir Christopher Owen, KCMG

Humphreys, *Prof.* Sir Colin John, Kt., CBE

Hunt, Sir John Leonard, Kt.

Hunt, *Dr* Sir Richard Timothy, Kt.

Hunt-Davis, *Brig.* Sir Miles Garth, GCVO, CBE

Hunte, *Hon. Dr* Sir Julian Robert, KCMG, OBE

Hunter, Sir Alistair John, KCMG

Hunter, *Prof.* Sir Laurence Colvin, Kt., CBE, FRSE

Hunter, *Dr* Sir Philip John, Kt., CBE

Hunter, Sir Thomas Blane, Kt.

Huntington-Whiteley, Sir John Miles, Bt. (1918), VRD

Hurn, Sir (Francis) Roger, Kt.

Hurst, Sir Geoffrey Charles, Kt., MBE

Husbands, Sir Clifford Straugh, GCMG

Hutchison, Sir Peter Craft, Bt. (1956), CBE

Hutchison, *Rt. Hon.* Sir Michael, Kt.

Hutchison, Sir Robert, Bt. (1939)

Hutt, Sir Dexter Walter, Kt.

Huxtable, *Gen.* Sir Charles Richard, KCB, CBE

Hytner, Sir Nicholas, Kt.

Iacobescu, Sir George, Kt., CBE

Ibbotson, *Vice-Adm.* Sir Richard Jeffrey, KBE, CB, DSC

Ife, *Prof.* Sir Barry William, Kt., CBE

Imbert-Terry, Sir Michael Edward Stanley, Bt. (1917)

Imray, Sir Colin Henry, KBE, CMG

Ingham, Sir Bernard, Kt.

Ingilby, Sir Thomas Colvin William, Bt. (1866)

Inglis of Glencorse, Sir Roderick John, Bt. (S. 1703)

Ingram, Sir James Herbert Charles, Bt. (1893)

Innes, Sir Alastair Charles Deverell, Bt. (NS 1686)

Innes of Edingight, Sir Malcolm Rognvald, KCVO

Innes, Sir Peter Alexander Berowald, Bt. (S. 1628)

Insall, Sir Donald William, Kt., CBE

Ipatas, *Hon.* Sir Peter, KBE

Irvine, Sir Donald Hamilton, Kt., CBE, MD, FRCGP

Irving, *Prof.* Sir Miles Horsfall, Kt., MD, FRCS, FRCSE

Irwin, *Lt.-Gen.* Sir Alistair Stuart Hastings, KCB, CBE

Irwin, *Rt. Hon.* Sir Stephen John, Kt.

Isaacs, Sir Jeremy Israel, Kt.

Isham, Sir Norman Murray Crawford, Bt. (1627), OBE

Italeli, *HE* Sir Iakoba Taeia, GCMG

Ive, Sir Jonathan Paul, KBE

Ivory, Sir Brian Gammell, Kt., CBE

Jack, Sir Malcolm Roy, KCB

Jack, *Hon.* Sir Raymond Evan, Kt.

Jackling, Sir Roger Tustin, KCB, CBE

Jackson, Sir Barry Trevor, Kt.

Jackson, Sir Kenneth Joseph, Kt.

Jackson, *Gen.* Sir Michael David, GCB, CBE

Jackson, Sir Nicholas Fane St George, Bt. (1913)

†Jackson, Sir Neil Keith, Bt. (1815)

Jackson, *Hon.* Sir Peter Arthur Brian, Kt.

Jackson, *Rt. Hon.* Sir Rupert Matthew, Kt.

Jackson, Sir Thomas Saint Felix, Bt. (1902)

Jackson, Sir (William) Roland Cedric, Bt. (1869)

Jacob, *Rt. Hon.* Sir Robert Raphael Hayim (Robin), Kt.

Jacobi, Sir Derek George, Kt., CBE

Jacobs, Sir Cecil Albert, Kt., CBE

Jacobs, *Rt. Hon.* Sir Francis Geoffrey, KCMG, QC

Jacobs, *Dr* Sir Michael Graham, Kt.

Jacomb, Sir Martin Wakefield, Kt.

Jaffray, Sir William Otho, Bt. (1892)

Jagger, Sir Michael Philip, Kt.

James, Sir Jeffrey Russell, KBE

James, Sir John Nigel Courtenay, KCVO, CBE

Jardine, Sir Andrew Colin Douglas, Bt. (1916)

Jardine of Applegirth, Sir William Murray, Bt. (S. 1672)

Jarman, *Prof.* Sir Brian, Kt., OBE

Jarratt, Sir Alexander Anthony, Kt., CB

Jawara, *Hon.* Sir Dawda Kairaba, Kt.

Jay, *Hon.* Sir Robert Maurice, Kt.

Jeewoolall, Sir Ramesh, Kt.

Jeffery, Sir Thomas Baird, Kt., CB

Jeffrey, Sir William Alexander, KCB

Jeffreys, *Prof.* Sir Alec John, Kt., CH, FRS

Jeffries, *Hon.* Sir John Francis, Kt.

Jehangir, Sir Cowasji, Bt. (1908)

Jejeebhoy, Sir Jamsetjee, Bt. (1857)

Jenkins, Sir Brian Garton, GBE

Jenkins, Sir Elgar Spencer, Kt., OBE

Jenkins, Sir James Christopher, KCB, QC

Jenkins, Sir John, KCMG, LVO

Jenkins, *Dr* Sir Karl William Pamp, Kt., CBE

Jenkins, Sir Michael Nicholas Howard, Kt., OBE

Jenkins, Sir Paul Christopher, KCB

Jenkins, Sir Simon, Kt.

Jenkinson, Sir John Banks, Bt. (1661)

Jenks, Sir (Richard) Peter, Bt. (1932)

Jenner, *Air Marshal* Sir Timothy Ivo, KCB

Jennings, Sir John Southwood, Kt., CBE, FRSE

Jennings, Sir Peter Neville Wake, Kt., CVO

Jephcott, Sir David Welbourn, Bt. (1962)

Jessel, Sir Charles John, Bt. (1883)

Jewkes, Sir Gordon Wesley, KCMG

Job, Sir Peter James Denton, Kt.

John, Sir David Glyndwr, KCMG

John, Sir Elton Hercules (Reginald Kenneth Dwight), Kt., CBE

Johns, *Vice-Adm.* Sir Adrian James, KCB, CBE, ADC

Johns, *Air Chief Marshal* Sir Richard Edward, GCB, KCVO, CBE

Johnson, Sir Colpoys Guy, Bt. (1755)

Johnson, *Gen.* Sir Garry Dene, KCB, OBE, MC

Johnson, Sir John Rodney, KCMG

†Johnson, Sir Patrick Eliot, Bt. (1818)

Johnson, *Hon.* Sir Robert Lionel, Kt.

Johnson-Ferguson, Sir Mark Edward, Bt. (1906)

Johnston, *Lt.-Gen.* Sir Maurice Robert, KCB, CVO, OBE

Johnston, Sir Thomas Alexander, Bt. (S. 1626)

Johnston, Sir William Ian Ridley, Kt., CBE, QPM

Johnstone, Sir Geoffrey Adams Dinwiddie, KCMG

Johnstone, Sir (George) Richard Douglas, Bt. (S. 1700)

Johnstone, Sir (John) Raymond, Kt., CBE

Jolliffe, Sir Anthony Stuart, GBE

Jolly, Sir Arthur Richard, KCMG

Jonas, Sir John Peter, Kt., CBE

Jones, Sir Alan Jeffrey, Kt.

Jones, Sir Bryn Terfel, Kt., CBE

Jones, Sir David Charles, Kt., CBE

Jones, Sir Derek William, KCB

Jones, Sir Harry George, Kt., CBE

†Jones, Sir James Peter Martin Benton, Bt. (1919)

Jones, *Rt. Revd* James Stuart, KBE

Jones, Sir John Francis, Kt.

Jones, Sir Kenneth Lloyd, Kt., QPM

Jones, Sir Lyndon, Kt.

Jones, Sir Mark Ellis Powell, Kt.

Jones, *Vice-Adm.* Sir Philip Andrew, KCB

Jones, Sir Richard Anthony Lloyd, KCB

Jones, Sir Robert Edward, Kt.

Jones, Sir Roger Spencer, Kt., OBE

†Joseph, *Hon.* Sir James Samuel, Bt. (1943)

Jowell, *Prof.* Sir Jeffrey Lionel, KCMG, QC

Jowitt, *Hon.* Sir Edwin Frank, Kt.

Jugnauth, *Rt. Hon.* Sir Anerood, KCMG

Jungius, *Vice-Adm.* Sir James George, KBE

Kaberry, *Hon.* Sir Christopher Donald, Bt. (1960)

Kabui, Sir Frank Utu Ofagioro, GCMG, OBE

Kadoorie, *Hon.* Sir Michael David, Kt.

Kakaraya, Sir Pato, KBE

Kamit, Sir Leonard Wilson, Kt., CBE

Kao, *Prof.* Sir Charles Kuen, KBE

Kapoor, Sir Anish Mikhail, Kt., CBE
Kaputin, Sir John Rumet, KBE, CMG
Kavali, Sir Thomas, Kt., OBE
Kay, *Rt. Hon.* Sir Maurice Ralph, Kt.
Kay, Sir Nicholas Peter, KCMG
Kaye, Sir Paul Henry Gordon, Bt. (1923)
Keane, Sir John Charles, Bt. (1801)
Kearney, *Hon.* Sir William John Francis, Kt., CBE
Keegan, *Dr* Sir Donal Arthur John, KCVO, OBE
Keehan, *Hon.* Sir Michael Joseph, Kt.
Keene, *Rt. Hon.* Sir David Wolfe, Kt.
Keith, *Hon.* Sir Brian Richard, Kt.
Keith, *Rt. Hon.* Sir Kenneth, KBE
†Kellett, Sir Stanley Charles, Bt. (1801)
Kelly, Sir Christopher William, KCB
Kelly, Sir David Robert Corbett, Kt., CBE
Kemakeza, Sir Allan, Kt.
Kemball, *Air Marshal* Sir (Richard) John, KCB, CBE
Kemp-Welch, Sir John, Kt.
Kendall, Sir Peter Ashley, Kt.
Kennaway, Sir John Lawrence, Bt. (1791)
Kennedy, *Hon.* Sir Ian Alexander, Kt.
Kennedy, *Prof.* Sir Ian McColl, Kt.
†Kennedy, Sir George Matthew Rae, Bt. (1836)
Kennedy, *Rt. Hon.* Sir Paul Joseph Morrow, Kt.
Kenny, Sir Anthony John Patrick, Kt., DPHIL, DLITT, FBA
Kenny, Sir Paul Stephen, Kt.
Kentridge, Sir Sydney Woolf, KCMG, QC
Kenyon, Sir Nicholas Roger, Kt., CBE
Keogh, *Prof.* Sir Bruce Edward, KBE
Kere, *Dr* Sir Nathan, KCMG
Kerr, *Adm.* Sir John Beverley, GCB
Kerr, Sir Ronald James, Kt., CBE
Kerr, *Hon.* Sir Timothy Julian, Kt.
Kershaw, *Prof.* Sir Ian, Kt.
Keswick, Sir Henry Neville Lindley, Kt.
Keswick, Sir John Chippendale Lindley, Kt.
Kevau, *Prof.* Sir Isi Henao, Kt., CBE
Khaw, *Prof.* Sir Peng Tee, Kt.
Kikau, *Ratu* Sir Jone Latianara, KBE
Kimber, Sir Rupert Edward Watkin, Bt. (1904)
King, *Prof.* Sir David Anthony, Kt., FRS
King, Sir James Henry Rupert, Bt. (1888)
King, Sir Julian Beresford, KCVO, CMG
King, *Hon.* Sir Timothy Roger Alan, Kt.
King, Sir Wayne Alexander, Bt. (1815)
Kingman, *Prof.* Sir John Frank Charles, Kt., FRS
Kingman, Sir John Oliver Frank, KCB
Kingsley, Sir Ben, Kt.
Kinloch, Sir David, Bt. (S. 1686)
Kinloch, Sir David Oliphant, Bt. (1873)
Kipalan, Sir Albert, Kt.
Kirch, Sir David Roderick, KBE

Kirkpatrick, Sir Ivone Elliott, Bt. (S. 1685)
Kiszely, *Lt.-Gen.* Sir John Panton, KCB, MC
Kitchin, *Rt. Hon.* Sir David James Tyson, Kt.
Kitson, *Gen.* Sir Frank Edward, GBE, KCB, MC
Kitson, Sir Timothy Peter Geoffrey, Kt.
Kleinwort, Sir Richard Drake, Bt. (1909)
Klug, Sir Aaron, Kt., OM
Knight, *Rt. Hon.* Sir Gregory, Kt.
Knight, Sir Kenneth John, Kt., CBE, QFSM
Knight, *Air Chief Marshal* Sir Michael William Patrick, KCB, AFC
Knight, *Prof.* Sir Peter, Kt.
Knill, Sir Thomas John Pugin Bartholomew, Bt. (1893)
Knowles, Sir Charles Francis, Bt. (1765)
Knowles, Sir Durward Randolph, Kt., OBE
Knowles, Sir Nigel Graham, Kt.
Knowles, *Hon.* Sir Robin St John, Kt.
Knox, Sir David Laidlaw, Kt.
Knox-Johnston, Sir William Robert Patrick (Sir Robin), Kt., CBE, RD
Koraea, Sir Thomas, Kt.
Kornberg, *Prof.* Sir Hans Leo, Kt., DSc, SCD, PHD, FRS
Korowi, Sir Wiwa, GCMG
Kulukundis, Sir Elias George (Eddie), Kt., OBE
Kulunga, Sir Toami, Kt., OBE, QPM
Kumar, Sir Harpal Singh, Kt.
Kwok-Po Li, *Dr* Sir David, Kt., OBE

Lachmann, *Prof.* Sir Peter Julius, Kt.
Lacon, Sir Edmund Richard Vere, Bt. (1818)
Lacy, Sir Patrick Brian Finucane, Bt. (1921)
Laing, Sir (John) Martin (Kirby), Kt., CBE
Laird, Sir Gavin Harry, Kt., CBE
Lake, Sir Edward Geoffrey, Bt. (1711)
Lakin, Sir Richard Anthony, Bt. (1909)
Lamb, Sir Albert Thomas, KBE, CMG, DFC
Lamb, *Lt.-Gen.* Sir Graeme Cameron Maxwell, KBE, CMG, DSO
Lambert, *Vice-Adm.* Sir Paul, KCB
†Lambert, Sir Peter John Biddulph, Bt. (1711)
Lambert, Sir Richard Peter, Kt.
Lampl, Sir Peter, Kt., OBE
Lamport, Sir Stephen Mark Jeffrey, KCVO
Lancashire, Sir Steve, Kt.
Landau, Sir Dennis Marcus, Kt.
Lander, Sir Stephen James, KCB
Lane, *Prof.* Sir David Philip, Kt.
Langham, Sir John Stephen, Bt. (1660)
Langlands, Sir Robert Alan, Kt.
Langley, *Hon.* Sir Gordon Julian Hugh, Kt.
Langrishe, Sir James Hercules, Bt. (I. 1777)
Langstaff, *Hon.* Sir Brian Frederick James, Kt.

Lankester, Sir Timothy Patrick, KCB
Lapli, Sir John Ini, GCMG
Lapthorne, Sir Richard Douglas, Kt., CBE
Large, Sir Andrew McLeod Brooks, Kt.
Latasi, *Rt. Hon.* Sir Kamuta, KCMG, OBE
Latham, *Rt. Hon.* Sir David Nicholas Ramsey, Kt.
Latham, Sir Michael Anthony, Kt.
Latham, Sir Richard Thomas Paul, Bt. (1919)
Laughton, Sir Anthony Seymour, Kt.
Laurence, *Vice-Adm.* Sir Timothy James Hamilton, KCVO, CB, ADC
Laurie, Sir Robert Bayley Emilius, Bt. (1834)
Lavender, *Hon.* Sir Nicholas, Kt.
Lawrence, Sir Clive Wyndham, Bt. (1906)
Lawrence, Sir Edmund Wickham, GCMG, OBE
Lawrence, Sir Henry Peter, Bt. (1858)
Lawrence, Sir Ivan John, Kt., QC
†Lawrence, Sir Aubrey Lyttelton Simon, Bt. (1867)
Lawrence-Jones, Sir Christopher, Bt. (1831)
Laws, *Rt. Hon.* Sir John Grant McKenzie, Kt.
Laws, Sir Stephen Charles, KCB
Lawson, Sir Charles John Patrick, Bt. (1900)
Lawson, *Gen.* Sir Richard George, KCB, DSO, OBE
Lawson-Tancred, Sir Andrew Peter, Bt. (1662)
Lawton, *Prof.* Sir John Hartley, Kt., CBE, FRS
Layard, *Adm.* Sir Michael Henry Gordon, KCB, CBE
Lea, Sir Thomas William, Bt. (1892)
Leahy, Sir Daniel Joseph, Kt.
Leahy, Sir Terence Patrick, Kt.
Learmont, *Gen.* Sir John Hartley, KCB, CBE
Leaver, Sir Christopher, GBE
Le Cheminant, *Air Chief Marshal* Sir Peter de Lacey, GBE, KCB, DFC
Lechler, *Prof.* Sir Robert Ian, Kt.
Lechmere, Sir Nicholas Anthony Hungerford, Bt. (1818)
†Leeds, Sir John Charles Hildyard, Bt. (1812)
Lees, Sir David Bryan, Kt.
Lees, Sir Christopher James, Bt. (1897), TD
Lees, Sir Thomas Harcourt Ivor, Bt. (1804)
Lees, Sir (William) Antony Clare, Bt. (1937)
Leese, Sir Richard Charles, Kt., CBE
Leeson, *Air Marshal* Sir Kevin James, KCB, CBE
le Fleming, Sir David Kelland, Bt. (1705)
Legard, Sir Charles Thomas, Bt. (1660)
Legg, Sir Thomas Stuart, KCB, QC
Leggatt, *Rt. Hon.* Sir Andrew Peter, Kt.
Leggatt, *Hon.* George Andrew Midsomer, Kt.
Leggett, *Prof.* Sir Anthony James, KBE

Le Grand, *Prof.* Sir Julian Ernest, Kt.
Leigh, Sir Edward Julian Egerton, Kt.
Leigh, Sir Geoffrey Norman, Kt.
Leigh, *Dr* Sir Michael, KCMG
Leigh, Sir Richard Henry, Bt. (1918)
Leighton, Sir John Mark Nicholas, Kt.
Leighton, Sir Michael John Bryan, Bt. (1693)
†Leith-Buchanan, Sir Gordon Kelly McNicol, Bt. (1775)
Le Marchant, Sir Piers Alfred, Bt. (1841)
Lennox-Boyd, *Hon.* Sir Mark Alexander, Kt.
Leon, Sir John Ronald, Bt. (1911)
Lepani, Sir Charles Watson, KBE
†Leslie, Sir Shaun Rudolph Christopher, Bt. (1876)
Lester, Sir James Theodore, Kt.
Lethbridge, Sir Thomas Periam Hector Noel, Bt. (1804)
Letwin, *Rt. Hon.* Sir Oliver, Kt.
Lever, Sir Jeremy Frederick, KCMG, QC
Lever, Sir Paul, KCMG
Lever, Sir (Tresham) Christopher Arthur Lindsay, Bt. (1911)
Leveson, *Rt. Hon.* Sir Brian Henry, Kt.
Levi, Sir Wasangula Noel, Kt., CBE
Levinge, Sir Richard George Robin, Bt. (I. 1704)
Lewinton, Sir Christopher, Kt.
Lewis, *Hon.* Sir Clive Buckland, Kt.
Lewis, Sir David Thomas Rowell, Kt.
Lewis, Sir John Anthony, Kt., OBE
Lewis, Sir Leigh Warren, KCB
Lewis, Sir Martyn John Dudley, Kt., CBE
Lewis, Sir Terence Murray, Kt., OBE, GM, QPM
Lewison, *Rt. Hon.* Sir Kim Martin Jordan, Kt.
†Ley, Sir Christopher Ian, Bt. (1905)
Li, Sir Ka-Shing, KBE
Lickiss, Sir Michael Gillam, Kt.
Liddington, Sir Bruce, Kt.
Lightman, *Hon.* Sir Gavin Anthony, Kt.
Lighton, Sir Thomas Hamilton, Bt. (I. 1791)
Likierman, *Prof.* Sir John Andrew, Kt.
Lilleyman, *Prof.* Sir John Stuart, Kt.
Lindblom, *Rt. Hon.* Sir Keith John, Kt.
†Lindsay, Sir James Martin Evelyn, Bt. (1962)
Lindsay, *Hon.* Sir John Edmund Frederic, Kt.
†Lindsay-Hogg, Sir Michael Edward, Bt. (1905)
Lipton, Sir Stuart Anthony, Kt.
Lipworth, Sir (Maurice) Sydney, Kt.
Lister, *Vice-Adm.* Sir Simon Robert, KCB, OBE
Lister-Kaye, Sir John Phillip Lister, Bt. (1812), OBE
Lithgow, Sir William James, Bt. (1925)
Llewellyn, Sir Roderic Victor, Bt. (1922)
Llewellyn-Smith, *Prof.* Sir Christopher Hubert, Kt.
Lloyd, *Prof.* Sir Geoffrey Ernest Richard, Kt., FBA
Lloyd, Sir Nicholas Markley, Kt.
Lloyd, *Rt. Hon.* Sir Peter Robert Cable, Kt.

Lloyd, Sir Richard Ernest Butler, Bt. (1960)
Lloyd, *Rt. Hon.* Sir Timothy Andrew Wigram, Kt.
Lloyd-Edwards, *Capt.* Sir Norman, KCVO, RD
Lloyd Jones, *Rt. Hon.* Sir David, Kt.
Loader, Air Marshal Sir Clive Robert, KCB, OBE
Lobban, Sir Iain Robert, KCMG, CB
Lockett, Sir Michael Vernon, KCVO
Lockhead, Sir Moir, Kt., OBE
Loder, Sir Edmund Jeune, Bt. (1887)
Logan, Sir David Brian Carleton, KCMG
Longley, *Hon.* Sir Hartman Godfrey, Kt.
Longmore, *Rt. Hon.* Sir Andrew Centlivres, Kt.
Lorimer, *Lt.-Gen.* Sir John Gordon, KCB, MBE, DSO
Lorimer, Sir (Thomas) Desmond, Kt.
Los, *Hon.* Sir Kubulan, Kt., CBE
Loughran, Sir Gerald Finbar, KCB
Lourdenadin, Sir Ninian Mogan, KCMG, KBE
Lovestone, *Prof.* Sir Simon, Kt.
Lovill, Sir John Roger, Kt., CBE
Low, *Dr* Sir John Menzies, Kt., CBE
Lowa, *Rt. Revd* Sir Samson, KBE
Lowcock, Sir Mark Andrew, KCB
Lowe, *Air Chief Marshal* Sir Douglas Charles, GCB, DFC, AFC
Lowe, Sir Frank Budge, Kt.
Lowe, Sir Philip Martin, KCMG
Lowe, Sir Thomas William Gordon, Bt. (1918), QC
Lowson, Sir Ian Patrick, Bt. (1951)
Lowther, *Col.* Sir Charles Douglas, Bt. (1824)
Lowry, Sir Frank, Kt.
Loyd, Sir Julian St John, KCVO
Lu, Sir Tseng Chi, Kt.
Lucas, *Prof.* Sir Colin Renshaw, Kt.
†Lucas, Sir Thomas Edward, Bt. (1887)
Lucas-Tooth, Sir (Hugh) John, Bt. (1920)
Luff, Sir Peter James, Kt.
Lumsden, Sir David James, Kt.
Lushington, Sir John Richard Castleman, Bt. (1791)
Lyall Grant, Sir Mark Justin, KCMG
Lyle, Sir Gavin Archibald, Bt. (1929)
Lynch-Blosse, *Capt.* Sir Richard Hely, Bt. (I. 1622)
Lynch-Robinson, Sir Dominick Christopher, Bt. (1920)
Lyne, *Rt. Hon.* Sir Roderic Michael John, KBE, CMG
Lyons, Sir John, Kt.
Lyons, Sir Michael Thomas, Kt.

McAllister, Sir Ian Gerald, Kt., CBE
McAlpine, *Hon.* Sir William Hepburn, Bt. (1918)
McCamley, Sir Graham Edward, KBE
McCanny, *Prof.* Sir John Vincent, Kt., CBE
McCarthy, Sir Callum, Kt.
McCartney, *Rt. Hon.* Sir Ian, Kt.
McCartney, Sir (James) Paul, Kt., CH, MBE

†Macartney, Sir John Ralph, Bt. (I. 1799)
McClement, *Vice-Admiral* Sir Timothy Pentreath, KCB, OBE
Macleod, Sir Iain, KCMG
McClintock, Sir Eric Paul, Kt.
McCloskey, *Hon.* Sir John Bernard, Kt.
McColl, Sir Colin Hugh Verel, KCMG
McColl, *Gen.* Sir John Chalmers, KCB, CBE, DSO
McCollum, *Rt. Hon.* Sir William, Kt.
McCombe, *Rt. Hon.* Sir Richard George Bramwell, Kt.
McConnell, Sir Robert Shean, Bt. (1900)
†McCowan, Sir David William, Bt. (1934)
McCoy, Sir Anthony Peter, Kt., OBE
McCullin, Sir Donald, Kt., CBE
MacCulloch, *Prof.* Sir Diarmaid Ninian John, Kt.
McCulloch, *Rt. Revd* Nigel Simeon, KCVO
McCullough, *Hon.* Sir (Iain) Charles (Robert), Kt.
MacDermott, *Rt. Hon.* Sir John Clarke, Kt.
Macdonald, Sir Alasdair Uist, Kt., CBE
MacDonald, *Hon.* Sir Alistair William Orchard, Kt.
Macdonald of Sleat, Sir Ian Godfrey Bosville, Bt. (S. 1625)
McDonald, *Prof.* Sir James, Kt.
Macdonald, Sir Kenneth Carmichael, KCB
McDonald, Sir Simon Gerard, KCMG, KCVO
McDonald, Sir Trevor, Kt., OBE
McDowell, Sir Eric Wallace, Kt., CBE
MacDuff, *Hon.* Sir Alistair Geoffrey, Kt.
Mace, *Lt.-Gen.* Sir John Airth, KBE, CB
McEwen, Sir John Roderick Hugh, Bt. (1953)
MacFadyen, *Air Marshal* Sir Ian David, KCVO, CB, OBE
McFarland, Sir John Talbot, Bt. (1914)
MacFarlane, *Prof.* Sir Alistair George James, Kt., CBE, FRS
McFarlane, *Rt. Hon.* Sir Andrew Ewart, Kt.
Macfarlane, Sir (David) Neil, Kt.
McGeechan, Sir Ian Robert, Kt., OBE
McGrath, Sir Harvey Andrew, Kt.
†Macgregor, Sir Ian Grant, Bt. (1828)
MacGregor of MacGregor, Sir Malcolm Gregor Charles, Bt. (1795)
McGrigor, Sir James Angus Rhoderick Neil, Bt. (1831)
McIntosh, Sir Neil William David, Kt., CBE
McIntosh, Sir Ronald Robert Duncan, KCB
McIntyre, Sir Donald Conroy, Kt., CBE
McIntyre, Sir Meredith Alister, Kt.
Mackay, *Hon.* Sir Colin Crichton, Kt.
MacKay, Sir Francis Henry, Kt.
McKay, Sir Neil Stuart, Kt., CB
McKay, Sir William Robert, KCB
Mackay-Dick, *Maj.-Gen.* Sir Iain Charles, KCVO, MBE
Mackechnie, Sir Alistair John, Kt.

McKellen, Sir Ian Murray, Kt., CH, CBE

†Mackenzie, Sir (James William) Guy, Bt. (1890)

Mackenzie, Gen. Sir Jeremy John George, GCB, OBE

†Mackenzie, Sir Peter Douglas, Bt. (S. 1673)

†Mackenzie, Sir Roderick McQuhae, Bt. (S. 1703)

Mackeson, Sir Rupert Henry, Bt. (1954)

McKibbin, Dr Sir Malcolm, KCB

McKillop, Sir Thomas Fulton Wilson, Kt.

McKinnon, Rt. Hon. Sir Donald Charles, GCVO

McKinnon, Hon. Sir Stuart Neil, Kt.

Mackintosh, Sir Cameron Anthony, Kt.

Mackworth, Sir Digby (John), Bt. (1776)

McLaughlin, Sir Richard, Kt.

Maclean of Dunconnel, Sir Charles Edward, Bt. (1957)

Maclean, Hon. Sir Lachlan Hector Charles, Bt., CVO (NS 1631)

Maclean, Sir Murdo, Kt.

†McLeod, Sir James Roderick Charles, Bt. (1925)

MacLeod, Hon. Sir (John) Maxwell Norman, Bt. (1924)

Macleod, Sir (Nathaniel William) Hamish, KBE

McLintock, Sir Michael William, Bt. (1934)

McLoughlin, Sir Francis, Kt., CBE

McLoughlin, Rt. Hon. Sir Patrick Allen, Kt.

Maclure, Sir John Robert Spencer, Bt. (1898)

McMahon, Sir Brian Patrick, Bt. (1817)

McMahon, Sir Christopher William, Kt.

McMaster, Sir Brian John, Kt., CBE

McMichael, Prof. Sir Andrew James, Kt., FRS

MacMillan, Very Revd Gilleasbuig Iain, KCVO

McMillan, Sir Iain Macleod, Kt., CBE

Macmillan, Dr Sir James Loy, Kt., CBE

MacMillan, Lt.-Gen. Sir John Richard Alexander, KCB, CBE

McMurtry, Sir David, Kt., CBE

Macnaghten, Sir Malcolm Francis, Bt. (1836)

McNair-Wilson, Sir Patrick Michael Ernest David, Kt.

McNee, Sir David Blackstock, Kt., QPM

McNulty, Sir (Robert William) Roy, Kt., CBE

MacPhail, Sir Bruce Dugald, Kt.

Macpherson of Cluny, Hon. Sir William Alan, Kt., TD

MacRae, Sir (Alastair) Christopher (Donald Summerhayes), KCMG

Macready, Sir Charles Nevil, Bt. (1923)

Mactaggart, Sir John Auld, Bt. (1938)

McVicar, Sir David, Kt.

McWilliam, Sir Michael Douglas, KCMG

McWilliams, Sir Francis, GBE

Madden, Sir Charles Jonathan, Bt. (1919)

Madden, Sir David Christopher Andrew, KCMG

Maddison, Hon. Sir David George, Kt.

Madejski, Sir John Robert, Kt., OBE

Madel, Sir (William) David, Kt.

Magee, Sir Ian Bernard Vaughan, Kt., CB

Magnus, Sir Laurence Henry Philip, Bt. (1917)

Maguire, Hon. Sir Paul Richard, Kt.

Mahon, Sir William Walter, Bt. (1819), LVO

Maiden, Sir Colin James, Kt., DPHIL

Maini, Prof. Sir Ravinder Nath, Kt.

Maino, Sir Charles, KBE

†Maitland, Sir Charles Alexander, Bt. (1818)

Major, Rt. Hon. Sir John, KG, CH

Malbon, Vice-Adm. Sir Fabian Michael, KBE

Malcolm, Sir Alexander James Elton, Bt. (S. 1665), OBE

Malcolm, Dr Noel Robert, Kt., FBA

Malet, Sir Harry Douglas St Lo, Bt. (1791)

Males, Hon. Sir Stephen Martin, Kt.

Mallaby, Sir Christopher Leslie George, GCMG, GCVO

Mallick, Prof. Sir Netar Prakash, Kt.

Mallinson, Sir William James, Bt. (1935)

Malpas, Sir Robert, Kt., CBE

Mander, Sir (Charles) Nicholas, Bt. (1911)

Manduell, Sir John, Kt., CBE

Mann, Hon. Sir George Anthony, Kt.

Mann, Sir Rupert Edward, Bt. (1905)

Manning, Sir David Geoffrey, GCMG, KCVO

Mano, Sir Koitaga, Kt., MBE

Mans, Lt.-Gen. Sir Mark Francis Noel, KCB, CBE

Mansel, Sir Philip, Bt. (1622)

Manuella, Sir Tulaga, GCMG, MBE

Mara, Sir Nambuga, KBE

Margetson, Sir John William Denys, KCMG

Margetts, Sir Robert John, Kt., CBE

Markesinis, Prof. Sir Basil Spyridonos, Kt., QC

Markham, Prof. Sir Alexander Fred, Kt.

Markham, Sir (Arthur) David, Bt. (1911)

Marling, Sir Charles William Somerset, Bt. (1882)

Marmot, Prof. Sir Michael Gideon, Kt.

Marr, Sir Leslie Lynn, Bt. (1919)

†Marsden, Sir Tadgh Orlando Denton, Bt. (1924)

Marsh, Prof. Sir John Stanley, Kt., CBE

Marshall, Sir Michael John, Kt., CBE

Marshall, Sir Paul, Kt.

Marshall, Sir Peter Harold Reginald, KCMG

Marshall, Prof. Emeritus Sir Woodville Kemble, Kt.

Martin, Sir Clive Haydon, Kt., OBE

Martin, Sir Gregory Michael Gerard, Kt.

Martin, Prof. Sir Laurence Woodward, Kt.

Martin, Sir (Robert) Bruce, Kt., QC

Masefield, Sir Charles Beech Gordon, Kt.

Mason, Hon. Sir Anthony Frank, KBE

Mason, Prof. Sir David Kean, Kt., CBE

Mason, Sir Peter James, KBE

Mason, Prof. Sir Ronald, KCB, FRS

Massey, Vice-Adm. Sir Alan, KCB, CBE, ADC

Massie, Sir Herbert William, Kt., CBE

Matane, HE Sir Paulias Nguna, GCMG, OBE

Matheson of Matheson, Sir Alexander Fergus, Bt. (1882)

Mathews, Vice-Adm. Sir Andrew David Hugh, KCB

Mathewson, Sir George Ross, Kt., CBE, PHD, FRSE

Matthews, Sir Terence Hedley, Kt., OBE

Maughan, Sir Deryck, Kt.

Mawer, Sir Philip John Courtney, Kt.

Maxwell, Sir Michael Eustace George, Bt. (S. 1681)

Maxwell Macdonald (formerly Stirling-Maxwell), Sir John Ronald, Bt. (NS 1682)

Maxwell-Scott, Sir Dominic James, Bt. (1642)

May, Rt. Hon. Sir Anthony Tristram Kenneth, Kt.

Mayall, Lt.-Gen. Sir Simon Vincent, KBE, CB

Mayfield, Sir Andrew Charles, Kt.

Meadow, Prof. Sir (Samuel) Roy, Kt., FRCP, FRCPE

Meale, Sir Joseph Alan, Kt.

Medlycott, Sir Mervyn Tregonwell, Bt. (1808)

Meeran, His Hon. Sir Goolam Hoosen Kader, Kt.

Meldrum, Sir Graham, Kt., CBE, QFSM

Melhuish, Sir Michael Ramsay, KBE, CMG

Mellars, Prof. Sir Paul Anthony, Kt., FBA

Mellon, Sir James, KCMG

Melmoth, Sir Graham John, Kt.

Melville, Prof. Sir David, Kt., CBE

Merifield, Sir Anthony James, KCVO, CB

Messenger, Gen. Sir Gordon Kenneth, KCB, DSO, OBE

Metcalf, Prof. Sir David Harry, Kt., CBE

†Meyer, Sir (Anthony) Ashley Frank, Bt. (1910)

Meyer, Sir Christopher John Rome, KCMG

†Meyrick, Sir Timothy Thomas Charlton, Bt. (1880)

Miakwe, Hon. Sir Akepa, KBE

Michael, Sir Duncan, Kt.

Michael, Dr Sir Jonathan, Kt.

Michael, Sir Peter Colin, Kt., CBE

Michels, Sir David Michael Charles, Kt.

Middleton, Sir John Maxwell, Kt.

Middleton, Sir Peter Edward, GCB

Miers, Sir (Henry) David Alastair Capel, KBE, CMG

Milbank, Sir Edward Mark Somerset, Bt. (1882)

Milborne-Swinnerton-Pilkington, Sir Thomas Henry, Bt. (S. 1635)
Milburn, Sir Anthony Rupert, Bt. (1905)
†Miles, Sir Philip John, Bt. (1859)
Millais, Sir Geoffroy Richard Everett, Bt. (1885)
Millar, *Prof.* Sir Fergus Graham Burtholme, Kt.
Miller, Sir Donald John, Kt., FRSE, FRENG
Miller, *Air Marshal* Sir Graham Anthony, KBE
Miller, Sir Anthony Thomas, Bt. (1705)
Miller, Sir Jonathan Wolfe, Kt., CBE
Miller, Sir Peter North, Kt.
Miller, Sir Robin Robert William, Kt.
Miller, Sir Ronald Andrew Baird, Kt., CBE
Miller of Glenlee, Sir Stephen William Macdonald, Bt. (1788)
Mills, Sir Ian, Kt.
Mills, Sir Jonathan Edward Harland (John), Kt., FRSE
Mills, Sir Keith Edward, GBE
Mills, Sir Peter Frederick Leighton, Bt. (1921)
Milman, Sir David Patrick, Bt. (1800)
Milne-Watson, Sir Andrew Michael, Bt. (1937)
Milner, Sir Timothy William Lycett, Bt. (1717)
Mirrlees, *Prof.* Sir James Alexander, Kt., FBA
Mitchell, *Rt. Hon.* Sir James FitzAllen, KCMG
Mitchell, *Very Revd* Patrick Reynolds, KCVO
Mitchell, *Hon.* Sir Stephen George, Kt.
Mitting, *Hon.* Sir John Edward, Kt.
Moate, Sir Roger Denis, Kt.
Moberly, Sir Patrick Hamilton, KCMG
Moir, Sir Christopher Ernest, Bt. (1916)
Molesworth-St Aubyn, Sir William, Bt. (1689)
Molony, Sir Peter John, Bt. (1925)
Moncada, *Prof.* Sir Salvador, Kt.
Montagu, Sir Nicholas Lionel John, KCB
†Montagu-Pollock, Sir Guy Maximillian, Bt. (1872)
Montague, Sir Adrian Alastair, Kt., CBE
Montgomery, Sir (Basil Henry) David, Bt. (1801), CVO
Montgomery, *Vice-Adm.* Sir Charles Percival Ross, KBE, ADC
Montgomery-Cuninghame, Sir John Christopher Foggo, Bt. (NS 1672)
Moody-Stuart, Sir Mark, KCMG
Moollan, Sir Abdool Hamid Adam, Kt.
Moon, Sir Roger, Bt. (1887)
Moor, *Hon.* Sir Philip Drury, Kt.
Moorcroft, Sir William, KBE
Moore, *Most Revd* Desmond Charles, KBE
Moore, Sir Francis Thomas, Kt.
Moore, *Vice Adm.* Sir Michael Antony Claës, KBE, LVO
Moore, Sir Peter Alan Cutlack, Bt. (1919)

Moore, Sir William Roger Clotworthy, Bt. (1932), TD
Moore-Bick, *Rt. Hon.* Sir Martin James, Kt.
Morauta, Sir Mekere, KCMG
Mordaunt, Sir Richard Nigel Charles, Bt. (1611)
Morgan, *Vice-Adm.* Sir Charles Christopher, KBE
Morgan, *Rt. Hon.* Sir (Charles) Declan, Kt.
Morgan, Sir Graham, Kt.
Morgan, *Hon.* Sir Paul Hyacinth, Kt.
Morgan, Sir Terence Keith, Kt., CBE
Morison, *Hon.* Sir Thomas Richard Atkin, Kt.
Moritz, Sir Michael Jonathan, KBE
Morland, *Hon.* Sir Michael, Kt.
Morland, Sir Robert Kenelm, Kt.
†Morris, Sir Allan Lindsay, Bt. (1806)
Morris, Sir Andrew Valentine, Kt., OBE
Morris, *Air Marshal* Sir Arnold Alec, KBE, CB
Morris, Sir Derek James, Kt.
Morris, Sir Keith Elliot Hedley, KBE, CMG
Morris, *Prof.* Sir Peter John, Kt.
Morris, *Hon.* Sir Stephen Nathan, Kt.
Morris, Sir Trefor Alfred, Kt., CBE, QPM
Morrison, Sir (Alexander) Fraser, Kt., CBE
Morrison, Sir George Ivan, Kt., OBE
Morrison, Sir Howard Andrew Clive, KCMG, CBE
Morrison-Bell, Sir William Hollin Dayrell, Bt. (1905)
Morrison-Low, Sir Richard Walter, Bt. (1908)
Morritt, *Rt. Hon.* Sir (Robert) Andrew, Kt., CVO
Morse, Sir Amyas Charles Edward, KCB
Moses, *Rt. Hon.* Sir Alan George, Kt.
Moses, *Very Revd* Dr John Henry, KCVO
Moss, Sir David Joseph, KCVO, CMG
Moss, Sir Stephen Alan, Kt.
Moss, Sir Stirling Craufurd, Kt., OBE
Mostyn, *Hon.* Sir Nicholas Anthony Joseph Ghislain, Kt.
Mostyn, Sir William Basil John, Bt. (1670)
Motion, Sir Andrew, Kt.
Mott, Sir David Hugh, Bt. (1930)
Mottram, Sir Richard Clive, GCB
†Mount, Sir (William Robert) Ferdinand, Bt. (1921)
Mountain, Sir Edward Brian Stanford, Bt. (1922)
Mowbray, Sir John Robert, Bt. (1880)
Moylan, *Rt. Hon.* Sir Andrew John Gregory, Kt.
Moynihan, *Dr* Sir Daniel, Kt.
†Muir, Sir Richard James Kay, Bt. (1892)
Muir-Mackenzie, Sir Alexander Alwyne Henry Charles Brinton, Bt. (1805)
Mulcahy, Sir Geoffrey John, Kt.
Mummery, *Rt. Hon.* Sir John Frank, Kt.
Munby, *Rt. Hon.* Sir James Lawrence, Kt.

Munro, Sir Alan Gordon, KCMG
†Munro, Sir Ian Kenneth, Bt. (S. 1634)
Munro, Sir Keith Gordon, Bt. (1825)
Muria, *Hon.* Sir Gilbert John Baptist, Kt.
Murphy, Sir Jonathan Michael, Kt., QPM
Murray, Sir Andrew, Kt., OBE
Murray, Sir David Edward, Kt.
Murray, *Rt. Hon.* Sir Donald Bruce, Kt.
Murray, Sir Nigel Andrew Digby, Bt. (S. 1628)
Murray, Sir Patrick Ian Keith, Bt. (S. 1673)
Murray, Sir Robert Sydney, Kt., CBE
Murray, Sir Robin MacGregor, Kt.
†Murray, Sir Rowland William, Bt. (S. 1630)
Muscatelli, *Prof.* Sir Vito Antonio, Kt., FRSE
Musgrave, Sir Christopher John Shane, Bt. (I. 1782)
Musgrave, Sir Christopher Patrick Charles, Bt. (1611)
Myers, Sir Derek John, Kt.
Myers, *Prof.* Sir Rupert Horace, KBE
Mynors, Sir Richard Baskerville, Bt. (1964)

Naipaul, Sir Vidiadhar Surajprasad, Kt.
Nairn, Sir Michael, Bt. (1904)
Naish, Sir (Charles) David, Kt.
Nalau, Sir Jerry Kasip, KBE
Nall, Sir Edward William Joseph, Bt. (1954)
Namaliu, *Rt. Hon.* Sir Rabbie Langanai, KCMG
Napier, Sir Charles Joseph, Bt. (1867)
Napier, Sir John Archibald Lennox, Bt. (S. 1627)
Narey, Sir Martin James, Kt.
Naylor, Sir Robert, Kt.
Naylor-Leyland, Sir Philip Vyvian, Bt. (1895)
Neal, Sir Eric James, Kt., CVO
Neave, Sir Paul Arundell, Bt. (1795)
Neill, *Rt. Hon.* Sir Brian Thomas, Kt.
Neill, Sir (James) Hugh, KCVO, CBE, TD
†Nelson, Sir Jamie Charles Vernon Hope, Bt. (1912)
Nelson, *Hon.* Sir Robert Franklyn, Kt.
New, *Maj.-Gen.* Sir Laurence Anthony Wallis, Kt., CB, CBE
Newbigging, Sir David Kennedy, Kt., OBE
Newby, *Prof.* Sir Howard Joseph, Kt., CBE
Newey, *Hon.* Sir Guy Richard, Kt.
Newington, Sir Michael John, KCMG
Newman, Sir Francis Hugh Cecil, Bt. (1912)
Newman, Sir Geoffrey Robert, Bt. (1836)
Newman, *Hon.* Sir George Michael, Kt.
Newman, *Vice-Adm.* Sir Roy Thomas, KCB
Newman Taylor, *Prof.* Sir Anthony John, Kt., CBE
Newsam, Sir Peter Anthony, Kt.
Newson-Smith, Sir Peter Frank Graham, Bt. (1944)

Newton, *Revd* George Peter Howgill, Bt. (1900)

Newton, Sir John Garnar, Bt. (1924)

Newton, *Lt.-Gen.* Sir Paul Raymond, KBE

Newton, *Hon.* Sir Roderick Brian, Kt.

Nice, Sir Geoffrey, Kt., QC

Nickell, *Prof.* Sir Stephen John, Kt., CBE, FBA

Nicol, *Hon.* Sir Andrew George Lindsay, Kt.

Nichol, Sir Duncan Kirkbride, Kt., CBE

Nicholas, Sir David, Kt., CBE

Nicholas, Sir John William, KCVO, CMG

Nicholson, Sir Bryan Hubert, GBE, Kt.

Nicholson, Sir Charles Christian, Bt. (1912)

Nicholson, Sir David, KCB, CBE

Nicholson, *Rt. Hon.* Sir Michael, Kt.

Nicholson, Sir Paul Douglas, KCVO, Kt.

Nicholson, Sir Robin Buchanan, Kt., PHD, FRS, FRENG

Nightingale, Sir Charles Manners Gamaliel, Bt. (1628)

†Nixon, Sir Simon Michael Christopher, Bt. (1906)

Noble, Sir David Brunel, Bt. (1902)

Noble, Sir Timothy Peter, Bt. (1923)

Nombri, Sir Joseph Karl, Kt., ISO, BEM

Norgrove, Sir David Ronald, Kt.

Norman, Sir Nigel James, Bt. (1915)

Norman, Sir Ronald, Kt., OBE

Norman, Sir Torquil Patrick Alexander, Kt., CBE

Normington, Sir David John, GCB

Norrington, Sir Roger Arthur Carver, Kt., CBE

Norris, *Hon.* Sir Alastair Hubert, Kt.

Norriss, *Air Marshal* Sir Peter Coulson, KBE, CB, AFC

North, *Air Marshal* Sir Barry Mark, KCB, OBE

North, Sir Peter Machin, Kt., CBE, QC, DCL, FBA

North, Sir Thomas Lindsay, Kt.

North, Sir (William) Jonathan (Frederick), Bt. (1920)

Norton, Barry, Kt.

Norton, *Maj.-Gen.* Sir George Pemberton Ross, KCVO, CBE

Norton-Griffiths, Sir Michael, Bt. (1922)

Nossal, Sir Gustav Joseph Victor, Kt., CBE

Nott, *Rt. Hon.* Sir John William Frederic, KCB

Nourse, *Rt. Hon.* Sir Martin Charles, Kt.

Novoselov, *Prof.* Sir Konstantin, Kt.

Nugee, *Hon.* Sir Christopher George, Kt.

†Nugent, Sir Nicholas Myles John, Bt. (I. 1795)

Nugent, Sir Christopher George Ridley, Bt. (1806)

Nugent, Sir (Walter) Richard Middleton, Bt. (1831)

Nunn, Sir Trevor Robert, Kt., CBE

Nunneley, Sir Charles Kenneth Roylance, Kt.

Nursaw, Sir James, KCB, QC

Nurse, Sir Paul Maxime, Kt.

Nuttall, Sir Harry, Bt. (1922)

Nutting, Sir John Grenfell, Bt. (1903), QC

Oakeley, Sir Robert John Atholl, Bt. (1790)

Oakes, Sir Christopher, Bt. (1939)

Oakshott, Sir Thomas Hendrie, Bt. (1959)

O'Brien, Sir Robert Stephen, Kt., CBE

O'Brien, *Rt. Hon.* Sir Stephen Rothwell, KBE

†O'Brien, Sir Timothy John, Bt. (1849)

O'Brien, Sir William, Kt.

O'Connell, Sir Bernard, Kt.

O'Connell, Sir Maurice James Donagh MacCarthy, Bt. (1869)

O'Connor, Sir Denis Francis, Kt., CBE, QPM

Odell, Sir Stanley John, Kt.

Odgers, Sir Graeme David William, Kt.

O'Donnell, Sir Christopher John, Kt.

O'Donoghue, *Lt.-Gen.* Sir Kevin, KCB, CBE

O'Dowd, Sir David Joseph, Kt., CBE, QPM

Ogden, *Dr* Sir Peter James, Kt.

Ogden, Sir Robert, Kt., CBE

Ogilvy, Sir Francis Gilbert Arthur, Bt. (S. 1626)

Ogilvy-Wedderburn, Sir Andrew John Alexander, Bt. (1803)

Ognall, *Hon.* Sir Harry Henry, Kt.

Ohlson, Sir Peter Michael, Bt. (1920)

Oldham, *Dr* Sir John, Kt., OBE

Oliver, Sir Craig Stewart, Kt.

Oliver, Sir James Michael Yorrick, Kt.

Oliver, Sir Stephen John Lindsay, Kt., QC

O'Hara, *Hon.* Sir John Ailbe

†O'Loghlen, Sir Michael, Bt. (1838)

Olver, Sir Richard Lake, Kt.

Omand, Sir David Bruce, GCB

Ondaatje, Sir Christopher, Kt., CBE

O'Nions, *Prof.* Sir Robert Keith, Kt., FRS, PHD

Onslow, Sir Richard Paul Atherton, Bt. (1797)

Oppenheimer, Sir Michael Bernard Grenville, Bt. (1921)

Openshaw, *Hon.* Sir Charles Peter Lawford, Kt.

O'Rahilly, *Prof.* Sir Stephen Patrick, Kt., FRS

Ord, Sir David Charles, Kt.

Orde, Sir Hugh Stephen Roden, Kt., OBE, QPM

O'Regan, *Dr* Sir Stephen Gerard (Tipene), Kt.

O'Reilly, Sir Anthony John Francis, Kt.

O'Reilly, *Prof.* Sir John James, Kt.

Orr, Sir John, Kt., OBE

Orr-Ewing, *Hon.* Sir (Alistair) Simon, Bt. (1963)

Orr-Ewing, Sir Archibald Donald, Bt. (1886)

Osborn, Sir Richard Henry Danvers, Bt. (1662)

Osborne, Sir Peter George, Bt. (I. 1629)

O'Shea, *Prof.* Sir Timothy Michael Martin, Kt.

Osmotherly, Sir Edward Benjamin Crofton, Kt., CB

Oswald, Sir (William Richard) Michael, KCVO

Ottaway, *Rt. Hon.* Sir Richard Geoffrey James, Kt.

Otton, Sir Geoffrey John, KCB

Otton, *Rt. Hon.* Sir Philip Howard, Kt.

Ouseley, *Hon.* Sir Duncan Brian Walter, Kt.

Outram, Sir Alan James, Bt. (1858)

Owen, Sir Geoffrey, Kt.

Owen, *Prof.* Sir Michael John, Kt.

Owen, *Hon.* Sir Robert Michael, Kt.

Owen-Jones, Sir Lindsay Harwood, KBE

Packer, Sir Richard John, KCB

Paget, Sir Henry James, Bt. (1871)

Paget, Sir Richard Herbert, Bt. (1886)

Paice, *Rt. Hon.* Sir James Edward Thornton, Kt.

Paine, Sir Christopher Hammon, Kt., FRCP, FRCR

Pakenham, *Hon.* Sir Michael Aiden, KBE, CMG

Palin, *Air Chief Marshal* Sir Roger Hewlett, KCB, OBE

Palmer, Sir Albert Rocky, Kt.

Palmer, Sir (Charles) Mark, Bt. (1886)

Palmer, Sir Geoffrey Christopher John, Bt. (1660)

Palmer, *Rt. Hon.* Sir Geoffrey Winston Russell, KCMG

Palmer, *Prof.* Sir Godfrey Henry Oliver, Kt, OBE

Palmer, Sir John Edward Somerset, Bt. (1791)

Panter, Sir Howard Hugh, Kt.

Pappano, Sir Antonio, Kt.

Parbo, Sir Arvi Hillar, Kt.

Park, *Hon.* Sir Andrew Edward Wilson, Kt.

Parker, Sir Alan, Kt.

Parker, Sir Alan William, Kt., CBE

Parker, *Rt. Hon.* Sir Jonathan Frederic, Kt.

Parker, *Hon.* Sir Kenneth Blades, Kt.

Parker, *Maj.* Sir Michael John, KCVO, CBE

Parker, *Gen.* Sir Nicholas Ralph, KCB, CBE

Parker, Sir Richard (William) Hyde, Bt. (1681)

Parker, Sir (Thomas) John, GBE

Parker, Sir William Peter Brian, Bt. (1844)

Parkes, Sir Edward Walter, Kt., FRENG

Parkinson, Sir Michael, Kt., CBE

Parry, *Prof.* Sir Eldryd Hugh Owen, KCMG, OBE

Parry, Sir Emyr Jones, GCMG

Parry-Evans, *Air Chief Marshal* Sir David, GCB, CBE

Parsons, Sir John Christopher, KCVO

Partridge, Sir Michael John Anthony, KCB

Partridge, Sir Nicholas Wyndham, Kt., OBE

Pascoe, *Gen.* Sir Robert Alan, KCB, MBE

Pasley, Sir Robert Killigrew Sabine, Bt. (1794)

Paston-Bedingfeld, Sir Henry Edgar, Bt. (1661)

Patey, Sir William Charters, KCMG

Patten, *Rt. Hon.* Sir Nicholas John, Kt.

Pattie, *Rt. Hon.* Sir Geoffrey Edwin, Kt.

Pattison, *Prof.* Sir John Ridley, Kt., DM, FRCPATH

Pattullo, Sir (David) Bruce, Kt., CBE

Pauncefort-Duncombe, Sir David Philip Henry, Bt. (1859)

Payne, *Prof.* Sir David Neil, Kt., CBE, FRS

Peace, Sir John Wilfrid, Kt.

Peach, *Air Chief Marshal* Sir Stuart William, GBE, KCB, ADC

Pearce, Sir (Daniel Norton) Idris, Kt., CBE, TD

Pears, Sir Trevor Stephen, Kt., CMG

Pearse, Sir Brian Gerald, Kt.

Pearson, Sir David Lee, Kt., CBE

Pearson, Sir Francis Nicholas Fraser, Bt. (1964)

Pearson, Sir Keith, Kt.

Pearson, *Gen.* Sir Thomas Cecil Hook, KCB, CBE, DSO

Peart, *Prof.* Sir William Stanley, Kt., MD, FRS

Pease, Sir Joseph Gurney, Bt. (1882)

Pease, Sir Richard Thorn, Bt. (1920)

Peat, Sir Gerrard Charles, KCVO

Peat, Sir Michael Charles Gerrard, GCVO

Peckham, *Prof.* Sir Michael John, Kt.,

Peek, Sir Richard Grenville, Bt. (1874)

Pelgen, Sir Harry Friedrich, Kt., MBE

Pelham, *Dr* Sir Hugh Reginald Brentnall, Kt., FRS

Pelly, Sir Richard John, Bt. (1840)

Pendry, *Prof.* Sir John Brian, Kt., FRS

Penny, *Dr* Nicholas Beaver, Kt., FBA

Penrose, *Prof.* Sir Roger, Kt., OM, FRS

Pepper, *Dr* Sir David Edwin, KCMG

Pepper, *Prof.* Sir Michael, Kt.

Pepys, *Prof.* Sir Mark Brian, Kt.

Perowne, *Vice-Adm.* Sir James Francis, KBE

Perring, Sir John Raymond, Bt. (1963), TD

Perris, Sir David (Arthur), Kt., MBE

Perry, Sir David Howard, KCB

Perry, Sir Michael Sydney, GBE

Pervez, Sir Mohammed Anwar, Kt., OBE

Petchey, Sir Jack, Kt., CBE

Peters, *Prof.* Sir David Keith, Kt., FRCP

Pethica, *Prof.* Sir John Bernard, Kt., FRS

Petit, Sir Dinshaw Manockjee, Bt. (1890)

†Peto, Sir Francis Michael Morton, Bt. (1855)

Peto, Sir Henry Christopher Morton Bampfylde, Bt. (1927)

Peto, *Prof.* Sir Richard, Kt., FRS

Petrie, Sir Peter Charles, Bt. (1918), CMG

†Philipson-Stow, Sir (Robert) Matthew, Bt. (1907)

Phillips, Sir (Gerald) Hayden, GCB

Phillips, Sir John David, Kt., QPM

Phillips, Sir Jonathan, KCB

Phillips, Sir Peter John, Kt., OBE

Phillips, Sir Robin Francis, Bt. (1912)

Phillips, *Hon.* Sir Stephen Edmund, Kt.

Phillips, Sir Tom Richard Vaughan, KCMG

Pickard, Sir (John) Michael, Kt.

Picken, *Hon.* Sir Simon Derek, Kt.

Pickles, *Rt. Hon.* Sir Eric Jack, Kt.

Pickthorn, Sir James Francis Mann, Bt. (1959)

†Piers, Sir James Desmond, Bt. (I. 1661)

Piggott-Brown, Sir William Brian, Bt. (1903)

Pigot, Sir George Hugh, Bt. (1764)

Pigott, *Lt.-Gen.* Sir Anthony David, KCB, CBE

†Pigott, Sir David John Berkeley, Bt. (1808)

Pike, *Lt.-Gen.* Sir Hew William Royston, KCB, DSO, MBE

Pike, Sir Michael Edmund, KCVO, CMG

Pilditch, Sir John Richard, Bt. (1929)

Pile, Sir Anthony John Devereux, Bt. (1900), MBE

Pill, *Rt. Hon.* Sir Malcolm Thomas, Kt.

Pilling, Sir Joseph Grant, KCB

Pinsent, Sir Matthew Clive, Kt., CBE

Pinsent, Sir Thomas Benjamin Roy, Bt. (1938)

Pirmohamed, *Prof.* Sir Hussein Munir, Kt.

Pissarides, *Prof.* Sir Christopher Antoniou, Kt., FBA

Pitcher, Sir Desmond Henry, Kt.

Pitchers, *Hon.* Sir Christopher (John), Kt.

Pitchford, *Rt. Hon.* Sir Christopher John, Kt.

Pitoi, Sir Sere, Kt., CBE

Pitt, Sir Michael Edward, Kt.

Plastow, Sir David Arnold Stuart, Kt.

Platt, Sir Martin Philip, Bt. (1959)

Pledger, *Air Chief Marshal* Sir Malcolm David, KCB, OBE, AFC

Plender, *Hon.* Sir Richard Owen, Kt.

Plumbly, Sir Derek John, KCMG

Pocock, *Dr* Sir Andrew John, KCMG

Poh, Sir Sang Chung, Kt., MBE

Pohai, Sir Timothy, Kt., MBE

Pole, Sir (John) Richard (Walter Reginald) Carew, Bt. (1628), OBE

Pole, Sir John Chandos, Bt. (1791)

Poliakoff, *Prof.* Sir Martyn, Kt., CBE

Polkinghorne, *Revd Canon* John Charlton, KBE

Pollard, Sir Charles, Kt.

†Pollen, Sir Richard John Hungerford, Bt. (1795)

Pollock, Sir David Frederick, Bt. (1866)

Pomeroy, Sir Brian Walter, Kt., CBE

Ponder, *Prof.* Sir Bruce Anthony John, Kt.

Ponsonby, Sir Charles Ashley, Bt. (1956)

Poon, Sir Dickson, Kt., CBE

†Poore, Sir Roger Ricardo, Bt. (1795)

Popplewell, *Hon.* Sir Andrew John, Kt.

Popplewell, *Hon.* Sir Oliver Bury, Kt.

Porritt, *Hon.* Sir Jonathon Espie, Bt. (1963), CBE

Portal, Sir Jonathan Francis, Bt. (1901)

Porter, *Prof.* Sir Keith Macdonald, Kt.

Potter, *Rt. Hon.* Sir Mark Howard, Kt.

Pound, Sir John David, Bt. (1905)

Povey, Sir Keith, Kt., QPM

Powell, Sir Ian Clifford, Kt.

Powell, Sir John Christopher, Kt.

Powell, Sir Nicholas Folliott Douglas, Bt. (1897)

Power, Sir Alastair John Cecil, Bt. (1924)

Pownall, Sir Michael Graham, KCB

Poya, Sir Nathaniel, Kt.

Prance, *Prof.* Sir Ghillean Tolmie, Kt., FRS

Prendergast, Sir (Walter) Kieran, KCVO, CMG

Prescott, Sir Mark, Bt. (1938)

Preston, Sir Philip Charles Henry Hulton, Bt. (1815)

Prevost, Sir Christopher Gerald, Bt. (1805)

Price, Sir Francis Caradoc Rose, Bt. (1815)

Price, Sir Frank Leslie, Kt.

†Prichard-Jones, Sir David John Walter, Bt. (1910)

†Primrose, Sir John Ure, Bt. (1903)

Pringle, *Hon.* Sir John Kenneth, Kt.

Pringle, Sir Norman Murray Archibald Macgregor, Bt. (S. 1683)

Proby, Sir William Henry, Bt. (1952), CBE

Proctor-Beauchamp, Sir Christopher Radstock, Bt. (1745)

Prosser, Sir David John, Kt.

Prosser, Sir Ian Maurice Gray, Kt.

Pryke, Sir Christopher Dudley, Bt. (1926)

Puapua, *Rt. Hon.* Sir Tomasi, GCMG, KBE

Pulford, *Air Chief Marshal* Sir Andrew Douglas, GCB, CBE, ADC

Purves, Sir William, Kt., CBE, DSO

Purvis, *Vice-Adm.* Sir Neville, KCB

Quan, Sir Henry (Francis), KBE

Quilter, Sir Guy Raymond Cuthbert, Bt. (1897)

Radcliffe, Sir Sebastian Everard, Bt. (1813)

Radda, *Prof.* Sir George Karoly, Kt., CBE, FRS

Rae, Sir William, Kt., QPM

Raeburn, Sir Michael Edward Norman, Bt. (1923)

Rake, Sir Michael Derek Vaughan, Kt.

Ralli, Sir David Charles, Bt. (1912)

Ramakrishnan, *Dr* Sir Venkatraman, Kt.

Ramdanee, Sir Mookteswar Baboolall Kailash, Kt.

Ramphal, Sir Shridath Surendranath, GCMG

Ramphul, Sir Baalkhristna, Kt.

Ramphul, Sir Induraduth, Kt.

Ramsay, Sir Alexander William Burnett, Bt. (1806)

Ramsay, Sir Allan John (Hepple), KBE, CMG

Ramsay-Fairfax-Lucy, Sir Edmund John William Hugh, Bt. (1836)
Ramsden, Sir David Edward John, Kt., CBE
Ramsden, Sir John Charles Josslyn, Bt. (1689)
Ramsey, *Dr* Sir Frank Cuthbert, KCMG
Ramsey, *Hon.* Sir Vivian Arthur, Kt.
Randall, *Rt. Hon.* Sir (Alexander) John, Kt.
Rankin, Sir Ian Niall, Bt. (1898)
Rasch, Sir Simon Anthony Carne, Bt. (1903)
Rashleigh, Sir Richard Harry, Bt. (1831)
Ratcliffe, *Prof.* Sir Peter John, Kt., FRS
Ratford, Sir David John Edward, KCMG, CVO
Rattee, *Hon.* Sir Donald Keith, Kt.
Rattle, Sir Simon Dennis, Kt., OM, CBE
Rawlins, *Hon.* Sir Hugh Anthony, Kt.
Rawlins, *Prof.* Sir Michael David, GBE, FRCP, FRCPED
Rawlinson, Sir Anthony Henry John, Bt. (1891)
Rea, *Prof.* Sir Desmond, Kt., OBE
Read, *Prof.* Sir David John, Kt.
Reardon-Smith, Sir (William) Antony (John), Bt. (1920)
Reddaway, Sir David Norman, KCMG, MBE
Redgrave, Sir Steven Geoffrey, Kt., CBE
Redmayne, Sir Giles Martin, Bt. (1964)
Redmond, Sir Anthony Gerard, Kt.
Redwood, Sir Peter Boverton, Bt. (1911)
Reed, *Prof.* Sir Alec Edward, Kt., CBE
Reedie, Sir Craig Collins, Kt., CBE
Rees, Sir David Allan, Kt., PHD, DSC, FRS
Rees, Sir Richard Ellis Meuric, Kt., CBE
Reffell, *Adm.* Sir Derek Roy, KCB
Reich, Sir Erich Arieh, Kt.
Reid, Sir Alexander James, Bt. (1897)
Reid, Sir David Edward, Kt.
Reid, *Rt. Hon.* Sir George, Kt.
Reid, Sir (Philip) Alan, GCVO
Reid, Sir Robert Paul, Kt.
Reid, Sir William Kennedy, KCB
Reiher, Sir Frederick Bernard Carl, KCMG, KBE
Renals, Sir Stanley, Bt. (1895)
Renouf, Sir Clement William Bailey, Kt.
Renshaw, Sir John David Bine, Bt. (1903)
Renwick, Sir Richard Eustace, Bt. (1921)
Reynolds, Sir James Francis, Bt. (1923)
Reynolds, Sir Peter William John, Kt., CBE
Rhodes, Sir John Christopher Douglas, Bt. (1919)
Ribat, *Most Revd* John Ribat, KBE
Rice, *Prof.* Sir Charles Duncan, Kt.
Rice, *Maj.-Gen.* Sir Desmond Hind Garrett, KCVO, CBE
Rice, Sir Timothy Miles Bindon, Kt.

Richard, Sir Cliff, Kt., OBE
Richards, Sir Brian Mansel, Kt., CBE, PHD
Richards, *Rt. Hon.* Sir David Anthony Stewart, Kt.
Richards, Sir David Gerald, Kt.
Richards, Sir Francis Neville, KCMG, CVO
Richards, *Prof.* Sir Michael Adrian, Kt., CBE
Richards, Sir Rex Edward, Kt., DSC, FRS
Richards, *Rt. Hon.* Sir Stephen Price, Kt.
Richardson, Sir Anthony Lewis, Bt. (1924)
Richardson, Sir John Patrick, KBE
Richardson, Sir Thomas Legh, KCMG
Richardson-Bunbury, Sir (Richard David) Michael, Bt. (I. 1787)
Richmond, Sir David Frank, KBE, CMG
Richmond, *Prof.* Sir Mark Henry, Kt., FRS
Ricketts, Sir Stephen Tristram, Bt. (1828)
Ricks, *Prof.* Sir Christopher Bruce, Kt.
Riddell, Sir Walter John Buchanan, Bt. (S. 1628)
Ridgway, *Lt.-Gen.* Sir Andrew Peter, KBE, CB
Ridley, Sir Adam (Nicholas), Kt.
Ridley, Sir Michael Kershaw, KCVO
Rifkind, *Rt. Hon.* Sir Malcolm Leslie, KCMG
Rigby, Sir Anthony John, Bt. (1929)
Rigby, Sir Peter, Kt.
Rimer, *Rt. Hon.* Sir Colin Percy Farquharson, Kt.
Ripley, Sir William Hugh, Bt. (1880)
Ritako, Sir Thomas Baha, Kt., MBE
Ritblat, Sir John Henry, Kt.
Ritchie, *Prof.* Sir Lewis Duthie, Kt., OBE
Rivett-Carnac, Sir Jonathan James, Bt. (1836)
Rix, *Rt. Hon.* Sir Bernard Anthony, Kt.
Robb, Sir John Weddell, Kt.
Roberts, Sir Derek Harry, Kt., CBE, FRS, FRENG
Roberts, *Prof.* Sir Edward Adam, KCMG
Roberts, Sir Gilbert Howland Rookehurst, Bt. (1809)
Roberts, Sir Hugh Ashley, GCVO
Roberts, Sir Ivor Anthony, KCMG
†Roberts, Sir James Elton Denby Buchanan, Bt. (1909)
Roberts, *Dr* Sir Richard John, Kt.
Roberts, Sir Samuel, Bt. (1919)
Roberts, *Maj.-Gen.* Sir Sebastian John Lechmere, KCVO, OBE
Robertson, *Rt. Hon.* Sir Hugh Michael, KCMG
Robertson, Sir Simon Manwaring, Kt.
Robey, Sir Simon Christopher Townsend, Kt.
Robins, Sir Ralph Harry, Kt., FRENG
Robinson, Sir Anthony, Kt.
Robinson, Sir Bruce, KCB
†Robinson, Sir Christopher Philipse, Bt. (1854)
Robinson, Sir Gerrard Jude, Kt.

Robinson, Sir Ian, Kt.
Robinson, Sir John James Michael Laud, Bt. (1660)
Robinson, *Dr* Sir Kenneth, Kt.
Robinson, Sir Peter Frank, Bt. (1908)
Robson, Sir Stephen Arthur, Kt., CB
Roch, *Rt. Hon.* Sir John Ormond, Kt.
Roche, Sir David O'Grady, Bt. (1838)
Roche, Sir Henry John, Kt.
Rodgers, Sir (Andrew) Piers (Wingate Aikin-Sneath), Bt. (1964)
Rogers, *Air Chief Marshal* Sir John Robson, KCB, CBE
Rogers, Sir Mark Ivan, KCMG
Rogers, Sir Peter, Kt.
Rollo, *Lt.-Gen.* Sir William Raoul, KCB, CBE
†Ropner, Sir Henry John William, Bt. (1952)
Ropner, Sir Robert Clinton, Bt. (1904)
Rose, Sir Arthur James, Kt., CBE
Rose, *Rt. Hon.* Sir Christopher Dudley Roger, Kt.
Rose, Sir Clive Martin, GCMG
†Rose, Sir David Lancaster, Bt. (1874)
Rose, *Gen.* Sir (Hugh) Michael, KCB, CBE, DSO, QGM
Rose, Sir John Edward Victor, Kt.
Rose, Sir Julian Day, Bt. (1872 and 1909)
Rosenthal, Sir Norman Leon, Kt.
Ross, *Maj.* Sir Andrew Charles Paterson, Bt. (1960)
Ross, *Lt.-Gen.* Sir Robert Jeremy, KCB, OBE
Ross, *Lt.-Col.* Sir Walter Hugh Malcolm, GCVO, OBE
Ross, Sir Walter Robert Alexander, KCVO
Rossi, Sir Hugh Alexis Louis, Kt.
Roth, *Hon.* Sir Peter Marcel, Kt.
Rothschild, Sir Evelyn Robert Adrian de, Kt.
Rowe, *Rear-Adm.* Sir Patrick Barton, KCVO, CBE
Rowe-Ham, Sir David Kenneth, GBE
Rowland, Sir Geoffrey Robert, Kt.
Rowland, Sir (John) David, Kt.
Rowley, Sir Richard Charles, Bt. (1786 and 1836)
Rowling, Sir John Reginald, Kt.
Rowlinson, *Prof.* Sir John Shipley, Kt., FRS
Royce, *Hon.* Sir Roger John, Kt.
†Royden, Sir John Michael Joseph, Bt. (1905)
Rubin, *Prof.* Sir Peter Charles, Kt.
Rudd, Sir (Anthony) Nigel (Russell), Kt.
Ruddock, Sir Paul, Kt.
Rudge, Sir Alan Walter, Kt., CBE, FRS
†Rugge-Price, Sir James Keith Peter, Bt. (1804)
Ruggles-Brise, Sir Timothy Edward, Bt. (1935)
Rumbold, Sir Henry John Sebastian, Bt. (1779)
Rushdie, Sir (Ahmed) Salman, Kt.
Russell, Sir Charles Dominic, Bt. (1916)
Russell, Sir George, Kt., CBE
Russell, Sir Muir, KCB
Russell, Sir Robert, Kt.

†Russell, Sir Stephen (Steve) Charles, Bt. (1812)

Rutter, *Prof.* Sir Michael Llewellyn, Kt., CBE, MD, FRS

Ryan, Sir Derek Gerald, Bt. (1919)

Rycroft, Sir Richard John, Bt. (1784)

Ryder, *Rt. Hon.* Sir Ernest Nigel, Kt., TD

Sacranie, Sir Iqbal Abdul Karim Mussa, Kt., OBE

Sainsbury, *Rt. Hon.* Sir Timothy Alan Davan, Kt.

St Clair-Ford, Sir William Sam, Bt. (1793)

St George, Sir John Avenel Bligh, Bt. (I. 1766)

St John-Mildmay, Sir Walter John Hugh, Bt. (1772)

St Paul, Sir Lyle Kevin, KCMG

Sainty, Sir John Christopher, KCB

Sakora, *Hon.* Sir, Bernard Berekia, KBE

Sales, *Rt. Hon.* Sir Philip James, Kt.

Salika, Sir Gibuna Gibbs, KBE

Salisbury, Sir Robert William, Kt.

Salt, Sir Patrick MacDonnell, Bt. (1869)

Salt, Sir (Thomas) Michael John, Bt. (1899)

Salusbury-Trelawny, Sir John William Richard, Bt. (1628)

Salz, Sir Anthony Michael Vaughan, Kt.

Samani, *Prof.* Sir Nilesh Jayantilal, Kt.

Sampson, Sir Colin, Kt., CBE, QPM

Samuel, Sir John Michael Glen, Bt. (1898)

Samuelson, Sir James Francis, Bt. (1884)

Samuelson, Sir Sydney Wylie, Kt., CBE

Samworth, Sir David Chetwode, Kt., CBE

Sanders, Sir Robert Tait, KBE, CMG

Sanders, Sir Ronald Michael, KCMG

Sanderson, Sir Frank Linton, Bt. (1920), OBE

Sands, Sir Roger Blakemore, KCB

Sants, Sir Hector William Hepburn, Kt.

Sargent, Sir William Desmond, Kt., CBE

Satchwell, Sir Kevin Joseph, Kt.

Saunders, Sir Bruce Joshua, KBE

Saunders, *Hon.* Sir John Henry Boulton, Kt.

Savill, *Prof.* Sir John Stewart, Kt.

Savory, Sir Michael Berry, Kt.

Sawers, Sir Robert John, GCMG

Saxby, *Prof.* Sir Robin Keith, Kt.

Scarlett, Sir John McLeod, KCMG, OBE

Schiemann, *Rt. Hon.* Sir Konrad Hermann Theodor, Kt.

Schiff, Sir András, Kt.

Scholar, Sir Michael Charles, KCB

Scholar, Sir Thomas Whinfield, KCB

Scholey, Sir David Gerald, Kt., CBE

Scipio, Sir Hudson Rupert, Kt.

Scott, Sir Anthony Percy, Bt. (1913)

Scott, Sir David Richard Alexander, Kt., CBE

Scott, *Prof.* Sir George Peter, Kt.

Scott, Sir James Jervoise, Bt. (1962)

Scott, Sir John Hamilton, KCVO

Scott, Sir Kenneth Bertram Adam, KCVO, CMG

Scott, Sir Christopher James Anderson, Bt. (1909)

Scott, Sir Ridley, Kt.

Scott, Sir Robert David Hillyer, Kt.

Scott, Sir Walter John, Bt. (1907)

Scott-Lee, Sir Paul Joseph, Kt., QPM

Scruton, *Prof.* Sir Roger Vernon, Kt.

Seale, Sir Clarence David, Kt.

Seale, Sir John Robert Charters, Bt. (1838)

Sealy, Sir Austin Llewellyn, Kt.

Seaton, HE Sir Samuel Weymouth Tapley, GCMG, CVO

†Sebright, Sir Rufus Hugo Giles, Bt. (1626)

Seconde, Sir Reginald Louis, KCMG, CVO

Sedley, *Rt. Hon.* Sir Stephen John, Kt.

Seely, Sir Nigel Edward, Bt. (1896)

Seeto, Sir Ling James, Kt., MBE

Seeyave, Sir Rene Sow Choung, Kt., CBE

Seldon, *Dr* Sir Anthony Francis, Kt.

Semple, Sir John Laughlin, KCB

Sergeant, Sir Patrick, Kt.

Serota, *Hon.* Sir Nicholas Andrew, Kt. CH

Setchell, Sir Marcus Edward, KCVO

†Seton, Sir Charles Wallace, Bt. (S. 1683)

Seton, Sir Iain Bruce, Bt. (S. 1663)

Seymour, Sir Julian Roger, Kt., CBE

Shadbolt, *Prof.* Sir Nigel Richard, Kt.

Shakerley, Sir Nicholas Simon Adam, Bt. (1838)

Shakespeare, Sir Thomas William, Bt. (1942)

Sharp, Sir Adrian, Bt. (1922)

†Sharp, Sir Fabian Alexander Sebastian, Bt. (1920)

Sharp, Sir Leslie, Kt., QPM

Sharples, Sir James, Kt., QPM

Shaw, Sir Charles De Vere, Bt. (1821)

Shaw, *Prof.* Sir John Calman, Kt., CBE

Shaw, Sir Neil McGowan, Kt.

Shaw-Stewart, Sir Ludovic Houston, Bt. (S. 1667)

Shebbeare, Sir Thomas Andrew, KCVO

Sheehy, Sir Patrick, Kt.

Sheffield, Sir Reginald Adrian Berkeley, Bt. (1755)

Shehadie, Sir Nicholas Michael, Kt., OBE

Sheil, *Rt. Hon.* Sir John, Kt.

Sheinwald, Sir Nigel Elton, GCMG

Shelley, Sir John Richard, Bt. (1611)

Shepherd, Sir Colin Ryley, Kt.

Shepherd, Sir John Alan, KCVO, CMG

Shepherd, Sir Richard Charles Scrimgeour, Kt.

Sher, Sir Antony, KBE

Sherlock, Sir Nigel, KCVO, OBE

Sherston-Baker, Sir Robert George Humphrey, Bt. (1796)

Shiffner, Sir Henry David, Bt. (1818)

Shinwell, Sir (Maurice) Adrian, Kt.

Shirreff, *Gen.* Sir Alexander Richard David, KCB, CBE

Shock, Sir Maurice, Kt.

Shortridge, Sir Jon Deacon, KCB

Shuckburgh, Sir James Rupert Charles, Bt. (1660)

Siedentop, *Dr* Sir Larry Alan, Kt., CBE

Sieff, *Hon.* Sir David, Kt.

Silber, *Rt. Hon.* Sir Stephen Robert, Kt.

Silk, Sir Evan Paul, KCB

†Simeon, Sir Stephen George Barrington, Bt. (1815)

Simmonds, *Rt. Hon. Dr* Sir Kennedy Alphonse, KCMG

Simmons, *Air Marshal* Sir Michael George, KCB, AFC

Simms, Sir Neville Ian, Kt., FRENG

Simon, *Rt. Hon.* Sir Peregrine Charles Hugh, Kt.

Simonet, Sir Louis Marcel Pierre, Kt., CBE

Simpson, Sir Peter Austin, Kt., OBE

Simpson, *Dr* Sir Peter Jeffery, Kt.

Sims, Sir Roger Edward, Kt.

Sinclair, Sir Clive Marles, Kt.

Sinclair, Sir William Robert Francis, Bt. (S. 1704)

Sinclair, Sir Robert John, Kt.

Sinclair-Lockhart, Sir Simon John Edward Francis, Bt. (S. 1636)

Singer, *Hon.* Sir Jan Peter, Kt.

Singh, Sir Pritpal, Kt.

Singh, *Hon.* Sir Rabinder, Kt.

Singleton, Sir Roger, Kt., CBE

Sione, Sir Tomu Malaefone, GCMG, OBE

†Sitwell, Sir George Reresby Sacheverell, Bt. (1808)

Skeggs, Sir Clifford George, Kt.

Skehel, Sir John James, Kt., FRS

Skingsley, *Air Chief Marshal* Sir Anthony Gerald, GBE, KCB

Skinner, Sir (Thomas) Keith (Hewitt), Bt. (1912)

Skipwith, Sir Alexander Sebastian Grey d'Estoteville, Bt. (1622)

Slack, Sir William Willatt, KCVO, FRCS

Slade, *Rt. Hon.* Sir Christopher John, Kt.

Slade, Sir Julian Benjamin Alfred, Bt. (1831)

Slater, *Adm.* Sir John (Jock) Cunningham Kirkwood, GCB, LVO

Sleight, Sir Richard, Bt. (1920)

Sloman, Sir David Morgan, Kt.

Smiley, *Lt.-Col.* Sir John Philip, Bt. (1903)

Smith, *Prof.* Sir Adrian Frederick Melhuish, Kt., FRS

Smith, *Hon.* Sir Andrew Charles, Kt.

Smith, Sir Andrew Thomas, Bt. (1897)

Smith, *Prof.* Sir David Cecil, Kt., FRS

Smith, Sir David Iser, KCVO

Smith, *Prof.* Sir Eric Brian, Kt., PHD

Smith, *Prof.* Sir James Cuthbert, Kt., FRS

Smith, Sir John Alfred, Kt., QPM

Smith, Sir Joseph William Grenville, Kt.

Smith, Sir Kevin, Kt., CBE

Smith, *Hon.* Sir Marcus Alexander, Kt.

Smith, Sir Martin Gregory, Kt.

Smith, Sir Michael John Llewellyn, KCVO, CMG

Smith, Sir (Norman) Brian, Kt., CBE, PHD

Smith, Sir Paul Brierley, Kt., CBE

Smith, *Hon.* Sir Peter Winston, Kt.

Smith, Sir Robert Courtney, Kt., CBE

Smith, Sir Robert Hill, Bt. (1945)

Smith, *Gen.* Sir Rupert Anthony, KCB, DSO, OBE, QGM

Smith, Sir Steven Murray, Kt.

Smith-Dodsworth, Sir David John, Bt. (1784)

Smith-Gordon, Sir (Lionel) Eldred (Peter), Bt. (1838)

Smith-Marriott, Sir Peter Francis, Bt. (1774)

Smurfit, *Dr* Sir Michael William Joseph, KBE

Smyth, Sir Timothy John, Bt. (1956)

Smyth-Osbourne, *Maj.-Gen.* Sir Edward Alexander, KCVO, CBE

Snowden, *Prof.* Sir Christopher Maxwell, Kt.

Snowden, *Hon.* Sir Richard Andrew, Kt.

Snyder, Sir Michael John, Kt.

Soames, *Rt. Hon.* Sir (Arthur) Nicholas Winston, Kt.

Soar, *Adm.* Sir Trevor Alan, KCB, OBE

Sobers, Sir Garfield St Auburn, Kt.

Solomon, Sir Harry, Kt.

Somare, *Rt. Hon.* Sir Michael Thomas, GCMG, CH

Somerville, *Brig.* Sir John Nicholas, Kt., CBE

Songo, Sir Bernard Paul, Kt., CMG, OBE

Soole, *Hon.* Sir Michael Alexander, Kt.

Sorabji, *Prof.* Sir Richard Rustom Kharsedji, Kt., CBE

Sorrell, Sir John William, Kt., CBE

Sorrell, Sir Martin Stuart, Kt.

Sosa, Sir Manuel, Kt.

Soulsby, Sir Peter Alfred, Kt.

Souter, Sir Brian, Kt.

Southby, Sir John Richard Bilbe, Bt. (1937)

Southern, *Prof.* Sir Edwin Mellor, Kt.

Southgate, Sir Colin Grieve, Kt.

Southgate, Sir William David, Kt.

Southward, *Dr* Sir Nigel Ralph, KCVO

Sowrey, *Air Marshal* Sir Frederick Beresford, KCB, CBE, AFC

Sparrow, Sir John, Kt.

Spearman, Sir Alexander Young Richard Mainwaring, Bt. (1840)

Speed, Sir (Herbert) Keith, Kt., RD

Spencer, Sir Derek Harold, Kt., QC

Spencer, *Vice-Adm.* Sir Peter, KCB

Spencer, *Hon.* Sir Robin Godfrey, Kt.

Spencer-Nairn, Sir Robert Arnold, Bt. (1933)

Spicer, Sir Nicholas Adrian Albert, Bt. (1906)

Spiegelhalter, *Prof.* Sir David John, Kt., OBE, FRS

Spiers, Sir Donald Maurice, Kt., CB, TD

Spooner, Sir James Douglas, Kt.

Spring, Sir Dryden Thomas, Kt.

Spurling, Sir John Damian, KCVO, OBE

Squire, *Air Chief Marshal* Sir Peter Ted, GCB, DFC, AFC, ADC

Stacey, *Air Marshal* Sir Graham Edward, KBE, CB

Stadlen, *Hon.* Sir Nicholas Felix, Kt.

Stagg, Sir Charles Richard Vernon, KCMG

Staite, Sir Richard John, Kt., OBE

Stamer, Sir Peter Tomlinson, Bt. (1809)

Stanhope, *Adm.* Sir Mark, GCB, OBE, ADC

Stanier, Sir Beville Douglas, Bt. (1917)

Stanley, *Rt. Hon.* Sir John Paul, Kt.

Starkey, Sir John Philip, Bt. (1935)

Starmer, *Rt. Hon.* Sir Keir, KCB, QC

Stear, *Air Chief Marshal* Sir Michael James Douglas, KCB, CBE

Steel, *Vice-Adm.* Sir David George, KBE

Steel, *Hon.* Sir David William, Kt.

Steer, Sir Alan William, Kt.

Stephen, *Rt. Hon.* Sir Ninian Martin, KG, GCMG, GCVO, KBE

Stephens, Sir (Edwin) Barrie, Kt.

Stephens, Sir Jonathan Andrew de Sievrac, KCB

Stephens, Sir William Benjamin Synge, Kt.

†Stephenson, Sir Henry Upton, Bt. (1936)

Stephenson, Sir Paul Robert, Kt., QPM

Sterling, Sir Michael John Howard, Kt.

Stevens, Sir Michael John, KCVO

Stevenson, Sir Hugh Alexander, Kt.

Stewart, Sir Alan d'Arcy, Bt. (I. 1623)

Stewart, Sir Alastair Robin, Bt. (1960)

Stewart, Sir Brian John, Kt., CBE

Stewart, Sir David James Henderson, Bt. (1957)

Stewart, Sir David John Christopher, Bt. (1803)

Stewart, Sir James Moray, KCB

Stewart, Sir (John) Simon (Watson), Bt. (1920)

Stewart, Sir John Young, Kt., OBE

Stewart, Sir Patrick, Kt., OBE

Stewart, *Lt.-Col.* Sir Robert Christie, KCVO, CBE, TD

Stewart, Sir Roderick David, Kt., CBE

Stewart, *Hon.* Sir Stephen Paul, Kt.

Stewart, *Prof.* Sir William Duncan Paterson, Kt., FRS, FRSE

Stewart-Clark, Sir John, Bt. (1918)

Stewart-Richardson, Sir Simon Alaisdair Ian Neile, Bt. (S. 1630)

Stheeman, Sir Robert Alexander Talma, Kt., CB

Stilgoe, Sir Richard Henry Simpson, Kt., OBE

Stirling, Sir Angus Duncan Aeneas, Kt.

Stirling of Garden, *Col.* Sir James, KCVO, CBE, TD

Stirling-Hamilton, Sir Malcolm William Bruce, Bt. (S. 1673)

Stockdale, Sir Thomas Minshull, Bt. (1960)

Stoddart, *Prof.* Sir James Fraser, Kt.

Stoller, Sir Norman Kelvin, Kt., CBE

Stone, Sir Christopher, Kt.

Stonhouse, *Revd* Michael Philip, Bt. (1628 and 1670)

Stonor, *Air Marshal* Sir Thomas Henry, KCB

Stoppard, Sir Thomas, Kt., OM, CBE

Storey, *Hon.* Sir Richard, Bt., CBE (1960)

Stothard, Sir Peter Michael, Kt.

Stott, Sir Adrian George Ellingham, Bt. (1920)

Stoute, Sir Michael Ronald, Kt.

Stracey, Sir John Simon, Bt. (1818)

Strachan, Sir Curtis Victor, Kt., CVO

Strachan, Sir Hew Francis Anthony, Kt.

†Strachey, Sir Henry Leofric Benvenuto, Bt. (1801)

Straker, Sir Louis Hilton, KCMG

Strang, *Prof.* Sir John Stanley, Kt.

Strang Steel, Sir (Fiennes) Michael, Bt. (1938), CBE

Stratton, *Prof.* Sir Michael Rudolf, Kt., FRS

Street, *Hon.* Sir Laurence Whistler, KCMG

Streeton, Sir Terence George, KBE, CMG

Strickland-Constable, Sir Frederic, Bt. (1641)

Stringer, Sir Donald Edgar, Kt., CBE

Stringer, Sir Howard, Kt.

Strong, Sir Roy Colin, Kt., CH, PHD, FSA

†Stronge, Sir James Anselan Maxwell, Bt. (1803)

†Stuart, Sir Geoffrey Phillip, Bt. (1660)

Stuart, Sir James Keith, Kt.

Stuart, Sir Kenneth Lamonte, Kt.

†Stuart-Forbes, Sir William Daniel, Bt. (S. 1626)

†Stuart-Menteth, Sir Charles Greaves, Bt. (1838)

Stuart-Paul, *Air Marshal* Sir Ronald Ian, KBE

Stuart-Smith, *Hon.* Sir Jeremy Hugh, Kt

Stuart-Smith, *Rt. Hon.* Sir Murray, KCMG

Stubbs, Sir William Hamilton, Kt., PHD

Stucley, *Lt.* Sir Hugh George Coplestone Bampfylde, Bt. (1859)

Studd, Sir Edward Fairfax, Bt. (1929)

Studholme, Sir Henry William, Bt. (1956)

Sturridge, Sir Nicholas Anthony, KCVO

Stuttard, Sir John Boothman, Kt.

†Style, Sir William Frederick, Bt. (1627)

Sullivan, *Rt. Hon.* Sir Jeremy Mirth, Kt.

Sullivan, Sir Richard Arthur, Bt. (1804)

Sulston, Sir John Edward, Kt., CH

Sunderland, Sir John Michael, Kt.

Supperstone, *Hon.* Sir Michael Alan, Kt.

Sutherland, Sir John Brewer, Bt. (1921)

Sutherland, Sir William George MacKenzie, Kt.

Sutton, Sir Richard Lexington, Bt. (1772)

Swan, Sir Conrad Marshall John Fisher, KCVO, PHD

Swan, Sir John William David, KBE

Swann, Sir Michael Christopher, Bt. (1906), TD

Swayne, *Rt. Hon.* Sir Desmond, Kt.,
TD
Sweeney, Sir George, Kt.
Sweeney, *Hon.* Sir Nigel Hamilton, Kt.
Sweeting, *Prof.* Sir Martin Nicholas,
Kt., OBE, FRS
Swinburn, *Lt.-Gen.* Sir Richard Hull,
KCB
Swinnerton-Dyer, *Prof.* Sir (Henry)
Peter (Francis), Bt. (1678), KBE,
FRS
Swinton, *Maj.-Gen.* Sir John, KCVO,
OBE
Swire, Sir Adrian Christopher, Kt.
Swire, *Rt. Hon.* Sir Hugo George
William, KCMG
Sykes, Sir David Michael, Bt. (1921)
Sykes, Sir Francis John Badcock, Bt.
(1781)
Sykes, Sir Hugh Ridley, Kt.
Sykes, *Prof.* Sir (Malcolm) Keith, Kt.
Sykes, Sir Richard, Kt.
Sykes, Sir Tatton Christopher Mark,
Bt. (1783)
Symons, *Vice-Adm.* Sir Patrick Jeremy,
KBE
†Synge, Sir Allen James Edward, Bt.
(1801)

Tanner, Sir David Whitlock, Kt., CBE
Tapps-Gervis-Meyrick, Sir George
Christopher Cadafael, Bt. (1791)
Tapsell, *Rt. Hon.* Sir Peter Hannay
Bailey, Kt.
†Tate, Sir Edward Nicolas, Bt. (1898)
Tate, *Dr* Sir Jeffrey Philip, Kt., CBE
Taureka, *Dr* Sir Reubeh, KBE
Tauvasa, Sir Joseph James, KBE
Taylor, Sir Cyril Julian Hebden, GBE
Taylor, Sir Edward Macmillan (Teddy),
Kt.
Taylor, Sir Hugh Henderson, KCB
Taylor, *Dr* Sir John Michael, Kt., OBE
Taylor, *Prof.* Sir Martin John, Kt., FRS
Taylor, Sir Nicholas Richard Stuart,
Bt. (1917)
Taylor, *Prof.* Sir William, Kt., CBE
Taylor, Sir William George, Kt.
Teagle, *Vice-Adm.* Sir Somerford
Francis, KBE
Teare, *Hon.* Sir Nigel John Martin, Kt.
Teasdale, *Prof.* Sir Graham Michael,
Kt.
Tebbit, Sir Kevin Reginald, KCB,
CMG
Temple, *Prof.* Sir John Graham, Kt.
Temple, Sir Richard Carnac Chartier,
Bt. (1876)
Temu, *Hon. Dr* Sir Puka, KBE, CMG
Tennyson-D'Eyncourt, Sir Mark
Gervais, Bt. (1930)
Terry, *Air Marshal* Sir Colin George,
KBE, CB
Terry, *Air Chief Marshal* Sir Peter
David George, GCB, AFC
Thatcher, *Hon.* Sir Mark, Bt. (1990)
Thomas, Sir David John Godfrey, Bt.
(1694)
Thomas, Sir Derek Morison David,
KCMG
Thomas, *Prof.* Sir Eric Jackson, Kt.
Thomas, Sir Gilbert Stanley, Kt., OBE
Thomas, Sir Jeremy Cashel, KCMG

Thomas, Sir (John) Alan, Kt.
Thomas, *Prof.* Sir John Meurig, Kt.,
FRS
Thomas, Sir Keith Vivian, Kt.
Thomas, *Dr* Sir Leton Felix, KCMG,
CBE
Thomas, Sir Philip Lloyd, KCVO,
CMG
Thomas, Sir Quentin Jeremy, Kt., CB
Thomas, Sir William Michael, Bt.
(1919)
Thompson, Sir Christopher Peile, Bt.
(1890)
Thompson, Sir Clive Malcolm, Kt.
Thompson, Sir David Albert, KCMG
Thompson, *Prof.* Sir Michael Warwick,
Kt., DSc
Thompson, Sir Nicholas Annesley, Bt.
(1963)
Thompson, Sir Nigel Cooper, KCMG,
CBE
Thompson, Sir Paul Anthony, Bt.
(1963)
Thompson, Sir Peter Anthony, Kt.
Thompson, *Dr* Sir Richard Paul
Hepworth, KCVO
Thompson, Sir Thomas d'Eyncourt
John, Bt. (1806)
Thomson, Sir Adam McClure, KCMG
Thomson, Sir (Frederick Douglas)
David, Bt. (1929)
Thomson, Sir John Adam, GCMG
Thomson, Sir Mark Wilfrid Home, Bt.
(1925)
Thorne, Sir Neil Gordon, Kt., OBE,
TD
Thornicroft, *Prof.* Sir Graham John, Kt.
Thornton, *Air Marshal* Sir Barry
Michael, KCB
Thornton, Sir (George) Malcolm, Kt.
Thornton, Sir Peter Ribblesdale, Kt.
†Thorold, Sir (Anthony) Oliver, Bt.
(1642)
Thorpe, *Rt. Hon.* Sir Mathew
Alexander, Kt.
Thrift, *Prof.* Sir Nigel John, Kt.
Thurecht, Sir Ramon Richard, Kt.,
OBE
Thwaites, Sir Bryan, Kt., PHD
Tickell, Sir Crispin Charles Cervantes,
GCMG, KCVO
Tidmarsh, Sir James Napier, KCVO,
MBE
Tilt, Sir Robin Richard, Kt.
Tiltman, Sir John Hessell, KCVO
Timmins, *Col.* Sir John Bradford,
KCVO, OBE, TD
Timpson, Sir William John Anthony,
Kt., CBE
Tims, Sir Michael David, KCVO
Tindle, Sir Ray Stanley, Kt., CBE
Tirvengadum, Sir Harry Krishnan, Kt.
Tod, *Vice-Adm.* Sir Jonathan James
Richard, KCB, CBE
Todd, *Prof.* Sir David, Kt., CBE
Toka, Sir Mahuru Dadi, Kt., MBE
Tollemache, Sir Lyonel Humphry
John, Bt. (1793)
Tomkys, Sir (William) Roger, KCMG
Tomlinson, Sir John Rowland, Kt.,
CBE
Tomlinson, Sir Michael John, Kt., CBE
Tomlinson, *Rt. Hon.*. Sir Stephen Miles,
Kt.

Tooke, *Prof.* Sir John Edward, Kt.
Tooley, Sir John, Kt.
ToRobert, Sir Henry Thomas, KBE
Torpy, *Air Chief Marshal* Sir Glenn
Lester, GCB, CBE, DSO
Torry, Sir Peter James, GCVO, KCMG
Touche, Sir Anthony George, Bt.
(1920)
†Touche, Sir Eric MacLellan, Bt.
(1962)
Tovadek, Sir Martin, Kt. CMG
Tovua, Sir Paul Joshua, KCMG
ToVue, Sir Ronald, Kt., OBE
Towneley, Sir Simon Peter Edmund
Cosmo William, KCVO
Townsley, Sir John Arthur, Kt.
Traill, Sir Alan Towers, GBE
Trawen, Sir Andrew Sean, Kt., CMG,
MBE
Trainor, *Prof.* Sir Richard Hughes,
KBE
Treacher, *Adm.* Sir John Devereux,
KCB
Treacy, *Rt. Hon.* Sir Colman Maurice,
Kt.
Treacy, *Hon.* Sir (James Mary) Seamus,
Kt.
Treisman, Sir Richard Henry, Kt., FRS
Treitel, *Prof.* Sir Guenter Heinz, Kt.,
FBA, QC
Trescowthick, Sir Donald Henry, KBE
†Trevelyan, Sir Peter John, Bt. (1662
and 1874)
Trezise, Sir Kenneth Bruce, Kt., OBE
Trippier, Sir David Austin, Kt., RD
Tritton, Sir Jeremy Ernest, Bt. (1905)
Trollope, Sir Anthony Simon, Bt.
(1642)
Trotter, Sir Neville Guthrie, Kt.
Troubridge, Sir Thomas Richard, Bt.
(1799)
Trousdell, *Lt.-Gen.* Sir Philip Charles
Cornwallis, KBE, CB
†Truscott, Sir Ralph Eric Nicholson,
Bt. (1909)
Tsang, Sir Donald Yam-keun, KBE
Tuck, Sir Bruce Adolph Reginald, Bt.
(1910)
Tucker, Sir Paul, Kt.
Tucker, *Hon.* Sir Richard Howard, Kt.
Tuckey, *Rt. Hon.* Sir Simon Lane, Kt.
Tugendhat, *Hon.* Sir Michael George,
Kt.
Tuite, Sir Christopher Hugh, Bt. (I.
1622), PHD
Tully, Sir William Mark, KBE
Tunstall, Sir Craig, Kt.
†Tupper, Sir Charles Hibbert, Bt.
(1888)
Turing, Sir John Dermot, Bt. (S. 1638)
Turnbull, *Prof.* Sir Douglass Matthew,
Kt.
Turner, *Hon.* Sir Mark George, Kt.
Turner, *Hon.* Sir Michael John, Kt.
Turnquest, Sir Orville Alton, GCMG,
QC
Tusa, Sir John, Kt.
Tweedie, *Prof.* Sir David Philip, Kt.
Tyrwhitt, Sir Reginald Thomas
Newman, Bt. (1919)

Udny-Lister, Sir Edward Julian, Kt.
Ullmann, Sir Anthony James, Kt.

Underhill, *Rt. Hon.* Sir Nicholas Edward, Kt.

Underwood, *Prof.* Sir James Cressee Elphinstone, Kt.

Unwin, Sir (James) Brian, KCB

Ure, Sir John Burns, KCMG, LVO

Uren, Sir John Michael Leal, Kt., CBE

Urquhart, Sir Brian Edward, KCMG, MBE

Usher, Sir Andrew John, Bt. (1899)

Utting, Sir William Benjamin, Kt., CB

Vardy, Sir Peter, Kt.

Varney, Sir David Robert, Kt.

Vassar-Smith, Sir John Rathbone, Bt. (1917)

Vavasour, Sir Eric Michael Joseph Marmaduke, Bt. (1828)

Veness, Sir David, Kt., CBE, QPM

Vereker, Sir John Michael Medlicott, KCB

Verey, Sir David John, Kt., CBE

Verity, Sir Gary Keith, Kt.

Verney, Sir Edmund Ralph, Bt. (1818)

†Verney, Sir John Sebastian, Bt. (1946)

Vernon, Sir James William, Bt. (1914)

Vestey, Sir Paul Edmund, Bt. (1921)

Vickers, *Prof.* Sir Brian William, Kt.

Vickers, Sir John Stuart, Kt.

Vickers, *Lt.-Gen.* Sir Richard Maurice Hilton, KCB, CVO, OBE

Vickers, Sir Roger Henry, KCVO

Viggers, *Lt.-Gen.* Sir Frederick Richard, KCB, CMG, MBE

Viggers, Sir Peter John, Kt.

Vincent, Sir William Percy Maxwell, Bt. (1936)

Vineall, Sir Anthony John Patrick, Kt.

Virdee, *Prof.* Sir Tejinder Singh, Kt.

Vos, *Rt. Hon.* Sir Geoffrey Charles, Kt.

Vuatha, Sir Tipo, Kt., LVO, MBE

†Vyvyan, Sir Ralph Ferrers Alexander, Bt. (1645)

Waena, Sir Nathaniel Rahumaea, GCMG

Waine, *Rt. Revd* John, KCVO

Waite, *Rt. Hon.* Sir John Douglas, Kt.

Waka, Sir Lucas Joseph, Kt., OBE

Wake, Sir Hereward, Bt. (1621), MC

Wakefield, Sir (Edward) Humphry (Tyrrell), Bt. (1962)

Wakefield, Sir Norman Edward, Kt.

Wakeford, Sir Geoffrey Michael Montgomery, Kt., OBE

Wakeham, *Prof.* Sir William Arnot, Kt.

†Wakeley, Sir Nicholas Jeremy, Bt. (1952)

Wald, *Prof.* Sir Nicholas John, Kt.

Wales, Sir Robert Andrew, Kt.

Waley-Cohen, Sir Stephen Harry, Bt. (1961)

Walker, *Gen.* Sir Antony Kenneth Frederick, KCB

Walker, Sir Christopher Robert Baldwin, Bt. (1856)

Walker, Sir David Alan, Kt.

Walker, *Air Vice-Marshal* Sir David Allan, KCVO, OBE

Walker, Sir Harold Berners, KCMG

Walker, Sir John Ernest, Kt., DPHIL, FRS

Walker, *Air Marshal* Sir John Robert, KCB, CBE, AFC

Walker, Sir Malcolm Conrad, Kt., CBE

Walker, Sir Miles Rawstron, Kt., CBE

Walker, Sir Patrick Jeremy, KCB

Walker, *Hon.* Sir Paul James, Kt.

Walker, Sir Rodney Myerscough, Kt.

Walker, Sir Roy Edward, Bt. (1906)

Walker, *Hon.* Sir Timothy Edward, Kt.

Walker, Sir Victor Stewart Heron, Bt. (1868)

Walker-Okeover, Sir Andrew Peter Monro, Bt. (1886)

Walker-Smith, *Hon.* Sir John Jonah, Bt. (1960)

Wall, Sir (John) Stephen, GCMG, LVO

Wall, *Gen.* Sir Peter Anthony, GCB, CBE, ADC

Wallace, *Prof.* Sir David James, Kt., CBE, FRS

Waller, *Rt. Hon.* Sir (George) Mark, Kt.

†Waller, Sir John Michael, Bt. (I. 1780)

Wallis, Sir Peter Gordon, KCVO

Wallis, Sir Timothy William, Kt.

Walmsley, *Vice-Adm.* Sir Robert, KCB

Walport, *Dr* Sir Mark Jeremy, Kt.

†Walsham, Sir Gerald Percy Robert, Bt. (1831)

Walters, Sir Dennis Murray, Kt., MBE

Walters, Sir Frederick Donald, Kt.

Walters, Sir Peter Ingram, Kt.

Wamiri, Sir Akapite, KBE

Warby, *Hon.* Sir Mark David John, Kt.

Ward, *Rt. Hon.* Sir Alan Hylton, Kt.

Ward, Sir Austin, Kt., QC

Ward, *Hon.* Sir (Frederik) Gordon (Roy), Kt., OBE

Ward, *Prof.* Sir John MacQueen, Kt., CBE

Ward, Sir Joseph James Laffey, Bt. (1911)

Ward, Sir Timothy James, Kt.

Wardale, Sir Geoffrey Charles, KCB

†Wardlaw, Sir Henry Justin, Bt. (NS. 1631)

Waring, Sir (Alfred) Holburt, Bt. (1935)

Warmington, Sir Rupert Marshall, Bt. (1908)

Warner, Sir Gerald Chierici, KCMG

Warner, Sir Philip Courtenay Thomas, Bt. (1910)

Warren, Sir David Alexander, KCMG

Warren, Sir (Frederick) Miles, KBE

Warren, Sir Kenneth Robin, Kt.

Warren, *Hon.*Sir Nicholas Roger, Kt.

Waterlow, Sir Christopher Rupert, Bt. (1873)

Waterlow, Sir (Thomas) James, Bt. (1930)

Waters, *Gen.* Sir (Charles) John, GCB, CBE

Waters, Sir David Mark Rylance (Mark Rylance), Kt.

Waters, Sir (Thomas) Neil (Morris), Kt.

Wates, Sir Christopher Stephen, Kt.

Watson, Sir Graham Robert, Kt.

Watson, Sir (James) Andrew, Bt. (1866)

Watson, *Prof.* Sir Robert Tony, Kt., CMG

Watson, Sir Ronald Matthew, Kt., CBE

Watt, *Gen.* Sir Charles Redmond, KCB, KCVO, CBE, ADC

Watts, Sir Philip Beverley, KCMG

Weatherall, *Prof.* Sir David John, GBE, FRS

Weatherall, *Vice-Adm.* Sir James Lamb, KCVO, KBE

Weatherup, *Hon.* Sir Ronald Eccles, Kt.

Webb, *Prof.* Sir Adrian Leonard, Kt.

Webb, *Rt. Hon.* Sir Steven John, Kt.

Webb-Carter, *Maj.-Gen.* Sir Evelyn John, KCVO, OBE

Webster, *Vice-Adm.* Sir John Morrison, KCB

Wedgwood, Sir Ralph Nicholas, Bt. (1942)

Weekes, Sir Everton DeCourcey, KCMG, OBE

Weinberg, Sir Mark Aubrey, Kt.

Weir, *Hon.* Sir Reginald George, Kt.

Weir, Sir Roderick Bignell, Kt.

Welby, Sir (Richard) Bruno Gregory, Bt. (1801)

Welch, Sir John Reader, Bt. (1957)

Weldon, Sir Anthony William, Bt. (I. 1723)

Wellend, *Prof.* Sir Mark Edward, Kt.

Weller, *Prof.* Sir Ian Vincent Derrick, Kt.

Weller, Sir Nicholas John, Kt.

†Wells, Sir Christopher Charles, Bt. (1944)

Wells, *Prof.* Sir Stanley William, Kt., CBE

Wells, Sir William Henry Weston, Kt., FRICS

Wenge, Rt. Revd Girege, KBE

Wessely, *Prof.* Sir Simon Charles, Kt.

Westmacott, Sir Peter John, GCMG, LVO

Weston, Sir Michael Charles Swift, KCMG, CVO

Weston, Sir (Philip) John, KCMG

Whalen, Sir Geoffrey Henry, Kt., CBE

Wheeler, *Rt. Hon.* Sir John Daniel, Kt.

Wheeler, Sir John Frederick, Bt. (1920)

Wheeler, *Gen.* Sir Roger Neil, GCB, CBE

Wheeler-Booth, Sir Michael Addison John, KCB

Wheler, Sir Trevor Woodford, Bt. (1660)

Whitaker, Sir John James Ingham (Jack), Bt. (1936)

Whitbread, Sir Samuel Charles, KCVO

Whitchurch, Sir Graeme Ian, Kt., OBE

White, Sir Adrian Edwin, Kt., CBE

White, *Prof.* Sir Christopher John, Kt., CVO

White, Sir David (David Jason), Kt., OBE

White, Sir David Harry, Kt.

White, Sir George Stanley James, Bt. (1904)

White, Sir John Woolmer, Bt. (1922)

White, *Prof.* Sir Nicholas John, KCMG, OBE

White, Sir Nicholas Peter Archibald, Bt. (1802)

White, Sir Willard Wentworth, Kt., CBE

White-Spunner, *Lt.-Gen.* Sir Barnabas William Benjamin, KCB, CBE

Whitehead, Sir Philip Henry Rathbone, Bt. (1889)
Whitfield, Sir William, Kt., CBE
Whitmore, Sir Clive Anthony, GCB, CVO
†Whitmore, Sir Jason, Bt. (1954)
Whitson, Sir Keith Roderick, Kt.
Whittam Smith, Sir Andreas, Kt., CBE
Wickerson, Sir John Michael, Kt.
Wicks, Sir Nigel Leonard, GCB, CVO, CBE
Wigan, Sir Michael Iain, Bt. (1898)
Wiggin, Sir Richard Edward John, Bt. (1892)
Wiggins, Sir Bradley Marc, Kt., CBE
Wigram, Sir John Woolmore, Bt. (1805)
Wilbraham, Sir Richard Baker, Bt. (1776)
Wild, Sir John Ralston, Kt., CBE
Wiles, *Prof.* Sir Andrew John, KBE
Wilkie, *Hon.* Sir Alan Fraser, Kt.
Wilkins, Sir Michael, Kt.
Wilkinson, Sir (David) Graham (Brook) Bt. (1941)
Willcocks, *Lt.-Gen.* Sir Michael Alan, KCB, CVO
Williams, Sir Anthony Geraint, Bt. (1953)
Williams, Sir (Arthur) Gareth Ludovic Emrys Rhys, Bt. (1918)
Williams, Sir Charles Othniel, Kt.
Williams, Sir Daniel Charles, GCMG, QC
Williams, Sir David Reeve, Kt., CBE
Williams, Sir Donald Mark, Bt. (1866)
Williams, *Prof.* Sir (Edward) Dillwyn, Kt., FRCP
Williams, Sir Francis Owen Garbett, Kt., CBE
Williams, *Hon.* Sir (John) Griffith, Kt.
Williams, Sir (Lawrence) Hugh, Bt. (1798)
Williams, Sir Nicholas Stephen, Kt.
Williams, *Prof.* Sir Norman Stanley, Kt.
Williams, Sir Paul Michael, Kt., OBE
Williams, Sir Peter Michael, Kt.
Williams, Sir (Robert) Philip Nathaniel, Bt. (1915)
Williams, *HE Dr* Sir Rodney Errey Lawrence, GCMG
Williams, *Prof.* Sir Roger, Kt.
Williams, Sir (William) Maxwell (Harries), Kt.
Williams, *Hon.* Sir Wyn Lewis, Kt.
Williams-Bulkeley, Sir Richard Thomas, Bt. (1661)
Williams-Wynn, Sir David Watkin, Bt. (1688)
Williamson, Sir George Malcolm, Kt.
Williamson, *Marshal of the Royal Air Force* Sir Keith Alec, GCB, AFC
Williamson, Sir Robert Brian, Kt., CBE
Willink, Sir Edward Daniel, Bt. (1957)
Wills, Sir David James Vernon, Bt. (1923)
Wills, Sir David Seton, Bt. (1904)

Wilmot, Sir Henry Robert, Bt. (1759)
Wilmut, *Prof.* Sir Ian, Kt., OBE
Wilsey, *Gen.* Sir John Finlay Willasey, GCB, CBE
Wilshaw, Sir Michael, Kt.
Wilson, *Prof.* Sir Alan Geoffrey, Kt.
Wilson, *Vice-Adm.* Sir Barry Nigel, KCB
Wilson, Sir David Mackenzie, Kt.
Wilson, Sir Franklyn Roosevelt Wilson, KCMG
Wilson, Sir James William Douglas, Bt. (1906)
Wilson, *Brig.* Sir Mathew John Anthony, Bt. (1874), OBE, MC
Wilson, *Prof.* Sir Robert James Timothy, Kt.
Wilson, *Rt. Hon.* Sir Nicholas Allan Roy, Kt. (Lord Wilson of Culworth)
Wilson, Sir Robert Peter, KCMG
Wilson, *Air Chief Marshal* Sir (Ronald) Andrew (Fellowes), KCB, AFC
Wilson, Sir Thomas David, Bt. (1920)
Winkley, Sir David Ross, Kt.
Winnington, Sir Anthony Edward, Bt. (1755)
Winship, Sir Peter James Joseph, Kt., CBE
Winsor, Sir Thomas Philip, Kt.
Winter, *Dr* Sir Gregory Winter, Kt., CBE
Winterton, Sir Nicholas Raymond, Kt.
Wiseman, Sir John William, Bt. (1628)
Witty, Sir Andrew, Kt.
Wolfendale, *Prof.* Sir Arnold Whittaker, Kt., FRS
Wolseley, Sir Charles Garnet Richard Mark, Bt. (1628)
†Wolseley, Sir James Douglas, Bt. (I. 1745)
†Wombwell, Sir George Philip Frederick, Bt. (1778)
Womersley, Sir Peter John Walter, Bt. (1945)
Woo, Sir Leo Joseph, Kt., MBE
Woo, Sir Po-Shing, Kt.
Wood, Sir Andrew Marley, GCMG
Wood, Sir Anthony John Page, Bt. (1837)
Wood, Sir Ian Clark, GBE
Wood, Sir James Sebastian Lamin, KCMG
Wood, Sir Martin Francis, Kt., OBE
Wood, Sir Michael Charles, KCMG
Wood, Sir Peter John, Kt., CBE
Wood, *Hon.* Sir Roderic Lionel James, Kt.
Woodard, *Rear Adm.* Sir Robert Nathaniel, KCVO
Woodhead, *Vice-Adm.* Sir (Anthony) Peter, KCB
Woods, *Prof.* Sir Kent Linton, Kt.
Woods, Sir Robert Kynnersley, Kt., CBE
Woodward, Sir Clive Ronald, Kt., OBE
Woodward, Sir Thomas Jones (Tom Jones), Kt., OBE

Wootton, Sir David Hugh, Kt.
Wormald, Sir Christopher Stephen, Kt.
Worsley, Sir William Ralph, Bt. (1838)
Worsthorne, Sir Peregrine Gerard, Kt.
Worthington, Sir Mark, Kt., OBE
Wratten, *Air Chief Marshal* Sir William John, GBE, CB, AFC
Wraxall, Sir Charles Frederick Lascelles, Bt. (1813)
Wrey, Sir George Richard Bourchier, Bt. (1628)
Wright, Sir Allan Frederick, KBE
Wright, Sir David John, GCMG, LVO
Wright, *Hon.* Sir (John) Michael, Kt.
Wright, *Prof.* Sir Nicholas Alcwyn, Kt.
Wright, Sir Peter Robert, Kt., CBE
Wright, *Air Marshal* Sir Robert Alfred, KBE, AFC
Wright, Sir Stephen John Leadbetter, KCMG
Wrightson, Sir Charles Mark Garmondsway, Bt. (1900)
Wrigley, *Prof.* Sir Edward Anthony (Sir Tony), Kt., PHD, PBA
Wrixon-Becher, Sir John William Michael, Bt. (1831)
Wroughton, Sir Philip Lavallin, KCVO
Wu, Sir Gordon Ying Sheung, KCMG
Wynne, Sir Graham Robert, Kt., CBE

Yacoub, *Prof.* Sir Magdi Habib, Kt., OM, FRCS
Yaki, Sir Roy, KBE
Yang, *Hon.* Sir Ti Liang, Kt.
Yarrow, Sir Alan Colin Drake, Kt.
Yarrow, Sir Eric Grant, Bt. (1916), MBE
Yassaie, *Dr* Sir Hossein, Kt.
Yoo Foo, Sir (François) Henri, Kt.
Young, Sir Colville Norbert, GCMG, MBE
Young, Sir Dennis Charles, KCMG
Young, Sir John Kenyon Roe, Bt. (1821)
Young, Sir John Robertson, GCMG
Young, Sir Leslie Clarence, Kt., CBE
Young, Sir Nicholas Charles, Kt.
Young, Sir Robin Urquhart, KCB
Young, Sir Stephen Stewart Templeton, Bt. (1945), QC
Young, Sir William Neil, Bt. (1769)
Younger, *Capt.* Sir John David Bingham, KCVO
Younger, Sir Julian William Richard, Bt. (1911)
Yuwi, Sir Matiabe, KBE

Zacca, *Rt. Hon.* Sir Edward, KCMG
Zahedi, *Prof.* Sir Mir Saeed, Kt., OBE
Zambellas, *Adm.* Sir George Michael, GCB, DSC, ADC
Zissman, Sir Bernard Philip, Kt.
Zumla, *Prof.* Sir Alimuddin, Kt.
Zunz, Sir Gerhard Jacob (Jack), Kt., FRENG
Zurenuoc, Sir Manasupe Zure, Kt., OBE
Zurenuoc, Sir Zibang, KBE

THE ORDER OF ST JOHN

THE MOST VENERABLE ORDER OF THE HOSPITAL
OF ST JOHN OF JERUSALEM (1888)

GCStJ	Bailiff/Dame Grand Cross
KStJ	Knight of Justice/Grace
DStJ	Dame of Justice/Grace
CStJ	Commander
OStJ	Officer
SBStJ	Serving Brother
SSStJ	Serving Sister

Motto, Pro Fide, Pro Utilitate Hominum
(For the faith and in the service of humanity)

The Order of St John, founded in the early 12th century in Jerusalem, was a religious order with a particular duty to care for the sick. In Britain the order was dissolved by Henry VIII in 1540 but the British branch was revived in the early 19th century. The branch was not accepted by the Grand Magistracy of the Order in Rome but its search for a role in the tradition of the hospitallers led to the founding of the St John Ambulance Association in 1877 and later the St John Ambulance Brigade; in 1882 the St John Ophthalmic Hospital was founded in Jerusalem. A royal charter was granted in 1888 establishing the Order of St John as a British Order of Chivalry with the sovereign as its head.

Since October 1999 the whole order worldwide has been governed by a Grand Council which includes a representative from each of the 11 priories (England, Scotland, Wales, Hong Kong, Kenya, Singapore, South Africa, New Zealand, Canada, Australia and the USA). In addition there are also five commanderies in Northern Ireland, Jersey, Guernsey, the Isle of Man and Western Australia. There are also branches in about 30 other Commonwealth countries. Apart from St John Ambulance, the Order is also responsible for the Eye Hospital in Jerusalem. Admission to the order is usually conferred in recognition of service to either one of these institutions. Membership does not confer any rank, style, title or precedence on a recipient.

SOVEREIGN HEAD OF THE ORDER
HM The Queen

GRAND PRIOR
HRH The Duke of Gloucester, KG, GCVO

Lord Prior, Lt.-Col. Sir Malcolm Ross, GCVO, OBE
Prelate, Rt. Revd Timothy Stevens, CBE
Chancellor, Patrick Burgess, OBE
Sub-Prior, John Mah, QC
Secretary-General, Vice-Adm. Sir Paul Lambert, KCB

International Office, 3 Charterhouse Mews, London EC1M 6BB
T 020-7251 3292 W www.stjohninternational.org

DAMES

Style, 'Dame' before forename and surname, followed by appropriate post-nominal initials. Where such an award is made to a lady already in possession of a higher title, the appropriate initials follow her name
Envelope, Dame F_ S_, followed by appropriate post-nominal letters. *Letter (formal),* Dear Madam; *(social),* Dear Dame F_. *Spoken,* Dame F_
Husband, Untitled

Dame Grand Cross and Dame Commander are the higher classes for women of the Order of the Bath, the Order of St Michael and St George, the Royal Victorian Order, and the Order of the British Empire. Dames Grand Cross rank after the wives of Baronets and before the wives of Knights Grand Cross. Dames Commanders rank after the wives of Knights Grand Cross and before the wives of Knights Commanders.

Honorary damehoods may be conferred on women who are citizens of countries of which the Queen is not head of state.

LIST OF DAMES   *as at 31 August 2017*

Women peers in their own right and life peers are not included in this list. Female members of the royal family are not included in this list; details of the orders they hold can be found within the Royal Family section.

If a dame has a double barrelled or hyphenated surname, she is listed under the first element of the name.

Abaijah, Dame Josephine, DBE
Abramsky, Dame Jennifer Gita, DBE
Acland Hood Gass, Lady (Elizabeth Periam), DCVO
Airlie, The Countess of, DCVO
Allen, *Hon.* Dame Anita Mildred, DBE
Allen, *Prof.* Dame Ingrid Victoria, DBE
Andrews, *Hon.* Dame Geraldine Mary, DBE
Andrews, Dame Julie, DBE
Angiolini, *Rt. Hon.* Dame Elish, DBE, QC
Anionwu, *Prof.* Dame Elizabeth Nneka, DBE
Anson, Lady (Elizabeth Audrey), DBE
Archer, *Dr* Dame Mary Doreen, DBE
Arden, *Rt. Hon.* Dame Mary Howarth (Mrs Mance), DBE
Ashcroft, *Prof.* Dame Frances Mary, DBE, FRS
Asplin, *Hon.* Dame Sarah Jane (Mrs Sherwin), DBE
Atkins, Dame Eileen, DBE
August, Dame Kathryn, DBE
Bacon, Dame Patricia Anne, DBE
Bailey, *Prof.* Dame Susan Mary, DBE
Baird, Dame Vera, DBE
Baker, Dame Janet Abbott (Mrs Shelley), CH, DBE
Barbour, Dame Margaret (Mrs Ash), DBE
Barker, Dame Katharine Mary, DBE
Barker-Welch, *Hon.* Dame Maizie Irene, DBE
Barrow, Dame Jocelyn Anita (Mrs Downer), DBE
Barstow, Dame Josephine Clare (Mrs Anderson), DBE
Bassey, Dame Shirley, DBE
Beale, Dame Inga Kristine, DBE
Beasley, *Prof.* Dame Christine Joan, DBE
Beaurepaire, Dame Beryl Edith, DBE
Beckett, *Rt. Hon.* Dame Margaret Mary, DBE
Beer, *Prof.* Dame Gillian Patricia Kempster, DBE, FBA
Begg, Dame Anne, DBE
Beral, *Prof.* Dame Valerie, DBE
Bertschinger, *Dr* Dame Claire, DBE
Bevan, Dame Yasmin, DBE
Bewley, Dame Beulah Rosemary, DBE
Bibby, Dame Enid, DBE
Black, *Prof.* Dame Carol Mary, DBE
Black, *Rt. Hon.* Dame Jill Margaret, DBE
Black, *Prof.* Dame Susan Margaret, DBE, FRSE
Blackadder, Dame Elizabeth Violet, DBE

Blaize, Dame Venetia Ursula, DBE
Blaxland, Dame Helen Frances, DBE
Blume, Dame Hilary Sharon Braverman, DBE
Booth, *Hon.* Dame Margaret Myfanwy Wood, DBE
Boulding, Dame Hilary, DBE
Bourne, Dame Susan Mary (Mrs Bourne), DBE
Bowe, *Dr* Dame (Mary) Colette, DBE
Bowtell, Dame Ann Elizabeth, DCB
Braddock, *Dr* Dame Christine, DBE
Brain, Dame Margaret Anne (Mrs Wheeler), DBE
Breakwell, *Prof.* Dame Glynis Marie, DBE
Brennan, Dame Maureen, DBE
Brennan, Dame Ursula, DCB
Brewer, *Dr* Dame Nicola Mary, DCMG
Bridges, Dame Mary Patricia, DBE
Brindley, Dame Lynne Janie, DBE
Brittan, Dame Diana (Lady Brittan of Spennithorne), DBE
Brooke, *Rt. Hon.* Dame Annette (Lesley), DBE
Bruce, Dame Susan Margaret, DBE
Bruce, *Prof.* Dame Victoria Geraldine, DBE, FBA, FRSE
Buckland, Dame Yvonne Helen Elaine, DBE
Burnell, *Prof.* Dame Susan Jocelyn Bell, DBE
Burslem, Dame Alexandra Vivien, DBE
Butler, Dame Rosemary Janet Mair, DBE
Byatt, Dame Antonia Susan, DBE, FRSL
Cairncross, Dame Frances Anne, DBE, FRSE
Caldicott, Dame Fiona, DBE, FRCP, FRCPSYCH
Callil, Dame Carmen Thérèse, DBE
Cameron, *Prof.* Dame Averil Millicent, DBE
Campbell-Preston, Dame Frances Olivia, DCVO
Carnall, Dame Ruth, DBE
Carnwath, Dame Alison Jane, DBE
Carr, *Hon.* Dame Sue Lascelles (Mrs Birch), DBE
Cartwright, Dame Silvia Rose, DBE
Casey, Dame Louise, DBE, CB
Cheema-Grubb, *Hon.* Dame Bobbie, DBE
Clancy, Dame Claire Elizabeth, DCB
Clark, *Prof.* Dame Jill MacLeod, DBE
Clark, *Prof.* Dame (Margaret) June, DBE, PHD
Cleverdon, Dame Julia Charity, DCVO, CBE
Coates, Dame Sally, DBE
Coia, *Dr* Dame Denise Assunta, DBE
Collarbone, Dame Patricia, DBE
Collins, Dame Joan Henrietta, DBE
Connolly, Dame Sarah Patricia, DBE
Contreras, *Prof.* Dame Marcela, DBE
Corner, *Prof.* Dame Jessica Lois, DBE
Corsar, *Hon.* Dame Mary Drummond, DBE
Courtice, Dame Veronica Anne (Polly), DBE, LVO
Coward, Dame Pamela Sarah, DBE
Cowley, *Prof.* Dame Sarah Ann, DBE
Cox, *Hon.* Dame Laura Mary, DBE
Cramp, *Prof.* Dame Rosemary Jean, DBE
Cullum, *Prof.* Dame Nicola Anne, DBE
Dacon, Dame Monica Jessie, DBE, CMG
Davies, *Prof.* Dame Kay Elizabeth, DBE
Davies, Dame Laura Jane, DBE
Davies, *Hon.* Dame Nicola Velfor, DBE
Davies, *Prof.* Dame Sally Claire, DBE
Davies, Dame Wendy Patricia, DBE
Davis, Dame Karlene Cecile, DBE
Dawson, *Prof.* Dame Sandra Jane Noble, DBE
de Havilland, Dame Olivia Mary, DBE
De Souza, Dame Rachel Mary, DBE
Dean, *Prof.* Dame Caroline, DBE, FRS
Dell, Dame Miriam Patricia, DBE
Dench, Dame Judith Olivia (Mrs Williams), CH, DBE
Descartes, Dame Marie Selipha Sesenne, DBE, BEM

Dethridge, Dame Kate, DBE
Digby, The Lady, DBE
Dobbs, *Hon.* Dame Linda Penelope, DBE
Docherty, Dame Jacqueline, DBE
Dominiczak, *Prof.* Dame Anna Felicja, DBE, FRSE
Donald, *Prof.* Dame Athene Margaret, DBE, FRS
Dowling, *Prof.* Dame Ann Patricia, OM, DBE
Duffield, Dame Vivien Louise, DBE
Duffy, Dame Carol Ann, DBE
Dumont, Dame Ivy Leona, DCMG
Dunnell, Dame Karen, DCB
Dyche, Dame Rachael Mary, DBE
Elcoat, Dame Catherine Elizabeth, DBE
Ellis, Dame Diana Margaret (Mrs Ellis), DBE
Ellison, Dame Jill, DBE
Elton, Dame Susan Richenda (Lady Elton), DCVO
Engel, Dame Pauline Frances (Sister Pauline Engel), DBE
Ennis-Hill, Dame Jessica, DBE
Esteve-Coll, Dame Elizabeth Anne Loosemore, DBE
Evans, Dame Anne Elizabeth Jane, DBE
Evans, Dame Madeline Glynne Dervel, DBE, CMG
Evans, Dame Oremi, DBE
Fagan, Dame (Florence) Mary, DCVO
Fallowfield, *Prof.* Dame Lesley Jean, DBE
Farnham, Dame Marion (Lady Farnham), DCVO
Fawcett, Dame Amelia Chilcott, DBE
Fielding, Dame Pauline, DBE
Finch, *Prof.* Dame Janet Valerie, DBE
Fisher, *Prof.* Dame Amanda Gray, DBE
Fisher, Dame Jacqueline, DBE
Forgan, Dame Elizabeth Anne Lucy, DBE
Furse, Dame Clara Hedwig Frances, DBE
Fradd, Dame Elizabeth, DBE
Francis, *Prof.* Dame Jane Elizabeth, DCMG
Fraser, Lady Antonia, DBE
Fraser, Dame Helen Jean Sutherland, DBE
Frost, Dame Barbara May, DBE
Fry, Dame Margaret Louise, DBE
Gaymer, Dame Janet Marion, DBE, QC
Ghosh, Dame Helen Frances, DCB
Gibb, Dame Moira Margaret, DBE
Glenn, *Prof.* Dame Hazel Gillian, DBE
Glennie, *Dr* Dame Evelyn Elizabeth Ann, CH, DBE
Gloster, *Rt. Hon.* Dame Elizabeth (Lady Popplewell), DBE
Glover, Dame Audrey Frances, DBE, CMG
Glover, *Prof.* Dame Lesley Anne, DBE, FRSE
Goad, Dame Sarah Jane Frances, DCVO
Goodall, *Dr* Dame (Valerie) Jane, DBE
Goodfellow, *Prof.* Dame Julia Mary, DBE
Gordon, Dame Minita Elmira, GCMG, GCVO
Gordon, *Hon.* Dame Pamela Felicity, DBE
Gow, Dame Jane Elizabeth (Mrs Whiteley), DBE
Grafton, Ann, The Duchess of, GCVO
Grainger, *Dr* Dame Katherine Jane, DBE
Grant, Dame Mavis, DBE
Green, Dame Pauline, DBE
Gretton, Lady Jennifer Ann, DCVO
Grey, Dame Beryl Elizabeth (Mrs Svenson), CH, DBE
Grimthorpe, Elizabeth, The Lady, DCVO
Guilfoyle, Dame Margaret Georgina Constance, DBE
Guthardt, *Revd Dr* Dame Phyllis Myra, DBE
Hackitt, Dame Judith Elizabeth, DBE
Hakin, *Dr* Dame Barbara Ann, DBE
Hall, *Prof.* Dame Wendy, DBE
Hallett, *Rt. Hon.* Dame Heather Carol, DBE
Hallett, Dame Nancy Karen, DBE
Hamilton, *Prof.* Dame Carolyn Paula, DBE
Harbison, Dame Joan Irene, DBE
Harper, Dame Elizabeth Margaret Way, DBE
Harris, Dame Pauline (Lady Harris of Peckham), DBE
Harris, Dame Philippa Jill Olivier, DBE
Hassan, Dame Anna Patricia Lucy, DBE
Hay, Dame Barbara Logan, DCMG, MBE

Henderson, Dame Fiona Douglas, DCVO
Hercus, *Hon.* Dame (Margaret) Ann, DCMG
Higgins, *Prof.* Dame Joan Margaret, DBE
Higgins, *Prof.* Dame Julia Stretton, DBE, FRS
Higgins, *Prof.* Dame Rosalyn, DBE, QC
Hill, *Air Cdre* Dame Felicity Barbara, DBE
Hill, *Prof.* Dame Judith Eileen, DBE
Hine, Dame Deirdre Joan, DBE, FRCP
Hodge, *Rt. Hon.* Dame Margaret (Eve), DBE
Hodgson, Dame Patricia Anne, DBE
Hogg, *Hon.* Dame Mary Claire (Mrs Koops), DBE
Hollows, Dame Sharon, DBE
Holmes, Dame Kelly, DBE
Holroyd, Lady (Margaret Drabble), DBE
Holt, Dame Denise Mary, DCMG
Homer, Dame Linda Margaret, DCB
Hoodless, Dame Elisabeth Anne, DBE
Hoyles, *Prof.* Dame Celia Mary, DBE
Hudson, Dame Alice, DBE
Hufton, *Prof.* Dame Olwen, DBE
Humphrey, *Prof.* Dame Caroline (Lady Rees of Ludlow), DBE
Husband, *Prof.* Dame Janet Elizabeth Siarey, DBE
Hussey, Dame Susan Katharine (Lady Hussey of North Bradley), GCVO
Hutton, Dame Deirdre Mary, DBE
Hyde, Dame Helen, DBE
Imison, Dame Tamsyn, DBE
Ion, *Dr* Dame Susan Elizabeth, DBE
Isaacs, Dame Albertha Madeline, DBE
James, Dame Naomi Christine (Mrs Haythorne), DBE
Jefford, *Hon.* Dame Nerys Angharad, DBE
Jiang, *Prof.* Dame Xiangqian (Jane), DBE
John, Dame Susan, DBE
Johnson, *Prof.* Dame Anne Mandall, DBE
Johnston, Dame Rotha Geraldine Diane, DBE
Jones, Dame Gwyneth (Mrs Haberfeld-Jones), DBE
Jordan, *Prof.* Dame Carole, DBE
Joseph, Dame Monica Theresa, DBE
Jowell, *Rt. Hon.* Dame Tessa Jane, DBE
Jowett, Dame Susan, DBE
Julius, *Dr* Dame DeAnne Shirley, DCMG, CBE
Karika, Dame Pauline Margaret Rakera George (Mrs Taripo), DBE
Keeble, *Dr* Dame Reena, DBE
Keegan, Dame Elizabeth Mary, DBE
Keegan, Dame Geraldine Mary Marcella, DBE
Keegan, *Hon.* Dame Siobhan Roisin, DBE
Keith, Dame Penelope Anne Constance (Mrs Timson), DBE
Kekedo, Dame Rosalina Violet, DBE
Kelleher, Dame Joan, DBE
Kelly, Dame Barbara Mary, DBE
Kelly, Dame Lorna May Boreland, DBE
Kendrick, Dame Fiona Marie, DBE
Kershaw, Dame Janet Elizabeth Murray (Dame Betty), DBE
Kharas, Dame Zarine, DBE
Khemka, Dame Asha, DBE
Kidu, Lady, DBE
King, *Rt. Hon.* Dame Eleanor Warwick, DBE
Kinnair, Dame Donna, DBE
Kirby, Dame Georgina Kamiria, DBE
Kirkby, Dame (Carolyn) Emma, DBE
Kirwan, *Prof.* Dame Frances Clare, DBE, FRS
Kumar, *Prof.* Dame Parveen June (Mrs Leaver), DBE
La Grenade, *HE* Dame Cécile Ellen Fleurette, GCMG, OBE
Laine, Dame Cleo (Clementine) Dinah (Lady Dankworth), DBE
Laing, *Hon.* Dame Elisabeth Mary Caroline, DBE
Lake-Tack, *HE* Dame Louise Agnetha, GCMG
Lamb, Dame Dawn Ruth, DBE
Lang, *Hon.* Dame Beverley Ann Mcnaughton, DBE
Lannon, *Dr* Dame Frances, DBE
Lansbury Shaw, Dame Angela Brigid, DBE

Lavender, *Prof.* Dame Tina, DBE
Leather, Dame Susan Catherine, DBE
Lee, *Prof.* Dame Hermione, DBE
Legge-Bourke, *Hon.* Dame Elizabeth Shân Josephine, DCVO
Lenehan, Dame Christine, DBE
Leslie, Dame Alison Mariot, DCMG
Leslie, Dame Ann Elizabeth Mary, DBE
Lewis, Dame Edna Leofrida (Lady Lewis), DBE
Leyser Day, *Prof.* Dame Henrietta Miriam Ottoline, DBE
Lively, Dame Penelope Margaret, DBE
Lott, Dame Felicity Ann Emwhyla (Mrs Woolf), DBE
Louisy, Dame (Calliopa) Pearlette, GCMG
Lynn, Dame Vera (Mrs Lewis), CH, DBE
Lynne, Dame Gillian Barbara, DBE
MacArthur, Dame Ellen Patricia, DBE
McBride, *Hon.* Dame Denise Anne, DBE
McCall, Dame Carolyn Julia, DBE
Macdonald, Dame Mary Beaton, DBE
McDonald, Dame Mavis, DCB
Mace, *Prof.* Dame Georgina, DBE
McGowan, *Hon.* Dame Maura Patricia, DBE
Macgregor, Dame Judith Anne, DCMG, LVO
McGuire, *Rt. Hon.* Dame Anne Catherine, DBE
MacIntyre, *Prof.* Dame Sarah Jane, DBE
Macur, *Rt. Hon.* Dame Julia Wendy, DBE
McVittie, Dame Joan Christine, DBE
Major, Dame Malvina Lorraine (Mrs Fleming), DBE
Major, Dame Norma Christina Elizabeth, DBE
Makin, *Dr* Dame Pamela Louise, DBE
Mantel, *Dr* Dame Hilary Mary, DBE
Marsden, *Dr* Dame Rosalind Mary, DCMG
Marsh, Dame Mary Elizabeth, DBE
Marteau, *Prof.* Dame Theresa Mary, DBE
Mason, Dame Monica Margaret, DBE
Massenet, Dame Natalie Sara, DBE
Matheson, Dame Jilian Norma, DCB
May, *Hon.* Dame Juliet Mary May, DBE
Mayhew Jonas, Dame Judith, DBE
Mellor, Dame Julie Thérèse Mellor, DBE
Metge, *Dr* Dame (Alice) Joan, DBE
Middleton, Dame Elaine Madoline, DCMG, MBE
Milburn, Dame Martina Jane, DCVO, CBE
Mills, *Prof.* Dame Anne Jane, DCMG, CBE
Mirren, Dame Helen, DBE
Monroe, *Prof.* Dame Barbara, DBE
Moore, Dame Henrietta Louise, DBE, FBA
Moore, Dame Julie, DBE
Moores, Dame Yvonne, DBE
Morgan, *Dr* Dame Gillian Margaret, DBE
Morgan, Dame Shan Elizabeth, DCMG
Morris, Dame Sylvia Ann, DBE
Morrison, *Hon.* Dame Mary Anne, GCVO
Morrissey, Dame Helena Louise, DBE
Muirhead, Dame Lorna Elizabeth Fox, DCVO, DBE
Mullally, *Rt. Revd* Dame Sarah Elisabeth, DBE
Murray, Dame Jennifer Susan, DBE
Nelson, *Prof.* Dame Janet Laughland, DBE
Nelson-Taylor, Dame Nicola Jane, DBE
Neville, Dame Elizabeth, DBE, QPM
Newell, Dame Priscilla Jane, DBE
O'Brien, Dame Una, DCB
O'Farrell, *Hon.* Dame Finola Mary, DBE
Ogilvie, Dame Bridget Margaret, DBE, PHD, DSc
Oliver, Dame Gillian Frances, DBE
Owers, Dame Anne Elizabeth (Mrs Cook), DBE
Oxenbury, Dame Shirley Ann, DBE
Palmer, Dame Felicity Joan, DBE
Paraskeva, *Rt. Hon.* Dame Janet, DBE
Park, Dame Merle Florence (Mrs Bloch), DBE
Parker, *Hon.* Dame Judith Mary Frances, DBE
Partridge, *Prof.* Dame Linda, DBE
Patel, Dame Indira, DBE
Paterson, Dame Vicki, DBE

Pauffley, *Hon.* Dame Anna Evelyn Hamilton, DBE
Peacock, Dame Alison Margaret, DBE
Pearce, *Prof.* Dame Shirley, DBE
Pereira, *Hon.* Dame Janice Mesadis, DBE
Penhaligon, Dame Annette (Mrs Egerton), DBE
Perkins, Dame Mary Lesley, DBE
Peters, Dame Mary Elizabeth, CH, DBE
Peyton-Jones, Dame Julia, DBE
Phillips, Dame Jane Elizabeth Ailwen (Sian), DBE
Pienaar, Dame Erica, DBE
Pindling, Lady (Marguerite Matilda), GCMG
Platt, Dame Denise, DBE
Plotnikoff, Dame Joyce Evelyn, DBE
Plowright, Dame Joan Ann, DBE
Plunket Greene, Dame Barbara Mary, DBE
Poole, Dame Avril Anne Barker, DBE
Porter, Dame Shirley (Lady Porter), DBE
Powell, Dame Sally Ann Vickers, DBE
Pringle, Dame Anne Fyfe, DCMG
Proudman, *Hon.* Dame Sonia Rosemary Susan, DBE
Pugh, *Dr* Dame Gillian Mary, DBE
Rabbatts, Dame Heather Victoria, DBE
Rafferty, *Rt. Hon.* Dame Anne Judith, DBE
Rantzen, Dame Esther Louise (Mrs Wilcox), DBE
Rawson, *Prof.* Dame Jessica Mary, DBE
Rees, *Prof.* Dame Judith Anne, DBE
Rees, *Prof.* Dame Lesley Howard, DBE
Rees, *Prof.* Dame Teresa Lesley, DBE
Reeves, Dame Helen May, DBE
Refson, Dame Benita, DBE
Rego, Dame Paula Figueiroa, DBE
Reid, Dame Seona Elizabeth, DBE
Reynolds, Dame Fiona Claire, DBE
Rhodes, Dame Zandra Lindsey, DBE
Richard, Dame Alison (Fettes), DBE
Richardson, Dame Mary, DBE
Rigg, Dame Diana, DBE
Rimington, Dame Stella, DCB
Ritterman, Dame Janet, DBE
Roberts, Dame Jane Elisabeth, DBE
Roberts, *Hon.* Dame Jennifer Mary, DBE
Roberts, *Hon.* Dame Priscilla Jane Stephanie (Lady Roberts), DCVO
Robins, Dame Ruth Laura, DBE
Robinson, *Prof.* Dame Carol Vivien, DBE
Robottom, Dame Marlene, DBE
Roe, Dame Marion Audrey, DBE
Roe, Dame Raigh Edith, DBE
Ronson, Dame Gail, DBE
Roscoe, *Dr* Dame Ingrid Mary, DCVO
Rose, *Hon.* Dame Vivien Judith, DBE
Ross-Wawrzynski, Dame Dana (Mrs Ross-Wawrzynski), DBE
Rothwell, *Prof.* Dame Nancy Jane, DBE
Routledge, Dame Katherine Patricia, DBE
Ruddock, *Rt. Hon.* Dame Joan Mary, DBE
Runciman of Doxford, The Viscountess, DBE
Russell, *Hon.* Dame Alison Hunter, DBE
Russell, *Dr* Dame Philippa Margaret, DBE
Sackler, Dame Theresa, DBE
Salmond, *Prof.* Dame Mary Anne, DBE
Savill, Dame Rosalind Joy, DBE
Sawyer, *Rt. Hon.* Dame Joan Augusta, DBE
Scardino, Dame Marjorie, DBE
Scott, Dame Catherine Margaret (Mrs Denton), DBE
Scott Thomas, Dame Kristin, DBE
Seward, Dame Margaret Helen Elizabeth, DBE
Shafik, *Dr* Dame Nemat Talaat, DBE
Sharp, *Rt. Hon.* Dame Victoria Madeleine, DBE
Shaw, *Prof.* Dame Pamela Jean, DBE
Sheldrick, *Dr* Dame Daphne Marjorie, DBE
Shirley, Dame Stephanie, CH, DBE
Shovelton, Dame Helena, DBE

Sibley, Dame Antoinette (Mrs Corbett), DBE
Sills, *Prof.* Dame Eileen, DBE
Silver, *Dr* Dame Ruth Muldoon, DBE
Simler, *Hon.* Dame Ingrid Ann (Mrs Bernstein), DBE
Slade, *Hon.* Dame Elizabeth Ann, DBE
Slingo, *Prof.* Dame Julia Mary, DBE
Smith, Dame Dela, DBE
Smith, *Rt. Hon.* Dame Janet Hilary (Mrs Mathieson), DBE
Smith, *Hon.* Dame Jennifer Meredith, DBE
Smith, Dame Margaret Natalie (Maggie) (Mrs Cross), CH, DBE
Snowball, Dame Priscilla (Cilla) Deborah, DBE
Southgate, *Prof.* Dame Lesley Jill, DBE
Spelman, *Rt. Hon.* Dame Caroline Alice, DBE
Spencer, Dame Rosemary Jane, DCMG
Stacey, Dame Glenys Jean (Mrs Kyle), DBE
Steel, *Hon.* Dame (Anne) Heather (Mrs Beattie), DBE
Stocking, Dame Barbara Mary, DBE
Storey, Dame Sarah Joanne, DBE
Strachan, Dame Valerie Patricia Marie, DCB
Strank, *Dr* Dame Angela Rosemary Emily, DBE
Strathern, *Prof.* Dame Anne Marilyn, DBE
Street, Dame Susan Ruth, DCB
Stringer, *Prof.* Dame Joan Kathleen, DBE
Sutherland, Dame Veronica Evelyn, DBE, CMG
Suzman, Dame Janet, DBE
Swift, *Hon.* Dame Caroline Jane (Mrs Openshaw), DBE
Symmonds, Dame Olga Patricia, DBE
Tanner, *Dr* Dame Mary Elizabeth, DBE
Taylor, Dame Meg, DBE
Te Kanawa, Dame Kiri Janette, DBE
Theis, *Hon.* Dame Lucy Morgan, DBE
Thirlwall, *Rt. Hon.* Dame Kathryn Mary, DBE
Thomas, *Prof.* Dame Jean Olwen, DBE
Thomas, Dame Maureen Elizabeth (Lady Thomas), DBE
Thompson, Dame Ila Dianne, DBE
Thornton, *Prof.* Dame Janet Maureen, DBE
Tickell, Dame Clare Oriana, DBE
Tinson, Dame Sue, DBE
Tizard, Dame Catherine Anne, GCMG, GCVO, DBE
Tokiel, Dame Rosa, DBE

Trotter, Dame Janet Olive, DBE
Twelftree, Dame Marcia, DBE
Uchida, Dame Mitsuko, DBE
Uprichard, Dame Mary Elizabeth, DBE
Varley, Dame Joan Fleetwood, DBE
Wagner, Dame Gillian Mary Millicent (Lady Wagner), DBE
Wallace, *Prof.* Dame Helen Sarah, DBE, CMG
Wallis, Dame Sheila Ann, DBE
Walter, Dame Harriet Mary, DBE
Walters, Dame Julie Mary, DBE
Warburton, Dame Arabella, DBE
Warner, *Prof.* Dame Marina Sarah, DBE, FBA
Waterhouse, *Dr* Dame Rachel Elizabeth, DBE
Waterman, *Dr* Dame Fanny, DBE
Watkins, *Prof.* Dame Caroline Leigh, DBE
Watkinson, Dame Angela Eileen, DBE
Webb, *Prof.* Dame Patricia, DBE
Weir, Dame Gillian Constance (Mrs Phelps), DBE
Weller, Dame Rita, DBE
Wells, Dame Rachel Anne, DCVO
Weston, Dame Margaret Kate, DBE
Westwood, Dame Vivienne Isabel, DBE
Whipple, *Hon.* Dame Philippa Jane Edwards, DBE
Whitehead, *Hon.* Dame Annabel Alice Hoyer, DCVO
Whitehead, *Prof.* Dame Margaret McRae, DBE
Whitfield, Dame June Rosemary, DBE
Williams, Dame Josephine, DBE
Willmot, Dame Glenis, DBE
Wilson, Dame Jacqueline, DBE
Wilton, Dame Penelope Alice, DBE
Wilson-Barnett, *Prof.* Dame Jenifer, DBE
Windsor, Dame Barbara, DBE
Winterton, *Rt. Hon.* Dame Rosalie, DBE
Wintour, Dame Anna, DBE
Wolfson de Botton, Dame Janet (Mrs Wolfson de Botton), DBE
Wong Yick-ming, Dame Rosanna, DBE
Woodward, Dame Barbara Janet, DCMG, OBE
Woolf, Dame Catherine Fiona, DBE
Wykes, *Prof.* Dame Til Hilary Margaret, DBE
Zaffar, Dame Naila, DBE

DECORATIONS AND MEDALS

PRINCIPAL DECORATIONS AND MEDALS IN ORDER OF WEAR

VICTORIA CROSS (VC), 1856 (*see* below)
GEORGE CROSS (GC), 1940 (*see* below)

BRITISH ORDERS OF KNIGHTHOOD
(*see also* Orders of Chivalry)
Order of the Garter
Order of the Thistle
Order of St Patrick
Order of the Bath
Order of Merit
Order of the Star of India
Order of St Michael and George
Order of the Indian Empire
Order of the Crown of India
Royal Victorian Order (Classes I, II and III)
Order of the British Empire (Classes I, II and III)
Order of the Companions of Honour
Distinguished Service Order
Royal Victorian Order (Class IV)
Order of the British Empire (Class IV)
Imperial Service Order
Royal Victorian Order (Class V)
Order of the British Empire (Class V)

BARONET'S BADGE

KNIGHT BACHELOR'S BADGE

INDIAN ORDER OF MERIT (MILITARY)

DECORATIONS
Conspicuous Gallantry Cross (CGC), 1995
Royal Red Cross Class I (RRC), 1883
Distinguished Service Cross (DSC), 1914
Military Cross (MC), December 1914
Distinguished Flying Cross (DFC), 1918
Air Force Cross (AFC), 1918
Royal Red Cross Class II (ARRC)
Order of British India
Kaisar-i-Hind Medal
Order of St John

MEDALS FOR GALLANTRY AND DISTINGUISHED CONDUCT
Union of South Africa Queen's Medal for Bravery, in Gold
Distinguished Conduct Medal (DCM), 1854
Conspicuous Gallantry Medal (CGM), 1874
Conspicuous Gallantry Medal (Flying)
George Medal (GM), 1940
Queen's Police Medal for Gallantry
Queen's Fire Service Medal for Gallantry
Royal West African Frontier Force Distinguished Conduct Medal
King's African Rifles Distinguished Conduct Medal
Indian Distinguished Service Medal
Union of South Africa Queen's Medal for Bravery, in Silver
Distinguished Service Medal (DSM), 1914
Military Medal (MM), 1916
Distinguished Flying Medal (DFM), 1918
Air Force Medal (AFM)
Constabulary Medal (Ireland)
Medal for Saving Life at Sea (Sea Gallantry Medal)
Indian Order of Merit (Civil)
Indian Police Medal for Gallantry
Ceylon Police Medal for Gallantry

Sierra Leone Police Medal for Gallantry
Sierra Leone Fire Brigades Medal for Gallantry
Overseas Territories Police Medal for Gallantry
Queen's Gallantry Medal (QGM), 1974
Royal Victorian Medal (RVM), Gold, Silver and Bronze
British Empire Medal (BEM)
Canada Medal
Queen's Police Medal for Distinguished Service (QPM)
Queen's Fire Service Medal for Distinguished Service (QFSM)
Queen's Volunteer Reserves Medal
Queen's Medal for Chiefs

CAMPAIGN MEDALS AND STARS
Including authorised United Nations, European Community/Union and North Atlantic Treaty Organisation medals (in order of date of campaign for which awarded).

Iraq Reconstruction Service Medal
Civilian Service Medal (Afghanistan)

POLAR MEDALS
in order of date

IMPERIAL SERVICE MEDAL

POLICE MEDALS FOR VALUABLE SERVICE
Indian Police Medal for Meritorious Service
Ceylon Police Medal for Merit
Sierra Leone Police Medal for Meritorious Service
Sierra Leone Fire Brigades Medal for Meritorious Service
Overseas Territories Police Medal for Meritorious Service

BADGE OF HONOUR

JUBILEE, CORONATION AND DURBAR MEDALS
Queen Victoria, King Edward VII, King George V, King George VI, Queen Elizabeth II, Visit Commemoration and Long and Faithful Service Medals

EFFICIENCY AND LONG SERVICE DECORATIONS AND MEDALS
Medal for Meritorious Service
Accumulated Campaign Service Medal
Medal for Long Service and Good Conduct (Military)
Naval Long Service and Good Conduct Medal
Medal for Meritorious Service (Royal Navy 1918–28)
Indian Long Service and Good Conduct Medal
Indian Meritorious Service Medal
Royal Marines Meritorious Service Medal (1849–1947)
Royal Air Force Meritorious Service Medal (1918–1928)
Royal Air Force Long Service and Good Conduct Medal
Medal for Long Service and Good Conduct (Ulster Defence Regiment)
Indian Long Service and Good Conduct Medal
Royal West African Frontier Force Long Service and Good Conduct Medal
Royal Sierra Leone Military Forces Long Service and Good Conduct Medal
King's African Rifles Long Service and Good Conduct Medal
Indian Meritorious Service Medal
Police Long Service and Good Conduct Medal
Fire Brigade Long Service and Good Conduct Medal
African Police Medal for Meritorious Service
Royal Canadian Mounted Police Long Service Medal
Ceylon Police Long Service Medal
Ceylon Fire Services Long Service Medal
Sierra Leone Police Long Service Medal
Overseas Territories Police Long Service Medal

Sierra Leone Fire Brigades Long Service Medal
Mauritius Police Long Service and Good Conduct Medal
Mauritius Fire Services Long Service and Good Conduct Medal
Mauritius Prisons Service Long Service and Good Conduct Medal
Overseas Territories Fire Brigades Long Service Medal
Overseas Territories Prison Service Medal
Hong Kong Disciplined Services Medal
Army Emergency Reserve Decoration (ERD)
Volunteer Officers' Decoration (VD)
Volunteer Long Service Medal
Volunteer Officers' Decoration (for India and the Colonies)
Volunteer Long Service Medal (for India and the Colonies)
Colonial Auxiliary Forces Officers' Decoration
Colonial Auxiliary Forces Long Service Medal
Medal for Good Shooting (Naval)
Militia Long Service Medal
Imperial Yeomanry Long Service Medal
Territorial Decoration (TD), 1908
Ceylon Armed Services Long Service Medal
Efficiency Decoration (ED)
Territorial Efficiency Medal
Efficiency Medal
Special Reserve Long Service and Good Conduct Medal
Decoration for Officers of the Royal Navy Reserve (RD), 1910
Decoration for Officers of the Royal Naval Volunteer Reserve
  (VRD)
Royal Naval Reserve Long Service and Good Conduct Medal
Royal Naval Volunteer Reserve Long Service and Good Conduct
  Medal
Royal Naval Auxiliary Sick Berth Reserve Long Service and Good
  Conduct Medal
Royal Fleet Reserve Long Service and Good Conduct Medal
Royal Naval Wireless Auxiliary Reserve Long Service and Good
  Conduct Medal
Royal Naval Auxiliary Service Medal
Air Efficiency Award (AE), 1942
Volunteer Reserves Service Medal
Ulster Defence Regiment Medal
Northern Ireland Home Service Medal
Queen's Medal (for Champion Shots of the RN and RM)
Queen's Medal (for Champion Shots of the New Zealand
  Naval Forces)
Queen's Medal (for Champion Shots in the Military Forces)
Queen's Medal (for Champion Shots of the Air Forces)
Cadet Forces Medal, 1950
HM Coastguard Long Service and Good Conduct Medal
Special Constabulary Long Service Medal
Canadian Forces Decoration
Royal Observer Corps Medal
Civil Defence Long Service Medal
Ambulance Service (Emergency Duties) Long Service and Good
  Conduct Medal
Royal Fleet Auxiliary Service Medal
Prison Services (Operational Duties) Long Service and Good
  Conduct Medal
Jersey Honorary Police Long Service and Good Conduct Medal
Merchant Navy Medal for Meritorious Service
Ebola Medal for Service in West Africa
National Crime Agency Long Service and Good Conduct Medal
Rhodesia Medal
Royal Ulster Constabulary Service Medal
Northern Ireland Prison Service Medal
Union of South Africa Commemoration Medal
Indian Independence Medal
Pakistan Medal
Ceylon Armed Services Inauguration Medal
Ceylon Police Independence Medal (1948)
Sierra Leone Independence Medal
Jamaica Independence Medal
Uganda Independence Medal
Malawi Independence Medal
Fiji Independence Medal
Papua New Guinea Independence Medal

Solomon Islands Independence Medal
Service Medal of the Order of St John
Badge of the Order of the League of Mercy
Voluntary Medical Service Medal (1932)
Women's Royal Voluntary Service Medal
South African Medal for War Services
Overseas Territories Special Constabulary Medal

HONORARY MEMBERSHIP OF COMMONWEALTH
ORDERS

OTHER COMMONWEALTH MEMBERS' ORDERS,
DECORATIONS AND MEDALS

FOREIGN ORDERS

FOREIGN DECORATIONS

FOREIGN MEDALS

THE VICTORIA CROSS (1856)

FOR CONSPICUOUS BRAVERY

VC

Ribbon, Crimson, for all Services (until 1918 it was blue for
the Royal Navy)

Instituted on 29 January 1856, the Victoria Cross was awarded
retrospectively to 1854, the first being held by Lt. C. D. Lucas,
RN, for bravery in the Baltic Sea on 21 June 1854 (gazetted
24 February 1857). The first 62 crosses were presented by
Queen Victoria in Hyde Park, London, on 26 June 1857.
  The Victoria Cross is worn before all other decorations, on
the left breast, and consists of a cross-pattée of bronze, 3.8cm
in diameter, with the royal crown surmounted by a lion in the
centre, and beneath there is the inscription *For Valour.* In July
2015 the tax-free annuity given to holders of the VC,
irrespective of need or other conditions, was increased to
£10,000. At the same time, further annual increases to the
annuity were linked to the CPI rate of inflation. In 1911, the
right to receive the cross was extended to Indian soldiers, and
in 1920 to matrons, sisters and nurses, the staff of the nursing
services and other services pertaining to hospitals and nursing,
and to civilians of either sex regularly or temporarily under the
orders, direction or supervision of the naval, military, or air
forces of the crown.

SURVIVING RECIPIENTS OF THE VICTORIA CROSS
as at 31 August 2017
Apiata, *Cpl.* B. H., VC (New Zealand Special Air Service)
  2004 *Afghanistan*
Beharry, *LSgt* J. G., VC (Princess of Wales's Royal Regiment)
  2005 *Iraq*
Cruickshank, *Flt Lt.* J. A., VC (RAFVR)
  1944 *World War*
Donaldson, *Cpl.* M. G. S., VC (Australian Special Air Service)
  2008 *Afghanistan*
Keighran, *Cpl.* D. A., VC (Royal Australian Regiment)
  2012 *Afghanistan*
Leakey, *Lance Cpl.* J. M., VC (Parachute Regiment)
  2015 *Afghanistan*
Payne, *WO* K., VC, DSC (USA) (Australian Army Training
  Team)
  1969 *Vietnam*
Rambahadur Limbu, *Capt.,* VC, MVO (10th Princess Mary's
  Gurkha Rifles)

1965 *Sarawak*
Roberts-Smith, *Cpl.* B., VC (Australian Special Air Service)
   2010 *Afghanistan*
Speakman, *Sgt.* W., VC (Black Watch, attached KOSB)
   1951 *Korea*

THE GEORGE CROSS (1940)

FOR GALLANTRY

GC

Ribbon, Dark blue, threaded through a bar adorned with
   laurel leaves
Instituted 24 September 1940 (with amendments,
   3 November 1942)

The George Cross is worn before all other decorations (except
the VC) on the left breast (when worn by a woman it may be
worn on the left shoulder from a ribbon of the same width and
colour fashioned into a bow). It consists of a plain silver cross
with four equal limbs, the cross having in the centre a circular
medallion bearing a design showing St George and the
Dragon. The inscription *For Gallantry* appears round the
medallion and in the angle of each limb of the cross is the royal
cypher 'G VI' forming a circle concentric with the medallion.
The reverse is plain and bears the name of the recipient and the
date of the award. The cross is suspended by a ring from a bar
adorned with laurel leaves on dark blue ribbon 3.8cm wide.

   The cross is intended primarily for civilians; awards to the
fighting services are confined to actions for which purely
military honours are not normally granted. It is awarded only
for acts of the greatest heroism or of the most conspicuous
courage in circumstances of extreme danger. In July 2015 the
tax-free annuity given to holders of the GC, irrespective of
need or other conditions, was increased to £10,000. At the
same time, further annual increases to the annuity were linked
to the CPI rate of inflation. The cross has twice been awarded
collectively rather than to an individual: to the island of Malta
(1942) and the Royal Ulster Constabulary (1999).

   In October 1971 all surviving holders of the Albert Medal
and the Edward Medal exchanged those decorations for the
George Cross.

SURVIVING RECIPIENTS OF THE GEORGE CROSS
as at 31 August 2017
If the recipient originally received the Albert Medal (AM) or
the Edward Medal (EM), this is indicated by the initials in
parentheses.

Bamford, J., GC, 1952
Beaton, J., GC, CVO, 1974
Croucher, *Lance Cpl.* M., GC, 2008
Finney, C., GC, 2003
Flintoff, H. H., GC (EM), 1944
Gledhill, A. J., GC, 1967
Haberfield, *CSgt.* K. H., GC, 2005
Hughes, *WO2* K. S., GC, 2010
Johnson, *WO1* (*SSM*) B., GC, 1990
Kinne, D. G., GC, 1954
Lowe, A. R., GC (AM), 1949
Norton, *Maj.* P. A., GC, 2006
Pratt, M. K., GC, 1978
Purves, Mrs M., GC (AM), 1949
Raweng, Awang anak, GC, 1951
Shephard, S. J., GC, 2014
Stevens, H. W., GC, 1958
Troulan, D., GC, QGM, 2017
Walker, C., GC, 1972

THE ELIZABETH CROSS (2009)

EC

Instituted 1 July 2009

The Elizabeth Cross consists of a silver cross with a laurel
wreath passing between the arms, which bear the floral
symbols of England (rose), Scotland (thistle), Ireland
(shamrock) and Wales (daffodil). The centre of the cross bears
the royal cypher and the reverse is inscribed with the name of
the person for whom it is in honour. The cross is accompanied
by a memorial scroll and a miniature.

   The cross was created to commemorate UK armed forces
personnel who have died on operations or as a result of an act
of terrorism. It may be granted to and worn by the next of kin
of any eligible personnel who died from 1 January 1948 to
date. It offers the wearer no precedence. Those that are eligible
include the next of kin of personnel who died while serving
on a medal earning operation, as a result of an act of terrorism,
or on a non-medal earning operation where death was caused
by the inherent high risk of the task.

   The Elizabeth Cross is not intended as a posthumous medal
for the fallen but as an emblem of national recognition of the
loss and sacrifice made by the personnel and their families.

CHIEFS OF CLANS IN SCOTLAND

Only chiefs of whole Names or Clans are included, except certain special instances (marked *) who, though not chiefs of a whole Name, were or are for some reason (eg the Macdonald forfeiture) independent. Under decision (*Campbell-Gray*, 1950) that a bearer of a 'double or triple-barrelled' surname cannot be held chief of a part of such, several others cannot be included in the list at present.

THE ROYAL HOUSE: HM The Queen

AGNEW: Sir Crispin Agnew of Lochnaw, Bt., QC
ANSTRUTHER: Tobias Anstruther of Anstruther and Balcaskie
ARBUTHNOTT: Viscount of Arbuthnott
BANNERMAN: Sir David Bannerman of Elsick, Bt.
BARCLAY: Peter C. Barclay of Towie Barclay and of that Ilk
BORTHWICK: Lord Borthwick
BOYLE: Earl of Glasgow
BRODIE: Alexander Brodie of Brodie
BROUN OF COLSTOUN: Sir Wayne Broun of Colstoun, Bt.
BRUCE: Earl of Elgin and Kincardine, KT
BUCHAN: David Buchan of Auchmacoy
BURNETT: James C. A. Burnett of Leys
CAMERON: Donald Cameron of Lochiel
CAMPBELL: Duke of Argyll
CARMICHAEL: Richard Carmichael of Carmichael
CARNEGIE: Duke of Fife
CATHCART: Earl Cathcart
CHARTERIS: Earl of Wemyss and March
CLAN CHATTAN: K. Mackintosh of Clan Chattan
CHISHOLM: Hamish Chisholm of Chisholm (*The Chisholm*)
COCHRANE: Earl of Dundonald
COLQUHOUN: Sir Malcolm Rory Colquhoun of Luss, Bt.
CRANSTOUN: David Cranstoun of that Ilk
CUMMING: Sir Alastair Cumming of Altyre, Bt.
DARROCH: Duncan Darroch of Gourock
DAVIDSON OF DAVIDSTON: Grant Davidson of Davidston
DEWAR: Michael Dewar of that Ilk and Vogrie
DRUMMOND: Earl of Perth
DUNBAR: Sir James Dunbar of Mochrum, Bt.
DUNDAS: David Dundas of Dundas
DURIE: Andrew Durie of Durie, CBE
ELIOTT: Mrs Margaret Eliott of Redheugh
ERSKINE: Earl of Mar and Kellie
FARQUHARSON: Capt. Alwyne Farquharson of Invercauld, MC
FERGUSSON: Sir Charles Fergusson of Kilkerran, Bt.
FORBES: Lord Forbes
FORSYTH: Alistair Forsyth of that Ilk
FRASER: Lady Saltoun
*FRASER (OF LOVAT): Lord Lovat
GAYRE: Reinold Gayre of Gayre and Nigg
GORDON: Marquess of Huntly
GRAHAM: Duke of Montrose
GRANT: Lord Strathspey
GUNN: Iain Gunn of Gunn
GUTHRIE: Alexander Guthrie of Guthrie
HAIG: Earl Haig
HALDANE: Martin Haldane of Gleneagles
HANNAY: David Hannay of Kirkdale and of that Ilk
HAY: Earl of Erroll
HENDERSON: Alistair Henderson of Fordell
HUNTER: Pauline Hunter of Hunterston
IRVINE OF DRUM: David Irvine of Drum
JARDINE: Sir William Jardine of Applegirth, Bt.

JOHNSTONE: Earl of Annandale and Hartfell
KEITH: Earl of Kintore
KENNEDY: Marquess of Ailsa
KERR: Marquess of Lothian, PC
KINCAID: Madam Arabella Kincaid of Kincaid
LAMONT: Revd Peter Lamont of that Ilk
LEASK: Jonathan Leask of that Ilk
LENNOX: Edward Lennox of that Ilk
LESLIE: Earl of Rothes
LINDSAY: Earl of Crawford and Balcarres, KT, GCVO, PC
LIVINGSTONE (or MACLEA): Niall Livingstone of the Bachuil
LUMSDEN: Gillem Lumsden of that Ilk and Blanerne
MACALESTER: William St J. McAlester of Loup and Kennox
MACARTHUR; John MacArthur of that Ilk
MCBAIN: James H. McBain of McBain
MACDONALD: Lord Macdonald (*The Macdonald of Macdonald*)
*MACDONALD OF CLANRANALD: Ranald Macdonald of Clanranald
*MACDONALD OF KEPPOCH: Ranald MacDonald of Keppoch
*MACDONALD OF SLEAT (CLAN HUSTEAIN): Sir Ian Macdonald of Sleat, Bt.
*MACDONELL OF GLENGARRY: Ranald MacDonell of Glengarry
MACDOUGALL: Morag MacDougall of MacDougall
MACDOWALL: Fergus Macdowall of Garthland
MACGREGOR: Sir Malcolm MacGregor of MacGregor, Bt.
MACINTYRE: Donald MacIntyre of Glenoe
MACKAY: Lord Reay
MACKENZIE: Earl of Cromartie
MACKINNON: Anne Mackinnon of Mackinnon
MACKINTOSH: John Mackintosh of Mackintosh (*The Mackintosh of Mackintosh*)
MACLACHLAN: Euan MacLachlan of MacLachlan
MACLAREN: Donald MacLaren of MacLaren and Achleskine
MACLEAN: Hon. Sir Lachlan Maclean of Duart, Bt., CVO
MACLENNAN: Ruaraidh MacLennan of MacLennan
MACLEOD: Hugh MacLeod of MacLeod
MACMILLAN: George MacMillan of MacMillan
MACNAB: James W. A. Macnab of Macnab (*The Macnab*)
MACNAGHTEN: Sir Malcolm Macnaghten of Macnaghten and Dundarave, Bt.
MACNEACAIL: John Macneacail of Macneacail and Scorrybreac
MACNEIL OF BARRA: Rory Macneil of Barra (*The Macneil of Barra*)
MACPHERSON: Hon. Sir William Macpherson of Cluny, TD
MACTAVISH: Steven MacTavish of Dunardry
MACTHOMAS: Andrew MacThomas of Finegand
MAITLAND: Earl of Lauderdale
MAKGILL: Viscount of Oxfuird
MALCOLM (MACCALLUM): Robin N. L. Malcolm of Poltalloch
MAR: Countess of Mar
MARJORIBANKS: Andrew Marjoribanks of that Ilk
MATHESON: Sir Alexander Matheson of Matheson, Bt.
MENZIES: David Menzies of Menzies
MOFFAT: Madam Moffat of that Ilk
MONCREIFFE: Hon. Peregrine Moncreiffe of that Ilk
MONTGOMERIE: Earl of Eglinton and Winton
MORRISON: Dr John Ruairidh Morrison of Ruchdi
MUNRO: Hector Munro of Foulis
MURRAY: Duke of Atholl

NESBITT (or NISBET): Mark Nesbitt of that Ilk
OGILVY: Earl of Airlie, KT, GCVO, PC
OLIPHANT: Richard Oliphant of that Ilk
RAMSAY: Earl of Dalhousie
RIDDELL: Sir Walter Riddell of Riddell, Bt.
ROBERTSON: Alexander Robertson of Struan *(Struan-Robertson)*
ROLLO: Lord Rollo
ROSS: David Ross of that Ilk and Balnagowan
RUTHVEN: Earl of Gowrie, PC
SCOTT: Duke of Buccleuch and Queensberry, KBE
SCRYMGEOUR: Earl of Dundee

SEMPILL: Lord Sempill
SHAW: John Shaw of Tordarroch
SINCLAIR: Earl of Caithness, PC
SKENE: Dugald Skene of Skene
STIRLING: Fraser Stirling of Cader
STRANGE: Maj. Timothy Strange of Balcaskie
SUTHERLAND: Countess of Sutherland
SWINTON: John Swinton of that Ilk
TROTTER: Alexander Trotter of Mortonhall, CVO
URQUHART: Wilkins F. Urquhart of Urquhart
WEDDERBURN: The Master of Dundee
WEMYSS: Michael Wemyss of that Ilk

THE PRIVY COUNCIL

The sovereign in council, or Privy Council, was the chief source of executive power until the system of cabinet government developed in the 18th century. Now the Privy Council's main functions are to advise the sovereign and to exercise its own statutory responsibilities independent of the sovereign in council.

Membership of the Privy Council is automatic upon appointment to certain government and judicial positions in the UK, eg cabinet ministers must be Privy Counsellors and are sworn in on first assuming office. Membership is also accorded by the Queen to eminent people in the UK and independent countries of the Commonwealth of which she is Queen, on the recommendation of the prime minister. Membership of the council is retained for life, except for very occasional removals.

The administrative functions of the Privy Council are carried out by the Privy Council Office under the direction of the president of the council, who is always a member of the cabinet. (*see also* Parliament)

President of the Council, Rt. Hon. Andrea Leadsom, MP

Clerk of the Council, Richard Tilbrook

Style The Right (or Rt.) Hon._
Envelope, The Right (or Rt.) Hon. F_ S_. Letter, Dear Mr/Miss/Mrs S_. *Spoken,* Mr/Miss/Mrs S_

It is incorrect to use the letters PC after the name in conjunction with the prefix The Right Hon., unless the Privy Counsellor is a peer below the rank of Marquess and so is styled The Right Hon. because of his/her rank.

MEMBERS *as at August 2017*

HRH The Duke of Edinburgh, 1951
HRH The Prince of Wales, 1977
HRH The Duke of Cambridge, 2016
HRH The Duchess of Cornwall, 2016

Abbott, Diane, 2017
Abernethy, *Hon.* Lord (Alastair Cameron), 2005
Adonis, Lord, 2009
Aikens, Sir Richard, 2008
Ainsworth, Robert, 2005
Airlie, Earl of, 1984
Aldous, Sir William, 1995
Alebua, Ezekiel, 1988
Alexander, Sir Danny, 2010
Alexander, Douglas, 2005
Amos, Baroness, 2003
Anderson of Swansea, Lord, 2000
Anelay of St Johns, Baroness, 2009
Angiolini, Dame Elish, 2006
Anthony, Douglas, 1971
Arbuthnot of Edrom, Lord, 1998
Arden, Dame Mary, 2000
Armstrong of Hill Top, Baroness, 1999
Arthur, *Hon.* Owen, 1995
Ashcroft, Lord, 2012
Ashdown of Norton-sub-Hamdon, Lord, 1989
Ashton of Upholland, Baroness, 2006
Astor of Hever, Lord, 2015
Atkins, Sir Robert, 1995
Auld, Sir Robin, 1995
Baker, Norman, 2014
Baker, Sir Thomas, 2002
Baker of Dorking, Lord, 1984
Baldry, Sir Tony, 2013
Balls, Ed, 2007
Barker of Battle, Lord, 2012
Barron, Sir Kevin, 2001
Barrow, Dean, 2016
Barwell, Gavin, 2017
Bassam of Brighton, Lord, 2009
Bates, Lord, 2015
Battle, John, 2002

Bean, Sir David, 2014
Beatson, Sir Jack, 2013
Beckett, Dame Margaret, 1993
Beith, Lord, 1992
Beldam, Sir Roy, 1989
Benn, Hilary, 2003
Benyon, Richard, 2017
Bercow, John, 2009
Birch, Sir William, 1992
Black, Dame Jill, 2010
Blackford, Ian, 2017
Blackstone, Baroness, 2001
Blair, Anthony, 1994
Blanchard, Peter, 1998
Blears, Hazel, 2005
Blencathra, Lord, 1995
Blunkett, Lord, 1997
Boateng, Lord, 1999
Bolger, James, 1991
Bonomy, *Hon.* Lord (Iain Bonomy), 2010
Boothroyd, Baroness, 1992
Bottomley of Nettlestone, Baroness, 1992
Boyd of Duncansby, Lord, 2000
Brabazon of Tara, Lord, 2013
Bracadale, *Hon.* Lord (Alistair Campbell), 2013
Bradley, Karen, 2016
Bradley, Lord, 2001
Bradshaw, Ben, 2009
Brake, Thomas, 2011
Briggs, Sir Michael, 2013
Brodie, *Hon.* Lord (Philip Brodie), 2013
Brokenshire, James, 2015
Brooke, Dame Annette, 2014
Brooke, Sir Henry, 1996
Brooke of Sutton Mandeville, Lord, 1988
Brown, Gordon, 1996
Brown, Nicholas, 1997
Brown, Sir Stephen, 1983
Brown of Eaton-under-Heywood, Lord, 1992

Browne of Ladyton, Lord, 2005
Browne-Wilkinson, Lord, 1983
Bruce of Bennachie, Lord, 2006
Burnett, Sir Ian, 2014
Burnham, Andy, 2007
Burns, Sir Simon, 2011
Burnton, Sir Stanley, 2008
Burstow, Paul, 2012
Burt, Alistair, 2013
Butler of Brockwell, Lord, 2004
Butler-Sloss, Baroness, 1988
Buxton, Sir Richard, 1997
Byers, Stephen, 1998
Byrne, Liam, 2008
Byron, Sir Dennis, 2004
Cable, Sir Vincent, 2010
Caborn, Richard, 1999
Cairns, Alun, 2016
Caithness, Earl of, 1990
Cameron, David, 2005
Cameron of Lochbroom, Lord, 1984
Camoys, Lord, 1997
Campbell, Alan, 2014
Campbell, Sir William, 1999
Campbell of Pittenweem, Lord, 1999
Canterbury, Archbishop of, 2013
Carey of Clifton, Lord, 1991
Carloway, *Hon.* Lord (Colin Sutherland), 2008
Carmichael, Alistair, 2010
Carnwath of Notting Hill, Lord, 2002
Carrington, Lord, 1959
Carswell, Lord, 1993
Chadwick, Sir John, 1997
Chalfont, Lord, 1964
Chalker of Wallasey, Baroness, 1987
Chan, Sir Julius, 1981
Chartres, Rt. Revd Richard, 1995
Chilcot, Sir John, 2004
Christie, Perry, 2004
Clark, Greg, 2010
Clark, Helen, 1990
Clark of Calton, Baroness, 2013
Clark of Windermere, Lord, 1997
Clarke, Charles, 2001

Clarke, Sir Christopher, 2013
Clarke, Kenneth, 1984
Clarke, *Hon.* Lord (Matthew Clarke), 2008
Clarke, Thomas, 1997
Clarke of Stone-Cum-Ebony, Lord, 1998
Clegg, Nicholas, 2008
Clinton-Davis, Lord, 1998
Clwyd, Ann, 2004
Coghlin, Sir Patrick, 2009
Collins of Mapesbury, Lord, 2007
Cooper, Yvette, 2007
Cope of Berkeley, Lord, 1988
Corbyn, Jeremy, 2015
Corston, Baroness, 2003
Cosgrove, *Hon.* Lady (Hazel Cosgrove), 2003
Crabb, Stephen, 2014
Crawford and Balcarres, Earl of, 1972
Creech, *Hon.* Wyatt, 1999
Crickhowell, Lord, 1979
Cullen of Whitekirk, Lord, 1997
Cunningham of Felling, Lord, 1993
Curry, David, 1996
Darling of Roulanish, Lord, 1997
Darzi of Denham, Lord, 2009
Davey, Sir Edward, 2012
Davidson, Ruth, 2016
Davies, Denzil, 1978
Davies, Ronald, 1997
Davies of Oldham, Lord, 2006
Davis, David, 1997
Davis, Sir Nigel, 2011
Davis, Terence, 1999
de la Bastide, Michael, 2004
de Silva, Sir Desmond, 2011
Dean of Thornton-le-Fylde, Baroness, 1998
Deben, Lord, 1985
Denham, John, 2000
Denham, Lord, 1981
Dholakia, Lord, 2010
Dobson, Frank, 1997
Dodds, Nigel, 2010
Donaldson, Sir Jeffrey, 2007
Dorrell, Stephen, 1994
Dorrian, *Hon.* Lady (Leona Dorrian), 2013
Douglas, *Dr* Denzil, 2011
Drayson, Lord, 2008
Drummond Young, *Hon.* Lord (James Drummond Young), 2013
D'Souza, Baroness, 2009
Duncan, Sir Alan, 2010
Duncan Smith, Iain, 2001
Dyson, Lord, 2001
Eassie, *Hon.* Lord (Ronald Mackay), 2006
East, Paul, 1998
Eden of Winton, Lord, 1972
Edward, Sir David, 2005
Eggar, Timothy, 1995
Eichelbaum, Sir Thomas, 1989
Elias, Sir Patrick, 2009
Elias, *Hon.* Dame Sian, 1999
Elis-Thomas, Lord, 2004
Ellwood, Tobias, 2017
Emslie, *Hon.* Lord (George Emslie), 2011
Esquivel, Manuel, 1986
Etherton, Sir Terence, 2008
Evans, Sir Anthony, 1992

Evans of Bowes Park, Baroness, 2016
Evennett, David, 2015
Falconer of Thoroton, Lord, 2003
Fallon, Sir Michael, 2012
Featherstone, Baroness, 2014
Feldman of Elstree, Lord, 2015
Fellowes, Lord, 1990
Fergusson, Sir Alexander, 2010
Field, Frank, 1997
Field, Mark, 2015
Flaux, Sir Julian, 2017
Flint, Caroline, 2008
Floyd, Sir Christopher, 2013
Forsyth of Drumlean, Lord, 1995
Foster, Arlene, 2016
Foster of Bath, Lord, 2010
Foster of Bishop Auckland, Lord, 1993
Foulkes of Cumnock, Lord, 2002
Fowler, Lord, 1979
Fox, Liam, 2010
Francois, Mark, 2010
Freedman, Sir Lawrence, 2009
Freeman, Lord, 1993
Freud, Lord, 2015
Fulford, Sir Adrian, 2013
Gage, Sir William, 2004
Garden of Frognal, Baroness, 2015
Garel-Jones, Lord, 1992
Garnier, Sir Edward, 2015
Gauke, David, 2016
Geidt, Sir Christopher, 2007
George, Bruce, 2000
Gibb, Nicolas, 2016
Gibson, Sir Peter, 1993
Gill, *Hon.* Lord (Brian Gill), 2002
Gillan, Cheryl, 2010
Gillen, Sir John, 2014
Girvan, Sir (Frederick) Paul, 2007
Glennie, *Hon.* Lord (Angus Glennie), 2016
Gloster, Dame Elizabeth, 2013
Goldring, Sir John, 2008
Goldsmith, Lord, 2002
Goodlad, Lord, 1992
Gove, Michael, 2010
Gowrie, Earl of, 1984
Graham, Sir Douglas, 1998
Graham of Edmonton, Lord, 1998
Grayling, Chris, 2010
Green, Damian, 2012
Greening, Justine, 2011
Grieve, Dominic, 2010
Grocott, Lord, 2002
Gross, Sir Peter, 2010
Gummer, Ben, 2016
Habgood, Lord, 1983
Hague of Richmond, Lord, 1995
Hailsham, Viscount, 1992
Hain, Lord, 2001
Hale of Richmond, Baroness, 1999
Halfon, Robert, 2015
Hallett, Dame Heather, 2005
Hamblen, Sir Nicholas, 2016
Hamilton, *Hon.* Lord (Arthur Hamilton), 2002
Hamilton of Epsom, Lord, 1991
Hammond, Philip, 2010
Hancock, Matthew, 2014
Hands, Gregory, 2014
Hanley, Sir Jeremy, 1994
Hanson, David, 2007
Hardie, Lord, 1997

Hardie Boys, Sir Michael, 1989
Harman, Harriet, 1997
Harper, Mark, 2015
Haselhurst, Sir Alan, 1999
Hattersley, Lord, 1975
Hayes, John, 2013
Hayman, Baroness, 2000
Heald, Sir Oliver, 2016
Healey, John, 2008
Heath, David, 2015
Heathcoat-Amory, David, 1996
Henderson, Sir Launcelot, 2016
Hendry, Charles, 2015
Henley, Lord, 2013
Henry, John, 1996
Herbert, Nick, 2010
Heseltine, Lord, 1979
Heseltine, Sir William, 1986
Hesketh, Lord, 1991
Hewitt, Patricia, 2001
Hickinbottom, Sir Gary, 2017
Higgins, Lord, 1979
Higgins, Sir Malachy, 2007
Hill, Keith, 2003
Hill of Oareford, Lord, 2013
Hodge, Dame Margaret, 2003
Hodge, Lord, 2013
Hoffmann, Lord, 1992
Hollis of Heigham, Baroness, 1999
Hoon, Geoffrey, 1999
Hooper, Sir Anthony, 2004
Hope of Craighead, Lord, 1989
Hope of Thornes, Lord, 1991
Hordern, Sir Peter, 1993
Howard of Lympne, Lord, 1990
Howarth, George, 2005
Howarth of Newport, Lord, 2000
Howe, Earl, 2013
Howell of Guildford, Lord, 1979
Howells, Kim, 2009
Hoyle, Lindsay, 2013
Hughes, Sir Simon, 2010
Hughes of Ombersley, Lord, 2006
Hughes of Stretford, Baroness, 2004
Hunt, Jeremy, 2010
Hunt, Jonathon, 1989
Hunt of Kings Heath, Lord, 2009
Hunt of Wirral, Lord, 1990
Hurd of Westwell, Lord, 1982
Hutchison, Sir Michael, 1995
Hutton, Lord, 1988
Hutton of Furness, Lord, 2001
Inge, Lord, 2004
Ingraham, Hubert, 1993
Ingram, Adam, 1999
Irvine of Lairg, Lord, 1997
Irwin, Sir Stephen, 2016
Jack, Michael, 1997
Jackson, Sir Rupert, 2008
Jacob, Sir Robert, 2004
Jacobs, Francis, 2005
Janvrin, Lord, 1998
Javid, Sajid, 2014
Jay of Paddington, Baroness, 1998
Johnson, Alan, 2003
Johnson, Boris, 2016
Jones, Carwyn, 2010
Jones, David, 2012
Jones, Lord, 1999
Jopling, Lord, 1979
Jowell, Baroness, 1998
Judge, Lord, 1996
Jugnauth, Sir Aneerood, 1987

Kakkar, Lord, 2014
Kay, Sir Maurice, 2004
Keene, Sir David, 2000
Keith, Sir Kenneth, 1998
Kelly, Ruth, 2004
Kennedy, Jane, 2003
Kennedy, Sir Paul, 1992
Kerr of Tonaghmore, Lord, 2004
Khan, Sadiq, 2009
King, Dame Eleanor, 2014
King of Bridgwater, Lord, 1979
Kingarth, *Hon.* Lord (Derek Emslie), 2006
Kinnock, Lord, 1983
Kitchin, Sir David, 2011
Knight, Sir Gregory, 1995
Knight of Weymouth, Lord, 2008
Kramer, Baroness, 2014
Lamb, Norman, 2014
Laming, Lord, 2014
Lammy, David, 2008
Lamont of Lerwick, Lord, 1986
Lang of Monkton, Lord, 1990
Lansley, Lord, 2010
Latasi, Sir Kamuta, 1996
Latham, Sir David, 2000
Laws, David, 2010
Laws, Sir John, 1999
Lawson of Blaby, Lord, 1981
Leadsom, Andrea, 2016
Leggatt, Sir Andrew, 1990
Letwin, Sir Oliver, 2002
Leveson, Sir Brian, 2006
Lewis, Brandon, 2016
Lewis, Dr Julian, 2015
Lewison, Sir Kim, 2011
Liddell of Coatdyke, Baroness, 1998
Lidington, David, 2010
Lilley, Peter, 1990
Lindblom, Sir Keith, 2015
Llewellyn of Steep, Lord, 2015
Lloyd, Sir Peter, 1994
Lloyd, Sir Timothy, 2005
Lloyd of Berwick, Lord, 1984
Lloyd Jones, Sir David, 2012
Llwyd, Elfyn, 2011
Longmore, Sir Andrew, 2001
Lothian, Marquess of, 1996
Luce, Lord, 1986
Lyne, Sir Roderic, 2009
McAvoy, Lord, 2003
McCartney, Sir Ian, 1999
McCollum, Sir Liam, 1997
McCombe, Sir Richard, 2012
McConnell of Glenscorrodale, Lord, 2001
MacDermott, Sir John, 1987
McDonnell, John, 2016
Macdonald of Tradeston, Lord, 1999
McFadden, Patrick, 2008
McFall of Alcluith, Lord, 2004
McFarlane, Sir Andrew, 2011
MacGregor of Pulham Market, Lord, 1985
McGuire, Dame Anne, 2008
Macintosh, Kenneth, 2016
Mackay, Andrew, 1998
Mackay of Clashfern, Lord, 1979
Mackay of Drumadoon, Lord, 1996
McKinnon, Sir Donald, 1992
Maclean, *Hon.* Lord (Ranald MacLean), 2001
McLeish, Henry, 2000

Maclennan of Rogart, Lord, 1997
McLoughlin, Sir Patrick, 2005
McNally, Lord, 2005
McNulty, Anthony, 2007
Mactaggart, Fiona, 2015
Macur, Dame Julia, 2013
McVey, Esther, 2014
Major, Sir John, 1987
Malcolm, *Hon.* Lord (Colin Campbell), 2015
Malloch-Brown, Lord, 2007
Mance, Lord, 1999
Mandelson, Lord, 1998
Marnoch, *Hon.* Lord (Michael Marnoch), 2001
Martin of Springburn, Lord, 2000
Marwick, Tricia, 2012
Mates, Michael, 2004
Maude of Horsham, Lord, 1992
Mawhinney, Lord, 1994
May, Sir Anthony, 1998
May, Theresa, 2003
Mellor, David, 1990
Menzies, *Hon.* Lord (Duncan Menzies), 2012
Michael, Alun, 1998
Milburn, Alan, 1998
Miliband, David, 2005
Miliband, Ed, 2007
Miller, Maria, 2012
Millett, Lord, 1994
Milton, Anne, 2015
Mitchell, Andrew, 2010
Mitchell, Sir James, 1985
Mitchell, Dr Keith, 2004
Moore, Michael, 1990
Moore, Michael, 2010
Moore of Lower Marsh, Lord, 1986
Moore-Bick, Sir Martin, 2005
Morgan, Sir Declan, 2009
Morgan, Nicky, 2014
Morris of Aberavon, Lord, 1970
Morris of Yardley, Baroness, 1999
Morritt, Sir Robert, 1994
Moses, Sir Alan, 2005
Moylan, Sir Andrew, 2017
Mulholland, Frank, 2011
Mummery, Sir John, 1996
Munby, Sir James, 2009
Mundell, David, 2010
Murphy, James, 2008
Murphy of Torfaen, Lord, 1999
Murray, Sir Donald, 1989
Musa, Wilbert, 2005
Namaliu, Sir Rabbie, 1989
Naseby, Lord, 1994
Needham, Sir Richard, 1994
Neill, Sir Brian, 1985
Neuberger of Abbotsbury, Lord, 2004
Neville-Jones, Baroness, 2010
Newby, Lord, 2014
Nicholls of Birkenhead, Lord, 1995
Nicholson, Sir Michael, 1995
Nimmo Smith, *Hon.* Lord (William Nimmo Smith), 2005
Northover, Baroness, 2015
Nott, Sir John, 1979
Nourse, Sir Martin, 1985
O'Brien, Mike, 2009
O'Brien, Sir Stephen, 2013
O'Donnell, Turlough, 1979
Oppenheim-Barnes, Baroness, 1979
Osborne, George, 2010

Osborne, *Hon.* Lord (Kenneth Osborne), 2001
Ottaway, Sir Richard, 2013
Otton, Sir Philip, 1995
Owen, Lord, 1976
Paeniu, Bikenibeu, 1991
Paice, Sir James, 2010
Palmer, Sir Geoffrey, 1986
Paraskeva, Dame Janet, 2010
Parker, Sir Jonathan, 2000
Patel, Priti, 2015
Paterson, Owen, 2010
Paton, *Hon.* Lady (Ann Paton), 2007
Patten, Lord, 1990
Patten, Sir Nicholas, 2009
Patten of Barnes, Lord, 1989
Patterson, Percival, 1993
Pattie, Sir Geoffrey, 1987
Paul, Lord, 2009
Peel, Earl, 2006
Pendry, Lord, 2000
Penning, Mike, 2014
Penrose, *Hon.* Lord (George Penrose), 2000
Peters, Winston, 1998
Philip, *Hon.* Lord (Alexander Philip), 2005
Phillips of Worth Matravers, Lord, 1995
Pickles, Sir Eric, 2010
Pill, Sir Malcolm, 1995
Pitchford, Sir Christopher, 2010
Portillo, Michael, 1992
Potter, Sir Mark, 1996
Prashar, Baroness, 2009
Primarolo, Baroness, 2002
Puapua, Sir Tomasi, 1982
Purnell, James, 2007
Quin, Baroness, 1998
Radice, Lord, 1999
Rafferty, Dame Anne, 2011
Ramsden, James, 1963
Randall, Sir John, 2010
Raynsford, Nick, 2001
Redwood, John, 1993
Reed, Lord, 2008
Reid, Sir George, 2004
Reid of Cardowan, Lord, 1998
Renton of Mount Harry, Lord, 1989
Richard, Lord, 1993
Richards, Sir David, 2016
Richards, Sir Stephen, 2005
Riddell, Peter, 2010
Rifkind, Sir Malcolm, 1986
Rimer, Sir Colin, 2007
Rix, Sir Bernard, 2000
Robathan, Lord, 2010
Robertson, Angus, 2015
Robertson, Sir Hugh, 2012
Robertson of Port Ellen, Lord, 1997
Robinson, Peter, 2007
Roch, Sir John, 1993
Rodgers of Quarry Bank, Lord, 1975
Rooker, Lord, 1999
Rose, Sir Christopher, 1992
Ross, *Hon.* Lord (Donald MacArthur), 1985
Royall of Blaisdon, Baroness, 2008
Rudd, Amber, 2015
Ruddock, Dame Joan, 2010
Ryan, Joan, 2007
Ryder, Sir Ernest, 2013
Ryder of Wensum, Lord, 1990

Sainsbury, Sir Timothy, 1992
Sales, Sir Philip, 2014
Salisbury, Marquess of, 1994
Salmond, Alex, 2007
Sandiford, Lloyd Erskine, 1989
Saville of Newdigate, Lord, 1994
Sawyer, Dame Joan, 2004
Schiemann, Sir Konrad, 1995
Scotland of Asthal, Baroness, 2001
Scott of Foscote, Lord, 1991
Seaga, Edward, 1981
Sedley, Sir Stephen, 1999
Selkirk of Douglas, Lord, 1996
Shapps, Grant, 2010
Sharp, Dame Victoria, 2013
Sheil, Sir John, 2005
Sheldon, Lord, 1977
Shephard of Northwold, Baroness, 1992
Shipley, Jennifer, 1998
Short, Clare, 1997
Shutt of Greetland, Lord, 2009
Simmonds, Sir Kennedy, 1984
Simmonds, Mark, 2014
Simon, Sir Peregrine, 2015
Simpson, Keith, 2015
Sinclair, Ian, 1977
Slade, Sir Christopher, 1982
Smith, Andrew, 1997
Smith, *Hon.* Lady (Anne Smith), 2013
Smith, Jacqueline, 2003
Smith, Dame Janet, 2002
Smith of Basildon, Baroness, 2009
Smith of Finsbury, Lord, 1997
Soames, Sir Nicholas, 2011
Somare, Sir Michael, 1977
Soubry, Anna, 2015
Spellar, John, 2001
Spelman, Dame Caroline, 2010
Spicer, Lord, 2013
Stanley, Sir John, 1984
Starmer, Sir Keir, 2017
Steel of Aikwood, Lord, 1977
Stephen, Sir Ninian, 1979
Stewartby, Lord, 1989
Steyn, Lord, 1992

Stowell of Beeston, Baroness, 2014
Strang, Gavin, 1997
Strathclyde, Lord, 1995
Straw, Jack, 1997
Stride, Melvyn, 2017
Stuart, Freundel, 2013
Stuart, Gisela, 2015
Stuart-Smith, Sir Murray, 1988
Stunell, Lord, 2012
Sturgeon, Nicola, 2014
Sullivan, Sir Jeremy, 2009
Sumption, Lord, 2011
Sutherland, *Hon.* Lord (Ranald Sutherland), 2000
Swayne, Sir Desmond, 2011
Swire, Sir Hugo, 2010
Symons of Vernham Dean, Baroness, 2001
Tapsell, Sir Peter, 2011
Taylor of Bolton, Baroness, 1997
Taylor of Holbeach, Lord, 2014
Tebbit, Lord, 1981
Thirlwall, Dame Kathryn, 2017
Thomas, Edmund, 1996
Thomas of Cwmgiedd, Lord, 2003
Thornberry, Emily, 2017
Thorpe, Sir Matthew, 1995
Thurso, Viscount, 2014
Timms, Stephen, 2006
Tipping, Andrew, 1998
Tomlinson, Sir Stephen, 2010
Touhig, Lord, 2006
Treacy, Sir Colman, 2012
Trefgarne, Lord, 1989
Trimble, Lord, 1997
Trumpington, Baroness, 1992
Truss, Elizabeth, 2014
Tuckey, Sir Simon, 1998
Turnbull, Lord, 2016
Tyler, Lord, 2014
Tyrie, Andrew, 2015
Ullswater, Viscount, 1994
Underhill, Sir Nicholas, 2013
Upton, Simon, 1999
Vadera, Baroness, 2009
Vaizey, Ed, 2016

Vaz, Keith, 2006
Villiers, Theresa, 2010
Vos, Sir Geoffrey, 2013
Waite, Sir John, 1993
Wakeham, Lord, 1983
Waldegrave of North Hill, Lord, 1990
Walker of Gestingthorpe, Lord, 1997
Wallace, Ben, 2017
Wallace of Saltaire, Lord, 2012
Wallace of Tankerness, Lord, 2000
Waller, Sir Mark, 1996
Ward, Sir Alan, 1995
Warner, Lord, 2006
Warsi, Baroness, 2010
Weatherup, Sir Ronald, 2016
Webb, Sir Steven, 2014
Weir, Sir Reginald, 2016
West of Spithead, Lord, 2010
Wheatley, *Hon.* Lord (John Wheatley), 2007
Wheeler, Sir John, 1993
Whittingdale, John, 2015
Whitty, Lord, 2005
Widdecombe, Ann, 1997
Wigley, Lord, 1997
Willetts, Lord, 2010
Williams of Crosby, Baroness, 1974
Williams of Elvel, Lord, 2013
Williams of Oystermouth, Lord, 2002
Williamson, Gavin, 2015
Willott, Jennifer, 2014
Wills, Lord, 2008
Wilson, Brian, 2003
Wilson of Culworth, Lord, 2005
Wingti, Paias, 1987
Winterton, Dame Rosie, 2006
Wolffe, James, 2016
Woodward, Shaun, 2007
Woolf, Lord, 1986
Wright, Jeremy, 2014
York, Archbishop of, 2005
Young of Cookham, Lord, 1993
Young of Graffham, Lord, 1984
Zacca, Sir Edward, 1992

PRIVY COUNCIL OF NORTHERN IRELAND

The Privy Council of Northern Ireland had responsibilities in Northern Ireland similar to those of the Privy Council in Great Britain until the Northern Ireland Act 1974. Membership of the Privy Council of Northern Ireland is retained for life. Since the Northern Ireland Constitution Act 1973 no further appointments have been made. The postnominal initials PC (NI) are used to differentiate its members from those of the Privy Council.

MEMBERS *as at August 2017*
Bailie, Robin, 1971
Dobson, John, 1969
Kilclooney, Lord, 1970

PARLIAMENT

The UK constitution is not contained in any single document but has evolved over time, formed by statute, common law and convention. A constitutional monarchy, the UK is governed by ministers of the crown in the name of the sovereign, who is head both of the state and of the government.

The organs of government are the legislature (parliament), the executive and the judiciary. The executive comprises HM government (the cabinet and other ministers), government departments and local authorities (see Government Departments, Public Bodies and Local Government). The judiciary (see Law Courts and Offices) pronounces on the law, both written and unwritten, interprets statutes and is responsible for the enforcement of the law; the judiciary is independent of both the legislature and the executive.

THE MONARCHY

The sovereign personifies the state and is, in law, an integral part of the legislature, head of the executive, head of the judiciary, commander-in-chief of all armed forces of the crown and supreme governor of the Church of England. In the Channel Islands and the Isle of Man, which are crown dependencies, the sovereign is represented by a lieutenant-governor. In the member states of the Commonwealth of which the sovereign is head of state, her representative is a governor-general; in UK overseas territories the sovereign is usually represented by a governor, who is responsible to the British government.

Although in practice the powers of the monarchy are now very limited, and restricted mainly to the advisory and ceremonial, there are important acts of government which require the participation of the sovereign. These include summoning, proroguing and dissolving parliament, giving royal assent to bills passed by parliament, appointing important office-holders, eg government ministers, judges, bishops and governors, conferring peerages, knighthoods and other honours, and granting pardon to a person wrongly convicted of a crime. The sovereign appoints the prime minister; by convention this office is held by the leader of the political party which enjoys, or can secure, a majority of votes in the House of Commons. In international affairs the sovereign, as head of state, has the power to declare war and make peace, to recognise foreign states and governments, to conclude treaties and to annex or cede territory. However, as the sovereign entrusts executive power to ministers of the crown and acts on the advice of her ministers, which she cannot ignore, royal prerogative powers are in practice exercised by ministers, who are responsible to parliament.

Ministerial responsibility does not diminish the sovereign's importance to the smooth working of government. She holds meetings of the Privy Council (see below), gives audiences to her ministers and other officials at home and overseas, receives accounts of cabinet decisions, reads dispatches and signs state papers; she must be informed and consulted on every aspect of national life; and she must show complete impartiality.

COUNSELLORS OF STATE

If the sovereign travels abroad for more than a few days or suffers from a temporary illness, it is necessary to appoint members of the royal family, known as counsellors of state, under letters patent to carry out the chief functions of the monarch, including the holding of Privy Councils and giving royal assent to acts passed by parliament. The normal procedure is to appoint three or four members of the royal family among those members remaining in the UK, provided they are over 21. There are currently five counsellors of state.

In the event of the sovereign on accession being under the age of 18 years, or by infirmity of mind or body, rendered incapable of performing the royal functions, provision is made for a regency.

THE PRIVY COUNCIL

The sovereign in council, or Privy Council, was the chief source of executive power until the system of cabinet government developed. Its main function today is to advise the sovereign on the approval of various statutory functions and acts of the royal prerogative. These powers are exercised through orders in council and royal proclamations, approved by the Queen at meetings of the Privy Council. The council is also able to exercise a number of statutory duties without approval from the sovereign, including powers of supervision over the registering bodies for the medical and allied professions. These duties are exercised through orders of council.

Although appointment as a privy counsellor is for life, only those who are currently government ministers are involved in the day-to-day business of the council. A full council is summoned only on the death of the sovereign or when the sovereign announces his or her intention to marry. (For a full list of privy counsellors, see the Privy Council section.)

There are a number of advisory Privy Council committees whose meetings the sovereign does not attend. Some are prerogative committees, such as those dealing with legislative matters submitted by the legislatures of the Channel Islands and the Isle of Man or with applications for charters of incorporation; and some are provided for by statute, eg those for the universities of Oxford and Cambridge and some Scottish universities.

Administrative work is carried out by the Privy Council Office under the direction of the Lord President of the Council, a cabinet minister.

JUDICIAL COMMITTEE OF THE PRIVY COUNCIL
Supreme Court Building, Parliament Square, London SW1P 3BD
T 020-7960 1500 W www.jcpc.uk

The Judicial Committee of the Privy Council is the court of final appeal from courts of the UK dependencies, courts of independent Commonwealth countries which have retained the right of appeal and courts of the Channel Islands and the Isle of Man. It also hears very occasional appeals from a number of ancient and ecclesiastical courts.

The committee is composed of privy counsellors who hold, or have held, high judicial office. Only three or five judges hear each case, and these are usually justices of the supreme court.
Chief Executive, Mark Ormerod

PARLIAMENT

Parliament is the supreme law-making authority and can legislate for the UK as a whole or for any parts of it separately (the Channel Islands and the Isle of Man are crown dependencies and not part of the UK). The main functions of parliament are to pass laws, to enable the government to raise taxes and to scrutinise government policy and administration, particularly proposals for expenditure. International treaties and agreements are customarily presented to parliament before ratification.

Parliament can trace its roots to two characteristics of Anglo-Saxon rule: the witan (a meeting of the king, nobles and advisors) and the moot (county meetings where local matters were discussed). However, it was the parliament that Simon de Montfort called in 1265 that is accepted as the forerunner to modern parliament, as it included non-noble representatives from counties, cities and towns alongside the nobility. The nucleus of early parliaments at the beginning of the 14th century were the officers of the king's household and the king's judges, joined by such ecclesiastical and lay magnates as the king might summon to form a prototype 'House of Lords', and occasionally by the knights of the shires, burgesses and proctors of the lower clergy. By the end of Edward III's reign a 'House of Commons' was beginning to appear; the first known Speaker was elected in 1377.

Parliamentary procedure is based on custom and precedent, partly formulated in the standing orders of both houses of parliament. Each house has the right to control its own internal proceedings and to commit for contempt. The system of debate in the two houses is similar; when a motion has been moved, the Speaker proposes the question as the subject of a debate. Members speak from wherever they have been sitting. Questions are decided by a vote on a simple majority. Draft legislation is introduced, in either house, as a bill. Bills can be introduced by a government minister or a private member, but in practice the majority of bills which become law are introduced by the government. To become law, a bill must be passed by each house (for parliamentary stages, *see* Parliamentary Information) and then sent to the sovereign for the royal assent, after which it becomes an act of parliament.

Proceedings of both houses are public, except on extremely rare occasions. The minutes (called *Votes and Proceedings,*in the Commons and *House of Lords Minutes of Proceedings* in the Lords) and the speeches *(The Official Report of Parliamentary Debates,* Hansard) are published daily. Proceedings are also recorded for transmission on radio and television and stored in the Parliamentary Recording Unit before transfer to the British Library Sound Archive. Television cameras have been allowed into the House of Lords since 1985 and into the House of Commons since 1989; committee meetings may also be televised.

The Fixed Term Parliament Act 2011 fixed the duration of a parliament at five years in normal circumstances, the term being reckoned from the date given on the writs for the new parliament. The term of a parliament has been prolonged by legislation in such rare circumstances as the two World Wars (31 January 1911 to 25 November 1918; 26 November 1935 to 15 June 1945). The life of a parliament is divided into sessions, usually of one year in length, beginning and ending most often in May.

DEVOLUTION

The Scottish parliament and the National Assembly for Wales have legislative power over all devolved matters, ie matters not reserved to Westminster or otherwise outside its powers. The Northern Ireland Assembly has legislative authority in the fields previously administered by the Northern Ireland departments. The assembly was suspended in October 2002 and dissolved in April 2003, before being reinstated on 8 May 2007. Following a snap election in March 2017, negotiations to form an executive have failed and as at September 2017 the Northern Ireland Assembly remains suspended. For further information, *see* Devolved Government

THE HOUSE OF LORDS

London SW1A 0PW
T 020-7219 3107
E hlinfo@parliament.uk W www.parliament.uk

The House of Lords is the second chamber, or 'Upper House', of the UK's bicameral parliament. Until the beginning of the 20th century, the House of Lords had considerable power, being able to veto any bill submitted to it by the House of Commons. Since the introduction of the Parliament Acts 1911 and 1949, however, it has no powers over money bills and its power of veto over public legislation has been reduced over time to the power to delay bills for up to one session of parliament (usually one year). Today the main functions of the House of Lords are to contribute to the legislative process, to act as a check on the government, and to provide a forum of expertise. Its judicial role as final court of appeal ended in 2009

with the establishment of a new UK Supreme Court (*see* Law Courts and Offices section).

The House of Lords has a number of select committees. Some relate to the internal affairs of the house – such as its House of Lords Commission – while others carry out important investigative work on matters of public interest. The main committees are: the Communications Committee; the Constitution Committee; the Economic Affairs Committee; the European Union Committee; and the Science and Technology Committee. House of Lords' investigative committees look at broad issues and do not mirror government departments as the select committees in the House of Commons do.

The Constitutional Reform Act 2005 significantly altered the judicial function of the House of Lords and the role of the Lord Chancellor as a judge and its presiding officer. The Lord Chancellor is no longer the presiding officer of the House of Lords nor head of the judiciary in England and Wales, but remains a cabinet minister (the Lord Chancellor and Secretary of State for Justice), and is currently a member of the House of Commons. The function of the presiding officer of the House of Lords was devolved to the newly created post of the Speaker of the House of Lords, commonly known as Lord Speaker. The first Lord Speaker elected by the House was the Rt. Hon. Baroness Hayman on 4 July 2006.

Membership of the House of Lords comprises mainly of life peers created under the Life Peerages Act 1958, along with 92 hereditary peers and a small number of Lords of Appeal in Ordinary, ie law lords, who were created under the Appellate Jurisdiction Act 1876*. The Archbishops of Canterbury and York, the Bishops of London, Durham and Winchester, and the 21 senior diocesan bishops of the Church of England are also members.

The House of Lords Act 1999 provides for 92 hereditary peers to remain in the House of Lords until further reform of the House has been carried out. Of these, 75 (42 Conservative, 28 crossbench, three Liberal Democrat and two Labour) were elected by hereditary peers in their political party or crossbench grouping. In addition, 15 office holders were elected by the whole house. Two hereditary peers with royal duties, the Earl Marshal and the Lord Great Chamberlain, have also remained members. Since November 2002, by-elections have been held to replace elected heriditary peers who have died, and since 2014 to replace those who retire permanently from the House. By-elections are held under the Alternative Vote System, and must take place within three months of a vacancy occurring. (*see also* The Peerage).

Peers are disqualified from sitting in the house if they are:

- aliens, ie any peer who is not a British citizen, a Commonwealth citizen (under the British Nationality Act 1981) or a citizen of the Republic of Ireland
- under the age of 21
- undischarged bankrupts or, in Scotland, those whose estate is sequestered
- holders of a disqualifying judicial office
- members of the European parliament
- convicted of treason

Bishops cease to be members of the house when they retire.

Members who do not wish to attend sittings of the House of Lords may apply for leave of absence for the duration of a parliament. Since the passage of the House of Lords Reform Act 2014, members of the House may also retire permanently by giving notice in writing to the Clerk of the Parliaments.

Members of the House of Lords, who are not paid a salary, may claim a daily allowance of £300 (or may elect to claim a reduced daily allowance of £150) per sitting day – but only if they attend a sitting of the House and/or committee proceedings.

* Although the office of Lord of Appeal in Ordinary no longer exists, law lords created under the Appellate Jurisdiction Act 1876 remain members of the House. Those in office at the time of the establishment of the Supreme Court became justices of the UK Supreme Court and are not permitted to sit or vote in the House of Lords until they retire.

COMPOSITION *as at 20 September 2017*

Archbishops and bishops	25
Life peers under the Appellate Jurisdiction Act 1876 and the Life Peerages Act 1958	682
Peers under the House of Lords Act 1999	91
Total	798

STATE OF THE PARTIES *as at 20 September 2017*†

Conservative	253
Labour	199
Liberal Democrat	100
Crossbench	176
Archbishops and bishops	25
Non-affiliated	30
Other parties	15
Total	798
† Excluding four peers on leave of absence	

HOUSE OF LORDS PAY FOR SENIOR STAFF 2016–17

Senior staff are placed in the following pay bands according to their level of responsibility and taking account of other factors such as experience and marketability.

Judicial group 4	£177,988
Senior band 3	£106,000–£139,829
Senior band 2	£87,000–£124,845
Senior band 1A	£71,000–£105,560
Senior band 1	£64,500–£93,380

OFFICERS AND OFFICIALS

The house is presided over by the Lord Speaker, whose powers differ from those of the Speaker of the House of Commons. The Lord Speaker has no power to rule on matters of order because the House of Lords is self-regulating. The maintenance of the rules of debate is the responsibility of all the members who are present.

A panel of deputy speakers is appointed by Royal Commission. The first deputy speaker is the Chair of Committees, a salaried officer of the house appointed at the beginning of each session. He or she chairs a number of 'domestic' committees relating to the internal affairs of the house . The first deputy speaker is assisted by a panel of deputy chairs, headed by the salaried Principal Deputy Chair of Committees, who is also chair of the European Union Committee of the house.

The Clerk of the Parliaments is the accounting officer and the chief permanent official responsible for the administration of the house. The Gentleman Usher of the Black Rod is responsible for security and other services and also has royal duties as secretary to the Lord Great Chamberlain.

Lord Speaker (£102,101), Rt. Hon. Lord Fowler
Senior Deputy Speaker of the House of Lords (£84,524), Rt. Hon. Lord McFall of Alcluith
Principal Deputy Chair (£79,076), Lord Boswell of Aynho
Clerk of the Parliaments (Judicial Group 4), Edward Ollard
Clerk Assistant (Senior Band 3), Simon Burton
Reading Clerk and Clerk of the Overseas Office (Senior Band 3), Jake Vaughan
Gentleman Usher of the Black Rod and Serjeant-at-Arms (Senior Band 2), Lt.-Gen. David Leakey, CMG, CBE
Yeoman Usher of the Black Rod and Deputy Serjeant-at-Arms, Neil Baverstock
Commissioner for Lords' Standards, Kathryn Stone
Counsel to the Chair of Committees (Senior Band 2), Peter Milledge; P. Hardy
Registrar of Lords' Interests (Senior Band 1A), Brendan Keith
Clerk of Committees (Senior Band 2), Dr F. P. Tudor

Legal Adviser to the Human Rights Committee (Senior Band 2), Murray Hunt
Director of Information Services and Librarian (Senior Band 2), vacant
Director of Facilities (Senior Band 2), Carl Woodall
Finance Director (Senior Band 1A), Andrew Makower
Director of Parliamentary Digital Service (Senior Band 1A), Rob Greig
Director of Human Resources (Senior Band 1A), Tom Mohan
Clerk of Legislation (Senior Band 1A), vacant
Principal Clerk of Select Committees (Senior Band 1A), Christopher Johnson, DPHIL
Director of Parliamentary Archives (Senior Band 1), Adrian Brown

LORD GREAT CHAMBERLAIN'S OFFICE

Lord Great Chamberlain, 7th Marquess of Cholmondeley, KCVO

SELECT COMMITTEES

The main House of Lords select committees, as at September 2017, are as follows:

Artificial Intelligence – Chair, Lord Clement-Jones, CBE; *Clerk,* Luke Hussey
Charities – Chair, Baroness Pitkeathley, OBE; *Clerk,* Matt Korris
Citizens and Civic Engagements – Chair, Lord Hodgson of Astley Abbotts,CBE; *Clerk,* Michael Collon
Communications – Chair, Rt. Hon.Lord Henley, PC; *Clerk,* Theodore Pembroke
Constitution – Chair, Rt. Hon Baroness Taylor of Bolton ; *Clerk,* Matt Korris
Delegated Powers and Regulatory Reform – Chair, Baroness Fookes, DBE;
Economic Affairs – Chair, Rt. Hon. Lord Forsyth of Drumlean *Clerk,* Ayeesha Waller
European Union – Chair, Lord Boswell of Aynho; *Principal Clerk,* Christopher Johnson, DPHIL; *Clerk,* Stuart Stoner
European Union – Sub-committees:
  Energy and Environment – Chair, Lord Teverson; *Clerk,* Breda Twomey
  External Affairs – Chair, Baroness Verma *Clerk,* Eva George
  Financial Affairs – Chair, Baroness Falkner of Margravine; *Clerk,* John Turner
  Home Affairs – Chair, Lord Jay of Ewelme, GCMG; *Clerk,* Tristan Stubbs
  Internal Market – Chair, Rt. Hon. Lord Whitty, PC; *Clerk,* Pippa Westwood
  Justice – Chair, Baroness Kennedy of the Shaws, QC; *Clerk,* Chris Clarke
Finance – Chair, Baroness Doocey, OBE; *Clerk,* Susannah Street
Financial Exclusion – Chair, Baroness Tyler of Enfield; *Clerk,* Matthew Smith
High Speed Rail (London – West Midlands) Bill – Chair, Rt. Hon.Lord Walker of Gestingthorpe, PC
House – Chair, Rt. Hon. Lord Fowler, PC; *Clerk,* Patrick Milner
Hybrid Instruments – Chair, Rt. Hon. Lord McFall of Alcluith
Intellectual Property (Unjust Threats) Bill – Chair,Rt Hon. Lord Saville of Newdigate; *Clerk,* Susannah Clarke
International Relations – Chair, Rt. Hon. Lord Howell of Guildford, PC; *Clerk,* James Whittle
Liaison – Chair, Rt. Hon. Lord McFall of Alcluith, PC; *Clerk,* Philippa Tudor
Licensing Act 2003 – Chair, Baroness McIntosh of Pickering; *Clerk,* Michael Collon
Long-Term Sustainability of the NHS – Chair, Lord Patel; *Clerk,* Patrick Milner
Lord's Conduct – Chair, Lord Brown of Eaton-under-Heywood, PC

National Policy for the Built Environment – Chair, Baroness O'Cathain, OBE; *Clerk*, Matthew Smith
Natural Environment and Rural Communities (NERC) Act 2006 – Chair,Lord Cameron of Dillington, FRICS; *Clerk*, Matthew Smith
Political Polling and Digital Media – Chair, Lord Lipsey *Clerk*, Helena Peacock
Privileges and Conduct – Chair, Rt. Hon. Lord McFall of Alcluith, PC; *Clerk*, Chloe Mawson
Procedure – Chair, Rt. Hon. Lord McFall of Alcluith, PC; *Clerk*, Chloe Mawson
Science and Technology – Chair, Lord Patel; *Clerk*, Anna Murphy
Secondary Legislation Scrutiny – Chair, Rt. Hon. Lord Trefgarne, PC
Selection Committee – Chair, Rt. Hon. Lord McFall of Alcluith, PC
Services – Chair, Rt. Hon. Lord Laming, CBE; *Clerk*, Susannah Street
Social Mobility – Chair, Rt. Hon. Baroness Corston, PC; *Clerk*, Luke Hussey
Standing Orders (Private Bills) – Chair, Rt. Hon. Lord McFall of Alcluith, PC

THE HOUSE OF COMMONS
London SW1A 0AA
T 020-7219 3000 W www.parliament.uk

HOUSE OF COMMONS ENQUIRY SERVICE
14 Tothill Street, London SW1H 9NB
T 020-7219 4272 E hcinfo@parliament.uk

The members of the House of Commons are elected by universal adult suffrage. For electoral purposes, the UK is divided into constituencies, each of which returns one member to the House of Commons, the member being the candidate who obtains the largest number of votes cast in the constituency. To ensure equitable representation, the four Boundary Commissions keep constituency boundaries under review and recommend any redistribution of seats which may seem necessary because of population movements etc. At the 2010 general election the number of seats increased from 646 to 650. Of the present 650 seats, there are 533 for England, 40 for Wales, 59 for Scotland and 18 for Northern Ireland.

NUMBER OF SEATS IN THE HOUSE OF COMMONS BY COUNTRY

	2005	2017
England	529	533
Wales	40	40
Scotland	59	59
Northern Ireland	18	18
Total	646	650

ELECTIONS
Elections are by secret ballot, each elector casting one vote; voting is not compulsory. (For entitlement to vote in parliamentary elections, *see* Legal Notes.) When a seat becomes vacant between general elections, a by-election is held.

British subjects and citizens of the Irish Republic can stand for election as MPs provided they are 18 or over and not subject to disqualification. Those disqualified from sitting in the house include:

- undischarged bankrupts
- people sentenced to more than one year's imprisonment
- members of the House of Lords (but hereditary peers not sitting in the Lords are eligible)
- holders of certain offices listed in the House of Commons Disqualification Act 1975, eg members of the judiciary, civil service, regular armed forces, police forces, some local government officers and some members of public corporations and government commissions

A candidate does not require any party backing but his or her nomination for election must be supported by the signatures of ten people registered in the constituency. A candidate must also deposit £500 with the returning officer, which is forfeit if the candidate does not receive more than 5 per cent of the votes cast. All election expenses at a general election, except the candidate's personal expenses, are subject to a statutory limit of £8,700, plus six pence for each elector in a borough constituency or nine pence for each elector in a county constituency.
See also members of parliament for a current alphabetical list.

STATE OF THE PARTIES *as at September 2017*

Party	Seats
Conservative	316
Labour	262
Scottish National Party	35
Liberal Democrats	12
Democratic Unionist Party	10
Sinn Fein (have not taken their seats)	7
Plaid Cymru	4
Independant	2
Green	1
The Speaker	1
Total	650

BUSINESS
The week's business of the house is outlined each Thursday by the leader of the house, after consultation between the chief government whip and the chief opposition whip. A quarter to a third of the time will be taken up by the government's legislative programme and the rest by other business. As a rule, bills likely to raise political controversy are introduced in the Commons before going on to the Lords, and the Commons claims exclusive control in respect of national taxation and expenditure. Bills such as the finance bill, which imposes taxation, and the consolidated fund bills, which authorise expenditure, must begin in the Commons. A bill of which the financial provisions are subsidiary may begin in the Lords, and the Commons may waive its rights in regard to Lords' amendments affecting finance.

The Commons has a public register of MPs' financial and certain other interests; this is published annually as a House of Commons paper. Members must also disclose any relevant financial interest or benefit in a matter before the house when taking part in a debate, in certain other proceedings of the house, or in consultations with other MPs, with ministers or with civil servants.

MEMBERS' PAY AND ALLOWANCES
Since 1911 members of the House of Commons have received salary payments; facilities for free travel were introduced in 1924. Salary rates for the last 30 years are as follows:

1987 Jan – £18,500	2001 Apr – £49,822
1988 Jan – £22,548	2002 Apr – £55,118
1989 Jan – £24,107	2003 Apr – £56,358
1990 Jan – £26,701	2004 Apr – £57,485
1991 Jan – £29,970	2005 Apr – £59,095
1992 Jan – £30,854	2006 Apr – £59,686
1993 Jan – £30,854	2007 Apr – £61,181
1994 Jan – £31,687	2008 Apr – £63,291
1995 Jan – £33,189	2009 Apr – £64,766
1995 Jan – £33,189	2010 Apr – £65,738
1996 Jan – £34,085	2011 Apr – £65,738
1996 Jul – £43,000	2012 Apr – £65,738
1997 Apr – £43,860	2013 Apr – £66,396
1998 Apr – £45,066	2014 Apr – £67,060
1999 Apr – £47,008	2015 May – £74,000
2000 Apr – £48,371	2016 Apr – £ 74,962
	2017 Apr – £76,011

The Independent Parliamentary Standards Authority (IPSA) was established under the Parliamentary Standards Act 2009 and is responsible for the independent regulation and administration of the MPs' Scheme of Business Costs and Expenses, as well as for paying the salaries of MPs and their staff members. Since May 2011, the IPSA has also been responsible for determining MPs' pay and setting the level of any increase to their salary.

For 2017–18, the office costs expenditure budget is £27,550 for London area MPs and £24,850 for non-London area MPs. The maximum annual staff budget for London area MPs is £161,5500 and £150,990 for non-London area MPs.

Since 1972 MPs have been able to claim reimbursement for the additional cost of staying overnight away from their main residence while on parliamentary business. This is not payable to London area MPs and those MPs who reside in 'grace and favour' accommodation. Accommodation expenses for MPs claiming rental payments in the London area is capped at £22,760 a year; outside of the London area each constituency is banded according to rental values in the area and capped at £15,850. For MPs who own their own homes, mortgage interest and associated expenses up to £5,000 are payable.

For ministerial salaries *see* Government Departments.

MEMBERS' PENSIONS

Pension arrangements for MPs were first introduced in 1964. Under the Parliamentary Contributory Pension Fund CARE (career-averaged revalued earnings) scheme, MPs receive a pension on retirement based upon their salary in their final year, and upon accumulating proportions of pensionable earnings over each year of membership. MPs contributions are payable at a rate of 11.09 per cent of pay. Exchequer contributions are paid at a rate recommended by the Government Actuary and meet the balance of the cost of providing MP's retirement benefits. Pensions are normally payable upon retirement at age 65 to those who are no longer MPS. Abated pensions may be payable to members aged 55 or over. Pensions are also payable to spouses and other qualifying partners of deceased scheme members at the rate of three-eighths of the deceased member's pension. In the case of members who die in service, an enhanced spouse's or partner's pension and a lump sum equal to two times pensionable salary is payable. There are also provisions in place for dependants and MPs of any age who retire due to ill health. All pensions are CPI index-linked.

The House of Commons Members' Fund provides for annual or lump sum grants to ex-MPs, their widows or widowers, and children of those who either ceased to serve as an MP prior to the PCPF being established or who are experiencing hardship. Members contribute £24 a year and the Exchequer £215,000 a year to the fund.

HOUSE OF COMMONS PAY BANDS FOR SENIOR STAFF

Senior Staff are placed in the following Senior Civil Service pay bands. These pay bands apply to the most senior staff in departments and agencies.

Pay Band 1	£64,640–£118,978
Pay Band 1A*	£67,600–£128,900
Pay Band 2	£87,870–£164,125
Pay Band 3	£107,060–£210,181
* Pay Band 1A is now effectively a closed grade, although existing staff will remain on this grade	

OFFICERS AND OFFICIALS

The House of Commons is presided over by the Speaker, who has considerable powers to maintain order. A deputy speaker, called the Chairman of Ways and Means, and two deputy chairs may preside over sittings of the House of Commons;

they are elected by the house, and, like the Speaker, neither speak nor vote other than in their official capacity.

The staff of the house are employed by a commission chaired by the Speaker. The heads of the six House of Commons departments are permanent officers of the house, not MPs. The Clerk of the House is the principal adviser to the Speaker on the privileges and procedures of the house, the conduct of the business of the house, and committees. The Serjeant-at-Arms is responsible for security and ceremonial functions of the house.

Speaker (£150,236)*, Rt. Hon. John Bercow, MP
Chairman of Ways and Means (£107,108), Rt. Hon. Lindsay Hoyle, MP
First Deputy Chairman of Ways and Means (£102,098), Eleanor Laing, MP
Second Deputy Chairman of Ways and Means (£102,098), Dame Rosie Winterton, MP
House of Commons Commission, Rt. Hon. John Bercow, MP *(chair)*; Ian Ailles; Sir Paul Beresford, MP; Rt. Hon. Tom Brake, MP; Dame Janet Gaymer; Stewart Hosie, MP; Rt. Hon. Andrea Leadsom, MP; Jane McCall; David Natzler; Valerie Vaz, MP; Rt. Hon. Dame Rosie Winterton, MP
Secretary of the Commission, Marianne Cwynarski

* Salaries in parentheses are the maximum available. The Speaker and Deputies have opted not to take the statutory increases awarded to them each year as office holders.

OFFICE OF THE SPEAKER
Speaker's Secretary, Peter Barratt
Trainbearer, Jim Davey
Speaker's Counsel, Saira Salimi
Chaplain to the Speaker, Revd Rose Hudson-Wilkin

OFFICE OF THE CLERK OF THE HOUSE
Clerk of the House, David Natzler

PARLIAMENTARY COMMISSIONER FOR STANDARDS
Parliamentary Commissioner for Standards, Kathryn Hudson
Registrar of Members' Financial Interests, Heather Wood

PARLIAMENTARY SECURITY DIRECTOR
Parliamentary Security Director, Eric Hepburn

GOVERNANCE OFFICE
Head of Office, Marianne Cwynarski
Corporate Risk Management Facilitator, Rachel Harrison
Head of Central Communications, Lee Bridges
Head of Internal Audit, vacant
Strategy, Planning and Performance Manager, Jane Hough

DEPARTMENT OF CHAMBER AND COMMITTEE SERVICES
Clerk Assistant and Director General, John Benger
Director of Departmental Services, Elizabeth Hunt

OVERSEAS OFFICE
Principal Clerk, Matthew Hamlyn
Delegation Secretary, Nick Wright
Inward Visits Manager, Alison Game, MBE
National Parliament Representative (Brussels), Alison Groves

COMMITTEE OFFICE
Clerk of Committees,
Principal Clerks of Select Committees, Mark Hutton; Colin Lee; Simon Patrick; Bob Twigger

DEPARTMENTAL SELECT COMMITTEES
Administration – Chair, vacant; *Clerk,* Sarah Heath
Backbench Business – Chair, Ian Mearns; *Clerk,* Ed Beale
Business, Innovation and Skills – Chair, Rachel Reeves; *Clerk,* Chris Shaw

Communities and Local Government – Chair, Clive Betts; Clerk, Ed Beale

Digital,Culture, Media and Sport – Chair, Damian Collins; Clerk, Elizabeth Flood

Defence – Chair, Rt. Hon. Dr Julian Lewis; Clerk, Mark Etherton

Education – Chair, Robert Halfton; Clerk, Richard Ward

Environment, Food and Rural Affairs – Chair, Neil Parish; Clerk, Eliot Barrass

Environmental Audit – Chair, Mary Creagh; Clerk, David Slater

European Scrutiny – Chair, vacant; Clerk, Eve Samson

Exiting the European Union – Chair, Rt. Hon. Hilary Benn, MP; Clerk, James Rhys

Finance – Chair, vacantClerk, Helen Wood

Foreign Affairs – Chair, Tom Tugendhat; Clerk, Chris Stanton

Health – Chair, Dr Sarah Wollaston; Clerk, Huw Yardley

High Speed Rail Bill – Chair, Robert Syms

Home Affairs – Chair, Rt. Hon. Yvette Cooper, MP; Clerk, Carol Oxborough

International Development – Chair, Stephen Twigg; Clerk, Fergus Reid

International Trade – Chair, Angus Bendan McNeil; Clerk, Lydia Menzies

Justice – Chair, Robert Neill; Clerk, Nick Walker

Liaison – Chair, vacant; Clerk, Sarah Hartwell-Naguiby

Northern Ireland Affairs – Chair, Dr Andrew Murrison; Clerk, Margaret McKinnon

Petitions – Chair, Helen Jones

Privileges – Chair, vacant; Clerk, Dr Lynn Gardner

Procedure – Chair, Charles Walker; Clerk, Martyn Atkins

Public Accounts – Chair, Meg Hillier; Clerk, Richard Cooke

Public Administration and Constitutional Affairs – Chair, Bernard Jenkin; Clerks, Dr Rebecca Davis and Rhiannon Hollis

Regulatory Reform – Chair, vacant; Clerk, Eliot Wilson

Science and Technology – Chair, Norman Lamb; Clerk, Simon Fiander

Scottish Affairs – Chair, Pete Wishart; Clerk, Jyoti Chandola

Selection (Committee of) – Chair, vacant; Clerks, Katy Stout and Clementine Brown

Standards – Chair, Sir Kevin Barron; Clerk, Dr Lynn Gardner

Standing Orders (Private Bills) – Chair, Rt. Hon. Lindsay Hoyle

Statutory Instruments – Chair, vacant; Clerk, Mike Winter

Transport – Chair, Lillian Greenwood; Clerk, Gordon Clarke

Treasury – Chair, Rt. Hon. Nicky Morgan; Clerk, Sarah Rees

Welsh Affairs – Chair, David T.C. Davies; Clerk, Sarah Thatcher

Women and Equalities – Chair, Rt. Hon. Maria Miller; Clerk, Judith Boyce

Work and Pensions – Chair, Rt. Hon. Frank Field; Clerk, Adam Mellows-Facer

SCRUTINY UNIT
Head of Unit, David Lloyd
Head of Financial Security, Larry Honeysett
Public Bill Committees, Ian Hook

VOTE OFFICE
Deliver of the Vote, Catherine Fogarty
Deputy Deliverer of the Vote, Owen Sweeney
Head of Procedural Publishing, Tom McVeagh
Procedural Publishing Operations Manager, Stuart Miller

CHAMBER BUSINESS DIRECTORATE
Clerk of Legislation, Liam Laurence Smyth
Principal Clerks: Philippa Helme (Table Office); Paul Evans (Journals)

OFFICIAL REPORT DIRECTORATE
Editor, Alex Newton
Director of Broadcasting, John Angeli

SERJEANT-AT-ARMS DIRECTORATE
Serjeant-at-Arms, Kamal El-Hajji
Deputy Serjeant-at-Arms, Richard Latham
Assistant Serjeant-at-Arms, Lesley Scott

DEPARTMENT OF FACILITIES
Director-General, John Borley, CB
Director of Business Management, Della Herd
Acting Parliamentary Director of Estates, Brian Finnimore
Director of Accommodation and Logistics Services, Fiona Channon
Executive Officer, Katie Phelan-Molloy
Director of Catering Services, Richard Tapner-Evans
Executive Chef, Mark Hill

DEPARTMENT OF FINANCE
Director of Finance, Myfanwy Barrett
Chief Accountant, Alex Mills
Head of Financial Planning, Amanda Colledge
Head of Financial Accounting, Debra Shirtcliffe
Head of Financial Services, Sam Rao

DEPARTMENT OF HUMAN RESOURCES AND CHANGE
Director-General of HR and Change, Andrew Walker
Head of Safety, Dr Marianne McDougall

DEPARTMENT OF INFORMATION SERVICES
Director-General and Librarian, Penny Young
Curator of Works of Art, Malcolm Hay
Deputy Curator, Melanie Unwin
Assistant Curator, Emma Gormley
Registrar of Collections, Emily Green
Collections Care Manager, Caroline Babington
Collections Information Manager, Therese Crawley
Administrators, Michelle Klein and Susan Reynolds
Head of Customer Services, Dr Patsy Richards

PARLIAMENTARY INFORMATION AND COMMUNICATION TECHNOLOGY (ICT)
Director of Parliamentary Digital Service, Rob Greig
Director of Technology, Steve O'Connor
Director of Live Services, Rob Sanders
Director of Resources, Tracey Jessup
Director of Programmes and Projects, Charlotte Simmonds
Head of the Strategy, Tracy Green

OTHER PRINCIPAL OFFICERS
Clerk of the Crown in Chancery, Richard Heaton, CB
Parliamentary and Health Service Ombudsman, Robert Behrens, CBE

NATIONAL AUDIT OFFICE
157–197 Buckingham Palace Road, London SW1W 9SP
T 020-7798 7000
E enquiries@nao.gsi.gov.uk W www.nao.org.uk

The National Audit Office came into existence under the National Audit Act 1983 to replace and continue the work of the former Exchequer and Audit Department. The act reinforced the office's total financial and operational independence from the government and brought its head, the Comptroller and Auditor-General, into a closer relationship with parliament as an officer of the House of Commons.

The National Audit Office (NAO) scrutinises public spending on behalf of parliament, helping it to hold government departments to account and helping public service managers improve performance and service delivery. The NAO audits the financial statements of all government departments and a wide range of other public bodies. It regularly publishes 'value for money' reports on the efficiency and effectiveness of how public resources are used.

Chair, Lord Bichard, KCB
Comptroller and Auditor-General, Sir Amyas Morse, KCB
Executive Leaders, Abdool Kara; Daniel Lambauer; Kate
   Mathers; Rebecca Sheeran; Stephen Smith; Max Tse; John
   Thorpe

PARLIAMENTARY INFORMATION

The following is a short glossary of aspects of the work of parliament. Unless otherwise stated, references are to House of Commons procedures.

BILL – Proposed legislation is termed a bill. The stages of a public bill (for private bills, see below) in the House of Commons are as follows:

First reading: This stage introduces the legislation to the house and, for government bills, merely constitutes an order to have the bill printed.

Second reading: The debate on the principles of the bill.

Committee stage: The detailed examination of a bill, clause by clause. In most cases this takes place in a public bill committee, or the whole house may act as a committee. Public bill committees may take evidence before embarking on detailed scrutiny of the bill. Very rarely, a bill may be examined by a select committee.

Report stage: Detailed review of a bill as amended in committee, on the floor of the house, and an opportunity to make further changes.

Third reading: Final debate on the full bill in the Commons.

Public bills go through the same stages in the House of Lords, but with important differences: the committee stage is taken in committee of the whole house or in a grand committee, in which any peer may participate. There are no time limits, all amendments are debated, and further amendments can be made at third reading.

A bill may start in either house, and has to pass through both houses to become law. Both houses have to agree the final text of a bill, so that amendments made by the second house are then considered in the originating house, and if not agreed, sent back or themselves amended, until agreement is reached.

CHILTERN HUNDREDS – A nominal office of profit under the crown, the acceptance of which requires an MP to vacate his/her seat. The Manor of Northstead is similar. These are the only means by which an MP may resign.

CONSOLIDATED FUND BILL – A bill to authorise the issue of money to maintain government services. The bill is dealt with without debate.

EARLY DAY MOTION – A motion put on the notice paper by an MP without, in general, the real prospect of its being debated. Such motions are expressions of back-bench opinion.

FATHER OF THE HOUSE – The MP whose continuous service in the House of Commons is the longest. The present Father of the House is the Rt. Hon. Kenneth Clarke, CH, QC, MP.

GRAND COMMITTEES – There are three grand committees in the House of Commons, one each for Northern Ireland, Scotland and Wales; they consider matters relating specifically to that country. In the House of Lords, bills may be sent to a grand committee instead of a committee of the whole house (see also Bill).

HOURS OF MEETING – The House of Commons normally meets on Mondays at 2.30pm, Tuesdays and Wednesdays at 11.30am, Thursdays at 9.30am and some Fridays at 9.30am. (See also Westminster Hall Sittings, below.) The House of Lords normally meets at 2.30pm Mondays and Tuesdays, 3pm on Wednesdays and at 11am on Thursdays. The House of Lords occasionally sits on Fridays at 10am.

LEADER OF THE OPPOSITION – In 1937 the office of leader of the opposition was recognised and a salary was assigned to the post. In 2017–18 this is £139,773 (including a parliamentary salary of £76,011). The present leader of the opposition is the Rt. Hon. Jeremy Corbyn, MP.

THE LORD CHANCELLOR – The office of Lord High Chancellor of Great Britain was significantly altered by the Constitutional Reform Act 2005. Previously, the Lord Chancellor was (ex officio) the Speaker of the House of Lords, and took part in debates and voted in divisions in the House of Lords. The Department for Constitutional Affairs was created in 2003, and became the Ministry of Justice in 2007, incorporating most of the responsibilities of the Lord Chancellor's department. The role of Speaker has been transferred to the post of Lord Speaker. The Constitutional Reform Act 2005 also brought to an end the Lord Chancellor's role as head of the judiciary. A Judicial Appointments Commission was created in April 2006, and a supreme court (separate from the House of Lords) was established in 2009.

THE LORD GREAT CHAMBERLAIN – The Lord Great Chamberlain is a Great Officer of State, the office being hereditary since the grant of Henry I to the family of De Vere, Earls of Oxford. It is now a joint hereditary office rotating on the death of the sovereign between the Cholmondeley, Carington and Ancaster families.

The Lord Great Chamberlain, currently the 7th Marquess of Cholmondeley, is responsible for the royal apartments in the Palace of Westminster, the Royal Gallery, the administration of the Chapel of St Mary Undercroft and, in conjunction with the Lord Speaker and the Speaker of the House of Commons, Westminster Hall. The Lord Great Chamberlain has the right to perform specific services at a coronation and has particular responsibility for the internal administrative arrangements within the House of Lords for state openings of parliament.

THE LORD SPEAKER – The first Lord Speaker of the House of Lords, the Rt. Hon. Baroness Hayman, took up office on 4 July 2006. The Lord Speaker is independent of the government and elected by members of the House of Lords rather than appointed by the prime minister. Although the Lord Speaker's primary role is to preside over proceedings in the House of Lords, she does not have the same powers as the Speaker of the House of Commons. For example, the Lord Speaker is not responsible for maintaining order during debates, as this is the responsibility of the house as a whole. The Lord Speaker sits in the Lords on one of the woolsacks, which are couches covered in red cloth and stuffed with wool.

OPPOSITION DAY – A day on which the topic for debate is chosen by the opposition. There are 20 such days in a normal session. On 17 days, subjects are chosen by the leader of the opposition; on the remaining three days by the leader of the next largest opposition party.

PARLIAMENT ACTS 1911 AND 1949 – Under these acts, bills may become law without the consent of the Lords, though the House of Lords has the power to delay a public bill for a parliamentary session.

PRIME MINISTER'S QUESTIONS – The prime minister answers questions from 12 to 12.30pm on Wednesdays.

PRIVATE BILL – A bill promoted by a body or an individual to give powers additional to, or in conflict with, the general law, and to which a special procedure applies to enable people affected to object.

PRIVATE MEMBER'S BILL – A public bill promoted by an MP or peer who is not a member of the government.

PRIVATE NOTICE QUESTION – A question adjudged of urgent importance on submission to the Speaker (in the Lords, the Lord Speaker), answered at the end of oral questions.

PRIVILEGE – The House of Commons has rights and immunities to protect it from obstruction in carrying out its duties. These are known as parliamentary privilege and enable Members of Parliament to debate freely. The most important privilege is that of freedom of speech. MPs cannot be prosecuted for sedition or sued for libel or slander over anything said during proceedings in the house. This enables them to raise in the house questions affecting the public good which might be difficult to raise outside owing to the possibility of legal action against them. The House of Lords has similar privileges.

QUESTION TIME – Oral questions are answered by ministers in the Commons from 2.30 to 3.30pm on Mondays, 11.30am to 12.30pm on Tuesdays and Wednesdays, and 9.30 to 10.30am on Thursdays. Questions are also taken for half an hour at the start of the Lords sittings.

ROYAL ASSENT – The royal assent is signified by letters patent to such bills and measures as have passed both Houses of Parliament (or bills which have been passed under the Parliament Acts 1911 and 1949). The sovereign has not given royal assent in person since 1854. On occasion, for instance in the prorogation of parliament, royal assent may be pronounced to the two houses by Lords Commissioners. More usually royal assent is notified to each house sitting separately in accordance with the Royal Assent Act 1967. The old French formulae for royal assent are then endorsed on the acts by the Clerk of the Parliaments.

The power to withhold assent resides with the sovereign but has not been exercised in the UK since 1707.

SELECT COMMITTEES – Consisting usually of 10 to 15 members of all parties, select committees are a means used by both houses in order to investigate certain matters.

Most select committees in the House of Commons are tied to departments: each committee investigates subjects within a government department's remit. There are other select committees dealing with matters such as public accounts (ie the spending by the government of money voted by parliament) and European legislation, and also committees advising on procedures and domestic administration of the house. Major select committees usually take evidence in public; their evidence and reports are published on the parliament website and in hard copy by The Stationery Office (TSO). House of Commons select committees are reconstituted after a general election.

In the House of Lords, select committees do not mirror government departments but cover broader issues. There is a select committee on the European Union (EU), which has six sub-committees dealing with specific areas of EU policy, a select committee on science and technology, a select committee on economic affairs and also one on the constitution. There is also a select committee on delegated powers and regulatory reform and one on privileges and conduct. In addition, *ad hoc* select committees have been set up from time to time to investigate specific subjects. There are also joint committees of the two houses, eg the committees on statutory instruments and on human rights.

THE SPEAKER – The Speaker of the House of Commons is the spokesperson and chair of the Chamber. He or she is elected by the house at the beginning of each parliament or when the previous Speaker retires or dies. The Speaker neither speaks in debates nor votes in divisions except when the voting is equal.

VACANT SEATS – When a vacancy occurs in the House of Commons during a session of parliament, the writ for the by-election is moved by a whip of the party to which the member whose seat has been vacated belonged. If the house is in recess, the Speaker can issue a warrant for a writ, should two members certify to him that a seat is vacant.

WESTMINSTER HALL SITTINGS – Following a report by the Modernisation of the House of Commons Select Committee, the Commons decided in May 1999 to set up a second debating forum. It is known as 'Westminster Hall' and sittings are in the Grand Committee Room on some Mondays from 4.30pm to 7.30pm, Tuesdays and Wednesdays from 9.30am to 11.30am and from 2.30pm to 5.30pm, and Thursdays from 1.30pm to 4.30pm. Sittings are open to the public at the times indicated.

WHIPS – In order to secure the attendance of members of a particular party in parliament, particularly on the occasion of an important vote, whips (originally known as 'whippers-in') are appointed. The written appeal or circular letter issued by them is also known as a 'whip', its urgency being denoted by the number of times it is underlined. Failure to respond to a three-line whip is tantamount in the Commons to secession (at any rate temporarily) from the party. Whips are provided with office accommodation in both houses, and government and some opposition whips receive salaries from public funds.

PARLIAMENTARY ARCHIVES

Houses of Parliament, London SW1A 0PW
T 020-7219 3074 E archives@parliament.uk W www.parliament.uk/archives

Since 1497, the records of parliament have been kept within the Palace of Westminster. They are in the custody of the Clerk of Parliaments. In 1946 the House of Lords Record Office, which became the Parliamentary Archives in 2006, was established to supervise their preservation and their availability to the public. Some 3 million documents are preserved, including acts of parliament from 1497, journals of the House of Lords from 1510, minutes and committee proceedings from 1610, and papers laid before parliament from 1531. Among the records are the Petition of Right, the death warrant of Charles I, the Declaration of Breda, and the Bill of Rights. Records are made available through a public search room.

Director of the Parliamentary Archives, Adrian Brown

GOVERNMENT OFFICE

The government is the body of ministers responsible for the administration of national affairs, determining policy and introducing into parliament any legislation necessary to give effect to government policy. The majority of ministers are members of the House of Commons but members of the House of Lords, or of neither house, may also hold ministerial responsibility. The prime minister is, by current convention, always a member of the House of Commons.

THE PRIME MINISTER

The office of prime minister, which had been in existence for nearly 200 years, was officially recognised in 1905 and its holder was granted a place in the table of precedence. The prime minister, by tradition also First Lord of the Treasury and Minister for the Civil Service, is appointed by the sovereign and is usually the leader of the party which enjoys, or can secure, a majority in the House of Commons. Other ministers are appointed by the sovereign on the recommendation of the prime minister, who also allocates functions among ministers and has the power to dismiss ministers from their posts.

The prime minister informs the sovereign on state and political matters, advises on the dissolution of parliament, and makes recommendations for important crown appointments, ie the award of honours, etc.

As the chair of cabinet meetings and leader of a political party, the prime minister is responsible for translating party policy into government activity. As leader of the government, the prime minister is responsible to parliament and to the electorate for the policies and their implementation.

The prime minister also represents the nation in international affairs, eg summit conferences.

THE CABINET

The cabinet developed during the 18th century as an inner committee of the Privy Council, which was the chief source of executive power until that time. The cabinet is composed of about 20 ministers chosen by the prime minister, usually the heads of government departments (generally known as secretaries of state unless they have a special title, eg Chancellor of the Exchequer), the leaders of the two houses of parliament, and the holders of various traditional offices.

The cabinet's functions are the final determination of policy, control of government and coordination of government departments. The exercise of its functions is dependent upon the incumbent party's (or parties') majority support in the House of Commons. Cabinet meetings are held in private, taking place once or twice a week during parliamentary sittings and less often during a recess. Proceedings are confidential, the members being bound by their oath as privy counsellors not to disclose information about the proceedings.

The convention of collective responsibility means that the cabinet acts unanimously even when cabinet ministers do not all agree on a subject. The policies of departmental ministers must be consistent with the policies of the government as a whole, and once the government's policy has been decided, each minister is expected to support it or resign.

The convention of ministerial responsibility holds a minister, as the political head of his or her department, accountable to parliament for the department's work. Departmental ministers usually decide all matters within their responsibility, although on matters of political importance they normally consult their colleagues collectively. A decision by a departmental minister is binding on the government as a whole.

POLITICAL PARTIES

Before the reign of William and Mary, the principal officers of state were chosen by and were responsible to the sovereign alone, and not to parliament or the nation at large. Such officers acted sometimes in concert with one another but more often independently, and the fall of one did not, of necessity, involve that of others, although all were liable to be dismissed at any moment.

In 1693 the Earl of Sunderland recommended to William III the advisability of selecting a ministry from the political party which enjoyed a majority in the House of Commons, and the first united ministry was drawn in 1696 from the Whigs, to which party the king owed his throne. This group became known as the 'junto' and was regarded with suspicion as a novelty in the political life of the nation, being a small section meeting in secret apart from the main body of ministers. It may be regarded as the forerunner of the cabinet and in the course of time it led to the establishment of the principle of joint responsibility of ministers, so that internal disagreement caused a change of personnel or resignation of the whole body of ministers.

The accession of George I, who was unfamiliar with the English language, led to a disinclination on the part of the sovereign to preside at meetings of his ministers and caused the emergence of a prime minister, a position first acquired by Robert Walpole in 1721 and retained by him without interruption for 20 years and 326 days. The office of prime minister was formally recognised in 1905 when it was established by royal warrant.

DEVELOPMENT OF PARTIES
In 1828 the Whigs became known as Liberals, a name originally given by opponents to imply laxity of principles, but gradually accepted by the party to indicate its claim to be pioneers and champions of political reform and progressive legislation. In 1861 a Liberal Registration Association was founded and Liberal Associations became widespread. In 1877 a National Liberal Federation was formed, with its headquarters in London. The Liberal Party was in power for long periods during the second half of the 19th century and for several years during the first quarter of the 20th century, but after a split in the party in 1931, the numbers elected remained small. In 1988 a majority of the Liberals agreed on a merger with the Social Democratic Party under the title Social and Liberal Democrats; since 1989 they have been known as the Liberal Democrats. A minority continue separately as the Liberal Party.

Soon after the change from Whig to Liberal, the Tory Party became known as Conservative, a name believed to have been invented by John Wilson Croker in 1830 and to have been generally adopted around the time of the passing of the Reform Act of 1832 – to indicate that the preservation of national institutions was the leading principle of the party. After the Home Rule crisis of 1886 the dissentient Liberals entered into a compact with the Conservatives, under which the latter undertook not to contest their seats, but a separate Liberal Unionist organisation was maintained until 1912, when it was united with the Conservatives.

Labour candidates for parliament made their first appearance at the general election of 1892, when there were 27 standing as Labour or Liberal-Labour. In 1900 the Labour Representation Committee (LRC) was set up in order to establish a distinct Labour group in parliament, with its own whips, its own policy, and a readiness to cooperate with any party which might be engaged in promoting legislation in the direct interests of labour. In 1906 the LRC became known as the Labour Party.

The Green Party was founded in 1973 and campaigns for social and environmental justice. The party began as 'People', was renamed the Ecology Party, and became the Green Party in 1985.

The UK Independence Party (UKIP) was founded in 1993 by members of the Anti-Federalist League. It is a right-wing populist party with one key policy – to leave the European Union. In the 2014 European elections, UKIP became the first party, other than the Conservatives or Labour to win a national election in over a century.

Plaid Cymru was founded in 1926 to provide an independent political voice for Wales and to campaign for self-government in Wales.

The Scottish National Party (SNP) was founded in 1934 to campaign for independence for Scotland and a referendum on the subject was held in September 2014 which culminated in a 'no' to independence result.

The Social Democratic and Labour Party (SDLP) was founded in 1970, emerging from the civil rights movement of the 1960s, with the aim of promoting reform, reconciliation and partnership across the sectarian divide in Northern Ireland, and of opposing violence from any quarter.

The Democratic Unionist Party (DUP) was founded in 1971 to resist moves by the Ulster Unionist Party which were considered a threat to the Union. Its aim is to maintain Northern Ireland as an integral part of the UK.

Sinn Fein first emerged in the 1900s as a federation of nationalist clubs. It is a left-wing republican and labour party that seeks to end British governance in Ireland and achieve a 32-county republic.

GOVERNMENT AND OPPOSITION
The government is formed by the party which wins the largest number of seats in the House of Commons at a general election, or which has the support of a majority of members in the House of Commons. By tradition, the leader of the majority party is asked by the sovereign to form a government, while the largest minority party becomes the official opposition with its own leader and a shadow cabinet. Leaders of the government and opposition sit on the front benches of the Commons with their supporters (the back-benchers) sitting behind them.

FINANCIAL SUPPORT
Financial support for opposition parties in the House of Commons was introduced in 1975 and is commonly known as Short Money, after Edward Short, the leader of the house at that time, who introduced the scheme. Short Money is only payable to those parties that secured at least two seats, or one seat and more than 150,000 votes, at the previous general election and is only intended to provide assistance for parliamentary duties. The amount payable is £16,938.16 for every seat won at the most recent general election plus £33.83 for every 200 votes gained by the party. Short Money allocations for 2016–17 were:

DUP	£166,661
Green	£212,100
Labour	£5,510,661
Liberal Democrats	£544,170
Plaid Cymru	£81,532
SDLP	£62,246
SNP	£1,194,540
UKIP	£212,100
UUP	£70,700

The sum paid to Sinn Fein and any other party that may choose not to take their seats in the House of Commons is calculated on the same basis as Short Money, but is know as Representative Money.

For the financial year which commenced on 1 April 2016, the leader of the opposition's office was allocated £789,146 for running costs.

Financial support for opposition parties in the House of Lords was introduced in 1996 and is commonly known as Cranborne Money, after former leader of the house, Viscount Cranborne.

The following list of political parties are those with at least one MP or sitting member of the House of Lords in the present parliament.

CONSERVATIVE PARTY

Conservative Campaign Headquarters, 4 Matthew Parker Street, London SW1H 9HQ
T 020-7222 9000 W www.conservatives.com

Parliamentary Party Leader, Rt. Hon. Theresa May, MP
Leader in the Lords, Rt. Hon. Baroness Evans of Bowes Park
Leader in the Commons and Lord President of the Council, Rt. Hon. Andrea Leadsom, MP
Deputy Leader in the Commons, Michael Ellis, MP
Chair, Rt. Hon. Sir Patrick McLoughlin, MP
Party Treasurer, Sir Mick Davies

GREEN PARTY

The Biscuit Factory, Unit 201 A Block, 100 Clements Road, London SE16 4DG
T 020-3691 9400 E office@greenparty.org.uk
W www.greenparty.org.uk

Party Leaders, Dr Caroline Lucas, MP and Jonathan Bartley
Deputy Leader, Amelia Womack
Chair, Clare Phipps
Finance Coordinator, Emma Carter

LABOUR PARTY

Labour Central, Kings Manor, Newcastle upon Tyne NE1 6PA
T 0845-092 2299 W www.labour.org.uk

General Secretary, Iain McNicol
General Secretary, Welsh Labour, Louise Magee
General Secretary, Scottish Labour Party, Brian Roy

SHADOW CABINET
Leader of the Opposition, Rt. Hon. Jeremy Corbyn, MP
Deputy Leader and Secretary of State for Culture, Media and Sport, Tom Watson, MP
Chancellor of the Exchequer, Rt. Hon. John McDonnell, MP
Foreign Secretary, Rt. Hon. Emily Thornberry, MP
Home Secretary, Rt. Hon. Diane Abbot, MP

Secretary of State for Business, Energy and Industrial Strategy, Rebecca Long-Bailey, MP
Secretary of State for Environment, Food and Rural Affairs, Sue Hayman, MP
Secretary of State for Communities and Local Government, Andrew Gwynne, MP
Secretary of State for Defence, Nia Griffith, MP
Secretary of State for Education, Angela Rayner, MP
Secretary of State for Exiting the European Union, Rt. Hon. Sir Keir Starmer, KCB, QC, MP
Secretary of State for Health, Jon Ashworth, MP
Secretary of State for Housing, Rt. Hon. John Healey, MP
Secretary of State for International Development, Kate Osamor, MP
Secretary of State for International Trade, Barry Gardiner, MP

Lord Chancellor and Secretary of State for Justice, Richard Burgon, MP
Secretary of State for Scotland, Lesley Laird, MP
Secretary of State for Transport, Andy McDonald, MP
Chief Secretary to the Treasury, Peter Dowd, MP
Secretary of State for Wales, Christina Rees, MP
Secretary of State for Northern Ireland, Owen Smith, MP
Secretary of State for Work and Pensions, Debbie Abrahams, MP
Minister for Diverse Communities, Dawn Butler, MP
Minister for Mental Health and Social Care, Barbara Keeley, MP
Minister for Voter Engagement and Youth Affairs, Cat Smith, MP
Minister for Women and Equalities, Dawn Butler, MP
Minister for the Cabinet Office, Ian Lavery, MP
Lord President of the Council and National Elections and Campaigns Coordinator, Jon Trickett, MP
Leader of the House of Commons, Valerie Vaz, MP
Leader of the House of Lords, Rt. Hon. Baroness Smith of Basildon
Attorney General, Rt. Hon. Baroness Chakrabarti, CBE

LABOUR WHIPS
Commons Chief Whip, Rt. Hon. Nick Brown, MP
Lords Chief Whip, Rt. Hon. Lord Bassam of Brighton

LIBERAL DEMOCRATS

8–10 Great George Street, London SW1P 3AE
T 020-7022 0988 E info@libdems.org.uk W www.libdems.org.uk

Parliamentary Party Leader, Rt. Hon. Sir Vince Cable, MP
Leader in the Lords, Rt. Hon. Lord Newby, OBE
President, Baroness Brinton

NORTHERN IRELAND DEMOCRATIC UNIONIST PARTY

91 Dundela Avenue, Belfast BT4 3BU
T 028-9047 1155
E info@mydup.com W www.mydup.com

Parliamentary Party Leader, Rt. Hon. Arlene Foster, MLA
Deputy Leader, Rt. Hon Nigel Dodds, OBE, MP, MLA
Chair, Lord Morrow, MLA

PLAID CYMRU – THE PARTY OF WALES

Ty Gwynfor, Anson Court, Atlantic Wharf, Caerdydd CF10 4AL
T 029-2047 2272 E post@plaidcymru.org W www.partyof.wales

Party Leader, Leanne Wood, AM
Hon. Party President, Rt. Hon. Lord Wigley
Parliamentary Group Leader, Liz Saville Roberts, MP
Chair, Dafydd Trystan Davies
Chief Executive, Gareth Clubb

SCOTTISH NATIONAL PARTY

Gordon Lamb House, 3 Jackson's Entry, Edinburgh EH8 8PJ
T 0800-633 5432 E info@snp.org W www.snp.org

Westminster Parliamentary Party Leader, Rt. Hon.Ian Blackford, MP
Westminster Parliamentary Party Chief Whip, Patrick Grady, MP
First Minister of Scotland and Leader of the SNP, Rt. Hon. Nicola Sturgeon, MSP
Deputy Leader, Rt. Hon. Angus Robertson
Party President, Ian Hudghton, MEP
National Treasurer, Colin Beattie, MSP
Chief Executive, Peter Murrell

SINN FEIN

53 Falls Road, Belfast BT12 4PD
T 028-9034 7350 E admin@sinnfein.ie W www.sinnfein.ie

Party President, Gerry Adams, TD
Vice-President, Mary Lou McDonald, TD
Chair, Declan Kearney, MLA

MEMBERS OF PARLIAMENT *as at July 2017*

KEY
* Previously an MP for this seat in the 2015–17 parliament
† Previously an MP for this seat in any parliament prior to the 2015–17 parliament
‡ Previously an MP for a different seat in any previous parliament
§ Currently suspended from the parliamentary Conservative Party

* **Abbott**, Rt. Hon. Diane (*b.* 1953) *Lab., Hackney North & Stoke Newington,* Maj. 35,139
* **Abrahams**, Debbie (*b.* 1960) *Lab., Oldham East & Saddleworth,* Maj. 8,182
* **Adams**, Nigel (*b.* 1966) *C., Selby & Ainsty,* Maj. 13,772
Afolami, Bim *C., Hitchin & Harpenden,* Maj. 12,031
* **Afriyie**, Adam (*b.* 1965) *C., Windsor,* Maj. 22,384
* **Aldous**, Peter (*b.* 1961) *C., Waveney,* Maj. 9,215
* **Alexander**, Heidi (*b.* 1975) *Lab., Lewisham East,* Maj. 21,213
* **Ali**, Rushanara (*b.* 1975) *Lab., Bethnal Green & Bow,* Maj. 35,393
* **Allan**, Lucy (*b.* 1964) *C., Telford,* Maj. 720
* **Allen**, Heidi (*b.* 1975) *C., Cambridgeshire South,* Maj. 15,952
* **Allin-Khan**, Dr Rosena (*b.* 1977) *Lab., Tooting,* Maj. 15,458
Amesbury, Mike *Lab., Weaver Vale,* Maj. 3,928
* **Amess**, Sir David (*b.* 1952) *C., Southend West,* Maj. 10,000
* **Andrew**, Stuart (*b.* 1971) *C., Pudsey,* Maj. 331
Antoniazzi, Tonia *Lab., Gower,* Maj. 3,269
* **Argar**, Edward (*b.* 1977) *C., Charnwood,* Maj. 16,341
* **Ashworth**, Jon (*b.* 1978) *Lab. Co-op, Leicester South,* Maj. 26,261
* **Atkins**, Victoria (*b.* 1976) *C., Louth & Horncastle,* Maj. 19,641
* **Austin**, Ian (*b.* 1965) *Lab., Dudley North,* Maj. 22
* **Bacon**, Richard (*b.* 1962) *C., Norfolk South,* Maj. 16,678
Badenoch, Kemi (*b.* 1980) *C., Saffron Walden,* Maj. 24,966
* **Bailey**, Adrian (*b.* 1945) *Lab. Co-op, West Bromwich West,* Maj. 4,460
* **Baker**, Steve (*b.* 1971) *C., Wycombe,* Maj. 6,578
* **Baldwin**, Harriett (*b.* 1960) *C., Worcestershire West,* Maj. 21,328
* **Barclay**, Stephen (*b.* 1972) *C., Cambridgeshire North East,* Maj. 21,270
* **Bardell**, Hannah (*b.* 1984) *SNP, Livingston,* Maj. 3,878
* **Baron**, John (*b.* 1959) *C., Basildon & Billericay,* Maj. 13,400
* **Barron**, Rt. Hon. Sir Kevin (*b.* 1946) *Lab., Rother Valley,* Maj. 3,882
* **Bebb**, Guto (*b.* 1968) *C., Aberconwy,* Maj. 635
* **Beckett**, Rt. Hon. Dame Margaret (*b.* 1943) *Lab., Derby South,* Maj. 11,248
* **Bellingham**, Sir Henry (*b.* 1955) *C., Norfolk North West,* Maj. 13,788
* **Benn**, Rt. Hon. Hilary (*b.* 1953) *Lab., Leeds Central,* Maj. 23,698
* **Benyon**, Rt. Hon. Richard (*b.* 1960) *C., Newbury,* Maj. 24,380
* **Bercow**, Rt. Hon. John (*b.* 1963) *Speaker, Buckingham,* Maj. 25,725
* **Beresford**, Sir Paul (*b.* 1946) *C., Mole Valley,* Maj. 24,137
* **Berger**, Luciana (*b.* 1981) *Lab. Co-op, Liverpool Wavertree,* Maj. 29,466
* **Berry**, Jake (*b.* 1978) *C., Rossendale & Darwen,* Maj. 3,216
* **Betts**, Clive (*b.* 1950) *Lab., Sheffield South East,* Maj. 11,798
* **Black**, Mhairi (*b.* 1994) *SNP, Paisley & Renfrewshire South,* Maj. 2,541
* **Blackford**, Ian (*b.* 1961) *SNP, Ross, Skye & Lochaber,* Maj. 5,919
* **Blackman**, Kirsty (*b.* 1986) *SNP, Aberdeen North,* Maj. 4,139
* **Blackman**, Bob (*b.* 1956) *C., Harrow East,* Maj. 1,757
* **Blackman-Woods**, Roberta, PHD (*b.* 1957) *Lab., Durham, City of,* Maj. 12,364

* **Blomfield**, Paul (*b.* 1953) *Lab., Sheffield Central,* Maj. 27,748
* **Blunt**, Crispin (*b.* 1960) *C., Reigate,* Maj. 17,614
* **Boles**, Nick (*b.* 1965) *C., Grantham & Stamford,* Maj. 20,094
* **Bone**, Peter (*b.* 1952) *C., Wellingborough,* Maj. 12,460
* **Bottomley**, Sir Peter (*b.* 1944) *C., Worthing West,* Maj. 12,090
Bowie, Andrew *C., Aberdeenshire West & Kincardine,* Maj. 7,950
* **Brabin**, Tracy (*b.* 1961) *Lab. Co-op, Batley & Spen,* Maj. 8,961
Bradley, Ben *C., Mansfield,* Maj. 1,057
* **Bradley**, Rt. Hon. Karen (*b.* 1970) *C., Staffordshire Moorlands,* Maj. 10,830
* **Bradshaw**, Rt. Hon. Ben (*b.* 1960) *Lab., Exeter,* Maj. 16,117
* **Brady**, Graham (*b.* 1967) *C., Altrincham & Sale West,* Maj. 6,426
* **Brady**, Mickey (*b.* 1950) *SF, Newry & Armagh,* Maj. 12,489
* **Brake**, Rt. Hon. Tom (*b.* 1962) *LD, Carshalton & Wallington,* Maj. 1,369
* **Brennan**, Kevin (*b.* 1959) *Lab., Cardiff West,* Maj. 12,551
Brereton, Jack (*b.* 1991) *C., Stoke-on-Trent South,* Maj. 663
* **Bridgen**, Andrew (*b.* 1964) *C., Leicestershire North West,* Maj. 13,286
* **Brine**, Steve (*b.* 1974) *C., Winchester,* Maj. 9,999
* **Brock**, Deidre (*b.* 1961) *SNP, Edinburgh North & Leith,* Maj. 1,625
* **Brokenshire**, Rt. Hon. James (*b.* 1968) *C., Old Bexley & Sidcup,* Maj. 15,466
* **Brown**, Alan (*b.* 1970) *SNP, Kilmarnock & Loudoun,* Maj. 6,269
* **Brown**, Rt. Hon. Nick (*b.* 1950) *Lab., Newcastle upon Tyne East,* Maj. 19,261
* **Brown**, Lyn (*b.* 1960) *Lab., West Ham,* Maj. 36,754
* **Bruce**, Fiona (*b.* 1957) *C., Congleton,* Maj. 12,619
* **Bryant**, Chris (*b.* 1962) *Lab., Rhondda,* Maj. 13,746
* **Buck**, Karen (*b.* 1958) *Lab., Westminster North,* Maj. 11,512
* **Buckland**, Robert (*b.* 1968) *C., Swindon South,* Maj. 2,464
* **Burden**, Richard (*b.* 1954) *Lab., Birmingham Northfield,* Maj. 4,667
Burghart, Alex (*b.* 1977) *C., Brentwood & Ongar,* Maj. 24,002
* **Burgon**, Richard (*b.* 1980) *Lab., Leeds East,* Maj. 12,752
* **Burns**, Conor (*b.* 1972) *C., Bournemouth West,* Maj. 7,711
* **Burt**, Rt. Hon. Alistair (*b.* 1955) *C., Bedfordshire North East,* Maj. 20,862
* **Butler**, Dawn (*b.* 1969) *Lab., Brent Central,* Maj. 27,997
* **Byrne**, Rt. Hon. Liam (*b.* 1970) *Lab., Birmingham Hodge Hill,* Maj. 31,026
† **Cable**, Rt. Hon. Vince, PHD (*b.* 1943) *LD, Twickenham,* Maj. 9,762
* **Cadbury**, Ruth (*b.* 1959) *Lab., Brentford & Isleworth,* Maj. 12,182
* **Cairns**, Rt. Hon. Alun (*b.* 1970) *C., Vale of Glamorgan,* Maj. 2,190
* **Cameron**, Dr Lisa (*b.* 1972) *SNP, East Kilbride, Strathaven & Lesmahagow,* Maj. 3,866
* **Campbell**, Ronnie (*b.* 1943) *Lab., Blyth Valley,* Maj. 7,915
* **Campbell**, Gregory (*b.* 1953) *DUP, Londonderry East,* Maj. 8,842
* **Campbell**, Rt. Hon. Alan (*b.* 1957) *Lab., Tynemouth,* Maj. 11,666
Carden, Dan (*b.* 1987) *Lab., Liverpool Walton,* Maj. 32,551
* **Carmichael**, Rt. Hon. Alistair (*b.* 1965) *LD, Orkney & Shetland,* Maj. 4,563
* **Cartlidge**, James (*b.* 1974) *C., Suffolk South,* Maj. 17,749
* **Cash**, Sir William (*b.* 1940) *C., Stone,* Maj. 17,495
* **Caulfield**, Maria (*b.* 1974) *C., Lewes,* Maj. 5,508
* **Chalk**, Alex (*b.* 1977) *C., Cheltenham,* Maj. 2,569
* **Champion**, Sarah (*b.* 1969) *Lab., Rotherham,* Maj. 11,387
* **Chapman**, Jenny (*b.* 1973) *Lab., Darlington,* Maj. 3,280
* **Chapman**, Douglas (*b.* 1955) *SNP, Dunfermline & Fife West,* Maj. 844

Charalambous, Bambos (*b.* 1967) *Lab., Enfield Southgate,* Maj. 4,355

* **Cherry**, Joanna (*b.* 1966) *SNP, Edinburgh South West,* Maj. 1,097

* **Chishti**, Rehman (*b.* 1978) *C., Gillingham & Rainham,* Maj. 9,430

* **Chope**, Christopher (*b.* 1947) *C., Christchurch,* Maj. 25,171

* **Churchill**, Jo (*b.* 1964) *C., Bury St Edmunds,* Maj. 18,441

Clark, Colin (*b.* 1968) *C., Gordon,* Maj. 2,607

* **Clark**, Rt. Hon. Greg, PHD (*b.* 1967) *C., Tunbridge Wells,* Maj. 16,465

Clarke, Simon *C., Middlesbrough South & Cleveland East,* Maj. 1,020

* **Clarke**, Rt. Hon. Kenneth (*b.* 1940) *C., Rushcliffe,* Maj. 8,010

* **Cleverly**, James (*b.* 1969) *C., Braintree,* Maj. 18,422

* **Clifton-Brown**, Geoffrey (*b.* 1953) *C., Cotswolds, The,* Maj. 25,499

* **Clwyd**, Rt. Hon. Ann (*b.* 1937) *Lab., Cynon Valley,* Maj. 13,238

* **Coaker**, Vernon (*b.* 1953) *Lab., Gedling,* Maj. 4,694

* **Coffey**, Ann (*b.* 1946) *Lab., Stockport,* Maj. 14,477

* **Coffey**, Therese, PHD (*b.* 1971) *C., Suffolk Coastal,* Maj. 16,012

* **Collins**, Damian (*b.* 1974) *C., Folkestone & Hythe,* Maj. 15,411

* **Cooper**, Julie (*b.* 1960) *Lab., Burnley,* Maj. 6,353

* **Cooper**, Rosie (*b.* 1950) *Lab., Lancashire West,* Maj. 11,689

* **Cooper**, Rt. Hon. Yvette (*b.* 1969) *Lab., Normanton, Pontefract & Castleford,* Maj. 14,499

* **Corbyn**, Rt. Hon. Jeremy (*b.* 1949) *Lab., Islington North,* Maj. 33,215

* **Costa**, Alberto (*b.* 1971) *C., Leicestershire South,* Maj. 18,631

* **Courts**, Robert (*b.* 1978) *C., Witney,* Maj. 21,241

* **Cowan**, Ronnie (*b.* 1959) *SNP, Inverclyde,* Maj. 384

* **Cox**, Geoffrey (*b.* 1960) *C., Devon West & Torridge,* Maj. 20,686

* **Coyle**, Neil (*b.* 1978) *Lab., Bermondsey & Old Southwark,* Maj. 12,972

* **Crabb**, Rt. Hon. Stephen (*b.* 1973) *C., Preseli Pembrokeshire,* Maj. 314

* **Crausby**, Sir David (*b.* 1946) *Lab., Bolton North East,* Maj. 3,797

* **Crawley**, Angela (*b.* 1987) *SNP, Lanark & Hamilton East,* Maj. 266

* **Creagh**, Mary (*b.* 1967) *Lab., Wakefield,* Maj. 2,176

* **Creasy**, Stella, PHD (*b.* 1977) *Lab. Co-op, Walthamstow,* Maj. 32,017

* **Crouch**, Tracey (*b.* 1975) *C., Chatham & Aylesford,* Maj. 10,458

* **Cruddas**, Jon (*b.* 1962) *Lab., Dagenham & Rainham,* Maj. 4,652

* **Cryer**, John (*b.* 1964) *Lab., Leyton & Wanstead,* Maj. 22,607

* **Cummins**, Judith (*b.* 1967) *Lab., Bradford South,* Maj. 6,700

* **Cunningham**, Jim (*b.* 1941) *Lab., Coventry South,* Maj. 7,947

* **Cunningham**, Alex (*b.* 1955) *Lab., Stockton North,* Maj. 8,715

* **Dakin**, Nic (*b.* 1955) *Lab., Scunthorpe,* Maj. 3,431

† **Davey**, Rt. Hon. Sir Edward (*b.* 1965) *LD, Kingston & Surbiton,* Maj. 4,124

* **David**, Wayne (*b.* 1957) *Lab., Caerphilly,* Maj. 12,078

* **Davies**, Chris (*b.* 1967) *C., Brecon & Radnorshire,* Maj. 8,038

* **Davies**, Mims (*b.* 1975) *C., Eastleigh,* Maj. 14,179

* **Davies**, David (*b.* 1970) *C., Monmouth,* Maj. 8,206

* **Davies**, Glyn (*b.* 1944) *C., Montgomeryshire,* Maj. 9,285

* **Davies**, Philip (*b.* 1972) *C., Shipley,* Maj. 4,681

* **Davies**, Geraint (*b.* 1960) *Lab. Co-op, Swansea West,* Maj. 10,598

* **Davis**, Rt. Hon. David (*b.* 1948) *C., Haltemprice & Howden,* Maj. 15,405

* **Day**, Martyn (*b.* 1971) *SNP, Linlithgow & Falkirk East,* Maj. 2,919

De Cordova, Marsha *Lab., Battersea,* Maj. 2,416

* **De Piero**, Gloria (*b.* 1972) *Lab., Ashfield,* Maj. 441

* **Debbonaire**, Thangam (*b.* 1966) *Lab., Bristol West,* Maj. 37,336

Dent Coad, Emma *Lab., Kensington,* Maj. 20

Dhesi, Tan *Lab., Slough,* Maj. 16,998

* **Dinenage**, Caroline (*b.* 1971) *C., Gosport,* Maj. 17,211

* **Djanogly**, Jonathan (*b.* 1965) *C., Huntingdon,* Maj. 14,475

Docherty, Leo (*b.* 1976) *C., Aldershot,* Maj. 11,478

* **Docherty**, Martin (*b.* 1971) *SNP, Dunbartonshire West,* Maj. 2,288

Dockerill, Julia *C., Hornchurch & Upminster,* Maj. 17,723

* **Dodds**, Rt. Hon. Nigel (*b.* 1958) *DUP, Belfast North,* Maj. 2,081

Dodds, Anneliese, PHD (*b.* 1978) *Lab. Co-op, Oxford East,* Maj. 23,284

* **Donaldson**, Rt. Hon. Sir Jeffrey (*b.* 1962) *DUP, Lagan Valley,* Maj. 19,229

* **Donelan**, Michelle (*b.* 1984) *C., Chippenham,* Maj. 16,630

* **Dorries**, Nadine (*b.* 1957) *C., Bedfordshire Mid,* Maj. 20,983

* **Double**, Steve (*b.* 1966) *C., St Austell & Newquay,* Maj. 11,142

* **Doughty**, Stephen (*b.* 1980) *Lab. Co-op, Cardiff South & Penarth,* Maj. 14,864

* **Dowd**, Peter (*b.* 1957) *Lab., Bootle,* Maj. 36,200

* **Dowden**, Oliver, CBE (*b.* 1978) *C., Hertsmere,* Maj. 16,951

* **Doyle-Price**, Jackie (*b.* 1969) *C., Thurrock,* Maj. 345

* **Drax**, Richard (*b.* 1958) *C., Dorset South,* Maj. 11,695

† **Drew**, David (*b.* 1952) *Lab. Co-op, Stroud,* Maj. 687

* **Dromey**, Jack (*b.* 1948) *Lab., Birmingham Erdington,* Maj. 7,285

* **Duddridge**, James (*b.* 1971) *C., Rochford & Southend East,* Maj. 5,548

Duffield, Rosie (*b.* 1971) *Lab., Canterbury,* Maj. 187

Duguid, David *C., Banff & Buchan,* Maj. 3,693

* **Duncan**, Rt. Hon. Sir Alan (*b.* 1957) *C., Rutland & Melton,* Maj. 23,104

* **Duncan Smith**, Rt. Hon. Iain (*b.* 1954) *C., Chingford & Woodford Green,* Maj. 2,438

* **Dunne**, Philip (*b.* 1958) *C., Ludlow,* Maj. 19,286

* **Eagle**, Maria (*b.* 1961) *Lab., Garston & Halewood,* Maj. 32,149

* **Eagle**, Angela (*b.* 1961) *Lab., Wallasey,* Maj. 23,320

* **Edwards**, Jonathan (*b.* 1976) *PC, Carmarthen East & Dinefwr,* Maj. 3,908

* **Efford**, Clive (*b.* 1958) *Lab., Eltham,* Maj. 6,296

* **Elliott**, Julie (*b.* 1963) *Lab., Sunderland Central,* Maj. 9,997

* **Ellis**, Michael (*b.* 1967) *C., Northampton North,* Maj. 807

* **Ellman**, Louise (*b.* 1945) *Lab. Co-op, Liverpool Riverside,* Maj. 35,947

* **Ellwood**, Rt. Hon. Tobias (*b.* 1966) *C., Bournemouth East,* Maj. 7,937

* **Elmore**, Chris (*b.* 1983) *Lab., Ogmore,* Maj. 13,871

* **Elphicke**, Charlie (*b.* 1971) *C., Dover,* Maj. 6,437

* **Esterson**, Bill (*b.* 1966) *Lab., Sefton Central,* Maj. 15,618

* **Eustice**, George (*b.* 1971) *C., Camborne & Redruth,* Maj. 1,577

* **Evans**, Chris (*b.* 1976) *Lab. Co-op, Islwyn,* Maj. 11,412

* **Evans**, Nigel (*b.* 1957) *C., Ribble Valley,* Maj. 13,199

* **Evennett**, Rt. Hon. David (*b.* 1949) *C., Bexleyheath & Crayford,* Maj. 9,073

* **Fabricant**, Michael (*b.* 1950) *C., Lichfield,* Maj. 18,581

* **Fallon**, Rt. Hon. Sir Michael, KCB (*b.* 1952) *C., Sevenoaks,* Maj. 21,917

* **Farrelly**, Paul (*b.* 1962) *Lab., Newcastle-under-Lyme,* Maj. 30

* **Farron**, Tim (*b.* 1970) *LD, Westmorland & Lonsdale,* Maj. 777

* **Fellows**, Marion (*b.* 1949) *SNP, Motherwell & Wishaw,* Maj. 318

* **Fernandes**, Suella (*b.* 1980) *C., Fareham,* Maj. 21,555

* **Field**, Rt. Hon. Frank (*b.* 1942) *Lab., Birkenhead,* Maj. 25,514

* **Field**, Rt. Hon. Mark (*b.* 1964) *C., Cities of London & Westminster,* Maj. 3,148

* **Fitzpatrick**, Jim (*b.* 1952) *Lab., Poplar & Limehouse,* Maj. 27,712

* **Fletcher**, Colleen (*b.* 1954) *Lab., Coventry North East,* Maj. 15,580

* **Flint**, Rt. Hon. Caroline (*b.* 1961) *Lab., Don Valley,* Maj. 5,169

* **Flynn**, Paul (*b.* 1935) *Lab., Newport West*, Maj. 5,658
Ford, Vicky (*b.* 1967) *C., Chelmsford*, Maj. 13,572
* **Foster**, Kevin (*b.* 1978) *C., Torbay*, Maj. 14,283
* **Fovargue**, Yvonne (*b.* 1956) *Lab., Makerfield*, Maj. 13,542
* **Fox**, Rt. Hon. Dr Liam (*b.* 1961) *C., Somerset North*, Maj. 17,103
* **Foxcroft**, Vicky (*b.* 1977) *Lab., Lewisham Deptford*, Maj. 34,899
* **Francois**, Rt. Hon. Mark (*b.* 1965) *C., Rayleigh & Wickford*, Maj. 23,450
* **Frazer**, Lucy (*b.* 1972) *C., Cambridgeshire South East*, Maj. 16,158
* **Freeman**, George (*b.* 1967) *C., Norfolk Mid*, Maj. 16,086
* **Freer**, Mike (*b.* 1960) *C., Finchley & Golders Green*, Maj. 1,657
Frith, James *Lab., Bury North*, Maj. 4,375
* **Furniss**, Gill (*b.* 1957) *Lab., Sheffield Brightside & Hillsborough*, Maj. 19,143
* **Fysh**, Marcus (*b.* 1970) *C., Yeovil*, Maj. 14,723
Gaffney, Hugh *Lab., Coatbridge, Chryston & Bellshill*, Maj. 1,586
* **Gale**, Sir Roger (*b.* 1943) *C., Thanet North*, Maj. 10,738
* **Gapes**, Mike (*b.* 1952) *Lab. Co-op, Ilford South*, Maj. 31,647
* **Gardiner**, Barry (*b.* 1957) *Lab., Brent North*, Maj. 17,061
* **Garnier**, Mark (*b.* 1963) *C., Wyre Forest*, Maj. 13,334
* **Gauke**, Rt. Hon. David (*b.* 1971) *C., Hertfordshire South West*, Maj. 19,550
George, Ruth *Lab., High Peak*, Maj. 2,322
* **Gethins**, Stephen (*b.* 1976) *SNP, Fife North East*, Maj. 2
* **Ghani**, Nus (*b.* 1972) *C., Wealden*, Maj. 23,628
* **Gibb**, Rt. Hon. Nick (*b.* 1960) *C., Bognor Regis & Littlehampton*, Maj. 17,494
† **Gildernew**, Michelle (*b.* 1970) *SF, Fermanagh & South Tyrone*, Maj. 875
Gill, Preet *Lab. Co-op, Birmingham Edgbaston*, Maj. 6,917
* **Gillan**, Rt. Hon. Cheryl (*b.* 1952) *C., Chesham & Amersham*, Maj. 22,140
Girvan, Paul (*b.* 1963) *DUP, Antrim South*, Maj. 3,208
* **Glen**, John (*b.* 1974) *C., Salisbury*, Maj. 17,333
* **Glindon**, Mary (*b.* 1957) *Lab., Tyneside North*, Maj. 19,284
* **Godsiff**, Roger (*b.* 1946) *Lab., Birmingham Hall Green*, Maj. 33,944
* **Goldsmith**, Zac (*b.* 1975) *C., Richmond Park*, Maj. 45
* **Goodman**, Helen (*b.* 1958) *Lab., Bishop Auckland*, Maj. 502
* **Goodwill**, Robert (*b.* 1956) *C., Scarborough & Whitby*, Maj. 3,435
* **Gove**, Rt. Hon. Michael (*b.* 1967) *C., Surrey Heath*, Maj. 24,943
* **Grady**, Patrick (*b.* 1980) *SNP, Glasgow North*, Maj. 1,060
* **Graham**, Richard (*b.* 1958) *C., Gloucester*, Maj. 5,520
Graham, Luke *C., Ochil & Perthshire South*, Maj. 3,359
Grant, Bill (*b.* 1951) *C., Ayr, Carrick & Cumnock*, Maj. 2,774
* **Grant**, Peter (*b.* 1961) *SNP, Glenrothes*, Maj. 3,267
* **Grant**, Helen (*b.* 1961) *C., Maidstone & The Weald*, Maj. 17,704
* **Gray**, Neil (*b.* 1986) *SNP, Airdrie & Shotts*, Maj. 195
* **Gray**, James (*b.* 1954) *C., Wiltshire North*, Maj. 22,877
* **Grayling**, Rt. Hon. Chris (*b.* 1962) *C., Epsom & Ewell*, Maj. 20,475
* **Green**, Rt. Hon. Damian (*b.* 1956) *C., Ashford*, Maj. 17,478
* **Green**, Chris (*b.* 1973) *C., Bolton West*, Maj. 936
* **Green**, Kate (*b.* 1960) *Lab., Stretford & Urmston*, Maj. 19,705
* **Greening**, Rt. Hon. Justine (*b.* 1969) *C., Putney*, Maj. 1,554
* **Greenwood**, Lilian (*b.* 1966) *Lab., Nottingham South*, Maj. 15,162
* **Greenwood**, Margaret (*b.* 1959) *Lab., Wirral West*, Maj. 5,365
* **Grieve**, Rt. Hon. Dominic (*b.* 1956) *C., Beaconsfield*, Maj. 24,543
* **Griffith**, Nia (*b.* 1956) *Lab., Llanelli*, Maj. 12,024
* **Griffiths**, Andrew (*b.* 1970) *C., Burton*, Maj. 10,047

‡ **Grogan**, John (*b.* 1956) *Lab., Keighley*, Maj. 249
* **Gwynne**, Andrew (*b.* 1974) *Lab., Denton & Reddish*, Maj. 14,077
* **Gyimah**, Sam (*b.* 1976) *C., Surrey East*, Maj. 23,914
* **Haigh**, Louise (*b.* 1987) *Lab., Sheffield Heeley*, Maj. 13,828
Hair, Kirstene (*b.* 1989) *C., Angus*, Maj. 2,645
* **Halfon**, Rt. Hon. Robert (*b.* 1969) *C., Harlow*, Maj. 7,031
* **Hall**, Luke (*b.* 1986) *C., Thornbury & Yate*, Maj. 12,071
* **Hamilton**, Fabian (*b.* 1955) *Lab., Leeds North East*, Maj. 16,991
* **Hammond**, Rt. Hon. Philip (*b.* 1955) *C., Runnymede & Weybridge*, Maj. 18,050
* **Hammond**, Stephen (*b.* 1962) *C., Wimbledon*, Maj. 5,622
* **Hancock**, Rt. Hon. Matt (*b.* 1978) *C., Suffolk West*, Maj. 17,063
* **Hands**, Rt. Hon. Greg (*b.* 1965) *C., Chelsea & Fulham*, Maj. 8,188
* **Hanson**, Rt. Hon. David (*b.* 1957) *Lab., Delyn*, Maj. 4,240
Hardy, Emma (*b.* 1980) *Lab., Hull West & Hessle*, Maj. 8,025
* **Harman**, Rt. Hon. Harriet (*b.* 1950) *Lab., Camberwell & Peckham*, Maj. 37,316
* **Harper**, Rt. Hon. Mark (*b.* 1970) *C., Forest of Dean*, Maj. 9,502
* **Harrington**, Richard (*b.* 1957) *C., Watford*, Maj. 2,092
* **Harris**, Rebecca (*b.* 1967) *C., Castle Point*, Maj. 18,872
* **Harris**, Carolyn (*b.* 1960) *Lab., Swansea East*, Maj. 13,168
* **Harrison**, Trudy (*b.* 1976) *C., Copeland*, Maj. 1,695
* **Hart**, Simon (*b.* 1963) *C., Carmarthen West & Pembrokeshire South*, Maj. 3,110
* **Hayes**, Helen (*b.* 1974) *Lab., Dulwich & West Norwood*, Maj. 28,156
* **Hayes**, Rt. Hon. John, CBE (*b.* 1958) *C., South Holland & The Deepings*, Maj. 24,897
* **Hayman**, Sue (*b.* 1962) *Lab., Workington*, Maj. 3,925
Hazzard, Chris (*b.* 1984) *SF, Down South*, Maj. 2,446
* **Heald**, Sir Oliver (*b.* 1954) *C., Hertfordshire North East*, Maj. 16,835
* **Healey**, Rt. Hon. Sir John (*b.* 1960) *Lab., Wentworth & Dearne*, Maj. 14,803
* **Heappey**, James (*b.* 1981) *C., Wells*, Maj. 7,582
* **Heaton-Harris**, Chris (*b.* 1967) *C., Daventry*, Maj. 21,734
* **Heaton-Jones**, Peter (*b.* 1963) *C., Devon North*, Maj. 4,332
* **Henderson**, Gordon (*b.* 1948) *C., Sittingbourne & Sheppey*, Maj. 15,211
* **Hendrick**, Mark (*b.* 1958) *Lab. Co-op, Preston*, Maj. 15,723
* **Hendry**, Drew (*b.* 1964) *SNP, Inverness, Nairn, Badenoch & Strathspey*, Maj. 4,924
* **Hepburn**, Stephen (*b.* 1959) *Lab., Jarrow*, Maj. 17,263
* **Herbert**, Rt. Hon. Nick, CBE (*b.* 1963) *C., Arundel & South Downs*, Maj. 23,883
* **Hermon**, Lady (Sylvia) (*b.* 1955) *Ind., Down North*, Maj. 1,208
Hill, Mike *Lab., Hartlepool*, Maj. 7,650
* **Hillier**, Meg (*b.* 1969) *Lab. Co-op, Hackney South & Shoreditch*, Maj. 37,931
* **Hinds**, Damian (*b.* 1969) *C., Hampshire East*, Maj. 25,852
* **Hoare**, Simon (*b.* 1969) *C., Dorset North*, Maj. 25,777
Hobhouse, Wera (*b.* 1960) *LD, Bath*, Maj. 5,694
* **Hodge**, Rt. Hon. Dame Margaret (*b.* 1944) *Lab., Barking*, Maj. 21,608
* **Hodgson**, Sharon (*b.* 1966) *Lab., Washington & Sunderland West*, Maj. 12,940
* **Hoey**, Kate (*b.* 1946) *Lab., Vauxhall*, Maj. 20,250
* **Hollern**, Kate (*b.* 1955) *Lab., Blackburn*, Maj. 20,368
* **Hollingbery**, George (*b.* 1963) *C., Meon Valley*, Maj. 25,692
* **Hollinrake**, Kevin (*b.* 1963) *C., Thirsk & Malton*, Maj. 19,001
* **Hollobone**, Philip (*b.* 1964) *C., Kettering*, Maj. 10,562
* **Holloway**, Adam (*b.* 1965) *C., Gravesham*, Maj. 9,347
* **Hopkins**, Kelvin (*b.* 1941) *Lab., Luton North*, Maj. 14,364
* **Hosie**, Stewart (*b.* 1963) *SNP, Dundee East*, Maj. 6,645
* **Howarth**, Rt. Hon. George (*b.* 1949) *Lab., Knowsley*, Maj. 42,214

* **Howell**, John (b. 1955) C., Henley, Maj. 22,294
* **Hoyle**, Rt. Hon. Lindsay (b. 1957) Lab., Chorley, Maj. 7,512
* **Huddleston**, Nigel (b. 1970) C., Worcestershire Mid, Maj. 23,326
Hughes, Eddie C., Walsall North, Maj. 2,601
* **Hunt**, Rt. Hon. Jeremy (b. 1966) C., Surrey South West, Maj. 21,590
* **Huq**, Dr Rupa (b. 1972) Lab., Ealing Central & Acton, Maj. 13,807
* **Hurd**, Nick (b. 1962) C., Ruislip, Northwood & Pinner, Maj. 13,980
* **Hussain**, Imran (b. 1978) Lab., Bradford East, Maj. 20,540
Jack, Alister (b. 1964) C., Dumfries & Galloway, Maj. 5,643
* **James**, Margot (b. 1957) C., Stourbridge, Maj. 7,654
Jardine, Christine LD, Edinburgh West, Maj. 2,988
* **Jarvis**, Dan (b. 1972) Lab., Barnsley Central, Maj. 15,546
* **Javid**, Rt. Hon. Sajid (b. 1969) C., Bromsgrove, Maj. 16,573
* **Jayawardena**, Ranil (b. 1986) C., Hampshire North East, Maj. 27,772
* **Jenkin**, Hon. Bernard (b. 1959) C., Harwich & Essex North, Maj. 14,356
* **Jenkyns**, Andrea (b. 1974) C., Morley & Outwood, Maj. 2,104
* **Jenrick**, Robert (b. 1982) C., Newark, Maj. 18,149
* **Johnson**, Gareth (b. 1969) C., Dartford, Maj. 13,186
* **Johnson**, Diana (b. 1966) Lab., Hull North, Maj. 14,262
* **Johnson**, Joseph (b. 1971) C., Orpington, Maj. 19,461
* **Johnson**, Caroline (b. 1977) C., Sleaford & North Hykeham, Maj. 25,237
* **Johnson**, Rt. Hon. Boris (b. 1964) C., Uxbridge & Ruislip South, Maj. 5,034
Jones, Darren (b. 1986) Lab., Bristol North West, Maj. 4,761
* **Jones**, Susan Elan (b. 1968) Lab., Clwyd South, Maj. 4,356
* **Jones**, Rt. Hon. David (b. 1952) C., Clwyd West, Maj. 3,437
Jones, Sarah (b. 1972) Lab., Croydon Central, Maj. 5,652
* **Jones**, Kevan (b. 1964) Lab., Durham North, Maj. 12,939
* **Jones**, Andrew (b. 1963) C., Harrogate & Knaresborough, Maj. 18,168
* **Jones**, Graham (b. 1966) Lab., Hyndburn, Maj. 5,815
* **Jones**, Gerald (b. 1970) Lab., Merthyr Tydfil & Rhymney, Maj. 16,334
* **Jones**, Marcus (b. 1974) C., Nuneaton, Maj. 4,739
* **Jones**, Helen (b. 1954) Lab., Warrington North, Maj. 9,582
* **Kane**, Mike (b. 1969) Lab., Wythenshawe & Sale East, Maj. 14,944
* **Kawczynski**, Daniel (b. 1972) C., Shrewsbury & Atcham, Maj. 6,627
Keegan, Gillian C., Chichester, Maj. 22,621
* **Keeley**, Barbara (b. 1952) Lab., Worsley & Eccles South, Maj. 8,379
* **Kendall**, Liz (b. 1971) Lab., Leicester West, Maj. 11,060
* **Kennedy**, Seema (b. 1974) C., South Ribble, Maj. 7,421
Kerr, Stephen (b. 1960) C., Stirling, Maj. 148
Khan, Afzal (b. 1958) Lab., Manchester Gorton, Maj. 31,730
Killen, Ged Lab. Co-op, Rutherglen & Hamilton West, Maj. 265
* **Kinnock**, Stephen (b. 1970) Lab., Aberavon, Maj. 16,761
* **Knight**, Julian (b. 1972) C., Solihull, Maj. 20,571
* **Knight**, Rt. Hon. Sir Greg (b. 1949) C., Yorkshire East, Maj. 15,006
* **Kwarteng**, Kwasi, PHD (b. 1975) C., Spelthorne, Maj. 13,425
* **Kyle**, Peter, DPHIL (b. 1970) Lab., Hove, Maj. 18,757
* **Laing**, Eleanor (b. 1958) C., Epping Forest, Maj. 18,243
Laird, Lesley (b. 1958) Lab., Kirkcaldy & Cowdenbeath, Maj. 259
Lake, Ben (b. 1993) PC, Ceredigion, Maj. 104
* **Lamb**, Rt. Hon. Norman (b. 1957) LD, Norfolk North, Maj. 3,512
* **Lammy**, Rt. Hon. David (b. 1972) Lab., Tottenham, Maj. 34,584
Lamont, John (b. 1976) C., Berwickshire, Roxburgh & Selkirk, Maj. 11,060
* **Lancaster**, Mark (b. 1970) C., Milton Keynes North, Maj. 1,915
* **Latham**, Pauline (b. 1948) C., Derbyshire Mid, Maj. 11,616

* **Lavery**, Ian (b. 1963) Lab., Wansbeck, Maj. 10,435
* **Law**, Chris (b. 1969) SNP, Dundee West, Maj. 5,262
* **Leadsom**, Rt. Hon. Andrea (b. 1963) C., Northamptonshire South, Maj. 22,840
* **Lee**, Dr Phillip (b. 1970) C., Bracknell, Maj. 16,016
Lee, Karen (b. 1961) Lab., Lincoln, Maj. 1,538
* **Lefroy**, Jeremy (b. 1959) C., Stafford, Maj. 7,729
* **Leigh**, Sir Edward (b. 1950) C., Gainsborough, Maj. 17,023
* **Leslie**, Chris (b. 1972) Lab. Co-op, Nottingham East, Maj. 19,590
* **Letwin**, Rt. Hon. Sir Oliver, PHD (b. 1956) C., Dorset West, Maj. 19,091
* **Lewell-Buck**, Emma (b. 1978) Lab., South Shields, Maj. 14,508
Lewer, Andrew (b. 1971) C., Northampton South, Maj. 1,159
* **Lewis**, Ivan (b. 1967) Lab., Bury South, Maj. 5,965
* **Lewis**, Brandon (b. 1971) C., Great Yarmouth, Maj. 7,973
* **Lewis**, Rt. Hon. Julian, DPHIL (b. 1951) C., New Forest East, Maj. 21,995
* **Lewis**, Clive (b. 1971) Lab., Norwich South, Maj. 15,596
* **Liddell-Grainger**, Ian (b. 1959) C., Bridgwater & Somerset West, Maj. 15,448
* **Lidington**, Rt. Hon. David, CBE (b. 1956) C., Aylesbury, Maj. 14,696
Linden, David SNP, Glasgow East, Maj. 75
Little Pengelly, Emma (b. 1979) DUP, Belfast South, Maj. 1,996
† **Lloyd**, Stephen (b. 1957) LD, Eastbourne, Maj. 1,609
‡ **Lloyd**, Tony (b. 1950) Lab., Rochdale, Maj. 14,819
* **Long Bailey**, Rebecca (b. 1979) Lab., Salford & Eccles, Maj. 19,132
* **Lopresti**, Jack (b. 1969) C., Filton & Bradley Stoke, Maj. 4,182
* **Lord**, Jonathan (b. 1962) C., Woking, Maj. 16,724
* **Loughton**, Tim (b. 1962) C., Worthing East & Shoreham, Maj. 5,106
* **Lucas**, Caroline, PHD (b. 1960) Green, Brighton Pavilion, Maj. 14,689
* **Lucas**, Ian (b. 1960) Lab., Wrexham, Maj. 1,832
* **Lynch**, Holly (b. 1986) Lab., Halifax, Maj. 5,376
* **McCabe**, Steve (b. 1955) Lab., Birmingham Selly Oak, Maj. 15,207
McCallion, Elisha (b. 1982) SF, Foyle, Maj. 169
* **McCarthy**, Kerry (b. 1965) Lab., Bristol East, Maj. 13,394
* **McDonagh**, Siobhain (b. 1960) Lab., Mitcham & Morden, Maj. 21,375
* **McDonald**, Stuart (b. 1978) SNP, Cumbernauld, Kilsyth & Kirkintilloch East, Maj. 4,264
* **McDonald**, Stewart (b. 1986) SNP, Glasgow South, Maj. 2,027
* **McDonald**, Andy (b. 1958) Lab., Middlesbrough, Maj. 13,873
* **McDonnell**, John (b. 1951) Lab., Hayes & Harlington, Maj. 18,115
McElduff, Barry (b. 1966) SF, Tyrone West, Maj. 10,342
* **McFadden**, Rt. Hon. Pat (b. 1965) Lab., Wolverhampton South East, Maj. 8,514
* **McGinn**, Conor (b. 1984) Lab., St Helens North, Maj. 18,406
* **McGovern**, Alison (b. 1980) Lab., Wirral South, Maj. 8,323
* **McInnes**, Liz (b. 1959) Lab., Heywood & Middleton, Maj. 7,617
* **Mackinlay**, Craig (b. 1966) C., Thanet South, Maj. 6,387
* **McKinnell**, Catherine (b. 1976) Lab., Newcastle upon Tyne North, Maj. 10,349
Maclean, Rachel (b. 1965) C., Redditch, Maj. 7,363
* **McLoughlin**, Rt. Hon. Sir Patrick (b. 1957) C., Derbyshire Dales, Maj. 14,327
* **McMahon**, Jim (b. 1980) Lab. Co-op, Oldham West & Royton, Maj. 17,198
McMorrin, Anna (b. 1971) Lab., Cardiff North, Maj. 4,174
* **McNally**, John (b. 1951) SNP, Falkirk, Maj. 4,923
* **MacNeil**, Angus (b. 1970) SNP, Na h-Eileanan an Iar, Maj. 1,007
* **McPartland**, Stephen (b. 1976) C., Stevenage, Maj. 3,384
‡ **McVey**, Rt. Hon. Esther (b. 1967) C., Tatton, Maj. 14,787

* **Madders**, Justin (*b.* 1972) *Lab., Ellesmere Port & Neston*, Maj. 11,390
* **Mahmood**, Shabana (*b.* 1980) *Lab., Birmingham Ladywood*, Maj. 28,714
* **Mahmood**, Khalid (*b.* 1961) *Lab., Birmingham Perry Barr*, Maj. 18,383
* **Main**, Anne (*b.* 1957) *C., St Albans*, Maj. 6,109
* **Mak**, Alan (*b.* 1983) *C., Havant*, Maj. 15,956
* **Malhotra**, Seema (*b.* 1972) *Lab. Co-op, Feltham & Heston*, Maj. 15,603
* **Malthouse**, Kit (*b.* 1966) *C., Hampshire North West*, Maj. 22,679
* **Mann**, John (*b.* 1960) *Lab., Bassetlaw*, Maj. 4,852
* **Mann**, Scott (*b.* 1977) *C., Cornwall North*, Maj. 7,200
* **Marsden**, Gordon (*b.* 1953) *Lab., Blackpool South*, Maj. 2,523
Martin, Sandy (*b.* 1957) *Lab., Ipswich*, Maj. 831
* **Maskell**, Rachael (*b.* 1972) *Lab. Co-op, York Central*, Maj. 18,575
* **Maskey**, Paul (*b.* 1967) *SF, Belfast West*, Maj. 21,652
Masterton, Paul *C., Renfrewshire East*, Maj. 4,712
* **Matheson**, Chris (*b.* 1968) *Lab., Chester, City of*, Maj. 9,176
* **May**, Rt. Hon. Theresa (*b.* 1956) *C., Maidenhead*, Maj. 26,457
* **Maynard**, Paul (*b.* 1975) *C., Blackpool North & Cleveleys*, Maj. 2,023
* **Mearns**, Ian (*b.* 1957) *Lab., Gateshead*, Maj. 17,350
* **Menzies**, Mark (*b.* 1971) *C., Fylde*, Maj. 11,805
* **Mercer**, Johnny (*b.* 1981) *C., Plymouth Moor View*, Maj. 5,019
* **Merriman**, Huw (*b.* 1973) *C., Bexhill & Battle*, Maj. 22,165
* **Metcalfe**, Stephen (*b.* 1966) *C., Basildon South & Thurrock East*, Maj. 11,490
* **Miliband**, Rt. Hon. Edward (*b.* 1969) *Lab., Doncaster North*, Maj. 14,024
* **Miller**, Rt. Hon. Maria (*b.* 1964) *C., Basingstoke*, Maj. 9,466
* **Milling**, Amanda (*b.* 1975) *C., Cannock Chase*, Maj. 8,391
* **Mills**, Nigel (*b.* 1974) *C., Amber Valley*, Maj. 8,300
* **Milton**, Rt. Hon. Anne (*b.* 1955) *C., Guildford*, Maj. 17,040
* **Mitchell**, Rt. Hon. Andrew (*b.* 1956) *C., Sutton Coldfield*, Maj. 15,339
* **Molloy**, Francie (*b.* 1950) *SF, Ulster Mid*, Maj. 12,890
* **Monaghan**, Carol (*b.* 1972) *SNP, Glasgow North West*, Maj. 2,561
* **Moon**, Madeleine (*b.* 1950) *Lab., Bridgend*, Maj. 4,700
Moore, Damien *C., Southport*, Maj. 2,914
Moran, Layla (*b.* 1982) *LD, Oxford West & Abingdon*, Maj. 816
* **Mordaunt**, Penny (*b.* 1973) *C., Portsmouth North*, Maj. 9,965
* **Morden**, Jessica (*b.* 1968) *Lab., Newport East*, Maj. 8,003
* **Morgan**, Rt. Hon. Nicky (*b.* 1972) *C., Loughborough*, Maj. 4,269
Morgan, Stephen (*b.* 1981) *Lab., Portsmouth South*, Maj. 1,554
* **Morris**, Grahame (*b.* 1961) *Lab., Easington*, Maj. 14,892
* **Morris**, James (*b.* 1967) *C., Halesowen & Rowley Regis*, Maj. 5,253
* **Morris**, David (*b.* 1966) *C., Morecambe & Lunesdale*, Maj. 1,399
*§ **Morris**, Anne Marie (*b.* 1957) *C., Newton Abbot*, Maj. 17,160
* **Morton**, Wendy (*b.* 1967) *C., Aldridge-Brownhills*, Maj. 14,307
* **Mundell**, Rt. Hon. David (*b.* 1962) *C., Dumfriesshire, Clydesdale & Tweeddale*, Maj. 9,441
* **Murray**, Sheryll (*b.* 1956) *C., Cornwall South East*, Maj. 17,443
* **Murray**, Ian (*b.* 1976) *Lab., Edinburgh South*, Maj. 15,514
* **Murrison**, Dr Andrew (*b.* 1961) *C., Wiltshire South West*, Maj. 18,326
* **Nandy**, Lisa (*b.* 1979) *Lab., Wigan*, Maj. 16,027
* **Neill**, Robert (*b.* 1952) *C., Bromley & Chislehurst*, Maj. 9,590
* **Newlands**, Gavin (*b.* 1980) *SNP, Paisley & Renfrewshire North*, Maj. 2,613
* **Newton**, Sarah (*b.* 1962) *C., Truro & Falmouth*, Maj. 3,792
* **Nokes**, Caroline (*b.* 1972) *C., Romsey & Southampton North*, Maj. 18,006
* **Norman**, Jesse (*b.* 1962) *C., Hereford & Herefordshire South*, Maj. 15,013

Norris, Alex *Lab. Co-op, Nottingham North*, Maj. 11,160
O'Brien, Neil *C., Harborough*, Maj. 12,429
* **Offord**, Matthew, PHD (*b.* 1969) *C., Hendon*, Maj. 1,072
* **O'Hara**, Brendan (*b.* 1963) *SNP, Argyll & Bute*, Maj. 1,328
O'Mara, Jared (*b.* 1981) *Lab., Sheffield Hallam*, Maj. 2,125
Onasanya, Fiona *Lab., Peterborough*, Maj. 607
* **Onn**, Melanie (*b.* 1979) *Lab., Great Grimsby*, Maj. 2,565
* **Onwurah**, Chi (*b.* 1965) *Lab., Newcastle upon Tyne Central*, Maj. 14,937
* **Opperman**, Guy (*b.* 1965) *C., Hexham*, Maj. 9,236
* **Osamor**, Kate (*b.* 1968) *Lab. Co-op, Edmonton*, Maj. 21,115
* **Owen**, Albert (*b.* 1959) *Lab., Ynys Mon*, Maj. 5,259
* **Paisley**, Hon. Ian (*b.* 1960) *DUP, Antrim North*, Maj. 20,643
* **Parish**, Neil (*b.* 1956) *C., Tiverton & Honiton*, Maj. 19,801
* **Patel**, Rt. Hon. Priti (*b.* 1972) *C., Witham*, Maj. 18,646
* **Paterson**, Rt. Hon. Owen (*b.* 1956) *C., Shropshire North*, Maj. 16,355
* **Pawsey**, Mark (*b.* 1957) *C., Rugby*, Maj. 8,212
Peacock, Stephanie (*b.* 1986) *Lab., Barnsley East*, Maj. 13,283
* **Pearce**, Teresa (*b.* 1955) *Lab., Erith & Thamesmead*, Maj. 10,014
* **Penning**, Rt. Hon. Mike (*b.* 1957) *C., Hemel Hempstead*, Maj. 9,445
* **Pennycook**, Matthew (*b.* 1982) *Lab., Greenwich & Woolwich*, Maj. 20,714
* **Penrose**, John (*b.* 1964) *C., Weston-Super-Mare*, Maj. 11,544
* **Percy**, Andrew (*b.* 1977) *C., Brigg & Goole*, Maj. 12,363
* **Perkins**, Toby (*b.* 1970) *Lab., Chesterfield*, Maj. 9,605
* **Perry**, Claire (*b.* 1964) *C., Devizes*, Maj. 21,136
* **Phillips**, Jess (*b.* 1981) *Lab., Birmingham Yardley*, Maj. 16,574
* **Phillipson**, Bridget (*b.* 1983) *Lab., Houghton & Sunderland South*, Maj. 12,341
* **Philp**, Chris (*b.* 1976) *C., Croydon South*, Maj. 11,406
Pidcock, Laura (*b.* 1988) *Lab., Durham North West*, Maj. 8,792
* **Pincher**, Christopher (*b.* 1969) *C., Tamworth*, Maj. 12,347
Platt, Jo *Lab. Co-op, Leigh*, Maj. 9,554
Pollard, Luke (*b.* 1980) *Lab. Co-op, Plymouth Sutton & Devonport*, Maj. 6,002
* **Poulter**, Dr Dan (*b.* 1978) *C., Suffolk Central & Ipswich North*, Maj. 17,185
* **Pound**, Stephen (*b.* 1948) *Lab., Ealing North*, Maj. 19,693
* **Pow**, Rebecca (*b.* 1960) *C., Taunton Deane*, Maj. 15,887
* **Powell**, Lucy (*b.* 1974) *Lab. Co-op, Manchester Central*, Maj. 31,445
* **Prentis**, Hon. Victoria (*b.* 1971) *C., Banbury*, Maj. 12,399
* **Prisk**, Mark (*b.* 1962) *C., Hertford & Stortford*, Maj. 19,035
* **Pritchard**, Mark (*b.* 1966) *C., Wrekin, The*, Maj. 9,564
* **Pursglove**, Tom (*b.* 1988) *C., Corby*, Maj. 2,690
* **Quin**, Jeremy (*b.* 1968) *C., Horsham*, Maj. 23,484
* **Quince**, Will (*b.* 1982) *C., Colchester*, Maj. 5,677
* **Qureshi**, Yasmin (*b.* 1963) *Lab., Bolton South East*, Maj. 13,126
* **Raab**, Dominic (*b.* 1974) *C., Esher & Walton*, Maj. 23,298
Rashid, Faisal *Lab., Warrington South*, Maj. 2,549
* **Rayner**, Angela (*b.* 1980) *Lab., Ashton Under Lyne*, Maj. 11,295
* **Redwood**, Rt. Hon. John, DPHIL (*b.* 1951) *C., Wokingham*, Maj. 18,798
* **Reed**, Steve (*b.* 1963) *Lab. Co-op, Croydon North*, Maj. 32,365
* **Rees**, Christina (*b.* 1954) *Lab. Co-op, Neath*, Maj. 12,631
* **Rees-Mogg**, Jacob (*b.* 1969) *C., Somerset North East*, Maj. 10,235
* **Reeves**, Rachel (*b.* 1979) *Lab., Leeds West*, Maj. 15,965
Reeves, Ellie *Lab., Lewisham West & Penge*, Maj. 23,162
* **Reynolds**, Jonathan (*b.* 1980) *Lab. Co-op, Stalybridge & Hyde*, Maj. 8,084
* **Reynolds**, Emma (*b.* 1977) *Lab., Wolverhampton North East*, Maj. 4,587
* **Rimmer**, Marie (*b.* 1947) *Lab., St Helens South & Whiston*, Maj. 24,343
* **Robertson**, Laurence (*b.* 1958) *C., Tewkesbury*, Maj. 22,574
* **Robinson**, Gavin (*b.* 1984) *DUP, Belfast East*, Maj. 8,474
* **Robinson**, Mary (*b.* 1955) *C., Cheadle*, Maj. 4,507

* **Robinson**, Geoffrey (b. 1938) Lab., Coventry North West, Maj. 8,580
Rodda, Matt (b. 1966) Lab., Reading East, Maj. 3,749
* **Rosindell**, Andrew (b. 1966) C., Romford, Maj. 13,778
Ross, Douglas (b. 1983) C., Moray, Maj. 4,159
Rowley, Lee (b. 1980) C., Derbyshire North East, Maj. 2,861
Rowley, Danielle Lab., Midlothian, Maj. 885
† **Ruane**, Chris (b. 1958) Lab., Vale of Clwyd, Maj. 2,379
* **Rudd**, Rt. Hon. Amber (b. 1963) C., Hastings & Rye, Maj. 346
Russell-Moyle, Lloyd (b. 1986) Lab. Co-op, Brighton Kemptown, Maj. 9,868
* **Rutley**, David (b. 1961) C., Macclesfield, Maj. 8,608
* **Ryan**, Rt. Hon. Joan (b. 1955) Lab., Enfield North, Maj. 10,247
* **Sandbach**, Antoinette (b. 1969) C., Eddisbury, Maj. 11,942
* **Saville Roberts**, Liz (b. 1964) PC, Dwyfor Meirionnydd, Maj. 4,850
* **Scully**, Paul (b. 1968) C., Sutton & Cheam, Maj. 12,698
Seely, Bob C., Isle of Wight, Maj. 21,069
* **Selous**, Andrew (b. 1962) C., Bedfordshire South West, Maj. 14,168
* **Shah**, Naz (b. 1973) Lab., Bradford West, Maj. 21,902
* **Shannon**, Jim (b. 1955) DUP, Strangford, Maj. 18,343
* **Shapps**, Rt. Hon. Grant (b. 1968) C., Welwyn Hatfield, Maj. 7,369
* **Sharma**, Virendra (b. 1947) Lab., Ealing Southall, Maj. 22,090
* **Sharma**, Alok (b. 1967) C., Reading West, Maj. 2,876
* **Sheerman**, Barry (b. 1940) Lab. Co-op, Huddersfield, Maj. 12,005
* **Shelbrooke**, Alec (b. 1976) C., Elmet & Rothwell, Maj. 9,805
* **Sheppard**, Tommy (b. 1959) SNP, Edinburgh East, Maj. 3,425
* **Sherriff**, Paula (b. 1975) Lab., Dewsbury, Maj. 3,321
* **Shuker**, Gavin (b. 1981) Lab. Co-op, Luton South, Maj. 13,925
* **Siddiq**, Tulip (b. 1982) Lab., Hampstead & Kilburn, Maj. 15,560
* **Simpson**, Rt. Hon. Keith (b. 1949) C., Broadland, Maj. 15,816
* **Simpson**, David (b. 1959) DUP, Upper Bann, Maj. 7,992
* **Skidmore**, Chris (b. 1981) C., Kingswood, Maj. 7,500
* **Skinner**, Dennis (b. 1932) Lab., Bolsover, Maj. 5,288
* **Slaughter**, Andy (b. 1960) Lab., Hammersmith, Maj. 18,651
* **Smeeth**, Ruth (b. 1979) Lab., Stoke-on-Trent North, Maj. 2,359
* **Smith**, Nick (b. 1960) Lab., Blaenau Gwent, Maj. 11,907
* **Smith**, Henry (b. 1969) C., Crawley, Maj. 2,457
Smith, Laura Lab., Crewe & Nantwich, Maj. 48
* **Smith**, Cat (b. 1985) Lab., Lancaster & Fleetwood, Maj. 6,661
* **Smith**, Jeff (b. 1963) Lab., Manchester Withington, Maj. 29,875
* **Smith**, Chloe (b. 1982) C., Norwich North, Maj. 507
* **Smith**, Angela (b. 1961) Lab., Penistone & Stocksbridge, Maj. 1,322
* **Smith**, Owen (b. 1970) Lab., Pontypridd, Maj. 11,448
* **Smith**, Julian (b. 1971) C., Skipton & Ripon, Maj. 19,985
* **Smith**, Royston (b. 1964) C., Southampton Itchen, Maj. 31
Smith, Eleanor Lab., Wolverhampton South West, Maj. 2,185
* **Smyth**, Karin (b. 1964) Lab., Bristol South, Maj. 15,987
* **Snell**, Gareth (b. 1986) Lab. Co-op, Stoke-on-Trent Central, Maj. 3,897
* **Soames**, Rt. Hon. Sir Nicholas (b. 1948) C., Sussex Mid, Maj. 19,673
Sobel, Alex Lab. Co-op, Leeds North West, Maj. 4,224
* **Soubry**, Rt. Hon. Anna (b. 1956) C., Broxtowe, Maj. 863
* **Spellar**, Rt. Hon. John (b. 1947) Lab., Warley, Maj. 16,483
* **Spelman**, Rt. Hon. Dame Caroline, DBE (b. 1958) C., Meriden, Maj. 19,198
* **Spencer**, Mark (b. 1970) C., Sherwood, Maj. 5,198
* **Starmer**, Rt. Hon. Sir Keir (b. 1962) Lab., Holborn & St Pancras, Maj. 30,509
* **Stephens**, Chris (b. 1973) SNP, Glasgow South West, Maj. 60
* **Stephenson**, Andrew (b. 1981) C., Pendle, Maj. 1,279
* **Stevens**, Jo (b. 1966) Lab., Cardiff Central, Maj. 17,196
* **Stevenson**, John (b. 1963) C., Carlisle, Maj. 2,599
* **Stewart**, Bob (b. 1949) C., Beckenham, Maj. 15,087

* **Stewart**, Iain (b. 1972) C., Milton Keynes South, Maj. 1,725
* **Stewart**, Rory (b. 1973) C., Penrith & The Border, Maj. 15,910
Stone, Jamie (b. 1954) LD, Caithness, Sutherland & Easter Ross, Maj. 2,044
* **Streeter**, Gary (b. 1955) C., Devon South West, Maj. 15,816
* **Streeting**, Wes (b. 1983) Lab., Ilford North, Maj. 9,639
* **Stride**, Rt. Hon. Mel (b. 1961) C., Devon Central, Maj. 15,680
* **Stringer**, Graham (b. 1950) Lab., Blackley & Broughton, Maj. 19,601
* **Stuart**, Graham (b. 1962) C., Beverley & Holderness, Maj. 14,042
* **Sturdy**, Julian (b. 1971) C., York Outer, Maj. 8,289
* **Sunak**, Rishi (b. 1980) C., Richmond (Yorks), Maj. 23,108
* **Swayne**, Rt. Hon. Sir Desmond (b. 1956) C., New Forest West, Maj. 23,431
Sweeney, Paul (b. 1989) Lab. Co-op, Glasgow North East, Maj. 242
† **Swinson**, Jo (b. 1980) LD, Dunbartonshire East, Maj. 5,339
* **Swire**, Rt. Hon. Sir Hugo, KCMG (b. 1959) C., Devon East, Maj. 8,036
* **Syms**, Robert (b. 1956) C., Poole, Maj. 14,209
* **Tami**, Mark (b. 1962) Lab., Alyn & Deeside, Maj. 5,235
* **Thewliss**, Alison (b. 1982) SNP, Glasgow Central, Maj. 2,267
* **Thomas**, Gareth (b. 1967) Lab. Co-op, Harrow West, Maj. 13,314
* **Thomas**, Derek (b. 1972) C., St Ives, Maj. 312
* **Thomas-Symonds**, Nick (b. 1980) Lab., Torfaen, Maj. 10,240
Thomson, Ross (b. 1987) C., Aberdeen South, Maj. 4,752
* **Thornberry**, Rt. Hon. Emily (b. 1960) Lab., Islington South & Finsbury, Maj. 20,263
* **Throup**, Maggie (b. 1957) C., Erewash, Maj. 4,534
* **Timms**, Rt. Hon. Stephen (b. 1955) Lab., East Ham, Maj. 39,883
* **Tolhurst**, Kelly (b. 1978) C., Rochester & Strood, Maj. 9,850
* **Tomlinson**, Michael (b. 1977) C., Dorset Mid & Poole North, Maj. 15,339
* **Tomlinson**, Justin (b. 1976) C., Swindon North, Maj. 8,335
* **Tracey**, Craig (b. 1974) C., Warwickshire North, Maj. 8,510
* **Tredinnick**, David (b. 1950) C., Bosworth, Maj. 18,351
* **Trevelyan**, Anne-Marie (b. 1969) C., Berwick-upon-Tweed, Maj. 11,781
* **Trickett**, Jon (b. 1950) Lab., Hemsworth, Maj. 10,174
* **Truss**, Rt. Hon. Elizabeth (b. 1975) C., Norfolk South West, Maj. 18,312
* **Tugendhat**, Tom (b. 1973) C., Tonbridge & Malling, Maj. 23,508
* **Turley**, Anna (b. 1978) Lab. Co-op, Redcar, Maj. 9,485
* **Turner**, Karl (b. 1971) Lab., Hull East, Maj. 10,396
* **Twigg**, Derek (b. 1959) Lab., Halton, Maj. 25,405
* **Twigg**, Stephen (b. 1966) Lab. Co-op, Liverpool West Derby, Maj. 32,908
Twist, Liz Lab., Blaydon, Maj. 13,477
* **Umunna**, Chuka (b. 1978) Lab., Streatham, Maj. 26,285
* **Vaizey**, Rt. Hon. Edward (b. 1968) C., Wantage, Maj. 17,380
* **Vara**, Shailesh (b. 1960) C., Cambridgeshire North West, Maj. 18,008
* **Vaz**, Rt. Hon. Keith (b. 1956) Lab., Leicester East, Maj. 22,428
* **Vaz**, Valerie (b. 1954) Lab., Walsall South, Maj. 8,892
* **Vickers**, Martin (b. 1950) C., Cleethorpes, Maj. 10,400
* **Villiers**, Rt. Hon. Theresa (b. 1968) C., Chipping Barnet, Maj. 353
* **Walker**, Charles (b. 1967) C., Broxbourne, Maj. 15,792
Walker, Thelma Lab., Colne Valley, Maj. 915
* **Walker**, Robin (b. 1978) C., Worcester, Maj. 2,508
* **Wallace**, Rt. Hon. Ben (b. 1970) C., Wyre & Preston North, Maj. 12,246
* **Warburton**, David (b. 1965) C., Somerton & Frome, Maj. 22,906
* **Warman**, Matt (b. 1981) C., Boston & Skegness, Maj. 16,572
Watling, Giles (b. 1953) C., Clacton, Maj. 15,828
* **Watson**, Tom (b. 1967) Lab., West Bromwich East, Maj. 7,713

* **West**, Catherine (*b.* 1966) *Lab., Hornsey & Wood Green*, Maj. 30,738

Western, Matt *Lab., Warwick & Leamington*, Maj. 1,206

* **Whately**, Helen (*b.* 1976) *C., Faversham & Kent Mid*, Maj. 17,413

* **Wheeler**, Heather (*b.* 1959) *C., Derbyshire South*, Maj. 11,970

* **Whitehead**, Alan, PHD (*b.* 1950) *Lab., Southampton Test*, Maj. 11,503

Whitfield, Martin (*b.* 1965) *Lab., East Lothian*, Maj. 3,083

* **Whitford**, Dr Philippa (*b.* 1958) *SNP, Ayrshire Central*, Maj. 1,267

* **Whittaker**, Craig (*b.* 1962) *C., Calder Valley*, Maj. 609

* **Whittingdale**, Rt. Hon. John (*b.* 1959) *C., Maldon*, Maj. 23,430

* **Wiggin**, Bill (*b.* 1966) *C., Herefordshire North*, Maj. 21,602

* **Williams**, Hywel (*b.* 1953) *PC, Arfon*, Maj. 92

Williams, Paul, PHD (*b.* 1972) *Lab., Stockton South*, Maj. 888

† **Williamson**, Chris (*b.* 1956) *Lab., Derby North*, Maj. 2,015

* **Williamson**, Rt. Hon. Gavin, CBE (*b.* 1976) *C., Staffordshire South*, Maj. 22,733

* **Wilson**, Sammy (*b.* 1953) *DUP, Antrim East*, Maj. 15,923

* **Wilson**, Phil (*b.* 1959) *Lab., Sedgefield*, Maj. 6,059

* **Winterton**, Rt. Hon. Dame Rosie, DBE (*b.* 1958) *Lab., Doncaster Central*, Maj. 10,131

* **Wishart**, Pete (*b.* 1962) *SNP, Perth & Perthshire North*, Maj. 21

* **Wollaston**, Dr Sarah (*b.* 1962) *C., Totnes*, Maj. 13,477

* **Wood**, Mike (*b.* 1976) *C., Dudley South*, Maj. 7,730

* **Woodcock**, John (*b.* 1978) *Lab. Co-op, Barrow & Furness*, Maj. 209

* **Wragg**, William (*b.* 1987) *C., Hazel Grove*, Maj. 5,514

* **Wright**, Rt. Hon. Jeremy (*b.* 1972) *C., Kenilworth & Southam*, Maj. 18,086

Yasin, Mohammad *Lab., Bedford*, Maj. 789

* **Zahawi**, Nadhim (*b.* 1967) *C., Stratford-on-Avon*, Maj. 20,958

* **Zeichner**, Daniel (*b.* 1956) *Lab., Cambridge*, Maj. 12,661

GENERAL ELECTION 2017 RESULTS

UK Turnout

Electorate (E.) 46,843,896 Turnout (T.). 32,181,757 (68.7%)

The results of voting in each of the 650 parliamentary constituencies at the general election on 8 June 2017 are given below.

KEY

* Previously an MP for this seat in the 2015–17 parliament

† Previously an MP for this seat in any parliament prior to the 2015–17 parliament

‡ Previously an MP for a different seat in any previous parliament

§ Currently suspended from the parliamentary Conservative Party

swing N/A indicates a constituency for which the swing data cannot be calculated because one of the top two parties in the 2015 General Election did not field a candidate in the seat in 2017.

ABBREVIATIONS OF POLITICAL PARTIES

Active Dem.	Movement for Active Democracy	Green Soc.	Alliance for Green Socialism	Rebooting	Rebooting Democracy
AD	Apolitical Democrats	Guildford	Guildford Greenbelt Group	Referendum	Scotland's Independence Referendum Party
Alliance	Alliance Party of Northern Ireland	Humanity	Humanity	Respect	The Respect Party
AP	All People's Party	Ind.	Independent	Rochdale	Rochdale First Party
APNI	APNI Party	IPP	Immigrants Political Party	Roman	The Roman Party
AWP	Animal Welfare Party			S. New	Something New
Blue	Blue Revolution	JACP	Justice & Anti- Corruption Party	SCP	Scottish Christian Party
BNP	British National Party			SDLP	Social Democratic and Labour Party
Bournemouth	Bournemouth Independent Alliance	Just	The Just Political Party		
		Lab.	Labour	SF	Sinn Fein
BPE	Bus-Pass Elvis Party	Lab. Alt	Labour Alternative	SNP	Scottish National Party
Bradford	Better for Bradford	Lab. Co-op	Labour and Co- operative	Soc.	Socialist Party
Bristol	Independents for Bristol			Soc. Dem.	Social Democratic Party
C.	Conservative	LD	Liberal Democrat	Soc. Lab.	Socialist Labour Party
Change	Alter Change	Lib.	The Liberal Party	Southampton	Southampton Independents
Ch. P.	The Christian Party	Lib. GB	Liberty Great Britain		
CISTA	Cannabis is Safer than Alcohol	Libertarian	Libertarian Party	Southend	Southend Independent Association
		Lincs Ind.	Lincolnshire Independents	Southport	The Southport Party
Citizens	Citizens Independent Social Thought Alliance			Sovereign	Independent Sovereign Democratic Britain
		Loony	Monster Raving Loony Party		
Comm.	Communist Party of Britain			Space	Space Navies Party
		Love	One Love Party	Speaker	The Speaker
Comm. Lge	Communist League	MC	The Magna Carta Party	SPGB	The Socialist Party of Great Britain
Community	Communities United Party	Money	Money Free Party		
		ND	No description	SSP	Scottish Socialist Party
Compass	Compass Party	NE	The North East Party	Thanet	Party for a United Thanet
Concordia	Concordia	NF	National Front		
CPA	Christian Peoples Alliance	NHAP	National Health Action Party	TUSC	Trade Unionist and Socialist Coalition
Croydon	Putting Croydon First	North	Putting North of England People First	TUV	Traditional Unionist Voice
CSP	Common Sense Party	Northern	Northern Party	UKIP	UK Independence Party
DDI	Demos Direct Initiative	Open	Open Borders Party	UUP	Ulster Unionist Party
Digital	Digital Democracy	Patria	Patria	Wessex Reg.	Wessex Regionalists
DUP	Democratic Unionist Party	PBP	People Before Profit Alliance	Wigan	Wigan Independents
				Women	Women's Equality Party
Eccentric	The Eccentric Party of Great Britain	PC	Plaid Cymru	Worth	The New Society of Worth
		Peace	Peace Party		
Elmo	Give Me Back Elmo	PF	People First	WP	Workers' Party
Elvis	Church of the Militant Elvis	Pilgrim	The Pilgrim Party	WRP	Workers' Revolutionary Party
		Pirate	Pirate Party UK		
Eng. Dem.	English Democrats	Poole	The Party for Poole People Ltd	WVPTFP	War Veteran's Pro- Traditional Family Party
Eng. Ind.	English Independence				
Friends	Friends Party	Populist	Populist Party	Yorks	Yorkshire First
GM Homeless	Greater Manchester Homeless Voice	PUP	Progressive Unionist Party	Yorkshire	The Yorkshire Party
				Young	Young People's Party UK
Good	The Common Good	Radical	The Radical Party		
Green	Green Party	Realist	The Realists' Party		

ENGLAND

ALDERSHOT
E. 76,205   T. 48,955 (64.24%)   C. hold
Leo Docherty, C.   26,955
Gary Puffett, Lab.   15,477
Alan Hilliar, LD   3,637
Roy Swales, UKIP   1,796
Donna Wallace, Green   1,090
C. majority 11,478 (23.45%)
4.41% swing C. to Lab.
(2015: C. majority 14,901 (32.26%))

ALDRIDGE-BROWNHILLS
E. 60,363   T. 40,235 (66.66%)   C. hold
*Wendy Morton, C.   26,317
John Fisher, Lab.   12,010
Ian Garrett, LD   1,343
Mark Beech, Loony   565
C. majority 14,307 (35.56%)
2.94% swing Lab. to C.
(2015: C. majority 11,723 (29.68%))

ALTRINCHAM & SALE WEST
E. 73,220   T. 52,790 (72.10%)   C. hold
*Graham Brady, C.   26,933
Andrew Western, Lab.   20,507
Jane Brophy, LD   4,051
Geraldine Coggins, Green   1,000
Neil Taylor, Lib.   299
C. majority 6,426 (12.17%)
7.07% swing C. to Lab.
(2015: C. majority 13,290 (26.31%))

AMBER VALLEY
E. 68,065   T. 45,811 (67.30%)   C. hold
*Nigel Mills, C.   25,905
James Dawson, Lab.   17,605
Kate Smith, LD   1,100
Matt McGuinness, Green   650
Daniel Bamford, Ind.   551
C. majority 8,300 (18.12%)
4.46% swing Lab. to C.
(2015: C. majority 4,205 (9.20%))

ARUNDEL & SOUTH DOWNS
E. 80,766   T. 60,256 (74.61%)   C. hold
*Nick Herbert, C.   37,573
Caroline Fife, Lab.   13,690
Shweta Kapadia, LD   4,783
Jo Prior, Green   2,542
John Wallace, UKIP   1,668
C. majority 23,883 (39.64%)
4.98% swing C. to Lab.
(2015: C. majority 26,177 (46.35%))

ASHFIELD
E. 78,099   T. 49,993 (64.01%)   Lab. hold
*Gloria De Piero, Lab.   21,285
Tony Harper, C.   20,844
Gail Turner, Ind.   4,612
Ray Young, UKIP   1,885
Bob Charlesworth, LD   969
Arran Rangi, Green   398
Lab. majority 441 (0.88%)
8.86% swing Lab. to C.
(2015: Lab. majority 8,820 (18.60%))

ASHFORD
E. 87,396   T. 59,879 (68.51%)   C. hold
*Damian Green, C.   35,318
Sally Gathern, Lab.   17,840
Adrian Gee-Turner, LD   3,101
Gerald O'Brien, UKIP   2,218
Mandy Rossi, Green   1,402
C. majority 17,478 (29.19%)
2.41% swing C. to Lab.
(2015: C. majority 19,296 (33.63%))

ASHTON-UNDER-LYNE
E. 67,674   T. 39,773 (58.77%)   Lab. hold
*Angela Rayner, Lab.   24,005
Jack Rankin, C.   12,710
Maurice Jackson, UKIP   1,878
Carly Hicks, LD   646
Andy Hunter-Rossall, Green   534
Lab. majority 11,295 (28.40%)
0.38% swing C. to Lab.
(2015: Lab. majority 10,756 (27.64%))

AYLESBURY
E. 82,546   T. 58,743 (71.16%)   C. hold
*David Lidington, C.   32,313
Mark Bateman, Lab.   17,617
Steven Lambert, LD   5,660
Vijay Srao, UKIP   1,296
Coral Simpson, Green   1,237
Kyle Michael, Ind.   620
C. majority 14,696 (25.02%)
5.26% swing C. to Lab.
(2015: C. majority 17,158 (30.96%))

BANBURY
E. 83,818   T. 61,562 (73.45%)   C. hold
*Victoria Prentis, C.   33,388
Sean Woodcock, Lab.   20,989
John Howson, LD   3,452
Dickie Bird, UKIP   1,581
Ian Middleton, Green   1,225
Roseanne Edwards, Ind.   927
C. majority 12,399 (20.14%)
5.79% swing C. to Lab.
(2015: C. majority 18,395 (31.71%))

BARKING
E. 77,020   T. 47,679 (61.90%)   Lab. hold
*Margaret Hodge, Lab.   32,319
Minesh Talati, C.   10,711
Roger Gravett, UKIP   3,031
Shannon Butterfield, Green   724
Pauline Pearce, LD   599
Noel Falvey, Ind.   295
Lab. majority 21,608 (45.32%)
1.97% swing C. to Lab.
(2015: Lab. majority 15,272 (35.50%))

BARNSLEY CENTRAL
E. 64,204   T. 39,089 (60.88%)   Lab. hold
*Dan Jarvis, Lab.   24,982
Amanda Ford, C.   9,436
Gavin Felton, UKIP   3,339
Richard Trotman, Green   572
David Ridgway, LD   549
Stephen Morris, Eng. Dem.   211
Lab. majority 15,546 (39.77%)
0.48% swing Lab. to C.
(2015: Lab. majority 12,435 (34.01%))

BARNSLEY EAST
E. 69,204   T. 40,776 (58.92%)   Lab. hold
Stephanie Peacock, Lab.   24,280
Andrew Lloyd, C.   10,997
James Dalton, UKIP   3,247
Tony Devoy, Yorkshire   1,215
Nicola Turner, LD   750
Kevin Riddiough, Eng. Dem.   287
Lab. majority 13,283 (32.58%)
3.78% swing Lab. to C.
(2015: Lab. majority 12,034 (31.24%))

BARROW & FURNESS
E. 69,474   T. 47,590 (68.50%)
                            Lab. Co-op hold
*John Woodcock, Lab.   22,592
Co-op
Simon Fell, C.   22,383
Loraine Birchall, LD   1,278
Alan Piper, UKIP   962
Rob O'Hara, Green   375
Lab. Co-op majority 209 (0.44%)
0.70% swing Lab. to C.
(2015: Lab. Co-op majority 795
(1.84%))

BASILDON & BILLERICAY
E. 69,149   T. 44,918 (64.96%)   C. hold
*John Baron, C.   27,381
Kayte Block, Lab.   13,981
Tina Hughes, UKIP   2,008
Antonia Harrison, LD   1,548
C. majority 13,400 (29.83%)
0.41% swing Lab. to C.
(2015: C. majority 12,482 (29.01%))

BASILDON SOUTH &
THURROCK EAST
E. 73,541   T. 47,120 (64.07%)   C. hold
*Stephen Metcalfe, C.   26,811
Byron Taylor, Lab.   15,321
Peter Whittle, UKIP   3,193
Reetendra Banerji, LD   732
Sim Harman, Green   680
Paul Borg, BNP   383
C. majority 11,490 (24.38%)
3.10% swing Lab. to C.
(2015: C. majority 7,691 (16.87%))

BASINGSTOKE
E. 81,873   T. 55,960 (68.35%)   C. hold
*Maria Miller, C.   29,510
Terry Bridgeman, Lab.   20,044
John Shaw, LD   3,406
Alan Stone, UKIP   1,681
Richard Winter, Green   1,106
Scott Neville, Libertarian   213
C. majority 9,466 (16.92%)
1.96% swing C. to Lab.
(2015: C. majority 11,063 (20.84%))

BASSETLAW
E. 78,535   T. 52,250 (66.53%)   Lab. hold
*John Mann, Lab.   27,467
Annette Simpson, C.   22,615
Leon Duveen, LD   1,154
Nigel Turner, Ind.   1,014
Lab. majority 4,852 (9.29%)
4.33% swing Lab. to C.
(2015: Lab. majority 8,843 (17.94%))

BATH
E. 66,769   T. 49,582 (74.26%)   LD gain
Wera Hobhouse, LD   23,436
*Ben Howlett, C.   17,742
Joe Rayment, Lab.   7,279
Eleanor Field, Green   1,125
LD majority 5,694 (11.48%)
9.81% swing C. to LD
(2015: C. majority 3,833 (8.13%))

BATLEY & SPEN
E. 80,153   T. 53,780 (67.10%)
                        Lab. Co-op hold
*Tracy Brabin, Lab. Co-op   29,844
Ann Myatt, C.   20,883
John Lawson, LD   1,224
Aleks Lukic, Ind.   1,076
Alan Freeman, Green   695
Mohammed Hanif, Ind.   58
Lab. Co-op majority 8,961 (16.66%)
2.33% swing C. to Lab.
(2015: Lab. majority 6,057 (12.00%))
(2016: Lab. majority 16,537 (81.09%))

BATTERSEA
E. 77,572   T. 55,058 (70.98%)   Lab. gain
Marsha De Cordova, Lab.   25,292
*Jane Ellison, C.   22,876
Richard Davis, LD   4,401
Chris Coghlan, Ind.   1,234
Lois Davis, Green   866
Eugene Power, UKIP   357
Daniel Lambert, SPGB   32
Lab. majority 2,416 (4.39%)
9.97% swing C. to Lab.
(2015: C. majority 7,938 (15.56%))

BEACONSFIELD
E. 77,534   T. 56,028 (72.26%)   C. hold
*Dominic Grieve, C.   36,559
James English, Lab.   12,016
Peter Chapman, LD   4,448
Jon Conway, UKIP   1,609
Russell Secker, Green   1,396
C. majority 24,543 (43.80%)
4.01% swing C. to Lab.
(2015: C. majority 26,311 (49.49%))

BECKENHAM
E. 67,928   T. 51,630 (76.01%)   C. hold
*Bob Stewart, C.   30,632
Marina Ahmad, Lab.   15,545
Julie Ireland, LD   4,073
Ruth Fabricant, Green   1,380
C. majority 15,087 (29.22%)
4.31% swing C. to Lab.
(2015: C. majority 18,471 (37.85%))

BEDFORD
E. 71,829   T. 48,480 (67.49%)   Lab. gain
Mohammad Yasin, Lab.   22,712
*Richard Fuller, C.   21,923
Henry Vann, LD   2,837
Lucy Bywater, Green   1,008
Lab. majority 789 (1.63%)
2.00% swing C. to Lab.
(2015: C. majority 1,097 (2.38%))

BEDFORDSHIRE MID
E. 83,800   T. 63,148 (75.36%)   C. hold
*Nadine Dorries, C.   38,936
Rhiannon Meades, Lab.   17,953
Lisa French, LD   3,798
Gareth Ellis, Green   1,794
Ann Kelly, Loony   667
C. majority 20,983 (33.23%)
3.47% swing C. to Lab.
(2015: C. majority 23,327 (40.18%))

BEDFORDSHIRE NORTH EAST
E. 86,988   T. 64,220 (73.83%)   C. hold
*Alistair Burt, C.   39,139
Julian Vaughan, Lab.   18,277
Stephen Rutherford, LD   3,693
Duncan Strachan, UKIP   1,896
Philippa Fleming, Green   1,215
C. majority 20,862 (32.49%)
5.61% swing C. to Lab.
(2015: C. majority 25,644 (43.71%))

BEDFORDSHIRE SOUTH WEST
E. 79,670   T. 55,635 (69.83%)   C. hold
*Andrew Selous, C.   32,961
Daniel Scott, Lab.   18,793
Daniel Norton, LD   2,630
Morvern Rennie, Green   950
Morenike Mafoh, CPA   301
C. majority 14,168 (25.47%)
4.63% swing C. to Lab.
(2015: C. majority 17,813 (34.72%))

BERMONDSEY & OLD SOUTHWARK
E. 87,227   T. 58,521 (67.09%)   Lab. hold
*Neil Coyle, Lab.   31,161
Simon Hughes, LD   18,189
Siobhan Baillie, C.   7,581
Elizabeth Jones, UKIP   838
John Tyson, Green   639
James Clarke, Ind.   113
Lab. majority 12,972 (22.17%)
6.72% swing LD to Lab.
(2015: Lab. majority 4,489 (8.73%))

BERWICK-UPON-TWEED
E. 58,774   T. 42,212 (71.82%)   C. hold
*Anne-Marie Trevelyan, C.   22,145
Scott Dickinson, Lab.   10,364
Julie Porksen, LD   8,916
Thomas Stewart, Green   787
C. majority 11,781 (27.91%)
0.89% swing Lab. to C.
(2015: C. majority 4,914 (12.16%))

BETHNAL GREEN & BOW
E. 86,071   T. 59,825 (69.51%)   Lab. hold
*Rushanara Ali, Lab.   42,969
Charlie Chirico, C.   7,576
Ajmal Masroor, Ind.   3,888
William Dyer, LD   2,982
Alistair Polson, Green   1,516
Ian de Wulverton, UKIP   894
Lab. majority 35,393 (59.16%)
6.61% swing C. to Lab.
(2015: Lab. majority 24,317 (45.95%))

BEVERLEY & HOLDERNESS
E. 80,657   T. 55,678 (69.03%)   C. hold
*Graham Stuart, C.   32,499
Johanna Boal, Lab.   18,457
Denis Healy, LD   2,808
Lee Walton, Yorkshire   1,158
Richard Howarth, Green   756
C. majority 14,042 (25.22%)
1.03% swing Lab. to C.
(2015: C. majority 12,203 (23.17%))

BEXHILL & BATTLE
E. 78,512   T. 59,472 (75.75%)   C. hold
*Huw Merriman, C.   36,854
Christine Bayliss, Lab.   14,689
Joel Kemp, LD   4,485
Geoffrey Bastin, UKIP   2,006
Jonathan Kent, Green   1,438
C. majority 22,165 (37.27%)
1.69% swing C. to Lab.
(2015: C. majority 20,075 (36.36%))

BEXLEYHEATH & CRAYFORD
E. 65,315   T. 45,189 (69.19%)   C. hold
*David Evennett, C.   25,113
Stef Borella, Lab.   16,040
Mike Ferro, UKIP   1,944
Simone Reynolds, LD   1,201
Ivor Lobo, Green   601
Peter Finch, BNP   290
C. majority 9,073 (20.08%)
0.48% swing C. to Lab.
(2015: C. majority 9,192 (21.04%))

BIRKENHEAD
E. 64,484   T. 43,663 (67.71%)   Lab. hold
*Frank Field, Lab.   33,558
Stewart Gardiner, C.   8,044
Allan Brame, LD   1,118
Jayne Clough, Green   943
Lab. majority 25,514 (58.43%)
1.81% swing C. to Lab.
(2015: Lab. majority 20,652 (54.81%))

BIRMINGHAM EDGBASTON
E. 68,091   T. 43,612 (64.05%)
                        Lab. Co-op hold
Preet Gill, Lab. Co-op   24,124
Caroline Squire, C.   17,207
Colin Green, LD   1,564
Alice Kiff, Green   562
Dick Rodgers, Good   155
Lab. Co-op majority 6,917 (15.86%)
4.65% swing C. to Lab.
(2015: Lab. majority 2,706 (6.55%))

BIRMINGHAM ERDINGTON
E. 65,067   T. 37,217 (57.20%)   Lab. hold
*Jack Dromey, Lab.   21,571
Robert Alden, C.   14,286
Ann Holtom, LD   750
James Lovatt, Green   610
Lab. majority 7,285 (19.57%)
2.39% swing C. to Lab.
(2015: Lab. majority 5,129 (14.79%))

BIRMINGHAM HALL GREEN
E. 78,271   T. 54,310 (69.39%)   Lab. hold
*Roger Godsiff, Lab.   42,143
Reena Ranger, C.   8,199
Jerry Evans, LD   3,137
Patrick Cox, Green   831
Lab. majority 33,944 (62.50%)
10.19% swing C. to Lab.
(2015: Lab. majority 19,818 (42.12%))

BIRMINGHAM HODGE HILL
E. 75,698   T. 46,394 (61.29%)   Lab. hold
*Liam Byrne, Lab.   37,606
Ahmereen Reza, C.   6,580
Mohammed Khan, UKIP   1,016
Phil Bennion, LD   805
Clare Thomas, Green   387
Lab. majority 31,026 (66.88%)
4.97% swing C. to Lab.
(2015: Lab. majority 23,362 (56.93%))

BIRMINGHAM LADYWOOD
E. 70,023   T. 41,307 (58.99%)   Lab. hold
*Shabana Mahmood, Lab.   34,166
Andrew Browning, C.   5,452
Lee Dargue, LD   1,156
Kefentse Dennis, Green   533
Lab. majority 28,714 (69.51%)
4.31% swing C. to Lab.
(2015: Lab. majority 21,868 (60.89%))

BIRMINGHAM NORTHFIELD
E. 72,322   T. 44,348 (61.32%)   Lab. hold
*Richard Burden, Lab.   23,596
Meg Powell-Chandler, C.   18,929
Roger Harmer, LD   959
Eleanor Masters, Green   864
Lab. majority 4,667 (10.52%)
2.31% swing C. to Lab.
(2015: Lab. majority 2,509 (5.91%))

BIRMINGHAM PERRY BARR
E. 70,106   T. 44,197 (63.04%)   Lab. hold
*Khalid Mahmood, Lab.   30,109
Charlotte Hodivala, C.   11,726
Harjun Singh, LD   1,080
Shangara Bhatoe, Soc. Lab.   592
Vijay Rana, Green   591
Harjinder Singh, Open   99
Lab. majority 18,383 (41.59%)
2.83% swing C. to Lab.
(2015: Lab. majority 14,828 (35.94%))

BIRMINGHAM SELLY OAK
E. 74,370   T. 48,985 (65.87%)   Lab. hold
*Steve McCabe, Lab.   30,836
Sophie Shrubsole, C.   15,629
David Radcliffe, LD   1,644
Julien Pritchard, Green   876
Lab. majority 15,207 (31.04%)
6.20% swing C. to Lab.
(2015: Lab. majority 8,447 (18.65%))

BIRMINGHAM YARDLEY
E. 72,581   T. 44,502 (61.31%)   Lab. hold
*Jess Phillips, Lab.   25,398
Mohammed Afzal, C.   8,824
John Hemming, LD   7,984
Paul Clayton, UKIP   1,916
Christopher Garghan, Green   280
Abu Nowshed, Ind.   100
Lab. majority 16,574 (37.24%)
4.81% swing C. to Lab.
(2015: Lab. majority 6,595 (16.03%))

BISHOP AUCKLAND
E. 67,661   T. 43,281 (63.97%)   Lab. hold
*Helen Goodman, Lab.   20,808
Christopher Adams, C.   20,306
Ciaran Morrissey, LD   1,176
Adam Walker, BNP   991
Lab. majority 502 (1.16%)
3.87% swing Lab. to C.
(2015: Lab. majority 3,508 (8.91%))

BLACKBURN
E. 70,657   T. 47,512 (67.24%)   Lab. hold
*Kate Hollern, Lab.   33,148
Bob Eastwood, C.   12,780
Duncan Miller, Ind.   875
Irfan Ahmed, LD   709
Lab. majority 20,368 (42.87%)
6.93% swing C. to Lab.
(2015: Lab. majority 12,760 (29.00%))

BLACKLEY & BROUGHTON
E. 71,648   T. 40,113 (55.99%)   Lab. hold
*Graham Stringer, Lab.   28,258
David Goss, C.   8,657
Martin Power, UKIP   1,825
Charles Gadsden, LD   737
David Jones, Green   462
Abi Ajoku, CPA   174
Lab. majority 19,601 (48.86%)
0.99% swing C. to Lab.
(2015: Lab. majority 16,874 (45.47%))

BLACKPOOL NORTH & CLEVELEYS
E. 63,967   T. 41,007 (64.11%)   C. hold
*Paul Maynard, C.   20,255
Chris Webb, Lab.   18,232
Paul White, UKIP   1,392
Sue Close, LD   747
Duncan Royle, Green   381
C. majority 2,023 (4.93%)
1.77% swing C. to Lab.
(2015: C. majority 3,340 (8.48%))

BLACKPOOL SOUTH
E. 58,450   T. 34,953 (59.80%)   Lab. hold
*Gordon Marsden, Lab.   17,581
Peter Anthony, C.   15,058
Noel Matthews, UKIP   1,339
Bill Greene, LD   634
John Peter Warnock, Green   341
Lab. majority 2,523 (7.22%)
0.38% swing Lab. to C.
(2015: Lab. majority 2,585 (7.97%))

BLAYDON
E. 68,459   T. 48,084 (70.24%)   Lab. hold
Liz Twist, Lab.   26,979
Thomas Smith, C.   13,502
Jonathan Wallace, LD   4,366
Ray Tolley, UKIP   2,459
Paul McNally, Green   583
Michael
Marchetti, Libertarian   114
Lisabela Marschild, Space   81
Lab. majority 13,477 (28.03%)
1.84% swing Lab. to C.
(2015: Lab. majority 14,227 (31.66%))

BLYTH VALLEY
E. 63,371   T. 42,490 (67.05%)   Lab. hold
*Ronnie Campbell, Lab.   23,770
Ian Levy, C.   15,855
Jeff Reid, LD   1,947
Dawn Furness, Green   918
Lab. majority 7,915 (18.63%)
2.99% swing Lab. to C.
(2015: Lab. majority 9,229 (24.00%))

BOGNOR REGIS & LITTLEHAMPTON
E. 75,827   T. 51,352 (67.72%)   C. hold
*Nick Gibb, C.   30,276
Alan Butcher, Lab.   12,782
Francis Oppler, LD   3,352
Paul Sanderson, Ind.   2,088
Patrick Lowe, UKIP   1,861
Andrew Bishop, Green   993
C. majority 17,494 (34.07%)
1.73% swing C. to Lab.
(2015: C. majority 13,944 (29.60%))

BOLSOVER
E. 73,429   T. 46,519 (63.35%)   Lab. hold
*Dennis Skinner, Lab.   24,153
Helen Harrison, C.   18,865
Philip Rose, UKIP   2,129
Ross Shipman, LD   1,372
Lab. majority 5,288 (11.37%)
7.70% swing Lab. to C.
(2015: Lab. majority 11,778 (26.77%))

BOLTON NORTH EAST
E. 67,233   T. 45,183 (67.20%)   Lab. hold
*David Crausby, Lab.   22,870
James Daly, C.   19,073
Harry Lamb, UKIP   1,567
Warren Fox, LD   1,316
Liz Spencer, Green   357
Lab. majority 3,797 (8.40%)
0.87% swing Lab. to C.
(2015: Lab. majority 4,377 (10.14%))

BOLTON SOUTH EAST
E. 68,886   T. 42,323 (61.44%)   Lab. hold
*Yasmin Qureshi, Lab.   25,676
Sarah Pochin, C.   12,550
Jeff Armstrong, UKIP   2,779
Frank Harasiwka, LD   781
Alan Johnson, Green   537
Lab. majority 13,126 (31.01%)
0.45% swing C. to Lab.
(2015: Lab. majority 10,928 (26.82%))

BOLTON WEST
E. 72,797   T. 51,054 (70.13%)   C. hold
*Chris Green, C.   24,459
Julie Hilling, Lab.   23,523
Martin Tighe, UKIP   1,587
Rebecca Forrest, LD   1,485
C. majority 936 (1.83%)
0.09% swing Lab. to C.
(2015: C. majority 801 (1.65%))

BOOTLE

E. 72,872   T. 50,288 (69.01%)   Lab. hold

*Peter Dowd, Lab.	42,259
Charles Fifield, C.	6,059
David Newman, LD	837
Alison Gibbon, Green	709
Kim Bryan, Soc. Lab.	424

Lab. majority 36,200 (71.99%)
2.79% swing C. to Lab.
(2015: Lab. majority 28,704 (63.57%))

BOSTON & SKEGNESS

E. 68,391   T. 42,879 (62.70%)   C. hold

*Matt Warman, C.	27,271
Paul Kenny, Lab.	10,699
Paul Nuttall, UKIP	3,308
Philip Smith, LD	771
Victoria Percival, Green	547
Mike Gilbert, Blue	283

C. majority 16,572 (38.65%)
5.67% swing Lab. to C.
(2015: C. majority 4,336 (10.00%))

BOSWORTH

E. 80,633   T. 56,168 (69.66%)   C. hold

*David Tredinnick, C.	31,864
Chris Kealey, Lab.	13,513
Michael Mullaney, LD	9,744
Mick Gregg, Green	1,047

C. majority 18,351 (32.67%)
3.66% swing Lab. to C.
(2015: C. majority 10,988 (20.51%))

BOURNEMOUTH EAST

E. 74,591   T. 48,618 (65.18%)   C. hold

*Tobias Ellwood, C.	25,221
Mel Semple, Lab.	17,284
Jon Nicholas, LD	3,168
David Hughes, UKIP	1,405
Alasdair Keddie, Green	1,236
Kieron Wilson, Ind.	304

C. majority 7,937 (16.33%)
8.14% swing C. to Lab.
(2015: C. majority 14,612 (32.60%))

BOURNEMOUTH WEST

E. 73,195   T. 44,507 (60.81%)   C. hold

*Conor Burns, C.	23,812
David Stokes, Lab.	16,101
Phil Dunn, LD	2,929
Simon Bull, Green	1,247
Jason Halsey, Pirate	418

C. majority 7,711 (17.33%)
6.62% swing C. to Lab.
(2015: C. majority 12,410 (29.71%))

BRACKNELL

E. 79,199   T. 55,892 (70.57%)   C. hold

*Phillip Lee, C.	32,882
Paul Bidwell, Lab.	16,866
Patrick Smith, LD	4,186
Len Amos, UKIP	1,521
Olivio Barreto, Ind.	437

C. majority 16,016 (28.66%)
5.12% swing C. to Lab.
(2015: C. majority 20,650 (38.90%))

BRADFORD EAST

E. 70,389   T. 45,622 (64.81%)   Lab. hold

*Imran Hussain, Lab.	29,831
Mark Trafford, C.	9,291
David Ward, Ind.	3,576
Jonathan Barras, UKIP	1,372
Mark Jewell, LD	843
Paul Parkins, Bradford	420
Andy Stanford, Green	289

Lab. majority 20,540 (45.02%)
4.84% swing C. to Lab.
(2015: Lab. majority 7,084 (17.11%))

BRADFORD SOUTH

E. 67,752   T. 41,049 (60.59%)   Lab. hold

*Judith Cummins, Lab.	22,364
Tanya Graham, C.	15,664
Stephen Place, UKIP	1,758
Stuart Thomas, LD	516
Therese Hirst, Eng. Dem.	377
Darren Parkinson, Green	370

Lab. majority 6,700 (16.32%)
0.42% swing Lab. to C.
(2015: Lab. majority 6,450 (17.15%))

BRADFORD WEST

E. 67,568   T. 45,528 (67.38%)   Lab. hold

*Naz Shah, Lab.	29,444
George Grant, C.	7,542
Salma Yaqoob, ND	6,345
Derrick Hodgson, UKIP	885
Alun Griffiths, LD	712
Celia Hickson, Green	481
Hussain Khadim, ND	65
Muhammad Hijazi, Ind.	54

Lab. majority 21,902 (48.11%)
swing N/A
(2015: Lab. majority 11,420 (28.34%))

BRAINTREE

E. 75,316   T. 52,326 (69.48%)   C. hold

*James Cleverly, C.	32,873
Malcolm Fincken, Lab.	14,451
Peter Turner, LD	2,251
Richard Bingley, UKIP	1,835
Thomas Pashby, Green	916

C. majority 18,422 (35.21%)
0.07% swing C. to Lab.
(2015: C. majority 17,610 (35.02%))

BRENT CENTRAL

E. 80,845   T. 52,296 (64.69%)   Lab. hold

*Dawn Butler, Lab.	38,208
Rahoul Bhansali, C.	10,211
Anton Georgiou, LD	2,519
Shaka Lish, Green	802
Janice North, UKIP	556

Lab. majority 27,997 (53.54%)
5.88% swing C. to Lab.
(2015: Lab. majority 19,649 (41.78%))

BRENT NORTH

E. 82,556   T. 56,444 (68.37%)   Lab. hold

*Barry Gardiner, Lab.	35,496
Ameet Jogia, C.	18,435
Paul Lorber, LD	1,614
Michaela Lichten, Green	660
Elcena Jeffers, Ind.	239

Lab. majority 17,061 (30.23%)
4.74% swing C. to Lab.
(2015: Lab. majority 10,834 (20.74%))

BRENTFORD & ISLEWORTH

E. 85,151   T. 61,629 (72.38%)   Lab. hold

*Ruth Cadbury, Lab.	35,364
Mary Macleod, C.	23,182
Joe Bourke, LD	3,083

Lab. majority 12,182 (19.77%)
9.48% swing C. to Lab.
(2015: Lab. majority 465 (0.81%))

BRENTWOOD & ONGAR

E. 74,911   T. 52,910 (70.63%)   C. hold

Alex Burghart, C.	34,811
Gareth Barrett, Lab.	10,809
Karen Chilvers, LD	4,426
Michael McGough, UKIP	1,845
Paul Jeater, Green	915
Louca Kousoulou, Ind.	104

C. majority 24,002 (45.36%)
0.48% swing C. to Lab.
(2015: C. majority 21,810 (42.03%))

BRIDGWATER & SOMERSET WEST

E. 89,294   T. 58,267 (65.25%)   C. hold

*Ian Liddell-Grainger, C.	32,111
Wes Hinckes, Lab.	16,663
Marcus Kravis, LD	6,332
Simon Smedley, UKIP	2,102
Kay Powell, Green	1,059

C. majority 15,448 (26.51%)
0.91% swing C. to Lab.
(2015: C. majority 14,583 (26.78%))

BRIGG & GOOLE

E. 66,069   T. 45,057 (68.20%)   C. hold

*Andrew Percy, C.	27,219
Terence Smith, Lab.	14,856
David Jeffreys, UKIP	1,596
Jerry Lonsdale, LD	836
Isabel Pires, Green	550

C. majority 12,363 (27.44%)
0.81% swing Lab. to C.
(2015: C. majority 11,176 (25.83%))

BRIGHTON KEMPTOWN

E. 67,893   T. 49,207 (72.48%)

Lab. Co-op gain

Lloyd Russell-Moyle, Lab. Co-op	28,703
*Simon Kirby, C.	18,835
Emily Tester, LD	1,457
Doktor Haze, ND	212

Lab. Co-op majority 9,868 (20.05%)
10.79% swing C. to Lab.
(2015: C. majority 690 (1.52%))

BRIGHTON PAVILION

E. 75,486   T. 57,677 (76.41%)

Green hold

*Caroline Lucas, Green	30,139
Solomon Curtis, Lab.	15,450
Emma Warman, C.	11,082
Ian Buchanan, UKIP	630
Nick Yeomans, Ind.	376

Green majority 14,689 (25.47%)
5.45% swing Lab. to Green
(2015: Green majority 7,967 (14.57%))

BRISTOL EAST
E. 72,414 T. 50,799 (70.15%) Lab. hold
*Kerry McCarthy, Lab.   30,847
Theo Clarke, C.   17,453
Chris Lucas, LD   1,389
Lorraine Francis, Green   1,110
Lab. majority 13,394 (26.37%)
8.88% swing C. to Lab.
(2015: Lab. majority 3,980 (8.61%))

BRISTOL NORTH WEST
E. 75,431 T. 54,096 (71.72%) Lab. gain
Darren Jones, Lab.   27,400
*Charlotte Leslie, C.   22,639
Celia Downie, LD   2,814
Sharmila Bousa, Green   1,243
Lab. majority 4,761 (8.80%)
9.17% swing C. to Lab.
(2015: C. majority 4,944 (9.54%))

BRISTOL SOUTH
E. 83,009 T. 54,382 (65.51%) Lab. hold
Karin Smyth, Lab.   32,666
Mark Weston, C.   16,679
Benjamin Nutland, LD   1,821
Ian Kealey, UKIP   1,672
Tony Dyer, Green   1,428
John Langley, Ind.   116
Lab. majority 15,987 (29.40%)
7.69% swing C. to Lab.
(2015: Lab. majority 7,128 (14.02%))

BRISTOL WEST
E. 92,986 T. 71,608 (77.01%) Lab. hold
*Thangam Debbonaire, Lab.   47,213
Annabel Tall, C.   9,877
Molly Scott Cato, Green   9,216
Stephen Williams, LD   5,201
Jodian Rodgers, Money   101
Lab. majority 37,336 (52.14%)
15.83% swing C. to Lab.
(2015: Lab. majority 5,673 (8.83%))

BROADLAND
E. 77,334 T. 55,971 (72.38%) C. hold
*Keith Simpson, C.   32,406
Iain Simpson, Lab.   16,590
Steve Riley, LD   4,449
David Moreland, UKIP   1,594
Andrew Boswell, Green   932
C. majority 15,816 (28.26%)
1.73% swing C. to Lab.
(2015: C. majority 16,838 (31.72%))

BROMLEY & CHISLEHURST
E. 65,113 T. 46,662 (71.66%) C. hold
*Robert Neill, C.   25,175
Sara Hyde, Lab.   15,585
Sam Webber, LD   3,369
Emmett Jenner, UKIP   1,383
Roisin Robertson, Green   1,150
C. majority 9,590 (20.55%)
5.11% swing C. to Lab.
(2015: C. majority 13,564 (30.78%))

BROMSGROVE
E. 73,571 T. 54,040 (73.45%) C. hold
*Sajid Javid, C.   33,493
Michael Thompson, Lab.   16,920
Neil Lewis, LD   2,488
Spoz Esposito, Green   1,139
C. majority 16,573 (30.67%)
0.48% swing C. to Lab.
(2015: C. majority 16,529 (31.64%))

BROXBOURNE
E. 73,502 T. 47,485 (64.60%) C. hold
*Charles Walker, C.   29,515
Selina Norgrove, Lab.   13,723
Tony Faulkner, UKIP   1,918
Andy Graham, LD   1,481
Tabitha Evans, Green   848
C. majority 15,792 (33.26%)
2.20% swing C. to Lab.
(2015: C. majority 16,723 (36.34%))

BROXTOWE
E. 74,017 T. 55,508 (74.99%) C. hold
*Anna Soubry, C.   25,983
Greg Marshall, Lab.   25,120
Tim Hallam, LD   2,247
Fran Loi, UKIP   1,477
Pat Morton, Green   681
C. majority 863 (1.55%)
3.23% swing C. to Lab.
(2015: C. majority 4,287 (8.02%))

BUCKINGHAM
E. 79,616 T. 52,679 (66.17%)
                                Speaker hold
*John Bercow, Speaker   34,299
Michael Sheppard, Green   8,574
Scott Raven, Ind.   5,638
Brian Mapletoft, UKIP   4,168
Speaker majority 25,725 (48.83%)
0.93% swing C. to Green
(2015: Speaker majority 22,942
(42.73%))

BURNLEY
E. 64,714 T. 40,290 (62.26%) Lab. hold
*Julie Cooper, Lab.   18,832
Paul White, C.   12,479
Gordon Birtwistle, LD   6,046
Tom Commis, UKIP   2,472
Laura Fisk, Green   461
Lab. majority 6,353 (15.77%)
4.16% swing Lab. to C.
(2015: Lab. majority 3,244 (8.16%))

BURTON
E. 73,954 T. 49,911 (67.49%) C. hold
*Andrew Griffiths, C.   28,936
John McKiernan, Lab.   18,889
Dominic Hardwick, LD   1,262
Simon Hales, Green   824
C. majority 10,047 (20.13%)
1.34% swing C. to Lab.
(2015: C. majority 11,252 (22.81%))

BURY NORTH
E. 67,587 T. 47,903 (70.88%) Lab. gain
James Frith, Lab.   25,683
*David Nuttall, C.   21,308
Richard Baum, LD   912
Lab. majority 4,375 (9.13%)
4.98% swing C. to Lab.
(2015: C. majority 378 (0.84%))

BURY ST EDMUNDS
E. 87,758 T. 62,160 (70.83%) C. hold
*Jo Churchill, C.   36,794
Bill Edwards, Lab.   18,353
Helen Korfanty, LD   3,565
Helen Geake, Green   2,596
Liam Byrne, Ind.   852
C. majority 18,441 (29.67%)
3.11% swing C. to Lab.
(2015: C. majority 21,301 (35.90%))

BURY SOUTH
E. 73,723 T. 50,990 (69.16%) Lab. hold
*Ivan Lewis, Lab.   27,165
Robert Largan, C.   21,200
Ian Henderson, UKIP   1,316
Andrew Page, LD   1,065
Peter Wright, Ind.   244
Lab. majority 5,965 (11.70%)
0.64% swing C. to Lab.
(2015: Lab. majority 4,922 (10.42%))

CALDER VALLEY
E. 79,045 T. 58,054 (73.44%) C. hold
*Craig Whittaker, C.   26,790
Josh Fenton-Glynn, Lab.   26,181
Janet Battye, LD   1,952
Paul Rogan, UKIP   1,466
Robert Holden, Ind.   1,034
Kieran Turner, Green   631
C. majority 609 (1.05%)
3.61% swing C. to Lab.
(2015: C. majority 4,427 (8.27%))

CAMBERWELL & PECKHAM
E. 85,586 T. 57,412 (67.08%) Lab. hold
*Harriet Harman, Lab.   44,665
Ben Spencer, C.   7,349
Michael Bukola, LD   3,413
Eleanor Margolies, Green   1,627
Ray Towey, CPA   227
Sellu Aminata, WRP   131
Lab. majority 37,316 (65.00%)
7.46% swing C. to Lab.
(2015: Lab. majority 25,824 (50.08%))

CAMBORNE & REDRUTH
E. 67,462 T. 48,456 (71.83%) C. hold
*George Eustice, C.   23,001
Graham Winter, Lab.   21,424
Geoff Williams, LD   2,979
Geoff Garbett, Green   1,052
C. majority 1,577 (3.25%)
6.01% swing C. to Lab.
(2015: C. majority 7,004 (15.27%))

CAMBRIDGE
E. 78,003 T. 55,934 (71.71%) Lab. hold
*Daniel Zeichner, Lab.   29,032
Julian Huppert, LD   16,371
John Hayward, C.   9,133
Stuart Tuckwood, Green   1,265
Keith Garrett, Reboot   133
Lab. majority 12,661 (22.64%)
10.74% swing LD to Lab.
(2015: Lab. majority 599 (1.16%))

CAMBRIDGESHIRE NORTH EAST
E. 84,404 T. 53,284 (63.13%) C. hold
*Stephen Barclay, C.   34,340
Ken Rustidge, Lab.   13,070
Darren Fower, LD   2,383
Robin Talbot, UKIP   2,174
Ruth Johnson, Green   1,024
Stephen Goldspink,   293
Eng. Dem.
C. majority 21,270 (39.92%)
0.37% swing C. to Lab.
(2015: C. majority 16,874 (32.59%))

CAMBRIDGESHIRE NORTH WEST

E. 93,223　T. 63,991 (68.64%)　C. hold
*Shailesh Vara, C.　37,529
Iain Ramsbottom, Lab.　19,521
Bridget Smith, LD　3,168
John Whitby, UKIP　2,518
Greg Guthrie, Green　1,255
C. majority 18,008 (28.14%)
3.23% swing C. to Lab.
(2015: C. majority 19,795 (32.40%))

CAMBRIDGESHIRE SOUTH

E. 85,257　T. 64,924 (76.15%)　C. hold
*Heidi Allen, C.　33,631
Dan Greef, Lab.　17,679
Susan van de Ven, LD　12,102
Simon Saggers, Green　1,512
C. majority 15,952 (24.57%)
4.45% swing C. to Lab.
(2015: C. majority 20,594 (33.46%))

CAMBRIDGESHIRE SOUTH EAST

E. 86,121　T. 63,002 (73.16%)　C. hold
*Lucy Frazer, C.　33,601
Huw Jones, Lab.　17,443
Lucy Nethsingha, LD　11,958
C. majority 16,158 (25.65%)
3.84% swing C. to Lab.
(2015: C. majority 16,837 (28.29%))

CANNOCK CHASE

E. 74,540　T. 47,872 (64.22%)　C. hold
*Amanda Milling, C.　26,318
Paul Dadge, Lab.　17,927
Paul Allen, UKIP　2,018
Paul Woodhead, Green　815
Nat Green, LD　794
C. majority 8,391 (17.53%)
3.54% swing Lab. to C.
(2015: C. majority 4,923 (10.45%))

CANTERBURY

E. 78,137　T. 56,800 (72.69%)　Lab. gain
Rosie Duffield, Lab.　25,572
*Julian Brazier, C.　25,385
James Flanagan, LD　4,561
Henry Stanton, Green　1,282
Lab. majority 187 (0.33%)
9.33% swing C. to Lab.
(2015: C. majority 9,798 (18.33%))

CARLISLE

E. 62,294　T. 43,056 (69.12%)　C. hold
*John Stevenson, C.　21,472
Ruth Alcroft, Lab.　18,873
Fiona Mills, UKIP　1,455
Peter Thornton, LD　1,256
C. majority 2,599 (6.04%)
0.24% swing C. to Lab.
(2015: C. majority 2,774 (6.51%))

CARSHALTON & WALLINGTON

E. 70,849　T. 50,753 (71.64%)　LD hold
*Tom Brake, LD　20,819
Matthew Maxwell Scott, C.　19,450
Emina Ibrahim, Lab.　9,360
Shasha Khan, Green　501
Nick Mattey, Ind.　434
Ashley Dickenson, CPA　189
LD majority 1,369 (2.70%)
0.24% swing LD to C.
(2015: LD majority 1,510 (3.17%))

CASTLE POINT

E. 69,470　T. 44,710 (64.36%)　C. hold
*Rebecca Harris, C.　30,076
Joe Cooke, Lab.　11,204
David Kurten, UKIP　2,381
Tom Holder, LD　1,049
C. majority 18,872 (42.21%)
2.59% swing Lab. to C.
(2015: C. majority 8,934 (19.66%))

CHARNWOOD

E. 78,071　T. 55,176 (70.67%)　C. hold
*Edward Argar, C.　33,318
Sean Kelly-Walsh, Lab.　16,977
Simon Sansome, LD　2,052
Victoria Connor, UKIP　1,471
Nick Cox, Green　1,036
Stephen Denham, BNP　322
C. majority 16,341 (29.62%)
1.39% swing C. to Lab.
(2015: C. majority 16,931 (32.40%))

CHATHAM & AYLESFORD

E. 70,419　T. 44,890 (63.75%)　C. hold
*Tracey Crouch, C.　25,587
Vince Maple, Lab.　15,129
Nicole Bushill, UKIP　2,225
Thomas Quinton, LD　1,116
Bernard Hyde, Green　573
John Gibson, CPA　260
C. majority 10,458 (23.30%)
1.65% swing C. to Lab.
(2015: C. majority 11,455 (26.59%))

CHEADLE

E. 72,780　T. 54,572 (74.98%)　C. hold
*Mary Robinson, C.　24,331
Mark Hunter, LD　19,824
Martin Miller, Lab.　10,417
C. majority 4,507 (8.26%)
1.95% swing C. to LD
(2015: C. majority 6,453 (12.15%))

CHELMSFORD

E. 81,045　T. 56,860 (70.16%)　C. hold
Vicky Ford, C.　30,525
Chris Vince, Lab.　16,953
Stephen Robinson, LD　6,916
Nigel Carter, UKIP　1,645
Hossain Reza, Green　821
C. majority 13,572 (23.87%)
5.02% swing C. to Lab.
(2015: C. majority 18,250 (33.91%))

CHELSEA & FULHAM

E. 63,728　T. 42,128 (66.11%)　C. hold
*Greg Hands, C.　22,179
Alan De'Ath, Lab.　13,991
Louise Rowntree, LD　4,627
Bill Cashmore, Green　807
Alasdair Seton-Marsden, UKIP　524
C. majority 8,188 (19.44%)
10.20% swing C. to Lab.
(2015: C. majority 16,022 (39.83%))

CHELTENHAM

E. 78,875　T. 57,012 (72.28%)　C. hold
*Alex Chalk, C.　26,615
Martin Horwood, LD　24,046
Keith White, Lab.　5,408
Adam Van Coevorden, Green　943
C. majority 2,569 (4.51%)
3.81% swing C. to LD
(2015: C. majority 6,516 (12.13%))

CHESHAM & AMERSHAM

E. 71,645　T. 55,252 (77.12%)　C. hold
*Cheryl Gillan, C.　33,514
Nina Dluzewska, Lab.　11,374
Peter Jones, LD　7,179
Alan Booth, Green　1,660
David Meacock, UKIP　1,525
C. majority 22,140 (40.07%)
3.13% swing C. to Lab.
(2015: C. majority 23,920 (45.36%))

CHESTER, CITY OF

E. 72,859　T. 56,421 (77.44%)　Lab. hold
*Chris Matheson, Lab.　32,023
Will Gallagher, C.　22,847
Lizzie Jewkes, LD　1,551
Lab. majority 9,176 (16.26%)
8.04% swing C. to Lab.
(2015: Lab. majority 93 (0.18%))

CHESTERFIELD

E. 72,063　T. 47,927 (66.51%)　Lab. hold
*Toby Perkins, Lab.　26,266
Spencer Pitfield, C.　16,661
Tom Snowdon, LD　2,612
Stuart Bent, UKIP　1,611
David Wadsworth, Green　777
Lab. majority 9,605 (20.04%)
4.90% swing Lab. to C.
(2015: Lab. majority 13,598 (29.84%))

CHICHESTER

E. 84,996　T. 59,918 (70.50%)　C. hold
Gillian Keegan, C.　36,032
Mark Farwell, Lab.　13,411
Jonathan Brown, LD　6,749
Heather Barrie, Green　1,992
Andrew Moncreiff, UKIP　1,650
Andrew Emerson, Patria　84
C. majority 22,621 (37.75%)
3.89% swing C. to Lab.
(2015: C. majority 24,413 (42.73%))

CHINGFORD & WOODFORD GREEN

E. 66,078　T. 46,961 (71.07%)　C. hold
*Iain Duncan Smith, C.　23,076
Bilal Mahmood, Lab.　20,638
Deborah Unger, LD　2,043
Sinead King, Green　1,204
C. majority 2,438 (5.19%)
6.98% swing C. to Lab.
(2015: C. majority 8,386 (19.14%))

CHIPPENHAM

E. 76,432　T. 57,140 (74.76%)　C. hold
*Michelle Donelan, C.　31,267
Helen Belcher, LD　14,637
Andrew Newman, Lab.　11,236
C. majority 16,630 (29.10%)
5.46% swing LD to C.
(2015: C. majority 10,076 (18.19%))

CHIPPING BARNET
E. 77,020 T. 55,423 (71.96%)   C. hold
*Theresa Villiers, C.   25,679
Emma Whysall, Lab.   25,326
Marisha Ray, LD   3,012
Phil Fletcher, Green   1,406
C. majority 353 (0.64%)
6.90% swing C. to Lab.
(2015: C. majority 7,656 (14.44%))

CHORLEY
E. 76,404 T. 55,634 (72.82%)   Lab. hold
*Lindsay Hoyle, Lab.   30,745
Caroline Moon, C.   23,233
Stephen Fenn, LD   1,126
Peter Lageard, Green   530
Lab. majority 7,512 (13.50%)
2.37% swing C. to Lab.
(2015: Lab. majority 4,530 (8.76%))

CHRISTCHURCH
E. 70,329 T. 50,633 (71.99%)   C. hold
*Christopher Chope, C.   35,230
Patrick Canavan, Lab.   10,059
Michael Cox, LD   4,020
Chris Rigby, Green   1,324
C. majority 25,171 (49.71%)
0.57% swing Lab. to C.
(2015: C. majority 18,224 (36.66%))

CITIES OF LONDON &
WESTMINSTER
E. 61,533 T. 38,654 (62.82%)   C. hold
*Mark Field, C.   18,005
Ibrahim Dogus, Lab.   14,857
Bridget Fox, LD   4,270
Lawrence McNally, Green   821
Anil Bhatti, UKIP   426
Tim Lord, ND   173
Ankit Love The Maharaja of
Kashmir, Ind.   59
Benjamin Weenen, Young   43
C. majority 3,148 (8.14%)
9.29% swing C. to Lab.
(2015: C. majority 9,671 (26.73%))

CLACTON
E. 69,263 T. 44,145 (63.74%)   C. gain
Giles Watling, C.   27,031
Tasha Osben, Lab.   11,203
Paul Oakley, UKIP   3,357
David Grace, LD   887
Chris Southall, Green   719
Caroline Shearer, Ind.   449
Robin Tilbrook, Eng. Dem.   289
Nick Martin, Ind.   210
C. majority 15,828 (35.85%)
30.70% swing UKIP to C.
(2015: UKIP majority 3,437 (7.77%))

CLEETHORPES
E. 73,047 T. 47,844 (65.50%)   C. hold
*Martin Vickers, C.   27,321
Peter Keith, Lab.   16,921
Tony Blake, UKIP   2,022
Roy Horobin, LD   1,110
Loyd Emmerson, Green   470
C. majority 10,400 (21.74%)
2.12% swing Lab. to C.
(2015: C. majority 7,893 (17.51%))

COLCHESTER
E. 79,996 T. 53,545 (66.93%)   C. hold
*Will Quince, C.   24,565
Tim Young, Lab.   18,888
Bob Russell, LD   9,087
Mark Goacher, Green   828
Robin Rennie, CPA   177
C. majority 5,677 (10.60%)
6.09% swing C. to Lab.
(2015: C. majority 5,575 (11.47%))

COLNE VALLEY
E. 84,381 T. 60,420 (71.60%)   Lab. gain
Thelma Walker, Lab.   28,818
*Jason McCartney, C.   27,903
Cahal Burke, LD   2,494
Sonia King, Green   892
Patricia Sadio, Ind.   313
Lab. majority 915 (1.51%)
5.49% swing C. to Lab.
(2015: C. majority 5,378 (9.47%))

CONGLETON
E. 76,694 T. 56,231 (73.32%)   C. hold
*Fiona Bruce, C.   31,830
Sam Corcoran, Lab.   19,211
Peter Hirst, LD   2,902
Mark Davies, UKIP   1,289
Alexander Heath, Green   999
C. majority 12,619 (22.44%)
5.23% swing C. to Lab.
(2015: C. majority 16,773 (32.90%))

COPELAND
E. 61,751 T. 42,927 (69.52%)   C. hold
*Trudy Harrison, C.   21,062
Gillian Troughton, Lab.   19,367
Rebecca Hanson, LD   1,404
Herbert Crossman, UKIP   1,094
C. majority 1,695 (3.95%)
5.21% swing Lab. to C.
(2015: Lab. majority 2,564 (6.47%))
(2017: C. majority 2,147 (6.91%))

CORBY
E. 82,439 T. 59,997 (72.78%)   C. hold
*Tom Pursglove, C.   29,534
Beth Miller, Lab.   26,844
Chris Stanbra, LD   1,545
Sam Watts, UKIP   1,495
Steven Scrutton, Green   579
C. majority 2,690 (4.48%)
0.09% swing Lab. to C.
(2015: C. majority 2,412 (4.29%))

CORNWALL NORTH
E. 68,850 T. 50,944 (73.99%)   C. hold
*Scott Mann, C.   25,835
Daniel Rogerson, LD   18,635
Joy Bassett, Lab.   6,151
John Allman, CPA   185
Robert Hawkins, Soc. Lab.   138
C. majority 7,200 (14.13%)
0.20% swing LD to C.
(2015: C. majority 6,621 (13.72%))

CORNWALL SOUTH EAST
E. 71,896 T. 53,214 (74.02%)   C. hold
*Sheryll Murray, C.   29,493
Gareth Derrick, Lab.   12,050
Phil Hutty, LD   10,336
Martin Corney, Green   1,335
C. majority 17,443 (32.78%)
4.23% swing C. to Lab.
(2015: C. majority 16,995 (33.65%))

COTSWOLDS, THE
E. 80,446 T. 59,702 (74.21%)   C. hold
*Geoffrey Clifton-Brown, C.   36,201
Mark Huband, Lab.   10,702
Andrew Gant, LD   9,748
Sabrina Poole, Green   1,747
Chris Harlow, UKIP   1,197
Sandy Steel, ND   107
C. majority 25,499 (42.71%)
2.30% swing C. to Lab.
(2015: C. majority 21,477 (37.90%))

COVENTRY NORTH EAST
E. 75,792 T. 46,508 (61.36%)   Lab. hold
*Colleen Fletcher, Lab.   29,499
Timothy Mayer, C.   13,919
Avtar Taggar, UKIP   1,350
Russell Field, LD   1,157
Matthew Handley, Green   502
Afzal Mahmood, Ind.   81
Lab. majority 15,580 (33.50%)
2.22% swing C. to Lab.
(2015: Lab. majority 12,274 (29.06%))

COVENTRY NORTH WEST
E. 75,214 T. 49,849 (66.28%)   Lab. hold
*Geoffrey Robinson, Lab.   26,894
Resham Kotecha, C.   18,314
Michael Gee, UKIP   1,525
Andrew Hilton, LD   1,286
Ciaran Norris, Ind.   1,164
Stephen Gray, Green   666
Lab. majority 8,580 (17.21%)
3.62% swing C. to Lab.
(2015: Lab. majority 4,509 (9.97%))

COVENTRY SOUTH
E. 70,754 T. 47,009 (66.44%)   Lab. hold
*Jim Cunningham, Lab.   25,874
Michelle Lowe, C.   17,927
Greg Judge, LD   1,343
Ian Rogers, UKIP   1,037
Aimee Challenor, Green   604
Sandra Findlay, Ind.   224
Lab. majority 7,947 (16.91%)
4.80% swing C. to Lab.
(2015: Lab. majority 3,188 (7.30%))

CRAWLEY
E. 73,424 T. 50,273 (68.47%)   C. hold
*Henry Smith, C.   25,426
Tim Lunnon, Lab.   22,969
Marko Scepanovic, LD   1,878
C. majority 2,457 (4.89%)
4.28% swing C. to Lab.
(2015: C. majority 6,526 (13.44%))

CREWE & NANTWICH
E. 78,895 T. 55,027 (69.75%) Lab. gain
Laura Smith, Lab. 25,928
*Edward Timpson, C. 25,880
Michael Stanley, UKIP 1,885
David Crowther, LD 1,334
Lab. majority 48 (0.09%)
3.67% swing C. to Lab.
(2015: C. majority 3,620 (7.26%))

CROYDON CENTRAL
E. 80,045 T. 57,091 (71.32%) Lab. gain
Sarah Jones, Lab. 29,873
*Gavin Barwell, C. 24,221
Gill Hickson, LD 1,083
Peter Staveley, UKIP 1,040
Tracey Hague, Green 626
John Boadu, CPA 177
Don Locke, Ind. 71
Lab. majority 5,652 (9.90%)
5.11% swing C. to Lab.
(2015: C. majority 165 (0.31%))

CROYDON NORTH
E. 87,461 T. 59,623 (68.17%)
                        Lab. Co-op hold
*Steve Reed, Lab. Co-op 44,213
Samuel Kasumu, C. 11,848
Maltby Pindar, LD 1,656
Peter Underwood, Green 983
Michael Swadling, UKIP 753
Lee Berks, Ind. 170
Lab. Co-op majority 32,365 (54.28%)
7.18% swing C. to Lab.
(2015: Lab. Co-op majority 21,364
(39.92%))

CROYDON SOUTH
E. 83,518 T. 61,257 (73.35%) C. hold
*Chris Philp, C. 33,334
Jennifer Brathwaite, Lab. 21,928
Anna Jones, LD 3,541
Catherine Shelley, Green 1,125
Kathleen Garner, UKIP 1,116
David Omamogho, CPA 213
C. majority 11,406 (18.62%)
5.54% swing C. to Lab.
(2015: C. majority 17,140 (29.70%))

DAGENHAM & RAINHAM
E. 70,620 T. 45,843 (64.92%) Lab. hold
*Jon Cruddas, Lab. 22,958
Julie Marson, C. 18,306
Peter Harris, UKIP 3,246
Denis Breading, Green 544
Jonathan Fryer, LD 465
Paul Sturdy, BNP 239
Terence London, Concordia 85
Lab. majority 4,652 (10.15%)
3.45% swing Lab. to C.
(2015: Lab. majority 4,980 (11.57%))

DARLINGTON
E. 66,341 T. 44,817 (67.56%) Lab. hold
*Jenny Chapman, Lab. 22,681
Peter Cuthbertson, C. 19,401
Kevin Brack, UKIP 1,180
Anne-Marie Curry, LD 1,031
Matthew Snedker, Green 524
Lab. majority 3,280 (7.32%)
0.18% swing Lab. to C.
(2015: Lab. majority 3,158 (7.68%))

DARTFORD
E. 78,506 T. 54,224 (69.07%) C. hold
*Gareth Johnson, C. 31,210
Bachchu Kaini, Lab. 18,024
Ben Fryer, UKIP 2,544
Simon Beard, LD 1,428
Andrew Blatchford, Green 807
Ola Adewunmi, Ind. 211
C. majority 13,186 (24.32%)
0.38% swing Lab. to C.
(2015: C. majority 12,345 (23.55%))

DAVENTRY
E. 75,335 T. 55,663 (73.89%) C. hold
*Chris Heaton-Harris, C. 35,464
Aiden Ramsey, Lab. 13,730
Andrew Simpson, LD 4,015
Ian Gibbins, UKIP 1,497
Jamie Wildman, Green 957
C. majority 21,734 (39.05%)
0.53% swing C. to Lab.
(2015: C. majority 21,059 (40.10%))

DENTON & REDDISH
E. 65,751 T. 39,599 (60.23%) Lab. hold
*Andrew Gwynne, Lab. 25,161
Rozila Kana, C. 11,084
Josh Seddon, UKIP 1,798
Catherine Ankers, LD 853
Gareth Hayes, Green 486
Farmin Lord Dave, Loony 217
Lab. majority 14,077 (35.55%)
4.19% swing C. to Lab.
(2015: Lab. majority 10,511 (27.17%))

DERBY NORTH
E. 69,919 T. 48,672 (69.61%) Lab. gain
†Chris Williamson, Lab. 23,622
*Amanda Solloway, C. 21,607
Lucy Care, LD 2,262
Bill Piper, UKIP 1,181
Lab. majority 2,015 (4.14%)
2.12% swing C. to Lab.
(2015: C. majority 41 (0.09%))

DERBY SOUTH
E. 69,918 T. 45,306 (64.80%) Lab. hold
*Margaret Beckett, Lab. 26,430
Evonne Williams, C. 15,182
Alan Graves, UKIP 2,011
Joe Naitta, LD 1,229
Ian Sleeman, Green 454
Lab. majority 11,248 (24.83%)
1.60% swing C. to Lab.
(2015: Lab. majority 8,828 (21.63%))

DERBYSHIRE DALES
E. 64,418 T. 49,571 (76.95%) C. hold
*Patrick McLoughlin, C. 29,744
Andy Botham, Lab. 15,417
Andrew Hollyer, LD 3,126
Matthew Buckler, Green 1,002
Robin Greenwood,
Humanity 282
C. majority 14,327 (28.90%)
0.38% swing C. to Lab.
(2015: C. majority 14,044 (29.65%))

DERBYSHIRE MID
E. 67,466 T. 50,371 (74.66%) C. hold
*Pauline Latham, C. 29,513
Alison Martin, Lab. 17,897
Adam Wain, LD 1,793
Sue Macfarlane, Green 1,168
C. majority 11,616 (23.06%)
1.85% swing C. to Lab.
(2015: C. majority 12,774 (26.76%))

DERBYSHIRE NORTH EAST
E. 72,097 T. 50,381 (69.88%) C. gain
Lee Rowley, C. 24,784
*Natascha Engel, Lab. 21,923
James Bush, UKIP 1,565
David Lomax, LD 1,390
David Kesteven, Green 719
C. majority 2,861 (5.68%)
4.80% swing Lab. to C.
(2015: Lab. majority 1,883 (3.93%))

DERBYSHIRE SOUTH
E. 76,341 T. 52,631 (68.94%) C. hold
*Heather Wheeler, C. 30,907
Robert Pearson, Lab. 18,937
Lorraine Johnson, LD 1,870
Marten Kats, Green 917
C. majority 11,970 (22.74%)
0.07% swing Lab. to C.
(2015: C. majority 11,471 (22.60%))

DEVIZES
E. 72,184 T. 50,593 (70.09%) C. hold
*Claire Perry, C. 31,744
Imtiyaz Shaikh, Lab. 10,608
Christopher Coleman, LD 4,706
Timothy Page, UKIP 1,706
Emma Dawnay, Green 1,606
Jim Gunter, Wessex Reg. 223
C. majority 21,136 (41.78%)
1.49% swing C. to Lab.
(2015: C. majority 20,751 (42.34%))

DEVON CENTRAL
E. 74,370 T. 57,844 (77.78%) C. hold
*Mel Stride, C. 31,278
Lisa Robillard Webb, Lab. 15,598
Alex White, LD 6,770
Andy Williamson, Green 1,531
Tim Matthews, UKIP 1,326
John Dean, NHAP 871
Lloyd Knight, Lib. 470
C. majority 15,680 (27.11%)
6.14% swing C. to Lab.
(2015: C. majority 21,265 (39.06%))

DEVON EAST
E. 82,382 T. 60,382 (73.30%) C. hold
*Hugo Swire, C. 29,306
Claire Wright, Ind. 21,270
Jan Ross, Lab. 6,857
Alison Eden, LD 1,468
Brigitte Graham, UKIP 1,203
Peter Faithfull, Ind. 150
Michael Val Davies, Ind. 128
C. majority 8,036 (13.31%)
4.55% swing C. to Ind.
(2015: C. majority 12,261 (22.41%))

DEVON NORTH
E. 75,784   T. 55,705 (73.50%)   C. hold
*Peter Heaton-Jones, C.   25,517
Nick Harvey, LD   21,185
Mark Cann, Lab.   7,063
Stephen Crowther, UKIP   1,187
Ricky Knight, Green   753
C. majority 4,332 (7.78%)
2.74% swing C. to LD
(2015: C. majority 6,936 (13.26%))

DEVON SOUTH WEST
E. 71,262   T. 52,857 (74.17%)   C. hold
*Gary Streeter, C.   31,634
Philippa Davey, Lab. Co-op   15,818
Caroline Voaden, LD   2,732
Ian Ross, UKIP   1,540
Win Scutt, Green   1,133
C. majority 15,816 (29.92%)
5.00% swing C. to Lab.
(2015: C. majority 20,109 (39.92%))

DEVON WEST & TORRIDGE
E. 80,527   T. 59,480 (73.86%)   C. hold
*Geoffrey Cox, C.   33,612
Vince Barry, Lab. Co-op   12,926
David Chalmers, LD   10,526
Chris Jordan, Green   1,622
Robin Julian, Ind.   794
C. majority 20,686 (34.78%)
2.72% swing C. to Lab.
(2015: C. majority 18,403 (32.52%))

DEWSBURY
E. 81,338   T. 56,545 (69.52%)   Lab. hold
*Paula Sherriff, Lab.   28,814
Beth Prescott, C.   25,493
Ednan Hussain, LD   1,214
Simon Cope, Green   1,024
Lab. majority 3,321 (5.87%)
1.58% swing C. to Lab.
(2015: Lab. majority 1,451 (2.71%))

DON VALLEY
E. 73,988   T. 45,988 (62.16%)   Lab. hold
*Caroline Flint, Lab.   24,351
Aaron Bell, C.   19,182
Stevie Manion, Yorkshire   1,599
Anthony Smith, LD   856
Lab. majority 5,169 (11.24%)
4.84% swing Lab. to C.
(2015: Lab. majority 8,885 (20.91%))

DONCASTER CENTRAL
E. 71,716   T. 43,024 (59.99%)   Lab. hold
*Rosie Winterton, Lab.   24,915
Tom Hunt, C.   14,784
Chris Whitwood, Yorkshire   1,346
Eddie Todd, Ind.   1,006
Alison Brelsford, LD   973
Lab. majority 10,131 (23.55%)
2.40% swing Lab. to C.
(2015: Lab. majority 10,093 (24.97%))

DONCASTER NORTH
E. 72,372   T. 42,312 (58.46%)   Lab. hold
*Ed Miliband, Lab.   25,711
Shade Adoh, C.   11,687
Kim Parkinson, UKIP   2,738
Charlie Bridges, Yorkshire   741
Robert Adamson, LD   706
Frank Calladine, Ind.   366
David Allen, Eng. Dem.   363
Lab. majority 14,024 (33.14%)
0.48% swing Lab. to C.
(2015: Lab. majority 11,780 (29.82%))

DORSET MID & POOLE NORTH
E. 65,054   T. 48,254 (74.18%)   C. hold
*Michael Tomlinson, C.   28,585
Vikki Slade, LD   13,246
Steve Brew, Lab.   6,423
C. majority 15,339 (31.79%)
4.57% swing LD to C.
(2015: C. majority 10,530 (22.65%))

DORSET NORTH
E. 76,385   T. 55,724 (72.95%)   C. hold
*Simon Hoare, C.   36,169
Pat Osborne, Lab.   10,392
Thomas Panton, LD   7,556
John Tutton, Green   1,607
C. majority 25,777 (46.26%)
0.70% swing C. to Lab.
(2015: C. majority 21,118 (39.56%))

DORSET SOUTH
E. 72,323   T. 51,906 (71.77%)   C. hold
*Richard Drax, C.   29,135
Tashi Warr, Lab.   17,440
Howard Legg, LD   3,053
Jon Orrell, Green   2,278
C. majority 11,695 (22.53%)
1.07% swing C. to Lab.
(2015: C. majority 11,994 (24.68%))

DORSET WEST
E. 79,043   T. 59,598 (75.40%)   C. hold
*Oliver Letwin, C.   33,081
Andy Canning, LD   13,990
Lee Rhodes, Lab.   10,896
Kelvin Clayton, Green   1,631
C. majority 19,091 (32.03%)
1.73% swing LD to C.
(2015: C. majority 16,130 (28.57%))

DOVER
E. 74,564   T. 51,966 (69.69%)   C. hold
*Charlie Elphicke, C.   27,211
Stacey Blair, Lab.   20,774
Piers Wauchope, UKIP   1,722
Simon Dodd, LD   1,336
Beccy Sawbridge, Green   923
C. majority 6,437 (12.39%)
0.07% swing C. to Lab.
(2015: C. majority 6,294 (12.53%))

DUDLEY NORTH
E. 62,043   T. 38,910 (62.71%)   Lab. hold
*Ian Austin, Lab.   18,090
Les Jones, C.   18,068
Bill Etheridge, UKIP   2,144
Ben France, LD   368
Andrew Nixon, Green   240
Lab. majority 22 (0.06%)
5.47% swing Lab. to C.
(2015: Lab. majority 4,181 (11.00%))

DUDLEY SOUTH
E. 61,323   T. 38,244 (62.36%)   C. hold
*Mike Wood, C.   21,588
Natasha Millward, Lab.   13,858
Mitch Bolton, UKIP   1,791
Jon Bramall, LD   625
Jenny Maxwell, Green   382
C. majority 7,730 (20.21%)
4.52% swing Lab. to C.
(2015: C. majority 4,270 (11.18%))

DULWICH & WEST NORWOOD
E. 77,947   T. 56,143 (72.03%)   Lab. hold
*Helen Hayes, Lab.   39,096
Rachel Wolf, C.   10,940
Gail Kent, LD   4,475
Rashid Nix, Green   1,408
Robin Lambert, Ind.   121
Yen Lin Chong, Ind.   103
Lab. majority 28,156 (50.15%)
9.38% swing C. to Lab.
(2015: Lab. majority 16,122 (31.39%))

DURHAM, CITY OF
E. 71,132   T. 48,324 (67.94%)   Lab. hold
*Roberta Blackman-Woods,
Lab.   26,772
Richard Lawrie, C.   14,408
Amanda Hopgood, LD   4,787
Malcolm Bint, UKIP   1,116
Jonathan Elmer, Green   797
Jim Clark, Ind.   399
Jon Collings, Young   45
Lab. majority 12,364 (25.59%)
0.27% swing C. to Lab.
(2015: Lab. majority 11,439 (25.05%))

DURHAM NORTH
E. 66,970   T. 43,284 (64.63%)   Lab. hold
*Kevan Jones, Lab.   25,917
Laetitia Glossop, C.   12,978
Kenneth Rollings, UKIP   2,408
Craig Martin, LD   1,981
Lab. majority 12,939 (29.89%)
2.05% swing Lab. to C.
(2015: Lab. majority 13,644 (33.99%))

DURHAM NORTH WEST
E. 71,982   T. 47,902 (66.55%)   Lab. hold
Laura Pidcock, Lab.   25,308
Sally-Ann Hart, C.   16,516
Owen Temple, LD   3,398
Alan Breeze, UKIP   2,150
Dominic Horsman, Green   530
Lab. majority 8,792 (18.35%)
2.57% swing Lab. to C.
(2015: Lab. majority 10,056 (23.49%))

EALING CENTRAL & ACTON
E. 74,200   T. 55,342 (74.58%)   Lab. hold
*Rupa Huq, Lab.   33,037
Joy Morrissey, C.   19,230
Jon Ball, LD   3,075
Lab. majority 13,807 (24.95%)
12.21% swing C. to Lab.
(2015: Lab. majority 274 (0.54%))

EALING NORTH
E. 74,764　T. 52,516 (70.24%)　Lab. hold
*Stephen Pound, Lab.　34,635
Isobel Grant, C.　14,942
Humaira Sanders, LD　1,275
Peter McIlvenna, UKIP　921
Meena Hans, Green　743
Lab. majority 19,693 (37.50%)
6.04% swing C. to Lab.
(2015: Lab. majority 12,326 (25.41%))

EALING SOUTHALL
E. 65,188　T. 45,145 (69.25%)　Lab. hold
*Virendra Sharma, Lab.　31,720
Fabio Conti, C.　9,630
Nigel Bakhai, LD　1,892
Peter Ward, Green　1,037
John Poynton, UKIP　504
Arjinder Thiara, WRP　362
Lab. majority 22,090 (48.93%)
2.81% swing C. to Lab.
(2015: Lab. majority 18,760 (43.30%))

EASINGTON
E. 62,385　T. 36,364 (58.29%)　Lab. hold
*Grahame Morris, Lab.　23,152
Barney Campbell, C.　8,260
Susan McDonnell, NE　2,355
Allyn Roberts, UKIP　1,727
Tom Hancock, LD　460
Martie Warin, Green　410
Lab. majority 14,892 (40.95%)
3.57% swing Lab. to C.
(2015: Lab. majority 14,641 (42.29%))

EAST HAM
E. 83,827　T. 56,633 (67.56%)　Lab. hold
*Stephen Timms, Lab.　47,124
Kirsty Finlayson, C.　7,241
Daniel Oxley, UKIP　697
Glanville Williams, LD　656
Chidi Oti-Obihara, Green　474
Choudhry Afzal, Friends　311
Mirza Rahman, Ind.　130
Lab. majority 39,883 (70.42%)
2.46% swing C. to Lab.
(2015: Lab. majority 34,252 (65.50%))

EASTBOURNE
E. 78,754　T. 57,420 (72.91%)　LD gain
†Stephen Lloyd, LD　26,924
*Caroline Ansell, C.　25,315
Jake Lambert, Lab.　4,671
Alex Hough, Green　510
LD majority 1,609 (2.80%)
2.09% swing C. to LD
(2015: C. majority 733 (1.39%))

EASTLEIGH
E. 81,213　T. 57,280 (70.53%)　C. hold
*Mims Davies, C.　28,889
Mike Thornton, LD　14,710
Jill Payne, Lab.　11,454
Malcolm Jones, UKIP　1,477
Ron Meldrum, Green　750
C. majority 14,179 (24.75%)
4.14% swing LD to C.
(2015: C. majority 9,147 (16.48%))

EDDISBURY
E. 70,272　T. 51,319 (73.03%)　C. hold
*Antoinette Sandbach, C.　29,192
Cathy Reynolds, Lab.　17,250
Ian Priestner, LD　2,804
John Bickley, UKIP　1,109
Mark Green, Green　785
Morgan Hill, Pirate　179
C. majority 11,942 (23.27%)
2.06% swing C. to Lab.
(2015: C. majority 12,974 (27.40%))

EDMONTON
E. 65,705　T. 43,678 (66.48%)
　　　　　　　　Lab. Co-op hold
*Kate Osamor, Lab. Co-op　31,221
Gonul Daniels, C.　10,106
Nigel Sussman, UKIP　860
David Schmitz, LD　858
Benjamin Gill, Green　633
Lab. Co-op majority 21,115 (48.34%)
5.52% swing C. to Lab.
(2015: Lab. Co-op majority 15,419 (37.30%))

ELLESMERE PORT & NESTON
E. 68,666　T. 50,939 (74.18%)　Lab. hold
*Justin Madders, Lab.　30,137
Nigel Jones, C.　18,747
Ed Gough, LD　892
Fred Fricker, UKIP　821
Steven Baker, Green　342
Lab. majority 11,390 (22.36%)
4.47% swing C. to Lab.
(2015: Lab. majority 6,275 (13.43%))

ELMET & ROTHWELL
E. 80,291　T. 59,542 (74.16%)　C. hold
*Alec Shelbrooke, C.　32,352
David Nagle, Lab.　22,547
Stewart Golton, LD　2,606
Matthew Clover, Yorkshire　1,042
Dylan Brown, Green　995
C. majority 9,805 (16.47%)
0.89% swing Lab. to C.
(2015: C. majority 8,490 (14.69%))

ELTHAM
E. 64,474　T. 46,155 (71.59%)　Lab. hold
*Clive Efford, Lab.　25,128
Matt Hartley, C.　18,832
David Hall-Matthews, LD　1,457
John Clarke, BNP　738
Lab. majority 6,296 (13.64%)
3.70% swing C. to Lab.
(2015: Lab. majority 2,693 (6.24%))

ENFIELD NORTH
E. 68,454　T. 48,565 (70.95%)　Lab. hold
*Joan Ryan, Lab.　28,177
Nick de Bois, C.　17,930
Nicholas da Costa, LD　1,036
Deborah Cairns, UKIP　848
Bill Linton, Green　574
Lab. majority 10,247 (21.10%)
9.37% swing C. to Lab.
(2015: Lab. majority 1,086 (2.35%))

ENFIELD SOUTHGATE
E. 65,137　T. 48,328 (74.19%)　Lab. gain
Bambos Charalambous, Lab.　24,989
*David Burrowes, C.　20,634
Pippa Morgan, LD　1,925
David Flint, Green　780
Lab. majority 4,355 (9.01%)
9.69% swing C. to Lab.
(2015: C. majority 4,753 (10.38%))

EPPING FOREST
E. 74,737　T. 50,779 (67.94%)　C. hold
*Eleanor Laing, C.　31,462
Liam Preston, Lab.　13,219
Jon Whitehouse, LD　2,884
Patrick O'Flynn, UKIP　1,871
Simon Heap, Green　1,233
Thomas Hall, Young　110
C. majority 18,243 (35.93%)
1.35% swing C. to Lab.
(2015: C. majority 17,978 (36.43%))

EPSOM & EWELL
E. 80,029　T. 59,266 (74.06%)　C. hold
*Chris Grayling, C.　35,313
Ed Mayne, Lab.　14,838
Steve Gee, LD　7,401
Janice Baker, Green　1,714
C. majority 20,475 (34.55%)
4.11% swing C. to Lab.
(2015: C. majority 24,443 (42.78%))

EREWASH
E. 72,991　T. 49,781 (68.20%)　C. hold
*Maggie Throup, C.　25,939
Catherine Atkinson, Lab.　21,405
Martin Garnett, LD　1,243
Ralph Hierons, Green　675
Roy Dunn, Ind.　519
C. majority 4,534 (9.11%)
0.85% swing Lab. to C.
(2015: C. majority 3,584 (7.42%))

ERITH & THAMESMEAD
E. 69,724　T. 44,464 (63.77%)　Lab. hold
*Teresa Pearce, Lab.　25,585
Edward Baxter, C.　15,571
Ronie Johnson, UKIP　1,728
Simon Waddington, LD　750
Claudine Letsae, Green　507
Temi Olodu, CPA　243
Doro Oddiri, Ind.　80
Lab. majority 10,014 (22.52%)
0.09% swing C. to Lab.
(2015: Lab. majority 9,525 (22.35%))

ESHER & WALTON
E. 80,938　T. 59,842 (73.94%)　C. hold
*Dominic Raab, C.　35,071
Lana Hylands, Lab.　11,773
Andrew Davis, LD　10,374
Olivia Palmer, Green　1,074
David Ions, UKIP　1,034
Baron Badger, Loony　318
Della Reynolds, Ind.　198
C. majority 23,298 (38.93%)
5.65% swing C. to Lab.
(2015: C. majority 28,616 (50.22%))

EXETER
E. 77,329 T. 55,423 (71.67%) Lab. hold
*Ben Bradshaw, Lab.   34,336
James Taghdissian, C.   18,219
Vanessa Newcombe, LD   1,562
Joe Levy, Green   1,027
Jonathan West, Ind.   212
Jonathan Bishop, ND   67
Lab. majority 16,117 (29.08%)
7.89% swing C. to Lab.
(2015: Lab. majority 7,183 (13.30%))

FAREHAM
E. 79,495 T. 57,014 (71.72%) C. hold
*Suella Fernandes, C.   35,915
Matthew Randall, Lab.   14,360
Matthew Winnington, LD   3,896
Tony Blewett, UKIP   1,541
Miles Grindey, Green   1,302
C. majority 21,555 (37.81%)
2.02% swing C. to Lab.
(2015: C. majority 22,262 (40.70%))

FAVERSHAM & KENT MID
E. 76,008 T. 49,749 (65.45%) C. hold
*Helen Whately, C.   30,390
Michael Desmond, Lab.   12,977
David Naghi, LD   3,249
Mark McGiffin, UKIP   1,702
Alastair Gould, Green   1,431
C. majority 17,413 (35.00%)
1.59% swing C. to Lab.
(2015: C. majority 16,652 (36.36%))

FELTHAM & HESTON
E. 81,707 T. 53,027 (64.90%)
                              Lab. Co-op hold
*Seema Malhotra, Lab. Co-   32,462
op
Samir Jassal, C.   16,859
Stuart Agnew, UKIP   1,510
Hina Malik, LD   1,387
Tony Firkins, Green   809
Lab. Co-op majority 15,603 (29.42%)
3.11% swing C. to Lab.
(2015: Lab. Co-op majority 11,463
(23.20%))

FILTON & BRADLEY STOKE
E. 72,569 T. 50,694 (69.86%) C. hold
*Jack Lopresti, C.   25,331
Naomi Rylatt, Lab.   21,149
Eva Fielding, LD   3,052
Diana Warner, Green   1,162
C. majority 4,182 (8.25%)
5.89% swing C. to Lab.
(2015: C. majority 9,838 (20.04%))

FINCHLEY & GOLDERS GREEN
E. 73,138 T. 52,385 (71.62%) C. hold
*Mike Freer, C.   24,599
Jeremy Newmark, Lab.   22,942
Jonathan Davies, LD   3,463
Adele Ward, Green   919
Andrew Price, UKIP   462
C. majority 1,657 (3.16%)
4.00% swing C. to Lab.
(2015: C. majority 5,662 (11.15%))

FOLKESTONE & HYTHE
E. 84,090 T. 58,875 (70.01%)   C. hold
*Damian Collins, C.   32,197
Laura Davison, Lab.   16,786
Lynne Beaumont, LD   4,222
Stephen Priestley, UKIP   2,565
Martin Whybrow, Green   2,498
David Plumstead, Ind.   493
Naomi Slade, Ind.   114
C. majority 15,411 (26.18%)
3.62% swing C. to Lab.
(2015: C. majority 13,797 (25.08%))

FOREST OF DEAN
E. 70,898 T. 51,767 (73.02%)   C. hold
*Mark Harper, C.   28,096
Shaun Stammers, Lab.   18,594
Janet Ellard, LD   2,029
James Greenwood, Green   1,241
Ernie Warrender, UKIP   1,237
Julian Burrett, Ind.   570
C. majority 9,502 (18.36%)
1.92% swing C. to Lab.
(2015: C. majority 10,987 (22.19%))

FYLDE
E. 65,937 T. 46,467 (70.47%)   C. hold
*Mark Menzies, C.   27,334
Jed Sullivan, Lab.   15,529
Freddie van Mierlo, LD   2,341
Tina Rothery, Green   1,263
C. majority 11,805 (25.41%)
2.48% swing C. to Lab.
(2015: C. majority 13,224 (30.36%))

GAINSBOROUGH
E. 75,893 T. 51,425 (67.76%)
*Edward Leigh, C.   31,790
Catherine Tite, Lab.   14,767
Lesley Rollings, LD   3,630
Vicky Pearson, Green   1,238
C. majority 17,023 (33.10%)
0.87% swing Lab. to C.
(2015: C. majority 15,449 (31.36%))

GARSTON & HALEWOOD
E. 75,248 T. 53,522 (71.13%) Lab. hold
*Maria Eagle, Lab.   41,599
Adam Marsden, C.   9,450
Anna Martin, LD   1,723
Lawrence Brown, Green   750
Lab. majority 32,149 (60.07%)
2.32% swing C. to Lab.
(2015: Lab. majority 27,146 (55.42%))

GATESHEAD
E. 65,186 T. 42,103 (64.59%) Lab. hold
*Ian Mearns, Lab.   27,426
Lauren Hankinson, C.   10,076
Mark Bell, UKIP   2,281
Frank Hindle, LD   1,709
Andy Redfern, Green   611
Lab. majority 17,350 (41.21%)
0.43% swing Lab. to C.
(2015: Lab. majority 14,784 (38.90%))

GEDLING
E. 71,221 T. 51,682 (72.57%) Lab. hold
*Vernon Coaker, Lab.   26,833
Carolyn Abbott, C.   22,139
Lee Waters, UKIP   1,143
Robert Swift, LD   1,052
Rebecca Connick, Green   515
Lab. majority 4,694 (9.08%)
1.43% swing C. to Lab.
(2015: Lab. majority 2,986 (6.22%))

GILLINGHAM & RAINHAM
E. 72,903 T. 48,868 (67.03%)   C. hold
*Rehman Chishti, C.   27,091
Andrew Stamp, Lab.   17,661
Martin Cook, UKIP   2,097
Paul Chaplin, LD   1,372
Clive Gregory, Green   520
Roger Peacock, CPA   127
C. majority 9,430 (19.30%)
1.54% swing C. to Lab.
(2015: C. majority 10,530 (22.37%))

GLOUCESTER
E. 82,963 T. 54,071 (65.17%)   C. hold
*Richard Graham, C.   27,208
Barry Kirby, Lab.   21,688
Jeremy Hilton, LD   2,716
Daniel Woolf, UKIP   1,495
Gerald Hartley, Green   754
George Ridgeon, Loony   210
C. majority 5,520 (10.21%)
1.79% swing C. to Lab.
(2015: C. majority 7,251 (13.79%))

GOSPORT
E. 73,886 T. 49,481 (66.97%)   C. hold
*Caroline Dinenage, C.   30,647
Alan Durrant, Lab.   13,436
Bruce Tennent, LD   2,328
Chloe Palmer, UKIP   1,790
Monica Cassidy, Green   1,024
Jeffrey Roberts, Ind.   256
C. majority 17,211 (34.78%)
3.00% swing C. to Lab.
(2015: C. majority 17,098 (35.87%))

GRANTHAM & STAMFORD
E. 81,762 T. 56,593 (69.22%)   C. hold
*Nick Boles, C.   35,090
Barrie Fairbairn, Lab.   14,996
Anita Day, LD   3,120
Marietta King, UKIP   1,745
Tariq Mahmood, Ind.   860
Becca Thackray, Green   782
C. majority 20,094 (35.51%)
0.23% swing C. to Lab.
(2015: C. majority 18,989 (35.33%))

GRAVESHAM
E. 72,948 T. 48,997 (67.17%)   C. hold
*Adam Holloway, C.   27,237
Mandy Garford, Lab.   17,890
Emmanuel Feyisetan, UKIP   1,742
James Willis, LD   1,210
Marna Gilligan, Green   723
Michael Rogan, Ind.   195
C. majority 9,347 (19.08%)
1.18% swing Lab. to C.
(2015: C. majority 8,370 (16.71%))

GREAT GRIMSBY
E. 61,743   T. 35,521 (57.53%)   Lab. hold
*Melanie Onn, Lab.   17,545
Jo Gideon, C.   14,980
Mike Hookem, UKIP   1,648
Steve Beasant, LD   954
Christina McGilligan-Fell,   394
Ind.
Lab. majority 2,565 (7.22%)
3.12% swing Lab. to C.
(2015: Lab. majority 4,540 (13.46%))

GREAT YARMOUTH
E. 71,408   T. 44,146 (61.82%)   C. hold
*Brandon Lewis, C.   23,901
Mike Smith-Clare, Lab.   15,928
Catherine Blaiklock, UKIP   2,767
James Joyce, LD   987
Harry Webb, Green   563
C. majority 7,973 (18.06%)
2.11% swing Lab. to C.
(2015: C. majority 6,154 (13.84%))

GREENWICH & WOOLWICH
E. 77,190   T. 53,106 (68.80%)   Lab. hold
*Matthew Pennycook, Lab.   34,215
Caroline Attfield, C.   13,501
Chris Adams, LD   3,785
Daniel Garrun, Green   1,605
Lab. majority 20,714 (39.01%)
6.72% swing C. to Lab.
(2015: Lab. majority 11,946 (25.57%))

GUILDFORD
E. 75,454   T. 55,509 (73.57%)   C. hold
*Anne Milton, C.   30,295
Zoe Franklin, LD   13,255
Howard Smith, Lab.   10,545
Mark Bray-Parry, Green   1,152
John Morris, Peace   205
Semi Essessi, ND   57
C. majority 17,040 (30.70%)
5.44% swing C. to LD
(2015: C. majority 22,448 (41.58%))

HACKNEY NORTH & STOKE NEWINGTON
E. 83,955   T. 56,298 (67.06%)   Lab. hold
*Diane Abbott, Lab.   42,265
Amy Gray, C.   7,126
Joe Richards, LD   3,817
Alastair Binnie-   2,606
Lubbock, Green
Jonathan Homan, AWP   222
Abraham Spielmann, Ind.   203
Coraline Corlis-   59
Khan, Friends
Lab. majority 35,139 (62.42%)
7.15% swing C. to Lab.
(2015: Lab. majority 24,008 (48.12%))

HACKNEY SOUTH & SHOREDITCH
E. 82,004   T. 55,354 (67.50%)
                          Lab. Co-op hold
*Meg Hillier, Lab. Co-op   43,974
Luke Parker, C.   6,043
Dave Raval, LD   3,168
Rebecca Johnson, Green   1,522
Vanessa Hudson, AWP   226
Russell Higgs, Ind.   143
Angel Watt, CPA   113
Jonty Leff, WRP   86
Hugo Sugg, Ind.   50
Dale Kalamazad, Ind.   29
Lab. Co-op majority 37,931 (68.52%)
8.80% swing C. to Lab.
(2015: Lab. Co-op majority 24,243
(50.92%))

HALESOWEN & ROWLEY REGIS
E. 68,856   T. 44,379 (64.45%)   C. hold
*James Morris, C.   23,012
Ian Cooper, Lab.   17,759
Stuart Henley, UKIP   2,126
Jamie Scott, LD   859
James Robertson, Green   440
Tim Weller, Ind.   183
C. majority 5,253 (11.84%)
2.40% swing Lab. to C.
(2015: C. majority 3,082 (7.03%))

HALIFAX
E. 71,224   T. 48,276 (67.78%)   Lab. hold
*Holly Lynch, Lab.   25,507
Chris Pearson, C.   20,131
Mark Weedon, UKIP   1,568
James Baker, LD   1,070
Lab. majority 5,376 (11.14%)
5.08% swing C. to Lab.
(2015: Lab. majority 428 (0.98%))

HALTEMPRICE & HOWDEN
E. 71,520   T. 51,440 (71.92%)   C. hold
*David Davis, C.   31,355
Hollie Devanney, Lab.   15,950
David Nolan, LD   2,482
Diana Wallis, Yorkshire   942
Carole Needham, Green   711
C. majority 15,405 (29.95%)
1.63% swing C. to Lab.
(2015: C. majority 16,195 (33.22%))

HALTON
E. 73,457   T. 49,518 (67.41%)   Lab. hold
*Derek Twigg, Lab.   36,115
Matthew Lloyd, C.   10,710
Glyn Redican, UKIP   1,488
Ryan Bate, LD   896
Vic Turton, Ind.   309
Lab. majority 25,405 (51.30%)
3.12% swing C. to Lab.
(2015: Lab. majority 20,285 (45.05%))

HAMMERSMITH
E. 72,803   T. 52,252 (71.77%)   Lab. hold
*Andy Slaughter, Lab.   33,375
Charlie Dewhirst, C.   14,724
Joyce Onstad, LD   2,802
Alex Horn, Green   800
Jack Bovill, UKIP   507
Jagdeosingh Hauzaree, Ind.   44
Lab. majority 18,651 (35.69%)
11.05% swing C. to Lab.
(2015: Lab. majority 6,518 (13.59%))

HAMPSHIRE EAST
E. 74,148   T. 55,408 (74.73%)   C. hold
*Damian Hinds, C.   35,263
Rohit Dasgupta, Lab.   9,411
Richard Robinson, LD   8,403
Richard Knight, Green   1,760
Susan Jerrard, JACP   571
C. majority 25,852 (46.66%)
1.95% swing C. to Lab.
(2015: C. majority 25,147 (48.69%))

HAMPSHIRE NORTH EAST
E. 75,476   T. 57,627 (76.35%)   C. hold
*Ranil Jayawardena, C.   37,754
Barry Jones, Lab.   9,982
Graham Cockarill, LD   6,987
Chas Spradbery, Green   1,476
Mike Gascoigne, UKIP   1,061
Robert Blay, Ind.   367
C. majority 27,772 (48.19%)
3.94% swing C. to Lab.
(2015: C. majority 29,916 (55.40%))

HAMPSHIRE NORTH WEST
E. 81,430   T. 58,772 (72.17%)   C. hold
*Kit Malthouse, C.   36,471
Andy Fitchet, Lab.   13,792
Alex Payton, LD   5,708
Roger Clark, UKIP   1,467
Dan Hill, Green   1,334
C. majority 22,679 (38.59%)
3.09% swing C. to Lab.
(2015: C. majority 23,943 (43.38%))

HAMPSTEAD & KILBURN
E. 82,957   T. 58,407 (70.41%)   Lab. hold
*Tulip Siddiq, Lab.   34,464
Claire-Louise Leyland, C.   18,904
Kirsty Allan, LD   4,100
John Mansook, Green   742
Hugh Easterbrook, Ind.   136
Rainbow George Weiss, Ind.   61
Lab. majority 15,560 (26.64%)
12.27% swing C. to Lab.
(2015: Lab. majority 1,138 (2.11%))

HARBOROUGH
E. 78,647   T. 57,598 (73.24%)   C. hold
Neil O'Brien, C.   30,135
Andy Thomas, Lab.   17,706
Zuffar Haq, LD   7,286
Teck Khong, UKIP   1,361
Darren Woodiwiss, Green   1,110
C. majority 12,429 (21.58%)
7.92% swing C. to Lab.
(2015: C. majority 19,632 (37.41%))

HARLOW
E. 67,697   T. 44,846 (66.25%)   C. hold
*Robert Halfon, C.   24,230
Phil Waite, Lab.   17,199
Mark Gough, UKIP   1,787
Geoffrey Seeff, LD   970
Hannah Clare, Green   660
C. majority 7,031 (15.68%)
1.60% swing C. to Lab.
(2015: C. majority 8,350 (18.87%))

HARROGATE & KNARESBOROUGH
E. 77,265   T. 56,740 (73.44%)   C. hold
*Andrew Jones, C.   31,477
Helen Flynn, LD   13,309
Mark Sewards, Lab.   11,395
Donald Fraser, Ind.   559
C. majority 18,168 (32.02%)
0.67% swing LD to C.
(2015: C. majority 16,371 (30.67%))

HARROW EAST
E. 71,757   T. 50,845 (70.86%)   C. hold
*Bob Blackman, C.   25,129
Navin Shah, Lab.   23,372
Adam Bernard, LD   1,573
Emma Wallace, Green   771
C. majority 1,757 (3.46%)
3.13% swing C. to Lab.
(2015: C. majority 4,757 (9.71%))

HARROW WEST
E. 69,798   T. 50,355 (72.14%)
                              Lab. Co-op hold
*Gareth Thomas, Lab. Co-op   30,640
Hannah David, C.   17,326
Christopher Noyce, LD   1,267
Rowan Langley, Green   652
Rathy Alagaratnam, UKIP   470
Lab. Co-op majority 13,314 (26.44%)
10.85% swing C. to Lab.
(2015: Lab. Co-op majority 2,208
(4.74%))

HARTLEPOOL
E. 70,718   T. 41,835 (59.16%)   Lab. hold
Mike Hill, Lab.   21,969
Carl Jackson, C.   14,319
Phillip Broughton, UKIP   4,801
Andy Hagon, LD   746
Lab. majority 7,650 (18.29%)
1.77% swing C. to Lab.
(2015: Lab. majority 3,024 (7.66%))

HARWICH & ESSEX NORTH
E. 71,294   T. 51,141 (71.73%)   C. hold
*Bernard Jenkin, C.   29,921
Rosalind Scott, Lab.   15,565
Dominic Graham, LD   2,787
Aaron Hammond, UKIP   1,685
Blake Roberts, Green   1,042
Stephen Todd, CPA   141
C. majority 14,356 (28.07%)
1.63% swing C. to Lab.
(2015: C. majority 15,174 (31.33%))

HASTINGS & RYE
E. 78,298   T. 54,766 (69.95%)   C. hold
*Amber Rudd, C.   25,668
Peter Chowney, Lab.   25,322
Nicholas Perry, LD   1,885
Michael Phillips, UKIP   1,479
Nicholas Wilson, Ind.   412
C. majority 346 (0.63%)
4.39% swing C. to Lab.
(2015: C. majority 4,796 (9.42%))

HAVANT
E. 72,464   T. 46,314 (63.91%)   C. hold
*Alan Mak, C.   27,676
Graham Giles, Lab.   11,720
Paul Gray, LD   2,801
John Perry, UKIP   2,011
Tim Dawes, Green   1,122
Ann Buckley, Ind.   984
C. majority 15,956 (34.45%)
0.63% swing C. to Lab.
(2015: C. majority 13,920 (31.05%))

HAYES & HARLINGTON
E. 73,268   T. 47,802 (65.24%)   Lab. hold
*John McDonnell, Lab.   31,796
Greg Smith, C.   13,681
Cliff Dixon, UKIP   1,153
Bill Newton Dunn, LD   601
John Bowman, Green   571
Lab. majority 18,115 (37.90%)
1.53% swing C. to Lab.
(2015: Lab. majority 15,700 (34.85%))

HAZEL GROVE
E. 62,684   T. 44,132 (70.40%)   C. hold
*William Wragg, C.   20,047
Lisa Smart, LD   14,533
Nav Mishra, Lab.   9,036
Robbie Lee, Green   516
C. majority 5,514 (12.49%)
1.33% swing C. to LD
(2015: C. majority 6,552 (15.16%))

HEMEL HEMPSTEAD
E. 75,011   T. 52,282 (69.70%)   C. hold
*Mike Penning, C.   28,735
Mandi Tattershall, Lab.   19,290
Sally Symington, LD   3,233
Sherief Hassan, Green   1,024
C. majority 9,445 (18.07%)
5.49% swing C. to Lab.
(2015: C. majority 14,420 (29.05%))

HEMSWORTH
E. 71,870   T. 45,944 (63.93%)   Lab. hold
*Jon Trickett, Lab.   25,740
Mike Jordan, C.   15,566
David Dews, UKIP   2,591
Martin Roberts, Yorkshire   1,135
Joan MacQueen, LD   912
Lab. majority 10,174 (22.14%)
3.17% swing Lab. to C.
(2015: Lab. majority 12,078 (28.48%))

HENDON
E. 76,329   T. 52,215 (68.41%)   C. hold
*Matthew Offord, C.   25,078
Mike Katz, Lab.   24,006
Alasdair Hill, LD   1,985
Carmen Legarda, Green   578
Sabriye Warsame, UKIP   568
C. majority 1,072 (2.05%)
2.73% swing C. to Lab.
(2015: C. majority 3,724 (7.50%))

HENLEY
E. 74,987   T. 57,099 (76.15%)   C. hold
*John Howell, C.   33,749
Oliver Kavanagh, Lab.   11,455
Laura Coyle, LD   8,485
Robin Bennett, Green   1,864
Tim Scott, UKIP   1,154
Patrick Gray, Radical   392
C. majority 22,294 (39.04%)
3.45% swing C. to Lab.
(2015: C. majority 25,375 (45.94%))

HEREFORD & HEREFORDSHIRE SOUTH
E. 74,088   T. 50,484 (71.02%)   C. hold
*Jesse Norman, C.   27,004
Anna Coda, Lab.   11,991
Jim Kenyon, Ind.   5,560
Lucy Hurds, LD   3,556
Diana Toynbee, Green   1,220
Gwyn Price, UKIP   1,153
C. majority 15,013 (29.74%)
5.02% swing C. to Lab.
(2015: C. majority 16,890 (35.74%))

HEREFORDSHIRE NORTH
E. 67,751   T. 50,177 (74.06%)   C. hold
*Bill Wiggin, C.   31,097
Roger Page, Lab.   9,495
Jeanie Falconer, LD   5,874
Ellie Chowns, Green   2,771
Sasha Norris, Ind.   577
Arthur Devine, Ind.   363
C. majority 21,602 (43.05%)
0.59% swing C. to Lab.
(2015: C. majority 19,996 (41.64%))

HERTFORD & STORTFORD
E. 82,429   T. 59,992 (72.78%)   C. hold
*Mark Prisk, C.   36,184
Katherine Chibah, Lab.   17,149
Mark Argent, LD   4,845
David Woollcombe, Green   1,814
C. majority 19,035 (31.73%)
3.25% swing C. to Lab.
(2015: C. majority 21,509 (38.22%))

HERTFORDSHIRE NORTH EAST
E. 75,967   T. 55,580 (73.16%)   C. hold
*Oliver Heald, C.   32,587
Doug Swanney, Lab.   15,752
Nicky Shepard, LD   4,276
Tim Lee, Green   2,965
C. majority 16,835 (30.29%)
3.10% swing C. to Lab.
(2015: C. majority 19,080 (36.49%))

HERTFORDSHIRE SOUTH WEST
E. 80,293   T. 60,653 (75.54%)   C. hold
*David Gauke, C.   35,128
Robert Wakely, Lab.   15,578
Christopher Townsend, LD   7,078
Paul De Hoest, Green   1,576
Mark Anderson, UKIP   1,293
C. majority 19,550 (32.23%)
4.19% swing C. to Lab.
(2015: C. majority 23,263 (40.62%))

HERTSMERE

E. 73,554   T. 52,253 (71.04%)   C. hold
*Oliver Dowden, C.   31,928
Fiona Smith, Lab.   14,977
Joe Jordan, LD   2,794
David Hoy, UKIP   1,564
Sophie Summerhayes, Green   990
C. majority 16,951 (32.44%)
2.21% swing C. to Lab.
(2015: C. majority 18,461 (36.85%))

HEXHAM

E. 61,012   T. 46,224 (75.76%)   C. hold
*Guy Opperman, C.   24,996
Stephen Powers, Lab.   15,760
Fiona Hall, LD   3,285
Wesley Foot, Green   1,253
Francis Miles, UKIP   930
C. majority 9,236 (19.98%)
3.89% swing C. to Lab.
(2015: C. majority 12,031 (27.76%))

HEYWOOD & MIDDLETON

E. 79,901   T. 49,865 (62.41%)   Lab. hold
*Liz McInnes, Lab.   26,578
Chris Clarkson, C.   18,961
Lee Seville, UKIP   3,239
Bill Winlow, LD   1,087
Lab. majority 7,617 (15.28%)
4.37% swing Lab. to C.
(2015: Lab. majority 5,299 (10.92%))

HIGH PEAK

E. 73,254   T. 53,853 (73.52%)   Lab. gain
Ruth George, Lab.   26,753
*Andrew Bingham, C.   24,431
Charles Lawley, LD   2,669
Lab. majority 2,322 (4.31%)
6.97% swing C. to Lab.
(2015: C. majority 4,894 (9.64%))

HITCHIN & HARPENDEN

E. 75,916   T. 58,783 (77.43%)   C. hold
Bim Afolami, C.   31,189
John Hayes, Lab.   19,158
Hugh Annand, LD   6,236
Richard Cano, Green   1,329
Ray Blake, Ind.   629
Sid Cordle, CPA   242
C. majority 12,031 (20.47%)
7.87% swing C. to Lab.
(2015: C. majority 20,055 (36.22%))

HOLBORN & ST PANCRAS

E. 88,088   T. 58,997 (66.98%)   Lab. hold
*Keir Starmer, Lab.   41,343
Tim Barnes, C.   10,834
Stephen Crosher, LD   4,020
Sian Berry, Green   1,980
Giles Game, UKIP   727
Janus Polenceus, Eng. Dem.   93
Lab. majority 30,509 (51.71%)
10.33% swing C. to Lab.
(2015: Lab. majority 17,048 (31.04%))

HORNCHURCH & UPMINSTER

E. 80,821   T. 56,107 (69.42%)   C. hold
Julia Dockerill, C.   33,750
Rocky Gill, Lab.   16,027
Lawrence Webb, UKIP   3,502
Jonathan Mitchell, LD   1,371
Peter Caton, Green   1,077
David Furness, BNP   380
C. majority 17,723 (31.59%)
1.36% swing Lab. to C.
(2015: C. majority 13,074 (23.67%))

HORNSEY & WOOD GREEN

E. 79,944   T. 62,293 (77.92%)   Lab. hold
*Catherine West, Lab.   40,738
Dawn Barnes, LD   10,000
Emma Lane, C.   9,246
Sam Hall, Green   1,181
Nimco Ali, Women   551
Ruth Price, UKIP   429
Helen Spiby-Vann, CPA   93
Anna Athow, WRP   55
Lab. majority 30,738 (49.34%)
15.10% swing LD to Lab.
(2015: Lab. majority 11,058 (19.14%))

HORSHAM

E. 82,773   T. 61,987 (74.89%)   C. hold
*Jeremy Quin, C.   36,906
Susannah Brady, Lab.   13,422
Morwen Millson, LD   7,644
Catherine Ross, Green   1,844
Roger Arthur, UKIP   1,533
James Smith, S. New   375
Jim Duggan, Peace   263
C. majority 23,484 (37.89%)
4.01% swing C. to Lab.
(2015: C. majority 24,658 (43.32%))

HOUGHTON & SUNDERLAND SOUTH

E. 68,123   T. 41,480 (60.89%)   Lab. hold
*Bridget Phillipson, Lab.   24,665
Paul Howell, C.   12,324
Michael Joyce, UKIP   2,379
Paul Edgeworth, LD   908
Richard Bradley, Green   725
Mick Watson, Ind.   479
Lab. majority 12,341 (29.75%)
3.46% swing Lab. to C.
(2015: Lab. majority 12,938 (33.61%))

HOVE

E. 74,236   T. 57,596 (77.58%)   Lab. hold
*Peter Kyle, Lab.   36,942
Kristy Adams, C.   18,185
Caroline Hynds, LD   1,311
Phelim Mac Cafferty, Green   971
Charley Sabel, Ind.   187
Lab. majority 18,757 (32.57%)
15.10% swing C. to Lab.
(2015: Lab. majority 1,236 (2.37%))

HUDDERSFIELD

E. 67,033   T. 43,834 (65.39%)
                         Lab. Co-op hold
*Barry Sheerman, Lab.   26,470
Co-op
Scott Benton, C.   14,465
Andrew Cooper, Green   1,395
Zulfiqar Ali, LD   1,155
Bikatshi Katenga, Yorkshire   274
Marteen
Thokkudubiyyapu, Ind.   75
Lab. Co-op majority 12,005 (27.39%)
4.62% swing C. to Lab.
(2015: Lab. Co-op majority 7,345 (18.15%))

HULL EAST

E. 65,959   T. 36,638 (55.55%)   Lab. hold
*Karl Turner, Lab.   21,355
Simon Burton, C.   10,959
Mark Fox, UKIP   2,573
Andrew Marchington, LD   1,258
Julia Brown, Green   493
Lab. majority 10,396 (28.37%)
3.72% swing Lab. to C.
(2015: Lab. majority 10,319 (29.36%))

HULL NORTH

E. 64,666   T. 37,102 (57.37%)   Lab. hold
*Diana Johnson, Lab.   23,625
Lia Nici-Townend, C.   9,363
Mike Ross, LD   1,869
John Kitchener, UKIP   1,601
Martin Deane, Green   644
Lab. majority 14,262 (38.44%)
0.32% swing C. to Lab.
(2015: Lab. majority 12,899 (36.50%))

HULL WEST & HESSLE

E. 60,181   T. 34,565 (57.44%)   Lab. hold
Emma Hardy, Lab.   18,342
Christine Mackay, C.   10,317
Claire Thomas, LD   2,210
Michelle Dewberry, Ind.   1,898
Gary Shores, UKIP   1,399
Mike Lammiman, Green   332
Will Taylor, Libertarian   67
Lab. majority 8,025 (23.22%)
4.25% swing Lab. to C.
(2015: Lab. majority 9,333 (29.35%))

HUNTINGDON

E. 84,320   T. 59,720 (70.83%)   C. hold
*Jonathan Djanogly, C.   32,915
Nik Johnson, Lab.   18,440
Rod Cantrill, LD   5,090
Paul Bullen, UKIP   2,180
Tom MacLennan, Green   1,095
C. majority 14,475 (24.24%)
5.23% swing C. to Lab.
(2015: C. majority 19,404 (34.70%))

HYNDBURN

E. 73,110   T. 45,202 (61.83%)   Lab. hold
*Graham Jones, Lab.   24,120
Kevin Horkin, C.   18,305
Janet Brown, UKIP   1,953
Les Jones, LD   824
Lab. majority 5,815 (12.86%)
1.30% swing C. to Lab.
(2015: Lab. majority 4,400 (10.26%))

ILFORD NORTH
E. 72,997   T. 52,941 (72.52%)   Lab. hold
*Wes Streeting, Lab.	30,589
Lee Scott, C.	20,950
Richard Clare, LD	1,034
Doris Osen, Ind.	368

Lab. majority 9,639 (18.21%)
8.50% swing C. to Lab.
(2015: Lab. majority 589 (1.20%))

ILFORD SOUTH
E. 85,358   T. 57,657 (67.55%)
                 Lab. Co-op hold
*Mike Gapes, Lab. Co-op	43,724
Chris Chapman, C.	12,077
Farid Ahmed, LD	772
Rosemary Warrington, Green	542
Tariq Saeed, UKIP	477
Kane Khan, Friends	65

Lab. Co-op majority 31,647 (54.89%)
8.40% swing C. to Lab.
(2015: Lab. Co-op majority 19,777 (38.10%))

IPSWICH
E. 74,799   T. 51,137 (68.37%)   Lab. gain
Sandy Martin, Lab.	24,224
*Ben Gummer, C.	23,393
Tony Gould, UKIP	1,372
Adrian Hyyrylainen-Trett, LD	1,187
Charlotte Armstrong, Green	840
David Tabane, Ind.	121

Lab. majority 831 (1.63%)
4.65% swing C. to Lab.
(2015: C. majority 3,733 (7.67%))

ISLE OF WIGHT
E. 110,697   T. 74,479 (67.28%)   C. hold
Bob Seely, C.	38,190
Julian Critchley, Lab.	17,121
Vix Lowthion, Green	12,915
Nick Belfitt, LD	2,740
Julie Jones-Evans, Ind.	1,592

C. majority 21,069 (28.29%)
0.20% swing Lab. to C.
(2015: C. majority 13,703 (19.49%))

ISLINGTON NORTH
E. 74,831   T. 54,928 (73.40%)   Lab. hold
*Jeremy Corbyn, Lab.	40,086
James Clark, C.	6,871
Keith Angus, LD	4,946
Caroline Russell, Green	2,229
Keith Fraser, UKIP	413
Michael Foster, ND	208
Knigel Knapp, Loony	106
Susanne Cameron-Blackie, Ind.	41
Bill Martin, SPGB	21
Andres Mendoza, Comm. Lge	7

Lab. majority 33,215 (60.47%)
8.71% swing C. to Lab.
(2015: Lab. majority 21,194 (43.05%))

ISLINGTON SOUTH & FINSBURY
E. 69,534   T. 48,049 (69.10%)   Lab. hold
*Emily Thornberry, Lab.	30,188
Jason Charalambous, C.	9,925
Alain Desmier, LD	5,809
Benali Hamdache, Green	1,198
Pete Muswell, UKIP	929

Lab. majority 20,263 (42.17%)
6.73% swing C. to Lab.
(2015: Lab. majority 12,708 (28.71%))

JARROW
E. 64,828   T. 43,023 (66.36%)   Lab. hold
*Stephen Hepburn, Lab.	28,020
Robin Gwynn, C.	10,757
James Askwith, UKIP	2,338
Peter Maughan, LD	1,163
David Herbert, Green	745

Lab. majority 17,263 (40.13%)
0.77% swing C. to Lab.
(2015: Lab. majority 13,881 (35.99%))

KEIGHLEY
E. 71,429   T. 51,724 (72.41%)
‡John Grogan, Lab.	24,066
*Kris Hopkins, C.	23,817
Paul Latham, UKIP	1,291
Matt Walker, LD	1,226
Ros Brown, Green	790
David Crabtree, Ind.	534

Lab. majority 249 (0.48%)
3.35% swing C. to Lab.
(2015: C. majority 3,053 (6.22%))

KENILWORTH & SOUTHAM
E. 66,323   T. 51,311 (77.37%)   C. hold
*Jeremy Wright, C.	31,207
Bally Singh, Lab.	13,121
Richard Dickson, LD	4,921
Rob Ballantyne, Green	1,133
Harry Cottam, UKIP	929

C. majority 18,086 (35.25%)
3.90% swing C. to Lab.
(2015: C. majority 21,002 (43.04%))

KENSINGTON
E. 60,594   T. 38,677 (63.83%)   Lab. gain
Emma Dent Coad, Lab.	16,333
*Lady (Victoria) Borwick, C.	16,313
Annabel Mullin, LD	4,724
Jennifer Nadel, Green	767
James Torrance, Ind.	393
Peter Marshall, Ind.	98
John Lloyd, Green Soc.	49

Lab. majority 20 (0.05%)
10.59% swing C. to Lab.
(2015: C. majority 7,361 (21.14%))

KETTERING
E. 71,523   T. 49,404 (69.07%)   C. hold
*Philip Hollobone, C.	28,616
Mick Scrimshaw, Lab.	18,054
Suzanna Austin, LD	1,618
Rob Reeves, Green	1,116

C. majority 10,562 (21.38%)
2.64% swing C. to Lab.
(2015: C. majority 12,590 (26.66%))

KINGSTON & SURBITON
E. 81,584   T. 62,178 (76.21%)   LD gain
†Edward Davey, LD	27,810
*James Berry, C.	23,686
Laurie South, Lab.	9,203
Graham Matthews, UKIP	675
Chris Walker, Green	536
Jason Chinnery, Loony	168
Michael Basman, Ind.	100

LD majority 4,124 (6.63%)
5.71% swing C. to LD
(2015: C. majority 2,834 (4.78%))

KINGSWOOD
E. 69,426   T. 48,741 (70.21%)   C. hold
*Chris Skidmore, C.	26,754
Mhairi Threlfall, Lab.	19,254
Karen Wilkinson, LD	1,749
Matt Furey-King, Green	984

C. majority 7,500 (15.39%)
1.66% swing C. to Lab.
(2015: C. majority 9,006 (18.71%))

KNOWSLEY
E. 81,751   T. 55,483 (67.87%)   Lab. hold
*George Howarth, Lab.	47,351
James Spencer, C.	5,137
Neil Miney, UKIP	1,285
Carl Cashman, LD	1,189
Steve Baines, Green	521

Lab. majority 42,214 (76.08%)
2.30% swing C. to Lab.
(2015: Lab. majority 34,655 (68.32%))

LANCASHIRE WEST
E. 73,258   T. 54,389 (74.24%)   Lab. hold
*Rosie Cooper, Lab.	32,030
Sam Currie, C.	20,341
Jo Barton, LD	1,069
Nate Higgins, Green	680
David Braid, WVPTFP	269

Lab. majority 11,689 (21.49%)
2.33% swing C. to Lab.
(2015: Lab. majority 8,360 (16.83%))

LANCASTER & FLEETWOOD
E. 67,171   T. 45,989 (68.47%)   Lab. hold
*Cat Smith, Lab.	25,342
Eric Ollerenshaw, C.	18,681
Robin Long, LD	1,170
Rebecca Novell, Green	796

Lab. majority 6,661 (14.48%)
5.73% swing C. to Lab.
(2015: Lab. majority 1,265 (3.03%))

LEEDS CENTRAL
E. 89,537   T. 47,673 (53.24%)   Lab. hold
*Hilary Benn, Lab.	33,453
Gareth Davies, C.	9,755
Bill Palfreman, UKIP	2,056
Ed Carlisle, Green	1,189
Andy Nash, LD	1,063
Alex Coetzee, CPA	157

Lab. majority 23,698 (49.71%)
6.02% swing C. to Lab.
(2015: Lab. majority 16,967 (37.66%))

LEEDS EAST
E. 65,950   T. 41,441 (62.84%)   Lab. hold

*Richard Burgon, Lab.	25,428
Matthew Robinson, C.	12,676
Paul Spivey, UKIP	1,742
Ed Sanderson, LD	739
Jaimes Moran, Green	434
John Otley, Yorkshire	422

Lab. majority 12,752 (30.77%)
1.02% swing Lab. to C.
(2015: Lab. majority 12,533 (32.81%))

LEEDS NORTH EAST
E. 70,112   T. 52,999 (75.59%)   Lab. hold

*Fabian Hamilton, Lab.	33,436
Ryan Stephenson, C.	16,445
Jon Hannah, LD	1,952
Ann Forsaith, Green	680
Tess Seddon, Yorkshire	303
Celia Foote, Green Soc.	116
Tim Mutamiri, CPA	67

Lab. majority 16,991 (32.06%)
8.52% swing C. to Lab.
(2015: Lab. majority 7,250 (15.01%))

LEEDS NORTH WEST
E. 68,152   T. 46,287 (67.92%)
Lab. Co-op gain

Alex Sobel, Lab. Co-op	20,416
*Greg Mulholland, LD	16,192
Alan Lamb, C.	9,097
Martin Hemingway, Green	582

Lab. Co-op majority 4,224 (9.13%)
7.92% swing LD to Lab.
(2015: LD majority 2,907 (6.70%))

LEEDS WEST
E. 67,955   T. 42,229 (62.14%)   Lab. hold

*Rachel Reeves, Lab.	27,013
Zoe Metcalfe, C.	11,048
Mark Thackray, UKIP	1,815
Andrew Pointon, Green	1,023
Alisdair McGregor, LD	905
Ed Jones, Yorkshire	378
Mike Davies, Green Soc.	47

Lab. majority 15,965 (37.81%)
4.94% swing C. to Lab.
(2015: Lab. majority 10,727 (27.92%))

LEICESTER EAST
E. 77,788   T. 52,424 (67.39%)   Lab. hold

*Keith Vaz, Lab.	35,116
Edward He, C.	12,688
Sujata Barot, Ind.	1,753
Nitesh Dave, LD	1,343
Melanie Wakley, Green	1,070
Ian Fox, Ind.	454

Lab. majority 22,428 (42.78%)
2.30% swing C. to Lab.
(2015: Lab. majority 18,352 (38.18%))

LEICESTER SOUTH
E. 75,534   T. 50,517 (66.88%)
Lab. Co-op hold

*Jon Ashworth, Lab. Co-op	37,157
Meera Sonecha, C.	10,896
Harrish Bisnauthsing, LD	1,287
Mags Lewis, Green	1,177

Lab. Co-op majority 26,261 (51.98%)
6.56% swing C. to Lab.
(2015: Lab. Co-op majority 17,845 (38.87%))

LEICESTER WEST
E. 64,834   T. 37,512 (57.86%)   Lab. hold

*Liz Kendall, Lab.	22,823
Jack Hickey, C.	11,763
Stuart Young, UKIP	1,406
Ian Bradwell, LD	792
Mel Gould, Green	607
David Bowley, Ind.	121

Lab. majority 11,060 (29.48%)
4.31% swing C. to Lab.
(2015: Lab. majority 7,203 (20.86%))

LEICESTERSHIRE NORTH WEST
E. 75,362   T. 53,541 (71.05%)   C. hold

*Andrew Bridgen, C.	31,153
Sean Sheahan, Lab.	17,867
Michael Wyatt, LD	3,420
Mia Woolley, Green	1,101

C. majority 13,286 (24.81%)
1.38% swing Lab. to C.
(2015: C. majority 11,373 (22.06%))

LEICESTERSHIRE SOUTH
E. 78,985   T. 56,689 (71.77%)   C. hold

*Alberto Costa, C.	34,795
Shabbir Aslam, Lab.	16,164
Gregory Webb, LD	2,403
Roger Helmer, UKIP	2,235
Mary Morgan, Green	1,092

C. majority 18,631 (32.87%)
0.83% swing Lab. to C.
(2015: C. majority 16,824 (31.20%))

LEIGH
E. 76,211   T. 46,874 (61.51%)
Lab. Co-op hold

Jo Platt, Lab. Co-op	26,347
James Grundy, C.	16,793
Mark Bradley, UKIP	2,783
Richard Kilpatrick, LD	951

Lab. Co-op majority 9,554 (20.38%)
5.43% swing Lab. to C.
(2015: Lab. majority 14,096 (31.24%))

LEWES
E. 70,947   T. 54,192 (76.38%)   C. hold

*Maria Caulfield, C.	26,820
Kelly-Marie Blundell, LD	21,312
Daniel Chapman, Lab.	6,060

C. majority 5,508 (10.16%)
4.01% swing LD to C.
(2015: C. majority 1,083 (2.14%))

LEWISHAM DEPTFORD
E. 78,472   T. 55,112 (70.23%)   Lab. hold

*Vicky Foxcroft, Lab.	42,461
Melanie McLean, C.	7,562
Bobby Dean, LD	2,911
John Coughlin, Green	1,640
Malcolm Martin, CPA	252
Laura McAnea, AWP	225
Jane Lawrence, Realist	61

Lab. majority 34,899 (63.32%)
8.98% swing C. to Lab.
(2015: Lab. majority 21,516 (45.37%))

LEWISHAM EAST
E. 68,126   T. 47,201 (69.28%)   Lab. hold

*Heidi Alexander, Lab.	32,072
Peter Fortune, C.	10,859
Emily Frith, LD	2,086
Storm Poorun, Green	803
Keith Forster, UKIP	798
Willow Winston, Ind.	355
Maureen Martin, CPA	228

Lab. majority 21,213 (44.94%)
5.77% swing C. to Lab.
(2015: Lab. majority 14,333 (33.39%))

LEWISHAM WEST & PENGE
E. 72,902   T. 53,196 (72.97%)   Lab. hold

Ellie Reeves, Lab.	35,411
Shaun Bailey, C.	12,249
John Russell, LD	3,317
Karen Wheller, Green	1,144
Hoong-Wai Cheah, UKIP	700
Katherine Hortense, CPA	325
Russell White, Populist	50

Lab. majority 23,162 (43.54%)
8.56% swing C. to Lab.
(2015: Lab. majority 12,714 (26.42%))

LEYTON & WANSTEAD
E. 65,285   T. 46,173 (70.73%)   Lab. hold

*John Cryer, Lab.	32,234
Laura Farris, C.	9,627
Ben Sims, LD	2,961
Ashley Gunstock, Green	1,351

Lab. majority 22,607 (48.96%)
6.15% swing C. to Lab.
(2015: Lab. majority 14,919 (36.65%))

LICHFIELD
E. 74,430   T. 53,524 (71.91%)   C. hold

*Michael Fabricant, C.	34,018
Chris Worsey, Lab.	15,437
Paul Ray, LD	2,653
Robert Pass, Green	1,416

C. majority 18,581 (34.72%)
0.31% swing C. to Lab.
(2015: C. majority 18,189 (35.34%))

LINCOLN
E. 73,111   T. 48,718 (66.64%)   Lab. gain

Karen Lee, Lab.	23,333
*Karl McCartney, C.	21,795
Nick Smith, UKIP	1,287
Caroline Kenyon, LD	1,284
Benjamin Loryman, Green	583
Phil Gray, Ind.	312
Iain Scott-Burdon, Ind.	124

Lab. majority 1,538 (3.16%)
3.12% swing C. to Lab.
(2015: C. majority 1,443 (3.08%))

LIVERPOOL RIVERSIDE
E. 76,332   T. 48,020 (62.91%)
Lab. Co-op hold

*Louise Ellman, Lab. Co-op	40,599
Pamela Hall, C.	4,652
Stephanie Pitchers, Green	1,582
Tom Sebire, LD	1,187

Lab. Co-op majority 35,947 (74.86%)
8.52% swing C. to Lab.
(2015: Lab. Co-op majority 24,463 (55.27%))

LIVERPOOL WALTON
E. 62,738   T. 42,197 (67.26%)   Lab. hold
Dan Carden, Lab.   36,175
Laura Evans, C.   3,624
Terry May, Ind.   1,237
Kris Brown, LD   638
Colm Feeley, Green   523
Lab. majority 32,551 (77.14%)
0.27% swing C. to Lab.
(2015: Lab. majority 27,777 (72.33%))

LIVERPOOL WAVERTREE
E. 62,411   T. 43,640 (69.92%)
                          Lab. Co-op hold
*Luciana Berger, Lab. Co-op   34,717
Denise Haddad, C.   5,251
Richard Kemp, LD   2,858
Ted Grant, Green   598
Adam Heatherington, ND   216
Lab. Co-op majority 29,466 (67.52%)
4.10% swing C. to Lab.
(2015: Lab. Co-op majority 24,303
(59.31%))

LIVERPOOL WEST DERBY
E. 65,164   T. 45,163 (69.31%)
                          Lab. Co-op hold
*Stephen Twigg, Lab. Co-op   37,371
Paul Richardson, C.   4,463
Steve Radford, Lib.   2,150
Paul Parr, LD   545
Will Ward, Green   329
Graham Hughes, Ind.   305
Lab. Co-op majority 32,908 (72.86%)
2.15% swing C. to Lab.
(2015: Lab. Co-op majority 27,367
(66.70%))

LOUGHBOROUGH
E. 79,607   T. 54,148 (68.02%)   C. hold
*Nicky Morgan, C.   27,022
Jewel Miah, Lab.   22,753
David Walker, LD   1,937
Andy McWilliam, UKIP   1,465
Philip Leicester, Green   971
C. majority 4,269 (7.88%)
4.88% swing C. to Lab.
(2015: C. majority 9,183 (17.65%))

LOUTH & HORNCASTLE
E. 79,006   T. 52,771 (66.79%)   C. hold
*Victoria Atkins, C.   33,733
Julie Speed, Lab.   14,092
Jonathan Noble, UKIP   2,460
Lisa Gabriel, LD   1,990
The Iconic Arty-Pole, Loony   496
C. majority 19,641 (37.22%)
2.04% swing Lab. to C.
(2015: C. majority 14,977 (29.75%))

LUDLOW
E. 68,034   T. 49,970 (73.45%)   C. hold
*Philip Dunne, C.   31,433
Julia Buckley, Lab.   12,147
Heather Kidd, LD   5,336
Hilary Wendt, Green   1,054
C. majority 19,286 (38.60%)
1.71% swing C. to Lab.
(2015: C. majority 18,929 (39.38%))

LUTON NORTH
E. 66,811   T. 46,622 (69.78%)   Lab. hold
*Kelvin Hopkins, Lab.   29,765
Caroline Kerswell, C.   15,401
Rabi Martins, LD   808
Simon Hall, Green   648
Lab. majority 14,364 (30.81%)
4.24% swing C. to Lab.
(2015: Lab. majority 9,504 (22.33%))

LUTON SOUTH
E. 67,188   T. 46,133 (68.66%)
                          Lab. Co-op hold
*Gavin Shuker, Lab. Co-op   28,804
Dean Russell, C.   14,879
Andrew Strange, LD   1,056
Ujjawal Ub, UKIP   795
Marc Scheimann, Green   439
Abid Ali, Ind.   160
Lab. Co-op majority 13,925 (30.18%)
8.33% swing C. to Lab.
(2015: Lab. Co-op majority 5,711
(13.53%))

MACCLESFIELD
E. 75,228   T. 54,307 (72.19%)   C. hold
*David Rutley, C.   28,595
Neil Puttick, Lab.   19,987
Richard Flowers, LD   3,350
James Booth, Green   1,213
Mark Johnson, Ind.   1,162
C. majority 8,608 (15.85%)
7.01% swing C. to Lab.
(2015: C. majority 14,811 (29.86%))

MAIDENHEAD
E. 76,276   T. 58,239 (76.35%)   C. hold
*Theresa May, C.   37,718
Pat McDonald, Lab.   11,261
Tony Hill, LD   6,540
Derek Wall, Green   907
Gerard Batten, UKIP   871
Andrew Knight, AWP   282
Lord Buckethead, ND   249
Grant Smith, Ind.   152
Howling 'Laud' Hope,
Loony   119
Edmonds Victor, CPA   69
Julian Reid, Just   52
Yemi Hailemariam, Ind.   16
Bobby Smith, ND   3
C. majority 26,457 (45.43%)
4.26% swing C. to Lab.
(2015: C. majority 29,059 (53.96%))

MAIDSTONE & THE WEALD
E. 75,334   T. 51,696 (68.62%)   C. hold
*Helen Grant, C.   29,136
Allen Simpson, Lab.   11,432
Emily Fermor, LD   8,455
Pamela Watts, UKIP   1,613
Stuart Jeffery, Green   888
Yolande Kenward, Ind.   172
C. majority 17,704 (34.25%)
0.35% swing C. to Lab.
(2015: C. majority 10,709 (21.41%))

MAKERFIELD
E. 74,259   T. 46,933 (63.20%)   Lab. hold
*Yvonne Fovargue, Lab.   28,245
Adam Carney, C.   14,703
Bob Brierley, Ind.   2,663
John Skipworth, LD   1,322
Lab. majority 13,542 (28.85%)
1.71% swing Lab. to C.
(2015: Lab. majority 13,155 (29.37%))

MALDON
E. 66,960   T. 50,202 (74.97%)   C. hold
*John Whittingdale, C.   34,111
Peter Edwards, Lab.   10,681
Zoe O'Connell, LD   2,181
Jesse Pryke, UKIP   1,899
Steven Betteridge, Green   1,073
Richard Perry, BNP   257
C. majority 23,430 (46.67%)
1.04% swing C. to Lab.
(2015: C. majority 22,070 (45.94%))

MANCHESTER CENTRAL
E. 90,261   T. 49,720 (55.08%)
                          Lab. Co-op hold
*Lucy Powell, Lab. Co-op   38,490
Xingan Wang, C.   7,045
John Bridges, LD   1,678
Kalvin Chapman, UKIP   1,469
Rachael Shah, Green   846
Neil Blackburn, Pirate   192
Lab. Co-op majority 31,445 (63.24%)
7.75% swing C. to Lab.
(2015: Lab. Co-op majority 21,639
(47.74%))

MANCHESTER GORTON
E. 75,362   T. 45,953 (60.98%)   Lab. hold
Afzal Khan, Lab.   35,085
Shaden Jaradat, C.   3,355
George Galloway, Ind.   2,615
Jackie Pearcey, LD   2,597
Jess Mayo, Green   1,038
Phil Eckersley, UKIP   952
Kemi Abidogun, CPA   233
David Hopkins, Ind.   51
Peter Clifford, Comm. Lge   27
Lab. majority 31,730 (69.05%)
5.82% swing C. to Lab.
(2015: Lab. majority 24,079 (57.31%))

MANCHESTER WITHINGTON
E. 74,553   T. 53,602 (71.90%)   Lab. hold
*Jeff Smith, Lab.   38,424
John Leech, LD   8,549
Sarah Heald, C.   5,530
Laura Bannister, Green   865
Sally Carr, Women   234
Lab. majority 29,875 (55.73%)
12.98% swing LD to Lab.
(2015: Lab. majority 14,873 (29.77%))

MANSFIELD
E. 77,811   T. 50,157 (64.46%)   C. gain
Ben Bradley, C.   23,392
*Sir Alan Meale, Lab.   22,335
Sid Pepper, UKIP   2,654
Philip Shields, Ind.   1,079
Anita Prabhakar, LD   697
C. majority 1,057 (2.11%)
6.68% swing Lab. to C.
(2015: Lab. majority 5,315 (11.26%))

MEON VALLEY
E. 74,246 T. 54,192 (72.99%) C. hold
*George Hollingbery, C.   35,624
Sheena King, Lab.   9,932
Martin Tod, LD   5,900
Paul Bailey, UKIP   1,435
Andrew Hayward, Green   1,301
C. majority 25,692 (47.41%)
1.36% swing C. to Lab.
(2015: C. majority 23,913 (46.24%))

MERIDEN
E. 81,437 T. 54,643 (67.10%) C. hold
*Caroline Spelman, C.   33,873
Tom McNeil, Lab.   14,675
Antony Rogers, LD   2,663
Leslie Kaye, UKIP   2,016
Alison Gavin, Green   1,416
C. majority 19,198 (35.13%)
0.30% swing C. to Lab.
(2015: C. majority 18,795 (35.73%))

MIDDLESBROUGH
E. 61,114 T. 35,637 (58.31%) Lab. hold
*Andy McDonald, Lab.   23,404
Jacob Young, C.   9,531
David Hodgson, UKIP   1,452
Terry Lawton, Ind.   632
Dawud Islam, LD   368
Carl Martinez, Green   250
Lab. majority 13,873 (38.93%)
0.71% swing Lab. to C.
(2015: Lab. majority 12,477 (38.15%))

MIDDLESBROUGH SOUTH & CLEVELAND EAST
E. 72,336 T. 47,620 (65.83%) C. gain
Simon Clarke, C.   23,643
Tracy Harvey, Lab.   22,623
Chris Foote-Wood, LD   1,354
C. majority 1,020 (2.14%)
3.55% swing Lab. to C.
(2015: Lab. majority 2,268 (4.97%))

MILTON KEYNES NORTH
E. 89,272 T. 63,864 (71.54%) C. hold
*Mark Lancaster, C.   30,307
Charlynne Pullen, Lab.   28,392
Imogen Shepherd-
Dubey, LD   2,499
Jeff Wyatt, UKIP   1,390
Alan Francis, Green   1,107
Venetia Sams, CPA   169
C. majority 1,915 (3.00%)
6.95% swing C. to Lab.
(2015: C. majority 9,753 (16.91%))

MILTON KEYNES SOUTH
E. 92,494 T. 64,486 (69.72%) C. hold
*Iain Stewart, C.   30,652
Hannah O'Neill, Lab.   28,927
Tahir Maher, LD   1,895
Vince Peddle, UKIP   1,833
Graham Findlay, Green   1,179
C. majority 1,725 (2.67%)
6.07% swing C. to Lab.
(2015: C. majority 8,742 (14.81%))

MITCHAM & MORDEN
E. 68,705 T. 48,118 (70.04%) Lab. hold
*Siobhain McDonagh, Lab.   33,039
Alicia Kearns, C.   11,664
Claire Mathys, LD   1,494
Richard Hilton, UKIP   1,054
Laura Collins, Green   644
Des Coke, CPA   223
Lab. majority 21,375 (44.42%)
3.47% swing C. to Lab.
(2015: Lab. majority 16,922 (37.49%))

MOLE VALLEY
E. 74,545 T. 56,726 (76.10%) C. hold
*Paul Beresford, C.   35,092
Paul Kennedy, LD   10,955
Marc Green, Lab.   7,864
Jacquetta Fewster, Green   1,463
Judy Moore, UKIP   1,352
C. majority 24,137 (42.55%)
1.81% swing C. to LD
(2015: C. majority 25,453 (46.16%))

MORECAMBE & LUNESDALE
E. 66,838 T. 45,657 (68.31%) C. hold
*David Morris, C.   21,773
Vikki Singleton, Lab.   20,374
Matthew Severn, LD   1,699
Robert Gillespie, UKIP   1,333
Cait Sinclair, Green   478
C. majority 1,399 (3.06%)
3.78% swing C. to Lab.
(2015: C. majority 4,590 (10.61%))

MORLEY & OUTWOOD
E. 76,495 T. 52,357 (68.44%) C. hold
*Andrea Jenkyns, C.   26,550
Neil Dawson, Lab. Co-op   24,446
Craig Dobson, LD   1,361
C. majority 2,104 (4.02%)
1.57% swing C. to Lab.
(2015: C. majority 422 (0.87%))

NEW FOREST EAST
E. 72,602 T. 51,366 (70.75%)
*Julian Lewis, C.   32,162
Julie Renyard, Lab.   10,167
David Harrison, LD   7,786
Henry Mellor, Green   1,251
C. majority 21,995 (42.82%)
0.63% swing C. to Lab.
(2015: C. majority 19,162 (38.75%))

NEW FOREST WEST
E. 68,787 T. 49,627 (72.15%) C. hold
*Desmond Swayne, C.   33,170
Jo Graham, Lab.   9,739
Terry Scriven, LD   4,781
Janet Richards, Green   1,454
Des Hjerling, Pirate   483
C. majority 23,431 (47.21%)
0.95% swing C. to Lab.
(2015: C. majority 20,604 (43.46%))

NEWARK
E. 75,526 T. 55,042 (72.88%) C. hold
*Robert Jenrick, C.   34,493
Chantal Lee, Lab.   16,344
David Watts, LD   2,786
Xandra Arundel, UKIP   1,419
C. majority 18,149 (32.97%)
1.17% swing C. to Lab.
(2015: C. majority 18,474 (35.32%))

NEWBURY
E. 82,923 T. 60,849 (73.38%) C. hold
*Richard Benyon, C.   37,399
Judith Bunting, LD   13,019
Alex Skirvin, Lab.   8,596
Paul Field, Green   1,531
Dave Yates, AD   304
C. majority 24,380 (40.07%)
2.98% swing C. to LD
(2015: C. majority 26,368 (46.02%))

NEWCASTLE-UNDER-LYME
E. 65,540 T. 43,842 (66.89%) Lab. hold
*Paul Farrelly, Lab.   21,124
Owen Meredith, C.   21,094
Nigel Jones, LD   1,624
Lab. majority 30 (0.07%)
0.72% swing Lab. to C.
(2015: Lab. majority 650 (1.51%))

NEWCASTLE UPON TYNE CENTRAL
E. 55,571 T. 37,094 (66.75%) Lab. hold
*Chi Onwurah, Lab.   24,071
Steve Kyte, C.   9,134
Nick Cott, LD   1,812
David Muat, UKIP   1,482
Peter Thomson, Green   595
Lab. majority 14,937 (40.27%)
2.07% swing C. to Lab.
(2015: Lab. majority 12,673 (36.12%))

NEWCASTLE UPON TYNE EAST
E. 62,333 T. 41,637 (66.80%) Lab. hold
*Nick Brown, Lab.   28,127
Simon Kitchen, C.   8,866
Wendy Taylor, LD   2,574
Tony Sanderson, UKIP   1,315
Alistair Ford, Green   755
Lab. majority 19,261 (46.26%)
7.20% swing C. to Lab.
(2015: Lab. majority 12,494 (31.85%))

NEWCASTLE UPON TYNE NORTH
E. 66,312 T. 48,288 (72.82%) Lab. hold
*Catherine McKinnell, Lab.   26,729
Duncan Crute, C.   16,380
Anita Lower, LD   2,533
Timothy Marron, UKIP   1,780
Alison Whalley, Green   513
Brian Moore, North   353
Lab. majority 10,349 (21.43%)
0.59% swing Lab. to C.
(2015: Lab. majority 10,153 (22.62%))

NEWTON ABBOT
E. 71,722 T. 51,637 (72.00%) C. hold
*§Anne Marie Morris, C.   28,635
James Osben, Lab.   11,475
Marie Chadwick, LD   10,601
Kathryn Driscoll, Green   926
C. majority 17,160 (33.23%)
2.12% swing C. to Lab.
(2015: C. majority 11,288 (23.42%))

NORFOLK MID
E. 80,026 T. 55,668 (69.56%)   C. hold
*George Freeman, C.   32,828
Sarah Simpson, Lab.   16,742
Fionna Tod, LD   2,848
Tracy Knowles, UKIP   2,092
Hannah Lester, Green   1,158
C. majority 16,086 (28.90%)
2.43% swing C. to Lab.
(2015: C. majority 17,276 (33.09%))

NORFOLK NORTH
E. 69,263 T. 52,188 (75.35%)   LD hold
*Norman Lamb, LD   25,260
James Wild, C.   21,748
Stephen Burke, Lab.   5,180
LD majority 3,512 (6.73%)
0.73% swing LD to C.
(2015: LD majority 4,043 (8.18%))

NORFOLK NORTH WEST
E. 72,062 T. 48,811 (67.73%)   C. hold
*Henry Bellingham, C.   29,408
Jo Rust, Lab.   15,620
Michael Stone, UKIP   1,539
Rupert Moss-Eccardt, LD   1,393
Andrew de Whalley, Green   851
C. majority 13,788 (28.25%)
0.60% swing C. to Lab.
(2015: C. majority 13,948 (29.44%))

NORFOLK SOUTH
E. 83,056 T. 61,111 (73.58%)   C. hold
*Richard Bacon, C.   35,580
Danielle Glavin, Lab.   18,902
Christopher Brown, LD   5,074
Catherine Rowett, Green   1,555
C. majority 16,678 (27.29%)
4.29% swing C. to Lab.
(2015: C. majority 20,493 (35.88%))

NORFOLK SOUTH WEST
E. 77,874 T. 52,416 (67.31%)   C. hold
*Elizabeth Truss, C.   32,894
Peter Smith, Lab.   14,582
David Williams, UKIP   2,575
Stephen Gordon, LD   2,365
C. majority 18,312 (34.94%)
0.64% swing Lab. to C.
(2015: C. majority 13,861 (27.66%))

NORMANTON, PONTEFRACT &
CASTLEFORD
E. 81,641 T. 49,191 (60.25%)   Lab. hold
*Yvette Cooper, Lab.   29,268
Andrew Lee, C.   14,769
Lewis Thompson, UKIP   3,030
Daniel Gascoigne, Yorkshire   1,431
Clarke Roberts, LD   693
Lab. majority 14,499 (29.47%)
2.31% swing Lab. to C.
(2015: Lab. majority 15,428 (33.61%))

NORTHAMPTON NORTH
E. 58,183 T. 40,378 (69.40%)   C. hold
*Michael Ellis, C.   19,065
Sally Keeble, Lab.   18,258
Jonathan Bullock, UKIP   1,404
George Smid, LD   1,015
Steve Miller, Green   636
C. majority 807 (2.00%)
3.12% swing C. to Lab.
(2015: C. majority 3,245 (8.23%))

NORTHAMPTON SOUTH
E. 60,993 T. 41,034 (67.28%)   C. hold
Andrew Lewer, C.   19,231
Kevin McKeever, Lab.   18,072
Rose Gibbins, UKIP   1,630
Jill Hope, LD   1,405
Scott Mabbutt, Green   696
C. majority 1,159 (2.82%)
3.47% swing C. to Lab.
(2015: C. majority 3,793 (9.75%))

NORTHAMPTONSHIRE SOUTH
E. 85,756 T. 64,998 (75.79%)   C. hold
*Andrea Leadsom, C.   40,599
Sophie Johnson, Lab.   17,759
Chris Lofts, LD   3,623
Nigel Wickens, UKIP   1,363
Denise Donaldson, Green   1,357
Josh Phillips, Ind.   297
C. majority 22,840 (35.14%)
4.13% swing C. to Lab.
(2015: C. majority 26,416 (43.40%))

NORWICH NORTH
E. 66,924 T. 45,895 (68.58%)   C. hold
*Chloe Smith, C.   21,900
Chris Jones, Lab.   21,393
Hugh Lanham, LD   1,480
Adrian Holmes, Green   782
Liam Matthews, Pirate   340
C. majority 507 (1.10%)
4.57% swing C. to Lab.
(2015: C. majority 4,463 (10.24%))

NORWICH SOUTH
E. 74,182 T. 51,359 (69.23%)   Lab. hold
*Clive Lewis, Lab.   31,311
Lana Hempsall, C.   15,715
James Wright, LD   2,841
Richard Bearman, Green   1,492
Lab. majority 15,596 (30.37%)
7.29% swing C. to Lab.
(2015: Lab. majority 7,654 (15.79%))

NOTTINGHAM EAST
E. 61,762 T. 39,327 (63.68%)
                          Lab. Co-op hold
*Chris Leslie, Lab. Co-op   28,102
Simon Murray, C.   8,512
Barry Holliday, LD   1,003
Robert Hall-Palmer, UKIP   817
Kat Boettge, Green   698
David Bishop, Elvis   195
Lab. Co-op majority 19,590 (49.81%)
8.02% swing C. to Lab.
(2015: Lab. Co-op majority 11,894
(33.78%))

NOTTINGHAM NORTH
E. 66,894 T. 38,319 (57.28%)
                          Lab. Co-op hold
Alex Norris, Lab. Co-op   23,067
Jack Tinley, C.   11,907
Stephen Crosby, UKIP   2,133
Tad Jones, LD   674
Kirsty Jones, Green   538
Lab. Co-op majority 11,160 (29.12%)
2.22% swing Lab. to C.
(2015: Lab. majority 11,860 (33.56%))

NOTTINGHAM SOUTH
E. 71,178 T. 48,129 (67.62%)   Lab. hold
*Lilian Greenwood, Lab.   30,013
Jane Hunt, C.   14,851
Tony Sutton, LD   1,564
David Hollas, UKIP   1,103
Adam McGregor, Green   598
Lab. majority 15,162 (31.50%)
7.77% swing C. to Lab.
(2015: Lab. majority 6,936 (15.96%))

NUNEATON
E. 69,201 T. 46,067 (66.57%)   C. hold
*Marcus Jones, C.   23,755
Philip Johnson, Lab.   19,016
Craig Carpenter, UKIP   1,619
Richard Brighton-Knight,
LD   914
Chris Brookes, Green   763
C. majority 4,739 (10.29%)
0.19% swing C. to Lab.
(2015: C. majority 4,882 (10.67%))

OLD BEXLEY & SIDCUP
E. 66,005 T. 48,042 (72.79%)   C. hold
*James Brokenshire, C.   29,545
Danny Hackett, Lab.   14,079
Freddy Vachha, UKIP   1,619
Drew Heffernan, LD   1,572
Derek Moran, Green   820
Michael Jones, BNP   324
Chinwe
Nwadikeduruibe, CPA   83
C. majority 15,466 (32.19%)
0.81% swing C. to Lab.
(2015: C. majority 15,803 (33.80%))

OLDHAM EAST & SADDLEWORTH
E. 72,223 T. 47,037 (65.13%)   Lab. hold
*Debbie Abrahams, Lab.   25,629
Kashif Ali, C.   17,447
Ian Bond, UKIP   2,278
Jonathan Smith, LD   1,683
Lab. majority 8,182 (17.39%)
1.95% swing C. to Lab.
(2015: Lab. majority 6,002 (13.49%))

OLDHAM WEST & ROYTON
E. 72,418 T. 45,788 (63.23%)
                          Lab. Co-op hold
*Jim McMahon, Lab. Co-op   29,846
Christopher Glenny, C.   12,648
Ruth Keating, UKIP   1,899
Garth Harkness, LD   956
Adam King, Green   439
Lab. Co-op majority 17,198 (37.56%)
0.88% swing C. to Lab.
(2015: Lab. majority 14,738 (34.17%))
(2015: Lab. majority 10,722 (38.70%))

ORPINGTON
E. 67,906 T. 50,461 (74.31%)   C. hold
*Joseph Johnson, C.   31,762
Nigel de Gruchy, Lab.   12,301
Alex Feakes, LD   3,315
Brian Philp, UKIP   2,023
Tamara Galloway, Green   1,060
C. majority 19,461 (38.57%)
1.63% swing C. to Lab.
(2015: C. majority 19,979 (40.75%))

OXFORD EAST
E. 78,360   T. 53,896 (68.78%)
Lab. Co-op hold

Anneliese Dodds, Lab. Co-op	35,118
Suzanne Bartington, C.	11,834
Kirsten Johnson, LD	4,904
Larry Sanders, Green	1,785
Chaka Artwell, Ind.	255

Lab. Co-op majority 23,284 (43.20%)
6.53% swing C. to Lab.
(2015: Lab. majority 15,280 (30.14%))

OXFORD WEST & ABINGDON
E. 79,289   T. 60,020 (75.70%)   LD gain

Layla Moran, LD	26,256
*Nicola Blackwood, C.	25,440
Marie Tidball, Lab.	7,573
Alan Harris, UKIP	751

LD majority 816 (1.36%)
9.05% swing C. to LD
(2015: C. majority 9,582 (16.74%))

PENDLE
E. 64,963   T. 44,854 (69.05%)   C. hold

*Andrew Stephenson, C.	21,986
Wayne Blackburn, Lab.	20,707
Gordon Lishman, LD	941
Brian Parker, BNP	718
Ian Barnett, Green	502

C. majority 1,279 (2.85%)
4.71% swing C. to Lab.
(2015: C. majority 5,453 (12.27%))

PENISTONE & STOCKSBRIDGE
E. 71,293   T. 49,787 (69.83%)   Lab. hold

*Angela Smith, Lab.	22,807
Nicola Wilson, C.	21,485
John Booker, UKIP	3,453
Penny Baker, LD	2,042

Lab. majority 1,322 (2.66%)
5.85% swing Lab. to C.
(2015: Lab. majority 6,723 (14.35%))

PENRITH & THE BORDER
E. 65,139   T. 46,470 (71.34%)   C. hold

*Rory Stewart, C.	28,078
Lola McEvoy, Lab.	12,168
Neil Hughes, LD	3,641
Kerryanne Wilde, UKIP	1,142
Douglas Lawson, Green	1,029
Jonathan Davies, Ind.	412

C. majority 15,910 (34.24%)
5.53% swing C. to Lab.
(2015: C. majority 19,894 (45.29%))

PETERBOROUGH
E. 71,522   T. 47,738 (66.75%)   Lab. gain

Fiona Onasanya, Lab.	22,950
*Stewart Jackson, C.	22,343
Beki Sellick, LD	1,597
Fiona Radic, Green	848

Lab. majority 607 (1.27%)
2.68% swing C. to Lab.
(2015: C. majority 1,925 (4.09%))

PLYMOUTH MOOR VIEW
E. 69,342   T. 45,417 (65.50%)   C. hold

*Johnny Mercer, C.	23,567
Sue Dann, Lab.	18,548
Wendy Noble, UKIP	1,849
Graham Reed, LD	917
Joshua Pope, Green	536

C. majority 5,019 (11.05%)
4.32% swing Lab. to C.
(2015: C. majority 1,026 (2.41%))

PLYMOUTH SUTTON & DEVONPORT
E. 76,584   T. 44,621 (58.26%)
Lab. Co-op gain

Luke Pollard, Lab. Co-op	23,808
*Oliver Colvile, C.	17,806
Richard Ellison, UKIP	1,148
Henrietta Bewley, LD	1,106
Daniel Sheaff, Green	540
Danny Bamping, Ind.	213

Lab. Co-op majority 6,002 (13.45%)
7.27% swing C. to Lab.
(2015: C. majority 523 (1.09%))

POOLE
E. 73,811   T. 49,850 (67.54%)   C. hold

*Robert Syms, C.	28,888
Katie Taylor, Lab.	14,679
Mike Plummer, LD	4,433
Adrian Oliver, Green	1,299
Marty Caine, DDI	551

C. majority 14,209 (28.50%)
4.36% swing C. to Lab.
(2015: C. majority 15,789 (33.32%))

POPLAR & LIMEHOUSE
E. 87,274   T. 58,814 (67.39%)   Lab. hold

*Jim Fitzpatrick, Lab.	39,558
Christopher Wilford, C.	11,846
Elaine Bagshaw, LD	3,959
Oliur Rahman, Ind.	1,477
Bethan Lant, Green	989
Nicholas McQueen, UKIP	849
David Barker, ND	136

Lab. majority 27,712 (47.12%)
6.98% swing C. to Lab.
(2015: Lab. majority 16,924 (33.16%))

PORTSMOUTH NORTH
E. 71,374   T. 47,210 (66.14%)   C. hold

*Penny Mordaunt, C.	25,860
Rumal Khan, Lab.	15,895
Darren Sanders, LD	2,608
Mike Fitzgerald, UKIP	1,926
Ken Hawkins, Green	791
Joe Jenkins, Libertarian	130

C. majority 9,965 (21.11%)
1.05% swing C. to Lab.
(2015: C. majority 10,537 (23.21%))

PORTSMOUTH SOUTH
E. 69,785   T. 44,566 (63.86%)   Lab. gain

Stephen Morgan, Lab.	18,290
*Flick Drummond, C.	16,736
Robert Vernon-Jackson, LD	7,699
Kevan Chippindall-Higgin, UKIP	1,129
Ian McCulloch, Green	712

Lab. majority 1,554 (3.49%)
9.38% swing C. to Lab.
(2015: C. majority 5,241 (12.51%))

PRESTON
E. 57,791   T. 35,597 (61.60%)
Lab. Co-op hold

*Mark Hendrick, Lab. Co-op	24,210
Kevin Beaty, C.	8,487
Simon Platt, UKIP	1,348
Neil Darby, LD	1,204
Anne Power, Green	348

Lab. Co-op majority 15,723 (44.17%)
4.06% swing C. to Lab.
(2015: Lab. Co-op majority 12,067 (36.05%))

PUDSEY
E. 72,622   T. 53,959 (74.30%)   C. hold

*Stuart Andrew, C.	25,550
Ian McCargo, Lab. Co-op	25,219
Allen Nixon, LD	1,761
Bob Buxton, Yorkshire	1,138
Michael Wharton, Ind.	291

C. majority 331 (0.61%)
4.11% swing C. to Lab.
(2015: C. majority 4,501 (8.84%))

PUTNEY
E. 65,026   T. 46,894 (72.12%)   C. hold

*Justine Greening, C.	20,679
Neeraj Patil, Lab.	19,125
Ryan Mercer, LD	5,448
Ben Fletcher, Green	1,107
Patricia Ward, UKIP	477
Lotta Quizeen, Ind.	58

C. majority 1,554 (3.31%)
10.23% swing C. to Lab.
(2015: C. majority 10,180 (23.78%))

RAYLEIGH & WICKFORD
E. 78,556   T. 55,323 (70.42%)

*Mark Francois, C.	36,914
Mark Daniels, Lab.	13,464
Peter Smith, UKIP	2,326
Ron Tindall, LD	1,557
Paul Hill, Green	1,062

C. majority 23,450 (42.39%)
0.16% swing Lab. to C.
(2015: C. majority 17,230 (32.38%))

READING EAST
E. 75,522   T. 55,238 (73.14%)   Lab. gain

Matt Rodda, Lab.	27,093
*Rob Wilson, C.	23,344
Jenny Woods, LD	3,378
Kizzi Johannessen, Green	1,093
Michael Turberville, Ind.	188
Andy Kirkwood, Active Dem.	142

Lab. majority 3,749 (6.79%)
9.85% swing C. to Lab.
(2015: C. majority 6,520 (12.91%))

READING WEST
E. 74,518   T. 51,766 (69.47%)   C. hold

*Alok Sharma, C.	25,311
Olivia Bailey, Lab.	22,435
Meri O'Connell, LD	3,041
Jamie Whitham, Green	979

C. majority 2,876 (5.56%)
4.09% swing C. to Lab.
(2015: C. majority 6,650 (13.74%))

REDCAR
E. 66,836   T. 42,560 (63.68%)
Lab. Co-op hold
*Anna Turley, Lab. Co-op   23,623
Peter Gibson, C.   14,138
Josh Mason, LD   2,849
Chris Gallacher, UKIP   1,950
Lab. Co-op majority 9,485 (22.29%)
2.68% swing Lab. to C.
(2015: Lab. Co-op majority 10,388
(25.39%))

REDDITCH
E. 64,334   T. 45,203 (70.26%)
Rachel Maclean, C.   23,652
Rebecca Blake, Lab.   16,289
Neal Stote, NHAP   2,239
Paul Swansborough, UKIP   1,371
Susan Juned, LD   1,173
Kevin White, Green   380
Sally Woodhall, Ind.   99
C. majority 7,363 (16.29%)
0.15% swing Lab. to C.
(2015: C. majority 7,054 (16.00%))

REIGATE
E. 74,628   T. 53,823 (72.12%)   C. hold
*Crispin Blunt, C.   30,896
Toby Brampton, Lab.   13,282
Anna Tarrant, LD   5,889
Jonathan Essex, Green   2,214
Joseph Fox, UKIP   1,542
C. majority 17,614 (32.73%)
5.62% swing C. to Lab.
(2015: C. majority 22,334 (43.49%))

RIBBLE VALLEY
E. 77,968   T. 55,200 (70.80%)   C. hold
*Nigel Evans, C.   31,919
David Hinder, Lab.   18,720
Allan Knox, LD   3,247
Graham Sowter, Green   1,314
C. majority 13,199 (23.91%)
1.07% swing C. to Lab.
(2015: C. majority 13,606 (26.04%))

RICHMOND (YORKS)
E. 80,920   T. 57,013 (70.46%)   C. hold
*Rishi Sunak, C.   36,458
Dan Perry, Lab.   13,350
Tobie Abel, LD   3,360
Chris Pearson, Yorkshire   2,106
Fiona Yorke, Green   1,739
C. majority 23,108 (40.53%)
1.17% swing Lab. to C.
(2015: C. majority 19,550 (36.20%))

RICHMOND PARK
E. 80,025   T. 63,330 (79.14%)   C. gain
*Zac Goldsmith, C.   28,588
*Sarah Olney, LD   28,543
Cate Tuitt, Lab.   5,773
Peter Jewell, UKIP   426
C. majority 45 (0.07%)
19.44% swing C. to LD
(2015: C. majority 23,015 (38.94%))
(2016: LD majority 1,872 (4.53%))

ROCHDALE
E. 78,064   T. 50,044 (64.11%)   Lab. gain
‡Tony Lloyd, Lab.   29,035
Jane Howard, C.   14,216
Andy Kelly, LD   4,027
Christopher Baksa, UKIP   1,641
*Simon Danczuk, ND   883
Andy Littlewood,
GM Homeless   242
Lab. majority 14,819 (29.61%)
0.26% swing C. to Lab.
(2015: Lab. majority 12,442 (27.39%))

ROCHESTER & STROOD
E. 82,702   T. 53,769 (65.02%)   C. hold
*Kelly Tolhurst, C.   29,232
Teresa Murray, Lab.   19,382
David Allen, UKIP   2,893
Bart Ricketts, LD   1,189
Sonia Hyner, Green   781
Steve Benson, CPA   163
Primerose Chiguri, Ind.   129
C. majority 9,850 (18.32%)
2.98% swing C. to Lab.
(2015: C. majority 7,133 (13.58%))

ROCHFORD & SOUTHEND EAST
E. 73,501   T. 47,248 (64.28%)   C. hold
*James Duddridge, C.   23,013
Ashley Dalton, Lab.   17,465
Ron Woodley, Ind.   2,924
Neil Hookway, UKIP   1,777
Peter Gwizdala, LD   1,265
Simon Cross, Green   804
C. majority 5,548 (11.74%)
4.99% swing C. to Lab.
(2015: C. majority 9,476 (21.73%))

ROMFORD
E. 73,516   T. 49,944 (67.94%)   C. hold
*Andrew Rosindell, C.   29,671
Angelina
Leatherbarrow, Lab.   15,893
Andrew Beadle, UKIP   2,350
Ian Sanderson, LD   1,215
David Hughes, Green   815
C. majority 13,778 (27.59%)
1.25% swing C. to Lab.
(2015: C. majority 13,859 (28.18%))

ROMSEY & SOUTHAMPTON NORTH
E. 67,186   T. 50,168 (74.67%)   C. hold
*Caroline Nokes, C.   28,668
Catherine Royce, LD   10,662
Darren Paffey, Lab.   9,614
Ian Callaghan, Green   953
Don Jerrard, JACP   271
C. majority 18,006 (35.89%)
0.35% swing C. to LD
(2015: C. majority 17,712 (36.60%))

ROSSENDALE & DARWEN
E. 72,495   T. 50,156 (69.19%)   C. hold
*Jake Berry, C.   25,499
Alyson Barnes, Lab.   22,283
Sean Bonner, LD   1,550
John Payne, Green   824
C. majority 3,216 (6.41%)
2.56% swing C. to Lab.
(2015: C. majority 5,654 (11.53%))

ROTHER VALLEY
E. 75,230   T. 49,488 (65.78%)   Lab. hold
*Kevin Barron, Lab.   23,821
Bethan Eddy, C.   19,939
Lee Hunter, UKIP   3,704
Katie Pruszynski, LD   1,155
Paul Martin, Green   869
Lab. majority 3,882 (7.84%)
6.24% swing Lab. to C.
(2015: Lab. majority 7,297 (15.52%))

ROTHERHAM
E. 63,237   T. 37,923 (59.97%)   Lab. hold
*Sarah Champion, Lab.   21,404
James Bellis, C.   10,017
Allen Cowles, UKIP   3,316
Adam Carter, LD   1,754
Mick Bower, Yorkshire   1,432
Lab. majority 11,387 (30.03%)
5.09% swing Lab. to C.
(2015: Lab. majority 8,446 (22.33%))

RUGBY
E. 72,175   T. 51,336 (71.13%)   C. hold
*Mark Pawsey, C.   27,872
Claire Edwards, Lab.   19,660
Jerry Roodhouse, LD   2,851
Graham Bliss, Green   953
C. majority 8,212 (16.00%)
2.56% swing C. to Lab.
(2015: C. majority 10,345 (21.11%))

RUISLIP, NORTHWOOD & PINNER
E. 73,425   T. 53,382 (72.70%)   C. hold
*Nick Hurd, C.   30,555
Rebecca Lury, Lab.   16,575
Alex Cunliffe, LD   3,813
Sarah Green, Green   1,268
Richard Braine, UKIP   1,171
C. majority 13,980 (26.19%)
6.65% swing C. to Lab.
(2015: C. majority 20,224 (39.48%))

RUNNYMEDE & WEYBRIDGE
E. 74,887   T. 51,609 (68.92%)   C. hold
*Philip Hammond, C.   31,436
Fiona Dent, Lab.   13,386
John Vincent, LD   3,765
Nicholas Wood, UKIP   1,675
Lee-Anne Lawrance, Green   1,347
C. majority 18,050 (34.97%)
4.62% swing C. to Lab.
(2015: C. majority 22,134 (44.22%))

RUSHCLIFFE
E. 74,740   T. 58,311 (78.02%)   C. hold
*Kenneth Clarke, C.   30,223
David Mellen, Lab.   22,213
Jayne Phoenix, LD   2,759
George Mallender, Green   1,626
Matthew Faithfull, UKIP   1,490
C. majority 8,010 (13.74%)
5.67% swing C. to Lab.
(2015: C. majority 13,829 (25.07%))

RUTLAND & MELTON
E. 78,463 T. 57,569 (73.37%)   C. hold
*Alan Duncan, C.   36,169
Heather Peto, Lab.   13,065
Ed Reynolds, LD   4,711
John Scutter, UKIP   1,869
Alastair McQuillan, Green   1,755
C. majority 23,104 (40.13%)
0.08% swing C. to Lab.
(2015: C. majority 21,705 (39.75%))

SAFFRON WALDEN
E. 83,690 T. 60,911 (72.78%)
Kemi Badenoch, C.   37,629   C. hold
Jane Berney, Lab.   12,663
Mike Hibbs, LD   8,528
Lorna Howe, UKIP   2,091
C. majority 24,966 (40.99%)
2.21% swing C. to Lab.
(2015: C. majority 24,991 (43.42%))

ST ALBANS
E. 72,811 T. 56,998 (78.28%)   C. hold
*Anne Main, C.   24,571
Daisy Cooper, LD   18,462
Kerry Pollard, Lab.   13,137
Jack Easton, Green   828
C. majority 6,109 (10.72%)
8.71% swing C. to LD
(2015: C. majority 12,732 (23.39%))

ST AUSTELL & NEWQUAY
E. 78,618 T. 54,212 (68.96%)   C. hold
*Steve Double, C.   26,856
Kevin Neil, Lab.   15,714
Stephen Gilbert, LD   11,642
C. majority 11,142 (20.55%)
4.72% swing C. to Lab.
(2015: C. majority 8,173 (16.23%))

ST HELENS NORTH
E. 76,088 T. 50,222 (66.01%)   Lab. hold
*Conor McGinn, Lab.   32,012
Jackson Ng, C.   13,606
Peter Peers, UKIP   2,097
Tom Morrison, LD   1,287
Rachel Parkinson, Green   1,220
Lab. majority 18,406 (36.65%)
0.37% swing Lab. to C.
(2015: Lab. majority 17,291 (37.38%))

ST HELENS SOUTH & WHISTON
E. 79,036 T. 52,886 (66.91%)   Lab. hold
*Marie Rimmer, Lab.   35,879
Ed McRandal, C.   11,536
Brian Spencer, LD   2,101
Mark Hitchen, UKIP   1,953
Jess Northey, Green   1,417
Lab. majority 24,343 (46.03%)
1.07% swing C. to Lab.
(2015: Lab. majority 21,243 (43.89%))

ST IVES
E. 67,462 T. 51,226 (75.93%)   C. hold
*Derek Thomas, C.   22,120
Andrew George, LD   21,808
Christopher Drew, Lab.   7,298
C. majority 312 (0.61%)
2.25% swing C. to LD
(2015: C. majority 2,469 (5.11%))

SALFORD & ECCLES
E. 78,082 T. 47,619 (60.99%)   Lab. hold
*Rebecca Long Bailey, Lab.   31,168
Jason Sugarman, C.   12,036
Christopher Barnes, UKIP   2,320
John Reid, LD   1,286
Wendy Olsen, Green   809
Lab. majority 19,132 (40.18%)
5.59% swing C. to Lab.
(2015: Lab. majority 12,541 (28.99%))

SALISBURY
E. 72,892 T. 53,311 (73.14%)   C. hold
*John Glen, C.   30,952
Tom Corbin, Lab.   13,619
Paul Sample, LD   5,982
Dean Palethorpe, UKIP   1,191
Brig Oubridge, Green   1,152
King Arthur Pendragon, Ind.   415
C. majority 17,333 (32.51%)
3.88% swing C. to Lab.
(2015: C. majority 20,421 (40.27%))

SCARBOROUGH & WHITBY
E. 73,593 T. 50,449 (68.55%)   C. hold
*Robert Goodwill, C.   24,401
Eric Broadbent, Lab.   20,966
Sam Cross, UKIP   1,682
Robert Lockwood, LD   1,354
David Malone, Green   915
John Freeman, Ind.   680
Bill Black, Yorkshire   369
Gordon Johnson, Ind.   82
C. majority 3,435 (6.81%)
3.09% swing C. to Lab.
(2015: C. majority 6,200 (12.99%))

SCUNTHORPE
E. 61,578 T. 40,202 (65.29%)   Lab. hold
*Nic Dakin, Lab.   20,916
Holly Mumby-Croft, C.   17,485
Andy Talliss, UKIP   1,247
Ryk Downes, LD   554
Lab. majority 3,431 (8.53%)
0.03% swing C. to Lab.
(2015: Lab. majority 3,134 (8.48%))

SEDGEFIELD
E. 63,890 T. 41,591 (65.10%)   Lab. hold
*Phil Wilson, Lab.   22,202
Dehenna Davison, C.   16,143
John Grant, UKIP   1,763
Stephen Psallidas, LD   797
Melissa Wilson, Green   686
Lab. majority 6,059 (14.57%)
1.55% swing Lab. to C.
(2015: Lab. majority 6,843 (17.67%))

SEFTON CENTRAL
E. 69,019 T. 52,079 (75.46%)   Lab. hold
*Bill Esterson, Lab.   32,830
Jade Marsden, C.   17,212
Daniel Lewis, LD   1,381
Mike Carter, Green   656
Lab. majority 15,618 (29.99%)
2.91% swing C. to Lab.
(2015: Lab. majority 11,846 (24.17%))

SELBY & AINSTY
E. 75,765 T. 56,076 (74.01%)   C. hold
*Nigel Adams, C.   32,921
David Bowgett, Lab.   19,149
Callum Delhoy, LD   2,293
Tony Pycroft, UKIP   1,713
C. majority 13,772 (24.56%)
0.56% swing C. to Lab.
(2015: C. majority 13,557 (25.67%))

SEVENOAKS
E. 71,061 T. 51,218 (72.08%)   C. hold
*Michael Fallon, C.   32,644
Chris Clark, Lab.   10,727
Alan Bullion, LD   4,280
Graham Cushway, UKIP   1,894
Philip Dodd, Green   1,673
C. majority 21,917 (42.79%)
0.63% swing C. to Lab.
(2015: C. majority 19,561 (39.03%))

SHEFFIELD BRIGHTSIDE & HILLSBOROUGH
E. 70,344 T. 41,870 (59.52%)   Lab. hold
*Gill Furniss, Lab.   28,193
Michael Naughton, C.   9,050
Shane Harper, UKIP   2,645
Simon Clement-Jones, LD   1,061
Christine Gilligan Kubo, Green   737
Mike Driver, WRP   137
Muzafar Rahman, Soc. Dem.   47
Lab. majority 19,143 (45.72%)
0.07% swing C. to Lab.
(2015: Lab. majority 13,807 (34.47%))
(2016: Lab. majority 9,590 (42.47%))

SHEFFIELD CENTRAL
E. 77,560 T. 47,877 (61.73%)   Lab. hold
*Paul Blomfield, Lab.   33,963
Stephanie Roe, C.   6,215
Natalie Bennett, Green   3,848
Shaffaq Mohammed, LD   2,465
Dominic Cook, UKIP   1,060
Jack Carrington, Yorkshire   197
Robert Moran, Pirate   91
Joe Westridge, Soc. Dem.   38
Lab. majority 27,748 (57.96%)
7.03% swing C. to Lab.
(2015: Lab. majority 17,309 (39.18%))

SHEFFIELD HALLAM
E. 73,455 T. 57,020 (77.63%)   Lab. gain
Jared O'Mara, Lab.   21,881
*Nick Clegg, LD   19,756
Ian Walker, C.   13,561
John Thurley, UKIP   929
Logan Robin, Green   823
Steven Winstone, Soc. Dem.   70
Lab. majority 2,125 (3.73%)
3.98% swing LD to Lab.
(2015: LD majority 2,353 (4.24%))

SHEFFIELD HEELEY
E. 68,040 T. 44,226 (65.00%)   Lab. hold
*Louise Haigh, Lab.   26,524
Gordon Gregory, C.   12,696
Joe Otten, LD   2,022
Howard Denby, UKIP   1,977
Declan Walsh, Green   943
Jaspreet Oberoi, Soc. Dem.   64
Lab. majority 13,828 (31.27%)
0.39% swing Lab. to C.
(2015: Lab. majority 12,954 (30.81%))

SHEFFIELD SOUTH EAST
E. 68,945 T. 43,596 (63.23%) Lab. hold
*Clive Betts, Lab. 25,520
Lindsey Cawrey, C. 13,722
Dennise Dawson, UKIP 2,820
Colin Ross, LD 1,432
Ishleen Oberoi, Soc. Dem. 102
Lab. majority 11,798 (27.06%)
3.50% swing Lab. to C.
(2015: Lab. majority 12,311 (29.53%))

SHERWOOD
E. 76,196 T. 53,364 (70.04%) C. hold
*Mark Spencer, C. 27,492
Mike Pringle, Lab. 22,294
Stuart Bestwick, UKIP 1,801
Becky Thomas, LD 1,113
Morris Findley, Green 664
C. majority 5,198 (9.74%)
0.29% swing Lab. to C.
(2015: C. majority 4,647 (9.17%))

SHIPLEY
E. 73,133 T. 53,395 (73.01%) C. hold
*Philip Davies, C. 27,417
Steve Clapcote, Lab. 22,736
Caroline Jones, LD 2,202
Sophie Walker, Women 1,040
C. majority 4,681 (8.77%)
5.14% swing C. to Lab.
(2015: C. majority 9,624 (19.04%))

SHREWSBURY & ATCHAM
E. 79,043 T. 58,203 (73.63%) C. hold
*Daniel Kawczynski, C. 29,073
Laura Davies, Lab. 22,446
Hannah Fraser, LD 4,254
Edward Higginbottom, UKIP 1,363
Emma Bullard, Green 1,067
C. majority 6,627 (11.39%)
3.15% swing C. to Lab.
(2015: C. majority 9,565 (17.68%))

SHROPSHIRE NORTH
E. 80,535 T. 55,599 (69.04%) C. hold
*Owen Paterson, C. 33,642
Graeme Currie, Lab. 17,287
Tom Thornhill, LD 2,948
Duncan Kerr, Green 1,722
C. majority 16,355 (29.42%)
0.98% swing C. to Lab.
(2015: C. majority 16,494 (31.37%))

SITTINGBOURNE & SHEPPEY
E. 81,715 T. 51,389 (62.89%) C. hold
*Gordon Henderson, C. 30,911
Mike Rolfe, Lab. 15,700
Mike Baldock, Ind. 2,133
Keith Nevols, LD 1,392
Mark Lindop, Green 558
Mad Mike Young, Loony 403
Lee McCall, Ind. 292
C. majority 15,211 (29.60%)
0.14% swing C. to Lab.
(2015: C. majority 12,168 (24.64%))

SKIPTON & RIPON
E. 78,108 T. 58,138 (74.43%) C. hold
*Julian Smith, C. 36,425
Alan Woodhead, Lab. 16,440
Andy Brown, Green 3,734
Jack Render, Yorkshire 1,539
C. majority 19,985 (34.38%)
1.84% swing C. to Lab.
(2015: C. majority 20,761 (38.05%))

SLEAFORD & NORTH HYKEHAM
E. 90,925 T. 65,797 (72.36%) C. hold
*Caroline Johnson, C. 42,245
Jim Clarke, Lab. 17,008
Ross Pepper, LD 2,722
Sally Chadd, UKIP 1,954
Fiona McKenna, Green 968
Paul Coyne, Ind. 900
C. majority 25,237 (38.36%)
0.29% swing C. to Lab.
(2015: C. majority 24,115 (38.93%))
(2016: C. majority 13,144 (40.03%))

SLOUGH
E. 83,272 T. 54,295 (65.20%) Lab. hold
Tan Dhesi, Lab. 34,170
Mark Vivis, C. 17,172
Tom McCann, LD 1,308
Karen Perez, UKIP 1,228
Paul Janik, Ind. 417
Lab. majority 16,998 (31.31%)
8.06% swing C. to Lab.
(2015: Lab. majority 7,336 (15.20%))

SOLIHULL
E. 77,784 T. 56,748 (72.96%) C. hold
*Julian Knight, C. 32,985
Nigel Knowles, Lab. 12,414
Ade Adeyemo, LD 8,901
Andrew Garcarz, UKIP 1,291
Max McLoughlin, Green 1,157
C. majority 20,571 (36.25%)
1.28% swing C. to Lab.
(2015: C. majority 12,902 (23.55%))

SOMERSET NORTH
E. 80,538 T. 61,994 (76.97%) C. hold
*Liam Fox, C. 33,605
Greg Chambers, Lab. 16,502
Richard Foord, LD 5,982
Donald Davies, Ind. 3,929
Charley Pattison, Green 1,976
C. majority 17,103 (27.59%)
5.80% swing C. to Lab.
(2015: C. majority 23,099 (39.19%))

SOMERSET NORTH EAST
E. 71,350 T. 54,043 (75.74%) C. hold
*Jacob Rees-Mogg, C. 28,992
Robin Moss, Lab. 18,757
Manda Rigby, LD 4,461
Sally Calverley, Green 1,245
Shaun Hughes, Ind. 588
C. majority 10,235 (18.94%)
3.00% swing C. to Lab.
(2015: C. majority 12,749 (24.94%))

SOMERTON & FROME
E. 84,435 T. 63,592 (75.31%) C. hold
*David Warburton, C. 36,231
Mark Blackburn, LD 13,325
Sean Dromgoole, Lab. 10,998
Theo Simon, Green 2,047
Richard Hadwin, Ind. 991
C. majority 22,906 (36.02%)
1.21% swing LD to C.
(2015: C. majority 20,268 (33.61%))

SOUTH HOLLAND & THE DEEPINGS
E. 76,381 T. 50,315 (65.87%) C. hold
*John Hayes, C. 35,179
Voyteck Kowalewski, Lab. 10,282
Nicola Smith, UKIP 2,185
Julia Cambridge, LD 1,433
Daniel Wilshire, Green 894
Rick Stringer, Ind. 342
C. majority 24,897 (49.48%)
1.19% swing Lab. to C.
(2015: C. majority 18,567 (37.73%))

SOUTH RIBBLE
E. 75,752 T. 54,834 (72.39%) C. hold
*Seema Kennedy, C. 28,980
Julie Gibson, Lab. 21,559
John Wright, LD 2,073
Mark Smith, UKIP 1,387
Andrew Wight, Green 494
Mark Jarnell, NHAP 341
C. majority 7,421 (13.53%)
1.09% swing Lab. to C.
(2015: C. majority 5,945 (11.35%))

SOUTH SHIELDS
E. 63,449 T. 40,772 (64.26%) Lab. hold
*Emma Lewell-Buck, Lab. 25,078
Felicity Buchan, C. 10,570
Richard Elvin, UKIP 3,006
Shirley Ford, Green 1,437
Gita Gordon, LD 681
Lab. majority 14,508 (35.58%)
0.46% swing C. to Lab.
(2015: Lab. majority 10,614 (29.27%))

SOUTHAMPTON ITCHEN
E. 71,716 T. 46,783 (65.23%) C. hold
*Royston Smith, C. 21,773
Simon Letts, Lab. 21,742
Eleanor Bell, LD 1,421
Kim Rose, UKIP 1,122
Rosie Pearce, Green 725
C. majority 31 (0.07%)
2.56% swing C. to Lab.
(2015: C. majority 2,316 (5.18%))

SOUTHAMPTON TEST
E. 70,194 T. 46,903 (66.82%) Lab. hold
*Alan Whitehead, Lab. 27,509
Paul Holmes, C. 16,006
Thomas Gravatt, LD 1,892
Andrew Pope, Southampton 816
Keith Morrell, Ind. 680
Lab. majority 11,503 (24.53%)
7.90% swing C. to Lab.
(2015: Lab. majority 3,810 (8.73%))

SOUTHEND WEST
E. 67,677   T. 47,191 (69.73%)   C. hold
*David Amess, C.   26,046
Julian Ware-Lane, Lab.   16,046
Lucy Salek, LD   2,110
John Stansfield, UKIP   1,666
Dominic Ellis, Green   831
Tino Callaghan, Southend   305
Jason Pilley, Ind.   187
C. majority 10,000 (21.19%)
5.16% swing C. to Lab.
(2015: C. majority 14,021 (31.50%))

SOUTHPORT
E. 69,400   T. 47,956 (69.10%)   C. gain
Damien Moore, C.   18,541
Liz Savage, Lab.   15,627
Sue McGuire, LD   12,661
Terry Durrance, UKIP   1,127
C. majority 2,914 (6.08%)
7.63% swing LD to C.
(2015: LD majority 1,322 (3.00%))

SPELTHORNE
E. 72,641   T. 50,115 (68.99%)   C. hold
*Kwasi Kwarteng, C.   28,692
Rebecca Geach, Lab.   15,267
Rosamund Shimell, LD   2,755
Redvers Cunningham, UKIP   2,296
Paul Jacobs, Green   1,105
C. majority 13,425 (26.79%)
2.16% swing C. to Lab.
(2015: C. majority 14,152 (28.84%))

STAFFORD
E. 68,445   T. 51,924 (75.86%)   C. hold
*Jeremy Lefroy, C.   28,424
David Williams, Lab.   20,695
Christine Tinker, LD   1,540
Tony Pearce, Green   1,265
C. majority 7,729 (14.89%)
1.97% swing C. to Lab.
(2015: C. majority 9,177 (18.82%))

STAFFORDSHIRE MOORLANDS
E. 66,009   T. 44,655 (67.65%)   C. hold
*Karen Bradley, C.   25,963
Dave Jones, Lab.   15,133
Nicholas Sheldon, ND   1,524
Henry Jebb, LD   1,494
Mike Shone, Green   541
C. majority 10,830 (24.25%)
0.18% swing Lab. to C.
(2015: C. majority 10,174 (23.89%))

STAFFORDSHIRE SOUTH
E. 73,453   T. 51,109 (69.58%)   C. hold
*Gavin Williamson, C.   35,656
Adam Freeman, Lab.   12,923
Hilary Myers, LD   1,348
Claire McIlvenna, Green   1,182
C. majority 22,733 (44.48%)
1.70% swing Lab. to C.
(2015: C. majority 20,371 (41.07%))

STALYBRIDGE & HYDE
E. 71,409   T. 42,457 (59.46%)
                          Lab. Co-op hold
*Jonathan Reynolds,
Lab. Co-op   24,277
Tom Dowse, C.   16,193
Paul Ankers, LD   996
Julie Wood, Green   991
Lab. Co-op majority 8,084 (19.04%)
1.37% swing C. to Lab.
(2015: Lab. Co-op majority 6,686
(16.29%))

STEVENAGE
E. 70,765   T. 49,329 (69.71%)   C. hold
*Stephen McPartland, C.   24,798
Sharon Taylor, Lab. Co-op   21,414
Barbara Gibson, LD   2,032
Victoria Snelling, Green   1,085
C. majority 3,384 (6.86%)
1.75% swing C. to Lab.
(2015: C. majority 4,955 (10.37%))

STOCKPORT
E. 63,425   T. 41,544 (65.50%)   Lab. hold
*Ann Coffey, Lab.   26,282
Daniel Hamilton, C.   11,805
Daniel Hawthorne, LD   1,778
John Kelly, UKIP   1,088
Gary Lawson, Green   591
Lab. majority 14,477 (34.85%)
4.74% swing C. to Lab.
(2015: Lab. majority 10,061 (25.38%))

STOCKTON NORTH
E. 66,279   T. 42,731 (64.47%)   Lab. hold
*Alex Cunningham, Lab.   24,304
Mark Fletcher, C.   15,589
Ted Strike, UKIP   1,834
Sarah Brown, LD   646
Emma Robson, Green   358
Lab. majority 8,715 (20.40%)
0.37% swing Lab. to C.
(2015: Lab. majority 8,367 (21.14%))

STOCKTON SOUTH
E. 75,619   T. 53,824 (71.18%)   Lab. gain
Paul Williams, Lab.   26,102
*James Wharton, C.   25,214
David Outterside, UKIP   1,186
Drew Durning, LD   951
Jo Fitzgerald, Green   371
Lab. majority 888 (1.65%)
5.70% swing C. to Lab.
(2015: C. majority 5,046 (9.74%))

STOKE-ON-TRENT CENTRAL
E. 58,196   T. 33,145 (56.95%)
                          Lab. Co-op hold
*Gareth Snell, Lab. Co-op   17,083
Daniel Jellyman, C.   13,186
Mick Harold, UKIP   1,608
Peter Andras, LD   680
Adam Colclough, Green   378
Barbara Fielding, Ind.   210
Lab. Co-op majority 3,897 (11.76%)
2.51% swing Lab. to C.
(2015: Lab. majority 5,179 (16.66%))
(2017: Lab. majority 2,620 (12.38%))

STOKE-ON-TRENT NORTH
E. 72,368   T. 41,786 (57.74%)   Lab. hold
*Ruth Smeeth, Lab.   21,272
Ben Adams, C.   18,913
Richard Whelan, LD   916
Douglas Rouxel, Green   685
Lab. majority 2,359 (5.65%)
3.43% swing Lab. to C.
(2015: Lab. majority 4,836 (12.51%))

STOKE-ON-TRENT SOUTH
E. 66,046   T. 41,690 (63.12%)   C. gain
Jack Brereton, C.   20,451
*Rob Flello, Lab.   19,788
Ian Wilkes, LD   808
Jan Zablocki, Green   643
C. majority 663 (1.59%)
4.04% swing Lab. to C.
(2015: Lab. majority 2,539 (6.49%))

STONE
E. 67,824   T. 50,032 (73.77%)   C. hold
*William Cash, C.   31,614
Sam Hale, Lab. Co-op   14,119
Martin Lewis, LD   2,222
Edward Whitfield, UKIP   1,370
Samantha Pancheri, Green   707
C. majority 17,495 (34.97%)
0.21% swing Lab. to C.
(2015: C. majority 16,250 (34.55%))

STOURBRIDGE
E. 70,215   T. 47,135 (67.13%)   C. hold
*Margot James, C.   25,706
Pete Lowe, Lab.   18,052
Glen Wilson, UKIP   1,801
Christoper Bramall, LD   1,083
Andi Mohr, Green   493
C. majority 7,654 (16.24%)
0.85% swing Lab. to C.
(2015: C. majority 6,694 (14.54%))

STRATFORD-ON-AVON
E. 72,609   T. 52,532 (72.35%)   C. hold
*Nadhim Zahawi, C.   32,657
Jeff Kenner, Lab.   11,699
Elizabeth Adams, LD   6,357
Dominic Giles, Green   1,345
Jandy Spurway, Ind.   255
Tom Darwood, Ind.   219
C. majority 20,958 (39.90%)
2.40% swing C. to Lab.
(2015: C. majority 22,876 (44.45%))

STREATHAM
E. 78,532   T. 55,795 (71.05%)   Lab. hold
*Chuka Umunna, Lab.   38,212
Kim Caddy, C.   11,927
Alex Davies, LD   3,611
Nicole Griffiths, Green   1,696
Robert Stephenson, UKIP   349
Lab. majority 26,285 (47.11%)
9.60% swing C. to Lab.
(2015: Lab. majority 13,934 (27.91%))

STRETFORD & URMSTON
E. 71,840 T. 50,191 (69.86%) Lab. hold
*Kate Green, Lab.   33,519
Lisa Cooke, C.   13,814
Andrew Beaumont, UKIP   1,094
Anna Fryer, LD   1,001
Michael Ingleson, Green   641
Rose Doman, CPA   122
Lab. majority 19,705 (39.26%)
7.03% swing C. to Lab.
(2015: Lab. majority 11,685 (25.19%))

STROUD
E. 82,849 T. 63,816 (77.03%)
                              Lab. Co-op gain
†David Drew, Lab. Co-op   29,994
*Neil Carmichael, C.   29,307
Max Wilkinson, LD   2,053
Sarah Lunnon, Green   1,423
Glenville Gogerly, UKIP   1,039
Lab. Co-op majority 687 (1.08%)
4.54% swing C. to Lab.
(2015: C. majority 4,866 (8.00%))

SUFFOLK CENTRAL & IPSWICH
NORTH
E. 78,116 T. 56,524 (72.36%) C. hold
*Dan Poulter, C.   33,992
Elizabeth Hughes, Lab.   16,807
Aidan Van de Weyer, LD   2,431
Regan Scott, Green   1,659
Stephen Searle, UKIP   1,635
C. majority 17,185 (30.40%)
3.42% swing C. to Lab.
(2015: C. majority 20,144 (37.24%))

SUFFOLK COASTAL
E. 79,366 T. 58,074 (73.17%) C. hold
*Therese Coffey, C.   33,713
Cameron Matthews, Lab.   17,701
James Sandbach, LD   4,048
Eamonn O'Nolan, Green   1,802
Philip Young, Ind.   810
C. majority 16,012 (27.57%)
3.16% swing C. to Lab.
(2015: C. majority 18,842 (33.89%))

SUFFOLK SOUTH
E. 75,967 T. 54,235 (71.39%) C. hold
*James Cartlidge, C.   32,829
Emma Bishton, Lab.   15,080
Andrew
Aalders-Dunthorne, LD   3,154
Robert Lindsay, Green   1,723
Aidan Powlesland, UKIP   1,449
C. majority 17,749 (32.73%)
0.54% swing C. to Lab.
(2015: C. majority 17,545 (33.80%))

SUFFOLK WEST
E. 76,984 T. 51,746 (67.22%) C. hold
*Matt Hancock, C.   31,649
Michael Jefferys, Lab.   14,586
Julian Flood, UKIP   2,396
Elfreda Tealby-Watson, LD   2,180
Donald Allwright, Green   935
C. majority 17,063 (32.97%)
0.86% swing C. to Lab.
(2015: C. majority 14,984 (30.44%))

SUNDERLAND CENTRAL
E. 72,728 T. 45,111 (62.03%) Lab. hold
*Julie Elliott, Lab.   25,056
Robert Oliver, C.   15,059
Gary Leighton, UKIP   2,209
Niall Hodson, LD   1,777
Rachel Featherstone, Green   705
Sean Cockburn, Ind.   305
Lab. majority 9,997 (22.16%)
2.30% swing Lab. to C.
(2015: Lab. majority 11,179 (26.77%))

SURREY EAST
E. 82,004 T. 59,203 (72.20%) C. hold
*Sam Gyimah, C.   35,310
Hitesh Tailor, Lab.   11,396
David Lee, LD   6,197
Andy Parr, Ind.   2,973
Helena Windsor, UKIP   2,227
Benedict Southworth, Green   1,100
C. majority 23,914 (40.39%)
2.60% swing C. to Lab.
(2015: C. majority 22,658 (40.39%))

SURREY HEATH
E. 80,537 T. 57,822 (71.80%) C. hold
*Michael Gove, C.   37,118
Laween Atroshi, Lab.   12,175
Anne-Marie Barker, LD   6,271
Sharon Galliford, Green   2,258
C. majority 24,943 (43.14%)
2.76% swing C. to Lab.
(2015: C. majority 24,804 (45.57%))

SURREY SOUTH WEST
E. 78,042 T. 60,432 (77.44%) C. hold
*Jeremy Hunt, C.   33,683
Louise Irvine, NHAP   12,093
David Black, Lab.   7,606
Ollie Purkiss, LD   5,967
Mark Webber, UKIP   1,083
C. majority 21,590 (35.73%)
7.83% swing C. to NHAP
(2015: C. majority 28,556 (49.99%))

SUSSEX MID
E. 83,747 T. 61,632 (73.59%) C. hold
*Nicholas Soames, C.   35,082
Greg Mountain, Lab.   15,409
Sarah Osborne, LD   7,855
Chris Jerrey, Green   1,571
Toby Brothers, UKIP   1,251
Baron Von
Thunderclap, Loony   464
C. majority 19,673 (31.92%)
5.16% swing C. to Lab.
(2015: C. majority 24,286 (42.24%))

SUTTON & CHEAM
E. 70,404 T. 51,970 (73.82%) C. hold
*Paul Scully, C.   26,567
Amna Ahmad, LD   13,869
Bonnie Craven, Lab.   10,663
Claire Jackson-Prior, Green   871
C. majority 12,698 (24.43%)
8.29% swing LD to C.
(2015: C. majority 3,921 (7.86%))

SUTTON COLDFIELD
E. 75,652 T. 52,858 (69.87%) C. hold
*Andrew Mitchell, C.   32,224
Rob Pocock, Lab.   16,885
Jennifer Wilkinson, LD   2,302
David Ratcliff, Green   965
Hannah Sophia, ND   482
C. majority 15,339 (29.02%)
1.63% swing C. to Lab.
(2015: C. majority 16,417 (32.28%))

SWINDON NORTH
E. 80,194 T. 54,911 (68.47%) C. hold
*Justin Tomlinson, C.   29,431
Mark Dempsey, Lab.   21,096
Liz Webster, LD   1,962
Steve Halden, UKIP   1,564
Andy Bentley, Green   858
C. majority 8,335 (15.18%)
3.69% swing C. to Lab.
(2015: C. majority 11,786 (22.56%))

SWINDON SOUTH
E. 72,391 T. 51,271 (70.83%) C. hold
*Robert Buckland, C.   24,809
Sarah Church, Lab. Co-op   22,345
Stan Pajak, LD   2,079
Martin Costello, UKIP   1,291
Talis Kimberley-Fairbourn,
Green   747
C. majority 2,464 (4.81%)
3.47% swing C. to Lab.
(2015: C. majority 5,785 (11.74%))

TAMWORTH
E. 71,319 T. 47,110 (66.06%) C. hold
*Christopher Pincher, C.   28,748
Andrew Hammond, Lab.   16,401
Jenny Pinkett, LD   1,961
C. majority 12,347 (26.21%)
1.13% swing Lab. to C.
(2015: C. majority 11,302 (23.96%))

TATTON
E. 67,874 T. 49,116 (72.36%) C. hold
‡Esther McVey, C.   28,764
Sam Rushworth, Lab.   13,977
Gareth Wilson, LD   4,431
Nigel Hennerley, Green   1,024
Quentin Abel, Ind.   920
C. majority 14,787 (30.11%)
5.08% swing C. to Lab.
(2015: C. majority 18,241 (40.27%))

TAUNTON DEANE
E. 85,466 T. 63,053 (73.78%) C. hold
*Rebecca Pow, C.   33,333
Gideon Amos, LD   17,446
Martin Jevon, Lab.   9,689
Alan Dimmick, UKIP   1,434
Clive Martin, Green   1,151
C. majority 15,887 (25.20%)
0.78% swing C. to LD
(2015: C. majority 15,491 (26.76%))

TELFORD
E. 68,164 T. 44,686 (65.56%) C. hold
*Lucy Allan, C.   21,717
Kuldip Sahota, Lab.   21,057
Susan King, LD   954
Luke Shirley, Green   898
C. majority 720 (1.61%)
0.09% swing C. to Lab.
(2015: C. majority 730 (1.80%))

TEWKESBURY
E. 81,442 T. 59,084 (72.55%) C. hold
*Laurence Robertson, C. 35,448
Manjinder Kang, Lab. 12,874
Cait Clucas, LD 7,981
Cate Cody, Green 1,576
Simon Collins, UKIP 1,205
C. majority 22,574 (38.21%)
0.75% swing C. to Lab.
(2015: C. majority 21,972 (39.70%))

THANET NORTH
E. 72,657 T. 48,325 (66.51%) C. hold
*Roger Gale, C. 27,163
Frances Rehal, Lab. 16,425
Clive Egan, UKIP 2,198
Martyn Pennington, LD 1,586
Ed Targett, Green 825
Iris White, CPA 128
C. majority 10,738 (22.22%)
4.44% swing C. to Lab.
(2015: C. majority 10,948 (23.27%))

THANET SOUTH
E. 72,342 T. 49,753 (68.77%) C. hold
*Craig Mackinlay, C. 25,262
Raushan Ara, Lab. 18,875
Stuart Piper, UKIP 2,997
Jordan Williams, LD 1,514
Trevor Roper, Green 809
Tim Garbutt, Ind. 181
Faith Fisher, CPA 115
C. majority 6,387 (12.84%)
0.77% swing C. to Lab.
(2015: C. majority 2,812 (5.69%))

THIRSK & MALTON
E. 78,670 T. 55,929 (71.09%) C. hold
*Kevin Hollinrake, C. 33,572
Alan Avery, Lab. 14,571
Dinah Keal, LD 3,859
Toby Horton, UKIP 1,532
Martin Brampton, Green 1,100
John Clark, Lib. 753
Philip Tate, Ind. 542
C. majority 19,001 (33.97%)
1.59% swing C. to Lab.
(2015: C. majority 19,456 (37.15%))

THORNBURY & YATE
E. 67,927 T. 50,690 (74.62%) C. hold
*Luke Hall, C. 28,008
Claire Young, LD 15,937
Brian Mead, Lab. 6,112
Iain Hamilton, Green 633
C. majority 12,071 (23.81%)
10.37% swing LD to C.
(2015: C. majority 1,495 (3.08%))

THURROCK
E. 78,153 T. 50,325 (64.39%) C. hold
*Jackie Doyle-Price, C. 19,880
John Kent, Lab. 19,535
Tim Aker, UKIP 10,112
Kevin McNamara, LD 798
C. majority 345 (0.69%)
0.20% swing C. to Lab.
(2015: C. majority 536 (1.08%))

TIVERTON & HONITON
E. 80,731 T. 57,815 (71.61%) C. hold
*Neil Parish, C. 35,471
Caroline Kolek, Lab. 15,670
Matthew Wilson, LD 4,639
Gill Westcott, Green 2,035
C. majority 19,801 (34.25%)
3.52% swing C. to Lab.
(2015: C. majority 20,173 (37.52%))

TONBRIDGE & MALLING
E. 77,234 T. 56,907 (73.68%) C. hold
*Tom Tugendhat, C. 36,218
Dylan Jones, Lab. 12,710
Keith Miller, LD 3,787
April Clark, Green 2,335
Colin Bullen, UKIP 1,857
C. majority 23,508 (41.31%)
1.97% swing C. to Lab.
(2015: C. majority 23,734 (44.22%))

TOOTING
E. 77,960 T. 58,171 (74.62%) Lab. hold
*Rosena Allin-Khan, Lab. 34,694
Dan Watkins, C. 19,236
Alexander Glassbrook, LD 3,057
Esther Obiri-Darko, Green 845
Ryan Coshall, UKIP 339
Lab. majority 15,458 (26.57%)
10.63% swing C. to Lab.
(2015: Lab. majority 2,842 (5.31%))
(2016: Lab. majority 6,357 (19.87%))

TORBAY
E. 75,936 T. 51,174 (67.39%) C. hold
*Kevin Foster, C. 27,141
Deborah Brewer, LD 12,858
Paul Raybould, Lab. 9,310
Tony McIntyre, UKIP 1,213
Sam Moss, Green 652
C. majority 14,283 (27.91%)
10.54% swing LD to C.
(2015: C. majority 3,286 (6.83%))

TOTNES
E. 68,913 T. 50,270 (72.95%) C. hold
*Sarah Wollaston, C. 26,972
Gerrie Messer, Lab. 13,495
Julian Brazil, LD 6,466
Jacqi Hodgson, Green 2,097
Steven Harvey, UKIP 1,240
C. majority 13,477 (26.81%)
6.72% swing C. to Lab.
(2015: C. majority 18,285 (38.82%))

TOTTENHAM
E. 72,883 T. 49,339 (67.70%) Lab. hold
*David Lammy, Lab. 40,249
Myles Stacey, C. 5,665
Brian Haley, LD 1,687
Jarelle Francis, Green 1,276
Patricia Rumble, UKIP 462
Lab. majority 34,584 (70.09%)
7.36% swing C. to Lab.
(2015: Lab. majority 23,564 (55.37%))

TRURO & FALMOUTH
E. 74,691 T. 56,647 (75.84%) C. hold
*Sarah Newton, C. 25,123
Jayne Kirkham, Lab. 21,331
Rob Nolan, LD 8,465
Duncan Odgers, UKIP 897
Amanda Pennington, Green 831
C. majority 3,792 (6.69%)
11.07% swing C. to Lab.
(2015: C. majority 14,000 (27.16%))

TUNBRIDGE WELLS
E. 75,138 T. 54,209 (72.15%) C. hold
*Greg Clark, C. 30,856
Charles Woodgate, Lab. 14,391
Rachel Sadler, LD 5,355
Chris Hoare, UKIP 1,464
Trevor Bisdee, Green 1,441
Celine Thomas, Women 702
C. majority 16,465 (30.37%)
7.05% swing C. to Lab.
(2015: C. majority 22,874 (44.48%))

TWICKENHAM
E. 83,362 T. 66,290 (79.52%) LD gain
†Vince Cable, LD 34,969
*Tania Mathias, C. 25,207
Katherine Dunne, Lab. 6,114
LD majority 9,762 (14.73%)
8.99% swing C. to LD
(2015: C. majority 2,017 (3.25%))

TYNEMOUTH
E. 77,434 T. 56,858 (73.43%) Lab. hold
*Alan Campbell, Lab. 32,395
Nick Varley, C. 20,729
John Appleby, LD 1,724
Stuart Houghton, UKIP 1,257
Julia Erskine, Green 629
Anthony The Durham
Cobbler Jull, ND 124
Lab. majority 11,666 (20.52%)
2.56% swing C. to Lab.
(2015: Lab. majority 8,240 (15.40%))

TYNESIDE NORTH
E. 78,914 T. 51,892 (65.76%) Lab. hold
*Mary Glindon, Lab. 33,456
Henry Newman, C. 14,172
Gary Legg, UKIP 2,101
Greg Stone, LD 1,494
Martin Collins, Green 669
Lab. majority 19,284 (37.16%)
0.22% swing C. to Lab.
(2015: Lab. majority 17,194 (36.73%))

UXBRIDGE & RUISLIP SOUTH
E. 69,938 T. 46,694 (66.76%)
*Boris Johnson, C. 23,716
Vincent Lo, Lab. 18,682
Rosina Robson, LD 1,835
Elizabeth Kemp, UKIP 1,577
Mark Keir, Green 884
C. majority 5,034 (10.78%)
6.54% swing C. to Lab.
(2015: C. majority 10,695 (23.87%))

VAUXHALL
E. 81,907 T. 55,042 (67.20%) Lab. hold
*Kate Hoey, Lab.   31,576
George Turner, LD   11,326
Dolly Theis, C.   10,277
Gulnar Hasnain, Green   1,152
Harini Iyengar, Women   539
Mark Chapman, Pirate   172
Lab. majority 20,250 (36.79%)
5.04% swing Lab. to LD
(2015: Lab. majority 12,708 (26.51%))

WAKEFIELD
E. 70,340 T. 46,284 (65.80%) Lab. hold
*Mary Creagh, Lab.   22,987
Antony Calvert, C.   20,811
Lucy Brown, Yorkshire   1,176
Denis Cronin, LD   943
Waj Ali, Ind.   367
Lab. majority 2,176 (4.70%)
0.69% swing Lab. to C.
(2015: Lab. majority 2,613 (6.08%))

WALLASEY
E. 67,454 T. 48,353 (71.68%) Lab. hold
*Angela Eagle, Lab.   34,552
Andy Livsey, C.   11,232
Debbie Caplin, UKIP   1,160
Paul Childs, LD   772
Lily Clough, Green   637
Lab. majority 23,320 (48.23%)
5.27% swing C. to Lab.
(2015: Lab. majority 16,348 (37.70%))

WALSALL NORTH
E. 67,309 T. 38,118 (56.63%) C. gain
Eddie Hughes, C.   18,919
*David Winnick, Lab.   16,318
Liz Hazell, UKIP   2,295
Isabelle Parasram, LD   586
C. majority 2,601 (6.82%)
6.04% swing Lab. to C.
(2015: Lab. majority 1,937 (5.25%))

WALSALL SOUTH
E. 67,417 T. 44,072 (65.37%) Lab. hold
*Valerie Vaz, Lab.   25,286
James Bird, C.   16,394
Derek Bennett, UKIP   1,805
Anna Wellings Purvis, LD   587
Lab. majority 8,892 (20.18%)
2.91% swing C. to Lab.
(2015: Lab. majority 6,007 (14.36%))

WALTHAMSTOW
E. 68,144 T. 48,143 (70.65%)
                        Lab. Co-op hold
*Stella Creasy, Lab. Co-op   38,793
Molly Samuel, C.   6,776
Ukonu Obasi, LD   1,384
Andrew Johns, Green   1,190
Lab. Co-op majority 32,017 (66.50%)
5.50% swing C. to Lab.
(2015: Lab. Co-op majority 23,195
(55.50%))

WANSBECK
E. 62,099 T. 42,454 (68.37%) Lab. hold
*Ian Lavery, Lab.   24,338
Chris Galley, C.   13,903
Joan Tebbutt, LD   2,015
Melanie Hurst, UKIP   1,483
Steven Leyland, Green   715
Lab. majority 10,435 (24.58%)
1.83% swing Lab. to C.
(2015: Lab. majority 10,881 (28.24%))

WANTAGE
E. 87,735 T. 63,602 (72.49%) C. hold
*Edward Vaizey, C.   34,459
Rachel Eden, Lab. Co-op   17,079
Chris Carrigan, LD   9,234
Sue Ap-Roberts, Green   1,546
David McLeod, UKIP   1,284
C. majority 17,380 (27.33%)
4.98% swing C. to Lab.
(2015: C. majority 21,749 (37.29%))

WARLEY
E. 63,724 T. 40,206 (63.09%) Lab. hold
*John Spellar, Lab.   27,004
Anthony Mangnall, C.   10,521
Darryl Magher, UKIP   1,349
Bryan Manley-Green, LD   777
Mark Redding, Green   555
Lab. majority 16,483 (41.00%)
1.07% swing C. to Lab.
(2015: Lab. majority 14,702 (38.86%))

WARRINGTON NORTH
E. 72,015 T. 48,517 (67.37%) Lab. hold
*Helen Jones, Lab.   27,356
Val Allen, C.   17,774
James Ashington, UKIP   1,561
Stefan Krizanac, LD   1,207
Lyndsay McAteer, Green   619
Lab. majority 9,582 (19.75%)
0.05% swing C. to Lab.
(2015: Lab. majority 8,923 (19.65%))

WARRINGTON SOUTH
E. 85,755 T. 61,995 (72.29%) Lab. gain
Faisal Rashid, Lab.   29,994
*David Mowat, C.   27,445
Bob Barr, LD   3,339
John Boulton, Ind.   1,217
Lab. majority 2,549 (4.11%)
4.37% swing C. to Lab.
(2015: C. majority 2,750 (4.63%))

WARWICK & LEAMINGTON
E. 74,237 T. 54,055 (72.81%) Lab. gain
Matt Western, Lab.   25,227
*Chris White, C.   24,021
Nick Solman, LD   2,810
Jonathan Chilvers, Green   1,198
Bob Dhillon, UKIP   799
Lab. majority 1,206 (2.23%)
7.65% swing C. to Lab.
(2015: C. majority 6,606 (13.06%))

WARWICKSHIRE NORTH
E. 72,277 T. 47,178 (65.27%) C. hold
*Craig Tracey, C.   26,860
Julie Jackson, Lab.   18,350
James Cox, LD   1,028
Keith Kondakor, Green   940
C. majority 8,510 (18.04%)
5.88% swing Lab. to C.
(2015: C. majority 2,973 (6.28%))

WASHINGTON & SUNDERLAND
WEST
E. 67,280 T. 40,574 (60.31%) Lab. hold
*Sharon Hodgson, Lab.   24,639
Jonathan Gullis, C.   11,699
Bryan Foster, UKIP   2,761
Tom Appleby, LD   961
Michal Chantkowski, Green   514
Lab. majority 12,940 (31.89%)
2.10% swing Lab. to C.
(2015: Lab. majority 13,157 (35.31%))

WATFORD
E. 86,507 T. 58,610 (67.75%) C. hold
*Richard Harrington, C.   26,731
Chris Ostrowski, Lab.   24,639
Ian Stotesbury, LD   5,335
Ian Green, UKIP   1,184
Alex Murray, Green   721
C. majority 2,092 (3.57%)
6.94% swing C. to Lab.
(2015: C. majority 9,794 (17.44%))

WAVENEY
E. 80,784 T. 52,674 (65.20%) C. hold
*Peter Aldous, C.   28,643
Sonia Barker, Lab.   19,428
Bert Poole, UKIP   1,933
Elfrede Brambley-Crawshaw,
Green   1,332
Jacky Howe, LD   1,012
Allyson Barron, Ind.   326
C. majority 9,215 (17.49%)
6.44% swing Lab. to C.
(2015: C. majority 2,408 (4.61%))

WEALDEN
E. 81,425 T. 60,464 (74.26%) C. hold
*Nus Ghani, C.   37,027
Angela Smith, Lab.   13,399
Chris Bowers, LD   6,281
Colin Stocks, Green   1,959
Nicola Burton, UKIP   1,798
C. majority 23,628 (39.08%)
3.56% swing C. to Lab.
(2015: C. majority 22,967 (40.28%))

WEAVER VALE
E. 69,016 T. 50,613 (73.34%) Lab. gain
Mike Amesbury, Lab.   26,066
*Graham Evans, C.   22,138
Paul Roberts, LD   1,623
Christopher
Copeman, Green   786
Lab. majority 3,928 (7.76%)
4.74% swing C. to Lab.
(2015: C. majority 806 (1.72%))

WELLINGBOROUGH
E. 79,258 T. 53,240 (67.17%) C. hold
*Peter Bone, C.   30,579
Andrea Watts, Lab.   18,119
Allan Shipham, UKIP   1,804
Chris Nelson, LD   1,782
Jonathan Hornett, Green   956
C. majority 12,460 (23.40%)
4.58% swing Lab. to C.
(2015: C. majority 16,397 (32.51%))

WELLS
E. 82,449   T. 60,843 (73.79%)   C. hold
*James Heappey, C.   30,488
Tessa Munt, LD   22,906
Andy Merryfield, Lab.   7,129
Lorna Corke, CPA   320
C. majority 7,582 (12.46%)
0.43% swing C. to LD
(2015: C. majority 7,585 (13.33%))

WELWYN HATFIELD
E. 72,888   T. 51,669 (70.89%)   C. hold
*Grant Shapps, C.   26,374
Anawar Miah, Lab.   19,005
Nigel Quinton, LD   3,836
Dean Milliken, UKIP   1,441
Christianne Sayers, Green   835
Melvyn Jones, Ind.   178
C. majority 7,369 (14.26%)
4.97% swing C. to Lab.
(2015: C. majority 12,153 (24.21%))

WENTWORTH & DEARNE
E. 74,890   T. 43,947 (58.68%)   Lab. hold
*John Healey, Lab.   28,547
Steven Jackson, C.   13,744
Janice Middleton, LD   1,656
Lab. majority 14,803 (33.68%)
4.15% swing Lab. to C.
(2015: Lab. majority 13,838 (32.04%))

WEST BROMWICH EAST
E. 63,833   T. 39,098 (61.25%)   Lab. hold
*Tom Watson, Lab.   22,664
Emma Crane, C.   14,951
Karen Trench, LD   625
John Macefield, Green   533
Colin Rankine, Ind.   325
Lab. majority 7,713 (19.73%)
2.77% swing Lab. to C.
(2015: Lab. majority 9,470 (25.26%))

WEST BROMWICH WEST
E. 65,956   T. 36,094 (54.72%)
                         Lab. Co-op hold
*Adrian Bailey, Lab. Co-op   18,789
Andrew Hardie, C.   14,329
Star Anderton, UKIP   2,320
Flo Clucas, LD   333
Robert Buckman, Ind.   323
Lab. Co-op majority 4,460 (12.36%)
5.55% swing Lab. to C.
(2015: Lab. Co-op majority 7,742
(22.10%))

WEST HAM
E. 92,243   T. 60,708 (65.81%)   Lab. hold
*Lyn Brown, Lab.   46,591
Patrick Spencer, C.   9,837
Paul Reynolds, LD   1,836
Rosamund Beattie, UKIP   1,134
Michael Spracklin, Green   957
Kayode Shedowo, CPA   353
Lab. majority 36,754 (60.54%)
3.77% swing C. to Lab.
(2015: Lab. majority 27,986 (53.01%))

WESTMINSTER NORTH
E. 63,846   T. 43,295 (67.81%)   Lab. hold
*Karen Buck, Lab.   25,934
Lindsey Hall, C.   14,422
Alex Harding, LD   2,253
Emmanuelle Tandy, Green   595
Abby Dharamsey, ND   91
Lab. majority 11,512 (26.59%)
10.79% swing C. to Lab.
(2015: Lab. majority 1,977 (5.00%))

WESTMORLAND & LONSDALE
E. 66,391   T. 51,687 (77.85%)   LD hold
*Tim Farron, LD   23,686
James Airey, C.   22,909
Eli Aldridge, Lab.   4,783
Mr Fishfinger, Ind.   309
LD majority 777 (1.50%)
8.39% swing LD to C.
(2015: LD majority 8,949 (18.29%))

WESTON-SUPER-MARE
E. 82,160   T. 56,415 (68.66%)   C. hold
*John Penrose, C.   29,982
Timothy Taylor, Lab.   18,438
Mike Bell, LD   5,175
Helen Hims, UKIP   1,932
Suneil Basu, Green   888
C. majority 11,544 (20.46%)
4.62% swing C. to Lab.
(2015: C. majority 15,609 (29.70%))

WIGAN
E. 75,359   T. 47,542 (63.09%)   Lab. hold
*Lisa Nandy, Lab.   29,575
Alexander Williams, C.   13,548
Nathan Ryding, UKIP   2,750
Mark Clayton, LD   916
William Patterson, Green   753
Lab. majority 16,027 (33.71%)
1.14% swing C. to Lab.
(2015: Lab. majority 14,236 (31.43%))

WILTSHIRE NORTH
E. 71,408   T. 53,706 (75.21%)   C. hold
*James Gray, C.   32,398
Brian Mathew, LD   9,521
Peter Baldrey, Lab.   9,399
Phil Chamberlain, Green   1,141
Paddy Singh, UKIP   871
Lisa Tweedie, Ind.   376
C. majority 22,877 (42.60%)
0.48% swing LD to C.
(2015: C. majority 21,046 (41.63%))

WILTSHIRE SOUTH WEST
E. 76,898   T. 54,751 (71.20%)   C. hold
*Andrew Murrison, C.   32,841
Laura Pictor, Lab.   14,515
Trevor Carbin, LD   5,360
Christopher Walford, Green   1,445
Liam Silcocks, Ind.   590
C. majority 18,326 (33.47%)
2.87% swing C. to Lab.
(2015: C. majority 18,168 (35.18%))

WIMBLEDON
E. 66,771   T. 51,526 (77.17%)   C. hold
*Stephen Hammond, C.   23,946
Imran Uddin, Lab.   18,324
Carl Quilliam, LD   7,472
Charles Barraball, Green   1,231
Strachan McDonald, UKIP   553
C. majority 5,622 (10.91%)
7.57% swing C. to Lab.
(2015: C. majority 12,619 (26.06%))

WINCHESTER
E. 72,497   T. 57,156 (78.84%)   C. hold
*Steve Brine, C.   29,729
Jackie Porter, LD   19,730
Mark Chaloner, Lab.   6,007
Andrew Wainwright, Green   846
Martin Lyon, UKIP   695
Teresa Skelton, JACP   149
C. majority 9,999 (17.49%)
6.54% swing C. to LD
(2015: C. majority 16,914 (30.58%))

WINDSOR
E. 73,595   T. 53,921 (73.27%)   C. hold
*Adam Afriyie, C.   34,718
Peter Shearman, Lab.   12,334
Julian Tisi, LD   5,434
Fintan McKeown, Green   1,435
C. majority 22,384 (41.51%)
4.25% swing C. to Lab.
(2015: C. majority 25,083 (50.01%))

WIRRAL SOUTH
E. 57,670   T. 45,195 (78.37%)   Lab. hold
*Alison McGovern, Lab.   25,871
Adam Sykes, C.   17,548
Chris Carubia, LD   1,322
Mandi Roberts, Green   454
Lab. majority 8,323 (18.42%)
3.71% swing C. to Lab.
(2015: Lab. majority 4,599 (10.99%))

WIRRAL WEST
E. 55,995   T. 43,951 (78.49%)   Lab. hold
*Margaret Greenwood, Lab.   23,866
Tony Caldeira, C.   18,501
Peter Reisdorf, LD   1,155
John Coyne, Green   429
Lab. majority 5,365 (12.21%)
5.61% swing C. to Lab.
(2015: Lab. majority 417 (1.00%))

WITHAM
E. 69,137   T. 49,241 (71.22%)   C. hold
*Priti Patel, C.   31,670
Phil Barlow, Lab.   13,024
Jo Hayes, LD   2,715
James Abbott, Green   1,832
C. majority 18,646 (37.87%)
1.90% swing C. to Lab.
(2015: C. majority 19,554 (41.46%))

WITNEY
E. 82,727   T. 60,927 (73.65%)   C. hold
*Robert Courts, C.   33,839
Laetisia Carter, Lab.   12,598
Liz Leffman, LD   12,457
Claire Lasko, Green   1,053
Alexander Craig, UKIP   980
C. majority 21,241 (34.86%)
4.08% swing C. to Lab.
(2015: C. majority 25,155 (43.01%))
(2016: C. majority 5,702 (14.83%))

WOKING
E. 76,167 T. 55,246 (72.53%)   C. hold
*Jonathan Lord, C.   29,903
Fiona Colley, Lab.   13,179
Will Forster, LD   9,711
Troy De Leon, UKIP   1,161
James Brierley, Green   1,092
Hassan Akberali, Ind.   200
C. majority 16,724 (30.27%)
4.89% swing C. to Lab.
(2015: C. majority 20,810 (40.05%))

WOKINGHAM
E. 79,879 T. 59,690 (74.73%)   C. hold
*John Redwood, C.   33,806
Andy Croy, Lab.   15,008
Clive Jones, LD   9,512
Russell Seymour, Green   1,364
C. majority 18,798 (31.49%)
5.86% swing C. to Lab.
(2015: C. majority 24,197 (43.21%))

WOLVERHAMPTON NORTH EAST
E. 60,799 T. 36,508 (60.05%)   Lab. hold
*Emma Reynolds, Lab.   19,282
Sarah Macken, C.   14,695
Graham Eardley, UKIP   1,479
Ian Jenkins, LD   570
Clive Wood, Green   482
Lab. majority 4,587 (12.56%)
1.80% swing Lab. to C.
(2015: Lab. majority 5,495 (16.16%))

WOLVERHAMPTON SOUTH EAST
E. 69,951 T. 36,304 (51.90%)   Lab. hold
*Pat McFadden, Lab.   21,137
Kieran Mullan, C.   12,623
Barry Hodgson, UKIP   1,675
Ben Mathis, LD   448
Amy Bertaut, Green   421
Lab. majority 8,514 (23.45%)
3.78% swing Lab. to C.
(2015: Lab. majority 10,778 (31.00%))

WOLVERHAMPTON SOUTH WEST
E. 60,003 T. 42,346 (70.57%)   Lab. hold
Eleanor Smith, Lab.   20,899
Paul Uppal, C.   18,714
Rob Jones, LD   1,012
Sarah Quarmby, LD   784
Andrea Cantrill, Green   579
Jagmeet Singh, Ind.   358
Lab. majority 2,185 (5.16%)
1.58% swing Lab. to C.
(2015: Lab. majority 801 (1.99%))

WORCESTER
E. 72,815 T. 51,423 (70.62%)   C. hold
*Robin Walker, C.   24,731
Joy Squires, Lab.   22,223
Stephen Kearney, LD   1,757
Paul Hickling, UKIP   1,354
Louis Stephen, Green   1,211
Alex Rugg, Ind.   109
Mark Shuker, Compass   38
C. majority 2,508 (4.88%)
3.24% swing C. to Lab.
(2015: C. majority 5,646 (11.35%))

WORCESTERSHIRE MID
E. 76,065 T. 55,089 (72.42%)   C. hold
*Nigel Huddleston, C.   35,967
Fred Grindrod, Lab.   12,641
Margaret Rowley, LD   3,450
David Greenwood, UKIP   1,660
Fay Whitfield, Green   1,371
C. majority 23,326 (42.34%)
0.10% swing C. to Lab.
(2015: C. majority 20,532 (39.31%))

WORCESTERSHIRE WEST
E. 74,385 T. 56,471 (75.92%)   C. hold
*Harriett Baldwin, C.   34,703
Samantha Charles, Lab.   13,375
Edward McMillan-Scott, LD   5,307
Natalie McVey, Green   1,605
Mike Savage, UKIP   1,481
C. majority 21,328 (37.77%)
2.46% swing C. to Lab.
(2015: C. majority 22,578 (41.73%))

WORKINGTON
E. 60,256 T. 41,676 (69.16%)   Lab. hold
*Sue Hayman, Lab.   21,317
Clark Vasey, C.   17,392
George Kemp, UKIP   1,556
Phill Roberts, LD   1,133
Roy Ivinson, Ind.   278
Lab. majority 3,925 (9.42%)
1.38% swing Lab. to C.
(2015: Lab. majority 4,686 (12.18%))

WORSLEY & ECCLES SOUTH
E. 73,692 T. 45,642 (61.94%)   Lab. hold
*Barbara Keeley, Lab.   26,046
Iain Lindley, C.   17,667
Kate Clarkson, LD   1,087
Tom Dylan, Green   842
Lab. majority 8,379 (18.36%)
2.11% swing C. to Lab.
(2015: Lab. majority 5,946 (14.14%))

WORTHING EAST & SHOREHAM
E. 75,543 T. 53,117 (70.31%)   C. hold
*Tim Loughton, C.   25,988
Sophie Cook, Lab.   20,882
Oli Henman, LD   2,523
Mike Glennon, UKIP   1,444
Leslie Groves   1,273
Williams, Green
Carl Walker, NHAP   575
Andy Lutwyche, Ind.   432
C. majority 5,106 (9.61%)
10.17% swing C. to Lab.
(2015: C. majority 14,949 (29.96%))

WORTHING WEST
E. 77,777 T. 54,503 (70.08%)   C. hold
*Peter Bottomley, C.   30,181
Beccy Cooper, Lab.   18,091
Hazel Thorpe, LD   2,982
Mark Withers, UKIP   1,635
Benjamin Cornish, Green   1,614
C. majority 12,090 (22.18%)
6.80% swing C. to Lab.
(2015: C. majority 16,855 (33.20%))

WREKIN, THE
E. 68,642 T. 49,523 (72.15%)   C. hold
*Mark Pritchard, C.   27,451
Dylan Harrison, Lab.   17,887
Denis Allen, UKIP   1,656
Rod Keyes, LD   1,345
Pat McCarthy, Green   804
Fay Easton, Ind.   380
C. majority 9,564 (19.31%)
2.17% swing C. to Lab.
(2015: C. majority 10,743 (23.64%))

WYCOMBE
E. 77,089 T. 53,493 (69.39%)   C. hold
*Steve Baker, C.   26,766
Rafiq Raja, Lab.   20,188
Steve Guy, LD   4,147
Richard Phoenix, UKIP   1,210
Peter Sims, Green   1,182
C. majority 6,578 (12.30%)
8.29% swing C. to Lab.
(2015: C. majority 14,856 (28.88%))

WYRE & PRESTON NORTH
E. 72,319 T. 52,646 (72.80%)   C. hold
*Ben Wallace, C.   30,684
Michelle Heaton-Bentley,
Lab.   18,438
John Potter, LD   2,551
Ruth Norbury, Green   973
C. majority 12,246 (23.26%)
2.55% swing C. to Lab.
(2015: C. majority 14,151 (28.36%))

WYRE FOREST
E. 77,734 T. 51,129 (65.77%)   C. hold
*Mark Garnier, C.   29,859
Matthew Lamb, Lab.   16,525
Shazu Miah, LD   1,943
George Connolly, UKIP   1,777
Brett Caulfield, Green   1,025
C. majority 13,334 (26.08%)
0.02% swing Lab. to C.
(2015: C. majority 12,871 (26.03%))

WYTHENSHAWE & SALE EAST
E. 76,361 T. 45,846 (60.04%)   Lab. hold
*Mike Kane, Lab.   28,525
Fiona Green, C.   13,581
William Jones, LD   1,504
Mike Bayley-Sanderson,
UKIP   1,475
Dan Jerrome, Green   576
Luckson Francis
Augustine, Ind.   185
Lab. majority 14,944 (32.60%)
4.08% swing C. to Lab.
(2015: Lab. majority 10,569 (24.43%))

YEOVIL
E. 82,911 T. 59,404 (71.65%)   C. hold
*Marcus Fysh, C.   32,369
Jo Roundell Greene, LD   17,646
Ian Martin, Lab.   7,418
Robert Wood, Green   1,052
Katy Pritchard, Ind.   919
C. majority 14,723 (24.78%)
7.73% swing LD to C.
(2015: C. majority 5,313 (9.33%))

YORK CENTRAL
E. 77,315 T. 53,088 (68.66%)
Lab. Co-op hold
*Rachael Maskell, Lab. Co-op 34,594
Ed Young, C. 16,019
Nick Love, LD 2,475
Lab. Co-op majority 18,575 (34.99%)
10.45% swing C. to Lab.
(2015: Lab. Co-op majority 6,716 (14.09%))

YORK OUTER
E. 75,856 T. 57,427 (75.71%) C. hold
*Julian Sturdy, C. 29,356
Luke Charters-Reid, Lab. 21,067
James Blanchard, LD 5,910
Bethan Vincent, Green 1,094
C. majority 8,289 (14.43%)
4.96% swing C. to Lab.
(2015: C. majority 13,129 (24.36%))

YORKSHIRE EAST
E. 81,065 T. 53,956 (66.56%) C. hold
*Greg Knight, C. 31,442
Alan Clark, Lab. 16,436
Carl Minns, LD 2,134
Andrew Dennis, UKIP 1,986
Timothy Norman, Yorkshire 1,015
Michael Jackson, Green 943
C. majority 15,006 (27.81%)
1.03% swing C. to Lab.
(2015: C. majority 14,933 (29.87%))

WALES

ABERAVON
E. 49,891 T. 33,268 (66.68%) Lab. hold
*Stephen Kinnock, Lab. 22,662
Sadie Vidal, C. 5,901
Andrew Bennison, PC 2,761
Caroline Jones, UKIP 1,345
Cen Phillips, LD 599
Lab. majority 16,761 (50.38%)
6.67% swing C. to Lab.
(2015: Lab. majority 10,445 (33.13%))

ABERCONWY
E. 45,251 T. 32,150 (71.05%) C. hold
*Guto Bebb, C. 14,337
Emily Owen, Lab. 13,702
Wyn Jones, PC 3,170
Sarah Lesiter-Burgess, LD 941
C. majority 635 (1.98%)
5.64% swing C. to Lab.
(2015: C. majority 3,999 (13.26%))

ALYN & DEESIDE
E. 63,041 T. 44,760 (71.00%) Lab. hold
*Mark Tami, Lab. 23,315
Laura Knightly, C. 18,080
Jacqui Hurst, PC 1,171
David Griffiths, UKIP 1,117
Pete Williams, LD 1,077
Lab. majority 5,235 (11.70%)
1.80% swing C. to Lab.
(2015: Lab. majority 3,343 (8.09%))

ARFON
E. 41,367 T. 28,208 (68.19%) PC hold
*Hywel Williams, PC 11,519
Mary Griffiths Clarke, Lab. 11,427
Phillippa Parry, C. 4,614
Calum Davies, LD 648
PC majority 92 (0.33%)
6.67% swing PC to Lab.
(2015: PC majority 3,668 (13.67%))

BLAENAU GWENT
E. 51,227 T. 32,384 (63.22%) Lab. hold
*Nick Smith, Lab. 18,787
Nigel Copner, PC 6,880
Tracey West, C. 4,783
Dennis May, UKIP 973
Vicki Browning, Ind. 666
Cameron Sullivan, LD 295
Lab. majority 11,907 (36.77%)
6.13% swing Lab. to PC
(2015: Lab. majority 12,703 (40.09%))

BRECON & RADNORSHIRE
E. 56,010 T. 41,334 (73.80%) C. hold
*Chris Davies, C. 20,081
James Gibson-Watt, LD 12,043
Dan Lodge, Lab. 7,335
Kate Heneghan, PC 1,299
Peter Gilbert, UKIP 576
C. majority 8,038 (19.45%)
3.36% swing LD to C.
(2015: C. majority 5,102 (12.73%))

BRIDGEND
E. 62,185 T. 43,255 (69.56%) Lab. hold
*Madeleine Moon, Lab. 21,913
Karen Robson, C. 17,213
Rhys Watkins, PC 1,783
Jonathan Pratt, LD 919
Alun Williams, UKIP 781
Isabel Robson, Ind. 646
Lab. majority 4,700 (10.87%)
2.99% swing C. to Lab.
(2015: Lab. majority 1,927 (4.88%))

CAERPHILLY
E. 64,381 T. 41,297 (64.14%) Lab. hold
*Wayne David, Lab. 22,491
Jane Pratt, C. 10,413
Lindsay Whittle, PC 5,962
Liz Wilks, UKIP 1,259
Kay David, LD 725
Andrew Creak, Green 447
Lab. majority 12,078 (29.25%)
0.75% swing C. to Lab.
(2015: Lab. majority 10,073 (25.01%))

CARDIFF CENTRAL
E. 59,288 T. 40,367 (68.09%) Lab. hold
*Jo Stevens, Lab. 25,193
Gregory Stafford, C. 7,997
Eluned Parrott, LD 5,415
Mark Hooper, PC 999
Benjamin Smith, Green 420
Sarul-Islam Mohammed, UKIP 343
Lab. majority 17,196 (42.60%)
8.64% swing C. to Lab.
(2015: Lab. majority 4,981 (12.89%))

CARDIFF NORTH
E. 67,221 T. 52,022 (77.39%) Lab. gain
Anna McMorrin, Lab. 26,081
*Craig Williams, C. 21,907
Steffan Webb, PC 1,738
Matthew Hemsley, LD 1,714
Gary Oldfield, UKIP 582
Lab. majority 4,174 (8.02%)
6.10% swing C. to Lab.
(2015: C. majority 2,137 (4.18%))

CARDIFF SOUTH & PENARTH
E. 76,499 T. 50,736 (66.32%)
Lab. Co-op hold
*Stephen Doughty, Lab. Co-op 30,182
Bill Rees, C. 15,318
Ian Titherington, PC 2,162
Emma Sands, LD 1,430
Andrew Bevan, UKIP 942
Anthony Slaughter, Green 532
Jeb Hedges, Pirate 170
Lab. Co-op majority 14,864 (29.30%)
6.66% swing C. to Lab.
(2015: Lab. Co-op majority 7,453 (15.97%))

CARDIFF WEST
E. 67,221 T. 46,629 (69.37%) Lab. hold
*Kevin Brennan, Lab. 26,425
Matt Smith, C. 13,874
Michael Deem, PC 4,418
Alex Meredith, LD 1,214
Richard Lewis, UKIP 698
Lab. majority 12,551 (26.92%)
5.71% swing C. to Lab.
(2015: Lab. majority 6,789 (15.50%))

CARMARTHEN EAST & DINEFWR
E. 55,976 T. 41,029 (73.30%) PC hold
*Jonathan Edwards, PC 16,127
David Darkin, Lab. 12,219
Havard Hughes, C. 10,778
Neil Hamilton, UKIP 985
Lesley Prosser, LD 920
PC majority 3,908 (9.52%)
2.34% swing PC to Lab.
(2015: PC majority 5,599 (14.21%))

CARMARTHEN WEST & PEMBROKESHIRE SOUTH
E. 58,548 T. 42,226 (72.12%) C. hold
*Simon Hart, C. 19,771
Marc Tierney, Lab. 16,661
Abi Thomas, PC 3,933
Alistair Cameron, LD 956
Phil Edwards, UKIP 905
C. majority 3,110 (7.37%)
3.82% swing C. to Lab.
(2015: C. majority 6,054 (15.00%))

CEREDIGION
E. 52,889   T. 39,767 (75.19%)   PC gain
Ben Lake, PC   11,623
*Mark Williams, LD   11,519
Dinah Mulholland, Lab.   8,017
Ruth Davis, C.   7,307
Tom Harrison, UKIP   602
Grenville Ham, Green   542
Crazed Sir Dudley, Loony   157
PC majority 104 (0.26%)
4.23% swing LD to PC
(2015: LD majority 3,067 (8.20%))

CLWYD SOUTH
E. 54,341   T. 37,474 (68.96%)   Lab. hold
*Susan Elan Jones, Lab.   19,002
Simon Baynes, C.   14,646
Christopher Allen, PC   2,293
Jeanette Bassford-
Barton, UKIP   802
Bruce Roberts, LD   731
Lab. majority 4,356 (11.62%)
2.39% swing C. to Lab.
(2015: Lab. majority 2,402 (6.85%))

CLWYD WEST
E. 58,263   T. 40,654 (69.78%)   C. hold
*David Jones, C.   19,541
Gareth Thomas, Lab.   16,104
Dilwyn Roberts, PC   3,918
Victor Babu, LD   1,091
C. majority 3,437 (8.45%)
4.62% swing C. to Lab.
(2015: C. majority 6,730 (17.70%))

CYNON VALLEY
E. 51,332   T. 31,802 (61.95%)   Lab. hold
*Ann Clwyd, Lab.   19,404
Keith Dewhurst, C.   6,166
Liz Walters, PC   4,376
Ian McLean, UKIP   1,271
Nicola Knight, LD   585
Lab. majority 13,238 (41.63%)
3.00% swing C. to Lab.
(2015: Lab. majority 9,406 (30.87%))

DELYN
E. 54,116   T. 39,418 (72.84%)   Lab. hold
*David Hanson, Lab.   20,573
Matt Wright, C.   16,333
Paul Rowlinson, PC   1,481
Tom Rippeth, LD   1,031
Lab. majority 4,240 (10.76%)
1.47% swing C. to Lab.
(2015: Lab. majority 2,930 (7.82%))

DWYFOR MEIRIONNYDD
E. 44,699   T. 30,348 (67.89%)   PC hold
*Liz Saville Roberts, PC   13,687
Neil Fairlamb, C.   8,837
Mathew Norman, Lab.   6,273
Stephen Churchman, LD   937
Frank Wykes, UKIP   614
PC majority 4,850 (15.98%)
1.11% swing PC to C.
(2015: PC majority 5,261 (18.20%))

GOWER
E. 62,163   T. 45,576 (73.32%)   Lab. gain
Tonia Antoniazzi, Lab.   22,727
*Byron Davies, C.   19,458
Harri Roberts, PC   1,669
Howard Evans, LD   931
Ross Ford, UKIP   642
Jason Winstanley, Pirate   149
Lab. majority 3,269 (7.17%)
3.62% swing C. to Lab.
(2015: C. majority 27 (0.06%))

ISLWYN
E. 56,256   T. 36,093 (64.16%)
                              Lab. Co-op hold
*Chris Evans, Lab. Co-op   21,238
Dan Thomas, C.   9,826
Darren Jones, PC   2,739
Joe Smyth, UKIP   1,605
Matthew Kidner, LD   685
Lab. Co-op majority 11,412 (31.62%)
1.10% swing Lab. to C.
(2015: Lab. Co-op majority 10,404
(29.39%))

LLANELLI
E. 59,434   T. 40,342 (67.88%)   Lab. hold
*Nia Griffith, Lab.   21,568
Stephen Davies, C.   9,544
Mari Arthur, PC   7,351
Ken Rees, UKIP   1,331
Rory Daniels, LD   548
Lab. majority 12,024 (29.81%)
1.40% swing C. to Lab.
(2015: Lab. majority 7,095 (18.39%))

MERTHYR TYDFIL & RHYMNEY
E. 55,463   T. 33,545 (60.48%)   Lab. hold
*Gerald Jones, Lab.   22,407
Pauline Jorgensen, C.   6,073
Amy Kitcher, PC   2,740
David Rowlands, UKIP   1,484
Bob Griffin, LD   841
Lab. majority 16,334 (48.69%)
2.45% swing C. to Lab.
(2015: Lab. majority 11,513 (35.19%))

MONMOUTH
E. 64,909   T. 49,734 (76.62%)   C. hold
*David Davies, C.   26,411
Ruth Jones, Lab.   18,205
Veronica German, LD   2,064
Carole Damon, PC   1,338
Ian Chandler, Green   954
Roy Neale, UKIP   762
C. majority 8,206 (16.50%)
3.32% swing C. to Lab.
(2015: C. majority 10,982 (23.14%))

MONTGOMERYSHIRE
E. 50,755   T. 34,891 (68.74%)   C. hold
*Glyn Davies, C.   18,075
Jane Dodds, LD   8,790
Iwan Jones, Lab.   5,542
Aled Hughes, PC   1,960
Richard Chaloner, Green   524
C. majority 9,285 (26.61%)
5.42% swing LD to C.
(2015: C. majority 5,325 (15.77%))

NEATH
E. 55,859   T. 38,285 (68.54%)
                              Lab. Co-op hold
*Christina Rees, Lab. Co-op   21,713
Orla Lowe, C.   9,082
Daniel Williams, PC   5,339
Richard Pritchard, UKIP   1,419
Frank Little, LD   732
Lab. Co-op majority 12,631 (32.99%)
2.25% swing C. to Lab.
(2015: Lab. majority 9,548 (25.71%))

NEWPORT EAST
E. 57,233   T. 36,820 (64.33%)   Lab. hold
*Jessica Morden, Lab.   20,804
Natasha Asghar, C.   12,801
Ian Gorman, UKIP   1,180
Pete Brown, LD   966
Cameron Wixcey, PC   881
Nadeem Ahmed, ND   188
Lab. majority 8,003 (21.74%)
4.17% swing C. to Lab.
(2015: Lab. majority 4,705 (13.40%))

NEWPORT WEST
E. 64,399   T. 43,438 (67.45%)   Lab. hold
*Paul Flynn, Lab.   22,723
Angela Jones-Evans, C.   17,065
Stan Edwards, UKIP   1,100
Morgan Bowler-Brown, PC   1,077
Sarah Lockyer, LD   976
Pippa Bartolotti, Green   497
Lab. majority 5,658 (13.03%)
2.16% swing C. to Lab.
(2015: Lab. majority 3,510 (8.70%))

OGMORE
E. 56,661   T. 37,204 (65.66%)   Lab. hold
*Chris Elmore, Lab.   23,225
Jamie Wallis, C.   9,354
Huw Marshall, PC   2,796
Glenda Davies, UKIP   1,235
Gerald Francis, LD   594
Lab. majority 13,871 (37.28%)
0.14% swing C. to Lab.
(2015: Lab. majority 13,043 (37.00%))
(2016: Lab. majority 8,575 (36.44%))

PONTYPRIDD
E. 60,566   T. 39,894 (65.87%)   Lab. hold
*Owen Smith, Lab.   22,103
Juliette Ash, C.   10,655
Fflur Elin, PC   4,102
Michael Powell, LD   1,963
Robin Hunter-Clarke, UKIP   1,071
Lab. majority 11,448 (28.70%)
2.49% swing C. to Lab.
(2015: Lab. majority 8,985 (23.72%))

PRESELI PEMBROKESHIRE
E. 58,540   T. 42,197 (72.08%)   C. hold
*Stephen Crabb, C.   18,302
Philippa Thompson, Lab.   17,988
Owain Williams, PC   2,711
Chris Overton, Ind.   1,209
Bob Kilmister, LD   1,106
Susan Bale, UKIP   850
Rodney Maile, Worth   31
C. majority 314 (0.74%)
5.75% swing C. to Lab.
(2015: C. majority 4,969 (12.25%))

RHONDDA
E. 50,513   T. 32,936 (65.20%)   Lab. hold
*Chris Bryant, Lab.   21,096
Branwen Cennard, PC   7,350
Virginia Crosbie, C.   3,333
Janet Kenrick, UKIP   880
Karen Roberts, LD   277
Lab. majority 13,746 (41.74%)
9.05% swing PC to Lab.
(2015: Lab. majority 7,455 (23.64%))

SWANSEA EAST
E. 58,521   T. 35,159 (60.08%)   Lab. hold
*Carolyn Harris, Lab.   22,307
Dan Boucher, C.   9,139
Steffan Phillips, PC   1,689
Clifford Johnson, UKIP   1,040
Charley Hasted, LD   625
Chris Evans, Green   359
Lab. majority 13,168 (37.45%)
0.11% swing Lab. to C.
(2015: Lab. majority 12,028 (35.78%))

SWANSEA WEST
E. 56,892   T. 37,282 (65.53%)
                              Lab. Co-op hold
*Geraint Davies, Lab. Co-op   22,278
Craig Lawton, C.   11,680
Rhydian Fitter, PC   1,529
Michael O'Carroll, LD   1,269
Mike Whittall, Green   434
Brian Johnson, SPGB   92
Lab. Co-op majority 10,598 (28.43%)
4.21% swing C. to Lab.
(2015: Lab. Co-op majority 7,036 (20.01%))

TORFAEN
E. 61,839   T. 38,429 (62.14%)   Lab. hold
*Nick Thomas-Symonds,   22,134
Lab.
Graham Smith, C.   11,894
Jeff Rees, PC   2,059
Ian Williams, UKIP   1,490
Andrew Best, LD   852
Lab. majority 10,240 (26.65%)
2.56% swing C. to Lab.
(2015: Lab. majority 8,169 (21.53%))

VALE OF CLWYD
E. 56,890   T. 38,684 (68.00%)   Lab. gain
†Chris Ruane, Lab.   19,423
*James Davies, C.   17,044
David Wyatt, PC   1,551
Gwyn Williams, LD   666
Lab. majority 2,379 (6.15%)
3.41% swing C. to Lab.
(2015: C. majority 237 (0.67%))

VALE OF GLAMORGAN
E. 73,958   T. 53,718 (72.63%)   C. hold
*Alun Cairns, C.   25,501
Camilla Beaven, Lab.   23,311
Ian Johnson, PC   2,295
Jennifer Geroni, LD   1,020
Melanie Hunter-   868
Clarke, UKIP
Stephen Davis-Barker, Green   419
Sharon Lovell, Women   177
David Elston, Pirate   127
C. majority 2,190 (4.08%)
4.67% swing C. to Lab.
(2015: C. majority 6,880 (13.41%))

WREXHAM
E. 50,422   T. 35,092 (69.60%)   Lab. hold
*Ian Lucas, Lab.   17,153
Andrew Atkinson, C.   15,321
Carrie Harper, PC   1,753
Carole O'Toole, LD   865
Lab. majority 1,832 (5.22%)
0.19% swing Lab. to C.
(2015: Lab. majority 1,831 (5.60%))

YNYS MON
E. 52,448   T. 37,367 (71.25%)   Lab. hold
*Albert Owen, Lab.   15,643
Tomos Davies, C.   10,384
Ieuan Wyn Jones, PC   10,237
James Turner, UKIP   624
Sarah Jackson, LD   479
Lab. majority 5,259 (14.07%)
2.06% swing C. to Lab.
(2015: Lab. majority 229 (0.66%))

SCOTLAND

ABERDEEN NORTH
E. 62,130   T. 36,757 (59.16%)
                                    SNP hold
*Kirsty Blackman, SNP   15,170
Orr Vinegold, Lab.   11,031
Grace O'Keeffe, C.   8,341
Isobel Davidson, LD   1,693
Richard Durkin, Ind.   522
SNP majority 4,139 (11.26%)
9.61% swing SNP to Lab.
(2015: SNP majority 13,396 (30.49%))

ABERDEEN SOUTH
E. 64,964   T. 44,483 (68.47%)   C. gain
Ross Thomson, C.   18,746
*Callum McCaig, SNP   13,994
Callum O'Dwyer, Lab.   9,143
Jenny Wilson, LD   2,600
C. majority 4,752 (10.68%)
14.75% swing SNP to C.
(2015: SNP majority 7,230 (14.89%))

ABERDEENSHIRE WEST &
KINCARDINE
E. 72,477   T. 51,625 (71.23%)   C. gain
Andrew Bowie, C.   24,704
*Stuart Donaldson, SNP   16,754
Barry Black, Lab.   5,706
John Waddell, LD   4,461
C. majority 7,950 (15.40%)
14.07% swing SNP to C.
(2015: SNP majority 7,033 (12.74%))

AIRDRIE & SHOTTS
E. 64,146   T. 38,002 (59.24%)
                                    SNP hold
*Neil Gray, SNP   14,291
Helen McFarlane, Lab.   14,096
Jennifer Donnellan, C.   8,813
Ewan McRobert, LD   802
SNP majority 195 (0.51%)
9.66% swing SNP to Lab.
(2015: SNP majority 8,779 (19.82%))

ANGUS
E. 63,840   T. 40,192 (62.96%)   C. gain
Kirstene Hair, C.   18,148
*Mike Weir, SNP   15,503
William Campbell, Lab.   5,233
Clive Sneddon, LD   1,308
C. majority 2,645 (6.58%)
15.91% swing SNP to C.
(2015: SNP majority 11,230 (25.24%))

ARGYLL & BUTE
E. 67,230   T. 48,069 (71.50%)
                                    SNP hold
*Brendan O'Hara, SNP   17,304
Gary Mulvaney, C.   15,976
Alan Reid, LD   8,745
Michael Kelly, Lab.   6,044
SNP majority 1,328 (2.76%)
13.29% swing SNP to C.
(2015: SNP majority 8,473 (16.33%))

AYR, CARRICK & CUMNOCK
E. 71,241   T. 46,222 (64.88%)   C. gain
Bill Grant, C.   18,550
*Corri Wilson, SNP   15,776
Carol Mochan, Lab.   11,024
Callum Leslie, LD   872
C. majority 2,774 (6.00%)
17.50% swing SNP to C.
(2015: SNP majority 11,265 (21.58%))

AYRSHIRE CENTRAL
E. 68,997   T. 45,087 (65.35%)
                                    SNP hold
*Philippa Whitford, SNP   16,771
Caroline Hollins Martin, C.   15,504
Nairn McDonald, Lab.   11,762
Tom Inglis, LD   1,050
SNP majority 1,267 (2.81%)
16.51% swing SNP to C.
(2015: SNP majority 13,589 (26.76%))

AYRSHIRE NORTH & ARRAN
E. 73,174   T. 47,433 (64.82%)
                                    SNP hold
*Patricia Gibson, SNP   18,451
David Rocks, C.   14,818
Chris Rimicans, Lab.   13,040
Mark Dickson, LD   1,124
SNP majority 3,633 (7.66%)
15.36% swing SNP to C.
(2015: SNP majority 13,573 (25.20%))

BANFF & BUCHAN
E. 67,601   T. 41,643 (61.60%)   C. gain

David Duguid, C.		19,976
*Eilidh Whiteford, SNP		16,283
Caitlin Stott, Lab.		3,936
Galen Milne, LD		1,448

C. majority 3,693 (8.87%)
20.15% swing SNP to C.
(2015: SNP majority 14,339 (31.43%))

BERWICKSHIRE, ROXBURGH & SELKIRK
E. 73,191   T. 52,367 (71.55%)   C. gain

John Lamont, C.		28,213
*Calum Kerr, SNP		17,153
Ian Davidson, Lab. Co-op		4,519
Caroline Burgess, LD		2,482

C. majority 11,060 (21.12%)
10.86% swing SNP to C.
(2015: SNP majority 328 (0.60%))

CAITHNESS, SUTHERLAND & EASTER ROSS
E. 46,868   T. 30,901 (65.93%)   LD gain

Jamie Stone, LD		11,061
*Paul Monaghan, SNP		9,017
Struan Mackie, C.		6,990
Olivia Bell, Lab.		3,833

LD majority 2,044 (6.61%)
8.93% swing SNP to LD
(2015: SNP majority 3,844 (11.24%))

COATBRIDGE, CHRYSTON & BELLSHILL
E. 71,198   T. 45,040 (63.26%)   Lab. gain

Hugh Gaffney, Lab.		19,193
*Phil Boswell, SNP		17,607
Robyn Halbert, C.		7,318
David Bennie, LD		922

Lab. majority 1,586 (3.52%)
13.10% swing SNP to Lab.
(2015: SNP majority 11,501 (22.69%))

CUMBERNAULD, KILSYTH & KIRKINTILLOCH EAST
E. 66,554   T. 43,833 (65.86%)

		SNP hold
*Stuart McDonald, SNP		19,122
Elisha Fisher, Lab.		14,858
Stephen Johnston, C.		8,010
Rod Ackland, LD		1,238
Carl Pearson, UKIP		605

SNP majority 4,264 (9.73%)
10.07% swing SNP to Lab.
(2015: SNP majority 14,752 (29.87%))

DUMFRIES & GALLOWAY
E. 74,206   T. 51,599 (69.53%)   C. gain

Alister Jack, C.		22,344
*Richard Arkless, SNP		16,701
Daniel Goodare, Lab.		10,775
Joan Mitchell, LD		1,241
Yen Hongmei Jin, ND		538

C. majority 5,643 (10.94%)
11.22% swing SNP to C.
(2015: SNP majority 6,514 (11.51%))

DUMFRIESSHIRE, CLYDESDALE & TWEEDDALE
E. 67,672   T. 48,964 (72.35%)   C. hold

*David Mundell, C.		24,177
Mairi McAllan, SNP		14,736
Douglas Beattie, Lab.		8,102
John Ferry, LD		1,949

C. majority 9,441 (19.28%)
8.88% swing SNP to C.
(2015: C. majority 798 (1.53%))

DUNBARTONSHIRE EAST
E. 66,300   T. 51,801 (78.13%)   LD gain

†Jo Swinson, LD		21,023
*John Nicolson, SNP		15,684
Sheila Mechan, C.		7,563
Callum McNally, Lab.		7,531

LD majority 5,339 (10.31%)
7.13% swing SNP to LD
(2015: SNP majority 2,167 (3.95%))

DUNBARTONSHIRE WEST
E. 67,602   T. 44,083 (65.21%)

		SNP hold
*Martin Docherty, SNP		18,890
Jean Anne Mitchell, Lab.		16,602
Penny Hutton, C.		7,582
Rebecca Plenderleith, LD		1,009

SNP majority 2,288 (5.19%)
11.26% swing SNP to Lab.
(2015: SNP majority 14,171 (27.71%))

DUNDEE EAST
E. 65,854   T. 42,928 (65.19%)

		SNP hold
*Stewart Hosie, SNP		18,391
Eleanor Price, C.		11,746
Lesley Brennan, Lab.		11,176
Christopher McIntyre, LD		1,615

SNP majority 6,645 (15.48%)
14.63% swing SNP to C.
(2015: SNP majority 19,162 (39.77%))

DUNDEE WEST
E. 62,644   T. 38,677 (61.74%)

		SNP hold
*Chris Law, SNP		18,045
Alan Cowan, Lab.		12,783
Darren Cormack, C.		6,257
Jenny Blain, LD		1,189
Sean Dobson, Ind.		403

SNP majority 5,262 (13.60%)
12.31% swing SNP to Lab.
(2015: SNP majority 17,092 (38.23%))

DUNFERMLINE & FIFE WEST
E. 75,672   T. 51,010 (67.41%)

		SNP hold
*Douglas Chapman, SNP		18,121
Cara Hilton, Lab. Co-op		17,277
Belinda Hacking, C.		12,593
James Calder, LD		3,019

SNP majority 844 (1.65%)
8.43% swing SNP to Lab.
(2015: SNP majority 10,352 (18.52%))

EAST KILBRIDE, STRATHAVEN & LESMAHAGOW
E. 80,442   T. 54,102 (67.26%)

		SNP hold
*Lisa Cameron, SNP		21,023
Monique McAdams, Lab.		17,157
Mark McGeever, C.		13,704
Paul McGarry, LD		1,590
Janice MacKay, UKIP		628

SNP majority 3,866 (7.15%)
10.08% swing SNP to Lab.
(2015: SNP majority 16,527 (27.30%))

EAST LOTHIAN
E. 79,093   T. 55,878 (70.65%)   Lab. gain

Martin Whitfield, Lab.		20,158
*George Kerevan, SNP		17,075
Sheila Low, C.		16,540
Elisabeth Wilson, LD		1,738
Mike Allan, Ind.		367

Lab. majority 3,083 (5.52%)
8.52% swing SNP to Lab.
(2015: SNP majority 6,803 (11.53%))

EDINBURGH EAST
E. 65,896   T. 43,523 (66.05%)

		SNP hold
*Tommy Sheppard, SNP		18,509
Patsy King, Lab.		15,084
Katie Mackie, C.		8,081
Tristan Gray, LD		1,849

SNP majority 3,425 (7.87%)
5.73% swing SNP to Lab.
(2015: SNP majority 9,106 (19.34%))

EDINBURGH NORTH & LEITH
E. 79,473   T. 56,552 (71.16%)

		SNP hold
*Deidre Brock, SNP		19,243
Gordon Munro, Lab. Co-op		17,618
Iain McGill, C.		15,385
Martin Veart, LD		2,579
Lorna Slater, Green		1,727

SNP majority 1,625 (2.87%)
3.39% swing SNP to Lab.
(2015: SNP majority 5,597 (9.65%))

EDINBURGH SOUTH
E. 64,553   T. 47,840 (74.11%)   Lab. hold

*Ian Murray, Lab.		26,269
Jim Eadie, SNP		10,755
Stephanie Smith, C.		9,428
Alan Beal, LD		1,388

Lab. majority 15,514 (32.43%)
13.54% swing SNP to Lab.
(2015: Lab. majority 2,637 (5.35%))

EDINBURGH SOUTH WEST
E. 71,178   T. 49,390 (69.39%)

		SNP hold
*Joanna Cherry, SNP		17,575
Miles Briggs, C.		16,478
Foysol Choudhury, Lab.		13,213
Aisha Mir, LD		2,124

SNP majority 1,097 (2.22%)
10.25% swing SNP to C.
(2015: SNP majority 8,135 (15.76%))

EDINBURGH WEST
E. 71,500   T. 52,795 (73.84%)   LD gain

Christine Jardine, LD	18,108
Toni Giugliano, SNP	15,120
Sandy Batho, C.	11,559
Mandy Telford, Lab.	7,876
Mark Whittet, Referendum	132

LD majority 2,988 (5.66%)
5.76% swing SNP to LD
(2015: SNP majority 3,210 (5.85%))

FALKIRK
E. 82,240   T. 53,809 (65.43%)
SNP hold

*John McNally, SNP	20,952
Craig Martin, Lab.	16,029
Callum Laidlaw, C.	14,088
Austin Reid, LD	1,120
Debra Pickering, Green	908
Stuart Martin, UKIP	712

SNP majority 4,923 (9.15%)
11.75% swing SNP to Lab.
(2015: SNP majority 19,701 (32.65%))

FIFE NORTH EAST
E. 58,685   T. 41,822 (71.27%)
SNP hold

*Stephen Gethins, SNP	13,743
Janet Riches, LD	13,741
Tony Miklinski, C.	10,088
Rosalind Garton, Lab.	4,026
Mike Scott-Hayward, Sovereign	224

SNP majority 2 (0.00%)
4.80% swing SNP to LD
(2015: SNP majority 4,344 (9.60%))

GLASGOW CENTRAL
E. 64,346   T. 35,984 (55.92%)
SNP hold

*Alison Thewliss, SNP	16,096
Faten Hameed, Lab.	13,829
Charlotte Fairbanks, C.	5,014
Isabel Nelson, LD	1,045

SNP majority 2,267 (6.30%)
6.59% swing SNP to Lab.
(2015: SNP majority 7,662 (19.49%))

GLASGOW EAST
E. 66,242   T. 36,175 (54.61%)
SNP hold

David Linden, SNP	14,024
Kate Watson, Lab.	13,949
Thomas Kerr, C.	6,816
Matthew Clark, LD	576
John Ferguson, UKIP	504
Karin Finegan, Ind.	158
Steven Marshall, Soc. Dem.	148

SNP majority 75 (0.21%)
12.14% swing SNP to Lab.
(2015: SNP majority 10,387 (24.49%))

GLASGOW NORTH
E. 53,863   T. 33,473 (62.14%)
SNP hold

*Patrick Grady, SNP	12,597
Pam Duncan-Glancy, Lab.	11,537
Stuart Cullen, C.	4,935
Patrick Harvie, Green	3,251
Calum Shepherd, LD	1,153

SNP majority 1,060 (3.17%)
11.00% swing SNP to Lab.
(2015: SNP majority 9,295 (25.17%))

GLASGOW NORTH EAST
E. 59,932   T. 31,775 (53.02%)
Lab. Co-op gain

Paul Sweeney, Lab. Co-op	13,637
*Anne McLaughlin, SNP	13,395
Jack Wylie, C.	4,106
Daniel Donaldson, LD	637

Lab. Co-op majority 242 (0.76%)
12.56% swing SNP to Lab.
(2015: SNP majority 9,222 (24.36%))

GLASGOW NORTH WEST
E. 63,773   T. 38,844 (60.91%)
SNP hold

*Carol Monaghan, SNP	16,508
Michael Shanks, Lab.	13,947
Christopher Land, C.	7,002
James Speirs, LD	1,387

SNP majority 2,561 (6.59%)
8.52% swing SNP to Lab.
(2015: SNP majority 10,364 (23.63%))

GLASGOW SOUTH
E. 69,126   T. 44,550 (64.45%)
SNP hold

*Stewart McDonald, SNP	18,312
Eileen Dinning, Lab.	16,285
Taylor Muir, C.	8,506
Ewan Hoyle, LD	1,447

SNP majority 2,027 (4.55%)
10.30% swing SNP to Lab.
(2015: SNP majority 12,269 (25.15%))

GLASGOW SOUTH WEST
E. 62,991   T. 35,378 (56.16%)
SNP hold

*Chris Stephens, SNP	14,386
Matt Kerr, Lab. Co-op	14,326
Thomas Haddow, C.	5,524
Ben Denton-Cardew, LD	661
Sarah Hemy, UKIP	481

SNP majority 60 (0.17%)
12.07% swing SNP to Lab.
(2015: SNP majority 9,950 (24.32%))

GLENROTHES
E. 66,378   T. 40,399 (60.86%)
SNP hold

*Peter Grant, SNP	17,291
Altany Craik, Lab.	14,024
Andrew Brown, C.	7,876
Rebecca Bell, LD	1,208

SNP majority 3,267 (8.09%)
10.55% swing SNP to Lab.
(2015: SNP majority 13,897 (29.20%))

GORDON
E. 78,531   T. 53,685 (68.36%)   C. gain

Colin Clark, C.	21,861
*Alex Salmond, SNP	19,254
Kirsten Muat, Lab.	6,340
David Evans, LD	6,230

C. majority 2,607 (4.86%)
20.40% swing SNP to C.
(2015: SNP majority 8,687 (14.94%))

INVERCLYDE
E. 58,853   T. 39,093 (66.42%)
SNP hold

*Ronnie Cowan, SNP	15,050
Martin McCluskey, Lab.	14,666
David Wilson, C.	8,399
David Stevens, LD	978

SNP majority 384 (0.98%)
11.91% swing SNP to Lab.
(2015: SNP majority 11,063 (24.80%))

INVERNESS, NAIRN, BADENOCH & STRATHSPEY
E. 76,844   T. 52,801 (68.71%)
SNP hold

*Drew Hendry, SNP	21,042
Nicholas Tulloch, C.	16,118
Mike Robb, Lab.	8,552
Ritchie Cunningham, LD	6,477
Donald Boyd, SCP	612

SNP majority 4,924 (9.33%)
17.41% swing SNP to C.
(2015: SNP majority 10,809 (18.76%))

KILMARNOCK & LOUDOUN
E. 73,327   T. 46,509 (63.43%)
SNP hold

*Alan Brown, SNP	19,690
Laura Dover, Lab.	13,421
Alison Harper, C.	12,404
Irene Lang, LD	994

SNP majority 6,269 (13.48%)
5.91% swing SNP to Lab.
(2015: SNP majority 13,638 (25.30%))

KIRKCALDY & COWDENBEATH
E. 72,721   T. 46,193 (63.52%)   Lab. gain

Lesley Laird, Lab.	17,016
*Roger Mullin, SNP	16,757
Dave Dempsey, C.	10,762
Malcolm Wood, LD	1,118
David Coburn, UKIP	540

Lab. majority 259 (0.56%)
9.71% swing SNP to Lab.
(2015: SNP majority 9,974 (18.86%))

LANARK & HAMILTON EAST
E. 77,313   T. 50,470 (65.28%)
SNP hold

*Angela Crawley, SNP	16,444
Poppy Corbett, C.	16,178
Andrew Hilland, Lab.	16,084
Colin Robb, LD	1,214
Donald Mackay, UKIP	550

SNP majority 266 (0.53%)
16.21% swing SNP to C.
(2015: SNP majority 10,100 (18.28%))

LINLITHGOW & FALKIRK EAST
E. 86,186   T. 56,094 (65.08%)
SNP hold

*Martyn Day, SNP	20,388
Joan Coombes, Lab.	17,469
Charles Kennedy, C.	16,311
Sally Pattle, LD	1,926

SNP majority 2,919 (5.20%)
7.90% swing SNP to Lab.
(2015: SNP majority 12,934 (21.00%))

LIVINGSTON
E. 81,208   T. 52,505 (64.65%)

		SNP hold
*Hannah Bardell, SNP		21,036
Rhea Wolfson, Lab.		17,158
Damian Timson, C.		12,799
Charles Dundas, LD		1,512

SNP majority 3,878 (7.39%)
10.94% swing SNP to Lab.
(2015: SNP majority 16,843 (29.27%))

MIDLOTHIAN
E. 68,328   T. 45,273 (66.26%)   Lab. gain

Danielle Rowley, Lab.	16,458
*Owen Thompson, SNP	15,573
Chris Donnelly, C.	11,521
Ross Laird, LD	1,721

Lab. majority 885 (1.95%)
11.18% swing SNP to Lab.
(2015: SNP majority 9,859 (20.40%))

MORAY
E. 70,649   T. 47,605 (67.38%)   C. gain

Douglas Ross, C.	22,637
*Angus Robertson, SNP	18,478
Jo Kirby, Lab.	5,208
Alex Linklater, LD	1,078
Anne Glen, Ind.	204

C. majority 4,159 (8.74%)
13.57% swing SNP to C.
(2015: SNP majority 9,065 (18.39%))

MOTHERWELL & WISHAW
E. 68,215   T. 41,926 (61.46%)

	SNP hold
*Marion Fellows, SNP	16,150
Angela Feeney, Lab.	15,832
Meghan Gallacher, C.	8,490
Yvonne Finlayson, LD	920
Neil Wilson, UKIP	534

SNP majority 318 (0.76%)
11.95% swing SNP to Lab.
(2015: SNP majority 11,898 (24.67%))

NA H-EILEANAN AN IAR
E. 21,301   T. 14,818 (69.56%)

	SNP hold
*Angus MacNeil, SNP	6,013
Ealasaid MacDonald, Lab.	5,006
Dan McCroskrie, C.	2,441
John Cormack, SCP	1,108
James Paterson, LD	250

SNP majority 1,007 (6.80%)
9.47% swing SNP to Lab.
(2015: SNP majority 4,102 (25.74%))

OCHIL & PERTHSHIRE SOUTH
E. 76,767   T. 54,168 (70.56%)   C. gain

Luke Graham, C.	22,469
*Tasmina Ahmed-Sheikh, SNP	19,110
Joanne Ross, Lab.	10,847
Iliyan Stefanov, LD	1,742

C. majority 3,359 (6.20%)
15.74% swing SNP to C.
(2015: SNP majority 10,168 (17.57%))

ORKNEY & SHETLAND
E. 34,164   T. 23,277 (68.13%)   LD hold

*Alistair Carmichael, LD	11,312
Miriam Brett, SNP	6,749
Robina Barton, Lab.	2,664
Jamie Halcro Johnston, C.	2,024
Robert Smith, UKIP	283
Stuart Hill, Ind.	245

LD majority 4,563 (19.60%)
8.00% swing SNP to LD
(2015: LD majority 817 (3.59%))

PAISLEY & RENFREWSHIRE NORTH
E. 67,436   T. 46,615 (69.12%)

	SNP hold
*Gavin Newlands, SNP	17,455
Alison Taylor, Lab.	14,842
David Gardiner, C.	12,842
John Boyd, LD	1,476

SNP majority 2,613 (5.61%)
6.19% swing SNP to Lab.
(2015: SNP majority 9,076 (17.99%))

PAISLEY & RENFREWSHIRE SOUTH
E. 61,344   T. 41,712 (68.00%)

	SNP hold
*Mhairi Black, SNP	16,964
Alison Dowling, Lab.	14,423
Amy Thomson, C.	8,122
Eileen McCartin, LD	1,327
Paul Mack, Ind.	876

SNP majority 2,541 (6.09%)
3.10% swing SNP to Lab.
(2015: SNP majority 5,684 (12.30%))

PERTH & PERTHSHIRE NORTH
E. 71,743   T. 51,525 (71.82%)

	SNP hold
*Pete Wishart, SNP	21,804
Ian Duncan, C.	21,783
David Roemmele, Lab.	5,349
Peter Barrett, LD	2,589

SNP majority 21 (0.04%)
8.87% swing SNP to C.
(2015: SNP majority 9,641 (17.79%))

RENFREWSHIRE EAST
E. 70,067   T. 53,738 (76.70%)   C. gain

Paul Masterton, C.	21,496
*Kirsten Oswald, SNP	16,784
Blair McDougall, Lab.	14,346
Aileen Morton, LD	1,112

C. majority 4,712 (8.77%)
13.68% swing SNP to C.
(2015: SNP majority 3,718 (6.55%))

ROSS, SKYE & LOCHABER
E. 53,638   T. 38,454 (71.69%)

	SNP hold
*Ian Blackford, SNP	15,480
Robert Mackenzie, C.	9,561
Jean Davis, LD	8,042
Peter O'Donnghaile, Lab.	4,695
Ronnie the Crofter Campbell, Ind.	499
Stick Sturrock, S New	177

SNP majority 5,919 (15.39%)
13.26% swing SNP to C.
(2015: SNP majority 5,124 (12.26%))

RUTHERGLEN & HAMILTON WEST
E. 80,098   T. 50,872 (63.51%)

	Lab. Co-op gain
Ged Killen, Lab. Co-op	19,101
*Margaret Ferrier, SNP	18,836
Ann Le Blond, C.	9,941
Robert Brown, LD	2,158
Caroline Santos, UKIP	465
Andy Dixon, Ind.	371

Lab. Co-op majority 265 (0.52%)
8.92% swing SNP to Lab.
(2015: SNP majority 9,975 (17.31%))

STIRLING
E. 66,415   T. 49,356 (74.31%)   C. gain

Stephen Kerr, C.	18,291
*Steven Paterson, SNP	18,143
Chris Kane, Lab.	10,902
Wendy Chamberlain, LD	1,683
Kirsten Rummery, Women	337

C. majority 148 (0.30%)
11.40% swing SNP to C.
(2015: SNP majority 10,480 (20.10%))

NORTHERN IRELAND

ANTRIM EAST
E. 62,908   T. 38,143 (60.63%)

	DUP hold
*Sammy Wilson, DUP	21,873
Stewart Dickson, Alliance	5,950
John Stewart, UUP	4,524
Oliver McMullan, SF	3,555
Margaret McKillop, SDLP	1,278
Mark Logan, C.	963

DUP majority 15,923 (41.75%)
10.30% swing Alliance to DUP
(2015: DUP majority 5,795 (17.30%))

ANTRIM NORTH
E. 75,657   T. 48,460 (64.05%)

	DUP hold
*Ian Paisley, DUP	28,521
Cara McShane, SF	7,878
Jackson Minford, UUP	3,482
Timothy Gaston, TUV	3,282
Patricia O'Lynn, Alliance	2,723
Declan O'Loan, SDLP	2,574

DUP majority 20,643 (42.60%)
5.83% swing SF to DUP
(2015: DUP majority 11,546 (27.55%))

ANTRIM SOUTH
E. 68,244   T. 43,170 (63.26%)

	DUP gain
Paul Girvan, DUP	16,508
*Danny Kinahan, UUP	13,300
Declan Kearney, SF	7,797
Neil Kelly, Alliance	3,203
Roisin Lynch, SDLP	2,362

DUP majority 3,208 (7.43%)
5.01% swing UUP to DUP
(2015: UUP majority 949 (2.60%))

BELFAST EAST
E. 63,495   T. 42,890 (67.55%)

		DUP hold
*Gavin Robinson, DUP		23,917
Naomi Long, Alliance		15,443
Hazel Legge, UUP		1,408
Mairead O'Donnell, SF		894
Georgina Milne, Green		561
Sheila Bodel, C.		446
Seamas de Faoite, SDLP		167
Bobby Beck, Ind.		54

DUP majority 8,474 (19.76%)
6.61% swing Alliance to DUP
(2015: DUP majority 2,597 (6.54%))

BELFAST NORTH
E. 68,249   T. 45,936 (67.31%)

		DUP hold
*Nigel Dodds, DUP		21,240
John Finucane, SF		19,159
Sam Nelson, Alliance		2,475
Martin McAuley, SDLP		2,058
Malachai O'Hara, Green		644
Gemma Weir, WP		360

DUP majority 2,081 (4.53%)
4.30% swing DUP to SF
(2015: DUP majority 5,326 (13.12%))

BELFAST SOUTH
E. 66,105   T. 43,705 (66.11%)

		DUP gain
Emma Little Pengelly, DUP		13,299
*Alasdair McDonnell, SDLP		11,303
Paula Bradshaw, Alliance		7,946
Mairtin O Muilleoir, SF		7,143
Clare Bailey, Green		2,241
Michael Henderson, UUP		1,527
Clare Salier, C.		246

DUP majority 1,996 (4.57%)
3.45% swing SDLP to DUP
(2015: SDLP majority 906 (2.33%))

BELFAST WEST
E. 62,423   T. 40,633 (65.09%)   SF hold

*Paul Maskey, SF		27,107
Frank McCoubrey, DUP		5,455
Gerry Carroll, PBP		4,132
Tim Attwood, SDLP		2,860
Sorcha Eastwood, Alliance		731
Conor Campbell, WP		348

SF majority 21,652 (53.29%)
3.45% swing DUP to SF
(2015: SF majority 12,365 (35.00%))

DOWN NORTH
E. 64,334   T. 39,185 (60.91%)   Ind. hold

*Lady (Sylvia) Hermon, Ind.		16,148
Alex Easton, DUP		14,940
Andrew Muir, Alliance		3,639
Steven Agnew, Green		2,549
Frank Shivers, C.		941
Therese McCartney, SF		531
Caoimhe McNeill, SDLP		400
Gavan Reynolds, Ind.		37

Ind. majority 1,208 (3.08%)
20.56% swing Ind. to Ind.
(2015: Ind. majority 9,202 (25.60%))

DOWN SOUTH
E. 75,685   T. 50,893 (67.24%)   SF gain

Chris Hazzard, SF		20,328
*Margaret Ritchie, SDLP		17,882
Diane Forsythe, DUP		8,867
Harold McKee, UUP		2,002
Andrew McMurray, Alliance		1,814

SF majority 2,446 (4.81%)
9.30% swing SDLP to SF
(2015: SDLP majority 5,891 (13.80%))

FERMANAGH & SOUTH TYRONE
E. 70,601   T. 53,481 (75.75%)   SF gain

†Michelle Gildernew, SF		25,230
*Tom Elliott, UUP		24,355
Mary Garrity, SDLP		2,587
Noreen Campbell, Alliance		886
Tanya Jones, Green		423

SF majority 875 (1.64%)
1.34% swing UUP to SF
(2015: UUP majority 530 (1.04%))

FOYLE
E. 70,324   T. 45,965 (65.36%)   SF gain

Elisha McCallion, SF		18,256
*Mark Durkan, SDLP		18,087
Gary Middleton, DUP		7,398
Shaun Harkin, PBP		1,377
John Doherty, Alliance		847

SF majority 169 (0.37%)
8.35% swing SDLP to SF
(2015: SDLP majority 6,046 (16.34%))

LAGAN VALLEY
E. 72,380   T. 44,926 (62.07%)

		DUP hold
*Jeffrey Donaldson, DUP		26,762
Robbie Butler, UUP		7,533
Aaron McIntyre, Alliance		4,996
Pat Catney, SDLP		3,384
Jacqui Russell, SF		1,567
Ian Nickels, C.		462
Jonny Orr, ND		222

DUP majority 19,229 (42.80%)
5.07% swing UUP to DUP
(2015: DUP majority 13,000 (32.67%))

LONDONDERRY EAST
E. 67,038   T. 41,030 (61.20%)

		DUP hold
*Gregory Campbell, DUP		19,723
Dermot Nicholl, SF		10,881
Stephanie Quigley, SDLP		4,423
Richard Holmes, UUP		3,135
Chris McCaw, Alliance		2,538
Liz St Clair-Legge, C.		330

DUP majority 8,842 (21.55%)
0.47% swing DUP to SF
(2015: DUP majority 7,804 (22.48%))

NEWRY & ARMAGH
E. 78,266   T. 53,579 (68.46%)   SF hold

*Mickey Brady, SF		25,666
William Irwin, DUP		13,177
Justin McNulty, SDLP		9,055
Sam Nicholson, UUP		4,425
Jackie Coade, Alliance		1,256

SF majority 12,489 (23.31%)
swing N/A
(2015: SF majority 4,176 (8.37%))

STRANGFORD
E. 64,327   T. 38,749 (60.24%)

		DUP hold
*Jim Shannon, DUP		24,036
Kellie Armstrong, Alliance		5,693
Mike Nesbitt, UUP		4,419
Joe Boyle, SDLP		2,404
Carole Murphy, SF		1,083
Ricky Bamford, Green		607
Claire Hiscott, C.		507

DUP majority 18,343 (47.34%)
8.39% swing Alliance to DUP
(2015: DUP majority 10,185 (30.02%))

TYRONE WEST
E. 64,009   T. 43,486 (67.94%)   SF hold

Barry McElduff, SF		22,060
Thomas Buchanan, DUP		11,718
Daniel McCrossan, SDLP		5,635
Alicia Clarke, UUP		2,253
Stephen Donnelly, Alliance		1,000
Ciaran McClean, Green		427
Barry Brown, Citizens		393

SF majority 10,342 (23.78%)
1.12% swing SF to DUP
(2015: SF majority 10,060 (26.03%))

ULSTER MID
E. 68,485   T. 46,694 (68.18%)   SF hold

*Francie Molloy, SF		25,455
Keith Buchanan, DUP		12,565
Malachy Quinn, SDLP		4,563
Mark Glasgow, UUP		3,017
Fay Watson, Alliance		1,094

SF majority 12,890 (27.61%)
3.88% swing SF to DUP
(2015: SF majority 13,617 (33.28%))

UPPER BANN
E. 80,168   T. 51,258 (63.94%)

		DUP hold
*David Simpson, DUP		22,317
John O'Dowd, SF		14,325
Doug Beattie, UUP		7,900
Declan McAlinden, SDLP		4,397
Tara Doyle, Alliance		2,319

DUP majority 7,992 (15.59%)
3.73% swing SF to DUP
(2015: DUP majority 2,264 (4.79%))

THE GOVERNMENT

THE CABINET

Prime Minister, First Lord of the Treasury and Minister for the Civil Service
Rt. Hon. Theresa May, MP
First Secretary of State and Minister for the Cabinet Office
Rt. Hon. Damian Green, MP
Chancellor of the Exchequer and Second Lord of the Treasury
Rt. Hon. Philip Hammond, MP
Secretary of State for the Home Department
Rt. Hon. Amber Rudd, MP
Secretary of State for Foreign and Commonwealth Affairs
Rt. Hon. Boris Johnson, MP
Secretary of State for Exiting the European Union
Rt. Hon. David Davis, MP
Secretary of State for Defence
Rt. Hon. Sir Michael Fallon, KCB, MP
Secretary of State for Health
Rt. Hon. Jeremy Hunt, MP
Lord Chancellor and Secretary of State for Justice
Rt. Hon. David Lidington , CBE, MP
Secretary of State for Education and Minister for Women and Equalities
Rt. Hon. Justine Greening, MP
Secretary of State for International Trade
Rt. Hon. Liam Fox, MP
Secretary of State for Business, Energy and Industrial Strategy
Rt. Hon. Greg Clark, MP
Secretary of State for Environment, Food and Rural Affairs
Rt. Hon. Michael Gove, MP
Secretary of State for Transport
Rt. Hon. Chris Grayling, MP
Secretary of State for Communities and Local Government
Rt. Hon. Sajid Javid, MP
Lord Privy Seal and Leader of the House of Lords
Rt. Hon. Baroness Evans of Bowes Park
Secretary of State for Scotland
Rt. Hon. David Mundell, MP
Secretary of State for Wales
Rt. Hon. Alun Cairns, MP
Secretary of State for Northern Ireland
Rt. Hon. James Brokenshire, MP
Secretary of State for International Development
Rt. Hon. Priti Patel, MP
Secretary of State for Digital, Culture, Media and Sport
Rt. Hon. Karen Bradley, MP
Secretary of State for Work and Pensions
Rt. Hon. David Gauke, MP
Chancellor of the Duchy of Lancaster
Rt. Hon. Sir Patrick McLoughlin, MP

ALSO ATTENDING CABINET MEETINGS

Chief Secretary to the Treasury
Rt. Hon. Liz Truss, MP
Lord President of the Council and Leader of the House of Commons
Rt. Hon. Andrea Leadsom, CBE, MP
Parliamentary Secretary to the Treasury and Chief Whip
Rt. Hon. Gavin Williamson, CBE, MP
Attorney-General
Rt. Hon. Jeremy Wright, QC, MP
Minister of State for Immigration
Rt. Hon. Brandon Lewis, MP

LAW OFFICERS

Attorney-General
Rt. Hon. Jeremy Wright, QC, MP
Solicitor-General
Robert Buckland, QC, MP
Advocate-General for Scotland
Rt. Hon. Lord Keen of Elie, QC

MINISTERS OF STATE

Business, Energy and Industrial Strategy
Jo Johnson, MP*
Claire Perry, MP
Communities and Local Government
Alok Sharma, MP
Defence
Rt. Hon. Earl Howe**
Mark Lancaster, MP
Digital, Media, Culture and Sport
Rt. Hon. Matthew Hancock, MP
Education
Rt. Hon. Nick Gibb, MP
Robert Goodwill, MP
Jo Johnson, MP†
Rt. Hon. Anne Milton, MP
Environment, Food and Rural Affairs
George Eustice, MP
Exiting the European Union
Rt. Hon. Baroness Anelay of St Johns, DBE
Foreign and Commonwealth Office
Lord Ahmad of Wimbledon
Rt. Hon. Alistair Burt, MP‡
Rt. Hon. Sir Alan Duncan, MP
Rt. Hon. Mark Field MP
Rory Stewart, OBE, MP‡
Health
Philip Dunne, MP
Home Office
Nick Hurd, MP
Brandon Lewis, MP
Ben Wallace, MP
Baroness Williams of Trafford
International Development
Rt. Hon. Lord Bates
Rt. Hon. Alistair Burt, MP§
Rory Stewart, OBE, MP§
International Trade
Rt. Hon. Greg Hands, MP
Lord Price, CVO
Justice
Dominic Raab, MP
Transport
Rt. Hon. John Hayes, CBE, MP
Work and Pensions
Damian Hinds, MP
Penny Mordaunt, MP

* position jointly held with the Department of Education
† position jointly held with the Department of Business, Energy and Industrial Strategy
‡ position jointly held with the Department of International Development
§ position jointly held with the Department of Education
** alongside role as Deputy Leader of the House of Lords

UNDER-SECRETARIES OF STATE

Business, Energy and Industrial Strategy
Margot James, MP
Richard Harrington, MP
Lord Prior of Brampton
Communities and Local Government
Jake Berry, MP
Lord Bourne of Aberystwyth*
Marcus Jones, MP
Defence
Harriett Baldwin, MP
Rt. Hon. Tobias Ellwood, MP
Digital, Culture, Media and Sport
Lord Ashton of Hyde
Tracey Crouch, MP
John Glen, MP
Education
Lord Nash
Environment, Food and Rural Affairs
Thérèse Coffey, MP
Lord Gardiner of Kimble
Exiting the European Union
Steve Baker, MP
Robin Walker, MP
Health
Steve Brine, MP
Jackie Doyle-Price, MP
Lord O'Shaughnessy
Home Office
Sarah Newton, MP
International Trade
Mark Garnier, MP
Justice
Sam Gyimah, MP
Phillip Lee, MP
Northern Ireland Office
Lord Bourne of Aberystwyth†
Chloe Smith, MP
Scotland Office
Rt. Hon. Lord Duncan of Springbank‡
Transport
Lord Callanan
Paul Maynard, MP
Jesse Norman, MP
Office for the Secretary of State for Wales
Guto Bebb, MP
Rt. Hon. Lord Duncan of Springbank§
Work and Pensions
Baroness Buscombe
Caroline Dinenage, MP
Guy Opperman, MP

* position jointly held with the Northern Ireland Office
† position jointly held with the Department of Communities and Local Government
‡ position jointly held with the Office for the Secretary of State for Wales
§ position jointly held with the Scotland Office

OTHER MINISTERS

Cabinet Office
Chris Skidmore, MP *(Minister for the Constitution and Parliamentary Secretary)*
Office of the Leader of the House of Commons
Michael Ellis, MP *(Parliamentary Secretary and Deputy Leader of the Commons)*
Caroline Nokes, MP *(Parliamentary Secretary)*
Office of the Leader of the House of Lords
Rt. Hon. Earl Howe *(Deputy Leader of the House of Lords)*
Treasury
Stephen Barclay, MP *(Economic Secretary)*
Rt. Hon. Mel Stride, MP *(Financial Secretary and Paymaster General)*
Rt. Hon. Liz Truss, MP *(Chief Secretary)*

GOVERNMENT WHIPS

HOUSE OF LORDS

Lords Chief Whip and Captain of the Honourable Corps of Gentlemen-at-Arms
Rt. Hon. Lord Taylor of Holbeach, CBE
Deputy Chief Whip and Captain of the Queen's Bodyguard of the Yeomen of the Guard
Earl of Courtown
Lords-in-Waiting
Rt. Hon.Lord Young of Cookham, CH
Viscount Younger of Leckie
Baronesses-in-Waiting
Baroness Chisholm of Owlpen
Baroness Goldie
Baroness Sugg, CBE
Baroness Vere of Norbiton

HOUSE OF COMMONS

Chief Whip and Parliamentary Secretary to the Treasury
Rt. Hon. Gavin Williamson, CBE, MP
Deputy Chief Whip and Treasurer of HM Household
Julian Smith, MP
Deputy Chief Whip and Comptroller of HM Household
Christopher Pincher, MP
Government Whip and Vice-Chamberlain of HM Household
Chris Heaton-Harris, MP
Lords Commissioners of HM Treasury (Whips)
Guto Bebb, MP*; Rt. Hon. David Evennett, MP; Andrew Griffiths, MP; David Rutley, MP; Mark Spencer, MP; Heather Wheeler, MP
Assistant Whips
Nigel Adams, MP; Stuart Andrew, MP; Mike Freer, MP; Rebecca Harris, MP; Chloe Smith, MP†; Graham Stuart, MP; Andrew Stephenson, MP; Craig Whittaker, MP

* alongside role as Secretary of State at the Office for the Secretary of State for Wales
† alongside role as Secretary of State at the Northern Ireland Office

GOVERNMENT DEPARTMENTS

THE CIVIL SERVICE

The civil service helps the government develop and deliver its policies as effectively as possible. It works in three types of organisations – departments, executive agencies, and non-departmental government bodies (NDPBs). Under the Next Steps programme, launched in 1988, many semi-autonomous executive agencies were established to carry out much of the work of the civil service. Executive agencies operate within a framework set by the responsible minister which specifies policies, objectives and available resources. All executive agencies are set annual performance targets by their minister. Each agency has a chief executive, who is responsible for the day-to-day operations of the agency and who is accountable to the minister for the use of resources and for meeting the agency's targets. The minister accounts to parliament for the work of the agency.

There are currently 321,163 civil servants on a full-time equivalent (FTE) basis and 419,399 on a headcount basis. FTE is a measure that counts staff according to the proportion of full-time hours that they work. Almost three-quarters of all civil servants work outside London and the south-east. All government departments and executive agencies are responsible for their own pay and grading systems for civil servants outside the senior civil service.

SALARIES 2017–18

MINISTERIAL SALARIES
Ministers who are members of the House of Commons receive a parliamentary salary of £74,962 in addition to their ministerial salary.

Prime minister	£75,440
Cabinet minister (Commons)	£67,505
Cabinet minister (Lords)	£101,038
Minister of state (Commons)	£31,680
Minister of state (Lords)	£78,891
Parliamentary under-secretary (Commons)	£22,375
Parliamentary under-secretary (Lords)	£68,710

SPECIAL ADVISERS' SALARIES
Special advisers to government ministers are paid out of public funds; their salaries are negotiated individually, but are usually in the range of £40,352 to £106,864.

CIVIL SERVICE SALARIES	
Senior Civil Servants	
Permanent secretary	£143,420–£202,000
Band 3	£107,060–£210,181
Band 2	£87,870–£164,125
Band 1	£64,640–£118,978

Staff are placed in pay bands according to their level of responsibility and taking account of other factors such as experience and marketability. Movement within and between bands is based on performance. Following the delegation of responsibility for pay and grading to government departments and agencies from 1 April 1996, it is no longer possible to show service-wide pay rates for staff outside the Senior Civil Service.

GOVERNMENT DEPARTMENTS

For more information on government departments, *see* W www.gov.uk/government/organisations

ATTORNEY-GENERAL'S OFFICE
Attorney-General's Office, 5–8 The Sanctuary, London SW1P 3JS
T 020-7271 2492 E correspondence@attorneygeneral.gsi.gov.uk
W www.gov.uk/government/organisations/attorney-generals-office

The law officers of the crown for England and Wales are the Attorney-General and the Solicitor-General. The Attorney-General, assisted by the Solicitor-General, is the chief legal adviser to the government and is also ultimately responsible for all crown litigation. He has overall responsibility for the work of the Law Officers' Departments (the Treasury Solicitor's Department, the Crown Prosecution Service – incorporating the Revenue and Customs Prosecutions Office – and the Serious Fraud Office). The Attorney-General also oversees the armed forces' prosecuting authority and the government legal service. He has a specific statutory duty to superintend the discharge of their duties by the Director of Public Prosecutions (who heads the Crown Prosecution Service) and the Director of the Serious Fraud Office. The Attorney-General has specific responsibilities for the enforcement of the criminal law and also performs certain public interest functions, eg protecting charities and appealing unduly lenient sentences. He also deals with questions of law arising in bills and with issues of legal policy.

Following the devolution of power to the Northern Ireland Assembly on 12 April 2010, the assembly now appoints the Attorney-General for Northern Ireland. The Attorney-General for England and Wales holds the office of Advocate-General for Northern Ireland, with significantly reduced responsibilities in Northern Ireland. The Attorney-General's Office is supported by four executive agencies and public bodies.

Attorney-General, Rt. Hon. Jeremy Wright, QC, MP
Principal Private Secretary, Josh Dodd
Deputy Principal Private Secretary, Andrea Dowsett
Assistant Private Secretary, Leeann Thayalanayagam
Solicitor-General, Robert Buckland, QC, MP

MANAGEMENT BOARD
Director-General, Rowena Collins Rice
Deputy Legal Secretary and Head of Operations, Michelle Crotty

DEPARTMENT FOR BUSINESS, ENERGY AND INDUSTRIAL STRATEGY
1 Victoria Street, London SW1H 0ET
T 020-7215 5000 E enquiries@beis.gov.uk W www.gov.uk/government/organisations/department-for-business-energy-and-industrial-strategy

The Department for Business, Energy and Industrial Strategy (BEIS) was established in July 2016 following the appointment of Theresa May as prime minister. It merged the Department of Business, Innovation and Skills and the Department of Energy and Climate Change. BEIS brings together responsibilities for business, industrial strategy, science, innovation, energy and climate change, and is supported by 47 executive agencies and public bodies. It is responsible for: developing and delivering a comprehensive industrial strategy and leading the government's relationship with business; ensuring that the UK has secure, reliable, affordable and clean energy supplies; ensuring the UK remains at the forefront of science, research and innovation; and tackling climate change.

Secretary of State for Business, Energy and Industrial Strategy, Rt. Hon. Greg Clark, MP
Parliamentary Private Secretary, Kelly Tolhurst, MP
Special Advisers, Glen Hall; Guy Newey; Jacob Wilmer
Minister of State, Jo Johnson, MP *(Universities, Science, Research and Innovation)**
Parliamentary Private Secretary, Rishi Sunak, MP
Minister of State, Claire Perry, MP *(Climate Change and Industry)*
Parliamentary Under-Secretary of State, Margot James, MP *(Small Business, Consumers and Corporate Responsibility)*
Parliamentary Under-Secretary of State, Richard Harrington, MP *(Industry and Energy)*
Parliamentary Under-Secretary of State, Lord Prior of Brampton
* Jointly with the Department for Education

MANAGEMENT BOARD
Permanent Secretary, Alex Chisholm
Members, Sam Beckett *(Director-General, International, Growth and Analysis);* Prof. Tim Dafforn *(Chief Entrepreneurial Adviser);* Gareth Davies *(Director-General, Business and Science);* Prof. John Loughhead, OBE *(BEIS Chief Scientific Adviser);* Clive Maxwell *(Director-General, Energy Transformation);* Jeremy Pocklington *(Director-General, Energy and Security);* Angie Ridgwell *(Director-General, Corporate Services);* Jaee Samant *(Director-General, Economics and Markets);*
Non-Executive Members, Archie Norman *(Lead);* Stephen Carter; Prof. Dame Ann Dowling, DBE; Dame Carolyn McCall, DBE; Kathryn Parsons; Charles Randell; Stuart Quickenden

BETTER REGULATION EXECUTIVE
1 Victoria Street, London SW1 0ET
T 020-7215 5000 E betterregulation@bis.gsi.gov.uk
W www.gov.uk/government/policy-teams/better-regulation-executive

The Better Regulation Executive (BRE) is a joint BEIS/Cabinet Office unit which leads on delivering the government's manifesto commitment to reduce the overall burden on business, in order to increase growth and create jobs. Each government department is however responsible for delivering its part of the deregulation agenda within the framework put in place by the BRE.

Non-Executive Chair, Lord Curry of Kirkharle, CBE
Chief Executive, Graham Turnock

CABINET OFFICE
70 Whitehall, London SW1A 2AS
T 020-7276 1234
W www.gov.uk/government/organisations/cabinet-office

The Cabinet Office, alongside the Treasury, sits at the centre of the government, with an overarching purpose of making government work better. It supports the prime minister and the cabinet, helping to ensure effective development, coordination and implementation of policy and operations across all government departments. The Cabinet Office also leads work to ensure that the Civil Service provides the most effective and efficient support to the government to meet its objectives. The department is headed by the Minister for the Cabinet Office. The Cabinet Office is responsible for: supporting collective government; supporting the National Security Council and the Joint Intelligence Organisation, coordinating the government's response to crises and managing the UK's cyber security; promoting efficiency and reform across government through innovation, better procurement and project management, and by transforming the delivery of services; promoting the release of government

data, and making the way government works more transparent; improving the capability and effectiveness of the Civil Service; and political constitution and reform.

The priorities of the Cabinet Office include: supporting the prime minister and cabinet to deliver the government's programme; driving efficiencies and reforms to improve the government's performance; creating a more united democracy; and strengthening and securing the UK at home and abroad. The Cabinet Office employs around 2,050 staff and is supported by 19 executive agencies and public bodies.

Prime Minister, First Lord of the Treasury and Minister for the Civil Service, Rt. Hon. Theresa May, MP
Parliamentary Private Secretaries, George Hollingbery, MP; Seema Kennedy, MP
Principal Private Secretary, Peter Hill
Special Advisers, Alex Dawson; Stephen Parkinson; Sheridan Westlake, OBE
First Secretary of State and Minister for the Cabinet Office, Rt. Hon. Damian Green, MP
Parliamentary Private Secretary, James Morris, MP
Special Advisers, Flora Rose; Dylan Sharpe
Chancellor of the Duchy of Lancaster, Rt. Hon. Sir Patrick McLoughlin, MP
Parliamentary Private Secretary, Edward Argar, MP
Lord President of the Council, Rt. Hon. Andrea Leadsom, MP
Parliamentary Private Secretary, Victoria Prentis, MP
Special Advisers. Lucia Hodgson; Marc Pooler
Parliamentary Under-Secretary of State, Chris Skidmore, MP *(Constitution)*
Parliamentary Under-Secretary of State, Caroline Nokes, MP *(Government Resilience and Efficiency)*

MANAGEMENT BOARD
Permanent Secretary and Chief Executive of the Civil Service, John Manzoni
Cabinet Secretary and Head of the Civil Service, Sir Jeremy Heywood
First Parliamentary Counsel, Elizabeth Gardiner
Head of UK Governance Group, Philip Rycroft
Executive Director, Implementation Group, James Quinault
Chief People Officer, Rupert McNeil
Director-General, Propriety and Ethics Team and Head of Private Offices Group, Sue Gray
National Security Adviser, Mark Sedwill
Chair of the Joint Intelligence Committee, Charles Farr
Director-General, Prime Minister's Office, Peter Hill
Government Chief Commercial Officer, Gareth Rhys Williams
Finance Director, Guy Lester
Human Resources Directors, Crystall Akass and Ruth Bailey
Executive Director, Government Communications, Alex Aiken
Director-General, Government Digital Service, Kevin Cunnington
Director-General, UK Governance, Lucy Smith (acting)
Non-Executive Directors, Catherine Brown; Sir Ian Cheshire; Paul Kirby; Amy Stirling

HONOURS AND APPOINTMENTS BOARD
Room G-39, Horse Guards Road, London SW1A 2HQ
T 020-7276 2777
Chair, Sir Jonathan Stephens, KCB

OFFICE OF THE LEADER OF THE HOUSE OF COMMONS
1 Horse Guards Road, London SW1A 2HQ
T 020-7276 1005 E commonsleader@cabinetoffice.gov.uk
W www.gov.uk/government/organisations/the-office-of-the-leader-of-the-house-of-commons

The Office of the Leader of the House of Commons is responsible for the arrangement of government business in the House of Commons and for planning and supervising the government's legislative programme. The Leader of the House of Commons upholds the rights and privileges of the house and acts as a spokesperson for the government as a whole.

The leader reports regularly to the cabinet on parliamentary business and the legislative programme. In his capacity as leader of the house, he is a member of the House of Commons Commission. He also chairs the cabinet committee on the legislative programme. As Lord President of the Council, he is a member of the cabinet and in charge of the Office of the Privy Council.

The Deputy Leader of the House of Commons supports the leader in handling the government's business in the house. He is responsible for monitoring MPs' and peers' correspondence.

Leader of the House of Commons and Lord Privy Seal, Rt. Hon. Andrea Leadsom, MP
Parliamentary Private Secretary, Victoria Prentis, MP
Special Advisers, Lucia Hodgson, Marc Pooler
Deputy Leader of the House of Commons, Michael Ellis, MP

OFFICE OF THE LEADER OF THE HOUSE OF LORDS
House of Lords, London SW1A 0PW
T 020-7219 3200 E psleaderofthelords@cabinet-office.x.gsi.gov.uk
W www.gov.uk/government/organisations/office-of-the-leader-of-the-house-of-lords

The Office of the Leader of the House of Lords provides support to the leader in their parliamentary and ministerial duties, which include leading the government benches in the House of Lords; the delivery of the government's business in the Lords; taking part in formal ceremonies such as the state opening of parliament; and giving guidance to the House of Lords on matters of procedure and order.

Lord Privy Seal and Leader of the House of Lords, Rt. Hon. Baroness Evans of Bowes Park
Parliamentary Private Secretary, Victoria Atkins, MP
Special Adviser, Katherine Howell
Deputy Leader of the House of Lords, Rt. Hon. Earl Howe

GOVERNMENT POLICY

PRIME MINISTER'S OFFICE
10 Downing Street, London SW1A 2AA
T 020-7930 4433
W www.number-10.gov.uk

Prime Minister, Rt. Hon. Theresa May, MP
Parliamentary Private Secretaries, George Hollingbery, MP; Seema Kennedy, MP
Special Advisers, Alex Dawson; Stephen Parkinson; Sheridan Westlake, OBE
Principal Private Secretary, Peter Hill
Director of Communications, Robbie Gibb
Director of Policy, James Marshall
Prime Minister's Official Spokesman, James Slack
Prime Minister's Official Speech Writer, Jessica Cunliffe
Chief of Staff, Gavin Barwell
Deputy Chief of Staff, Joanna Penn
Press Secretary, James Slack
Head of Briefing, Edward de Minckwitz
Head of Features, Liz Sanderson
Head of Policy Unit, James Marshall
Head of Implementation Unit, Peter Hill

IMPLEMENTATION GROUP
Executive Director, James Quinault

PRIVATE OFFICES GROUP
Director-General, Propriety and Ethics and Head of Private Offices Group, Sue Gray

UK GOVERNANCE GROUP
Head of UK Governance Group, Philip Rycroft

CABINET OFFICE CORPORATE SERVICES
Executive Director, Government Communications, Alex Aiken
Finance Director, Guy Lester
Human Resources Directors, Crystal Akass and Ruth Bailey

NATIONAL SECURITY
Comprises the National Security Secretariat and the Joint Intelligence Organisation. The National Security Secretariat is responsible for providing policy advice to the National Security Council, where ministers discuss national security issues at a strategic level; coordinating and developing foreign and defence policy across government; coordinating policy, ethical and legal issues across the intelligence community, managing its funding and priorities, and dealing with the Intelligence and Security Committee which calls it to account; developing effective protective security policies and capabilities for government; improving the UK's resilience to respond to and recover from emergencies, and maintaining facilities for the effective coordination of government response to crises; and providing strategic leadership for cyber security in the UK, in line with the National Cyber Security Strategy.

NATIONAL SECURITY SECRETARIAT
National Security Adviser, Mark Sedwill
Deputy National Security Advisers, Gwyn Jenkins; Paddy McGuinness

JOINT INTELLIGENCE ORGANISATION
Chair, Joint Intelligence Committee, Charles Farr

INDEPENDENT OFFICES

CIVIL SERVICE COMMISSION
1 Horse Guards Road, London SW1A 2HQ
T 020-7271 0831
W www.civilservicecommission.independent.gov.uk

The Civil Service Commission regulates the requirement that selection for appointment to the Civil Service must be on merit on the basis of fair and open competition; the commission publishes its recruitment principles and audit departments and agencies' performance against these. Commissioners personally chair competitions for the most senior jobs in the civil service. In addition, the commission hears complaints from civil servants under the Civil Service Code.

The commission was established as a statutory body in November 2010 under the provisions of the Constitutional Reform and Governance Act 2010.

Commissioners, Jonathan Baume; Jane Burgess; Jan Cameron; Natalie Campbell; Isabel Doverty; Margaret Edwards; Andrew Flanagan; Rosie Glazebrook; Sarah Laessig; June Milligan; Joe Montgomery; Ian Watmore; Kevin Woods

THE COMMISSIONER FOR PUBLIC APPOINTMENTS
G/8, 1 Horse Guards Road, London SW1A 2HQ
T 020-7271 0831 E publicappointments@csc.gsi.gov.uk
W http://publicappointmentscommissioner.independent.gov.uk

The Commissioner for Public Appointments is responsible for monitoring, regulating and reporting on ministerial appointments (including those made by Welsh government ministers) to public bodies. The commissioner can investigate complaints about the way in which appointments were made.

Commissioner for Public Appointments, Peter Riddell
Chief Executive Commission Secretariat, Peter Lawrence, OBE

OFFICE OF THE PARLIAMENTARY COUNSEL
1 Horse Guards Road, London SW1A 2HQ
T 02-7276 6586 E goodlaw@cabinet-office.gsi.gov.uk
W www.gov.uk/government/organisations/office-of-the-parliamentary-counsel

The Office of the Parliamentary Counsel is a group of government lawyers who specialise in drafting government bills; advising departments on the rules and procedures of Parliament; reviewing orders and regulations which amend

Acts of Parliament; and assisting the government on a range of legal and constitutional issues.

First Parliamentary Counsel, Elizabeth Gardiner
Chief Executive, Jim Barron, CBE

DEPARTMENT FOR COMMUNITIES AND LOCAL GOVERNMENT

2 Marsham Street, London SW1P 4DF
T 0303-444 0000 W www.gov.uk/government/organisations/department-for-communities-and-local-government

The Department for Communities and Local Government (DCLG) was formed in May 2006 with a remit to promote community cohesion and prevent extremism, and was given responsibility for housing, urban regeneration and planning. It unites the communities and civil renewal functions previously undertaken by the Home Office, with responsibility for regeneration, neighbourhood renewal and local government (previously held by the Office of the Deputy Prime Minister, which was abolished following a cabinet reshuffle in May 2006). The department ensures that the Fire and Rescue services have the resources they need to reduce the number of deaths from fire, promote fire prevention activity and respond swiftly to national emergencies. The department also has responsibility for equality policy on race and faith (functions that were previously split between several government departments).The DCLG is supported by eleven executive agencies and public bodies.

Secretary of State for Communities and Local Government, Rt. Hon. Sajid Javid, MP *(Ministerial Champion for the Midlands Engine)*
Parliamentary Private Secretary, Mims Davies, MP
Special Advisers, James Hedgeland; Nick King; Salma Shah
Minister of State, Alok Sharma, MP *(Housing and Planning)*
Parliamentary Private Secretary, Kevin Foster, MP
Parliamentary Under-Secretary of State, Jake Berry, MP *(Northern Powerhouse and Local Growth)*
Parliamentary Under-Secretary of State, Marcus Jones, MP *(Local Government)*
Parliamentary Under-Secretary of State, Lord Bourne of Aberystwyth *(Faith)**

* Jointly held with the Northern Ireland Office

MANAGEMENT BOARD
Permanent Secretary, Melanie Dawes, CB
Members, Jo Farrar *(Director-General, Local Government and Public Services)*; Christine Hewitt *(Director, People, Capability and Change)*; Jacinda Humphry *(Director, Finance)*; Helen MacNamara *(Director-General, Housing and Planning)*; Stephen Meek *(Director, Strategy, Communications and Private Office)*; Simon Ridley *(Director-General, Decentralisation and Growth)*
Non-Executive Members, Nick Markham *(Lead)*; Mary Ney; Grenville Turner

SPECIAL REPRESENTATIVES
UK Special Envoy for post-Holocaust Issues and Anti-Corruption Champion, Rt. Hon. Sir Eric Pickles

MINISTRY OF DEFENCE

Main Building, Whitehall, London SW1A 2HB
T 020-7218 9000 W www.gov.uk/government/organisations/ministry-of-defence

For further information on the responsibilities and remit of the MoD *see* the Defence Chapter.

Secretary of State for Defence, Rt. Hon. Sir Michael Fallon, KCB, MP
Parliamentary Private Secretary, Oliver Dowden, MP
Special Advisers, Rob Oxley; James Wild
Minister of State, Rt. Hon. Earl Howe *(Lords)*

Minister of State, Mark Lancaster, TD, MP *(Armed Forces)*
Parliamentary Private Secretary, Anne-Marie Trevelyan, MP
Parliamentary Under-Secretary of State and Minister for Defence Procurement, Harriett Baldwin, MP
Parliamentary Under-Secretary of State and Minister for Defence People and Veterans, Rt. Hon. Tobias Ellwood, MP

CHIEFS OF STAFF
Chief of the Defence Staff, Air Chief Marshal Sir Stuart Peach, GBE, KCB, ADC
Vice-Chief of the Defence Staff, Gen. Sir Gordon Messenger, KCB, DSO*, OBE, ADC
Chief of the Naval Staff and First Sea Lord, Adm. Sir Philip Jones, KCB, ADC
Chief of the General Staff, Gen. Sir Nicholas Carter, KCB, CBE, DSO, ADC
Chief of the Air Staff, Air Chief Marshal Sir Stephen Hillier, KCB, CBE, DFC, ADC
Commander of Joint Forces Command, Gen. Sir Chris Deverell, KCB, MBE, ADC

MANAGEMENT BOARD
Permanent Secretary, Stephen Lovegrove
Members, Julian Kelly *(Nuclear)*; Lt.-Gen. Richard Nugee, CVO, CBE *(Chief of Defence People)*; Julie Taylor *(Head Office and Commissioning Services)*; Louise Tulett, CBE *(Finance)*; Peter Watkins, CBE *(Security Policy)*
Non-Executive Members, Sir Gerry Grimstone *(Lead)*; Danuta Gray; Paul Skinner, CBE; Graham Williams

DEPARTMENT FOR DIGITAL, CULTURE, MEDIA AND SPORT

100 Parliament Street, London SW1A 2BQ
T 020-7211 6000 E enquiries@culture.gov.uk W www.gov.uk/government/organisations/department-for-culture-media-sport

The Department for Digital, Culture, Media and Sport (DCMS) was established in July 1997 (as the Department for Culture, Media and Sport) and aims to improve the quality of life for all those in the UK through cultural and sporting activities while championing the tourism, creative and leisure industries. It is responsible for government policy relating to the arts, sport, the National Lottery, tourism, libraries, museums and galleries, creative industries – including film and the music industry – press freedom and regulation, licensing, gambling, the historic environment, telecommunications and online and media ownership and mergers. In July 2017, the department was rebranded to reflect its growing commitment and responsibility regarding digital infrastructure, communication and cyber security.

The department is also responsible for 42 agencies and public bodies that help deliver the department's strategic aims and objectives, the listing of historic buildings and scheduling of ancient monuments, the export licensing of cultural goods, and the management of the Government Art Collection and the Royal Parks (its sole executive agency). It has the responsibility for humanitarian assistance in the event of a disaster, as well as for the organisation of the annual Remembrance Day ceremony at the Cenotaph. In September 2012, the Government Equalities Office became part of DCMS, having previously been part of the Home Office.

Secretary of State for Digital, Culture, Media and Sport, Rt. Hon. Karen Bradley, MP
Parliamentary Private Secretary, Matt Warman, MP
Special Adviser, Aidan Corley
Minister of State, Rt. Hon. Matthew Hancock, MP *(Digital)*
Parliamentary Private Secretary, Nigel Huddleston, MP
Parliamentary Under-Secretary of State, Tracey Crouch, MP *(Sport and Civil Society)*
Parliamentary Under-Secretary of State, John Glen, MP *(Arts, Heritage and Tourism)*
Parliamentary Under-Secretary of State, Lord Ashton of Hyde

MANAGEMENT BOARD

Permanent Secretary, Sue Owen

Members, Matthew Gould (Director-General, Digital and Media); Helen Judge (Director-General, Performance and Strategy); David Rossington (Director, Finance)

Non-Executive Members, Charles Alexander (Lead); Matthew Campbell-Hill; Neil Mendoza; Fields Wicker-Miurin, OBE

DEPARTMENT FOR EDUCATION

20 Great Smith Street, London SW1P 3BT
T 0370-000 2288
W www.gov.uk/government/organisations/department-for-education

The Department for Education (DfE) was established in May 2010 in place of the Department for Children, Schools and Families (DCSF), in order to refocus the department on its core purpose of supporting teaching and learning. The department is responsible for education and children's services, while the Department for Business, Innovation and Skills is responsible for higher education. The DfE is supported by 18 executive agencies and public bodies.

The department's objectives include the expansion of the academies programme, to allow schools to apply to become independent of their local authority, and the introduction of the free schools programme, to allow any suitable proposers, such as parents, businesses or charities, to set up their own school.

Secretary of State for Education and Minister for Women and Equalities, Rt. Hon. Justine Greening, MP

Parliamentary Private Secretary, Helen Whatley, MP

Special Advisers, Victoria Crawford; Peter Wilson

Minister of State, Rt. Hon. Nick Gibb, MP (School Standards; Equalities)

Parliamentary Private Secretary, Luke Hall, MP

Minister of State, Robert Goodwill, MP (Children and Families)

Minister of State, Jo Johnson, MP (Universities, Science, Research and Innovation)*

Minister of State, Rt. Hon. Anne Milton, MP (Apprenticeships and Skills; Women)

Parliamentary Under-Secretary of State, Lord Nash (School System)

* Jointly with the Department for Business, Energy and Industrial Strategy

MANAGEMENT BOARD

Permanent Secretary, Jonathan Slater

Members, Paul Kett (Director-General, Education Standards); Philippa Lloyd (Director-General, Higher and Further Education); Andrew McCully (Director-General, Infrastructure and Funding); Indra Morris (Director-General, Social Care, Mobility and Equalities); Howard Orme (Chief Financial and Operating Officer, Insight, Resources and Transformation)

Non-Executive Members, Ian Ferguson, CBE; Baroness Ruby McGregor-Smith, CBE; David Meller; Marion Plant, OBE

GOVERNMENT EQUALITIES OFFICE

Department for Education, 20 Great Smith Street, London SW1P 3BT T 0370-000 2288
W www.gov.uk/government/organisations/government-equalities-office

The Government Equalities Office (GEO) is responsible for the government's overall strategy on equality. Its work includes leading the development of a more integrated approach on equality across government with the aim of improving equality and reducing discrimination and disadvantage for all. The office is also responsible for leading policy on gender equality, sexual orientation and transgender equality matters.

Minister for Women and Equalities, Rt. Hon. Justine Greening, MP

Minister for Women, Rt. Hon Anne Milton, MP

Minister for Equalities, Nick Gibb, MP

Director, Hilary Spencer

DEPARTMENT FOR ENVIRONMENT, FOOD AND RURAL AFFAIRS

Nobel House, 17 Smith Square, London SW1P 3JR
T 03459-335577
E defra.helpline@defra.gsi.gov.uk W www.gov.uk/government/organisations/department-for-environment-food-rural-affairs

The Department for Environment, Food and Rural Affairs (DEFRA) is responsible for government policy on the environment, rural matters and farming and food production. In association with the agriculture departments of the Scottish government, the National Assembly for Wales and the Northern Ireland Office, the department is responsible for negotiations in the EU on the common agricultural and fisheries policies, and for single European market questions relating to its responsibilities. Its remit includes international agricultural and food trade policy.

The department's five strategic priorities are climate change adaptation; sustainable consumption and production; the protection of natural resources and the countryside; sustainable rural communities; and sustainable farming and food, including animal health and welfare. DEFRA, which is supported by 33 executive agencies and public bodies, is also the lead government department for emergencies in animal and plant diseases, flooding, food and water supply, dealing with the consequences of a chemical, biological, radiological or nuclear incident, and other threats to the environment.

Secretary of State for Environment, Food and Rural Affairs, Rt. Hon. Michael Gove, MP

Parliamentary Private Secretary, Kevin Hollinrake, MP

Special Adviser, Henry Cook

Minister of State, George Eustice, MP (Agriculture, Fisheries and Food)

Parliamentary Private Secretary, Rebecca Pow, MP

Parliamentary Under-Secretary of State, Thérèse Coffey, MP (Environment)

Parliamentary Under-Secretary of State, Lord Gardiner of Kimble (Rural Affairs and Biosecurity)

MANAGEMENT BOARD

Permanent Secretary, Clare Moriarty

Members, Betsy Bassis (Chief Operating Officer); Emma Howard Boyd; Prof. Ian Boyd (Chief Scientific Adviser); Nick Joicey (Strategy, EU Exit and Finance); David Kennedy (Food, Farming, Animal and Plant Health); Sonia Phippard (Marine, Natural Environment and Rural); Andrew Sells

Non-Executive Members, Peter Bonfield; Catherine Doran; Steve Holliday; Paul Rew

DEPARTMENT FOR EXITING THE EUROPEAN UNION

9 Downing Street, London SW1A 2AG
T 020-7276 0432
W www.gov.uk/government/organisations/department-for-exiting-the-european-union

The Department for Exiting the European Union (DEEU) was formed by the prime minister Theresa May in July 2016 after the UK voted to leave the European Union in a referendum on 23 June 2016. The DEEU is responsible for overseeing negotiations to leave the EU and establishing the future relationship of the UK with the EU.

The department has four main responsibilities: to support the UK's negotiations to leave the EU and to establish the future relationship between the UK and the EU; to work closely with the UK's devolved administrations, Parliament, and a range of other interested parties on the approach to the negotiations; to conduct the negotiations in support of the prime minister including supporting bilateral discussions on exiting the EU with other European countries; and to lead and coordinate cross-government work to seize the opportunities and ensure a smooth process of exit on positive terms.

Secretary of State for Exiting the European Union, Rt. Hon. David Davis, MP
Parliamentary Private Secretary, Gareth Johnson, MP
Special Advisers, Stewart Jackson; Raoul Ruparel; Tim Smith
Minister of State, Rt. Hon. Baroness Anelay of St Johns, DBE,
Parliamentary Private Secretary, Jeremy Quin, MP
Parliamentary Under-Secretary of State, Steve Baker, MP
Parliamentary Under-Secretary of State, Robin Walker, MP

MANAGEMENT BOARD
Permanent Secretary, Oliver Robbins
Second Permanent Secretary, Philip Rycroft
Members, Matt Baugh *(Director of the Negotiation Coordination Unit);* Alex Ellis, *(Director-General);* Sarah Healey *(Director-General);* Chris Jones *(Justice, Security and Migration);* Joanna Key *(Strategy and Planning);* Anthony Phillipson *(Trade and Partnerships);* Tom Shinner *(Cross-Government Policy Coordination);* Susannah Storey *(Planning and Analysis);* Catherine Webb *(Market Access and Budget)*
Non-Executive Members, Susan Hooper; Margaret Stephens

FOREIGN AND COMMONWEALTH OFFICE
King Charles Street, London SW1A 2AH
T 020-7008 1500 E fcocorrespondence@fco.gov.uk
W www.gov.uk/government/organisations/
foreign-commonwealth-office

The Foreign and Commonwealth Office (FCO) provides the means of communication between the British government and other governments – and international governmental organisations – on all matters falling within the field of international relations. The FCO employs over 14,000 people in nearly 270 places across the world through a network of embassies and consulates, which help to protect and promote national interests. FCO diplomats are skilled in understanding and influencing what is happening abroad, supporting British citizens who are travelling and living overseas, helping to manage migration into Britain, promoting British trade and other interests abroad and encouraging foreign investment in the UK. The FCO is supported by ten executive agencies and public bodies.

Secretary of State for Foreign and Commonwealth Affairs, Rt. Hon. Boris Johnson, MP
Parliamentary Private Secretary, Conor Burns, MP
Special Advisers, David Blair; David Frost; Ben Gascoigne; Liam Parker
Minister of State, Rt. Hon. Sir Alan Duncan, KCMG, MP *(Europe and the Americas)*
Minister of State, Rt. Hon. Alistair Burt, MP *(Middle East)**
Minister of State, Rory Stewart, OBE, MP *(Africa)**
Minister of State, Rt. Hon Mark Field, MP *(Asia and the Pacific)*
Minister of State, Lord Ahmad of Wimbledon *(Commonwealth and the UN)*
Parliamentary Private Secretary, Amanda Milling, MP
Special Representatives, Lord Ahmad of Wimbledon *(Prime Minister's Special Representative on Preventing Sexual Violence in Conflict);* Nick Bridge *(Climate Change);* Prof. Robin Grimes *(Chief Scientific Adviser);* Owen Jenkins *(Afghanistan and Pakistan);* Simon Mustard *(Special Envoy for the African Great Lakes and Head of Southern and Central African Department);* Rt. Hon. Sir Eric Pickles *(UK Special Envoy for Post-Holocaust Issues and Anti-Corruption Champion);* Joanna Roper, CMG *(Special Envoy for Gender Equality);* Chris Trott *(Sudan and South Sudan)*

* Jointly with the Department for International Development

MANAGEMENT BOARD
Permanent Under-Secretary and Head of the Diplomatic Service, Sir Simon McDonald, KCMG, KCVO
Members, Philip Barton *(Consular and Security);* Alison Blake *(Overseas Network Representative);* Helen Bower-Easton, CBE *(Communication);* Deborah Bronnert, CMG *(Economic and Global Issues);* Jill Gallard *(Human Resources);* Peter Jones *(Chief Operating Officer);* Sir Iain Macleod, KCMG *(Legal);* Karen Pierce, CMG *(Political);* Andrew Sanderson *(Finance);* Liane Saunders *(Strategy and Strategic Programmes Coordinator);* Christian Turner, CMG *(Deputy National Security Adviser)*
Non-Executive Members, Miranda Curtis *(Lead);* Julia Bond; Sir Edward Lister; Warren Tucker

DEPARTMENT OF HEALTH
Richmond House, 79 Whitehall, London SW1A 2NS
T 020-7210 4850 W www.gov.uk/government/organisations/
department-of-health

The Department of Health (DH) leads, shapes and funds health and care in England, making sure people have the support, care and treatment they need and that this is delivered in a compassionate, respectful and dignified manner.
   The DH leads across health and care by creating national policies and legislation to meet current and future challenges. It provides funding, assures the delivery and continuity of services and accounts to parliament in a way that represents the best interests of patients, the public and the taxpayer. The DH is supported by 29 executive agencies and public bodies.

Secretary of State for Health, Rt. Hon. Jeremy Hunt, MP
Parliamentary Private Secretary, Jo Churchill, MP
Special Adviser, Ed Jones
Minister of State, Philip Dunne, MP
Parliamentary Private Secretary, James Cartlidge, MP
Parliamentary Under-Secretary of State, Steve Brine, MP
Parliamentary Under-Secretary of State, Jackie Doyle-Price, MP
Parliamentary Under-Secretary of State, Lord O'Shaughnessy *(Lords)*

DEPARTMENTAL BOARD
Permanent Secretary, Sir Chris Wormald, KCB
Members, Prof. Dame Sally Davies, DBE *(Chief Medical Officer);* Tamara Finkelstein *(Community Care);* Lee McDonough *(Acute Care and Workforce);* Clara Swinson *(Global and Public Health);* Prof. Chris Whitty *(Chief Scientific Adviser);* David Williams *(Finance and Group Operations)*

HOME OFFICE
2 Marsham Street, London SW1P 4DF
T 020-7035 4848 E public.enquiries@homeoffice.gsi.gov.uk
W www.gov.uk/government/organisations/home-office

The Home Office deals with those internal affairs in England and Wales which have not been assigned to other government departments. The Secretary of State for the Home Department is the link between the Queen and the public, and exercises certain powers on her behalf, including that of the royal pardon.
   The Home Office aims to build a safe, just and tolerant society and to maintain and enhance public security and protection; to support and mobilise communities so that they are able to shape policy and improvement for their locality, overcome nuisance and anti-social behaviour, maintain and enhance social cohesion and enjoy their homes and public spaces peacefully; to deliver departmental policies and responsibilities fairly, effectively and efficiently; and to make the best use of resources. These objectives reflect the priorities of the government and the home secretary in areas of crime, citizenship and communities, namely to work on the problems caused by illegal drug use; shape the alcohol strategy, policy and licensing conditions; keep the UK safe from the threat of

terrorism; reduce and prevent crime, and ensure people feel safe in their homes and communities; secure the UK border and control immigration; consider applications to enter and stay in the UK; issue passports and visas; and to support visible, responsible and accountable policing by empowering the public and freeing up the police to fight crime.

The Home Office delivers these aims through the immigration services, its 28 executive agencies and non-departmental public bodies, and by working with partners in private, public and voluntary sectors, individuals and communities. The home secretary is also the link between the UK government and the governments of the Channel Islands and the Isle of Man.

Secretary of State for the Home Department, Rt. Hon. Amber Rudd, MP
Parliamentary Private Secretary, Robert Jenrick, MP
Special Advisers, Amy Fisher; Simon Glasson; Mo Hussein
Minister of State, Rt. Hon. Brandon Lewis, MP *(Immigration)*
Parliamentary Private Secretary, James Cleverly, MP
Special Adviser, Rupert Yorke
Minister of State, Rt. Hon. Ben Wallace, MP *(Security)*
Minister of State, Nick Hurd, MP *(Policing and the Fire Service)*
Minister of State, Baroness Williams of Trafford *(Countering Extremism)*
Parliamentary Private Secretaries, Nus Ghani, MP; Simon Hoare, MP
Parliamentary Under-Secretary of State, Sarah Newton, MP *(Crime, Safeguarding and Vulnerability)*

MANAGEMENT BOARD
Permanent Secretary, Philip Rutnam
Second Permanent Secretary, Patsy Wilkinson
Members, Peter Fish, CB *(Legal);* Tom Hurd *(Security and Counter-Terrorism);* Hugh Ind *(Immigration Enforcement);* Paula Leach *(Chief People Officer);* Paul Lincoln *(Crime, Policing and Fire Group);* Sir Charles Montgomery *(Border Force);* Mike Parsons *(Capabilities and Resources);* Mark Thomson *(UK Visas and Immigration; Director-General HM Passport Office)*
Non-Executive Members, Sue Langley, OBE *(Lead);* Adrian Joseph; Suzy Levy; Nicholas Shott; John Studzinski, CBE

DEPARTMENT FOR INTERNATIONAL DEVELOPMENT

22 Whitehall, London SW1A 2EG **T** 020-7023 0000
Abercrombie House, Eaglesham Road, East Kilbride, Glasgow G75 8EA **T** 01355-844000
Public Enquiries 0845-300 4100 **E** enquiry@dfid.gov.uk
W www.gov.uk/government/organisations/department-for-international-development

The Department for International Development (DFID) is responsible for promoting sustainable development and reducing poverty. The central focus of the government's policy, based on the 1997, 2000, 2006 and 2009 white papers on international development, is a commitment to the internationally agreed Millennium Development Goals, to be achieved by 2015. These seek to eradicate extreme poverty and hunger; achieve universal primary education; promote gender equality and empower women; reduce child mortality; improve maternal health; combat HIV/AIDS, malaria and other diseases; improve sanitation and access to clean water; ensure environmental sustainability; and encourage a global partnership for development.

DFID's assistance is concentrated in the poorest countries of sub-Saharan Africa and Asia, but also contributes to poverty reduction and sustainable development in middle-income countries, including those in Latin America and Eastern Europe. It also responds to overseas emergencies. The department works in partnership with governments of developing countries, charities, non-governmental organisations and businesses. It also works with multilateral institutions, including the World Bank, United Nations agencies and the European Commission. The department, which is supported by two executive agencies and public bodies, has headquarters in London and East Kilbride, offices in many developing countries, and staff based in British embassies and high commissions around the world.

Secretary of State for International Development, Rt. Hon. Priti Patel, MP
Parliamentary Private Secretary, Wendy Morton, MP
Special Adviser, Richard Parr
Minister of State, Rory Stewart, OBE, MP*
Minister of State, Rt. Hon. Alistair Burt, MP*
Minister of State, Rt. Hon. Lord Bates
Parliamentary Private Secretary, Michael Tomlinson, MP

*Jointly with the Foreign and Commonwealth Office

MANAGEMENT BOARD
Permanent Secretary, Nick Dyer
Members, Lindy Cameron *(Country Programmes);* Joy Hutcheon *(Finance and Corporate Performance)*
Non-Executive Members, Vivienne Cox, CBE *(Lead);* Sally Jones-Evans; Richard Keys; Tim Robinson

CDC GROUP

123 Victoria Street, London SW1E 6DE
T 020-7963 4700 **E** enquiries@cdcgroup.com
W www.cdcgroup.com

Founded in 1948, CDC is the UK's Development Finance Institution wholly owned by the UK government. It invests to create jobs and build businesses in developing countries in Africa and South Asia. In 2016 CDC's new investment commitments totalled £1.2bn to 653 businesses in Africa and 342 businesses in South Asia, helping to create 1.29 million new jobs across these regions. CDC is a public limited company with net assets of £4.8bn.

Chair, Graham Wrigley
Chief Executive, Nick O'Donohoe

DEPARTMENT FOR INTERNATIONAL TRADE

King Charles Street, Whitehall, London SW1A 2AH
T 020-7215 5000
W www.gov.uk/government/organisations/department-for-international-trade

The Department for International Trade was formed by the prime minister Theresa May in July 2016 following the UK referendum to leave the European Union. The department is responsible for promoting British trade around the world, striking and extending trade agreements between the UK and non-EU states. It is supported by two executive agencies and public bodies.

Secretary of State for International Trade and President of the Board of Trade, Rt. Hon. Liam Fox, MP
Parliamentary Private Secretary, Tom Pursglove, MP
Special Advisers, David Goss; Amy Tinley
Minister of State, Rt. Hon. Greg Hands, MP *(Trade and Investment)*
Minister of State, Lord Price, CVO *(Trade Policy)*
Parliamentary Under-Secretary of State, Mark Garnier, MP
Parliamentary Private Secretary, Mike Wood, MP

MANAGEMENT BOARD
Permanent Secretary, Antonia Romeo
Second Permanent Secretary, Crawford Falconer
Members, John Alty *(Trade Policy);* Alison Currie *(Finance and Corporate Services Director);* Paul McComb *(Transition Programme);* James Norton *(Human Resources and Organisational Development);* Dr Catherine Raines, FRSA *(International Trade and Investment);* Emma Squire

(Ministerial Strategy); Louis Taylor *(Chief Executive, UK Export Finance)*
Non-Executive Members, Simon Walker *(Lead);* Julie Currie, Noel Harwerth, Dr Pippa Malmgren

MINISTRY OF JUSTICE
102 Petty France, London SW1H 9AJ
T 020-3334 3555 E general.queries@justice.gsi.gov.uk
W www.gov.uk/government/organisations/ministry-of-justice

The Ministry of Justice (MoJ) was established in May 2007. MoJ is headed by the Lord Chancellor and Secretary of State for Justice who is responsible for improvements to the justice system so that it better serves the public. He is also responsible for some areas of constitutional policy.

The MoJ's key priorities are to reduce reoffending by using the skills of the public, private and voluntary sectors; reduce youth crime by putting education at the centre of youth justice; build a prison system that delivers maximum value for money; reduce the cost of legal aid and ensure it helps those cases that genuinely require it; and to improve the way the courts are run and put the needs of victims first. The MoJ has a budget of around £9bn and is supported by its executive agencies and public bodies to achieve its targets.

The Lord Chancellor and Secretary of State for Justice is the government minister responsible to parliament for the judiciary, the court system and prisons and probation. The Lord Chief Justice has been the head of the judiciary since 2006.

MoJ incorporates HM Prison and Probation Service; HM Courts and Tribunals Service; the Legal Aid Agency; and the Youth Justice Board.

Lord Chancellor and Secretary of State for Justice, Rt. Hon. David Lidington, CBE, MP
Parliamentary Private Secretary, Lucy Frazer, QC, MP
Special Advisers, Anita Boateng; Fraser Raleigh
Minister of State, Dominic Raab, MP
Parliamentary Private Secretary, Alan Mak, MP
Parliamentary Under-Secretary of State, Sam Gyimah, MP *(Prisons and Probation)*
Parliamentary Under-Secretary of State, Dr Phillip Lee, MP *(Youth Justice, Victims, Female Offenders and Offender Health)*
HM Advocate-General for Scotland and MoJ Spokesman for the Lords, Lord Keen of Elie, QC

MANAGEMENT BOARD
Permanent Secretary, Richard Heaton
Members, Matthew Coats, CB *(Chief Operating Officer);* Mike Driver *(Chief Financial Officer and Head of the Government Finance Function);* Scott McPhearson *(Justice and Courts Policy Group (acting));* Justin Russell *(Prisons, Offender and Youth Justice Policy);* Michael Spurr *(Chief Executive HM Prison and Probation Service)*
Non-Executive Members, Sir Theodore Agnew *(Lead);* Liz Doherty; Lizzie Noel

NORTHERN IRELAND OFFICE
1 Horse Guards Road, London SW1A 2HQ
Stormont House, Stormont Estate, Belfast BT4 3SH
T 028-9052 0700 E NIOwebEditor.mailbox@nio.gov.uk
W www.gov.uk/government/organisations/northern-ireland-office

The Northern Ireland Office was established in 1972, when the Northern Ireland (Temporary Provisions) Act transferred the legislative and executive powers of the Northern Ireland parliament and government to the UK parliament and a secretary of state. Under the terms of the 1998 Good Friday Agreement, power was devolved to the Northern Ireland Assembly in 1999. The assembly took on responsibility for the relevant areas of work previously undertaken by the departments of the Northern Ireland Office, covering agriculture and rural development, the environment, regional development, social development, education, higher education, training and employment, enterprise, trade and investment, culture, arts and leisure, health, social services, public safety and finance and personnel. In October 2002 the Northern Ireland Assembly was suspended and Northern Ireland returned to direct rule, but despite repeated setbacks, devolution was restored on 8 May 2007. On 9 January 2017 Martin McGuinness resigned as Deputy First Minister of Northern Ireland. Under the joint protocols that govern the power-sharing agreement, if either the first minister or the deputy resigns and a replacement is not nominated by the relevant party within seven days, then a snap election must be called. The assembly was formerly dissolved at midnight on 25 January 2017 and the most recent assembly elections were held on 2 March 2017. The assembly failed to appoint the executive committee of ministers in charge of the nine government departments within the three-week deadline following the election and, to date, the devolved government in Northern Ireland has yet to be restored. For further details, *see* Devolved Government.

The Northern Ireland Office is supported by three executive agencies and public bodies and is currently responsible for overseeing the devolution settlement; representing Northern Ireland interests within the UK government and similarly representing the UK government in Northern Ireland; working in partnership with the Northern Ireland Executive for a stable, prosperous Northern Ireland; and supporting and implementing political agreements to increase stability.

Secretary of State for Northern Ireland, Rt. Hon. James Brokenshire, MP
Parliamentary Private Secretary, David Morris, MP
Special Advisers, Jonathan Caine; Peter Cardwell
Parliamentary Under-Secretary of State, Chloe Smith, MP
Parliamentary Under-Secretary of State, Lord Bourne of Aberystwyth*
Permanent Secretary, Sir Jonathan Stephens

*Jointly with the Department for Communities and Local Government

OFFICE OF THE ADVOCATE-GENERAL FOR SCOTLAND
Dover House, Whitehall, London SW1A 2AU
T 020-7270 6770
Office of the Solicitor to the Advocate-General, Victoria Quay, Edinburgh EH6 6QQ
T 0131-244 0359 E enquiries@advocategeneral.gsi.gov.uk
W www.gov.uk/government/organisations/office-of-the-advocate-general-for-scotland

The Advocate-General for Scotland is one of the three law officers of the crown, alongside the Attorney-General and the Solicitor-General for England and Wales. He is the legal adviser to the UK government on Scottish law and is supported by staff in the Office of the Advocate-General for Scotland. The office is divided into the Legal Secretariat, based mainly in London, and the Office of the Solicitor to the Advocate-General, based in Edinburgh.

The post was created as a consequence of the constitutional changes set out in the Scotland Act 1998, which created a devolved Scottish parliament. The Lord Advocate and the Solicitor-General for Scotland then became part of the Scottish government and the Advocate-General took over their previous role as legal adviser to the UK government on Scots law. *See also* Devolved Government *and* Ministry of Justice.

HM Advocate-General for Scotland and MoJ Spokesman for the Lords, Lord Keen of Elie, QC
Private Secretary, Craig Chalcraft

MANAGEMENT BOARD
Head of Advisory and Legislation Division, Ruraidh Macniven
Members, Jim Logie *(Head of HMRC Division);* Fiona Robertson *(Head of Litigation Division);* Neil Taylor *(Legal Secretary to the Advocate-General)*

SCOTLAND OFFICE

Dover House, Whitehall, London SW1A 2AU
1 Melville Crescent, Edinburgh EH3 7HW
T 0131-244 9010 E enquiries@scotlandoffice.gsi.gov.uk
W www.gov.uk/government/organisations/scotland-office

The Scotland Office is the department of the Secretary of State for Scotland which represents Scottish interests within the UK government in matters reserved to the UK parliament. The Secretary of State for Scotland maintains the stability of the devolution settlement for Scotland; delivers secondary legislation under the Scotland Act 1998; is responsible for the conduct and funding of the Scottish parliament elections; manages the Scottish vote provision and authorises the monthly payment of funds from the UK consolidated fund to the Scottish consolidated fund; and publishes regular information on the state of the Scottish economy.

Matters reserved to the UK parliament include the constitution, foreign affairs, defence, international development, the civil service, financial and economic matters, national security, immigration and nationality, misuse of drugs, trade and industry, various aspects of energy regulation (eg coal, electricity, oil, gas and nuclear energy), various aspects of transport, social security, employment, abortion, genetics, surrogacy, medicines, broadcasting and equal opportunities. Devolved matters include health and social work, education and training, local government and housing, justice and police, agriculture, forestry, fisheries, the environment, tourism, sports, heritage, economic development and internal transport. It is supported by one public body. *See also* Devolved Government *and* Ministry of Justice.

Secretary of State for Scotland, Rt. Hon. David Mundell, MP
Parliamentary Private Secretary, Alberto Costa, MP
Special Adviser, Jenny Donelan
Principal Private Secretary, Julie Humphreys
Parliamentary Under-Secretary of State, Rt. Hon. Lord Duncan of Springbank*
* Jointly with the Office of the Secretary of State for Wales

MANAGEMENT BOARD
Director, Francesca Osowska, OBE
Members, Victoria Bowman, *(Corporate Services);* James Dowler *(Constitutional Policy);* Alyson King *(Policy Delivery, Relationship Management);* Flavia Paterson *(Communications)*

DEPARTMENT FOR TRANSPORT

Great Minster House, 33 Horseferry Road, London SW1P 4DR
T 0300-330 3000 W www.gov.uk/government/organisations/department-for-transport

The Department for Transport (DfT) works with its agencies and partners to support the transport network that helps the UK's businesses and gets people and goods travelling around the country. The DfT plans and invests in transport infrastructure to keep the UK on the move. DFT is supported by 19 executive agencies and public bodies.

Secretary of State for Transport, Rt. Hon. Chris Grayling, MP
Parliamentary Private Secretary, James Heappey, MP
Special Advisers, Emma Boon; Simon Jones
Minister of State, Rt. Hon. John Hayes, CBE, MP *(Transport Legislation and Maritime)*
Parliamentary Private Secretary, Scott Mann, MP
Parliamentary Under-Secretary of State, Paul Maynard, MP *(Rail, Accessibility and HS2)*
Parliamentary Under-Secretary of State, Jesse Norman, MP *(Roads, Local Transport and Devolution)*
Parliamentary Under-Secretary of State, Lord Callanan *(Aviation, International and Security)*

MANAGEMENT BOARD
Permanent Secretary, Bernadette Kelly, CB
Members, Prof. Phil Blythe *(Chief Scientific Adviser);* Lucy Chadwick *(International, Security and Environment Group);*

Tricia Hayes *(Roads, Devolution and Motoring Group);* Nick Joyce *(Rail Group);* Jonathan Moor, CBE *(Resources and Strategy Group);* Nick Olley *(General Counsel);* David Prout *(High Speed 2 Group)*
Non-Executive Members, Ed Smith, CBE *(Lead);* Richard Brown, CBE; Tony Poulter; Mary Reilly

HM TREASURY

1 Horse Guards Road, London SW1A 2HQ
T 020-7270 5000 E public.enquiries@hmtreasury.gsi.gov.uk
W www.gov.uk/government/organisations/hm-treasury

HM Treasury is the country's economics and finance ministry, and is responsible for formulating and implementing the government's financial and economic policy. It aims to raise the rate of sustainable growth, boost prosperity, and provide the conditions necessary for universal economic and employment opportunities. The Office of the Lord High Treasurer has been continuously in commission for over 200 years. The Lord High Commissioners of HM Treasury are the First Lord of the Treasury (who is also the prime minister), the Chancellor of the Exchequer and five junior lords. This board of commissioners is assisted at present by the chief secretary, the parliamentary secretary (who is also the government chief whip in the House of Commons), the financial secretary, the economic secretary, the exchequer secretary and the commercial secretary. The prime minister as first lord is not primarily concerned with the day-to-day aspects of Treasury business; neither are the parliamentary secretary and the junior lords as government whips. Treasury business is managed by the Chancellor of the Exchequer and the other Treasury ministers, assisted by the permanent secretary.

The chief secretary is responsible for public expenditure, including spending reviews and strategic planning; in-year control; public-sector pay and pensions; Annually Managed Expenditure and welfare reform; efficiency in public services; procurement and capital investment. He also has responsibility for the Treasury's interest in devolution.

The financial secretary has responsibility for financial services policy including banking and financial services reform and regulation; financial stability; city competitiveness; wholesale and retail markets in the UK, Europe and internationally; and the Financial Services Authority. His other responsibilities include banking support; bank lending; UK Financial Investments; Equitable Life; and personal savings and pensions policy. He also provides support to the chancellor on EU and wider international finance issues.

The exchequer secretary is a title only used occasionally, normally when the post of paymaster-general is allocated to a minister outside of the Treasury. The exchequer secretary's responsibilities include strategic oversight of the UK tax system; corporate and small business taxation, with input from the commercial secretary; departmental minister for HM Revenue and Customs and the Valuation Office Agency; and lead minister on European and international tax issues.

The economic secretary's responsibilities include environmental issues such as taxation of transport, international climate change and energy; North Sea oil taxation; tax credits and child poverty; assisting the chief secretary on welfare reform; charities and the voluntary sector; excise duties and gambling; stamp duty land tax; EU Budget; the Royal Mint; and departmental minister for HM Treasury Group.

HM Treasury is supported by 12 executive agencies and public bodies.

Prime Minister and First Lord of the Treasury, Rt. Hon. Theresa May, MP
Parliamentary Private Secretaries, George Hollingbery, MP; Seema Kennedy, MP
Special Advisers, Alex Dawson; Stephen Parkinson; Sheridan Westlake, OBE
Chancellor of the Exchequer, Rt. Hon. Philip Hammond, MP
Parliamentary Private Secretary, Kwasi Kwarteng, MP

Special Advisers, Duncan McCourt; Poppy Trowbridge; Giles Winn

Chief Secretary to the Treasury, Rt. Hon. Liz Truss, MP

Parliamentary Private Secretaries, Suella Fernandes, MP and Chris Philp, MP

Special Advisers, Jane Ellison; Tim Pitt; Karen Ward

Financial Secretary to the Treasury and Paymaster General, Rt. Hon. Mel Stride, MP

Economic Secretary to the Treasury, Stephen Barclay, MP

Exchequer Secretary to the Treasury, Andrew Jones, MP

Lords Commissioners of HM Treasury (Whips), Guto Bebb, MP; Rt. Hon. David Evennett, MP; Andrew Griffiths, MP; David Rutley, MP, Mark Spencer, MP; Heather Wheeler, MP

Assistant Whips, Nigel Adams, MP; Stuart Andrew, MP; Mike Freer, MP; Rebecca Harris, MP; Chloe Smith, MP; Andrew Stephenson, MP; Graham Stuart, MP; Craig Whittaker, MP

MANAGEMENT BOARD

Permanent Secretary, Sir Tom Scholar, KCB

Second Permanent Secretary, Charles Roxburgh

Executive Members, James Bowler *(Tax and Welfare);* Mark Bowman *(International and EU);* Katharine Braddick *(Financial Services);* Sir Dave Ramsden, CBE *(Chief Economic Adviser)*

Non-Executive Members, Dame Amelia Fawcett; Baroness Sarah Hogg; Richard Meddings; Tim Score

UK GOVERNMENT INVESTMENTS

1 Victoria Street, London SW1H 0ET

W www.gov.uk/government/organisations/uk-government-investments

UK Government Investments (UKGI) is the government's centre of expertise in corporate finance and corporate governance. UKGI Limited began operating on 1 April 2016 as a government company, wholly owned by HM Treasury, which brought together the functions of the Shareholder Executive (formerly part of the Department for Business, Innovation and Skills) and UK Financial Investments. UKGI's principle investments are to: prepare and execute all significant corporate asset sales by the UK government; advise on all major UK government financial interventions into corporate structures; act as shareholder for those arm's length bodies of the UK government that are structured to allow a meaningful shareholder function and for other UK government assets facing complex transformations; and to advise on major UK government negotiations with corporates.

Chief Executive, Mark Russell

Members, Roger Lowe; Justin Manson; Rachel Mortimer *(Chief Operating Officer);* Robert Razzell *(Chief Financial Officer);* Ceri Smith

OFFICE OF TAX SIMPLIFICATION

HM Treasury, 1 Horse Guards Road, London SW1A 2HQ

T 0300-0585 028 E ots@ots.gsi.gov.uk W www.gov.uk/government/organisations/office-of-tax-simplification

The chancellor and exchequer secretary to HM Treasury launched the Office of Tax Simplification (OTS) on 20 July 2010 to provide the government with independent advice on simplifying the UK tax system. The OTS is part of HM Treasury and provides the government with independent advice on simplifying the UK tax system. It carries out projects investigating complex areas of the tax system and makes recommendations to the chancellor in reports which are published on its website.

Chair, Angela Knight, CBE

Tax Director, Paul Morton

ROYAL MINT LTD

PO Box 500, Llantrisant, Pontyclun CF72 8YT

T 01443-222111 W www.royalmint.com

From 1975 the Royal Mint operated as a trading fund and was established as an executive agency in 1990. Since 2010 it has operated as Royal Mint Ltd, a company 100 per cent owned by HM Treasury, with an exclusive contract to supply all coinage for the UK.

The Royal Mint actively competes in world markets for a share of the available circulating coin business and about half of the coins and blanks it produces annually are exported. It is the leading export mint, accounting for around 15 per cent of the world market. The Royal Mint also manufactures special proof and uncirculated quality coins in gold, silver and other metals; military and civil decorations and medals; commemorative and prize medals; and royal and official seals.

Master of the Mint, Chancellor of the Exchequer *(ex officio)*

Chair, Peter Warry

Chief Executive, Adam Lawrence

UK EXPORT FINANCE

1 Horse Guards Road, London SW1A 2HQ

T 020-7271 8000 E contact-us@ukef.gsi.gov.uk

W www.gov.uk/government/organisations/uk-export-finance

UK Export Finance is the UK's export credit agency. It helps UK exporters by providing insurance to them and guarantees to banks to share the risks of providing export finance. Additionally, it can make loans to overseas buyers of goods and services from the UK. UK Export Finance is the operating name of the Export Credits Guarantee Department.

The priorities of UK Export Finance are to fulfil its statutory remit to support exports; operate within the policy and financial objectives established by the government, which includes international obligations; and to recover the maximum amount of debt in respect of claims paid, taking account of the government's policy on debt forgiveness. It is a ministerial department supported by one public body, the Export Guarantees Advisory Council.

Secretary of State for International Trade and President of the Board of Trade, Rt. Hon. Liam Fox, MP

Parliamentary Private Secretary, Tom Pursglove, MP

Special Advisers, David Goss; Amy Tinley

Minister of State, Rt. Hon. Greg Hands, MP *(Trade and Investment)*

MANAGEMENT BOARD

Chief Executive, Louis Taylor

Chair, Noel Harwerth

Members, Bhaskar Dasgupta *(Chief Operating Officer);* Cameron Fox *(Chief Financial Officer);* David Havelock *(Credit Risk Group);* Shane Lynch *(HR Director);* Davinder Mann *(Head of Legal Division);* Justin Manson *(UK Government Investments Representative);* Gordon Welsh *(Head of the Business Group)*

Non-Executive Members, Amin Mawji, OBE; Sir Eric Peacock; Oliver Peterken; Lawrence Weiss

OFFICE OF THE SECRETARY OF STATE FOR WALES

Gwydyr House, Whitehall, London SW1A 2NP

T 029-2092 4220 E correspondence@walesoffice.gsi.gov.uk

W www.gov.uk/wales-office

The Office of the Secretary of State for Wales, informally known as the Wales Office, was established in 1999 when most of the powers of the Welsh Office were handed over to the National Assembly for Wales. It is the department of the Secretary of State for Wales, who is the key government figure liaising with the devolved government in Wales and who represents Welsh interests in the cabinet and parliament. The secretary of state has the right to attend and speak at sessions of the National Assembly (and must consult the assembly on the government's legislative programme). *See also* Devolved Government *and* Ministry of Justice.

Secretary of State for Wales, Rt. Hon. Alun Cairns, MP
Parliamentary Private Secretary, Glyn Davies, MP
Special Advisers, Geraint Evans; Sophie Treherne
Principal Private Secretary, Michael Dynan-Oakley
Parliamentary Under-Secretary of State, Guto Bebb, MP
Parliamentary Under-Secretary of State, Lord Duncan of Springbank*
Director, Glynne Jones
Deputy Director, Geth Williams *(Constitution and Policy)*

* Jointly with the Scotland Office

DEPARTMENT FOR WORK AND PENSIONS

Caxton House, Tothill Street, London SW1H 9NA
T 020-7340 4000 E ministers@dwp.gsi.gov.uk
W www.gov.uk/government/organisations/
department-for-work-pensions

The Department for Work and Pensions was formed in June 2001 from parts of the former Department of Social Security, the Department for Education and Employment and the Employment Service. The department helps unemployed people of working age into work, helps employers to fill their vacancies and provides financial support to people unable to help themselves, through back-to-work programmes. The department also administers the child support system, social security benefits and the social fund. In addition, the department has reciprocal social security arrangements with other countries. The department is supported by 13 executive agencies and public bodies.

Secretary of State for Work and Pensions, Rt. Hon. David Gauke, MP
Parliamentary Private Secretary, Peter Heaton-Jones, MP
Special Adviser, James Dowling
Minister of State, Damian Hinds, MP *(Employment)*
Minister of State, Penny Mordaunt, MP *(Disabled People, Health and Work)*
Parliamentary Private Secretary, Huw Merriman, MP
Parliamentary Under-Secretary of State, Caroline Dinenage, MP *(Family Support, Housing and Child Maintenance)*
Parliamentary Under-Secretary of State, Guy Opperman, MP *(Pensions and Financial Inclusion)*
Parliamentary Under-Secretary of State, Baroness Buscombe *(Lords)*

MANAGEMENT BOARD
Permanent Secretary, Sir Robert Devereux, KCB
Members, Debbie Alder *(Human Resources);* Neil Couling, CBE *(Universal Credit Programme);* Jeremy Moore *(Strategy);* Mayank Prakash *(Digital Technology);* Andrew Rhodes *(Operations);* Peter Schofield *(Finance)*

EXECUTIVE AGENCIES

Executive agencies are well-defined business units that carry out services with a clear focus on delivering specific outputs within a framework of accountability to ministers. They can be set up or disbanded without legislation, and they are organisationally independent from the department they are answerable to. In the following list the agencies are shown in the accounts of their sponsor departments. Legally they act on behalf of the relevant secretary of state. Their chief executives also perform the role of accounting officers, which means they are responsible for the money spent by their organisations. Staff employed by agencies are civil servants.

DEPARTMENT FOR BUSINESS, ENERGY AND INDUSTRIAL STRATEGY

COMPANIES HOUSE
Crown Way, Cardiff CF14 3UZ
T 0303-123 4500 E enquiries@companies-house.gov.uk
W www.gov.uk/government/organisations/companies-house
Companies House incorporates and dissolves companies, examines and stores company information delivered under the Companies Act and related legislation; and makes this information available to the public.
Chief Executive, Ann Lewis

THE INSOLVENCY SERVICE
4 Abbey Orchard Street, London SW1P 2HT
T 020-7637 1110 E redundancyclaims@insolvency.gsi.gov.uk
W www.gov.uk/government/organisations/insolvency-service
The role of the service includes administration and investigation of the affairs of bankrupts, individuals subject to debt relief orders, partnerships and companies in compulsory liquidation; dealing with the disqualification of directors in all corporate failures; authorising and regulating the insolvency profession; providing banking and investment services for bankruptcy and liquidation estate funds; assessing and paying statutory entitlement to redundancy payments when an employer cannot, or will not, pay its employees; and advising ministers on insolvency, redundancy and related issues. The service has around 1,700 staff, operating from 22 locations across Great Britain.
Inspector-General and Chief Executive, Sarah Albon

INTELLECTUAL PROPERTY OFFICE
Concept House, Cardiff Road, Newport NP10 8QQ
T 0300-300 2000 E information@ipo.gov.uk
W www.gov.uk/government/organisations/
intellectual-property-office
The Intellectual Property Office (an operating name of the Patent Office) was set up in 1852 to act as the UK's sole office for the granting of patents. It was established as an executive agency in 1990 and became a trading fund in 1991. The office is responsible for the granting of intellectual property (IP) rights which include patents, trade marks, designs and copyright.
Comptroller-General and Chief Executive, Tim Moss

MET OFFICE
FitzRoy Road, Exeter, Devon EX1 3PB
T 01392-885680 E enquiries@metoffice.gov.uk
W www.metoffice.gov.uk
The Met Office is the UK's National Weather Service, operating as an executive agency of BEIS, having transferred from the MoD to the Department for Business, Innovation and Skills in July 2011. It is a world leader in providing weather and climate services, using over 10 million weather observations a day, and employs more than 1,700 people at 60 locations throughout the world.
Chief Executive, Rob Varley
Chief Scientist, Prof. Stephen Belcher

UK SPACE AGENCY
Polaris House, North Star Avenue, Swindon, Wiltshire SN2 1SZ
T 020-7215 5000 E info@ukspaceagency.bis.gsi.gov.uk
W www.gov.uk/government/organisations/uk-space-agency
The UK Space Agency was established on 23 March 2010 and became an executive agency on 1 April 2011. It was created to provide a single voice for UK space ambitions, and is responsible for all strategic decisions on the UK civil space programme. Responsibilities of the UK Space Agency include coordinating UK civil space activity; supporting academic research; nurturing the UK space industry; raising the profile of UK space activities at home and abroad; working to increase understanding of space science and its practical benefits; and inspiring the next generation of UK scientists and engineers. It aims to capture 10 per cent of the global market for space by 2030.
Chief Executive, Graham Turnock

CABINET OFFICE

CROWN COMMERCIAL SERVICE

Floor 9, The Capital Building, Old Hall Street, Liverpool L3 9PP
T 0345-410 2222 E info@crowncommercial.gov.uk
W www.gov.uk/government/organisations/
crown-commercial-service

The Crown Commercial Service (CCS) is an executive agency of the Cabinet Office, bringing together policy, advice and direct buying; providing commercial services to the public sector and saving money for the taxpayer. The CCS works with over 17,000 customer organisations in the public sector. A major priority is helping government departments save more money, with a target of between £240m–£330m.
Chief Executive, Malcolm Harrison

DEPARTMENT FOR COMMUNITIES AND LOCAL GOVERNMENT

PLANNING INSPECTORATE

Temple Quay House, 2 The Square, Temple Quay, Bristol BS1 6PN
T 0303-444 5000 E enquiries@pins.gsi.gov.uk
W www.gov.uk/government/organisations/planning-inspectorate

The main work of the inspectorate consists of national infrastructure planning under the Planning Act 2008 as amended by the Localism Act 2011, the processing of planning and enforcement appeals, and holding examinations into development plan documents. It also deals with listed building consent appeals; advertisement appeals; rights of way cases; cases arising from the Environmental Protection and Water acts, the Transport and Works Act 1992 and other highways legislation; and reporting on planning applications called in for decision by the Department for Communities and Local Government and the Welsh government.
Chief Executive, Sarah Richards

THE QUEEN ELIZABETH II CONFERENCE CENTRE

Broad Sanctuary, London SW1P 3EE
T 020-7798 4000 W www.qeiicc.co.uk

The centre provides secure conference facilities for national and international government and private sector use.
Chief Executive, Mark Taylor

DEPARTMENT FOR DIGITAL, CULTURE, MEDIA AND SPORT

THE ROYAL PARKS

The Old Police House, Hyde Park, London W2 2UH
T 0300-061 2000 E hq@royalparks.gsi.gov.uk
W www.royalparks.org.uk

Royal Parks is responsible for maintaining and developing over 2,000 hectares (5,000 acres) of urban parkland contained within the eight royal parks in London: Bushy Park (with the Longford river); Green Park; Greenwich Park; Hyde Park; Kensington Gardens; Regent's Park (with Primrose Hill); Richmond Park and St James's Park.
Chief Executive, Andrew Scattergood

MINISTRY OF DEFENCE

See also Defence Chapter.

DEFENCE ELECTRONICS AND COMPONENTS AGENCY

Welsh Road, Deeside, Flintshire CH5 2LS T 01244-847694
E decainfo@deca.mod.uk
W www.gov.uk/government/organisations/defence-electronics-and-components-agency

The Defence Electronics and Components Agency (DECA) provides maintenance, repair, overhaul, upgrade and procurement in avionics, electronics and components fields to support the MoD. As a 'trading' executive agency DECA is run along commercial lines with funding for DECA's activities being generated entirely by payments for delivery of services provided to the MoD and other private sector customers. DECA currently has an annual turnover of around £25m and employs approximately 430 staff across its head office and main operating centre in North Wales, a site in Stafford and various deployed locations across the UK.
Chief Executive, Geraint Spearing

DEFENCE SCIENCE AND TECHNOLOGY LABORATORY

Porton Down, Salisbury, Wiltshire SP4 0JQ T 01980-950000
E centralenquiries@dstl.gov.uk
W www.gov.uk/government/organisations/defence-science-and-technology-laboratory

The Defence Science and Technology Laboratory (DSTL) supplies specialist science and technology services to the MoD and wider government.
Chief Executive, Jonathan Lyle

UK HYDROGRAPHIC OFFICE

Admiralty Way, Taunton, Somerset TA1 2DN
T 01823-484444
E customerservices@ukho.gov.uk
W www.gov.uk/government/organisations/uk-hydrographic-office

The UK Hydrographic Office (UKHO) collects and supplies hydrographic and geospatial data for the Royal Navy and merchant shipping, to protect lives at sea. Working with other national hydrographic offices, UKHO sets and raises global standards of hydrography, cartography and navigation.
Chief Executive, John Humphrey

DEPARTMENT FOR EDUCATION

THE EDUCATION AND SKILLS FUNDING AGENCY

Sanctuary Buildings, 20 Great Smith Street, London SW1P 3BT
T 0370-000 2288 W www.gov.uk/government/organisations/education-and-skills-funding-agency

Formed on 1 April 2017 after a merger of the Education Funding Agency (EFA) and the Skills Funding Agency (SFA), the Education and Skills Funding Agency (ESFA)is the DFE's delivery agency for funding and compliance. It manages £61bn of funding each year to support all state-provided education and training for children and young people aged 3 to 19. The ESFA also supports the delivery of building and maintenance programmes for schools, academies, free schools and sixth-form colleges. It also administers the National Careers Service, the National Apprenticeship Service and the digital apprenticeship service.
Chief Executive, Eileen Milner

NATIONAL COLLEGE FOR TEACHING AND LEADERSHIP

Piccadilly Gate, Store Street, Manchester M1 2WD
T 0370-000 2288 E enquiries@nationalcollege.org.uk
W www.gov.uk/government/organisations/national-college-for-teaching-and-leadership

On 1 April 2013 the National College merged with the Teaching Agency to become the National College for Teaching and Leadership. It has two key aims: improving the quality of the workforce; and helping schools to help each other to improve. It is also the awarding body for Qualified Teacher Status (QTS).
Chair, Roger Pope

STANDARDS AND TESTING AGENCY

53–55 Butts Road, Earlsdon Park, Coventry CV1 3BH
T 0300-303 3013 E assessments@education.gov.uk
W www.gov.uk/government/organisations/standards-and-testing-agency

The Standards and Testing Agency (STA) opened on 1 October 2011 and is responsible for the development and delivery of all statutory assessments from early years to the end of Key Stage 2.
Chief Executive, Claire Burton

DEPARTMENT FOR ENVIRONMENT, FOOD AND RURAL AFFAIRS

ANIMAL AND PLANT HEALTH AGENCY
Woodham Lane, New Haw, Addlestone, Surrey KT15 3NB
T 01932-341 111 E enquiries@apha.gsi.gov.uk
W www.gov.uk/government/organisations/
animal-and-plant-health-agency
The Animal and Plant Health Agency (APHA) was launched on 1 October 2014. It merged the former Animal Health and Veterinary Laboratories Agency with parts of the Food and Environment Research Agency responsible for plant and bee health to create a single agency responsible for animal, plant and bee health.

APHA is responsible for identifying and controlling endemic and exotic diseases and pests in animals, plants and bees, and surveillance of new and emerging pests and diseases; scientific research in areas such as bacterial, viral, prion and parasitic diseases, vaccines and food safety and act as an international reference laboratory for many farm animal diseases; facilitating international trade in animals, products of animal origin, and plants; protecting endangered wildlife through licensing and registration; managing a programme of apiary inspections, diagnostics, research and development, training and advice; and regulating the safe disposal of animal by-products to reduce the risk of potentially dangerous substances entering the food chain.

The agency provides all or some of these services to DEFRA and the Scottish and Welsh governments.
Chief Executive, Chris Hadkiss

CENTRE FOR ENVIRONMENT, FISHERIES AND AQUACULTURE SCIENCE (CEFAS)
Pakefield Road, Lowestoft, Suffolk NR33 0HT
T 01502-562244 W www.gov.uk/government/organisations/
centre-for-environment-fisheries-and-aquaculture-science
Established in April 1997, the agency provides research and consultancy services in fisheries science and management, aquaculture, fish health and hygiene, environmental impact assessment, and environmental quality assessment.
Chief Executive, Tom Karsten

RURAL PAYMENTS AGENCY
PO Box 69, Reading RG1 3YD
T 0300-0200 301 E ruralpayments@defra.gsi.gov.uk
W www.gov.uk/government/organisations/rural-payments-agency
The RPA was established in 2001. It pays out over £2bn each year to support the farming and food sector and is responsible for Common Agricultural Policy (CAP) schemes in England. In addition it manages over 40 other rural economy and community schemes. It is also responsible for operating cattle tracing services across Great Britain; conducting inspections of farms, processing plants and fresh produce markets in England; and managing the Rural Land Register.
Chief Executive, Paul Caldwell

VETERINARY MEDICINES DIRECTORATE
Woodham Lane, New Haw, Addlestone, Surrey KT15 3LS
T 01932-336911 E postmaster@vmd.defra.gsi.gov.uk
W www.gov.uk/government/organisations/
veterinary-medicines-directorate
The Veterinary Medicines Directorate is responsible for all aspects of the authorisation and control of veterinary medicines, including post-authorisation surveillance of residues in animals and animal products. It is also responsible for the development and enforcement of legislation concerning veterinary medicines and the provision of policy advice to ministers.
Chief Executive, Prof. Peter Borriello

FOREIGN AND COMMONWEALTH OFFICE

FCO SERVICES
Hanslope Park, Milton Keynes MK19 7BH
T 01908-515 789
W www.fcoservices.gov.uk
FCO Services was established as an executive agency in April 2006 and became a trading fund in April 2008. It operates as the service delivery arm of the FCO, keeping their people, assets and information across the globe safe and secure from the threats they face. FCO Services also works with central government departments, law enforcement, HM government abroad, local government and the UK's critical national infrastructure.
Chief Executive, Danny Payne

WILTON PARK CONFERENCE CENTRE
Wiston House, Steyning, W. Sussex BN44 3DZ
T 01903-815020 W www.wiltonpark.org.uk
Wilton Park organises international affairs conferences and is hired out to government departments and commercial users.
Chair, Iain Ferguson
Chief Executive, Sharmila Nebhrajani, OBE

DEPARTMENT OF HEALTH

MEDICINES AND HEALTHCARE PRODUCTS REGULATORY AGENCY (MHRA)
151 Buckingham Palace Road, London SW1W 9SZ
E info@mhra.gsi.gov.uk W www.gov.uk/government/organisations/
medicines-and-healthcare-products-regulatory-agency
The MHRA is a centre of the Medicines and Healthcare Products Regulatory Agency which also includes the National Institute for Biological Standards and Control (NIBSC) and the Clinical Practice Research Datalink (CPRD). The MHRA is responsible for regulating all medicines and medical devices in the UK by ensuring they work and are acceptably safe.
Chair, Prof. Sir Michael Rawlins
Chief Executive, Dr Ian Hudson

PUBLIC HEALTH ENGLAND
Wellington House, 133–155 Waterloo Road, London SE1 8UG
T 020-7654 8000 E enquiries@phe.gov.uk
W www.gov.uk/government/organisations/public-health-england
Public Health England (PHE) began operating on 1 April 2013 with a remit to protect and improve the health and wellbeing of people within the UK, and reducing health inequalities. PHE employs 5,500 staff who are mostly scientists, researchers and public health professionals. It has 8 local centres and four regions in England and works closely with public health professionals in Wales, Scotland, Northern Ireland and internationally.
Chief Executive, Duncan Selbie

MINISTRY OF JUSTICE

CRIMINAL INJURIES COMPENSATION AUTHORITY (CICA)
Alexander Bain House, Atlantic Quay, 15 York Street, Glasgow G2 8JQ
T 0300-003 3601
W www.gov.uk/government/organisations/
criminal-injuries-compensation-authority
CICA is the executive agency responsible for administering the Criminal Injuries Compensation Scheme in England, Scotland and Wales (separate arrangements apply in Northern Ireland). CICA handles up to 40,000 applications for compensation each year, covering every aspect of compensation under the 1996, 2001 and 2008 Criminal Injuries Compensation Schemes. Appeals against decisions made by CICA can be put to the First-tier Tribunal (Criminal Injuries Compensation) *see* Tribunals.
Chief Executive, Carole Oatway

HM COURTS AND TRIBUNALS SERVICE
102 Petty France, London SW1H 9AJ
W www.gov.uk/government/organisations/hm-courts-and-
tribunals-service
HM Courts Service and the Tribunals Service merged on 1 April 2011 to form HM Courts and Tribunals Service, an

integrated agency providing support for the administration of justice in courts and tribunals. As an agency within the MoJ it operates as a partnership between the Lord Chancellor, the Lord Chief Justice and the Senior President of Tribunals. It is responsible for the administration of the criminal, civil and family courts and tribunals in England and Wales and non-devolved tribunals in Scotland and Northern Ireland. The agency's work is overseen by a board headed by an independent chair working with non-executive, executive and judicial members.
Chief Executive, Susan Acland-Hood

HM PRISON AND PROBATION SERVICE
Clive House, 70 Petty France, London SW1H 9EX
T 0203-193 5921 E public.enquiries@noms.gsi.gov.uk
W https://www.gov.uk/government/organisations/her-majestys-prison-and-probation-service
HM Prison and Probation Service (HMPPS) was established on 1 April 2017, responsible for the roll out of government policies concerning the welfare of offenders and communities and to reduce levels of re-offending by the rehabilitation of offenders through education and training schemes. HMPPS works closely with HM Prisons Service to oversee the management of public sector prisons and probation centres in England and Wales.
Chief Executive, Michael Spurr

HM PRISON SERVICE
Clive House, 70 Petty France, London SW1H 9EX
T 0300-047 6325 E public.enquiries@noms.gsi.gov.uk
W www.gov.uk/government/organisations/hm-prison-service
HM Prison Service is an executive agency responsible for keeping those sentenced to prison in custody, helping them lead law-abiding and useful lives, both while they are in prison and after they have been released. HM Prison Service works alongside courts, police and local councils, in addition to voluntary organisations to achieve their aims. The agency runs 109 of the 123 prisons in England and Wales. HM Prison Service is further responsible for managing prison and probation services, and supporting effective offender management.
Chief Executive, Phil Copple

LEGAL AID AGENCY
Berkley Way, Viking Business Park, Jarrow, South Tyneside NE31 1SF
T 0300-200 2020 E contactcivil@legalaid.gsi.gov.uk
W www.gov.uk/government/organisations/legal-aid-agency
The Legal Aid Agency provides civil and criminal legal aid and advice in England and Wales. Formed on 1 April 2013 as part of the Legal Aid, Sentencing and Punishment of Offenders Act 2012, the agency replaced the Legal Services Commission, a non-departmental public body of the MoJ.
Chief Executive, Shaun McNally, CBE

OFFICE OF THE PUBLIC GUARDIAN
PO Box 16185, Birmingham B2 2WH
T 0300-456 0300 E customerservices@publicguardian.gsi.gov.uk
W www.gov.uk/government/organisations/office-of-the-public-guardian
The Office of the Public Guardian (OPG) works within the Mental Capacity Act 2005 to support and protect those who lack the mental capacity to make decisions for themselves. It supports the Public Guardian in the registration of Enduring Powers of Attorney (EPA) and Lasting Powers of Attorney (LPA), and the supervision of deputies appointed by the Court of Protection. The OPG also has responsibility for investigating and acting on allegations of abuse by attorneys and deputies. The OPG's responsibility extends across England and Wales.
Chief Executive and Public Guardian, Alan Eccles, CBE

DEPARTMENT FOR TRANSPORT

DRIVER AND VEHICLE LICENSING AGENCY (DVLA)
Longview Road, Swansea SA6 7JL
W www.gov.uk/government/organisations/driver-and-vehicle-licensing-agency

The DVLA, established as an executive agency in 1990, maintains registers of drivers and vehicles in Great Britain. The information collated by the DVLA helps to improve road safety, reduce vehicle related crime, support environmental initiatives and limit vehicle tax evasion. The DVLA maintains over 45 million driver records and over 39 million vehicle records and collects over £6bn a year in vehicle tax.
Chief Executive, Oliver Morley, CBE

DRIVER AND VEHICLE STANDARDS AGENCY
Berkeley House, Croydon Street, Bristol BS5 0DA
T 0300-123 9000 E inform@vosa.gov.uk
W www.gov.uk/government/organisations/driver-and-vehicle-standards-agency
Formed by the merger of the Driving Standards Agency and the Vehicle and Operator Services Agency in 2014, the Driver and Vehicle Standards Agency (DVSA) is responsible for improving road safety in the UK by setting standards for driving and motorcycling, and ensuring drivers, vehicle operators and MOT garages understand and comply with roadworthiness standards. It additionally provides a range of licensing, testing, education and enforcement services.
Chief Executive, Gareth Llewellyn

MARITIME AND COASTGUARD AGENCY
Spring Place, 105 Commercial Road, Southampton SO15 1EG
T 020-3817 2000 W www.gov.uk/government/organisations/maritime-and-coastguard-agency
The agency's aims are to prevent loss of life, continuously improve maritime safety and protect the marine environment.
Chief Executive, Sir Alan Massey, KCB, CBE

VEHICLE CERTIFICATION AGENCY
1 Eastgate Office Centre, Eastgate Road, Bristol BS5 6XX
T 0300-330 5797 E enquiries@vca.gov.uk W www.dft.gov.uk/vca
The agency is the UK authority responsible for ensuring that new road vehicles, agricultural tractors, off-road vehicles and vehicle parts have been designed and constructed to meet internationally agreed standards of safety and environmental protection.
Chief Executive, Pia Wilkes

HM TREASURY

GOVERNMENT INTERNAL AUDIT AGENCY
1 Horse Guards Road, London SW1A 2HQ
E GIAAPMO@giaa.gsi.gov.uk W www.gov.uk/government/organisations/government-internal-audit-agency
Launched on 1 April 2015, the Government Internal Audit Agency (GIAA) helps ensure government and the wider public sector provide services effectively. GIAA offers quality assurance on organisation's systems and processes, based on an objective assessment of the governance, risk management and control arrangements in place.
Chief Executive, Jon Whitfield

UK DEBT MANAGEMENT OFFICE
Eastcheap Court, 11 Philpot Lane, London EC3M 8UD
T 020-7862 6500 W www.gov.uk/government/organisations/uk-debt-management-office
The UK Debt Management Office (DMO) was launched as an executive agency of HM Treasury in April 1998. The Chancellor of the Exchequer determines the policy and financial framework within which the DMO operates, but delegates operational decisions on debt and cash management and the day-to-day running of the office to the chief executive. The DMO's remit is to carry out the government's debt management policy of minimising financing costs over the long term, and to minimise the cost of offsetting the government's net cash flows over time, while operating at a level of risk approved by ministers in both cases. The DMO is also responsible for providing loans to local authorities through the Public Works Loan Board, and for managing the assets of certain public-sector bodies through the Commissioners for the Reduction of the National Debt.
Chief Executive, Sir Robert Stheeman, CB

NON-MINISTERIAL GOVERNMENT DEPARTMENTS

Non-ministerial government departments are part of central government but are not headed by a minister and are not funded by a sponsor department. They are created to implement specific legislation, but do not have the ability to change it. Departments may have links to a minister, but the minister is not responsible for the department's overall performance. Staff employed by non-ministerial departments are civil servants.

CHARITY COMMISSION

PO Box 1227, Liverpool L69 3UG
T 0845-300 0218 W www.gov.uk/government/organisations/charity-commission

The Charity Commission is established by law as the independent regulator and registrar of charities in England and Wales. Its aim is to provide the best possible regulation of these charities in order to ensure their legal compliance and increase their efficiency, accountability and effectiveness, as well as to encourage public trust and confidence in them. The commission maintains a register of over 160,000 charities. It is accountable to both parliament and the First-tier Tribunal (Charity), and the chamber of the Upper Tribunal or high court for decisions made in exercising the commission's legal powers. The Charity Commission has offices in London, Liverpool, Taunton and Newport.

Chair, William Shawcross, CVO
Chief Executive, Helen Stephenson, CBE

COMPETITION AND MARKETS AUTHORITY

Victoria House, Southampton Row, London WC1B 4AD
T 020-3738 6000 E general.enquiries@cma.gsi.gov.uk
W www.gov.uk/government/organisations/competition-and-markets-authority

The Competition and Markets Authority (CMA) is the UK's primary competition and consumer authority. It is an independent non-ministerial government department with responsibility for carrying out investigations into mergers, markets and the regulated industries and enforcing competition and consumer law. From 1 April 2014 it took over the functions of the Competition Commission and the competition and certain consumer functions of the Office of Fair Trading under the Enterprise Act 2002, as amended by the Enterprise and Regulatory Reform Act 2013.

Chair, David Currie
Chief Executive, Andrea Coscelli

CROWN PROSECUTION SERVICE

Rose Court, 2 Southwark Bridge Road, London SE1 9HS
T 020-3357 0000 E enquiries@cps.gsi.gov.uk
W www.cps.gov.uk

The Crown Prosecution Service (CPS) is the independent body responsible for prosecuting people in England and Wales. The CPS was established as a result of the Prosecution of Offences Act 1985. It works closely with the police to advise on lines of inquiry and to decide on appropriate charges and other disposals in all but minor cases. *See also* Law Courts and Offices.

Director of Public Prosecutions, Alison Saunders, CB
Chief Executive, Nick Folland

FOOD STANDARDS AGENCY

Aviation House, 125 Kingsway, London WC2B 6NH
T 020-7276 8829 E helpline@foodstandards.gsi.gov.uk
W www.food.gov.uk

Established in April 2000, the FSA is a UK-wide non-ministerial government body responsible for food safety and hygiene. The agency has the general function of developing policy in these areas and provides information and advice to the government, other public bodies and consumers. The FSA also works with local authorities to enforce food safety regulations and has staff working in UK meat plants to check that the requirements of the regulations are being met.

Chair, Heather Hancock
Chief Executive, Jason Feeney

FOOD STANDARDS AGENCY NORTHERN IRELAND, 10C Clarendon Road, Belfast BT1 3BG T 028-9041 7700 E infosani@foodstandards.gsi.gov.uk

FOOD STANDARDS AGENCY WALES, 11th Floor, South Gate House, Wood Street, Cardiff CF10 1EW T 029-2067 8999 E walesadminteam@foodstandards.gsi.gov.uk

FORESTRY COMMISSION

620 Bristol Business Park, Coldharbour Lane, Bristol BS16 1EJ
T 0300-067 4000 E fe.england@forestry.gsi.gov.uk
W www.forestry.gov.uk

The Forestry Commission is the government department responsible for forestry policy in England and Scotland. It is divided into Forestry Commission England and Forestry Commission Scotland, which report to forestry ministers (the Secretary of State for Environment, Food & Rural Affairs in the UK government, and to ministers in the Scottish government), to whom it is responsible for advice on and implementation of forestry policy. It has an agency, Forest Research, which carries out scientific research and technical development relevant to forestry. The public forests are managed through two additional executive agencies, known as Forest Enterprise England and Forest Enterprise Scotland.

On 1 April 2013 the functions of its Welsh division, Forestry Commission Wales, were subsumed into Natural Resources Wales, a new body established by the Welsh government to regulate and manage natural resources in Wales.

The commission's principal objectives are to protect and expand England's and Scotland's forests and woodlands; enhance the economic value of forest resources; conserve and improve the biodiversity, landscape and cultural heritage of forests and woodlands; develop opportunities for woodland recreation; and increase public understanding of, and community participation, in forestry. It does this by managing public forests in its care to implement these objectives; by supporting other woodland owners with grants, regulation, advice and tree felling licences; and, through its Forest Research agency, by carrying out scientific research and technical development in support of these objectives.

Chair (2014–20), Sir Harry Studholme, Bt.
Chief Executive, Forest Enterprise England, Simon Hodgson
Chief Executive, Forest Enterprise Scotland, Simon Hodge

FORESTRY COMMISSION ENGLAND, 620 Bristol Business Park, Coldharbour Lane, Bristol BS16 1EJ T 0117-906 6000

FORESTRY COMMISSION SCOTLAND, Silvan House, 231 Corstorphine Road, Edinburgh EH12 7AT T 0845-367 3787

GOVERNMENT ACTUARY'S DEPARTMENT

Finlaison House, 15–17 Furnival Street, London EC4A 1AB
T 020-7211 2601
Belford House, 59 Belford Road, Edinburgh EH4 3UE
T 0131-467 0324
E enquiries@gad.gov.uk W www.gov.uk/government/organisations/government-actuary-department

The Government Actuary's Department (GAD) was established in 1919 and provides actuarial advice to the public sector in the UK and overseas, and also to the private sector, where consistent with government policy. The GAD provides advice on occupational pension schemes, social security and National Insurance, investment and strategic risk management, insurance analysis and advice, financial risk management, and healthcare financing.

Government Actuary, Martin Clarke
Deputy Government Actuary, Colin Wilson

GOVERNMENT LEGAL DEPARTMENT

1 Kemble Street, London WC2B 4TS
T 020-7210 3000
E thetreasurysolicitor@governmentlegal.gov.uk
W www.gov.uk/government/organisations/
government-legal-department

The Treasury Solicitor's Department became the Government Legal Department (GLD) on 1 April 2015. The department provides legal advice to government on the development, design and implementation of government policies and decisions, and represents the government in court. It is superintended by the Attorney-General. The permanent secretary of the GLD, the Treasury Solicitor, is also the Queen's Proctor, and is responsible for collecting ownerless goods *(bona vacantia)* on behalf of the crown.

HM Procurator-General and Treasury Solicitor, Jonathan Jones
Directors-General, Stephen Braviner-Roman; Peter Fish, CB;
  Claire Johnston
Head of Bona Vacantia, Caroline Harold

HM REVENUE AND CUSTOMS (HMRC)

100 Parliament Street, London SW1A 2BQ
Income Tax Enquiries 0300-200 3300
National Insurance Enquiries 0300-200 3500
VAT Enquiries 0300-200 3700
W www.gov.uk/government/organisations/hm-revenue-customs

HMRC was formed following the integration of the Inland Revenue and HM Customs and Excise, which was made formal by parliament in April 2005. It collects and administers direct taxes (capital gains tax, corporation tax, income tax, inheritance tax and national insurance contributions) and indirect taxes (excise duties, insurance premium tax, petroleum revenue tax, stamp duty, stamp duty land tax, stamp duty reserve tax and value-added tax). HMRC also pays and administers child benefit, tax credits and the Child Trust Fund, in addition to being responsible for environmental taxes, national minimum wage enforcement, recovery of student loans, the climate change levy and landfill tax. HMRC also administers the Government Banking Service.

Chief Executive and Permanent Secretary, Jon Thompson
Executive Chair and Permanent Secretary, Edward Troup

VALUATION OFFICE AGENCY

Wingate House, 93–107 Shaftesbury Avenue, London W1D 5BU
T 0300-050 1501 W www.voa.gov.uk
Established in 1991, the Valuation Office is an executive agency of HM Revenue and Customs. It is responsible for compiling and maintaining the business rating and council tax valuation lists for England and Wales; valuing property throughout Great Britain for the purposes of taxes administered by HMRC; providing statutory and non-statutory property valuation services in England, Wales and Scotland; and giving policy advice to ministers on property valuation matters. In April 2009 the VOA assumed responsibility for the functions of The Rent Service, which provided a rental valuation service to local authorities in England, and fair rent determinations for landlords and tenants.

Chief Executive, Penny Ciniewicz

HM LAND REGISTRY

Trafalgar House, 1 Bedford Park, Croydon CR0 2AQ
T 0300-006 0411
W www.gov.uk/government/organisations/land-registry

A government department and trading fund of BEIS, HM Land Registry maintains the Land Register – the definitive source of information for more than 24 million property titles in England and Wales. The Land Register has been open to public inspection since 1990.

Chief Land Registrar and Chief Executive, Graham Farrant

NATIONAL ARCHIVES

NATIONAL ARCHIVES

Kew, Richmond, Surrey TW9 4DU
T 020-8876 3444 W www.nationalarchives.gov.uk

The National Archives is a non-ministerial government department of the Ministry of Justice. It incorporates the Public Record Office, Historical Manuscripts Commission, Office of Public Sector Information and Her Majesty's Stationery Office. As the official archive of the UK government, it preserves, protects and makes accessible the historical collection of official records.

The National Archives also manages digital information including the UK government web archive which contains over one billion digital documents, and devises solutions for keeping government records readable now and in the future.

The organisation administers the UK's public records system under the Public Records Acts of 1958 and 1967. The records it holds span 1,000 years – from the Domesday Book to the latest government papers to be released – and fill more than 167km (104 miles) of shelving.

Chief Executive and Keeper, Jeff James

NATIONAL CRIME AGENCY

Units 1–6 Citadel Place, Tinworth Street, London SE11 5EF
T 0370-496 7622 E communication@nca.x.gsi.gov.uk
W www.nationalcrimeagency.gov.uk

The National Crime Agency (NCA) is an operational crime fighting agency introduced under the Crime and Courts Act 2013, which became fully operational in October 2013. The NCA's remit is to fight organised crime, strengthen UK borders, tackle fraud and cyber crime and protect children and young people. The agency employs over 4,000 officers and provides leadership through its organised crime, border policing, economic crime and Child Exploitation and Online Protection Centre commands, the National Cyber Crime Unit and specialist capability teams.

Chair, Lynne Owens, CBE, QPM

NATIONAL SAVINGS AND INVESTMENTS

Glasgow G58 1SB
T 0500-007 007 W www.nsandi.com

NS&I (National Savings and Investments) came into being in 1861 when the Palmerston government set up the Post Office Savings Bank, a savings scheme which aimed to encourage ordinary wage earners 'to provide for themselves against adversity and ill health'. NS&I was established as a government department in 1969. It is responsible for the design, marketing and administration of savings and investment products for personal savers and investors. It has over 25 million customers and more than £147bn invested. *See also* Banking and Finance, National Savings.

Chief Executive, Ian Ackerley

OFFICE OF GAS AND ELECTRICITY MARKETS (OFGEM)

9 Millbank, London SW1P 3GE
T 020-7901 7000 W www.ofgem.gov.uk

OFGEM is the regulator for Britain's gas and electricity industries. Its role is to protect and advance the interests of consumers by promoting competition where possible, and through regulation only where necessary. OFGEM operates under the direction and governance of the Gas and Electricity Markets Authority, which makes all major decisions and sets policy priorities for OFGEM. OFGEM's powers are provided for under the Gas Act 1986 and the Electricity Act 1989, as amended by the Utilities Act 2000. It also has enforcement powers under the Competition Act 1998 and the Enterprise Act 2002.

Chair, David Gray
Chief Executive, Dermot Nolan

OFFICE OF RAIL AND ROAD
1 Kemble Street, London WC2B 4AN
T 020-7282 2000
W www.orr.gov.uk

The Office of the Rail and Road (ORR) is the operating name of the Office of Rail Regulation. The Office of Rail Regulation was established on 5 July 2004 under the Railways and Transport Safety Act 2003. It replaced the Office of the Rail Regulator.

On 1 April 2006, ORR assumed new responsibilities as a combined safety and economic regulator under the Railways Act 2005. It also has concurrent jurisdiction with the Competition and Market Authority under the Competition Act 1998 as the competition authority for the railways.

As the railway industry's independent health and safety and economic regulator, its principal functions are to: ensure that Network Rail and HS1 manage the national network efficiently and in a way that meets the needs of its users; encourage continuous health and safety performance; secure compliance with relevant health and safety law, including taking enforcement action as necessary; develop policy and enhance relevant railway health and safety legislation; and license operators of railway assets, setting the terms for access by operators to the network and other railway facilities, and enforce competition and consumer law in the rail sector.

On 1 April 2015, under the Infrastructure Act 2015, ORR assumed responsibility for monitoring Highways England's management and development of the strategic road network – the motorways and main 'A' roads in England. In this role ORR ensures that the network is managed efficiently, safely and sustainably, for the benefit of road users and the public.

On 16 March 2015, ORR signed an agreement with the French rail regulator ARAF to establish a collaborative regulatory approach for consistent independent regulation across the Channel tunnel network.

ORR is led by a board appointed by the Secretary of State for Transport.

Chair, Stephen Glaister
Chief Executive, Joanna Whittington

OFFICE OF QUALIFICATIONS AND EXAMINATIONS REGULATION (OFQUAL)
Spring Place, Herald Avenue, Coventry CV5 6UB
T 0300-303 3344 E public.enquiries@ofqual.gov.uk
W www.gov.uk/government/organisations/ofqual

OFQUAL became the independent regulator of qualifications, examinations and assessments on 1 April 2010. It is responsible for maintaining standards, improving confidence and distributing information about qualifications and examinations, as well as regulating general and vocational qualifications in England.

Chief Regulator, Sally Collier
Chair, Roger Taylor

OFFICE FOR STANDARDS IN EDUCATION, CHILDREN'S SERVICES AND SKILLS (OFSTED)
Piccadilly Gate, Store Street, Manchester M1 2WD
T 0300-123 1231 E enquiries@ofsted.gov.uk
W www.gov.uk/government/organisations/ofsted

Ofsted was established under the Education (Schools Act) 1992 and was relaunched on 1 April 2007 with a wider remit, bringing together four formerly separate inspectorates.

It works to raise standards in services through the inspection and regulation of care for children and young people, and inspects education and training for children of all ages. *See also* Education.

HM Chief Inspector, Amanda Speilman
Chair, Prof. Julius Weinburg

ORDNANCE SURVEY
Adanac Drive, Southampton SO16 0AS
T 0845-605 0505
E customerservices@os.uk
W www.ordnancesurvey.co.uk

Ordnance Survey is the national mapping agency for Great Britain. It is a government department and executive agency operating as a trading fund since 1999.

Director-General and Chief Executive, Nigel Clifford

SERIOUS FRAUD OFFICE
2–4 Cockspur Street, London SW1Y 5BS
T 020-7239 7272 E public.enquiries@sfo.gsi.gov.uk
W www.sfo.gov.uk

The Serious Fraud Office is an independent government department that investigates and, where appropriate, prosecutes serious or complex fraud, bribery and corruption. It is part of the UK criminal justice system with jurisdiction over England, Wales and Northern Ireland but not Scotland, the Isle of Man or the Channel Islands. The office is headed by a director who is superintended by the Attorney-General.

Director, David Green, CB, QC

SUPREME COURT OF THE UNITED KINGDOM
Parliament Square, London SW1P 3BD
T 020-7960 1900 E enquiries@supremecourt.uk
W www.supremecourt.uk

The Supreme Court of the United Kingdom is the highest domestic judicial authority; it replaced the appellate committee of the House of Lords (the house functioning in its judicial capacity) on 1 October 2009. It is the final court of appeal for cases heard in Great Britain and Northern Ireland (except for criminal cases from Scotland). Cases concerning the interpretation and application of European Union law, including preliminary rulings requested by British courts and tribunals, are decided by the Court of Justice of the European Union (CJEU), and the supreme court can make a reference to the CJEU in appropriate cases. Additionally, in giving effect to rights contained in the European Convention on Human Rights, the supreme court must take account of any decision of the European Court of Human Rights.

The supreme court also assumed jurisdiction in relation to devolution matters under the Scotland Act 1998 (now partly superseded by the Scotland Act 2012), the Northern Ireland Act 1988 and the Government of Wales Act 2006; these powers were transferred from the Judicial Committee of the Privy Council. Ten of the 12 Lords of Appeal in Ordinary (Law Lords) from the House of Lords transferred to the 12-member supreme court when it came into operation (at the same time one law lord retired and another was appointed Master of the Rolls). All new justices of the supreme court are now appointed by an independent selection commission, and, although styled Rt. Hon. Lord, are not members of the House of Lords. Peers who are members of the judiciary are disqualified from sitting or voting in the House of Lords until they retire from their judicial office.

Chief Executive, Mark Ormerod, CB

UK STATISTICS AUTHORITY

1 Drummond Gate, London SW1V 2QQ
T 0845-604 1857 E authority.enquiries@statistics.gsi.gov.uk
W www.statisticsauthority.gov.uk

The UK Statistics Authority was established on 1 April 2008 by the Statistics and Registration Service Act 2007 as an independent body operating at arm's length from government, reporting to the UK parliament and the devolved legislatures. Its overall objective is to promote and safeguard the production and publication of official statistics and ensure their quality and comprehensiveness. The authority's main functions are the oversight of the Office for National Statistics (ONS); monitoring and reporting on all UK official statistics, which includes around 30 central government departments and the devolved administrations; and the production of a code of practice for statistics and the assessment of official statistics against the code.

BOARD

Chair, Sir David Norgrove
Board Members, Prof. Sir Adrian Smith, FRS *(Deputy Chair);* Jonathan Athow *(Deputy National Statistician for Economic Statistics);* Sian Baldwin; Iain Bell *(Deputy National Statistician for Population and Public Policy);* Dame Colette Bowe, DBE; Dame Moira Gibb, DBE; Prof. David Hand, OBE; Prof. Jonathan Haskel; Ed Humpherson; David Levy; Nora Nanayakkara; John Pullinger, CB *(National Statistician);* Heather Savory *(Deputy National Statistician for Data Capability)*

OFFICE FOR NATIONAL STATISTICS (ONS)

Cardiff Road, Newport NP10 8XG
T 0845-601 3034 E info@ons.gsi.gov.uk W www.ons.gov.uk
The ONS was created in 1996 by the merger of the Central Statistical Office and the Office of Population Censuses and Surveys. On 1 April 2008 it became the executive office of the UK Statistics Authority. As part of these changes, the office's responsibility for the General Register Office transferred to HM Passport Office of the Home Office.

The ONS is responsible for preparing, interpreting and publishing key statistics on the government, economy and society of the UK. Its key responsibilities include designing, managing and running the Census and providing statistics on health and other demographic matters in England and Wales; the production of the UK National Accounts and other economic indicators; the organisation of population censuses in England and Wales and surveys for government departments and public bodies.

National Statistician, John Pullinger
Director-Generals, Jonathan Athowin Bell; Heather Savory

WATER SERVICES REGULATION AUTHORITY (OFWAT)

Centre City Tower, 7 Hill Street, Birmingham B5 4UA
T 0121-644 7500 E mailbox@ofwat.gsi.gov.uk
W www.ofwat.gov.uk

OFWAT is the independent economic regulator of the water and sewerage companies in England and Wales. It is responsible for ensuring that the water industry in England and Wales provides household and business customers with a good quality service and value for money. This is done by ensuring that the companies provide customers with a good quality, efficient service at a fair price; limiting the prices companies can charge; monitoring the companies' performance and taking action, including enforcement, to protect customers' interests; settting the companies efficiency targets; making sure the companies deliver the best for consumers and the environment in the long term; and encouraging competition where it benefits consumers.

Chair, Jonson Cox
Chief Executive, Cathryn Ross

PUBLIC BODIES

The following section is a listing of public bodies and other civil service organisations: it is not a complete list of these organisations.

Whereas executive agencies are either part of a government department or are one in their own right (*see* Government Departments), public bodies carry out their functions to a greater or lesser extent at arm's length from central government. Ministers are ultimately responsible to parliament for the activities of the public bodies sponsored by their department and in almost all cases (except where there is separate statutory provision) ministers make the appointments to their boards. Departments are responsible for funding and ensuring good governance of their public bodies.

The term 'public body' is a general one which includes public corporations, such as the BBC; NHS bodies; and non-departmental public bodies (NDPBs).

ADJUDICATOR'S OFFICE
PO Box 10280, Nottingham NG2 9PF
T 0300-057 1111 W www.adjudicatorsoffice.gov.uk

The Adjudicator's Office investigates complaints from individuals and businesses about the way that HM Revenue and Customs and the Valuation Office Agency have handled a person's affairs. The Adjudicator's Office will only consider a complaint after the respective organisation's internal complaints procedure has been exhausted.

The Adjudicator, Helen Megarry

ADVISORY, CONCILIATION AND ARBITRATION SERVICE (ACAS)
22nd Floor, Euston Tower, 286 Euston Road, London NW1 3JJ
T 0300-123 1100 W www.acas.org.uk

The Advisory, Conciliation and Arbitration Service was set up under the Employment Protection Act 1975 (the provisions now being found in the Trade Union and Labour Relations (Consolidation) Act 1992).

ACAS is largely funded by the Department for Business, Innovation and Skills. A council sets its strategic direction, policies and priorities, and ensures that the agreed strategic objectives and targets are met. It consists of a chair and 11 employer, trade union and independent members, appointed by the Secretary of State for Business, Energy and Industrial Strategy.

ACAS aims to improve organisations and working life through better employment relations, to provide up-to-date information, independent advice and high-quality training, and to work with employers and employees to solve problems and improve performance.

ACAS has regional offices, in Birmingham, Bristol, Bury St Edmunds, Cardiff, Fleet, Glasgow, Leeds, Liverpool, Manchester, Newcastle-upon-Tyne and Nottingham. The head office is in London.

Chair, Sir Brendan Barber
Chief Executive, Anne Sharp, CBE

ADVISORY COUNCIL ON NATIONAL RECORDS AND ARCHIVES
The National Archives, Kew, Surrey TW9 4DU
T 020-8392 5337
W http://www.nationalarchives.gov.uk/about/our-role/advisory-council/

The Advisory Council on National Records and Archives advises the Secretary of State for Digital, Culture, Media and Sport on issues relating to public records that are over 20 years old including public access to them. The council meets four times a year, and its main task is to consider requests for the extended closure of public records; it also reaches decisions regarding government departments that want to keep records.

The Forum on Historical Manuscripts and Academic Research, a sub-committee of the Advisory Council, provides advice to the Chief Executive of The National Archives and Keeper of Public Records on matters relating to historical manuscripts, records and archives, other than public records.

Chair, Rt. Hon. Sir Terence Etherton *(Master of the Rolls)*

AGRICULTURE AND HORTICULTURE DEVELOPMENT BOARD
Stoneleigh Park, Kenilworth, Warwickshire CV8 2TL
T 02476-692051 E info@ahdb.org.uk W www.ahdb.org.uk

The Agriculture and Horticulture Development Board (AHDB) is funded by the agriculture and horticulture industries through statutory levies, with the duty to improve efficiency and competitiveness within six sectors: pig meat in England; milk in Great Britain; beef and lamb in England; commercial horticulture in Great Britain; cereals and oilseeds in the UK; and potatoes in Great Britain. The AHDB represents about 75 per cent of total UK agricultural output. Levies raised from the six sectors are ring-fenced to ensure that they can only be used to the benefit of the sectors from which they were raised.

Chair, Sir Peter Kendall
Independent members, Prof. Ian Crute, CBE; Will Lifford; George Lyon
Sector members, Gary Taylor, MBE *(horticulture);* Adam Quinney *(beef and lamb);* Meryl Ward, MBE *(pig meat);* Fiona Fell *(potatoes);* Paul Temple *(cereals and oilseeds);* Gwyn Jones *(milk)*
Chief Executive, Jane King

ARCHITECTURE AND DESIGN SCOTLAND
Bakehouse Close, 146 Canongate, Edinburgh EH8 8DD
T 0131-556 6699 W www.ads.org.uk

Architecture and Design Scotland (A&DS) was established in 2005 by the Scottish government as the national champion for good architecture, urban design and planning in the built environment; it works with a wide range of organisations at national, regional and local levels.

Chair, Karen Anderson
Chief Executive, Jim MacDonald

ARMED FORCES' PAY REVIEW BODY
8th Floor, Fleetbank House, 2-6 Salisbury Square, London EC4Y 8JX
T 020-7211 8315 W www.ome.uk.com

The Armed Forces' Pay Review Body was appointed in 1971. It advises the prime minister and the Secretary of State for Defence on the pay and allowances of members of naval, military and air forces of the Crown.

Chair, John Steele
Members, Brendan Connor; Tim Flesher, CB; Paul Kernaghan, CBE, QPM; Prof. Ken Mayhew; Lesley Mercer; Vilma Patterson, MBE; Rear Admiral (retd) Jon Westbrook, CBE

ARTS COUNCIL ENGLAND

21 Bloomsbury Street, London WC1B 3HF
T 0845-300 6200
W www.artscouncil.org.uk

Arts Council England is the national development agency for the arts in England. Using public money from government and the National Lottery, it supports a range of artistic activities, including theatre, music, literature, dance, photography, digital art, carnival and crafts. Between 2015 and 2018, Arts Council England is investing £1.1bn of public money from the government and around £700m from the National Lottery.

The governing body, the national council, comprises 14 members, who are appointed by the Secretary of State for Culture, Media and Sport usually for a term of four years. There are also five councils, responsible for the agreement of area strategies, plans and priorities for action within the national framework.

National Council Chair, Sir Nicholas Serota, CH
National Council Members, Maria Balshaw, CBE; Matthew Bowcock, CBE; David Bryan; Prof. Jon Cook; Joe Docherty; Sheila Healy; David Joseph; Sir Nicholas Kenyon; Nazo Moosa; Peter Phillips; Alistair Spalding, CBE; Rosemary Squire, OBE; Veronica Wadley
Chief Executive, Darren Henley, OBE

ARTS COUNCIL OF NORTHERN IRELAND

77 Malone Road, Belfast BT9 6AQ
T 028-9038 5200 E info@artscouncil-ni.org
W www.artscouncil-ni.org

The Arts Council of Northern Ireland is the prime distributor of government funds in support of the arts in Northern Ireland. It is funded by the Department of Culture, Arts and Leisure and from National Lottery funds.

Chair, Bob Collins
Members, David Alderdice; Anna Carragher; Roisin Erskine; Dr Siún Hanrahan; Jarlath Kearney; Dr Leon Litvack; Noelle McAlinden; Katherine McCloskey; Paul Mullan; Dr Katy Radford, MBE; Cian Smyth
Chief Executive, Roisin McDonough

ARTS COUNCIL OF WALES

Bute Place, Cardiff CF10 5AL
T 0845-873 4900 E information@arts.wales
W www.arts.wales

The Arts Council of Wales was established in 1994 by royal charter and is the development body for the arts in Wales. It funds arts organisations with funding from the Welsh government and is the distributor of National Lottery funds to the arts in Wales.

Chair, Phil George
Members, Iwan Bala; Andy Eagle; Kate Eden; Michael Griffiths; Melanie Hawthorne; Dr Lesley Hodgson; Andrew Miller; Rachel O'Riordan; Dafyd Rhys; Richard Turner; Alan Watkin; Marian Wyn Jones
Chief Executive, Nick Capaldi

AUDIT SCOTLAND

102 West Port, Edinburgh EH3 9DN
T 0131-625 1500 E info@audit-scotland.gov.uk
W www.audit-scotland.gov.uk

Audit Scotland was set up in 2000 to provide services to the Accounts Commission and the Auditor-General for Scotland. Together they help to ensure that public-sector bodies in Scotland are held accountable for the proper, efficient and effective use of public funds.

Audit Scotland's work covers bodies including local authorities; health boards; further education colleges; Scottish Water; the Scottish government; government agencies such as the Prison Service and non-departmental public bodies such as the Scottish Police Authority and the Scottish Fire and Rescue Service. The organisation audited 329 sets of accounts in 2016–17.

Audit Scotland carries out financial and regularity audits to ensure that public-sector bodies adhere to the highest standards of financial management and governance. It also carries out performance audits to ensure that these bodies achieve the best value for money. All of Audit Scotland's work in connection with local authorities is carried out for the Accounts Commission; its other work is undertaken for the Auditor-General.

Chair, Ian Leitch, CBE
Auditor-General, Caroline Gardner
Chair of the Accounts Commission, Ronnie Hinds

BANK OF ENGLAND

Threadneedle Street, London EC2R 8AH
T 020-7601 4444 E enquiries@bankofengland.co.uk
W www.bankofengland.co.uk

The Bank of England was incorporated in 1694 under royal charter. It was nationalised in 1946 under the Bank of England Act of that year which gave HM Treasury statutory powers over the bank. It is the banker of the government and it manages the issue of banknotes. Since 1998 it has been operationally independent and its Monetary Policy Committee has been responsible for setting short-term interest rates to meet the government's inflation target. Its responsibility for banking supervision was transferred to the Financial Services Authority in the same year. As the central reserve bank of the country, the Bank of England keeps the accounts of British banks, and of most overseas central banks; the larger banks and building societies are required to maintain with it a proportion of their cash resources. The bank's core purposes are monetary stability and financial stability. The Banking Act 2009 increased the responsibilities of the bank, including giving it a new financial stability objective and creating a special resolution regime for dealing with failing banks.

In 2013, through the Prudential Regulation Authority (PRA), the bank became responsible for the prudential regulation and supervision of banks, building societies, credit unions, insurers and major investment firms.

Governor, Mark Carney
Deputy Governors, Dr Ben Broadbent; Sir Jon Cunliffe, CB; Joanna Place; Sir David Ramsden; Sam Woods
Court of Directors, The Governor; Anthony Habgood *(Chair of Court);* Dr Ben Broadbent; Sir Jon Cunliffe; Bradley Fried; Tim Frost; Baroness Harding of Winscombe; Dave Prentis; Don Robert; Dorothy Thompson; Sam Woods
Monetary Policy Committee, The Governor; Dr Ben Broadbent; Sir Jon Cunliffe; Andy Haldane; Ian McCafferty; Michael Saunders; Silvana Tenreyo; Dr Gertjan Vlieghe
Financial Policy Committee, The Governor; Andrew Bailey; Dr Ben Broadbent; Sir Jon Cunliffe; Alex Brazier; Dame Clara Furse, DBE; Anil Kashyap; Donald Kohn; Charles Roxburgh; Richard Sharp; Martin Taylor; Sam Woods
General Counsel, Sonya Branch
Director for Banknotes and Chief Cashier, Victoria Cleland
The Auditor, Stephen Brown

BIG LOTTERY FUND

1 Plough Place, London EC4A 1DE
T 020-7211 1800 **Advice Line** 0345-410 2030
E general.enquiries@biglotteryfund.org.uk
W www.biglotteryfund.org.uk

The Big Lottery Fund is responsible for distributing 40 per cent of all funds raised for good causes by the National Lottery, amounting to around £670m to 12,000 projects a year across the UK. It is responsible for supporting health, education, environmental and charitable projects.

Chair, Peter Ainsworth
Vice-Chair, Tony Burton, CBE
Regional Chairs, Julie Harrison *(Northern Ireland);* Maureen
  McGinn *(Scotland);* Nat Sloane, CBE *(England);* Sir Adrian
  Webb *(Wales)*
Chief Executive, Dawn Austwick, OBE

BOUNDARY COMMISSIONS

ENGLAND
2nd Floor, 35 Great Smith Street, London SW1P 3BQ
T 020-7276 1102
E information@boundarycommissionengland.gov.uk
W http://boundarycommissionforengland.independent.gov.uk

Deputy Chair, Hon. Mr Justice Nichol

WALES
Hastings House, Fitzalan Court, Cardiff CF24 0BL
T 029-2046 4819 E bcomm.wales@wales.gsi.gov.uk
W www.bcomm-wales.gov.uk

Deputy Chair, Hon. Mr Justice Lewis

SCOTLAND
Thistle House, 91 Haymarket Terrace, Edinburgh EH12 5HD
T 0131-538 7510 E bcs@scottishboundaries.gov.uk
W www.bcomm-scotland.independent.gov.uk

Deputy Chair, Hon. Lord Matthews

NORTHERN IRELAND
The Bungalow, Stormont House, Stormont Estate, Belfast BT4 3SH
T 028-9052 7821 E contact@boundarycommission.org.uk
W www.boundarycommission.org.uk

Deputy Chair, Hon. Ms Justice McBride, DBE

The commissions, established in 1944, are constituted under
the Parliamentary Constituencies Act 1986 (as amended). The
Speaker of the House of Commons is the *ex officio* chair of all
four commissions in the UK.
  The next reviews of UK parliament constituencies will be
undertaken using the electoral register from 1 December 2015;
these reviews must be submitted before 1 October 2018.

BRITISH BROADCASTING CORPORATION (BBC)
BBC Broadcasting House, Portland Place, London W1A 1AA
W www.bbc.co.uk

The BBC was incorporated under royal charter in 1926 as
successor to the British Broadcasting Company Ltd. The BBC's
current charter, which came into force on 1 January 2007 and
extends to 31 December 2016, recognises the BBC's editorial
independence and sets out its public purposes. The BBC Trust
was formed under the new charter and replaces the Board of
Governors; it sets the strategic direction of the BBC and has a
duty to represent the interests of licence fee payers. The chair,
vice-chair and other trustees are appointed by the Queen-in-
Council. The BBC is financed by television licence revenue and
by grant-in-aid from parliament for the World Service (radio).
See Broadcasting.

BBC TRUST MEMBERS

Chair, Rona Fairhead
National Trustees, Mark Florman *(England);* Aideen McGinley,
  OBE *(Northern Ireland);* Bill Matthews *(Scotland);* Elan
  Closs Stephens *(Wales)*
Trustees, Sonita Alleyne, OBE; Richard Ayre; Sir Roger Carr;
  Mark Damazer; Nicholas Prettejohn; Suzanne Taverne;
  Lord Williams of Baglan

EXECUTIVE BOARD
Director-General, Lord Hall of Birkenhead
Members, Anne Bulford, OBE *(Deputy Director-General);* Simon
  Burke *(Senior Independent Director);* David Clementi *(Chair);*
  Elan Closs Stephens *(Wales);* Tim Davie *(CEO: BBC
  Worldwide, Director: Global);* Baroness Grey-Thompson,
  DBE *(Non-Executive Director);* Ian Hargreaves *(Non-
  Executive Director);* Tom Ilube *(Non-Executive Director);* Ken
  McQuarrie *(Nations and Regions);* Steve Morrison *(Scotland);*
  Nicholas Serota *(Non-Executive Director);* Ashley Steel
  (England)

STATION CONTROLLERS
Director of BBC Content (BBC One), Charlotte Moore
BBC Two, Patrick Holland
BBC Three, Damian Kavanagh
CBBC, Cheryl Taylor
CBeebies, Kay Benbow
Business, Childrens, Jackie Myburgh
Comedy, Shane Allen
Drama, Piers Wenger
Entertainment, Kate Phillips
Factual, Alison Kirkham
Programming and Daytime, Dan McGolphin
Director of BBC Radio and BBC Music, Bob Shennan
Radio 1, 1Xtra and Asian Network, Ben Cooper
Radio 2, Lewis Carnie
Radio 3, Alan Davey
Radio 4 and 4 Extra, Gwyneth Williams
Radio 5 Live and 5 Live Sports Extra, Jonathan Wall
Radio 6 Music, Paul Rodgers
Radio and Music Multiplatform, Mark Friend
World Service English, Mark Hockaday

BRITISH COUNCIL
Bridgewater House, 58 Whitworth Street, Manchester M1 6BB
T 0161-957 7755 E general.enquiries@britishcouncil.org
W www.britishcouncil.org

The British Council was established in 1934, incorporated by
royal charter in 1940 and granted a supplemental charter in
1993. It is an independent, non-political organisation which
promotes Britain abroad and is the UK's international
organisation for educational and cultural relations. The British
Council is represented in over 100 countries.

Chair, Christopher Rodrigues, CBE
Chief Executive, Sir Ciarán Devane

BRITISH FILM INSTITUTE
21 Stephen Street, London W1T 1LN
T 020-7255 1444 W www.bfi.org.uk

The BFI, established in 1933, offers opportunities for people
throughout the UK to experience, learn and discover more
about the world of film and moving image culture. It
incorporates the BFI National Archive, the BFI Reuben
Library, BFI Southbank, BFI Distribution, the annual BFI
London Film Festival as well as the BFI FLARE: London LGBT
Film Festival, and the BFI IMAX cinema. It also publishes the
monthly *Sight and Sound* magazine and provides advice and
support for regional cinemas and film festivals across the UK.
  Following the closure of the UK Film Council in April 2011,
the BFI became the lead body for film in the UK, in charge of
allocating lottery money for the development and production
of new British films.

Chair, Josh Berger, CBE
Chief Executive, Amanda Nevill

BRITISH LIBRARY

96 Euston Road, London NW1 2DB
T 0843-208 1144 E customer-services@bl.uk
W www.bl.uk

The British Library was established in 1973. It is the UK's national library and one of the world's greatest research libraries. It aims to serve scholarship, research, industry, commerce and all other major users of information. The Library's collection has developed over 250 years and exceeds 150 million separate items, including books, journals, manuscripts, maps, stamps, music, patents, newspapers and sound recordings in all written and spoken languages. The library is now based at two sites: London St Pancras and Boston Spa, W. Yorks. The library's sponsoring department is the Department for Culture, Media and Sport. Up to 3 million digitised items are added to the collection each year.

BRITISH LIBRARY BOARD

Chair, Rt. Hon. Baroness Blackstone
Members, David Barclay; Dr Robert Black, CBE, FRSE; Jonathan Callaway; Tracey Chevalier, FRSL; Martin Dickson; Lord Janvrin, GCB, GCVO, QSO, PC; Roly Keating; Dr Stephen Page; Patrick Plant; Sir John Ritblat; Dr Simon Thurley, CBE; Prof. Dame Helen Wallace, DBE, CMG, FBA

EXECUTIVE

Chief Executive, Roly Keating
Chief Librarian, Caroline Brazier
Chief Operating Officer, Phil Spence

BRITISH LIBRARY, BOSTON SPA
Boston Spa, Wetherby, W. Yorks LS23 7BQ
T 01937-546070

BRITISH MUSEUM

Great Russell Street, London WC1B 3DG
T 020-7323 8000 E information@britishmuseum.org
W www.britishmuseum.org

The British Museum houses the national collection of antiquities, ethnography, coins and paper money, medals, prints and drawings. The British Museum dates from 7 June 1753, when parliament approved the holding of a public lottery to raise funds for the purchase of the collections of Sir Hans Sloane and the Harleian manuscripts, and for their proper housing and maintenance. The building (Montagu House) was opened in 1759. The existing buildings were erected between 1823 and the present day, and the original collection has increased to its current dimensions by gifts and purchases. Total government grant-in-aid for 2016–17 was £53.6m.

Chair, Sir Richard Lambert
Trustees, Hon. Nigel Boardman; Cheryl Carolus; Elizabeth Corley, CBE; Patricia Cumper, MBE; Clarissa Farr; Prof. Clive Gamble; Muriel Gray; Wasfi Kani, OBE; Prof. Nicola Lacey, FBA; Sir Richard Lambert; Sir Deryck Maughan; John Micklethwait, CBE; Sir Paul Nurse, PRS; Gavin Patterson; Mark Pears, CBE; Grayson Perry, CBE, RA; Sir Paul Ruddock; Rt. Hon. Lord Sassoon, KT; Prof. Amartya Sen; Dame Nemat (Minouche) Shafik; Ahdaf Soueif; Lord Stern of Brentford, FBA; Lord Turner of Ecchinswell; Baroness Wheatcroft

OFFICERS

Director, Dr Hartwig Fischer
Deputy Directors, Joanna Mackle; Marilyn Standley; Jonathan Williams; Christopher Yates

KEEPERS

Keeper of Africa, Oceania and the Americas, Lissant Bolton
Keeper of Ancient Egypt and Sudan, Neal Spencer
Keeper of Asia, Jane Portal
Keeper of Coins and Medals, Philip Attwood
Keeper of Greece and Rome, J. Lesley Fitton
Keeper of the Middle East, Jonathan Tubb
Deputy Keeper of Britain, Europe and Prehistory, Jill Cook
Keeper of Prints and Drawings, Hugo Chapman

BRITISH PHARMACOPOEIA COMMISSION

151 Buckingham Palace Road, London SW1W 9SZ
T 020-3080 6561 E bpcom@mhra.gsi.gov.uk
W www.pharmacopoeia.com

The British Pharmacopoeia Commission sets standards for medicinal products used in human and veterinary medicines and is responsible for publication of *British Pharmacopoeia* (a publicly available statement of the standard that a medicinal substance or product must meet throughout its shelf-life), *British Pharmacopoeia (Veterinary)* and *British Approved Names.* It has 17 members, including two lay members, who are appointed on behalf of the Secretary of State for Health by the Department of Health.

Chair, Prof. Kevin Taylor
Vice-Chair, Prof. Alastair Davidson

CARE QUALITY COMMISSION

Citygate, Gallowgate, Newcastle upon Tyne NE1 4PA
T 0300-061 6161 E enquiries@cqc.org.uk W www.cqc.org.uk

The Care Quality Commission (CQC) is the independent regulator of health and adult social care services in England, ensuring health and social care services provide people with safe, effective, compassionate, high-quality care and encouraging them to improve. CQC monitors, inspects and regulates services to make sure they meet fundamental standards of quality and safety and publishes performance ratings to help people choose care.

Chair, Peter Wyman, CBE
Board Members, Prof. Louis Appleby, CBE; Prof. Ted Baker; Paul Corrigan, CBE; Prof. Steve Field, CBE; Dr Malte Gerhold; Jora Gill; Jane Mordue ; Sir Robert Francis, QC; Paul Rew; Andrea Sutcliffe; Peter Wyman, CBE
Chief Executive, Sir David Behan, CBE

CENTRAL ARBITRATION COMMITTEE

22nd Floor, Euston Tower, 286 Euston Road, London NW1 3JJ
T 020-7904 2300 E enquiries@cac.gov.uk W www.cac.gov.uk

The Central Arbitration Committee (CAC) is a permanent independent body with statutory powers whose main function is to adjudicate on applications relating to the statutory recognition and de-recognition of trade unions for collective bargaining purposes, where such recognition or de-recognition cannot be agreed voluntarily. In addition, the CAC has a statutory role in determining disputes between trade unions and employers over the disclosure of information for collective bargaining purposes, and in resolving applications and complaints under the information and consultation regulations, and performs a similar role in relation to the legislation on the European Works Council, European companies, European cooperative societies and cross-border mergers. The CAC and its predecessors have also provided voluntary arbitration in collective disputes.

Chair, Sir Michael Burton
Chief Executive, James Jacob

CERTIFICATION OFFICE FOR TRADE UNIONS AND EMPLOYERS' ASSOCIATIONS

Euston Tower, 286 Euston Road, London NW1 3JJ
T 020-7210 3734 E info@certoffice.org
W www.gov.uk/certificationofficer

The Certification Office is an independent statutory authority. The Certification Officer is appointed by the Secretary of State for Business, Energy and Industrial Strategy and is responsible for maintaining a list of trade unions and employers' associations; ensuring compliance with statutory requirements and keeping available for public inspection annual returns from trade unions and employers' associations; determining complaints concerning trade union elections, certain ballots and certain breaches of trade union rules; ensuring observance of statutory requirements governing mergers between trade unions or employers' associations; overseeing the political funds and finances of trade unions and employers' associations; and for certifying the independence of trade unions.

Certification Officer, Gerard Walker

CHURCH COMMISSIONERS

Church House, Great Smith Street, London SW1P 3AZ
T 020-7898 1000 E commissioners.enquiry@churchofengland.org
W www.churchofengland.org/about-us/structure/
churchcommissioners

The Church Commissioners were established in 1948 by the amalgamation of Queen Anne's Bounty (established 1704) and the Ecclesiastical Commissioners (established 1836). They are responsible for the management of some of the Church of England's assets, the income from which is predominantly used to help pay for the stipend and pension of the clergy and to support the church's work throughout the country. The commissioners own UK and global company shares, over 120,000 acres of forestry estate, a residential estate in central London, and commercial property across Great Britain, plus an interest in overseas property via managed funds. They also carry out administrative duties in connection with pastoral reorganisation and closed churches.

The 33 commissioners are: the Archbishops of Canterbury and of York; eleven people elected by the General Synod, comprising four bishops, three clergy and four lay persons; three Church Estates Commissioners; two cathedral deans; nine people appointed by the crown and the archbishops; six holders of state office, comprising the Prime Minister, the Lord Chancellor, the Lord President of the Council, the Secretary of State for Culture, Media and Sport, the Speaker of the House of Commons and the Lord Speaker.

CHURCH ESTATES COMMISSIONERS
First, Loretta Minghella, OBE
Second, Rt. Hon. Dame Caroline Spelman, DBE, MP
Third, Andrew Mackie

OFFICERS
Chief Executive, Andrew Brown
Official Solicitor, Stephen Slack

COAL AUTHORITY

200 Lichfield Lane, Mansfield, Notts NG18 4RG
T 01623-637000 E thecoalauthority@coal.gov.uk
W www.gov.uk/government/organisations/the-coal-authority

The Coal Authority was established under the Coal Industry Act 1994 to manage certain functions previously undertaken by British Coal, including ownership of unworked coal. It is responsible for licensing coal mining operations and for providing information on coal reserves and past and future coal mining. It settles subsidence damage claims which are not the responsibility of licensed coal mining operators. It deals with the management and disposal of property, and with surface hazards such as abandoned coal mine entries and mine water discharges. The Coal Authority's powers were extended alongside the Energy Act 2011 to enable it to deal with metal mine subsidence issues and deliver a metal mine water treatment programme when the necessary funding is made available.

Chair, Stephen Dingle
Chief Executive, Philip Lawrence

COMMITTEE ON STANDARDS IN PUBLIC LIFE

1 Horseguards Road, London SW1A 2HQ
T 020-7271 2948 E public@public-standards.gov.uk
W www.gov.uk/government/organisations/
the-committee-on-standards-in-public-life

The Committee on Standards in Public Life (CSPL) was set up in October 1994. It is formed of 8 people appointed by the prime minister, comprising the chair, three political members nominated by the leaders of the three main political parties and four independent members. The CSPL advises the prime minister on ethical standards across the whole of public life in the UK. It monitors and reports on issues relating to the standards of conduct of all public office holders. It is responsible for promoting the 7 principles of public life, being: selflessness; integrity; objectivity; accountability; openness; honesty; and leadership.

Chair, Lord Bew
Members, Rt. Hon. Dame Margaret Beckett, DBE, MP; Sheila Drew Smith, OBE; Simon Hart, MP; Dr Jane Martin, CBE; Jane Ramsey; Monisha Shah; Sheila Drew Smith, OBE; The Rt. Hon. Lord Andrew Stunell, OBE

COMMONWEALTH WAR GRAVES COMMISSION

2 Marlow Road, Maidenhead, Berks SL6 7DX
T 01628-634221 W www.cwgc.org

The Commonwealth War Graves Commission (formerly Imperial War Graves Commission) was founded by royal charter in 1917. It is responsible for the commemoration of around 1.7 million members of the forces of the Commonwealth who lost their lives in the two world wars. More than one million graves are maintained in over 23,000 burial grounds across 154 countries. Over three-quarters of a million men and women who have no known grave or who were cremated are commemorated by name on memorials built by the commission.

The funds of the commission are derived from the six participating governments: the UK, Canada, Australia, New Zealand, South Africa and India.

President, HRH the Duke of Kent, KG, GCMG, GCVO, ADC
Chair, Secretary of State for Defence
Vice-Chair, Vice Adm. Sir Tim Laurence, KCB, CB, ADC(P)
Members, High Commissioners in London for Australia, Canada, India, New Zealand and South Africa; Edward Chaplin, CMG, OBE; Robert Fox, MBE; Kevan Jones, MP; Hon. Ros Kelly; Lt.-Gen. Sir William Rollo, KCB, CBE; Keith Simpson, MP; Prof. Sir Hew Strachan, FRSE; Air Marshal David Walker, CB, CBE, AFC, RAF (retd)
Director-General and Secretary to the Commission, Victoria Wallace
Director of Legal Services, Gillian Stedman

COMPETITION SERVICE

Victoria House, Bloomsbury Place, London WC1A 2EB
T 020-7979 7979 E info@catribunal.org.uk
W www.catribunal.org.uk

The Competition Service is the financial corporate body by which the Competition Appeal Tribunal is administered and through which it receives funding for the performance of its judicial functions.

Registrar, Charles Dhanowa, OBE

CONSUMER COUNCIL FOR WATER

1st Floor, Victoria Square House, Victoria Square, Birmingham, B2 4AJ
T 0121-345 1000 E enquiries@ccwater.org.uk
W www.ccwater.org.uk

The Consumer Council for Water was established in 2005 under the Water Act 2003 to represent consumers' interests in respect of price, service and value for money from their water and sewerage services, and to investigate complaints from customers about their water company. There are four regional committees in England and one in Wales.

Chair, Alan Lovell

CORPORATION OF TRINITY HOUSE

Trinity House, Tower Hill, London EC3N 4DH
T 020-7481 6900 E enquiries@trinityhouse.co.uk
W www.trinityhouse.co.uk

The Corporation of Trinity House of Deptford Strond is the UK's largest-endowed maritime charity, established formally by Royal Charter by Henry VIII in 1514, with statutory duties as the General Lighthouse Authority (GLA) for England, Wales, the Channel Islands and Gibraltar. Its remit is to assist the safe passage of a variety of vessels through some of the busiest sea-lanes in the world; it does this by deploying and maintaining approximately 600 aids to navigation, ranging from lighthouses to a satellite navigation service. The corporation also has certain statutory jurisdiction over aids to navigation maintained by local harbour authorities and is responsible for marking or dispersing wrecks dangerous to navigation, except those occurring within port limits or wrecks of HM ships.

The statutory duties of Trinity House are funded by the General Lighthouse Fund, which is provided from light dues levied on ships calling at ports of the UK and the Republic of Ireland. The corporation is a deep-sea pilotage authority, authorised by the Secretary of State for Transport to license deep-sea pilots. In addition Trinity House is a charitable organisation that maintains a number of retirement homes for mariners and their dependants, funds a four-year training scheme for those seeking a career in the merchant navy, and also dispenses grants to a wide range of maritime charities. The charity work is wholly funded by its own activities.

The corporation is controlled by a court of 41 Elder Brethren; a separate board controls the Lighthouse Service. The Elder Brethren also act as nautical assessors in marine cases in the Admiralty Division of the High Court.

ELDER BRETHREN

Master, HRH the Princess Royal, KG, KT, GCVO
Deputy Master, Capt. Ian McNaught
Wardens, Capt. Nigel Palmer, OBE *(Rental);* Rear-Adm. David Snelson, CB *(Nether)*
Elder Brethren, HRH the Duke of Edinburgh, KG, KT, OM, GBE; HRH the Prince of Wales, KG, KT, GCB; HRH the Duke of York, KG, GCVO, ADC; Capt. Roger Barker; Adm. Lord Boyce, KG, GCB, OBE; Lord Browne of Madingley, FRS, FRENG; Capt. John Burton-Hall, RD; Lord Carrington, KG, GCMG, CH, MC, PC; Viscount Cobham; Cdre Robert Dorey; Capt. Sir Malcolm Edge, KCVO; Capt. Ian Gibb, MBE; Malcolm Glaister; Capt. Duncan Glass, OBE; Capt. Stephen Gobbi; Lord Greenway, Bt.; Rear-Adm. Sir Jeremy de Halpert, KCVO, CB; Capt. Nigel Hope, RD; Lord Mackay of Clashfern, KT; Sir John Major, KG, CH; Capt. Peter Mason, CBE; Cdre. Peter Melson, CVO, CBE, RN; Capt. David Orr; Sir John Parker, GBE; Douglas Potter; Capt. Nigel Pryke; Richard Sadler; Capt. Derek Richards, RD; Lord Robertson of Port Ellen, KT, GCMG, PC; Rear-Adm. Sir Patrick Rowe, KCVO, CBE; Cdre. James Scorer; Simon Sherrard; Adm. Sir Jock Slater, GCB, LVO; Cdre. David Squire, CBE, RFA; Rear-Adm. Lord Sterling of Plaistow, GCVO, CBE, RNR; Capt. Colin Stewart, LVO; Sir Adrian Swire, AE; Capt. Thomas Woodfield, OBE; Capt. Richard Woodman, LVO; Cdre. William Walworth, CBE; Adm. Sir George Zambellas, GCB, DSC

OFFICERS

Secretary, Thomas Arculus
Director of Business Services, Ton Damen, RA
Director of Navigational Requirements, Capt. Roger Barker
Director of Operations, Cdre Rob Dorey

CREATIVE SCOTLAND

Waverley Gate, 2–4 Waterloo Place, Edinburgh EH1 3EG
T 0330-333 2000 E enquiries@creativescotland.com
W www.creativescotland.com

Creative Scotland is the organisation tasked with leading the development of the arts, creative and screen industries across Scotland. It was created in 2010 as an amalgamation of the Scottish Arts Council and Scottish Screen, and it encourages and sustains the arts through investment in the form of grants, bursaries, loans and equity. It aims to invest in talent; artistic production; audiences, access and participation; and the cultural economy. Total Scottish government grant-in-aid for 2016–17 is £44.3m.

Chair, Ben Thomson *(interim)*
Board, Ian Aitchison; David Brew; Karen Forbes; Erin Forster; Prof. Maggie Kinloch; Sheila Murray; Cate Nelson-Shaw; Barclay Price; Karthik Subramanya; Ruth Wishart
Chief Executive, Janet Archer

CRIMINAL CASES REVIEW COMMISSION

5 St Philip's Place, Birmingham B3 2PW
T 0121-233 1473 E info@ccrc.x.gsi.gov.uk
W www.ccrc.gov.uk

The Criminal Cases Review Commission is the independent body set up under the Criminal Appeal Act 1995. It is a non-departmental public body reporting to parliament via the Lord Chancellor and Secretary of State for Justice. It is responsible for investigating possible miscarriages of justice in England, Wales and Northern Ireland, and deciding whether or not to refer cases back to an appeal court. Members of the commission are appointed in accordance with the Commissioner for Public Appointments' code of practice.

Chair, Richard Foster, CBE
Members, Liz Calderbank; Celia Hughes; Stephen Leach, CB; Alexandra Marks, CBE; Dr Sharon Persaud; Andrew Rennison; David Smith; Ewen Smith; Ranjit Sondhi
Chief Executive, Karen Kneller

CROFTING COMMISSION

Great Glen House, Leachkin Road, Inverness IV3 8NW
T 01463-663439 E info@crofting.scotland.gov.uk
W www.crofting.scotland.gov.uk

The Crofting Commission was established on 1 April 2012, taking over the regulation of crofting from the Crofters Commission. The aim of the Crofting Commission is to regulate crofting, to promote the occupancy of crofts, active land use, and shared management of the land by crofters, as a means of sustaining and enhancing rural communities in Scotland.

Chief Executive, Bill Barron

CROWN ESTATE

St James's Market, London SW1Y 4AH
T 020-7851 5000 E enquiries@thecrownestate.co.uk
W www.thecrownestate.co.uk

The Crown Estate is part of the hereditary possessions of the sovereign 'in right of the crown', managed under the provisions of the Crown Estate Act 1961. It had a capital value of £13.1bn in 2017, and includes substantial blocks of urban property, primarily in London, almost 95,000 hectares of rural land, around half of the foreshore, and the seabed out to the 12 nautical mile territorial limit throughout the UK. The

Crown Estate has a duty to maintain and enhance the capital value of estate and the income obtained from it. Under the terms of the act, the estate pays its revenue surplus to the Treasury every year.

Chair and First Commissioner, Robin Budenberg, CBE
Chief Executive and Second Commissioner, Alison Nimmo, CBE, FRICS

DISCLOSURE AND BARRING SERVICE

PO Box 3961, Royal Wootton Bassett SN4 4HF
T 0300-020 0190 **E** customerservices@dbs.gsi.gov.uk
W www.gov.uk/government/organisations/
disclosure-and-barring-service

The Disclosure and Barring Service (DBS) is an executive non-departmental public body of the Home Office. It helps employers make safer recruitment decisions and prevent unsuitable people from working with vulnerable groups, including children. It was formed on 1 December 2012 and replaced the Criminal Records Bureau (CRB) and Independent Safeguarding Authority (ISA). The DBS is responsible for the children's barred list and adults' barred list for England, Wales and Northern Ireland.

Chair, Bill Griffiths
Chief Executive, Adele Downey

ENVIRONMENT AGENCY

PO Box 544, Rotherham S60 1BY
T 0370-850 6506 **E** enquiries@environment-agency.gov.uk
Incident Hotline 0800-807060
W www.environment-agency.gov.uk

Established in 1996 under the Environment Act 1995, the Environment Agency is a non-departmental public body sponsored by the Department for Environment, Food and Rural Affairs. On 1 April 2013, Natural Resources Wales took over the Environment Agency's responsibilities in Wales. Around 68 per cent of the agency's funding is from the government, with the rest raised from various charging schemes. The agency is responsible for pollution prevention and control in England and for the management and use of water resources, including flood defences, fisheries and navigation. Its remit also includes: scrutinising potentially hazardous business operations; helping businesses to use resources more efficiently; taking action against those who do not take environmental responsibilities seriously; looking after wildlife; working with farmers; helping people get the most out of their environment; and improving the quality of inner city areas and parks by restoring rivers and lakes.

The Environment Agency has head offices in Bristol and London has offices across England divided into 14 regions. Its total grant-in-aid for 2016–17 was £800m.

Chair, Emma Howard Boyd
Deputy Chair, Richard Macdonald
Board Members, Maria Adebowale-Schwarte; Peter Ainsworth; Karen Burrows; Clive Elphick; Lynne Frostick; Joanne Segan; John Varley; Gill Weeks
Chief Executive, Sir James Bevan

EQUALITY AND HUMAN RIGHTS COMMISSION

Arndale House, The Arndale Centre, Manchester M4 3AQ
T 0161-829 8100 **E** correspondence@equalityhumanrights.com
W www.equalityhumanrights.com

The Equality and Human Rights Commission (EHRC) is a statutory body, established under the Equality Act 2006 and launched in October 2007. It inherited the responsibilities of the Commission for Racial Equality, the Disability Rights Commission and the Equal Opportunities Commission. The EHRC's purpose is to reduce inequality, eliminate discrimination, strengthen relations between people, and promote and protect human rights. It enforces equality legislation on age, disability, gender reassignment, marriage and civil partnership, pregnancy and maternity, race, religion or belief, sex and sexual orientation, and encourages compliance with the Human Rights Act 1998 throughout England, Wales and Scotland.

Chair, David Isaac, CBE
Deputy Chair, Caroline Waters, OBE
Commissioners, Susan Johnson, OBE; Lorna McGregor; June Milligan *(Wales Commissioner);* Dr Lesley Sawers *(Scotland Commissioner);* Prof. Swaran Singh; Lord Shinkwin; Sarah Veale, CBE
Chief Executive, Rebecca Hilsenrath

EQUALITY COMMISSION FOR NORTHERN IRELAND

Equality House, 7–9 Shaftesbury Square, Belfast BT2 7DP
T 028-9050 0600**Textphone** 028-9050 0589
E information@equalityni.org **W** www.equalityni.org

The Equality Commission was set up in 1999 under the Northern Ireland Act 1998 and is responsible for promoting equality, keeping the relevant legislation under review, eliminating discrimination on the grounds of race, disability, sexual orientation, gender (including marital and civil partner status, gender reassignment, pregnancy and maternity), age, religion and political opinion and for overseeing the statutory duties on public authorities to promote equality of opportunity and good relations.

Chief Commissioner, Dr Michael Wardlow
Deputy Chief Commissioner, Revd Dr Lesley Carroll
Chief Executive, Evelyn Collins, CBE, FRSA

GAMBLING COMMISSION

Victoria Square House, Victoria Square, Birmingham B2 4BP
T 0121-230 6666
E info@gamblingcommission.gov.uk
W www.gamblingcommission.gov.uk

The Gambling Commission was established under the Gambling Act 2005, and took over the role previously occupied by the Gaming Board for Great Britain in regulating and licensing all commercial gambling – apart from spread betting and the National Lottery – ie casinos, bingo, betting, remote gambling, gaming machines and lotteries. It also advises local and central government on related issues, and is responsible for the protection of children and the vulnerable from being harmed by gambling. In October 2013, the Gambling Commission took over all the responsibilities of the National Lottery Commission in regulating the National Lottery. The commission is sponsored by the Department for Culture, Media and Sport, with its work funded by licence fees paid by the gambling industry.

Chair, Dr William Moyes
Chief Executive, Sarah Harrison, MBE

HEALTH AND SAFETY EXECUTIVE

Redgrave Court, Merton Road, Bootle, Merseyside L20 7HS
T 0845-300 9923 **W** www.hse.gov.uk

The Health and Safety Commission (HSC) and the Health and Safety Executive (HSE) merged on 1 April 2008 to form a single national regulatory body – the HSE – responsible for promoting the cause of better health and safety at work. The HSE is sponsored by the Department for Work and Pensions.

HSE regulates all industrial and commercial sectors except operations in the air and at sea. This includes agriculture, construction, manufacturing, services, transport, mines, offshore oil and gas, quarries and major hazard sites in chemicals and petrochemicals.

HSE is responsible for developing and enforcing health and safety law; providing guidance and advice; commissioning research; conducting inspections and accident and ill-health investigations; developing standards; and licensing or approving some work activities such as asbestos removal. The HSE's nuclear directorate merged with a number of other bodies on 1 April 2011 to form the Office for Nuclear Regulation, an agency of the HSE.

Chair, Martin Temple, CBE
Board Members, Nick Baldwin; Jonathan Baume; George Brechin; Janice Crawford; Isobel Garner; Susan Johnson; Sarah Pinch; Ken Robertson; Kevin Rowan; Martyn Thomas
Chief Executive, Richard Judge

HER MAJESTY'S OFFICERS OF ARMS

COLLEGE OF ARMS (HERALDS' COLLEGE)

130 Queen Victoria Street, London EC4V 4BT
T 020-7248 2762 W www.college-of-arms.gov.uk

The Sovereign's Officers of Arms (King's, Heralds and Pursuivants of Arms) were first incorporated by Richard III in 1484. The powers vested by the crown in the Earl Marshal (the Duke of Norfolk) with regard to state ceremonial are largely exercised through the college, The college is also the official repository of the arms and pedigrees of English, Welsh, Northern Irish and Commonwealth (except Canadian) families and their descendants, and its records include official copies of the records of the Ulster King of Arms, the originals of which remain in Dublin. The 13 officers of the college specialise in genealogical and heraldic work for their respective clients.

Arms have long been, and still are, granted by letters patent from the Kings of Arms. A right to arms can only be established by the registration in the official records of the College of Arms of a pedigree showing direct male line descent from an ancestor already appearing therein as being entitled to arms, or by making application through the College of Arms for a grant of arms. Grants are made to corporations as well as to individuals.
Earl Marshal, the Duke of Norfolk

KINGS OF ARMS
Garter, Thomas Woodcock, CVO, FSA
Clarenceux, Patric Dickinson, LVO
Norroy and Ulster, Timothy Duke

HERALDS
Lancaster, Robert Noel
Windsor, vacant
Somerset, David White
Richmond, Clive Cheesman, FSA
York, Michael O'Donoghue, FSA
Chester, vacant

PURSUIVANTS
Portcullis, Hon. Christopher Fletcher-Vane
Rouge Croix, John Allen-Petrie
Rouge Dragon, vacant
Bluemantle, vacant

COURT OF THE LORD LYON
HM New Register House, Edinburgh EH1 3YT
T 0131-556 7255 E lyonoffice@scotland.gsi.gov.uk
W www.lyon-court.com
Her Majesty's Officers of Arms in Scotland perform ceremonial duties and in addition may be consulted by members of the public on heraldic and genealogical matters in a professional capacity.

KING OF ARMS
Lord Lyon King of Arms, Dr Joseph Morrow, QC

HERALDS
Rothesay, Sir Crispin Agnew of Lochnaw, Bt., QC
Snawdoun, Elizabeth Roads, LVO, FSA, FSA SCOT
Marchmont, The Hon. Adam Bruce, WS

PURSUIVANTS
Ormond, Mark Dennis
Dingwall, Yvonne Holton
Unicorn, Liam Devlin

EXTRAORDINARY OFFICERS
Orkney Herald Extraordinary, Sir Malcolm Innes of Edingight, KCVO, WS
Angus Herald Extraordinary, Robin Blair, CVO, WS
Islay Herald Extraordinary, David Sellar, MVO

HIGHLANDS AND ISLANDS ENTERPRISE

An Lòchran, 10 Inverness Campus, Inverness IV2 5NA
T 01463-245245 E info@hient.co.uk W www.hie.co.uk

Highlands and Islands Enterprise (HIE) was set up under the Enterprise and New Towns (Scotland) Act 1991. Its role is to deliver community and economic development in line with the Scottish government economic strategy. It focuses on four priorities: supporting businesses and social enterprises; strengthening communities and fragile areas; developing growth sectors; and creating the conditions for a competitive and low carbon region. HIE's draft budget for 2017–18 is £66.7m.

Chair, Prof. Lorne Crerar
Chief Executive, Charlotte Wright

HISTORIC ENGLAND

1 Waterhouse Square, 138–142 Holborn, London EC1N 2ST
T 020-7973 3700 E customers@historicengland.org.uk
W www.historicengland.org.uk

Historic England was established as an executive non-departmental public body on 1 April 2015, having previously been known as English Heritage (following the National Heritage Act 1983). Its remit is to look after England's historic environment and has five key objectives: to champion historic places; to identify and protect England's heritage; to support change, including giving advice on over 20,000 applications for planning permission or listed building consent; to understand historic places; and to provide expertise at a local level. In 2016–17 Historic England received £87.8m in grant-in-aid from the Department for Culture, Media and Sport.

Chair, Sir Laurie Magnus
Commissioners, Sally Balcombe; Paul Baker; Alex Balfour; Nicholas Boys Smith; Prof. Martin Daunton; Prof. Michael Fulford, CBE; Victoria Harley; Rosemarie MacQueen, MBE; Neil Mendoza; Michael Morrison; Charles O'Brien
Chief Executive, Duncan Wilson, OBE

HISTORIC ENVIRONMENT SCOTLAND

Longmore House, Salisbury Place, Edinburgh EH9 1SH
T 0131-668 8600
W www.historicenvironment.scot

Historic Environment Scotland is the lead public body established to investigate, care for and promote Scotland's historic environment. It is the result of the bringing together of two of Scotland's leading heritage bodies, Historic Scotland and the Royal Commission on Ancient and Historical Monuments Scotland, and has been formed to help deliver the Our Place in Time strategy. It is responsible for more than 300 properties of national importance, including Edinburgh Castle, Skara Brae and Fort George, and for collections including more than 5 million drawings, photographs, negatives and manuscripts, along with Scotland's National Collection of Aerial Photography, containing more than 26 million aerial images. Total income from the Scottish government in 2017 is £40.8m.

Chair, Jane Ryder, OBE

Trustees, Ian Brennan; Dr Janet Brennan; Trudi Craggs; Andrew Holmes; Dr Coinneach Maclean; Dr Fiona McLean; Ian Robertson; Dr Paul Stollard; Dr Ken Thomson
Chief Executive, Alex Paterson

HISTORIC ROYAL PALACES
Apartment 39A, Hampton Court Palace, Surrey KT8 9AU
T 0203-166 6000 E operators@hrp.org.uk W www.hrp.org.uk

Historic Royal Palaces was established in 1998 as a royal charter body with charitable status and is contracted by the Secretary of State for Culture, Media and Sport to manage the palaces on his behalf. The palaces – the Tower of London, Hampton Court Palace, the Banqueting House, Kensington Palace and Kew Palace – are owned by the Queen on behalf of the nation. Since 1 April 2014, Historic Royal Palaces is also responsible for the management of Hillsborough Castle in Northern Ireland under contract with the Secretary of State for Northern Ireland.

The organisation is governed by a board comprising a chair and 11 non-executive trustees. The chief executive is accountable to the board of trustees and ultimately to parliament. Historic Royal Palaces receives no funding from the government or the Crown.

TRUSTEES
Chair, Rupert Gavin
Appointed by the Queen, Zeinab Badawi; Ajay Chowdhury; Jonathan Marsden, CVO, FSA; Sir Michael Stevens, KCVO
Appointed by the Secretary of State, Prof. Sir David Cannadine; Bruce Carnegie-Brown; Liz Cleaver; Jane Kennedy; Carole Souter, CBE; Louise Wilson, FRSA
Ex officio, Gen. Sir Nicholas Houghton, GCB, CBE *(160th Constable of the Tower of London)*

OFFICER
Chief Executive, John Barnes

HOMES AND COMMUNITIES AGENCY
Fry Building, 2 Marsham Street, London SW1P 4DF
T 0300-500 1234 E mail@homesandcommunities.co.uk
W www.gov.uk/hca

The Homes and Communities Agency (HCA) is the national housing regeneration agency for England. The HCA invests mostly in building new homes, but also in creating employment floorspace nationwide. The HCA regulates social housing. It also brings forward public land for development and increases the speed with which it is made available.

Chair, Sir Edward Lister
Chief Executive, Nick Walkley

HUMAN TISSUE AUTHORITY (HTA)
151 Buckingham Palace Road, London SW1W 9SZ
T 020-7269 1900 E enquiries@hta.gov.uk
W www.hta.gov.uk

The Human Tissue Authority (HTA) was established on 1 April 2005 under the Human Tissue Act 2004, and is sponsored and part-funded by the Department of Health. It regulates organisations that remove, store and use tissue for research, medical treatment, post-mortem examination, teaching and display in public. The HTA also gives approval for organ and bone marrow donations from living people. Under the EU tissues and cells directives, the HTA is one of the two designated competent authorities for the UK responsible for regulating tissues and cells. The HTA is also the sole competent authority for the UK under the EU organ donation directive.

Chair, Sharmila Nebhrajani, OBE
Chief Executive, Allan Marriott-Smith

IMPERIAL WAR MUSEUMS (IWM)
Lambeth Road, London SE1 6HZ
T 020-7416 5000 E mail@iwm.org.uk
W www.iwm.org.uk

IWM is the world's leading authority on conflict and its impact, focusing on Britain, its former empire and the Commonwealth, from the First World War to the present. IWM aims to enrich people's understanding of the causes, course and consequences of war and conflict.

IWM comprises the organisation's flagship, IWM London; IWM North in Trafford, Manchester; IWM Duxford in Cambridgeshire; the Churchill War Rooms in Whitehall; and HMS *Belfast* in the Pool of London.

The total grant-in-aid for 2016–17 was £32.14m.

OFFICERS
President, HRH the Duke of Kent, KG, GCMG, GCVO, ADC
Chair, Air Chief Marshal Sir Stuart Peach, GBE, KCB, ADC
Trustees, Rt. Hon. Lord Ashcroft, KCMG; HE Janice Charette; Elizabeth Cleaver; HE Hon. Alexander Downer; HE; Rear-Adm. Amjad Hussain, CB; HE Syed Ibne Abbas; Tim Marlow; HE Rt. Hon. Sir Jerry Mateparae; Dame Judith Mayhew Jonas, DBE; HE Obed Mlaba; Sir John Scarlett, KCMG, OBE; HE Y. K. Sinha; Prof. Sir Hew Strachan, FRSE; Tamsin Todd; Peter Watkins, CBE; Matthew Westerman; HE Amari Wijewardene
Director-General, Diane Lees, CBE
Directors, Keith Cameron; Jon Card; Paul Potts, CBE; Catherine Pusey; Rt. Hon. Tamsin Todd, KCMG

INFORMATION COMMISSIONER'S OFFICE
Wycliffe House, Water Lane, Wilmslow, Cheshire SK9 5AF
T 0303-123 1113 W www.ico.org.uk

The Information Commissioner's Office (ICO) oversees and enforces the Freedom of Information Act 2000 and the Data Protection Act 1998, with the objective of promoting public access to official information and protecting personal information.

The Data Protection Act 1998 sets out rules for the processing of personal information and applies to records held on computers and some paper files. The Freedom of Information Act 2000 is designed to help end the culture of unnecessary secrecy and open up the inner workings of the public sector to citizens and businesses.

The ICO also enforces and oversees the privacy and electronic communications regulations 2003 and the environmental regulations 2004. It also has limited responsibilities under the INSPIRE regulations 2009 and DRR regulations 2014.

The Information Commissioner reports annually to parliament on the performance of his/her functions under the acts and has obligations to assess breaches of the acts. As of April 2010, the ICO has been able to fine organisations up to £500,000 for serious breaches of the Data Protection Act.

Information Commissioner, Elizabeth Denham

INDUSTRIAL INJURIES ADVISORY COUNCIL
First Floor, Caxton House, Tothill Street, London SW1H 9NA
T 020-7449 5618 E iiac@dwp.gsi.gov.uk
W www.gov.uk/iiac

The Industrial Injuries Advisory Council was established under the National Insurance (Industrial Injuries) Act 1946, which came into effect on 5 July 1948. Statutory provisions governing its work are set out in the Social Security Administration Act 1992 and corresponding Northern Ireland legislation. The council currently consists of 17 members, including a chair, appointed by the Secretary of State for Work and Pensions, and has three roles: to advise on the prescription of diseases; to consider and advise on draft regulations and proposals concerning the industrial injuries disablement benefit scheme referred to it by the Secretary of State for Work and Pensions or the Department for Communities in Northern Ireland; and to advise on any other matter concerning the scheme or its administration.

Chair, Prof. Keith Palmer

JOINT NATURE CONSERVATION COMMITTEE
Monkstone House, City Road, Peterborough PE1 1JY
T 01733-562626 E comment@jncc.gov.uk
W www.jncc.defra.gov.uk

The committee was established under the Environmental Protection Act 1990 and was reconstituted by the Natural Environment and Rural Communities Act 2006. It advises the government and devolved administrations on UK and international nature conservation issues. Its work contributes to maintaining and enriching biological diversity, conserving geological features and sustaining natural systems.

Chair, Prof. Chris Gilligan, CBE
Chief Executive, Marcus Yeo

LAW COMMISSION
1st Floor, Tower, 52 Queen Anne's Gate, London SW1H 9AG
T 020-3334 0200 E enquiries@lawcommission.gsi.gov.uk
W www.lawcom.gov.uk

The Law Commission was set up under the Law Commissions Act 1965 to make proposals to the government for the examination of the law in England and Wales and for its revision where it is unsuited for modern requirements, obscure or otherwise unsatisfactory. It recommends to the lord chancellor programmes for the examination of different branches of the law and suggests whether the examination should be carried out by the commission itself or by some other body. The commission is also responsible for the preparation of Consolidation and Statute Law (Repeals) Bills.

Chair, Rt. Hon. Lord Justice Bean
Commissioners, Prof. Nicholas Hopkins; Stephen Lewis; Prof.
David Ormerod QC; Nicholas Paines, QC
Chief Executive, Phil Golding

NATIONAL ARMY MUSEUM
Royal Hospital Road, Chelsea, London SW3 4HT
T 020-7730 0717 E info@nam.ac.uk
W www.nam.ac.uk

The National Army Museum shares the stories of the British Army and its soldiers. It was established by royal charter in 1960 and moved to its current site in Chelsea in 1970. The museum re-opened in spring 2017 following a major redevelopment project. The new museum features five state-of-the-art galleries, housing a wide array of artefacts, paintings, photographs, uniforms and equipment; a café; a shop; and learning and research facilities.

Chair, Gen. Sir Richard Shirreff, KCB, CBE
Council Members, Patrick Aylmer; Keith Baldwin; Patrick
Bradley; Brig. Douglas Erskine Crum; Rt. Hon. Lord
Hamilton of Epsom; Jessica Spungin; William Wells
Director-General, Janice Murray, FRSA

NATIONAL GALLERIES OF SCOTLAND
73 Belford Road, Edinburgh EH4 3DS
T 0131-624 6200 E enquiries@nationalgalleries.org
W www.nationalgalleries.org

The National Galleries of Scotland comprise three galleries in Edinburgh: the National Gallery of Scotland, the Scottish National Portrait Gallery and the Scottish National Gallery of Modern Art. There are also partner galleries at Paxton House,

Berwickshire, and Duff House, Banffshire. It also owns the Granton Centre for Art, a purpose built storage facility.

TRUSTEES
Chair, Benny Higgins
Trustees, Tricia Bey; Alistair Dodds; Edward Green; Lesley
Knox; Tari Lang; Catherine Muirden; Prof. Nicholas
Pearce; Willy Watt; Nicky Wilson

OFFICERS
Director-General, Sir John Leighton
Directors, Christopher Baker *(Scottish National Portrait Gallery);*
Nicola Catterall *(Chief Operating Officer);* Jo Coomber
(Public Engagement); Dr Simon Groom *(Scottish National
Gallery of Modern Art);* Jacqueline Ridge *(Keeper of
Conservation)*

NATIONAL GALLERY
Trafalgar Square, London WC2N 5DN
T 020-7747 2885 E information@ng-london.org.uk
W www.nationalgallery.org.uk

The National Gallery, which houses a collection of paintings in the western European tradition from the 13th to the 20th century, was founded in 1824, following a parliamentary grant of £60,000 for the purchase and exhibition of the Angerstein collection of pictures. The present site was first occupied in 1838; an extension to the north of the building with a public entrance in Orange Street was opened in 1975; the Sainsbury Wing was opened in 1991; and the Getty Entrance opened off Trafalgar Square at the east end of the main building in 2004. Total government grant-in-aid for 2016–17 was £24.1m.

BOARD OF TRUSTEES
Chair, Hannah Rothschild
Trustees, Lance Batchelor; Prof. Dexter Dalwood; Katrin
Henkel; Prof. Anya Hurlbert; Lord King of Lothbury, KG,
GBE, FBA; Sir John Kingman; Rosemary Leith; David
Marks; John Nelson; Charles Sebag-Montefiore; John
Singer

OFFICERS
Director, Dr Gabriele Finaldi
Director of Public Engagement and Deputy Director, Dr Susan
Foister
Director of Finance and Operations, Chris Walker
Director of Collections, Dr Larry Keith

NATIONAL HERITAGE MEMORIAL FUND
7 Holbein Place, London SW1W 8NR
T 020-7591 6044 E NHMF_Enquiries@nhmf.org.uk
W www.nhmf.org.uk

The National Heritage Memorial Fund was set up under the National Heritage Act 1980 in memory of people who have given their lives for the United Kingdom. The fund provides grants to organisations based in the UK, mainly so that they can buy items of outstanding interest and of importance to the national heritage. These must either be at risk or have a memorial character. The fund is administered by a chair and 12 trustees who are appointed by the prime minister.

The National Heritage Memorial Fund receives an annual grant from the Department for Culture, Media and Sport. Under the National Lottery etc. Act 1993, the trustees of the fund became responsible for the distribution of funds for both the National Heritage Memorial Fund and the Heritage Lottery Fund. Total annual government grant-in-aid is £5m.

Chair, Sir Peter Luff
Trustees, Baroness Andrews, OBE, FSA; Anna Carragher; Sir
Neil Cossons, OBE; Sandie Dawe, CBE; Dr Angela Dean;
Jim Dixon; Perdita Hunt, OBE; Steve Miller; Richard
Morris, OBE; Atul Patel; Dame Seona Reid, DBE; Dr Tom
Tew
Chief Executive, Ros Kerslake, OBE

NATIONAL LIBRARY OF SCOTLAND

George IV Bridge, Edinburgh EH1 1EW
T 0131-623 3700 E enquiries@nls.uk W www.nls.uk

The library, which was founded as the Advocates' Library in 1682, became the National Library of Scotland in 1925. It contains over 24 million printed items: two million maps, 25,000 newspaper and magazine titles and over 100,000 manuscripts, including the John Murray Archive. The library receives around 300,000 new items every year and has material in 490 languages. It has an unrivalled Scottish collection as well as online catalogues and digital resources which can be accessed through the Library's website. Material can be consulted in the library branches in Edinburgh and Glasgow, which are open to anyone with a valid library card.

The National Library of Scotland Act 2012 modernised the make-up and responsibilities of the board. At present there are 14, one of whom is nominated by the Faculty of Advocates. All of them are appointed by the Scottish ministers.

Chair, Sir Kenneth Calman
National Librarian and Chief Executive, Dr John Scally
Heads of Department, John Coll *(Access);* Graeme Forbes *(Collection Management);* Anthony Gillespie *(Business Support);* Murat Guven *(Resources);* Stuart Lewis *(Digital);* Alexandra Miller *(External Relations & Governance);* Robin Smith *(Collections and Research)*

NATIONAL LIBRARY OF WALES/ LLYFRGELL GENEDLAETHOL CYMRU

Aberystwyth, Ceredigion, Wales SY23 3BU
T 01970-632800 E gofyn@llgc.org.uk W www.llgc.org.uk

The National Library of Wales was founded by royal charter in 1907, and is funded by the Welsh government. It contains about five million printed books, 40,000 manuscripts, four million deeds and documents, numerous maps, prints and drawings, and a sound and moving image collection. It specialises in manuscripts and books relating to Wales and the Celtic peoples. It is the repository for pre-1858 Welsh probate records, manorial records and tithe documents, and certain legal records. Admission is by reader's ticket to the reading rooms but entry to the exhibition programme is free.

Total grant-in-aid from the Welsh government for 2016–17 is £9.3m.

Trustees, Lord Aberdare; Philip Cooper; Eleri Davies; Iwan Davies; Susan Davies; Richard Houdmont; Dyfrig Jones; Gwilym Dyfri Jones; Elizabeth Siberry; Rhodri Thomas *(President);* Huw Williams; Steve Williams; Lee Yale-Helms *(Treasurer)*
Librarian and Chief Executive, Linda Tomos

NATIONAL MUSEUM OF THE ROYAL NAVY

HM Naval Base (PP66), Portsmouth PO1 3NH
T 023-9289 1370
W www.nmrn.org.uk

The National Museum of the Royal Navy comprises nine museums: HMS *Victory,* HMS *Caroline,* HMS *M.33,* the National Museum of the Royal Navy Portsmouth, the National Museum of the Royal Navy Hartlepool, the Fleet Air Arm Museum, the Royal Navy Submarine Museum, the Royal Marines Museum and Explosion! Museum of Naval Firepower. The Fleet Air Museum is located at RNAS Yeovilton, Somerset, and HMS Caroline is located at Alexandra Dock, Belfast, while the other five are situated in Portsmouth and Gosport.

Chair, Adm. Sir Jonathon Band, GCB
Trustees, M. Bedingfield; John Brookes, OBE; Capt. Dan Conley, OBE; Prof. John Craven, CBE; Sir Robert Crawford, CBE; M. Gambazzi; Vice-Adm. Sir Adrian Johns, KCB, CBE, ADC; Kim Marshall; Maj. Gen. Jeffrey

Mason, MBE; Tim Schadla-Hall; Gavin Whitter; Dr Caroline Williams, Charles Wilson
Director-General, Prof. Dominic Tweddle

NATIONAL MUSEUM WALES/ AMGUEDDFA CYMRU

Cathays Park, Cardiff CF10 3NP
T 029-2039 7951
W museum.wales

National Museum Wales (also known as Amgueddfa Cymru) is the body that runs Wales's seven national museums. It comprises National Museum Cardiff; St Fagans: National History Museum; Big Pit: National Coal Museum, Blaenafon; National Roman Legion Museum, Caerleon; National Slate Museum, Llanberis; National Wool Museum, Dre-fach Felindre; National Waterfront Museum, Swansea; and National Collections Centre, Nantgarw. Total funding from the Welsh government for 2015–16 was £25.3m.

Trustees, Elisabeth Elias *(President);* Dr Carol Bell *(Vice President);* Laurence Pavelin, CBE *(Treasurer);* Baroness Andrews, OBE; Prof. Tony Atkins; Dr Caroline Duigan; Carys Howell; Rachel Hughes; Hywel John; Dr Glenda Jones; Dr Hywel Jones, CMG; Prof. Robert Pickard; Michael Prior; Victoria Provis; Jessica Seaton; Keshav Singhal, MBE
Director-General, David Anderson, OBE

NATIONAL MUSEUMS LIVERPOOL

127 Dale Street, Liverpool L2 2JH
T 0151-207 0001 W www.liverpoolmuseums.org.uk

National Museums Liverpool is a group of museums and collections including the World Museum, the Merseyside Maritime Museum (also home to the Border Force National Museum), the Lady Lever Art Gallery, the Walker Art Gallery, Sudley House, the International Slavery Museum and the Museum of Liverpool.

Chair, Sir David Henshaw
Trustees, Carmel Booth; Laura Carstensen; James Chapman; Heather Lauder; Andrew McCluskey; Philip Price; Ian Rosenblatt, OBE; Virginia Tandy; Dr Nicola Thorp; Clive Wilson
Director, Dr David Fleming, OBE
Director of Art Galleries, Sandra Penketh
Director, World Museum Liverpool, Steve Judd
Director, Museum of Liverpool, Janet Dugdale
Head of International Slavery Museum, Dr Richard Benjamin

NATIONAL MUSEUMS NORTHERN IRELAND

Cultra, Holywood, Northern Ireland BT18 0EU
T 0845-608 0000 E info@nmni.com
W www.nmni.com

Across three unique sites National Museums Northern Ireland cares for and presents inspirational collections reflecting the creativity, innovation, history, culture and people of Northern Ireland and beyond.

Together the Ulster Museum, Ulster Folk and Transport Museum and Ulster American Folk Park offer a unique opportunity to experience the heritage and way of life of Northern Ireland.

Chair, Miceal McCoy
Trustees, Prof. Michael Catto; Prof. Garth Earls; Prof. Karen Fleming; Hazel Francey; Daphne Harshaw; Dr Rosemary Kelly; Dr Leon Litvack; Alan McFarland; Dr George McIlroy; Catherine Molloy; Annette Moor; Joseph Rice; Dr Margaret Ward
Chief Executive, Kathryn Thomson

NATIONAL MUSEUMS SCOTLAND

Chambers Street, Edinburgh EH1 1JF
T 0300-123 6789 E info@nms.ac.uk W www.nms.ac.uk

National Museums Scotland provides advice, expertise and support to the museums community across Scotland, and undertakes fieldwork that often involves collaboration at local, national and international levels. National Museums Scotland comprises the National Museum of Scotland, the National War Museum, the National Museum of Rural Life, the National Museum of Flight and the National Museums Collection Centre. Its collections represent more than two centuries of collecting and include Scottish and classical archaeology, decorative and applied arts, world cultures and social history and science, technology and the natural world.

Up to 15 trustees can be appointed by the Minister for Culture, Tourism and External Affairs for a term of four years, and may serve a second term.

Chair, Bruce Minto
Trustees, Ann Allen; Mary Bownes; Prof. Chris Breward; Adam Bruce; Gordon Drummond; Chris Fletcher; Dr Brian Lang, FRSE; Lynda Logan; Dr Catriona Macdonald; Miller McLean, FCIBS, FIB; Prof. Walter Nimmo, CBE, MD, FRCP, FRSED, FRCA, FRSE; Janet Stevenson; James Troughton, RIBA; Eilidh Wiseman
Director, Dr Gordon Rintoul, CBE

NATIONAL PORTRAIT GALLERY

St Martin's Place, London WC2H 0HE
T 020-7306 0055 W www.npg.org.uk

The National Portrait Gallery was established in 1856. Today the Gallery collects portraits of those who have made, or are making, a significant contribution to British history and culture. The Collection is free to visit, and includes works across all media, from painting and sculpture to photography and digital portraits. To complement the Collection, the Gallery stages exhibitions, displays, talks and events throughout the year which explore the nature of portraiture. The Gallery loans exhibitions, displays and individual portraits to organisations across the UK and internationally as part of its ongoing commitment to sharing the Collection as widely as possible.

Chair of the Board of Trustees, Sir William Proby, Bt., CBE
Director, Dr Nicholas Cullinan

NATURAL ENGLAND

County Hall, Spetchley Road, Worcester, WR5 2NP
T 0300-060 3900 E enquiries@naturalengland.org.uk
W www.gov.uk/natural-england

Natural England is the government's adviser on the natural environment, providing practical scientific advice on how to look after England's landscapes and wildlife.

The organisation's remit is to ensure sustainable stewardship of the land and sea so that people and nature can thrive.

Natural England works with farmers and land managers; business and industry; planners and developers; national and local government; charities and conservationists; interest groups and local communities to help them improve their local environment.

Chair, Andrew Sells
Chief Executive, James Cross

NATURAL HISTORY MUSEUM

Cromwell Road, London SW7 5BD
T 020-7942 5000 W www.nhm.ac.uk

The Natural History Museum, which houses 80 million natural history specimens, originates from the natural history departments of the British Museum, which grew extensively during the 19th century; in 1860 it was agreed that the natural history collections should be separated from the British Museum's collections of books, manuscripts and antiquities. Part of the site of the 1862 International Exhibition in South Kensington was acquired for the new museum, and the museum opened to the public in 1881. In 1963 the Natural History Museum became completely independent with its own board of trustees. The Natural History Museum at Tring, bequeathed by the second Lord Rothschild, has formed part of the museum since 1937. The Geological Museum merged with the Natural History Museum in 1985. In September 2009 the Natural History Museum opened the Darwin Centre, which contains public galleries, a high-tech interactive area known as the Attenborough Studio, scientific research facilities and storage for 28 million zoological specimens, 17 million entomology specimens and three million botanical specimens. Total budgeted government grant-in-aid for 2017–18 is £41.8m

Chair, Lord Green of Hurstpierpoint
Trustees, Prof. Sir John Beddington, CMG, FRS; Dame Frances Cairncross, DBE, FRSE; Prof. Christopher Gilligan; Prof. Sir John Holman; Anand Mahindra; Hilary Newiss; Robert Noel; Simon Patterson; Prof. Stephen Sparks, FRS, CBE; Prof. Dame Janet Thornton, DBE, FRS, FMedSci; Dr Kim Winser, OBE
Museum Director, Sir Michael Dixon
Directors, Neil Greenwood *(Finance and Corporate Services);* Fiona McWilliams *(Development and Communications);* Dr Justin Morris *(Public Engagement);* Prof. Ian Owens *(Science)*

NATURAL RESOURCES WALES

Ty Cambria, 29 Newport Road, Cardiff CF24 0TP
T 0300-065 3000 E enquiries@naturalresourceswales.gov.uk
W www.naturalresources.wales

Natural Resources Wales is the principal adviser to the Welsh government on the environment. It became operational on 1 April 2013 following a merger of the Countryside Council for Wales, Environment Agency Wales and the Forestry Commission Wales. It is responsible for ensuring that the natural resources of Wales are sustainably maintained, enhanced and used; now and in the future.

Chair, Diane McCrea, MBE
Board Members, Karen Balmer; Chris Blake; Howard Davies; Dr Ruth Hall; Elizabeth Haywood; Zoë Henderson; Dr Madeleine Havard; Andy Middleton; Nigel Reader, CBE; Dr Emyr Roberts; Sir Paul Williams, OBE
Chief Executive, Dr Emyr Roberts

NHS PAY REVIEW BODY

8th Floor, Fleetbank House, 2-6 Salisbury Square, London EC4Y 8JX
T 020-7211 8295 W www.gov.uk/government/organisations/nhs-pay-review-body

The NHS Pay Review Body (NHSPRB) makes recommendations to the prime minister, Secretary of State for Health and ministers in Scotland, Wales and Northern Ireland on the remuneration of all paid staff under agenda for change and employed in the NHS. The review body was established in 1983 for nurses and allied health professionals. Its remit has since expanded to cover over 1.5 million staff; ie almost all staff in the NHS, with the exception of dentists, doctors and very senior managers.

Chair, Philippa Hird
Members, Bronwen Curtis, CBE; Patricia Gordon; Joan Ingram; Shamaila Qureshi; Prof. David Ulph, CBE; Prof. Jonathan Wadsworth; Lorraine Zuleta

NORTHERN IRELAND HUMAN RIGHTS COMMISSION

Temple Court, 39 North Street, Belfast BT1 1NA
T 028-9024 3987 E info@nihrc.org W www.nihrc.org

The Northern Ireland Human Rights Commission is a non-departmental public body, established by the Northern Ireland Act 1998 and set up in March 1999. Its purpose is to protect and promote human rights in Northern Ireland. Its main functions include reviewing the law and practice relating to human rights, advising government and the Northern Ireland Assembly, and promoting an awareness of human rights. It can also investigate human rights violations and take cases to court. The members of the commission are appointed by the Secretary of State for Northern Ireland.

Chief Commissioner, Les Allamby
Commissioners, John Corey; Christine Collins; Milton Kerr, QPM; Grainia Long; Alan McBride; Marion Reynolds, MBE; Paul Yam, MBE
Chief Executive, Dr David Russell

NORTHERN LIGHTHOUSE BOARD
84 George Street, Edinburgh EH2 3DA
T 0131-473 3100 E enquiries@nlb.org.uk
W www.nlb.org.uk

The Northern Lighthouse Board is the general lighthouse authority for Scotland and the Isle of Man and owes its origin to an act of parliament passed in 1786. At present there are 19 commissioners who operate under the Merchant Shipping Act 1995.
The commissioners control 206 lighthouses, 165 lighted and unlighted buoys, four DGPS (differential global positioning system) stations and an ELORAN (long-range navigation) system. *See also* Transport.

Chair, Graham Crerar
Commissioners, Lord Advocate; Solicitor-General for Scotland; Lord Provosts of Edinburgh, Glasgow and Aberdeen; Convener of Highland Council; Provost of Argyll and Bute Council; Sheriffs-Principal of North Strathclyde, Tayside, Central and Fife, Grampian, Highlands and Islands, South Strathclyde, Dumfries and Galloway, Lothians and Borders and Glasgow and Strathkelvin; Capt. Alastair Beveridge; Capt. Michael Brew; Graham Crerar; Capt. H. Michael Close; Capt. Alistair Mackenzie; John Ross, CBE
Chief Executive, Mike Bullock, MBE

NUCLEAR DECOMMISSIONING AUTHORITY
Herdus House, Westlakes Science and Technology Park, Moor Row, Cumbria CA24 3HU
T 01925-802077 E enquiries@nda.gov.uk W www.nda.gov.uk

The Nuclear Decommissioning Authority (NDA) was created under the Energy Act 2004. It is a strategic authority that owns 17 sites plus associated civil nuclear liabilities and assets of the public sector, previously under the control of the UK Energy Authority and British Nuclear Fuels. The NDA's responsibilities include decommissioning and cleaning up civil nuclear facilities; ensuring the safe management of waste products, both radioactive and non-radioactive; implementing government policy on the long-term management of nuclear waste; and developing UK-wide low-level waste strategy plans.
Total planned expenditure for 2017–18 is £3.24bn, with total grant-in-aid standing at £2.36bn. The remaining £0.88bn will come from commercial operations.

Chair, Tom Smith
Chief Executive, David Peattie

OFFICE FOR BUDGET RESPONSIBILITY
14T, 102 Petty France, London SW1H 9AJ
T 020-3334 6337 E OBR.enquiries@obr.gsi.gov.uk
W budgetresponsibility.org.uk

The Office for Budget Responsibility (OBR) was created in 2010 to provide independent and authoritative analysis of the UK's public finances. It has five main roles: producing forecasts for the economy and public finances; judging progress towards the government's fiscal targets; evaluating fiscal risks; assessing the long-term sustainability of the public finances; and scrutinising HM Treasury's costing of tax and welfare spending measures.

Chair, Robert Chote
Committee Members, Prof. Sir Charles Bean; Graham Parker, CBE

OFFICE OF COMMUNICATIONS (OFCOM)
Riverside House, 2A Southwark Bridge Road, London SE1 9HA
T 0300-123 3000 W www.ofcom.org.uk

OFCOM was established in 2003 under the Office of Communications Act 2002 as the independent regulator and competition authority for the UK communications industries with responsibility for television, video-on-demand, radio, telecommunications and wireless communications services.
Following the passing of the Postal Services Act 2011, OFCOM has assumed regulatory responsibility for postal services from Postcomm, the Postal Services Commission.

Chair, Dame Patricia Hodgson, DBE
Deputy Chair, Baroness Noakes, DBE
Board Members, Dame Lynne Brindley, DBE; Graham Mather; Jonathan Oxley; Nick Pollard; Dr Stephen Unger; Ben Verwaayen
Chief Executive, Sharon White

OFFICE OF MANPOWER ECONOMICS (OME)
8th Floor, Fleetbank House, 2–6 Salisbury Square, London EC4Y 8JX
T 020-7211 8165 W www.gov.uk/government/organisations/office-of-manpower-economics

The Office of Manpower Economics (OME) was established in 1971. It is an independent non-statutory organisation which is responsible for servicing eight independent review bodies which make recommendations impacting 2.5m workers – around 45 per cent of public sector staff – and a pay bill of £100bn.

OME Director, Martin Williams
Directors, Mark Franks *(Chief Economist, Research and Analysis Group; Senior Salaries Review Body);* Stuart Sarson *(Prison Service Pay Review Body; Armed Forces' Pay Review Body; School Teachers' Review Body);* Edmund Quilty *(NHS Pay Review Body; Review Body on Doctors' and Dentists' Remuneration; National Crime Agency Remuneration Review Body; Police Remuneration Review Body)*

PARADES COMMISSION
Andras House, 60 Great Victoria Street, Belfast BT2 7BB
T 028-9089 5900 E info@paradescommissionni.org
W www.paradescommission.org

The Parades Commission was set up under the Public Processions (Northern Ireland) Act 1998. Its function is to encourage and facilitate local accommodation of contentious parades; where this is not possible, the commission is empowered to make legal determinations about such parades, which may include imposing conditions on aspects of the notified parade (such as restrictions on routes/areas and exclusion of certain groups with a record of bad behaviour).
The chair and members are appointed by the Secretary of State for Northern Ireland; the membership must, as far as is practicable, be representative of the community in Northern Ireland.

Chair, Anne Henderson
Members, Sarah Havlin; Paul Hutchinson; Colin Kennedy; Geraldine McGahey; Anne Marshall

PAROLE BOARD FOR ENGLAND AND WALES

52 Queen Anne's Gate, London SW1H 9AG
T 020-3334 4402 E info@paroleboard.gsi.gov.uk
W www.gov.uk/government/organisations/parole-board

The Parole Board was established in 1968 under the Criminal Justice Act 1967 and became an independent executive non-departmental public body on 1 July 1996 under the Criminal Justice and Public Order Act 1994. It is the body that protects the public by making risk assessments about prisoners to decide who may safely be released into the community and who must remain in, or be returned to, custody. Board decisions are taken at two main types of panels of up to three members: 'paper panels' for the majority of cases, or oral hearings for decisions concerning prisoners serving life or indeterminate sentences for public protection. The budget for 2017–18 is £19.2m.

Chair, Prof. Nick Hardwick
Chief Executive, Martin Jones

PAROLE BOARD FOR SCOTLAND

Saughton House, Broomhouse Drive, Edinburgh EH11 3XD
T 0131-244 8373 E paroleboardforscotland@gov.scot
W www.scottishparoleboard.gov.uk

The board directs and advises the Scottish ministers on the release of prisoners on licence, and related matters.

Chair, John Watt

PENSION PROTECTION FUND (PPF)

Renaissance, 12 Dingwall Road, Croydon CR0 2NA
T 0345-600 2541 E information@ppf.gsi.gov.uk
W www.pensionprotectionfund.org.uk

The PPF became operational in 2005. It was established to pay compensation to members of eligible defined-benefit pension schemes where a qualifying insolvency event in relation to the employer occurs and where there is a lack of sufficient assets in the pension scheme. The PPF also administers the Financial Assistance Scheme, which helps members whose schemes wound-up before 2005. It is also responsible for the Fraud Compensation Fund (which provides compensation to occupational pension schemes that suffer a loss that can be attributed to dishonesty). The chair and board of the PPF are appointed by, and accountable to, the Secretary of State for Work and Pensions, and are responsible for paying compensation, calculating annual levies (which help fund the PPF), and setting and overseeing investment strategy.

Chair, Arnold Wagner, OBE
Chief Executive, Alan Rubenstein

PENSIONS REGULATOR

Napier House, Trafalgar Place, Brighton BN1 4DW
T 0345-600 0707 E customersupport@tpr.gov.uk
W www.thepensionsregulator.gov.uk

The Pensions Regulator was established in 2005 as the regulator of work-based pension schemes in the UK, replacing the Occupational Pensions Regulatory Authority (OPRA). It aims to protect the benefits of occupational and personal pension scheme members by working with trustees, employers, pension providers and advisers. The regulator's work focuses on encouraging better management and administration of schemes, ensuring that final salary schemes have a sensible funding plan, and encouraging money purchase schemes to provide members with the information that they need to make informed choices about their pension fund. The Pensions Act 2004 and the Pensions Act 2008 gave the regulator a range of powers which can be used to protect scheme members, but a strong emphasis is placed on educating and enabling those responsible for managing pension schemes, and powers are used only where necessary. The regulator offers free online resources to help trustees, employers, professionals and advisers understand their role, duties and obligations.

Chair, Mark Boyle
Chief Executive, Lesley Titcomb

POLICE ADVISORY BOARD FOR ENGLAND AND WALES

Home Office, 6th Floor Fry, 2 Marsham Street, London SW1P 4DF
E PABEWsecretariat@homeoffice.gsi.gov.uk
W www.gov.uk/government/organisations/police-advisory-board-for-england-and-wales

The Police Advisory Board for England and Wales was established in 1965 and provides advice to the home secretary on general questions affecting the police in England and Wales. It also considers draft regulations which the secretary of state proposes to make with respect to matters other than hours of duty, leave, pay and allowances or the issue, use and return of police clothing, personal equipment and other effects.

Independent Chair, Elizabeth France

PRISON SERVICE PAY REVIEW BODY

8th Floor, Fleetbank House, 2-6 Salisbury Square, London EC4Y 8JX
T 020-7211 8259 W www.gov.uk/government/organisations/prison-services-pay-review-body

The Prison Service Pay Review Body was set up in 2001. It makes independent recommendations on the pay of prison governors, operational managers, prison officers and related grades for the Prison Service in England and Wales and for the Northern Ireland Prison Service.

Chair, Dr Peter Knight, CBE
Members, Roberta Brownlee; Nicholas Caton; Prof. Andy Dickerson; Peter Maddison, QPM; Leslie Manasseh, MBE; Paul West, QPM

PRIVY COUNCIL OFFICE

1 Horse Guards Road, London SW1A 2HQ
T 020-7271 3292 E enquiries@pco.gov.uk
W https://privycouncil.independent.gov.uk

The primary function of the office is to act as the secretariat to the Privy Council. It is responsible for the arrangements leading to the making of all royal proclamations and orders in council; for certain formalities connected with ministerial changes; for considering applications for the granting (or amendment) of royal charters; for the scrutiny and approval of by-laws and statutes of chartered institutions and of the governing instruments of universities and colleges; and for the appointment of high sheriffs and Privy Council appointments to governing bodies. Under the relevant acts, the office is responsible for the approval of certain regulations and rules made by the regulatory bodies of the medical and certain allied professions.

The Lord President of the Council is the ministerial head of the office and presides at meetings of the Privy Council. The Clerk of the Council is the administrative head of the Privy Council office.

Lord President of the Council and Leader of the House of Commons, Rt. Hon. Andrea Leadsom
Clerk of the Council, Richard Tilbrook
Head of Secretariat and Deputy Clerk, Ceri King
Deputy Clerk, Christopher Berry

REVIEW BODY ON DOCTORS' AND DENTISTS' REMUNERATION

8th Floor, Fleetbank House, 2-6 Salisbury Square, London EC4Y 8JX
T 020-7211 8809 W www.gov.uk/government/organisations/review-body-on-doctors-and-dentists-remuneration

The Review Body on Doctors' and Dentists' Remuneration was set up in 1971. It advises the prime minister, the secretary of state for health, first ministers in Scotland, Wales and

Northern Ireland, and the ministers for Health, in England, Scotland, Wales and Northern Ireland on the remuneration of doctors and dentists taking any part in the National Health Service.

Chair, Prof. Sir Paul Curnan
Members, David Bingham; Mehrunnisa Lalani; Prof. Kevin Lee; Prof. James Malcomson; John Matheson, CBE; Nigel Turner, OBE; Jane Williams

ROYAL AIR FORCE MUSEUM

Grahame Park Way, London NW9 5LL
T 020-8205 2266 E london@rafmuseum.org
W www.rafmuseum.org.uk

The museum has two sites, one at the former airfield at Hendon and the second at Cosford, in the West Midlands, both of which illustrate the development of aviation from before the Wright brothers to the present-day RAF. The museum's collection across both sites consists of over 170 aircraft, as well as artefacts, aviation memorabilia, fine art and photographs.

Chair, Air Chief Marshal Sir Glenn Torpy, GCB, CBE, DSO
Trustees, Peter Bateson; Laurie Benson; Dr Carol Cole; Alan Coppin; Dr Rodney Eastwood, MBE; Sir Gerry Grimstone; Richard Holman; Catriona Kempston; Julie McGarvey; Hon. John Michaelson; Andrew Reid; Nick Sanders; Michael Schindler; Robin Southwell, OBE; Alan Spence; Malcolm White, OBE
Chief Executive, Maggie Appleton, MBE

ROYAL BOTANIC GARDEN EDINBURGH

20A Inverleith Row, Edinburgh EH3 5LR
T 0131-552 7171 W www.rbge.org.uk

The Royal Botanic Garden Edinburgh (RBGE) originated as the Physic Garden, established in 1670 beside the Palace of Holyroodhouse. The garden moved to its present 28ha site at Inverleith, Edinburgh, in 1821. There are also three regional gardens: Benmore Botanic Garden, near Dunoon, Argyll; Logan Botanic Garden, near Stranraer, Wigtownshire; and Dawyck Botanic Garden, near Stobo, Peeblesshire. Since 1986 RBGE has been administered by a board of trustees established under the National Heritage (Scotland) Act 1985. It receives an annual grant from the Scottish government's Environment and Forestry Directorate.

The RBGE is an international centre for scientific research on plant diversity and for horticulture education and conservation. It has an extensive library, a herbarium with almost three million preserved plant specimens, and over 15,000 species in the living collections.

Chair, Sir Muir Russell, KCB, FRSE
Trustees, Prof. Beverley Glover; Dr David Hamilton; Patricia Henton, FRSE; Prof. Thomas Meagher; Diana Murray; Prof. Ian Wall, FRSE; Chris Wallace; Robert Wilson
Regius Keeper and Queen's Botanist in Scotland, Simon Milne, MBE

ROYAL BOTANIC GARDENS, KEW

Kew Gardens, Richmond, Surrey TW9 3AB
T 020-8332 5655 E info@kew.org
Wakehurst, Ardingly, W. Sussex RH17 6TN
T 01444-894066 E wakehurst@kew.org
W www.kew.org

Kew Gardens was originally laid out as a private garden for the now demolished White House for George III's mother, Princess Augusta, in 1759. The gardens were much enlarged in the 19th century, notably by the inclusion of the grounds of the former Richmond Lodge. In 1965 Kew acquired the gardens at Wakehurst on a long lease from the National Trust. Under the National Heritage Act 1983 a board of trustees was set up to administer the gardens, which in 1984 became an independent body supported by grant-in-aid from the Department for Environment, Food and Rural Affairs. Total grant in aid for 2016–17 was £33m.

The functions of RBG, Kew are to carry out research into plant sciences, to disseminate knowledge about plants and to provide the public with the opportunity to gain knowledge and enjoyment from the gardens' collections. There are extensive national reference collections of living and preserved plants and a comprehensive library and archive. The main emphasis is on plant conservation and biodiversity; Wakehurst houses the Millennium Seed Bank Partnership, which is the largest *ex situ* conservation project in the world – its aim is to save seed from 25 per cent of the earth's wild plant species by 2020.

Chair, Marcus Agius
Trustees, Nick Baird; Prof. Liam Dolan; Catherine Dugmore; Sarah Flannigan; Valerie Gooding; Prof. Sue Hartley; Ian Karet; Sir Henry Keswick; Sir Derek Myers; Prof. Malcolm Press
Director, Richard Deverell

ROYAL COMMISSION ON THE ANCIENT AND HISTORICAL MONUMENTS OF WALES

Ffordd Penglais, Aberystwyth SY23 3BU
T 01970-621200 E nmr.wales@rcahmw.gov.uk
W www.rcahmw.gov.uk

The Royal Commission on the Ancient and Historical Monuments of Wales, established in 1908, is the investigation body and national archive for the historic environment of Wales. It has the lead role in ensuring that Wales's archaeological, built and maritime heritage is authoritatively recorded, and seeks to promote the understanding and appreciation of this heritage nationally and internationally. The commission is funded by the Welsh government.

Chair, Dr Eurwyn Wiliam, FSA
Vice-Chair, Catherine Hardman, FSA
Commissioners, Caroline Crewe-Read, FRSA; Thomas Lloyd, OBE, FSA; Dr Mark Redknap, FSA; Prof. Christopher Williams, FRHISTS
Secretary, Christopher Catling

ROYAL MUSEUMS GREENWICH

National Maritime Museum, Greenwich, London SE10 9NF
T 020-8858 4422 E RMGenquiries@rmg.co.uk
W www.rmg.co.uk
Royal Museums Greenwich comprises the National Maritime Museum, the Queen's House and the Royal Observatory Greenwich. It also works in collaboration with the Cutty Sark Trust. The National Maritime Museum provides information on the maritime history of Great Britain and is the largest institution of its kind in the world, with over 2.5 million items in its collections related to seafaring, navigation and astronomy. Originally the home of Charles I's Queen, Henrietta Maria, the Queen's House was designed by Inigo Jones and built between 1616–18, although it was structurally altered between 1629–35. It now contains a fine-art collection. The Royal Observatory, Greenwich is the home of Greenwich Mean Time and the prime meridian of the world. It also contains London's only planetarium, Harrison's timekeepers and the UK's largest refracting telescope.

Chair, Sir Charles Dunstone
Trustees, Prof. Alison Bashford, CVO; Eleanor Boddington; Joyce Bridges, CBE; Dr Aminul Hoque, MBE; Prof. Christopher Lintott; Carol Marlow; Jonathan Ofer; Jeremy Penn; Eric Reynolds; Gerald Russell; Adm. Sir Mark Stanhope, GCB, OBE
Director, Kevin Fewster, FRSA

SCHOOL TEACHERS' REVIEW BODY

8th Floor, Fleetbank House, 2-6 Salisbury Square, London EC4Y 8JX
T 020-7211 8463 W www.gov.uk/government/organisations/
school-teachers-review-body

The School Teachers' Review Body was set up under the School Teachers' Pay and Conditions Act 1991. It is required to examine and report on such matters relating to the statutory conditions of employment of school teachers in England and Wales as may be referred to it by the education secretary.

Chair, Dr Patricia Rice
Members, Peter Batley; Sir Robert Burgess; Ken Clark; Mike Redhouse; Jeanne Watson

SCIENCE MUSEUM

Exhibition Road, London SW7 2DD
T 020-7942 4000 E info@sciencemuseum.ac.uk
W www.sciencemuseum.org.uk

The Science Museum, part of the Science Museum Group (SMG), houses the national collections of science, technology, industry and medicine. The museum began as the science collection of the South Kensington Museum and first opened in 1857. In 1883 it acquired the collections of the Patent Museum and in 1909 the science collections were transferred to the new Science Museum, leaving the art collections with the Victoria and Albert Museum. The Wellcome Wing was opened in July 2000.

The SMG also incorporates the National Railway Museum, York; the National Media Museum, Bradford; Locomotion: the National Railway Museum at Shildon; and the Museum of Science and Industry, Manchester.

Total government grant-in-aid for 2016–17 is £37.47m.

Chair, Dame Mary Archer, DBE
Trustees, Matthew D'Ancona; Prof. Brian Cantor; Dr Sarah Dry; Lord Faulkner of Worcester; Sharon Flood; Prof. Russell Foster, CBE, FRS, FMEDSCI; Andreas Goss; Lord Grade of Yarmouth, CBE; Prof. Ludmilla Jordanova; Simon Linnett; Lopa Patel; Prof. David Phoenix, OBE; Anton Valk, CBE; Rt. Hon. Lord Willetts; Dame Fiona Woolf, CBE
Director of Science Museum, Ian Blatchford
Director of Museum of Science & Industry, Sally MacDonald
Director of National Science and Media Museum, Jo Quinton-Tulloch
Director of National Railway Museum, Judith McNicol

SCOTTISH CRIMINAL CASES REVIEW COMMISSION

5th Floor, Portland House, 17 Renfield Street, Glasgow G2 5AH
T 0141-270 7030 E info@sccrc.org.uk W www.sccrc.org.uk

The commission is a non-departmental public body, funded by the Scottish Government Justice Directorate, and established by Act of Parliament in April 1999. It assumed the role previously performed by the Secretary of State for Scotland to consider alleged miscarriages of justice in Scotland and refer cases meeting the relevant criteria to the high court for determination. Members are appointed by the Queen on the recommendation of the first minister; senior executive staff are appointed by the commission.

Chair, Bill Matthews
Members, Dr Rajan Darjee; Colin Dunipace; Peter Ferguson, QC; Prof. Jim Fraser; Frances McMenamin, QC; Raymond McMenamin; Elaine Noad
Chief Executive, Gerard Sinclair

SCOTTISH ENTERPRISE

Atrium Court, 50 Waterloo Street, Glasgow G2 6HQ
T 0300-013 3385 E enquiries@scotent.co.uk
W www.scottish-enterprise.com

Scottish Enterprise was established in 1991 and its purpose is to stimulate the sustainable growth of Scotland's economy. It is mainly funded by the Scottish government and is responsible to the Scottish ministers. Working in partnership with the private and public sectors, Scottish Enterprise plan to invest £291.5m in 2017–18 to further the development of Scotland's economy by helping ambitious and innovative businesses grow and become more successful. Scottish Enterprise is particularly interested in supporting companies that provide renewable energy, encourage trade overseas, increase innovation, and those that will help Scotland become a low-carbon economy. Its anticipated grant-in-aid allocation (capital and resource allocation) for 2017–18 was £211.4m.

Chair, Bob Keiller
Chief Executive, Dr Lena Wilson

SCOTTISH ENVIRONMENT PROTECTION AGENCY (SEPA)

Erskine Court, Castle Business Park, Stirling FK9 4TZ
T 0300-996 699
W www.sepa.org.uk

SEPA was established in 1996 and is the public body responsible for environmental protection in Scotland. It regulates potential pollution to land, air and water; the storage, transport and disposal of controlled waste; and the safekeeping and disposal of radioactive materials. It does this within a complex legislative framework of acts of parliament, EU directives and regulations, granting licences to operations of industrial processes and waste disposal. SEPA also operates Floodline (T 0345-988 1188), a public service providing information on the possible risk of flooding 24 hours a day, 365 days a year.

Chair, Bob Downes
Chief Executive, Terry A'Hearn
Directors, Calum MacDonald *(Operations);* David Pirie *(Science and Strategy)*

SCOTTISH LAW COMMISSION

140 Causewayside, Edinburgh EH9 1PR
T 0131-668 2131 E info@scotlawcom.gsi.gov.uk
W www.scotlawcom.gov.uk

The Scottish Law Commission, established in 1965, keeps the law in Scotland under review and makes proposals for its development and reform. It is responsible to the Scottish ministers through the Scottish government constitution, law and courts directorate.

Chair, Hon. Lord Pentland
Chief Executive, Malcolm McMillan
Commissioners, Caroline Drummond; David Johnston, QC; Prof. Hector MacQueen; Dr Andrew Steven

SCOTTISH LEGAL AID BOARD

Thistle House, 91 Haymarket Terrace, Edinburgh EH12 5HE
T 0131-226 7061 Helpline 0845-122 8686
E general@slab.org.uk W www.slab.org.uk

The Scottish Legal Aid Board was set up under the Legal Aid (Scotland) Act 1986 to manage legal aid in Scotland. It reports to the Scottish government. Board members are appointed by Scottish ministers.

Chair, Ray MacFarlane
Members, Rani Dhir; Marieke Dwarshuis; Alastair Kinroy, QC; Tim McKay; Bill McQueen, CBE; Ros Micklem; Sarah O'Neill; Paul Reid; David Sheldon, QC; Sheriff Ray Small; Lesley Ward
Chief Executive, Colin Lancaster

SCOTTISH NATURAL HERITAGE (SNH)

Great Glen House, Leachkin Road, Inverness IV3 8NW
T 01463-725000 E enquiries@snh.gov.uk
W www.snh.gov.uk

SNH was established in 1992 under the Natural Heritage (Scotland) Act 1991. It is the government's adviser on all aspects of nature and landscape across Scotland and its role is to help the public understand, value and enjoy Scotland's nature, as well as to support those people and organisations that manage it.

Chair, Mike Cantlay
Chief Executive (interim), Joe Moore
Directors, Nick Halfhide *(Operations);* vacant *(Policy and Advice);* vacant *(Corporate Services)*

SEAFISH
18 Logie Mill, Logie Green Road, Edinburgh EH7 4HS
T 0131-558 3331 E seafish@seafish.co.uk
W www.seafish.org

Established under the Fisheries Act 1981, Seafish works with all sectors of the UK seafood industry to satisfy consumers, raise standards, improve efficiency and secure a sustainable and profitable future. Services range from research and development, economic consulting, market research and training and accreditation through to legislative advice for the seafood industry. It is sponsored by the four UK fisheries departments, which appoint the board, and receives 80 per cent of its funding through a levy on seafood.

Chair (acting), Brian Young
Chief Executive, Marcus Coleman

SECURITY AND INTELLIGENCE SERVICES

GOVERNMENT COMMUNICATIONS HEADQUARTERS (GCHQ)
Hubble Road, Cheltenham GL51 0EX
T 01242-221491
W www.gchq.gov.uk

GCHQ produces signals intelligence in support of national security and the UK's economic wellbeing, and in the prevention or detection of serious crime. Additionally, in 2017 GCHQ launched the National Cyber Security Centre, NCSC, replacing the CESG, CCA, CERT UK and the cyber related responsibilities of CPNI. It is the national authority for cyber security, and provides advice and assistance to government departments, the armed forces and other national infrastructure bodies on the security of their communications and information systems. GCHQ was placed on a statutory footing by the Intelligence Services Act 1994 and is headed by a director who is directly accountable to the foreign secretary.

Director, Jeremy Fleming

SECRET INTELLIGENCE SERVICE (MI6)
PO Box 1300, London SE1 1BD
Anti-Terrorist Hotline 0800-789 321 W www.sis.gov.uk

Established in 1909 as the Foreign Section of the Secret Service Bureau, the Secret Intelligence Service produces secret intelligence in support of the government's security, defence, foreign and economic policies. It was placed on a statutory footing by the Intelligence Services Act 1994 and is headed by a chief, known as 'C', who is directly accountable to the foreign secretary.

Chief, Alex Younger

SECURITY SERVICE (MI5)
PO Box 3255, London SW1P 1AE
T 0800-111 4645Anti-Terrorist Hotline 0800-789 321
W www.mi5.gov.uk

The Security Service is responsible for security intelligence work against covertly organised threats to the UK. It is organised into ten branches, each with dedicated areas of responsibility, which include countering terrorism, espionage and the proliferation of weapons of mass destruction. The Security Service also provides security advice to a wide range of organisations to help reduce vulnerability to threats from individuals, groups or countries hostile to UK interests. The home secretary has parliamentary accountability for the Security Service. There is a network of regional offices around the UK plus a Northern Ireland headquarters.

Director-General, Andrew Parker

SENIOR SALARIES REVIEW BODY
8th Floor, Fleetbank House, 2-6 Salisbury Square, London EC4Y 8JX
T 020-7211 8315 W www.ome.uk.com

The Senior Salaries Review Body (formerly the Top Salaries Review Body) was set up in 1971 to advise the prime minister on the remuneration of the judiciary, senior civil servants, senior officers of the armed forces and very senior managers in the NHS. In 1993 its remit was extended to cover the pay, pensions and allowances of MPs, ministers and others whose pay is determined by the Ministerial and Other Salaries Act 1975, and also the allowances of peers. If asked, it advises on the pay of officers and members of the devolved parliament and assemblies.

Chair, Dr Martin Read, CBE
Members, Margaret Edwards; Sir Adrian Johns, KCB, CBE; David Lebrecht; John Steele; Dr Peter Westaway; Sharon Witherspoon

STUDENT LOANS COMPANY LTD
100 Bothwell Street, Glasgow G2 7JD
T 0300-100 0611 W www.slc.co.uk

The Student Loans Company (SLC) is owned by the Department for Education. It processes and administers financial assistance, in the form of grants and loans, for undergraduates who have secured a place at university or college. The SLC also provides loans for tuition fees, which are paid directly to the university or college. In 2016 the SLC introduced the provision of loans to postgraduates in accordance with government policy. The SLC supports around 1.8 million students per year.

Chair, Christian Brodie
Chief Executive, Steve Lamey

TATE
W www.tate.org.uk

TATE BRITAIN
Millbank, London SW1P 4RG
T 020-7887 8888 E visiting.britain@tate.org.uk

TATE MODERN
Bankside, London SE1 9TG
T 020-7887 8888 E visiting.modern@tate.org.uk

TATE LIVERPOOL
Albert Dock, Liverpool L3 4BB
T 015-1702 7400 E visiting.liverpool@tate.org.uk

TATE ST IVES
Porthmeor Beach, St Ives, Cornwall TR26 1TG
T 01736-796226 E visiting.stives@tate.org.uk

Tate comprises four art galleries: Tate Britain and Tate Modern in London, Tate Liverpool and Tate St Ives.

Tate Britain, which opened in 1897, displays the national collection of British art from 1500 to the present day – with special attention and dedicated space given to Blake, Turner and Constable. A £45m renovation of Tate Britain was completed in 2013.

Opened in May 2000, Tate Modern displays the Tate collection of international modern art dating from 1900 to the present day. It includes works by Dalí, Picasso, Matisse and Warhol as well as many contemporary works. It is housed in the former Bankside Power Station in London, which was redesigned by the Swiss architects Herzog and de Meuron, and in the neighbouring and purpose-built Switch House, which was designed by Herzog and de Meuron and opened in 2016.

Tate Liverpool opened in 1988 and houses mainly 20th-century art and Tate St Ives, which features work by artists from and working in St Ives and includes the Barbara Hepworth Museum and Sculpture Garden, opened in 1993.

BOARD OF TRUSTEES
Chair (interim), Lionel Barber
Trustees, John Akomfrah; Dexter Dalwood; Tim Davie; Jayne-Anne Gadhia; Mala Gaonkar; Moya Greene; Maja Hoffman; Michael Lynton; Dame Seona Reid, DBE; Stephen Witherford

OFFICERS
Director, Tate, Maria Balshaw, CBE
Directors, Alex Farquharson *(Tate Britain);* Frances Morris *(Tate Modern);* Caroline Collier *(Partnerships and Programmes);* Anna Cutler *(Learning);* Andrea Nixon *(Tate Liverpool);* Mark Osterfield *(Tate St Ives)*

TOURISM BODIES
Visit Britain, Visit Scotland, Visit Wales and the Northern Ireland Tourist Board are responsible for developing and marketing the tourist industry in their respective regions. Visit Wales is not listed here as it is part of the Welsh government, within the Department for Heritage, and not a public body.

VISITBRITAIN
Sanctuary Buildings, 20 Great Smith Street, London SW1P 3BT
E industry.relations@visitbritain.org
W www.visitbritain.com
Chair, Steve Ridgway, CBE
Chief Executive, Sally Balcombe

VISIT SCOTLAND
Ocean Point One, 94 Ocean Drive Edinburgh EH6 6JH T 0131-472 2222 E info@visitscotland.com W www.visitscotland.com
Chair, Lord Thurso
Chief Executive, Malcolm Roughead, OBE

NORTHERN IRELAND TOURIST BOARD
Floors 10–12, Linum Chambers, Bedford Square, Bedford Street, Belfast BT2 7ES T 028-9023 1221
E info@tourismni.com W www.tourismni.com
Chair, Terence Brannigan
Chief Executive, John McGrillen

TRANSPORT FOR LONDON (TFL)
4th Floor, 14 Pier Walk, London SE10 0ES
T 0343-222 1234 W www.tfl.gov.uk

TfL was created in July 2000 and is the integrated body responsible for the capital's transport system. Its role is to implement the Mayor of London's transport strategy and manage the transport services across London for which the mayor has responsibility. These services include TFL Rail, London's buses, London Underground, London Overground, the Docklands Light Railway (DLR), Tramlink, London River Services and Victoria Coach Station. TfL also runs the Emirates Air Line and the London Transport Museum. In a joint venture with the Department for Transport, TfL is responsible for the construction of Crossrail - a new railway linking Maidenhead and Heathrow in the west, to Shenfield and Abbey Wood in the east. The central section of Crossrail is expected to be completed by the end of 2018. In 2017 Tfl announced plans for Crossrail 2, a railway running between Surrey and Hertfordshire.

TfL is responsible for managing the Congestion Charging scheme and for maintaining 360 miles (580km) of main roads and all of London's 6,000+ traffic lights. It also regulates the city's taxis and private hire vehicles. TfL runs the Santander Cycle Hire scheme, allowing customers to hire a bicycle from £2, and the Dial-a-ride scheme, a door-to-door service for disabled people unable to use buses, trams or the London Underground.

Chair, Rt. Hon. Sadiq Khan
Members, Kay Carberry, CBE; Prof. Greg Clark, CBE; Baroness Grey-Thompson, DBE; Bronwen Handyside; Ron Kalifa; Michael Liebreich; Anne McMeel; Dr Alice Maynard, CBE; Dr Mee Ling Ng, OBE; Dr Nelson Ogunshakin, OBE; Val Shawcross, CBE *(Deputy Chair);* Dr Nina Skorupska, CBE; Dr Lynn Sloman; Ben Story
Commissioner, Mike Brown, MVO

UK ATOMIC ENERGY AUTHORITY
Culham Science Centre, Abingdon, Oxfordshire OX14 3DB
T 01235-528822 W www.gov.uk/government/organisations/uk-atomic-energy-authority

The UK Atomic Energy Authority (UKAEA) was established by the Atomic Energy Authority Act 1954 and took over responsibility for the research and development of the civil nuclear power programme. The UKAEA reports to the Department for Business, Energy and Industrial Strategy and is responsible for managing UK fusion research including operating the Joint European Torus (JET) on behalf of the UKAEA's European partners at its site in Culham, Oxfordshire. Culham also houses the facilities for Materials Research, Remote Access in Challenging Environments and Oxford Advanced Skills. In October 2009, as part of the government's Operation Efficiency Programme, the authority sold its commercial arm, UKAEA Limited; as a result, the UKAEA no longer provides nuclear decommissioning services.

Chair, Prof. Roger Cashmore, CMG, FRS
Chief Executive, Prof. Ian Chapman

UK SPORT
21 Bloomsbury Street, London WC1B 3HF
T 020-7211 5100 E info@uksport.gov.uk W www.uksport.gov.uk

UK Sport was established by royal charter in 1997 and is accountable to parliament through the Department for Culture, Media and Sport. Its mission is to lead sport in the UK to world-class success. This means working with partner organisations to deliver medals at the Olympic and Paralympic Games and organising, bidding for and staging major sporting events in the UK; increasing the UK's sporting activity and influence overseas; and promoting sporting conduct, ethics and diversity in society. UK Sport is funded by a mix of grant-in-aid and National Lottery income.

Chair, Dame Katherine Grainger, DBE
Chief Executive, Liz Nicholl, OBE

VICTORIA AND ALBERT MUSEUM
Cromwell Road, London SW7 2RL
T 020-7942 2000 E contact@vam.ac.uk W www.vam.ac.uk

The Victoria and Albert Museum (V&A) is the national museum of art, design and performance. It descends directly from the Museum of Manufactures, which opened in Marlborough House in 1852 after the Great Exhibition of 1851. The museum was moved in 1857 to become part of the South Kensington Museum. It was renamed the Victoria and Albert Museum in 1899. It also houses the National Art Library and Print Room.

The museum's collections span over 5,000 years of human creativity, including paintings, sculpture, architecture, ceramics, furniture, fashion and textiles, theatre and performance, photography, glass, jewellery and metalwork. Materials relating to childhood are displayed at the V&A Museum of Childhood at Bethnal Green, which opened in 1872 and is the most important surviving example of the type of glass and iron construction used by Joseph Paxton for the Great Exhibition. The V&A also houses the National Art

Library which holds over 950,000 books dedicated to the study of fine and decorative arts from around the world.

Chair, Nicholas Coleridge, CBE

Trustees, Mark Damazer, CBE; Benjamin Elliot; Prof. Margot Finn; Robert Glick; Andrew Hochhauser, QC; Nick Hoffman; Stephen McGuckin; Steven Murphy; Prof. Lynda Nead; Dame Theresa Sackler, DBE; Mark Sebba; Caroline Silver; Sir John Sorrell; Dr Paul Thompson; Edmund de Waal, OBE; Nigel Webb

Director, Dr Tristram Hunt

WALLACE COLLECTION

Hertford House, Manchester Square, London W1U 3BN
T 020-7563 9500 E collection@wallacecollection.org
W www.wallacecollection.org

The Wallace Collection was bequeathed to the nation by the widow of Sir Richard Wallace, in 1897, and Hertford House was subsequently acquired by the government. The collection contains works by Titian and Rembrandt, and includes porcelain, furniture and an array of arms and armour.

Chair, António Horta-Osório

Trustees, Marilyn Berk; Prof. Frances Corner, OBE; Jennifer Eady, QC; Eric Ellul; Dounia Nadar; Jessica Pulay; Jemima Rellie; Sir Hugh Roberts, GCVO, FSA; Kate de Rothschild Agius; Dr Ashok Roy; Timothy Schroder

Director, Dr Xavier Bray

DEVOLVED GOVERNMENT

WALES

NATIONAL ASSEMBLY FOR WALES
Cardiff Bay, Cardiff CF99 1NA
T 0845-010 5500 W www.assemblywales.org

The National Assembly for Wales has been in existence since 1999, following a 'yes' vote in the 1997 referendum. However, the way the assembly is structured and its powers have changed over time.

The UK Act that created the assembly was the Government of Wales Act 1998. This stated that the Assembly was a 'corporate body' which meant that the Welsh government and the assembly were a single organisation. Also, it could not pass its own acts. It could, however make orders and regulations, known as secondary legislation.

The Government of Wales Act 2006 created a formal legal separation between:
- the legislative branch: the National Assembly for Wales, made up of 60 assembly members, and
- the executive branch: the Welsh government, made up of the First Minister, Welsh cabinet secretaries and the Counsel General

The act allowed the assembly to seek the power to make laws from the UK parliament. The laws were known as 'measures' of the National Assembly for Wales ('assembly measures'). The power to make laws ('legislative competence') was granted through clauses in Westminster bills or through legislative competence orders. These had to be approved by parliament and by the assembly. This is how the third assembly operated between 2007 and 2011.

The Government of Wales Act 2006 also contained provision for the assembly to make its own lawns without the permission of the UK parliament. These provisions could only be triggered by:
- two-thirds of all assembly members voting in favour of a referendum
- the approval of the UK government and parliament to hold a referendum
- a 'yes' vote in a referendum of the Welsh public

A referendum held on 3 March 2011 resulted in a 'yes' vote in favour of bringing into force part four of the Government of Wales Act 2006. This has meant that since the 2011 National Assembly of Wales election the assembly has been able to pass laws on all subjects in the devolved areas without first needing the agreement of the UK parliament.

During an assembly election, the people of Wales have two votes. One vote is for their constituency assembly member who represents local areas. Wales is divided into 40 constituencies and each is represented by one assembly member (AM).

The other vote is for a party or independent candidate to represent the voter's region. Wales is divided into five regions – North Wales, Mid and West Wales, South Wales West, South Wales East and South Wales Central.

This system means that the overall number of seats held by each political party more closely reflects the share of the vote that the party receives.

The 60 assembly members who are elected make decisions regarding many things that affect life in Wales – health, education, housing and transport. Their job is to make sure that the Welsh government's decisions are in the best interests of Wales and its people.

The National Assembly for Wales does this by:
- scrutinising the policies the Welsh government sets and the decisions it makes
- scrutinising suggestions for laws, proposing changes and voting on whether they should be passed

- asking questions to Welsh government and making suggestions about policies
- voting on how the Welsh government spends its budget every year

The assembly also makes laws for Wales. A law can be put forward by the Welsh government, an individual assembly member, or an assembly committee or the Assembly Commission. The majority of laws are put forward by the Welsh government.

The assembly operates in both Welsh and English and all its legislation is made bilingually.

ASSEMBLY COMMISSION
The Assembly Commission was created under the Government of Wales Act 2006 to ensure that the assembly is provided with the property, staff and services required for it to carry out its functions. The commission also sets the National Assembly's strategic aims, objectives, standards and values. The Assembly Commission consists of the presiding officer, plus four other assembly members, one nominated by each of the four party groups. The five commissioners are accountable to the National Assembly.
Presiding Officer, Elin Jones, AM
Deputy Presiding Officer, Ann Jones, AM
Commissioners, Suzy Davies, Caroline Jones, Adam Price, Joyce Watson
Chief Executive and Clerk of the Assembly, Manon Antoniazzi

ASSEMBLY COMMITTEES
The Business Committee, chaired by the Presiding Officer and established on 24 May 2016, is responsible for facilitating the effective organisation of assembly proceedings. The rest of the assembly committees *as at* August 2017 are:
Children, Young People and Education
  Chair, Lynne Neagle, AM
Climate Change, Environment and Rural Affairs
  Chair, Mark Reckless, AM
Constitutional and Legislative Affairs
  Chair, Huw Irranca-Davies, AM
Culture, Welsh Language and Communications
  Chair, Bethan Jenkins, AM
Economy, Infrastructure and Skills
  Chair, Russell George, AM
Equality, Local Government and Communities
  Chair, John Griffiths, AM
Finance
  Chair, Simon Thomas, AM
Health, Social Care and Sport
  Chair, Dai Lloyd, AM
Petitions
  Chair, David Rowlands, AM
Public Accounts
  Chair, Nick Ramsay, AM
External Affairs and Additional Legislation
  Chair, David Rees, AM
Committee for the Scrutiny of the First Minister
  Chair, Ann Jones, AM
Standards of Conduct
  Chair, Jayne Bryant, AM

SALARIES *2017–18*

First Minister*	£77,596
Presiding Officer*	£65,344
Cabinet Secretary*	£36,756
Minister/Deputy Presiding Officer*	£21,441
Assembly Commissioners*	£13,273
Assembly Member (AM)	£65,344

* In addition to the AM salary

MEMBERS OF THE NATIONAL ASSEMBLY FOR WALES *as at 31 July 2017*

Antoniw, Mick, *Lab., Pontypridd*, Maj. 5,327
ap Iorweth, Rhun, *PC, Ynys Môn*, Maj. 9,510
Asghar, Mohammad, *C., South Wales East region*
Bennett, Gareth, *UKIP, South Wales Central region*
Blythyn, Hannah, *Lab., Delyn*, Maj. 3,582
Bowden, Dawn, *Lab., Merthyr Tydfil and Rhymney*, Maj. 5,486
Brown, Michelle, *UKIP, North Wales region*
Bryant, Jayne, *Lab., Newport West*, Maj. 4,115
Burns, Angela, *C., Carmarthen West and South Pembrokeshire*, Maj. 3,373
David, Hefin, *Lab., Caerphilly*, Maj. 1,575
Davies, Alun, *Lab., Blaenau Gwent*, Maj. 650
Davies, Andrew R. T., *C., South Wales Central region*
Davies, Paul, *C., Preseli Pembrokeshire*, Maj. 3,930
Davies, Suzy, *C., South Wales West region*
Drakeford, Mark, *Lab., Cardiff West*, Maj. 1,176
***** **Elis-Thomas**, Rt. Hon. Lord, *Ind., Dwyfor Meirionnydd*, Maj. 6,406
Evans, Rebecca, *Lab., Gower*, Maj. 1,829
Finch-Saunders, Janet, *C., Aberconwy*, Maj. 754
George, Russell, *C., Montgomeryshire*, Maj. 3,339
Gething, Vaughan, *Lab., Cardiff South and Penarth*, Maj. 6,921
† **Gill**, Nathan, *Ind., North Wales region*
Griffiths, John, *Lab., Newport East*, Maj. 4,896
Griffiths, Lesley, *Lab., Wrexham*, Maj. 1,325
Gruffydd, Llyr, *PC, North Wales region*
Gwenllian, Sian, *PC, Arfon*, Maj. 4,162
Hamilton, Neil, *UKIP, Mid and West Wales region*
Hedges, Mike, *Lab., Swansea East*, Maj. 7,452
Howells, Vikki, *Lab., Cynon Valley*, Maj. 5, 994
Hutt, Jane, *Lab., Vale of Glamorgan*, Maj. 777
Irranca-Davies, Huw, *Lab., Ogmore*, Maj. 9,468
Isherwood, Mark, *C., North Wales region*
James, Julie, *Lab., Swansea West*, Maj. 5,080
Jenkins, Bethan, *PC, South Wales West region*
Jones, Ann, *Lab., Vale of Clwyd*, Maj. 768
Jones, Caroline, *UKIP, South Wales West region*
Jones, Rt. Hon. Carwyn, *Lab., Bridgend*, Maj. 5,623
Jones, Elin, *PC, Ceredigion*, Maj. 2,408
Lewis, Steffan, *PC, South Wales East region*
Lloyd, Dai, *PC, South Wales West region*
McEvoy, Neil, *PC, South Wales Central region*
Melding, David, *C. South Wales Central region*
Miles, Jeremy, *Lab. Neath*, Maj. 2,923
Millar, Darren, *C., Clwyd West*, Maj. 5,063
Morgan, Eluned *Lab., Mid and West Wales region*
Morgan, Julie, *Lab., Cardiff North*, Maj. 3,667
Neagle, Lynne, *Lab., Torfaen*, Maj. 4,498
Passmore, Rhianon, *Lab., Islwyn*, Maj. 5,106
Price, Adam, *PC, Carmarthen East and Dinefwr*, Maj. 8,700
Ramsay, Nick, *C., Monmouth*, Maj. 5,147
Rathbone, Jenny, *Lab., Cardiff Central*, Maj. 817
† **Reckless**, Mark, *C., South Wales East*
Rees, David, *Lab, Aberavon*, Maj. 6,402
Rowlands, David J., *UKIP, Sorth Wales East region*
Sargeant, Carl, *Lab., Alyn and Deeside* Maj. 5,364
Skates, Ken, *Lab., Clwyd South*, Maj. 3,016
Thomas, Simon, *PC, Mid and West Wales region*
Waters, Lee, *Lab., Llanelli*, Maj. 382
Watson, Joyce, *Lab., Mid and West Wales region*
Williams, Kirsty, *LD, Brecon and Radnorshire*, Maj. 8,170
Wood, Leanne, *PC, Rhondda*, Maj. 3,359

* Previously AM for PC
† Previously AM for UKIP

STATE OF THE PARTIES *as at 31 July 2017*

	Constituency AMs	Regional AMs	AM total
Labour (Lab.)	*27	2	29
Conservative (C.)	6	6	12
Plaid Cymru (PC)	†5	6	11
UKIP	0	5	5
Independent (Ind.)	1	1	2
Liberal Democrats (LD)	1	0	1
Total	40	20	60

* Includes the Deputy Presiding Officer
† Includes the Presiding Officer

WELSH GOVERNMENT

Cathays Park, Cardiff CF10 3NQ
T 0300-060 3300 W www.gov.wales

The Welsh government is the devolved government of Wales. It is accountable to the National Assembly for Wales, the Welsh legislature which represents the interests of the people of Wales, and makes laws for Wales. The Welsh government and the National Assembly for Wales were established as separate institutions under the Government of Wales Act 2006.

The Welsh government comprises the first minister, who is usually the leader of the largest party in the National Assembly for Wales; up to 14 cabinet secretaries and ministers and deputy ministers; and a counsel general (the chief legal adviser).

Following the referendum on 3 March 2011 on granting further law-making powers to the National Assembly, the Welsh government's functions now include the ability to propose bills to the National Assembly on subjects within 20 set areas of policy. Subject to limitations prescribed by the Government of Wales Act 2006, acts of the National Assembly may make any provision that could be made by act of parliament. The 20 areas of responsibility devolved to the National Assembly for Wales (and within which Welsh ministers exercise executive functions) are: agriculture, fisheries, forestry and rural development; ancient monuments and historic buildings; culture; economic development; education and training; environment; fire and rescue services and promotion of fire safety; food; health and health services; highways and transport; housing; local government; the National Assembly for Wales; public administration; social welfare; sport and recreation; tourism; town and county planning; water and flood defence; and the Welsh language.

First Minister of Wales, Rt. Hon. Carwyn Jones, AM
Cabinet Secretary for Communities and Children, Carl Sargeant, AM
Cabinet Secretary for Economy and Infrasructure, Ken Skates, AM
Cabinet Secretary Education, Kirsty Williams, AM
Cabinet Secretary for Environment and Rural Affairs, Lesley Griffiths, AM
Cabinet Secretary for Finance and Local Government, Prof. Mark Drakeford, AM
Cabinet Secretary for Health, Well-being and Sport, Vaughan Gething, AM
Counsel General for Wales, Mick Antoniw, AM
Leader of the House and Chief Whip, Jane Hutt, AM

Minister for Lifelong Learning and Welsh Language, Alun Davies, AM
Minister for Skills and Science, Julie James, AM
Minister for Social Services and Public Health, Rebecca Evans, AM

MANAGEMENT BOARD

Permanent Secretary, Shan Morgan, CMG
Deputy Permanent Secretary, Education and Public Services, Owen Evans

Deputy Permanent Secretary, Economy, Skills and Natural Resources, James Price

Director-General, Health, Social Services and Children and Chief Executive of NHS Wales, Dr Andrew Goodall

Director of Finance, Gawain Evans

Director of Governance, David Richards

Director of HR, Peter Kennedy

Director of Legal Services, Jeffrey Godfrey

Chief Executive of Children and Family Court Advisory and Support Service (CAFCASS) Cymru, Gillian Baranski

Non-Executive Directors, Ann Keen; Elan Closs Stephens; James Turner; Adrian Webb

DEPARTMENTS

DEPARTMENT FOR EDUCATION AND PUBLIC SERVICES

Chief Digital Officer; Education; Local government, Communities and Tackling Poverty; Housing and Regeneration; Welsh Language

DEPARTMENT FOR HEALTH AND SOCIAL SERVICES

DEPARTMENT FOR ECONOMY, SKILLS AND NATURAL RESOURCES

Economy and Infrastructure; Environment and Rural Affairs; Skills, Higher Education and Lifelong Learning, National Procurement Service

OFFICE OF THE FIRST MINISTER AND CABINET OFFICE

Constitutional Affairs and Inter-governmental Relations Division; European and External Affairs Division; Finance; HR and Corporate Services; Legal Services Department; Office of the First Minister; Welsh European Funding Office; Welsh Treasury

NATIONAL ASSEMBLY ELECTION RESULTS *as at 5 May 2016*

Electorate (E.) 2,248,050 Turnout (T.) 45.3%
See General Election Results for a list of party abbreviations

ABERAVON (S. WALES WEST)
E. 49,074 T. 20,852 (42.49%)

David Rees, Lab.	10,578
Bethan Jenkins, PC	4,176
Glenda Davies, UKIP	3,119
David Jenkins, C.	1,342
Helen Ceri Clarke, LD	1,248
Jonathan Tier, Green	389

Lab. majority 6,402 (30.70%)
9.31% swing Lab. to PC

ABERCONWY (WALES N.)
E. 44,960 T. 22,038 (49.02%)

Janet Finch-Saunders, C.	7,646
Trystan Lewis, PC	6,892
Mike Priestley, Lab.	6,039
Sarah Lesiter-Burgess, LD	781
Petra Haig, Green	680

C. majority 754 (3.42%)
2.15% swing C. to PC

ALYN AND DEESIDE (WALES N.)
E. 62,697 T. 21,696 (34.60%)

Carl Sargeant, Lab.	9,922
Mike Gibbs, C.	4,558
Michelle Brown, UKIP	3,765
Jacqui Hurst, PC	1,944
Pete Williams, LD	980
Martin Bennewith, Green	527

Lab. majority 5,364 (24.72%)
0.11% swing C. to Lab.

ARFON (WALES N.)
E. 39,269 T. 19,994 (50.92%)

Sian Gwenllian, PC	10,962
Sion Jones, Lab.	6,800
Martin Peet, C.	1,655
Sara Lloyd Williams, LD	577

PC majority 4,162 (20.82%)
4.86% swing PC to Lab.

BLAENAU GWENT (S. WALES EAST)
E. 50,574 T. 21,291 (42.10%)

Alun Davies, Lab.	8,442
Nigel Copner, PC	7,792
Kevin Boucher, UKIP	3,423
Tracey West, C.	1,334
Brendan D'Cruz, LD	300

Lab. majority 650 (3.05%)
27.73% swing Lab. to PC

**BRECON AND RADNORSHIRE
(WALES MID AND W.)**
E. 53,793 T. 30,367 (56.45%)

Kirsty Williams, LD	15,898
Gary Price, C.	7,728
Alex Thomas, Lab.	2,703
Thomas Turton, UKIP	2,161
Freddy Greaves, PC	1,180
Grenville Ham, Green	697

LD majority 8,170 (26.90%)
8.59% swing C. to LD

BRIDGEND (S. WALES WEST)
E. 60,195 T. 26,851 (44.61%)

Carwyn Jones, Lab.	12,166
George Jabbour, C.	6,543
Caroline Jones, UKIP	3,919
James Radcliffe, PC	2,569
Jonathan Pratt, LD	1,087
Charlie Barlow, Green	567

Lab. majority 5,623 (20.94%)
3.62% swing Lab. to C.

CAERPHILLY (S. WALES EAST)
E. 62,449 T. 27,115 (43.42%)

Hefin David, Lab.	9,584
Lindsay Whittle, PC	8,009
Sam Gould, UKIP	5,954
Jane Pratt, C.	2,412
Andrew Creak, Green	770
Aladdin Ayesh, LD	386

Lab. majority 1,575 (5.81%)
6.72% swing Lab. to PC

**CARDIFF CENTRAL (S. WALES
CENTRAL)**
E. 57,177 T. 26,068 (45.59%)

Jenny Rathbone, Lab.	10,016
Eluned Parrott, LD	9,199
Joel Williams, C.	2,317
Glyn Wise, PC	1,951
Mohammed Islam, UKIP	1,223
Amelia Womack, Green	1,150
Jane Croad, Ind.	212

Lab. majority 817 (3.13%)
1.49% swing LD to Lab.

**CARDIFF NORTH (S. WALES
CENTRAL)**
E. 65,927 T. 37,452 (56.81%)

Julie Morgan, Lab.	16,766
Jayne Cowan, C.	13,099
Haydn Rushworth, UKIP	2,509
Elin Walker Jones, PC	2,278
John Dixon, LD	1,130
Fiona Burt, Ind.	846
Chris von Ruhland, Green	824

Lab. majority 3,667 (9.79%)
2.31% swing C. to Lab.

**CARDIFF SOUTH AND PENARTH
(S. WALES CENTRAL)**
E. 76,110 T. 30,276 (39.78%)

Vaughan Gething, Lab.	13,274
Ben Gray, C.	6,353
Dafydd Davies, PC	4,320
Hugh Moelwyn Hughes, UKIP	3,716
Nigel Howells, LD	1,345
Anthony Slaughter, Green	1,268

Lab. majority 6,921 (22.86%)
0.04% swing C. to Lab.

**CARDIFF WEST (S. WALES
CENTRAL)**
E. 66,040 T. 31,960 (48.39%)

Mark Drakeford, Lab.	11,381
Neil McEvoy, PC	10,205
Sean Driscoll, C.	5,617
Gareth Bennett, UKIP	2,629
Hannah Pudner, Green	1,032
Cadan ap Tomos, LD	868
Eliot Freedman, Ind.	132
Lee Woolls, FTC	96

Lab. majority 1,176 (3.68%)
11.71% swing Lab. to PC

**CARMARTHEN EAST AND
DINEFWR (WALES MID AND W.)**
E. 55,395 T. 29,751 (53.71%)

Adam Price, PC	14,427
Stephen Jeacock, Lab.	5,727
Matthew Paul, C.	4,489
Neil Hamilton, UKIP	3,474
William Powell, LD	837
Freya Amsbury, Green	797

PC majority 8,700 (29.24%)
7.17% swing Lab. to PC

**CARMARTHEN WEST AND SOUTH
PEMBROKESHIRE (WALES MID
AND W.)**
E. 56,886 T. 29,237 (51.40%)

Angela Burns, C.	10,355
Marc Tierney, Lab.	6,982
Simon Thomas, PC	5,459
Allan Brookes, UKIP	3,300
Chris Overton, Ind.	1,638
Val Bradley, Green	804
Alistair Cameron, LD	699

C. majority 3,373 (11.54%)
3.10% swing Lab. to C.

**CEREDIGION (WALES MID AND
W.)**
E. 51,230 T. 29,485 (57.55%)

Elin T Jones, PC	12,014
Elizabeth Evans, LD	9,606
Gethin James, UKIP	2,665
Felix Aubel, C.	2,075
Iwan Wyn Jones, Lab.	1,902
Brian Williams, Green	1,223

PC majority 2,408 (8.17%)
1.03% swing LD to PC

CLWYD SOUTH (WALES N.)
E. 54,185 T. 22,159 (40.90%)

Ken Skates, Lab.	7,862
Simon Baynes, C.	4,846
Mabon ap Gwynfor, PC	3,861
Mandy Jones, UKIP	2,827
Aled Roberts, LD	2,289
Duncan Rees, Green	474

Lab. majority 3,016 (13.61%)
0.17% swing C. to Lab.

CLWYD WEST (WALES N.)
E. 57,657 T. 26,226 (45.49%)

Darren Millar, C.	10,831
Llyr Gruffydd, PC	5,768
Jo Thomas, Lab.	5,246
David Edwards, UKIP	2,985
Victor Babu, LD	831
Julian Mahy, Green	565

C. majority 5,063 (19.31%)
0.52% swing C. to PC

CYNON VALLEY (S. WALES CENTRAL)
E. 50,292 T. 19,236 (38.25%)

Vikki Howells, Lab.	9,830
Cerith Griffiths, PC	3,836
Liz Wilks, UKIP	3,460
Lyn Hudson, C.	1,177
John Matthews, Green	598
Michael Wallace, LD	335

Lab. majority 5,994 (31.16%)
1.78% swing Lab. to PC

DELYN (WALES N.)
E. 53,490 T. 23,159 (43.30%)

Hannah Blythyn, Lab.	9,480
Huw Williams, C.	5,898
Nigel Williams, UKIP	3,794
Paul Rowlinson, PC	2,269
Tom Rippeth, LD	1,718

Lab. majority 3,582 (15.47%)
1.52% swing C. to Lab.

DWYFOR MEIRONNYDD (WALES MID AND W.)
E. 43,304 T. 20,236 (46.73%)

Dafydd Elis-Thomas, PC	9,566
Neil Fairlamb, C.	3,160
Ian MacIntyre, Lab.	2,443
Frank Wykes, UKIP	2,149
Louise Hughes, Ind.	1,259
Steve Churchman, LD	916
Alice Hooker-Stroud, Green	743

PC majority 6,406 (31.66%)
2.77% swing C. to PC

GOWER (S. WALES WEST)
E. 60,631 T. 30,187 (49.79%)

Rebecca Evans, Lab.	11,982
Lyndon Jones, C.	10,153
Colin Beckett, UKIP	3,300
Harri Roberts, PC	2,982
Sheila Kingston-Jones, LD	1,033
Abi Cherry-Hamer, Green	737

Lab. majority 1,829 (6.06%)
6.05% swing Lab. to C.

ISLWYN (S. WALES EAST)
E. 54,465 T. 22,309 (40.96%)

Rhianon Passmore, Lab.	10,050
Joe Smyth, UKIP	4,944
Lyn Ackerman, PC	4,349
Paul Williams, C.	1,775
Matthew Kidner, LD	597
Katy Beddoe, Green	594

Lab. majority 5,106 (22.89%)

LLANELLI (WALES MID AND W.)
E. 59,651 T. 28,116 (47.13%)

Lee Waters, Lab.	10,267
Helen Mary Jones, PC	9,885
Ken Rees, UKIP	4,132
Stefan Ryszewski, C.	1,937
Sian Caiach, PF	1,113
Guy Smith, Green	427
Gemma Bowker, LD	355

Lab. majority 382 (1.36%)
0.53% swing PC to Lab.

MERTHYR TYDFIL AND RHYMNEY (S. WALES EAST)
E. 53,754 T. 20,683 (38.48%)

Dawn Bowden, Lab.	9,763
David Rowlands, UKIP	4,277
Brian Thomas, PC	3,721
Elizabeth Simon, C.	1,331
Bob Griffin, LD	1,122
Julie Colbran, Green	469

Lab. majority 5,486 (26.52%)

MONMOUTH (S. WALES EAST)
E. 64,197 T. 31,401 (48.91%)

Nick Ramsay, C.	13,585
Catherine Fookes, Lab.	8,438
Tim Price, UKIP	3,092
Debby Blakebrough, Ind.	1,932
Jonathan Clark, PC	1,824
Veronica German, LD	1,474
Chris Were, Green	910
Stephen Morris, Eng Dem	146

C. majority 5,147 (16.39%)
2.00% swing C. to Lab.

MONTGOMERYSHIRE (WALES MID AND W.)
E. 48,682 T. 23,600 (48.48%)

Russell George, C.	9,875
Jane Dodds, LD	6,536
Des Parkinson, UKIP	2,458
Aled Morgan Hughes, PC	2,410
Martyn Singleton, Lab.	1,389
Richard Chaloner, Green	932

C. majority 3,339 (14.15%)
2.01% swing LD to C.

NEATH (S. WALES WEST)
E. 55,395 T. 25,363 (45.79%)

Jeremy Miles, Lab.	9,468
Alun Llewelyn, PC	6,545
Richard Pritchard, UKIP	3,780
Peter Crocker-Jaques, C.	2,179
Steve Hunt, Ind.	2,056
Frank Little, LD	746
Lisa Rapado, Green	589

Lab. majority 2,923 (11.52%)
7.63% swing Lab. to PC

NEWPORT EAST (S. WALES EAST)
E. 55,499 T. 20,688 (37.28%)

John Griffiths, Lab.	9,229
James Peterson, UKIP	4,333
Munawar Mughal, C.	3,768
Paul Halliday, LD	1,481
Tony Salkeld, PC	1,386
Peter Varley, Green	491

Lab. majority 4,896 (23.67%)

NEWPORT WEST (S. WALES EAST)
E. 62,169 T. 27,751 (44.64%)

Jayne Bryant, Lab.	12,157
Matthew Evans, C.	8,042
Michael Ford, UKIP	3,842
Simon Coopey, PC	1,645
Liz Newton, LD	880
Pippa Bartolotti, Green	814
Bill Fearnley-Whittingstall, Ind.	333
Gruff Meredith, WSov	38

Lab. majority 4,115 (14.83%)
1.75% swing Lab. to C.

OGMORE (S. WALES WEST)
E. 54,502 T. 23,356 (42.85%)

Huw Irranca-Davies, Lab.	12,895
Tim Thomas, PC	3,427
Elizabeth Kendall, UKIP	3,233
Jamie Wallis, C.	2,587
Anita Davies, LD	698
Laurie Brophy, Green	516

Lab. majority 9,468 (40.54%)
3.36% swing Lab. to PC

PONTYPRIDD (S. WALES CENTRAL)
E. 58,277 T. 25,338 (43.48%)

Mick Antoniw, Lab.	9,986
Chad Rickard, PC	4,659
Joel James, C.	3,884
Edwin Allen, UKIP	3,322
Mike Powell, LD	2,979
Ken Barker, Green	508

Lab. majority 5,327 (21.02%)
8.18% swing Lab. to PC

PRESELI PEMBROKESHIRE (WALES MID AND W.)
E. 56,414 T. 28,397 (50.34%)

Paul Davies, C.	11,123
Dan Lodge, Lab.	7,193
John Osmond, PC	3,957
Howard Lillyman, UKIP	3,286
Bob Kilmister, LD	1,677
Frances Bryant, Green	1,161

C. majority 3,930 (13.84%)
2.92% swing Lab. to C.

RHONDDA (S. WALES CENTRAL)
E. 49,758 T. 23,486 (47.20%)

Leanne Wood, PC	11,891
Leighton Andrews, Lab.	8,432
Stephen Clee, UKIP	2,203
Maria Hill, C.	528
Pat Matthews, Green	259
Rhys Taylor, LD	173

PC majority 3,459 (14.73%)
24.19% swing Lab. to PC

SWANSEA EAST (S. WALES WEST)
E. 57,589 T. 20,576 (35.73%)

Mike Hedges, Lab.	10,726
Clifford Johnson, UKIP	3,274
Dic Jones, PC	2,744
Sadie Vidal, C.	1,729
Charlene Webster, LD	1,574
Tony Young, Green	529

Lab. majority 7,452 (36.22%)

SWANSEA WEST (S. WALES WEST)
E. 54,593 T. 22,202 (40.67%)

Julie James, Lab.	9,014
Craig Lawton, C.	3,934
Dai Lloyd, PC	3,225
Rosie Irwin, UKIP	3,058
Chris Holley, LD	2,012
Gareth Tucker, Green	883
Brian Johnson, SPGB	76

Lab. majority 5,080 (22.88%)
0.77% swing C. to Lab.

TORFAEN (S. WALES EAST)
E. 60,246 T. 22,978 (38.14%)

Lynne Neagle, Lab.	9,688
Susan Boucher, UKIP	5,190
Graham Smith, C.	3,931
Matthew Woolfall-Jones, PC	2,860
Steve Jenkins, Green	681
Alison Willott, LD	628

Lab. majority 4,498 (19.58%)

VALE OF CLWYD (WALES N.)
E. 56,322 T. 24,183 (42.94%)

Ann Jones, Lab.	9,560
Sam Rowlands, C.	8,792
Paul Davies-Cooke, UKIP	2,975
Mair Rowlands, PC	2,098
Gwyn Williams, LD	758

Lab. majority 768 (3.18%)
7.11% swing Lab. to C.

VALE OF GLAMORGAN (S. WALES CENTRAL)
E. 71,177 T. 37,798 (53.10%)

Jane Hutt, Lab.	14,655
Ross England, C.	13,878
Ian Johnson, PC	3,871
Lawrence Andrews, UKIP	3,662
Denis Campbell, LD	938
Alison Haden, Green	794

Lab. majority 777 (2.06%)
4.65% swing Lab. to C.

WREXHAM (WALES N.)
E. 51,567 T. 20,354 (39.47%)

Lesley Griffiths, Lab.	7,552
Andrew Atkinson, C.	6,227
Carrie Harper, PC	2,631
Jeanette Bassford-Barton, UKIP	2,393
Beryl Blackmore, LD	1,140
Alan Butterworth, Green	411

Lab. majority 1,325 (6.51%)
5.67% swing Lab. to C.

YNYS MON (WALES N.)
E. 50,345 T. 25,167 (49.99%)

Rhun ap Iorwerth, PC	13,788
Julia Dobson, Lab.	4,278
Simon Wall, UKIP	3,212
Clay Theakston, C.	2,904
Gerry Wolff, Green	389
Thomas Crofts, LD	334
Daniel ap Eifion Jones, Ind.	262

PC majority 9,510 (37.79%)
11.29% swing Lab. to PC

REGIONS *as at 5 May 2016*
E. 2,248,050 T. 45.3%

MID AND WEST WALES
E. 425,355 T. 215,840 (50.74%)

PC	56,754	(26.29%)
C.	44,461	(20.60%)
Lab.	41,975	(19.45%)
UKIP	25,042	(11.60%)
LD	23,554	(10.91%)
Abolish	10,707	(4.96%)
Green	8,222	(3.81%)
PF	1,496	(0.69%)
Ch. P.	1,103	(0.51%)
Loony	1,071	(0.50%)
Loc. Ind.	1,032	(0.48%)
Welsh Comm	423	(0.20%)

PC majority 12,293 (5.70%)
2.02% swing C. to PC (2011 PC majority 3,479)
ADDITIONAL MEMBERS
Joyce Watson, *Lab.*
Eluned Morgan, *Lab.*
Simon Thomas, *PC*
Neil Hamilton, *UKIP*

NORTH WALES
E. 470,492 T. 204,490 (43.46%)

Lab.	57,528	(28.13%)
PC	47,701	(23.33%)
C	45,468	(22.23%)
UKIP	25,518	(12.48%)
Abolish	9,409	(4.60%)
LD	9,345	(4.57%)
Green	4,789	(2.34%)
Loc Ind.	1,865	(0.91%)
Loony	1,355	(0.66%)
Ind.	926	(0.45%)
Welsh Comm	586	(0.29%)

Lab. majority 9,827 (4.81%)
2.98% swing Lab. to PC (2011 Lab. majority 10,476)
ADDITIONAL MEMBERS
Mark Isherwood, *C.*
Llyr Gruffydd, *PC*
Nathan Gill, *UKIP*
Michelle Brown, *UKIP*

SOUTH WALES CENTRAL
E. 494,758 T. 231,133 (46.72%)

Lab.	78,366	(33.91%)
PC	48,357	(20.92%)
C.	42,185	(18.25%)
UKIP	23,958	(10.37%)
LD	14,875	(6.44%)
Abolish	9,163	(3.96%)
Green	7,949	(3.44%)
Women	2,807	(1.21%)
Loony	1,096	(0.47%)
TUSC	736	(0.32%)
Ind.	651	(0.28%)
Comm	520	(0.22%)
FTC	470	(0.20%)

Lab. majority 30,009 (12.98%)
7.24% swing Lab. to PC (2011 Lab. majority 39,694)
ADDITIONAL MEMBERS
Andrew Davies, *C.*
David Melding, *C.*
Neil McEvoy, *PC*
Gareth Bennett, *UKIP*

SOUTH WALES EAST
E. 463,353 T. 194,091 (41.89%)

Lab.	74,424	(38.34%)
UKIP	34,524	(17.79%)
C.	33,318	(17.17%)
PC	29,686	(15.29%)
Abolish	7,870	(4.05%)
LD	6,784	(3.50%)
Green	4,831	(2.49%)
Loony	1,115	(0.57%)
TUSC	618	(0.32%)
Welsh Comm	492	(0.25%)
NF	429	(0.22%)

Lab. majority 39,900 (20.56%)
9.93% swing Lab. to UKIP (2011 Lab. majority 47,240)
ADDITIONAL MEMBERS
Oscar Asghar, *C.*
Steffan Lewis, *PC*
Mark Reckless, *UKIP*
David Rowlands, *UKIP*

SOUTH WALES WEST
E. 391,979 T. 169,189 (43.16%)

Lab.	66,903	(39.54%)
PC	29,050	(17.17%)
C.	25,414	(15.02%)
UKIP	23,096	(13.65%)
LD	10,946	(6.47%)
Abolish	7,137	(4.22%)
Green	4,420	(2.61%)
Loony	1,106	(0.65%)
TUSC	686	(0.41%)
Welsh Comm	431	(0.25%)

Lab. majority 37,853 (22.37%)
5.17% swing Lab. to PC (2011 Lab. majority 44,309)
ADDITIONAL MEMBERS
Suzy Davies, *C.*
Bethan Jenkins, *PC*
Dai Lloyd, *PC*
Caroline Jones, *UKIP*

SCOTLAND

SCOTTISH PARLIAMENT

Edinburgh EH99 1SP
T 0131-348 5000/ 0800-092 7500
E info@parliament.scot
W www.parliament.scot

In July 1997 the government announced plans to establish a Scottish parliament. In a referendum on 11 September 1997 about 60 per cent of the electorate voted. Of those who voted, 74.3 per cent voted in favour of the parliament and 63.5 per cent voted in support of granting the parliament having tax-raising powers. Elections are normally held every four years, but the current session is scheduled to last for five years. The first elections were held on 6 May 1999, when around 59 per cent of the electorate voted. The first meeting was held on 12 May 1999 and the Scottish parliament was officially opened on 1 July 1999 at the Assembly Hall, Edinburgh. A new building to house the parliament was opened, in the presence of the Queen, at Holyrood on 9 October 2004. On 5 May 2016 the fifth elections to the Scottish parliament took place.

The Scottish parliament has 129 members (including the presiding officer), comprising 73 constituency members and 56 additional regional members, drawn from the party lists. It can introduce primary legislation and has the power to set rates and bands for income tax on non-savings and non-dividend income for Scottish taxpayers.

Members of the Scottish parliament are elected using the additional member system, the same system used to elect London Assembly and Welsh Assembly members. Under the additional member system the electorate has two votes; the first to elect their constituency member via the 'first past the post' method of voting and the second to elect their regional member. The 56 regional seats are filled proportionally from the party's lists according to their share of the vote on the second ballot paper. By-elections are held for constituency seat vacancies but not for regional seat vacancies which are filled by the next candidate on the list from the same political party in which the vacancy arose.

The areas for which the Scottish parliament is responsible include: civil and criminal justice; education; health; environment; economic development; local government; housing; police; fire services; planning; financial assistance to industry; tourism; heritage and the arts; agriculture; social work; sports; public registers and records; forestry; food standards; some aspects of transport; and some areas of welfare.

SALARIES *as at 1 April 2017*

First Minister*	£89,493
Cabinet Secretary*	£46,426
Lord Advocate*	£60,653
Solicitor-General for Scotland*	£43,860
Minister*	£29,083
MSP†	£61,778
Presiding Officer*	£46,426
Deputy Presiding Officer*	£29,083

* In addition to the MSP salary
† Reduced by two-thirds if the member is also an MP or an MEP

MEMBERS OF THE SCOTTISH PARLIAMENT *as at 30 June 2017*

KEY
* Elected via by-election since the 2016 Scottish parliament election
† Replacement from the party list since the 2016 Scottish parliament election under the additional member system
‡ The Presiding Officer was elected as a regional member for Labour but has no party affiliation while in post

Adam, George, *SNP, Paisley,* Maj. 5,199
Adamson, Clare, *SNP, Motherwell and Wishaw,* Maj. 6,223
Allan, Alasdair, *SNP, Na h-Eileanan an Iar,* Maj. 3,496
Arthur, Tom, *SNP, Renfrewshire South,* Maj. 4,408
Baillie, Jackie, *Lab., Dumbarton,* Maj. 109
Baker, Claire, *Lab., Mid Scotland and Fife region*
Balfour, Jeremy, *C., Lothian region*
† **Ballantyne**, Michelle, *C., South Scotland region*
Beamish, Claudia, *Lab., South Scotland region*
Beattie, Colin, *SNP, Midlothian North and Musselburgh,* Maj. 7,035
Bibby, Neil, *Lab., West Scotland region*
† **Bowman**, Bill, *C., North East Scotland region*
Briggs, Miles, *C. Lothian region*
Brown, Keith, *SNP, Clackmannanshire and Dunblane,* Maj. 6,721
Burnett, Alexander, *C., Aberdeenshire West,* Maj. 900
Cameron, Donald, *C., Highlands and Islands region*
Campbell, Aileen, *SNP, Clydesdale,* Maj. 5,979
Carlaw, Jackson, *C., Eastwood,* Maj. 1.611
Carson, Finlay, *C., Galloway and West Dumfries,* Maj. 1,514
Chapman, Peter, *C., North East Scotland region*
Coffey, Willie, *SNP, Kilmarnock and Irvine Valley,* Maj. 11,194
Cole-Hamilton, Alex, *LD, Edinburgh Western,* Maj. 2,960
Constance, Angela, *SNP, Almond Valley,* Maj. 8,393
Corry, Maurice, *C., West Scotland region*
Crawford, Bruce, *SNP, Stirling,* Maj. 6,718
Cunningham, Roseanna, *SNP, Perthshire South and Kinross-shire,* Maj. 1,422
Davidson, Ruth, *C., Edinburgh Central,* Maj. 610
Denham, Ash, *SNP, Edinburgh Eastern,* Maj. 5,087
Dey, Graeme, *SNP, Angus South,* Maj. 4,304
Doris, Bob, *SNP, Glasgow Maryhill and Springburn,* Maj. 5,602
Dornan, James, *SNP, Glasgow Cathcart,* Maj. 9,390
Dugdale, Kezia, *Lab., Lothian region*
Evans, Mairi, *SNP, Angus North and Mearns,* Maj. 2,472
Ewing, Annabelle, *SNP, Cowdenbeath,* Maj. 3,041
Ewing, Fergus, *SNP, Inverness and Nairn,* Maj. 10,857
Fabiani, Linda, *SNP, East Kilbride,* Maj. 10,979
Fee, Mary, *Lab., West Scotland region*
Findlay, Neil, *Lab., Lothian region*
Finnie, John, *Green, Highlands and Islands region*
FitzPatrick, Joe, *SNP, Dundee City West,* Maj. 8,828
Forbes, Kate, *SNP, Skye, Lochaber and Badenoch,* Maj. 9,043
Fraser, Murdo, *C., Mid Scotland and Fife region*
Freeman, Jeane, *SNP, Carrick, Cumnock and Doon Valley,* Maj. 6,006
Gibson, Kenneth, *SNP, Cunninghame North,* Maj. 8,724
Gilruth, Jenny, *SNP, Mid Fife and Glenrothes,* Maj. 8,276
Golden, Maurice, *C., West Scotland region*
Grahame, Christine, *SNP, Midlothian South, Tweeddale and Lauderdale,* Maj. 5,868
Grant, Rhoda, *Lab., Highlands and Islands region*
Gray, Iain, *Lab., East Lothian,* Maj. 1,127
Greene, Jamie, *C., West Scotland region*
Greer, Ross, *Green, West Scotland region*
Griffin, Mark, *Lab., Central Scotland region*
† **Halcro Johnston**, Jamie, *C., Highlands and Islands region*
* **Hamilton**, Rachael, *C. Ettrick, Roxburgh and Berwickshire,* Maj. 9,338

Harper, Emma, *SNP, South Scotland region*
Harris, Alison, *C.,Central Scotland region*
Harvie, Patrick, *Green, Glasgow region*
Haughey, Clare, *SNP, Rutherglen,* Maj. 3,743
Hepburn, Jamie, *SNP, Cumbernauld and Kilsyth,* Maj. 9,478
Hyslop, Fiona, *SNP, Linlithgow,* Maj. 9,335
Johnson, Daniel, *Lab., Edinburgh Southern,* Maj. 1,123
Johnstone, Alison, *Green, Lothian region*
Kelly, James, *Lab. Glasgow region*
Kerr, Liam, *C. North East Scotland region*
Kidd, Bill, *SNP, Glasgow Anniesland,* Maj. 6,153
Lamont, Johann, *Lab., Glasgow region*
Lennon, Monica, *Lab., Central Scotland region*
Leonard, Richard, *Lab., Central Scotland region*
Lindhurst, Gordon, *C., Lothian region*
Lochhead, Richard, *SNP, Moray,* Maj. 2,875
Lockhart, Dean, *C., Mid Scotland and Fife region*
Lyle, Richard, *SNP, Uddingston and Bellshill,* Maj. 4,809
McAlpine, Joan, *SNP, South Scotland region*
McArthur, Liam, *LD, Orkney Islands,* Maj. 4,534
MacDonald, Angus, *SNP, Falkirk East,* Maj. 8,312
MacDonald, Gordon, *SNP, Edinburgh Pentlands,* Maj. 2,456
Macdonald, Lewis, *Lab., North East Scotland region*
McDonald, Mark, *SNP, Aberdeen Donside,* Maj. 11,630
MacGregor, Fulton, *SNP, Coatbridge and Chryston,* Maj. 3,779
‡ Macintosh, Ken, *no party affiliation, West Scotland region*
Mackay, Derek, *SNP, Renfrewshire North and West,* Maj. 7,373
Mackay, Rona, *SNP, Strathkelvin and Bearsden,* Maj. 8,100
McKee, Ivan, *SNP, Glasgow Provan,* Maj. 4,783
McKelvie, Christina, *SNP, Hamilton, Larkhall and Stonehouse,* Maj. 5,437
McMillan, Stuart, *SNP, Greenock and Inverclyde,* Maj. 8,230
McNeill, Pauline, *Lab., Glasgow region*
Macpherson, Ben, *SNP, Edinburgh Northern and Leith,* Maj. 6,746
Maguire, Ruth, *SNP, Cunninghame South,* Maj. 5,693
Marra, Jenny, *Lab., North East Scotland region*
Martin, Gillian, *SNP, Aberdeenshire East,* Maj. 5,837
Mason, John, *SNP, Glasgow Shettleston,* Maj. 7,323
† Mason, Tom, *C., North East Scotland region*
Matheson, Michael, *SNP, Falkirk West,* Maj. 11,280
Mitchell, Margaret, *C., Central Scotland region*
Mountain, Edward, *C., Highlands and Islands region*
Mundell, Oliver, *C., Dumfriesshire,* Maj. 1,230
Neil, Alex, *SNP, Airdrie and Shotts,* Maj. 6,192
Paterson, Gil, *SNP, Clydebank and Milngavie,* Maj. 8,432
Rennie, Willie, *LD, North East Fife,* Maj. 3,465
Robison, Shona, *SNP, Dundee City East,* Maj. 10,898
Ross, Gail, *SNP, Caithness, Sutherland and Ross,* Maj. 3,913
Rowley, Alex, *Lab., Mid Scotland and Fife region*
Rumbles, Mike, *LD, North East Scotland region*
Ruskell, Mark, *Green, Mid Scotland and Fife region*
Russell, Michael, *SNP, Argyll and Bute,* Maj. 5,978
Sarwar, Anas, *Lab., Glasgow region*
Scott, John, *C., Ayr,* Maj. 750
Scott, Tavish, *LD, Shetland Islands,* Maj. 4,895
Simpson, Graham, *C., Central Scotland region*
Smith, Elaine, *Lab., Central Scotland region*
Smith, Liz, *C., Mid Scotland and Fife region*
Smyth, Colin, *Lab., South Scotland region*
Somerville, Shirley-Anne, *SNP, Dunfermline,* Maj. 4,558
Stevenson, Stewart, *SNP, Banffshire and Buchan Coast,* Maj. 6,583
Stewart, Alexander, *C., Mid Scotland and Fife region*
Stewart, David, *Lab., Highlands and Islands region*
Stewart, Kevin, *SNP, Aberdeen Central,* Maj. 4,349
Sturgeon, Nicola, *SNP, Glasgow Southside,* Maj. 9,593
Swinney, John, *SNP, Perthshire North,* Maj. 3,336
Todd, Maree, *SNP, Highlands and Islands region*
Tomkins, Adam, *C., Glasgow region*
Torrance, David, *SNP, Kirkcaldy,* Maj. 7,395

Watt, Maureen, *SNP, Aberdeen South and North Kincardine,* Maj. 2,755
Wells, Annie, *C., Glasgow region*
Wheelhouse, Paul, *SNP, South Scotland region*
White, Sandra, *SNP, Glasgow Kelvin,* Maj. 4,048
Whittle, Brian, *C., South Scotland region*
Wightman, Andy, *Green, Lothian region*
Yousaf, Humza, *SNP, Glasgow Pollok,* Maj. 6,482

The Presiding Officer, Ken Macintosh, MSP
Deputy Presiding Officers, Linda Fabiani, MSP; Christine Grahame, MSP

STATE OF THE PARTIES *as at 30 June 2017*

	Constituency MSPs	Regional MSPs	Total
Scottish National Party (SNP)	59	4	63
Scottish Conservative and Unionist Party (C.)	7	24	31
Scottish Labour Party (Lab.)	3	20	23
Scottish Green Party (Green)	0	6	6
Scottish Liberal Democrats (LD)	4	1	5
*Presiding Officer	–	1	1
Total	73	56	129

SCOTTISH GOVERNMENT

St Andrew's House, Regent Road, Edinburgh EH1 3DG
T 0300-244 4000
E ceu@gov.scot W www.gov.scot

The devolved government for Scotland is responsible for most of the issues of day-to-day concern to the people of Scotland, including health, education, justice, rural affairs and transport.

The Scottish government was known as the Scottish executive when it was established in 1999, following the first elections to the Scottish parliament. There has been a majority Scottish National Party administration since the elections in May 2011.

The government is led by a first minister who is nominated by the parliament and in turn appoints the other Scottish ministers who make up the cabinet.

Civil servants in Scotland are accountable to Scottish ministers, who are themselves accountable to the Scottish parliament.

CABINET

First Minister, Rt. Hon. Nicola Sturgeon, MSP
Deputy First Minister and Cabinet Secretary for Education and Skills, John Swinney, MSP
Cabinet Secretary for Communities, Social Security and Equalities, Angela Constance, MSP
Cabinet Secretary for Culture, Tourism and External Affairs, Fiona Hyslop, MSP
Cabinet Secretary for Economy, Jobs and Fair Work, Keith Brown, MSP
Cabinet Secretary for the Environment, Climate Change and Land Reform, Roseanna Cunningham, MSP
Cabinet Secretary for Finance and the Constitution, Derek Mackay, MSP
Cabinet Secretary for Health and Sport, Shona Robison, MSP
Cabinet Secretary for Justice, Michael Matheson, MSP
Cabinet Secretary for Rural Economy and Connectivity, Fergus Ewing, MSP
Minister for Business, Innovation and Energy, Paul Wheelhouse, MSP
Minister for Community Safety and Legal Affairs, Annabelle Ewing, MSP
Minister for Employability and Training, Jamie Hepburn, MSP
Minister for Further Education, Higher Education and Science, Shirley-Anne Somerville, MSP

Minister for International Development and Europe, Alasdair Allan, MSP
Minister for Local Government and Housing, Kevin Stewart, MSP
Minister for Mental Health, Maureen Watt, MSP
Minister for Parliamentary Business, Joe Fitzpatrick, MSP
Minister for Public Health and Sport, Aileen Campbell, MSP
Minister for Social Security, Jeane Freeman, MSP
Minister for Transport and the Islands, Humza Yousaf, MSP

LAW OFFICERS
Lord Advocate, James Wolffe, QC
Solicitor-General for Scotland, Alison di Rollo

STRATEGIC BOARD
Permanent Secretary, Leslie Evans
Director-General Constitution and External Affairs, Ken Thomson
Director-General, Economy, Liz Ditchburn
Director-General, Education, Communities and Justice, Paul Johnston
Director-General, Finance, Alyson Stafford
Director-General, Health and Social Care, Paul Gray
Director-General, Organisational Development and Operations, Sarah Davidson

GOVERNMENT DEPARTMENTS

CONSTITUTION AND EXTERNAL AFFAIRS
St Andrew's House, Regent Road, Edinburgh EH1 3DG
Director-General, Ken Thomson
Directorates: External Affairs; Legal Services (Solicitor to the Scottish Government); Strategy and Constitution; Parliamentary Counsel

ECONOMY
St Andrew's House, Regent Road, Edinburgh EH1 3DG
Director-General, Liz Ditchburn
Directorates: Agriculture and Rural Economy; Chief Economist; Chief Scientific Adviser for Rural Affairs, Food and the Environment; Culture, Tourism and Major Events; Economic Development; Energy and Climate Change; Environment and Forestry; Fair Work, Employability and Skills; Marine Scotland; Scottish Development International
Executive Agencies
Accountant in Bankruptcy
Drinking Water Quality Regulator
James Hutton Institute
Moredun Research Institute
Scottish Agricultural College
Transport Scotland
Waterwatch Scotland

EDUCATION, COMMUNITIES AND JUSTICE
St Andrew's House, Regent Road, Edinburgh EH1 3DG
Director-General Paul Johnston
Directorates: Advance Learning and Science; Children and Families; Education Analytical Services; Housing and Social Justice; Justice; Learning; Local Government and Communities; Safer Communities
Executive Agencies
Disclosure Scotland
Education Scotland
HM Chief Inspector of Prosecution in Scotland
HM Inspectorate of Constabulary
HM Inspectorate of Prisons
Inspectorate of Prosecution in Scotland

Justice of the Peace Advisory Committee
Scottish Prison Service
Student Awards Agency for Scotland
Visiting Committees for Scottish Penal Establishments

FINANCE
Victoria Quay, Edinburgh, EH6 6QQ
Director-General, Alyson Stafford
Directorates: Financial Strategy; Internal Audit
Executive Agencies
Audit Scotland
Scottish Public Pensions Agency

HEALTH AND SOCIAL CARE
St Andrew's House, Regent Road, Edinburgh EH1 3DG
Director-General Health and Social Care and Chief Executive NHS Scotland, Paul Gray
Directorates: Chief Medical Officer; Chief Nursing Officer; Health Finance; Health Workforce and Strategic Change; Health and Social Care Integration; Healthcare Quality and Improvement; Office of the Chief Executive NHS Scotland; Performance and Delivery; Population Health
Executive Agency
Scottish Children's Reporters Administration

ORGANISATIONAL DEVELOPMENT AND OPERATIONS
St Andrew's House, Regent Road, Edinburgh EH1 3DG
Directorates: Communications and Ministerial Support; Digital; Financial Management; People; Social Security; Scottish Procurement and Commercial

NON-MINISTERIAL DEPARTMENTS

FOOD STANDARDS SCOTLAND
Pilgrim House, Old Ford Road, Aberdeen AB11 5RL T 01224-285100
Chief Executive, Geoff Ogle

NATIONAL RECORDS OF SCOTLAND
General Register House, 2 Princes Street, Edinburgh EH1 3YY
T 0131-535 1314 W www.nrscotland.gov.uk
Registrar General and Keeper of the Records of Scotland, Tim Ellis

OFFICE OF THE SCOTTISH CHARITY REGULATOR
2nd Floor, Quadrant House, 9 Riverside Drive, Dundee DD1 4NY
T 01382-220446 W www.oscr.org.uk
Chief Executive, David Robb

REGISTERS OF SCOTLAND
Meadowbank House, 153 London Road, Edinburgh, Midlothian
EH8 7AU T 0800-169 9391 W www.ros.gov.uk
Keeper, Sheenagh Adams

REVENUE SCOTLAND
PO Box 24068, Victoria Quay, Edinburgh EH6 9BR T 0300-020 0310
W www.revenue.scot
Chief Executive, Elaine Lorimer

SCOTTISH COURTS AND TRIBUNALS SERVICE
Saughton House, Broomhouse Drive, Edinburgh EH11 3XD
T 0131-444 3352 W www.scotcourts.gov.uk
Chief Executive, Eric McQueen

SCOTTISH HOUSING REGULATOR
Buchanan House, 58 Port Dundas Road, Glasgow G4 0HF
T 0141-242 5642 W www.scottishhousingregulator.gov.uk
Chief Executive, Michael Cameron

SCOTTISH PARLIAMENT ELECTION RESULTS *as at 5 May 2016*

Electorate (E.) 4,099,407 Turnout (T.) 55.6%
See General Election Results for a list of party abbreviations

ABERDEEN CENTRAL
(Scotland North East Region)
E. 57,195 T. 26,704 (46.69%)
Kevin Stewart, SNP	11,648
Lewis Macdonald, Lab.	7,299
Tom Mason, C.	6,022
Ken McLeod, LD	1,735

SNP majority 4,349 (16.29%)
6.92% swing Lab. to SNP

ABERDEEN DONSIDE
(Scotland North East Region)
E. 61,200 T. 30,981 (50.62%)
Mark McDonald, SNP	17,339
Liam Kerr, C.	5,709
Greg Williams, Lab.	5,672
Isobel Davidson, LD	2,261

SNP majority 11,630 (37.54%)
4.82% swing SNP to C.

ABERDEEN SOUTH & KINCARDINE NORTH
(Scotland North East Region)
E. 59,710 T. 32,340 (54.16%)
Maureen Watt, SNP	13,604
Ross Thomson, C.	10,849
Alison Evison, Lab.	5,603
John Waddell, LD	2,284

SNP majority 2,755 (8.52%)
9.49% swing SNP to C.

ABERDEENSHIRE EAST
(Scotland North East Region)
E. 62,844 T. 34,753 (55.30%)
Gillian Martin, SNP	15,912
Colin Clark, C.	10,075
Christine Jardine, LD	6,611
Sarah Flavell, Lab.	2,155

SNP majority 5,837 (16.80%)
16.90% swing SNP to C.

ABERDEENSHIRE WEST
(Scotland North East Region)
E. 59,576 T. 35,198 (59.08%)
Alexander Burnett, C.	13,400
Dennis Robertson, SNP	12,500
Mike Rumbles, LD	7,262
Sarah Christina Duncan, Lab.	2,036

C. majority 900 (2.56%)
12.03% swing SNP to C.

AIRDRIE & SHOTTS
(Scotland Central Region)
E. 53,899 T. 26,573 (49.30%)
Alex Neil, SNP	13,954
Richard Leonard, Lab.	7,762
Eric Holford, C.	4,164
Louise Young, LD	693

SNP majority 6,192 (23.30%)
7.46% swing Lab. to SNP

ALMOND VALLEY
(Lothian Region)
E. 64,901 T. 34,872 (53.73%)
Angela Constance, SNP	18,475
Neil Findlay, Lab.	10,082
Stephanie Smith, C.	5,308
Charles Dundas, LD	1,007

SNP majority 8,393 (24.07%)
3.02% swing Lab. to SNP

ANGUS NORTH & MEARNS
(Scotland North East Region)
E. 54,268 T. 29,379 (54.14%)
Mairi Evans, SNP	13,417
Alex Johnstone, C.	10,945
John Ruddy, Lab.	2,752
Euan Davidson, LD	2,265

SNP majority 2,472 (8.41%)
10.41% swing SNP to C.

ANGUS SOUTH
(Scotland North East Region)
E. 56,278 T. 31,929 (56.73%)
Graeme Dey, SNP	15,622
Kirstene Hair, C.	11,318
Joanne McFadden, Lab.	3,773
Clive Sneddon, LD	1,216

SNP majority 4,304 (13.48%)
12.40% swing SNP to C.

ARGYLL & BUTE
(Highlands and Islands Region)
E. 48,804 T. 29,476 (60.40%)
Michael Russell, SNP	13,561
Alan Reid, LD	7,583
Donald Cameron, C.	5,840
Mick Rice, Lab.	2,492

SNP majority 5,978 (20.28%)
9.07% swing SNP to LD

AYR
(Scotland South Region)
E. 61,558 T. 37,615 (61.10%)
John Scott, C.	16,183
Jennifer Dunn, SNP	15,433
Brian McGinley, Lab.	5,283
Robbie Simpson, LD	716

C. majority 750 (1.99%)
0.67% swing C. to SNP

BANFFSHIRE & BUCHAN COAST
(Scotland North East Region)
E. 59,155 T. 28,683 (48.49%)
Stewart Stevenson, SNP	15,802
Peter Chapman, C.	9,219
Nathan Morrison, Lab.	2,372
David Evans, LD	1,290

SNP majority 6,583 (22.95%)
12.96% swing SNP to C.

CAITHNESS, SUTHERLAND & ROSS
(Highlands and Islands Region)
E. 55,176 T. 32,207 (58.37%)
Gail Ross, SNP	13,937
Jamie Stone, LD	10,024
Struan Mackie, C.	4,912
Leah Franchetti, Lab.	3,334

SNP majority 3,913 (12.15%)
6.96% swing SNP to LD

CARRICK, CUMNOCK & DOON VALLEY
(Scotland South Region)
E. 58,548 T. 31,680 (54.11%)
Jeane Freeman, SNP	14,690
Carol Mochan, Lab.	8,684
Lee Lyons, C.	7,666
Dawud Islam, LD	640

SNP majority 6,006 (18.96%)
4.98% swing Lab. to SNP

CLACKMANNANSHIRE & DUNBLANE
(Mid Scotland and Fife Region)
E. 50,557 T. 29,746 (58.84%)
Keith Brown, SNP	14,147
Craig Miller, Lab.	7,426
Alexander Stewart, C.	6,915
Christopher McKinlay, LD	1,258

SNP majority 6,721 (22.59%)
4.72% swing Lab. to SNP

CLYDEBANK & MILNGAVIE
(Scotland West Region)
E. 54,761 T. 32,838 (59.97%)
Gil Paterson, SNP	16,158
Gail Casey, Lab.	7,726
Maurice Golden, C.	6,029
Frank Bowles, LD	2,925

SNP majority 8,432 (25.68%)
11.58% swing Lab. to SNP

CLYDESDALE
(Scotland South Region)
E. 58,471 T. 33,619 (57.50%)
Aileen Campbell, SNP	14,821
Alex Allison, C.	8,842
Claudia Beamish, Lab.	6,895
Danny Meikle, Ind.	1,332
Bev Gauld, CSSInd.	909
Jennifer Jamieson Ball, LD	820

SNP majority 5,979 (17.78%)
8.88% swing SNP to C.

COATBRIDGE & CHRYSTON
(Scotland Central Region)
E. 54,169 T. 28,334 (52.31%)
Fulton MacGregor, SNP		13,605
Elaine Smith, Lab.		9,826
Robyn Halbert, C.		2,868
John Wilson, Green		1,612
Jenni Lang, LD		423

SNP majority 3,779 (13.34%)
12.56% swing Lab. to SNP

COWDENBEATH
(Mid Scotland and Fife Region)
E. 54,596 T. 29,734 (54.46%)
Annabelle Ewing, SNP		13,715
Alex Rowley, Lab.		10,674
Dave Dempsey, C.		4,251
Bryn Jones, LD		1,094

SNP majority 3,041 (10.23%)
7.54% swing Lab. to SNP

CUMBERNAULD & KILSYTH
(Scotland Central Region)
E. 49,964 T. 28,308 (56.66%)
Jamie Hepburn, SNP		17,015
Mark Griffin, Lab.		7,537
Anthony Newman, C.		3,068
Irene Lang, LD		688

SNP majority 9,478 (33.48%)
9.89% swing Lab. to SNP

CUNNINGHAME NORTH
(Scotland West Region)
E. 55,647 T. 31,965 (57.44%)
Kenneth Gibson, SNP		16,587
Jamie Greene, C.		7,863
Johanna Baxter, Lab.		6,735
Charity Pierce, LD		780

SNP majority 8,724 (27.29%)
5.83% swing SNP to C.

CUNNINGHAME SOUTH
(Scotland South Region)
E. 50,215 T. 25,695 (51.17%)
Ruth Maguire, SNP		13,416
Joe Cullinane, Lab.		7,723
Billy McClure, C.		3,940
Ruby Kirkwood, LD		616

SNP majority 5,693 (22.16%)
5.76% swing Lab. to SNP

DUMBARTON
(Scotland West Region)
E. 55,098 T. 33,598 (60.98%)
Jackie Baillie, Lab.		13,522
Gail Robertson, SNP		13,413
Maurice Corry, C.		4,891
Aileen Morton, LD		1,131
Andrew Muir, Ind.		641

Lab. majority 109 (0.32%)
2.71% swing Lab. to SNP

DUMFRIESSHIRE
(Scotland South Region)
E. 60,698 T. 36,260 (59.74%)
Oliver Mundell, C.		13,536
Joan McAlpine, SNP		12,306
Elaine Murray, Lab.		9,151
Richard Brodie, LD		1,267

C. majority 1,230 (3.39%)
10.99% swing Lab. to C.

DUNDEE EAST
(Scotland North East Region)
E. 55,261 T. 28,437 (51.46%)
Shona Robison, SNP		16,509
Richard McCready, Lab.		5,611
Bill Bowman, C.		4,969
Craig Duncan, LD		911
Leah Ganley, TUSC		437

SNP majority 10,898 (38.32%)
1.57% swing SNP to Lab.

DUNDEE WEST
(Scotland North East Region)
E. 53,830 T. 27,788 (51.62%)
Joe FitzPatrick, SNP		16,070
Jenny Marra, Lab.		7,242
Nicola Ross, C.		2,826
Daniel Coleman, LD		1,008
Jim McFarlane, TUSC		642

SNP majority 8,828 (31.77%)
2.79% swing Lab. to SNP

DUNFERMLINE
(Scotland Mid and Fife Region)
E. 57,740 T. 32,909 (57.00%)
Shirley-Anne Somerville, SNP		14,257
Cara Hilton, Lab.		9,699
James Reekie, C.		5,797
James Calder, LD		3,156

SNP majority 4,558 (13.85%)
5.92% swing Lab. to SNP

EAST KILBRIDE
(Scotland Central Region)
E. 61,134 T. 34,629 (56.64%)
Linda Fabiani, SNP		19,371
LizAnne Handibode, Lab.		8,392
Graham Simpson, C.		5,857
Paul McGarry, LD		1,009

SNP majority 10,979 (31.70%)
12.59% swing Lab. to SNP

EAST LOTHIAN
(Scotland South Region)
E. 60,848 T. 37,913 (62.31%)
Iain Gray, Lab.		14,329
DJ Johnston-Smith, SNP		13,202
Rachael Hamilton, C.		9,045
Ettie Spencer, LD		1,337

Lab. majority 1,127 (2.97%)
1.25% swing SNP to Lab.

EASTWOOD
(Scotland West Region)
E. 53,085 T. 36,255 (68.30%)
Jackson Carlaw, C.		12,932
Stewart Maxwell, SNP		11,321
Ken Macintosh, Lab.		11,081
John Duncan, LD		921

C. majority 1,611 (4.44%)
5.70% swing Lab. to C.

EDINBURGH CENTRAL
(Lothian Region)
E. 59,581 T. 34,169 (57.35%)
Ruth Davidson, C.		10,399
Alison Dickie, SNP		9,789
Sarah Boyack, Lab.		7,546
Alison Johnstone, Green		4,644
Hannah Bettsworth, LD		1,672
Tom Laird, SLP		119

C. majority 610 (1.79%)
9.73% swing SNP to C.

EDINBURGH EASTERN
(Lothian Region)
E. 62,817 T. 35,397 (56.35%)
Ash Denham, SNP		16,760
Kezia Dugdale, Lab.		11,673
Nick Cook, C.		5,700
Cospatric D'Inverno, LD		1,264

SNP majority 5,087 (14.37%)
3.55% swing Lab. to SNP

EDINBURGH NORTHERN & LEITH
(Lothian Region)
E. 67,273 T. 37,102 (55.15%)
Ben Macpherson, SNP		17,322
Lesley Hinds, Lab.		10,576
Iain McGill, C.		6,081
Martin Veart, LD		1,779
Jack Caldwell, Ind.		1,344

SNP majority 6,746 (18.18%)
10.05% swing Lab. to SNP

EDINBURGH PENTLANDS
(Lothian Region)
E. 55,241 T. 33,353 (60.38%)
Gordon MacDonald, SNP		13,181
Gordon Lindhurst, C.		10,725
Blair Heary, Lab.		7,811
Emma Farthing-Sykes, LD		1,636

SNP majority 2,456 (7.36%)
0.76% swing C. to SNP

EDINBURGH SOUTHERN
(Lothian Region)
E. 59,587 T. 38,259 (64.21%)
Daniel Johnson, Lab.		13,597
Jim Eadie, SNP		12,474
Miles Briggs, C.		9,972
Pramod Subbaraman, LD		2,216

Lab. majority 1,123 (2.94%)
2.49% swing SNP to Lab.

EDINBURGH WESTERN
(Lothian Region)
E. 61,666 T. 39,766 (64.49%)

Alex Cole-Hamilton, LD	16,645
Toni Giugliano, SNP	13,685
Sandy Batho, C.	5,686
Cat Headley, Lab.	3,750

LD majority 2,960 (7.44%)
7.74% swing SNP to LD

ETTRICK, ROXBURGH & BERWICKSHIRE
(Scotland South Region)
E. 54,506 T. 33,095 (60.72%)

John Lamont, C.	18,257
Paul Wheelhouse, SNP	10,521
Jim Hume, LD	2,551
Barrie Cunning, Lab.	1,766

C. majority 7,736 (23.38%)
2.43% swing SNP to C.

FALKIRK EAST
(Scotland Central Region)
E. 60,271 T. 32,524 (53.96%)

Angus MacDonald, SNP	16,720
Craig Martin, Lab.	8,408
Callum Laidlaw, C.	6,342
James Munro, LD	1,054

SNP majority 8,312 (25.56%)
6.50% swing Lab. to SNP

FALKIRK WEST
(Scotland Central Region)
E. 59,812 T. 32,083 (53.64%)

Michael Matheson, SNP	18,260
Mandy Telford, Lab.	6,980
Alison Harris, C.	5,877
Gillian Cole-Hamilton, LD	966

SNP majority 11,280 (35.16%)
7.39% swing Lab. to SNP

FIFE MID & GLENROTHES
(Scotland Mid and Fife Region)
E. 53,241 T. 28,547 (53.62%)

Jenny Gilruth, SNP	15,555
Kay Morrison, Lab.	7,279
Alex Stewart-Clark, C.	4,427
Jane-Ann Liston, LD	1,286

SNP majority 8,276 (28.99%)
6.54% swing Lab. to SNP

FIFE NORTH EAST
(Scotland Mid and Fife Region)
E. 54,052 T. 34,063 (63.02%)

Willie Rennie, LD	14,928
Roderick Campbell, SNP	11,463
Huw Bell, C.	5,646
Rosalind Garton, Lab.	2,026

LD majority 3,465 (10.17%)
9.45% swing SNP to LD

GALLOWAY & WEST DUMFRIES
(Scotland South Region)
E. 56,321 T. 33,363 (59.24%)

Finlay Carson, C.	14,527
Aileen McLeod, SNP	13,013
Fiona O'Donnell, Lab.	4,876
Andrew Metcalf, LD	947

C. majority 1,514 (4.54%)
0.83% swing SNP to C.

GLASGOW ANNIESLAND
(Glasgow Region)
E. 57,884 T. 29,016 (50.13%)

Bill Kidd, SNP	15,007
Bill Butler, Lab.	8,854
Adam Tomkins, C.	4,057
James Speirs, LD	1,098

SNP majority 6,153 (21.21%)
10.59% swing Lab. to SNP

GLASGOW CATHCART
(Glasgow Region)
E. 60,871 T. 30,637 (50.33%)

James Dornan, SNP	16,200
Soryia Siddique, Lab.	6,810
Kyle Thornton, C.	4,514
Margot Clark, LD	1,703
Brian Smith, TUSC	909
Chris Creighton, Ind.	501

SNP majority 9,390 (30.65%)
12.29% swing Lab. to SNP

GLASGOW KELVIN
(Glasgow Region)
E. 62,203 T. 28,442 (45.72%)

Sandra White, SNP	10,964
Patrick Harvie, Green	6,916
Michael Shanks, Lab.	5,968
Sheila Mechan, C.	3,346
Carole Ford, LD	1,050
Tom Muirhead, Ind.	198

SNP majority 4,048 (14.23%)

GLASGOW MARYHILL & SPRINGBURN
(Glasgow Region)
E. 53,647 T. 23,612 (44.01%)

Bob Doris, SNP	13,109
Patricia Ferguson, Lab.	7,507
John Anderson, C.	2,305
James Harrison, LD	691

SNP majority 5,602 (23.73%)
15.01% swing Lab. to SNP

GLASGOW POLLOK
(Glasgow Region)
E. 61,350 T. 27,943 (45.55%)

Humza Yousaf, SNP	15,316
Johann Lamont, Lab.	8,834
Thomas Haddow, C.	2,653
Isabel Nelson, LD	585
Ian Leech, TUSC	555

SNP majority 6,482 (23.20%)
12.96% swing Lab. to SNP

GLASGOW PROVAN
(Glasgow Region)
E. 56,169 T. 24,077 (42.87%)

Ivan McKee, SNP	13,140
Paul Martin, Lab.	8,357
Annie Wells, C.	2,062
Tom Coleman, LD	518

SNP majority 4,783 (19.87%)
15.35% swing Lab. to SNP

GLASGOW SHETTLESTON
(Glasgow Region)
E. 58,021 T. 25,375 (43.73%)

John Mason, SNP	14,198
Thomas Rannachan, Lab.	6,875
Thomas Kerr, C.	3,151
Jamie Cocozza, TUSC	583
Giovanni Caccavello, LD	568

SNP majority 7,323 (28.86%)
13.05% swing Lab. to SNP

GLASGOW SOUTHSIDE
(Glasgow Region)
E. 52,141 T. 24,903 (47.76%)

Nicola Sturgeon, SNP	15,287
Fariha Thomas, Lab.	5,694
Graham Hutchison, C.	3,100
Kevin Lewsey, LD	822

SNP majority 9,593 (38.52%)
9.64% swing Lab. to SNP

GREENOCK & INVERCLYDE
(Scotland West Region)
E. 55,171 T. 31,725 (57.50%)

Stuart McMillan, SNP	17,032
Siobhan McCready, Lab.	8,802
Graeme Brooks, C.	4,487
John Watson, LD	1,404

SNP majority 8,230 (25.94%)
13.88% swing Lab. to SNP

HAMILTON, LARKHALL & STONEHOUSE
(Scotland Central Region)
E. 57,656 T. 28,885 (50.10%)

Christina McKelvie, SNP	13,945
Margaret McCulloch, Lab.	8,508
Margaret Mitchell, C.	5,596
Eileen Baxendale, LD	836

SNP majority 5,437 (18.82%)
5.05% swing Lab. to SNP

INVERNESS & NAIRN
(Highlands and Islands Region)
E. 66,619 T. 38,317 (57.52%)

Fergus Ewing, SNP	18,505
Edward Mountain, C.	7,648
David Stewart, Lab.	6,719
Carolyn Caddick, LD	5,445

SNP majority 10,857 (28.33%)
5.80% swing SNP to C.

KILMARNOCK & IRVINE VALLEY
(Scotland South Region)
E. 62,620 T. 34,385 (54.91%)

Willie Coffey, SNP	19,047
Dave Meechan, Lab.	7,853
Brian Whittle, C.	6,597
Rebecca Plenderleith, LD	888

SNP majority 11,194 (32.55%)
6.87% swing Lab. to SNP

KIRKCALDY
(Scotland Mid and Fife Region)
E. 59,533 T. 31,108 (52.25%)

David Torrance, SNP	16,358
Claire Baker, Lab.	8,963
Martin Laidlaw, C.	4,568
Lauren Jones, LD	1,219

SNP majority 7,395 (23.77%)
11.56% swing Lab. to SNP

LINLITHGOW
(Lothian Region)
E. 71,434 T. 38,407 (53.77%)

Fiona Hyslop, SNP	19,362
Angela Moohan, Lab.	10,027
Charles Kennedy, C.	7,699
Dan Farthing-Sykes, LD	1,319

SNP majority 9,335 (24.31%)
6.17% swing Lab. to SNP

MIDLOTHIAN NORTH & MUSSELBURGH
(Lothian Region)
E. 63,360 T. 34,685 (54.74%)

Colin Beattie, SNP	16,948
Bernard Harkins, Lab.	9,913
Jeremy Balfour, C.	6,267
Jacquie Bell, LD	1,557

SNP majority 7,035 (20.28%)
5.12% swing Lab. to SNP

MIDLOTHIAN SOUTH, TWEEDDALE & LAUDERDALE
(Scotland South Region)
E. 60,204 T. 35,581 (59.10%)

Christine Grahame, SNP	16,031
Michelle Ballantyne, C.	10,163
Fiona Dugdale, Lab.	5,701
Kris Chapman, LD	3,686

SNP majority 5,868 (16.49%)
7.63% swing SNP to C.

MORAY
(Highlands and Islands Region)
E. 61,969 T. 33,421 (53.93%)

Richard Lochhead, SNP	15,742
Douglas Ross, C.	12,867
Sean Morton, Lab.	3,547
Jamie Paterson, LD	1,265

SNP majority 2,875 (8.60%)
14.83% swing SNP to C.

MOTHERWELL & WISHAW
(Scotland Central Region)
E. 57,045 T. 29,111 (51.03%)

Clare Adamson, SNP	15,291
John Pentland, Lab.	9,068
Meghan Gallacher, C.	3,991
Yvonne Finlayson, LD	761

SNP majority 6,223 (21.38%)
11.89% swing Lab. to SNP

NA H-EILEANAN AN IAR
(Highlands and Islands Region)
E. 21,695 T. 13,206 (60.87%)

Alasdair Allan, SNP	6,874
Rhoda Grant, Lab.	3,378
Ranald Fraser, C.	1,499
John Cormack, SCP	1,162
Ken MacLeod, LD	293

SNP majority 3,496 (26.47%)
5.10% swing SNP to Lab.

ORKNEY
(Highlands and Islands Region)
E. 16,997 T. 10,534 (61.98%)

Liam McArthur, LD	7,096
Donna Heddle, SNP	2,562
Jamie Halcro Johnston, C.	435
Gerry McGarvey, Lab.	304
Paul Dawson, Ind.	137

LD majority 4,534 (43.04%)
16.20% swing SNP to LD

PAISLEY
(Scotland West Region)
E. 51,673 T. 29,464 (57.02%)

George Adam, SNP	14,682
Neil Bibby, Lab.	9,483
Paul Masterton, C.	3,533
Eileen McCartin, LD	1,766

SNP majority 5,199 (17.65%)
8.34% swing Lab. to SNP

PERTHSHIRE NORTH
(Scotland and Mid Fife Region)
E. 54,255 T. 34,025 (62.71%)

John Swinney, SNP	16,526
Murdo Fraser, C.	13,190
Anna McEwan, Lab.	2,604
Peter Barrett, LD	1,705

SNP majority 3,336 (9.80%)
12.38% swing SNP to C.

PERTHSHIRE SOUTH & KINROSS-SHIRE
(Scotland and Mid Fife Region)
E. 59,397 T. 36,149 (60.86%)

Roseanna Cunningham, SNP	15,315
Liz Smith, C.	13,893
Scott Nicholson, Lab.	3,389
Willie Robertson, LD	3,008
Craig Finlay, Community	544

SNP majority 1,422 (3.93%)
9.51% swing SNP to C.

RENFREWSHIRE NORTH & WEST
(Scotland West Region)
E. 50,555 T. 30,807 (60.94%)

Derek Mackay, SNP	14,718
David Wilson, C.	7,345
Mary Fee, Lab.	7,244
Rod Ackland, LD	888
Jim Halfpenny, TUSC	414
Peter Morton, Ind.	198

SNP majority 7,373 (23.93%)
1.02% swing C. to SNP

RENFREWSHIRE SOUTH
(Scotland West Region)
E. 49,422 T. 29,681 (60.06%)

Thomas Arthur, SNP	14,272
Paul O'Kane, Lab.	9,864
Ann Le Blond, C.	4,752
Tristan Gray, LD	793

SNP majority 4,408 (14.85%)
12.21% swing Lab. to SNP

RUTHERGLEN
(Glasgow Region)
E. 60,702 T. 32,952 (54.28%)

Clare Haughey, SNP	15,222
James Kelly, Lab.	11,479
Taylor Muir, C.	3,718
Robert Brown, LD	2,533

SNP majority 3,743 (11.36%)
8.96% swing Lab. to SNP

SHETLAND ISLANDS
(Highlands and Islands Region)
E. 17,784 T. 11,041 (62.08%)

Tavish Scott, LD	7,440
Danus Skene, SNP	2,545
Robina Barton, Lab.	651
Cameron Smith, C.	405

LD majority 4,895 (44.33%)
4.45% swing SNP to LD

SKYE, LOCHABER & BADENOCH
(Highlands and Islands Region)
E. 59,537 T. 36,505 (61.31%)

Kate Forbes, SNP	17,362
Angela MacLean, LD	8,319
Robbie Munro, C.	5,887
Linda Stewart, Lab.	3,821
Ronnie Campbell, Ind.	1,116

SNP majority 9,043 (24.77%)
4.56% swing LD to SNP

STIRLING
(Scotland and Mid Fife Region)
E. 55,785 T. 34,189 (61.29%)

Bruce Crawford, SNP	16,303
Dean Lockhart, C.	9,585
Rebecca Bell, Lab.	6,885
Elisabeth Wilson, LD	1,416

SNP majority 6,718 (19.65%)
7.03% swing SNP to C.

STRATHKELVIN & BEARSDEN
(Scotland West Region)
E. 62,598 T. 39,188 (62.60%)

Rona Mackay, SNP	17,060
Andrew Polson, C.	8,960
Margaret McCarthy, Lab.	8,288
Katy Gordon, LD	4,880

SNP majority 8,100 (20.67%)
4.21% swing SNP to C.

UDDINGSTON & BELLSHILL
(Central Scotland Region)
E. 57,556 T. 29,543 (51.33%)

Richard Lyle, SNP	14,424
Michael McMahon, Lab.	9,615
Andrew Morrison, C.	4,693
Kaitey Blair, LD	811

SNP majority 4,809 (16.28%)
9.57% swing Lab. to SNP

REGIONS *as at 5 May 2016*
E. 4,099,407 T. 55.6%

GLASGOW
E. 522,988 T. 248,109 (47.44%)

SNP	111,101	(44.78%)
Lab.	59,151	(23.84%)
C.	29,533	(11.90%)
Green	23,398	(9.43%)
LD	5,850	(2.36%)
UKIP	4,889	(1.97%)
Solidarity	3,593	(1.45%)
RISE	2,454	(0.99%)
UP	2,453	(0.99%)
Women	2,091	(0.84%)
Animal	1,819	(0.73%)
SCP	1,506	(0.61%)
Ind.	271	(0.11%)

SNP majority 51,950 (20.94%)
8.05% swing Lab. to SNP (2011 SNP majority 10,078)
ADDITIONAL MEMBERS

Adam Tomkins, C.	James Kelly, Lab.
Annie Wells, C.	Pauline McNeill, Lab.
Anas Sarwar, Lab.	Patrick Harvie, Green
Johann Lamont, Lab.	

HIGHLANDS AND ISLANDS
E. 348,581 T. 205,313 (58.90%)

SNP	81,600	(39.74%)
C.	44,693	(21.77%)
LD	27,223	(13.26%)
Lab.	22,894	(11.15%)
Green	14,781	(7.20%)
UKIP	5,344	(2.60%)
Ind.	3,689	(1.80%)
SCP	3,407	(1.66%)
RISE	889	(0.43%)
Solidarity	793	(0.39%)

SNP majority 36,907 (17.98%)
8.95% swing SNP to C. (2011 SNP majority 59,198)
ADDITIONAL MEMBERS

Douglas Ross, C.	David Steward, Lab.
Edward Mountain, C.	Maree Todd, SNP
Donald Cameron, C.	John Finnie, Green
Rhoda Grant, Lab.	

LOTHIAN
E. 565,860 T. 327,178 (57.82%)

SNP	118,546	(36.23%)
C.	74,972	(22.91%)
Lab.	67,991	(20.78%)
Green	34,551	(10.56%)
LD	18,479	(5.65%)
UKIP	5,802	(1.77%)
Women	3,877	(1.18%)
RISE	1,641	(0.50%)
Solidarity	1,319	(0.40%)

SNP majority 43,574 (13.32%)
7.10% swing SNP to C. (2011 SNP majority 40,409)
ADDITIONAL MEMBERS

Miles Briggs, C.	Neil Findlay, Lab.
Gordon Lindhurst, C.	Alison Johnstone, Green
Jeremy Balfour, C.	Andy Wightman, Green
Kezia Dugdale, Lab.	

SCOTLAND CENTRAL
E. 511,506 T. 270,706 (52.92%)

SNP	129,082	(47.68%)
Lab.	67,103	(24.79%)
C.	43,602	(16.11%)
Green	12,722	(4.70%)
UKIP	6,088	(2.25%)
LD	5,015	(1.85%)
Solidarity	2,684	(0.99%)
SCP	2,314	(0.85%)
RISE	1,636	(0.60%)
Ind.	460	(0.17%)

SNP majority 61,979 (22.90%)
5.92% swing Lab. to SNP (2011 SNP majority 25,802)
ADDITIONAL MEMBERS

Margaret Mitchell, C.	Monica Lennon, Lab.
Graham Simpson, C.	Mark Griffin, Lab.
Alison Harris, C.	Elaine Smith, Lab.
Richard Leonard, Lab.	

SCOTLAND MID AND FIFE
E. 499,156 T. 291,172 (58.33%)

SNP	120,128	(41.26%)
C.	73,293	(25.17%)
Lab.	51,373	(17.64%)
LD	20,401	(7.01%)
Green	17,860	(6.13%)
UKIP	5,345	(1.84%)
RISE	1,073	(0.37%)
Solidarity	1,049	(0.36%)
SLP	650	(0.22%)

SNP majority 46,835 (16.08%)
7.50% swing SNP to C. (2011 SNP majority 52,068)
ADDITIONAL MEMBERS

Murdo Fraser, C.	Alex Rowley, Lab.
Liz Smith, C.	Claire Baker, Lab.
Dean Lockhart, C.	Mark Ruskell, Green
Alexander Stewart, C.	

SCOTLAND NORTH EAST
E. 579,317 T. 307,006 (52.99%)

SNP	137,086	(44.65%)
C.	85,848	(27.96%)
Lab.	38,791	(12.64%)
LD	18,444	(6.01%)
Green	15,123	(4.93%)
UKIP	6,376	(2.08%)
SCP	2,068	(0.67%)
Solidarity	992	(0.32%)
Nat Front	617	(0.20%)
RISE	599	(0.20%)
SLP	552	(0.18%)
Comm Brit	510	(0.17%)

SNP majority 51,238 (16.69%)
10.95% swing SNP to C. (2011 SNP majority 96,856)
ADDITIONAL MEMBERS

Alex Johnstone, C.	Jenny Marra, Lab.
Ross Thomson, C.	Lewis Macdonald, Lab.
Peter Chapman, C.	Mike Rumbles, LD
Liam Kerr, C.	

SCOTLAND SOUTH
E. 533,774 T. 314,192 (58.86%)

SNP	120,217	(38.26%)
C.	100,753	(32.07%)
Lab.	56,072	(17.85%)
Green	14,773	(4.70%)
LD	11,775	(3.75%)
UKIP	6,726	(2.14%)
CSSInd.	1,485	(0.47%)
Solidarity	1,294	(0.41%)
RISE	1,097	(0.35%)

SNP majority 19,464 (6.19%)
7.65% swing SNP to C. (2011 SNP majority 43,675)
ADDITIONAL MEMBERS

Rachel Hamilton, C.	Joan McAlpine, SNP
Brian Whittle, C.	Emma Harper, SNP
Claudia Beamish, Lab.	Paul Wheelhouse, SNP
Colin Smyth, Lab.	

SCOTLAND WEST
E. 538,225 T. 322,076 (59.84%)

SNP	135,827	(42.17%)
Lab.	72,544	(22.52%)
C.	71,528	(22.21%)
Green	17,218	(5.35%)
LD	12,097	(3.76%)
UKIP	5,856	(1.82%)
Solidarity	2,609	(0.81%)
SCP	2,391	(0.74%)
RISE	1,522	(0.47%)
SLP	484	(0.15%)

SNP majority 63,283 (19.65%)
5.44% swing Lab. to SNP (2011 SNP majority 24,776)
ADDITIONAL MEMBERS

Jamie Green, C.	Mary Fee, Lab.
Maurice Golden, C.	Ken Macintosh, Lab.
Maurice Corry, C.	Ross Greer, Green
Neil Bibby, Lab.	

THE SCOTTISH INDEPENDENCE REFERENDUM 2014

THE ROAD TO REFERENDUM
Following the establishment of a majority Scottish National Party (SNP) government at Holyrood in May 2011, the SNP officially launched its independence bid at its annual party conference in October the same year. In May 2012 the UK government published the results of the Scottish referendum consultation, which showed strong levels of support for a single clear question on independence.

THE EDINBURGH AGREEMENT
A series of talks between the Scottish government's deputy first minister Nicola Sturgeon and the Secretary of State for Scotland Michael Moore resulted in the Edinburgh Agreement. The agreement was signed by prime minister David Cameron and first minister Alex Salmond on 15 October 2012 and set out a timetable for a referendum vote to be held in autumn 2014.

THOSE AGED 16 GET TO VOTE
On 12 March 2013 the Scottish independence referendum (franchise) bill was brought before parliament to ensure that all those aged 16 and over on the date of the referendum were entitled to vote.

REFERENDUM RESULTS 18 SEPTEMBER 2014
Should Scotland be an independent country?

NO	YES
2,001,926 votes	1,617,989 votes
(55.3%)	(44.7%)
Turnout 84.6%	

PERCENTAGE OF VOTE BY REGION
Only four of the 32 Scottish local authority areas voted in favour of independence: Dundee City, Glasgow, North Lanarkshire and West Dunbartonshire.

Local Authority Area	No (%)	Yes (%)
Aberdeen City	58.6	41.4
Aberdeenshire	60.4	39.6
Angus	56.3	43.7
Argyll and Bute	58.5	41.5
Clackmannanshire	53.8	46.2
Dumfries and Galloway	65.7	34.3
Dundee City	42.7	57.3
East Ayrshire	52.8	47.2
East Dunbartonshire	61.2	38.8
East Lothian	61.7	38.3
East Renfrewshire	63.2	36.8
Edinburgh City	61.1	38.9
Falkirk	53.5	46.5
Fife	55.0	45.0
Glasgow City	46.5	53.5
Highland	52.9	47.1
Inverclyde	50.1	49.9
Midlothian	56.3	43.7
Moray	57.6	42.4
North Ayrshire	51.0	49.0
North Lanarkshire	48.9	51.1
Orkney	67.2	32.8
Perth and Kinross	60.2	39.8
Renfrewshire	52.8	47.2
Scottish Borders	66.6	33.4
Shetland	63.7	36.3
South Ayrshire	57.9	42.1
South Lanarkshire	54.7	45.3
Stirling	59.8	40.2
West Dunbartonshire	46.0	54.0
Western Isles (Eilean Siar)	53.4	46.6
West Lothian	55.2	44.8

NORTHERN IRELAND

NORTHERN IRELAND ASSEMBLY
Parliament Buildings, Stormont, Belfast BT4 3XX
T 028-9052 1137 E info@niassembly.gov.uk
W www.niassembly.gov.uk

The Northern Ireland Assembly was established as a result of the Belfast Agreement (also known as the Good Friday Agreement) in April 1998. The agreement was endorsed through a referendum held in May 1998 and subsequently given legal force through the Northern Ireland Act 1998.

The Northern Ireland Assembly has full legislative and executive authority for all matters that are the responsibility of the government's Northern Ireland departments – known as transferred matters. Excepted and reserved matters are defined in schedules 2 and 3 of the Northern Ireland Act 1998 and remain the responsibility of UK parliament.

The first assembly election occurred on 25 June 1998 and the 108 members elected met for the first time on 1 July 1998.

On 29 November 1999 the assembly appointed ten ministers as well as the chairs and deputy chairs for the ten statutory departmental committees. Devolution of powers to the Northern Ireland Assembly occurred on 2 December 1999, following several delays concerned with Sinn Fein's inclusion in the executive while Irish Republican Army (IRA) weapons were yet to be decommissioned.

Since the devolution of powers, the assembly has been suspended by the Secretary of State for Northern Ireland on four occasions. The first was between 11 February and 30 May 2000, with two 24-hour suspensions on 10 August and 22 September 2001 – all owing to a lack of progress in decommissioning. The final suspension took place on 14 October 2002 after unionists walked out of the executive following a police raid on Sinn Fein's office investigating alleged intelligence gathering.

The assembly was formally dissolved in April 2003 in anticipation of an election, which eventually took place on 26 November 2003. The results of the election changed the balance of power between the political parties, with an increase in the number of seats held by the Democratic Unionist Party (DUP) and Sinn Fein (SF), so that they became the largest parties. The assembly was restored to a state of suspension following the November election while political parties engaged in a review of the Belfast Agreement aimed at fully restoring the devolved institutions.

In July 2005 the leadership of the IRA formally ordered an end to its armed campaign; it authorised a representative to engage with the Independent International Commission on Decommissioning in order to verifiably put the arms beyond use. On 26 September 2005 General John de Chastelain, the chair of the commission, along with two independent church witnesses confirmed that the IRA's entire arsenal of weapons had been decommissioned.

Following the passing of the Northern Ireland Act 2006 the secretary of state created a non-legislative fixed-term assembly, whose membership consisted of the 108 members elected in the 2003 election. It first met on 15 May 2006 with the remit of making preparations for the restoration of devolved government; its discussions informed the next round of talks called by the British and Irish governments held at St Andrews. The St Andrews agreement of 13 October 2006 led to the establishment of the transitional assembly.

The Northern Ireland (St Andrews Agreement) Act 2006 set out a timetable to restore devolution, and also set the date for the third election to the assembly as 7 March 2007. The DUP and SF again had the largest number of Members of the Legislative Assembly (MLAs) elected, and although the initial restoration deadline of 26 March was missed, the leaders of the DUP and SF (Revd Dr Ian Paisley and Gerry Adams respectively) took part in a historic meeting and made a joint commitment to establish an executive committee in the assembly to which devolved powers were restored on 8 May 2007.

RECENT DEVELOPMENTS
Assembly elections took place on 5 May 2016 to elect the 108 members of the legislative assembly for a fifth term. This assembly collapsed on 9 January 2017 when Martin McGuinness resigned as Deputy First Minister. Under the joint protocols that govern the power-sharing agreement, if either the first minister or the deputy resigns and a replacement is not nominated by the relevant party within seven days, then a snap election must be called. The assembly was formerly dissolved at midnight on 25 January 2017 and the most recent assembly elections were held on 2 March 2017 to elect the 90 members of the legislative assembly. Under the Assembly Members (Reduction of Numbers) Act Northern Ireland 2016, the number of assembly members was reduced from 108 to 90 – five members to be elected by each constituency, rather than six – for the first assembly election to take place after the 2016 election.

Following the March 2017 election, negotiations to form an executive have missed both the normal three week deadline and an extended deadline of 29 June 2017 set by the Secretary of State for Northern Ireland. As both deadlines have passed the Northern Ireland secretary has a duty to set a date for a new election. This duty is currently under review and the assembly remains suspended until an executive is formed.

THE SINGLE TRANSFERABLE VOTE SYSTEM
Members of the Northern Ireland Assembly are elected by the single transferable vote system from 18 constituencies – five per constituency. Under the single transferable vote system every voter has a single vote that can be transferred from one candidate to another. Voters number their candidates in order of preference. Where candidates reach their quota of votes and are elected, surplus votes are transferred to other candidates according to the next preference on each voter's ballot slip. The candidate in each round with the fewest votes is eliminated and their surplus votes are redistributed according to the voter's next preference. The process is repeated until the required number of members are elected.

SALARIES

	2017–18
First Minister/Deputy First Minister	£121,500
Minister	£87,500
Junior Minister	£55,500
MLA	£49,500

NORTHERN IRELAND ASSEMBLY
MEMBERS *elected on 2 March 2017*

Agnew, Steven, *Green, Down North*
Aiken, Steve, OBE, *UUP, Antrim South*
Allen, Andy, *UUP, Belfast East*
Allister, Jim, *TUV, Antrim North*
Archibald, Caoimhe, *SF, Londonderry East*
Armstrong, Kellie, *Alliance, Strangford*
Bailey, Clare, *Green, Belfast South*
Barton, Rosemary, *UUP, Fermanagh and South Tyrone*
Beattie, Doug, MC, *UUP, Upper Bann*
Beggs, Roy, *UUP, Antrim East*
Boylan, Cathal, *SF, Newry and Armagh*
Boyle, Michaela, *SF, Tyrone West*
Bradley, Maurice, *DUP, Londonderry East*
Bradley, Paula, *DUP, Belfast North*
Bradley, Sinéad, *SDLP, Down South*
Bradshaw, Paula, *Alliance, Belfast South*
Buchanan, Keith, *DUP, Ulster Mid*
Buchanan, Thomas, *DUP, Tyrone West*
Buckley, Jonathan, *DUP, Upper Bann*

Bunting, Joanne, *DUP, Belfast East*
Butler, Robbie, *UUP, Lagan Valley*
Cameron, Pam, *DUP, Antrim South*
Carroll, Gerry, *PBP, Belfast West*
Catney, Pat, *SDLP, Lagan Valley*
Chambers, Alan, *UUP, Down North*
Dallat, John, *SDLP, Londonderry East*
Dickson, Stewart, *Alliance, Antrim East*
Dillon, Linda, *SF, Ulster Mid*
Dolan, Jemma, *SF, Fermanagh and South Tyrone*
Dunne, Gordon, *DUP, Down North*
Durkan, Mark, *SDLP, Foyle*
Easton, Alex, *DUP, Down North*
Eastwood, Colum, *SDLP, Foyle*
Ennis, Sinéad, *SF, Down South*
Farry, Dr Stephen, *Alliance, Down North*
Fearon, Megan, *SF, Newry and Armagh*
Flynn, Órlaithí, *SF, Belfast West*
Ford, David, *Alliance, Antrim South*
Foster, Arlene, *DUP, Fermanagh and South Tyrone*
Frew, Paul, *DUP, Antrim North*
Gildernew, Michelle, *SF, Fermanagh and South Tyrone*
Girvan, Paul, *DUP, Antrim South*
Givan, Paul, *DUP, Lagan Valley*
Hamilton, Simon, *DUP, Strangford*
Hanna, Claire, *SDLP, Belfast South*
Hazzard, Chris, *SF, Down South*
Hilditch, David, *DUP, Antrim East*
Humphrey, William, *DUP, Belfast North*
Irwin, William, *DUP, Newry and Armagh*
Kearney, Declan, *SF, Antrim South*
Kelly, Dolores, *SDLP, Upper Bann*
Kelly, Gerry, *SF, Belfast North*
Lockhart, Carla, *DUP, Upper Bann*
Long, Naomi, *Alliance, Belfast East*
Lunn, Trevor, *Alliance, Lagan Valley*
Lynch, Seán, *SF, Fermanagh and South Tyrone*
Lyons, Gordon, *DUP, Antrim East*
Lyttle, Chris, *Alliance, Belfast East*
McAleer, Declan, *SF, Tyrone West*
McCallion, Elisha, *SF, Foyle*
McCann, Fra, *SF, Belfast West*
McCartney, Raymond, *SF, Foyle*
McCrossan, Daniel, *SDLP, Tyrone West*
McElduff, Barry, *SF, Tyrone West*
McGlone, Patsy, *SDLP, Ulster Mid*
McGrath, Colin, *SDLP, Down South*
McGuigan, Philip, *SF, Antrim North*
McIlveen, Michelle, *DUP, Strangford*
McNulty, Justin, *SDLP, Newry and Armagh*
Mallon, Nichola, *SDLP, Belfast North*
Maskey, Alex, *SF, Belfast West*
Middleton, Gary, *DUP, Foyle*
Milne, Ian, *SF, Ulster Mid*
Murphy, Conor, *SF, Newry and Armagh*
Nesbitt, Mike, *UUP, Strangford*
Newton, Robin, *DUP, Belfast East*
Ní Chuilín, Carál, *SF, Belfast North*
O'Dowd, John, *SF, Upper Bann*
O'Neill, Michelle, *SF, Ulster Mid*
Ó Muilleoir, Máirtín, *SF, Belfast South*
Poots, Edwin, *DUP, Lagan Valley*
Robinson, George, *DUP, Londonderry East*
Sheehan, Pat, *SF, Belfast West*
Stalford, Christopher, *DUP, Belfast South*
Stewart, John, *UUP, Antrim East*
Storey, Mervyn, *DUP, Antrim North*
Sugden, Claire, *Ind., Londonderry East*
Swann, Robin, *UUP, Antrim North*
Weir, Peter, *DUP, Down North*
Wells, Jim, *DUP, Down South*

STATE OF THE PARTIES *as at 2 March 2017 election*

Party	Seats
Democratic Unionist Party (DUP)	28
Sinn Fein (SF)	27
Social Democratic and Labour Party (SDLP)	12
Ulster Unionist Party (UUP)	10
Alliance Party of Northern Ireland (Alliance)	8
Green Party (Green)	2
People Before Profit Alliance (PBP)	1
Traditional Unionist Voice (TUV)	1
Independents (Ind.)	1
Total	90

NORTHERN IRELAND EXECUTIVE
Stormont Castle, Stormont, Belfast BT4 3TT
T 028-9052 8400
W www.northernireland.gov.uk

The Northern Ireland Executive comprises the first minister, deputy first minister, two junior ministers and eight departmental ministers.

The executive exercises authority on behalf of the Northern Ireland Assembly, and takes decisions on significant issues and matters which cut across the responsibility of two or more ministers.

The executive also agrees proposals put forward by ministers for new legislation in the form of 'executive bills' for consideration by the assembly. It is also responsible for drawing up a programme for government and an agreed budget for approval by the assembly. Ministers of the executive are nominated by the political parties in the Northern Ireland Assembly. The number of ministers which a party can nominate is determined by its share of seats in the assembly. The first minister and deputy first minister are nominated by the largest and second largest parties respectively and act as chairs of the executive. Each executive minister has responsibility for a specific Northern Ireland government department.

EXECUTIVE COMMITTEE OF MINISTERS
There are currently no executive ministers in post since the most recent assembly elections which took place on 2 March 2017. Negotiations to appoint the executive committee of ministers in charge of the nine government departments failed to meet both the three-week deadline following the election and an extended deadline of 29 June 2017 set by the Secretary of State for Northern Ireland. The assembly remains suspended until an executive is formed.

NORTHERN IRELAND EXECUTIVE DEPARTMENTS
THE EXECUTIVE OFFICE, Stormont Castle, Stormont, Belfast BT4 3TT T 028-9052 8400 W www.executiveoffice-ni.gov.uk
DEPARTMENT OF AGRICULTURE, ENVIRONMENT AND RURAL AFFAIRS, Dundonald House, Upper Newtownards Road, Belfast BT4 3SB T 0300-200 7850 W www.daera-ni.gov.uk
DEPARTMENT FOR COMMUNITIES, Causeway Exchange, 1–7 Bedford Street, Belfast BT2 7EG T 028-9082 9000 W www.communities-ni.gov.uk
DEPARTMENT FOR THE ECONOMY, Netherleigh, Massey Avenue, Belfast BT4 2JP T 028-9052 9900 W www.economy-ni.gov.uk
DEPARTMENT OF EDUCATION, Rathgael House, Balloo Road, Bangor, Co. Down BT19 7PR T 028-9127 9279 W www.education-ni.gov.uk
DEPARTMENT OF FINANCE, Clare House, 303 Airport Road, Belfast BT3 9ED T 028-9185 8111 W www.finance-ni.gov.uk
DEPARTMENT OF HEALTH, Castle Buildings, Stormont, Belfast BT4 3SQ T 028-9052 0500 W www.health-ni.gov.uk
DEPARTMENT FOR INFRASTRUCTURE, Clarence Court, 10–18 Adelaide Street, Belfast BT2 8GB T 028-9054 0540 W www.infrastructure-ni.gov.uk

DEPARTMENT OF JUSTICE, Block B, Castle Buildings, Stormont Estate, Belfast BT4 3SG **T** 028-9076 3000
W www.justice-ni.gov.uk

NORTHERN IRELAND AUDIT OFFICE

106 University Street, Belfast BT7 1EU
T 028-9025 1000 **E** info@niauditoffice.gov.uk
W www.niauditoffice.gov.uk

The Northern Ireland Audit Office supports the Comptroller and Auditor-General in fulfilling his responsibilities. He is responsible for authorising the issue of money from central government funds to Northern Ireland departments and for both financial and value for money audits of central government bodies in Northern Ireland, including, Northern Ireland departments, executive agencies, executive non-departmental public bodies and health and social care bodies.

Comptroller and Auditor-General, Kieran Donnelly

OFFICE OF THE ATTORNEY-GENERAL FOR NORTHERN IRELAND

PO Box 1272, Belfast BT1 9LU
T 028-9072 5333 **E** contact@attorneygeneralni.gov.uk
W www.attorneygeneralni.gov.uk

With the devolution of justice responsibilities on 12 April 2010, the Justice (Northern Ireland) Act 2002 was enacted which established a new post of Attorney-General for Northern Ireland. The Attorney-General acts as the chief legal adviser to the Northern Ireland executive for both civil and criminal matters that fall within the devolved powers of the assembly. He is the executive's most senior representative in the courts and responsible for protecting the public interest in matters of law; overseeing the legal work of the in-house advisers to the executive and its departments; and for the appointment of the director and deputy director of the Public Prosecution Service for Northern Ireland. The Attorney-General participates in the assembly proceedings to the extent permitted by its standing orders, but does not vote in the assembly.

The post of Attorney-General is statutorily independent of the first minister, deputy first minister, the executive and the executive departments.

Attorney-General for Northern Ireland, John Larkin, QC

NORTHERN IRELAND ASSEMBLY ELECTION RESULTS *as at 2 March 2017*

Electorate (E.) 1,254,709 Turnout (T.) 64.8%

First = number of first-preference votes

See General Election Results for a list of party abbreviations

ANTRIM EAST
E. 62,933 T. 37,836 (60.12%)

	First	Round Elected
David Hilditch, DUP	6,000	3
Roy Beggs, UUP	5,121	6
Stewart Dickson, Alliance, DUP	4,179	6
Gordon Lyons, DUP	3,851	8
Oliver McMullan, SF	3,701	
John Stewart, UUP	3,377	9
Stephen Ross, DUP	3,313	
Danny Donnelly, Alliance	1,817	
Noel Jordan, UKIP	1,579	
Ruth Wilson, TUV	1,534	
Margaret McKillop, SDLP	1,524	
Dawn Patterson, Green	777	
Conor Sheridan, Lab. Alt	393	
Alan Dunlop, Lab. C	152	
Ricky Best, Ind.	106	

ANTRIM NORTH
E. 76,739 T. 48,518 (63.22%)

	First	Round Elected
Philip McGuigan, SF	7,600	6
Paul Frew, DUP	6,975	7
Mervyn Storey, DUP	6,857	7
Jim Allister, TUV	6,214	7
Robin Swann, UUP	6,022	6
Phillip Logan, DUP	5,708	
Connor Duncan, SDLP	3,519	
Patricia O'Lynn, Alliance	2,616	
Timothy Gaston, TUV	1,505	
Mark Bailey, Green	530	
Monica Digney, Ind.	435	
Adam McBride, Ind.	113	

ANTRIM SOUTH
E. 68,475 T. 42,726 (62.40%)

	First	Round Elected
Declan Kearney, SF	6,891	4
Steve Aiken, UUP	6,287	5
David Ford, Alliance	5,278	7
Paul Girvan, DUP	5,152	8
Pam Cameron, DUP	4,604	8
Trevor Clarke, DUP	4,522	
Roisin Lynch, SDLP	4,024	
Adrian Cochrane-Watson, UUP	2,505	
Richard Cairns, TUV	1,353	
Ivanka Antova, PBP	530	
David McMaster, Ind.	503	
Eleanor Bailey, Green	501	
Mark Logan, C.	194	

BELFAST EAST
E. 64,788 T. 40,828 (63.02%)

	First	Round Elected
Naomi Long, Alliance	7,610	1
Joanne Bunting, DUP	6,007	9
Andy Allen, UUP	5,275	9
Chris Lyttle, Alliance	5,059	8
Robin Newton, DUP	4,729	11
David Douglas, DUP	4,431	
John Kyle, PUP	2,658	
Georgina Milne, Green	1,447	
Mairead O'Donnell, SF	1,173	
Andrew Girvin, TUV.	917	
Courtney Robinson, CCLA	442	
Sheila Bodel, C.	275	
Séamas de Faoite, SDLP	250	
Jordy McKeag, Ind.	84	

BELFAST NORTH
E. 68,187 T. 42,119 (61.77%)

	First	Round Elected
Gerry Kelly, SF	6,275	7
Caral Ni Chuilin, SF	5,929	7
Nichola Mallon, SDLP	5,431	7
Paula Bradley, DUP	4,835	6
William Humphrey, DUP	4,418	6
Nelson McCausland, DUP	4,056	
Nuala McAllister, Alliance	3,487	
Robert Foster, UUP	2,418	
Julie-Anne Corr-Johnston, PUP	2,053	
Fiona Ferguson, PBP	1,559	
Malachai O'Hara, Green	711	
Gemma Weir, WP	248	
Adam Millar, Ind.	66	

BELFAST SOUTH
E. 61,309 T. 43,465 (70.89%)

	First	Round Elected
Mairtin O Muilleoir, SF	7,610	1
Claire Hanna, SDLP	6,559	6
Paula Bradshaw, Alliance	5,595	6
Christopher Stalford, DUP	4,529	9
Emma Little-Pengelly, DUP	4,446	
Clare Bailey, Green	4,247	9
Michael Henderson, UUP	3,863	
Emmet McDonough-Brown, Alliance	2,053	
Naomh Gallagher, SDLP	1,794	
Padraigin Mervyn, PBP	760	
John Hiddleston, TUV	703	
Sean Burns, Lab. Alt	531	
George Jabbour, C.	200	
Lily Kerr, WP	163	

BELFAST WEST
E. 61,309 T. 40,930 (66.76%)

	First	Round Elected
Orlaithi Flynn, SF	6,918	1
Alex Maskey, SF	6,346	3
Fra McCann, SF	6,201	4
Pat Sheehan, SF	5,466	4
Gerry Carroll, PBP	4,903	3
Frank McCoubrey, DUP	4,063	
Alex Attwood, SDLP	3,452	
Michael Collins, PBP	1,096	
Sorcha Eastwood, Alliance	747	
Fred Rodgers, UUP	486	
Connor Campbell, WP	415	
Ellen Murray, Green	251	

DOWN NORTH
E. 64,461 T. 38,174 (59.22%)

	First	Round Elected
Alex Easton, DUP	8,034	1
Alan Chambers, UUP	7,151	1
Stephen Farry, Alliance	7,014	1
Gordon Dunne, DUP	6,118	2
Steven Agnew, Green	5,178	7
Melanie Kennedy, Ind.	1,246	
William Cudworth, UUP	964	
Caoimhe McNeill, SDLP	679	
Frank Shivers, C.	641	
Kieran Maxwell, SF	591	
Chris Carter, Ind.	92	
Gavan Reynolds, Ind.	31	

DOWN SOUTH
E. 75,415 T. 49,934 (66.21%)

	First	Round Elected
Sinead Ennis, SF	10,256	1
Chris Hazzard, SF	8,827	1
Jim Wells, DUP	7,786	5
Sinead Bradley, SDLP	7,323	3
Colin McGrath, SDLP	5,110	7
Patrick Brown, Alliance	4,535	
Harold McKee, UUP	4,172	
Lyle Rea, TUV	630	
Hannah George, Green	483	
Patrick Clarke, Ind.	192	
Gary Hynds, C.	85	

FERMANAGH AND SOUTH TYRONE
E. 73,100 T. 53,075 (72.61%)

	First	Round Elected
Arlene Foster, DUP	8,479	2
Michelle Gildernew, SF	7,987	3
Jemma Dolan, SF	7,767	3
Maurice Morrow, DUP	7,102	
Sean Lynch, SF	6,254	4
Rosemary Barton, UUP	6,060	4
Richie McPhillips, SDLP	5,134	
Noreen Campbell, Alliance	1,437	
Alex Elliott, TUV	780	
Donal O'Cofaigh, Lab. Alt	643	
Tanya Jones, Green	550	
Ricahrd Dunn, C.	70	

FOYLE
E. 69,718 T. 45,317 (65.00%)

	First	Round Elected
Elisha McCallion, SF	9,205	1
Colum Eastwood, SDLP	7,240	3
Raymond McCartney, SF	7,145	2
Mark H. Durkan, SDLP	6,948	5
Gary Middleton, DUP	5,975	6
Eamon McCann, PBP	4,760	
Julia Kee, UUP	1,660	
Colm Cavanagh, Alliance	1,124	
Shannon Downey, Green	242	
John Lindsay, CISTA	196	
Stuart Canning, C.	77	
Arthur McGuinness, Ind.	44	

LAGAN VALLEY
E. 72,621 T. 45,440 (62.50%)

	First	Round Elected
Paul Givan, DUP	8,035	1
Robbie Butler, UUP	6,846	7
Trevor Lunn, Alliance	6,105	7
Edwin Poots, DUP	6,013	8
Brenda Hale, DUP	4,566	
Jenny Palmer, UUP	4,492	
Pat Catney, SDLP	3,795	8
Peter Doran, SF	1,801	
Samuel Morrison, TUV	1,389	
Dan Barrios-O'Neill, Green	912	
Jonny Orr, Ind.	856	
Matthew Robinson, C.	183	
Keith John Gray, Ind.	76	

LONDONDERRY EAST
E. 67,392 T. 42,248 (62.69%)

	First	Round Elected
Caoimhe Archibald, SF	5,851	12
Maurice Bradley, DUP	5,444	9
Cathal ohOisin, SF	4,953	
Claire Sugden, Ind.	4,918	8
George Robinson, DUP	4,715	9
Adrian McQuillan, DUP	3,881	
John Dallat, SDLP	3,319	12
William McCandless, UUP	2,814	
Chris McCaw, Alliance	1,841	
Gerry Mullan, Ind.	1,204	
Jordan Armstrong, TUV	1,038	
Russell Watton, PUP	879	
Gavin Campbell, PBP	492	
Anthony Flynn, Green	305	
David Harding, C.	219	

NEWRY AND ARMAGH
E. 80,140 T. 55,625 (69.41%)

	First	Round Elected
William Irwin, DUP	9,760	1
Cathal Boylan, SF	9,197	1
Justin McNulty, SDLP	8,983	2
Megan Fearon, SF	8,881	2
Conor Murphy, SF	8,454	3
Danny Kennedy, UUP	7,256	
Jackie Coade, Alliance	1,418	
Emmet Crossan, CISTA	704	
Rowan Tunnicliffe, Green	265	

STRANGFORD
E. 64,393 T. 39,239 (60.94%)

	First	Round Elected
Simon Hamilton, DUP	6,221	5
Kellie Armstrong, Alliance	5,813	4
Michelle McIlveen, DUP	5,728	9
Mike Nesbitt, UUP	5,323	9
Peter Weir, DUP	3,543	11
Joe Boyle, SDLP	3,045	
Philip Smith, UUP	2,453	
Jimmy Menagh, Ind.	1,627	
Jonathan Bell, Ind.	1,479	
Stephen Cooper, TUV	1,330	
Dermot Kennedy, SF	1,110	
Ricky Bamford, Green	918	
Scott Benton, C.	195	

TYRONE WEST
E. 64,258 T. 44,907 (69.89%)

	First	Round Elected
Thomas Buchanan, DUP	9,064	1
Michaela Boyle, SF	7,714	1
Barry McElduff, SF	7,573	1
Daniel McCrossan, SDLP	6,283	5
Declan McAleer, SF	6,034	5
Alicia Clarke, UUP	3,654	
Stephen Donnelly, Alliance	1,252	
Sorcha McAnespy, Ind.	864	
Charlie Chittick, TUV	851	
Ciaran McClean, Green	412	
Barry Brown, CISTA	373	
Corey French, Ind.	98	
Roisin McMackin, Ind.	85	
Susan-Anne White, Ind.	41	
Roger Lomas, C.	27	

ULSTER MID
E. 69,396 T. 50,228 (72.38%)

	First	Round Elected
Michelle, O'Neill, SF	10,258	1
Keith Buchanan, DUP	9,568	1
Ian Milne, SF	8,143	2
Linda Dillon, SF	7,806	2
Patsy McGlone, SDLP	6,419	5
Sandra Overend, UUP	4,516	
Hannah Loughrin, TUV	1,244	
Fay Watson, Alliance	1,017	
Hugh McCloy, Ind.	247	
Stefan Taylor, Green	243	
Hugh Scullion, WP	217	

UPPER BANN
E. 83,431 T. 52,174 (62.54%)

	First	Round Elected
Carla Lockhart, DUP	9,140	1
John O'Dowd, SF	8,220	5
Jonathan Buckley, DUP	7,745	4
Nuala Toman, SF	6,108	
Doug Beattie, UUP	5,467	5
Jo-Anne Dobson, UUP	5,132	
Dolores Kelly, SDLP	5,127	6
Tara Doyle, Alliance	2,720	
Roy Ferguson, TUV	1,035	
Simon Lee, Green	555	
Colin Craig, WP	218	
Ian Nickels, C.	81	

REGIONAL GOVERNMENT

LONDON

GREATER LONDON AUTHORITY (GLA)

City Hall, The Queen's Walk, London SE1 2AA
T 020-7983 4000 E mayor@london.gov.uk W www.london.gov.uk

On 7 May 1998 London voted in favour of the formation of the Greater London Authority (GLA). The first elections to the GLA took place on 4 May 2000 and the new authority took over its responsibilities on 3 July 2000. In July 2002 the GLA moved to one of London's most spectacular buildings, newly built on a brownfield site on the south bank of the Thames, adjacent to Tower Bridge. The fifth and most recent election to the GLA took place on 5 May 2016.

The structure and objectives of the GLA stem from its main areas of responsibility: transport, policing, fire and emergency planning, economic development, planning, culture and health. There are four functional bodies which form part of the wider GLA group and report to the GLA: the Mayor's Office for Policing and Crime (MOPAC), Transport for London (TfL), the London Fire and Emergency Planning Authority (LFEPA) and the London Legacy Development Corporation, established in 2012.

The GLA consists of a directly elected mayor, the Mayor of London, and a separately elected assembly, the London Assembly. The mayor has the key role in decision making, with the assembly responsible for regulating and scrutinising these decisions, and investigating issues of importance to Londoners. In addition, the GLA has around 600 permanent staff to support the activities of the mayor and the assembly, which are overseen by a head of paid service. The mayor may appoint two political advisers and not more than ten other members of staff, though he does not necessarily exercise this power, but he does not appoint the chief executive, the monitoring officer or the chief finance officer. These must be appointed jointly by the assembly and the mayor.

Every aspect of the assembly and its activities must be open to public scrutiny and therefore accountable. The assembly holds the mayor to account through scrutiny of his strategies, decisions and actions. Mayor's Question Time, conducted on ten occasions a year at City Hall, is carried out by direct questioning at assembly meetings and by conducting detailed investigations in committee.

People's Question Time, held twice a year, and Talk London (W www.london.gov.uk/talk-london) give Londoners the chance to question and express their opinions to the mayor and the assembly about plans, priorities and policies for London.

The role of the mayor can be broken down into a number of key areas:
- to represent and promote London at home and abroad and speak up for Londoners
- to devise strategies and plans to tackle London-wide issues, such as crime, transport, housing, planning, economic development and regeneration, environment, public services, society and culture, sport and health; and to set budgets for TfL, MOPAC, LFEPA and the London Legacy Development Corporation
- the mayor is chair of TfL, and is responsible for the Metropolitan Police's priorities and performance

The role of the assembly can be broken down into a number of key areas:
- to hold the mayor to account by examining his decisions and actions
- to have the power to amend the mayor's budget by a majority of two-thirds
- to have the power to summon the mayor, senior staff of the GLA and functional bodies
- to investigate issues of London-wide significance and make proposals to appropriate stakeholders
- to examine the work of MOPAC and to review the police and crime plan for London through the Police and Crime Committee

MAYORAL TEAM

Mayor, Sadiq Khan
Deputy Mayors, Rajesh Agrawal *(Business);* Sophie Linden *(Policing and Crime);* Joanne McCartney, AM *(Education and Childcare);* James Murray *(Housing and Residential Development);* Jules Pipe *(Planning, Regeneration and Skills);* Matthew Ryder *(Social Integration, Social Mobility and Community Engagement);* Shirley Rodrigues *(Environment and Energy);* Val Shawcross, CBE *(Transport);* Justine Simons, OBE *(Culture and the Creative Industries)*
Chief of Staff, David Bellamy
Directors, Nick Bowes *(Policy);* Patrick Hennessy *(Communications);* Leah Kreitzman *(External and International Affairs);* Jack Stenner *(Political and Public Affairs)*
Special Appointments, Dr Tom Coffey, OBE *(Health Adviser);* Philip Kolvin, QC *(Chair of the Night Time Commission);* Amy Lamé *(Night Czar);* Dr Will Norman *(Walking and Cycling Commissioner);* Claire Waxman *(Victims Commissioner)*

ELECTIONS AND VOTING SYSTEMS

The assembly is elected every four years at the same time as the mayor, and consists of 25 members. There is one member from each of the 14 GLA constituencies topped up with 11 London-wide members who are either representatives of political parties or individuals standing as independent candidates. The last election was on 5 May 2016.

Two distinct voting systems are used to appoint the existing mayor and the assembly. The mayor is elected using the supplementary vote system (SVS). With SVS, electors have two votes: one to give a first choice for mayor and one to give a second choice; they cannot vote twice for the same candidate. If one candidate gets more than half of all the first-choice votes, he or she becomes mayor. If no candidate gets more than half of the first-choice votes, the two candidates with the most first-choice votes remain in the election and all the other candidates drop out. The second-choice votes on the ballot papers for the candidates who are then counted. Where these second-choice votes are for the two remaining candidates they are added to the first-choice votes these candidates already have. The candidate with the most first- and second-choice votes combined becomes the Mayor of London.

The assembly is appointed using the additional member system (AMS). Under AMS, electors have two votes. The first vote is for a constituency candidate. The second vote is for a party list or individual candidate contesting the London-wide assembly seats. The 14 constituency members are elected under the first-past-the-post system, the same system used in general and local elections. Electors vote for one candidate and the candidate with the most votes wins. The additional members are drawn from party lists or are independent candidates who stand as London members; they are chosen using a form of proportional representation.

The Greater London Returning Officer (GLRO) is the independent official responsible for running the election in London. He is supported in this by returning officers in each of the 14 London constituencies.
GLRO for 2016 Election, Jeff Jacobs

TRANSPORT FOR LONDON (TFL)

TfL is the integrated body responsible for London's transport system. Its role is to implement the mayor's transport strategy for London and manage transport services across the capital for which the mayor has responsibility. TfL is directed by a management board whose members are chosen for their understanding of transport matters and are appointed by the mayor, who chairs the board. TfL's role is:

- to manage the London Underground, buses, Croydon Tramlink, London Overground and the Docklands Light Railway (DLR)
- to manage a 580km network of main roads and all 6,000 of London's traffic lights
- to regulate taxis and minicabs
- to run the London River Services, Victoria Coach Station and London Transport Museum
- to help to coordinate the Dial-a-Ride, Capital Call and Taxicard schemes for door-to-door services for transport users with mobility problems

The London Borough Councils maintain the role of highway and traffic authorities for 95 per cent of London's roads. A congestion charge for motorists driving into central London between the hours of 7am and 6.30pm, Monday to Friday (excluding public holidays) was introduced on 17 February 2003. On 19 February 2007, the charge zone roughly doubled in size after a westward expansion and the charging hours were shortened, to finish at 6pm. On 4 January 2011, the westward expansion was removed from the charging zone and an automated payment system was also introduced. As at September 2016 the daily congestion charge was £11.50 (£10.50 if paid via the automated service).

TfL introduced a low emission zone (LEZ) for London on 4 February 2008 which is in constant operation. Following tougher emissions standards introduced on 3 January 2012 there is a daily charge for polluting vehicles entering the zone (which covers most of Greater London) that do not meet Euro 3 or Euro 4 emissions standards. With the exception of minibuses, vehicles over three-and-a-half tonnes such as lorries, buses and coaches, face a daily charge of £200. Vehicles up to three-and-a-half tonnes and minibuses (with more than eight passenger seats) up to five tonnes pay a daily charge of £100. For further information see W www.tfl.gov.uk/lez

Since 2 January 2009, Londoners over pensionable age (or over 60 if born before 1950) and those with eligible disabilities are entitled to free travel on the capital's transport network at any time. War veterans who are receiving ongoing payments under the war pensions scheme, or those receiving guaranteed income payments under the armed forces compensation scheme can travel free at any time on bus, underground, DLR, tram and London Overground services and at certain times on National Rail services.

In the summer of 2010, the London cycle hire scheme launched with 6,000 new bicycles for hire from 400 docking stations across eight boroughs, the City and the Royal parks. The scheme has been expanded and there are now around 11,500 bicycles available and over 750 docking stations.

Commissioner of TfL, Mike Brown, MVO

MAYOR'S OFFICE FOR POLICING AND CRIME (MOPAC)

The Mayor's Office for Policing and Crime (MOPAC) was set up in response to the Police Reform and Social Responsibility Act 2011, replacing the Metropolitan Police Authority. MOPAC is headed by the mayor, or the appointed statutory deputy mayor for policing and crime. Operational responsibility for policing in London belongs to the Metropolitan Police Commissioner. The major areas of focus of MOPAC are:

- operational policing and crime reduction including counter terrorism
- ensuring the Metropolitan Police effectively reduce gang crime and violence in London and coordinating support for

communities and local organisations to prevent gang activities
- criminal justice, including preventing reoffending, reducing crime and decreasing demand within the criminal justice system in addition to reducing alcohol and drug abuse.

The Police and Crime Committee consisting of nine elected members of the London Assembly scrutinises the work of MOPAC and meets regularly to hold to account the Deputy Mayor for Policing and Crime.

Deputy Mayor for Policing and Crime, Sophie Linden

LONDON FIRE AND EMERGENCY PLANNING AUTHORITY (LFEPA)

In July 2000 the London Fire and Civil Defence Authority became the London Fire and Emergency Planning Authority. It consists of 17 members, eight drawn from the assembly, seven from the London boroughs and two mayoral appointees. The role of the LFEPA is:

- to set the strategy for the provision of fire services
- to ensure that the fire brigade can meet all the normal requirements efficiently
- to ensure that effective arrangements are made for the fire brigade to receive emergency calls and deal with them promptly
- to ensure members of the fire brigade are properly trained and equipped
- to ensure that information useful to the development of the fire brigades is gathered
- to ensure arrangements for advice and guidance on fire protection are made

Chair, Dr Fiona Twycross, AM

LONDON LEGACY DEVELOPMENT CORPORATION

Following the London 2012 Olympic Games, the London Legacy Development Corporation was made responsible for the long-term planning, development, management and maintenance of the Queen Elizabeth Olympic Park (formerly the Olympic Park) and its facilities. The organisation is tasked with transforming the area into a thriving neighbourhood.

Chair, Sir Peter Hendy, CBE

SALARIES as at September 2017

Mayor	£145,350
Chief of Staff	£133,220
Deputy Mayors	
Housing and Residential Development	£126,250
Business	£126,250
Culture and the Creative Industries	£126,250
Transport	£126,250
Policing and Crime	£125,000
Education and Childcare	£100,180
(and Statutory Deputy Mayor)	
Chair of the Assembly	£66,830
Assembly Member	£55,713

LONDON ASSEMBLY COMMITTEES

Chair, Audit Panel, Peter Whittle
Chair, Budget and Performance Committee, Gareth Bacon
Chair, Budget Monitoring Sub-Committee, Gareth Bacon
Chair, Confirmation Hearings Committee, Andrew Boff
Chair, Economy Committee, Caroline Russell
Chair, Education Panel, Jennette Arnold, OBE
Chair, Environment Committee, Leonie Cooper
Chair, EU Exit Working Group, Len Duvall
Chair, GLA Oversight Committee, Len Duvall
Chair, Health Committee, Dr Onkar Sahota
Chair, Housing Committee, Sian Berry
Chair, Planning Committee, Nicky Gavron
Chair, Police and Crime Committee, Steve O'Connell
Chair, Regeneration Committee, Navin Shah
Chair, Transport Committee, Keith Prince

LONDON ASSEMBLY MEMBERS

as at September 2017

Arbour, Tony, *C., South West,* Maj. 21,444
Arnold, Jennette, OBE, *Lab., North East,* Maj. 101,742
Bacon, Gareth, *C., Bexley and Bromley,* Maj. 41,669
Bailey, Shaun, *C., London-wide*
Berry, Sian, *Green, London-wide*
Boff, Andrew, *C., London-wide*
Cooper, Leonie, *Lab., Merton and Wandsworth,* Maj. 4,301
Copley, Tom, *Lab., London-wide*
Desai, Unmesh, *Lab., City and East,* Maj. 89,629
Deverish, Tony, *C., West Central,* Maj. 14,564
Dismore, Andrew, *Lab., Barnet and Camden,* Maj. 16,240
Duvall, Len, *Lab., Greenwich and Lewisham,* Maj. 54,895
Eshalomi, Florence, *Lab., Lambeth and Southwark,* Maj. 62,243
Gavron, Nicky, *Lab., London-wide*
Hall, Susan, *C., London-wide*
Kurten, David, *UKIP, London-wide*
McCartney, Joanne, *Lab., Enfield and Haringey,* Maj. 51,152
O'Connell, Steve, *C., Croydon and Sutton,* Maj. 11,614
Pidgeon, Caroline, MBE, *LD, London-wide*
Prince, Keith, *C. Havering and Redbridge,* Maj. 1,438
Russell, Caroline, *Green, London-wide*
Sahota, Dr Onkar, *Lab., Ealing and Hillingdon,* Maj. 15,933
Shah, Navin, *Lab., Brent and Harrow,* Maj. 20,755
Twycross, Fiona, *Lab., London-wide*
Whittle, Peter, *UKIP, London-wide*

Chair of the London Assembly, Jennette Arnold, OBE, AM

STATE OF THE PARTIES *as at September 2017*

Party	Seats
Labour (Lab.)	12
Conservative (C.)	8
Green	2
UKIP	2
LD	1

MAYORAL ELECTION RESULTS

as at 5 May 2016

Electorate 5,739,011 Turnout 45.6%

First	Party	Votes	%
Sadiq Khan	Lab.	1,148,716	44.2
Zac Goldsmith	C.	909,755	35.0
Siân Berry	Green	150,673	5.8
Caroline Pidgeon	LD	120,005	4.6
Peter Whittle	UKIP	94,373	3.6
Sophie Walker	Women	53,055	2.0
George Galloway	Respect	37,007	1.4
Paul Golding	Brit. First	31,372	1.2
Lee Harris	CISTA	20,537	0.8
David Furness	BNP	13,325	0.5
Prince Zylinski	Ind.	13,202	0.5
Ankit Love	One Love	4,941	0.2
Second	*Party*	*Votes*	*%*
Sadiq Khan	Lab.	161,427	65.5
Zac Goldsmith	C.	84,859	34.5

LONDON ASSEMBLY ELECTION RESULTS *as at 5 May 2016*

E. Electorate T. Turnout
See General Election Results for a list of party abbreviations

CONSTITUENCIES
E. 5,739,011 T 45.6%

BARNET AND CAMDEN
E. 387,844 T. 47.44%

Andrew Dismore, Lab.	81,482
Daniel Thomas, C.	65,242
Stephen Taylor, Green	16,996
Zack Polanski, LD	11,204
Joseph Langton, UKIP	9,057

Lab. majority 16,240

BEXLEY AND BROMLEY
E. 404,342 T. 46.94%

Gareth Bacon, C.	87,460
Sam Russell, Lab.	45,791
Frank Gould, UKIP	30,485
Roisin Robertson, Green	12,685
Julie Ireland, LD	12,145
Veronica Obadara, APP	1,243

C. majority 41,669

BRENT AND HARROW
E. 381,778 T. 45.76%

Navin Shah, Lab.	79,902
Joel Davidson, C.	59,147
Anton Georgiou, LD	11,534
Jafar Hassan, Green	9,874
Rathy Alagaratnam, UKIP	9,074
Akib Mahmood, Respect GG	5,170

Lab. majority 20,755

CITY AND EAST
E. 503,301 T. 42.01%

Unmesh Desai, Lab.	122,175
Chris Chapman, C.	32,546
Rachel Collinson, Green	18,766
Peter Harris, UKIP	18,071
Elaine Bagshaw, LD	10,714
Rayne Mickail, Respect GG	6,772
Amina Gichinga, TBTC	1,368
Aaron D'Souza, APP	1,009

Lab. majority 89,629

CROYDON AND SUTTON
E. 401,660 T. 45.29%

Steve O'Connell, C.	70,156
Marina Ahmad, Lab.	58,542
Amna Ahmad, LD	18,859
Peter Staveley, UKIP	18,338
Tracey Hague, Green	13,513
Madonna Lewis, APP	1,386
Richard Edmonds, NF	1,106

C. majority 11,614

EALING AND HILLINGDON
E. 444,168 T. 45.25%

Onkar Sahota, Lab.	86,088
Dominic Gilham, C.	70,155
Alex Nieora, UKIP	15,832
Meena Hans, Green	15,758
Francesco Fruzza, LD	13,154

Lab. majority 15,933

ENFIELD AND HARINGEY
E. 377,060 T. 44.73%

Joanne McCartney, Lab.	91,075
Linda Kelly, C.	39,923
Ronald Stewart, Green	15,409
Nicholas da Costa, LD	12,038
Neville Watson, UKIP	9,042
Godson Azu, APP	1,172

Lab. majority 51,152

GREENWICH AND LEWISHAM
E. 362,376 T. 45.08%

Len Duvall, Lab.	85,735
Adam Thomas, C.	30,840
Imogen Solly, Green	20,520
Paul Oakley, UKIP	13,686
Julia Fletcher, LD	11,303
Ajaratu Bangura, APP	1,275

Lab. majority 54,895

HAVERING AND REDBRIDGE
E. 383,234 T. 44.63%

Keith Prince, C.	64,483
Ivana Bartoletti, Lab.	63,045
Lawrence Webb, UKIP	26,788
Lee Burkwood, Green	9,617
Ian Sanderson, LD	7,105

C. majority 1,438

LAMBETH AND SOUTHWARK
E. 426,966 T. 43.98%

Florence Eshalomi, Lab.	96,946
Robert Flint, C.	34,703
Rashid Nix, Green	25,793
Michael Bukola, LD	21,489
Idham Ramadi, UKIP	6,591
Kevin Parkin, SPGB	1,333
Amadu Kanumansa, APP	906

Lab. majority 62,243

MERTON AND WANDSWORTH
E. 374,126 T. 49.56%

Leonie Cooper, Lab.	77,340
David Dean, C.	73,039
Esther Obiri-Darko, Green	14,682
Adrian Hyyrylainen-Trett, LD	10,732
Elizabeth Jones, UKIP	8,478
Thamilini Kulendran, Ind.	1,142

Lab. majority 4,301

NORTH EAST
E. 500,432 T. 45.72%

Jennette Arnold, Lab.	134,307
Sam Malik, C.	32,565
Samir Jeraj, Green	29,401
Terry Stacy, LD	14,312
Freddy Vachha, UKIP	11,315
Tim Allen, Respect GG	5,068
Bill Martin, SPGB	1,293
Jonathan Silberman, Comm L	536

Lab. majority 101,742

SOUTH WEST
E. 435,877 T. 49.04%

Tony Arbour, C.	84,381
Martin Whelton, Lab.	62,937
Rosina Robson, LD	30,654
Andree Frieze, Green	19,745
Alexander Craig, UKIP	14,983
Adam Buick, SPGB	1,065

C. majority 21,444

WEST CENTRAL
E. 348,740 T. 43.96%

Tony Devenish, C.	67,775
Mandy Richards, Lab.	53,211
Jennifer Nadel, Green	14,050
Annabel Mullin, LD	10,577
Clive Egan, UKIP	7,708

C. majority 14,564

LONDON-WIDE MEMBERS

Conservative Party	*Labour Party*
Kemi Badenoch	Fiona Twycross
Andrew Boff	Tom Copley
Shaun Bailey	Nicky Gavron

Green Party	*UKIP*
Sian Berry	Peter Whittle
Caroline Russell	David Kurten

Liberal Democrats
Caroline Pidgeon

EUROPEAN PARLIAMENT

European parliament elections take place at five-yearly intervals; the first direct elections to the parliament were held in 1979. In mainland Britain, members of the European parliament (MEPs) were elected in all constituencies on a first-past-the-post basis until 1999, when a regional system of proportional representation was introduced; in Northern Ireland three MEPs have been elected by the single transferable vote system of proportional representation since 1979. Under the terms of the Lisbon Treaty, the UK gained an extra seat in December 2011, taking the total to 73. This seat was added to the West Midlands region and filled by the highest-ranked losing candidate standing for the region in the 2009 European parliament elections.

At the 2014 European parliament elections all UK MEPs were elected under a 'closed-list' regional system of proportional representation, with England being divided into nine regions (residents of Gibraltar vote in the South West region) and Scotland, Wales and Northern Ireland each constituting a single region each. Parties submitted a list of candidates for each region in their own order of preference. Votes were cast for a party or an independent candidate, and the first seat in each region was allocated to the party or candidate with the highest number of votes. The rest of the seats in each region were then allocated broadly in proportion to each party's share of the vote. Each region returned the following number of members: East Midlands, 5; Eastern, 7; London, 8; North East, 3; North West, 8; South East, 10; South West, 6; West Midlands, 7; Yorkshire and the Humber, 6; Wales, 4; Northern Ireland, 3; Scotland, 6.

If a vacancy occurs due to the resignation or death of an MEP, it is filled by the next available person on that party's list. If an independent MEP resigns or dies, a by-election is held. Where an MEP leaves the party on whose list he/she was elected, there is no requirement to resign the post of MEP.

British subjects and nationals of member states of the European Union are eligible for election to the European parliament provided they are aged 18 or over and not subject to disqualification. Since 1994, eligible citizens have had the right to vote in elections to the European parliament in the UK as long as they are entered on the electoral register.

In July 2009 an MEP statute introduced a uniform salary for all MEPs, set at a rate of 38.5 per cent of the basic salary of a European court of justice judge. As at June 2016 this equated to an annual salary of €96,246.36 (approximately £68,000, depending on the monthly exchange rate). Member states can also subject the salary to national taxes. In the UK the salary is taxed by HM Revenue and Customs in order to bring the total tax paid up to the level of taxation payable by a UK resident.

The next elections to the European parliament will take place in 2019. For further information visit the UK's European parliament website (W www.europarl.europa.eu/unitedkingdom).

UK MEMBERS *as at 15 September 2017*

KEY

* Denotes membership of the last European parliament
† Previously sat as a member of the Conservative Party
‡ Previously sat as a member of UKIP
§ Previously sat as a member of UCUNF

*Agnew, Stuart (*b.* 1949), *UKIP, Eastern*
Aker, Tim (*b.* 1985), *UKIP, Eastern*
Anderson, Lucy, *Lab., London*
*Anderson, Martina (*b.* 1962), *SF, Northern Ireland*
Arnott, Jonathan (*b.* 1981), *UKIP, North East*
*Ashworth, Richard (*b.* 1947), *C., South East*
Atkinson, Janice (*b.* 1962), *Ind., South East*
‡Bashir, Amjad (*b.* 1952), *C., Yorkshire and the Humber*

*Batten, Gerard (*b.* 1954), *UKIP, London*
*Bearder, Catherine (*b.* 1949), *LD, South East*
Bours, Louise (*b.* 1968), *UKIP, North West*
Brannen, Paul (*b.* 1962), *Lab., North East*
Bullock, Jonathan (*b.* 1963), *UKIP, East Midlands*
*‡Campbell Bannerman, David (*b.* 1960), *C., Eastern*
Carver, James (*b.* 1969), *UKIP, West Midlands*
Coburn, David (*b.* 1958), *UKIP, Scotland*
Collins, Jane (*b.* 1962), *UKIP, Yorkshire and the Humber*
Corbett, Richard (*b.* 1955), *Lab., Yorkshire and the Humber*
Dalton, Daniel (*b.* 1974), *C., West Midlands*
Dance, Seb (*b.* 1981), *Lab., London*
*Dartmouth, Earl of (*b.* 1949), *UKIP, South West*
*Deva, Nirj (*b.* 1948), *C., South East*
*Dodds, Diane (*b.* 1958), *DUP, Northern Ireland*
Etheridge, Bill (*b.* 1970), *UKIP, West Midlands*
*Evans, Jill (*b.* 1959), *PC, Wales*
*Farage, Nigel (*b.* 1964), *UKIP, South East*
Finch, Ray (*b.* 1963), *UKIP, South East*
Flack, John (*b.* 1957) *C., Eastern*
*Foster, Jacqueline (*b.* 1947), *C., North West*
*Fox, Ashley (*b.* 1969), *C., South West*
Gill, Nathan (*b.* 1973), *UKIP, Wales*
Gill, Neena, CBE (*b.* 1957), *Lab., West Midlands*
*Girling, Julie (*b.* 1956), *C., South West*
Griffin, Theresa (*b.* 1962), *Lab., North West*
*Hannan, Daniel (*b.* 1971), *C., South East*
*Honeyball, Mary (*b.* 1952), *Lab., London*
Hookem, Mike (*b.* 1953), *UKIP, Yorkshire and the Humber*
Howarth, John (*b.* 1958), *Lab., South East*
*Hudghton, Ian (*b.* 1951), *SNP, Scotland*
‡James, Diane (*b.* 1959), *Ind., South East*
*Kamall, Dr Syed (*b.* 1967), *C., London*
*Karim, Sajjad (*b.* 1970), *C., North West*
Khan, Wajid (*b.* 1978) *Lab., North West*
Kirton-Darling, Judith (*b.* 1977), *Lab., North East*
*Lambert, Jean (*b.* 1950), *Green, London*
*Martin, David (*b.* 1954), *Lab., Scotland*
Matthews, Rupert (*b.* 1961), *C., East Midlands*
Mayer, Alex (*b.* 1981), *Lab., Eastern*
*McAvan, Linda (*b.* 1962), *Lab., Yorkshire and the Humber*
*McClarkin, Emma (*b.* 1978), *C., East Midlands*
*McIntyre, Anthea (*b.* 1954), *C., West Midlands*
Mobarik, Baroness, CBE (*b.* 1975), *C., Scotland*
Moody, Clare (*b.* 1965), *Lab., South West*
*Moraes, Claude (*b.* 1965), *Lab., London*
*§Nicholson, James (*b.* 1945), *UUP, Northern Ireland*
*Nuttall, Paul (*b.* 1976), *UKIP, North West*
O'Flynn, Patrick (*b.* 1965), *UKIP, Eastern*
Parker, Margot (*b.* 1943), *UKIP, East Midlands*
Procter, John, (*b.* 1966), *C., Yorkshire and the Humber*
Reid, Julia (*b.* 1952), *UKIP, South West*
Scott Cato, Molly (*b.* 1963), *Green, South West*
Seymour, Jill (*b.* 1958), *UKIP, West Midlands*
Simon, Siôn (*b.* 1968), *Lab., West Midlands*
*Smith, Alyn (*b.* 1973), *SNP, Scotland*
*Stihler, Catherine (*b.* 1973), *Lab., Scotland*
*Swinburne, Dr Kay (*b.* 1967), *C., Wales*
*Tannock, Dr Charles (*b.* 1957), *C., London*
*Taylor, Keith (*b.* 1953), *Green, South East*
*Van Orden, Geoffrey (*b.* 1945), *C., Eastern*
*Vaughan, Derek (*b.* 1961), *Lab., Wales*
Ward, Julie (*b.* 1957), *Lab., North West*
*Willmott, Glenis (*b.* 1951), *Lab., East Midlands*
‡Woolfe, Steven (*b.* 1967), *Ind., North West*

STATE OF THE PARTIES *as at September 2017*

Party	Seats
UK Independence Party (UKIP)	20
Labour (Lab.)	20
Conservative (C.)	20
Green Party (Green)	3
Independent (Ind.)	3
Scottish National Party (SNP)	2
Others*	5
Total	73

* The Democratic Unionist Party (DUP), Liberal Democrats (LD), Plaid Cymru (PC), Ulster Unionist Party (UUP), and Sinn Fein (SF) have one seat each.

UK REGIONS AS AT 22 MAY 2014 ELECTION

Abbreviations

4FP	4 Freedoms Party (UK EPP)
AIFE	An Independence from Europe
AW	Animal Welfare
BF	Britain First
CPA	Christian Peoples Alliance
CUP	Communities United Party
EP	Europeans Party
Harmony	Harmony Party
Liberty	Liberty GB
NLP	National Liberal Party
NI21	NI21
No2EU	No2EU Yes to Democracy
Peace	Peace Party
Roman	Roman Party
SGB	Socialist Party of Great Britain
SLP	Socialist Labour Party
TUV	Traditional Unionist Voice (NI)
WDR	We Demand a Referendum
Your	YOURvoice
YF	Yorkshire First

For other abbreviations, *see* UK General Election Results.

E. 46,437,794 T.35.32%

EASTERN
(Bedfordshire, Cambridgeshire, Essex, Hertfordshire, Luton, Norfolk, Peterborough, Southend-on-Sea, Suffolk, Thurrock)
E. 4,369,382 T. 36.19%

UKIP	542,812 (34.5%)
C.	446,569 (28.4%)
Lab.	271,601 (17.2%)
Green	133,331 (8.5%)
LD	108,010 (6.9%)
AIFE	26,564 (1.7%)
Eng. Dem.	16,497 (1.0%)
BNP	12,465 (0.8%)
CPA	11,627 (0.7%)
No2EU	4,870 (0.3%)
UKIP majority	96,243

(June 2009, C. maj. 186,410)

MEMBERS ELECTED
1. P. O'Flynn, *UKIP* 2. *V. Ford, *C.* 3. *R. Howitt, *Lab.* 4. *S. Agnew, *UKIP* 5. *G. Van Orden, *C.* 6. T. Aker, *UKIP* 7. *‡ D. Campbell Bannerman, *C.*

EAST MIDLANDS
(Derby, Derbyshire, Leicester, Leicestershire, Lincolnshire, Northamptonshire, Nottingham, Nottinghamshire, Rutland)

E 3,437,794 T. 32.6%

UKIP	368,734 (32.9%)
C.	291,270 (26.0%)
Lab.	279,363 (24.9%)
Green	67,066 (6.0%)
LD	60,773 (5.4%)
AIFE	21,384 (1.9%)
BNP	18,326 (1.6%)
Eng. Dem.	11,612 (1.0%)
Harmony	2,194 (0.2%)
UKIP majority	77,464

(June 2009, C. maj. 163,330)

MEMBERS ELECTED
1. *†R. Helmer, *UKIP* 2.*E. McClarkin, *C.* 3. *G. Willmott, *Lab.* 4. M. Parker, *UKIP* 5. A. Lewer, *C.*

LONDON
E. 5,490,248 T. 40.5%

Lab.	806,959 (36.7%)
C.	495,639 (22.5%)
UKIP	371,133 (16.9%)
Green	196,419 (8.9%)
LD	148,013 (6.7%)
4FP	28,014 (1.3%)
AIFE	26,675 (1.2%)
CPA	23,702 (1.1%)
NHAP	23,253 (1.1%)
AW	21,092 (1.0%)
BNP	19,246 (0.9%)
EP	10,712 (0.5%)
Eng. Dem.	10,142 (0.5%)
CUP	6,951 (0.3%)
NLP	6,736 (0.3%)
No2EU	3,804 (0.2%)
Harmony	1,985 (0.1%)
Lab. majority	311,320

(June 2009, C. maj. 106,447)

MEMBERS ELECTED
1. *C. Moraes, *Lab.* 2. *S. Kamall, *C.* 3. *M. Honeyball, *Lab.* 4. *G. Batten, *UKIP* 5. L. Anderson, *Lab.* 6. *C. Tannock, *C.* 7. S. Dance, *Lab.* 8. *J. Lambert, *Green*

NORTH EAST
(Co. Durham, Darlington, Hartlepool, Middlesbrough, Northumberland, Redcar and Cleveland, Stockton-on-Tees, Tyne and Wear)

E. 1,968,780 T. 31.0%

Lab.	221,988 (36.5%)
UKIP	177,660 (29.2%)
C.	107,733 (17.7%)
LD	36,093 (5.9%)
Green	31,605 (5.2%)
AIFE	13,934 (2.3%)
BNP	10,360 (1.7%)
Eng. Dem.	9,279 (1.5%)
Lab. majority	44,328

(June 2009, Lab. maj. 30,427)

MEMBERS ELECTED
1. J. Kirton-Darling, *Lab.* 2. J. Arnott, *UKIP* 3. P. Brannen, *Lab.*

NORTHERN IRELAND
(Northern Ireland forms a three-member seat with a single transferable vote system)

E. 1,225,771 T. 51.84%

	1st Pref. Votes
Martina Anderson, *SF*	159,813 (25.5%)
Diane Dodds, *DUP*	131,163 (20.9%)
Jim Nicholson, *UUP*	83,438 (13.3%)
Alex Attwood, *SDLP*	81,594 (13%)
Jim Allister, *TUV*	75,806 (12.1%)
Anna Lo, *Alliance*	44,432 (7.1%)
Henry Reilly, *UKIP*	24,584 (3.9%)
Ross Brown, *Green*	10,598 (1.7%)
Tina McKenzie, *NI21*	10,553 (1.7%)
Mark Brotherston, *C.*	4,144 (0.7%)

MEMBERS ELECTED
1. *M. Anderson, *SF* 2. *D. Dodds, *DUP* 3. *§ J. Nicholson, *UUP*

NORTH WEST
(Blackburn-with-Darwen, Blackpool, Cheshire, Cumbria, Greater Manchester, Halton, Lancashire, Merseyside, Warrington)

E. 5,267,777 T. 33.68%

Lab.	594,063 (33.9%)
UKIP	481,932 (27.5%)
C.	351,985 (20.1%)
Green	123,075 (7.0%)
LD	105,487 (6.0%)
BNP	32,826 (1.9%)
AIFE	26,731 (1.5%)
Eng. Dem.	19,522 (1.1%)
Pirate	8,597 (0.5%)
No2EU	5,402 (0.3%)
SEP	5,067 (0.3%)
Lab. majority	112,131

(June 2009, C. maj. 86,343)

MEMBERS ELECTED
1. T. Griffin, Lab. 2.*P. Nuttall, UKIP 3. *J. Foster, C. 4. A. Khan, Lab. 5. L. Bours, UKIP 6. J. Ward, Lab. 7. *S. Karim, C. 8. S. Woolfe, UKIP

SCOTLAND
E. 4,016,735 T. 33.5%

SNP	389,503 (29.0%)
Lab.	348,219 (25.9%)
C.	231,330 (17.2%)
UKIP	140,534 (10.5%)
Green	108,305 (8.7%)
LD	95,319 (7.1%)
BF	13,639 (1.0%)
BNP	10,216 (0.8%)
No2EU	6,418 (0.5%)
SNP majority	41,284

(June 2009, SNP. maj. 91,154)

MEMBERS ELECTED
1. *I. Hudghton, SNP 2. *D. Martin, Lab. 3. I. Duncan, C. 4. *A. Smith, SNP 5. *C. Stihler, Lab. 6. D. Coburn, UKIP

SOUTH EAST
(Bracknell Forest, Brighton and Hove, Buckinghamshire, East Sussex, Hampshire, Isle of Wight, Kent, Medway, Milton Keynes, Newbury, Oxfordshire, Portsmouth, Reading, Slough, Southampton, Surrey, West Sussex, Windsor and Maidenhead, Wokingham)

E. 6,441,003 T. 36.46%

UKIP	751,439 (32.1%)
C.	723,571 (31.0%)
Lab.	342,775 (14.7%)
Green	211,706 (9.1%)
LD	187,876 (8.0%)
AIFE	45,199 (1.9%)
Eng. Dem.	17,771 (0.8%)
BNP	16,909 (0.7%)
CPA	14,893 (0.6%)
Peace	10,130 (0.4%)
SGB	5,454 (0.2%)
Roman	2,997 (0.1%)
Your	2,932 (0.1%)
Liberty	2,494 (0.1%)
Harmony	1,904 (0.1%)
UKIP majority	27,868

(June 2009, C. maj. 372,286)

MEMBERS ELECTED
1. *N. Farage, UKIP 2. *D. Hannan, C. 3. J. Atkinson, UKIP 4. *N. Deva, C. 5. A. Dodds, Lab. 6. D. James, UKIP 7. *R. Ashworth, C. 8. *K.Taylor, Green 9. * C. Bearder, LD 10. R. Finch, UKIP

SOUTH WEST
(Bath and North East Somerset, Bournemouth, Bristol, Cornwall, Devon, Dorset, Gloucestershire, North Somerset, Plymouth, Poole, Somerset, South Gloucestershire, Swindon, Torbay, Wiltshire, Isles of Scilly, Gibraltar)

E. 4,059,889 T. 37.03%

UKIP	484,184 (32.3%)
C.	433,151 (28.9%)
Lab.	206,124 (13.8%)
Green	166,447 (11.1%)
LD	160,376 (10.7%)
AIFE	23,169 (1.6%)
Eng. Dem.	15,081 (1.0%)
BNP	10,910 (0.7%)
UKIP majority	51,033

(June 2009, C. maj. 126,627)

MEMBERS ELECTED
1. *W. Dartmouth, UKIP 2. *A. Fox, C. 3. J. Reid, UKIP 4. *J. Girling, C. 5. C. Moody, Lab. 6. M. Scott Cato, Green

WALES
E. 2,327,175 T. 31.50%

Lab.	206,332 (28.2%)
UKIP	201,983 (27.6%)
C.	127,742 (17.4%)
PC	111,864 (15.3%)
Green	33,275 (4.5%)
LD	28,930 (4.0%)
BNP	7,655 (1.0%)
BF	6,633 (0.9%)
SLP	4,459 (0.6%)
No2EU	2,803 (0.4%)
SGB	1,384 (0.2%)
Lab. majority	4,349

(June 2004, Lab. maj. 120,039)

MEMBERS ELECTED
1. *D. Vaughan, Lab. 2. N. Gill, UKIP 3. *K. Swinburne, C. 4. *J. Evans, PC

WEST MIDLANDS
(Herefordshire, Shropshire, Staffordshire, Stoke-on-Trent, Telford and Wrekin, Warwickshire, West Midlands Metropolitan area, Worcestershire)

E. 4,105,305 T. 33.31%

UKIP	428,010 (28.1%)
Lab.	363,033 (21.3%)
C.	330,470 (17.0%)
LD	75,648 (12.0%)
Green	71,464 (8.6%)
AIFE	27,171 (6.2%)
WDR	23,426 (2.3%)
BNP	20,643 (1.3%)
Eng. Dem.	12,832 (1.0%)
No2EU	4,653 (0.9%)
Harmony	1,857 (0.6%)
UKIP majority	64,977

(June 2009, C. maj. 96,016)

MEMBERS ELECTED
1. J Seymour, UKIP 2. N. Gill, Lab. 3. *P. Bradbourn, C. 4. J. Carver, UKIP 5. S. Simon, Lab. 6. *A. McIntyre, C. 7. B. Etheridge, UKIP

YORKSHIRE AND THE HUMBER
(East Riding of Yorkshire, Kingston-upon-Hull, North East Lincolnshire, North Lincolnshire, North Yorkshire, South Yorkshire, West Yorkshire, York)

E. 3,905,726 T. 33.2%

UKIP	403,630 (31.1%)
Lab.	380,189 (29.3%)
C.	248,945 (19.2%)
Green	102,282 (7.9%)
LD	81,108 (6.3%)
AIFE	24,297 (1.9%)
BNP	20,138 (1.6%)
YF	19,017 (1.5%)
Eng. Dem.	13,288 (1.0%)
No2EU	3,807 (0.3%)
UKIP majority	23,441

(June 2009, C. maj. 69,793)

MEMBERS ELECTED
1. J. Collins, UKIP 2. *L. McAvan, Lab. 3. *T. Kirkhope, C. 4. A. Bashir, UKIP 5. R. Corbett, Lab. 6. M. Hookem, UKIP

LOCAL GOVERNMENT

Major changes in local government were introduced in England and Wales in 1974 and in Scotland in 1975 by the Local Government Act 1972 and the Local Government (Scotland) Act 1973. Further significant alterations were made in England by the Local Government Acts of 1985, 1992 and 2000.

The structure in England was based on two tiers of local authorities (county councils and district councils) in the non-metropolitan areas; and a single tier of metropolitan councils in the six metropolitan areas of England and London borough councils in London.

Following reviews of the structure of local government in England by the Local Government Commission (now the Boundary Commission for England), 46 unitary (all-purpose) authorities were created between April 1995 and April 1998 to cover certain areas in the non-metropolitan counties. The remaining county areas continue to have two tiers of local authorities. The county and district councils in the Isle of Wight were replaced by a single unitary authority on 1 April 1995; the former counties of Avon, Cleveland, Humberside and Berkshire were replaced by unitary authorities; and Hereford & Worcester was replaced by a new county council for Worcestershire (with district councils) and a unitary authority for Herefordshire. On 1 April 2009 the county areas of Cornwall, Durham, Northumberland, Shropshire and Wiltshire were given unitary status and two new unitary authorities were created for Bedfordshire (Bedford and Central Bedfordshire) and Cheshire (Cheshire East and Cheshire West & Chester) replacing the two-tier county/district system in these areas.

The Local Government (Wales) Act 1994 and the Local Government etc (Scotland) Act 1994 abolished the two-tier structure in Wales and Scotland with effect from 1 April 1996, replacing it with a single tier of unitary authorities.

In Northern Ireland a reform programme to reduce the number of local authorities from 26 to 11 began in 2012 when legislation finalising the boundaries of the new 11 local government district authorities was approved by the Northern Ireland Assembly. The Local Government Act (Northern Ireland) 2014 received royal assent on 12 May 2014, providing the legislative framework for the 11 new councils. On 1 April 2015 additional functions, previously the responsibility of the Northern Ireland executive, fully transferred to the new district authorities.

ELECTIONS

Local elections are normally held on the first Thursday in May. Generally, all citizens of the UK, the Republic of Ireland, Commonwealth and other European Union citizens who are 18 years or over and resident on the qualifying date in the area for which the election is being held, are entitled to vote at local government elections. A register of electors is prepared and published annually by local electoral registration officers.

A returning officer has the overall responsibility for an election. Voting takes place at polling stations, arranged by the local authority and under the supervision of a presiding officer specially appointed for the purpose. Candidates, who are subject to various statutory qualifications and disqualifications designed to ensure that they are suitable to hold office, must be nominated by electors for the electoral area concerned.

In England, the Local Government Boundary Commission for England is responsible for carrying out periodic reviews of electoral arrangements, to consider whether the boundaries of wards or divisions within a local authority need to be altered to take account of changes in electorate; structural reviews, to consider whether a single, unitary authority should be established in an area instead of an existing two-tier system;

and administrative boundary reviews of district or county authorities.

The Local Democracy and Boundary Commission for Wales, the Local Government Boundary Commission for Scotland and the local government boundary commissioner for Northern Ireland (appointed when required by the Boundary Commission for Northern Ireland) are responsible for reviewing the electoral arrangements and boundaries of local authorities within their respective regions.

The Local Government Act 2000 provided for the secretary of state to change the frequency and phasing of elections in England and Wales.

LOCAL GOVERNMENT BOUNDARY COMMISSION FOR ENGLAND, 14th Floor, Millbank Tower, London SW1P 4QP T 0330-500 1525 E reviews@lgbce.org.uk W www.lgbce.org.uk

LOCAL DEMOCRACY AND BOUNDARY COMMISSION FOR WALES, Ground Floor, Hastings House, Fitzalan Court, Cardiff CF24 0BL T 029-2046 4819 E ldbc.wales@wales.gsi.gov.uk W www.ldbc.gov.wales

LOCAL GOVERNMENT BOUNDARY COMMISSION FOR SCOTLAND, Thistle House, 91 Haymarket Terrace, Edinburgh EH12 5HD T 0131-244 2001 E lgbcs@scottishboundaries.gov.uk W www.lgbc-scotland.gov.uk

BOUNDARY COMMISSION FOR NORTHERN IRELAND, The Bungalow, Stormont House, Stormont Estate, Belfast BT4 3SH T 028-9052 7821 E contact@boundarycommission.org.uk W www.boundarycommission.org.uk

INTERNAL ORGANISATION

The council as a whole is the final decision-making body within any authority. Councils are free to a great extent to make their own internal organisational arrangements. The Local Government Act, given royal assent on 28 July 2000, allows councils to adopt one of three broad categories of constitution which include a separate executive:

- A directly elected mayor with a cabinet selected by that mayor
- A cabinet, either elected by the council or appointed by its leader
- A directly elected mayor and council manager

Normally, questions of policy are settled by the full council, while the administration of the various services is the responsibility of committees of councillors. Day-to-day decisions are delegated to the council's officers, who act within the policies laid down by the councillors.

FINANCE

Local government in England, Wales and Scotland is financed from four sources: council tax, non-domestic rates, government grants and income from fees and charges for services.

COUNCIL TAX

Council tax is a local tax levied by each local council. Liability for the council tax bill usually falls on the owner-occupier or tenant of a dwelling which is their sole or main residence. Council tax bills may be reduced because of the personal circumstances of people resident in a property and there are discounts in the case of dwellings occupied by fewer than two adults.

In England, unitary and metropolitan authorities are responsible for collecting their own council tax. In areas where there are two tiers of local authority, each county and district authority sets its own council tax rate; the district authorities collect the combined council tax and the county councils claim their share from the district councils' collection funds. In Wales and Scotland each unitary authority sets its own council tax rate and is responsible for collection.

The tax relates to the value of the dwelling. In England and Scotland each dwelling is placed in one of eight valuation bands, ranging from A to H, based on the property's estimated market value as at 1 April 1991. In Wales there are nine bands, ranging from A to I, based on the estimated market value of property as at 1 April 2003.

The valuation bands and ranges of values in England, Wales and Scotland are:

England

A	Up to £40,000	E	£88,001–£120,000
B	£40,001–£52,000	F	£120,001–£160,000
C	£52,001–£68,000	G	£160,001–£320,000
D	£68,001–£88,000	H	Over £320,001

Wales

A	Up to £44,000	F	£162,001–£223,000
B	£44,001–£65,000	G	£223,001–£324,000
C	£65,001–£91,000	H	£324,001–£424,000
D	£91,001–£123,000	I	Over £424,001
E	£123,001–£162,000		

Scotland

A	Up to £27,000	E	£58,001–£80,000
B	£27,001–£35,000	F	£80,001–£106,000
C	£35,001–£45,000	G	£106,001–£212,000
D	£45,001–£58,000	H	Over £212,001

The council tax within a local area varies between the different bands according to proportions laid down by law. The charge attributable to each band as a proportion of the Band D charge set by the council is approximately:

A	67%	F	144%
B	78%	G	167%
C	89%	H	200%
D	100%	I*	233%
E	122%		

* Wales only

The average Band D council tax bill for each authority area is given in the complete lists of local authorities for England, London, Wales and Scotland which follow. There may be variations from the given figure within each district council area because of different parish or community precepts being levied.

NON-DOMESTIC RATES

Non-domestic (business) rates are collected by billing authorities; these are the district councils in those areas of England with two tiers of local government and unitary authorities in other parts of England, in Wales and in Scotland. In respect of England and Wales, the Local Government Finance Act 1988 provides for liability for rates to be assessed on the basis of a poundage (multiplier) tax on the rateable value of property (hereditaments). Separate multipliers are set by the Department for Communities and Local Government (DCLG) in England, the Welsh government and the Scottish government. Rates are collected by the billing authority for the area where a property is located. Rate income collected by billing authorities is paid into a national non-domestic rating (NNDR) pool and redistributed to individual authorities on the basis of the adult population figure as prescribed by DCLG, the Welsh government or the Scottish government. The rates pools are maintained separately in England, Wales and Scotland. Actual payment of rates in certain cases is subject to transitional arrangements, to phase in the larger increases and reductions in rates resulting from the effects of the latest revaluation.

The most recent rating lists for England, Wales and Scotland came into effect on 1 April 2017. The rateable values on these lists are derived from the rental value of property as at 1 April 2015 and determined on certain statutory assumptions by the Valuation Office Agency in England and Wales, and by local area assessors in Scotland. New property which is added to the list, and significant changes to existing property, necessitate amendments to the rateable value on the same basis. Rating lists (valuation rolls in Scotland) remain in force until the next general revaluation, which usually takes place every five years to reflect changes in the property market.

A revaluation of non-domestic properties in Northern Ireland was completed at the start of 2015 and since 1 April 2015 the rateable value of all non-domestic properties in Northern Ireland is based on the rental value of the property as at 1 April 2013; there is no date scheduled for the next revaluation.

Certain types of property are exempt from rates, eg agricultural land and buildings, buildings used for the training or welfare of disabled people and buildings registered for public religious worship. Charities and other non-profit-making organisations may receive full or partial relief and relief schemes for small businesses are available in England, Wales, Scotland and Northern Ireland. Empty commercial property in England and Wales is exempt from business rates for the first three months that the property is vacant, empty industrial property for six months and listed buildings are exempt until re-occupied; after which full business rates are normally payable. In Scotland empty commercial property is entitled to a 50 per cent discount on business rates for the first three months and a 10 per cent discount thereafter, empty industrial buildings are entitled to full relief for six months and a 10 per cent discount thereafter and empty listed buildings and properties with a rateable value of less than £1,700 are entirely exempt.

COMPLAINTS

ENGLAND

In England the Local Government Ombudsman investigates complaints of injustice arising from maladministration by local authorities and certain other bodies. The Local Government Ombudsman will not usually consider a complaint unless the local authority concerned has had an opportunity to investigate and reply to a complainant.
LOCAL GOVERNMENT OMBUDSMAN, 53–55 Butts Road, Coventry CV1 3BH T 0300-061 0614 W www.lgo.org.uk
Ombudsman, Michael King

WALES

The office of Public Services Ombudsman for Wales came into force on 1 April 2006, incorporating the functions of the Local Government Ombudsman for Wales.
PUBLIC SERVICES OMBUDSMAN FOR WALES, 1 Ffordd yr Hen Gae, Pencoed CF35 5LJ T 0300-790 0203
W www.ombudsman-wales.org.uk
Ombudsman, Nick Bennett

SCOTLAND

The Scottish Public Services Ombudsman is responsible for complaints regarding the maladministration of local government in Scotland.
SCOTTISH PUBLIC SERVICES OMBUDSMAN, 4 Melville Street, Edinburgh EH3 7NS T 0800-377 7330
W www.spso.org.uk
Ombudsman, Rosemary Agnew

NORTHERN IRELAND

The Local Government Commissioner for Standards fulfils a similar function in Northern Ireland, investigating complaints about local authorities and certain public bodies. Complaints are made to the relevant local authority in the first instance but may also be made directly to the commissioner.

NORTHERN IRELAND LOCAL GOVERNMENT COMMISSIONER FOR STANDARDS, Progressive House, 33 Wellington Place, Belfast BT1 6HN T 028-9023 3821
E nipso@nipso.org.uk W www.nipso.org.uk
Local Government Commissioner for Standards, Marie Anderson

THE QUEEN'S REPRESENTATIVES

The lord-lieutenant of a county is the permanent local representative of the Crown in that county. The appointment of lord-lieutenants is now regulated by the Lieutenancies Act 1997. They are appointed by the sovereign on the recommendation of the prime minister. The retirement age is 75. The office of lord-lieutenant dates from 1551, and its holder was originally responsible for maintaining order and for local defence in the county. The duties of the post include attending on royalty during official visits to the county, performing certain duties in connection with the armed forces (and in particular the reserve forces), and making presentations of honours and awards on behalf of the Crown. In England, Wales and Northern Ireland, the lord-lieutenant usually also holds the office of *Custos Rotulorum.* As such, he or she acts as head of the county's commission of the peace (which recommends the appointment of magistrates).

The office of sheriff (from the Old English *shire-reeve*) of a county was created in the tenth century. The sheriff was the special nominee of the sovereign, and the office reached the peak of its influence under the Norman kings. The Provisions of Oxford (1258) laid down a yearly tenure of office. Since the mid-16th century the office has been purely civil, with military duties taken over by the lord-lieutenant of the county. The sheriff (commonly known as 'high sheriff') attends on royalty during official visits to the county, acts as the returning officer during parliamentary elections in county constituencies, attends the opening ceremony when a high court judge goes on circuit, executes high court writs, and appoints under-sheriffs to act as deputies. The appointments and duties of the sheriffs in England and Wales are laid down by the Sheriffs Act 1887.

The serving high sheriff submits a list of names of possible future sheriffs to a tribunal, which chooses three names to put to the sovereign. The tribunal nominates the high sheriff annually on 12 November and the sovereign picks the name of the sheriff to succeed in the following year. The term of office runs from 25 March to the following 24 March (the civil and legal year before 1752). No person may be chosen twice in three years if there is any other suitable person in the county.

CIVIC DIGNITIES

District councils in England and local councils in Wales may petition for a royal charter granting borough or 'city' status to the council.

In England and Wales the chair of a borough or county borough council may be called a mayor, and the chair of a city council may be called a lord mayor (if lord mayoralty has been conferred on that city). Parish councils in England and community councils in Wales may call themselves 'town councils', in which case their chair is the town mayor.

In Scotland the chair of a local council may be known as a convenor; a provost is the mayoral equivalent. The chair of the councils for the cities of Aberdeen, Dundee, Edinburgh and Glasgow are lord provosts.

ENGLAND

The country of England lies between 55° 46′ and 49° 57′ 30″ N. latitude (from a few miles north of the mouth of the Tweed to the Lizard), and between 1° 46′ E. and 5° 43′ W. longitude (from Lowestoft to Land's End). England is bounded on the north by the Cheviot Hills; on the south by the English Channel; on the east by the Straits of Dover (Pas de Calais) and the North Sea; and on the west by the Atlantic Ocean, Wales and the Irish Sea. It has a total area of 130,432 sq. km (50,360 sq. miles): land 130,279 sq. km (50,301 sq. miles); inland water 153 sq. km (59 sq. miles).

There are 27 counties, divided into 201 districts, 55 unitary authorities (plus the Isles of Scilly) and 36 metropolitan boroughs.

POPULATION

The population at the 2011 census was 53,012,456 (men 26,069,148; women 26,943,308). The average density of the population in 2011 was 406 persons per sq. km (1,053 per sq. mile).

The populations of most of the unitary authorities are in the range of 100,000 to 300,000. The district councils have populations broadly in the range of 60,000 to 150,000; some, however, have larger populations, because of the need to avoid dividing large towns, and some in mainly rural areas have smaller populations.

The main conurbations outside Greater London – Tyne and Wear, West Midlands, Merseyside, Greater Manchester, West Yorkshire and South Yorkshire – are divided into 36 metropolitan boroughs, most of which have a population of over 200,000.

ELECTIONS

For districts, counties and for 8,810 parishes, there are elected councils, consisting of directly elected councillors. The councillors elect one of their number as chair annually.

In general, councils can have whole council elections, elections by thirds or elections by halves. However all metropolitan authorities must hold elections by thirds. The electoral cycle of any new unitary authority is specified in the appropriate statutory order under which it is established.

COUNCIL FUNCTIONS

In areas with a two-tier system of local governance, functions are divided between the district and county authorities, with those functions affecting the larger area or population generally being the responsibility of the county council. A few functions continue to be exercised over the larger area by joint bodies, made up of councillors from each authority within the area.

Generally the allocation of functions is as follows:

County councils: education; strategic planning; traffic, transport and highways; fire service; consumer protection; refuse disposal; smallholdings; social care; libraries

District councils: local planning; housing; highways (maintenance of certain urban roads and off-street car parks); building regulations; environmental health; refuse collection; cemeteries and crematoria; collection of council tax and non-domestic rates

Unitary and metropolitan councils: their functions are all those listed above, except that the fire service is exercised by a joint body

Concurrently by county and district councils: recreation (parks, playing fields, swimming pools); museums; encouragement of the arts, tourism and industry

PARISH COUNCILS

Parish or town councils are the most local tier of government in England. There are currently 10,199 parishes in England, of which around 8,817 have councils. Since 15 February 2008 local councils have been able to create new parish councils without seeking approval from the government. Around 80 per cent of parish councils represent populations of less than 2,500; parishes with no parish council can be grouped with neighbouring parishes under a common parish council. A parish council comprises at least five members, the number being fixed by the district council. Elections are held every four years, at the time of the election of the district councillor for the ward including the parish. Full parish councils must be formed for those parishes with more than 999 electors – below this number, parish meetings comprising the electors of the parish must be held at least twice a year.

Parish council functions include: allotments; encouragement of arts and crafts; community halls, recreational facilities (eg open spaces, swimming pools), cemeteries and crematoria; and many minor functions. They must also be given an opportunity to comment on planning applications. They may, like county and district councils, spend limited sums for the general benefit of the parish. They levy a precept on the district councils for their funds. Parish precepts for 2017–18 total £485m, an increase of 9 per cent on 2016–17.

FINANCE

Local government revenue expenditure is budgeted to be £94.5bn in 2017–18; of this £27.6bn is to be raised through council tax, £14.7bn from the business rate retention scheme and £50.2bn from government grants. The remainder will be drawn down from local authority reserves.

Since April 2013 local authorities retain a share of business rates and keep the growth on that share (the 'rate retention scheme'). Revenue support grant is paid to local authorities to enable all authorities in the same class to broadly set the same council tax; in 2017–18 revenue support grant totals £3.9bn. In addition central government pays specific grants in support of revenue expenditure on particular services. Police grant totals £7.3bn in 2017–18. In 2017–18, local authorities were able to increase council tax by up to 3 per cent to fund adult social care; this is in addition to the usual funding of adult social care through council tax. Adult social care precept totals £552m in 2017–18.

In England, the average council tax per dwelling for 2017–18 is £1,185, an increase of 5.1 per cent from 2016–17. The average council tax bill for a Band D dwelling (occupied by two adults, including adult social care and parish precepts) for 2017–18 is £1,591, an increase of 4.0 per cent from 2016–17. The average Band D council tax is £1,662 in shire districts, £1,575 in metropolitan areas, £1,641 in unitary authority areas and £1,350 in London. Since 2006–7 the London figure has included a levy to fund the 2012 Olympic Games. This precept equated to £20 a year on a Band D property between 2006–7 and 2015–16. The precept was £8 in 2016–17 and will remain at this level for 2017–18.

The non-domestic rating multiplier for England for 2017–18 is 47.9p (46.6p for small businesses). The City of London is able to set a different multiplier from the rest of England; for 2017–18 this is 48.4p (47.1p for small businesses).

Under the Local Government and Housing Act 1989, local authorities have four main ways of paying for capital expenditure: borrowing and other forms of extended credit; capital grants from central government towards some types of capital expenditure; 'usable' capital receipts from the sale of land, houses and other assets; and revenue.

The amount of capital expenditure which a local authority can finance by borrowing (or other forms of credit) is effectively limited by the credit approvals issued to it by central government. Most credit approvals can be used for any kind of local authority capital expenditure; these are known as basic credit approvals. Others (supplementary credit approvals) can be used only for the kind of expenditure specified in the approval, and so are often given to fund particular projects or services.

Local authorities can use all capital receipts from the sale of property or assets for capital spending, except in the case of sales of council houses. Generally, the 'usable' part of a local authority's capital receipts consists of 25 per cent of receipts from the sale of council houses and 50 per cent of other housing assets such as shops or vacant land. The balance has to be set aside as provision for repaying debt and meeting other credit liabilities.

EXPENDITURE

Budgeted revenue expenditure for 2017–18 is:

Service	£ million
Education	33,343
Highways and transport	4,240
Social care	23,651
Public health	3,410
Housing (excluding HRA)	1,543
Cultural, environment and planning	8,332
Police	11,145
Fire and rescue	2,055
Central	2,987
Other	264
Total Service Expenditure	90,970
*Housing benefits	20,304
Parish precepts	486
†Levies	69
Trading account and other adjustments	(458)
Total Net Current Expenditure	111,370
Non-current Expenditure and External Receipts	
Capital expenditure charged to revenue account	1,785
Housing benefits subsidies	(20,308)
Community infrastructure levy	(138)
Capital financing and debt servicing	4,261
REVENUE EXPENDITURE	94,470

HRA = Housing Revenue Account

* Includes all mandatory and non-mandatory housing benefits

† Includes Integrated Transport Authority levy, Waste Disposal Authority levy, London Pensions Fund Authority levy and other levies

RELIEF

There is a marked division between the upland and lowland areas of England. In the extreme north the Cheviot Hills (highest point, the Cheviot, 815m/2,674ft) form a natural boundary with Scotland. Running south from the Cheviots, though divided from them by the Tyne Gap, is the Pennine range (highest point, Cross Fell, 893m/2,930ft), the main orological feature of the country. The Pennines culminate in the Peak District of Derbyshire (Kinder Scout, 636m/2,088ft). West of the Pennines are the Cumbrian mountains, which include Scafell Pike (978m/3,210ft), the highest peak in England, and to the east are the Yorkshire Moors, their highest point being Urra Moor (454m/1,490ft).

In the west, the foothills of the Welsh mountains extend into the bordering English counties of Shropshire (the Wrekin, 407m/1,334ft; Long Mynd, 516m/1,694ft) and Hereford and Worcester (the Malvern Hills – Worcestershire Beacon, 425m/1,394ft). Extensive areas of highland and moorland are also to be found in the south-western peninsula formed by Somerset, Devon and Cornwall, principally Exmoor (Dunkery Beacon, 519m/1,704ft), Dartmoor (High Willhays, 621m/2,038ft) and Bodmin Moor (Brown Willy, 420m/1,377ft). Ranges of low, undulating hills run across the south of the country, including the Cotswolds in the Midlands and south-west, the Chilterns to the north of London, and the North (Kent) and South (Sussex) Downs of the south-east coastal areas.

The lowlands of England lie in the Vale of York, East Anglia and the area around the Wash. The lowest-lying are the Cambridgeshire Fens in the valleys of the Great Ouse and the river Nene, which are below sea-level in places. Since the 17th century extensive drainage has brought much of the Fens under cultivation. The North Sea coast between the Thames and the Humber, low-lying and formed of sand and shingle for the most part, is subject to erosion and defences against further incursion have been built along many stretches.

HYDROGRAPHY

The Severn is the longest river in Great Britain, rising on the north-eastern slopes of Plynlimon (Wales) and entering England in Shropshire, with a total length of 354km (220 miles) from its source to its outflow into the Bristol Channel, where it receives the Bristol Avon on the east and the Wye on the west; its other tributaries are the Vyrnwy, Tern, Stour, Teme and Upper (or Warwickshire) Avon. The Severn is tidal below Gloucester, and a high bore or tidal wave sometimes reverses the flow as high as Tewkesbury (21.75km/13.5 miles above Gloucester). The scenery of the greater part of the river is very picturesque, and the Severn is a noted salmon river, with some of its tributaries being famous for trout. Navigation is assisted by the Gloucester and Berkeley Ship Canal (26km/16.25 miles), which admits vessels of 350 tons to Gloucester. The Severn Tunnel was begun in 1873 and completed in 1886 at a cost of £2m and after many difficulties caused by flooding. It is 7km (4 miles 628 yards) in length (of which 3.67km/2.25 miles are under the river). The Severn road bridge between Haysgate, Gwent, and Almondsbury, Glos, with a centre span of 988m (3,240ft), was opened in 1966.

The longest river wholly in England is the Thames, with a total length of 346km (215 miles) from its source in the Cotswold hills to the Nore, and is navigable by ocean-going ships to London Bridge. The Thames is tidal to Teddington (111km/69 miles from its mouth) and forms county boundaries almost throughout its course; on its banks are situated London, Windsor Castle, Eton College and Oxford University. Of the remaining English rivers, those flowing into the North Sea are the Tyne, Wear, Tees, Ouse and Trent from the Pennine Range, the Great Ouse (257km/160 miles), which rises in Northamptonshire, and the Orwell and Stour from the hills of East Anglia. Flowing into the English Channel are the Sussex Ouse from the Weald, the Itchen from the Hampshire hills, and the Axe, Teign, Dart, Tamar and Exe from the Devonian hills. Flowing into the Irish Sea are the Mersey, Ribble and Eden from the western slopes of the Pennines and the Derwent from the Cumbrian mountains.

The English Lakes, notable for their picturesque scenery and poetic associations, lie in Cumbria's Lake District; the largest are Windermere (14.7 sq. km/5.7 sq. miles), Ullswater (8.8 sq. km/3.4 sq. miles) and Derwent Water (5.3 sq. km/2.0 sq. miles).

FLAG

The flag of England is the cross of St George, a red cross on a white field (cross gules in a field argent). The cross of St George, the patron saint of England, has been used since the 13th century.

ISLANDS

The Isle of Wight is separated from Hampshire by the Solent. The capital, Newport, stands at the head of the estuary of the Medina, and Cowes (at the mouth) is the chief port. Other centres are Ryde, Sandown, Shanklin, Ventnor, Freshwater, Yarmouth, Totland Bay, Seaview and Bembridge.

Lundy (the name is derived from the Old Norse for 'puffin island'), 18km (11 miles) north-west of Hartland Point, Devon, is around 5km (3 miles) long and almost 1km (half a mile) wide on average, with a total area of around 452 hectares (1,116 acres), and a population of 27. It became the property of the National Trust in 1969 and is now principally a bird sanctuary and the UK's first marine conservation zone.

The Isles of Scilly comprise around 140 islands and skerries (total area, 10 sq. km/6 sq. miles) situated 45 km (28 miles)

south-west of Land's End in Cornwall. Only five are inhabited: St Mary's, St Agnes, Bryher, Tresco and St Martin's. The population at the 2011 census was 2,200. The entire group has been designated an Area of Outstanding Natural Beauty because of its unique flora and fauna. Tourism and the winter/spring flower trade for the home market form the basis of the economy of the islands. The island group is a recognised rural development area.

EARLY HISTORY

Archaeological evidence suggests that England has been inhabited since at least the Palaeolithic period, though the extent of the various Palaeolithic cultures was dependent upon the degree of glaciation. The succeeding Neolithic and Bronze Age cultures have left abundant remains throughout the country; the best-known of these are the henges and stone circles of Stonehenge (ten miles north of Salisbury, Wilts) and Avebury (Wilts), both of which are believed to have been of religious significance. In the latter part of the Bronze Age the Goidels, a people of the Celtic race, invaded the country and brought with them Celtic civilisation and dialects; as a result place names in England bear witness to the spread of the invasion across the whole region.

THE ROMAN CONQUEST

The Roman conquest of Gaul (57–50 BC) brought Britain into close contact with Roman civilisation, but although Julius Caesar raided the south of Britain in 55 and 54 BC, conquest was not undertaken until nearly 100 years later. In AD 43 the Emperor Claudius dispatched Aulus Plautius, with a well-equipped force of 40,000, and himself followed with reinforcements in the same year. Success was delayed by the resistance of Caratacus (Caractacus), the British leader from AD 48–51, who was finally captured and sent to Rome, and by a great revolt in AD 61 led by Boudicca (Boadicea), Queen of the Iceni, but the south of Britain was secured by AD 70, and Wales and the area north to the Tyne by about AD 80.

In AD 122, the Emperor Hadrian visited Britain and built a continuous rampart, since known as Hadrian's Wall, from Wallsend to Bowness (Tyne to Solway). The work was entrusted by the Emperor Hadrian to Aulus Platorius Nepos, legate of Britain from AD 122 to 126, and it was intended to form the northern frontier of the Roman Empire.

The Romans administered Britain as a province under a governor, with a well-defined system of local government, each Roman municipality ruling itself and its surrounding territory, while London was the centre of the road system and the seat of the financial officials of the Province of Britain. Colchester, Lincoln, York, Gloucester and St Albans stand on the sites of five Roman municipalities, and Wroxeter, Caerleon, Chester, Lincoln and York were at various times the sites of legionary fortresses. Well-preserved Roman towns have been uncovered at or near Silchester (Calleva Atrebatum), ten miles south of Reading, Wroxeter (Viroconium Cornoviorum), near Shrewsbury and St Albans (Verulamium) in Hertfordshire.

Four main groups of roads radiated from London, and a fifth (the Fosse) ran obliquely from Lincoln through Leicester, Cirencester and Bath to Exeter. Of the four groups radiating from London, one ran south-east to Canterbury and the coast of Kent, a second to Silchester and thence to parts of western Britain and south Wales, a third (later known as Watling Street) ran through St Albans to Chester, with various branches, and the fourth reached Colchester, Lincoln, York and the eastern counties.

In the fourth century Britain was subjected to raids along the east coast by Saxon pirates, which led to the establishment of a system of coastal defences from the Wash to Southampton Water, with forts at Brancaster, Burgh Castle (Yarmouth), Walton (Felixstowe), Bradwell, Reculver, Richborough, Dover, Lympne, Pevensey and Porchester (Portsmouth). The Irish (Scoti) and Picts in the north were also becoming aggressive and from around AD 350 incursions became more frequent and more formidable. As the Roman Empire came increasingly under attack towards the end of the fourth century, many troops were removed from Britain for service in other parts of the empire. The island was eventually cut off from Rome by the Teutonic conquest of Gaul, and with the withdrawal of the last Roman garrison early in the fifth century, the Romano-British were left to themselves.

SAXON SETTLEMENT

According to legend, the British King Vortigern called in the Saxons to defend his lands against the Picts. The Saxon chieftains Hengist and Horsa landed at Ebbsfleet, Kent, and established themselves in the Isle of Thanet, but the events during the one-and-a-half centuries between the final break with Rome and the re-establishment of Christianity are unclear. However, it would appear that over the course of this period the raids turned into large-scale settlement by invaders traditionally known as Angles (England north of the Wash and East Anglia), Saxons (Essex and southern England) and Jutes (Kent and the Weald), which pushed the Romano-British into the mountainous areas of the north and west. Celtic culture outside Wales and Cornwall survives only in topographical names. Various kingdoms established at this time attempted to claim overlordship of the whole country, hegemony finally being achieved by Wessex (with the capital at Winchester) in the ninth century. This century also saw the beginning of raids by the Vikings (Danes), which were resisted by Alfred the Great (871–899), who fixed a limit on the advance of Danish settlement by the Treaty of Wedmore (878), giving them the area north and east of Watling Street on the condition that they adopt Christianity.

In the tenth century the kings of Wessex recovered the whole of England from the Danes, but subsequent rulers were unable to resist a second wave of invaders. England paid tribute (Danegeld) for many years, and was invaded in 1013 by the Danes and ruled by Danish kings (including Cnut) from 1016 until 1042, when Edward the Confessor was recalled from exile in Normandy. On Edward's death in 1066 Harold Godwinson (brother-in-law of Edward and son of Earl Godwin of Wessex) was chosen to be King of England. After defeating (at Stamford Bridge, Yorkshire, 25 September 1066) an invading army under Harald Hadraada, King of Norway (aided by the outlawed Earl Tostig of Northumbria, Harold's brother), Harold was himself defeated at the Battle of Hastings on 14 October 1066, and the Norman conquest secured the throne of England for Duke William of Normandy, a cousin of Edward the Confessor.

CHRISTIANITY

Christianity reached the Roman province of Britain from Gaul in the third century (or possibly earlier). Alban, traditionally Britain's first martyr, was put to death as a Christian during the persecution of Diocletian (22 June 303) at his native town Verulamium, and the bishops of Londinium, Eboracum (York), and Lindum (Lincoln) attended the Council of Arles in 314. However, the Anglo-Saxon invasions submerged the Christian religion in England until the sixth century: conversion was undertaken in the north from 563 by Celtic missionaries from Ireland led by St Columba, and in the south by a mission sent from Rome in 597 which was led by St Augustine, who became the first archbishop of Canterbury. England appears to have been converted again by the end of the seventh century and followed, after the Council of Whitby in 663, the practices of the Roman Church, which brought the kingdom into the mainstream of European thought and culture.

PRINCIPAL CITIES

There are 51 cities in England and space constraints prevent us from including profiles of them all. Below is a selection of England's principal cities with the date on which city status was conferred in parentheses. Other cities are Bradford (pre-1900), Chelmsford (2012), Chichester (pre-1900), Coventry (pre-1900), Derby (1977), Ely (pre-1900), Exeter (pre-1900), Gloucester (pre-1900), Hereford (pre-1900), Kingston-upon-Hull (pre-1900), Lancaster (1937), Lichfield (pre-1900), London (pre-1900), Peterborough (pre-1900), Plymouth (1928), Portsmouth (1926), Preston (2002), Ripon (pre-1900), Salford (1926), Stoke-on-Trent (1925), Sunderland (1992), Truro (pre-1900), Wakefield (pre-1900), Wells (pre-1900), Westminster (pre-1900), Wolverhampton (2000) and Worcester (pre-1900).

Certain cities have also been granted a lord mayoralty – this grant confers no additional powers or functions and is purely honorific. Cities with lord mayors are Birmingham, Bradford, Bristol, Canterbury, Chester, Coventry, Exeter, Kingston-upon-Hull, Leeds, Leicester, Liverpool, London, Manchester, Newcastle-upon-Tyne, Norwich, Nottingham, Oxford, Plymouth, Portsmouth, Sheffield, Stoke-on-Trent, Westminster and York.

BATH (PRE-1900)

Bath stands on the river Avon between the Cotswold Hills to the north and the Mendips to the south, and was originally a small roman town *(Aquae Sulis)* with a baths and temple complex built around naturally occurring hot springs. In the early 18th century Bath became England's premier spa town where the rich and celebrated members of fashionable society gathered to 'take the waters' and enjoy the town's theatres and concert rooms. During this period the architect John Wood laid the foundations of a new Georgian city built using the honey-coloured stone for which Bath is famous today. Since 1987 the city has been listed as a UNESCO World Heritage Site.

Contemporary Bath is a thriving tourist destination and remains a leading cultural, religious and historical centre with many art galleries and historic sites including the Pump Room (1790); the Royal Crescent (1767); the Circus (1754); the 18th-century Assembly Rooms (housing the Museum of Costume); Pulteney Bridge (1771); the Guildhall and the Abbey, now over 500 years old, which is built on the site of a Saxon monastery. In 2006 the Bath Thermae Spa was completed and the hot springs reopened to the public for the first time since 1978.

BIRMINGHAM (PRE-1900)

Birmingham is Britain's second largest city, with a population of over one million. The generally accepted derivation of 'Birmingham' is the *ham* (dwelling-place) of the *ing* (family) of *Beorma*, presumed to have been Saxon. During the Industrial Revolution the town grew into a major manufacturing centre, known as the 'city of a thousand trades', and in 1889 was granted city status. By the 18th century, Birmingham was the main European producer of items such as buckles, medals and coins. Today, around 40 per cent of all the UK's handmade jewellery is produced in Birmingham's Jewellery Quarter. Another product of the Industrial Revolution are the city's 34 miles (56km) of canals.

Recent developments include Millennium Point, which houses Thinktank, the Birmingham science museum, and Brindleyplace, a development of shops, offices and leisure facilities on a former industrial site clustered around canals. In 2003 the Bullring shopping centre was officially opened as part of the city's urban regeneration programme.

The principal buildings are the Town Hall (1834–50), the Council House (1879), Victoria Law Courts (1891), the University of Birmingham (1906–9), the 13th-century church of St Martin in the Bull Ring (rebuilt 1873), the cathedral (formerly St Philip's Church) (1711), the Roman Catholic cathedral of St Chad (1839–41), the Assay Office (1773), the Rotunda (1964) and the National Exhibition Centre (1976).

BRIGHTON AND HOVE (2000)

Brighton and Hove is situated on the south coast of England, around 96km (60 miles) south of London. Originally a fishing village called Brighthelmstone, it was transformed into a fashionable seaside resort in the 18th century when Dr Richard Russell popularised the benefits of his 'sea-water cure'; as one of the closest beaches to London, Brighton began to attract wealthy visitors. One of these was the Prince Regent (the future King George IV), who first visited in 1783 and became so fond of the city that in 1807 he bought the former farmhouse he had been renting, and gradually turned it into Brighton's most recognisable building, the Royal Pavilion. The Pavilion is renowned for its Indo-Saracenic exterior, featuring minarets and an enormous central dome designed by John Nash, combined with the lavish chinoiserie of Frederick Crace's and Robert Jones' interiors. Queen Victoria sold the Pavilion to Brighton's municipal authority in 1850.

Brighton and Hove's Regency heritage can also be seen in the numerous elegant squares and crescents designed by Amon Wilds and Augustin Busby that dominate the seafront.

BRISTOL (PRE-1900)

Bristol was a royal borough before the Norman conquest. The earliest form of the name is *Bricgstow*. Due to the city's position close to the mouth of the River Avon, it was an important location for marine trade for centuries and prospered greatly from the transatlantic slave trade during the 18th century.

The principal buildings include the 12th-century cathedral with Norman chapter house and gateway; the 14th-century church of St Mary Redcliffe; Wesley's Chapel, Broadmead; the Merchant Venturers' Almshouses; the Council House (1956); the Guildhall; the Exchange (erected from the designs of John Wood in 1743); Cabot Tower; the university and Clifton College.

The Clifton Suspension Bridge, with a span of 214m (702ft) over the Avon, was projected by Isambard Kingdom Brunel in 1836 but was not completed until 1864. Brunel's SS *Great Britain,* the first ocean-going propeller-driven ship, now forms a museum at the western dockyard, from where she was originally launched in 1843. The docks themselves have been extensively restored and redeveloped; the 19th-century two-storey former tea warehouse is now the Arnolfini Centre for Contemporary Arts, and an 18th-century sail-loft houses the Architecture Centre. On Princes Wharf, 1950s transit sheds have been renovated and converted into the museum of Bristol, M Shed, which opened in 2011.

CAMBRIDGE (1951)

Cambridge, a settlement far older than its ancient university, lies on the River Cam (or Granta). Its industries include technology research and development, and biotechnology. Among its open spaces are Jesus Green, Sheep's Green, Coe Fen, Parker's Piece, Christ's Pieces, the University Botanic Garden, and the 'Backs' – lawns and gardens through which the Cam winds behind the principal line of college buildings. Historical sites east of the Cam include King's Parade, Great St Mary's Church, Gibbs' Senate House and King's College Chapel.

University and college buildings provide the outstanding features of Cambridge's architecture but several churches (especially St Benet's, the oldest building in the city, and Holy Sepulchre or the Round Church) are also notable. The Guildhall (1937) stands on a site of which at least part has held municipal buildings since 1224. In 2009 the University of Cambridge celebrated its 800th anniversary.

CANTERBURY (PRE-1900)

Canterbury, seat of the Archbishop of Canterbury, the primate of the Church of England, dates back to prehistoric times. It was the Roman *Durovernum Cantiacorum* and the Saxon *Cant-wara-byrig* (stronghold of the men of Kent). It was here in 597 that St Augustine began the conversion of the English to Christianity, when Ethelbert, King of Kent, was baptised.

Of the Benedictine St Augustine's Abbey, burial place of the Jutish kings of Kent, only ruins remain. According to Bede, St Martin's Church, on the eastern outskirts of the city, was the place of worship of Queen Bertha, the Christian wife of King

Ethelbert, before the advent of St Augustine. In 1170 the rivalry of Church and State culminated in the murder of Archbishop Thomas Becket in Canterbury Cathedral, by Henry II's knights. His shrine became a great centre of pilgrimage, as described in Chaucer's *Canterbury Tales*. After the Reformation pilgrimages ceased, the prosperity of the city was strengthened by an influx of Huguenot refugees, who introduced weaving. The poet and playwright Christopher Marlowe was born and raised in Canterbury and the city is home to the 1,200-seat Marlowe Theatre, which reopened to the public in 2011, following an extensive £25m rebuild.

The cathedral, its architecture ranging from the 11th to the 15th centuries, is famous worldwide. Visitors are attracted particularly to the Martyrdom, the Black Prince's Tomb and the Warriors' Chapel.

The medieval city walls are built on Roman foundations and the 14th-century West Gate is one of the finest buildings of its kind in the country.

CHESTER (PRE-1900)

Chester is situated on the River Dee. Its recorded history dates from the first century when the Romans founded the fortress of *Deva*. The city's name is derived from the latin *Castra* (a camp or encampment). During the middle ages, Chester was the principal port of north-west England but declined with the silting of the Dee estuary and competition from Liverpool. The city was also an important military centre, notably during Edward I's Welsh campaigns and the Elizabethan Irish campaigns. During the Civil War, Chester supported the king and was besieged from 1643 to 1646. Chester's first charter was granted *c.*1175 and the city was incorporated in 1506. The office of sheriff is the earliest created in the country (1120s), and in 1992 the mayor, who also enjoys the title 'Admiral of the Dee', was made a lord mayor.

The city's architectural features include the city walls (an almost complete two-mile circuit), the unique 13th-century Rows (covered galleries above the street-level shops), the Victorian Gothic town hall (1869), the castle (rebuilt 1788 and 1822) and numerous half-timbered buildings. The cathedral was a Benedictine abbey until the dissolution of the monasteries. Chester racecourse is the oldest racecourse in Britain, believed to have origins in the 13th century. The first recorded horserace was in 1539 during the reign of Henry VIII. Chester also houses the ruins of a Roman amphitheatre, built in the late first century AD.

DURHAM (PRE-1900)

The city of Durham's prominent Norman cathedral and castle are set high on a wooded peninsula overlooking the River Wear. The cathedral was founded as a shrine for the body of St Cuthbert in 995. The present building dates from 1093 and among its many treasures is the tomb of the Venerable Bede (673–735). Durham's prince bishops had unique powers up to 1836, being lay rulers as well as religious leaders. As a palatinate, Durham could have its own army, nobility, coinage and courts. The castle was the main seat of the prince bishops for nearly 800 years; it is now used as a college by the University of Durham. The university, founded in the early 19th century on the initiative of Bishop William Van Mildert, is England's third oldest.

Annual events include Durham's regatta in June (claimed to be the oldest rowing event in Britain) and the annual Gala (formerly Durham Miners' Gala) in July. Durham County Cricket Club was established in 1882.

LEEDS (PRE-1900)

Leeds, situated in the lower Aire valley, was first incorporated by Charles I in 1626. The earliest forms of the name are *Loidis* or *Ledes*, the origins of which are obscure.

The principal buildings are the Civic Hall (1933), the Town Hall (1858), the Municipal Buildings and Art Gallery (1884) with the Henry Moore Gallery (1982), the Corn Exchange (1863) and the university. The parish church of St Peter was

rebuilt in 1841 and granted minister status in 2012. The 17th-century St John's Church has a fine interior with a famous English Renaissance screen; the last remaining 18th-century church in the city is Holy Trinity in Boar Lane (1727). Kirkstall Abbey (about three miles from the centre of the city), founded by Henry de Lacy in 1152, is one of the most complete examples of a Cistercian house now remaining. The Royal Armouries Museum forms part of a group of museums that house the national collection of antique arms and armour. The Grand Theatre and Opera House is home to Northern Ballet and Opera North.

LEICESTER (1919)

Leicester is situated in central England. The city was an important Roman settlement and also one of the five 'burghs' or boroughs of the Danelaw. In 1485 Richard III was buried in Leicester following his death at the nearby Battle of Bosworth. In 1589 Queen Elizabeth I granted a charter to the city and the ancient title was confirmed by letters patent in 1919.

The textile industry was responsible for Leicester's early expansion and the city still maintains a strong manufacturing base. Cotton mills and factories are now undergoing extensive regeneration and are being converted into offices, apartments, bars and restaurants. The principal buildings include the two universities (the University of Leicester and De Montfort University), as well as the Town Hall, the 13th-century Guildhall, De Montfort Hall, Leicester Cathedral, the Jewry Wall (the UK's highest standing Roman wall), St Nicholas Church and St Mary de Castro church. The motte and Great Hall of Leicester can be seen from the castle gardens, situated next to the River Soar.

LINCOLN (PRE-1900)

Situated 64km (40 miles) inland on the river Witham, Lincoln derives its name from a contraction of *Lindum Colonia,* the settlement founded in AD 48 by the Romans to command the crossing of Ermine Street and Fosse Way. Sections of the third-century Roman city wall can be seen, including an extant gateway (Newport Arch). The Romans also drained the surrounding fenland and created a canal system, laying the foundations of Lincoln's agricultural prosperity and also the city's importance in the medieval wool trade as a port and staple town.

As one of the five 'burghs' or boroughs of the Danelaw, Lincoln was an important trading centre in the ninth and tenth centuries and prosperity from the wool trade lasted until the 14th century. This wealth enabled local merchants to build parish churches, of which three survive, and there are also remains of a 12th-century Jewish community. However, the removal of the staple to Boston in 1369 heralded a decline, from which the city only recovered fully in the 19th century, when improved fen drainage made Lincoln agriculturally important. Improved canal and rail links led to industrial development, mainly in the manufacture of machinery and engineering products.

The castle was built shortly after the Norman Conquest and is unusual in having two mounds; on one motte stands a keep (Lucy's Tower) added in the 12th century. It currently houses one of the four surviving copies of the Magna Carta. The cathedral was begun *c.*1073 but was mostly destroyed by fire and earthquake in the 12th century. Rebuilding was begun by St Hugh and completed over a century later. Other notable architectural features are the 12th-century High Bridge, the oldest in Britain still to carry buildings, and the Guildhall, situated above the 15th-century Stonebow gateway.

LIVERPOOL (PRE-1900)

Liverpool, on the north bank of the river Mersey, 5km (3 miles) from the Irish Sea, is the UK's foremost port for Atlantic trade.

There are 2,100 acres of dockland on both sides of the river and the Gladstone and Royal Seaforth Docks can accommodate tanker-sized vessels. Liverpool Free Port was opened in 1984.

Liverpool was created a free borough in 1207 and was given city status in 1880. From the early 18th century it expanded rapidly with the growth of industrialisation and the transatlantic slave trade. Surviving buildings from this period include the Bluecoat Chambers (1717, formerly the Bluecoat School), and the Town Hall (1754, rebuilt to the original design 1795). Notable from the 19th and 20th centuries are the Anglican cathedral (built from the designs of Sir Giles Gilbert Scott, it took 74 years to construct), and the Catholic Metropolitan Cathedral (designed by Sir Frederick Gibberd, consecrated 1967). Both of these cathedrals are situated on Hope Street, named after the merchant William Hope, which is the only street in the UK with a cathedral at either end. The refurbished Albert Dock (designed by Jesse Hartley) contains the Merseyside Maritime Museum, the International Slavery Museum, the Beatles Story and the Tate Liverpool art gallery. The Museum of Liverpool opened in 2011.

MANCHESTER (PRE-1900)

Manchester (the *Mamucium* of the Romans, who occupied it in AD 79) is a commercial and industrial centre connected with the sea by the Manchester Ship Canal, 57km (35.5 miles) long, opened in 1894 and accommodating ships up to 15,000 tons. During the Industrial Revolution the city had a thriving cotton industry and by 1853 there were over 100 cotton mills, which dominated the city's landscape.

The principal buildings are the Town Hall, erected in 1877 from the designs of Alfred Waterhouse, with a large extension of 1938; the Royal Exchange (1869, enlarged 1921); the Central Library (1934); Heaton Hall; the 17th-century Chetham Library; the Rylands Library (1900), which includes the Althorp collection; the university precinct; the 15th-century cathedral (formerly the parish church); the Manchester Central conference and exhibition centre and the Bridgewater Hall (1996) concert venue. Manchester is the home of the Hallé Orchestra, the Royal Northern College of Music, the Royal Exchange Theatre and numerous public art galleries.

The town received its first charter of incorporation in 1838 and was created a city in 1853.

NEWCASTLE UPON TYNE (PRE-1900)

Newcastle upon Tyne, on the north bank of the River Tyne, is 13km (8 miles) from the North Sea. A cathedral and university city, it is the administrative, commercial and cultural centre for north-east England and the principal port.

The principal buildings include the Castle Keep (12th century), Black Gate (13th century), Blackfriars (13th century), West Walls (13th century), St Nicholas Cathedral (15th century, fine lantern tower), St Andrew's Church (12th–14th century), St John's (14th–15th century), All Saints (1786 by Stephenson), St Mary's Roman Catholic Cathedral (1844), Trinity House (17th century), Sandhill (16th-century houses), Guildhall (Georgian), Grey Street (1834–9), Central Station (1846–50) and the Central Library (1969). Open spaces include the Town Moor (927 acres).

Numerous bridges span the Tyne at Newcastle, including the Tyne Bridge (1928) and the Tilting Millennium Bridge (2001) which links the city with Gateshead to the south.

The city's name is derived from the 'new castle' (1080) erected as a defence against the Scots. In 1265 defensive walls over two miles in length were built around the city as further protection; parts of these walls remain today and can be found to the west of the city centre.

NORWICH (PRE-1900)

Norwich grew from an early Anglo-Saxon settlement near the confluence of the rivers Yare and Wensum, and now serves as the provincial capital for the predominantly agricultural region of East Anglia. The name is thought to relate to the most northerly of a group of Anglo-Saxon villages or *wics*. The city's first known charter was granted in 1158 by Henry II.

Norwich serves its surrounding area as a market town and commercial centre. From the 14th century until the Industrial Revolution, Norwich was the regional centre of the woollen industry. Now the biggest single industry is financial services and principal trades are engineering, printing and shoemaking. The University of East Anglia is on the city's western boundary and admitted its first students in 1963. Norwich is accessible to seagoing vessels by means of the river Yare, entered at Great Yarmouth, 32km (20 miles) to the east.

Among many historic buildings are the cathedral (completed in the 12th century and surmounted by a 15th-century spire 96m (315ft) in height); the keep of the Norman castle (now a museum and art gallery); the 15th-century flint-walled Guildhall; some 30 medieval parish churches; St Andrew's and Blackfriars' Halls; the Tudor houses preserved in Elm Hill and the Georgian Assembly House.

NOTTINGHAM (PRE-1900)

Nottingham stands on the river Trent. *Snotingaham* or *Notingeham,* the 'homestead of the people of Snot', is the Anglo-Saxon name for the Celtic settlement of *Tigguocobauc,* or the house of caves. In 878, Nottingham became one of the five 'burghs' or boroughs of the Danelaw. William the Conqueror ordered the construction of Nottingham Castle, while the town itself developed rapidly under Norman rule. Its laws and rights were formally recognised by Henry II's charter in 1155. The castle became a favoured residence of King John. In 1642 Charles I raised his personal standard at Nottingham Castle at the start of the Civil War.

Architecturally, Nottingham has a wealth of notable buildings, particularly those designed in the Victorian era by T. C. Hine and Watson Fothergill. The city council owns the castle (of Norman origin but restored in 1878), Wollaton Hall (1580–8), Newstead Abbey (once the home of Lord Byron), the Guildhall (1888) and the Council House (1929). St Mary's, St Peter's and St Nicholas' churches are of interest, as is the Roman Catholic cathedral (Pugin, 1842–4). Nottingham was granted city status in 1897.

OXFORD (PRE-1900)

Oxford is a university city, an important industrial centre and a market town.

Oxford is known for its architecture, its oldest specimens being the reputedly Saxon tower of St Michael's Church, the remains of the Norman castle and city walls, and the Norman church at Iffley. It also has many Gothic buildings, such as the Divinity Schools, the Old Library at Merton College, William of Wykeham's New College, Magdalen and Christ Church colleges and many other college buildings. Later centuries are represented by the Laudian Quadrangle at St John's College, the Renaissance Sheldonian Theatre by Sir Christopher Wren, Trinity College Chapel, All Saints Church, Hawksmoor's mock-Gothic at All Souls College, and the 18th-century Queen's College. In addition to individual buildings, High Street and Radcliffe Square both form interesting architectural compositions. Most of the colleges have gardens, those of Magdalen, New College, St John's and Worcester being the largest.

The Oxford University Museum of Natural History, renowned for its spectacular neo-Gothic architecture, houses the university's scientific collections of zoological, entomological and geological specimens and is attached to the neighbouring Pitt Rivers Museum, which houses ethnographic and archaeological objects from around the world. The Ashmolean is the city's museum of art and archaeology and Modern Art Oxford hosts a programme of contemporary art exhibitions.

ST ALBANS (PRE-1900)

The origins of St Albans, situated on the river Ver, stem from the Roman town of *Verulamium.* Named after the first Christian martyr in Britain, who was executed there, St Albans has developed around the Norman abbey and the cathedral church (consecrated 1115), which was built partly of materials from the old Roman city. The museums house Iron Age and Roman artefacts and the Roman theatre, unique in Britain, has a stage as opposed to an amphitheatre. Archaeological excavations in the city centre have revealed evidence of pre-Roman, Saxon and medieval occupation.

The town's significance grew to the extent that it was a signatory and venue for the drafting of the Magna Carta. It was also the scene of riots during the Peasants' Revolt, the French King John was imprisoned there after the Battle of Poitiers, and heavy fighting took place there during the Wars of the Roses.

Previously controlled by the Abbot, the town achieved a charter in 1553 and city status in 1877. The street market, first established in 1553, is still an important feature of the city, as are many hotels and inns, surviving from the days when St Albans was an important coach stop. St Albans is also noted for its clock tower, built between 1403 and 1412, the only remaining medieval town belfry in England.

SALISBURY (PRE-1900)
The history of Salisbury centres around the cathedral and cathedral close. The city evolved from an Iron Age camp a mile to the north of its current position which was strengthened by the Romans and called *Serviodunum*. The Normans built a castle and cathedral on the site and renamed it Sarum. In 1220 Bishop Richard Poore and the architect Elias de Derham decided to build a new Gothic-style cathedral. The cathedral was completed 38 years later and a community known as New Sarum, now called Salisbury, grew around it. Originally the cathedral had a squat tower; the 123m (404ft) spire that makes the cathedral the tallest medieval structure in the world was added c.1315. A walled close with houses for the clergy was built around the cathedral; the Medieval Hall still stands today, alongside buildings dating from the 13th to the 20th century, including some designed by Sir Christopher Wren.

A prosperous wool and cloth trade allowed Salisbury to flourish until the 17th century. When the wool trade declined new crafts were established, including cutlery, leather and basket work, saddlery, lacemaking, joinery and malting. By 1750 it had become an important road junction and coaching centre and in the Victorian era the railways enabled a new age of expansion and prosperity.

SHEFFIELD (PRE-1900)
Sheffield is situated at the confluence of the rivers Sheaf, Porter, Rivelin and Loxley with the river Don and was created a city in 1893.

The parish church of St Peter and St Paul, founded in the 12th century, became the cathedral church of the diocese of Sheffield in 1914. The Roman Catholic Cathedral Church of St Marie (founded 1847) was made a cathedral for the new diocese of Hallam in 1980; parts of the present building date from c.1435. The principal buildings are the Town Hall (1897), the Cutlers' Hall (1832), City Hall (1932), Graves Art Gallery (1934), Mappin Art Gallery, the Crucible Theatre and the restored Lyceum Theatre, which dates from 1897 and was reopened in 1990. Three major sporting and entertainment venues were opened between 1990 and 1991: Sheffield Arena, Pond's Forge and Don Valley Stadium – which was closed and demolished in 2013, but the site is now being redeveloped as the Olympic Legacy Park. The Millennium Galleries opened in 2001. The Leadmill, Sheffield's longest-running independent live music venue, opened in 1980.

SOUTHAMPTON (1964)
Southampton is a major seaport on the south coast of England, situated between the mouths of the Test and Itchen rivers. Southampton's natural deep-water harbour has made the area an important settlement since the Romans built the first port (known as *Clausentum*) in the first century, and Southampton's port has witnessed several important departures, including those of Henry V in 1415 for the Battle of Agincourt, the *Mayflower* in 1620, and the RMS *Titanic* in 1912.

The city's strategic importance, not only as a seaport but also as a centre for aircraft production, meant that it was heavily bombed during the Second World War. However, many historically significant structures remain, including the Wool House, dating from 1417 and now used as the Maritime Museum; parts of the Norman city walls, which are among the most complete in the UK; the Bargate, which was originally the main gateway into the city; God's House Tower, now the Museum of Archaeology; St Michael's, the city's oldest church; and the Tudor Merchants Hall.

WINCHESTER (PRE-1900)
Winchester, the ancient capital of England, is situated on the river Itchen. The city is rich in architecture of all types, and especially notable is the cathedral. Built in 1079–93 the cathedral exhibits examples of Norman, early English and Perpendicular styles and is the burial place of author Jane Austen. Winchester College, founded in 1382, is one of the country's most famous public schools, and the original building (1393) remains largely unaltered. St Cross Hospital, another great medieval foundation, lies one mile south of the city. The almshouses were founded in 1136 by Bishop Henry de Blois, and Cardinal Henry Beaufort added a new almshouse of 'Noble Poverty' in 1446. The chapel and dwellings are of great architectural interest, and visitors may still receive the 'Wayfarer's Dole' of bread and ale, a tradition now 900 years old.

Excavations have done much to clarify the origins and development of Winchester. Part of the forum and several of the streets from the Roman town have been discovered. Excavations in the cathedral close have uncovered the entire site of the Anglo-Saxon cathedral (known as the Old Minster) and parts of the New Minster which was built by Alfred the Great's son, Edward the Elder, and is the burial place of the Alfredian dynasty. The original burial place of St Swithun, before his remains were translated to a site in the present cathedral, was also uncovered.

Excavations in other parts of the city have cast much light on Norman Winchester, notably on the site of the Royal Castle (adjacent to which the new Law Courts have been built) and in the grounds of Wolvesey Castle, where the great house built by bishops Giffard and Henry de Blois in the 12th century has been uncovered. The Great Hall, built by Henry III between 1222 and 1236, survives and houses the Arthurian Round Table.

YORK (PRE-1900)
The city of York is an archiepiscopal seat. Its recorded history dates from AD 71, when the Roman Ninth Legion established a base under Petilius Cerealis that would later become the fortress of *Eburacum*, or *Eboracum*. In Anglo-Saxon times the city was the royal and ecclesiastical centre of Northumbria, and after capture by a Viking army in AD 866 it became the capital of the Viking kingdom of Jorvik. By the 14th century the city had become a great mercantile centre, mainly because of its control of the wool trade, and was used as the chief base against the Scots. Under the Tudors its fortunes declined, although Henry VIII made it the headquarters of the Council of the North. Excavations on many sites, including Coppergate, have greatly expanded knowledge of Roman, Viking and medieval urban life. The JORVIK Viking Centre (reopened in 2017) takes visitors on a journey through a reconstructed 10th century Viking-age York.

The city is rich in examples of architecture of all periods. The earliest church was built in AD 627 and, from the 12th to 15th centuries, the present Minster was built in a succession of styles.

LORD-LIEUTENANTS AND HIGH SHERIFFS

Area	Lord-Lieutenant	High Sheriff (2017–18)
Bedfordshire	Helen Nellis	Vinod Tailor
Berkshire	James Puxley	Sarah Scrope
Bristol	Lois Golding, OBE	Anthony Brown
Buckinghamshire	Sir Henry Aubrey-Fletcher, Bt.	Peter Kara
Cambridgeshire	Julie Spence, OBE, QPM	Richard Pemberton
Cheshire	David Briggs, MBE	Sarah Beckett
Cornwall	Col. Edward Bolitho, OBE	Jane Hartley
Cumbria	Claire Hensman	Alistair Wannop
Derbyshire	William Tucker	Anne Hall
Devon	David Fursdon	Heleen Lindsay-Fynn
Dorset	Angus Campbell	Simon Young, MC
Durham	Susan Snowden	Caroline Peacock
East Riding of Yorkshire	Hon. Susan Cunliffe-Lister	Gillian Drewry
East Sussex	Peter Field	Maureen Chowen
Essex	Jennifer Tolhurst	Simon Hall, MBE
Gloucestershire	Dame Janet Trotter, DBE	Lt.-Col. Andrew Tabor
Greater London	Kenneth Olisa, OBE	William Furber
Greater Manchester	Warren Smith	Lady Joy Smith
Hampshire	Nigel Atkinson	Hon. Mary Montagu-Scott
Herefordshire	Countess of Darnley	Revd Lady Lisvane
Hertfordshire	Robert Voss, CBE	William Hobhouse
Isle of Wight	Maj.-Gen. Martin White, CB, CBE	Benedict Rouse
Kent	Viscount De L'Isle, MBE	George Jessel
Lancashire	Lord Shuttleworth, KG, KCVO	John Barnett, MBE
Leicestershire	Lady Gretton, DCVO	Timothy Maxted
Lincolnshire	Toby Dennis	Andrew Clark
Merseyside	Dame Lorna Fox Muirhead, DCVO, DBE	James Davies, OBE
Norfolk	Richard Jewson	Alfred Bagge
North Yorkshire	Barry Dodd, CBE	Simon Wrightson
Northamptonshire	David Laing	Rupert Fordham
Northumberland	Duchess of Northumberland	John Dickinson
Nottinghamshire	Sir John Peace	Col. David Sneath, TD
Oxfordshire	Tim Stevenson, OBE	Jane Cranston
Rutland	Dr Sir Laurence Howard, KCVO, OBE	Craig Mitchell
Shropshire	Sir Algernon Heber-Percy, KCVO	Charles Lillis
Somerset	Anne Maw	Richard Hickmet
South Yorkshire	Andrew Coombe	Stephen Ingram
Staffordshire	Ian Dudson, CBE	Humphrey Scott-Moncrieff
Suffolk	Countess of Euston	Geoffrey Probert
Surrey	Michael More-Molyneux	Robert Napier, CBE
Tyne and Wear	Susan Winfield, OBE	Lt-Gen. Robin Brims, CB, CBE, DSO
Warwickshire	Timothy Cox	Mark Davies
West Midlands	John Crabtree, OBE	John Hudson, OBE
West Sussex	Susan Pyper	Lady Barnard
West Yorkshire	Dame Dr Ingrid Roscoe, DCVO	Dr Terence Bramall, CBE
Wiltshire	Sarah Troughton	Lady Marland
Worcestershire	Lt.-Col. Patrick Holcroft, LVO, OBE	Stephen Betts

COUNTY COUNCILS

Council & Administrative HQ	Telephone	Population*	Council Tax†	Chief Executive‡
Buckinghamshire, Aylesbury	01296-395000	534,720	£1,218	Rachael Shimmin, OBE
Cambridgeshire, Cambridge	0345-045 5200	651,940	£1,190	Gillian Beasley
Cumbria, Carlisle	01228-606060	497,906	£1,281	Katherine Fairclough
Derbyshire, Matlock	01629-580000	785,765	£1,212	Ian Stephenson
Devon, Exeter	0345-155 1015	779,834	£1,268	Dr Phil Norrey
Dorset, Dorchester	01305-221000	422,727	£1,327	Debbie Ward
East Sussex, Lewes	0345-608 0190	547,797	£1,314	Becky Shaw
Essex, Chelmsford	0845-7430 430	1,455,340	£1,164	Gavin Jones
Gloucestershire, Gloucester	01452-425000	623,129	£1,179	Peter Bungard
Hampshire, Winchester	0300-555 1375	1,360,426	£1,133	John Coughlan, CBE
Hertfordshire, Hertford	0300-123 4040	1,176,720	£1,246	John Wood
Kent, Maidstone	0300-041 4141	1,541,893	£1,179	David Cockburn
Lancashire, Preston	0300-123 6701	1,198,798	£1,222	Jo Turton
Leicestershire, Leicester	0116-232 3232	682,957	£1,172	John Sinnott
Lincolnshire, Lincoln	01522-552222	743,143	£1,173	Tony McArdle
Norfolk, Norwich	0344-800 8020	892,870	£1,248	Dr Wendy Thomson, CBE
North Yorkshire, Northallerton	01609-780780	604,866	£1,190	Richard Flinton
Northamptonshire Northampton	0300-126 1000	733,128	£1,167	Paul Blantern
Nottinghamshire, Nottingham	0115-982 3823	810,710	£1,352	Anthony May
Oxfordshire, Oxford	01865-792422	683,169	£1,346	Peter Clark
Somerset, Taunton	0300-123 2224	549,447	£1,125	Patrick Flaherty
Staffordshire, Stafford	0300-111 8000	867,122	£1,143	John Henderson, CB
Suffolk, Ipswich	03456-606 6067	745,274	£1,184	Deborah Cadman, OBE
Surrey, Kingston upon Thames	0345-600 9009	1,176,549	£1,322	David McNulty
Warwickshire, Warwick	01926-410410	556,750	£1,299	David Carter & Monica Fogarty
West Sussex, Chichester	01243-777100	843,765	£1,256	Nathan Elvery
Worcestershire, Worcester	01905-763763	583,053	£1,155	Clare Marchant

* Source: Office for National Statistics – *Mid-2016 Population Estimates* (Crown copyright)

† Average 2017–18 Band D council tax in the county area inclusive of the adult social care precept, but exclusive of precepts for fire authorities and Police and Crime Commissioners. County councils claim their share of the combined council tax from the collection funds of the district authorities within their area. Band D council tax bills for the billing authority are given on the following pages

‡ Or equivalent postholder

DISTRICT COUNCILS

District Council	Telephone	Population*	Council Tax†	Chief Executive‡
Adur	01273-263000	63,506	£1,710	Alex Bailey
Allerdale	01900-702702	96,956	£1,728	Ian Frost
Amber Valley	01773-570222	124,645	£1,668	Sylvia Delahay & Julian Townsend
Arun	01903-737500	156,997	£1,649	Nigel Lynn
Ashfield	01623-450000	124,482	£1,800	Robert Mitchell
Ashford	01233-331111	126,151	£1,592	Tracey Kerly
Aylesbury Vale	01296-585858	193,113	£1,680	Andrew Grant
Babergh	01473-822801	89,498	£1,593	Arthur Charvonia
Barrow-in-Furness	01229-876543	67,321	£1,729	Phil Huck
Basildon	01268-533333	183,378	£1,659	Bala Mahendran
Basingstoke and Deane	01256-844844	178,588	£1,494	Melbourne Barrett
Bassetlaw	01909-533533	114,847	£1,805	Neil Taylor
Blaby	0116-275 0555	97,703	£1,663	Jane Toman
Bolsover	01246-242424	78,082	£1,754	Dan Swaine
Boston	01205-314200	67,564	£1,610	Phil Drury
Braintree	01376-552525	150,999	£1,597	Nicola Beach
Breckland	01362-656870	137,032	£1,630	Anna Graves
Brentwood	01277-312500	76,386	£1,582	Philip Ruck
Broadland	01603-431133	127,455	£1,656	Phil Kirby
Bromsgrove	01527-881288	96,796	£1,658	Kevin Dicks
Broxbourne	01992-785555	96,779	£1,521	Jeff Stack
Broxtowe	0115-917 7777	112,671	£1,797	Ruth Hyde, OBE
Burnley	01282-425011	87,522	£1,740	vacant
CAMBRIDGE	01223-457000	131,799	£1,631	Antoinette Jackson
Cannock Chase	01543-462621	98,534	£1,628	Tony McGovern
CANTERBURY	01227-862000	162,416	£1,623	Colin Carmichael
CARLISLE	01228-817000	108,409	£1,721	Dr Jason Gooding
Castle Point	01268-882200	89,731	£1,641	David Marchant
Charnwood	01509-263151	179,389	£1,613	Geoffrey Parker
CHELMSFORD	01245-606606	174,089	£1,611	Steve Packham
Cheltenham	01242-262626	117,530	£1,596	Pat Pratley
Cherwell	01295-227001	146,338	£1,730	Yvonne Rees
Chesterfield	01246-345345	104,440	£1,634	Huw Bowen
Chichester	01243-785166	118,175	£1,617	Diane Shepherd
Chiltern	01494-729000	95,103	£1,689	Bob Smith
Chorley	01257-515151	114,351	£1,652	Gary Hall
Christchurch	01202-495000	49,481	£1,788	David McIntosh
Colchester	01206-282222	186,635	£1,595	Adrian Pritchard
Copeland	01946-598300	69,307	£1,746	Mike Starkie
Corby	01536-464000	68,187	£1,570	Norman Stronach
Cotswold	01285-623000	85,756	£1,590	Christine Gore & Frank Wilson
Craven	01756-700600	56,308	£1,699	Paul Shevlin
Crawley	01293-438000	111,375	£1,604	Natalie Brahma-Pearl
Dacorum	01442-228000	152,692	£1,601	Sally Marshall
Dartford	01322-343434	105,543	£1,611	Graham Harris
Daventry	01327-871100	81,316	£1,602	Ian Vincent
Derbyshire Dales	01629-761100	71,288	£1,714	Dorcas Bunton
Dover	01304-821199	114,227	£1,649	Nadeem Aziz
East Cambridgeshire	01353-665555	87,825	£1,653	John Hill
East Devon	01395-516551	139,908	£1,715	Mark Williams
East Dorset	01202-886201	89,093	£1,861	David McIntosh
East Hampshire	01730-266551	117,955	£1,564	Sandy Hopkins
East Hertfordshire	01279-655261	146,309	£1,622	Liz Watts
East Lindsey	01507-601111	138,443	£1,563	Stuart Davy
East Northamptonshire	01832-742000	90,999	£1,606	David Oliver
East Staffordshire	01283-508000	116,701	£1,605	Andy O'Brien
Eastbourne	01323-410000	103,054	£1,790	Robert Cottrill
Eastleigh	023-8068 8000	129,635	£1,557	Nick Tustian
Eden	01768-817817	52,639	£1,738	Robin Hooper
Elmbridge	01372-474474	132,764	£1,768	Robert Moran
Epping Forest	01992-564000	130,321	£1,602	Glen Chipp
Epsom and Ewell	01372-732000	79,588	£1,743	Kathryn Beldon
Erewash	0115-907 2244	114,891	£1,650	Jeremy Jaroszek
EXETER	01392-277888	129,801	£1,671	Karime Hassan
Fareham	01329-236100	115,423	£1,513	Peter Grimwood
Fenland	01354-654321	100,182	£1,744	Paul Medd
Forest Heath	01638-719000	64,447	£1,590	Ian Gallin

Forest of Dean	01594-810000	85,385	£1,636	Sue Pangbourne
Fylde	01253-658658	77,990	£1,680	Allan Oldfield
Gedling	0115-901 3901	116,501	£1,786	John Robinson
GLOUCESTER	01452-396396	128,488	£1,591	Jon McGinty
Gosport	023-9258 4242	85,363	£1,575	David Williams
Gravesham	01474-564422	106,808	£1,610	David Hughes
Great Yarmouth	01493-856100	99,164	£1,630	Sheila Oxtoby
Guildford	01483-505050	148,020	£1,746	James Whiteman
Hambleton	01619-779977	90,537	£1,617	Dr Justin Ives
Harborough	01858-828282	90,416	£1,633	Beverley Jolly & Norman Proudfoot
Harlow	01279-446655	85,995	£1,662	Malcolm Morley, OBE
Harrogate	01423-500600	156,312	£1,721	Wallace Sampson
Hart	01252-622122	94,250	£1,600	Patricia Hughes & Daryl Phillips
Hastings	01424-451066	92,236	£1,807	Ross McLeod
Havant	023-9244 6019	123,640	£1,555	Sandy Hopkins
Hertsmere	020-8207 2277	103,528	£1,594	Dr Donald Graham
High Peak	0345-129 7777	91,662	£1,665	Simon Baker
Hinckley and Bosworth	01455-238141	110,102	£1,594	Bill Cullen
Horsham	01403-215100	138,018	£1,603	Tom Crowley
Huntingdonshire	01480-388388	175,666	£1,675	Jo Lancaster
Hyndburn	01254-388111	80,537	£1,689	David Welsby
Ipswich	01473-432000	135,908	£1,701	Russell Williams
Kettering	01536-410333	99,002	£1,602	David Cook, MBE
King's Lynn and West Norfolk	01553-616200	151,589	£1,639	Ray Harding
LANCASTER	01524-582000	143,517	£1,681	Susan Parsonage
Lewes	01273-471600	101,381	£1,842	Robert Cottrill
Lichfield	01543-308000	103,061	£1,604	Diane Tilley
LINCOLN	01522-881188	97,795	£1,638	Angela Andrews
Maidstone	01622-602000	166,360	£1,683	Alison Broom
Maldon	01621-854477	63,350	£1,635	Fiona Marshall
Malvern Hills	01684-862151	76,130	£1,638	Jack Hegarty
Mansfield	01623-463463	107,435	£1,799	Hayley Barsby *(interim)*
Melton	01664-502502	50,878	£1,645	Lynn Aisbett
Mendip	0300-3038588	112,545	£1,624	Stuart Brown
Mid Devon	01884-255255	79,789	£1,768	Stephen Walford
Mid Suffolk	01449-720711	100,014	£1,589	Arthur Charvonia
Mid Sussex	01444-458166	147,089	£1,629	Kathryn Hall
Mole Valley	01306-885001	86,223	£1,732	Yvonne Rees
New Forest	023-8028 5000	179,236	£1,604	Bob Jackson
Newark and Sherwood	01636-650000	119,570	£1,849	Andrew Muter
Newcastle-under-Lyme	01782-717717	128,467	£1,592	John Sellgren
North Devon	01271-327711	94,615	£1,753	Mike Mansell
North Dorset	01258-454111	71,064	£1,820	Matt Prosser
North East Derbyshire	01246-231111	100,423	£1,746	Dan Swaine
North Hertfordshire	01462-474000	132,747	£1,637	David Scholes
North Kesteven	01529-414155	113,297	£1,616	Ian Fytche
North Norfolk	01263-513811	103,752	£1,658	Nick Baker & Steve Blatch
North Warwickshire	01827-715341	63,229	£1,745	Jerry Hutchinson
North West Leicestershire	01530-454545	98,644	£1,654	Beverley Smith
Northampton	0300-330 7000	225,474	£1,605	David Kennedy
NORWICH	0344-980 3333	141,014	£1,714	Laura McGillivray
Nuneaton and Bedworth	024-7637 6376	127,019	£1,711	Alan Franks
Oadby and Wigston	0116-288 8961	55,825	£1,634	Mark Hall
OXFORD	01865-249811	161,291	£1,811	Gordon Mitchell *(interim)*
Pendle	01282-661661	90,588	£1,766	Dean Langton & Philip Mousdale
PRESTON	01772-906900	141,801	£1,755	Lorraine Norris
Purbeck	01929-556561	46,336	£1,852	Steve Mackenzie
Redditch	01527-64252	84,971	£1,652	Kevin Dicks
Reigate and Banstead	01737-276000	145,648	£1,777	John Jory
Ribble Valley	01200-425111	58,826	£1,616	Marshal Scott
Richmondshire	01748-829100	53,732	£1,714	Tony Clark
Rochford	01702-318111	85,670	£1,651	Nick Khan & Shaun Scrutton
Rossendale	01706-217777	69,886	£1,714	Stuart Sugarman
Rother	01424-787000	93,551	£1,787	Malcolm Johnston & Dr Anthony Leonard
Rugby	01788-533533	103,815	£1,690	Adam Norburn
Runnymede	01932-838383	86,889	£1,711	Paul Turrell
Rushcliffe	0115-981 9911	115,204	£1,804	Allen Graham
Rushmoor	01252-398398	96,327	£1,555	Paul Shackley
Ryedale	01653-600666	53,486	£1,708	Janet Waggott

ST ALBANS	01727-866100	146,282	£1,610	James Blake
St Edmundsbury	01284-763233	112,938	£1,598	Ian Gallin
Scarborough	01723-232323	107,824	£1,721	Jim Dillon
Sedgemoor	0845-408 2540	121,436	£1,595	Kerry Rickards
Selby	01757-705101	86,667	£1,704	Janet Waggott
Sevenoaks	01732-227000	119,142	£1,693	Dr Pav Ramewal
Shepway	01303-853000	111,190	£1,715	Alistair Stewart
South Bucks	01895-837200	69,636	£1,671	Bob Smith
South Cambridgeshire	0345-045 0500	156,468	£1,663	Alex Colyer *(acting)*
South Derbyshire	01283-595795	100,334	£1,645	Frank McArdle
South Hams	01803-861234	84,306	£1,737	Sophie Hosking & Steve Jorden
South Holland	01775-761161	92,387	£1,578	Anna Graves
South Kesteven	01476-406080	140,193	£1,562	Beverly Agass
South Lakeland	01539-733333	103,274	£1,722	Lawrence Conway
South Norfolk	01508-533633	132,837	£1,676	Sandra Dinneen
South Northamptonshire	01327-322322	89,959	£1,631	Yvonne Rees
South Oxfordshire	01235-520202	138,128	£1,711	David Hill
South Ribble	01772-421491	110,118	£1,672	Jean Hunter *(interim)*
South Somerset	01935-462462	165,645	£1,630	Alex Parmley
South Staffordshire	01902-696000	111,180	£1,553	Dave Heywood
Spelthorne	01784-451499	98,902	£1,749	Roberto Tambini
Stafford	01785-619000	134,155	£1,566	Ian Thompson
Staffordshire Moorlands	0345-605 3010	98,069	£1,584	Simon Baker
Stevenage	01438-242242	87,081	£1,596	Scott Crudgington
Stratford-on-Avon	01789-267575	122,278	£1,685	Dave Buckland & Dave Webb
Stroud	01453-766321	117,381	£1,667	David Hagg
Suffolk Coastal	01394-383789	125,955	£1,579	Stephen Baker
Surrey Heath	01276-707100	88,387	£1,782	Karen Whelan
Swale	01795-417850	145,042	£1,598	Mark Radford *(interim)*
Tamworth	01827-709709	76,955	£1,562	Tony Goodwin
Tandridge	01883-722000	86,665	£1,782	Louise Round
Taunton Deane	01823-356356	115,515	£1,557	Penny James
Teignbridge	01626-361101	129,856	£1,749	Phil Shears
Tendring	01255-686868	142,598	£1,582	Ian Davidson
Test Valley	01264-368000	122,044	£1,535	Roger Tetstall
Tewkesbury	01684-295010	88,589	£1,559	Michael Dawson
Thanet	01843-577000	140,652	£1,662	Madeline Homer
Three Rivers	01923-776611	92,533	£1,610	Dr Steven Halls
Tonbridge and Malling	01732-844522	127,293	£1,661	Julie Beilby
Torridge	01237-428700	66,977	£1,734	Jenny Wallace
Tunbridge Wells	01892-526121	117,069	£1,630	William Benson
Uttlesford	01799-510510	86,188	£1,615	Dawn French
Vale of White Horse	01235-520202	128,738	£1,711	David Hill
Warwick	01926-410410	140,411	£1,675	Chris Elliott
Watford	01923-226400	96,773	£1,653	Manny Lewis
Waveney	01502-562111	116,514	£1,583	Stephen Baker
Waverley	01483-523333	123,768	£1,782	Paul Wenham
Wealden	01323-443322	157,575	£1,834	Charles Lant
Wellingborough	01933-229777	78,191	£1,538	Liz Elliott *(interim)*
Welwyn & Hatfield	01707-357000	121,996	£1,640	Rob Bridge
West Devon	01822-813600	54,582	£1,809	Sophie Hosking & Steve Jorden
West Dorset	01305-251010	101,382	£1,822	Matt Prosser
West Lancashire	01695-577177	113,401	£1,661	Kim Webber
West Lindsey	01427-676676	93,734	£1,645	Manjeet Gill
West Oxfordshire	01993-861000	108,674	£1,689	Christine Gore & Frank Wilson
West Somerset	01643-703704	34,306	£1,609	Penny James
Weymouth and Portland	01305-838000	65,371	£1,891	Matt Prosser
WINCHESTER	01962-840222	121,965	£1,573	Laura Taylor
Woking	01483-755855	99,695	£1,783	Ray Morgan, OBE
WORCESTER	01905-722233	102,338	£1,604	David Blake
Worthing	01903-239999	108,605	£1,634	Alex Bailey
Wychavon	01386-565000	122,943	£1,590	Jack Hegarty
Wycombe	01494-461000	176,868	£1,626	Karen Satterford
Wyre	01253-891000	110,261	£1,659	Garry Payne
Wyre Forest	01562-732928	99,902	£1,659	Ian Miller

* *Source:* Office for National Statistics – *Mid-2016 Population Estimates* (Crown copyright)
† Band D council tax bill for 2017–18 inclusive of adult social care and parish precepts
‡ Or equivalent postholder
Councils in CAPITAL LETTERS have city status

METROPOLITAN BOROUGH COUNCILS

Metropolitan Borough Council	Telephone	Population*	Council Tax†	Chief Executive‡
Barnsley	01226-770770	241,218	£1,592	Diana Terris
BIRMINGHAM	0121-303 1111	1,128,569	£1,446	Stella Manzie *(interim)*
Bolton	01204-333333	283,115	£1,612	Margaret Asquith
BRADFORD	01274-432001	538,279	£1,482	Kersten England
Bury	0161-253 5000	118,669	£1,644	Pat Jones-Greenhalgh *(interim)*
Calderdale	01422-288001	209,770	£1,584	Merran McRae
COVENTRY	0500-834 333	352,991	£1,674	Dr Martin Reeves
Doncaster	01302-736000	306,391	£1,490	Jo Miller
Dudley	0300-555 2345	317,634	£1,391	Sarah Norman
Gateshead	0191-433 3000	201,592	£1,783	Sheena Ramsey
Kirklees	01484-221000	437,047	£1,601	Jacqui Gedman
Knowsley	0151-489 6000	147,915	£1,633	Mike Harden
LEEDS	0113-222 4444	781,743	£1,496	Tom Riordan
LIVERPOOL	0151-233 3000	484,578	£1,752	Joe Anderson *(interim)*
MANCHESTER	0161-234 5000	541,263	£1,502	Joanne Roney, OBE
NEWCASTLE UPON TYNE	0191-278 7878	296,478	£1,683	Pat Ritchie
North Tyneside	0191-643 5991	203,307	£1,626	Patrick Melia
Oldham	0161-770 3000	232,724	£1,729	Dr Carolyn Wilkins, OBE
Rochdale	01706-647474	216,165	£1,671	Steve Rumbelow
Rotherham	01709-382121	261,930	£1,659	Sharon Kemp
St Helens	01744-676789	178,455	£1,571	Mike Palin
SALFORD	0161-794 4711	248,726	£1,667	Jim Taylor
Sandwell	0121-569 2200	322,712	£1,457	Jan Britton
Sefton	0151-922 4040	274,261	£1,690	Margaret Carney
SHEFFIELD	0114-273 4567	575,424	£1,659	John Mothersole
Solihull	0121-704 8001	211,763	£1,459	Nick Page
South Tyneside	0191-427 7000	149,418	£1,612	Martin Swales
Stockport	0161-480 4949	290,557	£1,744	Pam Smith
SUNDERLAND	0191-520 5555	277,962	£1,472	Irene Lucas, CBE
Tameside	0161-342 8355	223,189	£1,569	Steven Pleasant
Trafford	0161-912 2000	234,673	£1,407	Theresa Grant
WAKEFIELD	0845-850 6506	336,834	£1,513	Andy Wallhead *(acting)*
Walsall	01922-650000	278,715	£1,744	Paul Sheehan
Wigan	01942-244991	323,060	£1,476	Donna Hall
Wirral	0151-606 2000	321,238	£1,636	Eric Robinson
WOLVERHAMPTON	01902-551155	256,621	£1,655	Keith Ireland

* *Source:* Office for National Statistics – *Mid-2016 Population Estimates* (Crown copyright)
† Band D council tax bill for 2017–18 inclusive of adult social care and parish precepts
‡ Or equivalent postholder
Councils in CAPITAL LETTERS have city status

UNITARY COUNCILS

Unitary Council	Telephone	Population*	Council Tax†	Chief Executive‡
Bath and North East Somerset	01225-477000	187,751	£1,573	Ashley Ayre
Bedford	01234-267422	168,751	£1,704	Philip Simpkins
Blackburn with Darwen	01254-585585	147,049	£1,619	Harry Catherall
Blackpool	01253-477477	139,195	£1,657	Neil Jack
Bournemouth	01202-451451	197,657	£1,623	Sue Ross
Bracknell Forest	01344-352000	119,447	£1,498	Timothy Wheadon
BRIGHTON AND HOVE	01273-290000	289,229	£1,705	Geoff Raw
BRISTOL	0117-922 2000	454,213	£1,800	Anna Klonowski
Central Bedfordshire	0300-300 8000	278,937	£1,795	Richard Carr
Cheshire East	0300-123 5500	376,695	£1,610	Kath O'Dwyer *(acting)*
Cheshire West and Chester	0300-123 8123	335,680	£1,645	Gerald Meehan
Cornwall	0300-123 4100	553,582	£1,686	Kate Kennally
Darlington	01325-380651	105,646	£1,651	Ada Burns
DERBY	01332-293111	256,233	£1,551	Paul Robinson
DURHAM	0300-026000	522,143	£1797	Terry Collins
East Riding of Yorkshire	01482-393939	337,696	£1,643	Caroline Lacey
Halton	0303-333 4300	126,903	£1,553	David Parr
Hartlepool	01429-266522	92,817	£1,835	Gill Alexander
Herefordshire	01432-260000	183,309	£1,702	Alistair Neill
Isle of Wight	01983-821000	139,798	£1,695	John Metcalfe
Isles of Scilly§	01720-424000	2,308	£1,346	Theo Leijser
KINGSTON-UPON-HULL	01482-609100	260,240	£1,536	Matt Jukes
LEICESTER	0116-254 1000	348,343	£1,672	Andy Keeling
Luton	01582-546000	216,791	£1,615	Trevor Holden
Medway	01634-333333	278,542	£1,532	Neil Davies
Middlesbrough	01642-245432	140,398	£1,780	Tony Parkinson *(interim)*
Milton Keynes	01908-691691	264,479	£1,579	Carole Mills
North East Lincolnshire	01472-313131	159,144	£1,698	Rob Walsh
North Lincolnshire	01724-296296	170,786	£1,659	Denise Hyde
North Somerset	01934-888888	211,681	£1,573	Mike Jackson
Northumberland	0345-600 6400	316,002	£1,737	Daljit Lally *(interim)*
NOTTINGHAM	0115-915 5555	325,282	£1,852	Ian Curryer
PETERBOROUGH	01733-747474	197,095	£1,496	Gillian Beasley
PLYMOUTH	01752-668000	264,199	£1,665	Tracey Lee
Poole	01202-633633	151,500	£1,586	Andrew Flockhart
PORTSMOUTH	023-9282 2251	214,832	£1,508	David Williams
Reading	0118-937 3787	162,666	£1,723	Simon Warren *(interim)*
Redcar and Cleveland	0164-277 4774	135,404	£1,761	Amanda Skelton
Rutland	01572-722577	38,606	£1,842	Helen Briggs
Shropshire	0345-678 9000	313,373	£1,611	Clive Wright
Slough	01753-475111	147,181	£1,512	Roger Parkin *(interim)*
South Gloucestershire	01454-868009	277,623	£1,686	Amanda Deeks
SOUTHAMPTON	023-8083 3000	254,275	£1,636	Dawn Baxendale
Southend-on-Sea	01702-215000	179,799	£1,499	Alison Griffin
Stockton-on-Tees	01642-393939	195,681	£1,759	Neil Schneider
STOKE-ON-TRENT	01782-234567	253,226	£1,472	David Sidaway
Swindon	01793-463000	217,905	£1,591	John Gilbert
Telford and Wrekin	01952-380000	172,976	£1,589	Richard Partington
Thurrock	01375-652652	167,025	£1,453	Lyn Carpenter
Torbay	01803-201201	133,833	£1,641	Steve Parrock
Warrington	01925-443322	208,809	£1,581	Prof. Steven Broomhead
West Berkshire	01635-42400	156,837	£1,675	Nick Carter
Wiltshire	0300-456 0100	488,409	£1,671	Dr Carlton Brand & Carolyn Godfrey
Windsor and Maidenhead	01628-683800	148,814	£1,214	Alison Alexander
Wokingham	0118-974 6000	161,878	£1,650	Andy Couldrick
YORK	01904-551550	208,367	£1,544	Mary Weastell

* *Source:* Office for National Statistics – *Mid-2016 Population Estimates* (Crown copyright)
† Band D council tax bill for 2017–18 inclusive of adult social care and parish precepts
‡ Or equivalent postholder
§ Under the Isles of Scilly Clause the council has additional functions to other unitary authorities
Councils in CAPITAL LETTERS have city status

MAP OF COUNCILS IN ENGLAND

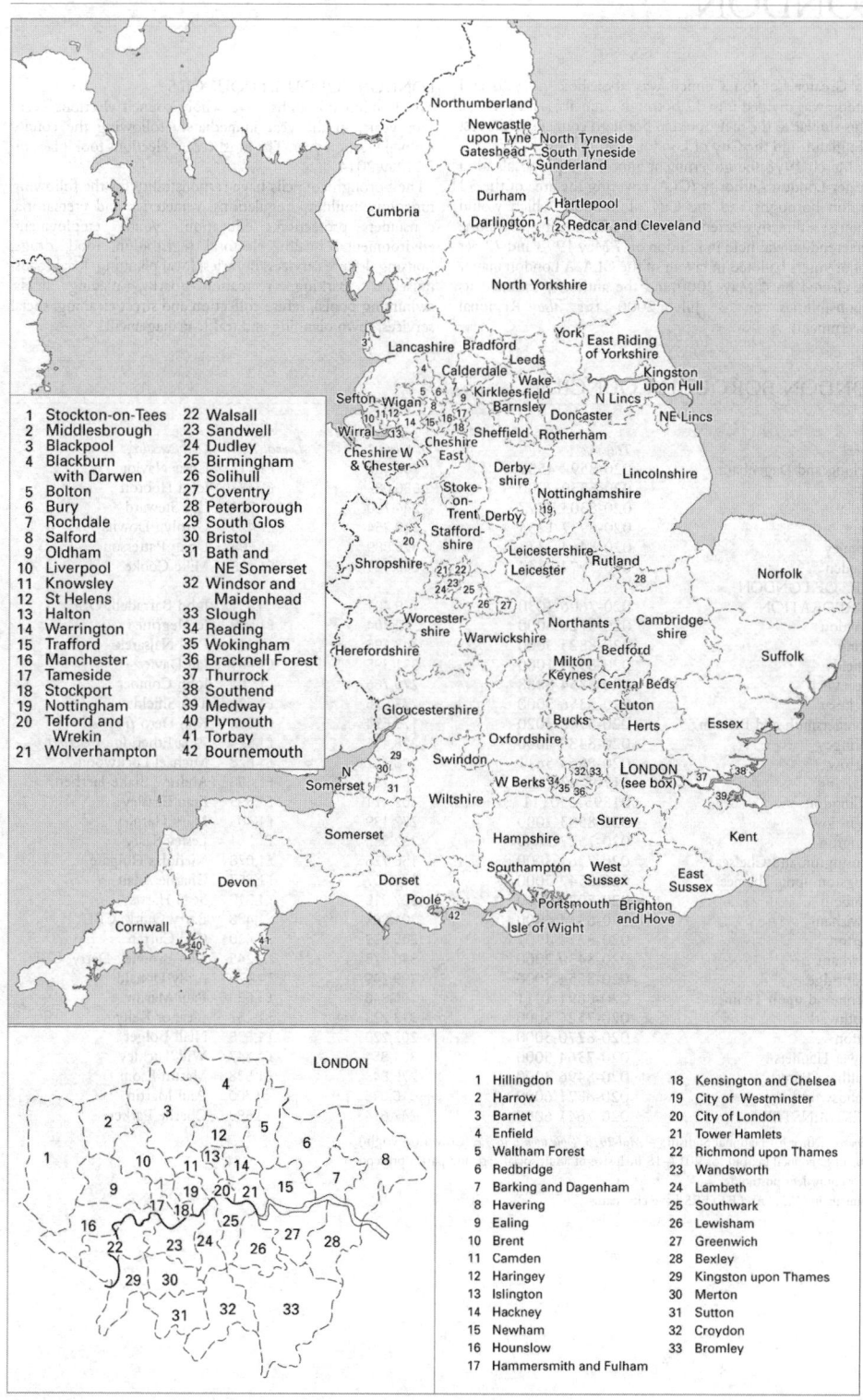

1	Stockton-on-Tees	22	Walsall
2	Middlesbrough	23	Sandwell
3	Blackpool	24	Dudley
4	Blackburn	25	Birmingham
	with Darwen	26	Solihull
5	Bolton	27	Coventry
6	Bury	28	Peterborough
7	Rochdale	29	South Glos
8	Salford	30	Bristol
9	Oldham	31	Bath and
10	Liverpool		NE Somerset
11	Knowsley	32	Windsor and
12	St Helens		Maidenhead
13	Halton	33	Slough
14	Warrington	34	Reading
15	Trafford	35	Wokingham
16	Manchester	36	Bracknell Forest
17	Tameside	37	Thurrock
18	Stockport	38	Southend
19	Nottingham	39	Medway
20	Telford and	40	Plymouth
	Wrekin	41	Torbay
21	Wolverhampton	42	Bournemouth

LONDON

1	Hillingdon	18	Kensington and Chelsea
2	Harrow	19	City of Westminster
3	Barnet	20	City of London
4	Enfield	21	Tower Hamlets
5	Waltham Forest	22	Richmond upon Thames
6	Redbridge	23	Wandsworth
7	Barking and Dagenham	24	Lambeth
8	Havering	25	Southwark
9	Ealing	26	Lewisham
10	Brent	27	Greenwich
11	Camden	28	Bexley
12	Haringey	29	Kingston upon Thames
13	Islington	30	Merton
14	Hackney	31	Sutton
15	Newham	32	Croydon
16	Hounslow	33	Bromley
17	Hammersmith and Fulham		

LONDON

The Greater London Council was abolished in 1986 and London was divided into 32 borough councils, which have a status similar to the metropolitan borough councils in the rest of England, and the City of London Corporation.

In March 1998 the government announced proposals for a Greater London Authority (GLA) covering the area of the 32 London boroughs and the City of London, which would comprise a directly elected mayor and a 25-member assembly. A referendum was held in London on 7 May 1998 and 72 per cent of voters balloted in favour of the GLA. A London mayor was elected on 4 May 2000 and the authority assumed its responsibilities on 3 July 2000 (*see also* Regional Government).

LONDON BOROUGH COUNCILS

The London boroughs have whole council elections every four years, in the year immediately following the county council election year. The most recent elections took place on 22 May 2014.

The borough councils have responsibility for the following functions: building regulations, cemeteries and crematoria, consumer protection, education, youth employment, environmental health, electoral registration, food, drugs, housing, leisure services, libraries, local planning, local roads, museums, parking, recreation (parks, playing fields, swimming pools), refuse collection and street cleaning, social services, town planning and traffic management.

LONDON BOROUGH COUNCILS

Council	Telephone	Population*	Council Tax†	Chief Executive‡
Barking and Dagenham	020-8592 4500	206,460	£1,412	Chris Naylor
Barnet	020-8359 2000	386,083	£1,432	John Hooton
Bexley	020-8303 7777	244,760	£1,524	Gill Steward
Brent	020-8937 1234	328,254	£1,425	Carolyn Downs
Bromley	020-8464 3333	326,889	£1,394	Doug Patterson
Camden	020-7974 4444	246,181	£1,418	Mike Cooke
CITY OF LONDON CORPORATION	020-7606 3030	9,401	£931	John Barradell, OBE
Croydon	020-8726 6000	382,304	£1,559	Jo Negrini
Ealing	020-8825 5000	343,196	£1,361	Paul Najsarek
Enfield	020-8379 1000	331,395	£1,481	Ian Davies
Greenwich	020-8854 8888	279,766	£1,351	John Comber
Hackney	020-8356 5000	273,526	£1,329	Tim Shields
Hammersmith and Fulham	020-8748 3020	179,654	£1,008	Kim Dero (*interim*)
Haringey	020-8489 0000	278,451	£1,524	Zina Etheridge (*interim*)
Harrow	020-8863 5611	248,752	£1,628	Michael Lockwood
Havering	01708-434343	252,783	£1,598	Andrew Blake-Herbert
Hillingdon	01895-250111	302,471	£1,393	Fran Beasley
Hounslow	020-8583 2000	272,139	£1,403	Mary Harpley
Islington	020-7527 2000	232,865	£1,351	Lesley Seary
Kensington and Chelsea	020-7361 3000	156,726	£1,078	Nicholas Holgate
Kingston upon Thames	020-8547 5000	176,107	£1,757	Charlie Adan
Lambeth	020-7926 1000	327,910	£1,310	Sean Harriss
Lewisham	020-8314 6000	301,867	£1,438	Barry Quirk, CBE
Merton	020-8274 4901	205,029	£1,420	Ged Curran
Newham	020-8430 2000	340,978	£1,245	Kim Bromley-Derry, CBE
Redbridge	020-8554 5000	299,249	£1,476	Andy Donald
Richmond upon Thames	020-8891 1411	195,846	£1,639	Paul Martin
Southwark	020-7525 5000	313,223	£1,257	Eleanor Kelly
Sutton	020-8770 5000	202,220	£1,538	Niall Bolger
Tower Hamlets	020-7364 5000	304,854	£1,247	Will Tuckley
Waltham Forest	020-8496 3000	275,843	£1,538	Martin Esom
Wandsworth	020-8871 6000	316,096	£700	Paul Martin
WESTMINSTER	020-7641 6000	247,614	£688	Charlie Parker

* *Source:* Office for National Statistics – *Mid-2016 Population Estimates* (Crown copyright)
† Band D council tax bill for 2017–18 inclusive of adult social care and parish precepts
‡ Or equivalent postholder
Councils in CAPITAL LETTERS have city status

CITY OF LONDON CORPORATION

The City of London Corporation is the local authority for the City of London. Its legal definition is the 'Mayor and Commonalty and Citizens of the City of London'. It is governed by the court of common council, which consists of the lord mayor, 24 other aldermen and 100 common councilmen. The lord mayor and two sheriffs are nominated annually by the City guilds (the livery companies) and elected by the court of aldermen. Aldermen and councilmen are elected from the 25 wards into which the City is divided; councilmen must stand for re-election every four years. The council is a legislative assembly, and there are no political parties.

The corporation has the same functions as the London borough councils. In addition, it runs the City of London Police; is the health authority for the Port of London; has health control of animal imports throughout Greater London, including at Heathrow airport; owns and manages public open spaces throughout Greater London; runs the central criminal court; and runs Billingsgate, New Spitalfields and Smithfield markets.

The City of London is the historic centre at the heart of London known as 'the square mile', around which the vast metropolis has grown over the centuries. The City's residential population was 7,400 at the 2011 census and in addition, around 400,000 people work in the City. The City is an international financial and business centre, generating about £30bn a year for the British economy. It includes the head offices of the principal banks, insurance companies and mercantile houses, in addition to buildings ranging from the historic Roman Wall and the 15th-century Guildhall, to the massive splendour of St Paul's Cathedral and the architectural beauty of Wren's spires.

The City of London was described by Tacitus in AD 62 as 'a busy emporium for trade and traders'. Under the Romans it became an important administration centre and hub of the road system. Little is known of London in Saxon times, when it formed part of the kingdom of the East Saxons. In 886 Alfred recovered London from the Danes and reconstituted it a burgh under his son-in-law. In 1066 the citizens submitted to William the Conqueror who in 1067 granted them a charter, which is still preserved, establishing them in the rights and privileges they had hitherto enjoyed.

THE MAYORALTY

The mayoralty was probably established about 1189, the first mayor being Henry Fitz Ailwyn who filled the office for 23 years and was succeeded by Fitz Alan (1212–14). A new charter was granted by King John in 1215, directing the mayor to be chosen annually, which has been done ever since, though in early times the same individual often held the office more than once. A familiar instance is that of 'Whittington, thrice Lord Mayor of London' (in reality four times: 1397, 1398, 1406 and 1419); and many modern cases have occurred. The earliest instance of the phrase 'lord mayor' in English is in 1414. It was used more generally in the latter part of the 15th century and became invariable from 1535 onwards. At Michaelmas the liverymen in Common Hall choose two aldermen who have served the office of sheriff for presentation to the Court of Aldermen, and one is chosen to be lord mayor for the following mayoral year.

LORD MAYOR'S DAY

The lord mayor of London was previously elected on the feast of St Simon and St Jude (28 October), and from the time of Edward I, at least, was presented to the King or to the Barons of the Exchequer on the following day, unless that day was a Sunday. The day of election was altered to 16 October in 1346, and after some further changes was fixed for Michaelmas Day in 1546, but the ceremonies of admittance and swearing-in of the lord mayor continued to take place on 28 and 29 October respectively until 1751. In 1752, at the reform of the calendar, the lord mayor was continued in office until 8 November, the 'new style' equivalent of 28 October. The lord mayor is now presented to the lord chief justice at the royal courts of justice on the second Saturday in November to make the final declaration of office, having been sworn in at Guildhall on the preceding day. The procession to the royal courts of justice is popularly known as the Lord Mayor's Show.

REPRESENTATIVES

Aldermen are mentioned in the 11th century and their office is of Saxon origin. They were elected annually between 1377 and 1394, when an act of parliament of Richard II directed them to be chosen for life. Aldermen now serve a six-year term of office before submitting themselves for re-election.

The Common Council was, at an early date, substituted for a popular assembly called the *Folkmote*. At first only two representatives were sent from each ward, but now each of the City's 25 wards is represented by an alderman and at least two Common Councilmen (the number depending on the size of the ward). Common Councilmen are elected every four years.

OFFICERS

Sheriffs were Saxon officers; their predecessors were the *wicreeves* and *portreeves* of London and Middlesex. At first they were officers of the Crown, and were named by the Barons of the Exchequer; but Henry I (in 1132) gave the citizens permission to choose their own sheriffs, and the annual election of sheriffs became fully operative under King John's charter of 1199. The citizens lost this privilege, as far as the election of the sheriff of Middlesex was concerned, by the Local Government Act 1888; but the liverymen continue to choose two sheriffs of the City of London, who are appointed on Midsummer Day and take office at Michaelmas.

The office of chamberlain is an ancient one, the first contemporary record of which is 1237. The town clerk (or common clerk) is first mentioned in 1274.

ACTIVITIES

The work of the City of London Corporation is assigned to a number of committees which present reports to the Court of Common Council. The commitees include: Audit and Risk Management; Barbican Centre; Barbican Residential; Board of Governors of the City of London Freeman's School, the City of London School, the City of London School for Girls and the Guildhall School of Music and Drama; City Bridge Trust; Community and Children's Services; Culture, Heritage and Libraries; Education; Epping Forest and Commons; Establishment; Finance; Freedom Applications; Gresham (City Side); Hampstead Heath, Highgate Wood and Queen's Park; Health and Wellbeing; Investment; Licensing; Markets; Open Spaces and City Gardens; Pensions Board; Planning and Transportation; Police; Policy and Resources; Port Health and Environmental Services; Standards Committee; and West Ham Park. There are numerous other sub-committees which report to the corporation's 'grand' committees.

The City's estate, in the possession of which the City of London Corporation differs from other municipalities, is largely managed by the property investment board.

The Honourable the Irish Society, which manages the City Corporation's estates in Ulster, consists of a governor, two other aldermen and 12 common councilmen.

THE LORD MAYOR 2017–18

The Rt. Hon. the Lord Mayor, Charles Bowman*
Executive Director of Mansion House and the Central Criminal Court, Vic Annells

* Provisional

THE SHERIFFS 2017–18

Alderman Timothy Hailes (Bassishaw); Neil Redcliffe

OFFICERS, ETC

Town Clerk, John Barradell
Chamberlain, Peter Kane
Chief Commoner (2017), Wendy Mead, OBE

Clerk, The Honourable the Irish Society, H. E. J. Montgomery, MBE

THE ALDERMEN

with office held and date of appointment to that office

Name and Ward	Common Councilman	Alderman	Sheriff	Lord Mayor
Ian Luder, *Castle Baynard*	1998	2005	2007	2008
Nicholas Anstee, *Aldersgate*	1987	1996	2003	2009
Sir Michael Bear, *Portsoken*	2003	2005	2007	2010
Sir David Wootton, *Langbourn*	2002	2005	2009	2011
Sir Roger Gifford, *Cordwainer*	–	2004	2008	2012
Dame Fiona Woolf, DBE, *Candlewick*	–	2007	2010	2013
Sir Alan Yarrow, *Bridge & Bridge Wt.*	–	2007	2011	2014
Lord Mountevans, *Cheap*	–	2007	2012	2015
Dr Andrew Parmley, *Vintry*	1992	2001	2014	2016
Charles Bowman, *Lime Street*	–	2013	2015	2017

All the above have passed the Civic Chair

	Common Councilman	Alderman	Sheriff
Alison Gowman, *Dowgate*	1991	2002	–
David Graves, *Cripplegate*	–	2008	–
John Garbutt, *Walbrook*	–	2009	–
Peter Hewitt, *Aldgate*	–	2012	–
Matthew Richardson, *Billingsgate*	2009	2012	–
William Russell, *Bread Street*	–	2013	–
Timothy Hailes, *Bassishaw*	–	2013	–
Prof. Michael Mainelli, *Broad Street*	–	2013	–
Vincent Keaveny, *Farringdon Wn*	–	2013	–
Peter Estlin, *Coleman Street*	–	2013	–
Baroness Scotland of Asthal, QC, *Bishopsgate*	–	2015	–
Robert Howard, *Cornhill*	2011	2015	–
Alistair King, *Queenhithe*	–	2016	–
Gregory Jones, QC, *Farringdon Wt.*	2013	2017	–

THE COMMON COUNCIL

Deputy: each common councilman so described serves as deputy to the alderman of her/his ward.

Abrahams, G. C. (2000) — *Farringdon Wt.*
Absalom, *Deputy* J. D. (1994) — *Farringdon Wt.*
Addy, C. K. (2017) — *Farringdon Wt.*
Ali, M. (2017) — *Portsoken*
Ameer, R. B. (2017) — *Vintry*
Anderson, R. K. (2013) — *Aldersgate*
Anderson, T. A. (2017) — *Farringdon Wn.*
Barr, A. R. M. (2017) — *Cordwainer*
Barrow, *Deputy* D. G. F. (2007) — *Aldgate*
Bastow, A. M. (2017) — *Aldersgate*
Bell, M. (2017) — *Farringdon Wn.*
Bennett, *Deputy* J. A. (2005) — *Broad Street*
Bensted-Smith, N. M. (2014) — *Cheap*
Boden, C. P. (2013) — *Castle Baynard*
Boleat, Sir Mark (2002) — *Cordwainer*
Bostock, R. M. (2017) — *Cripplegate*
Bottomley, *Deputy* K. D. F. (2015) — *Bridge & Bridge Wt.*
Bradshaw, *Deputy* D. J. (1991) — *Cripplegate Wn.*
Broeke, T. (2017) — *Cheap*
Cassidy, *Deputy* M. J., CBE (1980) — *Coleman Street*
Chadwick, *Deputy* R. A. H., OBE (1994) — *Tower*
Chapman, *Deputy* J. D. (2006) — *Langbourn*
Christian, D. G. (2016) — *Lime Street*
Clementi, T. C. (2017) — *Lime Street*
Colthurst, H. N. A. (2013) — *Lime Street*
Crossan, R. P. (2017) — *Aldersgate*

De Sausmarez, H. J. (2015) — *Candlewick*
Dostalova, K. H. (2013) — *Farringdon Wn.*
Duckworth, S. D., OBE (2000) — *Bishopsgate Wn.*
Dunphy, P. G. (2009) — *Cornhill*
Durcan, J. M. (2017) — *Cripplegate*
Edhem, E. (2014) — *Castle Baynard*
Everett, *Deputy* K. M. (1984) — *Candlewick*
Fairweather, A. H. (2016) — *Tower*
Fernandes, S. A. (2009) — *Coleman Street*
Fletcher, J. W. (2011) — *Portsoken*
Fraser, S. J., CBE (1993) — *Coleman Street*
Fredericks, M. B. (2008) — *Tower*
Goyal, P. B., OBE (2017) — *Bishopsgate*
Haines, C. W. (2017) — *Queenhithe*
Haines, *Deputy* Revd S. D. (2005) — *Cornhill*
Harrower, G. G. (2015) — *Bassishaw*
Hayward, C. M. (2013) — *Broad Street*
Hill, C. (2017) — *Farringdon Wn.*
Hoffman, *Deputy* T. D. D. (2002) — *Vintry*
Holmes, A. (2013) — *Farringdon Wn.*
Hudson, M. (2007) — *Castle Baynard*
Hyde, *Deputy* W. (2011) — *Bishopsgate Wt.*
Ingham Clark, *Deputy* J. (2013) — *Billingsgate*
James, *Deputy* C. (2008) — *Farringdon Wn.*
Jones, *Deputy* H. L. M. (2004) — *Portsoken*
Knowles-Cutler, A. (2017) — *Castle Baynard*
Lawrence, G. A. (2002) — *Farringdon Wn.*
Levene, T. C. (2017) — *Bridge and Bridge Wt.*
Littlechild, V. (2009) — *Cripplegate Wn.*
Lodge, O. A. W., TD (2009) — *Bread Street*
Lord, *Deputy* C. E., OBE (2001) — *Farringdon Wt.*
Lumley, Prof. J. S. P. (2013) — *Aldersgate*
Mayer, A. P. (2017) — *Bishopsgate*
McGuinness, *Deputy* C. S. (1997) — *Castle Baynard*
McMurtie, A. S. (2013) — *Coleman Street*
Martinelli, P. N. (2013) — *Farringdon Wt.*
Mayhew, J. P. (1996) — *Aldersgate*
Mead, *Chief Commoner* W., OBE (1997) — *Farringdon Wt.*
Merrett, *Deputy* R. A. (2009) — *Bassishaw*
Meyers, A. G. D. (2017) — *Aldgate*
Mooney, *Deputy* B. D. F. (1998) — *Queenhithe*
Morris, H. F. (2008) — *Aldgate*
Moss, *Deputy* A. M. (2013) — *Cheap*
Moys, S. D. (2001) — *Aldgate*
Nash, *Deputy* J. C., OBE (1983) — *Aldersgate*
Newman, B. P., CBE (1989) — *Aldersgate*
Packham, G. D. (2013) — *Castle Baynard*
Patel, D. (2013) — *Aldgate*
Pearson, S. J. (2017) — *Cripplegate*
Pimlott, W. (2017) — *Cripplegate*
Pleasance, J. L. (2013) — *Langbourn*
Pollard, *Deputy* J. H. G. (2002) — *Dowgate*
Priest, H. J. S. (2009) — *Castle Baynard*
Pritchard, J. P. (2017) — *Portsoken*
Punter, C. (1993) — *Cripplegate Wt.*
Quilter, S. D. (1998) — *Cripplegate Wt.*
Regan, *Deputy* R. D., OBE (1998) — *Farringdon Wn.*
Rogula, *Deputy* E. (2008) — *Lime Street*
Sayed, R. (2017) — *Farringdon Wt.*
Scott, J. G. S. (1999) — *Broad Street*
Seaton, I. C. N. (2009) — *Cornhill*
Sells, O. M., QC (2017) — *Farringdon Wt.*
Shilson, *Deputy*, G. R. E. (2009) — *Bread Street*
Simons, J. L. (2004) — *Castle Baynard*
Sleigh, T. C. C. (2013) — *Bishopsgate Wt.*
Smith, G. M. (2013) — *Farringdon Wt.*
Snyder, *Deputy* Sir Michael (1986) — *Cordwainer*
Starling, A. M. (2006) — *Cripplegate Wn.*
Tank, P. S. (2017) — *Bishopsgate*
Thompson, D. J. (2004) — *Aldgate*
Thomson, *Deputy* J. M. D. (2013) — *Walbrook*
Tomlinson, *Deputy* J. (2004) — *Cripplegate Wt.*

Tumbridge, J. R. (2009)	*Tower*
Upton, J. W. D. (2017)	*Farringdon Wt.*
Welbank, J. M., MBE (2005)	*Billingsgate*
Wheatley, M. R. P. H. D. (2013)	*Dowgate*
Woodhouse, *Deputy* P. J. (2013)	*Langbourn*

THE CITY GUILDS (LIVERY COMPANIES)

The livery companies of the City of London grew out of early medieval religious fraternities and began to emerge as trade and craft guilds, retaining their religious aspect, in the 12th century. From the early 14th century, only members of the trade and craft guilds could call themselves citizens of the City of London. The guilds began to be called livery companies, because of the distinctive livery worn by the most prosperous guild members on ceremonial occasions, in the late 15th century.

By the early 19th century the power of the companies within their trades had begun to wane, but those wearing the livery of a company continued to play an important role in the government of the City of London. Liverymen still have the right to nominate the Lord Mayor and sheriffs, and most members of the Court of Common Council are liverymen.

The constitution of the livery companies has been unchanged for centuries. There are three ranks of membership: freemen, liverymen and assistants. A person can become a freeman by patrimony (through a parent having been a freeman); by servitude (through having served an apprenticeship to a freeman); or by redemption (by purchase).

Election to the livery is the prerogative of the company, who can elect any of its freemen as liverymen. Assistants are usually elected from the livery and form a court of assistants which is the governing body of the company. The master (in some companies called the prime warden) is elected annually from the assistants.

The register for 2017–18 lists 25,644 liverymen of the guilds entitled to vote at elections at common hall.

The order of precedence, omitting extinct companies, is given in parentheses after the name of each company in the list below. In certain companies the election of master or prime warden for the year does not take place until the autumn. In such cases the master or prime warden for 2016–17, rather than 2017–18, is given.

The Twelve Great Companies are given in order of civic precedence and appear first in the list below; the remaining guilds are listed in alphabetical order. Parish clerks and watermen and lightermen have requested to remain with no livery and are marked with a '*'

MERCERS (1). *Hall*, Mercers' Hall, Ironmonger Lane, London EC2V 8HE *Livery*, 247.
Clerk, Rob Abernethy *Master*, Roddy Graham

GROCERS (2). *Hall*, Grocers' Hall, Princes Street, London EC2R 8AD *Livery*, 359.
Clerk, Brig. Greville Bibby, CBE *Master*, Rupert Gavin

DRAPERS (3). *Hall*, Drapers' Hall, Throgmorton Avenue, London EC2N 2DQ *Livery*, 321.
Clerk, Col. Richard Winstanley, OBE *Master*, Steven Beharrell

FISHMONGERS (4). *Hall*, Fishmongers' Hall, London Bridge, London EC4R 9EL *Livery*, 362.
Clerk, Cdre Toby Williamson, MVO
Prime Warden, HRH The Princess Royal, KG KT GCVO QSO

GOLDSMITHS (5). *Hall*, Goldsmiths' Hall, Foster Lane, London EC2V 6BN *Livery*, 285.
Clerk, Sir David Reddaway, KCMG, MBE
Prime Warden, Judith Cobham-Lowe, OBE

MERCHANT TAYLORS (6/7). *Hall*, Merchant Taylors' Hall, 30 Threadneedle Street, London EC2R 8JB *Livery*, 350.
Clerk, Rear-Adm. Nicholas Harris, CB, MBE
Master, Peter Magill

SKINNERS (6/7). *Hall*, Skinners' Hall, 8 Dowgate Hill, London EC4R 2SP *Livery*, 400.
Clerk, Maj.-Gen. Andrew Kennett, CB, CBE
Master, James Leahy

HABERDASHERS (8). *Hall*, Haberdashers' Hall, 18 West Smithfield, London EC1A 9HQ *Livery*, 318.
Clerk, Cdre Philip Thicknesse *Master*, Joff Hamilton

SALTERS (9). *Hall*, Salters' Hall, 4 London Wall Place, London EC2Y 5DE *Livery*, 176.
Clerk, Capt. David Morris, RN
Master, Revd. Prof. Michael Reiss

IRONMONGERS (10). *Hall*, Ironmongers' Hall, Shaftesbury Place, London EC2Y 8AA *Livery*, 146.
Clerk, Col. Hamon Massey *Master*, Richard Slade, QC

VINTNERS (11). *Hall*, Vintners' Hall, Upper Thames Street, London EC4V 3BG *Livery*, 383.
Clerk, Brig. Jonathan Bourne-May *Master*, Nicholas Arkell

CLOTHWORKERS (12). *Hall*, Clothworkers' Hall, Dunster Court, London EC3R 7AH *Livery*, 200.
Clerk, Jocelyn Stuart-Grumbar *Master*, Dr Carolyn Boulter

ACTUARIES (91). Cheapside House, 138 Cheapside, London EC2V 6BW *Livery*, 220.
Clerk, Lyndon Jones *Master*, Nick Dumbreck

AIR PILOTS AND AIR NAVIGATORS (81). *Hall*, Cobham House, 9 Warwick Court, London WC1R 5DJ *Livery*, 600.
Clerk, Paul Tacon *Master*, Capt. Chris Spurrier
Grand Master, HRH the Duke of York, KG, GCVO, ADC(P)

APOTHECARIES (58). *Hall*, Apothecaries' Hall, 14 Black Friars Lane, London EC4V 6EJ *Livery*, 1,215.
Clerk, Nick Royle *Master*, Prof. Charles Mackworth-Young

ARBITRATORS (93). 28 The Meadway, Cuffley EN6 4ES *Livery*, 180.
Clerk, Biagio Fraulo *Master*, Matthew Bastone

ARMOURERS AND BRASIERS (22). *Hall*, Armourers' Hall, 81 Coleman Street, London EC2R 5BJ *Livery*, 135.
Clerk, Peter Bateman *Master*, Julian Beare

ART SCHOLARS (110). 5 Queen Anne's Gate, White House Walk, Farnham GU9 9AN *Livery*, 85.
Clerk, Lt.-Col. Chris Booth
Master, Loyd Grossman, CBE, PHD, FSA

BAKERS (19). *Hall*, Bakers' Hall, 9 Harp Lane, London EC3R 6DP *Livery*, 220.
Clerk, Alan Willis *Master*, Patrick Wilkins

BARBERS (17). *Hall*, Barber-Surgeons' Hall, Monkwell Square, London EC2Y 5BL *Livery*, 230.
Clerk, Malachy Doran *Master*, Anthony Hoskinson

BASKETMAKERS (52). 30 Cadgwith Place, Port Solent, Portsmouth PO6 4TD *Livery*, 300.
Clerk, Fiona Janczur *Prime Warden*, Peter Allen

BLACKSMITHS (40). Painters' Hall, 9 Little Trinity Lane, London EC4V 2AD *Livery*, 246.
Clerk, Wg Cdr M. A. Heath *Prime Warden*, Jashvantrai Joshi

BOWYERS (38). Fosters Lodge, Duck Street, Warminster BA12 7AL *Livery*, 98.
Clerk, Lt Col Tony Marinos *Master*, Mr Antony Kench

BREWERS (14). *Hall*, Brewers' Hall, Aldermanbury Square, London EC2V 7HR *Livery*, 200.
Clerk, Col. Michael O'Dwyer, OBE *Master*, Paul Wells

BRODERERS (48). Ember House, 35–37 Creek Road, East Molesey KT8 9BE *Livery*, 120.
Clerk, Brig. Bill Aldridge, CBE *Master*, Roger Sanders, OBE

BUILDERS MERCHANTS (88). 4 College Hill, London EC4R 2RB *Livery*, 208.
Clerk, Virginia Rounding *Master*, Stuart Thompson

BUTCHERS (24). *Hall*, Butchers' Hall, 87 Bartholomew Close, London EC1A 7EB *Livery*, 650.
Clerk, Maj.-Gen. J. S. Mason, MBE *Master*, Geoff Gillo

CARMEN (77). Plaisterers' Hall, 1 London Wall, London EC2Y 5JU *Livery*, 500.
Clerk, Walter Gill *Master*, Marsha Rae Ratcliff

CARPENTERS (26). *Hall*, Carpenters' Hall, 1 Throgmorton Avenue, London EC2N 2JJ *Livery*, 150.
Clerk, Brig. Tim Gregson, MBE *Master*, Alistair Gregory-Smith

CHARTERED ACCOUNTANTS (86). 35 Ascot Way, Bicester OX26 1AG *Livery*, 365.
Clerk, Jonathan Grosvenor *Master*, Michael Jeans, MBE

CHARTERED ARCHITECTS (98). The Old Vicarage, Anchor Road, Calne SN11 8DR *Livery*, 165.
Clerk, Jonathan Soar *Master*, Richard Brindley

CHARTERED SECRETARIES AND ADMINISTRATORS (87). 3rd Floor, Saddlers' House, 40 Gutter Lane, London EC2V 6BR *Livery*, 240.
Clerk, Erica Lee *Master*, Christopher Hallam

CHARTERED SURVEYORS (85). 75 Meadway Drive, Woking GU21 4TF *Livery*, 365.
Clerk, Amanda Jackson *Master*, William Hill

CLOCKMAKERS (61). 1 Throgmorton Avenue, London EC2N 2BY *Livery*, 280.
Clerk, Lt.-Col. Oliver Bartrum, MBE *Master*, Roy Harris, FBHI

COACHMAKERS AND COACH-HARNESS MAKERS (72). The Old Barn, Church Lane, Glentham LN8 2EL *Livery*, 500.
Clerk, Cdr Mark Leaning, RN *Master*, Martin Payne

CONSTRUCTORS (99). 5 Delft Close, Southampton SO31 7TQ *Livery*, 170.
Clerk, Kim Tyrrell *Master*, Anthony Ward

COOKS (35). 18 Solent Drive, Southampton SO31 9HB *Livery*, 71.
Clerk, Vice-Adm. Peter Wilkinson, CB, CVO *Master*, Mark Grove

COOPERS (36). *Hall*, Coopers' Hall, 13 Devonshire Square, London EC2M 4TH *Livery*, 260.
Clerk, Lt.-Col. Adrian Carroll *Master*, Roy Campbell

CORDWAINERS (27). Clothworkers' Hall, Dunster Court, London EC3R 7AH *Livery*, 186.
Clerk, John Miller *Master*, Patrick Peal

CURRIERS (29). Oak Lodge, 4 Greenhill Lane, BH21 2RN *Livery*, 104.
Clerk, Adrian Rafferty *Master*, Maurice Blaber

CUTLERS (18). *Hall*, Cutlers' Hall, Warwick Lane, London EC4M 7BR *Livery*, 100.
Clerk, Rupert Meacher *Master*, Colin Evans

DISTILLERS (69). 1 The Sanctuary, London SW1P 3JT *Livery*, 260.
Clerk, Edward Macey-Dare *Master*, Richard Watling

DYERS (13). *Hall*, Dyers' Hall, 10 Dowgate Hill, London EC4R 2ST *Livery*, 140.
Clerk, Russell Vaizey *Prime Warden*, Gerald Rothwell

EDUCATORS (109). 8 Little Trinity Lane, London EC4V 2AN *Livery*, 310.
Clerk, Dr Misha Hebel *Master*, Susan Fey, OBE

ENGINEERS (94). Wax Chandlers' Hall, 6 Gresham Street, London EC2V 7AD *Livery*, 320.
Clerk, Caroline Gillett *Master*, Richard Groome

ENVIRONMENTAL CLEANERS (97). 64 Ravensfield Gardens, Epsom KT19 0SR *Livery*, 189.
Clerk, Maureen Marden *Master*, John Broadley

FAN MAKERS (76). Skinners' Hall, 8 Dowgate Hill, London EC4R 2SP *Livery*, 190.
Clerk, Martin Davies *Master*, Marshall Baker

FARMERS (80). *Hall*, The Farmers' and Fletchers' Hall, 3 Cloth Street, London EC1A 7LD *Livery*, 350.
Clerk, Graham Bamford *Master*, Philip Wynn

FARRIERS (55). 19 Queen Street, Kings Langley WD4 9BT *Livery*, 340.
Clerk, Charlotte Clifford *Master*, Brig. Neill O'Connor

FELTMAKERS (63). Post Cottage, Hook RG29 1DA *Livery*, 190.
Clerk, Maj. Jollyon Coombs *Master*, Jeremy Brassington

FIREFIGHTERS (103). The Insurance Hall, 20 Aldermanbury, London EC2V 7GF *Livery*, 121.
Clerk, Steven Tamcken *Master*, John Mansfield

FLETCHERS (39). *Hall*, The Farmers' and Fletchers' Hall, 3 Cloth Street, London EC1A 7LD *Livery*, 140.
Clerk, Kate Pink *Master*, Clare James

FOUNDERS (33). *Hall*, Founders' Hall, 1 Cloth Fair, London EC1A 7JQ *Livery*, 180.
Clerk, Andrew Bell *Master*, Michael Swan

FRAMEWORK KNITTERS (64). The Grange, Walton Road, Lutterworth LE17 5RU *Livery*, 200.
Clerk, Shaun Mackaness *Master*, Peter White

FRUITERERS (45). 3 Parsonage Vale, Marlborough SN8 3SZ *Livery*, 283.
Clerk, Lt.-Col. Philip Brown *Master*, Dennis Surgeon

FUELLERS (95). Skinners' Hall, 8 Dowgate Hill, London EC4R 2SP *Livery*, 141.
Clerk, Cdre Bill Walworth, CBE *Master*, Janet Harrison

FURNITURE MAKERS (83). *Hall*, Furniture Makers' Hall, 12 Austin Friars, London EC2N 2HE *Livery*, 250.
Clerk, Jonny Westbrooke *Master*, Tony Smart, MBE

GARDENERS (66). Ingrams, Ingram's Green, Midhurst EC2A 4AR *Livery*, 298.
Clerk, Maj. Jeremy Herrtage *Master*, David Green, CB, QC

GIRDLERS (23). *Hall*, Girdlers' Hall, Basinghall Avenue, London EC2V 5DD *Livery*, 80.
Clerk, Brig. Ian Rees *Master*, James Maitland

GLASS SELLERS (71). PO Box 241, Safron Walden *Livery*, 172.
Clerk, Lance Whitehouse *Master*, John Poulten

GLAZIERS AND PAINTERS OF GLASS (53). *Hall*, Glaziers' Hall, 9 Montague Close, London SE1 9DD *Livery*, 292.
Clerk, Cdr Andrew Gordon-Lennox, RN *Master*, Sir David Wooton

GLOVERS (62). Seniors Farmhouse, Shaftesbury SP7 9AX *Livery*, 250.
Clerk, Lt.-Col. Mark Butler *Master*, Jonathan Crossman, MBE

GOLD AND SILVER WYRE DRAWERS (74). Lye Green Forge, Lye Green, Crowborough TN6 1UU *Livery*, 275.
Clerk, Cdr. M. C. Dickens *Master*, Paul Constantinidi

GUNMAKERS (73). The Proof House, 48–50 Commercial Road, London E1 1LP *Livery*, 350.
Clerk, John Allen *Master*, Robert Pitcher

HACKNEY CARRIAGE DRIVERS (104). 25 The Grove, Latimer HP5 1UE *Livery*, 105.
Clerk, Mary Whitworth *Master*, Alan Roughan

HORNERS (54). 12 Coltsfoot Close, Ixworth IP31 2NJ *Livery*, 225.
Clerk, Jonathan Mead *Master*, Alison Gill

INFORMATION TECHNOLOGISTS (100). *Hall*, Information Technologists' Hall, 39A Bartholomew Close, London EC1A 7JN *Livery*, 365.
Clerk, Mike Jenkins *Master*, Dr Stefan Fafinski

INNHOLDERS (32). *Hall*, Innholders' Hall, 30 College Street, London EC4R 2RH *Livery*, 180.
Clerk, Dougal Bulger *Master*, Nicholas Rettie, MBE

INSURERS (92). Insurance Hall, 20 Aldermanbury, London EC2V 7HY *Livery*, 341.
Clerk, Sarah Clark *Master*, Stephen Riley

INTERNATIONAL BANKERS (106). 12 Austin Friars, London EC2N 2HE *Livery*, 210.
Clerk, Nicholas Westgarth *Master*, Peter Estlin

JOINERS AND CEILERS (41). 75 Meadway Drive, Woking GU21 4TF *Livery*, 11 5.
Clerk, Amanda Jackson *Master*, John Skarratt

LAUNDERERS (89). *Hall*, Launderers' Hall, 9 Montague Close, London SE1 9DD *Livery*, 175.
Clerk, Margaret Campbell *Master*, David Pantlin

LEATHERSELLERS (15). 7 St Helen's Place, London EC3A 6AB *Livery*, 150.
Clerk, Brig. David Santa-Olalla, DSO, MC *Master*, Antony Barrow

LIGHTMONGERS (96). 1 Manor House Garden, Wanstead E11 2RU *Livery*, 168.
Clerk, Phillip Hyde *Master*, Michael Simpson

LORINERS (57). 30 Elm Park, Royal Wootton Bassett SN4 7TA *Livery*, 400.
Clerk, Honor Page *Master*, Dr George Anderson

MAKERS OF PLAYING CARDS (75). 256 St David's Square, London E14 3WE *Livery*, 147.
Clerk, David Barrett *Master*, Richard Wells

MANAGEMENT CONSULTANTS (105). Skinners' Hall, 8 Dowgate Hill, London EC4R 2SP *Livery*, 180.
Clerk, Julie Fox *Master*, David Johnson

MARKETORS (90). Plaisterers' Hall, One London Wall, London EC2Y 5JU *Livery*, 250.
Clerk, John Hammond *Master*, Sue Garland Worthington, OBE

MASONS (30). 8 Little Trinity Lane, London EC4V 2AN *Livery*, 163.
Clerk, Maj. Giles Clapp *Master*, Peter Clark

MASTER MARINERS (78). *Hall*, HQS Wellington, Temple Stairs, London WC2R 2PN *Livery*, 186.
Clerk, Cdre Angus Menzies, RN *Master*, Capt. Martin Reed

MUSICIANS (50). 1 Speed Highwalk, Barbican EC2Y BDX *Livery*, 420.
Clerk, Hugh Lloyd *Master*, Sir Roger Gifford

NEEDLEMAKERS (65). PO Box 73635, London SW14 9BY *Livery*, 200.
Clerk, Fiona Sedgwick *Master*, Dame Elizabeth Fradd, DBE

PAINTER-STAINERS (28). *Hall*, Painters' Hall, 9 Little Trinity Lane, London EC4V 2AD *Livery*, 280.
Clerk, Christopher Twyman *Master*, James Lee

PATTENMAKERS (70). 3 The High Street, Sutton Valence ME17 3AG *Livery*, 203.
Clerk, Col. R. W. Murfin, TD *Master*, Richard Kottler

PAVIORS (56). Paviors' House, Charterhouse, London EC1M 6AN *Livery*, 285.
Clerk, John Freestone *Master*, Miles Ashley

PEWTERERS (16). *Hall*, Pewterers' Hall, Oat Lane, London EC2V 7DE *Livery*, 140.
Clerk, Capt. Paddy Watson, RN *Master*, Ann Buxton

PLAISTERERS (46). *Hall*, Plaisterers' Hall, 1 London Wall, London EC2Y 5JU *Livery*, 236.
Clerk, Nigel Bamping *Master*, Richard Hanney

PLUMBERS (31). Carpenters' Hall, 1 Throgmorton Avenue, London EC2N 2JJ *Livery*, 360.
Clerk, Cdre Pieter Cox *Master*, Brian Wadsworth

POULTERS (34). 20 Waltham Road, Woodford Green 1GB 8DN *Livery*, 204.
Clerk, Julie Pearce *Master*, George Harris

SADDLERS (25). *Hall*, Saddlers' Hall, 40 Gutter Lane, London EC2V 6BR *Livery*, 85.
Clerk, Brig. Philip Napier, OBE *Master*, Hugh Thomas

SCIENTIFIC INSTRUMENT MAKERS (84). Glaziers' Hall, 9 Montague Close, London SE1 9DD *Livery*, 185.
Clerk, Neville Watson *Master*, John Caunt

SCRIVENERS (44). HQS Wellington, Temple Stairs, London WC2R 2PN *Livery*, 191.
Clerk, Giles Cole *Master*, David Philip

SECURITY PROFESSIONALS (108). 34 Tye Green, Sudbury CO10 7RG *Livery*, 185.
Clerk, Patricia Boswell *Master*, Air Cdre Stephen Anderton

SHIPWRIGHTS (59). Ironmongers Hall, Shaftesbury Place, London EC2Y 8AA *Livery*, 425.
Clerk, Lt.-Col. Richard Cole-Mackintosh
Prime Warden, Archie Smith
Grand Master, HRH the Prince of Wales, KG, KT, GCB

SOLICITORS (79). 4 College Hill, London EC4R 2RB *Livery*, 350.
Clerk, Linzi James *Master*, David Graves

SPECTACLE MAKERS (60). Apothecaries' Hall, Black Friars Lane, London EC4V 6EL *Livery*, 400.
Clerk, Helen Perkins *Master*, Don Grocott, TD

STATIONERS AND NEWSPAPER MAKERS (47). *Hall*, Stationers' Hall, Ave Maria Lane, London EC4M 7DD *Livery*, 535.
Clerk, William Alden, MBE *Master*, Nick Steidl

TALLOW CHANDLERS (21). *Hall*, Tallow Chandlers' Hall, 4 Dowgate Hill, London EC4R 2SH *Livery*, 180.
Clerk, Brig. D. Homer, MBE *Master*, James Long

TAX ADVISERS (107). 191 West End Road, Ruislip HA4 6LD *Freemen*, 145.
Clerk, Paul Herbage, MBE *Master*, Kevin Thomas

TIN PLATE WORKERS (ALIAS WIRE WORKERS) (67). PO Box 71002, London W4 9FH *Livery*, 190.
Clerk, Piers Baker *Master*, Howard Reed

TOBACCO PIPE MAKERS AND TOBACCO BLENDERS (82). 14 Montpelier Road, Sutton SM1 4QE *Livery*, 138.
Clerk, Sandra Stocker *Master*, Ralph Edmonson

TURNERS (51). Skinner's Hall, 8 Dowgate Hill, London EC4R 2SP *Livery*, 185.
Clerk, Alex Robertson *Master*, Andrew Neill

TYLERS AND BRICKLAYERS (37). 3 Farmers' Way, Seer Green HP9 2YY *Livery*, 200.
Clerk, John Brooks *Master*, Jeff Fuller

UPHOLDERS (49). Pembroke Lodge, 162 Tonbridge Road, Hildenborough TN11 9HP *Livery*, 164.
Clerk, Susan Nevard *Master*, Judy Tayler-Smith, FSA SCOT

WATER CONSERVATORS (102). The Lark, Bell Lane, Bury St Edmunds IP28 8SE *Livery*, 201.
Clerk, Ralph Riley *Master*, Mike Williamson

WAX CHANDLERS (20). *Hall*, Wax Chandlers' Hall, 6 Gresham Street, London EC2V 7AD *Livery*, 120.
Clerk, Georgina Brown *Master*, Arthur Davey

WEAVERS (42). Saddlers' House, Gutter Lane, London EC2V 6BR *Livery*, 128.
Clerk, John Snowdon *Upper Bailiff*, John Garbutt, MBE

WHEELWRIGHTS (68). 90 Fernside Road, London SW12 8LJ *Livery*, 223.
Clerk, Susie Morris *Master*, Alan Culverhouse

WOOLMEN (43). 52 Cumberland Drive, Bexleyheath DA7 5LB *Livery*, 175.
Clerk, Maj. Steve Wake *Master*, Christopher Thierry

WORLD TRADERS (101). 13 Hall Gardens, St. Albans AL4 0QF *Livery*, 240.
Clerk, Gaye Duffy *Master*, Robert Woodthorpe Brown, MBE

PARISH CLERKS (No Livery*). Acreholt, 33 Medstead Road, Alton GU34 4AD *Members*, 88.
Clerk, Alana Coombes *Master*, Stephen Plumb

WATERMEN AND LIGHTERMEN (No Livery*). *Hall*, Watermen's Hall, 16–18 St Mary at Hill, London EC3R 8EF *Craft Owning Freemen*, 379.
Clerk, Colin Middlemiss *Master*, Simon McCarthy

WALES

Cymru

The principality of Wales (Cymru) occupies the extreme west of the central southern portion of the island of Great Britain, with a total area of 20,778 sq. km (8,022 sq. miles): land 20,733 sq. km (8,005 sq. miles); inland water 45 sq. km (17 sq. miles). It is bordered in the north by the Irish Sea, in the south by the Bristol Channel, in the east by the English counties of Cheshire West and Chester, Shropshire, Herefordshire and Gloucestershire, and in the west by St George's Channel.

Across the Menai Straits is Ynys Mon (Isle of Anglesey) (715 sq. km/276 sq. miles), communication with which is facilitated by the Menai Suspension Bridge (305m/1,000ft long) built by Telford in 1826, and by the Britannia Bridge (351m/1,151ft), a two-tier road and rail truss arch design, rebuilt in 1972 after a fire destroyed the original tubular railway bridge built by Stephenson in 1850. Holyhead harbour, on Holy Isle (north-west of Anglesey), provides ferry services to Dublin (113km/70 miles).

The Local Government (Wales) Act 1994 abolished the two-tier structure of eight county and 37 district councils which had existed since 1974, and replaced it, from 1 April 1996, with 22 unitary authorities. The new authorities were elected in May 1995. Each unitary authority inherited all the functions of the previous county and district councils, except fire services (which are provided by three combined fire authorities, composed of representatives from the unitary authorities) and national parks (which are the responsibility of three independent national park authorities).

POPULATION
The population at the 2011 census was 3,063,456 (men 1,504,228; women 1,559,228). The average density of population in 2011 was 147 persons per sq. km (382 per sq. mile).

COMMUNITY COUNCILS
In Wales communities are the equivalent of parishes in England. Unlike England, where many areas are not in any parish, communities have been established for the whole of Wales, approximately 865 communities in all. Community meetings may be convened as and when desired.

Community or town councils exist in around 730 of the communities and further councils may be established at the request of a community meeting. Community councils have broadly the same range of powers as English parish councils. Community councillors are elected for a term of four years.

ELECTIONS
Elections usually take place every four years; the last elections took place on 4 May 2017.

FINANCE
Total budgeted revenue expenditure for 2017–18 is £8bn, an increase of 1.4 per cent on 2016–17. Total budget requirement, which excludes expenditure financed by specific and special government grants and any use of reserves, is £6.2bn. This comprises revenue support grant of £3.2bn, support from the national non-domestic rate pool of £1.1bn, police grant of £211m and £1.7bn to be raised through council tax. The non-domestic rating multiplier for Wales for 2017–18 is 49.9p. The average Band D council tax levied in Wales for 2017–18 is £1,420, comprising unitary authorities £1,162, police and crime commissioners £227 and community councils £32.

EXPENDITURE
Local authority budgeted revenue expenditure for 2017–18 is:

Service	£ million
Education	2,598.9
Social services	1,728.7
Council fund housing	1,141.3
Local environmental services	373.8
Roads and transport	280.5
Libraries, culture, heritage, sport and recreation	203.9
Planning, economic and community development	84.9
Council tax collection	25.9
Debt financing	310.2
Central administrative and other revenue expenditure	360.9
Police	675.7
Fire	150.5
National parks	14.6
Gross revenue expenditure	7,950.0
Less specific and special government grants	(1,930.7)
Net revenue expenditure	6,019.3
Less appropriations from reserves	(103.3)
Council tax reduction scheme	258.0
BUDGET REQUIREMENT	6,174.0

RELIEF
Wales is a country of extensive tracts of high plateau and shorter stretches of mountain ranges deeply dissected by river valleys. Lower-lying ground is largely confined to the coastal belt and the lower parts of the valleys. The highest mountains are those of Snowdonia in the north-west (Snowdon, 1,085m/3,559ft and Aran Fawddwy, 906m/2,971ft). Snowdonia is also home to Cader Idris (Pen y Gadair, 892m/2,928ft). Other high peaks are to be found in the Cambrian range (Plynlimon, 752m/2,467ft), and the Black Mountains, Brecon Beacons and Black Forest ranges in the south-east (Pen y Fan, 886m/2,906ft; Waun Fâch, 811m/2,660ft; Carmarthen Van, 802m/2,630ft).

HYDROGRAPHY
The principal river in Wales is the Severn, which flows from the slopes of Plynlimon to the English border. The Wye (209km/130 miles) also rises on the slopes of Plynlimon. The Usk (90km/56 miles) flows into the Bristol Channel through Gwent. The Dee (113km/70 miles) rises in Bala Lake and flows through the Vale of Llangollen, where an aqueduct (built by Telford in 1805) carries the Pontcysyllte branch of the Shropshire Union Canal across the valley. The estuary of the Dee is the navigable portion; it is 23km (14 miles) in length and about 8km (5 miles) in breadth. The Towy (109km/68 miles), Teifi (80km/50 miles), Taff (64km/40 miles), Dovey (48km/30 miles), Taf (40km/25 miles) and Conway (39km/24 miles) are wholly Welsh rivers.

The largest natural lake is Bala (Llyn Tegid) in Gwynedd, nearly 7km (4 miles) long and 1.6km (1 mile) wide. Lake Vyrnwy is an artificial reservoir, about the size of Bala, and forms the water supply of Liverpool; Birmingham's water is supplied from reservoirs in the Elan and Claerwen valleys.

WELSH LANGUAGE

According to the 2011 census results, the percentage of people aged three years and over who are able to speak Welsh is:

Blaenau Gwent	7.8	Neath Port Talbot	15.3
Bridgend	9.7	Newport	9.3
Caerphilly	11.2	Pembrokeshire	19.2
Cardiff	11.1	Powys	18.6
Carmarthenshire	43.9	Rhondda Cynon Taf	12.3
Ceredigion	47.3	Swansea	11.4
Conwy	27.4	Torfaen	9.8
Denbighshire	24.6	Vale of Glamorgan	10.8
Flintshire	13.2	Wrexham	12.9
Gwynedd	65.4	Ynys Mon	
Merthyr Tydfil	8.9	(Isle of Anglesey)	57.2
Monmouthshire	9.9	*Total in Wales*	19.0

FLAG

The flag of Wales, the Red Dragon *(Y Ddraig Goch)*, is a red dragon on a field divided by white over green *(per fess argent and vert a dragon passant gules)*. The flag was augmented in 1953 by a royal badge on a shield encircled with a riband bearing the words *Ddraig Goch Ddyry Cychwyn* and imperially crowned, but this augmented flag is rarely used.

EARLY HISTORY

The earliest inhabitants of whom there is any record appear to have been subdued or exterminated by the Goidels (a people of Celtic race) in the Bronze Age. A further invasion of Celtic Brythons and Belgae followed in the ensuing Iron Age. The Roman conquest of southern Britain and Wales was for some time successfully opposed by Caratacus (Caractacus or Caradog), chieftain of the Catuvellauni and son of Cunobelinus (Cymbeline). South-east Wales was subjugated and the legionary fortress at Caerleon-on-Usk established by around AD 75–7; the conquest of Wales was completed by Agricola around AD 78. Communications were opened up by the construction of military roads from Chester to Caerleon-on-Usk and Caerwent, and from Chester to Conwy (and thence to Carmarthen and Neath). Christianity was introduced in the fourth century, during the Roman occupation.

ANGLO-SAXON ATTACKS

The Anglo-Saxon invaders of southern Britain drove the Celts into the mountain stronghold of Wales, and into Strathclyde (Cumberland and south-west Scotland) and Cornwall, giving them the name of *Waelisc* (Welsh), meaning 'foreign'. The West Saxons' victory of Deorham (AD 577) isolated Wales from Cornwall and the battle of Chester (AD 613) cut off communication with Strathclyde and northern Britain. In the eighth century the boundaries of the Welsh were further restricted by the annexations of Offa, King of Mercia, and counter-attacks were largely prevented by the construction of an artificial boundary from the Dee to the Wye (Offa's Dyke).

In the ninth century Rhodri Mawr (844–878) united the country and successfully resisted further incursions of the Saxons by land and raids of Norse and Danish pirates by sea, but at his death his three provinces of Gwynedd (north), Powys (central) and Deheubarth (south) were divided among his three sons, Anarawd, Mervyn and Cadell. Cadell's son Hywel Dda ruled a large part of Wales and codified its laws but the provinces were not united again until the rule of Llewelyn ap Seisyllt (husband of the heiress of Gwynedd) from 1018 to 1023.

THE NORMAN CONQUEST

After the Norman conquest of England, William I created palatine counties along the Welsh frontier, and the Norman barons began to make encroachments into Welsh territory.

The Welsh princes recovered many of their losses during the civil wars of Stephen's reign (1135–54), and in the early 13th century Owen Gruffydd, prince of Gwynedd, was the dominant figure in Wales. Under Llywelyn ap Iorwerth (1194–1240) the Welsh united in powerful resistance to English incursions and Llywelyn's privileges and *de facto* independence were recognised in the Magna Carta. His grandson, Llywelyn ap Gruffydd, was the last native prince; he was killed in 1282 during hostilities between the Welsh and English, allowing Edward I of England to establish his authority over the country. On 7 February 1301, Edward of Caernarvon, son of Edward I, was created Prince of Wales, a title subsequently borne by the eldest son of the sovereign.

Strong Welsh national feeling continued, expressed in the early 15th century in the rising led by Owain Glyndwr, but the situation was altered by the accession to the English throne in 1485 of Henry VII of the Welsh House of Tudor. Wales was politically annexed by England under the Act of Union of 1535, which extended English laws to the principality and gave it parliamentary representation for the first time.

EISTEDDFOD

The Welsh are a distinct nation, with a language and literature of their own; the national bardic festival (Eisteddfod), instituted by Prince Rhys ap Griffith in 1176, is still held annually.

PRINCIPAL CITIES

There are six cities in Wales (with date city status conferred): Bangor (pre-1900), Cardiff (1905), Newport (2002), St Asaph (2012), St David's (1994) and Swansea (1969). Cardiff and Swansea have also been granted lord mayoralities.

CARDIFF

Cardiff *(Caerdydd)*, at the mouth of the rivers Taff, Rhymney and Ely, is the capital city of Wales and at the 2011 census had a population of 346,090. The city has changed dramatically in recent years following the regeneration of Cardiff Bay and construction of a barrage, which has created a permanent freshwater lake and waterfront for the city. As the capital city, Cardiff is home to the National Assembly for Wales and is a major administrative, retail, business and cultural centre.

The city is home to many fine buildings, including the City Hall, Cardiff Castle, Llandaff Cathedral, the National Museum of Wales, university buildings, law courts and the Temple of Peace and Health. The Millennium Stadium opened in 1999 and has hosted high-profile events since 2001.

SWANSEA

Swansea *(Abertawe)* is a seaport with a population of 239,023 at the 2011 census. The Gower peninsula was brought within the city boundary under local government reform in 1974.

The principal buildings are the Norman castle (rebuilt *c*.1330), the Royal Institution of South Wales, founded in 1835 (including library), the University of Wales Swansea at Singleton and the Guildhall, containing Frank Brangwyn's British Empire panels. The Dylan Thomas Centre, formerly the old Guildhall, was restored in 1995. More recent buildings include the County Hall, the Maritime Quarter Marina, the Wales National Pool and the National Waterfront Museum. In 2017 Swansea council approved plans for a £500m regeneration of the city centre.

Swansea was chartered by the Earl of Warwick (1158–84), and further charters were granted by King John, Henry III, Edward II, Edward III and James II, Oliver Cromwell and the Marcher Lord William de Breos. It was formally invested with city status in 1969.

LORD-LIEUTENANTS AND HIGH SHERIFFS

Area	Lord-Lieutenant	High Sheriff (2017–18)
Clwyd	Henry Fetherstonhaugh, OBE	Charlotte Howard
Dyfed	Sara Edwards	Susan Balsom
Gwent	Brig. Robert Aiken, CBE	John Thomas
Gwynedd	Edmund Bailey	Prof. Sian Hope
Mid Glamorgan	Kate Thomas, CVO	David Davies
Powys	Hon. Dame Elizabeth Legge-Bourke, DCVO	Susan Thompson
S. Glamorgan	Morfudd Ann Meredith	Gilbert Lloyd
W. Glamorgan	D. Byron Lewis	Roberta Fleet

LOCAL COUNCILS

Council	Administrative Headquarters	Telephone	Population*	Council Tax†	Chief Executive
Blaenau Gwent	Ebbw Vale	01495-311556	69,628	£1,754	Stephen Gillingham (interim)
Bridgend	Bridgend	01656-643643	143,117	£1,593	Darren Mepham
Caerphilly	Hengoed	01443-815588	180,462	£1,252	Chris Burns
CARDIFF	Cardiff	029-2087 2087	361,468	£1,320	Paul Orders
Carmarthenshire	Carmarthen	01267-234567	185,610	£1,435	Mark James, CBE
Ceredigion	Aberaeron	01545-570881	74,146	£1,413	Bronwen Morgan
Conwy	Conwy	01492-574000	116,538	£1,401	Iwan Davies
Denbighshire	Ruthin	01824-706101	94,805	£1,487	Dr Mohammed Mehmet
Flintshire	Mold	01352-752121	154,419	£1,395	Colin Everett
Gwynedd	Caernarfon	01766-771000	123,627	£1,530	Dilwyn Williams
Merthyr Tydfil	Merthyr Tydfil	01685-725000	59,810	£1,660	Gareth Chapman
Monmouthshire	Cwmbran	01633-644644	92,843	£1,466	Paul Matthews
Neath Port Talbot	Port Talbot	01639-686868	141,588	£1,703	Stephen Phillips
NEWPORT	Newport	01633-656656	149,148	£1,242	Will Godfrey
Pembrokeshire	Haverfordwest	01437-764551	123,954	£1,128	Ian Westley
Powys	Llandrindod Wells	01597-827460	132,160	£1,397	Jeremy Patterson
Rhondda Cynon Taff	Tonypandy	01443-425005	238,306	£1,604	Chris Bradshaw
SWANSEA	Swansea	01792-636000	244,513	£1,437	Phil Roberts
Torfaen	Pontypool	01495-762200	92,052	£1,456	Alison Ward
Vale of Glamorgan	Barry	01446-700111	128,463	£1,404	Rob Thomas
Wrexham	Wrexham	01978-292000	136,710	£1,346	Dr Helen Paterson
Ynys Mon (Isle of Anglesey)	Ynys Mon	01248-750057	69,723	£1,377	Dr Gwynne Jones

* Source: Office for National Statistics – Mid-2016 Population Estimates (Crown copyright)
† Average Band D council tax bill 2017–18
Councils in CAPITAL LETTERS have city status

Key	Council	Key	Council
1	Anglesey (Ynys Mon)	12	Merthyr Tydfil
2	Blaenau Gwent	13	Monmouthshire
3	Bridgend	14	Neath Port Talbot
4	Caerphilly	15	Newport
5	Cardiff	16	Pembrokeshire
6	Carmarthenshire	17	Powys
7	Ceredigion	18	Rhondda Cynon Taff
8	Conwy	19	Swansea
9	Denbighshire	20	Torfaen
10	Flintshire	21	Vale of Glamorgan
11	Gwynedd	22	Wrexham

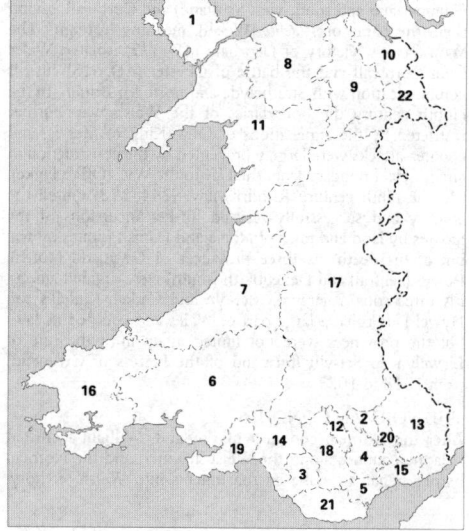

SCOTLAND

Scotland occupies the northern portion of the main island of Great Britain and includes the Inner and Outer Hebrides, Orkney, Shetland and many other islands. It lies between 60° 51′ 30″ and 54° 38′ N. latitude and between 1° 45′ 32″ and 6° 14′ W. longitude, with England to the south-east, the North Channel and the Irish Sea to the south-west, the Atlantic Ocean on the north and west, and the North Sea on the east.

The greatest length of the mainland (Cape Wrath to the Mull of Galloway) is 441km (274 miles), and the greatest breadth (Buchan Ness to Applecross) is 248km (154 miles). The customary measurement of the island of Great Britain is from the site of John o' Groats house, near Duncansby Head, Caithness, to Land's End, Cornwall, a total distance of 970km (603 miles) in a straight line and approximately 1,448km (900 miles) by road.

The Local Government etc (Scotland) Act 1994 abolished the two-tier structure of nine regional and 53 district councils which had existed since 1975 and replaced it, from 1 April 1996, with 29 unitary authorities on the mainland; the three islands councils remained. The new authorities were elected in April 1995.

In July 1999 the Scottish parliament assumed responsibility for legislation on local government.

The total area of Scotland is 78,807 sq. km (30,427 sq. miles): land 77,907 sq. km (30,080 sq. miles), inland water 900 sq. km (347 sq. miles).

POPULATION
The population at the 2011 census was 5,295,403 (men 2,567,444; women 2,727,959). The average density of the population in 2011 was 67 persons per sq. km (174 per sq. mile).

ELECTIONS
The unitary authorities consist of directly elected councillors. The Scottish Local Government (Elections) Act 2002 moved elections from a three-year to a four-year cycle. The last local authority elections took place in May 2017.

FUNCTIONS
The functions of the councils and islands councils are: education; social work; strategic planning; the provision of infrastructure such as roads; consumer protection; flood prevention; coast protection; valuation and rating; the police and fire services; civil defence; electoral registration; public transport; registration of births, deaths and marriages; housing; leisure and recreation; development and building control; environmental health; licensing; allotments; public conveniences; and the administration of district courts.

COMMUNITY COUNCILS
Scottish community councils differ from those in England and Wales. Their purpose as defined in statute is to ascertain and express the views of the communities they represent, and to take in the interests of their communities such action as appears to be expedient or practicable. Around 1,200 community councils have been established under schemes drawn up by local authorities in Scotland.

FINANCE
For 2017–18 Scotland's local authorities set a net revenue expenditure budget of £11.9bn for spending on all services; Education accounted for 41.8 per cent of the total budget and social work 26.7 per cent.

Budgeted total revenue support for 2017–18 is £11.8bn, comprising government grants (£6.9bn), council tax (£2.6bn), non-domestic rates and local authority reserves (£112m).

The non-domestic rate multiplier or poundage for 2017–18 is 46.6p. Larger businesses in 2017–18 (rateable value in excess of £51,000) pay a poundage supplement of 2.6p, which contributes towards the cost of the small business bonus scheme. Non-domestic properties with a rateable value of £15,000 or less do not have to pay business rates in 2017–18. The average Band D council tax for 2017–18 is £1,173.

EXPENDITURE
Local authority budgeted net revenue expenditure for 2017–18 is:

Service	£ million
Education	4,970
Cultural and related services	548
Social work services	3,174
Roads and transport	405
Environmental services	674
Planning and development services	237
Other	1,894
TOTAL	11,902

RELIEF
There are three natural orographic divisions of Scotland. The southern uplands have their highest points in Merrick (843m/ 2,766ft), Rhinns of Kells (814m/2,669ft) and Cairnsmuir of Carsphairn (797m/2,614ft), in the west; and the Tweedsmuir Hills in the east (Broad Law 840m/2,756ft; Dollar Law 817m/2,682ft; Hartfell 808m/2,651ft).

The central lowlands, formed by the valleys of the Clyde, Forth and Tay, divide the southern uplands from the Highlands, which extend from close to the extreme north of the mainland to the central lowlands, and are divided into a northern and a southern system by the Great Glen.

The Grampian Mountains, the southern Highland system, include in the west Ben Nevis (1,345m/4,412ft), the highest point in the British Isles, and in the east the Cairngorm Mountains (Ben Macdui 1,309m/4,296ft; Braeriach 1,295m/4,248ft; Cairn Gorm 1,245m/4,084ft). The north-west Highlands contain the mountains of Wester and Easter Ross (Carn Eige 1,183m/3,880ft; Sgurr na Lapaich 1,151m/ 3,775ft).

Created, like the central lowlands, by a major geological fault, the Great Glen (97km/60 miles long) runs between Inverness and Fort William, and contains Loch Ness, Loch Oich and Loch Lochy. These are linked to each other and to the north-east and south-west coasts of Scotland by the Caledonian Canal, providing a navigable passage between the Moray Firth and the Inner Hebrides.

HYDROGRAPHY
The western coast is fragmented by peninsulas and islands, and indented by fjords (sea-lochs), the longest of which is Loch Fyne (68km/42 miles long) in Argyll. Although the east coast tends to be less fractured and lower, there are several great drowned inlets (firths), including the Firth of Forth, Firth of Tay and the Moray Firth, as well as the Firth of Clyde in the west.

The lochs are the principal hydrographic feature. The largest in Scotland and in Britain is Loch Lomond (70 sq. km/27 sq. miles), in the Grampian valleys, and the longest and deepest is Loch Ness (39km/24 miles long and 244m/800ft deep), in the Great Glen.

The longest river is the Tay (188km/117 miles), noted for its salmon. It flows into the North Sea, with Dundee on the estuary, which is spanned by the Tay Bridge (3,136m/ 10,289ft) opened in 1887 and the Tay Road Bridge (2,245m/7,365ft) opened in 1966. Other noted salmon rivers are the Dee (145km/90 miles) which flows into the North Sea at Aberdeen, and the Spey (177km/110 miles), the swiftest flowing river in the British Isles, which flows into the Moray Firth. The Tweed, which gave its name to the woollen cloth produced along its banks, marks in the lower stretches of its 154km (96 mile) course the border between Scotland and England.

The most important river commercially is the Clyde (171km/106 miles), formed by the junction of the Daer and Portrail water, which flows through the city of Glasgow to the Firth of Clyde. During its course it passes over the picturesque Falls of Clyde, Bonnington Linn (9m/30ft), Corra Linn (26m/84ft), Dundaff Linn (3m/10ft) and Stonebyres Linn (24m/80ft), above and below Lanark. The Forth (106km/66 miles), upon which stands Edinburgh, the capital, is spanned by the Forth Railway Bridge (1890), which is 1,625m (5,330ft) long, and the Forth Road Bridge (1964), which has a total length of 1,876m (6,156ft) (over water) and a single span of 914m (3,000ft).

The highest waterfall in Scotland, and the British Isles, is Eas a'Chùal Aluinn with a total height of 201m (658ft), which falls from Glas Bheinn in Sutherland. The Falls of Glomach, on a head-stream of the Elchaig in Wester Ross, have a drop of 113m (370ft).

GAELIC LANGUAGE
According to the 2011 census, 1.1 per cent (58,000 people) of the population of Scotland aged three and over were able to speak the Scottish form of Gaelic. This was a slight decrease from the 1.2 per cent recorded at the 2001 census.

LOWLAND SCOTTISH LANGUAGE
Several regional lowland Scottish dialects, known variously as Scots, Lallans or Doric, are widely spoken. According to the 2011 census, 43 per cent of the population of Scotland aged three and over stated they could do one or a combination of read, write, speak or understand Scots. A question on Scots was not included in the 2001 census.

FLAG
The flag of Scotland is known as the Saltire. It is a white diagonal cross on a blue field (saltire argent in a field azure) and represents St Andrew, the patron saint of Scotland.

THE SCOTTISH ISLANDS

ORKNEY
The Orkney Islands (total area 972 sq. km/376 sq. miles) lie about 10km (six miles) north of the mainland, separated from it by the Pentland Firth. Of the 90 islands and islets (holms and skerries) in the group, about one-third are inhabited.

The total population at the 2011 census was 21,349; the 2011 populations of the islands shown here include those of smaller islands forming part of the same council district.

Mainland, 17,162	Inner Holm, 1
Auskerry, 4	Norh Ronaldsay, 72
Burray, 409	Papa Westray, 90
Eday, 160	Rousay, 216
Egilsay, 26	Sanday, 494
Flotta, 8	Shapinsay, 307
Gairsay, 3	South Ronaldsay, 909
Graemsay, 28	Stronsay, 349
Holm of Grimbister, 3	Westray, 588
Hoy, 419	Wyre, 29

The islands are rich in prehistoric and Scandinavian remains, the most notable being the Stone Age village of Skara Brae, the burial chamber of Maes Howe, the many brochs (towers) and the 12th-century St Magnus Cathedral. Scapa Flow, between the Mainland and Hoy, was the war station of the British Grand Fleet from 1914 to 1919 and the scene of the scuttling of the surrendered German High Seas Fleet (21 June 1919).

Most of the islands are low-lying and fertile, and farming (principally beef cattle) is the main industry. Flotta, to the south of Scapa Flow, is the site of the oil terminal for the Piper, Claymore and Tartan fields in the North Sea.

The capital is Kirkwall (population 7,045) situated on Mainland.

SHETLAND
The Shetland Islands have a total area of 1,427 sq. km (551 sq. miles) and had a population at the 2011 census of 23,167. They lie about 80km (50 miles) north of the Orkneys, with Fair Isle about half way between the two groups. Out Stack, off Muckle Flugga, 1.6km (one mile) north of Unst, is the most northerly part of the British Isles (60° 51′ 30″ N. lat.).

There are over 100 islands, of which 16 are inhabited. Populations at the 2011 census were:

Mainland, 18,765	Muckle Roe, 130
Bressay, 368	Papa Stour, 15
Bruray, 24	Trondra, 135
East Burra, 76	Unst, 632
Fair Isle, 68	Vaila, 2
Fetlar, 61	West Burra, 776
Foula, 38	Whalsay, 1,061
Housay, 50	Yell, 966

Shetland's many archaeological sites include Jarlshof, Mousa and Clickhimin, and its long connection with Scandinavia has resulted in a strong Norse influence on its place names and dialect.

Industries include fishing, knitwear and farming. In addition to the fishing fleet there are fish processing factories, and the traditional handknitting of Fair Isle and Unst is now supplemented with machine-knitted garments. Farming is mainly crofting, with sheep being raised on the moorland and hills of the islands. Latterly the islands have become a centre of the North Sea oil industry, with pipelines from the Brent and Ninian fields running to the terminal at Sullom Voe, the largest of its kind in Europe.

The capital is Lerwick (population 6,958) situated on Mainland. Lerwick is the main centre for supply services for offshore oil exploration and development.

THE HEBRIDES
Until the late 13th century the Hebrides included other Scottish islands in the Firth of Clyde, the peninsula of Kintyre (Argyll), the Isle of Man and the (Irish) Isle of Rathlin. The origin of the name is probably the Greek *Eboudai*, latinised as *Hebudes* by Pliny, and corrupted to its present form. The Norwegian name *Sudreyjar* (Southern Islands) was latinised as *Sodorenses*, a name that survives in the Anglican bishopric of Sodor and Man.

There are over 500 islands and islets, of which about 100 are inhabited, though mountainous terrain and extensive peat bogs mean that only a fraction of the total area is under cultivation. Stone, Bronze and Iron Age settlement has left many remains, including those at Callanish on Lewis, and Norse colonisation influenced language, customs and place names. Occupations include farming (mostly crofting and stock-raising), fishing and the manufacture of tweeds and other woollens. Tourism is also an important part of the economy.

The Inner Hebrides lie off the west coast of Scotland and are relatively close to the mainland. The largest and best-known is Skye (area 1,665 sq. km/643 sq. miles; pop. 10,008; chief town, Portree), which contains the Cuillin Hills (Sgurr Alasdair, 993m/3,257ft), Bla Bheinn (928m/3,046ft), the Storr (719m/2,358ft) and the Red Hills (Beinn na Caillich, 732m/2,403ft). Other islands in the Highland council area include Raasay (pop. 161), Eigg (pop. 83), Muck (pop. 27) and Rhum (pop. 22).

Further south the Inner Hebridean islands include Arran (pop. 4,629), containing Goat Fell (874m/2,868ft); Coll (pop. 195) and Tiree (pop. 653); Colonsay (pop. 124) and Oronsay (pop. 8); Easdale (pop. 59); Gigha (pop. 163); Islay (area 608 sq. km/235 sq. miles; pop. 3,228); Jura (area 414 sq. km/160 sq. miles; pop. 196), with a range of hills culminating in the Paps of Jura (Beinn-an-Oir, 785m/2,576ft, and Beinn Chaolais, 755m/2,477ft); Lismore (pop.

192); Luing (pop. 195); and Mull (area 950 sq. km/367 sq. miles; pop. 2,800; chief town Tobermory), containing Ben More (967m/3,171ft).

The Outer Hebrides, separated from the mainland by the Minch, now form the Eilean Siar (Western Isles) council area (area 2,897 sq. km/1,119 sq. miles; pop. 27,684). The main islands are Lewis with Harris (area 1,994 sq. km/770 sq. miles, pop. 21,031), whose chief town, Stornoway, is the administrative headquarters; North Uist (pop. 1,254); South Uist (pop. 1,754); Benbecula (pop. 1,303) and Barra (pop. 1,174). Other inhabited islands include Great Bernera (252), Berneray (138), Eriskay (143), Grimsay (169), Scalpay (291) and Vatersay (90).

EARLY HISTORY

There is evidence of human settlement in Scotland dating from the third millennium BC, the earliest settlers being Mesolithic hunters and fishermen. Early in the second millennium BC, Neolithic farmers began to cultivate crops and rear livestock; their settlements were on the west coast and in the north, and included Skara Brae and Maeshowe (Orkney). Settlement by the early Bronze Age 'Beaker Folk', so-called from the shape of their drinking vessels, in eastern Scotland dates from about 1800 BC. Further settlement is believed to have occurred from 700 BC onwards, as tribes were displaced from further south by new incursions from the Continent and the Roman invasions from AD 43.

Julius Agricola, the Roman governor of Britain AD 77–84, extended the Roman conquests in Britain by advancing into Caledonia, culminating with a victory at Mons Graupius, probably in AD 84; he was recalled to Rome shortly afterwards and his forward policy was not pursued. Hadrian's Wall, mostly completed by AD 30, marked the northern frontier of the Roman empire except for the period between about AD 144 and 190 when the frontier moved north to the Forth-Clyde isthmus and a turf wall, the Antonine Wall, was manned.

After the Roman withdrawal from Britain, there were centuries of warfare between the Picts, Scots, Britons, Angles and Vikings. The Picts, generally accepted to be descended from the indigenous Iron Age people of northern Scotland, occupied the area north of the Forth. The Scots, a Gaelic-speaking people of northern Ireland, colonised the area of Argyll and Bute (the kingdom of Dalriada) in the fifth century AD and then expanded eastwards and northwards. The Britons, speaking a Brythonic Celtic language, colonised Scotland from the south from the first century BC; they lost control of south-eastern Scotland (incorporated into the kingdom of Northumbria) to the Angles in the early seventh century but retained Strathclyde (south-western Scotland and Cumbria). Viking raids from the late eighth century were followed by Norse settlement in the western and northern isles, Argyll, Caithness and Sutherland from the mid-ninth century onwards.

UNIFICATION

The union of the areas which now comprise Scotland began in AD 843 when Kenneth MacAlpin, king of the Scots from c.834, also became king of the Picts, joining the two lands to form the kingdom of Alba (comprising Scotland north of a line between the Forth and Clyde rivers). Lothian, the eastern part of the area between the Forth and the Tweed, seems to have been leased to Kenneth II of Alba (reigned 971–995) by Edgar of England c.973, and Scottish possession was confirmed by Malcolm II's victory over a Northumbrian army at Carham c.1016. At about this time Malcolm II (reigned 1005–34) placed his grandson Duncan on the throne of the British kingdom of Strathclyde, bringing under Scots rule virtually all of what is now Scotland.

The Norse possessions were incorporated into the kingdom of Scotland from the 12th century onwards. An uprising in the mid-12th century drove the Norse from most of mainland Argyll. The Hebrides were ceded to Scotland by the Treaty of Perth in 1266 after a Norwegian expedition in 1263 failed to maintain Norse authority over the islands. Orkney and Shetland fell to Scotland in 1468–9 as a pledge for the unpaid dowry of Margaret of Denmark, wife of James III, although Danish claims of suzerainty were relinquished only with the marriage of Anne of Denmark to James VI in 1590.

From the 11th century, there were frequent wars between Scotland and England over territory and the extent of England's political influence. The failure of the Scottish royal line with the death of Margaret of Norway in 1290 led to disputes over the throne which were resolved by the adjudication of Edward I of England. He awarded the throne to John Balliol in 1292 but Balliol's refusal to be a puppet king led to war. Balliol surrendered to Edward I in 1296 and Edward attempted to rule Scotland himself. Resistance to Scotland's loss of independence was led by William Wallace, who defeated the English at Stirling Bridge (1297), and Robert Bruce, crowned in 1306, who held most of Scotland by 1311 and routed Edward II's army at Bannockburn (1314). England recognised the independence of Scotland in the Treaty of Northampton in 1328. Subsequent clashes include the disastrous battle of Flodden (1513) in which James IV and many of his nobles fell.

THE UNION

In 1603 James VI of Scotland succeeded Elizabeth I on the throne of England (his mother, Mary Queen of Scots, was the great-granddaughter of Henry VII), his successors reigning as sovereigns of Great Britain. Political union of the two countries did not occur until 1707.

THE JACOBITE REVOLTS

After the abdication (by flight) in 1688 of James VII and II, the crown devolved upon William III (grandson of Charles I) and Mary II (elder daughter of James VII and II). In 1689 Graham of Claverhouse roused the Highlands on behalf of James VII and II, but died after a military success at Killiecrankie.

After the death of Anne (younger daughter of James VII and II), the throne devolved upon George I (great-grandson of James VI and I). In 1715, armed risings on behalf of James Stuart (the Old Pretender, son of James VII and II) led to the indecisive battle of Sheriffmuir, and the Jacobite movement died down until 1745, when Charles Stuart (the Young Pretender) defeated the Royalist troops at Prestonpans and advanced to Derby (1746). From Derby, the adherents of 'James VIII and III' (the title claimed for his father by Charles Stuart) fell back on the defensive and were finally crushed at Culloden (16 April 1746) by an army led by the Duke of Cumberland, son of George II.

PRINCIPAL CITIES

ABERDEEN

Aberdeen, 209km (130 miles) north-east of Edinburgh, received its charter as a Royal Burgh in 1124. Scotland's third largest city, Aberdeen lies between two rivers, the Dee and the Don, facing the North Sea; the city has a strong maritime history and is today a major centre for offshore oil exploration and production. It is also an ancient university town and distinguished research centre. Other industries include engineering, food processing, textiles, paper manufacturing and chemicals.

Places of interest include King's College, St Machar's Cathedral, Brig o' Balgownie, Duthie Park and Winter Gardens, Hazlehead Park, the Kirk of St Nicholas, Mercat Cross, Marischal College and Marischal Museum, Provost Skene's House, Aberdeen Art Gallery, Gordon Highlanders Museum, Satrosphere Science Centre, and Aberdeen Maritime Museum.

DUNDEE

The Royal Burgh of Dundee is situated on the north bank of the Tay estuary. The city's port and dock installations are important to the offshore oil industry and the airport also provides servicing facilities. Principal industries include textiles, biotechnology and digital media, lasers, printing, tyre manufacture, food processing, engineering and tourism.

The unique City Churches – three churches under one roof, together with the 15th-century St Mary's Tower – are the most prominent architectural feature. Dundee is home to two historic ships: the Dundee-built RRS *Discovery* which took Capt. Scott to the Antarctic lies alongside Discovery Quay, and the frigate *Unicorn*, the only British-built wooden warship still afloat, is moored in Victoria Dock. Places of interest include Mills Public Observatory, the Tay road and rail bridges, Dundee Contemporary Arts centre, McManus Galleries, Claypotts Castle, Broughty Castle, Verdant Works (textile heritage centre) and the Sensation Science Centre.

EDINBURGH

Edinburgh is the capital city and seat of government in Scotland. The new Scottish parliament building designed by Enric Miralles was completed in 2004 and is open to visitors. The city is built on a group of hills and both the Old and New Towns are inscribed on the UNESCO World Cultural and Natural Heritage List for their cultural significance.

Other places of interest include the castle, which houses the Stone of Scone and also includes St Margaret's Chapel, the oldest building in Edinburgh, and near it, the Scottish National War Memorial; the Palace of Holyroodhouse, the Queen's official residence in Scotland; Parliament House, the present seat of the judicature; Princes Street; three universities (Edinburgh, Heriot-Watt, Napier); St Giles' Cathedral; St Mary's (Scottish Episcopal) Cathedral (Sir George Gilbert Scott); the General Register House (Robert Adam); the National and Signet libraries; the National Gallery of Scotland; the Royal Scottish Academy; the Scottish National Portrait Gallery and the Edinburgh International Conference Centre.

GLASGOW

Glasgow, a Royal Burgh, is Scotland's largest city and its principal commercial and industrial centre. The city occupies the north and south banks of the Clyde, formerly one of the chief commercial estuaries in the world. The main industries include engineering, electronics, finance, chemicals and printing. The city is also a key tourist and conference destination.

The chief buildings are the 13th-century Gothic cathedral, the university (Sir George Gilbert Scott), the City Chambers, the Royal Concert Hall, St Mungo Museum of Religious Life and Art, Pollok House, the School of Art (Charles Rennie Mackintosh), Kelvingrove Art Gallery and Museum, the Gallery of Modern Art, the Riverside Museum: Scotland's Museum of Transport and Travel (Zaha Hadid), the Burrell Collection museum and the Mitchell Library. The city is home to the Royal Scottish National Orchestra, Scottish Opera, Scottish Ballet, BBC Scotland and Scottish Television (STV).

INVERNESS

Inverness was granted city status in 2000. The city's name is derived from the Gaelic for 'the mouth of the Ness', referring to the river on which it lies. Inverness is recorded as being at the junction of trade routes since AD 565. Today the city is the main administrative centre for the north of Scotland and is the capital of the Highlands. Tourism is one of the city's main industries.

Among the city's most notable buildings is Abertarff House, built in 1593 and the oldest secular building remaining in Inverness. Balnain House, built as a town house in 1726, is a fine example of early Georgian architecture. The Old High Church, on St Michael's Mount, is the original parish church of Inverness and is built on the site of the earliest Christian church in the city. Parts of the church date back to the 14th century.

Stirling was granted city status in 2002 and Perth in 2012. Aberdeen, Dundee, Edinburgh and Glasgow have also been granted lord mayoralty/lord provostship.

LORD-LIEUTENANTS

Title	Name
Aberdeen City*	Lord Provost George Adam
Aberdeenshire	James Ingleby
Angus	Georgiana Osborne, CVO
Argyll and Bute	Patrick Stewart, MBE, WS
Ayrshire and Arran	John Duncan, CVO QPM
Banffshire	Clare Russell, CVO
Berwickshire	Jeannna Swan
Caithness	Margaret Annie Dunnett, CVO
Clackmannanshire	Lt.-Col. Johnny Stewart
Dumfries	Lady Fiona MacGregor of MacGregor (Fiona Armstrong)
Dunbartonshire	Rear-Adm. Michael Gregory, OBE
Dundee City*	Lord Provost Robert Duncan
East Lothian	Maj. Michael Williams, MBE
Edinburgh City*	Rt. Hon. Lord Provost Donald Wilson
Eilean Siar (Western Isles)	Donald Martin
Fife	Robert Balfour
Glasgow City*	Rt. Hon. Lord Provost Sadie Docherty
Inverness	Donald Cameron of Lochiel
Kincardineshire	Carol Kinghorn
Lanarkshire	Mushtaq Ahmad, OBE
Midlothian	Sir Robert Maxwell Clerk, Bt., OBE
Moray	Lt.-Col. Grenville Shaw Johnston, OBE, TD
Nairn	Ewen Brodie of Lethen, CVO
Orkney	Bill Spence
Perth and Kinross	Brig. Melville Jameson, CBE
Renfrewshire	Guy Clark
Ross and Cromarty	Janet Bowen
Roxburgh, Ettrick and Lauderdale	Duke of Buccleuch and Queensberry, KBE, FRSE
Shetland	Robert Hunter
Stirling and Falkirk	Alan Simpson, OBE
Sutherland	Dr Monica Main
The Stewartry of Kirkcudbright	Lt.-Col. Sir Malcolm Ross, GCVO, OBE
Tweeddale	Prof. Sir Hew Strachan
West Lothian	Isobel Brydie, CVO, MBE
Wigtown	Dr John Ross, CBE

* The Lord Provosts of the four cities of Aberdeen, Dundee, Edinburgh and Glasgow are Lord-Lieutenants *ex officio* for those districts

LOCAL COUNCILS

Council	Administrative Headquarters	Telephone	Population*	Council Tax†	Chief Executive
ABERDEEN	Aberdeen	01224-522000	229,840	£1,230	Angela Scott
Aberdeenshire	Aberdeen	08456-081207	262,190	£1,170	Jim Savege
Angus	Forfar	0845-277 7778	116,520	£1,104	Margo Williamson
Argyll and Bute	Lochgilphead	01546-602127	87,130	£1,213	Cleland Sneddon
Clackmannanshire	Alloa	01259-450000	51,350	£1,182	Elaine McPherson
Dumfries and Galloway	Dumfries	030-3333 3000	149,520	£1,080	Gavin Stevenson
DUNDEE	Dundee	01382-434000	148,270	£1,241	David Martin
East Ayrshire	Kilmarnock	01563-576000	122,200	£1,225	Fiona Lees
East Dunbartonshire	Kirkintilloch	0300-123 4510	107,540	£1,176	Gerry Cornes
East Lothian	Haddington	01620-827827	104,090	£1,151	Angela Leitch
East Renfrewshire	Giffnock	0141-577 3000	93,810	£1,160	Lorraine McMillan
EDINBURGH	Edinburgh	0131-200 2000	507,170	£1,204	Andrew Kerr
Eilean Siar (Western Isles)	Stornoway	01851-703773	26,900	£1,055	Malcolm Burr
Falkirk	Falkirk	01324-506070	159,380	£1,102	Mary Pitcaithly, OBE
Fife	Glenrothes	0345-155 0000	370,330	£1,152	Steve Grimmond
GLASGOW	Glasgow	0141-287 2000	615,070	£1,249	Annemarie O'Donnell
Highland	Inverness	01349-886606	234,770	£1,198	Steve Barron
Inverclyde	Greenock	01475-717171	79,160	£1,198	Aubrey Fawcett
Midlothian	Dalkeith	0131-270 7500	88,610	£1,246	Kenneth Lawrie
Moray	Elgin	01343-543451	96,070	£1,169	Roddy Burns
North Ayrshire	Irvine	0845-603 0590	135,890	£1,187	Elma Murray
North Lanarkshire	Motherwell	01698-403200	339,390	£1,098	Paul Jukes
Orkney	Kirkwall	01856-873535	21,850	£1,068	Alistair Buchan
Perth and Kinross	Perth	01738-475000	150,680	£1,181	Bernadette Malone
Renfrewshire	Paisley	0300-300 0300	175,930	£1,165	Sandra Black
Scottish Borders	Melrose	01835-824000	114,530	£1,117	Tracey Logan
Shetland	Lerwick	01595-693535	23,200	£1,085	Mark Boden
South Ayrshire	Ayr	0300-123 0900	112,470	£1,189	Eileen Howat
South Lanarkshire	Hamilton	0303-123 1015	317,100	£1,101	Lindsay Freeland
STIRLING	Stirling	0845-277 7000	93,750	£1,197	Stewart Carruth
West Dunbartonshire	Dumbarton	01389-737000	89,860	£1,163	Joyce White
West Lothian	Livingston	01506-280000	180,130	£1,128	Graham Hope

* *Source:* Office for National Statistics – *Mid-2016 Population Estimates* (Crown copyright)

† Average Band D council tax bill 2017–18. Council tax in Scotland has remained the same since 2007: the council tax freeze will be lifted from April 2017 and local authorities will be allowed to increase council tax up to a maximum of 3 per cent.

Councils in CAPITAL LETTERS have city status

Key	Council	Key	Council
1	Aberdeen City	17	Inverclyde
2	Aberdeenshire	18	Midlothian
3	Angus	19	Moray
4	Argyll and Bute	20	North Ayrshire
5	City of Edinburgh	21	North Lanarkshire
6	Clackmannanshire	22	Orkney
7	Dumfries and Galloway	23	Perth and Kinross
8	Dundee City	24	Renfrewshire
9	East Ayrshire	25	Scottish Borders
10	East Dunbartonshire	26	Shetland
11	East Lothian	27	South Ayrshire
12	East Renfrewshire	28	South Lanarkshire
13	Falkirk	29	Stirling
14	Fife	30	West Dunbartonshire
15	Glasgow City	31	Western Isles (Eilean Siar)
16	Highland	32	West Lothian

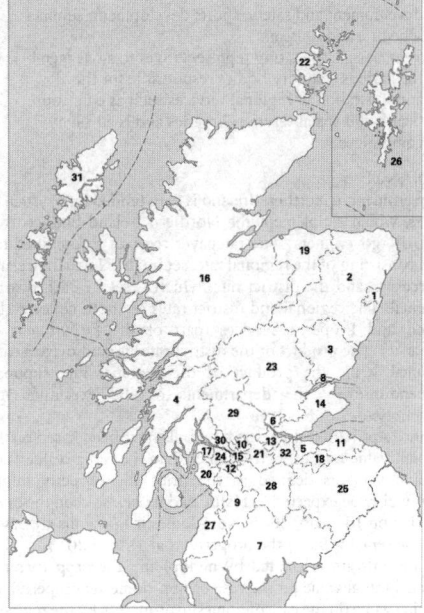

NORTHERN IRELAND

Northern Ireland has a total area of 14,149 sq. km (5,463 sq. miles): land, 13,576 sq. km (5,242 sq. miles); inland water, 573 sq. km (221 sq. miles).

In 2012 a reform programme began to reduce the number of district councils from 26 to 11. The Local Government Act (Northern Ireland) received royal assent on 12 May 2014 providing new governance arrangements for local councils and made transitional provisions for the transfer of staff, assets and liabilities etc to the new 11 councils. On 1 April 2015 additional functions, that were previously the responsibility of the Northern Ireland executive, fully transferred to the new district authorities.

POPULATION
The population of Northern Ireland at the 2011 census was 1,810,863 (men 887,323; women 923,540). The average density of population in 2011 was 128 persons per sq. km (331 per sq. mile).

ELECTIONS
Elections to the 11 councils took place on 22 May 2014.

FUNCTIONS
The councils are responsible for approving business and financial plans, setting domestic and non-domestic rates. Since April 2016 councils have also been responsible for urban regeneration and community development.

The district councils are responsible for:

Direct Service Provision of a wide range of local services, including: building control-inspection and the regulation of new buildings; byelaw enforcement; cemeteries; community centres; cultural facilities; dog control; environmental health; food safety; health and safety; local economic development; local planning; off-street parking (except park and ride schemes); parks, open spaces and playgrounds; public conveniences; recycling and waste management; registration of births, deaths and marriages; sport, leisure and recreational facilities; and street cleaning. District councils also have a role in community development and safety; sports development; summer schemes; and tourism.

Representation: nominating representatives to sit as members of the various statutory bodies responsible for the administration of regional services such as education, health and social services, libraries and road safety committees

FINANCE
Government in Northern Ireland is part-funded by a system of rates, which supplement the Northern Ireland budget from the UK government. The ratepayer receives a combined tax bill consisting of the regional rate, set by the Northern Ireland executive, and the district rate, which is set by each district council. The regional and district rates are both collected by Land and Property Services (part of the Department of Finance). The product of the district rates is paid over to each council while the product of the regional rate supports expenditure by the departments of the executive and assembly.

Since April 2007 domestic rates bills have been based on the capital value of a property, rather than the rental value. The capital value is defined as the price the property might reasonably be expected to realise had it been sold on the open market on 1 January 2005. Non-domestic rates bills are based on the rental value of the property as at 1 April 2013.

Rate bills are calculated by multiplying the property's net annual rental value (in the case of non-domestic property), or capital value (in the case of domestic property), by the regional and district rate poundages respectively.

For 2017–18 the overall average domestic poundage is 0.7735p compared to 0.7606p in 2016–17. The overall average non-domestic rate poundage in 2017–18 is 57.28p compared to 56.33p in 2016–17.

FLAG
The official national flag of Northern Ireland is the Union Flag.

PRINCIPAL CITIES
In addition to Belfast and Londonderry, three other places in Northern Ireland have been granted city status: Armagh (1994), Lisburn (2002) and Newry (2002).

BELFAST
Belfast, the administrative centre of Northern Ireland, is situated at the mouth of the River Lagan at its entrance to Belfast Lough. The city grew to be a great industrial centre, owing to its easy access by sea to Scottish coal and iron.

The principal buildings are of a relatively young age and include the parliament buildings at Stormont, the City Hall, Waterfront Hall, the Law Courts, the Public Library and the Museum and Art Gallery. In March 2012, a new museum, Titanic Belfast, opened on the banks of the Lagan River – the site where RMS *Titanic* was built and launched. The museum forms the centrepiece of a new mixed-use maritime quarter.

Belfast received its first charter of incorporation in 1613 and was created a city in 1888; the title of lord mayor was conferred in 1892.

LONDONDERRY
Londonderry (originally Derry) is situated on the River Foyle, and has important associations with the City of London. The Irish Society was created by the City of London in 1610, and under its royal charter of 1613 it fortified the city and was for a long time closely associated with its administration. Because of this connection the city was incorporated in 1613 under the new name of Londonderry.

The city is famous for the great siege of 1688–9, when for 105 days the town held out against the forces of James II. The city walls are still intact and form a circuit of 1.6 km (one mile) around the old city.

Interesting buildings are the Protestant cathedral of St Columb's (1633) and the Guildhall, reconstructed in 1912 and containing a number of beautiful stained glass windows, many of which were presented by the livery companies of London.

CONSTITUTIONAL HISTORY
Northern Ireland is subject to the same fundamental constitutional provisions which apply to the rest of the UK. It had its own parliament and government from 1921 to 1972, but after increasing civil unrest the Northern Ireland (Temporary Provisions) Act 1972 transferred the legislative and executive powers of the Northern Ireland parliament and government to the UK parliament and a secretary of state. The Northern Ireland Constitution Act 1973 provided for devolution in Northern Ireland through an assembly and executive, but a power-sharing executive formed by the Northern Ireland political parties in January 1974 collapsed in May 1974. Following the collapse of the power-sharing executive Northern Ireland returned to direct rule governance under the provisions of the Northern Ireland Act 1974, placing the Northern Ireland department under the direction and control of the Northern Ireland secretary.

In December 1993 the British and Irish governments published the Joint Declaration, complementing their political talks and making clear that any settlement would need to be founded on principles of democracy and consent.

On 12 January 1998 the British and Irish governments issued a joint document, *Propositions on Heads of Agreement,* proposing the establishment of various new cross-border bodies; further proposals were presented on 27 January. A draft peace settlement was issued by the talks' chairman, US Senator George Mitchell, on 6 April 1998 but was rejected by the Unionists the following day. On 10 April agreement was reached between the British and Irish governments and the eight Northern Ireland political parties still involved in the talks (the Good Friday Agreement). The agreement provided for an elected Northern Ireland Assembly, a North/South Ministerial Council, and a British-Irish Council comprising representatives of the British, Irish, Channel Islands and Isle of Man governments and members of the new assemblies for Scotland, Wales and Northern Ireland. Further points included the abandonment of the Republic of Ireland's constitutional claim to Northern Ireland, the decommissioning of weapons, the release of paramilitary prisoners and changes in policing.

The agreement was ratified in referendums held in Northern Ireland and the Republic of Ireland on 22 May 1998. In the UK, the Northern Ireland Act received royal assent in November 1998.

On 28 April 2003 the secretary of state again assumed responsibility for the direction of the Northern Ireland departments on the dissolution of the Northern Ireland Assembly, following its initial suspension from midnight on 14 October 2002. In 2006, following the passing of the Northern Ireland Act, the secretary of state created a non-legislative fixed-term assembly which would cease to operate either when the political parties agreed to restore devolution, or on 24 November 2006 (whichever occurred first). In October 2006 a timetable to restore devolution was drawn up (St Andrews Agreement) and a transitional Northern Ireland Assembly was formed on 24 November. The transitional assembly was dissolved in January 2007 in preparation for elections to be held on 7 March; following the elections a power-sharing executive was formed and the new 108-member Northern Ireland Assembly became operational on 8 May 2007.

See also Devolved Government.

LORD-LIEUTENANTS AND HIGH SHERIFFS

County	Lord-Lieutenant	High Sheriff (2017)
Antrim	Joan Christie, OBE	Miranda Tisdale
Armagh	Earl of Caledon, KCVO	Godfrey McCartney
Belfast City	Fionnuala Mary Jay-O'Boyle, CBE	Alderman Thomas Haire
Down	David Lindsay	Henry Catherwood
Fermanagh	Viscount Brookeborough	Selwyn Johnston
Londonderry	Denis Desmond, CBE	Jean Caulfield, MBE
Londonderry City	Dr Angela Josepha Garvey	Mary Bradley
Tyrone	Robert Scott, OBE	Jennifer Hawkes

LOCAL COUNCILS

Council	Telephone	Population*	Chief Executive
Antrim & Newtownabbey	028-9448 1311	141,032	Jacqui Dixon
Armagh, Banbridge & Craigavon	0300-030 0900	210,260	Roger Wilson
Belfast	028-9027 0549	339,579	Suzanne Wylie
Causeway Coast & Glens	028-7034 7034	143,525	David Jackson, MBE
Derry & Strabane	028-7138 2204	150,142	John Kelpie
Fermanagh & Omagh	0300-303 1777	115,799	Brendan Hegarty
Lisburn & Castlereagh	028-9250 9250	141,181	Dr Theresa Donaldson
Mid & East Antrim	028-9335 8000	137,821	Anne Donaghy
Mid Ulster	0300-013 2132	145,389	Anthony Tohill
Newry, Mourne & Down	028-3031 3037	177,816	Liam Hannaway
North Down & Ards	0300-013 3333	159,593	Stephen Reid

* Source: NISRA – Mid-year Population Estimates 2016

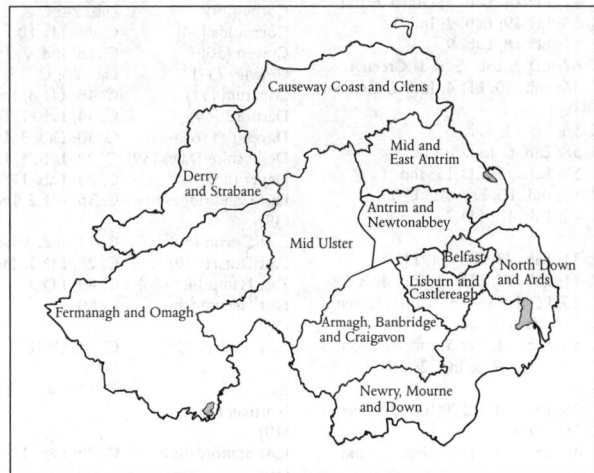

POLITICAL COMPOSITION OF LOCAL COUNCILS

as at 4 May 2017
Abbreviations

All.	Alliance
BNP	British National Party
C.	Conservative
DUP	Democratic Unionist Party
Green	Green
Ind.	Independent
Ind. Un.	Independent Unionist
Lab.	Labour
LD	Liberal Democrat
Lib.	Liberal
O.	Other
PC	Plaid Cymru
PUP	Progressive Unionist Party of Northern Ireland
R.	Residents Associations/Ratepayers
SD	Social Democrat
SDLP	Social Democratic and Labour Party
SF	Sinn Fein
SNP	Scottish National Party
Soc.	Socialist
TUV	Traditional Unionist Voice
UKIP	UK Independence Party
UUP	Ulster Unionist Party
v.	vacant

Total number of seats is given in parentheses after council name.

ENGLAND

COUNTY COUNCILS

Buckinghamshire (49)	C. 41; LD 4; Ind. 3; Lab. 1
Cambridgeshire (61)	C. 36; LD 15; Lab. 7; Ind. 3
Cumbria (84)	C. 37; Lab. 26; LD 16; Ind. 5
Derbyshire (64)	C. 37; Lab. 24; LD 3
Devon (60)	C. 42; Lab. 7; LD 7; Ind. 3; Green 1
Dorset (46)	C. 32; LD 11; Green 2; Lab. 1
East Sussex (50)	C. 30; LD 11; Ind. 5; Lab. 4
Essex (75)	C. 56; LD 7; Lab. 6; Ind. 4; R 1; Green 1
Gloucestershire (53)	C. 31; LD 14; Lab. 5; Green 2; Ind. 1
Hampshire (78)	C. 56; LD 19; Lab. 2; Ind. 1
Hertfordshire (78)	C. 51; LD 18; Lab. 9
Kent (81)	C. 67; LD 7; Lab. 5; R 1; Green 1
Lancashire (84)	C. 46; Lab. 30; LD 4; Ind. 2; Green 1; UKIP 1
Leicestershire (55)	C. 36; LD 13; Lab. 6
Lincolnshire (70)	C. 58; Lab. 6; Ind. 5; LD 1
Norfolk (84)	C. 55; Lab. 17; LD 11; Ind. 1
North Yorkshire (72)	C. 55; Ind. 10; Lab. 4; LD 3
Northamptonshire (57)	C. 43; Lab. 12; LD 2
Nottinghamshire (66)	C. 31; Lab. 23; Ind. 11; LD 1
Oxfordshire (63)	C. 31; Lab. 14; LD 13; Ind. 4; R 1
Somerset (55)	C. 35; LD 12; Ind. 3; Lab. 3; Green 2
Staffordshire (62)	C. 51; Lab. 10; Ind. 1
Suffolk (75)	C. 52; Lab. 11; LD 5; Ind. 4; Green 3
Surrey (81)	C. 60; LD 9; R 8; Ind. 2; Lab. 1; Green 1
Warwickshire (57)	C. 36; Lab. 10; LD 7; Ind. 2; Green 2
West Sussex (70)	C. 56; LD 9; Lab. 5
Worcestershire (57)	C. 40; Lab. 10; LD 3; Green 2; Ind. 1; O. 1

DISTRICT COUNCILS

Adur (29)	C. 16; UKIP 8; Lab. 3; Ind. 2
Allerdale (56)	Lab. 28; C. 17; Ind. 4; O. 4; UKIP 3
Amber Valley (45)	C. 23; Lab. 22
Arun (54)	C. 42; LD 5; UKIP 4; Ind. 2; Lab. 1
Ashfield (35)	Lab. 22; LD 5; C. 4; Ind. 3; O. 1
Ashford (43)	C. 34; Lab. 4; Ind. 3; LD 1; UKIP 1
Aylesbury Vale (59)	C. 43; LD 9; UKIP 4; Lab. 2; Ind. 1
Babergh (43)	C. 31; Ind. 8; LD 3; Lab. 1
Barrow-in-Furness (36)	Lab. 27; C. 9
Basildon (42)	C. 18; UKIP 10; Lab. 9; Ind. 5
Basingstoke and Deane (60)	C. 33; Lab. 19; LD 6; Ind. 2
Bassetlaw (48)	Lab. 33; C. 12; Ind. 3
Blaby (39)	C. 29; Lab. 6; LD 4
Bolsover (37)	Lab. 32; Ind. 4; O. 1
Boston (30)	C. 13; UKIP 12; Ind. 2; Lab. 2; O. 1
Braintree (49)	C. 44; Lab. 2; R. 2; Green 1
Breckland (49)	C. 42; UKIP 4; Lab. 2; Ind. 1
Brentwood (37)	C. 24; LD 10; Lab. 2; Ind. 1
Broadland (47)	C. 43; LD 4
Bromsgrove (31)	C. 18; Lab. 7; Ind. 3; R. 3
Broxbourne (30)	C. 26; Lab. 3; UKIP 1
Broxtowe (44)	C. 27; Lab. 12; LD 4; Ind. 1
Burnley (45)	Lab. 27; LD 13; C. 4; UKIP 1
Cambridge (42)	Lab. 26; LD 13; Ind. 2; Green 1
Cannock Chase (41)	Lab. 21; C. 13; UKIP 4; LD 1; Green 1; Ind. 1
Canterbury (39)	C. 31; Lab. 3; LD 3; UKIP 2
Carlisle (52)	Lab. 27; C. 20; Ind. 4; LD 1
Castle Point (41)	C. 22; Ind. 16; UKIP 3
Charnwood (52)	C. 41; Lab. 9; Ind. 1; LD 1
Chelmsford (57)	C. 52; LD 5
Cheltenham (40)	LD 29; C. 7; Ind. 4
Cherwell (48)	C. 38; Lab. 8; Ind. 2
Chesterfield (48)	Lab. 34; LD 11; Ind. 2; UKIP 1
Chichester (48)	C. 42; Ind. 3; LD 3
Chiltern (40)	C. 35; LD 3; Ind. 2
Chorley (47)	Lab. 31; C. 14; Ind. 2
Christchurch (24)	C. 21; Ind. 2; UKIP 1
Colchester (51)	C. 22; LD 15; Lab. 11; Ind. 3
Copeland (51)	Lab. 29; C. 17; Ind. 5
Corby (29)	Lab. 24; C. 5
Cotswolds (34)	C. 24; LD 10
Craven (30)	C. 18; Ind. 7; Lab. 3; LD 1; UKIP 1
Crawley (37)	Lab. 20; C. 17
Dacorum (51)	C. 46; LD 3; Lab. 2
Dartford (44)	C. 34; Lab. 7; R. 3
Daventry (36)	C. 30; Lab. 3; UKIP 2; LD 1
Derbyshire Dales (39)	C. 29; Lab. 5; LD 3; Ind. 1; O. 1
Dover (45)	C. 25; Lab. 17; UKIP 3
East Cambridgeshire (39)	C. 36; LD 2; Ind. 1
East Devon (59)	C. 37; Ind. 15; LD 6; O. 1
East Dorset (29)	C. 25; LD 3; Ind. 1
East Hampshire (44)	C. 42; LD 2
East Hertfordshire (50)	C. 50
East Lindsey (55)	C. 33; UKIP 8; Ind. 6; Lab. 4; O. 3; LD 1
East Northamptonshire (40)	C. 37; Ind. 2; LD 1
East Staffordshire (39)	C. 25; Lab. 12; LD 1; UKIP 1

Eastbourne (27) LD 18; C. 9
Eastleigh (44) LD 38; C. 6
Eden (38) C. 21; Ind. 10; LD 7
Elmbridge (48) C. 22; R 19; LD 7
Epping Forest (58) C. 36; R 13; LD 3; Green 2; Ind. 2; UKIP 2
Epsom and Ewell (38) R. 31; C. 4; Lab. 3
Erewash (47) C. 30; Lab. 17
Exeter (39) Lab. 30; C. 8; LD 1
Fareham (31) C. 24; LD 4; UKIP 2; Ind. 1
Fenland (39) C. 34; Ind. 3; LD 2
Forest Heath (27) C. 23; Ind. 2; Lab. 1; LD 1
Forest of Dean (48) C. 21; Lab. 13; UKIP 7; Ind. 5; Green 2
Fylde (51) C. 32; Ind. 12; LD 2; O. 2; R. 2; Lab. 1
Gedling (41) Lab. 25; C. 15; LD 1
Gloucester (39) C. 22; Lab. 10; LD 7
Gosport (34) C. 20; LD 9; Lab. 4; UKIP 1
Gravesham (44) C. 23; Lab. 21
Great Yarmouth (39) C. 14; UKIP 12; Lab. 11; Ind. 2
Guildford (48) C. 35; LD 9; O. 3; Lab. 1
Hambleton (28) C. 27; UKIP 1
Harborough (37) C. 29; LD 8
Harlow (33) Lab. 19; C. 12; UKIP 2
Harrogate (54) C. 37; LD 15; Ind. 2
Hart (33) C. 16; LD 8; R 8; Ind. 1
Hastings (32) Lab. 24; C. 8
Havant (38) C. 31; UKIP 4; Lab. 2; LD 1
Hertsmere (39) C. 37; Lab. 2
High Peak (43) C. 23; Lab. 17; LD 2; Ind. 1
Hinckley and Bosworth (34) C. 21; LD 12; Lab. 1
Horsham (44) C. 39; LD 4; Ind. 1
Huntingdonshire (52) C. 34; Ind. 7; LD 6; UKIP 3; Lab. 2
Hyndburn (35) Lab. 26; C. 7; UKIP 2
Ipswich (48) Lab. 33; C. 13; LD 2
Kettering (36) C. 25; Lab. 7; Ind. 1; v. 3
King's Lynn and West Norfolk (62) C. 50; Lab. 10; Ind. 2
Lancaster (60) Lab. 29; C. 19; Green 9; Ind. 2; O. 1
Lewes (41) C. 24; LD 11; Green 3; Ind. 2; UKIP 1
Lichfield (47) C. 41; Lab. 4; LD 1; UKIP 1
Lincoln City (33) Lab. 27; C. 6
Maidstone (55) C. 23; LD 22; Ind. 5; UKIP 3; Lab. 2
Maldon (31) C. 28; Ind. 2; UKIP 1
Malvern Hills (38) C. 23; Ind. 7; LD 5; Green 3
Mansfield (36) Lab. 18; Ind. 16; UKIP 2
Melton (28) C. 26; Ind. 2
Mendip (47) C. 32; LD 11; Green 3; Ind. 1
Mid Devon (42) C. 28; Ind. 6; LD 5; UKIP 2; Lib. 1
Mid Suffolk (40) C. 29; Green 5; LD 4; Ind. 2
Mid Sussex (54) C. 54
Mole Valley (41) C. 24; LD 12; Ind. 5
New Forest (60) C. 58; LD 2
Newark and Sherwood (39) C. 24; Lab. 12; Ind. 3
Newcastle-under-Lyme (60) Lab. 27; C. 21; Ind. 6; LD 3; UKIP 2; Green 1
North Devon (43) C. 19; LD 12; Ind. 10; O. 1; UKIP 1
North Dorset (33) C. 27; LD 4; Ind. 2
North East Derbyshire (53) Lab. 34; C. 18; Ind. 1
North Hertfordshire (49) C. 34; Lab. 12; LD 3
North Kesteven (43) C. 28; O. 15
North Norfolk (48) C. 33; LD 15
North Warwickshire (35) C. 22; Lab. 13
North West Leicestershire (38) C. 25; Lab. 10; Ind. 2; LD 1

Northampton (45) C. 26; Lab. 17; LD 2
Norwich (39) Lab. 26; Green 10; LD 3
Nuneaton and Bedworth (34) Lab. 25; C. 6; Green 2; Ind. 1
Oadby and Wigston (26) LD 19; C. 6; Lab. 1
Oxford (48) Lab. 34; LD 8; Green 4; Ind. 2
Pendle (49) C. 21; Lab. 17; LD 10; Ind. 1
Preston (57) Lab. 33; C. 19; LD 5
Purbeck (25) C. 20; LD 4; Ind. 1
Redditch (29) Lab. 15; C. 13; UKIP 1
Reigate and Banstead (51) C. 38; R 6; Green 3; LD 2; Ind. 1; UKIP 1
Ribble Valley (40) C. 35; LD 4; Lab. 1
Richmondshire (34) C. 21; Ind. 11; LD 2
Rochford (39) C. 21; R 6; UKIP 4; LD 4; Green 3; Ind. 1
Rossendale (36) Lab. 22; C. 13; Ind. 1
Rother (38) C. 31; O. 3; LD 2; Ind. 1; Lab. 1
Rugby (42) C. 21; LD 9; Lab. 9; Ind. 3
Runnymede (42) C. 36; Ind. 6
Rushcliffe (44) C. 34; Lab. 4; Green 2; Ind. 2; LD 2
Rushmoor (39) C. 26; Lab. 10; UKIP 2; v. 1
Ryedale (30) C. 20; Ind. 5; Lib. 3; LD 2
St Albans (58) C. 31; LD 17; Lab. 7; Ind. 2; Green 1
St Edmundsbury (46) C. 36; UKIP 4; Ind. 2; Lab. 2; Green 1; Ind. 1
Scarborough (50) C. 26; Lab. 14; UKIP 5; Ind. 3; Green 2
Sedgemoor (48) C. 35; Lab. 10; UKIP 2; LD 1
Selby (31) C. 22; Lab. 8; Ind. 1
Sevenoaks (54) C. 49; LD 2; Ind. 1; Lab. 1; UKIP 1
Shepway (30) C. 22; UKIP 7; Lab. 1
South Bucks (28) C. 27; Ind. 1
South Cambridgeshire (57) C. 36; LD 14; Ind. 6; Lab. 1
South Derbyshire (36) C. 24; Lab. 12
South Hams (31) C. 25; Green 3; LD 2; Lab. 1
South Holland (37) C. 28; Ind. 7; UKIP 2
South Kesteven (58) C. 45; Ind. 5; Lab. 3; O. 2; UKIP 1; v. 2
South Lakeland (51) LD 32; C. 16; Lab. 2; Ind. 1
South Norfolk (46) C. 40; LD 6
South Northamptonshire (42) C. 35; Lab. 4; LD 3
South Oxfordshire (36) C. 33; Lab. 1; LD 1; R 1
South Ribble (50) C. 29; Lab. 19; LD 2
South Somerset (60) LD 29; C. 28; Ind. 3
South Staffordshire (49) C. 43; Ind. 4; Lab. 1; UKIP 1
Spelthorne (39) C. 35; LD 3; Lab. 1
Stafford (40) C. 29; Lab. 9; Ind. 2
Staffordshire Moorlands (56) C. 41; Lab. 7; O. 6; LD 2
Stevenage (39) Lab. 29; C. 7; LD 3
Stratford-on-Avon (36) C. 31; LD 3; Ind. 1; Lab. 1
Stroud (51) C. 23; Lab. 18; Green 8; LD 2
Suffolk Coastal (42) C. 37; Ind. 2; LD 2; Lab. 1
Surrey Heath (40) C. 36; Ind. 2; Lab. 1; LD 1
Swale (47) C. 32; UKIP 9; Lab. 4; Ind. 2
Tamworth (30) C. 20; Lab. 7; UKIP 3
Tandridge (42) C. 33; LD 7; Ind. 1; R 1
Taunton Deane (56) C. 36; LD 14; Ind. 3; Lab. 2; UKIP 1
Teignbridge (46) C. 30; LD 11; Ind. 5
Tendring (60) C. 23; UKIP 16; Ind. 11; Lab. 4; R. 3; LD 1; O. 1; v. 1
Test Valley (48) C. 38; LD 9; Ind. 1
Tewkesbury (38) C. 33; Ind. 2; LD 2; O. 1
Thanet (56) UKIP 33; C. 18; Lab. 4; Ind. 1

Three Rivers (39) LD 19; C. 17; Lab. 3
Tonbridge and C. 48; LD 4; Ind. 2
Malling (54)
Torridge (36) C. 19; O. 10; UKIP 7
Tunbridge Wells (48) C. 43; LD 3; Lab. 2
Uttlesford (39) C. 23; O. 9; LD 6; Ind. 1
Vale of White Horse C. 29; LD 9
(38)
Warwick (46) C. 31; Lab. 9; R. 3; LD 2; Green 1
Watford (36) LD 25; Lab. 11
Waveney (48) C. 27; Lab. 20; Green 1
Waverley (57) C. 53; R. 3; Ind. 1
Wealden (55) C. 50; Ind. 5
Wellingborough (36) C. 27; Lab. 9
Welwyn and Hatfield C. 28; Lab. 15; LD 5
(48)
West Devon (31) C. 21; Ind. 9; LD 1
West Dorset (42) C. 30; LD 12
West Lancashire (54) Lab. 31; C. 22; Ind. 1
West Lindsey (36) C. 24; LD 7; Lab. 3; Ind. 2
West Oxfordshire C. 41; Lab. 4; LD 4
(49)
West Somerset (28) C. 21; Ind. 3; UKIP 3; Lab. 1
Weymouth and C. 14; Lab. 12; LD 6; Ind. 2; UKIP 1;
Portland (36) Green 1
Winchester (45) C. 25; LD 20
Woking (30) C. 17; LD 7; Ind. 3; Lab. 3
Worcester (35) C. 17; Lab. 16; Green 2
Worthing (37) C. 32; UKIP 2; LD 2; Green 1
Wychavon (45) C. 38; LD 5; UKIP 1; v. 1
Wycombe (60) C. 47; Lab. 6; O. 3; Ind. 2; LD 1;
UKIP 1
Wyre (50) C. 36; Lab. 14
Wyre Forest (33) C. 22; Ind. 5; Lab. 4; LD 2

LONDON BOROUGH COUNCILS

Barking and Lab. 51
Dagenham (51)
Barnet (63) C. 32; Lab. 30; LD 1
Bexley (63) C. 45; Lab. 15; UKIP 3
Brent (63) Lab. 56; C. 6; LD 1
Bromley (60) C. 51; Lab. 7; UKIP 2
Camden (54) Lab. 40; C. 12; Green 1; LD 1
Croydon (70) Lab. 40; C. 30
Ealing (69) Lab. 53; C. 12; LD 4
Enfield (63) Lab. 39; C. 22; Ind. 2
Greenwich (51) Lab. 43; C. 8
Hackney (57) Lab. 50; C. 4; LD 3
Hammersmith and Lab. 26; C. 20
Fulham (46)
Haringey (57) Lab. 48; LD 9
Harrow (63) Lab. 34; C. 26; Ind. 2; LD 1
Havering (54) Ind. 24; C. 22; UKIP 7; Lab. 1
Hillingdon (65) C. 42; Lab. 23
Hounslow (60) Lab. 47; C. 11; Ind. 1; v. 1
Islington (48) Lab. 47; Green 1
Kensington and C. 37; Lab. 12; LD 1
Chelsea (50)
Kingston upon C. 28; LD 18; Lab. 2
Thames (48)
Lambeth (63) Lab. 59; C. 3; Green 1
Lewisham (55) Lab. 54; Green 1
Merton (60) Lab. 36; C. 20; R. 3; O. 1
Newham (60) Lab. 60
Redbridge (63) Lab. 35; C. 25; LD 3
Richmond upon C. 39; LD 15
Thames (54)
Southwark (63) Lab. 48; LD 13; C. 2
Sutton (54) LD 43; C. 8; Ind. 2; v. 1
Tower Hamlets (45) Lab. 22; Ind. 17; C. 5; v. 1
Waltham Forest (60) Lab. 44; C. 16
Wandsworth (60) C. 39; Lab. 19; O. 2
Westminster (60) C. 44; Lab. 16

METROPOLITAN BOROUGHS

Barnsley (63) Lab. 55; C. 4; Ind. 4
Birmingham (120) Lab. 80; C. 29; LD 10; Ind. 1
Bolton (60) Lab. 37; C. 15; UKIP 5; LD 3
Bradford (90) Lab. 49; C. 21; LD 10; Ind. 6; Green
3; UKIP 1
Bury (51) Lab. 32; C. 16; LD 3
Calderdale (51) Lab. 23; C. 22; LD 5; Ind. 1
Coventry (54) Lab. 39; C. 15
Doncaster (55) Lab. 43; C. 7; Ind. 5
Dudley (72) Lab. 35; C. 29; UKIP 8
Gateshead (66) Lab. 54; LD 12
Kirklees (69) Lab. 34; C. 20; LD 9; Ind. 3; Green 3
Knowsley (45) Lab. 42; LD 3
Leeds (99) Lab. 64; C. 19; LD 9; Ind. 4; Green 3
Liverpool (90) Lab. 80; Green 4; LD 4; Lib 2
Manchester (96) Lab. 95; LD 1
Newcastle-upon-Tyne Lab. 55; LD 20; Ind. 3
(78)
North Tyneside (60) Lab. 51; C. 7; LD 1; Ind. 1
Oldham (60) Lab. 45; LD 9; C. 2; Ind. 2; UKIP 2
Rochdale (60) Lab. 48; C. 10; LD 2
Rotherham (63) Lab. 48; UKIP 14; Ind. 1
St Helens (48) Lab. 42; C. 3; LD 3
Salford (60) Lab. 51; C. 8; Ind. 1
Sandwell (72) Lab. 71; UKIP 1
Sefton (66) Lab. 38; LD 17; C. 7; Ind. 4
Sheffield (84) Lab. 57; LD 19; Green 4; UKIP 4
Solihull (51) C. 32; Green 10; LD 6; UKIP 2; Lab.
1
South Tyneside (54) Lab. 53; Ind. 1
Stockport (63) Lab. 22; LD 22; C. 14; R 5
Sunderland (75) Lab. 67; C. 6; Ind. 1; LD 1
Tameside (57) Lab. 51; C. 6
Trafford (63) C. 34; Lab. 25; LD 3; Ind. 1
Wakefield (63) Lab. 53; C. 7; UKIP 2; Ind. 1
Walsall (60) Lab. 28; C. 25; UKIP 3; LD 2; Ind. 2
Wigan (75) Lab. 65; Ind. 5; C. 5
Wirral (66) Lab. 39; C. 21; LD 5; Green 1
Wolverhampton (60) Lab. 49; C. 10; UKIP 1

UNITARY COUNCILS

Bath and North East C. 37; LD 15; Lab. 6; Ind. 5; Green 2
Somerset (65)
Bedford (40) C. 15; Lab. 14; LD 9; Ind. 2
Blackburn with Lab. 45; C. 16; LD 3
Darwen (64)
Blackpool (42) Lab. 29; C. 13; LD 1; v. 1
Bournemouth (54) C. 51; Green 1; Ind. 1; UKIP 1
Bracknell Forest (42) C. 41; Lab. 1
Brighton and Hove Lab. 23; C. 20; Green 11
(54)
Bristol (70) Lab. 37; C. 14; Green 11; LD 8
Central Bedfordshire C. 53; Ind. 3; Lab. 2; LD 1
(59)
Cheshire East (82) C. 53; Lab. 16; O. 7; R. 3; LD 2; Ind.
1
Cheshire West and Lab. 38; C. 36; Ind. 1
Chester (75)
Cornwall (123) C. 46; LD 37; Ind. 30; Lab. 5; O. 4;
v. 1
Darlington (50) Lab. 29; C. 17; LD 3; Ind. 1
Derby (51) Lab. 26; C. 17; LD 5; UKIP 3
Durham (126) Lab. 74; Ind. 28; LD. 14; C. 10
East Riding of C. 51; Lab. 6; Ind. 5; UKIP 3; LD 2
Yorkshire (67)
Halton (56) Lab. 52; LD 2; C. 2
Hartlepool (33) Lab. 21; UKIP 5; Ind. 4; C. 3
Herefordshire (58) C. 27; Ind. 13; O. 13; LD 3; Green 2
*Isles of Scilly (16) Ind. 9; O. 7
Isle of Wight (40) C. 25; Ind. 11; LD 2; Green 1; Lab. 1
Kingston-upon-Hull Lab. 39; LD 17; C. 2; Ind. 1
(59)

Leicester (54)	Lab. 52; C. 1; LD 1
Luton (48)	Lab. 35; LD 8; C. 5
Medway (55)	C. 36; Lab. 15; UKIP 3; Ind. 1
Middlesbrough (47)	Lab. 34; O. 6; C. 4; Ind. 3
Milton Keynes (56)	C. 22; Lab. 21; LD 13
North East Lincolnshire (42)	Lab. 18; C. 11; UKIP 5; LD 5; Ind. 2; v. 1
North Lincolnshire (43)	C. 26; Lab. 17
North Somerset (50)	C. 36; Ind. 7; LD 4; Lab. 3
Northumberland (67)	C. 33; Lab. 24; Ind. 7; LD. 3
Nottingham (55)	Lab. 52; C. 3
Peterborough (60)	C. 31; Lab. 14; LD 7; Lib 3; Ind. 3; UKIP 2
Plymouth (57)	C. 27; Lab. 27; UKIP 3
Poole (42)	C. 32; LD 6; O. 3; UKIP 1
Portsmouth (42)	C. 19; LD 15; UKIP 4; Lab. 2; Ind. 2
Reading (46)	Lab. 31; C. 10; Green 3; LD 2
Redcar and Cleveland (59)	Lab. 29; LD 11; C. 10; Ind. 8; UKIP 1
Rutland (26)	C. 17; Ind. 7; LD 2
Shropshire (74)	C. 49; LD. 12; Lab. 8; Ind. 3; Green 1, O. 1
Slough (42)	Lab. 33; C. 8; UKIP 1
South Gloucestershire (70)	C. 40; LD 16; Lab. 14
Southampton (48)	Lab. 25; C. 19; Ind. 4
Southend-on-Sea (51)	C. 24; Ind. 13; Lab. 10; UKIP 2; LD 2
Stockton-on-Tees (56)	Lab. 32; C. 13; O. 10; LD 1
Stoke-on-Trent (44)	Lab. 21; Ind. 14; C. 7; UKIP 2
Swindon (57)	C. 30; Lab. 25; LD 2
Telford and Wrekin (54)	Lab. 27; C. 22; LD 3; Ind. 2
Thurrock (49)	C. 17; UKIP 17; Lab. 14; Ind. 1
Torbay (37)	C. 26; LD 7; Ind. 3; UKIP 1
Warrington (58)	Lab. 45; LD 11; C. 2
West Berkshire (52)	C. 48; LD 4
Wiltshire (98)	C. 69; LD. 19; Ind. 7; Lab. 3
Windsor and Maidenhead (57)	C. 54; R. 2; LD 1
Wokingham (54)	C. 48; LD 5; Lab. 1
York (47)	Lab. 15; C. 14; LD 12; Green 4; Ind. 2

* Twelve councillors are elected by the residents of the isle of St Mary's and one councillor each are elected by the residents of the four other islands (Bryher, St Agnes, St Martins and Tresco)

WALES

Blaenau Gwent (42)	Ind. 28; Lab. 13; PC 1
Bridgend (54)	Lab. 26; Ind. 13; C. 11; PC 3; LD 1
Caerphilly (73)	Lab. 50; PC 18; Ind. 5
Cardiff (75)	Lab. 40; C. 20; LD 11; PC 3; Ind. 1
Carmarthenshire (74)	PC 36; Lab. 22; Ind. 16
Ceredigion (42)	PC 19; Ind. 13; LD 8; v. 1; Lab. 1
Conwy (59)	Ind. 21; C. 16; PC 10; Lab. 8; LD 4
Denbighshire (47)	C. 16; Lab. 13; PC 9; Ind. 8; LD 1
Flintshire (70)	Lab. 34; Ind. 25; C. 6; LD 5
Gwynedd (75)	PC 41; Ind. 26; O. 6; Lab. 1; LD 1
Merthyr Tydfil (33)	Ind. 16; Lab. 14; v. 3
Monmouthshire (43)	C. 25; Lab. 10; Ind. 5; LD 3
Neath Port Talbot (64)	Lab. 43; PC 15; Ind. 5; LD 1
Newport (50)	Lab. 31; C. 12; Ind. 5; LD 2
Pembrokeshire (60)	Ind. 35; C. 11; Lab. 7; PC 6; LD 1
Powys (73)	Ind. 30; C. 19; LD 13; Lab. 7; PC 2; v. 1; Green 1
Rhondda Cynon Taff (75)	Lab. 47; PC 18; Ind. 5; C. 4; LD 1
Swansea (72)	Lab. 48; Ind. 9; C. 8; LD 7
Torfaen (44)	Lab. 29; Ind. 11; C. 4
Vale of Glamorgan (47)	C. 23; Lab. 14; Ind. 6; PC 4
Wrexham (52)	Ind. 26; Lab. 12; C. 9; PC 3; LD 2
Ynys Mon (Isle of Anglesey) (30)	PC 14; Ind. 13; Lab. 2; LD 1

SCOTLAND

Aberdeen (45)	SNP 19; C. 11; Lab. 9; LD 4; Ind. 2
Aberdeenshire (70)	C. 23; SNP 21; LD 14; Ind. 10; Green 1; Lab. 1
Angus (28)	Ind. 9; SNP 9; C. 8; LD 2
Argyll and Bute (36)	SNP 11; Ind. 10; C. 9; LD 6
Clackmannanshire (18)	SNP 8; Lab. 5; C. 5
Dumfries and Galloway (43)	C. 16; Lab. 11; SNP 11; Ind. 4; LD 1
Dundee (29)	SNP 14; Lab. 9; C. 3; LD 2; Ind. 1
East Ayrshire (32)	SNP 14; Lab. 9; C. 6; Ind. 3
East Dunbartonshire (22)	SNP 7; C. 6; LD 6; Lab. 2; Ind. 1
East Lothian (22)	Lab. 9; C. 7; SNP 6
East Renfrewshire (18)	C. 7; SNP 5; Lab. 4; Ind. 2
Edinburgh (63)	SNP 19; C. 18; Lab. 12; Green 8; LD 6
Eilean Siar (Western Isles) (31)	Ind. 23; SNP 7; C. 1
Falkirk (30)	SNP 12; Lab. 9; C. 7; Ind. 2
Fife (75)	SNP 29; Lab. 24; C. 15; LD 7
Glasgow (85)	SNP 39; Lab. 31; C. 8; Green 7
Highland (74)	Ind. 28; SNP 22; LD 10; C. 10; Lab. 3; Green 1
Inverclyde (22)	Lab. 8; SNP 7; Ind. 4; C. 2; LD 1
Midlothian (18)	Lab. 7; SNP 6; C. 5
Moray (26)	SNP 9; Ind. 8; C. 8; Lab. 1
North Ayrshire (32)	Lab. 11; SNP 11; C. 7; Ind. 4
North Lanarkshire (77)	SNP 33; Lab. 32; C. 10; Ind. 2
Orkney Islands (21)	Ind. 20; Green 1
Perth and Kinross (40)	C. 17; SNP 15; LD 4; Ind. 3; Lab. 1
Renfrewshire (43)	SNP 19; Lab. 13; C. 8; Ind. 2; LD 1
Scottish Borders (34)	C. 15; SNP 9; Ind. 8; LD 2
Shetland Islands (22)	Ind. 21; SNP 1
South Ayrshire (28)	C. 12; SNP 9; Lab. 5; Ind. 2
South Lanarkshire (64)	SNP 27; Lab. 22; C. 14; LD 1
Stirling (23)	C. 9; SNP 9; Lab. 4; Green 1
West Dunbartonshire (22)	SNP 10; Lab. 8; Ind. 2; C. 2
West Lothian (33)	SNP 13; Lab. 12; C. 7; Ind. 1

NORTHERN IRELAND

Antrim and Newtownabbey (40)
DUP 15; UUP 11; All. 4; SDLP 4; SF 3; TUV 2; v. 1

Armagh, Banbridge and Craigavon (41)
DUP 13; UUP 12; SF 8; SDLP 6; Ind. 1; UKIP 1

Belfast (60)
SF 19; DUP 13; All. 8; SDLP 7; UUP 7; PUP 3; Green 1; O. 1; TUV 1

Causeway Coast and Glens (40)
DUP 11; UUP 9; SF 7; SDLP 6; TUV 3; All. 1; Ind. 1; Ind. Un. 1; PUP 1

Derry and Strabane (40)
SF 16; SDLP 10; DUP 8; Ind. 4; UUP 2

Fermanagh and Omagh (40)
SF 17; UUP 9; SDLP 8; DUP 5; Ind. 1

Lisburn and Castlereagh (40)
DUP 18; UUP 10; All. 7; SDLP 3; O. 1; TUV 1

Mid and East Antrim (40)
DUP 16; UUP 9; TUV 5; All. 3; SF 3; Ind. 2; SDLP 1; UKIP 1

Mid Ulster (40)
SF 18; DUP 8; UUP 7; SDLP 6; Ind. 1

Newry, Mourne and Down (41)
SF 14; SDLP 13; Ind. 5; DUP 4; UUP 3; All. 1; UKIP 1

North Down and Ards (40)
DUP 17; UUP 9; All. 7; Ind. 3; Green 2; SDLP 1; TUV 1

THE ISLE OF MAN

Ellan Vannin

The Isle of Man is an island situated in the Irish Sea, at latitude 54° 3'–54° 25' N. and longitude 4° 18'–4° 47' W., nearly equidistant from England, Scotland and Ireland. Although the early inhabitants were of Celtic origin, the Isle of Man was part of the Norwegian Kingdom of the Hebrides until 1266, when this was ceded to Scotland. Subsequently granted to the Stanleys (Earls of Derby) in the 15th century and later to the Dukes of Atholl, it was brought under the administration of the Crown in 1765. The island forms the bishopric of Sodor and Man.

The total land area is 572 sq. km (221 sq. miles). The 2016 census showed a resident population of 83,314 (men, 41,269; women, 42,045). The main language in use is English. Around 1,660 people are able to speak the Manx Gaelic language.

CAPITAL – ΨDouglas; population, 26,997 (2016). ΨCastletown (3,216) is the ancient capital; the other towns are ΨPeel (5,374) and ΨRamsey (7,845)

FLAG – A red flag charged with three conjoined armoured legs in white and gold

NATIONAL DAY – 5 July (Tynwald Day)

GOVERNMENT

The Isle of Man is a self-governing Crown dependency, with its own parliamentary, legal and administrative system. The British government is responsible for international relations and defence. Under the UK Act of Accession, Protocol 3, the island's relationship with the European Union is limited to trade alone and does not extend to financial aid. The Lieutenant-Governor is the Queen's personal representative on the island.

The legislature, Tynwald, is the oldest parliament in the world in continuous existence. It has two branches: the Legislative Council and the House of Keys. The council consists of the President of Tynwald, the Bishop of Sodor and Man, the Attorney-General (who does not have a vote) and eight members elected by the House of Keys. The House of Keys has 24 members, elected by universal adult suffrage. The branches sit separately to consider legislation and sit together, as Tynwald Court, for most other parliamentary purposes.

The presiding officer of Tynwald Court is the President of Tynwald, elected by the members, who also presides over sittings of the Legislative Council. The presiding officer of the House of Keys is the Speaker, who is elected by members of the house.

The principal members of the Manx government are the chief minister and eight departmental ministers, who comprise the Council of Ministers.

Lieutenant-Governor, HE Sir Richard Gozney, KCMG, CVO

President of Tynwald, Hon. Steve Rodan
Speaker, House of Keys, Hon. Juan Paul Watterson, SHK
Deputy Speaker, House of Keys, Chris Robertshaw, MHK
The First Deemster and Clerk of the Rolls, His Hon. David Doyle
Clerk of Tynwald, Secretary to the House of Keys and Counsel to the Speaker, Roger Phillips
Clerk of the Legislative Council and Deputy Clerk of Tynwald, Jonathan King
Attorney-General, John Quinn
Chief Minister, Hon. Howard Quayle, MHK
Chief Secretary, Will Greenhow

ECONOMY

Much of the income generated in the island is earned in the services sector with financial and professional services accounting for 40.4 per cent of the national income. Another significant sector is e-gaming, contributing 19.5 per cent to the national income. Under the terms of protocol 3, the island has tariff-free access to EU markets for the products of its engineering, farming and fishing industries.

In May 2017 the island's unemployment rate was 1 per cent and the rate of inflation for RPI and CPI respectively, was 8.4 per cent and 3.9 per cent.

FINANCE

The budget for 2017–18 provides for gross revenue expenditure of £1,030m. The principal sources of government revenue are taxes on income and expenditure. Income tax is payable at a rate of 10 per cent on the first £6,500 of taxable income for single resident individuals and 20 per cent on the balance, after personal allowances of £12,500. These bands are doubled for married couples. The rate of income tax for trading companies is zero per cent except for income from banking and major retail operations which is taxed at 10 per cent, and income from land and property which is taxed at 20 per cent. By agreement with the British government, the island keeps most of its rates of indirect taxation (VAT and duties) the same as those in the UK. However, VAT on tourist accommodation, property, repairs and renovations is charged at 5 per cent. Taxes are also charged on property (rates), but these are comparatively low.

The major government expenditure items are social care, health and education. The island makes an annual contribution to the UK for defence and other external services.

The island has a special relationship with the European Union and neither contributes money to nor receives funds from the EU budget.

Ψ = sea port

THE CHANNEL ISLANDS

The Channel Islands, situated off the north-west coast of France (at a distance of 16km (10 miles) at their closest point), are the only portions of the Dukedom of Normandy still belonging to the Crown, to which they have been attached since the Norman Conquest of 1066. They were the only British territory to come under German occupation during the Second World War, following invasion on 30 June and 1 July 1940. Guernsey and Jersey were relieved by British forces on 9 May 1945, Sark on 10 May 1945 and Alderney on 16 May 1945; 9 May (Liberation Day) is now observed as a bank and public holiday in Guernsey and Jersey.

The islands consist of Jersey (11,630ha/28,717 acres), Guernsey (6,340ha/15,654 acres), and the dependencies of Guernsey: Alderney (795ha/1,962 acres), Brecqhou (30ha/74 acres), Great Sark (419ha/1,035 acres), Little Sark (97ha/239 acres), Herm (130ha/320 acres), Jethou (18ha/44 acres) and Lihou (15ha/38 acres) – a total of 19,474ha/48,083 acres, or 195 sq. km/75 sq. miles.

The 2011 census (taken in March) showed the population of Jersey as 97,857. Guernsey uses a rolling electronic census system and the most recent figures (June 2016) showed the populations of Guernsey and Alderney to be 63,026 and 2,020 respectively. Sark's population is estimated to be around 600. The official language is English but French is often used for ceremonial purposes. A Norman-French *patois* is also spoken by a few in Jersey, Guernsey and Sark.

GOVERNMENT

The islands are Crown dependencies with their own legislative assemblies (the States of Jersey, the States of Alderney, the States of Deliberation in Guernsey and the Chief Pleas in Sark), systems of local administration and law, and their own courts. *Projets de Loi* (Acts) passed by the States require the sanction of the Queen-in-council. The UK government is responsible for defence and international relations, although the islands are increasingly entering into agreements with other countries in their own right. The Channel Islands are not members of the European Union but, under protocol 3 of the UK's Treaty of Accession, have trading rights with the free movement of goods within the EU. A common customs tariff, levies and agricultural and import measures apply to trade between the islands and non-member countries.

In both Jersey and Guernsey bailiwicks the Lieutenant-Governor and Commander-in-Chief, who is appointed by the Crown, is the personal representative of the Queen and the official channel of communication between the Crown (via the Privy Council) and the islands' governments.

The head of government in both Jersey and Guernsey is the Chief Minister. Jersey has a ministerial system of government; the executive comprises the Council of Ministers and consists of a chief minister and ten other ministers. The ministers are assisted by up to ten assistant ministers. Members of the States who are not in the executive are able to sit on a number of scrutiny panels and the Public Accounts Committee to examine the policy of the executive and hold ministers to account. Guernsey is administered by a number of committees. The Policy and Resources committee is the senior committee responsible for leadership and coordination of the work of the States and is presided over by the Chief Minister, in addition there are six principal committees with mandated responsibilities. The States of Deliberation is the island's parliamentary assembly. Alderney has a legislature comprising a President and ten members elected by universal suffrage. Sark has a directly elected legislature of 28 members *(conseillers)* who serve on a number of committees.

Justice is administered by the royal courts of Jersey and Guernsey, each consisting of the bailiff and 12 elected jurats. The bailiffs of Jersey and Guernsey, appointed by the Crown, are presidents of the royal courts of their respective islands. Each bailiff is the *ex-officio* presiding officer in their respective parliaments and, by convention, the civic head.

The Church of England in each bailiwick is under the jurisdiction of the Dean of Jersey and the Dean of Guernsey respectively. The Bishop of Dover (Diocese of Canterbury) has episcopal oversight of the Channel Islands.

ECONOMY

A mild climate and good soil have led to the development of intensive systems of agriculture and horticulture, which form a significant part of the economy. Equally important are earnings from tourism and banking and finance: the low rates of income and corporation tax and the absence of death duties make the islands an important offshore financial centre. The financial services sector contributes over 50 per cent of GDP in Jersey and around 33 per cent in Guernsey. In addition, there is no VAT or equivalent tax in Guernsey and only small goods and services tax in Jersey (5 per cent since 1 June 2011). The international stock exchange is located in Guernsey, which also has a thriving e-gaming sector.

Principal exports are agricultural produce and flowers; imports are chiefly machinery, manufactured goods, food, fuel and chemicals. Trade with the UK is regarded as internal.

British currency is legal tender in the Channel Islands but each bailiwick issues its own coins and notes (*see* Currency section). They also issue their own postage stamps; UK stamps are not valid.

JERSEY

Lieutenant-Governor and Commander-in-Chief of Jersey, HE Air
    Chief Marshal Sir Stephen Dalton, GCB, *from* 2017
Chief of Staff, Maj. Justin Oldridge
Bailiff of Jersey, Sir William J. Bailhache
Deputy Bailiff, Timothy J. Le Cocq
Attorney-General, Robert J. MacRae, QC
Receiver-General, David Pett
Solicitor-General, Mark Temple, QC
Greffier of the States, Mark Egan
States Treasurer, Richard Bell
Chief Minister, Senator Ian Gorst

FINANCE

	2015	2016
Revenue income	£691,700,000	£736,800,000
Revenue expenditure	£697,000,000	£698,500,000
Capital expenditure	£45,609,000	£40,856,000

CHIEF TOWN – ΨSt Helier, on the south coast
FLAG – A white field charged with a red saltire cross, and the arms of Jersey in the upper centre

GUERNSEY AND DEPENDENCIES

*Lieutenant-Governor and Commander-in-Chief of the Bailiwick of
    Guernsey and its Dependencies,* Vice-Adm. Sir Ian Corder,
    KBE, CB
*Presiding Officer of the Royal Court and of the States of
    Deliberation,* Bailiff Sir Richard Collas
*Deputy Presiding Officer of the Royal Court and States of
    Deliberation,* Deputy Bailiff Richard McMahon, QC
HM Procureur and Receiver-General (Attorney-General), Megan
    Pullum, QC
HM Comptroller (Solicitor-General), Robert Titterington, QC

GUERNSEY

Chief Minister, Deputy Gavin St Pier
Chief Executive, Paul Whitfield

FINANCE

	2015	2016
Revenue income	£379,817,000	£406,964,000
Revenue expenditure	£364,528,000	£363,133,000
Capital expenditure	£7,506,000	£7,696,000

CHIEF TOWNS – ΨSt Peter Port, on the east coast of Guernsey; St Anne on Alderney

FLAG – White, bearing a red cross of St George, with a gold cross of Normandy overall in the centre

ALDERNEY

President of the States, Stuart Trought
Chief Executive, Adrian Lewis
Greffier, Jonathan Anderson

SARK

Sark was the last European territory to abolish feudal parliamentary representation. Elections for a democratic legislative assembly took place in December 2008, with the *conseillers* taking their seats in the newly constituted Chief Pleas in January 2009.

Seigneur of Sark, Maj. Christopher Beaumont
Seneschal, Jeremy la Trobe-Bateman
President, Arthur Rolfe
Greffier, Trevor Hamon

OTHER DEPENDENCIES

Herm and Lihou are owned by the States of Guernsey; Herm is leased, Lihou is uninhabited. Jethou is leased by the Crown to the States of Guernsey and is sub-let by the States. Brecqhou is within the legislative and judicial territory of Sark.

Ψ = seaport

LAW COURTS AND OFFICES

SUPREME COURT OF THE UNITED KINGDOM

The Supreme Court of the United Kingdom is the highest domestic judicial authority; it replaced the appellate committee of the House of Lords (the house functioning in its judicial capacity) on 1 October 2009. It is the final court of appeal for cases heard in Great Britain and Northern Ireland (except for criminal cases from Scotland). Cases concerning the interpretation and application of European Union law, including preliminary rulings requested by British courts and tribunals, which are decided by the Court of Justice of the European Union (CJEU) (*see* European Union), and the supreme court can make a reference to the CJEU in appropriate cases. Additionally, in giving effect to rights contained in the European Convention on Human Rights, the supreme court must take account of any decision of the European Court of Human Rights.

The supreme court also assumed jurisdiction in relation to devolution matters under the Scotland Act 1998 (now partly superseded by the Scotland Act 2012), the Northern Ireland Act 1988 and the Government of Wales Act 2006; these powers were transferred from the Judicial Committee of the Privy Council. Ten of the 12 Lords of Appeal in Ordinary (Law Lords) from the House of Lords transferred to the 12-member supreme court when it came into operation (at the same time one law lord retired and another was appointed Master of the Rolls). All new justices of the supreme court are now appointed by an independent selection commission, and, although styled Rt. Hon. Lord, are not members of the House of Lords. Peers who are members of the judiciary are disqualified from sitting or voting in the House of Lords until they retire from their judicial office. *See* Life Peers for a list of such peers (§).

President of the Supreme Court (£225,091), Rt. Hon. Lady Hale of Richmond, *born* 1945, *apptd* 2017
Deputy President of the Supreme Court (£217,409), vacant

JUSTICES OF THE SUPREME COURT *as at October 2017* (each £217,409)
Style, The Rt. Hon. Lord/Lady–

Rt. Hon. Lord Mance, *born* 1943, *apptd* 2005
Rt. Hon. Lord Kerr of Tonaghmore, *born* 1948, *apptd* 2009
Rt. Hon. Lord Wilson of Culworth, *born* 1945, *apptd* 2011
Rt. Hon. Lord Sumption, *born* 1948, *apptd* 2012
Rt. Hon. Lord Reed, *born* 1956, *apptd* 2012
Rt. Hon. Lord Carnwath of Notting Hill, CVO, *born* 1945, *apptd* 2012
Rt. Hon. Lord Hughes of Ombersley, *born* 1948, *apptd* 2013
Rt. Hon. Lord Hodge, *born* 1953, *apptd* 2013
Rt. Hon. Dame Jill Black, DBE *born* 1954, *apptd* 2017
Rt. Hon. Sir David Lloyd Jones, *born* 1952, *apptd* 2017
Rt. Hon. Sir Michael Briggs, *born* 1954, *apptd* 2017

UNITED KINGDOM SUPREME COURT
Parliament Square, London SW1P 3BD T 020-7960 1900
Chief Executive, Mark Ormerod, CB

JUDICATURE OF ENGLAND AND WALES

The legal system in England and Wales is divided into criminal law and civil law. Criminal law is concerned with acts harmful to the community and the rules laid down by the state for the benefit of citizens, whereas civil law governs the relationships and transactions between individuals. Administrative law is a kind of civil law usually concerning the interaction of individuals and the state, and most cases are heard in tribunals specific to the subject (*see* Tribunals section). Scotland and Northern Ireland possess legal systems that differ from the system in England and Wales in law, judicial procedure and court structure, but retain the distinction between criminal and civil law.

Under the provisions of the Criminal Appeal Act 1995, a commission was set up to direct and supervise investigations into possible miscarriages of justice and to refer cases to the appeal courts on the grounds of conviction and sentence; these functions were formerly the responsibility of the home secretary.

HIERARCHY OF ENGLISH AND WELSH COURTS

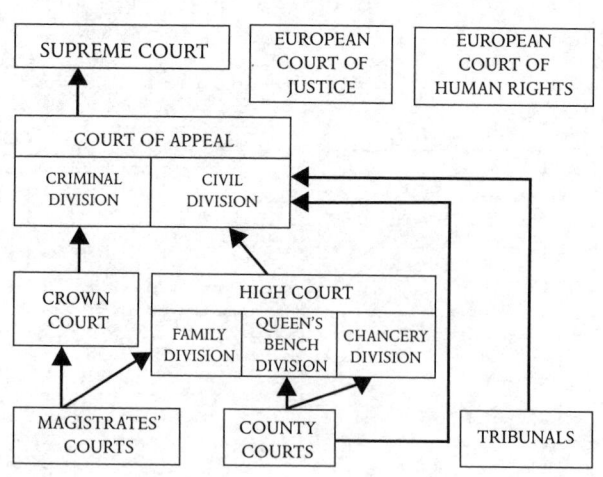

SENIOR COURTS OF ENGLAND AND WALES

The senior courts of England and Wales (until September 2009 known as the supreme court of judicature of England and Wales) comprise the high court, the crown court and the court of appeal. The President of the Courts of England and Wales, a new title given to the Lord Chief Justice under the Constitutional Reform Act 2005, is the head of the judiciary.

The high court was created in 1875 and combined many previously separate courts. Sittings are held at the royal courts of justice in London or at around 120 district registries outside the capital. It is the superior civil court and is split into three divisions – the chancery division, the Queen's bench division and the family division – each of which is further divided. The chancery division is headed by the Chancellor of the High Court and is concerned mainly with equity, trusts, tax and bankruptcy, while also including two specialist courts, the patents court and the companies court. The Queen's bench division (QBD) is the largest of the three divisions, and is headed by its own president. It deals with common law (ie tort, contract, debt and personal injuries), some tax law, eg VAT tribunal appeals, and encompasses the admiralty court and the commercial court. The QBD also administers the technology and construction court. The family division was created in 1970 and is headed by its own president, who is also Head of Family Justice, and hears cases concerning divorce, access to and custody of children, and other family matters. The divisional court of the high court sits in the family and chancery divisions, and hears appeals from the magistrates' courts and county courts.

The crown court was set up in 1972 and sits at 77 centres throughout England and Wales. It deals with more serious (indictable) criminal offences, which are triable before a judge and jury, including treason, murder, rape, kidnapping, armed robbery and Official Secrets Act offences. It also handles cases transferred from the magistrates' courts where the magistrate decides his or her own power of sentence is inadequate, or where someone appeals against a magistrate's decision, or in a case that is triable 'either way' where the accused has chosen a jury trial. The crown court centres are divided into three tiers: high court judges, circuit judges and sometimes recorders (part-time circuit judges), sit in first-tier centres, hearing the most serious criminal offences (eg murder, treason, rape, manslaughter) and some civil high court cases. The second-tier centres are presided over by high court judges, circuit judges or recorders and also deal with the most serious criminal cases. Third-tier courts deal with the remaining criminal offences, with circuit judges or recorders presiding.

The court of appeal hears appeals against both fact and law, and was last restructured in 1966 when it replaced the court of criminal appeal. It is split into the civil division (which hears appeals from the high court, tribunals and in certain cases, the county courts) and the criminal division (which hears appeals from the crown court). Cases are heard by Lords Justices of Appeal and high court judges if deemed suitable for reconsideration.

The Constitutional Reform Act 2005 instigated several key changes to the judiciary in England and Wales. These included the establishment of the independent supreme court, which opened in October 2009; the reform of the post of Lord Chancellor, transferring its judicial functions to the President of the Courts of England and Wales; a duty on government ministers to uphold the independence of the judiciary by barring them from trying to influence judicial decisions through any special access to judges; the formation of a fully transparent and independent Judicial Appointments Commission that is responsible for selecting candidates to recommend for judicial appointment to the Lord Chancellor and Secretary of State for Justice; and the creation of the post of Judicial Appointments and Conduct Ombudsman.

CRIMINAL CASES

In criminal matters the decision to prosecute (in the majority of cases) rests with the Crown Prosecution Service (CPS), which is the independent prosecuting body in England and Wales. The CPS is headed by the director of public prosecutions, who works under the superintendence of the Attorney-General. Certain categories of offence continue to require the Attorney-General's consent for prosecution.

Most minor criminal cases (summary offences) are dealt with in magistrates' courts, usually by a bench of three unpaid lay magistrates (justices of the peace) sitting without a jury and assisted on points of law and procedure by a legally trained clerk. There are approximately 23,000 justices of the peace. In some courts a full-time, salaried and legally qualified district judge (magistrates' court) – formerly known as a stipendiary judge – presides alone. There are 140 district judges and 170 deputy district judges operating in around 330 magistrates' courts in England and Wales. Magistrates' courts deal with 95 per cent of all criminal cases. Magistrates' courts also house some family proceedings courts (which deal with relationship breakdown and childcare cases) and youth courts. Cases of medium seriousness (known as 'offences triable either way') where the defendant pleads not guilty can be heard in the crown court for a trial by jury, if the defendant so chooses. Preliminary proceedings in a serious case to decide whether there is evidence to justify committal for trial in the crown court are dealt with in the magistrates' courts.

The 77 centres that the crown court sits in are divided into seven regions. There are over 600 circuit judges and 1,000 recorders (part-time circuit judges; expected to sit for 30 days a year. A jury is present in all trials that are contested.

Appeals from magistrates' courts against sentence or conviction are made to the crown court, and appeals upon a point of law are made to the high court, which may ultimately be appealed to the supreme court. Appeals from the crown court, either against sentence or conviction, are made to the court of appeal (criminal division). Again, these appeals may be brought to the supreme court if a point of law is contested, and if the house considers it is of sufficient importance.

CIVIL CASES

Most minor civil cases – including contract, tort (especially personal injuries), property, divorce and other family matters, bankruptcy etc – are dealt with by the county courts, of which there are around 200 (see W www.justice.gov.uk for further details). Cases are heard by circuit judges, recorders or district judges. For cases involving small claims (with certain exceptions, where the amount claimed is £5,000 or less) there are informal and simplified procedures designed to enable parties to present their cases themselves without recourse to lawyers. Where there are financial limits on county court jurisdiction, claims that exceed those limits may be tried in the county courts with the consent of the parties, subject to the court's agreement, or in certain circumstances on transfer from the high court. Outside London, bankruptcy proceedings can be heard in designated county courts. Magistrates' courts also deal with certain classes of civil case, and committees of magistrates license public houses, clubs and betting shops. For the implementation of the Children Act 1989, a new structure of hearing centres was set up in 1991 for family proceedings cases, involving magistrates' courts (family proceedings courts), divorce county courts, family hearing centres and care centres.

Appeals in certain family matters heard in the family proceedings courts go to the family division of the high court. Appeals from county courts may be heard in the court of appeal (civil division) or the high court, and may go on to the supreme court.

CORONERS' COURTS

Unlike the unified courts system, administered by HM Courts and Tribunals Service, there are 92 separate coroners' jurisdictions in England and Wales. Each jurisdiction is locally funded and resourced by local authorities. Coroners are barristers, solicitors or medical practitioners of not less than five years standing, who continue in their legal or medical practices when not sitting as coroners. Some 30 coroners are 'full-time' coroners and are paid an annual salary regardless of their caseload. The remainder are paid according to the number of cases referred to them. The coroner's jurisdiction is territorial – it is the location of the dead body which dictates which coroner has jurisdiction in any particular case.

The coroners' courts investigate violent and unnatural deaths or sudden deaths where the cause is unknown. Doctors, the police, various public authorities or members of the public may bring cases before a coroner. Where a death is sudden and the cause is unknown, the coroner may order a post-mortem examination to determine the cause of death rather than hold an inquest in court. An inquest must be held, however, if a person died in a violent or unnatural way, or died in prison or other unusual circumstances. If the coroner suspects murder, manslaughter or infanticide, then they must summon a jury.

Coroners are required to appoint a deputy or assistant deputy to act in their stead if they are out of the district or otherwise unable to act. Deputies and assistant deputies have the same professional qualifications as the coroner. In exceptionally high-profile or complex cases, a serving judge may be appointed as a deputy coroner.

SENIOR JUDICIARY OF ENGLAND AND WALES

Lord Chief Justice of England and Wales and Head of Criminal Justice (£252,079), Rt. Hon. Sir Ian Burnett, *born* 1958, *apptd* 2017
Master of the Rolls and Head of Civil Justice (£225,091), Rt. Hon. Sir Terence Etherton, *born* 1951, *apptd* 2016
President of the Queen's Bench Division (£217,409), Rt. Hon. Sir Brian Leveson, *born* 1949, *apptd* 2013
President of the Family Division and Head of Family Justice (£217,409), Rt. Hon. Sir James Munby, *born* 1948, *apptd* 2013
Chancellor of the High Court (£217,409), Rt. Hon. Sir Geoffrey Vos, *born* 1955, *apptd* 2016

SENIOR COURTS OF ENGLAND AND WALES

COURT OF APPEAL

Presiding Judge, Criminal Division, Lord Chief Justice of England and Wales
Presiding Judge, Civil Division, Master of the Rolls
Vice-President, Civil Division (£206,742), Rt. Hon. Dame Elizabeth Gloster, DBE *born* 1949, *apptd* 2016
Vice-President, Criminal Division (£206,742), Rt. Hon. Dame Heather Hallett, DBE, *born* 1949, *apptd* 2013

LORD JUSTICES OF APPEAL *as at November 2017* (each £206,742)
Style, The Rt. Hon. Lord/Lady Justice [surname]

Rt. Hon. Dame Mary Arden, DBE, *born* 1947, *apptd* 2000
Rt. Hon. Sir Andrew Longmore, *born* 1944, *apptd* 2001
Rt. Hon. Dame Heather Hallett, DBE, *born* 1949, *apptd* 2005
Rt. Hon. Sir Rupert Jackson, *born* 1948, *apptd* 2008
Rt. Hon. Sir Nicholas Patten, *born* 1950, *apptd* 2009
Rt. Hon. Sir Stephen Tomlinson, *born* 1952, *apptd* 2010
Rt. Hon. Sir Peter Gross, *born* 1952, *apptd* 2010
Rt. Hon. Dame Anne Rafferty, DBE, *born* 1950, *apptd* 2011
Rt. Hon. Sir Andrew McFarlane, *born* 1954, *apptd* 2011
Rt. Hon. Sir Nigel Davis, *born* 1951, *apptd* 2011
Rt. Hon. Sir Kim Lewison, *born* 1952, *apptd* 2011
Rt. Hon. Sir David Kitchin, *born* 1955, *apptd* 2011
Rt. Hon. Sir Colman Treacy, *born* 1949, *apptd* 2012
Rt. Hon. Sir Richard McCombe, *born* 1952, *apptd* 2012
Rt. Hon. Sir Jack Beatson, *born* 1948, *apptd* 2013
Rt. Hon. Dame Elizabeth Gloster, DBE, *born* 1949, *apptd* 2013
Rt. Hon. Sir Ernest Ryder, TD, *born* 1957, *apptd* 2013
Rt. Hon. Sir Nicholas Underhill, *born* 1952, *apptd* 2013
Rt. Hon. Sir Christopher Floyd, *born* 1951, *apptd* 2013
Rt. Hon. Sir Adrian Fulford, *born* 1953, *apptd* 2013

Rt. Hon. Dame Julia Macur, DBE, *born* 1957, *apptd* 2013
Rt. Hon. Dame Victoria Sharp, DBE, *born* 1956, *apptd* 2013
Rt. Hon. Sir David Bean, *born* 1954, *apptd* 2014
Rt. Hon. Dame Eleanor King, DBE, *born* 1957, *apptd* 2014
Rt. Hon. Sir Philip Sales, *born* 1962, *apptd* 2014
Rt. Hon. Sir Peregrine Simon, *born* 1950, *apptd* 2015
Rt. Hon. Sir Keith Lindblom, *born* 1956, *apptd* 2015
Rt. Hon. Sir David Richards, *born* 1951, *apptd* 2015
Rt. Hon. Sir Nicholas Hamblen, *born* 1957, *apptd* 2016
Rt. Hon. Sir Stephen Irwin, *born* 1953, *apptd* 2016
Rt. Hon. Sir Launcelot Henderson, *born* 1951, *apptd* 2016
Rt. Hon. Sir Julian Flaux, *born* 1955, *apptd* 2016
Rt. Hon. Dame Kathryn Thirlwall, DBE, *born* 1957, *apptd* 2017
Rt. Hon. Sir Gary Hickinbottom, *born* 1955, *apptd* 2017
Rt. Hon. Sir Andrew Moylan, *born* 1953, *apptd* 2017
Rt. Hon. Sir Peter Jackson, *born* 1955, *apptd* 2017

Ex Officio Judges, Lord Chief Justice of England and Wales; Master of the Rolls; President of the Queen's Bench Division; President of the Family Division; Chancellor of the High Court

COURTS-MARTIAL APPEAL COURT

Judges, Lord Chief Justice of England and Wales; Master of the Rolls; Lord Justices of Appeal; Judges of the High Court of Justice

HIGH COURT

CHANCERY DIVISION

Chancellor of the High Court (£217,409), Rt. Hon. Sir Geoffrey Vos, *born* 1955, *apptd* 2016
Senior Personal Secretary, Adam David
Private/Legal Secretary, Vannina Ettori
Clerk, Jessie Davidson

JUDGES *as at November 2017* (each £181,566)
Style, The Hon. Mr/Mrs Justice [surname]

Hon. Sir Peter Smith, *born* 1952, *apptd* 2002
Hon. Sir George Mann, *born* 1951, *apptd* 2004
Hon. Sir Nicholas Warren, *born* 1949, *apptd* 2005
Hon. Sir Paul Morgan, *born* 1952, *apptd* 2007
Hon. Sir Alastair Norris, *born* 1950, *apptd* 2007
Hon. Sir Gerald Barling, *born* 1949, *apptd* 2007
Hon. Dame Sonia Proudman, DBE, *born* 1949, *apptd* 2008
Hon. Sir Richard Arnold, *born* 1961, *apptd* 2008
Hon. Sir Peter Roth, *born* 1952, *apptd* 2009
Hon. Sir Guy Newey, *born* 1959, *apptd* 2010
Hon. Sir Robert Hildyard, *born* 1952, *apptd* 2011
Hon. Dame Sarah Asplin, DBE, *born* 1959, *apptd* 2012
Hon. Sir Colin Birss, *born* 1964, *apptd* 2013
Hon. Dame Vivien Rose, DBE, *born* 1960, *apptd* 2013
Hon. Sir Christopher Nugee, *born* 1959, *apptd* 2013
Hon. Sir Richard Snowden, *born* 1962, *apptd* 2015
Hon. Sir Henry Carr, *born* 1958, *apptd* 2015
Hon. Sir Marcus Smith, *born* 1967, *apptd* 2017
The Chancery Division also includes three specialist courts: the Companies Court, the Patents Court and the Bankruptcy Court.

QUEEN'S BENCH DIVISION

President (£217,409), Rt. Hon. Sir Brian Leveson, *born* 1949, *apptd* 2013
Vice-President (£206,742), Rt. Hon. Dame Victoria Sharp, DBE, *born* 1956, *apptd* 2016

JUDGES *as at November 2017* (each £181,566)
Style, The Hon. Mr/Mrs Justice [surname]

Hon. Sir (Arthur) William Charles, *born* 1948, *apptd* 1998
Hon. Sir Duncan Ouseley, *born* 1950, *apptd* 2000
Hon. Sir John Mitting, *born* 1947, *apptd* 2001
Hon. Sir Paul Walker, *born* 1954, *apptd* 2004
Hon. Sir Charles Openshaw, *born* 1947, *apptd* 2005
Hon. Sir Brian Langstaff, *born* 1948, *apptd* 2005

Hon. Sir Nigel Teare, *born* 1952, *apptd* 2006
Hon. Sir Timothy King, *born* 1949, *apptd* 2007
Hon. Sir David Foskett, *born* 1949, *apptd* 2007
Hon. Sir Nicholas Blake, *born* 1949, *apptd* 2007
Hon. Sir Peter Coulson, *born* 1958, *apptd* 2008
Hon. Sir William Blair, *born* 1950, *apptd* 2008
Hon. Sir Nigel Sweeney, *born* 1954, *apptd* 2008
Hon. Dame Elizabeth Slade, DBE, *born* 1949, *apptd* 2008
Hon. Sir Timothy Holroyde, *born* 1955, *apptd* 2009
Hon. Sir Andrew Nicol, *born* 1951, *apptd* 2009
Hon. Dame Nicola Davies, DBE, *born* 1953, *apptd* 2010
Hon. Sir Michael Supperstone, *born* 1950, *apptd* 2010
Hon. Sir Robin Spencer, *born* 1955, *apptd* 2010
Hon. Sir Henry Globe, *born* 1949, *apptd* 2011
Hon. Sir Andrew Popplewell, *born* 1959, *apptd* 2011
Hon. Sir Rabinder Singh, *born* 1964, *apptd* 2011
Hon. Dame Beverley Lang, DBE, *born* 1955, *apptd* 2011
Hon. Sir Charles Haddon-Cave, *born* 1956, *apptd* 2011
Hon. Sir Stephen Males, *born* 1955, *apptd* 2012
Hon. Sir Jeremy Stuart-Smith, *born* 1955, *apptd* 2012
Hon. Sir George Leggatt, *born* 1957, *apptd* 2012
Hon. Sir Mark Turner, *born* 1959, *apptd* 2013
Hon. Sir Jeremy Baker, *born* 1958, *apptd* 2013
Hon. Sir Stephen Stewart, *born* 1953, *apptd* 2013
Hon. Sir Robert Jay, *born* 1959, *apptd* 2013
Hon. Sir James Dingemans, *born* 1964, *apptd* 2013
Hon. Sir Clive Lewis, *born* 1960, *apptd* 2013
Hon. Dame Sue Carr, DBE, *born* 1964, *apptd* 2013
Hon. Sir Stephen Phillips, *born* 1961, *apptd* 2013
Hon. Dame Geraldine Andrews, DBE, *born* 1959, *apptd* 2013
Hon. Sir Nicholas Green, *born* 1958, *apptd* 2013
Hon. Dame Ingrid Simler, DBE, *born* 1963, *apptd* 2013
Hon. Dame Elisabeth Laing, DBE, *born* 1956, *apptd* 2014
Hon. Sir William Davis, *born* 1954, *apptd* 2014
Hon. Sir Mark Warby, *born* 1958, *apptd* 2014
Hon. Sir Andrew Edis, *born* 1957, *apptd* 2014
Hon. Sir James Goss, *born* 1953, *apptd* 2014
Hon. Dame Maura McGowan, DBE, *born* 1957, *apptd* 2014
Hon. Sir Robin Knowles, *born* 1960, *apptd* 2014
Hon. Sir Ian Dove, *born* 1963, *apptd* 2014
Hon. Sir Andrew Gilbart, *born* 1950, *apptd* 2014
Hon. Sir David Holgate, *born* 1956, *apptd* 2014
Hon. Sir Timothy Kerr, *born* 1958, *apptd* 2015
Hon. Sir Simon Picken, *born* 1966, *apptd* 2015
Hon. Dame Philippa Whipple, DBE, *born* 1966, *apptd* 2015
Hon. Sir Peter Fraser, *born* 1963, *apptd* 2015
Hon. Sir Neil Garnham, *born* 1959, *apptd* 2015
Hon. Dame Bobbie Cheema-Grubb, DBE *born* 1966, *apptd* 2015
Hon. Sir Michael Soole, *born* 1954, *apptd* 2015
Hon. Dame Juliet May, DBE, *born* 1961, *apptd* 2015
Hon. Sir Stephen Morris, *born* 1957, *apptd* 2016
Hon. Dame Nerys Jefford, DBE, *born* 1962, *apptd* 2016
Hon. Sir Nicholas Lavender, *born* 1964, *apptd* 2016
Hon. Dame Finola O'Farrell, DBE, *born* 1960, *apptd* 2016
Hon. Sir Andrew Baker, *born* 1965, *apptd* 2016
Hon. Sir Akhlaq Choudhury, *born* 1967, *apptd* 2017
Hon. Sir Julian Goose, *born* 1961, *apptd* 2017
Hon. Sir Simon Bryan, *born* 1965, *apptd* 2017
Hon. Sir Richard Lane, *born* 1953, *apptd* 2017
Hon. Sir Martin Spencer, *born* 1956, *apptd* 2017
Hon. Dame Sara Cockerill, *born* 1968, *apptd* 2017
The Queen's Bench Division also includes the Divisional Court, the Admiralty Court, Commercial Court and Technology and Construction Court.

FAMILY DIVISION
President (£217,409), Rt. Hon. Sir James Munby, *born* 1948, *apptd* 2013

JUDGES *as at November 2017* (each £181,566)
Style, The Hon. Mr/Mrs Justice [surname]

Hon. Sir Edward Holman, *born* 1947, *apptd* 1995

Hon. Sir David Bodey, *born* 1947, *apptd* 1999
Hon. Dame Anna Pauffley, DBE, *born* 1956, *apptd* 2003
Hon. Dame Judith Parker, DBE *born* 1950, *apptd* 2008
Hon. Sir Jonathan Baker, *born* 1955, *apptd* 2009
Hon. Sir Nicholas Mostyn, *born* 1957, *apptd* 2010
Hon. Dame Lucy Theis, DBE, *born* 1960, *apptd* 2010
Hon. Sir Philip Moor, *born* 1959, *apptd* 2011
Hon. Sir Stephen Cobb, *born* 1962, *apptd* 2013
Hon. Sir Michael Keehan, *born* 1960, *apptd* 2013
Hon. Sir Anthony Hayden, *born* 1961, *apptd* 2013
Hon. Dame Alison Russell, DBE, *born* 1958, *apptd* 2014
Hon. Roderick Newton, *born* 1958, *apptd* 2014
Hon. Dame Jennifer Roberts, DBE, *born* 1953, *apptd* 2014
Hon. Sir Alistair MacDonald, *born* 1970, *apptd* 2015
Hon. Sir Peter Francis, *born* 1958, *apptd* 2016
Hon. Dame Gwynneth Knowles, DBE *born* 1962, *apptd* 2017
Hon. Sir Jonathan Cohen, *born* 1951, *apptd* 2017

DEPARTMENTS AND OFFICES OF THE SENIOR COURTS OF ENGLAND AND WALES
Royal Courts of Justice, London WC2A 2LL
T 020-7947 6000

ADMINISTRATIVE COURT OFFICE
T 020-7947 6655
Judge in charge of the Administrative Court (£181,566), Hon. Mr Justice Supperstone
Master of the Crown Office, and Queen's Coroner and Attorney (£108,171), M. Egan, QC, *apptd* 2011

ADMIRALTY, COMMERCIAL AND LONDON MERCANTILE COURTS' OFFICE
Ground Floor, 7 Rolls Building, Fetter Lane, London EC4A 1NL T 020-7947 6112
Registrar (£108,171), J. Kay, QC
Admiralty Judge (£181,566), Hon. Mr Justice Teare
Judge in charge of the Commercial Court (£181,566), Hon. Mr Justice Blair

BANKRUPTCY AND COMPANIES COURT REGISTRY
7 Rolls Building, Fetter Lane, London EC4A 1NL T 020-7947 6294
Chief Bankruptcy Registrar (134,841), Chief Registrar Briggs *apptd* 2017
Bankruptcy Registrars (£108,171), Registrar Barber *apptd* 2009; Registrar Brougham *apptd* 2013; Registrar Derrett *apptd* 2002; Registrar Jones *apptd* 2012; Registrar Lawson *apptd* 2015

CENTRAL OFFICE OF THE QUEEN'S BENCH DIVISION
Senior Master and Queen's Remembrancer (£134,841), Senior Master Fontaine *apptd* 2014
Masters of the Queen's Bench Division (£108,171), Master Cook *apptd* 2011; Master Davison *apptd* 2016; Master Eastman *apptd* 2009; Master Gidden *apptd* 2012; Master Kay, QC; *apptd* 2009; Master McCloud *apptd* 2010; Master Roberts *apptd* 2009; Master Thornett *apptd* 2016; Master Yoxall *apptd* 2002

CHANCERY CHAMBERS
7 Rolls Building, Fetter Lane, London EC4A 1NL T 020-7947 7391
Chief Chancery Master (£134,841), Chief Master Marsh *apptd* 2014
Masters of Chancery (£108,171), Master Bowles *apptd* 1999; Master Clark *apptd* 2015; Master Matthews *apptd* 2015; Master Price *apptd* 1999; Master Teverson *apptd* 2005

COSTS OFFICE
T 020-7947 6423
Senior Costs Judge (Chief Taxing Master) (£134,841), Chief Master Gordon-Saker *apptd* 2014

Cost Judges (Taxing Masters) (£108,171), Master Brown *apptd* 2016; Master Haworth *apptd* 2006; Master James *apptd* 2015; Master Leonard *apptd* 2010; Master Nagalingam *apptd* 2017; Master Rowley *apptd* 2013; Master Whalan *apptd* 2015

COURT OF APPEAL CIVIL DIVISION
T 020-7947 6195

COURT OF APPEAL CRIMINAL DIVISION
T 020-7947 6011
Registrar (£108,171), M. Egan, QC

COURT OF PROTECTION
First Avenue House, 42–49 High Holborn, London WC1V 6NP
T 0300-456 4600
Senior Judge and Master of the Court of Protection (£134,841), Her Hon. Judge Hilder, *apptd* 2017

ELECTION PETITIONS OFFICE
Room E113, Royal Courts of Justice, Strand, London WC2A 2LL
T 020-7947 6877

The office accepts petitions and deals with all matters relating to the questioning of parliamentary, European parliament, local government and parish elections, and with applications for relief under the 'representation of the people' legislation.

Prescribed Officer, The Senior Master and Senior Remembrancer (£134,841), B. Fontaine

EXAMINERS OF THE COURT
Empowered to take examination of witnesses in all divisions of the High Court.

PRINCIPAL REGISTRY (FAMILY DIVISION)
First Avenue House, 42–49 High Holborn, London WC1V 6NP
T 020-7421 8594

TECHNOLOGY AND CONSTRUCTION COURT (TCC)
Ground Floor, 7 Rolls Building, Fetter Lane, London EC4A 1NL
T 020-7947 7156
Judge in charge of the TCC (£181,566), Hon. Mr Justice Coulson

COURT FUNDS OFFICE
Glasgow G58 1AB T 0300-020 0199

The Court Funds Office (CFO), established in 1726, provides a banking and administration service for the civil courts throughout England and Wales, including the High Court.

OFFICIAL SOLICITOR AND PUBLIC TRUSTEE
Victory House, 30–34 Kingsway, London WC2B 6EX
E enquiries@offsol.gsi.gov.uk

The Official Solicitor and the Public Trustee are independent statutory office holders. Their office (OSPT) is an arms-length body of the Ministry of Justice that exists to support their work. The Official Solicitor provides access to the justice system to those who are vulnerable by virtue of minority or lack of mental capacity. The Public Trustee acts as executor or administrator of estates and as the appointed trustee of settlements, providing an effective executor and trustee service of last resort.

Official Solicitor to the Senior Courts and the Public Trustee, Alistair Pitblado

PROBATE SERVICE
London Probate Department, 7th Floor, First Avenue House, 42–49 High Holborn, London WC1V 6NP T 020-7421 8509

The probate offices that issue grants of probate and grants of letters of administration are known as probate registries. The principal probate registry is situated in central London and there are 11 district probate registries in Birmingham,

Brighton, Bristol, Cardiff, Ipswich, Leeds, Liverpool, Manchester, Newcastle, Oxford and Winchester, and a further 18 probate sub-registries. Probate registries are administered by HM Courts Service.

JUDGE ADVOCATES GENERAL
The Judge Advocate General is the judicial head of the Service justice system, and the leader of the judges who preside over trials in the court martial and other Service courts. The defendants are service personnel from the Royal Navy, the army and the Royal Air Force, and civilians accompanying them overseas.

JUDGE ADVOCATE GENERAL OF THE FORCES
9th Floor, Thomas More Building, Royal Courts of Justice, Strand, London WC2A 2LL
T 020-7218 8089
Judge Advocate General (£145,614), His Hon. Judge Blackett
Vice-Judge Advocate General (£126,946), Judge Hunter
Assistant Judge Advocates General (£108,171), J. P. Camp; R. D. Hill; A. M. Large; A. J. B. McGrigor
Style, Judge [surname]

HIGH COURT AND CROWN COURT CENTRES
First-tier centres deal with both civil and criminal cases and are served by high court and circuit judges. Second-tier centres deal with criminal cases only and are served by high court and circuit judges. Third-tier centres deal with criminal cases only and are served only by circuit judges.

LONDON REGION

First-tier – None
Second-tier – Central Criminal Court
Third-tier – Blackfriars, Croydon, Harrow, Inner London, Isleworth, Kingston upon Thames, Snaresbrook, Southwark, Wood Green, Woolwich

The high court (first-tier) in Greater London sits at the Royal Courts of Justice.

MIDLANDS REGION

First-tier – Birmingham, Lincoln, Nottingham, Stafford, Warwick
Second-tier – Leicester, Northampton, Shrewsbury, Worcester, Wolverhampton
Third-tier – Coventry, Derby, Hereford, Stoke on Trent

NORTH-EAST REGION

First-tier – Leeds, Newcastle upon Tyne, Sheffield, Teesside
Second-tier – Bradford, York
Third-tier – Doncaster, Durham, Kingston upon Hull, Great Grimsby

NORTH-WEST REGION

First-tier – Carlisle, Chester, Liverpool, Manchester (Crown Square), Preston
Third-tier – Barrow in Furness, Bolton, Burnley, Knutsford, Lancaster, Manchester (Minshull Street), Warrington

SOUTH-EAST REGION

First-tier – Cambridge, Chelmsford, Lewes, Norwich, Oxford
Second-tier – Guildford, Ipswich, Luton, Maidstone, Reading, St Albans
Third-tier – Aylesbury, Basildon, Canterbury, Chichester, Croydon, King's Lynn, Peterborough, Southend

SOUTH-WEST REGION

First-tier – Bristol, Exeter, Truro, Winchester
Second-tier – Dorchester & Weymouth, Gloucester, Plymouth
Third-tier – Barnstaple, Bournemouth, Newport (IoW), Portsmouth, Salisbury, Southampton, Swindon, Taunton

WALES REGION

First-tier – Caernarfon, Cardiff, Merthyr Tydfil, Mold, Swansea
Second-tier – Carmarthen, Newport, Welshpool
Third-tier – Dolgellau, Haverfordwest

CIRCUIT JUDGES

Circuit judges are barristers of at least seven years' standing or recorders of at least five years' standing. Circuit judges serve in the county courts and the crown court.

Style, His/Her Hon. Judge [surname]
Senior Presiding Judge, Rt. Hon. Lady Justice Macur
Deputy Senior Presiding Judge, vacant
Senior Circuit Judges, each £145,614
Circuit Judges at the Central Criminal Court, London (Old Bailey Judges), each £145,614
Circuit Judges, each £134,841

MIDLAND CIRCUIT
Presiding Judges, Hon. Mr Justice Haddon-Cave; Hon. Mrs Justice Carr

NORTH-EASTERN CIRCUIT
Presiding Judges, Hon. Mr Justice Globe; Hon. Mr Justice Males

NORTHERN CIRCUIT
Presiding Judges, Hon. Mr Justice Turner; Hon. Mr Justice Davis

SOUTH-EASTERN CIRCUIT
Presiding Judges, Hon. Mr Justice Spencer; Hon. Mr Justice Stuart-Smith; Hon. Mr Justice McGowan; Hon. Mr Justice Green

WALES CIRCUIT
Presiding Judges, Hon. Mrs Justice Davies; Hon. Mr Justice Lewis

WESTERN CIRCUIT
Presiding Judges, Hon. Mr Justice Dingemans; Hon. Mrs Justice May

DISTRICT JUDGES

District judges, formerly known as registrars of the court, are solicitors of at least seven years' standing and serve in county courts.
District Judges, each £108,171

DISTRICT JUDGES (MAGISTRATES' COURTS)

District judges (magistrates' courts), formerly known as stipendiary magistrates, serve in magistrates courts where they hear criminal cases, youth cases and some civil proceedings. Many also hear family cases in the single family court. Some may be authorised to handle extradition proceedings and terrorist cases. District judges (magistrates' courts) are appointed following competition conducted by the Judicial Appointments Commission.
District Judges (Magistrates' Courts), each £108,171

OFFICE OF THE CHIEF MAGISTRATE
181 Marylebone Road, London NW1 5BR
T 020-3126 3100

The Chief Magistrate (senior district judge) is responsible for hearing many of the sensitive or complex cases – extradition and special jurisdiction cases in particular – in the magistrates' courts. The Chief Magistrate also supports and guides district judges (magistrates' courts), and liaises with the senior judiciary and presiding judges on matters pertaining to magistrates' courts.

The Office of the Chief Magistrate provides administration support to both the Chief Magistrate and to all the district judges sitting at magistrates' courts in England and Wales.
Chief Magistrate, Emma Arbuthnot
Deputy Chief Magistrate, Tanweer Ikram

CROWN PROSECUTION SERVICE
Rose Court, 2 Southwark Bridge Road, London SE1 9HS
T 020-3357 0000 E enquiries@cps.gsi.gov.uk W www.cps.gov.uk

The Crown Prosecution Service (CPS) is responsible for prosecuting cases investigated by the police in England and Wales, with the exception of cases conducted by the Serious Fraud Office and certain minor offences.

The CPS is headed by the director of public prosecutions (DPP), who works under the superintendence of the attorney-general. The service is divided into 13 areas across England and Wales, with each area led by a chief crown prosecutor.

Director of Public Prosecutions, Alison Saunders, CB
Chief Executive, Nick Folland
Directors, Jean Ashton, OBE *(Business Services);* Gregor McGill *(Legal Services);* Paul Staff *(Corporate Services)*

CPS AREAS
EAST MIDLANDS, 2 King Edward Court, King Edward Street, Nottingham NG1 1EL T 0115-852 3300
Chief Crown Prosecutor, Janine Smith
EAST, County House, 100 New London Road, Chelmsford, Essex CM2 0RG T 01245-455800
Chief Crown Prosecutor, Jenny Hopkins
LONDON, 5th Floor, Rose Court, 2 Southwark Bridge, London SE1 9HST 020-3357 7000
Chief Crown Prosecutor (London North), Ed Beltrami, CBE
Chief Crown Prosecutor (London South), Claire Lindley
MERSEY–CHESHIRE, 2nd Floor, Walker House, Exchange Flags, Liverpool L2 3YL T 0151-239 6400
Chief Crown Prosecutor, Siobhan Blake
NORTH EAST, St Ann's Quay, 112 Quayside, Newcastle Upon Tyne, NE1 3BD T 0191-260 4200
Chief Crown Prosecutor, Andrew Penhale
NORTH WEST, 1st Floor, Stocklund House, Castle Street, Carlisle CA3 8SY T 01228-882900
Chief Crown Prosecutor, Martin Goldman
SOUTH EAST, Riding Gate House, 37 Old Dover Road, Canterbury, Kent CT1 3JG T 01227-866000
Chief Crown Prosecutor, Jaswant Narwal
SOUTH WEST, 5th Floor, Kite Wing, Temple Quay House, 2 The Square, Bristol BS1 6PN T 0117-930 2800
Chief Crown Prosecutor, Chris Long
THAMES AND CHILTERN, Eaton Court, 112 Oxford Road, Reading, Berks RG1 7LL T 01727-798700
Chief Crown Prosecutor, Adrian Foster
WALES, 20th Floor, Capital Tower, Greyfriars Road, Cardiff CF10 3PL T 029-2080 3800
Chief Crown Prosecutor, Barry Hughes
WESSEX, 3rd Floor, Black Horse House, 8–10 Leigh Road, Eastleigh, Hants SO50 9FH T 02380-673 800
Chief Crown Prosecutor, Joanne Jakymec
WEST MIDLANDS, Colmore Gate, 2 Colmore Row, Birmingham B3 2QA T 0121-262 1300
Chief Crown Prosecutor, Grace Ononiwu, OBE
YORKSHIRE AND HUMBERSIDE, 27 Park Place, Leeds LS1 2SZ T 0113-290 2700
Chief Crown Prosecutor, Gerry Wareham

HER MAJESTY'S COURTS AND TRIBUNALS SERVICE
1st Floor, 102 Petty France, London SW1H 9AJ
W www.gov.uk/government/organisations/hm-courts-and-tribunals-service

Her Majesty's Courts Service and the Tribunals Service merged on 1 April 2011 to form HM Courts and Tribunals Service. It is an agency of the Ministry of Justice, operating as a partnership between the Lord Chancellor, the Lord Chief Justice and the Senior President of Tribunals. It is responsible for administering the criminal, civil and family courts and tribunals in England and Wales and non-devolved tribunals in Scotland and Northern Ireland.

Chief Executive, Susan Acland-Hood

JUDICIAL APPOINTMENTS COMMISSION
1st Floor, Zone A, 102 Petty France, London SW1H 9AJ
T 020-3334 0123 E jaas@jac.gsi.gov.uk
W https://jac.judiciary.gov.uk

The Judicial Appointments Commission was established as an independent non-departmental public body in April 2006 by the Constitutional Reform Act 2005. Its role is to select judicial office holders independently of government (a responsibility previously held by the Lord Chancellor) for courts and tribunals in England and Wales, and for some tribunals whose jurisdiction extends to Scotland or Northern Ireland. It has a statutory duty to encourage diversity in the range of persons available for selection and is sponsored by the Ministry of Justice and accountable to parliament through the Lord Chancellor. It is made up of 15 commissioners, including a chair.

Chair, Rt. Hon. Lord Kakkar
Commissioners, Judge Mathu Asokan; Emir Khan Feisal; Martin Forde, QC; Jane Furness, CBE; Her Hon. Judge Usha Karu; Andrew Kennon; Prof. Noel Lloyd, CBE; Alexandra Marks, CBE; Fiona Monk; Dame Valerie Strachan, DCB; His Hon. Judge Phillip Sycamore; Sir Simon Wessely
Chief Executive, Richard Jarvis

JUDICIAL OFFICE
The Judicial Office was established in April 2006 to support the judiciary in discharging its responsibilities under the Constitutional Reform Act 2005. It is led by a chief executive, who reports to the Lord Chief Justice rather than to ministers, and its work is directed by the judiciary rather than by the administration of the day. The Judicial Office incorporates the Judicial College, sponsorship of the Family and Civil Justice Councils, the Office for Judicial Complaints and Office of the Chief Coroner.

Chief Executive, Andrew Key

JUDICIAL COMMITTEE OF THE PRIVY COUNCIL
The Judicial Committee of the Privy Council is the final court of appeal for the United Kingdom overseas territories (*see* UK Overseas Territories section), crown dependencies and those independent Commonwealth countries which have retained this avenue of appeal and the sovereign base areas of Akrotiri and Dhekelia in Cyprus. The committee also hears appeals against pastoral schemes under the Pastoral Measure 1983, and deals with appeals from veterinary disciplinary bodies.

Until October 2009, the Judicial Committee of the Privy Council was the final arbiter in disputes as to the legal competence of matters done or proposed by the devolved legislative and executive authorities in Scotland, Wales and Northern Ireland. This is now the responsibility of the UK Supreme Court.

The members of the Judicial Committee are the justices of the supreme court, and Privy Counsellors who hold or have held high judicial office in the United Kingdom or in certain designated courts of Commonwealth countries from which appeals are taken to committee.

JUDICIAL COMMITTEE OF THE PRIVY COUNCIL
Parliament Square, London SW1P 3BD T 020-7960 1500
W www.jcpc.uk
Chief Executive, Mark Ormerod
Registrar of the Privy Council, Louise di Mambro

SCOTTISH JUDICATURE
Scotland has a legal system separate from, and differing greatly from, the English legal system in enacted law, judicial procedure and the structure of courts.

In Scotland the system of public prosecution is headed by the Lord Advocate and is independent of the police, who have no say in the decision to prosecute. The Lord Advocate, discharging his functions through the Crown Office in Edinburgh, is responsible for prosecutions in the high court, sheriff courts and justice of the peace courts. Prosecutions in the high court are prepared by the Crown Office and conducted in court by one of the law officers, by an advocate-depute, or by a solicitor advocate. In the inferior courts the decision to prosecute is made and prosecution is preferred by procurators fiscal, who are lawyers and full-time civil servants subject to the directions of the Crown Office. A permanent legally qualified civil servant, known as the crown agent, is responsible for the running of the Crown Office and the organisation of the Procurator Fiscal Service, of which he or she is the head.

Scotland is divided into six sheriffdoms, each with a full-time sheriff principal. The sheriffdoms are further divided into sheriff court districts, each of which has a legally qualified resident sheriff or sheriffs, who are the judges of the court.

In criminal cases sheriffs principal and sheriffs have the same powers; sitting with a jury of 15 members, they may try more serious cases on indictment, or, sitting alone, may try lesser cases under summary procedure. Minor summary offences are dealt with in justice of the peace courts, which replaced district courts formerly operated by local authorities, and presided over by lay justices of the peace (of whom some 500 regularly sit in court) and, in Glasgow only, by stipendiary magistrates. Juvenile offenders (children under 16) may be brought before an informal children's hearing comprising three local lay people. The superior criminal court is the high court of justiciary which is both a trial and an appeal court. Cases on indictment are tried by a high court judge, sitting with a jury of 15, in Edinburgh and on circuit in other towns. Appeals from the lower courts against conviction or sentence are also heard by the high court, which sits as an appeal court only in Edinburgh. There is no further appeal to the UK supreme court in criminal cases.

In civil cases the jurisdiction of the sheriff court extends to most kinds of action. Appeals against decisions of the sheriff may be made to the sheriff principal and thence to the court of session, or direct to the court of session, which sits only in Edinburgh. The court of session is divided into the inner and the outer house. The outer house is a court of first instance in which cases are heard by judges sitting singly, sometimes with a jury of 12. The inner house, itself subdivided into two divisions of equal status, is mainly an appeal court. Appeals may be made to the inner house from the outer house as well as from the sheriff court. An appeal may be made from the inner house to the UK supreme court.

The judges of the court of session are the same as those of the high court of justiciary, with the Lord President of the court of session also holding the office of Lord Justice General in the high court. Senators of the College of Justice are Lords Commissioners of Justiciary as well as judges of the court of session. On appointment, a senator takes a judicial title, which is retained for life. Although styled The Hon./Rt. Hon. Lord, the senator is not a peer, although some judges are peers in their own right.

The office of coroner does not exist in Scotland. The local procurator fiscal inquires privately into sudden or suspicious deaths and may report findings to the crown agent. In some cases a fatal accident inquiry may be held before the sheriff.

COURT OF SESSION AND HIGH COURT OF JUSTICIARY
The Lord President and Lord Justice General (£225,091), Rt. Hon. Lord Carloway, *born* 1954, *apptd* 2015
Private Secretary, Paul Gilmour

INNER HOUSE
Lords of Session (each £206,742)

FIRST DIVISION
The Lord President
Rt. Hon. Lord Menzies (Duncan Menzies), *born* 1953, *apptd* 2012
Rt. Hon. Lady Smith (Anne Smith), *born* 1955, *apptd* 2012
Rt. Hon. Lord Brodie (Philip Brodie), *born* 1950, *apptd* 2012
Rt. Hon. Lady Clark of Calton (Lynda Clark), *born* 1949, *apptd* 2013
Rt. Hon. Lord Glennie (Angus Glennie), *born* 1950, *apptd* 2016

SECOND DIVISION
Lord Justice Clerk (£217,409), Rt. Hon. Lady Dorrian (Leona Dorrian), *born* 1957, *apptd* 2016
Rt. Hon. Lady Paton (Ann Paton), *born* 1952, *apptd* 2007
Rt. Hon. Lord Drummond Young (James Drummond Young), *born* 1950, *apptd* 2013
Rt. Hon. Lord Malcolm (Colin M. Campbell), *born* 1953, *apptd* 2015
Hon. Lord Turnbull (Alan Turnbull), *born* 1958, *apptd* 2016

OUTER HOUSE
Lords of Session (each £181,566)
Hon. Lord Kinclaven (Alexander F. Wylie, OBE), *born* 1951, *apptd* 2005
Hon. Lord Brailsford (S. Neil Brailsford), *born* 1954, *apptd* 2006
Hon. Lord Uist (Roderick Macdonald), *born* 1951, *apptd* 2006
Hon. Lord Matthews (Hugh Matthews), *born* 1953, *apptd* 2007
Hon. Lord Woolman (Stephen Woolman), *born* 1953, *apptd* 2008
Hon. Lord Pentland (Paul Cullen), *born* 1957, *apptd* 2008
Hon. Lord Bannatyne (Iain Peebles, QC), *born* 1954, *apptd* 2008
Hon. Lady Stacey (Valerie E. Stacey), *born* 1954, *apptd* 2009
Hon. Lord Tyre (Colin Tyre, CBE), *born* 1956, *apptd* 2010
Hon. Lord Doherty (J. Raymond Doherty), *born* 1958, *apptd* 2010
Rt. Hon. Lord Boyd of Duncansby (Colin Boyd), *born* 1953, *apptd* 2012
Hon. Lord Burns (David Burns), *born* 1952, *apptd* 2012
Hon. Lady Scott (Margaret Scott), *born* 1960, *apptd* 2012
Hon. Lady Wise (Morag Wise), *born* 1963, *apptd* 2013
Hon. Lord Armstrong (Iain Armstrong), *born* 1956, *apptd* 2013
Hon. Lady Rae (Rita Rae), *born* 1950, *apptd* 2014
Hon. Lady Wolffe (Sarah Wolffe, QC), *apptd* 2014
Hon. Lord Beckett (John Beckett, QC), *apptd* 2016
Hon. Lord Clark (Alistair Clark, QC), *born* 1955, *apptd* 2016
Hon. Lord Ericht (Andrew Stewart, QC), *born* 1963, *apptd* 2016
Hon. Lady Carmichael (Ailsa Carmichael, QC), *born* 1969, *apptd* 2016
Rt. Hon. Lord Mulholland (Frank Mulholland, QC), *born* 1959, *apptd* 2016
Hon. Lord Summers (Alan Summers, QC), *born* 1964, *apptd* 2017
Hon. Lord Arthurson (Paul Arthurson, QC), *born* 1964, *apptd* 2017

COURT OF SESSION AND HIGH COURT OF JUSTICIARY
Parliament House, Parliament Square, Edinburgh EH1 1RQ
T 0131-225 2595

Principal Clerk of Session and Justiciary, Gillian Prentice
Deputy Principal Clerk of Session, Diane Machin
Deputy Principal Clerk of Justiciary, Joe Moyes
Depute in Charge of the Offices of the Court of Session, Yvonne Anderson
Depute in Charge of the Justiciary Office, Ross Martin
Keeper of the Rolls, Trish Fiddes

Assistant Keeper of the Rolls, Michael Stanners
Depute Clerk, Robyn Broome
Appeals Manager, David Cullen
Clerking Services Manager, Nicola Boyle

JUDICIAL APPOINTMENTS BOARD FOR SCOTLAND
Thistle House, 91 Haymarket Terrace, Edinburgh EH12 5HE
T 0131-528 5101 W www.judicialappointments.scot

The board's remit is to provide the first minister with the names of candidates recommended for appointment to the court posts of senator of the college of justice, chair of the Scottish Land Court, sheriff principal, sheriff and part-time sheriff. It is also responsible for recommending individuals to the office of vice-president of the Upper Tribunal; chamber and deputy chamber presidents of the First-tier Tribunal; and members of the Upper Tribunal and First-tier Tribunal.

Chair, Nicola Gordon

Chief Executive, Michael Garden

JUDICIAL OFFICE FOR SCOTLAND
Parliament House, Edinburgh EH1 1RQ
T 0131-240 6677 W www.scotland-judiciary.org.uk
The Judicial Office for Scotland came into being on 1 April 2010 as part of the changes introduced by the Judiciary and Courts (Scotland) Act 2008. It provides support for the Lord President in his role as head of the Scottish judiciary with responsibility for the training, welfare, deployment and conduct of judges and the efficient disposal of business in the courts.
Executive Director, Tim Barraclough

SCOTTISH COURTS AND TRIBUNALS SERVICE
Saughton House, Broomhouse Drive, Edinburgh EH11 3XD
T 0131-444 3300 W www.scotcourts.gov.uk

The Scottish Courts and Tribunals Service (SCTS) is an independent body which was established on 1 April 2010 under the Judiciary and Courts (Scotland) Act 2008. Its function is to provide administrative support to Scottish courts and tribunals and to the judiciary of courts, including the High Court of Justiciary, Court of Session, sheriff courts and justice of the peace courts, and to the Office of the Public Guardian and Accountant of Court.

Chief Executive, Eric McQueen

SCOTTISH GOVERNMENT JUSTICE DIRECTORATE
Legal System Division, Room 2W, St Andrew's House, Edinburgh EH1 3DG
T 0131-556 8400

The Justice Directorate is responsible for the appointment of judges and sheriffs to meet the needs of the business of the supreme and sheriffs court in Scotland. It is also responsible for providing resources for the efficient administration of certain specialist courts and tribunals.

Director (Justice), Neil Rennick

SCOTTISH LAND COURT
126 George Street, Edinburgh EH2 4HH
T 0131-271 4360 W www.scottish-land-court.org.uk

The court deals with disputes relating to agricultural and crofting land in Scotland.
Chair (£145,614), Hon. Lord Miningish (Roderick John MacLeod, QC)
Deputy Chair, Iain Maclean
Members, Tom Campbell; John Smith
Principal Clerk, Barbara Brown

SHERIFF COURTS

The majority of cases in Scotland are handled by one of the 39 sheriff courts. Criminal cases are heard by a sheriff and a jury (solemn procedure) but can be heard by a sheriff alone (summary procedure). Civil cases are heard by a single sheriff.

Scotland is split into six sheriffdoms, each headed by a sheriff principal.

SALARIES
Sheriff Principal, £145,614
Sheriff, £134,841

SHERIFFDOMS

GLASGOW AND STRATHKELVIN
Sheriff Principal, Craig Turnbull

GRAMPIAN, HIGHLAND AND ISLANDS
Sheriff Principal, Derek Pyle

LOTHIAN AND BORDERS
Sheriff Principal, Mhairi Stephen, QC

NORTH STRATHCLYDE
Sheriff Principal, Duncan Murray

SOUTH STRATHCLYDE, DUMFRIES AND GALLOWAY
Sheriff Principal, Ian Abercrombie, QC

TAYSIDE, CENTRAL AND FIFE
Sheriff Principal, Marysia Lewis

JUSTICE OF THE PEACE COURTS

Justice of the peace courts replaced district courts and are a unique feature of Scotland's judicial system. Justices of the peace are lay magistrates who either sit alone, or in a bench of three, and deal with summary crimes such as speeding and careless driving. In court, justices have access to solicitors, who fulfill the role of legal advisers or clerks of court.

A justice of the peace court can be presided over by a stipendiary magistrate – a legally qualified solicitor or advocate who sits alone. They deal with more serious summary business similar to sheriffs, such as drink driving and assault. All sheriffs principal have powers to appoint stipendiary magistrates, but at present there are no justice of the peace courts in the sheriff court districts of Lerwick, Kirkwall, Wick, Stornoway, Lochmaddy and Portree.

CROWN OFFICE AND PROCURATOR FISCAL SERVICE

25 Chambers Street, Edinburgh EH1 1LA
T 0300-020 3000 W www.copfs.gov.uk

The Crown Office and Procurator Fiscal Service (COPFS) is Scotland's prosecution service. COPFS receive reports about crimes from the police and other reporting agencies and then decide what action to take, including whether to prosecute someone. It is also responsible for looking into deaths that need further explanation and investigating allegations of criminal conduct against police officers.

Lord Advocate, James Wolffe, QC
Solicitor-General, Alison Di Rollo
Crown Agent, David Harvie

COURT OF THE LORD LYON

HM New Register House, Edinburgh EH1 3YT
T 0131-556 7255 W www.lyon-court.com

The Court of the Lord Lyon is the Scottish Court of Chivalry (including the genealogical jurisdiction of the *Ri-Sennachie* of Scotland's Celtic kings). The Lord Lyon King of Arms has jurisdiction, subject to appeal to the Court of Session and the House of Lords, in questions of heraldry and the right to bear arms. The court also administers the Public Register of All Arms and Bearings and the Public Register of All Genealogies in Scotland. Pedigrees are established by decrees of Lyon Court and by letters patent. As Royal Commissioner in Armory, the Lord Lyon grants patents of arms to virtuous and well-deserving Scots and to petitioners (personal or corporate) in the Queen's overseas realms of Scottish connection, and also issues birthbrieves. For information on Her Majesty's Officers of Arms in Scotland, *see* the Court of the Lord Lyon in the Public Bodies section.

Lord Lyon King of Arms, Dr Joseph Morrow, QC
Lyon Clerk and Keeper of the Records, Mrs C. G. W. Roads, LVO, FSA SCOT, FSA
Procurator Fiscal, Alexander M. S. Green

NORTHERN IRELAND JUDICATURE

In Northern Ireland the legal system and the structure of courts closely resemble those of England and Wales; there are, however, often differences in enacted law.

The court of judicature of Northern Ireland comprises the court of appeal, the high court of justice and the crown court. The practice and procedure of these courts is similar to that in England. The superior civil court is the high court of justice, from which an appeal lies to the Northern Ireland court of appeal; the UK supreme court is the final civil appeal court.

The crown court, served by high court and county court judges, deals with criminal trials on indictment. Cases are heard before a judge and, except those certified by the Director of Public Prosecutions under the Justice and Security Act 2007, a jury. Appeals from the crown court against conviction or sentence are heard by the Northern Ireland court of appeal; the UK supreme court is the final court of appeal.

The decision to prosecute in criminal cases in Northern Ireland rests with the Director of Public Prosecutions.

Minor criminal offences are dealt with in magistrates' courts by a legally qualified district judge (magistrates' courts) and, where an offender is under the age of 18, by youth courts each consisting of a district judge (magistrates' courts) and two lay magistrates (at least one of whom must be a woman). As at 1 September 2016 there were approximately 210 lay magistrates in Northern Ireland. Appeals from magistrates' courts are heard by the county court, or by the court of appeal on a point of law or an issue as to jurisdiction.

Magistrates' courts in Northern Ireland can deal with certain classes of civil case but most minor civil cases are dealt with in county courts. Judgments of all civil courts are enforceable through a centralised procedure administered by the Enforcement of Judgments Office.

COURT OF JUDICATURE

The Royal Courts of Justice, Chichester Street, Belfast BT1 3JF
T 028-9023 5111 W www.courtsni.gov.uk

Lord Chief Justice of Northern Ireland (£225,091), Rt. Hon. Sir Declan Morgan, *born* 1952, *apptd* 2009

LORDS JUSTICES OF APPEAL (£206,742)
Style, The Rt. Hon. Lord Justice [surname]
    Rt. Hon. Sir John Gillen, *born* 1947, *apptd* 2014
Rt. Hon. Sir Benjamin Stephens, *born* 1954, *apptd* 2017
Rt. Hon. Sir Donnell Deeny, *born* 1950, *apptd* 2017

HIGH COURT JUDGES (£181,566)
Style, The Hon. Mr Justice [surname]
Hon. Sir Seamus Treacy, *born* 1956, *apptd* 2007
Hon. Sir Bernard McCloskey, *born* 1956, *apptd* 2008
Hon. Sir Paul Maguire, *born* 1952, *apptd* 2012
Hon. Sir Mark Horner, *born* 1956, *apptd* 2012
Hon. Sir John O'Hara, *born* 1956, *apptd* 2013
Hon. Sir Adrian Colton, *born* 1959, *apptd* 2015

Hon. Dame Denise McBride, DBE, *apptd* 2015
Hon. Dame Siobhan Keegan, DBE, *born, apptd* 2015

MASTERS OF THE HIGH COURT (£108,171)
Master Bell, *apptd* 2006; Master Hardstaff, *apptd* 2014; Master Kelly, *apptd* 2005; Master McCorry, *apptd* 2001; Master McGivern *apptd* 2015; Master Sweeney, *apptd* 2015; Master Wells, *apptd* 2005

COUNTY COURTS

JUDGES (£145,614†)
Style, His/Her Hon. Judge [surname]

Judge Babington; Judge Crawford; Judge Devlin; Judge Fowler, QC; Judge Grant; Judge Kerr, QC; Judge Kinney; Judge Lynch, QC; Judge McCaffrey; Judge McColgan, QC; Judge McFarland; Judge McReynolds; Judge Marrinan; Judge Miller, QC; Judge Rafferty, QC; Judge Ramsay, QC; Judge Sherrard; Judge Smyth

† County court judges are paid £145,614 so long as they are required to carry out significantly different work from their counterparts elsewhere in the UK

RECORDERS
Belfast (£157,263), Judge McFarland
Londonderry (£145,614), Judge Babington

DISTRICT JUDGES (£108,171)
Only barristers and solicitors with ten years' standing are eligible to become district judges. There are four district judges in Northern Ireland:
District Judge Brownlie; District Judge Collins; District Judge Duncan; District Judge Gilpin

MAGISTRATES' COURTS

DISTRICT JUDGES (MAGISTRATES' COURTS) (£108,171)
There are usually 21 district judges (magistrates' courts) in Northern Ireland:
District Judge Bagnall; District Judge Bates; District Judge Brady; District Judge Broderick; District Judge Conner; District Judge Copeland; District Judge Hamill; District Judge Henderson; District Judge Kelly; District Judge E. King; District Judge P. King; District Judge McCourt; District Judge McElholm; District Judge McKibbin; District Judge McNally; District Judge Magill; District Judge Meehan; District Judge Mullan; District Judge Prytherch; District Judge Watters

NORTHERN IRELAND COURTS AND TRIBUNALS SERVICE
23–27 Oxford Street, Belfast BT1 3LA
T 0300-200 7812 W www.courtsni.gov.uk
Chief Executive (acting), Peter Luney

CROWN SOLICITOR'S OFFICE
Royal Courts of Justice, Chichester Street, Belfast BT1 3JE
T 028-9054 2555
Crown Solicitor, Fiona Chamberlain

PUBLIC PROSECUTION SERVICE
Belfast Chambers, 93 Chichester Street, Belfast BT1 3JR
T 028-9089 7100 W www.ppsni.gov.uk
Director of Public Prosecutions, Barra McGrory, QC

TRIBUNALS

Information on all the tribunals listed here, with the exception of the independent tribunals and the tribunals based in Scotland, Wales and Northern Ireland, can be found on the Ministry of Justice website (W www.justice.gov.uk/tribunals).

HM COURTS AND TRIBUNALS SERVICE

102 Petty France, London SW1H 9AJ
W www.gov.uk/government/organisations/
hm-courts-and-tribunals-service
W www.gov.uk/find-court-tribunal

HM Courts Service and the Tribunals Service merged on 1 April 2011 to form HM Courts and Tribunals Service, an integrated agency providing support for the administration of justice in courts and tribunals. It is an agency within the Ministry of Justice, operating as a partnership between the Lord Chancellor, the Lord Chief Justice and the Senior President of Tribunals. It is responsible for the administration of the criminal, civil and family courts and tribunals in England and Wales and non-devolved tribunals in Scotland and Northern

Ireland. The agency's work is overseen by a board headed by an independent chair working with non-executive, executive and judicial members.

A two-tier tribunal system, comprising the First-tier Tribunal and Upper Tribunal, was established on 3 November 2008 as a result of radical reform under the Tribunals, Courts and Enforcement Act 2007. Both of these tiers are split into a number of separate chambers. These chambers group together individual tribunals (also known as 'jurisdictions') which deal with similar work or require similar skills. Cases start in the First-tier Tribunal and there is a right of appeal to the Upper Tribunal. Some tribunals transferred to the new two-tier system immediately, with more transferring between 2009 and 2011. The exception is employment tribunals, which remain outside this structure. The Act also allowed legally qualified tribunal chairs and adjudicators to swear the judicial oath and become judges.

Senior President, Rt. Hon. Sir Ernest Ryder, TD
Chief Executive, Susan Acland-Hood

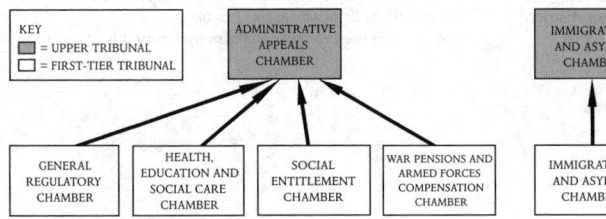

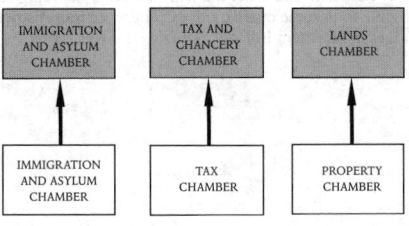

FIRST-TIER TRIBUNAL

The main function of the First-tier Tribunal is to hear appeals by citizens against decisions of the government. In most cases appeals are heard by a panel made up of one judge and two specialists in their relevant field, known as 'members'. Both judges and members are appointed through the Independent Judicial Appointments Commission. Most of the tribunals administered by central government are part of the First-tier Tribunal, which is split into seven separate chambers.

GENERAL REGULATORY CHAMBER
For all jurisdictions: General Regulatory Chamber, HMCTS, PO Box 9300, Leicester LE1 8DJ T 0300-123 4504 E grc@hmcts.gsi.gov.uk
Chamber President, Judge Lane

CHARITY
Under the Charities Act 2011 (only applicable to England and Wales), First-tier Tribunal (Charity) hears appeals against the decisions of the Charity Commission, applications for the review of decisions made by the Charity Commission and considers references from the Attorney-General or the Charity Commission on points of law.

CLAIMS MANAGEMENT SERVICES
Under section 13 of the Compensation Act 2006, Claims Management Services hears appeals pertaining to decisions made by the claims regulator, such as the regulator's decision to cancel or suspend a claims management licence, refuse authorisation for claims management services or add conditions to a claims management licence. Claims

management services include all companies and individuals that offer a service for people hoping to claim compensation for personal injury, mis-sold financial products and services, redundancy, criminal or industrial injury and housing disrepair.

COMMUNITY RIGHT TO BID
The Community Right to Bid jurisdiction of the General Regulatory Chamber was established in January 2013 and hears appeals against review decisions made by local authorities to list your property as a community asset and give local communities the right to bid for it if you decide to sell. Individuals have the right to appeal against a listing decision under the Localism Act 2011 and the assets of community value (England) regulations 2012.

CONVEYANCING
The professional regulation jurisdiction hears appeals against decisions made by the Council for Licensed Conveyancers under the Legal Services Act 2007.

COPYRIGHT LICENSING
Under the copyright (regulation of relevant licensing bodies) regulations 2014 a copyright licensing body may appeal to a First-tier Tribunal (Copyright Licensing) against a government decision to fine or impose a code of conduct on their organisation.

DRIVING INSTRUCTORS
First-tier Tribunal (Driving Instructors) hears appeals against decisions made by the Registrar of Approved Driving

Instructors under the Road Traffic Act 1988, Transport Act 2000 and the Motor Cars (Driving Instruction) Regulations 2005. Its jurisdiction covers England, Scotland and Wales.

ELECTRONIC COMMUNICATIONS AND POSTAL SERVICES

Hears appeals against decisions made by the Interception of Communications Commissioner under the Regulation of Investigatory Powers (Monetary Penalty Notices and Consents for Interceptions) Regulations 2011.

ENVIRONMENT

First-tier Tribunal (Environment) was created to decide appeals regarding civil sanctions made by environmental regulators. Established in April 2010, the jurisdiction of the tribunal extends to England and Wales.

ESTATE AGENTS

First-tier Tribunal (Estate Agents) hears appeals, under the Estate Agents Act 1979, against decisions made by the Office of Fair Trading pertaining to orders prohibiting a person from being employed as an estate agent when that person has been, for example, convicted of fraud or another offence involving dishonesty. The tribunal also hears appeals relating to decisions refusing to revoke or vary a prohibition order or warning order, as well as appeals regarding the issuing of a warning order when a person has not fulfilled their obligations under the Act.

EXAM BOARDS

Under the Education Act 1997 regulated awarding organisations can appeal to the Exam Board tribunal if they disagree with a decision by OFQUAL or the Welsh government to impose a fine, the amount of the fine, or to recover the costs of taking enforcement action. The board is an independent tribunal and hears appeals across England and Wales.

FOOD

The food jurisdiction of the General Regulatory Chamber was established in January 2013 and hears appeals against some of the decisions taken by the Food Standards Agency, Department for Environment, Food and Rural Affairs and local authority trading standards departments. It also deals with appeals against decisions under the Fish Labelling (England) Regulations.

GAMBLING

First-tier Tribunal (Gambling) hears and decides appeals against decisions made by the Gambling Commission under the Gambling Act 2005.

IMMIGRATION SERVICES

First-tier Tribunal (Immigration Services) is an independent judicial body established in 2000. It hears appeals against decisions made by the Office of the Immigration Services Commissioner and considers disciplinary charges brought against immigration advisers by the Commissioner. The tribunal does not deal with immigration and asylum cases.

INFORMATION RIGHTS

First-tier Tribunal (Information Rights) determines appeals against notices issued by the Information Commissioner under the Freedom of Information Act 2000 and other regulations.

When a minister of the crown issues a certificate on the grounds of national security, the appeal must be transferred to the Administrative Appeals Chamber of the Upper Tribunal on receipt.

LETTING OR MANAGING AGENTS

First-tier Tribunal (Letting or Managing Agents) hears appeals against a decision by a local authority or the Trading Standards

Office to impose a fine on an agent for not being a member of an approved complaints scheme or for not clearly publicising fees under The Redress Schemes for Lettings Agency Work and Property Management Work (Requirements to Belong to a Scheme etc) (England) Order 2014 and schedule 9 of the Consumer Rights Act 2015.

MICROCHIPPING DOGS

Established under the Microchipping of Dogs (England) Regulations 2015, appeals can be made to First-Tier Tribunal (Microchipping Dogs) against a decision by the Department for the Environment and Rural Affairs to ban or stop an individual from microchipping dogs or from running a database on microchipped dogs. Dog owners can also appeal against a notice to microchip their dog served by the police or local authority.

PENSIONS REGULATION

First-tier Tribunal (Pensions) hears appeals against decisions made by the Pensions Regulator under section 44 of the Pensions Act 2008. Appeals under section 102 of the Act are heard by the Tax and Chancery Chamber of the Upper Tribunal.

HEALTH, EDUCATION AND SOCIAL CARE CHAMBER

Chamber President, His Hon. Judge Sycamore

CARE STANDARDS

First-tier Tribunal (Care Standards), 1st Floor Darlington Magistrates' Court, Parkgate DL1 1RU
T 01325-289350 E cst@hmcts.gsi.gov.uk

First-tier Tribunal (Care Standards) was established under the Protection of Children Act 1999 and considers appeals in relation to decisions made by the Secretary of State for Education, the Secretary of State for Health, the Care Quality Commission, OFSTED or the Care Council for Wales about the inclusion of individuals' names on the list of those considered unsuitable to work with children or vulnerable adults, restrictions from teaching and employment in schools/ further education institutions, and the registration of independent schools. It also deals with general registration decisions made about care homes, children's homes, childcare providers, nurses' agencies, social workers, residential family centres, independent hospitals and fostering agencies.

MENTAL HEALTH

PO Box 8793, 5th Floor, Leicester LE1 8BN
T 0300-123 2201 E mhrtenquiries@hmcts.gsi.gov.uk

The First-tier Tribunal (Mental Health) hears applications and references for people detained under the Mental Health Act 1983 (as amended by the Mental Health Act 2007). There are separate mental health tribunals for Wales and Scotland.

PRIMARY HEALTH LISTS

First-tier Tribunal (Primary Health Lists), 1st Floor Darlington Magistrates' Court, Parkgate DL1 1RU
T 01325-289350

First-tier Tribunal (Primary Health Lists) hears appeals against decisions made by the NHS Commissioning Board to not include, to remove or to change the conditions of inclusion for medical practitioners and providers on the NHS medical, dental, ophthalmic or pharmaceutical lists.

SPECIAL EDUCATIONAL NEEDS AND DISABILITY

First-tier Tribunal (SEND), 1st Floor Darlington Magistrates' Court, Parkgate DL1 1RU
T 01325-289350 E sendistqueries@hmcts.gsi.gov.uk

First-tier Tribunal (Special Educational Needs and Disability) considers parents' appeals against the decisions of local authorities about children's special educational needs if parents cannot reach agreement with the local authority. It also considers claims of disability discrimination in schools.

IMMIGRATION AND ASYLUM CHAMBER
Chamber President, Judge Clements
PO Box 6987, Leicester LE1 6ZX
T 0300-123 1711 E customer.service@hmcts.gsi.gov.uk

The Immigration and Asylum Chamber is an independent tribunal dealing with appeals against decisions made by the Home Office concerning immigration, asylum and nationality matters.

PROPERTY CHAMBER
Chamber President, Judge McGrath
10 Alfred Place, London WC1E 7LR
T 020-7291 7250 E rplondon@hmcts.gsi.gov.uk

The First-tier Tribunal (Property Chamber) handles applications, appeals and references relating to disputes over property and land. It serves the private-rented and leasehold property market in England regarding rent increases, leasehold disputes, improvement notices under the Housing Act 2004, land registration matters and agricultural land and drainage matters.

SOCIAL ENTITLEMENT CHAMBER
Chamber President, His Hon. Judge Aitken

ASYLUM SUPPORT
2nd Floor, Anchorage House, 2 Clove Crescent, London E14 2BE
T 0800-681 6509

First-tier Tribunal (Asylum Support) deals with appeals against decisions made by the Home Office. The Home Office decides whether asylum seekers, failed asylum seekers and/or their dependants are entitled to support and accommodation on the grounds of destitution, as provided by the Immigration and Asylum Act 1999. The tribunal can only consider appeals against a refusal or termination of support. It can, if appropriate, require the Secretary of State for the Home Department to reconsider the original decision, substitute the original decision with the tribunal's own decision or dismiss the appeal.

CRIMINAL INJURIES COMPENSATION
3rd Floor Wellington House, 134–136 Wellington Street, Glasgow
G2 2XL T 0141-354 8555 E cic.enquiries@hmcts.gsi.gov.uk

First-tier Tribunal (Criminal Injuries Compensation) determines appeals against review decisions made by the Criminal Injuries Compensation Authority on applications for compensation made by victims of violent crime.

SOCIAL SECURITY AND CHILD SUPPORT
England and Wales, T 0300-123 1142
Scotland, T 0141-354 8400

First-tier Tribunal (Social Security and Child Support) arranges and hears appeals against decisions made by the Department for Work and Pensions and HM Revenue and Customs regarding social security benefits. Appeals considered include those concerned with: attendance, bereavement and carer's allowances; child benefit; child support; the compensation recovery scheme (including NHS recovery claims); diffuse mesotheliomia and the industrial injuries disablement benefit payment schemes; income support; jobseeker's allowance; tax credits; universal credit; and vaccine damage payment.

TAX CHAMBER
Chamber President, Judge Sinfield
PO Box 16972, Birmingham B16 6TZ
T 0300-123 1024 E taxappeals@hmcts.gsi.gov.uk

First-tier Tribunal Tax Chamber hears most appeals against decisions made by HM Revenue and Customs in relation to income tax, corporation tax, capital gains tax, inheritance tax, stamp duty land tax, statutory sick and maternity pay, national insurance contributions and VAT or duties. The tribunal also hears some appeals relating to goods seized by HM Revenue and Customs or Border Force and against some decisions made by the National Crime Agency. Appeals can be made by individuals or organisations, single taxpayers or large multinational companies. First-tier Tribunal (Tax) also hears appeals against certain decisions made by a compliance officer, an independent office holder appointed by the Independent Parliamentary Standards Authority, the organisation responsible for determining and paying MP expenses. Appeals can be made by current or former MPs under the Parliamentary Standards Act 2009. The jurisdiction is UK-wide.

WAR PENSIONS AND ARMED FORCES COMPENSATION CHAMBER
Chamber President, Hon. Sir William Charles
5th Floor, Fox Court, 14 Gray's Inn Road, London WC1X 8HN
T 020-3206 0701 E armedforces.chamber@hmcts.gsi.gov.uk

The War Pensions and Armed Forces Compensation Chamber of the First-tier Tribunal hears appeals brought by ex-servicemen and women against decisions by Veterans UK regarding pensions, compensation and other amounts under the war pensions legislation for injuries sustained before 5 April 2005, and under the armed forces compensation scheme for injuries after that date.

UPPER TRIBUNAL

Comprising four separate chambers, the Upper Tribunal deals mostly with appeals from, and enforcement of, decisions taken by the First-tier Tribunal, but it also handles some cases that do not go through the First-tier Tribunal. Additionally, it has assumed some of the supervisory powers of the courts to deal with the actions of tribunals, government departments and some other public authorities. All the decision-makers of the Upper Tribunal are judges or expert members sitting in a panel chaired by a judge, and are specialists in the areas of law they handle. Over time their decisions are expected to build comprehensive case law for each area covered by the tribunals.

ADMINISTRATIVE APPEALS CHAMBER
Chamber President, Hon. Sir William Charles
England and Wales, 5th Floor, 7 Rolls Building, Fetter Lane,
London EC4A 1NL T 020-7071 5662
E adminappeals@hmcts.gsi.gov.uk
Scotland, George House, 126 George Street, Edinburgh EH2 4HH
T 0131-271 4310 E UTAAmailbox@scotland.gsi.gov.uk
Northern Ireland, Tribunal Hearing Centre, 2nd Floor Royal Courts
of Justice, Chichester Street, Belfast BT1 3JF T 028-9072 4883
E tribunalsunit@courtsni.gov.uk

The Administrative Appeals Chamber appeals against decisions made by certain lower tribunals and organisations including: social security and child support, war pensions and armed forces compensation, mental health, special education needs or disabilities, disputes heard by the General Regulatory Chamber, decisions made by the Disclosure and Barring Service, decisions made by the Traffic Commissioner (or the Transport Regulation Unit in Northern Ireland), Special Education Needs Tribunal for Wales, Mental Health Review Tribunal for Wales and the Pensions Appeal Tribunal in Northern Ireland (only for assessment appeals under the War

Pensions Scheme). It also handles applications for judicial review of decisions made by: First-tier Tribunal (Criminal Injuries Compensation) and other first-tier tribunals where there is no right of appeal.

IMMIGRATION AND ASYLUM CHAMBER
Chamber President, Hon. Sir Bernard McCloskey
1A Field House, 15–25 Bream's Buildings, London EC4A 1DZ
T 0300-123 1711 E fieldhousecorrespondence@hmcts.gsi.gov.uk
The Immigration and Asylum Chamber hears appeals against decisions made by the First-tier Tribunal (Immigration and Asylum) relating to visa and asylum applications and the right to enter or stay in the UK. The chamber also deals with applications for judicial review of certain decisions made by the Home Office relating to immigration, asylum and human rights claims.

LANDS CHAMBER
Chamber President, Hon. Sir David Holgate
5th Floor, 7 Rolls Buildings, London EC4A 1NL
T 020-7612 9710 E lands@hmcts.gsi.gov.uk

The Lands Chamber is responsible for handling appeals against decisions made by the First-tier Tribunal (Property Chamber) (except decisions about land registration), the Residential Property Tribunal in Wales and the Leasehold Valuation Tribunal in Wales. It is also responsible for handling applications for cases regarding decisions about rates made by the Valuation Tribunal in England or Wales, compensation for the compulsory purchase of land, discharge or modification of land affected by a 'restrictive covenant', compensation for the effect on land affected by public works, a tree preservation order, compensation for damage to land damaged by subsidence from mining, the valuation of land or buildings for Capital Gains Tax or Inheritance Tax purposes and compensation for blighted land.

TAX AND CHANCERY CHAMBER
Chamber President, Hon. Dame Vivien Rose, DBE
5th Floor, 7 Rolls Buildings, London EC4A 1NL
T 020-7612 9700 E uttc@hmcts.gsi.gov.uk

The Tax and Chancery Chamber hears appeals against decisions made by the First-tier Tribunal (Tax), the land registration division of the First-tier Tribunal (Property Chamber) and the General Regulatory Chamber in cases relating to charities. The chamber also hears appeals against decisions issued by the Financial Conduct Authority, the Prudential Regulation Authority, the Pensions Regulator, the Bank of England, HM Treasury and OFGEM.

SPECIAL IMMIGRATION APPEALS COMMISSION
15–25 Bream's Buildings, London EC4A 1DZ
T 0300-123 1711

The commission was set up under the Special Immigration Appeals Commission Act 1997. It remains separate from the First-tier and Upper Tribunal structure but is part of HM Courts and Tribunals Service. Its main function is to consider appeals against orders for deportation or exclusion, or orders withdrawing or refusing British nationality, in cases which involve considerations of national security.
Chair, Rt. Hon. Sir Julian Flaux

EMPLOYMENT TRIBUNALS
Employment Tribunal Central Office England and Wales, PO Box 10218, Leicester LE1 8EG T 0300-123 1024
Employment Tribunal Central Office Scotland, PO Box 27105, Glasgow G2 9JR T 0141-354 8574

Employment tribunals hear claims regarding matters of employment law, redundancy, dismissal, contract disputes, sexual, racial and disability discrimination and related areas of dispute which may arise in the workplace.

President (England and Wales), Judge Doyle
President (Scotland), Judge Simon

EMPLOYMENT APPEAL TRIBUNAL
Employment Appeal Tribunal England and Wales, 2nd Floor, Fleetbank House, 2–6 Salisbury Square, London EC4Y 8AE
T 020-7273 1041 E londoneat@hmcts.gsi.gov.uk
Employment Appeal Tribunal Scotland, 52 Melville Street, Edinburgh EH3 7HF T 0131-225 3963
E edinburgheat@hmcts.gsi.gov.uk

The Employment Appeal Tribunal hears appeals (on points of law only) arising from decisions made by employment tribunals.

President, Hon. Dame Ingrid Simler, DBE

SCOTTISH COURTS AND TRIBUNALS SERVICE
Saughton House, Broomhouse Drive, Edinburgh EH11 3XD
T 0131-444 3300
W www.scotcourts.gov.uk
E enquiries@scotcourts.gov.uk

The Tribunals (Scotland) Act 2014 created a new, simplified statutory framework for tribunals in Scotland, bringing existing jurisdictions together and providing a structure for new ones. The Act created two new tribunals, the First-tier Tribunal for Scotland and the Upper Tribunal for Scotland.
The Lord President is the head of the Scottish Tribunals and has delegated various functions to the President of Scottish Tribunals.
President of Scottish Tribunals, Rt. Hon. Lady Smith (Anne Smith)

THE UPPER TRIBUNAL FOR SCOTLAND
4th Floor, 1 Atlantic Quay, 45 Robertson Street, Glasgow G2 8JB
T 0141-302 5880
E uppertribunalforscotland@scotcourtstribunals.gov.uk

The Upper Tribunal hears appeals on decisions of the chambers of the First-tier Tribunal.

THE FIRST-TIER TRIBUNAL FOR SCOTLAND
The First-tier Tribunal is organised into chambers. From 1 December 2016, the Housing and Property Chamber was established and took on the functions of the former Home Owner and Housing Panel and the Private Rented Housing Panel.
From 24 April 2017, the Tax Chamber was established and took on the functions of the former Tax Tribunals for Scotland.

HOUSING AND PROPERTY CHAMBER FIRST-TIER TRIBUNAL FOR SCOTLAND
4th Floor, 1 Atlantic Quay, 45 Robertson Street, Glasgow G2 8JB
T 0141-302 5900

TAX CHAMBER FIRST-TIER TRIBUNAL FOR SCOTLAND
George House, 126 George Street, Edinburgh EH2 4HH
T 0131-271 4385
E taxtribs@scotcourtstribunals.gov.uk

The Scottish Courts and Tribunals Service currently provides administrative support for the following Scottish tribunals:

THE ADDITIONAL SUPPORT NEEDS TRIBUNAL FOR
SCOTLAND, 4th Floor, 1 Atlantic Quay, 45 Robertson Street,

Glasgow G2 8JB **T** 0141-302 5860
E ASNTSAdmin@scotcourtstribunals.gov.uk
W www.asntscotland.gov.uk
President, May Dunsmuir

COUNCIL TAX REDUCTION REVIEW PANEL, 4th Floor,
1 Atlantic Quay, 45 Robertson Street, Glasgow G2 8JB
T 0141-302 5840 **E** ctrrpadmin@scotcourtstribunals.gov.uk
W www.counciltaxreductionreview.scotland.gov.uk

THE LANDS TRIBUNAL FOR SCOTLAND, George House,
126 George Street, Edinburgh EH2 4HH **T** 0131-271 4350
E LTS_mailbox@scotcourtstribunals.gov.uk
W www.lands-tribunal-scotland.org.uk
President, Hon. Lord Minginish (Roderick MacLeod)

THE MENTAL HEALTH TRIBUNAL FOR SCOTLAND,
Bothwell House, First Floor, Hamilton Business Park, Caird Park,
Hamilton ML3 0QA **T** 0800-345 7060
E mhtsTeam1@scotcourtstribunals.gov.uk
W www.mhtscotland.gov.uk
President, Dr Joe Morrow

THE PENSIONS APPEAL TRIBUNAL SCOTLAND,
George House, 126 George Street, Edinburgh EH2 4HH **T** 0131-
271 4340 **E** PAT_Info_Mailbox@scotcourtstribunals.gov.uk
W www.patscotland.org.uk
President, Marion Caldwell, QC

THE SCOTTISH CHARITY APPEALS PANEL, George
House, 126 George Street, Edinburgh EH2 4HH
T 0131-271 4340 **E** scap@scotcourtstribunals.gov.uk
W www.scap.gov.uk
Chairs, Aileen Devanny; Joseph Hughes; Gary McIlravey; John
Walker

NORTHERN IRELAND COURTS AND TRIBUNALS SERVICE

Laganside House, 23–27 Oxford Street, Belfast BT1 3LA
T 028-9032 8594 **W** www.courtsni.gov.uk
Lord Chief Justice of Northern Ireland, Rt. Hon. Sir Declan
Morgan

The Northern Ireland Courts and Tribunals Service currently
provides administrative support for the following Northern
Ireland tribunals. All the tribunals below, unless otherwise
specified, can be contacted at: 2nd Floor, Royal Courts of Justice,
Chichester Street, Belfast BT1 3JF **T** 0300-200 7812
E tribunalsunit@courtsni.gov.uk

THE APPEALS SERVICE, 6th Floor, Oyster House, 12
Wellington Place, Belfast BT1 6GE **T** 028-9054 4000
E appeals.service.belfast@dsdni.gov.uk

THE CARE TRIBUNAL
Chairs, Diane Drennan, Stephen Quinn

THE CHARITY TRIBUNAL

**CRIMINAL INJURIES COMPENSATION APPEALS
PANEL NORTHERN IRELAND,**
E cicapnicustomer@courtsni.gov.uk
Chair, Patricia McKaigue

LANDS TRIBUNAL, E landstribunal@courtsni.gov.uk
Registrar, Kevin McQuillan

MENTAL HEALTH REVIEW TRIBUNAL

**NORTHERN IRELAND HEALTH AND SAFETY
TRIBUNAL**

NORTHERN IRELAND TRAFFIC PENALTY TRIBUNAL

NORTHERN IRELAND VALUATION TRIBUNAL

**OFFICE OF SOCIAL SECURITY COMMISSIONERS AND
CHILD SUPPORT COMMISSIONERS**
Chief Commissioner, Dr Kenneth Mullan

**PAROLE COMMISSIONERS FOR NORTHERN
IRELAND,** Laganside Court, Mezzanine 1st Floor, Oxford
Street, Befast BT1 3LL **T** 028-9041 2969
E referrals@parolecomni.x.gsi.gov.uk
Chief Commissioner, Christine Glenn

PENSIONS APPEAL COMMISSIONERS

PENSIONS APPEAL TRIBUNALS

RENT ASSESSMENT PANEL, Cleaver House, 3 Donegall
Square North, Belfast BT1 5GA **T** 028-9051 8518
E appeals.service.belfast@dsdni.gov.uk

**SPECIAL EDUCATIONAL NEEDS AND DISABILITY
TRIBUNAL**

INDEPENDENT TRIBUNALS

The following represents a selection of tribunals not
administered by HM Courts and Tribunals Service.

CIVIL AVIATION AUTHORITY

CAA House, 45–59 Kingsway, London WC2B 6TE
T 0330-022 1500 **E** infoservices@caa.co.uk
W www.caa.co.uk

The Civil Aviation Authority (CAA) does not have a separate
tribunal department as such, but for certain purposes the CAA
must conform to tribunal requirements, for example, to deal
with appeals against the refusal or revocation of aviation
licences and certificates issued by the CAA, and the allocation
of routes outside of the EU to airlines.

The chair and five non-executive members who may sit on
panels for tribunal purposes are appointed by the Secretary of
State for Transport.

Chair, Dame Deirdre Hutton, DBE

COMPETITION APPEAL TRIBUNAL

Victoria House, Bloomsbury Place, London WC1A 2EB
T 020-7979 7979 **E** info@catribunal.org.uk
W www.catribunal.org.uk

The Competition Appeal Tribunal (CAT) is a specialist tribunal
established to hear certain cases in the sphere of UK
competition and economic regulatory law. It hears appeals
against decisions of the Competition and Markets Authority
(CMA) and the sectoral regulators in respect of infringements
of competition law and with respect to mergers and markets.
The CAT also has jurisdiction to award damages in respect of
infringements of EU or UK competition law and to hear
appeals against decisions of the Office of Communications
(OFCOM) in telecommunications matters.

President, Hon. Sir Peter Roth

COPYRIGHT TRIBUNAL

4 Abbey Orchard Street, London SW1P 2HT
T 020-7034 2836 **E** copyright.tribunal@ipo.gov.uk
W www.gov.uk/government/organisations/copyright-tribunal

The Copyright Tribunal resolves disputes over the terms and
conditions of licences offered by, or licensing schemes
operated by, collective management organisations in the
copyright and related rights area. Its decisions are appealable
to the high court on points of law only.

Chair, His Hon. Judge Hacon

INDUSTRIAL TRIBUNALS AND THE FAIR
EMPLOYMENT TRIBUNAL (NORTHERN IRELAND)

Killymeal House, 2 Cromac Quay, Ormeau Road, Belfast BT7 2JD
T 028-9032 7666 **E** mail@employmenttribunalsni.org
W www.employmenttribunalsni.org

The industrial tribunal system in Northern Ireland was set up
in 1965 and has a similar remit to the employment tribunals
in the rest of the UK. There is also a Fair Employment Tribunal,
which hears and determines individual cases of alleged
religious or political discrimination in employment. Employers
can appeal to the Fair Employment Tribunal if they consider
the directions of the Equality Commission to be unreasonable,
inappropriate or unnecessary, and the Equality Commission
can make application to the tribunal for the enforcement of

undertakings or directions with which an employer has not complied.

President, Eileen McBride, CBE

INVESTIGATORY POWERS TRIBUNAL
PO Box 33220, London SW1H 9ZQ
T 020-7035 3711 E info@ipt-uk.com W www.ipt-uk.com

The Investigatory Powers Tribunal replaced the Interception of Communications Tribunal, the Intelligence Services Tribunal, the Security Services Tribunal and the complaints function of the commissioner appointed under the Police Act 1997.

The Regulation of Investigatory Powers Act 2000 (RIPA) provides for a tribunal made up of senior members of the legal profession, independent of the government and appointed by the Queen, to consider all complaints against the intelligence services and those against public authorities in respect of powers covered by RIPA; and to consider proceedings brought under section 7 of the Human Rights Act 1998 against the intelligence services and law enforcement agencies in respect of these powers.

President, Sir Michael Burton

NATIONAL HEALTH SERVICE TRIBUNAL (SCOTLAND)
Anderson Strathern LLP, Lomond House, 9 George Square, Glasgow G2 1DY
T 0141-242 7974 E nhstribunal@nhs.net
W www.nhstribunal.scot.nhs.uk

The Scottish National Health Service Tribunal considers representations that the continued inclusion of a family health service practitioner (eg a doctor, dentist, optometrist or pharmacist) on a health board's list would be prejudicial to the efficiency of the service concerned, by virtue either of fraudulent practices or unsatisfactory personal or professional conduct. If this is established, the tribunal has the power to disqualify practitioners from working in the NHS family health services.

Chair, J. Michael Graham

SOLICITORS' DISCIPLINARY TRIBUNAL
3rd Floor, Gate House, 1 Farringdon Street, London EC4M 7LG
T 020-7329 4808 E enquiries@solicitorsdt.com
W www.solicitorstribunal.org.uk

The Solicitors' Disciplinary Tribunal is an independent statutory body whose members are appointed by the Master of the Rolls. The tribunal adjudicates upon alleged breaches of the rules and regulations applicable to solicitors and their firms, including the Solicitors' Code of Conduct 2007. It also decides applications by former solicitors for restoration to the Roll.

Chair, Edward Nally

SCOTTISH SOLICITORS' DISCIPLINE TRIBUNAL
Unit 3.5, The Granary Business Centre, Coal Road, Cupar, Fife KY15 5YQ
T 01334-659088 E enquiries@ssdt.org.uk W www.ssdt.org.uk

The Scottish Solicitors' Discipline Tribunal is an independent statutory body with a panel of 24 members, 12 of whom are solicitors appointed by the Lord President of the Court of Session. Its principal function is to consider complaints of misconduct against solicitors in Scotland.

Chair, Nicholas Whyte

TRAFFIC PENALTY TRIBUNAL
Springfield House, Water Lane, Wilmslow, Cheshire SK9 5BG
T 0800-160 1999 E help@trafficpenaltytribunal.gov.uk
W www.trafficpenaltytribunal.gov.uk

The Traffic Penalty Tribunal adjudicators consider appeals in relation to penalty charge notices issued by local authorities in England (outside London) and Wales for parking and bus lane contraventions and, additionally in Wales, moving traffic contraventions. The tribunal also considers appeals in relation to penalties issued by the Secretary of State for Transport for failing to pay a charge at the Dartford river crossing and by Durham County Council in the Durham congestion charging zone.

Chief Adjudicator, Caroline Sheppard

VALUATION TRIBUNAL FOR ENGLAND
2nd Floor, 120 Leman Street, London E1 8EU
T 020-7246 3900 W www.valuationtribunal.gov.uk

The Valuation Tribunal for England (VTE) came into being on 1 October 2009, replacing 56 valuation tribunals in England. Provision for the VTE was made in the Local Government and Public Involvement in Health Act 2007. The VTE hears appeals concerning council tax and non-domestic (business) rates, as well as a small number of appeals against drainage boards' assessments of drainage rates. A separate panel is constituted for each hearing, and consists of a chair and usually one or two other members.

The Valuation Tribunal Service (VTS) was created as a corporate body by the Local Government Act 2003, and is responsible for providing or arranging the services required for the operation of the Valuation Tribunal for England. The VTS board consists of a chair and members appointed by the secretary of state. The VTS is sponsored by the Department for Communities and Local Government.

President (VTE), Gary Garland
Chair (VTS), Anne Galbraith, CBE

VALUATION TRIBUNAL FOR WALES
Government Buildings, Block A (L1), Sarn Mynach, Llandudno Junction LL31 9RZ
T 0300-062 5350 E VTWalesnorth@vtw.gsi.gov.uk
W www.valuation-tribunals-wales.org.uk

The Valuation Tribunal for Wales (VTW) was established by the Valuation Tribunal for Wales Regulations 2010, and hears and determines appeals concerning council tax, non-domestic rating and drainage rates in Wales. The governing council, comprising the president, four regional representatives and one member who is appointed by the Welsh government, performs the management functions on behalf of the tribunal.

President, Carol Cobert

OMBUDSMAN SERVICES

The following section is a listing of selected ombudsman services. Ombudsmen are a free, independent and impartial means of resolving certain disputes outside of the courts. These disputes are, in the majority of cases, concerned with whether something has been badly or unfairly handled (for example owing to delay, neglect, inefficiency or failure to follow proper procedures). Most ombudsman schemes are established by statute; they cover various public and private bodies and generally examine matters only after the relevant body has been given a reasonable opportunity to deal with the complaint.

After conducting an investigation an ombudsman will usually issue a written report, which normally suggests a resolution to the dispute and often includes recommendations concerning the improvement of procedures.

OMBUDSMAN ASSOCIATION

PO Box 343, Carshalton, Surrey SM5 9BX
T 020-8894 9272 E secretary@ombudsmanassociation.org
W www.ombudsmanassociation.org

The Ombudsman Association was established in 1994 and exists to provide information to the government, public bodies and the public about ombudsmen and other complaint-handling services in the UK and Ireland. An ombudsman scheme must meet four criteria in order to attain full Ombudsman Association membership: independence from the organisations the ombudsman has the power to investigate, fairness, effectiveness and public accountability. Complaint Handler membership is open to complaint-handling bodies that do not meet these criteria in full. Ombudsmen schemes from the UK, Ireland, British crown dependencies and overseas territories may apply to the Ombudsman Association for membership. The Ombudsman Association publishes a triannual newsletter containing news about ombudsmen and complaint-handling services in the UK, Ireland and overseas, along with topical articles of interest to members of the Association.

Chair, Kieran FitzGerald

The following is a selection of organisations that are members of the Ombudsman Association.

FINANCIAL OMBUDSMAN SERVICE

Exchange Tower, London E14 9SR
T 020-7964 1000 E complaint.info@financial-ombudsman.org.uk
W www.financial-ombudsman.org.uk

The Financial Ombudsman Service settles individual disputes between businesses providing financial services and their customers. The service answers around a million enquiries every year and deals with over 250,000 disputes. The service examines complaints about most financial matters, including banking, insurance, mortgages, pensions, savings, loans and credit cards. *See also* Banking and Finance.

Chief Ombudsman and Chief Executive, Caroline Wayman

HOUSING OMBUDSMAN SERVICE

Exchange Tower, London E14 9GE
T 0300-111 3000 E info@housing-ombudsman.org.uk
W www.housing-ombudsman.org.uk

The Housing Ombudsman Service was established in 1997 to deal with complaints and disputes involving tenants and housing associations and social landlords, certain private-sector landlords and managing agents. The ombudsman has a statutory jurisdiction over all registered social landlords in England. Private and other landlords can join the service on a voluntary basis. On 1 April 2013 a new Housing Ombudsman Service was launched with an extended jurisdiction covering all housing associations and local authorities.

Ombudsman, Denise Fowler

INDEPENDENT POLICE COMPLAINTS COMMISSION (IPCC)

90 High Holborn, London WC1V 6BH
T 0300-020 0096 E enquiries@ipcc.gsi.gov.uk
W www.ipcc.gov.uk

The IPCC succeeded the Police Complaints Authority in 2004. It was established under the Police Reform Act 2002. The IPCC is responsible for carrying out independent investigations into serious incidents or allegations of misconduct by those serving with the police in England and Wales. The IPCC's chair and commissioners must not have worked for the police in any capacity prior to their appointment. It has the power to initiate, undertake and oversee investigations and is also responsible for the way in which complaints are handled by local police forces. The IPCC is also responsible for serious complaints and conduct matters relating to staff at the National Crime Agency (NCA), Her Majesty's Revenue and Customs (HMRC), and the Home Office immigration and enforcement staff. In 2011 the IPCC became responsible for investigating allegations against the Police and Crime Commissioner for each police force area in England and Wales (established 2011) and against the equivalent for the Metropolitan Police, the Mayor's Office for Policing and Crime (MOPAC), set up in 2012.

Chair, Dame Anne Owers, DBE
Deputy Chairs, Rachel Cerfontyne; Sarah Green
Chief Executive, Lesley Longstone

LEGAL OMBUDSMAN

Edward House, Quay Place, Birmingham B1 2RA
T 0300-555 0333 E enquiries@legalombudsman.org.uk
W www.legalombudsman.org.uk

The Legal Ombudsman was set up by the Office for Legal Complaints under the Legal Services Act 2007 and is the single body for all consumer legal complaints in England and Wales. It replaced the Office of the Legal Services Ombudsman in 2010. The Legal Ombudsman aims to resolve disputes between individuals and authorised legal practitioners, including barristers, law cost draftsmen, legal executives, licensed conveyancers, notaries, patent attorneys, probate practitioners, registered European lawyers, solicitors and trade mark attorneys. The Legal Ombudsman is an independent and impartial organisation and deals with various types of complaints against legal services, such as wills, family issues, personal injury and buying or selling a house.

Chief Ombudsman, Kathryn Stone, OBE

LOCAL GOVERNMENT OMBUDSMAN

PO Box 4771, Coventry CV4 0EH
T 0300-061 0614 W www.lgo.org.uk

The Local Government Ombudsman deals with complaints about councils and service failure by local authorities, schools and care providers.

There are two ombudsmen in England, each with responsibility for different regions; they aim to provide satisfactory redress for complainants and better administration by the authorities. The ombudsmen investigate complaints about most council matters, including housing, planning, education, social care, housing benefit, transport and highways, environment and waste, and council tax. *See also* Local Government.

Local Government Ombudsman, Michael King

NORTHERN IRELAND PUBLIC SERVICES OMBUDSMAN

33 Wellington Place, Belfast BT1 6HN
T 028-9023 3821 E nipso@nipso.org.uk
W www.nipso.org.uk

The Office of Northern Ireland Public Services Ombudsman (NIPSO) was established in April 2016, replacing and expanding the functions of the Northern Ireland Assembly Ombudsman and Commissioner for Complaints. NIPSO provides an independent review of complaints of members of the public, where they believe they have sustained an injustice or hardship as a result or inaction of a public service provider. NIPSO additionally ensures that public services improve as a result of the complaints brought to them by the public. The professional, independent and impartial service is provided free of charge to the citizens of Northern Ireland.

Ombudsman, Marie Anderson

OFFICE OF THE PENSIONS OMBUDSMAN

11 Belgrave Road, London SW1V 1RB
T 020-7630 2200 E enquiries@pensions-ombudsman.org.uk
W www.pensions-ombudsman.org.uk
The Pensions Ombudsman is appointed by the Secretary of State for Work and Pensions, under the Pension Schemes Act 1993 as amended by the Pensions Act 1995. He investigates and decides complaints and disputes about the way that personal and occupational pension schemes are run and between members of pensions schemes and their beneficiaries, employers, trustees, managers and scheme administrators. As the ombudsman for the Board of the Pension Protection Fund, he can deal with disputes about the decisions made by the board or the actions of their staff. He also deals with appeals against decisions made by the scheme manager under the Financial Assistance Scheme.

Pensions Ombudsman, Anthony Arter
Deputy Pensions Ombudsman, Karen Johnston

OMBUDSMAN SERVICES

3300 Daresbury Park, Warrington WA4 4HS
W www.ombudsman-services.org

Ombudsman Services was founded in 2002 and provides independent dispute resolution for the communications, copyright licensing, energy and property sectors.

Ombudsman Services: Communications investigates complaints from consumers about companies which provide communication services to the public.

Ombudsman Services: Copyright Licensing helps to resolve complaints about bodies that either own or administer, on behalf of third parties, the licensing of copyright materials.

Ombudsman Services: Energy helps to resolve complaints from consumers about energy (gas and electricity companies). This service is also responsible for handling investigations concerning the government's Green Deal policy, which launched in 2013, and offers long-term loans towards energy-saving home improvements.

Ombudsman Services: Property investigates complaints from consumers about chartered surveying companies, surveyors, estate agents and other property professionals.

Chair, Lord Tim Clement-Jones, CBE
Chief Ombudsman, Lewis Shand Smith

OMBUDSMAN SERVICES: COMMUNICATIONS
PO Box 730, Warrington WA4 6WU
T 0330-440 1614

OMBUDSMAN SERVICES: COPYRIGHT LICENSING
PO Box 1124, Warrington WA4 9GH
T 0330-440 1601

OMBUDSMAN SERVICES: ENERGY
PO Box 966, Warrington WA4 9DF
T 0330-440 1624

OMBUDSMAN SERVICES: PROPERTY
PO Box 1021, Warrington WA4 9FE
T 0330-440 1634

PARLIAMENTARY AND HEALTH SERVICE OMBUDSMAN

Millbank Tower, Millbank, London SW1P 4QP
T 0345-015 4033
W www.ombudsman.org.uk

The Parliamentary Commissioner for Administration (commonly known as the Parliamentary Ombudsman) is independent of government and is an officer of Parliament. She is responsible for investigating complaints referred to her by MPs from members of the public who claim to have sustained injustice in consequence of maladministration by or on behalf of government departments and certain non-departmental public bodies in the UK. Certain types of action by government departments or bodies are excluded from investigation.

The Health Service Ombudsman is responsible for investigating complaints about services funded by the National Health Service in England that have not been dealt with by the service providers to the satisfaction of the complainant. This includes complaints about doctors, dentists, pharmacists and opticians. Complaints can be referred directly by the member of the public who claims to have sustained injustice or hardship in consequence of the failure in a service provided by a relevant organisation.

The two offices of the Parliamentary and Health Service Ombudsman are traditionally held by the same person.

Parliamentary Ombudsman and Health Service Ombudsman, Robert Behrens, CBE

PRISONS AND PROBATION OMBUDSMAN

PO Box 70769, London SE1P 4XY
T 020-7633 4100 E mail@ppo.gsi.gov.uk
W www.ppo.gov.uk

The Prisons and Probation Ombudsman investigates complaints from prisoners, people on probation and immigration detainees, deaths of prisoners, residents of probation-service Approved Premises and those held in immigration removal centres. The ombudsman is appointed by the Secretary of State for Justice and works closely with the Ministry of Justice. All deaths that occur in prison are investigated and an anonymised fatal incident report is written after each investigation.

Ombudsman, Nigel Newcomen, CBE

PROPERTY OMBUDSMAN

Milford House, 43–55 Milford Street, Salisbury SP1 2BP
T 01722-333306
W www.tpos.co.uk

The Property Ombudsman (TPO) scheme was established in 1998 and provides a free, impartial and independent service for dealing with unresolved disputes between property agents and buyers, sellers, tenants and landlords of property in the UK.

The ombudsman's role is to consider complaints against the agents' obligation to act in accordance with the TPO codes of practice and to propose a full and final resolution to the dispute. Consumers are not bound by the Ombudsman's decision, but registered agents are.

With over 12,800 estate agent offices and 11,500 lettings offices registered, TPO is the primary dispute-resolution service for the property industry.

Ombudsman, Katrine Sporle, CBE

PUBLIC SERVICES OMBUDSMAN FOR WALES

1 Ffordd yr Hen Gae, Pencoed CF35 5LJ
T 0300-790 0203
W www.ombudsman-wales.org.uk

The office of Public Services Ombudsman for Wales was established, with effect from 1 April 2006, by the Public Services Ombudsman (Wales) Act 2005. The ombudsman, who is appointed by the Queen, investigates complaints of injustice caused by maladministration or service failure by public services such as the Assembly Commission (and public bodies sponsored by the assembly); Welsh government; National Health Service bodies, including GPs, family health service providers and hospitals; registered social landlords; local authorities, including community councils; fire and rescue authorities; police authorities; the Arts Council of Wales; national park authorities; and countryside and environmental organisations.

Ombudsman, Nick Bennett

REMOVALS INDUSTRY OMBUDSMAN SCHEME

PO Box 1535, High Wycombe HP12 9EE
T 020-8144 3790 E ombudsman@removalsombudsman.co.uk
W www.removalsombudsman.co.uk

The Removals Industry Ombudsman Scheme was established to resolve disputes between removal companies that are members of the scheme and their clients, both domestic and commercial. It comprises a board of four members, only one of whom has any connection with the removals industry. The ombudsman investigates complaints such as breaches of contract, unprofessional conduct, delays, excessive charges or breaches in the code of practice. The National Guild of Removers and Storers is currently the principal member.

Ombudsman, Tony Kaye

SCOTTISH PUBLIC SERVICES OMBUDSMAN

4 Melville Street, Edinburgh EH3 7NS
T 0800-377 7330
W www.spso.org.uk

The Scottish Public Services Ombudsman (SPSO) was established in 2002. The SPSO is the final stage for complaints about public services in Scotland. Its service is free and independent. SPSO investigates complaints about the Scottish government, its agencies and departments; the Scottish Parliamentary Corporate Body; colleges and universities; councils; housing associations; NHS Scotland; prisons; some water and sewerage service providers; and most other Scottish public bodies. The ombudsman looks at complaints regarding poor service or administrative failure and can usually only look at those that have been through the formal complaints process of the organisation concerned. It also has a statutory function in improving complaints handling in public services, which it carries out through its Complaints Standards Authority.

Scottish Public Services Ombudsman, Rosemary Agnew

WATERWAYS OMBUDSMAN

PO Box 854, Altrincham WA15 5JS
T 0161-980 4858 E enquiries@waterways-ombudsman.org
W www.waterways-ombudsman.org

Since July 2012, the Waterways Ombudsman has investigated complaints about the Canal and River Trust and its subsidiaries (such as British Waterways Marinas Limited). The ombudsman does not consider complaints about canals in Scotland, which are the responsibility of the Scottish Public Services Ombudsman.

Ombudsman, Andrew Walker

THE POLICE SERVICE

There are 45 police forces in the United Kingdom: 43 in England and Wales, including the Metropolitan Police and the City of London Police, Police Scotland and the Police Service of Northern Ireland. The Isle of Man, Jersey and Guernsey have their own forces responsible for policing in their respective islands and bailiwicks. The National Crime Agency, which became operational in October 2013, is responsible for preventing organised crime and strengthening UK borders.

Since 1964, police authorities – separate independent bodies for each police force – were responsible for the supervision of local policing in England and Wales. Following the government's white paper *Policing in the 21st Century* it was concluded that, in order to make the police more accountable, police authorities should be replaced with a directly elected commissioner for each force, supported by a police and crime panel. In November 2012, following the enactment of the Police Reform and Social Responsibility Act 2011, elections to install police and crime commissioners (PCCs) were held in 41 police force areas across England and Wales. The PCCs are responsible for appointing the chief constable of their force, establishing local priorities and setting budgets. The PCCs are not in place to run their local force but rather to hold them to account. The Mayor of London, supported by the Mayor's Office for Policing and Crime (MOPAC), acts as the PCC for the Metropolitan Police. The City of London Corporation acts as the police authority for the City of London Police.

In England the police and crime panels are made up of representatives from each local authority in a police force area. In Wales they are independent public bodies, established and maintained by the secretary of state, rather than local authority committees.

Under the Police and Fire Reform (Scotland) Act 2012, Police Scotland was established on 1 April 2013, merging the eight separate territorial police forces, the Scottish Crime and Drug Enforcement Agency and the Association of Chief Police Officers in Scotland. Responsible for policing the whole of Scotland, Police Scotland is the second largest force in the UK after the Metropolitan Police. The service is led by a chief constable who is supported by a team of four deputy constables, assistant chief constables and three directors. The Scottish Police Authority, established in October 2012, is responsible for maintaining policing, promoting policing principles, the continuous improvement of policing and holds the Chief Constable to account. In Northern Ireland, the Northern Ireland Policing Board, an independent public body consisting of 19 political and independent members, fulfils a similar role.

Police forces in England, Scotland and Wales are financed by central and local government grants and a precept on the council tax. The Police Service of Northern Ireland is wholly funded by central government.

The home secretary, the Scottish government and the Northern Ireland Minister of Justice are responsible for the organisation, administration and operation of the police service. They regulate police ranks, discipline, hours of duty and pay and allowances. All police forces are subject to inspection by HM Inspectorate of Constabulary, which reports to the home secretary and the Northern Ireland Minister of Justice. Police forces in Scotland are inspected by HM Inspectorate of Constabulary for Scotland which operates independently of the Scottish government.

COMPLAINTS

The Independent Police Complaints Commission (IPCC) was established under the Police Reform Act 2002. The IPCC is responsible for overseeing the whole of the police complaints system in England and Wales. It has the power to initiate, undertake and oversee investigations and is also responsible for the way in which complaints are handled by local police forces. In addition the IPCC is responsible for dealing with serious complaints and conduct matters relating to staff at the National Crime Agency, HM Revenue and Customs and Home Office immigration and enforcement staff. The most recent responsibility assigned to the IPCC is to decide whether investigations should be made regarding any allegations of criminal offence against MOPAC, the PCCs or their deputies.

Complaints about the police must first be recorded with the relevant police force; the local force will attempt to resolve complaints internally and an official investigation might not be required. Certain complaints, such as an allegation that an officer has seriously assaulted someone, are automatically referred to the IPCC. The IPCC or police force may refer the case to the Crown Prosecution Service, which will decide whether to bring criminal charges against the officer/s involved. An officer who is dismissed, required to resign or reduced in rank, whether as a result of a complaint or not, can appeal to a police appeals tribunal established by the relevant police authority.

On 1 April 2013, under the Police and Fire Reform (Scotland) Act 2012 which brought together Scotland's eight police services into the single Police Service of Scotland, the remit of the Police Complaints Commissioner for Scotland (PCCS) was expanded to include investigations into the most serious incidents concerning the police. To reflect this change, the PCCS was renamed the Police Investigations and Review Commissioner (PIRC).

The Police Ombudsman for Northern Ireland provides an independent police complaints system for Northern Ireland, dealing with all stages of the complaints procedure. Complaints that cannot be resolved informally are investigated and the ombudsman recommends a suitable course of action to the Chief Constable of the Police Service of Northern Ireland or the Northern Ireland Policing Board based on the investigation's findings. The ombudsman may recommend that a police officer be prosecuted, but the decision to prosecute a police officer rests with the Director of Public Prosecutions.

INDEPENDENT POLICE COMPLAINTS COMMISSION, PO Box 473, Sale M33 0BW T 0300-020 0096 E enquiries@ipcc.gsi.gov.uk W www.ipcc.gov.uk *Chair,* Dame Anne Owers, DBE

POLICE INVESTIGATIONS AND REVIEW COMMISSIONER, Hamilton House, Hamilton Business Park, Caird Park, Hamilton ML3 0QA T 01698-542900 E enquiries@pirc.gsi.gov.uk W www.pirc.scotland.gov.uk *Police Investigations and Review Commissioner,* Kate Frame

POLICE OMBUDSMAN FOR NORTHERN IRELAND, New Cathedral Buildings, Writers' Square, 11 Church Street, Belfast BT1 1PG T 028-9082 8600 E info@policeombudsman.org W www.policeombudsman.org *Police Ombudsman,* Dr Michael Maguire

POLICE SERVICES

COLLEGE OF POLICING

Leamington Road, Ryton-on-Dunsmore, Coventry CV8 3EN
T 0800-496 3322 E contactus@college.pnn.police.uk
W www.college.police.uk

The College of Policing was established in December 2012 as the first professional body set up for policing. It works on behalf of the public to raise professional standards in policing and to assist forces to reduce crime and protect the public. It engages with the public through the Police and Crime Commissioners to ensure that it is responsive to the issues of greatest concern.

The government has designated the college as a centre for reviewing and testing practices and interventions to identify which are effective in reducing crime. It makes this information accessible for all in policing, particularly frontline practitioners. The college also supports continuous professional development and sets national standards for promotion and progression.

Chief Executive, Alex Marshall, QPM
Chair, Millie Banerjee, CBE *(interim)*

NATIONAL CRIME AGENCY

Units 1–6 Citadel Place, Tinworth Street, London SE11 5EF
T 0370-496 7622
E communication@nca.x.gsi.gov.uk
W www.nationalcrimeagency.gov.uk

Established under the Crime and Courts Act 2013 the National Crime Agency (NCA) became fully operational in October 2013. The NCA is a non-ministerial government department.

In order to carry out its remit to fight organised crime, strengthen UK borders, tackle fraud and cyber crime and protect children and young people the agency is organised into four separate commands: Border Policing; Child Exploitation and Online Protection; the National Cyber Crime Unit; and Organised Crime.

The director-general has independent operational direction and control over the NCA's activities and, through the home secretary, is accountable to parliament.

Director-General, Lynne Owens, CBE, QPM

UK MISSING PERSONS BUREAU

Albert Day Building, Sunningdale Park, Ascot, Berks SL5 0QE T 0845-000 5481
E missingpersonsbureau@nca.x.gsi.gov.uk
W www.missingpersons.police.uk

The UK Missing Persons Bureau, which is now part of the National Crime Agency, acts as the centre for the exchange of information connected with the search for missing persons nationally and internationally alongside the police and other related organisations. The unit focuses on cross-matching missing persons with unidentified persons or bodies by maintaining records, including a dental index of ante-mortem chartings of long-term missing persons and post-mortem chartings from unidentified bodies.

Information is supplied and collected for all persons who have been missing in the UK for over 72 hours (or fewer where police deem appropriate), foreign nationals reported missing in the UK, UK nationals reported missing abroad and all unidentified bodies and persons found within the UK.

SPECIALIST FORCES

BRITISH TRANSPORT POLICE

25 Camden Road, London NW1 9LN T 0800-405040
W www.btp.police.uk
Strength (September 2016), 2.959

British Transport Police is the national police force for the railways in England, Wales and Scotland, including the London Underground system, Docklands Light Railway, Glasgow Subway, Midland Metro tram system, Sunderland Metro, London Tramlink and the Emirates Air Line cable car. The chief constable reports to the British Transport Police Authority. The members of the authority are appointed by the transport secretary and include representatives from the rail industry as well as independent members. Officers are paid the same salary as those in other police forces.

Chief Constable, Paul Crowther, OBE

CIVIL NUCLEAR CONSTABULARY

Building F6, Culham Science Centre, Abingdon,
Oxfordshire OX14 3DB T 0330-313 5400
W www.gov.uk/government/organisations/
civil-nuclear-constabulary
*Strength, c.*1,500

The Civil Nuclear Constabulary (CNC) operates under the strategic direction of the Department of Energy and Climate Change. The CNC is a specialised armed force that protects civil nuclear sites and nuclear materials. The constabulary is responsible for policing UK civil nuclear industry facilities and for escorting nuclear material between establishments within the UK and worldwide.

Chief Constable, Michael Griffiths, CBE
Deputy Chief Constable, Simon Chesterton, QPM

MINISTRY OF DEFENCE POLICE

Ministry of Defence Police HQ, Wethersfield, Braintree, Essex
CM7 4AZ T 01371-854000
W www.mod.police.uk
*Strength, c.*2,600

Part of the Ministry of Defence Police and Guarding Agency, the Ministry of Defence Police is a statutory civil police force with particular responsibility for the security and policing of the MoD environment. It contributes to the physical protection of property and personnel within its jurisdiction and provides a comprehensive police service to the MoD as a whole.

Chief Constable, vacant
Deputy Chief Constable, Andy Adams

THE SPECIAL CONSTABULARY

Darby House, 162 Bletchingley Road, Merstham, Surrey RH1 3DN
W www.policespecials.com
*Strength, c.*20,000

The Special Constabulary is a force of trained volunteers who support and work with their local police force, usually for a minimum of 16 hours a month. Special constables are thoroughly grounded in the basic aspects of police work, such as self-defence, powers of arrest, common crimes and preparing evidence for court, before they can begin to carry out any police duties. Once they have completed their training, they have the same powers as a regular officer and wear a similar uniform.

POLICE FORCES

The telephone number for each local police force in England, Wales, Scotland and Northern Ireland is T 101

Force	Strength†	Chief Constable	Police and Crime Commissioner
ENGLAND			
Avon and Somerset	2,517	Andy Marsh	Sue Mountstevens
Bedfordshire	1,030	Jon Boutcher, QPM	Kathryn Holloway
Cambridgeshire	1,308	Alec Wood	Jason Ablewhite
Cheshire	1,926	Janette McCormick (acting)	David Keane
Cleveland	1,118	Iain Spittal	Barry Coppinger
Cumbria	1,067	Jeremy Graham	Peter McCall
Derbyshire	1,685	Peter Goodman	Hardyal Dhindsa
Devon and Cornwall	2,901	Shaun Sawyer	Alison Hernandez
Dorset	1,153	Debbie Simpson, QPM	Martyn Underhill
Durham	1,077	Mike Barton, QPM	Ron Hogg
Essex	2,750	Stephen Kavanagh	Roger Hirst
Gloucestershire	1,043	Rod Hansen	Martin Surl
Greater Manchester	5,954	Ian Hopkins, QPM	Mayor of Greater Manchester
Hampshire	2,718	Olivia Pinkney	Michael Lane
Hertfordshire	1,828	Charlie Hall	David Lloyd
Humberside	1,522	Lee Freeman	Keith Hunter
Kent	3,090	Alan Pughsley, QPM	Matthew Scott
Lancashire	2,749	Andy Rhodes	Clive Grunshaw
Leicestershire	1,776	Simon Cole, QPM	Lord Willy Bach
Lincolnshire	1,028	Bill Skelly	Marc Jones
Merseyside	3,400	Andy Cooke, QPM	Jane Kennedy
Norfolk	1,473	Simon Bailey, QPM	Lorne Green
North Yorkshire	1,290	Dave Jones, QPM	Julia Mulligan
Northamptonshire	1,167	Simon Edens	Stephen Mold
Northumbria	3,221	Steve Ashman	Dame Vera Baird, DBE
Nottinghamshire	1,910	Craig Guilford	Paddy Tipping
South Yorkshire	2,385	Stephen Watson	Dr Alan Billings
Staffordshire	1,610	Gareth Morgan	Matthew Ellis
Suffolk	1,054	Gareth Wilson	Tim Passmore
Surrey	1,835	Nick Ephgrave	David Munro
Sussex	2,563	Giles York, QPM	Katy Bourne
Thames Valley	4,084	Francis Habgood	Anthony Stansfeld
Warwickshire	807	Martin Jelley, QPM	Philip Seccombe
West Mercia	2,009	Anthony Bangham	John Campion
West Midlands	6,636	Dave Thompson, QPM	David Jamieson
West Yorkshire	4,296	Dee Collins	Mark Burns-Williamson, OBE
Wiltshire	959	Mike Veale	Angus Macpherson
WALES			
Dyfed-Powys	1,103	Mark Collins	Dafydd Llywelyn
Gwent	1,062	Julian Williams	Jeff Cuthbert
North Wales	1,418	Mark Polin, QPM	Arfon Jones
South Wales	2,745	Peter Vaughan, QPM	Rt. Hon. Alun Michael
POLICE SCOTLAND	17,256	Philip Gormley, QPM	–
POLICE SERVICE OF NORTHERN IRELAND	6,827	George Hamilton, QPM	–

ISLANDS	Strength†	Chief Constable	Telephone
Isle of Man	210	Gary Roberts	01624-631212
States of Jersey	230	Mike Bowron, QPM	01534-612612
Guernsey	148	Patrick Rice	01481-725111

† Size of force (full-time equivalent; excluding long-term absentees) as at 31 March 2016

LONDON FORCES

CITY OF LONDON POLICE

Guildhall Yard East, London EC2V 5AE T 020-7601 2222
W www.cityoflondon.police.uk
Strength (May 2016), 699

The City of London has one of the most important financial centres in the world and the force has particular expertise in fraud investigation. The force concentrates on: economic crime, counter terrorism and community policing. It has a wholly elected police authority, the police committee of the City of London Corporation, which appoints the commissioner.

Commissioner, Ian Dyson, QPM
Assistant Commissioner, Alistair Sutherland
Commanders, Jane Gyford *(Operations);* David Clark *(National Coordinator for Economic Crime)*

METROPOLITAN POLICE SERVICE

New Scotland Yard, Broadway, London SW1H 0BG
T 020-7230 1212 W www.met.police.uk
Strength (September 2016), 32,469
Commissioner, Cressida Dick, CBE, QPM
Deputy Commissioner, Craig Mackey, QPM

The Metropolitan Police Service is divided into three main areas for operational purposes:

TERRITORIAL POLICING
Most of the day-to-day policing of London is carried out by 32 borough operational command units operating within the same boundaries as the London borough councils.
Assistant Commissioner, Martin Hewitt

SPECIALIST CRIME AND OPERATIONS (SC&O)
SC&O provides two main services: reducing the harm caused by serious crime and criminal networks and providing specialist policing services across London. SC&O provides specialist training to detectives, and conducts forensic examinations of crime scenes in the capital.
Assistant Commissioner, Patricia Gallan

SPECIALIST OPERATIONS
Counter Terrorism Command is responsible for the prevention and disruption of terrorist activity, domestic extremism and related offences within London and nationally. It provides an explosives disposal and chemical, biological, radiological and nuclear capability in London, assists the security services in fulfilling their roles and provides a point of contact for international partners
Protection Command is responsible for the protection and security of high-profile persons, including the royal family and the prime minister. It is also responsible for protecting royal residences and embassies, providing residential protection for visiting heads of state, heads of government and foreign ministers and advising the diplomatic community on security
Security Command works with authorities at the Houses of Parliament to provide security for peers, MPs, employees and visitors to the Palace of Westminster. It is also responsible for policing Heathrow and London City airports
Assistant Commissioner, Mark Rowley, QPM

PROFESSIONALISM
The Directorate of Professionalism's key aims are to uphold and improve professional standards across the Metropolitan Police Service. The directorate works with the IPCC to establish good practice, reduce bureaucracy and review decision making. It also works with the Crown Prosecution Service to ensure timely and professional investigations of complaints and conduct matters.
Temporary Assistant Commissioner, Fiona Taylor

STAFF ASSOCIATIONS

Police officers are not permitted to join a trade union or to take strike action. All ranks have their own staff associations.
NATIONAL POLICE CHIEFS' COUNCIL (NPCC), 10
  Victoria Street, London SW1H 0NN T 020-3276 3795
  W www.npcc.police.uk
Chair, Sara Thornton, CBE, QPM

ENGLAND AND WALES

POLICE FEDERATION OF ENGLAND AND WALES,
  Federation House, Highbury Drive, Leatherhead, Surrey
  KT22 7UY T 01372-352000 W www.polfed.org
General Secretary, Andy Fittes
POLICE SUPERINTENDENTS' ASSOCIATION OF
  ENGLAND AND WALES, 67A Reading Road, Pangbourne,
  Reading RG8 7JD T 0118-984 4005 W www.policesupers.com
National Secretary, Chief Supt. Dan Murphy

SCOTLAND

ASSOCIATION OF SCOTTISH POLICE
  SUPERINTENDENTS, Scottish Police College, Kincardine,
  Fife FK10 4BE T 01259-732122
  W www.scottishpolicesupers.org.uk
General Secretary, Craig Suttie
SCOTTISH POLICE FEDERATION, 5 Woodside Place,
  Glasgow G3 7QF T 0300-303 0027 W www.spf.org.uk
General Secretary, Calum Steele

NORTHERN IRELAND

POLICE FEDERATION FOR NORTHERN IRELAND, 77–
  79 Garnerville Road, Belfast BT4 2NX T 028-9076 4200
  W www.policefed-ni.org.uk
Secretary, Colin McCrum
SUPERINTENDENTS' ASSOCIATION OF NORTHERN
  IRELAND, PSNI College, Garnerville Road, Belfast BT4 2NX
  T 028-9092 2201 W www.psni.police.uk

RATES OF PAY FROM 1 SEPTEMBER 2017

Chief Constables of Greater Manchester and West Midlands*	£190,711
Chief Constable	£136,677–£178,000
Deputy Chief Constable	£114,428–£146,216
Assistant Chief Constable and Commanders	£98,539–£111,249
Chief Superintendent	£81,960–£86,460
Superintendent Range	£66,126–£78,108
in rank on or after 1 April 2014	
Superintendent	£66,126–£77,043
in rank before 1 April 2014	
Chief Inspector†	£54,969 (£57,162)– £58,167 (£60,342)
Inspector†	£49,665 (£51,840)– £53,868 (£56,061)
Sergeant	£40,086–£43,563
Constable *apptd on or after 1 April 2013*	£20,169–£38,760
Constable *apptd before 1 April 2013*	£24,687–£38,760

Metropolitan Police	
Commissioner	£273,354
Deputy Commissioner	£225,674
City of London Police	
Commissioner	£169,110
Assistant Commissioner	£139,483
Police Scotland	
Chief Constable	£214,404
Deputy Chief Constable	£174,741
Assistant Chief Constable	£118,485
Police Service of Northern Ireland	
Chief Constable	£203,422
Deputy Chief Constable	£165,277

* Also applicable to the four Assistant Commissioners of the Metropolitan Police Service

† London salary in parentheses. All other officers (not Metropolitan or City of London Commissioners) working in London receive an additional payment of £2,421 per annum

THE PRISON SERVICE

The prison services in the UK are the responsibility of the Secretary of State for Justice, the Scottish Secretary for Justice and the Minister of Justice in Northern Ireland. The chief executive (director-general in Northern Ireland), officers of HM Prison and Probation Service (HMPPS), the Scottish Prison Service (SPS) and the Northern Ireland Prison Service are responsible for the day-to-day running of the system.

There are 120 prison establishments in England and Wales, 15 in Scotland and three in Northern Ireland. Convicted prisoners are classified according to their assessed security risk and are housed in establishments appropriate to that level of security. There are no open prisons in Northern Ireland. Female prisoners are housed in women's establishments or in separate wings of mixed prisons. Remand prisoners are, where possible, housed separately from convicted prisoners. Offenders under the age of 21 are usually detained in a Young Offender Institution, which may be a separate establishment or part of a prison. Appellant and failed asylum seekers are held in Immigration Removal Centres, or in separate units of other prisons.

Fourteen prisons are now run by the private sector in England and Wales, and in England, Wales and Scotland all escort services have been contracted out to private companies. In Scotland, two prisons (Kilmarnock and Addiewell) were built and financed by the private sector and are being operated by private contractors.

There are independent prison inspectorates in England, Wales and Scotland which report annually on conditions and the treatment of prisoners. The Chief Inspector of Criminal Justice in Northern Ireland and HM Inspectorate of Prisons for England and Wales perform an inspectorate role for prisons in Northern Ireland. Every prison establishment also has an independent monitoring board made up of local volunteers.

Any prisoner whose complaint is not satisfied by the internal complaints procedures may complain to the prisons and probation ombudsman for England and Wales, the Scottish public services ombudsman or the prisoner ombudsman for Northern Ireland. The prisons and probation inspectors, the prisons ombudsman and the independent monitoring boards report to the home secretary and to the Minister of Justice in Northern Ireland.

PRISON STATISTICS

The projected 'high scenario' prison population for 2020 in England and Wales is 98,900; the 'low scenario' is 81,400.

PRISON POPULATION (UK) *AS AT JUNE 2016*

	Remand	Sentenced	Other
ENGLAND AND WALES	9,288	74,316	1,530
Male	8,764	71,008	1,500
Female	524	3,308	30
SCOTLAND*	1,148	6,102	–
Male	1,074	5,822	–
Female	74	280	–
N. IRELAND	407	1,117	–
Male	386	1,075	–
Female	21	42	–
UK TOTAL	10,843	81,535	1,530

* Figures from August 2016
Sources: MoJ; Scottish Prison Service; NI Prison Service

PRISON CAPACITY (ENGLAND AND WALES) *AS AT SEPTEMBER 2017*

Male prisoners	82,271
Female prisoners	3,964
Total	86,235
Useable operational capacity	87,228
Under home detention curfew supervision	2,033

Source: MoJ – *Prisons and Probation Statistics*

SENTENCED PRISON POPULATION BY SEX AND OFFENCE (ENGLAND AND WALES) *AS AT 30 JUNE 2016*

	Male	Female
Violence against the person	18,047	943
Sexual offences	12,423	108
Robbery	7,538	284
Theft offences	10,273	670
Criminal damage and arson	1,015	98
Fraud offences	1,185	188
Drugs offences	10,564	444
Possession of weapons	2,080	61
Public order offences	1,232	35
Miscellaneous crimes against society	3,324	214
Summary non-motoring	2,582	178
Summary motoring	388	17
Offence not recorded	269	54
Total	70,920	3,294

Source: MoJ – *Prisons and Probation Statistics*

SENTENCED POPULATION BY LENGTH OF SENTENCE (ENGLAND AND WALES) *AS AT 30 JUNE 2016*

	British	Other Nationalities or Not Recorded
Less than 12 months	5,549	762
12 months to less than 4 years	16,947	1,670
4 years to less than life	27,455	3,173
Indeterminate	10,395	964
*Total**	60,346	6,569

* Figures do not include civil (non-criminal) prisoners or fine defaulters
Source: MoJ – *Prisons and Probation Statistics*

AVERAGE DAILY POPULATION BY TYPE OF CUSTODY 2015–16 (SCOTLAND)

Remand: sub total	1,494
Persons under sentence: sub total	6,181
Under 4 years	3,353
4 years and over	2,828
Total	7,675

Source: SPS – *Annual Report and Accounts 2015–16*

SUICIDES IN PRISON IN 2015

(ENGLAND AND WALES)

Total	89

Source: MoJ

THE PRISON SERVICES

HM PRISON AND PROBATION SERVICE

Clive House, 70 Petty France, London SW1H 9EX
T 0203-193 5921 E public.enquiries@noms.gsi.gov.uk
W www.gov.uk/government/organisations/
her-majestys-prison-and-probation-service

HM Prison and Probation Service (HMPPS) was formed on 1 April 2017, incorporating the National Offender Management Service (NOMS) and HM Prisons. HMPPS is responsible for implementing government policy concerning the welfare of prison populations and local communities, working closely with HM Prison Service to oversee the management of public sector prisons in England and Wales.

SALARIES (ENGLAND AND WALES)
from 1 April 2017
All salary ranges given are for the average across England and Wales (includes inner and outer London salaries) and are based on a 37-hour-week inclusive of the required hours allowance (Governors, Deputy Governors and Heads of Function) or the additional 17 per cent unsocial hours payment for all other grades.

Governor	£65,810–£89,332
Deputy Governor	£46,674–£71,741
Head of Function	£40,028–£48,036
Custodial Manager	£30,326–£34,136
Supervising/Specialist Officer	£26,957–£29,981
Prison Officer	£21,219–£23,590
Operational Support Grade	£18,358–£19,276

HM PRISON AND PROBATION SERVICE BOARD
Chief Executive, Michael Spurr
Executive Director, HM Prisons, Phil Copple
Executive Director, HMPPS Wales and Estate Transformation, Simon Boddis
Director of Security, Order and Counter Terrorism, Claudia Stuart
Director of Probation and Women, Sonia Crozier
Director of Electronic Monitoring and Procurement, Adrian Scott
Director of Youth Custody, Sara Robinson
Director of Youth Custody Transition Service, Mark Read
Director of Rehabilitation and Assurance, Digby Griffith
Director of Community Interventions, Jim Barton
Director of Human Resources, Martin Beecroft
Director of Finance , Andrew Emmett
Director of Digital , Bryan Clarke
Director of Commercial, Kate Ellis

OPERATING COSTS OF NOMS 2016–17

Staff costs	£1,843,924,000
Operating income	(£297,750,000)
Total operating expenditure	£4,551,249,000
Net operating expenditure	£4,253,499,000

Source: NOMS – *Annual Report 2016–17* (NOMS was incorporated into HM Prison and Probation Service on 1 April 2017)

SCOTTISH PRISON SERVICE (SPS)

Calton House, 5 Redheughs Rigg, Edinburgh EH12 9HW
T 0131-330 3500 E gaolinfo@sps.pnn.gov.uk
W www.sps.gov.uk

SALARIES

Governor in Charge	£62,160–£70,509
Deputy Governor	£50,323–£58,424
Head of Operations	£40,654–£48,579
Unit Manager	£32,778–£41,269
First Line Manager	£26,717–£34,430
Residential Officer	£22,427–£28,891
Operations Officer	£17,521–£22,245

SPS BOARD
Chief Executive, Colin McConnell
Directors, James Kerr *(Operations);* Teresa Medhurst *(Strategy and Innovation);* Eric Murch *(Corperate Change);* Catherine Topley *(Corporate Services);*
Non-Executive Directors, S. Browell; A. McMillan; H. Monro; Z. Van Zwanenberg

OPERATING COSTS OF SPS 2016–17

Total income	(£7,351,000)
Total expenditure	£330,914,000
Staff costs	£168,884,000
Running costs	£131,850,000
Other current expenditure	£162,030,000
Operating cost	£1,073,183,000
Interest payable and similar charges	£2,723,000
Net operating cost	£331,038,000

Source: SPS – Annual Report and Accounts 2016-17

NORTHERN IRELAND PRISON SERVICE

Dundonald House, Upper Newtownards Road, Belfast BT4 3SU
T 028-9052 2922 E info@niprisonservice.gov.uk
W www.justice-ni.gov.uk/topics/prisons

SALARIES

Governing Governor	£75,120–£82,170
Governor in Charge	£64,900–£73,629
Head of Function	£53,300–£57,621
Head of Unit	£47,150–£51,566
Senior Prison Officer	£33,400–£38,380
Main Grade Prison Officer	£30,710–£38,116
Operational Support Grade	£20,500
Custody Prison Officer	£18,295–£26,005

MANAGEMENT BOARD
Chair, Ronnie Armour
Executive, Phil Wragg *(Operations);* Louise Cooper *(Rehabilitation);* Louise Blair *(Policy and Service Delivery);* Brendan Giffen *(Strategy and Governance);* Richard Stewart *(Press Office);* Phil Leighton, CBE, QPM

OPERATING COSTS OF NORTHERN IRELAND PRISON SERVICE 2015–16

Staff costs	£71,373,000
Operating income	(£2,636,000)
Total operating expenditure	£120,518,000
Net operating expenditure	£117,513,000

Source: NI Prison Service – Annual Report and Accounts 2015–16

PRISON ESTABLISHMENTS

ENGLAND AND WALES *AS AT SEPTEMBER 2017*

Prison	Address	Capacity	Prisoners	Governor/Director
ALTCOURSE (private prison)	Liverpool L9 7LH	1,033	1,004	Steve Williams
ASHFIELD (private prison)	Bristol BS16 9QJ	400	400	Vicky Pails
*‡ASKHAM GRANGE	York YO23 3FT	128	119	Susan Howard
‡AYLESBURY	Bucks HP20 1EH	444	440	Laura Sapwell
BEDFORD	Bedford MK40 1HG	261	476	Mary Bemment
BELMARSH	London SE28 0EB	910	846	Simon Cartwright
BIRMINGHAM	Birmingham B18 4AS	1,450	1,444	Peter Small
BLANTYRE HOUSE	Kent TN17 2NH	122	0	James Bourke
†‡BRINSFORD	Wolverhampton WV10 7PY	577	398	Heather Whithead
‡BRISTOL	Bristol BS7 8PS	614	549	Steve Cross
‡BRIXTON	London SW2 5XF	798	787	Dave Bamford
*BRONZEFIELD (private prison)	Middlesex TW15 3JZ	527	543	Ian Whiteside
BUCKLEY HALL	Lancs OL12 9DP	445	447	Rob Knight
BULLINGDON	Oxon OX25 1PZ	1,114	1,100	Ian Blakeman
BURE	Norfolk NR10 5GB	624	642	Sue Doolan
†CARDIFF	Cardiff CF24 0UG	820	770	Danny Kahn
CHANNINGS WOOD	Devon TQ12 6DW	724	696	Terry Witton
‡CHELMSFORD	Essex CM2 6LQ	745	708	Steve Rodford, OBE
COLDINGLEY	Surrey GU24 9EX	513	520	Jo Sims
‡COOKHAM WOOD	Kent ME1 3LU	178	144	Jonathan French
DARTMOOR	Devon PL20 6RR	640	634	Bridie Oakes-Richards
‡DEERBOLT	Co. Durham DL12 9BG	513	365	Gavin O'Malley
‡DONCASTER (private prison)	Doncaster DN5 8UX	1,145	961	Jerry Spencer
DOVEGATE (private prison)	Staffs ST14 8XR	1,060	1,102	John Hewitson
*DOWNVIEW	Surrey SM2 5PD	355	213	Robin Eldridge
*‡DRAKE HALL	Staffs ST21 6LQ	340	335	Carl Hardwick
DURHAM	Durham DH1 3HU	1,001	888	Tim Allen
*‡EAST SUTTON PARK	Kent ME17 3DF	100	97	Robin Eldridge
*EASTWOOD PARK	Glos GL12 8DB	442	365	Suzy Dymond-White
ELMLEY	Kent ME12 4DZ	1,252	1,249	Sara Pennington
ERLESTOKE	Wilts SN10 5TU	524	382	Tim Knight
†‡EXETER	Devon EX4 4EX	561	491	Pete Elbourn
FEATHERSTONE	Wolverhampton WV10 7PU	687	686	Babafemi Dada
†‡FELTHAM	Middx TW13 4ND	540	518	Glenn Knight
FORD	W. Sussex BN18 0BX	547	490	Stephen Fradley
‡FOREST BANK (private prison)	Manchester M27 8FB	1,460	1,452	Matt Spencer
*FOSTON HALL	Derby DE65 5DN	345	338	Andrea Black
FRANKLAND	Durham DH1 5YD	844	793	Norman Griddin
FULL SUTTON	York YO41 1PS	608	580	Ed Commell
GARTH	Preston PR26 8NE	845	836	Steve Pearson
GARTREE	Leics LE16 7RP	707	707	Ali Barker
GRENDON/SPRING HILL	Bucks HP18 0TL	238	543	Jamie Bennett
‡GUYS MARSH	Dorset SP7 0AH	579	548	Paul Millett
HAVERIGG	Cumbria LA18 4NA	286	604	Tony Corcoran
HEWELL	Worcs B97 6QS	1,279	1,200	Gareth Sands
HIGH DOWN	Surrey SM2 5PJ	1,023	1,002	Louise Spencer
HIGHPOINT	Suffolk CB8 9YG	1,116	1,257	Nigel Smith
†‡HINDLEY	Lancs WN2 5TH	664	501	Mark Livingston
‡HOLLESLEY BAY	Suffolk IP12 3JW	421	419	Declan Moore
HOLME HOUSE	Stockton-on-Tees TS18 2QU	1,210	1,157	Chris Dyer
‡HULL	Hull HU9 5LS	1,056	977	Rick Stuart
HUMBER	E. Yorks HU15	1,062	1,037	Marcella Goligher
‡HUNTERCOMBE	Oxon RG9 5SB	480	426	David Redhouse
ISIS	Thamesmead SE28 0NZ	628	617	Grahame Hawkings
ISLE OF WIGHT	Isle of Wight PO30 5RS	1,139	1,086	Andy Lattimore
KIRKHAM	Lancs PR4 2RN	657	638	Graham Beck
KIRKLEVINGTON GRANGE	Cleveland TS15 9PA	283	246	Angie Petit
†‡LANCASTER FARMS	Lancaster LA1 3QZ	549	538	Derek Harrison
LEEDS	Leeds LS12 2TJ	1,212	1,119	Steven Robson
LEICESTER	Leicester LE2 7AJ	408	335	Graham Batchford
‡LEWES	E. Sussex BN7 1EA	742	621	Jim Bourke
LEYHILL	Glos GL12 8BT	515	508	Helen Ryder
LINCOLN	Lincoln LN2 4BD	738	572	Peter Wright
LINDHOLME	Doncaster DN7 6EE	1,010	1,001	Simon Walters
LITTLEHEY	Cambs PE28 0SR	1,206	1,213	David Taylor
LIVERPOOL	Liverpool L9 3DF	1,300	978	Pete Francis
LONG LARTIN	Worcs WR11 8TZ	622	530	Clare Pearson
*‡LOW NEWTON	Durham DH1 5YA	336	234	Alan Richer
LOWDHAM GRANGE (private prison)	Notts NG14 7DA	888	916	Mark Hanson
MAIDSTONE	Kent ME14 1UZ	1,238	590	Dave Atkinson
MANCHESTER	Manchester M60 9AH	1,136	990	Terry Williams

Prison	Address	Average Daily	Maximum Number	Governor/Director
‡MOORLAND/HATFIELD	Doncaster DN7 6BW	1,006	977	Tim Beeston
§MORTON HALL	Lincoln LN6 9PT	392	373	Karen Head
MOUNT	Herts HP3 0NZ	1,028	1,014	Kevin Leggett
*‡NEW HALL	W. Yorks WF4 4XX	425	408	Susan Howard
NORTH SEA CAMP	Lincs PE22 0QX	420	369	Neil Richards
‡NORTHUMBERLAND	Northumberland NE65 9XG	1,348	1,325	David Gibbs
‡NORWICH	Norfolk NR1 4LU	769	733	Will Styles
NOTTINGHAM	Notts NG5 3AG	1,060	1,007	Tom Wheatley
OAKWOOD	W. Midlands WV10 7QD	1,604	1,632	John McLaughlin
ONLEY	Warks CV23 8AP	742	734	Darren Hughes
†‡PARC (private prison)	Bridgend CF35 6AP	1,336	1,702	Janet Wallsgrove
‡PENTONVILLE	London N7 8TT	1,310	1,294	Kevin Reilly
*†PETERBOROUGH (private prison)	Peterborough PE3 7PD	840	1,246	Damian Evans
‡PORTLAND	Dorset DT5 1DL	530	494	Steve Hodson
PRESTON	Lancs PR1 5AB	750	732	Steve Lawrence
RANBY	Notts DN22 8EU	1,038	1,022	Nigel Hirst
RISLEY	Cheshire WA3 6BP	1,095	1,095	Jerry Spencer
‡ROCHESTER	Kent ME1 3QS	744	730	James Carmichael
RYE HILL (private prison)	Warks CV23 8SZ	625	624	Dave Thompson, OBE
*SEND	Surrey GU23 7LJ	282	279	Carlene Dixon
STAFFORD	Stafford ST16 3AW	751	740	PJ Butler
STANDFORD HILL	Kent ME12 4AA	464	457	James Padley
STOCKEN	Rutland LE15 7RD	842	783	Neil Thomas
‡STOKE HEATH	Shropshire TF9 2JL	766	764	John Huntington
*‡STYAL	Cheshire SK9 4HR	486	484	Mahala McGuffie
SUDBURY	Derbys DE6 5HW	581	522	Adrian Turner
SWALESIDE	Kent ME12 4AX	1,112	1,046	Paul Newton
†‡SWANSEA	Swansea SA1 3SR	500	439	Graham Barrett
‡SWINFEN HALL	Staffs WS14 9QS	624	581	Ian West
THAMESIDE	London SE28 0FJ	1,232	1,204	Craig Thomson
‡THORN CROSS	Cheshire WA4 4RL	381	377	Mick Povall
USK/PRESCOED	Monmouthshire NP15 1XP	273	514	Darren Hughes
§VERNE	Dorset DT5 1EQ	607	469	David Bourne
WAKEFIELD	W. Yorks WF2 9AG	751	726	David Harding
WANDSWORTH	London SW18 3HU	1,877	1,608	Jeanne Bryant (acting)
‡WARREN HILL	Suffolk IP12 3JW	257	245	Sonia Walsh
WAYLAND	Norfolk IP25 6RL	1,017	944	Paul Cawkwell
WEALSTUN	W. Yorks LS23 7AZ	832	816	Diane Pellew
‡WERRINGTON	Stoke-on-Trent ST9 0DX	128	120	Pete Gormley
‡WETHERBY	W. Yorks LS22 5ED	336	244	Andrew Dickinson
WHATTON	Nottingham NG13 9FQ	841	837	Lynn Saunders, OBE
WHITEMOOR	Cambs PE15 0PR	458	438	Paul Cawkwell
WINCHESTER	Winchester SO22 5DF	706	632	David Rogers
WOODHILL	Bucks MK4 4DA	819	702	Rob Davis
WORMWOOD SCRUBS	London W12 0AE	1,279	1,285	Steve Bradford
WYMOTT	Preston PR26 8LW	1,176	1,158	John Illingsworth

SCOTLAND AS AT SEPTEMBER 2017

Prison	Address	Average Daily	Maximum Number	Governor/Director
ADDIEWELL(private prison)	West Lothian EH55 8QA	699	711	Ian Whitehead
†BARLINNIE	Glasgow G33 2QX	1,305	1,306	Michael Stoney
*†‡CORNTON VALE	Stirling FK9 5NU	126	226	Rhona Hotchkiss
†DUMFRIES	Dumfries DG2 9AX	80	100	Andy Hunstone (acting)
†EDINBURGH	Edinburgh EH11 3LN	870	900	Caroline Johnston
GLENOCHIL	Tullibody FK10 3AD	660	670	Nigel Ironside
GRAMPIAN	Peterhead AB42 2YY	412	500	Allister Purdie
†‡GREENOCK	Greenock PA16 9AH	223	370	William Stuart
*†INVERNESS	Inverness IV2 3HH	117	129	Stephen Coyle
†‡KILMARNOCK (private prison)	Kilmarnock KA1 5AA	500	510	Michael Guy
LOW MOSS	Glasgow G64 2PZ	747	784	David Abernethy
OPEN ESTATE – CASTLE HUNTLY	Dundee DD2 5HL	250	259	Gary Law
†PERTH	Perth PH2 8AT	678	678	Fraser Munro
†‡POLMONT	Falkirk FK2 0AB	486	509	Brenda Stewart
SHOTTS	Lanarkshire ML7 4LE	531	553	Jacquline Clinton

NORTHERN IRELAND AS AT SEPTEMBER 2017

Prison	Address	Prisoners	Governor/Director
*†‡HYDEBANK WOOD	Belfast BT8 8NA	162	Austin Treacy, OBE
†§MAGHABERRY	Co. Antrim BT28 2NF	840	Phil Wragg
MAGILLIGAN	Co. Londonderry BT49 0LR	465	David Eagleson

* Women's establishment or establishment with units for women
† Remand Centre or establishment with units for remand prisoners
‡ Young Offender Institution or establishment with units for young offenders
§ Immigration Removal Centre or establishment with units for immigration detainees

DEFENCE

The armed forces of the UK comprise the Royal Navy, the Army and the Royal Air Force (RAF). The Queen is Commander-in-Chief of all the armed forces. The Secretary of State for Defence is responsible for the formulation and content of defence policy and for providing the means by which it is conducted. The formal legal basis for the conduct of defence in the UK rests on a range of powers vested by statute and letters patent in the Defence Council, chaired by the Secretary of State for Defence. Beneath the ministers lies the top management of the Ministry of Defence (MoD), headed jointly by the Permanent Secretary and the Chief of Defence Staff. The Permanent Secretary is the government's principal civilian adviser on defence and has the primary responsibility for policy, finance, management and administration. The Permanent Secretary is also personally accountable to parliament for the expenditure of all public money allocated to defence purposes. The Chief of the Defence Staff is the professional head of the armed forces in the UK and the principal military adviser to the secretary of state and the government.

The Defence Board is the executive of the Defence Council. Chaired by the Permanent Secretary, it acts as the main executive board of the Ministry of Defence, providing senior level leadership and strategic management of defence.

The Central Staff, headed by the Vice-Chief of the Defence Staff and the Second Permanent Under-Secretary of State, is the policy core of the department. Defence Equipment and Support, headed by the Chief of Defence Materiel, is responsible for purchasing defence equipment and providing logistical support to the armed forces.

A permanent Joint Headquarters for the conduct of joint operations was set up at Northwood in 1996. The Joint Headquarters connects the policy and strategic functions of the MoD head office with the conduct of operations and is intended to strengthen the policy/executive division.

The UK pursues its defence and security policies through its membership of NATO (to which most of its armed forces are committed), the European Union, the Organisation for Security and Cooperation in Europe and the UN (see International Organisations section).

STRENGTH OF THE REGULAR ARMED FORCES

	Royal Navy	Army	RAF	All Services
1975 strength	76,200	167,100	95,000	338,300
2000 strength	42,850	110,050	54,720	207,620
2005 strength	39,940	109,290	51,870	201,100
2006 strength	39,390	107,730	48,730	195,850
2007 strength	38,850	106,340	45,480	190,670
2008 strength	38,560	104,980	43,370	186,910
2009 strength	38,340	106,700	43,560	188,600
2010 strength	38,730	108,920	44,050	191,700
2011 strength	37,660	106,240	42,460	186,360
2012 strength	35,540	104,250	40,000	179,800
2013 strength	33,960	99,730	37,030	170,710
2014 strength	33,330	91,070	35,230	159,630
2015 strength	32,740	87,060	33,930	153,720
2016 strength	32,500	85,040	33,460	151,000
2017 strength	32,544	83,561	33,261	149,366

Source: MoD – Defence Statistics (Tri-Service)

UK REGULAR ARMED FORCES BY RANK 2017
Officers	26,991
Other Ranks	122,375

Source: MoD – Defence Statistics (Tri-Service)

UK regular forces include trained and untrained personnel and nursing services, but exclude Gurkhas, full-time reserve service personnel, mobilised reservists and naval activated reservists. As at 1 April 2017 these groups numbered:

All Gurkhas	2,992
Full-time reserve service	4,889
Mobilised reservists	
Army	417
RAF	95
Naval activated reservists	36

Source: MoD – Defence Statistics (Tri-Service)

CIVILIAN PERSONNEL
2000 level	121,300
2001 level	118,200
2002 level	110,100
2003 level	107,600
2004 level	108,990
2005 level	107,680
2006 level	102,970
2007 level	95,790
2008 level	88,690
2009 level	86,620
2010 level	85,850
2011 level	83,060
2012 level	70,940
2013 level	65,400
2014 level	62,340
2015 level	58,200
2016 level	56,240
2017 level	56,680

Source: MoD – Defence Statistics (Tri-Service)

UK REGULAR FORCES: DEATHS
In 2016 there were a total of 72 deaths among the UK regular armed forces, of which 17 were serving in the Royal Navy and Royal Marines, 41 in the Army and 14 in the RAF. The largest single cause of death was cancers, which accounted for 21 deaths (29 per cent of the total) in 2016. Land transport accidents accounted for 12 deaths (17 per cent) and other accidents accounted for a further 19 deaths (26 per cent). There were no deaths as a result of hostile action. Suicides and open verdicts accounted for seven deaths.

NUMBER OF DEATHS AND MORTALITY RATES
	2012	2013	2014	2015	2016
Total number	130	86	68	60	72
Royal Navy	20	13	12	11	17
Army	95	63	40	39	41
RAF	15	10	16	10	14
Mortality rates per thousand					
Tri-service rate	0.72	0.50	0.42	0.39	0.47
Navy	0.59	0.42	0.35	0.32	0.52
Army	0.89	0.65	0.42	0.45	0.47
RAF	0.42	0.23	0.40	0.28	0.36

Source: MoD National Statistics

NUCLEAR FORCES
The Vanguard Class SSBN (ship submersible ballistic nuclear) provides the UK's strategic nuclear deterrent. Each Vanguard Class submarine is capable of carrying 16 Trident D5 missiles equipped with nuclear warheads.

There is a ballistic missile early warning system station at RAF Fylingdales in North Yorkshire.

ARMS CONTROL

The 1990 Conventional Armed Forces in Europe (CFE) Treaty, which commits all NATO and former Warsaw Pact members to limiting their holdings of five major classes of conventional weapons, has been adapted to reflect the changed geo-strategic environment and negotiations continue for its implementation. The Open Skies Treaty, which the UK signed in 1992 and entered into force in 2002, allows for the overflight of states parties by other states parties using unarmed observation aircraft.

The UN Convention on Certain Conventional Weapons (as amended 2001), which bans or restricts the use of specific types of weapons that are considered to cause unnecessary or unjustifiable suffering to combatants, or to affect civilians indiscriminately, was ratified by the UK in 1995. In 1968 the UK signed and ratified the Nuclear Non-Proliferation Treaty, which came into force in 1970 and was indefinitely and unconditionally extended in 1995. In 1996 the UK signed the Comprehensive Nuclear Test Ban Treaty and ratified it in 1998. The UK is a party to the 1972 Biological and Toxin Weapons Convention, which provides for a worldwide ban on biological weapons, and the 1993 Chemical Weapons Convention, which came into force in 1997 and provides for a verifiable worldwide ban on chemical weapons.

DEFENCE BUDGET

DEPARTMENTAL EXPENDITURE LIMITS
£ billion

	2017–18
Resource DEL	27.5
Capital DEL	8.5
Total	36.0

Source: HM Treasury – Spring Budget 2017 (Crown copyright)

MINISTRY OF DEFENCE

Main Building, Whitehall, London SW1A 2HB
T 020-7218 9000
W www.gov.uk/government/organisations/ministry-of-defence

Secretary of State for Defence, Rt. Hon. Sir Michael Fallon, KCB, MP
Parliamentary Private Secretary, Oliver Dowden, MP
Special Advisers, Rob Oxley; James Wild
Minister of State, Rt. Hon. Earl Howe (Lords)
Minister of State, Mark Lancaster, TD, MP (Armed Forces)
Parliamentary Private Secretary, Anne-Marie Trevelyan, MP
Parliamentary Under-Secretary of State and Minister for Defence Procurement, Harriett Baldwin, MP
Parliamentary Under-Secretary of State and Minister for Defence People and Veterans, Rt. Hon. Tobias Ellwood, MP

CHIEFS OF STAFF
Chief of the Defence Staff, Air Chief Marshal Sir Stuart Peach, GBE, KCB, ADC
Vice-Chief of the Defence Staff, Gen. Sir Gordon Messenger, KCB, DSO*, OBE, ADC
Chief of the Naval Staff and First Sea Lord, Adm. Sir Philip Jones, KCB, ADC
Second Sea Lord and Deputy Chief of Naval Staff, Vice-Adm. (Simon) Jonathan Woodcock, OBE
Chief of the General Staff, Gen. Sir Nicholas Carter, KCB, CBE, DSO, ADC
Assistant Chief of the General Staff, Maj.-Gen. Nicholas Welch, OBE
Chief of the Air Staff, Air Chief Marshal Sir Stephen Hillier, KCB, CBE, DFC, ADC
Assistant Chief of the Air Staff, Air Vice-Marshal Mike Wigston, CBE

SENIOR OFFICIALS
Permanent Secretary, Stephen Lovegrove
Chief Scientific Adviser, vacant
Director-General Finance, Louise Tulett, CBE

THE DEFENCE COUNCIL

The Defence Council is chaired by the Secretary of State, and comprises the other ministers, the Permanent Under-Secretary, the Chief of Defence Staff and senior service officers and officials who head the armed services and the department's major corporate functions. It provides the formal legal basis for the conduct of UK defence through a range of powers vested in it by statute and letters patent.

THE DEFENCE BOARD

The Defence Board is the main corporate board of the MoD, providing senior level leadership and strategic management of defence. The Defence Board is the highest committee in the MoD, responsible for the full range of defence business, other than the conduct of operations.

Permanent Secretary, Stephen Lovegrove
Members, Julian Kelly (Nuclear); Lt.-Gen. Richard Nugee, CVO, CBE (Chief of Defence People); Julie Taylor (Head Office and Commissioning Services); Louise Tulett, CBE (Finance); Peter Watkins, CBE (Security Policy)
Non-Executive Members, Sir Gerry Grimstone (Lead); Danuta Gray; Paul Skinner, CBE; Graham Williams

CENTRAL STAFF
Vice-Chief of the Defence Staff, Gen. Sir Gordon Messenger, KCB, DSO*, OBE, ADC

JOINT FORCES COMMAND
Commander of Joint Forces Command, Gen. Sir Chris Deverell, KCB, MBE, ADC
Chief of Joint Operations, Vice-Adm. Timothy Fraser, CB
Chief of Staff, Rear-Adm. Antony Radakin

FLEET COMMAND
First Sea Lord, Sir Philip Jones, KCB, ADC
Fleet Commander and Chief Naval Warfare Officer, Vice-Adm. Benjamin Key, CBE

NAVAL HOME COMMAND
Second Sea Lord, Vice-Adm. (Simon) Jonathan Woodcock, OBE

LAND FORCES
Commander Field Army, Lt.-Gen. Patrick Saunders, CBE, DSO
Deputy Commander Field Army, Maj.-Gen. Simon Brooks-Ward, CVO, OBE, TD, VR

AIR COMMAND
Deputy Commander Operations and Air Member for Operations, Air Marshal Stuart Atha, CB, DSO
Deputy Commander Capability and Air Member for Personnel and Capability, Air Marshal Sean Reynolds, CBE, DFC

DEFENCE EQUIPMENT AND SUPPORT
Chief Executive Tony Douglas
Chief of Materiel (Fleet), Vice-Adm. Simon Lister, CB, OBE
Chief of Materiel (Land), Lt.-Gen. Paul Jacques, CBE
Chief of Materiel (Air), Air Marshal Julian Young, CB, OBE

EXECUTIVE AGENCIES

DEFENCE ELECTRONICS AND COMPONENTS AGENCY
Welsh Road, Deeside, Flintshire CH5 2LS T 01244-847694
E decainfo@deca.mod.uk
W www.gov.uk/government/organisations/defence-electronics-and-components-agency

The Defence Electronics and Components Agency (DECA) provides maintenance, repair, overhaul, upgrade and procurement in avionics, electronics and components fields to support the MoD. As a 'trading' executive agency DECA is run along commercial lines with funding for DECA's activities being generated entirely by payments for delivery of services provided to the MoD and other private sector customers. DECA currently has an annual turnover of around £25m and employs approximately 430 staff across its head office and main operating centre in North Wales, a site in Stafford and various deployed locations across the UK.

Chief Executive, Geraint Spearing

DEFENCE SCIENCE AND TECHNOLOGY LABORATORY

Porton Down, Salisbury, Wiltshire SP4 0JQ **T** 01980-950000
E centralenquiries@dstl.gov.uk
W www.gov.uk/government/organisations/defence-science-and-technology-laboratory

The Defence Science and Technology Laboratory (DSTL) supplies specialist science and technology services to the MoD and wider government.

Chief Executive, Jonathan Lyle

UK HYDROGRAPHIC OFFICE

Admiralty Way, Taunton, Somerset TA1 2DN
T 01823-484444
E customerservices@ukho.gov.uk
W www.gov.uk/government/organisations/uk-hydrographic-office

The UK Hydrographic Office (UKHO) collects and supplies hydrographic and geospatial data for the Royal Navy and merchant shipping, to protect lives at sea. Working with other national hydrographic offices, UKHO sets and raises global standards of hydrography, cartography and navigation.

Chief Executive, John Humphrey

ARMED FORCES TRAINING AND RECRUITMENT

From Naval Bases at Plymouth, the Clyde in Scotland and a small team at Northwood in Middlesex, Flag Officer Sea Training (FOST) provides Operational Sea Training for all surface ships, submarines and Royal Fleet Auxiliaries of the Royal Navy. All aspects of naval training are offered by FOST including new entry, officer, Royal Marine, submarine, surface and aviation training. FOST also offers specialist training in a number of areas including hydrography, meteorology, oceanography, marine engineering and diving.

The Army Recruiting and Training Division (ARTD) is responsible for the four key areas of army training: soldier initial training, at the School of Infantry or at one of the army's four other facilities; officer initial training at the Royal Military Academy Sandhurst; trade training at one of the army's specialist facilities; and resettlement training for those about to leave the army. Trade training facilities include: the Armour Centre; the Infantry Battle School; the Infantry Training Centre, Catterick; the Royal School of Military Engineering and the Army Aviation Centre.

The Royal Air Force No. 22 (Training) Group is responsible for the recruitment, selection, initial and professional training of RAF personnel as well as providing trained specialist personnel to the armed forces as a whole, such as providing the army air corps with trained helicopter pilots. The group is split into five areas: RAF College Cranwell; the Air Cadet Organisation (ACO); the Directorate of Flying Training (DFT); the Directorate of Ground Training; and the Defence College of Technical Training.

The Defence College of Technical Training provides technical training to all three services and includes the Defence School of Aeronautical Engineering (DSAE); the Defence School of Communications and Information Systems (DSCIS); the Defence School of Electronic and Mechanical Engineering (DSEME); and the Defence School of Marine Engineering (DSMarE).

USEFUL WEBSITES

W www.royalnavy.mod.uk
W www.army.mod.uk
W www.raf.mod.uk

THE ROYAL NAVY

In Order of Seniority as at November 2017

LORD HIGH ADMIRAL OF THE UNITED KINGDOM
HRH The Prince Philip, Duke of Edinburgh, KG, KT, OM, GBE, AK, QSO, PC, *apptd* 2011

ADMIRALS OF THE FLEET
HRH The Prince Philip, Duke of Edinburgh, KG, KT, OM, GBE, AC, QSO, PC, *apptd* 1953
Sir Benjamin Bathurst, GCB, *apptd* 1995
HRH The Prince of Wales, KG, KT, GCB, OM, AK, QSO, PC, ADC, *apptd* 2012
Lord Boyce, KG, GCB, OBE, *apptd* 2014

ADMIRALS
(Former Chiefs or Vice Chiefs of Defence Staff and First Sea Lords who remain on the active list)
Slater, Sir Jock, GCB, LVO, *apptd* 1991
Essenhigh, Sir Nigel, GCB, *apptd* 1998
West of Spithead, Lord, GCB, DSC, PC, *apptd* 2000
Band, Sir Jonathon, GCB, *apptd* 2002
Stanhope, Sir Mark, GCB, OBE, *apptd* 2004
Zambellas, Sir George, GCB, DSC, *apptd* 2012

ADMIRALS
HRH The Princess Royal, KG, KT, GCVO, QSO *(Cdre-in-Chief Portsmouth)*
Jones, Sir Philip, KCB, ADC *(First Sea Lord and Chief of Naval Staff)*

VICE-ADMIRALS
HRH The Duke of York, KG, GCVO, ADC *(Adm. of the Sea Cadet Corps and Cdre-in-Chief Fleet Air Arm)*
Lister, Sir Simon, KCB, OBE *(Chief of Materiel (Submarines) and Chief Naval Engineering Officer)*
Potts, Duncan, CB *(Director-General Joint Force Development and Director Defence Academy)*
Woodcock, (Simon) Jonathan, OBE *(Second Sea Lord and Deputy Chief of Naval Staff)*
Johnstone, Clive, CB, CBE *(Cdr Maritime Command)*
Key, Benjamin, CBE *(Fleet Cdr and Chief Naval Warfare Officer)*
Fraser, Timothy, CB *(Chief of Joint Operations)*

REAR-ADMIRALS
Lowe, Timothy, CBE *(National Hydrographer and Deputy Chief Executive (Hydrography))*
Williams, Simon, CB, CVO *(Naval Secretary, Assistant Chief of Naval Staff (Personnel) and Flag Officer Reserves)*
Tarrant, Robert, CB *(Cdr Operations Study)*
Bennett, Paul, CB, OBE *(Assistant Chief of Naval Staff (Capability) and Chief of Staff Navy Command HQ)*
Kingwell, John, CBE *(Deputy Commandant Royal College of Defence Studies)*
Mackay, Graeme, CBE *(Director Carrier Strike)*
Clink, John, CBE *(Flag Officer Sea Training and Assistant Chief of the Naval Staff (Training))*
Burton, Alexander *(Cdr UK Maritime Forces and Rear-Adm. Surface Ships (Head of Fighting Arm))*
Beckett, Keith, CBE *(Chief Strategic Systems Executive)*
Radakin, Antony *(Chief of Staff Joint Forces Command)*
Stokes, Richard *(Assistant Chief of Naval Staff (Support))*
Weale, John, OBE *(Flag Officer Scotland & Northern Ireland, Assistant Chief of Naval Staff (Submarines) and Rear-Adm. Submarines (Head of Fighting Arm))*
Blount, Keith, OBE *(Assistant Chief of Naval Staff (Aviation, Amphibious Capability and Carriers) and Rear-Adm. Fleet Air Arm (Head of Fighting Arm))*

McAlpine, Paul, CBE *(Deputy Cdr Strike Force NATO)*
Hine, Nicholas *(Assistant Chief of Naval Staff (Policy))*
Gardner, Christopher, CBE *(Assistant Chief of Naval Staff (Ships) and Chief Naval Logistics Officer)*
Chivers, Paul, OBE *(Director Military Aviation Authority)*
Hodgson, Timothy, MBE *(Director Submarine Capability)*
Thompson, Richard, CBE *(Director (Technical) Military Aviation Authority)*
Hardern, Simon *(Deputy Chief of Staff Plans, Joint Forces Command Brunssum)*
Methven, Paul *(Director Submarines Acquisition)*
Entwisle, William, OBE, MVO *(Senior British Military Adviser, US Central Command)*
Pentreath, Jonathan, OBE *(Cdr Joint Helicopter Command)*
Halton, Paul, OBE *(Cdr Operations)*

MEDICAL
Walker, Alasdair, CB, OBE, QHS *(Surgeon Vice-Adm., Surgeon General)*

ROYAL MARINES

CAPTAIN-GENERAL
HRH The Prince Philip, Duke of Edinburgh, KG, KT, OM, GBE, AK, QSO, PC

GENERAL
Messenger, Sir Gordon, KCB, DSO*, OBE, ADC *(Vice-Chief of the Defence Staff)*

MAJOR-GENERAL
Smith, Martin, CB, MBE *(pending retirement)*
Bevis, Timothy, CBE *(Director Operations and Plans, International Military Staff)*
Magowan, Robert, CBE *(Cdr UK Amphibious Forces and Commandant-General Royal Marines)*

The Royal Marines were formed in 1664 and are part of the Naval Service. Their primary purpose is to conduct amphibious and land warfare. The principal operational units are:

- Three Commando Brigade, an amphibious all-arms brigade trained to operate in arduous environments (a core element of the UK's Joint Rapid Reaction Force). The commando units, 40 Commando, 42 Commando and 45 Commando each have a strength of around 700 and are based in Taunton, Plymouth and Arbroath, respectively. 43 Commando Fleet Protection Group is around 550 strong and is based at HM Naval Base Clyde on the west coast of Scotland.
- 1 Assault Group, which has its headquarters located in Devonport, Plymouth is responsible for ten landing craft training squadron at Poole, Dorset and 11 amphibious trials and training squadron at Instow, Devon

The Royal Marines also provide detachments for warships and land-based naval parties as required.

ROYAL MARINES RESERVES (RMR)
The Royal Marines Reserve is a commando-trained volunteer force with the principal role, when mobilised, of supporting the Royal Marines. The RMR consists of approximately 600 trained ranks who are distributed between the four RMR centres in the UK. Approximately 10 per cent of the RMR are working with the regular corps on long-term attachments within all of the Royal Marines regular units.

OTHER PARTS OF THE NAVAL SERVICE

FLEET AIR ARM
The Fleet Air Arm (FAA) provides the Royal Navy with a multi-role aviation combat capability able to operate autonomously at short notice worldwide in all environments, over the sea and land. The FAA numbers some 6,200 people, which comprises 11.5 per cent of the total Royal Naval strength. It operates some 200 combat aircraft and more than 50 support/training aircraft.

ROYAL FLEET AUXILIARY (RFA)
The Royal Fleet Auxiliary is a 1,620-strong civilian-manned flotilla of 13 ships owned by the MoD. Its primary role is to supply the Royal Navy and host nations while at sea with fuel, ammunition, food and spares, enabling them to maintain operations away from their home ports. It also provides amphibious support and secure sea transport for military units and their equipment. The ships routinely support and embark Royal Naval Air Squadrons.

ROYAL NAVAL RESERVE (RNR)
The Royal Naval Reserve is an integral part of the Naval Service. It is a part-time force of around 2,000 trained men and women who are deployed with the Royal Navy in times of tension, humanitarian crisis or conflict.

The Royal Naval Reserve has 18 units throughout the UK; 17 of these provide initial training while one other specialist unit, HMS Ferret, Bedford provides intelligence training. Basic training is provided at HMS Raleigh, Torpoint in Cornwall for ratings and at the Britannia Royal Naval College, Dartmouth in Devon for officers; both these and most other RNR courses are of two weeks' duration or less.

QUEEN ALEXANDRA'S ROYAL NAVAL NURSING SERVICE
The first nursing sisters were appointed to naval hospitals in 1884 and the Queen Alexandra's Royal Naval Nursing Service (QARNNS) gained its current title in 1902. Today QARNNS is a branch of the Royal Naval Medical Service that is committed to supporting the medical component of Royal Naval operational capability. QARNS trains and employs nurses in a wide variety of specialities including emergency nursing, intensive care, burns and plastics, trauma and orthopaedics, surgical, medical and ophthalmology.

QUARNS is ready to deploy anywhere in the world to support global naval operations; recent deployments have included fighting the Ebola outbreak in Sierra Leone and helping to save lives in the Mediterranean.

Patron, HRH Princess Alexandra, the Hon. Lady Ogilvy, KG, GCVO
Head of the Naval Nursing Service, Capt. Steve Spencer, QHNS, RN

HM FLEET
as at September 2017

Submarines	
Vanguard Class	Vanguard, Vengeance, Victorious, Vigilant
Trafalgar Class	Talent, Torbay, Trenchant, Triumph
Astute Class	Artful, Astute, Ambush
Aircraft Carrier	Queen Elizabeth
Landing Platform Helicopter Ship	Ocean
Landing Platform Dock	Albion, Bulwark
Destroyers	
Type 45	Daring, Dauntless, Defender, Diamond, Dragon, Duncan
Frigates	
Type 23	Argyll, Iron Duke, Kent, Lancaster, Monmouth, Montrose, Northumberland, Portland, Richmond, St Albans, Somerset, Sutherland, Westminster
Mine Warfare Vessels	
Hunt Class	Atherstone, Brocklesby, Cattistock, Chiddingfold, Hurworth, Ledbury, Middleton, Quorn
Sandown Class	Bangor, Blyth, Grimsby, Pembroke, Penzance, Ramsey, Shoreham
Patrol Vessels	
Archer Class P2000 Training Boats	Archer, Biter, Blazer, Charger, Dasher, Example, Exploit, Explorer, Express, Puncher, Pursuer, Raider, Ranger, Smiter, Tracker, Trumpeter
Gibraltar Squadron 16m Fast Patrol Boats	Sabre, Scimitar
River Class	Clyde, Mersey, Severn, Tyne
Survey Vessels	
Ice Patrol Ships	Protector
Ocean Survey Vessel	Scott
Coastal Survey Vessel	Gleaner
Multi-Role Survey Vessels	Echo, Enterprise

ROYAL FLEET AUXILIARY

Landing Ship Dock (Auxiliary)	RFA Cardigan Bay, RFA Mounts Bay, RFA Lyme Bay
Tide Class	RFA Tidespring
Wave Class	RFA Wave Knight, RFA Wave Ruler
Rover Class	RFA Black Rover, RFA Gold Rover
Fort Class	RFA Fort Austin, RFA Fort Rosalie, RFA Fort Victoria
Forward Repair Ship	RFA Diligence
Casualty Receiving Ship/ Aviation Training Facilities	RFA Argus

THE ARMY

In Order of Seniority as at November 2017

THE QUEEN

FIELD MARSHALS
HRH The Prince Philip, Duke of Edinburgh, KG, KT, OM, GBE, AK, QSO, PC, *apptd* 1953
Lord Bramall, KG, GCB, OBE, MC, *apptd* 1982
Lord Vincent of Coleshill, GBE, KCB, DSO, *apptd* 1991
Sir John Chapple, GCB, CBE, *apptd* 1992
HRH The Duke of Kent, KG, GCMG, GCVO, ADC, *apptd* 1993
Lord Inge, KG, GCB, PC, *apptd* 1994
HRH The Prince of Wales, KG, KT, GCB, OM, AK, QSO, PC, ADC, *apptd* 2012
Lord Guthrie of Craigiebank, GCB, LVO, OBE, *apptd* 2012
Lord Walker of Aldringham, GCB, CMG, CBE, *apptd* 2014

FORMER CHIEFS OF STAFF
Gen. Sir Roger Wheeler, GCB, CBE, *apptd* 1997
Gen. Sir Mike Jackson, GCB, CBE, DSO, *apptd* 2003
Gen. Sir Timothy Granville-Chapman, GBE, KCB, *apptd* 2005
Gen. Lord Dannatt, GCB, CBE, MC, *apptd* 2006
Gen. Lord Richards of Herstmonceux, GCB, CBE, DSO, ADC, *apptd* 2009
Gen. Sir Nicholas Houghton, GCB, CBE, ADC, *apptd* 2009
Gen. Sir Peter Wall, GCB, CBE, *apptd* 2010
Gen. Sir Richard Barrons, KCB, CBE, *apptd* 2013

GENERALS
Carter, Sir Nicholas, KCB, CBE, DSO, ADC *(Chief of the General Staff)*
Deverell, Sir Christopher, KCB, MBE *(Cdr Joint Forces Command)*
Everard, Sir James, KCB, CBE *(Deputy Supreme Allied Cdr Europe)*

LIEUTENANT-GENERALS
Lorimer, Sir John, KCB, MBE, DSO *(pending assignment: Defence Senior Adviser to the Middle East (January 2018))*
Poffley, M., OBE *(Deputy Chief of Defence Staff (Military Capability))*
Beckett, T., CBE *(Defence Senior Adviser to the Middle East (pending retirement January 2018))*
Bashall, J., CBE *(Cdr Home Command)*
Radford, T., CB, OBE, DSO *(Cdr Allied Rapid Reaction Corps)*
Pope, N., CBE *(Deputy Chief of the General Staff)*
Jaques, P., CBE *(Chief of Materiel (Land), Defence Equipment and Support)*
Storrie, A., CB, CBE *(pending retirement)*
Carleton-Smith, M., CBE *(Deputy Chief of Defence Staff (Military Strategy and Operations))*
Nugee, R., CVO, CBE *(Chief of Defence People)*
Norton, Sir George, KCVO, CBE *(UK National Military Representative to NATO and the European Union)*
Sanders, P., CBE, DSO *(Cdr Field Army)*
Felton, R., CBE *(Director-General Defence Safety Authority)*
Cripwell, R., CB, CBE *(Deputy Cdr Resolute Support)*

ACTING LIEUTENANT-GENERAL
Hooper, I. *(Acting Chief Executive Officer, Information Systems and Services)*

MAJOR-GENERALS
Foster, A., CMG, MBE *(pending retirement)*
Ashmore, N., CB, OBE *(pending retirement)*

Munro, R., CBE, TD, VR *(Assistant Chief of the Defence Staff (Reserves and Cadets))*
Chiswell, J., CBE, MC *(appointment withheld)*
Smyth-Osbourne, Sir Edward, KCVO, CBE *(Deputy Cdr NATO Rapid Deployable Corps – Italy)*
Urch, T., CBE *(GOC Force Troops Command)*
Crackett, J., CB, TD, VR *(Director Reserves)*
Hockenhull, J., OBE *(Cyber & Intelligence, Surveillance and Reconnaissance Cdr)*
Nitsch, R., CBE *(Director Personnel)*
Skeates, S., CBE *(Standing Joint Force Cdr)*
Tickell, C., CBE *(Director Capability)*
Semple, R., CBE *(Director Information)*
Talbot Rice, R. CBE *(pending retirement)*
Bathurst, B., CBE *(GOC London District and Maj.-Gen. The Household Division)*
Welch, N., OBE *(Assistant Chief of the General Staff)*
Fattorini, C. *(pending retirement)*
Coulter, D., CB, QHC, CF *(Revd Doctor – Chaplain-General)*
Patterson, J., CB *(Director Capability, Joint Forces Command)*
Fay, A. *(Assistant Chief of Defence Staff (Logistic Operations))*
Bruce, R., CBE, DSO *(Military Secretary and GOC Scotland)*
Gaunt, M., CB *(Director Support)*
Hill, G., CBE *(Assistant Chief of the Defence Staff (Defence Engagement))*
Stanford, R., MBE *(Senior British Loan Officer – Oman)*
Bramble, W., CBE *(Chief of Staff, HQ Allied Rapid Reaction Corps)*
Chalmers, D., DSO, OBE *(Deputy Commanding General-Support, Task Force PHANTOM)*
Cave, I., *(Deputy Chief of Staff (Plans), Joint Force Command Naples)*
Nanson, P., CBE *(Commandant Sandhurst Group)*
Wardlaw, R., OBE *(Director Army Basing and Infrastructure)*
Ridge, S. *(Director Army Legal Services)*
Brooks-Ward, S., CVO, OBE, TD, VR *(Deputy Cdr Field Army)*
Jones, I. *(Chief of Staff Field Army)*
Bricknell, M. QHP *(Director Medical Policy and Operational Capability)*
Swift, J., OBE *(Director Strategy)*
Mitchell, G., MBE *(Director Development, Concepts and Doctrine Centre)*
Cavanagh, N. *(Director Strategy and Planning, Defence Infrastructure Organisation)*
Jones, R., CBE *(pending assignment)*
Hyams, T., OBE *(GOC Recruiting and Training Division)*
Borton, N., DSO, MBE *(GOC 3rd (UK) Division)*
Illingworth, J., OBE *(Cdr British Forces Cyprus and Administrator of the Sovereign Base Areas)*
Gedney, F., OBE *(Deputy Commanding General-Support, HQ III (USA) Corps)*
Wooddisse, R., CBE, MC *(GOC 1st (UK) Division)*
Capps, D., CBE *(GOC Regional Command)*
Herbert, C., OBE *(Deputy Adviser Ministry of Interior, HQ Resolute Support)*
McClean, C., CBE *(Director Land Equipment, Defence Equipment and Support)*

CONSTITUTION OF THE ARMY

The army consists of the Regular Army, the Regular Reserve and the Army Reserve. It is commanded by the Chief of the General Staff, who is the professional Head of Service and Chair of the Executive Committee of the Army Board, which provides overall strategic policy and direction to the Commander Land Forces (formerly Commander-in-Chief, Land Forces). There are four subordinate commands that report to the Commander Land Forces: the Field Army; Support Command, headed by the Adjutant General; Force Development and Capability Command and the Joint Helicopter Command. The army is divided into functional arms and services, subdivided into regiments and corps (listed below in order of precedence). During 2008, as part of the Future Army Structure (FAS) reform programme, the infantry was re-structured into large multi-battalion regiments, which involved amalgamations and changes in title for some regiments. The 2010 Strategic Defence and Security Review laid out the commitments expected of the UK Armed Forces and, as a result, Army 2020 was created to replace FAS. The main changes at divisional, brigade and unit level occurred largely between mid-2014 and mid-2015.

All enquiries with regard to records of serving personnel (Regular and Reserve) should be directed to: The Army Personnel Centre Help Desk, Kentigern House, 65 Brown Street, Glasgow G2 8EX T 0345-600 9663. Enquirers should note that the Army is governed in the release of personal information by various acts of parliament.

ORDER OF PRECEDENCE OF CORPS AND REGIMENTS OF THE BRITISH ARMY

ARMS

HOUSEHOLD CAVALRY
    The Life Guards
    The Blues and Royals (Royal Horse Guards and 1st Dragoons)

ROYAL HORSE ARTILLERY
(when on parade, the Royal Horse Artillery take precedence over the Household Cavalry)

ROYAL ARMOURED CORPS
    1st the Queen's Dragoon Guards
    The Royal Scots Dragoon Guards (Carabiniers and Greys)
    The Royal Dragoon Guards
    The Queen's Royal Hussars (The Queen's Own and Royal Irish)
    The Royal Lancers
    The King's Royal Hussars
    The Light Dragoons
    Royal Tank Regiment

ROYAL REGIMENT OF ARTILLERY
(with the exception of the Royal Horse Artillery (see above))

CORPS OF ROYAL ENGINEERS

ROYAL CORPS OF SIGNALS

REGIMENTS OF FOOT GUARDS
    Grenadier Guards
    Coldstream Guards
    Scots Guards
    Irish Guards
    Welsh Guards

REGIMENTS OF INFANTRY
    The Royal Regiment of Scotland
    The Princess of Wales's Royal Regiment (Queen and Royal Hampshire's)
    The Duke of Lancaster's Regiment (King's, Lancashire and Border)
    The Royal Regiment of Fusiliers
    The Royal Anglian Regiment
    The Rifles
    The Yorkshire Regiment

The Mercian Regiment
The Royal Welsh
The Royal Irish Regiment
The Parachute Regiment
The Royal Gurkha Rifles

SPECIAL AIR SERVICE

ARMY AIR CORPS

SERVICES

ROYAL ARMY CHAPLAINS' DEPARTMENT

THE ROYAL LOGISTIC CORPS

ROYAL ARMY MEDICAL CORPS

CORPS OF ROYAL ELECTRICAL AND MECHANICAL ENGINEERS

ADJUTANT-GENERAL'S CORPS

ROYAL ARMY VETERINARY CORPS

SMALL ARMS SCHOOL CORPS

ROYAL ARMY DENTAL CORPS

INTELLIGENCE CORPS

ROYAL ARMY PHYSICAL TRAINING CORPS

QUEEN ALEXANDRA'S ROYAL ARMY NURSING CORPS

CORPS OF ARMY MUSIC

THE ROYAL MONMOUTHSHIRE ROYAL ENGINEERS (MILITIA) (THE ARMY RESERVE)

THE HONOURABLE ARTILLERY COMPANY (THE ARMY RESERVE)

REST OF THE ARMY RESERVE

THE ARMY RESERVE

The Army Reserve (formerly the Territorial Army (TA)) is part of the UK's reserve land forces and provides support to the regular army at home and overseas. The Army Reserve is divided into three types of unit: national, regional, and sponsored. Army Reserve soldiers serving in regional units complete a minimum of 27 days training a year, comprising some evenings, weekends and an annual two-week camp. National units normally specialise in a specific role or trade, such as logistics, IT, communications or medical services. Members of national units have a lower level of training commitment and complete 19 days training a year. Sponsored reserves are individuals who will serve, as members of the workforce of a company contracted to the MoD, in a military capacity and have agreed to accept a reserve liability to be called up for active service in a crisis. In 2012 the Secretary of State for Defence issued a consultation paper *Future Reserves 2020: Delivering the Nation's Security Together,* which outlined plans to invest an additional £1.8bn in the Reserve Forces over the next ten years, for the Reserve Forces to be more integrated with the regular forces and to have a more significant role within the armed forces as a whole.

QUEEN ALEXANDRA'S ROYAL ARMY NURSING CORPS

The Queen Alexandra's Royal Army Nursing Corps (QARANC) was founded in 1902 as Queen Alexandra's Imperial Military Nursing Service and gained its present title in 1949. The QARANC has trained nurses for the register since 1950 and also trains and employs healthcare assistants. Nursing officers, Nursing soldiers, healthcare assistants and student nurses of the QARANC deliver a high quality, adaptable and dedicated nursing care wherever the Army needs it and can find themselves working in a variety of settings. These can vary from NHS hospitals with military units, to ground based environments such as medical regiments and field hospitals. QARANC personnel deal with a wide range of medical situations, with civilian and military patients in the UK, to military casualties of war and conflict. Work locations vary between clinical roles and instructional positions at training bases. Currently Army nurses are based and deployed in the UK, Germany, Cyprus, Canada, Poland, Brunei, Nepal, Kenya and Sierra Leone.

Colonel-in-Chief, HRH The Countess of Wessex, GCVO
Colonels Commandant, Col. Sue Bush; Col. Jane Davis, OBE, QVRM, TD

THE ROYAL AIR FORCE

In Order of Seniority as at November 2017

THE QUEEN

MARSHALS OF THE ROYAL AIR FORCE
HRH The Prince Philip, Duke of Edinburgh, KG, KT, OM, GBE, AK, QSO, PC, *apptd* 1953
HRH The Prince of Wales, KG, KT, GCB, OM, AK, QSO, PC, ADC, *apptd* 2012

FORMER CHIEFS OF THE AIR STAFF

MARSHALS OF THE ROYAL AIR FORCE
Sir Keith Williamson, GCB, AFC, *apptd* 1985
Lord Craig of Radley, GCB, OBE, *apptd* 1988
Lord Stirrup, KG, GCB, AFC, *apptd* 2014

AIR CHIEF MARSHALS
Sir Michael Graydon, GCB, CBE, *apptd* 1991
Sir Richard Johns, GCB, KCVO, OBE, *apptd* 1994
Sir Peter Squire, GCB, DFC, AFC, *apptd* 1999
Sir Glenn Torpy, GCB, CBE, DSO, *apptd* 2006
Sir Stephen Dalton, GCB, *apptd* 2009
Sir Andrew Pulford, GCB, CBE, *apptd* 2013

AIR RANK LIST

AIR CHIEF MARSHALS
Peach, Sir Stuart, GBE, KCB, ADC *(Chief of the Defence Staff)*
Hillier, Sir Stephen, KCB, CBE, DFC, ADC *(Chief of the Air Staff)*

AIR MARSHALS
Stacey, Sir Graham, KBE, CB *(Chief of Staff to Supreme Allied Command Transformation)*
Osborne, P., CBE *(Chief of Defence Intelligence)*
Young, J., CB, OBE *(Chief of Materiel (Air) and Air Member for Materiel)*
Reynolds, S., CBE, DFC *(Deputy Cdr Capability and Air Member for Personnel and Capability)*
Atha, S., CB, DSO *(Deputy Cdr Operations and Air Member for Operations)*
Evans, S., CBE *(Deputy Cdr NATO Air Command, Ramstein)*

AIR VICE-MARSHALS
Morrison, I., CBE *(Director-General, Saudi Armed Forces Project)*
Farnell, G., CB, OBE *(General-Manager, NATO Eurofighter and Typhoon Management Agency)*
Stringer, E., CB, CBE *(Assistant Chief of the Defence Staff (Operations))*
Gray, S., CB, OBE *(Air Officer Commanding No. 38 Group)*
Turner, A., CBE *(Assistant Chief of the Defence Staff (Operations) Designate)*
Chaffey, J., QHC *(Chaplain-in-Chief (RAF) and Director-General Chaplaincy Services (RAF))*
Waterfall, G., CBE *(Chief of Staff (Operations), Permanent Joint HQ)*
Broadbridge, Hon. R., QHS *(Director Healthcare Delivery and Training)*
Wigston, M., CBE *(Assistant Chief of the Air Staff)*
Knighton, R. CB *(Assistant Chief of Defence Staff (Capability and Force Design))*
Parker, G., OBE *(Defence Attaché, Washington)*
Corbett, A., MBE *(Deputy Director Commonwealth Integration, Washington)*
Quigley, M. *(Director Safety & Environment, Quality & Technology, Defence Equipment and Support)*
Mayhew, G., CBE *(Air Officer Commanding No. 1 Group)*
Hedley, B., MBE *(Director Joint Warfare, Joint Forces Command)*

Tunnicliffe, G. *(Assistant Chief of the Defence Staff (Personnel Capability) and Defence Services Secretary)*
Bethell, K. *(Director Combat Air, Defence Equipment and Support)*
Elliot, C., CBE *(Chief of Staff Personnel and Air Secretary)*
Russell, G. *(Director Helicopters, Defence Equipment and Support)*
Shell, S., OBE *(Chief of Staff Operations), Air Command)*
Luck, C., MBE, DFC *(Commandant Joint Services Command and Staff College)*
Rochelle, S., OBE, DFC *(Chief of Staff Capability, Air Command)*
Mardell, A. *(Director Legal Services (RAF))*
James, W., CBE *(Air Officer Commanding No. 22 Group and Chief of Staff Training)*
Cooper, D., CBE *(Air Officer Commanding No 2. Group)*

CONSTITUTION OF THE RAF

CONSTITUTION OF THE ROYAL AIR FORCE
The RAF consists of a single command, Air Command, based at RAF High Wycombe. RAF Air Command was formed on 1 April 2007 from the amalgamation of Strike Command and Personnel and Training Command.

Air Command consists of three groups, each organised around specific operational duties. No. 1 Group is the coordinating organisation for the tactical fast-jet forces responsible for attack, offensive support and air defence operations. No. 2 Group provides air combat support including air transport and air-to-air refuelling; intelligence surveillance; targeting and reconnaissance; and force protection. No. 22 (Training) Group recruits personnel and provides trained specialist personnel to the RAF, as well as to the Royal Navy and the Army (*see also* Armed Forces Training and Recruitment).

RAF EQUIPMENT

AIRCRAFT

Combat Aircraft	Lightening II, Tornado GR4, Typhoon FGR4
Training Aircraft	Hawk T1, Hawk T2, King Air B200, Tucano T1, Tutor T1, Vigilant T1, Viking T1
Surveillance Aircraft	Reaper MQ9A RPAS, RC-135W Rivet Joint, Sentinel R1, E-3D Sentry AEW1, Shadow R1

HELICOPTERS

Helicopters	Chinook, Griffin HAR2, Merlin HC3, Puma HC2, Sea King HAR3/3A
Training Helicopters	Griffin HT1, Squirrel HT1

ROYAL AUXILIARY AIR FORCE

The Auxiliary Air Force was formed in 1924 to train an elite corps of civilians to serve their country in flying squadrons in their spare time. In 1947 the force was awarded the prefix 'royal' in recognition of its distinguished war service and the Sovereign's Colour for the RAuxAF was presented in 1989. The RAuxAF continues to recruit civilians who undertake military training in their spare time, with a standard minimum commitment of 27 days a year. With the amendments to the reserve service made under the Defence Reform Act 2014, reservists can now be employed to support the RAF across the full spectrum of military tasks. There are currently 27 squadrons with the RAuxAF, with a total establishment of just under 3,200 posts, with reservist posts being available in the majority of trades.

Air Commodore-in-Chief, HM The Queen
Commandant General, Air Vice-Marshal Lord Beaverbrook, ADC
Inspector, Gp Capt. Gavin Hellard, ADC

PRINCESS MARY'S ROYAL AIR FORCE NURSING SERVICE

The Princess Mary's Royal Air Force Nursing Service (PMRAFNS) was formed on 1 June 1918 as the Royal Air Force Nursing Service. In June 1923, His Majesty King George V gave his royal assent for the Royal Air Force Nursing Service to be known as the Princess Mary's Royal Air Force Nursing Service. The Princess Mary's Royal Air Force Nursing Service (PMRAFNS) is committed to providing a skilled, knowledgeable and able nursing workforce to deliver high quality care, whilst being responsive to the dynamic nature of RAF Nursing in peacetime and on operations.

Patron and Air Chief Commandant, HRH Princess Alexandra, The Hon. Lady Ogilvy, KG, GCVO
Matron-in-Chief, Gp Capt. Michael Priestley

SERVICE SALARIES

Pay16 was introduced on 1 April 2016, replacing the previous Pay 2000 scheme for all regular and reserve personnel on the main pay spines up to and including the rank of Commodore/ Brigadier/ Air Commodore (*see* following page for table of relative rank). Compared with Pay 2000 the total number of increments has been reduced and personnel, with the exception of Lieutenants, remain on the same salary for the first two years in rank.

The following rates of pay apply from 1 April 2017 and are rounded to the nearest pound.

The pay rates shown are for army personnel. The rates also apply to personnel of equivalent rank and pay band in the other services.

Rank	Annual Salary
Second Lieutenant	£25,984

LIEUTENANT	
On appointment	£31,232
After 1 year in rank	£32,329
After 2 years in rank	£33,425
After 3 years in rank	£34,522

CAPTAIN	
On appointment	£40,025
After 2 years in rank	£41,287
After 3 years in rank	£42,550
After 4 years in rank	£43,812
After 5 years in rank	£45,074
After 6 years in rank	£46,336
After 7 years in rank	£47,598

MAJOR	
On appointment	£50,417
After 2 years in rank	£52,078
After 3 years in rank	£53,739
After 4 years in rank	£55,399
After 5 years in rank	£57,060
After 6 years in rank	£58,721
After 7 years in rank	£60,381

LIEUTENANT-COLONEL	
On appointment	£70,760
After 2 years in rank	£72,628
After 3 years in rank	£74,485
After 4 years in rank	£76,347
After 5 years in rank	£78,209
After 6 years in rank	£80,072
After 7 years in rank	£81,934

COLONEL	
On appointment	£85,726
After 2 years in rank	£87,145
After 3 years in rank	£88,563
After 4 years in rank	£89,982
After 5 years in rank	£91,401
After 6 years in rank	£92,819
After 7 years in rank	£94,237

BRIGADIER	
On appointment	£102,159
After 2 years in rank	£103,192
After 3 years in rank	£104,226
After 4 years in rank	£105,259
After 5 years in rank	£106,293

PAY SYSTEM FOR SENIOR MILITARY OFFICERS

Pay rates effective from 1 April 2017 for all military officers of 2★ rank and above (excluding medical and dental officers). All pay rates are rounded to the nearest pound.

Rank	Annual Salary
MAJOR-GENERAL (2★)	
Scale 1	£113,810
Scale 2	£116,034
Scale 3	£118,303
Scale 4	£120,617
Scale 5	£122,979
Scale 6	£125,385
LIEUTENANT-GENERAL (3★)	
Scale 1	£132,420
Scale 2	£138,911
Scale 3	£145,727
Scale 4	£151,452
Scale 5	£155,917
Scale 6	£160,518
GENERAL (4★)	
Scale 1	£173,715
Scale 2	£178,058
Scale 3	£182,510
Scale 4	£187,072
Scale 5	£190,814
Scale 6	£194,630

Field Marshal – appointments to this rank will not usually be made in peacetime. The salary for holders of the rank is equivalent to the salary of a 5-star General, a salary created only in times of war. In peacetime, the equivalent rank to Field Marshal is the Chief of the Defence Staff. From 1 April 2017, the annual salary range for the Chief of the Defence Staff is £250,270–£265,588.

OFFICERS COMMISSIONED FROM THE SENIOR RANKS

Rank	Annual salary
Level 15	£53,499
Level 14	£53,149
Level 13	£52,781
Level 12	£52,068
Level 11	£51,359
Level 10	£50,642
Level 9	£49,928
Level 8	£49,215
Level 7★	£48,325
Level 6	£47,776
Level 5	£47,218
Level 4†	£46,116
Level 3	£45,567
Level 2	£45,005
Level 1‡	£43,907

★ Officers commissioned from the ranks with more than 15 years' service enter on level 7

† Officers commissioned from the ranks with between 12 and 15 years' service enter on level 4

‡ Officers commissioned from the ranks with less than 12 years' service enter on level 1

SOLDIERS' SALARIES

Pay16 was introduced on 1 April 2016, replacing the previous Pay 2000 scheme for all regular and reserve personnel on the main pay spines up to and including the rank of Commodore/ Brigadier/ Air Commodore (*see* below for table of relative rank). Rank remains the key determinant of pay, but the 'high' and 'low' bands under the Pay 2000 scheme were removed and replaced with 4 supplements *(Supp.)* under which trades are allocated. All ranks in a particular trade are treated the same for pay supplement purposes. Compared with Pay 2000 the total number of increments has been reduced and personnel remain on increment Level 1 for the first two years in rank, with the exception of Privates who remain on increment Level 2 for two years.

Rates of pay effective from 1 April 2017 (rounded to the nearest pound) are:

Rank	Supp. 1	Supp. 2	Supp. 3	Supp 4
PRIVATE				
Level 1	18,489	–	–	–
Level 2	19,831	–	–	–
Level 3	21,148	21,398	21,657	21,657
Level 4	22,255	22,503	22,839	23,151
Level 5	23,334	23,670	24,090	24,402
Level 6	24,414	24,899	25,409	25,733
LANCE CORPORAL				
(levels 7 to 9 also applicable to Privates)				
Level 7	25,525	26,118	26,628	27,092
Level 8	26,708	27,408	27,944	28,438
Level 9	27,949	28,721	29,327	29,899

CORPORAL				
Level 1	29,769	30,635	31,478	32,259
Level 2	30,565	31,449	32,316	33,096
Level 3	31,017	32,074	33,043	33,873
Level 4	31,441	32,513	33,739	34,685
Level 5	31,888	32,960	34,351	35,378
SERGEANT				
Level 1	33,490	34,618	36,081	37,266
Level 2	34,324	35,535	37,003	38,343
Level 3	35,188	36,495	37,912	39,354
Level 4	36,064	37,550	38,859	40,378
Level 5	36,948	38,504	39,854	41,441
STAFF SERGEANT				
Level 1	37,698	39,284	40,708	42,352
Level 2	38,292	39,969	41,437	43,040
Level 3	38,907	40,585	42,166	43,768
Level 4	39,501	41,178	42,915	44,517
Level 5	40,122	41,799	43,777	45,216
WARRANT OFFICER CLASS II				
(also applicable to Staff Sergeants)				
Level 1	41,002	42,903	45,014	46,482
Level 2	41,880	43,781	45,658	46,974
Level 3	42,711	44,388	45,985	47,325
Level 4	43,435	44,991	46,279	47,619
Level 5	44,175	45,576	46,556	47,895
WARRANT OFFICER CLASS I				
Level 1	47,488	–	–	48,865
Level 2	47,762	–	–	49,283
Level 3	47,830	–	–	49,756
Level 4	48,370	–	–	50,234
Level 5	49,354	–	–	50,685

RELATIVE RANK – ARMED FORCES

Royal Navy	*Army*	*Royal Air Force*
1 Admiral of the Fleet	1 Field Marshal	1 Marshal of the RAF
2 Admiral (Adm.)	2 General (Gen.)	2 Air Chief Marshal
3 Vice-Admiral (Vice-Adm.)	3 Lieutenant-General (Lt.-Gen.)	3 Air Marshal
4 Rear-Admiral (Rear-Adm.)	4 Major-General (Maj.-Gen.)	4 Air Vice-Marshal
5 Commodore (Cdre)	5 Brigadier (Brig.)	5 Air Commodore (Air Cdre)
6 Captain (Capt.)	6 Colonel (Col.)	6 Group Captain (Gp Capt.)
7 Commander (Cdr)	7 Lieutenant-Colonel (Lt.-Col.)	7 Wing Commander (Wg Cdr)
8 Lieutenant-Commander (Lt.-Cdr)	8 Major (Maj.)	8 Squadron Leader (Sqn Ldr)
9 Lieutenant (Lt.)	9 Captain (Capt.)	9 Flight Lieutenant (Flt Lt)
10 Sub-Lieutenant (Sub-Lt.)	10 Lieutenant (Lt.)	10 Flying Officer (FO)
11 Midshipman	11 Second Lieutenant (2nd Lt.)	11 Pilot Officer (PO)

EDUCATION

THE UK EDUCATION SYSTEM

The structure of the education system in the UK is a devolved matter with each of the countries of the UK having separate systems under separate governments. There are differences between the school systems in terms of the curriculum, examinations and final qualifications and, at university level, in terms of the nature of some degrees and in the matter of tuition fees. The systems in England, Wales and Northern Ireland are similar and have more in common with one another than the Scottish system, which differs significantly.

Education in England is overseen by the Department for Education (DfE).

Responsibility for education in Wales lies with the Department for Education and Skills (DfES) within the Welsh government. Ministers in the Scottish government are responsible for education in Scotland, led by the directorates of Learning and Lifelong Learning, while in Northern Ireland responsibility lies with the Department of Education (DfE) and the Department for the Economy (DE) within the Northern Ireland government.

DEPARTMENT FOR EDUCATION T 0370-000 2288
W www.gov.uk/government/organisations/
department-for-education

DEPARTMENT FOR EDUCATION AND SKILLS (DFES)
T 0300-060 3300 W www.gov.wales/topics/educationandskills

SCOTTISH GOVERNMENT – EDUCATION
T 0300-244 4000 W www.gov.scot/Topics/Education

DEPARTMENT OF EDUCATION (NI) T 028-9127 9279
W www.education-ni.gov.uk

DEPARTMENT FOR THE ECONOMY T 028-9052 9900
W www.economy-ni.gov.uk

RECENT DEVELOPMENTS

After a UK general election in June 2017, the Conservative government retained power in alliance with the Democratic Unionist Party. The new government's pledges for England include: ensuring that every child has the opportunity to attend a good school; fair funding for all schools; and a major reform of technical education to give people the skills necessary for the high-skilled, high-wage jobs of the future.

ENGLAND

- The Higher Education and Research Act was passed in April 2017, paving the way for a new single funding body, UK Research and Innovation, to bring together the seven existing Research Councils, Innovate UK and the research and knowledge exchange functions of the Higher Education Funding Council for England (HEFCE). A new body, Research England, will be responsible for quality-related research funding. A new Office for Students, replacing both HEFCE and the Office for Fair Access, will hold statutory responsibility for quality and standards, approve new entrants to the sector by managing the Register of Higher Education Providers and confer university title and degree awarding powers. All the new bodies are expected to start work in April 2018
- Results from the Teaching Excellence Framework (TEF) trial assessing higher education teaching quality, the learning environment and student outcomes were released in June 2017: 59 providers were rated 'gold', 116 rated 'silver' and 56 rated 'bronze'
- Until 2020, the government is expected to allow tuition fees to increase by the rate of inflation for universities participating in TEF and meeting minimum eligibility requirements. After 2020, fees may be linked to TEF

results. Universities will be able to charge higher annual fees for courses taught over a shorter period of time ('accelerated degrees')
- 12 'opportunity areas' in England will see local partnerships formed between early years providers, schools, colleges, universities, businesses, charities and local authorities, to help all children get the best start in life, no matter what their background, and ensure that they can access high-quality education at every stage
- A new Institute for Apprenticeships started work in April 2017. Independent from government, it will ensure that apprenticeships are of high quality and deliver the skills employers need. This will support the government's commitment to deliver 3 million apprenticeships by 2020
- Universities and colleges across England were awarded £4.5m to develop new degree apprenticeships for students starting in September 2017
- The Education Funding Agency and Skills Funding Agency merged in April 2017 to become the Education and Skills Funding Agency. The merged Agency oversees education funding for pupils aged 5 to 16, education and training for 16- to 19-year-olds, apprenticeships and adult education; it also manages school building programmes
- From September 2017 the government will increase the amount of childcare funded for working parents of 3- and 4-year-olds from 15 to 30 hours a week. Under a new scheme announced in April 2017, Tax-Free Childcare, working parents of children under 12 (or 17 for children with disabilities) can open an online account for registered childcare. For every £8 a parent pays in, the government will pay in an extra £2. Parents can receive up to £2,000 per child (£4,000 for children with disabilities) a year.

WALES

- A June 2017 consultation paper 'Public Good and a Prosperous Wales' proposes a new Tertiary Education and Research Commission for Wales to oversee the higher and further education sector. The new body would succeed the Higher Education Funding Council for Wales, regulate the skills sector and be responsible for funding research and innovation
- In April 2017 a review of government-funded research and innovation in Wales began looking at strengths, gaps and future potential
- Financial incentives of up to £20,000 to attract graduates into teaching subjects such as maths, chemistry, physics and computer science in Wales start in September 2017
- A 5-year plan on apprenticeships from 2016–22 will increase the number of apprentices aged 16–19, address skills shortages, develop higher-level skills and integrate apprenticeships into the wider education system
- £1m will be spent on developing a Foundation Phase Excellence Network, which will support the sharing of effective practice and work closely with the National Networks of Excellence in Science, Technology and Mathematics
- There are plans to launch a new National Academy for Educational Leadership by April 2018, to equip all leaders in the Welsh education system with the skills and knowledge to benefit pupils
- New online assessments will be phased in over three years from the 2018–19 academic year, to replace national reading and numeracy tests now taken by all pupils in years 2 to 9
- There will be a new £36m fund to reduce infant class sizes and raise standards
- The Additional Learning Needs and Education Tribunal (Wales) bill proposes to replace the current Special

Educational Needs (SEN) framework with a reformed system based on Additional Learning Needs (ALN) and provide universal, statutory individual development plans for all children and young people with ALN

SCOTLAND
• Sweeping reforms will put schools in charge of key decisions, giving them responsibility for: raising attainment and closing the poverty-related gap in their school; choosing school staff and management structure; deciding curriculum content, within a broad national framework; and controlling more school funding directly
• These new powers will be guaranteed in a statutory charter for headteachers. Young people and parents will also have a stronger voice in schools. Every school will have access to a 'home to school' link worker to support parents and families
• There will be enhanced career and development opportunities for teachers and continuing reform to Initial Teacher Education. New Regional Improvement Collaboratives will provide streamlined and strengthened support to teachers, including access to teams of attainment experts drawn from local authorities and Education Scotland
• Schools will have an educational support service from local councils, including payroll and HR, and councils will have democratic accountability for the number of schools in an area and the selection of headteachers
• There will be consultations on a proposed fair funding system, to allow schools to target resources better, raise attainment and close the poverty-related gap, and on financial support for college and university students
• Mandatory unit assessment will be removed: from 2017–18 for National 5 courses, from 2018–19 for Higher courses and from 2019–20 for Advanced Higher courses
• The General Teaching Council for Scotland, with other professional development bodies, will become the Education Workforce Council for Scotland
• A pilot programme to improve retention and attainment for students on FE college courses will be undertaken in five colleges during 2017–18 and 2018–19
• A research programme is planned to establish effective ways of raising school attainment and helping teachers, schools and local authorities make the most of existing data
• Scotland's spending on higher education research and development increased by 3.3 per cent in 2015 to £1,092m, the highest level since records began
• New courses will be established at two medical schools to assist more students from deprived backgrounds to enter the medical profession. The pre-entry courses will host 40 students during the 2017–18 academic year
• A new specialist group is to shape the government's science, technology, engineering and medicine strategy. The national STEM Reference Group will seek to inspire take up of STEM subjects and align existing efforts for maximum impact
• The number of Foundation Apprenticeship places available to young people will increase to 1,900 from August 2017 and to 5,000 by the end of 2019

NORTHERN IRELAND
• A record £749.6m was spent on research and development in Northern Ireland in 2015: £540.0m by businesses, £192.9m by the higher education sector and £16.7m by government
• Almost £3.6m was given to Queen's University Belfast for five partnership research projects in Energy, Sustainable Food Production and Processing, and Personalised Medicine
• A second round of the Schools Enhancement Programme was announced, with schools invited to apply for financial support for capital projects costing up to £4m

• £14m was given to schools to cover staff pay and retention costs in 2016–17

STATE SCHOOL SYSTEM

PRE-SCHOOL

Pre-school education is not compulsory. In England, a free place is available for every 3- and 4-year-old whose parents want one, although parents may use as little or as much of their entitlement as they choose. All 3- and 4-year-olds, and disadvantaged 2-year-olds, are entitled to 15 hours a week of free early education over 38 weeks of the year until they reach compulsory school age (the term following their fifth birthday). From September 2017 this will increase to 30 hours a week for 3- and 4-year-old children of working parents (*see* Recent Developments). Free places are funded by local authorities and are delivered by a range of approved providers in the maintained and non-maintained sectors – nursery schools; nursery classes in primary schools; private schools; private day nurseries; voluntary playgroups; pre-schools; and registered childminders. In order to receive funding, providers must be working towards the early learning goals and other features of the Early Years Foundation Stage curriculum, must be inspected on a regular basis by Ofsted and must meet any conditions set by the local authority.

In Wales, every child is entitled to receive free Foundation Phase education for a minimum of two hours a day from the term following their third birthday. The Flying Start scheme allows disadvantaged 2- to 3-year-olds 2.5 hours childcare a week for 39 weeks.

In Scotland, councils have a duty to provide a pre-school education for all 3- and 4-year-olds, and some disadvantaged 2- to 3-year-olds, whose parents request one. Education authorities must offer each child at least 600 hours of free pre-school education a year, although they may provide more if they choose.

In Northern Ireland, the Department of Education aims to provide a funded place for all 3- and 4-year-old children in their final pre-school year. All places offer 2.5 hours a day, five days a week for at least 38 weeks a year.

PRIMARY AND SECONDARY SCHOOLS

By law, full-time education starts at the age of five for children in England, Scotland and Wales and at the age of four in Northern Ireland. In practice, most children in the UK start school before their fifth birthday: in England all children are entitled to a primary school place from the September after their fourth birthday.

Children in England are required to stay in education or training until the end of the academic year in which they turn 18. In all other parts of the UK, compulsory schooling ends at age 16, but children born between certain dates may leave school before their 16th birthday; most young people stay in some form of education until 17 or 18.

Primary education consists mainly of infant schools for children aged 5 to 7, junior schools for those aged 7 to 11, and combined infant and junior schools for both age groups.

First schools in some parts of England cater for ages 5 to 10 as the first stage of a three-tier system of first (lower), middle and secondary (upper) schools. Scotland has only primary schools with no infant/junior division.

Children usually leave primary school and move on to secondary school at the age of 11 (or 12 in Scotland). In the few areas of England that have a three-tier system of schools, middle schools cater for children after they leave first schools for three to four years between the ages of 8 and 14, depending on the local authority.

Secondary schools cater for children aged 11 to 16 and, if they have a sixth form, for those who choose to stay on to the age of 18. From the age of 16, students may move instead to further education colleges or work-based training.

Most UK secondary schools are co-educational. The largest secondary schools have more than 1,500 pupils and around 60 per cent of secondary pupils in the UK are in schools that take more than 1,000 pupils.

Most state-maintained secondary schools in England, Wales and Scotland are comprehensive schools, which admit pupils without reference to ability. In England there remain some areas with grammar schools, catering for pupils aged 11 to 18, which select pupils on the basis of high academic ability. Over half of state secondary schools in England (2,109) are now academies: academies are funded directly by the state rather than being maintained by local authorities. Northern Ireland still has 66 grammar schools; the 11-plus has been officially discontinued but schools, or consortia of schools, use their own unregulated entry tests.

More than 90 per cent of pupils in the UK attend publicly funded schools and receive free education. The rest (6.5 per cent) attend privately funded 'independent' schools, which charge fees, or are educated at home.

The bulk of the UK government's expenditure on school education is through local authorities (Education and Library Boards (ELBs) in Northern Ireland), which pass on state funding to schools and other educational institutions.

SPECIAL EDUCATION

Schools and local authorities in England and Wales, Education and Library Boards (ELBs) in Northern Ireland and education authorities in Scotland are required to identify and secure provision for children with special educational needs and to involve parents in decisions. The majority of children with special educational needs are educated in ordinary mainstream schools, sometimes with supplementary help from outside specialists. Parents of children with special educational needs (referred to as additional support needs in Scotland) have a right of appeal to independent tribunals if their wishes are not met.

Special educational needs provision may be made in maintained special schools, special units attached to mainstream schools or in mainstream classes themselves, all funded by local authorities. There are also non-maintained special schools run by voluntary bodies, mainly charities, who may receive grants from central government for capital expenditure and equipment but whose other costs are met primarily from the fees charged to local authorities for pupils placed in the schools. Some independent schools also provide education wholly or mainly for children with special educational needs.

ADDITIONAL SUPPORT NEEDS TRIBUNALS FOR
  SCOTLAND T 0141-302 5860
  W www.asntscotland.gov.uk
FIRST-TIER TRIBUNAL (SPECIAL EDUCATIONAL
  NEEDS AND DISABILITY) T 020-7843 6958
  W www.gov.uk/special-educational-needs-disability-tribunal
INFORMATION ADVICE AND SUPPORT SERVICES
  NETWORK FOR SEND E iassn@ncb.org.uk
  W www.iassnetwork.org.uk
SPECIAL EDUCATIONAL NEEDS TRIBUNAL FOR
  WALES T 01597-829800 W www.sentw.gov.uk

HOME EDUCATION

In England and Wales parents have the right to educate their children at home and do not have to be qualified teachers to do so. Home-educated children do not have to follow the National Curriculum or take national tests nor do they need a fixed timetable, formal lessons or to observe school hours, days or terms. However, by law parents must ensure that the home education provided is full-time and suitable for the child's age, ability and aptitude and, if appropriate, for any special educational needs. Parents have no legal obligation to notify the local authority that a child is being educated at home, but if they take a child out of school, they must notify the school in writing and the school must report this to the local authority. Local authorities can make informal enquiries of parents to establish that a suitable education is being provided. For children in special schools, parents must seek the consent of the local authority before taking steps to educate them at home.

In Northern Ireland, ELBs monitor the quality of home provision and provide general guidance on appropriate materials and exam types through regular home visits.

The home schooling law in Scotland is similar to that of England. One difference, however, is that if parents wish to take a child out of school they must have permission from the local education authority.

HOME EDUCATION ADVISORY SERVICE
  T 01707-371854
  W www.heas.org.uk
HOME EDUCATION IN NORTHERN IRELAND
  W www.hedni.org
SCHOOLHOUSE HOME EDUCATION ASSOCIATION
  (SCOTLAND) T 01307-463120
  E contact@schoolhouse.org.uk W www.schoolhouse.org.uk

FURTHER EDUCATION

In the UK, further education (FE) is generally understood as post-secondary education, ie any education undertaken after an individual leaves school that is below higher education level. FE therefore embraces a wide range of general and vocational study undertaken by people of all ages from 16 upwards, full-time or part-time, who may be self-funded, employer-funded or state-funded.

FE in the UK is often undertaken at further education colleges, although some take place on employers' premises. Many of these colleges offer some courses at higher education level; some FE colleges teach certain subjects to 14- to 16-year-olds under collaborative arrangements with schools. Colleges' income comes from public funding, student fees and work for and with employers.

HIGHER EDUCATION

Higher education (HE) in the UK describes courses of study, provided in universities, specialist colleges of higher education and in some FE colleges, where the level of instruction is above that of A-level or equivalent exams.

All UK universities and colleges that provide HE are autonomous bodies with their own internal systems of governance. They are not owned by the state. However, most receive a portion of their income from state funds distributed by the separate HE funding councils for England, Scotland and Wales, and the Department for the Economy in Northern Ireland. The rest of their income comes from a number of sources including fees from home and overseas students, government funding for research, endowments and work with or for business.

EXPENDITURE

TOTAL-MANAGED EXPENDITURE ON EDUCATION
(Real terms adjusted to 2016–17 price levels) £bn

2012–13	84.4
2013–14	85.8
2014–15	90.5
2015–16	83.2
2016–17	89.7
2017–18 (est)	95.1

Source: HM Treasury – *Public Expenditure Statistical Analyses (PESA)* July 2017

SCHOOLS

ENGLAND AND WALES

In England and Wales, publicly funded schools are referred to as 'state schools'. Local authorities have a duty to ensure there is a suitable place for every school-age child resident in their area. Local authorities maintain four categories of state school – Community, Foundation, Voluntary-aided and Voluntary-controlled. Each school has a governing body, made up of volunteers elected or appointed by parents, staff, the community and the local authority, which is responsible for strategic management, ensuring accountability, monitoring school performance, setting budgets and appointing the headteacher and senior staff. The headteacher is responsible for the school's day-to-day management and operations and for decisions requiring professional teaching expertise.

In *Community schools,* which are non-denominational, local authorities are the employers of the staff, own the land and buildings and set the admissions criteria.

In *Foundation schools,* the governing body employs the staff and sets the admissions criteria. The land and buildings are usually owned by the governing body or a charitable foundation. A Foundation school may have a religious character, although most do not. A *Trust school* is a distinct type of foundation school that forms a charitable trust with an outside partner – for example, a business, a university, an educational charity or simply another school – that shares the school's aspirations.

Most *Voluntary-aided schools* are religious schools founded by Christian denominations or other faiths. As with Foundation schools, the governing body employs the staff and sets the admissions criteria, which may include priority for members of the faith or denomination. The school buildings and land are normally owned and provided by a charitable foundation, often a religious organisation, which appoints a majority of the school's governors and makes a small contribution to major building costs.

Voluntary-controlled schools are similar to Voluntary-aided schools in that they often have a particular religious ethos, commonly Church of England, and the school land and buildings are normally owned by a charity. However, as with Community schools, the local authority employs the school's staff, sets the admissions criteria and bears all the costs.

Among the local authority-maintained schools are some with particular characteristics:

- *Community and Foundation Special schools* cater for children with specific special educational needs, which may include physical disabilities or learning difficulties
- *Grammar schools* are secondary schools catering for pupils aged 11 to 18 that select all of their pupils based on academic ability. In England there are 164 grammar schools, concentrated in certain local authority areas. Wales has none
- *Maintained boarding schools* are state-funded and offer free tuition but charge fees for board and lodging

In Wales, Welsh-medium primary and secondary schools were first established in the 1950s and 1960s, originally in response to the wishes of Welsh-speaking parents who wanted their children to be educated through the medium of the Welsh language. Now, many children who are not from Welsh-speaking homes also attend Welsh-medium and bilingual schools throughout Wales. There are 428 Welsh-medium primary schools, where the main or sole medium of instruction is in the Welsh language, five Welsh-medium middle schools and 49 Welsh-medium secondary schools, where more than half of foundation subjects (other than English and Welsh) and religious education are taught wholly or partly in Welsh.

England now has increasing numbers of *Academies.* Those set up before the Academies Act 2010 were sponsored by business, faith or voluntary groups who contributed to funding their land and buildings, while the government covered the running costs at a level comparable to other local schools. The Academies Act 2010 streamlined the process of becoming an academy, enabled high-performing schools to convert without a sponsor and allowed primary and special schools to become academies. All academies now receive funding from central government at the level they would have received if still maintained by their local authority, with extra funding only to cover those services the local authority no longer provides. Academies have greater freedoms over how they use their budgets, set staff pay and conditions and deliver the curriculum. As at March 2017 there were 6,087 open academies, of which 3,707 were primary schools.

SCOTLAND

Most schools in Scotland, known as 'publicly funded' schools, are state-funded and charge no fees. Funding is met from resources raised by the Scottish local authorities and from an annual grant from the Scottish government. Scotland does not have school governing bodies like the rest of the UK: local authorities retain greater responsibility for the management and performance of publicly funded schools. Headteachers manage at least 80 per cent of a school's budget, covering staffing, furnishings, repairs, supplies, services and energy costs. Spending on new buildings, modernisation projects and equipment is financed by the local authority within the limits set by the Scottish government.

Scotland has 370 state-funded *faith schools,* the majority of which are Catholic. It has no grammar schools.

Integrated community schools form part of the Scottish government's strategy to promote social inclusion and to raise educational standards. They encourage closer and better joint working among education, health and social work agencies and professionals, greater pupil and parental involvement in schools, and improved support and service provision for vulnerable children and young people.

Scotland has eight *grant-aided schools* that are independent of local authorities but supported financially by the Scottish government. These schools are managed by boards and most of them provide education for children and young people with special educational needs.

NORTHERN IRELAND

Most schools in Northern Ireland are maintained by the state and generally charge no fees, though fees may be charged in preparatory departments of some grammar schools. There are different types of state-funded schools, each under the control of management committees, which also employ the teachers.

Controlled schools (nursery, primary, special, secondary and grammar schools) are managed by Northern Ireland's five ELBs through boards of governors consisting of teachers, parents, members of the ELB and transferor representatives (mainly from the Protestant churches).

Catholic maintained schools (nursery, primary, special and secondary) are under the management of boards of governors consisting of teachers, parents and members nominated by the employing authority, the Council for Catholic Maintained Schools (CCMS).

Other maintained schools (primary, special and secondary) are, in the main, Irish-medium schools that provide education in an Irish-speaking environment. The Department of Education has a duty to encourage and facilitate the development of Irish-medium education. Northern Ireland has 28 standalone Irish-medium schools, most of them primary schools, and 11 Irish-medium units attached to English-medium host schools.

Voluntary schools are mainly grammar schools (66 in 2016–17), which select most pupils according to academic ability. They are managed by boards of governors consisting of teachers, parents and, in most cases, representatives from the Department of Education and the ELB.

Integrated schools (primary and secondary) educate pupils from both the Protestant and Catholic communities as well as those of other faiths and no faith; each school is managed by a board of governors. There are at present 65 integrated schools maintained by the state, 27 of which are controlled schools.

Since 2013 all pupils are guaranteed access to a wide range of courses, with a minimum of 24 courses at Key Stage 4, and 27 at post-16. At least one-third of the courses on offer will be academic and another third will be vocational. Schools work with other schools, FE colleges and other providers to widen the range of courses on offer.

INDEPENDENT SCHOOLS

Around 6 per cent of UK schoolchildren are educated by privately funded 'independent' schools that charge fees and set their own admissions policies. Independent schools are required to meet certain minimum standards but need not teach the National Curriculum. *See also* Independent Schools.

UK SCHOOLS BY CATEGORY (2015–16)

	England	Wales
*Maintained nursery schools	406	13
†Maintained primary and secondary schools	14,963	1,522
Community	8,386	–
Voluntary-aided	3,415	–
Voluntary-controlled	2,197	–
Foundation	965	–
Pupil Referral Units	353	–
Maintained Special schools	973	39
‡Non-maintained Special schools	66	–
‡Academies	5,474	–
Independent schools	2,311	66
Total	24,546	1,640

* Includes one direct grant school in England
† Includes seven middle schools in Wales
‡ Includes City Technology Colleges, University Technology Colleges, studio schools and free schools; excludes voluntary and private pre-school education centres and academies and free schools alternative provision
Source: Department for Education; Welsh government

SCOTLAND

Publicly funded schools	2,531
Primary	2,031
Secondary	359
Special	141
Independent schools	101
Total	2,632

Source: Scottish government

NORTHERN IRELAND

State-maintained nursery schools	96
State-maintained primary and secondary schools	1,029
Controlled	436
Voluntary	61
Catholic maintained	438
Other maintained	31
Integrated	63
Special schools	39
Independent schools	14
Total	1,178

Source: DENI

INSPECTION

ENGLAND

The Office for Standards in Education, Children's Services and Skills (Ofsted) is the main body responsible for inspecting education in English schools. As well as inspecting all publicly funded and some independent schools, Ofsted inspects a range of other services in England, including childcare, children's homes, pupil referral units, local authority children's services, further education, initial teacher training and publicly funded adult skills training. Inspection reports, recommendations and statistical information are published on Ofsted's website.

Ofsted is an independent, non-ministerial government department that reports directly to parliament, headed by Her Majesty's Chief Inspector (HMCI). Ofsted is required to promote improvement in the public services that it inspects; ensure that these services focus on the interests of their users – children, parents, learners and employers; and see that these services are efficient, effective and promote value for money. A new 'common inspection regime' came into effect in September 2015 to make inspections of different settings with similar age groups more coherent.

From October half-term 2017, Ofsted intends to change the current system of giving all schools previously judged 'good' short (one-day) inspections. Where it is clear on the day that a full inspection is needed, the full inspection will be completed within 15 working days rather than 48 hours. Ofsted also proposes to select around 1 in 5 good schools for full inspections in advance.

OFFICE FOR STANDARDS IN EDUCATION, CHILDREN'S SERVICES AND SKILLS T 0300-123 1231
W www.gov.uk/government/organisations/ofsted

WALES

Estyn is the office of Her Majesty's Inspectorate for Education and Training in Wales. It is independent of, but funded by, the Welsh government and is led by Her Majesty's Chief Inspector of Education and Training in Wales.

Estyn's role is to inspect quality and standards in education and training in Wales, including in primary, secondary, special and independent schools, pupil referral units, publicly funded nursery schools and settings, further education, adult community-based and work-based learning, local authorities and teacher education and training.

Estyn also provides advice on quality and standards in education and training to the Welsh government and others and its remit includes making public good practice based on inspection evidence. Estyn publishes on its website the findings of its inspection reports, its recommendations and statistical information.

From September 2017, the inspection regime is changing. School inspections will focus on: standards; wellbeing and attitudes to learning; teaching and learning experiences; care, support and guidance; leadership and management; and a thematic area.

The current 4-point judgement scale remains but wording will be amended to focus on actions to be taken to support improvement:
• Excellent – Very strong, sustained performance and practice
• Good – Strong features, although minor aspects may require improvement
• Adequate and needs improvement – Strengths outweigh weaknesses, but important aspects require improvement
• Unsatisfactory and needs urgent improvement – Important weaknesses outweigh strengths

Reports will be shorter and there will no longer be an overall judgement on current performance or prospects for improvement. Many aspects currently in reports will only be included by exception, in particularly strong or weak cases. The notice period for inspections will be reduced to 15 days and inspections will typically take 4 days rather than 5. Follow-up work will be more supportive.

HER MAJESTY'S INSPECTORATE FOR EDUCATION AND TRAINING IN WALES T 029-2044 6446
W www.estyn.gov.uk

SCOTLAND

HM Inspectorate of Education (HMIE) merged with Learning and Teaching Scotland in July 2011 to become Education Scotland, an executive agency of the Scottish government. Education Scotland operates independently and impartially while being directly accountable to Scottish ministers for the standards of its work. The agency's core business is inspection and review. It is responsible for delivering measurable year-on-year improvements, with maximum efficiency, by promoting excellence, building on strengths, and identifying and addressing under-performance. Since August 2015, inspections take account of national expectations of progress in implementing Curriculum for Excellence.

Inspection reports and reviews, recommendations, examples of good practice and statistical information are published on Education Scotland's website.

EDUCATION SCOTLAND T 0131-244 4430
    W https://education.gov.scot

NORTHERN IRELAND

The Education and Training Inspectorate (ETINI) provides inspection services for the Department of Education and Employment and the Department for the Economy in Northern Ireland.

ETINI carries out inspections of all schools, pre-school services, special education, further education colleges, initial teacher training, training organisations, and curriculum advisory and support services. Since September 2013 regional colleges of further education have received four weeks' notification of inspection, while all other organisations have received two weeks' notification of inspection.

The inspectorate's role is to improve services and it provides evidence-based advice to ministers in order to assist in the formulation of policies. It publishes the findings of its inspection reports, its recommendations and statistical information on its website.

EDUCATION AND TRAINING INSPECTORATE T 028-
    9127 9726 W www.etini.gov.uk

THE NATIONAL CURRICULUM

ENGLAND

The National Curriculum, first introduced in 1988, is mandatory in all state schools for children from age 5 onwards.

Until age 5, or the end of Reception Year in primary school, children are in the Early Years Foundation Stage (EYFS), which has its own learning and development requirements for children in nursery and primary schools. Changes to the EYFS came into effect in 2012, 2014 and 2017. These included simplifying the statutory assessment of children's development at age five; reducing the number of early learning goals from 69 to 17; focusing on seven areas of learning and development (prime areas: communication and language, physical development and personal, social and emotional development; and specific areas: literacy, mathematics, understanding the world, expressive arts and design) and, for parents, a new progress check between age two and three on their child's development.

Following the EYFS, the National Curriculum is organised into 'Key Stages', and sets out the core subjects that must be taught and the standards or attainment targets for each subject at each Key Stage.

- Key Stage 1 covers Years 1 and 2 of primary school, for children aged 5–7
- Key Stage 2 covers Years 3 to 6 of primary school, for children aged 7–11
- Key Stage 3 covers Years 7 to 9 of secondary school, for children aged 11–14
- Key Stage 4 covers Years 10 and 11 of secondary school, for children aged 14–16

Within the framework of the National Curriculum, schools may plan and organise teaching and learning in the way that best meets the needs of their pupils, but maintained schools are expected to follow the programmes of study associated with particular subjects. The programmes of study describe the subject knowledge, skills and understanding that pupils are expected to have developed by the end of each Key Stage.

The government brought in a new National Curriculum for England for maintained primary and secondary schools from September 2014. From September 2017 schools must teach the new programmes of study to all pupils in all Key Stages.

KEY STAGES 1 AND 2 COMPULSORY SUBJECTS	
English	Design and technology
Mathematics	Geography
Science	History
Art and design	Music
Computing	Physical education (incl. swimming)

Foreign languages are compulsory in Key Stage 2, but not Key Stage 1: schools can choose from French, German, Italian, Mandarin, Spanish, Latin or Ancient Greek.

In Key Stage 3, compulsory subjects include those listed above for Key Stage 2 (though the language taught should be a modern foreign language) plus citizenship.

Pupils in Key Stage 4 study a mix of compulsory and optional subjects in preparation for national examinations such as GCSEs. The compulsory subjects are English, mathematics, science, citizenship, computing and physical education. Pupils at this key stage also have to undertake careers education and work-related learning. In addition, schools must offer at least one subject from each of four 'entitlement' areas: arts (art and design, music, dance, drama and media arts); design and technology; humanities (history and geography); and modern foreign languages. To meet the entitlement requirements, schools must ensure that courses in these areas lead to approved qualifications, and allow pupils to take courses in all four areas if they wish to do so.

Schools must teach religious education (RE) at all key stages, although parents have the right to withdraw children for all or part of the RE curriculum. Secondary schools must provide sex and relationship education.

ASSESSMENT

Statutory assessment must be undertaken for all pupils in publicly funded schools in the relevant years. It first takes place towards the end of the Early Years Foundation Stage, when children's level of development is compared to and recorded against a Foundation Stage Profile. This will continue to be statutory until the end of the 2017–18 academic year. Pupils receive a phonics screening check at the end of the first year in Key Stage 1, repeated the following year if necessary. Teacher assessments in English, mathematics and science take place at the end of Key Stage 1 (Year 2) and Key Stage 2 (Year 6); at the end of Key Stage 3 (Year 9) teachers assess progress in all subjects being studied. National tests in English and mathematics take place in Year 6. At Key Stage 4, national examinations are the main form of assessment.

The assessment process for English at the end of Key Stage 2 now involves three elements: English reading; English grammar, punctuation and spelling; and maths.

Key stage 2 results no longer use the previous system of levels. Instead, test results are converted into 'scaled scores', with a score of 100 being the expected standard. Any score below 100 means the pupil is working 'towards the expected standard'; any score above 100 means the pupil is working 'above the expected standard'. Previously the expected standard was a level 4.

Each year the Department for Education publishes on its website performance tables covering every school, college and local authority. The primary school tables are based mainly on the results of the tests taken by children at the end of Key Stage 2 when they are usually aged 11; since 2010 teacher assessment results are also included.

In performance tables, the English Baccalaureate (EBacc) shows how many students got a GCSE grade C or above in English, maths, two sciences, a language and history or geography. The tables for secondary schools and attainment post-16 rely mainly on the results of national examinations. All tables include indicators of the progress that pupils have made since their last assessment. From 2016 the tables will identify 'coasting' schools that are not pushing every pupil to reach their potential.

DEPARTMENT FOR EDUCATION T 0370-000 2288
   W www.education.gov.uk

WALES

A new curriculum for 3- to 16-year-olds in Wales will be phased in from September 2018 until 2021 (see below). For now a Foundation Phase curriculum for 3- to 7-year-olds, introduced in September 2008, places emphasis on learning by doing. Children's skills and knowledge are planned across seven areas of learning. They are:
- Personal and social development, well-being and cultural diversity
- Language, literacy and communication skills
- Mathematical development
- Welsh language development
- Knowledge and understanding of the world
- Physical development
- Creative development

Full details of the Foundation Phase can be found in *Framework for Children's Learning for 3- to 7-year-olds in Wales*, available on the Welsh government website (see below).

Currently the National Curriculum is for 7- to 16-year-olds. Originally it was broadly similar to that of England, with distinctive characteristics for Wales reflected in the programmes of study. From September 2008 a revised school curriculum was implemented, consisting of the National Curriculum subjects together with non-statutory frameworks for personal and social education, the world of work, religious education and skills.

The National Curriculum in Wales includes the following subjects:
- *Key Stage 2* – English, Welsh, mathematics, science, design and technology, ICT, history, geography, art and design, music, and physical education
- *Key Stage 3* – as Key Stage 2, plus a modern foreign language
- *Key Stage 4* – English, Welsh, mathematics, science and physical education

Welsh is compulsory for pupils at all key stages, either as a first or as a second language. In 2010, 16.5 per cent of pupils were taught Welsh as a first language. In April 2012, the Minister for Education and Skills approved the implementation of an action plan to raise standards and attainment in Welsh second language education.

Qualified for Life, the new curriculum for Wales from age 3 to 16, is being developed and was tested in 106 Pioneer schools in 2016 with the aim of making it available to all settings and schools by September 2018. The purpose of the curriculum in Wales is to develop children and young people as:
- Ambitious, capable learners, ready to learn throughout their lives
- Enterprising, creative contributors, ready to play a full part in life and work
- Ethical, informed citizens of Wales and the world
- Healthy, confident individuals, ready to lead fulfilling lives as valued members of society

The new curriculum will include:
- Six areas of learning and experience from 3 to 16 years old
- Three cross-curriculum responsibilities: literacy, numeracy and digital competence
- Progression reference points at ages 5, 8, 11, 14 and 16
- Achievement outcomes which describe expected achievements at each progression reference point

The six Areas of Learning and Experience will be:
- Expressive arts
- Health and well-being
- Humanities (including RE which should remain compulsory to age 16)
- Languages, literacy and communication (including Welsh, which should remain compulsory to age 16, and modern foreign languages)
- Mathematics and numeracy
- Science and technology (including computer science)

All teachers should be responsible for developing literacy, numeracy and digital competence across the curriculum.

From September 2016, the Pioneer schools had developed individual action plans and the Digital Competence Framework was available. From 2017 to 2021 the Welsh Assembly will help schools and teachers to prepare for the new curriculum. By September 2018, the new curriculum and assessment arrangements will be available, with new curriculum and assessment arrangements in place by September 2021.

ASSESSMENT

Statutory testing at the end of Key Stage 2 was removed for pupils in Wales from 2004–5, leaving only statutory teacher assessment. This takes place at the end of Key Stage 1 (the Foundation Phase) and Key Stage 3, and is being strengthened by moderation and accreditation arrangements.

A National Literacy and Numeracy Framework (LNF), outlining the skills 5- to 15-year-olds are expected to acquire, became statutory from September 2013. For literacy, this means children should become accomplished in reading for information, writing for information and expressing themselves fluently and grammatically in speech. In numeracy, children are expected to develop numerical reasoning and use number skills, measuring skills and data skills.

National reading and numeracy tests for pupils in Years 2 to 9 took place for the first time in Wales in May 2013. The tests are designed to give teachers a clearer insight into a learner's development and progress, to allow them to intervene at an earlier stage if learners are falling behind.

The reading test includes a statutory 'core' test, and a set of optional test materials to help teachers to investigate learners' strengths and development needs in more depth.

The numeracy test is split into two papers: numerical procedures and numerical reasoning. The procedural paper consists of a set of questions designed to assess the basic, essential numeracy skills such as addition, multiplication and division.

The numerical reasoning paper was introduced in May 2014. It will assess learners' ability to find the most effective ways to solve everyday numeracy problems.

Learners in Welsh medium schools will take a reading test in Welsh only in Years 2 and 3, but in both English and Welsh from Year 4 onwards. Schools will have the option to use both tests in Year 3. Learners will take the numeracy test in either English or Welsh.

THE WELSH GOVERNMENT – EDUCATION AND
   SKILLS W https://curriculumforwales.gov.wales
   W www.learning.wales.gov.uk

SCOTLAND

The curriculum in Scotland is not prescribed by statute but is the responsibility of education authorities and individual schools. However, schools and authorities are expected to follow the Scottish government's guidance on management and delivery of the curriculum, which is primarily through Education Scotland.

Scotland is now implementing *Curriculum for Excellence,* which aims to provide more autonomy for teachers, greater choice and opportunity for pupils and a single coherent curriculum for all children and young people aged 3 to 18.

The purpose of Curriculum for Excellence is encapsulated in 'the four capacities': to enable each child or young person to be a successful learner, a confident individual, a responsible citizen and an effective contributor. It focuses on providing a broad curriculum that develops skills for learning, skills for life and skills for work, with a sustained focus on literacy and numeracy. The period of education from pre-school through to the end of secondary stage 3, when pupils reach 14, aims to provide every young person in Scotland with this broad general education.

Curriculum for Excellence sets out 'experiences and outcomes', which describe broad areas of learning and what is to be achieved within them. They are:

- Expressive arts (including art and design, dance, drama, music)
- Health and wellbeing (including physical education, food and health, relationships and sexual health and mental, physical and social wellbeing)
- Languages
- Mathematics
- Religious and moral education
- Sciences
- Social studies (including history, geography, society and economy)
- Technologies (including business, computing, food and textiles, craft, design, engineering and graphics)

The experiences and outcomes are written at five levels with progression to examinations and qualifications during the senior phase, which covers secondary stages 4 to 6 when students are generally aged 14 to 17. The framework is designed to be flexible so that pupils can progress at their own pace.

Level	Stage
Early	The pre-school years and primary 1 (ages 3–5), or later for some
First	To the end of primary 4 (age 8), but earlier or later for some
Second	To the end of primary 7 (age 11), but earlier or later for some
Third and Fourth	Secondary 1 to secondary 3 (ages 12–14), but earlier for some. The fourth level experiences and outcomes are intended to allow choice, and young people's programmes will not include all of the fourth level outcomes
Senior phase	Secondary 4 to secondary 6 (ages 15–18), and college or other studies

Under the new curriculum, assessment of students' progress and achievements from ages 3 to 15 is carried out by teachers who base their assessment judgments on a range of evidence rather than single assessment instruments such as tests. Teachers have access to an online National Assessment Resource, which provides a range of assessment material and national exemplars across the curriculum areas.

In the senior phase, young people aged 16 to 18, including those studying outside school, build up a portfolio of national qualifications, awarded by the Scottish Qualifications Authority (SQA).

Provision is made for teaching in Gaelic in many parts of Scotland and the number of pupils in Gaelic-medium education, from nursery to secondary, is growing.

EDUCATION SCOTLAND T 0141-282 5000
W www.educationscotland.gov.uk

SCOTTISH QUALIFICATIONS AUTHORITY
T 0845-279 1000 W www.sqa.org.uk

NORTHERN IRELAND

In September 2009 Northern Ireland put in place across Years 1 to 12 a revised statutory curriculum placing greater emphasis on developing skills and preparing young people for life and work.

This curriculum includes a new Foundation Stage to cover Years 1 and 2 of primary school, to allow a more appropriate learning style for the youngest pupils and to ease the transition from pre-school. Key Stage 1 covers primary Years 3 and 4, until children are 8, and Key Stage 2 covers primary Years 5, 6 and 7, until children are 11. Post-primary, Key Stage 3 covers Years 8, 9 and 10 and Key Stage 4 covers Years 11 and 12.

The current primary curriculum is made up of the following areas of learning:

- Language and literacy
- Mathematics and numeracy
- The arts
- The world around us
- Personal development and mutual understanding
- Physical education
- Religious education

The current post-primary curriculum includes a new area of learning for life and work, made up of employability, personal development, local and global citizenship and home economics (at Key Stage 3). It is also made up of RE and the following areas of learning:

- Language and literacy
- Mathematics and numeracy
- Modern languages
- The arts
- Environment and society
- Physical education
- Science and technology

At Key Stage 4, there are nine areas of learning, but statutory requirements have been significantly reduced, to learning for life and work, physical education and RE. The aim is to provide greater choice and flexibility for pupils and allow them access to a wider range of academic and vocational courses provided under the revised curriculum's 'Entitlement Framework' (EF).

Since September 2013, schools have been required to provide pupils with access to at least 18 courses at Key Stage 4 and 21 courses at post-16. This increased to 24 and 27 courses respectively in September 2015. At least one third of the courses must be 'general' with one third 'applied'. The remaining third is at the discretion of each school. Individual pupils decide on the number and mix of courses they wish to follow.

RE is a compulsory part of the Northern Ireland curriculum, although parents have the right to withdraw their children from part or all of RE or collective worship. Schools have to provide RE in accordance with a core syllabus drawn up by the province's four main churches (Church of Ireland, Presbyterian, Methodist and Roman Catholic) and specified by the Department of Education.

Revised assessment and reporting arrangements were introduced when the curriculum was revised. The focus from Foundation to Key Stage 3 is on 'Assessment for Learning'. This programme includes classroom-based teacher assessment, computer-based assessment of literacy and numeracy and pupils deciding on their strengths and weaknesses and how they might progress to achieve their potential. Assessment information is given to parents in an annual report. Pupils at Key Stage 4 and beyond continue to be assessed through public examinations.

The Council for the Curriculum, Examinations and Assessment (CCEA), a non-departmental public body reporting to the Department of Education in Northern Ireland, is unique in the UK in combining the functions of a curriculum advisory body, an awarding body and a qualifications regulatory body. It advises the government on what should be taught in Northern Ireland's schools and colleges, ensures that the qualifications and examinations offered by awarding bodies in Northern Ireland are of an appropriate quality and standard and, as the leading awarding body itself, offers a range of qualifications including GCSEs, A-levels and AS-levels.

The CCEA hosts a dedicated curriculum website covering all aspects of the revised curriculum, assessment and reporting.

COUNCIL FOR THE CURRICULUM, EXAMINATIONS
AND ASSESSMENT T 028-9026 1200
W www.ccea.org.uk

NORTHERN IRELAND CURRICULUM T 028-9028 1200
W www.nicurriculum.org.uk

QUALIFICATIONS

ENGLAND, WALES AND NORTHERN IRELAND

There is a very wide range of public examinations and qualifications available, accredited by the Office of Qualifications and Examinations Regulation (OFQUAL) in England, Qualifications Wales in Wales, and the Council for the Curriculum, Examinations and Assessment (CCEA) in Northern Ireland. Up-to-date information on all accredited qualifications and awarding bodies is available online at the Register of Regulated Qualifications website.

The qualifications frameworks group all accredited qualifications into levels. All the qualifications within a level place similar demands on individuals as learners. Entry level, for example, covers basic knowledge and skills in English, maths and ICT not geared towards specific occupations, level 3 includes qualifications such as A-levels which are appropriate for those wishing to go on to higher education, level 7 covers Master's degrees and vocational qualifications appropriate for senior professionals and managers and level 8 is equivalent to a doctorate.

Young people aged 14 to 19 in schools or (post-16) colleges or apprenticeships may gain academic qualifications such as GCSEs, AS-levels and A-levels; qualifications linked to particular career fields, like diplomas; vocational qualifications such as BTECs and NVQs; and functional key or basic skills qualifications.

Both the National Qualifications Framework (NQF) formerly used in England, Wales and Northern Ireland and its succesor the Qualifications and Credit Framework (QCF) for England and Northern Ireland, have been replaced by the Regulated Qualifications Framework (RQF) for England and the Credit and Qualifications Framework for Wales (CQFW). In Northern Ireland the Council for the Curriculum, Examinations and Assessment (CCEA) regulates qualifications. There is also a Framework for Higher Education Qualifications (FHEQ) for England, Wales and Northern Ireland.

In England, Wales and Northern Ireland there are nine qualification levels:

Entry level – each entry-level qualification is available at three sub-levels: 1, 2 and 3, with level 3 the most difficult.

Entry-level qualifications are: entry-level award; entry-level certificate (ELC); entry-level diploma; entry-level English for speakers of other languages (ESOL); entry-level essential skills; entry-level functional skills; Skills for Life.

Level 1 qualifications are: first certificate; GCSE – grade D, E, F or G; level 1 award; level 1 certificate; level 1 diploma; level 1 ESOL; level 1 essential skills; level 1 functional skills; level 1 national vocational qualification (NVQ); music grades 1, 2 and 3.

Level 2 qualifications are: CSE – grade 1; GCSE – grade A*, A, B or C; intermediate apprenticeship; level 2 award; level 2 certificate; level 2 diploma; level 2 ESOL; level 2 essential skills; level 2 functional skills; level 2 national certificate; level

2 national diploma; level 2 NVQ; music grades 4 and 5; O level – grade A, B or C.

Level 3 qualifications are: A level – grade A, B, C, D or E; access to higher education; diploma; advanced apprenticeship; applied general; AS level; international Baccalaureate diploma; level 3 award; level 3 certificate; level 3 diploma; level 3 ESOL; level 3 national certificate; level 3 national diploma; level 3 NVQ; music grades 6, 7 and 8; tech level.

Level 4 qualifications are: certificate of higher education (CertHE); higher apprenticeship; higher national certificate (HNC); level 4 award; level 4 certificate; level 4 diploma; level 4 NVQ.

Level 5 qualifications are: diploma of higher education (DipHE); foundation degree; higher national diploma (HND); level 5 award; level 5 certificate; level 5 diploma; level 5 NVQ.

Level 6 qualifications are: degree apprenticeship; degree with honours – for example bachelor of arts (BA) with honours, bachelor of science (BSc) with honours; graduate certificate; graduate diploma; level 6 award; level 6 certificate; level 6 diploma; level 6 NVQ; ordinary degree without honours.

Level 7 qualifications are: integrated master's degree, for example master of engineering (MEng); level 7 award; level 7 certificate; level 7 diploma; level 7 NVQ; master's degree, for example master of arts (MA), master of science (MSc); postgraduate certificate; postgraduate certificate in education (PGCE); postgraduate diploma.

Level 8 qualifications are: doctorate, for example doctor of philosophy (PHD or DPHIL); level 8 award; level 8 certificate; level 8 diploma.

FRAMEWORK FOR HIGHER EDUCATION QUALIFICATIONS (FHEQ)

This framework applies to degrees, diplomas, certificates and other academic awards (other than honorary degrees and higher doctorates) granted by a higher education provider in the exercise of its degree awarding powers. It starts at RQF level 4 and goes up to level 8 and includes the following qualifications: Certificate of Higher Education; Diploma of Higher Education; Bachelor's degrees; Master's degrees; and Doctoral degrees.

COUNCIL FOR THE CURRICULUM, EXAMINATIONS
AND ASSESSMENT (NORTHERN IRELAND)
T 028-9026 1200
W www.ccea.org.uk

QUALIFICATIONS WALES T 0333-077 2701
W www.qualificationswales.org

REGISTER OF REGULATED QUALIFICATIONS W http://register.ofqual.gov.uk

OFFICE OF QUALIFICATIONS AND EXAMINATIONS
REGULATION (OFQUAL) T 0300-303 3344
W www.ofqual.gov.uk

GCSE

The vast majority of pupils in their last year of compulsory schooling in England, Wales and Northern Ireland take at least one General Certificate of Secondary Education (GCSE) exam, though GCSEs may be taken at any age. GCSEs assess the performance of pupils on a subject-specific basis and are mostly taken after a two-year course. They are available in more than 50 subjects, most of them academic subjects, though some, known as vocational or applied GCSEs, involve the study of a particular area of employment and the development of work-related skills. Some subjects are also offered as short-course qualifications, equivalent to half a standard GCSE, or as double awards, equivalent to two GCSEs.

For many years GCSEs were assessed on coursework completed by students during the course as well as exams at the end and GCSE certificates were awarded on an eight-point scale from A* to G. In most subjects two different papers, higher tier and foundation tier, were provided for different ranges of ability, with grades A*–D available to students taking the higher paper and grades C–G available from the foundation paper.

In England, all traditional GCSEs are being replaced by new GCSEs or, in some subjects, withdrawn. The new GCSEs no longer involve modules and coursework, just exam assessment at the end of the two-year course; a very few subjects (such as music technology) may include an element of non-exam assessment. Only maths, science and foreign language GCSEs will be tiered. New GCSEs are graded 9 to 1, rather than A* to G.

The changeover to new GCSEs is being phased in. In September 2015 schools began teaching revised GCSEs in English language, English literature and mathematics, for exams in 2017. Teaching of revised GCSEs in ancient and modern foreign languages, art and design, biology, chemistry, citizenship, computer science, double science, dance, drama, food preparation and nutrition, geography, history, music, physics, physical education and religious studies started in September 2016 for exams in 2018. Teaching in 14 other subjects started in September 2017 for exams in 2019.

In 2017 English language, English literature and maths were the first subjects to be graded from 9 to 1. Another 20 subjects will be graded 9 to 1 in 2018, with most others following in 2019. During this transition, students will receive a mixture of letter and number grades.

In Northern Ireland, new CCEA GCSEs will be introduced for first teaching in 2017, with first awards in 2019. They will be graded on a 9 grade system from A*-G with a new C* grade. W www.gov.uk/government/collections/gcse-subject-content

All GCSE specifications, assessments and grading procedures are monitored by OFQUAL, QW and the CCEA.

Since September 2010 state schools have been allowed to offer pupils International GCSE (iGCSE) qualifications in key subjects including English, mathematics, science and ICT. Though iGCSEs were considered more rigorous than traditional GCSEs, the government regards the new GCSEs in these subjects as superior, and has announced that iGCSE results will no longer count in school performance tables from 2017.

GCE A-LEVEL AND AS-LEVEL

GCE (General Certificate of Education) Advanced levels (A-levels) are the qualifications used by most young people in England, Wales and Northern Ireland to gain entry to university.

A-levels are subject-based qualifications. They are mostly taken by UK students aged 16 to 19 over a two-year course in school sixth forms or at college, but can be taken at any age. They are available in more than 45, mostly academic, subjects, though there are some A-levels in vocational areas, often termed 'applied A-levels'.

Traditionally, A-level qualifications consisted of two parts: advanced subsidiary (AS) and A2 units. The AS was a qualification assessed at the standard expected of a learner half way through an A-level course, normally consisting of two units that together contributed 50 per cent towards the full A-level. The A2 was the second half of a full A-level qualification. It was assessed at the standard expected of a learner at the end of a full A-level course, and normally consisted of two units that together made up the remaining 50 per cent of the full A-level qualification. Each unit was graded A–E, with an A* grade available to exceptional candidates since 2010.

An extended project was introduced in September 2008 as a separate qualification. It is a single piece of work on a topic of the student's own choosing that requires a high degree of planning, preparation, research and autonomous working. Awards are graded A–E and the extended project is accredited as half an A-level.

Since September 2013, students in England in their first or second year of A-level studies have not been allowed to sit A-level exams in January. A-levels are still examined unit by unit, but all exams are taken in the summer.

From 2015 until 2017, revised AS and A-levels have been introduced in phases. All assessment of the new A-levels now take place at the end of the two-year course and the AS has become a standalone qualification rather than contributing to a full A-level qualification.

Since September 2015, students have been taught the new-style AS-levels and A-levels in art and design, biology, business, chemistry, computer science, economics, English language, English language and literature, English literature, history, physics, psychology and sociology. New AS and A-levels in ancient languages, dance, drama and theatre, geography, modern foreign languages (French, German and Spanish), music, physical education and religious studies started to be taught in September 2016.

From September 2017, new-style A-levels are being introduced in: accounting, ancient history, archaeology, classical civilisation, design and technology, electronics, film studies, geology, government and politics, history of art, law, maths and further maths, media studies, music technology, philosophy and statistics.

W www.gov.uk/government/collections/gce-as-and-a-level-subject-content

INTERNATIONAL BACCALAUREATE

The International Baccalaureate (IB) offers four educational programmes for students aged 3 to 19: IB primary years programme, IB middle years programme, IB diploma programme, IB career-related certificate.

Some 155 'IB World Schools' in the UK offer at least one IB programme.

The IB diploma programme for students aged 16 to 19 is based around detailed academic study of a wide range of subjects, including languages, the arts, science, maths, history and geography, leading to a single qualification recognised by UK universities.

The IB diploma is made up of a compulsory 'core' plus six separate subjects where individuals have some choice over what they study. The compulsory core contains three elements: theory of knowledge; creativity, action and service; and a 4,000-word extended essay.

The IB diploma normally takes two years to complete and most of the assessment is done through externally marked examinations. Candidates are awarded points for each part of the programme, up to a maximum of 45. A candidate must score 24 points or more to achieve a full diploma.

Successfully completing the diploma earns points on the 'UCAS tariff', the UK system for allocating points to qualifications used for entry to higher education. An IB diploma total of 24 points is worth 260 UCAS points – the same as a B and two C grades at A-level. The maximum of 45 points earns 720 UCAS points – equivalent to six A-levels at grade A.

WELSH BACCALAUREATE

The Welsh Baccalaureate Qualification (WBQ), available for 14- to 19-year-olds in Wales, combines a compulsory core, which incorporates personal development skills, with options from existing academic and vocational qualifications, such as A-levels, GCSEs and NVQs, to make one broader award. The WBQ can be studied in English or Welsh, or a combination of the two. Candidates who meet the requirements of the compulsory core and options relevant to each level of the qualification are awarded the Welsh Baccalaureate Foundation, Intermediate or Advanced Diploma as appropriate.

WJEC (Welsh Joint Education Committee), which administers the WBQ, has also developed two new WBQs at level 1 and level 2 suitable for delivery over one year and with a particular focus on employability.

A revised and more rigorous Welsh Baccalaureate has been taught since September 2015. It is based on a Skills Challenge Certificate, which will be graded, and supporting qualifications. The aim is to enable learners to develop and demonstrate an understanding of, and proficiency in, essential and employability skills: communication, numeracy, digital literacy, planning and organisation, creativity and innovation, critical thinking and problem solving, and personal effectiveness. The emphasis is on applied and purposeful learning and opportunities for assessment in a range of real life contexts through three 'challenge briefs' and an individual project.

TECH LEVELS AND APPLIED GENERAL QUALIFICATIONS

Tech levels, first taught in schools from September 2014, are a new advanced qualification for students aged 16-19 who wish to specialise in a technical occupation. They take as long to complete as A-levels and, like A-levels, are at level 3; they lead to recognised occupations in, for example, engineering, IT, accounting or hospitality. They must be recognised by a relevant trade or professional body or at least five employers representative of the industry sector or occupation. Many higher education institutions have pledged support for Tech levels.

Tech levels count towards the TechBacc (Technical Baccalaureate) performance measure in the post-16 school and college performance tables from 2016. To achieve the TechBacc, students need an approved level 3 Tech level qualification, an approved level 3 mathematics qualification and the extended project qualification. Additional funding is provided for students who successfully complete a large TechBacc programme (960 guided learning hours or more).

The 2017 post-16 performance tables will also recognise Applied General Qualifications, which take the same time to complete as AS-levels and focus on broader study of a technical area. These are advanced (level 3) qualifications that allow 16 to 19 year old students to develop transferable knowledge and skills. They allow entry to a range of higher education courses, either by meeting the entry requirements in their own right or by adding value to other qualifications such as A-levels.

BTECS, OCR NATIONALS AND OTHER VOCATIONAL QUALIFICATIONS

Vocational qualifications can range from general qualifications where a person learns skills relevant to a variety of jobs, to specialist qualifications designed for a particular sector. They are available from several awarding bodies, such as City & Guilds, Edexcel and OCR, and can be taken at many different levels. All vocational and work-related qualifications fit into the Regulated Qualifications Framework (RQF).

BTEC qualifications and OCR Nationals are particular types of work-related qualifications, available in a wide range of subjects, including: art and design, business, health and social care, information technology, media, public services, science and sport. The qualifications offer a mix of theory and practice, can include work experience and can be part of an Apprenticeship. They can be studied full-time at college or school, or part-time at college.

Learners complete a range of assignments, case studies and practical activities, as well as a portfolio of evidence that shows what work has been completed.

Since 2016, the quality and assessment of all vocational courses offered by schools and colleges to 14- to 19-year-olds has been strengthened. The standards of reformed BTECs, along with Cambridge OCR National Certificates and Vocational Certificates (V-Certs), equal those of GCSE A*–C grades. All vocational qualifications are graded (previously many were simply pass/fail) and all have a 25 per cent externally examined component. New Substantial Vocational Qualifications at level 2 provide 16- to 19-year-old students seeking entry at a more basic level to a skilled trade or occupation with qualifications that are valued by employers.

NVQs

A National Vocational Qualification (NVQ) is a 'competence-based' qualification that is recognised by employers.

Individuals learn practical, work-related tasks designed to help them develop the skills and knowledge to do a particular job effectively. NVQs can be taken in school, at college or by people already in work. There are more than 1,300 different NVQs available from the vast majority of business sectors. NVQs exist at levels 1 to 5 on the RQF. A NVQ qualification at level 2 or 3 can also be taken as part of an Apprenticeship.

Functional Skills

Functional skills qualifications were launched during 2010, for all learners aged 14 and above. They test practical skills that allow people to work confidently, effectively and independently in life, and are available only in England. Wales and Northern Ireland have literacy and numeracy qualifications known as 'essential skills'.

Following a review by OFQUAL, the functional skills qualifications in English and mathematics are changing. Assessment materials are being improved, the risk of malpractice is being reduced and standard-setting procedures are being strengthened. There will be better evaluation of how well the qualifications meet user needs.

Apprenticeships

Apprenticeships combine on-the-job training with nationally recognised qualifications, allowing individuals to gain skills and qualifications while working and earning a wage. More than 200 different types of apprenticeships are available, offering over 1,500 job roles; they take between one and five years to complete. There are four levels available:

• Intermediate Apprenticeships – at level 2 on the Regulated Qualifications Framework (RQF), they are equivalent to five good GCSE passes
• Advanced Apprenticeships – at level 3 on the RQF, they are equivalent to two A-level passes
• Higher Apprenticeships – lead to qualifications at NVQ Level 4 or, in some cases, a foundation degree (RQF level 4)
• Degree Apprenticeships – added in 2015 (RQF level 6)

In England, the National Apprenticeship Service (NAS), launched in 2009, is responsible for the delivery of apprenticeships and provides an online vacancy matching system. There were 899,400 funded apprentices in the 2015–16 academic year. Some 18 groups of universities have developed new degree apprenticeships which began in September 2017 (*see* Recent Developments). The Welsh government and the Department for the Economy are responsible for the apprenticeship programmes in Wales and Northern Ireland respectively.

NATIONAL APPRENTICESHIP SERVICE (NAS)
 T 02476-826482
 W www.gov.uk/education/
 apprenticeships-traineeships-and-internships

REGISTER OF APPRENTICESHIP TRAINING
 PROVIDERS W www.gov.uk/guidance/
 register-of-apprenticeship-training-providers

SCOTLAND

Scotland has its own system of public examinations and qualifications. The Scottish Qualifications Authority (SQA) is Scotland's national body for qualifications, responsible for developing, accrediting, assessing and certificating all Scottish qualifications apart from university degrees and some professional body qualifications.

There are qualifications at all levels of attainment. Almost all school candidates gain SQA qualifications in the fourth year of secondary school and most obtain further qualifications in the fifth or sixth year or in further education colleges. Increasingly, people also take qualifications in the workplace.

SQA, with partners such as Universities Scotland, has introduced the Scottish Credit and Qualifications Framework (SCQF) as a way of comparing and understanding Scottish qualifications. It includes qualifications across academic and vocational sectors and compares them by giving a level and credit points. There are 12 levels in the SCQF, level 1 being the least difficult and level 12 the most difficult. The number of SCQF credit points shows how much learning has to be done to achieve the qualification. For instance, one SCQF credit point equals about 10 hours of learning including assessment.

- Standard Grades are taken over the third and fourth years at secondary school. Students often choose to study seven or eight subjects, of which Mathematics and English are compulsory. There are three levels of study at Standard Grade: Foundation, General and Credit. Students usually sit exams at two levels – either Foundation/General or General/Credit – to ensure they have the best chance of achieving as high a grade as possible.
- National Units are the building blocks of National Courses, but they are also recognised qualifications in their own right and are designed to take approximately 40 hours of teaching time to complete.
- National Courses usually comprise three National Units and an externally marked assessment. National Courses are available at a number of levels including Access 1, Access 2, Access 3, Intermediate 1, Intermediate 2, Higher and Advanced Higher.
- Skills for Work courses encourage school pupils to become familiar with the world of work. They involve a strong element of learning through involvement in practical and vocational activities and develop knowledge, skills and experience that are related to employment. They are available at a number of levels and are frequently delivered in partnership between schools and colleges.
- Wider Achievement qualifications provide young people with the opportunity to have learning and skills formally recognised, whether developed in or outside the classroom. Available at a number of levels in subjects including Employability, Leadership and Enterprise, these qualifications help schools deliver skills for learning, life and work.
- Scottish Baccalaureates consist of a coherent group of Higher and Advanced Higher qualifications and, uniquely, an interdisciplinary project of candidates' own choosing which is marked at Advanced Higher level in one of four broad topics – languages, science, expressive arts or social studies. Aimed at high-achieving candidates in their sixth year, the Scottish Baccalaureate is designed to encourage personalised in-depth study and interdisciplinary learning in the later stages of secondary school.

As part of the Curriculum for Excellence programme SQA developed revised National qualifications that became available in schools from August 2013, replacing Standard Grade, Intermediate and Access qualifications at all levels. New Higher qualifications became available from August 2014 and Advanced Higher qualifications from August 2015:

SCQF Level	New national qualifications	Replaces
1 and 2	National 1 and 2	Access 1 and Access 2
3	National 3	Access 3 Standard Grade (Foundation Level)
4	National 4	Standard Grade (General Level) Intermediate 1
5	National 5	Standard Grade (Credit Level) Intermediate 2
6	Higher (new)	Higher
7	Advanced Higher (new)	Advanced Higher

Revised qualifications were available alongside existing qualifications until 2015–16. Final results for existing Access, Intermediate, Higher and Advanced Higher qualifications were issued in August 2015.

From 2017–18 mandatory unit assessments are being removed from the National 5 qualification to reduce teacher and pupil workload (see Recent Developments). As a result, the course assessments for National 5 – a combination of exam and coursework – have been strengthened to maintain their integrity, breadth and standards.

Mandatory unit assessment will be removed for Higher courses from 2018–19 and from Advanced Higher courses from 2019–20. In addition, SQA will suspend the random sample element of unit verification for a further year (2017–18).

SQA has also developed five Awards – in modern languages, personal achievement, personal development, religion and wellbeing – that cover work from across different subject areas, and are shorter than traditional courses and recognise success across different levels of difficulty. These started in August 2012 and are marked and assessed by schools and colleges rather than by external assessment or exams. Awards in Cycling and Scottish Studies began in August 2013.

SQA QUALIFICATIONS
Higher National Certificates and Higher National Diplomas
Higher National Certificates and Higher National Diplomas (HNCs and HNDs) are offered by colleges, some universities and many other training providers, including employers. Both HNCs and HNDs are comprised of Higher National Units and cover a wide range of subject areas. Many HNDs allow the holder entry to the second or third year of a degree course. HNCs are available at SCQF level 7, HNDs at level 8.

National Qualification Group Awards
National Certificates and National Progression Awards are designed to prepare people for employment, career development or progression to more advanced study at HNC/HND level. They also aim to develop a range of transferable knowledge including core skills. These certificates are aimed at 16- to 18-year-olds or adults in full-time education and are at SCQF levels 2 to 6. Each one has specific aims relating to a subject or occupational area.

Scottish Vocational Qualifications
Scottish Vocational Qualifications (SVQs) are based on national standards drawn up by people from industry, commerce and education. Possession of an SVQ demonstrates ability to perform in a job to agreed national standards. Primarily delivered to candidates in full-time employment, SVQs are available at SCQF levels 4 to 12.

Professional Development Awards
Professional Development Awards (PDAs) are designed to develop and deliver high-level skills in a sharp, flexible and focused way. They are for people already in work who wish to extend or broaden their skills. Candidates often take a PDA after completing a degree or vocational qualification. PDAs are available at SCQF levels 6 to 12.

Foundation Apprenticeships
Foundation Apprenticeships are developed and delivered by Skills Development Scotland with support from the European Social Fund. The programme sees pupils complete the qualification over two years, usually beginning in the fifth year of school alongside studying for Highers and National 5 qualifications.

Foundation Apprenticeships offer work experience and a qualification in: business skills, civil engineering, creative and digital media, engineering, financial services, technology hardware, scientific technologies, social services and software development.

In August 2016, 351 young people started a Foundation Apprenticeship and from August 2017 the number of places available increased to 1,900. By the end of 2019, 5,000 places will be available for young people (see Recent Developments).

THE SCOTTISH QUALIFICATIONS AUTHORITY (SQA)
T 0345-279 1000
W www.sqa.org.uk

SCOTTISH CREDIT AND QUALIFICATIONS FRAMEWORK (SCQF) T 0845-270 7371
W www.scqf.org.uk

SKILLS DEVELOPMENT SCOTLAND (SDS)
T 0800-917 8000 W www.skillsdevelopmentscotland.co.uk

FURTHER EDUCATION AND LIFELONG LEARNING

ENGLAND

The further education (FE) system in England provides a wide range of education and training opportunities for young people and adults. From the age of 16, young people who wish to remain in education, but not in a school setting, can undertake further education (including skills training) in an FE college. There are two main types of college in the FE sector: sixth form colleges and general further education (GFE) colleges. Some FE colleges focus on a particular area, such as art and design or agriculture and horticulture. Each institution decides its own range of subjects and courses. Students at FE colleges can study for a wide and growing range of academic and/or work-related qualifications, from entry level to higher education level.

The Department for Business, Innovation and Skills was responsible for the FE sector and for funding adult FE until July 2016, when these responsibilities passed to the Department for Education, which already funded all education and training for 16- to 18-year-olds.

The proportion of 16- to 18-year-olds in education or training has risen steadily over recent years, driven by increases in state-funded schools and in higher education, and was expected to reach 100 per cent by 2015. The latest statistics for 2016, show 81.9 per cent of young people in full-time education.

The 'September Guarantee', introduced in 2007, offers a place in post-16 education or training to all 16- and 17-year-olds who want one. In 2016, 94.5 per cent of 16- and 17-year-olds in England received an offer of a place. An Education Funding Agency was established in April 2012 as an executive agency of the Department for Education (DfE), to be responsible for education funding for 16- to 19-year-olds as well as Academies.

The FE sector in England, as in other parts of the UK, also provides a range of opportunities for adults.

The Skills Funding Agency and the Education Funding Agency were replaced by the Education and Skills Funding Agency (ESFA) in April 2017 (see Recent Developments). The ESFA is accountable for £61bn of funding for the education and training sector, regulating academies, FE Colleges, employers and training providers, intervening where there is risk of failure or where there is evidence of mismanagement of public funds and delivering major projects in the education and skills sector, such as school capital programmes, the National Careers Service, the digital Apprenticeship Service and National Apprenticeship Service.

In November 2010, the government announced a new strategy for FE, including more adult apprenticeships (provision for 200,000 adults by 2014–15); fully-funded training for 19- to 24-year-olds undertaking their first full level 2 (GCSE equivalent) or first level 3 qualification; and fully funded basic skills training for people who left school without basic skills in reading, writing and mathematics. 'Train to Gain', the programme that funded trainees sponsored by employers, was replaced in July 2011 by a programme focused on helping small employers to train low-skilled staff. In April 2012 the National Careers Service was created.

In April 2013, the government announced plans to make the skills system more responsive and to create new traineeships.

There are currently 19 centres of training excellence called National Skills Academies, led, funded and designed by employers, in various stages of development. Each academy offers specialist training in a key sector of the economy, working in partnership with colleges, schools and independent training providers.

Among the many voluntary bodies providing adult education, the Workers' Educational Association (WEA) is the UK's largest, operating throughout England and Scotland. It provides part-time courses to adults in response to local need in community centres, village halls, schools, pubs or workplaces. Similar but separate WEA organisations operate in Wales and Northern Ireland.

In 2016, the National Institute of Adult Continuing Education (NIACE), a charitable non-governmental organisation, merged with the Centre for Economic and Social Inclusion to form the Learning and Work Institute, which promotes lifelong learning opportunities for adults in England and Wales.

LEARNING AND WORK INSTITUTE T 0116-204 4200
    W www.learningandwork.org.uk
THE EDUCATION AND SKILLS FUNDING AGENCY
    W www.gov.uk/government/organisations/
    education-and-skills-funding-agency
WORKERS' EDUCATIONAL ASSOCIATION (WEA)
    T 020-7426 3450 W www.wea.org.uk
EDUCATION AND TRAINING FOUNDATION
    T 020-3740 8280 W www.et-foundation.co.uk

WALES

In Wales, the aims and makeup of the FE system are similar to those outlined for England. The Welsh government funds a wide range of learning programmes for young people through its 15 FE colleges, local authorities and private organisations. The Welsh government has set out plans to improve learning opportunities for all post-16 learners in the shortest possible time, to increase the engagement of disadvantaged young people in the learning process, and to transform the learning network to increase learner choice, reduce duplication of provision and encourage higher-quality learning and teaching in all post-16 provision.

Responsibility for adult and continuing education lies with the Department for Education and Skills (DfES) within the Welsh government. Wales operates a range of programmes to support skills development, including subsidised work-based training courses for employees and the Workforce Development Programme, where employers can use the free services of experienced skills advisers to develop staff training plans.

COLLEGES WALES T 029-2052 2500
    W www.collegeswales.ac.uk
COLEG HARLECH WEA T 01248-353254
    W www.harlech.ac.uk/en
LEARNING AND WORK INSTITUTE T 029-2037 0900
    W www.learningandwork.wales
WEA SOUTH WALES T 029-2023 5277
    W www.swales.wea.org.uk

SCOTLAND

Following a series of mergers, Scotland now has 27 FE colleges (known simply as colleges), which are at the forefront of lifelong learning, education, training and skills in Scotland. Colleges cater for the needs of learners both in and out of employment, at all stages in their lives from middle secondary school and earlier to retirement. Colleges' courses span much of the range of learning needs, from specialised vocational education and training through to general educational programmes. The level of provision ranges from essential life skills and provision for students with learning difficulties to HNCs and HNDs. Some colleges, notably those in the Highlands and Islands, also deliver degrees and postgraduate qualifications.

A shift in study patterns is taking place within the college sector as colleges concentrate on full-time courses aimed at helping people gain employment and no longer fund short courses lasting less than ten hours. Overall figures are stable but this change has led to a decline in part-time study and an increase in full-time study.

The Scottish Funding Council (SFC) is the statutory body responsible for funding teaching and learning provision, research and other activities in Scotland's colleges. Overall strategic direction for the sector is provided by the Lifelong Learning Directorate of the Scottish government, which provides annual guidance to the SFC and liaises closely with bodies such as Colleges Scotland, the Scottish Qualifications Authority and the FE colleges themselves to ensure that policies remain relevant and practical.

The Scottish government takes responsibility for community learning and development in Scotland while Skills Development Scotland, a non-departmental public body, is charged with improving Scotland's skills performance by linking skills supply and demand and helping people and organisations to learn, develop and make use of these skills to greater effect. ILA Scotland is a Scottish government scheme delivered by Skills Development Scotland that provides funding for training to individuals over the age of 16 with an income of less than £22,000 a year. From October 2017 it will be replaced by Individual Training Accounts (ITAs), allowing eligible students up to £200 a year towards one course a year geared towards getting a job.

ILA SCOTLAND T 0800-917 8000
    W www.myworldofwork.co.uk/section/funding
COLLEGES SCOTLAND T 01786-892100
    W www.collegesscotland.ac.uk
SCOTTISH FUNDING COUNCIL T 0131-313 6500
    W www.sfc.ac.uk
SKILLS DEVELOPMENT SCOTLAND T 0800-917 8000
    W www.skillsdevelopmentscotland.co.uk

NORTHERN IRELAND

FE in Northern Ireland is provided through six regional multi-campus colleges and the College of Agriculture, Food and Rural Affairs. Most secondary schools also have a sixth form which students may attend for two additional years to complete their AS-levels and A-levels.

Colleges Northern Ireland acts as the representative body for the six FE colleges which, like their counterparts in the rest of the UK, are independent corporate bodies each managed by their own governing body. The range of courses that they offer spans essential skills, a wide choice of vocational and academic programmes and higher education programmes. Most full-time students in the six colleges are aged 16 to 19, while most part-time students are over 19.

The Department for the Economy is responsible for the policy, strategic development and financing of the statutory FE sector and for lifelong learning, and also provides support to a small number of non-statutory FE providers. The Educational Guidance Service for Adults, an independent, not-for-profit organisation, has a network of local offices based across Northern Ireland that provide services to adult learners, learning advisers, providers, employers and others interested in improving access to learning for adults.

COLLEGES NORTHERN IRELAND (CNI) T 028-9068 2296
    W www.collegesni.ac.uk
THE EDUCATIONAL GUIDANCE SERVICE FOR
    ADULTS T 01422-372222 W www.egsa.org.uk
WEA NORTHERN IRELAND T 028-9032 9718
    W www.wea-ni.com

FINANCIAL SUPPORT

England has a bursary scheme of up to £1,200 a year for full-time 16- to 19-year-old students facing financial hardship. Two types of bursary exist: vulnerable student bursary and discretionary bursary. Help with transport costs is also possible for some students. This scheme replaced the Education Maintenance Allowance (EMA), which gave 16- to 19-year-olds from low-income families a weekly allowance to continue in education.

There are EMA schemes in Scotland, Wales and Northern Ireland, but with slightly different eligibility conditions.

Students must apply to the EMA scheme for the part of the UK where they intend to study. In Northern Ireland 16- to 19-year-old students who meet the relevant criteria and live in a household that has an annual income of £20,500 or less a year (£22,500 more than one young person in the household qualifies for child benefit) automatically get £30 a week in 2017–18. There is a possibility of two £200 bonus payments too.

Colleges and learning providers award learner support funds directly to new students aged 19 and over.

Care to Learn is available in England to help young parents under the age of 20, who are caring for their own child or children while they are in some form of publicly funded learning (below higher education level), with the costs of childcare and travel. The scheme is not income-assessed and pays up to £160 a week (£175 in London) to cover costs.

Dance and Drama Awards (DaDA) are state-funded scholarships for students over the age of 16 enrolled at one of 19 private dance and drama schools in England, who are taking specified courses at National Certificate or National Diploma level. Awards, based on household income, cover some of students' tuition fees and up to £5,185 maintenance in 2017–18.

Young people studying away from home because their chosen course is not available locally may qualify for the *Residential Support Scheme.*

Information and advice on funding support and applications are available from the Learner Support helpline (T 0800-121 8989) or on the GOV.UK website (*see* below).

Discretionary Support Funds (DSF) are available in colleges and school sixth forms to help students who have trouble meeting the costs of participating in further education.

In Wales, students aged 19 or over on FE courses may be eligible for the *Welsh Government Learning Grant FE* (previously the Assembly Learning Grant for Further Education). This is a means-tested payment of up to £1,500 for full-time students and up to £750 for those studying part-time. *Discretionary Financial Contingency Funds* are also available to all students in Wales suffering hardship and are administered by the institutions themselves.

In Scotland, FE students can apply to their college for discretionary support in the form of *Further Education Bursaries,* which can include allowances for maintenance, travel, study, childcare and additional support needs; *Individual Training Accounts* (*see* above) may also be available.

In Northern Ireland, FE students may be eligible for *Further Education Awards,* non-refundable assistance administered on behalf of the five Education and Library Boards by the Western Education and Library Board.

UK FE students over 18 whose costs are not fully met from the grants described above may also be eligible for *Professional and Career Development Loans*. These loans – also available to HE students – cover up to 80 per cent of course fees (up to 100 per cent for those unemployed for three months); other course costs, such as books, travel and childcare; and living expenses, such as rent, food and clothing (for those who are unemployed or working fewer than 30 hours a week). The loans, of between £300 and £10,000, are available from participating high street banks. The government pays the interest on the loan while the student is studying and for one month afterwards. Once students complete their courses, they must pay interest at the rate fixed when they took out the loan, which will be competitive with other commercially available 'unsecured' personal loans.

CAREERS SCOTLAND W www.careers-scotland.org.uk/
    Education/Funding/Funding.asp
GOV.UK W www.gov.uk/further-education-courses/financial-help
STUDENT FINANCE WALES T 0845-602 8845
    W www.studentfinancewales.co.uk
WESTERN EDUCATION AND LIBRARY BOARD
    T 028-8241 1411 W www.welbni.org

HIGHER EDUCATION

Publicly funded higher education (HE) in the UK is provided in universities, higher education colleges and other specialist HE institutions, and in a significant number of FE colleges offering higher education courses.

The Higher Education Funding Council for England (HEFCE) funds 340 providers directly, of which 107 are universities or university colleges.

The Higher Education Funding Council for Wales (HEFCW) distributes funding for HE in Wales through Wales' 8 HEIs, the Open University in Wales and some FE colleges.

The Scottish Funding Council (SFC) – which is also responsible for FE in Scotland – is the national strategic body responsible for funding HE teaching and research in Scotland's 19 HEIs and 26 colleges.

In Northern Ireland, HE is provided by two universities, two university colleges, six regional institutes of further and higher education and the Open University (OU), which operates UK-wide. Unlike other parts of the UK, Northern Ireland has no higher education funding council; the Department for the Economy fulfils that role.

All UK universities and a number of HE colleges award their own degrees and other HE qualifications. HE providers who do not have their own degree-awarding powers offer degrees under 'validation arrangements' with other institutions that do have those powers. The OU, for example, runs a validation service which enables a number of other institutions to award OU degrees, after the OU has assured itself that the academic standards of their courses are as high as the OU's own standards.

Each HE institution is responsible for the standards of the awards it makes and the quality of the education it provides to its students, and each has its own internal quality assurance procedures. External quality assurance for HE institutions throughout the UK is provided by the Quality Assurance Agency for Higher Education (QAA).

The QAA is independent of government, funded by subscriptions from all publicly funded UK universities and colleges of HE. Its main role is to safeguard the standards of HE qualifications. It does this by defining standards for HE through a framework known as the academic infrastructure. QAA carries out reviews of the quality of UK HE institutions via a system known as 'institutional audits'. QAA also advises government on a range of HE quality issues, including applications for the grant of degree-awarding powers. It publishes reports on its review activities on its website.

Its future is in question as part of the changes proposed in the Higher Education and Research Act passed in April 2017 (*see* Recent Developments). The suggestion is that the new Office for Students will make the relevant decisions when it is established in April 2018.

DEPARTMENT FOR THE ECONOMY (NI)
T 028-9052 9900
W www.economy-ni.gov.uk

HIGHER EDUCATION FUNDING COUNCIL FOR ENGLAND T 0117-931 7317 W www.hefce.ac.uk
HIGHER EDUCATION FUNDING COUNCIL FOR WALES T 029-2076 1861 W www.hefcw.ac.uk
SCOTTISH FUNDING COUNCIL T 0131-313 6500
W www.sfc.ac.uk
THE QUALITY ASSURANCE AGENCY FOR HIGHER EDUCATION T 01452-557000 W www.qaa.ac.uk
See also Universities for information on the Research Excellence Framework (which replaced the Research Assessment Exercise) and listings of universities in the UK.

STUDENTS APPLYING TO UNIVERSITY			
	2016	2017	Difference
Total applicants by 30 June	674,890	649,700	3.7%
Source: UCAS			

STUDENTS IN HIGHER EDUCATION 2015–16*		
	Full-time	Part-time
HE students	1,740,540	540,285
Postgraduate students	305,120	227,850
Undergraduate students	1,435,420	312,435
* Includes UK, EU and non-EU students		

Source: Higher Education Statistics Agency (HESA) 2017

UK HIGHER EDUCATION QUALIFICATIONS AWARDED 2016–16		
	Full-time	Part-time
First degrees	367,240	32,580
Other undergraduate qualifications	46,335	34,415
Postgraduate Certificate in Education	19,760	1,040
Other postgraduate research and taught qualifications	166,810	74,545
Total qualifications awarded	151,415	39,800
Source: HESA 2017		

COURSES

HE institutions in the UK mainly offer courses leading to the following qualifications. These qualifications go from levels 4 to 8 on England's Regulated Qualifications Framework, levels 7 to 12 on Scotland's Credit and Qualifications Framework. Individual HEIs may not offer all of these.

Certificates of Higher Education (CertHE) are awarded after one year's full-time study (or equivalent). If available to students on longer courses, they certify that students have reached a minimum standard in their first year.

Diplomas of Higher Education (DipHE) and other *Higher Diplomas* are awarded after two to three years' full-time study (or equivalent). They certify that a student has achieved a minimum standard in first- and second-year courses and, in the case of nursing, third-year courses. They can often be used for entry to the third year of a related degree course.

Foundation degrees are awarded after two years of full-time study (or equivalent). These degrees combine academic study with work-based learning, and have been designed jointly by universities, colleges and employers with a particular area of work in mind. They are usually accepted as a basis for entry to the third year of a related degree course.

Bachelor's degrees, also referred to as *first degrees,* have different titles, Bachelor of Arts (BA) and Bachelor of Science (BSc) being the most common. In England, Wales and Northern Ireland most Bachelor's degree courses are 'with Honours' and awarded after three years of full-time study, although in some subjects the courses last longer. In Scotland, where young people may leave school and go to university a year younger, HE institutions typically offer Ordinary Bachelor's degrees after three years' study and Bachelor's degrees with Honours after four years. Honours degrees are graded as first, upper-second (2:1), lower second (2:2), or third. HEIs in England, Wales and Northern Ireland may allow students who fail the first year of an Honours degree by a small margin to transfer to an Ordinary degree course, if they have one. Ordinary degrees may also be awarded to Honours degree students who do not finish an Honours degree course but complete enough of it to earn a pass.

Postgraduate or *Higher degrees.* Graduates may go on to take *Master's degrees,* which involve one or two years' work and can be taught or research-based. They may also take one-year postgraduate diplomas and certificates, often linked to a specific profession, such as the *Postgraduate Certificate in Education* (PGCE) required to become a state school teacher. A *doctorate,* leading to a qualification such as Doctor of Philosophy – a PHD or DPHIL – usually involves at least three years of full-time research.

The framework for HE qualifications in England, Wales and Northern Ireland (FHEQ) and the framework for qualifications of HE institutions in Scotland can both be found on the QAA website, which describes the achievement represented by HE qualifications.

ADMISSIONS

When preparing to apply to a university or other HE college, individuals can compare facts and figures on institutions and courses using the government's Unistats website. This includes details of students' views from the annual National Student Survey.

For the vast majority of full-time undergraduate courses, individuals need to apply online through UCAS, the organisation responsible for managing applications to HE courses in the UK. More than half a million people wanting to study at a university or college each year use this UCAS service, which has useful online tools to help students find the right course.

UCAS also provides two specialist applications services used by more than 50,000 people each year: the Conservatoires UK Admissions Service (CUKAS), for those applying to UK music conservatoires, and the Graduate Teacher Training Registry (GTTR), for postgraduate applications for initial teacher training courses in England and Wales and some in Scotland. Details of initial teacher training courses in Scotland can also be obtained from Universities Scotland and from Teach in Scotland, the website created by the Scottish government to promote teaching.

Each university or college sets its own entry requirements. These can be in terms of particular exam grades or total points on the 'UCAS tariff' (UCAS's system for allocating points to different qualifications on a common basis), or be non-academic, like having a health check. HE institutions will make 'firm offers' to candidates who have already gained the qualifications they present for entry, and 'conditional offers' to those who have yet to take their exams or obtain their results. Conditional offers often require a minimum level of achievement in a specified subject, for example '300 points to include grade A at A-level Chemistry'. If candidates' achievements are lower than specified in their conditional offers, the university or college may not accept them; then, if they still wish to go into HE, they need to find another institution through the UCAS 'clearing' process.

The Open University conducts its own admissions. It is the UK's only university dedicated to distance learning and the UK's largest for part-time HE. Because it is designed to be 'open' to all, no qualifications are needed for entry to the majority of its courses.

Individuals can search thousands of UK postgraduate courses and research opportunities on UK graduate careers website Prospects. The application process for postgraduate places can vary between institutions. Most universities and colleges accept direct applications and many accept applications through UKPASS, a free, centralised online service run by UCAS that allows individuals to submit up to ten different applications, track their progress and attach supporting material, such as references.

UNISTATS W http://unistats.direct.gov.uk
UCAS T 0371-468 0468 W www.ucas.com
UNIVERSITIES SCOTLAND T 0131-226 1111
    W www.universities-scotland.ac.uk
TEACH IN SCOTLAND T 0845-345 4745
    W www.teachinginscotland.com
PROSPECTS T 0161-277 5200 W www.prospects.ac.uk
UKPASS T 0371-334 4447 W http://ukpass.ac.uk

TUITION FEES AND STUDENT SUPPORT

TUITION FEES

HE institutions (HEIs) in England, Wales and Northern Ireland charge tuition fees for full-time HE courses. Although students from outside the EU can be charged the full cost of their courses, the tuition fees that HEIs may charge students from the UK and other EU countries are capped. The maximum fee was set at £9,000 a year in September 2012, but increased to £9,250 in September 2017 universities have been able to charge up to £9,000 a year in tuition fees. In July 2016 a government statement setting out plans to link higher fees to better teaching declared an intention to increase the maximum fee to £9,250 from September 2017. Under the Higher Education and Research Act (*see* recent developments) the government plans to link higher fees to better teaching; allowing those HEIs with high quality teaching to increase tuition fees in line with inflation in subsequent years. The exact fee depends on the course studied and the institution attended.

Full-time students do not have to pay their fees themselves before or during their course, as tuition fee loans are available to cover the full cost; these do not have to be repaid until the student is working and earning more than a specified amount (*see* below).

In recent years, Scottish HE institutions have charged flat rate fees, set by the Scottish government, to undergraduate students classed as being ordinarily resident in England, Wales or Northern Ireland; though, as explained above, students can get repayable tuition fee loans to cover the cost. Since 2012 universities can set their own fees, up to £9,000 a year, for undergraduates starting courses. Undergraduate students classed as being ordinarily resident in Scotland or another EU country do not have to pay tuition fees at Scottish HE institutions. All tuition fees are paid on their behalf by the Scottish government through the Student Awards Agency for Scotland (SAAS); students must apply for this funding every year.

STUDENT LOANS, GRANTS AND BURSARIES

England

All students starting a full-time HE course in 2017–18 can apply through Student Finance England for financial support. Two student loans are available from the government: a *tuition fee loan* of up to £9,250 for 2017–18, or up to £6,165 for a private university or college; and a *maintenance loan* (for students aged under 60) to help with living expenses of up to £8,430 for those living away from home (£11,002 if studying away from home in London), or up to £7,907 for those living with their parents during term time, or up to £9,654 if living and studying abroad for a year.

The tuition fee loan is not affected by household income and is paid directly to the relevant HE institution. A proportion (currently 65 per cent) of the maximum maintenance loan is available irrespective of household income while the rest depends on an income assessment. Student Finance England usually pays the money into the student's own bank account in three instalments, one at the start of each term.

Repayment of both loans does not start until the April after the student has left university or college, or before they are earning over £21,000 a year.

At this point the individual's employer will deduct 9 per cent of any salary above the starting limit through the Pay As You Earn (PAYE) system. The self-employed make repayments through their tax returns. Student loans accrue interest from the date they are paid out, up until they are repaid in full. Generally, the interest rate for student loans is set in September each year. The latest rate can be found online (W www.studentloanrepayment.co.uk).

For all new full-time students starting HE from September 2016, maintenance grants are replaced by loans. Students whose family income is up to £42,620 will be able to apply in 2017–18 for maintenance loans of up to £8,430 a year (£11,002 in London) – the maximum amount applying only to students with a household income of less than £25,000 a year. Special support grants will also be replaced by maintenance loans.

Students needing extra help may also be entitled to receive disabled students' allowance, adult dependants' grant, childcare grant or parents' learning allowance.

Part-time Higher Education Students in England are entitled to tuition fee loans (which replaced grants) of up to £6,935 in 2017–18. Following government changes to student finance, the maximum universities and colleges can charge part-time students in tuition fees is £6,750. Part-time students who earn over £21,000 a year have to start paying back their loans after four years even if their course has not finished.

Details are available on the Student Finance England website (W www.gov.uk/student-finance/loans-and-grants) There is a student finance calculator on the website to work out what financial support is available.

Universities and other higher education providers offer their own grants and bursaries, with differing criteria. Bursaries do not have to be repaid. Students should always check with the institution they are planning to attend to find out what extra financial support may be available.

If the student's chosen HE institution runs the *additional fee support scheme*, it could provide extra financial help if the student is on a low income and in certain other circumstances. For students in financial difficulty help may also be available through the institution's *access to learning fund,*

Wales

Welsh students starting a full-time HE course in 2017–18 can apply through Student Finance Wales for the forms of financial support described below.

The system of tuition fee and maintenance loans and grants in Wales is similar to England's but Welsh students can also receive a substantial tuition *fee grant*. Maximum maintenance loans are: up to £6,922 for students living away from home (£9,697 if studying away from home in London) and up to £5,358 for those living with their parents during term time. From September 2017, eligible Welsh students can access a non means-tested tuition fee loan of up to £4,296 and grant of up to £4,954 to cover the exact amount that the institution charges for a course.

Welsh-domiciled students may apply for a *Welsh government learning grant* of up to £5,161 to help meet general living costs. This is paid in three instalments, one at the start of each term, like the student maintenance loan. The amount that a student gets depends on household income. The maximum grant is available to those with a household income of £18,370 or under. Those with an income of £50,020 or under receive a partial grant.

There is also a *special support grant* for single parents, student parents or those with disabilities, which is worth up to £5,161 a year in 2017–18. It is paid directly to students and is not offset against student loan borrowing.

Students needing extra help may also be entitled to adult dependants' grant, childcare grant, parents' learning allowance and disabled students' allowances.

Students can use the student finance calculator on the Student Finance Wales website to work out what financial support they may be entitled to.

Welsh HE institutions also hold financial contingency funds to provide discretionary assistance to students experiencing financial difficulties.

For 2017–18 part-time undergraduate higher education students and continuing students studying at least 25 per cent of an equivalent full-time course are entitled to receive a fee loan of £2,625 (£6,935 for a course at a publicly funded university or college elsewhere in the UK, or £4,625 at a private university or college).

A *course grant* of up to £1,155 for books, travel and other course-related costs is available for part-time students. This course grant depends on household income. Recipients must be studying at an average course intensity of at least 50 per cent to be eligible. The *course grant* is paid into the student's bank account in one lump sum. It is not usually available to those who already have a UK honours degree.

STUDENT FINANCE WALES T 0300-200 4050
    W www.studentfinancewales.co.uk

Scotland

All students starting a full-time HE course in 2017–18 can apply through the Student Awards Agency for Scotland for financial support. In 2017–18 students can receive tuition fee help of £1,285 for a HND/HNC, £1,820 for a degree or equivalent or £1,205 at a private university. Living cost support is mainly provided through a *student loan*, the majority of which is income-assessed. The maximum loan for 2017–18 is £6,750 for students classed as 'independent' of parental support.

The *young students' bursary* (YSB) is available to young students from low-income backgrounds and is non-repayable. Eligible students receive this bursary instead of part of the student loan, thus reducing their level of repayable debt. In 2017–18 the maximum annual support provided through YSB is £1,875 if household income is £18,999 or less a year.

The *independent students' bursary* (ISB) similarly replaces part of the loan and reduces repayable debt for low-income students independent of parental support. The maximum paid is £875 a year to those whose household income is £18,999 or less a year.

In 2017–18, students that have come from a care setting will be eligible to apply for a non means-tested bursary of £7,625 and a grant of £105 a week for accommodation costs. This new bursary replaces the current income-assessed living cost loan and bursary (ISB/YSB) package.

Travel expenses are included within the student loan. There are *supplementary grants* available to certain categories of students such as lone parents (£1,305) and those with dependants (£1,305). Extra help is also available to those who have a disability, learning difficulty or mental health problem.

STUDENT AWARDS AGENCY FOR SCOTLAND
    T 0300-555 0505
    W www.saas.gov.uk/forms/funding_guide.pdf

Northern Ireland

All students starting a full-time HE course in 2017–18 can apply through Student Finance Northern Ireland for financial support. The arrangements for both full-time and part-time students are similar to those for England. The main difference is that the income-assessed *maintenance grant* (or *special support grant* for students on certain income-assessed benefits) for new full-time students studying at UK universities and colleges is worth up to £3,925 (for household incomes of £19,203 or less).

Universities and colleges in Northern Ireland can charge up to £4,030 for tuition fees in academic year 2017–18. Students can get a loan to cover the full amount of tuition fees up to a maximum of £4,030. There are tuition fee loans of up to £9,250 for students studying in England, Scotland and Wales.

Loans are available for living costs: £3,750 for study in Northern Ireland, £4,840 for study elsewhere in the UK (£6,780 in London), £4,840 for study in the Republic of Ireland or £5,770 for study overseas.

STUDENT FINANCE NORTHERN IRELAND
    T 0300-100 0077 W www.studentfinanceni.co.uk

Disabled Students' Allowances

Disabled Students' Allowances (DSAs) are grants available throughout the UK to help meet the extra course costs that full-time, part-time and postgraduate (taught or research) students can face as a direct result of a disability, ongoing health condition, mental health condition or specific learning difficulty. They help disabled people to study in HE on an equal basis with other students. They are paid on top of the standard student finance package and do not have to be repaid. The amount that an individual gets depends on the type of extra help needed, not on household income.

In all parts of the UK, the following three allowances are available: a specialist equipment or large items allowance for the entire course (2017–18 maximum rates vary from £5,358 in England to £5,160 in Scotland); an annual non-medical helper allowance (2017–18 maximum rates for full-time students vary from £21,305 in England to £20,520 in Scotland); and an annual general or basic allowance (2017–18 maximum rates for full-time students vary from £1,790 in England to £1,725 in Scotland). Reasonable spending on extra disability-related travel costs can also be reimbursed. Eligible individuals should apply as early as possible to the relevant UK awarding authority.

POSTGRADUATE AWARDS

In general, postgraduate students do not qualify for mandatory support like student loans. An exception to this is students taking a Postgraduate Certificate in Education (PGCE), who can qualify for the finance package usually available only to undergraduates. There are also bursaries available for social work and some medical students.

There is heavy competition for any postgraduate funding available. Individuals can search for postgraduate awards and scholarships on two websites: Hot Courses and Prospects. They can also search for grants available from educational trusts, often reserved for students from poorer backgrounds or for those who have achieved academic excellence, on W www.gov.uk/grant-bursary-adult-learners or the Family Action website. Otherwise they need to fund their own fees and living expenses.

Postgraduates from Scotland, if they are full-time students aged under 50, can get £5,500 towards tuition fees and living cost loans of £4,500. No support for living costs is available to part-time postgraduates. In Northern Ireland, the Department for the Economy and the Education and Library Boards provide postgraduate funding for certain courses.

DEPARTMENT FOR THE ECONOMY (DE),
  NORTHERN IRELAND T 028-9052 9900
  W www.nidirect.gov.uk/articles/postgraduate-awards
FAMILY ACTION T 020-7254 6251
  W www.family-action.org.uk
HOT COURSES W www.hotcourses.com
SCHOLARSHIP SEARCH W www.scholarship-search.org.uk
PROSPECTS W www.prospects.ac.uk
STUDENT AWARDS AGENCY FOR SCOTLAND (SAAS)
  T 0300-555 0505 W www.student-support-saas.gov.uk

TEACHER TRAINING

See Professional Education/ Teaching.

EMPLOYEES AND SALARIES

EMPLOYEES

QUALIFIED TEACHERS IN MAINTAINED SCHOOLS
November 2015–16, Full-time equivalent, thousands

	England	Wales	Scotland	NI	UK
Nursery and primary schools	*222.4	13.6	24.9	8.4	269.3
Secondary schools	*208.2	12.1	23.0	9.3	252.6
Special schools	22.3	0.7	1.9	0.8	25.7
Total	452.9	26.4	49.8	18.5	547.6

* Includes academies and city technology colleges in England

SUPPORT STAFF IN MAINTAINED SCHOOLS,
ENGLAND AND WALES (2015–16)
Full-time equivalent, thousands

	England	Wales
Teaching assistants	265.6	–
Other support staff	*146.7	–
Total	*412.3	24.0

* Includes academies and city technology colleges in England

ACADEMIC STAFF IN UK HIGHER EDUCATION
INSTITUTIONS (2015–16)

	Full-time	Part-time	Total
Professors	15,960	4,015	19,975
Non-professors	119,055	62,350	181,405
Teaching only	13,405	39,185	52,590
Teaching and research	80,305	18,315	98,620
Research only	40,290	8,360	48,645
Neither teaching nor research	1,015	505	1,525

Source: HESA 2016

SALARIES

State school teachers in England and Wales are employed by local authorities or the governing bodies of their schools. All teachers are eligible for membership of the Teachers' Pension Scheme.

There are teaching and learning responsibility payments for specific posts, special needs work and recruitment and retention factors which may be awarded at the discretion of the school governing body or the local authority. There are separate pay ranges for Headteachers and other school leaders. Academies are free to set their own salaries.

In 2013 every school was required to revise its pay and appraisal policies, setting out how pay progression would, in future, be linked to a teacher's performance. The first decisions on pay progression under the new provisions were made in September 2014, based on appraisals at the end of the 2013–14 cycle. From September 2014, school governing bodies were also given more flexibility, within the national pay ranges, to determine the pay of headteachers and other school leaders. From September 2017 the pay of school leaders ranges from £39,374 to £109,366 (Headteachers £44,544 to £109,366) a year outside London and from £46,814 to £116,738 (Headteachers £51,991 to £116,738) a year in Inner London.

After completing initial teacher training and achieving qualified teacher status (QTS), newly qualified teachers (NQTs) in maintained schools can expect to start on a salary of £22,917 a year in England and Wales (or £28,660 in Inner London). The pay ranges for teachers in England and Wales from September 2017 are:

Main pay range (including NQTs)	
London fringe	£24,018–£34,934
Outer London	£26,662–£37,645
Inner London	£28,660–£39,006
Rest of England and Wales	£22,917–£33,824
Upper pay range	
London fringe	£37,017–£39,725
Outer London	£39,519–£42,498
Inner London	£43,616–£47,298
Rest of England and Wales	£35,927–£38,633

In October 2015 the Scottish Negotiating Committee for Teachers agreed a two-year pay deal. The agreement provided for pay increases of 1.5 per cent from 1 April 2015, followed by a 1 per cent increase from 1 April 2016. Teachers are paid on a seven-point scale where the entry point is for newly qualified teachers undertaking their probationary year. Experienced, ambitious teachers who reach the top of the main pay scale are eligible to become chartered teachers and earn more on a separate pay spine. However, to do so they must study for further professional qualifications. Headteachers and deputies have a separate pay spine as do 'principals' or heads of department. Additional allowances are payable to teachers under a range of circumstances, such as working in distant islands and remote schools.

Salary scales for teachers in Scotland as at 1 September 2017:

Headteacher/deputy headteacher	£44,223–£86,319
Principal teacher	£38,991–£50,319
Chartered teacher	£36,870–£43,845
Main grade	£22,416–£35,763

Teachers in Northern Ireland have broadly similar payscales to teachers in England and Wales. Classroom teachers who take on teaching and learning responsibilities outside their normal classroom duties may be awarded one of five teaching allowances. In July 2015 a 1 per cent increase to salary scales was announced; this increase was backdated to September 2014. A further 1 per cent pay increase was awarded from September 2016. As at 1 September 2017, salary scales in Northern Ireland are:

Principal (headteacher)	£43,664–£108,282
Classroom teacher (upper pay scale)	£35,217–£37,870
Classroom teacher (main pay scale)	£22,243–£32,509
Unqualified teacher	£14,151
Teaching allowances	£1,903–£12,272

Since 2007, most academic staff in HE across the UK are paid on a single national pay scale as a result of a national framework agreement negotiated by the HE unions and HE institutions. Staff are paid according to rates on a 51-point national pay spine and academic and academic-related staff are graded according to a national grading structure. As HE institutions are autonomous employers, precise job grades and salaries may vary but the following table outlines salaries that typically tally with certain job roles in HE.

Principal lecturer	£47,801–£55,389
Senior lecturer	£37,768–£46,414
Lecturer	£31,655–£36,672
Junior researcher	£25,023–£30,738

UNIVERSITIES

The following is a list of universities, which are those institutions that have been granted degree-awarding powers by either a royal charter or an act of parliament, or have been permitted to use the word 'university' (or 'university college') by the Privy Council. There are other recognised bodies in the UK with degree-awarding powers, as well as institutions offering courses leading to a degree from a recognised body. Further information is available at W www.gov.uk/recognised-uk-degrees

Student figures represent the number of undergraduate (UG) and postgraduate (PG) students based on information available at July 2017.

For information on tuition fees and student loans, *see* Education, Higher Education.

RESEARCH EXCELLENCE FRAMEWORK

The research excellence framework (REF) is the system for assessing the quality of research in UK higher education institutions. It replaced the research assessment exercise (RAE). The 2014 REF was conducted jointly by the Higher Education Funding Council for England (HEFCE), the Scottish Funding Council (SFC), the Higher Education Funding Council for Wales (HEFCW) and the Department for Employment and Learning (DEL), Northern Ireland. The primary purpose of REF 2014 was to assess the quality of research and produce outcomes for each submission made by institutions. The table below shows the top five universities or specialist colleges for each discipline based on the mean average ranking of the overall quality of their research.

Subject	Universities or university colleges
Agriculture, Veterinary & Food Science	Aberdeen (1), Warwick (2), Glasgow (3), Stirling (4), Queen's Belfast (5)
Anthropology	Oxford (1), Manchester: Anthropology (2), Manchester: Development Studies (3), UEA (4), LSE (5)
Architecture	Bath (1), Glasgow (1), Cambridge (3), Sheffield (4), Loughborough (5)
Area Studies	LSE(1), Birmingham (2), Exeter (3), London Met (4), UEA (5), Aston (5)
Art & Design	Reading (1), Courtauld (2), Westminster (3), St Andrews (4), York (5)
Biological Sciences	Institute of Cancer Research (1), Dundee (2), Edinburgh (3), Imperial (4), Oxford (5), Sheffield (5), Newcastle (5)
Business & Management	LSE (1), Cambridge (2), Imperial (3), Oxford (4), London Business School (5)
Chemistry	Cambridge (1), Liverpool (2), Oxford (3), Bristol (4), Durham (5)
Classics	Cambridge (1), Durham (2), St Andrews (2), Oxford (4), Birmingham (5)
Clinical Medicine	Oxford (1), Cambridge (2), King's (3), Imperial (4), Institute of Cancer Research (4)
Computer Science	UCL (1), Warwick (2), Imperial (3), Manchester (4), Sheffield (5)
Dentistry, Nursing & Pharmacy	Sheffield (1), Swansea (2), Southampton (3), Cardiff (4), Nottingham (4)
Earth Systems & Environmental Sciences	Oxford (1), Bristol (2), Cambridge (3), Southampton (4), Leeds (5)
Economics	UCL (1), LSE (2), Oxford (3), Cambridge (4), Warwick (5)
Education	Oxford (1), King's (2), Nottingham (3), Sheffield (4), Cambridge (5), Durham (5), Cardiff (5)
Engineering (Civil & Construction)	Cardiff (1), Imperial (2), Dundee (3), Sheffield (4), Manchester (5)
Engineering (Electronic)	Cambridge (1), Oxford (2), Imperial: Electrical and Electronic (3), Imperial: Metallurgy & Materials (4), Leeds (5)
Engineering (General)	Cambridge (1), Imperial (2), Manchester (3), Birmingham (4), Leeds (4)
English	Warwick (1), York (2), Newcastle (3), Durham (4), Queen Mary (5)
Geography, Environment & Archaeology	Bristol (1), Cambridge (2), Royal Holloway (2), LSE (4), St Andrews (5)
History	Birmingham (1), York (2), Southampton (3), Sheffield (3), King's (5), Hertfordshire (5)
Law	King's (1), LSE (2), Durham (3), Ulster (4), UCL (5), York (5)
Maths	Oxford (1), Cambridge (2), Warwick (3), Imperial (4), Bristol (5), Lancaster (5)
Modern Languages	Queen Mary (1), Edinburgh (2), Kent (3), Queen Margaret (3), Southampton (5), Queen's Belfast (5)
Philosophy	Oxford (1), Birmingham (2), King's (3), Warwick (4), St Andrew's (5), LSE (5)
Physics	Strathclyde (1), Oxford (2), Edinburgh (3), Nottingham (3), St Andrews (3)
Politics & International Studies	Essex (1), LSE (2), Sheffield (3), Oxford (4), UCL (5)
Psychology, Psychiatry & Neuroscience	Oxford (1), Cardiff (1), Cambridge (3), York (4), Birkbeck (5)
Public Health, Health Services & Primary Care	Oxford (1), Imperial (2), Cambridge (3), Bristol (4), Queen Mary (5)
Social Work and Social Policy	Oxford (1), LSE (2), York (3), UEA (4), Kent (5)
Sociology	York (1), Manchester (2), Cardiff (3), Lancaster (4), Oxford (5)
Sports-related subjects	Bristol (1), Liverpool John Moores (2), Leeds (3), Birmingham (4), Bath (5)
Theology & Religious Studies	Durham (1), Birmingham (2), Lancaster (3), Leeds (3), UCL (3)

UNIVERSITY OF ABERDEEN (1495)

King's College, Aberdeen AB24 3FX T 01224-272000
W www.abdn.ac.uk
Fee: £9,000 *Students:* 10,055 UG; 3,985 PG
Chancellor, HRH the Duchess of Rothesay, GCVO, PC
Vice-Chancellor, Prof. Sir Ian Diamond, FRSE
University Secretary, Caroline Inglis

UNIVERSITY OF ABERTAY DUNDEE (1994)

Bell Street, Dundee DD1 1HG T 01382-308000
E enquiries@abertay.ac.uk W www.abertay.ac.uk
Fee: £8,000 *Students:* 3,690 UG; 320 PG
Chancellor, Lord Cullen of Whitekirk, KT, PC, FRSE
Vice-Chancellor, Prof. Nigel Seaton, FRENG
University Secretary, Sheena Stewart

ABERYSTWYTH UNIVERSITY (1872)

Penglais, Aberystwyth SY23 3FL T 01970-62311 1
W www.aber.ac.uk
Fee: £9,000 *Students:* 7690 UG; 1,070 PG
Chancellor, Sir Emyr Jones Parry
Vice-Chancellor, Prof. Elizabeth Treasure
University Secretary, Geraint Pugh

ANGLIA RUSKIN UNIVERSITY (1992)
Chelmsford Campus, Bishop Hall Lane, Chelmsford CM1 1SQ
T 0845-271 3333 E answers@anglia.ac.uk W www.anglia.ac.uk
Fee: £9,250 *Students:* 17,270 UG; 3,665 PG
Chancellor, Lord Ashcroft, KCMG, PC
Vice-Chancellor, Prof. Iain Martin
Secretary and Clerk, Paul Bogle

ARTS UNIVERSITY BOURNEMOUTH (2012)
Wallisdown BH12 5HH T 01202-533011 W www.aub.ac.uk
Fee: £9,250 *Students:* 5,185 UG; 1,135 PG
Chancellor, Prof. Sir Christopher Frayling
Vice-Chancellor, Prof. Stuart Bartholomew, CBE
University Secretary, Jon Reynard

UNIVERSITY OF THE ARTS LONDON (2003) Formerly
The London Institute (1986), renamed 2004)
272 High Holborn, London WC1V 7EY T 020-7514 6000
E admissions@arts.ac.uk W www.arts.ac.uk
Fee: £9,250 *Students:* 14,800 UG; 3,405 PG
Chancellor, Greyson Perry, CBE
Vice-Chancellor, Nigel Carrington
Secretary and Registrar, Stephen Marshall

COLLEGES
CAMBERWELL COLLEGE OF ARTS (1898)
40–65 Peckham Road, London SE5 8UF
T 020-7514 6301
W www.arts.ac.uk/camberwell
Head of College, Prof. David Crow
CENTRAL SAINT MARTINS COLLEGE OF ART AND
DESIGN (1854)
Granary Building, 1 Granary Square, London N1C 4AA
T 020-7514 7444
W www.arts.ac.uk/csm
Head of College, Prof. Jeremy Till
CHELSEA COLLEGE OF ARTS (1895)
16 John Islip Street, London SW1P 4JU
T 020-7514 7751
W www.arts.ac.uk/chelsea
Head of College, Prof. David Crow
LONDON COLLEGE OF COMMUNICATION (1894)
Elephant and Castle, London SE1 6SB
T 020-7514 6500
W www.arts.ac.uk/cc
Head of College, Natalie Brett
LONDON COLLEGE OF FASHION (1963)
20 John Prince's Street, London W1G 0BJ
T 020-7514 7400
W www.arts.ac.uk/fashion
Head of College, Prof. Frances Corner, OBE
WIMBLEDON COLLEGE OF ART (1930)
Merton Hall Road, London SW19 3QA
T 020-7514 9641
W www.arts.ac.uk/wimbledon
Head of College, Prof. David Crow

ASTON UNIVERSITY (1966)
Aston Triangle, Birmingham B4 7ET T 0121-204 3000
W www.aston.ac.uk
Fee: £9,250 *Students:* 10,050 UG; 2,445 PG
Chancellor, Sir John Sunderland
Vice-Chancellor, Prof. Alec Cameron
Registrar, Alison Levey

BANGOR UNIVERSITY (1884)
Gwynedd LL57 2DG T 01248-3511 51 W www.bangor.ac.uk
Fee: £9,000 *Students:* 8,240 UG; 2,390 PG
Vice-Chancellor, Prof. John G. Hughes
University Secretary, Dr Kevin Mundy

UNIVERSITY OF BATH (1966)
Bath BA2 7AY T 01225-388388 W www.bath.ac.uk
Fee: £9,250 *Students:* 13,051 UG; 4,257PG
Chancellor, HRH the Earl of Wessex, KG, GCVO
Vice-Chancellor, Prof. Dame Glynis Breakwell, DBE, FRSA
University Secretary, Mark Humphriss

BATH SPA UNIVERSITY (2005)
Newton Park, Bath BA2 9BN T 01225-875875
E enquiries@bathspa.ac.uk W www.bathspa.ac.uk
Fee: £9,250 *Students:* 6,100 UG; 1,100 PG
Chancellor, Jeremy Irons
Vice-Chancellor (interim), Prof. Nick Foskett
Academic Registrar, Christopher Ellicott

UNIVERSITY OF BEDFORDSHIRE (1993)
University Square, Luton LU1 3JU T 01234-400400
W www.beds.ac.uk
Fee: £9,250 *Students:* 12,090 UG; 4,065 PG
Chancellor, Rt. Hon. John Bercow, MP
Vice-Chancellor, Bill Rammell
Registrar, Hugh Martin

UNIVERSITY OF BIRMINGHAM (1900)
Edgbaston, Birmingham B15 2TT T 0121-414 3344
W www.birmingham.ac.uk
Fee: £9,250 *Students:* 21,495 UG; 12,335 PG
Chancellor, Lord Bilimoria, CBE
Vice-Chancellor and Principal, Prof. Sir David Eastwood
Registrar and Secretary, Lee Sanders

BIRMINGHAM CITY UNIVERSITY (1992)
City North Campus, Birmingham B42 2SU T 0121-331 5000
W www.bcu.ac.uk
Fee: £9,250 *Students:* 19,715 UG; 4,345 PG
Chancellor, Sir Lenny Henry, CBE
Vice-Chancellor, Prof. Philip Plowden
University Secretary, Karen Stephenson

UNIVERSITY COLLEGE BIRMINGHAM (2012)
Summer Rowe, Birmingham B3 1JB T 0121-604 1000
E admissions@ucb.ac.uk W www.ucb.ac.uk
Fee: £9,076 *Students:* 4,570 UG; 455 PG
Vice-Chancellor and Principal, Prof. Ray Linforth

BISHOP GROSSETESTE UNIVERSITY (2013)
Longdales Road, Lincoln LN1 3DY T 01522-527347
E admissions@bton.ac.uk W www.bishopg.ac.uk
Fee: £9,250 *Students:* 1,855 UG; 385 PG
Chancellor, Dame Judith Mayhew, DBE
Vice-Chancellor, Revd. Canon Prof. Peter Neil
Registrar and University Secretary, Dr Anne Craven

UNIVERSITY OF BOLTON (2005)
Deane Road, Bolton BL3 5AB T 01204-900600
E enquiries@bolton.ac.uk W www.bolton.ac.uk
Fee: £9,250 *Students:* 5,185 UG; 1,135 PG
Chancellor, Earl of St Andrews
Vice-Chancellor, Prof. George E. Holmes, DL
Registrar and Secretary, Sue Duncan, LLD

BOURNEMOUTH UNIVERSITY (1992)
Fern Barrow, Poole BH12 5BB T 01202-52411 1
E askbu@bournemouth.ac.uk W www1.bournemouth.ac.uk
Fee: £9,250 *Students:* 15,225 UG; 3,820 PG
Chancellor, Lord Phillips of Worth Maltravers, KG, PC
Vice-Chancellor, Prof. John Vinney
Clerk, Deborah Wakeley

UNIVERSITY OF BRADFORD (1966)
Richmond Road, Bradford BD7 1DP **T** 01274-232323
E enquiries@bradford.ac.uk **W** www.bradford.ac.uk
Fee: £9,250 *Students:* 8,395 UG; 2,815 PG
Chancellor, Kate Swann
Vice-Chancellor and Principal, Prof. Brian Cantor, CBE
University Secretary, Alison Jones

UNIVERSITY OF BRIGHTON (1992)
Mithras House, Lewes Road, Brighton BN2 4AT **T** 01273-600900
E postmaster@bton.ac.uk **W** www.brighton.ac.uk
Fee: £9,250 *Students:* 17,170 UG; 3,965 PG
Vice-Chancellor, Prof. Debra Humphris
Secretary and Registrar, Stephen Dudderidge

UNIVERSITY OF BRISTOL (1909)
Senate House, Tyndall Avenue, Bristol BS8 1TH **T** 011 7-928 9000
W www.bristol.ac.uk
Fee: £9,250 *Students:* 16,730 UG; 5,175 PG
Chancellor, Sir Paul Nurse, FRS, FMEDSCI
Vice-Chancellor, Prof Hugh Brady
Registrar, Robin Geller

BRUNEL UNIVERSITY LONDON (1966)
Kingston Lane, Uxbridge UB8 3PH **T** 01895-274000
E admissions@brunel.ac.uk **W** www.brunel.ac.uk
Fee: £9,250 *Students:* 9,855 UG; 4,310 PG
Chancellor, Sir Richard Sykes
Vice-Chancellor, Prof. Julia Buckingham, PHD, DSC, FRSA
Academic Registrar, Jilly Court

UNIVERSITY OF BUCKINGHAM (1983)
Buckingham MK18 1EG **T** 01280-814080
E info@buckingham.ac.uk **W** www.buckingham.ac.uk
Fee: £12,444 *Students:* 1,263 UG; 1,354 PG
Chancellor, the Hon. Lady Keswick
Vice-Chancellor, Sir Anthony Seldon, PHD, FRSA
Registrar, Anne Miller

BUCKS NEW UNIVERSITY (2007)
High Wycombe Campus, Queen Alexandra Road, High Wycombe
HP11 2JZ **T** 01494-522141 **E** advice@bucks.ac.uk
W www.bucks.ac.uk
Fee: £9,250 *Students:* 7,660 UG; 980 PG
Vice-Chancellor, Prof. Rebecca Bunting

UNIVERSITY OF CAMBRIDGE (1209)
The Old Schools, Trinity Lane, Cambridge CB2 1TN
T 01223-337733 **W** www.cam.ac.uk
Fee: £9,250 *Students:* 12,220 UG; 7,440 PG
Chancellor, Lord Sainsbury of Turville, FRS (KING'S)
Vice-Chancellor, Prof. Stephen Toope
High Steward, Lord Watson of Richmond, CBE (JESUS)
Deputy High Steward, Mrs A. Lonsdale, CBE (Murray Edwards)
Commissary, Lord Judge, PC (Magdalene)
Pro-Vice-Chancellors, Prof. D. Maskell, FMedSci (Wolfson);
  Prof. G. J. Virgo, QC (Downing); Prof. E. L. Ferran, FBA
  (St Catharine's); Prof. C. Abell, FRS, FMedSci; Prof. A.
  Neely (Sidney Sussex)
Proctors (2017–18), T. Milner (Darwin); G. Burgess
  (Newnham)
Deputy Proctors (2017–18), G. Chesterman (St Edmund's); C.
  A. Ristuccia (Trinity Hall)
Orator, Dr R. J. E. Thompson (Selwyn)
Registrar, Dr J. W. Nicholls (Emmanuel)
Librarian, Dr J. Gardner (Selwyn)
Director of the Fitzwilliam Museum, T. Knox (Gonville and
  Caius)
Academic Secretary, (vacant)
Director of Finance, A. M. Reid (Wolfson)
Executive Director of Development, Ms A. Traub
Esquire Bedells, Mrs N. Hardy (Jesus); Ms S. V. Scarlett (Lucy
  Cavendish)
University Advocate, R. E. Thornton (Emmanuel)
Deputy University Advocate, J. K. Seymour (Sidney Sussex)

COLLEGES AND HALLS
(with dates of foundation)
CHRIST'S (1505)
Master, Prof. J. Stapleton, FBA
CHURCHILL (1960)
Master, Prof. Dame Athene Donald, DBE, FRS
CLARE (1326)
Master, Lord Grabiner, QC
CLARE HALL (1966)
President, Prof. D. J. Ibbetson, FBA
CORPUS CHRISTI (1352)
Master, S. Laing
DARWIN (1964)
Master, C. M. R. Fowler
DOWNING (1800)
Master, Prof. G. R. Grimmett
EMMANUEL (1584)
Master, Dame Fiona Reynolds, DBE
FITZWILLIAM (1966)
Master, Mrs N. M. Padfield
GIRTON (1869)
Mistress, Prof. S. J. Smith, FBA
GONVILLE AND CAIUS (1348)
Master, Dr. P. Rogerson
HOMERTON (1976)
Principal, Prof. G. Ward
HUGHES HALL (1885)
President, Dr Anthony Freeling
JESUS (1496)
Master, Prof. I. H. White
KING'S (1441)
Provost, Prof. M. R. E. Proctor, FRS
LUCY CAVENDISH (1965)
President, Jackie Ashley
MAGDALENE (1542)
Master, Rt. Revd Lord Williams of Oystermouth, PC,
DPHIL, FBA
MURRAY EDWARDS (1954)
President, Dame Barbara Stocking, DBE
NEWNHAM (1871)
Principal, Prof. Dame Carol Black, DBE, FRCP
PEMBROKE (1347)
Master, Lord Smith of Finsbury
PETERHOUSE (1284)
Master, Ms Bridget Kendall, MBE
QUEENS' (1448)
President, Prof. Lord Eatwell of Stratton St Margaret
ROBINSON (1977)
Warden, Prof. A. D. Yates
ST CATHARINE'S (1473)
Master, Prof. Sir Mark Welland, FRS, FREng
ST EDMUND'S (1896)
Master, Hon. Matthew Bullock
ST JOHN'S (1511)
Master, Prof. C. M. Dobson, FRS
SELWYN (1882)
Master, Roger Mosey
SIDNEY SUSSEX (1596)
Master, Prof. R. V. Penty
TRINITY (1546)
Master, Sir Gregory Winter, CBE, FRS
TRINITY HALL (1350)
Master, Revd. Dr Jeremy Morris
WOLFSON (1965)
President, Prof. Sir Richard Evans, FBA

CANTERBURY CHRIST CHURCH UNIVERSITY (2005)
North Holmes Road, Canterbury CT1 1QU T 01227-767700
E admissions@canterbury.co.uk W www.canterbury.ac.uk
Fee: £9,250 Students: 13,115 UG; 2,935 PG
Chancellor, Most Revd and Rt. Hon. Archbishop of Canterbury
Vice-Chancellor, Prof. Rama Thirunamachandran
Academic Registrar, Cathy Lambert

CARDIFF UNIVERSITY (1883)
Cardiff CF10 3XQ T 029-2087 4000 W www.cardiff.ac.uk
Fee: £9,000 Students: 21,905 UG; 8,775 PG
Vice-Chancellor, Prof. Colin Riordan
Chief Operating Officer, Jayne Sadgrove

CARDIFF METROPOLITAN UNIVERSITY (1865)
Western Avenue, Cardiff CF5 2YB T 029-2041 6070
W www.cardiffmet.ac.uk
Fee: £9,000 Students: 9,220 UG; 3,360 PG
President and Vice-Chancellor, Prof. Cara Carmichael Aitchison,
    FACSS, FRGS, FHEA
Chief Operating Officer, John Cappock

UNIVERSITY OF CENTRAL LANCASHIRE (1992)
Preston PR1 2HE T 01772-201201 E cenquiries@uclan.ac.uk
W www.uclan.ac.uk
Fee: £9,250 Students: 20,180 UG; 4,280 PG
Chancellor, Ranvir Singh
Vice-Chancellor, Prof. Mike Thomas
University Secretary, Ian Fisher

UNIVERSITY OF CHESTER (Founded in 1839 as Chester
Diocesan Training College; gained University status in
2005)
Parkgate Road, Chester CH1 4BJ T 01244-511 000
E enquiries@chester.ac.uk W www.chester.ac.uk
Fee: £9,250 Students: 10,830 UG; 4,085 PG
Chancellor, Gyles Brandreth
Vice-Chancellor, Canon Prof. Tim Wheeler
University Secretary, Adrian Lee

UNIVERSITY OF CHICHESTER (2005)
College Lane, Chichester PO19 6PE T 01243-816000
E help@chi.ac.uk W www.chi.ac.uk
Fee: £9,250 Students: 4,675 UG; 845 PG
Vice-Chancellor, Prof. Jane Longmore
University Secretary, Sophie Egleton

COVENTRY UNIVERSITY (1992)
Priory Street, Coventry CV1 5FB T 024-7688 7688
W www.coventry.ac.uk
Fee: £9,250 Students: 23,465 UG; 5,960 PG
Chancellor, Margaret Casely-Hayford
Vice-Chancellor, Prof. John Latham
Academic Registrar, Kate Quantrell

CRANFIELD UNIVERSITY (1969)
Cranfield MK43 0AL T 01234-75011 1 E info@cranfield.ac.uk
W www.cranfield.ac.uk
Students: 3,980 PG (postgraduate only)
Chancellor, Baroness Young of Old Scone
Vice-Chancellor, Prof. Sir Peter Gregson
University Secretary, Prof. William Stephens

UNIVERSITY FOR THE CREATIVE ARTS (2008)
Falkner Road, Farnham GU9 7DS T 01252-722441
W www.ucreative.ac.uk
Fee: £9,250 Students: 4,500 UG; 305 PG
Chancellor, Dame Zandra Rhodes, DBE
Vice-Chancellor, Prof. Bashir Makhoul
University Secretary, Marion Wilks

UNIVERSITY OF CUMBRIA (2007)
Fusehill Street, Carlisle CA1 2HH T 01228-616234
W www.cumbria.ac.uk
Fee: £9,250 Students: 6,995 UG; 1,795 PG
Chancellor, Most Revd and Rt. Hon. Archbishop of York
Vice-Chancellor, Prof. Julie Mennell
Registrar and Secretary, Neil Harris

DE MONTFORT UNIVERSITY (1992)
The Gateway, Leicester LE1 9BH T 011 6-255 1551
E enquiry@dmu.ac.uk W www.dmu.ac.uk
Fee: £9,250 Students: 17,140 UG; 3,765 PG
Chancellor, Baroness Lawrence of Clarendon, OBE
Vice-Chancellor, Prof. Dominic Shellard

UNIVERSITY OF DERBY (1992)
Kedleston Road, Derby DE22 1GB T 01332-590500
E askadmissions@derby.ac.uk W www.derby.ac.uk
Fee: £9,250 Students: 14,065 UG; 2,984 PG
Chancellor, Duke of Devonshire, KCVO, CBE
Vice-Chancellor and Principal, Prof. Kathryn Mitchell
Registrar, June Hughes

UNIVERSITY OF DUNDEE (1967)
Nethergate, Dundee DD1 4HN T 01382-383000
E university@dundee.ac.uk W www.dundee.ac.uk
Fee: £9,250 Students: 10,439UG; 5,742 PG
Chancellor, Lord Patel, KT, FRSE
Vice-Chancellor and Principal, Prof. Sir Pete Downes, OBE, FRSE
University Secretary, Dr James McGeorge

DURHAM UNIVERSITY (1832)
The Palatine Centre, Stockton Road, Durham DH1 3LE
T 0191-334 2000 W www.dur.ac.uk
Fee: £9,250 Students: 13,265 UG; 4,545 PG
Chancellor, Sir Thomas Allen, CBE
Vice-Chancellor, Prof. Stuart Corbridge
University Secretary, Jennifer Sewel

COLLEGES
COLLINGWOOD (1972)
Principal, Prof. J. Elliott
GREY (1959)
Master, Prof. T. Allen
HATFIELD (1846)
Master, Prof. A. M. MacLarnon
JOHN SNOW (2001)
Principal, Prof. C. Summerbell
JOSEPHINE BUTLER (2006)
Principal, A. Simpson
ST AIDAN'S (1947)
Principal, S. F. Frenk
ST CHAD'S (1904)
Principal, M. Masson
ST CUTHBERT'S SOCIETY (1888)
Principal, Prof. E. Archibald
ST HILD AND ST BEDE (1839)
Principal, Prof. J. Clarke
ST JOHN'S (1909)
Principal, Revd Dr D. Wilkinson
ST MARY'S (1899)
Principal, Prof. S. Hackett
STEPHENSON (2001)
Principal, Prof. J. Ashworth
TREVELYAN (1966)
Principal, Prof. H. M. Evans
UNIVERSITY (1832)
Master, Prof. D. Held

USTINOV (2003)
Principal, Prof. G. McGregor
VAN MILDERT (1965)
Principal, Prof. D. Harper

UNIVERSITY OF EAST ANGLIA (1963)
Norwich Research Park, Norwich NR4 7TJ **T** 01603-456161
E admissions@uea.ac.uk **W** www.uea.ac.uk
Fee: £9,250 *Students:* 11,741 UG; 4,467 PG
Chancellor, Karen Jones
Vice-Chancellor, Prof. David Richardson
Registrar and Secretary, Brian Summers

UNIVERSITY OF EAST LONDON (1898)
University Way, London E16 2RD **T** 020-8223 3000
E study@uel.ac.uk **W** www.uel.ac.uk
Fee: £9,250 *Students:* 10,300 UG; 3,300 PG
Chancellor, Shabir Randeree, CBE
Vice-Chancellor, Prof. John Joughin
Chief Operating Officer, David Tyndall

EDGE HILL UNIVERSITY (2006)
St Helens Road, Ormskirk L39 4QP **T** 01695-575171
W www.edgehill.ac.uk
Fee: £9,250 *Students:* 11,995 UG; 3,545 PG
Chancellor, Prof. Tanya Byron
Vice-Chancellor, Dr John Cater, CBE
University Secretary, Lynda Brady

UNIVERSITY OF EDINBURGH (1583)
Old College, South Bridge, Edinburgh EH8 9YL **T** 0131-650 1000
E communications.office@ed.ac.uk **W** www.ed.ac.uk
Fee: £9,000 *Students:* 21,338 UG; 7,794 PG
Chancellor, HRH the Princess Royal, KG, KT, GCVO
Vice-Chancellor and Principal, Prof. Sir Timothy O'Shea, FRSE
University Secretary, Sarah Smith

EDINBURGH NAPIER UNIVERSITY (1992)
Sighthill Campus, Edinburgh EH11 4BN **T** 0333-900 6040
W www.napier.ac.uk
Fee: £9,000 *Students:* 10,360 UG; 2,225 PG
Chancellor, David Eustace
Vice-Chancellor, Prof. Andrea Nolan, OBE
Secretary, Dr Gerry Webber

UNIVERSITY OF ESSEX (1965)
Wivenhoe Park, Colchester CO4 3SQ **T** 01206-873333
E enquiries@essex.ac.uk **W** www.essex.ac.uk
Fee: £9,250 *Students:* 10,701 UG; 2,493 PG
Chancellor, Rt. Hon. John Bercow, MP
Vice-Chancellor, Prof. Anthony Forster, DPHIL
Registrar, Bryn Morris

UNIVERSITY OF EXETER (1955)
Stocker Road, Exeter EX4 4PY **T** 01392-661000
W www.exeter.ac.uk
Fee: £9,250 *Students:* 17,375 UG; 4,295 PG
Chancellor, Lord Myners of Truro, CBE
Vice-Chancellor, Prof. Sir Steve Smith, PHD
Registrar and Secretary, Mike Shore-Nye

FALMOUTH UNIVERSITY (2012)
Falmouth Campus, Woodlane, Falmouth TR11 4RH
T 01326-211 077 **E** falmouthreception@falmouth.ac.uk
W www.falmouth.ac.uk
Fee: £9,250 *Students:* 4,410 UG; 240 PG
Chancellor, Dawn French
Vice-Chancellor, Prof. Anne Carlisle

UNIVERSITY OF GLASGOW (1451)
University Avenue, Glasgow G12 8QQ **T** 0141 330 2000
E student.recruitment@glasgow.ac.uk **W** www.gla.ac.uk
Fee: £9,250 *Students:* 19,230 UG; 7,990 PG
Chancellor, Prof. Sir Kenneth Calman, KCB, FRCS, FRSE
Vice-Chancellor, Prof. Anton Muscatelli, FRSE
Registrar, David Bennion

GLASGOW CALEDONIAN UNIVERSITY (1993)
City Campus, Cowcaddens Road, Glasgow G4 0BA
T 0141-331 3000 **E** ukroenquiries@gcu.ac.uk **W** www.gcu.ac.uk
Fee: £9,000 *Students:* 13,800 UG; 2,780 PG
Chancellor, Prof. Muhammed Yunus
Vice-Chancellor, Prof. Pamela Gillies, CBE, FRSE
University Secretary, Jan Hulme

UNIVERSITY OF GLOUCESTERSHIRE (2001)
The Park, Cheltenham GL50 2RH **T** 0844-801 0001
E admissions@glos.ac.uk **W** www.glos.ac.uk
Fee: £9,250 *Students:* 6,495 UG; 1,340 PG
Chancellor, Baroness Fritchie, DBE
Vice-Chancellor, Stephen Marston
Secretary and Registrar, Dr Matthew Andrews

GLYNDWR UNIVERSITY (2008)
Mold Road, Wrexham LL11 2AW **T** 01978-290666
E reception@glyndwr.ac.uk **W** www.glyndwr.ac.uk
Fee: £9,000 *Students:* 5,875 UG; 895 PG
Chancellor, Trefor Glyn Jones, CBE, CVO
Vice-Chancellor, Maria Hinfelaar

UNIVERSITY OF GREENWICH (1992)
Old Royal Naval College, Park Row, London SE10 9LS
T 020-8331 8000 **E** courseinfo@gre.ac.uk **W** www.gre.ac.uk
Fee: £9,250 *Students:* 16,045 UG; 4,600 PG
Chancellor, Baroness Scotland of Asthal, PC, QC
Vice-Chancellor, Prof. David Maguire
Secretary, Louise Nadal

HARPER ADAMS UNIVERSITY (2012)
Newport TF10 8NB **T** 01952-820280
E admissions@harper-adams.ac.uk **W** www.harper-adams.ac.uk
Fee: £9,250 *Students:* 6,495 UG; 595 PG
Chancellor, HRH the Princess Royal, KG, KT, GCVO
Vice-Chancellor, David Llewellyn
Academic Registrar, Abigail Hind

HERIOT-WATT UNIVERSITY (1966)
Edinburgh EH14 4AS **T** 0131-449 511 1 **E** enquiries@hw.ac.uk
W www.hw.ac.uk
Fee: £9,250 *Students:* 7,135 UG; 3,325 PG
Chancellor, Dr Robert Buchan
Vice-Chancellor, Prof. Richard A. Williams, OBE
University Secretary, Ann Marie Dalton-Pillay

UNIVERSITY OF HERTFORDSHIRE (1992)
Hatfield AL10 9AB **T** 01707-284000 **W** www.herts.ac.uk
Fee: £9,250 *Students:* 14,805 UG; 4,470 PG
Chancellor, Marquess of Salisbury, KCVO, PC
Vice-Chancellor, Prof. Quintin McKellar, CBE
Secretary and Registrar, Sue Grant

UNIVERSITY OF THE HIGHLANDS AND ISLANDS (2011)
Ness Walk, Inverness IV3 5SQ **T** 01463-279000 **W** www.uhi.ac.uk
Fee: £9,000 *Students:* 7,930 UG; 485 PG
Chancellor, HRH the Princess Royal, KG, KT, GCVO
Vice-Chancellor, Prof. Clive Mulholland
Academic Registrar, Rhiannon Tinsley

UNIVERSITY OF HUDDERSFIELD (1992)
Queensgate, Huddersfield HD1 3DH **T** 01484-422288
W www.hud.ac.uk
Fee: £9,250 *Students:* 14,805 UG; 4,4,470 PG
Chancellor, HRH the Duke Of York, KG, GCVO, ADC(P)
Vice-Chancellor, Prof. Bob Cryan, CBE, DL, FRENG
University Secretary, Michaela Boryslawskyj

UNIVERSITY OF HULL (1927)
Cottingham Road, Hull HU6 7RX **T** 01482-346311
W www.hull.ac.uk
Fee: £9,250 *Students:* 13,515 UG; 2,785 PG
Chancellor, Baroness Bottomley of Nettlestone, PC
Vice-Chancellor, Prof. Susan Lea, PHD
Registrar, Jeanette Strachan

IMPERIAL COLLEGE LONDON (1907)
South Kensington SW7 2AZ **T** 020-7589 511 1
W www.imperial.ac.uk
Fee: £9,250 *Students:* 9,2,40 UG; 7,795 PG
President, Prof. Alice Gast
Provost, Prof. James Stirling
Secretary and Registrar, John Neilson

KEELE UNIVERSITY (1962)
Keele ST5 5BG **T** 01782-732000 **E** admissions.ukeu@keele.ac.uk
W www.keele.ac.uk
Fee: £9,250 *Students:* 7,915 UG; 2,205 PG
Chancellor, Jonathon Porritt, CBE
Vice-Chancellor, Prof. Trevor McMillan
Academic Registrar, Dr Helen Galbraith

UNIVERSITY OF KENT (1965)
Canterbury CT2 7NZ **T** 01227-764000 **E** information@kent.ac.uk
W www.kent.ac.uk
Fee: £9,250 *Students:* 15,610 UG; PG 4,055
Chancellor, Gavin Esler
Vice-Chancellor & Principal, Prof. Karen Cox
Registrar, Mary Hughes

KINGSTON UNIVERSITY (1992)
River House, 53–57 High Street, Kingston upon Thames KT1 1LQ
T 020-8417 9000 **E** aps@kingston.ac.uk **W** www.kingston.ac.uk
Fee: £9,250 *Students:* 16,275 UG; 4,610 PG
Chancellor, Bonnie Greer, OBE
Vice-Chancellor, Prof. Stephen Spier
University Secretary, Matthew Hilton

UNIVERSITY OF LANCASTER (1964)
Bailrigg, Lancaster LA1 4YW **T** 01524-65201
W www.lancaster.ac.uk
Fee: £9,250 *Students:* 9,500 UG; 3,615 PG
Chancellor, Rt. Hon. Alan Milburn
Vice-Chancellor, Prof. Mark E. Smith, PHD
University Secretary, Fiona Aiken

UNIVERSITY OF LEEDS (1904)
Leeds LS2 9JT **T** 011 3-243 1751 **W** www.leeds.ac.uk
Fee: £9,250 *Students:* 23,565 UG; 8,225 PG
Chancellor, Lord Bragg
Vice-Chancellor, Sir Alan Langlands
University Secretary, Roger Gair

LEEDS BECKETT UNIVERSITY (1992)
City Campus, Leeds LS1 3HE **T** 011 3-812 0000
W www.leedsbeckett.ac.uk
Fee: £9,250 *Students:* 21,465 UG; 4,455 PG
Chancellor, Sir Bob Murray, CBE
Vice-Chancellor, Prof. Peter Slee
Secretary and Registrar, Jenny Share

LEEDS TRINITY UNIVERSITY (2012)
Brownberrie Lane, Leeds LS18 5HD **T** 011 3-283 7100
E enquiries@leedstrinity.ac.uk **W** www.leedstrinity.ac.uk
Fee: £9,250 *Students:* 2,865 UG; 850 PG
Chancellor, Gabby Logan
Vice-Chancellor, Prof. Margaret House
Chief Operating Officer, Denise McConnell

UNIVERSITY OF LEICESTER (1957)
University Road, Leicester LE1 7RH **T** 011 6-252 2522
W www.le.ac.uk
Fee: £9,250 *Students:* 11,505 UG; 6,315 PG
Chancellor, Lord Grocott, PC
Vice-Chancellor, Prof. Paul Boyle, CBE, FBA, FRSE
Registrar, David Hall

UNIVERSITY OF LINCOLN (1992)
Brayford Pool, Lincoln LN6 7TS **T** 01522-882000
E enquiries@lincoln.ac.uk **W** www.lincoln.ac.uk
Fee: £9,250 *Students:* 12,500 UG; 2,500 PG
Chancellor, Lord Adebowale, CBE
Vice-Chancellor, Prof. Mary Stuart
Registrar, Chris Spendlove

UNIVERSITY OF LIVERPOOL (1903)
Brownlow Hill, Liverpool L69 7ZX **T** 0151-794 2000
W www.liverpool.ac.uk
Fee: £9,250 *Students:* 19,595 UG; 5,185 PG
Chancellor, Colm Tóibín
Vice-Chancellor, Prof. Janet Beer

LIVERPOOL HOPE UNIVERSITY (2005)
Hope Park, Liverpool L16 9JD **T** 0151-291 3000
E enquiry@hope.ac.uk **W** www.hope.ac.uk
Fee: £9,250 *Students:* 3,935 UG; 1,005 PG
Chancellor, Lord Guthrie of Craigiebank, GCB, LVO, OBE
Vice-Chancellor and Rector, Prof. Gerald Pillay
University Secretary, Graham Donelan

LIVERPOOL JOHN MOORES UNIVERSITY (1992)
Kingsway House, 2nd Floor, Hatton Garden, Liverpool L3 2AJ
T 0151-231 2121 **E** courses@ljmu.ac.uk **W** www.ljmu.ac.uk
Fee: £9,250 *Students:* 18,375 UG; 3,500 PG
Chancellor, Rt. Hon. Sir Brian Leveson
Vice-Chancellor, Prof. Nigel Weatherill, DSC, FRENG
Registrar, Mark Power

UNIVERSITY OF LONDON (1836)
Senate House, Malet Street, London WC1E 7HU **T** 020-7862 8000
W www.london.ac.uk
Fee: £9,250
Chancellor, HRH the Princess Royal, KG, KT, GCVO
Vice-Chancellor, Prof. Sir Adrian Smith, FRS
University Secretary, Chris Cobb

COLLEGES
BIRKBECK
Malet Street, London WC1E 7HX
Students: 8,200 UG; 4,045 PG
President, Baroness Bakewell, DBE
Master, Prof. David Latchman, CBE
CITY
Northampton Square, London EC1V 0HB
Students: 9,830 UG; 9,170 PG
President, Prof. Sir Paul Curran
COURTAULD INSTITUTE OF ART
Somerset House, Strand, London WC2R 0RN
Students: 180 UG; 330 PG
Director, Prof. Deborah Swallow

GOLDSMITHS COLLEGE
New Cross, London SE14 6NW
Students, 5,655 UG; 2,870 PG
Warden, Patrick Loughrey

HEYTHROP COLLEGE
Kensington Square, London W8 5HN
Students, 255 UG; 355 PG
Principal, Prof. Claire Ozanne

INSTITUTE OF CANCER RESEARCH
15 Cotswold Road, Sutton, Surrey SM2 5NG
Students, 300 PG (postgraduate only)
Chief Executive, Prof. Paul Workman

KING'S COLLEGE LONDON
(includes Guy's, King's and St Thomas's Schools of
Medicine, Dentistry and Biomedical Sciences)
Strand, London WC2R 2LS
Students: 17,770 UG; 11,130 PG
Principal, Prof. Edward Byrne

LONDON BUSINESS SCHOOL
Regent's Park, London NW1 4SA
Students: 2,075 PG (postgraduate only)
Dean, François Ortalo-Magné

LONDON SCHOOL OF ECONOMICS AND POLITICAL
SCIENCE
Houghton Street, London WC2A 2AE
Students: 4,700 UG; 5,740 PG
Director, Dame Minouche Shafik

LONDON SCHOOL OF HYGIENE AND TROPICAL
MEDICINE
Keppel Street, London WC1E 7HT
Students: 1,200 PG (postgraduate only)
Director, Prof. Peter Piot, CMG, MD, PHD

QUEEN MARY
(incorporating St Bartholomew's and the London School of
Medicine and Dentistry)
Mile End Road, London E1 4NS
Students: 12,385 UG; 4,750 PG
Principal, Prof. Colin Bailey

ROYAL ACADEMY OF MUSIC
Marylebone Road, London NW1 5HT
Students: 375 UG; 385 PG
Principal, Prof. Jonathan Freeman-Attwood

ROYAL CENTRAL SCHOOL OF SPEECH AND DRAMA
Eton Avenue, London NW3 3HY
Students: 655 UG; 390 PG
Principal, Prof. Gavin Henderson, CBE

ROYAL HOLLOWAY
Egham Hill, Egham, Surrey TW20 0EX
Students: 7,475 UG; 2,510 PG
Principal, Prof. Paul Layzell

ROYAL VETERINARY COLLEGE
Royal College Street, London NW1 0TU
Students: 1,765 UG; 525 PG
Principal, Prof. Stuart Reid

ST GEORGE'S
Cranmer Terrace, London SW17 0RE
Students: 5,090 UG; 835 PG
Principal, Prof. Jenny Higham

SCHOOL OF ADVANCED STUDY
Senate House, Malet Street, London WC1E 7HU
Dean and Chief Executive, Prof. Rick Rylan

SCHOOL OF ORIENTAL AND AFRICAN STUDIES
Thornhaugh Street, Russell Square, London WC1H 0XG
Students: 3,220 UG; 2,850 PG
Director, Baroness Amos

UNIVERSITY COLLEGE LONDON
(including the Institute of Neurology, Eastman Dental
Institute, School of Pharmacy and Institute of Education)
Gower Street, London WC1E 6BT
Students: 17,910 UG; 19,225 PG
Provost and President, Prof. Michael Arthur, FRCP, FMedSci

UNIVERSITY OF LONDON INSTITUTE IN PARIS
9–11 rue de Constantine, 75340 Paris Cedex 07, France
Chief Executive, Dr Tim Gore, OBE

INSTITUTES

INSTITUTE OF ADVANCED LEGAL STUDIES
Charles Clore House, 17 Russell Square, London WC1B 5DR
Director, Jules Winterton

INSTITUTE OF CLASSICAL STUDIES
Senate House, Malet Street, London WC1E 7HU
Director, Prof. Greg Woolf, FSA

INSTITUTE OF COMMONWEALTH STUDIES
Senate House, Malet Street, London WC1E 7HU
Director, Prof. Philip Murphy

INSTITUTE OF ENGLISH STUDIES
Senate House, Malet Street, London WC1E 7HU
Director, Prof. Rick Rylance

INSTITUTE OF HISTORICAL RESEARCH
Senate House, Malet Street, London WC1E 7HU
Director, Prof. Jo Fox

INSTITUTE OF LATIN AMERICAN STUDIES
Senate House, Malet Street, London WC1E 7HU
Director, Prof. Linda Newson

INSTITUTE OF MODERN LANGUAGES RESEARCH
Senate House, Malet Street, London WC1E 7HU
Director, Prof. Catherine Davies

INSTITUTE OF PHILOSOPHY
Senate House, Malet Street, London WC1E 7HU
Director, Prof. Barry Smith

WARBURG INSTITUTE
Woburn Square, London WC1H 0AB
Director, Prof. Bill Sherman

LONDON METROPOLITAN UNIVERSITY (2002)
166–220 Holloway Road, London N7 8DB **T** 020-7423 0000
W www.londonmet.ac.uk
Fee: £9,250 *Students:* 9,945 UG; 2,915 PG
Patron, HRH the Duke of York, KG, GCVO, ADC(P)
Vice-Chancellor, Prof. John Raftery
University Secretary, Peter Garrod

LONDON SOUTH BANK UNIVERSITY (1992)
103 Borough Road, London SE1 0AA **T** 020-7815 7815
E course.enquiry@lsbu.ac.uk **W** www.lsbu.ac.uk
Fee: £9,250 *Students:* 12,620 UG; 4,985 PG
Chancellor, Richard Farleigh
Vice-Chancellor, Prof. David Phoenix
University Secretary, James Stevenson

LOUGHBOROUGH UNIVERSITY (1966)
Epinal Way, Loughborough LE11 3TU **T** 01509-222222
W www.lboro.ac.uk
Fee: £9,250 *Students:* 12,725 UG; 4,225 PG
Chancellor, Lord Coe, CH, OBE, MBE
Vice-Chancellor, Prof. Robert Allison
Chief Operating Officer, Richard Taylor

UNIVERSITY OF MANCHESTER (2004. Formed by the
amalgamation of Victoria University of Manchester (1851;
reorganised 1880 and 1903) and the University of
Manchester Institute of Science and Technology (1824))
Oxford Road, Manchester M13 9PL **T** 0161-306 6000
W www.manchester.ac.uk
Fee: £9,250 *Students:* 27,635 UG; 12,065 PG
Chancellor, Lemn Sissay, MBE
Vice-Chancellor, Prof. Dame Nancy Rothwell, DBE, FRS
Secretary and Registrar, Will Spinks

MANCHESTER METROPOLITAN UNIVERSITY (1992)
All Saints, Manchester M15 6BH **T** 0161-247 2000
W www.mmu.ac.uk
Fee: £9,250 *Students:* 26,835 UG; 5,650 PG
Chancellor, Rt. Hon. Lord Mandelson
Vice-Chancellor, Prof. Malcolm Press
Registrar, Prof. Karen Moore

MIDDLESEX UNIVERSITY (1992)
Hendon Campus, London NW4 4BT **T** 020-8411 5555
W www.mdx.ac.uk
Fee: £9,250 *Students:* 14,435 UG; 4,670 PG
Chancellor, Dame Janet Ritterman, DBE
Vice-Chancellor, Prof. Tim Blackman
Chief Operating Officer, Sophie Bowen, PHD

NEWCASTLE UNIVERSITY (1963)
Newcastle upon Tyne NE1 7RU **T** 0191-208 6000
W www.ncl.ac.uk
Fee: £9,250 *Students:* 17,720 UG; 6,070 PG
Chancellor, Prof. Sir Liam Donaldson
Vice-Chancellor, Prof. Chris Day, FRS, DPHIL
Registrar, Dr. John Hogan

NEWMAN UNIVERSITY, BIRMINGHAM (2013)
Genners Lane, Birmingham B32 3NT **T** 0121-476 11 81
E admissions@newman.ac.uk **W** www.newman.ac.uk
Fee: £9,250 *Students:* 2,250 UG; 560 PG
Chancellor, vacant
Vice-Chancellor, Prof. Scott Davidson
Secretary and Registrar, Andrea Bolshaw

UNIVERSITY OF NORTHAMPTON (2005)
Park Campus, Boughton Green Road, Northampton NN2 7AL
T 01604-735500 **E** study@northampton.ac.uk
W www.northampton.ac.uk
Fee: £9,250 *Students:* 10,670 UG; 2,315 PG
Chancellor, Baroness Falkner
Vice-Chancellor, Prof. Nick Petford, PHD, DSC
Chief Operating Officer, Terry Neville

NORTHUMBRIA UNIVERSITY AT NEWCASTLE (1992)
Ellison Building, Ellison Place, Newcastle upon Tyne NE1 8ST
T 0191-232 6002 **E** course.enquiries@northumbria.ac.uk
W www.northumbria.ac.uk
Fee: £9,250 *Students:* 22,415 UG; 4,750 PG
Chancellor, Baroness Grey-Thompson
Vice-Chancellor, Prof. Andrew Wathey, CBE, DPHIL
Chief Operating Officer, Chris Reilly

NORWICH UNIVERSITY OF THE ARTS (2012)
Francis House, 3–7 Redwell Street, Norwich NR2 4SN
T 01603-610561 **E** info@nua.ac.uk **W** www.nua.ac.uk
Fee: £9,250 *Students:* 1,920 UG; 75 PG
Chancellor, vacant
Vice-Chancellor, Prof. John Last
Academic Registrar, Angela Tubb

UNIVERSITY OF NOTTINGHAM (1948)
University Park, Nottingham NG7 2RD **T** 011 5-951 5151
E undergraduate-enquiries@nottingham.ac.uk
W www.nottingham.ac.uk
Fee: £9,250 *Students:* 23,935 UG; 8,185 PG
Chancellor, Sir Andrew Witty
Vice-Chancellor, Prof. David Greenaway
Registrar, Paul Greatrix

NOTTINGHAM TRENT UNIVERSITY (1992)
Burton Street, Nottingham NG1 4BU **T** 011 5-941 8418
E ask.ntu@ntu.ac.uk **W** www.ntu.ac.uk
Fee: £9,250 *Students:* 22,840 UG; 5,080 PG
Chancellor, Kevin Cahill, CBE
Vice-Chancellor, Prof. Edward Peck
Chief Operating Officer, Steve Denton

OPEN UNIVERSITY (1969)
Walton Hall, Milton Keynes MK7 6AA **T** 01908-274066
W www.open.ac.uk
Fee: £5,728 *Students:* 94,900 UG; 6,590 PG
Chancellor, Baroness Lane-Fox of Soho, CBE
Vice-Chancellor, Peter Horrocks, CBE
University Secretary, Keith Zimmerman

UNIVERSITY OF OXFORD (c.12th century)
University Offices, Wellington Square, Oxford OX1 2JD
T 01865-270000 **E** information.office@admin.ox.ac.uk
W www.ox.ac.uk
Fee: £9,250 *Students:* 11,728 UG; 10,941 PG
Chancellor, Lord Patten of Barnes, CH, PC
  (BALLIOL, ST ANTONY'S)
Vice-Chancellor, Prof. Louise Richardson, FRSE
Pro-Vice-Chancellors, Dr D. Prout, Prof. S. Whatmore (until
  January 2018) (Keble); Prof. A. Trefethen (St Cross); Prof.
  I. A. Walmsley (St Hugh's); Prof A. Buchan (Corpus
  Christi); Dr R. Surender (Green Templeton)
Academic Registrar, Emma Potts (Kellogg)
Public Orator, J. Katz (All Souls)
Director of University Library Services and Bodley's Librarian, R.
  Ovenden (Balliol)
Director of the Ashmolean Museum, Dr A. Sturgis (Worcester)
Director of the Museum of the History of Science, Dr Silke
  Ackermann (Linacre)
Director of the Pitt Rivers Museum, Dr Laura Van Broekhoven
  (Linacre)
Director of the University Museum of Natural History, Prof. Paul
  Smith (Kellogg)
Keeper of Archives, S. Bailey (Linacre)
Director of Estates, P. Goffin
Director of Finance, G. F. B. Kerr (Keble)

COLLEGES AND HALLS *(with dates of foundation)*
ALL SOULS (1438)
Warden, Prof. Sir John Vickers, FBA
BALLIOL (1263)
Master, Prof. Sir Drummond Bone, FRSE
BLACKFRIARS (1221)
Regent, Very Revd Dr Simon Gaine
BRASENOSE (1509)
Principal, John Bowers, QC
CAMPION HALL (1896)
Master, Revd James Hanvey
CHRIST CHURCH (1546)
Dean, Very Revd Prof. Martyn Percy
CORPUS CHRISTI (1517)
President, Prof. Stephen Cowley, FRS, FRENG
EXETER (1314)
Rector, Prof. Sir Rick Trainor, KBE
GREEN TEMPLETON (2008)
Principal, Prof. Denise Lievesley, CBE
HARRIS MANCHESTER (1889)
Principal, Revd Dr Ralph Waller, FRSE
HERTFORD (1740)
Principal, Will Hutton
JESUS (1571)
Principal, Prof. Sir Nigel Shadbolt, FRENG
KEBLE (1870)
Warden, Sir Jonathan Phillips, KCB

KELLOGG (1990)
President, Prof. Jonathan M. Michie
LADY MARGARET HALL (1878)
Principal, Alan Rusbridger
LINACRE (1962)
Principal, Dr Nick Brown
LINCOLN (1427)
Rector, Prof. Henry Woudhuysen, FBA
MAGDALEN (1458)
President, Prof. Sir David Clary, FRS
MANSFIELD (1886)
Principal, Baroness Kennedy of the Shaws, QC
MERTON (1264)
Warden, Prof. Sir Martin Taylor, FRS
NEW COLLEGE (1379)
Warden, Miles Young
NUFFIELD (1958)
Warden, Sir Andrew Dilnot, CBE
ORIEL (1326)
Provost, Moira Wallace, OBE
PEMBROKE (1624)
Master, Dame Lynne Brindley, DBE
QUEEN'S (1341)
Provost, Prof. Paul Madden, FRS, FRSE
REGENT'S PARK (1810)
Principal, Revd Dr Robert Ellis
ST ANNE'S (1878)
Principal, Helen King
ST ANTONY'S (1953)
Warden, Prof. Roger Goodman
ST BENET'S HALL (1897)
Master, Prof. Werner Jeanrond
ST CATHERINE'S (1963)
Master, Prof. Roger Ainsworth
ST CROSS (1965)
Master, Carole Souter, CBE
ST EDMUND HALL (C. 1278)
Principal, Prof. Keith Gull, CBE, FRS, FMEDSCI
ST HILDA'S (1893)
Principal, Prof. Sir Gordon Duff, FRCP, FRSE, FMEDSCI
ST HUGH'S (1886)
Principal, Dame Elish Angiolini, DBE, PC, QC
ST JOHN'S (1555)
President, Prof. Margaret J. Snowling, FBA, FMEDSCI
ST PETER'S (1929)
Principal, Mark Damazer, CBE
ST STEPHEN'S HOUSE (1876)
Principal, Revd Dr Robin Ward
SOMERVILLE (1879)
Principal, Baroness Royall of Blaisdon (from January 2018)
TRINITY (1554)
President, Dame Hilary Boulding, DBE
UNIVERSITY (1249)
Master, Sir Ivor Crewe
WADHAM (1610)
Warden, Lord Macdonald of River Glaven, QC
WOLFSON (1981)
President, Prof. Philomen Probert (*acting,* until mid-2018);
Tim Hitchens CMG, LVO (from mid-2018)
WORCESTER (1714)
Provost, Prof. Sir Jonathan Bate, CBE, FBA, FRSL
WYCLIFFE HALL (1877)
Principal, Revd Michael Lloyd

OXFORD BROOKES UNIVERSITY (1992)
Gipsy Lane, Oxford OX3 0BP T 01865-7411 11
E query@brookes.ac.uk W www.brookes.ac.uk
Fee: £9,250 *Students:* 13,905 UG; 3,935 PG
Chancellor, Dr Katherine Granger, CBE
Vice-Chancellor, Prof. Alistair Fitt
Registrar, Brendan Casey

UNIVERSITY OF PLYMOUTH (1992)
Drake Circus, Plymouth PL4 8AA T 01752-600600
E prospectus@plymouth.ac.uk W www.plymouth.ac.uk
Fee: £9,250 *Students:* 20,080 UG; 3,075 PG
Chancellor, Lord Kestenbaum
Vice-Chancellor, Prof. Judith Petts, CBE
University Secretary, Gordon Stewart

UNIVERSITY OF PORTSMOUTH (1992)
University House, Winston Churchill Avenue, Portsmouth PO1 2UP
T 023-9284 8484 E info.centre@port.ac.uk W www.port.ac.uk
Fee: £9,250 *Students:* 18,745 UG; 3,315 PG
Chancellor, Sandi Toksvig, OBE
Vice-Chancellor, Prof. Graham Galbraith, PHD
Chief Operating Officer, Bernie Topham

QUEEN MARGARET UNIVERSITY (2007)
Edinburgh EH21 6UU T 0131-474 0000 W www.qmu.ac.uk
Fee: £7,000 *Students:* 3,665 UG; 3,075 PG
Chancellor, Prue Leith, CBE
Vice-Chancellor, Prof. Petra Wend, FRSE
Secretary, Prof. Irene Hynd

QUEEN'S UNIVERSITY BELFAST (1908)
University Road, Belfast BT7 1NN T 028-9024 5133
E comms.office@qub.ac.uk W www.qub.ac.uk
Fee: £9,250 *Students:* 18,960 UG; 4,910 PG
Chancellor, Thomas J. Moran
Acting Vice-Chancellor, Prof. James McElnay
Registrar, James O'Kane

UNIVERSITY OF READING (1926)
Whiteknights, PO Box 217, Reading RG6 6AH T 011 8-987 5123
W www.reading.ac.uk
Fee: £9,250 *Students:* 10,315 UG; 4,665 PG
Chancellor, Rt. Hon. Lord Waldegrave of North Hill, PC
Vice-Chancellor, Sir David Bell, KCB
University Secretary, Dr Richard Messer

ROBERT GORDON UNIVERSITY (1992)
Schoolhill, Aberdeen AB10 1FR T 01224-262000
E admissions@rgu.ac.uk W www.rgu.ac.uk
Fee: £8,500 *Students:* 8,995 UG; 3,755 PG
Chancellor, Sir Ian Wood, GBE
Vice-Chancellor, Prof. Ferdinand von Prondzynski
Academic Registrar, Hilary Douglas

ROEHAMPTON UNIVERSITY (2004)
Erasmus House, Roehampton Lane, London SW15 5PU
T 020-8392 3000 E enquiries@roehampton.ac.uk
W www.roehampton.ac.uk
Fee: £9,250 *Students:* 7,050 UG; 1,700 PG
Chancellor, Dame Jacqueline Wilson, DBE, FRSL
Vice-Chancellor, Prof. Paul O'Prey
University Secretary, Andrew Skinner

ROYAL AGRICULTURAL UNIVERSITY (2013)
Stroud Road, Cirencester GL7 6JS T 01285-652531
E admissions@rau.ac.uk W www.rau.ac.uk
Fee: £9,250 *Students:* 965 UG; 235 PG
Vice-Chancellor, Prof. Joanna Price
Academic Registrar, Nigel Warner

ROYAL COLLEGE OF ART (1967)
Kensington Gore, London SW7 2EU T 020-7590 4444
E info@rca.ac.uk W www.rca.ac.uk
Students: 1,610 PG (postgraduate only)
Provost, Sir James Dyson, OM, CBE, FRS
Rector, Dr Paul Thompson
Chief Operating Officer, Richard Benson

UNIVERSITY OF ST ANDREWS (1413)
St Andrews KY16 9AJ T 01334-476161 W www.st-andrews.ac.uk
Fee: £9,250 *Students:* 8,035 UG; 2,710 PG
Chancellor, Rt. Hon. Lord Campbell of Pittenweem, CH,
CBE, QC
Vice-Chancellor, Prof. Sally Mapstone
Academic Registrar, Ester Ruskuc

UNIVERSITY OF ST MARK AND ST JOHN (2012)
Derriford Road, Plymouth PL6 8BH T 01752-636700
E admissions@marjon.ac.uk W www.marjon.ac.uk
Fee: £9,250 *Students:* 2,000 UG; 360 PG
Vice-Chancellor, Prof. Rob Warner
Registrar, Stephen Plant

ST MARY'S UNIVERSITY (2014)
Waldegrave Road, Strawberry Hill, Twickenham TW1 4SX
T 020-8240 4000 W www.stmarys.ac.uk
Fee: £9,250 *Students:* 4,120 UG; 1,415 PG
Chancellor, Cardinal Vincent Nichols
Vice-Chancellor, Prof. Francis Campbell
University Secretary, Simon Williams

UNIVERSITY OF SALFORD (1967)
The Crescent, Salford M5 4WT T 0161-295 5000
W www.salford.ac.uk
Fee: £9,250 *Students:* 15,725 UG; 4,790 PG
Chancellor, Jackie Kay, MBE
Vice-Chancellor, Prof. Helen Marshall
University Secretary, Alison Blackburn

UNIVERSITY OF SHEFFIELD (1905)
Western Bank, Sheffield S10 2TN T 011 4-222 2000
E ask@sheffield.ac.uk W www.sheffield.ac.uk
Fee: £9,250 *Students:* 19,661 UG; 8,286 PG
Chancellor, Rt. Hon. Justice Rafferty, DBE
President and Vice-Chancellor, Prof. Sir Keith Burnett, CBE,
DPHIL, FRS

SHEFFIELD HALLAM UNIVERSITY (1992)
City Campus, Howard Street, Sheffield S1 1WB T 011 4-225 5555
E enquiries@shu.ac.uk W www.shu.ac.uk
Fee: £9,250 *Students:* 24,705 UG; 6,775 PG
Chancellor, Prof. Lord Winston, FRCOG, FRCP, FMEDSCI
Vice-Chancellor, Prof. Chris Husbands
Chief Operating Officer, Richard Calvert

UNIVERSITY OF SOUTHAMPTON (1952)
University Road, Southampton SO17 1BJ T 023-8059 5000
W www.southampton.ac.uk
Fee: £9,250 *Students:* 17,485 UG; 7,390 PG
Chancellor, Dame Helen Alexander, DBE
Vice-Chancellor, Prof. Sir Christopher Snowden, FRS, FRENG
Chief Operating Officer, Ian Dunn

SOUTHAMPTON SOLENT UNIVERSITY (2005)
East Park Terrace, Southampton SO14 0YN T 023-8031 9039
E ask@solent.ac.uk W www.solent.ac.uk
Fee: £9,250 *Students:* 10,885 UG; 405 PG
Chancellor, Adm. Lord West of Spithead, GCB, DSC, PC
Vice-Chancellor, Prof. Graham Baldwin
Academic Registrar, Dave Dowland

UNIVERSITY OF SOUTH WALES (1992)
Pontypridd CF37 1DL T 0345-576 0101
E enquiries@southwales.ac.uk W www.southwales.ac.uk
Fee: £9,000 *Students:* 20,840 UG; 4,425 PG
Chancellor, Rt. Revd and Rt. Hon. Lord Williams of Oystermouth,
PC, DPHIL
Vice-Chancellor, Prof. Julie Lydon, OBE
Academic Registrar, Mary Hulford

STAFFORDSHIRE UNIVERSITY (1992)
College Road, Stoke-on-Trent ST4 2DE T 01782-294000
W www.staffs.ac.uk
Fee: £9,250 *Students:* 13,600 UG; 2,260 PG
Chancellor, Lord Stafford
Vice-Chancellor, Prof. Liz Barnes
Chief Operating Officer, Ian Blachford

UNIVERSITY OF STIRLING (1967)
Stirling FK9 4LA T 01786-473171 E externalaffairs@stir.ac.uk
W www.stir.ac.uk
Fee: £6,750 *Students:* 8,585 UG; 3,255 PG
Chancellor, James Naughtie, OBE
Vice-Chancellor, Prof. Gerry McCormac, FRSE
University Secretary, Eileen Schofield

UNIVERSITY OF STRATHCLYDE (1964)
16 Richmond Street, Glasgow G1 1XQ T 0141-552 4400
E corporatecomms@strath.ac.uk W www.strath.ac.uk
Fee: £9,250 *Students:* 14,965 UG; 6,505 PG
Chancellor, Lord Smith of Kelvin, KT, CH
Vice-Chancellor, Prof. Sir Jim McDonald, FRSE, FRENG
Academic Registrar, Dr Veena O'Halloran

UNIVERSITY OF SUFFOLK (2016)
Waterfront Building, Neptune Quay, Ipswich IP4 1QJ
T 01473-338000 W www.uos.ac.uk
Fee: £9,250 *Students:* 4,640 UG; 390 PG
Vice-Chancellor, Richard Lister
Secretary and Registrar, Tim Greenacre

UNIVERSITY OF SUNDERLAND (1992)
Edinburgh Building, Chester Road, Sunderland SR1 3SD
T 0191-515 2000 E student.helpline@sunderland.ac.uk
W www.sunderland.ac.uk
Fee: £9,250 *Students:* 10,575 UG; 2,425 PG
Chancellor, Steve Cram, MBE
Vice-Chancellor, Shirley Atkinson
Chief Operating Officer, Steve Knight

UNIVERSITY OF SURREY (1966) Guildford GU2 7XH
T 01483-300800 E studentdata@surrey.ac.uk W www.surrey.ac.uk
Fee: £9,250 *Students:* 12,114 UG; 3,605 PG
Chancellor, HRH the Duke of Kent, KG, GCMG, GCVO
Vice-Chancellor, Prof. G.Q. Max Lu
Registrar, Prof. Jane Powell

UNIVERSITY OF SUSSEX (1961)
Sussex House, Brighton BN1 9RH T 01273-606755
E information@sussex.ac.uk W www.sussex.ac.uk
Fee: £9,250 *Students:* 10,995 UG; 4,055 PG
Chancellor, Sanjeev Bhaskar, OBE
Vice-Chancellor, Prof. Adam Tickell
Academic Registrar, Sharon Jones

SWANSEA UNIVERSITY (1920)
Singleton Park, Swansea SA2 8PP T 01792-205678
W www.swansea.ac.uk
Fee: £9,000 *Students:* 14,680 UG; 2,765 PG
Chancellor, vacant
Vice-Chancellor, Prof. Richard B. Davies
Registrar, Raymond Ciborowski

TEESIDE UNIVERSITY (1992)
Middlesbrough TS1 3BA T 01642-218121 E enquiries@tees.ac.uk
W www.tees.ac.uk
Fee: £9,250 *Students:* 16,340 UG; 2,240 PG
Chancellor, Paul Drechsler, CBE
Vice-Chancellor, Prof. Paul Croney, CBE
Chief Operating Officer, Malcolm Page

UNIVERSITY OF ULSTER (1984)
Cromore Road, Coleraine BT52 1SA T 028-7012 3456
W www.ulster.ac.uk
Fee: £9,000 *Students:* 19,865 UG; 5,290 PG
Chancellor, James Nesbitt, OBE
Vice-Chancellor, Prof. Paddy Nixon
University Secretary, Eamon Mullan

UNIVERSITY OF WALES, TRINITY SAINT DAVID
(1828)
Carmarthen Campus, SA31 3EP T 01267-676767
W www.uwtsd.ac.uk
Fee: £9,000 *Students:* 8,420 UG; 1,510 PG
Vice-Chancellor, Prof. Medwin Hughes

UNIVERSITY OF WARWICK (1965)
Coventry CV4 7AL T 024-7652 3523 W www.warwick.ac.uk
Fee: £9,250 *Students:* 15,380 UG; 9,285 PG
Chancellor, Rt. Hon. Baroness Ashton of Upholland, GCMG, PC
Vice-Chancellor, Prof. Stuart Croft
Registrar, Rachel Sandby Thomas, CB

UNIVERSITY OF WEST LONDON (1992)
St Mary's Road, London W5 5RF T 0800-036 8888
W www.uwl.ac.uk
Fee: £9,250 *Students:* 9,050 UG; 1,360 PG
Chancellor, Laurence Geller, CBE
Vice-Chancellor, Prof. Peter John
University Secretary, Marion Lowe

UNIVERSITY OF WESTMINSTER (1992)
309 Regent Street, London W1B 2HW T 020-7911 5000
E course-enquiries@westminster.ac.uk W www.westminster.ac.uk
Fee: £9,250 *Students:* 16,035 UG; 4,160 PG
Chancellor, Lady Sorrell, OBE
Vice-Chancellor and Rector, Prof. Geoffrey Petts
Registrar and Secretary, Suzanne Enright

UNIVERSITY OF THE WEST OF ENGLAND (1992)
Frenchay Campus, Coldharbour Lane, Bristol BS16 1QY
T 011 7-965 6261 E infopoint@uwe.ac.uk W www.uwe.ac.uk
Fee: £9,250 *Students:* 21,070 UG; 6,650 PG
Chancellor, Sir Ian Carruthers, OBE
Vice-Chancellor, Prof. Steve West, CBE
Registrar, Rachel Cowie

UNIVERSITY OF THE WEST OF SCOTLAND (2007)
Paisley PA1 2BE T 0141-848 3000 E uni-direct@uws.ac.uk
W www.uws.ac.uk
Fee: £9,250 *Students:* 13,410 UG; 2,145 PG
Chancellor, Rt. Hon. Dame Elish Angiolini, QC, FRSA
Vice-Chancellor and Principal, Prof. Craig Mahoney
Chief Operating Officer, Susan Mitchell

UNIVERSITY OF WINCHESTER (2005)
Winchester SO22 4NR T 01962-841515
E course.enquiries@winchester.ac.uk W www.winchester.ac.uk
Fee: £9,250 *Students:* 6,125 UG; 1,415 PG
Chancellor, Alan Titchmarsh, MBE
Vice-Chancellor, Prof. Joy Carter
Registrar, Dee Povey

UNIVERSITY OF WOLVERHAMPTON (1992)
Wulfruna Street, Wolverhampton WV1 1LY T 01902-321000
E enquiries@wlv.ac.uk W www.wlv.ac.uk
Fee: £9,250 *Students:* 16,755 UG; 3,035 PG
Chancellor, Lord Paul of Marylebone, PC
Vice-Chancellor, Prof. Geoff Layer, OBE, FRSA
Academic Registrar, Chris Twine

UNIVERSITY OF WORCESTER (1946)
Henwick Grove, Worcester WR2 6AJ T 01905-855000
E study@worc.ac.uk W www.worcester.ac.uk
Fee: £9,250 *Students:* 8,865 UG; 1,595 PG
Chancellor, HRH the Duke of Gloucester, KG, GCVO
Vice Chancellor, Prof. David Green
Registrar, Kevin Pickess

WRITTLE UNIVERSITY COLLEGE (2016)
Lordship Road, Writtle CM1 3RR T 01245 424200
E info@writtle.ac.uk W www.writtle.ac.uk
Fee: £9,250 *Students:* 750 UG; 55 PG
Chancellor, Baroness Jenkin of Kennington
Vice-Chancellor, Prof. Sir Tim Middleton

UNIVERSITY OF YORK (1963)
York YO10 5DD T 01904-320000 W www.york.ac.uk
Fee: £9,250 *Students:* 13,090 UG; 4,065 PG
Chancellor, Prof. Sir Malcolm Grant, CBE
Vice-Chancellor, Prof. Koen Lamberts, PHD
Registrar and Secretary, Jo Horsburgh, PHD

YORK ST JOHN UNIVERSITY (2006)
Lord Mayor's Walk, York YO31 7EX T 01904-624624
E admissions@yorksj.ac.uk W www.yorksj.ac.uk
Fee: £9,250 *Students:* 5,265 UG; 715 PG
Chancellor, Most Revd and Rt. Hon. Archbishop of York
Vice-Chancellor, Prof. Karen Stanton
Registrar, Alison Kennel

PROFESSIONAL EDUCATION

The organisations selected below provide specialist training, conduct examinations or are responsible for maintaining a register of those with professional qualifications in their sector, thereby controlling entry into a profession.

EU RECOGNITION

It is possible for those with professional qualifications obtained in the UK to have these recognised in other European countries. Further information can be obtained from:

UK NARIC, Suffolk House, 68–70 Suffolk Road, Cheltenham GL50 2ED **T** 0871-330 7033 **W** www.ecctis.co.uk/naric

ACCOUNTANCY

Salary range for chartered accountants:
Certified £25,000 (starting), rising to £26,000–£50,000+ (qualified), £40,000–£100,000+ at senior levels
Management £28,000 (starting), £61,000 (average), £46,000–£129,000+ at senior levels
Public finance £18,000–£30,000 (starting), £32,000–£65,000 (qualified), £80,000+ at senior levels

Chartered Accountancy trainees can be school-leavers or graduates. They usually undertake a three-year training contract with an approved employer culminating in professional exams provided by ICAEW, ICAS or CAI. Success in the exams and membership of one of the professional bodies - which includes continuous professional development and regulation - allows them to use the designation 'chartered accountant' and the letters ACA, FCA or CA.

The Association of Chartered Certified Accountants (ACCA) is the global body for professional accountants. The ACCA aims to offer business-relevant qualifications to students in a range of business sectors and countries seeking a career in accountancy, finance and management. The ACCA Qualification consists of up to 14 examinations, practical experiences and a professional ethics module. Chartered certified accountants can use the designatory letters ACCA.

Chartered global management accountants focus on accounting for businesses, and most do not work in accountancy practices but in industry, commerce, not-for-profit and public-sector organisations. Graduates who have not studied a business or accounting degree must complete the Chartered Institute of Management Accountants (CIMA) Certificate in Business Accounting before progressing to the CIMA Professional Qualification, which requires three years of practical experience and twelve examinations. In May 2011, CIMA and the American Institute of Certified Public Accountants (AICPA) agreed on the creation of a new professional designation, the Chartered Global Management Accountant (CGMA), which represents a worldwide standard of professional excellence in management accounting.

The Chartered Institute of Public Finance and Accountancy (CIPFA) is the professional body for people working in public finance. Chartered public finance accountants usually work for public bodies, but they can also work in the private sector. To gain chartered public finance accountant status (CPFA), trainees must complete a professional qualification in public sector accountancy. In addition, CIPFA also offers a postgraduate diploma for those already working in leadership positions.

ASSOCIATION OF CHARTERED CERTIFIED ACCOUNTANTS (ACCA), The Adelphi, 1–11 John Adam Street, London WC2N 6AU **T** 0141-582 2000
E info@accaglobal.com **W** www.accaglobal.com
Chief Executive, Helen Brand, OBE

CHARTERED ACCOUNTANTS IRELAND (CAI), 47–49 Pearse Street, Dublin 2 **T** 0353-1637 7200
W www.charteredaccountants.ie
Chief Executive, Barry Dempsey

CHARTERED INSTITUTE OF MANAGEMENT ACCOUNTANTS (CIMA), The Helicon, One South Place, London EC2M 2RB **T** 020-8849 2251
E cima.contact@cimaglobal.com **W** www.cimaglobal.com
Chief Executive, Andrew Harding

CHARTERED INSTITUTE OF PUBLIC FINANCE AND ACCOUNTANCY (CIPFA), 77 Mansell Street, London E1 8AN **T** 020-7543 5600 **E** customerservices@cipfa.org
W www.cipfa.org
Chief Executive, Rob Whiteman

INSTITUTE OF CHARTERED ACCOUNTANTS IN ENGLAND AND WALES (ICAEW), Chartered Accountants' Hall, Moorgate Place, London EC2R 6EA
T 020-7920 8100 **E** generalenquiries@icaew.com
W www.icaew.com
Chief Executive, Michael Izza

INSTITUTE OF CHARTERED ACCOUNTANTS OF SCOTLAND (ICAS), CA House, 21 Haymarket Yards, Edinburgh EH12 5BH **T** 0131-347 0100 **E** enquiries@icas.org.uk
W www.icas.com
Chief Executive, Anton Colella

ACTUARIAL SCIENCE

Salary range: £25,000–£35,000 for graduate trainees; £40,000–£55,000 after qualification; £60,000–£100,000+ for senior roles; £185,000+ for senior directors

Actuaries apply financial and statistical theories to solve business problems. These problems usually involve analysing future financial events in order to assess investment risks. To qualify, graduate trainees must complete 15 exams and three years worth of actuarial work-based training; most graduate trainees take between three and six years to qualify. Students can become Associate members of the Institute and Faculty of Actuaries (IFoA) and gain the right to describe themselves as an actuary and to use the letters AIA or AFA. Members of the profession who wish to continue their studies to an advanced level, or who specialise in a particular actuarial field, may take further specialist exams to qualify as a Fellow and bear the designations FIA or FFA.

The IFoA is the UK's chartered professional body dedicated to educating, developing and regulating actuaries based both in the UK and internationally. The IFoA represent and regulate their 29,000 members and oversee their education at all stages of qualification and development throughout their careers.

The Financial Reporting Council (FRC) is the unified independent regulator for corporate reporting, auditing, actuarial practice, corporate governance and the professionalism of accountants and actuaries. The FRC's Board for Actuarial Standards sets and maintains technical actuarial standards independently of the profession, while the Professional Oversight Board of the FRC oversees the regulation of the accountancy and actuarial professions by their respective professional bodies. The Accountancy and Actuarial Discipline Board operates an investigation and discipline scheme for members of the profession who wish to raise issues affecting UK public interest.

FINANCIAL REPORTING COUNCIL (FRC), 8th Floor, 125 London Wall, London EC2Y 5AS **T** 020-7492 2300
E enquiries@frc.org.uk **W** www.frc.org.uk
Chief Executive, Stephen Haddrill

INSTITUTE AND FACULTY OF ACTUARIES (IFoA), 7th Floor, Holborn Gate, 326–330 High Holborn, London WC1V 7PP
T 020-7632 2100 E IFoA@actuaries.org.uk
W www.actuaries.org.uk
Chief Executive, Derek Cribb

ARCHITECTURE

Salary range: architectural assistant £24,000–£31,000; fully qualified £30,000–£45,000; senior associate, partner or director £90,000

It takes a minimum of seven years to become an architect, involving three stages: a three-year first degree, a two-year second degree or diploma and two years of professional experience followed by the successful completion of a professional practice examination.

The Architects Registration Board (ARB) is the independent regulator for the profession. It was set up by an act of parliament in 1997 and is responsible for maintaining the register of UK architects, prescribing qualifications that lead to registration as an architect, investigating complaints about the conduct and competence of architects and ensuring that only those who are registered with ARB offer their services as an architect. It is only following registration with ARB that an architect can apply for chartered membership of the Royal Institute of British Architects (RIBA). RIBA, the UK body for architecture and the architectural profession, received its royal charter in 1837 and validates courses at over 80 schools of architecture in the UK; it also validates overseas courses. RIBA provides support and guidance for its members in the form of training, technical services and events and sets standards for the education of architects.

The Chartered Institute of Architectural Technologists is the international qualifying body for Chartered Architectural Technologists (MCIAT) and Architectural Technicians (TCIAT).

ARCHITECTS REGISTRATION BOARD (ARB) 8 Weymouth Street, London W1W 5BU T 020-7580 5861
E info@arb.org.uk W www.arb.org.uk
Registrar and Chief Executive, Karen Holmes

CHARTERED INSTITUTE OF ARCHITECTURAL TECHNOLOGISTS 397 City Road, London EC1V 1NH
T 020-7278 2206 E info@ciat.org.uk W www.ciat.org.uk
Chief Executive, Francesca Berriman, MBE

ROYAL INCORPORATION OF ARCHITECTS IN SCOTLAND 15 Rutland Square, Edinburgh EH1 2BE
T 0131-229 7545 E info@rias.org.uk W www.rias.org.uk
Secretary and Treasurer, Neil Baxter, FRIBA

ROYAL INSTITUTE OF BRITISH ARCHITECTS (RIBA) 66 Portland Place, London W1B 1AD T 020-7580 5533
E info@riba.org W www.architecture.com
Chief Executive, Alan Vallance

ENGINEERING

Salary range:
Civil/structural £23,500–£30,000 (graduate); £49,793 (members of the Institution of Civil Engineers (ICE)); £81,447 (fellows of ICE)
Chemical £29,500 average (graduate); £70,000+ (chartered)
Electrical £20,000–£25,000 (graduate); £28,000–£40,000 with experience; £40,000–£60,000+ (chartered)

The Engineering Council holds the national registers of Engineering Technicians (EngTech), Incorporated Engineers (IEng), Chartered Engineers (CEng) and Information and Communication Technology Technicians (ICTTech). It also sets and maintains the internationally recognised standards of competence and ethics that govern the award and retention of these titles.

To apply for the EngTech, IEng, CEng or ICTTech titles, an individual must be a member of one of the 35 engineering institutions and societies (listed below) currently licensed by the Engineering Council to assess candidates. Applicants must demonstrate that they possess a range of technical and personal competences and are committed to keeping these up-to-date.

ENGINEERING COUNCIL, 5th Floor, Woolgate Exchange, 25 Basinghall Street, London EC2V 5HA T 020-3206 0500
W www.engc.org.uk
Chief Executive, Alasdair Coates

LICENSED MEMBERS

BCS – The Chartered Institute for IT
W www.bcs.org
British Institute of Non-Destructive Testing
W www.bindt.org
Chartered Institute of Plumbing and Heating Engineering
W www.ciphe.org.uk
Chartered Institution of Building Services Engineers
W www.cibse.org
Chartered Institution of Highways and Transportation
W www.ciht.org.uk
Chartered Institution of Water and Environmental Management
W www.ciwem.org.uk
Energy Institute
W www.energyinst.org
Institute of Acoustics
W www.ioa.org.uk
Institute of Cast Metals Engineers
W www.icme.org.uk
Institute of Healthcare Engineering and Estate Management
W www.iheem.org.uk
Institute of Highway Engineers
W www.theihe.org
Institute of Marine Engineering, Science and Technology
W www.imarest.org
Institute of Materials, Minerals and Mining
W www.iom3.org
Institute of Measurement and Control
W www.instmc.org.uk
Institute of Physics
W www.iop.org
Institute of Physics and Engineering in Medicine
W www.ipem.ac.uk
Institute of Water
W www.instituteofwater.org.uk
Institution of Agricultural Engineers
W www.iagre.org
Institution of Chemical Engineers
W www.icheme.org
Institution of Civil Engineers
W www.ice.org.uk
Institution of Engineering Designers
W www.ied.org.uk
Institution of Engineering and Technology
W www.theiet.org
Institution of Fire Engineers
W www.ife.org.uk
Institution of Gas Engineers and Managers
W www.igem.org.uk
Institution of Lighting Professionals
W www.theilp.org.uk
Institution of Mechanical Engineers
W www.imeche.org
Institution of Railway Signal Engineers
W www.irse.org
Institution of Royal Engineers
W www.instre.org
Institution of Structural Engineers
W www.istructe.org
Nuclear Institute
W www.nuclearinst.com
Royal Aeronautical Society
W www.aerosociety.com
Royal Institution of Naval Architects

W www.rina.org.uk
Society of Environmental Engineers
W www.environmental.org.uk
Society of Operations Engineers
W www.soe.org.uk
The Welding Institute
W www.theweldinginstitute.com

HEALTHCARE

CHIROPRACTIC

Salary range: £20,000–£40,000 starting salary; with own practice £50,000–£70,000

Chiropractors diagnose and treat conditions caused by problems with joints, ligaments, tendons and nerves of the body. The General Chiropractic Council (GCC) is the independent statutory regulatory body for chiropractors and its role and remit is defined in the Chiropractors Act 1994. The GCC sets the criteria for the recognition of chiropractic degrees and for standards of proficiency and conduct. Details of the institutions offering degree programmes are available on the GCC website (see below). It is illegal for anyone in the UK to use the title 'chiropractor' unless registered with the GCC.

The British Chiropractic Association, Scottish Chiropractic Association, McTimoney Chiropractic Association and United Chiropractic Association are the representative bodies for the profession and are sources of further information.

BRITISH CHIROPRACTIC ASSOCIATION, 59 Castle Street, Reading RG1 7SN T 0118-950 5950
  E enquiries@chiropractic-uk.co.uk W www.chiropractic-uk.co.uk
  Executive Director, Satjit Singh

GENERAL CHIROPRACTIC COUNCIL (GCC), 44 Wicklow Street, London WC1X 9HL T 020-7713 5155
  E enquiries@gcc-uk.org W www.gcc-uk.org
  Chief Executive and Registrar, Rosalyn Hayles

SCOTTISH CHIROPRACTIC ASSOCIATION, 1 Chisholm Avenue, Bishopton, Renfrewshire PA7 5LH T 0141-404 0260
  E admin@sca-chiropractic.org W www.sca-chiropractic.org
  Administrator, Morag Cairns

DENTISTRY

Salary range: see Health: Employees and Salaries

The General Dental Council (GDC) is the organisation that regulates dental professionals in the UK. All dentists, dental hygienists, dental therapists, dental technicians, clinical dental technicians, dental nurses and orthodontic therapists must be registered with the GDC to work in the UK.

There are various different routes to qualify for registration as a dentist, including holding a degree from a UK university, completing the GDC's qualifying examination or holding a relevant European Economic Area or overseas diploma. The GDC's purpose is to protect the public through the regulation of UK dental professionals. It keeps up-to-date registers of dental professionals, works to set standards of dental practice, behaviour and education, and helps to protect patients by hearing complaints and taking action against professionals where necessary.

Founded in 1880, the British Dental Association (BDA) is the professional association and trade union for dentists in the UK. It represents dentists working in general practice, in community and hospital settings, in academia, research and the armed forces, and includes dental students.

BRITISH DENTAL ASSOCIATION (BDA), 64 Wimpole Street, London W1G 8YS T 020-7935 0875 E enquiries@bda.org
  W www.bda.org
  Chief Executive, Peter Ward

GENERAL DENTAL COUNCIL (GDC), 37 Wimpole Street, London W1G 8DQ T 020-7167 6000 E information@gdc-uk.org
  W www.gdc-uk.org
  Chief Executive, Ian Brack

MEDICINE

Salary range: see Health: Employees and Salaries

The General Medical Council (GMC) regulates medical education and training in the UK. This covers undergraduate study (usually five years), the two-year foundation programme taken by doctors directly after graduation and all subsequent postgraduate study, including specialty and GP training.

All doctors must be registered with the GMC, which is responsible for protecting the public. It does this by promoting high standards of medical education and training, fostering good medical practice, keeping a register of qualified doctors and taking action where a doctor's fitness to practise is in doubt. Doctors are eligible for full registration upon successful completion of the first year of training after graduation.

Following the foundation programme, many doctors undertake specialist training (provided by the colleges and faculties listed below) to become either a consultant or a GP. Once specialist training has been completed, doctors are awarded the Certificate of Completion of Training (CCT) and are eligible to be placed on either the GMC's specialist register or its GP register.

GENERAL MEDICAL COUNCIL (GMC), Regents Place, 350 Euston Road, London NW1 3JN T 0161-923 6602
  E gmc@gmc-uk.org W www.gmc-uk.org
  Chief Executive, Charlie Massey

WORSHIPFUL SOCIETY OF APOTHECARIES OF LONDON, Black Friars Lane, London EC4V 6EJ
  T 020-7236 1189 E clerksec@apothecaries.org
  W www.apothecaries.org
  Master, Prof. Charles Mackworth-Young

SPECIALIST TRAINING COLLEGES AND FACULTIES

College of Emergency Medicine
W www.rcem.ac.uk
Faculty of Occupational Medicine
W www.facoccmed.ac.uk
Faculty of Public Health
W www.fph.org.uk
Joint Committee on Surgical Training
W www.jcst.org
Joint Royal Colleges of Physicians Training Board
W www.jrcptb.org.uk
Royal College of Anaesthetists
W www.rcoa.ac.uk
Royal College of General Practitioners
W www.rcgp.org.uk
Royal College of Obstetricians and Gynaecologists
W www.rcog.org.uk
Royal College of Opthalmologists
W www.rcophth.ac.uk
Royal College of Paediatrics and Child Health
W www.rcpch.ac.uk
Royal College of Pathologists
W www.rcpath.org
Royal College of Physicians, London
W www.rcplondon.ac.uk
Royal College of Psychiatrists
W www.rcpsych.ac.uk
Royal College of Radiologists
W www.rcr.ac.uk

MEDICINE, SUPPLEMENTARY PROFESSIONS

The standard of professional education for arts therapists, biomedical scientists, chiropodists and podiatrists, clinical scientists, dietitians, hearing aid dispensers, occupational therapists, operating department practitioners, orthoptists, paramedics, physiotherapists, practitioner psychologists, prosthetists and orthotists, radiographers, social workers in England and speech and language therapists are regulated by the Health and Care Professions Council (HCPC), which only registers those practitioners who meet certain standards of training, professional skills, behaviour and health. The HCPC can take action against professionals who do not meet these standards or falsely declare they are registered. Each profession regulated by the HCPC has at least one professional title that is protected by law.

HEALTH AND CARE PROFESSIONS COUNCIL (HCPC), Park House, 184 Kennington Park Road, London SE11 4BU T 0300-500 6184 E registration@hcpc-uk.org W www.hcpc-uk.org *Chief Executive and Registrar,* Marc Seale

ART, DRAMA AND MUSIC THERAPIES
Salary range: £26,000–£35,000 (starting); £31,000–£48,000 with experience

An art, drama or music therapist encourages people to express their feelings and emotions through art, such as painting and drawing, drama or music. A postgraduate qualification in the relevant therapy is required. Details of accredited training programmes in the UK can be obtained from the following organisations:

BRITISH ASSOCIATION FOR MUSIC THERAPY, 24–27 White Lion Street, London N1 9PD T 020-7837 6100 E info@bamt.org W www.bamt.org *Chair,* Ben Saul

BRITISH ASSOCIATION OF ART THERAPISTS, 24–27 White Lion Street, London N1 9PD T 020-7686 4216 E info@baat.org W www.baat.org *Chief Executive,* Val Huet

BRITISH ASSOCIATION OF DRAMATHERAPISTS, PO Box 1257, Cheltenham, Gloucestershire GL50 9YX T 0124-2235 5155 E info@badth.org.uk W www.badth.org.uk *Chair,* Alyson Coleman

BIOMEDICAL SCIENCES
Salary range: £21,000–£28,000 (starting); £26,000–£35,000 with experience; £31,500–48,000 for senior roles

The Institute of Biomedical Science (IBMS) is the professional body for biomedical scientists in the UK. Biomedical scientists carry out investigations on tissue and body fluid samples to diagnose disease and monitor the progress of a patient's treatment. The IBMS sets quality standards for the profession through training, education, assessments, examinations and continuous professional development.

INSTITUTE OF BIOMEDICAL SCIENCE (IBMS), 12 Coldbath Square, London EC1R 5HL T 020-7713 0214 E mail@ibms.org W www.ibms.org *Chief Executive,* Jill Rodney

CHIROPODY AND PODIATRY
Salary range: £22,000–£41,500

Chiropodists and podiatrists assess, diagnose and treat problems of the lower leg and foot. The Society of Chiropodists and Podiatrists is the professional body and trade union for the profession. Qualifications granted and degrees recognised by the society are approved by the HCPC. HCPC registration is required in order to use the titles chiropodist and podiatrist.

SOCIETY OF CHIROPODISTS AND PODIATRISTS, Quartz House, 207 Providence Square, Mill Street, London SE1 2EW T 020-7234 8620 E reception@scpod.org W www.scpod.org *Chief Executive,* Steve Jamieson

CLINICAL SCIENCE
Salary range: £25,000–£99,000

Clinical scientists conduct tests in laboratories in order to diagnose and manage disease. The Association of Clinical Scientists is responsible for setting the criteria for competence

of applicants to the HCPC's register and to present a Certificate of Attainment to candidates following a successful assessment. This certificate will allow direct registration with the HCPC.

ASSOCIATION OF CLINICAL SCIENTISTS, 130–132 Tooley Street, London SE1 2TU T 020-7940 8960 E info@assclinsci.org W www.assclinsci.org *Chair,* Prof. Richard Lerski

DIETETICS
Salary range: £22,000–£41,500

Dietitians advise patients on how to improve their health and counter specific health problems through diet. The British Dietetic Association, established in 1936, is the professional association for dietitians. Full membership is open to UK-registered dietitians, who must also be registered with the HCPC.

BRITISH DIETETIC ASSOCIATION, 5th Floor, Charles House, 148–149 Great Charles Street Queensway, Birmingham B3 3HT T 0121-200 8080 E info@bda.uk.com W www.bda.uk.com *Chief Executive,* Andy Burman

OCCUPATIONAL THERAPY
Salary range: £22,000–£41,500; £40,000–£58,000 for consultancy roles

Occupational therapists work with people who have physical, mental and/or social problems, either from birth or as a result of accident, illness or ageing, and aim to make them as independent as possible. The professional qualification and eligibility for registration may be obtained upon successful completion of a validated course in any of the educational institutions approved by the College of Occupational Therapists, which is the professional body for occupational therapy in the UK. The courses are normally degree-level and based in higher education institutions.

COLLEGE OF OCCUPATIONAL THERAPISTS, 106–114 Borough High Street, London SE1 1LB T 020-7357 6480 W www.rcot.co.uk *Chief Executive,* Julia Scott

MENTAL HEALTH
Salary range:
Clinical psychologist £26,000, rising to £46,000–£81,000 at senior levels
Counselling psychologist £26,000–£35,000 (starting), rising to £31,500–£41,500 (qualified) and up to £82,000 at senior levels
Educational psychologist £22,000, rising to £47,000 (fully qualified) and up to £65,000 at senior levels
Psychotherapist £21,600–£28,000 (starting), rising to £47,500 with experience

Psychologists and counsellors are mental health professionals who can work in a range of settings including prisons, schools and hospitals. The British Psychological Society (BPS) is the representative body for psychology and psychologists in the UK. The BPS is responsible for the development, promotion and application of psychology for the public good. The Association of Educational Psychologists (AEP) represents the interests of educational psychologists. The British Association for Counselling and Psychotherapy (BACP) sets educational standards and provides professional support to counsellors, psychotherapists and others working in counselling, psychotherapy or counselling-related roles. The BPS website provides more information on the different specialisations that may be pursued by psychologists.

ASSOCIATION OF EDUCATIONAL PSYCHOLOGISTS (AEP), 4 The Riverside Centre, Frankland Lane, Durham DH1 5TA T 0191-384 9512
E enquiries@aep.org.uk W www.aep.org.uk
President, vacant

BRITISH ASSOCIATION FOR COUNSELLING AND PSYCHOTHERAPY (BACP), BACP House, 15 St John's Business Park, Lutterworth, Leicestershire LE17 4HB T 01455-883300 E bacp@bacp.co.uk W www.bacp.co.uk
President, David Weaver

BRITISH PSYCHOLOGICAL SOCIETY (BPS), St Andrews House, 48 Princess Road East, Leicester LE1 7DR T 0116-254 9568 E enquiries@bps.org.uk W www.beta.bps.org.uk
President, Nicola Gale

ORTHOPTICS
Salary range: £21,500 (graduate), rising to £30,700–£81,500 in senior posts

Orthoptists undertake the diagnosis and treatment of all types of squint and other anomalies of binocular vision, working in close collaboration with ophthalmologists. The all-graduate workforce comes from three universities: the University of Liverpool, the University of Sheffield and Glasgow Caledonian University.

BRITISH AND IRISH ORTHOPTIC SOCIETY, Salisbury House, Station Road, Cambridge CB1 2LA T 0203-853 9797
E bios@orthoptics.org.uk W www.orthoptics.org.uk
Chair, Rowena McNamara

PARAMEDICAL SERVICES
Salary range: £22,000–£35,500; £56,000–£68,500 for consultancy roles

Paramedics deal with accidents and emergencies, assessing patients and carrying out any specialist treatment and care needed in the first instance. The body that represents ambulance professionals is the College of Paramedics.

COLLEGE OF PARAMEDICS, The Exchange, Express Park, Bristol Road, Bridgwater TA6 4RR T 01278-420014
E membership@collegeofparamedics.co.uk
W www.collegeofparamedics.co.uk
Chief Executive, Gerry Egan

PHYSIOTHERAPY
Salary range: £22,000–£41,500

Physiotherapists are concerned with movement and function and deal with problems arising from injury, illness and ageing. Full-time three- or four-year degree courses are available at around 36 higher education institutions in the UK. Information about courses leading to state registration is available from the Chartered Society of Physiotherapy.

CHARTERED SOCIETY OF PHYSIOTHERAPY, 14 Bedford Row, London WC1R 4ED T 020-7306 6666
W www.csp.org.uk
Chief Executive, Karen Middleton, CBE

PROSTHETICS AND ORTHOTICS
Salary range: £21,000 on qualification, up to £67,000 as a consultant

Prosthetists provide artificial limbs, while orthotists provide devices to support or control a part of the body. It is necessary to obtain an honours degree to become a prosthetist or orthotist. Training is centred at the University of Salford and the University of Strathclyde.

BRITISH ASSOCIATION OF PROSTHETISTS AND ORTHOTISTS, Unit 3010, Mile End Mill, Abbey Mill Business Centre, Paisley PA1 1JS T 0141-561 7217
E enquiries@bapo.com W www.bapo.com
Chair, Lynne Rowley

RADIOGRAPHY
Salary range: £21,000–£40,000, rising to £67,800 in consultancy posts

In order to practise both diagnostic and therapeutic radiography in the UK, it is necessary to have successfully completed a course of education and training recognised by the HCPC. Such courses are offered by around 24 universities throughout the UK and lead to the award of a degree in radiography. Further information is available from the Society of Radiographers, the trade union and professional body which represents the whole of the radiographic workforce in the UK.

SOCIETY OF RADIOGRAPHERS, 207 Providence Square, Mill Street, London SE1 2EW T 020-7740 7200
W www.sor.org
Chief Executive, Richard Evans, OBE

SPEECH AND LANGUAGE THERAPY
Salary range: £21,500–£40,500

Speech and language therapists (SLTs) work with people with communication, swallowing, eating and drinking problems. The Royal College of Speech and Language Therapists is the professional body for speech and language therapists and support workers. Alongside the HCPC, it accredits education and training courses leading to qualification.

ROYAL COLLEGE OF SPEECH AND LANGUAGE THERAPISTS, 2 White Hart Yard, London SE1 1NX
T 020-7378 1200
E info@rcslt.org W www.rcslt.org
Chief Executive, Kamini Gadhok, MBE

NURSING
Salary range: see Health: Employees and Salaries

In order to practise in the UK, all nurses and midwives must be registered with the Nursing and Midwifery Council (NMC). The NMC is a statutory regulatory body that establishes and maintains standards of education, training, conduct and performance for nursing and midwifery. Courses leading to registration are currently at a minimum of degree level. All take a minimum of three years if undertaken full-time. The NMC approves programmes run jointly by higher education institutions with their healthcare service partners who offer clinical placements. The nursing part of the register has four fields of practice: adult, children's (paediatric), learning disability and mental health nursing. In most cases students must select one specific field to study before applying to an institution. Some universities run courses which offer the simultaneous study of two nursing fields. In addition, those studying to become adult nurses gain experience of nursing in relation to medicine, surgery, maternity care and nursing in the home. The NMC also sets standards for programmes leading to registration as a midwife and a range of post-registration courses including specialist practice programmes, nurse prescribing and those for teachers of nursing and midwifery. The NMC has a part of the register for specialist community public health nurses and approves programmes for health visitors, occupational health nurses and school nurses.

The Royal College of Nursing is the largest professional union for nursing in the UK, representing qualified nurses, midwives, healthcare assistants and nursing students in the NHS and the independent sector.

NURSING AND MIDWIFERY COUNCIL (NMC), 23 Portland Place, London W1B 1PZ T 020-7637 7181
E ukenquiries@nmc-uk.org W www.nmc.org.uk
Chief Executive and Registrar, Jackie Smith

ROYAL COLLEGE OF NURSING, 20 Cavendish Square, London W1G 0RN T 020-7409 3333 W www.rcn.org.uk
Chief Executive and General Secretary, Janet Davies

OPTOMETRY AND DISPENSING OPTICS
Salary range:
Optometrist £19,00–£82,000 (NHS); £14,000–£60,000+ (private)
Dispensing Optician £16,000–£35,000+

There are various routes to qualification as a dispensing optician. Qualification takes three years in total, and can be completed by combining a distance learning course or day release while working as a trainee under the supervision of a qualified and registered optician. Alternatively, students can do a two-year full-time course followed by one year of supervised practice with a qualified and registered optician. Training must be done at a training establishment approved by the regulatory body – the General Optical Council (GOC). There are five training establishments which are approved by the GOC: ABDO (Association of British Dispensing Opticians) College, Anglia Ruskin University, Bradford College, City and Islington College and Glasgow Caledonian University. After the completion of training to fit contact lenses and attaining the ABDO Level 6 certificate in contact lens practice qualification, a Contact Lens Optician may apply to be included in the GOC Speciality Register. Students are also able to complete a Foundation or Undergraduate degree in Ophthalmic Dispensing, offered by ABDO in conjunction with Canterbury Christ Church University. All routes are concluded by professional qualifying examinations, successful completion of which leads to the awarding of the Level 6 Fellowship Diploma of the Association of British Dispensing Opticians (FBDO) by ABDO. FBDO holders are able to register with the GOC following the awarding of their diploma, with registration being compulsory for all practising dispensing opticians.

Continuing Education and Training (CET) is a statutory requirement for all registered dispensing opticians and contact lens opticians to retain GOC registration.

ASSOCIATION OF BRITISH DISPENSING OPTICIANS (ABDO), Godmersham Park, Godmersham, Canterbury, Kent CT4 7DT T 01227-733905
E general@abdo.org.uk W www.abdo.org.uk
General Secretary, Sir Anthony Garrett, CBE

COLLEGE OF OPTOMETRISTS, 42 Craven Street, London WC2N 5NG T 020-7839 6000 W www.college-optometrists.org
Chief Executive, Ian Humphreys

GENERAL OPTICAL COUNCIL (GOC), 10 Old Bailey, London EC4M 7NG T 020-7580 3898 E goc@optical.org
W www.optical.org
Chief Executive and Registrar, Vicky McDermott

OSTEOPATHY
Salary Range: £20,000–£100,000+

Osteopathy is a system of diagnosis and treatment for a wide range of conditions. It works with the structure and function of the body, and is based on the principle that the well-being of an individual depends on the skeleton, muscles, ligaments and connective tissues functioning smoothly together. The General Osteopathic Council (GOsC) regulates the practice of osteopathy in the UK and maintains a register of those entitled to practise. It is a criminal offence for anyone to describe themselves as an osteopath unless they are registered with the GOsC.

To gain entry to the register, applicants must hold a recognised qualification from an osteopathic education institute accredited by the GOsC; this involves a four-to five-year honours degree programme combined with clinical training.

GENERAL OSTEOPATHIC COUNCIL (GOsC), Osteopathy House, 176 Tower Bridge Road, London SE1 3LU
T 020-7357 6655
E info@osteopathy.org.uk W www.osteopathy.org.uk
Chief Executive and Registrar, Tim Walker

PHARMACY
Salary range: £20,000–£68,000+

Pharmacists are involved in the preparation and use of medicines, from the discovery of their active ingredients to their use by patients. Pharmacists also monitor the effects of medicines, both for patient care and for research purposes.

The General Pharmaceutical Council (GPhC) is the independent regulatory body for pharmacists in England, Scotland and Wales, having taken over the regulating function of the Royal Pharmaceutical Society in 2010. The GPhC maintains the register of pharmacists, pharmacy technicians and pharmacy premises; it also sets national standards for training, ethics, proficiency and continuing professional development. The Pharmaceutical Society of Northern Ireland (PSNI) performs the same role in Northern Ireland. In order to register, students must complete a four-year degree in pharmacy that is accredited by either the GPhC or the PSNI, followed by one year of pre-registration training at an approved pharmacy; they must then pass an entrance examination.

GENERAL PHARMACEUTICAL COUNCIL (GPhC), 25 Canada Square, London, E14 5LQ T 020-3713 8000
E info@pharmacyregulation.org
W www.pharmacyregulation.org
Chief Executive and Registrar, Duncan Rudkin

PHARMACEUTICAL SOCIETY OF NORTHERN IRELAND (PSNI), 73 University Street, Belfast BT7 1HL
T 028-9032 6927 E info@psni.org.uk W www.psni.org.uk
Chief Executive, Trevor Patterson

ROYAL PHARMACEUTICAL SOCIETY, 66 East Smithfield, London, E1W 1AW T 020-7572 2737 E support@rpharms.com
W www.rpharms.com
Chief Executive, Paul Bennett

INFORMATION MANAGEMENT
Salary range: Archivist £22,443 (newly qualified); £25,000–£38,000 (with experience); £55,000 in senior posts
Information Officer £17,000–£21,000 (starting); £21,000–£28,000 (newly qualified); £26,000–£50,000+ in senior and chartered posts
Librarian £19,800–£24,500 (newly qualified); £24,000–£30,000 (chartered); £32,000–£40,000 (senior); £45,000–£55,000 (head of service)

The Chartered Institute of Library and Information Professionals (CILIP) is the leading professional body for librarians, information specialists and knowledge managers. The Archives and Records Association is the professional body for archivists and record managers.

ARCHIVES AND RECORDS ASSOCIATION, Prioryfield House, 20 Canon Street, Taunton, Somerset TA1 1SW
T 01823-327077
E ara@archives.org.uk W www.archives.org.uk
Chief Executive, John Chambers

CHARTERED INSTITUTE OF LIBRARY AND INFORMATION PROFESSIONALS (CILIP), 7 Ridgmount Street, London WC1E 7AE T 020-7255 0500 E info@cilip.org.uk
W www.cilip.org.uk
Chief Executive, Nick Poole

JOURNALISM
Salary range: £12,000–£15,000 (trainee); £25,000 for established journalists, rising to £35,000–£40,000 for those with over a decade's experience

The National Council for the Training of Journalists (NCTJ) accredits 83 courses for journalists run by a number of different education providers throughout the United Kingdom; it also provides professional support to journalists.

The Broadcast Journalism Training Council (BJTC) is an association of the UK's main broadcast journalism employers and accredits courses in broadcast journalism.

BROADCAST JOURNALISM TRAINING COUNCIL (BJTC), Sterling House, 20 Station Road, Gerard's Cross, Buckinghamshire, SL9 8EL T 0845-600 8789
E sec@bjtc.org.uk W www.bjtc.org.uk
Chief Executive, Jon Godel

NATIONAL COUNCIL FOR THE TRAINING OF JOURNALISTS (NCTJ), The New Granary, Station Road, Newport, Saffron Walden, Essex CB11 3PL T 01799-544014
E info@nctj.com W www.nctj.com
Chief Executive, Joanne Butcher

LAW

There are three types of practising lawyers: barristers, notaries and solicitors. Solicitors tend to work as a group in firms, and can be approached directly by individuals. They advise on a variety of legal issues and must decide the most appropriate course of action, if any. Notaries have all the powers of a solicitor other than the conduct of litigation. Most of them are primarily concerned with the preparation and authentication of documents for use abroad. Barristers are usually self-employed. If a solicitor believes that a barrister is required, he or she will instruct one on behalf of the client; the client will not have contact with the barrister without the solicitor being present.

When specialist expertise is needed, barristers give opinions on complex matters of law, and when clients require representation in the higher courts (crown courts, the high court, the court of appeal and the supreme court), barristers provide a specialist advocacy service. However, solicitors – who represent their clients in the lower courts such as magistrates' courts and county courts – can also apply for advocacy rights in the higher courts instead of briefing a barrister.

THE BAR

Salary range: £12,000–£65,000 (pupillage); £25,000–£300,000 (qualified); £1,000,000+ with ten years experience

The governing body of the Bar of England and Wales is the General Council of the Bar, also known as the Bar Council. Since January 2006, the regulatory functions of the Bar Council (including regulating the education and training requirements for those wishing to enter the profession) have been undertaken by the Bar Standards Board.

In the first (or 'academic') stage of training, aspiring barristers must obtain a law degree of a good standard (at least second class). Alternatively, those with a non-law degree (at least second class) may complete a one-year full-time or two-year part-time Common Professional Examination (CPE) or Graduate Diploma in Law (GDL).

The second (vocational) stage is the completion of the Bar Professional Training Course (BPTC), which is available at a number of validated institutions in the UK and must be applied for around one year in advance. All barristers must join one of the four Inns of Court prior to commencing the BPTC.

Students are 'called to the Bar' by their Inn after completion of the vocational stage, but cannot practise as a barrister until completion of the third stage, which is called 'pupillage'. Being called to the Bar does not entitle a person to practise as a barrister – successful completion of pupillage is now a prerequisite. Pupillage lasts for two six-month periods: the 'first six' and the 'second six'. The former consists of shadowing an experienced barrister, while the latter involves appearing in court as a barrister. Chambers can then offer a long term 'tenancy' to students. Students who are not given 'tenancy' may take a 'third six'.

Admission to the Bar of Northern Ireland is controlled by the Bar of Northern Ireland; admission as an Advocate to the Scottish Bar is through the Faculty of Advocates.

BAR STANDARDS BOARD address as above
E contactus@barstandardsboard.org.uk
W www.barstandardsboard.org.uk

Chair of the Bar Council, Sir Andrew Burns, KCMG

FACULTY OF ADVOCATES, Parliament Square, Edinburgh EH1 1RF T 0131-226 5071 E info@advocates.org.uk
W www.advocates.org.uk
Dean, Gordon Jackson, QC

GENERAL COUNCIL OF THE BAR (THE BAR COUNCIL), 289–293 High Holborn, London WC1V 7HZ
T 020-7242 0082 E contactus@barcouncil.org.uk
W www.barcouncil.org.uk
Chief Executive, Malcolm Cree, CBE

THE BAR OF NORTHERN IRELAND, 91 Chichester Street, Belfast BT1 3JQ T 028-9024 1523 W www.barofni.com
Chief Executive, David Mulholland

THE INNS OF COURT

HONOURABLE SOCIETY OF GRAY'S INN, 8 South Square, London WC1R 5ET T 020-7458 7800
W www.graysinn.org.uk
Under-Treasurer, Brig. Anthony Harking, OBE

HONOURABLE SOCIETY OF LINCOLN'S INN, Treasury Office, Lincoln's Inn, London WC2A 3TL T 020-7405 1393
E mail@lincolnsinn.org.uk W www.lincolnsinn.org.uk
Under-Treasurer, Mary Kerr

HONOURABLE SOCIETY OF THE INNER TEMPLE, Inner Temple, London EC4Y 7HL T 020-7797 8250
E enquiries@innertemple.org.uk W www.innertemple.org.uk
Treasurer, David Pittaway, QC

HONOURABLE SOCIETY OF THE MIDDLE TEMPLE, Middle Temple Lane, London EC4Y 9AT T 020-7427 4800
E education@middletemple.org.uk
W www.middletemple.org.uk
Chief Executive, Guy Perricone

NOTARIES PUBLIC

Notaries are qualified lawyers with a postgraduate diploma in notarial practice. Once a potential notary has passed the postgraduate diploma, they can petition the Court of Faculties for a 'faculty'. After the faculty is granted, the notary is able to practise; however, for the first two years this must be under the supervision of an experienced notary. The admission and regulation of notaries in England and Wales is a statutory function of the Faculty Office. This jurisdiction was confirmed by the Courts and Legal Services Act 1990. The Notaries Society of England and Wales is the representative body for practising notaries.

THE FACULTY OFFICE, 1 The Sanctuary, Westminster, London SW1P 3JT T 020-7222 5381
E faculty.office@1thesanctuary.com W www.facultyoffice.org.uk
Registrars, Peter Beesley; Howard Dellar

THE NOTARIES SOCIETY OF ENGLAND AND WALES, PO Box 1023, Ipswich IP1 9XB
E admin@thenotariessociety.org.uk
W www.thenotariessociety.org.uk
Secretary, Christopher Vaughan

SOLICITORS

Salary range: Trainee solicitors paid at least the national minimum wage; £25,000–£75,000 after qualification; £100,000+ (associate or partner)

Graduates from any discipline can train to be a solicitor; however, if the undergraduate degree is not in law, a one-year conversion course – either the Common Professional Examination (CPE) or the Graduate Diploma in Law (GDL) – must be completed. The next stage, and the beginning of the vocational phase, is the Legal Practice Course (LPC), which takes one year and is obligatory for both law and non-law graduates. The LPC provides professional instruction for prospective solicitors and can be completed on a full-time or part-time basis. Trainee solicitors then enter the final stage, which is a paid period of supervised work that lasts two years for full-time contracts. The employer that provides the training contract must be authorised by the Solicitors Regulation Authority (SRA) (the regulatory body of the Law Society of England and Wales), the Law Society of Scotland or the Law Society of Northern Ireland. The SRA also monitors the training contract to ensure that it provides the trainee with the expertise to qualify as a solicitor.

Conveyancers are specialist property lawyers, dealing with the legal processes involved in transferring buildings, land and associated finances from one owner to another. This was the sole responsibility of solicitors until 1987 but under current legislation it is now possible for others to train as conveyancers.

COUNCIL FOR LICENSED CONVEYANCERS (CLC), CAN Mezzanine, 49–51 East Road, London N1 6AH
T 0207-250 8465
E clc@clc-uk.org W www.clc-uk.org
Chief Executive, Sheila Kumar

THE LAW SOCIETY OF ENGLAND AND WALES, The Law Society's Hall, 113 Chancery Lane, London WC2A 1PL
T 020-7242 1222 W www.lawsociety.org.uk
Chief Executive (interim), Paul Tennant, OBE

LAW SOCIETY OF NORTHERN IRELAND, 96 Victoria Street, Belfast BT1 3GN T 028-9023 1614 W www.lawsoc-ni.org
Chief Executive, Alan Hunter

LAW SOCIETY OF SCOTLAND, Atria One, 144 Morrison Street, Edinburgh EH3 8EX T 0131-226 7411
E lawscot@lawscot.org.uk W www.lawscot.org.uk
Chief Executive, Lorna Jack

SOLICITORS REGULATION AUTHORITY (SRA), The Cube, 199 Wharfside Street, Birmingham B1 1RN
T 0370-606 2555 W www.sra.org.uk
Chief Executive, Paul Philip

SOCIAL WORK

Salary range: £22,000 (newly qualified); £40,000 (with experience); £26,041–£34,876 (NHS)

Social workers tend to specialise in either adult or children's services. The HCPC obtained regulatory responsibility from the General Social Care Council in August 2012 and is responsible for setting standards of conduct and practice for social care workers and their employers; regulating the workforce and social work education and training. A degree or postgraduate qualification is needed in order to become a social worker. For more information *see* Social Welfare.

HEALTH AND CARE PROFESSIONS COUNCIL (HCPC), Park House, 184 Kennington Park Road, London SE11 4BU T 0845-300 6184 E registration@hcpc-uk.org
W www.hcpc-uk.org
Chief Executive and Registrar, Marc Seale

SURVEYING

Salary range: £18,500–£22,000 (starting); £45,000 (senior); up to £100,000 (partners and directors)

The Royal Institution of Chartered Surveyors (RICS) is the professional body that represents and regulates property professionals including land surveyors, valuers, auctioneers, quantity surveyors and project managers. Entry to the institution, following completion of a RICS-accredited degree, is through completion of the Assessment of Professional Competence (APC), which involves a period of practical training concluded by a final assessment of competence. Entry as a technical surveyor requires completion of the Assessment of Technical Competence (ATC), which mirrors the format of the APC. The different levels of RICS membership are MRICS (member) or FRICS (fellow) for chartered surveyors, and AssocRICS for associate members.

Relevant courses can also be accredited by the Chartered Institute of Building (CIOB), which represents managers working in a range of construction disciplines. The CIOB offers four levels of membership to those who satisfy its requirements: FCIOB (fellow), MCIOB (member), ICIOB (incorporated) and ACIOB (associate).

CHARTERED INSTITUTE OF BUILDING (CIOB), 1 Arlington Square, Downshire Way, Bracknell RG12 1WA T 01344-630700 E reception@ciob.org.uk W www.ciob.org
Chief Executive, Chris Blythe, OBE

ROYAL INSTITUTION OF CHARTERED SURVEYORS (RICS), Parliament Square, London SW1P 3AD T 024-7686 8555 E contactrics@rics.org W www.rics.org
Chief Executive, Sean Tompkins

TEACHING

Salary range: school teachers £22,000–£46,000; school leaders £38,500–£108,000 (for more detailed information *see* Education: Employees and Salaries)

The General Teaching Councils (GTCs) for Northern Ireland, Scotland and Wales maintain registers of qualified teachers in their respective countries, and registration is a legal requirement in order to teach in local authority schools. On 1 April 2013, the Teaching Agency merged with the National College to form the National College for Teaching and Leadership (NCTL), an executive agency of the Department for Education, which became the awarding body for Qualified Teacher Status (QTS). UCAS Teacher Training (UTT) has replaced the Graduate Teacher Training Registry (GTTR) as the body through which to apply for postgraduate teacher training in the UK. To become a qualified teacher, all entrants must have a degree and gain QTS, which includes a minimum of 24 weeks in at least two different schools and academic study of teaching. Another route is through School-centred Initial Teacher Training (SCITT), where practical, hands-on teacher training is delivered by experienced, practising teachers in their own government-approved school.

Many courses also award an academic qualification known as the Postgraduate Certificate in Education (PGCE) in England and Wales and the Professional Graduate Diploma in Education (PGDE) in Scotland. Once training is completed, applicants spend a year in school as a newly qualified teacher (NQT).

Teachers in Further Education (FE) need not have QTS, though new entrants to FE may be required to work towards a specified FE qualification by employers. A range of courses are offered and usually require one year of study in addition to 100 hours of teaching experience. Similarly, academic staff in Higher Education require no formal teaching qualification, but are expected to obtain a qualification that meets standards set by the Higher Education Academy.

Details of routes to gaining QTS are available in England from the NCTL, the Department for Education and UTT, in Wales from the Teacher Training & Education Recruitment Forum Wales, in Scotland from Teach in Scotland and in Northern Ireland from the Department of Education.

In July 2017, the College of Teaching became the Chartered College of Teaching. Under the terms of its royal charter, provides professional qualifications and membership to teachers and those involved in education in the UK and overseas.

CHARTERED COLLEGE OF TEACHING, 9–11 Endsleigh Gardens, London WC1H 0EH T 020-7911 5589
E hello@chartered.college W www.chartered.college
Chief Executive, Prof. Dame Alison Peacock, DBE

DEPARTMENT OF EDUCATION NORTHERN IRELAND, Rathgael House, Balloo Road, Rathgill, Bangor BT19 7PR T 028-9127 9279
E DE.DEWebMail@education-ni.gov.uk
W www.education-ni.gov.uk
Permanent Secretary, Derek Baker

EDUCATION WORKFORCE COUNCIL, 9th Floor, Eastgate House, 35–43 Newport Road, Cardiff CF24 0AB T 029-2046 0099 E information@ewc.wales W www.ewc.wales
Chair, Angela Jardine

GENERAL TEACHING COUNCIL FOR NORTHERN IRELAND, 4th Floor, Albany House, 73–75 Great Victoria Street, Belfast BT2 7AF T 028-9033 3390 E info@gtcni.org.uk W www.gtcni.org.uk
Chair, David Canning

GENERAL TEACHING COUNCIL FOR SCOTLAND, Clerwood House, 96 Clermiston Road, Edinburgh EH12 6UT T 0131-314 6000 E gtcs@gtcs.org.uk W www.gtcs.org.uk
Chief Executive, Ken Muir

HIGHER EDUCATION ACADEMY, Innovation Way, York Science Park, Heslington, York YO10 5BR T 01904-717500 E enquiries@heacademy.ac.uk W www.heacademy.ac.uk
Chief Executive, Prof. Stephanie Marshall

NATIONAL COLLEGE FOR TEACHING AND LEADERSHIP, Department for Education, Piccadilly Gate, Store Street, Manchester M1 2WD T 0370-000 2288 W www.gov.uk/government/organisations/national-college-for-teaching-and-leadership
Chair, Roger Pope

UCAS TEACHER TRAINING (UTT), Rosehill, New Barn Lane, Cheltenham GL52 3LZ T 0371-468 0469 W www.ucas.com/teacher-training
Chief Executive, Clare Marchant

VETERINARY MEDICINE

Salary range: £31,150 (newly qualified); £41,148–£44,142 (with experience); £70,000 (twenty years experience)

The regulatory body for veterinary surgeons in the UK is the Royal College of Veterinary Surgeons (RCVS), which keeps the register of those entitled to practise veterinary medicine, the register of veterinary nurses and veterinary practice premises (on behalf of the Veterinary Medicines Directorate). Holders of recognised degrees from any of the seven UK university veterinary schools that have been approved by the RCVS or from certain EU or overseas universities are entitled to be registered, and holders of certain other degrees may take a statutory membership examination. The UK's RCVS-approved veterinary schools are located at the University of Bristol, the University of Cambridge, the University of Edinburgh, the University of Glasgow, the University of Liverpool, Middlesex University and the Royal Veterinary College in London; all veterinary degrees last for five years except that offered at Cambridge, which lasts for six.

The British Veterinary Association is the national representative body for the UK veterinary profession. The British Veterinary Nursing Association is the professional body representing veterinary nurses.

BRITISH VETERINARY ASSOCIATION, 7 Mansfield Street, London W1G 9NQ T 020-7636 6541 E bvahq@bva.co.uk W www.bva.co.uk
Chief Executive, David Calpin

BRITISH VETERINARY NURSING ASSOCIATION, 79 Greenway Business Centre, Harlow Business Park, Harlow, Essex CM19 5QE T 01279-408644 E bvna@bvna.co.uk W www.bvna.org.uk
Honorary Secretary, Whilmari Worrow

ROYAL COLLEGE OF VETERINARY SURGEONS (RCVS), Belgravia House, 62–64 Horseferry Road, London SW1P 2AF T 020-7222 2001 E info@rcvs.org.uk W www.rcvs.org.uk
Chief Executive and Secretary, Nick Stace

INDEPENDENT SCHOOLS

Independent schools (non-maintained mainstream schools) charge fees and are owned privately or managed under special trusts, with profits being used for the benefit of the schools concerned. In 2015–16 there were 2,492 non-maintained mainstream schools in the UK, educating around 625,000 pupils, or around 6.5 per cent of the total school-age population. The number of pupils at non-maintained mainstream schools as at January 2017 was:

England	583,286
Wales	9,381
Scotland	30,238
Northern Ireland	658

The Independent Schools Council (ISC), formed in 1974, acts on behalf of the seven independent schools' associations which constitute it. These associations are:

Association of Governing Bodies of Independent Schools (AGBIS)
Girls' Schools Association (GSA)
Headmasters' & Headmistresses' Conference (HMC)
Independent Association of Prep Schools (IAPS)
Independent Schools Association (ISA)
Independent Schools' Bursars Association (ISBA)
The Society of Heads

In 2016–17 there were 522,879 pupils being educated in 1,301 schools in membership of associations within the Independent Schools Council (ISC). Most schools not in membership of an ISC association are likely to be privately owned. The Independent Schools Inspectorate (ISI) was demerged from ISC with effect from 1 January 2008 and is legally and operationally independent of ISC. ISI works as an accredited inspectorate of schools in membership of the ISC associations under a framework agreed with the Department for Education (DfE). A school must pass an ISI accreditation inspection to qualify for membership of an association within ISC.

In 2017 at GCSE 62.9 per cent of all exams taken by candidates in ISC associations' member schools achieved either an A/7 grade or higher (compared to the national average of 20 per cent), and at A-level 18.3 per cent of entries were awarded an A* grade (national average, 8.3 per cent). In 2016–17 a total of 168,025 (33 per cent) pupils at schools in ISC associations received help with their fees, mainly in the form of bursaries and scholarships from the schools. ISC schools provided more than £760m of assistance with fees.

INDEPENDENT SCHOOLS COUNCIL
First Floor, 27 Queen Anne's Gate, London SW1H 9BU
T 020-7766 7070 W www.isc.co.uk

The list of schools below was compiled from the *Independent Schools Yearbook 2016–17* (ed. Judy Mott, published by Bloomsbury Publishing) which includes schools whose heads are members of one of the ISC's five Heads' Associations. Further details are available online (W www.isyb.co.uk).

The fees shown below represent the upper limit payable for the year 2017–18 (marked with an asterisk), where these are not yet known, the fees below are the upper limit payable for 2016–17.

School	Web Address	Termly Fees Day	Board	Head
ENGLAND				
Abbey Gate College, Cheshire	www.abbeygatecollege.co.uk	£4,019	–	Mrs T. Pollard
*Abbots Bromley School, Staffs	www.abbotsbromleyschool.com	£5,119	£8,575	Mrs M. Shackleton
*Abbot's Hill School, Herts	www.abbotshill.herts.sch.uk	£5,998	–	Mrs E. Thomas
Abbotsholme School, Derbys	www.abbotsholme.co.uk	£7,080	£10,395	M. Boud-Self
Abingdon School, Oxon	www.abingdon.org.uk	£6,195	–	M. Windsor
Ackworth School, W. Yorks	www.ackworthschool.com	£4,395	£8,335	A. Maree
Adcote School, Shrops	www.adcoteschool.org.uk	£4,946	£9,032	Mrs D. Browne
*AKS Lytham, Lancs	www.arnoldkeqms.com	£3,778	–	M. Walton
*Aldenham School, Herts	www.aldenham.com	£7,338	£10,827	J. Fowler
Alderley Edge School for Girls, Cheshire	www.aesg.co.uk	£3,316	–	Mrs H. Jeys
Alleyn's School, London, SE22	www.alleyns.org.uk	£6,042	–	Dr G. Savage
Ampleforth College, N. Yorks	www.ampleforth.org.uk/college	£7,741	£11,130	Fr Wulstan Peterburs
*Ardingly College, W. Sussex	www.ardingly.com	£7,870	£11,140	B. Figgis
Ashford School, Kent	www.ashfordschool.co.uk	£5,600	£11,250	M. Buchanan
Ashville College, N. Yorks	www.ashville.co.uk	£4,600	£9,250	R. Marshall
*Austin Friars, Cumbria	www.austinfriars.co.uk	£4,715	–	M. Harris
Bablake School, W. Midlands	www.bablake.com	£3,660	–	J. Watson
*Badminton School, Bristol	www.badmintonschool.co.uk	£5,395	£12,220	Mrs R. Tear

*Bancroft's School, Essex	www.bancrofts.org	£5,794	–	S. Marshall
Barnard Castle School, Durham	www.barnardcastleschool.org.uk	£4,372	£7,842	A. Jackson
*Bedales School, Hants	www.bedales.org.uk	£9,272	£11,799	K. Budge
Bede's Senior School, E. Sussex	www.bedes.org	£6,975	£11,087	P. Goodyer
*Bedford Girls' School, Beds	www.bedfordgirlsschool.co.uk	£4,313	–	Miss J. MacKenzie
*Bedford Modern School, Beds	www.bedmod.co.uk	£4,346	–	A. Tate
*Bedford School, Beds	www.bedfordschool.org.uk	£6,159	£10,417	J. Hodgson
*Bedstone College, Shrops	www.bedstone.org	£4,885	£8,840	D. Gajadharsingh
Beechwood Sacred Heart School, Kent	www.beechwood.org.uk	£5,550	£9,250	A. Lennon
Benenden School, Kent	www.benenden.kent.sch.uk	–	£11,900	Mrs S. Price
Berkhamsted School, Herts	www.berkhamstedschool.org	£6,555	£10,442	R. Backhouse
Bethany School, Kent	www.bethanyschool.org.uk	£5,830	£9,915	M. Healy
Birkdale School, S. Yorks	www.birkdaleschool.org.uk	£4,000	–	Dr P. Owen
Birkenhead School, Merseyside	www.birkenheadschool.co.uk	£3,815	–	P. Vicars
*Bishop's Stortford College, Herts	www.bishopsstortfordcollege.org	£6,362	£9,708	J. Gladwin
*Blackheath High School, London, SE3	www.blackheathhighschool.gdst.net	£5,292	–	Mrs C. Chandler-Thompson
Bloxham School, Oxon	www.bloxhamschool.com	£8,210	£10,815	P. Sanderson
Blundell's School, Devon	www.blundells.org	£7,035	£10,955	Mrs N. Huggett
*Bolton School Boys' Division, Lancs	www.boltonschool.org/seniorboys	£3,912	–	P. Britton
*Bolton School Girls' Division, Lancs	www.boltonschool.org/seniorgirls	£3,912	–	Miss S. Hincks
Bootham School, N. Yorks	www.boothamschool.com	£5,840	£10,170	C. Jeffrey
*Bournemouth Collegiate School, Dorset	www.bournemouthcollegiateschool.co.uk	£4,715	£9,465	R. Slatford
*Box Hill School, Surrey	www.boxhillschool.com	£6,330	£11,250	C. Lowde
*Bradfield College, Berks	www.bradfieldcollege.org.uk	£9,684	£12,105	Dr C. Stevens
Bradford Grammar School, W. Yorks	www.bradfordgrammar.com	£4,107	–	Dr S. Hinchliffe
Bredon School, Glos	www.bredonschool.org	£6,145	£9,630	D. Ward
*Brentwood School, Essex	www.brentwoodschool.co.uk	£6,072	£11,900	D. Davies
*Brighton & Hove High School, E. Sussex	www.bhhs.gdst.net	£4,667	–	Ms J. Smith
Brighton College, E. Sussex	www.brightoncollege.org.uk	£7,600	£13,530	R. Cairns
Bristol Grammar School, Bristol	www.bristolgrammarschool.co.uk	£4,620	–	R. MacKinnon
*Bromley High School, Kent	www.bromleyhigh.gdst.net	£5,521	–	Mrs A. Drew
Bromsgrove School, Worcs	www.bromsgrove-school.co.uk	£5,140	£11,285	P. Clague
Bruton School for Girls, Somerset	www.brutonschool.co.uk	£5,300	£8,950	Mrs N. Botterill
*Bryanston School, Dorset	www.bryanston.co.uk	£10,109	£12,328	Ms S. Thomas
Burgess Hill Girls, W. Sussex	www.burgesshillgirls.com	£5,650	£10,150	Mrs K. Bell
Bury Grammar School Boys, Lancs	www.burygrammar.com	£3,480	–	D. Cassidy
Bury Grammar School Girls, Lancs	www.burygrammar.com	£3,480	–	Mrs J. Anderson
Caterham School, Surrey	www.caterhamschool.co.uk	£5,826	£10,954	C. Jones
Channing School, London, N6	www.channing.co.uk	£5,860	–	Mrs B. Elliott

*Charterhouse, Surrey	www.charterhouse.org.uk	–	£12,687	A. Turner
*Cheltenham College, Glos	www.cheltenhamcollege.org	£8,920	£11,900	Dr A. Peterken
Cheltenham Ladies' College, Glos	www.cheltladiescollege.org	£7,680	£11,440	Ms E. Jardine-Young
*Chetham's School of Music, Greater Manchester	www.chethams.com	£8,273	£10,677	A. Jones
*Chigwell School, Essex	www.chigwell-school.org	£5,665	£9,690	M. Punt
*Christ's Hospital, W. Sussex	www.christs-hospital.org.uk	£7,110	£10,930	S. Reid
Churcher's College, Hants	www.churcherscollege.com	£4,740	–	S. Williams
City of London Freemen's School, Surrey	www.freemens.org	£5,732	£9,289	R. Martin
*City of London School, London, EC4	www.cityoflondonschool.org.uk	£5,577	–	Dr R. Brookes
City of London School for Girls, London, EC2	www.clsg.org.uk	£5,352	–	Mrs E. Harrop
*Claremont Fan Court School, Surrey	www.claremontfancourt.co.uk	£5,695	–	J. Insall-Reid
Clayesmore School, Dorset	www.clayesmore.com	£8,340	£11,370	Mrs J. Thomson
*Clifton College, Bristol	www.cliftoncollege.com	£8,285	£12,750	Dr T. Greene
*Clifton High School, Bristol	www.cliftonhigh.bristol.sch.uk	£4,860	–	Dr A. Neill
Cobham Hall, Kent	www.cobhamhall.com	£7,052	£10,607	Dr S. Coates-Smith
Cokethorpe School, Oxon	www.cokethorpe.org.uk	£5,950	–	D. Ettinger
*Colfe's School, London, SE12	www.colfes.com	£5,478	–	R. Russell
*Colston's, Bristol	www.colstons.org	£4,535	–	J. McCullough
Concord College, Shrops	www.concordcollegeuk.com	£4,500	£12,000	N. Hawkins
*Cranford House, Oxon	www.cranfordhouse.net	£5,510	–	Dr J. Raymond
*Cranleigh School, Surrey	www.cranleigh.org	£9,995	£12,205	M. Reader
*Croydon High School, Surrey	www.croydonhigh.gdst.net	£5,378	–	Mrs E. Pattison
Culford School, Suffolk	www.culford.co.uk	£6,150	£9,995	J. Johnson-Munday
Dauntsey's School, Wilts	www.dauntseys.org	£5,980	£9,900	M. Lascelles
*Dean Close School, Glos	www.deanclose.org.uk	£7,772	£11,485	Mrs E. Taylor
Denstone College, Staffs	www.denstonecollege.org	£4,941	£8,603	D. Derbyshire
*Derby Grammar School, Derbys	www.derbygrammar.org	£4,331	–	Mrs L. Reynolds
Derby High School, Derbys	www.derbyhigh.derby.sch.uk	£3,999	–	Mrs D. Gould
Dodderhill School, Worcs	www.dodderhill.co.uk	£3,590	–	Mrs C. Mawston
Dover College, Kent	www.dovercollege.org.uk	£5,075	£9,640	G. Doodes
d'Overbroeck's, Oxon	www.doverbroecks.com	£7,450	£11,650	Mrs E. Henry
Downe House, Berks	www.downehouse.net	£8,480	£11,720	Mrs E. McKendrick
*Downside School, Somerset	www.downside.co.uk	£6,111	£10,905	J. Whitehead
*Dulwich College, London, SE21	www.dulwich.org.uk	£6,554	£13,680	Dr J. Spence
*Dunottar School, Surrey	www.dunottarschool.com	£5,164	–	M. Tottman
*Durham High School for Girls, Durham	www.dhsfg.org.uk	£4,245	–	Mrs L. Renwick
*Durham School, Durham	www.durhamschool.co.uk	£5,331	£9,846	K. McLaughlin
*Eastbourne College, E. Sussex	www.eastbourne-college.co.uk	£7,540	£11,440	T. Lawson
*Edgbaston High School, W. Midlands	www.edgbastonhigh.co.uk	£4,114	–	Dr R. Weeks
Ellesmere College, Shrops	www.ellesmere.com	£5,826	£10,296	B. Wignall
*Eltham College, London, SE9	www.elthamcollege.london	£5,686	–	G. Sanderson

Emanuel School, London, SW11	www.emanuel.org.uk	£5,858	–	R. Milne
Epsom College, Surrey	www.epsomcollege.org.uk	£7,824	£11,539	J. Piggott
Eton College, Berks	www.etoncollege.com	–	£12,354	S. Henderson
Ewell Castle School, Surrey	www.ewellcastle.co.uk	£5,075	–	P. Harris
Exeter School, Devon	www.exeterschool.org.uk	£4,105	–	B. Griffin
Farlington School, W. Sussex	www.farlingtonschool.net	£5,660	£9,600	Miss L. Higson
Farnborough Hill, Hants	www.farnborough-hill.org.uk	£4,569	–	Mrs A. Neil
Farringtons School, Kent	www.farringtons.org.uk	£4,700	£9,490	Mrs D. Nancekievill
*Felsted School, Essex	www.felsted.org	£7,575	£11,425	C. Townsend
Forest School, London, E17	www.forest.org.uk	£5,660	–	M. Hodges
Framlingham College, Suffolk	www.framcollege.co.uk	£6,212	£9,661	P. Taylor
Francis Holland School, London, NW1	www.fhs-nw1.org.uk	£6,130	–	C. Fillingham
Francis Holland School, London, SW1	www.fhs-sw1.org.uk	£6,390	–	Mrs L. Elphinstone
Frensham Heights, Surrey	www.frensham.org	£6,450	£9,595	A. Fisher
Fulneck School, W. Yorks	www.fulneckschool.co.uk	£4,120	£7,995	Mrs D. Newman
Gateways School, W. Yorks	www.gatewaysschool.co.uk	£4,240	–	Dr T. Johnson
Giggleswick School, N. Yorks	www.giggleswick.org.uk	£6,600	£10,600	M. Turnbull
Godolphin, Wilts	www.godolphin.org	£6,505	£9,880	Mrs E. Hattersley
*The Godolphin and Latymer School, London, W6	www.godolphinandlatymer.com	£6,716	–	Dr F. Ramsey
*The Grange School, Cheshire	www.grange.org.uk	£3,610	–	Mrs D. Leonard
*Gresham's School, Norfolk	www.greshams.com	£7,900	£11,320	D. Robb
Guildford High School, Surrey	www.guildfordhigh.surrey.sch.uk	£5,344	–	Mrs F. Boulton
The Haberdashers' Aske's Boys' School, Herts	www.habsboys.org.uk	£6,152	–	P. Hamilton
Haberdashers' Aske's School for Girls, Herts	www.habsgirls.org.uk	£5,482	–	Miss B. O'Connor
Halliford School, Middx	www.hallifordschool.co.uk	£4,900	–	J. Davies
Hampshire Collegiate School, Hants	www.hampshirecs.org.uk	£4,980	£9,370	C. Canning
Hampton School, Middx	hamptonschool.org.uk	£6,125	–	K. Knibbs
Harrogate Ladies' College, N. Yorks	www.hlc.org.uk	£7,920	£11,470	Mrs S. Brett
*Harrow School, Middx	www.harrowschool.org.uk	–	£12,850	J. Hawkins
*Headington School, Oxon	www.headington.org	£6,200	£12,330	Mrs C. Jordan
*Heathfield School, Berks	www.heathfieldschool.net	£7,305	£11,740	Mrs M. Legge
*Hereford Cathedral School, Herefords	www.herefordcs.com	£4,536	–	P. Smith
Hethersett Old Hall School, Norfolk	www.hohs.co.uk	£4,795	£8,980	S. Crump
*Highclare School, W. Midlands	www.highclareschool.co.uk	£4,070	–	Dr R. Luker
*Highgate School, London, N6	www.highgateschool.org.uk	£6,790	–	A. Pettitt
Hill House School, S. Yorks	www.hillhouse.doncaster.sch.uk	£4,100	–	D. Holland
*Hurstpierpoint College, W. Sussex	www.hppc.co.uk	£7,720	£11,500	T. Manly
Hymers College, E. Yorks	www.hymerscollege.co.uk	£3,534	–	D. Elstone
Immanuel College, Herts	www.immanuelcollege.co.uk	£5,500	–	G. Griffin

School	Website			Head
*Ipswich High School, Suffolk	www.ipswichhighschool.co.uk	£4,658	–	Ms O. Carlin
Ipswich School, Suffolk	www.ipswich.school	£4,801	£8,881	N. Weaver
James Allen's Girls' School (JAGS), London, SE22	www.jags.org.uk	£5,505	–	Mrs S. Huang
*The John Lyon School, Middx	www.johnlyon.org	£5,710	–	Miss K. Haynes
*Kent College, Canterbury, Kent	www.kentcollege.com	£5,985	£11,327	Dr D. Lamper
*Kent College, Pembury, Kent	www.kent-college.co.uk	£6,625	£10,577	Ms J. Lodrick
Kimbolton School, Cambs	www.kimbolton.cambs.sch.uk	£4,950	£8,235	J. Belbin
*King Edward VI High School for Girls, W. Midlands	www.kehs.org.uk	£4,134	–	Mrs A. Clark
*King Edward VI School, Hants	www.kes.hants.sch.uk	£5,170	–	J. Thould
King Edward's School, Somerset	www.kesbath.com	£4,525	–	M. Boden
*King Edward's School, W. Midlands	www.kes.org.uk	£4,245	–	Dr M. Fenton
*King Edward's Witley, Surrey	www.kesw.org	£6,650	£10,260	J. Attwater
*King Henry VIII School, W. Midlands	www.khviii.com	£3,784	–	J. Slack
*King William's College, Isle of Man	www.kwc.im	£7,200	£10,450	J. Buchanan
Kingham Hill School, Oxon	www.kinghamhill.org.uk	£6,075	£10,200	Revd Nick Seward
*King's College School, London, SW19	www.kcs.org.uk	£6,995	–	A. Halls
King's College, Taunton, Somerset	www.kings-taunton.co.uk	£6,995	£10,370	R. Biggs
King's Ely, Cambs	www.kingsely.org	£6,623	£9,588	Mrs S. Freestone
King's High School, Warks	www.kingshighwarwick.co.uk	£3,956	–	R. Nicholson
The King's School, Kent	www.kings-school.co.uk	£8,900	£11,765	P. Roberts
*The King's School, Chester, Cheshire	www.kingschester.co.uk	£4,425	–	G. Hartley
The King's School, Macclesfield, Cheshire	www.kingsmac.co.uk	£4,075	–	Dr S. Hyde
*King's Rochester, Kent	www.kings-rochester.co.uk	£6,235	£10,130	J. Walker
The King's School, Worcs	www.ksw.org.uk	£4,360	–	M. Armstrong
The Kingsley School, Warks	www.thekingsleyschool.com	£4,185	–	Ms H. Owens
*Kingsley School, Devon	www.kingsleyschoolbideford.co.uk	£4,395	£8,595	P. Last
*Kingston Grammar School, Surrey	www.kgs.org.uk	£6,225	–	S. Lehec
Kingswood School, Somerset	www.kingswood.bath.sch.uk	£4,794	£10,704	S. Morris
Kirkham Grammar School, Lancs	www.kirkhamgrammar.co.uk	£3,599	£6,831	D. Berry
The Lady Eleanor Holles School, Middx	www.lehs.org.uk	£6,315	–	Mrs H. Hanbury
*Lancing College, W. Sussex	www.lancingcollege.co.uk	£8,190	£11,645	D. Oliver
Langley School, Norfolk	www.langleyschool.co.uk	£4,845	£9,845	D. Findlay
Latymer Upper School, London, W6	www.latymer-upper.org	£6,170	–	D. Goodhew
*The Grammar School at Leeds, W. Yorks	www.gsal.org.uk	£4,425	–	Mrs S. Woodroofe
Leicester Grammar School, Leics	www.leicestergrammar.org.uk	£4,114	–	C. King
*Leicester High School for Girls, Leics	www.leicesterhigh.co.uk	£3,945	–	A. Whelpdale
*Leighton Park School, Berks	www.leightonpark.com	£7,218	£11,348	N. Williams

*Leweston School, Dorset	www.leweston.co.uk	£4,950	£10,400	Mrs K. Reynolds
The Leys, Cambs	www.theleys.net	£6,920	£10,345	M. Priestley
Lichfield Cathedral School, Staffs	www.lichfieldcathedralschool.com	£4,910	–	Mrs S. Hannam
*Lincoln Minster School, Lincolns	www.lincolnminsterschool.co.uk	£4,474	£10,350	M. Wallace
*Lingfield College, Surrey	www.lingfieldcollege.co.uk	£4,867	–	R. Bool
Longridge Towers School, Northumberland	www.lts.org.uk	£4,241	£8,636	J. Lee
*Lord Wandsworth College, Hants	www.lordwandsworth.org	£7,525	£10,700	A. Williams
Loughborough Grammar School, Leics	www.lesgrammar.org	£3,925	£8,643	D. Byrne
*Loughborough High School, Leics	www.leshigh.org	£3,996	–	Mrs G. Byrom
*Luckley House School, Berks	www.luckleyhouseschool.org	£5,405	£9,458	Mrs J. Tudor
*LVS Ascot, Berks	www.lvs.ascot.sch.uk	£5,801	£10,192	Mrs C. Cunniffe
*Magdalen College School, Oxon	www.mcsoxford.org	£5,928	–	Miss H. Pike
*Malvern College, Worcs	www.malverncollege.org.uk	£8,178	£12,739	A. Clark
The Manchester Grammar School, Greater Manchester	www.mgs.org	£3,990	–	Dr M. Boulton
*Manchester High School for Girls, Greater Manchester	www.manchesterhigh.co.uk	£3,824	–	Mrs C. Hewitt
*Manor House School, Bookham, Surrey	www.manorhouseschool.org	£5,621	–	Ms T. Fantham
*The Marist School, Berks	www.themarist.com	£4,680	–	K. McCloskey
*Marlborough College, Wilts	www.marlboroughcollege.org	£10,350	£12,175	J. Leigh
*Marymount International School, Surrey	www.marymountlondon.com	£7,620	£12,958	Mrs M. Frazier
*Mayfield School, E. Sussex	www.mayfieldgirls.org	£6,800	£10,975	Miss A. Beary
The Maynard School, Devon	www.maynard.co.uk	£4,195	–	Miss S. Dunn
Merchant Taylors' Boys' School, Merseyside	www.merchanttaylors.com	£3,650	–	D. Williams
Merchant Taylors' Girls' School, Merseyside	www.merchanttaylors.com	£3,650	–	Mrs L. Robinson
Merchant Taylors' School, Middx	www.mtsn.org.uk	£6,507	–	S. Everson
*Mill Hill School, London, NW7	www.millhill.org.uk	£6,875	£10,964	Mrs F. King
*Millfield, Somerset	millfieldschool.com	£8,270	£12,315	C. Considine
Milton Abbey School, Dorset	www.miltonabbey.co.uk	£5,965	£11,780	M. Bashaarat
Moira House Girls School, E. Sussex	www.moirahouse.co.uk	£5,760	£10,355	Mrs E. Vallantine
*Monkton School, Somerset	www.monktoncombeschool.com	£6,800	£10,845	C. Wheeler
*More House School, London, SW1	www.morehouse.org.uk	£6,310	–	Mrs A. Leach
Moreton Hall, Shrops	www.moretonhall.org	£8,980	£10,900	J. Forster
Mount House School, Herts	www.mounthouse.org.uk	£4,625	–	M. Burke
Mount Kelly, Devon	www.mountkelly.com	£5,570	£9,700	M. Semmence
Mount St Mary's College, Derbys	www.msmcollege.com	£4,307	£9,332	Dr N. Cuddihy
The Mount School, York, N. Yorks	www.mountschoolyork.co.uk	£5,694	£9,438	Miss A. Richmond
New Hall School, Essex	www.newhallschool.co.uk	£6,243	£9,585	Mrs K. Jeffrey
*Newcastle High School for Girls, Tyne and Wear	www.newcastlehigh.gdst.net	£4,204	–	Mrs H. French

*Newcastle School for Boys, Tyne and Wear	www.newcastleschool.co.uk	£4,440	–	D. Tickner
Newcastle-under-Lyme School, Staffs	www.nuls.org.uk	£3,838	–	D. Williamson
North London Collegiate School, Middx	www.nlcs.org.uk	£6,354	–	Mrs A. Wilson
*Northampton High School, Northants	www.northamptonhigh.gdst.net	£4,616	–	Dr H. Stringer
*Northwood College for Girls, Middx	www.northwoodcollege.gdst.net	£5,319	–	Miss J. Pain
*Norwich High School, Norfolk	www.norwichhigh.gdst.net	£4,690	–	Mrs K. Malaisé
Norwich School, Norfolk	www.norwich-school.org.uk	£5,020	–	S. Griffiths
*Notre Dame School, Surrey	www.notredame.co.uk	£5,360	–	Mrs A. King
*Notting Hill and Ealing High School, London, W13	www.nhehs.gdst.net	£5,978	–	M. Shoults
*Nottingham Girls' High School, Notts	www.nottinghamgirlshigh.gdst.net	£4,374	–	Miss J. Keller
*Nottingham High School, Notts	www.nottinghamhigh.co.uk	£4,769	–	K. Fear
Oakham School, Rutland	www.oakham.rutland.sch.uk	£6,450	£10,525	N. Lashbrook
Ockbrook School, Derbys	www.ockbrooksch.co.uk	£4,060	£8,405	T. Brooksby
Oldham Hulme Grammar School, Lancs	www.ohgs.co.uk	£3,582	–	C. Mairs
The Oratory School, Oxon	www.oratory.co.uk	£7,900	£10,865	J. Smith
*Oswestry School, Shrops	www.oswestryschool.org.uk	£5,050	£9,920	J. Noad
*Oundle School, Northants	www.oundleschool.org.uk	£7,595	£11,855	Mrs S. Kerr-Dineen
Our Lady's Abingdon Senior School, Oxon	www.olab.org.uk	£4,785	–	S. Oliver
*Oxford High School, Oxon	www.oxfordhigh.gdst.net	£4,985	–	Dr P. Hills
Palmers Green High School, London, N21	www.pghs.co.uk	£4,920	–	Mrs W. Kempster
Pangbourne College, Berks	www.pangbourne.com	£7,741	£10,949	T. Garnier
*The Perse Upper School, Cambs	www.perse.co.uk	£5,555	–	E. Elliott
*The Peterborough School, Cambs	www.thepeterboroughschool.co.uk	£5,018	–	A. Meadows
*Pipers Corner School, Bucks	www.piperscorner.co.uk	£5,850	–	Mrs H. Ness-Gifford
Pitsford School, Northants	www.pitsfordschool.com	£4,620	–	N. Toone
Plymouth College, Devon	www.plymouthcollege.com	£5,140	£9,930	J. Standen
*Pocklington School, E. Yorks	www.pocklingtonschool.com	£4,708	£9,176	M. Ronan
Portland Place School, London, W1B 1NJ	www.portland-place.co.uk	£6,665	–	D. Bradbury
The Portsmouth Grammar School, Hants	www.pgs.org.uk	£4,939	–	J. Priory
*Portsmouth High School, Hants	www.portsmouthhigh.co.uk	£4,549	–	Mrs J. Prescott
Princess Helena College, Herts	www.princesshelenacollege.co.uk	£6,325	£9,195	Mrs S. Wallace-Woodroffe
Princethorpe College, Warks	www.princethorpe.co.uk	£3,903	–	E. Hester
Prior Park College, Somerset	www.priorparkschools.com	£4,805	£9,815	J. Murphy-O'Connor
The Purcell School, Herts	www.purcell-school.org	£8,484	£10,833	S. Yeo
*Putney High School, London, SW15	www.putneyhigh.gdst.net	£6,064	–	Mrs S. Longstaff

School	Website	Day	Boarding	Head
Queen Anne's School, Berks	www.qas.org.uk	£7,375	£10,870	Mrs J. Harrington
*Queen Elizabeth's Hospital (QEH), Bristol	www.qehbristol.co.uk	£4,662	–	S. Holliday
Queen Mary's School, N. Yorks	www.queenmarys.org	£5,930	£7,710	Mrs C. Cameron
*Queen's College, London, London, W1G 8BT	www.qcl.org.uk	£6,135	–	R. Tillett
Queen's College, Somerset	www.queenscollege.org.uk	£5,800	£9,770	Dr L. Earps
Queen's Gate School, London, SW7	www.queensgate.org.uk	£6,300	–	Mrs R. Kamaryc
*Queenswood School, Herts	www.queenswood.org	£8,275	£11,250	Mrs J. Cameron
*Radley College, Oxon	www.radley.org.uk	–	£12,300	J. Moule
Ratcliffe College, Leics	www.ratcliffe-college.co.uk	£5,219	£8,236	G. Lloyd
*The Read School, N. Yorks	www.readschool.co.uk	£4,132	£9,482	J. Sweetman
*Reading Blue Coat School, Berks	www.rbcs.org.uk	£5,373	–	J. Elzinga
Reddam House Berkshire, Berks	www.reddamhouse.org.uk	£5,515	£10,315	Mrs T. Howard
Redmaids' High School, Bristol	www.redmaidshigh.co.uk	£4,440	–	Mrs I. Tobias
*Reed's School, Surrey	www.reeds.surrey.sch.uk	£7,950	£10,245	M. Hoskins
Reigate Grammar School, Surrey	www.reigategrammar.org	£5,820	–	S. Fenton
*Rendcomb College, Glos	www.rendcombcollege.org.uk	£7,550	£10,500	R. Jones
*Repton School, Derbys	www.repton.org.uk	£8,582	£11,569	A. Land
Rishworth School, W. Yorks	www.rishworth-school.co.uk	£4,020	£8,895	A. Gloag
*Roedean School, E. Sussex	www.roedean.co.uk	£6,955	£12,480	O. Blond
Rossall School, Lancs	www.rossall.org.uk	£4,150	£11,850	Ms E. Purves
*Royal Grammar School, Surrey	www.rgsg.co.uk	£5,865	–	Dr J. Cox
Royal Grammar School, Tyne and Wear	www.rgs.newcastle.sch.uk	£4,056	–	J. Fern
RGS Worcester, Worcs	www.rgsw.org.uk	£3,984	–	J. Pitt
*The Royal High School Bath, Somerset	www.royalhighbath.gdst.net	£4,542	£9,883	Mrs J. Duncan
*The Royal Hospital School, Suffolk	www.royalhospitalschool.org	£5,472	£10,395	S. Lockyer
The Royal Masonic School for Girls, Herts	www.royalmasonic.herts.sch.uk	£5,305	£9,380	K. Carson
*Royal Russell School, Surrey	www.royalrussell.co.uk	£5,945	£11,750	C. Hutchinson
*Rugby School, Warks	www.rugbyschool.co.uk	£7,268	£11,584	P. Green
*Ryde School with Upper Chine, Isle of Wight	www.rydeschool.org.uk	£4,125	–	M. Waldron
Rye St Antony, Oxon	www.ryestantony.co.uk	£4,725	£7,995	Miss A. Jones
*St Albans High School for Girls, Herts	www.stahs.org.uk	£5,910	–	Mrs J. Brown
St Albans School, Herts	www.st-albans.herts.sch.uk	£5,746	–	J. Gillespie
*St Augustine's Priory School, London, W5	www.sapriory.com	£5,054	–	Mrs S. Raffray
St Bede's College, Greater Manchester	www.sbcm.co.uk	£3,595	–	R. Robson
St Benedict's School, London, W5	www.stbenedicts.org.uk	£5,100	–	A. Johnson
*St Catherine's School, Surrey	www.stcatherines.info	£5,850	–	Mrs A. Phillips
St Catherine's School, Middx	www.stcatherineschool.co.uk	£4,674	–	Sister Paula Thomas
St Christopher School, Herts	www.stchris.co.uk	£5,785	£9,890	R. Palmer
St Columba's College, Herts	www.stcolumbascollege.org	£4,801	–	D. Buxton

St Dominic's Brewood, Staffs	www.stdominicsbrewood.co.uk	£4,032	£7,167	P. McNabb
St Dunstan's College, London, SE6	www.stdunstans.org.uk	£5,326	–	N. Hewlett
*St Edmund's College, Herts	www.stedmundscollege.org	£5,735	£9,955	P. Durán
St Edmund's School Canterbury, Kent	www.stedmunds.org.uk	£6,557	£10,572	Mrs L. Moelwyn-Hughes
St Edward's, Oxford, Oxon	www.stedwardsoxford.org	£9,515	£11,890	S. Jones
St Edward's School, Glos	www.stedwards.co.uk	£5,145	–	Mrs P. Clayfield
Saint Felix School, Suffolk	www.stfelix.co.uk	£5,150	£8,995	J. Harrison
St Gabriel's, Berks	www.stgabriels.co.uk	£5,420	–	R. Smith
St George's College, Weybridge, Surrey	www.stgeorgesweybridge.com	£5,915	–	Mrs R. Owens
*St George's, Ascot, Berks	www.stgeorges-ascot.org.uk	£7,300	£11,450	Mrs E. Hewer
St Helen & St Katharine, Oxon	www.shsk.org.uk	£4,915	–	Mrs R. Dougall
St Helen's School, Middx	www.sthelens.london	£5,326	–	Dr M. Short
*St James Senior Boys' School, Surrey	www.stjamesboys.co.uk	£6,040	–	D. Brazier
*St James Senior Girls' School, London, W14	www.stjamesgirls.co.uk	£6,410	–	Mrs S. Labram
*St John's College, Hants	www.stjohnscollege.co.uk	£3,895	£9,030	T. Bayley
St Joseph's College, Suffolk	www.stjos.co.uk	£4,635	£10,340	Mrs D. Clarke
*St Lawrence College, Kent	www.slcuk.com	£6,165	£11,545	A. Spencer
St Margaret's School, Bushey, Herts	www.stmargaretsbushey.co.uk	£5,259	£9,855	Mrs R. Hardy
Saint Martin's School, W. Midlands	www.saintmartins-school.com	£3,900	–	Miss N. Edgar
St Mary's Calne, Wilts	www.stmaryscalne.org	£9,050	£12,150	Dr F. Kirk
St Mary's School, Essex	www.stmaryscolchester.org.uk	£4,575	–	Mrs H. Vipond
St Mary's College, Merseyside	www.stmarys.ac	£3,541	–	M. Kennedy
St Mary's School, Bucks	www.stmarysschool.co.uk	£5,232	–	Mrs J. Ross
St Mary's School Ascot, Berks	www.st-marys-ascot.co.uk	£8,390	£11,790	Mrs M. Breen
St Mary's School, Dorset	www.stmarys.eu	£6,650	£9,840	Mrs M. Arnal
St Nicholas' School, Hants	www.st-nicholas.hants.sch.uk	£4,510	–	Mrs A. Whatmough
St Paul's Girls' School, London, W6	www.spgs.org	£8,247	–	Mrs S. Fletcher
*St Paul's School, London, SW13	www.stpaulsschool.org.uk	£8,101	–	Professor Mark Bailey
St Peter's School, York, N. Yorks	www.stpetersyork.org.uk	£5,645	£9,380	L. Winkley
*St Swithun's School, Hants	www.stswithuns.com	£6,721	£10,770	Ms J. Gandee
*Scarborough College, N. Yorks	www.scarboroughcollege.co.uk	£4,710	£7,949	C. Ellison
Seaford College, W. Sussex	www.seaford.org	£6,720	£10,395	J. Green
*Sevenoaks School, Kent	www.sevenoaksschool.org	£8,499	£12,969	Dr K. Ricks
Shebbear College, Devon	www.shebbearcollege.co.uk	£4,175	£8,250	S. Weale
*Sheffield High School for Girls, S. Yorks	www.sheffieldhighschool.org.uk	£4,189	–	Mrs V. Dunsford
Sherborne Girls, Dorset	www.sherborne.com	£6,580	£11,100	Mrs J. Dwyer
Sherborne School, Dorset	www.sherborne.org	£9,450	£11,675	D. Luckett
*Shiplake College, Oxon	www.shiplake.org.uk	£7,160	£10,650	A. Davies
*Shrewsbury School, Shrops	www.shrewsbury.org.uk	£8,130	£11,680	M. Turner

Sibford School, Oxon	www.sibfordschool.co.uk	£4,650	£9,035	T. Spence
Silcoates School, W. Yorks	www.silcoates.org.uk	£4,420	–	P. Rowe
*Solihull School, W. Midlands	www.solsch.org.uk	£4,195	–	D. Lloyd
*South Hampstead High School, London, NW3	www.shhs.gdst.net	£5,951	–	Mrs V. Bingham
*Stafford Grammar School, Staffs	www.staffordgrammar.co.uk	£4,039	–	M. Darley
*Stamford High School, Lincolns	www.ses.lincs.sch.uk	£4,922	£9,118	W. Phelan
*Stamford School, Lincolns	www.ses.lincs.sch.uk	£4,922	£9,118	W. Phelan
The Stephen Perse Foundation, Cambs	www.stephenperse.com	£5,325	–	Miss P. Kelleher
*Stockport Grammar School, Cheshire	www.stockportgrammar.co.uk	£3,798	–	A. Chicken
Stonar, Wilts	www.stonarschool.com	£5,265	£9,500	Dr S. Divall
Stonyhurst College, Lancs	www.stonyhurst.ac.uk	£6,205	£11,143	J. Browne
Stover School, Devon	www.stover.co.uk	£4,140	£8,480	R. Notman
Stowe School, Bucks	www.stowe.co.uk	£8,260	£11,490	Dr A. Wallersteiner
*Streatham & Clapham High School, London, SW16	www.schs.gdst.net	£5,676	–	Dr M. Sachania
*Sutton Valence School, Kent	www.svs.org.uk	£6,895	£10,740	B. Grindlay
*Sydenham High School, London, SE26	www.sydenhamhighschool.gdst.net	£5,417	–	Mrs K. Woodcock
Talbot Heath, Dorset	www.talbotheath.org	£4,444	£7,872	Mrs A. Holloway
Tettenhall College, W. Midlands	www.tettenhallcollege.co.uk	£4,330	£9,100	D. Williams
Thetford Grammar School, Norfolk	www.thetgram.norfolk.sch.uk	£4,424	–	M. Bedford
Tonbridge School, Kent	www.tonbridge-school.co.uk	£9,386	£12,513	T. Haynes
Tormead School, Surrey	www.tormeadschool.org.uk	£4,818	–	Mrs C. Foord
Tring Park School for the Performing Arts, Herts	www.tringpark.com	£7,470	£11,180	S. Anderson
*Trinity School, Surrey	www.trinity-school.org	£5,552	–	A. Kennedy
*Trinity School, Devon	www.trinityschool.co.uk	£3,980	£8,875	L. Coen
Truro High School for Girls, Cornwall	www.trurohigh.co.uk	£4,201	£8,205	Dr G. Moodie
*Truro School, Cornwall	www.truroschool.com	£4,540	£8,995	A. Gordon-Brown
*Tudor Hall, Oxon	www.tudorhallschool.com	£7,115	£11,370	Miss W. Griffiths
University College School, London, NW3	www.ucs.org.uk	£6,264	–	M. Beard
*Uppingham School, Rutland	www.uppingham.co.uk	£8,435	£12,050	Dr R. Maloney
*Walthamstow Hall, Kent	www.walthamstow-hall.co.uk	£6,460	–	Mrs J. Milner
Warminster School, Wilts	www.warminsterschool.org.uk	£4,910	£10,195	M. Mortimer
Warwick School, Warks	www.warwickschool.org	£4,061	£8,799	G. Lock
*Welbeck - The Defence Sixth Form College, Leics	www.dsfc.ac.uk	£6,500	–	J. Middleton
*Wellingborough School, Northants	www.wellingboroughschool.org	£4,970	–	G. Bowe
*Wellington College, Berks	www.wellingtoncollege.org.uk	£9,310	£12,740	J. Thomas
Wellington School, Somerset	www.wellington-school.org.uk	£4,785	£9,590	H. Price
Wells Cathedral School, Somerset	www.wells-cathedral-school.com	£5,965	£9,983	Mrs E. Cairncross
West Buckland School, Devon	www.westbuckland.com	£4,710	£10,325	P. Stapleton
*Westfield School, Tyne and Wear	www.westfield.newcastle.sch.uk	£4,355	–	N. Walker

*Westholme School, Lancs	www.westholmeschool.com	£3,550	–	Mrs L. Horner
*Westminster School, London, SW1	www.westminster.org.uk	£9,522	£12,580	P. Derham
Westonbirt School, Glos	www.westonbirt.org	£7,195	£11,430	Mrs N. Dangerfield
*Wimbledon High School, London, SW19	www.wimbledonhigh.gdst.net	£6,035	–	Mrs J. Lunnon
Winchester College, Hants	www.winchestercollege.org	–	£12,226	Dr T. Hands
Windermere School – Browhead, Cumbria	www.windermereschool.co.uk	£5,640	£9,990	I. Lavender
Wisbech Grammar School, Cambs	WisbechGrammar.com	£4,192	–	C. Staley
*Withington Girls' School, Greater Manchester	www.wgs.org	£3,973	–	Mrs S. Haslam
Woldingham School, Surrey	www.woldinghamschool.co.uk	£7,119	£11,371	Mrs A. Hutchinson
Wolverhampton Grammar School, W. Midlands	www.wgs.org.uk	£4,313	–	Mrs K. Crewe-Read
Woodbridge School, Suffolk	www.woodbridgeschool.org.uk	£5,210	£9,799	N. Tetley
*Woodhouse Grove School, W. Yorks	www.woodhousegrove.co.uk	£4,425	£8,995	J. Lockwood
*Worth School, W. Sussex	www.worthschool.org.uk	£7,570	£10,700	S. McPherson
Wrekin College, Shrops	www.wrekincollege.com	£5,675	£9,930	T. Firth
Wychwood School, Oxon	www.wychwoodschool.org	£4,900	£7,800	Mrs A. Johnson
Wycliffe College, Glos	www.wycliffe.co.uk	£6,330	£10,595	N. Gregory
*Wycombe Abbey, Bucks	www.wycombeabbey.com	–	£12,600	Mrs R. Wilkinson
Yarm School, Cleveland	www.yarmschool.org	£4,096	–	D. Dunn
*The Yehudi Menuhin School, Surrey	www.yehudimenuhinschool.co.uk	–	–	Dr R. Hillier

WALES

The Cathedral School Llandaff, Cardiff	www.cathedral-school.co.uk	£4,015	–	Mrs C. Sherwood
Christ College, Brecon	www.christcollegebrecon.com	£5,821	£8,994	G. Pearson
*Howell's School Llandaff, Cardiff	www.howells-cardiff.gdst.net	£4,563	–	Mrs S. Davis
Monmouth School for Boys, Monmouth	www.habs-monmouth.org	£4,969	£9,545	Dr A. Daniel
*Monmouth School for Girls, Monmouth	www.hmsg.co.uk	£4,782	£9,940	Mrs C. Pascoe
Myddelton College, Denbigh	www.myddeltoncollege.com	£3,333	£10,700	M. Roberts
Rougemont School, Newport	www.rougemontschool.co.uk	£4,232	–	R. Carnevale
Ruthin School, Ruthin	www.ruthinschool.co.uk	£4,333	£9,500	T. Belfield
Rydal Penrhos School, Colwyn Bay	www.rydalpenrhos.com	£5,380	£10,715	S. Smith

SCOTLAND

Dollar Academy, Dollar	www.dollaracademy.org.uk	£4,035	£9,336	D. Knapman
*The High School of Dundee, Dundee	www.highschoolofdundee.org.uk	£4,166	–	Dr J. Halliday
The Edinburgh Academy, Edinburgh	www.edinburghacademy.org.uk	£4,416	–	B. Welsh
Fettes College, Edinburgh	www.fettes.com	£8,515	£10,780	G. Stanford
*George Heriot's School, Edinburgh	www.george-heriots.com	£4,013	–	C. Wyllie
The Glasgow Academy, Glasgow	www.theglasgowacademy.org.uk	£11,063	–	P. Brodie
The High School of Glasgow, Glasgow	www.highschoolofglasgow.co.uk	£3,973	–	J. O'Neill
Glenalmond College, Perth	www.glenalmondcollege.co.uk	£7,318	£10,743	Ms E. Logan
Gordonstoun School, Elgin	www.gordonstoun.org.uk	£8,869	£11,974	Mrs L. Kerr

Hutchesons' Grammar School, Glasgow	www.hutchesons.org	£3,768	–	C. Gambles
*Kelvinside Academy, Glasgow	www.kelvinsideacademy.org.uk	£4,080	–	I. Munro
Kilgraston School, Bridge of Earn	www.kilgraston.com	£5,490	£9,380	Mrs D. MacGinty
Lomond School, Helensburgh	www.lomondschool.com	£3,700	£8,410	Mrs J. Urquhart
*Loretto School, Musselburgh	www.loretto.com	£7,625	£11,200	G. Hawley
*The Mary Erskine School, Edinburgh	www.esms.org.uk	£3,766	£7,556	D. Gray
*Merchiston Castle School, Edinburgh	www.merchiston.co.uk	£7,835	£10,550	A. Hunter
*Morrison's Academy, Crieff	www.morrisonsacademy.org	£4,223	–	G. Warren
*Robert Gordon's College, Aberdeen	www.rgc.aberdeen.sch.uk	£4,237	–	S. Mills
St Aloysius' College, Glasgow	www.staloysius.org	£3,738	–	M. Bartlett
St Columba's School, Kilmacolm	www.st-columbas.org	£3,748	–	Mrs A. Angus
St Leonards School, St Andrews	www.stleonards-fife.org	£4,379	£10,680	Dr M. Carslaw
*St Margaret's School for Girls, Aberdeen	www.st-margaret.aberdeen.sch.uk	£5,040	–	Miss A. Tomlinson
*Stewart's Melville College, Edinburgh	www.esms.org.uk	£3,766	£7,556	J. Gray
*Strathallan School, Perth	www.strathallan.co.uk	£7,249	£10,683	M. Lauder

NORTHERN IRELAND

*Bangor Grammar School, Bangor	www.bangorgrammarschool.com	–	–	Mrs E. Huddleson
Campbell College, Belfast	www.campbellcollege.co.uk	£0,838	£4,318	R. Robinson
The Royal School Dungannon, Dungannon	www.royaldungannon.com	£0,050	£3,200	D. Burnett
				Mrs R. Hardy

CHANNEL ISLANDS

Elizabeth College, Guernsey	www.elizabethcollege.gg	£3,585	–	Mrs J. Palmer
Victoria College, Jersey	www.victoriacollege.je	£1,770	–	A. Watkins

NATIONAL ACADEMIES OF SCHOLARSHIP

The national academies are self-governing bodies whose members are elected as a result of achievement and distinction in the academy's field. Within their discipline, the academies provide advice, support education and exceptional scholars, stimulate debate, promote UK research worldwide and collaborate with international counterparts.

The UK's four national academies – the Royal Society, the British Academy, the Royal Academy of Engineering and the Academy of Medical Sciences – receive funding from the Department for Business, Energy and Industrial Strategy (BEIS) for key programmes that help deliver government priorities. The total amount of resource funding allocated by BEIS to the four national academies for 2017–18 is £98m. The Royal Society of Edinburgh is aided by funds provided by the Scottish government. In addition to government funding, the national academies generate additional income from donations, membership contributions, trading and investments.

ACADEMY OF MEDICAL SCIENCES (1998)

41 Portland Place, London W1B 1QH
T 020-3141 3200 W www.acmedsci.ac.uk

Founded in 1998, the Academy of Medical Sciences is the independent body in the UK representing the diversity of medical science. The Academy seeks to improve health through research, as well as to promote medical science and its translation into benefits for society.

The academy is self-governing and receives funding from a variety of sources, including the fellowship, charitable donations, government and industry.

Fellows are elected from a broad range of medical sciences: biomedical, clinical and population based. The academy includes in its remit veterinary medicine, dentistry, nursing, medical law, economics, sociology and ethics. Elections are from nominations put forward by existing fellows.

There are around 1,202 fellows and 4 honorary fellows.

President, Prof. Sir Robert Lechler, PMEDSCI
Executive Director, Dr Helen Munn

BRITISH ACADEMY (1902)

10–11 Carlton House Terrace, London SW1Y 5AH
T 020-7969 5200 W www.britac.ac.uk

The British Academy is an independent, self-governing learned society for the promotion of the humanities and social sciences. It was founded in 1901 and granted a royal charter in 1902. The British Academy supports advanced academic research and is a channel for the government's support of research in those disciplines.

The fellows are scholars who have attained distinction in one of the branches of study that the academy exists to promote. Candidates must be nominated by existing fellows. There are just over 1,000 fellows, around 31 honorary fellows and 300 corresponding fellows overseas.

President, Prof. Sir David Cannadine
Chief Executive, Alun Evans

ROYAL ACADEMY OF ENGINEERING (1976)

3 Carlton House Terrace, London SW1Y 5DG
T 020-7766 0600 W www.raeng.org.uk

The Royal Academy of Engineering was established as the Fellowship of Engineering in 1976. It was granted a royal charter in 1983 and its present title in 1992. It is an independent, self-governing body whose object is the pursuit, encouragement and maintenance of excellence in the whole field of engineering, in order to promote the advancement of the science, art and practice of engineering for the benefit of the public.

Election to the fellowship is by invitation only, from nominations supported by the body of fellows. There are around 1,500 fellows, 40 honorary fellows and 100 international fellows. The Duke of Edinburgh is the senior fellow and the Princess Royal and the Duke of Kent are both royal fellows.

President, Dame Ann Dowling, DBE, FRENG, FRS
Chief Executive, Philip Greenish, CBE

ROYAL SOCIETY (1660)

6–9 Carlton House Terrace, London SW1Y 5AG
T 020-7451 2500 W www.royalsociety.org

The Royal Society is an independent academy promoting the natural and applied sciences. Founded in 1660 and granted a royal charter in 1662, the society has three roles: as the UK academy of science, as a learned society and as a funding agency. It is an independent, self-governing body under a royal charter, promoting and advancing all fields of physical and biological sciences, of mathematics and engineering, medical and agricultural sciences and their application.

Fellows are elected for their contributions to science, both in fundamental research resulting in greater understanding, and also in leading and directing scientific and technological progress in industry and research establishments. Each year up to 52 new fellows, who must be citizens or residents of the Commonwealth or Ireland, and up to ten foreign members may be elected. In addition one honorary fellow may also be elected annually from those not eligible for election as fellows or foreign members. There are around 1,600 fellows and foreign members and seven honorary members covering all scientific disciplines. The Queen is the patron of the Royal Society, and there are also five royal fellows.

President, Sir Venki Ramakrishnan, PRS
Executive Director, Dr Julie Maxton, CBE

ROYAL SOCIETY OF EDINBURGH (1783)

22–26 George Street, Edinburgh EH2 2PQ
T 0131-240 5000 W www.rse.org.uk

The Royal Society of Edinburgh (RSE) is an educational charity and Scotland's national academy. An independent body with charitable status, its multidisciplinary membership represents a knowledge resource for the people of Scotland. Granted its royal charter in 1783 for the 'advancement of learning and useful knowledge', the society organises conferences, debates and lectures; conducts independent inquiries; facilitates international collaboration and showcases the country's research and development capabilities; provides educational activities for primary and secondary school students; and awards prizes and medals. The society also awards over £2m annually to Scotland's top researchers and entrepreneurs working in Scotland.

There are just over 1,600 fellows, including 70 honorary fellows and 74 corresponding fellows overseas.

President, Prof. Dame Jocelyn Bell Burnell, DBE, FRS, FRSE
General Secretary, Prof. Alan Alexander, OBE, FRSE

PRIVATELY FUNDED ARTS ACADEMIES

The Royal Academy and the Royal Scottish Academy support the visual arts community in the UK, hold educational events and promote interest in the arts. They are entirely privately funded through contributions by 'friends' (regular donors who receive benefits such as free entry, previews and magazines), bequests, corporate donations and exhibitions.

ROYAL ACADEMY OF ARTS (1768)
Burlington House, Piccadilly, London W1J 0BD
T 020-7300 8000 W www.royalacademy.org.uk

Founded by George III in 1768, the Royal Academy of Arts is an independent, self-governing society devoted to the encouragement and promotion of the fine arts.

Membership of the academy is limited to 80 academicians, all of whom are either painters, engravers, printmakers, draughtsmen, sculptors or architects. There must always be at least 14 sculptors, 12 architects and eight printmakers among the academicians. Candidates must be professionally active in the UK and are nominated and elected by the existing academicians. The members are known as royal academicians (RAs) and are responsible for both the governance and direction of the academy. When RAs reach the age of 75, they become senior academicians and can no longer serve as officers or on the committees.

The title of honorary academician is awarded to a small number of distinguished artists who are not resident in the UK; as at September 2017, there were 30 honorary academicians. Unlike the RAs, they do not take part in the governance of the academy and are unable to vote.

President, Christopher Le Brun, PRA
Secretary and Chief Executive, Dr Charles Saumarez Smith, CBE

ROYAL SCOTTISH ACADEMY (1838)
The Mound, Edinburgh EH2 2EL
T 0131-225 6671 W www.royalscottishacademy.org

Founded in 1826 and led by a body of academicians comprising eminent artists and architects, the Royal Scottish Academy (RSA) is an independent voice for cultural advocacy and one of the largest supporters of artists in Scotland. The Academy administers a number of scholarships, awards and residencies and has a historic collection of Scottish artworks, recognised by the Scottish government as being of national significance. The Academy is independent from local or national government funding, relying instead on bequests, legacies, sponsorship and earned income.

Academicians have to be Scots by birth or domicile, and are elected from the disciplines of art and architecture following nominations put forward by the existing membership. There are also a small number of honorary academicians – distinguished artists and architects, writers, historians and musicians – who do not have to be Scottish. As at September 2017 there were 111 academicians and 30 honorary academicians.

President, Arthur Watson, PRSA
Secretary, Marion Smith, RSA
Treasurer, Gareth Fisher, RSA

RESEARCH COUNCILS

The government funds basic and applied civil science research, mostly through seven research councils, which are established under royal charter and supported by the Department for Business, Energy and Industrial Strategy (BEIS). Research Councils UK is the strategic partnership of these seven councils* (for further information *see* W www.rcuk.ac.uk). The councils support research and training in universities and other higher education and research facilities.

The Higher Education and Research Act was passed in April 2017, paving the way for a new single funding body, UK Research and Innovation, to bring together the seven existing Research Councils, Innovate UK and the research and knowledge exchange functions of the Higher Education Funding Council for England (HEFCE). A new body, Research England, will be responsible for quality-related research funding. A new Office for Students, replacing both HEFCE and the Office for Fair Access, will hold statutory responsibility for quality and standards, approve new entrants to the sector by managing the Register of Higher Education Providers and confer university title and degree awarding powers. All new bodies are expected to start work in April 2018.

The science budget, administered by BEIS, is the main source of public sector funding for research councils, with further public funds provided by the Higher Education Funding Council for England. Additional funds may also be provided by other government departments, devolved administrations, the European Commission and other international bodies. The councils also receive income for research specifically commissioned by government departments and the private sector, and income from charitable sources.

BEIS RESEARCH COUNCIL ALLOCATIONS
£ thousand

	2016–17	2017–18
Arts and Humanities Research Council	101,000	101,000
Biotechnology and Biological Sciences Research Council	417,000	419,000
Economic and Social Research Council	183,000	183,000
Engineering and Physical Sciences Research Council	859,000	848,000
Medical Research Council	614,000	627,000
Natural Environment Research Council	331,000	333,000
Science and Technology Facilities Council	512,000	513,000

Source: BEIS – The Allocation of Science and Research Funding 2016/17 to 2019/20

ARTS AND HUMANITIES RESEARCH COUNCIL*

Polaris House, North Star Avenue, Swindon SN2 1FL
T 01793-416000 W www.ahrc.ac.uk

The AHRC is the successor organisation to the Arts and Humanities Research Board and was incorporated by royal charter and established in 2005. It provides funding for postgraduate training and research in the arts and humanities; in any one year, the AHRC makes approximately 700 research awards and around 2,000 postgraduate scholarships. Awards are made after a rigorous peer review system, which ensures the quality of applications.

Chair, Prof. Sir Drummond Bone, FRSE
Chief Executive, Prof. Andrew Thompson, DPHIL

BIOTECHNOLOGY AND BIOLOGICAL SCIENCES RESEARCH COUNCIL*

Polaris House, North Star Avenue, Swindon SN2 1UH
T 01793-413200 W www.bbsrc.ac.uk

Established by royal charter in 1994, the BBSRC is the UK funding agency for research in the non-clinical life sciences. It funds research into how all living organisms function and behave, benefiting the agriculture, food, health, pharmaceutical and chemical sectors. To deliver its mission, the BBSRC supports research and training in universities and research centres throughout the UK, including providing strategic research grants to the eight institutes listed below. In June 2015, the institutes founded the National Institutes of Bioscience (NIB) partnership in order to increase the impact of bioscience research and to strengthen the UK's reputation in the field.

Chair, Prof. Sir Gordon Duff
Chief Executive (interim), Prof. Melanie Welham

INSTITUTES
BABRAHAM INSTITUTE, Babraham, Cambridge CB22 3AT
   T 01223-496000
Director, Prof. Michael Wakelam
INSTITUTE FOR BIOLOGICAL, ENVIRONMENTAL AND RURAL SCIENCES (ABERYSTWYTH UNIVERSITY), Penglais, Aberystwyth SY23 3DA
   T 01970-621986
Director, Prof. Mike Gooding
EARLHAM INSTITUTE, Norwich Research Park, Colney, Norwich NR4 7UZ T 01603-450001
Director, Prof. Neil Hall
JOHN INNES CENTRE, Norwich Research Park, Colney, Norwich NR4 7UH T 01603-450000
Director, Prof. Dale Sanders
PIRBRIGHT INSTITUTE, Pirbright Laboratory, Ash Road, Pirbright, Surrey GU24 0NF T 01483-232441
Director, Dr Bryan Charleston
QUADRAM INSTITUTE, Norwich Research Park, Norwich, Norfolk NR4 7UA T 01603-255000
Director, Prof. Ian Charles
ROSLIN INSTITUTE (UNIVERSITY OF EDINBURGH), Easter Bush, Midlothian EH25 9RG T 0131-651 9100
Director, Prof. Eleanor Riley
ROTHAMSTED RESEARCH, Harpenden, Herts AL5 2JQ T 01582-763133
Director, Prof. Achim Dobermann

ECONOMIC AND SOCIAL RESEARCH COUNCIL*

Polaris House, North Star Avenue, Swindon SN2 1UJ
T 01793-413000 W www.esrc.ac.uk

The ESRC was established by royal charter in 1965 as an organisation for funding and promoting research and postgraduate training in the social sciences. It supports independent research which has an impact on business, the public sector and civil society and also provides advice, disseminates knowledge and promotes public understanding in these areas.

The ESRC has a total budget of around £192m and provides funding to over 4,000 researchers and postgraduate students in academic institutions and independent research institutes.

Chair, Dr Alan Gillespie, CBE
Chief Executive (interim), Prof. Tony McEnery

ENGINEERING AND PHYSICAL SCIENCES RESEARCH COUNCIL*

Polaris House, North Star Avenue, Swindon SN2 1ET
T 01793-444000 W www.epsrc.ac.uk

Formed in 1994 by royal charter, the EPSRC is the UK government's main agency for funding research and training in engineering and the physical sciences in universities and other organisations throughout the UK. The EPSRC invests around £800m a year in a broad range of subjects – from mathematics to materials science, and from information technology to structural engineering. It also provides advice, disseminates knowledge and promotes public understanding in these areas.

Chair, Dr Paul Golby, CBE, FRENG
Chief Executive, Prof. Philip Nelson, FRENG

MEDICAL RESEARCH COUNCIL*

Polaris House, North Star Avenue, Swindon SN2 1FL
T 01793-416200 W www.mrc.ac.uk

The MRC is a publicly funded organisation dedicated to improving human health. The MRC supports research across the entire spectrum of medical sciences, in universities, hospitals, centres and institutes.

Chair, Donald Brydon, CBE
Chief Executive, Prof. Sir John Savill, FRS, FRSE
Chair, Infections and Immunity Board, Prof. Paul Moss
Chair, Molecular and Cellular Medicine Board, Prof. Anne Ferguson-Smith
Chair, Neurosciences and Mental Health Board, Prof. Patrick Chinnery
Chair, Population and Systems Medicine Board, Prof. Paul Elliott

MRC UNITS, CENTRES AND INSTITUTES

Asthma UK Centre in Allergic Mechanisms of Asthma
W www.asthma-allergy.ac.uk
Behavioural and Clinical Neuroscience Institute (BCNI)
W www.bcni.psychol.cam.ac.uk
Biostatistics Unit W www.mrc-bsu.cam.ac.uk
Brain Network Dynamics Unit W www.mrcbndu.ox.ac.uk
Cancer Unit W www.mrc-cu.cam.ac.uk
Centre for Ageing and Vitality W www.ncl.ac.uk/medicalsciences/research/centres/cav
Centre for Cognitive Ageing and Cognitive Epidemiology
W www.ccace.ed.ac.uk
Centre for Drug Safety Science W www.liverpool.ac.uk/drug-safety
Centre for Environment and Health
W www.environment-health.ac.uk
Centre for Immune Regulation W www.birmingham.ac.uk/research/activity/mds/centres/mrc-immune
Centre for Inflammation Research W www.ed.ac.uk/inflammation-research
Centre for Integrated Research into Musculoskeletal Ageing
W www.cimauk.org
Centre for Medical Mycology, W www.abdn.ac.uk/cmm
Centre for Molecular Bacteriology and Infection,
W www.imperial.ac.uk/mrc-centre-for-molecular-bacteriology-and-infection
Centre for Mouse Genetics W www.har.mrc.ac.uk
Centre for Musculoskeletal Ageing Research
W www.birmingham.ac.uk/generic/mrc-aruk
Centre for Musculoskeletal Health and Work
W www.mrc.soton.ac.uk/cmhw
Centre for Neurodevelopmental Disorders W https://devneuro.org/cndd
Centre for Neuromuscular Diseases W www.cnmd.ac.uk
Centre for Neuropsychiatric Genetics and Genomics
W www.cardiff.ac.uk/mrc-centre-neuropsychiatric-genetics-genomics

Centre for Outbreak Analysis and Modelling
W www.imperial.ac.uk/mrc-outbreaks
Centre for Regenerative Medicine W www.crm.ed.ac.uk
Centre for Reproductive Health W www.ed.ac.uk/centre-reproductive-health
Centre for Transplantation W http://transplantation.kcl.ac.uk
Centre for Virus Research W www.gla.ac.uk/researchinstitutes/iii/cvr
Clinical Trials Unit W www.ctu.mrc.ac.uk
Cognition and Brain Sciences Unit W www.mrc-cbu.cam.ac.uk
Elsie Widdowson Laboratory W www.mrc-ewl.cam.ac.uk
Epidemiology Unit W www.mrc-epid.cam.ac.uk
Francis Crick Institute W www.crick.ac.uk
Human Genetics Unit W www.ed.ac.uk/mrc-human-genetics-unit
Human Immunology Unit W www.imm.ox.ac.uk/mrc-human-immunology-unit
Institute of Hearing Research W www.nottingham.ac.uk/mrcihr
Institute of Genetics and Molecular Medicine W www.ed.ac.uk/igmm
Integrative Epidemiology Unit W www.bristol.ac.uk/integrative-epidemiology
Laboratory of Molecular Biology W www2.mrc-lmb.cam.ac.uk
Laboratory for Molecular Cell Biology W www.ucl.ac.uk/lmcb
Lifecourse Epidemiology Unit W www.mrc.soton.ac.uk
Lifelong Health and Ageing Unit W www.nshd.mrc.ac.uk
London Institute of Medical Sciences W https://lms.mrc.ac.uk
Metabolic Research Laboratories W www.mrl.ims.cam.ac.uk
Mitochondrial Biology Unit W www.mrc-mbu.cam.ac.uk
Molecular Haemotology Unit W www.imm.ox.ac.uk/mrc-molecular-haematology-unit
Oxford Institute for Radiation Oncology W www.rob.ox.ac.uk
Population Health Research Unit W www.mrc-phru.ox.ac.uk
Prion Unit W www.prion.ucl.ac.uk
Protein Phosphorylation and Ubiquitylation Unit
W www.ppu.mrc.ac.uk
Research Complex at Harwell W www.rc-harwell.ac.uk
Scottish Collaboration for Public Health Research and Policy
W www.scphrp.ac.uk
Social and Public Health Sciences Unit W www.gla.ac.uk/researchinstitutes/healthwellbeing/research/mrcsocialandpublichealthsciencesunit
Social, Genetic and Developmental Psychiatry Centre
W www.kcl.ac.uk/ioppn/depts/mrc
Stem Cell Institute W www.stemcells.cam.ac.uk
Toxicology Unit W www.tox.mrc.ac.uk
Weatherall Institute of Molecular Medicine (WIMM)
W www.imm.ox.ac.uk

MRC The Gambia W www.mrc.gm
Uganda Research Unit on AIDS W www.mrcuganda.org

NATIONAL PHYSICAL LABORATORY

Hampton Road, Teddington, Middx TW11 0LW
T 020-8977 3222 W www.npl.co.uk

The National Physical Laboratory (NPL) was established in 1900 and is the UK's national measurement institute. On 1 January 2015 it became a wholly owned government company, part of the Department for Business, Innovation and Skills (now BEIS). It develops, maintains and disseminates national measurement standards for physical quantities such as mass, length, time, temperature, voltage and force. It also conducts underpinning research on engineering materials and information technology, and disseminates good measurement practice.

Chief Executive, Peter Thompson

ASSOCIATION OF INNOVATION, RESEARCH AND TECHNOLOGY ORGANISATIONS LIMITED (AIRTO)

T 020-8943 6600 E enquiries@airto.co.uk W www.airto.co.uk

AIRTO is a membership body, based at the NPL, for organisations operating in the UK's innovation, research and technology sector and represents around 80 per cent of organisations in this sector. AIRTO's members deliver vital innovation and knowledge transfer services which include applied and collaborative research and development (frequently in conjunction with universities), consultancy, technology validation and testing, incubation of commercialisation opportunities and early stage financing. AIRTO members have a combined turnover of over £6.9bn from clients inside and outside the UK, and together employ around 57,200 scientists, technologists and engineers. For a full list of members, see AIRTO's website.

President, Prof. Richard Brook, OBE, FRENG

NATURAL ENVIRONMENT RESEARCH COUNCIL*

Polaris House, North Star Avenue, Swindon SN2 1EU
T 01793-411500 W www.nerc.ac.uk

NERC is the leading funder of independent research, training and innovation in environmental science in the UK. Its work covers the full range of atmospheric, earth, biological, terrestrial and aquatic sciences. NERC invests around £330m a year in research exploring how we can sustainably benefit from our natural resources, predict and respond to natural hazards and understand environmental change. NERC works closely with policymakers and industry to support sustainable economic growth in the UK and around the world.

Chair, Sir Anthony Cleaver
Chief Executive, Prof. Duncan Wingham

RESEARCH CENTRES
BRITISH ANTARCTIC SURVEY, High Cross, Madingley
    Road, Cambridge CB3 OET T 01223-221400
Director, Prof. Dame Jane Francis, DCMG
BRITISH GEOLOGICAL SURVEY, Kingsley Dunham Centre,
    Keyworth, Nottingham NG12 5GG T 0115-936 3100
Executive Director, Prof. John Ludden
CENTRE FOR ECOLOGY AND HYDROLOGY, Maclean
    Building, Benson Lane, Crowmarsh Gifford, Wallingford
    OX10 8BB T 01491-838800
Director, Prof. Mark Bailey

NATIONAL CENTRE FOR ATMOSPHERIC SCIENCE,
    NCAS Headquarters, School of Earth and Environment, University
    of Leeds, Leeds LS2 9JT T 0113-343 6408
Director, Prof. Stephen Mobbs
NATIONAL CENTRE FOR EARTH OBSERVATION,
    Michael Atiyah Building, University of Leicester, University Road,
    Leicester LE1 7RH T 0116-252 2016
Director, Prof. John Remedios
NATIONAL OCEANOGRAPHY CENTRE, University of
    Southampton Waterfront Campus, European Way,
    Southampton SO14 3ZH T 0238-059 6666
Director, Prof. Ed Hill, OBE

SCIENCE AND TECHNOLOGY FACILITIES COUNCIL*

Polaris House, North Star Avenue, Swindon SN2 1SZ
T 01793-442000 W www.stfc.ac.uk

Formed by royal charter in 2007, through the merger of the Council for the Central Laboratory of the Research Councils and the Particle Physics and Astronomy Research Council, the STFC is a non-departmental public body reporting to BEIS.

The STFC invests in large national and international research facilities, while delivering science and technology expertise for the UK. The council is involved in research projects such as the Diamond Light Source Synchrotron and the Large Hadron Collider, and develops new areas of science and technology. The EPSRC has transferred its responsibility for nuclear physics to the STFC.

Chair, Prof. Sir Michael Sterling, FRENG
Chief Executive, Dr Brian Bowsher

RESEARCH CENTRES
BOULBY UNDERGROUND SCIENCE FACILITY, Boulby
    Mine, Loftus, Saltburn-by-the-Sea, Cleveland TS13 4UZ
    T 01287-646300
CHILBOLTON OBSERVATORY, Chilbolton, Stockbridge,
    Hampshire SO20 6BJ T 01264-860391
DARESBURY LABORATORY, SciTech Daresbury, Keckwick
    Lane, Warrington WA4 4AD T 01925-603000
RUTHERFORD APPLETON LABORATORY, Harwell
    Campus, Didcot OX11 0QX T 01235-445000
UK ASTRONOMY TECHNOLOGY CENTRE, Royal
    Observatory Edinburgh, Blackford Hill, Edinburgh EH9 3HJ
    T 0131-668 8100

HEALTH

NATIONAL HEALTH SERVICE

The National Health Service (NHS) came into being on 5 July 1948 under the National Health Service Act 1946, covering England and Wales and, under separate legislation, Scotland and Northern Ireland. The NHS is now administered by the Secretary of State for Health (in England), the Welsh government, the Scottish government and the Northern Ireland Executive.

The function of the NHS is to provide a comprehensive health service designed to secure improvement in the physical and mental health of the people and to prevent, diagnose and treat illness. It was founded on the principle that treatment should be provided according to clinical need rather than ability to pay, and should be free at the point of delivery.

Hospital, mental, dental, nursing, ophthalmic and ambulance services and facilities for the care of expectant and nursing mothers and young children are provided by the NHS to meet all reasonable requirements. Rehabilitation services such as occupational therapy, physiotherapy, speech therapy and surgical and medical appliances are supplied where appropriate. Specialists and consultants who work in NHS hospitals can also engage in private practice, including the treatment of their private patients in NHS hospitals.

STRUCTURE

The structure of the NHS remained relatively stable for the first 30 years of its existence. In 1974, a three-tier management structure comprising regional health authorities, area health authorities and district management teams was introduced in England, and the NHS became responsible for community health services. In 1979, area health authorities were abolished and district management teams were replaced by district health authorities.

The National Health Service and Community Care Act 1990 provided for more streamlined regional health authorities and district health authorities, and for the establishment of family health services authorities (FHSAs) and NHS trusts. The concept of the 'internal market' was introduced into health care, whereby care was provided through NHS contracts where health authorities or boards and GP fundholders (the purchasers) were responsible for buying health care from hospitals, non-fundholding GPs, community services and ambulance services (the providers). The Act also paved the way for the community care reforms, which were introduced in April 1993, and changed the way care is administered for older people, the mentally ill, the physically disabled and people with learning disabilities.

ENGLAND

Under the Health and Social Care Act 2012, which gained royal assent in March 2012, the NHS in England is undergoing a complete operational and budgetary restructure at a cost of approximately £1.4bn. The full implementation of all the changes will not be complete for some time.

Hospitals will be extensively affected by the overhaul, with the cap on income from private hospital patients rising from 1.5 per cent to 49 per cent. All hospitals will become foundation trusts, competing for treatment contracts from clinical commissioning groups (CCGs).

On 1 April 2013 the new commissioning board, NHS England, took on full statutory responsibilities; at the same time, strategic health authorities (SHAs) and primary care trusts (PCTs) which, alongside the Department of Health (DoH), had been responsible for NHS planning and delivery, were abolished. NHS England is an executive non-departmental public body of the DoH with a remit to:

- provide national leadership to improve the quality of care
- oversee the operation of clinical commissioning groups
- allocate resources to clinical commissioning groups
- commission primary care and specialist services

The secretary of state has ultimate responsibility for the provision of a comprehensive health service in England and for ensuring the system works to its optimum capacity to meet the needs of its patients. The DoH is responsible for strategic leadership of the health and social care systems, but will cease to be the headquarters of the NHS, nor will it directly manage any NHS organisations.

In October 2014, NHS England published *Five Year Forward View* which committed the organisation to further change, including additional decentralisation and a greater emphasis on out-of-hospital care and preventative medicine.

NHS ENGLAND, PO Box 16738, Redditch B97 9PT
T 0300-311 2233
W www.england.nhs.uk
Chief Executive, Simon Stevens

CLINICAL COMMISSIONING GROUPS (CCGS)

On 1 April 2013, PCTs, which controlled 80 per cent of the NHS budget and commissioned most NHS services, were abolished. They were replaced with CCGs which took on many of the functions of the PCTs in addition to some functions previously assumed by the Department of Health. All GP practices now belong to a CCG which also includes other health professionals, such as nurses. CCGs commission most services, including:

- mental health and learning disability services
- planned hospital care
- rehabilitative care
- urgent and emergency care (including out-of-hours)
- most community health services

CCGs can commission any service provider that meets NHS standards and costs. These can be NHS hospitals, social enterprises, charities, or private-sector providers. There are around 200 CCGs, which together are responsible for around two-thirds of the NHS budget, around £73.6bn in 2017–18. In April 2015, 64 CCGs were approved to take on the additional responsibility for commissioning GP services within their area.

HEALTH AND WELLBEING BOARDS

Every upper-tier local authority has established a health and wellbeing board to act as a forum for local commissioners across the NHS, social care, public health and other services. There are more than 130 health and wellbeing boards in England, which are intended to:

- encourage integrated commissioning of health and social care services
- increase democratic input into strategic decisions about health and wellbeing services
- strengthen working relationships between health and social care

PUBLIC HEALTH ENGLAND (PHE)

This new organisation was established on 1 April 2013. It provides national leadership and expert services to support public health and also works with local government and the NHS to respond to emergencies. PHE's responsibilities are to:

- coordinate a national public health service
- support the public to make healthier choices
- provide leadership to the public health delivery system
- support the development of the public health workforce

REGULATION
Since the restructuring of the NHS in England began in April 2013, some elements of the regulation system have changed. Responsibility for the regulation of particular aspects of care is shared across a number of different bodies, including the Care Quality Commission (CQC), and individual professional regulatory bodies, such as the General Medical Council, Nursing and Midwifery Council, General Dental Council and the Health and Care Professions Council.

CARE QUALITY COMMISSION (CQC)
The CQC regulates all health and social care services in England, including those provided by the NHS, local authorities, private companies or voluntary organisations. In addition it protects the interests of people detained under the Mental Health Act. The CQC ensures that all essential standards of quality and safety are met where care is provided, from hospitals to private care homes. By law all NHS providers (such as hospitals and ambulance services) must register with the CQC to show they are protecting people from the risk of infection. The CQC possesses a range of legal powers and duties and will take action if providers do not meet essential standards of quality or safety.

NHS IMPROVEMENT
NHS Improvement is responsible for overseeing NHS foundation trusts, NHS trusts and independent providers, helping them give patients consistently high quality, safe and compassionate care within local health systems that are financially sustainable.

HEALTHWATCH
Healthwatch England was established in October 2012 following the restructuring of the NHS. The organisation functions at a national and local level as an independent consumer body, gathering and representing the views of the public about health and social care services in England.

CARE QUALITY COMMISSION, 151 Buckingham Palace Road, London SW1W 9SZ T 03000-616161
W www.cqc.org.uk
Chief Executive, David Behan, CBE
NHS IMPROVEMENTS, Wellington House, 133–155 Waterloo Road, London SE1 8UG T 0300-123 2257 W https://improvement.nhs.uk
Chief Executive, Jim Mackey
HEALTHWATCH, Citygate, Gallowgate, Newcastle upon Tyne NE1 4PA T 0300-068 3000 W www.healthwatch.co.uk
National Director, Imelda Redmond, CBE

AUTHORITIES AND TRUSTS
Overseen by NHS Improvements, all NHS trusts are expected to eventually become foundation trusts.

ACUTE TRUSTS
Hospitals in England are managed by acute trusts. There were 135 acute non-specialist trusts as at July 2017, of which 84 have foundation trust status and 17 acute specialist trusts, of which 16 have foundation trust status. Acute trusts ensure hospitals provide high-quality healthcare and spend money efficiently. They employ a large sector of the NHS workforce, including doctors, nurses, pharmacists, midwives and health visitors. Acute trusts also employ those in supplementary medical professions, such as physiotherapists, radiographers and podiatrists, in addition to many other non-medical staff.

AMBULANCE TRUSTS
There are 10 ambulance services (five foundation trusts) in England, providing emergency services to healthcare.

CLINICAL SENATES AND STRATEGIC CLINICAL NETWORKS
Clinical senates are advisory groups of experts from across health and social care. There are 12 senates covering England comprising clinical leaders from across the healthcare system, in addition to members from social care and public health.

There are 12 strategic clinical networks across England, comprising groups of clinical experts covering a particular disease, patient or professional group. They offer advice to CCGs and NHS England.

Neither organisation is a statutory body, and although they comment on CCG plans to NHS England, they are unable to veto them.

FOUNDATION TRUSTS
NHS foundation trusts are independent legal entities with unique governance arrangements. Each NHS foundation trust has a duty to consult and involve a board of governors in the strategic planning of its organisation. They have financial freedoms and can raise capital from both the public and private sectors within borrowing limits determined by projected cash flows and based on affordability.

MENTAL HEALTH TRUSTS
There are 54 mental health trusts in England, 42 of which have foundation trust status. They provide health and social care services for people with mental health problems.

SPECIAL HEALTH AUTHORITIES
There are 12 Special health authorities with a nationwide remit, including:
* The National Blood and Transplant Authority
* NHS Commissioning Board Authority
* NHS Trust Development Authority

WALES

The NHS Wales was reorganised according to Welsh Assembly commitments laid out in the *One Wales* strategy which came into effect in October 2009. There are now seven local health boards (LHBs) that are responsible for delivering all health care services within a geographical area, rather than the trust and local health board system that existed previously. Community health councils (CHCs) are statutory lay bodies that represent the public for the health service in their region. There are currently eight CHCs.

NHS TRUSTS
There are three NHS trusts in Wales. The Welsh Ambulance Services NHS Trust is for emergency services; the Velindre NHS Trust offers specialist services in cancer care; while Public Health Wales serves as a unified public health organisation for Wales.

LOCAL HEALTH BOARDS
The websites of the seven LHBs, and contact details for community health councils and NHS trusts, are available in the *NHS Wales Directory* on the NHS Wales website (W www.wales.nhs.uk).

ABERTAWE BRO MORGANNWG UNIVERSITY, One Talbot Gateway, Baglan Energy Park, Baglan, Port Talbot SA12 7BR T 01656-752752
Chief Executive (interim), Alex Howells
ANEURIN BEVAN, Headquarters, Lodge Road, Caerleon, Newport NP18 3XQ T 01873-732732
Chief Executive, Judith Paget
BETSI CADWALADR UNIVERSITY, Ysbyty Gwynedd, Penrhosgarnedd, Bangor, Gwynedd LL57 2PW T 01248-384384
Chief Executive, Gary Doherty

CARDIFF AND VALE UNIVERSITY, Cardigan House, University Hospital of Wales, Heath Park, Cardiff CF14 4XW T 029-2074 7747
Chief Executive, Len Richards

CWM TAF UNIVERSITY, Ynysmeurig House, Navigation Park, Abercynon CF45 4SN T 01443-744800
Chief Executive, Allison Williams

HYWEL DDA, Corporate Offices, Ystwyth Building, Hafan Derwen, Jobswell Road, Carmarthen SA31 3BB T 01267-235151
Chief Executive, Steve Moore

POWYS TEACHING, Glasbury House, Bronllys Hospital, Bronllys, Brecon, Powys LD3 0LS T 01874-771661
Chief Executive, Carol Shillabeer

SCOTLAND

The Scottish government Health and Social Care Directorates are responsible both for NHS Scotland and for the development and implementation of health and community care policy. The chief executive of NHS Scotland leads the central management of the NHS, is accountable to ministers for the efficiency and performance of the service and heads the Health Department which oversees the work of the 14 regional health boards. These boards provide strategic management for the entire local NHS system and are responsible for ensuring that services are delivered effectively and efficiently.

In addition to the 14 regional health boards there are a further seven special boards and one public health body, which provide national services, such as the Scottish ambulance service and NHS Health Scotland. Healthcare Improvement Scotland, was formed on 1 April 2011 by the Public Services Reform Act 2010 to improve the quality of Scottish healthcare.

REGIONAL HEALTH BOARDS

AYRSHIRE AND ARRAN, Eglinton House, Ailsa Hospital, Dalmellington Road, Ayr KA6 6AB T 0800-169 1441
W www.nhsaaa.net
Chief Executive, John Burns

BORDERS, Borders General Hospital, Melrose, Roxburghshire TD6 9BS T 01896-826000 W www.nhsborders.scot.nhs.uk
Chief Executive, Jane Davidson

DUMFRIES AND GALLOWAY, Crichton Hall, Dumfries DG1 4TG T 01387-246246 W www.nhsdg.scot.nhs.uk
Chief Executive, Jeff Ace

EILEAN SIAR (WESTERN ISLES), 37 South Beach Street, Stornoway, Isle of Lewis HS1 2BB T 01851-702997
W www.wihb.scot.nhs.uk
Chief Executive, Gordon Jamieson

FIFE, Hayfield House, Hayfield Road, Kirkcaldy, Fife KY2 5AH T 01592-643355 W www.nhsfife.org
Chief Executive, Paul Hawkins

FORTH VALLEY, Carseview House, Castle Business Park, Stirling FK9 4SW T 01786-463031 W www.nhsforthvalley.com
Chief Executive (interim), Fiona Ramsay

GRAMPIAN, Summerfield House, 2 Eday Road, Aberdeen AB15 6RE T 0345-456 6000 W www.nhsgrampian.org
Chief Executive, Malcolm Wright

GREATER GLASGOW AND CLYDE, J B Russell House, Gartnavel Royal Hospital Campus, 1055 Great Western Road, Glasgow G12 0XH T 0141-201 4444 W www.nhsgg.org.uk
Chief Executive, Jane Grant

HIGHLAND, Assynt House, Beechwood Park, Inverness IV2 3BW T 01463-717123 W www.nhshighland.scot.nhs.uk
Chief Executive, Elaine Mead

LANARKSHIRE, Kirklands, Fallside Road, Bothwell G71 8BB T 01236-748748 W www.nhslanarkshire.org.uk
Chief Executive, Calum Campbell

LOTHIAN, Waverley Gate, 2–4 Waterloo Place, Edinburgh EH1 3EG T 0131-536 9000 W www.nhslothian.scot.nhs.uk

Chief Executive, Tim Davison

ORKNEY, Garden House, New Scapa Road, Kirkwall, Orkney KW15 1BQ T 01856-888000 W www.ohb.scot.nhs.uk
Chief Executive, Cathie Cowan

SHETLAND, Upper Floor Montfield, Burgh Road, Lerwick ZE1 0LA T 01595-743060 W www.shb.scot.nhs.uk
Chief Executive, Ralph Roberts

TAYSIDE, Level 10, Ninewells Hospital, Dundee DD1 9SY T 01382-660111 W www.nhstayside.scot.nhs.uk
Chief Executive, Lesley McLay

NORTHERN IRELAND

On 1 April 2009 the four health and social services boards in Northern Ireland were replaced by a single health and social care board for the whole of Northern Ireland. The new board together with its local commissioning groups (whose boundaries are subject to review pending the outcome of local government reform) are responsible for improving the health and social wellbeing of people in the area for which they are responsible, planning and commissioning services, and coordinating the delivery of services in a cost-effective manner. In March 2016, the health minister announced plans to abolish the health and social care board, with all commissioning powers to be transferred to the Department of Health and a new group being established to hold the five Northern Ireland trusts to account.

HEALTH AND SOCIAL CARE BOARD, 12–22 Linenhall Street, Belfast BT2 8BS T 030-0555 0115
W www.hscboard.hscni.net
Chief Executive, Valerie Watts

FINANCE

The NHS is still funded mainly through general taxation, although in recent years more reliance has been placed on the NHS element of national insurance contributions, patient charges and other sources of income.

Funding for NHS England was set at £106bn for 2017–18. Expenditure for the NHS in Wales, Scotland and Northern Ireland is set by the devolved governments.

EMPLOYEES AND SALARIES

NHS ENGLAND HEALTH SERVICE STAFF 2017
Full-time equivalent

All hospital, community and dental staff	1,162,996
Consultants	46,574
Ambulance staff	20,066
Qualified nursing and midwifery staff	342,473
Qualified scientific, therapeutic and technical staff	148,412

Source: NHS Digital

SALARIES

Many general practitioners (GPs) are self-employed and hold contracts, either on their own or as part of a Clinical Commissioning Group (CCG). The profit of GPs varies according to the services they provide for their patients and the way they choose to provide these services. Salaried GPs who are part of a CCG earn between £56,525 and £85,298. Most NHS dentists are self-employed contractors. A contract for dentists was introduced on 1 April 2006 which provides dentists with an annual income in return for carrying out an agreed amount, or units, of work. A salaried dentist employed by the NHS, who works mainly with community dental services earn between £38,861 and £83,118.

BASIC SALARIES FOR HOSPITAL MEDICAL AND
DENTAL STAFF 2017–18

From 1 April 2017 to 31 March 2018 staff who are on the top salary in their pay band will receive a non-consolidated lump sum, payable in monthly instalments, of either 1 or 2 per cent of their basic pay dependent on the length of time they have been on the top salary in their pay band. The figures below do not include merit awards, discretionary points or banding supplements.

Consultant (2003 contract)	£76,761–£103,490
Specialist registrar	£31,931–£48,123
Speciality registrar (full)	£30,605–£48,123
Speciality registrar (fixed term)	£30,605–£40,491
Foundation doctor year 2	£28,640–£32,386
Foundation doctor year 1	£23,091–£25,973

NURSES

From 1 December 2004 the *Agenda for Change* pay system was introduced throughout the UK for all NHS staff with the exception of medical and dental staff, doctors in public health medicine and the community health service. Nurses' salaries are incorporated in the *Agenda for Change* nine band pay structure, which provides additional payments for flexible working such as providing out-of-hours services, working weekends and nights and being on-call. There is also additional payments for those staff who work in high-cost areas such as London.

SALARIES FOR NURSES AND MIDWIVES *from 1 April 2017*

Nurse/Midwife consultant	£40,428–£69,168
Modern matron	£40,428–£48,514
Nurse advanced/team manager	£31,696–£41,787
Midwife higher level	£31,696–£41,787
Nurse specialist/team leader	£26,565–£35,577
Hospital/community midwife	£26,565–£35,577
Registered nurse/entry level midwife*	£22,128–£28,746

*The starting salary in Wales is currently the same as in England. The starting salary is £22,440 in Scotland and £21,909 in Northern Ireland.

HEALTH SERVICES

PRIMARY CARE

Primary care comprises the services provided by general practitioners, community health centres, pharmacies, dental practices and opticians. Primary nursing care includes the work carried out by practice nurses, community nurses, community midwives and health visitors.

PRIMARY MEDICAL SERVICES

In England, primary medical services (PMS) are provided by 42,250 registerd GPs, working in around 7,500 GP practices, with 57.9 million registered patients.

In Wales, responsibility for primary medical services rests with local health boards (LHBs), in Scotland with the 14 regional health boards and in Northern Ireland with the Health and Social Care Board.

Any vocationally trained doctor may provide general or personal medical services. GPs may also have private fee-paying patients, but not if that patient is already an NHS patient on that doctor's patient list.

A person who is ordinarily resident in the UK is eligible to register with a GP (or PM/S provider) for free primary care treatment. Should a patient have difficulty in registering with a doctor, he or she should contact the local CCG for help. When a person is away from home he/she can still access primary care treatment from a GP if they ask to be treated as a temporary resident. In an emergency any doctor in the service will give treatment and advice.

GPs or CCGs are responsible for the care of their patients 24 hours a day, seven days a week, but can fulfil the terms of their contract by delegating or transferring responsibility for out-of-hours care to an accredited provider.

In addition, NHS walk-in centres (WICs) throughout England are usually open seven days a week, from early in the morning until late in the evening. They are nurse-led and provide treatment for minor illnesses and injuries, health information and self-help advice. Some WICs are not able to treat young children.

HEALTH COSTS

Some people are exempt from, or entitled to help with, health costs such as prescription charges, ophthalmic and dental costs, and in some cases help towards travel costs to and from hospital.

The following list is intended as a general guide to those who may be entitled to help, or who are exempt from some of the charges relating to the above:

- children under 16 and young people in full-time education who are under 19
- people aged 60 or over
- pregnant women and women who have had a baby in the last 12 months and have a valid maternity exemption certificate (MatEx)
- people, or their partners, who are in receipt of income support, income-based jobseeker's allowance and/or income-based employment and support allowance
- people in receipt of the pension credit
- diagnosed glaucoma patients, people who have been advised by an ophthalmologist that they are at risk of glaucoma and people aged 40 or over who have an immediate family member who is a diagnosed glaucoma patient
- NHS in-patients
- NHS out-patients for all prescribed contraceptives, medication given at a hospital, NHS walk-in centre, personally administered by a GP or supplied at a hospital or primary care trust clinic for the treatment of tuberculosis or a sexually transmissible infection
- out-patients of the NHS Hospital Dental Service
- people registered blind or partially sighted
- people who need complex lenses
- war pensioners whose treatment/prescription is for their accepted disablement and who have a valid exemption certificate
- people who are entitled to, or named on, a valid NHS tax credit exemption or HC2 certificate
- people who have a medical exemption (MedEx) certificate, including those with cancer or diabetes

People in other circumstances may also be eligible for help; *see* booklet HC12 (England) and HCS2 (Scotland) for further information.

WALES

On 1 April 2007 all prescription charges (including those for medical supports and appliances and wigs) for people living in Wales were abolished. The above guide still applies for NHS dental and optical charges although all people aged under 25 living in Wales are also entitled to free dental examinations.

SCOTLAND

On 1 April 2011 all prescription charges in Scotland were abolished. Those entitled to free prescriptions in Scotland include patients registered with a Scottish GP and receiving a prescription from a Scottish pharmacy, and Scottish patients who have an English GP and an entitlement card.

NORTHERN IRELAND

On 1 April 2010 all prescription charges in Northern Ireland were abolished. All prescriptions dispensed in Northern Ireland are free, even for patients visiting from England, Wales or Scotland.

PHARMACEUTICAL SERVICES

Patients may obtain medicines and appliances under the NHS from any pharmacy whose owner has entered into arrangements with the CCG to provide this service. There are also some suppliers who only provide special appliances. In rural areas, where access to a pharmacy may be difficult, patients may be able to obtain medicines, etc, from a dispensing doctor.

In England, a charge of £8.60 is payable for each item supplied (except for contraceptives for which there is no charge), unless the patient is exempt and the declaration on the back of the prescription form is completed. Prescription prepayment certificates (£29.10 valid for three months, £104.00 valid for a year) may be purchased by those patients not entitled to exemption who require frequent prescriptions.

DENTAL SERVICES

Dentists, like doctors, may take part in the NHS and also have private patients. Dentists are responsible to the local health provider in whose areas they provide services. Patients may go to any dentist who is taking part in the NHS and is willing to accept them. There is a three-tier payment system based on the individual course of treatment required.

NHS DENTAL CHARGES from 1 April 2017

	England/Wales
Band 1* – Examination, diagnosis, preventive care (eg x-rays, scale and polish)	£20.60/£14.00
Band 2 – Band 1 + basic additional treatment (eg fillings and extractions	£56.30/£44.00
Band 3 – Bands 1 and 2 + all other treatment (eg crowns, dentures and bridges)	£244.30/£190.00

* Urgent and out-of-hours treatment is also charged at this payment tier

The cost of individual treatment plans should be known prior to treatment and some dental practices may require payment in advance. There is no charge for writing a prescription or removing stitches and only one charge is payable for each course of treatment even if more than one visit to the dentist is required. If additional treatment is required within two months of visiting the dentist and this is covered by the course of treatment most recently paid for (eg payment was made for the second tier of treatment but an additional filling is required) then this will be provided free of charge.

SCOTLAND AND NORTHERN IRELAND

Scotland and Northern Ireland have yet to simplify their charging systems. NHS dental patients pay 80 per cent of the cost of the individual items of treatment provided up to a maximum of £384. Patients in Scotland are entitled to free basic and extensive examinations.

GENERAL OPHTHALMIC SERVICES

General ophthalmic services are administered by local health providers. Testing of sight may be carried out by any ophthalmic medical practitioner or ophthalmic optician (optometrist). The optician must give the prescription to the patient, who can take this to any supplier of glasses to have them dispensed. Only registered opticians can supply glasses to children and to people registered as blind or partially sighted.

Free eyesight tests and help towards the cost are available to people in certain circumstances. Help is also available for the purchase of glasses or contact lenses (see Health Costs). In Scotland eye examinations, which include a sight test, are free to all UK residents. Help is available for the purchase of glasses or contact lenses to those entitled to help with health costs in the same way it is available to those in England and Wales.

CHILD HEALTH SERVICES

Pre-school services at GP surgeries or child health clinics provide regular monitoring of children's physical, mental and emotional health and development and advise parents on their children's health and welfare.

NHS 111, NHS DIRECT AND NHS 24

NHS Direct Wales is a website and 24-hour nurse-led advice telephone service for Wales. It provides medical advice as well as directing people to the appropriate part of the NHS for treatment if necessary. (T 0845 46 47 W www.nhsdirect.wales.nhs.uk). NHS Direct had also operated in England but closed on 31 March 2014. Non-urgent 24-hour nurse-led advice in England can be accessed via the NHS 111 service (T 111).

NHS 24 provides an equivalent service for Scotland (T 111 W www.nhs24.com).

SECONDARY CARE AND OTHER SERVICES

HOSPITALS

NHS hospitals provide acute and specialist care services, treating conditions which normally cannot be dealt with by primary care specialists, and provide for medical emergencies.

NUMBER OF BEDS 2016–17

	Average daily	
	available beds	occupation of beds
England	131,060	116,598
Wales*	10,935	9,505
Scotland	15,495	12,861
Northern Ireland*	5,887	4,927

* Figures are for 2015–16
Sources: NHS England, Welsh government, ISD Scotland, Northern Ireland Executive

HOSPITAL CHARGES

Acute or foundation trusts can provide hospital accommodation in single rooms or small wards, if not required for patients who need privacy for medical reasons. The patient is still an NHS patient, but there may be a charge for these additional facilities. Acute or foundation trusts can charge for certain patient services that are considered to be additional treatments over and above the normal hospital service provision. There is no blanket policy to cover this and each case is considered in the light of the patient's clinical need. However, if an item or service is considered to be an integral part of a patient's treatment by their clinician, then a charge should not be made.

In some NHS hospitals, accommodation and services are available for the treatment of private patients where it does not interfere with care for NHS patients. Income generated by treating private patients is then put back into local NHS services. Private patients undertake to pay the full costs of medical treatment, accommodation, medication and other related services. Charges for private patients are set locally.

WAITING LISTS

England
During May 2017, 310,125 referral to treatment (RTT) patients started admitted treatment and 1,065,586 started non-admitted treatment. Of the admitted patients, 91.3 per cent were waiting up to 23 weeks, and for patients waiting to start treatment the median waiting time was six weeks.
Wales
In the quarter ending March 2017, 88 per cent of 434,536 patients were treated within 26 weeks and 95.5 per cent were treated within 36 weeks of the date the referral letter was received by the hospital. Neither the 26 and 36 week targets for new patients receiving treatment have been met since September 2011.
Scotland

In the quarter ending March 2017, 83.2 per cent of patients were seen within the 18 week RTT standard. 82.1 per cent of patients waiting for a new outpatient appointment in the same month had waited 12 weeks or less.

Northern Ireland
From March 2017 the aim was for at least 50 per cent of patients to wait no longer than nine weeks for a first outpatient appointment, with no patient waiting longer than 52 weeks. The total number of people waiting for a first outpatient appointment at the end of March 2017 was 253,093, of these 69.6 per cent had been waiting over nine weeks, compared with just 63.2 per cent at the end of March 2016. The number of people waiting to be admitted to hospital in Northern Ireland at the end of March 2017 was 71,483 – of these, 56 per cent had been waiting for more than 13 weeks.

AMBULANCE SERVICE
The NHS provides emergency ambulance services free of charge via the 999 emergency telephone service. Air ambulances, provided through local charities and partially funded by the NHS, are used throughout the UK. They assist with cases where access may be difficult or heavy traffic could hinder road progress. Non-emergency ambulance services are provided free to patients who are deemed to require them on medical grounds.

Since 1 April 2001 all services have had a system of call prioritisation. Since 2017, ambulances have been expected to reach Red 1 – calls requiring a defibrillator – and Red 2 emergency calls within seven minutes, at least 75 per cent of the time. Non-emergency calls are categorised as Green 1, 2, 3 or 4, with category Green 4 calls being the least serious. Green calls are generally responded to between 20 minutes and one hour.

In 2016 it was agreed that all ambulance staff were to be re-banded from a band 5 to a band 6 under the *Agenda for Change* pay scale. In 2017, the NHS employed 19,772 qualified ambulance staff in England earning between £16,968 (emergency care assistant) and £35,557 (senior paramedic).

BLOOD AND TRANSPLANT SERVICES
There are four national bodies which coordinate the blood donor programme and transplant and related services in the UK. Donors give blood at local centres on a voluntary basis.

NHS BLOOD AND TRANSPLANT, Oak House, Reeds Crescent, Watford, Herts WD24 4QN **T** 0300-123 2323 **W** www.nhsbt.nhs.uk

WELSH BLOOD SERVICE, Ely Valley Road, Talbot Green, Pontyclun CF72 9WB **T** 0800-252 2266 **W** www.welsh-blood.org.uk

SCOTTISH NATIONAL BLOOD TRANSFUSION SERVICE, 21 Ellen's Glen Road, Edinburgh EH17 7QT **T** 0131-314536 5510 **W** www.scotblood.co.uk

NORTHERN IRELAND BLOOD TRANSFUSION SERVICE, Lisburn Road, Belfast BT9 7TS **T** 028-9032 1414 **W** www.nibts.org

HOSPICES
Hospice or palliative care may be available for patients with life-threatening illnesses. It may be provided at the patient's home in a voluntary or NHS hospice or in hospital, and is intended to ensure the best possible quality of life for the patient, and to provide help and support to both the patient and the patient's family. The National Council for Palliative Care coordinates NHS and voluntary services in England, Wales and Northern Ireland; the Scottish Partnership for Palliative Care performs the same function in Scotland.

NATIONAL COUNCIL FOR PALLIATIVE CARE, Hospice House, 34–44 Britannia Street, London WC1X 9JG **T** 020-7697 1520 **W** www.ncpc.org.uk

SCOTTISH PARTNERSHIP FOR PALLIATIVE CARE, CBC House, 24 Canning Street, Edinburgh EH3 8EG **T** 0131-272 2735 **W** www.palliativecarescotland.org.uk

COMPLAINTS
Patient advice and liaison services (PALS) have been established for every NHS and PCT in England. PALS can give advice on local complaints procedure, or resolve concerns informally. If the case is not resolved locally or the complainant is not satisfied with the way a local NHS body or practice has dealt with their complaint, they may approach the Parliamentary and Health Service Ombudsman in England, the Scottish Public Services Ombudsman, Public Services Ombudsman for Wales or the Northern Ireland Commissioner for Complaints. *See* Ombudsman Services.

HEALTH ADVICE AND MEDICAL TREATMENT ABROAD

IMMUNISATION
Country-by-country guidance is set out on the website **W** www.fitfortravel.nhs.uk

RECIPROCAL ARRANGEMENTS
The European Health Insurance Card (EHIC) allows UK residents access to state-provided healthcare while temporarily travelling in all European Economic Area countries and Switzerland either free or at a reduced cost. A card is free, valid for up to five years and should be obtained before travelling. Applications can be made by telephone (**T** 0300 330 1350) online (**W** www.ehic.org.uk) or by post (a form is available from the post office).

The UK also has bilateral agreements with several other countries, including Australia and New Zealand, for the free provision of urgent medical treatment.

European Economic Area nationals visiting the UK and visitors from other countries with which the UK has bilateral health care agreements are able to receive emergency health care on the NHS on the same terms as is available to UK residents.

SOCIAL WELFARE

SOCIAL SERVICES

The Secretary of State for Health (in England), the Welsh government, the Scottish government and the Secretary of State for Northern Ireland are responsible, under the Local Authority Social Services Act 1970, for the provision of social services for older people, disabled people, families and children, and those with mental disorders. Personal social services are administered by local authorities according to policies, with standards set by central and devolved government. Each authority has a director and a committee responsible for the social services functions placed upon them. Local authorities provide, enable and commission care after assessing the needs of their population. The private and voluntary sectors also play an important role in the delivery of social services, and an estimated 7 million people in the UK provide substantial regular care for a member of their family.

The Care Quality Commission (CQC) was established in April 2009, bringing together the independent regulation of health, mental health and adult social care. Prior to 1 April 2009 this work was carried out by three separate organisations: the Healthcare Commission, the Mental Health Act Commission and the Commission for Social Care Inspection. The CQC is responsible for the registration of health and social care providers, the monitoring and inspection of all health and adult social care, issuing fines, public warnings or closures if standards are not met and for undertaking regular performance reviews. Since April 2007 the Office for Standards in Education, Children's Services and Skills (Ofsted) has been responsible for inspecting and regulating all care services for children and young people in England. Both Ofsted and CQC collate information on local care services and make this information available to the public.

The Care and Social Services Inspectorate Wales (CSSIW), an operationally independent part of the Welsh government, is responsible for the regulation and inspection of all social care services in Wales. A new unified body, the Care Inspectorate, was established on 1 April 2011, replacing the Scottish Commission for the Regulation of Care (the Care Commission) and is now the independent care services regulator for Scotland.

The Department of Health is responsible for social care in Northern Ireland.

CARE QUALITY COMMISSION (CQC), Citygate, Gallowgate, Newcastle upon Tyne NE1 4PA T 0300-061 6161 W www.cqc.org.uk

OFFICE FOR STANDARDS IN EDUCATION, CHILDREN'S SERVICES AND SKILLS (Ofsted), Piccadilly Gate, Store Street, Manchester M1 2WD T 0300-123 1231 E enquiries@ofsted.gov.uk W www.gov.uk/government/organisations/ofsted

CARE AND SOCIAL SERVICES INSPECTORATE WALES (CSSIW), Welsh Government Office, Rhydcar Business Park, Merthyr Tydfil CF48 1UZ T 0300-790 0126 E cssiw@wales.gsi.gov.uk W www.cssiw.org.uk

CARE INSPECTORATE, Compass House, 11 Riverside Drive, Dundee DD1 4NY T 0845-600 9527 E enquiries@careinspectorate.com W www.careinspectorate.com

DEPARTMENT OF HEALTH, Castle Buildings, Stormont, Belfast BT4 3SQ T 028-9052 0500 E webmaster@health-ni.gov.uk W www.health-ni.gov.uk

STAFF	
Total Social Services Staff (England, full-time)	120,200
Community	40,868
Residential	26,444
Other	25,242
Domiciliary	16,828
Day	10,818

Source: Health and Social Care Information Centre 2016

OLDER PEOPLE

Services for older people are designed to enable them to remain living in their own homes for as long as possible. Local authority services include advice, domestic help, meals in the home, alterations to the home to aid mobility, emergency alarm systems, day and/or night attendants, laundry services and the provision of day centres and recreational facilities. Charges may be made for these services. Respite care may also be provided in order to allow carers temporary relief from their responsibilities.

Local authorities and the private sector also provide 'sheltered housing' for older people, sometimes with resident wardens.

If an older person is admitted to a residential home, charges are made according to a means test; if the person cannot afford to pay, the costs are met by the local authority.

DISABLED PEOPLE

Services for disabled people are designed to enable them to remain living in their own homes wherever possible. Local authority services include advice, adaptations to the home, meals in the home, help with personal care, occupational therapy, educational facilities and recreational facilities. Respite care may also be provided in order to allow carers temporary relief from their responsibilities.

Special housing may be available for disabled people who can live independently, and residential accommodation for those who cannot.

FAMILIES AND CHILDREN

Local authorities are required to provide services aimed at safeguarding the welfare of children in need and, wherever possible, allowing them to be brought up by their families. Services include advice, counselling, help in the home and the provision of family centres. Many authorities also provide short-term refuge accommodation for women and children.

DAY CARE

In allocating day care places to children, local authorities give priority to children with special needs, whether in terms of their health, learning abilities or social needs. Since September 2001, Ofsted has been responsible for the regulation and registration of all early years childcare and education provision in England (previously the responsibility of the local authorities). All day care and childminding services that care for children under eight years of age for more than two hours a day must register with Ofsted and are inspected at least every two years. As at 31 March 2017, there were 81,400 providers in England.

CHILD PROTECTION

Children considered to be at risk of physical injury, neglect or sexual abuse are placed on the local authority's child protection register. Local authority social services staff, schools, health visitors and other agencies work together to prevent and detect cases of abuse. As at 31 March 2016, there was a total of 58,239 children on child protection registers or subject to a child protection plan in the UK. In England, there were 50,310 children on child protection registers, of these, 23,150 were at risk of neglect, 4,200 of physical abuse, 2,370 of sexual abuse and 17,770 of emotional abuse. At 31 March (July in Scotland) 2016 there were 3,060 children on child protection registers in Wales, 2,723 in Scotland and 2,146 in Northern Ireland.

LOCAL AUTHORITY CARE

Local authorities are required to provide accommodation for children who have no parents or guardians or whose parents or guardians are unable or unwilling to care for them. A family proceedings court may also issue a care order where a child is being neglected or abused, or is not attending school; the court must be satisfied that this would positively contribute to the well-being of the child.

The welfare of children in local authority care must be properly safeguarded. Children may be placed with foster families, who receive payments to cover the expenses of caring for the child or children, or in residential care.

Children's homes may be run by the local authority or by the private or voluntary sectors; all homes are subject to inspection procedures. As at 31 March 2016, 70,440 children in the UK were in the care of local authorities, of these, 51,850 were in foster placements and 7,600 were in children's homes, hostels or secure units.

ADOPTION

Local authorities are required to provide an adoption service, either directly or via approved voluntary societies. In 2015–16, 4,690 children in local authority care were adopted.

PEOPLE WITH LEARNING DISABILITIES

Services for people with learning disabilities are designed to enable them to remain living in the community wherever possible. Local authority services include short-term care, support in the home, the provision of day care centres, and help with other activities outside the home. Residential care is provided for the severely or profoundly disabled.

MENTALLY ILL PEOPLE

Under the care programme approach, mentally ill people should be assessed by specialist services and receive a care plan. A key worker should be appointed for each patient and regular reviews of the person's progress should be conducted. Local authorities provide help and advice to mentally ill people and their families, and places in day centres and social centres. Social workers can apply for a mentally disturbed person to be compulsorily detained in hospital. Where appropriate, mentally ill people are provided with accommodation in special hospitals, local authority accommodation, or at homes run by private or voluntary organisations. Patients who have been discharged from hospitals may be placed on a supervision register.

NATIONAL INSURANCE

The National Insurance (NI) scheme operates under the Social Security Contributions and Benefits Act 1992 and the Social Security Administration Act 1992, and orders and regulations made thereunder. The scheme is financed by contributions payable by earners, employers and others (*see* below). Money collected under the scheme is used to finance the National Insurance Fund (from which contributory benefits are paid) and to contribute to the cost of the National Health Service.

NATIONAL INSURANCE FUND

Estimated receipts, payments and statement of balances of the National Insurance Fund for 2017–18:

Receipts	£ million
Net national insurance contributions	99,217
Compensation from the Consolidated Fund for statutory sick, maternity, paternity and adoption pay recoveries	2,599
Income from investments	44
State scheme premiums	0
Other receipts	0
TOTAL RECEIPTS	101,860

Payments	£ million
Benefits	
At present rates	98,319
Increase due to proposed rate changes	1,952
Administration costs	841
Redundancy fund payments	274
Transfer to Northern Ireland	575
Other payments	177
TOTAL PAYMENTS	102,139

Balances	£ million
Balance at the beginning of the year	21,151
Excess of receipts over payments	(279)
BALANCE AT END OF YEAR	20,872

CONTRIBUTIONS

There are six classes of National Insurance contributions (NICs):

Class 1	paid by employees and their employers
Class 1A	paid by employers who provide employees with certain benefits in kind for private use, such as company cars
Class 1B	paid by employers who enter into a pay as you earn (PAYE) settlement agreement (PSA) with HM Revenue and Customs
Class 2	paid by self-employed people
Class 3	voluntary contributions paid to protect entitlement to the state pension for those who do not pay enough NI contributions in another class
Class 4	paid by the self-employed on their taxable profits over a set limit. These are normally paid by self-employed people in addition to class 2 contributions. Class 4 contributions do not count towards benefits.

The lower and upper earnings limits and the percentage rates referred to below apply from April 2017 to April 2018.

CLASS 1

Class 1 contributions are paid where a person:
- is an employed earner (employee), office holder (eg company director) or employed under a contract of service in Great Britain or Northern Ireland
- is 16 or over and under state pension age
- earns at or above the earnings threshold of £157.00 per week (including overtime pay, bonus, commission, etc, without deduction of superannuation contributions)

Class 1 contributions are made up of primary and secondary contributions. Primary contributions are those paid by the employee and these are deducted from earnings by the employer. Since 6 April 2001 the employee's and employer's earnings thresholds have been the same and are referred to as the earnings threshold. Primary contributions are not paid on earnings below the earnings threshold of £157.00 per week. However, between the lower earnings limit of £113.00 per week and the earnings threshold of £157.00 per week, NI contributions are treated as having been paid to protect the benefit entitlement position of lower earners. Contributions are payable at the rate of 12 per cent on earnings between the earnings threshold and the upper earnings limit of £866.00 per week. Above the upper earnings limit 2 per cent is payable.

Some married women or widows pay a reduced rate of 5.85 per cent on earnings between the earnings threshold and upper earnings limits and 2 per cent above this. It is no longer possible to elect to pay the reduced rate but those who had reduced liability before 12 May 1977 may retain it for as long as certain conditions are met.

Secondary contributions are paid by employers of employed earners at the rate of 13.8 per cent on all earnings above the earnings threshold of £157 per week. There is no upper earnings limit for employers' contributions.

CLASS 2

Class 2 contributions are paid where a person is self-employed and is 16 or over and under state pension age. Contributions are paid at a flat rate of £2.85 per week regardless of the amount earned. However, those with earnings of less than £6,025 a year can apply for small earnings exception. Those granted exemption from class 2 contributions may pay class 2 or class 3 contributions voluntarily. Self-employed earners (whether or not they pay class 2 contributions) may also be liable to pay class 4 contributions based on profits. There are special rules for those who are concurrently employed and self-employed.

Married women and widows can no longer choose not to pay class 2 contributions but those who elected not to pay class 2 contributions before 12 May 1977 may retain the right for as long as certain conditions are met.

Class 2 contributions are assessed and collected annually by HM Revenue and Customs (HMRC) as part of the self-assessment tax bill. For self-employed people that do not pay tax through self-assessment, a bill is issued by HMRC by the end of October.

CLASS 3

Class 3 contributions are voluntary flat-rate contributions of £14.25 per week payable by persons over the age of 16 who would otherwise be unable to qualify for retirement pension and certain other benefits because they have an insufficient record of class 1 or class 2 contributions. This may include those who are not working, those not liable for class 1 or class 2 contributions, or those excepted from class 2 contributions. Married women and widows who on or before 11 May 1977 elected not to pay class 1 (full rate) or class 2 contributions cannot pay class 3 contributions while they retain this right. Class 3 contributions are collected by HMRC by quarterly bills or monthly direct debit. One-off payments can also be made.

CLASS 4

Self-employed people whose profits and gains are over £8,164 a year pay class 4 contributions in addition to class 2 contributions. This applies to self-employed earners over 16 and under the state pension age. Class 4 contributions are calculated at 9 per cent of annual profits or gains between £8,164 and £45,000 and 2 per cent above. Class 4 contributions are assessed and collected annually by HMRC as part of the self-assessment tax bill. It is possible, in some circumstances, to apply for exceptions from liability to pay class 4 contributions or to have the amount of contribution reduced.

PENSIONS

Many people will qualify for a state pension; however, there are further pension choices available, such as workplace, personal and stakeholder pensions. There are also other non-pension savings and investment options.

STATE PENSION

From 6 April 2016, the system of basic and additional state pension was replaced with a new scheme for people reaching state pension age after that date (ie men born on or after 6 April 1951, and women born on or after 6 April 1953).

Those that reached state pension age before this date continue to receive their state pension in line with existing rules. Information about the new state pension can be found online (www.gov.uk/new-state-pension).

The state pension does not have to be claimed at state pension age, people can delay claiming it to earn weekly state pension or a lump sum payment. For the new state pension scheme from 6 April 2016 additional qualifying years can be added to a person's national insurance record until the person reaches the full new state pension amount or the state pension age – whichever is first.

STATE PENSION SCHEME FOR THOSE WHO REACHED STATE PENSION AGE BEFORE 6 APRIL 2016

The system consists of:
- basic state pension
- additional state pension

Basic State Pension
The amount of basic state pension paid is dependent on the number of 'qualifying years' a person has established during their working life. In 2017–18, the full basic state pension is £122.30 a week (*see also* Benefits, State Pension: Categories A and B).

NEW STATE PENSION

The full rate of the new state pension, for people reaching state pension age on or after 6 April 2016, is £159.55 for a single person in 2017–18. It is set at a level that is above the basic level of means-tested support, the standard minimum guarantee in pension credit.

The amounts of state pension people will receive under the new system will also be based on their NI record, with NI contributions or credits made prior to 6 April 2016 recognised under transitional arrangements.

NI contributions and credits will be used to calculate a 'starting amount' under the new system. An individual's starting amount will be the higher of either:
- the value of NI contributions under the current state pension rules (basic state pension, additional state pension and graduated retirement benefit)
- the value of NI contributions if the new state pension had been in place at the start of their working life

A deduction may be made to these amounts for periods an individual was contracted out of the additional state pension before 6 April 2016.

A minimum of 10 qualifying years will usually be needed to get any new state pension.

WORKING LIFE

The working life is from the start of the tax year (6 April) in which a person reaches 16 to the end of the tax year (5 April) before the one in which they reach state pension age (*see* State Pension Age).

QUALIFYING YEARS

A 'qualifying year' is a tax year in which a person has sufficient earnings upon which they have paid, are treated as having paid, or have been credited with national insurance (NI) contributions (*see* National Insurance Credits).

From 6 April 2016 a full new state pension (£159.55 in 2017–18) is payable to those individuals who have 35 qualifying years on their national insurance record. Individuals usually need at least ten qualifying years and will receive a proportion of the new state pension if they have between ten and 35 qualifying years.

Between 6 April 2010 and 5 April 2016, a person who has 30 qualifying years will be entitled to a full basic state pension. Someone with less than 30 qualifying years will be entitled to a proportion of the full basic state pension based on the number of qualifying years they have. Just one qualifying year, achieved through paid or credited contributions, will give entitlement to the basic state pension worth one-thirtieth of the full basic state pension.

Until 6 April 2010, women normally needed 39 qualifying years for a full basic state pension (£122.30 in 2017–18) and men normally needed 44 qualifying years. A reduced-rate basic state pension was payable if the number of qualifying years was less than 90 per cent of the working life, but to receive any basic state pension at all, a person must have had enough qualifying years, normally ten or 11, to receive a basic state pension of at least 25 per cent of the full rate.

NATIONAL INSURANCE CREDITS

Those in receipt of carer's allowance, working tax credit (with a disability premium), jobseeker's allowance, incapacity benefit, employment and support allowance, unemployability supplement, statutory sick pay, maternity allowance, statutory maternity, paternity or statutory adoption pay may have class 1 NI contributions credited to them each week. People may also get credits if they are unemployed and looking for work or too sick to work, even if they are not in receipt of any benefit, although the credits must be applied for in these circumstances. Since April 2010, spouses and civil partners of members of HM forces may get credits if they are on an accompanied assignment outside the UK. A new measure allows those who reach state pension age on or after 6 April 2016 to apply for NI credits for periods before April 2010 during which they were married to, or in a civil partnership with, a member of HM forces and accompanied them on a posting outside the UK. Persons undertaking certain training courses or jury service or who have been wrongly imprisoned for a conviction which is quashed on appeal may also get class 1 NI credits for each week they fulfill certain conditions. Class 1 credits may also be available to men approaching state pension age. Until 5 April 2010, these credits were awarded for the tax years in which they reached age 60 and continued until age 64, if they were not liable to pay contributions and were not absent from the UK for more than six months in any tax year. Since 6 April 2010 these credits are being phased out in line with the increase in women's state pension age. Class 1 NI credits count toward all future contributory benefits. A class 3 NI credit for basic state pension and bereavement benefit purposes is awarded, where required, for each week the working tax credit (without a disability premium) has been received or child benefit, for a child under 12, has been received. Class 3 credits may also be awarded, on application, to approved foster carers and people caring for at least 20 hours a week. Since 6 April 2011, class 3 credits have been available to adults under state pension age who care for a family member under 12. In certain cases people may also get a credit towards their state second pension.

STATE PENSION AGE

State pension age is currently 65 for men born before 6 December 1953 and 64 for women born before 6 July 1953. Women's state pension age will equalise with men's at 65 in 2018 and this will increase to age 66 for both men and women by October 2020. The Pensions Act 2014 makes provision for a regular review of state pension age. Reviews will take place at least once every six years and will take into account up-to-date life expectancy data and the findings of an independently led review, which will consider wider factors such as variation in life expectancy and employment opportunities for older workers. Further information can be obtained from the online state pension calculator (W www.gov.uk/state-pension-age).

USING THE NI CONTRIBUTION RECORD OF ANOTHER TO CLAIM A STATE PENSION

Married people or civil partners whose own NI record is incomplete may get a lower-rate basic state pension calculated using their partner's NI contribution record. This can be up to £73.30 a week in 2017–18, including any basic state pension of their own. Married men, members of married same-sex couples and civil partners may only qualify if their spouse or civil partner was born on or after 6 April 1950 (this rule does not apply to a married woman whose spouse has legally changed gender from male to female during the marriage). Widows, widowers, surviving civil partners, and people who are divorced or whose civil partnership has been dissolved may qualify for up to a full basic state pension based on their late or ex-spouse's/civil partner's NI contributions.

People who reached state pension age before 6 April 2016 will continue to be able to use these provisions, even if their spouse or civil partner reaches state pension age on or after that date. However, contributions their spouse or civil partner pays, or is credited with, following implementation of the new system will only count towards their own state pension. This means that only the NI record of the spouse or civil partner up to and including 2015–16 will be used to calculate any derived entitlement.

People who reached state pension age on or after 6 April 2016 will not be able to claim state pension on their spouse's or civil partner's NI record. There will be special arrangements for women who had opted to pay the married women's and widows reduced rate contributions before May 1977.

NON-CONTRIBUTORY STATE PENSIONS

A non-contributory state pension may be payable to those aged 80 or over who live in England, Scotland or Wales, and have done so for a total of ten years or more for any continuous period in the 20 years after their 60th birthday, if they are not entitled to another category of state pension, or are entitled to one below the rate of £73.30 a week in 2017–18 (see also Benefits, State Pension for people aged 80 and over).

GRADUATED RETIREMENT BENEFIT

Graduated Retirement Benefit (GRB) is based on the amount of graduated NI contributions paid into the GRB scheme between April 1961 and April 1975 (see also Benefits, Graduated Retirement Benefit). It is normally paid as an increase to a main state pension. For those reaching state pension age under the new state pension rules, it will be included in the calculation of their basic amount.

HOME RESPONSIBILITIES PROTECTION

From 6 April 1978 until 5 April 2010, it was possible for people who had low income or were unable to work because they cared for children or a sick or disabled person at home to reduce the number of qualifying years required for basic state pension. This was called home responsibilities protection (HRP); the number of years for which HRP was given was deducted from the number of qualifying years needed. HRP could, in some cases, also qualify the recipient for additional state pension. From April 2003 to April 2010 HRP was also available to approved foster carers.

From 6 April 2010, HRP was replaced by weekly credits for parents and carers. A class 3 national insurance credit is given, where eligible, towards basic state pension and bereavement benefits for spouses and civil partners. An earnings factor credit towards additional state pension is also awarded. Any years of HRP accrued before 6 April 2010 have been converted into qualifying years of credits for people reaching state pension age after that date, up to a maximum of 22 years for basic state pension purposes.

ADDITIONAL STATE PENSION

The amount of additional state pension paid depends on the amount of earnings a person has, or is treated as having, between the lower and upper earnings limits (from April 2009, the upper accruals point replaced the upper earnings limit for additional pension) for each complete tax year between 6 April 1978 (when the scheme started) and the tax year before they reach state pension age. The right to additional state pension does not depend on the person's right to basic state pension.

From 1978 to 2002, additional state pension was called the State Earnings-Related Pension Scheme (SERPS). SERPS covered all earnings by employees from 6 April 1978 to 5 April 1997 on which standard rate class 1 NI contributions had been paid, and earnings between 6 April 1997 and 5 April 2002 if the standard rate class 1 NI contributions had been contracted-in.

In 2002, SERPS was reformed through the state second pension, by improving the pension available to low and moderate earners and extending access to certain carers and people with long-term illness or disability. If earnings on which class 1 NI contributions have been paid or can be treated as paid are above the annual NI lower earnings limit (£5,876 for 2017–18) but below the statutory low earnings threshold (£8,164 for 2017–18), the state second pension regards this as earnings of £8,164 and it is treated as equivalent. Certain carers and people with long-term illness and disability will be considered as having earned at the low earnings threshold for each complete tax year since 2002–3 even if they do not work at all, or earn less than the annual NI lower earnings limit.

The amount of additional state pension paid also depends on when a person reaches state pension age; changes phased in from 6 April 1999 mean that pensions are calculated differently from that date.

ADDITIONAL STATE PENSION INHERITANCE

Men or women widowed before 6 October 2002 may inherit all of their late spouse's SERPS pension. From 6 October 2002, the maximum percentage of SERPS pension that a person can inherit from a late spouse or civil partner depends on their late spouse's or civil partner's date of birth:

Maximum SERPS entitlement	d.o.b (men)	d.o.b (women)
100%	5/10/37 or earlier	5/10/42 or earlier
90%	6/10/37 to 5/10/39	6/10/42 to 5/10/44
80%	6/10/39 to 5/10/41	6/10/44 to 5/10/46
70%	6/10/41 to 5/10/43	6/10/46 to 5/10/48
60%	6/10/43 to 5/10/45	6/10/48 to 5/7/50
50%	6/10/45 or later	6/7/50 or later

The maximum state second pension a person can inherit from a spouse or civil partner is 50 per cent. If a person is bereaved before they have reached their state pension age, inherited SERPS or state second pension can be paid as part of widowed parent's allowance (in the case of a person who has dependent children) or otherwise only from state pension age. If they remarry or form a new civil partnership before state pension age they lose the right to inherit any state pension.

NEW STATE PENSION INHERITANCE

A person who reached state pension age before 6 April 2016 will still be able to inherit additional state pension under the existing rules. However, if their late spouse or civil partner reaches state pension age on or after that date, the amount they can inherit will be based on the deceased's contributions up to 5 April 2016 only.

A person reaching state pension age on or after 6 April 2016 whose deceased spouse or civil partner reached state pension age or died before that date will be able to inherit additional state pension under the current rules. If the deceased spouse or civil partner is also in the new state pension the survivor may inherit half of any 'protected payment'. A person will have a protected payment if their state pension calculated under current rules is more than the full rate of new state pension at April 2016. The protected payment is the amount of the excess.

In order for a person reaching state pension age on or after 6 April 2016 to qualify for an inherited amount the marriage or civil partnership must have begun before that date; and, in the case of a person widowed under state pension age, they must not remarry or form a new civil partnership before state pension age.

STATE PENSION STATEMENTS

The Department for Work and Pensions provide state pension statements. These statements give an estimate of the state pension an individual may get based on their current NI contribution record.

There is also an online state pension calculator (W www.gov.uk/check-state-pension).

PRIVATE PENSIONS

CONTRACTED-OUT PENSIONS

From 6 April 2012, employees have not been able to contract-out of the state second pension through a money purchase (defined contribution) occupational pension scheme or a personal or stakeholder pension. Anyone contracted-out via these schemes, from that date, was automatically contracted back into the additional state pension. Although those rights built up before the abolition date can be used to provide pension benefits. These changes did not affect contracting-out via a salary-related occupational pension scheme (also known as contracted-out defined benefit (DB) or final salary schemes), which provide a pension related to earnings and the length of pensionable service. However, the introduction of the single-tier pension scheme in April 2016 closed the additional state pension for those reaching state pension age after this date, and contracting out on a DB basis ended.

STAKEHOLDER PENSION SCHEMES

Introduced in 2001, stakeholder pensions are available to everyone but are principally for moderate earners who do not have access to a good value company pension scheme. Stakeholder pensions must meet minimum standards to make sure they are flexible, portable and annual management charges are capped. The minimum contribution is £20.

AUTOMATIC ENROLMENT INTO WORKPLACE PENSIONS

Since October 2012, under the Pensions Act 2008, employers must automatically enrol their workers who meet the age and earnings criteria into a workplace pension. This applies to people who are not already in a qualifying workplace pension scheme and who:
- earn over £10,000 per annum (2017–18)
- are aged 22 or over
- are under state pension age
- ordinarily work in the UK

Employees who meet the above requirements are entitled to opt out of the scheme, if they wish to do so, within one calendar month of enrolment. Additionally certain employees can also choose to opt in to the scheme. Currently, employees can opt in if they are:
- aged 16 to 21, or state pension age to 74
- earning above £5,876 up to and including £10,000 per annum

If they remain in the scheme, they, together with their employer, will pay into it every month. The government will also contribute through tax relief. Employees can cease active membership from their workplace pension at any time after the opt-out period. Further information is available at W www.gov.uk/workplace-pensions

COMPLAINTS

The Pensions Advisory Service provides information and guidance to members of the public, on state, company, personal and stakeholder schemes. They also help any member of the public who has a problem, complaint or dispute with their occupational or personal pensions.

There are two bodies for pension complaints. The Financial Ombudsman Service deals with complaints which predominantly concern the sale and/or marketing of occupational, stakeholder and personal pensions. The Pensions Ombudsman deals with complaints which predominantly concern the management (after sale or marketing) of occupational, stakeholder and personal pensions.

The Pensions Regulator is the UK regulator for work-based pension schemes; it concentrates its resources on schemes where there is the greatest risk to the security of members' benefits, promotes good administration practice for all work-based schemes and works with trustees, employers and professional advisers to put things right when necessary.

WAR PENSIONS AND THE ARMED FORCES COMPENSATION SCHEME

Veterans UK is part of the Ministry of Defence. It was formed on 1 April 2007 to provide services to both serving personnel and veterans.

Veterans UK is responsible for the administration of the war pensions scheme and the armed forces compensation scheme (AFCS) to members of the armed forces in respect of disablement or death due to service. There is also a scheme for civilians and civil defence workers in respect of the Second World War, and other schemes for groups such as merchant seamen and Polish armed forces who served under British command during the Second World War. They are also responsible for the administration of the armed forces pension scheme (AFPS), which provides occupational pensions for ex-service personnel.

THE WAR PENSIONS SCHEME

War disablement pension is awarded for the disabling effects of any injury, wound or disease which was the result of, or was aggravated by, service in the armed forces prior to 6 April 2005. Claims are only considered once the person has left the armed forces. The amount of pension paid depends on the severity of disablement, which is assessed by comparing the health of the claimant with that of a healthy person of the same age and sex. The person's earning capacity or occupation are not taken into account in this assessment. A pension is awarded if the person has a disablement of 20 per cent or more and a lump sum is usually payable to those with a disablement of less than 20 per cent. No award is made for noise-induced sensorineural hearing loss where the assessment of disablement is less than 20 per cent. Where an assessment of disablement is at 40 per cent or more, an age addition is automatically given when the pensioner reaches 65.

A pension is payable to war widows, widowers and surviving civil partners where the spouse's or civil partner's death was due to, or hastened by, service in the armed forces prior to 6 April 2005 or where the spouse or civil partner was in receipt of a war disablement pension constant attendance allowance (or would have been if not in hospital) at the time of death. A pension is also payable to widows, widowers or surviving civil partners if the spouse or civil partner was receiving the war disablement pension at the 80 per cent rate or higher in conjunction with unemployability supplement at the time of death. War widows, widowers and surviving civil partners receive a standard rank-related rate, but a lower weekly rate is payable to war widows, widowers and surviving civil partners of personnel of the rank of Major or below who are under the age of 40, without children and capable of maintaining themselves. This is increased to the standard rate at age 40. Allowances are paid for children and adult dependants. An age allowance is automatically given when the widow, widower or surviving civil partner reaches 65 and increased at ages 70 and 80.

Pensioners living overseas receive the same pension rates as those living in the UK. All war disablement pensions and allowances and pensions for war widows, widowers and surviving civil partners are tax-free in the UK; this does not always apply in overseas countries due to different tax laws.

SUPPLEMENTARY ALLOWANCES

A number of supplementary allowances may be awarded to a war pensioner and are intended to meet various needs. The principal supplementary allowances are unemployability supplement, allowance for lowered standard of occupation, constant attendance allowance and war pensions mobility supplement. Others include exceptionally severe disablement allowance, severe disablement occupational allowance, treatment allowance, comforts allowance, clothing allowance, age allowance and widow/widower/surviving civil partner's age allowance. Rent and children's allowances are also available with pensions for war widows, widowers and surviving civil partners.

ARMED FORCES COMPENSATION SCHEME

The armed forces compensation scheme (AFCS) became effective on 6 April 2005 and covers all regular (including Gurkhas) and reserve personnel whose injury, ill health or death is caused predominantly by service on or after 6 April 2005. There are time limits under this scheme and generally claims must be made within seven years of the injury occurring or from first seeking medical advice about an illness. There are some exceptions to this time limit, the main one being for a late-onset illness. Claims for a late-onset illness can be made, after discharge, at any time after the event to which it relates, providing the claim is made within three years of medical advice being sought.

The AFCS provides compensation where service in the armed forces is the only or predominant cause of injury, illness or death. Any other personal accident cover held by the individual is not taken into account when determining an AFCS award. Under the terms of the scheme a tax-free lump sum is payable to service or ex-service personnel based on a 15-level tariff, graduated according to the seriousness of the injury. If multiple injuries are sustained in the same incident compensation for each injury, up to the scheme maximum, is awarded. For those with the most serious injuries and illness a tax-free, index-linked monthly payment – a guaranteed income payment or GIP – is paid for life from the point of discharge. A taxable survivor's GIP (SGIP) will also be paid to surviving spouses, civil partners and unmarried partners who meet certain criteria. GIP and SGIP are calculated by multiplying the pensionable pay of the service person by a factor that depends on the age at the person's last birthday. The younger the person, the higher the factor, because there are more years to normal retirement age.

ARMED FORCES INDEPENDENCE PAYMENT

Armed forces independence payment (AFIP) is designed to provide financial support for service personnel and veterans who have been seriously injured to cover the extra costs they may incur as a result of their injury. It is administered by Veterans UK as part of AFCS although payments are made by the Department for Work and Pensions (DWP). It is non-taxable and non-means-tested.

Service personnel and veterans awarded a GIP of 50 per cent or higher under the AFCS are eligible. Those eligible for AFIP are not required to undergo an assessment and will keep the payment for as long as they are entitled to receive a GIP of 50 per cent or higher.

DEPARTMENT FOR WORK AND PENSIONS
BENEFITS

Payments under the AFCS and the war pensions scheme may affect income related benefits from the DWP. In particular any supplementary allowances in payment with war pensions. Any state pension for which a war widow, widower or surviving civil partner qualifies for on their own NI contribution record can be paid in addition to monies received under the war pensions scheme.

CLAIMS AND QUESTIONS

Further information on the war pensions scheme, the AFCS and the nearest Veterans' Welfare Office can be obtained from Veterans UK (T 0808-191 4218, if calling from the UK or, if living overseas, T (+44) (1253) 866-043).

VETERANS UK, Norcross Lane, Thornton-Cleveleys FY5 3WP
E veterans-uk@mod.uk W www.gov.uk/government/organisations/veterans-uk

TAX CREDITS

Tax credits are administered by HM Revenue and Customs (HMRC). They are based on an individual's or couple's household income and current circumstances. Adjustments can be made during the year to reflect changes in income and/or circumstances. Further information regarding the qualifying conditions for tax credits, how to claim and the rates payable is available online at (W www.gov.uk/browse/benefits/tax-credits).

WORKING TAX CREDIT

Working tax credit is a payment from the government to support people on low incomes. It may be claimed by:
* those aged 25 or over who work at least 30 hours a week
* those aged 16 or over who work at least 16 hours a week, who are responsible for a child or young person, or have a disability that puts them at a disadvantage of getting a job
* those aged 60 or over, who work at least 16 hours a week
* couples who are responsible for a child or young person, who work at least 24 hours per week between them with one partner working at least 16 hours a week

The amount received depends on individual circumstances and income. The basic amount is up to £1,960 per annum and extra 'elements' are paid on top of this:

Element	Amount per annum
Couple applying together	up to £2,010
Single parent	up to £2,010
An individual working at least 30 hours a week	up to £810
An individual with a disability	up to £3,000
An individual with a severe disability	up to £1,290*

* Usually in addition to the disability element

CHILDCARE

In families with children where a lone parent works at least 16 hours a week, or couples who work at least 24 hours a week between them with one partner working at least 16 hours a week, or where one partner works at least 16 hours a week and the other is disabled, an in-patient in hospital, or in prison, the family is entitled to the childcare element of working tax credit. Depending on circumstances this payment can contribute up to £122.50 a week towards childcare costs for one child and up to £210 a week for two or more children. Families can only claim if they use an approved or registered childcare provider.

CHILD TAX CREDIT

Child tax credit combines all income-related support for children and is paid direct to the main carer. The credit is made up of a main 'family' element of up to £545 per year with an additional payment of up to £2,780 a year for each child in a household born before 6 April 2017. For children born after this date, only the child element of child tax credit will apply for the first two children in a household with no 'family element', however there are exceptions to this two-child rule. An additional payment is paid for children with a disability, plus a further payment for children who are severely disabled. Child tax credit is available to households where:

* there is at least one dependant under 16
* there is at least one dependant between 16 and 20 who is in relevant education or training or is registered for work, education or training with an approved body

BENEFITS

The following is intended as a general guide to the benefits system. Conditions of entitlement and benefit rates change annually and all prospective claimants should check exact entitlements and rates of benefit directly with their local Jobcentre Plus office, pension centre or online (W www.gov.uk). Leaflets relating to the various benefits and contribution conditions for different benefits are available from local Jobcentre Plus offices.

UNIVERSAL CREDIT

From 29 April 2013, universal credit began to gradually be introduced in certain local authority areas. Universal credit will replace a number of means tested benefits with a single monthly payment. The roll-out of universal credit to all local authority areas is due to be completed in September 2018.

For eligible claimants, the following benefits are set to be replaced by universal credit:

* Income-based jobseekers allowance
* Income-related employment support allowance
* Income support
* Child tax credit
* Working tax credit
* Housing benefit

The amount of universal credit awarded is determined by the circumstances of the claimant, this includes income and number of dependants in the household. It consists of a basic 'standard allowance' and additional payments as applicable to the claimant's circumstances. Universal credit can be claimed while working, but the monthly payment will reduce gradually as the claimant earns more.

Standard monthly allowance from April 2017

Single, under 25	£251.77
Single, over 25	£317.82
Couple, under 25	£395.20
Couple, over 25	£498.89

Maximum additional monthly payments from April 2017

Disability or health condition	£318.78
Carer allowance	£151.89
First child born before 6 April 2017	£277.07
First child born after 6 April 2017	£231.67
Second child	£231.67
Childcare for one child	£646.35
Childcare for two or more children	£1,108.04
Child with a disability	£372.30
Severely disabled child	£649.38

For more information and to check eligibility and local authority status visit W www.gov.uk/universal-credit

CONTRIBUTORY BENEFITS

Entitlement to contributory benefits depends on national insurance contribution conditions being satisfied either by the claimant or by someone on the claimant's behalf (depending on the kind of benefit). The class or classes of national insurance contribution relevant to each benefit are:

Jobseeker's allowance (contribution-based)	Class 1
Employment and Support Allowance (contributory)	Class 1 or 2
Widow's benefit and bereavement benefit	Class 1, 2 or 3
State pensions, categories A and B	Class 1, 2 or 3

The system of contribution conditions relates to yearly levels of earnings on which national insurance (NI) contributions have been paid.

JOBSEEKER'S ALLOWANCE

Jobseeker's allowance (JSA) replaced unemployment benefit and income support for unemployed people under state pension age from 7 October 1996. There are two routes of entitlement. Contribution-based JSA is paid at a personal rate (i.e. additional benefit for dependants is not paid) to those who have made sufficient NI contributions in two particular tax years. Savings and partner's earnings are not taken into account and payment can be made for up to six months. Rates of JSA correspond to income support rates.

Claims are made through Jobcentre Plus. A person wishing to claim JSA must generally be unemployed or working on average less than 16 hours a week, capable of work and available for any work which he or she can reasonably be expected to do, usually for at least 40 hours a week. The claimant must agree and sign a 'jobseeker's agreement', which will set out his or her plans to find work, and must actively seek work. If the claimant refuses work or training the benefit may be sanctioned for between one and 26 weeks.

A person will be sanctioned from JSA for up to 26 weeks if he or she has left a job voluntarily without just cause or through misconduct. In these circumstances, it may be possible to receive hardship payments, particularly where the claimant or the claimant's family is vulnerable, eg if sick or pregnant, or with children or caring responsibilities.

Weekly Rates from April 2017	
Person aged 18–24	£57.90
Person aged 25 to state pension age*	£73.10
* Since October 2003 people aged between 60 and state pension age can choose to claim pension credits instead of JSA	

EMPLOYMENT AND SUPPORT ALLOWANCE

From 27 October 2008, employment and support allowance (ESA) replaced incapacity benefit and income support paid on the grounds of incapacity or disability. The benefit consists of two strands, contribution-based benefit and income-related benefit, so that people no longer need to make two claims for benefit in order to gain their full entitlement. Contributory ESA is available to those who have limited capability for work but cannot get statutory sick pay from their employer. Those over pensionable age are not entitled to ESA. Apart from those who qualify under the special provisions for people incapacitated in youth, entitlement to contributory ESA is based on a person's NI contribution record. In order to qualify for contributory ESA, two contribution conditions, based on the last three years before the tax year in which benefit is claimed, must be satisfied. The amount of contributory ESA payable may be reduced where the person receives more than a specified amount of occupational or personal pension. Contributory ESA is paid only in respect of the person claiming the benefit – there are no additional amounts for dependants.

At the outset, new claimants are paid a basic allowance (the same rate as jobseeker's allowance) for 13 weeks while their medical condition is assessed and a work capability assessment is conducted. Following the completion of the assessment phase those claimants capable of engaging in work-related activities will receive a work-related activity component on top of the basic rate. The work-related activity component can be subject to sanctions if the claimant does not engage in the conditionality requirements without good reason. The maximum sanction is equal to the value of the work-related activity component of the benefit.

Those with the most severe health conditions or disabilities will receive the support component, which is more than the work-related activity component. Claimants in receipt of the support component are not required to engage in work-related activities, although they can volunteer to do so or undertake permitted work if their condition allows.

Weekly Rates from April 2017	
ESA plus work-related activity component	up to £102.15
ESA plus support component	up to £109.65

BEREAVEMENT BENEFITS

Bereavement benefits replaced widow's benefit on 9 April 2001. Those claiming widow's benefit before this date will continue to receive it under the old scheme for as long as they qualify. The new system provides bereavement benefits for widows, widowers and, from 5 December 2005, surviving civil partners (providing that their deceased spouse or civil partner paid NI contributions). The new system offers benefits in three forms:

- *Bereavement payment* – may be received by a man or woman who is under the state pension age at the time of their spouse or civil partner's death, or whose husband, wife or civil partner was not entitled to a category A retirement pension when he or she died. It is a single tax-free lump sum of £2,000 payable immediately on widowhood or loss of a civil partner
- *Widowed parent's allowance* – a taxable benefit payable to the surviving partner if he or she is entitled or treated as entitled to child benefit, or to a widow if she is expecting her husband's baby at the time of his death
- *Bereavement allowance* – a taxable weekly benefit paid for 52 weeks after the spouse or civil partner's death. If aged over 55 and under state pension age the full allowance is payable, if aged between 45 and 54 a percentage of the full rate is paid. A widow, widower or surviving civil partner may receive this allowance if his or her widowed parent's allowance ends before 52 weeks

It is not possible to receive widowed parent's allowance and bereavement allowance at the same time. Bereavement benefits and widow's benefit, in any form, cease upon remarriage or a new civil partnership or are suspended during a period of cohabitation as partners without being legally married or in a civil partnership.

Weekly Rates from April 2017	
Bereavement payment (lump sum)	£2,000
Widowed parent's allowance (or widowed mother's allowance)	£113.70
Bereavement allowance (or widow's pension), full entitlement (aged 55 and over at time of spouse's or civil partner's death)	£113.70

Amount of bereavement allowance (or widow's pension) by age of widow/widower or surviving civil partner at spouse's or civil partner's death:

aged 54	£105.74
aged 53	£97.78
aged 52	£89.82
aged 51	£81.86
aged 50	£73.91
aged 49	£65.95
aged 48	£57.99
aged 47	£50.03
aged 46	£42.07
aged 45	£34.11

NEW STATE PENSION
The new state pension is payable to men and women who reach state pension age on or after 6 April 2016 (ie men born on or after 6 April 1951 or women born on or after 6 April 1953). Those that reached state pension age before this date continue to receive state pension under the old rules outlined below.

The full new state pension of £159.55 a week in 2017–18 is payable to those individuals who have 35 qualifying years on their national insurance record. Individuals usually need at least ten qualifying years and will receive a proportion of the new state pension if they have between ten and 35 qualifying years. The starting amount is the higher of the amount receivable under the old state pension rules (category A and B) and the amount the individual would receive had the new state pension been in place at the start of their working life. The amount received includes a deduction for those who were contracted out of the additional state pension.

Each qualifying year on an individual's national insurance record after 5 April 2016 adds £4.56 a week to the new state pension. The exact amount can be calculated by dividing £159.55 by 35 and then multiplying by the number of qualifying years after 5 April 2016. Additional qualifying years can be added to a person's national insurance record until the person reaches the full new state pension amount or the state pension age – whichever is first.

Those individuals who have accrued an amount, before 5 April 2016, which is above the new full state pension – a 'protected payment' – have this paid on top of the full new state pension.

The new state pension increases each year by whichever is the highest:
• earnings – the average percentage growth in wages (in Great Britain)
• prices – the percentage growth in prices in the UK as measured by the Consumer Prices Index (CPI)
• 2.5 per cent
Any protected payment increases each year in line with the CPI.

Weekly Rate from April 2017	
Full new state pension	£159.55

STATE PENSION: CATEGORIES A AND B
Category A pension is payable for life to men and women who reach state pension age, who satisfy the contributions conditions and who claim for it. Category B pension may be payable to married women, married men and civil partners who are not entitled to a basic state pension on their own NI contributions or whose own basic state pension entitlement is less than £73.30 a week in 2017–18. It is based on their wife's, husband's or civil partner's NI contributions and is payable when both members of the couple have reached state pension age. Married men and civil partners may only be able to qualify for a category B pension if their wife or civil partner was born on or after 6 April 1950. Category B pension is also payable to widows, widowers and surviving civil partners

who are bereaved before state pension age if they were previously entitled to widowed parent's allowance or bereavement allowance based on their late spouse's or civil partner's NI contributions. If they were receiving widowed parent's allowance on reaching state pension age, they could qualify for a category B pension payable at the same rate as their widowed parent's allowance comprising a basic pension, plus, if applicable, the appropriate share of their late spouse's or late civil partner's additional state pension. If their widowed parent's allowance had stopped before they reached state pension age, or they had been getting bereavement allowance at any time before state pension age, their category B pension will consist of inheritable additional state pension only. No basic state pension is included, although they may qualify for a basic state pension or have their own basic state pension improved by substituting their late spouse's or late civil partner's NI records for their own.

Widows who are bereaved when over state pension age can qualify for a category B pension regardless of the age of their husband when he died. This is payable at the same rate as the basic state pension the widow's late husband was entitled to (or would have been entitled to) at the time of his death. It can also be paid to widowers and civil partners who are bereaved when over state pension age if their wife or civil partner had reached state pension age when they died. Widowers and surviving civil partners who reached state pension age on or after 6 April 2010 and bereaved when over state pension age can qualify for a category B pension regardless of the age of their wife or civil partner when they died.

Where a person is entitled to both a category A and category B pension then they can be combined to give a composite pension, but this cannot be more than the full rate pension. Where a person is entitled to more than one category A or category B pension then only one can be paid. In such cases the person can choose which to get; if no choice is made, the most favourable one is paid.

A person may defer claiming their pension beyond state pension age. In doing so they may earn increments which will increase the weekly amount paid by 1 per cent per five weeks of deferral (equivalent to 10.4 per cent/year) when they claim their state pension. If a person delays claiming for at least 12 months they are given the option of a one-off taxable lump sum, instead of a pension increase, based on the weekly pension deferred, plus interest of at least 2 per cent above the Bank of England base rate. Since 6 April 2010, a category B pension has been treated independently of the spouse's or partner's pension. It is possible to take a category B pension even if the spouse or partner has deferred theirs.

It is no longer possible to claim an increase on a state pension for another adult (known as adult dependency increase). Those who received the increase before April 2010 can keep receiving it until the conditions are no longer met or until 5 April 2020, whichever is first.

Provision for children is made through child tax credits. An age addition of 25p a week is payable with a state pension if a pensioner is aged 80 or over.

Since 1989 pensioners have been allowed to have unlimited earnings without affecting their state pension. *See* Pensions.

Weekly Rates from April 2017	
Category A or B pension for a single person	£122.30
Category B pension based on spouse or civil partner's NI contributions	£73.30

GRADUATED RETIREMENT BENEFIT
Graduated retirement benefit (GRB) is based on the amount of graduated NI contributions paid into the GRB scheme between April 1961 and April 1975; however, it is still paid in addition to any state pension to those who made the relevant contributions. A person will receive graduated retirement benefit based on their own contributions, even if not entitled to a basic state pension. Widows, widowers and

surviving civil partners may inherit half of their deceased spouse's or civil partner's entitlement, but none that the deceased spouse or civil partner may have been eligible for from a former spouse or civil partner. If a person defers making a claim beyond state pension age, they may earn an increase or a one-off lump sum payment in respect of their deferred graduated retirement benefit; calculated in the same way as for category A or B state pension.

NON-CONTRIBUTORY BENEFITS

These benefits are paid from general taxation and are not dependent on NI contributions.

JOBSEEKER'S ALLOWANCE (INCOME-BASED)

Those who do not qualify for contribution-based jobseeker's allowance (JSA), those who have exhausted their entitlement to contribution-based JSA or those for whom contribution-based JSA provides insufficient income may qualify for income-based JSA. The amount paid depends on age, whether they are single or a couple and amount of income and savings. To get income-based JSA the claimant must usually be aged 18 or over but below state pension age, although there are some exceptions for 16- or 17-year-olds. Since April 2003, child dependants have been provided for through the child tax credit system.

The rules of entitlement are the same as for contribution-based JSA.

If one person in a couple was born after 28 October 1957 and neither person in the couple has responsibility for a child or children, then the couple will have to make a joint claim for JSA if they wish to receive income-based JSA.

Weekly Rates from April 2017	
Person aged 16–24	£57.90
Person aged 25 to state pension age	£73.10
Couple, both aged 18 to state pension age	£114.85

MATERNITY ALLOWANCE

Maternity allowance (MA) is a benefit available for pregnant women who cannot get statutory maternity pay (SMP) from their employer or have been employed/self-employed during or close to their pregnancy. In order to qualify for payment, a woman must have been employed and/or self-employed for at least 26 weeks in the 66-week period up to and including the week before the baby is due (test period). These weeks do not have to be in a row and any part weeks worked will count towards the 26 weeks. She must also have an average weekly earning of at least £30 (maternity allowance threshold) over any 13 weeks of the woman's choice within the test period.

Self-employed women who pay class 2 NI contributions or who hold a small earnings exception certificate are deemed to have enough earnings to qualify for MA.

A woman can choose to start receiving MA from the 11th week before the week in which the baby is due (if she stops work before then) up to the day following the day of birth. The exact date MA starts will depend on when the woman stops work to have her baby or if the baby is born before she stops work. However, where the woman is absent from work wholly or partly due to her pregnancy in the four weeks before the week the baby is due to be born, MA will start the day following the first day of absence from work. MA is paid for a maximum of 39 weeks.

Women who are not eligible for statutory maternity pay or the higher amount of MA may be eligible for a reduced rate of MA for a 14-week period. For example, women who take part in the business of their self-employed spouse or civil partner, for at least 26 weeks in the 66 weeks before their baby is due, and the work they do is unpaid.

Weekly Rates from April 2017	
Standard rate	£140.98 or 90 per cent of the woman's average weekly earnings if less than £140.98
14-week reduced rate	£30

CHILD BENEFIT

Child benefit is payable for virtually all children aged under 16 and for those aged 16 and 17 if they are in relevant education or training or are registered for work, education or training with an approved body.

Weekly Rates from April 2017	
Eldest/only child	£20.70
Each subsequent child	£13.70

GUARDIAN'S ALLOWANCE

Guardian's allowance is payable to a person who is bringing up a child or young person because the child's parents have died, or in some circumstances, where only one parent has died. To receive the allowance the person must be in receipt of child benefit for the child or young person, although they do not have to be the child's legal guardian.

Weekly Rate (in addition to child benefit) from April 2017	
Each child	£16.70

CARER'S ALLOWANCE

Carer's allowance (CA) is a benefit payable to people who spend at least 35 hours a week caring for a severely disabled person. To qualify for CA a person must be caring for someone in receipt of one of the following benefits:

- attendance allowance
- disability living allowance
- personal independence payment
- constant attendance allowance, paid at not less than the normal maximum rate with an industrial injuries disablement payment or basic (full-day) rate, under the industrial injuries or war pension schemes.
- armed forces independence payment (AFIP)

Weekly Rate from April 2017	
Carer's allowance	£62.70

ATTENDANCE ALLOWANCE

This may be payable to people aged 65 or over who need help with personal care because they are physically or mentally disabled, and who have needed help for a period of at least six months. Attendance allowance has two rates: the lower rate is for day or night care, and the higher rate is for day and night care. People not expected to live for more than six months because of a progressive disease can receive the highest rate of attendance allowance straight away.

Weekly Rates from April 2017	
Higher rate	£83.10
Lower rate	£55.65

PERSONAL INDEPENDENCE PAYMENT (PIP)

Personal independence payment (PIP) replaced disability living allowance (DLA) for people aged 16 to 64 on 8 April 2013. PIP has two components: the daily living component and the mobility component, with each offering two different benefit rates: standard and enhanced. Whether one or both components are claimed depends on the requirements of the individual. Claimants are assessed on their ability to carry out everyday activities, with the majority of claims evaluated via an interview. Claimants with a terminal illness automatically receive the enhanced daily living component.

Weekly Rates from April 2017	
Daily living component	
Standard	£55.65
Enhanced	£83.10
Mobility component	
Standard	£22.00
Enhanced	£58.00

STATE PENSION FOR PEOPLE AGED 80 AND OVER

A state pension, also referred to as category D pension, is provided for people aged 80 and over if they are not entitled to another category of state pension or are entitled to a state pension that is less than £73.30 a week. The person must also live in Great Britain and have done so for a period of ten years or more in any continuous 20-year period since their 60th birthday.

Weekly Rate from April 2017	
Single person	£73.30
Age addition	£0.25

INCOME SUPPORT

Broadly speaking income support is a benefit for those between age 16 and the age they can receive pension credit, whose income is below a certain level, who work on average less than 16 hours a week and who are:

- bringing up children alone
- registered sick or disabled
- a student who is also a lone parent or disabled
- caring for someone who is sick or elderly

Income support is not payable if the claimant, or claimant and partner, have capital or savings in excess of £16,000 – and deductions are made for capital and savings in excess of £6,000. For people permanently in residential care and nursing homes deductions apply for capital over £10,000.

Sums payable depend on fixed allowances laid down by law for people in different circumstances. If both partners are eligible for income support, either may claim it for the couple. People receiving income support may be able to receive housing benefit, help with mortgage or home loan interest and help with healthcare. They may also be eligible for help with exceptional expenses from the Social Fund. Special rates may apply to some people living in residential care or nursing homes.

INCOME SUPPORT PREMIUMS

Income support premiums are extra weekly payments for those with additional needs. People qualifying for more than one premium will normally only receive the highest single premium for which they qualify. However, family premium, disabled child premium, severe disability premium and carer premium are payable in addition to other premiums.

Child tax credit replaced premiums for people with children for all new income support claims from 6 April 2004. People with children who were already in receipt of income support in April 2004 and have not claimed child tax credit may qualify for:

- the family premium if they have at least one child
- the disabled child premium if they have a child who receives disability living allowance or is registered blind
- the enhanced disability child premium if they have a child in receipt of the higher rate disability living allowance care component

Carers may qualify for:
- the carer premium if they or their partner are in receipt of carer's allowance

Long-term sick or disabled people may qualify for:
- the disability premium if they or their partner are receiving

certain benefits because they are disabled or cannot work; are registered blind; or if the claimant has been incapable of work or receiving statutory sick pay for at least 364 days (196 days if the person is terminally ill), including periods of incapacity separated by eight weeks or less
- the severe disability premium if the person lives alone and receives the middle or higher rate of disability living allowance care component and no one receives carer's allowance for caring for that person
- the enhanced disability premium if the person is in receipt of the higher rate disability living allowance care component

People with a partner aged over 60 may qualify for:

- the pensioner premium

WEEKLY RATES OF INCOME SUPPORT
from April 2017

Single person	
Aged under 18	£57.90
aged 25+	£73.10
Aged under 18 and a single parent	£57.90
Aged 18+ and a single parent	£73.10

Couples	
Both under 18	£57.90
Both under 18, in certain circumstances	£87.50
One under 18, one under 25	£57.90
One under 18, one aged 25+	£73.10
Both aged 18+	£114.85

Premiums	
Carer premium	£34.95
Severe disability premium	£62.45
Enhanced disability premium	
Single person	£15.90
Couples	£22.85
Pensioner premium (couple)	£128.40

PENSION CREDIT

Pension credit was introduced on 6 October 2003 and replaced income support for those aged 60 and over. Between April 2010 and April 2020 the pension credit qualifying age is increasing from 60 to 65 alongside the increase in women's state pension age.

There are two elements to pension credit:

THE GUARANTEE CREDIT

The guarantee credit guarantees a minimum income of £159.35 for single people and £243.25 for couples, with additional elements for people who have:
- eligible housing costs
- severe disabilities
- caring responsibilities

Income from state pension, private pensions, earnings, working tax credit and certain benefits are taken into account when calculating the pension credit. For savings and capital in excess of £10,000, £1 for every £500 or part of £500 held is taken into account as income when working out entitlement to pension credit.

People receiving the guarantee credit element of pension credit will be able to receive housing benefit, council tax benefit and help with healthcare costs.

Weekly Rates from April 2017	
Additional amount for severe disability	
Single person	£62.45
Couple (one qualifies)	£62.45
Couple (both qualify)	£124.90
Additional amount for carers	£34.95

THE SAVINGS CREDIT

Single people aged 65 or over (and couples where one member is 65 or over) may be entitled to a savings credit which provides additional support for pensioners who have made modest provision towards their retirement. The savings credit is calculated by taking into account any qualifying income above the savings credit threshold. For 2017–18 the threshold is £137.35 for single people and £218.42 for couples. The maximum savings credit is £13.20 a week (£14.90 a week for couples).

Income that qualifies towards the savings credit includes state pensions, earnings, second pensions and income taken into account from capital above £10,000.

Some people will be entitled to the guarantee credit, some to the savings credit and some to both.

Where only the savings credit is in payment, people need to claim standard housing benefit or council tax benefit. Although local authorities take any savings credit into account in the housing benefit or council tax benefit assessment, for people aged 65 and over housing benefit or council tax benefit is enhanced to ensure that gains in pension credit are not depleted.

HOUSING BENEFIT

Housing benefit is designed to help people with rent (including rent for accommodation in guesthouses, lodgings or hostels). It does not cover mortgage payments. The amount of benefit paid depends on:

- the income of the claimant, and partner if there is one, including earned income, unearned income (any other income including some other benefits) and savings
- number of dependants
- certain extra needs of the claimant, partner or any dependants
- number and gross income of people sharing the home who are not dependent on the claimant
- how much rent is paid

Housing benefit is not payable if the claimant, or claimant and partner, have savings in excess of £16,000. The amount of benefit is affected if savings held exceed £6,000 (£10,000 for people living in residential care and nursing homes). Housing benefit is not paid for meals, fuel or certain service charges that may be included in the rent. Deductions are also made for most non-dependants who live in the same accommodation as the claimant (and their partner). If the claimant is living with a partner or civil partner there can only be one claim.

The maximum amount of benefit (which is not necessarily the same as the amount of rent paid) may be paid where the claimant is in receipt of income support, income-based jobseeker's allowance, the guarantee element of pension credit or where the claimant's income is less than the amount allowed for their needs. Any income over that allowed for their needs will mean that their benefit is reduced.

LOCAL HOUSING ALLOWANCE

Local housing allowance (LHA), which was rolled out nationally from 7 April 2008, is a way of calculating the rent element of housing benefit based on the area in which a person lives and household size. It affects people in the deregulated private rented sector who make a new claim for housing benefit or existing recipients who move address.

LHA ensures that tenants in similar circumstances in the same area receive the same amount of financial support for their housing costs. It does not affect the way a person's income or capital is taken into account. LHA is paid to the tenant rather than the landlord in most circumstances. A weekly limit on payments is now in place so LHA does not exceed:

- £260.64 for a one bedroom property
- £302.33 for a two bedroom property
- £354.46 for a three bedroom property
- £417.02 for a four bedroom property

COUNCIL TAX REDUCTION

From April 2013, council tax benefit was replaced by council tax reduction. Nearly all the rules that apply to housing benefit apply to council tax reduction, which helps people on low incomes to pay council tax bills. The amount payable depends on how much council tax is paid and who lives with the claimant. The benefit may be available to those receiving income support, income-based jobseeker's allowance, the guarantee element of pension credit or to those whose income is less than that allowed for their needs. Any income over that allowed for their needs will mean that they will receive less help with their council tax reduction. Deductions are made for non-dependants.

A full council tax bill is based on at least two adults living in a home. Residents may receive a 25 per cent reduction on their bill if they count as an adult for council tax and live on their own. If the property is the resident's main home and there is no-one who counts as an adult, the reduction is 50 per cent.

THE SOCIAL FUND

REGULATED PAYMENTS

Sure Start Maternity Grant

Sure start maternity grant (SSMG) is a one-off payment of £500 to help people on low incomes pay for essential items for new babies that are expected, born, adopted, the subject of a parental order (following a surrogate birth) or, in certain circumstances, the subject of a residency order. SSMG can be claimed any time from within 11 weeks of the expected birth and up to three months after the birth, adoption or date of parental or residency order. Those eligible are people in receipt of income support, income-based jobseeker's allowance, pension credit, child tax credit at a rate higher than the family element or working tax credit where a disability or severe disability element is in payment. Since 11 April 2011, new rules have been applied for babies due, born or adopted on this date. These are that SSMG is only available if there are no other children under 16 in the family or in the case of a dependent child's new baby, SSMG is only available if the dependent is under the age of 20 and has no other children.

Funeral Payments

Payable to help cover the necessary cost of burial or cremation, a new burial plot with an exclusive right of burial (where burial is chosen), certain other expenses, and up to £700 for any other funeral expenses, such as the funeral director's fees, the coffin or flowers. Those eligible are people receiving income support, income-based jobseeker's allowance, pension credit, child tax credit at a higher rate than the family element, working tax credit where a disability or severe disability element is in payment, council tax benefit or housing benefit who have good reason for taking responsibility for the funeral expenses. These payments are recoverable from any estate of the deceased.

Cold Weather Payments

A payment of £25 per seven-day period between 1 November and 31 March when the average temperature is recorded at or forecast to be 0°C or below over seven consecutive days in the qualifying person's area. Payments are made to people on pension credit or child tax credit with a disability element, those on income support whose benefit includes a pensioner or disability premium, and those on income-based jobseeker's allowance or employment and support allowance who have a child who is disabled or under the age of five. Payments are made automatically and do not have to be repaid.

Winter Fuel Payments

For 2017–18 the winter fuel payment is £200 for households with someone born on or before 5 August 1953 and £300 for households with someone aged 80 or over. The rate paid is based on the person's age and circumstances in the 'qualifying week' between 18 and 24 September 2017. The majority of eligible people are paid automatically between November and December, although a few need to claim. Payments do not have to be repaid.

Christmas Bonus
The Christmas bonus is a one-off tax-free £10 payment made before Christmas to those people in receipt of a qualifying benefit in the qualifying week (usually the first full week of December).

DISCRETIONARY PAYMENTS

Finance Support – Northern Ireland
The Northern Ireland (Welfare Reform) Act 2016 introduced Finance Support to replace Crisis Loans and Community Care Grants on 31 October 2016. Since 31 October 2016, people suffering a financial crisis are able to apply for a discretionary support loan or short term benefit advance from the Finance Support Service (W www.nidirect.gov.uk/contacts/contacts-az/finance-support-service-times-crisis-and-need). To receive discretionary support, the applicant must have a crisis which places themselves or their family's health, safety or wellbeing at significant risk. Applicants must be a resident of Northern Ireland and be over 18-years-old (16-years-old if they do not have any parental support) and be earning less than £15,600 per annum (the national living wage). If eligibility conditions are met the applicant may be offered a discretionary support loan or grant; no more than three loans and one grant can be awarded within a 12-month period.

If the applicant is receiving one of the following benefits: jobseeker's allowance; employment and support allowance; income support; pension credit; state pension; carer's allowance, bereavement allowance, widowed parent's allowance, maternity allowance or incapacity benefit, they are able to apply for short-term benefit advance. It works on an advance of the benefit payment if they have an urgent financial need that may impact the applicant or their family's health, safety or wellbeing. The applicant must be able to afford to repay the advance within 12 weeks.

If an applicant's combined discretionary support and short-term benefit advance debt is £1,000 or more they will not be able to get further discretionary support until their debt falls below this limit.

Budgeting Loans
These are interest-free loans to people who have been receiving income support, income-based jobseeker's allowance or income-related employment and support allowance or pension credit for the past six months, for intermittent expenses that may be difficult to budget for. The smallest amount available to borrow is £100.

SAVINGS
Savings of £1,000 (£2,000 if the applicant or their partner is aged 63 or over) are taken into account for budgeting loans. Savings are not taken into account for sure start maternity grant, funeral payments, cold weather payments, winter fuel payments or the Christmas bonus.

INDUSTRIAL INJURIES AND DISABLEMENT BENEFITS
The Industrial Injuries Scheme, administered under the Social Security Contributions and Benefits Act 1992, provides a range of benefits designed to compensate for disablement resulting from an industrial accident (ie an accident arising out of and in the course of an earner's employment) or from a prescribed disease due to the nature of a person's employment. Those who are self-employed are not covered by this scheme.

INDUSTRIAL INJURIES DISABLEMENT BENEFIT
A person may be able to claim industrial injuries disablement benefit if they are ill or disabled due to an accident or incident that happened at work or in connection with work in England, Scotland or Wales. The amount of benefit awarded depends on the person's age and the degree of disability as assessed by a doctor.

The benefit is payable whether the person works or not and those who are incapable of work are entitled to draw other benefits, such as statutory sick pay or incapacity benefit, in addition to industrial injuries disablement benefit. It may also be possible to claim the following allowances:

- reduced earnings allowance for those who are unable to return to their regular work or work of the same standard and who had their accident (or whose disease started) before 1 October 1990. At state pension age this is converted to retirement allowance
- constant attendance allowance for those with a disablement of 100 per cent who need constant care. There are four rates of allowance depending on how much care the person needs
- exceptionally severe disablement allowance can be claimed in addition to constant care attendance allowance at one of the higher rates for those who need constant care permanently

Weekly Rates from April 2017

Degree of disablement	Aged 18+ or with dependants
100 per cent	£169.70
90	£152.73
80	£135.76
70	£118.79
60	£101.82
50	£84.85
40	£67.88
30	£50.91
20	£33.94
Unemployability supplement	£104.90
Reduced earnings allowance (maximum)	£67.88
Retirement allowance (maximum)	£16.97
Constant attendance allowance (normal maximum rate)	£67.90
Exceptionally severe disablement allowance	£67.90

OTHER BENEFITS
People who are disabled because of an accident or disease that was the result of work that they did before 5 July 1948 are not entitled to industrial injuries disablement benefit. They may, however, be entitled to payment under the Workmen's Compensation Scheme or the Pneumoconiosis, Byssinosis and Miscellaneous Diseases Benefit Scheme. People who suffer from certain industrial diseases caused by dust can make a claim for an additional payment under the Pneumoconiosis Act 1979 if they are unable to get damages from the employer who caused or contributed to the disease.

Diffuse Mesothelioma Payments (2008 Scheme)
Since 1 October 2008 any person suffering from the asbestos-related disease, diffuse mesothelioma, who is unable to make a claim under the Pneumoconiosis Act 1979, have not received payment in respect of the disease from an employer, via a civil claim or elsewhere, and are not entitled to compensation from a MoD scheme, can claim a one-off lump sum payment. The scheme covers people whose exposure to asbestos occurred in the UK and was not as a result of their work as an employee (ie they lived near a factory using asbestos). The amount paid depends on the age of the person when the disease was diagnosed, or the date of the claim if the diagnosis date is not known. The current rate is £87,473 for those aged 37 and under to £13,590 for persons aged 77 and over. From 1 October 2009 claims must be received within 12 months of the date of diagnosis. If the sufferer has died, their dependants may be able to claim, but must do so within 12 months of the date of death.

CLAIMS AND QUESTIONS

Entitlement to benefit and regulated Social Fund payments is determined by a decision maker on behalf of the Secretary of State for the Department for Work and Pensions. A claimant who is dissatisfied with that decision can ask for an explanation. He or she can dispute the decision by applying to have it revised or, in particular circumstances, superseded. The claimant can appeal to the First Tier-tribunal (Social Security and Child Support). There is a further right of appeal to the Administrative and Appeals Chamber of the Upper Tribunal (see Tribunals).

Decisions on claims and applications for housing benefit and council tax benefit are made by local authorities. The explanation, dispute and appeals process is the same as for other benefits.

All decisions on applications to the discretionary Social Fund are made by Jobcentre Plus Social Fund decision makers. Applicants can ask for a review of the decision within 28 days of the date on the decision letter. As above, the claimant has a right of appeal to the First-tier Tribunal (Social Security and Child Support).

EMPLOYER PAYMENTS

STATUTORY MATERNITY PAY

Employers pay statutory maternity pay (SMP) to pregnant women who have been employed by them full or part-time continuously for at least 26 weeks into the 15th week before the week the baby is due, and whose earnings on average at least equal the lower earnings limit applied to NI contributions (£113 a week if the end of the qualifying week is in the 2017–18 tax year). SMP can be paid for a maximum period of up to 39 weeks. If the qualifying conditions are met women will receive a payment of 90 per cent of their average earnings for the first six weeks, followed by 33 weeks at £140.98 or 90 per cent of the woman's average weekly earnings if this is less than £140.98. SMP can be paid, at the earliest, 11 weeks before the week in which the baby is due, up to the day following the birth. Women can decide when they wish their maternity leave and pay to start and can work until the baby is born. However, where the woman is absent from work wholly or partly due to her pregnancy in the four weeks before the week the baby is due to be born, SMP will start the day following the first day of absence from work.

Employers are reimbursed for 92 per cent of the SMP they pay. Small employers with annual gross NI payments of £45,000 or less recover 103 per cent of the SMP paid out.

STATUTORY PATERNITY PAY

Ordinary Statutory Paternity Pay

Employers pay ordinary statutory paternity pay (OSPP) to employees who are taking leave when a child is born or placed for adoption. To qualify the employee must:

- have responsibility for the child's upbringing
- be the biological father of the child (or the child's adopter), or the spouse/civil partner/partner of the mother or adopter
- have been employed by the same employer for at least 26 weeks ending with the 15th week before the baby is due (or the week in which the adopter is notified of having been matched with a child)
- continue working for the employer up to the child's birth (or placement for adoption)
- be earning an average of at least £113 a week (before tax)

Employees who meet these conditions receive payment of £140.98 or 90 per cent of the employee's average weekly earnings if this is less than £140.98. The employee can choose to be paid for one or two consecutive weeks. The earliest the OSPP period can begin is the date of the child's birth or placement for adoption. The OSPP period must be completed within eight weeks of that date. OSPP is not payable for any week in which the employee works. Employers are reimbursed in the same way as for statutory maternity pay.

Additional Paternity Leave and Pay

Regulations introduced on 6 April 2010 give parents greater flexibility in how they use their maternity and paternity provisions. For births from 3 April 2011, additional paternity leave (APL) entitles eligible fathers to take up to 26 weeks' additional paternity leave, allowing for up to a total of one year's leave to be shared between the couple. APL entitlement requires the mother to have returned to work; it must also be taken between 20 weeks and one year after the child is born. APL may be paid if taken during the mother's statutory maternity pay period or maternity allowance period.

The APL entitlement will also apply to husbands, partners or civil partners who are not the child's father but expect to have the main responsibility (apart from the mother) for the child's upbringing.

The current rate of additional statutory paternity pay is £140.98 a week or 90 per cent of the emplyee's average weekly earnings if this is less than £140.98.

STATUTORY ADOPTION PAY

Employers pay statutory adoption pay (SAP) to employees taking adoption leave from their employers. To qualify for SAP the employee must:

- be newly matched with a child by an adoption agency
- have been employed by the same employer for at least 26 weeks ending the week in which they have been notified of being matched with a child
- be earning an average of at least £113 a week (before tax)

Employees who meet these conditions receive payment of £140.98 or 90 per cent of their average weekly earnings if this is less than £140.98 for up to 39 weeks. The earliest SAP can be paid from is two weeks before the expected date of placement; the latest it can start is the date of the child's placement. Where a couple adopt a child, only one of them may receive SAP, the other may be able to receive statutory paternity pay if they meet the eligibility criteria. Employers are reimbursed in the same way as for statutory maternity pay.

The additional paternity leave entitlement (see above) will also apply to adoptions where adoptive parents are notified of a match on or after 3 April 2011.

STATUTORY SICK PAY

Employers pay statutory sick pay (SSP) for up to a maximum of 28 weeks to any employee incapable of work for four or more consecutive days. Employees must have done some work under their contract of service and have average weekly earnings of at least £113 from April 2017. SSP is a daily payment and is usually paid for the days that an employee would normally work, these days are known as qualifying days. SSP is not paid for the first three qualifying days in a period of sickness. SSP is paid at £89.35 per week and is subject to PAYE and NI contributions. Employees who cannot obtain SSP may be able to claim incapacity benefit. Employers may be able to recover some SSP costs.

THE WATER INDUSTRY

In the UK, the water industry provides clean and safe drinking water to over 64 million homes and has an annual turnover of around £10bn. It supplies around 17 billion litres of water a day to domestic and commercial customers and collects and treats more than 16 billion litres of wastewater a day. It also manages assets that include around 1,400 water treatment and 9,350 wastewater treatment works, 550 impounding reservoirs, over 6,500 service reservoirs/water towers and 800,000km of water mains and sewers.

Water services in England and Wales are provided by private companies. In Scotland and Northern Ireland there are single authorities, Scottish Water and Northern Ireland Water, that are publicly owned companies answerable to their respective governments. In drinking water quality tests carried out in 2017 by the Drinking Water Inspectorate, the water industry in England and Wales achieved 99.96 per cent compliance with the standards required by the EU Drinking Water Directive; Scotland achieved 99.91 per cent and Northern Ireland 99.86 per cent.

Water UK is the industry association that represents all UK water and wastewater service suppliers at national and European level and is funded directly by its members, who are the service suppliers for England, Scotland, Wales and Northern Ireland; every member has a seat on the Water UK Council.

WATER UK, 3rd Floor, 36 Broadway, London SW1H 0BH
T 020-7344 1844
W www.water.org.uk
Chief Executive, Michael Roberts

ENGLAND AND WALES

In England and Wales, the Secretary of State for Environment, Food and Rural Affairs and the Welsh government have overall responsibility for water policy and oversee environmental standards for the water industry.

The statutory consumer representative body for water services is the Consumer Council for Water.

CONSUMER COUNCIL FOR WATER, 1st Floor, Victoria Square House, Victoria Square, Birmingham B2 4AJ
T 0300-034 2222
E enquiries@ccwater.org.uk W www.ccwater.org.uk

REGULATORY BODIES

The Water Services Regulation Authority (OFWAT) was established in 1989 when the water and sewerage industry in England and Wales was privatised. Its statutory role and duties are laid out under the Water Industry Act 1991 and it is the independent economic regulator of the water and sewerage companies in England and Wales. OFWAT's main duties are to ensure that the companies can finance and carry out their statutory functions and to protect the interests of water customers. OFWAT is a non-ministerial government department headed by a board following a change in legislation introduced by the Water Act 2003.

Under the Competition Act 1998, from 1 March 2000 the Competition Appeal Tribunal has heard appeals against the regulator's decisions regarding anti-competitive agreements and abuse of a dominant position in the marketplace. The Water Act 2003 placed a new duty on OFWAT to contribute to the achievement of sustainable development.

The Environment Agency has statutory duties and powers in relation to water resources, pollution control, flood defence, fisheries, recreation, conservation and navigation in England and Wales. It is also responsible for issuing permits, licences, consents and registrations such as industrial licences to extract water and fishing licences.

The Drinking Water Inspectorate (DWI) is the drinking water quality regulator for England and Wales, responsible for assessing the quality of the drinking water supplied by the water companies and investigating any incidents affecting drinking water quality, initiating prosecution where necessary. The DWI science and strategy group provides scientific advice on drinking water policy issues to DEFRA and the Welsh government.

OFWAT, Centre City Tower, 7 Hill Street, Birmingham B5 4UA
T 0121-644 7500
E mailbox@ofwat.gsi.gov.uk W www.ofwat.gov.uk
Chair, Jonson Cox
Chief Executive, Cathryn Ross

METHODS OF CHARGING

In England and Wales, most domestic customers still pay for domestic water supply and sewerage services through charges based on the rateable value of their property. OFWAT estimated that the proportion of household customers in England and Wales to have metered supplies was over 50 per cent in 2016–17. Nearly all non-household customers are charged according to consumption.

Under the Water Industry Act 1999, water companies can continue basing their charges on the old rateable value of the property. Domestic customers can continue paying on an unmeasured basis unless they choose to pay according to consumption. After having a meter installed (which is free of charge), a customer can revert to unmeasured charging within 12 months. However, water companies may charge by meter for new homes, or homes where there is a high discretionary use of water. Domestic, school and hospital customers cannot be disconnected for non-payment.

In December 2014, OFWAT finalised its 2014 price review decisions for household water bills for the five-year period to 2020. With the exception of Bristol Water, all the water and sewerage, and water only companies confirmed acceptance of OFWAT's price decisions by the 12 February 2015 deadline. This means that average bills for water and waste-water customers in England and Wales will decrease by around 5 per cent, before adjustments for inflation, between 2015 and 2020; an average decrease of around £20, from £396 to £376 per annum.

AVERAGE HOUSEHOLD BILLS 2016–20 (£)
WATER AND SEWERAGE COMPANIES

	2016–17	2017–18	2019–20
	(£)	(£)	(£) estimated
Anglian	411	419	390
Dwr Cymru	438	439	416
Northumbrian	378	390	382
Severn Trent	329	341	316
South West	488	491	506
Southern	411	418	403
Thames	374	374	353
United Utilities	415	419	398
Wessex	460	470	442
Yorkshire	366	373	361

WATER ONLY COMPANIES

	2016–17	2017–18	2019–20
	(£)	(£)	(£) estimated
Affinity	185	185	163
Bristol	175	177	160
Cambridge	127	132	–
Dee Valley	145	150	149
Northumbrian	236	178	–
Portsmouth	98	100	96
Sembcorp Bournemouth	136	138	134
South East	198	206	194
South Staffordshire	142	144	135
Sutton and East Surrey	186	188	180

Source: OFWAT

SCOTLAND

In 2002 the three existing water authorities in Scotland (East of Scotland Water, North of Scotland Water and West of Scotland Water) merged to form Scottish Water. Scottish Water, which serves more than 2.4 million households and provides 1.34 billion litres of water per day while removing 847 million litres of waste water, is a public sector company, structured and managed like a private company, but remains answerable to the Scottish parliament. Scottish Water is regulated by the Water Industry Commission for Scotland (established under the Water Services (Scotland) Act 2005), the Scottish Environment Protection Agency (SEPA) and the Drinking Water Quality Regulator for Scotland. The Water Industry Commissioner is responsible for regulating all aspects of economic and customer service performance, including water and sewerage charges. SEPA, created under the Environment Act 1995, is responsible for environmental issues, including controlling pollution and promoting the cleanliness of Scotland's rivers, lochs and coastal waters. The Public Services Reform (Scotland) Act 2010 transferred the complaints handling function of Waterwatch Scotland regarding Scottish Water, to the Scottish Public Services Ombudsman. Consumer Futures represented the views and interests of Scottish Water customers but became part of Citizens Advice Scotland in 2014.

METHODS OF CHARGING

Scottish Water sets charges for domestic and non-domestic water and sewerage provision through charges schemes which are regulated by the Water Industry Commission for Scotland. In February 2004 the harmonisation of all household charges across the country was completed following the merger of the separate authorities under Scottish Water. In November 2014 the Water Industry Commission for Scotland published *The Strategic Review of Charges 2015–2021*, stating that annual price rises would not increase at a rate higher than that of consumer price inflation during this six-year period. For the year 2017–18, the combined service charge, covering the water supply and waste water collection, increased by a maximum of 1.6 per cent; resulting in an annual average household bill of £357.

CITIZENS ADVICE SCOTLAND, T 0808-800 9060
W www.cas.org.uk

DRINKING WATER QUALITY REGULATOR FOR SCOTLAND, Area 3-J South, Victoria Quay, Edinburgh EH6 6QQ **T** 0131-244 0190 **W** www.dwqr.scot

SCOTTISH ENVIRONMENT PROTECTION AGENCY, Third Floor,Silvan House, 231 Corstorphine Road, Edinburgh EH12 7AT **T** 0300-099 6699 **W** www.sepa.org.uk

SCOTTISH PUBLIC SERVICES OMBUDSMAN, 4 Melville Street, EdinburghEH3 7NS **T** 0800-377 7330
W www.spso.org.uk

SCOTTISH WATER, Castle House, 6 Castle Drive, Dunfermline KY11 8GG **T** 0800-077 8778 **W** www.scottishwater.co.uk
Chief Executive, Douglas Millican

WATER INDUSTRY COMMISSION FOR SCOTLAND, First Floor, Moray House, Forthside Way, Stirling FK8 1QZ **T** 01786-430200 **W** www.watercommission.co.uk

NORTHERN IRELAND

Formerly an executive agency of the Department for Regional Development, Northern Ireland Water is a government-owned company but with substantial independence from government. Northern Ireland Water was set up as a result of government reform of water and sewerage services in April 2007. It is responsible for policy and coordination with regard to the supply, distribution and cleanliness of water, and the provision and maintenance of sewerage services. It supplies 560 million litres of clean water a day to almost 1.8 million people and treats 320 million litres of waste water each day. The Northern Ireland Authority for Utility Regulation (known as the Utility Regulator) is responsible for regulating the water services provided by Northern Ireland Water. The Drinking Water Inspectorate, a unit in the Northern Ireland Environment Agency (NIEA), regulates drinking water quality. Another NIEA unit, the Water Management Unit, has responsibility for the protection of the aquatic environment. The Consumer Council for Northern Ireland is the consumer representative body for water services.

METHODS OF CHARGING

The water and sewerage used by domestic customers in Northern Ireland is currently paid for by the Department for Infrastructure (formerly known as the Regional Development (DRD)), however the future of the subsidy system is uncertain. Non-domestic customers in Northern Ireland became subject to water and sewerage charges and trade effluent charges where applicable in April 2008.

CONSUMER COUNCIL FOR NORTHERN IRELAND, Seatem House, 28–32 Alfred Street, Belfast BT2 8EN **T** 028-9025 1600
W www.consumercouncil.org.uk

NORTHERN IRELAND AUTHORITY FOR UTILITY REGULATION, Queens House, 14 Queen Street, Belfast BT1 6ED **T** 028-9031 1575 **W** www.uregni.gov.uk

NORTHERN IRELAND WATER, Westland House, 40 Old Westland Road, Belfast BT14 6TE **T** 0345-744 0088
W www.niwater.com
Chief Executive, Sara Venning

WATER SERVICE COMPANIES

WATER UK MEMBERS

AFFINITY WATER, Tamblin Way, Hatfield, Herts AL10 9EZ **T** 01707-268111 **W** www.affinitywater.co.uk

ALBION WATER, Harpdenden Hall, Southdown Road, Harpenden, Herts AL5 1TE **T** 0158-276 7720
W www.albionwater.co.uk

ANGLIAN WATER SERVICES LTD, Lancaster House, Lancaster Way, Huntington PE29 6YJ **T** 01480 32300
W www.anglianwater.co.uk

SEMBCORPBOURNEMOUTH WATER, George Jessel House, Francis Avenue, Bournemouth, Dorset BH11 8NX **T** 01202-591111 **W** www.bournemouthwater.co.uk

BRISTOL WATER PLC, Bridgwater Road, Bristol BS13 7AT **T** 0345-702 3797 **W** www.bristolwater.co.uk

CAMBRIDGE WATER COMPANY, PO Box 7040, Green Lane, Walsall WS1 9QG **T** 01223-706050
W www.cambridge-water.co.uk

DEE VALLEY WATER PLC, Packsaddle, Wrexham Road, Rhostyllen, Wrexham LL14 4EH **T** 01978-846946
W www.deevalleywater.co.uk

DWR CYMRU (WELSH WATER), Pentwyn Road, Nelson, Treharris, Mid Glamorgan CF46 6LY **T** 0800-052 0145
W www.dwrcymru.co.uk

ESSEX & SUFFOLK WATER PLC (subsidiary of Northumbrian Water Ltd), Customer Centre, PO Box 292, Durham DH1 9TX **T** 0845-782 0111 **W** www.eswater.co.uk

INDEPENDENT WATER NETWORKS, Driscoll 2, Ellen Street, Cardiff CF10 4BP T 02920-028711 W www.iwnl.co.uk

NORTHERN IRELAND WATER, PO Box 1026, Belfast BT1 9DJ T 0345-744 0088 W www.niwater.com

NORTHUMBRIAN WATER LTD, Abbey Road, Pity Me, Durham DH1 5FJ T 0845-604 7468 W www.nwl.co.uk

PEEL, Peel Dome, intu Trafford Centre, Manchester M17 8PL T 0161-629 8200 W www.peel.co.uk

PORTSMOUTH WATER PLC, PO Box 8, West Street, Havant, Hants PO9 1LG T 023-9249 9888 W www.portsmouthwater.co.uk

SCOTTISH WATER, Castle House, 6 Castle Drive, Carnegie Campus, Dunfermline KY11 8GG T 0345-601 8855 W www.scottishwater.co.uk

SEVERN TRENT WATER LTD, 2 St Johns Street, Coventry CV1 2LZ T 024-7771 5000 W www.stwater.co.uk

SOUTH EAST WATER LTD, Rocfort Road, Snodland, Kent ME6 5AH T 0333-000 0001 W www.southeastwater.co.uk

SOUTH STAFFORDSHIRE WATER PLC, Green Lane, Walsall WS2 7PD T 0845-607 0456 W www.south-staffs-water.co.uk

SOUTH WEST WATER LTD, Peninsula House, Rydon Lane, Exeter EX2 7HR T 01392-443020 W www.southwestwater.co.uk

SOUTHERN WATER SERVICES LTD, PO Box 41, Worthing BN13 3NZ T 01903-264444 W www.southernwater.co.uk

SSE, T 0345-078 3200 W www.sse.co.uk

SUTTON AND EAST SURREY WATER PLC, London Road, Redhill, Surrey RH1 1LJ T 01737-772000 W www.waterplc.com

THAMES WATER UTILITIES LTD, Clearwater Court, Vastern Road, Reading RG1 8DB T 0800-980 8800 W www.thameswater.co.uk

UNITED UTILITIES WATER PLC, Haweswater House, Lingley Mere Business Park, Great Sankey, Warrington WA5 3LP T 0845-746 2200 W www.unitedutilities.com

VEOLIA WATER PROJECTS, Kings Place, 90 York Way, London, N1 9AG T 020-784 38500 W www.veoliawater.co.uk

WESSEX WATER SERVICES LTD, Claverton Down, Bath BA2 7WW T 01225-526000 W www.wessexwater.co.uk

YORKSHIRE WATER SERVICES LTD, Western House, Western Way, Bradford BD6 2LZ T 01274-691111 W www.yorkshirewater.com

ASSOCIATE MEMBERS
(not members of Water UK)

GUERNSEY WATER, PO Box 30, Brickfield House, St Andrew, Guernsey GY1 3AS T 01481-239500 W www.water.gg

IRISH WATER (UISCE EIREANN), Colvill House, 24–26 Talbot Street, Dublin 1 W www.water.ie

JERSEY WATER, PO Box 69, Mulcaster House, Westmount Road, St Helier, Jersey JE1 1DG T 01534-707300 W www.jerseywater.je

ENERGY

The main primary sources of energy in Britain are coal, oil, natural gas, renewables and nuclear power. The main secondary sources are electricity, coke and smokeless fuels and petroleum products. The UK was a net importer of fuels in the 1970s, however as a result of growth in oil and gas production from the North Sea, the UK became a net exporter of energy for most of the 1980s. Output decreased in the late 1980s following the Piper Alpha disaster until the mid-1990s, after which the UK again became a net exporter. Since 2004, the UK reverted back to become a net importer of energy. In 2016, the UK net import gap decreased to 74 million tonnes of oil equivalent – from 78 million tonnes of oil equivalent in the previous year – accounting for 37.0 per cent of the total energy used in the UK. In value terms, on an Overseas Trade Statistics (OTS) basis, the total fuel deficit for 2016 was £10.5bn, 16 per cent less than in 2015, due to substantial reduction in crude oil prices. The deficit of crude oil and petroleum products, on the same basis, in 2016 was £4bn (27 per cent more than in 2015) compared with a £2.2bn surplus in 2004. The Department for Business, Energy and Industrial Strategy (BEIS) is responsible for promoting energy efficiency.

INDIGENOUS PRODUCTION OF PRIMARY FUELS
Million tonnes of oil equivalent

	2015	2016
Primary oils	49.5	52.0
Natural gas	38.8	39.8
Primary electricity	20.1	20.0
Coal	5.4	2.6
Bioenergy and waste	9.8	10.8
Total	123.7	125.1

Source: DBEIS

INLAND ENERGY CONSUMPTION BY PRIMARY FUEL
Million tonnes of oil equivalent, temperature adjusted

	2015	2016
Natural gas	68.1	76.7
Petroleum	67.3	68.0
Coal	25.1	12.4
Nuclear electricity	15.5	15.4
Bioenergy and waste	13.1	14.2
Wind and hydro electricity	4.7	4.6
Net Imports	1.8	1.5
Total	195.5	192.8

Source: DBEIS

TRADE IN FUELS AND RELATED MATERIALS (2016)

	Quantity, million tonnes of oil equivalent	Value £m
Imports		
Crude oil	53.4	11,675
Petroleum products	38.3	11,335
Natural gas	46.0	6,300
Coal and other solid fuel	10.4	955
Electricity	1.7	780
Total	149.7	31,050
Exports		
Crude oil	38.2	8,375
Petroleum products	26.7	8,050
Natural gas	10.0	1,350
Coal and other solid fuel	0.7	55
Electricity	0.2	105
Total	75.8	17,930

Source: DBEIS, ONS

OIL

Until the 1960s Britain imported almost all its oil supplies. In 1969 oil was discovered in the Arbroath field in the North Sea. The first oilfield to be brought into production was Argyll in 1975, and since the mid-1970s Britain has been a major producer of crude oil.

To date, the UK has produced around 3.7 billion tonnes of oil. It is estimated that there are around 515 million tonnes remaining to be produced. Licences for exploration and production are granted to companies by the Oil and Gas Authority. As at July 2017, 519 offshore production licences and 203 onshore petroleum exploration and development licences had been awarded. As of July 2017, there was a total of 325 offshore oil and gas fields in production. Total UK oil production peaked in 1999 but is now declining. Production stood at 47.9 million tonnes in 2016, just under a third of the 1999 level. Profits from oil production are subject to a special tax regime with different taxes applying depending on the date of approval of each field.

DRILLING ACTIVITY (2016)
by number of wells started

	Offshore	Onshore
Exploration	14	1
Appraisal	8	0
Exploration and appraisal	22	1
Development	87	4

Source: OGA

INDIGENOUS PRODUCTION AND REFINERY RECEIPTS
Thousand tonnes

	2015	2016
Indigenous production	45,698	47,872
Crude oil	42,826	44,306
*NGLs	2,462	3,139
Refinery receipts	61,391	60,363

* Natural Gas Liquids: condensates and petroleum gases derived at onshore treatment plants
Source: DBEIS

DELIVERIES OF PETROLEUM PRODUCTS FOR INLAND CONSUMPTION BY ENERGY USE
Thousand tonnes

	2015	2016
Transport	48,374	49,292
Industry	3,944	3,726
Domestic	2,273	2,275
Other	1,813	1,840
Total	56,404	57,133

Source: DBEIS

COAL

Mines were in private ownership until 1947 when they were nationalised and came under the management of the National Coal Board, later the British Coal Corporation. The corporation held a near monopoly on coal production until 1994 when the industry was restructured. Under the Coal Industry Act 1994, the Coal Authority was established to take over ownership of coal reserves and to issue licences to private mining companies. The Coal Authority is also responsible for the physical legacy of mining, eg subsidence damage claims that are not the responsibility of licensees, and for holding and making available all existing records. It also publishes current data on the coal industry on its website (W www.gov.uk/government/organisations/the-coal-authority).

The mines owned by the British Coal Corporation were sold as five separate businesses in 1994 and coal production is now undertaken entirely in the private sector. Coal output was around 50 million tonnes a year in 1994 but has since declined. In 2016, coal output stood at around 4.2 million tonnes, a decrease of 51 per cent. The decrease was due to the closure of Hatfield, Thoresby and Kellingley mines in 2015; three of the last remaining deep mines within the UK, combined with a steep reduction in demand as government policy and market forces reduced the use of coal for electricity generation. Deep mine production decreased by 99 per cent and surface production by 29 per cent. As at 31 December 2016, there were eight deep mines and 19 surface mines in production in the UK.

The main consumer of coal in the UK is the electricity supply industry. Coal still supplies over a third of the UK's electricity needs but as indigenous production has declined, imports have continued to make up the shortfall and now represent around 64 per cent of UK coal supply, 38 per cent of which is currently supplied from Russia.

UK government policy is to meet the long-term challenges posed by climate change while continuing to ensure secure, clean and affordable energy. Coal's availability, flexibility and reliability compared to other sources mean that it is expected to continue to play an important role in the future generating mix, but its carbon emissions will need to be managed through the introduction of abatement technologies including carbon capture and storage (CCS).

CCS attempts to mitigate the effects of global warming by capturing the carbon dioxide emissions from power stations that burn fossil fuels, preventing the gas from being released into the atmosphere, and storing it in underground geological formations. CCS is still in its infancy and only through its successful demonstration and development will it be possible for coal to remain a part of a low-carbon UK energy mix. The government is committed to public sector investment in CCS technology on four power stations and has made it clear that there can be no new coal power stations in England and Wales without CCS on a defined amount of capacity. As part of a wider package of reforms to the electricity market, the government will also be introducing an Emissions Performance Standard, which will limit the emissions from new fossil fuel power stations.

COAL PRODUCTION AND FOREIGN TRADE
Thousand tonnes

	2015	2016
Surface mining	5,814	4,156
Deep-mined	2,784	22
Imports	22,518	8,494
Exports	(385)	(443)
*Total supply	37,593	17,883
Total demand	37,612	17,889

* Includes stock change
Source: DBEIS

INLAND COAL USE
Thousand tonnes

	2015	2016
Fuel producers		
Electricity generators	29,330	12,058
Coke manufacture	3,673	1,821
Blast furnaces	1,544	1,364
Heat generation	213	213
Patent fuel manufacture	228	223
Final consumption		
Industry	2,043	1,615
Transport	13	15
Domestic	552	550
Public administration	4	20
Commercial	5	5
Agriculture	0	0
Miscellaneous	7	7

Source: DBEIS

GAS

From the late 18th century gas in Britain was produced from coal. In the 1960s town gas began to be produced from oil-based feedstocks using imported oil. In 1965 gas was discovered in the North Sea in the West Sole field, which became the first gasfield in production in 1967, and from the late 1960s natural gas began to replace town gas. From October 1998 Britain was connected to the continental European gas system via a pipeline from Bacton, Norfolk to Zeebrugge, Belgium. Gas is transported through 278,000km of mains pipeline including 7,600km of high-pressure gas pipelines owned and operated in the UK by National Grid Gas plc.

The gas industry in Britain was nationalised in 1949 and operated as the Gas Council. The Gas Council was replaced by the British Gas Corporation in 1972 and the industry became more centralised. The British Gas Corporation was privatised in 1986 as British Gas plc. In 1993 the Monopolies and Mergers Commission found that British Gas's integrated business in Great Britain as a gas trader and the owner of the gas transportation system could operate against the public interest. In February 1997, British Gas demerged its trading arm to become two separate companies, BG plc and Centrica plc. In February 2016, Royal Dutch Shell announced that it had acquired BG Group, whose principal business was finding and developing gas reserves and building gas markets. Its core operations are located in the UK, South America, Egypt, Trinidad and Tobago, Kazakhstan and India. Centrica runs the trading and services operations under the British Gas brand name in Great Britain. In October 2000 BG demerged its pipeline business, Transco, which became part of Lattice Group, finally merging with the National Grid Group in 2002 to become National Grid Transco plc.

In July 2005 National Grid Transco plc changed its name to National Grid plc and Transco plc became National Grid Gas plc. In the same year National Grid Gas also completed the sale of four of its eight gas distribution networks. The distribution networks transport gas at lower pressures, which eventually supply the consumers such as domestic customers. The Scotland and south-east of England networks were sold to Scotia Gas Networks. The Wales and south-west network was sold to Wales & West Utilities and the network in the north-east to Northern Gas Networks. This was the biggest change in the corporate structure of gas infrastructure since privatisation in 1986.

Competition was gradually introduced into the industrial gas market from 1986. Supply of gas to the domestic market was opened to companies other than British Gas, starting in April 1996 with a pilot project in the West Country and Wales, with the rest of the UK following soon after.

Declines in UK indigenous gas production and increasing demand led to the UK becoming a net importer of gas once more in 2004. With the depletion of the UK Continental Shelf reserves, UK gas production has seen growing rates of decline. As part of the Energy Act 2008, the government planned to strengthen regulation of the offshore gas supply infrastructure, to allow private sector investment to help maintain UK energy supplies.

In 2012, it was estimated that there could be over 200 trillion cubic feet of untapped gas underneath Lincolnshire. Trapped inside rock formations, the gas is known as shale gas and the process to release the gas is called hydraulic fracturing or fracking, whereby water, chemicals and sand are pumped into a drilled well at high pressure. A further investigation by the British Geological Survey in 2012 claimed that there could in fact be up to 1,300 trillion cubic feet of gas but opponents to the process raised concerns that fracking results in more greenhouse gas emissions than conventional gas, fracking damages the environment significantly and that it may cause seismic tremors.

CENTRICA PLC, Millstream, Maidenhead Road, Windsor,
Berkshire SL4 5GD **T** 01753-494000
W www.centrica.com
Chair, Rick Haythornthwaite
Chief Executive, Iain Conn

NATIONAL GRID PLC, National Grid House, Warwick
Technology Park, Gallows Hill, Warwick CV34 6DA
T 01926-653000 **W** www.nationalgrid.com
Chair, Sir Peter Gershon, CBE
Chief Executive, John Pettigrew

UK GAS CONSUMPTION BY INDUSTRY
GWh

	2015	2016
Domestic	297,582	311,375
Industry	99,211	98,006
Public administration	36,545	37,246
Commercial	44,097	46,459
Agriculture	983	946
Non-energy use	5,267	5,109
Miscellaneous	10,310	10,464
Total gas consumption	493,994	509,605

Source: DBEIS

ELECTRICITY

The first power station in Britain generating electricity for public supply began operating in 1882. In the 1930s a national transmission grid was developed and it was reconstructed and extended in the 1950s and 1960s. Power stations were operated by the Central Electricity Generating Board.

Under the Electricity Act 1989, 12 regional electricity companies, responsible for the distribution of electricity from the national grid to consumers, were formed from the former area electricity boards in England and Wales. Four companies were formed from the Central Electricity Generating Board: three generating companies (National Power plc, Nuclear Electric plc and Powergen plc) and the National Grid Company plc, which owned and operated the transmission system in England and Wales. National Power and Powergen were floated on the stock market in 1991.

National Power was demerged in October 2000 to form two separate companies: International Power plc and Innogy plc, which manages the bulk of National Power's UK assets. Nuclear Electric was split into two parts in 1996.

The National Grid Company was floated on the stock market in 1995 and formed a new holding company, National Grid Group. National Grid Group completed a merger with Lattice in 2002 to form National Grid Transco, a public limited company (*see* Gas).

Following privatisation, generators and suppliers in England and Wales traded via the Electricity Pool. A competitive wholesale trading market known as NETA (New Electricity Trading Arrangements) replaced the Electricity Pool in March 2001, and was extended to include Scotland via the British Electricity Transmissions and Trading Arrangements (BETTA) in 2005. As part of BETTA, National Grid became the system operator for all transmission. The introduction of competition into the domestic electricity market was completed in May 1999.

In Scotland, three new companies were formed under the Electricity Act 1989: Scottish Power plc and Scottish Hydro-Electric plc, which were responsible for generation, transmission, distribution and supply; and Scottish Nuclear Ltd. Scottish Power and Scottish Hydro-Electric were floated on the stock market in 1991. Scottish Hydro-Electric merged with Southern Electric in 1998 to become Scottish and Southern Energy plc. Scottish Nuclear was incorporated into British Energy in 1996.

In Northern Ireland, Northern Ireland Electricity plc (NIE) was set up in 1993 under a 1991 Order in Council. In 1993 it was floated on the stock market and in 1998 it became part of the Viridian Group and was responsible for distribution and supply until NIE was sold to ESB Independent Energy in December 2010. In June 2010, Airtricity became the first new electricity supplier since the Northern Ireland electricity market was opened to competition in 2007.

On 12 July 2011, the government published *Planning Our Electric Future: a White Paper for Secure, Affordable and Low-carbon Electricity* in response to the challenges set by increasing electricity demands. It was agreed that extensive investment is needed to update the grid and build new power stations. Currently, 21 per cent of the UK electricity generation comes from nuclear reactors, a process by which uranium atoms are split to produce heat through a chemical process known as fission. While nuclear power stations will close gradually over the next decade, with only one expected to produce power beyond 2025, there are plans in place for a new generation of reactors to be built, potentially running by 2019. Most of the UK's electricity comes from burning fossil fuels and in 2016 natural gas provided 42 per cent of electricity production, coal provided 9 per cent and under 1 per cent was provided from oil.

Interconnecting cables import and export electricity to Europe, in France, the Netherlands and Ireland. In 2016, the UK was a net importer from France and the Netherlands, accounting for 4.9 per cent of electricity supplied.

On 30 September 2003 the Electricity Association, the industry's main trade association, was replaced with three separate trade bodies: the Association of Electricity Producers; the Energy Networks Association; and the Energy Retail Association. In April 2012, following a merger between the Association of Electricity Producers, the Energy Retail Association and the UK Business Council for Sustainable Energy, Energy UK – the new trade association for the gas and electricity sector – was established.

ENERGY NETWORKS ASSOCIATION, 6th floor, Dean
Bradley House, 52 Horseferry Road, London SW1P 2AF
T 020-7706 5100
W www.energynetworks.org
Chief Executive, David Smith

ENERGY UK, Charles House, 5–11 Regent Street, London SW1Y
4LR **T** 020-7930 9390 **W** www.energy-uk.org.uk
Chief Executive, Lawrence Slade

ELECTRICITY PRODUCTION, SUPPLY AND CONSUMPTION
GWh

	2015	2016
Electricity produced		
Nuclear	70,345	71,726
Hydro	6,289	5,395
Wind, wave and solar photovoltaics	47,865	47,788
Coal	75,878	30,711
Oil	2,037	1,839
Gas	99,875	143,362
Other renewables	29,240	30,043
Other	4,639	5,574
Total	336,178	336,438
Electricity supplied		
Production	336,178	336,438
*Other sources	2,739	2,959
Imports	22,716	19,699
Exports	(1,778)	(2,153)
Total	359,855	356,943
Electricity consumed		
Industry	92,907	91,808
Transport	4,516	4,669
Other	206,026	207,318
Domestic	107,764	107,971
Public administration	19,371	19,827
Commercial	74,773	75,097
Agriculture	4,117	4,423
Total	3023,448	303,795

* Pumped storage production

Source: DBEIS

GAS AND ELECTRICITY SUPPLIERS

With the gas and electricity markets open, most suppliers offer their customers both services. The majority of gas/electricity companies have become part of larger multi-utility companies, often operating internationally.

As part of measures to reduce the UK's carbon output, the government has outlined plans to introduce 'smart meters' to all UK homes. Smart meters perform the traditional meter function of measuring energy consumption, in addition to more advanced functions such as allowing energy suppliers to communicate directly with their customers and removing the need for meter readings and bill estimates. The meters also allow domestic customers to have direct access to energy consumption information.

The following list comprises a selection of suppliers offering gas and electricity. In England, Scotland and Wales, the 'Big Six' are the largest energy suppliers in the UK, providing gas and electricity to around 50 million homes and businesses, and owning a 90 per cent share of the domestic customer market. Organisations in italics are subsidiaries of the companies listed in capital letters directly above.

ENGLAND, SCOTLAND AND WALES

CENTRICA PLC, Millstream, Maidenhead Road, Windsor, Berkshire SL4 5GD **T** 01753-494000 **W** www.centrica.com
British Gas, PO Box 4805, Worthing BN11 9QW **T** 0800-048 0202 **W** www.britishgas.co.uk
EDF ENERGY, Osprey House, Osprey Road, Exeter EX2 7WN **T** 0800-056 7777 **W** www.edfenergy.com
E.ON UK, Westward Way, Coventry, CV4 8LG **T** 024-7619 2000 **W** www.eonenergy.com
NPOWER, Windmill Business Park, Whitehill Way, Swindon SN5 6PB **T** 0800-073 3000 **W** www.npower.com
SCOTTISH POWER, 330-336 St Vincent Street, Glasgow G3 8UR **T** 0845-270 0072 **W** www.scottishpower.co.uk
SSE PLC, Inveralmond House, 200 Dunkeld Road, Perth PH1 3AQ **T** 0800-980 8831 **W** www.sse.co.uk

NORTHERN IRELAND

AIRTRICITY (a member of SSE plc), Red Oak South, South County Business Park, Dublin 18 **T** 0345-864 3546 **W** www.sseairtricity.com
ELECTRIC IRELAND, The Gasworks,1 Cromac Place, Belfast BT7 2JD **T** 0845-600 5335 **W** www.electricireland.ie
VIRIDIAN GROUP PLC, Greenwood House, 64 Newforge Lane, Belfast BT9 5NF **T** 028-9066 8416 **W** www.viridiangroup.co.uk
Energia, 3rd Floor, Mill House, Ashtowngate, Navan Road, Dublin 15 **T** 1850-363744 **W** www.energia.ie

REGULATION OF THE GAS AND ELECTRICITY INDUSTRIES

The Office of Gas and Electricity Markets (OFGEM) regulates the gas and electricity industries in Great Britain. It was formed in 1999 by the merger of the Office of Gas Supply and the Office of Electricity Regulation. OFGEM's overriding aim is to protect and promote the interests of all gas and electricity customers by promoting competition and regulating monopolies. It is governed by an authority and its powers are provided for under the Gas Act 1986, the Electricity Act 1989, the Competition Act 1998, the Utilities Act 2000 and the Enterprise Act 2002. Energywatch was the independent gas and electricity watchdog, set up in November 2000 through the Utility Act to protect and promote the interests of gas and electricity consumers. In October 2008 Energywatch merged with Postwatch and the National Consumer Council to form a new advocacy body, Consumer Focus. In October 2010, the government announced that Consumer Focus would be abolished and some of its functions would transfer to Citizens Advice, Citizens Advice Scotland and the Consumer Council for Northern Ireland. This transfer began in April 2013 and full responsibility was transferred to Citizens Advice following the abolition of Consumer Focus on 1 April 2014.

CITIZENS ADVICE, 3rd Floor North, 200 Aldersgate Street, London EC1A 4HD **T** 0300-023 1231 **W** www.citizensadvice.org.uk
CITIZENS ADVICE SCOTLAND, 1st Floor, Spectrum House, 2 Powderhall Road, Edinburgh EH7 4GB **T** 0131-550 1000 **W** www.cas.org.uk
CONSUMER COUNCIL FOR NORTHERN IRELAND, 3rd Floor, Seatem House, 28–32 Alfred Street, Belfast BT2 8EN **T** 028-9025 1600 **W** www.consumercouncil.org.uk
THE OFFICE OF GAS AND ELECTRICITY MARKETS (OFGEM), 9 Millbank, London SW1 3GE **T** 020-7901 7000 **W** www.ofgem.gov.uk

NUCLEAR POWER

Nuclear reactors began to supply electricity to the national grid in 1956. There are presently 15 reactors at eight sites which supply approximately 21 per cent of the UK's electricity generation or 20 per cent of supply. Approximately half of this capacity is due to end by 2025. In December 2015, the final magnox reactor (Wylfa 1) was shut down after 44 years of operation, which left seven advanced gas-cooled reactors (AGR) and one pressurised water reactor (PWR) Sizewell 'B' in Suffolk. The AGRs and PWR are owned by a private company, EDF Energy. Apart from Sizewell B, which first produced power in 1995, the seven other sites are expected to be shut down by 2035, however in June 2011, eight new sites across the UK were selected for locations of new nuclear power stations. The eight sites, which stemmed from the 2008 Energy bill, are: Bradwell, Hartlepool, Heysham, Hinkley Point, Oldbury, Sellafield, Sizewell and Wylfa. EDF Energy planned to construct four new European Pressurised Reactors, two of which are scheduled to be established at Hinkley Point, with the other two at Sizewell.

The four new reactors could supply 10 million homes with energy by 2025. Each year, EDF Energy spends around £600 million upgrading its eight sites.

Hinkley Point, which was designated as the first new nuclear power plant to be built in 20 years, was scheduled to be given the green light in the summer of 2016, but the Secretary of State for Business, Energy and Industrial Strategy, Greg Clark, delayed the decision. The French firm EDF Energy, which is set to finance two-thirds of the £18bn site (the other £6bn being funded by China), had approved the funding but critics of the planned nuclear site warned of environmental damage, increasing costs and implications of nuclear sites being built in the UK by foreign investors. However, in September 2016, Theresa May gave the go ahead for the nuclear power station at Hinkley Point after the government imposed significant new safeguards for future projects.

In April 2005 the responsibility for the decommissioning of civil nuclear reactors and other nuclear facilities used in research and development was handed to the Nuclear Decommissioning Authority (NDA). The NDA is a non-departmental public body, funded mainly by the Department for Business, Energy and Industrial Strategy. The total planned expenditure for the NDA in 2016–17 was £3.2bn. Until April 2007, UK Nirex was responsible for the disposal of intermediate and some low-level nuclear waste. After this date Nirex was integrated into the NDA and renamed the Radioactive Waste Management directorate.

There are currently 17 nuclear sites owned by the NDA that are in various stages of decommissioning, including the world's first commercial power station at Calder Hall on the Sellafield site in Cumbria and Windscale, which produced plutonium in the 1950s to be used for military reasons. The responsibilities of the NDA include: decommissioning and cleaning up nuclear facilities; ensuring that all waste, including radioactive and non-radioactive products are safely managed; developing nationwide strategies and plans for Low Level Waste; implementing a long-tem plan for the management of nuclear waste; and scrutinising EDF Energy's decommissioning plans, which includes the fleet of AGR nuclear stations.

In 2016 electricity supplied from nuclear sources accounted for 21 per cent of the total electricity generation, which equated to 70TWh of a total 338TWh produced or 20 per cent of supply, which equated to 65TWh of the total 324 supplied. A number of factors have led to government backing for nuclear power: domestic gas supplies are running low; oil and gas prices are high; carbon emissions must be cut to comply with EU legislation and meet global climate change targets; and a number of coal-fired power stations that fail to meet clean air requirements are due to be closed.

Nuclear power has its advantages: reactors emit virtually no carbon dioxide and uranium prices remain relatively steady. However, the advantages of low emissions are countered by the high costs of construction and difficulties in disposing of nuclear waste. Currently, the only method is to store it securely until it has slowly decayed to safe levels. Public distrust persists despite the advances in safety technology. Following the tsunami which struck Japan in March 2011 and the level 7 meltdowns of three reactors in the Fukushima Daiichi Nuclear Plant, the safety of nuclear reactors was brought further into public interest and became a government priority.

In 2016, following the UK vote to leave the EU, the Department of Energy and Climate Change was abolished and the UK's energy policy, which included the priority of establishing new nuclear sites, was transferred to the Department of Business, Energy and Industrial Strategy.

SAFETY AND REGULATION
The Office for Nuclear Regulation (ONR), a public corporation of the Department for Work and Pensions, is the nuclear industry's regulator. Operations at the 37 UK nuclear power stations are governed by a site licence which is issued under the Nuclear Installations Act. The ONR monitors compliance and has the jurisdiction to close down a reactor if the terms of the licence are breached. The Department for Business, Energy and Industrial Strategy is responsible for security at all the UK's nuclear power stations, which are policed by the Civil Nuclear Constabulary, a specialised armed force created in April 2005. In 2009 Magnox Electric Ltd was found guilty of breaking the Radioactive Substances Act 2003: it had left a radioactive leak on a holding tank at Bradwell power station, Essex, unchecked for 14 years.

RENEWABLE SOURCES

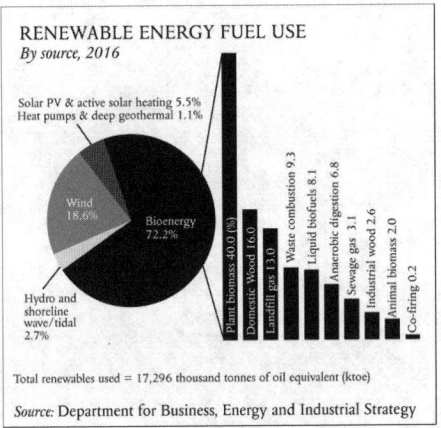

RENEWABLE ENERGY FUEL USE
By source, 2016

Solar PV & active solar heating 5.5%
Heat pumps & deep geothermal 1.1%

Wind 18.6%
Bioenergy 72.2%
Hydro and shoreline wave/tidal 2.7%

Plant biomass 40.0 (%)
Domestic Wood 16.0
Landfill gas 13.0
Waste combustion 9.3
Liquid biofuels 8.1
Anaerobic digestion 6.8
Sewage gas 3.1
Industrial wood 2.6
Animal biomass 2.0
Co-firing 0.2

Total renewables used = 17,296 thousand tonnes of oil equivalent (ktoe)

Source: Department for Business, Energy and Industrial Strategy

Progress was made towards the UK's target of consuming 15 per cent of energy from renewable sources introduced in the 2009 EU Renewable Directive, as 8.9 per cent of energy consumption came from renewable sources in 2016, up from 8.2 per cent in 2015. Renewable sources provided 24.5 per cent of the electricity generated in the UK in 2016, around the same as in 2015 (24.6 per cent). Lower rainfall and wind speeds resulted in lower hydro and wind generation, more than offsetting a 16 per cent increase in total capacity.

In 2016, for the second year running, solar photovoltaics were the leading technology in capacity terms, representing a third of total electricity capacity. This resulted in a 38 per cent increase in generation between 2015 and 2016. Generation from bioenergy sources also increased in 2016, by 2.7 per cent. Between 2015 and 2016, onshore and offshore wind generation fell by 8.4 per cent and 5.8 per cent respectively. Generation from hydro sources also fell by 14 per cent. Heat from renewable sources increased by 12 per cent during 2016 and renewable biofuels used for transport also increased, by 1.2 per cent.

The government's principal mechanisms for developing renewable energy sources are the Renewables Obligation (RO) and the Renewable Heat Incentive (RHI). The RO, since April 2002, has aimed to increase the contribution of electricity from renewables in the UK. There are separate RO schemes for England and Wales, Scotland and Northern Ireland. In England, Wales and Scotland, the RO is set so the number of ROCs (renewable obligation certificates) electricity suppliers are required to produce during 2017–18 is 0.409 ROCs per MWh. In Northern Ireland the RO is 0.167 ROCs per MWh for 2017–18.

In addition to the RO, in April 2010, the government launched a Feed-in Tariff (FIT) scheme in Great Britain to encourage the uptake of small-scale low carbon electricity generation technologies, principally renewables such as solar photovoltaics, wind and hydro-electricity. Over the years since, several reviews of the schemes have led to cuts in generation tariff levels, with the latest version of the scheme also subject to caps on deployment levels. An export tariff can be applied to sell any extra units not used by the owner, currently worth 5.03p per unit of electricity.

The RHI was originally introduced in November 2011 to provide a long-term financial incentive to support the uptake of renewable heat in the non-domestic sector. In April 2014, the RHI was extended to cover the domestic sector replacing the renewable heat premium payment scheme which closed in March 2013. Participants of the scheme receive tariff payments for the heat generated from an eligible renewable heating system which is heating a single dwelling.

The government approved an EU-wide agreement in March 2007 to generate 20 per cent of energy production from renewable sources by 2020. It has since negotiated down the national share in this target to 15 per cent of energy production by 2020. In July 2009 the government published a Renewable Energy Strategy in order to meet this target. Other impediments to the expansion of renewable energy production include planning restrictions, rising raw material prices, and the possible redirection of funds to develop CCS technology and nuclear energy sources.

TRANSPORT

CIVIL AVIATION

Since the privatisation of British Airways in 1987, UK airlines have been operated entirely by the private sector. In 2016, total capacity of British airlines amounted to 54 billion tonne-km, of which 49 billion tonne-km was on scheduled services. UK airlines carried around 154 million passengers; 143 million on scheduled services and 11 million on charter flights. Passenger traffic through UK airports increased by 7 per cent in 2016. Traffic at the six main London area airports (Gatwick, Heathrow, London City, Luton, Southend and Stansted) increased by 5 per cent over 2015 and other UK regional airports saw an increase of 9 per cent.

Leading British airlines include British Airways, EasyJet, Monarch, Thomas Cook Airlines, Thomson Airways and Virgin Atlantic. Irish airline Ryanair also operates frequent flights from the UK.

There are around 140 licensed civil aerodromes in Britain, with Heathrow and Gatwick handling the highest volume of passengers.

The Civil Aviation Authority (CAA), an independent statutory body, is responsible for the regulation of UK airlines. This includes economic and airspace regulation, air safety, consumer protection and environmental research and consultancy. All commercial airline companies must be granted an air operator's certificate, which is issued by the CAA to operators meeting the required safety standards. The CAA issues airport safety licences, which must be obtained by any airport used for public transport and training flights. All British-registered aircraft must be granted an airworthiness certificate, and the CAA issues professional licences to pilots, flight crew, ground engineers and air traffic controllers. The CAA also manages the Air Travel Organiser's Licence (ATOL), the UK's principal travel protection scheme. The CAA's costs are met entirely from charges on those whom it regulates; there is no direct government funding of the CAA's work.

The Transport Act 2000 separated the CAA from its subsidiary, National Air Traffic Services (NATS), which provides air traffic control services to aircraft flying in UK airspace and over the eastern part of the North Atlantic. NATS is a public private partnership (PPP) between the Airline Group (a consortium of UK airlines), which holds 42 per cent of the shares; NATS staff, who hold 5 per cent; UK airport operator LHR Airports Limited, which holds 4 per cent, and the government, which holds 49 per cent and a golden share. In 2017 NATS handled 2.45m flights, an increase of 7.6 per cent on 2016.

AIR PASSENGERS 2016

All UK Airports: Total	268,492,426
Aberdeen	2,955,338
Barra	12,820
Belfast City	2,665,139
Belfast International	5,147,546
Benbecula	32,467
Birmingham	11,645,334
Blackpool	36,269
Bournemouth	667,981
Bristol	7,610,780
Cambridge	591
Campbeltown	8,573
Cardiff	1,347,483
City of Derry (Eglinton)	290,671
Doncaster Sheffield	1,255,907
Dundee	37,647
Durham Tees Valley	132,369
East Midlands	4,653,818
Edinburgh	12,348,425
Exeter	847,257
Gatwick	43,119,628
Glasgow	9,327,193
Gloucestershire	12,365
Heathrow	75,711,130
Humberside	201,650
Inverness	783,017
Islay	28,339
Isle of Man	791,651
Isles of Scilly (St Mary's)	95,068
Kirkwall	163,029
Lands End (St Just)	64,804
Leeds Bradford	3,612,117
Lerwick (Tingwall)	4,438
Liverpool	4,778,939
London City	4,538,813
Luton	14,645,619
Lydd	509
Manchester	25,637,054
Newcastle	4,807,906
Newquay	371,500
Norwich	506,007
Oxford (Kidlington)	383
Prestwick	673,232
Scatsta	162,100
Shoreham	165
Southampton	1,947,052
Southend	874,549
Stansted	24,320,071
Stornoway	126,520
Sumburgh	250,407
Tiree	11,622
Wick	20,158
Channel Islands Airports	2,546,418
Alderney	57,595
Guernsey	874,118
Jersey	1,614,705

Source: Civil Aviation Authority

CAA, CAA House, 45–59 Kingsway, London WC2B 6TE
T 020-7379 7311
W www.caa.co.uk

Heathrow Airport	T 0844-335 1801
Gatwick Airport	T 0344-892 0322
Manchester Airport	T 0800-042 0213
Stansted Airport	T 0844-335 1803

BRITISH AIRLINES

BRITISH AIRWAYS, PO Box 365, Waterside, Harmondsworth UB7 0GB T 0344-493 0787 W www.britishairways.com

EASYJET, Hangar 89, London Luton Airport LU2 9PF
T 0330-365 5000 W www.easyjet.com

MONARCH, Prospect House, Prospect Way, London Luton Airport LU2 9NU T 0333-003 0100 W www.monarch.co.uk

THOMAS COOK AIRLINES, 3rd Floor, South Building, 200Algersgate, London, EC1A 4HD T 0800 916 0652
W www.thomascook.com

THOMSON AIRWAYS, Wigmore House, Wigmore Place, Wigmore Lane, Luton, Beds LU2 9TN T 0203-451 2688
W www.thomson.co.uk

VIRGIN ATLANTIC, The Office, Manor Royal, Crawley, W. Sussex RH10 9NU T 0844 811 0000 W www.virgin-atlantic.com

RAILWAYS

The railway network in Britain was developed by private companies in the 19th century. In 1948 the main railway companies were nationalised and were run by a public authority, the British Transport Commission. The commission was replaced by the British Railways Board in 1963, operating as British Rail. On 1 April 1994, responsibility for managing the track and railway infrastructure passed to a newly formed company, Railtrack plc. In October 2001 Railtrack was put into administration under the Railways Act 1993. In October 2002 Railtrack was taken out of administration and replaced by the not-for-profit company Network Rail. The British Railways Board continued as operator of all train services until 1996–7, when they were sold or franchised to the private sector.

The Strategic Rail Authority (SRA) was created to provide strategic leadership to the rail industry and formally came into being on 1 February 2001 following the passing of the Transport Act 2000. In January 2002 it published its first strategic plan, setting out the strategic priorities for Britain's railways over the next ten years. In addition to its coordinating role, the SRA was responsible for allocating government funding to the railways and awarding and monitoring the franchises for operating rail services.

On 15 July 2004 the transport secretary announced a new structure for the rail industry in the white paper *The Future of Rail*. These proposals were implemented under the Railways Act 2005, which abolished the SRA, passing most of its functions to the Department for Transport; established the Rail Passengers Council as a single national body, dissolving the regional committees; and gave devolved governments in Scotland and Wales more say in decisions at a local level. In addition, responsibility for railway safety regulation was transferred to the Office of Rail Regulation from the Health and Safety Executive.

OFFICE OF RAIL AND ROAD

The Office of Rail and Road (ORR), previously known as the Office of Rail Regulation, was established on 5 July 2004 by the Railways and Transport Safety Act 2003, replacing the Office of the Rail Regulator. In April 2015 it acquired responsibility for monitoring Highways England in addition to its existing role as the railway industry's economic and safety regulator and changed its name to better reflect its functions. The ORR regulates Network Rail's stewardship of the national network, licenses operators, approves network access agreements, and enforces domestic competition law. The ORR is led by a board appointed by the Secretary of State for Transport and chaired by Stephen Glaister.

SERVICES

For privatisation, under the Railways Act 1993, domestic passenger services were divided into 25 train operating units, which were franchised to private sector operators via a competitive tendering process. The train operators formed the Association of Train Operating Companies (ATOC) to act as the official voice of the passenger rail industry and provide its members with a range of services enabling them to comply with conditions imposed on them through their franchise agreements and operating licences.

As at September 2017 there were 31 passenger train operating companies: Arriva Trains Wales, c2c, Caledonian Sleeper, Chiltern Railways, CrossCountry, East Midlands Trains, Eurostar, Gatwick Express, Grand Central, Great Northern, Great Western Railway, Greater Anglia, Heathrow Connect, Heathrow Express, Hull Trains, Island Line, London Midland, London Overground, London Underground, Merseyrail, Northern, ScotRail, South Western Railway, Southeastern, Southern, Stansted Express, TfL Rail, Thameslink, TransPennine Express, Virgin Trains and Virgin Trains East Coast.

Network Rail publishes a national timetable which contains details of rail services operated over the UK network and sea ferry services which provide connections with Ireland, the Isle of Man, the Isle of Wight, the Channel Islands and some European destinations.

The national rail enquiries service offers information about train times and fares for any part of the country, Transport for London (TfL) provides London-specific travel information for all modes of travel and Eurostar provides information for international channel tunnel rail services:

NATIONAL RAIL ENQUIRIES
T 0345-748 4950 W www.nationalrail.co.uk
TRANSPORT FOR LONDON
T 0343-222 1234 W www.tfl.gov.uk
EUROSTAR
T 0343-218 6186 W www.eurostar.com

TRANSPORT FOCUS AND LONDON TRAVELWATCH

Previously known as Passenger Focus, Transport Focus is the national consumer watchdog for bus, tram, coach and rail passengers in England. Under The Infrastructure Act 2015 Transport Focus's role was expanded to also represent users of the strategic road network. The entity is funded by the Department for Transport and is an executive non-departmental public body.

Established in July 2000, London TravelWatch is the operating name of the official watchdog organisation representing the interests of transport users in and around the capital. Officially known as the London Transport Users' Committee, it is sponsored and funded by the London Assembly and is independent of the transport operators. London TravelWatch represents users of buses, the Underground, river and rail services in and around London, including Eurostar and Heathrow Express, Croydon Tramlink and the Docklands Light Railway. The interests of pedestrians, cyclists and motorists are also represented, as are those of taxi users.

FREIGHT

On privatisation in 1996, British Rail's bulk freight operations were sold to North and South Railways – subsequently called English, Welsh and Scottish Railways (EWS). In 2007, EWS was bought by Deutsche Bahn and in January 2009 was re-named DB Schenker. The other major companies in the rail freight sector are: Colas Rail, Direct Rail Services, Freightliner and GB Railfreight (GBRf). In 2015–16 total volume of freight moved by rail amounted to 17.8 billion net tonne-kilometres, a 20 per cent decrease from 2014–15.

NETWORK RAIL

Network Rail is responsible for the tracks, bridges, tunnels, level crossings, viaducts and 18 main stations that form Britain's rail network. In addition to providing the timetables for the passenger and freight operators, Network Rail is also responsible for all the signalling and electrical control equipment needed to operate the rail network and for monitoring and reporting performance across the industry.

In September 2014, Network Rail was reclassified as a public body after being privately run since 2002 as a commercial business which was directly accountable to its members. The members had similar rights to those of shareholders in a public company except they did not receive dividends or share capital and thereby had no financial interest in Network Rail. On 1 July 2015, the 46 public members were dismissed and the company is now accountable directly to parliament through the Secretary of State for Transport. Network Rail is regulated by the ORR and all of its profits are reinvested into maintaining and upgrading the rail infrastructure. In 2016–17 a total of 1.7 billion passenger journeys were made on the rail network.

LONDON TRAVELWATCH, 169 Union Street, London
SE1 0LL **T** 020-3176 2999
W www.londontravelwatch.org.uk

NETWORK RAIL, 1 Eversholt Street, London NW1 2DN
T 020-7557 8000 **W** www.networkrail.co.uk

OFFICE OF RAIL AND ROAD, 1 Kemble Street, London
WC2B 4AN **T** 020-7282 2000 **W** www.orr.gov.uk

TRANSPORT FOCUS, 2-6 Salisbury Square, London EC4Y 8JX
T 0300-123 0860 **W** www.transportfocus.org.uk

RAIL SAFETY
On 1 April 2006 responsibility for health and safety policy
and enforcement on the railways transferred from the Health
and Safety Executive to the Office of Rail Regulation (ORR).
  In 2016–17 a total of 39 passengers, railway staff and other
members of the public were fatally injured in all rail incidents
(excluding suicides).

ACCIDENTS ON RAILWAYS

	2015–16	2016–17
Rail incident fatalities	46	39
Passengers	8	5
Railway employees	0	1
Public	38	33
Rail incident major injuries	492	469
Passengers	294	266
Railway employees	160	164
Public	38	39

SUICIDES AND ATTEMPTED SUICIDES 2016–17
Fatalities   237

Source: RSSB – Annual Safety Performance Report 2016–17

OTHER RAIL SYSTEMS
Responsibility for the London Underground passed from the
government to the Mayor and Transport for London on 15
July 2003, with a public-private partnership already in place.
Plans for a public-private partnership for London
Underground were pushed through by the government in
February 2002 despite opposition from the Mayor of London
and a range of transport organisations. Under the PPP, long-
term contracts with private companies were estimated to
enable around £16bn to be invested in renewing and
upgrading the London Underground's infrastructure over 15
years. In July 2007, Metronet, which was responsible for two
of three PPP contracts, went into administration; TfL took
over both contracts. Responsibility for stations, trains,
operations, signalling and safety remains in the public sector.
In 2016–17 there were more than 1,350 million passenger
journeys on the London Underground.
  In addition to Glasgow Subway, which is classified as an
underground system (12.7 million passenger journeys in
2015–16), Britain has eight other light rail and tram systems:
Blackpool Tramway, Docklands Light Railway (DLR),
London Tramlink, Manchester Metrolink, Midland Metro,
Nottingham Express Transit (NET), Sheffield Supertram and
Tyne and Wear Metro.
  In 2015–16 there were 267.7 million passenger light rail
and tram journeys in Great Britain; an increase of 6.2 per cent
on 2014–15 figures.

THE CHANNEL TUNNEL
The earliest recorded scheme for a submarine transport
connection between Britain and France was in 1802.
Tunnelling began simultaneously on both sides of the
Channel three times: in 1881, in the early 1970s, and on 1
December 1987, when construction workers bored the first of
the three tunnels which form the Channel Tunnel. Engineers
'holed through' the first tunnel (the service tunnel) on 1
December 1990 and tunnelling was completed in June 1991.
The tunnel was officially inaugurated by the Queen and
President Mitterrand of France on 6 May 1994.
  The submarine link comprises two rail tunnels, each carrying
trains in one direction, which measure 7.6m (24.93ft) in

diameter. Between them lies a smaller service tunnel,
measuring 4.8m (15.75ft) in diameter. The service tunnel is
linked to the rail tunnels by 130 cross-passages for
maintenance and safety purposes. The tunnels are 50km (31
miles) long, 38km (24 miles) of which is under the seabed at
an average depth of 40m (132ft). The rail terminals are
situated at Folkestone and Calais, and the tunnels go
underground at Shakespeare Cliff, Dover and Sangatte, west
of Calais.

HIGH SPEED 1
The High Speed 1, the Channel Tunnel Rail Link, route runs
from Folkestone to St Pancras station, London, with
intermediate stations at Ashford and Ebbsfleet in Kent and
Stratford International in east London.
  Construction of the rail link was financed by the private
sector with a substantial government contribution. A private
sector consortium, London and Continental Railways Ltd
(LCR), comprising Union Railways and the UK operator of
Eurostar, owns the rail link and was responsible for its design
and construction. The rail link was constructed in two phases:
phase one, from the Channel Tunnel to Fawkham Junction,
Kent, began in October 1998 and opened to fare-paying
passengers on 28 September 2003; phase two, from
Southfleet Junction to St Pancras, was completed in
November 2007.
  Eurostar provides direct services from the UK to Avignon (5
hours 49 minutes), Calais (1 hour 2 minutes), Disneyland
Paris (2 hours 35 minutes), Lille (1 hour 20 minutes), Lyon (4
hours 41 minutes), Marseille (6 hours 27 minutes) and Paris
(2 hours 15 minutes) in France and Brussels (1 hour 51
minutes) in Belgium.

ROADS

HIGHWAY AUTHORITIES
The powers and responsibilities of highway authorities in
England and Wales are set out in the Highways Act 1980; for
Scotland there is separate legislation.
  Responsibility for motorways and other trunk roads in Great
Britain rests in England with the Secretary of State for
Transport, in Scotland with the Scottish government, and in
Wales with the Welsh government. The highway authority
for non-trunk roads in England, Wales and Scotland is, in
general, the local authority in whose area the roads lie. With
the establishment of the Greater London Authority in July
2000, Transport for London became the highway authority
for roads in London.
  In Northern Ireland the Department for Infrastructure is
responsible for public roads and their maintenance and
construction.

FINANCE
In England all aspects of trunk road and motorway funding
are provided directly by the government to Highways
England, which operates, maintains and improves a network
of motorways and trunk roads around 6,920km (4,300 miles)
long, on behalf of the secretary of state. Since 2001 the length
of the network that the Highways England is responsible for
has been decreasing owing to a policy of de-trunking, which
transfers responsibility for non-core roads to local authorities.
For the financial year 2017–18 Highways England's total
budget, excluding depreciation, is £3,458m. This includes
maintenance, major schemes, traffic management, technology
improvements, other programmes and administration costs.
  Government support for local authority capital expenditure
on roads and other transport infrastructure is provided
through grant and credit approvals as part of the Local
Transport Plan (LTP). Local authorities bid for resources on
the basis of a five-year programme built around delivering
integrated transport strategies. As well as covering the
structural maintenance of local roads and the construction of
major new road schemes, LTP funding also includes smaller-

scale safety and traffic management measures with associated improvements for public transport, cyclists and pedestrians.

Total budgeted expenditure by the Welsh government for 2016–17 to improve and maintain the motorway and trunk road network in Wales is £231.1m.

Since 1 July 1999 all decisions on Scottish transport expenditure have been devolved to the Scottish government. Total expenditure on motorways and trunk roads in Scotland during 2016–17 was £949m.

In Northern Ireland total expenditure by the Department for Infrastructure on all roads in 2016–17 was £142.8m with £73.6m spent on trunk roads and motorways. Planned expenditure for 2017–18 is £129.9m, of which £99.2m is allocated for trunk roads and motorways.

The Transport Act 2000 gave English and Welsh local authorities (outside London) powers to introduce road-user charging or workplace parking levy schemes. The act requires that the net revenue raised is used to improve local transport services and facilities for at least ten years. The aim is to reduce congestion and encourage greater use of alternative modes of transport. Schemes developed by local authorities require government approval. The UK's first toll road, the M6 Toll, opened in December 2003 and runs for 43.5km (27 miles) around Birmingham from junction 3a to junction 11a on the M6.

Charging schemes in London are allowed under the 1999 Greater London Authority Act. The Central London Congestion Charge Scheme began on 17 February 2003 (see also Regional Government London).

ROAD LENGTHS 2016
Miles

	England	Wales	Scotland	Great Britain
Major Roads	20,102	2,609	6,381	29,090
Motorways	1,896	88	283	2,268
Minor Roads	166,543	18,385	30,224	215,152
Total	188,541	21,082	36,888	246,510

Source: Department for Transport

BUSES
The majority of bus services outside London are provided on a commercial basis by private operators. Local authorities have powers to subsidise services where needs are not being met by a commercial service.

Since April 2008 men and women who have attained the state pension age and disabled people who qualify under the categories listed in the Transport Act 2000 have been able to travel for free on any local bus across England between 9.30am and 11pm Monday to Friday and all day on weekends and bank holidays. Local authorities recompense operators for the reduced fare revenue. The age of eligibility for concessionary travel is state pension age. A similar scheme from age 60 operates in Wales and within London, although there is no time restriction. In Scotland, people aged 60 and over and disabled people have been able to travel for free on any local or long-distance bus since April 2006.

In London, Transport for London (TfL) has overall responsibility for setting routes, service standards and fares for the bus network. Almost all routes are competitively tendered to commercial operators.

In Northern Ireland, passenger transport services are provided by Ulsterbus and Metro (formerly Citybus), two wholly owned subsidiaries of the Northern Ireland Transport Holding Company. Along with Northern Ireland Railways, Ulsterbus and Metro operate under the brand name of Translink and are publicly owned. Ulsterbus is responsible for virtually all bus services in Northern Ireland except Belfast city services, which are operated by Metro. People living in Northern Ireland aged 60 and over can travel on buses and trains for free once they have obtained a SmartPass from Translink.

LOCAL BUS PASSENGER JOURNEYS 2014–15
No. of journeys (millions)

England	4,700
London	2,390
Scotland	420
Wales	100
Total	5,220

Source: Department for Transport

TAXIS AND PRIVATE HIRE VEHICLES
A taxi is a public transport vehicle with fewer than nine passenger seats, which is licensed to 'ply for hire'. This distinguishes taxis from private hire vehicles (PHVs) which must be booked in advance through an operator. In London, taxis and private hire vehicles are licensed by the Public Carriage Office (PCO), part of TfL. There are currently around 22,500 taxis and 66,800 PHVs licensed in London. Outside London, local authorities are responsible for the licensing of taxis and private hire vehicles operational in their respective administrative areas. At the end of March 2015 there were 76,000 licensed taxis and 166,100 PHVs in England. In 2014 there were 34,519 taxis and PHVs licensed in Scotland.

ROAD TRAFFIC BY VEHICLE TYPE (GREAT BRITAIN) 2016

	Million vehicle miles
All motor vehicles	323,700
Cars	252,600
Light goods vehicles	49,100
Heavy goods vehicles	16,600
Other motor vehicles	5,400

Source: Department for Transport

ROAD SAFETY
In May 2011, the government published The Strategic Framework for Road Safety which identified key indicators at national and local level intended to monitor the progress towards improving safety and decreasing the number of fatalities and seriously injured casualties on Great Britain's roads.

The key findings from the Department for Transport's 2015 annual road casualty report found that despite a 1.6 per cent rise in traffic volume, the number of people killed in road accidents reported to the police had decreased by 2 per cent; from 1,775 in 2014 to 1,732 in 2015. The total number of reported casualties in Great Britain (slight injuries, serious injuries and fatalities) also decreased from 194,477 in 2014 to 186,209 in 2015. Total reported child casualties (0–15 years) decreased by 4 per cent, decreasing from 16,727 in 2014 to 16,101 in 2015.

ROAD ACCIDENT CASUALTIES 2015

	Killed	Serious	Slight	Total
Average for 2005–9	2,816	27,225	216,010	246,050
England	1,465	19,459	146,653	167,577
Wales	105	1,081	6,496	7,682
Scotland	162	1,597	9,191	10,950
Great Britain	1,732	22,137	162,340	186,209

Source: Department for Transport

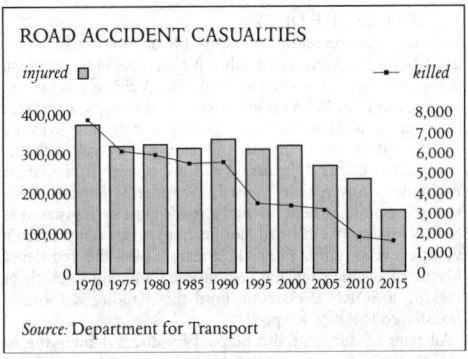

ROAD ACCIDENT CASUALTIES

injured □   ● killed

Source: Department for Transport

DRIVING LICENCE FEES *as at September 2017*

	fee online/postal
Provisional licence	
Car, motorcycle or moped	£34/£43
Bus or lorry	Free
After disqualification until passing re-test	Free
Changing a provisional licence to a full licence	Free
Renewal	
Renewing an expired licence (must be renewed every 10 years)	£14/£17
At age 70 and over	Free
For medical reasons	Free
Bus or lorry driver entitlement	Free
After disqualification	£65
After disqualification for some drink driving offences†	£90
After revocation (under the New Drivers Act)	£50
Replacing a lost, stolen, defaced or destroyed licence	£20/£20
Adding an entitlement to a full licence	Free
Removing expired endorsements	£20
Exchanging	
a paper licence for a photocard licence‡	£20/£20
a full Northern Ireland licence for a full GB licence	Free
a full GB licence for a full EU/EEA or other foreign licence (including Channel Islands and Isle of Man)	Free
a full EU/EEA or other foreign licence (including Channel Islands and Isle of Man) for a full GB licence	£43
Changing	
name or address (existing licence must be surrendered)†	Free
photo	£14/£17

* Not all services are available online; in these instances just the postal fee is shown. Licence fees differ in Northern Ireland (W www.nidirect.gov.uk/the-cost-of-a-driving-licence).
† For an alcohol-related offence where the DVLA need to arrange medical enquiries
‡ If a paper licence is exchanged for a photocard at the same time as name or address details are changed there is no charge

DRIVING LICENCES

It is necessary to hold a valid full licence in order to drive unaccompanied on public roads in the UK. Learner drivers must obtain a provisional driving licence before starting to learn to drive and must then pass theory and practical tests to obtain a full driving licence.

There are separate tests for driving motorcycles, cars, passenger-carrying vehicles (PCVs) and large goods vehicles (LGVs). Drivers must hold full car entitlement before they can apply for PCV or LGV entitlements.

The Driver and Vehicle Licensing Agency (DVLA) ceased the issue of paper licences in March 2000, but those currently in circulation will remain valid until they expire or the details on them change. The photocard driving licence was introduced to comply with the second EC directive on driving licences. This requires a photograph of the driver to be included on all UK licences issued from July 2001. The photocard licence must be renewed every ten years, with fines of up to £1,000 for failure to do so.

To apply for a first photocard driving licence, individuals are required to either apply online or complete the form *Application for a Driving Licence* (D1) and submit by post.

The minimum age for driving motor cars, light goods vehicles up to 3.5 tonnes and motorcycles is 17 (moped, 16). Since June 1997, drivers who collect six or more penalty points within two years of qualifying lose their licence and are required to take another test. Forms and leaflets are available from post offices and online (W www.gov.uk/dvlaforms or W www.gov.uk/government/organisations/driver-and-vehicle-licensing-agency).

The DVLA is responsible for issuing driving licences, registering and licensing vehicles, and collecting excise duty in Great Britain. The Driver and Vehicle Agency (DVA), has similar responsibilities in Northern Ireland.

DRIVING TESTS

The Driver and Vehicle Standards Agency (DVSA) is responsible for improving road safety in Great Britain by setting standards for driving and motorcycling and making sure drivers, vehicle operators and MOT garages understand and follow roadworthiness standards. The agency also provides a range of licensing, testing, education and enforcement services.

DRIVING TESTS TAKEN AND PASSED
April 2017–June 2017

	Number Taken	Percentage Passed
Practical Test		
Car	430,341	47.0
Motorcycle Module 1	17,775	73.1
Motorcycle Module 2	16,685	71.1
LGV/PCV	18,165	57.7
Driver CPC*	5,155	91.5
Theory Test		
Car	484,434	48.6
Motorcycle	23,941	72.3
LGV/PCV		
Multiple choice	13,287	63.5
Hazard perception	10,849	82.1
Driver CPC*	8,628	65.3

LGV = Large goods vehicle; PCV = Passenger-carrying vehicle
* Driver Certificate of Professional Competence – legal requirement for all professional bus, coach and lorry drivers
Source: DVSA

The theory and practical driving tests can be booked online (W www.gov.uk/book-driving-test) or by phone (T 0300-200 1122).

DRIVING TEST FEES

(WEEKDAY/EVENING* AND WEEKEND)
as at September 2017

Theory tests	
Car and motorcycle	£23.00/£23.00
Bus and lorry	
Multiple choice	£26.00/£26.00
Hazard perception	£11.00/£11.00
Driver CPC	£23.00/£23.00
Practical tests	
Car	£62.00/£75.00
Tractor and other specialist vehicles	£62.00/£75.00
Motorcycle	
Module 1 (off-road)	£15.50/£15.50
Module 2 (on-road)	£75.00/£88.50
Lorry and bus	£115.00/£141.00
Driver CPC	£55.00/£63.00
Car and trailer	£115.00/£141.00
Extended tests for disqualified drivers	
Car	£124.00/£150.00
Motorcycle Module 1 (on-road)	£150.00/£177.00

* After 4.30pm

VEHICLE LICENCES
Registration and first licensing of vehicles is through local offices of the DVLA in Swansea. Local facilities for relicensing are available at any post office which deals with vehicle licensing. Applicants will need to take their vehicle registration document (V55/5) or, if this is not available, the applicant must complete form V62. Forms are available at post offices and online (W www.gov.uk/dvlaforms)

MOTOR VEHICLES LICENSED (UK)
As at 30 June 2017

	Thousands
All cars	32,170
Light goods vehicles	3,982
Motorcycles	1,354
Heavy goods vehicles	523
Buses and coaches	167
Other vehicles*	774
Total	38,971

* Includes rear diggers, lift trucks, rollers, ambulances, Hackney Carriages, three-wheelers and agricultural vehicles

Source: Department for Transport

VEHICLE EXCISE DUTY
Details of the present duties chargeable on motor vehicles are available at post offices and online (W www.gov.uk/government/publications/rates-of-vehicle-tax-v149). The Vehicle Excise and Registration Act 1994 provides *inter alia* that any vehicle kept on a public road but not used on roads is chargeable to excise duty as if it were in use. All non-commercial vehicles constructed before 1 January 1973 are exempt from vehicle excise duty. Any vehicle licensed on or after 31 January 1998, not in use and not kept on public roads must be registered as SORN (Statutory Off Road Notification) to be exempted from vehicle excise duty. From 1 January 2004 the registered keeper of a vehicle remains responsible for taxing a vehicle or making a SORN declaration until that liability is formally transferred to a new keeper.

All rates of duty can also be paid by direct debit – the 6-month direct debit rate is slightly cheaper than the non-direct debit rate listed below. There is also the option to pay vehicle duty by direct debit monthly installments.

RATES OF DUTY *FROM 1 APRIL 2017*		
	6 month	12 months
Cars registered on or after 1 April 2017*†		
petrol/diesel car	£77.00	£140.00
alternative fuel car	£71.50	£130.00
Cars registered before 1 March 2001		
Under 1,549cc	£82.50	£150.00
Over 1,549cc	£134.75	£245.00
Light goods vehicles registered on or after 1 March 2001		
	£132.00	£240.00
Euro 4 light goods vehicles registered between 1 March 2003 and 31 December 2006		
	£77.00	£140.00
Euro 5 light goods vehicles registered between 1 January 2009 and 31 December 2010		
	£77.00	£140.00
Motorcycles (with or without sidecar)		
Not over 150cc	–	£18.00
151–400cc	–	£41.00
401–600cc	£34.10	£62.00
600cc+	£46.75	£85.00
Tricycles		
Not over 150cc	–	£18.00
All others	£46.75	£85.00

* Different first year licence rates based on CO_2 emissions are payable at first registration

† Cars with a list price of over £40,000 at first registration pay an additional £310 on the standard 12-month rate above for five years from the start of the second licence

RATES OF DUTY FOR CARS REGISTERED BETWEEN 1 MARCH 2001 AND 1 APRIL 2017

from 1 April 2017

	CO_2 Emissions	Petrol and Diesel Car		Alternative Fuel Car	
	(g/km)	6 months	12 months	6 months	12 months
A	Up to 100	–	£0.00	–	£0.00
B	101–110	–	£20.00	–	£10.00
C	111–120	–	£30.00	–	£20.00
D	121–130	£63.25	£115.00	£57.75	£105.00
E	131–140	£74.25	£135.00	£68.75	£125.00
F	141–150	£82.50	£150.00	£77.00	£140.00
G	151–165	£104.50	£190.00	£99.00	£180.00
H	166–175	£121.00	£220.00	£115.50	£210.00
I	176–185	£132.00	£240.00	£126.50	£230.00
J	186–200	£154.00	£280.00	£148.50	£270.00
K*	201–255	£167.75	£305.00	£162.25	£295.00
L	226–255	£286.00	£520.00	£280.50	£510.00
M	255+	£294.25	£535.00	£288.75	£525.00

* Includes cars that have a CO_2 emission figure over 225g/km but were registered before 23 March 2006

MOT TESTING

Cars, motorcycles, motor caravans, light goods and dual-purpose vehicles more than three years old must be covered by a current MOT test certificate. However, some vehicles (ie minibuses, ambulances and taxis) may require a certificate at one year old. All certificates must be renewed annually. Only MOT testing stations showing a blue sign with three triangles and an official 'MOT: Test: Fees and Appeals' poster may carry out an approved MOT. The MOT testing scheme is administered by the Driver and Vehicle Standards Agency (DVSA) on behalf of the Secretary of State for Transport.

A fee is payable to MOT testing stations. The current maximum fees are:

For cars, private hire and public service vehicles, motor caravans, dual purpose vehicles, ambulances and taxis (all up to eight passenger seats)	£54.85
For motorcycles	£29.65
For motorcycles with sidecar	£37.80
For three-wheeled vehicles (up to 450kg unladen weight)	£37.80

*Private passenger vehicles and ambulances with:

9–12 passenger seats	£57.30 (£64.00)
13–16 passenger seats	£59.55 (£80.50)
16+ passenger seats	£80.65 (£124.50)
Goods vehicles (3,000–3,500kg)	£58.60

* Figures in parentheses include seatbelt installation check

SHIPPING AND PORTS

Sea trade has always played a central role in Britain's economy. By the 17th century Britain had built up a substantial merchant fleet and by the early 20th century it dominated the world shipping industry. The UK registered trading fleet grew 6 per cent in 2016, to 14.4 million deadweight tonnes, and is now 14 per cent higher than the recent low in 2014. At the end of 2016, the UK registered trading fleet was over five times the size it was at the end of 1999, though it remains a small proportion of the world total – it was the 19th largest trading fleet in the world at the end of 2016, accounting for 0.8 per cent of the total measured by deadweight tonnage and 1.2 per cent when measured using gross tonnage.

Freight is carried by liner and bulk services, almost all scheduled liner services being containerised. About 95 per cent by weight of Britain's overseas trade is carried by sea. Passengers and vehicles are carried by roll-on, roll-off ferries, hovercraft, cruise ships and high-speed catamarans. In 2016 the number of international short sea passengers decreased by 5 per cent to 20 million compared to 21 million in 2015.

Lloyd's of London provides the most comprehensive shipping intelligence service in the world. *Lloyd's List* (www.lloydslistintelligence.com) lists 120,000 ocean-going vessels and gives the latest known report of each.

PORTS

There are 51 major ports in the UK. Overall freight tonnage handled by UK ports in 2016 was 484.0 million tonnes, a decrease of 3 per cent from 2015 . The largest ports in terms of freight tonnage in 2016 were Grimsby and Immingham (54.4 million tonnes), London (50.4 million tonnes), Southampton (36.0 million tonnes), Milford Haven (34.8 million tonnes) and Liverpool (31.9 million tonnes). Belfast (17.6 million tonnes) is the principal freight port in Northern Ireland.

Broadly speaking, ports are owned and operated by private companies, local authorities or self-owning bodies, known as trust ports. The largest operator is Associated British Ports which owns 21 ports.

MARINE SAFETY

The Maritime and Coastguard Agency (MCA) is an executive agency of the Department for Transport responsible for implementing the government's maritime safety policy in the UK and works to prevent the loss of life on the coast and at sea.

HM Coastguard maintains a 24-hour search and rescue response and coordination capability for the whole of the UK coast and the internationally agreed search and rescue region. HM Coastguard is responsible for mobilising and organising resources in response to people in distress at sea, or at risk of injury or death on the UK's cliffs or shoreline.

The MCA also inspects and surveys ships to ensure that they are meeting UK and international safety rules, provides certification to seafarers, registers vessels and responds to pollution from shipping and offshore installations.

Locations hazardous to shipping in coastal waters are marked by lighthouses and other lights and buoys. The lighthouse authorities are the Corporation of Trinity House (for England, Wales and the Channel Islands), the Northern Lighthouse Board (for Scotland and the Isle of Man), and the Commissioners of Irish Lights (for Northern Ireland and the Republic of Ireland). Trinity House maintains 66 lighthouses, nine light vessels/floats, 450 buoys, 21 beacons, 52 radar beacons, eight DGPS (differential global positioning system) stations* and three AIS (automatic identification system) stations. The Northern Lighthouse Board maintains 206 lighthouses, 165 buoys, 26 beacons, 29 radar beacons, 35 AIS stations, four DGPS stations and one LORAN (long-range navigation) station; and Irish Lights looks after 71 lighthouses, 117 buoys, 24 beacons, and three DGPS stations, with AIS in operation on 37 lighthouses.

Harbour authorities are responsible for pilotage within their harbour areas; and the Ports Act 1991 provides for the transfer of lights and buoys to harbour authorities where these are used mainly for local navigation.

* DGPS is a satellite-based navigation system

UK-OWNED TRADING VESSELS
500 gross tons and over, as at end 2016

Type of vessel	No.	Gross tonnage
Tankers	74	1,752,000
Fully cellular container	95	7,203,000
Dry bulk carriers	25	1,512,000
Ro-Ro (passenger)	62	824,000
Ro-Ro (cargo)	19	627,000
Passenger	15	806,000
Other general cargo	58	256,000
Specialised carriers	18	834,000
All vessels	366	13,814,000

Source: Department for Transport

UK SEA PASSENGER* MOVEMENTS 2015

Type of journey	No. of passenger movements
Passengers on short sea routes	21,005,000
Passengers on cruises beginning or ending at UK ports*	1,895,000
Passengers on long sea journeys	53,000
Total	22,954,000

* Passengers are included at both departure and arrival if their journeys begin and end at a UK seaport
Source: Department for Transport

UK SHIPPING FORECAST AREAS

Weather bulletins for shipping are broadcast daily on BBC Radio 4 at 00h 48m, 05h 20m, 12h 01m and 17h 54m. All transmissions are broadcast on long wave at 1515m (198kHz) and the 00h 48m and 05h 20m transmissions are also broadcast on FM. The bulletins consist of a gale warning summary, general synopsis, sea-area forecasts and coastal station reports. In addition, gale warnings are broadcast at the first available programme break after receipt. If this does not coincide with a news bulletin, the warning is repeated after the next news bulletin. Shipping forecasts and gale warnings are also available on the Met Office and BBC Weather websites.

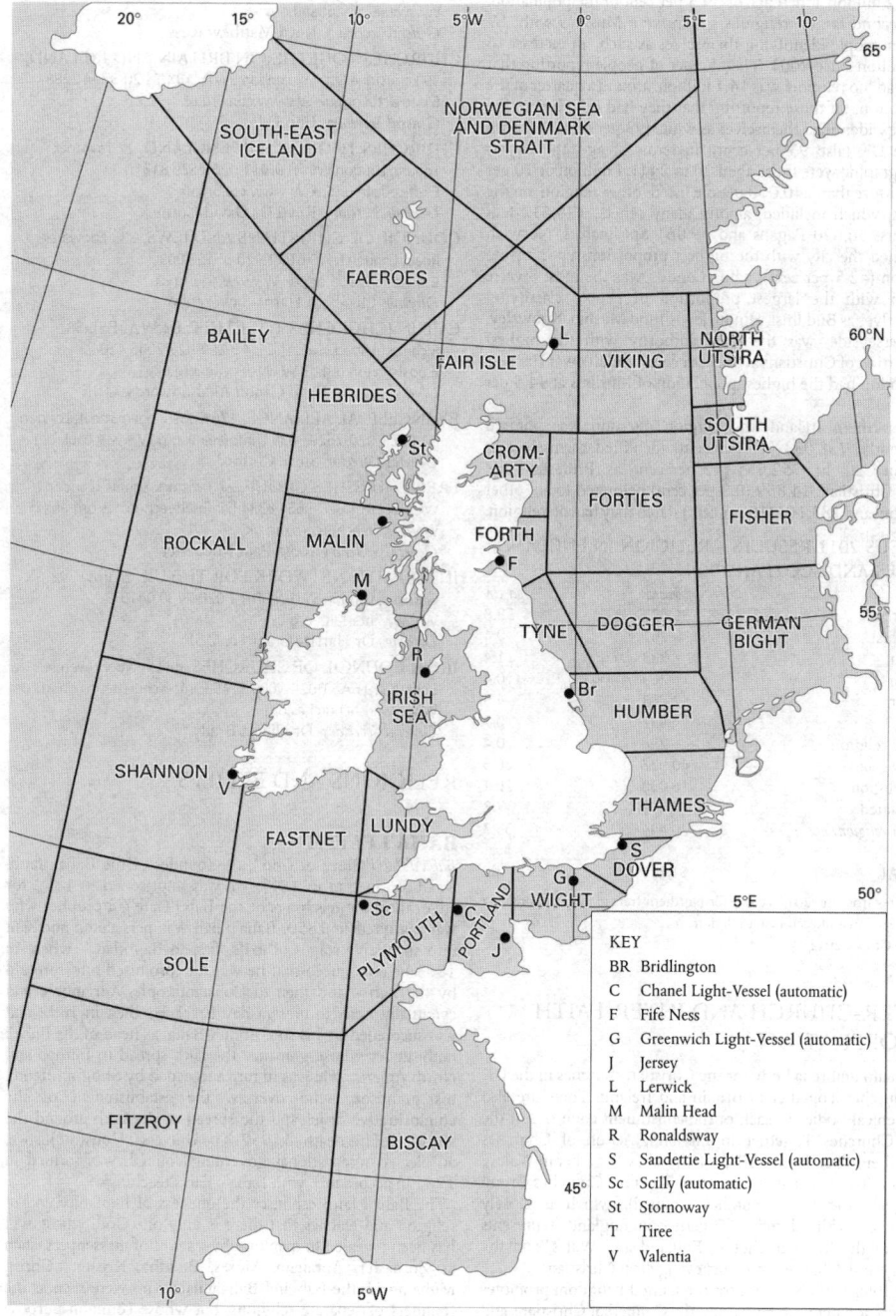

KEY

BR Bridlington
C   Chanel Light-Vessel (automatic)
F   Fife Ness
G   Greenwich Light-Vessel (automatic)
J   Jersey
L   Lerwick
M   Malin Head
R   Ronaldsway
S   Sandettie Light-Vessel (automatic)
Sc Scilly (automatic)
St Stornoway
T   Tiree
V   Valentia

RELIGION IN THE UK

The 2011 census in England and Wales included a voluntary question on religion; 92.8 per cent of the population chose to answer the question. Christianity remained the largest religion, despite a decrease of 4 million people from the 2001 census, to 33.2 million adherents, or 59.3 per cent of the population. The second largest religious group were Muslims with 2.7 million people identifying themselves as such, an increase of 1.2 million since 2001. The number of people reporting that they had 'no religion' was 14.1 million, around a quarter of the population. Of those reporting that they had no religion, the majority identified themselves as white (93 per cent) and born in the UK (also 93 per cent); in terms of age, the largest demographic were those aged 20 to 24 (1.4 million or 10 per cent). More than 240,000 people listed 'other religion' on the census, which included, among many others, 176,632 Jedi Knights, 56,620 Pagans and 39,061 Spiritualists. Norwich remained the city with the highest proportion reporting no religion (42.5 per cent), while London was the most diverse region with the largest proportion of people classifying themselves as Buddhist, Hindu, Jewish and Muslim. Knowsley, in Merseyside, was the local authority with the highest proportion of Christians at 80.9 per cent, while Tower Hamlets in London had the highest population of Muslims at 34.5 per cent.

In Northern Ireland, the religion question was phrased differently; 738,033 (41 per cent) identified themselves as Roman Catholic, 752,555 (42 per cent) as 'Protestant and other Christian', 14,859 (0.8 per cent) belonged to an 'other religion' and 183,164 (10 per cent) stated they had no religion.

CENSUS 2011 RESULTS – RELIGION IN ENGLAND, WALES AND SCOTLAND*

	thousands	per cent
Christian	36,093	58.8
Buddhist	261	0.4
Hindu	833	1.4
Jewish	269	0.4
Muslim	2,783	4.5
Sikh	432	0.7
Other religion	256	0.4
All religions	40,927	66.6
No religion	16,038	26.1
Not stated	4,406	7.2
All no religion/not stated	20,444	33.3
TOTAL	61,371	100

* Figures from the 2011 census for Northern Ireland did not contain a full breakdown of each major religion

Source: Census 2011

INTER-CHURCH AND INTER-FAITH COOPERATION

The main umbrella body for the Christian churches in the UK is Churches Together in Britain and Ireland. There are also ecumenical bodies in each of the constituent countries of the UK: Churches Together in England, Action of Churches Together in Scotland, CYTUN (Churches Together in Wales), and the Irish Council of Churches. The Free Churches Group (formerly the Free Churches Council), which is closely associated with Churches Together in England, represents most of the free churches in England and Wales, and the Evangelical Alliance represents evangelical Christians.

The Inter Faith Network for the United Kingdom promotes cooperation between faiths, and the Council of Christians and Jews works to improve relations between the two religions.

Churches Together in Britain and Ireland also has a commission on inter-faith relations.

ACTION OF CHURCHES TOGETHER IN SCOTLAND,
Jubilee House, Forthside Way, Stirling FK8 1QZ T 01259-216980
W www.acts-scotland.org
General Secretary, Revd Matthew Ross

CHURCHES TOGETHER IN BRITAIN AND IRELAND,
39 Ecclestone Square, London SW1V 1BX T 020-3794 2288
E info@ctbi.org.uk W www.ctbi.org.uk
General Secretary, Bob Fyffe

CHURCHES TOGETHER IN ENGLAND, 27 Tavistock Square, London WC1H 9HH T 020-7529 8131
E office@cte.org.uk W www.cte.org.uk
General Secretary, Revd Dr David Cornick

COUNCIL OF CHRISTIANS AND JEWS, 333 Edgware Road, London NW9 6TD T 020-3515 3003
E cjrelations@ccj.org.uk W www.ccj.org.uk
Director, Elizabeth Harris-Sawczenko

CYTUN (CHURCHES TOGETHER IN WALES), 58 Richmond Road, Cardiff CF24 3AT T 029-2046 4204
E post@cytun.org.uk W www.cytun.org.uk
Chief Executive, Revd Canon Aled Edwards, OBE

EVANGELICAL ALLIANCE, 176 Copenhagen Street, London N1 0ST T 020-7520 3830 E info@eauk.org W www.eauk.org
General Director, Steve Clifford

FREE CHURCHES GROUP, 27 Tavistock Square, London WC1H 9HH T 020-3651 8334 E info@freechurches.org.uk
W www.freechurches.org.uk
General Secretary, Revd Paul Rochester

INTERFAITH NETWORK FOR THE UK, 2 Grosvenor Gardens, London SW1W 0DH T 020-7730 0410
W www.interfaith.org.uk
Director, Dr Harriet Crabtree, OBE

IRISH COUNCIL OF CHURCHES, 48 Elmwood Avenue, Belfast BT9 6AZ T 028-9066 3145 E info@churchesinireland.com
W www.irishchurches.org
General Secretary, Dr Nicola Brady

RELIGIONS AND BELIEFS

BAHA'I FAITH

Baha'u'llah ('Glory of God'), the founder of the Baha'i faith, was born in Iran in 1817. He was imprisoned in 1852 for advocating the teachings of the Bab ('Gate'), a prophet who was martyred in 1850. Baha'u'llah was persecuted and sent into successive stages of exile, first to Baghdad – where in 1863 he announced that he was the 'promised one' foretold by the Bab – and then to Constantinople, Adrianople and eventually Acre, in present day Israel. He died in 1892 and was succeeded by his son, Abdu'l-Baha, as head of the Baha'i faith, under whose guidance the faith spread to Europe and North America. He was in turn succeeded by Shoghi Effendi, his grandson, who oversaw the establishment of the administrative order and the spread of the faith around the world until his death in 1957. The Universal House of Justice, an elected international governing council, was formed in 1963 in accordance with Baha'u'llah's teachings.

The Baha'i faith espouses the oneness of humanity and of religion and teaches that there is only one God, whose will has been revealed to mankind by a series of messengers, such as Zoroaster, Abraham, Moses, Buddha, Krishna, Christ, Muhammad, the Bab and Baha'u'llah, who were seen as the founders of separate religions, but whose common purpose was to bring God's message to mankind. The Baha'i faith attributes the differences in teachings between religions to humanity's changing needs. Baha'i teachings include that all races and both sexes are equal and deserving of equal opportunities and treatment, that education is a fundamental right and that extremes of wealth and poverty should be eliminated. In addition, the faith exhorts mankind to establish a world federal system to promote peace and unity.

In an effort to translate these principles into action, Baha'is have initiated an educational process across the world that seeks to raise the capacity of people of all ages and from all backgrounds to contribute towards the betterment of society. There is no clergy; each local community elects a local spiritual assembly to tend to its administrative needs. A national spiritual assembly is elected annually by locally elected delegates, and every five years the national spiritual assemblies meet together to elect the Universal House of Justice, the supreme international governing body of the Baha'i Faith. Worldwide there are over 13,000 local spiritual assemblies and more than 5 million members.

BAHA'I COMMUNITY OF THE UK, 27 Rutland Gate, London SW1 1PD T 020-7584 2566 E nsa@bahai.org.uk W www.bahai.org.uk
Director, Office of Public Affairs, Padideh Sabeti

BUDDHISM

Buddhism originated in what is now the Bihar area of northern India in the teachings of Siddhartha Gautama, who became the *Buddha* ('Enlightened One'). In the Thai or Suriyakati calendar the beginning of the Buddhist era is dated from the death of Buddha; the year 2018 is therefore 2561 by the Thai Buddhist reckoning.

Fundamental to Buddhism is the concept of rebirth, whereby each life carries with it the consequences of the conduct of earlier lives (known as the law of *karma)* and this cycle of death and rebirth is broken only when the state of *nirvana* has been reached. Buddhism steers a middle path between belief in personal continuity and the belief that death results in total extinction.

While doctrine does not have a pivotal position in Buddhism, a statement of four 'Noble Truths' is common to all its schools and varieties. These are: suffering is inescapable in even the most fortunate of existences; craving is the root cause of suffering; abandonment of the selfish mindset is the way to end suffering; and bodily and mental discipline, accompanied by the cultivation of wisdom and compassion, provides the spiritual path ('Noble Eightfold Path') to accomplish this. Buddhists deny the idea of a creator and prefer to emphasise the practical aspects of moral and spiritual development.

The schools of Buddhism can be broadly divided into three: *Theravada,* the generally monastic-led tradition practised in Sri Lanka and South East Asia; *Mahayana,* the philosophical and popular traditions of the Far East; and *Esoteric,* the Tantric-derived traditions found in Tibet and Mongolia and, to a lesser extent, China and Japan. The extensive Theravada scriptures are contained in the *Pali Canon,* which dates in its written form from the first century BC. Mahayana and Esoteric schools have Sanskrit-derived translations of these plus many more additional scriptures as well as exegetical material.

In the East the new and full moons and the lunar quarter days were (and to a certain extent, still are) significant in determining the religious calendar. Most private homes contain a shrine where offerings, worship and other spiritual practices (such as meditation, chanting or mantra recitation) take place on a daily basis. Buddhist festivals vary according to local traditions within the different schools and there is little uniformity – even in commemorating the birth, enlightenment and death of the Buddha.

There is no governing authority for Buddhism in the UK. Communities representing all schools of Buddhism operate independently. The Buddhist Society was established in 1924; it runs courses, lectures and meditation groups, and publishes books about Buddhism. The Network of Buddhist Organisations was founded in 1993 to promote fellowship and dialogue between Buddhist organisations and to facilitate cooperation in matters of common interest.

There are estimated to be at least 490 million Buddhists worldwide. Of the 248,000 Buddhists in England and Wales (according to the 2011 census), 72,000 are white British (the majority are converts), 49,000 Chinese, 93,000 'other Asian' and 36,000 are 'other ethnic'.

THE BUDDHIST SOCIETY, 58 Eccleston Square, London SW1V 1PH T 020-7834 5858 E info@thebuddhistsociety.org W www.thebuddhistsociety.org
President, Dr Desmond Biddulph, CBE

LONDON BUDDHIST CENTRE, 51 Roman Road, London E2 0HU T 020-8981 1225 E contact@lbc.org.uk W www.lbc.org.uk
Chair, Dharmachari Jnanavaca

THE NETWORK OF BUDDHIST ORGANISATIONS, PO Box 4147, Maidenhead SL60 1DN T 0845-345 8978 E secretary@nbo.org.uk W www.nbo.org.uk
Chair, Juliet Hackney

SOKA GAKKAI UK, Taplow Court Grand Cultural Centre, Cliveden Road, Taplow, Berkshire SL6 0ER T 01628-773163 W www.sgi-uk.org
General Director, Robert Harrap

TIBET HOUSE TRUST, Tibet House, 1 Culworth Street, London NW8 7AF T 020-7722 5378 E secretary@tibet-house-trust.co.uk W http://www.tibet-house-trust.co.uk
Secretary, Kunga Tenzin

CHRISTIANITY

Christianity is a monotheistic faith based on the person and teachings of Jesus Christ, and all Christian denominations claim his authority. Central to its teaching is the concept of God and his son Jesus Christ, who was crucified and resurrected in order to enable mankind to attain salvation.

The Jewish scriptures predicted the coming of a *Messiah,* an 'anointed one', who would bring salvation. To Christians, Jesus of Nazareth, a Jewish rabbi (teacher) who was born in Palestine, was the promised Messiah. Jesus' birth, teachings, crucifixion and subsequent resurrection are recorded in the *Gospels,* which, together with other scriptures that summarise Christian belief, form the *New Testament.* This, together with the Hebrew scriptures – entitled the *Old Testament* by Christians – makes up the Bible, the sacred texts of Christianity.

Christians believe that sin distanced mankind from God, and that Jesus was the son of God, sent to redeem mankind from sin by his death. In addition, many believe that Jesus will return again at some future date, triumph over evil and establish a kingdom on earth, thus inaugurating a new age. The Gospel assures Christians that those who believe in Jesus and obey his teachings will be forgiven their sins and will be resurrected from the dead.

The Apostles were Jesus' first converts and are recognised by Christians as the founders of the Christian community. Early Christianity spread rapidly throughout the eastern provinces of the Roman Empire but was subjected to great persecution until AD 313, when Emperor Constantine's Edict of Toleration confirmed its right to exist. Christianity was established as the religion of the Roman Empire in AD 381.

Between AD 325 and 787 there were seven Oecumenical Councils at which bishops from the entire Christian world assembled to resolve various doctrinal disputes. The estrangement between East and West began after Constantine moved the centre of the Roman Empire from Rome to Constantinople, and it grew after the division of the Roman Empire into eastern and western halves. Linguistic and cultural differences between Greek East and Latin West served to encourage separate ecclesiastical developments which became pronounced in the tenth and early 11th centuries. Administration of the church was divided between five ancient patriarchates: Rome and all the West, Constantinople (the imperial city – the 'New Rome'), Jerusalem and all of Palestine, Antioch and all the East, and Alexandria and all of Africa. Of these, only Rome was in the Latin West and after the schism in 1054, Rome developed a structure of authority centralised on the Papacy, while the Orthodox East maintained the style of localised administration. Papal authority over the doctrine and jurisdiction of the church in Western Europe was unrivalled after the split with the Eastern Orthodox Church until the Protestant Reformation in the 16th century.

Christian practices vary widely between different Christian churches, but prayer, charity and giving (for the maintenance of the church buildings, for the work of the church, and to those in need) are common to all. In addition, certain days of observance, ie the *Sabbath, Easter* and *Christmas,* are celebrated by most Christians. The Orthodox, Roman Catholic and Anglican churches celebrate many more days of observance, based on saints and significant events in the life of Jesus. The belief in sacraments, physical signs believed to have been ordained by Jesus Christ to symbolise and convey spiritual gifts, varies greatly between Christian denominations; *baptism* and the *Eucharist* are practised by most Christians. Baptism, symbolising repentance and faith in Jesus, is an act marking entry into the Christian community; the Eucharist, the ritual re-enactment of the Last Supper, Jesus' final meal with his disciples, is also practised by most denominations. Other sacraments, such as anointing the sick, the laying on of hands to symbolise the passing on of the office of priesthood or to heal the sick, and speaking in tongues, where it is believed that the person is possessed by the Holy Spirit, are less common. In denominations where infant baptism is practised, confirmation (where the person confirms the commitments made on their behalf in infancy) is common. Matrimony and the ordination of priests are also widely believed to be sacraments. Many Protestants regard only baptism and the Eucharist to be sacraments; the Quakers and the Salvation Army reject the use of sacraments.

See Churches for contact details of the Church of England, the Roman Catholic Church and other Christian churches in the UK.

HINDUISM

Hinduism has no historical founder but had become highly developed in India by *c.*2500 BC. Its adherents originally called themselves Aryans; Muslim invaders first called the Aryans 'Hindus' (derived from 'Sindhu', the name of the river Indus) in the eighth century.

Most Hindus hold that *satya* (truthfulness), honesty, sincerity and devotion to God are essential for good living. They believe in one supreme spirit *(Brahman),* and in the transmigration of *atman* (the soul). Most Hindus accept the doctrine of *karma* (consequences of actions), the concept of *samsara* (successive lives) and the possibility of all atmans achieving *moksha* (liberation from samsara) through *jnana* (knowledge), *yoga* (meditation), *karma* (work or action) and *bhakti* (devotion).

Most Hindus offer worship to *murtis* (images of deities) representing different incarnations or aspects of Brahman, and follow their *dharma* (religious and social duty) according to the traditions of their *varna* (social class), *ashrama* (stage in life), *jaiti* (caste) and *kula* (family).

Hinduism's sacred texts are divided into *shruti* ('that which is heard'), including the *Vedas,* and *smriti* ('that which is remembered'), including the *Ramayana,* the *Mahabharata,* the *Puranas* (ancient myths), and the sacred law books. Most Hindus recognise the authority of the *Vedas,* the oldest holy books, and accept the philosophical teachings of the *Upanishads,* the *Vedanta Sutras* and the *Bhagavad-Gita.*

Hindus believe Brahman to be omniscient, omnipotent, limitless and all-pervading. Brahman is usually worshipped in its deity form. Brahma, Vishnu and Shiva are the most important deities or aspects of Brahman worshipped by Hindus; their respective consorts are Saraswati, Lakshmi and Durga or Parvati, also known as Shakti. There are believed to have been ten *avatars* (incarnations) of Vishnu, of whom the most important are Rama and Krishna. Other popular gods are Ganesha, Hanuman and Subrahmanyam. All Hindu gods are seen as aspects of the supreme spirit (Brahman), not as competing deities.

Orthodox Hindus revere all gods and goddesses equally, but there are many denominations, including the Hare-Krishna movement (ISKCon), the Arya Samaj and the Swaminarayan Hindu mission, in which worship is concentrated on one deity. The *guru* (spiritual teacher) is seen as the source of spiritual guidance.

Hinduism does not have a centrally trained and ordained priesthood. The pronouncements of the *shankaracharyas* (heads of monasteries) of Shringeri, Puri, Dwarka and Badrinath are heeded by the orthodox but may be ignored by the various sects.

The commonest form of worship is *puja,* in which water, flowers, food, fruit, incense and light are offered to the deity. Puja may be done either in a home shrine or a *mandir* (temple). Many British Hindus celebrate *samskars* (purification rites), to name a baby, for the sacred thread (an initiation ceremony), marriage and cremation.

The largest communities of Hindus in Britain are in Leicester, London, Birmingham and Bradford, and developed as a result of immigration from India, eastern Africa and Sri Lanka.

There are an estimated 800 million Hindus worldwide; there are around 817,000 adherents, according to the 2011 census in England and Wales, and around 135 temples in the UK.

ARYA SAMAJ LONDON, 69 Argyle Road, London W13 0LY
  T 020-8991 1732 E aryasamajlondon@yahoo.co.uk
  W www.aryasamajlondon.org.uk
  General Secretary, Amrit Lal Bhardwaj
BHARATIYA VIDYA BHAVAN, 4A Castletown Road, London
  W14 9HE T 020-7381 3086 E info@bhavan.net
  W www.bhavan.net
  Executive Director, Dr M. N. Nandakumara
INTERNATIONAL SOCIETY FOR KRISHNA
  CONSCIOUSNESS (ISKCON), Bhaktivedanta Manor,
  Dharam Marg, Hilfield Lane, Aldenham, Watford, Herts
  WD25 8EZ T 01923-851000 E info@krishnatemple.com
  W www.krishnatemple.com
  Temple President, Sruti Dharma Das
NATIONAL COUNCIL OF HINDU TEMPLES (UK), c/o
  Shree Sanatan Mandir, 84 Weymouth Street, Leicester LE4 6FQ
  T 0771-781 4357 E info@nchtuk.org W www.nchtuk.org
  General Secretary, Satish K. Sharma
SWAMINARAYAN HINDU MISSION (SHRI
  SWAMINARAYAN MANDIR), 105–119 Brentfield Road,
  London NW10 8
  LD T 020-8965 2651 E info@londonmandir.baps.org
  W www.londonmandir.baps.org

HUMANISM

Humanism traces its roots back to ancient times, with Chinese, Greek, Indian and Roman philosophers expressing Humanist ideas some 2,500 years ago. Confucius, the Chinese philosopher who lived *c.*500 BC, believed that religious observances should be replaced with moral values as the basis of social and political order and that 'the true way' is based on reason and humanity. He also stressed the importance of benevolence and respect for others, and believed that the individual situation should be considered rather than the global application of traditional rules.

Humanists believe that there is no God or other supernatural being, that humans have only one life (Humanists do not believe in an afterlife or reincarnation) and that humans can live ethical and fulfilling lives without religious beliefs through a moral code derived from a shared history, personal experience and thought. There are no sacred Humanist texts. Particular emphasis is placed on science as the only reliable source of knowledge of the universe. Many Humanists recognise a need for ceremonies to mark important occasions in life and the British Humanist Association has a network of celebrants who are trained and accredited to conduct baby namings, weddings and funerals. The British Humanist Association's campaigns for a secular state (a state based on freedom of religious or non-religious belief with no privileges for any particular set of beliefs) are based on equality and human rights. The association also campaigns for inclusive schools that meet the needs of all parents and pupils, regardless of their religious or non-religious beliefs. According to figures from the 2011 census, there are just over 15,000 Humanists in England and Wales.

BRITISH HUMANIST ASSOCIATION, 39 Moreland Street, London EC1V 8BB **T** 020-7324 3060 **E** info@humanism.org.uk **W** www.humanism.org.uk
Chief Executive, Andrew Copson

ISLAM

Islam (which means 'peace arising from submission to the will of Allah' in Arabic) is a monotheistic religion which was taught in Arabia by the Prophet Muhammad, who was born in Mecca (Al-Makkah) in 570 AD. Islam spread to Egypt, north Africa, Spain and the borders of China in the century following the Prophet's death, and is now the predominant religion in Indonesia, the near and Middle East, northern and parts of western Africa, Pakistan, Bangladesh, Malaysia and some of the former Soviet republics. There are also large Muslim communities in other countries.

For Muslims (adherents of Islam), there is one God *(Allah)*, who holds absolute power. Muslims believe that Allah's commands were revealed to mankind through the prophets, who include Abraham, Moses and Jesus, but that Allah's message was gradually corrupted until revealed finally and in perfect form to Muhammad through the angel *Jibril* (Gabriel) over a period of 23 years. This last, incorruptible message is said to have been recorded in the *Qur'an* (Koran), which contains 114 divisions called *surahs,* each made up of *ayahs* of various lengths, and is held to be the essence of all previous scriptures. The *Ahadith* are the records of the Prophet Muhammad's deeds and sayings (the *Sunnah*) as practised and recounted by his immediate followers. A culture and a system of law and theology gradually developed to form a distinctive Islamic civilisation. Islam makes no distinction between sacred and worldly affairs and provides rules for every aspect of human life. The *Shariah* is the sacred law of Islam based primarily upon prescriptions derived from the *Qur'an* and the *Sunnah* of the Prophet.

The 'five pillars of Islam' are *shahadah* (a declaration of faith in the oneness and supremacy of Allah and the messengership of Muhammad); *salat* (formal prayer, to be performed five times a day facing the *Ka'bah* (the most sacred shrine in the holy city of Mecca)); *zakat* (welfare due, paid annually on all savings at the rate of 2.5 per cent); *sawm* (fasting during the month of Ramadan from dawn until sunset); and *hajj* (pilgrimage to Mecca made once in a lifetime if the believer is financially and physically able). Some Muslims would add *jihad* as the sixth pillar (striving for the cause of good and resistance to evil).

Two main groups developed among Muslims. *Sunni* Muslims accept the legitimacy of Muhammad's first four *caliphs* (successors as head of the Muslim community) and of the authority of the Muslim community as a whole. About 90 per cent of Muslims are Sunni Muslims.

Shi'ites recognise only Muhammad's son-in-law Ali as his rightful successor and the *Imams* (descendants of Ali, not to be confused with *imams,* who are prayer leaders or religious

teachers) as the principal legitimate religious authority. The largest group within Shi'ism is *Twelver Shi'ism,* which has been the official school of law and theology in Iran since the 16th century; other subsects include the *Ismailis,* the *Druze* and the *Alawis,* the latter two differing considerably from the main body of Muslims. The *Ibadis* of Oman are neither Sunni nor Shia, deriving from the strictly observant *Khariji* (Seceders). There is no organised priesthood, but learned men such as imams, *ulama,* and *ayatollahs* are accorded great respect. The *Sufis* are the mystics of Islam. Mosques are centres for worship and teaching and also for social and welfare activities.

Islam was first recorded in western Europe in the eighth century AD when 800 years of Muslim rule began in Spain. Later, Islam spread to eastern Europe. More recently, Muslims came to Europe from Africa, the Middle East and Asia in the late 19th century. Both the Sunni and Shia traditions are represented in Britain, but the majority of Muslims in Britain adhere to Sunni Islam. Efforts to establish a representative national body for Muslims in Britain resulted in the founding, in 1997, of the Muslim Council of Britain. In addition, there are many other Muslim organisations in the UK. There are around 1.6 billion Muslims worldwide, with around 2.8 million adherents in England, Wales and Scotland and about 1,500 mosques in the UK.

ISLAMIC CULTURAL CENTRE – THE LONDON CENTRAL MOSQUE, 146 Park Road, London NW8 7RG **T** 020-7724 3363 **E** info@iccuk.org **W** www.iccuk.org
Director-General, Dr Ahmad Al-Dubayan

MUSLIM COUNCIL OF BRITAIN, PO Box 57330, London E1 2WJ **T** 0845-262 6786 **E** admin@mcb.org.uk **W** www.mcb.org.uk
Secretary-General, Harun Rashid Khan

MUSLIM LAW (SHARIAH) COUNCIL UK, 20–22 Creffield Road, London W5 3RP **T** 0208-992 6636 **E** info@shariahcouncil.org **W** www.shariahcouncil.org
Chair, Dr Mohamed Benotman

MUSLIM WORLD LEAGUE LONDON, 46 Goodge Street, London W1T 4LU **T** 020-7636 7568 **E** info@mwllo.org.uk **W** www.mwllo.org.uk
Director, Dr Ahmed Makhdoom

JAINISM

Jainism traces its history to Vardhamana Jnatriputra, known as *Tirthankara Mahavira* ('the Great Hero') whose traditional dates were 599–527 BC. Jains believe he was the last of the current era in a series of 24 *Jinas* (those who overcome all passions and desires) or *Tirthankaras* (those who show a way across the ocean of life) stretching back to remote antiquity. Born to a noble family in north-eastern India (presently the state of Bihar), he renounced the world for the life of a wandering ascetic and after 12 years of austerity and meditation he attained enlightenment. He then preached his message until, at the age of 72, he left the mortal world and achieved total liberation *(moksha)* from the cycle of death and rebirth.

Jains declare that the Hindu rituals of transferring merit are not acceptable as each living being is responsible for its own actions. They recognise some of the minor deities of the Hindu pantheon, but the supreme objects of worship are the Tirthankaras. The pious Jain does not ask favours from the Tirthankaras, but seeks to emulate their example in his or her own life.

Jains believe that the universe is eternal and self-subsisting, that there is no omnipotent creator God ruling it and the destiny of the individual is in his or her own hands. *Karma,* the fruit of past actions, is believed to determine the place of every living being and rebirth may be in the heavens, on earth as a human, an animal or other lower being, or in the hells. The ultimate goal of existence for Jains is *moksha,* a state of perfect knowledge and tranquillity for each individual soul, which can be achieved only by gaining enlightenment.

The Jainist path to liberation is defined by the three jewels: *Samyak Darshan* (right perception), *Samyak Jnana* (right knowledge) and *Samyak Charitra* (right conduct). Of the five fundamental precepts of the Jains, *Ahimsa* (non-injury to any form of being, in any mode: thought, speech or action) is the first and foremost, and was popularised by Gandhi as *Ahimsa paramo dharma* (non-violence is the supreme religion).

The largest population of Jains can be found in India but there are approximately 30,000 Jains in Britain, with sizeable communities in North America, East Africa, Australia and smaller groups in many other countries.

INSTITUTE OF JAINOLOGY, Unit 18, Silicon Business Centre, 28 Wadsworth Road, Perivale, Greenford, Middx UB6 7JZ
T 020-8997 2300 E info@jainology.org W www.jainology.org
Chair, Dr Nemu Chandaria, OBE

JUDAISM

Judaism is the oldest monotheistic faith. The primary text of Judaism is the Hebrew bible or *Tanakh,* which records how the descendants of Abraham were led by Moses out of their slavery in Egypt to Mount Sinai where God's law *(Torah)* was revealed to them as the chosen people. The *Talmud,* which consists of commentaries on the *Mishnah* (the first text of rabbinical Judaism), is also held to be authoritative, and may be divided into two main categories: the *halakeh* dealing with legal and ritual matters) and the *aggadah* (dealing with theological and ethical matters not directly concerned with the regulation of conduct). The *midrash* comprises rabbinic writings containing biblical interpretations in the spirit of the aggadah. The halakah has become a source of division: orthodox Jews regard Jewish law as derived from God and therefore unalterable; progressive Jews seek to interpret it in the light of contemporary considerations; and conservative Jews aim to maintain most of the traditional rituals but to allow changes in accordance with tradition. Reconstructionist Judaism, a 20th-century movement, regards Judaism as a culture rather than a theological system and accepts all forms of Jewish practice.

The family is the basic unit of Jewish ritual, with the synagogue playing an important role as the centre for public worship and religious study. A synagogue is led by a group of laymen who are elected to office. The Rabbi is primarily a teacher and spiritual guide. The *Sabbath* is the central religious observance. Most British Jews are descendants of either the *Ashkenazim* of central and eastern Europe or the *Sephardim* of Spain, Portugal and the Middle East.

The Chief Rabbi of the United Hebrew Congregations of the Commonwealth is appointed by a Chief Rabbinate Conference, and is the rabbinical authority of the mainstream Orthodox sector of the Ashkenazi Jewish community, the largest body of which is the United Synagogue. His formal ecclesiastical authority is not recognised by the Reform Synagogues of Great Britain (the largest progressive group), the Union of Liberal and Progressive Synagogues, the Spanish and Portuguese Jews' Congregation or the Assembly of Masorti Synagogues. He is, however, generally recognised both outside the Jewish community and within it as the public religious representative of the totality of British Jewry. The Chief Rabbi is President of the London *Beth Din* (Court of Judgment), a rabbinic court. The *Dayanim* (Judges) adjudicate in disputes or on matters of Jewish law and tradition; they also oversee dietary law administration, marriage, divorce and issues of personal status.

The Board of Deputies of British Jews, established in 1760, is the representative body of British Jewry. The basis of representation is through the election of deputies by synagogues and communal organisations. It protects and promotes the interests of British Jewry, acts as the central voice of the community and seeks to counter anti-Jewish discrimination and anti-Semitic activities.

There are approximately 13.9 million Jews worldwide; in the UK there are an estimated 290,000 adherents and over 400 synagogues.

OFFICE OF THE CHIEF RABBI, 305 Ballards Lane, London N12 8GB T 020-8343 6301 E info@chiefrabbi.org
W www.chiefrabbi.org
Chief Rabbi, Ephraim Mirvis

BETH DIN (THE UNITED SYNAGOGUE), 305 Ballards Lane, London N12 8GB T 020-8343 6270 E info@bethdin.org.uk
W www.theus.org.uk
Registrar, David Frei
Dayanim, Yonason Abraham; Menachem Gelley *(Rosh Beth Din);* Ivan Binstock; Shmuel Simons

MASORTI JUDAISM, Alexander House, 3 Shakespeare Road, London N3 1XE T 020-8349 6650 E enquiries@masorti.org.uk
W www.masorti.org.uk
Executive Director, Matt Plen

BOARD OF DEPUTIES OF BRITISH JEWS, 1 Torriano Mews, London NW5 2RZ T 020-7543 5400 E info@bod.org.uk
W www.bod.org.uk
Chief Executive, Gillian Merron

FEDERATION OF SYNAGOGUES, 65 Watford Way, London NW4 3AQ T 020-8202 2263
E info@federationofsynagogues.com
W www.federationofsynagogues.com
Chief Executive, Rabbi Ari Lazarus

LIBERAL JUDAISM, The Montagu Centre, 21 Maple Street, London W1T 4BE T 020-7580 1663
E montagu@liberaljudaism.org W www.liberaljudaism.org
Chief Executive, Rabbi Danny Rich

THE MOVEMENT FOR REFORM JUDAISM, The Sternberg Centre for Judaism, 80 East End Road, London N3 2SY
T 020-8349 5640 E admin@reformjudaism.org.uk
W www.reformjudaism.org.uk
Senior Rabbi, Laura Janner-Klausner

THE SEPHARDI COMMUNITY, 2 Ashworth Road, London W9 1JY T 020-7289 2573 E admin@spsyn.org.uk
W www.sephardi.org.uk
Executive Director, Alison Rosen

UNITED SYNAGOGUE HEAD OFFICE, Adler House, 735 High Road, London N12 0US T 020-8343 8989
W www.theus.org.uk
Chief Executive, Dr Stephen Wilson

PAGANISM

Paganism draws on the ideas of the Celtic people of pre-Roman Europe and is closely linked to Druidism. The first historical record of Druidry comes from classical Greek and Roman writers of the third century BC, who noted the existence of Druids among a people called the Keltoi who inhabited central and southern Europe. The word druid may derive from the Indo-European 'dreo-vid', meaning 'one who knows the truth'. In practice it was probably understood to mean something like 'wise-one' or 'philosopher-priest'.

Paganism is a pantheistic nature-worshipping religion which incorporates beliefs and ritual practices from ancient times. Pagans place much emphasis on the natural world and the ongoing cycle of life and death is central to their beliefs. Most Pagans believe that they are part of nature and not separate from, or superior to it, and seek to live in a way that minimises harm to the natural environment (the word Pagan derives from the Latin *Paganus,* meaning 'rural'). Paganism strongly emphasises the equality of the sexes, with women playing a prominent role in the modern Pagan movement and goddess worship featuring in most ceremonies. Paganism cannot be defined by any principal beliefs because it is shaped by each individual's experiences.

The Pagan Federation was founded in 1971 to provide information on Paganism, campaigns on issues which affect Paganism and provides support to members of the Pagan community. Within the UK the Pagan Federation is divided into 12 districts each with a district manager and a regional coordinator. Local meetings are called 'moots' and take place in private homes, pubs or coffee bars. The Pagan Federation publishes a quarterly journal, *Pagan Dawn*, formerly *The Wiccan* (founded in 1968). The federation also publishes other material, arranges members-only and public events and maintains personal contact by letter with individual members and the wider Pagan community. Regional gatherings and conferences are held throughout the year.

THE PAGAN FEDERATION, Suite 1, The Werks, 45 Church Road, Hove BN3 2BE **E** info@paganfederation.co.uk
W www.paganfed.org
President, Robin Taylor

SIKHISM

The Sikh religion dates from the birth of Guru Nanak in the Punjab in 1469. 'Guru' means teacher but in Sikh tradition has come to represent the divine presence of God giving inner spiritual guidance. Nanak's role as the human vessel of the divine guru was passed on to nine successors, the last of whom (Guru Gobind Singh) died in 1708. The immortal guru is now held to reside in the sacred scripture, *Guru Granth Sahib,* and so to be present in all Sikh gatherings.

Guru Nanak taught that there is one God and that different religions are like different roads leading to the same destination. He condemned religious conflict, ritualism and caste prejudices. The fifth Guru, Guru Arjan Dev, largely compiled the Sikh Holy scripture, a collection of hymns *(gurbani)* known as the *Adi Granth.* It includes the writings of the first five gurus and the ninth guru, and selected writings of Hindu and Muslim saints whose views are in accord with the gurus' teachings. Guru Arjan Dev also built the Golden Temple at Amritsar, the centre of Sikhism. The tenth guru, Guru Gobind Singh, passed on the guruship to the sacred scripture, Guru Granth Sahib, and founded the *Khalsa,* an order intended to fight against tyranny and injustice. Male initiates to the order added 'Singh' to their given names and women added 'Kaur'. Guru Gobind Singh also made the wearing of five symbols obligatory: *kaccha* (a special undergarment), *kara* (a steel bangle), *kirpan* (a small sword), *kesh* (long unshorn hair, and consequently the wearing of a turban) and *kangha* (a comb). These practices are still compulsory for those Sikhs who are initiated into the Khalsa (the *Amritdharis*). Those who do not seek initiation are known as *Sehajdharis.*

There are no professional priests in Sikhism; anyone with a reasonable proficiency in the Punjabi language can conduct a service. Worship can be offered individually or communally, and in a private house or a *gurdwara* (temple). Sikhs are forbidden to eat meat prepared by ritual slaughter; they are also asked to abstain from smoking, alcohol and other intoxicants. Such abstention is compulsory for the Amritdharis.

There are about 24 million Sikhs worldwide and, according to the 2011 census, there are 432,000 adherents in England, Wales and Scotland. Every gurdwara manages its own affairs; there is no central body in the UK. The Sikh Missionary Society provides an information service.

SIKH MISSIONARY SOCIETY UK, 10 Featherstone Road, Southall, Middx UB2 5AA **T** 020-8574 1902
E info@sikhmissionarysociety.org
W www.sikhmissionarysociety.org
Hon. General Secretary, Bahadur Singh

ZOROASTRIANISM

Zoroastrians are followers of the Iranian prophet Spitaman Zarathushtra (or Zoroaster in its hellenised form) who lived *c.*1200–1500 BC. Zoroastrians were persecuted in Iran following the Arab invasion of Persia in the seventh century AD and a group (who are known as Parsis) migrated to India in the ninth century AD to avoid harassment and persecution. Zarathushtra's words are recorded in 17 hymns called the *Gathas,* which, together with other scriptures, form the *Avesta.*

Zoroastrianism teaches that there is one God, *Ahura Mazda* ('Wise Lord'), and that all creation stems ultimately from God; the Gathas teach that human beings have free will, are responsible for their own actions and can choose between good and evil. It is believed that choosing *Asha* (truth or righteousness), with the aid of *Vohu Manah* (good mind), leads to happiness for the individual and society, whereas choosing evil leads to unhappiness and conflict. The *Gathas* also encourage hard work, good deeds and charitable acts. Zoroastrians believe that after death the immortal soul is judged by God, and is then sent to paradise or hell, where it will stay until the end of time to be resurrected for the final judgment.

In Zoroastrian places of worship, an urn containing fire is the central feature; the fire symbolises purity, light and truth and is a visible symbol of the *Fravashi* or *Farohar* (spirit), the presence of Ahura Mazda in every human being. Zoroastrians respect nature and much importance is attached to cultivating land and protecting air, earth and water.

The Zoroastrian Trust Funds of Europe is the main body for Zoroastrians in the UK. Founded in 1861 as the Religious Funds of the Zoroastrians of Europe, it disseminates information on the Zoroastrian faith, provides a place of worship and maintains separate burial grounds for Zoroastrians. It also holds religious and social functions and provides assistance to Zoroastrians as considered necessary, including the provision of loans and grants to students of Zoroastrianism, and participates in inter-faith educational activities.

There are approximately 150,000 Zoroastrians worldwide, of which around 4,000 reside in England and Wales, mainly in London and the South East.

ZOROASTRIAN TRUST FUNDS OF EUROPE, Zoroastrian Centre, 440 Alexandra Avenue, Harrow, Middx HA2 9TL
T 020-8866 0765 **E** secretary@ztfe.com **W** www.ztfe.com
President, Malcolm Deboo

CHURCHES

There are two established (ie state) churches in the UK: the Church of England and the Church of Scotland. There are no established churches in Wales or Northern Ireland, though the Church in Wales, the Scottish Episcopal Church and the Church of Ireland are members of the Anglican Communion.

THE CHURCH OF ENGLAND

The Church of England is divided into the two provinces of Canterbury and York, each under an archbishop. The two provinces are subdivided into 42 dioceses, the newest of which came into existence on 20 April 2014. The new diocese is officially entitled the Diocese of Leeds – although known as the Diocese of West Yorkshire and the Dales – and was formed by the amalgamation of the former dioceses of Bradford, Ripon and Leeds and Wakefield.

Legislative provision for the Church of England is made by the General Synod, established in 1970. It also discusses and expresses opinion on any other matter of religious or public interest. The General Synod has 467 members in total, divided between three houses: the House of Bishops, the House of Clergy and the House of Laity. It is presided over jointly by the Archbishops of Canterbury and York and normally meets twice a year. The synod has the power, delegated by parliament, to frame statute law (known as a 'measure') on any matter concerning the Church of England. A measure must be laid before both houses of parliament, who may accept or reject it but cannot amend it. Once accepted the measure is submitted for royal assent and then has the full force of law. In addition to the General Synod, there are synods at diocesan level. The entire General Synod is re-elected once every five years. The tenth General Synod was inaugurated by the Queen on 23 November 2015.

THE ARCHBISHOPS' COUNCIL

The Archbishops' Council was established in January 1999. Its creation was the result of changes to the Church of England's national structure proposed in 1995 and subsequently approved by the synod and parliament. The council's purpose, set out in the National Institutions Measure 1998, is 'to coordinate, promote and further the work and mission of the Church of England'. It reports to the General Synod. The Archbishops' Council comprises the Archbishops of Canterbury and York, *ex officio*, the prolocutors elected by the convocations of Canterbury and York, the chair and vice-chair of the House of Laity, two bishops, two clergy and two lay persons elected by their respective houses of the General Synod, the Church Estates Commissioner, and up to six persons appointed jointly by the two archbishops.

There are also a number of national boards, councils and other bodies working on matters such as social responsibility, mission, Christian unity and education, which report to the General Synod through the Archbishops' Council.

GENERAL SYNOD OF THE CHURCH OF ENGLAND/ ARCHBISHOPS' COUNCIL, Church House, Great Smith Street, London SW1P 3AZ T 020-7898 1000

Secretary-General, William Nye

THE ORDINATION AND CONSECRATION OF WOMEN

The canon making it possible for women to be ordained to the priesthood was promulgated in the General Synod in February 1994 and the first 32 women priests were ordained on 12 March 1994.

On 14 July 2014 the General Synod approved the Bishops and Priests (Consecration and Ordination of Women) Measure which makes provision for the consecration of women as bishops and for the continuation of provision for the ordination of women. The Revd Elizabeth Lane was consecrated as the first female bishop on 26 January 2015 when she became Bishop Suffragan of Stockport in the diocese of Chester. The first female diocesan bishop, Rachel Treweek, was consecrated as the 41st Bishop of Gloucester on 22 July 2015.

PORVOO DECLARATION

The Porvoo Declaration was approved by the General Synod of the Church of England in July 1995. Churches that approve the declaration regard baptised members of each other's churches as members of their own, and allow free interchange of episcopally ordained ministers within the rules of each church.

MEMBERSHIP AND MINISTRY

	Full-time Diocesan Clergy 2015		Electoral Roll Membership 2015
	Male	Female	
Bath and Wells	131	55	29,900
Birmingham	110	38	15,200
Blackburn	138	25	27,500
Bristol	77	25	14,600
Canterbury	97	27	16,700
Carlisle	86	24	17,300
Chelmsford	241	81	41,300
Chester	155	49	38,400
Chichester	222	29	45,900
Coventry	83	18	15,200
Derby	97	40	14,800
Durham	109	47	18,600
Ely	77	44	17,200
Europe	160	35	10,800
Exeter	150	37	26,400
Gloucester	78	40	21,300
Guildford	123	42	26,300
Hereford	56	28	14,600
Leeds	223	92	38,300
Leicester	83	33	15,400
Lichfield	207	52	37,700
Lincoln	112	45	23,300
Liverpool	134	61	23,900
London	437	79	68,900
Manchester	135	65	27,400
Newcastle	88	31	13,700
Norwich	127	46	17,300
Oxford	266	94	51,300
Peterborough	98	46	17,700
Portsmouth	63	23	14,000
Rochester	160	41	25,700
St Albans	170	65	32,400
St Edmundsbury and Ipswich	80	37	19,700
Salisbury	129	62	34,900
Sheffield	98	30	15,100
Sodor and Man	18	4	2,000
Southwark	239	85	42,000
Southwell and Nottingham	78	41	16,400
Truro	56	28	13,200
Winchester	117	36	31,500
Worcester	73	33	14,400
York	147	51	28,400
Total	5,530	1,864	1,033,100

In 2015, 118,870 people were baptised, 44,670 people were married in parish churches, the Church of England had an electoral roll membership of 1.03 million, and each week an average 961,370 people attended services. As at December

2015 there were 15,685 churches and places of worship; 373 senior clergy (including bishops, archdeacons and cathedral clergy); 7,171 full-time equivalent parochial stipendiary clergy; 118 full-time equivalent non-parochial stipendiary clergy; 3,300 self-supporting ministers; 1,170 chaplains; 270 lay workers and 160 Church Army evangelists; 6,170 readers and licensed lay ministers; and 2,830 readers with permission to officiate and active emeriti.

STIPENDS
The stipends below are for those appointed on or after 1 April 2004; transitional arrangements are in place for those appointed prior to this date. The national minimum stipend from 1 April 2017 is £23,800; under common tenure all full-time office-holders must receive stipend, or stipend together with other income related to their office, of at least this amount.

	2017–18
Archbishop of Canterbury	£80,160
Archbishop of York	£68,700
Bishop of London	£62,970
Diocesan bishops	£43,510
Suffragan bishops	£35,500
Assistant bishops (full-time)	£34,360
Deans	£35,500
Archdeacons	£34,700
Residentiary canons	*£27,470
Incumbents and clergy of similar status	*£25,440

* National stipend benchmark: adjusted regionally to reflect variations in the cost of living

CANTERBURY

105TH ARCHBISHOP AND PRIMATE OF ALL ENGLAND
Most Revd and Rt. Hon. Justin Welby, *cons.* 2011, *apptd* 2013; Lambeth Palace, London SE1 7JU
Signs Justin Cantuar:

BISHOPS SUFFRAGAN
*Dover, Rt. Revd Trevor Willmott, *cons.* 2002, *apptd* 2009; Upway, St Martin's Hill, Canterbury, Kent CT1 1PR
*Ebbsfleet, Rt. Revd Jonathan Goodall, *cons.* 2013, *apptd* 2013; Hill House, Treetops, The Mount, Caversham, Reading RG4 7RE
*Richborough, Rt. Revd Norman Banks, *cons.* 2011, *apptd* 2011; Parkside House, Abbey Mill Lane, St Albans AL3 4HE
*Maidstone, Rt. Revd Roderick Thomas, *cons.* 2015, *apptd* 2015; The Bishop's Lodge, Church Road, Worth, Crawley RH10 7RT
*responsible for episcopal oversight of the Channel Islands

DEAN
Very Revd Robert Willis, *apptd* 2001

Dean of Jersey (A Peculiar), Very Revd Mike Keirle, *apptd* 2017
Dean of Guernsey (A Peculiar), Very Revd Tim Barker, *apptd* 2015

Organist (Canterbury Cathedral), David Flood, FRCO, *apptd* 1988

ARCHDEACONS
Ashford, Ven. Philip Down, *apptd* 2011
Canterbury, Ven. Jo Kelly Moore *apptd* 2017
Maidstone, Ven. Stephen Taylor, *apptd* 2011

Vicar-General of Province and Diocese, Chancellor Sheila Cameron, QC
Commissary-General, Morag Ellis, QC
Joint Registrars of the Province, Canon John Rees; Stephen Slack
Diocesan Registrar and Legal Adviser, Owen Carew Jones

Diocesan Secretary, Julian Hills, Diocesan House, Lady Wootton's Green, Canterbury CT1 1NQ T 01227-459401

YORK

97TH ARCHBISHOP AND PRIMATE OF ENGLAND
Most Revd and Rt. Hon. Dr John Sentamu, *cons.* 1996, *trans.* 2005; Bishopthorpe, York YO23 2GE
Signs Sentamu Ebor:

BISHOPS SUFFRAGAN
Hull, Rt. Revd Alison White, *cons.* 2015, *apptd* 2015; Hullen House, Woodfield Lane, Hessle, Hull HU13 0ES
Selby, Rt. Revd John Thomson, *cons.* 2014, *apptd* 2014; 6 Pinfold Garth, Malton YO17 7XQ
Whitby, Rt. Revd Paul Fergson, *cons.* 2014, *apptd* 2014; 21 Thornton Road, Stainton TS8 9DS

PRINCIPAL EPISCOPAL VISITOR
Beverley, Rt. Revd Glyn Webster, *cons.* 2013, *apptd* 2013; Holy Trinity Rectory, Micklegate, York YO1 6LE

DEAN
Very Revd Vivienne Faull, *apptd* 2012

Director of Music, Robert Sharpe, *apptd* 2008

ARCHDEACONS
Cleveland, Ven. Samantha Rushton, *apptd* 2015
East Riding, Ven. Andy Broom, *apptd* 2014
York, Ven. Sarah Bullock, *apptd* 2013

Chancellor of the Diocese, His Hon. Judge Collier, QC, *apptd* 2006
Registrar and Legal Secretary, Caroline Mockford
Diocesan Secretary, Canon Peter Warry, Diocesan House, Amy Johnson Way, York YO30 4XT T 01904-699500

LONDON (CANTERBURY)

133RD BISHOP
vacant

AREA BISHOPS
Edmonton, Rt. Revd Robert Wickham, *cons.* 2015, *apptd* 2015; 27 Thurlow Road, London NW3 5PP
Kensington, Rt. Revd Graham Tomlin, *cons.* 2015, *apptd* 2015; Dial House, Riverside, Twickenham TW1 3DT
Stepney, Rt. Revd Adrian Newman, *cons.* 2011, *apptd* 2011; 63 Coburn Road, London E3 2DB
Willesden, Rt. Revd Peter Broadbent, *cons.* 2001, *apptd* 2001; 173 Willesden Lane, London NW6 7YN

BISHOP SUFFRAGAN
Islington, Rt. Revd Ric Thorpe, *cons.* 2015, *apptd* 2015; St Edmund the King, Lombard Street, London, EC3V 9EA
Fulham, Rt. Revd Jonathan Baker, *cons.* 2011, *apptd* 2013; The Vicarage, 5 St Andrew Street, London EC4A 3AF

DEAN OF ST PAUL'S
Very Revd Dr David Ison, PHD, *apptd* 2012

Director of Music, Andrew Carwood, *apptd* 2007

ARCHDEACONS
Hackney, Ven. Liz Adekunle, *apptd* 2016
Hampstead, Ven. John Hawkins, *apptd* 2015
London, Ven. Luke Miller, *apptd* 2016
Middlesex, Ven. Stephan Welch, *apptd* 2006
Northolt, Ven. Duncan Green, *apptd* 2013

Chancellor, Nigel Seed, QC, *apptd* 2002
Registrar and Legal Secretary, Paul Morris
Diocesan Secretary, Richard Gough, London Diocesan House, 36 Causton Street, London SW1P 4AU T 020-7932 1100

DURHAM (YORK)

74TH BISHOP
Rt. Revd Paul Butler, *cons.* 2004, *trans.* 2013; Auckland Castle, Bishop Auckland DL14 7NR
Signs Paul Dunelm:

BISHOP SUFFRAGAN

Jarrow, Rt. Revd Mark Bryant, *cons.* 2007, *apptd* 2007;
Bishop's House, 25 Ivy Lane, Low Fell, Gateshead NE9 6QD

DEAN

Very Revd Andrew Tremlett, *apptd* 2015

Organist, James Lancelot, FRCO, *apptd* 1985

ARCHDEACONS

Auckland, vacant
Durham, Ven. Ian Jagger, *apptd* 2006
Sunderland, Ven. Stuart Bain, *apptd* 2002

Chancellor, His Hon. Judge Bursell, QC, *apptd* 1989
Registrar and Legal Secretary, Hilary Monckton-Milnes

Diocesan Secretary, Andrew Thurston, Diocesan Office, Cuthbert
House, Stonebridge, Durham DH1 3RY **T** 01388-660010

WINCHESTER (CANTERBURY)

97TH BISHOP

Rt. Revd Tim Dakin, cons. 2012, *apptd* 2011; Wolvesey,
Winchester SO23 9ND
Signs Tim Winton:

BISHOPS SUFFRAGAN

Basingstoke, Rt. Revd David Williams, *cons.* 2014, *apptd* 2014;
Bishop's Office, Old Alresford Place, Alresford, Hants SO24 9DH
Southampton, Rt. Revd Jonathan Frost, *cons.* 2010, *apptd*
2010; Bishop's House, St Mary's Church Close, Wessex Lane,
Southampton SO18 2ST

DEANS

Dean of Winchester, Very Revd Catherine Ogle, *apptd* 2017

Director of Music (Winchester Cathedral), Andrew Lumsden,
apptd 2002

ARCHDEACONS

Bournemouth, Ven. Dr Peter Rouch, *apptd* 2011
Winchester, Ven. Richard Brand, *apptd* 2016
For Mission Development, Ven. Paul Moore, *apptd* 2014

Chancellor, Cain Ormondroyd, *apptd* 2017
Registrar and Legal Secretary, Sue de Candole

Chief Executive, Andrew Robinson, Old Alresford Place,
Alresford, Hants SO24 9DH **T** 01962-737300

BATH AND WELLS (CANTERBURY)

79TH BISHOP

Rt. Revd Peter Hancock, *cons.* 2010, *apptd* 2014; The Bishop's
Palace, Wells, Somerset BA5 2PD
Signs Peter Bath & Wells:

BISHOP SUFFRAGAN

Taunton, Rt. Revd Ruth Worsley, *cons.* 2015, *apptd* 2015; The
Bishop's Palace, Market Place, Wells BA5 2PD

DEAN

Very Revd John Davies, *apptd* 2016

Organist, Matthew Owens, *apptd* 2005

ARCHDEACONS

Bath, Ven. Dr Adrian Youings, *apptd* 2017
Taunton, Ven. Simon Hill, *apptd* 2016
Wells, Ven. Anne Gell, *apptd* 2017

Chancellor, Timothy Briden, *apptd* 1993
Registrar and Legal Secretary, Roland Callaby

Diocesan Secretary, Nick May, The Old Deanery, St Andrew's
Street, Wells, Somerset BA5 2UG **T** 01749-670777

BIRMINGHAM (CANTERBURY)

9TH BISHOP

Rt. Revd David Urquhart, *cons.* 2000, *apptd* 2006; Bishop's
Croft, Old Church Road, Harborne, Birmingham B17 0BG
Signs David Birmingham:

BISHOP SUFFRAGAN

Aston, Anne Hollinghurst, *cons.* 2015, *apptd* 2015, Bishop's
Lodge, 16 Coleshill Street, Sutton Coldfield B72 1SH

DEAN

Very Revd Matt Thompson, *apptd* 2017

Director of Music, Marcus Huxley, FRCO, *apptd* 1986

ARCHDEACONS

Aston, Ven. Simon Heathfield, *apptd* 2014
Birmingham, Ven. Hayward Osborne, *apptd* 2001

Chancellor, Mark Powell, QC, *apptd* 2012
Registrar and Legal Secretary, Vicki Simpson

Diocesan Secretary, Andrew Halstead, 1 Colmore Row,
Birmingham B3 2BJ **T** 0121-426 0400

BLACKBURN (YORK)

9TH BISHOP

Rt. Revd Julian Henderson, *cons.* 2013, *apptd* 2013; Bishop's
House, Ribchester Road, Blackburn BB1 9EF
Signs Julian Blackburn

BISHOPS SUFFRAGAN

Burnley, Rt. Revd Philip North, *cons.* 2015, *apptd* 2015; Dean
House, 449 Padiham Road, Burnley BB12 6TE
Lancaster, vacant

DEAN

Very Revd Peter Howell-Jones, *apptd* 2016

Organist and Director of Music, Samuel Hudson, *apptd* 2011

ARCHDEACON

Blackburn, Ven. Mark Ireland, *apptd* 2015
Lancaster, Ven. Michael Everitt, *apptd* 2011

Chancellor, His Hon. Judge Bullimore, *apptd* 1990
Registrar and Legal Secretary, Stephen Crossley

Diocesan Secretary, Graeme Pollard, Diocesan Office, Clayton
House, Walker Office Park, Blackburn BB1 2QE **T** 01254-503070

BRISTOL (CANTERBURY)

56TH BISHOP

vacant; 58A High Street, Winterbourne, Bristol BS36 1JQ
Signs Michael Bristol

BISHOP SUFFRAGAN

Swindon, Rt. Revd Dr Lee Rayfield, *cons.* 2005, *apptd* 2005;
Mark House, Field Rise, Swindon, Wiltshire SN1 4HP

DEAN

Very Revd David Hoyle, *apptd* 2010

Organist and Director of Music, Mark Lee, *apptd* 1998

ARCHDEACONS

Bristol, Ven. Christine Froude *(acting)*
Malmesbury, Ven. Christine Froude, *apptd* 2011

Chancellor, The Worshipful Revd Justin Gau
Registrar and Legal Secretary, Roland Callaby

Diocesan Secretary, Oliver Home, First Floor, Hillside House, 1500
Parkway North, Stoke Gifford, Bristol BS34 8YU **T** 0117-9060100

CARLISLE (YORK)

67TH BISHOP
Rt. Revd James Newcome, *cons.* 2002, *apptd* 2009; Bishop's House, Ambleside Road, Keswick CA12 4DD
Signs James Carliol

BISHOP SUFFRAGAN
Penrith, Rt. Revd Robert Freeman, *cons.* 2011, *apptd* 2011; Holm Croft, 13 Castle Road, Kendal, Cumbria LA9 7AU

DEAN
Very Revd Mark Boyling, *apptd* 2004

Master of the Music, vacant

ARCHDEACONS
Carlisle, Ven. Lee Townend, *apptd* 2017
West Cumberland, Ven. Dr Richard Pratt, *apptd* 2009
Westmorland and Furness, Ven. Vernon Ross, *apptd* 2017

Chancellor, Geoffrey Tattersall, QC, *apptd* 2003
Registrar and Legal Secretary, Jane Lowdon
Diocesan Secretary, Derek Hurton, Church House, 19–24 Friargate, Penrith, Cumbria CA11 7XR **T** 01768-807777

CHELMSFORD (CANTERBURY)

10TH BISHOP
Rt. Revd Stephen Cottrell, *cons.* 2004, *apptd* 2010; Bishopscourt, Main Road, Margaretting, Ingatestone, Essex CM4 0HD
Signs Stephen Chelmsford

BISHOPS SUFFRAGAN
Barking, Rt. Revd Peter Hill, *cons.* 2014, *apptd* 2014; Barking Lodge, Verulam Avenue, London E17 8ES
Bradwell, vacant
Colchester, Rt. Revd Roger Morris, *cons.* 2014, *apptd* 2014; 1 Fitzwater Road, Colchester, Essex CO3 3SS

DEAN
Very Revd Nicholas Henshall, *apptd* 2013

Director of Music, James Davy, *apptd* 2012

ARCHDEACONS
Barking, Ven. Dr John Perumbalath, *apptd* 2013
Chelmsford, Ven. Elizabeth Snowden, *apptd* 2016
Colchester, Ven. Annette Cooper, *apptd* 2004
Harlow, Ven. Vanessa Herrick, *apptd* 2017
Southend, Ven. Mike Lodge, *apptd* 2017
Stansted, Ven. Robin King, *apptd* 2013
West Ham, Ven. Elwin Cockett, *apptd* 2007

Chancellor, George Pulman, QC, *apptd* 2001
Registrar and Legal Secretary, Aiden Hargreaves-Smith
Chief Executive, John Ball, 53 New Street, Chelmsford, Essex CM1 1AT **T** 01245-294400

CHESTER (YORK)

40TH BISHOP
Rt. Revd Peter Forster, PHD, *cons.* 1996, *apptd* 1996; Bishop's House, Abbey Square, Chester CH1 2JD
Signs Peter Cestr:

BISHOPS SUFFRAGAN
Birkenhead, Rt. Revd Keith Sinclair, *cons.* 2007, *apptd* 2007; Bishop's Lodge, 67 Bidston Road, Prenton CH43 6TR
Stockport, Rt. Revd Elizabeth Lane, *cons.* 2015, *apptd* 2015; Bishop's Lodge, Back Lane, Dunham, Altrincham WA14 4SG

DEAN
vacant

Organist and Director of Music, Philip Rushforth, FRCO, *apptd* 2008

ARCHDEACONS
Chester, Ven. Dr Michael Gilbertson, *apptd* 2010
Macclesfield, Ven. Ian Bishop, *apptd* 2011

Chancellor, His Hon. Judge Turner, QC, *apptd* 1998
Registrar and Legal Secretary, Lisa Moncur
Diocesan Secretary, George Colville, Church House, 5500 Daresbury Park, Daresbury, Warrington WA4 4GE **T** 01928-718834

CHICHESTER (CANTERBURY)

103RD BISHOP
Rt. Revd Dr Martin Warner, *cons.* 2010, *apptd* 2012; The Palace, Chichester PO19 1PY
Signs Martin Cicestr:

BISHOPS SUFFRAGAN
Horsham, Rt. Revd Mark Sowerby, *cons.* 2009, *apptd* 2009; 21 Guildford Road, Horsham, W. Sussex RH12 1LU
Lewes, Rt. Revd Richard Jackson, *cons.* 2014, *apptd* 2014; Ebenezer House, Kingston Ridge, Kingston, Lewes BN7 3JU

DEAN
Very Revd Stephen Waine, *apptd* 2015

Organist, Charles Harrison, *apptd* 2014

ARCHDEACONS
Brighton and Lewes, Ven. Martin Lloyd Williams, *apptd* 2015
Chichester, Ven. Douglas McKittrick, *apptd* 2002
Horsham, Ven. Fiona Windsor, *apptd* 2014
Hastings, Ven. Edward Dowler, *apptd* 2016

Chancellor, Prof. Mark Hill, QC
Registrar and Legal Secretary, Matthew Chinery
Diocesan Secretary, Gabrielle Higgins, Diocesan Church House, 211 New Church Road, Hove, E. Sussex BN3 4ED **T** 01273-421021

COVENTRY (CANTERBURY)

9TH BISHOP
Rt. Revd Dr Christopher Cocksworth, *cons.* 2008, *apptd* 2008; The Bishop's House, 23 Davenport Road, Coventry CV5 6PW
Signs Christopher Coventry

BISHOP SUFFRAGAN
Warwick, Rt. Revd John Stroyan, *cons.* 2005, *apptd* 2005; Warwick House, School Hill, Offchurch, Leamington Spa CV33 9AL

DEAN
Very Revd John Witcombe, *apptd* 2013

Director of Music, Mr Kerry Beaumont, *apptd* 2006

ARCHDEACONS
Archdeacon Pastor, Ven. John Green, CB, *apptd* 2013
Archdeacon Missioner, Ven. Morris Rodham, *apptd* 2010

Chancellor, His Hon. Judge Eyre, *apptd* 2009
Registrar and Legal Secretary, Mary Allanson
Diocesan Secretary, Ruth Marlow, Cathedral & Diocesan Offices, 1 Hilltop, Coventry CV1 5AB **T** 024-7652 1200

DERBY (CANTERBURY)

7TH BISHOP
Rt. Revd Dr Alastair Redfern, *cons.* 1997, *apptd* 2005; The Bishop's Office, King Street, Duffield DE56 4EU
Signs Alastair Derby

BISHOP SUFFRAGAN
Repton, Rt. Revd Jan McFarlane, *cons.* 2016, *apptd* 2016; Repton House, Lea, Matlock, Derby DE4 5JP

DEAN
vacant

Director of Music, Hugh Morris, *apptd* 2015

ARCHDEACONS
Chesterfield, vacant
Derby, Ven. Dr Christopher Cunliffe, *apptd* 2006

Chancellor, His Hon. Judge Bullimore, *apptd* 1981
Registrar and Legal Secretary, Nadine Waldron

Diocesan Secretary, vacant, Derby Church House, Full Street, Derby DE1 3DR T 01332-388650

ELY (CANTERBURY)

69TH BISHOP
Rt. Revd Stephen Conway, *cons.* 2006, *apptd* 2011; The Bishop's House, Ely CB7 4DW
Signs Stephen Ely

BISHOP SUFFRAGAN
Huntingdon, Rt. Revd David Thomson, DPHIL, *cons.* 2008, *apptd* 2008; 14 Lynn Road, Ely, Cambs CB6 1DA

DEAN
Very Revd Mark Bonney, *apptd* 2012

Director of Music, Paul Trepte, FRCO, *apptd* 1991

ARCHDEACONS
Cambridge, Ven. Dr Alex Hughes, *apptd* 2014
Huntingdon and Wisbech, Ven. Hugh McCurdy, *apptd* 2005

Chancellor, His Hon. Judge Leonard, QC
Registrar, Howard Dellar

Diocesan Secretary, Canon Paul Evans, Bishop Woodford House, Barton Road, Ely, Cambs CB7 4DX T 01353-652702

EXETER (CANTERBURY)

71ST BISHOP
Rt. Revd Robert Atwell, *cons.* 2008, *apptd* 2014; The Palace, Exeter EX1 1HY
Signs Robert Exon:

BISHOPS SUFFRAGAN
Crediton, Rt. Revd Dame Sarah Mullally, DBE, cons. 2015, apptd 2015: 32 The Avenue, Tiverton EX16 4HW

Plymouth, Rt. Revd Nick McKinnel, *cons.* 2012, *trans.* 2015; 108 Molesworth Road, Stoke, Plymouth PL3 4AQ

DEAN
vacant

Director of Music, Timothy Noon, *apptd* 2016

ARCHDEACONS
Barnstaple, Ven. Mark Butchers, *apptd* 2015
Exeter, Ven. Christopher Futcher, *apptd* 2012
Plymouth, Ven. Ian Chandler, *apptd* 2010
Totnes, Ven. Douglas Dettmer, *apptd* 2015

Chancellor, Hon. Sir Andrew McFarlane
Registrar and Legal Secretary, M. Follett

Diocesan Secretary, Stephen Hancock, The Old Deanery, The Cloisters, Exeter EX1 1HS T 01392-272686

GIBRALTAR IN EUROPE (CANTERBURY)

4TH BISHOP
Rt. Revd Robert Innes, PHD, *cons.* 2014, *apptd* 2014; 47, rue Capitaine Crespel – boite 49, 1050 Brussels, Belgium

BISHOP SUFFRAGAN
In Europe, Rt. Revd David Hamid, *cons.* 2002, *apptd* 2002; 14 Tufton Street, London SW1P 3QZ

Dean, Cathedral Church of the Holy Trinity, Gibraltar, Very Revd Dr John Paddock

Chancellor, Pro-Cathedral of St Paul, Valletta, Malta, Canon Simon Godfrey
Chancellor, Pro-Cathedral of the Holy Trinity, Brussels, Belgium, Ven. Dr Paul Vrolijk

ARCHDEACONS
Eastern, Ven. Colin Williams
North-West Europe, Ven. Dr Paul Vrolijk
France, Ven. Meurig Williams
Gibraltar, Canon Geoffrey Johnston
Italy and Malta, Ven. Vickie Sims
Germany and Northern Europe, Ven. Colin Williams
Switzerland, Canon Adèle Kelham

Chancellor, Prof. Mark Hill, QC
Registrar and Legal Secretary, Aiden Hargreaves-Smith

Diocesan Secretary, Adrian Mumford, 14 Tufton Street, London SW1P 3QZ T 020-7898 1155

GLOUCESTER (CANTERBURY)

41ST BISHOP
Rt. Revd Rachel Treweek, *cons.* 2015, *apptd* 2015; 2 College Green, Gloucester GL1 2LR
Signs Rachel Gloucestr

BISHOP SUFFRAGAN
Tewkesbury, Rt. Revd Robert Springett, *cons.* 2016, *apptd* 2016; 2 College Green, Gloucester GL1 2LR

DEAN
Very Revd Stephen Lake, *apptd* 2011

Director of Music, Adrian Partington, *apptd* 2007

ARCHDEACONS
Cheltenham, Ven. Phil Andrew, *apptd* 2017
Gloucester, Ven. Jackie Searle, *apptd* 2012

Chancellor and Vicar-General, June Rodgers, *apptd* 1990
Registrar and Legal Secretary, Jos Moule

Diocesan Secretary, Ben Preece Smith, Church House, College Green, Gloucester GL1 2LY T 01452-410022

GUILDFORD (CANTERBURY)

10TH BISHOP
Rt. Revd Andrew Watson, *cons.* 2008, *apptd* 2014; Willow Grange, Woking Road, Guildford, Surrey GU4 7QS
Signs Andrew Guildford

BISHOP SUFFRAGAN
Dorking, Rt Revd Jo Wells, *cons.* 2016, *apptd* 2016; Dayspring, 13 Pilgrim's Way, Guildford, Surrey GU4 8AD

DEAN
Very Revd Dianna Gwilliams, *apptd* 2013

Organist, Katherine Dienes-Williams, *apptd* 2007

ARCHDEACONS
Dorking, Ven. Paul Bryer, *apptd* 2014
Surrey, vacant

Chancellor, Andrew Jordan
Registrar and Legal Secretary, Howard Dellar

Diocesan Secretary, Peter Coles, Diocesan House, Quarry Street, Guildford GU1 3XG T 01483-790300

HEREFORD (CANTERBURY)

105TH BISHOP
Rt. Revd Richard Frith, cons. 1998, apptd 2014; Bishop's House, The Palace, Hereford HR4 9BN
Signs Richard Hereford

BISHOP SUFFRAGAN

Ludlow, Rt. Revd Alistair Magowan, *cons.* 2009, *apptd* 2009; Bishop's House, Corvedale Road, Craven Arms, Shropshire SY7 9BT

DEAN

Very Revd Michael Tavinor, *apptd* 2002

Organist and Director of Music, Geraint Bowen, FRCO, *apptd* 2001

ARCHDEACONS

Hereford, Ven. Paddy Benson, *apptd* 2011
Ludlow, Rt. Revd Alistair Magowan, *apptd* 2009

Chancellor, His Hon. Judge Kaye, QC
Registrar and Legal Secretary, Howard Dellar
Diocesan Secretary, Sam Pratley, The Palace, Hereford HR4 9BL T 01432-373300

LEEDS (YORK)

1ST BISHOP OF LEEDS

Rt. Revd Nicholas Baines, *cons.* 2003, *apptd* 2014; Hollin House, Weetwood Avenue, Leeds LS16 5NG
Signs Nicholas Leeds

AREA BISHOPS

Bradford, Rt. Revd Dr Toby Howarth, *cons.* 2014, *apptd* 2014; 47 Kirkgate, Shipley BD18 3EH
Huddersfield, Rt. Revd Jonathan Gibbs, *cons.* 2014, *apptd* 2014; University of Huddersfield, Ground Floor, Sir John Ramsden Court, Huddersfield HD1 3AQ
Ripon, vacant
Wakefield, Rt. Revd Anthony Robinson, *cons.* 2002, *apptd* 2014; Pontefract House 181A Manygates Lane, Sandal, Wakefield WF2 7DR

SUFFRAGAN BISHOP

Richmond, Rt. Revd Paul Slater, *cons.* 2015, apptd 2015; Church House, 17–19 York Place, Leeds LS1 2EX

DEANS

Bradford, Very Revd Jerry Lepine, *apptd* 2013
Ripon, Very Revd John Dobson, *apptd* 2014
Wakefield, Very Revd Jonathan Greener, *apptd* 2007

Directors of Music, Andrew Bryden (Ripon), *apptd* 2003; Thomas Moore (Wakefield), *apptd* 2010; Alex Berry (Bradford)

ARCHDEACONS

Bradford, Ven. Andrew Jolley, *apptd* 2016
Halifax, Ven. Dr Anne Dawtry, *apptd* 2011
Leeds, Ven. Paul Ayers, *apptd* 2017
Richmond and Craven, Ven. Beverley Mason, *apptd* 2016
Pontefract, Ven. Peter Townley, *apptd* 2008

Chancellor, Prof. Mark Hill, QC
Registrar and Legal Secretary, Peter Foskett
Joint Diocesan Secretaries, Debbie Child; Ashley Ellis Church House, 17–19 York Place, Leeds LS1 2EX T 0113-200 0540

LEICESTER (CANTERBURY)

7TH BISHOP

Rt Revd Martyn Snow, *cons.* 2013, *apptd* 2016; Bishop's Lodge, 10 Springfield Road, Leicester LE2 3BD
Signs Martyn Leicester

SUFFRAGAN BISHOP

Loughborough, Rt. Revd Guli Francis-Dehqani, *cons.* 2017, *apptd* 2017; c/o Bishop's Lodge, 10 Springfield Road, Leicester LE2 3BD

DEAN

Very Revd David Monteith, *apptd* 2013

Director of Music, Dr Christopher Johns

ARCHDEACONS

Leicester, Ven. Timothy Stratford, *apptd* 2012
Loughborough, Ven. Claire Wood, *apptd* 2017

Chancellor, Mark Blackett-Ord
Registrar and Legal Secretary, Revd Trevor Kirkman
Diocesan Secretary, Jonathan Kerry, St Martin's House, 7 Peacock Lane, Leicester LE1 5PZ T 0116-261 5200

LICHFIELD (CANTERBURY)

99TH BISHOP

Rt. Revd Dr Michael Ipgrave, OBE, *cons.* 2012, *apptd* 2016; 22 The Close, Lichfield, WS13 7LG
Signs Michael Lichfield

AREA BISHOPS

Shrewsbury, Rt. Revd Mark Rylands, *cons.* 2009, *apptd* 2009; Athlone House, 66 London Road, Shrewsbury SY2 6PG
Stafford, Rt. Revd Geoffrey Annas, *cons.* 2010, *apptd* 2010; Ash Garth, Broughton Crescent, Barlaston, Stoke-on-Trent ST12 9DD
Wolverhampton, Rt. Revd Clive Gregory, *cons.* 2007, *apptd* 2007; 61 Richmond Road, Wolverhampton WV3 9JH

DEAN

Very Revd Adrian Dorber, *apptd* 2005

Directors of Music, Ben and Cathy Lamb, *apptd* 2010
Organist, Martyn Rawles, *apptd* 2010

ARCHDEACONS

Lichfield, Ven. Simon Baker, *apptd* 2013
Salop, Ven. Paul Thomas, *apptd* 2011
Stoke-on-Trent, Ven. Matthew Parker, *apptd* 2013
Walsall, Ven. Dr Susan Weller, *apptd* 2015

Chancellor, His Hon. Judge Eyre, *apptd* 2012
Registrar and Legal Secretary, Niall Blackie
Diocesan Secretary, Julie Jones, St Mary's House, The Close, Lichfield, Staffs WS13 7LD T 01543-306030

LINCOLN (CANTERBURY)

72ND BISHOP

Rt. Revd Christopher Lowson, *cons.* 2011, *apptd* 2011; Bishop's Office, The Old Palace, Minster Yard, Lincoln LN2 1PU
Signs Christopher Lincoln

BISHOPS SUFFRAGAN

Grantham, Rt. Revd Dr Nicholas Chamberlain, *cons.* 2015, *apptd* 2015; The Old Palace, Minster Yard, Lincoln LN2 1PU
Grimsby, Rt. Revd Dr David Court, *cons.* 2014, *apptd* 2014; The Old Palace, Minster Yard, Lincoln LN2 1PU

DEAN

Very Revd Christine Wilson, *apptd* 2016

Director of Music, Aric Prentice, *apptd* 2003

ARCHDEACONS

Boston, Ven. Dr Justine Allain Chapman, *apptd* 2013
Lincoln, Ven. Gavin Kirk, *apptd* 2016
Stow and Lindsey, Ven. Mark Steadman, *apptd* 2015

Chancellor, His Hon. Judge Bishop
Registrar and Legal Secretary, Ian Blaney
Diocesan Secretary, Angela Sibson, OBE, Edward King House, Minster Yard, Lincoln LN2 1PU T 01522-504050

LIVERPOOL (YORK)

8TH BISHOP

Rt. Revd Paul Bayes, *cons.* 2010, *apptd* 2014; Bishop's Lodge, Woolton Park, Liverpool L25 6DT
Signs Paul Liverpool

BISHOP SUFFRAGAN

Warrington, Rt. Revd Richard Blackburn, *cons.* 2009, *apptd* 2009; St James' House, 20 St James Road, Liverpool L1 7BY

DEAN

vacant

Director of Music, Lee Ward, *apptd* 2017

ARCHDEACONS

Liverpool, Ven. Richard Panter, *apptd* 2002
Knowsley & Sefton, Ven. Pete Spiers *apptd* 2016
St Helens & Warrington, Ven. Peter Preece, *apptd* 2016
Wigan & West Lancashire, Ven. Jennifer McKenzie, *apptd* 2016

Chancellor, Sir Mark Hedley, QC
Registrar and Legal Secretary, Howard Dellar

Diocesan Secretary, Mike Eastwood, St James House, 20 St James Street, Liverpool L1 7BY **T** 0151-709 9722

MANCHESTER (YORK)

12TH BISHOP

Rt. Revd Dr David Walker, *cons.* 2000, *apptd* 2013; Bishopscourt, Bury New Road, Salford M7 4LE
Signs David Manchester

BISHOPS SUFFRAGAN

Bolton, Rt. Revd Mark Ashcroft, *cons.* 2016, *apptd* 2016; Bishop's Lodge, Walkenden Road, Walkenden M28 2WH
Middleton, Rt. Revd Mark Davies, *cons.* 2008, *apptd* 2008; The Hollies, Manchester Road, Rochdale OL11 3QY

DEAN

Very Revd Rogers Govender, *apptd* 2006

Organist, Christopher Stokes, *apptd* 1992

ARCHDEACONS

Bolton, Ven. David Bailey, *apptd* 2008
Manchester, Ven. Karen Lund, *apptd* 2017
Rochdale, Ven. Cherry Vann, *apptd* 2008
Salford, Ven. David Sharples, *apptd* 2009

Chancellor, Canon Geoffrey Tattersall, QC
Registrar and Legal Secretary, Jane Monks

Diocesan Secretary, Canon Martin Miller, Diocesan Church House, 90 Deansgate, Manchester M3 2GH **T** 0161-828 1400

NEWCASTLE (YORK)

12TH BISHOP

Rt. Revd Christine Elizabeth Hardman, *cons.* 2015, apptd 2015; Bishop's House, 29 Moor Road South, Gosforth, Newcastle upon Tyne NE3 1PA
Signs Christine Newcastle

SUFFRAGAN BISHOP

Berwick Rt. Revd Mark Tanner, *cons.* 2016, *apptd* 2016; Berwick House, Longhirst Road, Pegswood, Morpeth NE61 6XF

DEAN

Very Revd Christopher C. Dalliston, *apptd* 2003

Director of Music, Ian Roberts, *apptd* 2016

ARCHDEACONS

Lindisfarne, Ven. Dr Peter Robinson, *apptd* 2008
Northumberland, Ven. Geoffrey Miller, *apptd* 2004

Chancellor, Euan Duff, *apptd* 2013
Registrar and Legal Secretary, Jane Lowdon

Diocesan Secretary, Canon Shane Waddle, Church House, St John's Terrace, North Shields NE29 6HS **T** 0191-270 4100

NORWICH (CANTERBURY)

71ST BISHOP

Rt. Revd Graham R. James, *cons.* 1993, *apptd* 2000; Bishop's House, Norwich NR3 1SB
Signs Graham Norvic:

BISHOPS SUFFRAGAN

Lynn, Rt. Revd Jonathan Meyrick, *cons.* 2011, *apptd* 2011; The Old Vicarage, Castle Acre, King's Lynn PE32 2AA
Thetford, Rt. Revd Alan Winton, PHD, *cons.* 2009, *apptd* 2009; The Red House, 53 Norwich Road, Stoke Holy Cross, Norwich NR14 8AB

DEAN

Very Revd Jane Hedges, *apptd* 2014

Master of Music, Ashley Grote, *apptd* 2012

ARCHDEACONS

Lynn, Ven. John Ashe, *apptd* 2009
Norfolk, Ven. Steven Betts, *apptd* 2012
Norwich, Ven. Karen Hutchinson, *apptd* 2016

Chancellor, Ruth Arlow, *apptd* 2012
Registrar and Legal Secretary, Stuart Jones

Diocesan Secretary, Richard Butler, Diocesan House, 109 Dereham Road, Easton, Norwich, Norfolk NR9 5ES **T** 01603-880853

OXFORD (CANTERBURY)

44TH BISHOP

Rt. Revd Steven Croft, *cons.* 2009, *apptd* 2016; Church House Oxford, Langford Locks, Kidlington, Oxford OX5 1GF
Signs Steven Oxon:

AREA BISHOPS

Buckingham, Rt. Revd Dr Alan Wilson, *cons.* 2003, *apptd* 2003; Sheridan, Grimms Hill, Great Missenden, Bucks HP16 9BD
Dorchester, Rt. Revd Colin Fletcher, *cons.* 2000, *apptd* 2000; Arran House, Sandy Lane, Yarnton, Oxon OX5 1PB
Reading, Rt. Revd Andrew Proud, *cons.* 2011, *apptd* 2011; Bishop's House, Tidmarsh Lane, Tidmarsh, Reading RG8 8HA

DEAN OF CHRIST CHURCH

Very Revd Martyn Percy, PHD, *apptd* 2014

Organist, Dr Stephen Darlington, FRCO, *apptd* 1985

ARCHDEACONS

Berkshire, Ven. Olivia Graham, *apptd* 2013
Buckingham, Ven. Guy Elsmore, *apptd* 2016
Dorchester, Ven. Judy French, *apptd* 2014
Oxford, Ven. Martin Gorick, *apptd* 2013

Chancellor, Revd Alex McGregor, *apptd* 2013
Registrar and Legal Secretary, Revd Canon John Rees

Diocesan Secretary, Rosemary Pearce, Church House Oxford, Langford Locks, Kidlington, Oxford OX5 1GF **T** 01865-208202

PETERBOROUGH (CANTERBURY)

38TH BISHOP

Rt. Revd Donald Allister, *cons.* 2010, *apptd* 2009; Bishop's Lodging, The Palace, Peterborough PE1 1YA
Signs Donald Petriburg:

BISHOP SUFFRAGAN

Brixworth, Rt. Revd John Holbrook, *cons.* 2011, *apptd* 2011; Orchard Acre, 11 North Street, Mears Ashby, Northants NN6 0DW

DEAN
vacant

Director of Music, Stephen Grahl, *apptd* 2014

ARCHDEACONS
Northampton, Ven. Richard Ormston, *apptd* 2014
Oakham, Ven. Gordon Steele, *apptd* 2012

Chancellor, David Pittaway, QC, *apptd* 2005
Registrar and Legal Secretary, Anna Spriggs
Diocesan Secretary, Andrew Roberts, Diocesan Office, The Palace, Peterborough PE1 1YB **T** 01733-887000

PORTSMOUTH (CANTERBURY)

9TH BISHOP
Rt. Revd Christopher Foster, *cons.* 2010, *apptd* 2010; Bishopsgrove, 26 Osborn Road, Fareham, Hants PO16 7DQ
Signs Christopher Portsmouth

DEAN
Very Revd David Brindley, *apptd* 2002

Organist, David Price, *apptd* 1996

ARCHDEACONS
Isle of Wight, Ven. Peter Sutton, *apptd* 2012
Portsdown, Ven. Joanne Grenfell, *apptd* 2013
The Meon, Ven. Gavin Collins, *apptd* 2011

Chancellor, His Hon. Judge Waller, CBE
Registrar and Legal Secretary, Hilary Tyler
Diocesan Secretary, Wendy Kennedy, Diocesan Offices, 1st Floor, Peninsular House, Wharf Road, Portsmouth PO2 8HB **T** 023-9289 9664

ROCHESTER (CANTERBURY)

107TH BISHOP
Rt. Revd James Langstaff, *cons.* 2004, *apptd* 2010; Bishopscourt, 24 St Margaret's Street, Rochester ME1 1TS
Signs, James Roffen:

BISHOP SUFFRAGAN
Tonbridge, vacant

DEAN
Very Revd Dr Philip Hesketh, *apptd* 2016

Director of Music, Scott Farrell, *apptd* 2008

ARCHDEACONS
Bromley & Bexley, Ven. Dr Paul Wright, *apptd* 2003
Rochester, Ven. Simon Burton-Jones, *apptd* 2010
Tonbridge, Ven. Julie Conalty *apptd* 2017

Chancellor, The Worshipful John Gallagher
Registrar and Legal Secretary, Owen Carew-Jones
Diocesan Secretary, Geoff Marsh, St Nicholas Church, Boley Hill, Rochester ME1 1SL **T** 01634-560000

ST ALBANS (CANTERBURY)

10TH BISHOP
Rt. Revd Dr Alan Smith, *cons.* 2001, *apptd* 2009, *trans.* 2009; Abbey Gate House, St Albans AL3 4HD
Signs Alan St Albans

BISHOPS SUFFRAGAN
Bedford, Rt. Revd Richard Atkinson, OBE, *cons.* 2012, *apptd* 2012; Bishop's Lodge, Bedford Road, Cardington, Bedford MK44 3SS

Hertford, Rt. Revd Dr Michael Beasley, *cons.* 2015, *apptd* 2015; Bishopswood, 3 Stobarts Close, Knebworth SG3 6ND

DEAN
Very Revd Dr Jeffrey John, *apptd* 2004

Organist, Andrew Lucas, *apptd* 1998

ARCHDEACONS
Bedford, Ven. Paul Hughes, *apptd* 2003
Hertford, Ven. Janet Mackenzie, *apptd* 2016
St Albans, Ven. Jonathan Smith, *apptd* 2008

Chancellor, Roger Kaye, QC, *apptd* 2002
Registrar and Legal Secretary, Matthew Chinery, *apptd* 2015
Diocesan Secretary, Susan Pope, Holywell Lodge, 41 Holywell Hill, St Albans AL1 1HE **T** 01727-854532

ST EDMUNDSBURY AND IPSWICH (CANTERBURY)

11TH BISHOP
Rt. Revd Martin Seeley, *cons.* 2015, *apptd* 2015; The Bishop's House, 4 Park Road, Ipswich IP1 3ST
Signs Martin St Edmundsbury and Ipswich

BISHOP SUFFRAGAN
Dunwich, Rt. Revd Michael Harrison, PHD, *cons.* 2016, *apptd* 2015; Robin Hall, Chapel Lane, Mendlesham, Stowmarket IP14 5SQ

DEAN
Very Revd Frances Ward, *apptd* 2010

Director of Music, James Thomas, *apptd* 1997

ARCHDEACONS
Sudbury, Ven. Dr David Jenkins, *apptd* 2010
Suffolk, Ven. Ian Morgan, *apptd* 2012

Chancellor, David Etherington, QC
Registrar and Legal Secretary, James Hall
Diocesan Secretary, Anna Hughes, Diocesan Office, St Nicholas Centre, 4 Cutler Street, Ipswich IP1 1UQ **T** 01473-298500

SALISBURY (CANTERBURY)

78TH BISHOP
Rt. Revd Nicholas Holtam, *cons.* 2011, *apptd* 2011; South Canonry, 71 The Close, Salisbury SP1 2ER
Signs Nicholas Sarum

BISHOPS SUFFRAGAN
Ramsbury, Rt. Revd Edward Condry, DPHIL, *cons.* 2012, *apptd* 2012; Bishop's Office, Southbroom House, London Road, Devizes SN10 1LT

Sherborne, Rt. Revd Karen Gorham, *cons.* 2016, *apptd* 2015; The Sherborne Office, St Nicholas' Church Centre, 30 Wareham Road, Corfe Mullen BH21 3LE

DEAN
vacant

Director of Music, David Halls, *apptd* 2005

ARCHDEACONS
Dorset, Ven. Antony Macrow-Wood, *apptd* 2015
Sarum, Ven. Alan Jeans, *apptd* 2003
Sherborne, Ven. Paul Taylor, *apptd* 2004
Wilts, Ven. Sue Groom, *apptd* 2016

Chancellor, Canon Ruth Arlow, *apptd* 2016
Registrar and Legal Secretary, Sue de Candole
Diocesan Secretary, Lucinda Herklots, Church House, Crane Street, Salisbury SP1 2QB **T** 01722-411922

SHEFFIELD (YORK)

8TH BISHOP
Rt. Revd Dr Peter Wilcox, *cons.* 2017, *apptd* 2017;
Bishopscroft, Snaithing Lane, Sheffield S10 3LG
Signs Peter Sheffield

BISHOP SUFFRAGAN
Doncaster, Rt. Revd Peter Burrows, *cons.* 2012, *apptd* 2011;
Doncaster House, Church Lane, Fishlake, Doncaster DN7 5JW

DEAN
Very Revd Peter Bradley, *apptd* 2003

Master of Music, Thomas Corns, *apptd* 2017

ARCHDEACONS
Doncaster, Ven. Steve Wilcockson, *apptd* 2012
Sheffield and Rotherham, Ven. Malcolm Chamberlain, *apptd* 2013

Chancellor, Her Hon. Judge Sarah Singleton, QC, *apptd* 2014
Registrar and Legal Secretary, Andrew Vidler
Diocesan Secretary, Heidi Adcock, Church House, 95–99
Effingham Street, Rotherham S65 1BL **T** 01709-309100

SODOR AND MAN (YORK)

82ND BISHOP
Rt. Revd Peter Eagles, *cons.* 2017, *apptd* 2017; Thie yn Aspick,
4 The Falls, Douglas, Isle of Man IM4 4PZ
Signs Peter Sodor as Mannin

ARCHDEACON OF MAN
Ven. Andrew Brown, *apptd* 2011

Vicar-General and Chancellor, Geoffrey Tattersall, QC
Registrar, Louise Connacher
Diocesan Secretary, Andrew Swithinbank, c/o Thie yn Aspick, 4
The Falls, Douglas, Isle of Man IM4 4PZ **T** 07624-314590

SOUTHWARK (CANTERBURY)

10TH BISHOP
Rt. Revd Christopher Chessun, *cons.* 2005, *apptd* 2011;
Trinity House, 4 Chapel Court, Borough High Street, London
SE1 1HW
Signs Christopher Southwark

AREA BISHOPS
Croydon, Rt. Revd Jonathan Clark, *cons.* 2012, *apptd* 2012; St
Matthew's House, 100 George Street, London CR0 1PE
Kingston upon Thames, Rt. Revd Dr Richard Cheetham, *cons.*
2002, *apptd* 2002; 620 Kingston Road, Raynes Park, London
SW20 8DN
Woolwich, Rt. Revd Dr Karowei Dorga, *cons.* 2017, *apptd*
2017; Trinity House, 4 Chapel Court, Borough High Street,
London SE1 1HW

DEAN
Very Revd Andrew Nunn, *apptd* 2011

Organist, Peter Wright, FRCO, *apptd* 1989

ARCHDEACONS
Croydon, Ven. Christopher Skilton, *apptd* 2013
Lambeth, Ven. Simon Gates, *apptd* 2013
Lewisham & Greenwich, Ven. Alastair Cutting, *apptd* 2013
Reigate, Ven. Moira Astin, *apptd* 2016
Southwark, Ven. Dr Jane Steen, *apptd* 2013
Wandsworth, Ven. John Kiddle, *apptd* 2015

Chancellor, Philip Petchey
Registrar and Legal Secretary, Paul Morris
Diocesan Secretary, Ruth Martin, Trinity House, 4 Chapel Court,
Borough High Street, London SE1 1HW **T** 020-7939 9400

SOUTHWELL AND NOTTINGHAM (YORK)

12TH BISHOP
Rt. Revd Paul Williams, *cons.* 2009, *trans.* 2015; Bishop's
Manor, Southwell, Nottinghamshire NG25 0JR
Signs Paul Southwell and Nottingham

BISHOP SUFFRAGAN
Sherwood, Rt. Revd Anthony Porter, *cons.* 2006, *apptd* 2006;
Jubilee House, Westgate, Southwell NG25 0JH

DEAN
Very Revd Nicola Sullivan, *apptd* 2016

Rector Chori, Paul Provost, *apptd* 2017

ARCHDEACONS
Newark, Ven. David Picken, *apptd* 2012
Nottingham, Ven. Sarah Clark, *apptd* 2014

Chancellor, His Hon. Judge Ockelton
Registrar and Legal Secretary, Amanda Redgate
Chief Executive, Nigel Spraggins, Jubilee House, Westgate,
Southwell, Notts NG25 0JH **T** 01636-814331

TRURO (CANTERBURY)

16TH BISHOP
vacant

BISHOP SUFFRAGAN
St Germans, Rt. Revd Christopher Goldsmith, DPHIL, *cons.*
2013, *apptd* 2013; Vounder, Tresillian, Truro TR2 4BW

DEAN
Very Revd Roger Bush, *apptd* 2012

Organist and Director of Music, Chris Gray, *apptd* 2008

ARCHDEACONS
Bodmin, Ven. Audrey Elkington, *apptd* 2011
Cornwall, Ven. Bill Stuart-White, *apptd* 2012

Chancellor, Timothy Briden, *apptd* 1998
Registrar and Legal Secretary, Jos Moule
Diocesan Secretary, Esther Pollard, Church House, Woodlands
Court, Truro Business Park, Threemilestone, Truro TR4 9NH
T 01872-274351

WORCESTER (CANTERBURY)

113TH BISHOP
Rt. Revd Dr John Inge, *cons.* 2003, *apptd* 2007; The Bishop's
Office, The Old Palace, Deansway, Worcester WR1 2JE
Signs John Wigorn

SUFFRAGAN BISHOP
Dudley, Rt. Revd Graham Usher, *cons.* 2014, *apptd* 2014;
Bishop's House, 60 Bishop's Walk, Cradley Heath, West Midlands
B64 7RH

DEAN
Very Revd Peter Atkinson, *apptd* 2006

Organist, Dr Peter Nardone, *apptd* 2012

ARCHDEACONS
Dudley, Ven. Nikki Groarke, *apptd* 2014
Worcester, Ven. Robert Jones, *apptd* 2014

Chancellor, Charles Mynors, *apptd* 1999
Registrar and Legal Secretary, Stuart Ness
Diocesan Secretary, Robert Higham, The Old Palace, Deansway,
Worcester WR1 2JE **T** 01905-20537

ROYAL PECULIARS

WESTMINSTER
The Collegiate Church of St Peter

Dean, Very Revd Dr John Hall
Canon Steward, Revd Anthony Ball

Chapter Clerk, Receiver-General and Registrar, Sir Stephen Lamport, KCVO; Chapter Office, 20 Dean's Yard, London SW1P 3PA
Organist, James O'Donnell, *apptd* 2000
Legal Secretary, Christopher Vyse, *apptd* 2000

WINDSOR
The Queen's Free Chapel of St George within Her Castle of Windsor

Dean, Rt. Revd David Conner, KCVO, *apptd* 1998

Chapter Clerk, Charlotte Manley, LVO, OBE, *apptd* 2003; Chapter Office, The Cloisters, Windsor Castle, Windsor, Berks SL4 1NJ
Director of Music, James Vivian, *apptd* 2013

OTHER ANGLICAN CHURCHES

THE CHURCH IN WALES
The Anglican Church was the established church in Wales from the 16th century until 1920, when the estrangement of the majority of Welsh people from Anglicanism resulted in disestablishment. Since then the Church in Wales has been an autonomous province consisting of six sees. The bishops are elected by an electoral college comprising elected lay and clerical members, who also elect one of the diocesan bishops as Archbishop of Wales.

The legislative body of the Church in Wales is the Governing Body, which has 144 members divided between the three orders of bishops, clergy and laity. Its president is the Archbishop of Wales and it meets twice annually. Its decisions are binding upon all members of the church. The church's property and finances are the responsibility of the Representative Body. There are 46,580 members of the Church in Wales, with 417 stipendiary clergy and 690 parishes.

THE REPRESENTATIVE BODY OF THE CHURCH IN WALES, 39 Cathedral Road, Cardiff CF11 9XF
T 029-2034 8200
Secretary, Simon Lloyd
13TH ARCHBISHOP OF WALES, vacant

BISHOPS
Bangor (81st), Rt. Revd Andrew John, *b.* 1964, *cons.* 2008, *elected* 2008; Ty'r Esgob, Bangor, Gwynedd LL57 2SS
Signs Andrew Bangor. *Stipendiary clergy,* 47
Llandaff (103rd), Rt. Revd June Osborne, *b.* 1953, *cons.* 2017, *elected* 2017; Llys Esgob, The Cathedral Green, Llandaff, Cardiff CF5 2YE
Signs June Landav. *Stipendiary clergy,* 106
Monmouth (10th), Rt. Revd Richard Pain, *b.* 1956, *cons.* 2013, *elected* 2013; Bishopstow, Stow Hill, Newport NP20 4EA
Signs Richard Monmouth. *Stipendiary clergy,* 43
St Asaph (76th), Rt. Revd Gregory Cameron, *b.* 1959, *cons.* 2009, *elected* 2009; Esgobty, Upper Denbigh Road, St Asaph, Denbighshire LL17 0TW
Signs Gregory Llanelwy. *Stipendiary clergy,* 76
St David's (129th), Rt. Revd Joanna Penberthy, *b.* 1960, *cons.* 2017, *elected* 2016; Llys Esgob, Abergwili, Carmarthen SA31 2JG
Signs Joanna St Davids. *Stipendiary clergy,* 91
Swansea and Brecon (9th), Rt. Revd John Davies, *b.* 1953, *cons.* 2008, *elected* 2008; Ely Tower, Castle Square, Brecon, Powys LD3 9DJ
Signs John Swansea & Brecon. *Stipendiary clergy,* 54

The stipend for a diocesan bishop of the Church in Wales is £43,699 a year for 2017–18.

SCOTTISH EPISCOPAL CHURCH
The Scottish Episcopal Church was founded after the Act of Settlement (1690) established the presbyterian nature of the Church of Scotland. The Scottish Episcopal Church is a member of the worldwide Anglican Communion. The governing authority is the General Synod, which consists of the Church's seven bishops, the conveners of the provincial Standing Committee, the conveners of the boards, the Church's representatives on the Anglican Consultative Council and 124 elected members (62 from the clergy and 62 from the laity). The General Synod meets once a year. The bishop who convenes and presides at meetings of the General Synod is called the 'primus' and is elected by his fellow bishops.

There are around 30,000 members of the Scottish Episcopal Church, seven bishops, around 500 serving clergy and 300 churches and places of worship.

THE GENERAL SYNOD OF THE SCOTTISH EPISCOPAL CHURCH, 21 Grosvenor Crescent, Edinburgh EH12 5EE T 0131-225 6357
W www.scotland.anglican.org
Secretary-General, John Stuart

PRIMUS OF THE SCOTTISH EPISCOPAL CHURCH, Most Revd Mark Strange (Bishop of Moray, Ross and Caithness), *elected* 2017

BISHOPS
Aberdeen and Orkney, vacant. *Clergy,* 50
Argyll and the Isles, Rt. Revd Kevin Pearson, *b.* 1954, *cons.* 2011, *elected* 2010. *Clergy,* 25
Brechin, vacant. *Clergy,* 30
Edinburgh, Rt. Revd Dr John Armes, *b.* 1955, *cons.* 2012, *elected* 2012. *Clergy,* 160
Glasgow and Galloway, Rt. Revd Dr Gregor Duncan, *b.* 1950, *cons.* 2010, *elected* 2010. *Clergy,* 110
Moray, Ross and Caithness, Most Revd Mark Strange, *b.* 1961, *cons.* 2007, *elected* 2007. *Clergy,* 60
St Andrews, Dunkeld and Dunblane, vacant. *Clergy,* 75
The minimum stipend of a diocesan bishop of the Scottish Episcopal Church for 2017 is £38,160 (ie 1.5 times the standard clergy stipend of £25,440).

CHURCH OF IRELAND
The Anglican Church was the established church in Ireland from the 16th century but never secured the allegiance of the majority and was disestablished in 1871. The Church of Ireland is divided into the provinces of Armagh and Dublin, each under an archbishop. The provinces are subdivided into 12 dioceses.

The legislative body is the General Synod, which has 660 members in total, divided between the House of Bishops (12 members) and the House of Representatives (216 clergy and 432 laity). The Archbishop of Armagh is elected by the House of Bishops; other episcopal elections are made by an electoral college.

There are around 375,400 members of the Church of Ireland, 249,000 in Northern Ireland and 126,400 in the Republic of Ireland. There are two archbishops, ten bishops and 463 stipendiary clergy.

CENTRAL OFFICE, Church of Ireland House, Church Avenue, Rathmines, Dublin D06 CF67 T (+353) (1) 497 8422
Chief Officer and Secretary-General of the Representative Church Body, David Ritchie

PROVINCE OF ARMAGH
Archbishop of Armagh, Primate of all Ireland and Metropolitan, Most Revd Richard Clarke, PHD, *b.* 1949, *cons.* 1996, *trans.* 2012. *Clergy,* 41

BISHOPS
Clogher, Rt. Revd John McDowell, *b.* 1956, *cons.* 2011, *apptd* 2011. *Clergy,* 28

Connor, Rt. Revd Alan Abernethy, *b.* 1957, *cons.* 2007, *apptd* 2007. *Clergy,* 76

Derry and Raphoe, Rt. Revd Kenneth Good, *b.* 1952, *cons.* 2002, *apptd* 2002. *Clergy,* 44

Down and Dromore, Rt. Revd Harold Miller, *b.* 1950, *cons.* 1997, *apptd* 1997. *Clergy,* 81

Kilmore, Elphin and Ardagh, Rt. Revd Ferran Glenfield, *b.* 1954, *cons.* 2013, *apptd* 2013. *Clergy,* 17

Tuam, Killala and Achonry, Rt. Revd Patrick Rooke, *b.* 1955, *cons.* 2011, *apptd* 2011. *Clergy,* 12

PROVINCE OF DUBLIN

Archbishop of Dublin, Bishop of Glendalough, Primate of Ireland and Metropolitan, Most Revd Michael Jackson, PHD, DPHIL, *b.* 1956, *cons.* 2002, *trans.* 2011. *Clergy,* 68

BISHOPS

Cashel, Ferns and Ossory, Rt. Revd Michael Burrows, *b.* 1961, *cons.* 2006, *apptd* 2006. *Clergy,* 37

Cork, Cloyne and Ross, Rt. Revd Paul Colton, PHD, *b.* 1960, *cons.* 1999, *apptd* 1999. *Clergy,* 27

Limerick, Killaloe and Ardfert, Rt. Revd Kenneth Kearon, *b.* 1953, *cons.* 2015, *apptd* 2014. *Clergy,* 15

Meath and Kildare, Most Revd Patricia Storey, *b.* 1960, *cons.* 2013, *apptd* 2013. *Clergy,* 17

OVERSEAS

PRIMATES

Primate and Archbishop of Aotearoa, New Zealand and Polynesia, Most Revd Winston Halapua

Primate of Australia, Most Revd Phillip Freir

Primate of Brazil, Most Revd Francisco De Assis Da Silva

Archbishop of the Province of Burundi, Most Revd Martin Nyaboho

Primate of Canada, Most Revd Frederick Hiltz

Archbishop of the Province of Central Africa, Most Revd Albert Chama

Primate of the Central Region of America, Most Revd Sturdie Downs

Archbishop of the Province of Congo, Most Revd Zacharie Masimango Katanda

Archbishop of Hong Kong Sheng Kung Hui, Most Revd Paul Kwong

Archbishop of the Province of the Indian Ocean, Most Revd Ian Ernest

Primate of Japan (Nippon Sei Ko Kai), Most Revd Nathaniel Makoto Uematsu

Archbishop of Jerusalem and the Middle East, Most Revd Suheil Dawani

Primate and Archbishop of All Kenya, Most Revd Jackson Ole Sapit

Primate of Korea, Most Revd Onesimus Dongsin Park

Archbishop of Melanesia, Most Revd George Takeli

Presiding Bishop of Mexico, Most Revd Francisco Moreno

Archbishop of the Province of Myanmar (Burma), Most Revd Stephen Oo

Metropolitan and Primate of All Nigeria, Most Revd Nicholas Okoh

Archbishop of Papua New Guinea, Rt. Revd Allan Migi

Prime Bishop of the Philippines, Most Revd Renato Mag-Gay Abibico

Archbishop of the Province of Rwanda, Most Revd Onesphore Rwaje

Archbishop of the Province of South East Asia, Most Revd Ng Moon Hing

Primate of Southern Africa, Most Revd Dr Thabo Makgoba

Presiding Bishop of South America, Most Revd Gregory Venables

Archbishop of the Province of South Sudan, Most Revd Daniel Deng Bul Yak

Archbishop of the Province of Sudan, Most Revd Ezekiel Kumir Kondo

Archbishop of Tanzania, Most Revd Jacob Chimeledya

Archbishop of the Province of Uganda, Most Revd Stanley Ntagali

Presiding Bishop of the USA, Most Revd Michael Curry

Primate and Metropolitan of the Province of West Africa, Most Revd Dr Daniel Sarfo

Archbishop of the Province of the West Indies, Most Revd Dr John Holder

OTHER CHURCHES AND EXTRA-PROVINCIAL DIOCESES

Anglican Church of Bermuda, extra-provincial to Canterbury Bishop, Rt. Revd Nicholas Dill

Church of Ceylon, extra-provincial to Canterbury Bishop of Colombo, Rt. Revd Dhiloraj Canagasabey Bishop of Kurunagala, vacant

Episcopal Church of Cuba, Rt. Revd Griselda Del Carpio

Falkland Islands, extra-provincial to Canterbury Bishop, Rt. Revd Nigel Stock (Bishop to the Forces)

Lusitanian Church (Portuguese Episcopal Church), extra-provincial to Canterbury Bishop, Rt. Revd Jose Cabral

Reformed Episcopal Church of Spain, extra-provincial to Canterbury Bishop, Rt. Revd Carlos López-Lozano

MODERATION OF CHURCHES IN FULL COMMUNION WITH THE ANGLICAN COMMUNION

Church of Bangladesh, Most Revd Paul Sarker

Church of North India, Most Revd Pradeep Samantaroy

Church of South India, Most Revd Thomas Oommen

Church of Pakistan, Most Revd Humphrey Peters

CHURCH OF SCOTLAND

The Church of Scotland is the national church of Scotland. The church is reformed in doctrine, and presbyterian in constitution; ie based on a hierarchy of courts of ministers and elders and, since 1990, of members of a diaconate. At local level the Kirk Session consists of the parish minister and ruling elders. At district level the presbyteries, of which there are 44 in Britain, consist of all the ministers in the district, one ruling elder from each congregation, and those members of the diaconate who qualify for membership. The General Assembly is the supreme authority, and is presided over by a Moderator chosen annually by the Assembly. The sovereign, if not present in person, is represented by a Lord High Commissioner who is appointed each year by the Crown.

As at December 2015 the Church of Scotland had 363,597 members, 786 parish ministers and 30,301 elders. The majority of parishes are in Scotland, but there are also churches in England, Europe and overseas.

Lord High Commissioner (2017–18), HRH the Princess Royal, KG, KT, GCVO

Moderator of the General Assembly (2017–18), Rt. Revd Dr Derek Browning

Principal Clerk, Revd Dr George Whyte

Procurator, Laura Dunlop, QC

Law Agent and Solicitor of the Church, Mary Macleod

Parliamentary Officer, Chloe Clemmons

General Treasurer, Anne Macintosh

Secretary to the Council of Assembly, Revd Dr Martin Scott

CHURCH OFFICE, 121 George Street, Edinburgh EH2 4YN

T 0131-225 5722

PRESBYTERIES AND CLERKS

Aberdeen, Revd Dr John Ferguson

Abernethy, Revd James MacEwan

Angus, Revd Mike Goss

Annandale and Eskdale, Revd Bryan Haston

Ardrossan, Jean Hunter

Argyll, Dr Christopher Brett

Ayr, Revd Kenneth Elliott

Buchan, Revd Sheila Kirk
Caithness, Revd Ronald Johnstone
Dumbarton, Revd David Clark
Dumfries and Kirkcudbright, Revd William Hogg
Dundee, Revd Janet Foggie
Dunfermline, Revd Iain Greenshields
Dunkeld and Meigle, Revd John Russell
Duns, Revd Dr H. Dane Sherrard
Edinburgh, Revd Dr George Whyte
England, Revd Alistair Cimming
Europe, Revd Jim Sharp
Falkirk, Revd Andrew Sarle
Glasgow, Very Revd William Hewitt
Gordon, Revd Euan Glen
Greenock and Paisley, Revd Dr Peter McEnhill
Hamilton, Revd Dr Gordon McCracken
Inverness, Revd Trevor Hunt
Irvine and Kilmarnock, Steuart Dey
Jedburgh, Revd W. Frank Campbell
Kincardine and Deeside, Revd Hugh Conkey
Kirkcaldy, Revd Alan Kimmitt
Lanark, Revd Bryan Kerr
Lewis, John Cunningham
Lochaber, Revd Donald McCorkindale
Lochcarron-Skye, Revd John Murray
Lothian, John McCulloch
Melrose and Peebles, Revd Victoria Linford
Moray, Revd Alastair Gray
Orkney, Very Revd Dr David Lunan
Perth, Revd Colin Caskie
Ross, Ronald Gunstone
St Andrews, Revd Nigel Robb
Shetland, Revd Deborah Dobby
Stirling, Revd Alan Miller
Sutherland, Revd Stewart Goudie
Uist, vacant
West Lothian, Revd Duncan Shaw
Wigtown and Stranraer, Sam Scobie
The stipends for ministers in the Church of Scotland in 2017 range from £26,644–£32,743, depending on length of service.

ROMAN CATHOLIC CHURCH

The Roman Catholic Church is a worldwide Christian church acknowledging as its head the Bishop of Rome, known as the Pope (father). Despite its widespread usage, 'Pope' is actually an unofficial term. The *Annuario Pontificio,* (Pontifical Yearbook) lists eight official titles: Bishop of Rome, Vicar of Jesus Christ, Successor of the Prince of the Apostles, Supreme Pontiff of the Universal Church, Primate of Italy, Archbishop and Metropolitan of the Roman Province, Sovereign of the State of the Vatican City and Servant of the Servants of God.

The Pope leads a communion of followers of Christ, who believe they continue His presence in the world as servants of faith, hope and love to all society. The Pope is held to be the successor of St Peter and thus invested with the power which was entrusted to St Peter by Jesus Christ. A direct line of succession is therefore claimed from the earliest Christian communities. With the fall of the Roman Empire the Pope also became an important political leader. His territory is now limited to the 0.44 sq. km (0.17 sq. miles) of the Vatican City State, created to provide some independence to the Pope from Italy and other nations. The episcopal jurisdiction of the Roman Catholic Church is called the Holy See.

The Pope exercises spiritual authority over the church with the advice and assistance of the Sacred College of Cardinals, the supreme council of the church. The number of cardinals was fixed at 70 by Pope Sixtus V in 1586 but has increased steadily since the pontificate of John XXIII. On 28 February 2013, the date of Pope Benedict XVI's resignation, there were 207 cardinals.

Following the death or resignation of the Pope, the members of the College of Cardinals under the age of 80 are called to the Vatican to elect a successor. They are known as cardinal electors and form an assembly called the conclave. The conclave, which comprised 115 cardinal electors when it convened in March 2013, conducts a secret ballot in complete seclusion to elect the next Pope. A two-thirds majority is necessary before the vote can be accepted as final. When a cardinal receives the necessary number of votes, the Dean of the Sacred College formally asks him if he will accept election and the name by which he wishes to be known. On his acceptance of the office of Supreme Pontiff, the conclave is dissolved and the first Cardinal Deacon announces the election to the assembled crowd in St Peter's Square.

The Pope has full legislative, judicial and administrative power over the whole Roman Catholic Church. He is aided in his administration by the curia, which is made up of a number of departments. The Secretariat of State is the central office for carrying out the Pope's instructions and is presided over by the Cardinal Secretary of State. It maintains relations with the departments of the curia, with the episcopate, with the representatives of the Holy See in various countries, governments and private persons. The congregations and pontifical councils are the Pope's ministries and include departments such as the Congregation for the Doctrine of Faith, whose field of competence concerns faith and morals; the Congregation for the Clergy and the Congregation for the Evangelisation of Peoples, the Pontifical Council for the Family and the Pontifical Council for the Promotion of Christian Unity.

The Holy See, composed of the Pope and those who help him in his mission for the church, is recognised by the Conventions of Vienna as an international moral body. Apostolic nuncios are the Pope's diplomatic representatives; in countries where no formal diplomatic relations exist between the Holy See and that country, the papal representative is known as an apostolic delegate.

According to the 2017 Pontifical Yearbook the number of baptised Roman Catholics worldwide was 1,285 million in 2015; the number of bishops was around 5,250 and there were 415,656 priests.

SUPREME PONTIFF

His Holiness Pope Francis (Jorge Mario Bergoglio), *born* Buenos Aires, Argentina, 17 December 1936; *ordained priest* 13 December 1969; *appointed Archbishop* (of Buenos Aires), 28 February 1998; *created Cardinal* 21 February 2001; *assumed pontificate* 13 March 2013

PONTIFF EMERITUS

His Holiness Pope Benedict XVI (Joseph Ratzinger), *born* Bavaria, Germany, 16 April 1927; *ordained priest* 29 June 1951; *appointed Archbishop* (of Munich), 24 March 1977; *created Cardinal* 27 June 1977; *assumed pontificate* 19 April 2005; *resigned pontificate* 28 February 2013

SECRETARIAT OF STATE

Secretary of State, His Eminence Cardinal Pietro Parolin
First Section (General Affairs), Most Revd Giovanni Angelo Becciu (Titular Archbishop of Roselle)
Second Section (Relations with Other States), Most Revd Paul Gallagher (Titular Archbishop of Hodelm)

BISHOPS' CONFERENCE

The Catholic Bishops' Conference of England and Wales is the permanent assembly of Catholic Bishops and Ordinaries in the two member countries. The membership of the Conference comprises the Archbishops, Bishops and Auxiliary Bishops of the 22 Dioceses within England and Wales, the Bishop of the Forces (Military Ordinariate), the Apostolic Eparch of the Ukrainian Church in Great Britain, the Ordinary of the Personal Ordinariate of Our Lady of Walsingham, and the Apostolic Prefect of the Falkland Islands. The Conference is headed by a president and vice-president. There are six departments, each with an episcopal chair: Education and Formation, Christian Life and Worship, Christian

Responsibility and Citizenship, Dialogue and Unity, Evangelisation and Catechesis, and International Affairs.

The Bishops' Conference Standing Committee is made up of two directly elected bishops in addition to the Metropolitan Archbishops and chairs from each of the above departments. The committee has general responsibility for continuity of policy between the plenary sessions of the conference, preparing the conference agenda and implementing its decisions.

The administration of the Bishops' Conference is funded by a levy on each diocese, according to income. A general secretariat in London coordinates and supervises the Bishops' Conference administration activities. There are also other agencies and consultative bodies affiliated to the conference.

The Bishops' Conference of Scotland is the permanently constituted assembly of the eight bishops of Scotland. The conference is headed by the president (Most Revd Philip Tartaglia, Archbishop of Glasgow). The conference establishes various agencies which perform advisory functions in relation to the conference. The more important of these agencies are called commissions; each one is headed by a bishop president who, with the other members of the commissions, are appointed by the conference.

The Irish Catholic Bishops' Conference (also known as the Irish Episcopal Conference) has as its president the Most Revd Eamon Martin (Archbishop of Armagh). Its membership comprises all the archbishops and bishops of Ireland. It appoints various commissions and agencies to assist with the work of the Catholic Church in Ireland.

The Catholic Church in the UK has over 900,000 mass attendees, 5,500 priests and 4,550 churches.

Bishops' Conferences secretariats:

ENGLAND AND WALES, 39 Eccleston Square, London SW1V 1BX T 020-7630 8220 W www.cbcew.org.uk

General Secretary, Revd Christopher Thomas

SCOTLAND, 64 Aitken Street, Airdrie ML6 6LT T 01236-764061
  W www.bcos.org.uk

  General Secretary, Mgr Hugh Bradley

IRELAND, Columba Centre, Maynooth, County Kildare T (+353) (1) 505 3000 E columbacentre@iecon.ie
  W www.catholicbishops.ie

Episcopal Secretary, Most Revd Kieran O'Reilly (Archbishop of Cashel and Emly)

  Executive Secretary, Mgr Gearóid Dullea

GREAT BRITAIN

APOSTOLIC NUNCIO TO GREAT BRITAIN

Most Revd Edward Joseph Adams (Titular Archbishop of Scala), *apptd* 2017. *Apostolic Nunciature,* 54 Parkside, London SW19 5NE T 020-8944 7189

ENGLAND AND WALES

THE MOST REVD ARCHBISHOPS

Westminster, Cardinal Vincent Nichols, *cons.* 1992, *apptd* 2009 *Auxiliaries,* John Sherrington, *cons.* 2011; Nicholas Hudson, *cons.* 2014; Paul McAleenan, *cons.* 2016; John Wilson, *cons.* 2016. *Clergy,* 318. *Archbishop's House,* Ambrosden Avenue, London SW1P 1QJ T 020-7798 9033

Birmingham, Bernard Longley, *cons.* 2003, *apptd* 2009 *Auxiliaries,* William Kenney, *cons.* 1987; David McGough, *cons.* 2005; Robert Byrne, *cons.* 2014. *Clergy,* 430. *Archbishop's House,* 8 Shadwell Street, Birmingham B4 6EY T 0121-236 9090

Cardiff, George Stack, *cons.* 2001, *apptd* 2011. *Clergy,* 47. *Archbishop's House,* 41–43 Cathedral Road, Cardiff CF11 9HD T 029-2022 0411

Liverpool, Malcolm McMahon, *cons.* 2000, *apptd* 2014 *Auxiliary,* Thomas Williams, *cons.* 2003. *Clergy,* 402. *Archbishop's House,* 19 Salisbury Road, Cressington Park, Liverpool L19 0PH T 0151-494 0686

Southwark, Peter Smith, *cons.* 1995, *apptd* 2010 *Auxiliaries,* Patrick Lynch, *cons.* 2006; Paul Hendricks, *cons.* 2006; Paul Mason, *cons.* 2016. *Clergy,* 366. *Archbishop's House,* 150 St George's Road, London SE1 6HX T 020-7928 2495

THE RT. REVD BISHOPS

Arundel and Brighton, Richard Moth, *cons.* 2009, *apptd* 2015. *Clergy,* 95. *Bishop's House,* High Oaks, Old Brighton Road North, Pease Pottage RH11 9AJ T 01293-526428

Brentwood, Alan Williams, *cons.* 2014, *apptd* 2014. *Clergy,* 170. *Bishop's Office,* Cathedral House, Ingrave Road, Brentwood, Essex CM15 8AT T 01277-232266

Clifton, Declan Lang, *cons.* 2001, *apptd* 2001. *Clergy,* 153. *Bishop's House,* St Ambrose, North Road, Leigh Woods, Bristol BS8 3PW T 0117-973 3072

East Anglia, Alan Hopes, *cons.* 2003, *apptd* 2013. *Clergy,* 129. *Diocesan Curia,* The White House, 21 Upgate, Poringland, Norwich NR14 7SH T 01508-492202

Hallam, Ralph Heskett, *cons.* 2010, *apptd* 2014. *Clergy,* 71. *Bishop's House,* 75 Norfolk Road, Sheffield S2 2SZ T 0114-278 7988

Hexham and Newcastle, Seamus Cunningham, *cons.* 2009, *apptd* 2009. *Clergy,* 164. *Bishop's House,* 800 West Road, Newcastle upon Tyne NE5 2BJ T 0191-228 0003

Lancaster, Michael Campbell, *cons.* 2008, *apptd* 2009. *Clergy,* 97. *Bishop's Office,* The Pastoral Centre, Balmoral Road, Lancaster LA1 3BT T 01524-596050

Leeds, Marcus Stock, *cons.* 2014, *apptd* 2014. *Clergy,* 193. *Diocesan Curia,* Hinsley Hall, 62 Headingley Lane, Leeds LS6 2BX T 0113-230 4533

Menevia (Wales), Tom Burns, *cons.* 2002, *apptd* 2008. *Clergy,* 60. *Diocesan Curia,* 27 Convent Street, Swansea SA1 2BX T 01792-644017

Middlesbrough, Terence Drainey, *cons.* 2008, *apptd* 2007. *Clergy,* 50. *Diocesan Curia,* 16 Cambridge Road, Middlesbrough TS5 5NN T 01642-850505

Northampton, Peter Doyle, *cons.* 2005, *apptd* 2005. *Clergy,* 116. *Bishop's House,* Marriott Street, Northampton NN2 6AW T 01604-715635

Nottingham, Patrick McKinney, *cons.* 2015, *apptd* 2015. *Clergy,* 166. *Bishop's House,* 27 Cavendish Road East, The Park, Nottingham NG7 1BB T 0115-947 4786

Plymouth, Mark O'Toole, *cons.* 2014, *apptd* 2013. *Clergy,* 50. *Bishop's House,* 45 Cecil Street, Plymouth PL1 5HW T 01752-224414

Portsmouth, Philip Egan, *cons.* 2012, *apptd* 2012. *Clergy,* 214. *Bishop's House,* Bishop Crispian Way, Portsmouth, Hants PO1 3HG T 023-9282 0894

Salford, John Arnold, *cons.* 2006, *apptd* 2014. *Clergy,* 218. *Diocesan Curia,* Wardley Hall, Worsley, Manchester M28 2ND T 0161-794 2825

Shrewsbury, Mark Davies, *cons.* 2010, *apptd* 2010. *Clergy* 112. *Diocesan Curia,* 2 Park Road South, Prenton, Wirral CH43 4UX T 0151-652 9855

Wrexham (Wales), Peter Brignall, *cons.* 2012, *apptd* 2012. *Clergy,* 16. *Bishop's House,* Sontley Road, Wrexham LL13 7EW T 01978-262726

SCOTLAND

THE MOST REVD ARCHBISHOPS

St Andrews and Edinburgh, Leo Cushley, *cons.* 2013, *apptd* 2013. *Archbishop Emeritus,* HE Cardinal Keith O'Brien, *cons.* 1985, *elevated* 2003. *Clergy,* 50. *Archdiocesan Offices,* 100 Strathearn Road, Edinburgh EH9 1BB T 0131-623 8900

Glasgow, Philip Tartaglia, *cons.* 2005, *apptd* 2012. *Clergy,* 198. *Diocesan Curia,* 196 Clyde Street, Glasgow G1 4JY T 0141-226 5898

THE RT. REVD BISHOPS

Aberdeen, Hugh Gilbert, *cons.* 2011, *apptd* 2011. *Clergy,* 47. *Bishop's House,* 3 Queen's Cross, Aberdeen AB15 4XU T 01224-319154

Argyll and the Isles, Brian McGee, *cons.* 2016, *apptd* 2015. *Clergy,* 32. *Diocesan Office* Bishop's House, Esplanade, Oban, Argyll PA34 5AB T 01631-567436

Dunkeld, Stephen Robson, *cons.* 2012, *apptd* 2013. *Clergy,* 43. *Diocesan Curia,* 24–28 Lawside Road, Dundee DD3 6XY T 01382-225453

Galloway, William Nolan, *cons.* 2015, *apptd* 2014. *Clergy,* 19. *Diocesan Office,* 8 Corsehill Road, Ayr KA7 2ST T 01292-266750

Motherwell, Joseph Toal, *cons.* 2008, *trans.* 2014. *Clergy,* 123. *Diocesan Curia,* Coursington Road, Motherwell ML1 1PP T 01698-269114

Paisley, John Keenan, *cons.* 2014, *apptd* 2014. *Clergy,* 75. *Diocesan Curia,* Cathedral Precincts, Incle Street, Paisley PA1 1HR T 0141-847 6131

BISHOPRIC OF THE FORCES

vacant. *Administration,* RC Bishopric of the Forces, Wellington House, St Omer Barracks, Thornhill Road, Aldershot, Hants GU11 2BG T 01252-348234

IRELAND
There is one hierarchy for the whole of Ireland. Several of the dioceses have territory partly in the Republic of Ireland and partly in Northern Ireland.

APOSTOLIC NUNCIO TO IRELAND
Most Revd Jude Thaddeus Okolo (Titular Archbishop of Novica), *apptd* 2017. *Apostolic Nunciature,* 183 Navan Road, Dublin 7 T (+353) (1) 838 0577

THE MOST REVD ARCHBISHOPS

Armagh, Eamon Martin (*also* Primate of all Ireland), *cons.* 2013, *apptd* 2014. *Archbishop Emeritus,* HE Cardinal Seán Brady *cons.* 1995, *elevated* 2007. *Clergy,* 135. *Bishop's Residence,* Ara Coeli, Cathedral Road, Armagh BT61 7QY T 028-3752 2045

Cashel and Emly, Kieran O'Reilly, *cons.* 2010, *apptd* 2015. *Clergy,* 83. *Archbishop's House,* Thurles, Co. Tipperary T (+353) (504) 21512

Dublin, Diarmuid Martin (*also* Primate of Ireland), *cons.* 1999, *apptd Coadjutor Archbishop* 2003, *succeeded as Archbishop* 2004. *Auxiliaries,* Éamonn Walsh, *cons.* 1990; Raymond Field, *cons.* 1997. *Clergy,* 389. *Archbishop's House,* Drumcondra, Dublin 9 T (+353) (1) 837 3732

Tuam, Dr Michael Neary, *cons.* 1992, *apptd* 1995. *Clergy,* 110. *Archbishop's House,* Tuam, Co. Galway T (+353) (93) 24166

THE MOST REVD BISHOPS

Achonry, Brendan Kelly, *cons.* 2008, *apptd* 2007. *Clergy,* 50. *Bishop's House,* Edmondstown, Ballaghaderreen, Co. Roscommon T (+353) (94) 986 0021

Ardagh and Clonmacnois, Francis Duffy, *cons.* 2013, *apptd* 2013. *Clergy,* 60. *Diocesan Office,* St Mel's, Longford T (+353) (43) 334 6432

Clogher, vacant. *Clergy,* 74. *Bishop's House,* Monaghan T (+353) (47) 81019

Clonfert, John Kirby, *cons.* 1988, *apptd* 1988. *Clergy,* 37. *Bishop's House,* Coorheen, Loughrea, Co. Galway T (+353) (91) 841560

Cloyne, William Crean, *cons.* 2013, *apptd* 2013. *Clergy,* 126. *Diocesan Office,* Cobh, Co. Cork T (+353) (21) 481 1430

Cork and Ross, John Buckley, *cons.* 1984, *apptd* 1998. *Clergy,* 133. *Diocesan Office,* Cork and Ross Offices, Redemption Road, Cork T (+353) (21) 430 1717

Derry, Dónal McKeown, *cons.* 2001, *apptd* 2014. *Clergy,* 108. *Bishop's House,* PO Box 227, Derry BT48 9YG T 028-7126 2302

Down and Connor, Noël Treanor, *cons.* 2008, *apptd* 2008. *Clergy,* 199. *Bishop's Residence,* Lisbreen, 73 Somerton Road, Belfast, Co. Antrim BT15 4DE T 028-9077 6185

Dromore, John McAreavey, *cons.* 1999, *apptd* 1999. *Clergy,* 33. *Bishop's House,* 44 Armagh Road, Newry, Co. Down BT35 6PN T 028-3026 2444

Elphin, Kevin Doran, *cons.* 2014, *apptd* 2014. *Clergy,* 66. *Bishop's House,* Temple St, St Mary's, Sligo T (+353) (71) 915 0106

Ferns, Denis Brennan, *cons.* 2006, *apptd* 2006. *Clergy,* 88. *Bishop's House,* Summerhill, Wexford T (+353) (53) 912 2177

Galway, Kilmacduagh and Kilfenora, vacant. *Clergy,* 57. *Diocesan Office,* The Cathedral, Galway T (+353) (91) 563566

Kerry, Ray Browne, *cons.* 2013, *apptd* 2013. *Clergy,* 88. *Bishop's House,* Killarney, Co. Kerry T (+353) (64) 663 1168

Kildare and Leighlin, Denis Nulty, *cons.* 2013, *apptd* 2013. *Clergy,* 72. *Bishop's House,* Old Dublin Road, Carlow Town T (+353) (59) 917 6725

Killala, John Fleming, *cons.* 2002, *apptd* 2002. *Clergy,* 40. *Bishop's House,* Ballina, Co. Mayo T (+353) (96) 21518

Killaloe, Fintan Monahan, *cons.* 2016, *apptd* 2016. *Clergy,* 95. *Diocesan Office,* Westbourne, Ennis, Co. Clare T (+353) (65) 682 8638

Kilmore, Leo O'Reilly, *cons.* 1997, *apptd* 1998. *Clergy,* 67. *Bishop's House,* Cullies, Cavan, Co. Cavan T (+353) (49) 433 1496

Limerick, Brendan Leahy, *cons.* 2013, *apptd* 2013. *Clergy,* 109. *Diocesan Office,* Social Service Centre, Henry Street, Limerick T (+353) (61) 315856

Meath, Michael Smith, *cons.* 1984, *apptd* 1990. *Clergy,* 120. *Bishop's House,* Dublin Road, Mullingar, Co. Westmeath T (+353) (44) 934 8841

Ossory, vacant. *Clergy,* 81. *Diocesan Office,* James's Street, Kilkenny T (+353) (56) 776 2448

Raphoe, Dr Philip Boyce, *cons.* 1995, *apptd* 1995. *Clergy,* 80. *Bishop's House,* Ard Adhamhnáin, Letterkenny, Co. Donegal T (+353) (74) 912 1208

Waterford and Lismore, Alphonsus Cullinan, *cons.* 2015, *apptd* 2015. *Clergy,* 114. *Bishop's House,* John's Hill, Waterford T (+353) (51) 874463

OTHER CHURCHES IN THE UK

ASSOCIATED PRESBYTERIAN CHURCHES OF SCOTLAND
The Associated Presbyterian Churches came into being in 1989 as a result of a division within the Free Presbyterian Church of Scotland. The Associated Presbyterian Churches is reformed and evangelistic in nature and emphasises the importance of doctrine based primarily on the Bible and secondly on the Westminster Confession of Faith. There are an estimated 500 members, 8 ministers and 18 congregations in Scotland. There are also congregations in Canada.

ASSOCIATED PRESBYTERIAN CHURCHES OF SCOTLAND, Bruach Taibh, 2 Borve, Arnisort, Isle of Skye IV51 9PS T 01470-582264
W www.apchurches.org
Presbytery Clerk, Revd Ross Macaskill

BAPTIST CHURCH
Baptists trace their origins to John Smyth, who in 1609 in Amsterdam reinstituted the baptism of conscious believers as the basis of the fellowship of a gathered church. Members of Smyth's church established the first Baptist church in England in 1612. They came to be known as 'General' Baptists and their theology was Arminian, whereas a later group of Calvinists who adopted the baptism of believers came to be known as 'Particular' Baptists. The two sections of the Baptists were united into one body, the Baptist Union of Great Britain and Ireland, in 1891. In 1988 the title was changed to the Baptist Union of Great Britain.

Baptists emphasise the complete autonomy of the local church, although individual churches are linked in various kinds of associations. There are international bodies (such as the Baptist World Alliance) and national bodies, but some Baptist churches belong to neither. However, in Great Britain the majority of churches and associations belong to the Baptist

Union of Great Britain. There are also Baptist Unions in Wales, Scotland and Ireland, which are much smaller than the Baptist Union of Great Britain, and there is some overlap of membership.

There are currently around 135,000 members, 2,500 ministers and 2,080 churches associated with the Baptist Union of Great Britain. The Baptist Union of Great Britain is one of the founder members of the European Baptist Federation (1948) and the Baptist World Alliance (1905); the latter represents 42 million members worldwide.

In the Baptist Union of Wales (Undeb Bedyddwyr Cymru) there are 11,355 members, 88 pastors and 386 churches, including those in England.

In the Baptist Union of Scotland there are 11,500 members and 165 churches.

BAPTIST UNION OF GREAT BRITAIN, Baptist House, PO Box 44, 129 Broadway, Didcot, Oxon OX11 8RT
T 01235-517700
W www.baptist.org.uk
President (2017–18, Dianne Tidball
General Secretary, Revd Lynn Green

BAPTIST UNION OF WALES, Y Llwyfan, Trinity St David College, College Road, Carmarthen SA31 3EQ T 01267-245660
E mennajones@ubc.cymru W www.buw.org.uk
President of the Welsh Assembly (2017–18), Revd John Talfryn Jones
President of the English Assembly (2017–18), Revd Haydn Davies
General Secretary of the Baptist Union of Wales, Revd Judith Morris

BAPTIST UNION OF SCOTLAND, 48 Speirs Wharf, Glasgow G4 9TH T 0141-423 6169 E admin@scottishbaptist.org.uk
W www.scottishbaptist.com
General Director, Revd Alan Donaldson

THE BRETHREN

The Brethren was founded in Dublin in 1827–8, basing itself on the structures and practices of the early church and rejecting denominationalism and clericalism. Many groups sprang up; the group at Plymouth became the best known, resulting in its designation by others as the 'Plymouth Brethren'. Early worship had a prescribed form but quickly assumed an unstructured, non-liturgical format.

There are services devoted to worship, usually involving the breaking of bread, and separate preaching meetings. There is no salaried ministry.

A theological dispute led in 1848 to schism between the Open Brethren and the Closed or Exclusive Brethren, each branch later suffering further divisions.

Open Brethren churches are run by appointed elders and are completely independent, but freely cooperate with each other. Exclusive Brethren churches believe in a universal fellowship between congregations. They do not have appointed elders, but use respected members of their congregation to perform certain administrative functions.

The Brethren are established throughout the UK, Ireland, Europe, India, Africa and Australasia. In the UK there are over 70,000 members, 1,250 assembly halls and over 200 full-time Bible teachers, evangelists and administrators. There are a number of publishing houses that publish Brethren-related literature. Chapter Two is the main supplier of such literature in the UK; it also has a Brethren history archive which is available for use by appointment.

CHAPTER TWO, 3 Conduit Mews, London SE18 7AP T 020-8316 5389 E info@chaptertwobooks.org.uk
W www.chaptertwobooks.org.uk

CONGREGATIONAL FEDERATION

The Congregational Federation was founded by members of Congregational churches in England and Wales who did not join the United Reformed Church in 1972. There are also churches in Scotland and France affiliated to the federation. The federation exists to encourage congregations of believers to worship in free assembly, but it has no authority over them and emphasises their right to independence and self-governance.

The federation has around 7,000 members, 187 accredited ministers and 265 churches in England, Wales and Scotland.

CONGREGATIONAL FEDERATION, 8 Castle Gate, Nottingham NG1 7AS T 0115-911 1460
E admin@congregational.org.uk W www.congregational.org.uk
President of the Federation (2016–17), Paul Davis
General Secretary, Yvonne Campbell

FELLOWSHIP OF INDEPENDENT EVANGELICAL CHURCHES

The Fellowship of Independent Evangelical Churches (FIEC) was founded by Revd E. J. Poole-Connor (1872–1962) in 1922. In 1923 the fellowship published its first register of non-denominational pastors, evangelists and congregations who had accepted the doctrinal basis for the fellowship.

Members of the fellowship have two primary convictions: firstly to defend the evangelical faith, and secondly that evangelicalism is the bond that unites the fellowship, rather than forms of worship or church government.

The FIEC exists to promote the welfare of non-denominational Bible churches and to give expression to the fundamental doctrines of evangelical Christianity. It supports individual churches by gathering and disseminating information and resources and advising churches on current theological, moral, social and practical issues.

There are currently over 500 churches affiliated to the fellowship.

FELLOWSHIP OF INDEPENDENT EVANGELICAL CHURCHES, 39 The Point, Market Harborough, Leics LE16 7QU T 01858-434540
E admin@fiec.org.uk W www.fiec.org.uk
National Director, John Stevens

FREE CHURCH OF ENGLAND

The Free Church of England, otherwise called the Reformed Episcopal Church, is an independent episcopal church, constituted according to the historic faith, tradition and practice of the Church of England. Its roots lie in the 18th century, but it started to grow significantly from the 1840s onwards, as clergy and congregations joined it from the established church in protest against the Oxford Movement. The historic episcopate was conferred on the English church in 1876 through bishops of the Reformed Episcopal Church (which had broken away from the Protestant Episcopal Church in the USA in 1873). A branch of the Reformed Episcopal Church was founded in the UK and this merged with the Free Church of England in 1927 to create the present church. The Orders of the Free Church of England are recognised by the Church of England.

Worship is according to the *Book of Common Prayer* and some modern liturgy is permissable. Only men are ordained to the orders of deacon, presbyter and bishop.

The Free Church of England has two dioceses, 19 congregations and around 900 members in England. There is one congregation in St Petersburg, Russia and three congregations and six missions in Brazil.

THE FREE CHURCH OF ENGLAND, 329 Wolverhampton Road West, Willenhall, W. Midlands WV13 2RL T 01902-607335
W www.fcofe.org.uk
Bishop Primus, Rt. Revd Dr John Fenwick (Bishop of the Northern Diocese)
General Secretary, Rt. Revd Paul Hunt (Bishop of the Southern Diocese)

FREE CHURCH OF SCOTLAND

The Free Church of Scotland was formed in 1843 when over 400 ministers withdrew from the Church of Scotland as a result of interference in the internal affairs of the church by the civil authorities. In 1900, all but 26 ministers joined with others to form the United Free Church (most of which rejoined the Church of Scotland in 1929). In 1904 the remaining 26 ministers were recognised by the House of Lords as continuing the Free Church of Scotland.

The church maintains strict adherence to the Westminster Confession of Faith (1648) and accepts the Bible as the sole rule of faith and conduct. Its general assembly meets annually. It also has links with reformed churches overseas. The Free Church of Scotland has about 13,000 members, 90 ministers and 100 congregations.

FREE CHURCH OF SCOTLAND, 15 North Bank Street, The Mound, Edinburgh EH1 2LS **T** 0131-226 5286
E offices@freechurchofscotland.org.uk **W** www.freechurch.org
Chief Executive, Scott Matheson

FREE PRESBYTERIAN CHURCH OF SCOTLAND

The Free Presbyterian Church of Scotland was formed in 1893 by two ministers of the Free Church of Scotland who refused to accept a Declaratory Act passed by the Free Church General Assembly in 1892. The Free Presbyterian Church of Scotland is Calvinistic in doctrine and emphasises observance of the Sabbath. It adheres strictly to the Westminster Confession of Faith (1648).

The church has about 700 members in Scotland. It has 17 ministers and 40 churches in the UK.

FREE PRESBYTERIAN CHURCH OF SCOTLAND, 133 Woodlands Road, Glasgow G3 6LE **E** outreach@fpchurch.org.uk **W** www.fpchurch.org.uk
Moderator (2017–18), Revd J. MacLeod
Clerk of the Synod, Revd Keith Watkins

HOLY APOSTOLIC CATHOLIC ASSYRIAN CHURCH OF THE EAST

The Holy Apostolic Catholic Assyrian Church of the East traces its beginnings to the middle of the first century. It spread from Upper Mesopotamia throughout the territories of the Persian Empire. The Assyrian Church of the East became theologically separated from the rest of the Christian community following the Council of Ephesus in 431. The church is headed by the Catholicos Patriarch and is episcopal in government. The liturgical language is Syriac (Aramaic). The Assyrian Church of the East and the Roman Catholic Church agreed a common Christological declaration in 1994, and a process of dialogue between the Assyrian Church of the East and the Chaldean Catholic Church, which is in communion with Rome but shares the Syriac liturgy, was instituted in 1996.

The church has around 325,000 members in the Middle East, India, Russia, Europe, North America and Australasia. In Great Britain there is one parish, which is situated in London. The church in Great Britain forms part of the Diocese of Europe under HG Mar Odisho Oraham.

HOLY APOSTOLIC CATHOLIC ASSYRIAN CHURCH OF THE EAST, St Mary's Church Hall, 62 Greenford Avenue, Hanwell, London W7 3QP **T** 0786-873 7112

INDEPENDENT METHODIST CHURCHES

The Independent Methodist Churches were formed in 1805 and remained independent when the Methodist Church in Great Britain was formed in 1932. They are mainly concentrated in the industrial areas of the north of England.

The churches are Methodist in doctrine but their organisation is congregational. All the churches are members of the Independent Methodist Connexion of Churches. The controlling body of the Connexion is the Annual Meeting, to which churches send delegates. The Connexional President is elected every two years. Between annual meetings the affairs of the Connexion are handled by the Connexional Committee and departmental committees. Ministers are appointed by the churches and trained through the Connexion. The ministry is open to both men and women.

There are 1,600 members, 70 ministers and 74 churches in Great Britain.

INDEPENDENT METHODIST RESOURCE CENTRE, The Resource Centre, Fleet Street, Wigan WN5 0DS **T** 01942-223526 **E** resourcecentre@imcgb.org.uk **W** www.imcgb.org.uk
President, David McDonald
General Secretary, Brian Rowney

LUTHERAN CHURCH

Lutheranism is based on the teachings of Martin Luther, the German leader of the Protestant Reformation. The authority of the scriptures is held to be supreme over church tradition. The teachings of Lutheranism are explained in detail in 16th-century confessional writings, particularly the Augsburg Confession. Lutheranism is one of the largest Protestant denominations and it is particularly strong in northern Europe and the USA. Some Lutheran churches are episcopal, while others have a synodal form of organisation; unity is based on doctrine rather than structure. Most Lutheran churches are members of the Lutheran World Federation, based in Geneva.

Lutheran services in Great Britain are held in 15 languages to serve members of different nationalities. Services usually follow ancient liturgies. English-language congregations are members either of the Lutheran Church in Great Britain or of the Evangelical Lutheran Church of England. The Lutheran Church in Great Britain and other Lutheran churches in Britain are members of the Lutheran Council of Great Britain, which represents them and coordinates their common work.

There are around 70 million Lutherans worldwide, with around 180,000 members in Great Britain.

THE LUTHERAN COUNCIL OF GREAT BRITAIN, 30 Thanet Street, London WC1H 9QH **T** 020-7554 9753 **E** enquiries@lutheran.org.uk **W** www.lutheran.org.uk
Chair, Revd Torbjorn Holt
General Secretary, James Laing

METHODIST CHURCH

The Methodist movement started in England in 1729 when the Revd John Wesley, an Anglican priest, and his brother Charles met with others in Oxford and resolved to conduct their lives by 'rule and method'. In 1739 the Wesleys began evangelistic preaching and the first Methodist chapel was founded in Bristol in the same year. In 1744 the first annual conference was held, at which the Articles of Religion were drawn up. Doctrinal emphases included repentance, faith, the assurance of salvation, social concern and the priesthood of all believers. After John Wesley's death in 1791 the Methodists withdrew from the established church to form the Methodist Church. Methodists gradually drifted into many groups, but in 1932 the Wesleyan Methodist Church, the United Methodist Church and the Primitive Methodist Church united to form the Methodist Church in Britain.

The governing body is the Conference. The Conference meets annually and consists of two parts: the ministerial and representative sessions. The Methodist Church is structured as a 'Connexion' of churches, circuits and districts. The local churches in a defined area form a circuit, and a number of these 368 circuits make up each of the 31 districts. The latest 2017 *Statistics for Mission* show that as at 31 October 2016 the Methodist Church in Britain had 188,398 local church members, 3,459 ministers and 4,512 local churches.

THE METHODIST CHURCH IN BRITAIN, Methodist Church House, 25 Marylebone Road, London NW1 5JR **T** 020-7486 5502 **E** enquiries@methodistchurch.org.uk **W** www.methodist.org.uk
President of the Conference (2017–18), Revd Loraine Mellor
Vice-President of the Conference (2017–18), Jill Baker
Secretary of the Conference, Revd Canon Gareth Powell

THE METHODIST CHURCH IN IRELAND

The Methodist Church in Ireland is autonomous but has close links with British Methodism. As at December 2014 it had 45,828 members, 121 active ministers and 270 lay preachers.

METHODIST CHURCH IN IRELAND, 1 Fountainville Avenue, Belfast BT9 6AN T 028-9032 4554
E secretary@irishmethodist.org W www.irishmethodist.org
President of the Conference (2017–18), Revd Dr Laurence Graham
Lay Leader of the Conference (2016–19), Dr Fergus O'Ferrall
Secretary of the Conference, Revd John Stephens

ORTHODOX CHURCHES

EASTERN ORTHODOX CHURCH

The Eastern (or Byzantine) Orthodox Church is a communion of self-governing Christian churches that recognises the honorary primacy of the Ecumenical Patriarch of Constantinople.

The position of Orthodox Christians is that the faith was fully defined during the period of the Oecumenical Councils. In doctrine it is strongly trinitarian, and stresses the mystery and importance of the sacraments. It is episcopal in government. The structure of the Orthodox Christian year differs from that of western churches.

Orthodox Christians throughout the world are estimated to number about 300 million; there are around 300,000 in the UK.

GREEK ORTHODOX CHURCH (PATRIARCHATE OF ANTIOCH)

The church is led by John X, Patriarch of Antioch, who was enthroned in February 2013. The Archdiocese of the British Isles and Ireland has 18 parishes, including St George's Cathedral in London, and 27 clergy.

ANTIOCHIAN ORTHODOX ARCHDIOCESE OF THE BRITISH ISLES AND IRELAND, St George's Cathedral, 1A Redhill Street, London NW1 4BG T 020-7383 0403
E fr.s.gholam@antiochianorth.co.uk
W www.antiochian-orthodox.co.uk
Archbishop, Metropolitan Silouan Oner

GREEK ORTHODOX CHURCH (PATRIARCHATE OF CONSTANTINOPLE)

The presence of Greek Orthodox Christians in Britain dates back at least to 1677 when Archbishop Joseph Geogirenes of Samos fled from Turkish persecution and came to London. The present Greek cathedral in Moscow Road, Bayswater, was opened for public worship in 1879, and the Diocese of Thyateira and Great Britain was established in 1922. There are now around 100 parishes and one monastery in the UK, served by one archbishop, three bishops and around 120 clergy.

THE PATRIARCHATE OF CONSTANTINOPLE IN GREAT BRITAIN, Archdiocese of Thyateira and Great Britain, Thyateira House, 5 Craven Hill, London W2 3EN
T 020-7723 4787
E mail@thyateira.org.uk W www.thyateira.org.uk
Archbishop, Gregorios of Thyateira and Great Britain

THE RUSSIAN ORTHODOX CHURCH (PATRIARCHATE OF MOSCOW)

The records of Russian Orthodox Church activities in Britain date from the visit to England of Tsar Peter I in the early 18th century. Clergy were sent from Russia to serve the chapel established to minister to the staff of the Imperial Russian Embassy in London.

In 2007, after an 80-year division, the Russian Orthodox Church Outside Russia agreed to become an autonomous part of the Russian Orthodox Church, Patriarchate of Moscow. The reunification agreement was signed by Patriarch Alexy II, 15th Patriarch of Moscow and All Russia and Metropolitan Laurus,

leader of the Russian Orthodox Church Outside Russia on 17 May at a ceremony at Christ the Saviour Cathedral in Moscow. Patriarch Alexy II died on 5 December 2008. Metropolitan Kirill of Smolensk and Kaliningrad was enthroned as the 16th Patriarch of Moscow and All Russia on 1 February 2009, having been elected by a secret ballot of clergy on 27 January 2009.

The diocese of Sourozh is the diocese of the Russian Orthodox Church in Great Britain and Ireland and is led by Archbishop Elisey of Sourozh.

DIOCESE OF SOUROZH, Diocesan Office, Cathedral of the Dormition of the Mother of God and All Saints, 67 Ennismore Gardens, London SW7 1NH T 020-7584 0096
W www.sourozh.org
Diocesan Hierarch, Archbishop Elisey of Sourozh

SERBIAN ORTHODOX CHURCH (PATRIARCHATE OF SERBIA)

There are seven parishes in Great Britain and around 4,000 members. Great Britain is part of the Diocese of Great Britain and Scandinavia, which is led by Bishop Dositey. The church can be contacted via the church of St Sava in London.

SERBIAN ORTHODOX CHURCH IN GREAT BRITAIN, Church of Saint Sava, 89 Lancaster Road, London W11 1QQ
T 020-7727 8367
E crkva@spclondon.org W www.spclondon.org
Archpriest, Very Revd Goran Spaic

OTHER NATIONALITIES

The Patriarchates of Romania and Bulgaria (Diocese of Western Europe) have memberships estimated at 20,000 and 2,000 respectively, while the Georgian Orthodox Church has around 500 members. The Belarusian (membership estimated at 2,400) and Latvian (membership of around 100).

ORIENTAL ORTHODOX CHURCHES

The term 'Oriental Orthodox Churches' is now generally used to describe a group of six ancient eastern churches (Armenian, Coptic, Eritrean, Ethiopian, Indian (Malankara) and Syrian) which rejected the Christological definition of the Council of Chalcedon (AD 451). There are around 50 million members worldwide of the Oriental Orthodox Churches and over 20,000 in the UK.

ARMENIAN ORTHODOX CHURCH (CATHOLICOSATE OF ETCHMIADZIN)

The Armenian Orthodox Church is led by HH Karekin II, Catholicos of All Armenians. HG Bishop Hovakim Manukyan was appointed Primate of the Armenian Church in the UK and Ireland in 2015.

ARMENIAN CHURCH IN THE UK AND IRELAND, The Primate's Office, The Armenian Vicarage, Iverna Gardens, London W8 6TP T 020-8127 8364
E primatesoffice@armenianchurch.co.uk
W www.armenianchurch.co.uk
Primate, HG Bishop Hovakim Manukyan

COPTIC ORTHODOX CHURCH

The Coptic Orthodox Church is headed by Pope Tawadros II, who was appointed in November 2012. There are three dioceses in the UK: the Midlands, led by HG Bishop Missael; Ireland, Scotland and north-east England, led by HG Bishop Antony; and the Papal Diocese which is led by HG Bishop Angaelos and covers all the remaining parishes in the UK.

CATHEDRAL OF ST GEORGE AT THE COPTIC ORTHODOX CHURCH CENTRE, Shephalbury Manor, Broadhall Way, Stevenage, Herts SG2 8NP T 020-7993 9001
W www.copticcentre.com
Bishop, HG Bishop Angaelos

BRITISH ORTHODOX CHURCH

The British Orthodox Church is a small autonomous Orthodox jurisdiction, originally deriving from the Syrian Orthodox Church. It was canonically part of the Coptic Orthodox Patriarchate of Alexandria from 1994–2015. As it ministers to British people, all of its services are in English.

THE BRITISH ORTHODOX CHURCH, 10 Heathwood Gardens, Charlton, London SE7 8EP T 020-8854 3090
E info@britishorthodox.org W www.britishorthodox.org
Metropolitan, Abba Seraphim

ERITREAN ORTHODOX TEWAHEDO CHURCH

The Eritrean Orthodox Church was granted independence in 1994 by Pope Shenouda III, following the declaration of Eritrea's independence from Ethiopia in 1993. In 2006, the Eritrean government removed the third patriarch, Abune Antonios, from office and imprisoned him; the government replaced him with Abune Dioskoros in 2007, although the Oriental Orthodox Churches continue to recognise Antonios as the rightful patriarch. The diocesan bishop for North America, Europe and the Middle East is HG Abune Makarios.

ETHIOPIAN ORTHODOX TAWAHEDO CHURCH

The Ethiopian Orthodox Church was administratively part of the Coptic Orthodox Church of Alexandria until 1959, when it was granted its own patriarch by the Coptic Orthodox Pope of Alexandria and Patriarch of All Africa, Cyril VI. The current patriarch is HH Abune Mathias. The church in London was established in 1976.

ETHIOPIAN ORTHODOX TAWAHEDO CHURCH, St Mary of Zion, PO Box 56856, London N13 5US T 020-8807 5885
E pc@tserhasion.org.uk W www.stmaryofzion.co.uk
Priest-in-Charge, Melake Sion Habte Mariam

INDIAN ORTHODOX CHURCH

The Indian Orthodox Church, also known as the Malankara Orthodox Church, traces its origins to the first century. The head of the Malankara Orthodox Church is HH Baselios Marthoma Paulose II. The mother church of all the parishes in the UK and the Republic of Ireland is St Gregorios Church in London. The London parish has around 280 families as practising members.

INDIAN ORTHODOX CHURCH, St Gregorios Indian Orthodox Church, Cranfield Road, Brockley, London SE4 1UF
T 020-8691 9456
E ioclondon@gmail.com W www.ioclondon.co.uk
Diocesan Metropolitan, HG Dr Mathews Mar Thimothios
Vicar, Revd Fr Dr Ninan V. George

SYRIAN ORTHODOX CHURCH

The Syrian (Syriac) Orthodox Church of Antioch is an Oriental Orthodox Church based in the Eastern Mediterranean headed by HH Moran Mor Ignatius Aphrem II. The Patriarchate Vicariate in the UK is represented by HE Archbishop Mor Athanasius Toma Dawod.

SYRIAN ORTHODOX CHURCH IN THE UK, St Thomas Cathedral, 7–11 Armstrong Road, London W3 7JL
T 020-8749 5834
E enquiry-uk@syrianorthodoxchurch.net
W www.syrianorthodoxchurch.net
Archbishop, HE Mor Athanasius Toma Dawod

PENTECOSTAL CHURCHES

Pentecostalism is inspired by the descent of the Holy Spirit upon the apostles at Pentecost. The movement began in Los Angeles, USA, in 1906 and is characterised by baptism with the Holy Spirit, divine healing, speaking in tongues (glossolalia) and a literal interpretation of the scriptures.

The Pentecostal movement in Britain dates from 1907. Initially, groups of Pentecostalists were led by laymen and

did not organise formally. However, in 1915 the Elim Foursquare Gospel Alliance (more commonly called the Elim Pentecostal Church) was founded in Ireland by George Jeffreys and currently has about 550 churches, 68,500 adherents and 650 accredited ministers. In 1924 about 70 independent assemblies formed a fellowship called Assemblies of God in Great Britain and Ireland, which now incorporates around 600 churches, around 75,000 adherents and 1,000 ministers.

The Apostolic Church grew out of the 1904–5 Christian revivals in South Wales and was established in 1916. The Apostolic Church has around 110 churches, 7,180 adherents and 115 ministers in the UK. The New Testament Church of God was established in England in 1953 and has over 130 congregations, 11,000 members and over 300 ministers across England and Wales.

In recent years many aspects of Pentecostalism have been adopted by the growing charismatic movement within the Roman Catholic, Protestant and Eastern Orthodox churches. There are about 105 million Pentecostalists worldwide, with over 350,000 adherents in the UK.

THE APOSTOLIC CHURCH, Suite 105, Crystal House, New Bedford Road, Luton LU1 1HS T 020-7587 1802
E admin@apostolic-church.org W www.apostolic-church.org
National Leader, Jim Jack
ASSEMBLIES OF GOD, National Ministry Centre, Mattersey, Doncaster DN10 5HD T 017-7781 7663 E info@aog.org.uk
W www.aog.org.uk
National Leader, John Partington
THE ELIM PENTECOSTAL CHURCH, Elim International Centre, De Walden Road, Malvern WR14 4DF T 0345-302 6750
W www.elim.org.uk
General Superintendent, Chris Cartwright
THE NEW TESTAMENT CHURCH OF GOD, 3 Cheyne Walk, Northampton NN1 5PT T 01604-824222
E mmcc@ntcg.org.uk W www.ntcg.org.uk
Administrative Bishop, Donald Bolt

PRESBYTERIAN CHURCH IN IRELAND

Irish Presbyterianism traces its origins back to the Plantation of Ulster in 1606, when English and Scottish Protestants began to settle on the land confiscated from the Irish chieftains. The first presbytery was established in Ulster in 1642 by chaplains of a Scottish army that had been sent to crush a Catholic rebellion in 1641.

The Presbyterian Church in Ireland is reformed in doctrine and belongs to the World Alliance of Reformed Churches. Structurally, the 545 congregations are grouped in 19 presbyteries under the General Assembly. This body meets annually and is presided over by a moderator who is elected for one year. The ongoing work of the church is undertaken by 12 boards under which there are specialist committees.

There are over 240,000 members of Irish presbyterian churches in Ireland and Northern Ireland.

THE PRESBYTERIAN CHURCH IN IRELAND, Assembly Buildings, 2–10 Fisherwick Place, Belfast BT1 6DW
T 028-9032 2284 E info@presbyterianireland.org
W www.presbyterianireland.org
Moderator (2017–18), Rt. Revd Dr Noble McNeely
Clerk of Assembly and General Secretary, Revd Trevor Gribben

PRESBYTERIAN CHURCH OF WALES

The Presbyterian Church of Wales or Calvinistic Methodist Church of Wales is Calvinistic in doctrine and presbyterian in constitution. It was formed in 1811 when Welsh Calvinists severed the relationship with the established church by ordaining their own ministers. It secured its own confession of faith in 1823 and a Constitutional Deed in 1826, and since 1864 the General Assembly has met annually, presided over by a moderator elected for a year. The doctrine and constitutional structure of the Presbyterian Church of Wales was confirmed by act of parliament in 1931–2.

The Church has 20,000 members, 55 ministers and 600 congregations.

THE PRESBYTERIAN CHURCH OF WALES, Tabernacle Chapel, 81 Merthyr Road, Whitchurch, Cardiff CF14 1DD
T 029-2062 7465
E swyddfa.office@ebcpcw.org.uk W www.ebcpcw.cymru
Moderator (2017–18), Revd Brian Huw Jones
General Secretary, Revd Meirion Morris

RELIGIOUS SOCIETY OF FRIENDS (QUAKERS)

Quakerism is a religious denomination which was founded in the 17th century by George Fox and others in an attempt to revive what they saw as the original 'primitive Christianity'. The movement, at first called Friends of the Truth, started in the Midlands, Yorkshire and north-west England, but there are now Quakers all over the UK and in 36 countries around the world. The colony of Pennsylvania, founded by William Penn, was originally a Quaker settlement.

Quakers place an emphasis on the experience of God in daily life rather than on sacraments or religious occasions. There is no church calendar. Worship is largely silent and there are no appointed ministers; the responsibility for conducting a meeting is shared equally among those present. Religious tolerance and social reform have always been important to Quakers, together with a commitment to peace and non-violence in resolving disputes.

There are more than 23,000 'friends' or Quakers in Great Britain. There are around 475 places where Quaker meetings are held, many of them Quaker-owned Friends Meeting Houses. The Britain Yearly Meeting is the name given to the central organisation of Quakers in Britain.

THE RELIGIOUS SOCIETY OF FRIENDS (QUAKERS) IN BRITAIN, Friends House, 173–177 Euston Road, London NW1 2BJ T 020-7663 1000
E enquiries@quaker.org.uk W www.quaker.org.uk
Recording Clerk, Paul Parker

SALVATION ARMY

The Salvation Army is an international Christian organisation working in 126 countries worldwide. As a church and registered charity, The Salvation Army is funded through donations from its members, the general public and, where appropriate, government grants.

The Salvation Army was founded by Methodists William and Catherine Booth in the East End of London in 1865 and marked its 150th anniversary on 2 July 2015. It now has around 40,000 members and 1,067 Salvation Army Officers (full-time ministers) in the UK. There are over 700 local church and community centres, 62 residential support centres for homeless people, 16 care homes for older people and six substance-misuse centres. It also runs a clothing recycling programme, charity shops, foodbanks, a prison-visiting service and a family-tracing service. In 1878 it adopted a quasi-military command structure intended to inspire and regulate its endeavours and to reflect its view that the church was engaged in spiritual warfare.

UK TERRITORIAL HEADQUARTERS, 101 Newington Causeway, London SE1 6BN T 020-7367 4500
E info@salvationarmy.org.uk W www.salvationarmy.org.uk
UK Territorial Leaders, Commissioners Clive and Marianne Adams

SEVENTH-DAY ADVENTIST CHURCH

The Seventh-day Adventist Church is a worldwide Christian church marked by its observance of Saturday as the Sabbath and by its emphasis on the imminent second coming of Jesus Christ. Adventists summarise their faith in '28 fundamental beliefs'.

The church grew out of the Millerite movement in the USA during the mid-19th century and was formally established in 1863. The church has an ethnically and culturally diverse worldwide membership of over 17 million. In the UK and Ireland there are 34,048 members worshipping in around 300 churches and companies.

SEVENTH-DAY ADVENTIST CHURCH HQ, Stanborough Park, Watford WD25 9JZ T 01923-672251
E info@adventist.org.uk W www.adventist.org.uk
President, Pastor Ian Sweeney

THE (SWEDENBORGIAN) NEW CHURCH

The New Church is based on the teachings of the 18th-century Swedish scientist and theologian Emanuel Swedenborg (1688–1772), who believed that Jesus Christ appeared to him and instructed him to reveal the spiritual meaning of the Bible. He claimed to have visions of the spiritual world, including heaven and hell, and conversations with angels and spirits. He published several theological works, including descriptions of the spiritual world and a Bible commentary.

Swedenborgians believe that the second coming of Jesus Christ is taking place, being not an actual physical reappearance of Christ, but rather his return in spirit. It is also believed that concurrent with our life on earth is life in a parallel spiritual world, of which we are usually unconscious until death. There are around 30,000 Swedenborgians worldwide, with around 600 members, 18 churches and five ministers in the UK.

THE GENERAL CONFERENCE OF THE NEW CHURCH, Purley Chase Centre, Purley Chase Lane, Mancetter, Atherstone CV9 2RQ T 01827-712370
W www.generalconference.org.uk

UNDEB YR ANNIBYNWYR CYMRAEG

Undeb Yr Annibynwyr Cymraeg (the Union of Welsh Independents) was formed in 1872 and is a voluntary association of Welsh Congregational churches and personal members. It is mainly Welsh-speaking. Congregationalism in Wales dates back to 1639 when the first Welsh Congregational church was opened in Gwent.

Member churches are traditionally congregationalist in organisation and Calvinistic in doctrine, although a wide range of interpretations are permitted. Each church has complete independence in the governance and administration of its affairs.

The Union has around 24,000 members, 80 ministers and 440 member churches.

UNDEB YR ANNIBYNWYR CYMRAEG, 5 Axis Court, Riverside Business Park, Swansea Vale, Swansea SA7 0AJ
T 01792-795888
E undeb@annibynwyr.org W www.annibynwyr.org
President of the Union (2016–18), Revd Glyn Williams
General Secretary, Revd Dr Geraint Tudur

UNITED REFORMED CHURCH

The United Reformed Church (URC) was first formed by the union of most of the Congregational churches in England and Wales with the Presbyterian Church of England in 1972. It is Calvinistic in doctrine, and its followers form independent self-governing congregations bound under God by covenant, a principle laid down in the writings of Robert Browne (1550–1633). From the late 16th century the movement was driven underground by persecution, but the cause was defended at the Westminster Assembly in 1643 and the Savoy Declaration of 1658 laid down its principles. Congregational churches formed county associations for mutual support and in 1832 these associations merged to form the Congregational Union of England and Wales.

In the 1960s there was close cooperation locally and nationally between congregational and presbyterian churches. This led to union negotiations and a Scheme of Union, supported by an act of parliament in 1972. In 1981 a further unification took place, with the Reformed Association of Churches of Christ becoming part of the URC. In 2000 a third union took place, with the Congregational Union of Scotland. At its basis the URC reflects local church initiative and responsibility with a conciliar pattern of oversight.

The URC is divided into 13 synods, each with a synod moderator. There are around 1,500 churches which serve around 58,000 adults and around 41,000 children and young people. There are around 550 ministers in active service.

The General Assembly is the central body, and comprises around 400 representatives, mainly appointed by the synods, of which half are lay persons and half are ministers. Since 2010 the General Assembly has met biennially to elect two moderators (one lay and one ordained), who then become the public representatives of the URC.

UNITED REFORMED CHURCH, 86 Tavistock Place, London WC1H 9RT T 020-7916 2020
E urc@urc.org.uk W www.urc.org.uk
Moderators of the General Assembly 2016–18, Revd Kevin Watson; Alan Yates
General Secretary, Revd John Proctor

WESLEYAN REFORM UNION

The Wesleyan Reform Union was founded by Methodists who left or were expelled from Wesleyan Methodism in 1849 following a period of internal conflict. Its doctrine is conservative evangelical and its organisation is congregational, each church having complete independence in the government and administration of its affairs. The union has around 1,250 members, 20 ministers and 96 churches.

THE WESLEYAN REFORM UNION, Wesleyan Reform Church House, 123 Queen Street, Sheffield S1 2DU
T 0114-272 1938
E admin@thewru.co.uk W www.thewru.com
President (2017–18), Philip Hartshorn

NON-TRINITARIAN CHURCHES

CHRISTADELPHIAN

Christadelphians believe that the Bible is the word of God and that it reveals both God's dealings with mankind in the past and his plans for the future. These plans centre on the work of Jesus Christ, who it is believed will return to Earth to establish God's kingdom. The Christadelphian group was founded in the USA in the 1850s by the Englishman, Dr John Thomas.

THE CHRISTADELPHIAN MAGAZINE AND PUBLISHING ASSOCIATION, 404 Shaftmoor Lane, Hall Green, Birmingham B28 8SZ T 0121-777 6328
W www.thechristadelphian.com

CHURCH OF CHRIST, SCIENTIST

The Church of Christ, Scientist was founded by Mary Baker Eddy in the USA in 1879 to 'reinstate primitive Christianity and its lost element of healing'. Christian Science teaches the need for spiritual regeneration and salvation from sin, but it is best known for its reliance on prayer alone in the healing of sickness. Adherents believe that such healing is the result of divine laws, or divine science, and is in direct line with that practised by Jesus Christ (revered, not as God, but as the son of God) and by the early Christian church.

The denomination consists of The First Church of Christ, Scientist, in Boston, Massachusetts, USA ('The Mother Church') and its branch churches in almost 80 countries worldwide. The Bible and Mary Baker Eddy's book, *Science and Health with Key to the Scriptures,* are used for daily spiritual guidance and healing by all members and are read at services. There are no clergy; those engaged in full-time healing are called Christian Science practitioners, of whom there are around 1,500 worldwide.

No membership figures are available, since Mary Baker Eddy felt that numbers are no measure of spiritual vitality and ruled that such statistics should not be published. There are almost 2,000 branch churches worldwide, including 100 in the UK.

CHRISTIAN SCIENCE COMMITTEE ON PUBLICATION, 90 Long Acre, London WC2E 9RZ
T 020-8150 0245
E londoncs@csps.com W http://ukchristianscience.com
District Manager for the UK and Ireland, Robin Harragin Hussey

CHURCH OF JESUS CHRIST OF LATTER-DAY SAINTS

The Church of Jesus Christ of Latter-day Saints ('Mormons') was founded in New York State, USA, in 1830, and came to Britain in 1837. The oldest continuous congregation of the church is in Preston, Lancashire.

Mormons are Christians who claim to belong to the 'restored church' of Jesus Christ. They believe that true Christianity died when the last original apostle died, but that it was given back to the world by God and Jesus Christ through Joseph Smith, the church's founder and first president. They accept and use the Bible as scripture, but believe in continuing revelation from God; Mormons also use additional scriptures, including *The Book of Mormon: Another Testament of Jesus Christ.* The importance of the family is central to the church's beliefs and practices. Church members set aside Monday evenings as family home evenings when Christian family values are taught. Polygamy was formally discontinued in 1890.

The church has no paid ministry: local congregations are headed by a leader chosen from among their number. The world governing body, based in Utah, USA, is led by a president, believed to be the chosen prophet, and his two counsellors. There are over 15 million members worldwide, with 185,848 members and 333 congregations in the UK.

THE CHURCH OF JESUS CHRIST OF LATTER-DAY SAINTS, UK Headquarters, 751 Warwick Road, Solihull, W. Midlands B91 3DQ T 0121-712 1200
W www.lds.org.uk

JEHOVAH'S WITNESSES

The movement now known as Jehovah's Witnesses grew from a Bible study group formed by Charles Taze Russell in 1872 in Pennsylvania, USA. In 1896 it adopted the name of the Watch Tower Bible and Tract Society, and in 1931 its members became known as Jehovah's Witnesses.

Jehovah's (God's) Witnesses believe in the Bible as the word of God, and consider it to be inspired and historically accurate. They take the scriptures literally, except where there are obvious indications that they are figurative or symbolic, and reject the doctrine of the Trinity. Witnesses also believe that all those approved of by Jehovah will have eternal life on a cleansed and beautified earth; only 144,000 will go to heaven to rule with Jesus Christ. They believe that the second coming of Christ began in 1914, that his thousand-year reign over the earth is imminent, and that armageddon (a final battle in which evil will be defeated) will precede Christ's rule of peace. Jehovah's Witnesses refuse to take part in military service and do not accept blood transfusions.

The eight-member world governing body is based in New York, USA. There is no paid ministry, but each congregation has elders assigned to look after various duties and every Witness takes part in the public ministry in their neighbourhood. There are 8.3 million Jehovah's Witnesses worldwide, with around 136,000 Witnesses in Great Britain organised into around 1,500 congregations.

BRITISH HEADQUARTERS, The Ridgeway, London NW7 1RN
T 020-8906 2211
W www.jw.org

UNITARIAN AND FREE CHRISTIAN CHURCHES

Unitarianism has its historical roots in the Judaeo-Christian tradition but rejects the deity of Christ and the doctrine of the Trinity. It allows the individual to embrace insights from all of the world's faiths and philosophies, as there is no fixed creed. It is accepted that beliefs may evolve in the light of personal experience.

Unitarian communities first became established in Poland and Transylvania in the 16th century. The first avowedly Unitarian place of worship in the British Isles opened in London in 1774. The General Assembly of Unitarian and Free Christian Churches came into existence in 1928 as the result of the amalgamation of two earlier organisations.

There are around 3,400 Unitarians in Great Britain in 170 self-governing congregations and fellowship groups.

GENERAL ASSEMBLY OF UNITARIAN AND FREE CHRISTIAN CHURCHES, Essex Hall, 1–6 Essex Street, London WC2R 3HY T 020-7240 2384
E info@unitarian.org.uk W www.unitarian.org.uk
President (2017–18), Revd Charles VanDenBroeder
Chief Officer, Derek McAuley

COMMUNICATIONS

POSTAL SERVICES

Under the Postal Services Act 2011 Royal Mail was privatised on 15 October 2013 when it was listed on the London Stock Exchange. The government initially retained a 30 per cent stake in Royal Mail, however it sold its remaining shares in 2015. Royal Mail Group ltd operates Royal Mail, Parcelforce Worldwide and General Logistics Systems (GLS). Under the same 2011 Act, the Post Office became independent of Royal Mail Group on 1 April 2012. The government, through the Department for Business, Energy and Industrial Strategy (BEIS), holds a special share in Post Office ltd. The Post Office has a strategic agreement in place to continue to supply Royal Mail products and services through its network and also has the same group holding company (Royal Mail Holdings plc) which holds shares in both Post Office ltd and Royal Mail Group ltd. Neither Royal Mail Holdings plc, nor BEIS, have any involvement in the day-to-day operations of the Post Office.

Royal Mail is the sole provider of the 'universal service': postal products and associated minimum service standards that must be available to all addresses in the UK.

Following the passing of the Postal Services Act 2011, the Office of Communications (OFCOM) assumed regulatory responsibility for postal services. OFCOM's primary responsibility is to secure the provision of a universal postal service with regard to its financial sustainability.

ROYAL MAIL GROUP LTD, 100 Victoria Embankment, London EC4Y 0HQ **T** 0345-774 0740
W www.royalmailgroup.com

OFCOM, Riverside House, 2A Southwark Bridge Road, London SE1 9HA **T** 0207-981 3000 **W** www.ofcom.org.uk

PRICING IN PROPORTION

Since 2006 Royal Mail has priced mail according to its size as well as its weight. The system is intended to reflect the fact that larger, bulkier items cost more to handle than smaller, lighter ones. There are five basic categories of correspondence:

LETTER: *Length* up to 240mm, *width* up to 165mm, *thickness* up to 5mm, *weight* up to 100g; eg most cards and postcards

LARGE LETTER: *Length* up to 353mm, *width* up to 250mm, *thickness* up to 25mm, *weight* up to 750g; eg most A4 documents and magazines

SMALL PARCEL: *Length* up to 450mm, *width* up to 350mm, *thickness* up to 160mm, *weight* up to 2kg; eg books, clothes and gifts

MEDIUM PARCEL: *Length* up to 610mm, *width* up to 460mm, *thickness* up to 460mm, *weight* up to 20kg; eg gifts, shoes, heavy or bulky items

ROLLED OR CYLINDER SHAPED PARCEL: The length of the item plus twice the diameter must not exceed 104cm, with the greatest dimension being no more than 90cm; eg posters and prints

Items larger than those listed above can only be sent via Parcelforce:

STANDARD PARCELFORCE: *Length* up to 150cm, with a combined length and girth of less than 300cm, *weight* up to 30kg

LARGE PARCELFORCE*: *Length* up to 250cm, with a combined length and girth of less than 500cm, *weight* up to 30kg

* Only available at selected Post Office branches

INLAND POSTAL SERVICES

Following are the details of a number of popular postal services along with prices correct as at April 2017. For a full list of prices *see* W www.royalmail.com

FIRST AND SECOND CLASS

Format	Maximum weight	First class	Second class
Letter/postcard	100g	£0.65	£0.56
Large letter	100g	£0.98	£0.76
	250g	£1.30	£1.22
	500g	£1.74	£1.58
	750g	£2.52	£2.14
Small parcel	1,000g	£3.40	£2.90
	2,000g	£5.50	£2.90
Medium parcel	1,000g	£5.70	£5.00
	2,000g	£8.95	£5.00
	5,000g	£15.85	£13.75
	10,000g	£21.90	£20.25
	20,000g	£33.40	£28.55

First class post is normally delivered on the following working day and second class within three working days. Prices are exempt from VAT.

STANDARD PARCELFORCE

Maximum weight	Lowest tariff*
2kg	£11.99
5kg	£12.98
10kg	£16.40
15kg	£23.14
20kg	£28.51
25kg	£39.64
30kg	£43.78

* The rate listed includes VAT and is for delivery within 48 hours

OVERSEAS POSTAL SERVICES

For charging purposes Royal Mail divides the world into four zones: UK, Europe, World Zone 1 and World Zone 2. There is a complete listing on the Royal Mail website (W www.royalmail.com/international-zones)

Europe: Albania, Andorra, Armenia, Austria, Azerbaijan, Azores, Balearic Islands, Belarus, Belgium, Bosnia and Hercegovina, Bulgaria, Canary Islands, Corsica, Croatia, Cyprus, Czech Rep., Denmark, Estonia, Finland, France, Georgia, Germany, Gibraltar, Greece, Greenland, Hungary, Iceland, Ireland, Italy, Kazakhstan, Kosovo, Kyrgyzstan, Latvia, Liechtenstein, Lithuania, Luxembourg, Macedonia, Malta, Moldova, Monaco, Montenegro, Netherlands, Norway, Poland, Portugal, Romania, Russia, San Marino, Serbia, Slovakia, Slovenia, Spain, Sweden, Switzerland, Tajikistan, Turkey, Turkmenistan, Ukraine, Uzbekistan

World Zone 1: N. America, S. America, Africa, the Middle East, the Far East and S. E. Asia

World Zone 2: Australia, British Indian Ocean Territory, Fiji, French Polynesia, Kiribati, Laos, Macau, Nauru, New Caledonia, New Zealand, Palau, Papua New Guinea, Pitcairn Islands, Singapore, Solomon Islands, Tonga, Tuvalu, Samoa

INTERNATIONAL ECONOMY MAIL RATES*

Maximum weight	Standard tariff
Letters up to 100g†	
10g	£1.02
20g	£1.02
100g	£1.47

* Formerly Surface Mail

† Can only be sent by International Economy to destinations outside of Europe

Maximum weight	Large letters	Small parcels/ printed papers
100g	£2.50	£3.55
250g	£3.75	£3.85
500g	£5.10	£5.70
750g	£6.55	£7.10
1,000g	–	£8.50
2,000g	–	£13.35

Printed papers only add £1.15 for each additional 250g, or part thereof, up to 5,000g

INTERNATIONAL STANDARD MAIL RATES*

Weight up to and including	Europe	World Zone 1	World Zone 2
Letters			
10g	£1.17	£1.17	£1.17
20g	£1.17	£1.40	£1.40
100g	£1.57	£2.27	£2.27
Large letters			
100g	£2.55	£3.15	£3.30
250g	£3.80	£4.75	£5.05
500g	£5.15	£7.45	£7.90
750g	£6.60	£10.15	£10.75
Small parcels and printed papers			
100g	£3.80	£4.45	£4.80
250g	£4.10	£5.15	£5.60
500g	£5.80	£8.05	£8.70
750g	£7.20	£10.70	£11.40
1,000g	£8.60	£13.30	£14.05
2,000g	£13.45	£19.65	£21.40

Printed papers only add £1.15 for Europe, £1.70 for World Zone 1 or £1.90 for World Zone 2 for each additional 250g, or part thereof, up to 5,000g

* Formerly Airmail

SPECIAL DELIVERY SERVICES

INTERNATIONAL TRACKED AND SIGNED FOR SERVICES

There are various services available: *International Tracked & Signed* provides full end-to-end tracking, signature on delivery and online delivery confirmation to 65 destinations; *International Tracked* provides the same, but without a signature on delivery, to 50 destinations; and International Signed is tracked within the UK, a signature is taken on delivery and is available to 170 destinations. All Tracked and Signed For services deliver to Europe within 3–5 working days, and worldwide within 5–7 working days. Proof of posting and compensation up to £50 is provided as standard. Additional compensation up to £250 can be provided for an extra fee.

SAME DAY

A courier service which provides same day delivery of urgent items in most places in the UK. With collection within the hour of booking, satellite tracking, delivery confirmation and automatic compensation up to £2,500, and for an additional fee, up to £10,000, the service is charged for on a loaded mile basis T 0330-088 5522

SIGNED FOR

A service which offers proof of delivery including a signature from the receiver and compensation cover up to £50. The first

class service is delivered the next working day and prices vary from £1.75 to £34.40 depending on the size and weight of the item. The second class service allows two to three working days for delivery with charges of £1.66 to £29.55.

SPECIAL DELIVERY GUARANTEED

A guaranteed next working day delivery service by 9am or 1pm with a refund option guaranteed for late delivery. With many options available, Royal Mail offers a full list of prices online W www.royalmail.com/personal/uk-delivery/special-delivery

OTHER SERVICES

KEEPSAFE

Mail is held for up to two months while the addressee is away, and is delivered when the addressee returns. Prices start at £14.00 for 17 days up to £45.30 for 66 days.

PASSPORT CHECK & SEND

For a fee of £9.75 passport applications are checked to ensure they meet the requirements set by HM Passport Office and are dispatched by special delivery. For further information *see* W www.postoffice.co.uk

POST OFFICE BOX

A Post Office (PO) Box provides a short and memorable alternative address. Mail is held at a local delivery office until the addressee is ready to collect it, or delivered to a street address for an extra fee. Prices start at £147.00 for six months or £258.00 for a year or a monthly fee of £28.20.

POSTCODE FINDER

Customers can search an online database to find UK postcodes and addresses. For more information *see* Royal Mail's postcode finder W www.royalmail.com/postcode-finder

REDELIVERY

Customers can request a redelivery of an item for up to 18 days if it was unable to be delivered and the person is unable to collect from the address on the delivery notification card. A 48-hour notice period is required for redelivery. Redelivery can be arranged to the customer's house, an alternative local address or, for a fee of £0.70 payable on collection, to a local post office branch.

REDIRECTION

Customers may arrange the redirection of their mail via post, at the Post Office or online, subject to verification of their identity. The service is available for 0–3 months, 3–6 months or 6–12 months at varying prices depending on the location of delivery. A full price list is available at W www.royalmail.com/personal/receiving-mail/redirection

TRACK AND TRACE

An online service for customers to track the progress of items sent using any special delivery tracked and signed for service. It is accessible from W www.royalmail.com/track-your-item

CONTACTS

Parcelforce Worldwide T 0344-800 4466 W www.parcelforce.com
Post Office enquiries T 0345-611 2970 W www.postoffice.co.uk
Postcode enquiry line T 0906-302 1222/0845-711 1222

TELECOMMUNICATIONS

Mobile network technology has improved dramatically since the launch in 1985 of the first-generation global system for mobile communications (GSM), which offered little or no data capability. In 1992 Vodafone launched a new GSM network, usually referred to as 2G or second generation, which used digital encoding and allowed voice and low-speed data communications. This technology was extended, via the enhanced data transfer rate of 2.5G, to 3G – a family of mobile standards that provide high bandwidth support to applications such as voice- and video-calling, high-speed data transfer, television streaming and full internet access. Most recently, a 4G superfast mobile spectrum was rolled out, which delivers speeds of up to 100 megabits per second (Mbps), allowing for faster download speeds on a range of devices. In February 2015, OFCOM stated that 5G data connections could be available in the UK by 2020.

FOURTH GENERATION (4G) AND WI-FI
In March 2011 OFCOM announced plans for the auction of additional spectrum (the airwaves on which all communications rely) to provide the necessary capacity for 4G technology in the UK. OFCOM originally aimed to begin the auction in early 2012, but following a consultation regarding the proposals in 2011, the auction did not take place until February 2013. The spectrum was auctioned in two bands – 800 MHz and 2.6 GHz – which lie within the 'sweetspot', the frequency in greatest demand. This combination of low and high frequencies provides the potential to cope with high demand of 4G services. The auction raised £2.34bn for HM Treasury, less than the £3.5bn that was forecast by the Office for Budget Responsibility, and considerably less than the 3G auction in 2000 which raised £22bn. The winning bidders for the distribution of 4G mobile broadband were Everything Everywhere (EE), Hutchison 3G UK (3), Niche Spectrum Ventures (a BT subsidiary), Telefonica (O2) and Vodafone.

4G coverage was expected to cover 98 per cent of the UK population indoors and above that when outdoors. However, according to a survey taken by OpenSignal in conjunction with consumer watchdog Which? in April 2017, smartphone users in the UK could only access their 4G network 65 per cent of the time on average. The speeds offered by 4G are approximately four times faster than 3G networks which allows for higher quality and faster streaming of media such as TV and films. The average download speed of 4G across all four network providers is 22Mbps, whereas the figure for 3G is approximately 5Mbps.

EE was the first operator to launch 4G in late 2012 and by April 2013 the service was available in ten cities where the broadband speed was doubled to more than 20Mbps. O2 and Vodafone subsequently launched their 4G networks in late August 2013 while 3 began their service in December 2013. As at April 2017 EE provided the fastest 4G connection with an average download speed of 32Mbps; 3, Vodafone and O2 offered average download speeds of 23Mbps, 18Mbps and 15Mbps respectively.

The number of Wi-Fi hotspots around the world continued to increase in 2016 with approximately 262 million public hotspots available worldwide at the end of the year. There is Wi-Fi access at over 250 London Underground stations, available in ticket halls, corridors and platforms. Additionally Wi-Fi is also available at 79 London Overground stations.

FIXED-LINE SERVICES
The total number of fixed-line services in the UK remained fairly static in 2015 at a total of 33.2 million connections. However, fixed voice call minutes continued to decline, from 80 billion minutes in 2014 to 74 billion minutes in 2015; part of a steady decline from the 141 billion minutes recorded in 2008. Business customers continued to gravitate towards the use of mobile phones, emails and voice over internet protocol (VoIP) as opposed to business lines. Skype remained the most prominent provider of VoIP calls in 2015, despite a decline of 13 per cent in the proportion of VoIP callers choosing Skype as their provider.

The number of fixed broadband connections increased by 1 million from 23.7 in 2014 to 24.7 million in 2015, and the number of superfast connections (speeds of 30Mbps or more) jumped from 7.1 million to 9.2 million. In 2015 the average monthly household cost of telecommunications increased by £2.52 to £82.17 in real terms; this represents 3.5 per cent of total monthly household expenditure, the same proportion as in 2014. The proportion of connections in the UK with a headline speed of 30Mbps or higher increased from 33 per cent in 2014 to 42 per cent in 2015.

MOBILE COMMUNICATIONS
At the end of 2015 the total number of mobile subscriptions in the UK had increased by 1.6 million (1.8 per cent) to 91.5 million since the previous year. The volume of SMS and MMS messages sent continued to decline for the third year in a row, decreasing by 8 billion messages (7.6 per cent) to 101 billion messages in 2015. The decline in text messaging is likely to be a result of the increasing number of smartphones being used for communication, with social media platforms and instant messaging services such as Whatsapp and iMessenger, often pre-installed, providing alternatives to SMS. Total outgoing mobile calls increased by 5 billion minutes (3.9 per cent) in 2015.

By the end of 2015, 39.5 million mobile connections could access 4G, which represented an increase of 15.9 million (67.3 per cent) since the previous year and constituted 46 per cent of all UK mobile connections. 4G coverage continues to vary according to location, with 99.2 per cent of UK premises having outdoor coverage in urban areas, as opposed to 88.9 per cent in rural areas. In terms of retail subscriptions, 2015 saw EE retain their position as the predominant provider of mobile services with a market share of 29 per cent.

MOBILE PHONE USAGE
The mobile phone is the most popular device for using social media among adults (aged 16+) who use any social media during the course of a week. Of the total time spent by all adults on social media in 2016, 50 per cent was on mobile phones, 34 per cent on a computer and 13 per cent on a tablet.

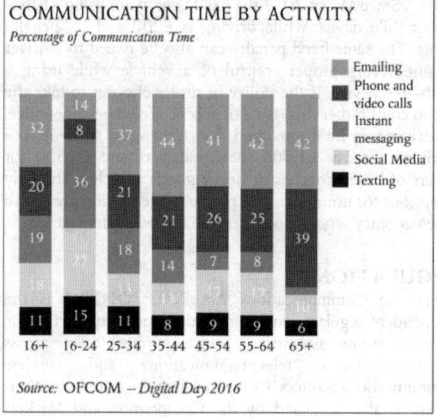

COMMUNICATION TIME BY ACTIVITY
Percentage of Communication Time

Source: OFCOM – Digital Day 2016

FIXED-LINE SERVICES

HEALTH
In 1999 the Independent Expert Group on Mobile Phones (IEGMP) was established to examine the possible effects on health of mobile phones, base stations and transmitters. The main findings of the IEGMP's report *Mobile Phones and Health*, published in May 2000, were:

- exposure to radio frequency radiation below guideline levels did not cause adverse health effects to the general population
- the use of mobile phones by drivers of any vehicle can increase the chance of accidents
- the widespread use of mobile phones by children for non-essential calls should be discouraged because if there are unrecognised adverse health effects children may be more vulnerable
- there is no general risk to the health of people living near to base stations on the basis that exposures are expected to be much lower than guidelines set by the International Commission on Non-Ionising Radiation Protection

The government set up the Mobile Telecommunications Health and Research (MTHR) programme in 2001 to undertake independent research into the possible health risks from mobile telephone technology. The MTHR programme published its report in September 2007 concluding that, in the short term, neither mobile phones nor base stations have been found to be associated with any biological or adverse health effects. An international cohort study into the possible long-term health effects of mobile phone use was launched by the MTHR in April 2010. The study is known as COSMOS and aims to follow the health of 250,000 mobile phone users from five countries over 20 to 30 years. Details of the study can be found on the COSMOS website (W www.ukcosmos.org).

A national measurement programme, to ensure that emissions from mobile phone base stations do not exceed the ICNIRP guideline levels, is overseen by OFCOM and annual audits of these levels can be found on the sitefinder part of its website. The Health Protection Agency (HPA), part of Public Health England from 1 April 2013, is responsible for providing information and advice in relation to the health effects of electromagnetic fields, including those emitted from mobile phones and base stations. In April 2012, the HPA's independent Advisory Group on Non-ionising Radiation published a report concluding that there was no convincing evidence that mobile phone technologies cause adverse effects on human health.

SAFETY WHILE DRIVING

Under legislation that came into effect in December 2003 it is illegal for drivers to use a hand-held mobile phone while driving. Since March 2017 the fixed penalty for using a hand-held mobile device while driving is £200 and six penalty points. The same fixed penalty can also be issued to a driver for not having proper control of a vehicle while using a hands-free device. If the police or driver chooses to take the case to court rather than issue or accept a fixed penalty notice, the driver may be disqualified from driving in addition to a maximum fine of £1,000 for car drivers and £2,500 for drivers of buses, coaches or heavy goods vehicles. The only exceptions for using a mobile phone while driving are to call the emergency services, or when the driver is safely parked.

REGULATION

Under the Communications Act 2003, OFCOM is the independent regulator and competition authority for the UK communications industries, with responsibilities across television, radio, telecommunications and wireless communications services. Competition in the communications market is also regulated by the Competition and Markets Authority, although OFCOM takes the lead in competition investigations in the UK market. The Competition Appeal Tribunal hears appeals against OFCOM's decisions.

CONTACTS

OFCOM, Riverside House, 2A Southwark Bridge Road, London SE1 9HA T 020-7981 3000 W www.ofcom.org.uk

INTERNET

As at August 2016, 81 per cent of UK adults (aged 16+) said they had broadband internet access at home, representing no change since 2015. Internet usage varies significantly according to age group, with 97 per cent of those aged 16 to 24 reporting they used the internet, as opposed to only 42 per cent of those aged over 75.

In terms of internet activity in 2016, 67 per cent of those who use the internet either at home or elsewhere stated they purchased items online; this was an increase of 5 per cent since 2015. Relatedly, 42 per cent of internet users claimed to use the same password for most, if not all websites.

In 2016, those aged 16 to 24 spent 27 per cent of their communication time on social networking sites, as opposed to using emails or phone calls. This is higher than for any other age group, and the average of 18 per cent for UK adults as a whole.

The youngest demographic represented, aged 16 to 24, were proportionally the largest users of many of the available internet activities, due to their familiarity with internet usage from an early age. This age group were most likely to engage in online activities including social networking, blogging, or downloading games, films or music. Those aged 25 to 34 engaged in more established activities such as personal banking and shopping.

The most visited search engine in March 2016 was Google with a digital audience of 39.3 million across all platforms, followed by Bing and Yahoo. For the same period in the UK, the most used online news outlet was the BBC, with an online audience of 27.6 million – the total UK audience is 50.3 million.

Posting photos on social media is an increasingly popular activity. A third of those who accessed the internet via mobile phone in April 2016 had deposited photos on one or more social media platforms.

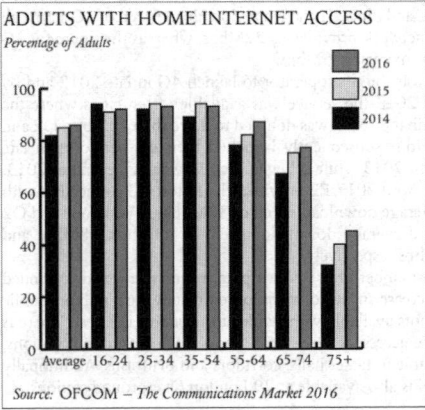

ADULTS WITH HOME INTERNET ACCESS
Percentage of Adults

Legend: 2016, 2015, 2014

Categories: Average, 16-24, 25-34, 35-54, 55-64, 65-74, 75+

Source: OFCOM – *The Communications Market 2016*

GLOSSARY OF TERMS

The following is a list of selected internet terms. It is by no means exhaustive but is intended to cover those that the average computer user might encounter.

BANNER AD: An advertisement on a web page that links to a corresponding website when clicked.

BLOG: Short for 'web log' – an online personal journal that is frequently updated and intended to be read by the public. Blogs are kept by 'bloggers' and are commonly available as RSS feeds.

BOOKMARKS: A method of storing links or automatic pathways within web browsers which allow a user to quickly return to a webpage. Referred to as 'Favourites' in Internet Explorer.

BROWSER: Typically refers to a 'web browser' program that allows a computer user to view web page content on their computer, eg Firefox, Internet Explorer or Safari.

CLICK-THROUGH: The number of times a web user 'clicks through' a paid advertisement link to the corresponding website.

CLOUD COMPUTING: The use of IT resources as an on-demand service across a network; through cloud computing, software, advanced computation and archived information can be accessed remotely, without the user needing local dedicated hardware.

COOKIE: A piece of information placed on a user's hard disk by a web server. Cookies contain data about the user's activity on a website, and are returned to the server whenever a browser makes further requests. They are important for remembering information such as login and registration details, 'shopping cart' data, user preferences etc, and are often set to expire after a fixed period.

DOMAIN: A set of words or letters, separated by dots, used to identify an internet server, eg
www.whitakersalmanack.com
where 'www' denotes a web (http) server, 'whitakersalmanack' denotes the organisation name and 'com' denotes that the organisation is a company.FIREWALL: A protection system designed to prevent unauthorised access to or from a private network.

FTP: File Transfer Protocol – a set of network rules enabling a user to exchange files with a remote server.

HACKER: A person who attempts to break or 'hack' into websites. Motives typically involve the desire to procure personal information such as addresses, passwords or credit card details. Hackers may also delete code or incorporate traces of malicious code to damage the functionality of a website.

HIT: A single request from a web browser for a single item from a web server. In order for a web browser to display a page that contains three graphics, four 'hits' would occur at the server: one for the HTML page and one for each of the three graphics. Therefore the number of hits on a website is not synonymous with the number of visitors.

HTML: HyperText Mark-up Language – a programming language used to denote or mark up how an internet page should be presented to a user from an HTTP server via a web browser.

HTTP: HyperText Transfer Protocol – an internet protocol whereby a web server sends web pages, images and files to a web browser.

HYPERLINK: A piece of specially coded text that users can click on to navigate to the web page, or element of a web page, associated with that link's code. Links are typically distinguished through the use of bold, underlined or differently coloured text.

JAVA: A programming language used widely on the internet.

MALWARE: A combination of the words 'malicious' and 'software'. Malware is software designed with the intention of infiltrating a computer and damaging its system.

OPEN-SOURCE: Describes a computer program that has its source code (the instructions that make up a program) freely available for viewing and modification.

PAGERANK: A link analysis algorithm used by search engines that assigns a numerical value based on a website's relevance and reputation. In general, a site with a higher pagerank has more traffic than a site with a lower one.

PHISHING: The fraudulent practice of sending emails to acquire personal information by masquerading as a legitimate company.

PODCAST: A form of audio and video broadcasting using the internet. Although the word is a portmanteau of 'iPod' and broadcasting, podcasting does not require the use of an iPod. A podcaster creates a list of files and makes it available in the RSS 2.0 format. The list can then be obtained using podcast 'retriever' software which makes the files available to digital devices (including iPods); users may then listen or watch at their convenience.

RSS FEED: Rich Site Summary or RDF Site Summary or Real Simple Syndication – a commonly used protocol for syndication and sharing of content, originally developed to facilitate the syndication of news articles, now widely used to share the content of blogs.

SEO: Search engine optimisation – the process of optimising the content of a web page to ensure that it is indexed by search engines.

SERVER: A node on a network that provides service to the terminals on the network. These computers have higher hardware specifications, ie more resources and greater speed, in order to handle large amounts of data.

SOCIAL NETWORKING: The practice of using a web-hosted service such as Facebook or Twitter to upload and share content and build friendship networks.

SPAM: A term used for unsolicited, generally junk, email.

TRAFFIC: The number of visitors to a website.

TWITTER: An online microblogging service that allows users to stay connected through the exchange of 140-character posts, known as 'tweets'.

URL: Uniform Resource Locator – address of a file accessible on the internet, eg http://www.whitakersalmanack.com

USER-GENERATED CONTENT (UGC): Refers to various media content produced or primarily influenced by end-users, as opposed to traditional media producers such as licensed broadcasters and production companies. These forms of media include digital video, blogging, podcasting, mobile phone photography and wikis.

CONSERVATION AND HERITAGE

NATIONAL PARKS

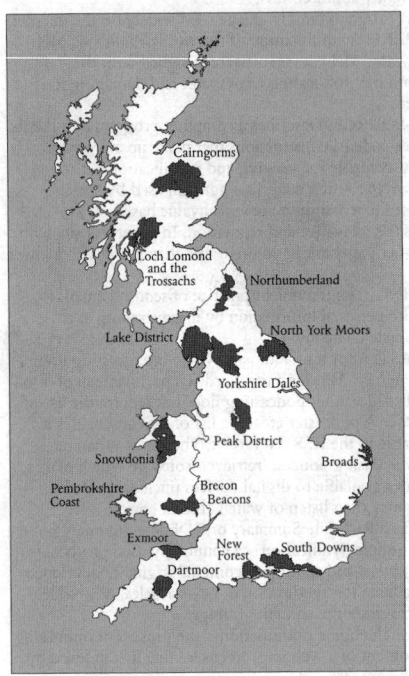

ENGLAND AND WALES

There are nine national parks in England, and three in Wales. In addition, the Norfolk and Suffolk Broads are considered to have equivalent status to a national park. Under the National Parks and Access to the Countryside Act 1949, as clarified by the Natural Environment and Rural Communities Act 2006, the two purposes of the national parks are to conserve and enhance the parks' natural beauty, wildlife and cultural heritage, and to promote opportunities for the understanding and enjoyment of the special qualities of national parks by the public. If there is a conflict between the two purposes, then conservation takes precedence.

Natural England is the statutory body that has the power to designate national parks in England, and Natural Resources Wales (formerly Countryside Council for Wales) is responsible for national parks in Wales. Designations in England are confirmed by the Secretary of State for Environment, Food and Rural Affairs and those in Wales by the Welsh government. The designation of a national park does not affect the ownership of the land or remove the rights of the local community. The majority of the land in the national parks is owned by private landowners (around 75 per cent) or by bodies such as the National Trust and the Forestry Commission. The national park authorities own only a small percentage of the land themselves.

The Environment Act 1995 replaced the existing national park boards and committees with free-standing national park authorities (NPAs). NPAs are the sole local planning authorities for their areas and as such influence land use and development, and deal with planning applications. NPAs are responsible for carrying out the statutory purposes of national parks stated above.

In pursuing these purposes they have a statutory duty to seek to foster the economic and social well-being of the communities within national parks. The NPAs publish management plans setting out overarching policies for their area and appoint their own officers and staff.

The Broads Authority was established under the Norfolk and Suffolk Broads Act 1988 and meets the requirement for the authority to have a navigation function in addition to a regard for the needs of agriculture, forestry and the economic and social interests of those who live or work in the Broads.

MEMBERSHIP

Membership of English NPAs comprises local authority appointees, members directly appointed by the Secretary of State for Environment, Food and Rural Affairs and members appointed by the secretary after consultation with local parishes. Under the Natural Environment and Rural Communities Act 2006 every district, county or unitary authority with land in a national park is entitled to appoint at least one member unless it chooses to opt out. The total number of local authority and parish members must exceed the number of national members.

Northumberland, Pembrokeshire Coast and Snowdonia NPAs have 18 members; Dartmoor has 19; the Lake District and North York Moors have 20; the Broads has 21; Exmoor, the New Forest 22; Brecon Beacons 24; Yorkshire Dales 25; South Downs 27; and the Peak District 30.

In Wales, two-thirds of NPA members are appointed by the constituent local authorities and one-third by the Welsh government, advised by Natural Resources Wales.

FUNDING

Core funding for the English NPAs and the Broads Authority is provided by central government through the Department for Environment, Food and Rural Affairs (DEFRA) National Park Grant.

In Wales, the three national parks are funded by the Welsh government and their constituent local authorities. Total budgeted revenue expenditure for 2016–17 is £13.8m.

All NPAs and the Broads Authority can take advantage of grants from other bodies including lottery and European grants.

The national parks (with date that designation was confirmed) are:

BRECON BEACONS (1957), Powys (66 per cent)/ Carmarthenshire/Rhondda, Cynon and Taff/Merthyr Tydfil/Blaenau Gwent/Monmouthshire, 1,344 sq. km/ 519 sq. miles – The park is centred on the Brecon Beacons mountain range, which includes the three highest mountains in southern Britain (Pen y Fan, Corn Du and Cribyn), but also includes the valleys of the rivers Usk and Wye, the Black Mountains to the east and the Black Mountain to the west. There are information centres at Abergavenny and Llandovery.
National Park Authority, Plas y Ffynnon, Cambrian Way, Brecon, Powys LD3 7HP **T** 01874-624437 **W** www.beacons-npa.gov.uk
Chief Executive, John Cook

BROADS (1989), Norfolk/Suffolk, 303 sq. km/117 sq. miles – The Broads is located between Norwich and Great Yarmouth on the flood plains of the six rivers flowing through the area to the sea. The area is one of fens, winding waterways, woodland and marsh. The 60 or so broads are man-made, and many are connected to the rivers by dykes, providing over 200km (125 miles) of navigable waterways. There are information centres at Hoveton, Whitlingham Country Park and How Hill National Nature Reserve. There are yacht stations at Norwich, Reedham and Great Yarmouth.

Broads Authority, Yare House, 62–64 Thorpe Road, Norwich
NR1 1RY **T** 01603-610734 **W** www.VisitTheBroads.co.uk
Chief Executive, Dr John Packman

DARTMOOR (1951), Devon, 953 sq. km / 368 sq. miles –
The park consists of moorland and rocky granite tors, and
is rich in prehistoric remains. There are visitor centres at
Haytor, Princetown (main visitor centre) and Postbridge.
National Park Authority, Parke, Bovey Tracey, Devon TQ13 9JQ
T 01626-832093 **E** hq@dartmoor.gov.uk
W www.dartmoor.gov.uk
Chief Executive, Kevin Bishop

EXMOOR (1954), Somerset (71 per cent)/Devon,
694 sq. km / 268 sq. miles – Exmoor is a moorland
plateau inhabited by wild Exmoor ponies and red deer.
There are many ancient remains and burial mounds. There
are national park centres at Dunster, Dulverton and
Lynmouth.
National Park Authority, Exmoor House, Dulverton, Somerset
TA22 9HL **T** 01398-323665 **E** info@exmoor-nationalpark.gov.uk
W www.exmoor-nationalpark.gov.uk
Chief Executive, Sarah Bryan

LAKE DISTRICT (1951), Cumbria, 2,362 sq. km / 912 sq.
miles – The Lake District includes England's highest
mountains (Scafell Pike, Helvellyn and Skiddaw) but it is
most famous for its glaciated lakes. There are national
park information centres at Bowness-on-Windermere,
Keswick, Ullswater and a visitor centre at Brockhole,
Windermere.
National Park Authority, Murley Moss, Oxenholme Road,
Kendal, Cumbria LA9 7RL **T** 01539-724555
E hq@lakedistrict.gov.uk **W** www.lakedistrict.gov.uk
Chief Executive, Richard Leafe

NEW FOREST (2005), Hampshire, 570 sq. km / 220 sq.
miles – The forest has been protected since 1079 when it
was declared a royal hunting forest. The area consists of
forest, ancient woodland, heathland, farmland, coastal
saltmarsh and mudflats. Much of the forest is managed by
the Forestry Commission, which provides several
campsites.
National Park Authority, Town Hall, Avenue Road, Lymington,
Hants SO41 9ZG **T** 01590-646600
E enquiries@newforestnpa.gov.uk **W** www.newforestnpa.gov.uk
Chief Executive, Alison Barnes

NORTH YORK MOORS (1952), North Yorkshire (96 per
cent)/Redcar and Cleveland, 1,434 sq. km / 554 sq. miles
– The park consists of dales woodland, moorland and
coast, and includes the Hambleton Hills and the
Cleveland Way. There are visitor centres at Danby and
Sutton Bank.
National Park Authority, The Old Vicarage, Bondgate, Helmsley,
York YO62 5BP **T** 01439-772700
E general@northyorkmoors.org.uk
W www.northyorkmoors.org.uk
Chief Executive, Andy Wilson

NORTHUMBERLAND (1956), Northumberland,
1,048 sq. km / 404 sq. miles – The park is an area of hill
country, comprising open moorland, blanket bogs and
very small patches of ancient woodland, stretching from
Hadrian's Wall to the Scottish border. There is an
information centre at Once Brewed.
National Park Authority, Eastburn, South Park, Hexham,
Northumberland NE46 1BS **T** 01434-605555
E enquiries@nnpa.org.uk
W www.northumberlandnationalpark.org.uk
Chief Executive, Tony Gates

PEAK DISTRICT (1951), Derbyshire (64 per cent)/
Staffordshire/South Yorkshire/Cheshire/West
Yorkshire/Greater Manchester, 1,437 sq. km / 555 sq.
miles – The Peak District includes the gritstone moors of
the Dark Peak, the limestone dales of the White Peak and
the crags and rolling farmland of the South West Peak.
There are information centres at Bakewell, Castleton,
Edale and Upper Derwent.
National Park Authority, Aldern House, Baslow Road, Bakewell,
Derbyshire DE45 1AE **T** 01629-816200
E customer.service@peakdistrict.gov.uk
W www.peakdistrict.gov.uk
Chief Executive, Sarah Fowler

PEMBROKESHIRE COAST (1952 and 1995),
Pembrokeshire, 621 sq. km / 236 sq. miles – The park
includes cliffs, moorland and a number of islands,
including Skomer and Ramsey, and the 186-mile
Pembrokeshire Coast Path National Trail. There is an
information centre in Newport and a gallery and visitor
centre, Oriel y Parc, in St Davids. The park also manages
Castell Henllys Iron Age Village, Carew Castle and Tidal
Mill.
National Park Authority, Llanion Park, Pembroke Dock,
Pembrokeshire SA72 6DY **T** 01606-624800
E info@pembrokeshirecoast.org.uk
W www.pembrokeshirecoast.wales
Chief Executive, Tegryn Jones

SNOWDONIA/ERYRI (1951), Gwynedd/Conwy,
2,176 sq. km / 840 sq. miles – Snowdonia, which takes its
name from Snowdon, is an area of deep valleys and
rugged mountains. There are information centres at
Aberdyfi, Beddgelert, Betws y Coed and Dolgellau.
National Park Authority, Penrhyndeudraeth, Gwynedd LL48 6LF
T 01766-770274 **E** parc@eyri-npa.gov.uk
W www.eyri-npa.gov.uk
Chief Executive, Emyr Williams

THE SOUTH DOWNS (2010), West Sussex/
Hampshire,1,624 sq. km / 627 sq. miles – The South
Downs contains a diversity of natural habitats, including
flower-studded chalk grassland, ancient woodland, flood
meadow, lowland heath and rare chalk heathland. There
are visitor centres at Beachy Head, Queen Elizabeth
Country Park in Hampshire and Seven Sisters Country
Park in East Sussex.
National Park Authority, North Street, Midhurst, W. Sussex
GU29 9DH **T** 01730-814810 **W** www.southdowns.gov.uk
Chief Executive, Trevor Beattie

YORKSHIRE DALES (1954), North Yorkshire (71 per
cent)/Cumbria (28 per cent)/Lancashire (1 per cent),
2,179 sq. km / 841 sq. miles – The Yorkshire Dales is
composed primarily of limestone overlaid in places by
millstone grit. The three peaks of Ingleborough,
Whernside and Pen-y-ghent are within the park. There
are information centres at Grassington, Hawes, Aysgarth
Falls, Malham and Reeth.
National Park Authority, Yoredale, Bainbridge, Leyburn, N.
Yorks DL8 3EL **T** 0300-456 0030 **E** info@yorkshiredales.org.uk
W www.yorkshiredales.org.uk
Chief Executive, David Butterworth

SCOTLAND

On 9 August 2000 the national parks (Scotland) bill received
royal assent, giving parliament the ability to create national
parks in Scotland. The Act gives Scottish parks wider powers
than in England and Wales, including statutory responsibilities
for the local economy and rural communities. The board of the
Cairngorms NPA comprises 19 members; seven appointed by
the Scottish ministers, a further seven nominated to the board
by the five local authorities in the park area and five locally
elected members. The board of Loch Lomond and the
Trossachs NPA comprises 17 members; five elected by the
community and 12 appointed by Scottish Ministers, six of
whom are nominated by local authorities. In Scotland, the
national parks are central government bodies and are wholly
funded by the Scottish government. The draft budget for
2017–18 totalled £12.4m.

CAIRNGORMS (2003), North-East Scotland, 4,528 sq. km/1,748 sq. miles – The Cairngorms national park is the largest in the UK, covering around 6 per cent of Scotland. It displays a vast collection of landforms, including five of the six highest mountains in the UK and contains 25 per cent of Britain's threatened species. The near natural woodlands contain remnants of the original ancient Caledonian pine forest. There are nine visitor centres within the park.
National Park Authority, 14 The Square, Grantown-on-Spey, Morayshire PH26 3HG T 01479-873535
E enquiries@cairngorms.co.uk W www.cairngorms.co.uk
Chief Executive, Grant Moir

LOCH LOMOND AND THE TROSSACHS (2002), Argyll and Bute/Perth and Kinross/Stirling/West Dunbartonshire, 1,865 sq. km/720 sq. miles – The park boundaries encompass lochs, rivers, forests, 21 mountains above 914m (3,000ft) including Ben More and a further 19 mountains between 762m (2,500ft) and 914m (3,000ft). There is a national park centre in Balmaha. There are also seven visitor centres administered by VisitScotland.
National Park Authority, Carrochan, Carrochan Road, Balloch G83 8EG T 01389-722600 E info@lochlomond-trossachs.org
W www.lochlomond-trossachs.org
Chief Executive, Gordon Watson

NORTHERN IRELAND

There is a power to designate national parks in Northern Ireland under the Nature Conservation and Amenity Lands Order (Northern Ireland) 1985, but there are currently no national parks in Northern Ireland.

AREAS OF OUTSTANDING NATURAL BEAUTY

ENGLAND AND WALES

Under the National Parks and Access to the Countryside Act 1949, provision was made for the designation of areas of outstanding natural beauty (AONBs). Natural England is responsible for AONBs in England and Natural Resources Wales for the Welsh AONBs. Designations in England are confirmed by the Secretary of State for Environment, Food and Rural Affairs and those in Wales by the Welsh government. The Countryside and Rights of Way (CROW) Act 2000 placed greater responsibility on local authorities to protect AONBs and made it a statutory duty for relevant authorities to produce a management plan for their AONB area. The CROW Act also provided for the creation of conservation boards for larger and more complex AONBs.

The primary objective of the AONB designation is to conserve and enhance the natural beauty of the area. Where an AONB has a conservation board, it has the additional purpose of increasing public understanding and enjoyment of the special qualities of the area; the board has greater weight should there be a conflict of interests between the two. In addition, the board is also required to foster the economic and social well-being of the local communities but without incurring significant expenditure in doing so. Overall responsibility for AONBs lies with the relevant local authorities or conservation board. To coordinate planning and management responsibilities between local authorities in whose area they fall, AONBs are overseen by a joint advisory committee (or similar body) which includes representatives from the local authorities, landowners, farmers, residents and conservation and recreation groups. Core funding for AONBs is provided by central government through DEFRA, local authorities and Natural Resources Wales.

The 38 AONBs (with date designation confirmed) are:

ARNSIDE AND SILVERDALE (1972), Cumbria/Lancashire, 75 sq. km/29 sq. miles

BLACKDOWN HILLS (1991), Devon/Somerset, 370 sq. km/143 sq. miles

CANNOCK CHASE (1958), Staffordshire, 68 sq. km/26 sq. miles

CHICHESTER HARBOUR (1964), Hampshire/West Sussex, 74 sq. km/29 sq. miles

CHILTERNS (1965; extended 1990), Bedfordshire/Buckinghamshire/Herefordshire/Oxfordshire, 839 sq. km/324 sq. miles

CLWYDIAN RANGE AND DEE VALLEY (1985; extended 2011), Denbighshire/Flintshire, 389 sq. km/150 sq. miles

CORNWALL (1959; Camel Estuary 1983), 958 sq. km/370 sq. miles

COTSWOLDS (1966; extended 1990), Gloucestershire/Oxfordshire/Warwickshire/Wiltshire/Worcestershire, 2,046 sq. km/790 sq. miles

CRANBORNE CHASE AND WEST WILTSHIRE DOWNS (1983), Dorset/Hampshire/Somerset/Wiltshire, 983 sq. km/380 sq. miles

DEDHAM VALE (1970; extended 1978, 1991), Essex/Suffolk, 90 sq. km/35 sq. miles

DORSET (1959), Dorset/Somerset, 1,129 sq. km/436 sq. miles

EAST DEVON (1963), 268 sq. km/103 sq. miles

FOREST OF BOWLAND (1964), Lancashire/North Yorkshire, 803 sq. km/310 sq. miles

GOWER (1956), Swansea, 188 sq. km/73 sq. miles

HIGH WEALD (1983), East Sussex/Kent/Surrey/West Sussex, 1,461 sq. km/564 sq. miles

HOWARDIAN HILLS (1987), North Yorkshire, 204 sq. km/79 sq. miles

ISLE OF WIGHT (1963), 189 sq. km/73 sq. miles

ISLES OF SCILLY (1976), 16 sq. km/6 sq. miles

KENT DOWNS (1968), 878 sq. km/339 sq. miles

LINCOLNSHIRE WOLDS (1973), 558 sq. km/215 sq. miles

LLYN (1957), Gwynedd, 155 sq. km/60 sq. miles

MALVERN HILLS (1959), Gloucestershire/Worcestershire, 105 sq. km/41 sq. miles

MENDIP HILLS (1972; extended 1989), Somerset, 198 sq. km/76 sq. miles

NIDDERDALE (1994), North Yorkshire, 603 sq. km/233 sq. miles

NORFOLK COAST (1968), 451 sq. km/174 sq. miles

NORTH DEVON (1960), 171 sq. km/66 sq. miles

NORTH PENNINES (1988), Cumbria/Durham/North Yorkshire/Northumberland, 1,983 sq. km/766 sq. miles

NORTH WESSEX DOWNS (1972), Hampshire/Oxfordshire/Wiltshire, 1,730 sq. km/668 sq. miles

NORTHUMBERLAND COAST (1958), 138 sq. km/64 sq. miles

QUANTOCK HILLS (1957), Somerset, 99 sq. km/38 sq. miles

SHROPSHIRE HILLS (1959), 804 sq. km/310 sq. miles

SOLWAY COAST (1964), Cumbria, 115 sq. km/44 sq. miles

SOUTH DEVON (1960), 337 sq. km/130 sq. miles

SUFFOLK COAST AND HEATHS (1970), 403 sq. km/156 sq. miles

SURREY HILLS (1958), 419 sq. km/162 sq. miles

TAMAR VALLEY (1995), Cornwall/Devon, 190 sq. km/73 sq. miles

WYE VALLEY (1971), Gloucestershire/Herefordshire/Monmouthshire, 326 sq. km/126 sq. miles

YNYS MON (ISLE OF ANGLESEY) (1967), 221 sq. km/85 sq. miles

NORTHERN IRELAND

The Department of the Environment for Northern Ireland, with advice from the Council for Nature Conservation and the Countryside, designates AONBs in Northern Ireland. Dates given are those of designation.

ANTRIM COAST AND GLENS (1988), Co. Antrim, 725 sq. km/280 sq. miles

BINEVENAGH (2006), Co. Londonderry, 166 sq. km/64 sq. miles

CAUSEWAY COAST (1989), Co. Antrim, 42 sq. km/ 16 sq. miles

LAGAN VALLEY (1965), Co. Down, 39 sq. km/15 sq. miles

MOURNE (1986), Co. Down, 580 sq. km/224 sq. miles

RING OF GULLION (1991), Co. Armagh, 153 sq. km/59 sq. miles

SPERRIN (1968; extended 2008), Co. Tyrone/Co. Londonderry, 1,182 sq. km/456 sq. miles

STRANGFORD LOUGH AND LECALE (2010), Co. Down, 528 sq. km/204 sq. miles

NATIONAL SCENIC AREAS

In Scotland, national scenic areas have a broadly equivalent status to AONBs. Scottish Natural Heritage recognises areas of national scenic significance. As at June 2017, there were 40, covering a land area of 1,021,600 hectares (2,524,400 acres) and a marine area of 359,500 hectares (888,300 acres).

Development within national scenic areas is dealt with by local authorities, who are required to consult Scottish Natural Heritage concerning certain categories of development. Disagreements between Scottish Natural Heritage and local authorities are referred to the Scottish government. Land management uses can also be modified in the interest of scenic conservation.

ASSYNT-COIGACH, Highland, 90,200ha/222,884 acres

BEN NEVIS AND GLEN COE, Highland, 101,600ha/251,053 acres

CAIRNGORM MOUNTAINS, Highland/Aberdeenshire/Moray, 67,200ha/166,051 acres

CUILLIN HILLS, Highland, 21,900ha/54,115 acres

DEESIDE AND LOCHNAGAR, Aberdeenshire, 40,000ha/98,840 acres

DORNOCH FIRTH, Highland, 7,500ha/18,532 acres

EAST STEWARTRY COAST, Dumfries and Galloway, 4,500ha/11,119 acres

EILDON AND LEADERFOOT, Borders, 3,600ha/8,896 acres

FLEET VALLEY, Dumfries and Galloway, 5,300ha/13,096 acres

GLEN AFFRIC, Highland, 19,300ha/47,690 acres

GLEN STRATHFARRAR, Highland, 3,800ha/9,390 acres

HOY AND WEST MAINLAND, Orkney Islands, 14,800ha/36,571 acres

JURA, Argyll and Bute, 21,800ha/53,868 acres

KINTAIL, Highland, 15,500ha/38,300 acres

KNAPDALE, Argyll and Bute, 19,800ha/48,926 acres

KNOYDART, Highland, 39,500ha/97,604 acres

KYLE OF TONGUE, Highland, 18,500ha/45,713 acres

KYLES OF BUTE, Argyll and Bute, 4,400ha/10,872 acres

LOCH LOMOND, Argyll and Bute, 27,400ha/67,705 acres

LOCH NA KEAL, Mull, Argyll and Bute, 12,700ha/31,382 acres

LOCH RANNOCH AND GLEN LYON, Perthshire and Kinross, 48,400ha/119,596 acres

LOCH SHIEL, Highland, 13,400ha/33,111 acres

LOCH TUMMEL, Perthshire and Kinross, 9,200ha/22,733 acres

LYNN OF LORN, Argyll and Bute, 4,800ha/11,861 acres

MORAR, MOIDART AND ARDNAMURCHAN, Highland, 13,500ha/33,358 acres

NITH ESTUARY, Dumfries and Galloway, 9,300ha/22,980 acres

NORTH ARRAN, North Ayrshire, 23,800ha/58,810 acres

NORTH-WEST SUTHERLAND, Highland, 20,500ha/50,655 acres

RIVER EARN, Perthshire and Kinross, 3,000ha/7,413 acres

RIVER TAY, Perthshire and Kinross, 5,600ha/13,838 acres

ST KILDA, Eilean Siar (Western Isles), 900ha/2,224 acres

SCARBA, LUNGA AND THE GARVELLACHS, Argyll and Bute, 1,900ha/4,695 acres

SHETLAND, Shetland Isles, 11,600ha/28,664 acres

SMALL ISLANDS, Highland, 15,500ha/38,300 acres

SOUTH LEWIS, HARRIS AND NORTH UIST, Eilean Siar (Western Isles), 109,600ha/270,822 acres

SOUTH UIST MACHAIR, Eilean Siar (Western Isles), 6,100ha/15,073 acres

THE TROSSACHS, Stirling, 4,600ha/11,367 acres

TROTTERNISH, Highland, 5,000ha/12,355 acres

UPPER TWEEDDALE, Borders, 10,500ha/25,945 acres

WESTER ROSS, Highland, 145,300ha/359,036 acres

THE NATIONAL FOREST

The National Forest is one of the UK's biggest environmental projects, creating a forest across 518.5 sq. km (200.2 sq. miles) of Derbyshire, Leicestershire and Staffordshire. Since the early 1990s, more than 8.5 million trees have been planted to create over 6,700ha of new woodland landscapes. Forest cover has increased from 6 per cent to 20 per cent, with the aim of eventually covering approximately one-third of the designated area.

Since its establishment in 1995, the National Forest leads the project and is responsible for delivery of the government-approved National Forest Strategy, sponsored by DEFRA. Priorities include continued forest creation and management, economic development of the area for recreation and tourism, and engaging local communities in the forest to improve quality of life.

NATIONAL FOREST COMPANY, Bath Yard, Moira, Swadlincote, Derbyshire DE12 6BA T 01283-551211 E enquiries@nationalforest.org W www.nationalforest.org

Chief Executive, John Everitt

SITES OF SPECIAL SCIENTIFIC INTEREST

Site of Special Scientific Interest (SSSI) is a legal notification applied to land in England, Scotland or Wales which Natural England (NE), Scottish Natural Heritage (SNH) or the Natural Resources Wales (NRW) identifies as being of special interest because of its flora, fauna, geological, geomorphological or physiographical features. In some cases, SSSIs are managed as nature reserves.

NE, SNH and NRW must notify the designation of an SSSI to the local planning authority, every owner/occupier of the land, and the environment secretary, the Scottish ministers or the National Assembly for Wales. The Environment Agency (in England), water companies and internal drainage authorities and a number of other interested parties are also formally notified.

Objections to the notification of an SSSI can be made and ultimately considered at a full meeting of the board of NE or, in Wales, a subgroup of the NRW board. In Scotland an objection will be dealt with by the main board of SNH or an appropriate subgroup.

The protection of these sites depends on the cooperation of individual landowners and occupiers. Owner/occupiers must consult NE, SNH or NRW and gain written consent before they can undertake certain listed activities on the site. Funds are available through management agreements and grants to assist owners and occupiers in conserving sites' interests. Sites can also be protected by management schemes, management notices and other enforcement mechanisms. As a last resort a site can be purchased.

SSSIs in Britain as at June 2017:

	Number	Hectares	Acres
England	4,123	1,093,315	2,701,636
Scotland	1,423	1,022,393	2,526,388
Wales	1,067	261,267	645,605

NORTHERN IRELAND

In Northern Ireland 360 areas of special scientific interest (ASSIs) have been declared by the Department of the Environment for Northern Ireland.

NATIONAL NATURE RESERVES

National Nature Reserves are defined in the National Parks and Access to the Countryside Act 1949 as modified by the Natural Environment and Rural Communities Act 2006. National Nature Reserves may be managed solely for the purpose of conservation, or for both the purposes of conservation and recreation, providing this does not compromise the conservation purpose.

NE, SNH or NRW can declare as a national nature reserve land which is held and managed as a nature reserve under an agreement; land held and managed by NE, SNH or NRW; or land held and managed as a nature reserve by an approved body. NE, SNH or NRW can make by-laws to protect reserves from undesirable activities; these are subject to confirmation by the Secretary of State for Environment, Food and Rural Affairs, the National Assembly for Wales or the Scottish ministers.

National nature reserves in Britain as at June 2017:

	Number	Hectares	Acres
England	224	94,563	233,670
Scotland	41	119,112	294,332
Wales	76	26,127	64,561

NORTHERN IRELAND

Nature reserves are established and managed by the Department of the Environment for Northern Ireland, with advice from the Council for Nature Conservation and the Countryside. Nature reserves are declared under the Nature Conservation and Amenity Lands (Northern Ireland) Order 1985; to date, 47 nature reserves have been declared.

LOCAL NATURE RESERVES

Local Nature Reserves are defined in the National Parks and Access to the Countryside Act 1949 (as amended by the Natural Environment and Rural Communities Act 2006) as land designated for the study and preservation of flora and fauna, or of geological or physiographical features. Local Nature Reserves also have a statutory obligation to provide opportunities for the enjoyment of nature or open air recreation, providing this does not compromise the conservation purpose of the reserve. Local authorities in England, Scotland and Wales have the power to acquire, declare and manage reserves in consultation with NE, SNH and NRW. There is similar legislation in Northern Ireland, where the consulting organisation is the Environment Agency.

Any organisation, such as water companies, educational trusts, local amenity groups and charitable nature conservation bodies, such as wildlife trusts, may manage local nature reserves, provided that a local authority has a legal interest in the land. This means that the local authority must either own it, lease it or have a management agreement with the landowner.

Designated local nature reserves in Britain as at June 2017:

	Number	Hectares	Acres
England	1,612	41,661	102,946
Scotland	74	10,777	26,631
Wales	95	6,187	15,288

There are 24 local nature reserves in Northern Ireland.

FOREST RESERVES

The Forestry Commission is the government department responsible for forestry policy throughout Great Britain. Forestry is a devolved matter, with the separate Forestry Commissions for England, Scotland and Wales reporting directly to their appropriate minister. The equivalent body in Northern Ireland is the Forest Service, an agency of the Department of Agriculture and Rural Development for Northern Ireland. The Forestry Commission in each country is led by a director who is also a member of the GB Board of Commissioners. As at March 2016, UK woodland certified by the Forestry Commission (including Forestry Commission-managed woodland) amounted to around 1,350,000ha (3,335,923 acres): 337,000ha (832,745 acres) in England, 141,000ha (348,419 acres) in Wales, 807,000ha (1,994,140 acres) in Scotland and 65,000ha (160,619 acres) in Northern Ireland. For more information, see W www.forestry.gov.uk

There are 37 forest nature reserves in Northern Ireland, covering 1,751 hectares (4,327 acres), designated and administered by the Forest Service.

MARINE NATURE RESERVES

Marine protected areas provide protection for marine flora and fauna, and geological and physiographical features on land covered by tidal waters or parts of the sea in or adjacent to the UK. These areas also provide opportunities for study and research.

ENGLAND AND WALES

The Marine and Coastal Access Act 2009 created a new kind of statutory protection for marine protected areas in England and Wales, marine conservation zones (MCZs), which are designed to increase the protection of species and habitats deemed to be of national importance. The Secretary of State for Environment, Food and Rural Affairs and the National Assembly for Wales have the power to designate MCZs. Individual MCZs can have varying levels of protection: some include specific activities that are appropriately managed, while others prohibit all damaging and disturbing activities. The act converted the waters around Lundy Island, a former marine protected area, to MCZ status in 2010.

In 2009, Natural England and the Joint Nature Conservation Committee (JNCC) gave sea-users and stakeholders the ability to recommend potential MCZs to the UK government by establishing four regional projects. On 21 November 2013, the government announced the creation of 27 new MCZs, covering an area of around 9,700 sq. km, to protect wildlife including seahorses, coral reefs and oyster beds from dredging and bottom-trawling. In January 2016, 23 new MCZs were designated, which extended the area of protection to 20,700 sq. km. The new MCZ designations means that 20 per cent of English waters are considered protected. The 50 MCZs (with date designation confirmed) are:

Inshore Sites
ALLONBY BAY (2016), Cumbria, 40 sq. km
ALN ESTUARY (2013), Northumberland, 0.39 sq. km
BLACKWATER, CROUCH, ROACH AND COLNE
    ESTUARIES (2013), Essex, 284 sq. km
BEACHY HEAD WEST (2013), E. Sussex, 24 sq. km
BIDEFORD TO FORELAND POINT (2016), Devon, 104
    sq. km
CHESIL BEACH AND STENNIS LEDGES (2013), Dorset,
    37 sq. km
COQUET TO ST. MARYS (2016), Northumberland, 192
    sq. km
CROMER SHOAL CHALK BEDS (2016), Norfolk, 321 sq.
    km
CUMBRIA COAST (2013), Cumbria, 18 sq. km
DOVER TO DEAL (2016), Kent, 10 sq. km
DOVER TO FOLKESTONE (2016), Kent, 20 sq. km
FARNES EAST (2016), Northumberland, 945 sq. km

FOLKESTONE POMERANIA (2013), Kent, 34 sq. km
FYLDE (2013), Lancs, 260 sq. km
HARTLAND POINT TO TINTAGEL (2016), Devon/
 Cornwall, 304 sq. km
HOLDERNESS INSHORE (2016), Yorkshire, 309 sq. km
ISLES OF SCILLY (2013), 30 sq. km
KINGMERE (2013), Sussex, 47 sq. km
LUNDY (2010 and 2013), Bristol Channel, 31 sq. km
THE MANACLES (2013), Cornwall, 3.5 sq. km
MEDWAY ESTUARY (2013), Kent, 60 sq. km
MOUNTS BAY (2016), Cornwall, 12 sq. km
THE NEEDLES (2016), Isle of Wight, 11 sq. km
NEWQUAY AND THE GANNEL (2016), Cornwall, 9 sq.
 km
PADSTOW BAY AND SURROUNDS (2013), Cornwall, 90
 sq. km
PAGHAM HARBOUR (2013), Sussex, 3 sq. km
POOLE ROCKS (2013), Dorset, 4 sq. km
RUNNEL STONE (2016), Cornwall, 20 sq. km
RUNSWICK BAY (2016), Yorkshire, 68 sq. km
SKERRIES BANK AND SURROUNDS (2013), Devon, 250
 sq. km
SOUTH DORSET (2013), 193 sq. km
THE SWALE ESTUARY (2016), Kent, 51 sq. km
TAMAR ESTUARY (2013), Devon/Cornwall, 15 sq. km
THANET COAST (2013), Kent, 64 sq. km
TORBAY (2013), Devon, 20 sq. km
UPPER FOWEY AND PONT PILL (2013), Cornwall, 2 sq.
 km
UTOPIA (2016), Isle of Wight, 3 sq. km
WEST OF WALNEY (2016), Cumbria, 388 sq. km
WHITSAND AND LOOE BAY (2013), Cornwall, 52 sq. km
Offshore Sites
THE CANYONS (2013), Cornwall, 661 sq. km
EAST OF HAIG FRAS (2013), Cornwall, 400 sq. km
FULMAR (2016), Northumberland, 2,439 sq. km
GREATER HAIG FRAS (2016), Cornwall, 2,048 sq. km
NORTH EAST OF FARNES DEEP (2013),
 Northumberland, 492 sq. km
NORTH-WEST OF JONES BANK (2016), Cornwall, 400
 sq. km
OFFSHORE BRIGHTON (2016), Sussex, 861 sq. km
OFFSHORE OVERFALLS (2016), Isle of Wight, 594 sq.
 km
SOUTH-WEST DEEPS (WEST) (2013), Cornwall, 1,800 sq.
 km
SWALLOW SAND (2013), Northumberland, 4,746 sq. km
WESTERN CHANNEL (2016), Cornwall, 1,614 sq. km

SCOTLAND

In July 2014, under the Marine (Scotland) Act 2010, the Scottish government designated 17 marine protected areas (MPAs) in Scottish inshore territorial waters (Clyde Sea Sill; East Caithness Cliffs; Fetlar to Haroldswick; Loch Creran; Loch Sunart; Loch Sunart to the Sound of Jura; Loch Sween; Lochs Duich, Long and Alsh; Monarch Isles; Mousa to Boddam; Noss Head; Papa Westray; Small Isles; South Arran; Upper Loch Fyne and Loch Goil; Wester Ross; and Wyre and Rousay Sounds). A further 13, also in July 2014, were designated in offshore waters under the UK Marine and Coastal Access Act 2009. These are: Central Fladen; East of Gannet and Montrose Fields; Faroe–Shetland Sponge Belt; Firth of Forth Banks Complex; Geikie Slide and Hebridean Slope; Hatton–Rockall Basin; North-east Faroe Shetland Channel; North-west Orkney; Norwegian Boundary Sediment Plain; Rosemary Bank Seamount; The Barra Fan and Hebrides Terrace Seamount; Turbot Bank; and West Shetland Shelf.

NORTHERN IRELAND

The Marine Act (Northern Ireland) 2013 includes provisions for establishing Marine Conservation Zones (MCZs), as well as a system of marine planning, fisheries management and marine licensing. MCZs may be designated for various purposes including the conservation of marine species and habitats, taking fully into account any economic, cultural or

social consequences of doing so. The Act also allows the NI Department of the Environment to make byelaws to protect MCZs from damage caused by unregulated activities such as anchoring, kite surfing or jet skiing. It is an offence to intentionally or recklessly destroy or damage a protected feature of an MCZ.

As at June 2017 there were five MCZs in Northern Ireland. Strangford Lough was Northern Ireland's only marine nature reserve, established in 1995 under the Nature Conservation and Amenity Lands Order (Northern Ireland) 1985, but it was redesignated as Northern Ireland's first MCZ on the introduction of the Marine Act (Northern Ireland) 2013. After a consultation period, the NI Department of Agriculture, Environment and Rural Affairs announced four new MCZ's in December 2016; Carlingford Lough, Outer Belfast Lough, Rathlin and Waterfoot.

INTERNATIONAL CONVENTIONS

The UK is party to a number of international conventions.

BERN CONVENTION

The 1979 Bern Convention on the Conservation of European Wildlife and Natural Habitats came into force in the UK in June 1982. There are 51 contracting parties and a number of other states attend meetings as observers.

The aims are to conserve wild flora and fauna and their habitats, especially where this requires the cooperation of several countries, and to promote such cooperation. The convention imposes legal obligations on contracting parties, protecting over 500 wild plant species and more than 1,000 wild animal species.

All parties to the convention must promote national conservation policies and take account of the conservation of wild flora and fauna when setting planning and development policies. Reports on contracting parties' conservation policies must be submitted to the standing committee every four years.
SECRETARIAT OF THE BERN CONVENTION
 STANDING COMMITTEE, Council of Europe, Avenue de
 L'Europe, 67075 Strasbourg-Cedex, France
 W www.coe.int/bernconvention

BIOLOGICAL DIVERSITY

The UK ratified the Convention on Biological Diversity (CBD) in June 1994. As at May 2017 there were 196 parties to the convention.

There are seven programmes addressing agricultural biodiversity, marine and coastal biodiversity and the biodiversity of inland waters, dry and sub-humid lands, islands, mountains and forests. On 29 January 2000 the Conference of the Parties adopted a supplementary agreement to the convention known as the Cartagena Protocol on Biosafety. The protocol seeks to protect biological diversity from potential risks that may be posed by introducing modified living organisms, resulting from biotechnology, into the environment. As at May 2017, 170 countries were party to the protocol; the UK joined on 17 February 2004. The Nagoya Protocol on Access and Benefit-sharing was adopted in October 2010 and entered into force on 12 October 2014. It provides international rules and procedure on liability and redress for damage to biodiversity resulting from living modified organisms. As at May 2017, 96 countries were party to the protocol.

The UK Biodiversity Action Plan (UKBAP), published in 1994, was the UK government's response to the CBD at the 1992 Rio Earth Summit. The UK Post-2010 Biodiversity Framework replaced UKBAP when it was published in 2012 by DEFRA and the devolved administrations. The framework covers the period 2011–20 and forms the UK government's response to the strategic plan of the CBD. It includes five internationally agreed strategic goals to be achieved by 2020: to address the underlying causes of biodiversity loss by making biodiversity a mainstream issue across government and society; to reduce the direct pressures on biodiversity and promote sustainable use; to safeguard ecosystems, species and genetic diversity; to enhance the benefits to all from biodiversity and ecosystem services; and to enhance implementation through participatory planning, knowledge management and capacity building. The list of priority species and habitats under the biodiversity framework covers 1,150 species and 65 habitats.

Secretariat of the Convention on Biological Diversity, 413, Saint Jacques Street, suite 800, Montreal, QC H2Y 1N9 Canada T +1514-288 2220 E secretariat@cbd.int W www.cbd.int
JNCC, Monkstone House, City Road, Peterborough PE1 1JY T 01733-555948 W www.jncc.defra.gov.uk

BONN CONVENTION

The 1979 Convention on Conservation of Migratory Species of Wild Animals (also known as the CMS or Bonn Convention) came into force in the UK in October 1985. As at 1 May 2017, 124 countries were party to the convention.

It requires the protection of listed endangered migratory species and encourages international agreements covering these and other threatened species.

Seven agreements have been concluded to date under the convention. They aim to conserve seals in the Wadden Sea; bat populations in Europe; small cetaceans of the Baltic, north-east Atlantic, Irish and North Seas; cetaceans of the Mediterranean Sea, Black Sea and contiguous Atlantic area; African-Eurasian migratory waterbirds; albatrosses and petrels; and gorillas and their habitats. A further 19 memorandums of understanding have been agreed for the Siberian crane, slender-billed curlew, marine turtles of the Atlantic coast of Africa, Indian Ocean and South East Asia, the middle-European population of the great bustard, bukhara deer, aquatic warbler, West-African populations of the African elephant, saiga antelope, cetaceans of the Pacific Islands, dugongs (large marine mammals), eastern-Atlantic populations of the Mediterranean monk seals, ruddy-headed goose, grassland birds of southern South America, birds of prey of Africa and Eurasia, small cetaceans and manatees of West Africa, sharks, huemuls (Andean deer) and high Andean flamingoes. In addition, there are three special species initiatives: the central Asian flyway, the central Asian mammals initiative and Sahelo–Saharan megafauna plan.

UNEP/CMS SECRETARIAT, Platz der Vereinten Nationen 1, 53113 Bonn, Germany T (+49) (228) 815 2401
E secretariat@cms.int W www.cms.int

CITES

The 1973 Convention on International Trade in Endangered Species of Wild Fauna and Flora (CITES), which entered into force in 1975, is an agreement between governments to ensure that international trade in specimens of wild animals and plants does not threaten their survival. The convention came into force in the UK in October 1976 and there are currently 183 member countries. Countries party to the convention ban commercial international trade in an agreed list of endangered species and regulate and monitor trade in other species that might become endangered. The convention accords varying degrees of protection to more than 35,000 species of animals and plants whether they are traded as live specimens or as products derived from them.

The Conference of the Parties to CITES meets every two to three years to review the convention's implementation. The Animal and Plant Health Agency at the Department for Environment, Food and Rural Affairs carries out the government's responsibilities under CITES.

CITES is implemented in the EU through a series of EC regulations known as the Wildlife Trade Regulations.

CITES SECRETARIAT, International Environment House, 11 Chemin des Anémones, CH-1219 Châtelaine, Geneva, Switzerland T (+41) (22) 917 8139/40 E info@cites.org
W www.cites.org

INTERNATIONAL CONVENTION FOR THE REGULATION OF WHALING

The International Convention for the Regulation of Whaling was signed in Washington DC in 1946 and currently has 88 member countries.

The measures in the convention provide for the complete protection of certain species; designate specified areas as whale sanctuaries; set limits on the numbers and size of whales which may be taken; prescribe open and closed seasons and areas for whaling; and prohibit the capture of suckling calves and female whales accompanied by calves. The International Whaling Commission meets annually to review and revise these measures.

THE INTERNATIONAL WHALING COMMISSION, The Red House, 135 Station Road, Impington, Cambridge, Cambridgeshire CB24 9NP T 01223-233 971 W www.iwc.int

OSPAR

The Convention for the Protection of the Marine Environment of the North-East Atlantic (the OSPAR Convention) was adopted in Paris, France in September 1992 and entered into force in March 1998. The OSPAR Convention replaced both the Oslo Convention (1972) and the Paris Convention (1974), with the intention of providing a comprehensive approach to addressing all sources of pollution which may affect the maritime area, and matters relating to the protection of the maritime environment. An annex on biodiversity and ecosystems was adopted in 1998 to cover non-polluting human activities that can adversely affect the sea.

Fifteen countries plus the European Union are party to the convention; the UK ratified OSPAR in 1998. The OSPAR Commission makes decisions and recommendations and sets out actions to be taken by the contracting parties. The OSPAR Secretariat administers the work under the convention, coordinates the work of the contracting parties and runs the formal meeting schedule of OSPAR.

OSPAR SECRETARIAT, Victoria House, 37–63 Southampton Row, London WC1B 4DA T 020-7430 5200
E secretariat@ospar.org W www.ospar.org

RAMSAR CONVENTION

The 1971 Convention on Wetlands of National Importance, called the Ramsar Convention, is an inter-governmental treaty that provides for the conservation and sustainable use of wetlands and their resources. The Convention entered into force in the UK in 1976.

Governments that are contracting parties to the convention must designate wetlands for inclusion in the List of Wetlands of International Importance (the 'Ramsar List') and include wetland conservation considerations in their land-use planning. As at July 2017, the Convention's 174 contracting parties had designated 2,279 wetland sites, covering 220,453,050 hectares. The UK currently has 170 designated sites covering 1,281,989 hectares.

The contracting parties meet every three years to assess progress. The 13th Meeting of the Conference of the Contracting Parties to the Ramsar Convention on Wetlands will take place in Dubai, UAE in October 2018.

At the 12th meeting of the Convention, held in Uruguay in June 2015, a new Ramsar Strategic Plan was adopted for the years 2016–24. The four priorities central to the new plan are: to address the factors driving the loss and degradation of wetlands; to renew country commitment to conserve and protect the Ramsar site network; to promote wise use of wetlands and to restore wetlands that are relevant for biodiversity conservation, disaster risk reduction, livelihoods and climate change mitigation; and to improve the implementation of the Convention.

RAMSAR CONVENTION SECRETARIAT, Rue Mauverney 28, CH-1196 Gland, Switzerland T (+41) (22) 999 0170
E ramsar@ramsar.org W www.ramsar.org

UK LEGISLATION

The Wildlife and Countryside Act 1981 gives legal protection to a wide range of wild animals and plants. Every five years the statutory nature conservation agencies (Natural England, Natural Resources Wales and Scottish Natural Heritage), working jointly through the JNCC, are required to review schedules 5 (animals, other than birds) and 8 (plants) of the Wildlife and Countryside Act 1981. They make recommendations to the Secretary of State for Environment, Food and Rural Affairs, the National Assembly for Wales and the Scottish government for changes to these schedules. The most recent variations of schedules 5 and 8 for England came into effect on 1 October 2011, following the fifth quinquennial review. The sixth review is currently underway.

Under section 9 of the act it is an offence to kill, injure, take, possess or sell (whether alive or dead) any wild animal included in schedule 5 of the act and to disturb its place of shelter and protection or to destroy that place. However certain species listed on schedule 5 are protected against some, but not all, of these activities.

Under section 13 of the act it is illegal without a licence to pick, uproot, sell or destroy plants listed in schedule 8. Since January 2001, under the Countryside and Rights of Way Act 2000, persons found guilty of an offence under part 1 of the Wildlife and Countryside Act 1981 face a maximum penalty of up to £5,000 and/or up to a six-month custodial sentence per specimen.

BIRDS

The act lays down a close season for birds (listed on Schedule 2, part 1) from 1 February to 31 August inclusive, each year. Variations to these dates are made for:

Black grouse – 10 December to 20 August (10 December – 1 September for Somerset, Devon and New Forest)
Capercaillie – 1 February to 30 September (England and Wales only)
Grey partridge – 1 February to 1 September
Pheasant – 1 February to 1 October
Ptarmigan and Red grouse – 10 December to 12 August
Red-legged partridge – 1 February to 1 September
Snipe – 1 February to 11 August
Woodcock – 1 February to 30 September (England and Wales); 1 February to 31 August (Scotland)
Birds listed on schedule 2, part 1 (below high water mark) (see below) – 21 February to 31 August
Wild duck and wild geese, in or over any area below the high-water mark of ordinary spring tides – 21 February to 31 August
Sundays and Christmas Day in Scotland, and Sundays for any area of England or Wales prescribed by the Secretary of State.

Birds listed on schedule 2, part 1, which may be killed or taken outside the close season are: capercaillie (England and Wales only); coot; certain wild duck (gadwall, goldeneye, mallard, Northern pintail, common pochard, Northern shoveler, teal, tufted duck, Eurasian wigeon); certain wild geese (Canada, greylag, pink-footed, white-fronted (in England and Wales only); golden plover; moorhen; snipe; and woodcock.

Section 16 of the 1981 act allows licences to be issued on either an individual or general basis, to allow the killing, taking and sale of certain birds for specified reasons such as public health and safety. All other wild birds are fully protected by law throughout the year.

ANIMALS PROTECTED BY SCHEDULE 5

Adder (Vipera berus)
Anemone, Ivell's Sea (Edwardsia ivelli)
Anemone, Starlet Sea (Nematosella vectensis)
Bat, Horseshoe, all species (Rhinolophidae)
Bat, Typical, all species (Vespertilionidae)
Beetle (Hypebaeus flavipes)
Beetle, Bembridge Water (Paracymus aeneus)
Beetle, Lesser Silver Water (Hydrochara caraboides)
Beetle, Mire Pill (Curimopsis nigrita)
Beetle, Moccas (Hypebaeus flavipes)
Beetle, Rainbow Leaf (Chrysolina cerealis)
Beetle, Spangled Water (Graphoderus zonatus)
Beetle, Stag (Lucanus cervus)
Beetle, Violet Click (Limoniscus violaceus)
Beetle, Water (Paracymus aeneus)
Burbot (Lota lota)
Butterfly, Adonis Blue (Lysandra bellargus)
Butterfly, Black Hairstreak (Strymonidia pruni)
Butterfly, Brown Hairstreak (Thecla betulae)
Butterfly, Chalkhill Blue (Lysandra coridon)
Butterfly, Chequered Skipper (Carterocephalus palaemon)
Butterfly, Duke of Burgundy Fritillary (Hamearis lucina)
Butterfly, Glanville Fritillary (Melitaea cinxia)
Butterfly, Heath Fritillary (Mellicta athalia or Melitaea athalia)
Butterfly, High Brown Fritillary (Argynnis adippe)
Butterfly, Large Blue (Maculinea arion)
Butterfly, Large Copper (Lycaena dispar)
Butterfly, Large Heath (Coenonympha tullia)
Butterfly, Large Tortoiseshell (Nymphalis polychloros)
Butterfly, Lulworth Skipper (Thymelicus acteon)
Butterfly, Marsh Fritillary (Eurodryas aurinia)
Butterfly, Mountain Ringlet (Erebia epiphron)
Butterfly, Northern Brown Argus (Aricia artaxerxes)
Butterfly, Pearl-bordered Fritillary (Boloria euphrosyne)
Butterfly, Purple Emperor (Apatura iris)
Butterfly, Silver Spotted Skipper (Hesperia comma)
Butterfly, Silver-studded Blue (Plebejus argus)
Butterfly, Small Blue (Cupido minimus)
Butterfly, Swallowtail (Papilio machaon)
Butterfly, White Letter Hairstreak (Stymonida w-album)
Butterfly, Wood White (Leptidea sinapis)
Cat, Wild (Felis silvestris)
Cicada, New Forest (Cicadetta montana)
Crayfish, Atlantic Stream (Austropotamobius pallipes)
Cricket, Field (Gryllus campestris)
Cricket, Mole (Gryllotalpa gryllotalpa)
Cricket, Wart-biter (Decticus verrucivorus)
Damselfly, Southern (Coenagrion mercuriale)
Dolphin, all species (Cetacea)
Dormouse (Muscardinus avellanarius)
Dragonfly, Norfolk Aeshna (Aeshna isosceles)
Frog, Common (Rana temporaria)
Frog, Pool, Northern Clade (Pelophylax lessonae)
Goby, Couch's (Gobius couchii)
Goby, Giant (Gobius cobitis)
Hatchet Shell, Northern (Thyasira gouldi)
Hydroid, Marine (Clavopsella navis)
Lagoon Snail, De Folin's (Caecum armoricum)
Lagoon Worm, Tentacled (Alkmaria romijni)
Leech, Medicinal (Hirudo medicinalis)
Lizard, Sand (Lacerta agilis)
Lizard, Viviparous (Lacerta vivipara)
Marten, Pine (Martes martes)
Moth, Barberry Carpet (Pareulype berberata)
Moth, Black-veined (Siona lineata or Idaea lineata)
Moth, Fiery Clearwing (Bembecia chrysidiformis)
Moth, Fisher's Estuarine (Gortyna borelii)
Moth, New Forest Burnet (Zygaena viciae)
Moth, Reddish Buff (Acosmetia caliginosa)
Moth, Slender Scotch Burnet (Zygaena loti)
Moth, Sussex Emerald (Thalera fimbrialis)
Moth, Talisker Burnet (Zygaena lonicerae)
Mussel, Fan (Atrina fragilis)
Mussel, Freshwater Pearl (Margaritifera margaritifera)
Newt, Great Crested (or Warty) (Triturus cristatus)
Newt, Palmate (Triturus helveticus)
Newt, Smooth (Triturus vulgaris)
Otter, Common (Lutra lutra)
Porpoise, all species (Cetacea)
Sandworm, Lagoon (Armandia cirrhosa)

Sea Fan, Pink *(Eunicella verrucosa)*
Sea Slug, Lagoon *(Tenellia adspersa)*
Sea-mat, Trembling *(Victorella pavida)*
Seahorse, Short Snouted (England only) *(Hippocampus hippocampus)*
Seahorse, Spiny (England only) *(Hippocampus guttulatus)*
Shad, Allis *(Alosa alosa)*
Shad, Twaite *(Alosa fallax)*
Shark, Angel (England only) *(Squatina squatina)*
Shark, Basking *(Cetorhinus maximus)*
Shrimp, Fairy *(Chirocephalus diaphanus)*
Shrimp, Lagoon Sand *(Gammarus insensibilis)*
Shrimp, Tadpole (Apus) *(Triops cancriformis)*
Skate, White *(Rostroraja alba)*
Slow-worm *(Anguis fragilis)*
Snail, Glutinous *(Myxas glutinosa)*
Snail, Roman (England only) *(Helix pomatia)*
Snail, Sandbowl *(Catinella arenaria)*
Snake, Grass *(Natrix natrix* or *Natrix helvetica)*
Snake, Smooth *(Coronella austriaca)*
Spider, Fen Raft *(Dolomedes plantarius)*
Spider, Ladybird *(Eresus niger)*
Squirrel, Red *(Sciurus vulgaris)*
Sturgeon *(Acipenser sturio)*
Toad, Common *(Bufo bufo)*
Toad, Natterjack *(Bufo calamita)*
Turtle, Flatback *(Cheloniidae/Natator Depressus)*
Turtle, Green Sea *(Chelonia mydas)*
Turtle, Hawksbill *(Eretmochelys imbricate)*
Turtle, Kemp's Ridley Sea *(Lepidochelys kempii)*
Turtle, Leatherback Sea *(Dermochelys coriacea)*
Turtle, Loggerhead Sea *(Caretta caretta)*
Turtle, Olive Ridley *(Lepidochelys olivacea)*
Vendace *(Coregonus albula)*
Vole, Water *(Arvicola terrestris)*
Walrus *(Odobenus rosmarus)*
Whale, all species *(Cetacea)*
Whitefish *(Coregonus lavaretus)*

PLANTS PROTECTED BY SCHEDULE 8

Adder's Tongue, Least *(Ophioglossum lusitanicum)*
Alison, Small *(Alyssum alyssoides)*
Anomodon, Long-leaved *(Anomodon longifolius)*
Beech-lichen, New Forest *(Enterographa elaborata)*
Blackwort *(Southbya nigrella)*
Bluebell *(Hyacinthoides non-scripta)*
Bolete, Royal *(Boletus regius)*
Broomrape, Bedstraw *(Orobanche caryophyllacea)*
Broomrape, Oxtongue *(Orobanche loricata)*
Broomrape, Thistle *(Orobanche reticulata)*
Cabbage, Lundy *(Rhynchosinapis wrightii)*
Calamint, Wood *(Calamintha sylvatica)*
Caloplaca, Snow *(Caloplaca nivalis)*
Catapyrenium, Tree *(Catapyrenium psoromoides)*
Catchfly, Alpine *(Lychnis alpina)*
Catillaria, Laurer's *(Catellaria laureri)*
Centaury, Slender *(Centaurium tenuiflorum)*
Cinquefoil, Rock *(Potentilla rupestris)*
Cladonia, Convoluted *(Cladonia convoluta)*
Cladonia, Upright Mountain *(Cladonia stricta)*
Clary, Meadow *(Salvia pratensis)*
Club-rush, Triangular *(Scirpus triquetrus)*
Colt's-foot, Purple *(Homogyne alpina)*
Cotoneaster, Wild *(Cotoneaster integerrimus)*
Cottongrass, Slender *(Eriophorum gracile)*
Cow-wheat, Field *(Melampyrum arvense)*
Crocus, Sand *(Romulea columnae)*
Crystalwort, Lizard *(Riccia bifurca)*
Cudweed, Broad-leaved *(Filago pyramidata)*
Cudweed, Jersey *(Gnaphalium luteoalbum)*
Cudweed, Red-tipped *(Filago lutescens)*
Cut-grass *(Leersia oryzoides)*
Diapensia *(Diapensia lapponica)*

Dock, Shore *(Rumex rupestris)*
Earwort, Marsh *(Jamesoniella undulifolia)*
Eryngo, Field *(Eryngium campestre)*
Fern, Dickie's Bladder *(Cystopteris dickieana)*
Fern, Killarney *(Trichomanes speciosum)*
Flapwort, Norfolk *(Leiocolea rutheana)*
Fleabane, Alpine *(Erigeron borealis)*
Fleabane, Small *(Pulicaria vulgaris)*
Fleawort, South Stack *(Tephroseris integrifolia ssp maritima)*
Frostwort, Pointed *(Gymnomitrion apiculatum)*
Fungus, Hedgehog *(Hericium erinaceum)*
Galingale, Brown *(Cyperus fuscus)*
Gentian, Alpine *(Gentiana nivalis)*
Gentian, Dune *(Gentianella uliginosa)*
Gentian, Early *(Gentianella anglica)*
Gentian, Fringed *(Gentianella ciliata)*
Gentian, Spring *(Gentiana verna)*
Germander, Cut-leaved *(Teucrium botrys)*
Germander, Water *(Teucrium scordium)*
Gladiolus, Wild *(Gladiolus illyricus)*
Goblin Lights *(Catolechia wahlenbergii)*
Goosefoot, Stinking *(Chenopodium vulvaria)*
Grass-poly *(Lythrum hyssopifolia)*
Grimmia, Blunt-leaved *(Grimmia unicolor)*
Gyalecta, Elm *(Gyalecta ulmi)*
Hare's-ear, Sickle-leaved *(Bupleurum falcatum)*
Hare's-ear, Small *(Bupleurum baldense)*
Hawk's-beard, Stinking *(Crepis foetida)*
Hawkweed, Northroe *(Hieracium northroense)*
Hawkweed, Shetland *(Hieracium zetlandicum)*
Hawkweed, Weak-leaved *(Hieracium attenuatifolium)*
Heath, Blue *(Phyllodoce caerulea)*
Helleborine, Red *(Cephalanthera rubra)*
Horsetail, Branched *(Equisetum ramosissimum)*
Hound's-tongue, Green *(Cynoglossum germanicum)*
Knawel, Perennial *(Scleranthus perennis)*
Knotgrass, Sea *(Polygonum maritimum)*
Lady's-slipper *(Cypripedium calceolus)*
Lecanora, Tarn *(Lecanora archariana)*
Lecidea, Copper *(Lecidea inops)*
Leek, Round-headed *(Allium sphaerocephalon)*
Lettuce, Least *(Lactuca saligna)*
Lichen, Arctic Kidney *(Nephroma arcticum)*
Lichen, Ciliate Strap *(Heterodermia leucomelos)*
Lichen, Coralloid Rosette *(Heterodermia propagulifera)*
Lichen, Ear-lobed Dog *(Peltigera lepidophora)*
Lichen, Forked Hair *(Bryoria furcellata)*
Lichen, Golden Hair *(Teloschistes flavicans)*
Lichen, Orange-fruited Elm *(Caloplaca luteoalba)*
Lichen, River Jelly *(Collema dichotomum)*
Lichen, Scaly Breck *(Squamarina lentigera)*
Lichen, Starry Breck *(Buellia asterella)*
Lily, Snowdon *(Lloydia serotina)*
Liverwort, Lindenberg's Leafy *(Adelanthus lindenbergianus)*
Lungwort, Tree *(Lobaria pulmonaria)*
Marsh-mallow, Rough *(Althaea hirsuta)*
Marshwort, Creeping *(Apium repens)*
Milk-parsley, Cambridge *(Selinum carvifolia)*
Moss *(Drepanocladius vernicosus)*
Moss, Alpine Copper *(Mielichoferia mielichoferi)*
Moss, Baltic Bog *(Sphagnum balticum)*
Moss, Blue Dew *(Saelania glaucescens)*
Moss, Blunt-leaved Bristle *(Orthotrichum obtusifolium)*
Moss, Bright Green Cave *(Cyclodictyon laetevirens)*
Moss, Cordate Beard *(Barbula cordata)*
Moss, Cornish Path *(Ditrichum cornubicum)*
Moss, Derbyshire Feather *(Thamnobryum angustifolium)*
Moss, Flamingo *(Desmatodon cernuus)*
Moss, Glaucous Beard *(Barbula glauca)*
Moss, Green Shield *(Buxbaumia viridis)*
Moss, Hair Silk *(Plagiothecium piliferum)*
Moss, Knothole *(Zygodon forsteri)*
Moss, Large Yellow Feather *(Scorpidium turgescens)*

Moss, Millimetre *(Micromitrium tenerum)*
Moss, Multi-fruited River *(Cryphaea lamyana)*
Moss, Nowell's Limestone *(Zygodon gracilis)*
Moss, Polar Feather *(Hygrohypnum polare)*
Moss, Rigid Apple *(Bartramia stricta)*
Moss, Round-leaved Feather *(Rhyncostegium rotundifolium)*
Moss, Schleicher's Thread *(Bryum schleicheri)*
Moss, Slender Green Feather *(Drepanocladus vernicosus)*
Moss, Triangular Pygmy *(Acaulon triquetrum)*
Moss, Vaucher's Feather *(Hypnum vaucheri)*
Mudwort, Welsh *(Limosella australis)*
Naiad, Holly-leaved *(Najas marina)*
Naiad, Slender *(Najas flexilis)*
Nail, Rock *(Calicium corynellum)*
Orache, Stalked *(Halimione pedunculata)*
Orchid, Early Spider *(Ophrys sphegodes)*
Orchid, Fen *(Liparis loeselii)*
Orchid, Ghost *(Epipogium aphyllum)*
Orchid, Lapland Marsh *(Dactylorhiza lapponica)*
Orchid, Late Spider *(Ophrys fuciflora)*
Orchid, Lizard *(Himantoglossum hircinum)*
Orchid, Military *(Orchis militaris)*
Orchid, Monkey *(Orchis simia)*
Pannaria, Caledonia *(Panneria ignobilis)*
Parmelia, New Forest *(Parmelia minarum)*
Parmentaria, Oil Stain *(Parmentaria chilensis)*
Pear, Plymouth *(Pyrus cordata)*
Penny-cress, Perfoliate *(Thlaspi perfoliatum)*
Pennyroyal *(Mentha pulegium)*
Pertusaria, Alpine Moss *(Pertusaria bryontha)*
Petalwort *(Petallophyllum ralfsi)*
Physcia, Southern Grey *(Physcia tribacioides)*
Pigmyweed *(Crassula aquatica)*
Pine, Ground *(Ajuga chamaepitys)*
Pink, Cheddar *(Dianthus gratianopolitanus)*
Pink, Childing *(Petroraghia nanteuilii)*
Pink, Deptford (England and Wales only) *(Dianthus armeria)*
Polypore, Oak *(Buglossoporus pulvinus)*
Pseudocyphellaria, Ragged *(Pseudocyphellaria lacerata)*

Psora, Rusty Alpine *(Psora rubiformis)*
Puffball, Sandy Stilt *(Battarraea phalloides)*
Ragwort, Fen *(Senecio paludosus)*
Ramping-fumitory, Martin's *(Fumaria martinii)*
Rampion, Spiked *(Phyteuma spicatum)*
Restharrow, Small *(Ononis reclinata)*
Rock-cress, Alpine *(Arabis alpina)*
Rock-cress, Bristol *(Arabis stricta)*
Rustwort, Western *(Marsupella profunda)*
Sandwort, Norwegian *(Arenaria norvegica)*
Sandwort, Teesdale *(Minuartia stricta)*
Saxifrage, Drooping *(Saxifraga cernua)*
Saxifrage, Tufted *(Saxifraga cespitosa)*
Saxifrage, Yellow Marsh *(Saxifrage hirulus)*
Solenopsora, Serpentine *(Solenopsora liparina)*
Solomon's-seal, Whorled *(Polygonatum verticillatum)*
Sow-thistle, Alpine *(Cicerbita alpina)*
Spearwort, Adder's-tongue *(Ranunculus ophioglossifolius)*
Speedwell, Fingered *(Veronica triphyllos)*
Speedwell, Spiked *(Veronica spicata)*
Spike-rush, Dwarf *(Eleocharis parvula)*
Star-of-Bethlehem, Early *(Gagea bohemica)*
Starfruit *(Damasonium alisma)*
Stonewort, Bearded *(Chara canescens)*
Stonewort, Foxtail *(Lamprothamnium papulosum)*
Strapwort *(Corrigiola litoralis)*
Sulphur-tresses, Alpine *(Alectoria ochroleuca)*
Turpswort *(Geocalyx graveolens)*
Violet, Fen *(Viola persicifolia)*
Viper's-grass *(Scorzonera humilis)*
Water-plantain, Floating *(Luronium natans)*
Water-plantain, Ribbon-leaved *(Alisma gramineum)*
Wood-sedge, Starved *(Carex depauperata)*
Woodsia, Alpine *(Woodsia alpina)*
Woodsia, Oblong *(Woodsia ilvenis)*
Wormwood, Field *(Artemisia campestris)*
Woundwort, Downy *(Stachys germanica)*
Woundwort, Limestone *(Stachys alpina)*
Yellow-rattle, Greater *(Rhinanthus serotinus)*

WORLD HERITAGE SITES

The Convention Concerning the Protection of the World Cultural and Natural Heritage was adopted by the United Nations Educational, Scientific and Cultural Organization (UNESCO) in 1972 and ratified by the UK in 1984. As at July 2017, 193 states were party to the convention. The convention provides for the identification, protection and conservation of cultural and natural sites of outstanding universal value.

Cultural sites may be:
- an extraordinary exponent of human creative genius
- sites representing architectural and technological innovation or cultural interchange
- sites of artistic, historic, aesthetic, archaeological, scientific, ethnologic or anthropologic value
- 'cultural landscapes', ie sites whose characteristics are marked by significant interactions between human populations and their natural environment
- exceptional examples of a traditional settlement or land- or sea-use, especially those threatened by irreversible changes.
- unique or exceptional examples of a cultural tradition or a civilisation either still present or extinct

Natural sites may be:
- those displaying critical periods of earth's history
- superlative examples of on-going ecological and biological processes in the evolution of ecosystems
- those exhibiting remarkable natural beauty and aesthetic significance or those where extraordinary natural phenomena are witnessed
- the habitat of threatened species and plants

Governments which are party to the convention nominate sites in their country for inclusion in the World Heritage List. Nominations are considered by the World Heritage Committee, an inter-governmental committee composed of 21 representatives of the parties to the convention. The committee is advised by the International Council on Monuments and Sites (ICOMOS), the International Centre for the Study of the Preservation and Restoration of Cultural Property (ICCROM) and the International Union for the Conservation of Nature (IUCN). ICOMOS evaluates and reports on proposed cultural and mixed sites, ICCROM provides expert advice and training on how to conserve and restore cultural property and IUCN provides technical evaluations of natural heritage sites and reports on the state of conservation of listed sites.

A prerequisite for inclusion in the World Heritage List is the existence of an effective legal protection system in the country in which the site is situated and a detailed management plan to ensure the conservation of the site. Inclusion in the list does not confer any greater degree of protection on the site than that offered by the national protection framework.

If a site is considered to be in serious danger of decay or damage, the committee may add it to the World Heritage in Danger List. Sites on this list may benefit from particular attention or emergency measures to allay threats and allow them to retain their world heritage status, or in extreme cases of damage or neglect they may lose their world heritage status completely. As at July 2017, there were 54 sites on the World Heritage in Danger List, the two most recent additions being the historic centre of Vienna and the Hebron/Al-Khalil Old Town in Palestine.

Financial support for the conservation of sites on the World Heritage List is provided by the World Heritage Fund, administered by the World Heritage Committee. The fund's income is derived from compulsory and voluntary contributions from the states party to the convention and from private donations.

WORLD HERITAGE CENTRE, UNESCO, 7 Place de
Fontenoy, 75352 Paris 07 SP, France E wh-info@unesco.org
W whc.unesco.org

DESIGNATED SITES

As at 12 July 2017, following the 41st session of the World Heritage Committee, 1,073 sites across 167 countries were on the World Heritage List. Of these, 27 are in the UK and four in UK overseas territories; 26 are listed for their cultural significance (†), four for their natural significance (*) and one for both cultural and natural significance. Liverpool's Maritime Mercantile City is the only UK site on the List of World Heritage in Danger. The year in which sites were designated appears in the first set of parentheses. The number in the second set of parentheses denotes the position of each site on the map below.

WORLD HERITAGE SITES IN THE UK

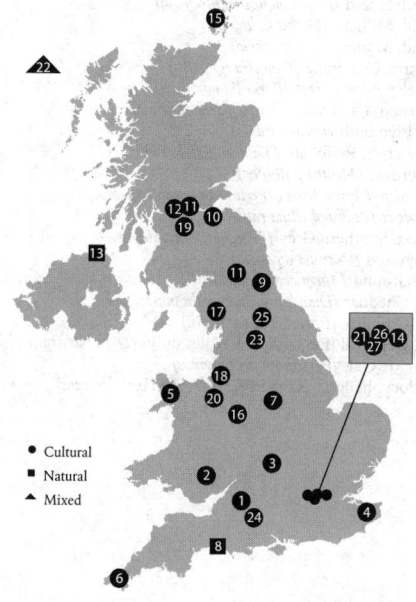

UNITED KINGDOM

†Bath – the city (1987). (1)

†Blaenarvon industrial landscape, Wales (2000). (2)

†Blenheim Palace and Park, Oxfordshire (1987). (3)

†Canterbury Cathedral, St Augustine's Abbey, St Martin's Church, Kent (1988). (4)

†Castle and town walls of King Edward I, north Wales – Beaumaris, Caernarfon Castle, Conwy Castle, Harlech Castle (1986). (5)

†Cornwall and west Devon mining landscape (2006). (6)

†Derwent Valley Mills, Derbyshire (2001). (7)

*Dorset and east Devon coast (2001). (8)

†Durham Cathedral and Castle (1986). (9)

†Edinburgh old and new towns (1995). (10)

†Forth Bridge, Firth of Forth, Scotland (2015). (11)

†Frontiers of the Roman Empire– Hadrian's Wall, northern England; Antonine Wall, central Scotland (1987, 2005, 2008). (12)

*Giant's Causeway and Causeway coast, Co. Antrim (1986). (13)

†Greenwich, London – maritime Greenwich, including the Royal Naval College, Old Royal Observatory, Queen's House, town centre (1997). (14)

†Heart of Neolithic Orkney (1999). (15)
†Ironbridge Gorge, Shropshire – the world's first iron bridge and other early industrial sites (1986). (16)
†Lake District, Cumbria (2017). (17)
†Liverpool – six areas of the maritime mercantile city (2004). (18)
†New Lanark, South Lanarkshire, Scotland (2001). (19)
†Pontcysyllte Aqueduct and Canal, Wrexham, Wales (2009). (20)
†Royal Botanic Gardens, Kew (2003). (21)
†*St Kilda, Eilean Siar (Western Isles) (1986). (22)
†Saltaire, West Yorkshire (2001). (23)
†Stonehenge, Avebury and related megalithic sites, Wiltshire (1986). (24)

†Studley Royal Park, Fountains Abbey, St Mary's Church, N. Yorkshire (1986). (25)
†Tower of London (1988). (26)
†Westminster Abbey, Palace of Westminster, St Margaret's Church, London (1987). (27)

UK OVERSEAS TERRITORIES
*Henderson Island, Pitcairn Islands, South Pacific Ocean (1988)
*Gough Island and Inaccessible Island (part of Tristan da Cunha), South Atlantic Ocean (1995)
†Historic town of St George and related fortifications, Bermuda (2000)
†Gorham's Cave Complex, Gibraltar (2016)

HISTORIC BUILDINGS AND MONUMENTS

ENGLAND

Under the Planning (Listed Buildings and Conservation Areas) Act 1990, the Secretary of State for Culture, Media and Sport has a statutory duty to approve buildings or groups of buildings in England that are of special architectural or historic interest. Since April 2015 the list of such buildings is maintained by Historic England who are also responsible for making recommendations to the secretary of state for additions, removals and amendments to the list. Under the Ancient Monuments and Archaeological Areas Act 1979 as amended by the National Heritage Act 1983, the secretary of state is also responsible for compiling a schedule of ancient monuments. Decisions are taken on the advice of Historic England. A searchable database of all nationally designated heritage assets, The National Heritage List for England (NHLE), is available online: W www.historicengland.org.uk/listing/the-list.

LISTED BUILDINGS

Listed buildings are classified into Grade I, Grade II* and Grade II. There are 377,414 listed buildings in England, of which approximately 90 per cent are Grade II listed. Almost all pre-1700 buildings are listed, as are most buildings of 1700 to 1840. Historic England surveys particular types of buildings with a view to making recommendations for listing. The main purpose of listing is to ensure that care is taken in deciding the future of a building. No changes which affect the architectural or historic character of a listed building can be made without listed building consent (in addition to planning permission where relevant). Applications for consent are normally dealt with by the local planning authority, although Historic England is always consulted about proposals affecting Grade I and Grade II* properties. It is a criminal offence to demolish a listed building, or alter it in such a way as to affect its character, without consent.

SCHEDULED MONUMENTS

There are 19,856 scheduled monuments in England. All monuments proposed for scheduling are considered to be of national importance. Where buildings are both scheduled and listed, ancient monuments legislation takes precedence. The main purpose of scheduling a monument is to preserve it for the future and to protect it from damage, destruction or any unnecessary interference. Once a monument has been scheduled, scheduled monument consent is required before any works can be carried out. The scope of the control is more extensive and more detailed than that applied to listed buildings, but certain minor works, as detailed in the Ancient Monuments (Class Consents) Order 1994, may be carried out without consent. It is a criminal offence to carry out unauthorised work to scheduled monuments.

WALES

Under the Planning (Listed Buildings and Conservation Areas) Act 1990 and the Ancient Monuments and Archaeological Areas Act 1979, the National Assembly for Wales is responsible for listing buildings and scheduling monuments in Wales on the advice of Cadw (the Welsh government's historic environment division) and the Royal Commission on the Ancient and Historical Monuments of Wales (RCAHMW). The criteria for evaluating buildings are similar to those in England and the same listing system is used. As at 31 March 2017, there were 29,994 listed buildings and 4,185 scheduled monuments in Wales.

SCOTLAND

Under the Planning (Listed Buildings and Conservation Areas) (Scotland) Act 1997 and the Ancient Monuments and Archaeological Areas Act 1979, Scottish ministers are responsible for listing buildings and scheduling monuments in Scotland on the advice of Historic Environment Scotland. The Historic Environment Scotland Act 2014 sets out Historic Environment Scotland's role and legal status. The criteria for evaluating buildings are similar to those in England but an A, B, C categorisation is used. As at 31 March 2017 there were 47,073 listed buildings and 8,145 scheduled monuments in Scotland.

NORTHERN IRELAND

Under the Planning (Northern Ireland) Act 2011 and the Historic Monuments and Archaeological Objects (Northern Ireland) Order 1995, the Historic Environment Division (part of the Department for Communities, Northern Ireland) is responsible for listing buildings and scheduling monuments. The Historic Buildings Council for Northern Ireland and the relevant district council must be consulted on listing proposals, and the Historic Monuments Council for Northern Ireland must be consulted on scheduling proposals. The criteria for evaluating buildings are similar to those in England but an A, B+, B1 and B2 categorisation is used. As at 31 March 2017 there were 8,864 listed buildings and 1,992 scheduled monuments in Northern Ireland.

ENGLAND

English Heritage cares for over 400 historic monuments, buildings and places. For more information on English Heritage properties, including those listed below, the official website is W www.english-heritage.org.uk

For more information on National Trust properties in England, including those listed below, the official website is W www.nationaltrust.org.uk

KEY
(EH) English Heritage property
(NT) National Trust property
* UNESCO World Heritage Site (see also World Heritage Sites)

A LA RONDE (NT), Exmouth, Devon EX8 5BD T 01395-265514
 Unique 16-sided house completed c.1796
ALNWICK CASTLE, Alnwick, Northumberland NE66 1NQ
 T 01665-511100 W www.alnwickcastle.com
 Seat of the Dukes of Northumberland since 1309; Italian Renaissance-style interior; gardens with spectacular water features
ALTHORP, Northants NN7 4HQ T 01604-770006
 W www.spencerofalthorp.com
 Spencer family seat; permanent Diana, Princess of Wales exhibition
ANGLESEY ABBEY (NT), Lode, Cambs CB25 9EJ
 T 01223-810080
 Jacobean house (c.1600) with gardens and a working watermill (Lode Mill) on the site of a 12th-century priory; fine furnishings and a unique clock collection
ARUNDEL CASTLE, Arundel, W. Sussex BN18 9AB
 T 01903-882173 W www.arundelcastle.org
 Castle dating from the Norman Conquest; seat of the Dukes of Norfolk
AVEBURY (EH/NT), Wilts SN8 1RF T 01672-539250
 Remains of stone circles constructed 4,000 years ago enclosing part of the later village of Avebury
BANQUETING HOUSE, Whitehall, London SW1A 2ER
 T 0844-482 7770 W www.hrp.org.uk/banquetinghouse

Designed by Inigo Jones in 1619; ceiling paintings by Rubens; site of the execution of Charles I

BASILDON PARK (NT), Reading, Berks RG8 9NR
T 01491-672382
Palladian mansion built in 1776–83 by John Carr

BATTLE ABBEY (EH), Battle, E. Sussex TN33 0AD
T 01424-775705
Remains of the abbey founded by William the Conqueror on the site of the Battle of Hastings

BEESTON CASTLE (EH), Cheshire CW6 9TX T 01829-260464
Built in the 13th century by Ranulf, sixth Earl of Chester on the site of an Iron Age hillfort

BELVOIR CASTLE, Grantham, Lincs NG32 1PE
T 01476-871001 W www.belvoircastle.com
Seat of the Dukes of Rutland; 19th-century Gothic-style castle; notable art collection

BERKELEY CASTLE, Glos GL13 9BQ T 01453-810303
W www.berkeley-castle.com
Completed late 12th century; site of the murder of Edward II (1327)

BIRDOSWALD ROMAN FORT (EH), Brampton, Cumbria CA8 7DD T 01697-747602
Stretch of Hadrian's Wall with Roman wall fort, turret and milecastle

*****BLENHEIM PALACE**, Woodstock, Oxon OX20 1PP
T 01993-810530 W www.blenheimpalace.com
Seat of the Dukes of Marlborough and Winston Churchill's birthplace; house designed by Vanbrugh; landscaped parkland by Capability Brown

BLICKLING ESTATE (NT), Blickling, Norfolk NR11 6NF
T 01263-738030
Jacobean house with state rooms; extensive gardens, temple and 18th-century orangery

BODIAM CASTLE (NT), Bodiam, E. Sussex TN32 5UA
T 01580-830196
Well-preserved medieval moated castle built in 1385

BOLSOVER CASTLE (EH), Bolsover, Derbys S44 6PR
T 01246-822844
17th-century castle on site of medieval fortress

BOSCOBEL HOUSE (EH), Bishops Wood, Shrops ST19 9AR
T 01902-850244
Timber-framed 17th-century hunting lodge; refuge of fugitive Charles II from parliamentary troops

BOUGHTON HOUSE, Kettering, Northants NN14 1BJ
T 01536-515731 W www.boughtonhouse.org.uk
17th-century house with French-style additions; home of the Dukes of Buccleuch and Queensbury

BOWOOD HOUSE, Calne, Wilts SN11 0LZ T 01249-812102
W www.bowood.org/bowood-house
18th-century house in Capability Brown park, featuring Robert Adam orangery and renowned pinetum and arboretum

BUCKFAST ABBEY, Buckfastleigh, Devon TQ11 0EE
T 01364-645500 W www.buckfast.org.uk
Benedictine monastery on medieval foundations

BUCKINGHAM PALACE, London SW1A 1AA
T 020-7766 7300 W www.royalcollection.org.uk
Purchased by George III in 1761, and the Sovereign's official London residence since 1837; 19 state rooms, including the Throne Room, and Queen's Gallery

BUCKLAND ABBEY (NT), Yelverton, Devon PL20 6EY
T 01822-853607
13th-century Cistercian monastery; home of Sir Francis Drake

BURGHLEY HOUSE, Stamford, Lincs PE9 3JY T 01780-752451
W www.burghley.co.uk
Late Elizabethan house built by William Cecil, first Lord Burghley

CARISBROOKE CASTLE (EH), Newport, Isle of Wight
PO30 1XY T 01983-523112
W www.carisbrookecastlemuseum.org.uk
Norman castle; museum; prison of Charles I 1647–8

CARLISLE CASTLE (EH), Carlisle, Cumbria CA3 8UR
T 01228-591922

Medieval castle; prison of Mary Queen of Scots

CASTLE ACRE PRIORY (EH), King's Lynn, Norfolk PE32 2XD
T 01760-755394
Remains include 12th-century church and prior's lodgings

CASTLE DROGO (NT), Drewsteignton, Devon EX6 6PB
T 01647-433306
Granite castle designed by Lutyens in 1911

CASTLE HOWARD, N. Yorks YO60 7DA T 01653-648333
W www.castlehoward.co.uk
Designed by Vanbrugh 1699–1726; mausoleum designed by Hawksmoor

CASTLE RISING CASTLE (EH), King's Lynn, Norfolk
PE31 6AH T 01553-631330 W www.castlerising.co.uk
12th-century keep with gatehouse and bridge, surrounded by 20 acres of defensive earthworks

CHARLES DARWIN'S HOUSE (DOWN HOUSE) (EH),
Downe, Kent BR6 7JT T 01689-859119
The family home where Darwin wrote *On the Origin of Species*

CHARTWELL (NT), Westerham, Kent TN16 1PS
T 01732-868381
Home and studio of Sir Winston Churchill

CHATSWORTH, Bakewell, Derbys DE45 1PP T 01246-565300
W www.chatsworth.org
Tudor mansion set in magnificent parkland; seat of the Dukes of Devonshire

CHESTERS ROMAN FORT (EH), Chollerford,
Northumberland NE46 4EU T 01434-681379
Roman cavalry fort built to guard Hadrian's Wall

CHYSAUSTER ANCIENT VILLAGE (EH), Penzance,
Cornwall TR20 8XA T 07831-757934
Remains of nearly 2,000-year-old Celtic settlement; eight stone-walled homesteads

CLIFFORD'S TOWER (EH), York YO1 9SA T 01904-646940
13th-century keep built on a mound; remains of a castle built by William the Conqueror

CORBRIDGE ROMAN SITE (EH), Corbridge,
Northumberland NE45 5NT T 01434-632349
Excavated central area of a Roman garrison town

CORFE CASTLE (NT), Wareham, Dorset BH20 5EZ
T 01929-481294
Former royal castle dating from the 11th century and partially ruined during the English Civil War

CROFT CASTLE AND PARKLAND (NT), Yarpole,
Herefordshire HR6 9PW T 01568-780246
17th-century quadrangular manor house with Georgian-Gothic interior; built close to ruin of pre-Conquest border castle

DEAL CASTLE (EH), Deal, Kent CT14 7BA T 01304-372762
Largest of the coastal defence forts built by Henry VIII; shaped like a rose with six inner and outer bastions

*****DERWENT VALLEY MILLS**, Belper, Derbyshire
T 01629-536831 W www.derwentvalleymills.org
Series of 18th- and 19th-century cotton mills; birthplace of the modern factory

DOVER CASTLE (EH), Dover, Kent CT16 1HU T 01304-211067
Castle with Roman, Saxon and Norman features; tunnels used as wartime operations rooms

DR JOHNSON'S HOUSE, Gough Square, London EC4A 3DE
T 020-7353 3745 W www.drjohnsonshouse.org
Home of Samuel Johnson 1748–59

DUNSTANBURGH CASTLE (EH/NT), Craster, nr Alnwick,
Northumberland NE66 3TT T 01665-576231
14th-century castle ruins on a cliff with a substantial twin-towered gatehouse-keep

ELTHAM PALACE (EH), Eltham, London SE9 5QE
T 02082-94 2548
Art Deco house next to remains of medieval palace once occupied by Henry VIII; moated gardens

FARLEIGH HUNGERFORD CASTLE (EH), Bath, Somerset
BA2 7RS T 01225-754026
Late 14th-century castle with inner and outer courts; chapel with rare medieval wall paintings

FARNHAM CASTLE KEEP (EH), Farnham, Surrey GU9 0AG
T 01252-721194 W www.farnhamcastle.com
Large 12th-century castle keep with motte and bailey wall

FISHBOURNE ROMAN PALACE, Fishbourne, Chichester, W.
Sussex PO19 3QR T 01243-785859 W www.sussexpast.co.uk
Excavated Roman palace with largest collection of in-situ
mosaics in Britain

*FOUNTAINS ABBEY (NT), nr Ripon, N. Yorks HG4 3DY
T 01765-608888
Ruined Cistercian monastery and corn mill; site includes
Studley Royal, a Georgian water garden and deer park

FRAMLINGHAM CASTLE (EH), Framlingham, Suffolk
IP13 9BP T 01728-724189
Castle (c.1200) with high curtain walls enclosing an
almshouse (1639); once the refuge of Mary Tudor

FURNESS ABBEY (EH), Barrow-in-Furness, Cumbria LA13 0PJ
T 01229-823420
Remains of church and cloister buildings founded in
1123

GLASTONBURY ABBEY, Glastonbury, Somerset BA6 9EL
T 01458-832267 W www.glastonburyabbey.com
12th-century abbey destroyed by fire in 1184 and later
rebuilt; ruined in 1539 during dissolution of monasteries;
site of an early Christian settlement

GOODRICH CASTLE (EH), Ross-on-Wye, Herefordshire
HR9 6HY T 01600-890538
Remains of 12th- and 13th-century castle; contains a
famous mortar that ruined the castle in 1646

GREENWAY (NT), nr Brixham, Devon TQ5 0ES T 01803-842382
Agatha Christie's holiday home which inspired several of
the settings in her books, including the murder in *Dead
Man's Folly*; large woodland; walled garden

GREENWICH, London SE10 9NF T 0870-608 2000
W www.visitgreenwich.org.uk
Former Royal Observatory (founded 1675) housing the
time ball and zero meridian of longitude; the Queen's
House, designed for Queen Anne, wife of James I, by
Inigo Jones; Painted Hall and neoclassical Chapel (Old
Royal Naval College)

GRIMES GRAVES (EH), Brandon, Norfolk IP26 5DE
T 01842-810656
Neolithic flint mines; one shaft can be descended

GUILDHALL, London EC2V 7HH T 020-7332 1313
W www.guildhall.cityoflondon.gov.uk
Centre of civic government of the City built c.1441;
facade built 1788–9

HADDON HALL, Bakewell, Derbys DE45 1LA T 01629-812855
W www.haddonhall.co.uk
Well-preserved 12th-century manor house

HAILES ABBEY (EH), Cheltenham, Glos GL54 5PB
T 01242-602398
Ruins of a 13th-century Cistercian monastery

HAM HOUSE AND GARDEN (NT), Richmond-upon-Thames,
Surrey TW10 7RS T 020-8940 1950
Stuart house with lavish interiors and formal gardens

HAMPTON COURT PALACE, East Molesey, Surrey KT8 9AU
T 0844-482 7777 W www.hrp.org.uk
16th-century palace originally built for Cardinal Wolsey
with 17th- and 18th-century additions by Wren; Royal
Tennis Court and world-renowned maze

HARDWICK HALL (NT), Chesterfield, Derbys S44 5QJ
T 01246-850430
Elizabethan house built for Bess of Hardwick

HARDY'S BIRTHPLACE (NT), Higher Bockhampton, Dorset
DT2 8QJ T 01305-262366
Birthplace and home of Thomas Hardy

HAREWOOD HOUSE, Harewood, W. Yorks LS17 9LG
T 0113-218 1010 W www.harewood.org
18th-century house designed by John Carr and Robert
Adam; park by Capability Brown

HATFIELD HOUSE, Hatfield, Herts AL9 5NQ T 01707-287000
W www.hatfield-house.co.uk

Jacobean house built by Robert Cecil; features surviving
wing of Royal Palace of Hatfield (c.1485), the childhood
home of Elizabeth I

HELMSLEY CASTLE (EH), Helmsley, N. Yorks YO62 5AB
T 01439-770442
12th-century keep and curtain wall with 16th-century
buildings; spectacular earthwork defences

HEVER CASTLE, nr Edenbridge, Kent TN8 7NG
T 01732-865224 W www.hevercastle.co.uk
13th-century double-moated castle; childhood home of
Anne Boleyn

HOLKHAM HALL, Wells-next-the-Sea, Norfolk NR23 1AB
T 01328-710227 W www.holkham.co.uk
Palladian mansion; notable fine art collection

HOUSESTEADS ROMAN FORT (EH), Hexham,
Northumberland NE47 6NN T 01434-344363
Excavated Roman infantry fort on Hadrian's Wall with
museum

*IRONBRIDGE GORGE, Ironbridge, Shropshire
W www.ironbridgeguide.info
Important Industrial Revolution site, featuring the world's
first iron bridge

KEDLESTON HALL (NT), Derbys DE22 5JH T 01332-842191
Palladian mansion built 1759–65; complete Robert Adam
interiors; museum of Asian artefacts

KELMSCOTT MANOR, nr Lechlade, Glos GL7 3HJ
T 01367-252486 W www.sal.org.uk/kelmscott-manor/
Built c.1600; summer home of William Morris, with
products of Morris and Co.

KENILWORTH CASTLE (EH), Kenilworth, Warks CV8 1NE
T 01926-852078
Largest castle ruin in England; Norman keep with 13th-
century outer walls

KENSINGTON PALACE, Kensington Gardens, London W8 4PX
T 0844-482 7777 W www.hrp.org.uk
Built in 1605 and enlarged by Wren; birthplace of Queen
Victoria

KENWOOD HOUSE (EH), Hampstead Lane, London NW3 7JR
T 020-8348 1286
Neoclassical villa housing the Iveagh bequest of paintings
and furniture

KEW PALACE, Richmond-upon-Thames, Surrey TW9 3AB
T 0844-482 7777 W www.hrp.org.uk
Red-brick mansion (c.1631); includes Queen Charlotte's
Cottage, used by King George III and family as a
summerhouse

KINGSTON LACY (NT), Wimborne Minster, Dorset BH21 4EA
T 01202-883402
17th-century mansion with 19th-century alterations;
important art collection

KNEBWORTH HOUSE, Knebworth, Herts SG3 6PY
T 01438-812661 W www.knebworthhouse.com
Tudor manor house concealed by 19th-century Gothic
decoration; Lutyens gardens

KNOLE (NT), Sevenoaks, Kent TN15 0RP T 01732-462100
House built in 1456 set in 1,000-acre deer park; fine art
and furniture collection; birthplace of Vita Sackville-West

LAMBETH PALACE, London SE1 7JU T 020-7898 1200
W www.archbishopofcanterbury.org
Official residence of the Archbishop of Canterbury since
the 13th century

LANERCOST PRIORY (EH), Brampton, Cumbria CA8 2HQ
T 01697-73030 W www.lanercostpriory.org.uk
The nave of the Augustinian priory's church, c.1166, is
still used; remains of other claustral buildings

LANHYDROCK (NT), Bodmin, Cornwall PL30 5AD
T 01208-265950
House dating from the 17th century; 50 rooms, including
kitchen and nursery

LEEDS CASTLE, nr Maidstone, Kent ME17 1PL T 01622-765400
W www.leeds-castle.com
Castle dating from the 12th century, situated on two
islands in a lake; used as a royal palace by Henry VIII

LEVENS HALL, Kendal, Cumbria LA8 0PD T 01539-560321
W www.levenshall.co.uk
Elizabethan house with unique topiary garden (1694);
steam engine collection

LINCOLN CASTLE, Lincoln, Lincs LN1 3AA T 01522-554559
W www.lincolncastle.com
Built by William the Conqueror in 1068 on a Roman site;
one of only two double-motted castles in Britain

LINDISFARNE PRIORY (EH), Holy Island, Northumberland
TD15 2RX T 01289-389200
Founded in AD 635; re-established in the 12th century as
a Benedictine priory, now ruined

LITTLE MORETON HALL (NT), Congleton, Cheshire
CW12 4SD T 01260-272018
Iconic timber-framed moated Tudor manor house with
knot garden

LONGLEAT HOUSE, Warminster, Wilts BA12 7NW
T 01985-844400 W www.longleat.co.uk
Elizabethan house in Italian Renaissance style; Capability
Brown parkland with lakes; safari park

LULLINGSTONE ROMAN VILLA (EH), Eynsford, Kent
DA4 0JA T 01322-863467
Large villa occupied for much of the Roman period; fine
mosaics and unique Christian paintings

MIDDLEHAM CASTLE (EH), Middleham, N. Yorks DL8 4QG
T 01969-623899
12th-century keep within later fortifications; childhood
home of Richard III

MONTACUTE HOUSE (NT), Montacute, Somerset TA15 6XP
T 01935-823289
Elizabethan mansion with National Portrait Gallery
collection of portraits from the period

MOUNT GRACE PRIORY (EH), Northallerton, N. Yorks
DL6 3JG T 01609-883494
Carthusian priory with remains of monastic buildings

OLD SARUM (EH), Salisbury, Wilts SP1 3SD T 01722-335398
Iron Age hill fort enclosing remains of Norman castle and
cathedral

ORFORD CASTLE (EH), Orford, Suffolk IP12 2ND
T 01394-450472
Polygonal tower keep of c.1170 and remains of coastal
defence castle built by Henry II

OSBORNE HOUSE (EH), East Cowes, Isle of Wight PO32 6JX
T 01983-200022
Queen Victoria's seaside residence; built by Thomas
Cubitt in Italian Renaissance style; summer house, Swiss
Cottage and museum

OSTERLEY PARK (NT), Isleworth, Middx TW7 4RB
T 020-8232 5050
18th-century neoclassical mansion with Tudor stable
block

PENDENNIS CASTLE (EH), Falmouth, Cornwall TR11 4LP
T 01326 316594
Well-preserved 16th-century coastal defence castle

PENSHURST PLACE, Penshurst, Kent TN11 8DG
T 01892-870307 W www.penshurstplace.com
Medieval house featuring Baron's Hall (1341) and
gardens (1346); toy museum

PETWORTH HOUSE (NT), Petworth, W. Sussex GU28 0AE
T 01798-342207
Late 17th-century house set in Capability Brown
landscaped deer park; fine art collection

PEVENSEY CASTLE (EH), Pevensey, E. Sussex BN24 5LE
T 01323-762604
Walls of a fourth-century Roman fort; remains of an 11th-
century castle

PEVERIL CASTLE (EH), Castleton, Derbys S33 8WQ
T 01433-620613
Remains of a 12th-century castle defended on two sides
by precipitous rocks

POLESDEN LACEY (NT), nr Dorking, Surrey RH5 6BD
T 01372-452048
Regency villa remodelled in the Edwardian era; fine
paintings and furnishings; walled rose garden

PORTCHESTER CASTLE (EH), Portchester, Hants PO16 9QW
T 02392-378291
Walls of a late Roman fort enclosing a Norman keep and
an Augustinian priory church

POWDERHAM CASTLE, Kenton, Devon EX6 8JQ
T 01626-890243 W www.powderham.co.uk
Medieval castle with 18th- and 19th-century alterations,
including James Wyatt music room

RABY CASTLE, Staindrop, Co. Durham DL2 3AH
T 01833-660202 W www.rabycastle.com
14th-century castle with walled gardens

RAGLEY HALL, Alcester, Warks B49 5NJ T 01789-762090
W www.ragleyhall.com
17th-century Palladian house with gardens and lake

RICHBOROUGH ROMAN FORT (EH), Richborough, Kent
CT13 9JW T 01304-612013
Remains of a Roman Saxon Shore fortress; landing-site of
the Claudian invasion in AD 43

RICHMOND CASTLE (EH), Richmond, N. Yorks DL10 4QW
T 01748-822493
12th-century keep with 11th-century curtain wall

RIEVAULX ABBEY (EH), nr Helmsley, N. Yorks YO62 5LB
T 01439-798228
Remains of a Cistercian abbey founded c.1132

ROCHESTER CASTLE (EH), Rochester, Kent ME1 1SW
T 01634-335882
11th-century castle partly on the Roman city wall, with a
well-preserved square keep of c.1127

ROCKINGHAM CASTLE, Market Harborough, Leics LE16 8TH
T 01536-770240 W www.rockinghamcastle.com
Built by William the Conqueror; formal gardens and 400-
year-old 'elephant' hedge

ROMAN BATHS, Pump Room, Stall Street, Bath BA1 1LZ T
01225-477785 W www.romanbaths.co.uk
Extensive remains of a Roman temple and bathing
complex which still flows with natural thermal water;
museum

ROYAL PAVILION, Brighton BN1 1EE T 03000-290900
W www.brighton-hove-rpml.org.uk
Unique palace of George IV, in indo-gothic style with
chinoiserie interiors and Regency gardens

ST AUGUSTINE'S ABBEY (EH), Canterbury, Kent CT1 1PF
T 01227-767345
Remains of Benedictine monastery founded c.597

ST MAWES CASTLE (EH), St Mawes, Cornwall TR2 5DE
T 01326-270526
Coastal defence castle built by Henry VIII

ST MICHAEL'S MOUNT (NT), Marazion, Cornwall TR17 0HS
T 01736-710265 W www.stmichaelsmount.co.uk
12th-century church and castle with later additions,
situated on an iconic rocky island

*SALTAIRE VILLAGE, nr Shipley, W. Yorks
W www.saltairevillage.info
Victorian industrial village founded by mill owner Titus
Salt for his workers see also World Heritage Sites

SANDRINGHAM, Norfolk PE35 6EN T 01485-545400
W www.sandringhamestate.co.uk
The Queen's private residence; neo-Jacobean house built
in 1870 with gardens and country park

SCARBOROUGH CASTLE (EH), Scarborough, N. Yorks
YO11 1HY T 01723-372451
Remains of 12th-century keep and curtain walls

SHERBORNE CASTLE, Sherborne, Dorset DT9 5NR
T 01935-812072 W www.sherbornecastle.com
16th-century castle built by Sir Walter Raleigh set in
Capability Brown landscaped gardens

SHUGBOROUGH ESTATE (NT), Milford, Staffs ST17 0XB
T 01889-880160 W www.shugborough.org.uk
Late 17th century house in 18th-century park with
monuments, temples and pavilions in the Greek Revival
style; seat of the Earls of Lichfield

SISSINGHURST CASTLE GARDEN (NT), Nr Cranbrook,
Kent TN17 2AB T 01580-710700

Early 14th century site, purchased by Vita Sackville-West in the 1930's where the writer, poet and Bloomsbury Group member created the famous gardens.

SKIPTON CASTLE, Skipton, N. Yorks BD23 1AW
T 01756-792442 W www.skiptoncastle.co.uk
Well-preserved D-shaped medieval castle with six round towers and inner courtyard

SMALLHYTHE PLACE (NT), Tenterden, Kent TN30 7NG
T 01580-762334
Half-timbered 16th-century house

*STONEHENGE (EH), nr Amesbury, Wilts SP4 7DE
T 0370-333 1181
World-famous prehistoric monument comprising concentric stone circles surrounded by a ditch and bank

STONOR PARK, Henley-on-Thames, Oxon RG9 6HF
T 01491-638587 W www.stonor.com
Medieval house with Georgian facade; refuge for Catholic recusants after the Reformation

STOURHEAD (NT), Stourton, Wilts BA12 6QD T 01747-841152
18th-century Palladian mansion with world-renowned landscape gardens; King Alfred's Tower

STRATFIELD SAYE HOUSE, Hants RG7 2BT T 01256-882694
W www.wellingtonestates.co.uk
House built 1630–40; home of the Dukes of Wellington since 1817

STRATFORD-UPON-AVON, Warks T 01789-868191
W www.stratford-upon-avon.co.uk
Shakespeare's Birthplace Trust with Shakespeare Centre; Anne Hathaway's Cottage; Holy Trinity Church, where Shakespeare is buried

SUDELEY CASTLE, Winchcombe, Glos GL54 5JD
T 01242-604244 W www.sudeleycastle.co.uk
Castle built in 1442; once owned by Richard III and former home to Catherine Parr, sixth wife of Henry VIII; restored in the 19th century

SULGRAVE MANOR, nr Banbury, Oxon OX17 2SD
T 01295-760205 W www.sulgravemanor.org.uk
Home of George Washington's family

SUTTON HOUSE (NT), Hackney, London E9 6JQ
T 020-8986 2264
Tudor house, built in 1535 by Sir Ralph Sadleir

SYON HOUSE, Brentford, Middx TW8 8JF T 020-8560 0882
W www.syonhouse.co.uk
Built on the site of a former monastery; Robert Adam interior; Capability Brown park

TINTAGEL CASTLE (EH), Tintagel, Cornwall PL34 0HE
T 01840-770328
13th-century cliff-top castle and 5th–6th-century Celtic settlement; linked with Arthurian legend

TOWER OF LONDON, London EC3N 4AB T 0844-482 7777
W www.hrp.org.uk
Royal palace and fortress begun by William the Conqueror in 1078; houses the Crown Jewels

TYNEMOUTH PRIORY AND CASTLE (EH), Tyne and Wear NE30 4BZ T 0191-257 1090
Remains of a Benedictine priory, founded c.1090, moated castle-towers, a gatehouse and keep on Saxon monastic site

UPPARK (NT), South Harting, W. Sussex GU31 5QR
T 01730-825415
17th-century house, restored after fire; Fetherstonhaugh art collection; 18th-century dolls' house

WALMER CASTLE (EH), Walmer, Kent CT14 7LJ
T 01304-364288
One of Henry VIII's coastal defence castles, now the residence of the Lord Warden of the Cinque Ports

WARKWORTH CASTLE (EH), Warkworth, Northumberland NE65 0UJ T 01665-711423
14th-century keep amid earlier ruins, with hermitage upstream

WHITBY ABBEY (EH), Whitby, N. Yorks YO22 4JT
T 01947-603568
Remains of Norman church on the site of a monastery founded in AD 657

WILTON HOUSE, nr Salisbury, Wilts SP2 0BJ T 01722-746714
W www.wiltonhouse.co.uk
17th-century house on the site of a Tudor house and ninth-century nunnery; Palladian bridge

WINDSOR CASTLE, Windsor, Berks SL4 1NJ T 020-7766 7304
W www.royalcollection.org.uk
Official residence of the Queen; oldest royal residence still in regular use; largest inhabited castle in the world. Also St George's Chapel; Queen Mary's Dolls' House

WOBURN ABBEY, Woburn, Beds MK17 9WA T 01525-290333
W www.woburn.co.uk
Built on the site of a Cistercian abbey; seat of the Dukes of Bedford; art collection; antiques centre

WROXETER ROMAN CITY (EH), nr Shrewsbury, Shropshire SY5 6PH T 01743-761330
Second-century public baths and part of the forum of the Roman town of *Viroconium*

WALES

For more information on Cadw properties, including those listed below, the official website is W www.cadw.wales.gov.uk For more information on National Trust properties in Wales, including those listed below, the official website is W www.nationaltrust.org.uk

KEY
(C) Property of Cadw: Welsh Historic Monuments
(NT) National Trust property
* UNESCO World Heritage Site (*see also* World Heritage Sites)

*BEAUMARIS CASTLE (C), Anglesey LL58 8AP
T 01248-810361
Concentrically planned 13th-century castle, still virtually intact

*BLAENAVON, Church Road, Blaenavon NP4 9AS T 01495-742333 W www.visitblaenavon.co.uk
18th- and 19th-century industrial landscape associated with coal and iron production

CAERLEON ROMAN BATHS AND AMPHITHEATRE (C), Newport NP18 1AE T 01633-422518
Rare example of a legionary bath-house and late first-century arena surrounded by bank for spectators

*CAERNARFON CASTLE (C), Gwynedd LL55 2AY
T 01286-677617 W www.caernarfon-castle.co.uk
Huge fortress with polygonal towers built between 1283 and 1330, initially for King Edward I of England; setting for the investiture of Prince Charles in 1969

CAERPHILLY CASTLE (C), Caerphilly CF83 1JD
T 029-2088 3143
Concentrically planned castle (c.1270) notable for its scale and use of water defences

CARDIFF CASTLE, Cardiff CF10 3RB T 029-2087 8100
W www.cardiffcastle.com
Norman keep built on site of Roman fort; 'fairytale' gothic-revival mansion added in the 19th century

CASTELL COCH (C), Tongwynlais, Cardiff CF15 7JS
T 029-2081 0101
'Fairytale'-style castle, rebuilt 1875–90 on medieval foundations

CHEPSTOW CASTLE (C), Monmouthshire NP16 5EY
T 01291-624065
Rectangular keep amid extensive fortifications; developed throughout the Middle Ages

*CONWY CASTLE (C), Gwynedd LL32 8AY T 01492-592358
Built for Edward I in 1283–7 on narrow rocky outcrop; features eight towers and two barbicans

CRICCIETH CASTLE (C), Gwynedd LL52 0DP
T 01766-522227
Native Welsh 13th-century castle, taken and altered by Edward I and Edward II

DENBIGH CASTLE (C), Denbighshire LL16 3NB
T 01745-813385
Remains of the castle (begun 1282), including triple-towered gatehouses

DYFFRYN GARDENS (NT), St Nicholas, Cardiff CF5 6SU
T 029-2059 3328
Edwardian gardens designed by Thomas Mawson, overlooked by a grand Edwardian mansion
*HARLECH CASTLE (C), Gwynedd LL46 2YH T 01766-780552
Well-preserved castle, constructed 1283–95, on an outcrop above the former shoreline; withstood seven-year siege 1461–8
PEMBROKE CASTLE, Pembrokeshire SA71 4LA
T 01646-681510 W www.pembroke-castle.co.uk
Castle founded in 1093; Great Tower built in late 12th century; birthplace of King Henry VII
PENRHYN CASTLE (NT), Bangor, Gwynedd LL57 4HN
T 01248-353084
Neo-Norman castle built in the 19th century; railway and dolls' museums; private art collection
*PONTCYSYLLTE AQUEDUCT AND CANAL,Trevor, Wrexham LL20 7TG T 01978-292015
W www.pontcysyllte-aqueduct.co.uk
Longest and highest aqueduct in Great Britain; designed by Thomas Telford and finished in 1805
POWIS CASTLE (NT), Welshpool, Powys SY21 8RF
T 01938-551944
Medieval castle with interior in variety of styles; 17th-century gardens; Clive of India museum
RAGLAN CASTLE (C), Monmouthshire NP15 2BT
T 01291-690228
Remains of 15th-century castle with moated hexagonal keep
ST DAVIDS BISHOP'S PALACE (C), Pembrokeshire SA62 6PE
T 01437-720517
Remains of residence of Bishops of St Davids built 1328–47
TINTERN ABBEY (C), nr Chepstow, Monmouthshire NP16 6SE
T 01291-689251
Remains of 13th-century church and conventual buildings of a 12th-century Cistercian monastery
TRETOWER COURT AND CASTLE (C), Nr Crickhowell, Powys NP8 1RD T 01874-730279
Medieval manor house rebuilt in the 15th century, with remains of 12th-century castle near by

SCOTLAND
For more information on Historic Environment Scotland properties, including those listed below, the official website is W www.historicenvironment.scot
For more information on National Trust for Scotland properties, including those listed below, the official website is W www.nts.org.uk

KEY
(HES) Historic Environment Scotland property
(NTS) National Trust for Scotland property
* Part of the Heart of Neolithic Orkney UNESCO World Heritage Site

ABBOTSFORD HOUSE, Melrose, Roxburghshire TD6 9BQ T 01896-752043 W www.scottsabbotsford.co.uk
Home of Sir Walter Scott; features historic Scottish relics and formal gardens
BALMORAL CASTLE, Ballater, Aberdeenshire AB35 5TB
T 01339-742534 W www.balmoralcastle.com
Baronial-style castle built for Victoria and Albert; the Queen's private residence
BLACKHOUSE, ARNOL (HES), Lewis, Western Isles HS2 9DB
T 01851-710395
Traditional Lewis thatched house
BLAIR CASTLE, Blair Atholl, Perthshire PH18 5TL
T 01796-481207 W www.blair-castle.co.uk
Mid-18th-century mansion with 13th-century tower; seat of the Dukes and Earls of Atholl
BOWHILL, Selkirk, Scottish Borders TD7 5ET T 01750-22204
W www.bowhillhouse.co.uk
Present house dates mainly from 1812; Seat of the Dukes of Buccleuch and Queensberry; fine collection of paintings

BROUGH OF BIRSAY (HES), Orkney KW17 2LX
T 01856-841815
Remains of Norse and Pictish village on the tidal island of Birsay
CAERLAVEROCK CASTLE (HES), Glencaple, Dumfries and Galloway DG1 4RU T 01387-770244
Unique triangular 13th-century moated castle with classical Renaissance additions
CAIRNPAPPLE HILL (HES), Torphichen, West Lothian
T 01315-507603
Neolithic ceremonial site and Bronze Age burial chambers
CALANAIS STANDING STONES (HES), Lewis, Western Isles HS2 9DY T 01851-621422
Standing stones in a cross-shaped setting, dating from between 2900 and 2600 BC
CATERTHUNS (BROWN AND WHITE) (HES), Menmuir, nr Brechin, Angus
Two large Iron Age hill forts
CAWDOR CASTLE, Nairn, Moray IV12 5RD T 01667-404401
W www.cawdorcastle.com
14th-century keep with 15th- and 17th-century additions
CLAVA CAIRNS (HES), nr Inverness, Inverness-shire IV2 5EU
T 01667-460232
Bronze Age cemetery complex of cairns and standing stones
CRATHES CASTLE (NTS), nr Banchory, Aberdeenshire AB31 5QJ T 01330-844525
16th-century baronial castle in woodland, fields and gardens
CULZEAN CASTLE (NTS), Maybole, Ayrshire KA19 8LE
T 01655-884455
18th-century Robert Adam castle with oval staircase and circular saloon
DRYBURGH ABBEY (HES), nr Melrose, Roxburghshire TD6 0RQ T 01835-822381
12th-century abbey containing the tomb of Sir Walter Scott
DUNVEGAN CASTLE, Skye IV55 8WF T 01470-521206
W www.dunvegancastle.com
13th-century castle with later additions; home of the chiefs of the Clan MacLeod
EDINBURGH CASTLE (HES), EH1 2NG T 0131-225 9846
W www.edinburghcastle.gov.uk
Fortress perched on extinct volcano; includes the Scottish Crown Jewels, Scottish National War Memorial, Scottish United Services Museum
EDZELL CASTLE (HES), nr Brechin, Angus DD9 7UE
T 01356-648631
Ruined 16th-century tower house on medieval foundations; early 17th-century walled garden
EILEAN DONAN CASTLE, Dornie, Ross and Cromarty IV40 8DX T 01599-555202 W www.eileandonancastle.com
13th-century castle situated at the meeting point of three sea lochs; Jacobite relics
ELGIN CATHEDRAL (HES), Moray IV30 1HU T 01343-547171
13th-century cathedral and octagonal chapterhouse
FLOORS CASTLE, Kelso, Roxburghshire TD5 7SF
T 01573-223333 W www.floorscastle.com
Largest inhabited castle in Scotland; seat of the Dukes of Roxburghe; built in the 1720s by William Adam
FORT GEORGE (HES), Ardersier, Inverness-shire IV2 7TD
T 01667-460232
18th-century fort; still a working army barracks
GLAMIS CASTLE, Forfar, Angus DD8 1RJ T 01307-840393
W www.glamis-castle.co.uk
Seat of the Lyon family (later Earls of Strathmore and Kinghorne) since 1372; the setting for Shakespeare's *Macbeth*
GLASGOW CATHEDRAL (HES), Lanarkshire G4 0QZ
T 0141-552 8198 W www.glasgowcathedral.org.uk
Late 12th-century cathedral with vaulted crypt
GLENELG BROCHS (HES), Glenelg, Ross and Cromarty
T 01667-460232
Two broch towers (Dun Telve and Dun Troddan) with well-preserved structural features

HOPETOUN HOUSE, South Queensferry, West Lothian
EH30 9SL T 0131-331 2451 W www.hopetoun.co.uk
Designed by Sir William Bruce in 1699 and enlarged by
William Adam 1721–48

HUNTLY CASTLE (HES), Aberdeenshire AB54 4SH
T 01466-793191
Ruin of a 16th- and 17th-century baronial residence

INVERARAY CASTLE, Argyll PA32 8XE T 01499-302203
W www.inveraray-castle.com
Gothic-style 18th-century castle designed by William
Adam and Roger Morris; seat of the Dukes of Argyll

IONA ABBEY (HES), Iona, Inner Hebrides PA76 6SQ
T 01681-700512
Monastery founded by St Columba in AD 563

JARLSHOF (HES), Sumburgh Head, Shetland ZE3 9JN
T 01950-460112
Prehistoric settlement with later ninth-century Norse
additions

JEDBURGH ABBEY (HES), Scottish Borders TD8 6JQ
T 01835-863925
Ruined Augustinian abbey founded c.1138

KISIMUL CASTLE (HES), Castlebay, Barra, Western Isles
HS9 5UZ T 01871-810313
Medieval island home of the Clan MacNeil

LINLITHGOW PALACE (HES), Kirkgate, Linlithgow, West
Lothian EH49 7AL T 01506-842896
Ruined royal palace, founded in 1424, set in park;
birthplace of James V and Mary, Queen of Scots

*MAESHOWE (HES), Stenness, Orkney KW16 3HH
T 01856-761606
Neolithic chambered tomb with Viking runes

MEIGLE SCULPTURED STONES (HES), Meigle, Perthshire
PH12 8SB T 01828-640612
Twenty-six carved Pictish stones dating from the late 8th
to the late 10th centuries

MELROSE ABBEY (HES), Melrose, Roxburghshire TD6 9LG
T 01896-822562
Ruin of Cistercian abbey founded c.1136 by David I;
museum of medieval objects

MOUSA BROCH (HES), Island of Mousa, Shetland ZE2 9HP
Finest surviving Iron Age broch tower

NEW ABBEY CORN MILL (HES), Dumfriesshire DG2 8BX
T 01387-850260
Working water-powered mill built in the late 18th
century

*NEW LANARK, South Lanarkshire ML11 9DB T 01555-661 345
18th-century village built around a cotton mill

PALACE OF HOLYROODHOUSE, Edinburgh EH8 8DX
T 0303-5123 7306 W www.royalcollection.org.uk
The Queen's official Scottish residence; home to Mary,
Queen of Scots; main part of the palace built 1671–9
close to ruined 12th-century Augustinian abbey

*RING O' BRODGAR (HES), Stenness, Orkney KW16
T 01856-841815
Neolithic circle of upright stones surrounded by circular
ditch

ROSSLYN CHAPEL, Roslin, Midlothian EH25 9PU
T 0131-440 2159 W www.rosslynchapel.org.uk
Historic church built between 1446 and 1484 with
unique stone carvings

ST ANDREWS CASTLE AND CATHEDRAL (HES), Fife
KY16 9AR (castle); 9QL (cathedral) T 01334-477196 (castle);
01334-472563 (cathedral)
Ruins of 13th-century castle, the former residence of
bishops of St Andrews, and remains of the largest
cathedral in Scotland; museum

SCONE PALACE, Perth, Perthshire PH2 6BD T 01738-552300
W www.scone-palace.co.uk
Georgian-Gothic house built 1802–12

*SKARA BRAE (HES), nr Stromness, Orkney KW16 3LR T
01856-841815
Neolithic village with adjacent replica house

SMAILHOLM TOWER (HES), nr Kelso, Roxburghshire
TD5 7PG T 01573-460365

Well-preserved 15th-century tower-house

STIRLING CASTLE (HES), Stirlingshire FK8 1EJ
T 01786-450000 W www.stirlingcastle.gov.uk
Great Hall and gatehouse built for James IV c.1500;
palace built for James V in 1538; site of coronations
including Mary, Queen of Scots

*STONES OF STENNESS, Stenness, Orkney T 01856 841815
Four surviving Neolithic standing stones and the uprights
of a three-stone dolmen

TANTALLON CASTLE (HES), North Berwick, East Lothian
EH39 5PN T 01620-892727
Ruined 14th-century curtain wall with towers

THREAVE CASTLE (HES), Castle Douglas, Kirkcudbrightshire
DG7 1TJ T 07711-223101
Ruined late 14th-century tower on an island; accessible
only by boat

URQUHART CASTLE (HES), Drumnadrochit, Inverness-shire
IV63 6XJ T 01456-450551
13th-century castle remains on the banks of Loch Ness

NORTHERN IRELAND

For the Northern Ireland Environment Agency, the official
website is W www.doeni.gov.uk/niea
For more information on National Trust properties in Northern
Ireland, including those listed below, the official website is
W www.nationaltrust.org.uk

KEY
(NIEA) Property in the care of the Northern Ireland
Environment Agency
(NT) National Trust property

CARRICKFERGUS CASTLE (NIEA), Carrickfergus, Co.
Antrim BT38 7BG T 028-9335 1273
Castle built in 1177 and taken by King John in 1210;
garrisoned until 1928

CASTLE COOLE (NT), Enniskillen, Co. Fermanagh BT74 6JY
T 028-6632 2690
18th-century neoclassical mansion in parkland; designed
by James Wyatt

CASTLE WARD (NT), Strangford, Co. Down BT30 7LS
T 028-4488 1204
18th-century house with Classical and Gothic facades

DEVENISH MONASTIC SITE (NIEA), nr Enniskillen, Co.
Fermanagh T 028-6862 1588
Island monastery founded in the sixth century by St
Molaise; church dating from 13th century

DOWNHILL DEMESNE AND HEZLETT HOUSE (NT),
Castlerock, Co. Londonderry BT51 4RP T 028-7084 8728
Ruins of 18th-century mansion and a 17th-century
cottage in landscaped estate including Mussenden Temple

DUNLUCE CASTLE (NIEA), Bushmills, Co. Antrim BT57 8UY
T 028-2073 1938
Ruins of medieval stronghold of the McDonnells

FLORENCE COURT (NT), Enniskillen, Co. Fermanagh
BT92 1DB T 028-6634 8249
Mid-18th-century house with Rococo decoration

GREY ABBEY (NIEA), Greyabbey, Co. Down BT22 2NQ
T 028-9181 1491
Substantial remains of a Cistercian abbey founded in
1193 set in landscaped parkland

MOUNT STEWART (NT), Newtownards, Co. Down BT22 2AD
T 028-4278 8387
18th-century house; octagonal Temple of the Winds

NENDRUM MONASTIC SITE (NIEA), Mahee Island, Co.
Down T 028-9054 3037
Island monastery founded in the fifth century by St
Machaoi

PATTERSON'S SPADE MILL (NT), Templepatrick, Co. Antrim
BT39 0AP T 028-9443 3619
Last working water-driven spade mill in the UK

TULLY CASTLE (NIEA), Co. Fermanagh T 028-6862 1588
Fortified house and bawn built c.1619

MUSEUMS AND GALLERIES

There are approximately 2,500 museums and galleries in the UK. As at April 2017, 1,552 of these were fully accredited by Arts Council England. Accreditation indicates that the museum or gallery has an appropriate constitution, is soundly financed, has adequate collection management standards and public services and has access to professional curatorial advice. A further 170 museums hold provisional accreditation and another 92 have applied for, or are in the process of obtaining accreditation. These applications are assessed by either Arts Council England; the Museums, Archives and Libraries division of the Welsh government; Museums Galleries Scotland or the Northern Ireland Museums Council.

The following is a selection of museums and art galleries in the UK. Opening hours and admission charges vary. Further information about museums and galleries in the UK is available from the Museums Association (W www.museumsassociation.org T 020-7566 7800).

W www.culture24.org.uk includes a database of all the museums and galleries in the UK.

ENGLAND
* England's national museums and galleries, which receive funding from a government department, such as the DCMS or MoD. These institutions are deemed to have collections of national importance, and the government is able to call upon their staff for expert advice.

ALTON
Jane Austen's House Museum, Chawton, Hants GU34 1SD
   T 01420-83262 W www.jane-austens-house-museum.org.uk
   17th-century house which tells the author's story
BARNARD CASTLE
The Bowes Museum, Co. Durham DL12 8NP T 01833-690606
   W www.bowesmuseum.org.uk
   Public gallery in a French châteaux style featuring archaeology, fashion and ceramics. Houses one of the largest collections of Spanish art in the country
BATH
American Museum, Claverton Manor BA2 7BD T 01225-460503
   W www.americanmuseum.org
   American decorative arts from the 17th to 20th centuries; American heritage exhibition
Fashion Museum, Bennett Street BA1 2QH T 01225-477789
   W www.museumofcostume.co.uk
   Fashion from the 17th century to the present day
Victoria Art Gallery, Bridge Street BA2 4AT T 01225-477233
   W www.victoriagal.org.uk
   European Old Masters and British art since the 15th century
BEAMISH
Beamish Museum, Co. Durham DH9 0RG T 0191-370 4000
   W www.beamish.org.uk
   Living working museum of a northern industrial town during Georgian, Victorian and Edwardian times
BEAULIEU
National Motor Museum, Hants SO42 7ZN T 01590-612345
   W www.beaulieu.co.uk
   Former royal estate within the New Forest national park home to Beaulieu Abbey, Palace House and the National Motor Museum
BIRMINGHAM
Aston Hall, Trinity Road B6 6JD T 0121-348 8100
   W www.birminghammuseums.org.uk/aston
   Jacobean House containing paintings, furniture and tapestries from the 17th to 19th centuries
Barber Institute of Fine Arts, University of Birmingham, Edgbaston B15 2TS T 0121-414 7333 W www.barber.org.uk
   Extensive coin collection; fine arts, including Old Masters

Birmingham Museum and Art Gallery, Chamberlain Square B3 3DH
   T 0121-348 8038 W www.bmag.org.uk
   Includes notable collection of Pre-Raphaelite art
Museum of the Jewellery Quarter, Vyse Street, Hockley B18 6HA
   T 0121-348 8140 W www.birminghammuseums.org.uk/jewellery
   Preserved jewellery workshop
Thinktank, Curzon Street B4 7XG T 0121-348 8000
   W www.thinktank.ac
   Science museum featuring over 200 hands-on displays and a Planetarium
BOURNEMOUTH
Russell-Cotes Art Gallery and Museum, East Cliff Promenade BH1 3AA T 01202-451858 W www.russellcotes.com
   Seaside villa housing 19th- and 20th-century art and sculptures from around the world
BOVINGTON
Tank Museum, Dorset BH20 6JG T 01929-405096
   W www.tankmuseum.org
   Collection of 300 tanks from their invention in 1915 to the modern conflict in Afghanistan
BRADFORD
Bradford Industrial Museum, Moorside Mills, Moorside Road, Eccleshill BD2 3HP T 01274-435900
   W www.bradfordmuseums.org
   Steam power, machinery and motor vehicle exhibits
Cartwright Hall Art Gallery, Lister Park BD9 4NS T 01274-431212
   W www.bradfordmuseums.org
   British 19th- and 20th-century fine art, contemporary prints and south Asian art
**National Media Museum*, BD1 1NQ T 0844-856 3797
   W www.nationalmediamuseum.org.uk
   Photography, film and television interactive exhibits; features an IMAX cinema and the only permanent Cinerama screen in Europe
BRIGHTON
Booth Museum of Natural History, Dyke Road BN1 5AA
   T 03000-290900 W www.brightonmuseums.org.uk/booth
   Zoology, botany and geology collections; British birds in recreated habitats
Brighton Museum and Art Gallery, Royal Pavilion Gardens BN1 1EE
   T 03000-290900 W www.brightonmuseums.org.uk/brighton
   Includes fine art and design, fashion, world art; Sussex history
BRISTOL
Arnolfini, Narrow Quay BS1 4QA T 0117-917 2300
   W www.arnolfini.org.uk
   Experimental contemporary visual arts, dance, performance, music; talks and workshops
Blaise Castle House Museum, Henbury Road BS10 7QS
   T 0117-903 9818 W www.bristolmuseums.org.uk/blaise-castle-house-museum
   18th-century mansion; social history collections
Bristol Museum and Art Gallery, Queen's Road BS8 1RL
   T 0117-922 3571 W www.bristolmuseums.org.uk/bristol-museum-and-art-gallery
   Includes Victorian, Edwardian and French fine art; archaeology, local history and natural sciencies
M Shed, Prince's Wharf BS1 4RN T 0117-352 6600
   W www.mshed.org
   The story of Bristol's heritage of engineering, transport, music and industry
CAMBRIDGE
Fitzwilliam Museum, Trumpington Street CB2 1RB
   T 01223-332900 W www.fitzmuseum.cam.ac.uk
   Antiquities, fine and applied arts, clocks, ceramics, manuscripts, furniture, sculpture, coins and medals

Imperial War Museum Duxford, Duxford CB22 4QR
T 01223-835000 W www.iwm.org.uk/visits/iwm-duxford
Displays of military and civil aircraft, tanks and naval exhibits

Museum of Archaeology and Anthropology, Downing Street
CB2 3DZ T 01223-333516 W www.maa.cam.ac.uk
Global archaeological and anthropological collections; photography and modern art collections

Sedgwick Museum of Earth Sciences, Downing Street CB2 3EQ
T 01223-333456 W www.sedgwickmuseum.org
Extensive geological collection

Whipple Museum of the History of Science, Free School Lane
CB2 3RH T 01223-330906 W www.hps.cam.ac.uk/whipple
Scientific instruments from the 14th century to the present

CARLISLE
Tullie House Museum and Art Gallery, Castle Street CA3 8TP
T 01228-618718 W www.tulliehouse.co.uk
Jacobean house with fine art, local social history, prehistoric archaeology and natural sciences including Hadrian's Wall exhibit

CHATHAM
The Historic Dockyard, ME4 4TE T 01634-823800
W www.thedockyard.co.uk
Maritime attractions including HMS *Cavalier*, the UK's last Second World War destroyer

Royal Engineers Museum, Prince Arthur Road, Gillingham ME4 4UG
T 01634-822839 W www.re-museum.co.uk
Regimental history, ethnography, decorative art and photography

CHELTENHAM
The Wilson Art Gallery and Museum, Clarence Street GL50 3JT
T 01242-237431 W www.cheltenhammuseum.org.uk
Arts and crafts, local heroes, fine art and natural history

CHESTER
Grosvenor Museum, Grosvenor Street CH1 2DD T 01244-972197
W www.grosvenormuseum.co.uk
Roman collections, natural history, art, Chester silver, local history and costume

CHICHESTER
Weald and Downland Open Air Museum, Singleton PO18 0EU
T 01243-811363 W www.wealddown.co.uk
Rebuilt vernacular buildings from south-east England; includes medieval houses and a working watermill; craft demonstrations, Tudor kitchen and cooking

COLCHESTER
Colchester Castle Museum, Castle Park CO1 1TJ T 01206-282939
W www.visitcolchester.com
Largest Norman keep in Europe standing on foundations of the Roman Temple of Claudius

COVENTRY
Coventry Transport Museum, Hales Street CV1 1JD
T 024-7623 4270 W www.transport-museum.com
Extensive collection of motor vehicles and bicycles; land speed record-holding car

Herbert Art Gallery and Museum, Jordan Well CV1 5QP
T 024-7623 7521 W www.theherbert.org
Local history, archaeology, industry and visual arts

DERBY
Derby Museum and Art Gallery, The Strand DE1 1BS
T 01332-641901 W www.derbymuseums.org/museumartgallery
Includes paintings by Joseph Wright of Derby, origins of Derby and military history

Derby Silk Mill, Silk Mill Lane DE1 3AF T 01332-641901
W www.derbymuseums.org/locations/the-silk-mill
Built on the site of the world's first factory; wildlife gallery, fine art, Bonnie Prince Charlie Room

Pickford's House Museum, Friar Gate DE1 1DA T 01332-641901
W www.derbymuseums.org/pickfords-house
Georgian town house designed by architect Joseph Pickford; museum of Georgian life and costume

DEVIZES
Wiltshire Museum, Library and Gallery, Long Street SN10 1NS
T 01380-727369 W www.wiltshiremuseum.org.uk

Natural and local history; art gallery; archaeological finds from prehistoric, Roman and Saxon sites

DORCHESTER
Dorset County Museum, High West Street DT1 1XA
T 01305-262735 W www.dorsetcountymuseum.org
Includes a collection of Thomas Hardy's manuscripts, books, notebooks and drawings; local history, geology and Roman mosaics

DOVER
Dover Museum, Market Square CT16 1PH T 01304-201066
W www.dovermuseum.co.uk
Contains the Dover Bronze Age Boat Gallery and archaeological finds from Bronze Age, Roman and Saxon sites

EXETER
Royal Albert Memorial Museum and Art Gallery, Queen Street
EX4 3RX T 01392-265858 W www.rammuseum.org.uk
Natural history; archaeology; worldwide fine and decorative art including Exeter silver

GATESHEAD
Baltic Centre for Contemporary Art, South Shore Road NE8 3BA
T 0191-478 1810 W www.balticmill.com
Contemporary art exhibitions and events

Shipley Art Gallery, Prince Consort Road NE8 4JB T 0191-477 1495
W www.twmuseums.org.uk/shipley
Contemporary crafts

GAYDON
Heritage Motor Centre, Banbury Road, Warks CV35 0BJ
T 01926-641188 W www.heritage-motor-centre.co.uk
The world's largest collection of British cars with nearly 300 vehicles spanning the classic, vintage and veteran eras

GLOUCESTER
Gloucester Waterways Museum, Gloucester Docks GL1 2EH
T 01452-318200 W www.canalrivertrust.org.uk/gloucester-waterways-museum
200-year history of Britain's canals and inland waterways

GOSPORT
Royal Navy Submarine Museum, Haslar Jetty Road, Hants PO12 2AS
T 023-9251 0354 W www.submarine-museum.co.uk
Underwater warfare exhibition, including submarines HMS *Alliance* and HMS *Holland 1* – the Royal Navy's first submarine

GRASMERE
Dove Cottage and the *Wordsworth Museum*, Cumbria LA22 9SH
T 015394-35544 W www.wordsworth.org.uk
William Wordsworth's manuscripts, home and garden

HOVE
Hove Museum and Art Gallery, New Church Road BN3 4AB
T 03000-290900 W www.brightonmuseums.org.uk/hove
Toys, cinema, local history and fine art collections

HULL
Ferens Art Gallery, Queen Victoria Square HU1 3RA
T 01482-300300 W www.hullcc.gov.uk/ferens
European Old Masters, Victorian, Edwardian and contemporary British art

Hull Maritime Museum, Queen Victoria Square HU1 3DX
T 01482-300300 W www.hullcc.gov.uk
Hull's maritime heritage including whaling, fishing, navigation and merchant trade

HUNTINGDON
The Cromwell Museum, Grammar School Walk PE29 3LF
T 01480-375830 W www.cromwellmuseum.org
Portraits and memorabilia relating to Oliver Cromwell

IPSWICH
Christchurch Mansion and *Wolsey Art Gallery*, Christchurch Park
IP4 2BE T 01473-433554 W www.cimuseums.org.uk
Tudor house with paintings by Gainsborough, Constable and other Suffolk artists; furniture and 18th-century ceramics; temporary exhibitions

KEIGHLEY
The Brontë Parsonage Museum, Haworth, W. Yorks BD22 8DR
T 01535-642323 W www.bronte.org.uk
The former home of the literary Brontë family

KESWICK

Pencil Museum, Southey Works CA12 5NG T 01768-773626
W www.pencilmuseum.co.uk
500-year history of the pencil; demonstration events and
workshops throughout the year

LEEDS

Armley Mills, Leeds Industrial Museum, Canal Road, Armley
LS12 2QF T 0113-378 3173 W www.leeds.gov.uk/armleymills
Once the world's largest woollen mill, now a museum for
textiles and Leeds' industrial heritage

Leeds Art Gallery, The Headrow LS1 3AA T 0113-378 5350
W www.leeds.gov.uk/artgallery
Includes English watercolours, sculpture, contemporary
art and prints from the region's artists

Royal Armouries Museum, Armouries Drive LS10 1LT
T 0113-220 1999 W www.royalarmouries.org
National collection of over 8,500 items of arms and
armour from BC to present over five galleries: War,
Tournament, Oriental, Self Defence and Hunting

LEICESTER

Jewry Wall Museum, St Nicholas Circle LE1 4LB T 0116-225 4971
W www.leicester.gov.uk/leisure-and-culture/
museums-and-galleries
Archaeology; Roman Jewry Wall and baths; mosaics

New Walk Museum and Art Gallery, 53 New Walk LE1 7EA
T 0116-255 4900 W www.leicester.gov.uk/leisure-and-culture/
museums-and-galleries
Natural and cultural history; ancient Egypt gallery;
European art including works by the German
expressionists and ceramics by Picasso

LINCOLN

The Collection, Danes Terrace LN2 1LP T 01522-782040
W www.thecollectionmuseum.com
Artefacts from the Stone Age to the Roman, Viking and
Medieval eras; adjacent art gallery; collections of
contemporary art and craft, sculpture, porcelain, clocks
and watches

Museum of Lincolnshire Life, Burton Road LN1 3LY
T 01522-782040 W www.lincolnshire.gov.uk/
museumoflincolnshirelife
Social history; agricultural, industrial, military and
commercial exhibits

LIVERPOOL

International Slavery Museum, Albert Dock L3 4AX
T 0151-478 4499 W www.liverpoolmuseums.org.uk/ism
Explores historical and contemporary aspects of slavery

Lady Lever Art Gallery, Wirral CH62 5EQ T 0151-478 4136
W www.liverpoolmuseums.org.uk/ladylever
Paintings, furniture and porcelain

Merseyside Maritime Museum, Albert Dock L3 4AQ
T 0151-478 4499 W www.liverpoolmuseums.org.uk/maritime
Floating exhibits, working displays and craft
demonstrations; incorporates the *UK Border Agency
National Museum*

Museum of Liverpool, Pier Head L3 1DG T 0151-478 4545
W www.liverpoolmuseums.org.uk/mol
Explores the significance of the city's geography, history
and culture

Sudley House, Mossley Hill Road L18 8BX T 0151-478 4016
W www.liverpoolmuseums.org.uk/sudley
Late 18th- and 19th-century paintings in former
shipowner's home

Tate Liverpool, Albert Dock L3 4BB T 0151-1702 7400
W www.tate.org.uk/liverpool
20th-century paintings and sculpture

Walker Art Gallery, William Brown Street L3 8EL
T 0151-478 4199 W www.liverpoolmuseums.org.uk/walker
Paintings and decorative arts from the 13th century to the
present day

World Museum Liverpool, William Brown Street L3 8EN
T 0151-478 4393 W www.liverpoolmuseums.org.uk/wml
Includes Egyptian mummies, weapons and classical
sculpture; planetarium, aquarium, vivarium and natural
history centre

LONDON: GALLERIES

Barbican Art Gallery, Barbican Centre, Silk Street EC2Y 8DS
T 020-7638 4141 W www.barbican.org.uk
Art, music, theatre, dance and film exhibitions

Courtauld Institute of Art Gallery, Somerset House, Strand WC2R
0RN T 020-7848 2526 W www.courtauld.ac.uk
Fine art from the early renaissance to the 20th century,
including impressionist and post-impressionist paintings

Dennis Severs' House, 18 Folgate Street E1 6BX T 020-7247 4013
W www.dennissevershouse.co.uk
Candlelit recreation of a Huguenot silk weaver's home

Dulwich Picture Gallery, Gallery Road SE21 7AD T 020-8693 5254
W www.dulwichpicturegallery.org.uk
England's first public art gallery; designed by Sir John
Soane to house 17th- and 18th-century paintings

Estorick Collection of Modern Italian Art, Canonbury Square
N1 2AN T 020-7704 9522 W www.estorickcollection.com
Early 20th-century Italian drawings, paintings, sculptures
and etchings, with an emphasis on Futurism

National Gallery, Trafalgar Square WC2N 5DN T 020-7747 2885
W www.nationalgallery.org.uk
Western painting from the 13th to 19th centuries; early
Renaissance collection in the Sainsbury Wing

National Portrait Gallery, St Martin's Place WC2H 0HE
T 020-7306 0055 W www.npg.org.uk
Portraits of eminent people in British history

Photographers' Gallery, Ramillies Street W1F 7LW T 020-7087 9300
W www.thephotographersgallery.org.uk
Temporary exhibitions; permanent camera obscura

The Queen's Gallery, Buckingham Palace SW1A 1AA
T 020-7766 7300 W www.royalcollection.org.uk
Art from the Royal Collection

Royal Academy of Arts, Burlington House, Piccadilly W1J 0BD
T 020-7300 8000 W www.royalacademy.org.uk
British art since 1750 and temporary exhibitions; annual
Summer Exhibition

Saatchi Gallery, Duke of York's HQ, King's Road SW3 4RY
T 020-7823 2363 W www.saatchi-gallery.co.uk
Contemporary art including paintings, photographs,
sculpture and installations

Serpentine Gallery, Kensington Gardens W2 3XA T 020-7402 6075
W www.serpentinegallery.org
Temporary exhibitions of British and international
contemporary art

Tate Britain, Millbank SW1P 4RG T 020-7887 8888
W www.tate.org.uk/britain
British art from the 16th century to the present;
international modern art

Tate Modern, Bankside SE1 9TG T 020-7887 8888
W www.tate.org.uk/modern
International modern art from 1900 to the present

Wallace Collection, Manchester Square W1U 3BN
T 020-7563 9500 W www.wallacecollection.org
Old Masters; French 18th-century paintings, furniture,
armour, porcelain, clocks and sculpture

Whitechapel Art Gallery, Whitechapel High Street E1 7QX
T 020-7522 7888 W www.whitechapelgallery.org
Temporary exhibitions of modern art

LONDON: MUSEUMS

Bank of England Museum, Threadneedle Street EC2R 8AH
(entrance on Bartholomew Lane) T 020-7601 5545
W www.bankofengland.co.uk/museum
History of the Bank of England since 1694

British Museum, Great Russell Street WC1B 3DG T 020-7323 8181
W www.britishmuseum.org
Collection of art and antiquities spanning 2 million years
of human history; temporary exhibitions; houses the Elgin
Marbles from the Parthenon

Brunel Museum, Rotherhithe SE16 4LF T 020-7231 3840
W www.brunel-museum.org.uk
Explores the engineering achievements of Isambard
Kingdom Brunel and his father, Marc Brunel

Cartoon Museum, Little Russell Street WC1A 2HH T 020-7580 8155
W www.cartoonmuseum.org

British cartoons, caricature and comic art from the 18th century to the present

Charles Dickens Museum, Doughty Street WC1N 2LX
T 020-7405 2127 W www.dickensmuseum.com
Dickens's home from 1837–9; manuscripts, personal items and paintings

Churchill War Rooms, King Charles Street SW1A 2AQ
T 020-7416 5000 W www.iwm.org.uk/visits/churchill-war-rooms
Underground rooms used by Churchill and the government during the Second World War

Cutty Sark, King William Walk SE10 9HT T 020-8858 4422
W www.rmg.co.uk/cuttysark
The world's last remaining tea clipper; re-opened in April 2012 following extensive restoration

Design Museum, Kensington High Street W8 6AG T 020-3862 5900
W www.designmuseum.org
The development of design and the mass-production of consumer objects

Garden Museum, Lambeth Palace Road SE1 7LB T 020-7401 8865
W www.gardenmuseum.org.uk
History and development of gardens and gardening; temporary exhibitions, symposia and events

Geffrye Museum, Kingsland Road E2 8EA T 020-7739 9893
W www.geffrye-museum.org.uk
English urban domestic interiors from 1600 to the present day; also paintings, furniture, decorative arts, walled herb garden and period garden rooms

HMS Belfast, The Queen's Walk SE1 2JH T 020-7940 6300
W www.iwm.org.uk/hms-belfast
Life and work on board a Second World War cruiser

Horniman Museum, London Road SE23 3PQ T 020-8699 1872
W www.horniman.ac.uk
Museum of anthropology, musical instruments and natural history; aquarium; reference library; gardens

Imperial War Museum, Lambeth Road SE1 6HZ T 020-7416 5000
W www.iwm.org.uk
All aspects of the two World Wars and other military operations involving Britain and the Commonwealth since 1914

Jewish Museum, Albert Street NW1 7NB T 020-7284 7384
W www.jewishmuseum.org.uk
Jewish life, history, art and religion

Migration Museum, Lambeth High Street SE1 7AG
E info@migrationmuseum.org W www.migrationmuseum.org
Opened in 2017, tells the story of migration through the ages and how it has affected and transformed Britain

London Metropolitan Archives, Northampton Road EC1R 0HB
T 020-7332 3820 W www.cityoflondon.gov.uk/lma
Material on the history of London and its people dating from 1067 to the present day

London Museum of Water and Steam, Green Dragon Lane TW8 0EN
T 020-8568 4757 W www.waterandsteam.org.uk
Large collection of steam engines; reopened in 2014 after refurbishment

London Transport Museum, Covent Garden Piazza WC2E 7BB
T 020-7379 6344 W www.ltmuseum.co.uk
Vehicles, photographs and graphic art relating to the history of transport in London

MCC Museum, Lord's Cricket Ground, St John's Wood NW8 8QN
T 020-7616 8656 W www.lords.org/mcc
Cricket exhibits including the Ashes, kits, paintings and W. G. Grace exhibit; guided tours by appointment

Museum of Childhood (V&A), Cambridge Heath Road E2 9PA
T 020-8983 5200 W www.museumofchildhood.org.uk
Toys, games and exhibits relating to the social history of childhood from the 17th century to the present

Museum of London, London Wall EC2Y 5HN T 020-7001 9844
W www.museumoflondon.org.uk
History of London from prehistoric times to the present day; Galleries of Modern London

Museum of London Docklands, West India Quay, Canary Wharf
E14 4AL T 020-7001 9844 W www.museumoflondon.org.uk/docklands

Explores the story of London's river, port and people over 2,000 years; includes the London Sugar Slavery Gallery

National Archives Museum, Kew TW9 4DU T 020-8876 3444
W www.nationalarchives.gov.uk/museum
Displays treasures from the archives, including the Domesday Book and Magna Carta

National Army Museum, Royal Hospital Road SW3 4HT
T 020-7730 0717 W www.nam.ac.uk
Five-hundred-year history of the British soldier; exhibits include model of the Battle of Waterloo and recreated First World War trench

National Maritime Museum, Romney Road SE10 9NF
T 020-8858 4422 W www.rmg.co.uk/national-maritime-museum
Maritime history of Britain; collections include globes, clocks, telescopes and paintings; comprises the main building, the Royal Observatory and the Queen's House

Natural History Museum, Cromwell Road SW7 5BD
T 020-7942 5000 W www.nhm.ac.uk
Natural history collections and interactive Darwin Centre

Petrie Museum of Egyptian Archaeology, University College London, Malet Place WC1E 6BT T 020-7679 2884 W www.ucl.ac.uk/museums/petrie
Egyptian and Sudanese archaeology featuring around 80,000 objects

Royal Air Force Museum, Hendon NW9 5LL T 020-8205 2266
W www.rafmuseum.org.uk
Aviation from before the Wright brothers to the present

Royal Mews, Buckingham Palace SW1W 1QH T 020-7766 7302
W www.royalcollection.org.uk/visit/royalmews
State vehicles, including the Queen's gold state coach; home to the Queen's horses; guided tours

Science Museum, Exhibition Road SW7 2DD T 020-7942 4000
W www.sciencemuseum.org.uk
Science, technology, industry and medicine exhibitions; children's interactive gallery; IMAX cinema

Shakespeare's Globe Exhibition, New Globe Walk, Bankside SE1 9DT
T 020-7902 1400 W www.shakespearesglobe.com
Recreation of Elizabethan theatre using 16th-century techniques; includes a tour of the theatre

Sir John Soane's Museum, Lincoln's Inn Fields WC2A 3BP
T 020-7405 2107 W www.soane.org
Art and antiquities collected by Soane throughout his lifetime; authentic Georgian and Victorian interior

Tower Bridge Exhibition, SE1 2UP T 020-7403 3761
W www.towerbridge.org.uk
History of the bridge and display of Victorian steam machinery; panoramic views from walkways

Victoria and Albert Museum, Cromwell Road SW7 2RL
T 020-7942 2000 W www.vam.ac.uk
Includes the National Art Library and the Gilbert Collection; fine and applied art and design; furniture, glass, textiles, theatre and dress collections; temporary exhibitions

Wellcome Collection, Euston Road NW1 2BE T 020-7611 2222
W www.wellcomecollection.org
Contemporary and historic exhibitions and collections including the Wellcome Library

Wimbledon Lawn Tennis Museum, Church Road SW19 5AE
T 020-8944 1066 W www.wimbledon.com/museum
Tennis trophies, fashion and memorabilia; view of Centre Court

MALTON

Eden Camp, N. Yorks YO17 6RT T 01653-697777
W www.edencamp.co.uk
Restored POW camp and Second World War memorabilia

MANCHESTER

Gallery of Costume, Platt Hall, Rusholme M14 5LL T 0161-245 7245
W www.manchestergalleries.org
Exhibits from the 17th century to the present day

Imperial War Museum North, Trafford Wharf Road M17 1TZ
T 0161-836 4000 W www.iwm.org.uk/north

History of war from the 20th century to the present

Manchester Art Gallery, Mosley Street M2 3JL T 0161-235 8888
W www.manchestergalleries.org
European fine and decorative art from the 17th to 20th
centuries

Manchester Museum, Oxford Road M13 9PL T 0161-275 2648
W www.museum.manchester.ac.uk
Collections include decorative arts, natural history and
zoology; three Ancient Worlds galleries

*Museum of Science and Industry, Liverpool Road M3 4FP
T 0161-832 2244 W www.mosi.org.uk
On site of world's oldest passenger railway station;
galleries relating to space, energy, power, transport,
aviation, textiles and social history

National Football Museum, Cathedral Gardens M4 3BG
T 0161-605 8200 W www.nationalfootballmuseum.com
Home to the FIFA, FA and Football League collections
including the 1966 World Cup final ball

People's History Museum, Left Bank, Spinningfields M3 3ER
T 0161-838 9190 W www.phm.org.uk
History of British political and working life

Whitworth Art Gallery, Oxford Road M15 6ER T 0161-275 7450
W www.whitworth.manchester.ac.uk
Fine and modern art, wallpapers, prints, textiles and
sculptures

MILTON KEYNES

Bletchley Park National Codes Centre, Bucks MK3 6EB
T 01908-640404 W www.bletchleypark.org.uk
Home of British codebreaking during the Second World
War; Enigma machine; computer museum and Alan
Turing gallery

The National Museum of Computing Block H, Bletchley Park,
MK3 6EB T 01908-374708 W www.tnmoc.org
Charts the development of computing from the 1940s
onwards and houses the world's largest collection of
functional historical computers, including the Colossus
and the WITCH

MONKWEARMOUTH

Monkwearmouth Station Museum, North Bridge Street, Sunderland
SR5 1AP T 0191-567 7075 W www.seeitdoitsunderland.co.uk/
monkwearmouth-station-museum
Victorian train station; interactive galleries

NEWCASTLE UPON TYNE

Discovery Museum, Blandford Square NE1 4JA T 0191-232 6789
W www.twmuseums.org.uk/discovery
Science and industry, local history, fashion; Tyneside's
maritime history; digital jukebox of 2,000 film and TV
titles from the BFI National Archive

Great North Museum: Hancock, Barras Bridge NE2 4PT
T 0191-222 6765 W www.twmuseums.org.uk/
greatnorthmuseum
Natural and ancient history; planetarium; Living Planet
display incorporates live animal tanks and aquaria

Laing Art Gallery, New Bridge Street NE1 8AG T 0191-278 1611
W www.twmuseums.org.uk/laing
19th and 20th century art including local painters;
ceramics, glass, Japanese decorative arts and prints

NEWMARKET

National Horseracing Museum, High Street CB8 8JH
T 01638-667314 W www.nhrm.co.uk
The story of people and horses involved in racing;
temporary exhibitions

NORTH SHIELDS

Stephenson Railway Museum, Middle Engine Lane NE29 8DX
T 0191-200 7146 W www.twmuseums.org.uk/stephenson
Locomotive engines and rolling stock; open April through
November and school holidays outside this period

NOTTINGHAM

Museum of Nottingham Life, Brewhouse Yard, Castle Boulevard
NG7 1FB T 0115-876 1400 W www.nottinghamcity.gov.uk
Social history from the 17th to 20th centuries

Natural History Museum, Wollaton Hall, Wollaton NG8 2AE
T 0115-876 3100 W www.nottinghamcity.gov.uk

Geology, botany and zoology specimens housed in an
Elizabethan mansion

Nottingham Castle and Art Gallery, Lenton Road NG1 6EL
T 0115-876 1400 W www.mynottingham.gov.uk/
nottinghamcastle
Paintings, ceramics, silver, glass and jewellery; history of
Nottingham

OXFORD

Ashmolean Museum, Beaumont Street OX1 2PH T 01865-278000
W www.ashmolean.org
Art and archaeology including Egyptian, Minoan, Anglo-
Saxon and Chinese exhibits; largest collection of Raphael
drawings in the world

Modern Art Oxford, Pembroke Street OX1 1BP T 01865-722733
W www.modernartoxford.org.uk
Temporary exhibitions

Museum of the History of Science, Broad Street OX1 3AZ
T 01865-277280 W www.mhs.ox.ac.uk
Displays include early scientific instruments, chemical
apparatus, clocks and watches

Oxford University Museum of Natural History, Parks Road
OX1 3PW T 01865-272950 W www.oum.ox.ac.uk
Entomology, geology, mineralogy and petrology, and
zoology

Pitt Rivers Museum, South Parks Road OX1 3PP T 01865-270927
W www.prm.ox.ac.uk
Anthropological and archaeological artefacts

PLYMOUTH

City Museum and Art Gallery, Drake Circus PL4 8AJ
T 01752-304774 W www.plymouthmuseum.gov.uk
Local and natural history; ceramics; silver; Old Masters;
world artefacts; temporary exhibitions

PORTSMOUTH

Charles Dickens Birthplace, Old Commercial Road PO1 4QL
T 023-9282 1879 W www.charlesdickensbirthplace.co.uk
Reproduction Regency house; Dickens memorabilia

D-Day Museum, Clarence Esplanade, Southsea PO5 3NT
T 023-9282 6722 W www.ddaymuseum.co.uk
Includes the Overlord embroidery

Portsmouth Historic Dockyard, HM Naval Base PO1 3LJ
T 023-9283 9766 W www.historicdockyard.co.uk
Incorporates the **National Museum of the Royal Navy* (PO1
3NH T 023-9272 7574 W www.nmrn.org.uk), *HMS Victory* –
restoration work open to the public (PO1 3NH
T 023-9283 9766 W www.hms-victory.com), *HMS Warrior*
(PO1 3QX T 023-9277 8600 W www.hmswarrior.org), *Mary
Rose* (PO1 3LX T 023-9281 2931 W www.maryrose.org) and
Action Stations (PO1 3LJ T 023-9289 3338
W www.actionstations.org)
History of the Royal Navy and of the dockyard; warships
and technology spanning 500 years

PRESTON

Harris Museum and Art Gallery, Market Square PR1 2PP
T 01772-258248 W www.harrismuseum.org.uk
British art since the 18th century; ceramics, glass, costume
and local history; contemporary exhibitions

ST ALBANS

Verulamium Museum, St Michael's Street AL3 4SW
T 01727-751810 W www.stalbansmuseums.org.uk
Remains of Iron Age settlement and the third-largest city
in Roman Britain; moving to a new site in 2017

ST IVES

*Tate St Ives, Porthmeor Beach, Cornwall TR26 1TG
T 01736-796226 W www.tate.org.uk/stives
Modern art, much by artists associated with St Ives;
includes the Barbara Hepworth Museum and Sculpture
Garden; open after 2014 part closure

SALISBURY

Salisbury & South Wiltshire Museum, The Close SP1 2EN
T 01722-332151 W www.salisburymuseum.org.uk
Local history and archaeology; Stonehenge exhibits

SHEFFIELD

Graves Gallery, Surrey Street S1 1XZ T 0114-278 2600
W www.museums-sheffield.org.uk

Twentieth-century British art; European art spanning four centuries

Millennium Galleries, Arundel Gate S1 2PP **T** 0114-278 2600 **W** www.museums-sheffield.org.uk
Incorporates four different galleries: the Special Exhibition Gallery, the Craft and Design Gallery, the Metalwork Gallery and the Ruskin Gallery, which houses John Ruskin's collection of paintings, drawings, books and medieval manuscripts

Weston Park Museum, Western Bank S10 2TP **T** 0114-278 2600 **W** www.museums-sheffield.org.uk
World and local history; art and temporary exhibitions

SOUTHAMPTON

City Art Gallery, Commercial Road SO14 7LP **T** 023-8083 3007 **W** www.southamptoncityartgallery.com
Western art from the Renaissance to the present

SeaCity Museum, Havelock Road SO14 7FY **T** 023-8083 3007 **W** www.seacitymuseum.co.uk
Opened in 2012, the museum tells the story of the city's maritime past and present

SOUTH SHIELDS

Arbeia Roman Fort, Baring Street NE33 2BB **T** 0191-456 1369 **W** www.twmuseums.org.uk/arbeia
Excavated ruins; reconstructions of original buildings

South Shields Museum and Art Gallery, Ocean Road NE33 2JA **T** 0191-277 1410 **W** www.twmuseums.org.uk/southshields
South Tyneside history; interactive art gallery

STOKE-ON-TRENT

Etruria Industrial Museum, Lower Bedford Street ST4 7AF **T** 01782-233144 **W** www.etruriamuseum.org.uk
Britain's sole surviving steam-powered potter's mill

Gladstone Pottery Museum, Uttoxeter Road, Longton ST3 1PQ **T** 01782-237777 **W** www.stokemuseums.org.uk/visit/gpm
The last complete Victorian pottery factory in Britain

Potteries Museum and Art Gallery, Bethesda Street ST1 3DW **T** 01782-232323 **W** www.stokemuseums.org.uk/visit/pmag
Pottery, china and porcelain collections and a Mark XVI Spitfire

The Wedgwood Museum, Barlaston ST12 9ER **T** 01782-371900 **W** www.wedgwoodmuseum.org.uk
The story of Josiah Wedgwood and the company he founded

SUNDERLAND

Sunderland Museum and Winter Gardens, Burdon Road SR1 1PP **T** 0191-553 2323 **W** www.seeitdoitsunderland.co.uk/sunderland-museum-winter-gardens
Fine and decorative art, local history and gardens

TELFORD

Ironbridge Gorge Museums, TF8 7DQ **T** 01952-433424 **W** www.ironbridge.org.uk
Ten museums including The Museum of the Gorge; The Iron Bridge and Tollhouse; Blists Hill (late Victorian working town); Brosely Pipeworks; Coalbrookdale Museum of Iron; Coalport China Museum; Jackfield Tile Museum; Tar Tunnel; Darby Houses

WAKEFIELD

Hepworth Wakefield, Gallery Walk WF1 5AW **T** 01924-247360 **W** www.hepworthwakefield.org
Historic and modern art; temporary exhibitions of contemporary art

National Coal Mining Museum for England, New Road, Overton WF4 4RH **T** 01924-848806 **W** www.ncm.org.uk
Includes underground tours of one of Britain's oldest working mines

Yorkshire Sculpture Park, West Bretton WF4 4LG **T** 01924-832631 **W** www.ysp.co.uk
Open-air sculpture gallery including works by Henry Moore, Barbara Hepworth and others in 500 acres of parkland

WEYBRIDGE

Brooklands Museum, Brooklands Road KT13 0QN **T** 01932-857381 **W** www.brooklandsmuseum.com
Birthplace of British motorsport; world's first purpose-built motor racing circuit

WILMSLOW

Quarry Bank Mill and Styal Estate, Wilmslow SK9 4LA **T** 01625-527468 **W** www.quarrybankmill.org.uk
Europe's most powerful working waterwheel owned by the National Trust illustrating history of cotton industry; costumed guides at restored Apprentice House

WINCHESTER

Winchester Science Centre and Planetarium, Telegraph Way, Hants SO21 1HZ **T** 01962-863791 **W** www.winchestersciencecentre.org
Interactive science centre and planetarium

WORCESTER

City Art Gallery and Museum, Foregate Street WR1 1DT **T** 01905-25371 **W** www.worcestershire.gov.uk/museums
Includes the Regimental museum, 19th-century chemist shop and changing art exhibitions

Museum of Royal Worcester, Severn Street WR1 2ND **T** 01905-21247 **W** www.museumofroyalworcester.org
Worcester porcelain from 1751 to the present day

YEOVIL

Fleet Air Arm Museum, RNAS Yeovilton, Somerset BA22 8HT **T** 01935-840565 **W** www.fleetairarm.com
History of naval aviation; historic aircraft, including Concorde 002

YORK

Beningbrough Hall, Beningbrough YO30 1DD **T** 01904-472027 **W** www.nationaltrust.org.uk/beningbrough-hall
18th-century house with portraits from the National Portrait Gallery; parklands and gardens

JORVIK Viking Centre, Coppergate YO1 9WT **T** 01904-615505 **W** www.jorvik-viking-centre.co.uk
Reconstruction of Viking York based on archaeological evidence

*National Railway Museum, Leeman Road YO26 4XJ **T** 0844-815 3139 **W** www.nrm.org.uk
Includes locomotives, rolling stock and carriages

York Art Gallery, Exhibition Square, YO1 7EW **T** 01904 687687 **W** www.yorkartgallery.org.uk
600 years of British and European painting; ceramics and sculpture

York Castle Museum, Eye of York YO1 9RY **T** 01904-687687 **W** www.yorkcastlemuseum.org.uk
Includes Kirkgate, a reconstructed Victorian street; costume and military collections

Yorkshire Museum, Museum Gardens YO1 7FR **T** 01904-687687 **W** www.yorkshiremuseum.org.uk
Yorkshire life from Roman to medieval times; geology and biology; York observatory

WALES

* Members of National Museum Wales, a public body that receives its core funding from the Welsh government

ABERYSTWYTH

Ceredigion Museum, Terrace Road SY23 2AQ **T** 01970-633088 **W** www.ceredigion.gov.uk
Local history, housed in a restored Edwardian theatre

Silver Mountain Experience, Ponterwyd SY23 3AB **T** 01970-890620 **W** www.silvermountainexperience.co.uk
Tours of an 18th-century silver mine, with interactive challenges and games for children

BLAENAFON

*Big Pit National Coal Museum, Torfaen NP4 9XP **T** 030-0111 2333 **W** www.museumwales.ac.uk/en/bigpit
Colliery with an underground tour and exhibitions of modern mining equipment

BODELWYDDAN

Bodelwyddan Castle, Denbighshire LL18 5YA **T** 01745-584060 **W** www.bodelwyddan-castle.co.uk
Art gallery within an historic house; features temporary art exhibits

CAERLEON

*National Roman Legion Museum, NP18 1AE **T** 030-0111 2333 **W** www.museumwales.ac.uk/en/roman

Features the oldest recorded piece of writing in Wales; pottery, Roman era gemstones

CARDIFF

*National Museum Cardiff, Cathays Park CF10 3NP T 030-0111 2333 W www.museumwales.ac.uk/en/cardiff
Houses Wales's national art, archaeology and natural history collections

*St Fagans: National History Museum, St Fagans CF5 6XB T 029-2057 3500 W www.museumwales.ac.uk/en/stfagans
Open-air museum with re-erected buildings, agricultural equipment and costume

TECHNIQUEST, Stuart Street CF10 5BW T 029-2047 5475 W www.techniquest.org
Interactive science exhibits, planetarium and science theatre

CRICCIETH

Lloyd George Museum, Llanystumdwy LL52 0SH T 01766-522071 W www.gwynedd.gov.uk
Childhood home of David Lloyd George

DRE-FACH FELINDRE

*National Wool Museum, Llandysul SA44 5UP T 030-0111 2333 W www.museumwales.ac.uk/en/wool
Exhibitions, a working woollen mill and craft workshops

LLANBERIS

*National Slate Museum, Gwynedd LL55 4TY T 030-0111 2333 W www.museumwales.ac.uk/en/slate
Former slate quarry with original machinery and plant; slate crafts demonstrations; working waterwheel

LLANDRINDOD WELLS

National Cycle Collection, Automobile Palace, Temple Street LD1 5DL T 01597-825531 W www.cyclemuseum.org.uk
Approximately 250 bicycles on display, from 1819 to the present

PRESTEIGNE

Judge's Lodging Museum, Broad Street LD8 2AD T 01544-260650 W www.judgeslodging.org.uk
Restored apartments, courtroom, cells and servants' quarters

SWANSEA

Glynn Vivian Art Gallery, Alexandra Road SA1 5DZ T 01792-516900 W www.swansea.gov.uk/glynnvivian
Fine art and ceramics from 1700 to the present

*National Waterfront Museum, Oystermouth Road SA1 3RD T 030-0111 2333 W www.museumwales.ac.uk/en/swansea
Wales during the Industrial Revolution

Swansea Museum, Victoria Road SA1 1SN T 01792-653763 W www.swansea.gov.uk/swanseamuseum
Paintings, Egyptian artifacts, transport and nautical collections; war time Swansea

TENBY

Tenby Museum and Art Gallery, Castle Hill SA70 7BP T 01834-842809 W www.tenbymuseum.org.uk
Local archaeology, history, geology and art

SCOTLAND

* Members of National Museums Scotland or National Galleries of Scotland, which are non-departmental public bodies funded by, and accountable to, the Scottish government

ABERDEEN

Aberdeen Art Gallery, Schoolhill AB10 1FQ T 01224-523666 W www.aagm.co.uk
Paintings, sculptures and graphics; temporary exhibitions

Aberdeen Maritime Museum, Shiprow AB11 5BY T 01224-337700 W www.aagm.co.uk
Maritime history, including shipbuilding and North Sea oil

AYR

Robert Burns Birthplace Museum, Murdoch's Lone, Alloway KA7 4PQ T 0129-244 3700 W www.burnsmuseum.org.uk
Comprises Burns Cottage, birthplace of the poet, gardens and a museum

EDINBURGH

Britannia, Leith EH6 6JJ T 0131-555 5566 W www.royalyachtbritannia.co.uk
Former royal yacht with royal barge and royal family picture gallery

City Art Centre, Market Street EH1 1DE T 0131-529 3993 W www.edinburghmuseums.org.uk
Rolling programme of exhibitions including historic and modern photography; contemporary art, design and architecture

Museum of Childhood, High Street EH1 1TG T 0131-529 4142 W www.edinburghmuseums.org.uk
Toys, games, clothes and exhibits relating to the social history of childhood

Museum of Edinburgh, Canongate, Royal Mile EH8 8DD T 0131-529 4143 W www.edinburghmuseums.org.uk
Local history, silver, glass and Scottish pottery

*National Museum of Flight, East Fortune Airfield, East Lothian EH39 5LF T 0300-123 6789 W www.nms.ac.uk/flight
Aviation from the early 20th century to the present

*National Museum of Scotland, Chambers Street EH1 1JF T 0300-123 6789 W www.nms.ac.uk/scotland
Scottish history; world cultures; natural world; art and design; science and technology

*National War Museum of Scotland, Edinburgh Castle EH1 2NG T 0300-123 6789 W www.nms.ac.uk/war
Scotland's military history housed within Edinburgh Castle

*Scottish National Gallery, The Mound EH2 2EL T 0131-624 6200 W www.nationalgalleries.org
Fine art from the early Renaissance to the end of the 19th century

*Scottish National Gallery of Modern Art, Belford Road EH4 3DR T 0131-624 6200 W www.nationalgalleries.org
Contemporary art featuring British, French and Russian collections; outdoor sculpture park

*Scottish National Portrait Gallery, Queen Street EH2 1JD T 0131-624 6200 W www.nationalgalleries.org/portraitgallery
Portraits of eminent people in Scottish history; Photography Gallery; Victorian Library

The Writers' Museum, Lady Stair's Close EH1 2PA T 0131-529 4901 W www.edinburghmuseums.org.uk
Exhibitions relating to Robert Burns, Sir Walter Scott and Robert Louis Stevenson

FORT WILLIAM

West Highland Museum, Cameron Square PH33 6AJ T 01397-702169 W www.westhighlandmuseum.org.uk
Highland life; Military, Victorian and Jacobite collections

GLASGOW

Burrell Collection, Pollokshaws Road G43 1AT T 0141-287 2550 W www.glasgowlife.org.uk/museums
Paintings by major artists; medieval art, Chinese and Islamic art

Gallery of Modern Art, Royal Exchange Square G1 3AH T 0141-287 3005 W www.glasgowlife.org.uk/museums
Collection of contemporary Scottish and world art

Hunterian, University of Glasgow G12 8QQ T 0141-330 4221 W www.gla.ac.uk/hunterian
Rennie Mackintosh and Whistler collections; coins; Scottish paintings; Pacific ethnographic collection; archaeology; medicine

Kelvingrove Art Gallery & Museum, Argyle Street G3 8AG T 0141-276 9500 W www.glasgowlife.org.uk/museums
Includes Old Masters; natural history; arms and armour

Museum of Piping, McPhater Street G4 0HW T 0141-353 0220 W www.thepipingcentre.co.uk
The history and origins of bagpiping

*Museum of Rural Life, Philipshill Road, East Kilbride G76 9HR T 0300-123 6789 W www.nms.ac.uk/rural
History of rural life and work

People's Palace and Winter Gardens, Glasgow Green G40 1AT T 0141-276 0788 W www.glasgowlife.org.uk/museums
Social history of Glasgow since 1750

Riverside Museum, 100 Pointhouse Place G3 8RS **T** 0141-287 2720
W www.glasgowlife.org.uk/museums
Scotland's museum of transport and travel; the Tall Ship *Glenlee*, a Clyde-built sailing ship, is berthed alongside

St Mungo Museum of Religious Art and Life, Castle Street G4 0RH
T 0141-276 1625 **W** www.glasgowlife.org.uk/museums
Exhibits detailing the world's major religions; oldest Zen garden in Britain

NORTHERN IRELAND

* Members of National Museums Northern Ireland, a public body sponsored by the Department for Communities, Northern Ireland executive.

ARMAGH

★Armagh County Museum, The Mall East BT61 9BE
T 028-3752 3070 **W** www.nmni.com/acm
Local history; fine art; archaeology; crafts

BANGOR

North Down Museum, Town Hall BT20 4BT **T** 028-9127 1200
W www.northdownmuseum.com
Presents the history of North Down, including its early-Christian monastery and Plantation-era maps

BELFAST

Titanic Belfast, Queen's Road, Titanic Quarter BT3 9EP
T 028-9076 6386 **W** www.titanicbelfast.com
The story of RMS *Titanic* from her conception to demise; Shipyard ride and ocean exploration centre

★Ulster Museum, Botanic Gardens BT9 5AB **T** 0845-608 0000
W www.nmni.com/um

Irish antiquities; natural and local history; fine and applied arts

★W5, Queen's Quay BT3 9QQ **T** 028-9046 7700
W www.w5online.co.uk
Interactive science and technology centre

HOLYWOOD

★Ulster Folk and Transport Museum, Cultra BT18 0EU
T 028-9042 8428 **W** www.nmni.com/uftm
Open-air museum with original buildings from Ulster town and rural life *c.*1900; indoor galleries including Irish rail and road transport

LONDONDERRY

The Tower Museum, Union Hall Place BT48 6LU **T** 028-7137 2411
W www.derrystrabane.com/towermuseum
Tells the story of Ireland through the history of Londonderry

NEWTOWNARDS

The Somme Heritage Centre, Bangor Road BT23 7PH
T 028-9182 3202 **W** www.sommeassociation.com
Commemorates the part played by Irish forces in the First World War

OMAGH

★Ulster American Folk Park, Castletown, Co. Tyrone BT78 5QU
T 028-8224 3292 **W** www.nmni.com/uafp
Open-air museum telling the story of Ulster's emigrants to America; restored or recreated dwellings and workshops; ship and dockside gallery

SIGHTS OF LONDON

For historic buildings, museums and galleries in London, *see* the Historic Buildings and Monuments, and Museums and Galleries sections.

BRIDGES

The bridges over the Thames in London, from east to west, are:

Tower Bridge (268m/880ft by 18m/60ft), architect: Horace Jones, engineer: John Wolfe Barry, opened 1894

London Bridge (262m/860ft by 32m/105ft), original 13th-century stone bridge rebuilt and opened 1831 (engineer: John Rennie), reconstructed in Arizona when current London Bridge opened 1973 (architect: Lord Holford, engineer: Mott, Hay and Anderson)

Cannon Street Railway Bridge (261m/855ft), engineers: John Hawkshaw and John Wolfe Barry, originally named Alexandra Bridge, opened 1866; renovated 1979–82

Southwark Bridge (244m/800ft by 17m/56ft), engineer: John Rennie, originally named Queen Street Bridge, opened 1819; rebuilt 1912–21 (architect: Ernest George, engineer: Mott, Hay and Anderson)

Millennium Bridge (325m/1,066ft by 4m/13ft), architect: Foster and Partners, engineer: Ove Arup and Partners, opened 2000; reopened after modification 2002

Blackfriars Railway Bridge (284m/933ft), engineers: John Wolfe Barry and Henri Marc Brunel, orginally named St Paul's Railway Bridge, opened 1886

Blackfriars Bridge (294m/963ft by 32m/105ft), engineer: Robert Mylne, opened 1769; rebuilt 1869 (engineer: Joseph Cubitt); widened 1909

Waterloo Bridge (366m/1,200ft by 24m/80ft), engineer: John Rennie, opened 1817; rebuilt 1945 (architect: Sir Giles Gilbert Scott, engineer: Rendel, Palmer and Triton)

Golden Jubilee Bridges (325m/1,066ft by 4.7m/15ft), architect: Lifschutz Davidson, engineer: WSP Group, opened 2002; commonly known as the Hungerford Footbridges

Hungerford Railway Bridge (366m/1,200ft), engineer: Isambard Kingdom Brunel, suspension bridge opened 1845; present railway bridge opened 1864 (engineer: John Hawkshaw); widened in 1886

Westminster Bridge (228m/748ft by 26m/85ft), engineer: Charles Labelye, opened 1750; rebuilt 1862 (architect: Charles Barry, engineer: Thomas Page)

Lambeth Bridge (237m/776ft by 18m/60ft), engineer: Peter W. Barlow, original suspension bridge opened 1862; current structure opened 1932 (architect: Reginald Blomfield, engineer: George W. Humphreys)

Vauxhall Bridge (231m/759ft by 24m/80ft), engineer: James Walker, opened 1816; redesigned and opened 1906 (architect: William Edward Riley, engineers: Alexander Binnie and Maurice Fitzmaurice)

Grosvenor Railway Bridge (213m/699ft), engineer: John Fowler, opened 1860; rebuilt 1965; also known as the Victoria Railway Bridge

Chelsea Bridge (213m/699ft by 25m/83ft), original suspension bridge opened 1858 (engineer: Thomas Page); rebuilt 1937 (architects: George Topham Forrest and E. P. Wheeler, engineer: Rendel, Palmer and Triton)

Albert Bridge (216m/710ft by 12m/40ft), engineer: Rowland M. Ordish, opened 1873; restructured 1884 (engineer: Joseph Bazalgette); strengthened 1971–3

Battersea Bridge (204m/670ft by 17m/56ft), engineer: Henry Holland, opened 1771; rebuilt 1890 (engineer: Joseph Bazalgette)

Battersea Railway Bridge (204m/670ft), engineer: William Baker, opened 1863; also known as Cremorne Bridge

Wandsworth Bridge (189m/619ft by 18m/60ft), engineer: Julian Tolmé, opened 1873; rebuilt 1940 (architect: E. P. Wheeler, engineer: T. Pierson Frank)

Putney Railway Bridge (229m/750ft), engineers: W. H. Thomas and William Jacomb, opened 1889; also known as the Fulham Railway Bridge or the Iron Bridge – it has no official name

Putney Bridge (213m/699ft by 23m/74ft), architect: Jacob Ackworth, original wooden bridge opened 1729; current granite structure completed in 1886 (engineer: Joseph Bazalgette). The starting point of the Boat Race.

Hammersmith Bridge (210m/688ft by 10m/33ft), engineer: William Tierney Clarke; the first suspension bridge in London, originally built 1827; rebuilt 1887 (engineer: Joseph Bazalgette)

Barnes Railway Bridge (also footbridge, 110m/360ft), engineer: Joseph Locke, opened 1849; rebuilt 1895 (engineers: London and South Western Railway); the original structure stands unused

Chiswick Bridge (137m/450ft by 21m/70ft), architect: Herbert Baker, engineer: Alfred Dryland, opened 1933. The bridge marks the end point of the Boat Race.

Kew Railway Bridge (175m/575ft), engineer: W. R. Galbraith, opened 1869

Kew Bridge (110m/360ft by 17m/56ft), engineer: Robert Tunstall, original timber bridge built 1759; replaced by a Portland stone structure in 1789 (engineer: James Paine); current granite bridge renamed King Edward VII Bridge in 1903, but still known as Kew Bridge (engineers: John Wolfe Barry and Cuthbert Brereton)

Richmond Lock (91m/300ft by 11m/36ft), engineer: F. G. M. Stoney, lock and footbridge opened 1894

Twickenham Bridge (85m/280ft by 21m/70ft), architect: Maxwell Ayrton, engineer: Alfred Dryland, opened 1933

Richmond Railway Bridge (91m/300ft), engineer: Joseph Locke, opened 1848; rebuilt 1906–8 (engineer: J. W. Jacomb-Hood)

Richmond Bridge (85m/280ft by 10m/33ft), architect: James Paine, engineer: Kenton Couse, built 1777; widened 1939

Teddington Lock (198m/650ft), engineer: G. Pooley, two footbridges opened 1889; marks the end of the tidal reach of the Thames

Kingston Railway Bridge architects: J. E. Errington and W. R. Galbraith, engineer: Thomas Brassey, opened 1863

Kingston Bridge (116m/382ft), engineer: Edward Lapidge, built 1825–8; widened 1911–14 (engineers: Basil Mott and David Hay) and 1999–2001

Hampton Court Bridge, engineers: Samuel Stevens and Benjamin Ludgator, built 1753; replaced by iron bridge 1865; present bridge opened 1933 (architect: Edwin Lutyens, engineer: W. P. Robinson)

CEMETERIES

In 1832, in response to the overcrowding of burial grounds in London, the government authorised the establishment of seven non-denominational cemeteries that would encircle the city. These large cemeteries, known as the 'magnificent seven', were seen by many Victorian families as places in which to demonstrate their wealth and stature, and as a result there are some highly ornate graves and tombs.

THE MAGNIFICENT SEVEN

Abney Park, Stoke Newington, N16 (13ha/32 acres), established 1840; tomb of William and Catherine Booth, founders of the Salvation Army, and memorials to many nonconformists and dissenters

Brompton, Old Brompton Road, SW10 (16.5ha/40 acres), established 1840; graves of Sir Henry Cole, Emmeline Pankhurst, John Wisden

Highgate, Swains Lane, N6 (15ha/38 acres), established 1839; graves of Douglas Adams, George Eliot, Eric Hobsbawm, Michael Faraday, Karl Marx, Ralph Miliband and Christina Rossetti

Kensal Green, Harrow Road, W10 (29ha/72 acres), established 1833; tombs of Charles Babbage, Isambard Kingdom Brunel, Wilkie Collins, George Cruikshank, Tom Hood, Leigh Hunt, Harold Pinter, William Makepeace Thackeray, Anthony Trollope

Nunhead, Linden Grove, SE15 (21ha/52 acres), established 1840; closed in 1969, restored and opened for burials

Tower Hamlets, Southern Grove, E3 (11ha/27 acres), established 1841, 350,000 interments; bombed heavily during the Second World War and closed to burials in 1966; now a nature reserve

West Norwood Cemetery and Crematorium, Norwood High Street, SE27 (17ha/42 acres), established 1837; tombs of C. W. Alcock, Mrs Beeton, Sir Henry Tate and Joseph Whitaker *(Whitaker's Almanack)*

OTHER CEMETERIES

Bunhill Fields, City Road, EC1 (1.6ha/4 acres), 17th-century nonconformist burial ground containing the graves of William Blake, John Bunyan and Daniel Defoe

City of London Cemetery and Crematorium, Aldersbrook Road, E12 (81ha/200 acres), established 1856; grave of Bobby Moore

Golders Green Crematorium, Hoop Lane, NW11 (5ha/12 acres), established 1902; retains the ashes of Kingsley Amis, Lionel Bart, Enid Blyton, Marc Bolan, Sigmund Freud, Keith Moon, Ivor Novello, Bram Stoker and H. G. Wells

Hampstead, Fortune Green Road, NW6 (10.5ha/26 acres), established 1876; graves of Alan Coren, Kate Greenaway, Joseph Lister and Marie Lloyd

MARKETS

Billingsgate, Trafalgar Way, E14 (fish), a market site for over 1,000 years, with the Lower Thames Street site dating from 1876; moved to the Isle of Dogs in 1982; owned and run by the City of London Corporation

Borough, Southwark Street, SE1 (vegetables, fruit, meat, dairy, bread), established on present site in 1756; privately owned and run

Brick Lane, E1 (jewellery, vintage clothes, bric-a-brac, food), open Sunday

Brixton, SW9 (African-Caribbean food, music, clothing), open Monday to Saturday

Broadway, E8 (food, fashion, crafts), re-established in 2004, open Saturday

Camden Lock, NW1 (second-hand clothing, jewellery, alternative fashion, crafts), established in 1973

Columbia Road, E2 (flowers), dates from 19th century; became dedicated flower market in the 20th century

Covent Garden, WC2 (antiques, handicrafts, jewellery, clothing, food), originally a fruit and vegetable market (*see* New Covent Garden market); it has been trading in its current form since 1980

Grays, Davies Street, W1K (antiques), indoor market in listed building, established 1977

Greenwich, SE10 (crafts, fashion, food), market revived in the 1980s

Leadenhall, Gracechurch Street, EC3V (meat, poultry, cheese, clothing), site of market since 14th century; present hall built 1881; owned and run by the City of London Corporation

New Covent Garden, SW8 (wholesale vegetables, fruit, flowers), established in 1670 under a charter of Charles II; relocated from central London in 1974

New Spitalfields, E10 (vegetables, fruit), established 1682, modernised 1928, moved out of the City to Leyton in 1991

Old Spitalfields, E1 (arts, crafts, books, clothes, organic food, antiques), continues to trade on the original Spitalfields site on Commercial Street

Petticoat Lane, Middlesex Street, E1, a market has existed on the site for over 500 years, now a Sunday morning market selling almost anything

Portobello Road, W11, originally for herbs and horse-trading from 1870; became famous for antiques after the closure of the Caledonian Market in 1948

Smithfield, EC1 (meat, poultry), built 1866–8, refurbished 1993–4; the site of St Bartholomew's Fair from 12th to 19th century; owned and run by the City of London Corporation

MONUMENTS
CENOTAPH

Whitehall, SW1. The Cenotaph (from the Greek meaning 'empty tomb') was built to commemorate 'The Glorious Dead' and is a memorial to all ranks of the sea, land and air forces who gave their lives in the service of the Empire during the First World War. Designed by Sir Edwin Lutyens and constructed in plaster as a temporary memorial in 1919, it was replaced by a permanent structure of Portland stone and unveiled by George V on 11 November 1920, Armistice Day. An additional inscription was made in 1946 to commemorate those who gave their lives in the Second World War

FOURTH PLINTH

Trafalgar Square, WC2. The fourth plinth (1841) was designed for an equestrian statue that was never built due to lack of funds. From 1999 temporary works have been displayed on the plinth including *Ecce Homo* (Mark Wallinger), *Monument* (Rachel Whiteread), *Alison Lapper Pregnant* (Marc Quinn), *One & Other* (Antony Gormley) and *Hahn/Cock* (Katharina Fritsch). Since September 2016 *Really Good* (David Shrigley), a 10m-high bronze sculpture of a human hand in the 'thumbs-up' gesture, has occupied the plinth. This will be followed in March 2018 by *The Invisible Enemy Should Not Exist* (Michael Rakowitz), a recreation of the Lamassu, a winged bull and protective deity that stood at the entrance to the Nergal Gate of Nineveh from *c.*700 BC, but was destroyed by Islamic State in 2015. The Lamassu will be made of empty Iraqi date syrup cans, representative of a once-renowned industry decimated by the Iraq Wars

LONDON MONUMENT

(Commonly called the Monument), Monument Street, EC3. Built to designs by Sir Christopher Wren and Robert Hooke between 1671 and 1677, the Monument commemorates the Great Fire of London, which broke out in Pudding Lane on 2 September 1666. The fluted Doric column is 36.6m (120ft) high, the moulded cylinder above the balcony supporting a flaming vase of gilt bronze is an additional 12.8m (42ft), and the column is based on a square plinth 12.2m (40ft) high (with fine carvings on the west face), making a total height of 61.6m (202ft) – the tallest isolated stone column in the world, with views of London from a gallery at the top (311 steps)

OTHER MONUMENTS

(sculptor's name in parentheses):

7 July Memorial (Carmody Groarke), Hyde Park

Afghanistan and Iraq War Memorial (Day), Victoria Embankment

Viscount Alanbrooke (Roberts-Jones), Whitehall

Albert Memorial (Scott), Kensington Gore

Battle of Britain (Day), Victoria Embankment

Beatty (Wheeler), Trafalgar Square

Belgian Gratitude (setting by Blomfield, statue by Rousseau), Victoria Embankment

Boadicea (or Boudicca), *Queen of the Iceni* (Thornycroft), Westminster Bridge

Brunel (Marochetti), Victoria Embankment

Burghers of Calais (Rodin), Victoria Tower Gardens, Westminster

Burns (Steell), Embankment Gardens
Canada Memorial (Granche), Green Park
Carlyle (Boehm), Chelsea Embankment
Cavalry (Jones), Hyde Park
Edith Cavell (Frampton), St Martin's Place
Charles I (Le Sueur), Trafalgar Square
Charles II (Gibbons), Royal Hospital, Chelsea
Churchill (Roberts-Jones), Parliament Square
Cleopatra's Needle (20.9m/68.5ft high, *c*.1500 BC, erected in London in 1878; the sphinxes are Victorian), Thames Embankment
Clive (Tweed), King Charles Street
Captain Cook (Brock), The Mall
Oliver Cromwell (Thornycroft), outside Westminster Hall
Cunningham (Belsky), Trafalgar Square
Gen. Charles de Gaulle (Conner), Carlton Gardens
Diana, Princess of Wales Memorial Fountain (Gustafson Porter), Hyde Park
Disraeli, Earl of Beaconsfield (Raggi), Parliament Square
Lord Dowding (Winter), Strand
Duke of Cambridge (Jones), Whitehall
Duke of York (37.8m/124ft column, with statue by Westmacott), Carlton House Terrace
Edward VII (Mackennal), Waterloo Place
Elizabeth I (Kerwin, 1586, oldest outdoor statue in London; from Ludgate), Fleet Street
Eros (Shaftesbury Memorial) (Gilbert), Piccadilly Circus
Marechal/Marshall Foch (Mallisard, copy of one in Cassel, France), Grosvenor Gardens
Charles James Fox (Westmacott), Bloomsbury Square
Yuri Gagarin (Novikov, copy of Russian statue), The Mall
Mahatma Gandhi (Jackson), Parliament Square
George III (Cotes Wyatt), Cockspur Street
George IV (Chantrey), Trafalgar Square
George V (Reid Dick and Scott), Old Palace Yard
George VI (McMillan), Carlton Gardens
Gladstone (Thornycroft), Strand
Guards' (Crimea; Bell), Waterloo Place
Guards Division (Ledward, figures, Bradshaw, cenotaph), Horse Guards' Parade
Haig (Hardiman), Whitehall
Sir Arthur (Bomber) Harris (Winter), Strand
Gen. Henry Havelock (Behnes), Trafalgar Square
International Brigades Memorial (Spanish Civil War) (Ian Walters), Jubilee Gardens, South Bank
Irving (Brock), north side of National Portrait Gallery
Isis (Gudgeon), Hyde Park
James II (Gibbons), Trafalgar Square
Jellicoe (McMillan), Trafalgar Square
Samuel Johnson (Fitzgerald), opposite St Clement Danes
Kitchener (Tweed), Horse Guards' Parade
Abraham Lincoln (Saint-Gaudens, copy of one in Chicago), Parliament Square
Mandela (Walters), Parliament Square
Milton (Montford), St Giles, Cripplegate
Mountbatten (Belsky), Foreign Office Green
Gen. Charles James Napier (Adams), Trafalgar Square
Nelson (Railton), Trafalgar Square, with Landseer's lions (cast from guns recovered from the wreck of the *Royal George*)
Florence Nightingale (Walker), Waterloo Place
Palmerston (Woolner), Parliament Square
Sir Keith Park (Johnson), Waterloo Place
Peel (Noble), Parliament Square
Pitt (Chantrey), Hanover Square
Portal (Nemon), Embankment Gardens
Prince Albert (Bacon), Holborn Circus
Queen Elizabeth Gate (Lund and Wynne), Hyde Park Corner
Queen Mother (Jackson), Carlton Gardens
Raleigh (McMillan), Greenwich
Richard I (Coeur de Lion) (Marochetti), Old Palace Yard
Roberts (Bates), Horse Guards' Parade
Franklin D. Roosevelt (Reid Dick), Grosvenor Square
Royal Air Force (Blomfield), Victoria Embankment

Royal Air Force Bomber Command Memorial (O'Connor), Green Park
Royal Artillery (Great War) (Jagger and Pearson), Hyde Park Corner
Royal Artillery (South Africa) (Colton), The Mall
Captain Scott (Lady Scott), Waterloo Place
Shackleton (Jagger), Kensington Gore
Shakespeare (Fontana, copy of one by Scheemakers in Westminster Abbey), Leicester Square
Smuts (Epstein), Parliament Square
Sullivan (Goscombe John), Victoria Embankment
Trenchard (McMillan), Victoria Embankment
Victoria Memorial (Webb and Brock), in front of Buckingham Palace
Raoul Wallenberg (Jackson), Great Cumberland Place
George Washington (Houdon copy), Trafalgar Square
Wellington (Boehm), Hyde Park Corner
Wellington (Chantrey), outside Royal Exchange
John Wesley (Adams Acton), City Road
Westminster School (Crimea) (Scott), Broad Sanctuary
William III (Bacon), St James's Square
Wolseley (Goscombe John), Horse Guards' Parade

PARKS, GARDENS AND OPEN SPACES

CITY OF LONDON CORPORATION OPEN SPACES
W www.cityoflondon.gov.uk
Ashtead Common (202ha/500 acres), Surrey
Burnham Beeches and *Fleet Wood* (220ha/540 acres), Bucks. Acquired by the City of London for the benefit of the public in 1880, Fleet Wood (26ha/65 acres) being presented in 1921
Coulsdon Common (51ha/127 acres), Surrey
Epping Forest (2,476ha/6,118 acres), Essex. Acquired by the City of London in 1878 and opened to the public in 1882. The Queen Elizabeth Hunting Lodge, built for Henry VIII in 1543, lies at the edge of the forest. The present forest is 19.3km (12 miles) long by around 3km (2 miles) wide, approximately one-tenth of its original area
**Epping Forest Buffer Land* (718ha/1,774 acres), Waltham Abbey/Epping
Farthing Downs and New Hill (95ha/235 acres), Surrey
Hampstead Heath (275ha/680 acres), NW3. Including Golders Hill (15ha/36 acres) and Parliament Hill (110ha/271 acres)
Highgate Wood (28ha/70 acres), N6/N10
Kenley Common (56ha/139 acres), Surrey
Queen's Park (12ha/30 acres), NW6
Riddlesdown (43ha/104 acres), Surrey
Spring Park (20ha/50 acres), Kent
Stoke Common (80ha/198 acres), Bucks. Ownership was transferred to the City of London in 2007
West Ham Park (31ha/77 acres), E15
West Wickham Common (10ha/26 acres), Kent
Also over 150 smaller open spaces within the City of London, including *Finsbury Circus* and *St Dunstan-in-the-East*
* Includes Copped Hall Park, Woodredon Estate and Warlies Park

OTHER PARKS AND GARDENS
CHELSEA PHYSIC GARDEN, 66 Royal Hospital Road SW3 4HS T 020-7352 5646 W www.chelseaphysicgarden.co.uk
A garden of general botanical research and education, maintaining a wide range of rare and unusual plants; established in 1673 by the Society of Apothecaries
HAMPTON COURT PARK AND GARDENS (304ha/750 acres), Surrey KT8 9AU T 0844-482 7777 W www.hrp.org.uk
Also known as Home Park, the park lies beyond the palace's formal gardens. It contains a herd of deer and a 750-year-old oak tree from the original park
HOLLAND PARK (22ha/54 acres), Ilchester Place W8 T 020-7361 3000 W www.rbkc.gov.uk The largest park in the Royal Borough of Kensington and Chelsea, includes the Kyoto Garden

KEW, ROYAL BOTANIC GARDENS (120ha/300 acres), Richmond, Surrey TW9 3AB T 020-8332 5655 W www.kew.org
Founded in 1759 and declared a UNESCO World Heritage Site in 2003

THAMES BARRIER PARK (9ha/22acres), North Woolwich Road E16 2HP T 020-7476 3741 Opened in 2000, landscaped gardens with spectacular views of the Thames Barrier

ROYAL PARKS
W www.royalparks.org.uk

Bushy Park (450ha/1,099 acres), Middx. Adjoins Hampton Court; contains an avenue of horse-chestnuts enclosed in a fourfold avenue of limes planted by William III

Green Park (19ha/47 acres), W1. Between Piccadilly and St James's Park, with Constitution Hill leading to Hyde Park Corner

Greenwich Park (74ha/183 acres), SE10. Enclosed by Humphrey, Duke of Gloucester, and laid out by Charles II from the designs of Le Nôtre. On a hill in Greenwich Park is the Royal Observatory (founded 1675). Its buildings are now managed by the National Maritime Museum (T 020-8858 4422 W www.rmg.co.uk) and the earliest building is named Flamsteed House, after John Flamsteed (1646–1719), the first astronomer royal

Hyde Park (142ha/350 acres), W1/W2. From Park Lane to Kensington Gardens and incorporating the Serpentine lake, Apsley House, the Achilles Statue, Rotten Row and the Ladies' Mile; fine gateway at Hyde Park Corner. To the north-east is Marble Arch, originally erected by George IV at the entrance to Buckingham Palace and re-erected in the present position in 1851. At Hyde Park Corner stands Wellington Arch, built in 1825–7, it opened to the public in 2012 following major renovation

Kensington Gardens (111ha/275 acres), W2/W8. From the western boundary of Hyde Park to Kensington Palace; contains the Albert Memorial, Serpentine Gallery and Peter Pan statue

The Regent's Park and *Primrose Hill* (197ha/487 acres), NW1. From Marylebone Road to Primrose Hill surrounded by the Outer Circle; divided by the Broad Walk leading to the Zoological Gardens

Richmond Park (1,000ha/2,500 acres), Surrey. Designated a National Nature Reserve, a Site of Special Scientific Interest and a Special Area of Conservation

St James's Park (23ha/58 acres), SW1. From Whitehall to Buckingham Palace; ornamental lake of 4.9ha (12 acres); the Mall leads from Admiralty Arch to Buckingham Palace

PLACES OF HISTORICAL AND CULTURAL INTEREST

1 Canada Square
Canary Wharf E14 5AB T 020-7418 2000
W www.canarywharf.com
Also known as 'Canary Wharf', the steel and glass skyscraper is designed to sway 35cm in the strongest winds

20 Fenchurch Street
W www.20fenchurchstreet.co.uk
Designed by architect Rafael Viñoly the skyscraper was completed in March 2014 and is nicknamed the 'Walkie-Talkie' because of its shape. The top three floors include a large viewing platform and are open to the public

30 St Mary Axe
EC3A 8EP W www.30stmaryaxe.com
Completed in 2004 and commonly known as the 'Gherkin', each of the floors rotates five degrees from the one below

122 Leadenhall Street
EC3V 4AB W www.theleadenhallbuilding.com
The distinctive 225m (737ft) asymmetrical Leadenhall Building, designed by architects Rogers Stirk Harbour & Partners, was completed in 2014.

Alexandra Palace
Alexandra Palace Way N22 7AY T 020-8365 2121
W www.alexandrapalace.com
The Victorian palace was severely damaged by fire in 1980 but was restored, and reopened in 1988. Alexandra Palace now provides modern facilities for exhibitions, conferences, banquets and leisure activities. There is a winter ice rink, a boating lake and a conservation area

Barbican Centre
Silk Street EC2Y 8DS T 020-7638 4141 W www.barbican.org.uk
Owned, funded and managed by the City of London Corporation, the Barbican Centre opened in 1982 and houses the Barbican Theatre, a studio theatre called The Pit and the Barbican Hall; it is also home to the London Symphony Orchestra. There are three cinemas, six conference rooms, two art galleries, a sculpture court, a lending library, trade and banqueting facilities and a conservatory

British Library
St Pancras, 96 Euston Road NW1 2DB T 0330-333 1144
W www.bl.uk
The largest building constructed in the UK in the 20th century with basements extending 24.5m underground. Holdings include the *Magna Carta*, the Gutenburg Bible, Shakespeare's First Folio, Beatles manuscripts and the first edition of *The Times* from 1788. Holds temporary exhibitions on a range of topics

Central Criminal Court
Old Bailey EC4M 7EH T 020-7248 3277
W www.cityoflondon.gov.uk
The highest criminal court in the UK, the 'Old Bailey' is located on the site of the old Newgate Prison. Trials held here have included those of Oscar Wilde, Dr Crippen and the Yorkshire Ripper. The courthouse has been rebuilt several times since 1674; Edward VII officially opened the current neo-baroque building in 1907

Charterhouse
Charterhouse Square EC1M 6AN T 020-7253 9503
W www.thecharterhouse.org
A Carthusian monastery from 1371 to 1538, purchased in 1611 by Thomas Sutton, who endowed it as a residence for aged men 'of gentle birth' and a school for poor scholars (removed to Godalming in 1872)

Downing Street
SW1A 2AA W www.number10.gov.uk
Number 10 Downing Street is the official town residence of the prime minister, number 11 of the Chancellor of the Exchequer and number 12 is the office of the government whips. The street was named after Sir George Downing, Bt., soldier and diplomat, who was MP for Morpeth 1660–84

George Inn
The George Inn Yard SE1 1NH T 020-7407 2056
W www.nationaltrust.org.uk/george-inn
The last galleried inn in London, built in 1677. Now owned by the National Trust and run as an ordinary public house

Horse Guards
Whitehall SW1
Archway and offices built about 1753. The changing of the guard takes place daily at 11am (10am on Sundays) and the inspection at 4pm. Only those with the Queen's permission may drive through the gates and archway into *Horse Guards Parade*, where the colour is 'trooped' on the Queen's official birthday

HOUSES OF PARLIAMENT W www.parliament.uk
House of Commons, Westminster SW1A 0AA T 020-7219 4272
House of Lords, Westminster SW1A 0PW T 020-7219 3107
The royal palace of Westminster, originally built by Edward the Confessor, was the normal meeting place of Parliament from about 1340. St Stephen's Chapel was used from about 1550 for the meetings of the House of Commons, which had previously been held in the

Chapter House or Refectory of Westminster Abbey. The House of Lords met in an apartment of the royal palace. The fire of 1834 destroyed much of the palace, and the present Houses of Parliament were erected on the site from the designs of Sir Charles Barry and Augustus Welby Pugin between 1840 and 1867. The chamber of the House of Commons was destroyed by bombing in 1941, and a new chamber designed by Sir Giles Gilbert Scott was used for the first time in 1950. *Westminster Hall and the Crypt Chapel* was the only part of the old palace of Westminster to survive the fire of 1834. It was built by William II from 1097 to 1099 and altered by Richard II between 1394 and 1399. The hammerbeam roof of carved oak dates from 1396–8. The Hall was the scene of the trial of Charles I. *The Victoria Tower* of the House of Lords is 98.5m (323ft) high and *The Elizabeth Tower* of the House of Commons is 96.3m (316ft) high and contains 'Big Ben', the hour bell said to be named after Sir Benjamin Hall, First Commissioner of Works when the original bell was cast in 1856. This bell, which weighed 16 tons 11 cwt, was found to be cracked in 1857. The present bell (13.5 tons) is a recasting of the original and was first brought into use in 1859. The dials of the clock are 7m (23ft) in diameter, the hands being 2.7m (9ft) and 4.3m (14ft) long (including balance piece).

During session, tours of the Houses of Parliament are only available to UK residents who have made advance arrangements through an MP or peer. Overseas visitors are no longer provided with permits to tour the Houses of Parliament during session, although they can tour on Saturdays and during the summer opening and attend debates for both houses in the Strangers' Galleries. During the summer recess, tickets for tours of the Houses of Parliament can be booked by telephone (T 020-7219 4114) or bought on site at the ticket office on Abingdon Green opposite Parliament and the Victoria Tower Gardens. The Strangers' Gallery of the House of Commons is open to the public when the house is sitting. To acquire tickets in advance, UK residents should write to their local MP and overseas visitors should apply to their embassy or high commission in the UK for a permit. If none of these arrangements has been made, visitors should join the public queue outside St Stephen's Entrance, where there is also a queue for entry to the House of Lords Gallery

INNS OF COURT

The Inns of Court are ancient unincorporated bodies of lawyers which for more than five centuries have had the power to call to the Bar those of their members who have qualified for the rank or degree of Barrister-at-Law. There are four Inns of Court as well as many lesser inns:

Lincoln's Inn, WC2A 3TL T 020-7405 1393 W www.lincolnsinn.org.uk
The most ancient of the inns with records dating back to 1422. The hall and library buildings are from 1845, although the library is first mentioned in 1474; the old hall (late 15th century) and the chapel were rebuilt c.1619–23

Inner Temple, King's Bench Walk EC4Y 7HL T 020-7797 8250 W www.innertemple.org.uk
Middle Temple, Middle Temple Lane EC4Y 9BT T 020-7427 4800 W www.middletemple.org.uk
Records for the Inner and Middle Temple date back to the beginning of the 16th century. The site was originally occupied by the Order of Knights Templar c.1160–1312. The two inns have separate halls thought to have been formed c.1350. The division between the two societies was formalised in 1732 with Temple Church and the Masters House remaining in common. The Inner Temple Garden is normally open to the public on weekdays between 12.30pm and 3pm

Temple Church, EC4Y 7BB T 020-7353 8559 W www.templechurch.com
The nave forms one of five remaining round churches in England

Gray's Inn, South Square WC1R 5ET T 020-7458 7800 W www.graysinn.info
Founded early 14th century; hall 1556–8
No other 'Inns' are active, but there are remains of *Staple Inn,* a gabled front on Holborn (opposite Gray's Inn Road). *Clement's Inn* (near St Clement Danes Church), *Clifford's Inn,* Fleet Street, and *Thavies Inn,* Holborn Circus, are all rebuilt. *Serjeants' Inn,* Fleet Street, and another (demolished 1910) of the same name in Chancery Lane, were composed of Serjeants-at-Law, the last of whom died in 1922

Institute of Contemporary Arts
The Mall SW1Y 5AH T 020-7930 3647 W www.ica.org.uk
Exhibitions of modern art in the fields of film, theatre, new media and the visual arts

Lloyd's
Lime Street EC3M 7HA T 020-7327 1000 W www.lloyds.com
International insurance market which evolved during the 17th century from Lloyd's Coffee House. The present building was opened for business in May 1986, and houses the Lutine Bell. Underwriting is on three floors with a total area of 10,591 sq. m (114,000 sq. ft). The Lloyd's building is not open to the general public

London Central Mosque and the Islamic Cultural Centre
Park Road NW8 7RG T 020-7724 3363 W www.iccuk.org
The focus for London's Muslims; established in 1944 but not completed until 1977, the mosque can accommodate about 5,000 worshippers; guided tours are available

London Eye
South Bank SE1 7PB T 0870-990 8883 W www.londoneye.com
Opened in March 2000 as London's millennium landmark, this 137m (450ft) observation wheel is the tallest cantilevered observation wheel in the world. The wheel provides a 30-minute ride offering panoramic views of the capital

London Zoo
Regent's Park NW1 4RY T 0344-225 1826 W www.zsl.org

Madame Tussauds
Marylebone Road NW1 5LR T 0871-894 3000 W www.madametussauds.com
Waxwork exhibition

Mansion House
Cannon Street EC4N 8BH T 020-7626 2500 W www.cityoflondon.gov.uk
The official residence of the Lord Mayor. Built in the 18th century in the Palladian style. Open to groups by appointment only

Marlborough House
Pall Mall SW1Y 5HX T 020-7747 6500 W www.thecommonwealth.org
Built by Wren for the first Duke of Marlborough and completed in 1711, the house reverted to the Crown in 1835. In 1863 it became the London house of the Prince of Wales and was the London home of Queen Mary until her death in 1953. In 1959 Marlborough House was given by the Queen as the headquarters for the Commonwealth Secretariat and it was opened as such in 1965. The Queen's Chapel, Marlborough Gate, was begun in 1623 from the designs of Inigo Jones for the Infanta Maria of Spain, and completed for Queen Henrietta Maria. Marlborough House is not open to the public

Neasden Temple
BAPS Shri Swaminarayan Mandir, Brentfield Road, Neasden NW10 8LD T 020-8965 2651 W http://londonmandir.baps.org
The first and largest traditional Hindu Mandir outside of India; opened in 1995

Port of London
Port of London Authority, Royal Pier Road, Kent DA12 2BG T 01474-562200 W www.pla.co.uk
The Port of London covers the tidal section of the river Thames from Teddington to the seaward limit (the outer Tongue buoy and the Sunk light vessel), a distance of 150km (93 miles). The governing body is the Port of

London Authority (PLA). Cargo is handled at privately operated riverside terminals between Fulham and Canvey Island, including the enclosed dock at Tilbury, 40km (25 miles) below London Bridge. Passenger vessels and cruise liners can be handled at moorings at Greenwich, Tower Bridge and Tilbury

Queen Elizabeth Olympic Park
Stratford E20 **T** 0800-072 2110
W www.queenelizabetholympicpark.co.uk
Built for the London 2012 Olympic and Paralympic Games, the park, which included the Olympic Stadium, Velodrome and Aquatics Centre has been redeveloped to provide 227ha (560 acres) of parkland with play areas, outside arts and theatre spaces, waterways and wetlands. The north of the park, which includes the Copper Box Arena sport venue, re-opened to the public in 2013. The south of the park, which re-opened in April 2014, incorporates three venues for arts and sports events and the *ArcelorMittal Orbit*, designed by Sir Anish Kapoor and Cecil Balmond; it is the UK's tallest sculpture (114.5m/ 376ft) and has two accessible observation floors

Roman Remains
The city wall of Roman *Londinium* was largely rebuilt during the medieval period but sections may be seen near the White Tower in the Tower of London; at Tower Hill; at Coopers' Row; at All Hallows, London Wall, its vestry being built on the remains of a semi-circular Roman bastion; at St Alphage, London Wall, showing a succession of building repairs from the Roman until the late medieval period; and at St Giles, Cripplegate. Sections of the great forum and basilica, more than 165 sq. m (1,776 sq. ft), have been encountered during excavations in the area of Leadenhall, Gracechurch Street and Lombard Street. Traces of Roman activity along the river include a massive riverside wall built in the late Roman period, and a succession of Roman timber quays along Lower and Upper Thames Street. Finds from these sites can be seen at the Museum of London.
Other major buildings are the amphitheatre at Guildhall, remains of bath-buildings in Upper and Lower Thames Street, and the temple of Mithras in Walbrook

Royal Albert Hall
Kensington Gore SW7 2AP **T** 0845-401 5045
W www.royalalberthall.com
The elliptical hall, one of the largest in the world, was completed in 1871; since 1941 it has been the venue each summer for the Promenade Concerts founded in 1895 by Sir Henry Wood. Other events include pop and classical music concerts, dance, opera, sporting events, conferences and banquets

Royal Courts of Justice
Strand WC2A 2LL **T** 020-7947 7726 **W** www.justice.gov.uk
Victorian Gothic building that is home to the high court. Visitors are free to watch proceedings

Royal Hospital, Chelsea
Royal Hospital Road SW3 4SR **T** 020-7881 5200
W www.chelsea-pensioners.co.uk
Founded by Charles II in 1682, and built by Wren; opened in 1692 for old and disabled soldiers. The extensive grounds include the former Ranelagh Gardens and are the venue for the Chelsea Flower Show each May

Royal Naval College
Greenwich SE10 9NN **T** 020-8269 4747 **W** www.ornc.org
The building was the Greenwich Hospital until 1869. It was built by Charles II, largely from designs by John Webb, and by Queen Mary II and William III, from designs by Wren. It stands on the site of an ancient abbey, a royal house and Greenwich Palace, which was constructed by Henry VII. Henry VIII, Mary I and Elizabeth I were born in the royal palace and Edward VI died there

Royal Opera House
Covent Garden WC2E 9DD **T** 020-7240 1200 **W** www.roh.org.uk

Home of The Royal Ballet (1931) and The Royal Opera (1946). The Royal Opera House is the third theatre to be built on the site, opening 1858; the first was opened in 1732

St James's Palace
Pall Mall SW1A 1BQ **W** www.royal.gov.uk
Built by Henry VIII, only the Gatehouse and Presence Chamber remain; later alterations were made by Wren and Kent. Representatives of foreign powers are still accredited 'to the Court of St James's'. *Clarence House* (1825), the official London residence of the Prince of Wales, stands within the St James's Palace estate

St Paul's Cathedral
St Paul's Churchyard EC4M 8AD **T** 020-7246 8350
W www.stpauls.co.uk
Built 1675–1710. The cross on the dome is 111m (365ft) above ground level, the inner cupola 66.4m (218ft) above the floor. 'Great Paul' in the south-west tower weighs nearly 17 tons. The organ by Father Smith (enlarged by Willis and rebuilt by Mander) is in a case carved by Grinling Gibbons, who also carved the choir stalls

Shakespeare's Globe
New Globe Walk SE1 9DT **T** 020-7902 1400
W www.shakespearesglobe.com
Reconstructed in 1997, the open-air playhouse is a unique resource for the works of William Shakespeare through perfomance and education; a new indoor replica Jacobean theatre staged its first public performance in January 2014

Shard
London Bridge SE1 **T** 020-7493 5311 **W** www.the-shard.com
Completed in May 2012, the skyscraper stands at 310m (1,016ft) and possesses a unique facade of 11,000 glass panels and a 360-degree viewing gallery

Somerset House
Strand WC2R 1LA **T** 020-7845 4600
W www.somersethouse.org.uk
The river facade (183m/600ft long) was built in 1776–1801 from the designs of Sir William Chambers; the eastern extension, which houses part of King's College, was built by Smirke in 1829–35. Somerset House was the property of Lord Protector Somerset, at whose attainder in 1552 the palace passed to the Crown, and it was a royal residence until 1692. Somerset House has recently undergone extensive renovation and is home to the Embankment Galleries and the Courtauld Gallery. Open-air concerts and ice-skating (Dec–Jan) are held in the courtyard

SOUTH BANK, SE1
Arts complex on the south bank of the river Thames which consists of:
BFI Southbank **T** 020-7928 3232 **W** www.bfi.org.uk
Opened in 1952 and administered by the British Film Institute, has four auditoria of varying capacities. Venue for the annual London Film Festival.
The *Royal Festival Hall* **T** 020-7960 4200
W www.southbankcentre.co.uk
Opened in 1951 for the Festival of Britain, adjacent are the *Queen Elizabeth Hall,* the *Purcell Room* and the *Hayward Gallery*
The *Royal National Theatre,* **T** 020-7452 3000
W www.nationaltheatre.org.uk
Opened in 1976; comprises the Olivier, the Lyttelton and Dorfman theatres. The Cottesloe Theatre closed in February 2013 and, following refurbishment reopened in 2014 as the Dorfman Theatre

Southwark Cathedral
London Bridge SE1 9DA **T** 020-7367 6700
W www.cathedral.southwark.anglican.org
Mainly 13th century, but the nave is largely rebuilt. The tomb of John Bunyan (1330–1408) is between the Bunyan and Chaucer memorial windows in the north aisle; Shakespeare's effigy, backed by a view of Southwark and the Globe Theatre, is in the south aisle; the tomb of

Bishop Andrewes (d.1626) is near the screen. The Lady Chapel was the scene of the consistory courts of the reign of Mary (Gardiner and Bonner) and is still used as a consistory court. John Harvard, after whom Harvard University is named, was baptised here in 1607, and the chapel by the north choir aisle is his memorial chapel

Thames Embankments

Sir Joseph Bazalgette (1819–91) constructed the *Victoria Embankment,* on the north side from Westminster to Blackfriars for the Metropolitan Board of Works, 1864–70; (the seats, of which the supports of some are a kneeling camel, laden with spicery, and of others a winged sphinx, were presented by the Grocers' Company and by W. H. Smith, MP, in 1874); the *Albert Embankment,* on the south side from Westminster Bridge to Vauxhall, 1866–9, and the Chelsea Embankment, 1871–4. The total cost exceeded £2m. Bazalgette also inaugurated the London main drainage system, 1858–65. A medallion *(Flumini vincula posuit)* has been placed on a pier of the *Victoria Embankment* to commemorate the engineer

Thames Flood Barrier

W www.environment-agency.gov.uk

Officially opened in May 1984, though first used in February 1983, the barrier consists of ten rising sector gates which span approximately 520m from bank to bank of the Thames at Woolwich Reach. When not in use the gates lie horizontally, allowing shipping to navigate the river normally; when the barrier is closed, the gates turn through 90 degrees to stand vertically more than 50 feet above the river bed. The barrier took eight years to complete and can be raised within about 90 minutes

Trafalgar Tavern

Park Row, Greenwich SE10 9NW T 020-8858 2909

W www.trafalgartavern.co.uk

Regency-period riverside public house built in 1837. Charles Dickens and William Gladstone were patrons

Wembley Stadium

Wembley HA9 0WS T 0844-980 8001

W www.wembleystadium.com

The second largest stadium in Europe; hosts major sporting events and music concerts

Westminster Abbey

SW1P 3PA T 020-7222 5152 W www.westminster-abbey.org

Founded as a Benedictine monastery over 1,000 years ago, the church was rebuilt by Edward the Confessor in 1065 and again by Henry III in the 13th century. The abbey is the resting place for monarchs including Edward I, Henry III, Henry V, Henry VII, Elizabeth I, Mary I and Mary, Queen of Scots, and has been the setting of coronations since that of William the Conqueror in 1066. In Poets' Corner there are memorials to many literary figures, and many scientists and musicians are also remembered here. The grave of the Unknown Warrior is to be found in the nave

Westminster Cathedral

Francis Street SW1P 1QW T 020-7798 9055

W www.westminstercathedral.org.uk

Roman Catholic cathedral built 1895–1903 from the designs of John Francis Bentley. The campanile is 83m (273ft) high

Wimbledon All England Lawn Tennis Club

Church Road SW19 5AE T 020-8944 1066

W www.wimbledon.com

Venue for the Wimbledon Championships. Includes the Wimbledon Lawn Tennis Museum

HALLMARKS

Hallmarks are the symbols stamped on gold, silver, palladium or platinum articles to indicate that they have been tested at an official Assay Office and that they conform to one of the legal standards. The marking of gold and silver articles to identify the maker was instituted in England in 1363 under a statute of Edward III. In 1478 the Assay Office in Goldsmiths' Hall was established and all gold and silversmiths were required to bring their wares to be date-marked by the Hall, hence the term 'hallmarked'.

With certain exceptions, all gold, silver, palladium or platinum articles are required by law to be hallmarked before they are offered for sale. Current hallmarking requirements come under the UK Hallmarking Act 1973 and subsequent amendments. The act is built around the principle of description, where it is an offence for any person to apply to an unhallmarked article a description indicating that it is wholly or partly made of gold, silver, palladium or platinum. There is an exemption by weight: compulsory hallmarks are not needed on gold and palladium under 1g, silver under 7.78g and platinum under 0.5g. Also, some descriptions, such as rolled gold and gold plate, are permissible. The British Hallmarking Council is a statutory body created as a result of the Hallmarking Act. It ensures adequate provision for assaying and hallmarking, supervises the assay offices and ensures the enforcement of hallmarking legislation. The four assay offices at London, Birmingham, Sheffield and Edinburgh operate under the act.

BRITISH HALLMARKING COUNCIL Secretariat, 1 Colmore Square, Birmingham B4 6AA T 0870-763 1455 W www.gov.uk/government/organisations/british-hallmarking-council

COMPULSORY MARKS

Since January 1999 UK hallmarks have consisted of three compulsory symbols – the sponsor's mark, the millesimal fineness (purity) mark and the assay office mark. The distinction between UK and foreign articles has been removed, and more finenesses are now legal, reflecting the more common finenesses elsewhere in Europe.

SPONSOR'S MARK

Formerly known as the maker's mark, the sponsor's mark was instituted in England in 1363. Originally a device such as a bird or fleur-de-lis, now it consists of a combination of at least two initials (usually a shortened form of the manufacturer's name) and a shield design. The London Assay Office offers 45 standard shield designs but other designs are possible by arrangement.

MILLESIMAL FINENESS MARK

The millesimal fineness (purity) mark indicates the number of parts per thousand of pure metal in the alloy. The current finenesses allowed in the UK are:

Gold	999; 990; 916 (22 carat); 750 (18 carat); 585 (14 carat); 375 (9 carat)
Silver	999; 958 (Britannia); 925 (sterling); 800
Palladium	999; 950; 500
Platinum	999; 950; 900; 850

ASSAY OFFICE MARK

This mark identifies the particular assay office at which the article was tested and marked. The British assay offices are:

 LONDON, Goldsmiths' Hall, Gutter Lane, London EC2V 8AQ T 020-7606 8971 W www.thegoldsmiths.co.uk

 BIRMINGHAM, PO Box 151, Newhall Street, Birmingham B3 1SB T 0121-236 6951 W www.theassayoffice.co.uk

 SHEFFIELD, Guardians' Hall, Beulah Road, Hillsborough, Sheffield S6 2AN T 0114-231 2121 W www.assayoffice.co.uk

 EDINBURGH, Goldsmiths' Hall, 24 Broughton Street, Edinburgh EH1 3RH T 0131-556 1144 W www.edinburghassayoffice.co.uk

Assay offices formerly existed in other towns, eg Chester, Exeter, Glasgow, Newcastle, Norwich and York, each having its own distinguishing mark.

OPTIONAL MARKS

Since 1999 traditional pictorial marks such as a crown for gold, the Britannia for 958 silver, the lion passant for 925 Sterling silver (lion rampant in Scotland) and the orb for 950 platinum may be added voluntarily to the millesimal mark. In 2010 a pictorial mark of the Greek goddess Pallas Athene was introduced for 950 palladium.

 Gold – a crown

 Britannia silver

 Sterling silver (England)

 Sterling silver (Scotland)

 Platinum – an orb

 Palladium – the Greek goddess Pallas Athene

OTHER MARKS

FOREIGN GOODS

Foreign goods imported into the UK are required to be hallmarked before sale, unless they already bear a convention mark or a hallmark struck by an independent assay office in the European Economic Area which is deemed to be equivalent to a UK hallmark.

The following are the assay office marks used for gold imported articles until the end of 1998. For silver and platinum the symbols remain the same but the shields differ in shape.

 London   Sheffield

 Birmingham   Edinburgh

CONVENTION HALLMARKS

The UK has been a signatory to the International Convention on Hallmarks since 1972. A convention hallmark struck by the UK assay offices is recognised by all member countries in the convention and, similarly, convention marks from member countries are legally recognised in the UK. There are currently 19 members of the hallmarking convention: Austria, Cyprus, Czech Republic, Denmark, Finland, Hungary, Ireland, Israel, Latvia, Lithuania, the Netherlands, Norway, Poland, Portugal, Slovakia, Slovenia, Sweden, Switzerland, and the UK.

A convention hallmark comprises four marks: a sponsor's mark, a common control mark, a fineness mark, and an assay office mark.

Examples of common control marks (figures differ according to fineness, but the style of each mark remains the same for each article):

GOLD	SILVER	PALLADIUM	PLATINUM

COMMEMORATIVE MARKS

There are other marks to commemorate special events: the silver jubilee of King George V and Queen Mary in 1935, the coronation of Queen Elizabeth II in 1953, her silver jubilee in 1977, and her golden jubilee in 2002. During 1999 and 2000 there was a voluntary additional Millennium Mark. A mark to commemorate the Queen's diamond jubilee in 2012 was available from July 2011 to October 2012:

   Diamond Jubilee Hallmark ·

DATE LETTER

The date letter shows the year in which an article was assayed and hallmarked. Each alphabetical cycle has a distinctive style of lettering or shape of shield. The date letters were different at the various assay offices and the particular office must be established from the assay office mark before reference is made to tables of date letters. Date letter marks became voluntary from 1 January 1999.

The table which follows shows one specimen shield and letter used by the London Assay Office on silver articles for each alphabetical cycle from 1498. The same letters are found on gold articles but the surrounding shield may differ. Until 1 January 1975, each hallmark covered two calendar years as the letter changed annually in May on St Dunstan's Day (the patron saint of silversmiths). Since 1 January 1975, each date letter has indicated a calendar year from January to December and each office has used the same style of date letter and shield for all articles.

	1498–9	1517–18			1756–7	1775–6
	1518–19	1537–8			1776–7	1795–6
	1538–9	1557–8			1796–7	1815–16
	1558–9	1577–8			1816–17	1835–6
	1578–9	1597–8			1836–7	1855–6
	1598–9	1617–18			1856–7	1875–6
	1618–19	1637–8			1876–7 (A to M square shield, N to Z as shown)	1895–6
	1638–9	1657–8			1896–7	1915–16
	1658–9	1677–8			1916–17	1935–6
	1678–9	1696–7			1936–7	1955–6
	1697 (from March, 1697 only)	1715–16			1956–7	1974
	1716–17	1735–6			1975	1999
	1736–7	1738–9			2000	
	1739–40	1755–6				

BRITISH CURRENCY

The unit of currency is the pound sterling (£) of 100 pence. The decimal system was introduced on 15 February 1971.

COIN

Gold Coins
One hundred pounds £100*
Fifty pounds £50*
Twenty-five pounds £25*
Ten pounds £10*
Five pounds £5
Two pounds £2
Sovereign £1
Half-sovereign 50p

Silver Coins
(Britannia coins)*
Two pounds £2
One pound £1
50 pence 50p
Twenty pence 20p

Maundy Money†
Fourpence 4p
Threepence 3p
Twopence 2p
Penny 1p

Bi-colour Coins‡
Two pounds £2
One pound £1§

Nickel-Brass Coins
Two pounds £2 (pre-1997)₵
One pound £1

Cupro-Nickel Coins
Crown £5 (since 1990)₵
50 pence 50p
Crown 25p (pre-1990)₵
20 pence 20p

*Nickel-plated Steel Coins***
10 pence 10p
5 pence 5p

Bronze Coins
2 pence 2p
1 penny 1p

Copper-plated Steel Coins††
2 pence 2p
1 penny 1p

* Britannia coins: gold bullion introduced 1987; silver, 1997
† Ceremonial money given annually by the sovereign on Maundy Thursday to as many elderly men and women as there are years in the sovereign's age
‡ Cupro-nickel centre and nickel-brass outer ring
§ The 12-sided £1 entered circulation on 28 March 2017
₵ Commemorative coins; not intended for general circulation
** Since September 1992; in 1998 the 2p was additionally struck in bronze
†† Pre-2012 the 10p and 5p coins were struck in cupro-nickel

GOLD COIN

Gold ceased to circulate during the First World War. Since then controls on buying, selling and holding gold coin have been imposed at various times but have subsequently been revoked. Under the Exchange Control (Gold Coins Exemption) Order 1979, gold coins may now be imported and exported without restriction, except gold coins which are more than 50 years old and valued at a sum in excess of £8,000.

Value Added Taxation on the sale of gold coins was revoked in 2000.

SILVER COIN

Prior to 1920 silver coins were struck from sterling silver, an alloy of which 925 parts in 1,000 were silver. In 1920 the proportion of silver was reduced to 500 parts. Since 1947 all 'silver' coins, except Maundy money, have been struck from cupro-nickel, an alloy of 75 parts copper and 25 parts nickel, except for the 20p, composed of 84 parts copper, 16 parts nickel. Maundy coins continue to be struck from sterling silver.

BRONZE COIN

Bronze, introduced in 1860 to replace copper, is an alloy consisting mainly of copper with small amounts of zinc and tin. Bronze was replaced by copper-plated steel in September

1992 with the exception of 1998 when the 2p was made in both copper-plated steel and bronze.

LEGAL TENDER *as at July 2017*

	Legal up to
Gold*	any amount
£2	any amount
£1	any amount
50p	£10
20p	£10
10p	£5
5p	£5
2p	20p
1p	20p

* Dated 1838 onwards, if not below least current weight

£5 (Crown since 1990) and 25p (Crown pre-1990) up to £10 are also legal tender under the Coinage Act 1971 but, as for all commemorative coins, are not designed for general circulation and are unlikely to be accepted by banks and shops.

VALUE AND NUMBER OF COINS IN CIRCULATION
estimated at 31 March 2016

Denomination	Face value (£m)	Number of pieces (millions)
£2	957.036	479
£1	1,671.328	1,671
50p	526.153	1,053
20p	600.828	3,004
10p	171.312	1,713
5p	203.764	4,075
2p	134.273	6,714
1p	114.299	11,430

The following coins have ceased to be legal tender:

Farthing	31 Dec 1960
Halfpenny (½d)	31 Jul 1969
Half-crown	31 Dec 1969
Threepence	31 Aug 1971
Penny (1d)	31 Aug 1971
Sixpence	30 Jun 1980
Halfpenny (½p)	31 Dec 1984
Old 5 pence	31 Dec 1990
Old 10 pence	30 Jun 1993
Old 50 pence	28 Feb 1998
Old £1 (nickel-brass/round)	15 Oct 2017

The Channel Islands and the Isle of Man issue their own coinage, which is legal tender only in the island of issue.

COIN STANDARDS

	Metal	Standard weight (g)	Standard diameter (mm)
1p	bronze	3.56	20.3
1p	copper-plated steel	3.56	20.3
2p	bronze	7.12	25.9
2p	copper-plated steel	7.12	25.9
5p	nickel-plated steel	3.25	18.0
10p	nickel-plated steel	6.50	24.5
20p	cupro-nickel	5.00	21.4
25p Crown	cupro-nickel	28.28	38.6
50p	cupro-nickel	8.00	27.3
£1	cupro-nickel, nickel-brass	8.75	23.4
£2	nickel-brass	15.98	28.4
£2	cupro-nickel, nickel-brass	12.00	28.4
£5 Crown	cupro-nickel	28.28	38.6

The 'remedy' is the amount of variation from standard permitted in weight and fineness of coins when first issued from the Royal Mint.

THE TRIAL OF THE PYX

The Trial of the Pyx is the examination by a jury to ascertain that coins made by the Royal Mint, which have been set aside in the pyx (or box), are of the proper weight, diameter and composition required by law. The trial is held annually, presided over by the Queen's Remembrancer, with a jury of freemen of the Company of Goldsmiths.

BANKNOTES

Bank of England notes are issued in denominations of £5, £10, £20 and £50 for the amount of the fiduciary note issue, and are legal tender in England and Wales. No £1 notes have been issued since 1984 and in March 1998 the outstanding notes were written off in accordance with the provision of the Currency Act 1983.

The E series of notes was introduced from June 1990, replacing the D series (*see* below). A new-style £20 note, the first in series F, was introduced in March 2007. A £50 note, the second in the F series, and the first banknote issued by the Bank of England to feature two portraits on the reverse, was issued in November 2011. The first polymer G series banknote, a £5 note featuring Sir Winston Churchill, was issued in September 2016. The historical figures portrayed in these series are:

£5	Sep 2016–date	Sir Winston Churchill
£5	May 2002–2017	Elizabeth Fry*
£5	Jun 1990–2003	George Stephenson*
£10	from Sep 2017	Jane Austen
£10	Nov 2000–date	Charles Darwin
£10	Apr 1992–2003	Charles Dickens*
£20	Mar 2007–date	Adam Smith
£20	Jun 1999–2010	Sir Edward Elgar*
£20	Jun 1991–2001	Michael Faraday*
£50	Nov 2011–date	Matthew Boulton and James Watt
£50	Apr 1994–2014	Sir John Houblon*

* These notes have been withdrawn from circulation

NOTE CIRCULATION

Note circulation is highest at the two peak spending periods of the year: around Christmas and during the summer holiday period.

The value of notes in circulation (£ million) at the end of February 2016 and 2017 was:

	2016	2017
£5	1,645	1,912
£10	7,767	8,006
£20	41,037	43,357
£50	13,157	15,601
Other notes*	4,212	4,322
Total	67,819	73,198

* Includes higher value notes used as backing for the note issues of authorised banks in Scotland and Northern Ireland

LEGAL TENDER

Banknotes which are no longer legal tender are payable when presented at the head office of the Bank of England in London.

The white notes for £10, £20, £50, £100, £500 and £1,000, which were issued until April 1943, ceased to be legal tender in May 1945, and the white £5 note in March 1946.

The white £5 note issued between October 1945 and September 1956, the £5 notes issued between 1957 and 1963 (bearing a portrait of Britannia) and the first series to bear a portrait of the Queen, issued between 1963 and 1971, ceased to be legal tender in March 1961, June 1967 and September 1973 respectively.

The series of £1 notes issued during the years 1928 to 1960 and the 10 shilling notes issued from 1928 to 1961 (those without the royal portrait) ceased to be legal tender in May and October 1962 respectively. The £1 note first issued in March 1960 (bearing on the back a representation of Britannia) and the £10 note first issued in February 1964 (bearing a lion on the back), both bearing a portrait of the Queen on the front, ceased to be legal tender in June 1979. The £1 note first issued in 1978 ceased to be legal tender on 11 March 1988. The 10 shilling note was replaced by the 50p coin in October 1969, and ceased to be legal tender on 21 November 1970.

The D series of banknotes was introduced from 1970 and ceased to be legal tender from the dates shown below. The predominant identifying feature of each note was the portrayal on the back of a prominent figure from British history:

£1	Feb 1978–Mar 1988	Sir Isaac Newton
£5	Nov 1971–Nov 1991	Duke of Wellington
£10	Feb 1975–May 1994	Florence Nightingale
£20	Jul 1970–Mar 1993	William Shakespeare
£50	Mar 1981–Sep 1996	Sir Christopher Wren

The £1 coin was introduced on 21 April 1983 to replace the £1 note.

OTHER BANKNOTES

Scotland – Banknotes are issued by three Scottish banks. The Royal Bank of Scotland issues notes for £1, £5, £10, £20, £50 and £100. Bank of Scotland and the Clydesdale Bank issue notes for £5, £10, £20, £50 and £100. Scottish notes are not legal tender in the UK but they are an authorised currency.

Northern Ireland – Banknotes are issued by four banks in Northern Ireland. The Bank of Ireland and the Ulster Bank issue notes for £5, £10, £20, £50 and £100. The First Trust Bank issue notes for £10, £20, £50 and £100 and Danske Bank (formerly Northern Bank) issue notes for £10 and £20. Northern Ireland notes are not legal tender in the UK but they are an authorised currency.

Channel Islands – The States of Guernsey issues its own currency notes and coinage. The notes are for £1, £5, £10, £20 and £50, and the coins are for 1p, 2p, 5p, 10p, 20p, 50p, £1 and £2.

The States of Jersey issues its own currency notes and coinage. The notes are for £1, £5, £10, £20, £50 and £100, and the coins are for 1p, 2p, 5p, 10p, 20p, 50p, £1 and £2.

The Isle of Man – The Isle of Man government issues notes for £1, £5, £10, £20 and £50. Although these notes are only legal tender in the Isle of Man, they may be exchanged at face value at certain UK banks at their discretion. The Isle of Man issues coins for 1p, 2p, 5p, 10p, 20p, 50p, £1, £2 and £5.

Although none of the series of notes specified above is legal tender in the UK, they are generally accepted by banks irrespective of their place of issue. At one time banks made a commission charge for handling Scottish and Irish notes but this was abolished some years ago.

BANK FAMILY TREE

Includes the major retail banks operating in the UK as at April 2017. For financial results for these banks *see* Banking and Personal Finance. Building societies are only included in instances where they demutualised to become a bank.

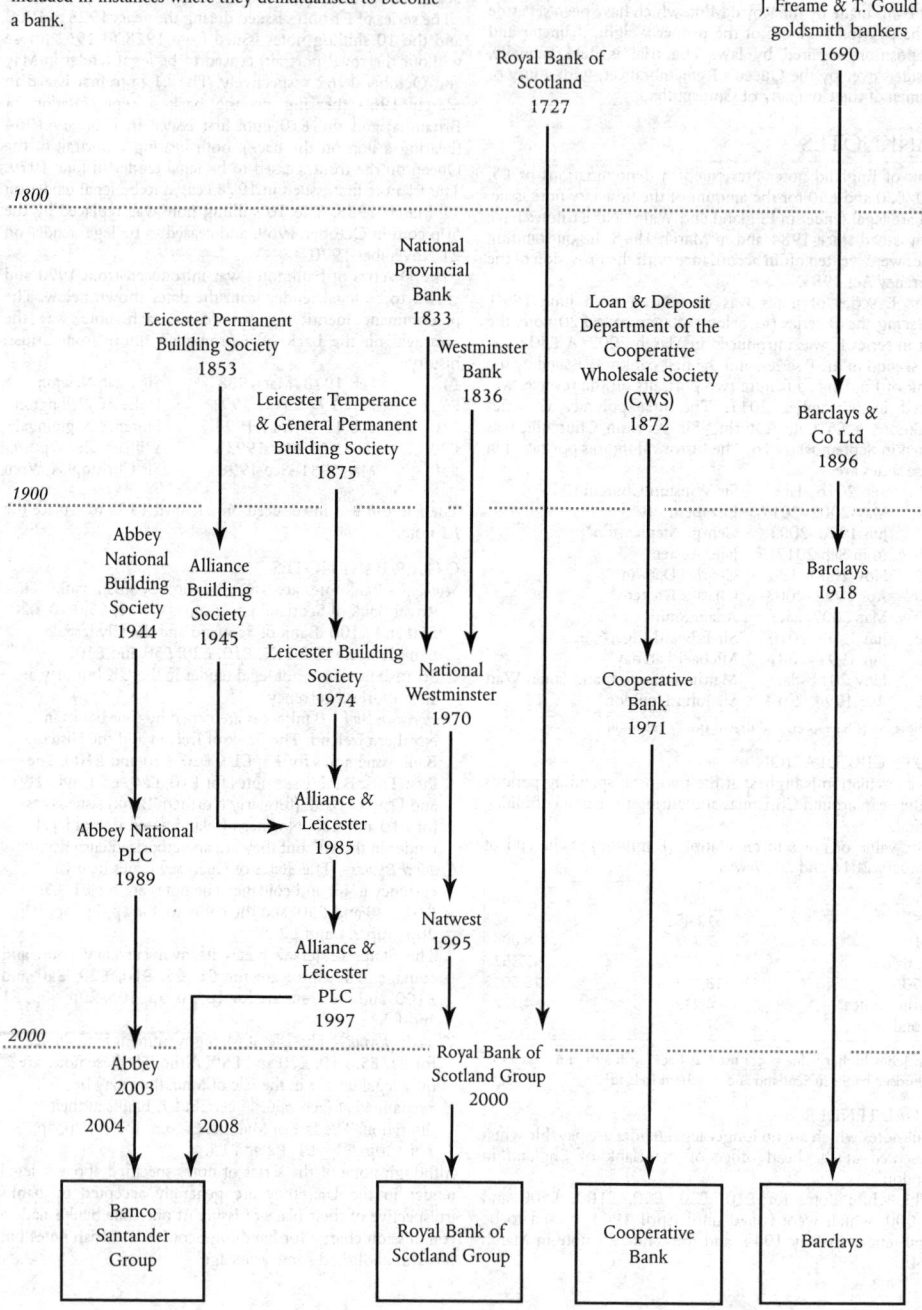

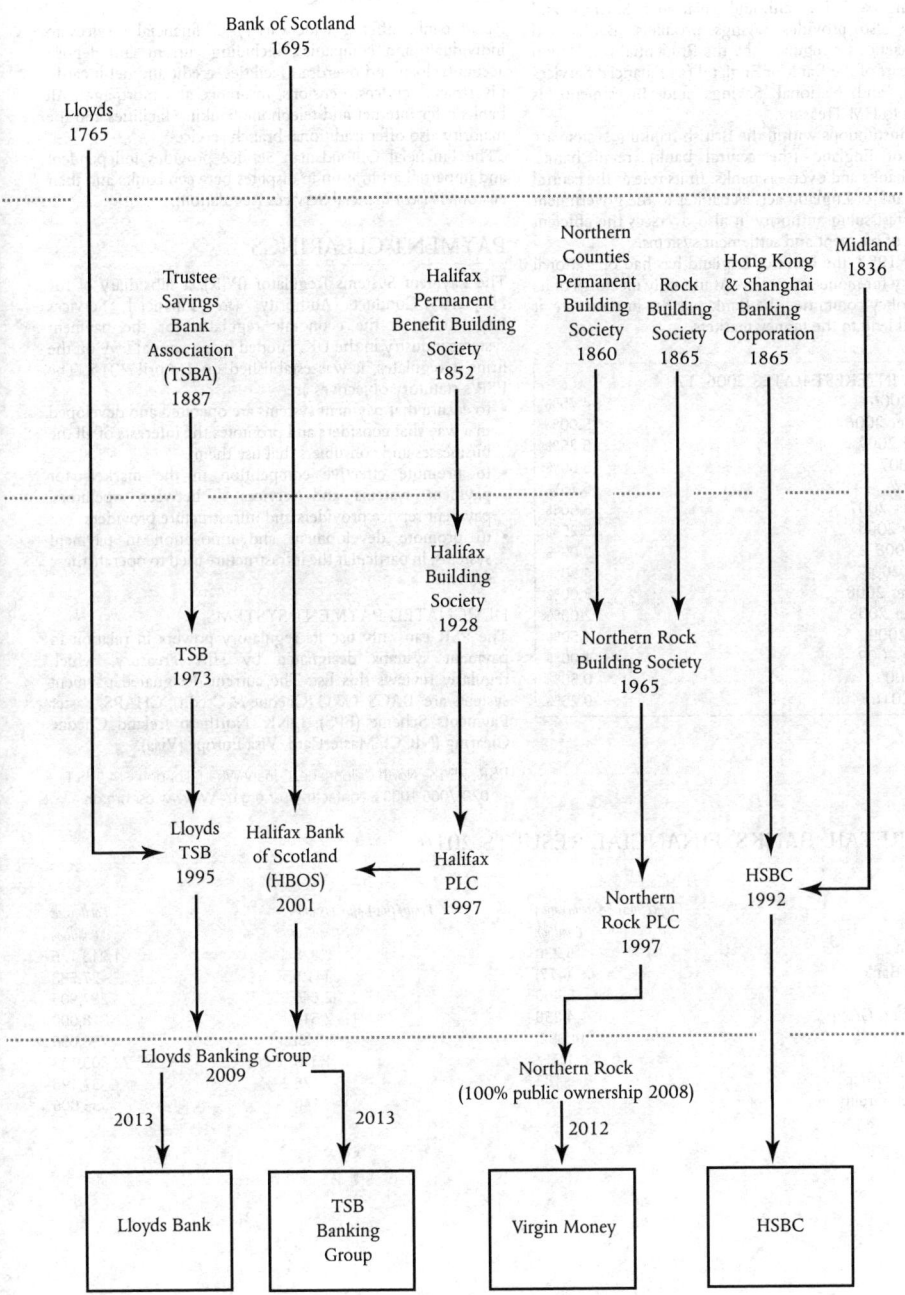

BANKING AND PERSONAL FINANCE

There are two main types of deposit-taking institutions: banks and building societies, although National Savings and Investments also provides savings products. Banks and building societies are regulated by the Prudential Regulation Authority, part of the Bank of England (*see* Financial Services Regulation), and National Savings and Investments is accountable to HM Treasury.

The main institutions within the British banking system are the Bank of England (the central bank), retail banks, investment banks and overseas banks. In its role as the central bank, the Bank of England acts as banker to the government and as a note-issuing authority; it also oversees the efficient functioning of payment and settlement systems.

Since May 1997, the Bank of England has had operational responsibility for monetary policy. At monthly meetings of its monetary policy committee the Bank sets the interest rate at which it will lend to the money markets.

OFFICIAL INTEREST RATES 2006–17	
3 August 2006	4.75%
9 November 2006	5.00%
11 January 2007	5.25%
10 May 2007	5.50%
5 July 2007	5.75%
6 December 2007	5.50%
7 February 2008	5.25%
10 April 2008	5.00%
8 October 2008	4.50%
6 November 2008	3.00%
4 December 2008	2.00%
8 January 2009	1.50%
5 February 2009	1.00%
5 March 2009	0.50%
4 August 2016	0.25%

RETAIL BANKING

Retail banks offer a wide variety of financial services to individuals and companies, including current and deposit accounts, loan and overdraft facilities, credit and debit cards, investment services, pensions, insurance and mortgages. All banks offer internet and telephone banking facilities and the majority also offer traditional branch services.

The Financial Ombudsman Service provides independent and impartial arbitration in disputes between banks and their customers (*see* Financial Services Regulation).

PAYMENT CLEARINGS

The Payment Systems Regulator (PSR), a subsidiary of the Financial Conduct Authority (*see* Financial Services Regulation), is the economic regulator for the payment systems industry in the UK. Funded by an annual levy on the firms it regulates, it was established on 1 April 2015. The PSR's statutory objectives are:

- to ensure that payment systems are operated and developed in a way that considers and promotes the interests of all the businesses and consumers that use them
- to promote effective competition in the markets for payment systems and services – between operators, payment service providers and infrastructure providers
- to promote development and innovation in payment systems, in particular the infrastructure used to operate these systems

DESIGNATED PAYMENT SYSTEMS

The PSR can only use its regulatory powers in relation to payment systems designated by HM Treasury, which regularly reviews this list. The current designated payment systems are: BACS, C&C (Cheque & Credit), CHAPS, Faster Payments Scheme (FPS), LINK, Northern Ireland Cheque Clearing (NICC), MasterCard, Visa Europe (Visa).

PSR, 25 The North Colonnade, Canary Wharf, London E14 5HS **T** 020-7066 1000 **E** contactus@psr.org.uk **W** www.psr.org.uk

MAJOR RETAIL BANKS' FINANCIAL RESULTS 2016

Bank group	Profit/(loss) before taxation £ million	Profit/(loss) after taxation £ million	Total assets £ million
Barclays Bank	3,230	2,828	1,213,126
Cooperative Bank	(477)	(419)	27,588
HSBC Bank	5,460	2,646	287,905
Lloyds Banking Group	4,238	2,514	818,000
RBS Group	(4,082)	(5,248)	798,656
Santander UK	1,917	1,319	303,142
TSB Banking Group	182	128	37,196
Virgin Money Group	194	140	35,006

GLOSSARY OF FINANCIAL TERMS

AER (ANNUAL EQUIVALENT RATE) – A notional rate quoted on savings and investment products which demonstrates the return on interest, when compounded and paid annually.

APR (ANNUAL PERCENTAGE RATE) – Calculates the total amount of interest payable over the whole term of a product (such as investment or loan), allowing consumers to compare rival products on a like-for-like basis. Companies offering loans, credit cards, mortgages or overdrafts are required by law to provide the APR rate. Where typical APR is shown, it refers to the company's typical borrower and so is given as a best example; rate and costs may vary depending on individual circumstances.

ANNUITY – A type of insurance policy that provides regular income in exchange for a lump sum. The annuity can be bought from a company other than the existing pension provider.

ASU – Accident, sickness and unemployment insurance taken out by a borrower to protect against being unable to work for these reasons. The policy will usually pay a percentage of the normal monthly mortgage repayment if the borrower is unable to work.

ATM (AUTOMATED TELLER MACHINES) – Commonly referred to as cash machines. Users can access their bank accounts using a card for simple transactions such as withdrawing money and viewing an account balance. Some banks and independent ATM deployers charge for transactions.

BANKER'S DRAFT – A cheque drawn on a bank against a cash deposit. Considered to be a secure way of receiving money in instances where a cheque could 'bounce' or where it is not desirable to receive cash.

BASE RATE – The interest rate set by the Bank of England at which it will lend to financial institutions. This acts as a benchmark for all other interest rates.

BASIS POINT – Unit of measure (usually one-hundredth of a percentage point) used to express movements in interest rates, foreign rates or bond yields.

BUY-TO-LET – The purchase of a residential property for the sole purpose of letting to a tenant. Not all lenders provide mortgage finance for this purpose. Buy-to-let lenders assess projected rental income (typical expectations are between 125 and 130 per cent of the monthly interest payment) in addition to, or instead of, the borrower's income. Buy-to-let mortgages are available as either interest only or repayment.

CAPITAL GAIN/LOSS – Increase/decrease in the value of a capital asset when it is sold or transferred compared to its initial worth.

CAPPED RATE MORTGAGE – The interest rate applied to a loan is guaranteed not to rise above a certain rate for a set period of time; the rate can therefore fall but will not rise above the capped rate. The level at which the cap is fixed is usually higher than for a fixed rate mortgage for a comparable period of time. The lender normally imposes early redemption penalties within the first few years.

CASH CARD – Issued by banks and building societies for withdrawing cash from ATMs.

CHARGE CARD – Charge cards, eg American Express and Diners Club, can be used in a similar way to credit cards but the debt must be settled in full each month.

CHIP AND PIN CARD – A credit/debit card which incorporates an embedded chip containing unique owner details. When used with a PIN, such cards offer greater security as they are less prone to fraud. Since 14 February 2006, most card transactions in the UK have required the use of a chip and pin card.

CREDIT CARD – Normally issued with a credit limit, credit cards can be used for purchases until the limit is reached. There is normally an interest-free period on the outstanding balance of up to 56 days. Charges can be avoided if the balance is paid off in full within the interest-free period. Alternatively part of the balance can be paid and in most cases there is a minimum amount set by the issuer (normally a percentage of the outstanding balance) which must be paid on a monthly basis. Some card issuers charge an annual fee and most issuers belong to at least one major credit card network, eg Mastercard or Visa.

CREDIT RATING – Overall credit worthiness of a borrower based on information from a credit reference agency, such as Experian or Equifax, which holds details of credit agreements, payment records, county court judgements etc for all adults in the UK. This information is supplied to lenders who use it in their credit scoring or underwriting systems to calculate the risk of granting a loan to an individual and the probability that it will be repaid. Each lender sets their own criteria for credit worthiness and may accept or reject a credit application based on an individual's credit rating.

CRITICAL ILLNESS COVER – Insurance that covers borrowers against critical illnesses such as stroke, heart attack or cancer and is designed to protect mortgage or other loan payments.

DEBIT CARD – Debit cards were introduced on a large scale in the UK in the mid-1980s, replacing cash and cheques to purchase goods and services. They can be used to withdraw cash from ATMs in the UK and abroad and may also function as a cheque guarantee card. Funds are automatically withdrawn from an individual's bank account after making a purchase and no interest is charged.

DIRECT DEBIT – An instruction from a customer to their bank, which authorises the payee to charge costs to the customer's bank account.

DISCOUNTED MORTGAGE – Discounted mortgages guarantee an interest rate set at a margin below the standard variable rate for a period of time. The discounted rate will move up or down with the standard variable rate, but the payment rate will retain the agreed differential below the standard variable rate. The lender normally imposes early redemption penalties within the first few years.

EARLY REDEMPTION PENALTY – *see* Redemption Penalty

ENDOWMENT MORTGAGE – Only the interest on a property loan is paid back to the lender each month as long as an endowment life insurance policy is taken out for an agreed amount of time, typically 25 years. When the policy matures the lender will take repayment of the money owed on the property loan and any surplus goes to the policyholder. If the endowment policy shows a shortfall on projected returns, the policy holder must make further provision to pay off the mortgage.

EQUITY – When applied to real estate, equity is the difference between the value of a property and the amount outstanding on any loan secured against it. Negative equity occurs when the loan is greater than the market value of the property.

FIXED RATE MORTGAGE – A repayment mortgage where the interest rate on the loan is fixed for a set amount of time, normally a period of between one and ten years. The interest rate does not vary with changes to the base rate resulting in the monthly mortgage payment remaining the same for the duration of the fixed period. The lender normally imposes early redemption penalties within the first few years.

ISA (INDIVIDUAL SAVINGS ACCOUNT) – A means by which investors can save (in a cash ISA) and invest (in a stocks and shares ISA) without paying any tax on the proceeds. There are limits on the amount that can be invested during any given tax year (*see* Taxation).

INTEREST ONLY MORTGAGE – Only interest is paid by the borrower and capital remains constant for the term of the loan. The onus is on the borrower to make provision to repay the capital at the end of the term. This is usually achieved through an investment vehicle such as an endowment policy or pension.

LOAN TO VALUE (LTV) – This is the ratio between the size of a mortgage loan sought and the mortgage lender's valuation. On a loan of £55,000, for example, on a property valued at £100,000, the loan to value is 55 per cent. This means that there is sufficient equity in the property for the lender to be reassured that if interest or capital repayments were stopped, it could sell the property and recoup the money owed. Fewer options are available to borrowers requiring high LTV.

LONDON INTERBANK OFFERED RATE (LIBOR) – Is the interest rate that London banks charge when lending to one another on the wholesale money market. LIBOR is set by supply and demand of money as banks lend to each other in order to balance their books on a daily basis.

MIG (MORTGAGE INDEMNITY GUARANTEE) – An insurance for the lender paid by the borrower on high LTV mortgages (typically more than 90 per cent). It is a policy designed to protect the lender against loss in the event of the borrower defaulting or ceasing to repay a mortgage and is usually paid as a one-off premium or can be added to the value of the loan. It offers no protection to the borrower. Not all lenders charge MIG premiums.

OVERDRAFT – An 'authorised' overdraft is an arrangement made between customer and bank allowing the balance of the customer's account to go below zero; interest is normally charged at an agreed rate and sometimes an arrangement fee is charged. If the negative balance exceeds the agreed terms or a prior arrangement for an overdraft facility has not been made (an 'unauthorised' overdraft) then additional penalty fees may be charged and higher interest rates may apply. Interest-free overdrafts are available for customers in certain circumstances, such as full-time higher education students and recent graduates.

PERSONAL PENSION PLAN (PPP) – Designed for the self-employed or those in non-pensionable employment. Contributions made to a PPP are exempt from tax and the retirement age may be selected at any time, usually from age 55. Up to 25 per cent of the pension fund may be taken as a tax-free cash sum on retirement.

PHISHING – A fraudulent attempt to obtain bank account details and security codes through an email. The email purports to come from a *bona fide* bank or building society and attempts to steer the recipient, usually under the pretext that the banking institution is updating its security arrangements, to a website which requests personal details.

PIN (PERSONAL IDENTIFICATION NUMBER) – A PIN is issued alongside a cash card to allow the user to access a bank account via an ATM. PINs are also issued with smart, credit and debit cards and, since 14 February 2006, have been compulsory as a security measure in the majority of purchases.

PORTABLE MORTGAGE – A mortgage product that can be transferred to a different property in the event of a house move. Preferable where early redemption penalties are charged.

REDEMPTION PENALTY – A charge levied for paying off a loan, debt balance or mortgage before a date agreed with the lender.

REPAYMENT MORTGAGE – In contrast to the interest only mortgage, the monthly repayment includes an element of the capital sum borrowed in addition to the interest charged.

SHARE – A share is a divided-up unit of the value of a company. If a company is worth £100m, and there are 50 million shares in issue, then each share is worth £2 (usually listed as pence). As the overall value of the company fluctuates so does the share price.

STANDING ORDER – An instruction made by the customer to their bank, which allows the transfer of a set amount to a payee at regular intervals.

UNIT TRUST – A 'pooled' fund of assets, usually shares, owned by a number of individuals. Managed by professional, authorised fund-management groups, unit trusts have traditionally delivered better returns than average cash deposits, but do rise and fall in value as their underlying investment varies in value.

VARIABLE RATE MORTGAGE – Repayment mortgages where the interest rate set by the lender increases or decreases in relation to the base interest rate which can result in fluctuating monthly repayments.

WITH-PROFITS – Usually applies to pensions, endowments, savings schemes or bonds. The intention is to smooth out the rises and falls in the stock market for the benefit of the investor. Actuaries working for the insurance company, or fund managers, hold back some profits in good years in order to make up the difference in years when shares perform badly.

FINANCIAL SERVICES REGULATION

Under the Financial Services and Markets Act 2000, as amended by the Financial Services Act (2012), the Financial Conduct Authority and the Prudential Regulation Authority are responsible for financial regulation in the UK.

FINANCIAL CONDUCT AUTHORITY

The Financial Conduct Authority (FCA) is responsible for supervising the conduct of over 56,000 financial services firms and financial markets in the UK and for regulating the prudential standards of those firms – over 18,000 – not regulated by the Prudential Regulation authority. The FCA has three statutory objectives:

- to secure an appropriate degree of protection for consumers
- to protect and enhance the integrity of the UK financial system
- to promote effective market competition in the interests of consumers

The FCA is accountable to HM Treasury and therefore to parliament, but is operationally independent of the government and is funded entirely by the firms which it regulates. The FCA is governed by a board appointed by HM Treasury, but day-to-day decisions and staff management are the responsibility of the executive committee.

The FCA's annual budget for ongoing regulatory activity (ORA) in 2017–18 is £508m, a 1 per cent increase from 2016–17. The 2017–18 annual funding requirement totals £526.9m, an increase of 1.5 per cent due to the increase in the ORA budget and an additional £2.5m allocated for the costs associated with withdrawing from the European Union.

THE FINANCIAL SERVICES REGISTER

The Financial Services Register lists financial services firms and individuals in the UK who are authorised by the FCA to do business and specifies which activity each firm or individual is regulated to undertake and what products or services each is approved to provide.

FINANCIAL CONDUCT AUTHORITY, 25 The North Colonnade, Canary Wharf, London E14 5HS T 020-7066 1000
W www.fca.org.uk
Chair, John Griffith-Jones
Chief Executive, Andrew Bailey

PRUDENTIAL REGULATION AUTHORITY

The Prudential Regulation Authority (PRA), part of the Bank of England, works alongside the FCA and is responsible for the prudential regulation and supervision of around 1,500 banks, building societies, credit unions, insurers and major investment firms. The PRA has three statutory objectives:

- to promote the safety and soundness of the firms it regulates
- to contribute to securing an appropriate degree of protection for those who are, or may become, insurance policyholders
- to facilitate effective competition

The PRA's committee is chaired by the Governor of the Bank of England. Five members are Bank of England staff including the Governor and four Deputy Governors. The committee has a majority of external members, including the chief executive of the FCA and six others selected for their experience and expertise in financial services.

The PRA's budget for 2017–18 is £288m. The budget includes two amendments approved after the start of the financial year: the first in relation to the emerging EU withdrawal implementation costs (£3m); and the second to accommodate the impact of market conditions on pension costs and further costs in relation to EU withdrawal (£10m).

PRUDENTIAL REGULATION AUTHORITY, 20 Moorgate, London EC2R 6DA T 020-7601 4444
E enquiries@bankofengland.co.uk
W www.bankofengland.co.uk/pra
Chief Executive, Sam Woods

COMPENSATION

Created under the Financial Services and Markets Act (2000), the Financial Services Compensation Scheme (FSCS) is the UK's statutory fund of last resort for customers of authorised financial services firms. It provides compensation if a firm authorised by the FCA or PRA is unable, or likely to be unable, to pay claims against it. In general this is when a firm has stopped trading and has insufficient assets to meet claims, or is in insolvency. The FSCS covers deposits, insurance policies, insurance broking, investment business and mortgage advice and arranging. The FSCS is independent of the UK regulators (FCA and PRA), with separate staff and premises. However, the FCA and PRA appoint the directors. The chair's appointment (and removal) is subject to Treasury approval. The FSCS is funded by annual levies on authorised firms.

The Pension Protection Fund (PPF) is a statutory fund established under the Pensions Act 2004 and became operational on 6 April 2005. The fund was set up to pay compensation to members of eligible defined benefit pension schemes, where there is a qualifying insolvency event in relation to the employer and where there are insufficient assets in the pension scheme to cover PPF levels of compensation. Compulsory annual levies are charged on all eligible schemes to help fund the PPF, in addition to investment of PPF assets. The PPF is also responsible for the Fraud Compensation Fund – a fund that will provide compensation to occupational pension schemes that suffer a loss attributable to dishonesty.

FINANCIAL SERVICES COMPENSATION SCHEME, PO Box 300, Mitcheldean GL17 1DY T 020-7741 4100/0800-678 1100
W www.fscs.org.uk
Chair, Lawrence Churchill, CBE
Chief Executive, Mark Neale

PENSION PROTECTION FUND, Renaissance, 12 Dingwall Road, Croydon CR0 2NA T 0345-600 2541
E information@ppf.gsi.gov.uk
W www.pensionprotectionfund.org.uk
Chair, Arnold Wagner, OBE
Chief Executive, Alan Rubenstein

DESIGNATED PROFESSIONAL BODIES

Professional firms are exempt from requiring direct regulation by the FCA if they carry out only certain restricted activities that arise out of, or are complementary to, the provision of professional services, such as arranging the sale of shares on the instructions of executors or trustees, or providing services to small, private companies. These firms are, however, supervised by designated professional bodies (DPBs). There are a number of safeguards to protect consumers dealing with firms that do not require direct regulation. These arrangements include:

- the FCA's power to ban a specific firm from taking advantage of the exemption and to restrict the regulated activities permitted to the firms
- rules which require professional firms to ensure that their clients are aware that they are not authorised persons
- a requirement for the DPBs to supervise and regulate the firms and inform the FCA on how the professional firms carry on their regulated activities

See Professional Education section for contact details of the following DPBs:

Association of Chartered Certified Accountants
Council for Licensed Conveyancers
Institute of Actuaries
Institute of Chartered Accountants in England and Wales
Institute of Chartered Accountants in Ireland
Institute of Chartered Accountants of Scotland
Law Society of England and Wales
Law Society of Northern Ireland
Law Society of Scotland
Royal Institution of Chartered Surveyors

RECOGNISED INVESTMENT EXCHANGES

The FCA currently supervises seven recognised investment exchanges (RIEs) in the UK; recognition confers an exemption from the need to be authorised to carry out regulated activities in the UK. The RIEs are organised markets on which member firms can trade investments such as equities and derivatives. The RIEs are listed with their year of recognition in parentheses:

BATS TRADING (2013), 6th Floor, 10 Lower Thames Street, London EC3R 6AF T 020-7012 8900
W www.bats.com

CME EUROPE (2014)*, 1 New Change, London EC4M 9AF
T 020-3379 3700 W www.cmegroup.com/europe

EURONEXT LONDON (2014), 10th Floor, 110 Cannon Street, London EC4N 6EU T 020-7076 0900
W www.euronext.com/en

ICE FUTURES EUROPE (2001), 5th Floor Milton Gate, 60 Chiswell Street, London EC1Y 4SA T 020-7065 7700
W www.theice.com

LONDON METAL EXCHANGE (2001), 10 Finsbury Square, London EC2A 1AJ T 020-7113 8888 W www.lme.com

LONDON STOCK EXCHANGE (2001), 10 Paternoster Square, London EC4M 7LS T 020-7797 1000
W www.londonstockexchange.com

NEX EXCHANGE (2007), 2 Broadgate, London EC2M 7UR
T 020-7818 9774 W www.nexexchange.com

RECOGNISED CLEARING HOUSES

The Bank of England is responsible for recognising and supervising recognised clearing houses (RCHs), which organise the settlement of transactions on recognised investment exchanges. There are currently five UK RCHs:

CME CLEARING EUROPE (2010)*, 1 New Change, London EC4M 9AF T 020-3379 3100
W www.cmegroup.com/europe/clearing-europe

EUROCLEAR UK AND IRELAND (2001), 33 Cannon Street, London EC4M 5SB T 020-7849 0000 W www.euroclear.com

ICE CLEAR EUROPE (2008), 5th Floor, Milton Gate, 60 Chiswell Street, London EC1Y 4SA T 020-7065 7600
W www.theice.com/clear_europe

LCH (LONDON CLEARING HOUSE) CLEARNET (2001), Aldgate House, 33 Aldgate High Street, London EC3N 1EA T 020-7426 7000 W www.lch.com

LME (LONDON METAL EXCHANGE) CLEAR (2014), 10 Finsbury Square, London EC2A 1AJ T 020-7113 8888
W www.lme.com/LME-Clear

* CME Group announced on 12 April 2017 that it intends to close CME Europe and CME Clearing Europe by the end of 2017

OMBUDSMAN SCHEMES

The Financial Ombudsman Service was set up by the Financial Services and Markets Act 2000 to provide consumers with a free, independent service for resolving disputes with authorised financial firms. The Financial Ombudsman Service can consider complaints about most financial matters including: banking; credit cards and store cards; financial advice; hire purchase and pawnbroking; insurance; loans and credit; money transfer; mortgages; payday lending and debt collecting; payment protection insurance; pensions; savings and investments; stocks, shares, unit trusts and bonds.

Complainants must first complain to the firm involved. They do not have to accept the ombudsman's decision and are free to go to court if they wish, but if a decision is accepted, it is binding for both the complainant and the firm.

The Pensions Ombudsman can investigate and decide complaints and disputes regarding the way occupational and personal pension schemes are administered and managed. Unless there are special circumstances, this only usually includes issues and disputes that have arisen within the past three years. The Pensions Ombudsman is also the Ombudsman for the Pension Protection Fund (PPF) and the Financial Assistance Scheme (which offers help to those who were a member of an under-funded defined benefit pension scheme that started to wind-up in specific financial circumstances between 1 January 1997 and 5 April 2005).

FINANCIAL OMBUDSMAN SERVICE, Exchange Tower, London E14 9SR Helpline 0800-023 4567 T 020-7964 1000
E complaint.info@financial-ombudsman.org.uk
W www.financial-ombudsman.org.uk
Chief Ombudsman, Caroline Wayman

PENSIONS OMBUDSMAN, 11 Belgrave Road, London SW1V 1RB T 020-7630 2200 E enquiries@pensions-ombudsman.org.uk
W www.pensions-ombudsman.org.uk
Pensions Ombudsman, Anthony Arter
   Deputy Pensions Ombudsman, Karen Johnston

THE TAKEOVER PANEL

The Panel on Takeovers and Mergers is an independent body, established in 1968, whose main functions are to issue and administer the City code and to ensure equality of treatment and opportunity for all shareholders in takeover bids and mergers. The panel's statutory functions are set out in the Companies Act 2006.

The panel comprises up to 36 members representing a spread of expertise in takeovers, securities markets, industry and commerce. The chair, deputy chair and up to 20 other members are nominated by the panel's own nomination committee. The remaining members are nominated by professional bodies representing the financial advice, insurance, investment, pension and accountancy industries; the Association for Financial Markets in Europe; the Confederation of British Industry; the Quoted Companies Alliance; and UK Finance.

THE TAKEOVER PANEL, 10 Paternoster Square, London EC4M 7DY T 020-7382 9026
E info@thetakeoverpanel.org.uk
W www.thetakeoverpanel.org.uk
Chair, Michael Crane, QC

NATIONAL SAVINGS AND INVESTMENTS

NS&I (National Savings and Investments) is both a non-ministerial government department and an executive agency of the Chancellor of the Exchequer. It is one of the UK's largest savings organisations, with 25 million customers and over £147bn invested. When people invest in NS&I they are lending money to the government which pays them interest or prizes in return. All deposits are 100 per cent financially secure because they are guaranteed by HM Treasury.

TAX-FREE PRODUCTS

PREMIUM BONDS
Introduced in 1956, premium bonds enable savers to enter a regular draw for tax-free prizes, while retaining the right to get their money back. A sum equivalent to interest on each bond is put into a prize fund and distributed by monthly prize draws. The prizes are drawn by ERNIE (electronic random number indicator equipment) and are free of all UK income tax and capital gains tax. Two £1m jackpots are drawn each month in addition to other tax-free prizes ranging in value from £25 to £100,000.

Bonds are in units of £1, with a minimum purchase of £100 (£50 by standing order or electronic transfer), up to a maximum holding limit of £50,000 per person. Bonds become eligible for prizes once they have been held for one clear calendar month following the month of purchase. Each £1 unit can win only one prize per draw, but it will be awarded the highest for which it is drawn. Bonds remain eligible for prizes until they are repaid.

The scheme offers a facility to reinvest prize wins automatically. Upon completion of an automatic prize reinvestment mandate, holders receive new bonds which are immediately eligible for future prize draws. Bonds can only be held in the name of an individual and not by organisations.

CHILDREN'S BONDS
Children's bonus bonds were introduced in 1991. In September 2012 changes were made to the product; including a change in name to Children's Bonds, which reflects the way interest is paid. Any amount between £25 and £3,000 (per child per issue) can be invested. Interest is calculated on a daily basis at the rate fixed on investment and is added on the anniversary of the investment. Children's bonds are designed to be held for five years at a time. They can be bought by parents, guardians and grandparents (including great grandparents) for any child under 16, but the investment must be managed by a parent or guardian. All returns are totally exempt from UK income tax.

INDIVIDUAL SAVINGS ACCOUNTS
Since April 1999 NS&I has offered cash individual savings accounts (ISAs). Its Direct ISA, launched in April 2006, can be opened and managed online and by telephone with a minimum investment of £1 and a maximum investment of £20,000 in the 2017–18 tax year. Interest for the Direct ISA is calculated daily and is free of tax.

OTHER PRODUCTS

SAVINGS AND INVESTMENT ACCOUNTS
The direct saver account was launched in March 2010. Customers are able to invest between £1 and £2m per person. The account can be managed online or by telephone. Interest is paid without deduction of tax at source.

The investment account is a postal-only account which pays tiered rates of interest. It can be opened with a minimum balance of £20 and has a maximum limit of £1m. The interest is paid without deduction of tax at source.

INCOME BONDS
NS&I income bonds were introduced in 1982. They are suitable for those who want to receive regular monthly payments of interest while preserving the full cash value of their capital. The minimum holding for each investment is £500 and the maximum £1m per person. A variable rate of interest is calculated on a day-to-day basis and paid monthly. Interest is taxable but is paid without deduction of tax at source.

INVESTMENT GUARANTEED GROWTH BONDS
Investment guaranteed growth bonds, announced by the chancellor in the 2016 Autumn Statement, offer a lump sum investment that earns a fixed rate of interest over three years. The minimum holding is £100 to a maximum of £3,000 per person (£6,000 jointly). Interest is calculated daily and added to the bond on each anniversary of the investment. Interest is taxable but is paid without deduction of tax at source.

FURTHER INFORMATION
Further information regarding products and their current availability can be obtained online (W www.nsandi.com) and by telephone (T 080-8500 7007).

THE NATIONAL DEBT

HISTORY

The early 1700s saw the meteoric rise of the banking and financial markets in Great Britain, with the emerging stock market revolving around government funds. The ability to raise money by means of creating debt through the issue of bills and bonds heralded the beginning of the national debt.

The war years of 1914–18 saw an increase in the national debt from £650m at the start of the war to £7,500m by 1919. The Treasury developed new expertise in foreign exchange, currency, credit and price control in order to manage the post-war economy. The slump of the 1930s necessitated the restructuring of the UK economy following the Second World War (the national debt stood at £21bn by its end) and the emphasis was placed on economic planning and financial relations.

The relatively high period of inflation in the 1970s and 1980s led to the rise of the national debt in nominal terms from £36bn in 1972 to £197bn in 1987 and then to £419bn in March 1998. Although in nominal terms the national debt has risen sharply in recent years, as a percentage of GDP it has decreased dramatically since the end of the Second World War, when it stood at 250 per cent of GDP (for current figures, *see* table below).

THE UK DEBT MANAGEMENT OFFICE

The decision in 1997 to transfer monetary policy to the Bank of England, while the Treasury retained control of fiscal policy, led to the creation of the UK Debt Management Office (DMO) as an executive agency of HM Treasury in April 1998. Initially the DMO was responsible only for the management of government marketable debt and for issuing gilts. In April 2000 responsibility for exchequer cash management and for issuing Treasury bills (short-dated securities with maturities of less than one year) was transferred from the Bank of England to the DMO. The national debt also includes the (non-marketable) liabilities of National Savings and Investments and other public sector and foreign currency debt.

In 2002 the operations of the long-standing statutory functions of the Public Works Loan Board, which lends capital to local authorities, and the Commissioners for the Reduction of the National Debt, which manages the investment portfolios of certain public funds, were integrated within the DMO (*see also* Government Departments).

UK PUBLIC SECTOR NET DEBT

	£ billion	per cent of GDP
2015–16 (outturn)	1,606	83.6
2016–17 (forecast)	1,730	86.6
2017–18 (forecast)	1,830	88.8

Source: HM Treasury – *Spring Budget 2017* (Crown copyright)

THE LONDON STOCK EXCHANGE

The London Stock Exchange Group (LSEG) serves the needs of companies by providing facilities for raising capital. It also operates marketplaces for members to trade financial instruments. including equities, bonds and derivatives, on behalf of investors and institutions such as pension funds and insurers.

LSEG's key subsidiary companies are the London Stock Exchange, Borsa Italiana, MTS (an electronic platform for the trading of European government and corporate bonds), Turquoise (a trading platform for European equities) and FTSE (a global index provider).

Headquartered in London, with significant operations in Italy, France, North America and Sri Lanka, the group employs around 4,700 people.

HISTORY

The London Stock Exchange is one of the world's oldest stock exchanges, dating back more than 300 years to its origins in the coffee houses of 17th-century London. It was formally established as a membership organisation in 1801.

MAJOR DEVELOPMENTS

'BIG BANG'

In 1986 a package of reforms which are now known as 'Big Bang' transformed the London Stock Exchange and the City of London, liberalising the way in which banks and stock-broking firms operated and facilitating greater foreign investment. The London Stock Exchange ceased granting voting rights to individual members and became a private company. The 'Big Bang' also saw the start of a move towards fully electronic trading and the closure of the trading floor.

INTRODUCTION OF SETS

In October 1997, the Exchange introduced SETS, its electronic order book. The system enhanced the efficiency and transparency of trading on the Exchange, allowing trades to be executed automatically and anonymously rather than negotiated by telephone.

DEMUTUALISATION AND LISTING

The London Stock Exchange demutualised in 2000 and listed on its own main market in 2001.

MERGER WITH BORSA ITALIANA

In October 2007 the London Stock Exchange merged with the Italian stock exchange, Borsa Italiana, creating London Stock Exchange Group (LSEG).

DIVERSIFICATION

Since 2009 LSEG has diversified its business beyond the listing and trading of UK and Italian equities:
• In 2009 LSEG purchased Sri Lankan technology company

MillenniumIT which provides technology to stock exchanges, brokerages and regulators around the world. It also supplies the trading technology to LSEG's own markets
• In 2010 LSEG acquired a majority stake in Turquoise, a platform facilitating the trading of stocks listed in 19 European countries and the USA
• In 2011 LSEG became the owner of FTSE, the international business which creates and manages financial indices
• In 2013 LSEG purchased a majority stake in LCH (London Clearing House) Clearnet (*see also* Financial Services Regulation, Recognised Clearing Houses)

UK EQUITY MARKETS

LSEG offers a range of listing options for companies, according to their size, history and requirements:
• The Main Market has the highest standards of regulation and disclosure obligations and is overseen by the UK Listing Authority (UKLA), a division of the Financial Conduct Authority (FCA). A Main Market listing enables established companies to raise capital, widen their investor base and have their shares traded alongside global peers. They are also eligible for inclusion in key indices, such as the FTSE 100 and the FTSE 250
• The Alternative Investment Market (AIM), established in June 1995, is specially designed to meet the needs of small and growing companies. It enables them to raise capital and broaden their investor base in a more flexible regulatory environment, while still being traded on an internationally recognised market. AIM companies retain an experienced Nominated Adviser (or 'Nomad') firm, which is responsible for ensuring the company's suitability for the market
• The Professional Securities Market (PSM), established in July 2005, allows companies to target professional investors only, on a market that offers greater flexibility in accounting standards
• The Specialist Fund Market (SFM), established in November 2007, is a market for highly specialised investment entities, such as hedge funds or private equity funds, that wish to target institutional investors only
As at 31 July 2017 there were 5,501 companies listed on LSEG's primary markets, with a combined market value of £1,923,802m: 1,710 on the Main Market (1,324 on the UK main market and 368 on the international main market), 3,741 on the AIM, 15 on the PSM and 35 entities on the SFM.

LONDON STOCK EXCHANGE, 10 Paternoster Square, London EC4M 7LS T 020-7797 1000
W www.lseg.com
Chair, Donald Brydon, CBE
Chief Executive, Xavier Rolet, KBE

ECONOMIC STATISTICS

THE SPRING BUDGET 2017

GOVERNMENT EXPENDITURE

DEPARTMENTAL EXPENDITURE LIMITS (£bn)

	Plans 2017–18
Resource DEL	
Education	61.4
Health (incl. NHS)	117.6
Transport	2.1
Exiting the EU	0.1
Business, Energy and Industrial Strategy	2.0
DCLG Communities	3.1
DCLG Local Government	6.5
Home Office	10.8
Justice	6.6
Law Officers' Departments	0.5
Defence	27.5
Single Intelligence Account	1.8
Foreign and Commonwealth Office	1.2
International Development	8.0
International Trade	0.3
Environment, Food and Rural Affairs	1.6
HM Revenue and Customs	3.5
HM Treasury	0.1
Digital, Culture, Media and Sport	1.4
Work and Pensions	6.3
Scotland	14.2
Wales	13.4
Northern Ireland	10.0
Cabinet Office	0.3
Small and Independent bodies	1.4
Reserves	5.1
Adjustment for budget exchange	(0.4)
TOTAL RESOURCE DEL	306.1
*OBR Allowance for shortfall	(0.8)
OBR Resource DEL	305.4
Capital DEL	
Education	5.3
Health (incl. NHS)	6.1
Transport	6.4
Exiting the EU	0.0
Business, Energy and Industrial Strategy	10.8
DCLG Communities	6.2
DCLG Local Government	0.0
Home Office	0.6
Justice	0.7
Law Officers' Departments	0.0
Defence	8.5
Single Intelligence Account	0.6
Foreign and Commonwealth Office	0.1
International Development	3.6
International Trade	0.0
Environment, Food and Rural Affairs	0.7
HM Revenue and Customs	0.2
HM Treasury	0.2
Digital, Culture, Media and Sport	0.5
Work and Pensions	0.4
Scotland	3.4
Wales	1.6
Northern Ireland	1.2
Cabinet Office	0.0
Small and Independent bodies	0.1
Reserves	1.2
Adjustment for budget exchange	(0.5)
TOTAL CAPITAL DEL	58.0
*OBR Allowance for shortfall	(1.5)
OBR Capital DEL	56.5
TOTAL DEL	361.9

* OBR = Office for Budget Responsibility

Source: HM Treasury – Spring Budget 2017 (Crown copyright)

TOTAL MANAGED EXPENDITURE (£bn)

	2016–17	Plans 2017–18	Plans 2018–19
Current Expenditure			
Resource Annually Managed Expenditure (AME)	363.6	392.2	400.7
Resource DEL	305.3	305.4	307.4
Ring-fenced depreciation	26.2	21.9	22.8
Public Sector Current Expenditure	695.1	719.5	730.9
Capital Expenditure			
Capital AME	24.7	26.4	27.7
Capital DEL	53.0	56.5	58.6
Public Sector Gross Investment	77.7	82.9	86.3
TOTAL MANAGED EXPENDITURE	772.8	802.4	817.2
Total Managed Expenditure (% GDP)	39.3	39.6	39.0

Source: HM Treasury – Budget Spring 2017 (Crown copyright)

GOVERNMENT RECEIPTS (£bn)

	Outturn 2015–16	Forecast 2016–17	Forecast 2017–18
Income tax (gross of tax credits)[1]	168.9	174.7	174.9
Pay as you earn	146.2	148.5	153.3
Self assessment	24.3	28.7	24.8
National insurance contributions (NICs)	114.1	125.0	130.3
Value added tax	116.4	120.7	125.4
Corporation tax	45.6	53.6	54.1
Petroleum revenue tax	(0.6)	(0.6)	(0.5)
Fuel duties	27.6	27.9	27.5
Business rates	28.8	28.8	29.6
Council tax	29.0	30.4	32.1
VAT refunds	14.1	13.8	13.8
Capital gains tax	7.1	8.7	9.1
Inheritance tax	4.7	4.7	5.0
Stamp duty land tax	10.9	11.6	13.1
Stamp taxes on shares	3.3	3.6	3.4
Tobacco duties	9.1	8.7	8.9
Spirits duties	3.1	3.3	3.6
Wine duties	4.0	4.1	4.4
Beer and cider duties	3.6	3.6	3.8
Air passenger duty	3.0	3.2	3.4
Insurance premium tax	3.7	5.0	5.7
Climate change levy	1.8	1.9	1.8
Other HMRC taxes[2]	7.1	7.4	7.3
Vehicle excise duties	5.7	5.8	6.0
Bank levy	3.2	3.0	2.9
Bank surcharge	0.4	1.5	1.4
Apprenticeship levy	0.0	0.0	2.6
Licence fee receipts	3.1	3.2	3.2
Enviromental levies	4.6	6.9	8.7
EU ETS* Auction receipts	0.5	0.5	0.4
Scottish taxes	0.6	0.6	0.7
Diverted profits tax	0.0	0.1	0.1
Other taxes	6.7	7.2	7.5
Total National Accounts Taxes	630.0	668.6	690.3

Less own resources			
contribution to EU	(3.1)	(3.3)	(3.5)
Interest and dividends	6.2	5.6	6.1
Gross operating surplus	46.4	47.9	49.3
Other receipts	2.7	2.2	2.0
CURRENT RECEIPTS	682.3	721.1	744.2
UK oil and gas revenues[3]	(0.2)	0.1	0.9

* ETS = Emissions Trading System
[1] Income tax includes PAYE and Self Assessment receipts, tax on savings income and other minor income tax components
[2] Consists of landfill tax (excluding Scotland), aggregates levy, betting and gaming duties and customs duties
[3] Consists of offshore corporation tax and petroleum revenue tax
Source: HM Treasury – *Spring Budget 2017* (Crown copyright)

TRADE

TRADE IN GOODS
£ million

	Exports	Imports	Balance
2010	270,196	367,580	(97,384)
2011	308,171	403,126	(94,955)
2012	301,621	412,528	(110,907)
2013	303,147	423,811	(120,664)
2014	292,894	415,469	(122,575)
2015	287,584	407,304	(119,720)
2016	301,405	435,472	(134,067)

Source: ONS (Crown copyright)

BALANCE OF PAYMENTS, 2016

Current Account	*£ million*
Trade in goods and services	
Trade in goods	(134,067)
Trade in services	97,041
Total trade in goods and services	(37,026)
Income	
Compensation of employees	(271)
Investment income	(21,710)
Other	(1,148)
Total income	(23,129)
Total secondary income	(24,349)
TOTAL (CURRENT BALANCE)	(84,504)

Source: ONS (Crown copyright)

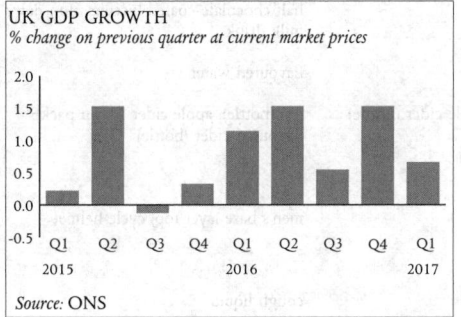

UK GDP GROWTH
% change on previous quarter at current market prices

Q1 Q2 Q3 Q4 (2015) Q1 Q2 Q3 Q4 (2016) Q1 (2017)

Source: ONS

UK EMPLOYMENT

DISTRIBUTION OF THE WORKFORCE

	Mar 2016	Mar 2017
Workforce jobs	34,368,000	34,831,000
HM forces	158,000	157,000
Self-employment jobs	4,431,000	4,508,000
Employees jobs	29,711,000	30,105,000
Government-supported trainees	67,000	61,000

Source: ONS – *Labour Market Statistics 2017* (Crown copyright)

EMPLOYED AND UNEMPLOYED
thousands, all aged 16+

	Apr–Jun 2016		Apr–Jun 2017	
	Number	Rate (%)	Number	Rate (%)
Employed	31,750	74.5	32,073	75.1
Unemployed	1,641	4.9	1,484	4.4

Source: ONS – *Labour Market Statistics 2017* (Crown copyright)

DURATION OF UNEMPLOYMENT, APR–JUN 2017

All unemployed	1,484,000
Less than 6 months	876,000
6 months–1 year	234,000
1 year +	374,000
2 years +	197.000

Source: ONS – *Labour Market Statistics 2017* (Crown copyright)

MEDIAN EARNINGS, 2016
full-time, £

	All	Male	Female
Gross annual earnings	28,213	30,567	24,833
Weekly earnings*	519.80	552.40	476.00
Hourly earnings*	13.59	14.16	12.82

* Excluding overtime
Source: ONS (Crown copyright)

LABOUR STOPPAGES BY DURATION, 2016

Under 5 days	65
5–10 days	23
11–20 days	5
21–30 days	2
31–50	4
50+	2
All stoppages	101

Source: ONS (Crown copyright)

LABOUR DISPUTES BY INDUSTRY, 2016

Industry Group	Working Days Lost
Mining, quarrying, electricity, gas	3,100
Manufacturing	5,700
Sewage, waste management, water supply	1,700
Construction	1,300
Motor vehicle repair, accommodation, food services	2,300
Transport & storage	49,100
Information & Communication	1,900
Financial, professional, scientific, administration	4,700
Public administration & defence	10,800
Education	105,400
Human health and social work	131,500
Other	4,800
All industries & services	322,300

Source: ONS (Crown copyright)

TRADE UNIONS

Year	No. of unions	Total membership
2012–13	166	7,197,415
2013–14	166	7,086,116
2014–15	160	7,010,527
2015–16	160	6,948,725
2016–17	151	6,865,056

Source: Annual Report of the Certification Officer 2016–17

COST OF LIVING AND INFLATION RATES

The first cost of living index to be calculated took July 1914 as 100 and was based on the pattern of expenditure of working-class families in 1914. The cost of living index was superseded in 1947 by the general index of retail prices (RPI), although the older term is still popularly applied.

The Harmonised Index of Consumer Prices (HICP) was introduced in 1997 to enable comparisons within the European Union using an agreed methodology. In 2003 the National Statistician renamed the HICP the Consumer Prices Index (CPI) to reflect its role as the main target measure of inflation for macroeconomic purposes. In March 2013 CPIH, an additional index which includes owner-occupiers' housing costs, was introduced.

The RPI and indices based on it continue to be published alongside the CPI. Private-sector pensions and index-linked gilts continue to be calculated with reference to RPI or its derivatives.

CPI AND RPI

The CPI and RPI measure the changes month by month in the average level of prices of goods and services purchased by households in the UK. The indices are compiled using a selection of around 700 goods and services, and the prices charged for these items are collected at regular intervals at about 140 locations throughout the country, from the internet and via phone. The Office for National Statistics (ONS) reviews the components of the indices once a year to reflect changes in consumer preferences and the establishment of new products. The table below shows changes made by the ONS to the CPI 'shopping basket' in 2017.

The CPI excludes a number of items that are included in the RPI, mainly related to housing, such as council tax, and a range of owner-occupier housing costs, such as mortgage payments. The CPI covers all private households, whereas the RPI excludes the top 4 per cent by income and pensioner households which derive at least three-quarters of their income from state benefits. The two indices use different methodologies to combine the prices of goods and services, which means that since 1996 the CPI inflation measure is less than the RPI inflation measure.

INFLATION RATE

The 12-monthly percentage change in the 'all items' index of the RPI or CPI is referred to as the rate of inflation. As the most familiar measure of inflation, the RPI is often referred to as the 'headline rate of inflation'. The CPI is the main measure of inflation for macroeconomic purposes and forms the basis of the government's inflation target, which is currently 2 per cent. The percentage change in prices between any two months/years can be obtained using this formula:

$$\frac{\text{Later date RPI/CPI} - \text{Earlier date RPI/CPI}}{\text{Earlier date RPI/CPI}} \times 100$$

For example, to find the CPI rate of inflation for 2006, using the annual averages for 2005 and 2006:

$$\frac{102.3 - 100.0}{100.0} \times 100 = 2.3$$

CHANGES TO THE 'SHOPPING BASKET' OF GOODS AND SERVICES IN 2017

The table below shows changes to the CPI* basket of goods and services made by the ONS in 2017 in order to reflect changes in consumer preferences and the establishment of new products.

Goods and services group	Removed items	New items
Food	–	half chocolate-coated biscuits; non-dairy milk drink
Non-alcoholic beverages	–	flavoured water
Alcoholic beverages (off sales)	spirit based drink; apple cider (bottle)	gin (bottle); apple cider (4 can pack); flavoured cider (bottle)
Tobacco	mentholated cigarettes	–
Clothing	–	men's base layer top; cycle helmet
Furniture, furnishings & carpet	single drainer sink	–
Medical products, appliances & equipment	–	cough liquid
Operation of personal transport equipment	brake pads	–
Telephone & telefax equipment & services	mobile phone handset	–
Recreational items, gardens & pets	child's swing	child's scooter; jigsaw
Catering services	apple cider	cider
Financial services	fee for stopping a cheque	–

* RPI goods and services are grouped together under different classifications

From 14 February 2006 the reference year for the CPI was re-based to 2005=100 to improve price comparison clarity across the EU. None of the underlying data, from which the re-referenced series was calculated, was revised. Historical rates of change (such as annual inflation figures), calculated from the re-based rounded index levels, were revised due to the effect of rounding. The CPI rate of inflation figure given in the table below may differ by plus or minus 0.1 percentage points from the figure calculated by the above equation. The change of reference period and revision due to rounding does not apply to the RPI, which remains unchanged.
The RPI and CPI figures are published on either the second or third Tuesday of each month in an indices bulletin on the ONS website (**W** www.ons.gov.uk).

PURCHASING POWER OF THE POUND

Changes in the internal purchasing power of the pound may be defined as the 'inverse' of changes in the level of prices: when prices go up, the amount which can be purchased with a given sum of money goes down. To find the purchasing power of the pound in one month or year, given that it was 100p in a previous month or year, the calculation would be:

$$100p \times \frac{\text{Earlier month/year RPI}}{\text{Later month/year RPI}}$$

Thus, if the purchasing power of the pound is taken to be 100p in 1975, the comparable purchasing power in 2000 would be:

$$100p \times \frac{34.2}{170.3} = 20.1p$$

For longer term comparisons, it has been the practice to use an index which has been constructed by linking together the RPI for the period 1962 to date; an index derived from the consumers' expenditure deflator for the period from 1938 to 1962; and the pre-war 'cost of living' index for the period 1914 to 1938. This long-term index enables the internal purchasing power of the pound to be calculated for any year from 1914 onwards. It should be noted that these figures can only be approximate.

	Annual average RPI (1987 = 100)	*Purchasing power of £ (1998 = 1.00)*	*Annual average CPI (2015 = 100)**	*Annual average CPIH† (2015=100)**	*Rate of inflation (RPI/CPI/CPIH)†*
1914	2.8	58.18			
1915	3.5	46.54			
1920	7.0	23.27			
1925	5.0	32.58			
1930	4.5	36.20			
1935	4.0	40.72			
1938	4.4	37.02			
There are no official figures for 1939–45					
1946	7.4	22.01			
1950	9.0	18.10			
1955	11.2	14.54			
1960	12.6	12.93			
1965	14.8	11.00			
1970	18.5	8.80			
1975	34.2	4.76			
1980	66.8	2.44			
1985	94.6	1.72			
1990	126.1	1.29			9.5/7.0
1995	149.1	1.09			3.5/2.6
1998	162.9	1.00	71.2		3.4/1.6
2000	170.3	0.96	72.7		3.0/0.8
2005	192.0	0.85	78.1	79.4	2.8/2.1
2006	198.1	0.82	79.9	81.3	3.2/2.3/2.4
2007	206.6	0.79	81.8	83.2	4.3/2.3/2.4
2008	214.8	0.76	84.7	86.1	4.0/3.6/3.5
2009	213.7	0.76	86.6	87.8	–0.5/2.2/1.9
2010	223.6	0.73	89.4	90.0	4.6/3.3/2.5
2011	235.2	0.69	93.4	93.5	5.2/4.5/3.9
2012	242.7	0.67	96.1	96.0	3.2/2.8/2.6
2013	250.1	0.65	98.5	98.2	3.0/2.6/2.3
2014	256.0	0.64	100.0	99.6	2.4/1.5/1.5
2015	258.5	0.63	100.0	100.0	1.0/0.0/0.4
2016	263.1	0.62	100.7	100.1	1.8/0.7/1.0

* All CPI indices were re-based to 2015=100 on 16 February 2016, replacing the 2005=100 series
† Due to changes in methodology figures for the CPIH index were revised back to 2005 in February 2015

INSURANCE

AUTHORISATION AND REGULATION OF INSURANCE COMPANIES

Since April 2013, under the Financial Services Act 2012, the prudential supervision of banks and insurers is the responsibility of the Prudential Regulation Authority (PRA), an operationally independent subsidiary of the Bank of England. The Financial Conduct Authority (FCA) is responsible for consumer protection and markets oversight. All life insurers, general insurers, reinsurers, insurance and reinsurance brokers, financial advisers and composite firms are statutorily regulated. *See also* Financial Services Regulation.

Firms wishing to effect or carry out contracts of insurance must be granted authorisation to do so. The PRA assesses applicant insurers from a prudential perspective, using the same framework that is employed for supervision of existing insurers. The FCA then assesses applicants from a conduct perspective. Although the PRA manages the authorisation process, an insurer will be granted authorisation only where both the FCA and the PRA are satisfied that they meet their relevant requirements.

There are around 700 insurance organisations and friendly societies with authorisation to transact one or more classes of insurance business in the UK. However, the single European insurance market, established in 1994, gave insurers authorised in any other European Union country automatic UK authorisation without further formality. The number of insurers operating within the single European market has been decreasing since 2010 and currently stands at around 3,700.

COMPLAINTS

Disputes between consumers and financial businesses can be referred to the Financial Ombudsman Service (FOS). Consumers with a complaint about any form of money matter, including bank accounts, insurance, mortgages, savings and credit, must first take the matter to the highest level within the provider. If it remains unresolved consumers can refer the complaint, free of charge, to the FOS. The FOS can tell a financial business to compensate up to a maximum limit of £150,000, excluding any interest and costs (£100,000 for complaints received before 1 January 2012). If the FOS decides that fair compensation exceeds £150,000 the provider is only bound to accept the FOS decision up to the limit. Businesses falling under the EU definition of a micro enterprise (businesses with a turnover of up to €2m (£1.7m) and fewer than ten employees) may also refer a matter to the FOS. In 2015–16, 63 per cent of new complaints about financial services companies related to payment protection insurance. Other types of insurance, such as motor, buildings and life insurance, accounted for just 9 per cent of the total number of complaints received. *See also* Financial Services Regulation.

ASSOCIATION OF BRITISH INSURERS

Over 90 per cent of the domestic business of UK insurance companies is transacted by the 250 members of the Association of British Insurers (ABI). The ABI is a trade association which protects and promotes the interests of all its insurance company members. Only insurers authorised in the EU are eligible for membership. Brokers, intermediaries, financial advisers and claims handlers may not join the ABI but may have their own trade associations. Since November 2015 legal firms, consultants, price comparison websites and other firms which help insurers deliver their services can join the ABI as associate members.

ASSOCIATION OF BRITISH INSURERS (ABI), One America Square, 17 Crosswall, London EC3N 2LB
T 020-7600 3333 W www.abi.org.uk
Chair, Andy Briggs (Chief Executive AVIVA UK)
Director-General, Huw Evans

BALANCE OF PAYMENTS

The financial services industry contributes 9.9 per cent to the UK's gross domestic product (GDP). In 2015 the UK trade surplus for insurance and pensions was around £12.8bn.

WORLDWIDE MARKET

In 2016 the UK insurance industry was the largest in Europe and the fourth largest in the world behind the USA, Japan and China. China has the fastest growing insurance market, moving from eighth largest in 2006 to third in 2016.

Market	Premium income (€bn)
USA	1,125
Japan	399
China	365
UK	232

TAKEOVERS AND MERGERS

Record-breaking activity in 2015, including the £28bn takeover of Chubb Insurance, the availability of cheap capital and low interest rates heightened speculation at the beginning of 2016 that it would be another busy year for takeovers and mergers. In the event, the political and economic uncertainty stemming from the Brexit referendum result and the new US administration resulted in a decrease of 13 per cent in the total number of takeovers and mergers completed in 2016 compared with 2015.

Among the deals that were completed French insurer AXA sold its Sun Life protection business and UK pensions division to Phoenix for £375m in May. This saw around 850,000 protection policies and around £12bn held in individual and corporate pensions transferred. The sale completed AXA's withdrawal from the UK life and savings market following the sale of its Elevate fund platform to Standard Life and its Isle of Man offshore investment division to the LCCG Group.

In the Lloyd's market, Japanese insurer Mitsui Sumitomo completed its £3.5bn acquisition of catastrophe, marine and aviation insurer Amlin. This was one of a number of overseas purchases by Japanese insurers pursuing businesses outside of Japan where a shrinking population has stifled growth.

INDUSTRY ISSUES

SOLVENCY II
After more than ten years of negotiations, several postponements and over 3,200 pages of regulatory text, the Solvency II directive was finally implemented on 1 January 2016.

The directive (2009/138/EC) codifies and harmonises EU insurance regulation. Primarily establishing an EU-wide set of requirements for capital adequacy and management standards to reduce the risk of insolvency. In general terms the directive requires firms to hold enough capital to survive a one in 200-year stress on their balance sheet.

The compliance process for insurers was far from easy or popular, took ten years and cost an estimated £3bn so the Brexit decision in June 2016 reignited much of the uncertainty just when insurers were looking for a period of stability to bed in the provisions. In September 2016 the

Treasury select committee launched an inquiry into EU insurance regulation and improvements that might be made following Brexit. Although there was no appetite for scrapping Solvency II, Brexit will offer the opportunity to ensure that future regulation is more specifically geared to UK requirements, particularly during the business challenges that Brexit will present.

BREXIT

Membership of the European Union guaranteed British insurers the right to do business in 27 other countries on an equal footing. This was advantageous to the UK as more insurance and long-term savings products were sold to the rest of the EU than within the UK. As a result, the industry lobbied for a 'remain' vote in the referendum.

The result in June 2016 and the UK's subsequent withdrawal from the EU will not mean UK insurers will no longer be able to trade in EU states, but there is a risk that, without the current 'passport' system (which allows an insurer authorised in any EU member state to transact business in any other, without further formality) they will need to set up locally authorised branches in each country if they are to continue operations. In addition, international insurers who currently have their European headquarters in the UK may also need to consider moving out of the UK to a nearby EU member state to retain access to the European markets.

The UK insurance industry has made clear to the government that their priorities for the Brexit negotiations are:

- to retain the ability to 'passport' out of and into the UK
- avoidance of the need for a whole new data protection regime
- a migration policy that will continue to allow highly skilled insurance professionals from both within and outside the EU to work in the UK industry
- swift trade deals with overseas financial services markets, particularly in India and China
- a secure regulatory environment

Although a survey by the Chartered Insurance Institute in January 2017 found that nearly half (48 per cent) of those working in insurance expected the economy to deteriorate in 2017. The longer term view was that the industry was robust enough to survive Brexit.

THE INSURANCE ACT 2015

The Insurance Act 2015, which applies to all classes of non-consumer insurance and reinsurance and, in part, to consumer insurances, came into effect on 12 August 2016. The government described it as 'the biggest reform to insurance contract law in more than a century'.

The Act updates and replaces the existing 'duty of disclosure' – the responsibility for non-consumer policyholders to disclose risk information to insurers when entering into, renewing or altering insurance contracts – with clear guidelines as to what information has to be disclosed and which staff should be involved.

The Act also changes the position on warranties in policies; including those in consumer contracts. Warranties are specific policy conditions, for example, that a burglar alarm has to be in operation when the premises are unoccupied. In the past, if there was a breach of the warranty, all cover ceased. Now the cover is only suspended while the breach is occurring and re-starts when the breach is rectified.

Fraud is also covered under the Act, which confirms that if a policyholder makes a fraudulent claim, the entire claim is forfeit, including any honest part of the claim, and the insurer can keep the premium paid. The insurer will remain liable for any genuine claims before the fraud, but has the option to terminate the policy from the date of the fraud.

Brokers and direct insurers will advise clients in detail as to how their policies are affected by the new law which applies to relevant contracts formed, altered or renewed after 12 August 2016.

GENERAL INSURANCE

The 2016 year began in much the same way as 2015 with the UK hit by flooding and storm damage. Storms Desmond, Eva and Frank hit various parts of the UK in quick succession and caused damage to over 15,300 properties and 6,600 vehicles. The insurance bill amounted to over £1.3bn for this period alone. In November 2016 further flooding hit parts of the UK. The final cost of claims from the November storms are not yet known.

After five years of negotiations and planning, 4 April 2016 saw the launch of Flood Re, a not-for-profit reinsurance fund, owned and managed by the insurance industry. Flood Re is designed to provide flood insurance at affordable levels for homes in high flood risk areas. In practice policyholders will not deal directly with Flood Re, it will be their insurers who will be able to 'lay off' the increased risk and if a claim occurs they can re-coup their outlay from Flood Re. As this facility will reduce the risk involved, the insurer will be able to charge the client a lower premium.

In October 1994 the government introduced insurance premium tax (IPT). Between 1994 and 2011 the rate rose from 2.5 per cent to 6 per cent. The former chancellor George Osborne announced an increase from 6 per cent to 9.5 per cent in the Summer Budget in July 2015, which came into effect in November of the same year. The rate was increased again to 10 per cent in the March 2016 Budget and a third increase in November 2016, to 12 per cent, means the tax has doubled in less than 18 months. The government claimed a proposed consultation on reducing the level of whiplash claims would offset the increased costs the IPT rise would impose. This was strongly refuted by the industry as the consultation mentioned had not even gone before parliament.

The industry has also been considering the insurance implications of the development of driverless cars. At present, the liability section of a motor insurance policy provides compensation for bodily injuries or damage to the property of others (third parties) caused by the negligence of the driver of the insured vehicle. Driverless cars raise the question of the need for insurance and whether it should be the driver or the vehicle manufacturer who is covered. Although some vehicle autonomy is available now, such as cruise control, anti-lock brakes and automatic parking, it is not expected that fully automated driving technology (ADT) will be commercially available until at least 2021. To begin exploring the issue the Department for Transport issued a consultation document in July 2016. The industry responded in September 2016 and although there is still much work to be done before the insurance position is clear and legislation can be passed, the arrival of this technology on our roads is inevitable and with 90 per cent of motor accidents attributable to human error it could have far reaching effects.

TOP FIVE GENERAL INSURANCE COMPANIES BY GROSS WRITTEN PREMIUMS

Insurance Company (2014 position)	2014 (£bn)	2015 (£bn)
1. AVIVA (1)	4.4	5.5
2. AIG (8)	1.6	4.8
3. RSA Insurance Group (4)	2.9	3.9
4. AXA UK (2)	3.2	3.3
5. Direct Line Group (3)	3.2	3.1

LONDON INSURANCE MARKET

In recent years it has become increasingly difficult to define the London Insurance Market business. Many businesses operate in London as branch offices of parent companies located elsewhere in the EU and may no longer separately identify London Market premiums. What is acknowledged is that London is the world's leading market for internationally traded insurance and reinsurance, its business comprising mainly overseas non-life large and high-exposure risks. The market is centred on the square mile of the City of London, which provides the required financial, banking, legal and other support services. Around 53 per cent of London market business is transacted at Lloyd's of London, the remainder through insurance companies and protection and indemnity clubs. In 2014 the market had a written gross premium income of around £48.2bn. Around 200 Lloyd's brokers service the market.

The trade association for the international insurers and reinsurers writing primarily non-marine insurance and all classes of reinsurance business in the London market is the International Underwriting Association (IUA).

INTERNATIONAL UNDERWRITING ASSOCIATION,
1 Minster Court, Mincing Lane, London EC3R 7AA
T 020-7617 4444 W www.iua.co.uk
Chair, Malcolm Newman
Chief Executive, Dave Matcham

BRITISH INSURANCE COMPANIES

The following insurance company figures refer to members and certain non-members of the ABI.

DOMESTIC PROPERTY CLAIMS STATISTICS 2015

Type	Payment (£m)
Theft	386
Fire	474
Weather	593
Escape of water	771
Domestic subsidence	119
Accidental damage	326
other domestic claims	327
Total	2,996

WORLDWIDE GENERAL BUSINESS TRADING RESULTS (£m)

	2014	2015
Net written premiums	47,179	42,515
Underwriting results	1,539	1,132
Investment income	4,162	2,103
Overall trading profit	2,820	3,235
Profit as percentage of premium income	12.1%	7.6%

LLOYD'S OF LONDON

Lloyd's of London is an international market for almost all types of general insurance. Lloyd's currently has the capacity to accept insurance premiums of around £25bn. Much of this business comes from outside the UK and makes a valuable contribution to the balance of payments.

A policy is underwritten at Lloyd's by a mixture of private and corporate members. Specialist underwriters accept insurance risks at Lloyd's on behalf of members (referred to as 'Names') grouped in syndicates. There are currently 84 syndicates of varying sizes, each managed by one of the 59 underwriting agents approved by the Council of Lloyd's.

Members divide into three categories: corporate organisations, individuals who have no limit to their liability for losses, and those who have an agreed limit (known as NameCos).

Lloyd's is incorporated by an act of parliament (Lloyd's Acts 1871 onwards) and is governed by an 18-person council, made up of six working, six external and six nominated members. The structure immediately below this changed when, in 2002, Lloyd's members voted at an extraordinary general meeting to implement a new franchise system for the market with the aim of improving profitability. The first move was the introduction of a new governance structure, replacing the Lloyd's Market Board and the Lloyd's Regulatory Board with an 11-person Lloyd's Franchise Board. Four main committees report to this board.

The corporation is a non-profit making body chiefly financed by its members' subscriptions. It provides the premises, administrative staff and services for Lloyd's underwriting syndicates. It does not, however, assume corporate liability for the risks accepted by its members. Individual members are responsible to the full extent of their personal means for their underwriting affairs unless they have converted to limited liability companies.

Lloyd's syndicates have no direct contact with the public. All business is transacted through insurance brokers accredited by the Corporation of Lloyd's. In addition, non-Lloyd's brokers in the UK, when guaranteed by Lloyd's brokers, are able to deal directly with Lloyd's motor syndicates, a facility that has made the Lloyd's market more accessible to the insuring public.

Under the Financial Services and Markets Act 2000, Lloyds is regulated by the FCA and the PRA. However, in situations where Lloyd's internal regulatory and compensation arrangements are more far-reaching – as for example with the Lloyd's Central Fund which safeguards claim payments to policyholders – the regulatory role is delegated to the Council of Lloyd's.

DEVELOPMENTS IN 2016

In 2016 the Lloyd's market result was a profit of £2.1bn, the same overall figure as for 2015. However the make up of the profits was very different. The underwriting profit of £2.0bn in 2015 substantially reduced to £0.5bn with the combined ratio, the losses and expenses incurred as a proportion of premiums earned, increasing from 90 per cent to 97.7 per cent.

The saving grace for Lloyd's results was foreign exchange gains, mainly caused by the fall in the value of sterling and vastly improved investment income driven by a downward yield shift in the bond markets. Lloyd's investment income more than tripled from £0.4bn to £1.3bn.

Lloyd's described the conditions throughout the year as 'extremely challenging' with premium levels under continuous pressure.

A dominant factor in the 2016 underwriting result was the cost of aggregate major claims, which reached £2.1bn – the fifth highest level since the turn of the century – due primarily to Hurricane Matthew, which struck the Caribbean, southeastern USA and eastern Canada, and the Fort McMurray wildfire in Canada.

Only the aviation account recorded an improvement in underwriting result during the year. Property and marine figures moved from profits of £501m and £108m to losses of £202m and £129m respectively. Losses for casualty and motor business worsened and even the extremely small life account (with a gross premium income of £81m) recorded an increased loss.

On the day of the publication of Lloyd's results for 2016, it was also announced that Lloyd's of London plans to have a new Brussels office up and running by the middle of 2018. The Society had been lobbying the UK government to guarantee continuation of passporting rights (which allows insurers to do business in the EU) but they felt the prospects of this had not improved and believed they could not delay any further establishing a Brussels office.

LLOYD'S OF LONDON, One Lime Street, London EC3M 7HA
T 020-7327 1000 W www.lloyds.com
Chair, John Nelson
Chief Executive, Dame Inga Beale, DBE

LLOYD'S MEMBERSHIP

	2015	2016
Individual	321	290
Corporate	1,771	1,760

LLOYD'S SEGMENTAL RESULTS 2015 (£m)

	Gross written premiums	Net earned premiums	Underwriting result
Reinsurance	9,408	7,154	548
Casualty	7,131	5,343	(146)
Property	7,988	5,859	(202)
Marine	2,470	2,075	(129)
Motor	1,047	893	(103)
Energy	1,110	795	59
Aviation	627	464	71
Life	81	77	(8)
Total from syndicate operations	29,862	22,660	90

LIFE AND LONG-TERM INSURANCE AND PENSIONS

The challenging operating environment faced by life insurers, savings and pension companies continued during 2016. Adapting to the new Solvency II regime, low investment returns and an uncertain economic climate were all factors.

In 2015 changes came into effect, which enabled anyone aged over 55 to withdraw up to 100 per cent (25 per cent tax free) of their private 'defined contribution' or 'money purchase' pension as a lump sum, if they wished. Initially, it was feared that the changes would lead to large numbers of 100 per cent withdrawals to purchase consumer goods or holidays. In fact, research by ABI in August 2016 found that more than half of all pension 'pots' had less than 1 per cent withdrawn a quarter, which suggested that most people were taking a sensible approach. A small number (around 4 per cent) were showing withdrawals of more than 10 per cent. Further research suggested that, far from buying cars or holidays, withdrawals were being used to pay off debts like loans, mortgages or credit cards.

In March 2015, as another part of reforms to pensions, the government also announced plans for a 'secondary annuity market'. This would allow anyone who had purchased an annuity to 'sell' it for a cash lump sum. The market was planned to launch in April 2017 and was intended to expand choice among retirees. However, in October 2016, following lobbying by the industry the government abandoned the plans as it was felt there would not be enough companies willing to purchase annuities to create competition in the market.

With an average individual changing jobs 11 times during their working life it has always been difficult to keep track of the various private and company pension schemes they may have contributed to over the years. In the 2016 Budget the chancellor announced plans for a 'pensions dashboard', a website giving any individual access to a full list of the details and values of the pension contributions they have made. In November a cross-industry project group reporting to HM Treasury, who will oversee the project, began work. The chancellor made the somewhat optimistic commitment in the 2016 Budget to launch the pensions dashboard by 2019.

PROTECTION INSURANCE CLAIMS 2016

Type of product	No. of claims paid*	% of new claims paid	% of new claims declined	Total value paid (£ thousand)	Average claim paid (£)
Critical illness	15,464	92.20	7.80	1,047,435	67,733.74
Life	36,814	98.30	1.70	2,763,324	75,061.78
Total permanent disability	531	69.50	30.50	30,357	57,169.49
Whole of life	85,860	99.99	0.01	407,696	4,748.38
Income protection	28,023	84.70	15.30	499,316	17,818.08
All protection products	166,692	97.30	2.70	4,748,128	–

* Figures are for new claims, as well as all income protection claims in payment

UK LONG-TERM INSURANCE NET PREMIUM INCOME

Year	Life & annuities	Individual pensions	Occupational pensions	Income protection & other business	Total
2005	36,590	22,702	58,868	2,034	120,194
2006	42,058	35,874	65,071	2,048	145,050
2007	49,866	35,252	98,575	1,660	185,353
2008	36,300	30,523	62,820	1,541	131,183
2009	20,336	27,725	68,988	1,473	118,521
2010	19,241	28,218	64,033	1,482	112,975
2011	16,008	27,401	71,680	1,456	116,545
2012	14,893	33,219	71,148	1,862	121,122
2013	9,944	25,119	80,192	1,457	116,712
2014	10,042	23,788	70,826	1,460	106,116
2015	10,617	35,297	76,188	1,461	123,563

TAXATION

The government raises money to pay for public services such as education, health and the social welfare system through tax. Each year the Chancellor of the Exchequer's Budget sets out how much it will cost to provide these services and how much tax is therefore needed to pay for them. HM Revenue and Customs (HMRC) is the government department that collects it. There are several different types of tax. The varieties that individuals may have to pay include income tax payable on earnings, pensions, state benefits, savings and investments; capital gains tax (CGT) payable on the disposal of certain assets; inheritance tax (IHT) payable on estates upon death and certain lifetime gifts; stamp duty payable when purchasing property and shares; and value added tax (VAT) payable on goods and services, plus certain other duties such as fuel duty on petrol and excise duty on alcohol and tobacco. Government funds are also raised from companies and small businesses through corporation tax.

New taxation measures and changes to the administration of the taxation system are normally announced by the incumbent Chancellor of the Exchequer in the government's annual Budget. In November 2016 the Chancellor announced that the Budget will be delivered in the autumn from autumn 2017, with a spring statement on government spending forecasts from spring 2018.

The government has a stated policy of investing manpower and funding into reducing tax evasion and avoidance by both individuals and companies. Information and updates on the latest measures can be found on the government's website (W www.gov.uk/government/policies/tax-evasion-and-avoidance).

The government also has an ongoing drive to simplify the UK tax system via the Office of Tax Simplification (OTS). Details of the OTS and its work can also be found on the government's website (W www.gov.uk/government/organisations/office-of-tax-simplification). The OTS welcomes views from individuals and can be contacted via email (E ots@ots.gsi.gov.uk).

HELP AND INFORMATION ON TAXATION

For information and help on any aspect of personal taxation, individuals may contact their local tax office or call the HMRC helpline (T 0300-200 3300).

HMRC closed its network of enquiry centres in 2014 because visitor numbers had dropped dramatically. To help the estimated 1.5 million customers identified as needing extra help to get their taxes and entitlements right, HMRC introduced a new service offering more in-depth support on the phone and a mobile advisory service if a face-to-face appointment is required.

The HMRC website (W www.gov.uk/government/organisations/hm-revenue-customs) provides wide-ranging information online. All HMRC forms, leaflets and guides are listed on, and can be downloaded from, the website or ordered by telephone. A list of all HMRC telephone helplines and order lines is also on the website. Those most relevant to topics covered in this section on taxation are included at pertinent points throughout.

INCOME TAX

Income tax is levied on different sorts of income. Not all types of income are taxable, however, and individuals are only taxed on their 'taxable income' above a certain level. Reliefs and allowances can also reduce or, in some cases, cancel out an individual's income tax bill.

An individual's taxable income is assessed each tax year, starting on 6 April and ending on 5 April the following year. The information below relates specifically to the year of assessment 2017–18, ending on 5 April 2018, and has only limited application to earlier years. Changes due to come into operation at a later date are briefly mentioned where information is available. Types of income that are taxable include:

- earnings from employment or profits from self-employment
- most pensions income, including state, company and personal pensions
- interest on most savings
- income (dividends) from shares
- income from property
- income received from a trust
- certain state benefits
- an individual's share of any joint income

There are certain sorts of income on which individuals never pay tax. These are ignored altogether when working out how much income tax an individual may need to pay. Types of income that are not taxable include:

- certain state benefits and tax credits, such as child benefit, working tax credit, child tax credit, pension credit, attendance allowance, personal independence payment, housing benefit and maternity allowance
- winter fuel payments
- income from National Savings and Investments savings certificates
- interest, dividends and other income from various tax-free investments, notably individual savings accounts (ISAs)
- premium bond and national lottery prizes

PERSONAL ALLOWANCE

Every individual resident in the UK has a 'personal allowance' for tax purposes. This is the amount of taxable income that an individual can earn or receive each year tax-free. This tax year (2017–18) the basic personal allowance or tax-free amount is £11,500, an increase of £500 from the 2016–17 figure of £11,000. The personal allowance is for all taxpayers regardless of age; previous differences in the amount of personal allowance dependent on age ceased from 2016–17.

Income tax is only due on an individual's taxable income that is above his or her tax-free allowance. Spouses and civil partners are taxed separately, with each entitled to his or her personal allowance. Each spouse or civil partner may obtain other allowances and reliefs where the required conditions are satisfied.

The personal allowance is subject to a single income limit of £100,000, meaning that the personal allowance is reduced for individuals with an 'adjusted net income' (see below) over £100,000. Those individuals with an 'adjusted net income' below or equal to the £100,000 limit are entitled to the full amount of personal allowance. However, where an individual's adjusted net income is above the £100,000 limit, their personal allowance is reduced by half the amount (£1 for every £2) they have over that limit until their personal allowance is reduced to nil.

An individual's 'adjusted net income' is calculated in a series of steps. The starting point is 'net income', which is the total of the individual's income subject to income tax less specified deductions such as payments made gross to pension schemes or trading losses. This net income is then reduced by the grossed-up amount of the individual's Gift Aid contributions to charities and the grossed-up amount of the individual's pension contributions that have received tax relief at source. The final step is to add back any relief for payments to trade unions or police organisations deducted in arriving at the individual's net income. The result is the individual's adjusted net income.

MARRIAGE ALLOWANCE
Some married couples and civil partners, made up of one non-taxpayer and one basic-rate taxpayer, are eligible for a new marriage allowance, which allows them to share some of the non-taxpayer's unused annual income tax allowance. In the 2017–18 tax year, the allowance allows a spouse or civil partner with an income less than £11,500 to transfer up to £1,150 of their unused personal allowance to their higher-income partner. So long as the person receiving the transfer is a basic-rate taxpayer, which, in most cases, means having an income of between £11,500 and £45,000 (£43,000 in Scotland), this transferable tax allowance is worth up to £230 in 2017–18.

BLIND PERSON'S ALLOWANCE
If an individual is registered blind or is unable to perform any work for which eyesight is essential, he or she can claim blind person's allowance, an extra amount of tax-free income added to the personal allowance. In 2017–18 the blind person's allowance is £2,320. It is the same for everyone who can claim it and is not dependent on age or level of income. If an individual is married or in a civil partnership and cannot use all of his or her blind person's allowance because of insufficient income, the unused part of the allowance can be passed to the spouse or civil partner.

PROPERTY AND TRADING ALLOWANCES
It was announced in the 2016 Budget that two new tax-free £1,000 allowances would be introduced, to benefit 'micro-entrepreneurs'. These allowances are available to individuals who use one or more of a wide range of money-making activities to supplement their income. Since April 2017, individuals with property or trading income do not need to declare or pay tax on the first £1,000 they earn from each source per year. Should they earn more than that amount they will have to declare it to HMRC, but they can still take advantage of the allowance.

Property income qualifying for relief under the property allowance could be any income that an individual makes from renting out a residence, home, building, property or land – even from renting out a driveway as a parking space, for example, or renting out a room to visiting tourists via websites like Airbnb.

Trading income qualifying for the allowance can be income from any sale of goods or services. An individual could do tasks such as cleaning or odd jobs, hiring out their own equipment such as power tools, or selling goods through websites like eBay or Etsy.

INCOME TAX ALLOWANCES

	2016–17	2017–18
Personal allowance	£11,000	£11,500
Income limit for personal allowance	£100,000	£100,000
Marriage allowance	£1,100	£1,150
Blind person's allowance	£2,290	£2,320
Property allowance	–	£1,000
Trading allowance	–	£1,000

CALCULATING INCOME TAX DUE
Individuals' liability to pay income tax is determined by establishing their level of taxable income for the year. For married couples and civil partners, income must be allocated between the couple by reference to the individual who is beneficially entitled to that income. Where income arises from jointly held assets, it is normally apportioned equally between the partners. If, however, the beneficial interests in jointly held assets are not equal, in most cases couples can make a special declaration to have income apportioned by reference to the actual interests in that income.

To work out an individual's liability for tax, his or her taxable income must be allocated between three different types: earned income (excluding income from savings and dividends); income from savings; and company dividends from shares and other equity-based investments.

After the tax-free personal allowance plus any deductible allowances and reliefs have been taken into account, the amount of tax an individual pays is calculated using different tax rates and a series of tax bands. The tax band applies to an individual's income after tax allowances and any reliefs have been taken into account.

SCOTLAND
In the tax year 2016–17, residents of Scotland paid the 'Scottish rate of income tax'. This was the same rate of income tax as the rest of the UK but 10 per cent of the tax raised was paid to the Scottish government.

From the tax year 2017–18, the Scottish government is able to set the rates and bands for tax on income from earnings, pensions and most other taxable income in Scotland. The tax raised is paid to the Scottish government.

Income from savings and dividend interest continues to be taxed at the same rate as in the rest of the UK.

UK INCOME TAX BANDS AND RATES

	Band 2017–18	Rate 2017–18
Basic rate	£0–33,500	20%
(Scotland*)	(31,500)	
Higher rate	£33,501 (31,501)–	40%
(Scotland*)	150,000	
Additional rate	£150,000+	45%

* Figures for Scotland (in parentheses) are given only where they differ from the bands or rates in the rest of the UK

The first calculation is applied to earned income, which includes income from employment or self-employment, most pension income and rental income, plus the value of a wide range of employee 'benefits in kind' such as company cars, living accommodation and private medical insurance (for more information on benefits in kind, see later section on payment of income tax). In working out the amount of an individual's net taxable earnings, all expenses incurred 'wholly, exclusively and necessarily' in the performance of his or her work duties, together with the cost of business travel, may be deducted. Fees and subscriptions to certain professional bodies may also be deducted. Redundancy payments and other sums paid on the termination of an employment are assessable income, but the first £30,000 is normally tax-free provided the payment is not linked with the recipient's retirement or performance.

The first £33,500 of taxable income remaining after the tax-free allowance plus any deductible allowances and reliefs have been taken into account, is taxed at the basic rate of 20 per cent. Taxable income between £33,501 and £150,000 is taxed at the higher rate of 40 per cent. Taxable income above £150,001 is taxed at the additional rate of 45 per cent.

Savings and dividends income is added to an individual's other taxable income and taxed last. This means that tax on such sorts of income is based on an individual's highest income tax band.

SAVINGS INCOME
The second calculation is applied to any income from savings received by an individual. Savings income includes interest paid on bank and building society accounts, interest paid on accounts from providers like credit unions or National Savings and Investments, interest distributions (but not dividend distributions) from authorised unit trusts, open-ended investment companies and investment trusts, interest from peer-to-peer lending, government or company bonds and life annuity payments.

The appropriate rate at which savings income must be taxed is determined by adding income from savings to an individual's other taxable income (excluding dividends).

Savings interest may be set against the personal allowance (if that is not used up on income from employment or pension), the starting rate for savings income and the personal savings allowance (introduced in April 2016).

The starting rate of tax for savings income allows an individual to earn up to £5,000 of interest tax-free in 2017–18, provided their other income is less than £16,500. The £5,000 allowance is reduced by £1 for every £1 of their non-savings income above the personal allowance threshold.

The personal savings allowance (PSA) allows a basic rate taxpayer to earn their first £1,000 of savings income tax-free. A higher rate taxpayer may earn their first £500 of savings income tax-free. Additional rate taxpayers do not get a PSA.

With the introduction of the PSA in April 2016, banks and building societies stopped automatically deducting 20 per cent tax from savings interest before it was paid to individuals. This means that non-taxpayers no longer have to apply to have their savings interest paid gross. It is now an individual's responsibility to inform HMRC if they earn savings income above the PSA on which tax is payable; any tax owed will normally be collected via the individual's tax code.

Tax on interest over the allowance is paid at the individual's usual rate of income tax, ie 20 per cent for basic rate taxpayers, 40 per cent for higher rate taxpayers and 45 per cent for additional rate taxpayers. If savings income falls on both sides of a tax band, the relevant amounts are taxed at the rates for each tax band.

DIVIDEND INCOME

The third and final income tax calculation is on UK dividends, which means income from shares in UK companies and other share-based investments.

A major change in the way dividend income is taxed came into effect on 6 April 2016. All taxpayers now have a £5,000 tax-free dividend allowance. This means that individuals do not have to pay tax on the first £5,000 of their dividend income, no matter what non-dividend income they have. The allowance is available to anyone who has dividend income.

Dividends received that exceed the £5,000 allowance are treated as the top band of income. This means that if an individual's divided income takes them from one income tax band into the next, they will then pay the higher dividend rate on that portion of income.

TAX RATES ON DIVIDENDS OVER £5,000

Band	2017–18
Basic rate	7.5%
Higher rate	32.5%
Additional rate	38.1%

If there is significant change to an individual's savings or other income, whatever his or her current tax bracket, it is the individual's responsibility to contact the relevant tax office immediately, even if he or she does not normally complete a tax return. This enables the tax office to work out whether extra or less tax should be paid.

TAX FREE SAVINGS

There is a small selection of savings and investment products that are tax-free. This means that there is no tax to pay on any income generated in the form of interest or dividends, nor on any increase in the value of the capital invested. Their tax-efficient status has been granted by the government in order to give people an incentive to save more. For this reason there are usually limits and restrictions on the amount of money an individual may invest in such savings and investments.

Individual savings accounts (ISAs) are the best known among tax-efficient savings and investments. There are four types: cash ISAs, stocks and shares, innovative finance ISAs (earning interest and capital gains free of tax on loans made via peer-to-peer lending platforms) and lifetime ISAs. Money may be invested in one of each type of ISA each tax year, up to an overall annual subscription limit, which is £20,000 in 2017–18. This may be paid into one ISA or split between some or all of the other types, although no more than £4,000 may be paid into a lifetime ISA in one tax year.

To be eligible to invest in ISAs and receive all profits free of tax, individuals must be:

- aged 16 or over to hold a cash ISA
- aged 18 or over for a stocks and shares or innovative finance ISA
- aged 18 or over but under 40 for a lifetime ISA
- resident in the UK or, if not resident in the UK, a Crown servant or their spouse or civil partner

An ISA must be in an individual's name and cannot be held jointly with another person, but spouses and civil partners may inherit their partner's ISA allowance after death.

The lifetime ISA introduced in April 2017 may be opened by UK residents between the ages of 18 and 40, and allows individuals to save up to £4,000 a year between the ages of 18 and 50. Savings put into the account before their 50th birthday will qualify for a government bonus of 25 per cent, up to £1,000 a year. An individual may use their savings and bonus towards the purchase of a first-time home worth up to £450,000. Alternatively, they may choose to keep the account as retirement savings until their 60th birthday, after which date they can withdraw all the money tax-free.

There are also long-term, tax-free savings accounts for children called Junior ISAs. The investment limit for these in 2017–18 is £4,128 per child. Parents or guardians with parental responsibility can open Junior ISAs for children aged under 18 who live in the UK. However, while parents can open and manage Junior ISAs for their children, the invested money belongs to the child, who can take control of their account when they are 16 and withdraw the money when they are 18. Children aged 16 and 17 can open their own Junior ISA as well as an adult cash ISA. Junior ISAs automatically turn into an adult ISA when the child turns 18.

The Help to Buy ISA, introduced in autumn 2015, is one of a number of government measures to help individuals save towards buying their first home. Aspiring first-time buyers aged 16 or over may save up to £200 a month in a Help to Buy ISA and the government boosts their savings by 25 per cent, up to a maximum of £3,000 per person. If, therefore, an individual saves £12,000, the government bonus boosts their total savings to £15,000. Savers can start an account with a lump-sum deposit of up to £1,200. The minimum government bonus is £400, meaning that the individual must save at least £1,600 to qualify for the scheme, but there is no monthly minimum investment.

Savings held in a Help to Buy ISA can be accessed at any time but the government payment is only added if and when the savings are used as a deposit on a first and only home in the UK. The bonus is available on home purchases of up to £450,000 in London and up to £250,000 outside London. Qualifying properties must be purchased with a mortgage and must be lived in by the purchaser and not rented out.

Individuals are able to open a Help to Buy ISA until 30 November 2019, after which they will no longer be available to new savers. Those who open an account before the cut-off date may continue saving into their account but must claim their bonus by 1 December 2030.

Further details about ISAs are available via the HMRC's savings helpline (T 0300-200 3312).

DEDUCTIBLE ALLOWANCES AND RELIEF

Income taxpayers may be entitled to certain tax-deductible allowances and reliefs as well as their personal allowances. Examples include the married couple's allowance and maintenance payments relief, see below. Unlike the tax-free allowances, these are not amounts of income that an individual can receive tax-free but amounts by which their tax bill can be reduced.

MARRIED COUPLE'S ALLOWANCE

A married couple's allowance (MCA) is available to taxpayers who are married or are in a civil partnership where at least one partner was born before 6 April 1935 and they usually live together. Eligible couples can start to claim the MCA from the year of marriage or civil partnership registration.

The MCA is restricted to give relief at a fixed rate of 10 per cent, which means that – unlike the personal allowance – it is not income that can be received without paying tax. Instead, it reduces an individual's tax bill by up to a fixed amount calculated as 10 per cent of the amount of the allowance to which they are entitled.

In 2017–18, the MCA is £8,445 at 10 per cent, worth up to £844.50 off a couple's tax bill. The MCA is made up of two parts. There is a minimum amount (£3,260 in 2017–18) which will always be due. The remaining amount (£8,445 in 2017–18) can be reduced if the highest earner's income exceeds certain limits. Whatever the level of the highest earner's income, the MCA can never be reduced below the minimum amount.

For marriages before 5 December 2005, the allowance is based on the husband's income; for marriages and civil partnerships after that date, the allowance is based on the income of the highest earner. A couple can decide to have the minimum amount of the allowance split equally between them or transfer the whole of the minimum MCA from one to the other. If an individual does not have enough income to use all of his or her share of the MCA, the unused part of it can be transferred to his or her spouse or civil partner. A couple must inform their tax office of their decision before the start of the new tax year in which they want the decision to take effect.

MAINTENANCE PAYMENTS RELIEF
An allowance is available to reduce an individual's tax bill for maintenance payments he or she makes to his or her ex-spouse or former civil partner in certain circumstances. To be eligible one or other partner must have been born before 6 April 1935; the couple must be legally separated or divorced; the maintenance payments being made must be under a court order; and the payments must be for the maintenance of an ex-spouse or former civil partner (provided he or she is not now remarried or in a new civil partnership) or for children who are under 21. For the tax year 2017–18, this allowance can reduce an individual's tax bill by:

- 10 per cent of £3,260 (maximum £326) – this applies where an individual makes maintenance payments of £3,260 or more a year
- 10 per cent of the amount the individual has actually paid – this applies where an individual makes maintenance payments of less than £3,260 a year

An individual cannot claim a tax reduction for any voluntary payments he or she makes for a child, ex-spouse or former civil partner. To claim maintenance payments relief, individuals should contact their tax office.

TAX RELIEF FOR LANDLORDS
Individual landlords were able to deduct their costs, including mortgage interest, from their profits before they paid tax, enabling wealthier landlords to receive tax relief at 40 per cent and 45 per cent. The calculation of this relief is to change, so that property profits and other income will be assessed and then relief will be applied at the basic rate of income tax. The changes are being phased in between April 2017 and April 2020.

CHARITABLE DONATIONS
A number of charitable donations qualify for tax relief. Individuals can increase the value of regular or one-off charitable gifts of money, however small, by using the Gift Aid scheme that allows charities or community amateur sports clubs (CASCs) to reclaim 20 per cent basic rate tax relief on donations they receive. If a taxpayer gives £10 using Gift Aid, for example, the donation is worth £12.50 to the charity or CASC.

Individuals who pay 40 per cent higher rate income tax can claim back the difference between the 40 per cent and the 20 per cent basic rate of income tax on the total (gross) value of their donations. For example, a 40 per cent tax payer donates £100; the total value of this donation to the charity or CASC is £125, of which the individual can claim back 20 per cent (£25) for themselves. Similarly, those who pay 45 per cent additional rate income tax can claim back the difference between the 45 per cent and the 20 per cent basic rate on the total (gross) value of their donations. On a £100 donation, this means they can claim back £31.25.

In order to make a Gift Aid donation, individuals need to make a Gift Aid declaration. The charity or CASC will normally ask an individual to complete a simple form. One form can cover every gift made to the same charity or CASC for whatever period chosen, including both gifts made in the past and in the future. Charities are able to claim a Gift Aid-type tax refund on small, ad-hoc donations up to a total of £5,000 a year per charity, without the need for donors to fill in any forms at all. This means Gift Aid can be claimed on the contents of collecting tins, for example. If a charity collects the full £5,000, it will get £1,250 back.

Individuals can use Gift Aid provided the amount of income tax and/or capital gains tax they have paid in the tax year in which their donations are made is at least equal to the amount of basic rate tax the charity or CASC is reclaiming on their gifts. It is the responsibility of the individual to make sure this is the case. If an individual makes Gift Aid donations and has not paid sufficient tax, they may have to pay the shortfall to HMRC. The Gift Aid scheme is not suitable for non-taxpayers.

Individuals who complete a tax return and are due a tax refund can ask HMRC to treat all or part of it as a Gift Aid donation.

For employees or those in receipt of an occupational pension, a tax-efficient way of making regular donations to charities is to use the payroll giving scheme. It allows the donations to be paid from a salary or pension before income tax is deducted. This effectively reduces the cost of giving for donors, which may allow them to give more.

For example, it costs a basic-rate taxpayer only £8 in take-home pay to give £10 to charity from their pre-tax pay. Where a donor pays 40 per cent higher rate tax, that same £10 donation costs the taxpayer £6, and for donors who pay the additional 45 per cent rate tax, it costs £5.50.

Anyone who pays tax through the pay as you earn (PAYE) system (see Payment of Income Tax) can give to any charity of their choosing in this way, providing their employer or pension provider offers the payroll giving scheme. There is no limit to the amount individuals can donate.

Details of tax-efficient charitable giving methods can be found at W www.gov.uk/donating-to-charity

TAX RELIEF ON PENSION CONTRIBUTIONS
Pensions are long-term investments designed to help ensure that people have enough income in retirement. The government encourages individuals to save towards a pension by offering tax relief on their contributions. Tax relief reduces an individual's tax bill or increases their pension fund.

The way tax relief is given on pension contributions depends on whether an individual pays into a company, public service or personal pension scheme.

For employees who pay into a company or public service pension scheme, most employers take the pension contributions from the employee's pay before deducting tax, which means that the individual – whether they pay income tax at the basic or higher rate – gets full tax relief straight away. Some employers, however, use the same method of paying pension contributions as that used by personal pension scheme payers described below.

Individuals who pay into a personal pension scheme normally make contributions from their net salary; that is, after tax has been deducted. For each pound that individuals contribute to their pension from net salary, the pension provider claims tax back from the government at the basic rate of 20 per cent and reinvests it on behalf of the individual into the scheme. In practice this means that for every £80 an individual pays into their pension, they receive £100 in their pension fund.

Higher rate taxpayers currently get 40 per cent tax relief on money they put into a pension. On contributions made from net salary, the first 20 per cent is claimed back from HMRC by the pension scheme in the same way as for a lower rate taxpayer. It is then up to individuals to claim back the other 20 per cent from their tax office, either when they fill in their annual tax return or by telephone or letter. In a similar fashion, individuals subject to the 45 per cent additional rate of income tax can get 45 per cent tax relief on their pension contributions.

Non-taxpayers can still pay into a personal pension scheme and benefit from 20 per cent basic rate relief on the first £2,880 a year they contribute. In practice this means that the government tops up their £2,880 contribution to make it £3,600, which is the current universal pension allowance. Such pension contributions may be made on behalf of a non-taxpayer by another individual. An individual may, for example, contribute to a pension on behalf of a husband, wife, civil partner, child or grandchild. Tax relief will be added to their contribution at the basic rate, again on up to £2,880 a year benefiting the recipient, but their own tax bill will not be affected.

In any one tax year, individuals can get tax relief on pension contributions made into any number and type of registered pension schemes of up to 100 per cent of their annual earnings, irrespective of age, up to a maximum 'annual allowance'. For the tax year 2017–18 the annual allowance for most individuals is £40,000. Since April 2016 this £40,000 annual allowance for those earning above £150,000 is reduced by £1 for every £2 of income between £150,000 and £210,000, so that those earning £210,000 and over have a £10,000 annual allowance.

Everyone also has a 'lifetime allowance' which defines the total amount a taxpayer can save in their pension fund and still get tax relief at their highest rate of income tax on all their contributions. Since April 2016 the lifetime allowance is £1m, reduced from £1.25m in 2015–16.

For information on pensions and tax relief visit W www.gov.uk/browse/working. Another useful source of information and advice is the Pensions Advisory Service (TPAS), an independent voluntary organisation grant-aided by the government, at W www.pensionsadvisoryservice.org.uk; its pensions helpline is on T 0300-123 1047.

PAYMENT OF INCOME TAX
Employees have their income tax deducted from their wages throughout the year by their employer, who sends it on to HMRC. Those in receipt of a company pension have their due tax deducted in the same way by their pension provider. This system of collecting income tax is known as 'pay as you earn' (PAYE).

BENEFITS IN KIND
The PAYE system is also used to collect tax on certain company benefits or 'benefits in kind' that employees or directors receive from their employer but are not included in their salary. These include company cars, living accommodation, private medical insurance paid for by the employer or cheap or free loans from the employer. Some company benefits are tax-free, including employer-paid contributions into an employee's pension fund, cheap or free canteen meals, works buses, in-house sports facilities, reasonable relocation expenses, provision of a mobile phone and workplace nursery places provided for the children of employees. For taxable company benefits, tax is paid on the 'taxable value' of the benefit.

Employers submit returns for individual employees to the tax office on the form P11D, with details of any company benefits they have been given. Employees should get a copy

of this form by 6 July following the end of the tax year and must enter the value of the company benefits they have received on their tax return for the relevant year, even if tax has already been paid on them under PAYE. Company benefits may be taxed under PAYE by being offset against personal tax allowances in an individual's PAYE code. Otherwise tax will be collected after the end of the tax year by the issue of an assessment on the company benefits.

SELF-ASSESSMENT
Individuals who are not on PAYE, notably the self-employed, need to complete a self-assessment tax return each year, in paper form or online (W www.gov.uk/log-in-file-self-assessment-tax-return), and pay any income tax owed in twice-yearly instalments. Some individuals with more complex tax affairs, such as those who earn money from rents or investments above a certain level, may also need to fill out a self-assessment return even if they are on PAYE. HMRC uses the figures supplied on the tax return to work out the individual's tax bill, or they can choose to work it out themselves. It is called 'self-assessment' because individuals are responsible for making sure the details they provide are correct.

Tax returns are usually sent out in early April, following the end of the tax year to which they apply. They may also go out at other times, for example if an individual wants to claim an allowance or repayment or to register for self-assessment for the first time.

Central to the self-assessment system is the requirement for individuals to contact their tax office if they do not receive a self-assessment return but think they should or if their financial circumstances change. Individuals have six months from when the tax year ends to report any new income, for example. If an individual becomes self-employed, they have three months after the calendar month in which they began self-employed work to let HMRC know. This can be done by telephoning the helpline number for the newly self-employed on T 0300-200 3500.

TAX RETURN FILING AND PAYMENT DEADLINES
There are also key deadlines for filing (sending in) completed tax returns and paying the tax due. Failure to do so can incur penalties, interest charges and surcharges.

KEY FILING DATES FOR SELF-ASSESSMENT RETURNS

Date	Why the date is important
31 Oct*	Deadline for filing paper returns* for tax year ending the previous 5 April
30 Dec	Deadline for online filing where the amount owed for tax year ending the previous 5 April is less than £3,000 and the taxpayer wants HMRC to collect any tax due through their PAYE tax code
31 Jan†	Deadline for online filing of returns for tax year ending the previous 5 April

* Or three months from the date the return was requested if this was after 31 July

† Or three months from the date the return was requested if this was after 31 October

KEY SELF-ASSESSMENT PAYMENT DATES

Date	What payment is due?
31 Jan	Deadline for paying the balance of any tax owed – the 'balancing payment' – for the tax year ending the previous 5 April. It is also the date by which a taxpayer must make any first 'payment on account' (advance payment) for the current tax year. For example, on 31 January 2018 a taxpayer may have to pay both the balancing payment for the year 2017–18 and the first payment on account for 2018–19.
31 Jul	Deadline for making a second payment on account for the current tax year

LATE FILING AND PAYMENT PENALTIES

Late filing of tax returns incurs an automatic £100 penalty although individuals may appeal against the penalty if they have a reasonable excuse. For late filing of 2015–16 tax returns the following penalties also apply:

- Over three months late – £10 each day, up to a maximum of £900, in addition to the penalty above
- Over six months late – an additional £300 or 5 per cent of the tax due, whichever is the higher, in addition to the penalty above
- Over 12 months late – a further £300 or 5 per cent of the tax due, whichever is the higher. In serious cases HMRC reserve the right to ask for 100 per cent of the tax due instead. In both instances this is in addition to the penalty above

Late payment of tax owing for 2015–16 incurs the following penalties:

- Over 30 days – 5 per cent of the tax unpaid at that date
- Over six months – an additional 5 per cent of the tax unpaid at that date
- Over 12 months – a further 5 per cent of the tax unpaid at that date

Interest is due on all outstanding amounts, including any unpaid penalties, until payment is received in full. Individuals may calculate the penalties they owe for late self-assessment tax returns and payments online (W www.gov.uk/ estimate-self-assessment-penalties).

PERSONAL TAX ACCOUNTS

The government has announced that it intends to abolish the annual tax return for millions of individuals and small businesses through the introduction of digital tax accounts as part of its aim to modernise and simplify the taxation system. At the end of 2015, HMRC launched the new system of digital personal tax accounts which will eventually replace annual tax returns. Since April 2016 all personal taxpayers have been able to access their personal tax account at W www.gov.uk/personal-tax-account The plan is that by 2020 the system, which operates in a way akin to online banking, will allow taxpayers to register, file, pay and update tax information at any time using the digital device of their choice, and will be mandatory for every individual taxpayer and business.

TAX CREDITS

Child tax credit, working tax credit and the new universal credit are paid to qualifying individuals. Although the titles of these credits incorporate the word 'tax', they do not affect the amount of income tax payable or repayable. They are forms of social security benefits. *See* Social Welfare.

CAPITAL GAINS TAX

Capital gains tax (CGT) is a tax on the gain or profit that an individual makes when they sell, give away or otherwise dispose of an asset – that is, something they own such as shares, land or buildings. An individual potentially has to pay CGT on gains they make from any disposal of assets during a tax year. There is, however, a tax-free allowance and some additional reliefs that may reduce an individual's CGT bill. The following information relates to the tax year 2017–18 ending on 5 April 2018.

CGT is paid by individuals who are either resident or ordinarily resident in the UK for the tax year, executors or administrators – 'personal representatives' – responsible for a deceased person's financial affairs and trustees of a settlement. Non-residents are not usually liable to CGT unless they carry on a business in the UK through a branch or agency. However, from April 2015, the government introduced a CGT charge on future gains made by non-residents disposing of UK residential property. Special CGT rules apply to individuals who used to live and work in the UK but have since left the country.

CAPITAL GAINS CHARGEABLE TO CGT

Typically, individuals have made a gain if they sell an asset for more than they paid for it. It is the gain that is taxed, not the amount the individual receives for the asset. For example, a man buys shares for £1,000 and later sells them for £3,000. He has made a gain of £2,000 (£3,000 less £1,000). If someone gives an asset away, the gain will be based on the difference between what the asset was worth when originally acquired compared with its worth at the time of disposal. The same is true when an asset is sold for less than its full worth in order to give away part of the value. For example, a woman buys a property for £120,000 and three years later, when the property's market value has risen to £180,000, she gives it to her son. The son may pay nothing for the property or pay less than its true worth, eg £100,000. Either way, she has made a gain of £60,000 (£180,000 less £120,000).

If an individual disposes of an asset he or she received as a gift, the gain is worked out according to the market value of the asset when it was received. For example, a man gives his sister a painting worth £8,000. She pays nothing for it. Later she sells the painting for £10,000. For CGT purposes, she is treated as making a gain of £2,000 (£10,000 less £8,000). If an individual inherits an asset, the estate of the person who died does not pay CGT at the time. If the inheritor later disposes of the asset, the gain is worked out by looking at the market value at the time of the death. For example, a woman acquires some shares for £5,000 and leaves them to her niece when she dies. No CGT is payable at the time of death when the shares are worth £8,000. Later the niece sells the shares for £10,000. She has made a gain of £2,000 (£10,000 less £8,000).

Individuals may also have to pay CGT if they dispose of part of an asset or exchange one asset for another. Similarly, CGT may be payable if an individual receives a capital sum of money from an asset without disposing of it, for example where he or she receives compensation when an asset is damaged.

Assets that may lead to a CGT charge when they are disposed of include:

- shares in a company that are not held in an ISA or PEP
- units in a unit trust
- land and buildings (though not normally an individual's main home – *see* 'Disposal of a home' section for details)
- personal possessions, including jewellery, paintings, antiques and other personal effects, individually worth £6,000 or more
- business assets

EXEMPT GAINS

Certain kinds of assets do not give rise to a chargeable gain when they are disposed of. Assets exempt from CGT include:

- an individual's private car
- an individual's main home, if certain conditions are met
- tax-free investments such as assets held in an ISA or PEP
- UK government gilts or 'bonds' (including premium bonds)
- personal belongings, including jewellery, paintings and antiques, individually worth £6,000 or less
- betting, lottery or pools winnings

DISPOSAL OF A HOME: PRIVATE RESIDENCE RELIEF

When an individual sells their own home they automatically qualify for private residence relief, which means they do not have to pay any CGT provided that:

- the property has been their only home or main residence since they bought it, and
- they have used it as their home and for no other purpose

Even if an individual has not lived in the property for all of the time that they owned it, they may still be entitled to the full relief.

Under the relief rules, the final 18 months of ownership are always treated as if the individual lived in the property even if they did not. This means that if an individual moves out of one home and into a new one, they have up to 18 months in which to sell their former home without incurring any CGT on the sale proceeds.

Full relief is granted to individuals when they sell their home if they could not live in it for periods because they were working abroad. Full relief is also granted if an individual is prevented from living in the home for periods totalling a maximum of four years because their job requires them to work elsewhere in the UK. In both cases, however, for the property to qualify for full relief, the general rule is that it must have been the individual's only or main home both before and after they worked away.

Individuals can also get full relief when they sell their home if they have lived away from it for reasons other than working away provided all of the following apply:

• they were not living away from the home for more than three years in total during the time they owned the property
• they were not entitled to private residence relief on any other property during that time
• the property was their only or main home both before and after they lived elsewhere

There are instances when individuals may not get the full amount of private residence relief when they sell their home. These include if:

• the grounds, including all buildings, are larger than 5,000 square metres
• any part of the home has been used exclusively for business purposes
• all or part of the home has been let out (or more than one lodger has been taken in at a time). The owner may, however, be entitled to another form of CGT relief – letting relief – instead
• the main reason the property was bought was to make a profit from a quick sale

If an individual lives in – not just owns – more than one property, they can 'nominate' which should be treated as their main home for private residence relief purposes. Married couples or those in a civil partnership must make such a nomination jointly as they are only entitled to private residence relief on one house between them.

Certain other kinds of disposal similarly do not give rise to a chargeable gain. For example, individuals who are married or in a civil partnership and who live together may sell or give assets to their spouse or civil partner without having to pay CGT. Individuals may not, however, give or sell assets cheaply to their children without having to consider CGT. There is no CGT to pay on assets given to a registered charity.

There is a calculator to help individuals work out how much private residence relief they may be entitled to when selling their main residence at W www.gov.uk/tax-relief-selling-home.

CALCULATING CGT

CGT is worked out for each tax year and is charged on the total of an individual's taxable gains after taking into account certain costs and reliefs that can reduce or defer chargeable gains, allowable losses made on assets to which CGT normally applies and an annual exempt (tax-free) amount that applies to every individual. If the total of an individual's net gains in a tax year is less than the annual exempt amount (AEA), the individual will not have to pay CGT. For the tax year 2017–18 the AEA is £11,300. If an individual's net gains are more than the AEA, they pay CGT on the excess. Should any part of the exemption remain unused, this cannot be carried forward to a future year.

There are certain reliefs available that may eliminate, reduce or defer CGT. Some reliefs are available to many people while others are available only in special circumstances. Some reliefs are given automatically while others are given only if they are claimed. Some of the costs of buying, selling and improving assets may be deducted from total gains when working out an individual's chargeable gain.

RATES OF TAX

The net gains remaining, if any, calculated after subtracting the AEA, deducting costs and taking into account all CGT reliefs, incur liability to capital gains tax. Individuals pay CGT at a rate of 10 per cent on gains up to the unused amount of the basic rate income tax band (if any) and at 20 per cent on gains above that amount. Rates for individuals for gains on residential property not eligible for private residence relief (see above) are charged at a rate of 18 per cent up to any unused amount of the basic rate income tax band and at 28 per cent on gains above that amount. The CGT rate charged to trustees and personal representatives is 28 per cent on residential property and 20 per cent on other chargeable assets.

CGT for 2017–18 is due for payment in full on 31 January 2019; payments on account for 2018–19 can be made on 31 January and 31 July 2019. If payment is delayed, interest or surcharges may be imposed. A husband and wife or registered civil partners who live together are separately assessed for CGT. Each partner must independently calculate his or her gains and losses, with each entitled to the AEA of £11,300 for 2017–18.

VALUATION OF ASSETS

The disposal proceeds – ie the amount received as consideration for the disposal of an asset – are the sum used to establish the gain or loss once certain allowable costs have been deducted. In most cases this is straightforward because the disposal proceeds are the amount actually received for disposing of the asset. This may include cash payable now or in the future and the value of any asset received in exchange for the asset disposed of. However, in certain circumstances, the disposal proceeds may not accurately reflect the value of the asset and the individual may be treated as disposing of an asset for an amount other than the actual amount (if any) that they received. This applies, in particular, where an asset is transferred as a gift or sold for a price known to be below market value. Disposal proceeds in such transactions are deemed to be equal to the market value of the asset at the time it was disposed of rather than the actual amount (if any) received for it.

Market value represents the price that an asset might reasonably be expected to fetch upon sale in the open market. In the case of unquoted shares or securities, it is to be assumed that the hypothetical purchaser in the open market would have available all the information that a prudent prospective purchaser of shares or securities might reasonably require if that person were proposing to purchase them from a willing vendor by private treaty and at arm's length. The market value of unquoted shares or securities will often be established following negotiations with the specialist HMRC Shares and Assets Valuation department. The valuation of land and interests in land in the UK is dealt with by the Valuation Office Agency. Special rules apply to determine the market value of shares quoted on the London Stock Exchange.

ALLOWABLE COSTS

When working out a chargeable gain, once the actual or notional disposal proceeds have been determined, certain allowable costs may be deducted. There is a general rule that no costs that could be taken into account when working out income or losses for income tax purposes may be deducted. Subject to this, allowable costs are:

• acquisition costs – the actual amount spent on acquiring the asset or, in certain circumstances, the equivalent market value

- incidental costs of acquiring the asset, such as fees paid for professional advice, valuation costs, stamp duty and advertising costs to find a seller
- enhancement costs – incurred for the purpose of enhancing the value of the asset (not including normal maintenance and repair costs)
- expenditure on defending or establishing a person's rights over the asset
- incidental costs of disposing of the asset, such as fees paid for professional advice, valuation costs, stamp duty and advertising costs to find a buyer

If an individual disposes of part of his or her interest in an asset, or part of a holding of shares of the same class in the same company, or part of a holding of units in the same unit trust, he or she can deduct part of the allowable costs of the asset or holding when working out the chargeable gain. Allowable costs may also be reduced by some reliefs.

ENTREPRENEURS' RELIEF

Entrepreneurs' relief allows individuals in business and some trustees to claim relief on the first £10m of gains made on the disposal of any of the following: all or part of a business; the assets of a business after it has ceased; and shares in a company. The relief is available to taxpayers as individuals if they are in business, for example as a sole trader or as a partner in a trading business, or if they hold shares in their own personal trading company. This relief is not available for companies.

Depending on the type of disposal, certain qualifying conditions need to be met throughout a qualifying one-year period. For example, if an individual is selling all or part of their business, they must have owned the business during a one-year period that ends on the date of the disposal.

Where all gains qualify for entrepreneurs' relief, CGT is charged at 10 per cent. An individual can make claims for this relief on more than one occasion as long as the lifetime total of all their claims does not exceed £10m of gains qualifying for relief.

BUSINESS ASSET ROLL-OVER RELIEF

When certain types of business asset are sold or disposed of and the proceeds reinvested in new qualifying trading assets, business asset rollover relief makes it possible to 'rollover' or postpone the payment of any CGT that would normally be due. The gain is deducted from the base cost of the new asset and only becomes chargeable to CGT on the eventual disposal of that replacement asset, unless a further rollover situation then develops. Full relief is available if all the proceeds from the original asset are reinvested in the qualifying replacement asset.

For example, a trader sells a freehold office for £75,000 and makes a gain of £30,000. All of the proceeds are reinvested in a new freehold business premises costing £90,000. The trader can postpone the whole of the £30,000 gain made on the sale of the old office, as all of the proceeds have been reinvested. When the trader eventually sells the new business premises and the CGT bill becomes payable, the cost of the new premises will be treated as £60,000 (£90,000 less the £30,000 gain).

If only part of the proceeds from the disposal of an old asset is reinvested in a new one, different rules may apply but it may still be possible to postpone paying tax on part of the gain until the eventual disposal of the new asset.

Relief is only available if the acquisition of the new asset takes place within a period between 12 months before and 36 months after the disposal of the old asset. However, HMRC may extend this time limit at their discretion where there is a clear intention to acquire a replacement asset. The most common types of business asset that qualify for rollover relief are land, buildings occupied and used for the purposes of trade, and fixed plant and machinery. Assets used for the commercial letting of furnished holiday accommodation qualify if certain conditions are satisfied.

GIFT HOLD-OVER RELIEF

The gift of an asset is treated as a disposal made for a consideration equal to market value, with a corresponding acquisition by the transferee at an identical value. In the case of gifts of business assets made by individuals and a limited range of trustees, a form of hold-over relief may be available. This relief, which must be claimed, in effect enables liability for CGT to be deferred and passed to the person to whom the gift is made. Relief is limited to the transfer of certain assets, including the following:

- gifts of assets used for the purposes of a business carried on by the donor or his or her personal company
- gifts of shares in trading companies that are not listed on a stock exchange
- gifts of shares or securities in the donor's personal trading company
- gifts of agricultural land and buildings that would qualify for inheritance tax agricultural property relief
- gifts that are chargeable transfers for inheritance tax purposes
- certain types of gifts that are specifically exempt from inheritance tax

Hold-over relief is automatically due on certain sorts of gifts, including gifts to charities and community amateur sports clubs, and gifts of works of art where certain undertakings have been given. There are certain rules to prevent gifts hold-over relief being used for tax-avoidance purposes. For example, restrictions may apply where an individual gifts assets to trustees administering a trust in which the individual retains an interest or the assets transferred comprise a dwelling-house. Subject to these exceptions, the effect of a valid claim for hold-over relief is similar to a claim for roll-over relief on the disposal of business assets.

OTHER CGT RELIEFS

There are certain other CGT reliefs available on the disposal of property, shares and business assets. For detailed information on all CGT reliefs and for more general guidance on CGT visit **W** www.gov.uk/personal-tax/capital-gains-tax

REPORTING AND PAYING CGT

Individuals are responsible for telling HMRC about capital gains on which they have to pay tax. Individuals who receive a self-assessment tax return may report capital gains by filling in the capital gains supplementary pages – the return explains how to obtain these pages if needed.

Individuals who do not normally complete a tax return but who need to report capital gains or losses should contact their local tax office.

There is a time limit for claiming capital losses. The deadline is four years from 31 January after the end of the tax year in which the loss was made.

INHERITANCE TAX

Inheritance tax (IHT) is a tax on the value of a person's estate on death and on certain gifts made by an individual during his or her lifetime, usually payable within six months of death. Broadly speaking, a person's estate is everything he or she owned at the time of death, including property, possessions, money and investments, less his or her debts. Not everyone pays IHT. It only applies if the taxable value of an estate is above the current IHT threshold. If an estate, including any assets held in trust and gifts made within seven years of death, is less than the threshold (ie in the nil rate band), no IHT will be due.

A claim can be made to transfer any unused IHT nil-rate band on a person's death to the estate of their surviving spouse or civil partner. This applies where the IHT nil-rate band of the first deceased spouse or civil partner was not fully used in calculating the IHT liability of their estate. When the surviving spouse or civil partner dies, the unused amount may be added to their own nil-rate band (*see* below for details).

IHT used to be something only very wealthy individuals needed to consider. This is no longer the case. The fact that the IHT threshold has not kept pace with house price inflation in recent years means that the estates of some 'ordinary' taxpayers are now liable for IHT purely because of the value of their home. However, there are a number of ways that individuals – while still alive – can legally reduce the IHT bill that will apply to their estates on death. Several valuable IHT exemptions are (explained further below) which allow individuals to pass on assets during their lifetime or in their will without any IHT being due. Detailed information on IHT is available at W www.gov.uk/inheritance-tax. Further help is also available from the probate and inheritance tax helpline (T 0300-123 1072).

DOMICILE

Liability to IHT depends on an individual's domicile at the time of any gift or on death. Domicile is a complex legal concept and what follows explains some of the main issues. An individual is domiciled in the country where he or she has a permanent home. Domicile is different from nationality or residence, and an individual can only have one domicile at any given time.

A 'domicile of origin' is normally acquired from the individual's father on birth, though this may not be the country in which he or she is born. For example, a child born in Germany while his or her father is working there, but whose permanent home is in the UK, will have the UK as his or her domicile of origin. Until a person legally changes his or her domicile, it will be the same as that of the person on whom they are legally dependent.

Individuals can legally acquire a new domicile – a 'domicile of choice' – from the age of 16 by leaving the current country of domicile and settling in another country and providing strong evidence of intention to live there permanently or indefinitely. Women who were married before 1974 acquired their husband's domicile and still retain it until they legally acquire a new domicile.

For IHT purposes, there is a concept of 'deemed domicile'. This means that even if a person is not domiciled in the UK under general law, he or she is treated as domiciled in the UK at the time of a transfer (ie at the time of a lifetime gift or on death) if he or she was:

- domiciled in the UK at any time in the three years immediately before the transfer, or
- 'resident' in the UK in at least 17 of the 20 income tax years of assessment ending with the year in which a transfer is made

Where a person is domiciled, or treated as domiciled, in the UK at the time of a gift or on death, the location of assets is immaterial and full liability to IHT arises. A non-UK domiciled individual is also liable to IHT but only on chargeable property in the UK.

In 2015 the government announced a major reform to non-domicile taxation under which non-UK domiciled individuals (non-doms) would be deemed UK domiciled for all tax purposes after they have been resident for 15 out of the past 20 tax years; individuals who were born in the UK and who have a UK domicile of origin would revert to their UK domiciled status for tax purposes while resident in the UK; and IHT would be charged on all UK residential property indirectly held through an offshore structure. These provisions, intended to come into effect from April 2017, were dropped from the Finance bill enacted in April 2017 because a General Election was called. Further details can be found at W www.gov.uk/government/consultations/reforms-to-the-taxation-of-non-domiciles.

The assets of spouses and registered civil partners are not merged for IHT purposes, except that the IHT value of assets owned by one spouse or civil partner may be affected if the other also owns similar assets (eg shares in the same company or a share in their jointly owned house). Each spouse or partner is treated as a separate individual entitled to receive the benefit of his or her exemptions, reliefs and rates of tax.

IHT EXEMPTIONS

There are some important exemptions that allow individuals to legally pass assets on to others, both before and after their death – without being subject to IHT.

Exempt Beneficiaries

Assets can be given away to certain people and organisations without any IHT having to be paid. These gifts, which are exempt whether individuals make them during their lifetime or in their will, include gifts to:

- a spouse or civil partner, even if the couple is legally separated (but not if they are divorced or the civil partnership has been dissolved). Note that gifts to an unmarried partner or a partner with whom the donor has not formed a civil partnership are not exempt
- a 'qualifying' charity established in the EU or another specified country
- some national institutions, including national museums, universities and the National Trust
- UK political parties

Annual Exemption

The first £3,000 of gifts made each tax year by each individual is exempt from IHT. If this exemption is not used, or not wholly used in any year, the balance may be carried forward to the following year only. A couple, therefore, may give away a total of £6,000 per tax year between them or £12,000 if they have not used their previous year's annual exemptions.

Wedding Gifts/Civil Partnership Ceremony Gifts

Some gifts are exempt from IHT because of the type of gift or reason for making it. Wedding or civil partnership ceremony gifts made to either of the couple are exempt from IHT up to certain amounts:

- gifts by a parent or step-parent, £5,000
- gifts by a grandparent or great-grandparent, £2,500
- gifts by anyone else, £1,000

The gift must be made on or shortly before the date of the wedding or civil partnership ceremony. If the ceremony is called off but the gift is made, this exemption will not apply.

Small Gifts

An individual can make small gifts, up to the value of £250, to any number of people in any one tax year without them being liable for IHT. However, a larger sum such as £500 cannot be given and exemption claimed for the first £250. In addition, this exemption cannot be used with any other exemption when giving to the same person. For example, a parent cannot combine a 'small gifts exemption' with a 'wedding/civil partnership ceremony gift exemption' to give a child £5,250 when he or she gets married or forms a civil partnership. Neither may an individual combine a 'small gifts exemption' with the 'annual exemption' to give someone £3,250. Note that it is possible to use the 'annual exemption' with any other exemption, such as the 'wedding/civil partnership ceremony gift exemption'. For example, if a child marries or forms a civil partnership, the parent can give him or her a total IHT-free gift of £8,000 by combining £5,000 under the wedding/civil partnership gift exemption and £3,000 under the annual exemption.

Normal Expenditure

Any gifts made out of an individual's after-tax income (not capital) are exempt from IHT if they are part of their normal expenditure and do not result in a fall in their standard of living. These can include regular payments to someone, such as an allowance or gifts for Christmas or a birthday, and regular premiums paid on a life insurance policy for someone else.

Maintenance Gifts

An individual can make IHT-free maintenance payments to his or her spouse or registered civil partner, ex-spouse or former civil partner, relatives dependent because of old age or infirmity, and children (including adopted children and step-children) who are under 18 or in full-time education.

POTENTIALLY EXEMPT TRANSFERS

If an individual makes a gift to either another individual or certain types of trust and it is not covered by one of the above exemptions, it is known as a 'potentially exempt transfer' (PET). A PET is only free of IHT on two strict conditions:

- the gift must be made at least seven years before the donor's death; if the donor does not survive seven years after making the gift, it will be liable for IHT
- the gift must be made as a true gift with no strings attached (technically known as a 'gift with reservation of benefit'). This means that the donor must give up all rights to the gift and stop benefiting from it in any way

If a gift is made and the donor does retain some benefit from it, then it will still count as part of his or her estate no matter how long he or she lives after making it. For example, a father could make a lifetime gift of his home to his child. However, HMRC would not accept this as a true gift if the father continued to live in the home (unless he paid his child a full commercial rent to do so) because he would be considered to still have a material interest in the gifted home. Its value, therefore, would still be liable for IHT.

In some circumstances a gift with strings attached might give rise to an income tax charge on the donor based on the value of the benefit he or she retains. In this case the donor can choose whether to pay the income tax or have the gift treated as a gift with reservation.

CHARGEABLE TRANSFERS

Any remaining lifetime gifts that are not (potentially or otherwise) exempt transfers are chargeable transfers or 'chargeable gifts', meaning that they incur liability to IHT. Chargeable transfers comprise mainly gifts to or from companies and gifts to particular types of trust. There is an immediate claim for IHT on chargeable gifts, and additional tax may be payable if the donor dies within seven years of making a chargeable gift.

DEATH

Immediately before the time of death an individual is deemed to make a transfer of value. This transfer will comprise the value of assets forming part of the deceased's estate after subtracting most liabilities. Any exempt transfers may be excluded, such as transfers for the benefit of a surviving spouse or civil partner and charities. Death may also trigger three additional liabilities:

- a PET made within the seven years before the death loses its potential status and becomes chargeable to IHT
- the value of gifts made with reservation may incur liability if any benefit was enjoyed within the seven years before the death
- additional tax may become payable for chargeable lifetime transfers made within the seven years before the death

The 'personal representative' (the person nominated to handle the affairs of the deceased person) arranges to value the estate and pay any IHT that is due. One or more personal representatives can be nominated in a person's will, in which case they are known as the 'executors'. If a person dies without leaving a will a court can nominate the personal representative, who is then known as the 'administrator'. Valuing the deceased person's estate is one of the first things his or her personal representative needs to do. The representative will not normally be able to take over management of the estate (called 'applying for probate') until all or some of any IHT that is due has been paid.

VALUATIONS

When valuing a deceased person's estate, all assets (property, possessions and money) owned at the time of death and certain assets given away during the seven years before death must be included. The valuation must accurately reflect what those assets would reasonably fetch in the open market at the date of death. The value of all of the assets that the deceased owned should include:

- his or her share of any assets owned jointly with someone else, for example a house owned with a partner
- any assets that are held in a trust, from which the deceased had the right to benefit
- any assets given away, but in which he or she kept an interest (gifts with reservation)
- PETs given away within the last seven years

Most estate assets can be valued quite easily, for example money in bank accounts or stocks and shares. In other instances the help of a professional valuer may be needed. Advice on how to value different assets, including joint or trust assets, is available at W www.gov.uk/valuing-estate-of-someone-who-died.

When valuing an estate, special relief is made available for certain assets. The two main reliefs are agricultural property relief and business relief, outlined below. Once all assets have been valued, the next step is to deduct from the total assets everything that the deceased person owed, such as unpaid bills, outstanding mortgages and other loans plus their funeral expenses.

The value of all of the assets, less the deductible debts, is their estate. IHT is only payable on any value above the threshold for the tax year. It is payable at the current rate of 40 per cent; for the estate of someone who has died since 6 April 2012, this rate is reduced to 36 per cent where 10 per cent or more of a net estate (after deducting IHT exemptions, reliefs and the nil-rate band) is left to charity.

RELIEF FOR SELECTED ASSETS

Agricultural Property

If an individual owns agricultural property and it is part of a working farm, it is possible to pass on some of this property free of IHT, either during that individual's lifetime or on their death. Agricultural property generally includes land or pasture used in the growing of crops or intensive rearing of animals for food consumption. It can also include farmhouses and farm cottages. The agricultural property can be owner-occupied or let. Relief is only due if the transferor has owned the property and it has been occupied for agricultural purposes for a minimum period.

The chargeable value transferred, either in a lifetime gift or on death, must be determined. This value may then be reduced by a percentage. Depending on the type of property, it will normally qualify for relief of 100 per cent.

Business Relief

Business relief is available on transfers of certain types of business and of business assets if they qualify as relevant business property and the transferor has owned them for a minimum period. The relief can be claimed for transfers made during the person's lifetime or on their death. Where the chargeable value transferred is attributable to relevant business property, the business relief reduces that value by a percentage of either 50 or 100 per cent, depending on the type of asset. Business relief may be claimed on relevant business property, including property and buildings or assets such as unlisted shares or machinery.

It is a general requirement that the property must have been retained for a period of two years before the transfer or death, and restrictions may be necessary if the property has not been used wholly for business purposes. The same property cannot obtain both business property relief and the relief available for agricultural property.

CALCULATION OF TAX PAYABLE

The calculation of IHT payable adopts the use of a cumulative or 'running' total. Each chargeable lifetime transfer is added to the total if it was made within seven years of the donor's death. To the running total this produces is added the total value of the estate at death. If the total exceeds the inheritance tax threshold (the 'nil-rate band') IHT becomes payable. The rate of tax that is paid is determined by the element that causes the estate to exceed the threshold; gifts use up all or part of the nil-rate band first.

Lifetime Chargeable Transfers

The value transferred by total chargeable transfers during the deceased's lifetime must be added to the seven-year running total to calculate whether any IHT is due. If the nil-rate band is exceeded, tax will be imposed on the excess at the rate of 20 per cent. However, if the donor dies within a period of seven years from the date of the chargeable lifetime transfer, additional tax may be due. This is calculated by applying tax at the full rate of 40 per cent (rather than 20 per cent). The amount of tax is then reduced by applying taper relief, which is percentage of the full rate of 40 per cent. This percentage is governed by the number of years from the date of the lifetime gift to the date of death, as follows:

TAPER RELIEF

Years between transfer and death	Taper relief %
More than 3 but not more than 4	20%
More than 4 but not more than 5	40%
More than 5 but not more than 6	60%
More than 6 but not more than 7	80%

Should this exercise produce liability greater than that previously paid at the 20 per cent rate on the lifetime transfer, additional tax, representing the difference, must be paid. Where the calculation shows an amount falling below tax paid on the lifetime transfer, no additional liability can arise nor will the shortfall become repayable.

Taper relief is only available if the calculation discloses a liability to IHT. There is no liability if the lifetime transfer falls within the nil-rate band.

Potentially Exempt Transfers

Where a PET loses immunity from liability to IHT because the donor dies within seven years of making the transfer, the value transferred enters into the running total. Any liability to IHT will be calculated by applying the full rate of 40 per cent, reduced to the percentage governed by taper relief if the original transfer occurred more than three years before death. Again, liability to IHT can only arise if the nil-rate band is exceeded.

Death

On death, IHT is due on the value of the deceased's estate plus the running total of gifts made in the seven years before death if they come to more than the nil-rate band. IHT is then charged at the full rate of 40 per cent on the amount in excess of the nil-rate band.

Settled Property and Trusts

Trusts are special legal arrangements that can be used by individuals to control how their assets are distributed to their beneficiaries and minimise their IHT liability. Complex rules apply to establish IHT liability on 'settled property' which includes property held in trust, and individuals are advised to take expert legal advice when setting up trusts.

RATES OF TAX

There are four rates:

- a nil rate
- a lifetime rate of 20 per cent
- a full rate of 40 per cent
- a reduced rate of 36 per cent applicable to taxable estates where 10 per cent of the net estate has been left to charity (see above)

The basic nil-rate band threshold is £325,000 for 2017–18. In 2015 the government announced that the nil-rate band would remain at this figure until April 2021. Any excess over this level is taxable at 20 per cent, 40 per cent or 36 per cent as the case may be.

ADDITIONAL THRESHOLD (RNRB)

The additional threshold (or residence nil-rate band) was introduced from April 2017, applying where a residence the deceased owns and has lived in passes on their death to direct descendants. The additional threshold is £100,000 in 2017–18, £125,000 in 2018–19, £150,000 in 2019–20 and £175,000 in 2020–21. It will increase in line with the consumer prices index (CPI) from 2021–22 onwards. Any unused nil-rate band may be transferred to the surviving spouse or civil partner.

The RNRB will also be available when an individual downsizes or ceases to own a home and other assets of an equivalent value are passed on death to direct descendants. These changes apply for deaths on or after 6 April 2017 where the deceased downsized or disposed of a property after 7 July 2015.

There will be a tapered withdrawal of the RNRB for estates with a net value of more than £2m. This will be at a rate of £1 for every £2 over the additional threshold. Guidance on the additional threshold can be found at W www.gov.uk/guidance/inheritance-tax-residence-nil-rate-band.

TRANSFER OF NIL-RATE BAND

Transfers of property between spouses or civil partners are generally exempt from IHT. This means that someone who dies leaving some or all of their property to their spouse or civil partner may not have fully used up their nil-rate band. Under rules introduced in autumn 2007, any nil-rate band unused on the first death can be used when the surviving spouse or civil partner dies. A transfer of unused nil-rate band from a deceased spouse or civil partner (no matter what the date of their death) may be made to the estate of their surviving spouse or civil partner.

Where a valid claim to transfer unused nil-rate band is made, the nil-rate band that is available when the surviving spouse or civil partner dies is increased by the proportion of the nil-rate band unused on the first death. For example, if on the first death the chargeable estate is £150,000 and the nil-rate band is £300,000, 50 per cent of the nil-rate band would be unused. If the nil-rate band when the survivor dies is £329,000, then that would be increased by 50 per cent to £493,500. The amount of the nil-rate band that can be transferred does not depend on the value of the first spouse or civil partner's estate. Whatever proportion of the nil-rate band is unused on the first death is available for transfer to the survivor.

The amount of additional nil-rate band that can be accumulated by any one surviving spouse or civil partner is limited to the value of the nil-rate band in force at the time of their death. This may be relevant where a person dies having survived more than one spouse or civil partner.

Where these rules have effect, personal representatives do not have to claim for the unused nil-rate band to be transferred at the time of the first death. Any claims for transfer of unused nil-rate band amounts are made by the personal representatives of the estate of the second spouse or civil partner to die when they make an IHT return.

Guidance on how to transfer the nil-rate band can be found at W www.gov.uk/inheritance-tax

PAYMENT OF TAX

IHT is normally due six months after the end of the month in which the death occurs or the chargeable transaction takes place. This is referred to as the 'due date'. Tax on some assets, such as business property, certain shares and securities and land and buildings (including the deceased person's home), can be deferred and paid in equal instalments over ten years, though interest will be charged in most cases. If IHT is due on lifetime gifts and transfers, the person or transferee who received the gift or assets is normally liable to pay the IHT, though any IHT already paid at the time of a transfer into a trust or company will be taken into account. If tax owed is not paid by the due date, interest is charged on any unpaid IHT, no matter what caused the delay in payment.

HMRC is developing an online service to support the administration of IHT. This does away with the need to complete paper forms and enables individuals to proceed with their application for probate and submit IHT accounts online. A beta version of the online service was available from the end of March 2017.

CORPORATION TAX

Corporation tax is a tax on a company's profits, including all its income and gains. This tax is payable by UK resident companies and by non-resident companies carrying on a trade in the UK through a permanent establishment. The following comments are confined to companies resident in the UK. The word 'company' is also used to include:

- members' clubs, societies and associations
- trade associations
- housing associations
- groups of individuals carrying on a business but not as a partnership (for example, cooperatives)

A company's taxable income is charged by reference to income or gains arising in its 'accounting period', which is normally 12 months long. In some circumstances accounting periods can be shorter than 12 months, but never longer. The accounting period is also normally the period for which a company's accounts are drawn up, but the two periods do not have to coincide.

If a company is liable to pay corporation tax on its profits, several things must be done. HMRC must be informed that the company exists and is liable for tax. A self-assessment company tax return plus full accounts and calculation of tax liability must be filed by the statutory filing date, normally 12 months after the end of the accounting period. Companies have to work out their own tax liability and have to pay their tax without prior assessment by HMRC. Records of all company expenditure and income must be kept in order to work out the tax liability correctly. Companies are liable to penalties if they fail to carry out these obligations.

A radically simpler way for small self-employed businesses, such as sole traders and partnerships, to calculate their tax was introduced with effect from the 2013–14 tax year. Such businesses with receipts of £150,000 or less are able to work out their income on a cash basis and use simplified expenses rules, rather than having to follow the rules for larger businesses. Limited companies and limited liability partnerships can not use cash basis. If a small business uses cash basis accounting and the business grows during the tax year, it can stay in the scheme up to a total business turnover of £300,000 a year.

Corporation tax information is available at W www.gov.uk/browse/business/business-tax and companies may file their company tax returns online (W www.gov.uk/file-your-company-accounts-and-tax-return).

RATE OF TAX

The rate of corporation tax is fixed for a financial year starting on 1 April and ending on the following 31 March. If a company's accounting period does not coincide with the financial year, its profits must be apportioned between the financial years and the tax rates for each financial year applied to those profits. The corporation tax liability is the total tax for both financial years.

For many years before 2015–16, corporation tax rates were based on three thresholds. Small companies with taxable profits up to £300,000 were taxed at the small profits rate, companies with taxable profits between £300,001 and £1,500,000 were taxed at the marginal rate and companies with taxable profits over £1,500,000 were taxed at the main rate of corporation tax.

From 1 April 2015, the main rate of corporation tax was reduced to 20 per cent, thereby unifying the small profits rate and the main rate, eliminating marginal relief and giving UK companies a single 20 per cent rate of corporation tax. Following the 2016 Budget announcement that the corporation tax rate would be reduced by 1 per cent in 2017 and again in 2020, the rate became 19 per cent from 1 April 2017.

ALLOWANCES AND RELIEFS

Businesses can claim tax allowances, called capital allowances, on certain purchases or investments. This means that a proportion of these costs can be deducted from a business' taxable profits and reduce its tax bill. Capital allowances are currently available on plant and machinery such as equipment and business vehicles. Reliefs are also available for research and development and on profits from patented inventions and certain creative industries. The amount of the allowance or relief depends on what is being claimed for.

Detailed information on allowances and reliefs is available at W www.gov.uk/corporation-tax-rates/allowances-and-reliefs

PAYMENT OF TAX

Corporation tax liabilities are normally due and payable in a single lump sum not later than nine months and one day after the end of the accounting period. For 'large' companies – those with profits over £1.5m – there is a requirement to pay corporation tax in four quarterly instalments. Where a company is a member of a group, the profits of the entire group must be merged to establish whether the company is 'large'.

HMRC runs a Business Payment Support Service (BPSS) which allows businesses facing temporary financial difficulties more time to pay their tax bills. Traders concerned about their ability to meet corporation tax, VAT or other payments owed to HMRC can call the BPSS Line (T 0300-200 3835) seven days a week. This helpline is for new enquiries only, not for traders who have already been contacted by HMRC about an overdue payment. For details of the service, visit W www.gov.uk/government/organisations/hm-revenue-customs/contact/business-payment-support-service

CAPITAL GAINS

Chargeable gains arising to a company are calculated in a manner similar to that used for individuals. However, companies are not entitled to the CGT annual exemption. Companies do not suffer CGT on chargeable gains but incur liability to corporation tax instead. Tax is due on the full chargeable gain of an accounting period after subtracting relief for any losses.

GROUPS OF COMPANIES

Each company within a group is separately charged corporation tax on profits, gains and income. However, where one group member realises a loss for which special rules apply, other than a capital loss, a claim may be made to offset the deficiency against profits of some other member of the same group. The transfer of capital assets from one member of a group to a fellow member will usually incur no liability to tax on chargeable gains.

SPORTS CLUBS

Though corporation tax is payable by unincorporated associations, including most sports clubs, on their profits, a substantial exemption from liability to corporation tax is available to qualifying registered community amateur sports clubs (CASCs). Sports clubs that are registered as CASCs are exempt from liability to corporation tax on:

- profits from trading where the turnover of the trade is less than £50,000 in a 12-month period
- income from letting property where the gross rental income is less than £30,000 in a 12-month period

- bank and building society interest received
- chargeable gains
- any Gift Aid donations

All of the exemptions depend upon the club having been a registered CASC for the whole of the relevant accounting period and the income or gains being used only for qualifying purposes. If the club has only been a registered CASC for part of an accounting period the exemption amounts of £50,000 (for trading) and £30,000 (for income from property) are reduced proportionately. Only interest and gains received after the club is registered are exempted. Some of the rules for CASCs changed on 1 April 2015. Full details can be found at W www.gov.uk/government/publications/community-amateur-sports-clubs-detailed-guidance-notes

Charities are also generally exempt from corporation tax where they operate through a company structure.

VALUE ADDED TAX

Value added tax (VAT) is a tax on consumer expenditure charged when an individual buys goods and services in the European Union, including the UK. It is normally included in the sale price of goods and services and paid at the point of purchase. Each EU country has its own rate of VAT. From a business point of view, VAT is charged on most business transactions involving the supply of goods and services by a registered trader in the UK and Isle of Man. It is also charged on goods and some services imported from places outside the EU and on goods and some services coming into the UK from the other EU countries. VAT is administered by HMRC. A wide range of information on VAT, including VAT forms, is available online (W www.gov.uk/topic/business-tax/vat). HMRC also runs a VAT enquiries helpline (T 0300-200 3700).

RATES OF TAX

There are three rates of VAT in the UK. The standard rate, payable on most goods and services in the UK, is 20 per cent.

The reduced rate – currently 5 per cent – is payable on certain goods and services, including, for example, domestic fuel and power, children's car seats, women's sanitary products, smoking cessation products and the installation of energy-saving materials such as wall insulation and solar panels.

A zero, or nil, rate applies to certain items, including, for example, children's clothes, books, newspapers, most food and drink, and drugs and aids for disabled people. There are numerous exceptions to the zero-rated categories, however. While most food and drink is zero-rated, items such as ice creams, chocolates, sweets, potato crisps and alcoholic drinks are not. Neither are drinks or items sold for consumption in a restaurant or cafe. Takeaway cold items such as sandwiches are zero-rated, while takeaway hot foods like fish and chips are not.

REGISTRATION

All traders, including professional persons and companies, must register for VAT if they are making 'taxable supplies' of a value exceeding stated limits. All goods and services that are VAT-rated are defined as 'taxable supplies', including zero-rated items, which must be included when calculating the total value of a trader's taxable supplies – his or her 'taxable turnover'. The limits that govern mandatory registration are amended periodically.

An unregistered trader must register for VAT if:

- at the end of any month the total value of his or her taxable turnover (not just profit) for the past 12 months or less is more than the current VAT threshold of £85,000

and

- at any time he or she has reasonable grounds to expect that his or her taxable turnover will be more than the current registration threshold of £85,000 in the next 30 days alone

To register for VAT, one or more forms must be completed and sent to HMRC within 30 days of any of the above. Basic VAT registration can currently be completed online (W www.gov.uk/vat-registration/how-to-register). Traders who do not register at the correct time can be fined. Traders must charge VAT on their taxable supplies from the date they first need to be registered. Traders who only supply zero-rated goods may not have to register for VAT even if their taxable turnover goes above the registration threshold. However, a trader in this position must inform HMRC first and apply to be 'exempt from registration'. A trader whose taxable turnover does not reach the mandatory registration limit may choose to register for VAT voluntarily if what he or she does counts as a business for VAT purposes. This step may be thought advisable to recover input tax (*see* below) or to compete with other registered traders. Registered traders may submit an application for deregistration if their taxable turnover subsequently falls. An application for deregistration can be made if the taxable turnover for the 12 months beginning on the application date is not expected to exceed £83,000.

INPUT TAX

Registered traders suffer input tax when buying in goods or services for the purposes of their business. It is the VAT that traders pay out to their suppliers on goods and services coming *in* to their business. Relief can usually be obtained for input tax suffered, either by setting that tax against output tax due or by repayment. Most items of input tax can be relieved in this manner. Where a registered trader makes both exempt supplies and taxable supplies to his customers or clients, there may be some restriction in the amount of input tax that can be recovered.

OUTPUT TAX

When making a taxable supply of goods or services, registered traders must account for output tax, if any, on the value of that supply. Output tax is the term used to describe the VAT on the goods and services that they supply or sell – the VAT on supplies going *out* of the business and collected from customers on each sale made. Usually the price charged by the registered trader will be increased by adding VAT, but failure to make the required addition will not remove liability to account for output tax. The liability to account for output tax, and also relief for input tax, may be affected where a trader is using a special secondhand goods scheme.

EXEMPT SUPPLIES

VAT is not chargeable on certain goods and services because the law deems them 'exempt' from VAT. These include the provision of burial and cremation facilities, insurance, loans of money, certain types of education and training and some property transactions. The granting of a lease to occupy land or the sale of land will usually comprise an exempt supply, for example, but there are numerous exceptions. Exempt supplies do not enter into the calculation of taxable turnover that governs liability to mandatory registration (*see* above). Such supplies made by a registered trader may, however, limit the amount of input tax that can be relieved. It is for this reason that the exemption may be useful.

COLLECTION OF TAX

Registered traders submit VAT returns for accounting periods usually of three months in duration, but arrangements can be made to submit returns on a monthly basis. Very large traders – those whose annual VAT liability exceeds £2.3m – must make payments on account on a monthly basis, with the three-monthly return used to determine the balancing payment. The return will show both the output tax due for supplies made by the trader in the accounting period and also the input tax for which relief is claimed. If the output tax exceeds input tax the balance must be remitted with the VAT return. Where input tax suffered exceeds the output tax due, the registered trader may claim the excess from HMRC.

This basis for collecting tax explains the structure of VAT. Where supplies are made between registered traders the supplier will account for an amount of tax that will usually be identical to the tax recovered by the person to whom the supply is made. However, where the supply is made to a person who is not a registered trader there can be no recovery of input tax and it is on this person that the final burden of VAT eventually falls. Where goods are acquired by a UK trader from a supplier within the EU, the trader must also account for the tax due on acquisition. There are a number of simplified arrangements to make VAT accounting easier for businesses, particularly small businesses, and there is advice on the HMRC website about how to choose the most appropriate scheme for a business:

Cash Accounting Scheme
This scheme allows businesses to only pay VAT on the basis of payments received from their customers rather than on invoice dates or time of supply. It can therefore be useful for businesses with cash flow problems that cannot pay their VAT as a result. Businesses may use the cash accounting scheme if estimated taxable turnover is £1.35m or less for the next 12 months. There is no need to apply for the scheme – eligible businesses may start using it at the beginning of a new tax period. If a trader opts to use this scheme, he or she can do so until the taxable turnover reaches £1.6m.

Annual Accounting Scheme
If estimated taxable turnover is £1.35m or less in the next 12 months, the trader may join the annual accounting scheme which allows them to make nine monthly or three quarterly instalments during the year based on an estimate of their total annual VAT bill. At the end of the year they submit a single return and any balance due. The advantages of this scheme for businesses are easier budgeting and cash flow planning because fixed payments are spread regularly throughout the year. Once a trader has joined the annual accounting scheme, membership may continue until the annual taxable turnover reaches £1.6m.

Flat Rate Scheme
This scheme allows small businesses with an annual taxable turnover of £150,000 or less to save on administration by paying VAT as a set flat percentage of their annual turnover instead of accounting internally for VAT on each individual 'in and out'. The percentage rate used is governed by the trade sector into which the business falls. The scheme can no longer be used once annual income exceeds £230,000.

Retail Schemes
There are special schemes that offer retailers an alternative if it is impractical for them to issue invoices for a large number of supplies direct to the public. These schemes include a provision to claim relief from VAT on bad debts where goods or services are supplied to a customer who does not pay for them.

VAT FACT SUMMARY *from 1 April 2017*

Standard rate	20%
Reduced rate	5%
Registration (last 12 months or next 30 days)	over £85,000
Deregistration (next 12 months)	under £83,000
Cash accounting scheme	up to £1,350,000
Annual accounting scheme	up to £1,350,000
Flat rate scheme	up to £150,000

STAMP DUTY

Stamp duty is payable by the buyer as a way of raising revenue for the government based on the purchase price of a property, stocks and shares. For the majority of people, contact with stamp duty arises when they buy a property. This section aims to provide a broad overview of stamp duty as it may affect the average person.

STAMP DUTY LAND TAX

Stamp duty land tax (SDLT) was introduced on 1 December 2003 and covers the purchase of houses, flats and other land, buildings and certain leases in the UK.

Before 1 December 2003 property purchasers had to submit documents providing all details of the purchase to the Stamp Office for 'stamping'. The purchaser's solicitor or licensed conveyancer would then send the stamped documentation to the appropriate land registry to register ownership of the property. Under stamp duty land tax, purchasers do not have to send documents for stamping. Instead, a land transaction return form, SDLT1, which contains all information regarding the purchase that is relevant to HMRC, is signed by the purchaser. Buyers of property are responsible for completing the land transaction return and payment of stamp duty, though the solicitor or licensed conveyancer acting for them in a land transaction will normally complete the relevant paperwork. Once HMRC has received the completed land transaction return and the payment of any stamp duty due, a certificate, SDLT5, will be issued that enables a solicitor or licensed conveyancer to register the property in the new owner's name at the land registry.

The threshold for notification of residential property is currently £40,000. This means that taxpayers entering into a transaction involving residential or non-residential property where the chargeable consideration is less than £40,000 do not need to notify HMRC about the transaction.

Since 1 April 2015 stamp duty has no longer applied to land transactions in Scotland. These are now subject to land and buildings transaction tax, details of which can be found online (W www.gov.uk/sdlt-scottish-transactions).

RATES OF STAMP DUTY LAND TAX

Stamp duty is charged at different rates and has thresholds for different types of property and different values of transaction. The tax rate and payment threshold can vary according to whether the property is in residential or non-residential use and whether it is freehold or leasehold.

Stamp duty on purchases of residential property is charged at increasing rates for each portion of the price.

STAMP DUTY ON RESIDENTIAL PROPERTY PURCHASES 2017–18

Portion of the transaction value	Stamp duty is charged at
Up to £125,000	zero
Between £125,001 and £250,000	2 per cent
Between £250,001 and £925,000	5 per cent
Between £925,001 and £1,500,000	10 per cent
Over £1,500,000	12 per cent

For example, on a property bought for £275,000, a total of £3,750 is payable in stamp duty. This is made up of: nothing on the first £125,000, £2,500 (2 per cent) on the next £125,000, and £1,250 (5 per cent) on the remaining £25,000.

Since 1 April 2016, higher rates of stamp duty may be applied to purchases of additional residential properties such as second homes and buy-to-let properties. The higher rates are 3 per cent above the standard rates of stamp duty. They do not apply to purchases of property under £40,000 or purchases of caravans, mobile homes and houseboats.

HIGHER RATE STAMP DUTY ON ADDITIONAL RESIDENTIAL PROPERTY PURCHASES 2017–18

Portion of the transaction value	Stamp duty is charged at
Up to £125,000	3 per cent
Between £125,001 and £250,000	5 per cent
Between £250,001 and £925,000	8 per cent
Between £925,001 and £1,500,000	13 per cent
Over £1,500,000	15 per cent

Each of these higher rates again applies to the portion of the consideration that falls within each rate band. For example, on a buy-to-let property bought for £300,000, a total of £14,000 is payable in higher rate stamp duty. This is made up of: £3,750 (3 per cent) on the first £125,000, £6,250 (5 per cent) on the next £125,000, and £4,000 (8 per cent) on the remaining £50,000.

A new way of calculating stamp duty payable on purchases of non-residential and mixed-use properties was introduced for all transactions completed on or after 17 March 2016. Previously, stamp duty was charged at a single rate on the entire purchase price of the property. Since 17 March 2016, the stamp duty on purchases of non-residential and mixed-use property has been charged at increasing rates for each portion of the price (in the same way that it is charged on purchases of residential property).

STAMP DUTY ON NON-RESIDENTIAL AND MIXED USE PROPERTY PURCHASES 2017–18

Portion of the transaction value	Stamp duty is charged at
Up to £150,000	zero
Between £150,001 and £250,000	2 per cent
Over £250,001	5 per cent

To work out the amount of stamp duty payable on residential or non-residential property, a stamp duty land tax calculator is available online (W www.tax.service.gov.uk/calculate-stamp-duty-land-tax/#/intro).

STAMP DUTY RESERVE TAX

Stamp duty or stamp duty reserve tax (SDRT) is payable at the rate of 0.5 per cent when shares are purchased. Stamp duty is payable when the shares are transferred using a stock transfer form, whereas SDRT is payable on 'paperless' share transactions where the shares are transferred electronically without using a stock transfer form. Most share transactions nowadays are paperless and settled by stockbrokers through CREST (the electronic settlement and registration system). SDRT therefore now accounts for the majority of taxation collected on share transactions effected through the London Stock Exchange.

The flat rate of 0.5 per cent is based on the amount paid for the shares, not what they are worth. If, for example, shares are bought for £2,000, £10 SDRT is payable, whatever the value of the shares themselves. If shares are transferred for free, no SDRT is payable.

A higher rate of 1.5 per cent is payable where shares are transferred into a 'depositary receipt scheme' or a 'clearance service'. These are special arrangements where the shares are held by a third party.

CREST automatically deducts the SDRT and sends it to HMRC. A stockbroker will settle up with CREST for the cost of the shares and the SDRT and then bill the purchaser for these and the broker's fees. If shares are not purchased through CREST, the stamp duty must be paid by the purchaser to HMRC.

UK stamp duty or SDRT is not payable on the purchase of foreign shares, though there may be foreign taxes to pay. SDRT is already accounted for in the price paid for units in unit trusts or shares in open-ended investment companies.

HELP AND INFORMATION

Further information on stamp duty land tax and SDRT is available via the stamp taxes helpline on T 0300-200 3510 or the government information website (W www.gov.uk/topic/business-tax).

LEGAL NOTES

These notes outline certain aspects of the law as they might affect the average person. They are intended only as a broad guideline and are by no means definitive. The law is constantly changing so expert advice should always be taken. In some cases, sources of further information are given in these notes.

It is always advisable to consult a solicitor without delay. Anyone who does not have a solicitor can contact the following for assistance in finding one: Citizens Advice (W www.citizensadvice.org.uk), the Community Legal Service (W www.gov.uk) or the Law Society of England and Wales. For assistance in Scotland, contact Citizens Advice Scotland (W www.cas.org.uk) or the Law Society of Scotland.

Legal aid schemes exist to make the help of a lawyer available to those who would not otherwise be able to afford one. Entitlement for most types of legal aid depends on an individual's means but a solicitor or Citizens Advice will be able to advise on this.

LAW SOCIETY OF ENGLAND AND WALES, 113 Chancery Lane, London WC2A 1PL **T** 020-7242 1222
  W www.lawsociety.org.uk

LAW SOCIETY OF SCOTLAND, Atria One, 144 Morrison Street, Edinburgh EH8 8EX **T** 0131-226 7411
  W www.lawscot.org.uk

ABORTION

Abortion is governed by the Abortion Act 1967. Under its provisions, a legally induced abortion must be:
- performed by a registered medical practitioner
- carried out in an NHS hospital or other approved premises
- certified by two registered medical practitioners as justified on one or more of the following grounds:
1. that the pregnancy has not exceeded its 24th week and that the continuance of the pregnancy would involve risk, greater than if the pregnancy were terminated, of injury to the physical or mental health of the pregnant woman or any existing children of her family
2. that the termination is necessary to prevent grave permanent injury to the physical or mental health of the pregnant woman
3. that the continuance of the pregnancy would involve risk to the life of the pregnant woman, greater than if the pregnancy were terminated
4. that there is a substantial risk that if the child were born it would suffer from such physical or mental abnormalities as to be seriously handicapped.

In determining whether the continuance of a pregnancy would involve such risk of injury to health as is mentioned in grounds (1) or (2), account may be taken of the pregnant woman's actual or reasonably foreseeable environment.

The requirements relating to the opinion of two registered medical practitioners and to the performance of the abortion at an NHS hospital or other approved place cease to apply in circumstances where a registered medical practitioner is of the opinion, formed in good faith, that a termination is immediately necessary to save the life, or to prevent grave permanent injury to the physical or mental health, of the pregnant woman.

The Abortion Act 1967 does not apply to Northern Ireland, where abortion is not legal.

FAMILY PLANNING ASSOCIATION (UK), 23–28 Penn Street, London N1 5DL **T** 020-7608 5240
  W www.fpa.org.uk

BRITISH PREGNANCY ADVISORY SERVICE (BPAS), 20 Timothys Bridge Road, Stratford-upon-Avon CV37 9BF
  T 0345-365 5050 **W** www.bpas.org

ADOPTION OF CHILDREN

The Adoption and Children Act 2002 reformed the framework for domestic and intercountry adoption in England and Wales and some parts of it extend to Scotland and Northern Ireland. The Children and Adoption Act 2006, recently amended by the Children and Families Act 2014, introduced further provisions for adoptions involving a foreign element.

WHO MAY APPLY FOR AN ADOPTION ORDER
A couple (whether married or two people living as partners in an enduring family relationship) may apply for an adoption order where both of them are over 21 or where one is only 18 but the natural parent and the other is 21. An adoption order may be made for one applicant where that person is 21 and: a) the court is satisfied that person is the partner of a parent of the person to be adopted; or b) they are not married and are not civil partners; or c) married or in a civil partnership but they are separated from their spouse or civil partner and living apart with the separation likely to be permanent; or d) their spouse/civil partner is either unable to be found, or their spouse/civil partner is incapable by reason of ill-health of making an application. There are certain qualifying conditions an applicant must meet, eg residency in the British Isles.

ARRANGING AN ADOPTION
Adoptions may generally only be arranged by an adoption agency or by way of an order from the high court; breach of the restrictions on who may arrange an adoption would constitute a criminal offence. When deciding whether a child should be placed for adoption, the court or adoption agency must consider all the factors set out in the 'welfare checklist' – the paramount consideration being the child's welfare, throughout his or her life. These factors include the child's wishes, needs, age, sex, background and any harm which the child has suffered or is likely to suffer. At all times, the court or adoption agency must bear in mind that delay is likely to prejudice a child's welfare.

ADOPTION ORDER
Once an adoption has been arranged, a court order is necessary to make it legal; this may be obtained from the high court, county court or magistrates' court (including the family proceedings court). An adoption order may not be given unless the court is satisfied that the consent of the child's natural parents (or guardians) has been given correctly. Consent can be dispensed with on two grounds: where the parent or guardian cannot be found or is incapable of giving consent, or where the welfare of the child so demands.

An adoption order extinguishes the parental responsibility that a person other than the adopters (or adopter) has for the child. Where an order is made on the application of the partner of the parent, that parent keeps parental responsibility. Once adopted, the child has the same status as a child born to the adoptive parents, but may lose rights to the estates of those losing their parental responsibility.

REGISTRATION AND CERTIFICATES
All adoption orders made in England and Wales are required to be registered in the Adopted Children Register which also contains particulars of children adopted under registrable foreign adoptions. The General Register Office keeps this register from which certificates may be obtained in a similar way to birth certificates. The General Register Office also has equivalents in Scotland and Northern Ireland.

TRACING NATURAL PARENTS OR CHILDREN WHO HAVE BEEN ADOPTED

An adult adopted person may apply to the Registrar-General to obtain a certified copy of his/her birth certificate. Adoption agencies and adoption support agencies should provide services to adopted persons to assist them in obtaining information about their adoption and facilitate contact with their relatives. There is an Adoption Contact Register which provides a safe and confidential way for birth parents and other relatives to assure an adopted person that contact would be welcome. CoramBAAF (*see* below) can provide addresses of organisations which offer advice, information and counselling to adopted people, adoptive parents and people who have had their children adopted.

CORAMBAAF ADOPTION AND FOSTERING

ACADEMY, 41 Brunswick Square, London WC1N 1AF
T 020-7421 2600
W www.corambaaf.org.uk

SCOTLAND

The relevant legislation is the Adoption and Children (Scotland) Act 2007 which came into force on 28 September 2009. In addition, adoptions with a foreign element are governed by the Adoptions with a Foreign Element (Scotland) Regulations 2009. Pre-2009 adoptions are governed by Part IV of the Adoption (Scotland) Act 1978. The provisions of the 2007 act are similar to those described above. In Scotland, petitions for adoption are made to the sheriff court or the court of session.

ADOPTION AND FOSTERING ALLIANCE SCOTLAND,

Conference House, The Exchange, 152 Morrison Street, Edinburgh EH3 8EB **T** 0131-248 2403

BIRTHS (REGISTRATION)

It is the duty of the parents of a child born in England or Wales to register the birth within 42 days of the date of birth at the register office in the district in which the baby was born. If it is inconvenient to go to the district where the birth took place, the information for the registration may be given to a registrar in another district, who will send your details to the appropriate register office. Failure to register the birth within 42 days without reasonable cause may leave the parents liable to a penalty. If a birth has not been registered within 12 months of its occurrence it is possible for the late registration of the birth to be authorised by the Registrar-General, provided documentary evidence of the precise date and place of birth are satisfactory.

Births that take place in England may only be registered in English, but births that take place in Wales may be registered bilingually in Welsh and English. In order to do this, the details must be given in Welsh and the registrar must be able to understand and write in Welsh.

If the parents of the child were married to each other at the time of the birth (or conception), either the mother or the father may register the birth alone. If the parents were not married to each other at the time of the child's birth (or conception), the father's particulars may be entered in the register only where he attends the register office with the mother and they sign the birth register together. Where an unmarried parent is unable to attend the register office, either parent may submit to the registrar a statutory declaration of acknowledgement of parentage (this form may be obtained from any registrar in England or Wales or online at **W** www.gro.gov.uk); alternatively a parental responsibility agreement or appropriate court order may be produced to the registrar.

If the father's details are not included in the birth register, it may be possible to re-register the birth at a later date. If the parents do not register the birth of their child the following people may do so:

- an occupier of the house or an administrative member of staff of the hospital where the child was born
- a person who was present at the birth
- a person who is responsible for the child

Upon registration of the birth a short certificate is issued for free. It may be possible to register the birth while still at hospital. Hospitals will advise individually whether this is possible.

SAME-SEX COUPLES

Male couples must get a parental order from the court before they can be registered as parents. Female couples can include both of their names on the child's birth certificate when registering the birth; however the rules differ depending on whether or not they are in a civil partnership.

In the case of female civil partners, either woman can register the birth on her own if all of the following are true:

- the mother had the child by donor insemination or fertility treatment
- she was married or in a civil partnership at the time of the treatment
- her civil partner is the child's legal parent

When a mother is not in a civil partnership, her partner can be seen as the child's second parent if both women:

- were treated together in the UK by a licensed clinic
- have made a 'parenthood agreement'

However, for both parents' details to be recorded on the birth certificate, the parents must do one of the following:

- register the birth jointly
- complete a 'statutory declaration of acknowledgement of parentage' form and one parent takes the signed form when she registers the birth
- get a document from the court (eg a court order) giving the second female parent parental responsibility and one parent shows the document when she registers the birth

BIRTHS ABROAD

There are certain countries where birth registrations may be made for British citizens overseas (for more details on British citizenship *see* below). The British consul or high commission may register the births and issue certificates which are then sent to the General Register Office. If a birth is registered by the British consul or high commission, the registration would show the person's claim to British citizenship, British overseas territories citizenship or British overseas citizenship. All consular birth registrations are now performed at the Foreign and Commonwealth Office's facility.

SCOTLAND

In Scotland the birth of a child must be registered within 21 days at the registration office of any registration district in Scotland.

If the child is born, either in or out of Scotland, on a ship, aircraft or land vehicle that ends its journey at any place in Scotland, the child, in most cases, will be registered as if born in that place.

CERTIFICATES OF BIRTHS, DEATHS OR MARRIAGES

Certificates of births, marriages and deaths that have taken place in England and Wales since 1837 can be obtained from the General Register Office (GRO).

Marriage or death certificates may also be obtained from the minister of the church in which the marriage or funeral took place. Any register office can advise about the best way to obtain certificates.

The fees for certificates are:

Online application:

- full certificate of birth, marriage, death or adoption, £9.25
- full certificate of birth, marriage, death or adoption with GRO reference supplied, £9.25

By postal/phone/fax application:

- full certificate of birth, marriage, death or adoption, £9.25
- full certificate of birth, marriage, death or adoption with GRO reference supplied, £9.25
- extra copies of the same birth, marriage or death certificate issued at the same time, £9.25

A priority service is available for a fee of £23.40.

A complete set of the GRO indexes including births, deaths and marriages, civil partnerships, adoptions and provisional indexes for births and deaths are available at the British Library, City of Westminster Archives Centre, Manchester Central Library, Newcastle City Library, Library of Birmingham, Bridgend Reference and Information Library and Plymouth Central Library. Copies of GRO indexes may also be held at some libraries, family history societies, local records offices and The Church of Jesus Christ of Latter Day Saints family history centres. Some organisations may not hold a complete record of indexes and a small fee may be charged by some of them. GRO indexes are also available online.

The Society of Genealogists has many records of baptisms, marriages and deaths prior to 1837.

SCOTLAND

Certificates of births, deaths or marriages that have taken place in Scotland since 1855 can be obtained from the National Records of Scotland (formerly the General Register Office for Scotland) or from the appropriate local registrar.

Applicable fees – local registrar:

- each extract or abbreviated certificate of birth, death, marriage, civil partnership or adoption within a month of registration, £10.00
- each extract or abbreviated certificate of birth, death, marriage, civil partnership or adoption outwith a month of registration, £15.00

A priority service is available for an additional fee.

The National Records of Scotland also keeps the Register of Divorces (including decrees of declaration of nullity of marriage), and holds parish registers dating from before 1855.

Applicable fees – National Records of Scotland:

- personal application, or postal, telephone or fax order: £15.00

A priority service for a response within 24 hours is available for an additional fee of £15.00.

A search of birth, death and marriage records including records of Church of Scotland parishes and other statutory records can be done at the Scotland's People Centre. There are also indexes to some of the old parish registers death and burial records in the library at the centre and indexes and images of census records from 1841–1911 are available. The charges for such searches are as follows:

- full or part-day search pass, £15.00
- quarterly search pass, £490.00
- annual search pass, £1,450.00

Online searching is also available. For more information, visit W www.scotlandspeople.gov.uk

THE GENERAL REGISTER OFFICE, General Register Office, Certificate Services Section, PO Box 2, Southport PR8 2JD
T 0300-123 1837
W www.gro.gov.uk/gro/content/certificates

THE NATIONAL RECORDS OF SCOTLAND, New Register House, 3 West Register Street, Edinburgh EH1 3YT
T 0131-334 0380 W www.nrscotland.gov.uk

SCOTLAND'S PEOPLE CENTRE, General Register House, 2 Princes Street, Edinburgh EH1 3YY T 0131-314 4300
W www.scotlandspeoplehub.gov.uk

THE SOCIETY OF GENEALOGISTS, 14 Charterhouse Buildings, Goswell Road, London EC1M 7BA T 020-7251 8799
W www.sog.org.uk

BRITISH NATIONALITY

There are different types of British nationality status: British citizenship; British overseas citizenship; British national (overseas); British overseas territories citizenship; British protected persons; and British subjects. The most widely held of these is British citizenship. Everyone born in the UK before 1 January 1983 became a British citizen when the British Nationality Act 1981 came into force, with the exception of children born to certain diplomatic staff working in the UK at the time. Individuals born outside the UK before 1 January 1983 but who at that date were citizens of the UK and colonies and had a right of abode in the UK also became British citizens. British citizens have the right to live permanently in the UK and are free to leave and re-enter the UK at any time.

A person born on or after 1 January 1983 in the UK (including, for this purpose, the Channel Islands and the Isle of Man) is entitled to British citizenship if he/she falls into one of the following categories:

- he/she has a parent who is a British citizen
- he/she has a parent who is settled in the UK
- he/she is a newborn infant found abandoned in the UK
- his/her parents subsequently settle in the UK or become British citizens and an application is made before he/she is 18
- he/she lives in the UK for the first ten years of his/her life and is not absent for more than 90 days in each of those years
- he/she is adopted in the UK and one of the adopters is a British citizen
- the home secretary consents to his/her registration while he/she is a minor
- if he/she has always been stateless and lives in the UK for a period of five years before his/her 22nd birthday
- if he/she has been born on or after 13 January 2010 to a parent who is a member of the UK armed forces
- if he/she has been born on or after 13 January 2010 and a parent becomes a member of the UK armed forces, and an application is made before he/she is 18

A person born outside the UK may acquire British citizenship if he/she falls into one of the following categories:

- he/she has a parent who is a British citizen otherwise than by descent, eg a parent who was born in the UK
- he/she has a parent who is a British citizen serving the crown or a European community institution overseas and was recruited to that service in the UK (including qualifying territories for those born on or after 21 May 2002) or in the European Community (for services within an EU institution); or if the applicant himself/herself has at any time been in crown, or similar, service under the government of a British overseas territory
- if he/she has been born on or after 13 January 2010 to a parent who is a member of the UK armed forces serving outside the UK and qualifying territories, is of good character and (if he/she is a minor at the time of application) all parents then alive consent in signed writing
- the home secretary consents to his/her registration while he/she is a minor
- he/she is a British overseas territories citizen, a British overseas citizen, a British subject or a British protected person and has been lawfully resident in the UK for five years
- he/she is a British overseas territories citizen who acquired that citizenship from a connection with Gibraltar
- he/she is adopted or naturalised

Where parents are married, the status of either may confer citizenship on their child. Since July 2006, both parents are able to pass on nationality even if they are not married, provided that there is satisfactory evidence of paternity. For children born before July 2006, it must be shown that there is parental consent and that the child would have an automatic claim to citizenship or entitlement to registration had the parents been married. Where parents are not married, the status of the mother determines the child's citizenship.

Under the 1981 act, Commonwealth citizens and citizens of the Republic of Ireland were entitled to registration as British citizens before 1 January 1983. In 1983, citizens of the Falkland Islands were granted British citizenship.

Renunciation of British citizenship must be registered with the home secretary and will be revoked if no new citizenship or nationality is acquired within six months. If the renunciation was required in order to retain or acquire another citizenship or nationality, the citizenship may be reacquired only once. If the renunciation was for another reason, the home secretary may allow reacquisition more than once, depending on the circumstances. The secretary of state may deprive a person of a citizenship status if he or she is satisfied that the person has done anything seriously prejudicial to the vital interests of the UK, or a British overseas territory, unless making the order would have the effect of rendering such a person stateless. A person may also be deprived of a citizenship status which results from his registration or naturalisation if the secretary of state is satisfied that the registration or naturalisation was obtained by fraud, false representation or concealment of a material fact.

BRITISH DEPENDENT TERRITORIES CITIZENSHIP

Since 26 February 2002, this category of nationality no longer exists and has been replaced by British overseas territory citizenship.

If a person had this class of nationality only by reason of a connection to the territory of Hong Kong, they lost it automatically when Hong Kong was returned to the People's Republic of China. However, if after 30 June 1997, they had no other nationality and would have become stateless, or were born after 30 June 1997 and would have been born stateless (but had a parent who was a British national (overseas) or a British overseas citizen), they became a British overseas citizen.

BRITISH OVERSEAS CITIZENSHIP

Under the 1981 act, as amended by the British Overseas Territories Act 2002, this type of citizenship was conferred on any UK and colonies citizens who did not become either a British citizen or a British overseas territories citizen on 1 January 1983 and as such is now, for most purposes, only acquired by persons who would otherwise be stateless.

BRITISH OVERSEAS TERRITORIES CITIZENSHIP

This category of nationality replaced British dependent territories citizenship. Most commonly, this form of nationality is acquired where, after 31 December 1982, a person was a citizen of the UK and colonies and did not become a British citizen, and that person, and their parents or grandparents, were born, registered or naturalised in the specified British overseas territory. However, on 21 May 2002, people became British citizens if they had British overseas territories citizenship by connection with any British overseas territory, except for the sovereign base areas of Akrotiri and Dhekelia in Cyprus.

RESIDUAL CATEGORIES

British subjects, British protected persons and British nationals (overseas) may be entitled to registration as British citizens on completion of five years' legal residence in the UK.

Citizens of the Republic of Ireland who were also British subjects before 1 January 1949 can retain that status if they fulfil certain conditions.

EUROPEAN UNION CITIZENSHIP

British citizens (including Gibraltarians who are registered for this purpose) are also EU citizens and are entitled to travel freely to other EU countries to work, study, reside and set up a business. EU citizens have the same rights with respect to the UK. At the time of writing, it is not known whether the UK's decision to withdraw from the EU will affect these rights.

NATURALISATION

Naturalisation is granted at the discretion of the home secretary. The basic requirements are lawful residence in the UK in the five years immediately preceding application (three years if the applicant is married to, or is the civil partner of a British citizen), good character, adequate knowledge of the English, Welsh or Scottish Gaelic language, passing the UK citizenship test and an intention to reside permanently in the UK.

STATUS OF ALIENS

Aliens, being persons without any of the above forms of British nationality, may not hold public office or vote in Britain and they may not own a British ship or aircraft. Citizens of the Republic of Ireland and Commonwealth citizens are not deemed to be aliens. Certain provisions of the Immigration and Asylum Act 1999 make provision about immigration and asylum and about procedures in connection with marriage by superintendent registrar's certificate.

CONSUMER LAW

SALE OF GOODS

The law in this area is enacted to protect buyers who deal as 'consumers' (where the seller is selling in the course of a business, the goods are of a type ordinarily bought for private use and the goods are purchased by a buyer who is not a business buyer).

A sale of goods contract is the most common type of contract. These are governed by the Consumer Rights Act 2015 (CRA), which was designed to modernise and simplify the law in this area by codifying consumer legislation, most notably incorporating the Sale of Goods Act 1979.

The CRA provides protection for buyers by implying terms into every business-to-consumer sale of goods contract. These terms include:

- where the seller sells goods by reference to a description, an implied term that the goods will match that description and, where the sale is by sample and description, it will not be sufficient that the bulk of the goods correspond with the sample if the goods do not also correspond with the description
- an implied term that the goods will be of satisfactory quality ie they meet the standard that a reasonable person would regard as satisfactory, taking into account any description of the goods, the price, and all other relevant circumstances. The quality of the goods includes their state and condition, relevant aspects being whether they are fit for all the purposes for which such goods are commonly supplied, their appearance and finish, freedom from minor defects and their safety and durability. This term will not be implied, however, if a buyer has examined the goods (including in a sale by sample) and should have noticed the defect or if the seller specifically drew the buyer's attention to the defect
- where the consumer makes a specific purpose known to a seller, there will be an implied term that any goods subsequently purchased will be fit for such purpose. It is irrelevant that the goods in question might not usually be sold to fulfil that purpose, unless the consumer does not rely, or it is unreasonable for the consumer to rely, on the seller's judgement
- where goods are sold by sample, implied terms that the bulk of the sample will correspond with the sample in quality, and that the goods are free from any defect rendering them unsatisfactory which would not have been apparent on a reasonable examination of the sample. Equally, where goods have been marketed by way of a model, then those goods must match it, unless the seller has given notice of any differences that might arise
- where goods have digital content included within them, then the goods as a whole will not be deemed to conform to the contract where the digital content is unsatisfactory

Under the CRA, which draws together and slightly amends the pre-existing rules under the Unfair Contract Terms Act 1977 and the Unfair Terms in Consumer Contracts Regulations 1999, these terms can not be excluded from contracts by the seller.

In a sale of secondhand goods by auction (at which individuals have the opportunity of attending the sale in person), a buyer does not deal as a consumer.

HIRE-PURCHASE AGREEMENTS

Terms similar to those implied in contracts of sales of goods are implied into contracts of hire-purchase, under the CRA. The act limits the exclusion of these implied terms as before.

SUPPLY OF GOODS AND SERVICES

Before the CRA, the Supply of Goods and Services Act 1982 regulated other types of contracts (including for services, contracts under which ownership of goods pass and contracts for hire of goods). This act has now also been amalgamated into the CRA. Similar terms to those above are implied into such contracts, however there are additional terms including:

- that the supplier will use reasonable care and skill in carrying out the service
- that the supplier will carry out the service in a reasonable time (unless the time has been agreed)
- that the supplier will make a reasonable charge (unless the charge or mechanism for its calculation has already been agreed)

The CRA act limits the exclusion of these implied terms in a similar manner as before.

DIGITAL CONTENT

The CRA is the first statute to address the sale and supply of digital products, defined as 'data which are produced and supplied in digital form.' The act applies to any digital content which is purchased or that which comes free alongside purchased services or goods. As above, implied terms for quality, fitness for purpose and adherence to description will be imposed on all consumer contracts. However, there is an extra term for contracts for digital content: that the seller has the right to provide such content.

These terms also apply to any future update or modification of the content. Should such future alterations fail to meet these standards, then the breach will be treated as having occurred at the time of supply rather than the point at which it was adapted.

Where digital content causes damage to other digital content or devices, and this could have been prevented where the seller had exercised reasonable skill and care, then that seller will be required to remedy the breach.

UNFAIR TERMS

The CRA has also consolidated the provisions of the Unfair Terms in Consumer Contracts Regulations 1999 that protected consumers against the imposition of unfair consumer contract terms. Where the terms have not been individually negotiated (ie where the terms were drafted in advance so that the consumer was unable to influence those terms), a term will be deemed unfair if it operates to the detriment of the consumer (ie causes a significant imbalance in the parties' rights and obligations arising under the contract). An unfair term does not bind the consumer but the contract may continue to bind the parties if it is capable of existing without the unfair term. The CRA contains a non-exhaustive list of terms that are regarded as potentially unfair. When a term does not fall into such a category, whether it will be regarded as fair or not will depend on many factors, including the nature of the goods or services, the surrounding circumstances (such as the bargaining strength of both parties) and the other terms in the contract.

CONSUMER PROTECTION

The Consumer Protection from Unfair Trading Regulations 2008 (CPRs) replaced much previous consumer protection regulation, including the majority of the Trade Descriptions Act 1968. The CPRs prohibit 31 specific practices, including pyramid schemes. In addition the CPRs prohibit business sellers from making misleading actions and misleading omissions, which cause, or are likely to cause, the average consumer to take a different transactional decision. There is also a general duty not to trade unfairly. The CPRs were amended by the Consumer Protection (Amendment) Regulations 2014, which entered into force on 1 October 2014 and introduced a new direct civil right of redress for consumers against businesses for misleading and aggressive practices, as well as extending the CPRs to cover misleading and aggressive demands for payment.

Under the Consumer Protection Act 1987, producers of goods are liable for any injury, death or damage to any property exceeding £275 caused by a defect in their product (subject to certain defences).

Consumers are also afforded protection under the Consumer Contracts (Information, Cancellation and Additional Charges) Regulations 2013, which came into force on 13 June 2014.

CONSUMER CREDIT

In matters relating to the provision of credit (or the supply of goods on hire or hire-purchase), consumers are also protected by the Consumer Credit Act 1974 (as amended by the Consumer Credit Act 2006). The act was most recently amended by a number of statutory instruments made under the Financial Services and Markets Act 2000. These came into force on 1 April 2014 and represent a major overhaul of the consumer credit regime which was carried out in order to implement the recent EU Consumer Credit Directive. Under the new regime, responsibility for consumer credit regulation has been transferred from the Office of Fair Trading (OFT), which has ceased to exist, to the Financial Conduct Authority (FCA). Previously, a licence issued by the OFT was required in order to conduct a consumer credit, consumer hire or an ancillary credit business, subject to certain exemptions. The requirement to obtain a licence from the OFT has been replaced by the need to obtain authorisation from the FCA to carry out a consumer credit 'regulated' activity, likewise subject to certain exemptions. Provisions of the 1974 Act as amended include:

- in order for a creditor to enforce a regulated agreement, the agreement must comply with certain formalities and must be properly executed. An improperly executed regulated agreement is enforceable only on an order of the court. The debtor must also be given specified information by the creditor or his/her broker or agent during the negotiations which take place before the signing of the agreement. The agreement must also state certain information to ensure that the debtor or hirer is aware of the rights and duties conferred or imposed on him/her and the protection and remedies available to him/her under the act
- the right to withdraw from or cancel some contracts depending on the circumstances. For example, subject to certain exceptions, a borrower may withdraw from a regulated credit agreement within 14 days without giving any reason. The exceptions include agreements for credit exceeding £60,260 and agreements secured on land. The right to withdraw applies only to the credit agreement itself and not to goods or services purchased with it. The borrower must also repay the credit and any interest
- if the debtor is in breach of the agreement, the creditor must serve a default notice before taking any action such as repossessing the goods
- if the agreement is a hire purchase or conditional sale agreement, the creditor cannot repossess the goods without a court order if the debtor has paid one third of the total price of the goods
- in agreements where the relationship between the creditor and the debtor is unfair to the debtor, the court may alter or set aside some of the terms of the agreement

It is intended that the statutory basis of consumer credit regulation, under the 1974 Act, will be replaced by a rules-based approach under the new regime. The FCA will be reviewing the statutory framework over the next few years and will develop rule-based alternatives where possible.

SCOTLAND

The legislation governing the sale and supply of goods applies to Scotland as follows:
- the Consumer Rights Act 2015 (with the exception of chapter three)
- the Sale of Goods Act 1979 applies with some modifications and it has been amended by the Sale and Supply of Goods Act 1994
- the Supply of Goods (Implied Terms) Act 1973 applies
- the Supply of Goods and Services Act 1982 does not extend to Scotland but some of its provisions were introduced by the Sale and Supply of Goods Act 1994
- only Parts II and III of the Unfair Contract Terms Act 1977 apply
- the Trade Descriptions Act 1968 applies with minor modifications
- the Consumer Credit Act 1974 applies
- the Consumer Credit Act 2006 applies
- the Consumer Protection Act 1987 applies
- the General Product Safety Regulations 2005 apply
- the Unfair Terms in Consumer Contracts (Amendment) Regulations 2001 apply
- the Consumer Protection (Distance Selling) Regulations 2000 apply
- the Consumer Protection from Unfair Trading Regulations 2008 apply

PROCEEDINGS AGAINST THE CROWN

Until 1947, proceedings against the Crown were generally possible only by a procedure known as a petition of right, which put the private litigant at a considerable disadvantage. The Crown Proceedings Act 1947 placed the Crown (not the sovereign in his/her private capacity, but as the embodiment of the state) largely in the same position as a private individual and made proceedings in the high court involving the Crown subject to the same rules as any other case. The act did not, however, extinguish or limit the Crown's prerogative or statutory powers, and it continued the immunity of HM ships and aircraft. It also left certain Crown privileges unaffected. The act largely abolished the special procedures which previously applied to civil proceedings by and against the Crown. Civil proceedings may be initiated against the appropriate government department or, if there is doubt regarding which is the appropriate department, against the attorney-general.

In Scotland proceedings against the Crown founded on breach of contract could be taken before the 1947 act and no special procedures applied. The Crown could, however, claim certain special pleas. The 1947 act applies in part to Scotland and brings the practice of the two countries as closely together as the different legal systems permit. As a result of the Scotland Act 1998, actions against government departments should be raised against the Lord Advocate or the advocate-general. Actions should be raised against the Lord Advocate where the department involved administers a devolved matter. Devolved matters include agriculture, education, housing, local government, health and justice. Actions should be raised against the advocate-general where the department is dealing with a reserved matter. Reserved matters include defence, foreign affairs and social security.

DEATHS

WHEN A DEATH OCCURS

If the death (including stillbirth) was expected, the doctor who attended the deceased during their final illness should be contacted. If the death was sudden or unexpected, the family doctor (if known) and police should be contacted. If the cause of death is quite clear, the doctor will provide:

- a medical certificate that shows the cause of death
- a formal notice that states that the doctor has signed the medical certificate and that explains how to get the death registered
- if the death was known to be caused by a natural illness but the doctor wishes to know more about the cause of death, he/she may ask the relatives for permission to carry out a post-mortem examination

In England and Wales a coroner is responsible for investigating deaths occurring:
- when there is no doctor who can issue a medical certificate of cause of death
- no doctor has treated the deceased during his or her last illness or when the doctor attending the patient did not see him or her within 14 days before death, or after death
- the death occurred during an operation or before recovery from the effect of an anaesthetic
- the death was sudden and unexplained or attended by suspicious circumstances
- the death might be due to an industrial injury or disease, or to accident, violence, neglect or abortion
- the death occurred in prison or in police custody

The doctor will write on the formal notice that the death has been referred to the coroner; if the post-mortem shows that death was due to natural causes, the coroner may issue a notification which gives the cause of death so that the death can be registered. If the cause of death was violent or unnatural, is still undetermined after a post-mortem, or took place in prison or police custody, the coroner must hold an inquest. The coroner must hold an inquest in these circumstances even if the death occurred abroad (and the body has been returned to England or Wales).

In Scotland the office of coroner does not exist. The local procurator fiscal inquires into sudden or suspicious deaths. A fatal accident inquiry will be held before the sheriff where the death has resulted from an accident during the course of the employment of the person who has died, or where the person who has died was in legal custody or a child required to be kept or detained in secure accommodation, or where the Lord Advocate deems it in the public interest that an inquiry be held.

REGISTERING A DEATH

In England and Wales the death can be registered at any register office, although if it is registered by the registrar of births and deaths for the district in which it occurred, the necessary documents can be obtained on the same day. A death which occurs in Scotland can be registered in any registration district in Scotland. Information concerning a death can be given before any registrar of births and deaths in England and Wales. The registrar will pass the relevant details to the registrar for the district where the death occurred, who will then register the death.

In England and Wales the death must normally be registered within five days (unless the registrar says this period can be extended); in Scotland within eight days. If the death has been referred to the coroner/local procurator fiscal it cannot be registered until the registrar has received authority from the coroner/local procurator fiscal to do so. Failure to register a death involves a penalty in England and Wales and may lead to a court decree being granted by a sheriff in Scotland. A stillbirth normally needs to be registered within 42 days, and at the latest within three months. In many cases this can be done at the hospital or at the local register office. In Scotland this must be done within 21 days.

If the death occurred at a house or hospital, the death may be registered by:
- any relative of the deceased
- any person present at the death
- the owner or occupier of the house or hospital if he/she knew of the occurrence of the death
- any person making the funeral arrangements with the funeral director

- an administrator from the hospital
- in Scotland, the deceased's executor or legal representative

For deaths that took place elsewhere, the death may be registered by:

- any relative of the deceased
- someone present at the death
- someone who found the body
- a person in charge of the body
- any person making the funeral arrangements with the funeral director

The majority of deaths are registered by a relative of the deceased. The registrar would normally allow one of the other listed persons to register the death only if there were no relatives available.

The person registering the death should take the medical certificate of the cause of death (signed by a doctor) with them; it is also useful, though not essential, to take the deceased's birth and marriage/civil partnership certificates, council tax bill, driving licence, passport, NHS medical card, pension documentation and life assurance details. The details given to the registrar must be absolutely correct, otherwise it may be difficult to change them later. The person registering the death should check the entry carefully before it is signed. The registrar will issue a certificate for burial or cremation, and a certificate of registration of death (commonly known as a 'death certificate' which is issued for social security purposes if the deceased received a state pension or benefits) – both free of charge. A death certificate is a certified copy of the entry in the death register; copies can be provided on payment of a fee and may be required for the following purposes, in particular by the executor or administrator when sorting out the deceased's affairs:

- the will
- bank and building society accounts
- savings bank certificates and premium bonds
- insurance policies
- pension claims

If the death occurred abroad or on a foreign ship or aircraft, the death should be registered according to the local regulations of the relevant country and a death certificate should be obtained. In many countries the death can also be registered with the British consulate in that country and a record will be kept at the General Register Office. This avoids the expense of bringing the body back.

After 12 months (three months in Scotland) of death or the finding of a dead body, no death can be registered without the written authority of the registrar-general.

BURIAL AND CREMATION

In most circumstances in England and Wales a certificate for burial or cremation must be obtained from the registrar before the burial or cremation can take place. If the death has been referred to the coroner, an order for burial or a certificate for cremation must be obtained. In Scotland a death or still birth must be registered in order that the appropriate certificate can be obtained to allow burial or cremation of the body.

Funeral costs can normally be repaid out of the deceased's estate and should be given priority over any other claims. If the deceased has left a will it may contain directions concerning the funeral; however, these directions need not be followed by the executor.

The deceased's papers should also indicate whether a grave space had already been arranged. This information will be contained in a document known as a 'Deed of Grant'. Most town churchyards and many suburban churchyards are no longer open for burial because they are full. Most cemeteries are non-denominational and may be owned by local authorities or private companies; fees vary.

If the body is to be cremated, an application form, two cremation certificates (for which there is a charge) or a certificate for cremation if the death was referred to the coroner, and a certificate signed by the medical referee must be completed in addition to the certificate for burial or cremation (the form is not required if the coroner has issued a certificate for cremation). All the forms are available from the funeral director or crematorium. Most crematoria are run by local authorities; the fees can include the medical referee's fee and the use of the chapel. Ashes may be scattered, buried in a churchyard or cemetery, or kept.

The registrar must be notified of the date, place and means of disposal of the body within 96 hours (England and Wales) or three days (Scotland).

If the death occurred abroad or on a foreign ship or aircraft, a local burial or cremation may be arranged. If the body is to be brought back to England or Wales, a death certificate from the relevant country or an authorisation for the removal of the body from the country of death from the coroner or relevant authority, together with a certificate of embalming, will be required. The British consulate can help to arrange this documentation. To arrange a funeral in England or Wales, an authenticated translation of a foreign death certificate or a death certificate issued in Scotland or Northern Ireland which must show the cause of death, is needed, together with a certificate of no liability to register from the registrar in England and Wales in whose sub-district it is intended to bury or cremate the body. If it is intended to cremate the body, a cremation order will be required from the Home Office or a certificate for cremation. If the body is to be cremated in Scotland, a certificate permitting this must be obtained from the Death Certification Review Service run by Healthcare Improvement Scotland.

THE GENERAL REGISTER OFFICE, General Register Office, PO Box 2, Southport PR8 2JD **T** 0300-123 1837 **W** www.gro.gov.uk/gro/content/certificates

THE NATIONAL RECORDS OF SCOTLAND, New Register House, 3 West Register Street, Edinburgh EH1 3YT **T** 0131-334 0380 **W** www.nrscotland.gov.uk

DIVORCE, DISSOLUTION AND RELATED MATTERS

Divorce is the legal process which ends a marriage. The process is the same whether the parties are of the opposite or same sex pursuant to the Marriage (Same Sex Couples) Act 2013. Dissolution is a similar process which ends a civil partnership. Divorce and dissolution should be distinguished from judicial separation which does not legally dissolve the marriage/civil partnership but removes the legal requirement for a married couple to live together.

DIVORCE

An application for a matrimonial order for divorce may only be presented to the court after one year of marriage and it must be based on matters which occurred within that time. The spouse who lodges this document is known as the 'petitioner' throughout the divorce proceedings and the other spouse is the 'respondent'.

Whether the English court may or may not have jurisdiction to deal with any divorce will depend on where the parties spent their married life and whether or not one party has retained their residence or domicile in England (and Wales). If there is a dispute as to which of two jurisdictions should host the divorce, where the two jurisdictions likely to be relevant are EU countries then the usual rule is that the divorce takes place in the country where the petition is filed first. The exception to this rule is Denmark, which opted out of the EU regulation which determines forums in this way.

If the two countries are not within the EU, or one of them is Denmark, then the forum of divorce may be determined by which is the more appropriate or convenient. An election of a country in a pre-nuptial agreement can be very important in resolving that dispute, although it cannot override the 'first in time' rule between EU countries (except Denmark) referred to above (save in the case of maintenance claims).

Some EU countries have signed up to a convention which would allow a couple to elect a choice of law even in EU countries whereby one country would be required to apply the law of another. For the time being, England has not signed up to that convention and would apply English law only.

There is only one ground for divorce, namely that the marriage has broken down irretrievably. This ground must be 'proved' by one of the following facts:

• the respondent has committed adultery and the petitioner finds it intolerable to live with him/her
• the respondent has behaved in such a way that the petitioner cannot reasonably be expected to live with him/her
• the respondent has deserted the petitioner for a continuous period of at least two years immediately prior to the petition
• the two spouses have lived apart for at least two years immediately prior to the petition and the respondent agrees to a divorce
• the two spouses have lived apart for at least five years immediately prior to the petition

If the court is satisfied that the petitioner has proved one of those facts then it must grant a decree nisi (see below) unless it is satisfied that the marriage has not broken down.

DECREE NISI

If the judge is satisfied that the petitioner has proved the contents of the divorce petition, a date will be set for the pronouncement of the decree nisi in open court. The decree nisi is a preliminary decree of divorce; the marriage will not be legally dissolved until the decree absolute. Neither party needs to attend and all the proceedings up to this point are usually carried out on paper.

DECREE ABSOLUTE

The final step in the divorce procedure is to obtain a decree absolute which formally ends the marriage. The petitioner can apply for this six weeks and one day after the date of the decree nisi. If the petitioner does not apply the respondent can apply, but only after three months from the earliest date on which the petitioner could have applied.

A decree absolute will not usually be granted until the parties have agreed, or the court has dealt with, the parties' financial situation (see below for details of financial provision).

DISSOLUTION OF CIVIL PARTNERSHIPS

The legal process for dissolution of a civil partnership follows a model closely based on divorce. Irretrievable breakdown of the partnership is the sole ground for dissolution. The facts to be proved to establish this are the same as for divorce, with the exception of adultery which, due to its legal definition, can only apply to opposite sex couples. Adultery can, however, be used as an example of unreasonable behaviour.

FINANCIAL RELIEF ANCILLARY TO DIVORCE, NULLITY AND JUDICIAL SEPARATION

Following a petition for divorce, nullity or judicial separation, it is open to either spouse or former spouse to make a claim for financial provision provided they have not remarried. It is common practice for such an application to be made at the same time, or shortly after, a divorce petition has been issued. The courts have wide powers to make financial provision where a marriage breaks down. Orders can be made for:

• spousal maintenance (periodical payments) which can be capitalised into a lump sum
• lump sum payments
• adjustment or transfer of interests in property
• adjustment of interests in trusts and settlements
• orders relating to pensions

EXERCISE OF THE COURT'S POWERS TO ORDER FINANCIAL PROVISION

The court must exercise its powers so as to achieve an outcome which is fair between the parties, although it has a wide discretion in determining what is a fair financial outcome. It will consider the worldwide assets of both parties, whether liquid or illiquid. In exercising its discretion, the court has to consider a range of statutory factors including:

• the income, earning capacity, property and other financial resources which either party has or is likely to have in the foreseeable future, including, in the case of earning capacity, any increase in that capacity which it would in the opinion of the court be reasonable to expect a party to the marriage to take steps to acquire
• the financial needs, obligations and responsibilities which each of the parties to the marriage has or is likely to have in the foreseeable future
• the standard of living enjoyed by the family before the breakdown of the marriage
• the age of each party to the marriage and the duration of the marriage
• any physical or mental disability of either of the parties to the marriage
• the contribution which each of the parties has made or is likely to make in the foreseeable future to the welfare of the family, including any contribution by looking after the home or caring for the family
• the conduct of each of the parties, if that conduct is such that it would in the opinion of the court be inequitable to disregard it
• the value to each of the parties to the marriage of any benefit which, by reason of the dissolution of that marriage, that party will lose the chance of acquiring

When considering the above factors, the court must give first consideration to the welfare of any child of the family.

The court has a wide discretion in considering these factors in order to achieve an outcome it considers to be fair. The court's approach changed dramatically following the House of Lords decision of White v White in October 2000 where it was said that, after providing for the parties' reasonable needs, the remaining assets should be shared.

In the House of Lords cases of Miller and McFarlane the court refined the thinking in the White case to say that the court should strive to achieve a fair result by considering three strands:

• the needs of the parties going forward
• compensation for any economic disparity between the parties (such as where one party has sacrificed their career to become a full-time parent)
• sharing

In October 2010, the supreme court gave judgment in Radmacher v Granatino which made it clear that a person now entering into a pre-nuptial agreement will be considered to have intended to be held to that agreement. However, the court will still be able to decide as to whether the agreement is fair and whether the terms setting out the financial provision on divorce should be enforced in whole or in part. The supreme court gave some guidelines on when a pre-nuptial agreement would be considered 'fair', but ultimately it depends on the facts of the individual case.

The Law Commission's Marital Property, Needs and Agreements Report, published in February 2014, proposed the introduction of 'qualifying nuptial agreements' which would be enforceable contracts allowing couples to make binding agreements concerning the financial consequences of divorce or dissolution. In order for an agreement to qualify, certain procedural safeguards would need to be met. Agreements could not be used by parties to contract out of meeting the financial needs of the other or of any children. The report is currently awaiting the government's response.

FINANCIAL PROVISION ON DISSOLUTION OF A CIVIL PARTNERSHIP

The Civil Partnership Act 2004 makes provisions for financial relief for civil partners generally and extends the same rights and responsibilities invoked by marriage. Again the court must consider a number of factors when exercising its discretion and must take into account all of the circumstances of the case while giving first consideration to the welfare of any child of the family who is under 18. The list of statutory factors the court must consider resemble those for marriage and it is likely that the interpretation of these factors will be based on the courts' interpretation of the factors relating to marriage.

COHABITING COUPLES

There is no such thing as a common law spouse. Unmarried couples do not benefit from the same statutory protection afforded to married couples. Instead, the rights of cohabitees are based on property law and trust interests. Therefore, it is advisable to consider entering into a contract, or 'cohabitation agreement', which establishes how money and property should be divided in the event of a relationship breakdown.

The cohabitation rights bill 2014–15, which sought to introduce certain protections for cohabitees during their lifetime and on death, was introduced in October 2013 but made no progress. It was reintroduced as the cohabitation rights bill 2015–16 (receiving its first reading in the House of Lords on 4 June 2015) and again, in its present form, as the cohabitation rights bill 2016–17 (receiving its first reading in the Lords on 4 June 2016), but has made no further progress. Thus, cohabitation agreements continue to be governed by the same general principles of property, trust, and contract law.

FINANCIAL PROVISION FOR CHILDREN

All parents are under a legal obligation to support their children financially. A parent who does not have day-to-day care of a child is under a duty to pay child maintenance to the parent who does.

Parents can arrange child maintenance themselves or through the Child Maintenance Service (CMS), (formerly the Child Support Agency (CSA)).

There are three different methods of calculating child support under the child maintenance schemes:
• the 'old' scheme (for all applications up until 3 March 2003
• the net income scheme (for applications from 3 March 2003)
• the gross income scheme (for all new applications since 25 November 2013)

By 2017, all child maintenance calculations will be dealt with under the gross income scheme. CMS uses the paying parent's gross annual income from the latest available tax year as a starting point to work out child maintenance with reference to the gross income maximum of £156,000. Once the gross income information is received, the CMS applies a specific formula to work out the level of child maintenance payable.

Under the gross income scheme, it is mandatory for parents to have a conversation with the Child Maintenance Options (CMO) team to discuss their choices and consider alternatives before they proceed with their application. The CMO will discuss the various options available to parents if they cannot agree a so-called 'family-based arrangement' between themselves:
• 'Direct Pay' (known as 'Maintenance Direct' under a CSA arrangement) which enables parents to keep control of making and receiving payments. The statutory service works out the payment amounts for parents but will not be involved in other areas, such as collection and enforcement
• 'Collect and Pay' (known as the 'calculation and collection services' under a CSA arrangement) whereby the CSA or CMS calculates how much maintenance the paying parent owes. If payments are not made on time, a range of enforcement actions can be taken

Within 72 hours of a payment being missed, the CMS will contact the paying parent to seek continuing payments. Where there is persistent non-payment, the CMS is able to take money directly from the paying parent, either from their earnings or bank account, or to take court action.

Provision is also made under Schedule 1 of the Children Act 1989 for unmarried parents to apply to the court for lump sum and property adjustment orders and, in limited circumstances, orders for child maintenance.

SCOTLAND

Although some provisions are similar to those for England and Wales, there is separate legislation for Scotland covering nullity of marriage, judicial separation, divorce and ancillary matters. The principal legislation in relation to family law in Scotland is the Family Law (Scotland) Act 1985. The Family Law (Scotland) Act 2006 came in to force on 4 May 2006, and introduced reforms to various aspects of Scottish family law. The following is confined to major points on which the law in Scotland differs from that of England and Wales.

An action for judicial separation or divorce may be raised in the court of session; it may also be raised in the sheriff court if either party was resident in the sheriffdom for 40 days immediately before the date of the action or for 40 days ending not more than 40 days before the date of the action and has no known residence in Scotland at that date. The fee for starting a divorce petition in the sheriff court is £150.

The grounds for raising an action of divorce in Scotland are set down in The Divorce (Scotland) Act 1976 and have been subject to reform in terms of the 2006 act. The current grounds for divorce are:
• the defender has committed adultery. When adultery is cited as proof that the marriage has broken down irretrievably, it is not necessary in Scotland to prove that it is also intolerable for the pursuer to live with the defender
• the defender's behaviour is such that the pursuer cannot reasonably be expected to cohabit with the defender
• there has been no cohabitation between the parties for one year prior to the raising of the action for divorce, and the defender consents to the granting of decree of divorce
• there has been no cohabitation between the parties for two years prior to the raising of the action for divorce
• the marriage has broken down irretrievably
• an interim gender recognition certificate under the Gender Recognition Act 2004 has, after the date of marriage, been issued to either party to the marriage. However, as a result of changes under the Marriage and Civil Partnership (Scotland) Act 2014, this ground of divorce will sometimes not be available where a full gender recognition certificate has been issued under the 2004 Act

The previously available ground of desertion was abolished by the 2006 Act.

A simplified procedure for 'do-it-yourself divorce' was introduced in 1983 for certain divorces. If the action is based on one or two years' separation and will not be opposed or because a gender recognition certificate has been issued; there are no children under 16; no financial claims; there is no sign that the applicant's spouse is unable to manage his or her affairs through mental illness or handicap; and there are no other court proceedings underway which might result in the end of the marriage, the applicant can access the appropriate forms to enable him or her to proceed on the Scottish Courts and Tribunals' website. From 1 April 2017 the fee is £120, however the applicant may be exempt from paying the fee if they are in receipt of certain benefits; or if legal advice and assistance is being provided by a solicitor in terms of the Legal Aid (Scotland) Act 1986.

Where a divorce action has been raised, it may be put on hold for a variety of reasons. In all actions for divorce an extract decree, which brings the marriage to an end, will be made available 14 days after the divorce has been granted. Unlike in England, there is no decree nisi, only a final decree of divorce. Parties must ensure that all financial issues have been resolved prior to divorce, as it is not possible to seek further financial provision after divorce has been granted.

FINANCIAL PROVISION

In relation to financial provision on divorce, the first, and most important, principle is fair sharing of the matrimonial property. There is a presumption that fair share means an equal share of the matrimonial property, which can be departed from if justified by special circumstances. In terms of Scots law matrimonial property is defined as all property acquired by either spouse from the date of marriage up to the date of separation. Property acquired before the marriage is not deemed to be matrimonial unless it was acquired for use by the parties as a family home or as furniture for that home. Property acquired after the date of separation is not matrimonial property. Any property acquired by either of the parties by way of gift or inheritance during the marriage is excluded and does not form part of the matrimonial property.

When considering whether to make an award of financial provision a court shall also take account of any economic advantage derived by either party to the marriage as a result of contributions, financial or otherwise, by the other, and of any economic disadvantage suffered by either party for the benefit of the other party. The court must also ensure that the economic burden of caring for a child under the age of 16 is shared fairly between the parties.

A court can also consider making an order requiring one party to pay the other party a periodical allowance for a certain period of time following divorce. Such an order may be appropriate in cases where there is insufficient capital to effect a fair sharing of the matrimonial property. Orders for periodical allowance are uncommon, as courts will favour a 'clean break' where possible.

CHILDREN
The court has the power to award a residence order in respect of any children of the marriage or to make an order regulating the child's contact with the non-resident parent. The court will only make such orders if it is deemed better for the child to do so than to make no order at all, and the welfare of the children is of paramount importance. The fact that a spouse has caused the breakdown of the marriage does not in itself preclude him/her from being awarded residence.

NULLITY
An action for 'declaration of nullity' can be brought if someone with a legitimate interest is able to show that the marriage is void or voidable. Although the grounds on which a marriage may be void or voidable are similar to those on which a marriage can be declared invalid in England, there are some differences. Where a spouse is capable of sexual intercourse but refuses to consummate the marriage, this is not a ground for nullity in Scots law, though it could be a ground for divorce. Where a spouse was suffering from venereal disease at the time of marriage and the other spouse did not know, this is not a ground for nullity in Scots law, neither is the fact that a wife was pregnant by another man at the time of marriage without the knowledge of her husband.

COHABITING COUPLES
The law in Scotland now provides certain financial and property rights for cohabiting couples in terms of the Family Law (Scotland) Act 2006, or 'the 2006 Act'. The relevant 2006 Act provisions do not place cohabitants in Scotland on an equal footing with married couples or civil partners, but provide some rights for cohabitants in the event that the relationship is terminated by separation or death. The provisions relate to couples who cease to cohabit after 4 May 2006.

The legislation provides for a presumption that most contents of the home shared by the cohabitants are owned in equal shares. A former cohabitant can also seek financial provision on termination of the relationship in the form of a capital payment if they can successfully demonstrate that they have been financially disadvantaged, and that conversely the other cohabitant has been financially advantaged, as a consequence of contributions made (financial or otherwise). An order can also be made in respect of the economic burden of caring for a child of whom the cohabitants are the parents. Such a claim must be made no later than one year after the day on which the cohabitants cease to cohabit.

The 2006 Act also provides that a cohabitant may make a claim on their partner's estate in the event of that partner's death, providing that there is no will. A claim of this nature must be made no later than six months after the date of the partner's death.

THE CENTRAL FAMILY COURT, First Avenue House, 42–49 High Holborn, London WC1 6NP T 020-7421 8594

THE COURT OF SESSION, Parliament House, Parliament Square, Edinburgh EH1 1RQ T 0131-225 2595 W www.scotcourts.gov.uk

THE CHILD SUPPORT AGENCY, T 0345-713 3133 W www.csa.gov.uk

EMPLOYMENT LAW

EMPLOYEES
A fundamental distinction in UK employment law is that drawn between an employee and someone who is self-employed. Further, there is an important, intermediate category introduced by legislation: 'workers' covers all employees but also catches others who do not have full employment status. An 'employee' is someone who has entered into or works under a contract of employment, while a 'worker' has entered into or works under a contract whereby he undertakes to do or perform personally any work or services for another party whose status is not that of a client or customer. Whether or not someone is an employee or a worker as opposed to being genuinely self-employed is an important and complex question, for it determines that person's statutory rights and protections. For certain purposes, such as protection against discrimination, protection extends to some genuinely self-employed people as well as workers and employees.

The greater the level of control that the employer has over the work carried out, the greater the depth of integration of the employee in the employer's business, and the closer the obligations to provide and perform work between the parties, the more likely it is that the parties will be employer and employee.

PAY AND CONDITIONS
The Employment Rights Act 1996 consolidated the statutory provisions relating to employees' rights. Employers must give each employee employed for one month or more a written statement containing the following information:
- names of employer and employee
- date when employment began and the date on which the employee's period of *continuous* employment began (taking into account any employment with a previous employer which counts towards that period)
- the scale, rate or other method of calculating remuneration and intervals at which it will be paid
- job title or description of job
- hours and the permitted place(s) of work and, where there are several such places, the address of the employer
- holiday entitlement and holiday pay
- provisions concerning incapacity for work due to sickness and injury, including provisions for sick pay
- details of pension scheme(s)
- length of notice the employee is obliged to give and entitled to receive in order to terminate the contract of employment
- if the employment is not intended to be permanent, the period for which it is expected to continue or, if it is for a fixed term, the end date of the contract
- details of any collective agreement (including the parties to the agreement) which directly affects the terms of employment
- details of disciplinary and grievance procedures (including the individual to whom a complaint should be made and the process of making that complaint)
- if the employee is to work outside the UK for more than one month, the period of such work and the currency in which payment is made and any additional remuneration or benefits payable to them

- a note stating whether a contracting-out certificate is in force

This must be given to the employee within two months of the start of their employment.

If the employer does not provide the written statement within two months (or a statement of any changes to these particulars within one month of the changes being made) then the employee can complain to an employment tribunal, which can specify the information that the employer should have given. When, in the context of an employee's successful tribunal claim, the employer is also found to have been in breach of the duty to provide the written statement at the time proceedings were commenced, the tribunal must award the employee two weeks' pay, and may award four weeks' pay, subject to the statutory cap, unless it would be unjust or inequitable to do so.

The Working Time Regulations 1998, the National Minimum Wage Act 1998, Employment Relations Act 1999, the Employment Act 2002 and the Employment Act 2008 now supplement the 1996 act.

FLEXIBLE WORKING

The Flexible Working Regulations 2014 gives all employees, from 30 June 2014, the right to apply for flexible working after working for the same employer for at least 26 weeks. An employer must consider and decide upon a request within three months and must have a sound business reason for rejecting any request. If an application under the act is not dealt with in accordance with a prescribed procedure, or is rejected on other than specific grounds, the employee may complain to an employment tribunal.

SICK PAY

Employees absent from work through illness or injury are entitled to receive Statutory Sick Pay (SSP) from the employer from the fourth day of absence for a maximum period of 28 weeks. The right to SSP will cease where an employee has had linked periods of sickness that have spanned a period of three years.

MATERNITY AND PARENTAL RIGHTS

Under the Employment Relations Act 1999, the Employment Act 2002, the Maternity and Parental Leave Regulations 1999 (as amended in 2002, 2006 and 2014), the Paternity and Adoption Leave Regulations 2002 and 2003, the Additional Paternity Leave Regulations 2010 and the Shared Parental Leave Regulations 2014, both men and women are entitled to take leave when they become a parent (including by adoption). Women are protected from discrimination, detriment or dismissal by reason of their pregnancy or maternity, including discrimination by association and by perception. Men and adoptive parents are protected from suffering a detriment or dismissal for taking paternity, adoption or parental leave.

Any woman who needs to attend an antenatal appointment on the advice of a registered medical professional is entitled to paid leave from work to attend. All pregnant women are entitled to a maximum period of maternity leave of 52 weeks. This comprises 26 weeks' ordinary maternity leave, followed immediately by 26 weeks' additional maternity leave. A woman who takes ordinary maternity leave normally has the right to return to the job in which she was employed before her absence. If she takes additional maternity leave, she is entitled to return to the same job or, if that is not reasonably practicable, to another job that is suitable and appropriate for her to do. There is a two-week period of compulsory maternity leave, immediately following the birth of the child, wherein the employer is not permitted to allow the mother to work.

A woman will qualify for Statutory Maternity Pay (SMP), which is payable for up to 39 weeks, if she has been continuously employed for not less than 26 weeks prior to the 15th week before the expected week of childbirth. For further information see Social Welfare, Employer Payments.

Employees are entitled to adoption leave and adoption pay (at the same rates as SMP) subject to fulfilment of similar criteria to those in relation to maternity leave and pay, but note that there is a 26-week qualifying period for adoption leave. Where

a couple is adopting a child, either one (but not both) of the parents may take adoption leave, and the other may take paternity leave.

Certain employees are entitled to paternity leave on the birth or adoption of a child. To be eligible, the employee must be the child's father, or the partner of the mother or adopter, and meet other conditions. These conditions are, firstly, that they must have been continuously employed for not less than 26 weeks prior to the 15th week before the expected week of childbirth (or, in the case of adoptions, 26 weeks ending with the week in which notification of the adoption match is given) and, secondly, that the employee must have or expect to have responsibility for the upbringing of the child. The employee may take either one week's leave, or two consecutive weeks' leave. This leave may be taken at any time between the date of the child's birth (or placement for adoption) and 56 days later. A statutory payment is available during this period.

For births and adoptions from 3 April 2011 but before 5 April 2015, an eligible employee has been able to take additional paternity leave at the end of the mother's or adopter's leave period provided the child is at least 20 weeks old or was placed for adoption at least 20 weeks previously. The maximum period of leave is 26 weeks and leave cannot extend beyond the child's first birthday.

For births on or after 5 April 2015, eligible parents are entitled to shared parental leave (SPL) whereby they will be able to share a pot of leave of up to 50 weeks and 27 weeks of pay, after the initial two weeks of maternity leave that is compulsory for the mother. During that 50 week period, parents can decide to be off work at the same time and/or take it in turns to have periods of leave to look after their child. To be eligible, the employee must be the child's mother, father, partner of the mother or adopter, and must have worked for the same employer for not less than 26 weeks prior to the 15th week before the expected week of childbirth (or, in case of adoptions, 26 weeks ending with the week in which notification of the adoption match is given). The amount of leave available is calculated using the mother's entitlement to maternity leave. If a mother reduces maternity leave she and/or her partner may opt to take SPL for the remaining weeks. On taking SPL, a woman will be entitled to statutory shared parental pay at the same rate as SMP.

For more information see Social Welfare, Employer Payments.

Any employee with one year's service who has, or expects to have, responsibility for a child may take parental leave to care for the child. Each parent is entitled to a total of 18 weeks parental leave for each child or adopted child. This leave must be taken (at the rate of no more than four weeks a year, and in blocks of whole weeks only) before the child's 18th birthday.

SUNDAY TRADING

The Sunday Trading Act 1994 allows shops to open on Sunday. The Employment Rights Act 1996 gives shop workers and betting workers the right not to be dismissed, selected for redundancy or to suffer any detriment (such as the denial of overtime, promotion or training) if they refuse to work on Sundays. This does not apply to those who, under their contracts, are employed to work on Sundays.

TERMINATION OF EMPLOYMENT

An employee may be dismissed without notice if guilty of gross misconduct but in other cases a period of notice must be given by the employer. The minimum periods of notice specified in the Employment Rights Act 1996 are:

- one week if the employee has been continuously employed for one month or more but for less than two years
- one week for each complete year of continuous employment, if the employee has been employed for two years or more, up to a maximum of 12 weeks' notice
- longer periods apply if these are specified in the contract of employment

If an employee is dismissed with less notice than he/she is entitled to by statute, or under their contract if longer, he/she will have a wrongful dismissal claim (unless the employer paid the employee in lieu of notice in accordance with a contractual provision entitling it to do so). This claim for wrongful dismissal can be brought by the employee either in the civil courts or the employment tribunal, but if brought in the tribunal the maximum amount that can be awarded is £25,000.

REDUNDANCY

An employee dismissed because of redundancy may be entitled to redundancy pay. This applies if:

• the employment commenced before 6 April 2012 and the employee has at least one year's continuous service or the employment commenced on or after 6 April 2012 and the employee has at least two years' continuous service
• the employee is dismissed by the employer by reason of redundancy (this can include cases of voluntary redundancy)

Redundancy can mean closure of the entire business, closure of a particular site of the business, or a reduction in the need for employees to carry out work of a particular kind.

An employee may not be entitled to a redundancy payment if offered a suitable alternative job by the same employer. The amount of statutory redundancy pay depends on the length of service, age, and their earnings, subject to a weekly maximum of (currently) £489. The maximum payment that can be awarded is £14,670. The redundancy payment is guaranteed by the government in cases where the employer becomes insolvent.

UNFAIR DISMISSAL

Complaints of unfair dismissal are dealt with by an employment tribunal. Any employee whose employment commenced before 6 April 2012 with at least one year's continuous service or any employee whose employment commenced on or after 6 April 2012 with at least two year's continuous service (subject to exceptions, including in relation to whistleblowers – see below) can make a complaint to the tribunal. At the tribunal, it is for the employee to show that the employer dismissed them either expressly or constructively and it is for the employer to prove that the dismissal was due to one or more potentially fair reasons: a statutory restriction preventing the continuation of the employee's contract; the employee's capability or qualifications for the job he/she was employed to do; the employee's conduct; redundancy; or some other substantial reason.

If the employer succeeds in showing this, the tribunal must then decide whether the employer acted reasonably in dismissing the employee for that reason. If the employee is found to have been unfairly dismissed, the tribunal can order that he/she be reinstated, re-engaged or compensated. Any person believing that they may have been unfairly dismissed should contact their local Citizens Advice bureau or seek legal advice. A claim must be brought within three months of the date of effective termination of employment.

The normal maximum compensatory award for unfair dismissal is £80,541 (as at April 2017). If the dismissal occurred after 6 April 2009 and the employer unreasonably failed to follow the ACAS Code of Practice on Disciplinary and Grievance Procedures in carrying out the dismissal, the tribunal may increase the employee's compensation by up to 25 per cent.

WHISTLEBLOWING

Under the whistleblowing legislation (Public Interest Disclosure Act 1998, which inserted provisions into the Employment Rights Act 1996) dismissal of an employee is automatically unfair if the reason or principal reason for the dismissal is that the employee has made a protected disclosure. The legislation also makes it unlawful to subject workers (a broad category that includes employees and certain other individuals, such as agency workers) who have made a protected disclosure to any detriment on the ground that they have done so.

For a disclosure to qualify for protection, the claimant must show that he or she has disclosed information, which in his or her reasonable belief tends to show one or more of the following six categories of wrongdoing: criminal offences; breach of any legal obligation; miscarriages of justice; danger to the health and safety of any individual; damage to the environment; or the deliberate concealing of information about any of the other categories. The malpractices can be past, present, prospective or merely alleged.

A qualifying disclosure will only be protected if the manner of the disclosure fulfils certain conditions, which varies according to the type of disclosure. With effect from 25 June 2013, there is no requirement for the disclosure to have been made in 'good faith', although where it appears to the tribunal that the protected disclosure was not made in good faith, the tribunal may reduce any compensatory award it makes by up to 25 per cent if it considers that it is just and equitable to do so in all the circumstances.

Any whistleblower claim in the employment tribunal must normally be brought within three months of the date of dismissal or other act leading to a detriment.

An individual does not need to have been working with the employer for any particular period of time to be able to bring such a claim and compensation is uncapped (and can include an amount for injury to feelings).

DISCRIMINATION

Discrimination in employment on the grounds of sex (including gender reassignment), sexual orientation, being pregnant or on maternity leave, race, colour, nationality, ethnic or national origins, religion or belief, marital or civil partnership status, age or disability is unlawful. Discrimination legislation generally covers direct discrimination, indirect discrimination, harassment and victimisation. Only in limited circumstances can such discrimination be justified (rendering it lawful).

An individual does not need to be employed for any particular period of time to be able to claim discrimination (discrimination can be alleged at the recruitment phase), and discrimination compensation is uncapped (and can include an amount for injury to feelings). These features distinguish the discrimination laws from, for example, the unfair dismissal laws.

The Equality Act 2010 was passed on 8 April 2010 and the main provisions came into force on 1 October 2010. The act unifies several pieces of discrimination legislation, providing one definition of direct discrimination, indirect discrimination, harassment and victimisation. The Equality Act applies to those employed in Great Britain but not to employees in Northern Ireland or (subject to EC exceptions) to those who work mainly abroad, and provides that:

• it is unlawful to discriminate on the grounds of sex, gender reassignment or marital/civil partner status, being pregnant or on maternity leave, including discrimination by association and by perception. This covers all aspects of employment (including advertising for jobs), but there are some limited exceptions, such as where the essential nature of the job requires it to be given to someone of a particular sex, or where decency and privacy requires it. The act entitles men and women to equality of remuneration for equivalent work or work of the same value
• individuals have the right not to be discriminated against on the grounds of race, colour, nationality, or ethnic or national origins and this applies to all aspects of employment. Employers may also take lawful positive action, including in relation to recruitment and promotion
• discrimination against a disabled person in all aspects of employment is unlawful. This includes protecting carers from discrimination by association with the disabled persons that they look after. The act also imposes a duty on employers to make 'reasonable adjustments' to the arrangements and physical features of the workplace if these place disabled people at a substantial disadvantage compared with those who are not disabled. The definition of a 'disabled person' is wide and includes people diagnosed with HIV, cancer and multiple sclerosis

- discrimination against a person on the grounds of religion or belief (or lack of belief) including discrimination by association and by perception, in all aspects of employment, is unlawful
- discrimination against an individual on the grounds of sexual orientation, including discrimination by association and by perception, in all aspects of employment, is unlawful
- age discrimination in the workplace is unlawful, and an employer may no longer dismiss an employee by reason of retirement once they have reached a certain age. However, it is lawful to discriminate because of age in relation to benefits based on length of service, redundancy pay, national minimum wage and insurance benefits.

The responsibility for monitoring equality in society rests with the Equality and Human Rights Commission.

In Northern Ireland similar provisions exist to those that were in force in Great Britain prior to the coming into force of the Equality Act but are contained in separate legislation (although the Disability Discrimination Act does extend to Northern Ireland).

In Northern Ireland there is one combined body working towards equality and eliminating discrimination, the Equality Commission for Northern Ireland.

WORKING TIME

The Working Time Regulations 1998 impose rules that limit working hours and provide for rest breaks and holidays. The regulations apply to workers and so cover not only employees but also other individuals who undertake to perform personally any work or services (eg freelancers). The regulations are complex and subject to various exceptions and qualifications but the basic provisions relating to adult day workers are as follows:

- No worker is permitted to work more than an average of 48 hours per week (unless they have made a genuine voluntary opt-out of this limit – it is not sufficient to make it a term of the contract that the worker opts out), and a worker is entitled to, but is not required to take, the following breaks:
- 11 consecutive hours' uninterrupted rest in every 24-hour period
- an uninterrupted rest period of 24 hours in each 7-day period or 48 hours in each fortnight (in addition to the daily rest period)
- 20 minutes' rest break provided that the working day is longer than 6 hours
- 5.6 weeks' paid annual leave (28 days full-time). This equates to 4 weeks plus public holidays

There are specific provisions relating to night work, young workers (ie those over school leaving age but under 18) and a variety of workers in specialised sectors (such as off-shore oil rig workers).

HUMAN RIGHTS

On 2 October 2000 the Human Rights Act 1998 came into force in the UK. This act incorporates the European Convention on Human Rights into the law of the UK. The main principles of the act are as follows:

- all legislation must be interpreted and given effect by the courts as compatible with the Convention so far as it is possible to do so. Before the second reading of a new bill the minister responsible for the bill must provide a statement regarding its compatibility with the Human Rights Act
- subordinate legislation (eg statutory instruments) which is incompatible with the Convention can be struck down by the courts
- primary legislation (eg an act of parliament) which is incompatible with the Convention cannot be struck down by a court, but the higher courts can make a declaration of incompatibility which is a signal to parliament to change the law
- all public authorities (including courts and tribunals) must not act in a way which is incompatible with the Convention

- individuals whose Convention rights have been infringed by a public authority may bring proceedings against that authority, but the act is not intended to create new rights as between individuals

The main human rights protected by the Convention are the right to life (article 2); protection from torture and inhuman or degrading treatment (article 3); protection from slavery or forced labour (article 4); the right to liberty and security of the person (article 5); the right to a fair trial (article 6); the right not to be subject to retrospective criminal offences (article 7); the right to respect for private and family life (article 8); freedom of thought, conscience and religion (article 9); freedom of expression (article 10); freedom of peaceful association and assembly (article 11); the right to marry and found a family (article 12); protection from discrimination (article 14); the right to protection of property (article 1 protocol No.1); the right to education (article 2 protocol No.1); and the right to free elections (article 3 protocol No.1). Most of the Convention rights are subject to limitations which deem the breach of the right acceptable on the basis it is 'necessary in a democratic society'.

Human rights are also enshrined in the common law (of tort). Although this is of historical significance, the common law (for example the duty of confidentiality) remains especially important regarding violations of human rights that occur between private parties, where the Human Rights Act 1998 does not apply.

PARENTAL RESPONSIBILITY

The Children Act 1989 (as amended by the Children and Families Act 2014) gives both the mother and father parental responsibility for the child if the parents are married to each other at the time of the child's birth. If the parents are not married, only the mother has parental responsibility. The father may acquire it in accordance with the provisions of section 4 of the Children Act 1989. He can do this in one of several ways, including: by being registered as the father on the child's birth certificate with the consent of the mother (only for fathers of children born after 1 December 2003, following changes to the Adoption and Children Act 2002); by applying to the court for a parental responsibility order; by entering into a parental responsibility agreement with the mother which must be in the prescribed form; or by marrying the mother of the child.

Following changes to the Children Act 1989 (introduced by the Children and Families Act 2014), if a court makes a child arrangements order in favour of a father, providing that the child lives with that father, the court must make a parental responsibility order in his favour. If the child arrangements order provides that the child spend time or otherwise have contact with the father, the court must consider whether to make a parental responsibility order (residence orders were replaced by child arrangement orders under the Children and Families Act 2014, but if obtained prior to 22 April 2014 are still valid).

Where a child's parent, who has parental responsibility, marries or enters into a civil partnership with a person who is not the child's parent, the child's parent(s) with parental responsibility can agree for the step-parent to have parental responsibility, or the step-parent may acquire parental responsibility by order of the court (section 4A(1) Children Act 1989).

If a child is born to female civil partners or female same-sex spouses as a result of IVF or AID treatment received after 5 April 2009, both individuals will have parental responsibility for that child. From 1 September 2009 a female, who is not in a civil partnership or same-sex marriage with the mother at the date of the child's birth, but is the child's other parent (under the Human Fertilisation and Embryology Act 2008), can acquire parental responsibility in the same way as set out above in relation to a father. Parental responsibility will also be acquired if the mother and the child's other parent enter into a civil partnership or (from 13 March 2014) a same-sex marriage after the mother's date of birth.

Where the court makes a child arrangements order and a person (who is not the parent or guardian of the child) is named in the order as a person with whom the child is to spend time or otherwise have contact (but not named as a person with whom the child is to live), the court may provide in the order for that person to have parental responsibility for the child.

An adoption order gives parental responsibility for the child to the adopters. It extinguishes parental responsibility that any person had for the child immediately before the making of the order.

In Scotland, the relevant legislation is the Children (Scotland) Act 1995, which gives the mother parental rights and responsibilities for her child whether or not she is married to the child's father. A father who is married to the mother, either at the time of the child's conception or subsequently, will also have automatic parental rights and responsibilities. Section 3 of the 2006 act provides that an unmarried father will obtain automatic parental responsibilities and rights if he is registered as the father on the child's birth certificate. For unmarried fathers who are not named on the birth certificate, or whose children were born before the 2006 act came into force, it is possible to acquire parental responsibilities and rights by applying to the court or by entering into a parental responsibilities and rights agreement with the mother. The father of any child, regardless of parental rights, has a duty to aliment that child until he/she is 18 (or under 25 if the child is still at an educational establishment or training for employment or for a trade, profession or vocation).

LEGITIMATION

Under the Legitimacy Act 1976, an illegitimate person automatically becomes legitimate when his/her parents marry. This applies even where one of the parents was married to a third person at the time of the birth. In such cases it is necessary to re-register the birth of the child. In Scotland, the status of illegitimacy has been abolished by section 21 of the 2006 act. The Law Reform Act 1987 reformed the law so as to remove so far as possible the legal disadvantages of illegitimacy.

JURY SERVICE

In England and Wales, the law concerning juries is largely consolidated in the Juries Act 1974 (as amended by the Criminal Justice and Courts Act 2015). In England and Wales, a person charged with a serious criminal offence is entitled to have their trial heard by a jury in a crown court, except in cases where there is a danger of jury tampering or where jury tampering has taken place.

In civil cases, there is a right to a jury in the Queen's Bench Division of the high court in cases where the person applying for a jury has been accused of fraud, as well as in cases of malicious prosecution or false imprisonment. The same applies to the county court. In all other cases in the Queen's Bench Division only the judge has discretion to order trial with a jury, though such an order is seldom made. In the chancery division of the high court a jury is never used. The same is true in the family division of the high court.

No right to a jury trial exists in Scotland, although more serious offences are heard before a jury. In England and Wales criminal cases and civil cases in the high court are generally heard by a jury of 12 members, but in the county court the jury is smaller, normally consisting of eight members. In the event that a juror is excused the trial can proceed so long as there are at least seven remaining jurors in the county court and nine in the case of the high court or crown court. At an inquest, there must be at least seven and no more than 11 members. In Scotland there are 12 members of a jury in a civil case in the court of session and certain sheriff court cases, and 15 in a criminal trial in the high court of justiciary. Jurors are normally asked to serve for ten working days, during which time they could sit on more than one case. Jurors selected for longer cases are expected to sit for the duration of the trial.

In England and Wales, every 'registered' parliamentary or local government elector between the ages of 18 and 75 who has lived in the UK (including, for this purpose, the Channel Islands and the Isle of Man) for any period of at least five years since reaching the age of 13 is qualified to serve on a jury unless he/she is 'mentally disordered' or disqualified.

Those disqualified from jury service include:

* those who have at any time been sentenced by a court in the UK (including, for this purpose, the Channel Islands and the Isle of Man) to a term of imprisonment or youth custody of five years or more
* those who have within the previous ten years served any part of a sentence of imprisonment, youth custody or detention, been detained in a young offenders' institution, received a suspended sentence of imprisonment or order for detention, or received a community order
* those who are on bail in criminal proceedings
* those who have been convicted of a jury misconduct offence
* those who are liable to be detained, who are under guardianship or who are under a community treatment order under the Mental Health Act 1983 or who are in resident in a hospital on account of mental disorder
* Those who lack capacity, as defined under the Mental Capacity Act 2005, to serve as a juror

The court has the discretion to excuse a juror from service, or defer the date of service, if the juror can show there is good reason why he/she should be excused from attending or good reason why his/her attendance should be deferred. It is an offence (punishable by a fine) to fail to attend when summoned, to serve knowing that you are disqualified from service, or to make false representations in an attempt to evade service. If a juror fails to turn up for service, or attends but cannot serve due to being under the influence of drink or drugs, this is punishable as contempt of court. Any party can object to any juror if he/she can show cause to the trial judge.

It may be appropriate for a judge to excuse a juror from a particular case if he is personally concerned in the facts of the particular case, or closely connected with a party to the proceedings or with a prospective witness. The judge may also discharge any juror who, from a mental or physical incapacity, temporary or permanent, or alternatively due to linguistic difficulties, cannot pay proper attention to the evidence.

An individual juror (or the entire jury) can be discharged if it is shown that they or any of their number have, among other things, separated from the rest of the jury without the leave of the court; talked to any person out of court who is not a member of the jury; determined the verdict of the trial by drawing lots; come to a compromise on the verdict; been drunk, or otherwise incapacitated, while carrying out their duties as a juror; exerted improper pressure on the other members of the jury (eg harassment or bullying); declined to take part in the jury's functions; displayed actual or apparent bias (eg racism, sexism or other discriminatory or deliberate hostility); or inadvertently possessed knowledge of the bad character of a party to the proceedings which has not been adduced as evidence in the proceedings. The factual situations that arise are many, and include falling asleep during the trial, asking friends on Facebook for help in making a decision, consulting an ouija board in the course of deliberations, making telephone calls after retirement, and lunching with a barrister not connected with the proceedings.

The Criminal Justice and Courts Act 2015 has introduced four new offences of juror misconduct with a penalty of up to two years in prison. A juror commits an offence if he: (a) intentionally seeks information during a trial where he knows, or ought to reasonably know, that the information sought is or may be relevant to the case; (b) passes on to another juror information obtained through such research; (c) engages in conduct from which it may reasonably be concluded that he intends to try the issue otherwise than on the basis of the evidence presented in the proceedings on the issue; and (d) discloses information about the jury's deliberations, subject to specified exceptions. A person who has been convicted of one of the above offences within the last ten years will be disqualified from jury duty. A judge now has a discretionary power to order members of a jury to surrender their electronic communication devices for a period of time, and a court security officer is authorised to search a juror for a device that a judge has ordered be surrendered.

In England and Wales, the jury's verdict need not be unanimous. In criminal proceedings, and civil proceedings in the high court, the agreement of ten jurors will suffice when there are not fewer than 11 people on the jury (or nine in a jury of ten). In civil proceedings in the county court the agreement of seven or eight jurors will suffice. Where a majority verdict is given, the court must be satisfied that the jury had reasonable time to consider its verdict based on the nature and complexity of the case. In criminal proceedings this must be no less than two hours and ten minutes (allowing time for the jury to settle after retiring).

A juror is immune from prosecution or civil claim in respect of anything said or done by him or her in the discharge of their office. It is an offence for a juror to disclose what happened in the jury room even after the trial is over. A juror may claim travelling expenses, a subsistence allowance and an allowance for other financial loss (eg loss of earnings or benefits, fees paid to carers or child-minders) up to a stated limit. For more information on jury service, visit W www.gov.uk/jury-service/overview

SCOTLAND

Qualification criteria for jury service in Scotland are similar to those in England and Wales, except that members of the judiciary are ineligible for ten years after ceasing to hold their post, and others concerned with the administration of justice are only eligible for service five years after ceasing to hold office. Certain persons have the right to apply to be excused – full-time members of the medical, dental, nursing, veterinary and pharmaceutical professions, full-time members of the armed forces, ministers of religion, persons who have served on a jury within the previous five years, persons who have attended court to serve on a jury but were not selected by ballot within the previous two years, members of the Scottish parliament, members of the Scottish government, junior Scottish ministers and those aged 71 years or over. Those who are incapable by reason of a mental disorder may also be excused. Such an application will be accepted if the application is made within 7 days of the person being notified that they may have to serve. For civil trials there is an age limit of 65 years. Those convicted of a crime and sentenced to a period of imprisonment of 5 years or more are automatically disqualified. The maximum fine for a person serving on a jury while knowing himself/herself to be ineligible is £1,000. The maximum fine for failing to attend without good cause in criminal trials is also £1,000, however in civil proceedings the maximum fine is £200.

HER MAJESTY'S COURTS AND TRIBUNALS SERVICE, 102 Petty France, London SW1H 9AJ T 0845-456 8770

JURY CENTRAL SUMMONING BUREAU, Freepost LON 19669, Pocock Street, London SE1 0YG T 0845-803 8003 E jurysummoning@hmcts.gsi.gov.uk

SCOTTISH COURTS AND TRIBUNALS SERVICE, Saughton House, Broomhouse Drive, Edinburgh EH11 3XD T 0131-444 3300 W www.scotcourts.gov.uk

THE CLERK OF JUSTICIARY, Parliament House, Parliament Square, Edinburgh EH1 1RQ T 0131-240 6915

LANDLORD AND TENANT

RESIDENTIAL LETTINGS

The provisions outlined here apply only where the tenant lives in a separate dwelling from the landlord and where the dwelling is the tenant's only or main home. It does not apply to licensees such as lodgers, guests or service occupiers.

The 1996 Housing Act radically changed certain aspects of the legislation referred to below; in particular, the grant of assured and assured shorthold tenancies under the Housing Act 1988.

ASSURED SHORTHOLD TENANCIES

If a tenancy was granted on or after 15 January 1989 and before 28 February 1997, the tenant would have an assured tenancy unless the landlord served notice under section 20 in the prescribed form prior to the commencement of the tenancy, stating that the tenancy is to be an assured shorthold tenancy and the tenancy is for a minimum fixed term period of six months (see below). An assured tenancy gives that tenant greater security. The tenant could, for example, stay in possession of the dwelling for as long as the tenant observed the terms of the tenancy. The landlord cannot obtain possession from such a tenant unless the landlord can establish a specific ground for possession (set out in the Housing Act 1988) and obtains a court order. The rent payable is that agreed with the landlord at the start of the tenancy. The landlord has the right to increase the rent annually by serving a notice. If that happens the tenant can apply to have the rent fixed by the rent assessment committee of the local authority. The tenant or the landlord may request that the committee sets the rent in line with open market rents for that type of property.

Under the Housing Act 1996, all new lettings (below an annual rent threshold of £100,000 since October 2010 in England or December 2011 in Wales) entered into on or after 28 February 1997 (for whatever term) will be assured shorthold tenancies unless the landlord serves a notice stating that the tenancy is not to be an assured shorthold tenancy. This means that the landlord is entitled to possession at the end of the tenancy provided he serves a notice under section 21 Housing Act 1988 and commences the proceedings in accordance with the correct procedure. The landlord must obtain a court order, however, to obtain possession if the tenant refuses to vacate at the end of the tenancy. If the tenancy is an assured shorthold tenancy, the court must grant the order.

REGULATED TENANCIES

Before the Housing Act 1988 came into force on 15 January 1989 there were regulated tenancies; some are still in existence and are protected by the Rent Act 1977. Under this act it is possible for the landlord or the tenant to apply to the local rent officer to have a 'fair' rent registered. The fair rent is then the maximum rent payable.

SECURE TENANCIES

Secure tenancies are generally given to tenants of local authorities, housing associations (before 15 January 1989) and certain other bodies. This gives the tenant security of tenure unless the terms of the agreement are broken by the tenant and it is reasonable to make an order for possession. Those with secure tenancies may have the right to buy their property. In practice this right is generally only available to council tenants. However, the Housing and Planning Act 2016 will enable housing associations voluntarily to extend the right to buy. Though the 2016 act is now in force, a roll out of the extended right to buy regime will not take place until the Department for Communities and Local Government publishes guidance, which has been delayed until at least April 2018.

The Prevention of Social Housing Fraud Act came into force in October 2013. It creates criminal offences for unlawful sub-letting by secure and assured tenants of social housing.

AGRICULTURAL PROPERTY

Tenancies in agricultural properties are governed by the Agricultural Holdings Act 1986, the Agricultural Tenancies Act 1995 (both amended by the Regulatory Reform (Agricultural Tenancies) (England and Wales) Order 2006), the Tribunals, Courts and Enforcement Act 2007, the Legal

Services Act 2007 and the Rent (Agriculture) Act 1976, which give similar protections to those described above, eg security of tenure, right to compensation for disturbance, etc. Similar provisions are applied to Scotland by the Agricultural Holdings (Scotland) Act 2003 for those leases entered into on or after 27 November 2003. The Agricultural Holdings (Scotland) Act 1991 continues to apply to those leases in Scotland entered into prior to this date and in certain other circumstances outlined by the 2003 act. However, one distinction to note between the 1991 act and the 2003 act is that those leases governed by the former have full security of tenure, subject to certain exceptions, whereas leases under the 2003 act are fixed term arrangements of various durations.

EVICTION
The Protection from Eviction Act 1977 (as amended by the Housing Act 1988 and Nationality, Immigration and Asylum Act 2002) sets out the procedure a landlord must follow in order to obtain possession of property. It is unlawful for a landlord to evict a tenant otherwise than in accordance with the law. For common law tenancies and for Rent Act tenants a notice to quit in the prescribed form giving 28 days notice is required. For secure and assured tenancies a notice seeking possession must be served. It is unlawful for the landlord to evict a person by putting their belongings on to the street, by changing the locks and so on. It is also unlawful for a landlord to harass a tenant in any way in order to persuade him/her to give up the tenancy. The tenant may be able to obtain an injunction to restrain the actions of the landlord and get back into the property and be awarded damages.

LANDLORD RESPONSIBILITIES
Under the Landlord and Tenant Act 1985, where the term of the lease is less than seven years, the landlord is responsible for maintaining the structure and exterior of the property, for sanitation, for heating and hot water, and all installations for the supply of water, gas and electricity.

While the responsibility of maintaining the premises remains intact, since July 2012 landlords are no longer permitted to enter the rental premises for the purpose of viewing their state and condition. This power of entry was revoked by the Protection of Freedoms Act 2012.

LEASEHOLDERS
Strictly speaking, leaseholders have bought a long lease rather than a property and in certain limited circumstances the landlord can end the tenancy. Under the Leasehold Reform Act 1967 (as amended by the Housing Acts 1969, 1974, 1980 and 1985), leaseholders of houses, as opposed to flats, may have the right to buy the freehold or to take an extended lease for a term of 50 years. This applies to leases where the term of the lease is over 21 years, at a low rent, and where the leaseholder has occupied the house as his/her only or main residence for the last two years, or for a total of two years over the last ten. The tenant must give the landlord written notice of his desire to acquire the freehold or extend the leasehold.

The Leasehold Reform, Housing and Urban Development Act came into force in 1993 and allows the leaseholders of flats in certain circumstances to buy the freehold of the building in which they live. Owners of certain long leases of flats may also have the right to take an extended act of 90 years plus the unexpired residue of their current lease: although technically a grant of a new lease, these are commonly called 'lease extensions'.

Responsibility for maintenance of the structure, exterior and interior of the building should be set out in the lease. Usually the upkeep of the interior of his/her part of the property is the responsibility of the leaseholder, and responsibility for the structure, exterior and common interior areas is shared between the freeholder and the leaseholder(s).

If leaseholders are dissatisfied with charges made in respect of lease extensions, they are entitled to have their situation evaluated by the First-tier Tribunal (Property Chamber).

The Commonhold and Leasehold Reform Act 2002 makes provision for the freehold estate in land to be registered as commonhold land and for the legal interest in the land to be vested in a 'commonhold association', ie a private limited company.

BUSINESS LETTINGS
The Landlord and Tenant Acts 1927 and 1954 (as amended) give security of tenure to the tenants of most business premises. The landlord can only evict the tenant on one of the grounds laid down in the 1954 act, and in some cases where the landlord repossesses the property the tenant may be entitled to compensation. However, it is commonplace for landlords and tenants to agree that these provisions will not apply to their lease, meaning that no security or tenure is granted.

SCOTLAND
In Scotland assured and short assured tenancies exist for residential lettings entered into after 2 January 1989 and are similar to assured shorthold tenancies in England and Wales. The relevant legislation is the Housing (Scotland) Act 1988. However, once the provisions of the Private Housing (Tenancies) (Scotland) Act 2016 come into force, assured and short assured tenancies will be abolished and replaced by a new private rental tenancy which will provide more security for tenants as the current 'no fault ground of repossession' (the equivalent of recovering possession under section 21 of the Housing Act 1988 in England) will be abolished. The act will also introduce a model tenancy agreement, rent controls and move the adjudication of disputes from the sheriff court to the housing tribunal.

Most tenancies created before 2 January 1989 were regulated tenancies and the Rent (Scotland) Act 1984 still applies where these exist. The act defines, among other things, the circumstances in which a landlord can increase the rent when improvements are made to the property. It does not apply to tenancies where the landlord is the Crown, a local authority or a housing corporation.

The Antisocial Behaviour etc (Scotland) Act 2004 provides that all private landlords letting property in Scotland must register with the local authority in which the let property is situated, unless the landlord is a local authority, or a registered social landlord. Exceptions also apply to holiday lets, owner-occupied accommodation and agricultural holdings. The act applies to partnerships, trusts and companies as well as to individuals.

Tenancy Deposit Schemes (Scotland) Regulations 2011 require that a landlord must pay deposits taken from tenants into an approved scheme and ensure that the money is held by an approved scheme for the duration of the tenancy. Evidence of registration with the relevant local authority in terms of the 2004 Act must be provided when the deposit is paid over.

Landlords who provide an assured or short assured tenancy must provide new tenants with a Tenant Information Pack. The Tenant Information Pack includes information on the Repairing Standard, and its provision satisfies the separate obligation of a landlord to provide a tenant with written information about the landlord's duty to repair and maintain in terms of the Housing (Scotland) Act 2006.

The Housing (Scotland) Acts of 1987 and 2001 relate to local authority and registered social landlord responsibilities for housing, the right to buy, and local authority secured tenancies. The provisions are broadly similar to England and Wales. The Housing (Scotland) Act 2010 reformed right-to-buy provisions, modernised social housing regulation, introduced the Scottish social housing charter and replaced the regulatory framework established by the 2001 act.

In Scotland, business premises are not controlled by statute to the same extent as in England and Wales, although the Tenancy of Shops (Scotland) Act 1949 gives some security to tenants of shops. Tenants of shops can apply to the sheriff, within 21 days of being served a notice to quit, for a renewal of tenancy if threatened with eviction. This application may be dismissed on various grounds, including where the landlord has offered to sell the property to the tenant at an agreed price or, in the absence of agreement as to price, at a price fixed by a single arbiter appointed by the parties or the sheriff. The act extends to properties where the Crown or government departments are the landlords or the tenants.

Under the Leases Act 1449 the landlord's successors (either purchasers or creditors) are bound by the agreement made with any tenants so long as the following conditions are met:
- the lease, if for more than one year, must be in writing
- there must be a rent
- there must be a term of expiry
- the tenant must have entered into possession
- the subjects of the lease must be land
- the landlord, if owner, must be the proprietor with a recorded title, ie the title deeds recorded in the Register of Sasines or registered in the Land Register

On 28 November 2015 certain leases which were granted for more than 175 years and under which the rent does not exceed £100 a year, converted to heritable titles. Therefore the tenants under these leases will become the owners of the property. Conversion of the lease will be automatic, provided certain conditions are met, unless the tenant opts out. It is possible for the landlord to claim compensation for their loss of income.

LEGAL AID

The Access to Justice Act 1999 transformed what used to be known as the Legal Aid system. The Legal Aid Board was replaced by the Legal Services Commission, which was responsible for the development and administration of two legal funding schemes in England and Wales, namely the Criminal Defence Service and the Community Legal Service. The Criminal Defence Service assisted people who were under police investigation or facing criminal charges. The Community Legal Service was designed to increase access to legal information and advice by involving a much wider network of funders and providers in giving publicly funded legal services. In Scotland, provision of legal aid is governed by the Legal Aid (Scotland) Act 1986, the Legal Profession and Legal Aid (Scotland) Act 2007 and the Scottish Civil Justice Council and Criminal Legal Assistance Act 2013, and administered by the Scottish Legal Aid Board.

Under the Legal Aid, Sentencing and Punishment of Offenders Act 2012 (LASPO), which came into force on 1 April 2013, the Legal Services Commission was abolished and replaced by the newly created Legal Aid Agency. The act has also limited the areas of law that fall within the scope of legal aid funding, especially those related to civil legal services. However, the act does include provisions for funding in exceptional cases, such as where failure to provide legal aid would result in a violation of an individual's human rights or where providing legal aid would serve a wider public interest. Further, the act allows for areas of law to be added or omitted from the scope of legal aid independently, without subsequent legislation.

LASPO took whole areas of law out of scope for legal aid; some areas only qualify if they meet certain criteria. Broadly, the following categories of cases are now out of such scope: (a) family cases where there is no proof of domestic violence, forced marriage or child abduction; (b) immigration cases that do not involve asylum or detention; (c) housing and debt matters unless they constitute an immediate risk to the home; (d) welfare benefit cases except appeals to the upper tribunal or high court; (e) almost all clinical negligence cases; and (f) employment cases that do not involve human trafficking or a contravention of the Equality Act 2010.

LEGAL AID AGENCY, W www.gov.uk/government/ organisations/legal-aid-agency

CIVIL LEGAL AID

From 1 January 2000, only organisations (such as solicitors or Citizens Advice) with a contract with the Legal Services Commission (now Legal Aid Agency) have been able to give initial help in any civil matter. Moreover, from that date decisions about funding were devolved from the Legal Services Commission to contracted organisations in relation to any level of publicly funded service in family and immigration cases. For other types of case, applications for public funding are made through a solicitor (or other contracted legal services providers) in much the same way as the former Legal Aid.

Under the civil funding scheme there are broadly six levels of service available:
- legal help
- help at court
- family help – either family help (lower) or family help (higher)
- legal representation – either investigative help or full representation
- family mediation
- such other services as authorised by specific orders

ELIGIBILITY

Eligibility for funding from the Legal Aid Agency depends broadly on five factors:
- the level of service sought (*see* above)
- whether the applicant qualifies financially
- the merits of the applicant's case
- a costs-benefits analysis (if the costs are likely to outweigh any benefit that might be gained from the proceedings, funding may be refused)
- whether there is any public interest in the case being litigated (ie whether the case has a wider public interest beyond that of the parties involved, eg a human rights case)

The limits on capital and income above which a person is not entitled to public funding vary with the type of service sought. As of Spring 2017, there is a consultation on government proposals seeking to amend the legal financial eligibility system to accommodate the expansion of Universal Credit.

The 2012 act also amended the merits criteria so that legal aid may be refused where the case is suitable for alternative funding, such as Conditional Fee Agreements. Children, and individuals on certain welfare benefits, may be relieved from means testing and from the liability to make contributions

CONTRIBUTIONS

Some of those who qualify for Legal Aid Agency funding will have to contribute towards their legal costs. Contributions must be paid by anyone who has a disposable income or disposable capital exceeding a prescribed amount. The rules relating to applicable contributions are complex and detailed information can be obtained from the Legal Aid Agency.

STATUTORY CHARGE

A statutory charge is made if a person keeps or gains money or property in a case for which they have received legal aid. This means that the amount paid by the Legal Aid Agency fund on their behalf is deducted from the amount that the person receives. This does not apply if the court has ordered that the costs be paid by the other party (unless the amount paid by the other party does not cover all of the costs). In certain circumstances, the Legal Aid Agency may waive or postpone payment.

CONTINGENCY OR CONDITIONAL FEES

This system was introduced by the Courts and Legal Services Act 1990. It can offer legal representation on a 'no win, no fee' basis. It provides an alternative form of assistance, especially for those cases which are ineligible for funding by the Legal Aid Agency. The main area for such work is in the field of personal injuries.

Not all solicitors offer such a scheme and different solicitors may well have different terms. The effect of the agreement is that solicitors may not make any charges, or may waive some of their charges, until the case is concluded successfully. If a case is won then the losing party will usually have to pay towards costs, with the winning party contributing around one third.

SCOTLAND
Civil legal aid is available for cases in the following:
- the sheriff courts
- the court of session
- the supreme court
- the lands valuation appeal court
- the Scottish land court
- the sheriff appeal court
- the Lands Tribunal for Scotland
- the employment appeal tribunals
- the Proscribed Organisations Appeal Commission
- certain appeals before the Social Security Commissioners

Civil legal aid is not available for election petitions, some simple procedure actions, simplified divorce procedures or petitions by a debtor for his own sequestration. In defamation actions additional criteria must be met in order for legal aid to be available.

Eligibility for civil legal aid is assessed in a similar way to that in England and Wales, though the financial limits differ in some respects. A person shall be eligible for civil legal aid if their disposable income does not exceed £26,239 a year. A person may be refused civil legal aid if their disposable capital exceeds £13,017 and it appears to the Legal Aid board that they can afford to pay without legal aid. Additionally:
- if disposable capital is between £7,853 and £13,017, the applicant will be required to pay a contribution which will be equal to the difference between £7,853 and their disposable capital
- if disposable income is between £3,522 and £11,540, a contribution of one third of the difference between £3,522 and the disposable income may be payable
- if disposable income is between £11,541 and £15,743, one third of the difference between £3,522 and £11,540 plus half the difference between £11,541 and the disposable income may be payable
- if disposable income is between £15,744 and £26,239, a contribution of the following: one third of the difference between £3,522 and £11,540, plus half the difference between £11,541 and £15,743, plus all the remaining disposable income between £15,744 and £26,239 – will be payable

CRIMINAL LEGAL AID
The Legal Aid Agency provides defendants facing criminal charges with free legal representation if they pass a merits test and a means test.

Criminal legal aid covers the cost of preparing a case and legal representation in criminal proceedings. It is also available for appeals against verdicts or sentences in magistrates' courts, the crown court or the court of appeal. It is not available for bringing a private prosecution in a criminal court.

If granted criminal legal aid, either the person may choose their own solicitor or the court will assign one. Contributions to the legal costs may be required. The rules relating to applicable contributions are complex and detailed information can be obtained from the Legal Aid Agency.

DUTY SOLICITORS
LASPO also provides for free initial advice and initial assistance to anyone questioned by the police (whether under arrest or helping the police with their enquiries). No means test or contributions are required for this.

SCOTLAND
Legal advice and assistance operates in a similar way in Scotland. A person is eligible:
- if disposable income does not exceed £245 a week. If

disposable income is between £105 and £245 a week, contributions are payable
- if disposable capital does not exceed £1,716 (if the person has dependent relatives, the savings allowance is higher)
- if receiving income support or income-related job seeker's allowance they qualify automatically provided their disposable capital is not over the limit

The procedure for application for criminal legal aid depends on the circumstances of each case. In solemn cases (more serious cases, such as murder) heard before a jury, a person is automatically entitled to criminal legal aid until they are given bail or placed in custody. Thereafter, it is for the court to decide whether to grant legal aid. The court will do this if the person accused cannot meet the expenses of the case without undue hardship on him or his dependants. In less serious cases the procedure depends on whether the person is in custody:
- anyone taken into custody has the right to free legal aid from the duty solicitor up to and including the first court appearance
- if the person is not in custody and wishes to plead guilty, they are not entitled to criminal legal aid but may be entitled to legal advice and assistance, including assistance by way of representation

However, regardless of whether the person is in custody if they wish to plead not guilty, they can apply for criminal legal aid. This must be done within 14 days of the first court appearance at which they made the plea.

The criteria used to assess whether or not criminal legal aid should be granted is similar to the criteria for England and Wales. When meeting with your solicitor, take evidence of your financial position such as details of savings, bank statements, pay slips, pension book or benefits book.

Under the relevant provisions of the Scottish Civil Justice Council and Criminal Legal Assistance Act 2013, a person in receipt of criminal legal aid or criminal assistance by way of representation will be required, in most circumstances, to make contributions where their weekly disposable income is £82 or above or if their disposable capital is £750 or more. The Scottish government has delayed the implementation of these provisions and no timetable has yet been proposed.

THE SCOTTISH LEGAL AID BOARD, Thistle House, 91 Haymarket Terrace, Edinburgh EH12 5HE T 0131-226 7061 W www.slab.org.uk

MARRIAGE

Any two persons may marry provided that:
- they are at least 16 years old on the day of the marriage (in England and Wales persons under the age of 18 must generally obtain the consent of their parents or guardian; if consent is refused an appeal may be made to the high court or the family court)
- they are not related to one another in a way which would prevent their marrying
- they are unmarried (a person who has already been married must produce documentary evidence that the previous marriage has been ended by death, divorce or annulment)
- they are capable of understanding the nature of a marriage ceremony and of consenting to marriage

It is now lawful for same sex couples to marry by way of civil or religious ceremony following the passing of the Marriage (Same Sex Couples) Act 2013, which came into force in March 2014. In addition, an existing marriage will now be able to continue where one or both parties change their legal gender and both parties wish to remain married. The act also makes provision for civil partners to convert their civil partnership into a marriage if they wish to do so.

The parties should check the marriage will be recognised as valid in their home country if either is not a British citizen.

DEGREES OF RELATIONSHIP
A marriage between persons within the prohibited degrees of consanguinity, affinity or adoption is void.

Neither party may marry his or her parent, child, grandparent, grandchild, sibling, parent's sibling, sibling's child, adoptive parent, former adoptive parent, adoptive child or former adoptive child. All references to siblings include half-brothers/sisters.

Under the Marriage (Prohibited Degrees of Relationship) Act 1986, some exceptions to the law permit a person to marry certain step-relatives or in-laws.

In addition to the above, a person may not marry a child of their former civil partner, a child of a former spouse, the former civil partner of a grandparent, the former civil partner of a parent, the former spouse of a grandparent, the former spouse of a parent, the grandchild of a former civil partner or the grandchild of a former spouse, unless that relationship is the only reason they cannot marry and both persons are over 21 and the younger party has not at any time before attaining the age of 18 been a child of the family in relation to the other party.

ENGLAND AND WALES

TYPES OF MARRIAGE CEREMONY

It is possible to marry by either religious or civil ceremony. A religious ceremony can take place at a church or chapel of the Church of England or the Church in Wales, or at any other place of worship which has been formally registered by the Registrar-General. Same-sex marriages can also take place in a religious building, provided that the premises have been registered for the marriage of same-sex couples and the relevant governing authority in relation to the building has provided written consent. It is not possible, however, for same-sex marriages to take place in an Anglican church.

A civil ceremony can take place at a register office, a venue approved by the local authority or any religious premises where permission has been given by the relevant organisation and is approved by the local authority.

An application for an approved premises licence must be made by the owners or trustees of the building concerned; it cannot be made by the prospective marriage couple. Approved premises must be regularly open to the public for marriages and civil partnerships; the venue must be deemed to be a permanent and immovable structure. Open-air ceremonies are prohibited.

Non-Anglican marriages may also be solemnised following the issue of a Registrar-General's licence in other premises where one of the parties is seriously ill, is not expected to recover, and cannot be moved to premises where the marriage could normally be solemnised. Detained and housebound persons may also be married at their place of residence on the authority of a superintendent registrar's certificates with proper notice and consents.

MARRIAGE IN THE CHURCH OF ENGLAND OR THE CHURCH IN WALES

Marriage by banns
The marriage can take place in a parish in which one of the parties lives, or in a church in another parish if it is the usual place of worship of either or both of the parties. Further to regulations introduced in October 2008 also, marriages can also take place in a parish where one of the parties has a 'qualifying connection', ie in: a parish where one of the parties was baptised (but not if combined rite) or confirmed (and where the confirmation was entered into that church or chapel's register book); a parish where one of the parties lived or habitually attended worship for six months or more; a parish where one of the parents of either of the parties lived for six months or more in the child's lifetime; a parish where one of the parents of either of the parties has habitually attended public worship for six months or more in the child's lifetime; or a parish where a parent or grandparent of either of the parties was married. The banns (ie the announcement of the marriage ceremony) must be called in the parish in which the marriage is to take place on three Sundays before

the day of the ceremony; if either or both of the parties lives in a different parish the banns must also be called there. After three months the banns are no longer valid. The minister will not perform the marriage unless satisfied that the banns have been properly called.

Marriage by common licence
The couple and the member of the church who is to conduct the marriage will arrange for a common licence to be issued by the local diocese; this dispenses with the necessity for banns. One of the parties must reside in the parish, must usually worship at the parish church or authorised chapel of that parish, or otherwise have a 'qualifying connection' to the parish. Any further eligibility requirements vary from diocese to diocese. The licence is valid for three months.

Marriage by special licence
A special licence is granted by the Archbishop of Canterbury where a party has a genuine connection to a particular church or chapel but does not satisfy the legal requirements to marry there. The parties are usually required to demonstrate that they have a worshipping connection to the church or chapel. The special licence will usually expire after three months, but will not usually be issued until one to three weeks prior to the date of the wedding. Application must be made to the registrar of the Faculty Office: 1 The Sanctuary, London SW1P 3JT T 020-7222 5381.

Marriage by certificate
The marriage can be conducted on the authority of a superintendent registrar's certificates, provided that the consent of the minister of the church or chapel where the marriage is to take place is obtained. Usually one of the parties must live in the parish or must usually worship at the church/chapel, but for non-EU nationals marriage by certificate will be allowed in any situation where the couple could otherwise have qualified for marriage by banns.

MARRIAGE BY OTHER RELIGIOUS CEREMONY

One of the parties must normally live in the registration district where the marriage is to take place or usually worship in the building where they wish to be married. If the building where the parties wish to be married has not been registered, the couple can still have a religious ceremony there, but this will have to follow a separate civil ceremony for the marriage to be valid. If the building is registered, in addition to giving notice to the superintendent registrar it may also be necessary to book a registrar, or authorised person to be present at the ceremony.

CIVIL MARRIAGE

A marriage may be solemnised at any register office, registered building or approved premises in England and Wales, without either of the parties being resident in the same district. The superintendent registrar of the district should be contacted and given notice, and, if the marriage is to take place at approved premises, the necessary arrangements at the venue must also be made.

NOTICE OF MARRIAGE

Where a marriage is intended to take place on the authority of a superintendent registrar's certificates, a notice of the marriage must be given in person to the superintendent registrar of the relevant district.

Both parties must have lived in a registration district in England or Wales for at least seven days immediately before giving notice personally at the local register office. If they live in different registration districts, notice must be given in both districts by the respective party in person. The marriage can take place in any register office or other approved premises in England and Wales no sooner than 28 days after notice has been given, when the superintendent registrar issues a certificate

It should be possible to make an advance (provisional) booking for 12 months before the ceremony. When giving notice of the marriage it is necessary to produce official proof, if relevant, that any previous marriage has ended in divorce or death by producing the original decree absolute or death certificate (or a certified copy); it is also necessary for each of the parties to provide evidence of name and surname, date of birth, place of residence and nationality, for example, with a passport or birth certificate and a recent bank statement. If either party is under 18 years old, evidence of consent by their parent or guardian is required. There are special procedures for those wishing to get married in the UK that are subject to immigration control; the register office will be able to advise on these.

SOLEMNISATION OF THE MARRIAGE

On the day of the wedding there must be at least two other people present who are prepared to act as witnesses and sign the marriage register. A registrar of marriages must be present at a marriage in a register office or at approved premises, but an authorised person may act in the capacity of registrar in a registered building.

If the marriage takes place at approved premises, the room must be separate from any other activity on the premises at the time of the ceremony, and no food or drink can be sold or consumed in the room during the ceremony or for one hour beforehand.

The marriage must be solemnised with open doors. At some time during the ceremony the parties must make a declaration that they know of no legal impediment to the marriage and they must also say the contracting words; the declaratory and contracting words may vary according to the form of service. A civil marriage cannot contain any religious aspects, but it may be possible for non-religious music and/or readings to be included. It may also be possible to embellish the marriage vows taken by the couple.

CIVIL FEES

Notice and registration of Marriage at a Register Office
By superintendent registrar's certificate, £35 per person for the notice of the marriage (which is not refundable if the marriage does not in fact take place) and £46 for the registration of the marriage.

Marriage at a Register Office/Approved Premises
Fees for marriage at a register office are set by the local authority responsible. An additional fee will also be payable for the registrar's attendance at the marriage on an approved premises. This is also set locally by the local authority responsible. A further charge is likely to be made by the owners of the building for the use of the premises. For marriages taking place in a registered religious building, an additional fee of £86 is payable for the registrar's attendance at the marriage unless an 'authorised person' has agreed to register the marriage. Additional fees may be charged by the trustees and/or proprietors of the building for the wedding and by the person who performs the ceremony.

ECCLESIASTICAL FEES
(Church of England and Church in Wales)

Marriage by banns
For publication of banns, £28*
For certificate of banns issued at time of publication, £13*
For marriage service, £424*
For marriage certificate at time of registration £4 and £10 thereafter
* These fees are revised from 1 January each calendar year. Some may not apply to the Church in Wales

SCOTLAND

REGULAR MARRIAGES
A regular marriage is one which is celebrated by a minister of religion or authorised registrar or other celebrant. Each of the parties must complete a marriage notice form and return it to the district registrar for the area in which they are to be married, irrespective of where they live, within the three

month period prior to the date of the marriage and not later than 29 days prior to that date. The district registrar must then enter the date of receipt and certain details in a marriage book kept for this purpose, and must also enter the names of the parties and the proposed date of marriage in a list which is displayed in a conspicuous place at the registration office until the date of the marriage has passed. All persons wishing to enter into a regular marriage in Scotland must follow the same preliminary procedure regardless of whether they intend to have a religious or civil ceremony. Before the marriage ceremony takes place any person may submit an objection in writing to the district registrar.

A marriage schedule, which is prepared by the registrar, will be issued to one or both of the parties in person up to seven days before a religious marriage; for a civil marriage the schedule will be available at the ceremony. The schedule must be handed to the celebrant before the ceremony starts and it must be signed immediately after the wedding. For religious marriages the schedule must be sent within three days by the parties to the district registrar who must register the marriage as soon as possible thereafter. In civil marriages, the district registrar must register the marriage as soon as possible.

The authority to conduct a religious marriage is deemed to be vested in the authorised celebrant rather than the building in which it takes place; open-air religious ceremonies are therefore permissible in Scotland.

From 10 June 2002 it has been possible, under the Marriage (Scotland) Act 2002, for venues or couples to apply to the local council for a licence to allow a civil ceremony to take place at a venue other than a registration office. To obtain further information, a venue or couple should contact the district registrar in the area they wish to marry.

MARRIAGE BY COHABITATION WITH HABIT AND REPUTE
Prior to the enactment of the Family Law (Scotland) Act 2006, if two people had lived together constantly as husband and wife and were generally held to be such by the neighbourhood and among their friends and relations, a presumption could arise from which marriage could be inferred. Before such a marriage could be registered, however, a decree of declarator of marriage had to be obtained from the court of session. Section 3 of the 2006 act provides that it will no longer be possible for a marriage to be constituted by cohabitation with habit and repute, but it will still be possible for couples whose period of cohabitation began before commencement of the 2006 act to seek a declarator under the old rule of law.

SAME-SEX MARRIAGES
On 12 March 2014 the Scottish government passed the Marriage and Civil Partnership (Scotland) Act 2014. This permits same-sex couples to get married, either in a civil ceremony or a 'religious or belief' ceremony where the religious or belief body has opted-in to solemnising same-sex marriage. Also, certain same-sex couples who have entered into a civil partnership have the option under the act to change their civil partnership to a marriage.

It is still possible for same-sex couples to enter into a civil partnership and this may be a 'religious or belief' civil partnership if the religious or belief body has agreed to perform these.

CIVIL FEES
The fee for submitting a notice of marriage to the district registrar is £30.00 per person. Solemnisation of a civil marriage costs £55.00, while the extract of the entry in the register of marriages attracts a fee of £10.00. The costs of religious marriage ceremonies can vary.

THE GENERAL REGISTER OFFICE, PO Box 2, Southport
  PR8 2JD T 0845-603 7788
  W www.gro.gov.uk/gro/content/certificates

THE NATIONAL RECORDS OF SCOTLAND, New Register House, 3 West Register Street, Edinburgh EH1 3YT
T 0131-314 0380 **W** www.nrscotland.gov.uk

TOWN AND COUNTRY PLANNING

There are a number of acts governing the development of land and buildings in England and Wales and advice should always be sought from Citizens Advice or the local planning authority before undertaking building works on any land or property. If development takes place which requires planning permission without permission being given, enforcement action may take place and the situation may need to be rectified. Planning law in Scotland is similar but certain Scotland-specific legislation applies so advice should always be sought.

PLANNING PERMISSION

Planning permission is needed if the work involves:
- making a material change in use, such as dividing off part of the house or garden so that it can be used as a separate home or dividing off part of the house for commercial use, eg for a workshop
- going against the terms of the original planning permission, eg there may be a restriction on fences in front gardens on an open-plan estate
- building, engineering or mining, except for the permitted developments below
- new or wider access to a main road
- additions or extensions to flats or maisonettes
- work which might obstruct the view of road users

Planning permission is not needed to carry out internal alterations or work which does not affect the external appearance of the building, and are not works for making good war damage or works begun after 5 December 1968 for the alteration of a building by providing additional space in it underground.

Under regulations which came into effect on 15 April 2015, there are certain types of development for which the Secretary of State for the Environment, Food and Rural Affairs has granted general permissions (permitted development rights). These include house extensions and additions, outbuildings and garages, other ancillary garden buildings such as swimming pools or ponds, and laying patios, paths or driveways for domestic use. All developments are subject to a number of conditions.

Before carrying out any of the above permitted developments you should contact your local planning authority to find out whether the general permission has been modified in your area. For more information, visit **W** www.planningportal.gov.uk

OTHER RESTRICTIONS

It may be necessary to obtain other types of permissions before carrying out any development. These permissions are separate from planning permission and apply regardless of whether or not planning permission is needed, eg:
- building regulations will probably apply if a new building is to be erected, if an existing one is to be altered or extended, or if the work involves building over a drain or sewer. The building control department of the local authority will advise on this
- any alterations to a listed building or the grounds of a listed building must be approved by the local authority. Listing will include not only the main building but everything in the curtilage of the building
- local authority approval is necessary if a building (or, in some circumstances, gates, walls, fences or railings) in a conservation area is to be demolished; each local authority keeps a register of all local buildings that are in conservation areas
- many trees are protected by tree preservation orders and must not be pruned or taken down without local authority consent
- bats and many other species are protected, and Natural England, Natural Resources Wales or Scottish Natural Heritage must be notified before any work is carried out that will affect the habitat of protected species, eg timber treatment, renovation or extensions of lofts
- developments in areas with special designations, such as National Parks, Areas of Outstanding Natural Beauty, National Scenic Areas or in the Norfolk or Suffolk Broads, are subject to greater restrictions. The local planning authority will advise or refer enquirers to the relevant authority

There may also be restrictions contained in the title to the property which require you to get someone else's agreement before carrying out certain developments, and which should be considered when works are planned.

VOTERS' QUALIFICATIONS

Those entitled to vote at parliamentary and local government elections are those who, at the date of taking the poll, are:
- on the electoral roll
- aged 18 years or older (although for Scottish parliament and local government elections in Scotland those aged 16 and older can vote)
- British citizens, Commonwealth citizens or citizens of the Irish Republic who are resident in the UK
- those who suffer from no other legal bar to voting (eg prisoners). It should be noted that there is some uncertainty regarding the future of the legal bar on prisoners' voting following a decision taken by the European Court of Human Rights
- in Northern Ireland electors must have been resident in Northern Ireland during the whole of the three-month period prior to the relevant date
- citizens of any EU member state may vote in local elections if they meet the criteria listed above (save for the nationality requirements). There is some uncertainty regarding future voting rights of EU citizens in light of Brexit. However, it should be noted that there will be no change to the voting rights of EU citizens living in the UK while the UK remains in the EU

British citizens resident abroad are entitled to vote, provided they have been registered to vote in the UK within the last 15 years, as overseas electors in domestic parliamentary elections in the constituency in which they were last resident if they are on the electoral roll of the relevant constituency. The government released a policy statement in October 2016 proposing to abolish the current 15 year time limit for British citizens registering as overseas electors although it is unclear when this proposal will be legislated for. Members of the armed forces and their spouses or civil partners, Crown servants and employees of the British Council who are overseas, along with their spouses and civil partners, are entitled to vote regardless of how long they have been abroad. British citizens who had never been registered as an elector in the UK are not eligible to register as an overseas voter unless they left the UK before they were 18, providing they left the country no more than 15 years ago. Overseas electors may opt to vote by proxy or by postal vote. Overseas voters may not vote in local government elections.

The main categories of people who are not entitled to vote at general elections are:
- sitting peers in the House of Lords
- convicted persons detained in pursuance of their sentences (though remand prisoners, unconvicted prisoners and civil prisoners can vote if on the electoral register). This is currently subject to review, as detailed above
- those convicted within the previous five years of corrupt or illegal election practices
- EU citizens (who may only vote in EU and local government elections)

Under the Representation of the People Act 2000, several new groups of people are permitted to vote for the first time.

These include: people who live on barges; people in mental health hospitals (other than those with criminal convictions) and homeless people who have made a 'declaration of local connection'.

REGISTERING TO VOTE

Voters must be entered on an electoral register. The Electoral Registration Officer (ERO) for each council area is responsible for preparing and publishing the register for his area by 1 December each year. Names may be added to the register to reflect changes in people's circumstances as they occur and each month during December to August, the ERO publishes a list of alterations to the published register.

On 10 May 2012, the government introduced the electoral registration and administration bill, which received royal assent on 31 January 2013. The act replaced household registration with individual elector registration, meaning each elector must apply individually to be registered to vote. Individuals will also be asked for identifying information such as date of birth and national insurance number. The act also introduced a number of changes relating to electoral administration and the conduct of elections. Anyone failing to supply information to the ERO when requested, or supplying false information, may be fined by up to £1,000. Further, the ERO may impose a civil penalty on those who fail to make an application for registration when required to do so by the ERO. Application forms and more information are available from the Electoral Commission (W www.aboutmyvote.co.uk).

VOTING

Voting is not compulsory in the UK. Those who wish to vote do so in person at the allotted polling station. Postal votes are now available to anyone on request and you do not need to give a reason for using a postal vote.

A proxy (whereby the voter nominates someone to vote in person on their behalf) can be appointed to act in a specific election, for a specified period of time or indefinitely. For the appointment of an indefinite or long-term proxy, the voter needs to specify physical employment, study reasons or a disability to explain why they are making an application. With proxy votes where a particular election is specified, the voter needs to provide details of the circumstances by which they cannot reasonably be expected to go to the polling station. Applications for a proxy are normally available up to six working days before an election, but should the voter fall ill on election day, it is possible to appoint a proxy up until polling day.

WILLS

A will is used to appoint executors (who will administer the estate), give directions as to the disposal of the body, appoint guardians for children and determine how and to whom property is to be passed. A well-drafted will can operate to reduce the level of inheritance tax which the estate pays. It is best to have a will drawn up by a solicitor, but if a solicitor is not employed the following points must be taken into account:

- if possible the will must not be prepared on behalf of another person by someone who is to benefit from it or who is a close relative of a major beneficiary
- the language used must be clear and unambiguous and it is better to avoid the use of legal terms where the same thing can be expressed in plain language
- it is better to rewrite the whole document if a mistake is made. If necessary, alterations can be made by striking through the words with a pen, and the signature or initials of the testator and the witnesses must be put in the margin opposite the alteration. No alteration of any kind should be made after the will has been executed
- if the person later wishes to change the will or part of it, it is better to write a new will revoking the old. The use of codicils (documents written as supplements or containing modifications to the will) should be left to a solicitor

- the will should be typed or printed, or if handwritten be legible and preferably in ink

The form of a will varies to suit different cases, a solicitor will be able to advise as to wording, however, 'DIY' will-writing kits can be purchased from good stationery shops and many banks offer a will-writing service.

LAPSED LEGATEES

If a person who has been left property in a will dies before the person who made the will, the gift fails and will pass to the person entitled to everything not otherwise disposed of (the residuary estate). If the beneficiary of the residuary estate dies before the person who made the will, the gift of the residuary estate also fails and passes to the closest relative(s) of the testator in accordance with the intestacy rules.

It is always better to draw up a new will if a beneficiary predeceases the person who made the will.

EXECUTORS

It is usual to appoint two executors, although one is sufficient. No more than four persons can deal with the estate of the person who has died. The name and address of each executor should be given in full (the addresses are not essential but including them adds clarity to the document). Executors should be 18 years of age or over. An executor may be a beneficiary of the will.

WITNESSES

A person who is a beneficiary of a will, or the spouse or civil partner of a beneficiary at the time the will is signed, must not act as a witness or else he/she will be unable to take his/her gift. There is nothing preventing the spouse or civil partner of the person making the will from acting as a witness, but as it is rare for a spouse or civil partner not to benefit from the will of his/her spouse or civil partner, an independent witness is usually better.

It is also better that a person does not act as an executor and as a witness, as he/she can take no benefit (including remuneration) under a will to which he/she is witness. In relation to deaths on or after 1 February 2001, however, a professional executor who is also a witness can receive payments due to him or her under a term in the will for services provided as executor.

The identity of the witnesses should be made as explicit as possible, such as by stating their names, addresses, and occupations.

EXECUTION OF A WILL

The person making the will should sign his/her name in the presence of the two witnesses. It is advisable to sign at the foot of the document, so as to avoid uncertainty about the testator's intention. The witnesses must then sign their names while the person making the will looks on. If this procedure is not adhered to, the will may be considered invalid. There are certain exceptional circumstances where these rules are relaxed, eg where the person may be too ill to sign.

CAPACITY TO MAKE A WILL

Anyone aged 18 or over can make a will. However, if there is any suspicion that the person making the will is not, through reasons of infirmity or age, fully in command of his/her faculties, it is advisable to arrange for a medical practitioner to examine the person making the will as near to the time that the testator gives instructions for the will and to when the will is executed (to verify his/her mental capacity and to record that medical opinion in writing), and to ask the examining practitioner to act as a witness. If a person is not mentally able to make a will, the court of protection may do this for him/her by virtue of the Mental Capacity Act 2005.

REVOCATION

A will may be revoked or cancelled in a number of ways:
- a later will revokes an earlier one if it says so; otherwise the earlier will is by implication revoked by the later one to the extent that it contradicts or repeats the earlier one

- a will is revoked if the original physical document on which it is written is destroyed by the person whose will it is. There must be an intention to revoke the will and an act of destruction. It may not be sufficient to obliterate the will with a pen
- a will is revoked by the testator making a written declaration to this effect executed in the same way as a will
- a will is also revoked when the person marries or forms a civil partnership, unless it is clear from the will that the person intended the will to stand after that particular marriage or civil partnership. A will is not revoked, however, by the conversion of a civil partnership to a marriage, or when the testator is treated as having formed a civil partnership on 5 December 2005 because he/she registered a recognised overseas relationship before that date.
- where a marriage or civil partnership ends in divorce or dissolution or is annulled or declared void, gifts to the spouse or civil partner and the appointment of the spouse or civil partner as executor fail unless the will says that this is not to happen. A former spouse or civil partner is treated as having predeceased the testator. A separation does not change the effect of a married person or civil partner's will.

PROBATE AND LETTERS OF ADMINISTRATION
The grant of probate is granted to the executors named in a will and once granted, the executors are obliged to carry out the instructions of the will. Letters of administration are granted where the deceased died intestate or did not leave a valid will. Letters of administration with will annexed are granted when the deceased did not appoint an executor in the will or the appointed executor(s) are not able or willing to act. The letters of administration give a person, often the next of kin, similar powers and duties to those of an executor.

Applications for the grant of probate or for letters of administration can be made to the Principal Registry of the Family Division, to a district probate registry or to a probate sub-registry. Applicants not using a solicitor will need to send the following documents to the main probate registry of choice: the Probate Application Form (PA1); the original will and codicils (if any) and three copies of the same; an official copy of the death certificate; and the appropriate tax form (an 'IHT 205' if no inheritance tax is owed; otherwise an 'IHT 421' stamped by HMRC confirming payment of inheritance tax), in addition to a cheque for the relevant probate fee. The applicant will then be invited to an interview at the probate registry of choice where they will swear an oath. Where an applicant is using a solicitor, the PA1 is not necessary and the appropriate oath (for executors or administrators) will be included in the documents to be sent to the probate registry; there is no interview. In both cases, where the estate of the deceased is below £5,000, there is no probate fee to pay. Certain property, up to the value of £5,000, may be disposed of without a grant of probate or letters of administration, as can assets that do not pass under the will such as jointly owned assets which pass automatically on the death of one of the joint holders to the survivor, life policies written in trust, or discretionary pension death benefits.

WHERE TO FIND A PROVED WILL
Since 1858 wills which have been proved, that is wills on which probate or letters of administration have been granted, must have been proved at the Principal Registry of the Family Division or at a district probate registry. The Lord Chancellor has power to direct where the original documents are kept but most are filed where they were proved and may be inspected there and a copy obtained. You can search for a probate record online or by post. The Principal Registry also holds copies of all wills proved at district probate registries and these may be inspected at First Avenue House, High Holborn, London. An index of all grants, both of probate and of letters of administration, is compiled by the Principal Registry and may be seen either at the Principal Registry or at a district probate registry.

It is also possible to discover when a grant of probate or letters of administration is issued by requesting a standing search. In response to a request and for a small fee, a district probate registry will supply the names and addresses of executors or administrators and the registry in which the grant was made, of any grant in the estate of a specified person made in the previous six months or following six months.

PRINCIPAL REGISTRY (FAMILY DIVISION), 7th Floor, 42–49 High Holborn, First Avenue House, London WC1V 6NP T 020-7421 8509

INTESTACY
Intestacy occurs when someone dies without leaving a will or leaves a will which is invalid or which does not take effect for some reason. Intestacy can be partial, for instance, if there is a valid will which disposes of some but not all of the testator's property. In such cases the person's estate (property, possessions, other assets following the payment of debts) passes to certain members of the family. If a will has been written that disposes of only part of a person's property, these rules apply to the part which is undisposed of.

Some types of property do not follow the intestacy rules, for example, property held as joint tenants, insurance policies taken out for specified individuals or assigned into trust during the testator's lifetime and death benefits under a pension scheme.

Following a lengthy review by the Law Commission, the intestacy rules changed on 1 October 2014.

If the person (intestate) leaves a spouse or a civil partner who survives for 28 days and children (legitimate, illegitimate and adopted children and other descendants), the estate is divided as follows:
- if the estate is worth more than £250,000, the spouse or civil partner takes the 'personal chattels' (household articles, including cars, but nothing used for business purposes or held solely as an investment), £250,000 and half of the rest of the estate absolutely
- the rest of the estate goes to the children*

If the intestate leaves a spouse or civil partner who survives for 28 days but no children, the spouse or civil partner will take the estate in its entirety, regardless of its value.

If there is no surviving spouse or civil partner, the estate is distributed among those who survive the intestate as follows (these provisions remained unchanged at 1 October 2014):
- to surviving children*, but if none to
- parents (equally, if both alive), but if none to
- brothers and sisters of the whole blood* (including issue of deceased ones), but if none to
- brothers and sisters of the half blood* (including issue of deceased ones), but if none to
- grandparents (equally, if more than one), but if none to
- aunts and uncles of the whole blood*, but if none to
- aunts and uncles of the half blood*, but if none to
- the Crown, Duchy of Lancaster or the Duke of Cornwall (bona vacantia)

* To inherit, a member of these groups must survive the intestate and attain the age of 18, or marry under that age. If they die under the age of 18 (unless married under that age), their share goes to others, if any, in the same group. If any member of these groups predeceases the intestate leaving children, their share is divided equally among their children.

In England and Wales the provisions of the Inheritance (Provision for Family and Dependants) Act 1975 may allow other people to claim provision from the deceased's assets. This act also applies to cases where a will has been made and allows a person to apply to the court if they feel that the will or rules of intestacy (or both) do not make adequate provision for them. The court can order payment from the deceased's assets or the transfer of property from them if the applicant's claim is accepted. The application must be made within six months of the grant of probate or letters of administration and the following people can make an application:
- the spouse or civil partner
- a former spouse or civil partner who has not remarried or formed a subsequent civil partnership

- a child of the deceased
- someone treated as a child of the deceased's family where the deceased stood in the role of a parent to the applicant
- someone maintained wholly or partly by the deceased
- where the deceased died on or after 1 January 1996, someone who has cohabited for two years before the death in the same household as the deceased and was living as the husband or wife or civil partner of the deceased

SCOTLAND

In Scotland any person over 12 and of sound mind can make a will. The person making the will can only freely dispose of the heritage and what is known as the 'dead's part' of the estate because:

- the spouse or civil partner has the right to inherit one-third of the moveable estate if there are children or other descendants, and one-half of it if there are not
- children are entitled to one-third of the moveable estate if there is a surviving spouse or civil partner, and one-half of it if there is not

The remaining portion of the moveable estate is the dead's part, and legacies and bequests are payable from this. Debts are payable out of the whole estate before any division. The Scottish government has indicated that it intends to reform the law in this area to remove the distinction which currently applies in relation to the treatment of heritable and moveable property.

From August 1995, wills no longer needed to be 'holographed' and it is now only necessary to have one witness. The person making the will still needs to sign each page. It is better that the will is not witnessed by a beneficiary although the attestation would still be sound and the beneficiary would not have to relinquish the gift.

As a result of the changes brought in by the Succession (Scotland) Act 2016, from 1 November 2016 a divorce, dissolution or annulment (granted by a UK court) will revoke any provision in a will which confers a benefit or power of appointment on the former spouse or civil partner unless the will expressly provides that the benefit or appointment should still apply in the event of a divorce, dissolution or annulment. Subsequent marriage or civil partnership does not revoke a will but the birth of a child who is not provided for may do so. A will may be revoked by a subsequent will, either expressly or by implication, but in so far as the two can be read together both have effect. If a subsequent will is revoked, the earlier will may be revived provided it was not physically destroyed.

Wills may be registered in the sheriff court Books of the Sheriffdom in which the deceased lived or in the Books of Council and Session at the Registers of Scotland.

CONFIRMATION

Confirmation (the Scottish equivalent of probate) is obtained in the sheriff court of the sheriffdom in which the deceased was domiciled at the time of death. Executors are either 'nominate' (named by the deceased in the will) or 'dative' (appointed by the court in cases where no executor is named in a will or in cases of intestacy). Applicants for confirmation must first provide an inventory of the deceased's estate and a schedule of debts, with an affidavit. In estates under £36,000 gross, confirmation can be obtained under a simplified procedure at reduced fees, with no need for a solicitor. The local sheriff clerk's office can provide assistance.

PRINCIPAL REGISTRY (FAMILY DIVISION), First Avenue House, 42–49 High Holborn, London WC1 6NP
T 020-7947 6000
REGISTERS OF SCOTLAND, Meadowbank House, 153 London Road, Edinburgh EH8 7AU T 0845-607 0161

INTESTACY

The rules of distribution are contained in the Succession (Scotland) Act 1964 and are extended to include civil partners by the Civil Partnership Act 2004.

A surviving spouse or civil partner is entitled to 'prior rights'. Once the provisions of the Marriage and Civil Partnership Act 2014 come into force references to people who are or were married are to be read as referring to both opposite and same-sex marriage. Prior rights mean that if certain conditions are met the spouse or civil partner has the right to inherit:

- the matrimonial or family home up to a value of £473,000, or one matrimonial or family home if there is more than one, or, in certain circumstances, the value of the home
- the furnishings and contents of that home, up to the value of £29,000
- a cash sum of £50,000 if the deceased left children or other descendants, or £89,000 if not

These figures are increased from time to time by regulations.

Once prior rights have been satisfied legal rights are settled. Legal rights are:

- *Jus relicti(ae) and rights under the section 131 of the Civil Partnership Act 2004* – the right of a surviving spouse or civil partner to one-half of the net moveable estate, after satisfaction of prior rights, if there are no surviving children; if there are surviving children, the spouse or civil partner is entitled to one-third of the net moveable estate
- *Legitim and rights under the section 131 of the Civil Partnership Act 2004* – the right of surviving children to one-half of the net moveable estate if there is no surviving spouse or civil partner; if there is a surviving spouse or civil partner, the children are entitled to one-third of the net moveable estate after the satisfaction of prior rights

Once prior and legal rights have been satisfied, the remaining estate will be distributed in the following order:

- to descendants
- if no descendants, then to collaterals (ie brothers and sisters) and parents with each being entitled to half of the estate, or if only either parents or collaterals survive, the whole of the estate
- surviving spouse or civil partner
- if no collaterals, parents, spouse or civil partner, then to ascendants collaterals (ie aunts and uncles), and so on in an ascending scale
- if all lines of succession fail, the estate passes to the Crown

Relatives of the whole blood are preferred to relatives of the half blood. Also the right of representation, ie the right of the issue of a person who would have succeeded if he/she had survived the intestate, applies.

The Family Law (Scotland) Act 2006 makes provision to allow an unmarried cohabitant to make a financial claim against the estate of a cohabitant who dies intestate. In general a claim must be made within six months of the deceased's death. The court must take into account certain factors when considering such a claim. If the claim is successful the court has the power to order payment of a capital sum and transfer of property.

INTELLECTUAL PROPERTY

Intellectual property is a broad term covering a number of legal rights provided by the government to help people protect their creative works and encourage further innovation. By using these legal rights people can own the things they create and control the way in which others use their innovations. Intellectual property owners can take legal action to stop others using their intellectual property, they can license their intellectual property to others or they can sell it on. Different types of intellectual property utilise different forms of protection including copyright, designs, patents and trade marks, which are all covered below in more detail.

CHANGES TO INTELLECTUAL PROPERTY LAW

Reforms to the Copyright, Designs and Patents Act 1988 came into force on 1 June 2014 giving a number of sectors a legal framework suitable for the digital age, removing unnecessary regulations and enabling these sectors to better preserve and use copyright material. Under the reforms, disabled people and disability groups can make accessible copies of copyright material (eg music, film, books) when no commercial alternative exists, researchers benefit from the introduction of a new text and data mining exception for non-commercial research and schools, colleges and universities can obtain a licence to use copyright material on interactive whiteboards and in presentations without accidentally infringing copyright. An existing preservation exception was expanded to cover all types of copyright work, and now applies to museums and galleries as well as libraries and archives.

An online patent renewal service (W www.gov.uk/renew-patent) was launched on 1 July 2014, designed to make renewing over 400,000 patents each year simpler, quicker and cheaper for businesses and inventors.

The Intellectual Property Act 2014 came into effect on 1 October 2014. The act modernised intellectual property law to help UK businesses better protect their rights. The act also implemented reforms to design legislation and introduced a number of changes to patent law making it cheaper and easier to use and defend patents.

Additional patent rule changes came into effect on 1 October 2016 and 6 April 2017. The changes streamlined the application process, made procedures more flexible and increased the legal certainty of patents that are granted.

COPYRIGHT

Copyright protects all original literary, dramatic, musical and artistic works, as well as sound and film recordings and broadcasts. Among the works covered by copyright are novels, computer programs, newspaper articles, sculptures, technical drawings, websites, maps and photographs. Under copyright the creators of these works can control the various ways in which their material may be exploited, the rights broadly covering copying, adapting, issuing (including renting and lending) copies to the public, performing in public, and broadcasting the material. The transfer of copyright works to formats accessible to visually impaired persons without infringement of copyright was enacted in 2002.

Copyright protection in the UK is automatic and there is no official registration system. The creator of a work can help to protect it by including the copyright symbol ©, the name of the copyright owner, and the year in which the work was created. In addition, steps can be taken by the work's creator to provide evidence that he/she had the work at a particular time (eg by depositing a copy with a bank or solicitor). The main legislation is the Copyright, Designs and Patents Act 1988 (as amended). As a result of an EU directive effective from January 1996, the term of copyright protection for literary, dramatic, musical (including song lyrics and musical

compositions) and artistic works lasts for 70 years after the death of the creator. For film, copyright lasts for 70 years after the director, authors of the screenplay and dialogue, or the composer of any music specially created for the film have all died. Sound recordings are protected for 50 years after their publication (or their first performance if they are not published), and broadcasts for 50 years from the end of the year in which the broadcast/transmission was made. The typographical arrangement of published editions remains under copyright protection for 25 years from the end of the year in which the particular edition was published.

The main international treaties protecting copyright are the Berne Convention for the Protection of Literary and Artistic Works (administered by the World Intellectual Property Organization (WIPO)), the Rome Convention for the Protection of Performers, Producers of Phonograms and Broadcasting Organisations (administered by the United Nations Educational, Scientific and Cultural Organization (UNESCO), the International Labour Organisation and WIPO), the Geneva Phonograms Convention (administered by WIPO), and the Universal Copyright Convention (developed by UNESCO); the UK is a signatory to these conventions. Copyright material created by UK nationals or residents is protected in the countries that have signed one of the above-named conventions by the national law of that country. A list of participating countries may be obtained from the UK Intellectual Property Office. The World Trade Organization's Trade-Related Aspects of Intellectual Property Rights (TRIPS) agreement, signed in 1995, may also provide copyright protection abroad.

Two treaties which strengthen and update international standards of protection, particularly in relation to new technologies, were agreed in December 1996: the WIPO Copyright Treaty, and the WIPO Performances and Phonograms Treaty. In May 2001 the European Union passed a new directive (which in 2003 became law in the UK) aimed at harmonising copyright law throughout the EU to take account of the internet and other technologies. More information can be found online (W www.ipo.gov.uk).

LICENSING

Use of copyright material without seeking permission in each instance may be permitted under 'blanket' licences available from national copyright licensing agencies. The International Federation of Reproduction Rights Organisations facilitates agreements between its member licensing agencies and on behalf of its members with organisations such as WIPO, UNESCO, the European Union and the Council of Europe. More information can be found online (W www.ifrro.org).

DESIGN PROTECTION

Design protection covers the outward appearance of an article and in the UK takes two forms: registered design and design right, which are not mutually exclusive. Registered design protects the aesthetic appearance of an article, including shape, configuration, pattern or ornament; artistic works such as sculptures are excluded, being generally protected by copyright. To achieve design protection the owner of the design must apply to the Intellectual Property Office. In order to qualify for protection, a design must be new and materially different from earlier UK published designs. Initial registration lasts for five years and can be extended in five-year increments to a maximum of 25 years. The current legislation is the Registered Designs Act 1949 which has been amended several times, most recently by the Regulatory Reform Order 2006.

UK applicants wishing to protect their designs in the EU can do so by applying for a Registered Community Design with the Office for Harmonization in the Internal Market. Outside the EU separate applications must be made in each country in which protection is sought.

Design right is an automatic right which applies to the shape or configuration of articles and does not require registration. Unlike registered design, two-dimensional designs do not qualify for protection but designs of electronic circuits are protected by design right. Designs must be original and non-commonplace. The term of design right is ten years from first marketing of the design, or 15 years after the creation of the design, whichever is earlier. This right is effective only in the UK. After five years anyone is entitled to apply for a licence of right, which allows others to make and sell products copying the design. The current legislation is Part 3 of the Copyright, Designs and Patents Act 1988.

PATENTS

A patent is a document issued by the UK Intellectual Property Office relating to an invention. It gives the proprietor the right for a limited period to stop others from making, using, importing or selling the invention without the inventor's permission. In return the patentee pays a fee to cover the costs of processing the patent and publicly discloses details of the invention.

To qualify for a patent an invention must be new, must be functional or technical, must exhibit an inventive step, and must be capable of industrial application. The patent is valid for a maximum of 20 years from the date on which the application was filed, subject to payment of annual fees from the end of the fifth year.

The UK Intellectual Property Office, established in 1852, is responsible for ensuring that all stages of an application comply with the Patents Act 1977, and that the invention meets the criteria for a patent.

WIPO is responsible for administering many of the international conventions on intellectual property. The Patent Cooperation Treaty allows inventors to file a single application for patent rights in some or all of the contracting states. This application is searched by an International Searching Authority to confirm the invention is novel and that the same concept has not already been made publicly available. The application and search report are then published by the International Bureau of WIPO. It may also be the subject of an (optional) international preliminary examination. Applicants must then deal directly with the patent offices in the countries where they are seeking patent rights. The European Patent Convention allows inventors to obtain patent rights in all the contracting states by filing a single application with the European Patent Office. More information can be found online (W www.ipo.gov.uk).

RESEARCH DISCLOSURES

Research disclosures are publicly disclosed details of inventions. Once published, an invention is considered no longer novel and becomes 'prior art'. Publishing a disclosure is significantly cheaper than applying for a patent; however, unlike a patent, it does not entitle the author to exclusive rights to use or license the invention. Instead, research disclosures are primarily published to ensure the inventor the freedom to use the invention. This works because publishing legally prevents other parties from patenting the disclosed innovation and in the UK, patent law dictates that by disclosing details of an invention, even the inventor relinquishes their right to a patent.

In theory, publishing details of an invention anywhere should be enough to constitute a research disclosure. However, to be effective, a research disclosure needs to be published in a location which patent examiners will include in their prior art searches. To ensure global legal precedent it must be included in a publication with a recognised date stamp and made publicly available throughout the world.

Research Disclosure, established in 1960 and operated by Questel Ireland Ltd, is the primary publisher of research disclosures. It is the only disclosure service recognised by the Patent Cooperation Treaty as a mandatory search resource which must be consulted by the international search authorities. More information can be found online (W www.researchdisclosure.com).

TRADE MARKS

Trade marks are a means of identification, enabling traders to make their goods and services readily distinguishable from those supplied by others. Trade marks can take the form of words, a logo or a combination of both. Registration prevents other traders using the same or similar trade marks for similar products or services.

In the UK trade marks are registered at the UK Intellectual Property Office. In order to qualify for registration a trade mark must be capable of distinguishing its proprietor's goods or services from those of other undertakings; it should be non-deceptive, should not describe the goods and services or any characteristics of them, should not be contrary to law or morality and should not be similar or identical to any earlier trade marks for the same or similar goods or services. The owner of a registered trade mark may include an ® symbol next to it, and must renew their registration every ten years to keep it in force. The relevant current legislation is the Trade Marks Act 1994 (as amended).

It is possible to obtain an international trade mark registration, effective in 92 countries, under the Madrid system for the international registration of marks, to which the UK is party. British companies can obtain international trade mark registration in those countries party to the system through a single application to WIPO.

EU trade mark regulation is administered by the European Union Intellectual Property Office in Alicante, Spain. The office registers Community trade marks, which are valid throughout the European Union. The registration of trade marks in individual member states continues in parallel with EU trade mark standards.

DOMAIN NAMES

An internet domain name (eg www.whitakersalmanack.com) has to be registered separately from a trade mark, and this can be done through a number of registrars which charge varying rates and compete for business. For each top-level domain name (eg uk.com), there is a central registry to store the unique internet names and addresses using that suffix. A list of accredited registrars can be found online (W www.icann.org).

CONTACTS

COPYRIGHT LICENSING AGENCY LTD, Barnard's Inn, 86 Fetter Lane, London EC4A 1EN T 020-7400 3100 W www.cla.co.uk

EUROPEAN PATENT OFFICE, 80298 Munich, Germany T (+49) 89 2399-0 W www.epo.org

INTELLECTUAL PROPERTY OFFICE, Concept House, Cardiff Road, Newport NP10 8QQ T 0300-300 2000 W www.ipo.gov.uk

WORLD INTELLECTUAL PROPERTY ORGANIZATION, 34 chemin des Colombettes, CH-1211 Geneva 20, Switzerland T (+41) 22 338 9111 W www.wipo.int

THE MEDIA

CROSS-MEDIA OWNERSHIP

The rules surrounding cross-media ownership were overhauled as part of the 2003 Communications Act. The act simplified and relaxed existing rules to encourage dispersion of ownership and new market entry while preventing the most influential media in any community being controlled by too narrow a range of interests. However, transfers and mergers are not solely subject to examination on competition grounds by the competition authorities. The Secretary of State for Culture, Media and Sport has a broad remit to decide if a transaction is permissible and can intervene on public interest grounds (relating both to newspapers and cross-media criteria, if broadcasting interests are also involved). The Office of Communications (OFCOM) has an advisory role in this context. Government and parliamentary assurances were given that any intervention into local newspaper transfers would be rare and exceptional. Following a request from the Secretary of State for Culture, Media and Sport in June 2010 for a removal of all restrictions from the ownership of local media, OFCOM recommended the liberalisation of local cross-media regulations to enable a single owner to control newspapers, a TV licence and radio stations in one area.

REGULATION

OFCOM is the regulator for the communication industries in the UK and has responsibility for television, radio, telecommunications and wireless communications services. OFCOM is required to report annually to parliament and exists to further the interests of consumers by balancing choice and competition with the duty to foster plurality; protect viewers and listeners and promote cultural diversity in the media; and to ensure full and fair competition between communications providers.

OFFICE OF COMMUNICATIONS (OFCOM), Riverside House, 2A Southwark Bridge Road, London SE1 9HA
T 020-7981 3000
W www.ofcom.org.uk
Chief Executive, Sharon White

COMPLAINTS

Under the Communications Act 2003 OFCOM's licensees are obliged to adhere to the provisions of its codes (including advertising, programme standards, fairness, privacy and sponsorship). Complainants should contact the broadcaster in the first instance (details can be found on OFCOM's website); however, if the complainant wishes the complaint to be considered by OFCOM, it will do so. Complaints should be made within a reasonable time, as broadcasters are only required to keep recordings for the following periods: radio, 42 days; television, 90 days; and cable and satellite, 60 days. OFCOM can fine a broadcaster, revoke a licence or take programmes off the air. Since November 2004 complaints relating to individual advertisements on TV or radio have been dealt with by the Advertising Standards Authority.

ADVERTISING STANDARDS AUTHORITY Mid City Place, 71 High Holborn, London WC1V 6QT T 020-7492 2222
W www.asa.org.uk
Chief Executive, Guy Parker

TELEVISION

There are six major television channel owners who are responsible for the biggest audience share. They are the British Broadcasting Corporation (BBC), Independent Television (ITV), Channel 4, Channel 5, Sky and UKTV. Overall there are around 480 channels available to viewers, through free-to-air, free-to-view and subscription-based services. Following the completion of the switchover to a digital format in October 2012, analogue transmissions ended and digital-only content was broadcast through a range of services, including terrestrial, satellite, cable and IP.

Beginning as a radio station in 1922, the BBC is the oldest broadcaster in the world. The corporation began a London-only television service from Alexandra Palace in 1936 and achieved nationwide coverage 15 years later. A second station, BBC Two, was launched in 1964. The BBC's other free-to-air channels available in the UK comprise BBC Four, BBC News, BBC Parliament, the children's channels, CBeebies and CBBC, and regional channels including BBC Alba. Many of the BBC's channels have a corresponding HD (high definition) service and there are additionally several local channels. BBC's iPlayer service was launched on Christmas Day 2007 and allows users to view and listen to content instantly, stream live television and download programmes on to a computer, tablet or mobile device for up to 30 days. An integrated service for radio was launched in June 2008. In 2009, iPlayer was extended to more than 20 devices, including mobile phones and games consoles, and an HD service was launched. The BBC services are funded by the licence fee. The corporation also has a commercial arm, BBC Worldwide, which was formed in 1994 and exists to maximise the value of the BBC's programme and publishing assets for the benefit of the licence payer. Its businesses include international programming distribution, magazines, other licensed products, live events and media monitoring.

The ITV (Independent Television) network began broadcasting in 1955 on Channel 3 in the London area, under the Television Act 1954 which made provision for commercial television in the UK. The ITV network originally comprised a number of independent licensees, the majority of which have now merged to form ITV plc. The network generates funds through broadcasting television advertisements. The ITV network channels now include ITV2, ITV3, ITV4, ITVBe, ITV Encore and CiTV, while the network also owns UTV Ireland. The majority of ITV channels have corresponding HD services. ITV Player, similar to iPlayer, was launched December 2008. ITV Network Centre is wholly owned by the ITV companies and undertakes commissioning and scheduling of programmes shown across the ITV network and, as with the other terrestrial channels, 25 per cent of programmes must come from independent producers.

Channel 4 and S4C (Sianel Pedwar Cymru – Channel Four Wales) were launched in 1982 to provide programmes with a distinctive character that appeal to interests not catered for by ITV. Channel 4 has a remit to be innovative, experimental and distinctive. Although publicly owned, Channel 4 receives no public funding and is financed predominantly through advertising, but unlike ITV, Channel 4 is not shareholder-owned. It has expanded to create the stations E4, More4, Film4, 4Music and, in July 2012, catchup channel 4seven. All 4 is Channel 4's online service which enables viewers to download and revisit programmes from the last 30 days as well as access an older archive of footage. All 4 replaced Channel 4's first online platform 4oD (launched in 2006) in March 2015. S4C, the Welsh language public service broadcaster, receives annual funding from the Department for Digital, Culture, Media and Sport (DCMS), which was maintained in 2016–17 at the same level established in 2015–16; it now receives £6.8m per year. Amid funding concerns for the future of S4C, it was agreed that the BBC would fund most of S4C's activities from the licence fee, contributing £74.5m per year until at least 2018. S4C will remain independent and be entitled to receive UK government funding and generate its own revenue. The on-demand service is called S4C Clic.

Channel 5 began broadcasting in 1997. It was rebranded Five in 2002 but reverted to its original name, Channel 5, after the station was acquired by Northern & Shell in July 2010. Digital stations 5USA and 5Star (formerly Five Life, then Fiver) were launched in October 2006. My5 (formerly Demand 5) is an online service, launched in June 2008, where viewers can watch and download content from the last 30 days on various platforms.

BSkyB was formed after the merger in 1990 of Sky Television and British Sky Broadcasting. Now known as Sky plc, the company operates across five countries: Italy, Germany, Austria, the UK and Ireland and serves 22 million customers. In addition to television services, Sky provides broadband and fixed line telephone services and is the UK's largest pay-TV broadcaster, with 12.5 million customers in 2017. In 2007, Freeview overtook Sky as the UK's most popular digital service. In 2014, BSkyB acquired Sky Italia and a 90.04 per cent majority interest in Sky Deutschland. 21st Century Fox owns a 39.14 per cent controlling stake in the company. In the UK, the company changed its operations name to Sky UK Limited but continued to trade under the name Sky. Its television service includes Sky Sports, Sky Cinema and Sky Arts.

In February 2011, a new version of OFCOM's Broadcasting Code came into force, permitting product placement for the first time in UK-produced television programmes. A large 'P' logo designed by OFCOM and broadcasters is displayed at the beginning and end of each programme containing product placement. The first instance of product placement occurred on 28 February 2011.

THE TELEVISION LICENCE

In the UK and its dependencies, a television licence is required to receive any publicly broadcast television service, regardless of its source, including commercial, satellite and cable programming. A TV licence registered to a home address allows the viewer to watch television on laptops, tablets and mobile phones outside the place of residence. From 1 September 2016, new legislation required a TV licence to be needed for viewers using services such as BBC iPlayer, even if the programme was not being watched live. The BBC hoped that the new legislation would fill a £150m gap in its finances, which had been caused by the increasing number of viewers only using the iPlayer service.

The TV licence is classified as a tax, therefore non-payment is a criminal offence. A fine of up to £1,000 can be imposed on those successfully prosecuted. The TV licence is issued on behalf of the BBC as the licensing authority under the Communications Act 2003. In 2016–17 income from licence fees totalled £3,787m, an increase from £3,743m the previous year. In 2017, the TV licence fee increased for the first time since 2010 with an annual colour television licence costing £147 and a black and white licence £49. Concessions are available for the elderly and people with disabilities. Further details can be found at W www.tvlicensing.co.uk/information

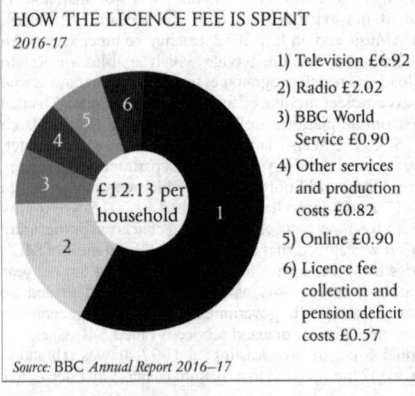

HOW THE LICENCE FEE IS SPENT
2016-17

£12.13 per household

1) Television £6.92
2) Radio £2.02
3) BBC World Service £0.90
4) Other services and production costs £0.82
5) Online £0.90
6) Licence fee collection and pension deficit costs £0.57

Source: BBC *Annual Report 2016–17*

DIGITAL TELEVISION

The Broadcasting Act 1996 provided for the licensing of 20 or more digital terrestrial television (DTT) channels (on six frequency channels or 'multiplexes'). The first digital services went on air in autumn 1998.

In June 2002, following the collapse of ITV Digital, the digital terrestrial television licence was awarded to a consortium made up of the BBC, BSkyB and transmitter company Crown Castle by the Independent Television Commission. Freeview was launched on 30 October 2002 with 25 free-to-air channels: it now offers over 60 digital channels, up to 15 HD channels and 25 radio stations and requires the one-off purchase of a set-top box, but is subsequently free of charge with no subscription. In Autumn 2005 ITV and Channel 4 officially became shareholders, each taking a 20 per cent stake. As at 2017, around 20 million homes use Freeview on at least one set, amounting to around 30 per cent of UK households. There is an additional Freeview+ service which works in a similar fashion to Sky+, allowing viewers to record programmes. Over 97 per cent of UK homes have access to digital television.

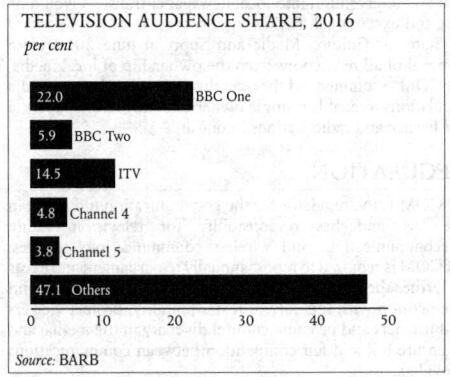

TELEVISION AUDIENCE SHARE, 2016
per cent

22.0	BBC One
5.9	BBC Two
14.5	ITV
4.8	Channel 4
3.8	Channel 5
47.1	Others

0   10   20   30   40   50

Source: BARB

RECENT DEVELOPMENTS

The internet has now firmly established itself as an alternative to live and programmed TV, particularly for those aged 16 to 34. Since the launch of 4oD in 2006 and BBC iPlayer in 2007, there has been a noticeable shift in the way viewers can watch their favourite programmes. Technological advancements have also contributed to this new phenomenon; more than half of the UK population uses a tablet, over 90 per cent of UK homes and businesses have access to superfast broadband and there are millions of public Wi-Fi hotspots across the UK. There is now a much bigger emphasis on catch-up, on-demand and streaming services than previously, with 315 million TV and radio requests in January 2016 alone, an increase of 2 per cent month-on-month. Streaming services such as Netflix have experienced a surge in popularity, with subscribers able to stream programmes through computers, mobiles, tablets and games consoles on up to four devices at a time for a monthly subscription fee. Netflix also commissions and distributes its own programmes, available exclusively to their subscribers, contributing to their popularity; as at 2017, Netflix has an estimated 6.5 million subscribers in the UK and is estimated to rise to 9.5 million by 2020. The BBC has provided exclusive content and programmes on the iPlayer since 2014 and in 2016 moved BBC Three to an online-only service. These transitions indicate that online catch-up and streaming services are now becoming competitive TV destinations in their own right.

Set-top boxes have also adapted to this viewing shift. YouView, in partnership with BBC, ITV, Channel Four, Channel Five, BT, Talk Talk and Arqiva, launched in July 2012. Subscribers are able to watch programmes (including on-demand), pause and rewind live TV and listen to digital radio via a hybrid set-top box connected to broadband.

Originally envisaged as free-to-air, it has drawn criticism for tying customers into broadband services and subscriptions with BT and Talk Talk, with the one-off payment for the YouView box more expensive than the Freeview box. In June 2014, Freeview announced plans for a Freeview Connect service, which launched as Freeview Play – offering over 60 TV channels and up to 15 HD channels, allowing viewers to watch programmes broadcast over the past seven days via an internet connection.

Despite the rise in the popularity of tablets, traditional TV sets are still the most popular way to watch television. HD TV provides more vibrant colours and greater detail and picture clarity, along with improved sound quality. An HD television screen uses 1,280 by 720 pixels up to 1,920 by 1,080 pixels. HD Ready TVs operate at 720p while full HD TVs tend to operate on 1080p or 1080i; the differences between these three settings are down to the number of lines in the resolution and the type of scanning technology. 'HD Ready' simply means the TV will only operate a higher definition once plugged into a decoder, whereas full HD has this built in. In 2016, the average screen size in the UK was 34.5 inches wide, indicating a trend towards bigger screens. Sales of Smart TVs, which can access apps, browse the internet and stream video, are rising with around 38 per cent of UK households owning a Smart TV in 2017.

In April 2010, Samsung released the first consumer 3D TV; in the same month Sky launched the UK's first dedicated 3D channel. Several sporting events have been broadcast in 3D including the Wimbledon Championships. The BBC began a two-year 3D trial in 2011 but announced in July 2013 it would suspend 3D programming for an indefinite period of time due to a lack of public appetite for the technology. Of the estimated 1.5 million 3D TV sets in the UK, just 5 per cent used 3D to watch the Queen's Christmas Speech 2013 and in the past two years the number of 3D TVs sold in the UK has begun to decline leading companies like LG and Sony to announce in 2017 their intention to discontinue their lines of 3D TVs.

In September 2012, OFCOM awarded its first local TV licences after announcing plans to broadcast 21 channels in total. In November 2013, Estuary TV, based in Grimsby, was the first to be launched. The government has backed the local TV initiative and the channels broadcast on channel 7 on Freeview in England and Northern Ireland and channel 8 in Scotland and Wales. In March 2013, OFCOM announced plans for a further 30 areas to invite bids for local television services but none had been launched as of September 2017.

CONTACTS

THE BRITISH BROADCASTING CORPORATION (BBC)

BBC Broadcasting House, Portland Place, London W1A 1AA
  W www.bbc.co.uk
BBC North, Media City UK, Bridge House, Salford Quays, Manchester M50 2BH
  Chair, BBC Board, Sir David Clementi
  Director-General, Baron Hall of Birkenhead
BBC Worldwide, 1 Television Centre, Wood Lane, London W12 7FA **W** www.bbcworldwide.com

INDEPENDENT TELEVISION (ITV)

London Television Centre, 72 Upper Ground, London SE1 9LT **W** www.itv.com
  Chair, Sir Peter Bazalgette
  Managing Director (ITV Studios), Julian Bellamy

INDEPENDENT TELEVISION (ITV) REGIONS

Anglia (eastern England), **W** www.itv.com/anglia
Border (Borders and the Isle of Man), **W** www.itv.com/border
Calendar (Yorkshire), **W** www.itv.com/calendar
Central (east, west and south Midlands), **W** www.itv.com/central
Channel (Channel Islands), **W** www.itv.com/channel
Granada (north-west England), **W** www.itv.com/granada
London, **W** www.itv.com/london

Meridian (south and south-east England), **W** www.itv.com/meridian
STV (Scotland), **W** www.stv.tv
Tyne Tees (north-east England), **W** www.itv.com/tynetees
Ulster (Northern Ireland), **W** www.itv.com/utv
Wales, **W** www.itv.com/wales
West, **W** www.itv.com/west

OTHER TELEVISION COMPANIES

Channel 4 Television, 124 Horseferry Road, London SW1P 2TX **T** 020-7396 4444 **W** www.channel4.com
Channel 5 Broadcasting Ltd, 10 Lower Thames Street, London EC3R 6EN **T** 020-8612 7700 **W** www.channel5.com
Independent Television Network (ITN), 200 Gray's Inn Road, London WC1X 8XZ **T** 020-7833 3000 **W** www.itn.co.uk
Provides news programming and services for ITV, Channel 4 and Channel 5. as well as content for international news
Sianel Pedwar Cymru (S4/C), Parc Ty Glas, Llanishen, Cardiff CF14 5DU **T** 0870-600 4141 **W** www.s4c.cymru
Freeview, DTV Services Ltd, 27 Mortimer Street, London W1T 3JF **W** www.freeview.co.uk

DIRECT BROADCASTING BY SATELLITE TELEVISION

Sky plc, Grant Way, Isleworth, Isleworth TW7 5QD **T** 033-3100 0333 **W** www.sky.com
  Chair, James Murdoch

RADIO

UK domestic radio services are broadcast across three wavebands: FM, medium wave and long wave (used by BBC Radio 4). In the UK the FM waveband extends in frequency from 87.5MHz to 108MHz and the medium waveband from 531kHz to 1602kHz. A number of radio stations are broadcast in both analogue and digital as well as a growing number in digital alone. As at June 2017, the BBC Radio network controlled around 52.3 per cent of the listening market (*see* BBC Radio section), and the independent sector (*see* Independent Radio section) 45 per cent. As at June 2017, a listener tunes into an average of 20 hours of radio per week.

ESTIMATED AUDIENCE SHARE

			Percentage
	Apr–Jun 2015	Apr–Jun 2016	Apr–Jun 2017
BBC Radio 1	6.4	5.7	6.2
BBC Radio 2	17.6	17.2	16.8
BBC Radio 3	1.3	1.2	1.2
BBC Radio 4	11.7	11.2	12.3
BBC Radio Five Live	3.5	3.9	3.4
Five Live Sports Extra	0.6	0.3	0.3
BBC 6 Music	1.8	2.1	1.9
BBC Asian Network UK	0.4	0.4	0.3
1Xtra	0.5	0.5	0.5
BBC Local/Regional	7.5	7.0	7.3
BBC World Service	0.7	0.7	0.9
All BBC	53.0	52.2	52.3
All independent	44.4	45.2	45.0
All national independent	14.5	15.8	16.7
All local independent	29.8	29.6	28.4
Other	2.6	2.6	2.8

Source: RAJAR

DIGITAL RADIO

The UK has the world's largest digital radio network, with 103 transmitters, two national Digital Audio Broadcasting (DAB) ensembles and a total of 48 local and regional DAB ensembles, which broadcast around 250 independent and 34 BBC radio stations. The BBC began test transmissions of the DAB Eureka 147 digital radio service in 1990 from the Crystal Palace transmitting station and the service was publicly launched in 1995. As well as DAB, digital televisions, car radios, games consoles, mobile devices and the internet are commonly employed as platforms to listen to radio in the UK. One of the major benefits of DAB is better sound quality than analogue radio, and the availability of a wider choice of stations, in addition to the lack of interference experienced by other broadcast media.

The UK government intends to migrate the majority of AM and FM analogue radio services to digital between 2015–19, based on certain conditions being met such as coverage, listening figures and agreements in relation to funding. In the second quarter of 2016, 45.3 per cent of all radio listening hours in the UK were through digital platforms. From this 45.3 per cent, DAB made up the majority of listenership with 71 per cent. In 2016, over 55 per cent of all UK households were believed to have access to DAB radio.

The BBC's national DAB ensemble has coverage across the UK of around 97 per cent and broadcasts on the frequency 225.648 MHz. Owned and operated by the BBC, the multiplex of broadcasts is transmitted across the UK from a number of sites. Local and regional ensembles, which cover 71.7 per cent of the UK, are transmitted through a number of DAB multiplex operators across the UK, including Digital One and Sound Digital – the two national operators – in addition to local multiplex operators.

There are two criteria that must be met for digital migration to occur:

- at least 50 per cent of radio listening is digital
- national DAB coverage is comparable to FM coverage, and local DAB reaches 90 per cent of the population and all major roads

LICENSING

The Broadcasting Act 1996 provided for the licensing of digital radio services (on multiplexes, where a number of stations share one frequency to transmit their services). To allocate the multiplexes, OFCOM advertises licences for which interested parties can bid. Once the licence has been awarded, the new owner seeks out services to broadcast on the multiplex. The BBC has a separate national multiplex for its services. There are local multiplexes around the country, each broadcasting an average of seven services, plus the local BBC station.

INNOVATIONS

The internet offers a number of advantages compared to other digital platforms such as DAB, including higher sound quality, a greater range of channel availability and flexibility in listening opportunity. Listeners can tune in to the majority of radio stations live on the internet or listen again online generally up to seven days after broadcast. DAB radio does not allow the same interactivity: the data is only able to travel one-way from broadcaster to listener whereas the internet allows a two-way flow of information.

Increases in Wi-Fi hotspots also means listening to radio, podcasts and catch-up programmes is easy to do through tablets and mobile phones; in 2016, over 45 per cent of all reported radio listening was via a digital platform. The increase in music streaming services and radio-related apps has had a major effect on music discovery and sharing. In the UK in 2016 the number of streams per week averaged around 500 million. Since 6 July 2014 the UK Official Charts Company has included streaming services in its compilation, with 100 streams the equivalent to one purchase.

Since 2005 most radio stations offer all or part of their programmes as downloadable files, known as podcasts, to listen to on computers, mobiles or tablets. Podcasting technology allows listeners to subscribe in order to receive automatically the latest episodes of regularly transmitted programmes as soon as they become available.

The relationship between radio stations and their audiences is also undergoing change. The quantity and availability of music on the internet has led to the creation of shows dedicated entirely to music sent in by listeners. Another new development in internet-based radio is personalised radio stations, such as Soundcloud and Spotify. Soundcloud allows users to upload, record, promote and share their music and sounds. Artists who upload their music are given a URL, allowing their music to be embedded anywhere, making it easier to share through social media platforms such as Twitter and Facebook. Users can also create their own playlists and link them to social media platforms. Spotify, available as an app on most smart phones and tablets as well as online, allows listeners access to the track, artist or genre of their choice, or to share and create playlists. It has seen steady growth in popularity since its launch in 2008, with 60 million paying subscribers and 140 million active users globally, as at June 2017. Spotify 'learns as you listen' and makes associated recommendations based on user choices. Radioplayer (W www.radioplayer.co.uk), a not-for-profit company backed by the BBC, Global Radio, Bauer Media and RadioCentre, allows audiences to listen to live and catch-up radio from one place. Over 6 million people per month use the Radioplayer service. There are over 400 stations available and a 'recommended' service which offers station suggestions depending on location, what is trending and the type of music the user likes. Radioplayer launched as a mobile app in 2012 and a tablet app in 2013. Through the tablet app, users sample an average of 4.6 stations a week in comparison with just 2.1 for analogue users.

BBC RADIO

BBC Radio broadcasts network services to the UK, Isle of Man and the Channel Islands, with around 34.7 million listeners each week. There is also a tier of national services in Wales, Scotland and Northern Ireland and around 40 local radio stations in England and the Channel Islands. In Wales and Scotland there are also dedicated language services in Welsh and Gaelic respectively. The frequency allocated for digital BBC broadcasts is 225.648MHz.

BBC Radio, Broadcasting House, Portland Place, London W1A 1AA
W www.bbc.co.uk/radio

BBC NETWORK RADIO STATIONS

Radio 1 (contemporary pop music and entertainment news) – 24 hours a day, *Frequencies:* 97–99 FM and digital

Radio 2 (popular music, entertainment, comedy and the arts) – 24 hours a day, *Frequencies:* 88–91 FM and digital

Radio 3 (classical music, classic drama, documentaries and features) – 24 hours a day, *Frequencies:* 90–93 FM and digital

Radio 4 (news, documentaries, drama, entertainment and cricket on long wave in season) – 5.20am–1am daily, with BBC World Service overnight, *Frequencies:* 92–95 FM/103–105 FM and 198 LW and digital

Radio Five Live (news and sport) – 24 hours a day, *Frequencies:* 909/693 MW and digital*Five Live Sports Extra* (live sport) – schedule varies, digital only

6 Music (contemporary and classic pop and rock music) – 24 hours a day, digital only

Asian Network (news, music and sport) – 5am–1am, with Radio Five Live overnight, *Frequencies:* various MW frequencies in Midlands and digital

BBC NATIONAL RADIO STATIONS

Radio Cymru (Welsh-language), *Frequencies:* 92–105 FM and digital

Radio Foyle, Frequencies: 93.1 FM and 792 MW and digital

Radio nan Gaidheal (Gaelic service), *Frequencies:* 103–105 FM and digital

Radio Scotland, Frequencies: 92–95 FM and 810 MW and digital. Local programmes for Orkney, Shetland and Highlands and Islands

Radio Ulster, Frequencies: 1341 MW and 92–95 FM and digital. Local programmes on Radio Foyle

Radio Wales, Frequencies: 657/882 MW and 93–104 FM and digital

BBC WORLD SERVICE

The BBC World Service broadcasts to an estimated weekly audience of 1.3 million people in the UK and 210 million worldwide, in 31 languages including English, and is now available in around 150 capital cities. It no longer broadcasts in Dutch, French for Europe, German, Hebrew, Italian, Japanese or Malay because it was found that most speakers of these languages preferred to listen to the English broadcasts. In 2006 services in ten languages (Bulgarian, Croatian, Czech, Greek, Hungarian, Kazakh, Polish, Slovak, Slovene and Thai) were terminated to provide funding for a new Arabic television channel, which was launched in March 2008. In August 2008 the BBC's Romanian World Service broadcasts were discontinued after 68 years. In January 2011 the BBC announced five more language services would be terminated: Albanian, Caribbean English, Macedonian, Portuguese for Africa and Serbian. The BBC World Service website offers interactive news services in 28 languages including English, Arabic, Chinese, Hindi, Persian, Portuguese for Brazil, Russian, Spanish and Urdu with audiostreaming available.

LANGUAGES
Arabic, Azeri, Bengali, Burmese, Cantonese, English, French, Hausa, Hindi, Indonesian, Kinyarwanda, Kirundi, Kyrgyz, Nepali, Nigerian Pidgin, Pashto, Persian, Portuguese, Russian, Sinhala, Somali, Spanish, Swahili, Tamil, Turkish, Ukrainian, Urdu, Uzbek, Yoruba and Vietnamese.

UK frequencies: digital; overnight on BBC Radio 4.
BBC Learning English teaches English worldwide through radio, television and a wide range of published and online courses.
BBC Media Action is a registered charity established in 1999 by BBC World Service, known as the BBC World Service Trust until December 2011. It promotes development through the innovative use of the media in the developing world.
BBC Monitoring tracks the global media for the latest news reports emerging around the world.

BBC WORLD SERVICE, Broadcasting House, Portland Place, London W1A 1AA **W** www.bbc.co.uk/worldservice

INDEPENDENT RADIO

Until 1973, the BBC had a legal monopoly on radio broadcasting in the UK. During this time, the corporation's only competition came from pirate stations located abroad, such as Radio Luxembourg. Christopher Chataway, Minister for Post and Telecommunications, changed this by creating the first licences for commercial radio stations. The Independent Broadcasting Authority (IBA) awarded the first of these licences to the London Broadcasting Company (LBC) to provide London's news and information service. LBC was followed by Capital Radio, to offer the city's entertainment service, Radio Clyde in Glasgow and BRMB in Birmingham.

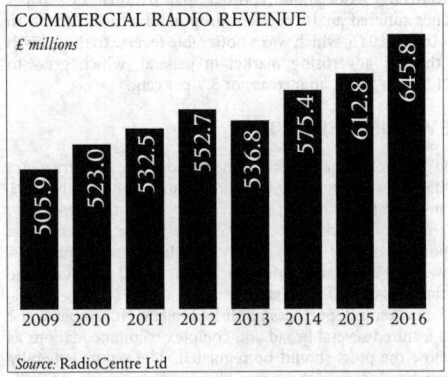

COMMERCIAL RADIO REVENUE
£ millions

2009	2010	2011	2012	2013	2014	2015	2016
505.9	523.0	532.5	552.7	536.8	575.4	612.8	645.8

Source: RadioCentre Ltd

The IBA was dissolved when the Broadcasting Act of 1990 de-regulated broadcasting, to be succeeded by the less rigid Radio Authority (RA). The RA began advertising new licences for the development of independent radio in January 1991. It awarded national and local radio, satellite and cable services licences, and long-term restricted service licences for stations serving non-commercial establishments such as hospitals and universities. The first national commercial digital multiplex licence was awarded in October 1998 and a number of local digital multiplex licences followed. At the end of 2003 the RA was replaced by OFCOM, which now carries out the licensing administration.

RadioCentre was formed in July 2006 as a result of the merger between the Radio Advertising Bureau (RAB) and the Commercial Radio Companies Association (CRCA), the former non-profit trade body for commercial radio companies in the UK, to operate essentially as a union for commercial radio stations.

RadioCentre, 6th Floor, 55 New Oxford Street, London WC1A 1BS
T 020-7010 0600
W www.radiocentre.org
Chief Executive, Siobhan Kenny

THE PRESS

The newspaper and periodical press in the UK is large and diverse, catering for a wide variety of views and interests. There is no state control or censorship of the press; however, it is subject to the laws on publication.

The press is not state-subsidised and receives few tax concessions. The income of most newspapers and periodicals is derived largely from sales and from advertising. The Advertising Association reported that national newspaper brands suffered an 10 per cent drop in advertising spend to £1.1bn in 2016, which was a noticeable reverse to the growth of the UK advertising market in general, which grew to £21.3bn in 2016, an increase of 3.7 per cent.

LEVESON REPORT

The Leveson Inquiry, established under the Inquiries Act 2005, was announced by the prime minister on 13 July 2011 to investigate the role of press and police in the News of the World phone-hacking scandal. Lord Justice Leveson was appointed as chair of the inquiry. The hearings began on 14 November 2011 and ended on 24 July 2012 following the testimonies of 650 witnesses.

The Leveson Report was published in late November 2012 and featured several broad and complex recommendations as to how the press should be regulated. The report generally recommended that the press should continue to be self-regulated, with the government allowed no direct power over what is published, and that a new press standards body, with a new code of conduct, should be established by legislation in order to ensure regulation is independent and effective. Lord Justice Leveson concluded that this arrangement should give the public confidence that their complaints would be dealt with seriously and ensure the press would be protected from interference.

SELF-REGULATION

Following the publication of the Leveson Report the Press Complaints Commission (PCC), which had been established in January 1991 as a non-statutory body to operate the press's self-regulation, was closed and replaced by the Independent Press Standards Organisation (IPSO) on 8 September 2014. While the majority of newspapers have signed up to the new regulator, several have not, including The Guardian, the Financial Times and the London Evening Standard.

In 2013 a royal charter on press regulation was granted by the Privy Council to create a watchdog to oversee a new regulator. On 3 November 2014, a fully independent body, the Press Recognition Panel (PRP) was established to consider whether press regulators meet the criteria recommended in the Leveson Report and, if so, to afford these regulators official recognition.

IPSO has not sought recognition from the PRP, but another regulator, IMPRESS, established by a group of free speech campaigners, is aiming to become compliant with the requirements of the Leveson Report and announced in May 2015 its intention to seek recognition from the PRP.

INDEPENDENT PRESS STANDARDS ORGANISATION,
Gate House, 1 Farringdon Street, London EC4M 7LH
T 0300-123 2220
E inquiries@ipso.co.uk W www.ipso.co.uk
Chair, Rt. Hon. Sir Alan Moses

PRESS RECOGNITION PANEL, Mappin House, 4 Winsley Street, London W1W 8HF
E contact@pressrecognitionpanel.org.uk
W www.pressrecognitionpanel.org.uk
Chair, Dr David Wolfe, QC

NEWSPAPERS

Newspapers are mostly financially independent of any political party, though most adopt a political stance in their editorial comments, usually reflecting proprietorial influence. Ownership of the national and regional daily newspapers is concentrated in the hands of large corporations whose interests cover publishing and communications, although The Guardian and The Observer are owned by the Scott Trust, formed in 1936 to protect the financial and editorial independence of The Guardian in perpetuity. The rules on cross-media ownership, as amended by the Broadcasting Act 1996, which limited the extent to which newspaper organisations may become involved in broadcasting, have been relaxed by the Communications Act 2003: newspapers with over a 20 per cent share of national circulation may own national and/or local radio licences.

In October 2010, The Independent launched a concise newspaper, i, the first new daily newspaper since 1986 but the final editions of The Independent and The Independent on Sunday were published in March 2016 as the paper moved to digital only. In July 2011, News of the World was closed by its parent company, News International, following accusations of phone-hacking. In February 2012 News International printed the first edition of The Sun on Sunday, a Sunday format of the daily tabloid paper The Sun. In February 2016, Trinity Mirror launched a compact daily newspaper, The New Day – the first new standalone paper since The Independent in 1986 – but it ceased publication in May 2016 after a sharp drop in circulation. There are 11 daily and Sunday national papers and several hundred local papers that are published daily, weekly or twice-weekly. Scotland, Wales and Northern Ireland all have at least one daily and one Sunday national paper.

UK CIRCULATION

National Daily Newspapers	June 2016	June 2017	% +/–
The Sun	1,755,331	1,571,168	–10.49
Daily Mail	1,548,349	1,440,392	–6.97
Daily Mirror	770,714	640,747	–16.86
Daily Star	513,452	426,154	–17.0
The Daily Telegraph	496,286	484,010	–2.47
The Times	449,151	458,381	2.05
Daily Express	421,057	381,467	–9.4
i	294,223	270,990	–7.9
Financial Times	199,359	193,029	–3.18
The Guardian	171,723	159,007	–7.4
Daily Record	167,865	145,724	–13.19

National Sunday Newspapers	June 2016	June 2017	% +/–
The Sun on Sunday	1,479,144	1,344,894	–9.08
The Mail on Sunday	1,361,228	1,236,839	–9.14
The Sunday Times	806,375	792,081	–1.77
Sunday Mirror	696,504	555,800	–20.2
The Sunday Telegraph	383,898	355,539	–7.15
Sunday Express	372,247	328,559	–11.74
Daily Star Sunday	336,618	250,248	–25.66
Sunday People	273,029	224,652	–17.72
The Observer	205,007	192,889	–5.91
Sunday Mail	177,277	153,427	–13.45
Sunday Post	151,861	135,747	–10.61

Source: Audit Bureau of Circulations Ltd

Newspapers are usually published in either broadsheet or smaller, tabloid format. The 'quality' daily papers – ie those providing detailed coverage of a wide range of public matters – have traditionally been broadsheets, the more populist newspapers tabloid. In 2004 this correlation between format and content was redefined when two traditionally broadsheet newspapers, *The Times* and *The Independent*, switched to tabloid-sized editions, while *The Guardian* launched a 'Berliner' format in September 2005. In October 2005 *The Independent on Sunday* became the first Sunday broadsheet to be published in the tabloid (or 'compact') size, and *The Observer*, like its daily counterpart *The Guardian*, began publishing in the Berliner format in January 2006.

NEWSPAPERS ONLINE

The demand to read news instantly and while on the move has increased the popularity of newspaper websites. Most newspapers now operate their own websites in line with their print editions, often including the same material as seen in daily printed editions but can also include video and audio features. Many articles and columns additionally have the option of reader contributions and debate. Certain newspapers charge a subscription fee to access their websites but the majority are free to browse.

NATIONAL PRESS WEBSITE DAILY AVERAGE BROWSERS

National Press Website	June 2016	June 2017	% +/-
MailOnline	15,053,614	15,406,452	2.3
theguardian.com	10,304,181	–	–
Mirror Group Nationals	5,032,799	5,641,634	12.1
Telegraph	5,623,053	5,013,911	-10.83
The Independent	4,382,722	6,157,038	40.48
express.co.uk	1,851,337	2,091,497	12.97
dailystar.co.uk	818,188	909,923	11.21

Source: Audit Bureau of Circulations Ltd

NATIONAL DAILY NEWSPAPERS

DAILY EXPRESS
Northern & Shell Building, 10 Lower Thames Street, London EC3R 6EN T 020-8612 7000 W www.express.co.uk
Editor, Hugh Whittow

DAILY MAIL
Northcliffe House, 2 Derry Street, London W8 5TT T 020-7938 6000 W www.dailymail.co.uk
Editor, Paul Dacre

DAILY MIRROR
1 Canada Square, Canary Wharf, London E14 5AP T 020-7293 3000 W www.mirror.co.uk
Editor, Lloyd Embley

DAILY RECORD
1 Central Quay, Glasgow G3 8DA T 0141-309 3000 W www.dailyrecord.co.uk
Editor, Murray Foote

DAILY STAR
Northern & Shell Building, 10 Lower Thames Street, London EC3R 6EN T 020-8612 7000 W www.dailystar.co.uk
Editor, Dawn Neesom

THE DAILY TELEGRAPH
111 Buckingham Palace Road, London SW1W 0DT T 020-7931 2000 W www.telegraph.co.uk
Editor, Chris Evans

FINANCIAL TIMES
1 Southwark Bridge, London SE1 9HL T 020-7873 3000 W www.ft.com
Editor, Lionel Barber

THE GUARDIAN
Kings Place, 90 York Way, London N1 9GU T 020-3353 2000 W www.theguardian.com
Editor, Katharine Viner

THE HERALD
200 Renfield Street, Glasgow G2 3QB T 0141-302 7000 W www.heraldscotland.com
Editor, Graeme Smith

i
2 Derry Street, London W8 5HF T 020-7005 2000 W www.inews.co.uk
Editor, Oliver Duff

THE SCOTSMAN
Orchard Brae House, 30 Queensferry Road, Edinburgh EH4 2HS T 0131-311 7311 W www.scotsman.com
Editorial Director, Frank O'Donnell

THE SUN
1 London Bridge Street, London SE1 9GF T 020-7782 4000 W www.thesun.co.uk
Editor, Tony Gallagher

THE TIMES
1 London Bridge Street, London SE1 9GF T 020-7782 5000 W www.thetimes.co.uk
Editor, John Witherow

WEEKLY NEWSPAPERS

DAILY STAR SUNDAY
Northern & Shell Building, 10 Lower Thames Street, London EC3R 6EN T 020-8612 7000 W www.dailystar.co.uk/sunday
Editor, Stuart James

MAIL ON SUNDAY
Northcliffe House, 2 Derry Street, London W8 HFT T 020-7938 6000 W www.mailonsunday.co.uk
Editor, Geordie Greig

THE OBSERVER
Kings Place, 90 York Way, London N1 9GU T 020-3353 2000 W www.theguardian.com/observer
Editor, John Mulholland

THE SUNDAY PEOPLE
1 Canada Square, Canary Wharf, London E14 5AP T 020-7293 3000 W www.people.co.uk
Editor, Gary Jones

SCOTLAND ON SUNDAY
Orchard Brae House, 30 Queensferry Road, Edinburgh EH4 2HS T 0131-311 7311 W www.scotlandonsunday.com
Editorial Director, Frank O'Donnell

THE SUN ON SUNDAY
1 London Bridge Street, London SE1 9GF T 020-7782 4000 W www.thesun.co.uk
Editor, Victoria Newton

SUNDAY EXPRESS
Northern & Shell Building, 10 Lower Thames Street, London EC4R 6EN T 020-8612 7000 W www.sundayexpress.co.uk
Editor, Martin Townsend

SUNDAY HERALD
200 Renfield Street, Glasgow G2 3QB T 0141-302 7000 W www.sundayherald.com
Executive Editor, Neil McKay

SUNDAY MAIL
1 Central Quay, Glasgow G3 8DA T 0141-309 3000 W www.sundaymail.com
Editor, Jim Wilson

SUNDAY MIRROR
1 Canada Square, Canary Wharf, London E14 5AP **T** 020-7293
3000 **W** www.sundaymirror.co.uk
Editor, Gary Jones

SUNDAY POST
2 Albert Square, Dundee, DD1 1DD **T** 01382-223131
W www.sundaypost.com
Editor, Richard Prest

SUNDAY TELEGRAPH
111 Buckingham Palace Road, London SW1W 0DT **T** 020-7931
2000 **W** www.telegraph.co.uk
Editor, Allister Heath

THE SUNDAY TIMES
1 London Bridge Street, London SE1 9GF **T** 020-7782 5000
W www.thesundaytimes.co.uk
Editor, Martin Ivens

REGIONAL NEWSPAPERS

EAST ANGLIA

CAMBRIDGE NEWS
Winship Road, Milton, Cambs. CB24 6PP **T** 01223-434434
W www.cambridge-news.co.uk
Editor, David Bartlett

EAST ANGLIAN DAILY TIMES
Portman House, 120 Princes Street, Ipswich IP1 1RS **T** 01473-
230023 **W** www.eadt.co.uk
Editor, Terry Hunt

EASTERN DAILY PRESS
Prospect House, Rouen Road, Norwich NR1 1RE **T** 01603-628311
W www.edp24.co.uk
Editor, David Powles

IPSWICH STAR
Lower Brook Street, Ipswich, Suffolk IP4 1AN **T** 01473-230023
W www.ipswichstar.co.uk
Editor, Brad Jones

NORWICH EVENING NEWS
Prospect House, Rouen Road, Norwich NR1 1RE **T** 01603-628311
W www.eveningnews24.co.uk
Editor, David Powles

EAST MIDLANDS

BURTON MAIL
Milton House, Worthington Way, Burton upon Trent DE14 1BQ **T**
01283-245000 **W** www.burtonmail.co.uk
Editor, Emma Turton

DERBY TELEGRAPH
2 Siddals Road, Derby DE1 2PB **T** 01332-411888
W www.derbytelegraph.co.uk
Editor, Steve Hall

THE LEICESTER MERCURY
St George Street, Leicester LE1 9FQ **T** 0116-251 2512
W www.leicestermercury.co.uk
Editor, George Oliver

LINCOLNSHIRE ECHO
Witham Wharf, Brayford Wharf East, Lincoln LN5 7AY
T 01522-804300 **W** www.lincolnshirelive.co.uk
Editor, Charles Walker

NORTHAMPTON CHRONICLE & ECHO
Albert House, Victoria Street, Northants NN1 3NR **T** 01604-467000
W www.northamptonchron.co.uk
Editor, David Summers

NOTTINGHAM POST
City Gate, Tollhouse Hill, Notts NG1 5FS **T** 0115-948 2000
W www.nottinghampost.com
Editor, Mike Sassi

LONDON

EVENING STANDARD
Northcliffe House, 2 Derry Street, London W8 5TT **T** 020-3367 7000
W www.standard.co.uk
Editor, George Osborne

METRO
Northcliffe House, 2 Derry Street, London W8 5TT **T** 020-3615 3480
W www.metro.co.uk
Editor, Ted Young

NORTH EAST

EVENING CHRONICLE
Groat Market, Newcastle upon Tyne NE1 1ED **T** 0191-232 7500
W www.chroniclelive.co.uk
Editor, Darren Thwaites

HARTLEPOOL MAIL
9–13 Scarborough Street, Hartlepool TS24 7DA **T** 01429-235197
W www.hartlepoolmail.co.uk
Editor, Joy Yates

THE JOURNAL
Groat Market, Newcastle upon Tyne NE1 1ED **T** 0191-201 6491
W www.thejournal.co.uk
Editor, Darren Thwaites

THE NORTHERN ECHO
PO Box 14, Priestgate, Darlington, Co. Durham DL1 1NF **T** 01325-
381313 **W** www.thenorthernecho.co.uk
Editor, Andy Richardson

THE SHIELDS GAZETTE
7 Beach Road, South Shields, Tyne & Wear NE33 2QA **T** 0191-501
7436 **W** www.shieldsgazette.com
Editor, Joy Yates

THE SUNDAY SUN
Groat Market, Newcastle upon Tyne NE1 1ED **T** 0191-232 7500
W www.sundaysun.co.uk
Editor, Matt McKenzie

SUNDERLAND ECHO
Echo House, Pennywell, Sunderland SR4 9ER **T** 0191-501 5800
W www.sunderlandecho.com
Editor, Joy Yates

TEESIDE GAZETTE
1st Floor, Hudson Quay, The Halyard, Middlehaven, Middlesbrough
TS3 6RT **T** 01642-234262 **W** www.gazettelive.co.uk
Editor, Chris Styles

NORTH WEST

THE BLACKPOOL GAZETTE
Avroe House, Avroe Crescent, Blackpool FY4 2DP **T** 01253-400888
W www.blackpoolgazette.co.uk
Editor, Gillian Parkinson

THE BOLTON NEWS
The Wellsprings, Victoria Square, Bolton BL1 1AR T 01204-522345
W www.theboltonnews.co.uk
Editor, Ian Savage

CARLISLE NEWS AND STAR
Newspaper House, Dalston Road, Carlisle CA2 5UA
T 01228-612600 W www.newsandstar.co.uk

LANCASHIRE EVENING POST
Stuart House, 89 Caxton Road, Fulwood, Preston PR2 9ZB
T 01772-254841 W www.lep.co.uk
Editor, Gillian Parkinson

LANCASHIRE TELEGRAPH
50–54 Church Street, Blackburn, Lancs. BB1 5AL T 01254 678678
W www.lancashiretelegraph.co.uk
Editor, Steven Thompson

LIVERPOOL ECHO
PO Box 48, Old Hall Street, Liverpool L69 3EB T 0151-227 2000
W www.liverpoolecho.co.uk
Editor, Alastair Machray

MANCHESTER EVENING NEWS
Mitchell Henry House, Hollinwood Avenue, Chadderton OL9 8EF
T 0161-832 7200 W www.manchestereveningnews.co.uk
Editor, Rob Irvine

NORTH-WEST EVENING MAIL
Abbey Road, Barrow-in-Furness, Cumbria LA14 5QS
T 01229-840100 W www.nwemail.co.uk
Editor, James Higgins

SOUTH EAST

THE ARGUS
Dolphin House, 2–5 Manchester Street, Brighton BN2 1TF
T 01273-021400 W www.theargus.co.uk
Editor, Aaron Hendy

ECHO
Newspaper House, Chester Hall Lane, Basildon, Essex SS14 3BL
T 01268-522792 W www.echo-news.co.uk
Editor, Chris Hatton

MEDWAY MESSENGER
Medway House, Ginsbury Close, Sir Thomas Longley Road, Strood,
Kent ME2 4DU T 01634-227800 W www.kentonline.co.uk/
medway
Editor, Matt Ramsden

THE NEWS, PORTSMOUTH
1000 Lakeside, North Harbour, Portsmouth PO6 3EN
T 023-9266 4488 W www.portsmouth.co.uk
Editor, Mark Waldron

OXFORD MAIL
Newsquest Oxfordshire & Wiltshire, Osney Mead, Oxford OX2 0EJ
T 01865-425262 W www.oxfordmail.co.uk
Managing Editor, Sara Taylor

READING CHRONICLE
2–10 Bridge Street, Reading, Berks. RG1 2LU T 0118-955 3333
W www.readingchronicle.co.uk
Group Editor, Samantha Harman

THE SOUTHERN DAILY ECHO
Newspaper House, Test Lane, Redbridge, Southampton SO16 9JX T
023-8042 4777 W www.dailyecho.co.uk
Editor, Gordon Sutter

SOUTH WEST

BRISTOL POST
Temple Way, Bristol BS2 0BY T 0117-934 3000
W www.bristolpost.co.uk
Editor, Mike Norton

BOURNEMOUTH ECHO
Richmond Hill, Bournemouth BH2 6HH T 01202-554601
W www.bournemouthecho.co.uk
Editor, Andy Martin

DORSET ECHO
Fleet House, Hampshire Road, Weymouth, Dorset DT4 9XD
T 01305-830930 W www.dorsetecho.co.uk
Editor, Diarmuid MacDonagh

EXETER EXPRESS & ECHO
Heron Road, Sowton, Exeter EX2 7NF T 01392-442220
W www.exeterexpressandecho.co.uk
Editor, Jim Parker

GLOUCESTER CITIZEN
St James's Square, Cheltenham GL50 3PR T 01242-278000
W www.gloucestershirelive.co.uk
Editor, Jenny Eastwood

GLOUCESTERSHIRE ECHO
St James's Square, Cheltenham GL50 3PR T 01242-278000
W www.gloucestershirelive.co.uk
Editor, Matt Holmes

THE HERALD
3rd Floor, Millbay Road, Plymouth PL1 3LF T 01752-293000
W www.plymouthherald.co.uk
Editor, Paul Burton

SUNDAY INDEPENDENT
Oakland Mews, Owen Sivell Close, Liskeard PL14 3UX
T 01579-556972 W www.sundayindependent.co.uk
Editor, John Collings

SWINDON ADVERTISER
100 Victoria Road, Old Town, Swindon SN1 3BE T 01793-528144
W www.swindonadvertiser.co.uk
Editor, Gary Lawrence

TORQUAY HERALD EXPRESS
Barton Hill Road, Torquay, Devon TQ2 8JN T 01803-676000
W www.torquayheraldexpress.co.uk
Editor, Jim Parker

WESTERN DAILY PRESS
Temple Way, Bristol BS99 7HD T 0117-934 3000
W www.somersetlive.co.uk
Editor, Gavin Thompson

THE WESTERN MORNING NEWS
3rd Floor, Millbay Road, Plymouth PL1 3LF T 01752-293000
W www.westernmorningnews.co.uk
Editor, Bill Martin

WEST MIDLANDS

BIRMINGHAM MAIL
6th Floor, Fort Dunlop, Fort Parkway, Birmingham B24 9FF
T 0121-234 5536 W www.birminghammail.co.uk
Editor-in-Chief, Marc Reeves

THE BIRMINGHAM POST
6th Floor, Fort Dunlop, Fort Parkway, Birmingham B24 9FF **T** 0121-236 5000
W www.birminghampost.co.uk
Editor-in-Chief, Marc Reeves

COVENTRY TELEGRAPH
Corporation Street, Coventry CV1 1FP **T** 024-7663 3633
W www.coventrytelegraph.net
Editor, Keith Perry

EXPRESS & STAR
51–53 Queen Street, Wolverhampton WV1 1ES **T** 01902-313131
W www.expressandstar.com
Editor, Keith Harrison

THE SENTINEL
Sentinel House, Bethesda Street, Stoke-on-Trent ST1 3GN
T 01782-864100 **W** www.stokesentinel.co.uk
Editor, Martin Tideswell

SHROPSHIRE STAR
Waterloo Road, Ketley, Telford TF1 5HU **T** 01952-242424
W www.shropshirestar.com
Editor, Martin Wright

WORCESTER NEWS
Berrows House, Hylton Road, Worcester WR2 5JX **T** 01905-748200
W www.worcesternews.co.uk
Editor, Peter John

YORKSHIRE AND HUMBERSIDE

GRIMSBY TELEGRAPH
80 Cleethorpe Road, Grimsby, Lincs DN31 3EH **T** 01472-360360
W www.grimsbytelegraph.co.uk

HALIFAX COURIER
PO Box 19, King Cross Street, Halifax HX1 2SF **T** 01422-260200
W www.halifaxcourier.co.uk
Editor, John Kenealy

THE HUDDERSFIELD DAILY EXAMINER
Pennine Business Park, Longbow Close, Bradley Road, Huddersfield HD2 1GQ **T** 01484-430000 **W** www.examiner.co.uk
Editor, Wayne Ankers

HULL DAILY MAIL
Blundell's Corner, Beverley Road, Hull HU3 1XS **T** 01482-327111
W www.hulldailymail.co.uk
Editor, Neil Hodgkinson

THE PRESS
PO Box 29, 76–86 Walmgate, York YO1 9YN **T** 01904-567131
W www.yorkpress.co.uk
Editor (acting), Nigel Burton

SCARBOROUGH NEWS
17–23 Aberdeen Walk, Scarborough, N. Yorks YO11 1BB
T 01723-60100 **W** www.thescarboroughnews.co.uk
Editor, Ed Asquith

SHEFFIELD STAR
York Street, Sheffield S1 1PU **T** 0114-276 7676
W www.thestar.co.uk
Editor, Nancy Fielder

TELEGRAPH & ARGUS
Hall Ings, Bradford BD1 1JR **T** 01274-729511
W www.thetelegraphandargus.co.uk
Editor (acting), Nigel Burton

YORKSHIRE EVENING POST
26 Whitehall Road, Leeds LS12 1BE **T** 0113-243 2701
W www.yorkshireeveningpost.co.uk
Editor, Hannah Thaxter

YORKSHIRE POST
26 Whitehall Road, Leeds LS12 1BE **T** 0113-243 2701
W www.yorkshirepost.co.uk
Editor, James Mitchinson

SCOTLAND

THE COURIER
80 Kingsway East, Dundee DD4 8SL **T** 01382-223131
W www.thecourier.co.uk
Editor (acting), Catriona MacInnes

DUNDEE EVENING TELEGRAPH
2 Albert Square, Dundee DD1 1DD **T** 01382-575950
W www.eveningtelegraph.co.uk
Editor, Andrew Kellock

EDINBURGH EVENING NEWS
Orchard Brae House, 30 Queensferry Road, Edinburgh EH4 2HS
T 0131-311 7311 **W** www.edinburghnews.scotsman.com
Editorial Director, Frank O'Donnell

EVENING EXPRESS
Aberdeen Journals Ltd, Lang Stracht, Mastrick, Aberdeen AB15 6DF
T 01224-691212 **W** www.eveningexpress.co.uk
Editor, Craig Walker

GLASGOW EVENING TIMES
200 Renfield Street, Glasgow G2 3QB **T** 0141-302 7000
W www.eveningtimes.co.uk
Editor, Graham Shields

INVERNESS COURIER
New Century House, Stadium Road, Inverness IV1 1FF
T 01463-233059 **W** www.inverness-courier.co.uk

PAISLEY DAILY EXPRESS
1 Central Quay, Glasgow G3 8DA **T** 0141-887 7911
W www.paisleydailyexpress.co.uk
Editor, Cheryl McEvoy

THE PRESS AND JOURNAL
Lang Stracht, Aberdeen AB15 6DF **T** 01224-690222
W www.pressandjournal.co.uk
Editor, Damian Bates

WALES

THE LEADER
Mold Business Park, Mold, Flintshire CH7 1XY **T** 01352-707707
W www.leaderlive.co.uk
Editor, Barrie Jones

SOUTH WALES ARGUS
Cardiff Road, Maesglas, Newport NP20 3QN **T** 01633-810000
W www.southwalesargus.co.uk
Editor, Nicole Garnon

SOUTH WALES ECHO
6 Park Street, Cardiff CF10 1XR **T** 029-2024 3630
W www.walesonline.co.uk
Editor, Tryst Williams

SOUTH WALES EVENING POST
Urban Village, High Street, Swansea SA1 1NW **T** 01792-545500
W www.southwales-eveningpost.co.uk
Editor, Jonathan Roberts

WESTERN MAIL
6 Park Street, Cardiff CF10 1XR **T** 029-2024 3630
W www.walesonline.co.uk
Editor, Catrin Pascoe

NORTHERN IRELAND

BELFAST TELEGRAPH
124–144 Royal Avenue, Belfast BT1 1DN **T** 028-9026 4000
W www.belfasttelegraph.co.uk
Editor, Gail Walker

IRISH NEWS
113–117 Donegall Street, Belfast BT1 2GE **T** 028-9032 2226
W www.irishnews.com
Editor, Noel Doran

NEWS LETTER
Ground Floor, Metro Building, 6–9 Donegall Sq. South, Belfast BT1
5JA **T** 028-3839 5577 **W** www.newsletter.co.uk
Editor, Alistair Bushe

SUNDAY LIFE
124–144 Royal Avenue, Belfast BT1 1EB **T** 028-9026 4000
W www.belfasttelegraph.co.uk/sunday-life
Editor, Martin Breen

CHANNEL ISLANDS

GUERNSEY PRESS
PO Box 57, Braye Road, Vale, Guernsey GY1 3BW **T** 01481-240240
W www.guernseypress.com
Editor, Shaun Green

JERSEY EVENING POST
Guiton House, Five Oaks, St Saviour, Jersey JE4 8XQ
T 01534-611611 **W** www.jerseyeveningpost.com
Editor, Andy Sibcy

PERIODICALS

ART

AESTHETICA
PO Box 371, York YO23 1WL **T** 01904-629137
W www.aestheticamagazine.com
Editor, Cherie Federico

APOLLO
22 Old Queen Street, London SW1H 9HP **T** 020-7961 0150
W www.apollo-magazine.com
Editor, Thomas Marks

ART MONTHLY
30 Charing Cross Road, London WC2H 0DE **T** 020-7240 0389
W www.artmonthly.co.uk
Editor, Patricia Bickers

ARTREVIEW
1 Honduras Street, London EC1Y 0TH **T** 020-7490 8138
W www.artreview.com
Editor, Mark Rappolt

TATE ETC.
Tate, Millbank, London SW1P 4RG **T** 020-7887 8724
W www.tate.org.uk
Editor, Simon Grant

BUSINESS AND FINANCE

THE ECONOMIST
20 Cabot Square, London E14 4QW **T** 020-7576 8000
W www.economist.com
Editor, Zanny Minton Beddoes

MANAGEMENT TODAY
Bridge House, 69 London Road, Twickenham TW1 3SP
T 020-8267 5000 **W** www.managementtoday.co.uk
Editor, Matthew Gwyther

MARKETING WEEK
79 Wells Street, London W1T 3QN **T** 020-7292 3711
W www.marketingweek.co.uk
Editor, Russell Parsons

MONEYWEEK
2nd Floor, Crowne House, 56–58 Southwark Street, London SE1
1UN **T** 020-7633 3780 **W** www.moneyweek.com
Editor-in-Chief, Merryn Somerset Webb

PUBLIC FINANCE
78 Chamber Street, London E1 8BL **T** 020-7880 6200
W www.publicfinance.co.uk
Managing Editor, Vivienne Russell

CELEBRITY

CLOSER
Endeavour House, 189 Shaftesbury Avenue, London WC2H 8JG
T 020-7859 8463 **W** www.closeronline.co.uk
Editor, Lisa Burrow

HEAT
Endeavour House, 189 Shaftesbury Avenue, London WC2H 8JG
T 020-7437 9011 **W** www.heatworld.com
Editor, Lucie Cave

HELLO!
Wellington House, 69–71 Upper Ground, London SE1 9PQ
T 020-7667 8901 **W** www.hellomagazine.com
Editor, Rosie Nixon

OK!
10 Lower Thames Street, London EC3R 6EN **T** 020-8612 7000
W www.ok.co.uk
Editor, Kirsty Tyler

CHILDREN'S AND FAMILY

THE BEANO
185 Fleet Street, London EC4A 2HS **W** www.beano.com
Editor, Craig Graham

MOTHER & BABY
Bauer Media Group, Media House, Lynchwood, Peterborough
Business Park, Peterborough PE2 6EA **T** 01733- 468000
W www.motherandbaby.co.uk
Editor, Sally Saunders

YOUR CAT
BPG Media, 1-6 Buckminster Yard, Main Street, Buckminster,
Grantham, Lincs NG33 5SA **T** 0844-848-8257
W www.yourcat.co.uk
Editor-in-Chief, Sarah Wright

YOUR DOG
BPG Media, 1-6 Buckminster Yard, Main Street, Buckminster,
Grantham, Lincs NG33 5SA **T** 0844-848 8257
W www.yourdog.co.uk
Editor, Sarah Wright

YOUR HORSE
Media House, Peterborough Business Park, Lynch Wood,
Peterborough PE2 6EA T 01733-468000 W www.yourhorse.co.uk
Editor, Imogen Johnson

CLASSICAL MUSIC AND OPERA

BBC MUSIC
Immediate Media Company Bristol Ltd, Tower House, Fairfax Street,
Bristol BS1 3BN T 0117-927 9009 W www.classical-music.com
Editor, Oliver Condy

CLASSICAL MUSIC
Rhinegold House, 20 Rugby Street, London WC1N 3QZ
T 020-7333 1729 W www.classicalmusicmagazine.org
Consultant Editor, Keith Clarke

GRAMOPHONE
c/o Mark Allen Group, St Jude's Church, Dulwich Road, London
SE24 0PB T 020-7738 5454 W www.gramophone.co.uk
Editor, Martin Cullingford

OPERA
36 Black Lion Lane, London W6 9BE T 020-8563 8893
W www.opera.co.uk
Editor, John Allison

COMPUTERS AND TECHNOLOGY

PC PRO
Dennis Technology, 30 Cleveland Street, London W1T 4JD
T 020-7907 6000 W www.alphr.com
Editor-in-Chief, Tim Danton

STUFF
Bridge House, 69 London Road, Twickenham TW1 3SP
T 020-8267 5036 W www.stuff.tv
Global Editor-in-Chief, Guy Cocker

T3
T3.com, 5 Pinesway Industrial Estate, Bath BA2 3QS
W www.t3.com
Editor, Dan Grabham

WEB USER
Dennis Publishing, 30 Cleveland Street, London W1T 4JD
T 020-7907 6000 W www.webuser.co.uk
Group Editor, Daniel Booth

WIRED
Condé Nast, Vogue House, Hanover Square, London W1S 1JU
T 0844-848 5202 W www.wired.co.uk
Editor, Greg Williams

CRAFT

CARDMAKING & PAPERCRAFT
Immediate Media, Vineyard House, 44 Brook Green, London W6
7BT T 0117-933 8081 W www.cardmakingandpapercraft.com
Editor, Sienna Parulis-Cook

SIMPLY KNITTING
Immediate Media, Vineyard House, 44 Brook Green, London W6
7BT T 0117-3008 253 W www.simplyknitting.co.uk
Commissioning Editor, Kirstie McLeod

THE WORLD OF CROSS STITCHING
Immediate Media, Vineyard House, 44 Brook Green, London W6
7BT T 0117-314 8351 W www.cross-stitching.com
Editor, Ruth Southorn

ENTERTAINMENT

EMPIRE
Endeavour House, 189 Shaftesbury Avenue, London WC2H 8JG
T 020-7437 9011 W www.empireonline.com
Editor-in-Chief, Terri White

RADIO TIMES
Vineyard House, 44 Brook Green, London W6 7BT
T 020-7150 5800 W www.radiotimes.com
Editorial Director, Mark Frith

SIGHT & SOUND
BFI, 21 Stephen Street, London W1T 1LN T 020-7255 1444
W www.bfi.org.uk/sightandsound
Editor, Nick James

TIME OUT LONDON
4th Floor, 125 Shaftesbury Avenue, London WC2H 8AD
T 020-7813 3000 W www.timeout.com
Editor, Caroline McGinn

TOTAL FILM
Future Publishing Ltd, 1–10 Praed Mews, London W2 1QY
T 020-7042 4831 W www.gamesradar.com/totalfilm
Editor, Jane Crowther

FASHION AND BEAUTY

COSMOPOLITAN
Hearst Magazines, 33 Broadwick Street, London W1F 0DQ
T 020-7439 5000 W www.cosmopolitan.co.uk
Editor, Farrah Storr

ELLE
Hearst Magazines, 72 Broadwick Street, London W1F 9EP
T 020-7150 7000 W www.elleuk.com
Editor-in-Chief, Anne-Marie Curtis

GLAMOUR
Condé Nast, Vogue House, Hanover Square, London W1S 1JU
T 020-7499 9080 W www.glamourmagazine.co.uk
Editor-in-Chief, Jo Elvin

GRAZIA
Endeavour House, 189 Shaftesbury Avenue, London WC2H 8JG
T 0845-601 1356 W www.graziadaily.co.uk
Editor, Natasha Pearlman

HARPER'S BAZAAR
Hearst Magazines, 72 Broadwick Street, London W1F 9EP
T 0844-848 5203 W www.harpersbazaar.co.uk
Editor-in-Chief, Justine Picardie

MARIE CLAIRE
Blue Fin Building, 110 Southwark Street, London SE1 4SU
T 020-3148 5000 W www.marieclaire.co.uk
Editor-in-Chief, Trish Halpin

VOGUE
Condé Nast, Vogue House, Hanover Square, London W1S 1JU
T 0844-848 5202 W www.vogue.co.uk
Editor, Edward Enninful

FOOD AND DRINK

FOOD AND TRAVEL
Suite 51, The Business Centre, Ingate Place, London SW8 3NS
T 020-7501 0511 W www.foodandtravel.com
Editor, Mark Sansom

GOOD FOOD
44 Vineyard House, Brook Green, London W6 7BT
T 020-7150 5022 W www.bbcgoodfood.com
Editorial Director, Gillian Carter

JAMIE
Hearst Magazines, 72 Broadwick Street, London W1F 9EP
T 020-7312 3087 W www.jamieoliver.com/magazine
Editor, Emma Ventura

OLIVE
Vineyard House, 44 Brook Green, London W6 7BT
T 020-7150 5024 W www.olivemagazine.com
Editor, Laura Rowe

WHISKY
6 Woolgate Court, St Benedicts Street, Norwich NR2 4AP
T 01603-633 808 W www.whiskymag.com
Editor, Rob Allanson

GENERAL INTEREST

BBC HISTORY
Tower House, Fairfax Street, Bristol BS1 3BN T 0117-927 9009
W www.historyextra.com
Editor, Rob Attar

BOOKSELLER
Floor 10, Westminster Tower, 3 Albert Embankment, London SE1
7SP T 020-3358 0365 W www.thebookseller.com
Editor, Philip Jones

HISTORY TODAY
2nd Floor, 9 Staple Inn, London WC1V 7QH T 020-3219 7810
W www.historytoday.com
Editor, Paul Lay

LITERARY REVIEW
44 Lexington Street, London W1F 0LW T 020-7437 9392
W www.literaryreview.co.uk
Editor, Nancy Sladek

NEW STATESMAN
John Carpenter House, 7 Carmelite Street, Blackfriars, London
EC4Y 0AN T 020-7936 6400 W www.newstatesman.com
Editor, Jason Cowley

PRIVATE EYE
6 Carlisle Street, London W1D 3BN T 020-7437 4017
W www.private-eye.co.uk
Editor, Ian Hislop

PROSPECT
5th Floor, 23 Savile Row, London W1S 2ET T 020-7255 1281
W www.prospectmagazine.co.uk
Editor, Tom Clark

RAILWAY
Mortons Media Ltd, Horncastle, Lincs LN9 6JR T 01507-529529
W www.railwaymagazine.co.uk
Editor, Chris Milner

READER'S DIGEST
The Maltings, West Street, Bourne BH24 9PH T 0330-333 2220
W www.readersdigest.co.uk
Editor, Fiona Hicks

SAGA
Saga Publishing Ltd, Enbrook Park, Folkestone, Kent CT20 3SE
T 01303-771111 W www.saga.co.uk
Editor, Katy Bravery

THE SPECTATOR
22 Old Queen Street, London SW1H 9HP T 020-7961 0200
W www.spectator.co.uk
Editor, Fraser Nelson

TLS (THE TIMES LITERARY SUPPLEMENT)
1 London Bridge Street, London SE1 9GF T 020-7782 5000
W www.the-tls.co.uk
Editor, Stig Abell

THE WEEK
31–32 Alfred Place, London WC1E 7DP T 020-3890 3890
W www.theweek.co.uk
Editor-in-Chief, Jeremy O'Grady

WHO DO YOU THINK YOU ARE?
Tower House, Fairfax Street, Bristol BS1 3BN T 0117-314 7400
W www.whodoyouthinkyouaremagazine.com
Editor, Sarah Williams

HEALTH AND FITNESS

MEN'S FITNESS
31–32 Alfred Place, London WC1E 7DP T 020-3890 3890
W www.coachmag.co.uk
Editor, Jonathan Shannon

MEN'S HEALTH
Hearst Magazines, 72 Broadwick Street, London W1F 9EP
T 01858-438851 W www.menshealth.co.uk
Editor, Toby Wiseman

RUNNER'S WORLD
33 Broadwick Street, London W1F 9EP T 020-7339 4409
W www.runnersworld.co.uk
Editor, Andy Dixon

WEIGHT WATCHERS
The River Group, 1 Neal Street, London WC2H 9QL
T 020-7306 0304 W www.weightwatchers.co.uk

WOMEN'S FITNESS
31–32 Alfred Place, London WC1E 7DP T 020-3890 3890
W www.womensfitness.co.uk
Editor, Joanna Knight

HOBBIES AND GAMES

AIRFIX MODEL WORLD
Key Publishing Ltd, PO Box 100, Stamford PE9 1XQ
T 01780-755131 W www.airfixmodelworld.com
Editor, Chris Clifford

ANGLING TIMES
Bauer Media Group, Media House, Lynchwood, Peterborough
Business Park, Peterborough PE2 6EA T 01733-395097
W www.gofishing.co.uk
Editor-in-Chief, Steve Fitzpatrick

BRITISH RAILWAY MODELLING
Warners Group Publications, The Maltings, West Street, Bourne,
Lincs PE10 9PH T 01778-391000 W www.model-railways-live.co.uk

CHESS
Chess & Bridge Ltd, 44 Baker Street, London W1U 7RT
T 020-7486 7015 W www.chess.co.uk

COIN NEWS
Token Publishing Ltd, 40 Southernhay East, Exeter, Devon EX1 1PE
T 01404-46972 W www.tokenpublishing.com
Editor, John Mussell

HORNBY
Key Publishing Ltd, PO Box 100, Stamford PE9 1XQ
T 01780-755131 W www.hornbymagazine.com
Editor, Mike Wild

HOME AND GARDEN

GARDENERS' WORLD
Immediate Media, 5th Floor, Vineyard House, 44 Brook Green,
London W6 7BT T 020-7150 5700 W www.gardenersworld.com
Editor, Lucy Hall

GOOD HOUSEKEEPING
Hearst Magazines, 72 Broadwick Street, London W1F 9EP
T 020-7439 5000 W www.goodhousekeeping.co.uk
Editorial Director, Lindsay Nicholson

HOUSE & GARDEN
Condé Nast Publications, Vogue House, Hanover Square, London
W1S 1JU T 020-7499 9080 W www.houseandgarden.co.uk
Editor, Hatta Byng

LIVING ETC
IPC Media, Blue Fin Building, 110 Southwark Street, London SE1
0SU T 020-3148 7443 W www.housetohome.co.uk/livingetc
Editor, Suzanne Imre

MEN'S LIFESTYLE

ATTITUDE
Attitude Media, 33 Peartree Street, London EC1V 3AG
T 020-7608 6363 W www.attitude.co.uk
Editor-in-Chief, Matt Cain

ESQUIRE
Hearst Magazines, 72 Broadwick Street, London W1F 9EP
T 020-7439 5000 W www.esquire.co.uk
Editor, Alex Bilmes

GAY TIMES
Millivres Prowler Group, Spectrum House, 32-34 Gordon House
Road, London NW5 1LP T 020-7424 7400 W www.gaytimes.co.uk
Editor, Darren Scott

GQ
Vogue House, 1 Hanover Square, London W1S 1JU
T 020-7499 9080 W www.gq-magazine.co.uk
Editor, Dylan Jones

LOADED
114 The Strand, London WC2R 0AG T 020-8900 4590
W www.loaded.co.uk
Head of Traffic, Aaron Tinney

MOTORING

BIKE
Bauer Media, Media House, Lynchwood, Peterborough PE2 6EA
T 01733-468000 W www.bikemagazine.co.uk
Editor, Hugo Wilson

CARAVAN
Warners Group Publications, The Maltings, West Street, Bourne,
Lincs PE10 9PH T 01778-392450 W www.outandaboutlive.co.uk
Editor, John Sootheran

F1 RACING
Haymarket, Teddington Studios, Broom Road, Teddington TW11
9BE T 020-8267 5806 W www.f1racing.co.uk
Editorial Director, Anthony Rowlinson

OCTANE
Dennis Publishing Ltd, 31–32 Alfred Place, London WC1E 7DP
T 020-3890 3890 W www.classicandperformancecar.com
Editorial Director, David Lillywhite

PRACTICAL CARAVAN
Haymarket Ltd, Bridge House, 69 London Road, Twickenham TW1
3SP T 020-8267 5712 W www.practicalcaravan.com
Group Editor, Alastair Clement

TOP GEAR
Energy Centre, Media Centre, 201 Wood Lane, London W12 7TQ
T 020-7150 5558 W www.topgear.com
Editor, Charlie Turner

PHOTOGRAPHY

AMATEUR PHOTOGRAPHER
Pinehurst 2, Pinehurst Road, Farnborough, Hants. GU14 7BF
T 01252-555213 W www.amateurphotographer.co.uk
Group Editor, Nigel Atherton

DIGITAL CAMERA
Future Publishing Ltd Quay House, The Ambury, Bath BA1 1UA
W www.digitalcameraworld.com
Editor, Ben Brain

DIGITAL PHOTOGRAPHER
Future Publishing Ltd, Quay House, The Ambury, Bath BA1 1UA
T 01202-586200 W www.dphotographer.co.uk
Editor-in-Chief, Amy Squibb

POPULAR MUSIC

CLASH
Studio 86, Hackney Downs Studios, 17 Amhurst Terrace, London E8
2BT T 020-7628 2312 W www.clashmusic.com
Editor-in-Chief, Simon Harper

CLASSIC ROCK
Future Publishing Ltd, Quay House, The Ambury, Bath BA1 1UA
W www.classicrock.teamrock.com
Editor, Siân Llewellyn

DIY
2nd Floor, Unit 23, Tileyard Studios, Tileyard Road, London N7 9AH
W www.diymag.com
Founding Editor, Emma Swann

GUITARIST
Future Publishing Ltd, Beauford Court, 30 Monmouth Street, Bath
BA1 2BW T 01225-442244 W www.musicradar.com/guitarist
Editor, Mick Taylor

KERRANG!
W www.kerrang.com
Editor, James McMahon

MOJO
Endeavour House, 189 Shaftesbury Avenue, London WC2H 8JG
T 020-7208 3443 W www.mojo4music.com
Editor, Phil Alexander

NME
9th Floor, Blue Fin Building, 110 Southwark Street, London SE1 0SU
T 0845-676 7778 W www.nme.com
Editor-in-Chief, Mike Williams

Q
Endeavour House, 189 Shaftesbury Avenue, London WC2H 8JG
T 020-7295 5000 W www.qthemusic.com
Editor-in-Chief, Phil Alexander

UNCUT
Blue Fin Building, 110 Southwark Street, London SE1 0SU
T 020-3148 5000 **W** www.uncut.co.uk
Editor, John Mulvey

SCIENCE AND NATURE

BBC WILDLIFE
4th Floor, Tower House, Fairfax Street, Bristol BS1 3BN
T 0117-314 7366 **W** www.discoverwildlife.com
Editor, Sheena Harvey

BIRD WATCHING
Bauer Media, Media House, Lynch Wood, Peterborough PE2 6EA
T 01733-468000 **W** www.birdwatching.co.uk
Editor, Matthew Merritt

COUNTRYFILE
9th Floor, Tower House, Fairfax Street, Bristol BS1 3BN
T 0117-927 9009 **W** www.countryfile.com
Editor, Fergus Collins

FOCUS
Immediate Media, 9th Floor, Tower House, Fairfax Street, Bristol
BS1 3BN **T** 0117-314 7388 **W** www.sciencefocus.com

HOW IT WORKS
Future Publishing Limited Quay House, The Ambury, Bath BA1 1UA
W www.howitworksdaily.com
Editor-in-Chief, Dave Harfield

NEW SCIENTIST
110 High Holborn, London WC1V 6EU **T** 020-7611 1206
W www.newscientist.com
Editor-in-Chief, Sumit Paul-Choudhury

SKY AT NIGHT
Immediate Media Co., Tower House, Fairfax Street, Bristol BS1 3BN
T 0117-314 8758 **W** www.skyatnightmagazine.com
Editor, Chris Bramley

SPORT

ALL OUT CRICKET
TriNorth Ltd, Unit 3.40 Canterbury Court, 1–3 Brixton Road, London
SW9 6DE **T** 020-3176 0187 **W** www.alloutcricket.com
Editor, Phil Walker

BOXING MONTHLY
Topwave Ltd, 40 Morpeth Road, London E9 7LD **T** 020-8986 4141
W www.boxing-monthly.co.uk
Editor, Graham Houston

COUNTRY WALKING
Bauer Media, Media House, Peterborough Business Park,
Peterborough PE2 6EA **T** 01733-468205
W www.livefortheoutdoors.com
Editor, Guy Procter

THE CRICKETER
120 New Cavendish Street, London W1W 6XX **T** 020-3198 1359
W www.thecricketer.com
Editor, Simon Hughes

FOURFOURTWO
Haymarket Ltd, Bridge House, 69 London Road, Twickenham TW1
3SP **T** 020-8267 5000 **W** www.fourfourtwo.com
Editor, Hitesh Ratna

GOLF MONTHLY
Time Inc. (UK), Pinehurst 2, Pinehurst Road, Farnborough Business
Park, Farnborough, Hants GU14 7BF **T** 01252-555197
W www.golf-monthly.co.uk
Editor, Michael Harris

HORSE & HOUND
Time Inc. (UK), Pinehurst 2, Pinehurst Road, Farnborough Business
Park, Farnborough, Hants GU14 7BF **T** 01252-555029
W www.horseandhound.co.uk
Content Director, Sarah Jenkins

MATCH
Kelsey Media, Cudham Tithe Barn, Berrys Hill, Cudham, Kent, TN16
3AG **T** 01733-353358 **W** www.matchfootball.co.uk
Editor, Stephen Fishlock

RUGBY WORLD
Time Inc (UK) Ltd, 2nd Floor, Pinehurst 2, Pinehurst Road,
Farnborough Business Park, Farnborough, Hants GU14 7BF
T 01252-555271 **W** www.rugbyworld.com
Editor, Owain Jones

TENNISHEAD
Advantage Publishing (UK) Ltd, Suite 142, 61 Victoria Road,
Surbiton KT6 4JX **T** 020-8408 7148 **W** www.tennishead.net

WORLD SOCCER
Time Inc (UK) Ltd, 2nd Floor, Pinehurst 2, Pinehurst Road,
Farnborough Business Park, Farnborough, Hants GU14 7BF
T 020-3148 4817 **W** www.worldsoccer.com
Editor, Gavin Hamilton

TRAVEL

CONDÉ NAST TRAVELLER
Vogue House, Hanover Square, London W1S 1JU **T** 0844-848 2851
W www.cntraveller.com
Editor, Melinda Stevens

FRANCE
Archant House, 3 Oriel Road, Cheltenham GL50 1BB
T 01242-216050 **W** www.completefrance.com
Editor, Lara Dunn

LONELY PLANET
240 Blackfriars Road, London SE1 8NW **W** www.lonelyplanet.com
Editor, Peter Grunert

NATIONAL GEOGRAPHIC TRAVELLER
APL Media Ltd, Unit 310 Highgate Studios, 53–79 Highgate Road,
London NW5 1TL **T** 020-7253 9906 **W** www.natgeotraveller.co.uk
Editor, Pat Riddell

TRADE AND PROFESSIONAL BODIES

The following is a list of employers' and trade associations and other professional bodies in the UK. It does not represent a comprehensive list. For further professional bodies *see* Professional Education.

ASSOCIATIONS

ABTA – THE TRAVEL ASSOCIATION 30 Park Street, London SE1 9EQ T 020-311 70500 E abta@abta.co.uk W www.abta.com
Chief Executive, Mark Tanzer

ADVERTISING ASSOCIATION 7th Floor North, Artillery House, London SW1P 1RT T 020-7340 1100
E aa@adassoc.org.uk W www.adassoc.org.uk
Chief Executive, Stephen Woodford

AEROSPACE DEFENCE SECURITY Salamanca Square, 9 Albert Embankment, London SE1 7SP T 020-7091 4500
E enquiries@adsgroup.org.uk W www.adsgroup.org.uk
Chief Executive, Paul Everitt

AGRICULTURAL ENGINEERS ASSOCIATION Samuelson House, 62 Forder Way, Peterborough PE7 8JB T 0845-644 8748
E ab@aea.uk.com W www.aea.uk.com
Chief Executive, Ruth Bailey

ASBESTOS REMOVAL CONTRACTORS ASSOCIATION Unit 1, Stretton Business Park 2, Brunel Drive, Stretton DE13 0BY
T 01283-566467 E info@arca.org.uk W www.arca.org.uk
Chief Executive, Steve Sadley

ASSOCIATION FOR CONSULTANCY AND ENGINEERING Alliance House, 12 Caxton Street, London SW1H 0QL T 020-7222 6557 E consult@acenet.co.uk
W www.acenet.co.uk
Chief Executive, Dr Nelson Ogunshakin, OBE

ASSOCIATION OF ACCOUNTING TECHNICIANS 140 Aldersgate Street, London EC1A 4HY T 020-3735 2468
E aat@aat.org.uk W www.aat.org.uk
Chief Executive, Mark Farrar

ASSOCIATION OF ANAESTHETISTS OF GREAT BRITAIN AND IRELAND 21 Portland Place, London W1B 1PY T 020-7631 1650 E info@aagbi.org W www.aagbi.org
President, Dr Paul Clyburn

ASSOCIATION OF BRITISH INSURERS One America Square, London EC3N 2LB T 020-7600 3333 E info@abi.org.uk
W www.abi.org.uk
Director-General, Huw Evans

ASSOCIATION OF BUSINESS RECOVERY PROFESSIONALS 8th Floor, 120 Aldersgate Street, London EC1A 4JQ T 020-7566 4200 E association@r3.org.uk
W www.r3.org.uk
Chief Executive, vacant

ASSOCIATION OF CONSULTING SCIENTISTS 5 Willow Heights, Cradley Heath B64 7PL T 0121-602 3515
E secretary@consultingscientists.co.uk
Secretary, Dr Stuart Guy

ASSOCIATION OF CONVENIENCE STORES LTD Federation House, 17 Farnborough Street, Farnborough GU14 8AG T 01252-515001 E acs@acs.org.uk
W www.acs.org.uk
Chief Executive, James Lowman

ASSOCIATION OF CORPORATE TREASURERS 68 King William Street, London EC4N 7DZ T 020-7847 2540
E enquiries@treasurers.org W www.treasurers.org
Chief Executive, Caroline Stockmann

ASSOCIATION OF DRAINAGE AUTHORITIES Rural Innovation Centre, Avenue H, Stoneleigh Park CV8 2LG
T 024-7699 2889 E admin@ada.org.uk W www.ada.org.uk
Chief Executive, Innes Thomson, CENG

BOOKSELLERS ASSOCIATION 6 Bell Yard, London WC2A 2JR T 020-7421 4640 E mail@booksellers.org.uk
W www.booksellers.org.uk
Chief Executive, T. E. Godfray

BRITISH ANTIQUE DEALERS' ASSOCIATION 14 Dufferin Street, London EC1Y 8PD T 020-7589 4128 E info@bada.org
W www.bada.org
Secretary-General, Mark Dodgson

BRITISH ASSOCIATION OF SOCIAL WORKERS 16 Kent Street, Birmingham B5 6RD T 0121-622 3911
E online@basw.co.uk W www.basw.co.uk
Chief Executive, Ruth Allen

BRITISH BEER & PUB ASSOCIATION Ground Floor, Brewers' Hall, Aldermanbury Square, London EC2V 7HR
T 020-7627 9191 E contact@beerandpub.com
W www.beerandpub.com
Chief Executive, Brigid Simmonds, OBE

BRITISH CHAMBERS OF COMMERCE 65 Petty France, London SW1H 9EU T 020-7654 5800
W www.britishchambers.org.uk
Director-General, Adam Marshall

BRITISH ELECTROTECHNICAL AND ALLIED MANUFACTURERS ASSOCIATION (BEAMA) Westminster Tower, 3 Albert Embankment, London SE1 7SL
T 020-7793 3000 E info@beama.org.uk W www.beama.org.uk
Chief Executive, Dr Howard Porter

BRITISH HOROLOGICAL INSTITUTE Upton Hall, Upton, Newark NG23 5TE T 01636-813795 E info@bhi.co.uk
W www.bhi.co.uk
Chairman, Stella Haward

BRITISH HOSPITALITY ASSOCIATION Augustine House, 6a Austin Friars, London EC2N 2HA T 020-7404 7744
E bha@bha.org.uk W www.bha.org.uk
Chief Executive, Ufi Ibrahim

BRITISH INSTITUTE OF PROFESSIONAL PHOTOGRAPHY The Coach House, The Firs, High Street, Aylesbury HP22 4SJ T 01296-642020 E info@bipp.com
W www.bipp.com
Chief Executive, Chris Harper

BRITISH INSURANCE BROKERS' ASSOCIATION 8th Floor, John Stow House, 18 Bevis Marks, London EC3A 7JB
T 0344-770 0266 E enquiries@biba.org.uk W www.biba.org.uk
Chief Executive, Steve White

BRITISH MARINE FEDERATION Marine House, Thorpe Lea Road, Egham TW20 8BF T 01784-473377
E info@britishmarine.co.uk W www.britishmarine.co.uk
Chief Executive, Howard Pridding

BRITISH MEDICAL ASSOCIATION BMA House, Tavistock Square, London WC1H 9JP T 020-7387 4499
W www.bma.org.uk
Chief Executive, Keith Ward

BRITISH OFFICE SUPPLIES AND SERVICES (BOSS) FEDERATION c/o British Printing Industries Federation, 2 Villiers Court, Copse Drive CV5 9RN T 01676-526030
E liz@bossfederation.co.uk W www.bossfederation.co.uk
Chief Executive, Philip Lawson

BPI (BRITISH PHONOGRAPHIC INDUSTRY) Riverside Building, County Hall, Westminster Bridge Road, London SE1 7JA **T** 020-7803 1300 **E** general@bpi.co.uk **W** www.bpi.co.uk
Chief Executive, Geoff Taylor

BRITISH PLASTICS FEDERATION 6 Bath Place, London EC2A 3JE **T** 020-7457 5000 **E** reception@bpf.co.uk **W** www.bpf.co.uk
Director-General, Philip Law

BRITISH PORTS ASSOCIATION 1st Floor, 30 Park Street, London SE1 9EQ **T** 020-7260 1780 **E** info@britishports.org.uk **W** www.britishports.org.uk
Chief Executive, Richard Ballantyne

BRITISH PRINTING INDUSTRIES FEDERATION Unit 2, Villiers Court, Meriden Business Park CV5 9RN **T** 01676-526030 **W** www.britishprint.com
Chief Executive, Charles Jarrold

BRITISH PROPERTY FEDERATION 5th Floor, St Albans House, 57–59 Haymarket, London SW1Y 4QX **T** 020-7828 0111 **E** info@bpf.org.uk **W** www.bpf.org.uk
Chief Executive, Melanie Leech

BRITISH RETAIL CONSORTIUM 2 London Bridge, London SE1 9RA **T** 020-7854 8900 **E** info@brc.org.uk **W** www.brc.org.uk
Director-General, Helen Dickinson, OBE

BRITISH TYRE MANUFACTURERS' ASSOCIATION LTD 5 Berewyk Hall Court, White Colne, Colchester CO6 2QB **T** 01787-226995 **E** mail@btmauk.com **W** www.btmauk.com
Chief Executive, Graham Willson

BUILDING SOCIETIES ASSOCIATION 6th Floor, York House, London WC2B 6UJ **T** 020-7520 5900 **E** simon.rex@bsa.org.uk **W** www.bsa.org.uk
Chief Executive, Robin Fieth

CHARTERED ASSOCIATION OF BUILDING ENGINEERS Lutyens House, Billing Brook Road, Northampton NN3 8NW **T** 01604-404121 **W** www.cbuilde.com
Chief Executive, Dr John Hooper

CHARTERED INSTITUTE FOR ARCHAEOLOGISTS Miller Building, Reading RG6 6AB **T** 0118-378 6446 **E** admin@archaeologists.net **W** www.archaeologists.net
Chief Executive, Peter Hinton

CHARTERED INSTITUTE OF ENVIRONMENTAL HEALTH Chadwick Court, 15 Hatfields, London SE1 8DJ **T** 020-7928 6006 **E** information@cieh.org **W** www.cieh.org
Chief Executive, Anne Godfrey

CHARTERED INSTITUTE OF JOURNALISTS 2 Dock Offices, Surrey Quays Road, London SE16 2XU **T** 020-7252 1187 **E** memberservices@cioj.co.uk **W** www.cioj.co.uk
General Secretary, Dominic Cooper

CHARTERED INSTITUTE OF PURCHASING AND SUPPLY Easton House, Church Street, Stamford PE9 3NZ **T** 01780-756777 **W** www.cips.org
Chief Executive (interim), Gerry Walsh

CHARTERED INSTITUTE OF TAXATION 1st Floor Artillery House, 11–19 Artillery Row, London SW1P 1RT **T** 020-7340 0550 **E** comms@tax.org.uk **W** www.tax.org.uk
Chief Executive, Peter Fanning

CHARTERED INSURANCE INSTITUTE The Insurance Hall, 20 Aldermanbury, London EC2V 7HY **T** 020-8989 8464 **E** customer.serv@cii.co.uk **W** www.cii.co.uk
Chief Executive, Sian Fisher

CHARTERED MANAGEMENT INSTITUTE Management House, Cottingham Road, Corby NN17 1TT **T** 01536-207360 **E** enquiries@managers.org.uk **W** www.managers.org.uk
Chief Executive, Anne Francke

CHARTERED QUALITY INSTITUTE 2nd Floor North, Chancery Exchange, London EC4A 1AB **T** 020-7245 6722 **E** membership@quality.org **W** www.quality.org
Chief Executive (acting), Vincent Desmond

CHARTERED TRADING STANDARDS INSTITUTE 1 Sylvan Court, Sylvan Way, Basildon SS15 6TH **T** 01268-582200 **E** institute@tsi.org.uk **W** www.tradingstandards.uk
Chief Executive, Leon Livermore

CHEMICAL INDUSTRIES ASSOCIATION Kings Buildings, Smith Square, London SW1P 3JJ **T** 020-7834 3399 **E** enquiries@cia.org.uk **W** www.cia.org.uk
Chief Executive, Steve Elliott

CONFEDERATION OF PAPER INDUSTRIES 1 Rivenhall Road, Swindon SN5 7BD **T** 01793-889600 **E** cpi@paper.org.uk **W** www.paper.org.uk
Director-General, Andrew Large

CONFEDERATION OF PASSENGER TRANSPORT UK Fifth Floor Offices (South), Chancery House, London WC2A 1QS **T** 020-7240 3131 **E** admin@cpt-uk.org **W** www.cpt-uk.org
Chief Executive, Simon Posner

CONSTRUCTION PRODUCTS ASSOCIATION The Building Centre, 26 Store Street, London WC1E 7BT **T** 020-7323 3770 **W** www.constructionproducts.org.uk
Chief Executive, Diana Montgomery

DAIRY UK 6th Floor, London WC1V 7EP **T** 020-7405 1484 **E** info@dairyuk.org **W** www.dairyuk.org
Chief Executive, Dr Judith Bryans

EEF, THE MANUFACTURERS' ORGANISATION Broadway House, Tothill Street, London SW1H 9NQ **T** 020-7222 7777 **E** enquiries@eef.org.uk **W** www.eef.org.uk
Chief Executive, Terry Scuoler

ENERGY UK Charles House, 5–11 Regent Street, London SW1Y 4LR **T** 020-7930 9390 **W** www.energy-uk.org.uk
Chief Executive, Lawrence Slade

FEDERATION OF BAKERS 6th Floor, 10 Bloomsbury Way, London WC1A 2SL **T** 020-7420 7190 **E** info@fob.uk.com **W** www.fob.uk.com
Director, Gordon Polson

FEDERATION OF MASTER BUILDERS David Croft House, 25 Ely Place, London EC1N 6TD **T** 0330-333 7777 **W** www.fmb.org.uk
Chief Executive, Brian Berry

FSPA (FEDERATION OF SPORTS AND PLAY ASSOCIATIONS) Office 8, Rural Innovation Centre, Unit 169 – Avenue H, Kenilworth CV8 2LG **T** 024-7641 4999 **E** info@sportsandplay.com **W** www.sportsandplay.com
Managing Director, Jane Montgomery

FINANCE AND LEASING ASSOCIATION 2nd Floor, Imperial House, 15–19 Kingsway, London WC2B 6UN **T** 020-7836 6511 **E** info@fla.org.uk **W** www.fla.org.uk
Director-General, Stephen Sklaroff

FOOD AND DRINK FEDERATION 6th Floor, London WC1A 2SL **T** 020-7836 2460 **W** www.fdf.org.uk
Director-General, Ian Wright

FREIGHT TRANSPORT ASSOCIATION LTD Hermes House, St John's Road, Tunbridge Wells TN4 9UZ **T** 01892-526171 **E** enquiry@fta.co.uk **W** www.fta.co.uk
Chief Executive, David Wells

GLASGOW CHAMBER OF COMMERCE 30 George Square, Glasgow G2 1EQ **T** 0141-204 2121 **E** chamber@glasgowchamberofcommerce.com **W** www.glasgowchamberofcommerce.com
Chief Executive, Stuart Patrick

INSTITUTE OF BREWING AND DISTILLING 44A Curlew Street, London SE1 2ND T 020-7499 8144
E enquiries@ibd.org.uk W www.ibd.org.uk
Chief Executive, Jerry Avis

INSTITUTE OF BRITISH ORGAN BUILDING 13 Ryefields, Bury St Edmunds IP31 3TD T 01359-233433
E administrator@ibo.co.uk W www.ibo.co.uk
President, Dr Christopher Batchelor

INSTITUTE OF CHARTERED FORESTERS 59 George Street, Edinburgh EH2 2JG T 0131-240 1425
E icf@charteredforesters.org W www.charteredforesters.org
Executive Director, Shireen Chambers

INSTITUTE OF CHARTERED SECRETARIES AND ADMINISTRATORS Saffron House, 6–10 Kirby Street, London EC1N 8TS T 020-7580 4741 E info@icsa.org.uk
W www.icsa.org.uk
Chief Executive, Simon Osborne

INSTITUTE OF CHARTERED SHIPBROKERS 85 Gracechurch Street, London EC3V 0AA T 020-7623 1111
E enquiries@ics.org.uk W www.ics.org.uk
Director, Julie Lithgow

INSTITUTE OF DIRECTORS 116 Pall Mall, London SW1Y 5ED T 020-7766 8888 E enquiries@iod.com
W www.iod.com
Director-General, Stephen Martin

INSTITUTE OF EXPORT AND INTERNATIONAL TRADE Export House, Minerva Business Park, Peterborough PE2 6FT T 01733-404400 W www.export.org.uk
Director-General, Lesley Batchelor, OBE

INSTITUTE OF FINANCIAL ACCOUNTANTS The Podium, 1 Eversholt Street, London NW1 2DN T 020-7554 0730
E mail@ifa.org.uk W www.ifa.org.uk
Chief Executive, John Edwards

INSTITUTE OF HEALTHCARE MANAGEMENT 33 Cavendish Square, London W1G 0PW T 020-7182 4066
E contact@ihm.org.uk W www.ihm.org.uk
Chief Executive, Jill de Bene

INSTITUTE OF HOSPITALITY Trinity Court, 34 West Street, Surrey SM1 1SH T 020-8661 4900
W www.instituteofhospitality.org
Chief Executive, Peter Ducker

INSTITUTE OF INTERNAL COMMUNICATION Suite G10, Gemini House, Sunrise Parkway, MK14 6PW
T 01908-232168 E enquiries@ioic.org.uk W www.ioic.org.uk
Chief Executive, Jennifer Sproul

INSTITUTE OF MANAGEMENT SERVICES Brooke House, 24 Dam Street, Lichfield WS13 6AA T 01543-266909
E admin@ims-productivity.com W www.ims-productivity.com
Chair, Julian Cutler

INSTITUTE OF QUARRYING McPherson House, 8A Regan Way, Chilwell NG9 6RZ T 0115-972 9995 E mail@quarrying.org
W www.quarrying.org
Chief Executive, James Thorne

INSTITUTE OF THE MOTOR INDUSTRY Fanshaws, Hertford SG13 8PQ T 01992-511 521 E comms@theimi.org.uk
W www.theimi.org.uk
Chief Executive, Steve Nash

INSTITUTION OF OCCUPATIONAL SAFETY AND HEALTH The Grange, Highfield Drive, Wigston LE18 1NN
T 0116-257 3100 E reception@iosh.co.uk W www.iosh.co.uk
Chief Executive, Bev Messinger

IP FEDERATION 5th Floor, 63–66 Hatton Garden, London EC1N 8LE T 020-7242 3923 E admin@ipfederation.com
W www.ipfederation.com
President, James Hayles

MAGISTRATES' ASSOCIATION 28 Fitzroy Square, London W1T 6DD T 020-7387 2353
E information@magistrates-association.org.uk
W www.magistrates-association.org.uk
Chief Executive, vacant

MANAGEMENT CONSULTANCIES ASSOCIATION 5th Floor, 36–38 Cornhill, London EC3V 3NG T 020-7645 7950
E info@mca.org.uk W www.mca.org.uk
Chief Executive, Alan Leaman, OBE

MASTER LOCKSMITHS ASSOCIATION 5D Great Central Way, Daventry NN11 3PZ T 01327-262255
E enquiries@locksmiths.co.uk W www.locksmiths.co.uk
Director of Development, Dr Steffan George

NATIONAL ASSOCIATION OF BRITISH MARKET AUTHORITIES The Guildhall, Shrops SY11 1PZ
T 01691-680713 E nabma@nabma.com W www.nabma.com
Chief Executive, Graham Wilson, OBE

NATIONAL ASSOCIATION OF ESTATE AGENTS Arbon House, 6 Tournament Court, Warwick CV34 6LG
T 01926-496800 E help@propertymark.co.uk
W www.naea.co.uk
President, David Mackie

NATIONAL FARMERS' UNION (NFU) Agriculture House, Stoneleigh Park, Stoneleigh CV8 2LZ T 024-7685 8500
W www.nfuonline.com
Director-General, Terry Jones

NATIONAL FEDERATION OF RETAIL NEWSAGENTS Yeoman House, Sekforde Street, London EC1R 0HF
T 020-7253 4225 E connect@nfrnonline.com
W www.nfrnonline.com
Chief Executive, Paul Baxter

NATIONAL LANDLORDS ASSOCIATION 2nd Floor, 200 Union Street, London SE1 0LX T 020-7840 8900
E info@landlords.org.uk W www.landlords.org.uk
Chief Executive, Richard Lambert

NATIONAL MARKET TRADERS FEDERATION Hampton House, Hawshaw Lane, Barnsley S74 0HA T 01226-749021
E genoffice@nmtf.co.uk W www.nmtf.co.uk
Chief Executive, Joe Harrison

NATIONAL PHARMACY ASSOCIATION Mallinson House, 38–42 St Peter's Street, Herts AL1 3NP T 01727-858687
E npa@npa.co.uk W www.npa.co.uk
Chief Executive, vacant

NEWS MEDIA ASSOCIATION 292 Vauxhall Bridge Road, London SW1V 1AE T 020-7963 7480 E nma@newsmediauk.org
W www.newsmediauk.org
Chief Executive, David Newell

OIL AND GAS UK 6th Floor East, Portland House, London SW1E 5BH T 020-7802 2400 E info@oilandgasuk.co.uk
W www.oilandgasuk.co.uk
Chief Executive, Deirdre Michie

PROPERTY CARE ASSOCIATION 11 Ramsay Court, Kingfisher Way, Huntingdon PE29 6FY T 0844-375 4301
E pca@property-care.org W www.property-care.org
Chief Executive, Stephen Hodgson

PUBLISHERS ASSOCIATION 50 Southwark Street, London SE1 1UN T 020-7378 0504 E mail@publishers.org.uk
W www.publishers.org.uk
Chief Executive, Stephen Lotinga

RADIOCENTRE 6th Floor, 55 New Oxford Street, London WC1A 1BS T 020-7010 0600 E info@radiocentre.org
W www.radiocentre.org
Chief Executive, Siobhan Kenny

ROAD HAULAGE ASSOCIATION LTD Roadway House,
Bretton Way, Bretton PE3 8DD **T** 01274-863100
W www.rha.uk.net
Chief Executive, Richard Burnett

ROYAL ASSOCIATION OF BRITISH DAIRY FARMERS*
Dairy House, Unit 31, Abbey Park, Kenilworth CV8 2LY
T 024-7663 9317 **E** office@rabdf.co.uk **W** www.rabdf.co.uk
Managing Director, Matthew Knight

ROYAL FACULTY OF PROCURATORS IN GLASGOW
12 Nelson Mandela Place, Glasgow G2 1BT **T** 0141-332 3593
E library@rfpg.org **W** www.rfpg.org
Chief Executive, John McKenzie

SHELLFISH ASSOCIATION OF GREAT BRITAIN
Fishmongers' Hall, London Bridge, London EC4R 9EL
T 020-7283 8305 **E** projects@shellfish.org.uk
W www.shellfish.org.uk
Director, David Jarrad

SOCIETY OF LOCAL AUTHORITY CHIEF EXECUTIVES
AND SENIOR MANAGERS (SOLACE) Suite 1.3A, 1st
Floor, Millbank Tower, London SW1P 4QP **T** 0845-652 4010
E info@solace.org.uk **W** www.solace.org.uk
Directors, Graeme McDonald; Terry McDougall

SOCIETY OF MOTOR MANUFACTURERS AND
TRADERS LTD 71 Great Peter Street, London SW1P 2BN
T 020-7235 7000 **E** communications@smmt.co.uk
W www.smmt.co.uk
Chief Executive, Mike Hawes

TIMBER TRADE FEDERATION The Building Centre, 26
Store Street, London WC1E 7BT **T** 020-3205 0067 **E** ttf@ttf.co.uk
W www.ttf.co.uk
Managing Director, David Hopkins

UK CHAMBER OF SHIPPING 30 Park Street, London
SE1 9EQ **T** 020-7417 2800 **E** query@ukchamberofshipping.com
W www.ukchamberofshipping.com
Chief Executive, Guy Platten

UK FASHION AND TEXTILE ASSOCIATION 3 Queen
Square, London WC1N 3AR **T** 020-7843 9460 **E** info@ukft.org
W www.ukft.org
Chief Executive, Adam Mansell

UK FINANCE 5th Floor, 1 Angel Court, London EC2R 7HJ
T 020-7706 3333 **E** membership@ukfinance.org.uk
W www.ukfinance.org.uk
Chief Executive, Stephen Jones

UK LEATHER FEDERATION Leather Trade House, Kings Park
Road, Northampton NN3 6JD **T** 01604-679999 **E** info@uklf.org
W www.ukleather.org
Director, Dr Kerry Senior

UK PETROLEUM INDUSTRY ASSOCIATION LTD
Quality House, Quality Court, London WC2A 1HP
T 020-7269 7600 **E** info@ukpia.com **W** www.ukpia.com
Director-General, Chris Hunt

ULSTER FARMERS' UNION 475 Antrim Road, Belfast
BT15 3DA **T** 028-9037 0222 **E** info@ufuhq.com
W www.ufuni.org
Chief Executive, Wesley Aston

THE WINE AND SPIRIT TRADE ASSOCIATION
International Wine and Spirit Centre, 39–45 Bermondsey Street,
London SE1 3XF **T** 020-7089 3877 **E** info@wsta.co.uk
W www.wsta.co.uk
Chief Executive, Miles Beale

CBI

Cannon Place, 78 Cannon Street, London EC4N 6HN
T 020-7379 7400 **E** enquiries@cbi.org.uk **W** www.cbi.org.uk

The CBI was founded in 1965 and is an independent non-party political body financed by industry and commerce. It works with the UK government, international legislators and policymakers to help UK businesses compete effectively. It is the recognised spokesman for the business viewpoint and is consulted as such by the government.

The CBI speaks for some 190,000 businesses that together employ approximately one-third of the private sector workforce. Member companies, which decide all policy positions, include FTSE 100 index listed companies, small-and medium-size firms, micro businesses, private and family owned businesses, start-ups and trade associations.

The CBI board is chaired by the president and meets four times a year. It is assisted by 14 expert standing committees which advise on the main aspects of policy. There are nine regional councils for England and three national councils for, Wales, Scotland and Northern Ireland. There are also offices in Beijing, Brussels, New Delhi and Washington DC.

President, Paul Drechsler, CBE
Director-General, Carolyn Fairbairn

WALES, 2 Caspian Point, Caspian Way, Cardiff Bay, Cardiff
CF10 4DQ **T** 029-2097 7600
E wales.mail@cbi.org.uk
Regional Director, Ian Price

SCOTLAND, 160 West George Street, Glasgow G2 2HQ
T 0141-222 2184 **E** scot.mail@cbi.org.uk
Regional Director, Hugh Aitken

NORTHERN IRELAND, Hamilton House, 3 Joy Street, Belfast
BT2 8LE **T** 028-9010 1100 **E** ni.mail@cbi.org.uk
Regional Director, Angela McGowan

TRADE UNIONS

A trade union is an organisation of workers formed for the purpose of collective bargaining over pay and working conditions. Trade unions may also provide legal and financial advice, sickness benefits and education facilities to their members. Legally any employee has the right to join a trade union, but not all employers recognise all or any trade unions. Conversely an employee also has the right not to join a trade union, in particular since the practice of a 'closed shop' system, where all employees have to join the employer's preferred union, is no longer permitted.

THE CENTRAL ARBITRATION COMMITTEE

Fleetbank House, 2–6 Salisbury Square, London EC4Y 8JX
T 020-7904 2300 E enquiries@cac.gov.uk
W www.gov.uk/government/organisations/
central-arbitration-committee

The Central Arbitration Committee's main role is concerned with requests for trade union recognition and de-recognition under the statutory procedures of Schedule A1 of the Employment Rights Act 1999. It also determines disclosure of information complaints under the Trade Union and Labour Relations (Consolidation) Act 1992, considers applications and complaints under the Information and Consultation Regulations 2004, and performs a similar role in relation to European works councils, companies, cooperative societies and cross-border mergers.

Chair, Sir Michael Burton
Chief Executive, James Jacob

TRADES UNION CONGRESS (TUC)

Congress House, 23–28 Great Russell Street, London WC1B 3LS
T 020-7636 4030 E info@tuc.org.uk
W www.tuc.org.uk

The Trades Union Congress (TUC), founded in 1868, is an independent association of trade unions. The TUC promotes the rights and welfare of those in work and helps the unemployed. The TUC brings Britain's unions together to draw up common polices; lobbies the government to implement policies that will benefit people at work; campaigns on economic and social issues; represents working people on public bodies, in the European Union and at the UN employment body – the International Labour Organisation; carries out research on employment-related issues; runs training and education programmes for union representatives; helps unions to develop new services for their members and negotiate with each other; and builds links with other trade union bodies worldwide.

The governing body of the TUC is the annual congress which sets policy. Between congresses, business is conducted by a 56-member general council, which meets every two months to oversee the TUC's work programme and sanction new policy initiatives. Each year, at its first post-congress meeting, the general council appoints an executive committee and the TUC president for that congress year. The executive committee meets monthly to implement and develop policy, manage TUC financial affairs and deal with any urgent business. The president chairs general council and executive meetings and is consulted by the General Secretary on all major issues.

There are 50 affiliated unions, with a total membership of 5.6 million.

President (2017–18), Sally Hunt
General Secretary, Frances O'Grady

SCOTTISH TRADES UNION CONGRESS (STUC)

333 Woodlands Road, Glasgow G3 6NG T 0141-337 8100
E info@stuc.org.uk W www.stuc.org.uk

The congress was formed in 1897 and acts as a national centre for the trade union movement in Scotland. The STUC promotes the rights to welfare of those in work and helps the unemployed. It helps its member unions to promote membership in new areas and industries, and campaigns for rights at work for all employees, including part-time and temporary workers, whether union members or not. It also makes representations to government and employers. In 2016 the STUC had over 580,000 members from 39 affiliated unions and 20 trade union councils.

The annual congress in April elects a 36-member general council on the basis of six sections.

President (2017–18), Satnam Ner
General Secretary, Grahame Smith

WALES TUC

Unite House, 1 Cathedral Road, Cardiff CF11 9SD
T 029-2034 7010 E wtuc@tuc.org.uk
W www.tuc.org.uk/wales

The Wales TUC was established in 1974 to ensure that the role of the TUC was effectively undertaken in Wales. Its structure reflects the four economic regions of Wales and matches the regional committee areas of the National Assembly of Wales. The regional committees oversee the implementation of Wales TUC policy and campaigns in the relevant regions, and liaise with local government, training organisations and regional economic development bodies. The Wales TUC seeks to reduce unemployment, increase the levels of skill and pay, and eliminate discrimination.

The governing body of Wales TUC is the conference, which meets annually in May and elects a general council (usually of around 50 people) that oversees the work of the TUC throughout the year.

There are over 50 affiliated unions representing almost 500,000 workers.

President (2017–18), Mike Jenkins
General Secretary, Martin Mansfield

TUC-AFFILIATED UNIONS
As at May 2017

ACCORD Simmons House, 46 Old Bath Road, Reading
RG10 9QR T 0118-934 1808 E info@accordhq.org
W www.accord-myunion.org
General Secretary, Ged Nichols
Membership: 22,798

ADVANCE 2nd Floor, 16–17 High Street, Tring HP23 5AH
T 01442-891122 E info@advance-union.org
W www.advance-union.org
General Secretary, Linda Rolph
Membership: 7,220

AEGIS THE UNION 1–3 Lochside Crescent, Edinburgh
EH12 9SE T 0131-549 5474 E members@aegistheunion.co.uk
W www.aegistheunion.co.uk
General Secretary, Brian Linn
Membership: 4,876

AEP (ASSOCIATION OF EDUCATIONAL PSYCHOLOGISTS) 4 The Riverside Centre, Durham DH1 5TA T 0191-384 9512 E enquiries@aep.org.uk W www.aep.org.uk
General Secretary, Kate Fallon
Membership: 3,343

AFA (ASSOCIATION OF FLIGHT ATTENDANTS) 32 Wingford Road, London SW2 4DS T 020-8276 6723 E afalhr@unitedafa.org W www.afacwa.org
Membership: 500

ASLEF (ASSOCIATED SOCIETY OF LOCOMOTIVE ENGINEERS AND FIREMEN) 77 St John Street, London EC1M 4NN T 020-7324 2400 E info@aslef.org.uk W www.aslef.org.uk
General Secretary, Mick Whelan
Membership: 21,354

BALPA (BRITISH AIRLINE PILOTS ASSOCIATION) BALPA House, 5 Heathrow Boulevard, 278 Bath Road, West Drayton UB7 0DQ T 020-8476 4000 E balpa@balpa.org W www.balpa.org
General Secretary, Jim McAuslan
Membership: 7,800

BDA (BRITISH DIETETIC ASSOCIATION) 5th Floor, Charles House, 148–149 Great Charles Street, Birmingham B3 3HT T 0121-200 8021 E info@bda.uk.com W www.bda.uk.com
Chief Executive, Andy Burman
Membership: 8,563

BFAWU (BAKERS, FOOD AND ALLIED WORKERS' UNION) Stanborough House, Great North Road, Welwyn Garden City AL8 7TA T 01707-260150 E info@bfawu.org W www.bfawu.org
General Secretary, Ronnie Draper
Membership: 19,070

BOS TU (BRITISH ORTHOPTIC SOCIETY TRADE UNION) Salisbury House, Station Road, Cambridge CB1 2LA T 01353-665541 E bios@orthoptics.org.uk W www.orthoptics.org.uk
Chair, Rowena McNamara
Membership: 1,081

BSU (BRITANNIA STAFF UNION) Court Lodge, Leonard Street, Leek ST13 5JP T 01538-399627 E bsu@themail.co.uk W www.britanniasu.org.uk
General Secretary, John Stoddard
Membership: 1,449

COMMUNITY 465C Caledonian Road, London N7 9GX T 020-7420 4000 E info@community-tu.org W www.community-tu.org
General Secretary, Roy Rickhuss
Membership: 31,886

CSP (CHARTERED SOCIETY OF PHYSIOTHERAPY) 14 Bedford Row, London WC1R 4ED T 020-7306 6666 E enquiries@csp.org.uk W www.csp.org.uk
Chief Executive, Karen Middleton, CBE
Membership: 40,050

CWU (COMMUNICATION WORKERS UNION) 150 The Broadway, London SW19 1RX T 020-8971 7200 E info@cwu.org W www.cwu.org
General Secretary, Dave Ward
Membership: 192,508

EIS (EDUCATIONAL INSTITUTE OF SCOTLAND) 46 Moray Place, Edinburgh EH3 6BH T 0131-225 6244 E enquiries@eis.org.uk W www.eis.org.uk
General Secretary, Larry Flanagan
Membership: 53,015

EQUITY Guild House, Upper St Martin's Lane, London WC2H 9EG T 020-7379 6000 E info@equity.org.uk W www.equity.org.uk
General Secretary, Christine Payne
Membership: 40,451

FBU (FIRE BRIGADES UNION) Bradley House, 68 Coombe Road, Kingston upon Thames KT2 7AE T 020-8541 1765 E office@fbu.org.uk W www.fbu.org.uk
General Secretary, Matt Wrack
Membership: 35,810

FDA 8 Leake Street, London SE1 7NN T 020-7401 5555 E info@fda.org.uk W www.fda.org.uk
General Secretary, Dave Penman
Membership: 16,734

GMB 22 Stephenson Way, London NW1 2HD T 020-7391 6700 E info@gmb.org.uk W www.gmb.org.uk
General Secretary, Tim Roache
Membership: 610,098

HCSA (HOSPITAL CONSULTANTS' AND SPECIALISTS' ASSOCIATION) 1 Kingsclere Road, Basingstoke RG25 3JA T 01256-771777 E conspec@hcsa.com W www.hcsa.com
Chief Executive, Eddie Saville
Membership: 3,069

MU (MUSICIANS' UNION) 60–62 Clapham Road, London SW9 0JJ T 020-7582 5566 E info@theMU.org W www.musiciansunion.org.uk
General Secretary, John F. Smith
Membership: 30,595

NACO (NATIONAL ASSOCIATION OF COOPERATIVE OFFICIALS) 6A Clarendon Place, Hyde SK14 2QZ T 0161-351 7900 E info@naco.coop W www.naco.coop
General Secretary, Bob Lister (interim)
Membership: 1,388

NAHT (NATIONAL ASSOCIATION OF HEAD TEACHERS) 1 Heath Square, Haywards Heath RH16 1BL T 0300-303 0333 E info@naht.org.uk W www.naht.org.uk
General Secretary, Russell Hobby
Membership: 28,855

NAPO (TRADE UNION AND PROFESSIONAL ASSOCIATION FOR FAMILY COURT AND PROBATION STAFF) 160 Falcon Road, London SW11 2NY T 020-7223 4887 E info@napo.org.uk W www.napo.org.uk
General Secretary, Ian Lawrence
Membership: 6,762

NASS (NATIONAL ASSOCIATION OF STABLE STAFF) The New Astley Club, Fred Archer Way, Newmarket CB8 8NT T 01638-663411 E admin@naoss.co.uk W www.naoss.co.uk
Chief Executive, George McGrath
Membership: 2,005

NASUWT (NATIONAL ASSOCIATION OF SCHOOLMASTERS/ UNION OF WOMEN TEACHERS) Hillscourt Education Centre, Rose Hill, Birmingham B45 8RS T 0121-453 6150 E nasuwt@mail.nasuwt.org.uk W www.nasuwt.org.uk
General Secretary, Ms Chris Keates
Membership: 295,565

NAUTILUS INTERNATIONAL 1–2 The Shrubberies, George Lane, London E18 1BD T 020-8989 6677 E enquiries@nautilusint.org W www.nautilusint.org
General Secretary, Mark Dickinson
Membership: 15,043

NEU (NATIONAL EDUCATION UNION) Hamilton House, Mabledon Place, London WC1H 9BD T 020-7388 6191 W www.neu.org.uk
General Secretaries, Dr Mary Bousted; Kevin Courtney
Membership: 459,519

NGSU (NATIONWIDE GROUP STAFF UNION) Middleton Farmhouse, 37 Main Road, Middleton Cheney OX17 2QT T 01295-710767 E ngsu@ngsu.org.uk W www.ngsu.co.uk
General Secretary, Tim Poil
Membership: 12,197

NUJ (NATIONAL UNION OF JOURNALISTS) 72 Acton
Street, London WC1X 9NB T 020-7843 3700 E info@nuj.org.uk
W www.nuj.org.uk
General Secretary, Michelle Stanistreet
Membership: 30,250

NUM (NATIONAL UNION OF MINEWORKERS) Miners'
Offices, 2 Huddersfield Road, Barnsley S70 2LS T 01226-215555
E chris.kitchen@num.org.uk W www.num.org.uk
National Secretary, Chris Kitchen
Membership: 1,065

PCS (PUBLIC AND COMMERCIAL SERVICES UNION)
160 Falcon Road, London SW11 2LN T 020-7924 2727
W www.pcs.org.uk
General Secretary, Mark Serwotka
Membership: 195,091

PFA (PROFESSIONAL FOOTBALLERS' ASSOCIATION)
20 Oxford Court, Manchester M2 3WQ T 0161-236 0575
E info@thepfa.co.uk W www.thepfa.com
Chief Executive, Gordon Taylor, OBE
Membership: 3,051

POA (PROFESSIONAL TRADE UNION FOR PRISON,
CORRECTIONAL AND SECURE PSYCHIATRIC
WORKERS) Cronin House, 245 Church Street, London
N9 9HW T 020-8803 0255 E general@poauk.org.uk
W www.poauk.org.uk
General Secretary, Steve Gillan
Membership: 30,103

PROSPECT New Prospect House, 8 Leake Street, London
SE1 7NN T 020-7902 6600 E enquiries@prospect.org.uk
W www.prospect.org.uk
General Secretary, Mike Clancy
Membership: 139,778

RCM (ROYAL COLLEGE OF MIDWIVES) 15 Mansfield
Street, London W1G 9NH T 030-0303 0444 E info@rcm.org.uk
W www.rcm.org.uk
General Secretary, Gill Walton
Membership: 32,813

RMT (NATIONAL UNION OF RAIL, MARITIME AND
TRANSPORT WORKERS) Unity House, 39 Chalton Street,
London NW1 1JD T 020-7387 4771 E info@rmt.org.uk
W www.rmt.org.uk
General Secretary, Mick Cash
Membership: 83,854

SCP (SOCIETY OF CHIROPODISTS AND
PODIATRISTS) Quartz House, London SE1 2EW
T 020-7234 8620 E reception@scpod.org W www.scpod.org
General Secretary (interim), Rosemary Gillespie
Membership: 9,367

SOR (SOCIETY OF RADIOGRAPHERS) 207 Providence
Square, Mill Street, London SE1 2EW T 020-7740 7200
W www.sor.org
Chief Executive, Richard Evans
Membership: 21,744

STAFF UNION WEST BROMWICH BUILDING
SOCIETY 2 Providence Place, West Bromwich B70 8AF
T 0121-796 7720 E staffunion@westbrom.co.uk
General Secretary, vacant
Membership: 500

TSSA (TRANSPORT SALARIED STAFFS' ASSOCIATION)
Walkden House, 10 Melton Street, London NW1 2EJ
T 020-7387 2101 E enquiries@tssa.org.uk W www.tssa.org.uk
General Secretary, Manuel Cortes
Membership: 19,238

UCAC (UNDEB CENEDLAETHOL ATHRAWON
CYMRU/ NATIONAL UNION OF THE TEACHERS OF
WALES) Prif Swyddfa UCAC, Ffordd Penglais, Aberystwyth
SY23 2EU T 01970-639950 E ucac@ucac.cymru
W www.athrawon.com
General Secretary, Elaine Edwards
Membership: 4,148

UCU (UNIVERSITY AND COLLEGE UNION) Carlow
Street, London NW1 7LH T 020-7756 2500 E hq@ucu.org.uk
W www.ucu.org.uk
General Secretary, Sally Hunt
Membership: 105,371

UNISON 130 Euston Road, London NW1 2AY T 0800-085 7857
W www.unison.org.uk
General Secretary, Dave Prentis
Membership: 1,216,659

UNITE 128 Theobald's Road, London WC1X 8TN
T 020-7611 2500 W www.unitetheunion.org
General Secretary, Len McCluskey
Membership: 1,340,841

URTU (UNITED ROAD TRANSPORT UNION) Almond
House, Oak Green, Cheadle, Hulme SK8 6QL T 0800-526 639
E info@urtu.com W www.urtu.com
General Secretary, Robert Monks
Membership: 10,615

USDAW (UNION OF SHOP, DISTRIBUTIVE AND
ALLIED WORKERS) 188 Wilmslow Road, Manchester
M14 6LJ T 0161-224 2804 E enquiries@usdaw.org.uk
W www.usdaw.org.uk
General Secretary, John Hannett
Membership: 440,603

WGGB (WRITERS' GUILD OF GREAT BRITAIN) 134
Tooley Street, London SE1 2TU T 020-7833 0777
E admin@writersguild.org.uk W www.writersguild.org.uk
General Secretary (acting), Ellie Peers
Membership: 1,319

NON-AFFILIATED UNIONS
As at May 2017

ASCL (ASSOCIATION OF SCHOOL AND COLLEGE
LEADERS) 130 Regent Road, Leicester LE1 7PG
T 0116-299 1122 E info@ascl.org.uk W www.ascl.org.uk
General Secretary, Geoff Barton
Membership: around 18,000

BDA (BRITISH DENTAL ASSOCIATION) 64 Wimpole
Street, London W1G 8YS T 020-7935 0875 E enquiries@bda.org
W www.bda.org
Chief Executive, Peter Ward
Membership: around 19,200

CIOJ (CHARTERED INSTITUTE OF JOURNALISTS) 2
Dock Offices, Surrey Quays Road, London SE16 2XU
T 020-7252 1187 E memberservices@cioj.co.uk
W www.cioj.co.uk
General Secretary, Dominic Cooper
Membership: around 2,000

NSEAD (NATIONAL SOCIETY FOR EDUCATION IN
ART AND DESIGN) 3 Mason's Wharf, Potley Lane, Corsham
SN13 9FY T 01225-810134 E info@nsead.org W www.nsead.org
General Secretary, Mrs Lesley Butterworth
Membership: around 2,000

SOCIETY OF AUTHORS 84 Drayton Gardens, London
SW10 9SB T 020-7373 6642 E info@societyofauthors.org
W www.societyofauthors.org
Chief Executive, Nicola Solomon
Membership: around 9,400

SSTA (SCOTTISH SECONDARY TEACHERS'
ASSOCIATION) West End House, 14 West End Place,
Edinburgh EH11 2ED T 0131-313 7300 E info@ssta.org.uk
W www.ssta.org.uk
General Secretary, Seamus Searson
Membership: around 8,500

SPORTS BODIES

SPORTS COUNCILS

SPORT AND RECREATION ALLIANCE Burwood House, 14 Caxton Street, London SW1H 0QT T 020-7976 3900 E info@sportandrecreation.org.uk W www.sportandrecreation.org.uk
Chief Executive, Emma Boggis
SPORT ENGLAND 21 Bloomsbury Street, London WC1B 3HF T 020-7273 1551 E info@sportengland.org W www.sportengland.org
Chief Executive, Jennie Price
SPORT NORTHERN IRELAND House of Sport, 2A Upper Malone Road, Belfast BT9 5LA T 028-9038 1222 E info@sportni.net W www.sportni.net
Chief Executive, vacant
SPORTSCOTLAND Doges, Templeton on the Green, 62 Templeton Street, Glasgow G40 1DA T 0141-534 6500 E website@sportscotland.org.uk W www.sportscotland.org.uk
Chief Executive, Stewart Harris
SPORT WALES Sophia Gardens, Cardiff CF11 9SW T 0300-300 3111 E info@sportwales.org.uk W www.sportwales.org.uk
Chief Executive, Sarah Powell
UK SPORT 21 Bloomsbury Street, London WC1B 3HF T 020-7211 5100 E info@uksport.gov.uk W www.uksport.gov.uk
Chief Executive, Liz Nicholl, CBE

AMERICAN FOOTBALL

BRITISH AMERICAN FOOTBALL ASSOCIATION 1 Franchise Street, Kidderminster DY11 6RE E human.resources@britishamericanfootball.org W www.britishamericanfootball.org
Chair, Martin Cockerill

ANGLING

ANGLING TRUST Eastwood House, 6 Rainbow Street, Herefordshire HR6 8DQ T 0156-862 0447 E admin@anglingtrust.net W www.anglingtrust.net
Chief Executive, Mark Lloyd

ARCHERY

ARCHERY GB Lilleshall National Sports Centre, Newport TF10 9AT T 0195-267 7888 E enquiries@archerygb.org W www.archerygb.org
Chief Executive, Neil Armitage

ASSOCIATION FOOTBALL

ENGLISH FOOTBALL LEAGUE EFL House, 10-12 West Cliff, Preston PR1 8HU T 01772-325800 E enquiries@efl.com W www.efl.com
Chief Executive, Shaun Harvey
FOOTBALL ASSOCIATION Wembley Stadium, PO Box 1966, London SW1P 9EQ T 0800-169 1863 E info@thefa.com W www.thefa.com
Chief Executive, Martin Glenn
FOOTBALL ASSOCIATION OF WALES 11–12 Neptune Court, Vanguard Way, Cardiff CF24 5PJ T 029-2043 5830 E info@faw.co.uk W www.faw.org.uk
Chief Executive, Jonathan Ford
IRISH FOOTBALL ASSOCIATION Donegal Avenue, Belfast BT12 6LU T 028-9066 9458 E info@irishfa.com W www.irishfa.com
Chief Executive, Patrick Nelson

PREMIER LEAGUE 30 Gloucester Place, London W1U 8PL T 020-7864 9000 E info@premierleague.com W www.premierleague.com
Chief Executive, Richard Scudamore
SCOTTISH FOOTBALL ASSOCIATION Hampden Park, Glasgow G42 9AY T 0141-616 6000 E info@scottishfa.co.uk W www.scottishfa.co.uk
Chief Executive, Stewart Regan
SCOTTISH PROFESSIONAL FOOTBALL LEAGUE Hampden Park, Glasgow G42 9DE T 0141-620 4140 E info@spfl.co.uk W www.spfl.co.uk
Chief Executive, Neil Doncaster

ATHLETICS

BRITISH ATHLETICS Athletics House, Alexander Stadium, Birmingham B42 2BE T 0121-713 8400 E enquiries@englandathletics.org W www.britishathletics.org.uk
Chief Executive, Niels de Vos
ATHLETICS NORTHERN IRELAND Athletics House, Old Coach Road, Belfast BT9 5PR T 028-9060 2707 E info@athleticsni.org W www.athleticsni.org
General Secretary, John Allen
SCOTTISH ATHLETICS Caledonia House, Edinburgh EH12 9DQ T 0131-539 7320 E admin@scottishathletics.org.uk W www.scottishathletics.org.uk
Chief Executive, Mark Munro
WELSH ATHLETICS Cardiff International Sports Stadium, Leckwith Road, Cardiff CF11 8AZ T 029-2064 4870 E office@welshathletics.org W www.welshathletics.org
Chief Executive, Matt Newman

BADMINTON

BADMINTON ENGLAND National Badminton Centre, Bradwell Road, Milton Keynes MK8 9LA T 01908-268400 E enquiries@badmintonengland.co.uk W www.badmintonengland.co.uk
Chief Executive, Adrian Christy
BADMINTON SCOTLAND Cockburn Centre, 40 Bogmoor Place, Glasgow G51 4TQ T 0141-445 1218 E enquiries@badmintonscotland.org.uk W www.badmintonscotland.org.uk
Chief Executive, Anne Smillie
BADMINTON WALES Sport Wales National Centre, Sophia Gardens, Cardiff CF11 9SW T 0300-300 3124 E manuel.belanche@badminton.wales W www.badminton.wales
General Manager, Gareth Hall

BASEBALL

BASEBALLSOFTBALL UK Ariel House, 74A Charlotte Street, London W1T 4QJ T 020-7453 7055 W www.baseballsoftballuk.com
Chief Executive, Jenny Fromer
BRITISH BASEBALL FEDERATION Ariel House, 74A Charlotte Street, London W1T 4QJ T 207-453 7055 W www.britishbaseball.org
President, Gerry Perez

BASKETBALL

BASKETBALL ENGLAND English Institute of Sport, Sheffield S9 5DA T 0114-284 1060 E info@basketballengland.co.uk W www.basketballengland.co.uk
Chief Executive, Stewart Kellett
BASKETBALL SCOTLAND Caledonia House, Edinburgh EH12 9DQ T 0131-317 7260 E enquiries@basketball-scotland.com W www.basketballscotland.co.uk
Chief Executive, Kevin Pringle

BILLIARDS AND SNOOKER

WORLD SNOOKER 75 Whiteladies Road, Bristol BS8 2NT
T 0117-317 8200 E info@worldsnooker.com
W www.worldsnooker.com
Chair, Jason Ferguson

BOBSLEIGH

BRITISH BOBSLEIGH & SKELETON ASSOCIATION
University of Bath, Claverton Down, Bath BA2 7AY
T 01225-384343 E office@thebbsa.co.uk W www.thebbsa.co.uk
Chief Executive, Richard Parker

BOWLS

BOWLS ENGLAND Riverside House, Milverton Hill, Royal
Leamington Spa CV32 5HZ T 01926-334609
E enquiries@bowlsengland.com W www.bowlsengland.com
Chief Executive, Tony Allcock, MBE
BRITISH ISLES BOWLS COUNCIL
E bibcsecretary@aol.co.uk W www.britishislesbowls.com
President (2017), Jim Humphreys
ENGLISH INDOOR BOWLING ASSOCIATION David
Cornwell House, Bowling Green, Melton Mowbray LE13 0FA
T 01664-481900 E enquiries@eiba.co.uk W www.eiba.co.uk
Chief Executive, Peter Thompson

BOXING

BRITISH BOXING BOARD OF CONTROL 14 North Road,
Cardiff CF10 3DY T 029-2036 7000 E admin@bbbofc.com
W www.bbbofc.com
General Secretary, Robert Smith
ENGLAND BOXING English Institute of Sport, Coleridge Road,
Sheffield S9 5DA T 0114-223 5654
E enquiries@englandboxing.org W www.abae.co.uk
Chief Executive, Paul Porter

CANOEING

BRITISH CANOEING National Water Sport Centre, Adbolton
Lane, Nottingham NG12 2LU T 0300-0119 500
E info@britishcanoeing.org.uk W www.britishcanoeing.org.uk
Chief Executive, David Joy

CHESS

ENGLISH CHESS FEDERATION The Watch Oak, Chain Lane,
Battle TN33 0YD T 01424-775222 E office@englishchess.org.uk
W www.englishchess.org.uk
Chief Executive, Mike Truran

CRICKET

ENGLAND AND WALES CRICKET BOARD Lord's Cricket
Ground, St John's Wood Road, London NW8 8QZ
T 020-7432 1200 W www.ecb.co.uk
Chief Executive Officer, Tom Harrison
MCC Lord's Cricket Ground, London NW8 8QN T 020-7616 8500
E reception@mcc.org.uk W www.lords.org
Chief Executive and Secretary, Derek Brewer

CROQUET

CROQUET ASSOCIATION Old Bath Road, Cheltenham
GL53 7DF T 01242-242318 E caoffice@croquet.org.uk
W www.croquet.org.uk
Manager, Elizabeth Larsson

CURLING

BRITISH CURLING c/o The Royal Caledonian Curling Club,
Ochil House, Stirling FK7 7XE E info@britishcurling.com
W www.britishcurling.org.uk
Chief Operating Officer, Bruce Crawford

ROYAL CALEDONIAN CURLING CLUB Ochil House,
Stirling FK7 7XE T 0131-333 3003
E office@royalcaledoniancurlingclub.org
W www.royalcaledoniancurlingclub.org
Chief Executive, Bruce Crawford

CYCLING

BRITISH CYCLING FEDERATION Stuart Street, Manchester
M11 4DQ T 0161-274 2000 E info@britishcycling.org.uk
W www.britishcycling.org.uk
Chief Executive, Julie Harrington

DARTS

BRITISH DARTS ORGANISATION Unit 4, Glan-y-Llyn
Industrial Estate, Cardiff CF15 7JD T 029-2081 1815
E contact@bdodarts.com W www.bdodarts.com
Chairman, Barry Gilbey

EQUESTRIANISM

BRITISH EQUESTRIAN FEDERATION Abbey Park,
Kenilworth CV8 2RH T 024-7669 8871 E info@bef.co.uk
W www.bef.co.uk
Chief Executive, Clare Salmon
BRITISH EVENTING Abbey Park, Kenilworth CV8 2RN
T 024-7669 8856 E info@britisheventing.com
W www.britisheventing.com
Chief Executive, David Holmes

ETON FIVES

ETON FIVES ASSOCIATION 45 Sandhills Crescent, Solihull
B91 3UE T 07833-600230 W www.etonfives.com
Chair, Richard Black

FENCING

BRITISH FENCING 1 Baron's Gate, 33 Rothschild Road,
London W4 5HT T 020-8742 3032
E headoffice@britishfencing.com W www.britishfencing.com
Chief Executive, Georgina Usher

GLIDING

BRITISH GLIDING ASSOCIATION 8 Merus Court, Meridian
Business Park, Leicester LE19 1RJ T 0116-289 2956
E office@gliding.co.uk W www.gliding.co.uk
Chief Executive, Pete Stratten

GOLF

ENGLAND GOLF The National Golf Centre, Woodhall Spa
LN10 6PU T 01526-354500 E info@englandgolf.org
W www.englandgolf.org
Chief Executive, Nick Pink
THE ROYAL AND ANCIENT GOLF CLUB Golf Place, St
Andrews KY16 9JD T 01334-460000
E thesecretary@randagc.org W www.randa.org
Chief Executive, Martin Slumbers

GYMNASTICS

BRITISH GYMNASTICS Ford Hall, Lilleshall National Sports
Centre, Newport TF10 9NB T 0345-129 7129
E information@british-gymnastics.org
W www.british-gymnastics.org
Chief Executive, Jane Allen

HANDBALL

ENGLAND HANDBALL The Halliwell Jones Stadium, Winwick
Road, Warrington WA2 7NE T 01925-246482
E office@englandhandball.com W www.englandhandball.com
Chief Executive, David Meli

HOCKEY

ENGLAND HOCKEY Bisham Abbey National Sports Centre, Marlow SL7 1RR **T** 01628-897500 **E** info@englandhockey.co.uk **W** www.englandhockey.co.uk
Chief Executive, Sally Munday
HOCKEY WALES Sport Wales National Centre, Sophia Gardens, Cardiff CF11 9SW **T** 0300-300 3126 **E** info@hockeywales.org.uk **W** www.hockeywales.org.uk
Chief Executive, David Phenis
SCOTTISH HOCKEY UNION Glasgow National Hockey Centre, 8 King's Drive, Glasgow G40 1HB **T** 0141-550 5999 **W** www.scottish-hockey.org.uk
Chief Executive, David Sweetman

HORSERACING

BRITISH HORSERACING AUTHORITY 75 High Holborn, London WC1V 6LS **T** 020-7152 0000
E info@britishhorseracing.com **W** www.britishhorseracing.com
Chief Executive, Nick Rust
THE JOCKEY CLUB 75 High Holborn, London WC1V 6LS
T 020-7611 1800 **E** info@thejockeyclub.co.uk
W www.thejockeyclub.co.uk
Chief Executive, Simon Bazalgette

ICE SKATING

NATIONAL ICE SKATING ASSOCIATION Grains Building, High Cross Street, Nottingham NG1 3AX **T** 0115-988 8060
E info@iceskating.org.uk **W** www.iceskating.org.uk
Chief Executive, Jackie Sheldon

LACROSSE

ENGLISH LACROSSE ASSOCIATION National Squash Centre and Regional Area, Gate 13, Manchester M11 3FF
T 0161-231 1357 **E** info@englishlacrosse.co.uk
W www.englishlacrosse.co.uk
Chief Executive, Mark Coups

LAWN TENNIS

LAWN TENNIS ASSOCIATION National Tennis Centre, 100 Priory Lane, London SW15 5JQ **T** 020-8487 7000
E info@lta.org.uk **W** www.lta.org.uk
Chief Executive, Michael Downey

MARTIAL ARTS

BRITISH JUDO ASSOCIATION Suite B, Loughborough Technology Centre, Epinal Way, Loughborough LE11 3GE
T 01509-637680 **E** bja@britishjudo.org.uk
W www.britishjudo.org.uk
Chief Executive, Andrew Scoular
BRITISH JU JITSU ASSOCIATION 5 Avenue Parade, Accrington BB5 6PN **T** 03333-202039 **E** bjjagb@icloud.com
W www.bjjagb.com
Chairman, Prof. Martin Dixon
BRITISH TAEKWONDO The Business Place, Park Road, Mansfield Woodhouse NG19 8ER **T** 01623-665005
E admin@britishtaekwondo.org.uk
W www.britishtaekwondo.org.uk
Chief Executive, Mark Abberley

MODERN PENTATHLON

PENTATHLON GB Sports Training Village, University of Bath, Bath BA2 7AY **T** 01225-386808 **E** admin@pentathlongb.org
W www.pentathlongb.org
Chief Executive, Danielle Every

MOTOR SPORTS

AUTO-CYCLE UNION ACU House, Rugby CV21 2YX
T 01788-566400 **E** admin@acu.org.uk **W** www.acu.org.uk
General Secretary, Gary Thompson, MBE

MOTOR SPORTS ASSOCIATION Motor Sports House, Riverside Park, SL3 0HG **T** 01753-765000 **W** www.msauk.org
Chief Executive, Rob Jones
SCOTTISH AUTO CYCLE UNION 28 West Main Street, Uphall EH52 5DW **T** 01506-858354 **E** office@sacu.co.uk
W www.sacu.co.uk
Chair, Sandy Mack

MOUNTAINEERING

BRITISH MOUNTAINEERING COUNCIL The Old Church, 177–179 Burton Road, Manchester M20 2BB **T** 0161-445 6111
E office@thebmc.co.uk **W** www.thebmc.co.uk
Chief Executive, Dave Turnbull

MULTI-SPORTS BODIES

BRITISH OLYMPIC ASSOCIATION 60 Charlotte Street, London W1T 2NU **T** 020-7842 5700 **E** club@teamgb.com
W www.teamgb.com
Chief Executive, Bill Sweeney
BRITISH PARALYMPIC ASSOCIATION 60 Charlotte Street, London W1T 2NU **T** 020-7842 5789 **E** info@paralympics.org.uk
W www.paralympics.org.uk
Chief Executive, Tim Hollingsworth, OBE
BRITISH UNIVERSITIES AND COLLEGES SPORT 20–24 Kings Bench Street, London SE1 0QX **T** 020-7633 5080
W www.bucs.org.uk
Chief Executive, Vince Mayne
COMMONWEALTH GAMES ENGLAND 307–308 High Holborn, London WC1V 7LL **T** 020-7831 3444
E info@weareengland.org **W** www.weareengland.org
Chief Executive, Paul Blanchard
COMMONWEALTH GAMES FEDERATION Quadrant House, 55–58 Pall Mall, London SW1Y 5JH **T** 020-7104 6427
E info@thecgf.com **W** www.thecgf.com
Chief Executive, David Grevemberg, CBE
ENGLISH FEDERATION OF DISABILITY SPORT Loughborough University, 3 Oakwood Drive, LE11 3QF
T 01509-227750 **W** www.efds.co.uk
Chief Executive, Barry Horne

NETBALL

ENGLAND NETBALL Netball House, 1–12 Old Park Road, Hitchin SG5 2JR **T** 01462-442344 **E** info@englandnetball.co.uk
W www.englandnetball.co.uk
Chief Executive, Joanna Adams
NETBALL NI Unit F, Curley Pavilion, Portside Business Park, Belfast BT3 9ED **T** 028-9073 6320
E bookingsandadmin@netballni.org **W** www.netballni.org
President, Michaela Diver
NETBALL SCOTLAND Emirates Arena, 1000 London Road, Glasgow G40 3HY **T** 0141-428 3460
E membership@netballscotland.com
W www.netballscotland.com
Chief Executive, Claire Nelson
WELSH NETBALL ASSOCIATION Sport Wales National Centre, Sophia Gardens, Cardiff CF11 9SW **T** 029-2033 4950
E welshnetball@welshnetball.com **W** www.welshnetball.co.uk
Chief Executive, Sarah Jones

ORIENTEERING

BRITISH ORIENTEERING Scholes Mill, Old Coach Road, Matlock DE4 5FY **T** 01629-583037
E info@britishorienteering.org.uk
W www.britishorienteering.org.uk
Chief Executive, Mike Hamilton

POLO

THE HURLINGHAM POLO ASSOCIATION Manor Farm, Little Coxwell, Faringdon SN7 7LW **T** 01367-242828
E enquiries@hpa-polo.co.uk **W** www.hpa-polo.co.uk
Chief Executive, David Woodd

RACKETS AND REAL TENNIS

TENNIS AND RACKETS ASSOCIATION c/o The Queen's Club, Palliser Road, London W14 9EQ T 020-7835 6937 E office@tennisandrackets.com W www.tennisandrackets.com
Chief Executive, C. S. Davies

ROWING

BRITISH ROWING 6 Lower Mall, London W6 9DJ T 020-8237 6700 E info@gbrowingteam.org.uk W www.britishrowing.org
Chief Executive, Andy Parkinson

HENLEY ROYAL REGATTA Regatta Headquarters, Henley-on-Thames RG9 2LY T 01491-572153 W www.hrr.co.uk
Secretary, D. G. M. Grist

RUGBY LEAGUE

BRITISH AMATEUR RUGBY LEAGUE ASSOCIATION West Yorkshire House, 4 New North Parade, Huddersfield HD1 5JP T 01484-599113 E secretary@barla.org.uk W www.barla.org.uk
Chair, Sue Taylor

RUGBY FOOTBALL LEAGUE Red Hall, Red Hall Lane, Leeds LS17 8NB T 0844-477 7113 E enquiries@rfl.uk.com W www.rugby-league.com
Chief Executive, Nigel Wood

RUGBY UNION

IRISH RUGBY FOOTBALL UNION 10–12 Lansdowne Road, Dublin 4 T (+353) 1647 3800 E info@irishrugby.ie W www.irishrugby.ie
Chief Executive, Philip Browne

RUGBY FOOTBALL UNION Rugby House, Twickenham Stadium, 200 Whitton Road, Twickenham TW2 7BA T 0871-222 2120 E enquiries@therfu.com W www.englandrugby.com
Chief Executive, Ian Ritchie

RUGBY FOOTBALL UNION FOR WOMEN Rugby House, Twickenham Stadium, 200 Whitton Road, TW2 7BA T 0871-222 2120 E enquiries@therfu.com W www.englandrugby.com
Managing Director, Rosie Williams

SCOTTISH RUGBY UNION Murrayfield, Edinburgh EH12 5PJ T 0131-346 5000 E feedback@sru.org.uk W www.scottishrugby.org
Chief Executive, Mark Dodson

SCOTTISH WOMEN'S RUGBY UNION Scottish Rugby Union, Edinburgh EH12 5PJ T 0131-346 5000 E feedback@sru.org.uk W www.scottishrugby.org
Chief Executive, Mark Dodson

WELSH RUGBY UNION Principality Stadium, Westgate Street, Cardiff CF10 1NS T 0844-249 1999 E info@wru.co.uk W www.wru.co.uk
Chief Executive, Martyn Phillips

SHOOTING

BRITISH SHOOTING Bisham Abbey National Sports Centre, Marlow Road, Marlow SL7 1RR T 01628-488800 E secretary@britishshooting.org.uk W www.britishshooting.org.uk
Chief Executive, Hamish McInnes

CLAY PIGEON SHOOTING ASSOCIATION Edmonton House, National Shooting Centre, Brookwood, Woking GU24 0NP T 01483-485400 E info@cpsa.co.uk W www.cpsa.co.uk
Chief Executive, Nick Fellows

NATIONAL RIFLE ASSOCIATION Bisley Camp, GU24 0PB T 01483-797777 E info@nra.org.uk W www.nra.org.uk
Chief Executive, Andrew Mercer

NATIONAL SMALL-BORE RIFLE ASSOCIATION Lord Roberts Centre, Bisley Camp, Woking GU24 0NP T 01483-485502 W www.nsra.co.uk
Chief Executive, Iain Root

SKIING AND SNOWBOARDING

BRITISH SKI AND SNOWBOARD 60 Charlotte Street, London W1T 2NU T 020-7842 5764 E bss@teambss.org.uk W www.teambss.org.uk
Chief Executive, Dave Edwards

SPEEDWAY

BRITISH SPEEDWAY ACU Headquarters, Wood Street, Rugby CV21 2YX T 01788-560648 E office@speedwaygb.co W www.speedwaygb.co
Chair, Keith Chapman

SQUASH

ENGLAND SQUASH National Squash Centre, Manchester M11 3FF T 0161-231 4499 W www.englandsquash.com
Chief Executive, Keir Worth

SCOTTISH SQUASH AND RACKETBALL LIMITED Caledonia House, 1 Redheughs Rigg, Edinburgh EH12 9DQ T 0131-625 4425 E info@scottishsquash.org W www.scottishsquash.org
Chief Executive, Maggie Still

WALES SQUASH AND RACKETBALL Sport Wales National Centre, Sophia Close, Cardiff CF11 9SW T 0300-300 3121 W www.walessquashandracketball.co.uk
Chair, Phil Brailey

SUB-AQUA

BRITISH SUB-AQUA CLUB Telford's Quay, South Pier Road, Ellesmere Port CH65 4FL T 0151-350 6200 E info@bsac.com W www.bsac.com
Chief Executive, Mary Tetley

SWIMMING

SWIM ENGLAND Pavilion 3, Sport Park, Loughborough LE11 3QF T 01509-618700 E customerservices@swimming.org W www.swimming.org
Chief Executive, Jane Nickerson

SCOTTISH SWIMMING National Swimming Academy, University of Stirling, FK9 4LA T 01786-466520 E info@scottishswimming.com W www.scottishswimming.com
Chief Executive, Forbes Dunlop

SWIM WALES WNPS, Sketty Lane, Swansea SA2 8QG T 01792-513636 W www.swimwales.org
Chief Executive, Fergus Feeney

TABLE TENNIS

TABLE TENNIS ENGLAND Norfolk House, 88 Saxon Gate West, Milton Keynes MK9 2DL T 01908-208860 E help@tabletennisengland.co.uk W www.tabletennisengland.co.uk
Chief Executive, Sara Sutcliffe

TABLE TENNIS SCOTLAND Caledonia House, South Gyle, Edinburgh EH12 9DQ T 0131-317 8077 E ttsadmin@btconnect.com W www.tabletennisscotland.co.uk
Chair, Terry McLernon, MBE

TABLE TENNIS WALES Glanrhyd, Ebbw View, Ebbw Vale NP23 5NU T 01244-571335 W www.tabletennis.wales
Chair, Bernard Carter

TRIATHLON

BRITISH TRIATHLON PO Box 25, Loughborough LE11 3WX T 01509-226161 E info@britishtriathlon.org W www.britishtriathlon.org
Chief Executive, Jack Buckner

VOLLEYBALL

NORTHERN IRELAND VOLLEYBALL ASSOCIATION 7 Greengage Cottages, Ballymoney BT53 6GZ
W www.nivolleyball.com
General Secretary, Paddy Elder

SCOTTISH VOLLEYBALL ASSOCIATION 48 The Pleasance, Edinburgh EH8 9TJ **T** 0131-556 4633
E info@scottishvolleyball.org **W** www.scottishvolleyball.org
Chief Executive, Margaret Ann Fleming

VOLLEYBALL ENGLAND SportPark, Loughborough University, 3 Oakwood Drive, Loughborough LE11 3QF **T** 01509-227722
E info@volleyballengland.org **W** www.volleyballengland.org
Chief Executive, Janet Inman

VOLLEYBALL WALES 13 Beckgrove Close, Cardiff CF24 2SE
T 029-2041 6537 **E** ysaker@cardiffmet.ac.uk
W www.volleyballwales.org
Chair, Yvonne Saker

WALKING

RACE WALKING ASSOCIATION Hufflers, Heard's Lane, Brentwood CM15 0SF **T** 01277-220687
E racewalkingassociation@btinternet.com
W www.racewalkingassociation.org.uk
Hon. General Secretary, Peter Cassidy

WATER SKIING

BRITISH WATER SKI AND WAKEBOARD The Forum, Hanworth Lane, Chertsey KT16 9JX **T** 01932-560007
E info@bwsf.co.uk **W** www.bwsw.org.uk
Chief Executive, Patrick Donovan

BRITISH WATER SKI AND WAKEBOARD The Forum, Hanworth Lane, Chertsey KT16 9JX **T** 01932-560007
E info@bwsf.co.uk **W** www.bwsw.org.uk
Chief Executive, Patrick Donovan

WEIGHTLIFTING

BRITISH WEIGHT LIFTING St Ann's Mill, Kirkstall Road, Leeds LS5 3AE **T** 0113-224 9402
E enquiries@britishweightlifting.org
W www.britishweightlifting.org
Chief Executive, Ashley Metcalfe

WRESTLING

BRITISH WRESTLING ASSOCIATION 41 Great Clowes St, Salford M7 1RQ **T** 0161-8352112 **E** admin@britishwrestling.org
W www.britishwrestling.org
Chief Executive, Colin Nicholson

YACHTING

ROYAL YACHTING ASSOCIATION RYA House, Ensign Way, Southampton SO31 4YA **T** 023-8060 4100
W www.rya.org.uk
Chief Executive, Sarah Treseder

CLUBS

Originally called gentlemen's clubs, these organisations are permanent institutions with a fixed clubhouse, which usually includes restaurants, bars, a library and overnight accommodation. Members are fee-paying and typically vetted for their suitability.

Gentlemen's clubs were created for males of the English upper class and grew out of the 17th-century fashion for coffee houses which enjoyed enormous popularity, despite opposition from Charles II, who believed they encouraged the spreading of royal disaffection. The first of the London clubs – White's – was founded in 1693 by Francesco Bianco in St James's Street, in the area that quickly became known as 'clubland'. Membership to the first of the clubs was a matter of hereditary privilege or special favour, a deliberately exclusionary measure which prompted an enormous growth in the number of clubs throughout the 19th century, fed by a burgeoning and aspirational middle class.

At the turn of the 20th century, there were more than 200 gentlemen's clubs in London alone, half of which had been founded since 1870. Inevitably, this level of competition could not be sustained, particularly given the number of men killed in two world wars. Financial restrictions necessitated greater provision for women and the relaxation of the social qualifications needed for membership. Nevertheless, waiting lists still exist for the leading clubs and a recommendation from at least one current member is almost always required to join.
* Men only †Women only

ARMY AND NAVY CLUB (1837), 36 Pall Mall, London
SW1Y 5JN T 020-7930 9721 E secretary@therag.co.uk
W www.armynavyclub.co.uk
Chief Executive and Secretary, Ayres de Souza
Former member: The Duke of Wellington

ARTS CLUB (1863), 40 Dover Street, London W1S 4NP
T 020-7499 8581 E reservations@theartsclub.co.uk
W www.theartsclub.co.uk
Chief Operating Officer, Rémy Lysé
Former members: Charles Dickens, Algernon Charles Swinburne, Ivan Turgenev

ATHENAEUM (1797), Church Alley, Liverpool L1 3DD
T 0151-709 7770 E reception@theathenaeum.org.uk
W www.theathenaeum.org.uk
Former members: William H. Duncan, William Roscoe

ATHENAEUM (1824), 107 Pall Mall, London SW1Y 5ER
T 020-7930 4843 E library@hellenist.org.uk
W www.athenaeumclub.co.uk
Former members: Matthew Arnold, Michael Faraday, Anthony Trollope

AUTHORS' CLUB (1891), c/o National Liberal Club, Whitehall Place, London SW1A 2HE T 020-7287 3381
E info@authorsclub.co.uk W www.authorsclub.co.uk
Honorary Secretary, Dinah Wiener
Former members: Arthur Conan Doyle, Graham Greene, Thomas Hardy, H. G. Wells, Oscar Wilde

BEEFSTEAK CLUB* (1876), 9 Irving Street, London
WC2H 7AH T 020-7930 5722 E office@thebeefsteakclub.co.uk
Secretary, Maria Hibbert
Former members: John Betjeman, Rudyard Kipling, Harold Macmillan

BOODLE'S* (1762), 28 St James's Street, London SW1A 1HJ
T 020-7930 7166 E secretary@boodles.org
Former members: Winston Churchill, Ian Fleming

BROOKS'S* (1764), St James's Street, London SW1A 1LN
T 020-7493 4411 E kay.emerson@brooksclub.org
Secretary, Ian Faul
Former members: Edward Gibbon, Roy Jenkins, William Pitt

BUCK'S CLUB (1919), 18 Clifford Street, London W1S 3RF
T 020-7734 2337 E secretary@bucksclub.co.uk
Secretary, Major Rupert Lendrum

CALEDONIAN CLUB (1891), 9 Halkin Street, London
SW1X 7DR T 020-7235 5162 E admin@caledonianclub.com
W www.caledonianclub.com
Secretary, David Balden

CANNING CLUB (1910), 4 St James's Square, London
SW1Y 4JU T 020-7827 5768 E canningclub@theinandout.co.uk
W www.theinandout.co.uk

CARLTON CLUB (1832), 69 St James's Street, London
SW1A 1PJ T 020-7493 1164 E info@carltonclub.co.uk
W www.carltonclub.co.uk
Secretary, Simon Robinson
Former members: Stanley Baldwin, Benjamin Disraeli, Harold Macmillan, John Major, Margaret Thatcher

CAVALRY AND GUARDS CLUB (1890), 127 Piccadilly, London W1J 7PX T 020-7499 1261 E secretary@cavgds.co.uk
W www.cavgds.co.uk
Secretary, David Cowdery
Former member: Lawrence Oates

CHELSEA ARTS CLUB (1891), 143 Old Church Street, London SW3 6EB T 020-7376 3311 E office@chelseaartsclub.com
W www.chelseaartsclub.com
Secretary, Geoffrey Matthews
Former members: Laurie Lee, John Singer Sargent, Walter Sickert, James McNeill Whistler

CITY LIVERY CLUB (1914), Bell Wharf Lane, Upper Thames Street, London EC4R 3TB T 020-7248 0620
E clerk@cityliveryclub.com W www.cityliveryclub.com
Hon. Secretary, Adèle Thorpe

CITY OF LONDON CLUB (1832), 19 Old Broad Street, London EC2N 1DS T 020 7588 7991
E secretary@cityoflondonclub.com
W www.cityoflondonclub.com
Former members: Robert Peel, Duke of Wellington

CITY UNIVERSITY CLUB (1895), 50 Cornhill, London
EC3V 3PD T 020-7626 8571 E secretary@cityuniversityclub.co.uk
W www.cityuniversityclub.co.uk

EAST INDIA CLUB* (1849), 16 St James's Square, London
SW1Y 4LH T 020-7930 1000 E secretary@eastindiaclub.co.uk
W www.eastindiaclub.co.uk
Secretary, Alex Bray

FARMERS CLUB (1842), 3 Whitehall Court, London
SW1A 2EL T 020-7930 3557 E reception@thefarmersclub.com
W www.thefarmersclub.com
Chief Executive and Secretary, Andrei Spence

FOX CLUB (2003), 46 Clarges Street, London W1J 7ER
T 020-7495 3656 E info@foxclublondon.com
W www.foxclublondon.com
General Manager, Bethan Seaton

GARRICK CLUB* (1831), 15 Garrick Street, London
WC2E 9AY T 020-7379 6478 E hallporters@garrickclub.co.uk
W www.garrickclub.co.uk
Secretary, Ann Robbie
Former members: Charles Dickens, William Thackeray

GROUCHO CLUB (1985), 45 Dean Street, London W1D 4QB
T 020-7439 4685 E reception@thegrouchoclub.com
W www.thegrouchoclub.com
Managing Director, Matthew Hobbs

HURLINGHAM CLUB (1869), Ranelagh Gardens, London
SW6 3PR **T** 020-7610 7400
E main.reception@hurlinghamclub.org.uk
W www.hurlinghamclub.org.uk
Secretary and Chief Executive, Alan Flitcroft

IN & OUT (NAVAL AND MILITARY CLUB) (1862), 4 St
James's Square, London SW1Y 4JU **T** 020-7827 5757
E club@theinandout.co.uk **W** www.theinandout.co.uk
Secretary, Anthony Lee
Former member: Robert Falcon Scott

LANSDOWNE CLUB (1935), 9 Fitzmaurice Place, London
W1J 5JD **T** 020-7629 7200 **E** secretary@LansdowneClub.com
W www.lansdowneclub.com
Secretary, Tim Cagney

LONDON PRESS CLUB (1882), 7–10 Adam Street, London
WC2N 6AA **T** 020-7520 9082 **E** info@londonpressclub.co.uk
W www.londonpressclub.co.uk
Secretary, Adam Cannon
Former members: Lord Astor, Lord Rothermere

NATIONAL LIBERAL CLUB (1882), Whitehall Place, London
SW1A 2HE **T** 020-7930 9871 **E** secretary@nlc.org.uk
W www.nlc.org.uk
Secretary, Simon Roberts
Former members: Winston Churchill, William Gladstone,
Ramsay MacDonald, George Bernard Shaw, H. G. Wells

NEW CAVENDISH CLUB (1920), 44 Great Cumberland
Place, London W1H 7BS **T** 07503-504639
E info@newcavendishclub.co.uk
W www.newcavendishclub.co.uk
Club Manager, Alex Maitland
Former member: Lady Bonham-Carter

NEW CLUB (1787), 86 Princes Street, Edinburgh EH2 2BB
T 0131-226 4881 **E** info@newclub.co.uk **W** www.newclub.co.uk
Secretary, Col. A. P. W. Campbell
Former members: Alec Douglas-Home, Walter Scott

NEW CLUB (1874), 2 Montpellier Parade, Cheltenham
GL50 1UD **T** 01242-541121 **E** secretary@thenewclub.co.uk
W www.thenewclub.co.uk

NORFOLK CLUB (1770), 17 Upper King Street, Norwich
NR3 1RB **T** 01603-626767 **E** clubsecretary@thenorfolkclub.co.uk
W www.thenorfolkclub.co.uk
Club Secretary, Baroness van Till

NORTHERN COUNTIES CLUB (1829), 11 Hood Street,
Newcastle upon Tyne NE1 6LH **T** 0191-232 2744
E secretary@northerncountiesclub.co.uk
W www.northerncountiesclub.co.uk

ORIENTAL CLUB (1824), Stratford House, Stratford Place,
London W1C 1ES **T** 020-7629 5126 **E** sec@orientalclub.org.uk
W www.orientalclub.org.uk
Secretary, M. Rivett

OXFORD AND CAMBRIDGE CLUB (1830), 71 Pall Mall,
London SW1Y 5HD **T** 020-7930 5151 **E** club@oandc.uk.com
W www.oxfordandcambridgeclub.co.uk
Secretary, Alistair Telfer

PORTLAND CLUB (1816), 36 Pall Mall, London SW1Y
T 020-7930 0444

PRATT'S CLUB* (1841), 14 Park Place, London SW1A 1LP
T 020-7493 0397 **E** secretary@prattsclub.org
Former member: Winston Churchill

REFORM CLUB (1836), 104–105 Pall Mall, London
SW1Y 5EW **T** 020-7930 9374 **E** generaloffice@reformclub.com
W www.reformclub.com
Secretary (acting), Ian Kenworthy
Former members: Isambard Kingdom Brunel, Guy Burgess,
Arthur Conan Doyle, Henry James, David Lloyd George

ROYAL AIR FORCE CLUB (1918), 128 Piccadilly, London
W1J 7PY **T** 020-7399 1000 **E** admin@rafclub.org.uk
W www.rafclub.org.uk
Secretary, Miles Pooley

ROYAL AUTOMOBILE CLUB (1897), 89 Pall Mall, London
SW1Y 5HS **T** 020-7930 2345
E secretary@royalautomobileclub.co.uk
W www.royalautomobileclub.co.uk
Secretary, Miles Wade, CBE
Former members: Winston Churchill, Rudyard Kipling,
Charles Rolls

ROYAL NORTHERN & UNIVERSITY CLUB* (1854), 9
Albyn Place, Aberdeen AB10 1YE **T** 01224-583292
E secretary@rnuc.org.uk **W** www.rnuc.org.uk
Club Secretary, Sharon Findlater

ROYAL OVER-SEAS LEAGUE (1910), Over-Seas House, Park
Place, London SW1A 1LR **T** 0207 408 0214 **E** info@rosl.org.uk
W www.rosl.org.uk

SAVAGE CLUB* (1857), 1 Whitehall Place, London SW1A 2HD
T 020-7930 8118 **E** secretary@savageclub.com
W www.savageclub.com

SAVILE CLUB* (1868), 69 Brook Street, London W1K 4ER
T 020-7629 5462 **W** www.savileclub.co.uk
Secretary, Julian Malone-Lee
Former members: Max Beerbohm, Thomas Hardy,
Robert Louis Stevenson

SCOTTISH ARTS CLUB (1872), 24 Rutland Square,
Edinburgh EH1 2BW **T** 0131-229 8157
E office@scottishartsclub.co.uk **W** www.scottishartsclub.co.uk
President, Marilyn Jeffcoat

SLOANE CLUB (1976), Lower Sloane Street, London
SW1W 8BS **T** 020-7730 9131 **E** reservations@sloaneclub.co.uk
W www.sloaneclub.co.uk
Membership Secretary, Fran Bremner

TRAVELLERS CLUB* (1819), 106 Pall Mall, London
SW1Y 5EP **T** 020-7930 8688
E secretary@thetravellersclub.org.uk
W www.thetravellersclub.org.uk
Secretary, David Broadhead
Former members: Arthur Balfour, Alec Douglas-Home,
Anthony Powell, Sir Patrick Leigh-Fermor

TURF CLUB (1868), 5 Carlton House Terrace, London
SW1Y 5AQ **T** 020-7930 8555 **E** mail@turfclub.co.uk
Secretary, Col. A. J. E. Malcolm, OBE

ULSTER REFORM CLUB (1885), 4 Royal Avenue, Belfast
BT1 1DA **T** 028-9032 3411 **E** info@ulsterreformclub.com
W www.ulsterreformclub.com
Chief Executive, A. W. Graham

UNIVERSITY WOMEN'S CLUB† (1886), 2 Audley Square,
London W1K 1DB **T** 020-7499 2268
E reservations@uwc-london.com
W www.universitywomensclub.com

VINCENT'S (1863), 1A King Edward Street, Oxford OX1 4HS
T 01865-722984 **E** bursar@vincents.org **W** www.vincents.org
Bursar, Colin Ryde
Former members: Roger Bannister, King Edward VIII

WESTERN CLUB (1825), 32 Royal Exchange Square, Glasgow
G1 3AB **T** 0141-221 2016 **E** secretary@westernclub.co.uk
W www.westernclub.co.uk
Secretary, Douglas Gifford

WHITE'S* (1693), 37–38 St James's Street, London SW1A 1JG
T 020-7493 6671
Former members: David Cameron, Evelyn Waugh

TIME AND SPACE

ASTRONOMY

The following pages give astronomical data for each month of the year 2018. There are four pages of data for each month. All data are given for 0h Greenwich Mean Time (GMT), ie at midnight at the beginning of the day named. This applies also to data for the months when British Summer Time is in operation (for dates, *see* below).

The astronomical data are given in a form suitable for observation with the naked eye or with a small telescope. These data do not attempt to replace the *Astronomical Almanac* for professional astronomers. Positions are given for the equinox of J2000.0 to match the coordinates used in most current atlases.

A fuller explanation of how to use the astronomical data is given on pages 630–632.

CALENDAR FOR EACH MONTH

The calendar for each month comprises dates of general interest plus the dates of birth or death of well-known people. The theme for this edition is 'European Politics and Power'. For key religious, civil and legal dates *see* page 9. For details of flag-flying days *see* page 23. For royal birthdays *see* pages 23 and 24–5. For public holidays *see also* pages 10 and 11.

Fuller explanations of the various calendars can be found under Time Measurement and Calendars.

The zodiacal signs through which the Sun is passing each month are illustrated.

JULIAN DATE

The Julian date on 2018 January 0.0 is 2458118.5. To find the Julian date for any other date in 2018 (at 0h GMT), add the day-of-the-year number on the extreme right of the calendar for each month to the Julian date for January 0.0.

BRITISH SUMMER TIME

British Summer Time is the legal time for general purposes during the period in which it is in operation (*see also* pages 634–635). During this period, clocks are kept one hour ahead of Greenwich Mean Time. The hour of changeover is 01h Greenwich Mean Time. The duration of Summer Time in 2018 is from March 25 01h GMT to October 28 01h GMT.

SEASONS

The seasons are defined astronomically as follows:

Spring from the vernal equinox to the summer solstice
Summer from the summer solstice to the autumnal equinox
Autumn from the autumnal equinox to the winter solstice
Winter from the winter solstice to the vernal equinox

The time when seasons start on 2017 are:

Northern Hemisphere
Vernal Equinox	March 20d 16h 15m GMT
Summer Solstice	June 21d 10h 07m GMT
Autumnal Equinox	September 23d 01h 54m GMT
Winter Solstice	December 21d 22h 23m GMT

Southern Hemisphere
Autumnal Equinox	March 20d 16h 15m GMT
Winter Solstice	June 21d 10h 07m GMT
Vernal Equinox	September 23d 01h 54m
Summer Solstice	December 21d 22h 23m

The longest day of the year, measured from sunrise to sunset, is at the summer solstice. The longest day in the UK will fall on 21 June in 2018.

The shortest day of the year, measured from sunrise to sunset, is at the winter solstice. The shortest day in the UK will fall on 21 December in 2018.

The equinox is the point at which day and night are of equal length all over the world.

In popular parlance, the seasons in the northern hemisphere comprise the following months:

Spring	March, April, May
Summer	June, July, August
Autumn	September, October, November
Winter	December, January, February

The March equinox can fall as early as 19 March but this has not happened since 1796 and it will not happen again until 2044. This equinox in 2007 was on 21 March, however in 2008 it occurred on 20 March and will not revert to 21 March again until 2102.

In 2008 the June solstice occurred on 20 June, the first time since 1897. The June solstice in 1975 was on 22 June, but it will not occur on this date again until 2203.

January 2018

FIRST MONTH, 31 DAYS. *Janus,* god of the portal, facing two ways, past and future

1	*Monday*	The UK formally joins the European Economic Community (EEC) 1973	week 1 day 1
2	*Tuesday*	Christian forces take control of Granada and expell the Moors from Spain 1492	2
3	*Wednesday*	William Joyce, ('Lord Haw-Haw'), is executed at Wandsworth Prison for broadcasting Nazi propaganda 1946	3
4	*Thursday*	Louis Braille, French educator and creator of the braille alphabet *b.* 1809	4
5	*Friday*	The German Workers' Party, precursor to the Nazi party, is founded in Munich 1919	5
6	*Saturday*	Kent Kirk, a Danish trawler captain, is arrested for entering British waters 1983	6
7	*Sunday*	Catherine of Aragon, first wife of King Henry VIII, divorced in 1533 *d.* 1536	7

8	*Monday*	François Mitterand. France's 21st and longest-serving president *d.* 1996	week 2 day 8
9	*Tuesday*	Two days after the Charlie Hebdo attack a gunman takes several people hostage at a Paris supermarket 2015	9
10	*Wednesday*	The Treaty of Versailles officially comes into effect 1920	10
11	*Thursday*	Jaak Aaviksoo, Estonian physicist and former Minister of Defence *b.* 1954	11
12	*Friday*	Edmund Burke, Irish philosopher and Whig politician who opposed the French Revolution *b.* 1729	12
13	*Saturday*	Soviet forces drive tanks through Vilinus and seize the television broadcast center of Lithuania 1991	13
14	*Sunday*	European regulations on six agricultural products are agreed following 140 hours of negotiations 1962	14

15	*Monday*	The headquarters of the European Union Police Mission (EUPM) open in Sarajevo 2003	week 3. day 15
16	*Tuesday*	Jan Palach, a student, sets himself on fire in protest of the Soviet invasions of Czechoslovakia 1969	16
17	*Wednesday*	Captain James Cook's ship, The Resolution, is the first to cross the Antarctic Circle 1773	17
18	*Thursday*	William I of Prussia is proclaimed German emperor at Versailles 1871	18
19	*Friday*	The city of Rouen surrenders to King Henry V who annexes Normandy as part of England 1419	19
20	*Saturday*	Christian II is deposed from the thrones of Denmark and Norway 1532	20
21	*Sunday*	Louis XVI, the last king of France, is executed at the guillotine 1793	21

22	*Monday*	Henry VIII of England and Francis I of France declare war on Holy Roman Emperor Charles V 1528	week 4 day 22
23	*Tuesday*	The European Union officially adopts an oil embargo against Iran as a reaction to its nuclear programme 2012	23
24	*Wednesday*	Frederick II (Frederick the Great), who introduced the potato to the Kingdom of Prussia *b.* 1712	24
25	*Thursday*	Russia mistakes a Norwegian/American research rocket for a US Trident missile 1995	25
26	*Friday*	The Treaty of Karlowitz ends the Austro-Ottoman War 1699	26
27	*Saturday*	Soviet troops liberate the Auschwitz concentration camp 1945	27
28	*Sunday*	James Dozier, a US Brigadier General, is liberated from Red Brigade captivity in Padua 1982	28

29	*Monday*	President Jacques Chirac announces that France will no longer test nuclear weapons 1996	week 5. day 29
30	*Tuesday*	The state funeral of Winston Churchill takes place 1965	30
31	*Wednesday*	Guy Fawkes leaps to his death from the gallows before he could be hung for treason 1606	31

ASTRONOMICAL PHENOMENA

d	h	
1	20	Mercury greatest elongation West
1	22	Moon closest Perigee
3	6	Earth at perihelion
7	4	Jupiter 0.2° North of Mars
11	6	Jupiter 4° South of the Moon
11	10	Mars 5° South of the Moon
13	7	Saturn 0.6° North of Mercury
15	2	Moon furthest Apogee
15	2	Saturn 3° South of the Moon
15	7	Mercury 3° South of the Moon
17	8	Venus 2° South of the Moon
20	20	Neptune 1.6° North of the Moon
31	13	Ceres at opposition

MINIMA OF ALGOL

d	h	d	h	d	h
1	16.2	13	3.5	24	14.7
4	13.0	16	0.3	27	11.6
7	9.8	18	21.1	30	8.4
10	6.6	21	17.9		

CONSTELLATIONS

The following constellations are near the meridian at

	d	h		d	h
December	1	24	January	16	21
December	16	23	February	1	20
January	1	22	February	15	19

Draco (below the Pole), Ursa Minor (below the Pole), Camelopardalis, Perseus, Auriga, Taurus, Orion, Eridanus and Lepus

THE MOON

Phases, Apsides and Node	d	h	m
○ Full Moon	2	2	24
◐ Last Quarter	8	22	25
● New Moon	17	2	17
◑ First Quarter	24	22	20
○ Full Moon	31	13	27
Perigee (356,565 km)	1	21	49
Apogee (406,464 km)	15	2	10
Perigee (358,994 km)	30	9	57
Mean longitude of the ascending node on 1st, 137°			

THE SUN

Diam. 32.5′

Day	Right Ascension			Dec. −	Equation of time		Rise 52°		56°		Transit		Set 52°		56°		Sidereal time			Transit of first point of Aries		
	h	m	s	°	m	s	h	m	h	m	h	m	h	m	h	m	h	m	s	h	m	s
1	18	45	45	23.0	−3	22	8	08	8	30	12	04	16	00	15	37	6	42	24	17	17	36
2	18	50	10	22.9	−3	50	8	08	8	30	12	04	16	01	15	38	6	46	20	17	13	40
3	18	54	34	22.8	−4	18	8	07	8	30	12	05	16	02	15	39	6	50	17	17	09	43
4	18	58	58	22.7	−4	45	8	07	8	29	12	05	16	03	15	41	6	54	13	17	05	47
5	19	03	22	22.6	−5	12	8	07	8	29	12	05	16	04	15	42	6	58	10	17	01	50
6	19	07	45	22.5	−5	39	8	07	8	28	12	06	16	05	15	44	7	02	07	16	57	53
7	19	12	08	22.4	−6	05	8	06	8	28	12	06	16	07	15	45	7	06	03	16	53	57
8	19	16	30	22.3	−6	31	8	06	8	27	12	07	16	08	15	47	7	10	00	16	50	00
9	19	20	52	22.1	−6	56	8	05	8	26	12	07	16	09	15	48	7	13	56	16	46	04
10	19	25	13	22.0	−7	21	8	05	8	26	12	08	16	11	15	50	7	17	53	16	42	07
11	19	29	34	21.8	−7	45	8	04	8	25	12	08	16	12	15	51	7	21	49	16	38	11
12	19	33	54	21.7	−8	09	8	03	8	24	12	08	16	14	15	53	7	25	46	16	34	14
13	19	38	13	21.5	−8	32	8	03	8	23	12	09	16	15	15	55	7	29	42	16	30	18
14	19	42	32	21.3	−8	54	8	02	8	22	12	09	16	17	15	57	7	33	39	16	26	21
15	19	46	51	21.2	−9	16	8	01	8	21	12	09	16	18	15	58	7	37	36	16	22	24
16	19	51	08	21.0	−9	37	8	00	8	20	12	10	16	20	16	00	7	41	32	16	18	28
17	19	55	25	20.8	−9	57	7	59	8	19	12	10	16	22	16	02	7	45	29	16	14	31
18	19	59	42	20.6	−10	17	7	58	8	17	12	10	16	23	16	04	7	49	25	16	10	35
19	20	03	57	20.4	−10	36	7	57	8	16	12	11	16	25	16	06	7	53	22	16	06	38
20	20	08	12	20.2	−10	54	7	56	8	15	12	11	16	26	16	08	7	57	18	16	02	42
21	20	12	26	20.0	−11	12	7	55	8	13	12	11	16	28	16	10	8	01	15	15	58	45
22	20	16	39	19.7	−11	29	7	54	8	12	12	12	16	30	16	12	8	05	11	15	54	49
23	20	20	52	19.5	−11	45	7	53	8	10	12	12	16	32	16	14	8	09	08	15	50	52
24	20	25	04	19.3	−12	00	7	51	8	09	12	12	16	33	16	16	8	13	05	15	46	55
25	20	29	15	19.0	−12	14	7	50	8	07	12	12	16	35	16	18	8	17	01	15	42	59
26	20	33	25	18.8	−12	28	7	49	8	06	12	13	16	37	16	20	8	20	58	15	39	02
27	20	37	34	18.5	−12	40	7	47	8	04	12	13	16	39	16	22	8	24	54	15	35	06
28	20	41	42	18.3	−12	52	7	46	8	02	12	13	16	40	16	24	8	28	51	15	31	09
29	20	45	50	18.0	−13	03	7	45	8	00	12	13	16	42	16	27	8	32	47	15	27	13
30	20	49	57	17.7	−13	14	7	43	7	59	12	13	16	44	16	29	8	36	44	15	23	16
31	20	54	03	17.5	−13	23	7	42	7	57	12	13	16	46	16	31	8	40	40	15	19	20

DURATION OF TWILIGHT (IN MINUTES)

Latitude	52°	56°	52°	56°	52°	56°	52°	56°
	1 January		11 January		21 January		31 January	
Civil	41	47	40	45	38	43	37	41
Nautical	84	96	82	93	80	90	78	87
Astronomical	125	141	123	138	120	134	117	130

THE NIGHT SKY

Mercury is at greatest elongation west on the 1st when it rises nearly two hours before the Sun. The opportunity to spot it lessens each day until the planet is lost to view around the end of the third week of January. There's a close pairing of Mercury and Saturn on the 13th, with the Moon nearby on the 15th.

Venus is an evening object after superior conjunction on the 9th but sets less than a half hour after the Sun for the rest of the month so an easy sighting can be discounted.

Mars opens the year in Libra and rises roughly 4.5 hours before the Sun all month. It brightens slightly from magnitude 1.5 to 1.2 but the disk remains rather small. Mars is within 0.5° of Jupiter on the 7th and the Moon is nearby on the 11th.

Jupiter (magnitude −1.9), in Libra, rises around the same time as Mars on January 1st but is up an hour earlier than the Red Planet by the 31st.

Saturn (magnitude 0.5), in Sagittarius, slowly emerges from the dawn to rise two hours before the Sun by the 31st.

January has two Full Moons and that of January 2nd is the closest of the year, or what is popularly called a 'Supermoon'. The most extreme lunar apogee of 2018 occurs on January 15th (406,464 km).

Full Moon on January 31st coincides with a total lunar eclipse that is visible from Asia, Australia, the Pacific, and western North America.

THE MOON

Day	R.A.		Dec	Hor Par	Diam	Sun Co-Long	PA of Br. limb	Ph.	Age	Rise				Transit		Set			
										52°		56°				52°		56°	
	h	m	°	'	'	°	°	%	d	h	m	h	m	h	m	h	m	h	m
1	5	38	+19.3	61.3	33.4	76	254	98	13.4	15	44	15	23	23	56	7	03	7	24
2	6	43	+20.1	61.5	33.5	88	210	100	14.4	16	50	16	29	—		8	09	8	30
3	7	48	+19.3	61.3	33.4	100	108	99	15.4	18	05	17	47	1	00	9	03	9	22
4	8	51	+17.2	60.8	33.1	112	107	95	16.4	19	23	19	09	2	01	9	46	10	01
5	9	51	+14.0	60.0	32.7	125	109	88	17.4	20	42	20	32	2	59	10	21	10	32
6	10	47	+10.1	59.1	32.2	137	111	80	18.4	21	59	21	53	3	53	10	50	10	56
7	11	40	+5.7	58.1	31.7	149	112	70	19.4	23	12	23	11	4	43	11	14	11	17
8	12	30	+1.2	57.1	31.1	161	112	60	20.4	—		—		5	31	11	37	11	36
9	13	19	−3.2	56.3	30.7	173	112	49	21.4	0	23	0	26	6	16	11	59	11	55
10	14	06	−7.4	55.5	30.3	185	111	39	22.4	1	31	1	38	7	01	12	22	12	14
11	14	54	−11.1	54.9	29.9	197	109	30	23.4	2	38	2	48	7	46	12	47	12	35
12	15	42	−14.4	54.5	29.7	210	107	22	24.4	3	42	3	56	8	31	13	14	13	00
13	16	30	−16.9	54.2	29.5	222	104	14	25.4	4	44	5	00	9	18	13	46	13	29
14	17	19	−18.8	54.0	29.4	234	101	08	26.4	5	42	6	01	10	05	14	24	14	05
15	18	09	−19.8	53.9	29.4	246	98	04	27.4	6	36	6	55	10	52	15	09	14	48
16	18	59	−20.0	54.0	29.4	258	97	01	28.4	7	23	7	43	11	40	16	00	15	39
17	19	50	−19.3	54.1	29.5	271	138	00	29.4	8	04	8	23	12	28	16	57	16	38
18	20	40	−17.7	54.3	29.6	283	251	01	0.9	8	39	8	55	13	15	17	58	17	42
19	21	29	−15.3	54.6	29.8	295	253	03	1.9	9	09	9	22	14	02	19	02	18	50
20	22	17	−12.3	55.0	29.9	307	251	08	2.9	9	35	9	45	14	47	20	09	20	01
21	23	05	−8.6	55.4	30.2	319	250	14	3.9	9	59	10	04	15	32	21	17	21	12
22	23	53	−4.6	55.9	30.5	331	249	21	4.9	10	21	10	23	16	18	22	26	22	26
23	0	41	−0.3	56.5	30.8	344	249	30	5.9	10	43	10	42	17	04	23	38	23	41
24	1	30	+4.2	57.2	31.2	356	249	40	6.9	11	06	11	01	17	52	—		—	
25	2	21	+8.5	58.0	31.6	8	251	51	7.9	11	32	11	23	18	42	0	51	0	58
26	3	14	+12.5	58.8	32.0	20	253	62	8.9	12	03	11	49	19	36	2	06	2	18
27	4	11	+16.0	59.6	32.5	32	257	73	9.9	12	40	12	23	20	34	3	23	3	39
28	5	11	+18.5	60.3	32.8	44	261	82	10.9	13	26	13	07	21	34	4	38	4	56
29	6	13	+19.9	60.8	33.1	57	266	91	11.9	14	24	14	05	22	37	5	46	6	07
30	7	17	+19.8	61.1	33.3	69	272	96	12.9	15	34	15	14	23	39	6	46	7	06
31	8	21	+18.4	61.0	33.3	81	275	100	13.9	16	51	16	35	—		7	36	7	52

MERCURY

Day	R.A.		Dec	Mag.	Diam.	Phase	Rise		Transit		Set	
	h	m	°		"	%	h	m	h	m	h	m
1	17	07.4	−20.9	−0.3	7	62	6	26	10	23	14	21
3	17	15.9	−21.3	−0.3	6	66	6	30	10	24	14	18
5	17	25.4	−21.8	−0.3	6	70	6	35	10	26	14	17
7	17	35.6	−22.2	−0.3	6	74	6	40	10	29	14	16
9	17	46.4	−22.6	−0.3	6	77	6	46	10	32	14	17
11	17	57.7	−22.9	−0.3	6	80	6	52	10	35	14	18
13	18	09.4	−23.1	−0.3	6	82	6	58	10	39	14	20
15	18	21.5	−23.3	−0.3	5	84	7	04	10	43	14	23
17	18	33.8	−23.5	−0.3	5	86	7	09	10	48	14	27
19	18	46.4	−23.5	−0.3	5	88	7	14	10	53	14	31
21	18	59.2	−23.5	−0.3	5	89	7	19	10	58	14	37
23	19	12.2	−23.3	−0.4	5	90	7	23	11	03	14	43
25	19	25.3	−23.1	−0.4	5	92	7	26	11	08	14	50
27	19	38.6	−22.8	−0.4	5	93	7	30	11	14	14	58
29	19	51.9	−22.5	−0.5	5	94	7	32	11	19	15	06
31	20	05.4	−22.0	−0.5	5	95	7	34	11	25	15	15

Rising and setting times are for latitude 54°

VENUS

Day	R.A.		Dec	Mag.	Diam.	Phase	Rise		Transit		Set	
	h	m	°		"	%	h	m	h	m	h	m
1	18	36.2	−23.6	−3.9	10	100	8	16	11	53	15	31
6	19	03.6	−23.3	−3.9	10	100	8	20	12	01	15	42
11	19	30.8	−22.6	−3.9	10	100	8	23	12	08	15	54
16	19	57.6	−21.7	−3.9	10	100	8	23	12	16	16	08
21	20	24.1	−20.5	−3.9	10	100	8	21	12	22	16	24
26	20	50.0	−19.0	−3.9	11	100	8	17	12	28	16	41
31	21	15.5	−17.3	−3.9	11	100	8	11	12	34	16	58

MARS

Day	R.A.		Dec	Mag.	Diam.	Phase	Rise		Transit		Set	
	h	m	°		"	%	h	m	h	m	h	m
1	14	47.0	−15.2	+1.5	5	93	3	28	8	04	12	40
6	14	59.3	−16.1	+1.4	5	93	3	26	7	56	12	26
11	15	11.7	−17.0	+1.4	5	93	3	25	7	49	12	13
16	15	24.3	−17.8	+1.3	5	92	3	23	7	42	12	01
21	15	36.9	−18.6	+1.3	5	92	3	21	7	35	11	48
26	15	49.5	−19.3	+1.2	5	91	3	19	7	28	11	36
31	16	02.2	−20.0	+1.2	6	91	3	17	7	21	11	25

SUNRISE AND SUNSET

	London				Bristol				Birmingham				Manchester				Newcastle				Glasgow				Belfast			
	0°	05′	51°	30′	2°	35′	51°	28′	1°	55′	52°	28′	2°	15′	53°	28′	1°	37′	54°	59′	4°	14′	55°	52′	5°	56′	54°	35′
d	h	m	h	m	h	m	h	m	h	m	h	m	h	m	h	m	h	m	h	m	h	m	h	m	h	m	h	m
1	8	06	16	02	8	16	16	12	8	18	16	04	8	25	16	00	8	31	15	49	8	47	15	54	8	46	16	09
2	8	06	16	03	8	16	16	13	8	18	16	06	8	25	16	02	8	31	15	50	8	47	15	55	8	46	16	10
3	8	06	16	04	8	15	16	14	8	18	16	07	8	24	16	03	8	31	15	52	8	47	15	57	8	46	16	11
4	8	05	16	05	8	15	16	16	8	18	16	08	8	24	16	04	8	30	15	53	8	46	15	58	8	45	16	12
5	8	05	16	07	8	15	16	17	8	17	16	09	8	24	16	05	8	30	15	54	8	46	15	59	8	45	16	14
6	8	05	16	08	8	15	16	18	8	17	16	10	8	23	16	07	8	29	15	56	8	45	16	01	8	44	16	15
7	8	04	16	09	8	14	16	19	8	16	16	12	8	23	16	08	8	29	15	57	8	45	16	02	8	44	16	17
8	8	04	16	10	8	14	16	21	8	16	16	13	8	22	16	09	8	28	15	59	8	44	16	04	8	43	16	18
9	8	03	16	12	8	13	16	22	8	15	16	15	8	22	16	11	8	27	16	00	8	43	16	05	8	42	16	20
10	8	03	16	13	8	13	16	23	8	15	16	16	8	21	16	12	8	27	16	02	8	42	16	07	8	42	16	21
11	8	02	16	15	8	12	16	25	8	14	16	17	8	20	16	14	8	26	16	03	8	41	16	09	8	41	16	23
12	8	02	16	16	8	11	16	26	8	13	16	19	8	20	16	15	8	25	16	05	8	41	16	10	8	40	16	24
13	8	01	16	18	8	11	16	28	8	13	16	20	8	19	16	17	8	24	16	07	8	40	16	12	8	39	16	26
14	8	00	16	19	8	10	16	29	8	12	16	22	8	18	16	19	8	23	16	08	8	39	16	14	8	38	16	28
15	7	59	16	21	8	09	16	31	8	11	16	24	8	17	16	20	8	22	16	10	8	37	16	16	8	37	16	29
16	7	58	16	22	8	08	16	32	8	10	16	25	8	16	16	22	8	21	16	12	8	36	16	18	8	36	16	31
17	7	58	16	24	8	07	16	34	8	09	16	27	8	15	16	24	8	20	16	14	8	35	16	19	8	35	16	33
18	7	57	16	25	8	06	16	36	8	08	16	29	8	14	16	25	8	19	16	16	8	34	16	21	8	34	16	35
19	7	56	16	27	8	05	16	37	8	07	16	30	8	13	16	27	8	17	16	17	8	32	16	23	8	33	16	37
20	7	55	16	29	8	04	16	39	8	06	16	32	8	12	16	29	8	16	16	19	8	31	16	25	8	31	16	39
21	7	53	16	30	8	03	16	41	8	05	16	34	8	10	16	31	8	15	16	21	8	30	16	27	8	30	16	40
22	7	52	16	32	8	02	16	42	8	03	16	36	8	09	16	33	8	13	16	23	8	28	16	29	8	29	16	42
23	7	51	16	34	8	01	16	44	8	02	16	37	8	08	16	34	8	12	16	25	8	27	16	31	8	27	16	44
24	7	50	16	36	8	00	16	46	8	01	16	39	8	06	16	36	8	11	16	27	8	25	16	33	8	26	16	46
25	7	49	16	37	7	58	16	47	8	00	16	41	8	05	16	38	8	09	16	29	8	24	16	36	8	25	16	48
26	7	47	16	39	7	57	16	49	7	58	16	43	8	04	16	40	8	07	16	31	8	22	16	38	8	23	16	50
27	7	46	16	41	7	56	16	51	7	57	16	45	8	02	16	42	8	06	16	33	8	20	16	40	8	21	16	52
28	7	45	16	43	7	54	16	53	7	55	16	46	8	01	16	44	8	04	16	35	8	19	16	42	8	20	16	54
29	7	43	16	44	7	53	16	54	7	54	16	48	7	59	16	46	8	03	16	37	8	17	16	44	8	18	16	56
30	7	42	16	46	7	52	16	56	7	52	16	50	7	57	16	48	8	01	16	39	8	15	16	46	8	16	16	58
31	7	40	16	48	7	50	16	58	7	51	16	52	7	56	16	50	7	59	16	41	8	13	16	48	8	15	17	00

JUPITER

Day	R.A.		Dec	Mag.	Diam.	Rise		Transit		Set	
	h	m	°		″	h	m	h	m	h	m
1	14	58.1	−15.8	−1.8	33	3	43	8	14	12	46
11	15	04.6	−16.2	−1.9	34	3	12	7	42	12	11
21	15	10.3	−16.6	−1.9	35	2	41	7	08	11	35
31	15	15.1	−16.9	−2.0	36	2	09	6	33	10	58

Equatorial Diam. 33″, Polar Diam. 31″

SATURN

Day	R.A.		Dec	Mag.	Diam.	Rise		Transit		Set	
	h	m	°		″	h	m	h	m	h	m
1	18	05.0	−22.5	+0.5	15	7	35	11	21	15	07
11	18	10.0	−22.5	+0.5	15	7	01	10	46	14	32
21	18	14.8	−22.5	+0.5	15	6	26	10	12	13	58
31	18	19.4	−22.5	+0.6	15	5	51	9	37	13	23

Equatorial Diam. 15″, Polar Diam. 14″
Rings − major axis 34″ minor axis 15″, Tilt 26°

URANUS

Day	R.A.		Dec	Mag.	Diam.	Rise		Transit		Set	
	h	m	°		″	h	m	h	m	h	m
1	1	30.9	+8.9	+5.8	4	11	53	18	45	1	42
11	1	31.0	+8.9	+5.8	4	11	14	18	06	1	03
21	1	31.5	+9.0	+5.8	4	10	34	17	27	0	24
31	1	32.2	+9.0	+5.8	3	9	55	16	49	23	42

NEPTUNE

Day	R.A.		Dec	Mag.	Diam.	Rise		Transit		Set	
	h	m	°		″	h	m	h	m	h	m
1	22	53.7	−8.0	+7.9	2	10	50	16	09	21	27
11	22	54.6	−7.9	+7.9	2	10	11	15	30	20	49
21	22	55.7	−7.8	+7.9	2	9	33	14	52	20	11
31	22	56.9	−7.7	+8.0	2	8	54	14	14	19	34

February 2018

SECOND MONTH, 28 or 29 DAYS. *Februa*, Roman festival of Purification

1	*Thursday*	France declares war on Britain and the Netherlands 1793	day 32
2	*Friday*	German forces surrender at the Battle of Stalingrad 1943	33
3	*Saturday*	Sweyn Forkbeard, first Danish King of England, who ruled briefly beginnning 1013 *d.* 1014	34
4	*Sunday*	The 'big three' Allied leaders discuss postwar reorganisation at the Yalta conference 1945	35

5	*Monday*	Leopold II of Belgium establishes himself as Sovereign of the Congo Free State 1885	week 6 day 36
6	*Tuesday*	Klaus Barbie, Nazi war criminal, arrives in France to face his trial following his extradition from Bolivia 1983	37
7	*Wednesday*	The European Union is established with the signing of the Maastricht Treaty 1992	38
8	*Thursday*	A protest in Paris in support of Algerian independence becomes a riot and ends in 8 deaths 1962	39
9	*Friday*	Lithuania holds a referendum for independence which is approved by a clear majority 1991	40
10	*Saturday*	Gen. Jozef Haller performs a symbolic 'wedding ceremony' between Poland' and the Baltic Sea 1920	41
11	*Sunday*	Guy Burgess and Donald Maclean, members of the Cambridge spy ring, reappear in the Soviet Union 1956	42

12	*Monday*	Emmanuel Kant, German philosopher and critic of direct democracy *d.* 1804	week 7. day 43
13	*Tuesday*	The Siege of Budapest ends as the city unconditionally surrenders to Soviet forces 1945	44
14	*Wednesday*	The city of Dresden is devastated by bombs dropped by British and American aircrafts 1945	45
15	*Thursday*	Protesters assemble across Europe to demonstrate against imminent war in Iraq 2003	46
16	*Friday*	Ferdinand Buisson, French politician, advocate of secular education and Nobel Peace Prize recipient *d.* 1932	47
17	*Saturday*	Roman Emperor Jovian *d.* 364	48
18	*Sunday*	Victor Emmanuel II becomes the first king of a united Italy since the 6th century 1861	49

19	*Monday*	Adam Adami, German monk and diplomat *d.* 1603	week 8 day 50
20	*Tuesday*	Anthony Eden resigns as foreign secretary from Neville Chamberlain's cabinet 1938	51
21	*Wednesday*	The Battle of Verdun, the longest battle of the First World War, begins 1916	52
22	*Thursday*	Anna Kingsford, English doctor, feminist and animal rights activist *d.* 1888	53
23	*Friday*	Lt.- Col. Antonio Tejero Molina leads a coup on the Spanish parliament 1981	54
24	*Saturday*	Mexico declares independence from Spain during the Mexican War of Independence 1821	55
25	*Sunday*	Soviet powers take control of Czechoslovakia in a military coup 1948	56

26	*Monday*	The Treaty of Nice is signed, accommodating up to 13 new EU member states 2001	week 9 day 57
27	*Tuesday*	The Treaty of Berwick is signed, expelling the French from Scotland 1560	58
28	*Wednesday*	Olof Palme, prime minister of Sweden (1969–76), is assasinated 1986	59

ASTRONOMICAL PHENOMENA

d	h	
7	20	Jupiter 4° South of the Moon
9	5	Mars 4° South of the Moon
11	14	Saturn 2° South of the Moon
15	19	Mercury 1° South of the Moon
16	16	Venus 0.6° North of the Moon
17	3	Neptune 2° North of the Moon
20	8	Uranus 5° North of the Moon
21	14	Neptune 0.6° North of Venus
25	10	Neptune 0.5° North of Mercury

MINIMA OF ALGOL

d	h	d	h	d	h
2	5.2	13	16.5	25	3.8
5	2.0	16	13.3	28	0.6
7	22.9	19	10.2		
10	19.7	22	7.0		

CONSTELLATIONS

The following constellations are near the meridian at

	d	h		d	h
January	1	24	February	15	21
January	16	23	March	1	20
February	1	22	March	16	19

Draco (below the Pole), Camelopardalis, Auriga, Taurus, Gemini, Orion, Canis Minor, Monoceros, Lepus, Canis Major and Puppis

THE MOON

Phases, Apsides and Node	d	h	m
◑ Last Quarter	7	15	54
● New Moon	15	21	5
◐ First Quarter	23	8	9
Apogee (405,700 km)	11	14	16
Perigee (363,933 km)	27	14	39

Mean longitude of the ascending node on 1st, 135°

THE SUN

Diam. 32.5′

Day	Right Ascension			Dec.	Equation of time		Rise 52°		56°		Transit		Set 52°		56°		Sidereal time			Transit of first point of Aries		
	h	m	s	°	m	s	h	m	h	m	h	m	h	m	h	m	h	m	s	h	m	s
1	20	58	08	17.2	−13	32	7	40	7	55	12	14	16	48	16	33	8	44	37	15	15	23
2	21	02	12	16.9	−13	39	7	38	7	53	12	14	16	50	16	35	8	48	34	15	11	26
3	21	06	16	16.6	−13	46	7	37	7	51	12	14	16	51	16	37	8	52	30	15	07	30
4	21	10	19	16.3	−13	53	7	35	7	49	12	14	16	53	16	39	8	56	27	15	03	33
5	21	14	21	16.0	−13	58	7	34	7	47	12	14	16	55	16	42	9	00	23	14	59	37
6	21	18	22	15.7	−14	03	7	32	7	45	12	14	16	57	16	44	9	04	20	14	55	40
7	21	22	22	15.4	−14	06	7	30	7	43	12	14	16	59	16	46	9	08	16	14	51	44
8	21	26	22	15.1	−14	10	7	28	7	41	12	14	17	01	16	48	9	12	13	14	47	47
9	21	30	21	14.8	−14	12	7	27	7	39	12	14	17	03	16	50	9	16	09	14	43	51
10	21	34	19	14.4	−14	13	7	25	7	37	12	14	17	05	16	53	9	20	06	14	39	54
11	21	38	16	14.1	−14	14	7	23	7	34	12	14	17	06	16	55	9	24	03	14	35	57
12	21	42	12	13.8	−14	14	7	21	7	32	12	14	17	08	16	57	9	27	59	14	32	01
13	21	46	08	13.4	−14	13	7	19	7	30	12	14	17	10	16	59	9	31	56	14	28	04
14	21	50	03	13.1	−14	12	7	17	7	28	12	14	17	12	17	01	9	35	52	14	24	08
15	21	53	58	12.8	−14	09	7	15	7	25	12	14	17	14	17	04	9	39	49	14	20	11
16	21	57	51	12.4	−14	07	7	13	7	23	12	14	17	16	17	06	9	43	45	14	16	15
17	22	01	44	12.1	−14	03	7	11	7	21	12	14	17	18	17	08	9	47	42	14	12	18
18	22	05	36	11.7	−13	59	7	09	7	19	12	14	17	19	17	10	9	51	38	14	08	22
19	22	09	28	11.4	−13	53	7	07	7	16	12	14	17	21	17	12	9	55	35	14	04	25
20	22	13	19	11.0	−13	48	7	05	7	14	12	14	17	23	17	15	9	59	32	14	00	28
21	22	17	09	10.7	−13	41	7	03	7	11	12	14	17	25	17	17	10	03	28	13	56	32
22	22	20	58	10.3	−13	34	7	01	7	09	12	13	17	27	17	19	10	07	25	13	52	35
23	22	24	47	9.9	−13	26	6	59	7	07	12	13	17	29	17	21	10	11	21	13	48	39
24	22	28	35	9.6	−13	18	6	57	7	04	12	13	17	30	17	23	10	15	18	13	44	42
25	22	32	23	9.2	−13	09	6	55	7	02	12	13	17	32	17	25	10	19	14	13	40	46
26	22	36	10	8.8	−12	59	6	53	6	59	12	13	17	34	17	28	10	23	11	13	36	49
27	22	39	56	8.4	−12	49	6	50	6	57	12	13	17	36	17	30	10	27	07	13	32	53
28	22	43	42	8.1	−12	38	6	48	6	54	12	13	17	38	17	32	10	31	04	13	28	56

DURATION OF TWILIGHT (IN MINUTES)

Latitude	52°	56°	52°	56°	52°	56°	52°	56°
	1 February		11 February		21 February		31 February	
Civil	37	41	35	39	34	38	34	37
Nautical	77	86	75	83	74	81	73	80
Astronomical	117	130	114	126	113	124	112	124

THE NIGHT SKY

Mercury is at superior conjunction on the 17th and then moves into the evening sky where it might be seen the last few days. It lies about 2.5° from Venus on the 28th but is hugging the horizon as dusk falls.

Venus should be picked up after sunset the second half of February but it stays stubbornly low. The planet is occulted by the crescent Moon on the 17th, but only for observers in Atlantic-bordering countries of the southern hemisphere. Bright twilight thwarts any chance of seeing Venus and Neptune 0.5° apart on the 21st.

Mars brightens further during February, from magnitude 1.2 to 0.8, and rises during the early hours. It opens the month in Scorpius but soon crosses into Ophiuchus. The Moon is close by on the 9th and the planet then passes about 5° from Antares on the 11th when just a little dimmer than its stellar rival.

Jupiter (magnitude −2.0 to −2.2) rises not long after the witching hour and plods slowly across Libra. It is at western quadrature this month when telescope users will note a not quite full disk. The Moon is near Jupiter on the 8th.

Saturn (magnitude 0.6) is now much better placed in the morning sky and can be found in Sagittarius rising 2¾ hours before the Sun. The Moon is nearby on the 11th.

There's a partial solar eclipse on the 15th which will only be seen from Antarctica and southern South America. The maximum eclipse magnitude is 0.599.

THE MOON

Day	R.A. h	R.A. m	Dec °	Hor Par '	Diam '	Sun Co-Long °	PA of Br. limb °	Ph. %	Age d	Rise 52° h	Rise 52° m	Rise 56° h	Rise 56° m	Transit h	Transit m	Set 52° h	Set 52° m	Set 56° h	Set 56° m
1	9	23	+15.7	60.7	33.1	93	105	100	14.9	18	12	18	00	0	40	8	15	8	29
2	10	22	+12.0	60.1	32.7	105	107	97	15.9	19	31	19	24	1	37	8	47	8	56
3	11	18	+7.6	59.3	32.3	117	109	92	16.9	20	49	20	46	2	30	9	15	9	20
4	12	11	+3.0	58.3	31.8	129	110	85	17.9	22	04	22	05	3	21	9	39	9	40
5	13	02	−1.6	57.4	31.3	141	110	76	18.9	23	16	23	21	4	09	10	02	10	00
6	13	51	−6.0	56.5	30.8	154	109	66	19.9	—		—		4	56	10	25	10	19
7	14	39	−10.0	55.7	30.4	166	107	57	20.9	0	25	0	34	5	42	10	50	10	39
8	15	28	−13.4	55.0	30.0	178	105	47	21.9	1	31	1	44	6	27	11	17	11	04
9	16	16	−16.2	54.6	29.7	190	101	37	22.9	2	35	2	50	7	14	11	47	11	30
10	17	05	−18.3	54.2	29.6	202	98	28	23.9	3	35	3	53	8	00	12	23	12	05
11	17	55	−19.6	54.1	29.5	214	93	20	24.9	4	30	4	50	8	48	13	05	12	44
12	18	45	−20.0	54.1	29.5	227	89	13	25.9	5	20	5	40	9	36	13	54	13	33
13	19	36	−19.6	54.2	29.5	239	84	08	26.9	6	02	6	22	10	24	14	48	14	29
14	20	26	−18.2	54.4	29.6	251	79	03	27.9	6	40	6	56	11	11	15	48	15	32
15	21	16	−16.0	54.7	29.8	263	72	01	28.9	7	12	7	26	11	58	16	53	16	39
16	22	05	−13.1	55.1	30.0	275	292	00	0.4	7	39	7	50	12	45	18	00	17	50
17	22	53	−9.6	55.5	30.2	288	258	01	1.4	8	04	8	11	13	31	19	08	19	02
18	23	42	−5.6	55.9	30.5	300	254	05	2.4	8	27	8	30	14	16	20	18	20	16
19	0	30	−1.3	56.4	30.7	312	252	10	3.4	8	49	8	49	15	02	21	29	21	31
20	1	19	+3.2	56.9	31.0	324	252	17	4.4	9	12	9	08	15	49	22	41	22	47
21	2	09	+7.6	57.5	31.3	336	253	25	5.4	9	36	9	28	16	38	23	55	—	
22	3	01	+11.6	58.0	31.6	349	255	35	6.4	10	04	9	53	17	30	—		0	05
23	3	55	+15.2	58.6	31.9	1	258	46	7.4	10	38	10	22	18	25	1	09	1	24
24	4	53	+17.9	59.1	32.2	13	263	58	8.4	11	19	11	01	19	22	2	22	2	40
25	5	52	+19.6	59.6	32.5	25	268	69	9.4	12	10	11	50	20	22	3	32	3	51
26	6	53	+20.0	60.0	32.7	37	273	79	10.4	13	12	12	52	21	22	4	33	4	53
27	7	55	+19.2	60.2	32.8	49	279	88	11.4	14	24	14	06	22	22	5	25	5	44
28	8	57	+17.0	60.2	32.8	62	286	94	12.4	15	41	15	27	23	20	6	08	6	23

MERCURY

Day	R.A. h m	Dec °	Mag.	Diam. "	Phase %	Rise h m	Transit h m	Set h m
1	20 12.1	−21.7	−0.6	5	95	7 35	11 27	15 20
3	20 25.7	−21.1	−0.7	5	96	7 36	11 33	15 31
5	20 39.3	−20.4	−0.7	5	97	7 37	11 39	15 42
7	20 53.0	−19.6	−0.8	5	98	7 37	11 45	15 53
9	21 06.7	−18.7	−1.0	5	98	7 37	11 51	16 05
11	21 20.5	−17.7	−1.1	5	99	7 36	11 57	16 18
13	21 34.3	−16.6	−1.2	5	99	7 34	12 02	16 31
15	21 48.1	−15.5	−1.4	5	100	7 33	12 08	16 45
17	22 02.0	−14.2	−1.5	5	100	7 31	12 14	16 59
19	22 15.9	−12.8	−1.6	5	100	7 28	12 20	17 14
21	22 29.7	−11.3	−1.5	5	99	7 26	12 26	17 28
23	22 43.6	−9.8	−1.5	5	99	7 22	12 32	17 44
25	22 57.4	−8.2	−1.4	5	97	7 19	12 38	17 59
27	23 11.1	−6.5	−1.4	5	96	7 15	12 44	18 14

Rising and setting times are for latitude 54°

VENUS

Day	R.A. h m	Dec °	Mag.	Diam. "	Phase %	Rise h m	Transit h m	Set h m
1	21 20.5	−16.9	−3.9	11	100	8 10	12 35	17 01
6	21 45.3	−15.0	−3.9	11	99	8 02	12 40	17 19
11	22 09.6	−12.9	−3.9	11	99	7 54	12 45	17 36
16	22 33.5	−10.7	−3.9	11	99	7 45	12 49	17 54
21	22 57.0	−8.3	−3.9	11	98	7 35	12 53	18 11
26	23 20.1	−5.8	−3.9	11	98	7 24	12 56	18 29

MARS

Day	R.A. h m	Dec °	Mag.	Diam. "	Phase %	Rise h m	Transit h m	Set h m
1	16 04.8	−20.1	+1.2	6	91	3 16	7 19	11 22
6	16 17.6	−20.8	+1.1	6	91	3 14	7 13	11 11
11	16 30.4	−21.3	+1.1	6	90	3 11	7 06	11 00
16	16 43.2	−21.8	+1.0	6	90	3 07	6 59	10 50
21	16 56.1	−22.2	+0.9	6	90	3 04	6 52	10 40
26	17 08.9	−22.6	+0.9	7	89	3 00	6 45	10 31

SUNRISE AND SUNSET

	London				Bristol				Birmingham				Manchester				Newcastle				Glasgow				Belfast			
	0°	05'	51°	30'	2°	35'	51°	28'	1°	55'	52°	28'	2°	15'	53°	28'	1°	37'	54°	59'	4°	14'	55°	52'	5°	56'	54°	35'
d	h	m	h	m	h	m	h	m	h	m	h	m	h	m	h	m	h	m	h	m	h	m	h	m	h	m	h	m
1	7	39	16	50	7	49	17	00	7	49	16	54	7	54	16	52	7	57	16	43	8	11	16	50	8	13	17	02
2	7	37	16	52	7	47	17	02	7	48	16	56	7	52	16	54	7	56	16	46	8	09	16	53	8	11	17	04
3	7	36	16	53	7	45	17	03	7	46	16	58	7	51	16	56	7	54	16	48	8	07	16	55	8	09	17	06
4	7	34	16	55	7	44	17	05	7	44	16	59	7	49	16	58	7	52	16	50	8	06	16	57	8	08	17	08
5	7	32	16	57	7	42	17	07	7	43	17	01	7	47	17	00	7	50	16	52	8	04	16	59	8	06	17	10
6	7	31	16	59	7	41	17	09	7	41	17	03	7	45	17	02	7	48	16	54	8	01	17	01	8	04	17	13
7	7	29	17	01	7	39	17	11	7	39	17	05	7	43	17	03	7	46	16	56	7	59	17	03	8	02	17	15
8	7	27	17	02	7	37	17	13	7	37	17	07	7	42	17	05	7	44	16	58	7	57	17	06	8	00	17	17
9	7	25	17	04	7	35	17	14	7	35	17	09	7	40	17	07	7	42	17	00	7	55	17	08	7	58	17	19
10	7	24	17	06	7	34	17	16	7	34	17	11	7	38	17	09	7	40	17	02	7	53	17	10	7	56	17	21
11	7	22	17	08	7	32	17	18	7	32	17	13	7	36	17	11	7	38	17	04	7	51	17	12	7	54	17	23
12	7	20	17	10	7	30	17	20	7	30	17	15	7	34	17	13	7	36	17	07	7	49	17	14	7	52	17	25
13	7	18	17	12	7	28	17	22	7	28	17	17	7	32	17	15	7	33	17	09	7	47	17	17	7	50	17	27
14	7	16	17	13	7	26	17	24	7	26	17	18	7	30	17	17	7	31	17	11	7	44	17	19	7	47	17	29
15	7	14	17	15	7	24	17	25	7	24	17	20	7	28	17	19	7	29	17	13	7	42	17	21	7	45	17	31
16	7	12	17	17	7	22	17	27	7	22	17	22	7	26	17	21	7	27	17	15	7	40	17	23	7	43	17	33
17	7	10	17	19	7	20	17	29	7	20	17	24	7	24	17	23	7	25	17	17	7	37	17	25	7	41	17	35
18	7	09	17	21	7	18	17	31	7	18	17	26	7	21	17	25	7	22	17	25	7	35	17	27	7	39	17	37
19	7	07	17	23	7	16	17	33	7	16	17	28	7	19	17	27	7	20	17	27	7	33	17	30	7	37	17	40
20	7	05	17	24	7	14	17	34	7	14	17	30	7	17	17	29	7	18	17	29	7	30	17	32	7	34	17	42
21	7	03	17	26	7	12	17	36	7	12	17	32	7	15	17	31	7	16	17	31	7	28	17	34	7	32	17	44
22	7	00	17	28	7	10	17	38	7	10	17	34	7	13	17	33	7	13	17	33	7	26	17	36	7	30	17	46
23	6	58	17	30	7	08	17	40	7	07	17	35	7	11	17	35	7	11	17	35	7	23	17	38	7	27	17	48
24	6	56	17	32	7	06	17	42	7	05	17	37	7	08	17	37	7	09	17	32	7	21	17	40	7	25	17	50
25	6	54	17	33	7	04	17	43	7	03	17	39	7	06	17	39	7	06	17	34	7	18	17	43	7	23	17	52
26	6	52	17	35	7	02	17	45	7	01	17	41	7	04	17	41	7	04	17	41	7	16	17	45	7	20	17	54
27	6	50	17	37	7	00	17	47	6	59	17	43	7	02	17	43	7	01	17	38	7	13	17	47	7	18	17	56
28	6	48	17	39	6	58	17	49	6	57	17	45	6	59	17	45	6	59	17	40	7	11	17	49	7	16	17	58

JUPITER

Day	R.A.		Dec	Mag.	Diam.	Rise		Transit		Set	
	h	m	°		"	h	m	h	m	h	m
1	15	15.5	−16.9	−2.0	36	2	05	6	30	10	55
11	15	19.2	−17.1	−2.0	37	1	31	5	54	10	18
21	15	21.9	−17.3	−2.1	38	0	55	5	18	9	40

Equatorial Diam. 36", Polar Diam. 34"

SATURN

Day	R.A.		Dec	Mag.	Diam.	Rise		Transit		Set	
	h	m	°		"	h	m	h	m	h	m
1	18	19.9	−22.5	+0.6	15	5	48	9	34	13	20
11	18	24.1	−22.4	+0.6	16	5	12	8	59	12	45
21	18	27.9	−22.4	+0.6	16	4	36	8	23	12	10

Equatorial Diam. 16", Polar Diam. 14"
Rings – major axis 35" minor axis 15", Tilt 26°

URANUS

Day	R.A.		Dec	Mag.	Diam.	Rise		Transit		Set	
	h	m	°		"	h	m	h	m	h	m
1	1	32.3	+9.1	+5.8	3	9	51	16	45	23	39
11	1	33.4	+9.2	+5.9	3	9	13	16	07	23	01
21	1	34.7	+9.3	+5.9	3	8	34	15	29	22	24

NEPTUNE

Day	R.A.		Dec	Mag.	Diam.	Rise		Transit		Set	
	h	m	°		"	h	m	h	m	h	m
1	22	57.0	−7.7	+8.0	2	8	50	14	10	19	30
11	22	58.3	−7.6	+8.0	2	8	11	13	32	18	53
21	22	59.7	−7.4	+8.0	2	7	32	12	54	18	16

March 2018

THIRD MONTH, 31 DAYS. *Mars,* Roman god of battle

1	*Thursday*	The European Space Agency launches Envisat, an Earth observation satellite, from French Guiana 2002	day 60
2	*Friday*	Soviet troops capture Tuppura Island from Finland 1940	61
3	*Saturday*	The Statute of Rhuddlan introduces the English common law system to Wales 1234	62
4	*Sunday*	In Frankfurt, Frederick Barbarossa (Frederick I) is elected King of Germany 1152	63

5	*Monday*	Winston Churchill gives his 'Iron Curtain' speech, condemning the Soviet Union's policy 1946	week 10 day 64
6	*Tuesday*	John of Gaunt *b.* 1340	65
7	*Wednesday*	Charles de Gaulle withdraws France from NATO's integrated military command 1966	66
8	*Thursday*	The European Union vets' committee agrees to lift the ban on the exports of British beef 2006	67
9	*Friday*	David Rizzio, Italian private secretary of Mary, Queen of Scots, is brutally murdered 1566	68
10	*Saturday*	The French Foreign Legion is established 1831	69
11	*Sunday*	Four commuter trains filled with civilians in Madrid are hit by a series of explosions 2004	70

12	*Monday*	The *Anschluss* begins when Nazi troops march into Austria 1938	week 11 day 71
13	*Tuesday*	The European Monetary System comes into operation 1979	72
14	*Wednesday*	Gerry Adams, president of Sinn Fein, is injured in an assasination attempt 1984	73
15	*Thursday*	Julius Caesar, dictator of the Roman Republic, is assassinated on the Ides of March 44BC	74
16	*Friday*	The European Court of Justice annuls the registration of 'feta' as a protected designation of origin 1999	75
17	*Saturday*	The establishment of the kingdom of Italy is proclaimed in Turin 1861	76
18	*Sunday*	The Paris Commune is established after the end of the Franco-Prussian War 1871	77

19	*Monday*	Egon Krenz, the last Communist leader of East Germany *b.* 1937	week 12 day78
20	*Tuesday*	Napoleon Bonaparte enters Paris and begins his 100 day rule 1815	79
21	*Wednesday*	Otto von Bismark is appointed as the first chancellor of the German Empire 1871	80
22	*Thursday*	Philippa of Lancaster, sister of King Henry IV, who married King John I of Portugal *b.* 1360	81
23	*Friday*	Margaret of Anjou, wife of King Henry VI and a principal figure during the Wars of the Roses *b.* 1430	82
24	*Saturday*	King James IV of Scotland becomes King James I of England; unifying the two crowns 1603	83
25	*Sunday*	British Summer Time begins. The European Economic Community (EEC) is formed 1957	84

26	*Monday*	Conrad II is crowned Holy Roman Emperor 1027	week 13 day 85
27	*Tuesday*	The European fighter jet makes its maiden flight 1994	86
28	*Wednesday*	The Spanish Civil War ends with the Republican surrender of Madrid 1939	87
29	*Thursday*	The UK formally notifies the European Council of its decision to leave the EU by triggering article 50 2017	88
30	*Friday*	The European Parliament (EP) is given its name 1962	89
31	*Saturday*	King Francis I *d.* 1547	90

ASTRONOMICAL PHENOMENA

d	h	
5	18	Venus 1.4° South of Mercury
7	7	Jupiter 4° South of the Moon
10	1	Mars 4° South of the Moon
11	2	Saturn 2° South of the Moon
15	15	Mercury greatest elongation East
16	12	Neptune 2° North of the Moon
18	1	Venus 4° South of Mercury
18	19	Venus 4° North of the Moon
19	16	Uranus 5° North of the Moon
20	16	Equinox
29	0	Uranus 0.1° North of Venus

MINIMA OF ALGOL

d	h	d	h	d	h
2	21.4	14	8.7	25	20.0
5	18.3	17	5.6	28	16.8
8	15.1	20	2.4	31	13.7
11	11.9	22	23.2		

CONSTELLATIONS

The following constellations are near the meridian at

	d	h		d	h
February	1	24	March	16	21
February	15	23	April	1	20
March	1	22	April	15	19

Cepheus (below the Pole), Camelopardalis, Lynx, Gemini, Cancer, Leo, Canis Minor, Hydra, Monoceros, Canis Major and Puppis

THE MOON

Phases, Apsides and Node	d	h	m
○ Full Moon	2	0	51
◑ Last Quarter	9	11	20
● New Moon	17	13	12
◐ First Quarter	24	15	35
○ Full Moon	31	12	37
Apogee (404,678 km)	11	9	14
Perigee (369,106 km)	26	17	17

Mean longitude of the ascending node on 1st, 134°

THE SUN

Diam. 32.3′

Day	Right Ascension			Dec.	Equation of time		Rise 52°		Rise 56°		Transit		Set 52°		Set 56°		Sidereal time			Transit of first point of Aries		
	h	m	s	°	m	s	h	m	h	m	h	m	h	m	h	m	h	m	s	h	m	s
1	22	47	27	−7.7	−12	27	6	46	6	52	12	12	17	40	17	34	10	35	01	13	24	59
2	22	51	12	−7.3	−12	15	6	44	6	49	12	12	17	41	17	36	10	38	57	13	21	03
3	22	54	56	−6.9	−12	03	6	42	6	47	12	12	17	43	17	38	10	42	54	13	17	06
4	22	58	40	−6.5	−11	50	6	39	6	44	12	12	17	45	17	40	10	46	50	13	13	10
5	23	02	23	−6.2	−11	37	6	37	6	42	12	11	17	47	17	42	10	50	47	13	09	13
6	23	06	06	−5.8	−11	24	6	35	6	39	12	11	17	48	17	45	10	54	43	13	05	17
7	23	09	49	−5.4	−11	09	6	33	6	37	12	11	17	50	17	47	10	58	40	13	01	20
8	23	13	31	−5.0	−10	55	6	31	6	34	12	11	17	52	17	49	11	02	36	12	57	24
9	23	17	13	−4.6	−10	40	6	28	6	31	12	11	17	54	17	51	11	06	33	12	53	27
10	23	20	54	−4.2	−10	25	6	26	6	29	12	10	17	56	17	53	11	10	30	12	49	30
11	23	24	35	−3.8	−10	10	6	24	6	26	12	10	17	57	17	55	11	14	26	12	45	34
12	23	28	16	−3.4	−9	54	6	21	6	24	12	10	17	59	17	57	11	18	23	12	41	37
13	23	31	56	−3.0	−9	38	6	19	6	21	12	09	18	01	17	59	11	22	19	12	37	41
14	23	35	37	−2.6	−9	22	6	17	6	18	12	09	18	03	18	01	11	26	16	12	33	44
15	23	39	17	−2.2	−9	05	6	15	6	16	12	09	18	04	18	03	11	30	12	12	29	48
16	23	42	56	−1.8	−8	48	6	12	6	13	12	09	18	06	18	05	11	34	09	12	25	51
17	23	46	36	−1.5	−8	31	6	10	6	10	12	08	18	08	18	07	11	38	05	12	21	55
18	23	50	15	−1.1	−8	14	6	08	6	08	12	08	18	10	18	09	11	42	02	12	17	58
19	23	53	55	−0.7	−7	57	6	05	6	05	12	08	18	11	18	12	11	45	59	12	14	01
20	23	57	34	−0.3	−7	39	6	03	6	03	12	07	18	13	18	14	11	49	55	12	10	05
21	0	01	12	+0.1	−7	22	6	01	6	00	12	07	18	15	18	16	11	53	52	12	06	08
22	0	04	51	+0.5	−7	04	5	58	5	57	12	07	18	16	18	18	11	57	48	12	02	12
23	0	08	30	+0.9	−6	46	5	56	5	55	12	07	18	18	18	20	12	01	45	11	58	15
24	0	12	08	+1.3	−6	28	5	54	5	52	12	06	18	20	18	22	12	05	41	11	54	19
25	0	15	47	+1.7	−6	10	5	51	5	49	12	06	18	22	18	24	12	09	38	11	50	22
26	0	19	25	+2.1	−5	52	5	49	5	47	12	06	18	23	18	26	12	13	34	11	46	26
27	0	23	04	+2.5	−5	33	5	47	5	44	12	05	18	25	18	28	12	17	31	11	42	29
28	0	26	42	+2.9	−5	15	5	44	5	41	12	05	18	27	18	30	12	21	28	11	38	32
29	0	30	20	+3.3	−4	57	5	42	5	39	12	05	18	28	18	32	12	25	24	11	34	36
30	0	33	59	+3.7	−4	39	5	40	5	36	12	04	18	30	18	34	12	29	21	11	30	39
31	0	37	37	+4.1	−4	21	5	38	5	34	12	04	18	32	18	36	12	33	17	11	26	43

DURATION OF TWILIGHT (IN MINUTES)

Latitude	52°	56°	52°	56°	52°	56°	52°	56°
	1 March		11 March		21 March		31 March	
Civil	34	37	34	37	34	37	34	38
Nautical	73	80	73	80	74	81	75	84
Astronomical	112	124	113	125	115	128	120	135

THE NIGHT SKY

Mercury can be seen these evenings up to around the 28th. It passes about 1° from Venus on the 3rd and is highest at greatest elongation east on the 15th. A young Moon joins the pair on the 18th. Over the following few days Mercury will be seen to lose altitude while Venus gains in height.

Venus (magnitude −3.9) continues to sparkle these evenings. Use binoculars to spot Uranus (magnitude 5.9) in the same low-power field as Venus on the 28th.

Mars (magnitude 0.8 to 0.3) rises in the early hours and crosses into Sagittarius on the 11th, coming within 1° of the Lagoon Nebula (M8) on the 19th. Mars is near the Moon on the 10th and ends March less than 2° from Saturn.

Jupiter (magnitude −2.2 to −2.4) is up around midnight soon after the beginning of the month and by late evening on the 30th. It also begins to retrograde, travelling 10° westward across Libra between now and mid-July. Jupiter is just below the Moon when they both rise on the 7th.

Saturn (magnitude 0.5) reaches western quadrature this month when the globe's shadow may be seen cast on the rings. It rises roughly three hours before the Sun and lies near the globular cluster M22 in Sagittarius. The Moon is nearby on the 11th.

March is another calendrical Blue Moon month following January's. The next occasion two Blue Moon months fall in the same year is 2037.

Neptune is at solar conjunction on March 4th.

THE MOON

Day	R.A.		Dec	Hor Par	Diam	Sun Co-Long	PA of Br. limb	Ph.	Age	Rise				Transit		Set			
										52°		56°				52°		56°	
	h	m	°	'	'	°	°	%	d	h	m	h	m	h	m	h	m	h	m
1	9	56	+13.7	60.0	32.7	74	294	99	13.4	17	02	16	52	—		6	43	6	54
2	10	53	+9.6	59.6	32.5	86	10	100	14.4	18	21	18	16	0	15	7	13	7	20
3	11	47	+5.1	59.0	32.1	98	99	99	15.4	19	38	19	37	1	07	7	39	7	41
4	12	40	+0.3	58.2	31.7	110	104	95	16.4	20	53	20	56	1	57	8	03	8	02
5	13	31	−4.3	57.4	31.3	122	105	89	17.4	22	05	22	13	2	45	8	26	8	21
6	14	21	−8.6	56.6	30.8	134	105	82	18.4	23	15	23	26	3	33	8	50	8	41
7	15	10	−12.3	55.8	30.4	147	103	73	19.4	—		—		4	20	9	16	9	05
8	16	00	−15.5	55.2	30.1	159	100	64	20.4	0	22	0	36	5	07	9	46	9	30
9	16	49	−17.8	54.7	29.8	171	97	55	21.4	1	24	1	42	5	54	10	20	10	02
10	17	39	−19.4	54.3	29.6	183	92	45	22.4	2	22	2	42	6	42	11	00	10	39
11	18	30	−20.1	54.2	29.5	195	88	36	23.4	3	14	3	35	7	30	11	45	11	25
12	19	20	−19.9	54.2	29.5	207	83	27	24.4	3	59	4	20	8	18	12	38	12	18
13	20	10	−18.8	54.4	29.6	220	79	19	25.4	4	39	4	56	9	05	13	36	13	19
14	21	00	−16.9	54.7	29.8	232	74	12	26.4	5	12	5	28	9	52	14	39	14	25
15	21	49	−14.1	55.1	30.0	244	69	07	27.4	5	41	5	53	10	39	15	45	15	34
16	22	38	−10.7	55.6	30.3	256	62	02	28.4	6	07	6	16	11	26	16	54	16	47
17	23	27	−6.8	56.1	30.6	268	42	00	29.4	6	31	6	35	12	12	18	05	18	02
18	0	16	−2.5	56.7	30.9	281	282	00	0.8	6	53	6	54	12	59	19	17	19	18
19	1	06	+2.1	57.2	31.2	293	261	02	1.8	7	16	7	13	13	46	20	30	20	36
20	1	56	+6.6	57.7	31.4	305	258	07	2.8	7	40	7	33	14	35	21	45	21	54
21	2	49	+10.8	58.1	31.7	317	258	13	3.8	8	07	7	57	15	27	23	00	23	14
22	3	43	+14.6	58.5	31.9	329	260	22	4.8	8	38	8	24	16	21	—		—	
23	4	39	+17.5	58.8	32.0	342	264	32	5.8	9	17	9	00	17	17	0	14	0	32
24	5	38	+19.5	59.1	32.2	354	268	43	6.8	10	05	9	44	18	15	1	24	1	44
25	6	38	+20.2	59.3	32.3	6	274	54	7.8	11	02	10	41	19	14	2	27	2	48
26	7	38	+19.7	59.4	32.4	18	279	65	8.8	12	08	11	49	20	12	3	21	3	41
27	8	38	+17.9	59.4	32.4	30	284	76	9.8	13	22	13	06	21	08	4	05	4	22
28	9	36	+15.0	59.3	32.3	43	289	85	10.8	14	39	14	27	22	03	4	42	4	55
29	10	32	+11.2	59.1	32.2	55	295	92	11.8	15	57	15	49	22	55	5	12	5	21
30	11	27	+6.9	58.7	32.0	67	302	97	12.8	17	14	17	11	23	45	5	39	5	44
31	12	19	+2.2	58.2	31.7	79	323	100	13.8	18	30	18	31	—		6	03	6	04

MERCURY

Day	R.A.		Dec	Mag.	Diam.	Phase	Rise		Transit		Set	
	h	m	°		"	%	h	m	h	m	h	m
1	23	24.6	−4.7	−1.3	5	93	7	11	12	50	18	30
3	23	37.9	−3.0	−1.3	5	89	7	06	12	55	18	45
5	23	50.8	−1.2	−1.2	6	85	7	01	13	00	18	59
7	0	03.1	+0.6	−1.1	6	79	6	56	13	04	19	13
9	0	14.6	+2.3	−1.0	6	72	6	50	13	07	19	25
11	0	25.2	+3.9	−0.8	6	64	6	44	13	09	19	36
13	0	34.5	+5.4	−0.6	7	56	6	37	13	10	19	45
15	0	42.4	+6.7	−0.3	7	47	6	29	13	10	19	51
17	0	48.6	+7.8	+0.0	8	39	6	21	13	08	19	54
19	0	53.1	+8.7	+0.4	8	30	6	13	13	03	19	53
21	0	55.6	+9.3	+0.9	9	23	6	04	12	57	19	50
23	0	56.3	+9.6	+1.5	9	16	5	55	12	50	19	42
25	0	55.2	+9.6	+2.2	10	10	5	46	12	40	19	32
27	0	52.4	+9.3	+3.0	10	6	5	37	12	29	19	18
29	0	48.3	+8.8	+3.8	11	3	5	28	12	17	19	02
31	0	43.3	+8.0	+4.7	11	1	5	20	12	04	18	44

Rising and setting times are for latitude 54°

VENUS

Day	R.A.		Dec	Mag.	Diam.	Phase	Rise		Transit		Set	
	h	m	°		"	%	h	m	h	m	h	m
1	23	33.9	−4.3	−3.9	11	98	7	18	12	58	18	39
6	23	56.6	−1.8	−3.9	11	97	7	07	13	01	18	56
11	0	19.3	+0.8	−3.9	11	97	6	56	13	04	19	13
16	0	41.9	+3.4	−3.9	11	96	6	44	13	07	19	30
21	1	04.6	+5.9	−3.9	11	96	6	33	13	10	19	47
26	1	27.4	+8.4	−3.9	11	95	6	22	13	13	20	05
31	1	50.5	+10.8	−3.9	11	94	6	11	13	16	20	22

MARS

Day	R.A.		Dec	Mag.	Diam.	Phase	Rise		Transit		Set	
	h	m	°		"	%	h	m	h	m	h	m
1	17	16.6	−22.8	+0.8	7	89	2	57	6	41	10	25
6	17	29.4	−23.0	+0.7	7	89	2	52	6	34	10	16
11	17	42.1	−23.3	+0.7	7	89	2	47	6	27	10	08
16	17	54.7	−23.4	+0.6	7	88	2	41	6	20	9	59
21	18	07.1	−23.5	+0.5	8	88	2	34	6	13	9	51
26	18	19.5	−23.6	+0.4	8	88	2	27	6	06	9	44
31	18	31.6	−23.6	+0.3	8	88	2	20	5	58	9	36

SUNRISE AND SUNSET

	London				Bristol				Birmingham				Manchester				Newcastle				Glasgow				Belfast			
	0°	05′	51°	30′	2°	35′	51°	28′	1°	55′	52°	28′	2°	15′	53°	28′	1°	37′	54°	59′	4°	14′	55°	52′	5°	56′	54°	35′
d	h	m	h	m	h	m	h	m	h	m	h	m	h	m	h	m	h	m	h	m	h	m	h	m	h	m	h	m
1	6	46	17	40	6	56	17	51	6	54	17	47	6	57	17	47	6	57	17	42	7	08	17	51	7	13	18	00
2	6	44	17	42	6	54	17	52	6	52	17	48	6	55	17	49	6	54	17	44	7	06	17	53	7	11	18	02
3	6	41	17	44	6	51	17	54	6	50	17	50	6	52	17	50	6	52	17	46	7	03	17	55	7	08	18	04
4	6	39	17	46	6	49	17	56	6	48	17	52	6	50	17	52	6	49	17	48	7	01	17	57	7	06	18	06
5	6	37	17	47	6	47	17	58	6	45	17	54	6	48	17	54	6	47	17	50	6	58	18	00	7	04	18	08
6	6	35	17	49	6	45	17	59	6	43	17	56	6	45	17	56	6	44	17	52	6	56	18	02	7	01	18	10
7	6	33	17	51	6	43	18	01	6	41	17	58	6	43	17	58	6	42	17	54	6	53	18	04	6	59	18	12
8	6	30	17	53	6	40	18	03	6	39	17	59	6	41	18	00	6	39	17	56	6	51	18	06	6	56	18	14
9	6	28	17	54	6	38	18	04	6	36	18	01	6	38	18	02	6	37	17	58	6	48	18	08	6	54	18	16
10	6	26	17	56	6	36	18	06	6	34	18	03	6	36	18	04	6	34	18	00	6	46	18	10	6	51	18	18
11	6	24	17	58	6	34	18	08	6	32	18	05	6	34	18	05	6	32	18	02	6	43	18	12	6	49	18	20
12	6	21	18	00	6	31	18	10	6	29	18	06	6	31	18	07	6	29	18	04	6	40	18	14	6	46	18	22
13	6	19	18	01	6	29	18	11	6	27	18	08	6	29	18	09	6	27	18	06	6	38	18	16	6	44	18	23
14	6	17	18	03	6	27	18	13	6	25	18	10	6	26	18	11	6	24	18	08	6	35	18	18	6	41	18	25
15	6	15	18	05	6	25	18	15	6	22	18	12	6	24	18	13	6	22	18	10	6	33	18	20	6	39	18	27
16	6	12	18	06	6	22	18	16	6	20	18	14	6	22	18	15	6	19	18	12	6	30	18	22	6	36	18	29
17	6	10	18	08	6	20	18	18	6	18	18	15	6	19	18	17	6	17	18	14	6	27	18	24	6	34	18	31
18	6	08	18	10	6	18	18	20	6	15	18	17	6	17	18	19	6	14	18	16	6	25	18	26	6	31	18	33
19	6	06	18	12	6	16	18	22	6	13	18	19	6	14	18	20	6	12	18	18	6	22	18	28	6	29	18	35
20	6	03	18	13	6	13	18	23	6	11	18	21	6	12	18	22	6	09	18	20	6	20	18	30	6	26	18	37
21	6	01	18	15	6	11	18	25	6	08	18	22	6	09	18	24	6	07	18	22	6	17	18	33	6	24	18	39
22	5	59	18	17	6	09	18	27	6	06	18	24	6	07	18	26	6	04	18	24	6	14	18	35	6	21	18	41
23	5	57	18	18	6	07	18	28	6	04	18	26	6	05	18	28	6	02	18	26	6	12	18	37	6	19	18	43
24	5	54	18	20	6	04	18	30	6	01	18	28	6	02	18	30	5	59	18	28	6	09	18	39	6	16	18	45
25	5	52	18	22	6	02	18	32	5	59	18	30	6	00	18	31	5	56	18	30	6	06	18	41	6	14	18	47
26	5	50	18	23	6	00	18	33	5	57	18	31	5	57	18	33	5	54	18	32	6	04	18	43	6	11	18	49
27	5	47	18	25	5	57	18	35	5	54	18	33	5	55	18	35	5	51	18	34	6	01	18	45	6	09	18	51
28	5	45	18	27	5	55	18	37	5	52	18	35	5	52	18	37	5	49	18	36	5	59	18	47	6	06	18	52
29	5	43	18	28	5	53	18	38	5	49	18	37	5	50	18	39	5	46	18	37	5	56	18	49	6	04	18	54
30	5	41	18	30	5	51	18	40	5	47	18	38	5	48	18	40	5	44	18	39	5	53	18	51	6	01	18	56
31	5	38	18	32	5	48	18	42	5	45	18	40	5	45	18	42	5	41	18	41	5	51	18	53	5	59	18	58

JUPITER

Day	R.A.		Dec	Mag.	Diam.	Rise		Transit		Set	
	h	m	°		″	h	m	h	m	h	m
1	15	23.1	−17.3	−2.2	39	0	25	4	47	9	09
11	15	23.5	−17.3	−2.2	40	23	43	4	08	8	30
21	15	22.7	−17.3	−2.3	41	23	02	3	28	7	51
31	15	20.6	−17.1	−2.4	43	22	20	2	47	7	10

Equatorial Diam. 39″, Polar Diam. 36″

SATURN

Day	R.A.		Dec	Mag.	Diam.	Rise		Transit		Set	
	h	m	°		″	h	m	h	m	h	m
1	18	30.6	−22.4	+0.6	16	4	07	7	54	11	41
11	18	33.4	−22.3	+0.6	16	3	31	7	18	11	05
21	18	35.7	−22.3	+0.6	16	2	53	6	41	10	28
31	18	37.3	−22.3	+0.5	17	2	15	6	03	9	51

Equatorial Diam. 16″, Polar Diam. 15″
Rings – major axis 37″ minor axis 16″, Tilt 26°

URANUS

Day	R.A.		Dec	Mag.	Diam.	Rise		Transit		Set	
	h	m	°		″	h	m	h	m	h	m
1	1	36.0	+9.4	+5.9	3	8	03	14	59	21	54
11	1	37.7	+9.6	+5.9	3	7	24	14	21	21	18
21	1	39.7	+9.8	+5.9	3	6	46	13	44	20	41
31	1	41.7	+10.0	+5.9	3	6	07	13	06	20	05

NEPTUNE

Day	R.A.		Dec	Mag.	Diam.	Rise		Transit		Set	
	h	m	°		″	h	m	h	m	h	m
1	23	00.8	−7.3	+8.0	2	7	01	12	24	17	46
11	23	02.2	−7.2	+8.0	2	6	23	11	46	17	09
21	23	03.6	−7.0	+8.0	2	5	44	11	08	16	32
31	23	04.9	−6.9	+8.0	2	5	05	10	30	15	55

April 2018

FOURTH MONTH, 30 DAYS. *Aperire*, to open; Earth opens to receive seed.

1	*Sunday*	The first legal same sex marriage ceremony is performed in Amsterdam 2001	day 91

2	*Monday*	George Pompidou, prime minister and later president of France *d.* 1974	week 14 day 92
3	*Tuesday*	Joseph Stalin is appointed head of the Russian Communist Party by Vladimir Lenin 1922	93
4	*Wednesday*	Napoleon abdicates naming his son Napoleon II, Emperor of France 1814	94
5	*Thursday*	Count von Spreti, Ambassador for W. Germany in Guatemala, is found dead after being held hostage 1970	95
6	*Friday*	Germany invades Greece and Yugoslavia 1941	96
7	*Saturday*	William Wordsworth, Romantic poet and supporter of the French Revolution in his youth, *b.* 1770	97
8	*Sunday*	Bartolomeo Prignano is elected as Pope Urban VI 1378	98

9	*Monday*	John Major wins the general election and is elected Prime Minister of the United Kingdom 1992	week 15 day 99
10	*Tuesday*	Northern Ireland peace talks culminate in the Good Friday Agreement 1998	100
11	*Wednesday*	Adolf Eichmann's trial for war crimes begins in Israel 1961	101
12	*Thursday*	Joanna the Mad, Queen of Castile and Aragon *d.* 1553	102
13	*Friday*	King Charles I recalls parliament forming the Short Parliament 1640	103
14	*Saturday*	Students rally in West Germany culminating in violent clashes between protesters and police officers 1968	104
15	*Sunday*	The European Bank for Reconstruction and Development is inaugurated in London 1991	105

16	*Monday*	The Treaty of Rapallo is signed between Germany and Russia 1922	week 16 day 106
17	*Tuesday*	The Easter Rebellion starts in Verona against French Occupation 1797	107
18	*Wednesday*	The European Coal and Steel Community (ECSC) is formed 1951	108
19	*Thursday*	The Treaty of London is signed recognising the independence of Belgium and Luxembourg 1839	109
20	*Friday*	The documents outlining the European Common Agricultural Policy (CAP) are released 1962	110
21	*Saturday*	The Soviet Red Army enters the outskirts of Berlin 1945	111
22	*Sunday*	2nd Battle of Ypres begins on the Western Front 1915	112

23	*Monday*	Exeter is bombed in the first of Germany's Baedeker air raids 1942	week 17 day 113
24	*Tuesday*	Philippe Pétain, Chief of State of Vichy France (1940-4), who was convicted of treason *b.* 1856	114
25	*Wednesday*	Elizabeth Petrovna is crowned Empress of Russia 1742	115
26	*Thursday*	Paul von Hindenburg becomes the first directly elected president of the Weimar Republic 1925	116
27	*Friday*	Benito Mussolini is captured in Dongo disguised as a member of the Luftwaffe 1945	117
28	*Saturday*	Dmitry Sipyagin, a Russian statesman, is assassinated by a socialist revolutionary 1902	118
29	*Sunday*	US troops liberate the Dachau concentration camp in Germany 1945	119

30	*Monday*	Adolf Hitler and his wife Eva Braun commit suicide in the Fürerbunker, Berlin 1945	week 18 day 120

ASTRONOMICAL PHENOMENA

d	*h*	
2	12	Saturn 1.3° North of Mars
3	14	Jupiter 4° South of the Moon
7	13	Saturn 2° South of the Moon
7	18	Mars 3° South of the Moon
12	23	Neptune 2° North of the Moon
14	9	Mercury 4° North of the Moon
17	19	Venus 5° North of the Moon
29	18	Mercury greatest elongation West
30	17	Jupiter 4° South of the Moon

MINIMA OF ALGOL

d	*h*	*d*	*h*	*d*	*h*
3	10.5	14	21.8	26	9.1
6	7.3	17	18.6	29	5.9
9	4.1	20	15.4		
12	1.0	23	12.2		

CONSTELLATIONS

The following constellations are near the meridian at

	d	*h*		*d*	*h*
March	1	24	April	15	21
March	16	23	May	1	20
April	1	22	May	16	19

Cepheus (below the Pole), Cassiopeia (below the Pole), Ursa Major, Leo Minor, Leo., Sextans, Hydra and Crater

THE MOON

Phases, Apsides and Node	*d*	*h*	*m*
◐ Last Quarter	8	7	18
● New Moon	16	1	57
◑ First Quarter	22	21	46
○ Full Moon	30	0	58
Apogee (404,144 km)	8	5	31
Perigee (368,714 km)	20	14	41

Mean longitude of the ascending node on 1st, 132°

THE SUN

Diam. 32.0′

Day	Right Ascension			Dec. +	Equation of time		Rise 52°		56°		Transit		Set 52°		56°		Sidereal time			Transit of first point of Aries		
	h	m	s	°	m	s	h	m	h	m	h	m	h	m	h	m	h	m	s	h	m	s
1	0	41	16	4.4	−4	03	5	35	5	31	12	04	18	34	18	38	12	37	14	11	22	46
2	0	44	55	4.8	−3	45	5	33	5	28	12	04	18	35	18	40	12	41	10	11	18	50
3	0	48	33	5.2	−3	27	5	31	5	26	12	03	18	37	18	42	12	45	07	11	14	53
4	0	52	12	5.6	−3	10	5	28	5	23	12	03	18	39	18	44	12	49	03	11	10	57
5	0	55	51	6.0	−2	52	5	26	5	21	12	03	18	40	18	46	12	53	00	11	07	00
6	0	59	31	6.4	−2	35	5	24	5	18	12	02	18	42	18	48	12	56	57	11	03	03
7	1	03	10	6.7	−2	18	5	22	5	15	12	02	18	44	18	50	13	00	53	10	59	07
8	1	06	50	7.1	−2	01	5	19	5	13	12	02	18	46	18	52	13	04	50	10	55	10
9	1	10	30	7.5	−1	45	5	17	5	10	12	02	18	47	18	54	13	08	46	10	51	14
10	1	14	10	7.8	−1	28	5	15	5	08	12	01	18	49	18	56	13	12	43	10	47	17
11	1	17	51	8.2	−1	12	5	13	5	05	12	01	18	51	18	58	13	16	39	10	43	21
12	1	21	32	8.6	−0	57	5	10	5	02	12	01	18	52	19	00	13	20	36	10	39	24
13	1	25	13	9.0	−0	41	5	08	5	00	12	01	18	54	19	03	13	24	32	10	35	28
14	1	28	54	9.3	−0	26	5	06	4	57	12	00	18	56	19	05	13	28	29	10	31	31
15	1	32	36	9.7	−0	11	5	04	4	55	12	00	18	58	19	07	13	32	26	10	27	34
16	1	36	18	10.0	+0	03	5	01	4	52	12	00	18	59	19	09	13	36	22	10	23	38
17	1	40	01	10.4	+0	17	4	59	4	50	12	00	19	01	19	11	13	40	19	10	19	41
18	1	43	44	10.7	+0	31	4	57	4	47	11	59	19	03	19	13	13	44	15	10	15	45
19	1	47	27	11.1	+0	44	4	55	4	45	11	59	19	04	19	15	13	48	12	10	11	48
20	1	51	11	11.4	+0	57	4	53	4	42	11	59	19	06	19	17	13	52	08	10	07	52
21	1	54	55	11.8	+1	09	4	51	4	40	11	59	19	08	19	19	13	56	05	10	03	55
22	1	58	39	12.1	+1	21	4	49	4	38	11	59	19	10	19	21	14	00	01	9	59	59
23	2	02	24	12.4	+1	33	4	47	4	35	11	58	19	11	19	23	14	03	58	9	56	02
24	2	06	10	12.8	+1	44	4	45	4	33	11	58	19	13	19	25	14	07	55	9	52	05
25	2	09	56	13.1	+1	55	4	42	4	30	11	58	19	15	19	27	14	11	51	9	48	09
26	2	13	42	13.4	+2	05	4	40	4	28	11	58	19	16	19	29	14	15	48	9	44	12
27	2	17	29	13.8	+2	15	4	38	4	26	11	58	19	18	19	31	14	19	44	9	40	16
28	2	21	16	14.1	+2	24	4	36	4	23	11	58	19	20	19	33	14	23	41	9	36	19
29	2	25	04	14.4	+2	33	4	34	4	21	11	57	19	21	19	35	14	27	37	9	32	23
30	2	28	52	14.7	+2	41	4	33	4	19	11	57	19	23	19	37	14	31	34	9	28	26

DURATION OF TWILIGHT (IN MINUTES)

Latitude	52°	56°	52°	56°	52°	56°	52°	56°
	1 April		11 April		21 April		31 April	
Civil	34	38	35	39	37	42	39	44
Nautical	76	84	79	89	83	96	89	106
Astronomical	120	136	127	147	137	165	152	204

THE NIGHT SKY

Mercury is at inferior conjunction on the 1st and then moves into the morning sky. However, it remains too deep in twilight all month to be seen.

Venus is now a prominent evening 'star' above the western skyline and is attractively paired with the young Moon on the 17th. Venus approaches and passes the Pleiades during the last week of April.

Mars surges in brightness this month, from magnitude 0.3 to −0.3, while telescopically the disk widens to 10 arc-seconds. It overtakes Saturn at the beginning of April and they are 3° apart when the Moon is in the area on the mornings of the 7th and 8th. Both rise about 02h in Sagittarius on April 1st but the wider gap between the two by the 30th means the Red Planet lags an hour behind Saturn's time of rise.

Jupiter (magnitude −2.5) rises late evening in Libra on April 1st but not long after sunset at the end of the month as the giant planet nears its early May opposition date. The Full Moon and Jupiter are 3.5° apart as both rise on the 30th.

Saturn (magnitude 0.4) is stationary in Sagittarius mid-month – and also at aphelion – before beginning to retrograde. The northern aspect of its magnificent ring system is presently tipped about 25.5° earthward and their wide-open aspect contributes almost one full magnitude to the planet's overall apparent brightness. Saturn rises just after midnight at the end of April.

Uranus is at solar conjunction on the 18th.

THE MOON

Day	R.A.		Dec	Hor Par	Diam	Sun Co-Long	PA of Br. limb	Ph.	Age	Rise				Transit		Set			
										52°		56°				52°		56°	
	h	m	°	′	′	°	°	%	d	h	m	h	m	h	m	h	m	h	m
1	13	10	−2.5	57.6	31.4	91	75	100	14.8	19	44	19	49	0	34	6	26	6	23
2	14	01	−7.0	57.0	31.1	103	96	97	15.8	20	55	21	05	1	22	6	50	6	43
3	14	51	−11.1	56.3	30.7	116	98	93	16.8	22	05	22	18	2	10	7	15	7	05
4	15	41	−14.5	55.7	30.3	128	98	87	17.8	23	11	23	28	2	58	7	43	7	29
5	16	31	−17.3	55.1	30.0	140	95	80	18.8	—		—		3	46	8	15	7	59
6	17	22	−19.1	54.7	29.8	152	92	71	19.8	0	12	0	31	4	34	8	53	8	33
7	18	13	−20.2	54.4	29.6	164	88	62	20.8	1	07	1	28	5	22	9	36	9	16
8	19	03	−20.3	54.3	29.6	176	84	53	21.8	1	55	2	16	6	10	10	26	10	07
9	19	53	−19.5	54.3	29.6	189	79	44	22.8	2	37	2	56	6	58	11	23	11	04
10	20	43	−17.8	54.5	29.7	201	75	34	23.8	3	12	3	29	7	45	12	24	12	08
11	21	33	−15.3	54.9	29.9	213	71	26	24.8	3	43	3	56	8	32	13	28	13	16
12	22	21	−12.1	55.4	30.2	225	67	17	25.8	4	09	4	20	9	18	14	36	14	27
13	23	10	−8.3	56.0	30.5	237	64	10	26.8	4	33	4	40	10	04	15	46	15	41
14	23	59	−4.1	56.7	30.9	250	59	05	27.8	4	56	4	58	10	51	16	58	16	57
15	0	48	+0.5	57.4	31.3	262	50	01	28.8	5	18	5	17	11	39	18	12	18	16
16	1	39	+5.2	58.0	31.6	274	351	00	0.3	5	42	5	37	12	28	19	29	19	37
17	2	32	+9.7	58.6	31.9	286	274	01	1.3	6	08	5	59	13	20	20	46	20	58
18	3	27	+13.7	59.0	32.2	299	266	05	2.3	6	38	6	25	14	14	22	03	22	20
19	4	24	+17.0	59.3	32.3	311	266	11	3.3	7	15	6	58	15	11	23	17	23	37
20	5	24	+19.3	59.4	32.4	323	269	19	4.3	8	00	7	39	16	10	—		—	
21	6	24	+20.4	59.5	32.4	335	274	29	5.3	8	55	8	33	17	09	0	24	0	45
22	7	25	+20.1	59.4	32.4	347	279	40	6.3	9	59	9	38	18	07	1	21	1	41
23	8	25	+18.6	59.2	32.2	360	284	51	7.3	11	10	10	53	19	04	2	07	2	26
24	9	23	+16.0	58.9	32.1	12	288	62	8.3	12	25	12	12	19	58	2	45	2	59
25	10	18	+12.5	58.6	31.9	24	292	73	9.3	13	42	13	32	20	49	3	16	3	27
26	11	12	+8.3	58.2	31.7	36	295	82	10.3	14	58	14	53	21	39	3	43	3	49
27	12	03	+3.7	57.8	31.5	48	298	90	11.3	16	12	16	12	22	27	4	07	4	09
28	12	54	−1.0	57.4	31.3	61	302	95	12.3	17	26	17	30	23	15	4	29	4	28
29	13	44	−5.5	56.8	31.0	73	312	99	13.3	18	38	18	46	—		4	52	4	46
30	14	33	−9.8	56.3	30.7	85	13	100	14.3	19	48	20	00	0	02	5	16	5	07

MERCURY

Day	R.A.		Dec	Mag.	Diam.	Phase	Rise		Transit		Set	
	h	m	°		″	%	h	m	h	m	h	m
1	0	40.6	+7.6	+5.1	11	0	5	16	11	57	18	34
3	0	35.1	+6.6	+5.1	11	1	5	08	11	44	18	16
5	0	29.8	+5.6	+4.4	11	2	5	01	11	31	17	57
7	0	25.2	+4.5	+3.6	11	4	4	54	11	19	17	39
9	0	21.5	+3.5	+3.0	11	7	4	48	11	07	17	23
11	0	18.9	+2.6	+2.5	11	10	4	43	10	57	17	09
13	0	17.5	+1.9	+2.0	11	14	4	38	10	49	16	57
15	0	17.4	+1.4	+1.7	10	17	4	33	10	41	16	47
17	0	18.5	+1.0	+1.4	10	21	4	28	10	35	16	39
19	0	20.8	+0.8	+1.2	10	25	4	24	10	29	16	34
21	0	24.2	+0.7	+1.0	9	29	4	20	10	25	16	30
23	0	28.5	+0.8	+0.8	9	32	4	15	10	22	16	28
25	0	33.8	+1.1	+0.7	9	36	4	11	10	20	16	27
27	0	39.8	+1.5	+0.6	8	39	4	07	10	18	16	28
29	0	46.6	+2.0	+0.5	8	43	4	03	10	17	16	31

Rising and setting times are for latitude 54°

VENUS

Day	R.A.		Dec	Mag.	Diam.	Phase	Rise		Transit		Set	
	h	m	°		″	%	h	m	h	m	h	m
1	1	55.1	+11.3	−3.9	11	94	6	09	13	17	20	26
6	2	18.6	+13.6	−3.9	11	93	5	59	13	21	20	43
11	2	42.4	+15.7	−3.9	12	93	5	50	13	25	21	01
16	3	06.6	+17.7	−3.9	12	92	5	41	13	29	21	19
21	3	31.2	+19.5	−3.9	12	91	5	34	13	34	21	36
26	3	56.3	+21.0	−3.9	12	90	5	28	13	40	21	53

MARS

Day	R.A.		Dec	Mag.	Diam.	Phase	Rise		Transit		Set	
	h	m	°		″	%	h	m	h	m	h	m
1	18	34.0	−23.6	+0.3	8	88	2	18	5	56	9	35
6	18	45.9	−23.5	+0.2	9	88	2	10	5	49	9	28
11	18	57.6	−23.4	+0.1	9	88	2	01	5	41	9	20
16	19	09.0	−23.3	0.0	10	88	1	52	5	32	9	13
21	19	20.0	−23.1	−0.1	10	88	1	42	5	24	9	06
26	19	30.7	−22.9	−0.3	11	88	1	32	5	15	8	58

SUNRISE AND SUNSET

d	London 0° 05' h m	51° 30' h m	Bristol 2° 35' h m	51° 28' h m	Birmingham 1° 55' h m	52° 28' h m	Manchester 2° 15' h m	53° 28' h m	Newcastle 1° 37' h m	54° 59' h m	Glasgow 4° 14' h m	55° 52' h m	Belfast 5° 56' h m	54° 35' h m
1	5 36	18 33	5 46	18 43	5 42	18 42	5 43	18 44	5 39	18 43	5 48	18 55	5 56	19 00
2	5 34	18 35	5 44	18 45	5 40	18 43	5 40	18 46	5 36	18 45	5 45	18 57	5 54	19 02
3	5 32	18 37	5 42	18 47	5 38	18 45	5 38	18 48	5 34	18 47	5 43	18 59	5 51	19 04
4	5 29	18 38	5 39	18 48	5 35	18 47	5 36	18 50	5 31	18 49	5 40	19 01	5 49	19 06
5	5 27	18 40	5 37	18 50	5 33	18 49	5 33	18 51	5 29	18 51	5 38	19 03	5 46	19 08
6	5 25	18 42	5 35	18 52	5 31	18 50	5 31	18 53	5 26	18 53	5 35	19 05	5 44	19 10
7	5 23	18 43	5 33	18 53	5 29	18 52	5 28	18 55	5 23	18 55	5 32	19 07	5 41	19 12
8	5 20	18 45	5 30	18 55	5 26	18 54	5 26	18 57	5 21	18 57	5 30	19 09	5 39	19 13
9	5 18	18 47	5 28	18 57	5 24	18 56	5 24	18 59	5 18	18 59	5 27	19 11	5 36	19 15
10	5 16	18 48	5 26	18 58	5 22	18 57	5 21	19 01	5 16	19 01	5 25	19 13	5 34	19 17
11	5 14	18 50	5 24	19 00	5 19	18 59	5 19	19 02	5 14	19 03	5 22	19 15	5 32	19 19
12	5 12	18 52	5 22	19 02	5 17	19 01	5 17	19 04	5 11	19 05	5 20	19 17	5 29	19 21
13	5 09	18 54	5 19	19 03	5 15	19 03	5 14	19 06	5 09	19 07	5 17	19 19	5 27	19 23
14	5 07	18 55	5 17	19 05	5 13	19 04	5 12	19 08	5 06	19 09	5 15	19 21	5 24	19 25
15	5 05	18 57	5 15	19 07	5 10	19 06	5 10	19 10	5 04	19 11	5 12	19 23	5 22	19 27
16	5 03	18 59	5 13	19 08	5 08	19 08	5 07	19 11	5 01	19 12	5 10	19 25	5 20	19 29
17	5 01	19 00	5 11	19 10	5 06	19 10	5 05	19 13	4 59	19 14	5 07	19 27	5 17	19 31
18	4 59	19 02	5 09	19 12	5 04	19 11	5 03	19 15	4 57	19 16	5 05	19 29	5 15	19 33
19	4 57	19 04	5 07	19 13	5 02	19 13	5 01	19 17	4 54	19 18	5 02	19 31	5 12	19 35
20	4 54	19 05	5 04	19 15	4 59	19 15	4 58	19 19	4 52	19 20	5 00	19 33	5 10	19 36
21	4 52	19 07	5 02	19 17	4 57	19 17	4 56	19 21	4 49	19 22	4 57	19 35	5 08	19 38
22	4 50	19 09	5 00	19 18	4 55	19 18	4 54	19 22	4 47	19 24	4 55	19 37	5 05	19 40
23	4 48	19 10	4 58	19 20	4 53	19 20	4 52	19 24	4 45	19 26	4 52	19 39	5 03	19 42
24	4 46	19 12	4 56	19 22	4 51	19 22	4 50	19 26	4 42	19 28	4 50	19 41	5 01	19 44
25	4 44	19 13	4 54	19 23	4 49	19 24	4 47	19 28	4 40	19 30	4 48	19 43	4 59	19 46
26	4 42	19 15	4 52	19 25	4 47	19 25	4 45	19 30	4 38	19 32	4 45	19 45	4 56	19 48
27	4 40	19 17	4 50	19 27	4 45	19 27	4 43	19 31	4 36	19 34	4 43	19 48	4 54	19 50
28	4 38	19 18	4 48	19 28	4 43	19 29	4 41	19 33	4 33	19 36	4 41	19 50	4 52	19 52
29	4 36	19 20	4 46	19 30	4 41	19 30	4 39	19 35	4 31	19 38	4 38	19 52	4 50	19 54
30	4 34	19 22	4 45	19 32	4 39	19 32	4 37	19 37	4 29	19 40	4 36	19 54	4 48	19 56

JUPITER

Day	R.A. h m	Dec °	Mag.	Diam. "	Rise h m	Transit h m	Set h m
1	15 20.4	−17.1	−2.4	43	22 16	2 43	7 06
11	15 17.1	−16.9	−2.4	44	21 32	2 00	6 25
21	15 12.9	−16.6	−2.5	44	20 46	1 17	5 44

Equatorial Diam. 43″, Polar Diam. 40″

SATURN

Day	R.A. h m	Dec °	Mag.	Diam. "	Rise h m	Transit h m	Set h m
1	18 37.4	−22.3	+0.5	17	2 12	5 59	9 47
11	18 38.3	−22.3	+0.5	17	1 33	5 21	9 09
21	18 38.4	−22.3	+0.4	17	0 54	4 42	8 29

Equatorial Diam. 17″, Polar Diam. 16″
Rings – major axis 39″ minor axis 17″, Tilt 25°

URANUS

Day	R.A. h m	Dec °	Mag.	Diam. "	Rise h m	Transit h m	Set h m
1	1 41.9	+10.0	+5.9	3	6 03	13 03	20 02
11	1 44.0	+10.2	+5.9	3	5 25	12 25	19 26
21	1 46.2	+10.4	+5.9	3	4 47	11 48	18 50

NEPTUNE

Day	R.A. h m	Dec °	Mag.	Diam. "	Rise h m	Transit h m	Set h m
1	23 05.1	−6.9	+8.0	2	5 01	10 26	15 51
11	23 06.3	−6.7	+8.0	2	4 22	9 48	15 14
21	23 07.5	−6.6	+7.9	2	3 44	9 10	14 36

May 2018

   ♊

FIFTH MONTH, 31 DAYS. *Maia*, goddess of growth and increase

1	*Tuesday*	The Acts of Union takes effect unifying England and Scotland under a single Parliament 1707	day 121
2	*Wednesday*	Catherine the Great, Empress and longest ruling female leader of Russia *b.* 1729	122
3	*Thursday*	The May Uprising takes place in Dresden, Germany 1848	123
4	*Friday*	The 5 year German occupation of Denmark ends 1945	124
5	*Saturday*	Napoleon Bonaparte dies having spent six years of his life in exile on the island of St Helena 1821	125
6	*Sunday*	Queen Elizabeth II and French president François Mitterand open the Channel Tunnel 1994	126

7	*Monday*	HMS *Victory* is launched, 40 years before the Battle of Trafalgar 1765	week 19 day 127
8	*Tuesday*	Winston Churchill officially announces the end of war with Germany 1945	128
9	*Wednesday*	Richard Wagner, German composer, flees Dresden following his involvement in a failed uprising 1849	129
10	*Thursday*	Winston Churchill replaces Neville Chamberlain as prime minister following his resignation 1940	130
11	*Friday*	Potrugal completes 107 hours of using only renewable sources to provide the country's electricity 2016	131
12	Saturday	The USSR lifts its blockade on Berlin 1949	132
13	*Sunday*	Marie Curie becomes the first woman to teach at the Sorbonne 1906	133

14	*Monday*	The Soviet Union establishes the Warsaw Pact with its Eastern Bloc allies 1955	week 20 day134
15	*Tuesday*	Édith Cresson becomes the first woman to be appointed Prime Minister of France 1991	135
16	*Wednesday*	Marie Antoinette marries the future King Louis XVI of France 1770	136
17	*Thursday*	The 'Dambusters' air raids (RAF Operation Chastise) begins over the Ruhr valley, Germany 1943	137
18	*Friday*	Napoleon Bonaparte is declared Napoleon I, Emperor of the French 1804	138
19	Saturday	Queen Elizabeth I of England orders for the arrest of Mary, Queen of Scots 1568	139
20	*Sunday*	German forces first reach the English channel during the Second World War 1940	140

21	*Monday*	Otto III is crowned Holy Roman Emperor 996	week 21 day 141
22	*Tuesday*	The Good Friday agreement is ratified in Ireland and Northern Ireland 1998	142
23	Wednesday	Pope Paul II installs an inquisition in Portugal 1536	143
24	*Thursday*	The Eurovision Song Contest is hosted for the first time in Switzerland 1956	144
25	*Friday*	Celtic becomes the first British football team to win the European Cup 1967	145
26	*Saturday*	Allied soldiers begin the evacuation of Dunkirk (Operation Dynamo) 1940	146
27	*Sunday*	Denmark and Sweden sign the Treaty of Copenhagen ending the 2nd Northern War 1660	147

28	*Monday*	Belgium surrender to Germany 1940	week 22 day 148
29	*Tuesday*	The Fall of Constantinople, bringing an end to the Byzantine Empire 1453	149
30	*Wednesday*	A summit is held in Italy celebrating the ten year anniversary of the Treaty of Rome 1967	150
31	*Thursday*	The Battle of Jutland, the largest naval battle of the First World War, begins 1916	151

ASTRONOMICAL PHENOMENA

d	h	
4	20	Saturn 2° South of the Moon
6	7	Mars 3° South of the Moon
9	1	Jupiter at opposition
10	9	Neptune 2° North of the Moon
12	21	Uranus 2° North of Mercury
13	17	Mercury 2° North of the Moon
17	18	Venus 5° North of the Moon
27	18	Jupiter 4° South of the Moon

MINIMA OF ALGOL

d	h	d	h	d	h
2	2.7	13	14.0	25	1.2
4	23.5	16	10.8	27	22.0
7	20.3	19	7.6	30	18.9
10	17.1	22	4.4		

CONSTELLATIONS

The following constellations are near the meridian at

	d	h		d	h
April	1	24	May	16	21
April	15	23	June	1	20
May	1	22	June	15	19

Cepheus (below the Pole), Cassiopeia (below the Pole), Ursa Minor, Ursa Major, Canes Venatici, Coma Berenices, Bootes, Leo, Virgo, Crater, Corvus and Hydra

THE MOON

Phases, Apsides and Node	d	h	m
◑ Last Quarter	8	2	9
● New Moon	15	11	48
◐ First Quarter	22	3	49
○ Full Moon	29	14	20
Apogee (404,457 km)	6	0	35
Perigee (363,776 km)	17	21	5

Mean longitude of the ascending node on 1st, 131°

THE SUN

Diam. 31.8′

Day	Right Ascension			Dec. +	Equation of time		Rise 52°		Rise 56°		Transit		Set 52°		Set 56°		Sidereal time			Transit of first point of Aries		
	h	m	s	°	m	s	h	m	h	m	h	m	h	m	h	m	h	m	s	h	m	s
1	2	32	41	15.0	+2	49	4	31	4	16	11	57	19	25	19	39	14	35	30	9	24	30
2	2	36	30	15.3	+2	56	4	29	4	14	11	57	19	26	19	41	14	39	27	9	20	33
3	2	40	20	15.6	+3	03	4	27	4	12	11	57	19	28	19	43	14	43	24	9	16	36
4	2	44	10	15.9	+3	09	4	25	4	10	11	57	19	30	19	45	14	47	20	9	12	40
5	2	48	01	16.2	+3	14	4	23	4	08	11	57	19	31	19	47	14	51	17	9	08	43
6	2	51	53	16.5	+3	19	4	21	4	05	11	57	19	33	19	49	14	55	13	9	04	47
7	2	55	45	16.7	+3	24	4	20	4	03	11	57	19	35	19	51	14	59	10	9	00	50
8	2	59	38	17.0	+3	28	4	18	4	01	11	56	19	36	19	53	15	03	06	8	56	54
9	3	03	31	17.3	+3	31	4	16	3	59	11	56	19	38	19	55	15	07	03	8	52	57
10	3	07	25	17.6	+3	33	4	14	3	57	11	56	19	39	19	57	15	10	59	8	49	01
11	3	11	20	17.8	+3	35	4	13	3	55	11	56	19	41	19	59	15	14	56	8	45	04
12	3	15	15	18.1	+3	37	4	11	3	53	11	56	19	43	20	01	15	18	53	8	41	07
13	3	19	10	18.3	+3	38	4	10	3	51	11	56	19	44	20	03	15	22	49	8	37	11
14	3	23	07	18.6	+3	38	4	08	3	50	11	56	19	46	20	04	15	26	46	8	33	14
15	3	27	04	18.8	+3	38	4	06	3	48	11	56	19	47	20	06	15	30	42	8	29	18
16	3	31	01	19.0	+3	37	4	05	3	46	11	56	19	49	20	08	15	34	39	8	25	21
17	3	34	59	19.3	+3	35	4	04	3	44	11	56	19	50	20	10	15	38	35	8	21	25
18	3	38	58	19.5	+3	33	4	02	3	42	11	56	19	52	20	12	15	42	32	8	17	28
19	3	42	57	19.7	+3	31	4	01	3	41	11	56	19	53	20	13	15	46	28	8	13	32
20	3	46	56	19.9	+3	28	3	59	3	39	11	57	19	55	20	15	15	50	25	8	09	35
21	3	50	56	20.1	+3	24	3	58	3	37	11	57	19	56	20	17	15	54	22	8	05	38
22	3	54	57	20.3	+3	20	3	57	3	36	11	57	19	57	20	19	15	58	18	8	01	42
23	3	58	58	20.5	+3	16	3	56	3	34	11	57	19	59	20	20	16	02	15	7	57	45
24	4	03	00	20.7	+3	11	3	54	3	33	11	57	20	00	20	22	16	06	11	7	53	49
25	4	07	02	20.9	+3	05	3	53	3	32	11	57	20	01	20	23	16	10	08	7	49	52
26	4	11	05	21.1	+2	59	3	52	3	30	11	57	20	03	20	25	16	14	04	7	45	56
27	4	15	08	21.3	+2	52	3	51	3	29	11	57	20	04	20	26	16	18	01	7	41	59
28	4	19	11	21.4	+2	45	3	50	3	28	11	57	20	05	20	28	16	21	57	7	38	03
29	4	23	15	21.6	+2	38	3	49	3	26	11	57	20	06	20	29	16	25	54	7	34	06
30	4	27	20	21.7	+2	30	3	48	3	25	11	58	20	07	20	31	16	29	51	7	30	09
31	4	31	25	21.9	+2	22	3	47	3	24	11	58	20	09	20	32	16	33	47	7	26	13

DURATION OF TWILIGHT

Latitude	52°	56°	52°	56°	52°	56°	52°	56°
		1 May		11 May		21 May		31 May
Civil	39	44	41	48	44	53	46	57
Nautical	89	106	97	120	106	141	115	187
Astronomical	152	204	176	TAN	TAN	TAN	TAN	TAN

THE NIGHT SKY

Mercury remains poorly placed for viewing in the morning sky this month.

Venus (magnitude −3.9) is highest mid-month for this evening sky apparition. Some interesting encounters occur when it is close to the binocular group NGC 1746 in Taurus on the 8th (although the planet's brilliance might overpower the cluster) and M35 in Gemini on the 20th. Venus is just about equidistant from the two stars marking the 'horns' of Taurus on the 13th, and it lies about 5.5° from the Moon on the 17th.

Mars rises just after 01h at the beginning of May and smoulders at magnitude −0.4 in Sagittarius. It crosses into Capricornus mid-month where it will be stoked up to magnitude −1.2 by the 31st. A small telescope now easily shows its polar caps and dusky surface features. The waning gibbous Moon is near Mars on the 5th.

Jupiter (magnitude −2.5) is at opposition in Libra on the 9th and vies with Venus for attention at first, before Mars comes into view. The planet is now on view all night, albeit setting by 03h on the 31st due to Jupiter's low arc across the sky as seen from Greenwich and our shortening summer nights. The Moon is 3° from Jupiter on the 27th.

Saturn (magnitude 0.3 to 0.2) rises around midnight on the 1st in Sagittarius but by late evening at the end of the month. The Moon is near Saturn on the night of the 4th and less than 2° away on the 31st.

THE MOON

Day	R.A.		Dec	Hor Par	Diam	Sun Co-Long	PA of Br. limb	Ph.	Age	Rise 52°		Rise 56°		Transit		Set 52°		Set 56°	
	h	m	°	'	'	°	°	%	d	h	m	h	m	h	m	h	m	h	m
1	15	23	−13.5	55.8	30.4	97	82	99	15.3	20	56	21	12	0	49	5	42	5	29
2	16	14	−16.6	55.3	30.1	109	90	96	16.3	21	59	22	19	1	37	6	12	5	56
3	17	04	−18.8	54.9	29.9	121	90	91	17.3	22	58	23	19	2	26	6	47	6	28
4	17	56	−20.1	54.5	29.7	134	87	85	18.3	23	50	—		3	15	7	28	7	08
5	18	46	−20.6	54.3	29.6	146	84	78	19.3	—		0	12	4	03	8	16	7	56
6	19	37	−20.1	54.2	29.5	158	80	70	20.3	0	35	0	55	4	51	9	10	8	50
7	20	27	−18.7	54.3	29.6	170	76	61	21.3	1	13	1	31	5	38	10	09	9	52
8	21	16	−16.5	54.5	29.7	182	73	51	22.3	1	45	1	59	6	25	11	12	10	58
9	22	05	−13.6	55.0	29.9	195	69	41	23.3	2	12	2	24	7	11	12	18	12	07
10	22	53	−10.0	55.5	30.3	207	67	32	24.3	2	37	2	45	7	56	13	26	13	19
11	23	41	−5.9	56.2	30.6	219	64	23	25.3	2	59	3	03	8	42	14	36	14	33
12	0	29	−1.4	57.0	31.1	231	63	15	26.3	3	21	3	21	9	28	15	49	15	50
13	1	19	+3.3	57.8	31.5	244	61	08	27.3	3	43	3	40	10	17	17	05	17	10
14	2	11	+7.9	58.6	32.0	256	57	03	28.3	4	08	4	01	11	08	18	23	18	33
15	3	06	+12.3	59.3	32.3	268	37	00	29.3	4	36	4	24	12	02	19	42	19	56
16	4	03	+16.0	59.9	32.6	280	293	00	0.8	5	10	4	54	12	59	20	59	21	19
17	5	04	+18.8	60.2	32.8	293	275	03	1.8	5	52	5	32	13	59	22	13	22	34
18	6	06	+20.4	60.3	32.8	305	275	09	2.8	6	44	6	23	15	00	23	16	23	37
19	7	08	+20.6	60.1	32.8	317	278	17	3.8	7	47	7	26	16	01	—		—	
20	8	10	+19.4	59.8	32.6	329	283	26	4.8	8	59	8	39	16	59	0	07	0	27
21	9	10	+16.9	59.4	32.4	341	287	37	5.8	10	14	10	00	17	55	0	49	1	04
22	10	06	+13.6	58.9	32.1	354	290	48	6.8	11	31	11	20	18	47	1	22	1	34
23	11	00	+9.5	58.3	31.8	6	293	60	7.8	12	47	12	40	19	37	1	49	1	57
24	11	52	+5.0	57.7	31.5	18	295	70	8.8	14	01	13	59	20	25	2	14	2	17
25	12	42	+0.3	57.1	31.1	30	296	79	9.8	15	14	15	16	21	12	2	36	2	36
26	13	31	−4.3	56.6	30.9	42	297	87	10.8	16	25	16	32	21	58	2	58	2	54
27	14	20	−8.6	56.1	30.6	55	298	93	11.8	17	36	17	46	22	44	3	20	3	12
28	15	09	−12.5	55.6	30.3	67	300	97	12.8	18	44	18	58	23	32	3	45	3	33
29	15	59	−15.7	55.2	30.1	79	316	100	13.8	19	49	20	07	—		4	13	3	58
30	16	49	−18.3	54.8	29.9	91	55	100	14.8	20	50	21	10	0	20	4	45	4	27
31	17	40	−19.9	54.5	29.7	103	80	98	15.8	21	45	22	06	1	08	5	23	5	04

MERCURY

Day	R.A.		Dec	Mag.	Diam.	Phase	Rise		Transit		Set	
	h	m	°		"	%	h	m	h	m	h	m
1	0	54.1	+2.7	+0.4	8	46	3	59	10	17	16	35
3	1	02.2	+3.4	+0.3	8	49	3	55	10	17	16	40
5	1	11.0	+4.3	+0.2	7	52	3	52	10	18	16	46
7	1	20.3	+5.2	+0.2	7	55	3	48	10	20	16	53
9	1	30.2	+6.3	+0.1	7	58	3	44	10	22	17	01
11	1	40.6	+7.4	+0.0	7	61	3	40	10	25	17	10
13	1	51.6	+8.5	−0.1	6	65	3	37	10	28	17	21
15	2	03.1	+9.7	−0.2	6	68	3	33	10	32	17	32
17	2	15.3	+11.0	−0.3	6	71	3	30	10	36	17	44
19	2	28.1	+12.3	−0.5	6	75	3	27	10	41	17	57
21	2	41.5	+13.7	−0.6	6	79	3	24	10	47	18	11
23	2	55.6	+15.0	−0.8	6	82	3	22	10	53	18	27
25	3	10.4	+16.4	−0.9	5	86	3	20	11	01	18	43
27	3	26.0	+17.7	−1.1	5	89	3	19	11	08	19	00
29	3	42.3	+19.0	−1.3	5	93	3	19	11	17	19	18
31	3	59.4	+20.2	−1.5	5	96	3	19	11	26	19	36

Rising and setting times are for latitude 54°

VENUS

Day	R.A.		Dec	Mag.	Diam.	Phase	Rise		Transit		Set	
	h	m	°		"	%	h	m	h	m	h	m
1	4	21.8	+22.4	−3.9	12	88	5	23	13	46	22	09
6	4	47.7	+23.5	−3.9	13	87	5	21	13	52	22	23
11	5	13.8	+24.3	−3.9	13	86	5	21	13	58	22	36
16	5	40.2	+24.8	−4.0	13	85	5	23	14	05	22	47
21	6	06.6	+25.0	−4.0	13	83	5	28	14	11	22	55
26	6	32.9	+25.0	−4.0	14	82	5	35	14	18	23	01
31	6	59.0	+24.6	−4.0	14	81	5	44	14	24	23	04

MARS

Day	R.A.		Dec	Mag.	Diam.	Phase	Rise		Transit		Set	
	h	m	°		"	%	h	m	h	m	h	m
1	19	41.0	−22.7	−0.4	11	88	1	21	5	05	8	50
6	19	50.9	−22.5	−0.5	12	88	1	09	4	56	8	42
11	20	00.3	−22.3	−0.6	12	89	0	58	4	45	8	34
16	20	09.1	−22.2	−0.8	13	89	0	45	4	34	8	24
21	20	17.3	−22.0	−0.9	14	90	0	33	4	23	8	14
26	20	24.8	−21.9	−1.0	14	90	0	20	4	11	8	03
31	20	31.6	−21.8	−1.2	15	91	0	05	3	58	7	51

SUNRISE AND SUNSET

	London		Bristol		Birmingham		Manchester		Newcastle		Glasgow		Belfast	
	0° 05′	51° 30′	2° 35′	51° 28′	1° 55′	52° 28′	2° 15′	53° 28′	1° 37′	54° 59′	4° 14′	55° 52′	5° 56′	54° 35′
d	h m	h m	h m	h m	h m	h m	h m	h m	h m	h m	h m	h m	h m	h m
1	4 33	19 23	4 43	19 33	4 37	19 34	4 35	19 39	4 27	19 42	4 34	19 56	4 46	19 57
2	4 31	19 25	4 41	19 35	4 35	19 36	4 33	19 40	4 25	19 44	4 32	19 58	4 43	19 59
3	4 29	19 27	4 39	19 37	4 33	19 37	4 31	19 42	4 23	19 45	4 29	20 00	4 41	20 01
4	4 27	19 28	4 37	19 38	4 31	19 39	4 29	19 44	4 20	19 47	4 27	20 02	4 39	20 03
5	4 25	19 30	4 35	19 40	4 29	19 41	4 27	19 46	4 18	19 49	4 25	20 03	4 37	20 05
6	4 23	19 32	4 34	19 41	4 27	19 42	4 25	19 47	4 16	19 51	4 23	20 05	4 35	20 07
7	4 22	19 33	4 32	19 43	4 26	19 44	4 23	19 49	4 14	19 53	4 21	20 07	4 33	20 09
8	4 20	19 35	4 30	19 45	4 24	19 46	4 21	19 51	4 12	19 55	4 19	20 09	4 31	20 10
9	4 18	19 36	4 28	19 46	4 22	19 47	4 19	19 53	4 10	19 57	4 17	20 11	4 29	20 12
10	4 17	19 38	4 27	19 48	4 20	19 49	4 18	19 54	4 08	19 59	4 15	20 13	4 27	20 14
11	4 15	19 39	4 25	19 49	4 19	19 51	4 16	19 56	4 06	20 00	4 13	20 15	4 26	20 16
12	4 13	19 41	4 24	19 51	4 17	19 52	4 14	19 58	4 05	20 02	4 11	20 17	4 24	20 18
13	4 12	19 43	4 22	19 52	4 15	19 54	4 12	19 59	4 03	20 04	4 09	20 19	4 22	20 19
14	4 10	19 44	4 20	19 54	4 14	19 55	4 11	20 01	4 01	20 06	4 07	20 21	4 20	20 21
15	4 09	19 46	4 19	19 55	4 12	19 57	4 09	20 03	3 59	20 08	4 05	20 23	4 18	20 23
16	4 07	19 47	4 17	19 57	4 11	19 59	4 07	20 04	3 57	20 09	4 03	20 25	4 17	20 25
17	4 06	19 49	4 16	19 58	4 09	20 00	4 06	20 06	3 56	20 11	4 02	20 26	4 15	20 26
18	4 04	19 50	4 15	20 00	4 08	20 02	4 04	20 08	3 54	20 13	4 00	20 28	4 13	20 28
19	4 03	19 51	4 13	20 01	4 06	20 03	4 03	20 09	3 52	20 15	3 58	20 30	4 12	20 30
20	4 02	19 53	4 12	20 03	4 05	20 05	4 01	20 11	3 51	20 16	3 56	20 32	4 10	20 31
21	4 01	19 54	4 11	20 04	4 03	20 06	4 00	20 12	3 49	20 18	3 55	20 33	4 09	20 33
22	3 59	19 56	4 09	20 05	4 02	20 08	3 58	20 14	3 48	20 19	3 53	20 35	4 07	20 35
23	3 58	19 57	4 08	20 07	4 01	20 09	3 57	20 15	3 46	20 21	3 52	20 37	4 06	20 36
24	3 57	19 58	4 07	20 08	4 00	20 10	3 56	20 17	3 45	20 23	3 50	20 38	4 04	20 38
25	3 56	20 00	4 06	20 09	3 58	20 12	3 55	20 18	3 44	20 24	3 49	20 40	4 03	20 39
26	3 55	20 01	4 05	20 11	3 57	20 13	3 53	20 20	3 42	20 26	3 47	20 42	4 02	20 41
27	3 54	20 02	4 04	20 12	3 56	20 14	3 52	20 21	3 41	20 27	3 46	20 43	4 01	20 42
28	3 53	20 03	4 03	20 13	3 55	20 16	3 51	20 22	3 40	20 29	3 45	20 45	3 59	20 43
29	3 52	20 05	4 02	20 14	3 54	20 17	3 50	20 24	3 39	20 30	3 43	20 46	3 58	20 45
30	3 51	20 06	4 01	20 16	3 53	20 18	3 49	20 25	3 37	20 31	3 42	20 48	3 57	20 46
31	3 50	20 07	4 00	20 17	3 52	20 19	3 48	20 26	3 36	20 33	3 41	20 49	3 56	20 47

JUPITER

Day	R.A. h	m	Dec °	Mag.	Diam. ″	Rise h	m	Transit h	m	Set h	m
1	15	08.1	−16.3	−2.5	45	20	00	0	33	5	01
11	15	03.0	−15.9	−2.5	45	19	14	23	45	4	19
21	14	58.0	−15.6	−2.5	45	18	27	23	00	3	37
31	14	53.4	−15.3	−2.5	44	17	41	22	16	2	55

Equatorial Diam. 45″, Polar Diam. 42″

SATURN

Day	R.A. h	m	Dec °	Mag.	Diam. ″	Rise h	m	Transit h	m	Set h	m
1	18	37.9	−22.3	+0.4	17	0	10	4	02	7	49
11	18	36.7	−22.3	+0.3	18	23	30	3	21	7	09
21	18	34.8	−22.3	+0.2	18	22	49	2	40	6	27
31	18	32.4	−22.3	+0.2	18	22	08	1	58	5	45

Equatorial Diam. 18″, Polar Diam. 16″
Rings – major axis 40″ minor axis 17″, Tilt 26°

URANUS

Day	R.A. h	m	Dec °	Mag.	Diam. ″	Rise h	m	Transit h	m	Set h	m
1	1	48.4	+10.6	+5.9	3	4	08	11	11	18	14
11	1	50.5	+10.8	+5.9	3	3	30	10	34	17	38
21	1	52.5	+11.0	+5.9	3	2	52	9	57	17	02
31	1	54.4	+11.2	+5.9	3	2	13	9	19	16	25

NEPTUNE

Day	R.A. h	m	Dec °	Mag.	Diam. ″	Rise h	m	Transit h	m	Set h	m
1	23	08.5	−6.5	+7.9	2	3	05	8	32	13	58
11	23	09.3	−6.4	+7.9	2	2	26	7	53	13	20
21	23	10.0	−6.4	+7.9	2	1	47	7	14	12	42
31	23	10.5	−6.3	+7.9	2	1	08	6	36	12	03

 II **June 2018**

SIXTH MONTH, 30 DAYS. *Junius,* Roman *gens* (family)

1	*Friday*	Victor Hugo, politician and author of *Les Misérables,* is given a national funeral in Paris 1885	day 152
2	*Saturday*	As a display of resistance to German nationalism the first Prague Slavic Congress begins 1848	153
3	*Sunday*	Saint Clotilda, Queen of the Franks *d.* 548	154

4	*Monday*	Allied forces complete their evacuation from Dunkirk 1940	week 23 day155
5	*Tuesday*	Pope Clement V is elected and moves the Curia from Rome to Avignon 1305	156
6	*Wednesday*	The UK votes to stay in the European Economic Community in the 1975 referendum	157
7	*Thursday*	The first elections to the European Parliament (EP) take place 1979	158
8	*Friday*	Vikings raid St Cuthbert's monastery on Lindisfarne Island 793	159
9	*Saturday*	Roman Emperor Nero commits suicide, ending the Julio-Claudian dynasty AD 68	160
10	*Sunday*	The Spanish government requests a eurozone rescue loan of around €100bn 2012	161

11	*Monday*	Henry VIII marries Catherine of Aragon, his brother's Spanish widow 1509	week 24 day 162
12	*Tuesday*	Ireland votes against the ratification of the Lisbon treaty 2008	163
13	*Wednesday*	Charles the Fat, great-grandson of Charlemagn and the last Carolingian Emperor *b.* AD 839	164
14	*Thursday*	The Schengen agreement is signed by five states, abolishing internal border controls 1985	165
15	*Friday*	King John of England signs the Magna Carta 1215	166
16	*Saturday*	The Battle of Quatre Bras, which precedes Waterloo, ends in a practical draw 1815	167
17	*Sunday*	The Erasmus programme is launched and over 3,000 students participate in the first exchange 1987	168

18	*Monday*	The Duke of Wellington leads the Seventh Coalition to victory at the Battle of Waterloo 1815	week 25 day 169
19	*Tuesday*	The Metropolitan Police Act, introduced to parliament by Sir Robert Peel, receives royal assent 1829	170
20	*Wednesday*	The French national assembly swear to pursue a constitution after meeting in a tennis court 1789	171
21	*Thursday*	Niccolò Machiavelli, author of *The Prince,* from whom the word 'Machiavellanism' originates *d.* 1527	172
22	*Friday*	Germany, Italy and Romania declare war on the Soviet Union 1941	173
23	*Saturday*	The UK votes to leave the EU in a referendum 2016	174
24	*Sunday*	The first republican constitution is accepted by the French National Convention 1793	175

25	*Monday*	George Orwell, author known for '1984' and essayist of 'Toward European Unity' *b.* 1903	week 26 day 176
26	*Tuesday*	Representatives of 50 countries sign the United Nations Charter 1945	177
27	*Wednesday*	Yugoslav troops move into Slovenia after it declares independence 1991	178
28	*Thursday*	The Archduke Franz Ferdinand of Austria is assassinated by Gavrilo Princip in Sarajevo 1914	179
29	*Friday*	Accession negotiations begin towards an EU partnership with Montenegro 2012	180
30	*Saturday*	The European Commission sign the Kennedy round of the General Agreement on Tariffs and Trade 1967	181

ASTRONOMICAL PHENOMENA

d	h	
1	1	Saturn 2° South of the Moon
3	12	Mars 3° South of the Moon
6	18	Neptune 2° North of the Moon
10	3	Uranus 5° North of the Moon
16	13	Venus 2° North of the Moon
19	20	Vesta at opposition
21	10	Solstice
23	19	Jupiter 4° South of the Moon
25	16	Pollux 5° North of Mercury
27	13	Saturn at opposition
28	4	Saturn 2° South of the Moon

MINIMA OF ALGOL

d	h	d	h	d	h
2	15.7	14	2.9	25	14.2
5	12.5	16	23.7	28	11.0
8	9.3	19	20.6		
11	6.1	22	17.4		

CONSTELLATIONS

The following constellations are near the meridian at

	d	h		d	h
May	1	24	June	15	21
May	16	23	July	1	20
June	1	22	July	16	19

Cassiopeia (below the Pole), Ursa Minor, Draco, Ursa Major, Canes Venatici, Bootes, Corona, Serpens, Virgo and Libra

THE MOON

Phases, Apsides and Node	d	h	m
◑ Last Quarter	6	18	32
● New Moon	13	19	43
◐ First Quarter	20	10	51
○ Full Moon	28	4	53
Apogee (405,317 km)	2	16	35
Perigee (359,503 km)	14	23	53
Apogee (406,061 km)	30	2	43

Mean longitude of the ascending node on 1st, 129°

THE SUN

Diam. 31.6′

Day	Right Ascension			Dec. +	Equation of time		Rise 52°		Rise 56°		Transit		Set 52°		Set 56°		Sidereal time			Transit of first point of Aries		
	h	m	s	°	m	s	h	m	h	m	h	m	h	m	h	m	h	m	s	h	m	s
1	4	35	30	22.0	+2	13	3	47	3	23	11	58	20	10	20	33	16	37	44	7	22	16
2	4	39	36	22.2	+2	04	3	46	3	22	11	58	20	11	20	35	16	41	40	7	18	20
3	4	43	42	22.3	+1	54	3	45	3	21	11	58	20	12	20	36	16	45	37	7	14	23
4	4	47	48	22.4	+1	44	3	44	3	20	11	58	20	13	20	37	16	49	33	7	10	27
5	4	51	55	22.5	+1	34	3	44	3	19	11	59	20	14	20	38	16	53	30	7	06	30
6	4	56	02	22.6	+1	23	3	43	3	19	11	59	20	15	20	39	16	57	26	7	02	34
7	5	00	10	22.7	+1	12	3	43	3	18	11	59	20	16	20	40	17	01	23	6	58	37
8	5	04	18	22.8	+1	01	3	42	3	17	11	59	20	16	20	41	17	05	20	6	54	40
9	5	08	26	22.9	+0	50	3	42	3	17	11	59	20	17	20	42	17	09	16	6	50	44
10	5	12	34	23.0	+0	38	3	41	3	16	11	59	20	18	20	43	17	13	13	6	46	47
11	5	16	43	23.1	+0	26	3	41	3	16	12	00	20	19	20	44	17	17	09	6	42	51
12	5	20	52	23.1	+0	13	3	41	3	15	12	00	20	19	20	45	17	21	06	6	38	54
13	5	25	01	23.2	+0	01	3	41	3	15	12	00	20	20	20	45	17	25	02	6	34	58
14	5	29	10	23.2	−0	12	3	40	3	15	12	00	20	20	20	46	17	28	59	6	31	01
15	5	33	19	23.3	−0	25	3	40	3	15	12	01	20	21	20	47	17	32	55	6	27	05
16	5	37	29	23.3	−0	38	3	40	3	14	12	01	20	21	20	47	17	36	52	6	23	08
17	5	41	38	23.4	−0	51	3	40	3	14	12	01	20	22	20	48	17	40	49	6	19	11
18	5	45	48	23.4	−1	04	3	40	3	14	12	01	20	22	20	48	17	44	45	6	15	15
19	5	49	58	23.4	−1	17	3	40	3	14	12	01	20	23	20	48	17	48	42	6	11	18
20	5	54	07	23.4	−1	30	3	40	3	14	12	02	20	23	20	49	17	52	38	6	07	22
21	5	58	17	23.4	−1	43	3	41	3	15	12	02	20	23	20	49	17	56	35	6	03	25
22	6	02	27	23.4	−1	56	3	41	3	15	12	02	20	23	20	49	18	00	31	5	59	29
23	6	06	36	23.4	−2	09	3	41	3	15	12	02	20	23	20	49	18	04	28	5	55	32
24	6	10	46	23.4	−2	22	3	41	3	16	12	02	20	23	20	49	18	08	24	5	51	36
25	6	14	55	23.4	−2	35	3	42	3	16	12	03	20	23	20	49	18	12	21	5	47	39
26	6	19	04	23.4	−2	47	3	42	3	16	12	03	20	23	20	49	18	16	18	5	43	42
27	6	23	13	23.3	−3	00	3	43	3	17	12	03	20	23	20	49	18	20	14	5	39	46
28	6	27	22	23.3	−3	12	3	43	3	18	12	03	20	23	20	49	18	24	11	5	35	49
29	6	31	31	23.2	−3	24	3	44	3	18	12	03	20	23	20	48	18	28	07	5	31	53
30	6	35	39	23.2	−3	36	3	44	3	19	12	04	20	23	20	48	18	32	04	5	27	56

DURATION OF TWILIGHT

Latitude	52°	56°	52°	56°	52°	56°	52°	56°
		1 June		11 June		21 June		31 June
Civil	46	58	48	61	49	63	48	61
Nautical	116	TAN	124	TAN	127	TAN	124	TAN
Astronomical	TAN	TAN	TAN	TAN	TAN	TAN	TAN	TAN

THE NIGHT SKY

Mercury is at superior conjunction on the 6th and then moves into the evening sky where it might be seen low in the northwest during the last week.

Venus (magnitude −4.0) remains a brilliant evening object and crosses from Gemini into Cancer this month, skirting the northern edge of the Beehive Cluster (M44) on the 19th and 20th. Venus and the Moon are 5.5° apart on the 16th.

Mars gains nearly another whole magnitude, brightening from −1.2 to −2.1, as the disk swells to more than 20 arc-seconds wide. It's up around midnight at the start of June but almost two hours earlier by the 31st. The Moon is near Mars as both rise the night of the 3rd and is close again on the 30th.

Jupiter (magnitude −2.5 to −2.3) shines bright in the south-eastern sky after sunset at the start of June but is setting by 01h by the end of the month. The Moon is 3° from Jupiter on the 23rd.

Saturn (magnitude 0.0) is at opposition on the 27th in Sagittarius with the Full Moon just 3° away the same night. The northern aspect of the rings are tipped 26° towards us at present and a beautiful sight.

The asteroid (4) Vesta has a very favourable opposition on the 20th and at magnitude 5.4 is about as bright as it ever gets. That makes it a naked eye object, but it lies in a star-rich area of Sagittarius and is rather low from more northerly latitudes.

THE MOON

Day	R.A. h	R.A. m	Dec °	Hor Par '	Diam '	Sun Co-Long °	PA of Br. limb °	Ph. %	Age d	Rise 52° h	Rise 52° m	Rise 56° h	Rise 56° m	Transit h	Transit m	Set 52° h	Set 52° m	Set 56° h	Set 56° m
1	18	31	−20.7	54.3	29.6	116	82	95	16.8	22	33	22	53	1	57	6	09	5	47
2	19	22	−20.5	54.1	29.5	128	80	90	17.8	23	13	23	33	2	46	7	01	6	39
3	20	12	−19.4	54.1	29.5	140	77	83	18.8	23	47	—		3	33	7	58	7	38
4	21	01	−17.5	54.2	29.5	152	74	76	19.8	—		0	03	4	20	8	59	8	42
5	21	50	−14.8	54.5	29.7	164	71	67	20.8	0	16	0	29	5	05	10	03	9	50
6	22	37	−11.4	54.9	29.9	177	69	58	21.8	0	41	0	51	5	50	11	09	11	01
7	23	24	−7.6	55.5	30.2	189	67	48	22.8	1	03	1	09	6	35	12	17	12	12
8	0	12	−3.3	56.2	30.6	201	65	38	23.8	1	25	1	27	7	20	13	27	13	26
9	1	00	+1.3	57.1	31.1	213	65	28	24.8	1	46	1	44	8	06	14	40	14	43
10	1	50	+5.9	58.0	31.6	226	65	19	25.8	2	08	2	03	8	55	15	55	16	03
11	2	43	+10.4	58.9	32.1	238	66	11	26.8	2	34	2	24	9	46	17	14	17	27
12	3	39	+14.5	59.7	32.6	250	66	05	27.8	3	04	2	51	10	42	18	34	18	50
13	4	38	+17.8	60.4	32.9	262	62	01	28.8	3	42	3	24	11	41	19	51	20	11
14	5	40	+20.0	60.8	33.2	275	322	00	0.2	4	29	4	09	12	43	21	00	21	23
15	6	45	+20.8	61.0	33.2	287	282	02	1.2	5	29	5	08	13	46	21	59	22	21
16	7	49	+20.1	60.8	33.2	299	282	07	2.2	6	39	6	19	14	48	22	47	23	04
17	8	51	+18.0	60.4	32.9	311	285	14	3.2	7	56	7	39	15	47	23	25	23	38
18	9	51	+14.8	59.8	32.6	324	289	24	4.2	9	15	9	03	16	43	23	55	—	
19	10	47	+10.8	59.1	32.2	336	291	34	5.2	10	34	10	26	17	34	—		0	04
20	11	40	+6.3	58.3	31.8	348	293	45	6.2	11	50	11	47	18	23	0	20	0	25
21	12	31	+1.6	57.5	31.4	0	294	56	7.2	13	04	13	05	19	11	0	43	0	44
22	13	20	−3.1	56.8	31.0	12	294	67	8.2	14	16	14	21	19	57	1	05	1	02
23	14	09	−7.5	56.2	30.6	25	293	76	9.2	15	26	15	35	20	43	1	26	1	20
24	14	57	−11.5	55.7	30.3	37	291	84	10.2	16	34	16	47	21	29	1	50	1	40
25	15	46	−14.9	55.1	30.0	49	289	91	11.2	17	40	17	56	22	16	2	16	2	03
26	16	36	−17.7	54.7	29.8	61	288	95	12.2	18	43	19	01	23	04	2	47	2	29
27	17	26	−19.6	54.4	29.7	73	288	99	13.2	19	40	20	00	23	53	3	22	3	03
28	18	17	−20.6	54.2	29.5	86	319	100	14.2	20	30	20	51	—		4	05	3	43
29	19	08	−20.7	54.1	29.5	98	72	99	15.2	21	13	21	34	0	41	4	54	4	32
30	19	59	−19.9	54.0	29.4	110	77	97	16.2	21	49	22	07	1	29	5	49	5	29

MERCURY

Day	R.A. h m	Dec °	Mag.	Diam. "	Phase %	Rise h m	Transit h m	Set h m
1	4 08.1	+20.8	−1.7	5	97	3 20	11 31	19 45
3	4 26.2	+21.9	−1.9	5	99	3 22	11 42	20 03
5	4 44.7	+22.9	−2.2	5	100	3 25	11 52	20 21
7	5 03.6	+23.7	−2.2	5	100	3 29	12 03	20 39
9	5 22.7	+24.3	−1.9	5	99	3 35	12 15	20 55
11	5 41.7	+24.8	−1.7	5	97	3 43	12 26	21 09
13	6 00.5	+25.1	−1.4	5	94	3 51	12 36	21 22
15	6 18.8	+25.2	−1.2	5	91	4 01	12 47	21 32
17	6 36.6	+25.1	−1.0	5	87	4 12	12 57	21 41
19	6 53.8	+24.8	−0.9	6	83	4 23	13 06	21 47
21	7 10.2	+24.5	−0.7	6	79	4 35	13 14	21 52
23	7 25.8	+23.9	−0.5	6	75	4 47	13 21	21 55
25	7 40.6	+23.3	−0.4	6	72	4 59	13 28	21 56
27	7 54.6	+22.6	−0.3	6	68	5 10	13 34	21 56
29	8 07.7	+21.8	−0.2	6	64	5 22	13 39	21 55

Rising and setting times are for latitude 54°

VENUS

Day	R.A. h m	Dec °	Mag.	Diam. "	Phase %	Rise h m	Transit h m	Set h m
1	7 04.2	+24.5	−4.0	14	80	5 47	14 26	23 05
6	7 29.9	+23.8	−4.0	14	79	5 58	14 31	23 05
11	7 55.1	+22.9	−4.0	15	77	6 11	14 37	23 02
16	8 19.7	+21.6	−4.0	15	75	6 26	14 42	22 57
21	8 43.8	+20.2	−4.0	16	74	6 41	14 46	22 51
26	9 07.2	+18.5	−4.0	16	72	6 56	14 50	22 42

MARS

Day	R.A. h m	Dec °	Mag.	Diam. "	Phase %	Rise h m	Transit h m	Set h m
1	20 32.8	−21.8	−1.2	15	91	0 02	3 55	7 48
6	20 38.5	−21.8	−1.4	16	92	23 48	3 41	7 34
11	20 43.3	−21.8	−1.5	17	93	23 34	3 26	7 19
16	20 47.0	−22.0	−1.7	18	94	23 19	3 10	7 02
21	20 49.5	−22.2	−1.8	19	95	23 03	2 53	6 44
26	20 50.8	−22.5	−2.0	20	96	22 47	2 35	6 23

SUNRISE AND SUNSET

	London				Bristol				Birmingham				Manchester				Newcastle				Glasgow				Belfast			
	0°	05′	51°	30′	2°	35′	51°	28′	1°	55′	52°	28′	2°	15′	53°	28′	1°	37′	54°	59′	4°	14′	55°	52′	5°	56′	54°	35′
d	h	m	h	m	h	m	h	m	h	m	h	m	h	m	h	m	h	m	h	m	h	m	h	m	h	m	h	m
1	3	49	20	08	3	59	20	18	3	51	20	20	3	47	20	27	3	35	20	34	3	40	20	50	3	55	20	49
2	3	48	20	09	3	58	20	19	3	50	20	21	3	46	20	28	3	34	20	35	3	39	20	52	3	54	20	50
3	3	48	20	10	3	58	20	20	3	50	20	23	3	45	20	30	3	34	20	36	3	38	20	53	3	53	20	51
4	3	47	20	11	3	57	20	21	3	49	20	24	3	45	20	31	3	33	20	38	3	37	20	54	3	52	20	52
5	3	46	20	12	3	56	20	22	3	48	20	25	3	44	20	32	3	32	20	39	3	36	20	55	3	52	20	53
6	3	46	20	13	3	56	20	23	3	48	20	26	3	43	20	33	3	31	20	40	3	35	20	56	3	51	20	54
7	3	45	20	14	3	55	20	24	3	47	20	26	3	43	20	34	3	30	20	41	3	35	20	57	3	50	20	55
8	3	45	20	15	3	55	20	24	3	47	20	27	3	42	20	35	3	30	20	42	3	34	20	58	3	50	20	56
9	3	44	20	15	3	54	20	25	3	46	20	28	3	42	20	35	3	29	20	43	3	33	20	59	3	49	20	57
10	3	44	20	16	3	54	20	26	3	46	20	29	3	41	20	36	3	29	20	44	3	33	21	00	3	49	20	58
11	3	43	20	17	3	54	20	27	3	45	20	30	3	41	20	37	3	28	20	44	3	32	21	01	3	48	20	59
12	3	43	20	17	3	53	20	27	3	45	20	30	3	40	20	38	3	28	20	45	3	32	21	02	3	48	21	00
13	3	43	20	18	3	53	20	28	3	45	20	31	3	40	20	38	3	28	20	46	3	32	21	03	3	48	21	00
14	3	43	20	19	3	53	20	28	3	45	20	32	3	40	20	39	3	27	20	46	3	31	21	03	3	47	21	01
15	3	43	20	19	3	53	20	29	3	44	20	32	3	40	20	39	3	27	20	47	3	31	21	04	3	47	21	02
16	3	43	20	20	3	53	20	29	3	44	20	33	3	40	20	40	3	27	20	48	3	31	21	05	3	47	21	02
17	3	43	20	20	3	53	20	30	3	44	20	33	3	40	20	40	3	27	20	48	3	31	21	05	3	47	21	03
18	3	43	20	20	3	53	20	30	3	44	20	33	3	40	20	41	3	27	20	48	3	31	21	05	3	47	21	03
19	3	43	20	21	3	53	20	31	3	44	20	34	3	40	20	41	3	27	20	49	3	31	21	06	3	47	21	03
20	3	43	20	21	3	53	20	31	3	45	20	34	3	40	20	41	3	27	20	49	3	31	21	06	3	47	21	04
21	3	43	20	21	3	53	20	31	3	45	20	34	3	40	20	42	3	27	20	49	3	31	21	06	3	47	21	04
22	3	43	20	21	3	53	20	31	3	45	20	34	3	40	20	42	3	27	20	49	3	31	21	06	3	47	21	04
23	3	44	20	22	3	54	20	31	3	45	20	34	3	41	20	42	3	28	20	50	3	32	21	07	3	48	21	04
24	3	44	20	22	3	54	20	31	3	46	20	35	3	41	20	42	3	28	20	50	3	32	21	07	3	48	21	04
25	3	44	20	22	3	54	20	31	3	46	20	35	3	41	20	42	3	28	20	50	3	32	21	07	3	49	21	04
26	3	45	20	22	3	55	20	31	3	46	20	34	3	42	20	42	3	29	20	49	3	33	21	06	3	49	21	04
27	3	45	20	21	3	55	20	31	3	47	20	34	3	42	20	42	3	29	20	49	3	34	21	06	3	50	21	04
28	3	46	20	21	3	56	20	31	3	47	20	34	3	43	20	42	3	30	20	49	3	34	21	06	3	50	21	04
29	3	46	20	21	3	56	20	31	3	48	20	34	3	43	20	41	3	31	20	49	3	35	21	06	3	51	21	03
30	3	47	20	21	3	57	20	31	3	49	20	34	3	44	20	41	3	31	20	48	3	36	21	05	3	51	21	03

JUPITER

Day	R.A.		Dec	Mag.	Diam.	Rise		Transit		Set	
	h	m	°		″	h	m	h	m	h	m
1	14	53.0	−15.3	−2.5	44	17	37	22	12	2	51
11	14	49.1	−15.0	−2.4	43	16	52	21	29	2	09
21	14	46.3	−14.8	−2.4	42	16	09	20	47	1	28

Equatorial Diam. 44″, Polar Diam. 41″

SATURN

Day	R.A.		Dec	Mag.	Diam.	Rise		Transit		Set	
	h	m	°		″	h	m	h	m	h	m
1	18	32.2	−22.4	+0.2	18	22	03	1	54	5	41
11	18	29.4	−22.4	+0.1	18	21	22	1	12	4	59
21	18	26.3	−22.4	+0.1	18	20	40	0	30	4	16

Equatorial Diam. 18″, Polar Diam. 17″
Rings – major axis 41″ minor axis 18″, Tilt 26°

URANUS

Day	R.A.		Dec	Mag.	Diam.	Rise		Transit		Set	
	h	m	°		″	h	m	h	m	h	m
1	1	54.6	+11.2	+5.9	3	2	09	9	15	16	21
11	1	56.3	+11.3	+5.9	3	1	31	8	38	15	45
21	1	57.8	+11.5	+5.9	3	0	52	8	00	15	08

NEPTUNE

Day	R.A.		Dec	Mag.	Diam.	Rise		Transit		Set	
	h	m	°		″	h	m	h	m	h	m
1	23	10.5	−6.3	+7.9	2	1	04	6	32	12	00
11	23	10.8	−6.3	+7.9	2	0	25	5	53	11	21
21	23	10.8	−6.3	+7.9	2	23	41	5	13	10	41

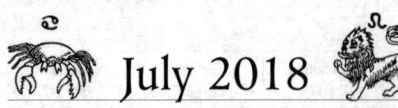

July 2018

SEVENTH MONTH, 31 DAYS. *Julius* Caesar, formerly *Quintilis*, fifth month of Roman pre-Julian calendar

1	*Sunday*	Croatia becomes a member state of the European Union 2013	day 182

2	*Monday*	Elie Wiesel, Holocaust survivor, Nobel Peace Prize winning political activist and author *d.* 2016	week 27 day 183
3	*Tuesday*	French troops enter Rome to restore Pope Pius IX to power over the Papal States 1849	184
4	*Wednesday*	Giuseppe Garibaldi, Italian military leader and revolutionary *b.* 1807	185
5	*Thursday*	Venezuela declares its independence from Spain 1811	186
6	*Friday*	Maximilian I Emperor of Mexico (1864–7), brother of Austrian Emperor Francis Joseph I, *b.* 1832	187
7	*Saturday*	Emperor Napolean and Tsar Alexander I sign the Treaty of Tilsit 1807	188
8	*Sunday*	Sweden is defeated by Russia at the Battle of Poltava, Ukraine 1709	189

9	*Monday*	King Henry VIII annuls his marriage to Anne of Cleves 1540	week 28 day 190
10	*Tuesday*	The Luftwaffe attack shipping convoys off the south-east coast of Britain 1940	191
11	*Wednesday*	Robert the Bruce, King of Scots who fought for Scotland's independence *b.* 1274	192
12	*Thursday*	William of Orange defeats King James II of Great Britain at Battle of the Boyne 1690	193
13	*Friday*	Real Madrid wins the first European Champions Cup final in Paris 1956	194
14	*Saturday*	Crowds storm the Bastille, marking the beginning of the French Revolution 1789	195
15	*Sunday*	Jean-Claude Juncker is elected president of the European Commission 2014	196

16	*Monday*	Richard of Bordeaux is crowned Richard II of England 1377	week 29. day 197
17	*Tuesday*	King George V issues a proclamation changing the royal surname to Windsor 1917	198
18	*Wednesday*	The Great Fire of Rome breaks out and begins to destroy much of the city 64	199
19	*Thursday*	Winston Churchill launches the 'V for Victory' propaganda campaign 1941	200
20	*Friday*	Otto John, the head of West Germany's intelligence service, defects to East Germany 1954	201
21	*Saturday*	A constitutional monarchy is established in Belgium as Leopold I becomes king 1831	202
22	*Sunday*	British, Spanish and Portuguese forces defeat the French at Salamanca 1812	203

23	*Monday*	Adam Czerniakow, head of the Warsaw Ghetto Jewish Council, swallows a cyanide capsule 1942	week 30 day 204
24	*Tuesday*	The first air raids of RAF Operation Gomorrah begin over Hamburg, Germany 1917	205
25	*Wednesday*	Louis Blériot becomes the first to cross the English Channel in an aeroplane, landing after 37 minutes 1909	206
26	*Thursday*	Clement Attlee becomes prime minister in the General Election 1945	207
27	*Friday*	Belarus declares independence from the Soviet Union 1990	208
28	*Saturday*	Maximilien Robespierre, French revolutionary, and 21 of his supporters are executed 1794	209
29	*Sunday*	Margaret Thatcher and François Mitterand ratify the Channel Tunnel treaty 1987	210

30	*Monday*	Otto von Bismarck, first chancellor of Germany *d.* 1898	week 31 day 211
31	*Tuesday*	Operation Banner, the British Armed Forces' operation in Northern Ireland ends after 38 years 2007	212

ASTRONOMICAL PHENOMENA

d	*h*	
4	0	Neptune 3° North of the Moon
6	17	Earth at aphelion
7	14	Uranus 5° North of the Moon
9	20	Regulus 1° South of Venus
12	5	Mercury greatest elongation East
14	22	Mercury 2° South of the Moon
16	4	Venus 2° South of the Moon
21	0	Jupiter 4° South of the Moon
25	6	Saturn 2° South of the Moon
27	5	Mars at opposition
27	20	Total Lunar Eclipse
31	5	Neptune 3° North of the Moon

MINIMA OF ALGOL

d	*h*	*d*	*h*	*d*	*h*
1	7.8	12	19.1	24	6.3
4	4.6	15	15.9	27	3.1
7	1.4	18	12.7	29	23.9
9	22.2	21	9.5		

CONSTELLATIONS

The following constellations are near the meridian at

	d	*h*			*d*	*h*
June	1	24		July	16	21
June	15	23		August	1	20
July	1	22		August	16	19

Ursa Minor, Draco, Corona, Hercules, Lyra, Serpens, Ophiuchus, Libra, Scorpius and Sagittarius

THE MOON

Phases, Apsides and Node	*d*	*h*	*m*
◑ Last Quarter	6	7	51
● New Moon	13	2	48
◐ First Quarter	19	19	52
○ Full Moon	27	20	20
Perigee (357,431 km)	13	8	25
Apogee (406,223 km)	27	5	44

Mean longitude of the ascending node on 1st, 127°

THE SUN

Diam. 31.5′

Day	Right Ascension			Dec. +	Equation of time		Rise 52°		56°		Transit		Set 52°		56°		Sidereal time			Transit of first point of Aries		
	h	m	s	°	m	s	h	m	h	m	h	m	h	m	h	m	h	m	s	h	m	s
1	6	39	48	23.1	−3	48	3	45	3	20	12	04	20	22	20	48	18	36	00	5	24	00
2	6	43	56	23.1	−4	00	3	46	3	20	12	04	20	22	20	47	18	39	57	5	20	03
3	6	48	03	23.0	−4	11	3	46	3	21	12	04	20	22	20	47	18	43	53	5	16	07
4	6	52	11	22.9	−4	22	3	47	3	22	12	04	20	21	20	46	18	47	50	5	12	10
5	6	56	18	22.8	−4	32	3	48	3	23	12	05	20	21	20	45	18	51	47	5	08	13
6	7	00	25	22.7	−4	43	3	49	3	24	12	05	20	20	20	45	18	55	43	5	04	17
7	7	04	31	22.6	−4	53	3	50	3	25	12	05	20	20	20	44	18	59	40	5	00	20
8	7	08	38	22.5	−5	02	3	51	3	26	12	05	20	19	20	43	19	03	36	4	56	24
9	7	12	44	22.4	−5	12	3	52	3	28	12	05	20	18	20	42	19	07	33	4	52	27
10	7	16	49	22.3	−5	20	3	53	3	29	12	05	20	18	20	41	19	11	29	4	48	31
11	7	20	54	22.1	−5	29	3	54	3	30	12	06	20	17	20	40	19	15	26	4	44	34
12	7	24	59	22.0	−5	37	3	55	3	31	12	06	20	16	20	39	19	19	22	4	40	38
13	7	29	03	21.9	−5	44	3	56	3	33	12	06	20	15	20	38	19	23	19	4	36	41
14	7	33	06	21.7	−5	52	3	57	3	34	12	06	20	14	20	37	19	27	16	4	32	44
15	7	37	09	21.6	−5	58	3	58	3	36	12	06	20	13	20	36	19	31	12	4	28	48
16	7	41	12	21.4	−6	04	3	59	3	37	12	06	20	12	20	34	19	35	09	4	24	51
17	7	45	14	21.2	−6	10	4	01	3	38	12	06	20	11	20	33	19	39	05	4	20	55
18	7	49	16	21.1	−6	15	4	02	3	40	12	06	20	10	20	32	19	43	02	4	16	58
19	7	53	17	20.9	−6	19	4	03	3	42	12	06	20	09	20	30	19	46	58	4	13	02
20	7	57	17	20.7	−6	23	4	05	3	43	12	06	20	07	20	29	19	50	55	4	09	05
21	8	01	17	20.5	−6	27	4	06	3	45	12	06	20	06	20	27	19	54	51	4	05	09
22	8	05	17	20.3	−6	29	4	07	3	46	12	06	20	05	20	26	19	58	48	4	01	12
23	8	09	15	20.1	−6	31	4	09	3	48	12	07	20	04	20	24	20	02	45	3	57	15
24	8	13	13	19.9	−6	33	4	10	3	50	12	07	20	02	20	22	20	06	41	3	53	19
25	8	17	11	19.7	−6	34	4	11	3	51	12	07	20	01	20	21	20	10	38	3	49	22
26	8	21	08	19.5	−6	34	4	13	3	53	12	07	19	59	20	19	20	14	34	3	45	26
27	8	25	04	19.3	−6	34	4	14	3	55	12	07	19	58	20	17	20	18	31	3	41	29
28	8	29	00	19.0	−6	33	4	16	3	57	12	07	19	56	20	15	20	22	27	3	37	33
29	8	32	55	18.8	−6	32	4	17	3	58	12	07	19	55	20	13	20	26	24	3	33	36
30	8	36	49	18.6	−6	30	4	19	4	00	12	06	19	53	20	11	20	30	20	3	29	40
31	8	40	43	18.3	−6	27	4	20	4	02	12	06	19	52	20	10	20	34	17	3	25	43

DURATION OF TWILIGHT

Latitude	52°	56°	52°	56°	52°	56°	52°	56°
	1 July		11 July		21 July		31 July	
Civil	48	61	47	58	44	53	42	49
Nautical	124	TAN	117	TAN	107	146	98	123
Astronomical	TAN	TAN	TAN	TAN	TAN	TAN	182	TAN

THE NIGHT SKY

Mercury is best placed at the beginning of July but is somewhat low these evenings. Greatest eastern elongation is on the 12th with the planet then being lost to view a couple of days later.

Venus (magnitude −4.1 to −4.3) is now slipping lower in the western sky but will dawdle a while longer on the evening stage until curtain fall in early September. Venus passes 1° from Regulus on the 9th, while the Moon is nearby on the 15th.

Mars (magnitude −2.8) reaches opposition in Capricornus on July 27th – its best since August 2003 – with the 24 arc-second wide disk showing a wealth of detail in a telescope. The planet also enjoys a rare opportunity to outshine Jupiter, which it does until early September.

Jupiter (magnitude −2.3 to −2.1) is stationary in Libra this month before its direct motion resumes. The planet sets before midnight by the 31st. The Moon is nearby on the 20th.

Saturn (magnitude 0.0 to 0.2) lies above the Teapot asterism in Sagittarius these evenings and doesn't set until the early hours. The Moon is close to Saturn on the 24th.

The dwarf planet Pluto (magnitude 14.2) is at opposition in Sagittarius on July 12th.

A partial solar eclipse on July 13th is visible from south Australia and the Southern Ocean. The maximum eclipse magnitude is 0.337.

A total lunar eclipse on July 27th is visible from South America, Europe, Africa, Asia, and Australia. The eclipse is in progress at moonrise from the British Isles.

THE MOON

Day	R.A. h	m	Dec °	Hor Par '	Diam '	Sun Co-Long °	PA of Br. limb °	Ph. %	Age d	Rise 52° h	m	Rise 56° h	m	Transit h	m	Set 52° h	m	Set 56° h	m
1	20	48	−18.2	54.0	29.4	122	75	93	17.2	22	20	22	35	2	16	6	49	6	31
2	21	37	−15.7	54.2	29.5	134	73	88	18.2	22	46	22	57	3	02	7	52	7	38
3	22	24	−12.6	54.5	29.7	147	71	81	19.2	23	09	23	17	3	47	8	57	8	47
4	23	11	−8.9	54.9	29.9	159	69	73	20.2	23	30	23	34	4	31	10	04	9	57
5	23	57	−4.8	55.4	30.2	171	68	63	21.2	23	50	23	51	5	15	11	11	11	09
6	0	44	−0.4	56.1	30.6	183	67	54	22.2	—		—		5	59	12	21	12	23
7	1	32	+4.1	56.9	31.0	196	68	43	23.2	0	12	0	08	6	45	13	33	13	39
8	2	23	+8.6	57.8	31.5	208	69	33	24.2	0	35	0	27	7	34	14	48	14	58
9	3	16	+12.8	58.8	32.0	220	71	23	25.2	1	02	0	50	8	26	16	05	16	21
10	4	12	+16.4	59.7	32.5	232	75	14	26.2	1	34	1	18	9	23	17	24	17	42
11	5	13	+19.1	60.5	33.0	244	79	07	27.2	2	16	1	57	10	23	18	38	18	58
12	6	16	+20.6	61.0	33.3	257	82	02	28.2	3	09	2	47	11	26	19	43	20	04
13	7	21	+20.6	61.3	33.4	269	55	00	29.2	4	14	3	53	12	29	20	38	20	56
14	8	25	+19.1	61.3	33.4	281	284	01	0.7	5	29	5	11	13	32	21	21	21	36
15	9	28	+16.2	60.9	33.2	293	286	05	1.7	6	51	6	36	14	31	21	55	22	06
16	10	27	+12.4	60.3	32.8	306	289	12	2.7	8	13	8	03	15	26	22	23	22	30
17	11	23	+7.9	59.5	32.4	318	291	21	3.7	9	33	9	28	16	18	22	48	22	50
18	12	16	+3.1	58.6	31.9	330	292	31	4.7	10	50	10	49	17	07	23	10	23	09
19	13	07	−1.7	57.7	31.4	342	292	41	5.7	12	04	12	08	17	54	23	32	23	27
20	13	57	−6.3	56.8	31.0	355	291	52	6.7	13	16	13	24	18	41	23	56	23	46
21	14	46	−10.5	56.0	30.5	7	289	62	7.7	14	25	14	37	19	27	—		—	
22	15	35	−14.1	55.4	30.2	19	286	72	8.7	15	32	15	47	20	14	0	21	0	08
23	16	24	−17.0	54.8	29.9	31	283	80	9.7	16	36	16	54	21	02	0	50	0	33
24	17	14	−19.1	54.5	29.7	44	279	87	10.7	17	34	17	54	21	50	1	23	1	05
25	18	05	−20.4	54.2	29.5	56	275	93	11.7	18	27	18	48	22	38	2	04	1	42
26	18	55	−20.7	54.0	29.5	68	270	97	12.7	19	12	19	33	23	26	2	50	2	28
27	19	46	−20.2	54.0	29.4	80	266	99	13.7	19	51	20	09	—		3	43	3	22
28	20	36	−18.7	54.0	29.4	92	78	100	14.7	20	23	20	39	0	14	4	41	4	23
29	21	25	−16.4	54.1	29.5	105	77	99	15.7	20	50	21	03	1	00	5	44	5	28
30	22	13	−13.4	54.3	29.6	117	74	96	16.7	21	14	21	23	1	45	6	48	6	37
31	22	59	−9.9	54.6	29.8	129	72	91	17.7	21	36	21	41	2	30	7	54	7	47

MERCURY

Day	R.A. h	m	Dec °	Mag.	Diam. "	Phase %	Rise h	m	Transit h	m	Set h	m
1	8	20.0	+21.0	+0.0	7	61	5	32	13	43	21	53
3	8	31.4	+20.0	+0.1	7	58	5	42	13	46	21	49
5	8	42.1	+19.1	+0.2	7	54	5	52	13	49	21	45
7	8	51.8	+18.2	+0.3	7	51	6	00	13	50	21	40
9	9	00.8	+17.2	+0.4	8	48	6	07	13	51	21	34
11	9	08.8	+16.2	+0.5	8	45	6	14	13	51	21	27
13	9	16.0	+15.3	+0.6	8	41	6	19	13	50	21	20
15	9	22.2	+14.4	+0.7	8	38	6	23	13	48	21	12
17	9	27.5	+13.5	+0.8	9	35	6	26	13	45	21	04
19	9	31.7	+12.7	+0.9	9	31	6	27	13	41	20	55
21	9	34.8	+11.9	+1.1	9	28	6	26	13	36	20	45
23	9	36.8	+11.3	+1.3	10	24	6	24	13	29	20	35
25	9	37.6	+10.7	+1.5	10	20	6	20	13	22	20	25
27	9	37.2	+10.3	+1.8	10	17	6	13	13	13	20	14
29	9	35.5	+10.1	+2.1	11	13	6	05	13	03	20	02
31	9	32.6	+9.9	+2.5	11	10	5	55	12	52	19	51

Rising and setting times are for latitude 54°

VENUS

Day	R.A. h	m	Dec °	Mag.	Diam. "	Phase %	Rise h	m	Transit h	m	Set h	m
1	9	29.9	+16.7	−4.1	17	70	7	12	14	52	22	33
6	9	51.9	+14.7	−4.1	18	68	7	27	14	55	22	22
11	10	13.3	+12.5	−4.1	18	66	7	42	14	56	22	10
16	10	34.0	+10.3	−4.1	19	64	7	56	14	57	21	57
21	10	54.1	+7.9	−4.1	20	62	8	10	14	57	21	44
26	11	13.7	+5.5	−4.2	21	60	8	24	14	57	21	30
31	11	32.7	+3.1	−4.2	22	57	8	37	14	56	21	16

MARS

Day	R.A. h	m	Dec °	Mag.	Diam. "	Phase %	Rise h	m	Transit h	m	Set h	m
1	20	50.8	−22.9	−2.2	21	97	22	31	2	15	6	01
6	20	49.5	−23.3	−2.3	22	98	22	13	1	54	5	36
11	20	46.9	−23.8	−2.5	23	98	21	55	1	32	5	10
16	20	43.1	−24.4	−2.6	23	99	21	36	1	08	4	42
21	20	38.3	−24.9	−2.7	24	100	21	16	0	44	4	13
26	20	32.9	−25.4	−2.8	24	100	20	56	0	18	3	43
31	20	27.2	−25.9	−2.8	24	100	20	34	23	59	3	14

SUNRISE AND SUNSET

	London				Bristol				Birmingham				Manchester				Newcastle				Glasgow				Belfast			
	0°	05′	51°	30′	2°	35′	51°	28′	1°	55′	52°	28′	2°	15′	53°	28′	1°	37′	54°	59′	4°	14′	55°	52′	5°	56′	54°	35′
d	h	m	h	m	h	m	h	m	h	m	h	m	h	m	h	m	h	m	h	m	h	m	h	m	h	m	h	m
1	3	47	20	21	3	58	20	30	3	49	20	33	3	45	20	41	3	32	20	48	3	36	21	05	3	52	21	03
2	3	48	20	20	3	58	20	30	3	50	20	33	3	45	20	40	3	33	20	48	3	37	21	04	3	53	21	02
3	3	49	20	20	3	59	20	30	3	51	20	33	3	46	20	40	3	34	20	47	3	38	21	04	3	54	21	02
4	3	50	20	19	4	00	20	29	3	52	20	32	3	47	20	39	3	35	20	46	3	39	21	03	3	55	21	01
5	3	50	20	19	4	01	20	29	3	52	20	32	3	48	20	39	3	36	20	46	3	40	21	02	3	56	21	00
6	3	51	20	18	4	02	20	28	3	53	20	31	3	49	20	38	3	37	20	45	3	41	21	02	3	57	21	00
7	3	52	20	18	4	02	20	28	3	54	20	30	3	50	20	37	3	38	20	44	3	42	21	01	3	58	20	59
8	3	53	20	17	4	03	20	27	3	55	20	30	3	51	20	37	3	39	20	44	3	43	21	00	3	59	20	58
9	3	54	20	16	4	04	20	26	3	56	20	29	3	52	20	36	3	40	20	43	3	44	20	59	4	00	20	57
10	3	55	20	16	4	05	20	25	3	57	20	28	3	53	20	35	3	41	20	42	3	46	20	58	4	01	20	56
11	3	56	20	15	4	06	20	25	3	58	20	27	3	54	20	34	3	42	20	41	3	47	20	57	4	02	20	56
12	3	57	20	14	4	07	20	24	4	00	20	26	3	55	20	33	3	44	20	40	3	48	20	56	4	03	20	54
13	3	58	20	13	4	09	20	23	4	01	20	25	3	57	20	32	3	45	20	39	3	50	20	55	4	05	20	53
14	4	00	20	12	4	10	20	22	4	02	20	24	3	58	20	31	3	46	20	37	3	51	20	54	4	06	20	52
15	4	01	20	11	4	11	20	21	4	03	20	23	3	59	20	30	3	48	20	36	3	53	20	52	4	07	20	51
16	4	02	20	10	4	12	20	20	4	04	20	22	4	00	20	29	3	49	20	35	3	54	20	51	4	09	20	50
17	4	03	20	09	4	13	20	19	4	06	20	21	4	02	20	28	3	51	20	34	3	56	20	50	4	10	20	49
18	4	04	20	08	4	15	20	18	4	07	20	20	4	03	20	27	3	52	20	32	3	57	20	48	4	12	20	47
19	4	06	20	07	4	16	20	17	4	08	20	19	4	05	20	25	3	54	20	31	3	59	20	47	4	13	20	46
20	4	07	20	06	4	17	20	16	4	10	20	18	4	06	20	24	3	55	20	30	4	00	20	45	4	15	20	45
21	4	08	20	04	4	18	20	14	4	11	20	16	4	07	20	23	3	57	20	28	4	02	20	44	4	16	20	43
22	4	10	20	03	4	20	20	13	4	12	20	15	4	09	20	21	3	58	20	27	4	04	20	42	4	18	20	42
23	4	11	20	02	4	21	20	12	4	14	20	14	4	10	20	20	4	00	20	25	4	05	20	40	4	19	20	40
24	4	12	20	01	4	22	20	10	4	15	20	12	4	12	20	18	4	01	20	23	4	07	20	39	4	21	20	39
25	4	14	19	59	4	24	20	09	4	17	20	11	4	13	20	17	4	03	20	22	4	09	20	37	4	23	20	37
26	4	15	19	58	4	25	20	08	4	18	20	09	4	15	20	15	4	05	20	20	4	10	20	35	4	24	20	35
27	4	17	19	56	4	27	20	06	4	20	20	08	4	16	20	14	4	06	20	18	4	12	20	33	4	26	20	34
28	4	18	19	55	4	28	20	05	4	21	20	06	4	18	20	12	4	08	20	17	4	14	20	32	4	27	20	32
29	4	19	19	53	4	30	20	03	4	23	20	05	4	20	20	10	4	10	20	15	4	16	20	30	4	29	20	30
30	4	21	19	52	4	31	20	02	4	24	20	03	4	21	20	09	4	12	20	13	4	18	20	28	4	31	20	28
31	4	22	19	50	4	33	20	00	4	25	20	01	4	23	20	07	4	13	20	11	4	20	20	26	4	33	20	26

JUPITER

Day	R.A.		Dec	Mag.	Diam.	Rise		Transit		Set	
	h	m	°		″	h	m	h	m	h	m
1	14	44.5	−14.8	−2.3	41	15	27	20	05	0	48
11	14	43.9	−14.8	−2.2	40	14	47	19	26	0	08
21	14	44.4	−14.8	−2.2	39	14	09	18	47	23	25
31	14	46.2	−15.0	−2.1	38	13	32	18	09	22	46

Equatorial Diam. 41″, Polar Diam. 39″

SATURN

Day	R.A.		Dec	Mag.	Diam.	Rise		Transit		Set	
	h	m	°		″	h	m	h	m	h	m
1	18	23.1	−22.5	0.0	18	19	57	23	43	3	33
11	18	20.0	−22.5	+0.1	18	19	15	23	01	2	50
21	18	17.1	−22.6	+0.1	18	18	33	22	19	2	08
31	18	14.5	−22.6	+0.2	18	17	52	21	37	1	26

Equatorial Diam. 18″, Polar Diam. 17″
Rings – major axis 41″ minor axis 18″, Tilt 26°

URANUS

Day	R.A.		Dec	Mag.	Diam.	Rise		Transit		Set	
	h	m	°		″	h	m	h	m	h	m
1	1	59.1	+11.6	+5.9	3	0	13	7	22	14	30
11	2	00.0	+11.7	+5.8	4	23	35	6	44	13	53
21	2	00.7	+11.7	+5.8	4	22	56	6	05	13	14
31	2	01.1	+11.8	+5.8	4	22	16	5	26	12	36

NEPTUNE

Day	R.A.		Dec	Mag.	Diam.	Rise		Transit		Set	
	h	m	°		″	h	m	h	m	h	m
1	23	10.7	−6.3	+7.9	2	23	02	4	34	10	02
11	23	10.4	−6.4	+7.9	2	22	23	3	54	9	22
21	23	09.9	−6.4	+7.8	2	21	43	3	14	8	42
31	23	09.2	−6.5	+7.8	2	21	04	2	35	8	01

 # August 2018

EIGHTH MONTH, 31 DAYS. *Augustus*, formerly *Sextilis*, sixth month of Roman pre-Julian calendar

1	*Wednesday*	The Warsaw uprising begins in Poland 1914	day 213
2	*Thursday*	A large bomb blast leaves dozens dead in Bologna 1980	214
3	*Friday*	Germany and France declare war 1914	215
4	*Saturday*	Gibraltar is captured by English and Dutch ships during the War of Spanish Succession 1704	216
5	*Sunday*	The provisional government of Lithuania is dissolved following German invasion 1941	217
6	*Monday*	The USSR launches a cosmonaut into space for an entire day 1961	week 32 day 218
7	*Tuesday*	The German army takes the Citadel of Liège 1914	219
8	*Wednesday*	The Battle of Amiens begins 1918	220
9	*Thursday*	Northern Ireland activates an internment law under the Civil Authorities Act 1971	221
10	*Friday*	Byrhtnoth, Ealdorman of Essex is defeated by Viking invaders at the Battle of Maldon 991	222
11	*Saturday*	John Henry Newman, a leader of the Oxford Movement d. 1890	223
12	*Sunday*	The East German army begins to close the border with West Berlin 1961	224
13	*Monday*	The Berlin wall is erected 1961	week 33 day 225
14	*Tuesday*	British troops are sent into Northern Ireland to restore law and order 1969	226
15	*Wednesday*	Following the surrender of Japan the Allied nations celebrate Victory in Japan (VJ) Day 1945	227
16	*Thursday*	Cyprus gains independence from the United Kingdom 1960	228
17	*Friday*	Napoleon Bonaparte leads France to victory against the Russians at Smolensk 1812	229
18	*Saturday*	William Cavendish, 1st Duke of Devonshire and Whig politician d. 1707	230
19	*Sunday*	The Allied Forces launch a beach raid on Dieppe 1942	231
20	*Monday*	Bulgaria wins a decisive victory against the Byzantine empire at the Battle of Anchialus 917	week 34 day 232
21	*Tuesday*	A coup d'état by Gustav III ends the Age of Liberty and parliamentary rule in Sweden 1772	233
22	*Wednesday*	Ida Siekmann becomes the first person to die while attempting to cross the Berlin wall 1961	234
23	*Thursday*	The Baltic Way, a 2 million-strong human chain demonstration against Soviet occupation occurs 1989	235
24	*Friday*	St Bartholomew's Day massacre begins in Paris 1572	236
25	*Saturday*	Riots break out in Brussels following a performance of Auber's opera *La Muette de Portici* 1830	237
26	*Sunday*	The English are victorious at the Battle of Crécy 1346	238
27	*Monday*	Romania declares war on Austria-Hungary and enters the First World War 1916	week 35 239
28	*Tuesday*	The first naval Battle of Heligoland Bight takes place 1914	240
29	*Wednesday*	Astrid Bernadotte, Queen consort of the Belgians d. 1935	241
30	*Thursday*	Samuel Whitbread, English brewer and MP b. 1720	242
31	*Friday*	The IRA announces a complete cessation of military operations 1994	243

ASTRONOMICAL PHENOMENA

d	h	
3	21	Uranus 5° North of the Moon
11	1	Mercury 6° South of the Moon
12	19	Peak of the Perseid meteor shower
14	13	Venus 6° South of the Moon
17	10	Jupiter 5° South of the Moon
17	18	Venus greatest elongation East
21	9	Saturn 2° South of the Moon
26	21	Mercury greatest elongation West
27	10	Neptune 2° North of the Moon
31	3	Uranus 5° North of the Moon

MINIMA OF ALGOL

d	h	d	h	d	h
1	20.7	13	8.0	24	19.2
4	17.5	16	4.8	27	16.0
7	14.4	19	1.6	30	12.8
10	11.2	21	22.4		

CONSTELLATIONS

The following constellations are near the meridian at

	d	h		d	h
July	1	24	August	16	21
July	16	23	September	1	20
August	1	22	September	15	19

Draco, Hercules, Lyra, Cygnus, Sagitta, Ophiuchus, Serpens, Aquila and Sagittarius

THE MOON

Phases, Apsides and Node	d	h	m
◑ Last Quarter	4	18	18
● New Moon	11	9	58
◐ First Quarter	18	7	49
○ Full Moon	26	11	56
Perigee (358,078 km)	10	18	7
Apogee (405,746 km)	23	11	23

Mean longitude of the ascending node on 1st, 126°

THE SUN

Diam. 31.5′

Day	Right Ascension h	m	s	Dec. + °	Equation of time m	s	Rise 52° h	m	Rise 56° h	m	Transit h	m	Set 52° h	m	Set 56° h	m	Sidereal time h	m	s	Transit of first point of Aries h	m	s
1	8	44	37	18.1	-6	24	4	22	4	04	12	06	19	50	20	08	20	38	14	3	21	46
2	8	48	29	17.8	-6	20	4	23	4	06	12	06	19	48	20	06	20	42	10	3	17	50
3	8	52	22	17.6	-6	16	4	25	4	08	12	06	19	47	20	04	20	46	07	3	13	53
4	8	56	13	17.3	-6	11	4	26	4	10	12	06	19	45	20	01	20	50	03	3	09	57
5	9	00	04	17.0	-6	05	4	28	4	11	12	06	19	43	19	59	20	54	00	3	06	00
6	9	03	54	16.8	-5	59	4	29	4	13	12	06	19	41	19	57	20	57	56	3	02	04
7	9	07	44	16.5	-5	52	4	31	4	15	12	06	19	40	19	55	21	01	53	2	58	07
8	9	11	33	16.2	-5	45	4	33	4	17	12	06	19	38	19	53	21	05	49	2	54	11
9	9	15	22	15.9	-5	37	4	34	4	19	12	06	19	36	19	51	21	09	46	2	50	14
10	9	19	10	15.6	-5	28	4	36	4	21	12	05	19	34	19	48	21	13	43	2	46	17
11	9	22	58	15.3	-5	19	4	37	4	23	12	05	19	32	19	46	21	17	39	2	42	21
12	9	26	45	15.0	-5	10	4	39	4	25	12	05	19	30	19	44	21	21	36	2	38	24
13	9	30	31	14.7	-5	00	4	41	4	27	12	05	19	28	19	42	21	25	32	2	34	28
14	9	34	17	14.4	-4	49	4	42	4	29	12	05	19	26	19	39	21	29	29	2	30	31
15	9	38	02	14.1	-4	38	4	44	4	31	12	05	19	24	19	37	21	33	25	2	26	35
16	9	41	47	13.8	-4	26	4	45	4	33	12	04	19	22	19	35	21	37	22	2	22	38
17	9	45	31	13.5	-4	13	4	47	4	35	12	04	19	20	19	32	21	41	18	2	18	42
18	9	49	15	13.2	-4	00	4	49	4	37	12	04	19	18	19	30	21	45	15	2	14	45
19	9	52	58	12.9	-3	47	4	50	4	39	12	04	19	16	19	27	21	49	12	2	10	48
20	9	56	40	12.5	-3	33	4	52	4	41	12	03	19	14	19	25	21	53	08	2	06	52
21	10	00	22	12.2	-3	19	4	54	4	42	12	03	19	12	19	23	21	57	05	2	02	55
22	10	04	04	11.9	-3	04	4	55	4	44	12	03	19	09	19	20	22	01	01	1	58	59
23	10	07	45	11.5	-2	48	4	57	4	46	12	03	19	07	19	18	22	04	58	1	55	02
24	10	11	26	11.2	-2	32	4	58	4	48	12	02	19	05	19	15	22	08	54	1	51	06
25	10	15	06	10.8	-2	16	5	00	4	50	12	02	19	03	19	13	22	12	51	1	47	09
26	10	18	46	10.5	-1	59	5	02	4	52	12	02	19	01	19	10	22	16	47	1	43	13
27	10	22	25	10.2	-1	42	5	03	4	54	12	02	18	59	19	08	22	20	44	1	39	16
28	10	26	05	9.8	-1	25	5	05	4	56	12	01	18	56	19	05	22	24	41	1	35	19
29	10	29	43	9.4	-1	07	5	07	4	58	12	01	18	54	19	02	22	28	37	1	31	23
30	10	33	22	9.1	-0	49	5	08	5	00	12	01	18	52	19	00	22	32	34	1	27	26
31	10	37	00	8.7	-0	30	5	10	5	02	12	00	18	50	18	57	22	36	30	1	23	30

DURATION OF TWILIGHT

Latitude	52°	56°	52°	56°	52°	56°	52°	56°
	1 August		11 August		21 August		31 August	
Civil	41	49	39	45	37	42	35	40
Nautical	97	121	90	107	84	97	79	90
Astronomical	179	TAN	154	210	139	168	128	148

THE NIGHT SKY

Mercury moves into the morning sky after inferior conjunction on the 9th and is visible during the second half of the month, gaining altitude each day until standing highest for this apparition on the 28th/29th.

Venus (magnitude −4.3 to −4.6) sets 1.5 hours after the Sun on the 1st but less than one hour after by the 31st. The disk shows a half phase mid-month and thereafter will narrow while growing in apparent size. The 34.5 hour-old Moon is close by on the 12th and the planet is at greatest elongation east on the 17th.

Mars (magnitude −2.5 to −2.1) tapers a little in brightness as it recedes from Earth but still is not setting until the early hours. Mars crosses into Sagittarius in late August and is stationary on the 28th when direct motion resumes. The Moon is nearby on the 23rd.

Jupiter (magnitude −2.1 to −1.9) loiters near Alpha Librae mid-month and is 0.5° from the star on the 17th – the Moon is 5° away on the same night. Jupiter sets mid-evening by the end of August.

Saturn (magnitude 0.3) remains a fine sight this month and doesn't set until around midnight. The Moon is nearby on the 20th and 21st.

A partial solar eclipse on August 11th is visible from northern Europe and northeast Asia. The maximum eclipse magnitude is 0.736. The Sun is less than 2 per cent covered from the northern tip of Scotland.

The Perseid meteor shower has favourable conditions for maximum on August 12th.

THE MOON

Day	R.A.		Dec	Hor Par	Diam	Sun Co-Long	PA of Br. limb	Ph.	Age	Rise				Transit		Set			
										52°		56°				52°		56°	
	h	m	°	′	′	°	°	%	d	h	m	h	m	h	m	h	m	h	m
1	23	46	−5.9	55.0	30.0	141	70	85	18.7	21	56	21	58	3	13	9	02	8	58
2	0	32	−1.6	55.5	30.2	153	70	77	19.7	22	17	22	15	3	57	10	10	10	10
3	1	19	+2.9	56.1	30.6	166	70	68	20.7	22	38	22	32	4	41	11	20	11	24
4	2	08	+7.3	56.8	31.0	178	71	58	21.7	23	03	22	53	5	28	12	32	12	40
5	2	58	+11.5	57.6	31.4	190	73	48	22.7	23	31	23	18	6	17	13	45	13	58
6	3	52	+15.2	58.5	31.9	202	76	37	23.7	—		23	50	7	10	15	00	15	18
7	4	49	+18.2	59.4	32.3	214	81	26	24.7	0	08	—		8	06	16	15	16	35
8	5	50	+20.1	60.1	32.8	227	86	17	25.7	0	53	0	32	9	06	17	23	17	45
9	6	53	+20.8	60.8	33.1	239	92	09	26.7	1	51	1	29	10	08	18	23	18	43
10	7	57	+19.9	61.1	33.3	251	99	03	27.7	3	01	2	40	11	11	19	11	19	29
11	9	00	+17.7	61.2	33.4	263	112	00	28.7	4	20	4	03	12	12	19	50	20	03
12	10	02	+14.2	61.0	33.2	276	277	01	0.2	5	43	5	30	13	10	20	22	20	31
13	11	00	+9.8	60.5	32.9	288	285	04	1.2	7	06	6	59	14	05	20	48	20	53
14	11	56	+5.0	59.7	32.5	300	288	10	2.2	8	27	8	24	14	57	21	13	21	13
15	12	49	+0.0	58.8	32.0	312	289	17	3.2	9	45	9	47	15	47	21	35	21	32
16	13	40	−4.9	57.8	31.5	325	288	27	4.2	11	00	11	06	16	35	21	59	21	51
17	14	31	−9.3	56.9	31.0	337	287	37	5.2	12	13	12	23	17	23	22	23	22	12
18	15	21	−13.2	56.1	30.6	349	284	47	6.2	13	22	13	36	18	10	22	52	22	36
19	16	11	−16.3	55.4	30.2	1	281	57	7.2	14	28	14	45	18	58	23	23	23	06
20	17	01	−18.7	54.8	29.9	13	277	66	8.2	15	28	15	48	19	46	—		23	41
21	17	52	−20.2	54.4	29.7	26	273	75	9.2	16	23	16	44	20	35	0	02	—	
22	18	42	−20.8	54.2	29.5	38	268	83	10.2	17	10	17	32	21	23	0	46	0	24
23	19	33	−20.4	54.1	29.5	50	263	89	11.2	17	51	18	11	22	11	1	37	1	16
24	20	23	−19.2	54.1	29.5	62	257	94	12.2	18	26	18	42	22	57	2	33	2	15
25	21	12	−17.1	54.2	29.5	74	250	98	13.2	18	54	19	08	23	43	3	35	3	19
26	22	00	−14.2	54.4	29.6	87	231	100	14.2	19	19	19	30	—		4	39	4	27
27	22	48	−10.8	54.6	29.8	99	95	100	15.2	19	42	19	48	0	28	5	46	5	37
28	23	35	−6.8	55.0	30.0	111	79	98	16.2	20	02	20	05	1	12	6	53	6	48
29	0	21	−2.5	55.4	30.2	123	75	94	17.2	20	23	20	22	1	56	8	01	8	00
30	1	08	+1.9	55.8	30.4	135	73	88	18.2	20	44	20	39	2	40	9	11	9	14
31	1	56	+6.3	56.4	30.7	148	74	81	19.2	21	07	20	58	3	26	10	22	10	29

MERCURY

Day	R.A.		Dec	Mag.	Diam.	Phase	Rise		Transit		Set	
	h	m	°		″	%	h	m	h	m	h	m
1	9	30.8	+9.9	+2.8	11	8	5	49	12	46	19	45
3	9	26.3	+10.1	+3.3	11	5	5	36	12	33	19	33
5	9	20.9	+10.4	+3.9	11	3	5	21	12	20	19	22
7	9	15.1	+10.8	+4.5	11	2	5	04	12	06	19	11
9	9	09.1	+11.4	+4.8	11	1	4	47	11	53	19	01
11	9	03.4	+12.0	+4.5	11	2	4	30	11	39	18	52
13	8	58.4	+12.7	+3.8	11	3	4	13	11	27	18	44
15	8	54.6	+13.4	+3.1	10	6	3	57	11	16	18	37
17	8	52.3	+14.1	+2.3	10	10	3	43	11	06	18	32
19	8	51.8	+14.8	+1.7	9	15	3	31	10	59	18	28
21	8	53.3	+15.3	+1.1	9	21	3	22	10	53	18	26
23	8	56.8	+15.6	+0.6	8	28	3	16	10	49	18	25
25	9	02.4	+15.9	+0.2	8	36	3	12	10	47	18	24
27	9	09.8	+15.9	−0.1	7	44	3	12	10	47	18	24
29	9	19.1	+15.7	−0.4	7	52	3	15	10	49	18	25
31	9	29.9	+15.3	−0.7	7	61	3	20	10	53	18	25

Rising and setting times are for latitude 54°

VENUS

Day	R.A.		Dec	Mag.	Diam.	Phase	Rise		Transit		Set	
	h	m	°		″	%	h	m	h	m	h	m
1	11	36.4	+2.6	−4.2	22	57	8	39	14	56	21	13
6	11	54.8	+0.2	−4.2	23	55	8	51	14	55	20	58
11	12	12.7	−2.3	−4.3	24	52	9	03	14	53	20	42
16	12	30.0	−4.7	−4.3	26	50	9	13	14	50	20	26
21	12	46.7	−7.1	−4.4	27	47	9	24	14	47	20	10
26	13	02.9	−9.4	−4.4	29	44	9	33	14	43	19	53
31	13	18.2	−11.6	−4.4	31	41	9	41	14	38	19	35

MARS

Day	R.A.		Dec	Mag.	Diam.	Phase	Rise		Transit		Set	
	h	m	°		″	%	h	m	h	m	h	m
1	20	26.1	−26.0	−2.8	24	100	20	30	23	54	3	08
6	20	20.5	−26.3	−2.7	24	99	20	07	23	28	2	40
11	20	15.5	−26.5	−2.6	24	99	19	44	23	03	2	14
16	20	11.5	−26.6	−2.5	23	98	19	21	22	39	1	49
21	20	08.7	−26.5	−2.4	23	97	18	58	22	16	1	27
26	20	07.3	−26.3	−2.3	22	96	18	35	21	54	1	07
31	20	07.3	−26.1	−2.1	21	94	18	13	21	34	0	49

SUNRISE AND SUNSET

	London 0° 05′	51° 30′	Bristol 2° 35′	51° 28′	Birmingham 1° 55′	52° 28′	Manchester 2° 15′	53° 28′	Newcastle 1° 37′	54° 59′	Glasgow 4° 14′	55° 52′	Belfast 5° 56′	54° 35′
d	h m	h m	h m	h m	h m	h m	h m	h m	h m	h m	h m	h m	h m	h m
1	4 24	19 48	4 34	19 58	4 27	20 00	4 25	20 05	4 15	20 09	4 21	20 24	4 34	20 25
2	4 25	19 47	4 36	19 57	4 29	19 58	4 26	20 03	4 17	20 07	4 23	20 22	4 36	20 23
3	4 27	19 45	4 37	19 55	4 31	19 56	4 28	20 01	4 19	20 05	4 25	20 20	4 38	20 21
4	4 28	19 43	4 39	19 53	4 32	19 54	4 30	20 00	4 21	20 03	4 27	20 18	4 40	20 19
5	4 30	19 42	4 40	19 52	4 34	19 53	4 31	19 58	4 22	20 01	4 29	20 16	4 41	20 17
6	4 32	19 40	4 42	19 50	4 35	19 51	4 33	19 56	4 24	19 59	4 31	20 14	4 43	20 15
7	4 33	19 38	4 43	19 48	4 37	19 49	4 35	19 54	4 26	19 57	4 33	20 11	4 45	20 13
8	4 35	19 36	4 45	19 46	4 39	19 47	4 36	19 52	4 28	19 55	4 35	20 09	4 47	20 11
9	4 36	19 34	4 46	19 44	4 40	19 45	4 38	19 50	4 30	19 53	4 37	20 07	4 49	20 09
10	4 38	19 33	4 48	19 42	4 42	19 43	4 40	19 48	4 32	19 51	4 38	20 05	4 50	20 07
11	4 39	19 31	4 49	19 41	4 44	19 41	4 41	19 46	4 33	19 49	4 40	20 03	4 52	20 04
12	4 41	19 29	4 51	19 39	4 45	19 39	4 43	19 44	4 35	19 47	4 42	20 00	4 54	20 02
13	4 42	19 27	4 53	19 37	4 47	19 37	4 45	19 42	4 37	19 44	4 44	19 58	4 56	20 00
14	4 44	19 25	4 54	19 35	4 48	19 35	4 47	19 40	4 39	19 42	4 46	19 56	4 58	19 58
15	4 46	19 23	4 56	19 33	4 50	19 33	4 48	19 37	4 41	19 40	4 48	19 53	4 59	19 56
16	4 47	19 21	4 57	19 31	4 52	19 31	4 50	19 35	4 43	19 38	4 50	19 51	5 01	19 54
17	4 49	19 19	4 59	19 29	4 53	19 29	4 52	19 33	4 45	19 35	4 52	19 49	5 03	19 51
18	4 50	19 17	5 01	19 27	4 55	19 27	4 54	19 31	4 46	19 33	4 54	19 46	5 05	19 49
19	4 52	19 15	5 02	19 25	4 57	19 25	4 55	19 29	4 48	19 31	4 56	19 44	5 07	19 47
20	4 54	19 13	5 04	19 23	4 58	19 23	4 57	19 27	4 50	19 28	4 58	19 41	5 09	19 44
21	4 55	19 11	5 05	19 21	5 00	19 20	4 59	19 24	4 52	19 26	5 00	19 39	5 10	19 42
22	4 57	19 09	5 07	19 18	5 02	19 18	5 01	19 22	4 54	19 24	5 02	19 37	5 12	19 40
23	4 58	19 06	5 08	19 16	5 03	19 16	5 02	19 20	4 56	19 21	5 04	19 34	5 14	19 37
24	5 00	19 04	5 10	19 14	5 05	19 14	5 04	19 18	4 58	19 19	5 06	19 32	5 16	19 35
25	5 02	19 02	5 12	19 12	5 07	19 12	5 06	19 15	4 59	19 16	5 08	19 29	5 18	19 33
26	5 03	19 00	5 13	19 10	5 08	19 09	5 07	19 13	5 01	19 14	5 10	19 27	5 20	19 30
27	5 05	18 58	5 15	19 08	5 10	19 07	5 09	19 11	5 03	19 11	5 11	19 24	5 21	19 28
28	5 06	18 56	5 16	19 06	5 12	19 05	5 11	19 08	5 05	19 09	5 13	19 22	5 23	19 25
29	5 08	18 54	5 18	19 03	5 13	19 03	5 13	19 06	5 07	19 07	5 15	19 19	5 25	19 23
30	5 09	18 51	5 20	19 01	5 15	19 00	5 14	19 04	5 09	19 04	5 17	19 16	5 27	19 21
31	5 11	18 49	5 21	18 59	5 17	18 58	5 16	19 01	5 11	19 02	5 19	19 14	5 29	19 18

JUPITER

Day	R.A. h m	Dec °	Mag.	Diam. ″	Rise h m	Transit h m	Set h m
1	14 46.4	−15.0	−2.1	38	13 29	18 05	22 42
11	14 49.4	−15.3	−2.0	37	12 54	17 29	22 04
21	14 53.3	−15.6	−2.0	36	12 21	16 54	21 27
31	14 58.3	−16.0	−1.9	35	11 49	16 19	20 50

Equatorial Diam. 38″, Polar Diam. 35″

SATURN

Day	R.A. h m	Dec °	Mag.	Diam. ″	Rise h m	Transit h m	Set h m
1	18 14.3	−22.6	+0.2	18	17 48	21 33	1 22
11	18 12.3	−22.6	+0.3	18	17 07	20 51	0 40
21	18 10.8	−22.7	+0.3	18	16 26	20 11	23 59
31	18 10.0	−22.7	+0.4	17	15 46	19 30	23 15

Equatorial Diam. 18″, Polar Diam. 16″
Rings – major axis 40″ minor axis 18″, Tilt 27°

URANUS

Day	R.A. h m	Dec °	Mag.	Diam. ″	Rise h m	Transit h m	Set h m
1	2 01.2	+11.8	+5.8	4	22 13	5 22	12 32
11	2 01.2	+11.8	+5.8	4	21 33	4 43	11 52
21	2 01.0	+11.7	+5.8	4	20 54	4 03	11 13
31	2 00.4	+11.7	+5.7	4	20 14	3 23	10 32

NEPTUNE

Day	R.A. h m	Dec °	Mag.	Diam. ″	Rise h m	Transit h m	Set h m
1	23 09.1	−6.5	+7.8	2	21 00	2 30	7 57
11	23 08.3	−6.6	+7.8	2	20 20	1 50	7 17
21	23 07.4	−6.7	+7.8	2	19 40	1 10	6 36
31	23 06.4	−6.8	+7.8	2	19 01	0 30	5 55

 # September 2018

NINTH MONTH, 30 DAYS. *Septem* (seven), seventh month of Roman pre-Julian calendar

1	*Saturday*	Germany invades Poland 1939	day 244
2	*Sunday*	King George II marries Princess Caroline of Brandenburg-Ansbach 1705	245

3	*Monday*	Britain and France declare war on Germany 1939	week 36 day 246
4	*Tuesday*	Queen Wilhemina of the Netherlands abdicates from the throne 1948	247
5	*Wednesday*	The Hilton hotel in London is bombed by the IRA 1975	248
6	*Thursday*	Lithuania's independence is officially recognised by the Soviet Union 1991	249
7	*Friday*	Baudouin I, king of the Belgians (1951–93) *b*. 1930	250
8	*Saturday*	A Bulgarian republic is established following a referendum 1946	251
9	*Sunday*	25 English football fans involved in the Heysel stadium disaster arrive in Belgium to stand trial 1987	252

10	*Monday*	Pablo Picasso's painting *Guernica* is returned to Spain 1981	week 37 253
11	*Tuesday*	The French army of Louis XIV was defeated at the battle of Malplaquet 1709	254
12	*Wednesday*	Scotland votes in favour of home rule in a referendum on Scottish governance 1997	255
13	*Thursday*	Miguel Primo de Rivera overthrows the Spanish government, after a military coup 1923	256
14	*Friday*	The USSR expels 25 British nationals in response to the British expulsion of alleged Soviet spies 1985	257
15	*Saturday*	Battle of Britain Day: the RAF defended Britain against a massive Luftwaffe assault 1940	258
16	*Sunday*	The United Kingdom suspends its membership of the European Exchange Rate Mechanism 1992	259

17	*Monday*	Jan Peder Syse, Norwegian politician and prime minister of Norway (1989–90) *d*. 1997	week 38 260
18	*Tuesday*	The Treaty of Belgrade ends the war between the Ottomans and the Habsburgs 1739	261
19	*Wednesday*	The Soviet Union and Finland sign the Moscow Armistice 1944	262
20	*Thursday*	The French defeat the Prussians at the Battle of Valmy 1792	263
21	*Friday*	The National Convention declares France a republic and abolishes its absolute monarchy 1792	264
22	*Saturday*	George III is crowned 1761	265
23	*Sunday*	Negotiations on the Karlstad Treaty end with an agreement to disunite Sweden and Norway 1905	266

24	*Monday*	Alfonso IX, king of León and Galicia (188–1230) *d*. 1230	week 39 267
25	*Tuesday*	King Harold II defeats Norwegian king Harald Hardrada at the Battle of Stamford Bridge 1066	268
26	*Wednesday*	Pope Paul VI (1963–78) *b*. 1897	269
27	*Thursday*	Louis XIII, king of France (1610–43) *b*. 1601	270
28	*Friday*	A referendum establishes a French community of states, linking France with its former colonies 1958	271
29	*Saturday*	Lech Walesa, president of Poland and Nobel Peace Prize laureate *b*. 1943	272
30	*Sunday*	Neville Chamberlain makes his 'peace for our time' speech on the Munich Agreement 1938	273

ASTRONOMICAL PHENOMENA

d	*h*	
2	9	Spica 1.5° North of Venus
7	18	Neptune at opposition
8	22	Mercury 1° South of the Moon
14	2	Jupiter 4° South of the Moon
17	16	Saturn 2° South of the Moon
20	6	Mars 5° South of the Moon
23	1	Equinox
23	16	Neptune 2° North of the Moon
27	3	Vesta 3° South of Saturn
27	7	Uranus 5° North of the Moon

MINIMA OF ALGOL

d	*h*	*d*	*h*	*d*	*h*
2	9.6	13	20.9	25	8.1
5	6.5	16	17.7	28	4.9
8	3.3	19	14.5		
11	0.1	22	11.3		

CONSTELLATIONS

The following constellations are near the meridian at

	d	*h*		*d*	*h*
August	1	24	September	15	21
August	16	23	October	1	20
September	1	22	October	16	19

Draco, Cepheus, Lyra, Cygnus, Vulpecula, Sagitta, Delphinus, Equuleus, Aquila, Aquarius and Capricornus

THE MOON

Phases, Apsides and Node	*d*	*h*	*m*
◑ Last Quarter	3	2	37
● New Moon	9	18	1
◐ First Quarter	16	23	15
○ Full Moon	25	2	52
Perigee (361,351 km)	8	1	20
Apogee (404,876 km)	20	0	53

Mean longitude of the ascending node on 1st, 124°

THE SUN

Diam. 31.7′

Day	Right Ascension			Dec.	Equation of time		Rise 52°		Rise 56°		Transit		Set 52°		Set 56°		Sidereal time			Transit of first point of Aries		
	h	m	s	°	m	s	h	m	h	m	h	m	h	m	h	m	h	m	s	h	m	s
1	10	40	37	+8.4	−0	11	5	12	5	04	12	00	18	47	18	55	22	40	27	1	19	33
2	10	44	15	+8.0	+0	08	5	13	5	06	12	00	18	45	18	52	22	44	23	1	15	37
3	10	47	52	+7.6	+0	27	5	15	5	08	11	59	18	43	18	50	22	48	20	1	11	40
4	10	51	29	+7.3	+0	47	5	16	5	10	11	59	18	41	18	47	22	52	16	1	07	44
5	10	55	06	+6.9	+1	06	5	18	5	12	11	59	18	38	18	44	22	56	13	1	03	47
6	10	58	42	+6.5	+1	26	5	20	5	14	11	58	18	36	18	42	23	00	10	0	59	50
7	11	02	19	+6.2	+1	47	5	21	5	16	11	58	18	34	18	39	23	04	06	0	55	54
8	11	05	55	+5.8	+2	07	5	23	5	18	11	58	18	31	18	36	23	08	03	0	51	57
9	11	09	31	+5.4	+2	28	5	25	5	20	11	57	18	29	18	34	23	11	59	0	48	01
10	11	13	06	+5.0	+2	49	5	26	5	22	11	57	18	27	18	31	23	15	56	0	44	04
11	11	16	42	+4.7	+3	09	5	28	5	23	11	57	18	24	18	29	23	19	52	0	40	08
12	11	20	18	+4.3	+3	30	5	29	5	25	11	56	18	22	18	26	23	23	49	0	36	11
13	11	23	53	+3.9	+3	52	5	31	5	27	11	56	18	20	18	23	23	27	45	0	32	15
14	11	27	28	+3.5	+4	13	5	33	5	29	11	56	18	17	18	21	23	31	42	0	28	18
15	11	31	03	+3.1	+4	34	5	34	5	31	11	55	18	15	18	18	23	35	39	0	24	21
16	11	34	39	+2.7	+4	56	5	36	5	33	11	55	18	13	18	15	23	39	35	0	20	25
17	11	38	14	+2.4	+5	17	5	38	5	35	11	55	18	10	18	13	23	43	32	0	16	28
18	11	41	49	+2.0	+5	38	5	39	5	37	11	54	18	08	18	10	23	47	28	0	12	32
19	11	45	24	+1.6	+6	00	5	41	5	39	11	54	18	06	18	07	23	51	25	0	08	35
20	11	48	59	+1.2	+6	21	5	42	5	41	11	53	18	03	18	05	23	55	21	0	04	39
21	11	52	34	+0.8	+6	43	5	44	5	43	11	53	18	01	18	02	23	59	18	0	00	42
22	11	56	10	+0.4	+7	04	5	46	5	45	11	53	17	59	17	59	0	03	14	23	56	46
23	11	59	45	+0.0	+7	25	5	47	5	47	11	52	17	56	17	57	0	07	11	23	52	49
24	12	03	20	−0.4	+7	46	5	49	5	49	11	52	17	54	17	54	0	11	08	23	48	52
25	12	06	56	−0.8	+8	07	5	51	5	51	11	52	17	52	17	51	0	15	04	23	44	56
26	12	10	32	−1.1	+8	28	5	52	5	53	11	51	17	49	17	49	0	19	01	23	40	59
27	12	14	08	−1.5	+8	49	5	54	5	55	11	51	17	47	17	46	0	22	57	23	37	03
28	12	17	44	−1.9	+9	09	5	56	5	57	11	51	17	45	17	43	0	26	54	23	33	06
29	12	21	20	−2.3	+9	29	5	57	5	59	11	50	17	42	17	41	0	30	50	23	29	10
30	12	24	57	−2.7	+9	49	5	59	6	01	11	50	17	40	17	38	0	34	47	23	25	13

DURATION OF TWILIGHT

Latitude	52°	56°	52°	56°	52°	56°	52°	56°
	1 September		11 September		21 September		31 September	
Civil	35	39	34	38	34	37	34	37
Nautical	79	89	76	85	74	82	73	80
Astronomical	127	147	120	136	116	129	113	125

THE NIGHT SKY

Mercury rises nearly two hours before the Sun on the 1st but then quickly dips back into the solar glare to be lost around mid-month. It is 1° from Regulus on the 6th and the Moon is 36.5 hours from New when 8.5° to Mercury's upper right on the 8th. Mercury is at superior conjunction on the 21st.

Venus (magnitude −4.7) may be spotted the first ten days of the month before being lost to view until November. It lies just over 1° from Spica on the 1st.

Mars (magnitude −2.1 to −1.3) still has plenty to offer the telescope user even though the apparent disk size is getting smaller. It crosses into Capricornus at the beginning of September, with the planet setting by midnight on the 30th. The Moon is nearby on the 19th.

Jupiter (magnitude −1.8) sets earlier and earlier these evenings, with it departing 1.5 hours after the Sun on the 30th. The Moon is near the giant planet on the 13th.

Saturn (magnitude 0.5) is stationary on the 6th after which direct motion resumes. This brings it within 2° of the Lagoon Nebula (M8) on the 8th. The Moon is close by on the 17th and two days later the rings are tipped their maximum earthward (26.61°) for 2018. Saturn is at eastern quadrature this month too, so you'll see the globe's shadow cast. The Ringed Planet is setting late-evening by the end of September.

Neptune (magnitude 7.8) is at opposition on September 7th in Aquarius.

THE MOON

Day	R.A. h	R.A. m	Dec °	Hor Par '	Diam '	Sun Co-Long °	PA of Br. limb °	Ph. %	Age d	Rise 52° h	Rise 52° m	Rise 56° h	Rise 56° m	Transit h	Transit m	Set 52° h	Set 52° m	Set 56° h	Set 56° m
1	2	45	+10.6	57.0	31.0	160	75	72	20.2	21	33	21	20	4	13	11	34	11	45
2	3	37	+14.4	57.6	31.4	172	78	62	21.2	22	06	21	49	5	04	12	47	13	02
3	4	32	+17.5	58.3	31.8	184	82	51	22.2	22	45	22	25	5	57	13	59	14	19
4	5	30	+19.7	59.0	32.1	196	86	40	23.2	23	36	23	15	6	53	15	08	15	30
5	6	30	+20.8	59.6	32.5	209	92	29	24.2	—		—		7	53	16	09	16	32
6	7	32	+20.5	60.2	32.8	221	98	19	25.2	0	39	0	17	8	54	17	01	17	21
7	8	34	+18.8	60.5	33.0	233	104	11	26.2	1	52	1	33	9	54	17	44	17	59
8	9	35	+15.8	60.7	33.1	245	112	04	27.2	3	12	2	58	10	53	18	18	18	30
9	10	35	+11.8	60.6	33.0	257	126	01	28.2	4	35	4	25	11	49	18	47	18	54
10	11	32	+7.1	60.2	32.8	270	246	00	29.2	5	58	5	53	12	43	19	12	19	15
11	12	26	+2.0	59.6	32.5	282	279	02	0.6	7	19	7	19	13	34	19	36	19	34
12	13	19	−3.0	58.8	32.0	294	284	07	1.6	8	37	8	42	14	24	19	59	19	53
13	14	11	−7.8	57.9	31.6	306	284	14	2.6	9	53	10	01	15	14	20	24	20	14
14	15	03	−12.0	57.0	31.1	319	283	22	3.6	11	06	11	19	16	02	20	51	20	37
15	15	54	−15.5	56.2	30.6	331	280	31	4.6	12	15	12	32	16	51	21	22	21	05
16	16	45	−18.2	55.5	30.2	343	277	41	5.6	13	19	13	39	17	40	21	58	21	37
17	17	36	−20.0	54.9	29.9	355	272	50	6.6	14	17	14	38	18	29	22	40	22	18
18	18	27	−20.8	54.5	29.7	7	268	60	7.6	15	07	15	29	19	18	23	29	23	08
19	19	18	−20.7	54.2	29.6	20	263	69	8.6	15	50	16	11	20	06	—		—	
20	20	09	−19.7	54.2	29.5	32	258	77	9.6	16	27	16	45	20	53	0	24	0	05
21	20	58	−17.8	54.2	29.5	44	253	85	10.6	16	57	17	12	21	39	1	24	1	07
22	21	47	−15.2	54.4	29.7	56	248	91	11.6	17	23	17	35	22	24	2	28	2	14
23	22	34	−11.8	54.7	29.8	68	242	96	12.6	17	46	17	54	23	09	3	34	3	24
24	23	22	−8.0	55.1	30.0	81	232	99	13.6	18	07	18	11	23	53	4	42	4	35
25	0	09	−3.7	55.5	30.3	93	175	100	14.6	18	28	18	28	—		5	51	5	48
26	0	56	+0.8	56.0	30.5	105	92	99	15.6	18	49	18	45	0	38	7	01	7	03
27	1	44	+5.4	56.5	30.8	117	81	96	16.6	19	11	19	03	1	24	8	12	8	18
28	2	34	+9.8	57.0	31.0	129	79	91	17.6	19	36	19	24	2	11	9	25	9	36
29	3	25	+13.7	57.5	31.3	141	80	84	18.6	20	06	19	51	3	01	10	39	10	53
30	4	19	+17.1	57.9	31.6	154	83	76	19.6	20	43	20	24	3	53	11	52	12	10

MERCURY

Day	R.A. h	R.A. m	Dec °	Mag.	Diam. "	Phase %	Rise h	Rise m	Transit h	Transit m	Set h	Set m
1	9	35.7	+15.1	−0.8	6	65	3	24	10	55	18	25
3	9	48.3	+14.4	−0.9	6	72	3	33	11	00	18	26
5	10	01.8	+13.5	−1.1	6	79	3	44	11	05	18	26
7	10	15.8	+12.4	−1.2	6	85	3	57	11	12	18	25
9	10	30.0	+11.2	−1.3	5	90	4	11	11	18	18	24
11	10	44.4	+9.9	−1.4	5	93	4	25	11	25	18	23
13	10	58.7	+8.5	−1.4	5	96	4	40	11	31	18	21
15	11	12.9	+7.0	−1.5	5	98	4	55	11	37	18	18
17	11	26.8	+5.5	−1.6	5	99	5	10	11	43	18	15
19	11	40.4	+3.9	−1.6	5	100	5	24	11	49	18	12
21	11	53.8	+2.3	−1.6	5	100	5	39	11	54	18	09
23	12	06.8	+0.7	−1.5	5	100	5	52	12	00	18	05
25	12	19.7	−0.8	−1.3	5	99	6	06	12	05	18	02
27	12	32.2	−2.4	−1.2	5	99	6	19	12	09	17	58
29	12	44.6	−3.9	−1.0	5	98	6	32	12	14	17	54

Rising and setting times are for latitude 54°

VENUS

Day	R.A. h	R.A. m	Dec °	Mag.	Diam. "	Phase %	Rise h	Rise m	Transit h	Transit m	Set h	Set m
1	13	21.2	−12.0	−4.4	31	40	9	42	14	37	19	32
6	13	35.4	−14.1	−4.5	34	37	9	49	14	31	19	14
11	13	48.5	−16.0	−4.5	36	34	9	54	14	24	18	55
16	14	00.1	−17.7	−4.5	39	30	9	56	14	15	18	35
21	14	09.9	−19.2	−4.6	42	26	9	56	14	05	18	15
26	14	17.3	−20.4	−4.6	46	22	9	51	13	52	17	53

MARS

Day	R.A. h	R.A. m	Dec °	Mag.	Diam. "	Phase %	Rise h	Rise m	Transit h	Transit m	Set h	Set m
1	20	07.5	−26.0	−2.1	21	94	18	09	21	30	0	46
6	20	09.2	−25.6	−2.0	20	93	17	48	21	12	0	31
11	20	12.3	−25.2	−1.8	19	92	17	27	20	55	0	18
16	20	16.7	−24.6	−1.7	18	91	17	07	20	39	0	07
21	20	22.3	−24.0	−1.6	17	90	16	48	20	24	23	58
26	20	28.9	−23.3	−1.4	17	89	16	29	20	11	23	50

SUNRISE AND SUNSET

	London 0° 05′	51° 30′	Bristol 2° 35′	51° 28′	Birmingham 1° 55′	52° 28′	Manchester 2° 15′	53° 28′	Newcastle 1° 37′	54° 59′	Glasgow 4° 14′	55° 52′	Belfast 5° 56′	54° 35′
d	h m	h m	h m	h m	h m	h m	h m	h m	h m	h m	h m	h m	h m	h m
1	5 13	18 47	5 23	18 57	5 18	18 56	5 18	18 59	5 13	18 59	5 21	19 11	5 31	19 16
2	5 14	18 45	5 24	18 55	5 20	18 54	5 20	18 57	5 14	18 57	5 23	19 09	5 32	19 13
3	5 16	18 42	5 26	18 52	5 22	18 51	5 21	18 54	5 16	18 54	5 25	19 06	5 34	19 11
4	5 17	18 40	5 28	18 50	5 23	18 49	5 23	18 52	5 18	18 52	5 27	19 04	5 36	19 08
5	5 19	18 38	5 29	18 48	5 25	18 47	5 25	18 49	5 20	18 49	5 29	19 01	5 38	19 06
6	5 21	18 36	5 31	18 46	5 27	18 44	5 27	18 47	5 22	18 47	5 31	18 58	5 40	19 03
7	5 22	18 33	5 32	18 43	5 28	18 42	5 28	18 45	5 24	18 44	5 33	18 56	5 42	19 01
8	5 24	18 31	5 34	18 41	5 30	18 40	5 30	18 42	5 26	18 42	5 35	18 53	5 43	18 58
9	5 25	18 29	5 35	18 39	5 32	18 37	5 32	18 40	5 27	18 39	5 37	18 51	5 45	18 56
10	5 27	18 27	5 37	18 37	5 33	18 35	5 34	18 37	5 29	18 36	5 39	18 48	5 47	18 53
11	5 29	18 24	5 39	18 34	5 35	18 33	5 35	18 35	5 31	18 34	5 41	18 45	5 49	18 51
12	5 30	18 22	5 40	18 32	5 37	18 30	5 37	18 32	5 33	18 31	5 43	18 43	5 51	18 48
13	5 32	18 20	5 42	18 30	5 38	18 28	5 39	18 30	5 35	18 29	5 45	18 40	5 53	18 46
14	5 33	18 17	5 43	18 27	5 40	18 25	5 41	18 27	5 37	18 26	5 46	18 37	5 54	18 43
15	5 35	18 15	5 45	18 25	5 42	18 23	5 42	18 25	5 39	18 24	5 48	18 35	5 56	18 41
16	5 37	18 13	5 47	18 23	5 43	18 21	5 44	18 23	5 40	18 21	5 50	18 32	5 58	18 38
17	5 38	18 10	5 48	18 20	5 45	18 18	5 46	18 20	5 42	18 18	5 52	18 29	6 00	18 35
18	5 40	18 08	5 50	18 18	5 47	18 16	5 48	18 18	5 44	18 16	5 54	18 27	6 02	18 33
19	5 41	18 06	5 51	18 16	5 48	18 14	5 49	18 15	5 46	18 13	5 56	18 24	6 04	18 30
20	5 43	18 04	5 53	18 14	5 50	18 11	5 51	18 13	5 48	18 11	5 58	18 21	6 05	18 28
21	5 45	18 01	5 55	18 11	5 52	18 09	5 53	18 10	5 50	18 08	6 00	18 19	6 07	18 25
22	5 46	17 59	5 56	18 09	5 53	18 06	5 55	18 08	5 52	18 06	6 02	18 16	6 09	18 23
23	5 48	17 57	5 58	18 07	5 55	18 04	5 56	18 05	5 54	18 03	6 04	18 14	6 11	18 20
24	5 49	17 54	5 59	18 04	5 57	18 02	5 58	18 03	5 55	18 00	6 06	18 11	6 13	18 18
25	5 51	17 52	6 01	18 02	5 58	17 59	6 00	18 01	5 57	17 58	6 08	18 08	6 15	18 15
26	5 53	17 50	6 03	18 00	6 00	17 57	6 01	17 58	5 59	17 55	6 10	18 06	6 16	18 13
27	5 54	17 47	6 04	17 57	6 02	17 55	6 03	17 56	6 01	17 53	6 12	18 03	6 18	18 10
28	5 56	17 45	6 06	17 55	6 03	17 52	6 05	17 53	6 03	17 50	6 14	18 00	6 20	18 08
29	5 57	17 43	6 07	17 53	6 05	17 50	6 07	17 51	6 05	17 48	6 16	17 58	6 22	18 05
30	5 59	17 41	6 09	17 51	6 07	17 48	6 09	17 48	6 07	17 45	6 18	17 55	6 24	18 03

JUPITER

Day	R.A. h m	Dec °	Mag.	Diam. ″	Rise h m	Transit h m	Set h m
1	14 58.8	−16.1	−1.9	35	11 46	16 16	20 46
11	15 04.6	−16.5	−1.9	34	11 15	15 42	20 10
21	15 11.2	−17.0	−1.8	33	10 45	15 10	19 34

Equatorial Diam. 35″, Polar Diam. 32″

SATURN

Day	R.A. h m	Dec °	Mag.	Diam. ″	Rise h m	Transit h m	Set h m
1	18 10.0	−22.7	+0.4	17	15 42	19 26	23 11
11	18 10.0	−22.7	+0.4	17	15 03	18 47	22 32
21	18 10.7	−22.7	+0.5	17	14 25	18 08	21 53

Equatorial Diam. 17″, Polar Diam. 15″
Rings – major axis 38″ minor axis 17″, Tilt 27°

URANUS

Day	R.A. h m	Dec °	Mag.	Diam. ″	Rise h m	Transit h m	Set h m
1	2 00.3	+11.7	+5.7	4	20 10	3 19	10 28
11	1 59.5	+11.6	+5.7	4	19 31	2 39	9 48
21	1 58.3	+11.5	+5.7	4	18 51	1 59	9 07

NEPTUNE

Day	R.A. h m	Dec °	Mag.	Diam. ″	Rise h m	Transit h m	Set h m
1	23 06.3	−6.8	+7.8	2	18 57	0 26	5 51
11	23 05.3	−6.9	+7.8	2	18 17	23 42	5 10
21	23 04.3	−7.0	+7.8	2	17 37	23 01	4 29

October 2018

TENTH MONTH, 31 DAYS. *Octo* (eighth), eighth month of Roman pre-Julian calendar

1	*Monday*	General Franco becomes Spain's head of state 1936	week 40 day 274
2	*Tuesday*	The Amsterdam Treaty is signed, extending the powers of the EU 1997	275
3	*Wednesday*	The reunification of East and West Germany is formerly completed and celebrated 1990	276
4	*Thursday*	Richard Cromwell, Lord Protector of England (1658-9) *b.* 1626	277
5	*Friday*	The Yugoslav parliament in Belgrade is stormed by opposition protesters 2000	278
6	*Saturday*	Swedish poet Tomas Tranströmer wins the Nobel Prize in Literature 2011	279
7	*Sunday*	Frederick I, king of Denmark and Norway (1523–33) *b.* 1471	280
8	*Monday*	Britain's first day as a member of the Exchange Rate Mechanism of the European Monetary System 1990	week 41. 281
9	*Tuesday*	King Alexander I of Yugoslavia is assassinated 1934	282
10	*Wednesday*	Radu Vasile, Romanian prime minister (1998–9) *b.* 1942	283
11	*Thursday*	Edward White Benson, Archbishop of Canterbury (1883–96) *d.* 1896	284
12	*Friday*	Christopher Columbus, Italian explorer, and his Spanish crew disembark at the Bahamas 1492	285
13	*Saturday*	Italy declares war on Germany 1943	286
14	*Sunday*	William, Duke of Normandy defeats King Harold Godwinson at the Battle of Hastings 1066	287
15	*Monday*	Engineers hole through the eastern passage of the 35-mile-long Gotthard Base Tunnel 2010	week 42 day 288
16	*Tuesday*	Ten Nazi war criminals are executed following sentencing at the Nuremberg trials 1946	289
17	*Wednesday*	Queen Elizabeth II becomes the first British monarch to make a state visit to the Vatican 1980	290
18	*Thursday*	Erich Honecker, the Communist leader of East Germany, steps down 1989	291
19	*Friday*	King Ferdinand II of Aragon marries Queen Isabella of Castile unifing Spain 1469	292
20	*Saturday*	George I is crowned 1714	293
21	*Sunday*	The Royal Navy defeats the combined fleets of the French and Spanish at the Battle of Trafalgar 1805	294
22	*Monday*	Double agent George Blake escapes from prison in London 1966	week 43 day 295
23	*Tuesday*	Thousands attend a rally in Budapest, Hungary to demand an end to Soviet rule 1956	296
24	*Wednesday*	The treaty of Westphalia is signed, signalling the end of the Thirty Years' War 1648	297
25	*Thursday*	The Light Brigade charges Russian guns at Balaclava during the Crimean War 1854	298
26	*Friday*	Austria is recognised as an independent sovereign state 1955	299
27	*Saturday*	Edmund I succeeds Athelstan as king of England 939	300
28	*Sunday*	British Summer Time ends. Bohemia, Moravia, Slovakia and Ruthenia form Czechoslovakia 1918	301
29	*Monday*	King Victor Emmanuel III hands over power to Bennito Mussolini 1922	week 44 day 302
30	*Tuesday*	Tsar Nicholas II issues the October Manifesto promising an elected parliament 1905	303
31	*Wednesday*	Martin Luther, German theologian, nails his 95 theses to the door of Wittenburg Cathedral 1517	304

ASTRONOMICAL PHENOMENA

d	h	
5	18	Spica 2° South of Mercury
10	1	Mercury 6° South of the Moon
11	21	Jupiter 4° South of the Moon
15	3	Saturn 2° South of the Moon
18	13	Mars 2° South of the Moon
20	22	Neptune 3° North of the Moon
24	1	Uranus at opposition
24	13	Uranus 5° North of the Moon
30	4	Jupiter 3° North of Mercury

MINIMA OF ALGOL

d	h	d	h	d	h
1	1.8	12	13.0	24	0.3
3	22.6	15	9.8	26	21.1
6	19.4	18	6.6	29	17.9
9	16.2	21	3.4		

The following constellations are near the meridian at

CONSTELLATIONS

	d	h		d	h
September	1	24	October	16	21
September	15	23	November	1	20
October	1	22	November	15	19

Ursa Major (below the Pole), Cepheus, Cassiopeia, Cygnus, Lacerta, Andromeda, Pegasus, Capricornus, Aquarius and Piscis Austrinus

THE MOON

Phases, Apsides and Node	d	h	m
◑ Last Quarter	2	9	45
● New Moon	9	3	47
◐ First Quarter	16	18	2
○ Full Moon	24	16	45
◑ Last Quarter	31	16	40
Perigee (366,392 km)	5	22	27
Apogee (404,227 km)	17	19	16
Perigee (370,204 km)	31	20	23

Mean longitude of the ascending node on 1st, 122°

THE SUN

Diam. 32.0′

Day	Right Ascension			Dec.	Equation of time		Rise 52°		Rise 56°		Transit		Set 52°		Set 56°		Sidereal time			Transit of first point of Aries		
	h	m	s	°	m	s	h	m	h	m	h	m	h	m	h	m	h	m	s	h	m	s
1	12	28	34	3.1	+10	09	6	01	6	03	11	50	17	38	17	36	0	38	43	23	21	17
2	12	32	11	3.5	+10	28	6	02	6	05	11	49	17	35	17	33	0	42	40	23	17	20
3	12	35	48	3.9	+10	47	6	04	6	07	11	49	17	33	17	30	0	46	37	23	13	23
4	12	39	26	4.2	+11	06	6	06	6	09	11	49	17	31	17	28	0	50	33	23	09	27
5	12	43	04	4.6	+11	24	6	07	6	11	11	48	17	29	17	25	0	54	30	23	05	30
6	12	46	43	5.0	+11	42	6	09	6	13	11	48	17	26	17	23	0	58	26	23	01	34
7	12	50	22	5.4	+12	00	6	11	6	15	11	48	17	24	17	20	1	02	23	22	57	37
8	12	54	01	5.8	+12	17	6	12	6	17	11	48	17	22	17	17	1	06	19	22	53	41
9	12	57	41	6.2	+12	34	6	14	6	19	11	47	17	20	17	15	1	10	16	22	49	44
10	13	01	22	6.5	+12	50	6	16	6	21	11	47	17	17	17	12	1	14	12	22	45	48
11	13	05	02	6.9	+13	06	6	18	6	23	11	47	17	15	17	10	1	18	09	22	41	51
12	13	08	44	7.3	+13	21	6	19	6	25	11	47	17	13	17	07	1	22	06	22	37	54
13	13	12	25	7.7	+13	36	6	21	6	27	11	46	17	11	17	05	1	26	02	22	33	58
14	13	16	07	8.0	+13	50	6	23	6	29	11	46	17	08	17	02	1	29	59	22	30	01
15	13	19	50	8.4	+14	04	6	24	6	31	11	46	17	06	17	00	1	33	55	22	26	05
16	13	23	33	8.8	+14	17	6	26	6	33	11	46	17	04	16	57	1	37	52	22	22	08
17	13	27	17	9.2	+14	30	6	28	6	35	11	45	17	02	16	55	1	41	48	22	18	12
18	13	31	02	9.5	+14	42	6	30	6	37	11	45	17	00	16	52	1	45	45	22	14	15
19	13	34	47	9.9	+14	54	6	31	6	39	11	45	16	58	16	50	1	49	41	22	10	19
20	13	38	32	10.2	+15	05	6	33	6	41	11	45	16	56	16	47	1	53	38	22	06	22
21	13	42	18	10.6	+15	15	6	35	6	43	11	45	16	53	16	45	1	57	35	22	02	25
22	13	46	05	11.0	+15	25	6	37	6	46	11	44	16	51	16	43	2	01	31	21	58	29
23	13	49	53	11.3	+15	34	6	39	6	48	11	44	16	49	16	40	2	05	28	21	54	32
24	13	53	41	11.7	+15	42	6	40	6	50	11	44	16	47	16	38	2	09	24	21	50	36
25	13	57	30	12.0	+15	50	6	42	6	52	11	44	16	45	16	35	2	13	21	21	46	39
26	14	01	19	12.3	+15	57	6	44	6	54	11	44	16	43	16	33	2	17	17	21	42	43
27	14	05	10	12.7	+16	03	6	46	6	56	11	44	16	41	16	31	2	21	14	21	38	46
28	14	09	01	13.0	+16	09	6	47	6	58	11	44	16	39	16	29	2	25	10	21	34	50
29	14	12	53	13.3	+16	14	6	49	7	00	11	44	16	37	16	26	2	29	07	21	30	53
30	14	16	45	13.7	+16	17	6	51	7	02	11	44	16	36	16	24	2	33	04	21	26	56
31	14	20	39	14.0	+16	20	6	53	7	05	11	44	16	34	16	22	2	37	00	21	23	00

DURATION OF TWILIGHT

Latitude	52°	56°	52°	56°	52°	56°	52°	56°
	1 October		11 October		21 October		31 October	
Civil	34	37	34	37	34	38	35	39
Nautical	73	80	73	80	74	81	75	83
Astronomical	113	125	112	124	113	124	114	126

THE NIGHT SKY

Mercury is in the evening sky but is not favourably placed for observation at higher northern latitudes.

Venus is also an evening object but lies well south of the ecliptic and will not be seen this month. It passes through inferior conjunction on the 26th, after which Venus moves into the morning sky.

Mars sets just before midnight all month and slowly fades from magnitude −1.3 to −0.6 during the period. Although It still far outshines the stars of Capricornus where it currently lies. By late October the apparent size of the disk is only half that of three months ago. The Moon is 3° from Mars on the 18th.

Jupiter (magnitude −1.8) is getting lower each evening and sets less than an hour after the Sun by the 31st. The two-day old Moon is nearby on the 11th.

Saturn (magnitude 0.5) sets four hours after the Sun at the beginning of the month and an hour earlier by the 31st. The planet lies in a region of Sagittarius that has a surfeit of bright Messier objects to explore with binoculars. The Moon is close to Saturn on the 14th and 15th.

Uranus (magnitude 5.7) is at opposition on the 24th in Aries. Observers below about latitude 20° S can potentially see all the solar system planets in one sweep an hour after sunset mid-October, although some optical aid will be needed for Uranus and Neptune. The dwarf planet Pluto (magnitude 14.3) in Sagittarius will be more challenging to spot.

THE MOON

Day	R.A.		Dec	Hor Par	Diam	Sun Co-Long	PA of Br. limb	Ph.	Age	Rise				Transit		Set			
										52°		56°				52°		56°	
	h	m	°	′	′	°	°	%	d	h	m	h	m	h	m	h	m	h	m
1	5	16	+19.5	58.4	31.8	166	87	66	20.6	21	29	21	08	4	48	13	00	13	23
2	6	15	+20.8	58.8	32.1	178	92	55	21.6	22	26	22	05	5	45	14	03	14	26
3	7	15	+20.9	59.2	32.3	190	97	43	22.6	23	34	23	14	6	44	14	57	15	18
4	8	15	+19.6	59.6	32.5	202	103	32	23.6	—		—		7	43	15	41	15	58
5	9	15	+17.1	59.8	32.6	215	108	22	24.6	0	50	0	33	8	40	16	17	16	30
6	10	13	+13.5	59.8	32.6	227	113	13	25.6	2	10	1	58	9	36	16	46	16	55
7	11	10	+9.0	59.7	32.6	239	119	06	26.6	3	31	3	24	10	30	17	12	17	17
8	12	04	+4.1	59.4	32.4	251	128	02	27.6	4	52	4	49	11	21	17	36	17	36
9	12	57	−1.0	59.0	32.1	263	179	00	28.6	6	11	6	13	12	12	17	59	17	55
10	13	50	−5.9	58.4	31.8	276	266	01	0.1	7	29	7	36	13	02	18	23	18	15
11	14	42	−10.5	57.6	31.4	288	277	04	1.1	8	45	8	55	13	51	18	49	18	36
12	15	34	−14.4	56.9	31.0	300	277	10	2.1	9	57	10	12	14	41	19	18	19	02
13	16	26	−17.5	56.1	30.6	312	275	17	3.1	11	05	11	24	15	31	19	52	19	33
14	17	18	−19.7	55.5	30.2	324	272	25	4.1	12	07	12	29	16	21	20	32	20	11
15	18	10	−20.9	54.9	29.9	337	268	34	5.1	13	01	13	24	17	10	21	19	20	58
16	19	02	−21.1	54.5	29.7	349	264	43	6.1	13	48	14	10	17	59	22	13	21	52
17	19	53	−20.4	54.3	29.6	1	259	52	7.1	14	27	14	46	18	47	23	11	22	52
18	20	42	−18.8	54.2	29.6	13	255	62	8.1	14	59	15	16	19	33	—		23	59
19	21	31	−16.3	54.4	29.6	25	251	71	9.1	15	27	15	40	20	19	0	14	—	
20	22	19	−13.2	54.6	29.8	38	247	79	10.1	15	50	15	59	21	03	1	19	1	07
21	23	06	−9.4	55.0	30.0	50	244	86	11.1	16	12	16	18	21	48	2	26	2	18
22	23	53	−5.2	55.5	30.3	62	240	92	12.1	16	32	16	34	22	32	3	34	3	31
23	0	40	−0.7	56.1	30.6	74	235	97	13.1	16	53	16	50	23	18	4	45	4	45
24	1	29	+4.0	56.7	30.9	86	219	99	14.1	17	14	17	08	—		5	57	6	01
25	2	19	+8.6	57.3	31.2	98	124	100	15.1	17	38	17	28	0	05	7	11	7	20
26	3	11	+12.8	57.8	31.5	111	90	98	16.1	18	07	17	53	0	55	8	27	8	40
27	4	05	+16.5	58.3	31.8	123	87	94	17.1	18	42	18	23	1	48	9	42	9	59
28	5	02	+19.2	58.6	32.0	135	88	87	18.1	19	25	19	05	2	43	10	54	11	16
29	6	01	+20.9	58.9	32.1	147	92	79	19.1	20	19	19	58	3	41	12	00	12	23
30	7	02	+21.3	59.1	32.2	159	97	69	20.1	21	24	21	03	4	39	12	56	13	19
31	8	02	+20.3	59.2	32.3	171	102	58	21.1	22	36	22	18	5	38	13	43	14	01

MERCURY

Day	R.A.	Dec	Mag.	Diam.	Phase	Rise	Transit	Set
	h m	°		″	%	h m	h m	h m
1	12 56.8	−5.5	−0.9	5	98	6 45	12 18	17 49
3	13 08.8	−6.9	−0.8	5	97	6 57	12 22	17 45
5	13 20.7	−8.4	−0.7	5	96	7 10	12 26	17 41
7	13 32.4	−9.8	−0.6	5	95	7 21	12 30	17 37
9	13 44.1	−11.1	−0.5	5	94	7 33	12 33	17 33
11	13 55.6	−12.5	−0.4	5	93	7 45	12 37	17 28
13	14 07.1	−13.7	−0.4	5	92	7 56	12 41	17 24
15	14 18.5	−14.9	−0.3	5	90	8 07	12 44	17 20
17	14 29.9	−16.1	−0.3	5	89	8 18	12 47	17 16
19	14 41.2	−17.2	−0.3	5	88	8 28	12 51	17 13
21	14 52.4	−18.3	−0.2	5	86	8 39	12 54	17 09
23	15 03.6	−19.3	−0.2	5	84	8 48	12 57	17 06
25	15 14.6	−20.2	−0.2	5	82	8 58	13 00	17 02
27	15 25.6	−21.0	−0.2	6	80	9 07	13 03	16 59
29	15 36.3	−21.8	−0.2	6	78	9 15	13 06	16 56
31	15 46.9	−22.5	−0.2	6	75	9 23	13 09	16 54

Rising and setting times are for latitude 54°

VENUS

Day	R.A.	Dec	Mag.	Diam.	Phase	Rise	Transit	Set
	h m	°		″	%	h m	h m	h m
1	14 21.8	−21.3	−4.5	50	17	9 41	13 35	17 31
6	14 23.0	−21.8	−4.5	54	13	9 26	13 16	17 09
11	14 20.5	−21.9	−4.4	58	8	9 03	12 53	16 46
16	14 14.4	−21.3	−4.3	62	5	8 32	12 27	16 25
21	14 05.4	−20.2	−4.2	64	2	7 55	11 58	16 05
26	13 54.9	−18.6	−4.0	66	1	7 14	11 28	15 46
31	13 44.6	−16.6	−4.1	65	1	6 31	10 59	15 30

MARS

Day	R.A.	Dec	Mag.	Diam.	Phase	Rise	Transit	Set
	h m	°		″	%	h m	h m	h m
1	20 36.3	−22.6	−1.3	16	88	16 11	19 58	23 43
6	20 44.6	−21.8	−1.2	15	88	15 54	19 47	23 40
11	20 53.5	−21.0	−1.1	14	87	15 36	19 36	23 35
16	21 03.0	−20.0	−1.0	14	87	15 20	19 25	23 31
21	21 13.0	−19.1	−0.8	13	87	15 03	19 15	23 28
26	21 23.4	−18.0	−0.7	13	86	14 47	19 06	23 26
31	21 34.1	−16.9	−0.6	12	86	14 30	18 57	23 24

SUNRISE AND SUNSET

	London			Bristol			Birmingham			Manchester			Newcastle			Glasgow			Belfast		
	0°	05′ | 51°	30′	2°	35′ | 51°	28′	1°	55′ | 52°	28′	2°	15′ | 53°	28′	1°	37′ | 54°	59′	4°	14′ | 55°	52′	5°	56′ | 54°	35′
d	h	m	h	m	h	m	h	m	h	m	h	m	h	m	h	m	h	m	h	m	h	m
1	6 01	17 38	6 11	17 48	6 09	17 45	6 10	17 46	6 09	17 43	6 20	17 53	6 26	18 00
2	6 02	17 36	6 12	17 46	6 10	17 43	6 12	17 44	6 10	17 40	6 22	17 50	6 28	17 58
3	6 04	17 34	6 14	17 44	6 12	17 41	6 14	17 41	6 12	17 38	6 23	17 47	6 29	17 55
4	6 06	17 32	6 16	17 42	6 14	17 38	6 16	17 39	6 14	17 35	6 25	17 45	6 31	17 53
5	6 07	17 29	6 17	17 39	6 15	17 36	6 17	17 36	6 16	17 33	6 27	17 42	6 33	17 50
6	6 09	17 27	6 19	17 37	6 17	17 34	6 19	17 34	6 18	17 30	6 29	17 40	6 35	17 48
7	6 11	17 25	6 21	17 35	6 19	17 31	6 21	17 32	6 20	17 28	6 31	17 37	6 37	17 45
8	6 12	17 23	6 22	17 33	6 21	17 29	6 23	17 29	6 22	17 25	6 33	17 34	6 39	17 43
9	6 14	17 20	6 24	17 30	6 22	17 27	6 25	17 27	6 24	17 23	6 36	17 32	6 41	17 40
10	6 16	17 18	6 26	17 28	6 24	17 24	6 27	17 25	6 26	17 20	6 38	17 29	6 43	17 38
11	6 17	17 16	6 27	17 26	6 26	17 22	6 28	17 22	6 28	17 18	6 40	17 27	6 45	17 35
12	6 19	17 14	6 29	17 24	6 28	17 20	6 30	17 20	6 30	17 15	6 42	17 24	6 47	17 33
13	6 21	17 12	6 31	17 22	6 29	17 18	6 32	17 18	6 32	17 13	6 44	17 22	6 48	17 31
14	6 22	17 09	6 32	17 19	6 31	17 15	6 34	17 15	6 34	17 10	6 46	17 19	6 50	17 28
15	6 24	17 07	6 34	17 17	6 33	17 13	6 36	17 13	6 36	17 08	6 48	17 17	6 52	17 26
16	6 26	17 05	6 36	17 15	6 35	17 11	6 38	17 11	6 38	17 05	6 50	17 14	6 54	17 23
17	6 27	17 03	6 37	17 13	6 36	17 09	6 39	17 08	6 40	17 03	6 52	17 12	6 56	17 21
18	6 29	17 01	6 39	17 11	6 38	17 07	6 41	17 06	6 42	17 01	6 54	17 09	6 58	17 19
19	6 31	16 59	6 41	17 09	6 40	17 04	6 43	17 04	6 44	16 58	6 56	17 07	7 00	17 16
20	6 33	16 57	6 43	17 07	6 42	17 02	6 45	17 02	6 46	16 56	6 58	17 05	7 02	17 14
21	6 34	16 55	6 44	17 05	6 44	17 00	6 47	17 00	6 48	16 54	7 00	17 02	7 04	17 12
22	6 36	16 53	6 46	17 03	6 45	16 58	6 49	16 57	6 50	16 51	7 02	17 00	7 06	17 10
23	6 38	16 51	6 48	17 01	6 47	16 56	6 51	16 55	6 52	16 49	7 04	16 57	7 08	17 07
24	6 40	16 49	6 50	16 59	6 49	16 54	6 53	16 53	6 54	16 47	7 06	16 55	7 10	17 05
25	6 41	16 47	6 51	16 57	6 51	16 52	6 54	16 51	6 56	16 45	7 08	16 53	7 12	17 03
26	6 43	16 45	6 53	16 55	6 53	16 50	6 56	16 49	6 58	16 42	7 11	16 50	7 14	17 01
27	6 45	16 43	6 55	16 53	6 54	16 48	6 58	16 47	7 00	16 40	7 13	16 48	7 16	16 58
28	6 47	16 41	6 56	16 51	6 56	16 46	7 00	16 45	7 02	16 38	7 15	16 46	7 18	16 56
29	6 48	16 39	6 58	16 49	6 58	16 44	7 02	16 43	7 04	16 36	7 17	16 44	7 20	16 54
30	6 50	16 37	7 00	16 47	7 00	16 42	7 04	16 41	7 06	16 34	7 19	16 41	7 22	16 52
31	6 52	16 35	7 02	16 45	7 02	16 40	7 06	16 39	7 08	16 32	7 21	16 39	7 24	16 50

JUPITER

Day	R.A.		Dec	Mag.	Diam.	Rise		Transit		Set	
	h	m	°		″	h	m	h	m	h	m
1	15	18.4	−17.5	−1.8	33	10	16	14	37	18	59
11	15	26.2	−18.0	−1.8	32	9	48	14	06	18	24
21	15	34.5	−18.5	−1.8	32	9	21	13	35	17	49
31	15	43.2	−19.0	−1.7	31	8	53	13	04	17	15

Equatorial Diam. 33″, Polar Diam. 30″

SATURN

Day	R.A.		Dec	Mag.	Diam.	Rise		Transit		Set	
	h	m	°		″	h	m	h	m	h	m
1	18	12.0	−22.8	+0.5	16	13	47	17	31	21	15
11	18	14.1	−22.8	+0.5	16	13	09	16	53	20	37
21	18	16.7	−22.8	+0.6	16	12	33	16	17	20	01
31	18	20.0	−22.8	+0.6	16	11	57	15	40	19	24

Equatorial Diam. 16″, Polar Diam. 15″
Rings – major axis 36″ minor axis 16″, Tilt 27°

URANUS

Day	R.A.		Dec	Mag.	Diam.	Rise		Transit		Set	
	h	m	°		″	h	m	h	m	h	m
1	1	57.0	+11.4	+5.7	4	18	07	1	18	8	25
11	1	55.6	+11.2	+5.7	4	17	27	0	37	7	44
21	1	54.0	+11.1	+5.7	4	16	47	23	53	7	02
31	1	52.5	+10.9	+5.7	4	16	07	23	12	6	20

NEPTUNE

Day	R.A.		Dec	Mag.	Diam.	Rise		Transit		Set	
	h	m	°		″	h	m	h	m	h	m
1	23	03.3	−7.1	+7.8	2	16	58	22	21	3	48
11	23	02.5	−7.2	+7.8	2	16	18	21	41	3	08
21	23	01.7	−7.3	+7.8	2	15	38	21	01	2	27
31	23	01.1	−7.4	+7.8	2	14	59	20	21	1	47

November 2018

ELEVENTH MONTH, 30 DAYS. *Novem* (nine), ninth month of Roman pre-Julian calendar

1	Thursday	The Maastricht Treaty is signed formally creating the European Union (EU) 1993	day 305
2	Friday	The office of the satirical magazine Charlie Hebdo in Paris is destroyed in a petrol-bomb attack 2011	306
3	Saturday	Thousands of truck drivers barricade Calais port to protest for better working hours and conditions 1997	307
4	Sunday	The Soviet military suppresses the Hungarian uprising 1956	308

5	Monday	The Battle of Inkerman ended in British and French victory over Russian forces 1854	week 45 day 309
6	Tuesday	Allied forces declare a ceasefire in the Suez Canal Crisis 1956	310
7	Wednesday	The Greek parliament passes a number of austerity measures 2012	311
8	Thursday	Mary Robinson becomes Ireland's first female president 1990	312
9	Friday	The dismantling of the Berlin Wall begins and border crossings are opened 1989	313
10	Saturday	Michael Foot is elected Labour Party leader 1980	314
11	Sunday	Armistice is agreed between Germany and the Allies signalling the end of WWI 1918	315

12	Monday	King Cnut (Canute), ruler of England (1016–1035) and also King of Denmark and Norway d. 1035	week 46 day 316
13	Tuesday	Lady Jane Grey and Archbishop Thomas Cranmer stand trial for treason 1553	317
14	Wednesday	Alexander Nevsky, Grand Prince of Kiev and Novgorod (1236–52) and Vladimir (1252–63) d. 1263	318
15	Thursday	The European Monetary Institute (EMI) determines the seven denominations of Euro banknotes 1994	319
16	Friday	Protestant leader Gustavus II of Sweden is killed at the Battle of Lützen 1635	320
17	Saturday	The French defeat the Austrians at the Battle of the Bridge of Arcole 1796	321
18	Sunday	Latvian independence is established 1918	322

19	Monday	James FitzGerald, 1st Duke of Leinster, Irish politician d. 1773	week 47 day 323
20	Tuesday	General Francisco Franco who ruled Spain for 35 years d. 1975	324
21	Wednesday	Voltaire, French Enlightenment writer, political philosopher and playwright b. 1694	325
22	Thursday	Angela Merkel becomes Germany's first female chancellor 2005	326
23	Friday	William III, king of the Netherlands (1849–90) d. 1890	327
24	Saturday	The leadership of the communist party in Czechoslovakia resigns to make way for democratic changes 1989	328
25	Sunday	The Greek government is overthrown by the country's armed forces 1973	329

26	Monday	René Goblet, French politician and prime minister of France (1886–7) b.1828	week 48 day 330
27	Tuesday	Alexander Dubcek, leader of Czechoslovakia (1968–9) b. 1921	331
28	Wednesday	In a referendum voters in Norway reject joining the European Union 1994	332
29	Thursday	Jaques Chirac, former president and prime minister of France b. 1932	333
30	Friday	The Soviet Union invades Finland 1939	334

ASTRONOMICAL PHENOMENA

d	h	
6	16	Mercury greatest elongation East
8	18	Jupiter 4° South of the Moon
9	6	Antares 2° South of Mercury
11	16	Saturn 1.5° South of the Moon
16	4	Mars 1° North of the Moon
17	6	Neptune 3° North of the Moon
20	20	Uranus 5° North of the Moon
24	2	Antares 4° South of Mercury
28	0	Jupiter 0.5° South of Mercury
30		Venus most brilliant (Mag -4.87)

MINIMA OF ALGOL

d	h	d	h	d	h
1	14.7	13	2.0	24	13.2
4	11.5	15	22.8	27	10.1
7	8.3	18	19.6	30	6.9
10	5.2	21	16.4		

The following constellations are near the meridian at

CONSTELLATIONS

	d	h		d	h
October	1	24	November	15	21
October	16	23	December	1	20
November	1	22	December	16	19

Ursa Major (below the Pole), Cepheus, Cassiopeia, Andromeda, Pegasus, Pisces, Aquarius and Cetus

THE MOON

Phases, Apsides and Node	d	h	m
● New Moon	7	16	2
◐ First Quarter	15	14	54
○ Full Moon	23	5	39
◑ Last Quarter	30	0	19
Apogee (404,339 km)	14	15	56
Perigee (366,620 km)	26	12	12

Mean longitude of the ascending node on 1st, 121°

THE SUN

Diam. 32.2′

Day	Right Ascension			Dec.	Equation of time		Rise 52°		Rise 56°		Transit		Set 52°		Set 56°		Sidereal time			Transit of first point of Aries		
	h	m	s	°	m	s	h	m	h	m	h	m	h	m	h	m	h	m	s	h	m	s
1	14	24	33	14.3	+16	23	6	55	7	07	11	44	16	32	16	20	2	40	57	21	19	03
2	14	28	28	14.7	+16	24	6	56	7	09	11	44	16	30	16	18	2	44	53	21	15	07
3	14	32	24	15.0	+16	25	6	58	7	11	11	44	16	28	16	15	2	48	50	21	11	10
4	14	36	21	15.3	+16	25	7	00	7	13	11	44	16	26	16	13	2	52	46	21	07	14
5	14	40	18	15.6	+16	24	7	02	7	15	11	44	16	25	16	11	2	56	43	21	03	17
6	14	44	17	15.9	+16	22	7	04	7	17	11	44	16	23	16	09	3	00	39	20	59	21
7	14	48	16	16.2	+16	19	7	05	7	19	11	44	16	21	16	07	3	04	36	20	55	24
8	14	52	16	16.5	+16	16	7	07	7	22	11	44	16	20	16	05	3	08	33	20	51	27
9	14	56	17	16.8	+16	11	7	09	7	24	11	44	16	18	16	03	3	12	29	20	47	31
10	15	00	19	17.1	+16	06	7	11	7	26	11	44	16	16	16	01	3	16	26	20	43	34
11	15	04	21	17.3	+16	00	7	13	7	28	11	44	16	15	16	00	3	20	22	20	39	38
12	15	08	25	17.6	+15	53	7	14	7	30	11	44	16	13	15	58	3	24	19	20	35	41
13	15	12	29	17.9	+15	46	7	16	7	32	11	44	16	12	15	56	3	28	15	20	31	45
14	15	16	34	18.2	+15	37	7	18	7	34	11	44	16	10	15	54	3	32	12	20	27	48
15	15	20	40	18.4	+15	28	7	20	7	36	11	45	16	09	15	52	3	36	08	20	23	52
16	15	24	47	18.7	+15	17	7	21	7	38	11	45	16	08	15	51	3	40	05	20	19	55
17	15	28	54	18.9	+15	06	7	23	7	40	11	45	16	06	15	49	3	44	02	20	15	58
18	15	33	03	19.2	+14	55	7	25	7	42	11	45	16	05	15	48	3	47	58	20	12	02
19	15	37	12	19.4	+14	42	7	26	7	44	11	45	16	04	15	46	3	51	55	20	08	05
20	15	41	22	19.6	+14	28	7	28	7	46	11	46	16	03	15	45	3	55	51	20	04	09
21	15	45	33	19.9	+14	14	7	30	7	48	11	46	16	01	15	43	3	59	48	20	00	12
22	15	49	44	20.1	+13	59	7	31	7	50	11	46	16	00	15	42	4	03	44	19	56	16
23	15	53	57	20.3	+13	43	7	33	7	52	11	46	15	59	15	40	4	07	41	19	52	19
24	15	58	10	20.5	+13	27	7	35	7	54	11	47	15	58	15	39	4	11	37	19	48	23
25	16	02	24	20.7	+13	09	7	36	7	56	11	47	15	57	15	38	4	15	34	19	44	26
26	16	06	39	20.9	+12	51	7	38	7	57	11	47	15	56	15	37	4	19	31	19	40	29
27	16	10	54	21.1	+12	32	7	39	7	59	11	48	15	56	15	35	4	23	27	19	36	33
28	16	15	10	21.3	+12	12	7	41	8	01	11	48	15	55	15	34	4	27	24	19	32	36
29	16	19	27	21.4	+11	52	7	42	8	03	11	48	15	54	15	33	4	31	20	19	28	40
30	16	23	45	21.6	+11	31	7	44	8	04	11	49	15	53	15	32	4	35	17	19	24	43

DURATION OF TWILIGHT

Latitude	52°	56°	52°	56°	52°	56°	52°	56°
	1 November		11 November		21 November		31 November	
Civil	36	40	37	41	38	43	40	45
Nautical	75	84	78	87	80	90	82	93
Astronomical	115	127	117	130	120	134	123	138

THE NIGHT SKY

Mercury is still too poorly placed to be seen from more northern latitudes this month. It is at greatest eastern elongation on the 6th and in inferior conjunction on the 27th.

Venus (magnitude −4.2 to −4.9) should be picked up in the eastern sky before sunrise towards the end of the first week. It's up almost four hours before the Sun by the 30th when also near greatest brilliancy, and is a lovely slender crescent all month in a small telescope. The Moon is only 32.5 hours from New when near Venus on the 6th and the planet's trajectory sees it climb towards Spica – they are closest on the 14th when just over 1° separates the two.

Mars (magnitude −0.6 to −0.1) moves from Capricornus into Aquarius early in the month and doesn't set until just before midnight. Telescope users will note the disk has now shrunk to around 10 arc-seconds wide. The Moon lies near Mars on the 15th and 16th, with an occultation of the planet on the 16th only visible from the southern tip of South America and Antarctica.

Jupiter is in conjunction with the Sun on the 26th and is more or less lost to view this month.

Saturn (magnitude 0.5) sets three hours after the Sun at the beginning of November and an hour earlier at the end of the month. That time difference between sunset and Saturn's departure will rapidly diminish next month. The Moon is within 1.5° of Saturn on the 11th.

THE MOON

Day	R.A.		Dec	Hor Par	Diam	Sun Co-Long	PA of Br. limb	Ph.	Age	Rise				Transit		Set			
										52°		56°				52°		56°	
	h	m	°	′	′	°	°	%	d	h	m	h	m	h	m	h	m	h	m
1	9	01	+18.1	59.2	32.3	183	106	47	22.1	23	54	23	40	6	35	14	20	14	35
2	9	58	+14.7	59.2	32.2	196	111	35	23.1	—		—		7	30	14	50	15	01
3	10	54	+10.6	59.0	32.2	208	114	25	24.1	1	13	1	04	8	22	15	16	15	23
4	11	47	+5.8	58.8	32.1	220	117	16	25.1	2	32	2	27	9	13	15	39	15	41
5	12	39	+0.8	58.5	31.9	232	120	08	26.1	3	50	3	50	10	03	16	02	15	59
6	13	31	−4.2	58.1	31.7	244	124	03	27.1	5	07	5	12	10	52	16	24	16	18
7	14	22	−8.9	57.6	31.4	257	140	01	28.1	6	23	6	32	11	41	16	48	16	37
8	15	14	−13.1	57.0	31.1	269	236	00	29.1	7	37	7	50	12	30	17	15	17	01
9	16	06	−16.6	56.4	30.7	281	267	02	0.6	8	48	9	05	13	21	17	47	17	29
10	16	59	−19.2	55.8	30.4	293	269	06	1.6	9	53	10	14	14	11	18	24	18	04
11	17	51	−20.8	55.3	30.1	305	268	11	2.6	10	53	11	15	15	01	19	09	18	46
12	18	44	−21.4	54.8	29.9	318	264	18	3.6	11	44	12	06	15	51	20	01	19	37
13	19	36	−21.0	54.5	29.7	330	260	26	4.6	12	26	12	47	16	40	20	57	20	36
14	20	26	−19.7	54.3	29.6	342	256	35	5.6	13	00	13	19	17	27	21	59	21	41
15	21	15	−17.5	54.2	29.6	354	253	44	6.6	13	30	13	45	18	12	23	03	22	48
16	22	03	−14.6	54.4	29.6	6	250	54	7.6	13	54	14	05	18	57	—		23	58
17	22	50	−11.0	54.7	29.8	19	247	63	8.6	14	16	14	24	19	41	0	08	—	
18	23	36	−7.0	55.2	30.1	31	245	72	9.6	14	37	14	40	20	24	1	15	1	10
19	0	23	−2.6	55.8	30.4	43	243	81	10.6	14	56	14	56	21	09	2	24	2	23
20	1	10	+2.1	56.5	30.8	55	242	88	11.6	15	17	15	13	21	56	3	35	3	38
21	1	59	+6.8	57.3	31.2	67	240	94	12.6	15	39	15	31	22	44	4	49	4	56
22	2	51	+11.3	58.0	31.6	79	236	98	13.6	16	06	15	53	23	37	6	05	6	17
23	3	45	+15.3	58.7	32.0	91	202	100	14.6	16	38	16	21	—		7	23	7	39
24	4	43	+18.5	59.2	32.3	104	102	99	15.6	17	18	16	59	0	32	8	39	8	58
25	5	43	+20.7	59.6	32.5	116	95	96	16.6	18	10	17	47	1	31	9	50	10	13
26	6	45	+21.5	59.8	32.6	128	97	90	17.6	19	13	18	51	2	31	10	52	11	16
27	7	47	+20.9	59.8	32.6	140	101	82	18.6	20	25	20	06	3	32	11	44	12	04
28	8	48	+18.9	59.6	32.5	152	105	73	19.6	21	42	21	26	4	31	12	24	12	41
29	9	46	+15.8	59.4	32.3	164	109	62	20.6	23	02	22	50	5	27	12	56	13	08
30	10	42	+11.8	59.0	32.2	176	112	50	21.6	—		—		6	20	13	23	13	31

MERCURY

Day	R.A.		Dec	Mag.	Diam.	Phase	Rise		Transit		Set	
	h	m	°		″	%	h	m	h	m	h	m
1	15	52.0	−22.8	−0.2	6	74	9	27	13	10	16	53
3	16	02.0	−23.4	−0.2	6	70	9	33	13	12	16	50
5	16	11.6	−23.9	−0.2	6	67	9	38	13	13	16	48
7	16	20.5	−24.3	−0.2	7	62	9	42	13	14	16	46
9	16	28.5	−24.6	−0.1	7	57	9	44	13	14	16	44
11	16	35.4	−24.7	−0.1	7	52	9	44	13	12	16	41
13	16	40.9	−24.8	+0.0	8	46	9	41	13	09	16	38
15	16	44.7	−24.7	+0.2	8	39	9	35	13	04	16	34
17	16	46.2	−24.4	+0.5	8	31	9	26	12	57	16	30
19	16	45.1	−24.0	+0.9	9	23	9	13	12	47	16	23
21	16	41.1	−23.4	+1.5	9	15	8	56	12	35	16	16
23	16	34.3	−22.5	+2.5	10	8	8	34	12	19	16	07
25	16	25.0	−21.5	+3.7	10	2	8	09	12	02	15	57
27	16	14.3	−20.4	+5.3	10	0	7	42	11	43	15	46
29	16	03.4	−19.3	+4.2	10	1	7	16	11	25	15	36

Rising and setting times are for latitude 54°

VENUS

Day	R.A.		Dec	Mag.	Diam.	Phase	Rise		Transit		Set	
	h	m	°		″	%	h	m	h	m	h	m
1	13	42.8	−16.1	−4.1	65	1	6	23	10	53	15	27
6	13	35.2	−14.1	−4.3	63	4	5	45	10	27	15	13
11	13	30.9	−12.4	−4.5	59	8	5	11	10	04	15	00
16	13	30.5	−11.0	−4.6	56	12	4	44	9	45	14	48
21	13	33.6	−10.2	−4.6	51	17	4	24	9	29	14	37
26	13	40.0	−9.8	−4.6	47	21	4	09	9	17	14	26

MARS

Day	R.A.		Dec	Mag.	Diam.	Phase	Rise		Transit		Set	
	h	m	°		″	%	h	m	h	m	h	m
1	21	36.3	−16.7	−0.6	12	86	14	27	18	55	23	23
6	21	47.3	−15.6	−0.5	11	86	14	11	18	46	23	22
11	21	58.5	−14.4	−0.4	11	86	13	55	18	37	23	20
16	22	09.9	−13.1	−0.3	10	86	13	39	18	29	23	20
21	22	21.5	−11.8	−0.2	10	86	13	23	18	21	23	19
26	22	33.2	−10.5	−0.1	10	86	13	07	18	13	23	19

SUNRISE AND SUNSET

	London 0° 05′ | 51° 30′				Bristol 2° 35′ | 51° 28′				Birmingham 1° 55′ | 52° 28′				Manchester 2° 15′ | 53° 28′				Newcastle 1° 37′ | 54° 59′				Glasgow 4° 14′ | 55° 52′				Belfast 5° 56′ | 54° 35′			
d	h	m	h	m	h	m	h	m	h	m	h	m	h	m	h	m	h	m	h	m	h	m	h	m	h	m	h	m
1	6	54	16	34	7	03	16	44	7	04	16	38	7	08	16	37	7	10	16	29	7	23	16	37	7	26	16	48
2	6	55	16	32	7	05	16	42	7	05	16	36	7	10	16	35	7	12	16	27	7	25	16	35	7	28	16	46
3	6	57	16	30	7	07	16	40	7	07	16	34	7	12	16	33	7	14	16	25	7	27	16	33	7	30	16	44
4	6	59	16	28	7	09	16	38	7	09	16	33	7	13	16	31	7	16	16	23	7	30	16	31	7	32	16	42
5	7	01	16	27	7	11	16	37	7	11	16	31	7	15	16	29	7	18	16	21	7	32	16	29	7	34	16	40
6	7	02	16	25	7	12	16	35	7	13	16	29	7	17	16	27	7	20	16	19	7	34	16	27	7	36	16	38
7	7	04	16	23	7	14	16	33	7	15	16	27	7	19	16	25	7	22	16	17	7	36	16	25	7	38	16	36
8	7	06	16	22	7	16	16	32	7	16	16	26	7	21	16	24	7	24	16	16	7	38	16	23	7	40	16	34
9	7	08	16	20	7	18	16	30	7	18	16	24	7	23	16	22	7	26	16	14	7	40	16	21	7	42	16	33
10	7	09	16	18	7	19	16	29	7	20	16	22	7	25	16	20	7	28	16	12	7	42	16	19	7	44	16	31
11	7	11	16	17	7	21	16	27	7	22	16	21	7	27	16	19	7	30	16	10	7	44	16	17	7	46	16	29
12	7	13	16	15	7	23	16	26	7	24	16	19	7	29	16	17	7	32	16	08	7	46	16	15	7	48	16	27
13	7	15	16	14	7	25	16	24	7	25	16	18	7	31	16	15	7	34	16	07	7	48	16	13	7	50	16	26
14	7	16	16	13	7	26	16	23	7	27	16	16	7	32	16	14	7	36	16	05	7	51	16	11	7	52	16	24
15	7	18	16	11	7	28	16	21	7	29	16	15	7	34	16	12	7	38	16	03	7	53	16	10	7	54	16	22
16	7	20	16	10	7	30	16	20	7	31	16	13	7	36	16	11	7	40	16	02	7	55	16	08	7	56	16	21
17	7	22	16	08	7	31	16	19	7	33	16	12	7	38	16	09	7	42	16	00	7	57	16	06	7	58	16	19
18	7	23	16	07	7	33	16	17	7	34	16	11	7	40	16	08	7	44	15	59	7	59	16	05	7	59	16	18
19	7	25	16	06	7	35	16	16	7	36	16	09	7	42	16	07	7	46	15	57	8	01	16	03	8	01	16	16
20	7	27	16	05	7	36	16	15	7	38	16	08	7	43	16	05	7	48	15	56	8	03	16	02	8	03	16	15
21	7	28	16	04	7	38	16	14	7	39	16	07	7	45	16	04	7	50	15	54	8	05	16	00	8	05	16	14
22	7	30	16	03	7	40	16	13	7	41	16	06	7	47	16	03	7	52	15	53	8	07	15	59	8	07	16	12
23	7	31	16	02	7	41	16	12	7	43	16	05	7	49	16	02	7	53	15	52	8	08	15	58	8	09	16	11
24	7	33	16	01	7	43	16	11	7	44	16	04	7	50	16	01	7	55	15	51	8	10	15	56	8	10	16	10
25	7	35	16	00	7	44	16	10	7	46	16	03	7	52	15	59	7	57	15	49	8	12	15	55	8	12	16	09
26	7	36	15	59	7	46	16	09	7	48	16	02	7	54	15	58	7	59	15	48	8	14	15	54	8	14	16	08
27	7	38	15	58	7	47	16	08	7	49	16	01	7	55	15	57	8	01	15	47	8	16	15	53	8	16	16	07
28	7	39	15	57	7	49	16	07	7	51	16	00	7	57	15	57	8	02	15	46	8	18	15	52	8	17	16	06
29	7	41	15	56	7	50	16	06	7	52	15	59	7	59	15	56	8	04	15	45	8	19	15	51	8	19	16	05
30	7	42	15	56	7	52	16	06	7	54	15	58	8	00	15	55	8	06	15	44	8	21	15	50	8	21	16	04

JUPITER

Day	R.A. h	m	Dec °	Mag.	Diam. ″	Rise h	m	Transit h	m	Set h	m
1	15	44.1	−19.1	−1.7	31	8	51	13	01	17	12
11	15	53.1	−19.5	−1.7	31	8	24	12	31	16	38
21	16	02.3	−20.0	−1.7	31	7	57	12	01	16	05

Equatorial Diam. 31″, Polar Diam. 29″

SATURN

Day	R.A. h	m	Dec °	Mag.	Diam. ″	Rise h	m	Transit h	m	Set h	m
1	18	20.3	−22.8	+0.6	16	11	53	15	37	19	21
11	18	24.1	−22.8	+0.6	16	11	17	15	01	18	45
21	18	28.3	−22.7	+0.6	15	10	42	14	26	18	10

Equatorial Diam. 15″, Polar Diam. 14″
Rings – major axis 35″ minor axis 16″, Tilt 26°

URANUS

Day	R.A. h	m	Dec °	Mag.	Diam. ″	Rise h	m	Transit h	m	Set h	m
1	1	52.3	+10.9	+5.7	4	16	03	23	08	6	16
11	1	50.8	+10.8	+5.7	4	15	23	22	27	5	35
21	1	49.4	+10.7	+5.7	4	14	43	21	46	4	53

NEPTUNE

Day	R.A. h	m	Dec °	Mag.	Diam. ″	Rise h	m	Transit h	m	Set h	m
1	23	01.1	−7.4	+7.8	2	14	55	20	17	1	43
11	23	00.7	−7.4	+7.9	2	14	15	19	37	1	03
21	23	00.5	−7.4	+7.9	2	13	36	18	58	0	23

December 2018

TWELFTH MONTH, 31 DAYS. *Decem* (ten), tenth month of Roman pre-Julian calendar

1	*Saturday*	The Locarno Treaties are formally signed 1925	day 335
2	*Sunday*	Napoleon III declares a second French empire 1852	336

3	*Monday*	The Malta summit brings the Cold War to a close 1989	week 49 day 337
4	*Tuesday*	Francisco Franco, autocratic head of Spain from 1939 until his death in 1975 *b.* 1892	338
5	*Wednesday*	The UK declares war on Finland, Hungary and Romania 1941	339
6	*Thursday*	The Anglo–Irish treaty partitions Northern Ireland from the Republic of Ireland 1921	340
7	*Friday*	Clement Attlee resigns as Labour leader 1955	341
8	*Saturday*	Ronald Reagan and Mikhail Gorbachev sign the Intermediate-Range Nuclear Forces Treaty 1987	342
9	*Sunday*	A European Council agrees on the draft Treaty on the European Union in Maastricht 1991	343

10	*Monday*	Formal negotations on the North Atlantic Treaty begin 1948	week 50 day 344
11	*Tuesday*	Mussolini declares Italy's withdrawal from the League of Nations 1937	345
12	*Wednesday*	Switzerland abolishes border control at land borders 2008	346
13	*Thursday*	Robert Kalina's designs for Euro banknotes are unveiled 1996	347
14	*Friday*	Leaders of Bosnia, Serbia and Croatia sign the Dayton Accord to end war in the Balkans 1995	348
15	*Saturday*	The gates separating Spain from Gibraltar are opened after 13 years 1982	349
16	*Sunday*	Henry VI of England is crowned king of France 1431	350

17	*Monday*	Pope Paul III excommunicates Henry VIII from the Catholic Church 1538	week 51 day 351
18	*Tuesday*	Vaclav Havel, the first president and last Communist leader of Romania *d.* 1989	352
19	*Wednesday*	Philip V, King of Spain (1700–46), first Spanish king from the House of Bourbon *b.* 1683	353
20	*Thursday*	Luis Carrero Blanco, the prime minister in Spain, is assasinated in Madrid 1973	354
21	*Friday*	General Charles de Gaulle is elected President of France 1958	355
22	*Saturday*	The Romanian government falls in an anti-communist coup 1989	356
23	*Sunday*	Sir Thomas Smith English scholar, parliamentarian and diplomat *b.* 1513	357

24	*Monday*	The 10 nation European Space Agency (ESA) launches its first rocket Ariane 1 1979	358
25	*Tuesday*	Allied and German soldiers play football in No-Mans-Land after an unofficial ceasefire 1914	week 52 day 359
26	*Wednesday*	Étienne Constantin de Gerlache, first prime minister of Belgium *b.* 1785	360
27	*Thursday*	Viktor Yushchenko is declared President of Ukraine in an election re-run 2004	361
28	*Friday*	The European Space Agency (ESA) launches Giove A, the first test satellite in its Galileo programme 2005	362
29	*Saturday*	Elizabeth of Russia, daughter of Peter the Great, Empress of Russia (1741–62) *b.* 1709	363
30	*Sunday*	Richard, Duke of York is killed and his army defeated at the Battle of Wakefield 1460	364

31	*Monday*	Vladimir Putin takes over from Boris Yeltsin as President of Russia 1999	week 1 day 365

ASTRONOMICAL PHENOMENA

d	h	
3	19	Venus 4° South of the Moon
5	21	Mercury 2° South of the Moon
6	13	Jupiter 3° South of the Moon
7	15	Neptune 0.04° South of Mars
9	5	Saturn 1° South of the Moon
14	6	Peak of the Geminid meteor shower
14	14	Neptune 3° North of the Moon
14	23	Mars 4° North of the Moon
15	11	Mercury greatest elongation West
18	4	Uranus 5° North of the Moon
21	15	Jupiter 1° South of Mercury
21	22	Solstice

MINIMA OF ALGOL

d	h	d	h	d	h
3	3.7	14	15.0	26	2.2
6	0.5	17	11.8	28	23.1
8	21.3	20	8.6	31	19.9
11	18.1	23	5.4		

CONSTELLATIONS

The following constellations are near the meridian at

	d	h		d	h
November	1	24	December	16	21
November	15	23	January	1	20
December	1	22	January	16	19

Ursa Major (below the Pole), Ursa Minor (below the Pole), Cassiopeia, Andromeda, Perseus, Triangulum, Aries, Taurus, Cetus and Eridanus

THE MOON

Phases, Apsides and Node	d	h	m
● New Moon	7	7	20
◗ First Quarter	15	11	49
○ Full Moon	22	17	49
◖ Last Quarter	29	9	34
Apogee (405,177 km)	12	12	25
Perigee (361,061 km)	24	9	49

Mean longitude of the ascending node on 1st, 119°

THE SUN

Diam. 32.5'

Day	Right Ascension			Dec. −	Equation of time		Rise 52°		56°		Transit		Set 52°		56°		Sidereal time			Transit of first point of Aries		
	h	m	s	°	m	s	h	m	h	m	h	m	h	m	h	m	h	m	s	h	m	s
1	16	28	03	21.8	+11	09	7	45	8	06	11	49	15	53	15	32	4	39	13	19	20	47
2	16	32	22	21.9	+10	47	7	46	8	08	11	49	15	52	15	31	4	43	10	19	16	50
3	16	36	42	22.1	+10	23	7	48	8	09	11	50	15	51	15	30	4	47	06	19	12	54
4	16	41	02	22.2	+10	00	7	49	8	11	11	50	15	51	15	29	4	51	03	19	08	57
5	16	45	23	22.3	+9	35	7	50	8	12	11	51	15	50	15	29	4	55	00	19	05	00
6	16	49	45	22.5	+9	10	7	52	8	14	11	51	15	50	15	28	4	58	56	19	01	04
7	16	54	07	22.6	+8	45	7	53	8	15	11	51	15	50	15	28	5	02	53	18	57	07
8	16	58	29	22.7	+8	19	7	54	8	16	11	52	15	49	15	27	5	06	49	18	53	11
9	17	02	52	22.8	+7	52	7	55	8	18	11	52	15	49	15	27	5	10	46	18	49	14
10	17	07	16	22.9	+7	26	7	56	8	19	11	53	15	49	15	26	5	14	42	18	45	18
11	17	11	40	23.0	+6	58	7	57	8	20	11	53	15	49	15	26	5	18	39	18	41	21
12	17	16	04	23.1	+6	30	7	58	8	21	11	54	15	49	15	26	5	22	35	18	37	25
13	17	20	29	23.1	+6	02	7	59	8	22	11	54	15	49	15	26	5	26	32	18	33	28
14	17	24	54	23.2	+5	34	8	00	8	23	11	55	15	49	15	26	5	30	29	18	29	31
15	17	29	19	23.2	+5	05	8	01	8	24	11	55	15	49	15	26	5	34	25	18	25	35
16	17	33	44	23.3	+4	36	8	02	8	25	11	56	15	49	15	26	5	38	22	18	21	38
17	17	38	10	23.3	+4	07	8	03	8	26	11	56	15	49	15	26	5	42	18	18	17	42
18	17	42	36	23.4	+3	38	8	03	8	27	11	57	15	50	15	26	5	46	15	18	13	45
19	17	47	02	23.4	+3	09	8	04	8	27	11	57	15	50	15	27	5	50	11	18	09	49
20	17	51	28	23.4	+2	39	8	05	8	28	11	58	15	50	15	27	5	54	08	18	05	52
21	17	55	54	23.4	+2	09	8	05	8	29	11	58	15	51	15	28	5	58	04	18	01	56
22	18	00	20	23.4	+1	40	8	06	8	29	11	59	15	51	15	28	6	02	01	17	57	59
23	18	04	47	23.4	+1	10	8	06	8	30	11	59	15	52	15	29	6	05	58	17	54	02
24	18	09	13	23.4	+0	40	8	07	8	30	12	00	15	53	15	29	6	09	54	17	50	06
25	18	13	39	23.4	+0	10	8	07	8	30	12	00	15	53	15	30	6	13	51	17	46	09
26	18	18	06	23.4	−0	19	8	07	8	30	12	01	15	54	15	31	6	17	47	17	42	13
27	18	22	32	23.3	−0	49	8	07	8	31	12	01	15	55	15	32	6	21	44	17	38	16
28	18	26	58	23.3	−1	18	8	08	8	31	12	02	15	56	15	32	6	25	40	17	34	20
29	18	31	24	23.2	−1	48	8	08	8	31	12	02	15	56	15	33	6	29	37	17	30	23
30	18	35	49	23.2	−2	17	8	08	8	31	12	03	15	57	15	34	6	33	33	17	26	27
31	18	40	15	23.1	−2	46	8	08	8	31	12	03	15	58	15	36	6	37	30	17	22	30

DURATION OF TWILIGHT

Latitude	52°	56°	52°	56°	52°	56°	52°	56°
	1 December		11 December		21 December		31 December	
Civil	40	45	41	47	41	47	41	47
Nautical	82	93	84	96	85	97	84	96
Astronomical	123	138	125	141	126	142	125	141

THE NIGHT SKY

Mercury is a morning object and highest (at Greenwich) on the 12th when up two hours before the Sun. Greatest western elongation occurs on the 15th. The waning crescent Moon is between Mercury and Jupiter on the 6th.

Venus (magnitude −4.9 to −4.6) rises four hours before the Sun during December. The Moon is nearby on the 4th.

Mars (magnitude 0.0 to 0.4) spends most of December in Aquarius but crosses into Pisces later. It is also at eastern quadrature so the disk appears gibbous. Mars is less than five arc-minutes from Neptune (magnitude 7.9) on the 7th and the Moon is nearby on the 14th and 15th.

Jupiter (magnitude −1.8) returns to the morning sky after the first week and ends 2018 rising two hours before the Sun. It is less than 1° from Mercury on the 21st.

Saturn (magnitude 0.5) is an evening object but will be lost to view after the third week. The Moon is nearby on the 8th and 9th. An occultation of Saturn on the 9th is visible from Siberia.

The Geminids enjoy a dark sky period once the Moon sets before local midnight on the 14th.

The short period comet 46P/Wirtanen passes 0.0777 AU (11.62 million km) from Earth on December 16th and may appear as a small diffuse glow to the naked eye this month.

On 2019 January 01 the New Horizons spacecraft will give us our first close up of a classical Kuiper Belt object during its flyby of 2014 MU69.

THE MOON

Day	R.A.		Dec	Hor Par	Diam	Sun Co-Long	PA of Br. limb	Ph.	Age	Rise				Transit		Set			
										52°		56°				52°		56°	
	h	m	°	'	'	°	°	%	d	h	m	h	m	h	m	h	m	h	m
1	11	35	+7.2	58.6	31.9	189	114	39	22.6	0	20	0	13	7	11	13	46	13	50
2	12	27	+2.3	58.2	31.7	201	116	29	23.6	1	37	1	35	7	59	14	08	14	07
3	13	17	−2.7	57.7	31.4	213	116	19	24.6	2	53	2	55	8	47	14	29	14	24
4	14	07	−7.4	57.2	31.2	225	116	11	25.6	4	07	4	15	9	35	14	52	14	43
5	14	58	−11.8	56.7	30.9	237	116	06	26.6	5	21	5	33	10	23	15	17	15	04
6	15	49	−15.5	56.3	30.7	249	118	02	27.6	6	32	6	48	11	12	15	45	15	29
7	16	41	−18.4	55.8	30.4	262	144	00	28.6	7	40	7	59	12	02	16	20	16	01
8	17	34	−20.4	55.3	30.1	274	253	00	0.0	8	42	9	04	12	53	17	02	16	39
9	18	26	−21.4	54.9	29.9	286	262	03	1.0	9	37	9	59	13	43	17	50	17	26
10	19	18	−21.4	54.5	29.7	298	261	07	2.0	10	24	10	45	14	33	18	44	18	23
11	20	10	−20.4	54.3	29.6	310	258	12	3.0	11	01	11	21	15	20	19	44	19	25
12	20	59	−18.5	54.1	29.5	323	255	19	4.0	11	33	11	49	16	07	20	47	20	32
13	21	48	−15.8	54.1	29.5	335	252	27	5.0	11	58	12	12	16	51	21	52	21	40
14	22	34	−12.5	54.3	29.6	347	249	36	6.0	12	21	12	30	17	35	22	58	22	50
15	23	20	−8.6	54.6	29.8	359	247	45	7.0	12	41	12	47	18	18	—		—	
16	0	06	−4.4	55.1	30.0	11	246	55	8.0	13	01	13	02	19	01	0	05	0	01
17	0	52	+0.1	55.8	30.4	23	246	65	9.0	13	20	13	18	19	45	1	14	1	14
18	1	39	+4.7	56.6	30.8	36	246	74	10.0	13	41	13	34	20	32	2	25	2	29
19	2	29	+9.3	57.4	31.3	48	247	83	11.0	14	04	13	54	21	22	3	38	3	47
20	3	22	+13.5	58.4	31.8	60	249	90	12.0	14	33	14	18	22	16	4	54	5	08
21	4	18	+17.2	59.2	32.3	72	251	96	13.0	15	09	14	50	23	14	6	12	6	31
22	5	17	+19.9	59.9	32.7	84	249	99	14.0	15	56	15	33	—		7	29	7	50
23	6	20	+21.4	60.5	32.9	96	121	100	15.0	16	55	16	31	0	15	8	38	9	00
24	7	24	+21.4	60.7	33.1	108	100	98	16.0	18	05	17	43	1	17	9	36	9	57
25	8	27	+19.8	60.7	33.1	120	103	93	17.0	19	23	19	07	2	19	10	23	10	41
26	9	29	+17.0	60.4	32.9	133	106	86	18.0	20	45	20	32	3	19	10	58	11	13
27	10	27	+13.1	59.9	32.7	145	110	76	19.0	22	07	21	59	4	15	11	28	11	38
28	11	23	+8.5	59.3	32.3	157	112	66	20.0	23	25	23	22	5	08	11	53	11	58
29	12	15	+3.6	58.6	31.9	169	113	55	21.0	—		—		5	57	12	15	12	16
30	13	06	−1.4	57.9	31.6	181	113	44	22.0	0	42	0	44	6	46	12	36	12	33
31	13	56	−6.3	57.3	31.2	193	112	33	23.0	1	57	2	03	7	33	12	58	12	50

MERCURY

Day	R.A.		Dec	Mag.	Diam.	Phase	Rise		Transit		Set	
	h	m	°		"	%	h	m	h	m	h	m
1	15	54.0	−18.3	+2.7	10	6	6	53	11	08	15	26
3	15	46.9	−17.5	+1.6	9	13	6	34	10	54	15	16
5	15	42.7	−17.0	+0.9	9	22	6	20	10	43	15	08
7	15	41.5	−16.9	+0.4	8	31	6	10	10	35	15	00
9	15	43.0	−16.9	+0.0	8	40	6	05	10	29	14	54
11	15	46.8	−17.2	−0.2	7	48	6	03	10	26	14	48
13	15	52.5	−17.7	−0.3	7	55	6	04	10	24	14	43
15	15	59.7	−18.2	−0.4	7	62	6	08	10	24	14	39
17	16	08.1	−18.8	−0.4	6	67	6	13	10	24	14	36
19	16	17.5	−19.5	−0.4	6	72	6	19	10	26	14	33
21	16	27.6	−20.1	−0.4	6	76	6	26	10	29	14	31
23	16	38.4	−20.8	−0.4	6	79	6	33	10	32	14	30
25	16	49.7	−21.4	−0.4	6	82	6	41	10	35	14	29
27	17	01.4	−22.0	−0.4	6	84	6	49	10	39	14	29
29	17	13.5	−22.5	−0.4	5	87	6	57	10	43	14	29
31	17	25.8	−23.0	−0.4	5	88	7	05	10	48	14	30

Rising and setting times are for latitude 54°

VENUS

Day	R.A.		Dec	Mag.	Diam.	Phase	Rise		Transit		Set	
	h	m	°		"	%	h	m	h	m	h	m
1	13	49.2	−9.8	−4.7	44	26	3	59	9	07	14	16
6	14	00.8	−10.2	−4.6	40	30	3	53	8	59	14	06
11	14	14.4	−10.8	−4.6	37	34	3	51	8	53	13	56
16	14	29.6	−11.7	−4.6	35	37	3	52	8	49	13	46
21	14	46.2	−12.7	−4.6	32	41	3	55	8	46	13	37
26	15	04.0	−13.8	−4.5	30	44	4	01	8	44	13	28
31	15	23.0	−15.0	−4.5	29	47	4	07	8	44	13	21

MARS

Day	R.A.		Dec	Mag.	Diam.	Phase	Rise		Transit		Set	
	h	m	°		"	%	h	m	h	m	h	m
1	22	44.9	−9.2	0.0	9	86	12	52	18	05	23	18
6	22	56.8	−7.8	+0.1	9	86	12	36	17	57	23	18
11	23	08.7	−6.4	+0.1	9	86	12	20	17	49	23	18
16	23	20.7	−5.0	+0.2	8	87	12	04	17	41	23	18
21	23	32.7	−3.6	+0.3	8	87	11	49	17	33	23	18
26	23	44.7	−2.1	+0.4	8	87	11	33	17	26	23	18
31	23	56.9	−0.7	+0.4	7	87	11	18	17	18	23	19

SUNRISE AND SUNSET

	London			Bristol			Birmingham			Manchester			Newcastle			Glasgow			Belfast		
	0°	05′	51°	30′	2°	35′	51°	28′	1°	55′	52°	28′	2°	15′	53°	28′	1°	37′	54°	59′	4°	14′	55°	52′	5°	56′	54°	35′
d	h	m	h	m	h	m	h	m	h	m	h	m	h	m	h	m	h	m	h	m	h	m	h	m	h	m	h	m
1	7 43	15 55	7 53	16 05	7 55	15 58	8 02	15 54	8 07	15 43	8 23	15 49	8 22	16 03
2	7 45	15 54	7 55	16 04	7 57	15 57	8 03	15 53	8 09	15 43	8 24	15 48	8 24	16 02
3	7 46	15 54	7 56	16 04	7 58	15 56	8 04	15 53	8 10	15 42	8 26	15 47	8 25	16 01
4	7 47	15 53	7 57	16 03	7 59	15 56	8 06	15 52	8 12	15 41	8 27	15 46	8 27	16 01
5	7 49	15 53	7 59	16 03	8 01	15 55	8 07	15 52	8 13	15 41	8 29	15 46	8 28	16 00
6	7 50	15 52	8 00	16 03	8 02	15 55	8 09	15 51	8 15	15 40	8 30	15 45	8 30	16 00
7	7 51	15 52	8 01	16 02	8 03	15 55	8 10	15 51	8 16	15 40	8 32	15 45	8 31	15 59
8	7 52	15 52	8 02	16 02	8 05	15 54	8 11	15 50	8 17	15 39	8 33	15 44	8 32	15 59
9	7 54	15 52	8 03	16 02	8 06	15 54	8 12	15 50	8 19	15 39	8 35	15 44	8 33	15 58
10	7 55	15 51	8 04	16 02	8 07	15 54	8 13	15 50	8 20	15 39	8 36	15 43	8 35	15 58
11	7 56	15 51	8 05	16 01	8 08	15 54	8 15	15 50	8 21	15 38	8 37	15 43	8 36	15 58
12	7 57	15 51	8 06	16 01	8 09	15 54	8 16	15 50	8 22	15 38	8 38	15 43	8 37	15 58
13	7 58	15 51	8 07	16 01	8 10	15 54	8 17	15 50	8 23	15 38	8 39	15 43	8 38	15 58
14	7 59	15 51	8 08	16 01	8 11	15 54	8 18	15 50	8 24	15 38	8 40	15 43	8 39	15 58
15	7 59	15 51	8 09	16 02	8 12	15 54	8 19	15 50	8 25	15 38	8 41	15 43	8 40	15 58
16	8 00	15 52	8 10	16 02	8 13	15 54	8 19	15 50	8 26	15 38	8 42	15 43	8 41	15 58
17	8 01	15 52	8 11	16 02	8 13	15 54	8 20	15 50	8 27	15 38	8 43	15 43	8 42	15 58
18	8 02	15 52	8 11	16 02	8 14	15 54	8 21	15 50	8 28	15 39	8 44	15 43	8 42	15 58
19	8 02	15 52	8 12	16 03	8 15	15 55	8 22	15 51	8 28	15 39	8 44	15 44	8 43	15 59
20	8 03	15 53	8 13	16 03	8 15	15 55	8 22	15 51	8 29	15 39	8 45	15 44	8 44	15 59
21	8 03	15 53	8 13	16 03	8 16	15 56	8 23	15 51	8 29	15 40	8 46	15 44	8 44	15 59
22	8 04	15 54	8 14	16 04	8 16	15 56	8 23	15 52	8 30	15 40	8 46	15 45	8 45	16 00
23	8 04	15 54	8 14	16 05	8 17	15 57	8 24	15 52	8 30	15 41	8 47	15 46	8 45	16 01
24	8 05	15 55	8 15	16 05	8 17	15 57	8 24	15 53	8 31	15 41	8 47	15 46	8 45	16 01
25	8 05	15 56	8 15	16 06	8 18	15 58	8 24	15 54	8 31	15 42	8 47	15 47	8 46	16 02
26	8 05	15 56	8 15	16 07	8 18	15 59	8 25	15 55	8 31	15 43	8 47	15 48	8 46	16 03
27	8 06	15 57	8 15	16 07	8 18	15 59	8 25	15 55	8 31	15 44	8 47	15 48	8 46	16 03
28	8 06	15 58	8 16	16 08	8 18	16 00	8 25	15 56	8 31	15 45	8 48	15 49	8 46	16 04
29	8 06	15 59	8 16	16 09	8 18	16 01	8 25	15 57	8 32	15 46	8 48	15 50	8 46	16 05
30	8 06	16 00	8 16	16 10	8 18	16 02	8 25	15 58	8 31	15 47	8 48	15 51	8 46	16 06
31	8 06	16 01	8 16	16 11	8 18	16 03	8 25	15 59	8 31	15 48	8 47	15 53	8 46	16 07

JUPITER

Day	R.A.		Dec	Mag.	Diam.	Rise		Transit		Set	
	h	m	°		″	h	m	h	m	h	m
1	16	11.6	−20.4	−1.7	31	7 30		11 31		15 32	
11	16	21.0	−20.8	−1.7	31	7 03		11 01		14 59	
21	16	30.3	−21.2	−1.8	31	6 35		10 31		14 26	
31	16	39.4	−21.5	−1.8	32	6 07		10 00		13 54	

Equatorial Diam. 31″, Polar Diam. 29″

SATURN

Day	R.A.		Dec	Mag.	Diam.	Rise		Transit		Set	
	h	m	°		″	h	m	h	m	h	m
1	18	32.8	−22.7	+0.6	15	10 07		13 51		17 36	
11	18	37.6	−22.6	+0.5	15	9 32		13 17		17 02	
21	18	42.6	−22.6	+0.5	15	8 57		12 43		16 28	
31	18	47.7	−22.5	+0.5	15	8 22		12 08		15 54	

Equatorial Diam. 15″, Polar Diam. 14″
Rings – major axis 34″ minor axis 16″, Tilt 26°

URANUS

Day	R.A.		Dec	Mag.	Diam.	Rise		Transit		Set	
	h	m	°		″	h	m	h	m	h	m
1	1	48.2	+10.6	+5.7	4	14 03		21 06		4 12	
11	1	47.2	+10.5	+5.7	4	13 23		20 25		3 31	
21	1	46.5	+10.4	+5.8	4	12 44		19 45		2 51	
31	1	46.2	+10.4	+5.8	4	12 04		19 06		2 11	

NEPTUNE

Day	R.A.		Dec	Mag.	Diam.	Rise		Transit		Set	
	h	m	°		″	h	m	h	m	h	m
1	23	00.5	−7.4	+7.9	2	12 56		18 18		23 40	
11	23	00.7	−7.4	+7.9	2	12 17		17 39		23 01	
21	23	01.2	−7.3	+7.9	2	11 38		17 00		22 23	
31	23	01.8	−7.3	+7.9	2	10 59		16 22		21 44	

ECLIPSES 2018

During 2018 there will be five eclipses, three of the Sun and two of the Moon.

1. A total lunar eclipse on 31 January is visible in north and east Europe, Asia, Australasia, north-east Africa, North America, north-west South America, the Pacific and the Indian Ocean.
2. A partial solar eclipse on 15 February is visible in the south of South America, southern Pacific and Antarctica.
3. A partial solar eclipse on 13 July is visible in the extreme south of Australia.
4. A total lunar eclipse on 27 July is visible in South America, Europe, Africa, Asia and Australia. Details for London are:

	h/m
Moonrise	19:49
Max. eclipse	20:22
Moon exits totality	21:14
Moon exits umbra	22:19
Moon exits penumbra	23:30
Penumbral Duration	3h 41.3m
Umbral duration	2h 30.2m
Duration of totality	1h 24.5m
Magnitude	1.614

5. Partial solar eclipse on 11 August visible in north Europe and northeast Asia.

MEAN AND SIDEREAL TIME

The length of a sidereal day in mean time is 23h 56m 04s.09. Hence 1h MT = 1h+9^s.86 ST and 1h ST = 1h − 9^s.83 MT.

Acceleration					Retardation				
h	m	s	m	s	h	m	s	m	s
1	0	10	0	00	1	0	10	0	00
2	0	20	3	02	2	0	20	3	03
3	0	30	9	07	3	0	29	9	09
4	0	39	15	13	4	0	39	15	15
5	0	49	21	18	5	0	49	21	21
6	0	59	27	23	6	0	59	27	28
7	1	09	33	28	7	1	09	33	34
8	1	19	39	34	8	1	19	39	40
9	1	29	45	39	9	1	28	45	46
10	1	39	51	44	10	1	38	51	53
11	1	48	57	49	11	1	48	57	59
12	1	58	60	00	12	1	58	60	00
13	2	08			13	2	08		
14	2	18			14	2	18		
15	2	28			15	2	27		
16	2	38			16	2	37		
17	2	48			17	2	47		
18	2	57			18	2	57		
19	3	07			19	3	07		
20	3	17			20	3	17		
21	3	27			21	3	26		
22	3	37			22	3	36		
23	3	47			23	3	46		
24	3	57			24	3	56		

The middle critical-table columns read (Acceleration): 0, 1, 2, 3, 4, 5, 6, 7, 8, 9, 10; (Retardation): 0, 1, 2, 3, 4, 5, 6, 7, 8, 9, 10.

To convert an interval of mean time to the corresponding interval of sidereal time, enter the acceleration table with the given mean time (taking the hours and the minutes and seconds separately) and add the acceleration obtained to the given mean time. To convert an interval of sidereal time to the corresponding interval of mean time, take out the retardation for the given sidereal time and subtract.

The columns for the minutes and seconds of the argument are in the form known as critical tables. To use these tables, find in the appropriate left-hand column the two entries between which the given number of minutes and seconds lies; the quantity in the right-hand column between these two entries is the required acceleration or retardation. Thus the acceleration for 11m 26s (which lies between the entries 9m 07s and 15m 13s) is 2s. If the given number of minutes and seconds is a tabular

entry, the required acceleration or retardation is the entry in the right-hand column above the given tabular entry, eg the retardation for 45m 46s is 7s.

Example − Convert 14h 27m 35s from ST to MT:

	h	m	s
Given ST	14	27	35
Retardation for 14h		2	18
Retardation for 27m 35s			5
Corresponding MT	14	25	12

For further explanation *see* pages 633 and 635.

EXPLANATION OF ASTRONOMICAL DATA

Positions of the heavenly bodies are given only to the degree of accuracy required by amateur astronomers for setting telescopes, or for plotting on celestial globes or star atlases. Where intermediate positions are required, linear interpolation may be employed.

Detailed definitions of the terms used cannot be given here. They must be sought in astronomical literature, the internet or textbooks.

A special feature has been made of the times when the various heavenly bodies are visible in the British Isles. Since two columns, calculated for latitudes 52° and 56°, are devoted to risings and settings, the range 50° to 58° can be covered by interpolation and extrapolation. The times given in these columns are Greenwich Mean Times for the meridian of Greenwich. An observer west of this meridian must add his/her longitude (in time) and vice versa.

In accordance with the usual convention in astronomy, + and − indicate respectively north and south latitudes or declinations.

All data are, unless otherwise stated, for 0h Greenwich Mean Time (GMT), ie at the midnight at the beginning of the day named. Allowance must be made for British Summer Time during the period that this is in operation.

PAGE ONE OF EACH MONTH

The calendar for each month is explained on page 1055.

Under the heading Astronomical Phenomena will be found particulars of the more important conjunctions of the Sun, Moon and planets with each other, and also the dates of other astronomical phenomena of special interest.

Times of Minima of Algol are approximate times of the middle of the period of diminished light.

The Constellations listed each month are those that are near the meridian at the beginning of the month at 22h local mean time. Allowance must be made for British Summer Time if necessary. The fact that any star crosses the meridian 4m earlier each night or 2h earlier each month may be used, in conjunction with the lists given each month, to find what constellations are favourably placed at any moment.

The principal phases of the Moon are the GMTs when the difference between the longitude of the Moon and that of the Sun is 0°, 90°, 180° or 270°. The times of perigee and apogee are those when the Moon is nearest to, and farthest from, the Earth, respectively. The nodes or points of intersection of the Moon's orbit and the ecliptic make a complete retrograde circuit of the ecliptic in about 19 years. From a knowledge of the longitude of the ascending node and the inclination, whose value does not vary much from 5°, the path of the Moon among the stars may be plotted on a celestial globe or star atlas.

PAGE TWO OF EACH MONTH

The Sun's diameter, in arc minutes, is given once a month.

The right ascension and declination (Dec.) is that of the true Sun. The right ascension of the mean Sun is obtained by applying the equation of time, with the sign given, to the right ascension of the true Sun, or, more easily, by applying 12h to the Sidereal Time. The direction in which the equation of time has to be applied in different problems is a frequent source of confusion and error. Apparent Solar Time is equal to the Mean Solar Time plus the Equation of Time. For example, at 12h GMT on August 8 the Equation of Time is −5m 45s and thus at 12h Mean Time on that day the Apparent Time is 12h − 5m 45s = 11h 54m 15s.

The Greenwich Sidereal Time at 0h and the Transit of the First Point of Aries (which is really the mean time when the sidereal time is 0h) are used for converting mean time to sidereal time and vice versa.

The GMT of transit of the Sun at Greenwich may also be taken as the local mean time (LMT) of transit in any longitude. It is independent of latitude. The GMT of transit in any longitude is obtained by adding the longitude to the time given if west, and vice versa.

LIGHTING-UP TIME

The legal importance of sunrise and sunset is that the Road Vehicles Lighting Regulations 1989 (SI 1989 No. 1796) as amended, make the use of front and rear position lamps on vehicles compulsory during the period between sunset and sunrise. Headlamps on vehicles are required to be used during the hours of darkness on unlit roads, on lit roads with a speed limit exceeding 30mph, or whenever visibility is seriously reduced. The hours of darkness are defined in these regulations as the period between half an hour after sunset and half an hour before sunrise.

In all laws and regulations 'sunset' refers to the local sunset, ie the time at which the Sun sets at the place in question. This common-sense interpretation has been upheld by legal tribunals.

MAGNITUDE

Magnitudes of astronomical objects are measured in what may be considered the reverse to the obvious. Magnitude +3 is brighter than +4, magnitude −2 is brighter than magnitude −1. So from brighter to dimmer: −4, −3, −2, −1, 0, +1, +2, +3 etc, with +6 being the dimmest considered visible with the naked eye in very dark skies. Each magnitude is roughly 2.5 times brighter than the next, so a magnitude +1 object is 100 times brighter than a magnitude +6 object.

SUNRISE AND SUNSET

The times of sunrise and sunset are those when the Sun's upper limb, as affected by refraction, is on the true horizon of an observer at sea-level. Assuming the mean refraction to be 34′, and the Sun's semi-diameter to be 16′, the time given is that when the true zenith distance of the Sun's centre is 90°+34′+16′ or 90° 50′, or, in other words, when the depression of the Sun's centre below the true horizon is 50′. The upper limb is then 34′ below the true horizon, but is brought there by refraction. An observer on a ship might see the Sun for a minute or so longer, because of the dip of the horizon, while another viewing the sunset over hills or mountains would record an earlier time. Nevertheless, the moment when the true zenith distance of the Sun's centre is 90° 50′ is a precise time dependent only on the latitude and longitude of the place, and independent of its altitude above sea-level, the contour of its horizon, the vagaries of refraction or the small seasonal change in the Sun's diameter; this moment is suitable in every way as a definition of sunset (or sunrise) for all statutory purposes. For further information, *see* Sunrise, Sunset, Moonrise and Moonset on page 632.

TWILIGHT

Light reaches us before sunrise and continues to reach us for some time after sunset. The interval between darkness and sunrise or sunset and darkness is called twilight. Astronomically speaking, twilight is considered to begin or end when the Sun's centre is 18° below the horizon, as no light from the Sun can then reach the observer. As thus defined twilight may last several hours; in high latitudes at the summer

solstice the depression of 18° is not reached, and twilight lasts from sunset to sunrise. The duration of twilight data is given in minutes.

The need for some sub-division of twilight is met by dividing the gathering darkness into four stages.
(1) *Sunrise or Sunset*, defined as above
(2) *Civil twilight*, which begins or ends when the Sun's centre is 6° below the horizon. This marks the time when operations requiring daylight may commence or must cease. In England it varies from about 30 to 60 minutes after sunset and the same interval before sunrise
(3) *Nautical twilight*, which begins or ends when the Sun's centre is 12° below the horizon. This marks the time when it is, to all intents and purposes, completely dark
(4) *Astronomical twilight*, which begins or ends when the Sun's centre is 18° below the horizon. This marks theoretical perfect darkness. It is of little practical importance, especially if nautical twilight is tabulated
To assist observers the durations of civil, nautical and astronomical twilights are given at intervals of ten days. The beginning of a particular twilight is found by subtracting the duration from the time of sunrise, while the end is found by adding the duration to the time of sunset. Thus the beginning of astronomical twilight in latitude 52°, on the Greenwich meridian, on March 11 is found as 06h 23m − 113m = 04h 30m and similarly the end of civil twilight as 17h 58m +34m = 18h 32m. The letters TAN (twilight all night) are printed when twilight lasts all night.

Under the heading The Night Sky will be found notes describing the position and visibility of the planets and other phenomena.

PAGE THREE OF EACH MONTH

The Moon moves so rapidly among the stars that its position is given only to the degree of accuracy that permits linear interpolation. The right ascension (RA) and declination (Dec.) are geocentric, ie for an imaginary observer at the centre of the Earth. To an observer on the surface of the Earth the position is always different, as the altitude is always less on account of parallax, which may reach 1°.

The lunar terminator is the line separating the bright from the dark part of the Moon's disk. Apart from irregularities of the lunar surface, the terminator is elliptical, because it is a circle seen in projection. It becomes the full circle forming the limb, or edge, of the Moon at New and Full Moon. The selenographic longitude of the terminator is measured from the mean centre of the visible disk, which may differ from the visible centre by as much as 8°, because of libration.

Instead of the longitude of the terminator the Sun's selenographic co-longitude (Sun's co-long.) is tabulated. It is numerically equal to the selenographic longitude of the morning terminator, measured eastwards from the mean centre of the disk. Thus its value is approximately 270° at New Moon, 360° at First Quarter, 90° at Full Moon and 180° at Last Quarter.

The Position Angle (PA) of the Bright Limb is the position angle of the midpoint of the illuminated limb, measured eastwards from the north point on the disk. The Phase column shows the percentage of the area of the Moon's disk illuminated; this is also the illuminated percentage of the diameter at right angles to the line of cusps. The terminator is a semi-ellipse whose major axis is the line of cusps, and whose semi-minor axis is determined by the tabulated percentage; from New Moon to Full Moon the east limb is dark, and vice versa.

The times given as moonrise and moonset are those when the upper limb of the Moon is on the horizon of an observer at sea-level. The Sun's horizontal parallax (Hor. par.) is about 9″, and is negligible when considering sunrise and sunset, but that of the Moon averages about 57′. Hence the computed time represents the moment when the true zenith distance of the Moon is 90° 50′ (as for the Sun) minus the horizontal parallax. The time required for the Sun or Moon to rise or set is about four minutes (except in high latitudes). *See also* Sunrise, Sunset, Moonrise and Moonset below.

The GMT of transit of the Moon over the meridian of Greenwich is given; these times are independent of latitude but must be corrected for longitude. For places in the British Isles it suffices to add the longitude if west, and vice versa. For other places a further correction is necessary because of the rapid movement of the Moon relative to the stars. The entire correction is conveniently determined by first finding the west longitude λ of the place. If the place is in west longitude, λ is the ordinary west longitude; if the place is in east longitude λ is the complement to 24h (or 360°) of the longitude and will be greater than 12h (or 180°). The correction then consists of two positive portions, namely λ and the fraction $\lambda/24$ (or $\lambda°/360$) multiplied by the difference between consecutive transits. Thus for Christchurch, New Zealand, the longitude is 11h 31m east, so $\lambda = 12$h 29m and the fraction $\lambda/24$ is 0.52. The transit on the local date 14 January 2018 is found as follows:

		d	h	m
GMT of transit at Greenwich	January	13	9	18
λ			12	29
0.52 x (10h 05m − 09h 18m)				47
GMT of transit at Christchurch		13	22	34
Corr. to NZ Standard Time			12	00
Local standard time of transit	January	14	10	34

As is evident, for any given place the quantities λ and the correction to local standard time may be combined permanently, being here 24h 29m.

Positions of Mercury are given for every second day, and those of Venus and Mars for every fifth day; they may be interpolated linearly. The diameter (Diam.) is given in seconds of arc. The phase is the illuminated percentage of the disk. In the case of the inner planets this approaches 100 at superior conjunction and 0 at inferior conjunction. When the phase is less than 50 the planet is crescent-shaped or horned; for greater phases it is gibbous. In the case of the exterior planet Mars, the phase approaches 100 at conjunction and opposition, and is a minimum at the quadratures.

To determine if a planet is visible or not, the transit time should be examined. If the transit time coincides with hours of darkness the planet should be easy to find, provided it is bright enough. If the time of transit is between 00h and 12h the planet should be visible above the eastern horizon; if between 12h and 24h, above the western horizon. The closer the transit time to midnight (0h) the longer it will be visible.

The inner planets – Mercury and Venus can never transit at midnight because they are too close to the Sun. If they transit close to noon (12h) then they will be too close to the Sun to be visible except during a large solar eclipse. The rise or set times should be examined to see if either is near sunrise or sunset. If this also coincides with a large positive declination (Dec.) then conditions are favourable for viewing.

Consulting The Night Sky paragraphs will also help determine observability.

PAGE FOUR OF EACH MONTH

The GMTs of sunrise and sunset for seven cities, whose adopted positions in longitude (W.) and latitude (N.) are given immediately below the name, may be used not only for these phenomena, but also for lighting-up times *(see* page 631 for a fuller explanation).

The particulars for the four outer planets resemble those for the planets on Page Three of each month, except that, because of the inferior brightness of Uranus and Neptune, these two planets require optical aids such as binoculars or a small telescope. The diameters given for the rings of Saturn are those of the major axis (in the plane of the planet's equator) and the minor axis respectively. The former has a small seasonal change due to the slightly varying distance of the Earth from Saturn, but the latter varies from zero when the Earth passes through the ring plane every 15 years to its

maximum opening half-way between these periods. The rings were last open at their widest extent (and Saturn at its brightest) in 2017. The Earth passed through the ring plane in 2009.

SUNRISE, SUNSET, MOONRISE AND MOONSET

The tables have been constructed for the meridian of Greenwich and for latitudes 52° and 56°. They give Greenwich Mean Time (GMT) throughout the year. To obtain the GMT of the phenomenon as seen from any other latitude and longitude in the British Isles, first interpolate or extrapolate for latitude by the usual rules of proportion. To the time thus found, the longitude (expressed in time) is to be added if west (as it usually is in Great Britain) or subtracted if east. If the longitude is expressed in degrees and minutes of arc, it must be converted to time at the rate of 1° = 4m and 15′ = 1m.

The GMT at which the planet transits the Greenwich meridian is also given. The times of transit are to be corrected to local meridians in the usual way, as already described.

TIME

From the earliest ages, the natural division of time into recurring periods of day and night has provided the practical time-scale for the everyday activities of the human race. Indeed, if any alternative means of time measurement is adopted, it must be capable of adjustment so as to remain in general agreement with the natural time-scale defined by the diurnal rotation of the Earth on its axis. Ideally the rotation should be measured against a fixed frame of reference; in practice it must be measured against the background provided by the celestial bodies. If the Sun is chosen as the reference point, we obtain Apparent Solar Time, which is the time indicated by a sundial. It is not a uniform time but is subject to variations which amount to as much as a quarter of an hour in each direction. Such wide variations cannot be tolerated in a practical time-scale, and this has led to the concept of Mean Solar Time in which all the days are exactly the same length and equal to the average length of the Apparent Solar Day.

The positions of the stars in the sky are specified in relation to a fictitious reference point in the sky known as the First Point of Aries (or the Vernal Equinox). It is therefore convenient to adopt this same reference point when considering the rotation of the Earth against the background of the stars. The time-scale so obtained is known as Apparent Sidereal Time.

GREENWICH MEAN TIME

The daily rotation of the Earth on its axis causes the Sun and the other heavenly bodies to appear to cross the sky from east to west. It is convenient to represent this relative motion as if the Sun really performed a daily circuit around a fixed Earth. Noon in Apparent Solar Time may then be defined as the time at which the Sun transits across the observer's meridian. In Mean Solar Time, noon is similarly defined by the meridian transit of a fictitious Mean Sun moving uniformly in the sky with the same average speed as the true Sun. Mean Solar Time observed on the meridian of the transit circle telescope of the Royal Observatory at Greenwich is called Greenwich Mean Time (GMT). The mean solar day is divided into 24 hours and, for astronomical and other scientific purposes, these are numbered 0 to 23, commencing at midnight. Civil time is usually reckoned in two periods of 12 hours, designated am *(ante meridiem,* ie before noon) and pm *(post meridiem,* ie after noon), although the 24 hour clock is increasingly being used.

UNIVERSAL TIME

Before 1925 January 1, GMT was reckoned in 24 hours commencing at noon; since that date it has been reckoned from midnight. To avoid confusion in the use of the designation

GMT before and after 1925, since 1928 astronomers have tended to use the term Universal Time (UT) or Weltzeit (WZ) to denote GMT measured from Greenwich Mean Midnight.

In precision work it is necessary to take account of small variations in Universal Time. These arise from small irregularities in the rotation of the Earth. Observed astronomical time is designated UT0. Observed time corrected for the effects of the motion of the poles (giving rise to a 'wandering' in longitude) is designated UT1. There is also a seasonal fluctuation in the rate of rotation of the Earth arising from meteorological causes, often called the annual fluctuation. UT1 corrected for this effect is designated UT2 and provides a time-scale free from short-period fluctuations. It is still subject to small secular and irregular changes.

APPARENT SOLAR TIME

As mentioned above, the time shown by a sundial is called Apparent Solar Time. It differs from Mean Solar Time by an amount known as the Equation of Time, which is the total effect of two causes which make the length of the apparent solar day non-uniform. One cause of variation is that the orbit of the Earth is not a circle but an ellipse, having the Sun at one focus. As a consequence, the angular speed of the Earth in its orbit is not constant; it is greatest at the beginning of January when the Earth is nearest the Sun.

The other cause is due to the obliquity of the ecliptic; the plane of the equator (which is at right angles to the axis of rotation of the Earth) does not coincide with the ecliptic (the plane defined by the apparent annual motion of the Sun around the celestial sphere) but is inclined to it at an angle of $23°\ 26'$. As a result, the apparent solar day is shorter than average at the equinoxes and longer at the solstices. From the combined effects of the components due to obliquity and eccentricity, the equation of time reaches its maximum values in February (-14 minutes) and early November ($+16$ minutes). It has a zero value on four dates during the year, and it is only on these dates (approximately April 15, June 14, September 1 and December 25) that a sundial shows Mean Solar Time.

SIDEREAL TIME

A sidereal day is the duration of a complete rotation of the Earth with reference to the First Point of Aries. The term sidereal (or 'star') time is a little misleading since the time-scale so defined is not exactly the same as that which would be defined by successive transits of a selected star, as there is a small progressive motion between the stars and the First Point of Aries due to the precession of the Earth's axis. This makes the length of the sidereal day shorter than the true period of rotation by 0.008 seconds. Superimposed on this steady precessional motion are small oscillations (nutation), giving rise to fluctuations in apparent sidereal time amounting to as much as 1.2 seconds. It is therefore customary to employ Mean Sidereal Time, from which these fluctuations have been removed. The conversion of GMT to Greenwich sidereal time (GST) may be performed by adding the value of the GST at 0h on the day in question to the GMT converted to sidereal time using the Mean and Sidereal Time table.

Example – To find the GST at August 8d 02h 41m 11s GMT:

	h	m	s
	21	05	49
GST at 0h	21	05	49
GMT	2	41	11
Acceleration for 2h			20
Acceleration for 41m 11s			7
Sum = GST =	23	47	27

If the observer is not on the Greenwich meridian then their longitude, measured positively westwards from Greenwich, must be subtracted from the GST to obtain Local Sidereal Time (LST). Thus, in the above example, an observer 5h east of Greenwich, or 19h west, would find the LST as 2h 05m 49s.

EPHEMERIS TIME

An analysis of observations of the positions of the Sun, Moon and planets taken over an extended period is used in preparing ephemerides. (An ephemeris is a table giving the apparent position of a heavenly body at regular intervals of time, eg one day or ten days, and may be used to compare current observations with tabulated positions.) Discrepancies between the positions of heavenly bodies observed over a 300-year period and their predicted positions arose because the time-scale to which the observations were related was based on the assumption that the rate of rotation of the Earth is uniform. It is now known that this rate of rotation is variable. A revised time-scale, Ephemeris Time (ET), was devised to bring the ephemerides into agreement with the observations.

The second of ET is defined in terms of the annual motion of the Earth in its orbit around the Sun ($1/31556925.9747$ of the tropical year for 1900 January 0d 12h ET). The precise determination of ET from astronomical observations is a lengthy process as the requisite standard of accuracy can only be achieved by averaging over a number of years.

In 1976 the International Astronomical Union adopted Terrestrial Dynamical Time (TDT), a new dynamical time-scale for general use whose scale unit is the SI second (*see* Atomic Time, below). TDT was renamed Terrestrial Time (TT) in 1991. ET is now of little more than historical interest.

TERRESTRIAL TIME

The uniform time system used in computing the ephemerides of the solar system is Terrestrial Time (TT), which has replaced ET for this purpose. Except for the most rigorous astronomical calculations, it may be assumed to be the same as ET. In June 2018 the difference TT − UT is estimated to be 69.2 seconds. This is known as Delta T.

ATOMIC TIME

The fundamental standards of time and frequency must be defined in terms of a periodic motion adequately uniform, enduring and measurable. Progress has made it possible to use natural standards, such as atomic or molecular oscillations. Continuous oscillations are generated in an electrical circuit, the frequency of which is then compared or brought into coincidence with the frequency characteristic of the absorption or emission by the atoms or molecules when they change between two selected energy levels. Since the 13th General Conference on Weights and Measures in October 1967, the unit of time, the second, has been defined in the International System of units (SI) as 'the duration of 9 192 631 770 periods of the radiation corresponding to the transition between the two hyperfine levels of the ground state of the caesium-133 atom'.

In the UK, the national time scale is maintained by the National Physical Laboratory (NPL), using an ensemble of atomic clocks based on either caesium or hydrogen atoms. In addition the NPL (along with several other national laboratories) has constructed and operates caesium fountain primary frequency standards, which utilise the cooling of caesium atoms by laser light to determine the duration of the SI second at the highest attainable level of accuracy. Caesium fountain primary standards typically achieve an accuracy of around 2 parts in 10 000 000 000 000 000, which is equivalent to one second in 158 million years.

Timekeeping worldwide is based on two closely related atomic time scales that are established through international collaboration. International Atomic Time (TAI) is formed by combining the readings of more than 400 atomic clocks located in more than 70 institutes and was set close to the astronomically based Universal Time (UT) near the beginning of 1958. It was formally recognised in 1971 and since 1988 January 1 has been maintained by the International Bureau of Weights and Measures (BIPM). Civil time in almost all countries is now based on Coordinated Universal Time (UTC), which differs from TAI by 37 seconds and was designed to make both atomic time and UT available with accuracy appropriate for most users. On 1 January 1972 UTC was set to be exactly 10 seconds behind TAI, and since then the UTC time-scale has been adjusted by the insertion (or, in principle, omission) of leap seconds in order to keep it within ±0.9 s of UT. These leap seconds are introduced, when necessary, at the same instant throughout the world, either at the end of December or at the end of June. The last leap second occurred immediately prior to 0h UTC on 2017 January 1, and was the 27th leap second. All leap seconds so far have been positive, with 61 seconds in the final minute of the UTC month. The time 23h 59m 60s UTC is followed one second later by 0h 0m 00s of the first day of the following month. Notices concerning the insertion of leap seconds are issued by the International Earth Rotation and Reference Systems Service (IERS).

The computation of UTC is carried out monthly by the BIPM and takes place in three stages. First, a weighted average known as Echelle Atomique Libre (EAL) is calculated from all of the contributing atomic clocks. In the second stage, TAI is generated by applying small corrections, derived from the results contributed by primary frequency standards, to the scale interval of EAL to maintain its value close to that of the SI second. Finally, UTC is formed from TAI by the addition of an integer number of seconds. The results are published monthly in the BIPM Circular T in the form of offsets at 5-day intervals between UTC and the time scales of contributing organisations.

RADIO TIME-SIGNALS

UTC is made generally available through time-signals and standard frequency broadcasts such as MSF in the UK, CHU in Canada and WWV and WWVH in the USA. These are based on national time-scales that are maintained in close agreement with UTC and provide traceability to the national time-scale and to UTC. The markers of seconds in the UTC scale coincide with those of TAI.

To disseminate the national time-scale in the UK, special signals (call-sign MSF) are broadcast by the National Physical Laboratory. From April 1, 2007 the MSF service, previously broadcast from British Telecom's radio station at Rugby, has been transmitted from Anthorn radio station in Cumbria. The signals are controlled from a caesium beam atomic frequency standard and consist of a precise frequency carrier of 60 kHz which is switched off, after being on for at least half a second, to mark every second. The first second of the minute begins with a period of 500 ms with the carrier switched off, to serve as a minute marker. In the other seconds the carrier is always off for at least one tenth of a second at the start and then it carries an on-off code giving the British clock time and date, together with information identifying the start of the next minute. Changes to and from summer time are made following government announcements. Leap seconds are inserted as announced by the IERS and information provided by them on the difference between UTC and UT is also signalled. Other broadcast signals in the UK include the BBC six pips signal, the BT Timeline ('speaking clock'), the NPL telephone and internet time services for computers, and a coded time-signal on the BBC 198 kHz transmitters which is used for timing in the electricity supply industry. From 1972 January 1 the six pips on the BBC have consisted of five short pips from second 55 to second 59 (six pips in the case of a leap second) followed by one lengthened pip, the start of which indicates the exact minute. From 1990 February 5 these signals have been controlled by the BBC with seconds markers referenced to the satellite-based US navigation system GPS (Global Positioning System) and time and day referenced to the MSF transmitter. Formerly they were generated by the Royal Greenwich Observatory. The NPL telephone and internet time services are directly connected to the national time scale.

Accurate timing may also be obtained from the signals of international navigation systems such as the ground-based eLORAN, or the satellite-based American GPS or Russian GLONASS systems.

STANDARD TIME

Since 1880 the standard time in Britain has been Greenwich Mean Time (GMT); a statute that year enacted that the word 'time' when used in any legal document relating to Britain meant, unless otherwise specifically stated, the mean time of the Greenwich meridian. Greenwich was adopted as the universal meridian on 13 October 1884. A system of standard time by zones is used worldwide, standard time in each zone differing from that of the Greenwich meridian by an integral number of hours or, exceptionally, half-hours or quarter-hours, either fast or slow. The large territories of the USA and Canada are divided into zones approximately 7.5° on either side of central meridians.

Variations from the standard time of some countries occur during part of the year; they are decided annually and are usually referred to as Summer Time or Daylight Saving Time.

At the 180th meridian the time can be either 12 hours fast on Greenwich Mean Time or 12 hours slow, and a change of date occurs. The internationally recognised date or calendar line is a modification of the 180th meridian, drawn so as to include islands of any one group on the same side of the line, or for political reasons. The line is indicated by joining up the following coordinates:

Lat.	Long.	Lat.	Long.
90° S.	180°	48° N.	180°
51° S.	180°	53° N.	170° E.
45° S.	172.5° W.	65.5° N.	169° W.
15° S.	172.5° W.	68° N.	169° W.
5° S.	180°	90° N.	180°

Changes to the date line would require an international conference.

BRITISH SUMMER TIME

In 1916 an Act ordained that during a defined period of that year the legal time for general purposes in Great Britain should be one hour in advance of Greenwich Mean Time. The Summer Time Acts 1922 and 1925 defined the period during which Summer Time was to be in force, stabilising practice until the Second World War.

During the Second World War (1941–5) and in 1947 Double Summer Time (two hours in advance of Greenwich Mean Time) was used for the period in which ordinary Summer Time would have been in force. During these years clocks were also kept one hour in advance of Greenwich Mean Time in the winter. After the war, ordinary Summer Time was invoked each year from 1948–68.

Between 1968 October 27 and 1971 October 31 clocks were kept one hour ahead of Greenwich Mean Time throughout the year. This was known as British Standard Time.

The most recent legislation is the Summer Time Act 1972, which enacted that 'the period of summer time for the purposes of this Act is the period beginning at two o'clock, Greenwich Mean Time, in the morning of the day after the third Saturday in March or, if that day is Easter Day, the day after the second Saturday in March, and ending at two o'clock, Greenwich Mean Time, in the morning of the day after the fourth Saturday in October.'

The duration of Summer Time can be varied by Order in Council and in recent years alterations have been made to synchronise the period of Summer Time in Britain with that used in Europe. The rule for 1981–94 defined the period of Summer Time in the UK as from the last Sunday in March to the day following the fourth Saturday in October and the hour of changeover was altered to 01h Greenwich Mean Time.

There was no rule for the dates of Summer Time between 1995–7. Since 1998 the 9th European Parliament and Council Directive on Summer Time has harmonised the dates on which Summer Time begins and ends across member states as the last Sundays in March and October respectively. Under the directive Summer Time begins and ends at 01hr Greenwich Mean Time in each member state. Amendments to the Summer Time Act to implement the directive came into force on 11 March 2002.

The duration of Summer Time in 2018 is:
March 25 01h GMT to October 28 01h GMT

MEAN REFRACTION

Alt. ° ′	Ref. ′	Alt. ° ′	Ref. ′	Alt. ° ′	Ref. ′
1 20	21	3 12	13	7 54	6
1 30	20	3 34	12	9 27	5
1 41	19	4 00	11	11 39	4
1 52	18	4 30	10	15 00	3
2 05	17	5 06	9	20 42	2
2 19	16	5 50	8	32 20	
2 35	15	6 44	7	62 17	1
2 52	14	7 54		90 00	0
3 12					

The refraction table is in the form of a critical table (see page 630).

ASTRONOMICAL CONSTANTS

Solar parallax	8″.794
Astronomical unit	149597870 km
Annual precession in longitude	50″.288
Precession in right ascension	3ˢ.075
Precession in declination	20″.043
Constant of nutation	9″.202
Constant of aberration	20″.496
Mean obliquity of ecliptic (2018)	23° 26′ 13″
Moon's equatorial hor. parallax	57′ 02″.70
Velocity of light in vacuo per second	299792.5 km
Solar motion per second	20.0 km
Equatorial radius of the Earth	6378.137 km
Polar radius of the Earth	6356.752 km
North galactic pole	
(IAU standard)	RA 12h 51m (2000.0). Dec + 27°.1 N.
Solar apex	RA 18h 04m Dec. + 30°

Length of year (in mean solar days)

Tropical	365.24219
Sidereal	365.25636
Anomalistic (perihelion to perihelion)	365.25964
Eclipse	346.62003

Length of month (mean values)

	d	h	m	s
Synodic (new Moon to new Moon)	29	12	44	02.0
Sidereal	27	07	43	43.2
Anomalistic (perigee to perigee)	27	13	18	51.8

THE EARTH

The shape of the Earth is that of an oblate spheroid or solid of revolution whose meridian sections are ellipses not differing much from circles, while the sections at right angles are circles. The length of the equatorial axis is about 12,756 km, and that of the polar axis is 12,714 km. The mean density of the Earth is 5.5 times that of water, although that of the surface layer is less. The Earth and Moon revolve about their common centre of gravity in a lunar month; this centre in turn revolves round the Sun in a plane known as the ecliptic, that passes through the Sun's centre. The Earth's equator is inclined to this plane at an angle of 23.4°. This tilt is the cause of the seasons. In mid-latitudes, and when the Sun is high above the Equator, not only does the high noon altitude make the days longer, but the Sun's rays fall more directly on the Earth's surface; these effects combine to produce summer. In equatorial regions the noon altitude is large throughout the year, and there is little variation in the length of the day. In higher latitudes the noon altitude is lower, and the days in summer are appreciably longer than those in winter.

The average velocity of the Earth in its orbit is 30km a second. It makes a complete rotation on its axis in about 23h 56m of mean time, which is the sidereal day. Because of its annual revolution round the Sun, the rotation with respect to the Sun, or the solar day, is more than this by about four minutes. The extremity of the axis of rotation, or the North Pole of the Earth, is not rigidly fixed, but wanders over an area roughly 20 metres in diameter.

Perihelion is when the Earth is closest to the Sun, and aphelion when the Earth is furthest from the Sun:

Perihelion January 2018 3d 05h 35m
　　　　　　　(147,097,232km, 0.983284268au)
Aphelion July 2018　6d 16h 48m
　　　　　　　(152,095,564km, 1.016696059au)

TERRESTRIAL MAGNETISM

The Earth's main magnetic field corresponds approximately to that of a very strong small bar magnet near the centre of the Earth, but with appreciable smooth spatial departures. The origin of the main field is generally ascribed to electric currents associated with fluid motions in the Earth's core. As a result not only does the main field vary in strength and direction from place to place, but also with time. Superimposed on the main field are local and regional anomalies whose magnitudes may in places approach that of the main field; these are due to the influence of mineral deposits in the Earth's crust. A small proportion of the field is of external origin, mostly associated with electric currents in the ionosphere and magnetosphere. The configuration of the external field and the ionisation of the atmosphere depend on the incident particle and radiation flux from the Sun. There are, therefore, short-term and non-periodic as well as diurnal, 27-day, seasonal and approximate 11-year periodic changes in the magnetic field, dependent upon the position of the Sun, the degree of solar activity and the magnetic field embedded in the solar wind.

A magnetic compass points along the horizontal component of a magnetic line of force. These lines of force converge on the 'magnetic dip-poles', the places where the Earth's magnetic field is vertical. These poles move with time, and their present approximate adopted mean positions are 86.5° N., 178.8° W. and 64.2° S., 136.1° E. Compasses do not point directly, ie via great circle routes, to the dip-poles.

There is also a 'magnetic equator', at all points of which the vertical component of the Earth's magnetic field is zero and a magnetised needle remains horizontal. This line runs between 2° and 12° north of the geographical equator in Asia and Africa, turns sharply south in the Atlantic Ocean and crosses South America south of the geographical equator; it re-crosses the geographical equator in mid-Pacific.

Reference has already been made to secular changes in the Earth's field. The following table indicates the changes in magnetic declination (or variation of the compass relative to true north). Declination is the angle in the horizontal plane between the direction of true north and that in which a magnetic compass points. Similar, though much smaller, changes have occurred in 'dip' or magnetic inclination. Secular changes differ throughout the world.

London (Greenwich)

1580	11°	15′	E.	1900	16° 29′	W.
1622	5°	56′	E.	1925	13° 10′	W.
1665	1°	22′	W.	1950	9° 07′	W.
1730	13°	00′	W.	1975	6° 39′	W.
1773	21°	09′	W.	1998	3° 32′	W.
1850	22°	24′	W.			

In Great Britain, lines of equal declination (isogonics) now run approximately north–northeast to south–southwest. Though there are considerable local deviations due to geological causes, a rough value of magnetic declination may be obtained by assuming that at 50° N. on the meridian of Greenwich, the value in 2018 is 0° 9' west and allowing an increase of 11' for each degree of latitude northwards and one of 22' for each degree of longitude westwards. For example, at 53° N., 5° W., declination will be about 0° 9' + 33' + 110', ie 2° 32' west. The average annual change at the present time is about 12' decrease. For navigation by compass using maps with the north lines from the British National Grid (as opposed to lines of equal longitude), account has to be taken of the difference between true north and grid north. This angle can be several degrees.

The number of magnetic observatories is about 170, irregularly distributed over the globe. There are three in the UK, run by the British Geological Survey: at Hartland, north Devon; at Eskdalemuir, Dumfries and Galloway; and at Lerwick, Shetland Islands. Some recent annual mean values of the magnetic elements for Hartland:

Year	Declination West		Dip or inclination		Horizontal intensity	Vertical intensity
	°	'	°	'	nT	nT
1960	9	58.8	66	43.9	18707	43504
1970	9	06.5	66	26.1	19033	43636
1980	7	43.8	66	10.3	19330	43768
1990	6	15.0	66	09.7	19539	43896
2000	4	43.6	66	06.9	19508	44051
2016	2	7.2	65	59.5	19756	44356

nT = nanoTesla

The magnetic field is also observed by a series of specialised satellites, the latest being a mission called Swarm. Three satellites were successfully launched by the European Space Agency in November 2013, each equipped with magnetometers and star cameras for accurate orientation. With the data from these satellites the Earth's magnetic field and its changes in time continue to be mapped to unprecedented accuracy.

Reliance on the Earth's magnetic field for navigation by compass is not restricted to land, maritime or aeronautical navigation (in the latter two usually as a fail-safe back-up system). It also extends underground with the oil industry using magnetic survey tools when drilling well-bores. Very accurate estimates of the local magnetic field are required for this, taking into account the crustal and external fields.

MAGNETIC STORMS

Occasionally, sometimes with great suddenness, the Earth's magnetic field is subject for several hours to marked disturbance. During a severe storm in October 2003 the declination at Eskdalemuir changed by over 5° in six minutes. In many instances such disturbances are accompanied by widespread displays of auroras, marked changes in the incidence of cosmic rays, an increase in the reception of 'noise' from the Sun at radio frequencies, and rapid changes in the ionosphere and induced electric currents within the Earth. These can adversely affect satellite operations, telecommunications and electric power transmission systems. The disturbances are caused by changes in the stream of ionised particles which emanates from the Sun and through which the Earth is continuously passing. Some of these changes are associated with visible eruptions on the Sun, usually in the region of sun-spots. There is some tendency for disturbances to recur after intervals of about 27 days, the period of rotation of the Sun on its axis as seen from the Earth. But the sources of many disturbances are shorter lived than this. Predicting such disturbances with any useful accuracy remains challenging. The year 2018 is expected to be about four years after the most recent maximum of the approximate 11-year solar activity cycle. The peak in magnetic activity usually lags that in solar activity by at least two years.

ELEMENTS OF THE SOLAR SYSTEM

Orb	Mean distance from Sun (Earth = 1)	km 10⁶	Sidereal period days	Synodic period days	Incl. of orbit to ecliptic ° '	Diameter km	Mass (Earth = 1)	Period of rotation on axis days
Sun	—	—	—	—	—	1,392,000	332,981	25–35*
Mercury	0.39	58	88.0	116	7 00	4,879	0.0553	58.646
Venus	0.72	108	224.7	584	3 24	12,104	0.8150	243.019r
Earth	1.00	150	365.3	—	—	12,756e	1.0000	0.997
Mars	1.52	228	687.0	780	1 51	6,794e	0.1074	1.026
Jupiter	5.20	778	4,334.4	399	1 18	142,984e 133,708p	317.83	0.410e
Saturn	9.55	1429	10,787.9	378	2 29	120,536e 108,728p	95.16	0.426e
Uranus	19.22	2875	30,773.3	370	0 46	51,118e	14.54	0.718r
Neptune	30.11	4504	60,349.2	367	1 46	49,528e	17.15	0.671
Pluto †	39.80	5954	91,708.2	367	17 09	2,390	0.002	6.387

e equatorial, p polar, r retrograde, * depending on latitude, † reclassified as a dwarf planet since August 2006

THE SATELLITES

Name		Star mag.	Mean distance from primary km	Sidereal period of revolution d
EARTH				
I	Moon	—	384,400	27.322
MARS				
I	Phobos	11	9,378	0.319
II	Deimos	12	23,459	1.262
JUPITER				
XVI	Metis	17	127,960	0.295
XV	Adrastea	19	128,980	0.298
V	Amalthea	14	181,300	0.498
XIV	Thebe	16	221,900	0.675
I	Io	5	421,600	1.769
II	Europa	5	670,900	3.551
III	Ganymede	5	1,070,000	7.155
IV	Callisto	6	1,883,000	16.689
XIII	Leda	20	11,165,000	240.92
VI	Himalia	15	11,460,000	250.57
X	Lysithea	18	11,717,000	259.22
VII	Elara	17	11,741,000	259.65
XII	Ananke	19	21,276,000	629.77r
XI	Carme	18	23,404,000	734.17r
VIII	Pasiphae	17	23,624,000	743.68r
IX	Sinope	18	23,939,000	758.90r
SATURN				
XVIII	Pan	20	133,583	0.575
XV	Atlas	18	137,640	0.602
XVI	Prometheus	16	139,353	0.613
XVII	Pandora	16	141,700	0.629
XI	Epimetheus	15	151,422	0.694
X	Janus	14	151,472	0.695
I	Mimas	13	185,520	0.942
II	Enceladus	12	238,020	1.370
III	Tethys	10	294,660	1.888
XIII	Telesto	19	294,660	1.888
XIV	Calypso	19	294,660	1.888
IV	Dione	10	377,400	2.737
XII	Helene	18	377,400	2.737
V	Rhea	10	527,040	4.518
VI	Titan	8	1,221,850	15.945

Name		Star mag.	Mean distance from primary km	Sidereal period of revolution d
SATURN				
VII	Hyperion	14	1,481,000	21.277
VIII	Iapetus	11	3,561,300	79.330
IX	Phoebe	16	12,952,000	550.48r
URANUS				
VI	Cordelia	24	49,770	0.335
VII	Ophelia	24	53,790	0.376
VIII	Bianca	23	59,170	0.435
IX	Cressida	22	61,780	0.464
X	Desdemona	22	62,680	0.474
XI	Juliet	21	64,350	0.493
XII	Portia	21	66,090	0.513
XIII	Rosalind	22	66,940	0.558
XIV	Belinda	22	75,260	0.624
XV	Puck	20	86,010	0.762
V	Miranda	16	129,390	1.413
I	Ariel	14	191,020	2.520
II	Umbriel	15	266,300	4.144
III	Titania	14	435,910	8.706
IV	Oberon	14	583,520	13.463
XVI	Caliban	22	7,230,000	579.5r
XX	Stephano	24	8,002,000	676.5r
XVII	Sycorax	21	12,179,000	1,283.4r
XVIII	Prospero	23	16,418,000	1,992.8r
XIX	Setebos	23	17,459,000	2,202.2r
NEPTUNE				
III	Naiad	25	48,230	0.294
IV	Thalassa	24	50,080	0.311
V	Despina	23	52,530	0.335
VI	Galatea	22	61,950	0.429
VII	Larissa	22	73,550	0.555
VIII	Proteus	20	117,650	1.122
I	Triton	13	354,760	5.877
II	Nereid	19	5,513,400	360.136
PLUTO				
I	Charon	17	19,600	6.387

The total number of satellites known so far for the outer planets are: Jupiter 67, Saturn 62, Uranus 27, Neptune 14, Pluto 5.

TIME MEASUREMENT AND CALENDARS

MEASUREMENTS OF TIME

Measurements of time are based on the time taken by the Earth to rotate on its axis (day); by the Moon to revolve around the Earth (month); and by the Earth to revolve around the Sun (year). From these, which are not commensurable, certain average or mean intervals have been adopted for ordinary use.

THE DAY

The day begins at midnight and is divided into 24 hours of 60 minutes, each of 60 seconds. The hours are counted from midnight up to 12 noon (when the Sun crosses the meridian), and these hours are designated am *(ante meridiem);* and again from noon up to 12 midnight, which hours are designated pm *(post meridiem),* except when the 24-hour reckoning is employed. The 24-hour reckoning ignores am and pm, numbering the hours 0 to 23 from midnight.

Colloquially the 24 hours are divided into day and night, day being the time while the Sun is above the horizon (including the four stages of twilight defined in the Astronomy section). Day is subdivided into morning, ending at noon; afternoon, from noon to about 6pm; and evening, which may be said to extend from 6pm until midnight. Night begins at the close of astronomical twilight (*see* the Astronomy section) and extends beyond midnight to sunrise the next day.

The names of the days are derived from Old English translations or adaptations of the Roman titles.

Sunday	Sol	Sun
Monday	Luna	Moon
Tuesday	Tiw/Tyr (god of war)	Mars
Wednesday	Woden/Odin	Mercury
Thursday	Thor	Jupiter
Friday	Frigga/Freyja (goddess of love)	Venus
Saturday	Saeterne	Saturn

THE MONTH

The month in the ordinary calendar is approximately the twelfth part of a year, but the lengths of the different months vary from 28 (or 29) days to 31.

THE YEAR

The equinoctial or tropical year is the time that the Earth takes to revolve around the Sun from equinox to equinox, ie 365.24219 mean solar days, or 365 days 5 hours 48 minutes and 45 seconds.

The calendar year usually consists of 365 days but a year containing 366 days is called a bissextile (*see* Roman calendar) or leap year, one day being added to the month of February so that a date 'leaps over' a day of the week. In the Roman calendar the day that was repeated was the sixth day before the beginning of March, the equivalent of 24 February.

A year is a leap year if the date of the year is divisible by four without remainder, unless it is the last year of the century. The last year of a century is a leap year only if its number is divisible by 400 without remainder, eg the years 1800 and 1900 had only 365 days but the year 2000 had 366 days.

THE SOLSTICE

A solstice is the point in the tropical year at which the Sun attains its greatest distance, north or south, from the Equator. In the northern hemisphere the furthest point north of the Equator marks the summer solstice and the furthest point south marks the winter solstice.

The date of the solstice varies according to locality. For example, if the summer solstice falls on 21 June late in the day by Greenwich time, that day will be the longest of the year at Greenwich, but it will fall on 22 June, local date, in Japan, and so 22 June will be the longest day there. The date of the solstice is also affected by the length of the tropical year, which is 365 days 6 hours less about 11 minutes 15 seconds. If a solstice happens late on 21 June in one year, it will be nearly 6 hours later in the next (unless the next year is a leap year), ie early on 22 June, and that will be the longest day.

This delay of the solstice does not continue because the extra day in a leap year brings it back a day in the calendar. However, because of the 11 minutes 15 seconds mentioned above, the additional day in a leap year brings the solstice back too far by 45 minutes, and the time of the solstice in the calendar is earlier, in a four-year pattern, as the century progresses. The last year of a century is in most cases not a leap year, and the omission of the extra day puts the date of the solstice later by about 6 hours. Compensation for this is made by the fourth centennial year being a leap year. The solstice became earlier in date throughout the last century and, because the year 2000 was a leap year, the solstice will get earlier still throughout the 21st century. The date of the winter solstice, the shortest day of the year, is affected by same factors as the longest day.

At Greenwich the Sun sets at its earliest by the clock about ten days before the shortest day. The daily change in the time of sunset is due in the first place to the Sun's movement southwards at this time of the year, which diminishes the interval between the Sun's transit and its setting. However, the daily decrease of the Equation of Time causes the time of apparent noon to be continuously later day by day, which to some extent counteracts the first effect. The rates of change of these two quantities are not equal or uniform; their combination causes the date of earliest sunset to be 12 or 13 December at Greenwich. In more southerly latitudes the effect of the movement of the Sun is less, and the change in the time of sunset depends on that of the Equation of Time to a greater degree, and the date of earliest sunset is earlier than it is at Greenwich, eg on the Equator it is about 1 November.

THE EQUINOX

The equinox is the point at which the Sun crosses the Equator and day and night are of equal length all over the world. This occurs in March and September.

DOG DAYS

The days about the heliacal rising of the Dog Star, noted from ancient times as the hottest period of the year in the northern hemisphere, are called the Dog Days. Their incidence has been variously calculated as depending on the Greater or Lesser Dog Star (Sirius or Procyon) and their duration has been reckoned as from 30 to 54 days. A generally accepted period is from 3 July to 15 August.

CHRISTIAN CALENDAR

In the Christian chronological system the years are distinguished by cardinal numbers before or after the birth of Christ, the period being denoted by the letters BC (Before Christ) or, more rarely, AC *(Ante Christum),* and AD *(Anno Domini* – In the Year of Our Lord); BCE (Before the Christian Era) and CE (Christian Era) are now sometimes used instead of BC and AD. The correlative dates of the epoch are the fourth year of the 194th Olympiad, the 753rd year from the foundation of Rome, AM 3761 in Jewish chronology, and the 4,714th year of the Julian period.

The system was introduced into Italy in the sixth century. Though first used in France in the seventh century, it was not universally established there until about the eighth century. It has been said that the system was introduced into England by St Augustine (AD 596), but it was probably not generally used until some centuries later. It was ordered to be used by the bishops at the Council of Chelsea (AD 816).

THE JULIAN CALENDAR

In the Julian calendar (adopted by the Roman Empire in 45 BC) all the centennial years were leap years, and for this reason towards the close of the 16th century there was a difference of ten days between the tropical and calendar years; the equinox fell on 11 March of the calendar, whereas at the time of the Council of Nicaea (AD 325), it had fallen on 21 March. In 1582 Pope Gregory ordained that 5 October should be called 15 October and that of the end-century years only the fourth should be a leap year.

THE GREGORIAN CALENDAR

The Gregorian calendar was adopted by Italy, France, Spain and Portugal in 1582, by Prussia, the Roman Catholic German states, Switzerland, Holland and Flanders on 1 January 1583, by Poland in 1586, Hungary in 1587, the Protestant German and Netherland states and Denmark in 1700, and by Great Britain and its Dominions (including the North American colonies) in 1752, by the omission of 11 days (3 September being reckoned as 14 September). Sweden omitted the leap day in 1700 but observed leap days in 1704

and 1708, and reverted to the Julian calendar by having two leap days in 1712; the Gregorian calendar was adopted in 1753 by the omission of 11 days (18 February being reckoned as 1 March). Japan adopted the calendar in 1872, China in 1912, Bulgaria in 1916, Turkey and Soviet Russia in 1918, Yugoslavia and Romania in 1919, and Greece in 1923.

In the same year that the change was made in England from the Julian to the Gregorian calendar, the start of the new year was also changed from 25 March to 1 January.

THE ORTHODOX CHURCHES

Some Orthodox churches still use the Julian reckoning but the majority of Greek Orthodox churches and the Romanian Orthodox Church have adopted a modified 'New Calendar', observing the Gregorian calendar for fixed feasts and the Julian for movable feasts.

The Orthodox Church year begins on 1 September. There are four fast periods and, in addition to Pascha (Easter), twelve great feasts, as well as numerous commemorations of the saints of the Old and New Testaments throughout the year.

EASTER DAYS AND DOMINICAL LETTERS 1500 TO 2040

Dates up to and including 1752 are according to the Julian calendar. For dominical letters in leap years, *see* note below

		1500–1599	1600–1699	1700–1799	1800–1899	1900–1999	2000–2040
March							
d	22	1573	1668	1761	1818		
e	23	1505/16	1600	1788	1845/56	1913	2008
f	24		1611/95	1706/99		1940	
g	25	1543/54	1627/38/49	1722/33/44	1883/94	1951	2035
A	26	1559/70/81/92	1654/65/76	1749/58/69/80	1815/26/37	1967/78/89	
b	27	1502/13/24/97	1608/87/92	1785/96	1842/53/64	1910/21/32	2005/16
c	28	1529/35/40	1619/24/30	1703/14/25	1869/75/80	1937/48	2027/32
d	29	1551/62	1635/46/57	1719/30/41/52	1807/12/91	1959/64/70	
e	30	1567/78/89	1651/62/73/84	1746/55/66/77	1823/34	1902/75/86/97	
f	31	1510/21/32/83/94	1605/16/78/89	1700/71/82/93	1839/50/61/72	1907/18/29/91	2002/13/24
April							
g	1	1526/37/48	1621/32	1711/16	1804/66/77/88	1923/34/45/56	2018/29/40
A	2	1553/64	1643/48	1727/38	1809/20/93/99	1961/72	
b	3	1575/80/86	1659/70/81	1743/63/68/74	1825/31/36	1904/83/88/94	
c	4	1507/18/91	1602/13/75/86/97	1708/79/90	1847/58	1915/20/26/99	2010/21
d	5	1523/34/45/56	1607/18/29/40	1702/13/24/95	1801/63/74/85/96	1931/42/53	2015/26/37
e	6	1539/50/61/72	1634/45/56	1729/35/40/60	1806/17/28/90	1947/58/69/80	
f	7	1504/77/88	1667/72	1751/65/76	1822/33/44	1901/12/85/96	
g	8	1509/15/20/99	1604/10/83/94	1705/87/92/98	1849/55/60	1917/28	2007/12
A	9	1531/42	1615/26/37/99	1710/21/32	1871/82	1939/44/50	2023/34
b	10	1547/58/69	1631/42/53/64	1726/37/48/57	1803/14/87/98	1955/66/77	2039
c	11	1501/12/63/74/85/96	1658/69/80	1762/73/84	1819/30/41/52	1909/71/82/93	2004
d	12	1506/17/28	1601/12/91/96	1789	1846/57/68	1903/14/25/36/98	2009/20
e	13	1533/44	1623/28	1707/18	1800/73/79/84	1941/52	2031/36
f	14	1555/60/66	1639/50/61	1723/34/45/54	1805/11/16/95	1963/68/74	
g	15	1571/82/93	1655/66/77/88	1750/59/70/81	1827/38	1900/06/79/90	2001
A	16	1503/14/25/36/87/98	1609/20/82/93	1704/75/86/97	1843/54/65/76	1911/22/33/95	2006/17/28
b	17	1530/41/52	1625/36	1715/20	1808/70/81/92	1927/38/49/60	2022/33
c	18	1557/68	1647/52	1731/42/56	1802/13/24/97	1954/65/76	
d	19	1500/79/84/90	1663/74/85	1747/67/72/78	1829/35/40	1908/81/87/92	
e	20	1511/22/95	1606/17/79/90	1701/12/83/94	1851/62	1919/24/30	2003/14/25
f	21	1527/38/49	1622/33/44	1717/28	1867/78/89	1935/46/57	2019/30
g	22	1565/76	1660	1739/53/64	1810/21/32	1962/73/84	
A	23	1508	1671		1848	1905/16	2000
b	24	1519	1603/14/98	1709/91	1859		2011
c	25	1546	1641	1736	1886	1943	2038

No dominical letter is placed against the intercalary day 29 February, but since it is still counted as a weekday and given a name, the series of letters moves back one day every leap year after intercalation. Thus, a leap year beginning with the dominical letter C will change to a year with the dominical letter B on 1 March

MOVEABLE FEASTS TO THE YEAR 2040

Year	Ash Wednesday	Easter	Ascension	Pentecost (Whit Sunday)	Advent Sunday
2018	14 February	1 April	10 May	20 May	2 December
2019	6 March	21 April	30 May	9 June	1 December
2020	26 February	12 April	21 May	31 May	29 November
2021	17 February	4 April	13 May	23 May	28 November
2022	2 March	17 April	26 May	5 June	27 November
2023	22 February	9 April	18 May	28 May	3 December
2024	14 February	31 March	9 May	19 May	1 December
2025	5 March	20 April	29 May	8 June	30 November
2026	18 February	5 April	14 May	24 May	29 November
2027	10 February	28 March	6 May	16 May	28 November
2028	1 March	16 April	25 May	4 June	3 December
2029	14 February	1 April	10 May	20 May	2 December
2030	6 March	21 April	30 May	9 June	1 December
2031	26 February	13 April	22 May	1 June	30 November
2032	11 February	28 March	6 May	16 May	28 November
2033	2 March	17 April	26 May	5 June	27 November
2034	22 February	9 April	18 May	28 May	3 December
2035	7 February	25 March	3 May	13 May	2 December
2036	27 February	13 April	22 May	1 June	30 November
2037	18 February	5 April	14 May	24 May	29 November
2038	10 March	25 April	3 June	13 June	28 November
2039	23 February	10 April	19 May	29 May	27 November
2040	15 February	1 April	10 May	20 May	2 December

NOTES

Ash Wednesday (first day in Lent) can fall at earliest on 4 February and at latest on 10 March

Mothering Sunday (fourth Sunday in Lent) can fall at earliest on 1 March and at latest on 4 April

Easter Day can fall at earliest on 22 March and at latest on 25 April

Ascension Day is forty days after Easter Day and can fall at earliest on 30 April and at latest on 3 June

Pentecost (Whit Sunday) is seven weeks after Easter and can fall at earliest on 10 May and at latest on 13 June

Trinity Sunday is the Sunday after Whit Sunday

Corpus Christi falls on the Thursday after Trinity Sunday

Sundays after Pentecost – there are not less than 18 and not more than 23

Advent Sunday is the Sunday nearest to 30 November

THE DOMINICAL LETTER

The dominical letter is one of the letters A–G which are used to denote the Sundays in successive years. If the first day of the year is a Sunday the letter is A; if the second, B; the third, C; and so on. A leap year requires two letters, the first for 1 January to 29 February, the second for 1 March to 31 December. The dominical letter for 2018, which is not a leap year, is G (*see also* page 9).

EPIPHANY

The feast of the Epiphany, commemorating the manifestation of Christ, later became associated with the offering of gifts by the Magi. The day was of great importance from the time of the Council of Nicaea (AD 325), as the primate of Alexandria was charged at every Epiphany feast with the announcement in a letter to the churches of the date of the forthcoming Easter. The day was also of importance in Britain as it influenced dates, ecclesiastical and lay, eg Plough Monday, when work was resumed in the fields, fell on the Monday in the first full week after Epiphany.

LENT

The Teutonic word *Lent,* which denotes the fast preceding Easter, originally meant no more than the spring season; but from Anglo-Saxon times, at least, it has been used as the equivalent of the more significant Latin term *Quadragesima,* meaning the 'forty days' or, more literally, the fortieth day. Ash Wednesday is the first day of Lent, which ends at midnight before Easter Day.

PALM SUNDAY

Palm Sunday, the Sunday before Easter and the beginning of Holy Week, commemorates the triumphal entry of Christ into Jerusalem.

MAUNDY THURSDAY

Maundy Thursday is the day before Good Friday, the name itself being a corruption of *dies mandati* (day of the mandate) when Christ washed the feet of the disciples and gave them the mandate to love one another.

EASTER DAY

Easter Day is the first Sunday after the full moon which happens on, or next after, the 21st day of March; if the full moon happens on a Sunday, Easter Day is the Sunday after.

This definition is contained in an Act of Parliament (24 Geo. II ch. 23) and explanation is given in the preamble to the Act that the day of full moon depends on certain tables that have been prepared. These tables are summarised in the early pages of the Book of Common Prayer. The moon referred to is not the real Moon of the heavens, but a hypothetical moon on whose 'full' the date of Easter depends, and the lunations of this 'calendar' moon consist of 29 and 30 days alternately, with certain necessary modifications to make the date of its full agree as nearly as possible with that of the real Moon, which is known as the Paschal Full Moon.

A FIXED EASTER

In 1928 the House of Commons agreed to a motion for the third reading of a bill proposing that Easter Day shall, in the calendar year next but one after the commencement of the Act and in all subsequent years, be the first Sunday after the second Saturday in April. Easter would thus fall on the second or third Sunday in April, ie between 9 and 15 April (inclusive). A clause in the bill provided that before it shall come into operation, regard shall be had to any opinion expressed officially by the various Christian churches. Efforts by the World Council of Churches to secure a unanimous choice of date for Easter by its member churches have so far been unsuccessful.

ROGATION DAYS

Rogation Days are the Monday, Tuesday and Wednesday preceding Ascension Day and from the fifth century were observed as public fasts with solemn processions and supplications. The processions were discontinued as religious observances at the Reformation, but survive in the ceremony known as 'beating the parish bounds'. Rogation Sunday is the Sunday before Ascension Day.

EMBER DAYS

The Ember days occur on the Wednesday, Friday and Saturday of the same week, four times a year. Used for the ordination of clergy, these days are set aside for fasting and prayer. The weeks in which they fall are: (a) after the third Sunday in Advent, (b) before the second Sunday in Lent, (c) before Trinity Sunday and (d) after Holy Cross day.

TRINITY SUNDAY

Trinity Sunday is eight weeks after Easter Day, on the Sunday following Pentecost (Whit Sunday). Subsequent Sundays are reckoned in the Book of Common Prayer calendar of the Church of England as 'after Trinity'.

Thomas Becket (1118–70) was consecrated Archbishop of Canterbury on the Sunday after Whit Sunday and his first act was to ordain that the day of his consecration should be held as a new festival in honour of the Holy Trinity.

HINDU CALENDAR

The Hindu calendar is a luni-solar calendar of 12 months, each containing 29 days, 12 hours. Each month is divided into a light fortnight (Shukla or Shuddha) and a dark fortnight (Krishna or Vadya) based on the waxing and waning of the Moon. In most parts of India the month starts with the light fortnight, ie the day after the new moon, although in some regions it begins with the dark fortnight, ie the day after the full moon.

The new year according to the civil calendar begins on the first day of the month of Chaitra (March/April) and ends in the month of Phalgun (March). The financial new year begins on the first day of Kartik (Diwali day). For most Hindus, the first day of Chaitra and the first day of Kartik are equally important.

The 12 months – Chaitra, Vaishakh, Jyeshtha, Ashadh, Shravan, Bhadrapad, Ashvin, Kartik, Margashirsh, Paush, Magh and Phalgun – have Sanskrit names derived from 12 asterisms (constellations). There are regional variations to the names of the months but the Sanskrit names are understood throughout India.

Every lunar month that has a solar transit is termed pure *(shuddha)*. The lunar month without a solar transit is impure *(mala)* and called an intercalary month. An intercalary month occurs approximately every 32 lunar months, whenever the difference between the Hindu year of 360 lunar days (354 days 8 hours solar time) and the 365 days 6 hours of the solar year reaches the length of one Hindu lunar month (29 days 12 hours).

The leap month, often referred to as Adhik Maas (extra month), may be added at any point in the Hindu year. The name given to the month varies according to when it occurs but is taken from the month immediately following it. The leap month in 2018 is Jyeshtha.

The days of the week are called Raviwar (Sunday), Somawar (Monday), Mangalwar (Tuesday), Budhawar (Wednesday), Guruwar (Thursday), Shukrawar (Friday) and Shaniwar (Saturday). The names are derived from the Sanskrit names of the Sun, the Moon and five planets, Mars, Mercury, Jupiter, Venus and Saturn.

Most fasts and festivals are based on the lunar calendar but a few are determined by the apparent movement of the Sun, eg Makar Sankranti and Pongal (in southern India), which are celebrated on 14/15 January to mark the start of the Sun's apparent journey northwards and a change of season.

Festivals celebrated throughout India are Chaitra (the New Year), Raksha-bandhan (the renewal of the kinship bond between brothers and sisters), Navaratri (a nine-night festival dedicated to the goddess Parvati), Dussehra (the victory of Rama over the demon army), Diwali (a festival of lights), Makar Sankranti, Shivaratri (dedicated to Shiva), and Holi (a spring festival). British Hindus commonly celebrate the festival of Diwali as the start of the financial new year.

Regional festivals are Durga-puja (dedicated to the goddess Durga (Parvati)), Sarasvati Puja (dedicated to the goddess Sarasvati), Ganesh Chaturthi (worship of Ganesh on the fourth day (Chaturthi) of the light half of Bhadrapad), Ram Navami (the birth festival of the god Rama) and Krishna Janmashtami (the birth festival of the god Krishna).

The main festivals celebrated in Britain are Navaratri, Dussehra, Durga-puja, Diwali, Holi, Sarasvati Puja, Ganesh Chaturthi, Raksha-bandhan, Ram Navami and Krishna Janmashtami. For dates of the main festivals in 2018, *see* page 9.

JEWISH CALENDAR

The story of the Flood in the Book of Genesis indicates the use of a calendar of some kind and that the writers recognised 30 days as the length of a lunation. However, after the diaspora, Jewish communities were left in considerable doubt as to the times of fasts and festivals. This led to the formation of the Jewish calendar as used today. It is said that this was done in AD 358 by Rabbi Hillel II, though some assert that it did not happen until much later.

The calendar is luni-solar, and is based on the lengths of the lunation and of the tropical year as found by Hipparchus (c.120 BC), which differ little from those adopted at the present day. The year AM 5777 (2016–17) is the 1st year of the 305th Metonic (Minor or Lunar) cycle of 19 years and the 9th year of the 207th Solar (or Major) cycle of 28 years since the Era of the Creation. Jews hold that the Creation occurred at the time of the autumnal equinox in the year known in the Christian calendar as 3760 BC (954 of the Julian period). The epoch or starting point of Jewish chronology corresponds to 7 October 3761 BC. At the beginning of each solar cycle, the Tekufah of Nisan (the vernal equinox) returns to the same day and hour.

The hour is divided into 1,080 minims, and the month between one new moon and the next is reckoned as 29 days 12 hours 793 minims. The normal calendar year, called a regular common year, consists of 12 months of 30 days and 29 days alternately. Since 12 months such as these comprise only 354 days, in order that each of them shall not diverge greatly from an average place in the solar year, a 13th month is occasionally added after the fifth month of the civil year (which commences on the first day of the month Tishri), or as the penultimate month of the ecclesiastical year (which commences on the first day of the month Nisan). The years when this happens are called Embolismic or leap years.

Of the 19 years that form a Metonic cycle, seven are leap years; they occur at places in the cycle indicated by the numbers 3, 6, 8, 11, 14, 17 and 19, these places being chosen so that the accumulated excesses of the solar years should be as small as possible.

A Jewish year is of one of the following six types:

minimal common	353 days
regular common	354 days
full common	355 days
minimal leap	383 days
regular leap	384 days
full leap	385 days

The regular year has alternate months of 30 and 29 days. In a full year, Marcheshvan, the second month of the civil year, has 30 days instead of 29; in minimal years Kislev, the third month, has 29 instead of 30. The additional month in leap years is called Adar Sheni (Adar II) and follows the month called Adar Rishon; the usual Adar festivals are observed in Adar Sheni. In a leap year Adar I has 30 days, in all other years it has 29. None of the variations mentioned are allowed to change the number of days in the other months, which still follow the alternation of the normal 12.

These are the main features of the Jewish calendar, which must be considered permanent because as a Jewish law it cannot be altered except by a Great Sanhedrin.

The Jewish day begins between sunset and nightfall. The time used is that of the meridian of Jerusalem, which is 2h 21m in advance of Greenwich Mean Time. Rules for the beginning of sabbaths and festivals were laid down for the latitude of London in the 18th century and hours for nightfall are fixed annually by the Chief Rabbi.

JEWISH CALENDAR 5778–79

AM 5778 is a regular common year of 12 months, 51 sabbaths and 354 days. AM 5779 is a full leap year of 13 months, 55 sabbaths and 385 days.

Month (length)	AM 5778	AM 5779
Tishri 1 (30)	21 Sep 2017	10 Sep 2018
Marcheshvan 1 (29/30)	21 Oct	10 Oct
Kislev 1 (30/30)	19 Nov	9 Nov
Tebet 1 (29)	19 Dec	9 Dec
Shebat 1 (30)	17 Jan 2018	7 Jan 2019
Adar Rishon 1 (29)	16 Feb	
Nisan 1 (30)	17 Mar	
Iyar 1 (29)	16 Apr	
Sivan 1 (30)	15 May	
Tammuz 1 (29)	14 Jun	
Ab 1 (30)	13 Jul	
Elul 1 (29)	12 Aug	

JEWISH FASTS AND FESTIVALS

For dates of principal festivals in 2018, *see* page 9.

Tishri 1–2	Rosh Hashanah (New Year)
Tishri 3	*Fast of Gedaliah
Tishri 10	Yom Kippur (Day of Atonement)
Tishri 15–21	Succot (Feast of Tabernacles)
Tishri 21	Hoshana Rabba
Tishri 22	Shemini Atseret (Solemn Assembly)
Tishri 23	Simchat Torah (Rejoicing of the Law)
Kislev 25	Hanukkah (Dedication of the Temple) begins
Tebet 10	Fast of Tebet
†Adar 13	§Fast of Esther
†Adar 14	Purim
†Adar 15	Shushan Purim
Nisan 15–22	Pesach (Passover)
Sivan 6–7	Shavuot (Feast of Weeks)
Tammuz 17	*Fast of Tammuz
Ab 9	*Fast of Ab

* If these dates fall on the sabbath the fast is kept on the following day
† Adar Sheni in leap years
§ This fast is observed on Adar 11 (or Adar Sheni 11 in leap years) if Adar 13 falls on a sabbath

MUSLIM CALENDAR

The Muslim era is dated from the *Hijrah*, or flight of the Prophet Muhammad from Mecca to Medina, the corresponding date of which in the Julian calendar is 16 July AD 622. The lunar *hijri* calendar is used principally in Iran, Egypt, Malaysia, Pakistan, Mauritania, various Arab states and certain parts of India. Iran uses the solar hijri calendar as well as the lunar hijri calendar. The dating system was adopted about AD 639, commencing with the first day of the month Muharram.

The lunar calendar consists of 12 months of either 30 or 29 days, with the intercalation of one day at the end of the 12th month at stated intervals in each cycle of 30 years. The object of the intercalation is to reconcile the date of the first day of the month with the date of the actual new moon.

Some adherents still take the date of the evening of the first physical sighting of the crescent of the new moon as that of the first of the month. If cloud obscures the Moon the present

month may be extended to 30 days, after which the new month will begin automatically regardless of whether the Moon has been seen. (Under religious law a month must have less than 31 days.) This means that the beginning of a new month and the date of religious festivals can vary from the published calendars.

In each cycle of 30 years, 19 years are common and contain 354 days, and 11 years are intercalary (leap years) of 355 days, the latter being called *kabisah*. The mean length of the Hijrah years is 354 days 8 hours 48 minutes and the period of mean lunation is 29 days 12 hours 44 minutes.

To ascertain if a year is common or kabisah, divide it by 30: the quotient gives the number of completed cycles and the remainder shows the place of the year in the current cycle. If the remainder is 2, 5, 7, 10, 13, 16, 18, 21, 24, 26 or 29, the year is kabisah and consists of 355 days.

MUSLIM CALENDAR 1439–40

Hijrah 1439 (remainder 29) is a kabisah year, while Hijrah 1440, which has no remainder, is a common year. Calendar dates below are estimates based on calculations of moon phases.

Month (length)	1439 AH	1440 AH
Muharram 1 (30/29)	21 Sep 2017	11 Sep 2018
Safar 1 (29/30)	21 Oct	10 Oct
Rabi'I 1 (30/29)	19 Nov	9 Nov
Rabi'II 1 (30/30)	19 Dec	8 Dec
Jumada I 1 (30/30)	18 Jan 2018	7 Jan 2019
Jumada II 1 (29)	17 Feb	
Rajab 1 (30)	18 Mar	
Sha'ban 1 (29)	17 Apr	
Ramadan 1 (30)	16 May	
Shawwal 1 (29)	15 Jun	
Dhu'l Qa'da 1 (29)	14 Jul	
Dhu'l Hijjah 1 (30)	12 Aug	

MUSLIM FESTIVALS

Ramadan is a month of fasting for all Muslims because it is the month in which the revelation of the *Qur'an* (Koran) began. During Ramadan, Muslims abstain from food, drink and sexual pleasure from dawn until after sunset.

The two major festivals are *Eid-ul-Fitr* and *Eid-ul-Adha*. Eid-ul-Fitr marks the end of the Ramadan fast and is celebrated on the day after the sighting of the new moon of the following month. Eid-ul-Adha, the festival of sacrifice (also known as the great festival), celebrates the submission of the Prophet Ibrahim (Abraham) to God. Eid-ul-Adha falls on the tenth day of Dhu'l-Hijjah, coinciding with the day when those on *hajj* (pilgrimage to Mecca) sacrifice animals.

Other days accorded special recognition are:

Muharram 1	New Year's Day
Muharram 10	Ashura (the day Prophet Noah left the Ark and Prophet Moses was saved from Pharaoh (Sunni), the death of the Prophet's grandson Husain (Shi'ite))
Rabi'u-l-Awwal (Rabi' I) 12	Mawlid ul-Nabi (birthday of the Prophet Muhammad)
Rajab 27	Laylat ul-Isra' wa'l-Mi'raj (The Night of Journey and Ascension)
Ramadan*	Laylat ul-Qadr (Night of Power)

*Moveable feast

For dates of the major celebrations in 2017–18, *see* page 9.

SIKH CALENDAR

The Sikh calendar is a lunar calendar of 365 days divided into 12 months. The length of the months varies between 29 and 32 days.

There are no prescribed feast days and no fasting periods. The main celebrations are Baisakhi (the new year and the anniversary of the founding of the Khalsa), Diwali Mela (festival of light), Hola Mohalla Mela (a spring festival held in the Punjab), and the Gurpurbs (anniversaries associated with the ten Gurus).

For dates of the major celebrations in 2018, *see* page 9.

THAI CALENDAR

Thailand adopted the Suriyakati calendar, a modified version of the Gregorian calendar, during the reign of King Rama V in 1888, using 1 April as the first day of the year. In 1940 the date of the new year was changed to 1 January. The years are counted from the beginning of the Buddhist era (BE), which is calculated to have commenced upon the death of the Lord Buddha, taken to have occurred in 543 BC, so AD 2018 is BE 2561. The Chinese system of associating years with one of twelve animals is also in use in Thailand. The Chantarakati lunar calendar is used to determine religious holidays; the new year begins on the first day of the waxing moon in November or, if there is a leap month, in December.

CIVIL AND LEGAL CALENDAR

THE HISTORICAL YEAR
Before 1752, two calendar systems were used in England. The civil or legal year began on 25 March and the historical year on 1 January. Thus the civil or legal date 24 March 1658 was the same day as the historical date 24 March 1659; a date in that portion of the year is written as 24 March 1658/9, the earlier date showing the civil or legal year.

THE NEW YEAR
In England in the seventh century, and as late as the 13th, the year was reckoned from Christmas Day, but in the 12th century the Church in England began the year with the feast of the Annunciation of the Blessed Virgin ('Lady Day') on 25 March, and this practice was adopted generally in the 14th century. The civil or legal year in the British dominions (exclusive of Scotland) began with Lady Day until 1751. But in and since 1752 the civil year has begun with 1 January. New Year's Day in Scotland was changed from 25 March to 1 January in 1600.

Elsewhere in Europe, 1 January was adopted as the first day of the year by Venice in 1522, German states in 1544, Spain, Portugal and the Roman Catholic Netherlands in 1556, Prussia, Denmark and Sweden in 1559, France in 1564, Lorraine in 1579, the Protestant Netherlands in 1583, Russia in 1725, and Tuscany in 1751.

REGNAL YEARS
Regnal years are the years of a sovereign's reign and each begins on the anniversary of his or her accession, eg regnal year 67 of the present queen begins on 6 February 2018.

The system was used for dating Acts of Parliament until 1962. The Summer Time Act 1925, for example, is quoted as 15 and 16 Geo. V ch. 64, because it became law in the parliamentary session which extended over part of both of these regnal years. Acts of a parliamentary session during which a sovereign died were usually given two year numbers, the regnal year of the deceased sovereign and the regnal year of his or her successor, eg those passed in 1952 were dated 16 Geo. VI and 1 Elizabeth II. Since 1962 Acts of Parliament have been dated by the calendar year.

QUARTER AND TERM DAYS
Holy days and saints days were the usual means in early times for setting the dates of future and recurrent appointments. The quarter days in England and Wales are the feast of the Nativity (25 December), the feast of the Annunciation (25 March), the feast of St John the Baptist (24 June) and the feast of St Michael and All Angels (29 September).

The term days in Scotland are Candlemas (the feast of the Purification), Whitsunday, Lammas (Loaf Mass) and Martinmas (St Martin's Day). These fell on 2 February, 15 May, 1 August and 11 November respectively. However, by the Term and Quarter Days (Scotland) Act 1990, the dates of the term days were changed to 28 February (Candlemas), 28 May (Whitsunday), 28 August (Lammas) and 28 November (Martinmas).

RED-LETTER DAYS
Red-letter days were originally the holy days and saints days indicated in early ecclesiastical calendars by letters printed in red ink. The days to be distinguished in this way were approved at the Council of Nicaea in AD 325.

These days still have a legal significance, as judges of the Queen's Bench Division wear scarlet robes on red-letter days falling during the law sittings. The days designated as red-letter days for this purpose are:

Holy and saints days
The Conversion of St Paul, the Purification, Ash Wednesday, the Annunciation, the Ascension, the feasts of St Mark, SS Philip and James, St Matthias, St Barnabas, St John the Baptist, St Peter, St Thomas, St James, St Luke, SS Simon and Jude, All Saints, St Andrew.

Civil calendar (for dates, *see* page 9)
Includes the anniversaries of the Queen's accession, the Queen's birthday and the Queen's coronation, the Queen's official birthday, the birthday of the Duke of Edinburgh, the birthday of the Prince of Wales, St David's Day and Lord Mayor's Day.

PUBLIC HOLIDAYS
Public holidays are divided into two categories, common law and statutory. Common law holidays are holidays 'by habit and custom'; in England, Wales and Northern Ireland these are Good Friday and Christmas Day.

Statutory public holidays, known as bank holidays, were first established by the Bank Holidays Act 1871. They were, literally, days on which the banks (and other public institutions) were closed and financial obligations due on that day were payable the following day. The legislation currently governing public holidays in the UK, which is the Banking and Financial Dealings Act 1971, stipulates the days that are to be public holidays in England, Wales, Scotland and Northern Ireland.

If a public holiday falls on a Saturday or a Sunday then another day will be given in lieu, usually the following Monday. For dates of public holidays in 2018 and 2019, *see* pages 10 and 11.

CHRONOLOGICAL CYCLES AND ERAS

SOLAR (OR MAJOR) CYCLE
The solar cycle is a period of 28 years; in any corresponding year of each cycle the days of the week recur on the same day of the month.

METONIC (LUNAR, OR MINOR) CYCLE
In 432 BC, Meton, an Athenian astronomer, found that 235 lunations are very nearly, though not exactly, equal in duration to 19 solar years and so after 19 years the phases of the Moon recur approximately on the same days of the month. The dates of full moon in a cycle of 19 years were inscribed in figures of gold on public monuments in Athens, and the number showing the position of a year in the cycle is called the golden number of that year.

JULIAN PERIOD
The Julian period was proposed by Joseph Scaliger in 1582. The period is 7,980 Julian years, and its first year coincides with the year 4713 BC. The figure of 7,980 is the product of the number of years in the solar cycle, the Metonic cycle and the cycle of the Roman indiction (28 x 19 x 15).

ROMAN INDICTION
The Roman indiction is a period of 15 years, instituted for fiscal purposes about AD 300.

EPACT
The epact is the age of the calendar Moon, diminished by one day, on 1 January, in the ecclesiastical lunar calendar.

CHINESE CALENDAR

A lunar calendar was the sole calendar in use in China until 1911, when the government adopted the new (Gregorian) calendar for official and most business activities. The Chinese tend to follow both calendars, the lunar calendar playing an important part in personal life, eg birth celebrations, festivals, marriages; in rural villages the lunar calendar dictates the cycle of activities, denoting the change of weather and farming activities.

The lunar calendar is used in Hong Kong, Singapore, Malaysia, Tibet and elsewhere in south-east Asia. The calendar has a cycle of 60 years. The new year begins at the first new moon after the sun enters the sign of Aquarius, ie the new year falls between 21 January and 19 February in the Gregorian calendar.

Each year in the Chinese calendar is associated with one of 12 animals: the rat, the ox, the tiger, the rabbit, the dragon, the snake, the horse, the sheep, the monkey, the chicken or rooster, the dog, and the pig.

The date of the Chinese new year and the astrological sign for the years 2018–21 are:

2018	16 February	Dog
2019	5 February	Pig
2020	25 January	Rat
2021	12 February	Ox

COPTIC CALENDAR

In the Coptic calendar, which is used in parts of Egypt and Ethiopia, the year is made up of 12 months of 30 days each, followed, in general, by five complementary days. Every fourth year is an intercalary or leap year and in these years there are six complementary days. The intercalary year of the Coptic calendar immediately precedes the leap year of the Julian calendar. The era is that of Diocletian or the Martyrs, the origin of which is fixed at 29 August AD 284 (Julian date).

INDIAN ERAS

In addition to the Muslim reckoning, other eras are used in India. The Saka era of southern India, dating from 3 March AD 78, was declared the national calendar of the Republic of India with effect from 22 March 1957, to be used concurrently with the Gregorian calendar. As revised, the year of the new Saka era begins at the spring equinox, with five successive months of 31 days and seven of 30 days in ordinary years, and six months of each length in leap years. The year AD 2018 is 1940 of the revised Saka era.

The year AD 2018 corresponds to the following years in other eras:

Year 2075 of the Vikram Samvat era
Year 1425 of the Bengali San era
Year 1194 of the Kollam era
Year 5119 of the Kaliyuga era
Year 2561 of the Buddha Nirvana era

JAPANESE CALENDAR

The Japanese calendar is essentially the same as the Gregorian calendar, the years, months and weeks being of the same length and beginning on the same days as those of the Gregorian calendar. The numeration of the years is different, based on a system of epochs or periods, each of which begins at the accession of an emperor or other important occurrence. The method is not unlike the British system of regnal years, except that each year of a period closes on 31 December. The Japanese chronology begins about AD 650 and the three latest epochs are defined by the reigns of emperors, whose actual names are not necessarily used:

Epoch
Taisho – 1 August 1912 to 25 December 1926
Showa – 26 December 1926 to 7 January 1989
Heisei – 8 January 1989
The year Heisei 30 begins on 1 January 2018.

The months are known as First Month, Second Month, etc, First Month being equivalent to January. The days of the week are Nichiyobi (Sun-day), Getsuyobi (Moon-day), Kayobi (Fire-day), Suiyobi (Water-day), Mokuyobi (Wood-day), Kinyobi (Metal-day) and Doyobi (Earth-day).

THE MASONIC YEAR

Two dates are quoted in warrants, dispensations, etc, issued by the United Grand Lodge of England, those for the current year being expressed as *Anno Domini* 2018 – *Anno Lucis* 6018. This *Anno Lucis* (year of light) is based on the Book of Genesis 1:3, the 4,000-year difference being derived, in modified form, from *Ussher's Notation*, published in 1654, which places the Creation of the World in 4004 BC.

OLYMPIADS

Ancient Greek chronology was reckoned in Olympiads, cycles of four years corresponding with the Olympic Games held on the plain of Olympia, in Elis. The intervening years were the first, second, etc, of the Olympiad, which received the name of the victor at the Games. The first recorded Olympiad is that of Choroebus, 776 BC.

ZOROASTRIAN CALENDAR

Zoroastrians, followers of the Iranian prophet Zarathushtra (known to the Greeks as Zoroaster) are mostly to be found in Iran and in India, where they are known as Parsees.

The Zoroastrian era dates from the coronation of the last Zoroastrian Sasanian king in AD 631. The Zoroastrian calendar is divided into 12 months, each comprising 30 days, followed by five holy days of the Gathas at the end of each year to make the year consist of 365 days.

In order to synchronise the calendar with the solar year of 365 days, an extra month was intercalated once every 120 years. However, this intercalation ceased in the 12th century and the new year, which had fallen in the spring, slipped back to August. Because intercalation ceased at different times in Iran and India, there was one month's difference between the calendar followed in Iran (Kadmi calendar) and that followed by the Parsees (Shenshai calendar). In 1906 a group of Zoroastrians decided to bring the calendar back in line with the seasons again and restore the new year to 21 March each year (Fasli calendar).

The Shenshai calendar (new year in August) is mainly used by Parsees. The Fasli calendar (new year, 21 March) is mainly used by Zoroastrians living in Iran, in the Indian subcontinent, or elsewhere.

ROMAN CALENDAR

Roman historians adopted as an epoch the foundation of Rome, which is believed to have happened in the year 753 BC. The ordinal number of the years in Roman reckoning is followed by the letters AUC *(ab urbe condita),* so that the year 2018 is 2771 AUC (MMDCCLXXI). The calendar that we know has developed from one said to have been established by Romulus using a year of 304 days divided into ten months, beginning with March. To this Numa added January and February, making the year consist of 12 months of 30 and 29 days alternately, with an additional day so that the total was 355. It is also said that Numa ordered an intercalary month of 22 or 23 days in alternate years, making 90 days in eight years, to be inserted after 23 February.

However, there is some doubt as to the origination and the details of the intercalation in the Roman calendar. In the year 46 BC Julius Caesar found that the calendar had been allowed to fall into some confusion. He sought the help of Egyptian astronomer Sosigenes, which led to the construction and adoption (45 BC) of the Julian calendar, and, by a slight alteration, to the Gregorian calendar now in use. The year 46 BC was made to consist of 445 days and is called the Year of Confusion.

In the Roman (Julian) calendar, the days of the month were counted backwards from three fixed points, or days, and an intervening day was said to be so many days before the next coming point, the first and last being counted. These three points were the Kalends, the Nones and the Ides. The year containing 366 days was called *bissextilis annus,* as it had a doubled sixth day *(bissextus dies)* before the March Kalends on 24 February – *ante diem sextum Kalendas Martias,* or a.d. VI Kal. Mart.

Present days of the month	March, May, July, October have thirty-one days		January, August, December have thirty-one days		April, June, September, November have thirty days		February has twenty-eight days, and in leap year twenty-nine	
1	Kalendis		Kalendis		Kalendis		Kalendis	
2	VI	⎫ ante	IV	⎫ ante	IV	⎫ ante	IV	⎫ ante
3	V	⎬	III	⎭ Nonas	III	⎭ Nonas	III	⎭ Nonas
4	IV	⎬ ante Nonas	pridie Nonas		pridie Nonas		pridie Nonas	
5	III	⎭	Nonis		Nonis		Nonis	
6	pridie Nonas		VIII	⎫	VIII	⎫	VIII	⎫
7	Nonis		VII	⎬	VII	⎬	VII	⎬
8	VIII	⎫	VI	⎬ ante	VI	⎬ ante	VI	⎬ ante
9	VII	⎬	V	⎭ Idus	V	⎭ Idus	V	⎭ Idus
10	VI	⎬ ante	IV		IV		IV	
11	V	⎭ Idus	III		III		III	
12	IV	⎬	pridie Idus		pridie Idus		pridie Idus	
13	III	⎭	Idibus		Idibus		Idibus	
14	pridie Idus		XIX	⎫	XVIII	⎫	XVI	⎫
15	Idibus		XVIII	⎬	XVII	⎬	XV	⎬
16	XVII	⎫	XVII	⎬	XVI	⎬	XIV	⎬
17	XVI	⎬	XVI	⎬	XV	⎬	XIII	⎬
18	XV	⎬	XV	⎬	XIV	⎬	XII	⎬
19	XIV	⎬	XIV	⎬	XIII	⎬	XI	⎬
20	XIII	⎬	XIII	⎬	XII	⎬ ante Kalendas	X	⎬ ante Kalendas
21	XII	⎬	XII	⎬ ante Kalendas	XI	⎬ (of the month	IX	⎭ Martias
22	XI	⎬ ante Kalendas	XI	⎬ (of the month	X	⎬ following)	VIII	
23	X	⎬ (of the month	X	⎬ following)	IX	⎬	VII	
24	IX	⎬ following)	IX	⎬	VIII	⎬	*VI	
25	VIII	⎬	VIII	⎬	VII	⎬	V	
26	VII	⎬	VII	⎬	VI	⎬	IV	
27	VI	⎬	VI	⎬	V	⎬	III	
28	V	⎬	V	⎬	IV	⎬	pridie Kalendas	
29	IV	⎬	IV	⎬	III	⎭	Martias	
30	III	⎭	III	⎭	pridie Kalendas			
31	pridie Kalendas (Aprilis, Iunias, Sextilis, Novembris)		pridie Kalendas (Februarias, Septembris, Ianuarias)		(Maias, Quinctilis, Octobris, Decembris)			

* Repeated in leap year

CALENDAR FOR ANY YEAR 1780–2040

To select the correct calendar for any year between 1780 and 2040, consult the index below

* leap year

1780 N*	1813 K	1846 I	1879 G	1912 D*	1945 C	1978 A	2011 M
1781 C	1814 M	1847 K	1880 J*	1913 G	1946 E	1979 C	2012 B*
1782 E	1815 A	1848 N*	1881 M	1914 I	1947 G	1980 F*	2013 E
1783 G	1816 D*	1849 C	1882 A	1915 K	1948 J*	1981 I	2014 G
1784 J*	1817 G	1850 E	1883 C	1916 N*	1949 M	1982 K	2015 I
1785 M	1818 I	1851 G	1884 F*	1917 C	1950 A	1983 M	2016 L*
1786 A	1819 K	1852 J*	1885 I	1918 E	1951 C	1984 B*	2017 A
1787 C	1820 N*	1853 M	1886 K	1919 G	1952 F*	1985 E	2018 C
1788 F*	1821 C	1854 A	1887 M	1920 J*	1953 I	1986 G	2019 E
1789 I	1822 E	1855 C	1888 B*	1921 M	1954 K	1987 I	2020 H*
1790 K	1823 G	1856 F*	1889 E	1922 A	1955 M	1988 L*	2021 K
1791 M	1824 J*	1857 I	1890 G	1923 C	1956 B*	1989 A	2022 M
1792 B*	1825 M	1858 K	1891 I	1924 F*	1957 E	1990 C	2023 A
1793 E	1826 A	1859 M	1892 L*	1925 I	1958 G	1991 E	2024 D*
1794 G	1827 C	1860 B*	1893 A	1926 K	1959 I	1992 H*	2025 G
1795 I	1828 F*	1861 E	1894 C	1927 M	1960 L*	1993 K	2026 I
1796 L*	1829 I	1862 G	1895 E	1928 B*	1961 A	1994 M	2027 K
1797 A	1830 K	1863 I	1896 H*	1929 E	1962 C	1995 A	2028 N*
1798 C	1831 M	1864 L*	1897 K	1930 G	1963 E	1996 D*	2029 C
1799 E	1832 B*	1865 A	1898 M	1931 I	1964 H*	1997 G	2030 E
1800 G	1833 E	1866 C	1899 A	1932 L*	1965 K	1998 I	2031 G
1801 I	1834 G	1867 E	1900 C	1933 A	1966 M	1999 K	2032 J*
1802 K	1835 I	1868 H*	1901 E	1934 C	1967 A	2000 N*	2033 M
1803 M	1836 L*	1869 K	1902 G	1935 E	1968 D*	2001 C	2034 A
1804 B*	1837 A	1870 M	1903 I	1936 H*	1969 G	2002 E	2035 C
1805 E	1838 C	1871 A	1904 L*	1937 K	1970 I	2003 G	2036 F*
1806 G	1839 E	1872 D*	1905 A	1938 M	1971 K	2004 J*	2037 I
1807 I	1840 H*	1873 G	1906 C	1939 A	1972 N*	2005 M	2038 K
1808 L*	1841 K	1874 I	1907 E	1940 D*	1973 C	2006 A	2039 M
1809 A	1842 M	1875 K	1908 H*	1941 G	1974 E	2007 C	2040 B*
1810 C	1843 A	1876 N*	1909 K	1942 I	1975 G	2008 F*	
1811 E	1844 D*	1877 C	1910 M	1943 K	1976 J*	2009 I	
1812 H*	1845 G	1878 E	1911 A	1944 N*	1977 M	2010 K	

A

	January	February	March
Sun.	1 8 15 22 29	5 12 19 26	5 12 19 26
Mon.	2 9 16 23 30	6 13 20 27	6 13 20 27
Tue.	3 10 17 24 31	7 14 21 28	7 14 21 28
Wed.	4 11 18 25	1 8 15 22	1 8 15 22 29
Thur.	5 12 19 26	2 9 16 23	2 9 16 23 30
Fri.	6 13 20 27	3 10 17 24	3 10 17 24 31
Sat.	7 14 21 28	4 11 18 25	4 11 18 25

	April	May	June
Sun.	2 9 16 23 30	7 14 21 28	4 11 18 25
Mon.	3 10 17 24	1 8 15 22 29	5 12 19 26
Tue.	4 11 18 25	2 9 16 23 30	6 13 20 27
Wed.	5 12 19 26	3 10 17 24 31	7 14 21 28
Thur.	6 13 20 27	4 11 18 25	1 8 15 22 29
Fri.	7 14 21 28	5 12 19 26	2 9 16 23 30
Sat.	1 8 15 22 29	6 13 20 27	3 10 17 24

	July	August	September
Sun.	2 9 16 23 30	6 13 20 27	3 10 17 24
Mon.	3 10 17 24 31	7 14 21 28	4 11 18 25
Tue.	4 11 18 25	1 8 15 22 29	5 12 19 26
Wed.	5 12 19 26	2 9 16 23 30	6 13 20 27
Thur.	6 13 20 27	3 10 17 24 31	7 14 21 28
Fri.	7 14 21 28	4 11 18 25	1 8 15 22 29
Sat.	1 8 15 22 29	5 12 19 26	2 9 16 23 30

	October	November	December
Sun.	1 8 15 22 29	5 12 19 26	3 10 17 24 31
Mon.	2 9 16 23 30	6 13 20 27	4 11 18 25
Tue.	3 10 17 24 31	7 14 21 28	5 12 19 26
Wed.	4 11 18 25	1 8 15 22 29	6 13 20 27
Thur.	5 12 19 26	2 9 16 23 30	7 14 21 28
Fri.	6 13 20 27	3 10 17 24	1 8 15 22 29
Sat.	7 14 21 28	4 11 18 25	2 9 16 23 30

EASTER DAYS

March 26	1815, 1826, 1837, 1967, 1978, 1989
April 2	1809, 1893, 1899, 1961
April 9	1871, 1882, 1939, 1950, 2023, 2034
April 16	1786, 1797, 1843, 1854, 1865, 1911, 1922, 1933, 1995, 2006, 2017
April 23	1905

B (LEAP YEAR)

	January	February	March
Sun.	1 8 15 22 29	5 12 19 26	4 11 18 25
Mon.	2 9 16 23 30	6 13 20 27	5 12 19 26
Tue.	3 10 17 24 31	7 14 21 28	6 13 20 27
Wed.	4 11 18 25	1 8 15 22 29	7 14 21 28
Thur.	5 12 19 26	2 9 16 23	1 8 15 22 29
Fri.	6 13 20 27	3 10 17 24	2 9 16 23 30
Sat.	7 14 21 28	4 11 18 25	3 10 17 24 31

	April	May	June
Sun.	1 8 15 22 29	6 13 20 27	3 10 17 24
Mon.	2 9 16 23 30	7 14 21 28	4 11 18 25
Tue.	3 10 17 24	1 8 15 22 29	5 12 19 26
Wed.	4 11 18 25	2 9 16 23 30	6 13 20 27
Thur.	5 12 19 26	3 10 17 24 31	7 14 21 28
Fri.	6 13 20 27	4 11 18 25	1 8 15 22 29
Sat.	7 14 21 28	5 12 19 26	2 9 16 23 30

	July	August	September
Sun.	1 8 15 22 29	5 12 19 26	2 9 16 23 30
Mon.	2 9 16 23 30	6 13 20 27	3 10 17 24
Tue.	3 10 17 24 31	7 14 21 28	4 11 18 25
Wed.	4 11 18 25	1 8 15 22 29	5 12 19 26
Thur.	5 12 19 26	2 9 16 23 30	6 13 20 27
Fri.	6 13 20 27	3 10 17 24 31	7 14 21 28
Sat.	7 14 21 28	4 11 18 25	1 8 15 22 29

	October	November	December
Sun.	7 14 21 28	4 11 18 25	2 9 16 23 30
Mon.	1 8 15 22 29	5 12 19 26	3 10 17 24 31
Tue.	2 9 16 23 30	6 13 20 27	4 11 18 25
Wed.	3 10 17 24 31	7 14 21 28	5 12 19 26
Thur.	4 11 18 25	1 8 15 22 29	6 13 20 27
Fri.	5 12 19 26	2 9 16 23 30	7 14 21 28
Sat.	6 13 20 27	3 10 17 24	1 8 15 22 29

EASTER DAYS

April 1	1804, 1888, 1956, 2040
April 8	1792, 1860, 1928, 2012
April 22	1832, 1984

C

	January	February	March
Sun.	7 14 21 28	4 11 18 25	4 11 18 25
Mon.	1 8 15 22 29	5 12 19 26	5 12 19 26
Tue.	2 9 16 23 30	6 13 20 27	6 13 20 27
Wed.	3 10 17 24 31	7 14 21 28	7 14 21 28
Thur.	4 11 18 25	1 8 15 22	1 8 15 22 29
Fri.	5 12 19 26	2 9 16 23	2 9 16 23 30
Sat.	6 13 20 27	3 10 17 24	3 10 17 24 31

	April	May	June
Sun.	1 8 15 22 29	6 13 20 27	3 10 17 24
Mon.	2 9 16 23 30	7 14 21 28	4 11 18 25
Tue.	3 10 17 24	1 8 15 22 29	5 12 19 26
Wed.	4 11 18 25	2 9 16 23 30	6 13 20 27
Thur.	5 12 19 26	3 10 17 24 31	7 14 21 28
Fri.	6 13 20 27	4 11 18 25	1 8 15 22 29
Sat.	7 14 21 28	5 12 19 26	2 9 16 23 30

	July	August	September
Sun.	1 8 15 22 29	5 12 19 26	2 9 16 23 30
Mon.	2 9 16 23 30	6 13 20 27	3 10 17 24
Tue.	3 10 17 24 31	7 14 21 28	4 11 18 25
Wed.	4 11 18 25	1 8 15 22 29	5 12 19 26
Thur.	5 12 19 26	2 9 16 23 30	6 13 20 27
Fri.	6 13 20 27	3 10 17 24 31	7 14 21 28
Sat.	7 14 21 28	4 11 18 25	1 8 15 22 29

	October	November	December
Sun.	7 14 21 28	4 11 18 25	2 9 16 23 30
Mon.	1 8 15 22 29	5 12 19 26	3 10 17 24 31
Tue.	2 9 16 23 30	6 13 20 27	4 11 18 25
Wed.	3 10 17 24 31	7 14 21 28	5 12 19 26
Thur.	4 11 18 25	1 8 15 22 29	6 13 20 27
Fri.	5 12 19 26	2 9 16 23 30	7 14 21 28
Sat.	6 13 20 27	3 10 17 24	1 8 15 22 29

EASTER DAYS

March 25	1883, 1894, 1951, 2035
April 1	1866, 1877, 1923, 1934, 1945, 2018, 2029
April 8	1787, 1798, 1849, 1855, 1917, 2007
April 15	1781, 1827, 1838, 1900, 1906, 1979, 1990, 2001
April 22	1810, 1821, 1962, 1973

D (LEAP YEAR)

	January	February	March
Sun.	7 14 21 28	4 11 18 25	3 10 17 24 31
Mon.	1 8 15 22 29	5 12 19 26	4 11 18 25
Tue.	2 9 16 23 30	6 13 20 27	5 12 19 26
Wed.	3 10 17 24 31	7 14 21 28	6 13 20 27
Thur.	4 11 18 25	1 8 15 22 29	7 14 21 28
Fri.	5 12 19 26	2 9 16 23	1 8 15 22 29
Sat.	6 13 20 27	3 10 17 24	2 9 16 23 30

	April	May	June
Sun.	7 14 21 28	5 12 19 26	2 9 16 23 30
Mon.	1 8 15 22 29	6 13 20 27	3 10 17 24
Tue.	2 9 16 23 30	7 14 21 28	4 11 18 25
Wed.	3 10 17 24	1 8 15 22 29	5 12 19 26
Thur.	4 11 18 25	2 9 16 23 30	6 13 20 27
Fri.	5 12 19 26	3 10 17 24 31	7 14 21 28
Sat.	6 13 20 27	4 11 18 25	1 8 15 22 29

	July	August	September
Sun.	7 14 21 28	4 11 18 25	1 8 15 22 29
Mon.	1 8 15 22 29	5 12 19 26	2 9 16 23 30
Tue.	2 9 16 23 30	6 13 20 27	3 10 17 24
Wed.	3 10 17 24 31	7 14 21 28	4 11 18 25
Thur.	4 11 18 25	1 8 15 22 29	5 12 19 26
Fri.	5 12 19 26	2 9 16 23 30	6 13 20 27
Sat.	6 13 20 27	3 10 17 24 31	7 14 21 28

	October	November	December
Sun.	6 13 20 27	3 10 17 24	1 8 15 22 29
Mon.	7 14 21 28	4 11 18 25	2 9 16 23 30
Tue.	1 8 15 22 29	5 12 19 26	3 10 17 24 31
Wed.	2 9 16 23 30	6 13 20 27	4 11 18 25
Thur.	3 10 17 24 31	7 14 21 28	5 12 19 26
Fri.	4 11 18 25	1 8 15 22 29	6 13 20 27
Sat.	5 12 19 26	2 9 16 23 30	7 14 21 28

EASTER DAYS

March 24	1940
March 31	1872, 2024
April 7	1844, 1912, 1996
April 14	1816, 1968

E

	January	February	March
Sun.	6 13 20 27	3 10 17 24	3 10 17 24 31
Mon.	7 14 21 28	4 11 18 25	4 11 18 25
Tue.	1 8 15 22 29	5 12 19 26	5 12 19 26
Wed.	2 9 16 23 30	6 13 20 27	6 13 20 27
Thur.	3 10 17 24 31	7 14 21 28	7 14 21 28
Fri.	4 11 18 25	1 8 15 22	1 8 15 22 29
Sat.	5 12 19 26	2 9 16 23	2 9 16 23 30

	April	May	June
Sun.	7 14 21 28	5 12 19 26	2 9 16 23 30
Mon.	1 8 15 22 29	6 13 20 27	3 10 17 24
Tue.	2 9 16 23 30	7 14 21 28	4 11 18 25
Wed.	3 10 17 24	1 8 15 22 29	5 12 19 26
Thur.	4 11 18 25	2 9 16 23 30	6 13 20 27
Fri.	5 12 19 26	3 10 17 24 31	7 14 21 28
Sat.	6 13 20 27	4 11 18 25	1 8 15 22 29

	July	August	September
Sun.	7 14 21 28	4 11 18 25	1 8 15 22 29
Mon.	1 8 15 22 29	5 12 19 26	2 9 16 23 30
Tue.	2 9 16 23 30	6 13 20 27	3 10 17 24
Wed.	3 10 17 24 31	7 14 21 28	4 11 18 25
Thur.	4 11 18 25	1 8 15 22 29	5 12 19 26
Fri.	5 12 19 26	2 9 16 23 30	6 13 20 27
Sat.	6 13 20 27	3 10 17 24 31	7 14 21 28

	October	November	December
Sun.	6 13 20 27	3 10 17 24	1 8 15 22 29
Mon.	7 14 21 28	4 11 18 25	2 9 16 23 30
Tue.	1 8 15 22 29	5 12 19 26	3 10 17 24 31
Wed.	2 9 16 23 30	6 13 20 27	4 11 18 25
Thur.	3 10 17 24 31	7 14 21 28	5 12 19 26
Fri.	4 11 18 25	1 8 15 22 29	6 13 20 27
Sat.	5 12 19 26	2 9 16 23 30	7 14 21 28

EASTER DAYS

March 24	1799
March 31	1782, 1793, 1839, 1850, 1861, 1907,
	1918, 1929, 1991, 2002, 2013
April 7	1822, 1833, 1901, 1985
April 14	1805, 1811, 1895, 1963, 1974
April 21	1867, 1878, 1889, 1935, 1946, 1957, 2019, 2030

F (LEAP YEAR)

	January	February	March
Sun.	6 13 20 27	3 10 17 24	2 9 16 23 30
Mon.	7 14 21 28	4 11 18 25	3 10 17 24 31
Tue.	1 8 15 22 29	5 12 19 26	4 11 18 25
Wed.	2 9 16 23 30	6 13 20 27	5 12 19 26
Thur.	3 10 17 24 31	7 14 21 28	6 13 20 27
Fri.	4 11 18 25	1 8 15 22 29	7 14 21 28
Sat.	5 12 19 26	2 9 16 23	1 8 15 22 29

	April	May	June
Sun.	6 13 20 27	4 11 18 25	1 8 15 22 29
Mon.	7 14 21 28	5 12 19 26	2 9 16 23 30
Tue.	1 8 15 22 29	6 13 20 27	3 10 17 24
Wed.	2 9 16 23 30	7 14 21 28	4 11 18 25
Thur.	3 10 17 24	1 8 15 22 29	5 12 19 26
Fri.	4 11 18 25	2 9 16 23 30	6 13 20 27
Sat.	5 12 19 26	3 10 17 24 31	7 14 21 28

	July	August	September
Sun.	6 13 20 27	3 10 17 24 31	7 14 21 28
Mon.	7 14 21 28	4 11 18 25	1 8 15 22 29
Tue.	1 8 15 22 29	5 12 19 26	2 9 16 23 30
Wed.	2 9 16 23 30	6 13 20 27	3 10 17 24
Thur.	3 10 17 24 31	7 14 21 28	4 11 18 25
Fri.	4 11 18 25	1 8 15 22 29	5 12 19 26
Sat.	5 12 19 26	2 9 16 23 30	6 13 20 27

	October	November	December
Sun.	5 12 19 26	2 9 16 23 30	7 14 21 28
Mon.	6 13 20 27	3 10 17 24	1 8 15 22 29
Tue.	7 14 21 28	4 11 18 25	2 9 16 23 30
Wed.	1 8 15 22 29	5 12 19 26	3 10 17 24 31
Thur.	2 9 16 23 30	6 13 20 27	4 11 18 25
Fri.	3 10 17 24 31	7 14 21 28	5 12 19 26
Sat.	4 11 18 25	1 8 15 22 29	6 13 20 27

EASTER DAYS

March 23	1788, 1856, 2008
April 6	1828, 1980
April 13	1884, 1952, 2036
April 20	1924

G

	January	February	March
Sun.	5 12 19 26	2 9 16 23	2 9 16 23 30
Mon.	6 13 20 27	3 10 17 24	3 10 17 24 31
Tue.	7 14 21 28	4 11 18 25	4 11 18 25
Wed.	1 8 15 22 29	5 12 19 26	5 12 19 26
Thur.	2 9 16 23 30	6 13 20 27	6 13 20 27
Fri.	3 10 17 24 31	7 14 21 28	7 14 21 28
Sat.	4 11 18 25	1 8 15 22	1 8 15 22 29

	April	May	June
Sun.	6 13 20 27	4 11 18 25	1 8 15 22 29
Mon.	7 14 21 28	5 12 19 26	2 9 16 23 30
Tue.	1 8 15 22 29	6 13 20 27	3 10 17 24
Wed.	2 9 16 23 30	7 14 21 28	4 11 18 25
Thur.	3 10 17 24	1 8 15 22 29	5 12 19 26
Fri.	4 11 18 25	2 9 16 23 30	6 13 20 27
Sat.	5 12 19 26	3 10 17 24 31	7 14 21 28

	July	August	September
Sun.	6 13 20 27	3 10 17 24 31	7 14 21 28
Mon.	7 14 21 28	4 11 18 25	1 8 15 22 29
Tue.	1 8 15 22 29	5 12 19 26	2 9 16 23 30
Wed.	2 9 16 23 30	6 13 20 27	3 10 17 24
Thur.	3 10 17 24 31	7 14 21 28	4 11 18 25
Fri.	4 11 18 25	1 8 15 22 29	5 12 19 26
Sat.	5 12 19 26	2 9 16 23 30	6 13 20 27

	October	November	December
Sun.	5 12 19 26	2 9 16 23 30	7 14 21 28
Mon.	6 13 20 27	3 10 17 24	1 8 15 22 29
Tue.	7 14 21 28	4 11 18 25	2 9 16 23 30
Wed.	1 8 15 22 29	5 12 19 26	3 10 17 24 31
Thur.	2 9 16 23 30	6 13 20 27	4 11 18 25
Fri.	3 10 17 24 31	7 14 21 28	5 12 19 26
Sat.	4 11 18 25	1 8 15 22 29	6 13 20 27

EASTER DAYS

March 23	1845, 1913
March 30	1823, 1834, 1902, 1975, 1986, 1997
April 6	1806, 1817, 1890, 1947, 1958, 1969
April 13	1800, 1873, 1879, 1941, 2031
April 20	1783, 1794, 1851, 1862, 1919, 1930, 2003, 2014, 2025

I

	January	February	March
Sun.	4 11 18 25	1 8 15 22	1 8 15 22 29
Mon.	5 12 19 26	2 9 16 23	2 9 16 23 30
Tue.	6 13 20 27	3 10 17 24	3 10 17 24 31
Wed.	7 14 21 28	4 11 18 25	4 11 18 25
Thur.	1 8 15 22 29	5 12 19 26	5 12 19 26
Fri.	2 9 16 23 30	6 13 20 27	6 13 20 27
Sat.	3 10 17 24 31	7 14 21 28	7 14 21 28

	April	May	June
Sun.	5 12 19 26	3 10 17 24 31	7 14 21 28
Mon.	6 13 20 27	4 11 18 25	1 8 15 22 29
Tue.	7 14 21 28	5 12 19 26	2 9 16 23 30
Wed.	1 8 15 22 29	6 13 20 27	3 10 17 24
Thur.	2 9 16 23 30	7 14 21 28	4 11 18 25
Fri.	3 10 17 24	1 8 15 22 29	5 12 19 26
Sat.	4 11 18 25	2 9 16 23 30	6 13 20 27

	July	August	September
Sun.	5 12 19 26	2 9 16 23 30	6 13 20 27
Mon.	6 13 20 27	3 10 17 24 31	7 14 21 28
Tue.	7 14 21 28	4 11 18 25	1 8 15 22 29
Wed.	1 8 15 22 29	5 12 19 26	2 9 16 23 30
Thur.	2 9 16 23 30	6 13 20 27	3 10 17 24
Fri.	3 10 17 24 31	7 14 21 28	4 11 18 25
Sat.	4 11 18 25	1 8 15 22 29	5 12 19 26

	October	November	December
Sun.	4 11 18 25	1 8 15 22 29	6 13 20 27
Mon.	5 12 19 26	2 9 16 23 30	7 14 21 28
Tue.	6 13 20 27	3 10 17 24	1 8 15 22 29
Wed.	7 14 21 28	4 11 18 25	2 9 16 23 30
Thur.	1 8 15 22 29	5 12 19 26	3 10 17 24 31
Fri.	2 9 16 23 30	6 13 20 27	4 11 18 25
Sat.	3 10 17 24 31	7 14 21 28	5 12 19 26

EASTER DAYS

March 22	1818
March 29	1807, 1891, 1959, 1970
April 5	1795, 1801, 1863, 1874, 1885, 1931, 1942, 1953, 2015, 2026, 2037
April 12	1789, 1846, 1857, 1903, 1914, 1925, 1998, 2009
April 19	1829, 1835, 1981, 1987

H (LEAP YEAR)

	January	February	March
Sun.	5 12 19 26	2 9 16 23	1 8 15 22 29
Mon.	6 13 20 27	3 10 17 24	2 9 16 23 30
Tue.	7 14 21 28	4 11 18 25	3 10 17 24 31
Wed.	1 8 15 22 29	5 12 19 26	4 11 18 25
Thur.	2 9 16 23 30	6 13 20 27	5 12 19 26
Fri.	3 10 17 24 31	7 14 21 28	6 13 20 27
Sat.	4 11 18 25	1 8 15 22 29	7 14 21 28

	April	May	June
Sun.	5 12 19 26	3 10 17 24 31	7 14 21 28
Mon.	6 13 20 27	4 11 18 25	1 8 15 22 29
Tue.	7 14 21 28	5 12 19 26	2 9 16 23 30
Wed.	1 8 15 22 29	6 13 20 27	3 10 17 24
Thur.	2 9 16 23 30	7 14 21 28	4 11 18 25
Fri.	3 10 17 24	1 8 15 22 29	5 12 19 26
Sat.	4 11 18 25	2 9 16 23 30	6 13 20 27

	July	August	September
Sun.	5 12 19 26	2 9 16 23 30	6 13 20 27
Mon.	6 13 20 27	3 10 17 24 31	7 14 21 28
Tue.	7 14 21 28	4 11 18 25	1 8 15 22 29
Wed.	1 8 15 22 29	5 12 19 26	2 9 16 23 30
Thur.	2 9 16 23 30	6 13 20 27	3 10 17 24
Fri.	3 10 17 24 31	7 14 21 28	4 11 18 25
Sat.	4 11 18 25	1 8 15 22 29	5 12 19 26

	October	November	December
Sun.	4 11 18 25	1 8 15 22 29	6 13 20 27
Mon.	5 12 19 26	2 9 16 23 30	7 14 21 28
Tue.	6 13 20 27	3 10 17 24	1 8 15 22 29
Wed.	7 14 21 28	4 11 18 25	2 9 16 23 30
Thur.	1 8 15 22 29	5 12 19 26	3 10 17 24 31
Fri.	2 9 16 23 30	6 13 20 27	4 11 18 25
Sat.	3 10 17 24 31	7 14 21 28	5 12 19 26

EASTER DAYS

March 29	1812, 1964
April 5	1896
April 12	1868, 1936, 2020
April 19	1840, 1908, 1992

J (LEAP YEAR)

	January	February	March
Sun.	4 11 18 25	1 8 15 22 29	7 14 21 28
Mon.	5 12 19 26	2 9 16 23	1 8 15 22 29
Tue.	6 13 20 27	3 10 17 24	2 9 16 23 30
Wed.	7 14 21 28	4 11 18 25	3 10 17 24 31
Thur.	1 8 15 22 29	5 12 19 26	4 11 18 25
Fri.	2 9 16 23 30	6 13 20 27	5 12 19 26
Sat.	3 10 17 24 31	7 14 21 28	6 13 20 27

	April	May	June
Sun.	4 11 18 25	2 9 16 23 30	6 13 20 27
Mon.	5 12 19 26	3 10 17 24 31	7 14 21 28
Tue.	6 13 20 27	4 11 18 25	1 8 15 22 29
Wed.	7 14 21 28	5 12 19 26	2 9 16 23 30
Thur.	1 8 15 22 29	6 13 20 27	3 10 17 24
Fri.	2 9 16 23 30	7 14 21 28	4 11 18 25
Sat.	3 10 17 24	1 8 15 22 29	5 12 19 26

	July	August	September
Sun.	4 11 18 25	1 8 15 22 29	5 12 19 26
Mon.	5 12 19 26	2 9 16 23 30	6 13 20 27
Tue.	6 13 20 27	3 10 17 24 31	7 14 21 28
Wed.	7 14 21 28	4 11 18 25	1 8 15 22 29
Thur.	1 8 15 22 29	5 12 19 26	2 9 16 23 30
Fri.	2 9 16 23 30	6 13 20 27	3 10 17 24
Sat.	3 10 17 24 31	7 14 21 28	4 11 18 25

	October	November	December
Sun.	3 10 17 24 31	7 14 21 28	5 12 19 26
Mon.	4 11 18 25	1 8 15 22 29	6 13 20 27
Tue.	5 12 19 26	2 9 16 23 30	7 14 21 28
Wed.	6 13 20 27	3 10 17 24	1 8 15 22 29
Thur.	7 14 21 28	4 11 18 25	2 9 16 23 30
Fri.	1 8 15 22 29	5 12 19 26	3 10 17 24 31
Sat.	2 9 16 23 30	6 13 20 27	4 11 18 25

EASTER DAYS

March 28	1880, 1948, 2032
April 4	1920
April 11	1784, 1852, 2004
April 18	1824, 1976

K

	January	February	March
Sun.	3 10 17 24 31	7 14 21 28	7 14 21 28
Mon.	4 11 18 25	1 8 15 22	1 8 15 22 29
Tue.	5 12 19 26	2 9 16 23	2 9 16 23 30
Wed.	6 13 20 27	3 10 17 24	3 10 17 24 31
Thur.	7 14 21 28	4 11 18 25	4 11 18 25
Fri.	1 8 15 22 29	5 12 19 26	5 12 19 26
Sat.	2 9 16 23 30	6 13 20 27	6 13 20 27

	April	May	June
Sun.	4 11 18 25	2 9 16 23 30	6 13 20 27
Mon.	5 12 19 26	3 10 17 24 31	7 14 21 28
Tue.	6 13 20 27	4 11 18 25	1 8 15 22 29
Wed.	7 14 21 28	5 12 19 26	2 9 16 23 30
Thur.	1 8 15 22 29	6 13 20 27	3 10 17 24
Fri.	2 9 16 23 30	7 14 21 28	4 11 18 25
Sat.	3 10 17 24	1 8 15 22 29	5 12 19 26

	July	August	September
Sun.	4 11 18 25	1 8 15 22 29	5 12 19 26
Mon.	5 12 19 26	2 9 16 23 30	6 13 20 27
Tue.	6 13 20 27	3 10 17 24 31	7 14 21 28
Wed.	7 14 21 28	4 11 18 25	1 8 15 22 29
Thur.	1 8 15 22 29	5 12 19 26	2 9 16 23 30
Fri.	2 9 16 23 30	6 13 20 27	3 10 17 24
Sat.	3 10 17 24 31	7 14 21 28	4 11 18 25

	October	November	December
Sun.	3 10 17 24 31	7 14 21 28	5 12 19 26
Mon.	4 11 18 25	1 8 15 22 29	6 13 20 27
Tue.	5 12 19 26	2 9 16 23 30	7 14 21 28
Wed.	6 13 20 27	3 10 17 24	1 8 15 22 29
Thur.	7 14 21 28	4 11 18 25	2 9 16 23 30
Fri.	1 8 15 22 29	5 12 19 26	3 10 17 24 31
Sat.	2 9 16 23 30	6 13 20 27	4 11 18 25

EASTER DAYS
March 28   1869, 1875, 1937, 2027
April 4   1790, 1847, 1858, 1915, 1926, 1999, 2010, 2021
April 11   1819, 1830, 1841, 1909, 1971, 1982, 1993
April 18   1802, 1813, 1897, 1954, 1965
April 25   1886, 1943, 2038

M

	January	February	March
Sun.	2 9 16 23 30	6 13 20 27	6 13 20 27
Mon.	3 10 17 24 31	7 14 21 28	7 14 21 28
Tue.	4 11 18 25	1 8 15 22	1 8 15 22 29
Wed.	5 12 19 26	2 9 16 23	2 9 16 23 30
Thur.	6 13 20 27	3 10 17 24	3 10 17 24 31
Fri.	7 14 21 28	4 11 18 25	4 11 18 25
Sat.	1 8 15 22 29	5 12 19 26	5 12 19 26

	April	May	June
Sun.	3 10 17 24	1 8 15 22 29	5 12 19 26
Mon.	4 11 18 25	2 9 16 23 30	6 13 20 27
Tue.	5 12 19 26	3 10 17 24 31	7 14 21 28
Wed.	6 13 20 27	4 11 18 25	1 8 15 22 29
Thur.	7 14 21 28	5 12 19 26	2 9 16 23 30
Fri.	1 8 15 22 29	6 13 20 27	3 10 17 24
Sat.	2 9 16 23 30	7 14 21 28	4 11 18 25

	July	August	September
Sun.	3 10 17 24 31	7 14 21 28	4 11 18 25
Mon.	4 11 18 25	1 8 15 22 29	5 12 19 26
Tue.	5 12 19 26	2 9 16 23 30	6 13 20 27
Wed.	6 13 20 27	3 10 17 24 31	7 14 21 28
Thur.	7 14 21 28	4 11 18 25	1 8 15 22 29
Fri.	1 8 15 22 29	5 12 19 26	2 9 16 23 30
Sat.	2 9 16 23 30	6 13 20 27	3 10 17 24

	October	November	December
Sun.	2 9 16 23 30	6 13 20 27	4 11 18 25
Mon.	3 10 17 24 31	7 14 21 28	5 12 19 26
Tue.	4 11 18 25	1 8 15 22 29	6 13 20 27
Wed.	5 12 19 26	2 9 16 23 30	7 14 21 28
Thur.	6 13 20 27	3 10 17 24	1 8 15 22 29
Fri.	7 14 21 28	4 11 18 25	2 9 16 23 30
Sat.	1 8 15 22 29	5 12 19 26	3 10 17 24 31

EASTER DAYS
March 27   1785, 1842, 1853, 1910, 1921, 2005
April 3   1825, 1831, 1983, 1994
April 10   1803, 1814, 1887, 1898, 1955, 1966, 1977, 2039
April 17   1870, 1881, 1927, 1938, 1949, 2022, 2033
April 24   1791, 1859, 2011

L (LEAP YEAR)

	January	February	March
Sun.	3 10 17 24 31	7 14 21 28	6 13 20 27
Mon.	4 11 18 25	1 8 15 22 29	7 14 21 28
Tue.	5 12 19 26	2 9 16 23	1 8 15 22 29
Wed.	6 13 20 27	3 10 17 24	2 9 16 23 30
Thur.	7 14 21 28	4 11 18 25	3 10 17 24 31
Fri.	1 8 15 22 29	5 12 19 26	4 11 18 25
Sat.	2 9 16 23 30	6 13 20 27	5 12 19 26

	April	May	June
Sun.	3 10 17 24	1 8 15 22 29	5 12 19 26
Mon.	4 11 18 25	2 9 16 23 30	6 13 20 27
Tue.	5 12 19 26	3 10 17 24 31	7 14 21 28
Wed.	6 13 20 27	4 11 18 25	1 8 15 22 29
Thur.	7 14 21 28	5 12 19 26	2 9 16 23 30
Fri.	1 8 15 22 29	6 13 20 27	3 10 17 24
Sat.	2 9 16 23 30	7 14 21 28	4 11 18 25

	July	August	September
Sun.	3 10 17 24 31	7 14 21 28	4 11 18 25
Mon.	4 11 18 25	1 8 15 22 29	5 12 19 26
Tue.	5 12 19 26	2 9 16 23 30	6 13 20 27
Wed.	6 13 20 27	3 10 17 24 31	7 14 21 28
Thur.	7 14 21 28	4 11 18 25	1 8 15 22 29
Fri.	1 8 15 22 29	5 12 19 26	2 9 16 23 30
Sat.	2 9 16 23 30	6 13 20 27	3 10 17 24

	October	November	December
Sun.	2 9 16 23 30	6 13 20 27	4 11 18 25
Mon.	3 10 17 24 31	7 14 21 28	5 12 19 26
Tue.	4 11 18 25	1 8 15 22 29	6 13 20 27
Wed.	5 12 19 26	2 9 16 23 30	7 14 21 28
Thur.	6 13 20 27	3 10 17 24	1 8 15 22 29
Fri.	7 14 21 28	4 11 18 25	2 9 16 23 30
Sat.	1 8 15 22 29	5 12 19 26	3 10 17 24 31

EASTER DAYS
March 27   1796, 1864, 1932, 2016
April 3   1836, 1904, 1988
April 17   1808, 1892, 1960

N (LEAP YEAR)

	January	February	March
Sun.	2 9 16 23 30	6 13 20 27	5 12 19 26
Mon.	3 10 17 24 31	7 14 21 28	6 13 20 27
Tue.	4 11 18 25	1 8 15 22 29	7 14 21 28
Wed.	5 12 19 26	2 9 16 23	1 8 15 22 29
Thur.	6 13 20 27	3 10 17 24	2 9 16 23 30
Fri.	7 14 21 28	4 11 18 25	3 10 17 24 31
Sat.	1 8 15 22 29	5 12 19 26	4 11 18 25

	April	May	June
Sun.	2 9 16 23 30	7 14 21 28	4 11 18 25
Mon.	3 10 17 24	1 8 15 22 29	5 12 19 26
Tue.	4 11 18 25	2 9 16 23 30	6 13 20 27
Wed.	5 12 19 26	3 10 17 24 31	7 14 21 28
Thur.	6 13 20 27	4 11 18 25	1 8 15 22 29
Fri.	7 14 21 28	5 12 19 26	2 9 16 23 30
Sat.	1 8 15 22 29	6 13 20 27	3 10 17 24

	July	August	September
Sun.	2 9 16 23 30	6 13 20 27	3 10 17 24
Mon.	3 10 17 24 31	7 14 21 28	4 11 18 25
Tue.	4 11 18 25	1 8 15 22 29	5 12 19 26
Wed.	5 12 19 26	2 9 16 23 30	6 13 20 27
Thur.	6 13 20 27	3 10 17 24 31	7 14 21 28
Fri.	7 14 21 28	4 11 18 25	1 8 15 22 29
Sat.	1 8 15 22 29	5 12 19 26	2 9 16 23 30

	October	November	December
Sun.	1 8 15 22 29	5 12 19 26	3 10 17 24 31
Mon.	2 9 16 23 30	6 13 20 27	4 11 18 25
Tue.	3 10 17 24 31	7 14 21 28	5 12 19 26
Wed.	4 11 18 25	1 8 15 22 29	6 13 20 27
Thur.	5 12 19 26	2 9 16 23 30	7 14 21 28
Fri.	6 13 20 27	3 10 17 24	1 8 15 22 29
Sat.	7 14 21 28	4 11 18 25	2 9 16 23 30

EASTER DAYS
March 26   1780
April 2   1820, 1972
April 9   1944
April 16   1876, 2028
April 23   1848, 1916, 2000

GEOLOGICAL TIME

Era	Period	Epoch	Dates*	Evolutionary Stages
Cenozoic	Quaternary	Holocene	11,700 BP†–present	First humans } Majority of still existing species
		Pleistocene	2,588,000–11,700 BP	
	Neogene	Pliocene	5.332–2.588 Mya ‡	
		Miocene	23.03–5.332 Mya	
	Palaeogene	Oligocene	33.9–23.03 Mya	} First modern mammals
		Eocene	55.8–33.9 Mya	
		Palaeocene	65.5–55.8 Mya	
Mesozoic	Cretaceous		145.5–65.5 Mya	First birds
	Jurassic		199.6–145.5 Mya	
	Triassic		251–199.6 Mya	First mammals
Palaeozoic	Permian		299–251 Mya	First reptiles
	Carboniferous		359.2–299 Mya	} First traces of land-living creatures
	Devonian		416–359.2 Mya	
	Silurian		443.7–416 Mya	
	Ordovician		488.3–443.7 Mya	First fish
	Cambrian		542–488.3 Mya	First invertebrates
Precambrian	Proterozoic		2,500–542 Mya	First primitive life forms, eg algae and bacteria
	Archaean		3,800–2,500 Mya	} Earth uninhabited
	Hadean		4,600–3,800 Mya	

* approximate † BP = Before Present ‡ Mya = million years ago

PALAEOZOIC ('ANCIENT LIFE')

Cambrian – Mainly sandstones, slate and shales; limestones in Scotland. Shelled fossils and invertebrates, eg trilobites and brachiopods, and the earliest known vertebrates (jawless fish) appear

Ordovician – Mainly shales and mudstones, eg in north Wales; limestones in Scotland. First fish

Silurian – Shales, mudstones and some limestones, found mostly in Wales and southern Scotland

Devonian – Old red sandstone, shale, limestone and slate, eg in south Wales and the West Country

Carboniferous – Coal-bearing rocks, millstone grit, limestone and shale. First traces of land-living creatures

Permian – Marls, sandstones and clays. First reptile fossils

There were two great phases of mountain building in the Palaeozoic era: the Caledonian, characterised in Britain by NE–SW lines of hills and valleys; and the later Hercynian, widespread in west Germany and adjacent areas, and in Britain exemplified in E–W lines of hills and valleys.

The end of the Palaeozoic era was marked by the extensive glaciations of the Permian period in the southern continents and the decline of amphibians. It was succeeded by an era of warm conditions.

MESOZOIC ('MIDDLE FORMS OF LIFE')

Triassic – Mostly sandstone, eg in the W. Midlands; primitive mammals appear

Jurassic – Mainly limestones and clays, typically displayed in the Jura mountains, and in England in a NE–SW belt from Lincolnshire and the Wash to the Severn and the Dorset coast

Cretaceous – Mainly chalk, clay and sands, eg in Kent and Sussex

Giant reptiles were dominant during the Mesozoic era; marsupial mammals first appeared, as well as *Archaeopteryx lithographica,* the earliest known species of bird. Coniferous trees and flowering plants also developed during the era and, with the birds and the mammals, were the main species to survive into the Cenozoic era. The giant reptiles became extinct.

CENOZOIC ('RECENT LIFE')

Palaeocene/ Eocene – The emergence of new forms of life, including existing species; primates appear

Oligocene – Fossils of a few still existing species

Miocene – Fossil remains show a balance of existing and extinct species

Piliocene/ Pleistocene – Fossil remains show a majority of still existing species

Holocene – The present, post-glacial period. Existing species only, except for a few exterminated by humans

In the last 25 million years, from the Miocene through the Pliocene periods, the Alpine-Himalayan and the circum-Pacific phases of mountain building reached their climax. During the Pleistocene period ice-sheets locked up masses of water as land ice, lowering the sea level by 100–200m. The glaciations and interglacials of the Ice Age are difficult to date and classify, but recent scientific opinion considers the Pleistocene period to have begun *c.*1.64 Mya. The last glacial retreat, merging into the Holocene period, was *c.*10,000 years ago.

HUMAN DEVELOPMENT

All members of the human race belong to one species of animal, *Homo sapiens,* the definition of a species being in biological terms that all its members can interbreed. As a species of mammal it is possible to group humans with other similar types, known as the primates. Amongst these is found a sub-group, the apes, which includes, in addition to humans, the chimpanzees, gorillas, orangutans and gibbons. All lack a tail, have shoulder blades at the back, and a Y-shaped chewing pattern on the surface of their molars, as well as showing the more general primate characteristics of four incisors, a thumb which is able to touch the fingers of the same hand, and finger and toe nails instead of claws. However, there once lived creatures, now extinct, which were closer to modern man than the chimpanzees and gorillas, and which shared with modern man the characteristics of having flat faces (ie the absence of a pronounced muzzle), being bipedal, and possessing large brains.

The debate surrounding evidence for the oldest human ancestors is ongoing. The earliest putative hominin for which there is significant fossil evidence is *Ardipithecus ramidus,* for which an almost complete skeleton, dating to at least 4.4 million years ago (Mya), was discovered in the Afar Rift, Ethiopia in 1992. Analysis of the *Ardipithecus ramidus* skeleton suggests the creature had characteristics of both humans and apes; able to climb trees and walk on two feet.

The subsequent Australopithecines have left more numerous remains in south and east Africa, among which sub-groups may be detected. Living between 4.2 and 1.5 Mya, they were relatives of modern humans in the respect that they walked upright, did not have an extensive muzzle and had similar types of pre-molars. The first australopithecine remains were recognised at Taung in South Africa in 1924 and named *Australopithecus africanus,* dating between 3.3 and 2.3 Mya. The most impressive discovery was made at Hadar, Ethiopia, in 1974 when about half a skeleton of *Australopithecus afarensis,* known as 'Lucy', was found. Some 3.2 Mya, 'Lucy' (who is now considered to be male) certainly walked upright.

Also in east Africa, especially at Olduvai Gorge in Tanzania, between 2.5 and 1.8 Mya, lived a hominid group which not only walked upright, had a flat face, and a large brain case, but also made simple pebble and flake stone tools. Due to their distinctive characteristics, they have been grouped as a separate sub-species, now extinct, of the genus *Homo* and are known as *Homo habilis* or 'handy man'.

The use of fire, again a human characteristic, is associated with another group of extinct hominids whose remains, about a million years old, are found in south and east Africa, China, Indonesia, north Africa and Europe. The ability to make fire probably helped the colonisation of the colder northern areas and in this respect the site of Vertesszollos in Hungary is of particular importance. *Homo ergaster* in Africa and *Homo erectus* in Asia are the names given to this group of fossils and they relate to a number of famous individual discoveries, eg Solo Man, Heidelberg Man, and especially Peking Man who lived at the cave site at Choukoutien which has yielded evidence of fire and burnt bone.

The well-known group the Neanderthals, or *Homo neanderthalensis,* is an extinct form of human that lived between *c.*350,000 and *c.*24,000 years ago, spanning the last Ice Age and living alongside modern humans. The Neanderthals' ability to adapt to the cold climate on the edge of the ice-sheets is one of their characteristic features, with remains being found only in Europe, Asia and the Middle East. Complete Neanderthal skeletons were found during excavations at Tabun in Israel, together with evidence of tool-making and the use of fire. Distinguished by very large brains, it seems that Neanderthals were the first to develop recognisable social customs, especially deliberate burial rites.

Why the Neanderthals became extinct is not clear but it may be connected with the climatic changes at the end of the Ice Ages, which would have seriously affected their food supplies; possibly they became too specialised for their own good.

The shin bone of Boxgrove Man found in 1993 – *Homo heidelbergensis* – and the Swanscombe skull are the best known early human fossil remains found in England. Some specialists prefer to group Swanscombe Man (or, more probably, woman) together with the Steinheim skull from Germany, seeing both as a separate sub-species. There is too little evidence as yet on which to form a final judgement.

Anatomically modern humans – *Homo sapiens sapiens* ('doubly wise man') – had evolved to our present physical condition and had colonised much of the world by about 40,000 years ago. There are many previously distinguished individual specimens, eg Cromagnon Man, the first early *Homo sapiens sapiens* of the European Upper Palaeolithic.

The discovery of the structure of DNA in 1953 has come to have a profound effect upon the study of human evolution. For example, it was claimed in 1987 that a common ancestor of all human beings was a person who lived in Africa some 200,000 years ago, thus encouraging the 'out of Africa' theory of hominid migration from east Africa to the Middle East and then throughout the world.

CULTURAL DEVELOPMENT

The Three Age system, whereby prehistory was divided into a Stone Age, a Bronze Age and an Iron Age, was devised by Christian Thomsen, curator of the National Museum of Denmark in the early 19th century, to facilitate the classification of the museum's collections. The adjectives referred to the materials from which the implements and weapons were made and came to be regarded as the dominant features of the societies to which they related. The Three Age system remains a generally accepted concept in the popular mind. However, it is now seen by archaeologists as an inadequate model for human development. Common sense suggests that there were no complete breaks between one so-called Age and another. Nor can the Three Age system be applied universally. In some areas it is necessary to insert a Copper Age, while in South Africa there would seem to be no Bronze Age at all; in Australia, Old Stone Age societies survived, while in South America, New Stone Age communities exist into modern times.

The concept of the 'Neolithic revolution', associated with the domestication of plants and animals, was a development of particular importance in the human cultural pattern. It reflected a gradual change from the hunter-gatherer economies to a more settled agricultural way of life and therefore, so the argument goes, made possible the development of urban civilisation. Though it appears that the cultivation of wheat and barley was first undertaken, together with the domestication of cattle and goats/sheep, around 10,000 years ago in the Fertile Crescent (the area bounded by the rivers Tigris and Euphrates), there is evidence that sorghum was first domesticated in Africa, rice was first deliberately planted and pigs domesticated in South East Asia, maize first cultivated in Central America and llamas first domesticated in South America. Cultural change took place independently in different parts of the world at different rates and different times.

The Neolithic period of cultural development has been difficult to date reliably because it took place long before writing was invented. With the development and refinement of radio-carbon dating and other scientific methods of producing absolute chronologies, it may eventually be possible to obtain a reliable chronological framework, in terms of years, against which the cultural development of any particular area may be set.

TIDES AND TIDAL PREDICTIONS

Tides are the periodic rise and fall of the sea-level caused mainly by the gravitational pull of the Moon and the Sun. This generates the tide raising force (TRF), of which the Moon accounts for approximately 70 per cent and the Sun 30 per cent. Routinely when the Moon and the Sun are in line with the Earth they are said to be 'in conjunction' (or syzygy) and their TRFs combine. This produces the largest rise and fall of the tide, known as spring tides; they occur each month just after a full or new Moon. This is amplified when the Moon is at perigee, its closest point to the Earth. When coincident with spring tides (about once every 18 months) this gives rise to very high proxigean tides. The opposite effect, just after the Moon's first and last quarters, when the Sun and Moon are at an angle of 90°, produces neap tides, with a relatively small tidal range between high and low water. There is an 18-year interval between the astronomical conditions – the Sun and Moon aligning with the Earth at perigee with zero declination – which generates the maximum TRF. Within this cycle there are times when zero solar declination (equinox) and lunar perigee occur almost simultaneously with zero lunar declination. This last occurred on 27 September 2015 and will occur again on 8 April 2020.

A lunar day is about 24 hours and 50 minutes, giving two complete tidal cycles, with about 12 hours and 25 minutes between successive high waters. These are known as semi-diurnal tides and are applicable in the Atlantic Ocean and around the coasts of north-west Europe. Other parts of the world have diurnal tides, with only one high water and one low water each (lunar) day, or mixed tides which are partly diurnal and partly semi-diurnal.

Land and seabed conditions influence the tides locally. On the south coast of England, for example, double high waters occur between Swanage and Selsey Bill, and low water is much more sharply defined than high water. Tides can also be greatly affected by the Coriolis force, which is induced by the Earth's rotation and, in the northern hemisphere, tends to deflect any moving object to the right. Thus the easterly flood tidal stream in the English Channel is deflected towards the French coast causing higher high waters; on the ebb the opposite happens causing lower low waters. This, coupled with local geography, means that the mean spring range of the tide at St Malo is nearly 11m while the range on the English coast at Portland, 120 miles to the north, is a mere 2m.

Meteorological conditions such as prolonged strong winds and unusually high (or low) atmospheric pressure can significantly lower (or raise) the height of the tide; the drag of the wind alone (wind stress) can affect the predicted times of high and low water by as much as an hour. Variation of pressure by 34 millibars from the norm can cause a height difference of 0.3m.

STORM SURGES AND SEICHES

On the east and west coasts of the UK there are about 20 events each year when surge levels exceed 0.6m. The semicentennial surge is 1m in the Hebrides and at Land's End but up to 3m in the Thames estuary. Infrequently, surge peaks coincide with high water. The North Sea and the Thames estuary experience the most profound effects, often when a deep depression tracks south–easterly across the UK. Negative surges occur when strong southerly winds in the North Sea may lower tidal levels by 2m below prediction in these areas and the Dover Strait. Intense minor depressions, line squalls, or other abrupt changes in the weather can cause wave oscillations known as seiches. The wave period of a seiche varies from a few minutes to about two hours, with heights of up to a metre. Wick on the north-east coast of Scotland and Fishguard in south-west Wales are particularly prone to these.

TIDAL STREAMS

Tidal streams are the horizontal movements of water caused by the rise and fall of the tide. They normally change direction about every six hours. Tidal streams should not be confused with ocean currents, such as the Gulf Stream, which run continuously in the same direction. The rate, or set, of the stream at any particular place is proportional to the range of the tide. Thus, the rate during spring tides is greater than that at neaps. In the central English Channel the maximum spring rate is nearly 5 knots while the neap rate at the same position is just 3 knots. As with tidal heights, local geography plays a significant role in the rate of the tidal stream. In the narrow waters of the Pentland Firth between mainland Scotland and the Orkney Islands, rates of 16 knots have been recorded.

The tidal stream does not necessarily turn at the same time as high or low water. In the English Channel the stream turns at approximately high and low water at Dover. However, high water at Dover is at about the same time as low water at Plymouth, and vice versa.

Around the UK, the main flood tidal stream sets eastward up the English Channel, north-east into the Bristol Channel, and north up the west coasts of Ireland and Scotland. However, the flood sets south-east through the North Channel and south into the Irish Sea, where it meets the northerly flood through St George's Channel at the Isle of Man. Off the east coasts of Scotland and England the stream sets south as far as the Thames estuary before meeting the north-going stream from the eastern part of the Dover Strait.

DEFINITIONS

Highest Astronomical Tide (HAT) and **Lowest Astronomical Tide (LAT)** are the highest and lowest tide levels predicted to occur under average meteorological, and any combination of astronomical, conditions. For a given area, **Chart Datum (CD)** is the level, as close as possible to LAT, below which charted depths are given. It is also the reference for tidal predictions: the total depth at a given time being equal to the charted depth plus the height of the tide. **Ordnance Datum (OD)** at Newlyn is the datum level of land survey on mainland England, Scotland and Wales, from which heights on UK land maps are measured. CD depends on the tidal range and varies around the UK from about 5m above OD to about 6.5m below. The differences are noted in tide tables, allowing comparison of the tide levels along the coast and reference to Ordnance Survey data. **Duration** of the tide is the interval between low water and the next high water. It can be used to calculate the approximate time of low water when only the time of high water is known. **Mean Sea Level (MSL or ML)** is the average level of the sea's surface over a long period, normally observed over 18.6 years. The **Range** of the tide is the difference in height between successive high and low waters. It is greatest at spring tides, least at neaps. The range may be indicated by **Tidal Coefficients** which are proportional to, but not the same as, the range on a particular day. A coefficient of 95 indicates an average spring tide, while 45 is an average neap tide.

PREDICTIONS

The following tidal prediction data gives the daily time (Greenwich Mean Time) and height of high water at four ports. When British Summer Time applies the one hour time difference should be added. The datum of predictions is the difference of height, in metres, of CD from Ordnance datum (Newlyn).

Tidal predictions for London Bridge, Liverpool, Greenock and Leith © Crown Copyright and/or database rights. Reproduced by permission of the Controller of Her Majesty's Stationery Office and the UK Hydrographic Office (W www.gov.uk/ukho). The section was compiled with the assistance of Chris Stevens and Perrin Towler.

JANUARY 2018 *High Water GMT*

		LONDON BRIDGE Datum 3.2m below						LIVERPOOL (Gladstone Dock) Datum 4.93 below						GREENOCK Datum 1.62 below						LEITH Datum 2.90 below					
		hr	m	ht	hr	m	ht	hr	m	ht	hr	m	ht	hr	m	ht	hr	m	ht	hr	m	ht	hr	m	ht
M	1	00	29	7.0	12	53	7.3	10	07	9.4	22	31	9.6	11	28	3.6	-		-	01	18	5.6	13	47	5.7
Tu	2	01	24	7.1	13	46	7.5	10	57	9.7	23	22	9.8	00	02	3.6	12	17	3.7	02	09	5.8	14	33	5.8
W	3	02	15	7.2	14	37	7.6	11	45	9.9	-		-	00	55	3.6	13	03	3.8	02	58	5.9	15	20	5.9
Th	4	03	05	7.2	15	27	7.6	00	12	9.8	12	34	9.9	01	47	3.6	13	49	3.9	03	47	6.0	16	08	5.9
F	5	03	52	7.2	16	15	7.5	01	02	9.6	13	23	9.7	02	37	3.6	14	34	3.9	04	37	5.8	16	57	5.8
Sa	6	04	38	7.1	17	03	7.3	01	51	9.3	14	11	9.5	03	25	3.5	15	19	3.9	05	28	5.6	17	49	5.6
Su	7	05	24	6.9	17	51	7.0	02	39	8.9	15	01	9.1	04	13	3.4	16	05	3.7	06	21	5.4	18	45	5.4
M	8	06	10	6.7	18	41	6.7	03	30	8.5	15	53	8.6	05	01	3.2	16	52	3.6	07	18	5.1	19	45	5.1
Tu	9	07	00	6.5	19	34	6.4	04	24	8.0	16	51	8.2	05	52	3.1	17	42	3.4	08	17	4.8	20	47	4.9
W	10	07	57	6.3	20	31	6.2	05	27	7.7	17	57	7.8	06	48	3.0	18	39	3.2	09	17	4.6	21	49	4.7
Th	11	08	59	6.1	21	32	6.1	06	36	7.6	19	07	7.7	07	54	2.9	19	47	3.1	10	19	4.6	22	53	4.7
F	12	10	04	6.1	22	39	6.1	07	45	7.7	20	13	7.8	09	06	3.0	21	05	3.0	11	22	4.6	23	56	4.7
Sa	13	11	10	6.2	22	43	6.3	08	43	8.0	21	08	8.0	10	07	3.1	22	13	3.1	12	23	4.8	-		-
Su	14	12	09	6.5	-		-	09	30	8.3	21	54	8.3	10	56	3.3	23	05	3.1	00	53	4.8	13	13	4.9
M	15	00	36	6.5	12	58	6.7	10	11	8.6	22	33	8.5	11	39	3.4	23	49	3.2	01	39	5.0	13	53	5.1
Tu	16	01	20	6.7	13	40	6.8	10	47	8.8	23	09	8.7	12	17	3.5	-		-	02	19	5.1	14	29	5.2
W	17	01	58	6.8	14	17	6.9	11	22	9.0	23	42	8.8	00	26	3.2	12	51	3.6	02	53	5.2	15	02	5.3
Th	18	02	33	6.8	14	51	6.9	11	55	9.1	-		-	01	02	3.3	13	23	3.6	03	26	5.2	15	34	5.4
F	19	03	05	6.9	15	22	6.9	00	14	8.8	12	28	9.1	01	36	3.3	13	54	3.6	03	59	5.3	16	07	5.4
Sa	20	03	37	6.9	15	55	6.9	00	47	8.8	13	02	9.1	02	11	3.3	14	27	3.6	04	33	5.2	16	40	5.3
Su	21	04	09	6.8	16	29	6.9	01	20	8.7	13	36	8.9	02	47	3.3	15	01	3.6	05	09	5.2	17	15	5.3
M	22	04	43	6.7	17	05	6.7	01	55	8.5	14	12	8.8	03	25	3.3	15	39	3.6	05	47	5.1	17	52	5.2
Tu	23	05	18	6.6	17	44	6.6	02	32	8.4	14	52	8.6	04	04	3.3	16	18	3.5	06	29	5.0	18	34	5.1
W	24	05	57	6.5	18	28	6.4	03	16	8.1	15	40	8.4	04	45	3.2	17	02	3.3	07	15	4.8	19	22	4.9
Th	25	06	43	6.4	19	20	6.2	04	10	7.9	16	40	8.1	05	30	3.1	17	53	3.2	08	10	4.7	20	21	4.8
F	26	07	40	6.3	20	31	6.1	05	19	7.7	17	54	8.0	06	23	3.0	19	01	3.1	09	17	4.7	21	37	4.8
Sa	27	09	00	6.3	21	52	6.2	06	38	7.8	19	12	8.1	07	35	3.0	20	29	3.0	10	29	4.7	22	55	4.9
Su	28	10	23	6.5	23	04	6.4	07	53	8.2	20	24	8.5	09	05	3.0	21	52	3.1	11	38	4.9	-		-
M	29	11	34	6.8	-		-	08	58	8.7	21	27	8.9	10	18	3.2	22	58	3.3	00	05	5.1	12	39	5.2
Tu	30	00	12	6.7	12	39	7.1	09	55	9.2	22	23	9.3	11	15	3.4	23	55	3.4	01	06	5.4	13	32	5.5
W	31	01	12	7.0	13	36	7.3	10	47	9.6	23	14	9.6	12	05	3.6	-		-	01	58	5.7	14	21	5.8

FEBRUARY 2018 *High Water GMT*

		LONDON BRIDGE						LIVERPOOL (Gladstone Dock)						GREENOCK						LEITH					
Th	1	02	05	7.1	14	27	7.5	11	35	9.9	-		-	00	48	3.5	12	53	3.7	02	47	5.9	15	07	5.9
F	2	02	53	7.3	15	15	7.6	00	02	9.8	12	22	10.0	01	38	3.5	13	38	3.8	03	34	5.9	15	53	6.0
Sa	3	03	37	7.3	16	00	7.5	00	48	9.7	13	06	9.9	02	24	3.5	14	22	3.8	04	21	5.8	16	40	5.9
Su	4	04	20	7.3	16	44	7.4	01	31	9.5	13	49	9.6	03	08	3.4	15	04	3.8	05	07	5.6	17	28	5.7
M	5	05	01	7.2	17	26	7.1	02	12	9.1	14	31	9.2	03	49	3.4	15	45	3.7	05	54	5.4	18	16	5.4
Tu	6	05	41	6.9	18	08	6.7	02	54	8.6	15	14	8.7	04	28	3.3	16	26	3.6	06	42	5.1	19	08	5.1
W	7	06	22	6.6	18	50	6.4	03	38	8.2	16	02	8.1	05	08	3.1	17	08	3.4	07	33	4.8	20	04	4.8
Th	8	07	08	6.3	19	38	6.1	04	31	7.7	17	02	7.6	05	52	3.0	17	53	3.1	08	28	4.5	21	03	4.6
F	9	08	05	6.0	20	36	5.8	05	37	7.3	18	16	7.3	06	44	2.9	18	45	2.9	09	26	4.4	22	07	4.4
Sa	10	09	13	5.8	21	45	5.8	06	55	7.2	19	36	7.3	07	55	2.8	19	55	2.8	10	31	4.3	23	19	4.4
Su	11	10	27	5.9	23	02	5.9	08	08	7.5	20	44	7.6	09	27	2.9	21	41	2.8	11	44	4.5	-		-
M	12	11	38	6.2	-		-	09	05	7.9	21	35	7.9	10	31	3.1	22	48	2.9	00	28	4.6	12	48	4.7
Tu	13	00	07	6.2	12	34	6.5	09	50	8.3	22	16	8.3	11	18	3.3	23	33	3.1	01	20	4.8	13	33	4.9
W	14	00	56	6.5	13	19	6.7	10	28	8.7	22	51	8.6	11	58	3.4	-		-	02	00	5.0	14	10	5.1
Th	15	01	38	6.7	13	58	6.8	11	03	9.0	23	23	8.8	00	12	3.1	12	34	3.5	02	34	5.1	14	44	5.3
F	16	02	14	6.8	14	32	6.9	11	35	9.1	23	55	8.9	00	47	3.2	13	05	3.5	03	06	5.3	15	16	5.4
Sa	17	02	48	6.9	15	04	6.9	12	08	9.3	-		-	01	20	3.2	13	35	3.5	03	38	5.3	15	47	5.4
Su	18	03	20	7.0	15	36	7.0	00	26	9.0	12	41	9.3	01	52	3.3	14	07	3.5	04	11	5.4	16	19	5.5
M	19	03	51	7.0	16	09	7.0	00	59	9.0	13	14	9.2	02	25	3.3	14	41	3.6	04	45	5.3	16	53	5.4
Tu	20	04	24	7.0	16	45	6.9	01	32	8.9	13	49	9.1	03	00	3.4	15	18	3.6	05	22	5.3	17	29	5.4
W	21	04	59	6.9	17	22	6.7	02	08	8.7	14	27	8.9	03	37	3.4	15	57	3.5	06	01	5.1	18	10	5.3
Th	22	05	37	6.8	18	03	6.4	02	49	8.5	15	13	8.6	04	15	3.3	16	38	3.4	06	45	5.0	18	57	5.1
F	23	06	20	6.6	18	52	6.2	03	39	8.1	16	10	8.2	04	55	3.2	17	24	3.2	07	36	4.8	19	54	4.8
Sa	24	07	15	6.4	19	58	6.0	04	45	7.8	17	27	7.9	05	43	3.1	18	24	3.0	08	41	4.6	21	10	4.7
Su	25	08	31	6.2	21	25	6.0	06	11	7.6	18	54	7.8	06	45	2.9	20	03	2.8	10	00	4.6	22	36	4.7
M	26	10	02	6.3	22	46	6.2	07	36	7.9	20	14	8.2	08	34	2.9	21	48	3.0	11	18	4.7	23	53	5.0
Tu	27	11	20	6.6	-		-	08	47	8.4	21	20	8.7	10	04	3.1	22	55	3.2	12	25	5.1	-		-
W	28	00	01	6.5	12	30	6.9	09	45	9.0	22	15	9.2	11	03	3.3	23	49	3.3	00	56	5.3	13	20	5.4

MARCH 2018 *High Water* GMT

		LONDON BRIDGE					LIVERPOOL (Gladstone Dock)					GREENOCK					LEITH				
		Datum of Predictions 3.2m below					Datum of Predictions 4.93 below					Datum of Predictions 1.62 below					Datum of Predictions 2.90 below				
		hr	m	ht	hr	m	ht	hr	m	ht	hr	m	ht	hr	m	ht	hr	m	ht	hr	m	ht
Th	1	01	02	6.9	13	26	7.2	10	35	9.5	23	02	9.5	11	53	3.5	-	-	01	47	5.6	14	07	5.7
F	2	01	52	7.1	14	15	7.4	11	21	9.8	23	46	9.7	00	38	3.4	12	39	3.6	02	33	5.8	14	51	5.9
Sa	3	02	37	7.3	14	59	7.4	12	04	9.9	-	-	01	23	3.4	13	23	3.7	03	17	5.8	15	35	5.9
Su	4	03	18	7.4	15	40	7.4	00	27	9.7	12	44	9.8	02	05	3.4	14	05	3.7	04	00	5.8	16	19	5.9
M	5	03	56	7.4	16	19	7.3	01	05	9.5	13	22	9.6	02	43	3.4	14	44	3.7	04	42	5.6	17	03	5.7
Tu	6	04	34	7.3	16	56	7.0	01	42	9.2	13	59	9.2	03	18	3.4	15	21	3.6	05	24	5.4	17	47	5.4
W	7	05	10	7.0	17	31	6.7	02	17	8.8	14	36	8.7	03	52	3.3	15	59	3.5	06	06	5.1	18	32	5.1
Th	8	05	47	6.7	18	07	6.3	02	56	8.3	15	18	8.1	04	29	3.2	16	37	3.3	06	50	4.8	19	21	4.8
F	9	06	26	6.4	18	46	6.0	03	42	7.8	16	10	7.5	05	08	3.0	17	18	3.1	07	39	4.5	20	17	4.5
Sa	10	07	13	6.0	19	38	5.7	04	42	7.3	17	22	7.0	05	54	2.9	18	06	2.8	08	35	4.3	21	19	4.2
Su	11	08	20	5.7	20	50	5.5	06	01	7.0	18	52	6.9	06	53	2.7	19	05	2.6	09	39	4.2	22	29	4.2
M	12	09	42	5.6	22	15	5.6	07	25	7.2	20	13	7.2	08	25	2.7	20	45	2.6	10	51	4.2	23	52	4.3
Tu	13	11	00	5.9	23	29	6.0	08	32	7.6	21	09	7.7	09	58	2.9	22	23	2.8	12	10	4.5	-	-
W	14	12	02	6.3	-	-	09	21	8.1	21	50	8.1	10	49	3.1	23	10	3.0	00	52	4.6	13	04	4.8
Th	15	00	25	6.4	12	50	6.6	10	01	8.5	22	26	8.5	11	31	3.3	23	49	3.1	01	33	4.9	13	43	5.0
F	16	01	09	6.6	13	30	6.8	10	36	8.9	22	58	8.8	12	07	3.3	-	-	02	08	5.1	14	18	5.2
Sa	17	01	47	6.8	14	05	6.9	11	09	9.2	23	29	9.1	00	24	3.2	12	40	3.4	02	40	5.3	14	50	5.4
Su	18	02	22	7.0	14	38	7.0	11	42	9.4	-	-	00	57	3.2	13	12	3.4	03	12	5.4	15	22	5.5
M	19	02	56	7.1	15	13	7.1	00	01	9.2	12	17	9.5	01	28	3.3	13	45	3.5	03	45	5.5	15	55	5.6
Tu	20	03	30	7.2	15	48	7.1	00	35	9.3	12	52	9.5	02	00	3.4	14	21	3.5	04	20	5.5	16	30	5.6
W	21	04	04	7.2	16	24	6.9	01	10	9.2	13	29	9.3	02	35	3.5	14	59	3.5	04	57	5.4	17	09	5.5
Th	22	04	40	7.1	17	02	6.7	01	47	9.0	14	09	9.1	03	11	3.5	15	39	3.5	05	37	5.3	17	52	5.4
F	23	05	20	6.9	17	43	6.4	02	29	8.7	14	56	8.6	03	49	3.4	16	20	3.3	06	21	5.1	18	41	5.1
Sa	24	06	05	6.7	18	33	6.2	03	20	8.2	15	55	8.1	04	30	3.3	17	07	3.1	07	11	4.8	19	40	4.9
Su	25	07	01	6.4	19	39	5.9	04	29	7.8	17	15	7.7	05	17	3.1	18	02	2.9	08	17	4.6	20	58	4.6
M	26	08	20	6.2	21	07	5.9	05	57	7.6	18	44	7.7	06	17	2.9	20	01	2.7	09	42	4.5	22	26	4.7
Tu	27	09	49	6.3	22	32	6.1	07	22	7.9	20	05	8.1	08	15	2.8	21	46	2.9	11	03	4.7	23	43	4.9
W	28	11	09	6.5	23	48	6.5	08	33	8.4	21	09	8.6	09	49	3.0	22	46	3.1	12	11	5.0	-	-
Th	29	12	18	6.9	-	-	09	31	8.9	22	01	9.1	10	47	3.3	23	35	3.3	00	44	5.2	13	05	5.3
F	30	00	47	6.8	13	12	7.1	10	19	9.3	22	45	9.4	11	35	3.5	-	-	01	33	5.4	13	51	5.6
Sa	31	01	35	7.1	13	57	7.2	11	01	9.6	23	25	9.5	00	20	3.4	12	21	3.6	02	15	5.6	14	33	5.7

APRIL 2018 *High Water* GMT

		LONDON BRIDGE					LIVERPOOL (Gladstone Dock)					GREENOCK					LEITH				
Su	1	02	16	7.2	14	37	7.3	11	41	9.7	-	-	01	03	3.4	13	03	3.6	02	56	5.7	15	15	5.8
M	2	02	53	7.3	15	15	7.3	00	02	9.5	12	19	9.6	01	40	3.4	13	43	3.6	03	36	5.6	15	57	5.7
Tu	3	03	29	7.4	15	50	7.2	00	38	9.4	12	54	9.4	02	14	3.4	14	20	3.6	04	16	5.5	16	38	5.5
W	4	04	05	7.3	16	24	7.0	01	11	9.2	13	29	9.0	02	46	3.4	14	55	3.5	04	54	5.3	17	19	5.3
Th	5	04	40	7.1	16	56	6.7	01	45	8.8	14	03	8.6	03	19	3.4	15	31	3.4	05	33	5.1	18	00	5.0
F	6	05	15	6.7	17	28	6.3	02	21	8.4	14	42	8.1	03	54	3.3	16	09	3.2	06	12	4.8	18	45	4.7
Sa	7	05	51	6.4	18	03	6.0	03	03	7.9	15	29	7.5	04	32	3.1	16	50	3.0	06	57	4.6	19	36	4.4
Su	8	06	31	6.0	18	46	5.7	03	56	7.4	16	33	7.0	05	15	2.9	17	37	2.8	07	49	4.3	20	34	4.2
M	9	07	24	5.7	19	49	5.5	05	10	7.0	18	00	6.8	06	09	2.8	18	34	2.6	08	51	4.2	21	39	4.2
Tu	10	08	49	5.5	21	24	5.4	06	34	7.0	19	27	7.0	07	23	2.7	19	53	2.6	10	00	4.2	22	52	4.2
W	11	10	11	5.7	22	43	5.8	07	47	7.4	20	29	7.5	09	07	2.8	21	38	2.7	11	13	4.3	-	-
Th	12	11	17	6.1	23	43	6.2	08	41	7.9	21	14	8.0	10	09	3.0	22	33	2.9	00	04	4.5	12	18	4.6
F	13	12	09	6.5	-	-	09	24	8.4	21	51	8.4	10	54	3.1	23	16	3.1	00	54	4.8	13	05	4.9
Sa	14	00	31	6.6	12	53	6.8	10	02	8.8	22	25	8.8	11	32	3.2	23	53	3.2	01	33	5.1	13	44	5.2
Su	15	01	13	6.8	13	32	6.9	10	38	9.2	22	59	9.1	12	07	3.3	-	-	02	08	5.3	14	20	5.4
M	16	01	51	7.0	14	10	7.0	11	14	9.4	23	34	9.4	00	27	3.3	12	43	3.4	02	43	5.5	14	55	5.6
Tu	17	02	29	7.2	14	48	7.1	11	51	9.6	-	-	01	00	3.3	13	22	3.4	03	19	5.6	15	31	5.7
W	18	03	07	7.3	15	27	7.1	00	11	9.4	12	30	9.6	01	35	3.5	14	02	3.5	03	55	5.6	16	10	5.7
Th	19	03	45	7.3	16	06	6.9	00	50	9.4	13	11	9.4	02	12	3.5	14	43	3.5	04	34	5.5	16	52	5.6
F	20	04	25	7.2	16	47	6.7	01	31	9.2	13	56	9.1	02	50	3.6	15	25	3.4	05	16	5.4	17	38	5.4
Sa	21	05	08	7.0	17	31	6.4	02	17	8.8	14	47	8.7	03	30	3.5	16	11	3.3	06	03	5.2	18	31	5.2
Su	22	05	57	6.8	18	23	6.2	03	12	8.4	15	50	8.1	04	12	3.4	17	02	3.1	06	56	4.9	19	33	4.9
M	23	06	57	6.5	19	32	6.0	04	23	8.0	17	09	7.8	05	01	3.2	18	12	2.8	08	05	4.7	20	52	4.7
Tu	24	08	16	6.3	20	55	6.0	05	46	7.8	18	33	7.8	06	04	3.0	20	05	2.8	09	29	4.6	22	13	4.7
W	25	09	35	6.4	22	14	6.2	07	05	8.0	19	49	8.1	07	59	2.9	21	30	2.9	10	45	4.8	23	26	4.9
Th	26	10	51	6.6	23	26	6.5	08	14	8.4	20	50	8.5	09	26	3.1	22	26	3.1	11	51	5.0	-	-
F	27	11	58	6.8	-	-	09	10	8.8	21	40	8.9	10	24	3.3	23	14	3.3	00	26	5.1	12	45	5.2
Sa	28	00	28	6.8	12	53	7.0	09	57	9.1	22	22	9.2	11	12	3.4	23	57	3.3	01	14	5.3	13	31	5.3
Su	29	01	11	7.0	13	35	7.1	10	38	9.3	23	00	9.3	11	57	3.4	-	-	01	55	5.4	14	13	5.5
M	30	01	51	7.1	14	13	7.1	11	17	9.3	23	36	9.3	00	36	3.4	12	39	3.4	02	34	5.5	14	55	5.6

MAY 2018   *High Water* GMT

	LONDON BRIDGE (Datum 3.2m below)						LIVERPOOL (Gladstone Dock) (Datum 4.93 below)						GREENOCK (Datum 1.62 below)						LEITH (Datum 2.90 below)					
	hr	m	ht	hr	m	ht	hr	m	ht	hr	m	ht	hr	m	ht	hr	m	ht	hr	m	ht	hr	m	ht
Tu 1	02	27	7.2	14	48	7.1	11	53	9.2	-	-		01	12	3.4	13	17	3.4	03	12	5.5	15	35	5.5
W 2	03	02	7.3	15	21	7.0	00	10	9.2	12	28	9.1	01	44	3.4	13	53	3.4	03	50	5.4	16	15	5.4
Th 3	03	38	7.2	15	54	6.9	00	43	9.1	13	02	8.8	02	16	3.4	14	29	3.3	04	27	5.2	16	54	5.2
F 4	04	13	7.0	16	26	6.7	01	17	8.8	13	37	8.5	02	49	3.4	15	05	3.3	05	03	5.1	17	33	5.0
Sa 5	04	47	6.7	16	57	6.4	01	52	8.5	14	14	8.1	03	24	3.4	15	43	3.2	05	40	4.9	18	15	4.8
Su 6	05	22	6.4	17	30	6.2	02	32	8.1	14	57	7.6	04	00	3.2	16	25	3.0	06	22	4.7	19	01	4.5
M 7	06	00	6.1	18	09	5.9	03	20	7.7	15	51	7.2	04	41	3.1	17	12	2.9	07	10	4.5	19	53	4.4
Tu 8	06	45	5.8	19	00	5.7	04	22	7.3	17	03	6.9	05	30	2.9	18	07	2.7	08	07	4.3	20	53	4.3
W 9	07	47	5.6	20	17	5.5	05	38	7.2	18	24	7.0	06	34	2.7	19	13	2.7	09	12	4.3	21	58	4.3
Th 10	09	15	5.7	21	49	5.7	06	50	7.4	19	33	7.3	07	55	2.7	20	35	2.8	10	19	4.4	23	04	4.5
F 11	10	23	6.0	22	53	6.1	07	50	7.8	20	25	7.8	09	13	2.9	21	44	2.9	11	23	4.6	-	-	
Sa 12	11	21	6.4	23	47	6.5	08	39	8.3	21	09	8.3	10	06	3.0	22	33	3.1	00	03	4.8	12	19	4.8
Su 13	12	12	6.7	-	-		09	22	8.7	21	49	8.8	10	50	3.2	23	15	3.2	00	52	5.0	13	05	5.1
M 14	00	35	6.9	12	59	6.9	10	04	9.1	22	28	9.2	11	31	3.3	23	54	3.3	01	34	5.3	13	47	5.4
Tu 15	01	20	7.1	13	43	7.1	10	45	9.4	23	08	9.4	12	14	3.4	-	-		02	14	5.5	14	27	5.6
W 16	02	03	7.3	14	27	7.1	11	28	9.6	23	50	9.5	00	32	3.4	12	59	3.4	02	53	5.6	15	09	5.7
Th 17	02	46	7.4	15	10	7.1	12	12	9.6	-	-		01	13	3.5	13	45	3.5	03	33	5.7	15	53	5.8
F 18	03	30	7.5	15	54	7.0	00	33	9.5	12	59	9.5	01	53	3.6	14	31	3.5	04	15	5.6	16	39	5.7
Sa 19	04	15	7.4	16	39	6.8	01	20	9.3	13	48	9.2	02	34	3.7	15	18	3.4	05	01	5.5	17	29	5.5
Su 20	05	02	7.1	17	26	6.5	02	10	9.0	14	43	8.7	03	16	3.6	16	09	3.2	05	50	5.3	18	24	5.3
M 21	05	54	6.9	18	20	6.3	03	08	8.6	15	46	8.3	04	02	3.5	17	07	3.1	06	47	5.1	19	27	5.0
Tu 22	06	56	6.7	19	25	6.2	04	15	8.3	16	56	8.0	04	53	3.3	18	19	2.9	07	56	4.9	20	40	4.8
W 23	08	05	6.5	20	37	6.2	05	28	8.1	18	11	7.9	06	00	3.1	19	45	2.9	09	12	4.8	21	53	4.8
Th 24	09	14	6.5	21	47	6.3	06	39	8.1	19	22	8.1	07	33	3.0	20	59	3.0	10	22	4.9	23	00	4.9
F 25	10	23	6.6	22	55	6.5	07	46	8.3	20	23	8.3	08	54	3.1	21	56	3.1	11	26	5.0	-	-	
Sa 26	11	29	6.7	23	55	6.7	08	43	8.6	21	14	8.6	09	55	3.2	22	45	3.2	00	00	5.0	12	22	5.1
Su 27	12	25	6.8	-	-		09	32	8.7	21	57	8.8	10	46	3.3	23	29	3.3	00	51	5.1	13	11	5.2
M 28	00	44	6.9	13	10	6.9	10	15	8.9	22	35	9.0	11	32	3.3	-	-		01	34	5.2	13	55	5.3
Tu 29	01	26	7.0	13	49	6.9	10	54	8.9	23	11	9.0	00	09	3.3	12	14	3.3	02	13	5.3	14	37	5.3
W 30	02	04	7.1	14	24	6.9	11	30	8.9	23	46	9.0	00	45	3.4	12	52	3.3	02	51	5.3	15	16	5.3
Th 31	02	40	7.2	14	57	6.9	12	06	8.8	-	-		01	18	3.4	13	28	3.2	03	28	5.3	15	55	5.2

JUNE 2018   *High Water* GMT

	LONDON BRIDGE						LIVERPOOL (Gladstone Dock)						GREENOCK						LEITH					
	hr	m	ht	hr	m	ht	hr	m	ht	hr	m	ht	hr	m	ht	hr	m	ht	hr	m	ht	hr	m	ht
F 1	03	15	7.1	15	29	6.8	00	19	9.0	12	40	8.6	01	50	3.5	14	03	3.2	04	03	5.2	16	32	5.1
Sa 2	03	50	7.0	16	02	6.7	00	54	8.8	13	15	8.4	02	23	3.5	14	40	3.2	04	38	5.1	17	09	5.0
Su 3	04	25	6.7	16	35	6.5	01	30	8.6	13	51	8.2	02	57	3.4	15	19	3.1	05	14	5.0	17	48	4.9
M 4	04	59	6.5	17	09	6.3	02	08	8.3	14	31	7.8	03	33	3.3	16	01	3.1	05	54	4.8	18	31	4.7
Tu 5	05	36	6.3	17	46	6.1	02	50	8.0	15	16	7.5	04	11	3.2	16	46	3.0	06	38	4.7	19	18	4.5
W 6	06	17	6.1	18	31	5.9	03	41	7.7	16	12	7.3	04	55	3.0	17	37	2.9	07	27	4.5	20	11	4.4
Th 7	07	07	5.9	19	27	5.8	04	43	7.5	17	19	7.2	05	49	2.9	18	33	2.8	08	24	4.5	21	10	4.4
F 8	08	15	5.9	20	46	5.8	05	50	7.6	18	28	7.4	06	54	2.8	19	36	2.8	09	28	4.5	22	13	4.5
Sa 9	09	32	6.0	22	03	6.1	06	54	7.8	19	31	7.8	08	07	2.9	20	43	2.9	10	33	4.6	23	15	4.7
Su 10	10	36	6.4	23	05	6.5	07	52	8.2	20	25	8.2	09	13	3.0	21	44	3.0	11	33	4.8	-	-	
M 11	11	34	6.7	-	-		08	44	8.6	21	14	8.7	10	09	3.1	22	36	3.2	00	11	5.0	12	28	5.1
Tu 12	00	00	6.9	12	29	6.9	09	33	9.0	22	00	9.1	11	00	3.3	23	23	3.3	01	01	5.3	13	18	5.4
W 13	00	52	7.2	13	20	7.1	10	22	9.3	22	46	9.4	11	50	3.3	-	-		01	47	5.5	14	05	5.6
Th 14	01	42	7.4	14	09	7.1	11	10	9.5	23	33	9.6	00	09	3.5	12	41	3.4	02	30	5.6	14	51	5.8
F 15	02	30	7.5	14	57	7.1	11	59	9.6	-	-		00	54	3.6	13	32	3.4	03	14	5.7	15	39	5.8
Sa 16	03	19	7.5	15	45	7.1	00	21	9.6	12	50	9.5	01	38	3.7	14	23	3.4	04	00	5.7	16	28	5.8
Su 17	04	07	7.5	16	32	7.0	01	11	9.5	13	41	9.3	02	22	3.7	15	14	3.3	04	48	5.7	17	19	5.6
M 18	04	57	7.3	17	20	6.8	02	03	9.3	14	35	8.9	03	07	3.7	16	08	3.3	05	39	5.5	18	14	5.4
Tu 19	05	48	7.1	18	11	6.6	02	58	9.0	15	32	8.6	03	54	3.6	17	04	3.1	06	36	5.3	19	14	5.2
W 20	06	44	6.9	19	08	6.5	03	57	8.6	16	33	8.2	04	45	3.4	18	04	3.0	07	41	5.1	20	19	5.0
Th 21	07	44	6.7	20	10	6.4	05	00	8.3	17	38	8.0	05	44	3.2	19	09	3.0	08	49	5.0	21	24	4.8
F 22	08	46	6.6	21	14	6.4	06	06	8.2	18	46	7.9	06	55	3.1	20	16	2.9	09	54	4.9	22	27	4.8
Sa 23	09	49	6.5	22	18	6.5	07	13	8.1	19	50	8.0	08	12	3.0	21	18	3.0	10	56	4.9	23	28	4.8
Su 24	10	54	6.5	23	20	6.6	08	14	8.2	20	45	8.2	09	21	3.1	22	13	3.1	11	56	4.9	-	-	
M 25	11	54	6.6	-	-		09	07	8.3	21	32	8.5	10	18	3.1	23	01	3.2	00	24	4.9	12	51	5.0
Tu 26	00	16	6.7	12	45	6.7	09	54	8.4	22	13	8.7	11	08	3.1	23	44	3.3	01	13	5.0	13	38	5.1
W 27	01	03	6.8	13	28	6.7	10	35	8.5	22	51	8.8	11	51	3.1	-	-		01	55	5.1	14	21	5.1
Th 28	01	45	7.0	14	05	6.8	11	12	8.6	23	26	8.9	00	22	3.4	12	30	3.1	02	33	5.2	15	00	5.2
F 29	02	23	7.0	14	40	6.8	11	48	8.6	-	-		00	57	3.4	13	06	3.1	03	09	5.2	15	36	5.2
Sa 30	03	00	7.0	15	13	6.8	00	00	8.9	12	22	8.6	01	29	3.5	13	41	3.1	03	43	5.2	16	11	5.1

JULY 2018 *High Water* GMT

		LONDON BRIDGE (Datum 3.2m below)				LIVERPOOL (Gladstone Dock) (Datum 4.93 below)				GREENOCK (Datum 1.62 below)				LEITH (Datum 2.90 below)			
		hr m	ht m	hr m	ht m	hr m	ht m	hr m	ht m	hr m	ht m	hr m	ht m	hr m	ht m	hr m	ht m
Su	1	03 34	6.9	15 46	6.8	00 35	8.9	12 56	8.5	02 01	3.5	14 17	3.1	04 17	5.2	16 46	5.1
M	2	04 07	6.8	16 18	6.7	01 10	8.7	13 31	8.3	02 34	3.5	14 55	3.1	04 52	5.1	17 23	5.0
Tu	3	04 40	6.7	16 52	6.5	01 46	8.6	14 07	8.2	03 08	3.4	15 36	3.1	05 29	5.0	18 02	4.9
W	4	05 15	6.5	17 27	6.4	02 24	8.4	14 46	7.9	03 44	3.3	16 18	3.1	06 08	4.9	18 45	4.8
Th	5	05 53	6.4	18 07	6.2	03 05	8.1	15 31	7.7	04 24	3.2	17 03	3.0	06 51	4.8	19 32	4.7
F	6	06 36	6.2	18 52	6.1	03 55	7.9	16 25	7.6	05 10	3.1	17 52	3.0	07 40	4.7	20 26	4.6
Sa	7	07 29	6.1	19 50	6.0	04 54	7.8	17 30	7.6	06 06	3.0	18 46	2.9	08 37	4.6	21 28	4.6
Su	8	08 41	6.0	21 11	6.1	06 01	7.9	18 40	7.7	07 13	2.9	19 48	2.9	09 45	4.7	22 32	4.7
M	9	09 56	6.2	22 26	6.4	07 08	8.1	19 46	8.1	08 28	3.0	20 57	3.0	10 53	4.8	23 35	4.9
Tu	10	11 02	6.5	23 30	6.8	08 12	8.4	20 45	8.6	09 37	3.1	22 02	3.1	11 57	5.0	-	-
W	11	12 04	6.8	-	-	09 10	8.8	21 39	9.0	10 38	3.2	22 59	3.3	00 32	5.2	12 55	5.3
Th	12	00 29	7.1	13 02	7.0	10 05	9.2	22 31	9.4	11 34	3.3	23 50	3.5	01 24	5.4	13 47	5.6
F	13	01 25	7.4	13 55	7.1	10 58	9.5	23 21	9.6	12 28	3.4	-	-	02 12	5.6	14 37	5.8
Sa	14	02 17	7.5	14 45	7.2	11 49	9.6	-	-	00 39	3.6	13 22	3.4	02 59	5.8	15 26	5.9
Su	15	03 08	7.6	15 33	7.2	00 10	9.8	12 40	9.6	01 26	3.7	14 15	3.4	03 46	5.9	16 15	5.9
M	16	03 56	7.6	16 20	7.2	01 00	9.8	13 29	9.5	02 12	3.8	15 06	3.3	04 34	5.8	17 05	5.8
Tu	17	04 45	7.5	17 06	7.1	01 49	9.6	14 18	9.2	02 57	3.8	15 56	3.3	05 25	5.7	17 57	5.5
W	18	05 33	7.3	17 52	6.9	02 38	9.3	15 07	8.8	03 43	3.7	16 45	3.2	06 18	5.5	18 51	5.3
Th	19	06 22	7.0	18 41	6.7	03 29	8.9	15 59	8.3	04 29	3.5	17 33	3.1	07 16	5.3	19 49	5.0
F	20	07 14	6.7	19 35	6.5	04 24	8.4	16 57	7.9	05 18	3.3	18 24	3.0	08 18	5.0	20 48	4.8
Sa	21	08 10	6.4	20 34	6.4	05 26	8.0	18 02	7.7	06 11	3.1	19 20	2.9	09 20	4.8	21 49	4.6
Su	22	09 08	6.3	21 37	6.3	06 34	7.7	19 12	7.7	07 15	3.0	20 28	2.9	10 23	4.7	22 51	4.6
M	23	10 13	6.2	22 43	6.3	07 44	7.7	20 16	7.8	08 35	2.9	21 37	2.9	11 28	4.7	23 55	4.7
Tu	24	11 20	6.3	23 48	6.5	08 45	7.9	21 09	8.1	09 52	2.9	22 35	3.1	12 30	4.8	-	-
W	25	12 19	6.5	-	-	09 36	8.1	21 54	8.4	10 50	3.0	23 22	3.2	00 51	4.9	13 23	4.9
Th	26	00 42	6.7	13 07	6.6	10 19	8.3	22 33	8.7	11 36	3.0	-	-	01 38	5.0	14 06	5.0
F	27	01 28	6.9	13 48	6.8	10 57	8.5	23 08	8.9	00 03	3.4	12 15	3.0	02 17	5.1	14 43	5.1
Sa	28	02 08	6.9	14 25	6.8	11 31	8.6	23 42	9.0	00 40	3.4	12 49	3.1	02 51	5.2	15 17	5.2
Su	29	02 45	6.9	14 59	6.9	12 03	8.7	-	-	01 11	3.5	13 22	3.1	03 24	5.3	15 49	5.2
M	30	03 17	6.9	15 30	6.9	00 16	9.0	12 36	8.7	01 41	3.5	13 55	3.1	03 56	5.3	16 22	5.2
Tu	31	03 48	6.9	16 01	6.9	00 49	9.0	13 08	8.6	02 12	3.5	14 31	3.2	04 30	5.3	16 57	5.2

AUGUST 2018 *High Water* GMT

		LONDON BRIDGE				LIVERPOOL (Gladstone Dock)				GREENOCK				LEITH			
		hr m	ht m	hr m	ht m	hr m	ht m	hr m	ht m	hr m	ht m	hr m	ht m	hr m	ht m	hr m	ht m
W	1	04 19	6.8	16 33	6.8	01 22	8.9	13 41	8.5	02 45	3.5	15 08	3.2	05 04	5.2	17 34	5.1
Th	2	04 52	6.7	17 06	6.6	01 56	8.7	14 16	8.3	03 20	3.5	15 47	3.2	05 40	5.2	18 13	5.0
F	3	05 28	6.5	17 42	6.5	02 33	8.5	14 56	8.1	03 57	3.4	16 27	3.2	06 19	5.0	18 57	4.9
Sa	4	06 07	6.3	18 22	6.4	03 16	8.3	15 43	7.9	04 38	3.3	17 11	3.1	07 03	4.9	19 46	4.7
Su	5	06 53	6.1	19 13	6.3	04 09	8.1	16 43	7.7	05 25	3.1	18 00	3.0	07 56	4.8	20 45	4.7
M	6	07 54	6.0	20 22	6.2	05 17	7.9	17 59	7.7	06 26	3.0	18 59	3.0	09 03	4.7	21 55	4.7
Tu	7	09 18	6.0	21 51	6.3	06 35	7.9	19 17	7.9	07 48	2.9	20 15	3.0	10 21	4.7	23 06	4.8
W	8	10 34	6.3	23 05	6.6	07 50	8.2	20 26	8.4	09 15	3.0	21 36	3.1	11 34	5.0	-	-
Th	9	11 44	6.6	-	-	08 57	8.6	21 26	8.9	10 27	3.1	22 42	3.3	00 10	5.1	12 39	5.3
F	10	00 12	7.0	12 47	6.9	09 55	9.1	22 19	9.4	11 26	3.3	23 36	3.5	01 07	5.4	13 34	5.6
Sa	11	01 12	7.3	13 42	7.1	10 48	9.5	23 09	9.8	12 20	3.3	-	-	01 57	5.7	14 24	5.8
Su	12	02 05	7.5	14 31	7.3	11 37	9.7	23 56	9.9	00 26	3.6	13 12	3.4	02 43	5.9	15 11	6.0
M	13	02 54	7.6	15 17	7.4	12 24	9.7	-	-	01 13	3.7	14 02	3.4	03 29	6.0	15 58	6.0
Tu	14	03 40	7.6	16 01	7.4	00 42	10.0	13 10	9.6	01 59	3.8	14 48	3.3	04 16	6.0	16 45	5.8
W	15	04 25	7.5	16 43	7.3	01 28	9.8	13 53	9.3	02 42	3.8	15 32	3.3	05 03	5.9	17 32	5.6
Th	16	05 09	7.3	17 25	7.1	02 11	9.4	14 36	8.9	03 24	3.7	16 12	3.2	05 53	5.6	18 21	5.3
F	17	05 52	6.9	18 07	6.8	02 55	8.9	15 20	8.4	04 05	3.6	16 52	3.2	06 45	5.3	19 12	5.0
Sa	18	06 36	6.5	18 53	6.5	03 43	8.3	16 11	7.9	04 46	3.4	17 34	3.0	07 42	5.0	20 07	4.7
Su	19	07 24	6.2	19 47	6.2	04 39	7.8	17 13	7.5	05 31	3.2	18 21	2.9	08 42	4.7	21 06	4.5
M	20	08 19	5.9	20 52	6.0	05 51	7.4	18 29	7.3	06 21	2.9	19 21	2.8	09 46	4.5	22 09	4.4
Tu	21	09 25	5.8	22 05	6.0	07 12	7.3	19 45	7.5	07 28	2.7	20 51	2.8	10 56	4.5	23 19	4.5
W	22	10 41	5.9	23 18	6.2	08 24	7.5	20 46	7.9	09 25	2.7	22 08	3.0	12 08	4.6	-	-
Th	23	11 50	6.2	-	-	09 19	7.9	21 34	8.3	10 36	2.8	23 00	3.2	00 27	4.7	13 05	4.8
F	24	00 18	6.5	12 43	6.5	10 02	8.2	22 13	8.7	11 21	3.0	23 42	3.4	01 17	4.9	13 47	5.0
Sa	25	01 07	6.8	13 26	6.7	10 38	8.5	22 48	8.9	11 58	3.1	-	-	01 56	5.1	14 22	5.1
Su	26	01 47	6.9	14 03	6.8	11 10	8.7	23 21	9.1	00 19	3.5	12 33	3.2	02 30	5.3	14 54	5.3
M	27	02 23	6.9	14 37	6.9	11 41	8.9	23 53	9.2	00 51	3.5	13 02	3.2	03 01	5.4	15 25	5.3
Tu	28	02 54	6.9	15 08	7.0	12 12	8.9	-	-	01 20	3.5	13 32	3.2	03 33	5.4	15 57	5.4
W	29	03 24	7.0	15 38	7.0	00 24	9.2	12 43	8.9	01 49	3.5	14 04	3.3	04 05	5.5	16 30	5.4
Th	30	03 54	6.9	16 09	7.0	00 57	9.2	13 15	8.8	02 21	3.5	14 39	3.3	04 38	5.4	17 06	5.3
F	31	04 27	6.8	16 42	6.8	01 29	9.0	13 48	8.7	02 57	3.5	15 16	3.4	05 12	5.4	17 43	5.2

SEPTEMBER 2018 *High Water* GMT

		LONDON BRIDGE						LIVERPOOL (Gladstone Dock)						GREENOCK						LEITH					
		Datum of Predictions 3.2m below						Datum of Predictions 4.93 below						Datum of Predictions 1.62 below						Datum of Predictions 2.90 below					
		hr	m	ht hr	m	ht m		hr	m	ht hr	m	ht m		hr	m	ht hr	m	ht m		hr	m	ht hr	m	ht m	
Sa	1	05	02	6.6 17	17	6.7		02	05	8.8 14	26	8.5		03	34	3.5 15	54	3.3		05	51	5.2 18	25	5.0	
Su	2	05	39	6.4 17	58	6.6		02	46	8.5 15	11	8.2		04	12	3.4 16	35	3.3		06	35	5.1 19	12	4.9	
M	3	06	23	6.2 18	46	6.4		03	38	8.2 16	10	7.8		04	55	3.2 17	21	3.1		07	28	4.9 20	10	4.7	
Tu	4	07	19	5.9 19	52	6.2		04	48	7.8 17	32	7.6		05	51	3.0 18	18	3.0		08	36	4.7 21	24	4.6	
W	5	08	43	5.8 21	25	6.2		06	15	7.7 18	59	7.8		07	17	2.8 19	38	3.0		10	01	4.7 22	44	4.7	
Th	6	10	11	6.0 22	47	6.5		07	39	8.0 20	14	8.3		09	08	2.9 21	19	3.1		11	21	4.9 23	54	5.0	
F	7	11	28	6.4 23	58	6.9		08	49	8.6 21	15	8.9		10	25	3.1 22	29	3.3		12	27	5.2 -	-		
Sa	8	12	33	6.8 -	-			09	47	9.1 22	07	9.5		11	21	3.3 23	22	3.5		00	51	5.4 13	22	5.6	
Su	9	00	58	7.2 13	27	7.1		10	36	9.5 22	54	9.8		12	10	3.4 -	-			01	40	5.7 14	08	5.8	
M	10	01	50	7.4 14	13	7.3		11	21	9.8 23	38	10.0		00	11	3.7 12	57	3.4		02	25	5.9 14	52	5.9	
Tu	11	02	36	7.5 14	56	7.4		12	04	9.8 -	-			00	57	3.8 13	41	3.4		03	09	6.1 15	36	5.9	
W	12	03	19	7.5 15	36	7.5		00	20	10.0 12	45	9.7		01	40	3.8 14	22	3.4		03	54	6.0 16	20	5.8	
Th	13	04	00	7.4 16	15	7.4		01	01	9.8 13	23	9.4		02	21	3.8 14	59	3.4		04	39	5.9 17	04	5.6	
F	14	04	39	7.2 16	53	7.2		01	40	9.4 14	01	8.9		03	00	3.7 15	34	3.3		05	25	5.6 17	48	5.3	
Sa	15	05	17	6.8 17	32	6.9		02	19	8.8 14	40	8.5		03	38	3.6 16	11	3.3		06	13	5.3 18	34	5.0	
Su	16	05	53	6.4 18	12	6.5		03	01	8.2 15	26	7.9		04	16	3.4 16	50	3.2		07	05	4.9 19	25	4.7	
M	17	06	32	6.0 18	58	6.1		03	53	7.6 16	24	7.5		04	58	3.2 17	35	3.0		08	03	4.6 20	22	4.5	
Tu	18	07	20	5.7 20	01	5.8		05	04	7.1 17	42	7.2		05	45	2.9 18	30	2.9		09	05	4.4 21	25	4.3	
W	19	08	30	5.5 21	22	5.7		06	35	6.9 19	07	7.3		06	45	2.7 19	50	2.8		10	15	4.3 22	35	4.4	
Th	20	09	56	5.5 22	41	5.9		07	58	7.2 20	16	7.7		08	32	2.6 21	34	3.0		11	36	4.4 23	51	4.6	
F	21	11	12	5.9 23	46	6.3		08	56	7.7 21	06	8.2		10	13	2.8 22	30	3.2		12	38	4.7 -	-		
Sa	22	12	10	6.3 -	-			09	38	8.2 21	46	8.6		10	56	3.0 23	13	3.4		00	47	4.9 13	21	5.0	
Su	23	00	36	6.6 12	55	6.6		10	13	8.6 22	21	9.0		11	33	3.2 23	50	3.5		01	28	5.1 13	55	5.2	
M	24	01	18	6.8 13	34	6.8		10	44	8.8 22	53	9.2		12	06	3.2 -	-			02	02	5.3 14	26	5.3	
Tu	25	01	53	6.9 14	08	6.9		11	14	9.0 23	25	9.4		00	23	3.5 12	37	3.3		02	34	5.4 14	57	5.5	
W	26	02	24	6.9 14	40	7.0		11	44	9.2 23	57	9.4		00	53	3.5 13	06	3.3		03	05	5.5 15	29	5.5	
Th	27	02	55	7.0 15	11	7.1		12	16	9.2 -	-			01	24	3.5 13	37	3.4		03	38	5.6 16	03	5.5	
F	28	03	28	7.0 15	44	7.1		00	30	9.4 12	49	9.1		01	59	3.6 14	11	3.5		04	12	5.6 16	38	5.5	
Sa	29	04	02	6.9 16	19	7.0		01	05	9.2 13	24	9.0		02	36	3.6 14	48	3.5		04	48	5.5 17	16	5.3	
Su	30	04	38	6.7 16	56	6.9		01	43	9.0 14	03	8.7		03	14	3.6 15	26	3.5		05	29	5.4 17	57	5.2	

OCTOBER 2018 *High Water* GMT

		LONDON BRIDGE						LIVERPOOL (Gladstone Dock)						GREENOCK						LEITH					
M	1	05	16	6.4 17	38	6.7		02	27	8.6 14	49	8.3		03	54	3.4 16	07	3.4		06	16	5.2 18	45	4.9	
Tu	2	06	00	6.1 18	29	6.4		03	21	8.2 15	52	7.9		04	37	3.2 16	53	3.3		07	11	4.9 19	45	4.7	
W	3	06	57	5.9 19	36	6.2		04	35	7.7 17	18	7.7		05	33	3.0 17	49	3.1		08	22	4.7 21	04	4.6	
Th	4	08	20	5.7 21	09	6.2		06	06	7.7 18	47	7.9		07	07	2.8 19	14	3.0		09	49	4.7 22	27	4.8	
F	5	09	52	5.9 22	31	6.5		07	31	8.0 20	01	8.4		09	12	2.9 21	05	3.1		11	09	4.9 23	38	5.1	
Sa	6	11	12	6.3 23	43	6.9		08	39	8.6 21	01	9.0		10	18	3.2 22	13	3.4		12	14	5.3 -	-		
Su	7	12	16	6.7 -	-			09	33	9.1 21	51	9.5		11	08	3.4 23	05	3.6		00	34	5.4 13	06	5.6	
M	8	00	42	7.2 13	08	7.0		10	19	9.5 22	35	9.8		11	53	3.5 23	51	3.7		01	22	5.7 13	50	5.8	
Tu	9	01	31	7.3 13	51	7.2		11	01	9.7 23	17	9.9		12	36	3.5 -	-			02	05	5.9 14	31	5.9	
W	10	02	14	7.4 14	31	7.4		11	40	9.7 23	56	9.8		00	36	3.8 13	16	3.5		02	48	6.0 15	12	5.8	
Th	11	02	54	7.4 15	09	7.5		12	17	9.6 -	-			01	18	3.8 13	52	3.5		03	31	5.9 15	53	5.7	
F	12	03	31	7.3 15	46	7.4		00	34	9.6 12	53	9.4		01	57	3.7 14	25	3.5		04	15	5.8 16	35	5.5	
Sa	13	04	07	7.1 16	23	7.2		01	11	9.2 13	28	9.0		02	35	3.7 14	59	3.5		04	59	5.5 17	15	5.3	
Su	14	04	41	6.7 16	59	6.9		01	47	8.7 14	05	8.6		03	11	3.6 15	35	3.4		05	44	5.2 17	57	5.0	
M	15	05	14	6.4 17	37	6.5		02	26	8.2 14	47	8.1		03	49	3.4 16	14	3.3		06	31	4.9 18	43	4.7	
Tu	16	05	47	6.1 18	17	6.1		03	13	7.6 15	40	7.6		04	30	3.2 16	58	3.2		07	24	4.6 19	37	4.5	
W	17	06	27	5.7 19	08	5.7		04	17	7.1 16	54	7.2		05	17	2.9 17	51	3.0		08	23	4.3 20	39	4.4	
Th	18	07	24	5.4 20	28	5.5		05	46	6.8 18	19	7.2		06	16	2.7 19	00	2.9		09	28	4.3 21	46	4.3	
F	19	08	59	5.3 21	53	5.6		07	15	7.0 19	33	7.5		07	40	2.7 20	39	3.0		10	41	4.3 22	58	4.5	
Sa	20	10	23	5.6 23	00	6.0		08	18	7.5 20	28	8.0		09	27	2.9 21	49	3.2		11	53	4.6 -	-		
Su	21	11	26	6.1 23	54	6.4		09	03	8.0 21	11	8.5		10	19	3.1 22	35	3.3		00	04	4.7 12	41	4.9	
M	22	12	15	6.5 -	-			09	39	8.5 21	47	8.9		10	59	3.3 23	14	3.4		00	49	5.0 13	18	5.2	
Tu	23	00	38	6.7 12	55	6.7		10	12	8.9 22	22	9.2		11	35	3.4 23	49	3.5		01	27	5.3 13	53	5.4	
W	24	01	16	6.9 13	33	6.9		10	43	9.1 22	56	9.4		12	07	3.4 -	-			02	02	5.4 14	27	5.5	
Th	25	01	51	7.0 14	09	7.1		11	16	9.3 23	30	9.5		00	23	3.5 12	38	3.5		02	36	5.6 15	01	5.6	
F	26	02	27	7.0 14	45	7.2		11	50	9.4 -	-			01	00	3.6 13	12	3.6		03	11	5.7 15	36	5.7	
Sa	27	03	04	7.0 15	22	7.3		00	07	9.5 12	26	9.4		01	38	3.6 13	48	3.7		03	48	5.7 16	13	5.6	
Su	28	03	41	6.9 16	00	7.2		00	46	9.4 13	05	9.2		02	18	3.6 14	26	3.7		04	29	5.6 16	52	5.5	
M	29	04	19	6.7 16	41	7.0		01	29	9.1 13	48	8.9		02	59	3.6 15	06	3.7		05	13	5.5 17	36	5.3	
Tu	30	05	00	6.5 17	26	6.8		02	17	8.7 14	39	8.5		03	43	3.5 15	48	3.6		06	03	5.3 18	27	5.1	
W	31	05	46	6.2 18	21	6.5		03	15	8.2 15	45	8.1		04	30	3.3 16	35	3.4		07	01	5.0 19	28	4.8	

NOVEMBER 2018 *High Water* GMT

	LONDON BRIDGE				LIVERPOOL (Gladstone Dock)				GREENOCK				LEITH			
	Datum of Predictions 3.2m below				Datum of Predictions 4.93 below				Datum of Predictions 1.62 below				Datum of Predictions 2.90 below			
	hr	m	hr	m ht	hr	m	hr	m ht	hr	m	hr	m ht	hr	m	hr	m ht
Th 1	06 45	5.9	19 31	6.3	04 30	7.8	17 08	7.9	05 32	3.0	17 34	3.3	08 14	4.8	20 49	4.7
F 2	08 07	5.8	20 55	6.3	05 55	7.8	18 30	8.0	07 14	2.9	19 01	3.1	09 37	4.8	22 10	4.8
Sa 3	09 33	6.0	22 11	6.5	07 15	8.1	19 42	8.5	08 58	3.0	20 43	3.2	10 52	5.0	23 18	5.1
Su 4	10 48	6.3	23 21	6.8	08 21	8.5	20 41	8.9	09 59	3.3	21 50	3.4	11 55	5.2	-	-
M 5	11 52	6.7	-	-	09 14	9.0	21 31	9.3	10 47	3.4	22 42	3.6	00 14	5.4	12 47	5.4
Tu 6	00 20	7.0	12 44	6.9	09 59	9.3	22 14	9.5	11 31	3.5	23 29	3.7	01 03	5.6	13 30	5.6
W 7	01 09	7.1	13 27	7.1	10 39	9.5	22 55	9.6	12 11	3.6	-	-	01 46	5.7	14 10	5.7
Th 8	01 51	7.1	14 06	7.2	11 16	9.5	23 33	9.5	00 13	3.7	12 49	3.6	02 29	5.8	14 50	5.7
F 9	02 28	7.1	14 42	7.3	11 52	9.5	-	-	00 55	3.7	13 23	3.6	03 11	5.7	15 29	5.6
Sa 10	03 03	7.1	15 19	7.3	00 10	9.3	12 27	9.3	01 33	3.6	13 56	3.6	03 54	5.6	16 08	5.5
Su 11	03 37	7.0	15 56	7.1	00 46	9.0	13 01	9.0	02 10	3.6	14 31	3.6	04 36	5.4	16 46	5.3
M 12	04 10	6.7	16 32	6.8	01 21	8.6	13 37	8.7	02 47	3.5	15 07	3.6	05 17	5.1	17 25	5.1
Tu 13	04 42	6.4	17 08	6.5	01 59	8.2	14 16	8.3	03 26	3.4	15 45	3.5	06 01	4.9	18 07	4.8
W 14	05 14	6.2	17 45	6.2	02 41	7.7	15 04	7.9	04 07	3.2	16 27	3.3	06 48	4.6	18 55	4.6
Th 15	05 49	5.9	18 28	5.9	03 35	7.3	16 06	7.5	04 54	3.0	17 15	3.2	07 40	4.4	19 52	4.5
F 16	06 35	5.7	19 24	5.6	04 47	7.0	17 22	7.3	05 49	2.9	18 15	3.0	08 39	4.3	20 56	4.4
Sa 17	07 39	5.4	20 49	5.6	06 09	7.0	18 35	7.4	06 58	2.8	19 30	3.0	09 42	4.4	22 02	4.5
Su 18	09 22	5.5	22 02	5.9	07 21	7.3	19 37	7.8	08 23	2.9	20 49	3.1	10 47	4.5	23 05	4.6
M 19	10 32	5.9	23 01	6.2	08 15	7.8	20 26	8.3	09 30	3.1	21 46	3.2	11 47	4.8	-	-
Tu 20	11 27	6.3	23 52	6.6	08 57	8.3	21 09	8.7	10 19	3.3	22 32	3.4	00 04	4.9	12 35	5.1
W 21	12 15	6.7	-	-	09 35	8.7	21 48	9.0	11 00	3.4	23 13	3.5	00 48	5.1	13 17	5.3
Th 22	00 37	6.8	12 59	7.0	10 12	9.1	22 27	9.3	11 37	3.5	23 54	3.5	01 29	5.4	13 56	5.5
F 23	01 21	7.0	13 41	7.2	10 49	9.4	23 07	9.5	12 12	3.6	-	-	02 09	5.6	14 34	5.7
Sa 24	02 03	7.0	14 22	7.3	11 28	9.5	23 48	9.6	00 37	3.6	12 50	3.7	02 49	5.7	15 12	5.7
Su 25	02 46	7.0	15 05	7.4	12 09	9.5	-	-	01 21	3.6	13 30	3.8	03 30	5.8	15 52	5.7
M 26	03 28	7.0	15 48	7.3	00 33	9.5	12 53	9.4	02 06	3.6	14 11	3.8	04 14	5.7	16 35	5.6
Tu 27	04 10	6.8	16 33	7.2	01 20	9.2	13 41	9.2	02 51	3.6	14 53	3.8	05 02	5.6	17 21	5.4
W 28	04 54	6.6	17 22	7.0	02 12	8.9	14 35	8.8	03 38	3.4	15 37	3.7	05 54	5.4	18 14	5.2
Th 29	05 43	6.3	18 18	6.7	03 11	8.5	15 39	8.5	04 31	3.3	16 26	3.6	06 52	5.1	19 16	5.0
F 30	06 41	6.2	19 25	6.5	04 19	8.1	16 51	8.3	05 36	3.1	17 25	3.4	08 02	4.9	20 32	4.9

DECEMBER 2018 *High Water* GMT

	LONDON BRIDGE				LIVERPOOL (Gladstone Dock)				GREENOCK				LEITH			
Sa 1	07 54	6.1	20 36	6.5	05 34	8.0	18 05	8.2	07 01	3.0	18 43	3.3	09 17	4.9	21 47	4.9
Su 2	09 09	6.2	21 45	6.5	06 48	8.1	19 14	8.4	08 25	3.1	20 10	3.3	10 27	4.9	22 53	5.1
M 3	10 18	6.4	22 53	6.7	07 54	8.3	20 16	8.7	09 29	3.2	21 20	3.4	11 29	5.1	23 52	5.2
Tu 4	11 22	6.6	23 55	6.8	08 50	8.7	21 08	8.9	10 20	3.4	22 17	3.5	12 23	5.2	-	-
W 5	12 17	6.8	-	-	09 36	8.9	21 54	9.0	11 06	3.5	23 07	3.5	00 43	5.3	13 10	5.4
Th 6	00 45	6.9	13 04	6.9	10 18	9.1	22 36	9.1	11 47	3.6	23 52	3.5	01 31	5.4	13 52	5.5
F 7	01 29	6.9	13 45	7.0	10 56	9.2	23 15	9.1	12 25	3.6	-	-	02 14	5.5	14 32	5.5
Sa 8	02 07	6.9	14 22	7.1	11 32	9.2	23 52	9.0	00 34	3.5	13 01	3.6	02 57	5.5	15 10	5.5
Su 9	02 41	6.9	14 59	7.1	12 06	9.2	-	-	01 13	3.5	13 34	3.7	03 37	5.4	15 47	5.4
M 10	03 14	6.9	15 35	7.0	00 27	8.8	12 41	9.0	01 49	3.4	14 08	3.7	04 16	5.3	16 23	5.3
Tu 11	03 47	6.7	16 11	6.8	01 02	8.6	13 16	8.8	02 26	3.4	14 44	3.7	04 54	5.1	16 58	5.1
W 12	04 20	6.5	16 45	6.6	01 37	8.3	13 53	8.5	03 05	3.3	15 21	3.6	05 33	5.0	17 37	5.0
Th 13	04 52	6.4	17 20	6.4	02 16	8.0	14 34	8.2	03 46	3.2	16 00	3.5	06 15	4.8	18 19	4.8
F 14	05 27	6.2	17 59	6.2	03 00	7.7	15 23	7.9	04 30	3.1	16 42	3.3	07 01	4.6	19 08	4.7
Sa 15	06 07	6.0	18 44	6.0	03 52	7.4	16 21	7.6	05 19	3.0	17 32	3.2	07 52	4.5	20 03	4.5
Su 16	06 55	5.8	19 40	5.8	04 56	7.2	17 28	7.5	06 14	3.0	18 32	3.1	08 49	4.4	21 05	4.5
M 17	07 59	5.7	20 57	5.8	06 07	7.2	18 34	7.7	07 18	2.9	19 39	3.0	09 51	4.5	22 10	4.6
Tu 18	09 29	5.8	22 07	6.1	07 13	7.5	19 34	8.0	08 28	3.0	20 48	3.1	10 53	4.7	23 12	4.7
W 19	10 37	6.2	23 08	6.4	08 09	8.0	20 27	8.4	09 31	3.1	21 48	3.2	11 51	4.9	-	-
Th 20	11 35	6.6	-	-	08 58	8.5	21 16	8.8	10 23	3.3	22 41	3.4	00 08	5.0	12 43	5.1
F 21	00 04	6.7	12 28	6.9	09 43	8.9	22 03	9.2	11 08	3.4	23 31	3.5	00 59	5.2	13 29	5.4
Sa 22	00 56	6.9	13 17	7.2	10 28	9.3	22 49	9.4	11 50	3.6	-	-	01 46	5.5	14 11	5.6
Su 23	01 45	7.0	14 06	7.4	11 12	9.6	23 36	9.6	00 20	3.5	12 33	3.6	02 31	5.7	15 05	5.8
M 24	02 33	7.1	14 53	7.5	11 58	9.7	-	-	01 09	3.6	13 16	3.8	03 16	5.8	15 36	5.8
Tu 25	03 19	7.1	15 41	7.5	00 24	9.6	12 45	9.7	01 58	3.6	14 00	3.9	04 03	5.8	16 22	5.8
W 26	04 05	7.0	16 29	7.4	01 14	9.5	13 35	9.5	02 46	3.5	14 44	3.9	04 51	5.7	17 10	5.7
Th 27	04 51	6.9	17 18	7.2	02 05	9.2	14 27	9.3	03 36	3.4	15 30	3.8	05 43	5.6	18 02	5.5
F 28	05 39	6.7	18 11	7.0	03 00	8.8	15 24	8.9	04 28	3.3	16 19	3.7	06 38	5.3	19 00	5.3
Sa 29	06 31	6.5	19 08	6.7	03 58	8.4	16 24	8.6	05 25	3.2	17 13	3.6	07 41	5.1	20 09	5.1
Su 30	07 31	6.4	20 10	6.6	05 01	8.1	17 30	8.3	06 28	3.1	18 14	3.4	08 48	4.9	21 18	5.0
M 31	08 37	6.4	-	-	06 10	7.9	-	-	07 38	3.0	-	-	09 54	4.8	-	-

ABBREVIATIONS AND ACRONYMS

A

AAA	Amateur Athletic Association
ABA	Amateur Boxing Association
abr	abridged
ac	alternating current
AC	*ante Christum* before Christ
	Companion, Order of Australia
ADC	Aide-de-Camp
ADC (P)	Personal ADC to the Queen
Adj.	Adjutant
Adj. Gen.	Adjutant General
Adm.	Admiral
AE	Air Efficiency award
AEM	Air Efficiency Medal
aet	after extra time
AFC	Air Force Cross
AFM	Air Force Medal
AG	Attorney-General
AH	*anno Hegirae* in the year of the Hegira
AM	Assembly Member (Wales)
ANC	African National Congress
AO	Air Officer
	Officer, Order of Australia
AOC	Air Officer Commanding
apptd	appointed
APR	annual percentage rate
ASBO	antisocial behaviour order
AUC	*ab urbe condita* from the foundation of Rome
	anno urbis conditae from the founding of the city

B

b.	born
	bowled (cricket)
BAF	British Athletics Federation
BAFTA	British Academy of Film and Television Arts
BAS	Bachelor in Agricultural Science
	British Antarctic Survey
BBA	British Bankers' Association
BBFC	British Board of Film Classification
BCH (D)	Bachelor of (Dental) Surgery
BCL	Bachelor of Civil Law
BCOM	Bachelor of Commerce
BD	Bachelor of Divinity
BDA	British Dental Association
BDS	Bachelor of Dental Surgery
BED	Bachelor of Education
BEM	British Empire Medal
BENG	Bachelor of Engineering
BFPO	British Forces Post Office
BLIT	Bachelor of Literature
BLITT	Bachelor of Letters
BM	Bachelor of Medicine
BMA	British Medical Association
BMUS	Bachelor of Music
Bp	Bishop
BPHARM	Bachelor of Pharmacy
BPHIL	Bachelor of Philosophy
BPS	British Psychological Society
Brig.	Brigadier
BSI	British Standards Institution
BST	British Summer Time
Bt.	Baronet
BTEC	Business and Technology Education Council
BVMS	Bachelor of Veterinary Medicine and Surgery

C

c.	*circa* about
C.	Conservative
Cantuar:	of Canterbury (Archbishop)
Capt.	Captain
Carliol	of Carlisle (Bishop)
CB	Companion, Order of the Bath
CBE	Commander, Order of the British Empire
CC	Companion, Order of Canada
CCF	Combined Cadet Force
CCHEM	chartered chemist
CD	Civil Defence
	Corps Diplomatique
Cdr	Commander
Cdre	Commodore
CDS	Chief of the Defence Staff
CE	civil engineer
	Common (or Christian) Era
CENG	chartered engineer
Cestr:	of Chester (Bishop)
CET	Central European Time
cf	*confer* compare
CGC	Conspicuous Gallantry Cross
CGEOL	chartered geologist
CGM	Conspicuous Gallantry Medal
CGS	Chief of General Staff
CH	Companion of Honour
CHB/M	Bachelor/Master of Surgery
CI	Channel Islands
Cicestr:	of Chichester (Bishop)
CID	Criminal Investigation Department
CIE	Companion, Order of the Indian Empire
C-in-C	Commander-in-Chief
CILIP	Chartered Institute of Library and Information Professionals
CIPFA	Chartered Institute of Public Finance and Accountancy
CIS	Commonwealth of Independent States
CLJ	Commander, Order of St Lazarus of Jerusalem
CM	*Chirurgiae Magister* Master of Surgery
CMG	Companion, Order of St Michael and St George
CO	Commanding Officer
C of E	Church of England
Col.	Colonel
cons.	consecrated
Cpl.	Corporal
CPM	Colonial Police Medal
CPS	Crown Prosecution Service
CSI	Companion, Order of the Star of India
CVO	Commander, Royal Victorian Order

D

d	*denarius* penny
d.	died
DAB	Digital Audio Broadcasting
DBE	Dame Commander, Order of the British Empire
DCB	Dame Commander, Order of the Bath
D CH	*Doctor Chirurgiae* Doctor of Surgery
DCL	Doctor of Civil Law
DCM	Distinguished Conduct Medal
DCMG	Dame Commander, Order of St Michael and St George
DCVO	Dame Commander, Royal Victorian Order
DD	Doctor of Divinity
DDS	Doctor of Dental Surgery
DDT	dichlorodiphenyl trichloroethane
DFC	Distinguished Flying Cross
DFM	Distinguished Flying Medal
DIP ED	Diploma in Education
DIP HE	Diploma in Higher Education
DL	Deputy Lieutenant
DLIT	Doctor of Literature
DLITT	Doctor of Letters
DLR	Docklands Light Railway

DMUS	Doctor of Music
DNA	deoxyribonucleic acid
DPH *or*	Doctor of Philosophy
DPHIL	
DPP	Director of Public Prosecutions
DSC	Distinguished Service Cross
DSc	Doctor of Science
DSM	Distinguished Service Medal
DSO	Companion, Distinguished Service Order
Dunelm:	of Durham (Bishop)
DUP	Democratic Unionist Party

E

Ebor:	of York (Archbishop)
EC	Elizabeth Cross
	European Community
ECG	electrocardiogram
ED	Efficiency Decoration
EEG	electroencephalogram
EEU	Eurasian Economic Union
EIB	European Investment Bank
ER	*Elizabetha Regina* Queen Elizabeth
ERM	exchange rate mechanism
ESA	European Space Agency
ETA	*Euzkadi ta Askatasuna* Basque separatist organisation
et seq	*et sequentia* and the following
Exon:	of Exeter (Bishop)

F

FANY	First Aid Nursing Yeomanry
FAQ	frequently asked questions
FARC	*Fuerzas Armadas Revolucionarias de Colombia* Revolutionary Armed Forces of Colombia
FBA	Fellow, British Academy
FBAA	Fellow, British Association of Accountants and Auditors
FBS	Fellow, Botanical Society
FBU	Fire Brigades Union
FCA	Fellow, Institute of Chartered Accountants in England and Wales
FCCA	Fellow, Chartered Association of Certified Accountants
FCGI	Fellow, City and Guilds of London Institute
FCIA	Fellow, Corporation of Insurance Agents
FCIARB	Fellow, Chartered Institute of Arbitrators
FCIB	Fellow, Chartered Institute of Bankers
	Fellow, Corporation of Insurance Brokers
FCIBSE	Fellow, Chartered Institution of Building Services Engineers
FCII	Fellow, Chartered Insurance Institute
FCIPS	Fellow, Chartered Institute of Purchasing and Supply
FCIS	Fellow, Institute of Chartered Secretaries and Administrators
FCIT	Fellow, Chartered Institute of Transport
FCMA	Fellow, Chartered Institute of Management Accountants
FCP	Fellow, College of Preceptors
FD	*Fidei Defensor* Defender of the Faith
FE	further education
FFA	Fellow, Faculty of Actuaries (Scotland)
	Fellow, Institute of Financial Accountants
FFAS	Fellow, Faculty of Architects and Surveyors
FFCM	Fellow, Faculty of Community Medicine
FFPHM	Fellow, Faculty of Public Health Medicine
FGS	Fellow, Geological Society
FHS	Fellow, Heraldry Society
FHSM	Fellow, Institute of Health Service Management
FIA	Fellow, Institute of Actuaries
FIBIOL	Fellow, Institute of Biology
FICE	Fellow, Institution of Civil Engineers
FICS	Fellow, Institution of Chartered Shipbrokers
FIEE	Fellow, Institution of Electrical Engineers

FIERE	Fellow, Institution of Electronic and Radio Engineers
FIM	Fellow, Institute of Metals
FIMGT	Fellow, Institute of Management
FIMM	Fellow, Institution of Mining and Metallurgy
FINSTF	Fellow, Institute of Fuel
FINSTP	Fellow, Institute of Physics
FIQS	Fellow, Institute of Quantity Surveyors
FIS	Fellow, Institute of Statisticians
FJI	Fellow, Institute of Journalists
FLS	Fellow, Linnean Society
FMEDSCI	Fellow, Academy of Medical Sciences
fo	folio
FPHS	Fellow, Philosophical Society
FRAD	Fellow, Royal Academy of Dancing
FRAES	Fellow, Royal Aeronautical Society
FRAGS	Fellow, Royal Agricultural Societies
FRAI	Fellow, Royal Anthropological Institute
FRAM	Fellow, Royal Academy of Music
FRAS	Fellow, Royal Asiatic Society
	Fellow, Royal Astronomical Society
FRBS	Fellow, Royal Botanic Society
	Fellow, Royal Society of British Sculptors
FRCA	Fellow, Royal College of Anaesthetists
FRCGP	Fellow, Royal College of General Practitioners
FRCM	Fellow, Royal College of Music
FRCO	Fellow, Royal College of Organists
FRCOG	Fellow, Royal College of Obstetricians and Gynaecologists
FRCP	Fellow, Royal College of Physicians, London
FRCPATH	Fellow, Royal College of Pathologists
FRCPE *or*	Fellow, Royal College of Physicians, Edinburgh
FRCPED	
FRCPI	Fellow, Royal College of Physicians, Ireland
FRCPSYCH	Fellow, Royal College of Psychiatrists
FRCR	Fellow, Royal College of Radiologists
FRCS	Fellow, Royal College of Surgeons of England
FRCSE *or*	Fellow, Royal College of Surgeons of Edinburgh
FRCSED	
FRCSGLAS	Fellow, Royal College of Physicians and Surgeons of Glasgow
FRCSI	Fellow, Royal College of Surgeons in Ireland
FRCVS	Fellow, Royal College of Veterinary Surgeons
FRECONS	Fellow, Royal Economic Society
FRENG	Fellow, Royal Academy of Engineering
FRGS	Fellow, Royal Geographical Society
FRHISTS	Fellow, Royal Historical Society
FRHS	Fellow, Royal Horticultural Society
FRIBA	Fellow, Royal Institute of British Architects
FRICS	Fellow, Royal Institution of Chartered Surveyors
FRMETS	Fellow, Royal Meteorological Society
FRMS	Fellow, Royal Microscopical Society
FRNS	Fellow, Royal Numismatic Society
FRPHARMS	Fellow, Royal Pharmaceutical Society
FRPS	Fellow, Royal Photographic Society
FRS	Fellow, Royal Society
FRSA	Fellow, Royal Society of Arts
FRSC	Fellow, Royal Society of Chemistry
FRSE	Fellow, Royal Society of Edinburgh
FRSH	Fellow, Royal Society of Health
FRSL	Fellow, Royal Society of Literature
FRTPI	Fellow, Royal Town Planning Institute
FSA	Fellow, Society of Antiquaries
FSS	Fellow, Royal Statistical Society
FSVA	Fellow, Incorporated Society of Valuers and Auctioneers
FTI	Fellow, Textile Institute
FTII	Fellow, Chartered Institute of Taxation
FZS	Fellow, Zoological Society

G

GBE	Dame/Knight Grand Cross, Order of the British Empire
GC	George Cross
GCB	Dame/Knight Grand Cross, Order of the Bath

GCLJ	Knight Grand Cross, Order of St Lazarus of Jerusalem
GCMG	Dame/Knight Grand Cross, Order of St Michael and St George
GCSI	Knight Grand Commander, Order of the Star of India
GCVO	Dame/Knight Grand Cross, Royal Victorian Order
Gen.	General
GHQ	general headquarters
GLA	Greater London Authority
GM	George Medal
GMB	Britain's General Union
GOC	General Officer Commanding
Gp Capt.	Group Captain
GPS	Global Positioning System

H

HB	His Beatitude
HBM	Her/His Britannic Majesty('s)
HCF	Honorary Chaplain to the Forces
HE	Her/His Excellency
	higher education
	His Eminence
HH	Her/His Highness
	Her/His Honour
	His Holiness
HIM	Her/His Imperial Majesty
HJS	*hic jacet sepultus* here lies buried
HM	Her/His Majesty('s)
HMAS	Her/His Majesty's Australian Ship
HMC	Headmasters' and Headmistresses' Conference
HMI	Her/His Majesty's Inspector
HMS	Her/His Majesty's Ship
Hon.	Honorary
	Honourable
HRH	Her/His Royal Highness
HRT	hormone replacement therapy
HSE	*hic sepultus est* here is buried
HSH	Her/His Serene Highness

I

IB	International Baccalaureate
IBF	International Boxing Federation
ICC	International Cricket Council
	International Criminal Court
ICJ	International Court of Justice
id	*idem* the same
IP	intellectual property
	internet protocol
IPSA	Independent Parliamentary Standards Authority
iPSC	induced pluripotent stem cell
IRA	Irish Republican Army
IRB	International Rugby Board
IRC	International Rescue Committee
Is	Islands
IS	Islamic State
ISO	Imperial Service Order
	International Organisation for Standardisation
ISP	internet service provider
ISSN	International Standard Serial Number
ITU	International Telecommunication Union

J

J	Judge
	Justice
JP	Justice of the Peace

K

KBE	Knight Commander, Order of the British Empire
KCB	Knight Commander, Order of the Bath
KCLJ	Knight Commander, Order of St Lazarus of Jerusalem

KCMG	Knight Commander, Order of St Michael and St George
KCSI	Knight Commander, Order of the Star of India
KCVO	Knight Commander, Royal Victorian Order
KG	Knight of the Garter
KGB	*Komitet Gosudarstvennoi Bezopasnosti* Committee of State Security (USSR)
KLJ	Knight, Order of St Lazarus of Jerusalem
KP	Knight, Order of St Patrick
KStJ	Knight, Order of St John of Jerusalem
Kt.	Knight
KT	Knight of the Thistle

L

Lab.	Labour
Lat.	Latitude
lbw	leg before wicket (cricket)
lc	lower case (printing)
LCJ	Lord Chief Justice
LCM	least/lowest common multiple
LD	Liberal Democrat
LDS	Licentiate in Dental Surgery
LHD	*Literarum Humaniorum Doctor* Doctor of Humane Letters/Literature
Lib.	Liberal
LITT D	Doctor of Letters
LJ	Lord Justice
LLB	Bachelor of Laws
LLD	Doctor of Laws
LLM	Master of Laws
loc cit	*loco citato* in the place cited
Londin:	of London (Bishop)
Long.	longitude
lsd	*librae, solidi, denarii* pounds, shillings and pence
Lt.	Lieutenant
LTA	Lawn Tennis Association
LVO	Lieutenant, Royal Victorian Order

M

m.	married
M	Monsieur
Maj.	Major
MB	*Medicinae Baccalaureus* Bachelor of Medicine
MBA	Master of Business Administration
MBC	Metropolitan Borough Council
MBE	Member, Order of the British Empire
MBO	management buy-out
MC	Master of Ceremonies
	Military Cross
MCB	Muslim Council of Britain
MCC	Marylebone Cricket Club
MCH(D)	Master of (Dental) Surgery
MDS	Master of Dental Surgery
ME	Middle English
	myalgic encephalomyelitis
MED	Master of Education
Mgr	Monsignor
MIT	Massachusetts Institute of Technology
MLA	Member of Legislative Assembly (NI)
	Museums, Libraries and Archives Council
MLITT	Master of Letters
Mlle	Mademoiselle
MM	Military Medal
Mme	Madame
MMR	measles, mumps and rubella (vaccine)
MN	Merchant Navy
MPHIL	Master of Philosophy
MR	Master of the Rolls
MRI	magnetic resonance imaging
MRSA	methicillin-resistant staphylococcus aureus
MS	manuscript (*pl* MSS)
	Master of Surgery
	multiple sclerosis
MSP	Member of Scottish Parliament
MUSB/D	Bachelor/Doctor of Music
MVO	Member, Royal Victorian Order

N

NAAFI	Navy, Army and Air Force Institutes
NAFTA	North American Free Trade Agreement
NAO	National Audit Office
NCO	non-commissioned officer
NDPB	non-departmental public body
NFU	National Farmers' Union
non seq	*non sequitur* it does not follow
Norvic:	of Norwich (Bishop)
NP	Notary Public
NSW	New South Wales (Australia)
NUJ	National Union of Journalists
NUS	National Union of Students
NUT	National Union of Teachers

O

Ob *or* obit	died
OBE	Officer, Order of the British Empire
OBR	Office for Budget Responsibility
OE	Old English
OED	*Oxford English Dictionary*
OHMS	On Her/His Majesty's Service
OM	Order of Merit
ono	or near(est) offer
op	*opus* work
op cit	*opere citato* in the work cited
OS	Ordnance Survey
OStJ	Officer, Order of St John of Jerusalem

P

PC	Plaid Cymru
	Police Constable
	Privy Counsellor
Petriburg:	of Peterborough (Bishop)
PG	parental guidance
	postgraduate
PHD	Doctor of Philosophy
pl	plural
PLO	Palestine Liberation Organisation
PM	post mortem
	Prime Minister
PO	Petty Officer
	Pilot Officer
	post office
	postal order
	per procurationem by proxy
PPS	Parliamentary Private Secretary
PR	proportional representation
PRA	President of the Royal Academy
pro tem	*pro tempore* for the time being
prox	*proximo* next month
PRS	President of the Royal Society
PRSE	President of the Royal Society of Edinburgh
Pte.	Private

Q

QBD	Queen's Bench Division
QC	Queen's Counsel
QE	quantitative easing
QED	*quod erat demonstrandum* which was to be proved
QGM	Queen's Gallantry Medal
QHC	Queen's Honorary Chaplain
QHDS	Queen's Honorary Dental Surgeon
QHNS	Queen's Honorary Nursing Sister
QHP	Queen's Honorary Physician
QHS	Queen's Honorary Surgeon
QMG	Quartermaster-General
QPM	Queen's Police Medal
QSO	quasi-stellar object *(quasar)*
	Queen's Service Order
quango	quasi-autonomous non-governmental organisation
qv	*quod vide* which see

R

r.	*recto* on the right-hand page
R	*Regina* Queen
	Rex King
RA	Royal Academy/Academician
	Royal Artillery
RAC	Royal Armoured Corps
	Royal Automobile Club
RADA	Royal Academy of Dramatic Art
RADC	Royal Army Dental Corps
RAEC	Royal Army Educational Corps
RAES	Royal Aeronautical Society
	Royal Academy of Music
RAMC	Royal Army Medical Corps
RAN	Royal Australian Navy
RAOC	Royal Army Ordnance Corps
RAPC	Royal Army Pay Corps
RAVC	Royal Army Veterinary Corps
RBS	Royal Society of British Sculptors
RC	Red Cross
	Roman Catholic
RCN	Royal College of Nursing
RCT	Royal Corps of Transport
RD	Royal Naval and Royal Marine Forces Reserve Decoration
	Rural Dean
RE	Royal Engineers
REME	Royal Electrical and Mechanical Engineers
Rep	Republican
Rep.	Republic
Revd	Reverend
RGS	Royal Geographical Society
RHS	Royal Horticultural Society
RI	Royal Institute of Painters in Watercolours
	Royal Institution
RIR	Royal Irish Regiment
RM	Royal Marines
RMA	Royal Military Academy
RMT	National Union of Rail, Maritime and Transport Workers
RNIB	Royal National Institute of Blind People
RNID	Royal National Institute for Deaf People
RNR	Royal Naval Reserve
RNVR	Royal Naval Volunteer Reserve
RNXS	Royal Naval Auxiliary Service
Roffen:	of Rochester (Bishop)
RPA	Rural Payments Agency
RSA	Royal Scottish Academician
	Royal Society of Arts
RSC	Royal Shakespeare Company
RSE	Royal Society of Edinburgh
Rt. Hon.	Right Honourable
RUC	Royal Ulster Constabulary

S

s	section (Public Acts)
	solidus shilling
Salop	Shropshire
Sarum:	of Salisbury (Bishop)
SCD	Doctor of Science
SDLP	Social Democratic and Labour Party
SEAQ	Stock Exchange Automated Quotations system
SEN	special educational needs
	State Enrolled Nurse
SF	Sinn Fein
SFO	Serious Fraud Office
SI	statutory instrument
	Système International d'Unités International System of Units
sic	*sic* so written
sig	signature
	Signor
SLD	Social and Liberal Democrats
SOE	Special Operations Executive

sp	*sine prole* without issue
Sr	Senior
	Sister (title)
SS	steamship
SSN	standard serial number
stet	*stet* let it stand (printing)
Sub Lt.	sub-lieutenant

T

TD	Territorial Decoration
TEFL	teaching English as a foreign language
TNT	trinitrotoluene (explosive)
trans.	translated
TRH	Their Royal Highnesses
trs	transpose (printing)

U

U	Unionist
uc	upper case (printing)
UDA	Ulster Defence Association
UG	undergraduate
USB	universal serial bus
UTC	*Temps Universel Coordonné* coordinated universal time
UVF	Ulster Volunteer Force

V

v	*versus* against
v.	*verso* on the left-hand page
VAD	Voluntary Aid Detachment (nursing)

VC	Victoria Cross
VD	Volunteer Officers' Decoration
Ven	Venerable
VR	Volunteer Reserve
VRD	Royal Naval Volunteer
	Reserve Officers' Decoration
VSO	Voluntary Service Overseas

W

w.	widowed
WBC	World Boxing Council
WBO	World Boxing Organisation
WCC	World Council of Churches
WFTU	World Federation of Trade Unions
Winton:	of Winchester (Bishop)
WO	Warrant Officer
WRAC	Women's Royal Army Corps
WRAF	Women's Royal Air Force
WRNS	Women's Royal Naval Service
WRVS	Women's Royal Voluntary Service
WS	Writer to the Signet

Y

YMCA	Young Men's Christian Association
YWCA	Young Women's Christian Association

Z

ZANU-PF	Zimbabwean African National Union-Patriotic Front

INDEX